The **Shelly Cashman** Se

Microsoft® 365® & Office

First Edition

Intermediate

Victoria Kaye
Susan L. Sebok
Mark Shellman
Misty E. Vermaat
Jill West

Cengage

Australia • Brazil • Canada • Mexico • Singapore • United Kingdom • United States

Cengage

***The Shelly Cashman Series® Microsoft® 365® & Office® Intermediate*, First Edition**

Victoria Kaye, Susan L. Sebok, Mark Shellman, Misty E. Vermaat, Jill West

SVP, Product Management: Cheryl Costantini

VP, Product Management & Marketing: Thais Alencar

Senior Product Director, Portfolio Product Management: Mark Santee

Portfolio Product Director: Rita Lombard

Senior Portfolio Product Manager: Amy Savino

Senior Product Assistant: Ciara Boynton

Learning Designer: Zenya Molnar

Senior Content Manager: Anne Orgren

Digital Project Manager: Jim Vaughey

Developmental Editors: Mary-Terese Cozzola, Deb Kaufmann, Lyn Markowicz

Senior Director, Product Marketing: Danae April

Senior Marketing Manager: Mackenzie Paine

Portfolio Specialist: Matt Schiesl

Content Acquisition Analyst: Callum Panno

Production Service: Lumina Datamatics Ltd.

Senior Designer: Erin Griffin

Cover Image Source: Milos Plazacic/Shutterstock.com

Mac Users: If you're working through this product using a Mac, some of the steps may vary. Additional information for Mac users is included with the Data files for this product.

Disclaimer: This text is intended for instructional purposes only; data is fictional and does not belong to any real persons or companies.

Disclaimer: The material in this text was written using Microsoft Windows 11 and Office 365 Professional Plus and was Quality Assurance tested before the publication date. As Microsoft continually updates the Windows operating system and Office 365, your software experience may vary slightly from what is presented in the printed text.

Previous edition(s): © 2023, © 2020, © 2017

For product information and technology assistance, contact us at
Cengage Customer & Sales Support, 1-800-354-9706
or support.cengage.com.

For permission to use material from this text or product, submit all requests online at **www.copyright.com.**

Library of Congress Control Number: 2024920551

Student Edition ISBN: 978-0-357-88144-6

Loose-Leaf Edition ISBN: 978-0-357-88145-3

K12 Edition ISBN: 978-0-357-88146-0

Cengage
5191 Natorp Boulevard
Mason, OH 45040
USA

Cengage is a leading provider of customized learning solutions. Our employees reside in nearly 40 different countries and serve digital learners in 165 countries around the world. Find your local representative at **www.cengage.com.**

To learn more about Cengage platforms and services, register or access your online learning solution, or purchase materials for your course, visit **www.cengage.com.**

Notice to the Reader

Printed at CLDPC, USA, 10-24

Brief Contents

Contents

PowerPoint

Module 5: Collaborating and Adding Animation ....PPT 5-1

Module 6: Formatting Tables and Charts ....PPT 6-1

Excel

Access

Preface: The Shelly Cashman Series®: Microsoft® 365® & Office®

The Shelly Cashman Series® offers application-specific comprehensive print titles for Word®, Excel®, PowerPoint®, Access®, Publisher®, Outlook®, and Windows®. The modules (chapters) of the four main Microsoft® applications (Word®, Excel®, PowerPoint®, and Access®) are also offered together in each of three print titles organized by level: introductory, intermediate, and advanced. The MindTap Collection includes all of the preceding content, plus additional digital-only content for Teams®, the Mac operating system, and more.

About the Authors

Word: Misty E. Vermaat has more than 30 years of experience in the field of computer and information technology. In addition to consulting in the field, she was an Associate Professor at Purdue University Calumet, teaching or developing courses in Microsoft® Office, computer concepts, database management, systems analysis and design, and programming. Since 1990, she has led the development of the Shelly Cashman Series and has authored and co-authored numerous series textbooks, including many editions of Discovering Computers, Discovering Computers Fundamentals, Microsoft® Publisher®, and Microsoft® Word® books.

PowerPoint: Susan L. Sebok is a retired professor at South Suburban College in South Holland, Illinois, and is also a licensed attorney. Working with the leading Shelly Cashman Series® since 1993, she has co-authored several successful textbooks, including multiple versions of Discovering Computers and Microsoft® PowerPoint®. She holds both Master of Arts and Juris Doctor degrees.

Excel: Victoria Kaye brings her industry knowledge and instructor experience to Cengage Group for the Shelly Cashman Series. As an avid Excel user with Microsoft teaching experience ranging from secondary to undergraduate levels, she is thrilled to be part of the esteemed Shelly Cashman Excel Series legacy.

Dr. Mark Shellman is an instructor and Chair of the Information Technology Department at Gaston College in Dallas, North Carolina. Dr. Mark, as his students call him, prides himself on being student-centered and loves learning himself. His favorite subjects in the information technology realm include databases and programming languages. Dr. Mark has been teaching for more than 30 years and has co-authored several texts in the New Perspective series on Microsoft® Office 365 & Access®, along with a textbook on Structured Query Language.

Access: Jill West authors Cengage courses for CompTIA Cloud+, CompTIA Network+, Data Communications, Technology for Success, and the popular Shelly Cashman Series. She has taught kindergarten through college and currently teaches computer technology courses at Georgia Northwestern Technical College. Jill specializes in designing innovative, critical-thinking activities and building courses that teach popular IT certifications. She regularly presents at conferences and webinars on preparing for CompTIA certifications, teaching cloud computing and computer networking, and mentoring lifelong student learners in IT. She's a member of the 2019 inaugural cohort of Faculty Ambassadors for AWS Educate and is currently an AWS Academy Accredited Educator. Jill and her husband, Mike, live in northwest Georgia with two children at home and two off to college.

Windows 11: Steven M. Freund serves as a lead instructor of various Microsoft® Office, computer concepts, programming, and Internet technology courses throughout central Florida. An integral author for the successful Shelly Cashman Series since 2001, he has presented at the annual customer conference, the Shelly Cashman Series Institute, and other customer events. Freund has co-authored multiple editions of Discovering Computers, Mozilla Firefox, Windows® Internet Explorer, Windows® Office, and Dreamweaver books. In addition, he has written numerous successful instructor supplements. He attended the University of Central Florida.

Preface for the Instructor

Shelly Cashman's trademark step-by-step, screen-by-screen, project-based approach encourages students to expand their understanding of Office applications through hands-on experimentation and critical thinking. Module learning objectives are mapped to Microsoft Office Specialist certification objectives, reinforcing the critical skills needed for success in college and career. Other Ways boxes help users identify alternate click paths to achieve a step, while BTW sidebars offer helpful hints as readers work through projects, enabling them to make the most of Microsoft Office tools. MindTap and updated SAM (Skills Assessment Manager) online resources are also available to guide additional study to maximize results.

Shelly Cashman prepares students for success in the real world by using current and relevant scenarios that apply to everyday life and careers. It also prepares students to take the Microsoft Office Specialist (MOS) exam, which they can leverage in their careers.

Shelly Cashman is designed for students at two- and four-year schools as well as in continuing education programs. Skill levels can range from experienced — for those with a foundational understanding from prior exposure to technology — to introductory — for those using a computer or technology device for the first time.

The Shelly Cashman Series® offers application-specific comprehensive print titles for Word®, Excel®, PowerPoint®, Access®, Publisher®, Outlook®, and Windows®. The modules (chapters) of the four main Microsoft® applications (Word®, Excel®, PowerPoint®, and Access®) are also offered together in each of three print titles organized by level: introductory, intermediate, and advanced. The MindTap Collection includes all of the preceding content, plus additional digital-only content for Teams®, the Mac operating system, and more.

Market research is conducted semi-annually with both current Cengage users and those who use other learning materials. The focus of the market research is to gain insights into the user experience and overall learner needs so we can continuously evolve our content to exceed user expectations. We survey hundreds of instructors to ensure we gather information from a large and varied demographic.

New to This Edition

Shelly Cashman provides thoroughly updated coverage that reflects current Microsoft® 365® features. Narrative content has been authored using Microsoft® 365 Business Standard. Module projects incorporate career topics that apply diversity, equity, and inclusion principles and ensure accessibility. All projects, assignments, and lessons have been refreshed with authentic case scenarios that focus on practical skills and employability.

Word: New features in the Word content include the enhanced Accessibility Checker, which identifies potential accessibility issues and presents suggestions to make documents more inclusive. The Word coverage also introduces Focus mode, the updated collaboration experience, Microsoft's expanded search tool, and voice options. The Immersive Reader is covered, as is the ability to create a private document copy and use Word's screen reader.

PowerPoint: The PowerPoint content introduces the new commenting experience, which lets users display comments in contextual view or the Comments pane. The comment anchor helps reviewers identify specific slide elements with comments and place the comment bubble anywhere on the slide. With the revised search feature, users can enter a word or phrase in the Search box to find the definition. Microsoft Search also provides support articles to help perform tasks. Users can record and save a presentation that includes digital inking to capture text, drawings, and annotations, and then play back animated drawings. The Speaker Coach uses artificial intelligence (AI) to improve presentation skills by giving feedback on body language, the use of sensitive and filler words, and perceived mispronounced words.

Excel: With the Excel modules, students learn both long-standing Excel functions and tools as well as the most recent innovations. Updates to the Excel content include the new XLOOKUP and LET functions, dynamic arrays, and the Analyze Data feature. Also covered is the Accessibility Checker, which identifies issues and offers solutions to produce an accessible workbook.

Access: New features in the Access coverage include updated, real-world scenarios from a variety of industries that illustrate the relevance of Access databases in today's businesses. Completely updated projects use gapped Start and Solution files to ensure students use new, authentic files for each project from one module to the next. Module projects alternate between two sets of scenarios for expanded relevance and practicality. Further, an off-module scenario database receives updates comparable to the on-module scenario so students see similar progression in all databases. A Solutions to Critical Thinking Questions document for each module guides instructors on what to look for in student work. Critical Thinking Questions invite students to engage with the module's skills and information at a conceptual level, and to reflect on their learning, thinking processes, and the relevance of learned skills to their chosen careers.

Windows: The updates to the Windows modules reflect the changes from Windows 10 to Windows 11. New end-of-module exercises incorporate current terminology and features. Module projects have been updated with the latest Windows 11 features, including widgets, the revised Start and Search menus, and the Immersive Reader.

Organization of the Text

The *Shelly Cashman Series: Microsoft 365 & Office, First Edition* is a comprehensive introduction to Microsoft applications and is intended for students in introductory computing courses. Each application is divided into modules within the three levels — introductory, intermediate, and advanced. Each module introduces a topic through a real-world project and presents content that aligns directly with the learning objectives listed at the beginning of the module. To enable students to practice and apply skills learned, each module ends with a summary and a Consider This: Plan Ahead master planning guide that students use as they complete assignments and create projects on their own. Lastly, the end-of-module assignments are related to the top 25 industries for each application and include critical thinking questions. To increase students' confidence in their abilities, the assignments build from applying skills to experimenting beyond the module content to implementing a solution using creative thinking and problem-solving approaches.

Features of the Text

The features of the text, which are found consistently throughout all modules, are designed to aid the student in a specific way.

The projects are focused on employability based on current research and data. They use authentic case scenarios and a step-by-step approach to be as engaging, comprehensive, and easy to use as possible.

Heading levels organize topics within a module. Unique to the Shelly Cashman Series are "To-Do" heading levels for step-by-step task sequences. A To-Do head lead-in paragraph may include a **Why?** element to clarify why students are performing the steps.

To Display a Different Tab on the Ribbon

When you start Word, the ribbon displays 11 main tabs: File, Home, Insert, Draw, Design, Layout, References, Mailings, Review, View, and Help. (Note that depending on the type of computer or device you are using, the Draw tab may not appear.) The tab currently displayed is called the active tab. To display a different tab on the ribbon, you click the tab. The following step displays the View tab, that is, makes it the active tab. **Why?** When working with Word, you may need to switch tabs to access other options for working with a document or to verify settings.

Step-by-step sequences include the following features:

Q&A boxes provide troubleshooting information, equivalent touch instructions, or an additional explanation for a step.

Experiment steps encourage students to explore a feature such as the Themes gallery.

2

- If necessary, scroll to and then point to Facet in the Themes gallery to display a Live Preview of that theme applied to the document (Figure 1–37).
- **Experiment:** Point to various themes in the Themes gallery to display a Live Preview of the various themes applied to the document in the document window.

Q&A What is Live Preview?
Recall from the discussion earlier in this module that Live Preview is a feature that allows you to point to a gallery choice and see its effect in the document — without actually selecting the choice.

Can I use Live Preview on a touch screen?
Live Preview may not be available on all touch screens.

Other Ways provide additional methods to accomplish the tasks covered in specific To-Do steps.

Other Ways

1. Right-click paragraph (or if using touch, tap 'Show Context Menu' button on Mini toolbar), click Paragraph on shortcut menu, click Indents and Spacing tab (Paragraph dialog box), click Alignment arrow, click Centered, click OK
2. Click Paragraph Dialog Box Launcher (Home tab or Layout tab | Paragraph group), click Indents and Spacing tab (Paragraph dialog box), click Alignment arrow, click Centered, click OK
3. Press CTRL+E

By the Way (BTW) boxes are short marginal elements that add value for students by expanding on information in the module.

BTW
Printing Document Properties
To print document properties, click File on the ribbon to open Backstage view, click Print in Backstage view to display the Print screen, click the first button in the Settings area to display a list of options specifying what you can print, click Document Info in the list to specify you want to print the document properties instead of the actual document, and then click the Print button in the Print screen to print the document properties on the currently selected printer.

Other in-text pedagogical elements include the following:

Key terms are bold and blue in the running text. In the MindTap, each bolded key term is linked to its definition in the Master Glossary.

> Calibri and Calibri Light are **sans serif fonts**, which are fonts that do not
> ends of their characters. Other fonts such as Calisto MT are **serif fonts**,

Consider This is a pedagogical sidebar in the form of a question and answer that appears within the module and in the end-of-module student assignments. The question addresses conceptual or critical thinking topics, general information about the app, or other important information students should know.

> **Consider This**
>
> **How do you use the touch keyboard with a touch screen?**
> To display the on-screen touch keyboard, tap the Touch Keyboard button on the Windows taskbar. When finished using the touch keyboard, tap the X button on the touch keyboard to close the keyboard.

Break Point is a note to students that indicates a good place to take a break. Every module includes at least one break point.

> **Break Point:** If you want to take a break, this is a good place to do so. You can exit Word now. To resume later, start Word and continue following the steps from this location forward.

SAM Upload and Download icons are for SAM users. A SAM download icon appears next to any step where students download a data file to begin a SAM Project.

> 1
> - sam Click the Start button on the Windows taskbar to display the Start

A SAM upload icon appears next to any step where students submit a file to SAM for a completed SAM Project.

> 3
> - Click the 'Clear Search String' button to remove the search string and redisplay all objects.
>
> **Q&A** Did I have to click the button to redisplay all objects? Could I simply have erased the current string to achieve the same result?
> You did not have to click the button. You could have used DEL or BACKSPACE to erase the current search string.
>
> - If desired, sign out of your Microsoft account.
> - sam Exit Access.

Figure callouts point to important parts of a screen and include two types:

Action/navigation callouts point to commands or buttons used in the step. Action/navigation callout boxes are a different color from explanatory callouts to help students easily locate screen elements referenced in step instructions.

Explanatory callouts direct students to other significant screen elements in the figure.

1. With the text selected (shown in Figure 1–55), click the Font Size arrow (Home tab | Font group) to display the Font Size gallery.
2. Click 20 in the Font Size gallery to increase the font size of the selected text.
3. Click anywhere in the document window to remove the selection from the text (Figure 1–56).

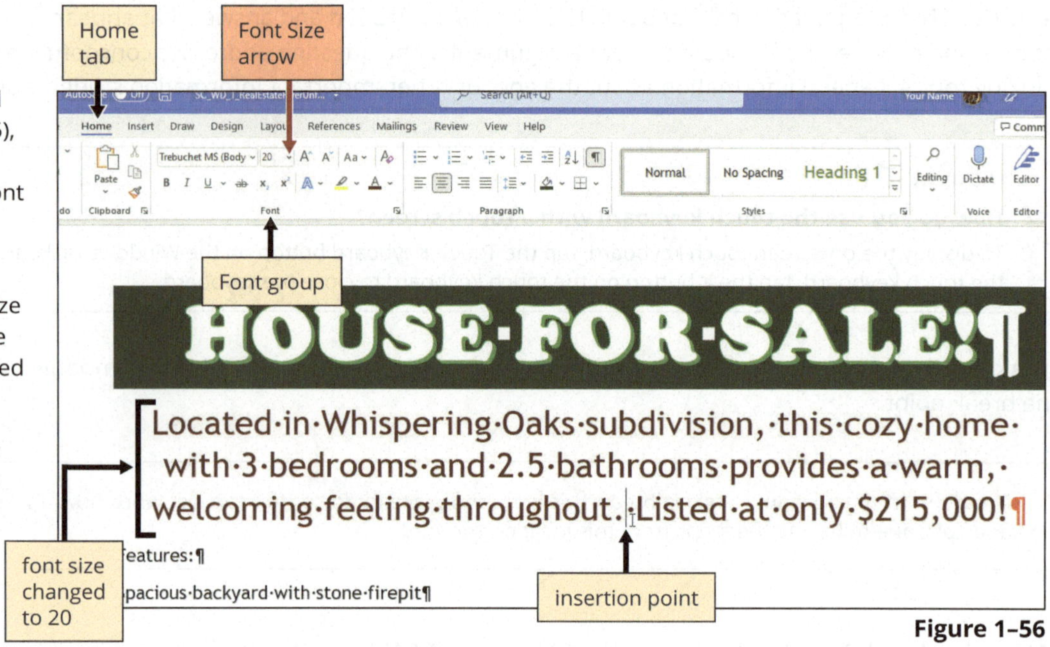

Figure 1–56

Course Solutions

Online Learning Platform: MindTap with SAM

The Shelly Cashman Series MindTap Collection, powered by SAM (Skills Assessment Manager), enables proficiency in Microsoft Office and computing concepts for your Introductory Computing courses. With a library of renowned course materials, including ready-to-assign, auto-graded learning modules, you can easily adapt your course to best prepare students for the evolving job market. In addition to an eReader that includes the full content of the printed book, The Shelly Cashman Series, First Edition MindTap course includes the following:

- SAM Textbook Projects: Follow the steps and scenarios outlined in the textbook readings; enable students to complete projects based on a real-world scenario live in Microsoft Office applications and submit them in SAM for automatic grading and feedback.
- SAM Training and Exam: Trainings teach students to complete specific skills in a simulated Microsoft application environment while exams allow students to demonstrate their proficiency (also in a simulated environment).
- SAM Projects: Students complete projects based on real-world scenarios live in Microsoft applications and submit the projects in SAM for automatic grading and feedback. SAM offers several types of projects, each with a unique purpose: 1A and 1B, critical thinking, end of module, capstone, and integration.

- Microsoft Office Specialist (MOS) resources: Training and exams are based on the Microsoft Office 365 Objective Domains for the MOS Exam and exam simulation that replicates the test-taking environment of the MOS exam for Word, Excel, Access, PowerPoint, and Outlook.

To learn more, go to: https://www.cengage.com/mindtap-collections/

Ancillary Package

Additional instructor and student resources for this product are available online. Instructor assets include an Instructor Manual, an Educator Guide, PowerPoint® slides, a Guide to Teaching Online, Solution Files, a test bank powered by Cognero®, and a Transition Guide. Student assets include data files and a glossary. Sign up or sign in at www.cengage.com to search for and access this product and its online resources. The instructor and student companion sites contain ancillary material for the full Shelly Cashman Series Collection, along with instructions on how to find specific content within the companion site.

- Instructor Manual: This guide provides additional instructional material to assist in class preparation, including module objectives, module outlines, discussion questions, and additional activities and assignments. Each outline corresponds directly with the content in the module, and additional discussion questions and activities are aligned to headings in the book.
- Educator Guide: The MindTap Educator Guide contains a detailed outline of the corresponding MindTap course, including activity types and time on task. The SAM Educator Guide explains how to use SAM functionality to maximize your course.
- PowerPoint slides: The slides may be used to guide classroom presentations, to provide to students for module review, or to print as classroom handouts. The slides align closely with the book while activities and the self-assessment align with module learning objectives and supplement the content in the book.
- Guide to Teaching Online: This guide presents technological and pedagogical considerations and suggestions for teaching the Introductory Computing course when you can't be in the same room with students.
- Solution and Answer Guide: The answers to the critical thinking questions are written by the author and correspond to critical thinking questions in the end-of-module activities.
- Solution files: These files provide solutions to all textbook projects for instructors to use to grade student work.
  - Instructors using SAM do not need solution files since projects are auto-graded within SAM.
  - Solution files are provided on the instructor companion site for instructors *not* using SAM.
- Data files: These files are provided for students to complete the projects in each module.
  - Students using SAM to complete the projects download the required data files directly from SAM.
  - Students who are *not* using SAM to complete the projects can find data files on the student companion site and within MindTap.
- Test banks: A comprehensive test bank, offered in Cognero, Word, Blackboard, Moodle, Desire2Learn, Canvas, and SAM formats, contains questions aligned with each module's learning objectives and is written by subject matter experts. Powered by Cognero, Cengage Testing is a flexible, online system that allows you to author, edit, and manage test bank content from multiple Cengage solutions and to create multiple test versions that you can deliver from your LMS, your classroom, or wherever you want.
- Transition Guide: This guide highlights all of the changes in the text and in the digital offerings from the previous edition to the current one so that instructors know what to expect.

Acknowledgments

Jill West: It's always a privilege to work with the incredible teams Cengage puts together, and this course is no exception. I've worked on many projects under the energetic and resourceful leadership of Amy Savino, whom I greatly admire and will forever be thankful for her vote of confidence in me when I needed it most. I've thoroughly enjoyed getting to know Anne Orgren, who has been our attentive and supportive content manager, providing just enough guidance exactly when needed. I can't say enough good things about MT Cozzola, developmental editor for this project. With her diversity of talents and skills, she has been a learner advocate, bringing the student's perspective to every conversation and providing synergistic insight. And I'm grateful for another opportunity to work with learning designer Zenya Molnar, who brings creative solutions to design challenges. Many other folks worked diligently behind the scenes to ensure consistency of quality, design, and innovation — their efforts are enthusiastically noted and greatly appreciated.

I owe a special thanks to my husband, Mike, for his tireless support and encouragement. And thanks to my kiddos: Winn, Sarah, Daniel, and Zack.

Victoria Kaye: Thank you for the many individuals who have made this edition possible. A text like this is not done without great effort, teamwork, and planning. Thank you to those individuals who contributed their expertise to this text, and an extra special thank you to developmental editors Barbara Clemens and MT Cozzola. Without your vast knowledge and careful consideration, this edition would not be possible. Thank you to the editorial team and their staff: Amy Savino, Senior Portfolio Product Manager; Anne Orgren, Senior Content Manager; and Zenya Molnar, Learning Designer. It is simply not possible to sum up the value of your contributions.

Getting to Know Microsoft Office Versions

Cengage is proud to bring you the next edition of Microsoft Office. This edition was designed to provide a robust learning experience that is not dependent upon a specific version of Office.

Microsoft supports several versions and editions of Office: (Refer to Table 1 below for more information)

- **Microsoft 365 (formerly known as Office 365):** A service that delivers the most up-to-date, feature-rich, modern Microsoft productivity applications direct to your device. There are several combinations of Microsoft 365 programs for business, educational, and personal use. Microsoft 365 is cloud-based, meaning it is stored, managed, and processed on a network of remote servers hosted on the Internet, rather than on local servers or personal computers. Microsoft 365 offers extra online storage and cloud-connected features, as well as updates with the latest features, fixes, and security updates. Microsoft 365 is purchased for a monthly subscription fee that keeps your software up to date with the latest features.
- **Office 2021:** The Microsoft "on-premises" version of the Office apps, available for both PCs and Macintosh computers, offered as a static, one-time purchase and outside of the subscription model. Unlike Microsoft 365, Office 2021 does not include online product updates with new features.
- **Microsoft 365 Online (formerly known as Office Online):** A free, simplified version of Microsoft web applications (Teams, Access, Word, Excel, PowerPoint, and OneNote) that lets users create and edit files collaboratively.
- **Office 365 Education:** A free subscription including Word, Excel, PowerPoint, OneNote, and now Microsoft Teams, plus additional classroom tools. Only available for students and educators at select institutions.

Table 1 Microsoft Office applications — uses and availability

Application	Use	Availability/Editions
Word	Create documents and improve your writing with intelligent assistance features.	Microsoft 365 Family, Home, Business, Office 2021, Office 365 Education
Excel	Simplify complex data into easy-to-read spreadsheets.	Microsoft 365 Personal, Home, Business, Office 2021, Office 365 Education
PowerPoint	Create presentations that stand out.	Home, Business, Office 2021, Office 365 Education
OneNote	A digital notebook for all your note-taking needs.	Home, Office 365 Education
OneDrive	Save and share your files and photos wherever you are.	Home, Business
Outlook	Manage your email, calendar, tasks, and contacts all in one place.	Home, Business
SharePoint	Create team sites to share information, files, and resources.	Business
Publisher	Create polished, professional layouts without the hassle.	Home, Business, Office 2021 (PC only)
Access	Create your own database apps easily in formats that serve your business best.	Home, Business, Office 2021 (PC only)
Teams	Bring everyone together in one place to meet, chat, call, and collaborate.	Business, Office 365 Education
Exchange	Business-class email and calendaring.	Business

Over time, the Microsoft 365 cloud interface will continuously update using its web connection, offering new application features and functions, while Office 2021 will remain static.

Because Microsoft 365 releases updates continuously, your onscreen experience may differ from what you see in this product. For example, the more advanced features and functionalities covered in this product may not be available in Microsoft 365 Online, may have updated from what you see in Office 2021, or may be from a post-publication update of Microsoft 365.

For up-to-date information on the differences between Microsoft 365, Office 2021, and Microsoft 365 Online, please visit the Microsoft Support website.

Cengage is committed to providing high-quality learning solutions for you to gain the knowledge and skills that will empower you throughout your educational and professional careers.

Thank you for using our product, and we look forward to exploring the future of Microsoft Office with you!

Using SAM Projects and Textbook Projects

SAM (Skills Assessment Manager) **Projects** allow you to actively apply the skills you learned in Microsoft Word, Excel, PowerPoint, or Access. You can also submit your work to SAM for online grading. You can use SAM Projects to become a more productive student and use these skills throughout your career.

To complete SAM Textbook Projects, please follow these steps:

SAM Textbook Projects allow you to complete a project as you follow along with the steps in the textbook. As you read the module, look for icons that indicate when you should download your SAM Start file(s) and when to upload your solution file to SAM for grading.

Everything you need to complete this project is provided within SAM. You can launch the eBook directly from SAM, which will allow you to take notes, highlight, and create a custom study guide, or you can use a print textbook or your mobile app. Download IOS or Download Android.

To get started, launch your SAM Project assignment from SAM, MindTap, or a link within your learning management system.

1. Step 1:
   Download Files
   - Click the "Download All" button or the individual links to download your **Start File** and **Support File(s)** (when available). You must use the SAM Start file.
   - Click the Instructions link to launch the eBook (or use the print textbook or mobile app).
   - Disregard any steps in the textbook that ask you to create a new file or to use a file from a location outside of SAM.
   - Look for the SAM Download icon to begin working with your start file.
   - Follow the module's step-by-step instructions until you reach the SAM Upload icon.
   - Save and close the file.

2. Step 2:
   Save Work to SAM
   - Ensure you rename your project file to match the Expected File Name.
   - Upload your in-progress or completed file to SAM. You can download the file to continue working or submit it for grading in the next step.
3. Step 3:
   Submit for Grading
   - Upload your completed solution file to SAM for immediate feedback and to view the available Reports.
     - The **Graded Summary Report** provides a detailed list of project steps, your score, and feedback to aid you in revising and resubmitting the project.
     - The **Study Guide** provides your score for each project step and links to the associated training and textbook pages.
   - If additional attempts are allowed, use your reports to assist with revising and resubmitting your project.
   - To re-submit your project, download the file you saved in step 2.
   - Edit, save, and close the file, then re-upload and submit it again.

For all other SAM Projects, please follow these steps:

To get started, launch your SAM Project assignment from SAM, MindTap, or a link within your learning management system.

1. Step 1:
   Download Files
   - Click the "Download All" button or the individual links to download your **Instruction File**, **Start File**, and **Support File(s)** (when available). You must use the SAM Start file.
   - Open the Instruction file and follow the step-by-step instructions. Ensure you rename your project file to match the Expected File Name (change _1 to _2 at the end of the file name).

2. Step 2:
   Save Work to SAM
   - Upload your in-progress or completed file to SAM. You can download the file to continue working or submit it for grading in the next step.

3. Step 3:
   Submit for Grading
   - Upload the completed file to SAM for immediate feedback and to view available Reports.
     - The **Graded Summary Report** provides a detailed list of project steps, your score, and feedback to aid you in revising and resubmitting the project.
     - The **Study Guide** provides your score for each project step and links to the associated training and textbook pages.
   - If additional attempts are allowed, use your reports to assist with revising and resubmitting your project.
   - To re-submit the project, download the file saved in step 2.
   - Edit, save, and close the file, then re-upload and submit it again.

For additional tips to successfully complete your SAM Projects, please view our SAM Video Tutorials.

Creating a Multipage Document

Objectives

After completing this module, you will be able to:

- Insert a cover page
- Insert text in and delete content controls
- Modify text, paragraph, and page formatting
- Modify print settings
- Insert and edit formatted headers and footers
- Format page numbers
- Select and format the bullet character for a list
- Create and edit a multilevel list
- Define a new bullet character or number format for a list level
- Sort paragraphs
- Edit and format Word tables
- Sort table data
- Insert a formula in a table
- Create a watermark

Introduction

During your business and personal endeavors, you may want or need to provide a recommendation to a person or group of people for their consideration. You might suggest they purchase a product, such as a vehicle or food, or contract a service, such as veterinary services or website design services. Or, you might try to convince an audience to take an action, such as visiting an establishment or donating to a cause. You may be asked to request funds for a new program or to promote an idea, such as a benefits package to company employees or a budget plan to upper management. To present these types of recommendations, you may find yourself writing a proposal.

A proposal generally is one of three types: sales, research, or planning. A **sales proposal** sells an idea, a product, or a service. A **research proposal** usually requests funding for a research project. A **planning proposal** offers solutions to a problem or improvement to a situation.

Project: Sales Proposal

Sales proposals describe the features and value of products and services being offered, with the intent of eliciting a positive response from the reader. Desired outcomes include the reader accepting ideas, purchasing products, contracting services, volunteering time, contributing to a cause, or taking an action. A well-written proposal can be the key to obtaining the desired results.

The project in this module follows generally accepted guidelines for writing short sales proposals and uses Word to create the sales proposal shown in Figure 4–1. The sales proposal in

Figure 4–1(a): Cover Page

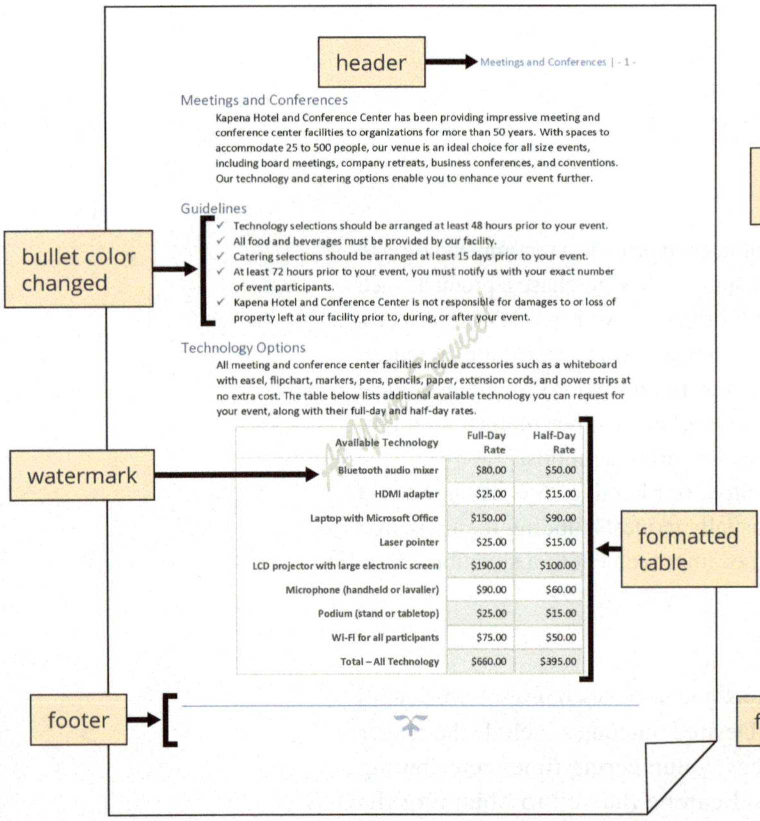

Figure 4–1(b): First Page of Body of Proposal

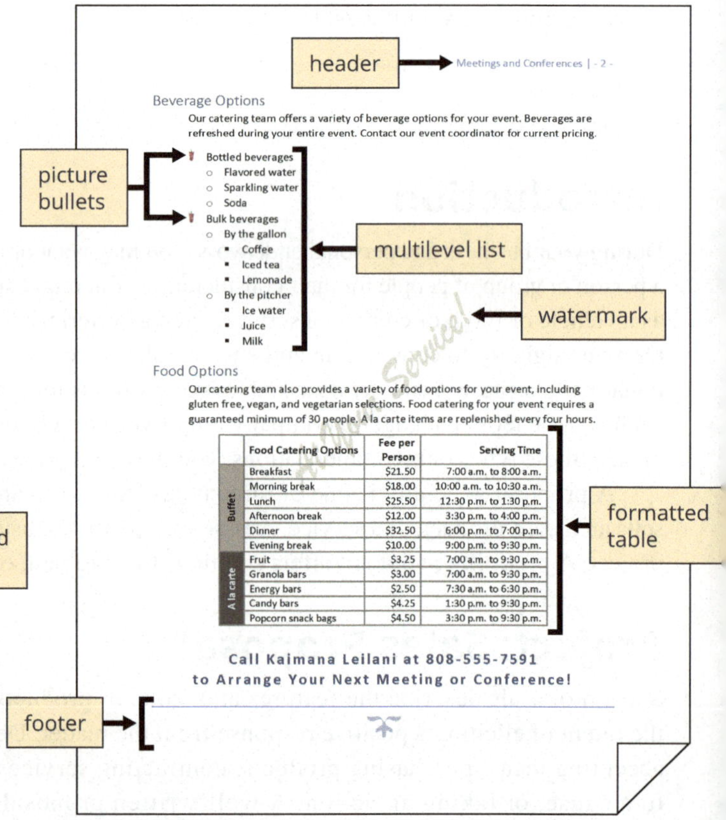

Figure 4–1(c): Second Page of Body of Proposal

this module, written by the administrative assistant to the event coordinator at Kapena Hotel and Conference Center, is designed to persuade organizations to use its venue to host their meetings and conferences. The proposal has a pleasing cover page to attract readers' attention. To add impact, the sales proposal has a watermark consisting of the phrase, At Your Service!, positioned behind the content on each page. The proposal also uses lists and tables to summarize and highlight important data.

In this module, you will learn how to create the sales proposal shown in Figure 4–1. You will perform the following general tasks as you progress through this module:

1. Create a cover page for the proposal.
2. Modify page formatting in the proposal.
3. Edit and format lists in the proposal.
4. Edit and format tables in the proposal.
5. Create a watermark in the proposal.

To Start Word, Open a Draft File, Save It with a New File Name, and Specify Settings

Assume you already have prepared a draft of the body of the proposal, which is located in the Data Files. Please contact your instructor for information about accessing the Data Files. To convert the draft into a final document, you will fix formatting issues, modify page formatting, format an existing list, create a new list, edit and format existing tables, and add a watermark.

The following steps start Word, open the proposal draft file, save it with a new file name, display formatting marks, change the zoom to page width, and display rulers on the screen. If you are using a computer to step through the project in this module and you want your screens to match the figures in this book, you should change your screen's resolution to 1366 × 768.

If your instructor wants you to submit your work as a SAM Project for automatic grading, you must download the Data Files from the assignment launch page.

1. sam Start Word and open the file called SC_WD_4-1.docx from the Data Files. If necessary, maximize the Word window.
2. Save the file on your hard drive, OneDrive, or other storage location using the file name, SC_WD_4_Meetings_Sales_Proposal (Figure 4–2).
3. If the Print Layout button on the status bar is not selected, click it so that your screen is in Print Layout view.
4. If the 'Show/Hide ¶' button (Home tab | Paragraph group) is not selected already, click it to display formatting marks on the screen.
5. To display the page the same width as the document window, if necessary, click the Page Width button (View tab | Zoom group).
6. To display rulers on the screen, if necessary, click the Ruler check box (View tab | Show group).

BTW
The Ribbon and Screen Resolution
Word may change how the groups and buttons within the groups appear on the ribbon, depending on the screen resolution of your computer. Thus, your ribbon may look different from the ones in this book if you are using a screen resolution other than 1366 × 768. For information about how to change a computer's resolution, use the search text, change resolution, in your operating system's Help files.

BTW
Touch Mode Differences
The Office and Windows interfaces may vary if you are using Touch mode. For this reason, you might notice that the function or appearance of your touch screen differs slightly from this module's presentation.

7 If you are using a mouse and you want your screens to match the figures in the book, verify that you are using Mouse mode by doing the following: display the Quick Access Toolbar, if necessary, by clicking the 'Ribbon Display Options' button at the right edge of the ribbon and then clicking 'Show Quick Access Toolbar' on the menu; clicking the 'Touch/Mouse Mode' button on the Quick Access Toolbar and then, if necessary, clicking Mouse on the menu (if your Quick Access Toolbar does not display the 'Touch/Mouse Mode' button, click the 'Customize Quick Access Toolbar' button on the Quick Access Toolbar and then click Touch/Mouse Mode on the menu to add the button to the Quick Access Toolbar); then hide the Quick Access Toolbar by clicking the 'Ribbon Display Options' button at the right edge of the ribbon and then clicking 'Hide Quick Access Toolbar' on the menu.

BTW
Normal Style
If your screen settings differ from Figure 4–2, it is possible the default settings in your Normal style have been changed. Normal style settings are saved in a file called normal.dotm. To restore the original Normal style settings, exit Word and use File Explorer to locate the normal.dotm file (be sure that hidden files and folders are displayed, and include system and hidden files in your search — you may need to use Help to assist you with these tasks). Rename the normal.dotm file as oldnormal.dotm. After renaming the normal.dotm file, it no longer will exist as normal.dotm. The next time you start Word, it will re-create a normal.dotm file using the original default settings.

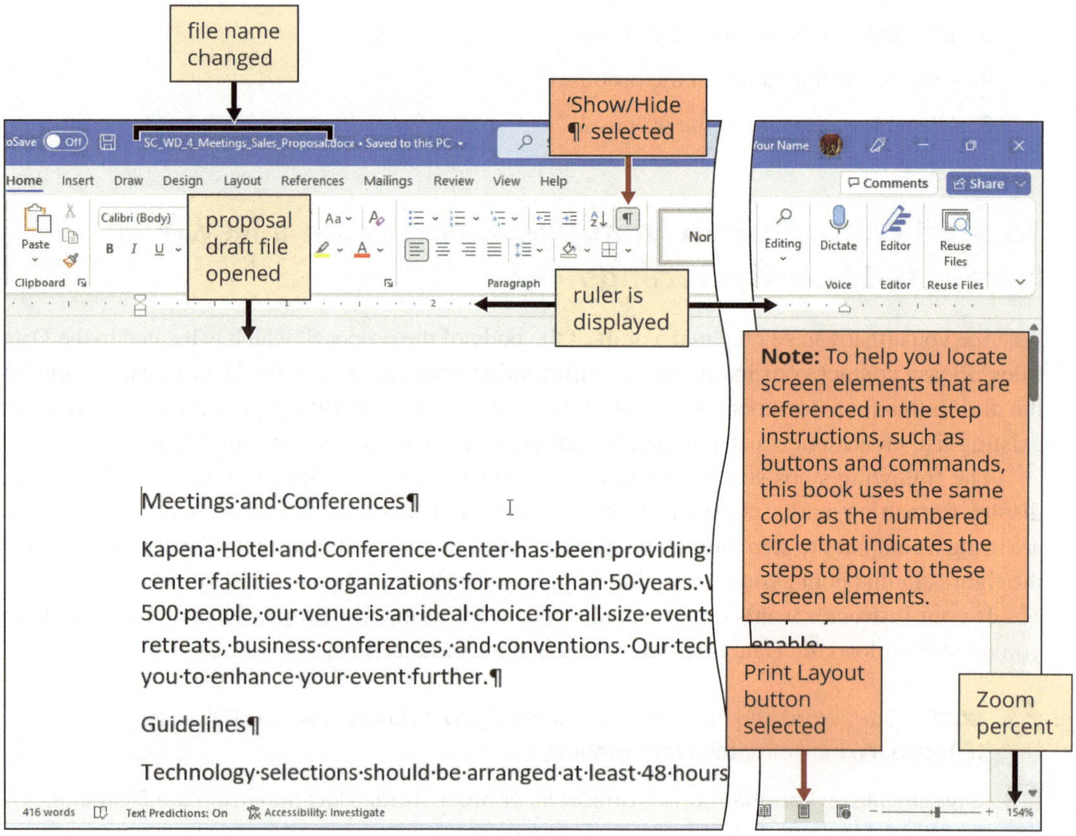

Figure 4–2

Creating a Cover Page

A **cover page** is a separate title page in a multipage document that contains, at a minimum, the title of a document, and often the writer's name and sometimes the date. For a sales proposal, the cover page usually is the first page of the document. Solicited proposals often have a specific format for the cover page. Guidelines for the cover page of a solicited proposal may stipulate the margins, spacing, layout, and required contents, such as title, sponsor name, author name, date, etc. With an unsolicited proposal, by contrast, you can design the cover page in a way that best presents its message.

Consider This

How do you design an effective cover page?

The cover page is the first section a reader encounters on a sales proposal. Thus, it is important that the cover page appropriately reflects the goal of the sales proposal. When designing the cover page, consider its content.

- **Use concise, descriptive text.** The cover page should contain a short, descriptive title that accurately reflects the message of the sales proposal. The cover page also may include a theme or slogan. Do not place a page number on the cover page.
- **Identify appropriate fonts, font sizes, and colors for the text.** Use fonts that are easy to read. Avoid using more than three different fonts because too many fonts can make the cover page visually confusing. Use larger font sizes to add impact to the cover page. To give the title more emphasis, its font size should be larger than any other text on the cover page. Use colors that complement one another and convey the meaning of the proposal.
- **Use graphics, if desired, to reinforce the goal.** Select simple graphics that clearly communicate the fundamental nature of the proposal. Possible graphics include shapes, pictures, and logos.
- **Use colors that complement text colors.** Be aware that too many graphics and colors can be distracting. Arrange graphics with the text so that the cover page is attractive and uncluttered.

The cover page of the sales proposal in this module (shown in Figure 4–1a) contains text, colors, and the faded phrase, At Your Service!, in the background. The steps in the next section create the cover page. The faded phrase, At Your Service!, is added to all pages at the end of this module.

To Insert a Cover Page

Word has many predefined cover page formats that you can use for the cover page in a document. When you insert a predefined cover page, Word inserts it at the top of the document by default. The following steps insert a cover page. **Why?** The predefined cover pages use complementary colors and fonts for a document's cover page.

1

- Display the Insert tab.
- Click the Cover Page button (Insert tab | Pages group) to display the Cover Page gallery.
- **Experiment:** Scroll through the Cover Page gallery to see the variety of available predefined cover pages. When finished, display the Filigree cover page in the Cover Page gallery, as shown in Figure 4–3.

Q&A Does it matter where I position the insertion point before inserting a cover page?
No. By default, Word inserts the cover page as the first page in a document.

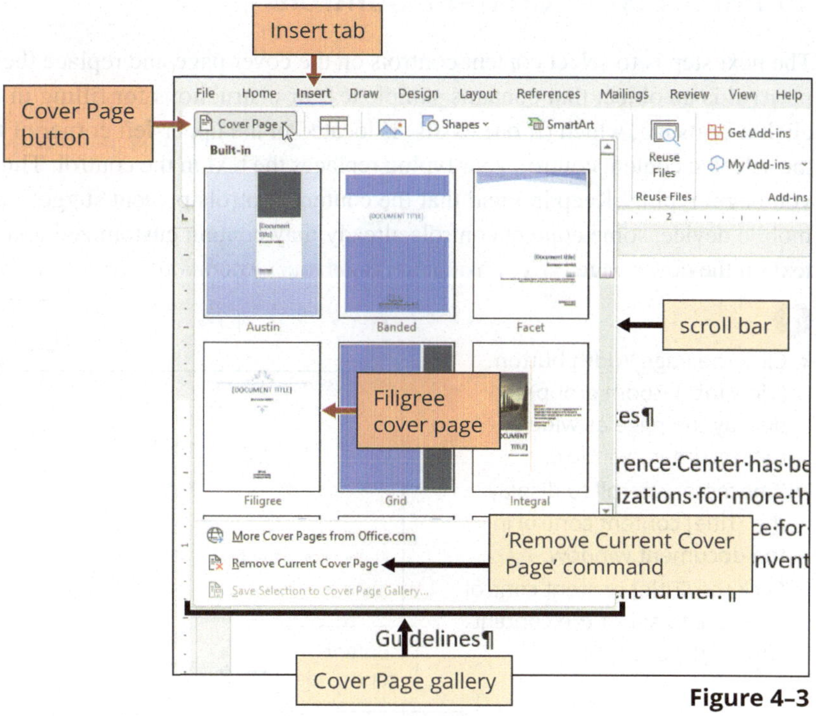

Figure 4–3

2

- Click Filigree in the Cover Page gallery to insert the selected cover page as the first page in the current document.
- Display the View tab. Click the One Page button (View tab | Zoom group) to display the entire cover page in the document window (Figure 4–4).

Q&A Does the cover page have to be the first page?
No. You can right-click the desired cover page in the Cover Page gallery and then click the desired location on the submenu.

How would I delete a cover page?
You would click the Cover Page button (Insert tab | Pages group) and then click 'Remove Current Cover Page' in the Cover Page gallery (shown in Figure 4–3).

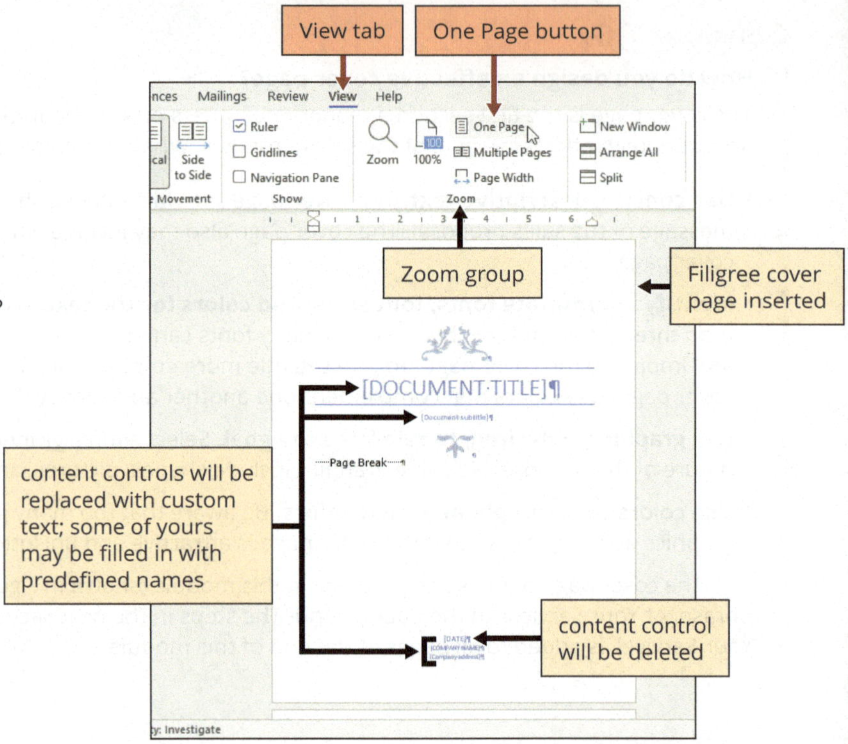

Figure 4–4

Other Ways

1. Click 'Explore Quick Parts' button (Insert tab | Text group), click 'Building Blocks Organizer' on Explore Quick Parts menu, select desired cover page building block (Building Blocks Organizer dialog box), click Insert button, click Close

To Enter Text in Content Controls

The next step is to select content controls on the cover page and replace their text with the cover page information. A **content control** is an object that contains sample text or instructions for filling in text and graphics. To select a content control, you click it or its tag, which (if one exists) is located in the upper-left corner of the content control. As soon as you begin typing in the selected content control, your typing replaces the text in the control. Thus, you do not need to delete the selected text before you begin typing. Keep in mind that the content controls present suggested text. Depending on settings on your computer or mobile device, some content controls already may contain customized text, which you will change. The following steps enter text on the cover page. **Why?** You want to replace the content controls with customized text.

1

- Click the Page Width button (View tab | Zoom group) to display the page as wide as the document window.
- If necessary, scroll to display the [Title] content control in the document window.
- Click the [Title] content control or its tag to select the content control (Figure 4–5).

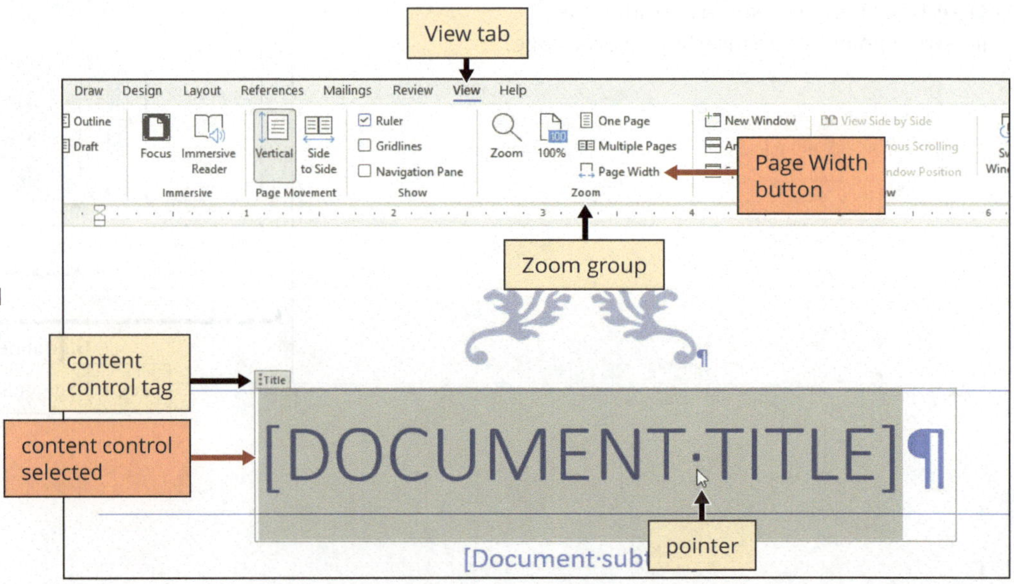

Figure 4–5

2

- Type **Meetings and Conferences** as the document title.

Q&A Why is my document title text capitalized?
Word automatically changes the text to uppercase letters.

- Click the [Subtitle] content control or its tag to select the content control (Figure 4–6).

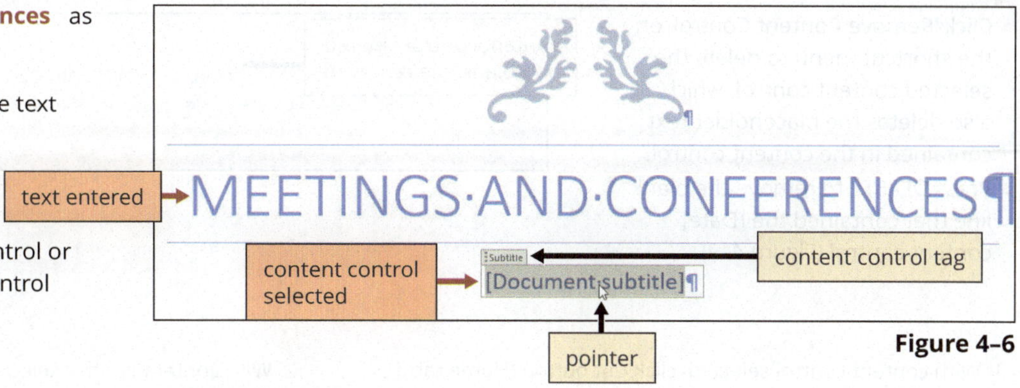

Figure 4–6

3

- Type **Your Satisfaction Is Our Priority** as the document subtitle.
- Scroll to the bottom of the cover page to display the company content control in the document window.
- Select the company content control and then type **Kapena Hotel and Conference Center** as the text.

Q&A Why is my company content control filled in?
Depending on settings, your content control already may display a company name.

- Select the address content control and then type **8510 Orchid Street, Honolulu, HI 96816; 808-555-7500; www.kapenahcc.com** as the text.
- Press END to deselect the content control (Figure 4–7).

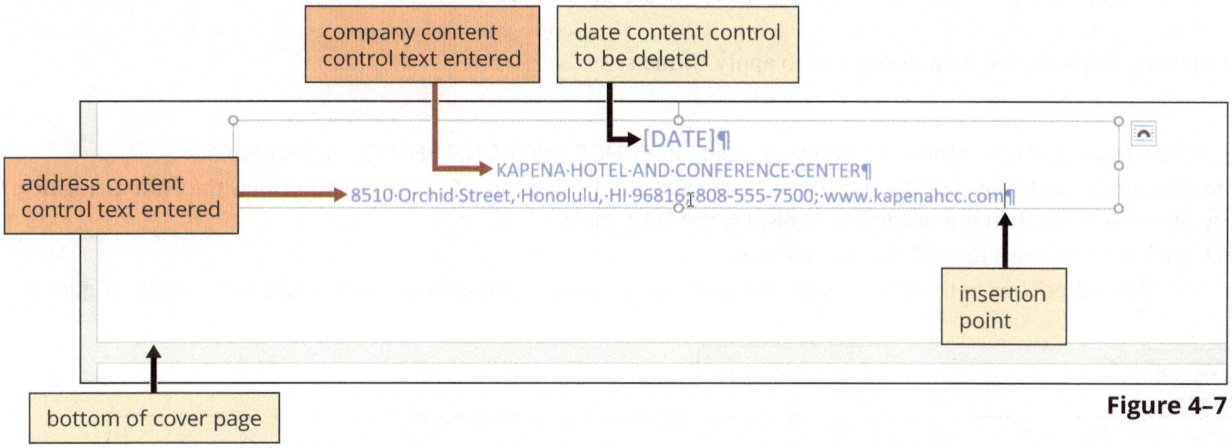

Figure 4–7

To Remove a Content Control

The following steps delete the [Date] content control. **Why?** You do not want the date to appear on the cover page.

1

- Right-click the [Date] content control to display a shortcut menu (Figure 4–8).

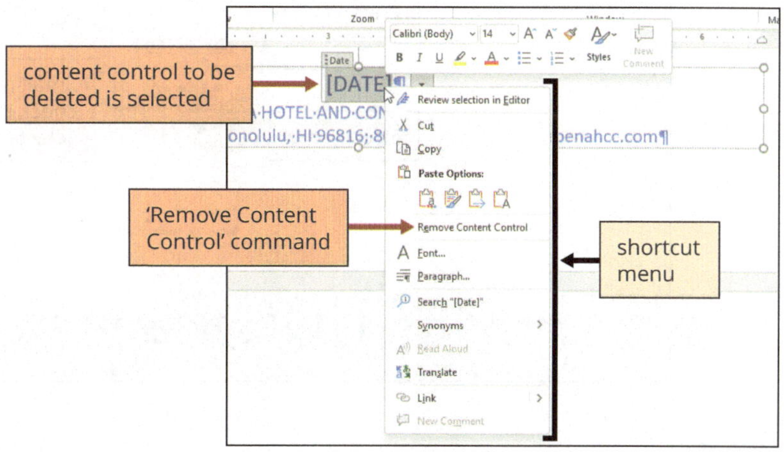

Figure 4–8

2

- Click 'Remove Content Control' on the shortcut menu to delete the selected content control, which also deletes the placeholder text contained in the content control.
- Press DELETE to remove the blank line that contained the [Date] content control (Figure 4–9).

Figure 4–9

Other Ways

1. With content control selected, click Cut button (Home tab | Clipboard group)
2. With content control selected, press CTRL+X or DELETE or BACKSPACE

To Format Characters in Small Caps and Modify Character Spacing

The next step in this project is to enter and format the document title text at the top of the cover page. Its characters are to be bold, and each letter in this text is formatted in **small caps**, which are letters that look like uppercase letters but are smaller than other uppercase letters in the document. Also, you want extra space between each character so that the text spans the width of the page.

Thus, the next steps apply the formats mentioned above using the Font dialog box. **Why?** Although you could use buttons on the Home tab to apply some of these formats, the small caps effect and expanded spacing are applied using the Font dialog box. The following steps use the Font dialog box to apply formats.

1

- Scroll up, if necessary, and select the text to be formatted, MEETINGS AND CONFERENCES, in this case.
- Display the Home tab and then click the Font Dialog Box Launcher (Home tab | Font group) to display the Font dialog box. If necessary, click the Font tab in the dialog box to display the Font sheet.
- Click Bold in the Font style list to bold the selected text.
- Click the Small caps check box in the Effects area so that each character is displayed as a small uppercase letter (Figure 4–10).

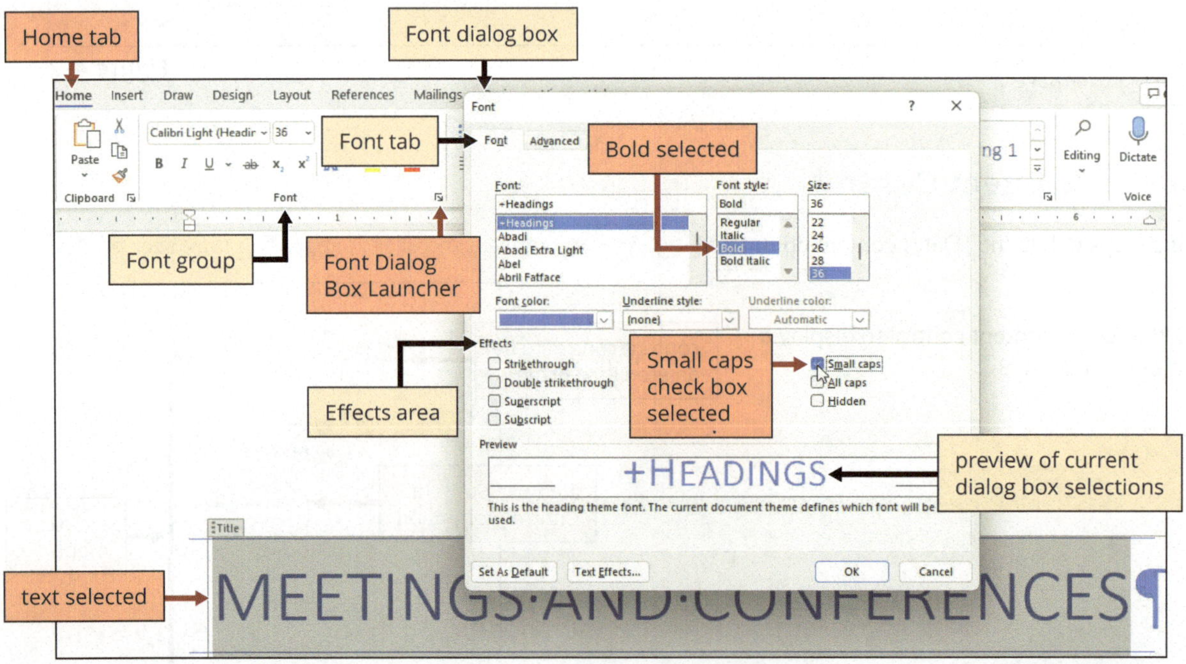

Figure 4–10

2

- Click the Advanced tab (Font dialog box) to display the Advanced sheet in the Font dialog box.
- Click the Spacing arrow in the Character Spacing area and then click Expanded to increase the amount of space between characters by 1 pt, which is the default.
- Double-click the value in the Spacing By box to select it and then type 4 because you want this amount of blank space to be displayed between each character.
- Click in any box in the dialog box for the change to take effect and display a preview of the entered value in the Preview area (Figure 4–11).

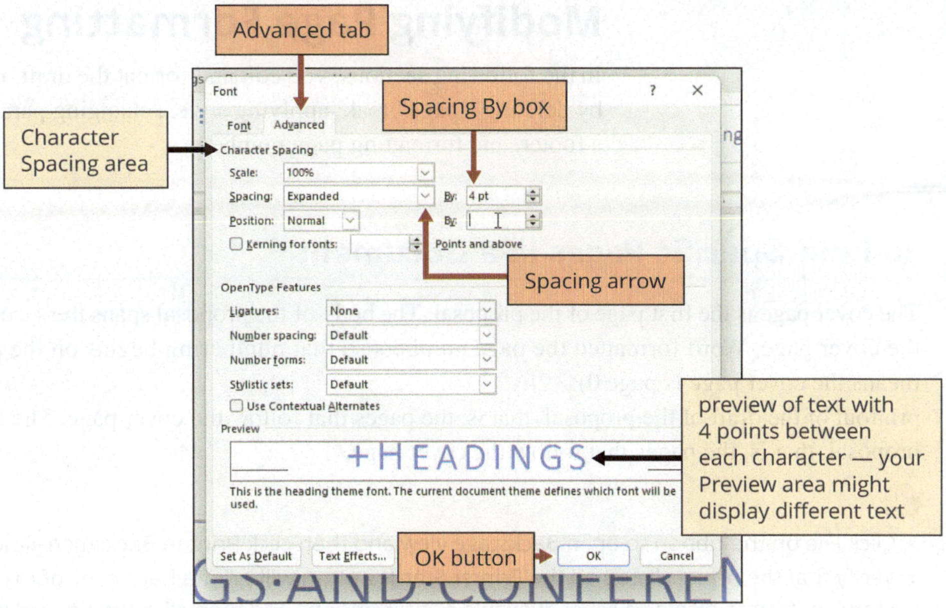

Figure 4–11

Q&A Can I click the Spacing By arrows instead of typing a value in the box?

Yes.

3

- Click OK to apply font changes to the selected text.
- Click anywhere to remove the selection from the text (Figure 4–12).

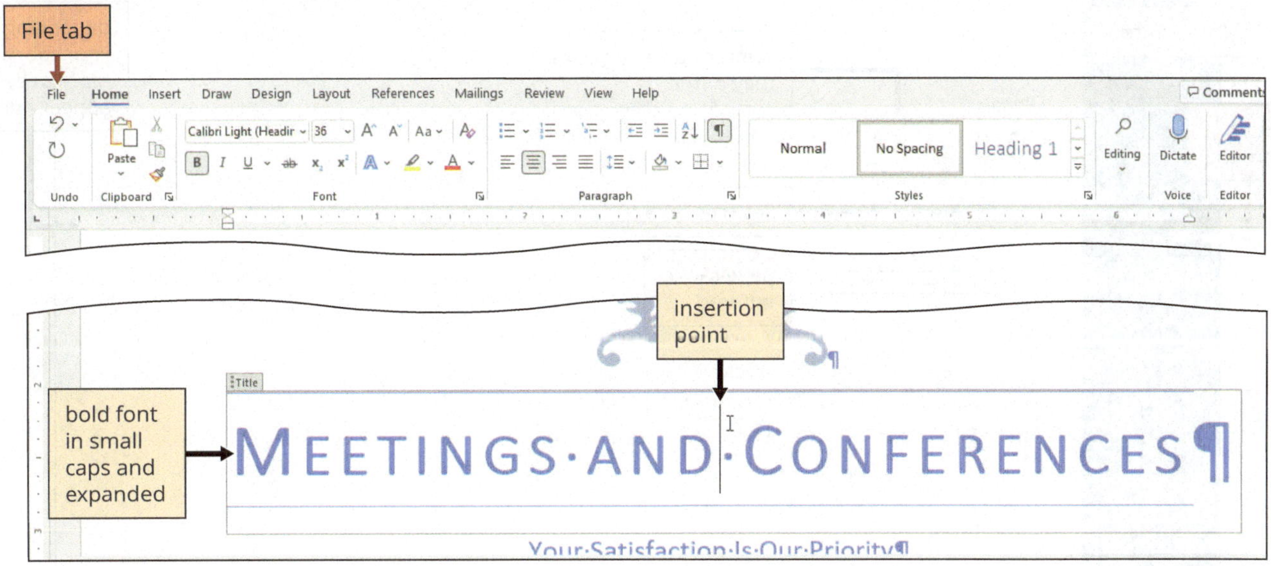

Figure 4–12

Other Ways

1. Right-click selected text (or, if using touch, tap 'Show Context Menu' button on Mini toolbar), click Font on shortcut menu, select formats (Font dialog box), click OK
2. Press CTRL+D, select formats (Font dialog box), click OK

Modifying Page Formatting

In the following sections, you edit and format the draft of the proposal that follows the cover page by deleting a page break, applying styles, changing paragraph indentation, inserting a header and a footer, and formatting page numbers.

To Print Specific Pages in a Document

The cover page is the first page of the proposal. The body of the proposal spans the second and third pages, but when you inserted the cover page, Word formatted the page numbers so that numbering begins on the page that follows the cover page (which means the cover page is page 0). **Why?** Cover pages typically do not have a page number on them. You would like to review a printout of the draft of the proposal, that is, the pages that follow the cover page. The following steps print only the body of the proposal, that is, the pages that follow the cover page.

1

- Click File on the ribbon to open Backstage view and then click Print in Backstage view to display the Print screen.
- Verify that the printer listed on the Printer Status button will print a hard copy of the document. If necessary, click the Printer Status button to display a list of available printer options and then click the desired printer to change the selected printer.
- Type **1–2** in the Pages text box in the Settings area of the Print screen (Figure 4–13).

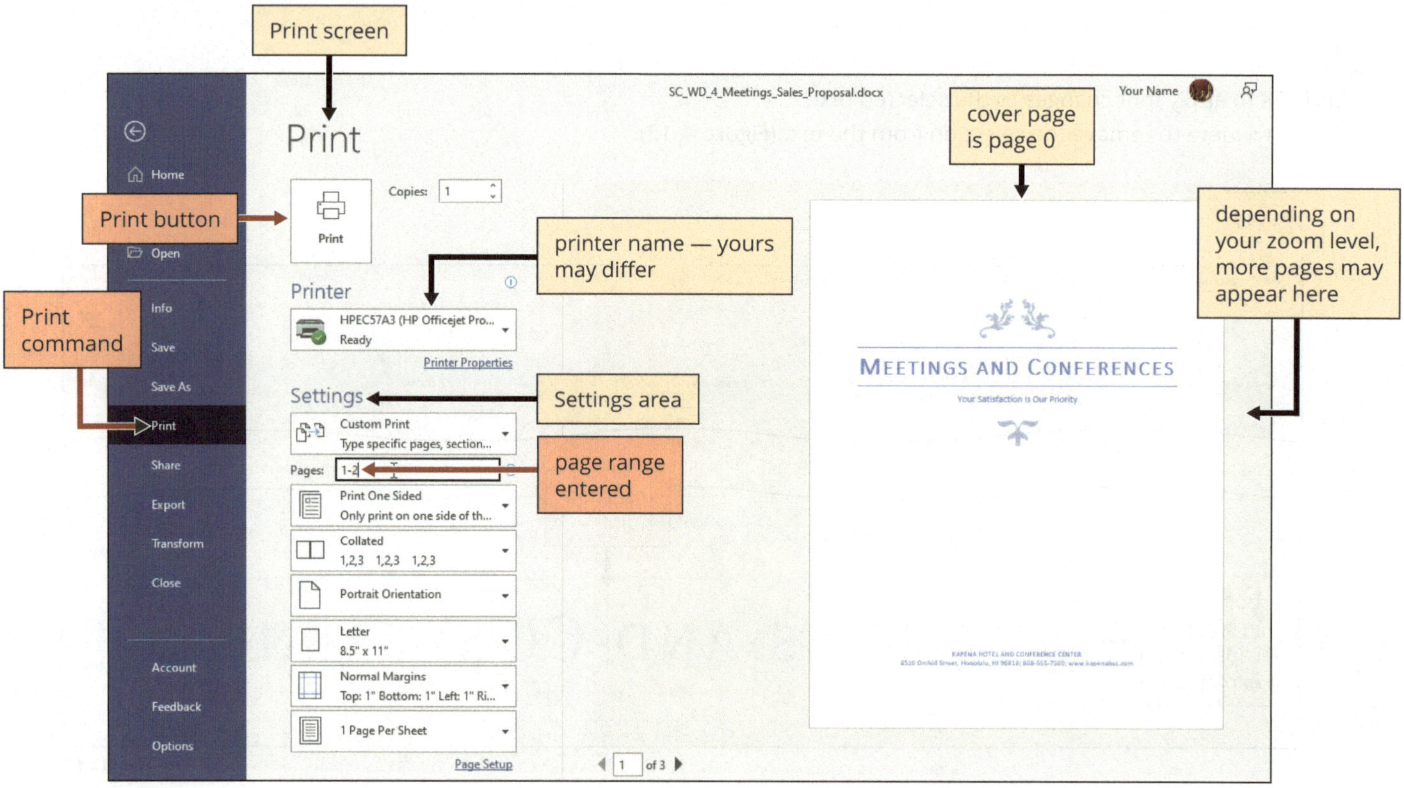

Figure 4–13

2

- Click the Print button to print the specified pages of the sales proposal (Figure 4–14).

Q&A How would I print pages from a certain point to the end of a document or just selected text?
You would enter the page number followed by a dash in the Pages text box. For example, 5- will print from page 5 to the end of the document. To print up to a certain page, put the dash first (e.g., -5 will print pages 1 through 5). To print part of a document, select the text or objects to be printed before opening Backstage view, click the first button in the Settings area, and then click Print Selection in the list.

Why does my document wrap on different words than Figure 4–14?
Differences in wordwrap may be related to the printer used by your computer.

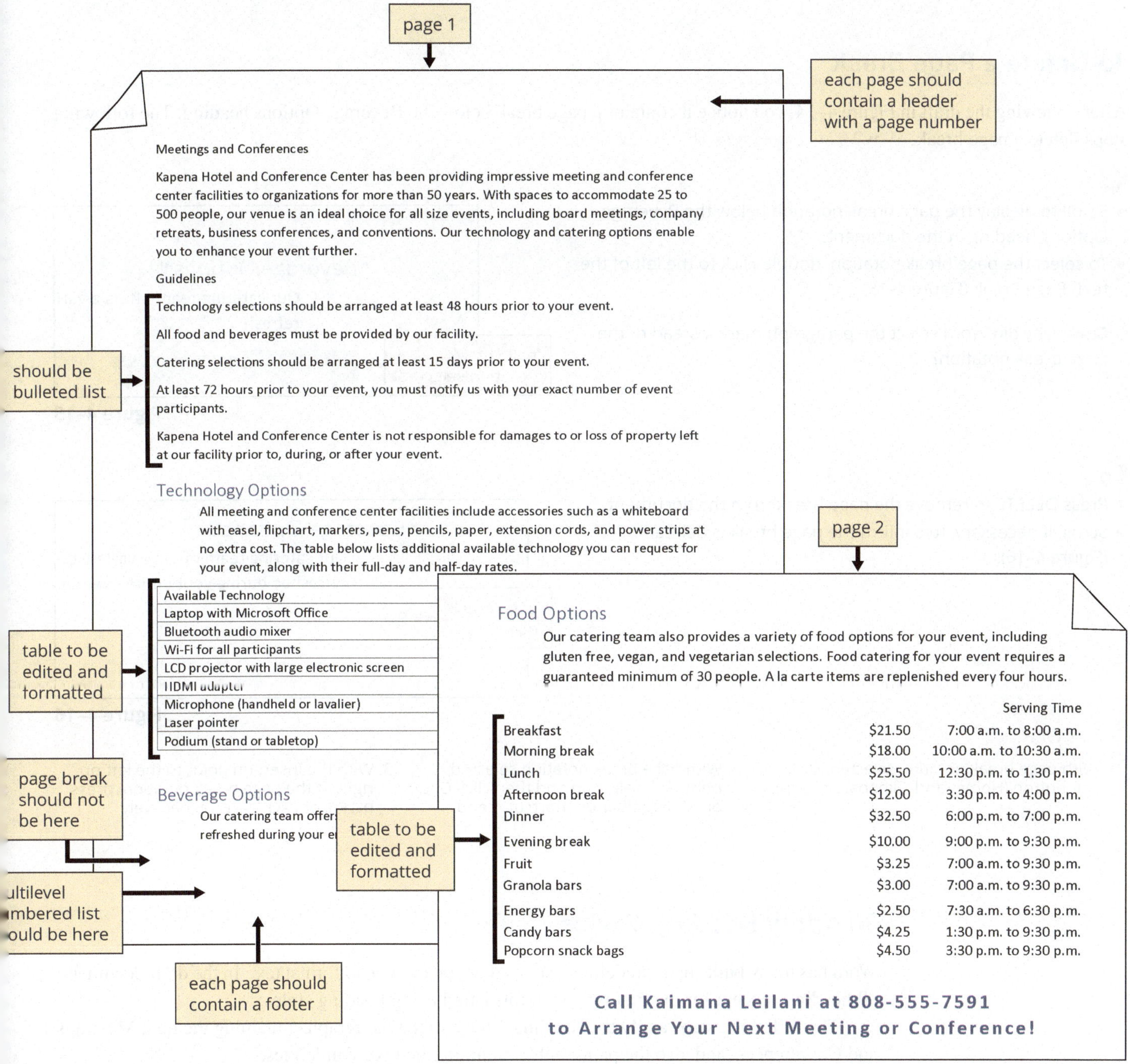

Meetings and Conferences

Kapena Hotel and Conference Center has been providing impressive meeting and conference center facilities to organizations for more than 50 years. With spaces to accommodate 25 to 500 people, our venue is an ideal choice for all size events, including board meetings, company retreats, business conferences, and conventions. Our technology and catering options enable you to enhance your event further.

Guidelines

Technology selections should be arranged at least 48 hours prior to your event.

All food and beverages must be provided by our facility.

Catering selections should be arranged at least 15 days prior to your event.

At least 72 hours prior to your event, you must notify us with your exact number of event participants.

Kapena Hotel and Conference Center is not responsible for damages to or loss of property left at our facility prior to, during, or after your event.

Technology Options

All meeting and conference center facilities include accessories such as a whiteboard with easel, flipchart, markers, pens, pencils, paper, extension cords, and power strips at no extra cost. The table below lists additional available technology you can request for your event, along with their full-day and half-day rates.

Available Technology
Laptop with Microsoft Office
Bluetooth audio mixer
Wi-Fi for all participants
LCD projector with large electronic screen
HDMI adapter
Microphone (handheld or lavalier)
Laser pointer
Podium (stand or tabletop)

Beverage Options

Our catering team offer[s] ... refreshed during your e[vent] ...

Food Options

Our catering team also provides a variety of food options for your event, including gluten free, vegan, and vegetarian selections. Food catering for your event requires a guaranteed minimum of 30 people. A la carte items are replenished every four hours.

		Serving Time
Breakfast	$21.50	7:00 a.m. to 8:00 a.m.
Morning break	$18.00	10:00 a.m. to 10:30 a.m.
Lunch	$25.50	12:30 p.m. to 1:30 p.m.
Afternoon break	$12.00	3:30 p.m. to 4:00 p.m.
Dinner	$32.50	6:00 p.m. to 7:00 p.m.
Evening break	$10.00	9:00 p.m. to 9:30 p.m.
Fruit	$3.25	7:00 a.m. to 9:30 p.m.
Granola bars	$3.00	7:00 a.m. to 9:30 p.m.
Energy bars	$2.50	7:30 a.m. to 6:30 p.m.
Candy bars	$4.25	1:30 p.m. to 9:30 p.m.
Popcorn snack bags	$4.50	3:30 p.m. to 9:30 p.m.

Call Kaimana Leilani at 808-555-7591
to Arrange Your Next Meeting or Conference!

Figure 4–14

Other Ways

1. Press CTRL+P; press ENTER

Consider This

What elements should the body of a sales proposal contain?

Be sure to include basic elements in your sales proposals:

- **Include an introduction, body, and conclusion.** The introduction could contain the subject, purpose, statement of problem, need, background, or scope. The body may include costs, benefits, supporting documentation, available or required facilities, feasibility, methods, timetable, materials, or equipment. The conclusion summarizes key points or requests an action.
- **Use headers and footers.** Headers and footers help to identify every page. A page number should be in either the header or footer. If the sales proposal should become disassembled, the reader can use the page numbers in the headers or footers to determine the order and pieces of your proposal.

To Delete a Page Break

After reviewing the draft in Figure 4–14, you notice it contains a page break below the Beverage Options heading. The following steps delete a page break. **Why?** This page break should not be in the proposal.

1

- Scroll to display the page break notation below the Beverage Options heading in the document.
- To select the page break notation, double-click to the left of the text, Page Break (Figure 4–15).

Q&A Why did Word select the paragraph mark instead of the page break notation?
You clicked to the right of the text, Page Break. Repeat Step 1.

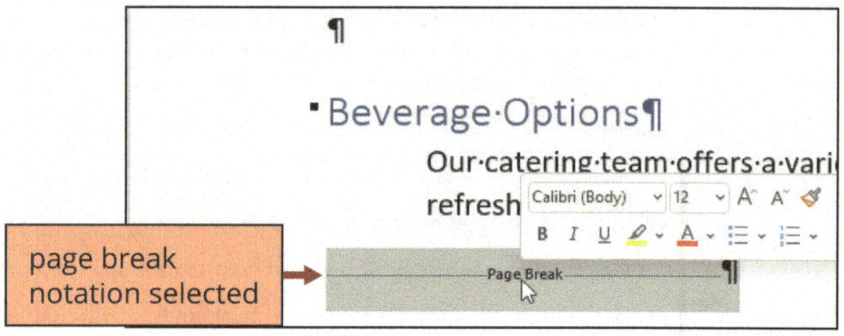

Figure 4–15

2

- Press DELETE to remove the page break from the document.
- Scroll, if necessary, to confirm the page break is deleted (Figure 4–16).

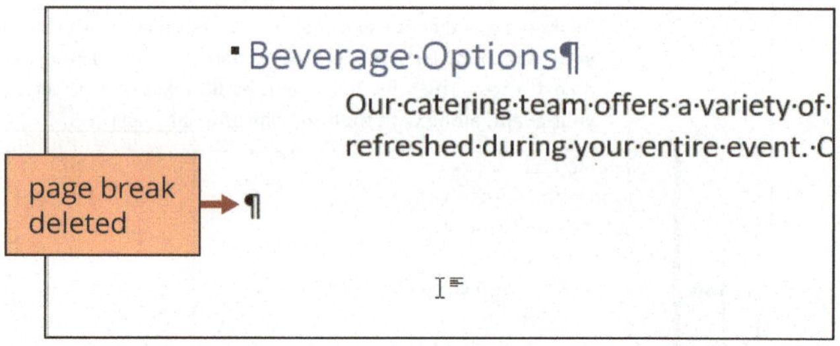

Figure 4–16

Other Ways

1. With page break notation selected, click Cut button (Home tab | Clipboard group)
2. With page break notation selected, right-click selection and then click Cut on Mini toolbar or shortcut menu
3. With the insertion point to the left or right of the page break notation, press DELETE or BACKSPACE, respectively

To Apply Heading Styles

Word has many built-in, or predefined, styles that you can use to format text. In the draft document, all headings except for the first two were formatted using heading styles.

The following steps apply the Heading 1 style to the paragraph containing the text, Meetings and Conferences, and also the paragraph containing the text, Guidelines.

1 Scroll to, if necessary, and then position the insertion point in the paragraph to be formatted with the Heading 1 style, in this case, the first line on the page below the cover page with the text, Meetings and Conferences.

2 Click Heading 1 in the Styles gallery (Home tab | Styles group) to apply the selected style to the paragraph containing the insertion point.

Q&A Why did a square appear on the screen near the left edge of the paragraph formatted with the Heading 1 style?

The square is a nonprinting character, like the paragraph mark, that indicates text to its right has a special paragraph format applied to it.

3 Position the insertion point in the next paragraph to be formatted with the Heading 1 style, in this case, the line containing the text, Guidelines.

4 Click Heading 1 in the Styles gallery (Home tab | Styles group) to apply the selected style to the paragraph containing the insertion point (Figure 4–17).

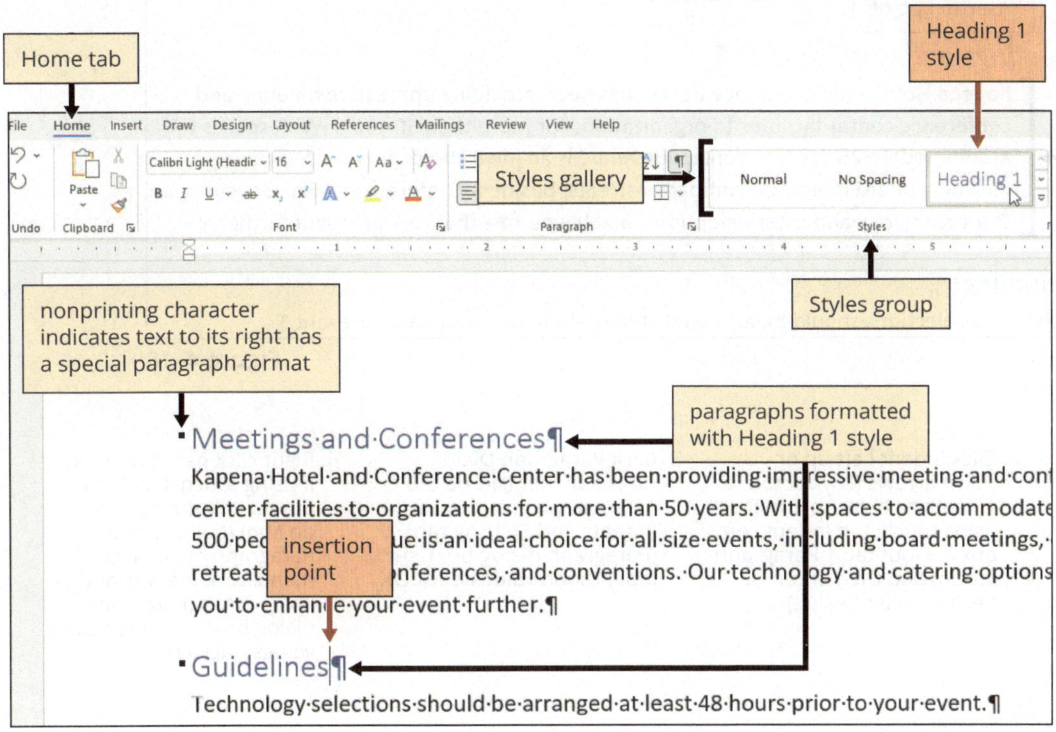

Figure 4–17

To Change the Left Paragraph Indent

The paragraphs in the proposal are indented from the left margin by one-half inch. **Why?** You want the headings to begin at the left margin and the paragraphs to be indented from the left margin. The Increase Indent and Decrease Indent buttons (Home tab | Paragraph group) change the left indent by one-half inch, respectively. The following step changes the left paragraph indent of the first paragraph in the proposal.

1

- Position the insertion point in the paragraph to indent, in this case, the paragraph that begins "Kapena Hotel and Conference Center has been..."
- Click the Increase Indent button (Home tab | Paragraph group) to indent the paragraph one-half inch from the left margin (Figure 4–18).
- **Experiment:** Repeatedly click the Increase Indent and Decrease Indent buttons (Home tab | Paragraph group) and watch the left edge of the current paragraph move in the document window. When you have finished experimenting, set the left indent so that it is one-half inch from the left margin as shown in Figure 4–18.

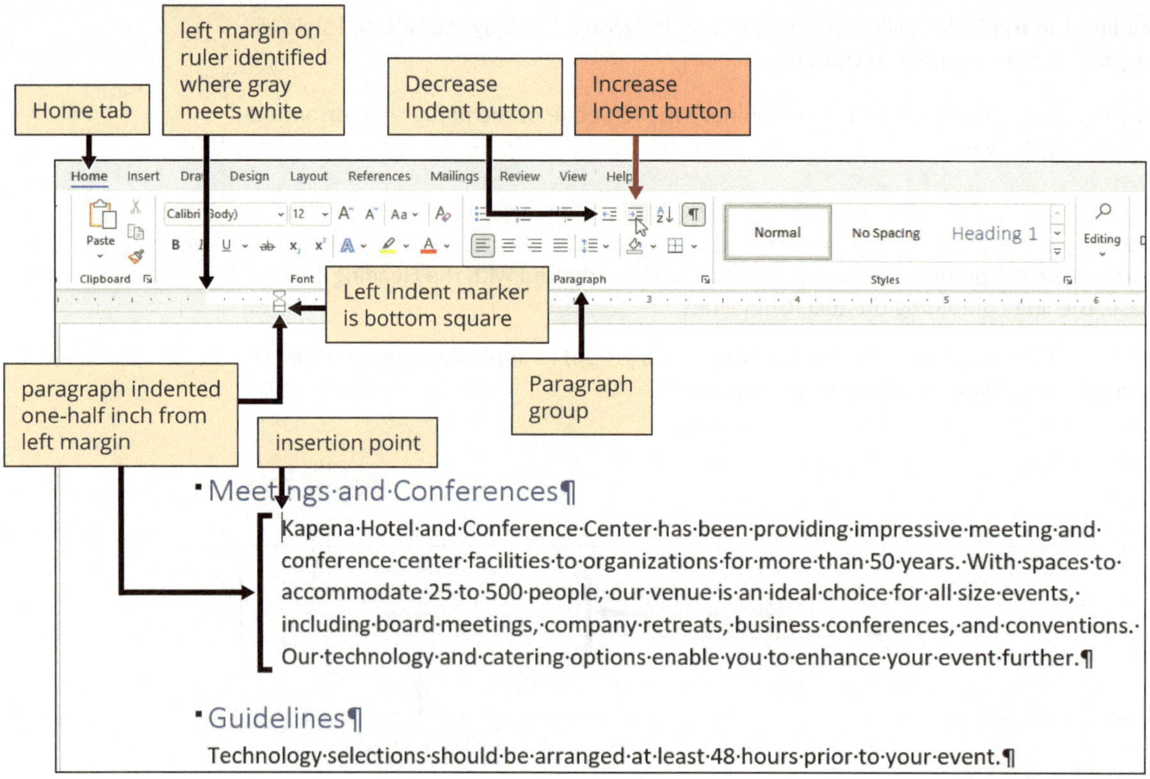

Figure 4–18

Other Ways

1. Drag Left Indent marker on ruler
2. Click Indent Left up or down arrows (Layout tab | Paragraph group) (or, if using touch, tap Indent Left box (Layout tab | Paragraph group) and then enter desired indent value)
3. Click Paragraph Dialog Box Launcher (Home tab | Paragraph group), click Indents and Spacing tab (Paragraph dialog box), set indentation values, click OK
4. Right-click paragraph (or, if using touch, tap 'Show Context Menu' button on Mini toolbar), click Paragraph on shortcut menu, click Indents and Spacing tab (Paragraph dialog box), set indentation values, click OK

To Insert a Different First Page Formatted Header

A header is information that appears at the top of each page in the document. A footer is information that appears at the bottom of each page. In this proposal, you want the header and footer you insert to appear on each page after the cover page. **Why?** You do not want the header to appear on the cover page. In Word, you can instruct the header and footer not to appear on the first page in a document. Word also provides several built-in preformatted header designs for you to insert in documents. The following steps insert a formatted header that does not appear on the first page of a document.

1

- Display the Insert tab.
- Click the Header button (Insert tab | Header & Footer group) to display the Header gallery.
- **Experiment:** Scroll through the list of built-in headers to see the variety of available formatted header designs. When finished, display the Filigree header design in the Header gallery, as shown in Figure 4–19.

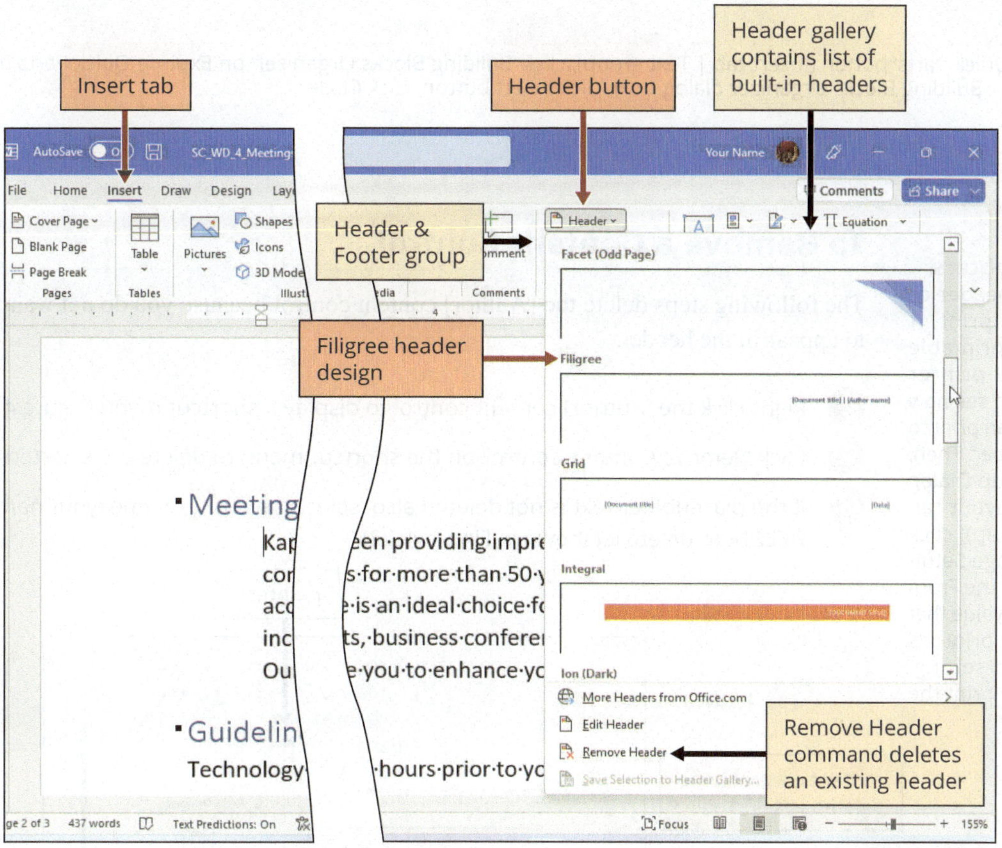

Figure 4–19

2

- Scroll to, if necessary, and then click the Filigree header design in the Header gallery to insert the formatted header, which contains the title and author content controls, at the top of the page.

Q&A Why choose the Filigree header design?
You want to use the same theme throughout the document, and the cover page used the Filigree design.

- If the 'Different First Page' check box (Header & Footer tab | Options group) is not selected, click it to select it so that this header does not appear on the cover page (Figure 4–20).

Q&A How would I delete a header?
You would click Remove Header in the Header gallery (shown in Figure 4–19).

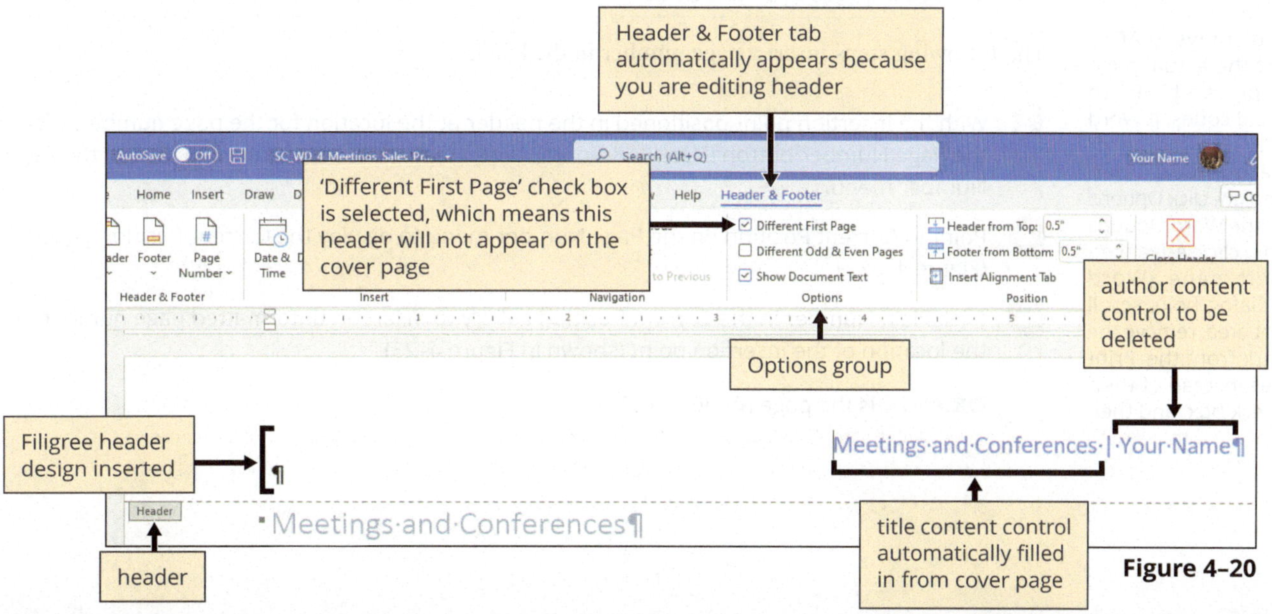

Figure 4–20

Other Ways

1. Click 'Explore Quick Parts' button (Insert tab | Text group), click 'Building Blocks Organizer' on Explore Quick Parts menu, select desired header (Building Blocks Organizer dialog box), click Insert button, click Close

BTW

Headers and Footers

If a portion of a header or footer does not print, it may be in a nonprintable area. Check the printer user instructions to see how close the printer can print to the edge of the paper. Then, click the Page Setup Dialog Box Launcher (Layout tab | Page Setup group), click the Layout tab (Page Setup dialog box), adjust the From edge text box to a value that is larger than the printer's minimum margin setting, click OK, and then print the document again.

To Remove a Content Control

The following steps delete the [Author] content control because you do not want the author name to appear in the header.

1. Right-click the [Author] content control to display a shortcut menu (Figure 4–21).
2. Click 'Remove Content Control' on the shortcut menu to delete the selected content control.
3. If the placeholder text is not deleted also, select the author name (your name) and press DELETE to delete it (shown in Figure 4–22).

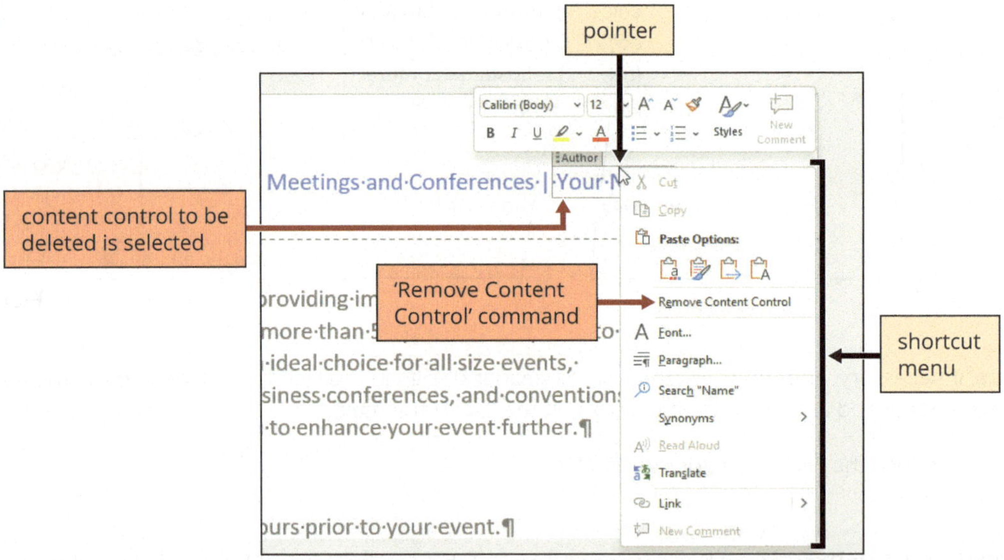

Figure 4–21

BTW

Page Numbers

If Word displays {PAGE} instead of the actual page number, press ALT+F9 to turn off field codes. If Word prints {PAGE} instead of the page number, open Backstage view, click Options to display the Word Options dialog box, click Advanced in the left pane (Word Options dialog box), scroll to the Print area, remove the check mark from the 'Print field codes instead of their values' check box, and then click OK.

To Insert Page Numbers

The following steps insert a page number in the header.

1. With the insertion point positioned in the header at the location for the page number, click the Page Number button (Header & Footer tab | Header & Footer group) to display the Page Number menu.
2. Point to Current Position on the Page Number menu to display the Current Position gallery (Figure 4–22).
3. Click Plain Number in the Current Position gallery to insert an unformatted page number at the location of the insertion point (shown in Figure 4–23).

Q&A Why is the page number a 1?

When you inserted the cover page, Word automatically removed the page number from the first page because numbering typically begins on the page after the cover page.

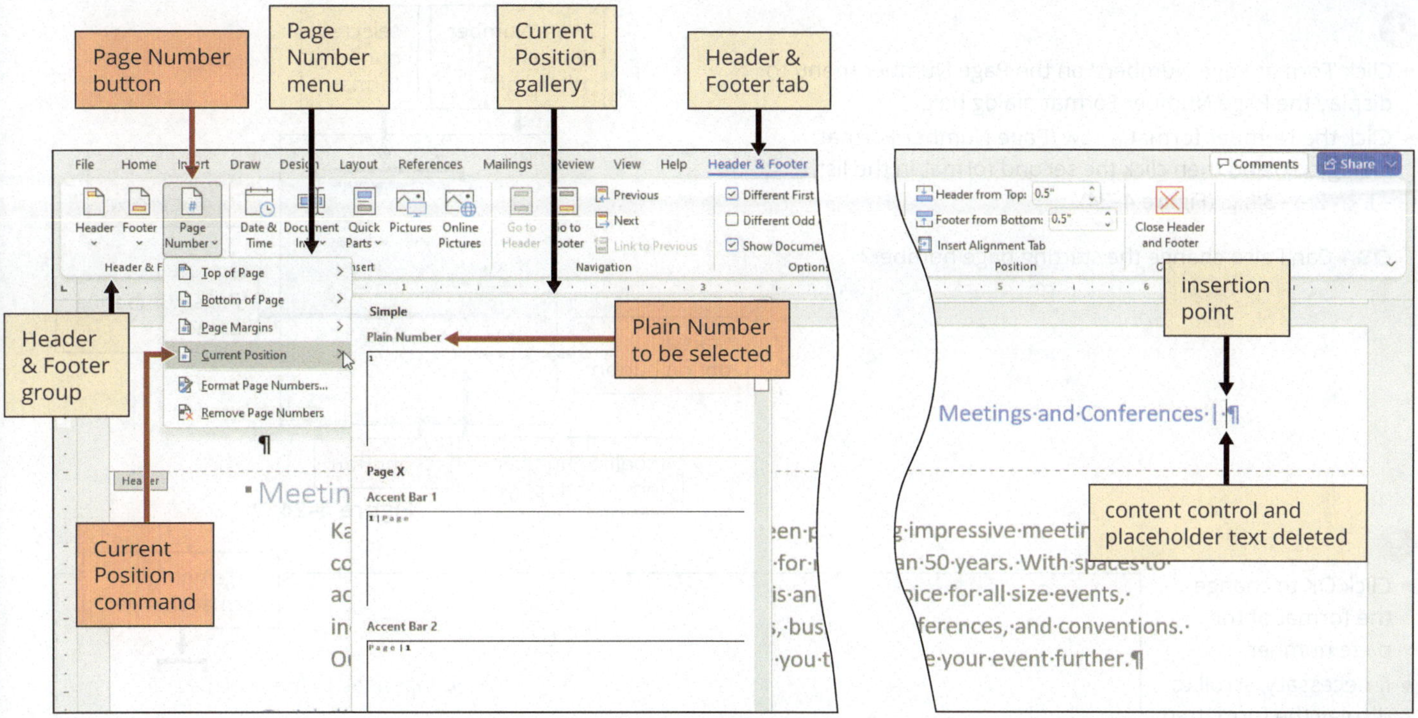

Figure 4–22

To Format Page Numbers

You would like the page number to display with dashes around it, - 1 -, instead of just the single number, 1. **Why?** You want the page number to be more noticeable. The following steps format the page numbers.

1

- Click the Page Number button (Header & Footer tab | Header & Footer group) to display the Page Number menu (Figure 4–23).

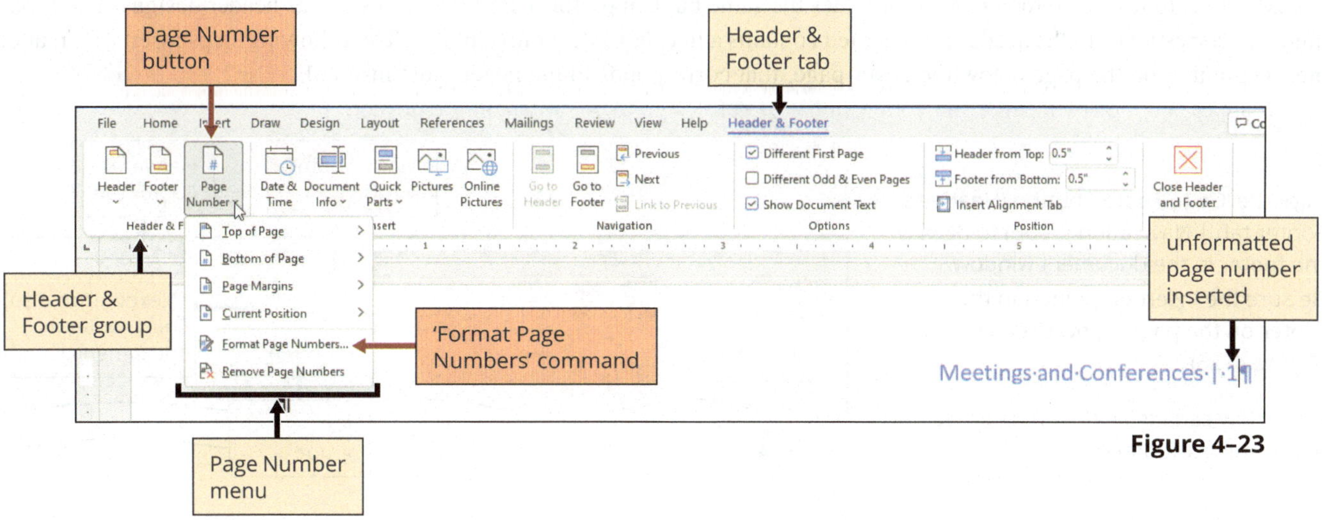

Figure 4–23

2

- Click 'Format Page Numbers' on the Page Number menu to display the Page Number Format dialog box.
- Click the Number format arrow (Page Number Format dialog box) and then click the second format in the list, - 1 -, - 2 -, - 3 -, ... (Figure 4–24).

Q&A Can I also change the starting page number?
Yes. Click the Start at option button in the Page numbering area (Page Number Format dialog box) and then enter the desired starting page number for the current page in the document.

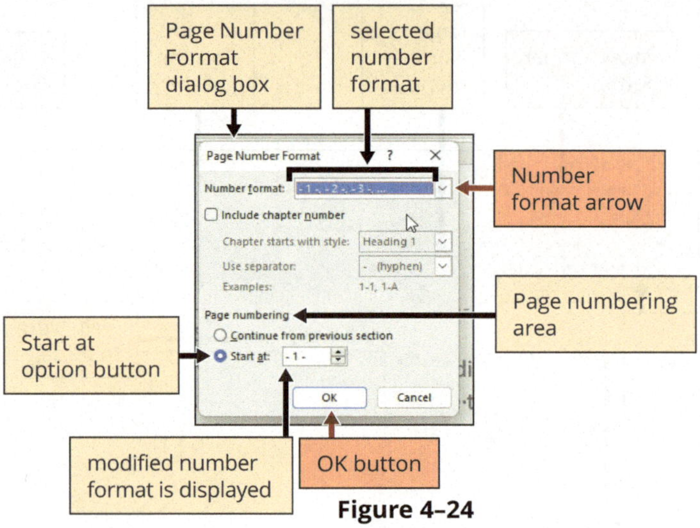

Figure 4–24

3

- Click OK to change the format of the page number.
- If necessary, scroll to display the formatted page number in the document window and then click in the header (Figure 4–25).

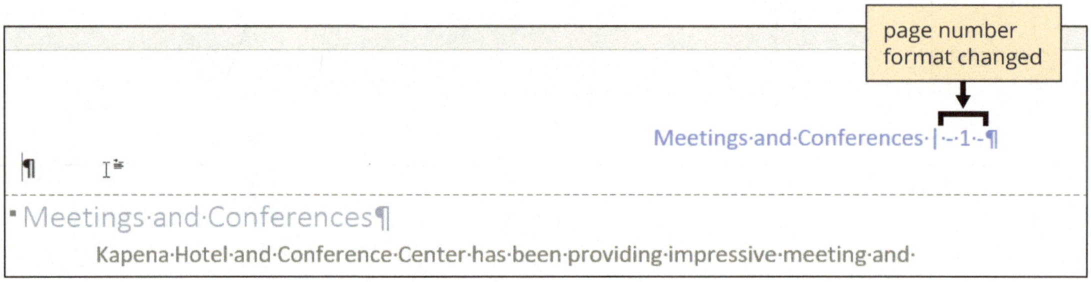

Figure 4–25

Other Ways

1. Click Page Number button (Insert tab | Header & Footer group), click 'Format Page Numbers' on Page Number menu, set page formats (Page Number Format dialog box), click OK

To Insert a Different First Page Formatted Footer

The next step is to insert the footer. Word provides the same built-in preformatted footer designs as header designs. The footer design that corresponds to the header just inserted contains a line and a decorative image. The following steps insert a formatted footer, beginning on the page below the cover page, that corresponds to the header just inserted. **Why?** You do not want the footer to appear on the cover page, and you want the footer design to complement the header.

1

- Click the 'Go to Footer' button (Header & Footer tab | Navigation group) to display the footer in the document window.
- Be sure the insertion point is in the footer on the page below the cover page (Figure 4–26).

Q&A How can I tell if the insertion point is in the correct footer?
If your footer label says 'First Page Footer' instead of just the text, Footer, click the Next button (Header & Footer tab | Navigation group) to position the insertion point in the next footer.

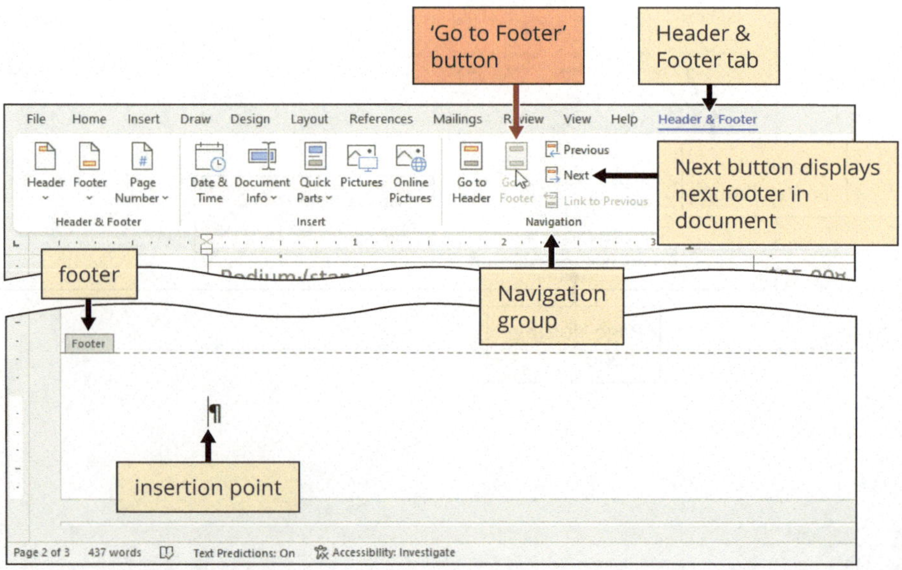

Figure 4–26

2

- Click the Footer button (Header & Footer tab | Header & Footer group) to display the Footer gallery.
- **Experiment:** Scroll through the list of built-in footers to see the variety of available formatted footer designs. When finished, display the Filigree footer design in the Footer gallery, as shown in Figure 4–27.

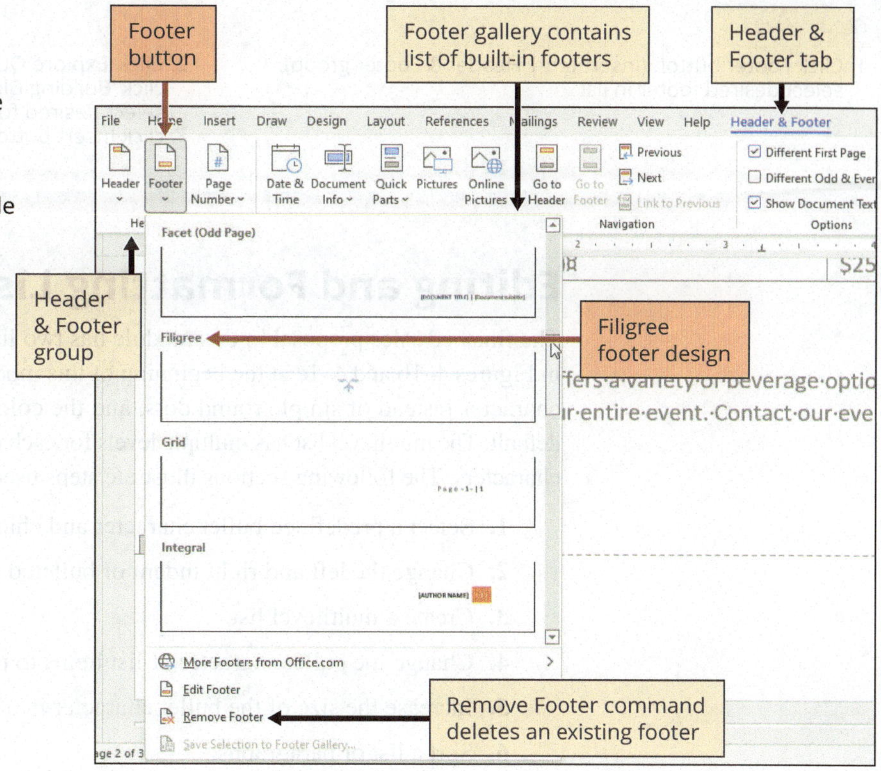

Figure 4–27

3

- Click the Filigree footer design to insert the formatted footer in the document.
- If the 'Different First Page' check box (Header & Footer tab | Options group) is not selected, click it to select the button so that this footer does not appear on the cover page (Figure 4–28).

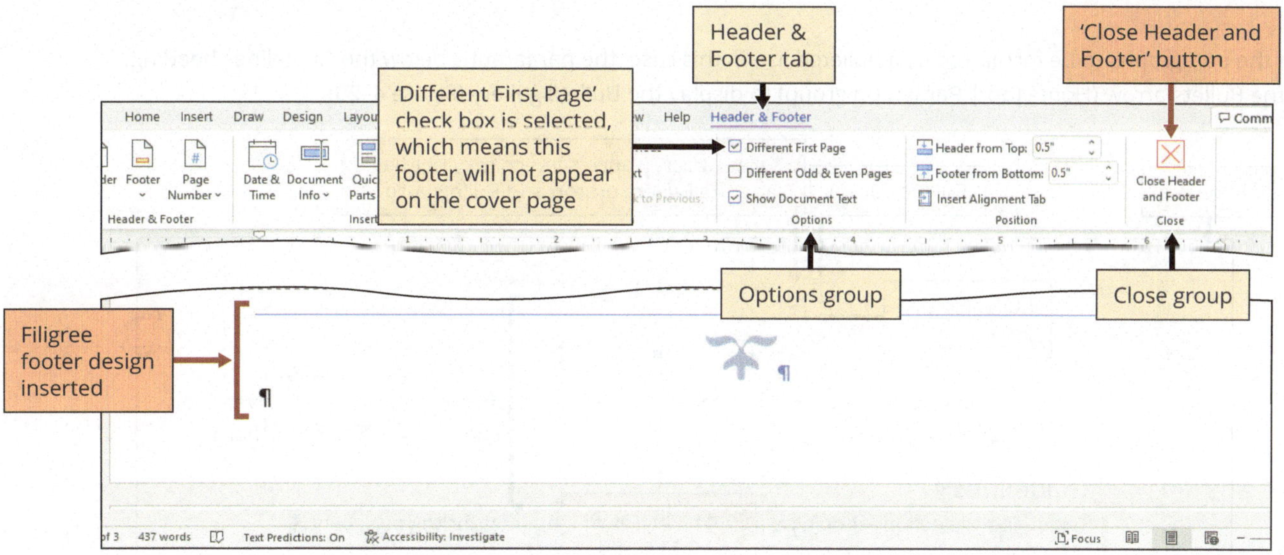

Figure 4–28

4

- Click the 'Close Header and Footer' button (Header & Footer tab | Close group) to close the header and footer.

Q&A How would I delete a footer?
You would click Remove Footer in the Footer gallery (shown in Figure 4–27).

- Save the sales proposal again with the same file name in the same storage location.

Other Ways

1. Click Footer button (Insert tab | Header & Footer group), select desired footer in list
2. Click 'Explore Quick Parts' button (Insert tab | Text group), click 'Building Blocks Organizer' on Explore Quick Parts menu, select desired footer (Building Blocks Organizer dialog box), click Insert button, click Close

Editing and Formatting Lists

The finished sales proposal in this module has two lists: a bulleted list and a multilevel list (shown in Figures 4–1b and 4–1c at the beginning of this module). The bulleted list uses a predefined bullet character instead of simple round dots, and the color of the bullet character is changed from the default. The multilevel list has multiple levels for each item and also uses a picture for one of the bullet characters. The following sections illustrate steps used to edit and format the lists in the proposal:

1. Select a predefined bullet character and change its color.
2. Change the left and right indent of bulleted paragraphs.
3. Create a multilevel list.
4. Change the bullet character of list items to picture bullets.
5. Increase the size of the bullet character in a multilevel list.
6. Sort a list of paragraphs.

To Select a Predefined Bullet Character for a List

The paragraphs below the heading, Guidelines, should be a bulleted list. Instead of simply clicking the Bullets button to apply the default bullet character, you will select a predefined character for the bulleted list. **Why?** You want to use a more visually appealing bullet for this list. The following steps format the bullets in a list from the default round dot to a predefined bullet character.

1

- Select the paragraphs to be formatted as a bulleted list, in this case, the paragraphs below the Guidelines heading.
- Click the Bullets arrow (Home tab | Paragraph group) to display the Bullets gallery (Figure 4–29).

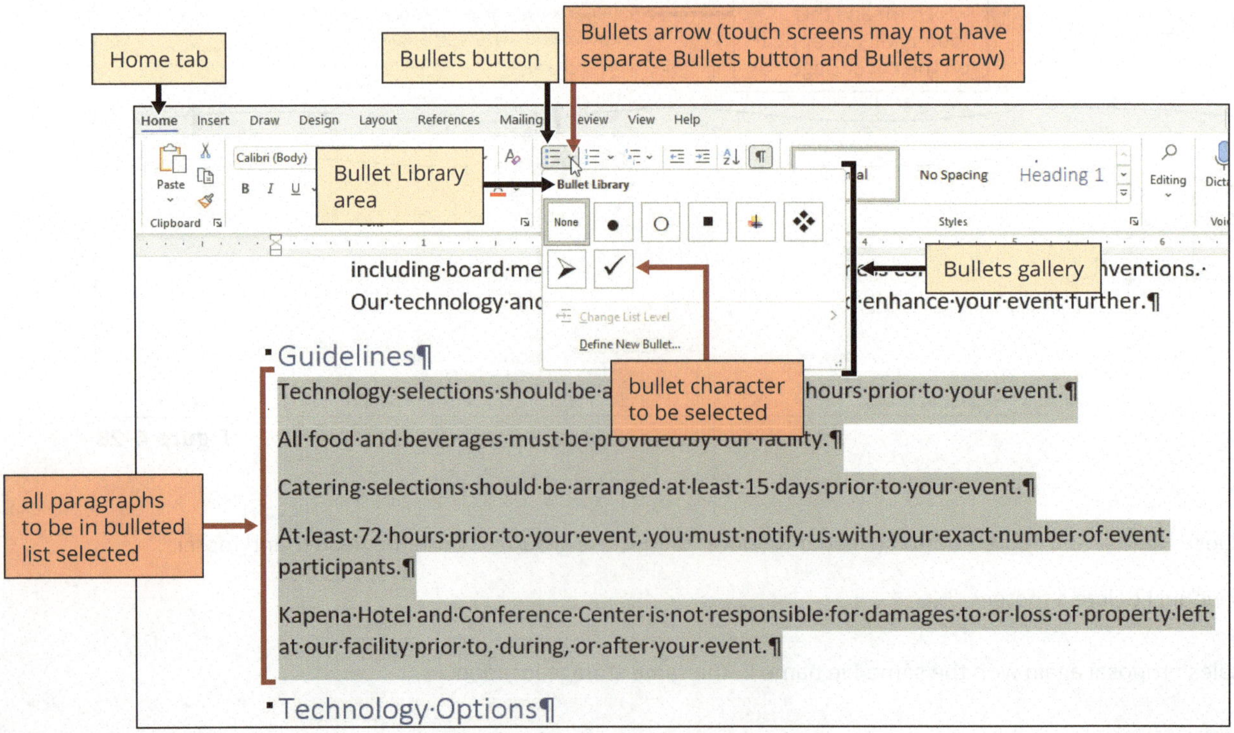

Figure 4–29

2

- Click the desired predefined bullet character in the Bullet Library area, in this case, the checkmark symbol, to format the selected paragraphs with the selected bullet character (shown in Figure 4–30).

To Change the Bullet Color

The predefined bullet character is colored blue in the proposal. **Why?** You want the bullet character color to complement the cover page and header and footer colors. The following steps change the color of bullet characters in a list.

1

- With the bulleted list selected, click the Bullets arrow (Home tab | Paragraph group) to display the Bullets gallery again (Figure 4–30).

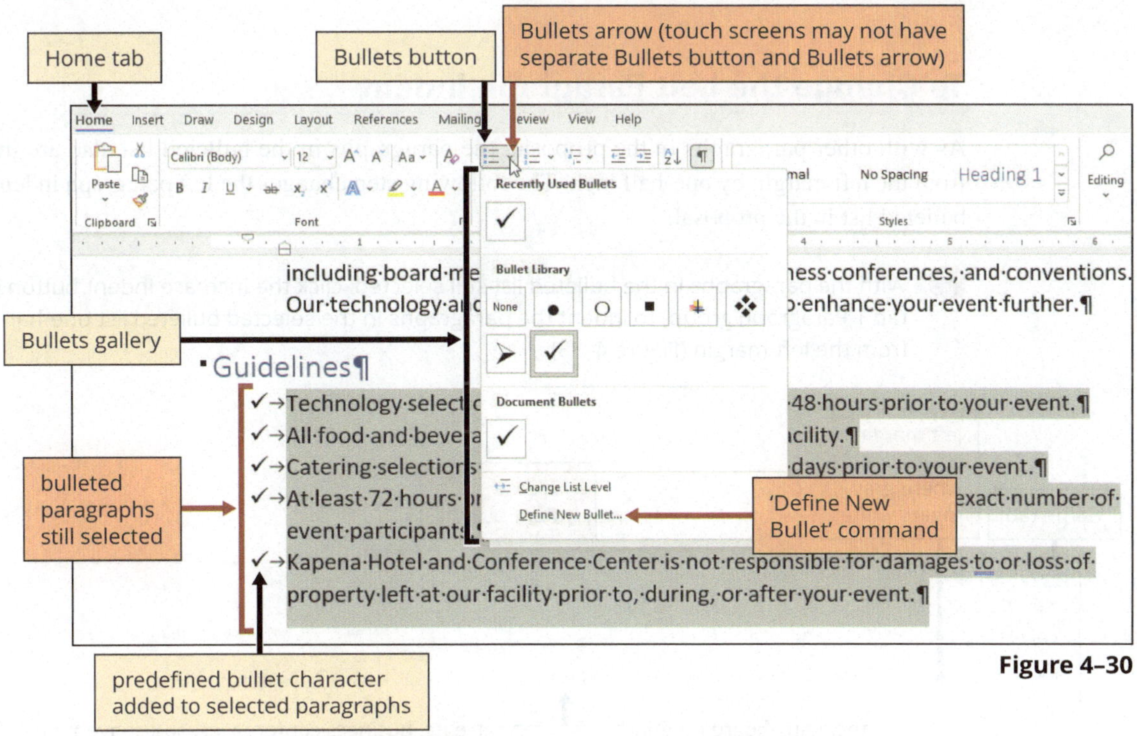

Figure 4–30

2

- Click 'Define New Bullet' in the Bullets gallery to display the Define New Bullet dialog box.
- Click the Font button (Define New Bullet dialog box) to display the Font dialog box.
- Click the Font color arrow (Font dialog box) and then click 'Blue, Accent 1, Darker 25%' (fifth color in fifth row) in the color gallery (Figure 4–31).

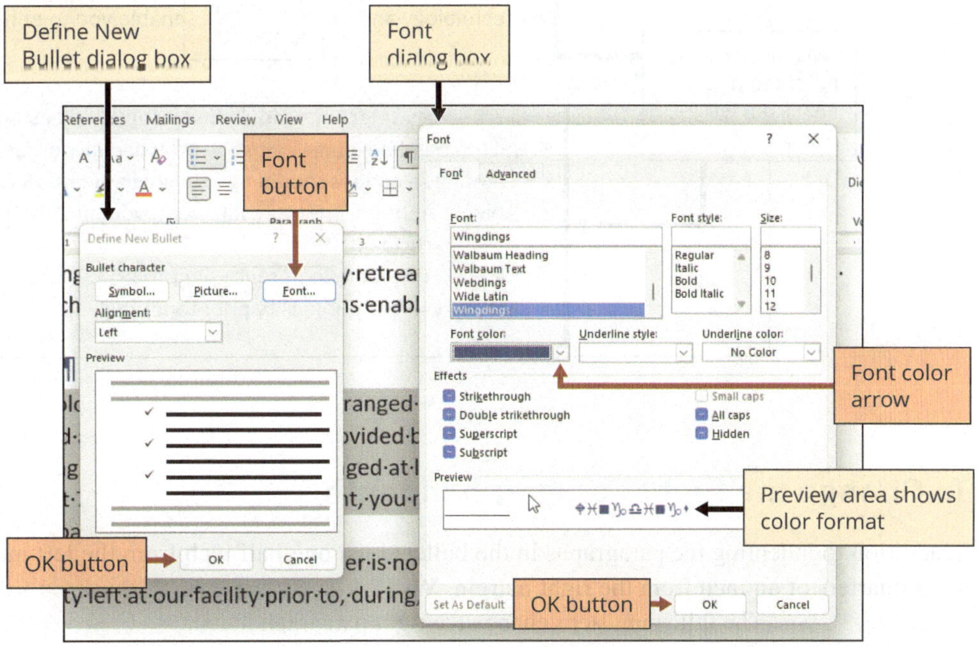

Figure 4–31

3

- Click OK (Font dialog box) to change the color of the bullet character to the selected color.
- Click OK (Define New Bullet dialog box) to change the color of the bullet character in the selected list in the document (Figure 4–32).

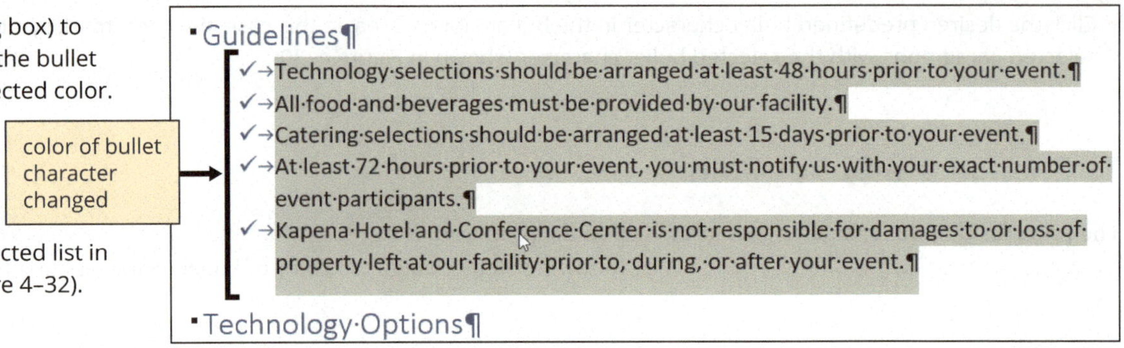

Figure 4–32

To Change the Left Paragraph Indent

As with other paragraphs in the proposal, the paragraphs in the bulleted list also are indented from the left margin by one-half inch. The following step changes the left paragraph indent of the bulleted list in the proposal.

1 With the paragraphs in the bulleted list still selected, click the Increase Indent button (Home tab | Paragraph group) to indent the paragraphs in the selected bulleted list one-half inch from the left margin (Figure 4–33).

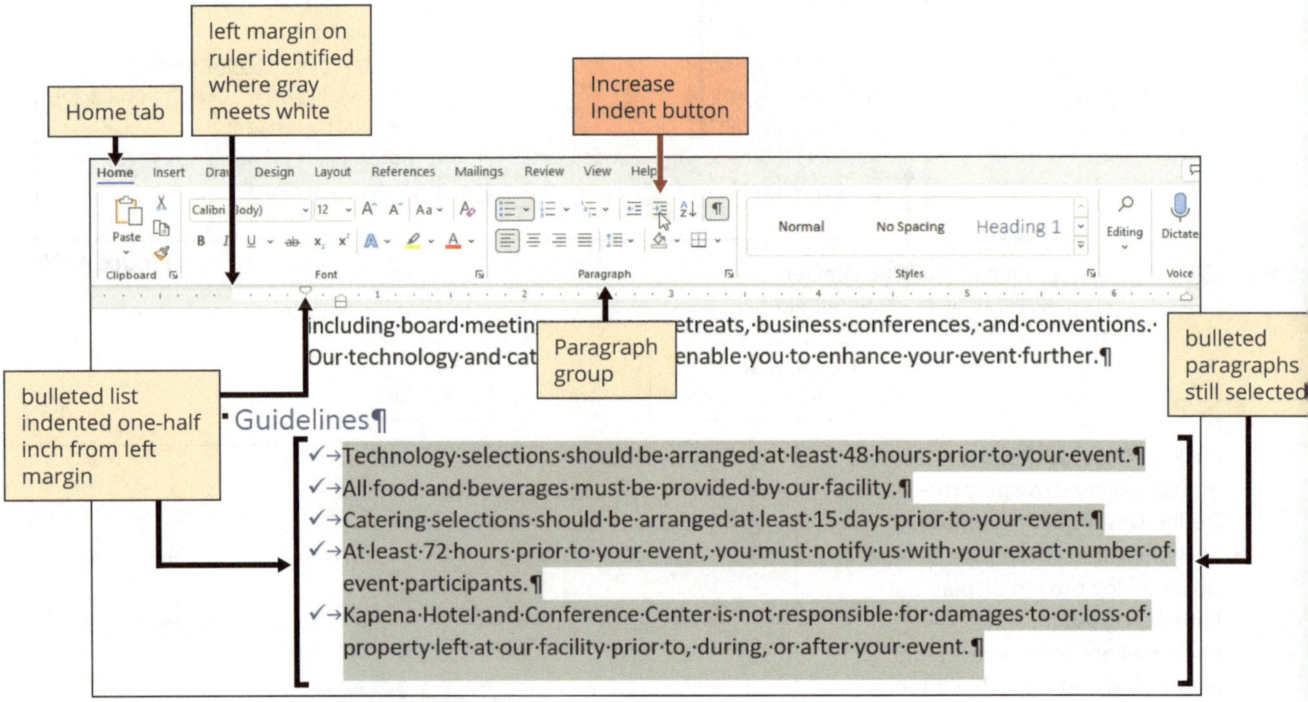

Figure 4–33

To Change the Right Paragraph Indent

In addition to indenting the paragraphs in the bulleted list one-half inch from the left margin, you also want to indent them three-quarters of an inch from the right margin. **Why?** You do not want the bulleted list paragraphs to extend as far as the paragraphs of text. The following steps change the right paragraph indent.

1

- With the paragraphs to format still selected, position the pointer on the Right Indent marker on the ruler (Figure 4–34).

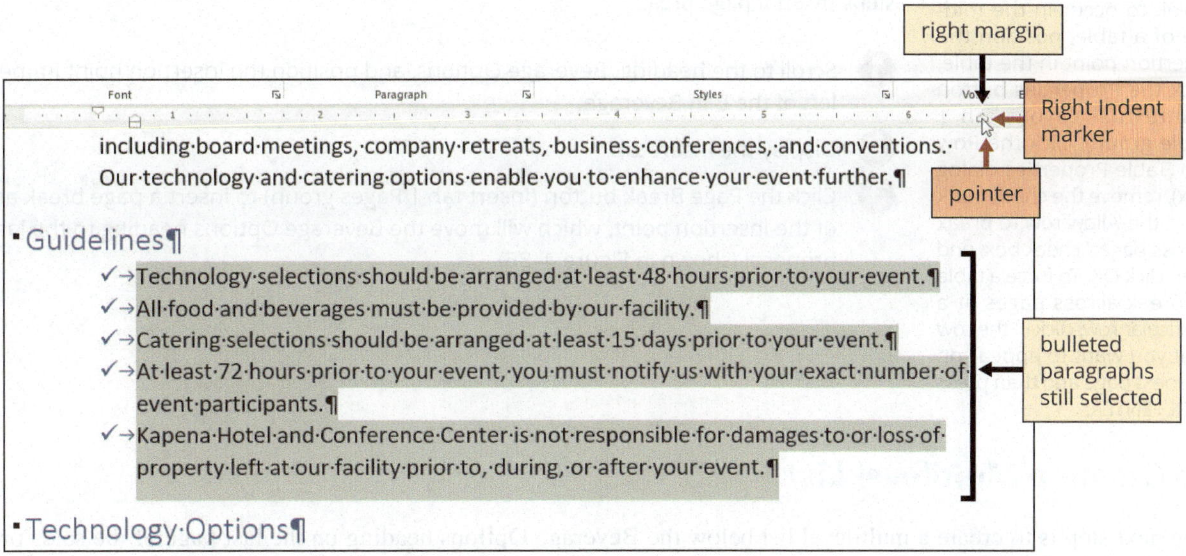

Figure 4–34

2

- Drag the Right Indent marker inward to the 6.25" mark on the ruler (Figure 4–35).

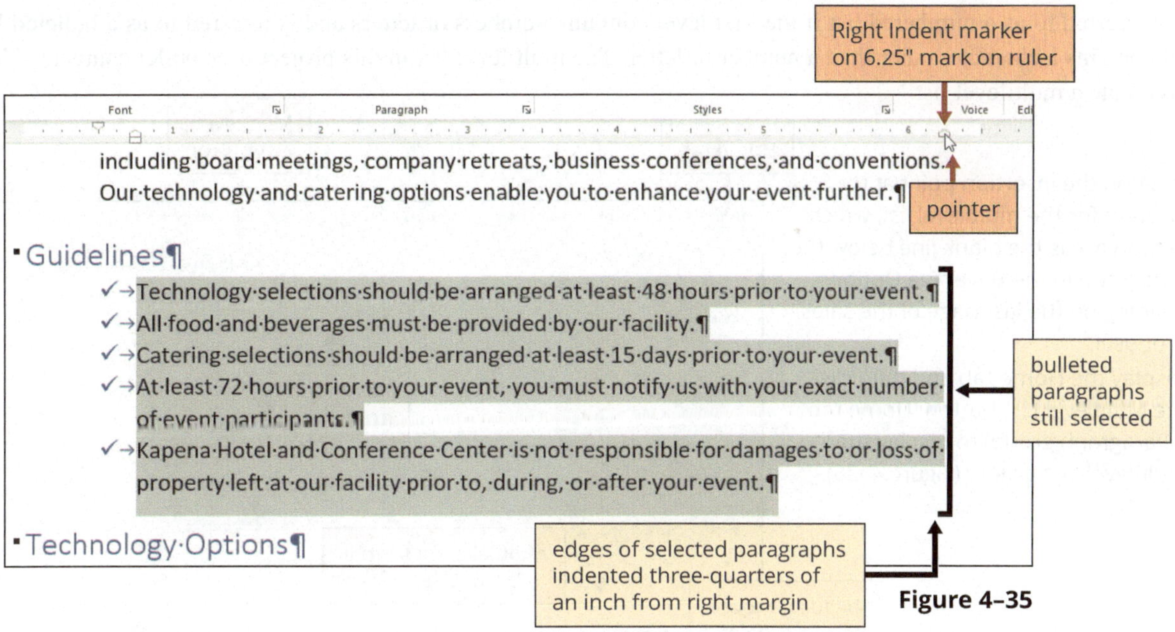

Figure 4–35

Other Ways

1. Click Indent Right up or down arrows (Layout tab | Paragraph group) (or, if using touch, tap Indent Right box (Layout tab | Paragraph group) and then enter desired indent value)
2. Click Paragraph Dialog Box Launcher (Home tab | Paragraph group), click Indents and Spacing tab (Paragraph dialog box), set indentation values, click OK
3. Right-click paragraph (or, if using touch, tap 'Show Context Menu' button on Mini toolbar), click Paragraph on shortcut menu, click Indents and Spacing tab (Paragraph dialog box), set indentation values, click OK

BTW

Page Breaks and Tables

If you do not want a page break to occur in the middle of a table, position the insertion point in the table, click the Properties button (contextual Layout tab | Table group), click the Row tab (Table Properties dialog box), remove the check mark from the 'Allow row to break across pages' check box, and then click OK. To force a table to break across pages at a particular row, click in the row that you want to appear on the next page and then press CTRL+ENTER.

To Insert a Page Break

The Beverage Options heading should appear at the beginning of the next page. The following steps insert a page break.

1. Scroll to the heading, Beverage Options, and position the insertion point immediately to the left of the B in Beverage.
2. Display the Insert tab.
3. Click the Page Break button (Insert tab | Pages group) to insert a page break at the location of the insertion point, which will move the Beverage Options heading to the last page of the proposal (shown in Figure 4–36).

To Create a Multilevel List

The next step is to create a multilevel list below the Beverage Options heading on the last page of the sales proposal in this module (shown in Figure 4–1c at the beginning of this module). **Why?** You would like to list the bottled and bulk beverages offered by the catering team.

A **multilevel list** is a list that contains several levels of list items, with each lower level displaying a different numeric, alphabetic, or bullet character. In a multilevel list, the first level is displayed at the left edge of the list and subsequent levels are indented; that is, the second level is indented below the first, the third level is indented below the second level, and so on. The list is referred to as a numbered list if the first level contains numbers or letters and is referred to as a bulleted list if the first level contains a character other than a number or letter. The multilevel list in this project uses bullet characters. The following steps create a multilevel list.

1

- Position the insertion point at the location for the multilevel list, which in this case is the blank line below the paragraph in the Beverage Options heading on the last page of the sales proposal.
- Display the Home tab and then click the Multilevel List button (Home tab | Paragraph group) to display the Multilevel List gallery (Figure 4–36).

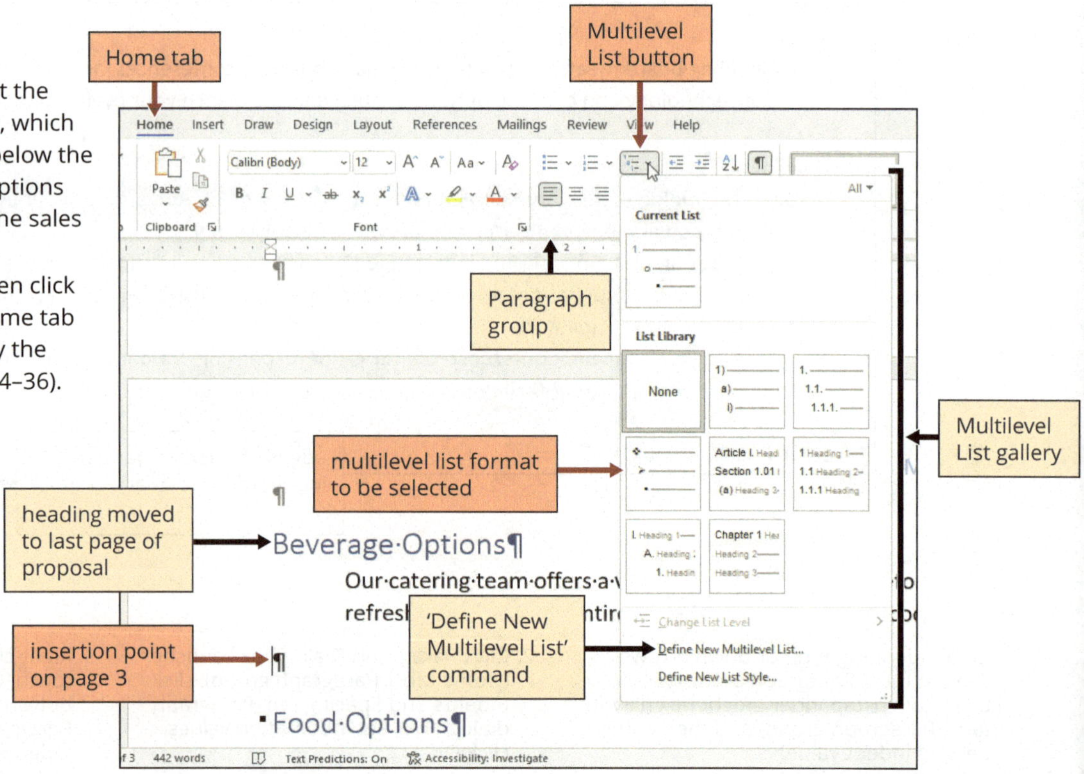

Figure 4–36

2

- Click the desired format in the Multilevel List gallery (shown in Figure 4–36) to display the current paragraph as a multilevel list item using the selected multilevel list format.
- Click the Increase Indent button (Home tab | Paragraph group) to indent the list one-half inch from the left margin.

Q&A What if I wanted a different number format?
You would click the Multilevel List button (Home tab | Paragraph group) and then select the desired format in the Multilevel List gallery, or click 'Define New Multilevel List' in the Multilevel List gallery (shown in Figure 4–36) to define your own format.

- Type **Bottled beverages** as a first-level list item and then press ENTER, which automatically places the next bullet for the current level at the beginning of the next line (Figure 4–37).

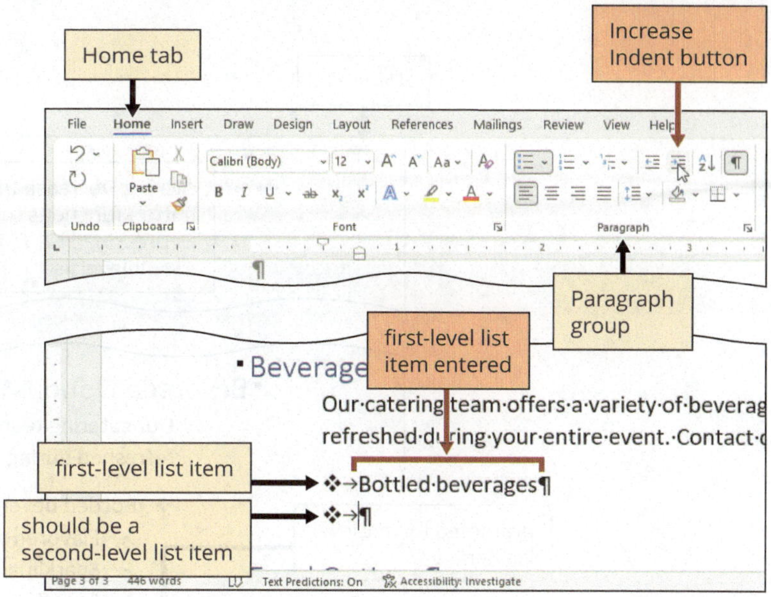

Figure 4–37

3

- Press TAB to demote the current list item to the next lower level, which is indented below the higher-level list item.

4

- Type **Flavored water** as a second-level list item and then press ENTER, which automatically places the next sequential list item for the current level on the next line.
- Type **Sparkling water** as a second-level list item and then press ENTER.
- Type **Soda** as a second-level list item and then press ENTER (Figure 4–38).

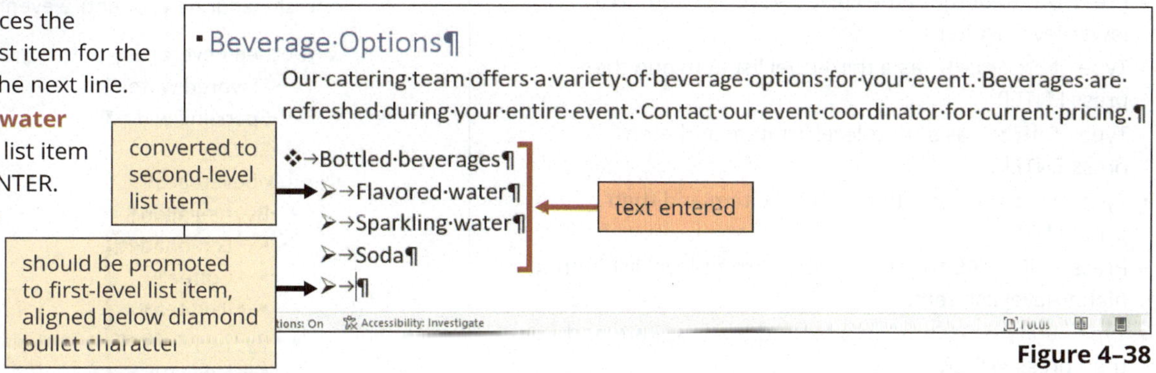

Figure 4–38

5

- Press SHIFT+TAB to promote the current-level list item to a higher-level list item.

Q&A Can I use buttons on the ribbon instead of pressing TAB or SHIFT+TAB to promote and demote list items?
Yes. With the insertion point in the item to adjust, you can click the Increase Indent or Decrease Indent button (Home tab | Paragraph group) or right-click the list item, click 'Adjust List Indents' on the shortcut menu, and select the desired options in the dialog box.

6

- Type **Bulk beverages** as a first-level list item and then press ENTER.
- Press TAB to demote the current level list item to a lower-level list item.
- Type **By the gallon** as a second-level list item and then press ENTER (Figure 4–39).

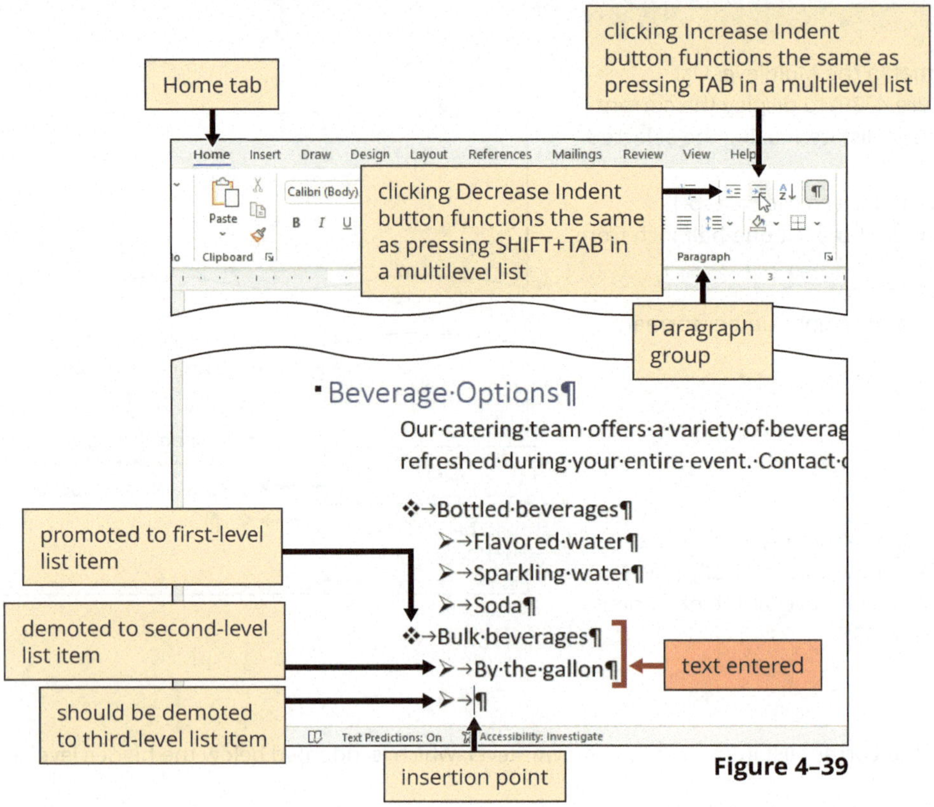

Figure 4–39

7

- Press TAB to demote the current-level list item to a lower-level list item.
- Type **Lemonade** as a third-level list item and then press ENTER.
- Type **Coffee** as a third-level list item and then press ENTER.
- Type **Iced tea** as a third-level list item and then press ENTER.
- Press SHIFT+TAB to promote the current-level list item to a higher-level list item.
- Type **By the pitcher** as a second-level list item and then press ENTER.
- Press TAB to demote the current-level list item to a lower-level list item.
- Type **Ice water** as a third-level list item and then press ENTER.
- Type **Juice** as a third-level list item and then press ENTER.
- Type **Milk** as a third-level list item (Figure 4–40).

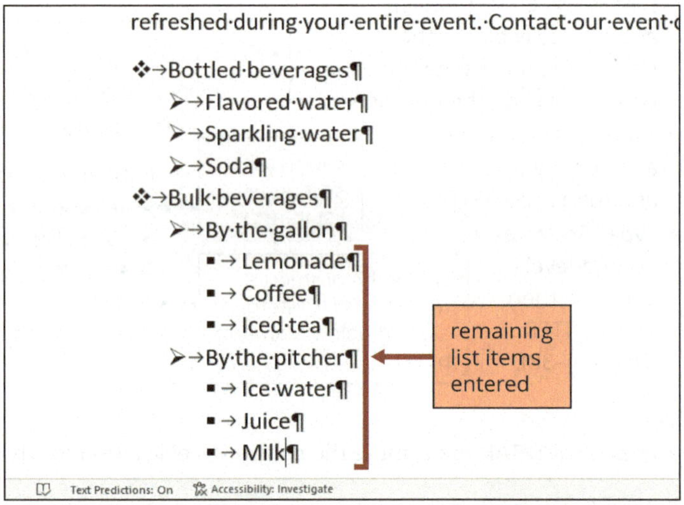

Figure 4–40

To Change the Bullet Character to Picture Bullets

The multilevel list in the sales proposal draft uses default bullet characters. The following steps change the first-level bullets in the multilevel list from the default to picture bullets. **Why?** You want to use a more visually appealing bullet that represents beverages.

1

- Position the insertion point in the paragraph containing the bullet you want to change to a picture bullet, in this case, the first bulleted item in the multilevel list.
- Click the Bullets arrow (Home tab | Paragraph group) to display the Bullets gallery (Figure 4–41).

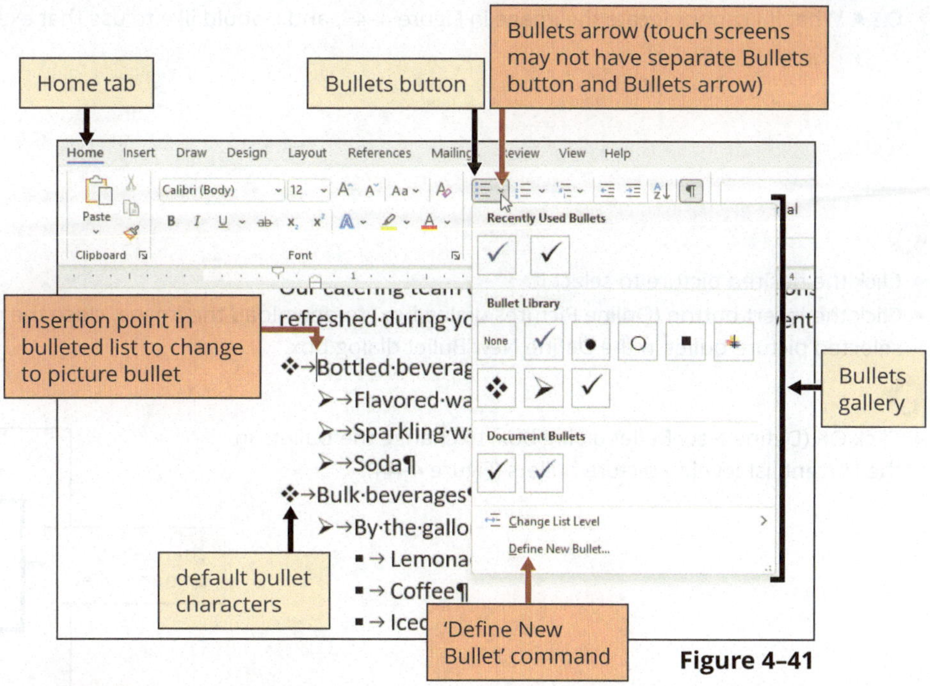

Figure 4–41

2

- Click 'Define New Bullet' in the Bullets gallery to display the Define New Bullet dialog box.
- Click the Picture button (Define New Bullet dialog box) to display the Insert Pictures dialog box.
- Type **beverage cup** in the Bing Image Search box (Insert Pictures dialog box) (Figure 4–42).

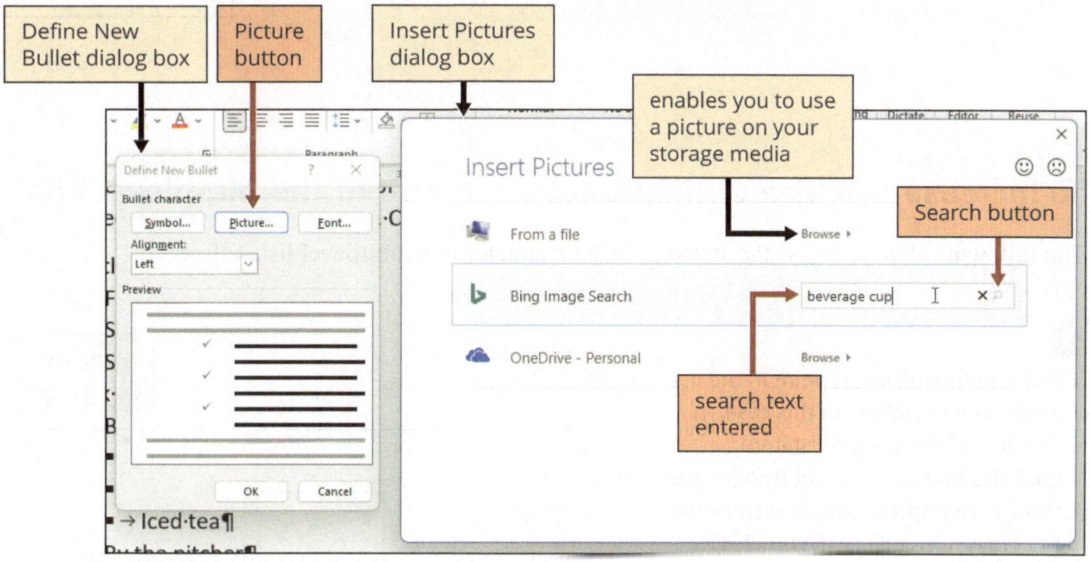

Figure 4–42

3

- Click the Search button to display a list of pictures (Online Pictures dialog box) that matches the entered search text.
- Scroll through the list of pictures to locate the one shown in Figure 4–43, or a similar image.

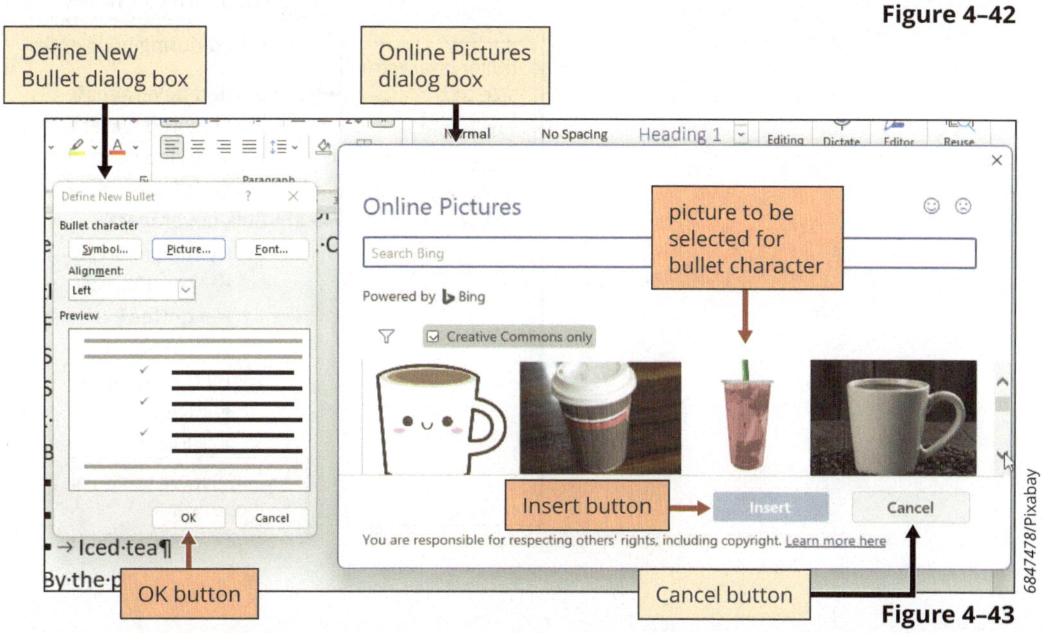

Figure 4–43

Q&A What if I cannot locate the image in Figure 4–43, and I would like to use that exact image?
The image is located in the Data Files. You can click Cancel (Online Pictures dialog box), click the Picture button (Define New Bullet dialog box) to display the Insert Pictures dialog box again, click Browse in the Insert Pictures dialog box, navigate to the file called Support_WD_4_BeverageCup.png in the Data Files, select the file, and then click the Insert button (Insert Picture dialog box) to show a preview of the selected picture bullet in the Define New Bullet dialog box. Proceed to Step 5.

4

- Click the desired picture to select it.
- Click the Insert button (Online Pictures dialog box) to download the image, close the dialog box, and show a preview of the selected picture bullet in the Define New Bullet dialog box.

5

- Click OK (Define New Bullet dialog box) to change the bullets in the current list level to picture bullets (Figure 4–44).

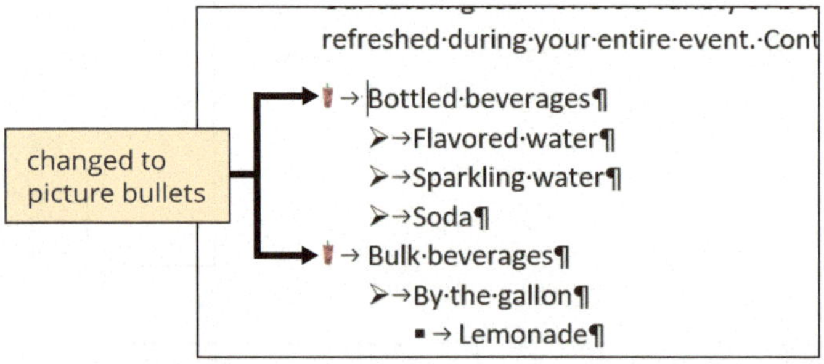

Figure 4–44

To Increase the Size of the Bullet Character in the Multilevel List

The following steps increase the size of a bullet character in a multilevel list. **Why?** The beverage cup bullet character would have more impact if it were a bit larger.

1

- Position the insertion point in the list item to be modified, in this case, in the Bottled beverages list item.
- Click the Multilevel List button (Home tab | Paragraph group) to display the Multilevel List gallery (Figure 4–45).

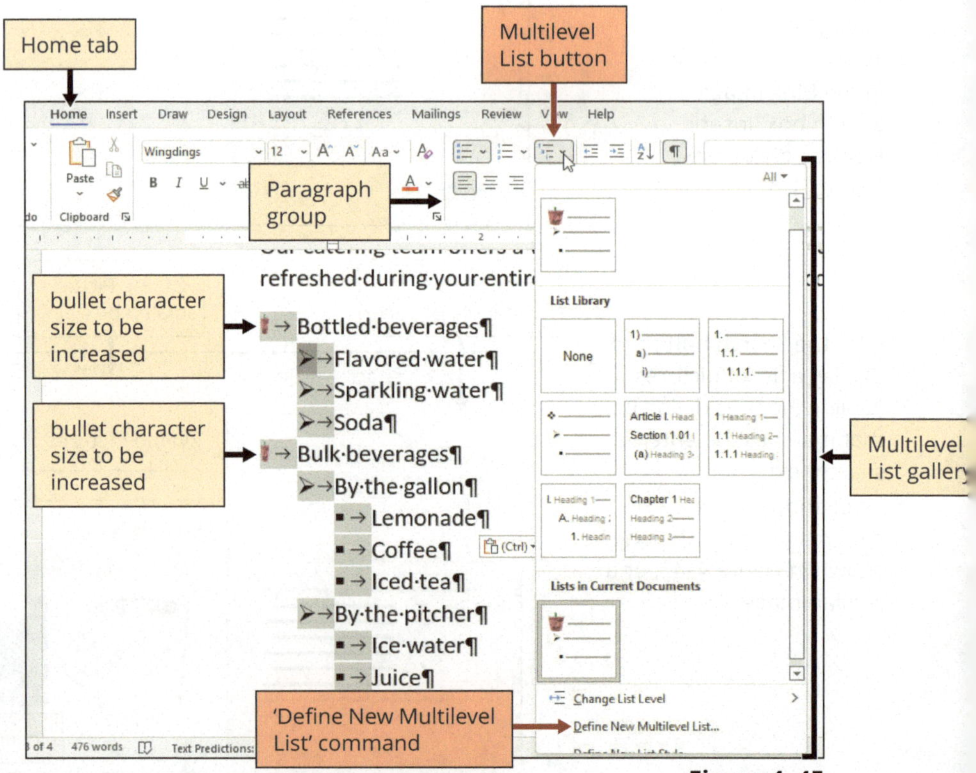

Figure 4–45

2

- Click 'Define New Multilevel List' in the Multilevel List gallery to display the Define new Multilevel list dialog box.
- Be sure level 1 is selected in the dialog box and then click the Font button (Define new Multilevel list dialog box) to display the Font dialog box.
- Scroll to and then click 14 in the Size list (Font dialog box) to change the font size for the bullet character in the selected level (Figure 4–46).

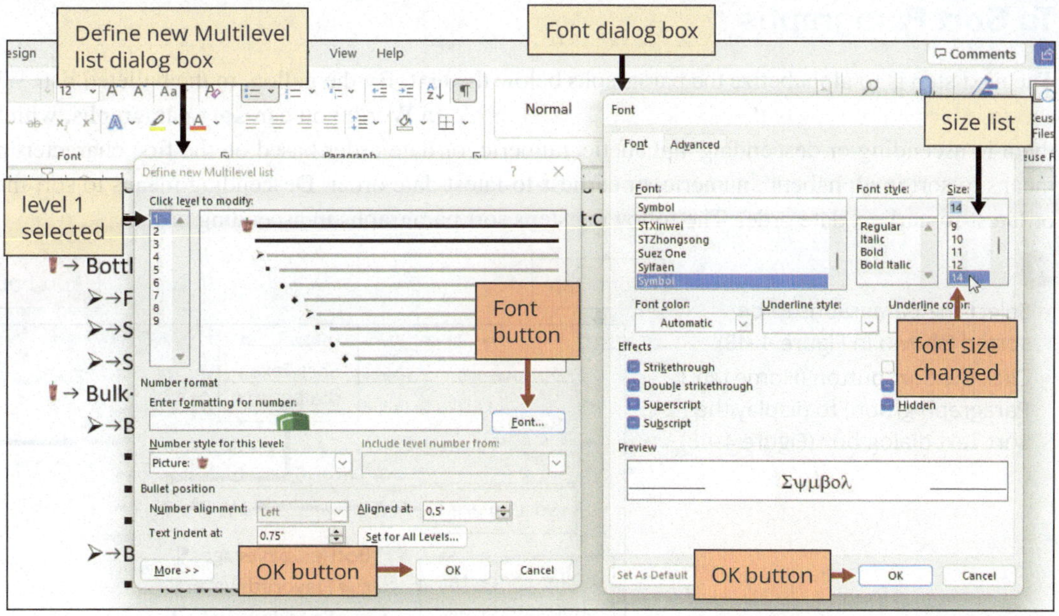

Figure 4–46

Q&A Why should level 1 be selected in the dialog box?
The picture bullets you want to modify are the first level in the multilevel list.

3

- Click OK in each open dialog box to increase the font size of the picture bullets (shown in Figure 4–47).

To Change the Bullet Character to a Predefined Bullet Character

You would like to change the bullet character for the second-level list items in the multilevel list to an open circle, which is a predefined bullet character. The following steps format bullets to a predefined bullet character.

1. Position the insertion point in the paragraph containing the bullet you want to change, in this case, the Flavored water bulleted paragraph.
2. Click the Bullets arrow (Home tab | Paragraph group) to display the Bullets gallery (Figure 4–47).
3. Click the desired predefined bullet character in the Bullet Library area, in this case, the open circle, to format current list level paragraphs with the selected bullet character (shown in Figure 4–48).

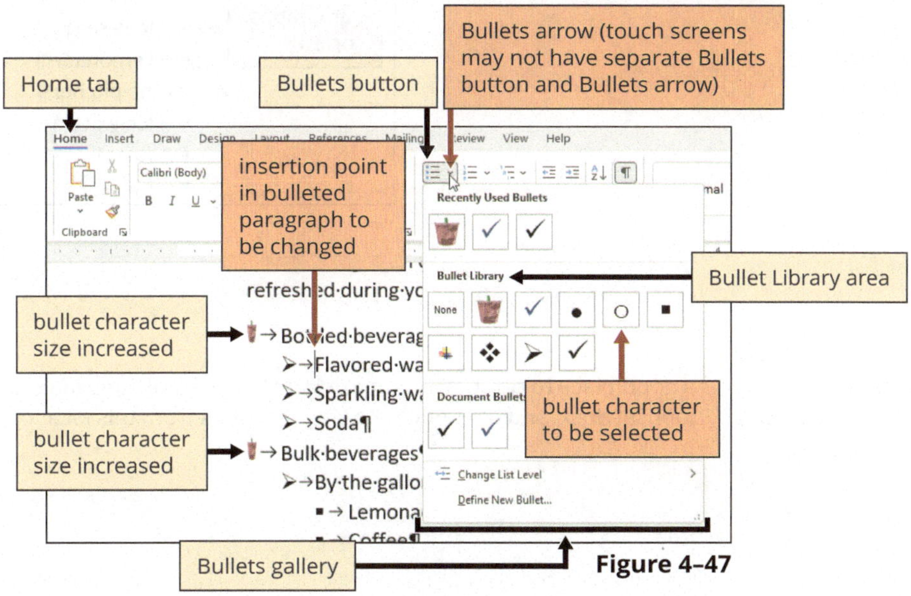

Figure 4–47

BTW
Bullets
In addition to selecting from a variety of bullet symbols and changing font attributes of a bullet by clicking 'Define New Bullet' in the Bullets gallery and then clicking the desired button in the Define New Bullet dialog box, you also can change the level of a bullet by pointing to 'Change List Level' in the Bullets gallery and then clicking the desired level.

To Sort Paragraphs

The next step is to alphabetize the paragraphs below the text, By the gallon, in the bulleted list. **Why?** It is easier for readers to locate information in lists that are in alphabetical order. In Word, you can **sort** paragraphs, which is the process of arranging them in ascending or descending alphabetic, numeric, or date order based on the first character in each paragraph. Ascending means to sort in alphabetic, numeric, or earliest-to-latest date order. Descending means to sort in reverse alphabetic, numeric, or latest-to-earliest date order. The following steps sort paragraphs in ascending order.

1

- Select the paragraphs to be sorted (shown in Figure 4–48).
- Click the Sort button (Home tab | Paragraph group) to display the Sort Text dialog box (Figure 4–48).

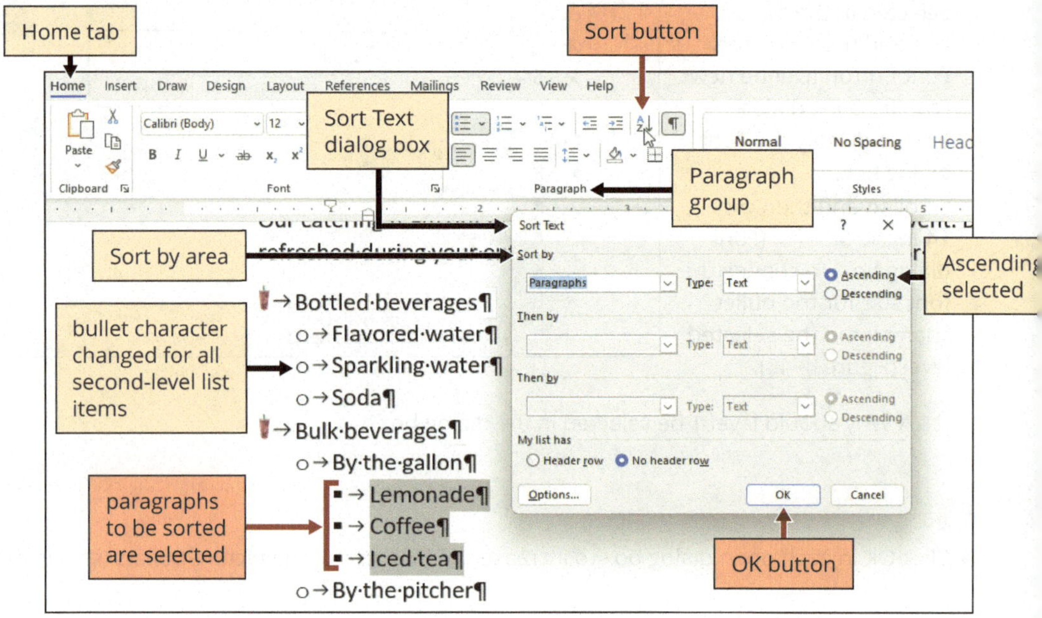

Figure 4–48

2

- Make sure the Ascending option button in the Sort by area is selected and then click OK (Sort Text dialog box) to instruct Word to alphabetize the selected paragraphs.
- Click anywhere to remove the selection from the text (Figure 4–49).
- Save the sales proposal again with the same file name in the same storage location.

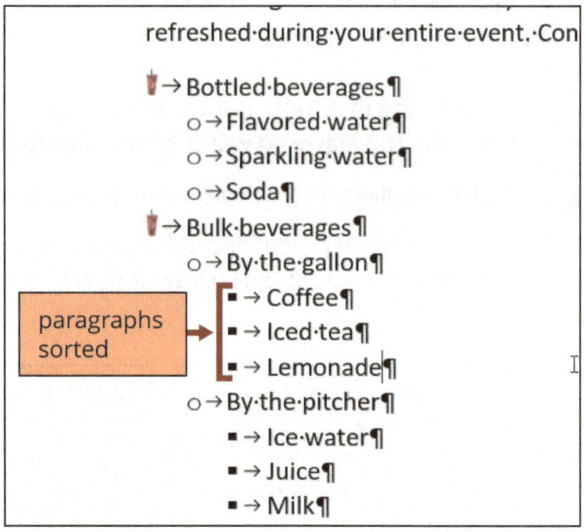

Figure 4–49

Break Point: If you want to take a break, this is a good place to do so. You can exit Word now. To resume later, start Word, open the file called SC_WD_4_Meetings_Sales_Proposal.docx, and continue following the steps from this location forward.

Editing and Formatting Tables

The sales proposal draft contains two Word tables: the available technology table and the food catering options table (shown earlier in the module in Figure 4–14). The available technology table shows the full-day and half-day rates for various available technology options, and the food catering options table shows costs and serving times for buffet and a la carte food catering options. In this section, you will make several modifications to these two tables so that they appear as shown in Figure 4–1 at the beginning of this module.

The following pages explain how to modify the tables in the sales proposal draft:

1. Available technology table
   a. Change the table column widths.
   b. Change the table row heights.
   c. Center the table.
   d. Align data in the table cells.
   e. Sort data in the table.
   f. Insert a formula in the table.
   g. Change cell spacing.
   h. Change margins in the table cells.
   i. Distribute table columns.
2. Food catering options table
   a. Split table cells.
   b. Move a cell boundary.
   c. Distribute table rows.
   d. Merge table cells.
   e. Change the direction of text in table cells.
   f. Resize table columns using AutoFit.
   g. Shade table cells.
   h. Add a table border.

BTW

Moving Tables

If you wanted to move a table to a new location, you would click in the table to display the table move handle in the upper-left corner of the table (shown in Figure 4–50) and then drag the table move handle to move the entire table to a new location.

Consider This

Why should you include visuals in a sales proposal?

Studies have shown that people tend to prefer images to text. Use tables to clarify ideas and illustrate points. Be aware, however, that too many visuals can clutter a document.

To Change Column Width

Notice in Figure 4–50 that the columns in the available technology table are much wider than their contents. Thus, you will change the widths of the columns. **Why?** You want the columns to be narrower to reduce the amount of white space between the end of the text in the columns and the column boundaries. The following steps change column widths.

1

- Position the insertion point somewhere in the table to be formatted.
- Position the pointer on the column boundary to the right of the column to adjust (in this case, to the right of the first column) so that the pointer changes to a double-headed arrow split by two vertical bars (Figure 4–50).

Q&A What is the column boundary?
You can drag a **column boundary**, the border to the right of a column, until the column is the desired width. Similarly, you can resize a row by dragging the **row boundary**, the border at the bottom of a row, until the row is the desired height. You also can resize the entire table by dragging the **table resize handle**, which is a small square that appears when you point to a corner of the table.

What causes the table move handle and table resize handle to appear and disappear from the table?
They appear whenever you position the pointer in the table.

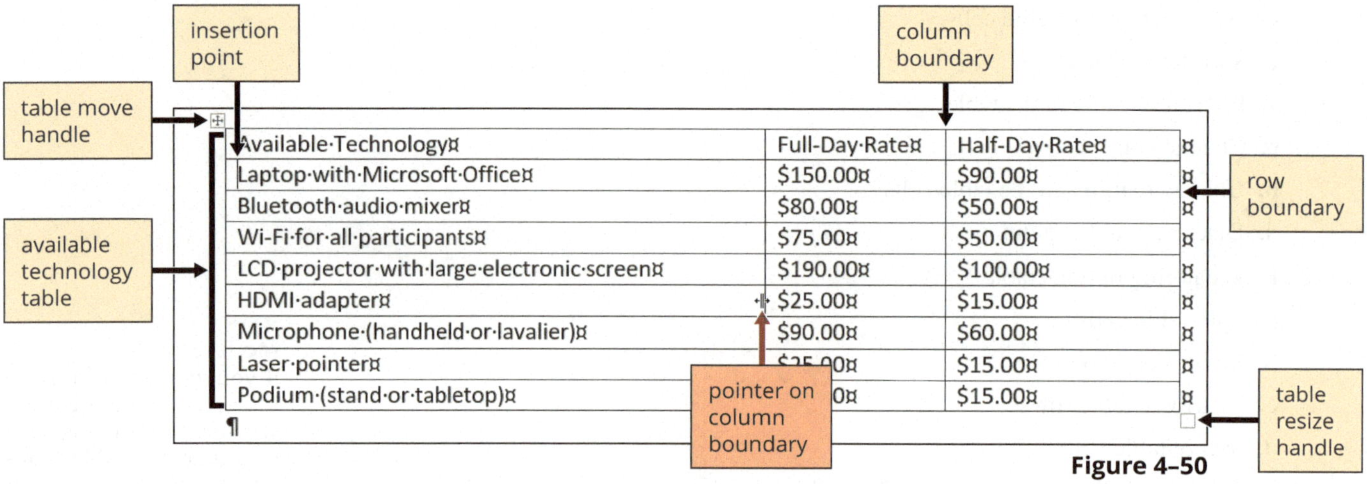
Available·Technology¤	Full-Day·Rate¤	Half-Day·Rate¤
Laptop·with·Microsoft·Office¤	$150.00¤	$90.00¤
Bluetooth·audio·mixer¤	$80.00¤	$50.00¤
Wi-Fi·for·all·participants¤	$75.00¤	$50.00¤
LCD·projector·with·large·electronic·screen¤	$190.00¤	$100.00¤
HDMI·adapter¤	$25.00¤	$15.00¤
Microphone·(handheld·or·lavalier)¤	$90.00¤	$60.00¤
Laser·pointer¤	$25.00¤	$15.00¤
Podium·(stand·or·tabletop)¤	0¤	$15.00¤

Figure 4–50

2

- Double-click the column boundary so that Word adjusts the column width to the width of the column's contents.
- Position the pointer on the column boundary to the right of the next column to adjust (in this case, to the right of the second column) so that the pointer changes to a double-headed arrow split by two vertical bars (Figure 4–51).

Q&A What if I am using a touch screen?
Position the insertion point in the column to adjust, tap the AutoFit button (contextual Layout tab | Cell Size group), and then tap AutoFit Contents on the AutoFit menu.

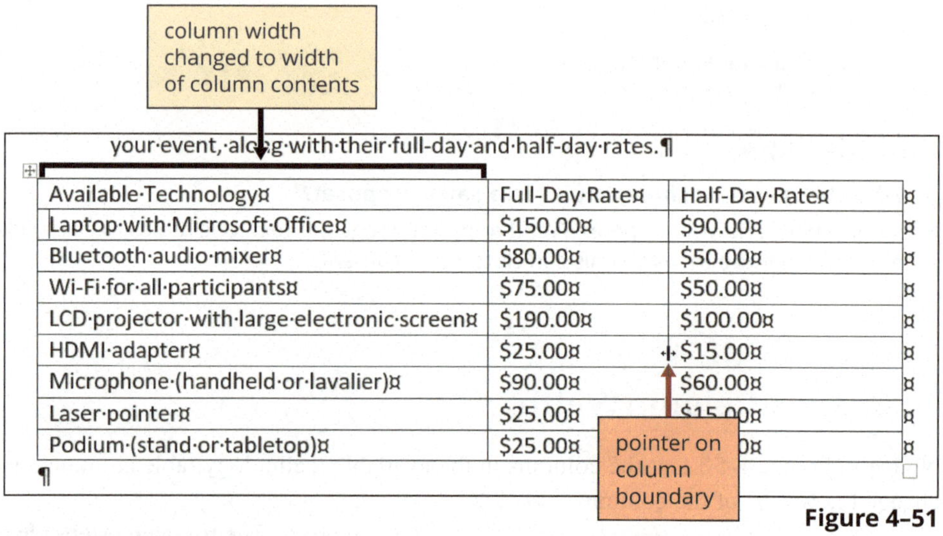
your·event,·along·with·their·full-day·and·half-day·rates.¶

Available·Technology¤	Full-Day·Rate¤	Half-Day·Rate¤
Laptop·with·Microsoft·Office¤	$150.00¤	$90.00¤
Bluetooth·audio·mixer¤	$80.00¤	$50.00¤
Wi-Fi·for·all·participants¤	$75.00¤	$50.00¤
LCD·projector·with·large·electronic·screen¤	$190.00¤	$100.00¤
HDMI·adapter¤	$25.00¤	$15.00¤
Microphone·(handheld·or·lavalier)¤	$90.00¤	$60.00¤
Laser·pointer¤	$25.00¤	$15.00¤
Podium·(stand·or·tabletop)¤	$25.00¤	0¤

Figure 4–51

3

- Drag the column boundary to the left so that Word adjusts the column width so that the column heading wraps to two lines (Figure 4–52).

Q&A Why drag the column boundary instead of double-clicking it?

When you double-click the column boundary, Word adjusts the width of the column to the column contents, usually adjusting the width to the widest item in the column, which, in this case, is the text, Full-Day Rate. To make the column even narrower and cause the text, Full-Day Rate, to wrap to two lines, you drag the column to make it narrower than the column heading.

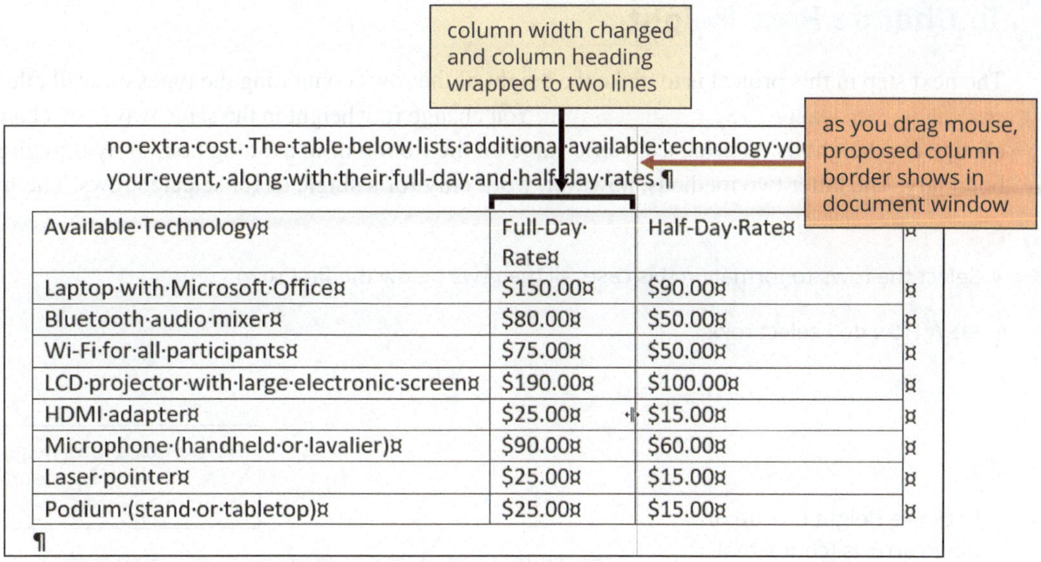

Figure 4–52

4

- Click Layout to display the contextual Layout tab on the ribbon.

Q&A Is the contextual Layout tab different from the main Layout tab?

Yes. The main Layout tab, which always appears on the ribbon, is used to change page setup, format paragraphs, and arrange objects in a document. The contextual Layout tab appears only when you are working in a table and is used to change the properties and organization of a table and its rows, columns, and cells.

- **Experiment:** Practice changing the column widths in the table using other techniques: drag the 'Move Table Column' marker on the horizontal ruler to the right and then to the left. Click the Width box up and down arrows (contextual Layout tab | Cell Size group).
- When you have finished experimenting, position the insertion point in the first column and then type **3** in the Width box (contextual Layout tab | Cell Size group) to specify the column width, position the insertion point in the second column and then type **.95** in the Width box (contextual Layout tab | Cell Size group) to specify the column width, and position the insertion point in the third column and then type **1** to specify the column width (Figure 4–53).

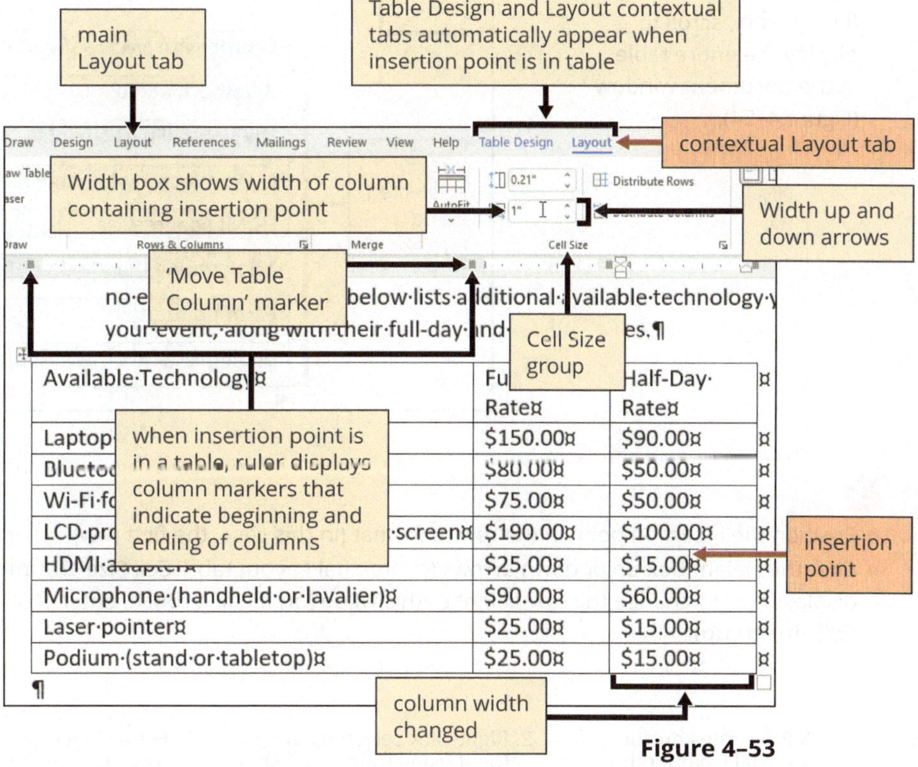

Figure 4–53

Other Ways

1. Drag 'Move Table Column' marker on horizontal ruler to desired width
2. Enter desired value in Width box (contextual Layout tab | Cell Size group)
3. Click Properties button (contextual Layout tab | Table group), click Column tab (Table Properties dialog box), enter width, click OK

To Change Row Height

The next step in this project is to make the height of the rows containing the types of available technology taller. **Why?** For ease of reading, you want more space in the rows. You change row height in the same ways you change column width. That is, you can change row height by entering a specific value on the ribbon or in a dialog box, or by dragging a marker on the ruler or the row boundary. The latter two methods, however, work only for a single or for selected rows. The following steps change row height.

1

- Select the rows to format (in this case, all the rows below the first row).

Q&A How do I select rows?
Point to the left of the first row and then drag downward when the pointer changes to a right-pointing arrow (or, if using touch, drag through the rows).

2

- Click the Height box up or down arrows (contextual Layout tab | Cell Size group) as many times as necessary until the box displays 0.3" to change the row height to this value (or, if using touch, enter **0.3** in the Height box (contextual Layout tab | Cell Size group)).
- If necessary, scroll to display the entire table in the document window (Figure 4–54).

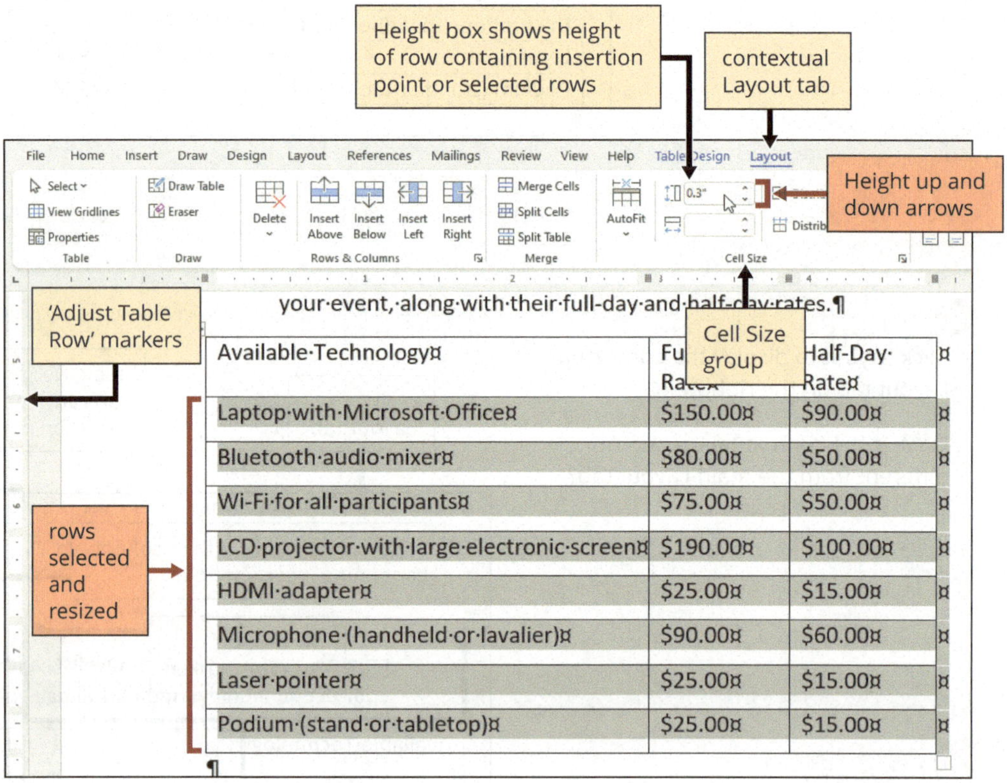

Figure 4–54

3

- Position the insertion point in the row to format (in this case, the first row).
- Click the Height box up or down arrows (contextual Layout tab | Cell Size group) as many times as necessary until the box displays 0.4" to change the row height to this value (or, if using touch, enter **0.4** in the Height box (contextual Layout tab | Cell Size group)).

Other Ways

1. Click Properties button (contextual Layout tab | Table group), click Row tab (Table Properties dialog box), enter row height, click OK
2. Right-click selected row (or, if using touch, tap 'Show Context Menu' button on Mini toolbar), click Table Properties on shortcut menu, click Row tab, enter row height (Table Properties dialog box), click OK
3. For a single row or selected rows, drag row boundary (horizontal gridline at bottom of row in table) to desired height
4. Drag 'Adjust Table Row' marker on vertical ruler to desired height

To Apply a Table Style

The following steps apply a table style to the table so that the table is more visually appealing.

1. Display the Table Design tab.

Q&A What if the Table Design tab no longer appears on the ribbon?
Click in the table and then display the Table Design tab.

2. With the insertion point in the table, click the More button in the Table Styles gallery (Table Design tab | Table Styles group) to expand the gallery and then click 'Grid Table 3 - Accent 3' in the Table Styles gallery to apply the selected style to the table in the document (Figure 4–55).

3. If the First Column check box in the Table Style Options group (Table Design tab) does not contain a check mark, click the check box to add a check mark because you want the first column in the table formatted differently from the rest of the table. Be sure the remaining check marks match those in the Table Style Options group (Table Design tab) as shown in Figure 4–55.

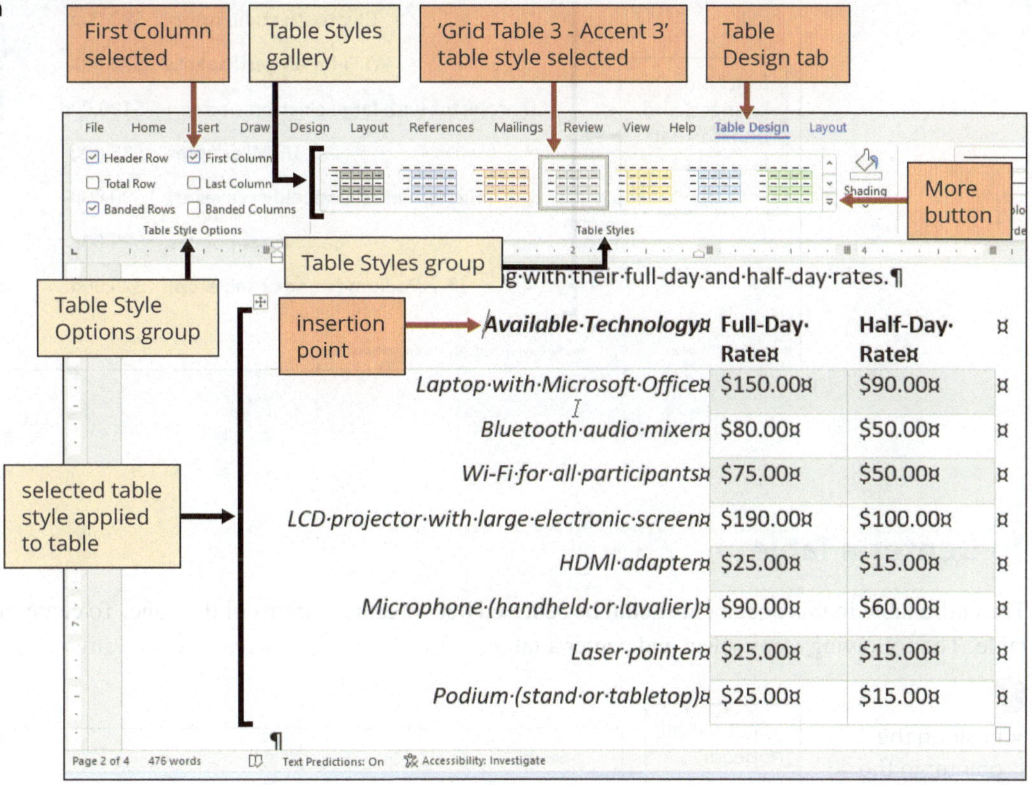

Figure 4–55

BTW
Table Wrapping
If you want text to wrap around a table, instead of displaying above and below the table, do the following: either right-click the table and then click Table Properties on the shortcut menu, or click the Properties button (contextual Layout tab | Table group), click the Table tab (Table Properties dialog box), click Around in the Text wrapping area, and then click OK.

To Format Table Cell Data

1. Select the first column in the table and remove the italic format.
2. Select all rows below the column headings and change their font to 11 point.
3. Select the column headings, if necessary, bold the headings, and change their font color to 'Light Gray, Background 2, Darker 75%' (third color in fifth row).
4. Select the row headings and change their font color also to 'Light Gray, Background 2, Darker 75%' (third color in fifth row).
5. Click anywhere to remove the selection from the table cells (Figure 4–56).

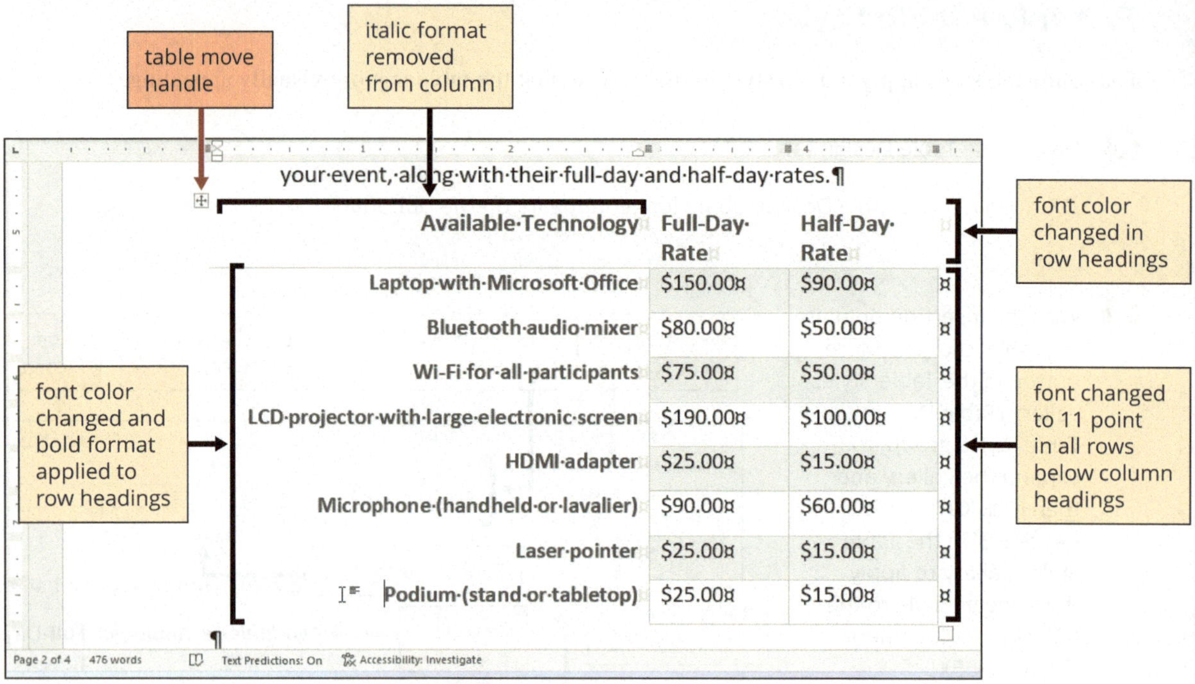

Figure 4–56

To Center a Table

The entire table in this document should be centered between the margins of the page. To center a table, you first select the entire table. The following steps select and center a table. **Why?** The table currently is left-aligned, and you would like it centered.

1

- Position the pointer in the table so that the table move handle appears (shown in Figure 4–56) and then click the table move handle to select the entire table (Figure 4–57).

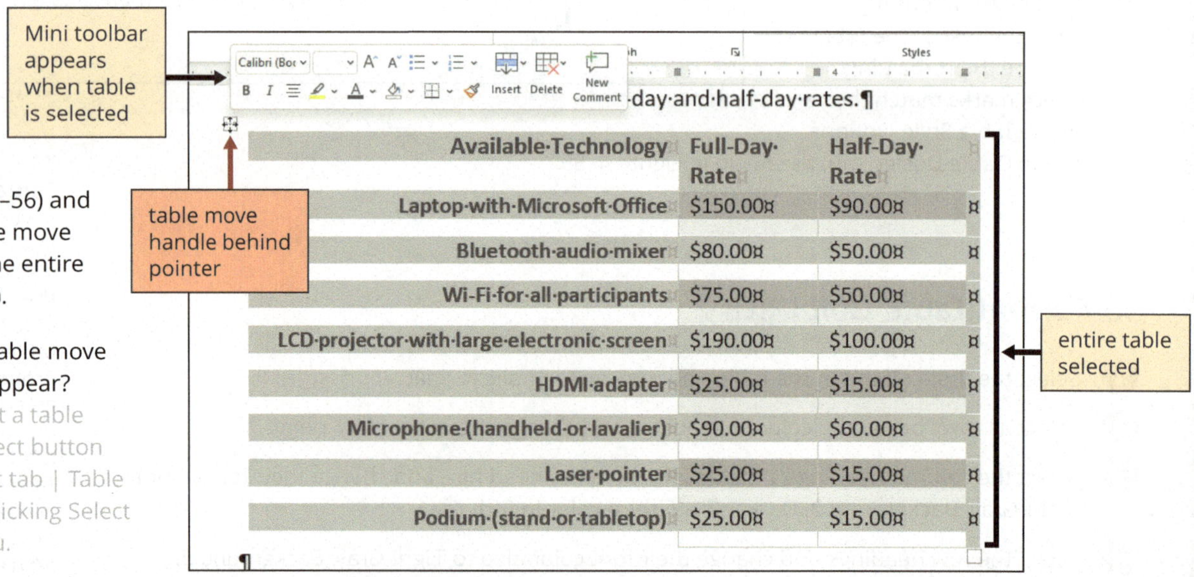

Figure 4–57

Q&A What if the table move handle does not appear?

You also can select a table by clicking the Select button (contextual Layout tab | Table group) and then clicking Select Table on the menu.

What if I am using a touch screen?

Tap the Select button (contextual Layout tab | Table group) and then tap Select Table on the Select menu to select the table.

2

- Click the Center button (Home tab | Paragraph group) to center the selected table between the left and right page margins (Figure 4–58).

Q&A Could I have clicked the Center button on the Mini toolbar?

Yes.

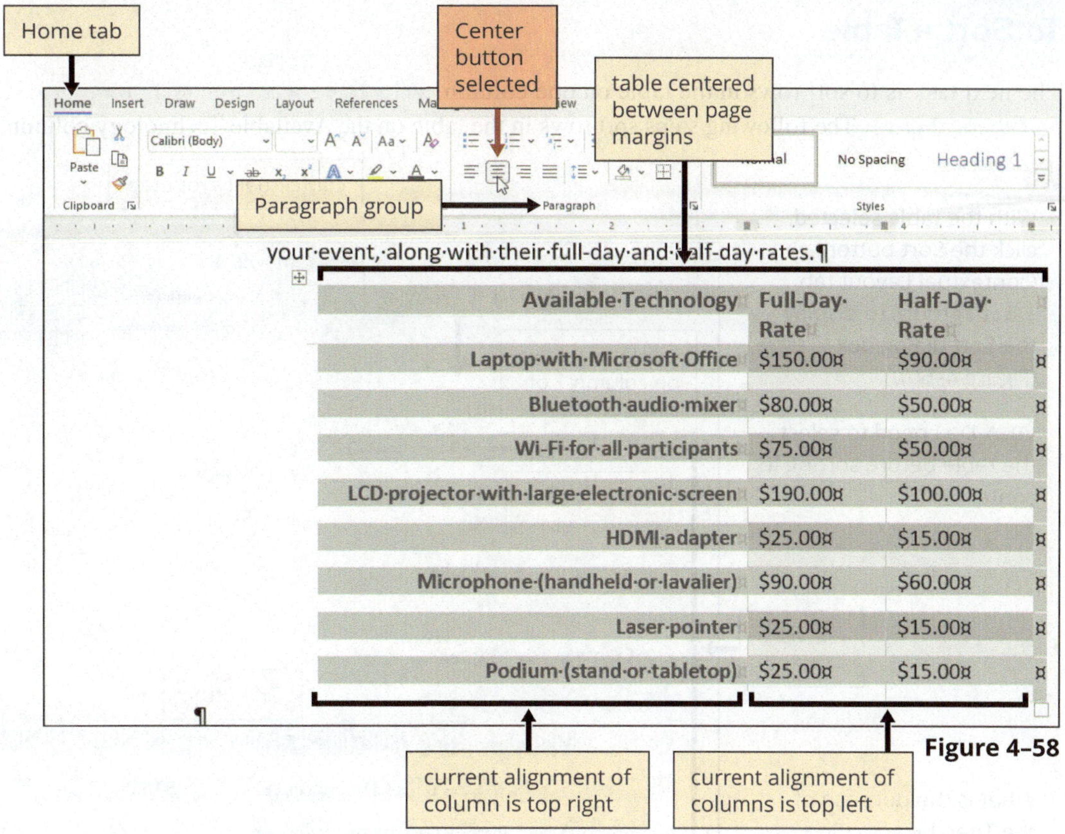

Figure 4–58

To Align Data in Cells

The next step is to change the alignment of the data in cells in the table. **Why?** *In addition to aligning text horizontally in a cell (left, center, or right), you can align it vertically within a cell (top, center, bottom). When the height of the cell is close to the same height as the text, however, differences in vertical alignment are not readily apparent. Because the rows are taller in this table, you will vertically center the data in the cells.* The cells in the left column are aligned top right, and the cells in the middle and right column area are aligned top left (shown in Figure 4–58). You would like all cells to be aligned center right, that is, vertically in the cell and right-aligned. The following step aligns data in cells.

1

- Display the contextual Layout tab.
- With the table still selected, as shown in Figure 4–58, click the desired alignment, in this case, the 'Align Center Right' button (contextual Layout tab | Alignment group) to align the contents of the selected cells (Figure 4–59).

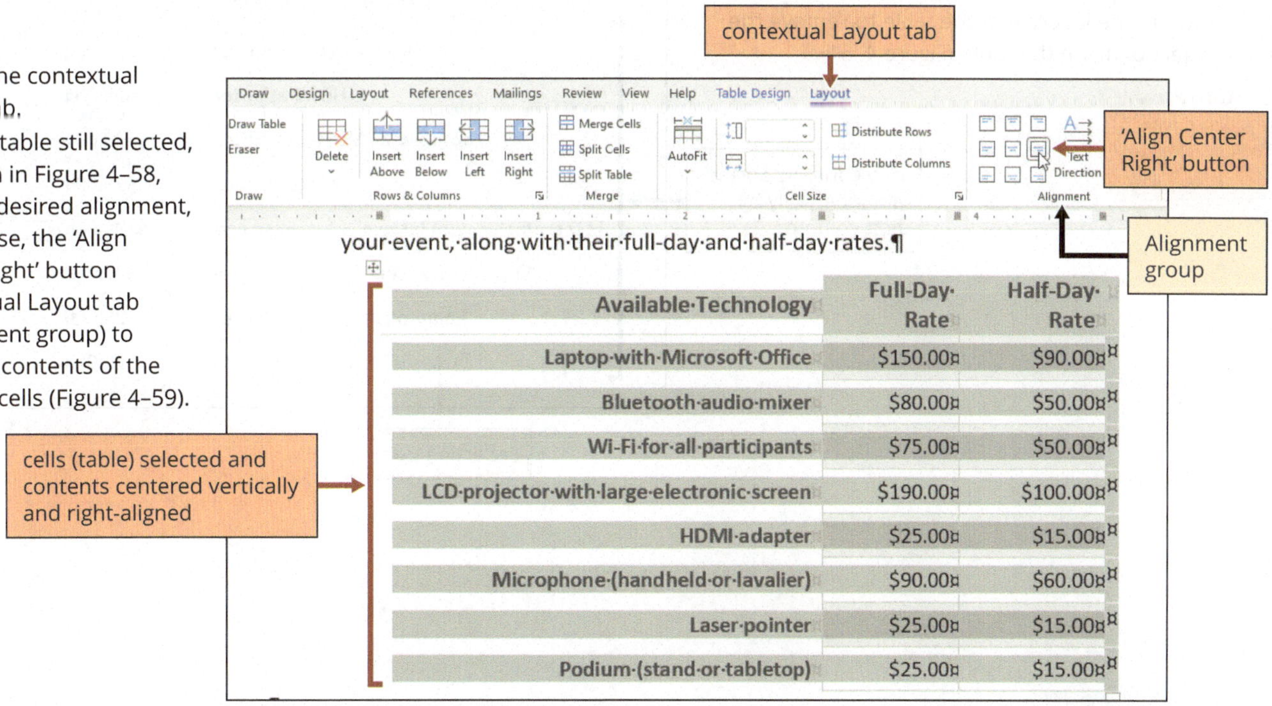

Figure 4–59

To Sort a Table

The next task is to sort rows in the table on one column. **Why?** The available technology row headings should be listed in alphabetical order. The following steps sort rows in the table on the Available Technology column.

1

- With the table selected, click the Sort button (contextual Layout tab | Data group) to display the Sort dialog box (Figure 4–60).

Q&A Do I need to select the table before sorting its contents?

No, you can also place the insertion point anywhere in the table instead of selecting it. If you want to sort only certain rows, select those rows first.

What is the purpose of the Then by area (Sort dialog box)?

If you have multiple values for a particular column, you can sort on multiple columns by sorting on columns within columns. For example, if the table had a city column and a last name column, you could sort by last names within cities.

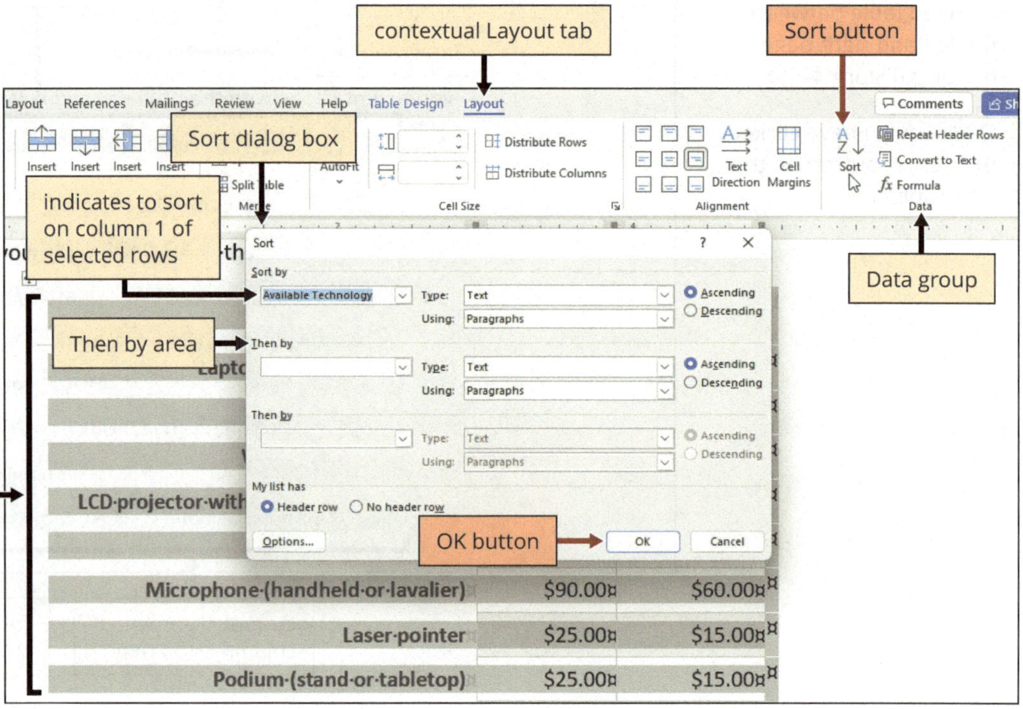

Figure 4–60

2

- Click OK (Sort dialog box) to instruct Word to alphabetize the selected rows.
- Click in the last row of the table to remove the selection from the table (Figure 4–61).

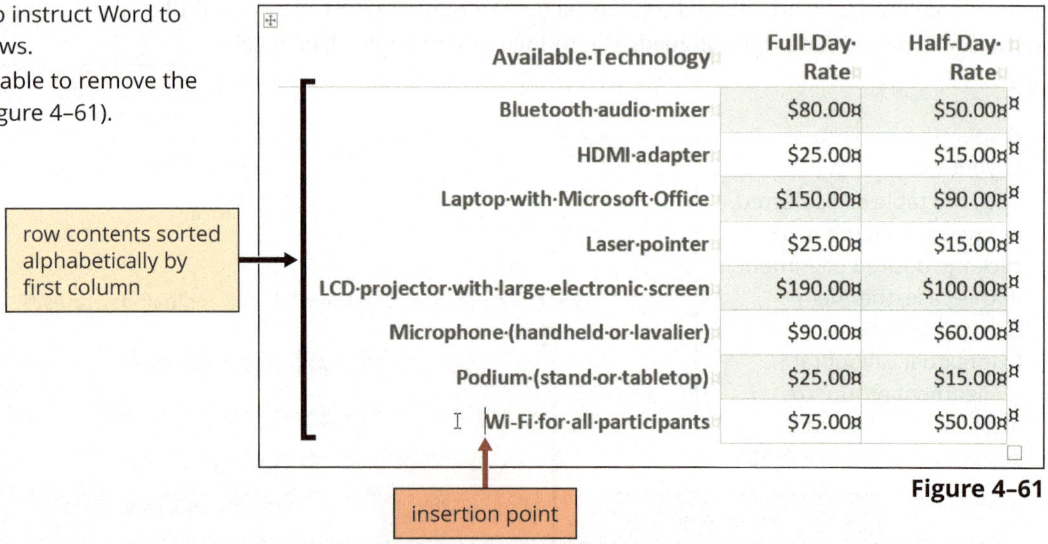

Available·Technology	Full-Day·Rate	Half-Day·Rate
Bluetooth·audio·mixer	$80.00	$50.00
HDMI·adapter	$25.00	$15.00
Laptop·with·Microsoft·Office	$150.00	$90.00
Laser·pointer	$25.00	$15.00
LCD·projector·with·large·electronic·screen	$190.00	$100.00
Microphone·(handheld·or·lavalier)	$90.00	$60.00
Podium·(stand·or·tabletop)	$25.00	$15.00
Wi-Fi·for·all·participants	$75.00	$50.00

Figure 4–61

To Add a Row to a Table

The next step is to insert a row at the bottom of the table because you want to add totals to the bottom of the two right columns. You can add a row at the end of a table by positioning the insertion point in the bottom-right corner cell and then pressing TAB. Or, you can use the Insert Below command (contextual Layout tab | Rows & Columns group) or the Insert Control. The following steps insert a row at the bottom of a table.

1. Position the insertion point somewhere in the last row of the table because you want to insert a row below this row (shown in Figure 4–61).

2. Click the Insert Below button (contextual Layout tab | Rows & Columns group) to insert a row below the row containing the insertion point and then select the newly inserted row.

3. Click in the leftmost column of the added row and then type **Total - All Technology** (shown in Figure 4–62).

Q&A Why did the hyphen I entered in Step 3 change to an en dash?
As you type text in a document, Word automatically formats some of it for you. If your entered hyphen did not automatically change to an en dash, you can enter an en dash by clicking the Symbol button (Insert tab | Symbols group), clicking More Symbols in the Symbol gallery, clicking the Special Characters tab (Symbol dialog box), clicking En Dash in the Character list, clicking the Insert button, and then closing the dialog box.

To Delete a Row in a Table If you wanted to delete a row, you would perform the following tasks.

1. Position the insertion point in the row to be deleted; click the Delete button (contextual Layout tab | Rows & Columns group) and then click Delete Rows on the Delete menu.

   or

2. If using touch, press and hold row to delete, tap Delete button on Mini toolbar, and then tap Delete Rows.

   or

3. Right-click the row to delete, click Delete Cells on the shortcut menu, click 'Delete entire row' (Delete Cells dialog box), and then click OK.

   or

4. Select the row to be deleted, right-click the selected row, and then click Delete Rows on the shortcut menu.

BTW
Table Headings
If a table continues on the next page, you can instruct Word to repeat the table headings at the top of the subsequent page(s) containing the table. To do this, select the first row in the table and then click the 'Repeat Header Rows' button (contextual Layout tab | Data group).

To Insert a Formula in a Table

Word can calculate the totals of rows and columns. The following steps sum the right two columns in the table. **Why?** In this project, the last row should display the sum (total) of the values in the Full-Day Rate and Half-Day Rate columns.

1
- Position the insertion point in the cell to contain the sum (last row, Full-Day Rate column).

2

- Click the Formula button (contextual Layout tab | Data group) to display the Formula dialog box (Figure 4–62).

Q&A What is the formula that shows in the Formula box, and can I change it?

Word places a default formula in the Formula box, depending on the location of the numbers in surrounding cells. In this case, because numbers are above the current cell, Word displays a formula that will add the numbers above the current cell. You can change the formula that Word proposes, or you can type a different formula. For example, instead of summing numbers you can multiply them.

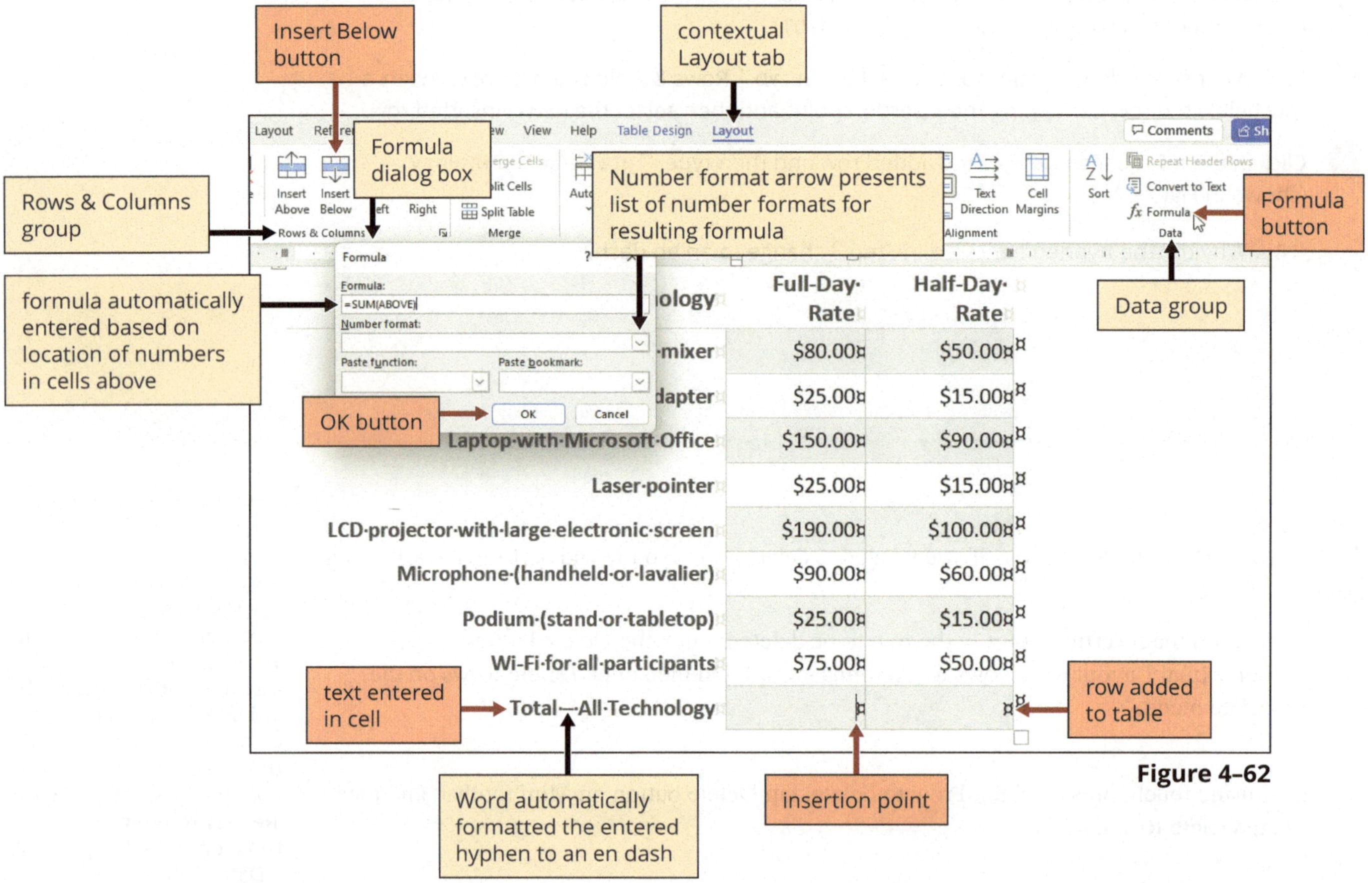

Figure 4–62

3

- Click OK (Formula dialog box) to place the sum of the numbers in the current cell (Figure 4–63).

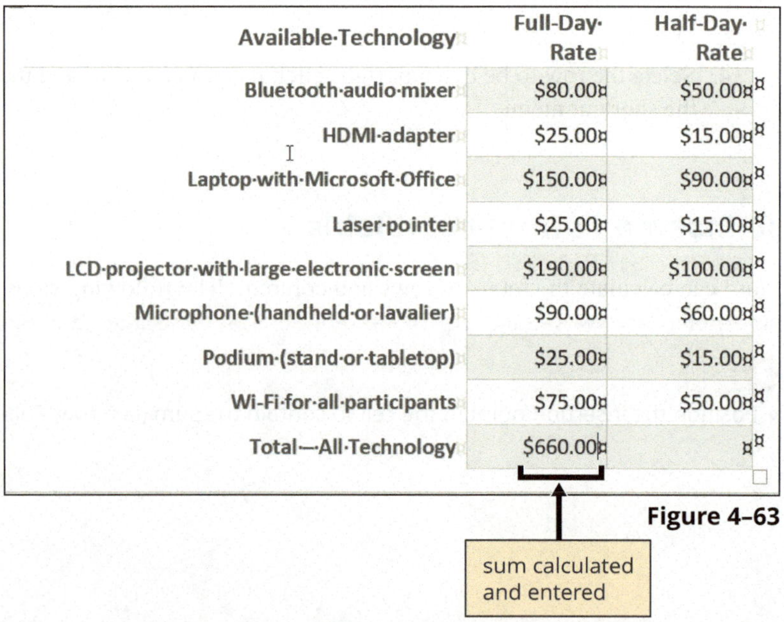

Figure 4–63

4

- Position the insertion point in the cell to contain the sum (last row, Half-Day Rate column).
- Click the Formula button (contextual Layout tab | Data group) to display the Formula dialog box and then click OK (Formula dialog box) to place the sum of the numbers in the current cell (shown in Figure 4–64).

Q&A Can I change the format of the displayed result?
Yes. Click the Number format arrow (Formula dialog box) and select the desired format, or type the desired format in the Number format box. The # symbol in the Number format list means to display a blank if the number has a value of zero. The format in the parenthesis is for negative numbers.

Can I sum a row instead of a column?
Yes. You would position the insertion point in an empty cell at the right edge of the row before clicking the Formula button.

If I make a change to a number in a table, does Word automatically recalculate the sum?
No. You will need to update the field by right-clicking it and then clicking Update Field on the shortcut menu or by selecting the field and then pressing F9.

To Change Cell Spacing

The next step in formatting the available technology table is to place a small amount of additional white space between every cell in the table. **Why?** You feel the table would be easier to read with more white space surrounding each cell. The following steps change spacing between cells.

1

- With the insertion point somewhere in the table, click the Cell Margins button (contextual Layout tab | Alignment group) to display the Table Options dialog box.
- Place a check mark in the 'Allow spacing between cells' check box and then ensure that 0.01" is displayed in this box, because you want to increase space between cells by this value (Figure 4–64).

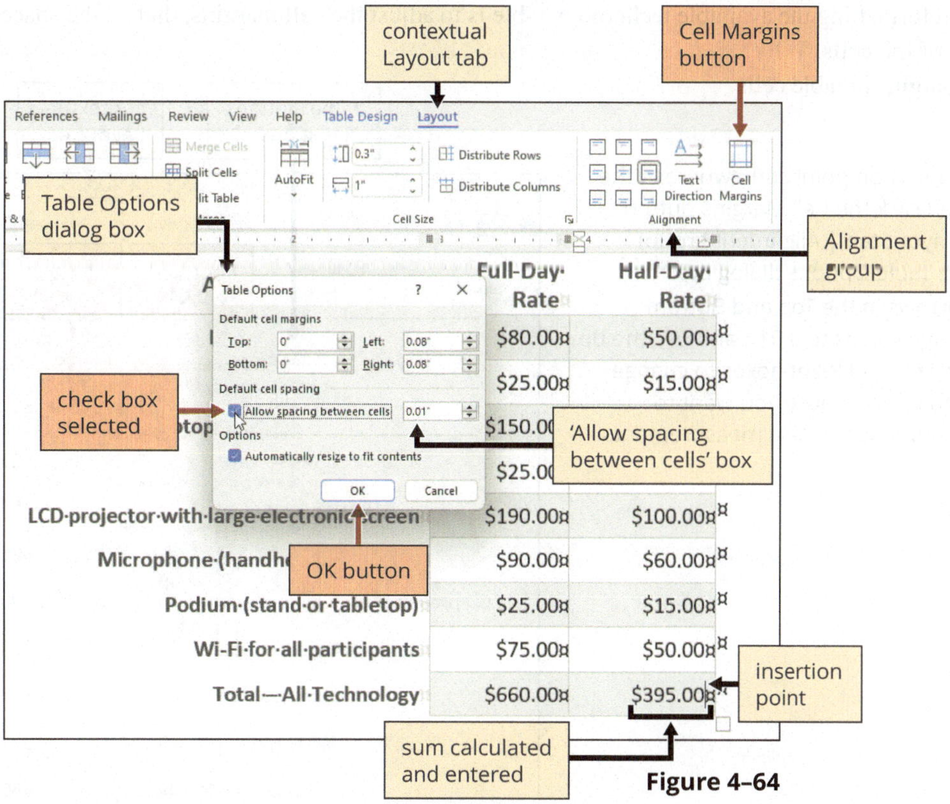

Figure 4–64

2

- Click OK (Table Options dialog box) to apply the cell spacing changes to the current table (Figure 4–65).

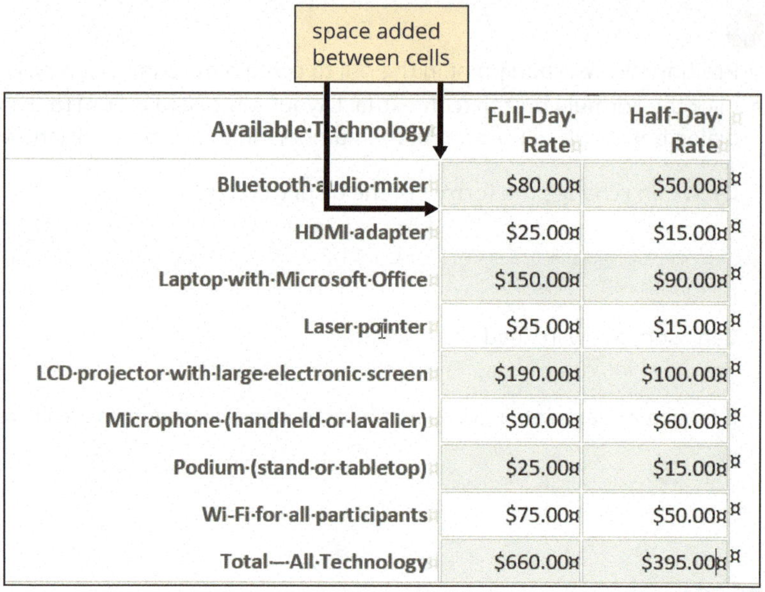

Figure 4–65

Other Ways

1. Click Properties button (contextual Layout tab | Table group), click Table tab (Table Properties dialog box), click Options button, select desired options (Table Options dialog box), click OK in each dialog box
2. Right-click table (or, if using touch, tap 'Show Context Menu' button on Mini toolbar), click Table Properties on shortcut menu, click Table tab (Table Properties dialog box), click Options button, select desired options (Table Options dialog box), click OK in each dialog box

To Change Margins in Table Cells

The next step in formatting the available technology table is to adjust the cell margins, that is, the space at the top, bottom, left, and right edge of the cells. **Why?** You feel the table would be easier to read with bigger margins in the cells. The following steps change margins in table cells.

1

- Position the insertion point somewhere in the table and then click the Cell Margins button (contextual Layout tab | Alignment group) to display the Table Options dialog box.
- Use the up arrows in the Top and Bottom boxes to change values to 0.01", and use the up arrows in the Left and Right boxes to change their values to 0.1", because you want to increase cell margins to these measurements (Figure 4–66).

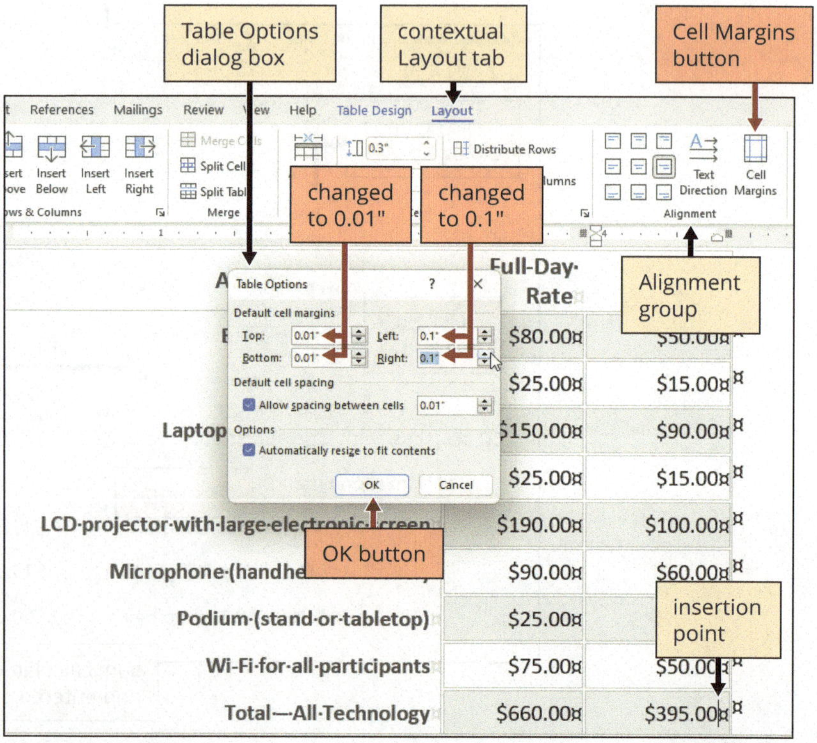

Figure 4–66

2

- Click OK (Table Options dialog box) to apply the cell margin changes to the current table (shown in Figure 4–67).

Q&A Why is there an extra page in my document?
The increased table margins may have added an extra page in the document. If this occurred, the blank page will be deleted after the next steps.

Other Ways

1. Click Properties button (contextual Layout tab | Table group), click Table tab (Table Properties dialog box), click Options button, select desired options (Table Options dialog box), click OK in each dialog box
2. Right-click table (or, if using touch, tap 'Show Context Menu' button on Mini toolbar), click Table Properties on shortcut menu, click Table tab (Table Properties dialog box), click Options button, select desired options (Table Options dialog box), click OK in each dialog box

To Distribute Columns

The last step in formatting the available technology table is to make the width of the second and third columns uniform, that is, the same width. The following step distributes selected columns. **Why?** Instead of checking and adjusting the width of each column individually, you can format multiple columns to a uniform size at the same time.

1

- Select the columns to format, in this case, the second and third columns.
- Click the Distribute Columns button (contextual Layout tab | Cell Size group) to make the width of the selected columns uniform (Figure 4–67).

Q&A How would I make all columns in the table uniform?
Simply place the insertion point somewhere in the table before clicking the Distribute Columns button.

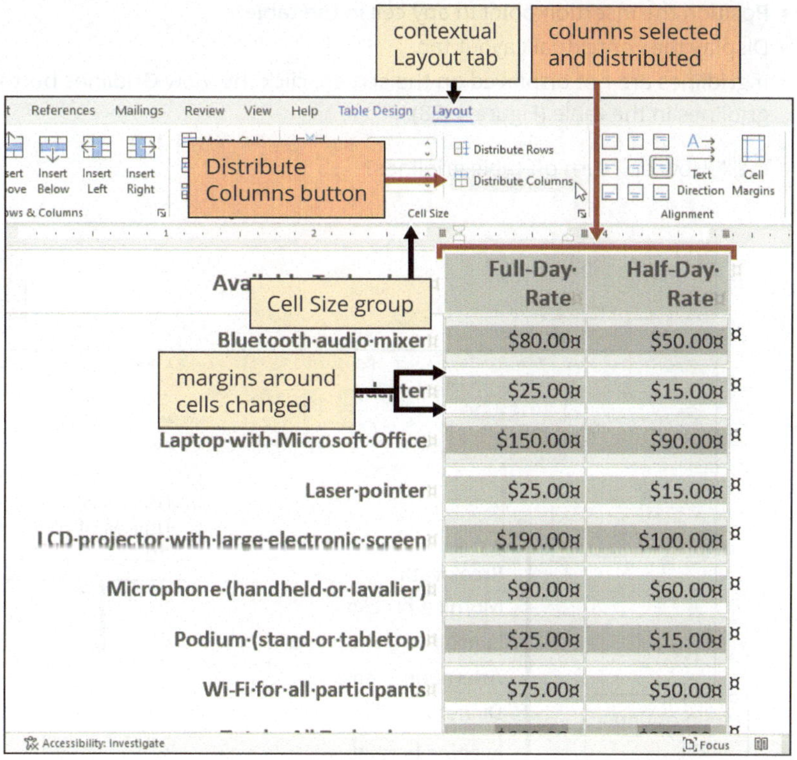

Figure 4–67

Other Ways

1. Right-click selected columns, click 'Distribute Columns Evenly' on shortcut menu (or, if using touch, tap 'Show Context Menu' button on Mini toolbar)

To Delete a Blank Paragraph

If you notice an extra paragraph mark below the available technology table that is causing an extra blank page in the document, you should delete the blank paragraph. If necessary, the following steps delete a blank paragraph.

1. If a blank paragraph appears below the available technology table, position the insertion point on the blank paragraph mark below the table.
2. If necessary, press DELETE to remove the extra blank paragraph and delete the blank page.

To Show Gridlines

When a table contains no borders or light borders, it may be difficult to see the individual cells in the table. Thus, the following step shows gridlines. **Why?** To help identify the location of cells in the food catering options table, you can display gridlines, which show cell outlines on the screen. **Gridlines** are formatting marks that show cell boundaries but do not print.

1

- If necessary, scroll to display the table to be edited in the document window (in this case, the table below the Food Options heading on the second page of the proposal).
- Position the insertion point in any cell in the table.
- Display the contextual Layout tab.
- If gridlines are not displayed on the screen, click the View Gridlines button (contextual Layout tab | Table group) to show gridlines in the table (Figure 4–68).

Q&A How do I turn off table gridlines?
Click the View Gridlines button again.

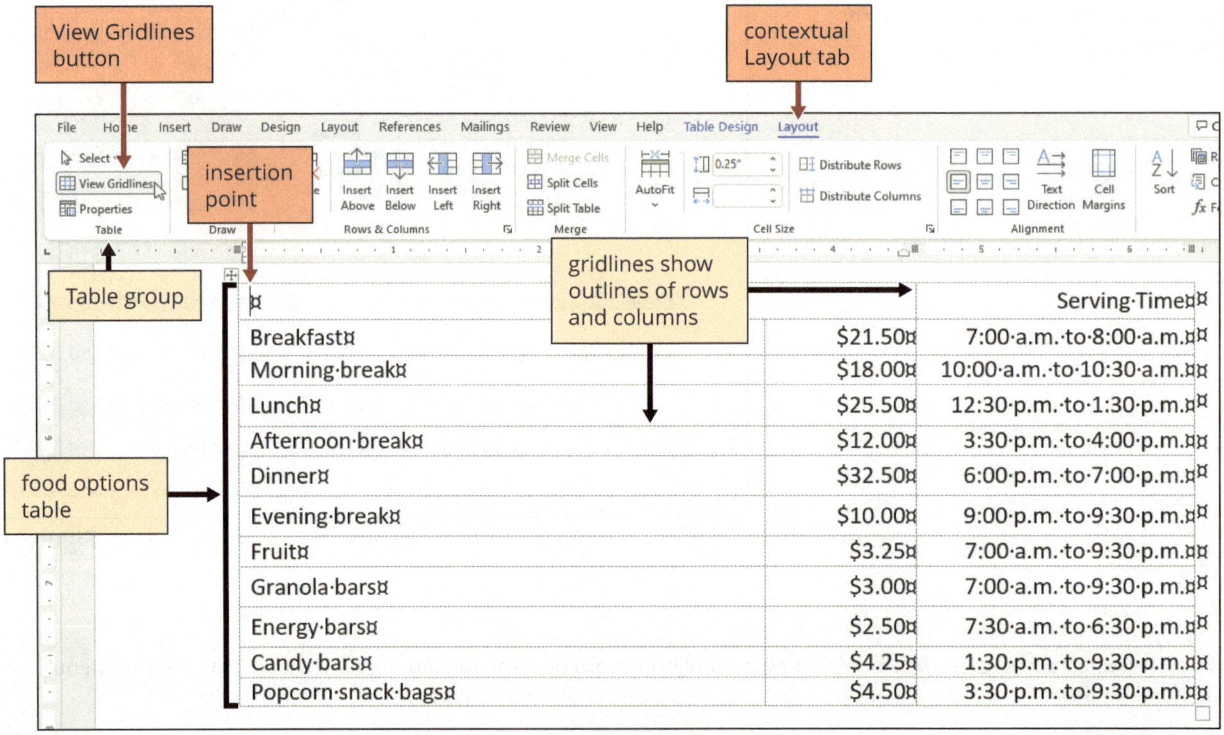

Figure 4–68

To Split a Table Cell

The top, left cell of the table contains one long cell that appears above two columns (the options and fees columns). The heading, Food Catering Options, should be above the first column, and the heading, Fee per Person, should be above the second column. Thus, you will split the cell into two cells. **Why?** With the cell split, you can enter a heading above each of the first two columns. The following steps split a single cell into two separate cells.

1

- Position the insertion point in the cell to split, in this case, the top left cell as shown in Figure 4–69.
- Click the Split Cells button (contextual Layout tab | Merge group) to display the Split Cells dialog box (Figure 4–69).

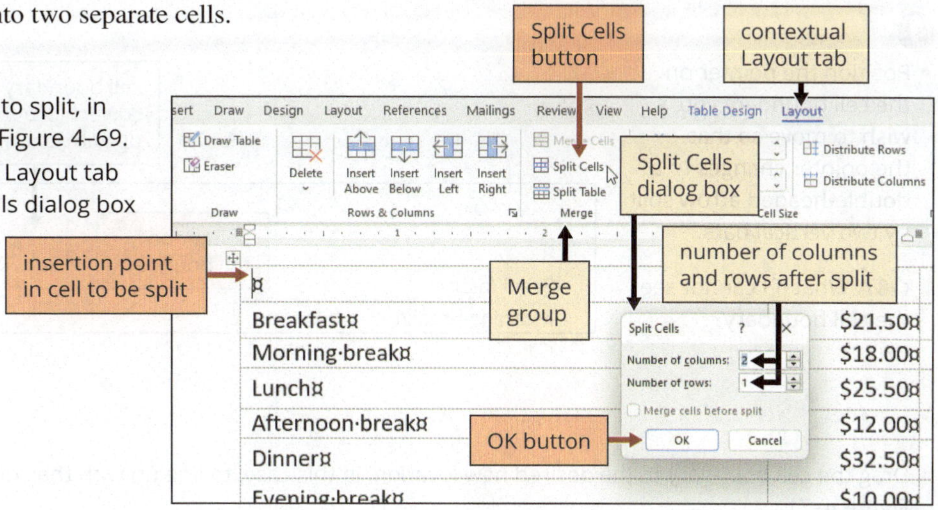

Figure 4–69

2

- Verify the number of columns and rows into which you want the cell split, in this case, 2 columns and 1 row.
- Click OK (Split Cells dialog box) to split the one cell into two columns (Figure 4–70).
- Click in the table to remove the selection from the cells.

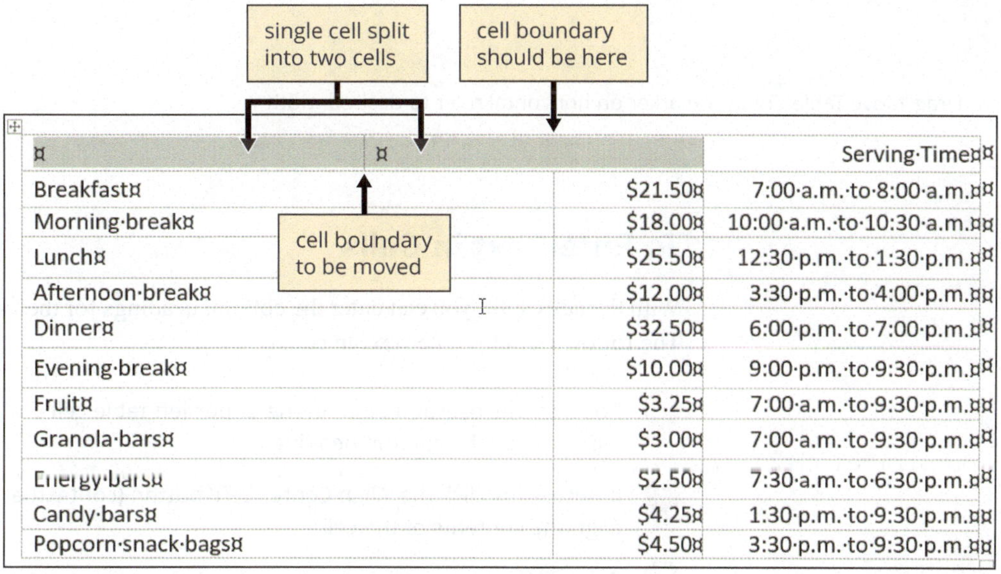

Figure 4–70

Other Ways

1. Right-click cell, click Split Cells on shortcut menu (or, if using touch, tap 'Show Context Menu' button on Mini toolbar)

To Split a Table Instead of splitting table cells into multiple cells, sometimes you want to split a single table into multiple tables. If you wanted to split a table, you would perform the following steps.

1. Position the insertion point in the cell where you want the table to be split.
2. Click the Split Table button (contextual Layout tab | Merge group) to split the table into two tables at the location of the insertion point.

To Move a Cell Boundary

Notice in Figure 4–70 that the cell boundary above the second column does not line up with the rest of the cells in the second column. **Why not?** This is because when you split a cell, Word divides the cell into evenly sized cells. If you want the boundary to line up with other column boundaries, drag it to the desired location. The following step moves a cell boundary.

1

- Position the pointer on the cell boundary you wish to move so that the pointer changes to a double-headed arrow split by two vertical bars.

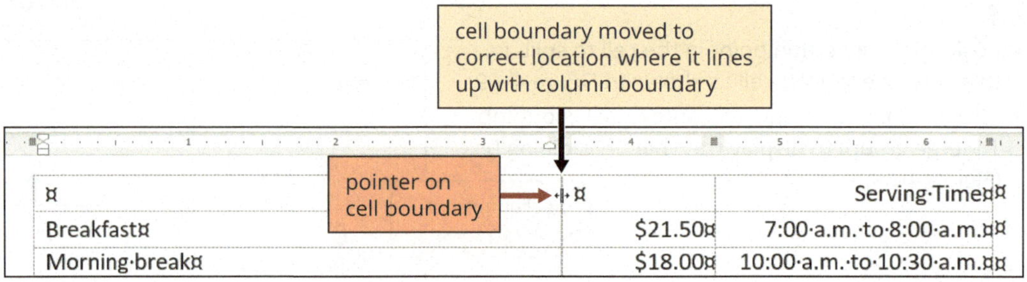

Figure 4–71

Q&A What if I cannot see the cell boundary?
Be sure that table gridlines are showing by using the View Gridlines button (contextual Layout tab | Table group).

- Drag the cell boundary to the desired new location, in this case, to line up with the column boundary to its right, as shown in Figure 4–71.

Q&A What if I am using a touch screen?
Position the insertion point in the upper-left cell and then type **3.6** in the Width box (contextual Layout tab | Cell Size group).

Other Ways

1. Drag 'Move Table Column' marker on horizontal ruler to desired width

To Enter Text in Cells

With the cells split, you can enter the column headings for the first and second column in the table. The following steps enter text in cells.

1. Position the insertion point in the upper-left table cell and then type **Food Catering Options** as the column heading.
2. If necessary, click the 'Align Center Left' button (contextual Layout tab | Alignment group) to align the contents of the cell.
3. Press TAB and then click the 'Align Center Right' button (contextual Layout tab | Alignment group) to align the contents of the cell.
4. Type **Fee per** as the first line of the heading, press ENTER, type **Person** as the heading (shown in Figure 4–72).

To Distribute Rows

The next step in formatting the food catering options table is to make the height of the rows below the column headings uniform, that is, the same height. The following step distributes selected rows. **Why?** Instead of checking and adjusting the width of each row individually, you can format multiple rows to a uniform size at the same time.

1

- Select the rows to format, in this case, all rows below the column headings.
- Click the Distribute Rows button (contextual Layout tab | Cell Size group) to make the height of the selected rows uniform (Figure 4–72).

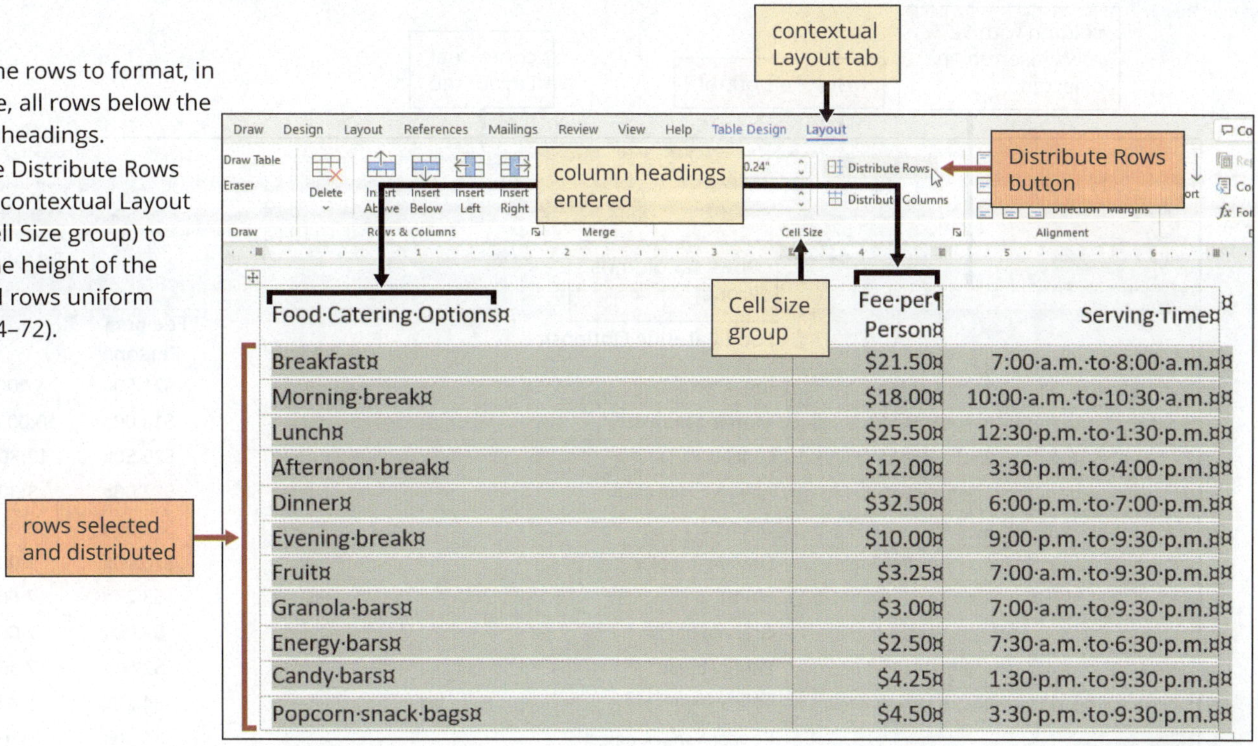

Figure 4–72

Other Ways

1. Right-click selected rows, click 'Distribute Rows Evenly' on shortcut menu (or, if using touch, tap 'Show Context Menu' button on Mini toolbar)

To Change Font Size of Cell Data

The cells below the column headings should be a smaller font size than the headings. Thus, the following step changes font size of the selected rows.

1 With the rows below the column headings selected, change their font size to 11 point (shown in Figure 4–74).

To Insert a Column

In this project, the left edge of the food catering options table has a column that displays the labels, Buffet and A la carte. Thus, the following steps insert a column at the left edge of the table.

1 Position the insertion point somewhere in the first column of the table.

2 If necessary, display the contextual Layout tab.

3 Click the Insert Left button (contextual Layout tab | Rows & Columns group) to insert a column to the left of the column containing the insertion point (Figure 4–73).

4 Click anywhere in the table to remove the selection.

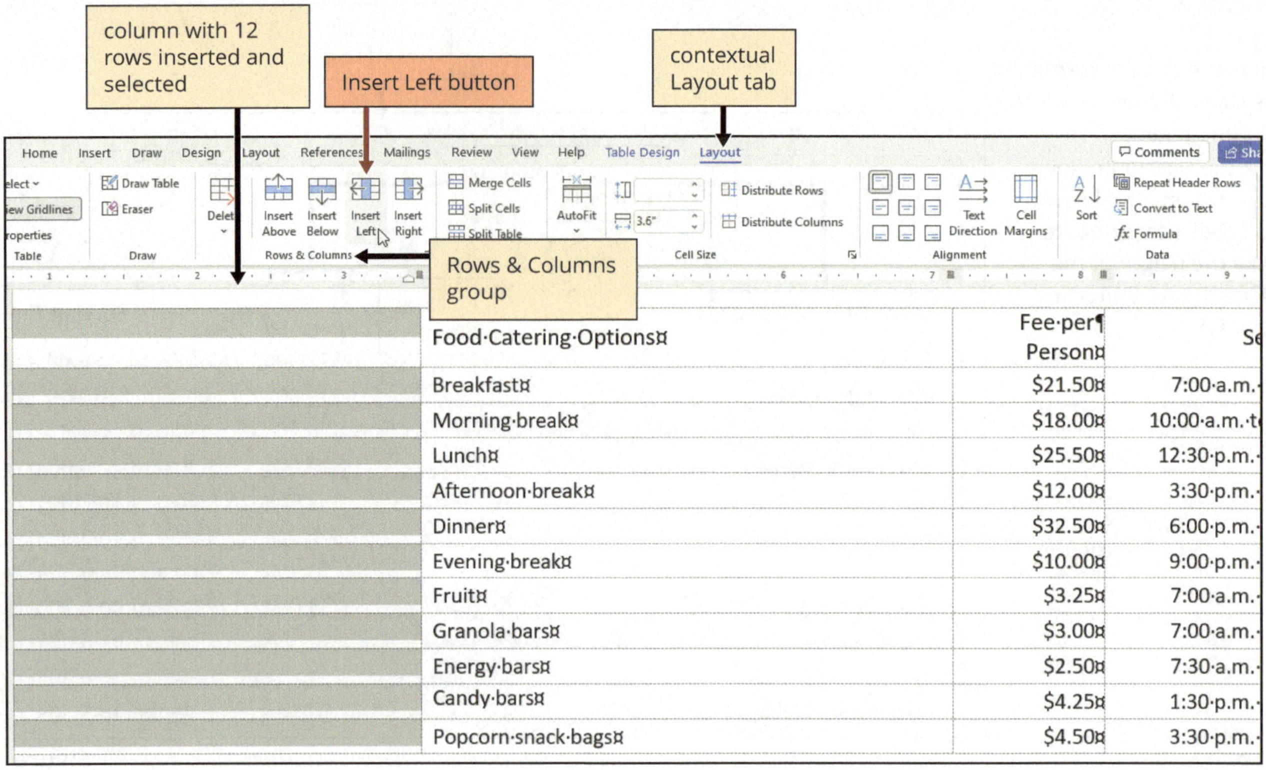

Figure 4–73

BTW
Deleting Table Cells
If you wanted to delete the contents of a table cell, you would select the cell contents and then press DELETE or BACKSPACE. To delete one or more cells entirely from a table, position the insertion point in the cell or select the cells to delete, click the Delete button (contextual Layout tab | Rows & Columns group), click Delete Cells on the Delete menu, select the desired option in the Delete Cells dialog box, and then click OK.

To Delete a Column If you wanted to delete a column, you would perform the following tasks.

1. Position the insertion point in the column to be deleted, click the Delete button (contextual Layout tab | Rows & Columns group), and then click Delete Columns on the Delete menu.

   or

2. If using touch, press and hold row to delete, tap Delete button on Mini toolbar, tap Delete Columns.

   or

3. Right-click the column to delete, click Delete Cells on the shortcut menu, click 'Delete entire column' (Delete Cells dialog box), and then click OK.

   or

4. Select the column to be deleted, right-click the selected column, and then click Delete Columns on the shortcut menu.

To Merge Table Cells

The column just inserted has one cell for each row, in this case, 12 cells (shown in Figure 4–73). The six rows in the first column below the title row should be a single cell with the label, Buffet, and the last five rows in the first column should be a single cell with the label A la carte. **Why?** The row heading, Buffet, should span six rows, and the row heading, A la carte, should span five rows. Thus, the following steps merge cells.

1

- Select the cells to merge, in this case, the second, third, fourth, fifth, sixth, and seventh cells in the first column to the left of the food catering options (Figure 4–74).

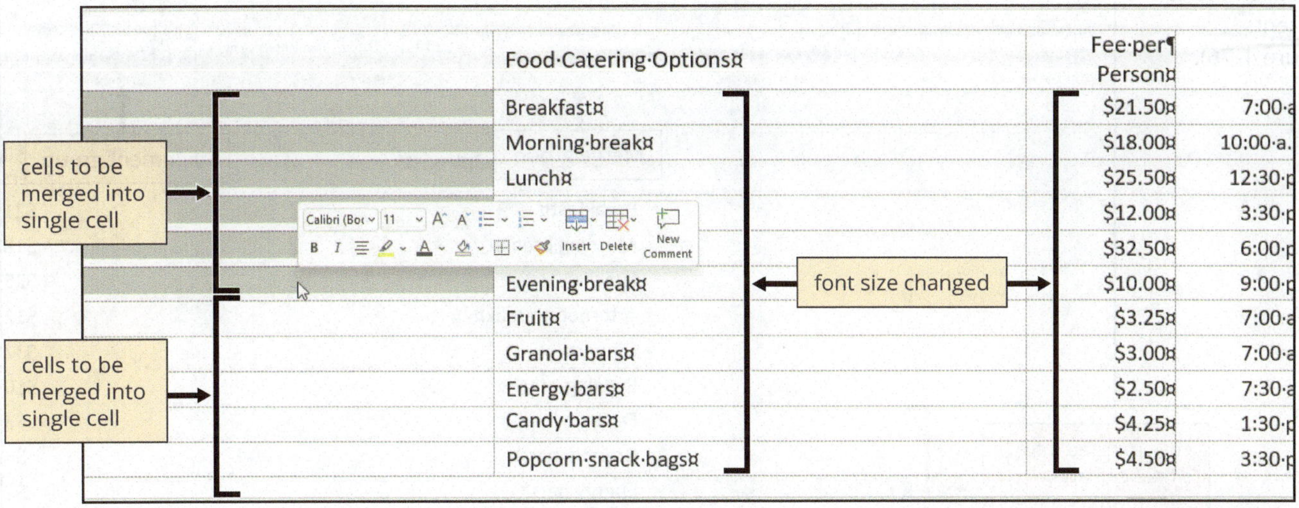

Figure 4–74

2

- With the cells to merge selected, click the Merge Cells button (contextual Layout tab | Merge group) to merge the selected cells into a single cell.
- Click the Align Center button (contextual Layout tab | Alignment group) to realign the cell contents (Figure 4–75).

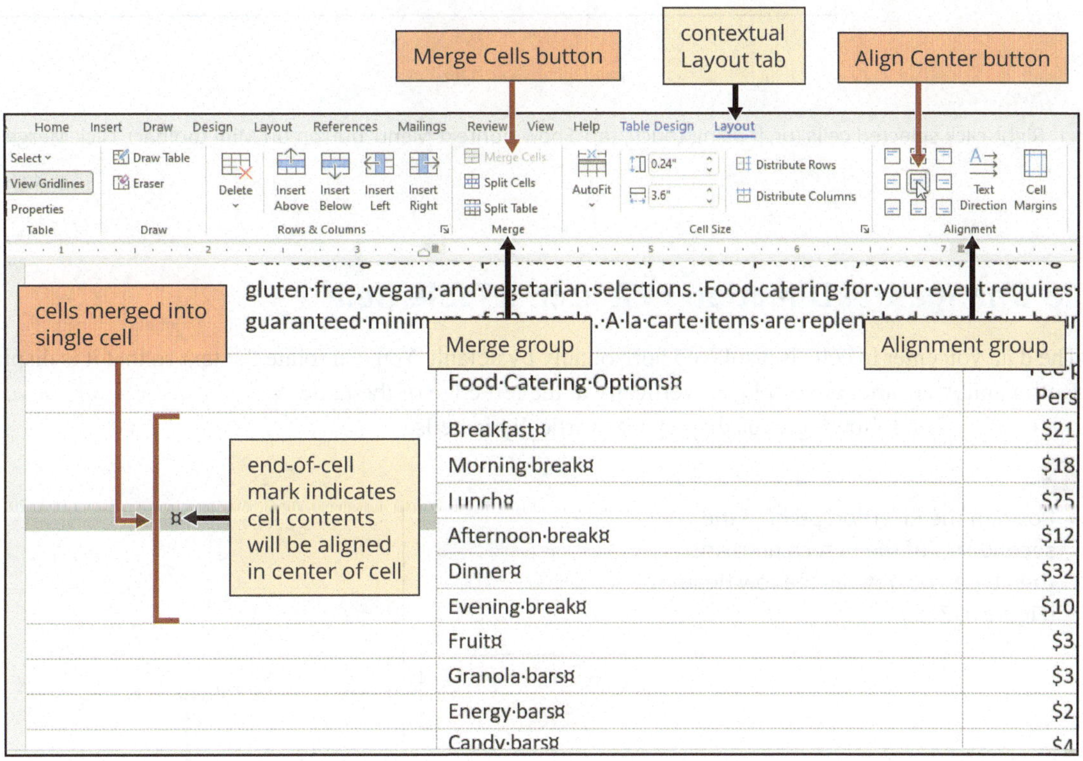

Figure 4–75

3

- Select the cells to merge, in this case, the bottom five cells in the first column to the left of the food catering options.
- With the cells to merge selected, click the Merge Cells button (contextual Layout tab | Merge group) to merge the selected cells into a single cell.

- Click the Align Center button (contextual Layout tab | Alignment group) to realign the cell contents (Figure 4–76).

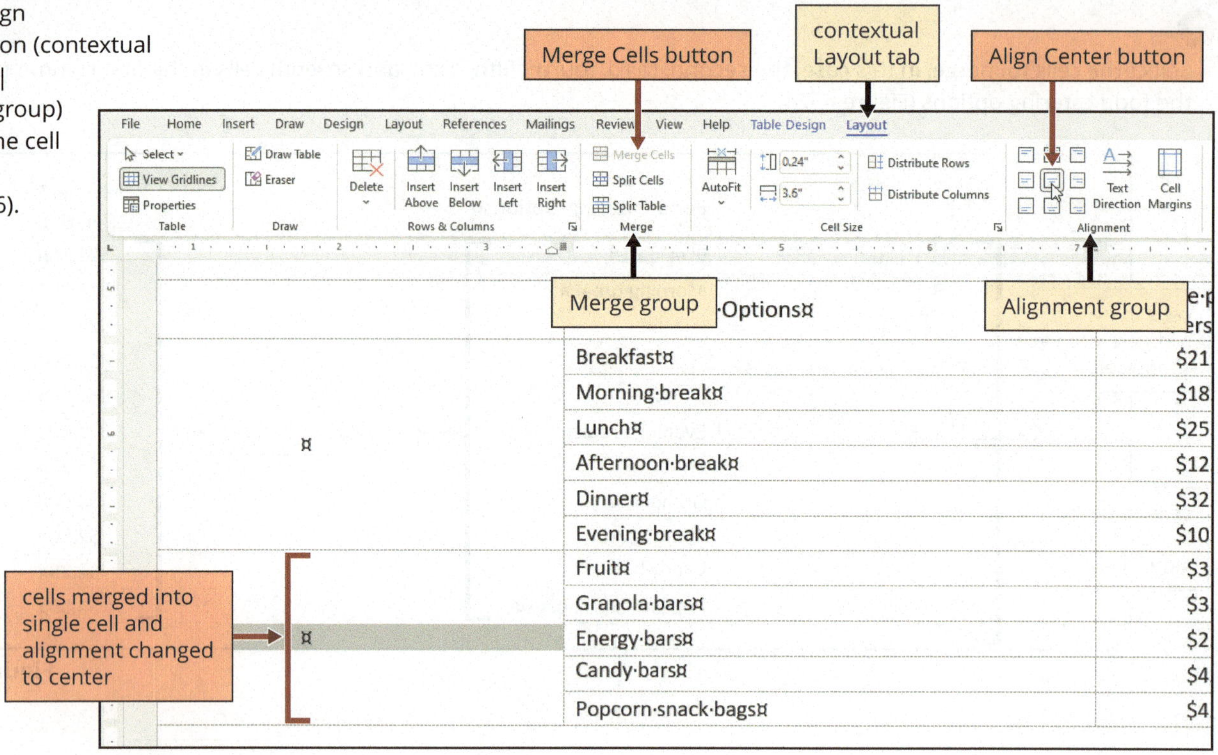

Figure 4–76

Other Ways

1. Right-click selected cells (or, if using touch, tap 'Show Context Menu' button on Mini toolbar), click Merge Cells on shortcut menu

To Change the Direction of Text in a Table Cell

The data you enter in cells is displayed horizontally by default. You can rotate the text so that it is displayed vertically. The labels, Buffet and A la carte, are displayed vertically at the left edge of the table. **Why?** Changing the direction of text adds variety to your tables. The following steps display text vertically in cells.

1

- Position the insertion point in the second row of the first column and then type **Buffet** as the row heading (Figure 4–77).

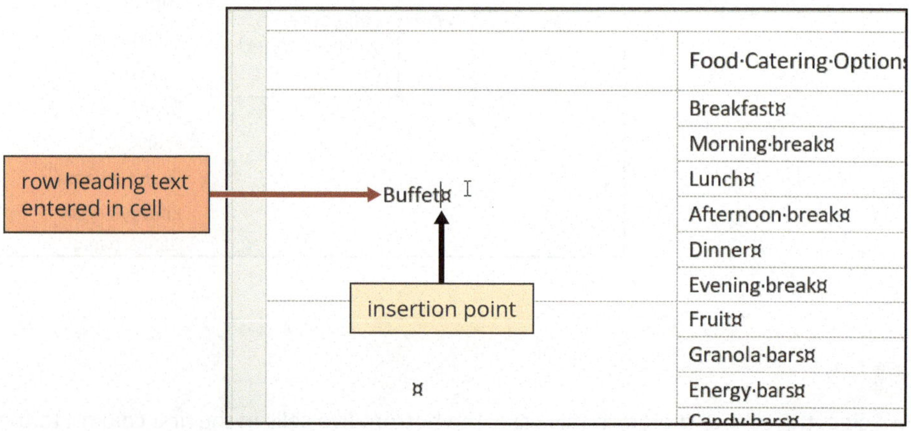

Figure 4–77

2

- With the insertion point in the cell that contains the text to rotate (in this case, Buffet), click the Text Direction button twice (contextual Layout tab | Alignment group) so that the text reads from bottom to top in the cell (Figure 4–78).

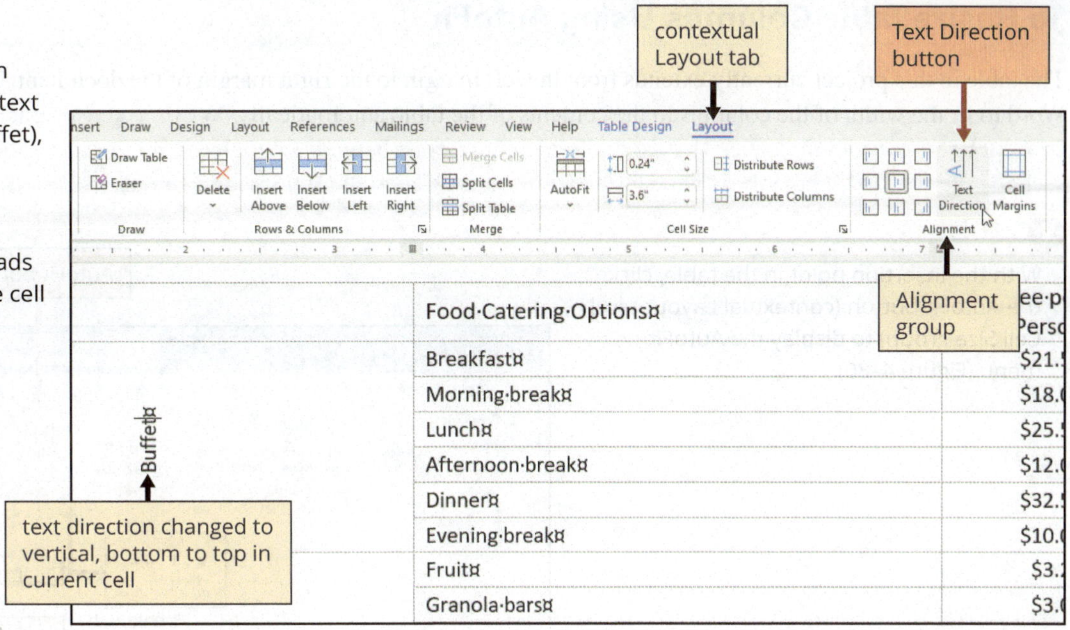

Figure 4–78

Q&A Why click the Text Direction button twice?
The first time you click the Text Direction button (contextual Layout tab | Alignment group), the text in the cell reads from top to bottom. The second time you click it, the text is displayed so that it reads from bottom to top (as shown in Figure 4–78). If you were to click the button a third time, the text would be displayed horizontally again.

3

- Position the insertion point in the third row of the first column and then type **A la carte** as the row heading.
- With the insertion point in the cell that contains the text to rotate (in this case, A la carte), click the Text Direction button twice (contextual Layout tab | Alignment group) so that the text reads from bottom to top in the cell (Figure 4–79).

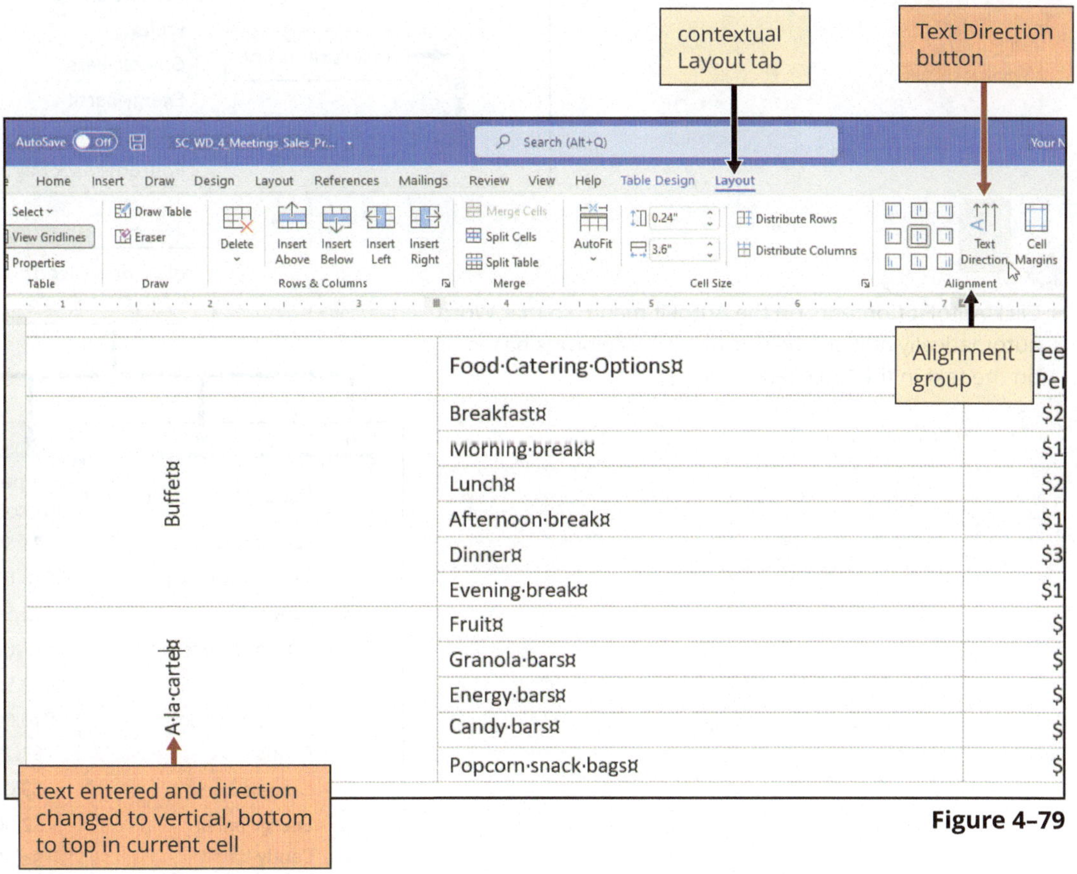

Figure 4–79

To Resize Table Columns Using AutoFit

The table in this project currently extends from the left margin to the right margin of the document. The following steps instruct Word to fit the width of the columns to the contents of the table automatically. **Why?** You want each column to be only as wide as the longest entry in the table. That is, the first column must be wide enough to accommodate the words, A la carte, and the second column should be only as wide as the words, Food Catering Options, and so on.

1

- With the insertion point in the table, click the AutoFit button (contextual Layout tab | Cell Size group) to display the AutoFit menu (Figure 4–80).

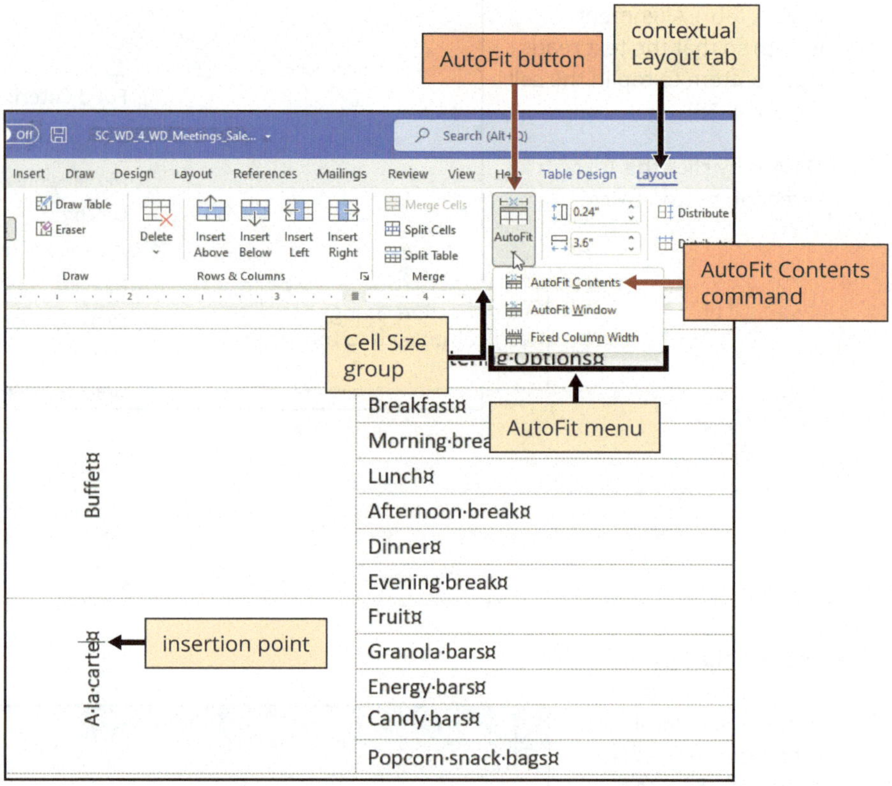

Figure 4–80

2

- Click AutoFit Contents on the AutoFit menu, so that Word automatically adjusts the widths of the columns based on the text in the table (Figure 4–81).

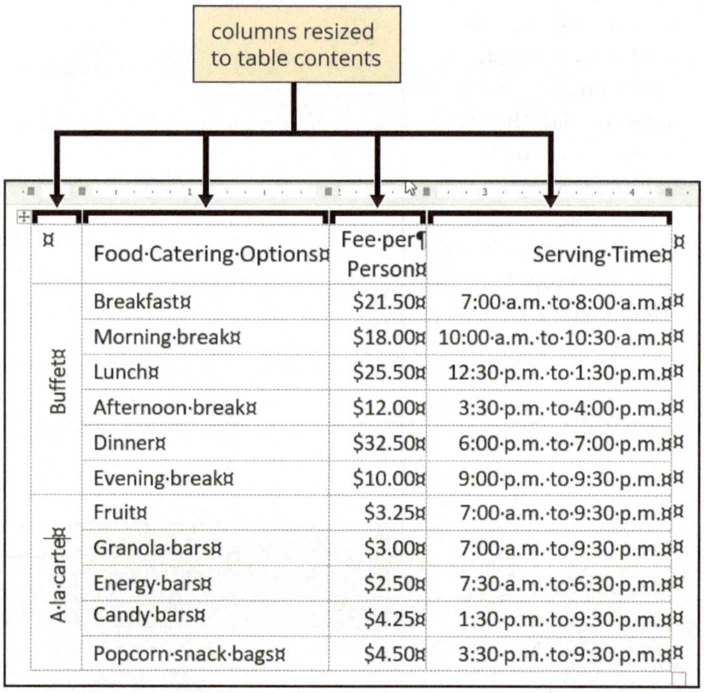

Figure 4–81

Other Ways

1. Double-click column boundary

To Change Column Widths

You would like the Fee per Person and Serving Time columns slightly wider. Thus, the next step is to change the width of these column. The following steps change column widths.

1. Position the insertion point in the column to format, in this case, the Fee per Person column.
2. Type .8 in the Width box (contextual Layout tab | Cell Size group) and then press ENTER to change the width of the column containing the insertion point.
3. Position the insertion point in the column to format, in this case, the Serving Time column.
4. Type 1.8 in the Width box (contextual Layout tab | Cell Size group) and then press ENTER to change the width of the column containing the insertion point (Figure 4–82).

Q&A What if I am using a touch screen?
Position the insertion point in the column to adjust. Tap the Width box (contextual Layout tab | Cell Size group), type the column width value, and then press ENTER.

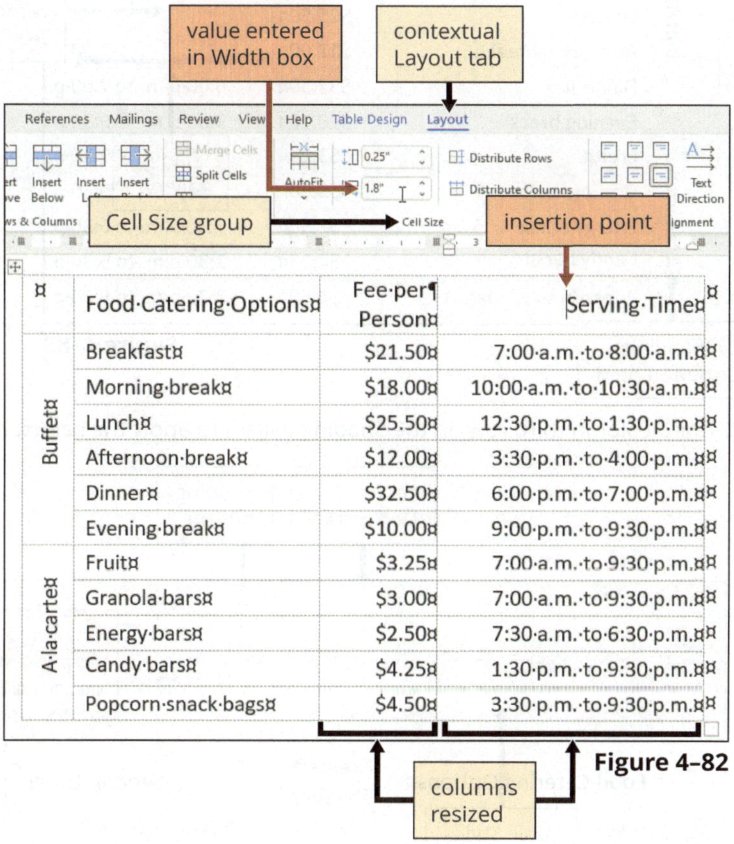

Figure 4–82

BTW
Table Columns
If you hold down ALT while dragging a column marker on the ruler or a column boundary in the table, the width measurements of all columns appear on the ruler as you drag the column marker or boundary.

To Bold Cell Contents

You would like the column and row headings to be formatted in bold. The following steps bold text.

1. Select the column headings and bold them.
2. Select the row headings (Buffet and A la carte) and bold them (shown in Figure 4–83).

To Shade Table Cells

In this table, the cells containing the row headers, Buffet and A la carte, are to be shaded gray. **Why?** You want the cell shading color to complement the colors on the cover page and headers and footers. The following steps shade cells.

1

- Position the insertion point in the cell to shade (in this case, the cell containing the Buffet row heading).
- Display the Table Design tab.
- Click the Shading arrow (Table Design tab | Table Styles group) to display the Shading gallery (Figure 4–83).

- **Experiment:** Point to various colors in the Shading gallery and watch the shading color of the current cell change.

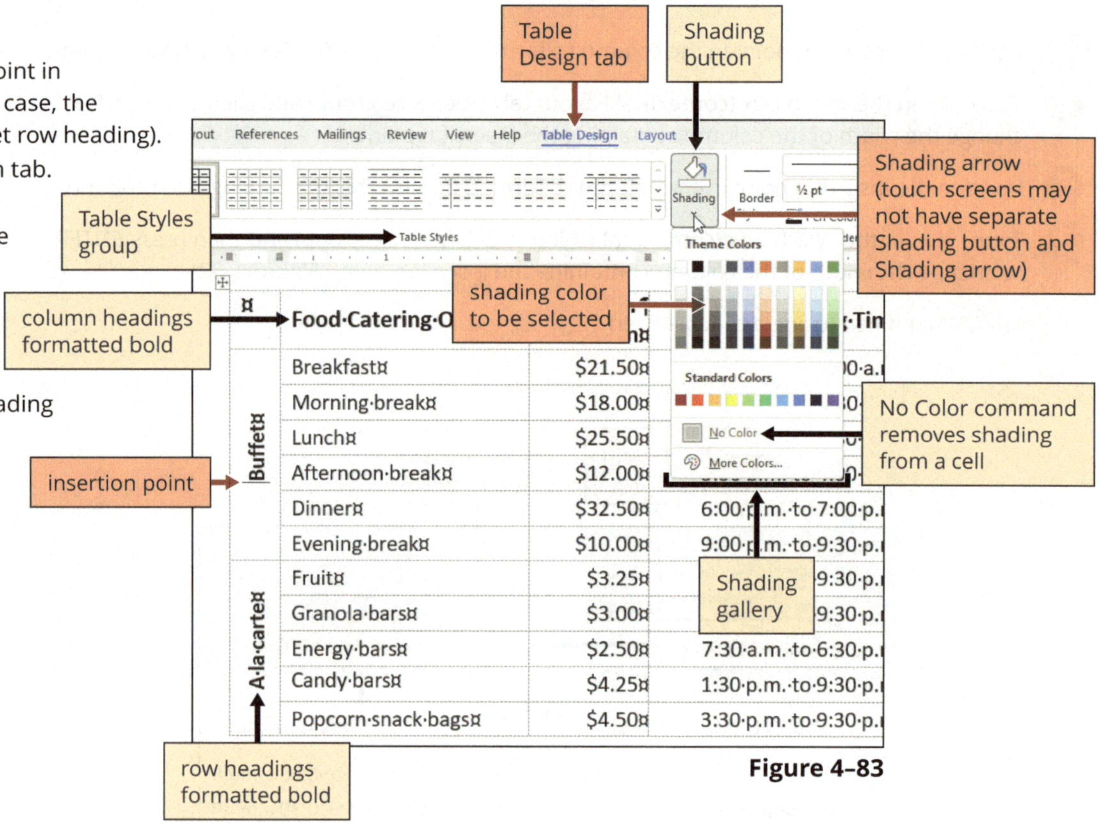

Figure 4–83

2

- Click 'Light Gray, Background 2, Darker 25%' (third color in third row) in the Shading gallery to apply the selected shading color to the current cell.

3

- Position the insertion point in the cell to shade (in this case, the cell containing the row header, A la carte).
- Click the Shading arrow (Table Design tab | Table Styles group) to display the Shading gallery and then click 'Light Gray, Background 2, Darker 75%' (third color in fifth row) in the Shading gallery to apply the selected shading color to the current cell (Figure 4–84).

Q&A Why did the text, A la carte, change to white in the cell?

When text color is too dark to be read on a shaded background, Word automatically changes the text color to white for ease of readability.

What happens if I click the Shading button (Table Design tab | Table Styles group) instead?

Word applies the most recently selected shading color to the current cell.

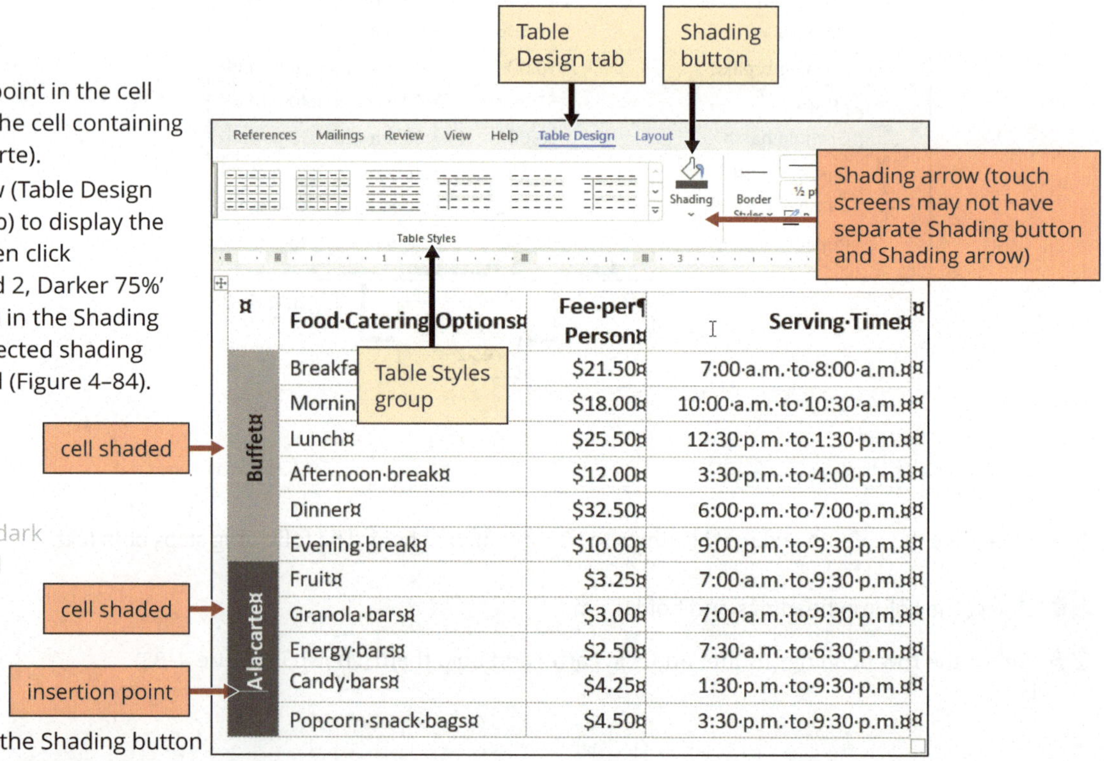

Figure 4–84

To Change Row Height

The next step in this project is to decrease the height of the cells below the column headings and to the right of the row headings. The following steps change row height.

1. Select the cells to format (in this case, the cells to the right of the row headings and below the column headings, as shown in Figure 4–85).
2. Display the contextual Layout tab.
3. Type **.2** in the Height box (contextual Layout tab | Cell Size group) and then press ENTER to change the row height to this value (Figure 4–85).

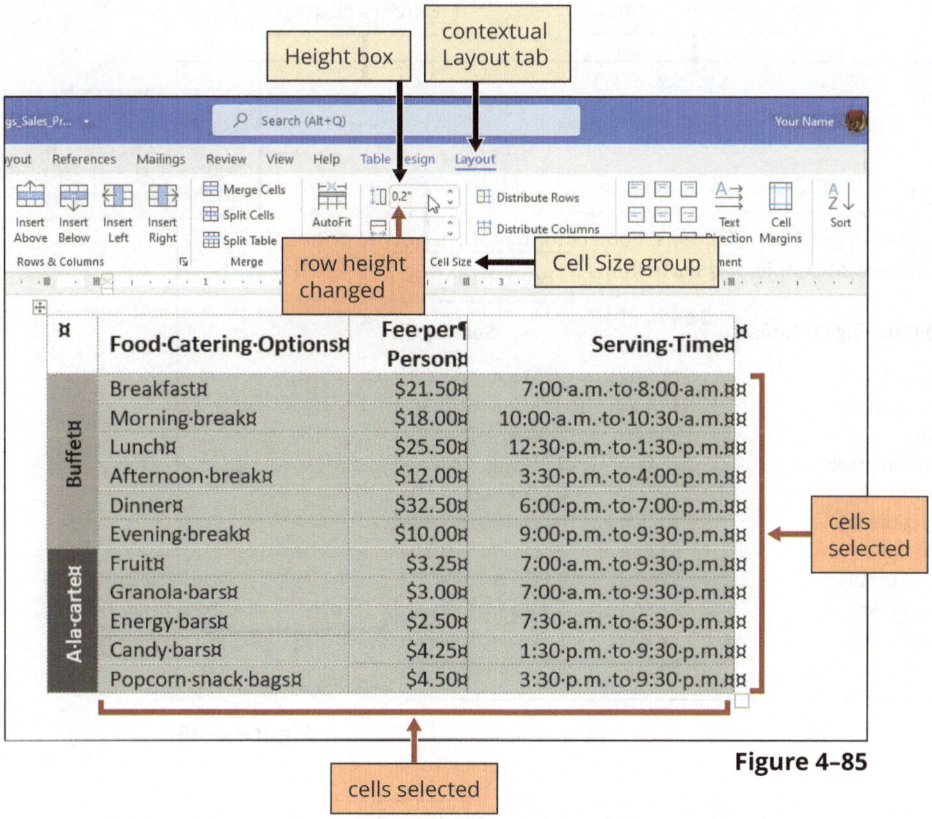

Figure 4–85

BTW
Draw Table
If you want to draw the boundary, rows, and columns of a table, click the Table button (Insert tab | Tables group) and then click Draw Table in the Table gallery. Use the pencil-shaped pointer to draw the perimeter of the table and the inside rows and columns. Use the Eraser button (contextual Layout tab | Draw group) to erase lines in the table. To continue drawing, click the Draw Table button (Table Design tab | Draw group).

To Hide Gridlines

You no longer need to see the gridlines in the table. Thus, you can hide the gridlines. The following steps hide gridlines.

1. If necessary, position the insertion point in a table cell.
2. Click the View Gridlines button (contextual Layout tab | Table group) to hide gridlines in the table on the screen.

To Add a Table Border

The table in this project has a ¼-point, gray, double-line border around all cells. The following steps change the border color in a table using the Borders and Shading dialog box. **Why?** Because the table border should be a double line with a gray color, you will use the Borders and Shading dialog box to specify the border settings for the table.

1

- If necessary, position the insertion point somewhere in the table.
- Display the Table Design tab.
- Click the Borders arrow (Table Design tab | Borders group) to display the Borders gallery (Figure 4–86).

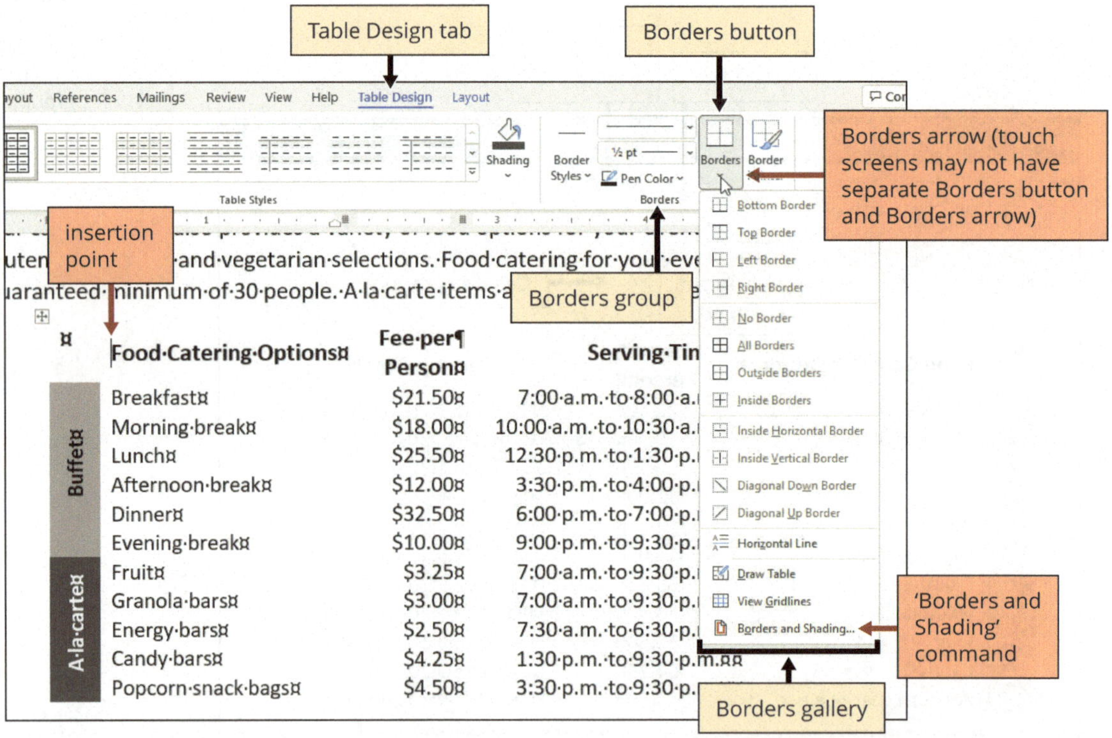

Figure 4–86

2

- Click 'Borders and Shading' in the Borders gallery to display the Borders and Shading dialog box.
- Click All in the Setting area (Borders and Shading dialog box), which will place a border on every cell in the table.
- Scroll to and then click the double line in the Style list.
- Click the Color arrow and then click 'Gray, Accent 3, Darker 25%' (seventh color in fifth row) in the Color palette to specify the border color.
- Click the Width arrow and then ¼ pt in the Width list to specify the border width (Figure 4–87).

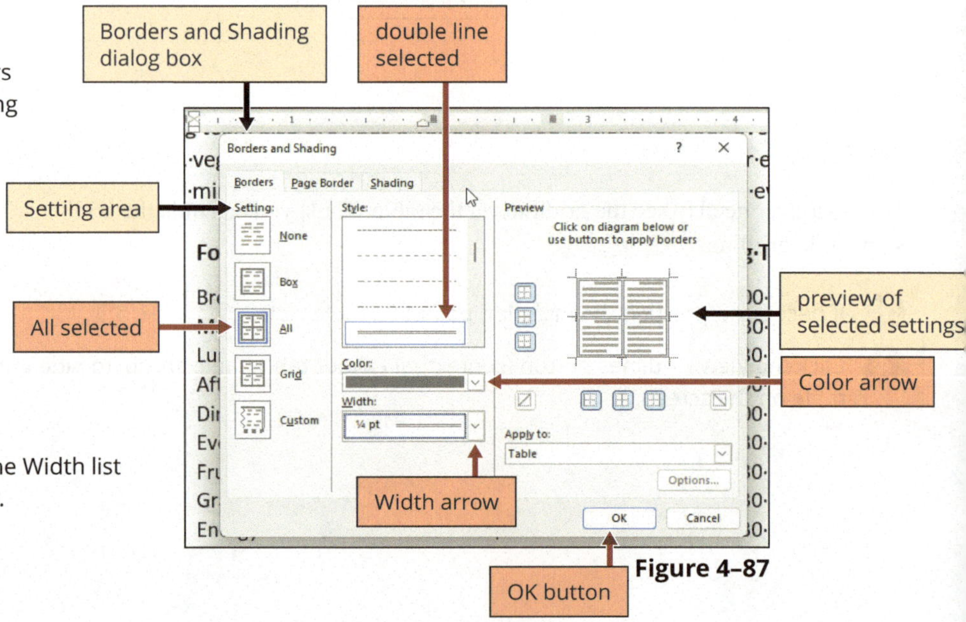

Figure 4–87

3

- Click OK to place the border shown in the preview area of the dialog box around the table cells in the document (Figure 4–88).
- If the entire sales proposal does not fit on three pages as shown in Figure 4–1 at the beginning of this module, remove space above and below paragraphs until the entire proposal fits on three pages.

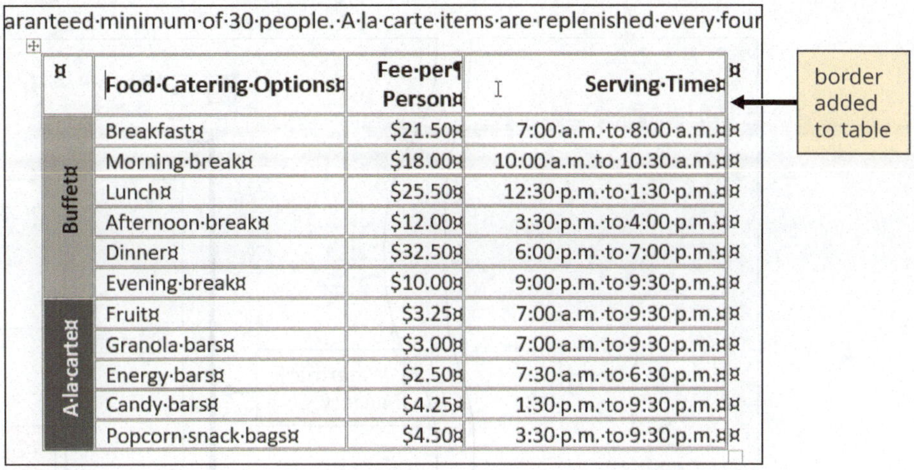
aranteed·minimum·of·30·people.·A·la·carte·items·are·replenished·every·four

¤	Food·Catering·Options¤	Fee·per¶ Person¤	Serving·Time¤
Buffet¤	Breakfast¤	$21.50¤	7:00·a.m.·to·8:00·a.m.¤
	Morning·break¤	$18.00¤	10:00·a.m.·to·10:30·a.m.¤
	Lunch¤	$25.50¤	12:30·p.m.·to·1:30·p.m.¤
	Afternoon·break¤	$12.00¤	3:30·p.m.·to·4:00·p.m.¤
	Dinner¤	$32.50¤	6:00·p.m.·to·7:00·p.m.¤
	Evening·break¤	$10.00¤	9:00·p.m.·to·9:30·p.m.¤
A·la·carte¤	Fruit¤	$3.25¤	7:00·a.m.·to·9:30·p.m.¤
	Granola·bars¤	$3.00¤	7:00·a.m.·to·9:30·p.m.¤
	Energy·bars¤	$2.50¤	7:30·a.m.·to·6:30·p.m.¤
	Candy·bars¤	$4.25¤	1:30·p.m.·to·9:30·p.m.¤
	Popcorn·snack·bags¤	$4.50¤	3:30·p.m.·to·9:30·p.m.¤

Figure 4–88

Creating a Watermark

The final task in this project is to create a watermark for the pages of the sales proposal. A **watermark** is text or a graphic, often semitransparent, that is displayed on top of or behind the text in a document. For example, a catalog may print the words, Sold Out, on top of sold-out items. The first draft of a five-year plan may have the word, Draft, printed behind the text of the document. Some companies use their logos or other graphics as watermarks to add visual appeal to their documents.

To Change the Zoom to Multiple Pages

The following steps display multiple pages in their entirety in the document window as large as possible, so that you can see the position of the watermark as you create it.

1 Display the View tab.

2 Click the Multiple Pages button (View tab | Zoom group) to display all three pages in the document window as large as possible (shown in Figure 4–89).

To Create a Watermark

In this project, the text, At Your Service!, is displayed behind all content in the proposal as a watermark. **Why?** The text adds visual appeal to the document, enticing readers to review its contents. The following steps create a watermark.

1

- Display the Design tab.
- Click the Watermark button (Design tab | Page Background group) to display the Watermark gallery (Figure 4–89).

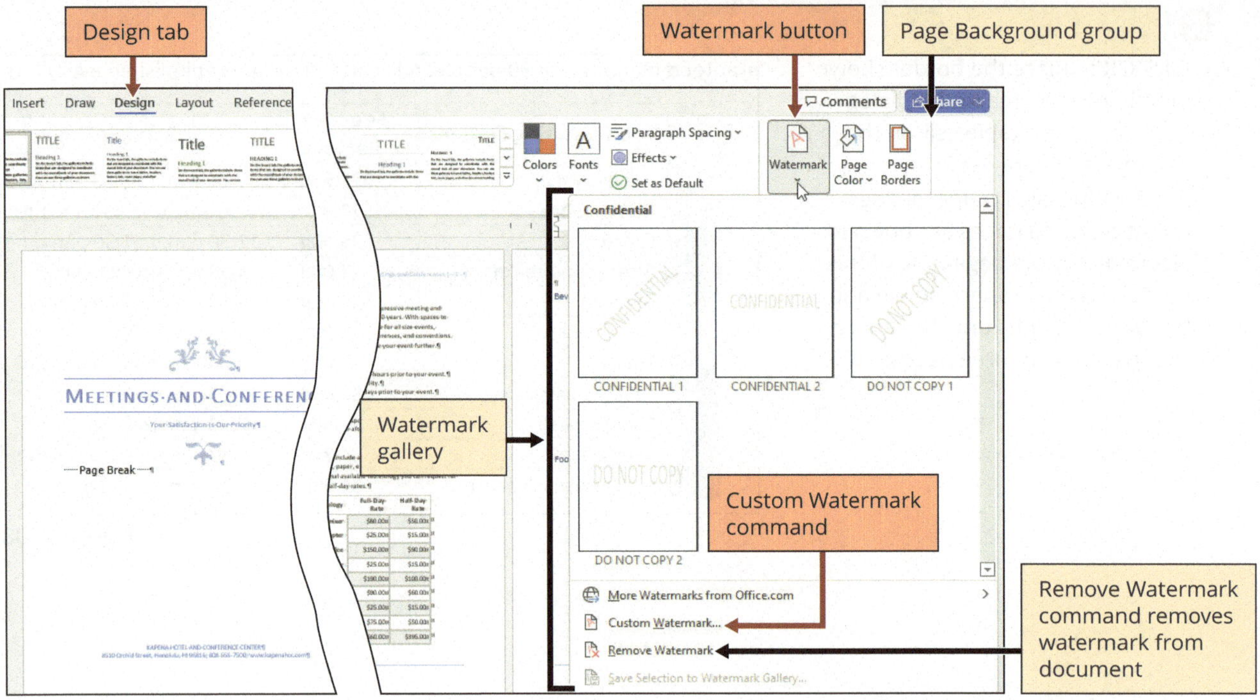

Figure 4–89

2

- Click Custom Watermark in the Watermark gallery to display the Printed Watermark dialog box.
- Click the Text watermark option button to select it (Printed Watermark dialog box), which enables you to enter or select text for the watermark.
- Select the text in the Text box and type **At Your Service!** in the Text box to replace the text.
- Click the Font arrow to display the list of fonts, scroll to and then click 'Brush Script MT' to select the font for the text watermark.
- Click the Font Size arrow to display the list of font sizes, scroll to and then click 44 to select the font size for the text watermark.
- If necessary, click Diagonal to specify the direction for the text watermark.
- Click the Apply button to show a preview of the watermark on the pages in the document window (Figure 4–90).

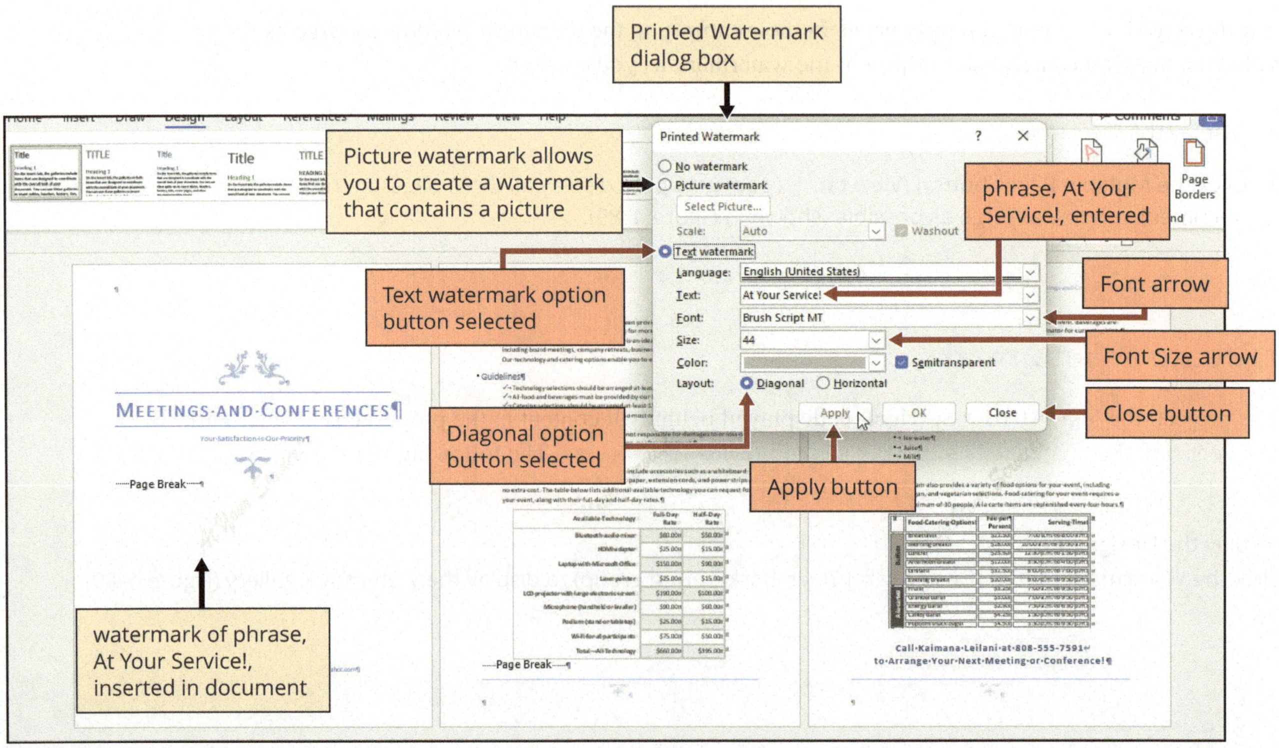

Figure 4–90

3

- Click Close to close the dialog box.

Q&A How do I remove a watermark from a document?
Click the Watermark button (Design tab | Page Background group) and then click Remove Watermark in the Watermark gallery (shown in Figure 4–89).

How do I create a picture watermark?
Click Picture watermark in the Printed Watermark dialog box (shown in Figure 4–90), click the Select Picture button to display the Insert Pictures dialog box, locate the desired picture, click the Insert button, click the Apply button, and then click Close.

Other Ways

1. Click 'Explore Quick Parts' button (Insert tab | Text group), click 'Building Blocks Organizer' on Explore Quick Parts menu, select desired watermark (Building Blocks Organizer dialog box), click Insert button

To Change the Zoom to Page Width

The following steps change the zoom to 100% so that you can see the watermark behind the first table in the proposal.

1 Display the View tab.

2 Click the 100% button (View tab | Zoom group) to display the pages at 100% in the document window (shown in Figure 4–91).

Q&A Why does my screen display two pages side-by-side in the document window?
Depending on screen resolution and other settings, your screen may display two pages in the document window. If this occurs, adjust the zoom percentage as necessary until only one page is displayed in the document window.

To Remove Table Shading

Watermarks do not show up behind shaded text or objects, which is why the watermark is not entirely visible behind the available technology table (shown in Figure 4–91). The following steps remove shading from cells in the table. **Why?** Even though it appears that the cells in the first column of the table are not shaded, they actually are shaded in white. To see the watermark, you will need to remove this shading. The following steps remove shading in table cells.

1

- Scroll to display the first table in the proposal in the document window.
- Select the cells in which you want to remove shading (in this case, the first column).
- Display the Table Design tab.
- Click the Shading arrow (Table Design tab | Table Styles group) to display the Shading gallery (Figure 4–91).

Q&A What if I want to remove shading from just one cell?
You do not need to select the cell. Just position the insertion point in the cell from which you would like to remove shading.

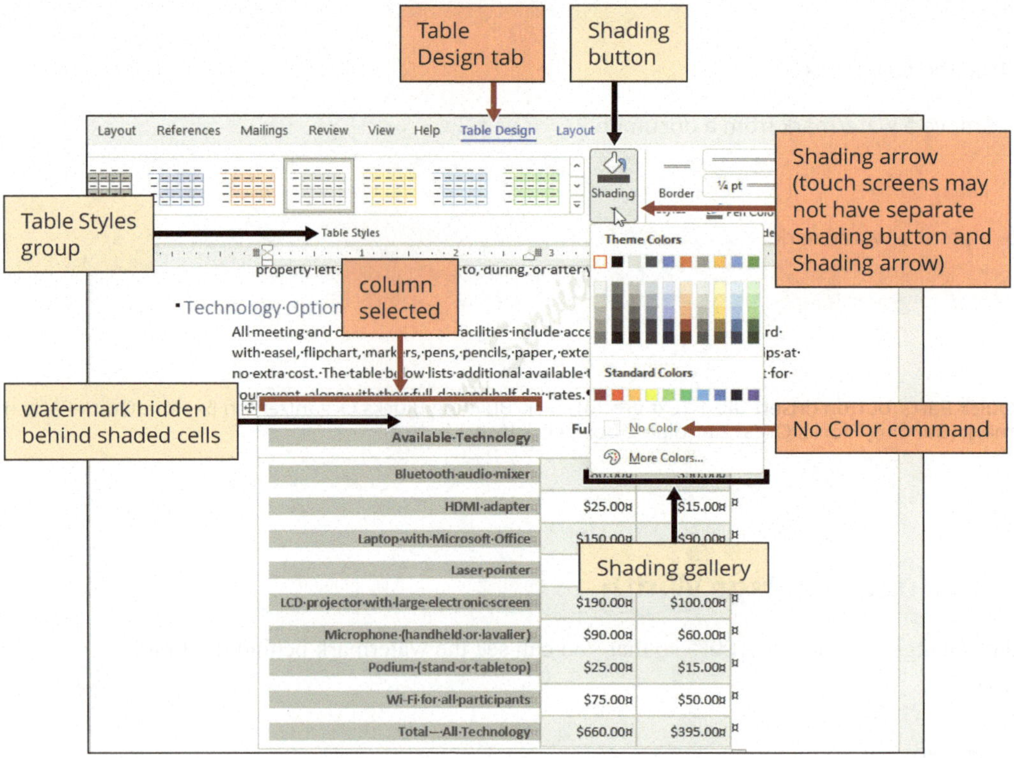

Figure 4–91

2

- Click No Color in the Shading gallery to remove the shading from the selected cells.
- Click anywhere to remove the selection from the table and notice the watermark now is visible behind the table (Figure 4–92).

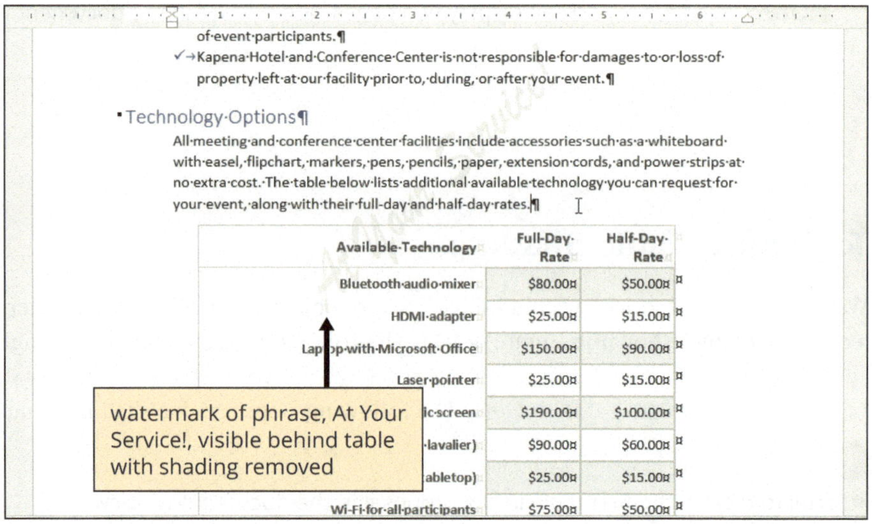

Figure 4–92

To Check and Fix Accessibility Issues

Recall that Word includes an Accessibility Checker that identifies potential accessibility issues and presents suggestions to make your documents more inclusive. Notice that instead of the phrase, Good to go, the Accessibility button on the status bar shows the word, Investigate. The following steps use the Accessibility Checker.

1 Click the Accessibility button on the status bar to open the Accessibility pane.

2 If necessary, click the arrow to the left of 'Missing alternative text' in the Accessibility pane to expand the description, which suggests three pictures should have alternative text. (**Note:** Instead of 'Missing alternative text', your version of Word may display 'Suggested alternative text' or 'Missing Object Description' or some other wording.)

3 One at a time, click the arrow to the right of each picture label to display the Recommended Actions menu and then click 'Mark as decorative' on the Recommended Actions menu because the pictures in the proposal add visual appeal but do not convey any meaning.

4 If necessary, click the arrow to the left of 'Image or object not inline' in the Accessibility pane to expand the description (which identifies a text box), click the arrow to the right of the text box label to display the Recommended Actions menu, and then click 'Mark as decorative' on the Recommended Actions menu.

5 Leave the last warning identified by the Accessibility Checker for merged or split cells in table.

Q&A How would I remove the last warning?

For purposes of illustrating Word's table commands and features, the Buffet and A la carte cells will remain as merged with vertical text for this project, but if you wanted to remove the accessibility warning, you would do the following: change the text direction of Buffet and A la carte from vertical to horizontal, split the Buffet cell into 1 column/6 rows (which will place Buffet in the top row), and then split the A la carte cell into 1 column/5 rows (which will place A la carte in the top row).

What if I find the small caps on the title page difficult to read?

For purposes of illustrating Word's small caps features, the title on the cover page will remain in small caps for this project, but if you wanted to remove the small caps, you would do this following: select the title on the cover page, display the Font sheet in the Font dialog box, remove the check mark from the Small caps check box (Font dialog box), and then click OK.

6 Click the Close button in the Accessibility pane to close the pane.

BTW

Print Scaling

If you wanted to ensure a document prints on a certain paper size, you can scale the document by opening Backstage view, clicking Print, clicking the bottom option in the Settings area of the Print screen, pointing to 'Scale to Paper Size', and then clicking the desired paper size before printing the document.

BTW

Conserving Ink and Toner

If you want to conserve ink or toner, you can instruct Word to print draft-quality documents by clicking File on the ribbon to open Backstage view, clicking Options in Backstage view to display the Word Options dialog box, clicking Advanced in the left pane (Word Options dialog box), scrolling to the Print area in the right pane, placing a check mark in the 'Use draft quality' check box, and then clicking OK. Then, use Backstage view to print the document as usual.

To Check Spelling, Save, Print, and Exit Word

The following steps check the spelling of the document, save and print the document, and then exit Word.

1 Display the Review tab. Click the Spelling and Grammar button or Editor button (Review tab | Proofing group) to begin the spelling and grammar check. Correct any misspelled words. Ignore proper names.

2 sam Save the sales proposal again with the same file name.

3 If requested by your instructor, print the sales proposal (shown in Figure 4–1 at the beginning of this module).

4 Exit Word.

BTW

Distributing a Document

Instead of printing and distributing a hard copy of a document, you can distribute the document electronically. Options include sending the document via email; posting it on cloud storage (such as OneDrive) and sharing the file with others; posting it on social media, a blog, or other website; and sharing a link associated with an online location of the document. You also can create and share a PDF or XPS image of the document, so that users can view the file in Adobe Acrobat Reader or XPS Viewer instead of in Word.

Summary

In this module, you learned how to insert a cover page, insert text in content controls, apply character effects, change paragraph indentation, insert formatted headers and footers, format page numbers, sort lists and tables, format bullet characters, create a multilevel list, edit and format Word tables, insert a formula in a table, and insert a watermark.

Consider This: Plan Ahead

What decisions will you need to make when creating your next proposal?

Use these guidelines as you complete the assignments in this module and create your own proposals outside of this class.

1. **Identify the nature of the proposal.**
   a) If someone else requests that you develop the proposal, it is a **solicited proposal**. Be sure to include all requested information in a solicited proposal.
   b) When you write a proposal because you recognize a need, it is considered an **unsolicited proposal**. With an unsolicited proposal, you must gather information you believe will be relevant and of interest to the intended audience.
2. **Design an eye-catching cover page.**
   a) The cover page should convey the overall message of the sales proposal.
   b) Use text, graphics, formats, and colors that reflect the goals of the sales proposal.
   c) Be sure to include a title.
3. **Compose the text of the sales proposal.**
   a) Sales proposals vary in length, style, and formality, but all should be designed to elicit acceptance from the reader.
   b) The sales proposal should have a neat, organized appearance.
   c) A successful sales proposal uses succinct wording and includes lists for textual messages.
   d) Write text using active voice, instead of passive voice.
   e) Assume that readers of unsolicited sales proposals have no previous knowledge about the topic.
   f) Be sure the goal of the proposal is clear.
   g) Establish a theme and carry it throughout the proposal.
4. **Enhance the sales proposal with appropriate visuals.**
   a) Use visuals to add interest, clarify ideas, and illustrate points.
   b) Visuals include tables, charts, and graphical images (i.e., photos, etc.).
5. **Proofread and edit the proposal.**
   a) Carefully review the sales proposal to be sure it contains no spelling, grammar, mathematical, or other errors.
   b) Check that transitions between sentences and paragraphs are smooth. Ensure that the purpose of the proposal is stated clearly.
   c) Ask others to review the proposal and give you suggestions for improvements.

BTW
Printing Document Properties
To print document properties, click File on the ribbon to open Backstage view, click Print in Backstage view to display the Print screen, click the first button in the Settings area to display a list of options specifying what you can print, click Document Info in the list to specify you want to print the document properties instead of the actual document, and then click the Print button on the Print screen to print the document properties on the currently selected printer.

Student Assignments

Apply Your Knowledge

Reinforce the skills and apply the concepts you learned in this module.

Working with Headers, Multilevel Lists, Tables, and Footers

Note: To complete this assignment, you will be required to use the Data Files. Please contact your instructor for information about accessing the Data Files.

Instructions: Start Word. Open the document, SC_WD_4-2.docx, which is located in the Data Files. The document is a draft for a proposal that presents the schedule and other information for Camden Park District summer camps. The park district manager, who created the draft, has asked you to delete its watermark; modify the header, footer, and table; and insert a multilevel list to create the finished document shown in Figure 4–93.

Perform the following tasks:

1. Click File on the ribbon and then click Save As and save the document using the new file name, SC_WD_4_SummerCampProposal.
2. Remove the watermark. (**Hint:** Use the Watermark button (Design tab | Page Background group).)
3. Apply the Heading 1 style to the first line of text that reads: General Information.
4. Remove the current header from the document. (**Hint:** Use the Header button (Insert tab | Header & Footer group).)
5. Add the predefined header called Banded to the document. Insert the text, Summer Camp!, in the Title content control in the header.
6. Format the text, Summer Camp!, in the header as small caps, bold the text, change its font size to 18 point, and expand its character spacing by 5 points. (**Hint:** Use the Font dialog box.)
7. Increase by one-half inch the left indent of the first paragraph of text that begins, Camden Park District offers…. (**Hint:** Use the Increase Indent button, the Left Indent marker on the ruler, the Layout tab on the ribbon, or the Paragraph dialog box.)
8. Increase by one-half inch the right indent of the first paragraph of text that begins, Camden Park District offers…. (**Hint:** Use the Right Indent marker on the ruler, the Layout tab on the ribbon, or the Paragraph dialog box.)
9. On the blank line above the table, create the following multilevel list using the number style shown. Increase the indent of the multilevel list so the 1) in the first list item is lined up with the left indent of the paragraphs above and below it. (That is, the 1 should be at the .5" mark on the ribbon.) Be sure to promote and demote the list items as shown below.

    1) Bring these essentials
        a) Bedding
            i) Sleeping bag or blanket and sheets
            ii) Pillow
        b) Hygiene items
            i) Toothbrush and toothpaste
            ii) Washcloth and soap
            iii) Shampoo
            iv) Bath towels
            v) Plastic bag for dirty clothes

Continued on next page

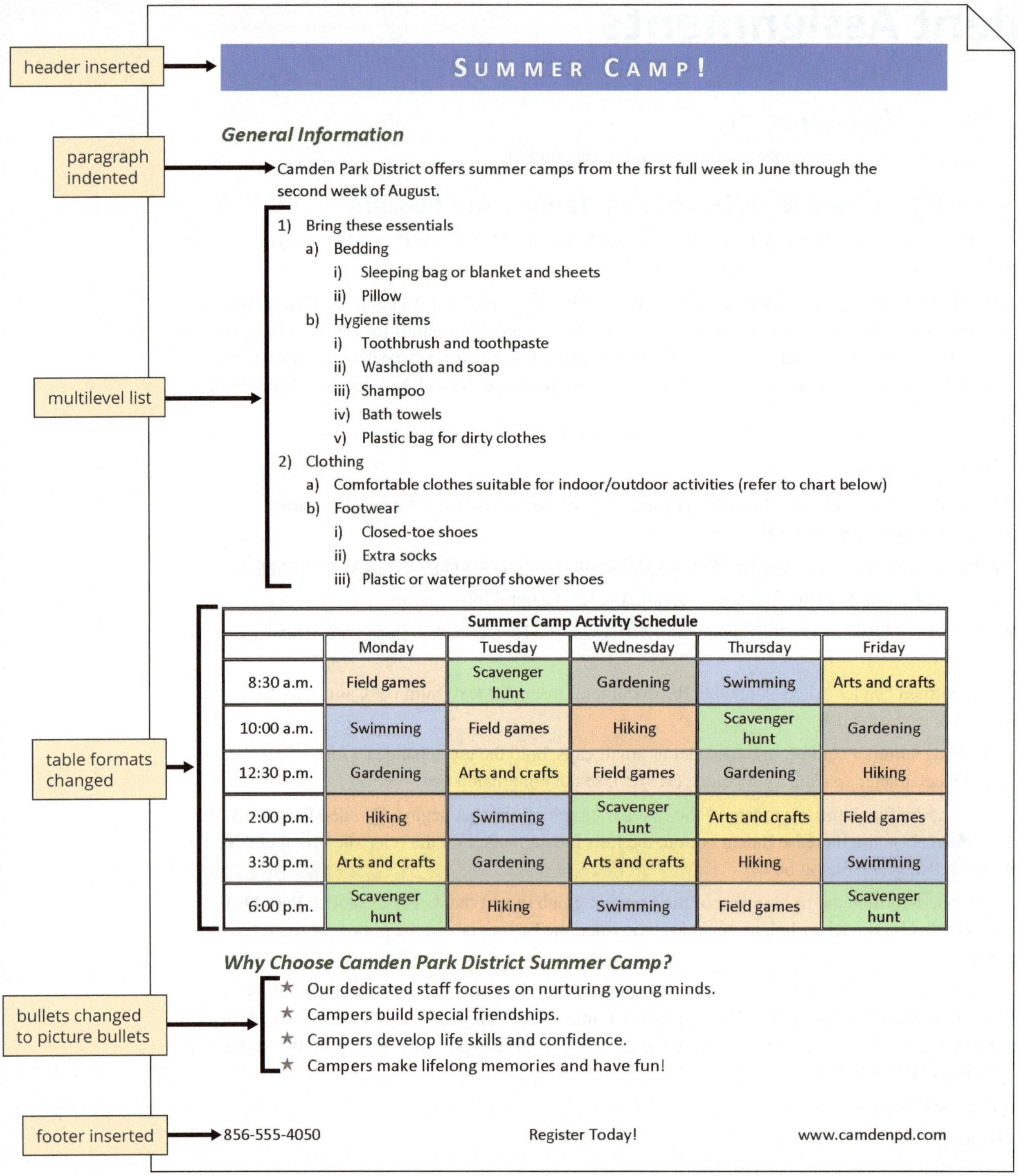

SUMMER CAMP!

General Information

Camden Park District offers summer camps from the first full week in June through the second week of August.

1) Bring these essentials
   a) Bedding
      i) Sleeping bag or blanket and sheets
      ii) Pillow
   b) Hygiene items
      i) Toothbrush and toothpaste
      ii) Washcloth and soap
      iii) Shampoo
      iv) Bath towels
      v) Plastic bag for dirty clothes
2) Clothing
   a) Comfortable clothes suitable for indoor/outdoor activities (refer to chart below)
   b) Footwear
      i) Closed-toe shoes
      ii) Extra socks
      iii) Plastic or waterproof shower shoes

Summer Camp Activity Schedule					
	Monday	Tuesday	Wednesday	Thursday	Friday
8:30 a.m.	Field games	Scavenger hunt	Gardening	Swimming	Arts and crafts
10:00 a.m.	Swimming	Field games	Hiking	Scavenger hunt	Gardening
12:30 p.m.	Gardening	Arts and crafts	Field games	Gardening	Hiking
2:00 p.m.	Hiking	Swimming	Scavenger hunt	Arts and crafts	Field games
3:30 p.m.	Arts and crafts	Gardening	Arts and crafts	Hiking	Swimming
6:00 p.m.	Scavenger hunt	Hiking	Swimming	Field games	Scavenger hunt

Why Choose Camden Park District Summer Camp?

- ★ Our dedicated staff focuses on nurturing young minds.
- ★ Campers build special friendships.
- ★ Campers develop life skills and confidence.
- ★ Campers make lifelong memories and have fun!

856-555-4050 Register Today! www.camdenpd.com

Figure 4–93

2) Clothing
   a) Comfortable clothes suitable for indoor/outdoor activities (refer to chart below)
   b) Footwear
      i) Closed-toe shoes
      ii) Extra socks
      iii) Plastic or waterproof shower shoes

10. Delete the page break below the table.
11. Use the Distribute Rows command to evenly space the rows below the column headings in the table. (**Hint:** Select the rows first.)
12. Use the Distribute Columns command to evenly space the columns containing the days of the week in the table. (**Hint:** Select the columns first.)
13. Use the AutoFit Contents command to change the cell widths so that they are as wide as the longest content of each column in the table.
14. Change the width of the column containing the times to .9".
15. Select the rows below the column headings and change the row height to .35".
16. Change the alignment of the cells that contain the days of the week and the activities to Align Center.
17. Change the alignment of the cells containing times to 'Align Center Right'.
18. Center the entire table across the width of the page.
19. Shade the cell intersecting the Monday column and the 3:30 row so that it is 'Gold, Accent 4, Lighter 60%'.
20. Shade the cell intersecting the Thursday column and the 10:00 a.m. row so that it is Green, Accent 6, Lighter 60%.
21. Add a row to the top of the table. Merge all cells in the first row into a single cell. Enter the title, Summer Camp Activity Schedule, formatted in bold as the table title. Change the alignment of the entered text to Align Center. Make sure the row height is .19".
22. Change the cell spacing for the table to allow 0.01" spacing between cells.
23. Change the cell margins so that the top and bottom cell margins are 0.01" and the left and right cell margins are 0.09".
24. Change the bullets in the bulleted list at the bottom of the page to picture bullets using a star picture (or use the image in the file called Support_WD_4_Star.png in the Data Files).
25. Delete the current footer from the document. (**Hint:** Use the Footer button (Insert tab | Header & Footer group).)
26. Insert the Blank (Three Columns) footer in the document. Enter the text, 856-555-4050, in the left placeholder text; the text, Register Today!, in the middle placeholder text; and the text, www.camdenpd.com, in the right placeholder text.
27. If requested by your instructor, insert your last name in front of the text, Summer Camp!, in the header.
28. This entire assignment should fit on a single page. If it does not, delete blank lines and adjust spacing above and below paragraphs as necessary. Check and fix accessibility issues, marking images as decorative and leaving the merged cells warning for this assignment. Save the document again with the same file name.
29. Submit the modified document, shown in Figure 4–93, in the format specified by your instructor.
30. Exit Word.
31. **Consider This:** This proposal contains a multilevel numbered list. How would you change the font size and font color of the numbers and letters at the beginning of each list item?

Extend Your Knowledge

Extend the skills you learned in this module and experiment with new skills. You may need to use Help to complete the assignment.

Working with Lists, Picture Watermarks, and Word's Draw Table Feature

Note: To complete this assignment, you will be required to use the Data Files. Please contact your instructor for information about accessing the Data Files.

Continued on next page

Instructions: Start Word. Open the document, SC_WD_4-3.docx, which is located in the Data Files. The document is a draft for a proposal that presents information about seminars offered by Pine Hill Financials to the public. The marketing coordinator, who created the draft, has asked you to delete the cover page, format the lists, add a table using Word's Draw Table feature, and insert a picture watermark.

Perform the following tasks:

1. Use Help to learn about Draw Table and picture watermarks.
2. Click File on the ribbon and then click Save As and save the document using the new file name, SC_WD_4_FinancialSeminarsProposal.
3. If requested by your instructor, use the Print command to print only the second page of this document. Then select just a bulleted list in the document and use the Print command to print just the selected text.
4. Remove the cover page from the document. (**Hint:** Use the Cover Page button (Insert tab | Pages group).)
5. Sort the paragraphs in the bulleted list at the top of the document.
6. Change the color of the bullets in the bulleted list to a color of your choice.
7. Draw the table shown in Figure 4–94 below the paragraph in the Details section (above the General Information heading). (**Hint:** Click Table button (Insert tab | Tables group) and then click Draw Table and then draw the table.) If necessary, use the Eraser button (contextual Layout tab | Draw group) to erase lines you do not need. Switch back to drawing the table anytime by clicking the Draw Table button (contextual Layout tab | Draw group).

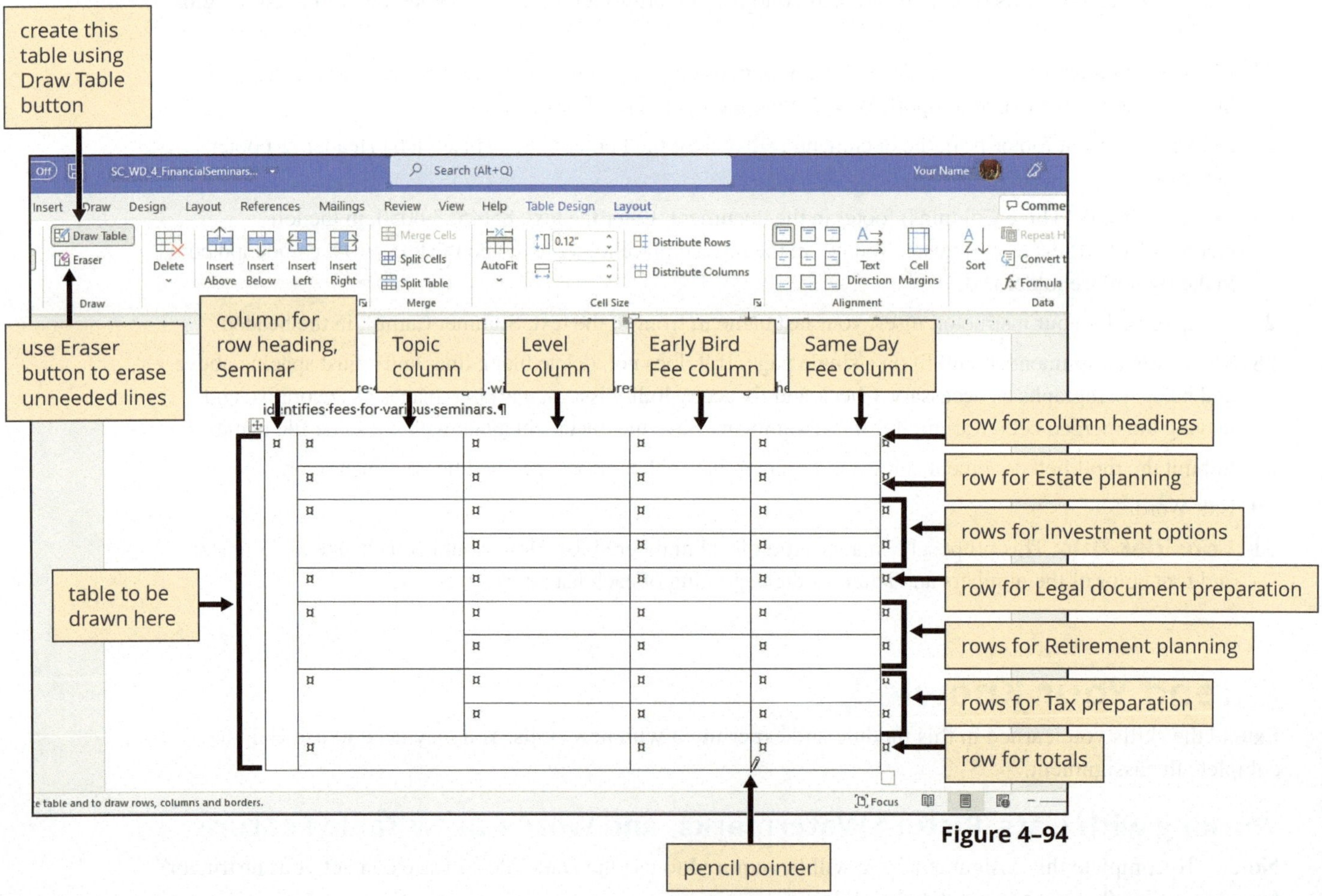

Figure 4–94

8. Show table gridlines, if they are not showing.
9. In the top row, enter these headings in the four rightmost columns: Topic, Level, Early Bird Fee, Same Day Fee.
10. In the leftmost column of the table, enter the text, Seminar, and then change its direction so that it displays vertically in the cell. Change the alignment to center.
11. In the second column of the table titled Topic, enter these labels: Estate planning, Investment options, Legal document preparation, Retirement planning, Tax preparation, Total for all seminars.
12. In the third column of the table titled Level, enter this text: Basic, Basic, Advanced, Basic, Basic, Advanced, Basic, Advanced.
13. In the fourth column of the table titled Early Bird Fee, enter these values: $ 65, $ 50, $ 65, $ 85, $ 50, $ 65, $ 65, $ 85.
14. In the fifth column of the table titled Same Day Fee, enter these values: $ 75, $ 60, $ 75, $ 95, $ 60, $ 75, $ 75, $ 95.
15. Resize table columns and rows as you deem appropriate.
16. Center the table between the page margins.
17. Distribute the last two columns containing monetary amounts so that they are evenly spaced.
18. Use the Formula button (contextual Layout tab | Data group) to place totals in the bottom row for the Early Bird Fee and Same Day Fee columns. The totals should be formatted to display dollar signs (no cents). (**Hint:** You will need to edit the formula number format and remove the .00 from the end of it.)
19. Change the values for Legal document preparation to $ 80 and $ 90 (for Early Bird Fee and Same Day Fee, respectively).
20. Update the fields containing the formulas by selecting the cells containing the formulas and then pressing F9, or right-clicking the cell and then clicking Update Field on the shortcut menu.
21. Select the table and change the spacing after each paragraph to 4 point. (**Hint:** Use the options in the Paragraph group in the Layout tab.)
22. Change the alignment of all cells containing numbers to Align Center. Align all other cells as you deem appropriate.
23. Shade the table cells, along with any other relevant enhancements, as you deem appropriate.
24. Set the column widths for the table to fixed column width. (**Hint:** Use the AutoFit button (contextual Layout tab | Cell Size group).)
25. Position the insertion point in the bottom-right cell in the table. Practice deleting a cell by clicking the Delete button (contextual Layout tab | Rows & Columns group), clicking Delete Cells on the Delete menu, clicking 'Shift cells left' (Delete Cells dialog box), and then clicking OK. Press CTRL+Z to undo the deletion. Hide gridlines.
26. Change the number style in the list at the bottom of the page to a style of your choice.
27. In the last line on the page, indent the left margin by one-half inch so that the paragraph shading starts one-half inch from the left margin. Then, adjust the right paragraph indent by one-half inch so that the paragraph shading ends one-half inch from the right margin.
28. Add an appropriate picture watermark to the document (or use the image in the file called Support_WD_4_DollarSigns.png in the Data Files). Change the scale in the Printed Watermark dialog box as necessary so that the watermark fills the entire page.
29. If requested by your instructor, change the name of the financial firm to include your last name.
30. Save the revised document again with the same name and then submit it in the format specified by your instructor.
31. **Consider This:** Which alignment and shading for the table cells did you choose and why?

Expand Your World

Create a solution that uses cloud or web technologies by learning and investigating on your own from general guidance.

Using Word Online to Create a Table

Instructions: You will use Word Online to create a table and then you will download the table to your desktop version of Word to edit it further. As HR specialist for River Valley School District, while attending a conference, you use Word Online to create a table for a proposal that you are developing for volunteer needs at the upcoming charity auction being hosted by your school. Then, when back at your office, you download the table and edit it further in your desktop version of Word.

Perform the following tasks:

1. Start a browser. Search for the text, Word Online, using a search engine. Visit several websites to learn about Word Online. Navigate to the Office Online website. You will need to sign in to your OneDrive account.
2. Create a new blank Word document using Word Online. Name the document SC_WD_4_VolunteersNeeded.
3. Create the table and enter the data shown in Figure 4–95.

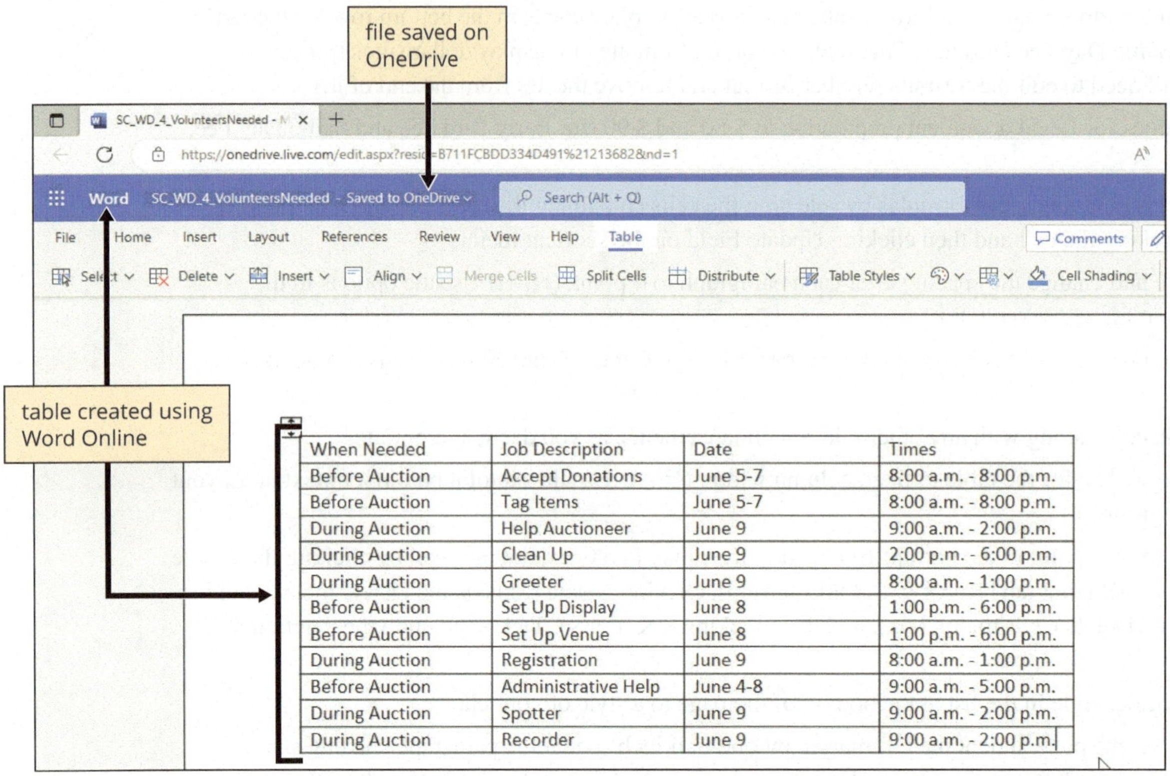

When Needed	Job Description	Date	Times
Before Auction	Accept Donations	June 5-7	8:00 a.m. - 8:00 p.m.
Before Auction	Tag Items	June 5-7	8:00 a.m. - 8:00 p.m.
During Auction	Help Auctioneer	June 9	9:00 a.m. - 2:00 p.m.
During Auction	Clean Up	June 9	2:00 p.m. - 6:00 p.m.
During Auction	Greeter	June 9	8:00 a.m. - 1:00 p.m.
Before Auction	Set Up Display	June 8	1:00 p.m. - 6:00 p.m.
Before Auction	Set Up Venue	June 8	1:00 p.m. - 6:00 p.m.
During Auction	Registration	June 9	8:00 a.m. - 1:00 p.m.
Before Auction	Administrative Help	June 4-8	9:00 a.m. - 5:00 p.m.
During Auction	Spotter	June 9	9:00 a.m. - 2:00 p.m.
During Auction	Recorder	June 9	9:00 a.m. - 2:00 p.m.

Figure 4–95

4. Apply the 'Grid Table 5 Dark - Accent 1' table style to the table.
5. Make sure Header Row and First Column are selected in the Table Style Options.
6. Change the colors of the table to a color of your choice.
7. Change the alignment of the Date column to Align Center.
8. Change the alignment of the Times column to Align Center.
9. Adjust the column widths so that the contents better fit the columns. How did you adjust the column width?

10. Open the document in Word using the Editing button on the ribbon and then select 'Open in Desktop App'. (Note that the AutoSave button may become enabled if you are saving the file on OneDrive.)
11. Distribute the rows in the table so that they are evenly spaced.
12. Remove the first column shading. (**Hint:** Use the check boxes in the Table Style Options group in the Table Design tab.)
13. Split the cell in the Job Description column with the description, Spotter, into two columns and one row. Enter the text, Runner, in the empty cell.
14. Split the cell in the Job Description column with the description, Greeter, into two columns and one row. Enter the text, Seating, in the empty cell.
15. Position the insertion point in the column headings and then click the 'Repeat Header Rows' button (contextual Layout tab | Data group) to repeat header rows if the table continues to a second page.
16. Sort the table on the Job Description column only with the beginning of the alphabet at the top. Did you use ascending or descending order?
17. Sort the table on the When Needed column and then by the Job Description column.
18. Add a border to all cells in the table. In the Borders and Shading dialog box, select a border style, color, and width of your choice.
19. Split the table where the When Needed column changes from Before Auction to During Auction so that one table is the Before Auction and the other table is the After Auction.
20. Copy the row containing the column headings from the first table to the second table. If necessary, use the format painter to copy formats from the column headings in the first table to the column headings second table, or apply borders again so that the column headings in the two tables are the same.
21. If requested by your instructor, add your name on a line below the second table.
22. Check and fix accessibility issues, except leave the split cells. Save the document again and submit it in the format requested by your instructor. Sign out of your OneDrive account.
23. **Consider This:** Which table features that are covered in the module are not available in Word Online? Answer the questions posed in #9 and #16.

In the Lab

Design and implement a solution using creative thinking and problem-solving skills.

Create a Proposal for a Tutoring Center

Note: To complete this assignment, you will be required to use the Data Files. Please contact your instructor for information about accessing the Data Files.

Problem: As administrative specialist for Top Notch Tutoring, you have been asked to design a multipage sales proposal that presents information about the tutoring center's services to the public and potential clients.

Part 1: The source content for the proposal is in a file called SC_WD_4-4.docx, which is located in the Data Files. The proposal should contain a cover page, followed by two pages of information about the tutoring center. Using the concepts and techniques presented in this module, along with the source content in the Data Files, create and format the sales proposal. While creating the proposal, be sure to do the following:

1. Insert an appropriate cover page. If requested by your instructor, include your name on the cover page.
2. Insert a formatted header and footer. The header or footer should contain page numbers. Format the page number so that it is in the format of - 1 -, - 2 -, etc.
3. Arrange content in a meaningful order.
4. Format headings and indent paragraphs appropriately.
5. Organize and format bulleted lists. Include a multilevel list. Sort paragraphs in lists as needed.

Continued on next page

6. Format the table(s) as needed and sort table contents appropriately.
7. Include an appropriate text watermark.
8. Be sure to check the spelling, grammar, and accessibility of the finished document.

When you are finished with the proposal, save it with the file name, SC_WD_4_TutoringCenterProposal. Submit your assignment and answers to the Part 2 critical thinking questions in the format specified by your instructor.

Part 2: **Consider This:** You made several decisions while creating the sales proposal in this assignment: how to organize elements on the cover page and the body of the proposal, which cover page to use and how to format its text, how to organize and format the tables and lists, and which text watermark to use and how to format it. What was the rationale behind each of these decisions? When you proofread the document, what further revisions did you make and why?

Creating a Resume and Sharing Documents

Objectives

After completing this module, you will be able to:

- Use a template to create a document
- Modify page setup
- Modify document, paragraph, and text formatting
- Create custom themes
- Edit a table
- Create, modify, and insert a building block
- Create and modify a style
- Export a Word document to a PDF file
- Open a PDF file in Word for editing
- Check document compatibility
- Save a Word document in an alternative file format
- Share a document on OneDrive
- Send a Word document using email
- Save a Word document as a webpage
- Format text as a hyperlink

Introduction

Some people prefer to use their own creative skills to design and compose Word documents. Using Word, for example, you can develop the content and decide the location of each item in a document. On occasion, however, you may have difficulty composing a particular type of document. To assist with the task of creating certain types of documents, such as resumes and letters, Word provides templates. A **template** is a file with a theme applied and that may contain formatted placeholder text in content controls, headers and footers, and graphics that you replace with your own information. After Word creates a document from a template, you fill in the blanks or replace placeholder text or content controls in the document.

Once you have created a document, such as a resume, you often share it with others electronically via email, webpages, or links.

Project: Resume

At some time, you almost certainly will prepare a resume to send to prospective employers. A **resume** usually contains the applicant's personal information, educational background, and job experience. Employers review many resumes for each vacant position. Thus, you should design your resume carefully so that it presents you as the best candidate for the job.

The project in this module follows generally accepted guidelines for creating resumes and uses Word to create the resume shown in Figure 5–1. The resume for Turan Schorel, an upcoming graduate of a business administration program who is seeking employment as a real estate agent with a national real estate franchise, uses a Word template to present relevant information to a potential employer.

TURAN SCHOREL

8523 Vada Road, Bainbridge, GA 39817 | 229-555-3698
tschorel05@cengage.net | linkedin.com/in/turan-schorel-agent

OBJECTIVE

To obtain a real estate agent position with a national real estate franchise that will allow me to grow in residential and commercial sales.

EDUCATION

September 2027-May 2029 B.S. Business Administration, Bainbridge, GA, *Coastal Plains College*
- GPA 3.7/4.0

September 2025-May 2027 A.A. Real Estate Studies, Bainbridge, GA, *Bass Capitol Community College*
- GPA 3.8/4.0

EXPERIENCE

November 2027-Present Real Estate Intern, Bainbridge, GA, *Piedmont Real Estate*

Show homes to prospective buyers, advise clients on current market trends, prepare purchase agreements, evaluate mortgage options with clients, assist with promoting active listings on social media platforms

CREDENTIALS

Licensed Real Estate Agent, GA
National Association of Realtors, member
Notary Public

PROFESSIONAL SKILLS

- Excellent communication skills, including negotiations and presentations
- Fluent in English, Spanish, and Persian languages
- Proficient with MLS (multiple listing service) database
- Extensive knowledge of market trend analysis techniques

Figure 5–1

In this module, you will learn how to create the resume shown in Figure 5–1. You will perform the following general tasks as you progress through this module:

1. Create a new resume document from a Word template.
2. Modify and format the resume template.
3. Save the resume document in other formats so that you can share it with others.
4. Make the resume document available online so that others can access it.
5. Create a webpage from the resume Word document.
6. Format the resume webpage.

To Start Word and Specify Settings

The following steps start Word, display formatting marks, change the zoom to page width, and verify ruler and Mouse mode settings. If you are using a computer to step through the project in this module and you want your screens to match the figures in this book, you should change your screen's resolution to 1366 × 768.

1. Start Word and create a blank document in the Word window. If necessary, maximize the Word window.
2. If the Print Layout button on the status bar is not selected (shown in Figure 5–4), click it so that your screen is in Print Layout view.
3. If the 'Show/Hide ¶' button (Home tab | Paragraph group) is not selected already, click it to display formatting marks on the screen.
4. To display the page the same width as the document window, if necessary, click the Page Width button (View tab | Zoom group).
5. Verify that the Ruler check box (View tab | Show group) is not selected. (If it is selected, click it to remove the selection because you do not want the rulers to appear on the screen.)
6. If you are using a mouse and you want your screens to match the figures in the book, verify that you are using Mouse mode by doing the following: display the Quick Access Toolbar, if necessary, by clicking the 'Ribbon Display Options' button at the right edge of the ribbon and then clicking 'Show Quick Access Toolbar' on the menu; clicking the 'Touch/Mouse Mode' button on the Quick Access Toolbar and then, if necessary, clicking Mouse on the menu (if your Quick Access Toolbar does not display the 'Touch/Mouse Mode' button, click the 'Customize Quick Access Toolbar' button on the Quick Access Toolbar and then click Touch/Mouse Mode on the menu to add the button to the Quick Access Toolbar); then hide the Quick Access Toolbar by clicking the 'Ribbon Display Options' button at the right edge of the ribbon and then clicking 'Hide Quick Access Toolbar' on the menu.

Using a Template to Create a Resume

Although you could compose a resume in a blank document window, this module shows how to use a template instead, where Word formats the resume with appropriate headings and spacing. You then customize the resume that the template generated by filling in blanks and by selecting and replacing text.

To Create a New Document from an Online Template

Word has a variety of templates available online to assist you with creating documents. Available online templates include agendas, award certificates, calendars, expense reports, greeting cards, invitations, invoices, letters, meeting minutes, memos, resumes, statements, and more. When you select an online template, Word downloads (or copies) it from the Office.com website to your computer or mobile device. Many of the templates use the same design or style. **Why?** If you create related documents, such as a resume and a cover letter, you can use the same template design or style so that the documents complement one another. Because the Word window already is open, the following steps use Backstage view to create a resume using the Resume template.

1

- sam Click File on the ribbon (shown in Figure 5–4) to open Backstage view and then click New in Backstage view to display the New screen, which initially lists several featured templates.
- Type **resume** in the 'Search for online templates' box and then click the Start searching button to display a list of online resume templates.
- If necessary, scroll through the list of templates to display the Resume thumbnail (Figure 5–2).

Q&A Can I select a template from the Word start screen that appears when I initially start Word?
Yes, instead of selecting Blank document from the Word start screen, you can select any of the available templates.

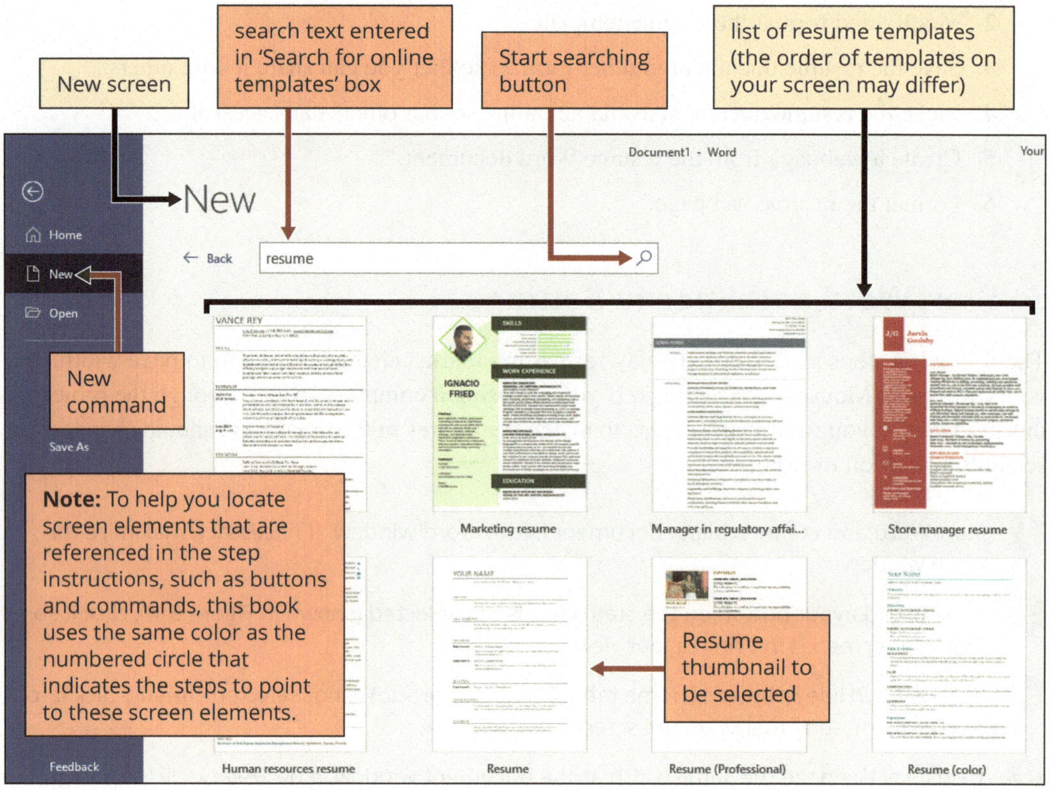

Figure 5–2

2

- Click the Resume thumbnail to select the template and display it in a preview window (Figure 5–3).
- **Experiment:** Click the Back and Forward buttons on the sides of the preview window to view previews of other templates. When finished, display the Resume thumbnail in the preview window.

Q&A What if I cannot locate the Resume template?
Close Backstage view, open the document called Support_WD_5_ResumeTemplate from the Data Files (please contact your instructor for information about accessing the Data Files), and then skip Steps 2 and 3.

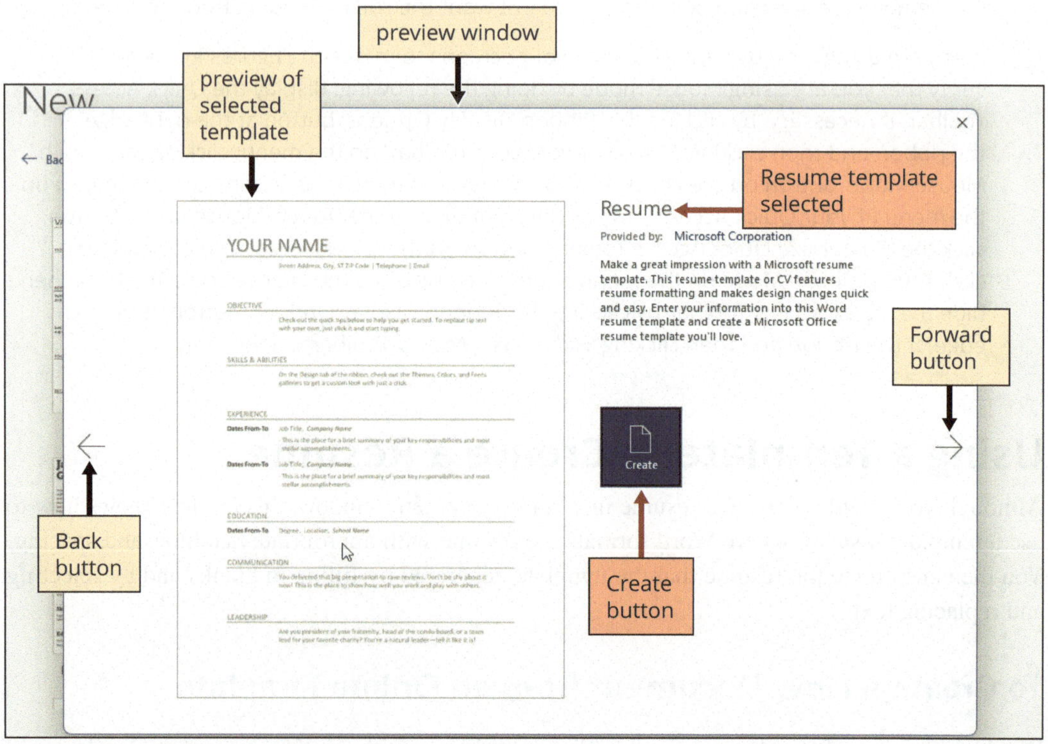

Figure 5–3

3

- Click the Create button to create a new document based on the selected template (Figure 5–4).
- If the resume template displays your name instead of the text, YOUR NAME, as shown in Figure 5–4, press CTRL+Z to reset the content control.

Q&A What is the Resume Assistant?

The Resume Assistant pane, available in some earlier versions of Office 365, provides examples of wording you can use in your resume.

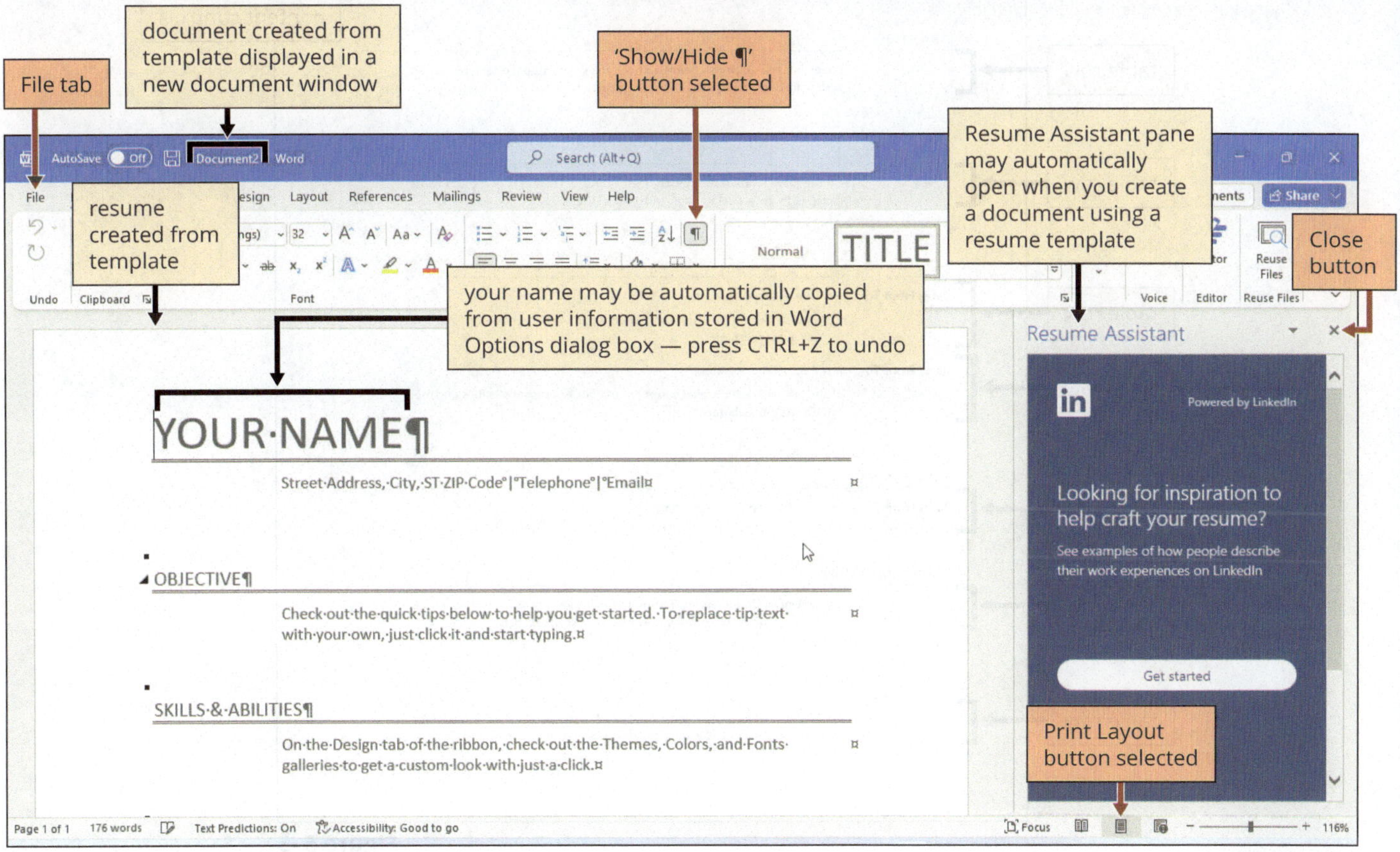

Figure 5–4

4

- If requested by your instructor, print the resume template so that you can view the entire document created by using the Resume template (Figure 5–5).

5

- If your screen opens the Resume Assistant pane, close the pane by clicking its Close button (shown in Figure 5–4).

6

- Save the resume on your hard drive, OneDrive, or other storage location using the file name, SC_WD_5_SchorelResume.

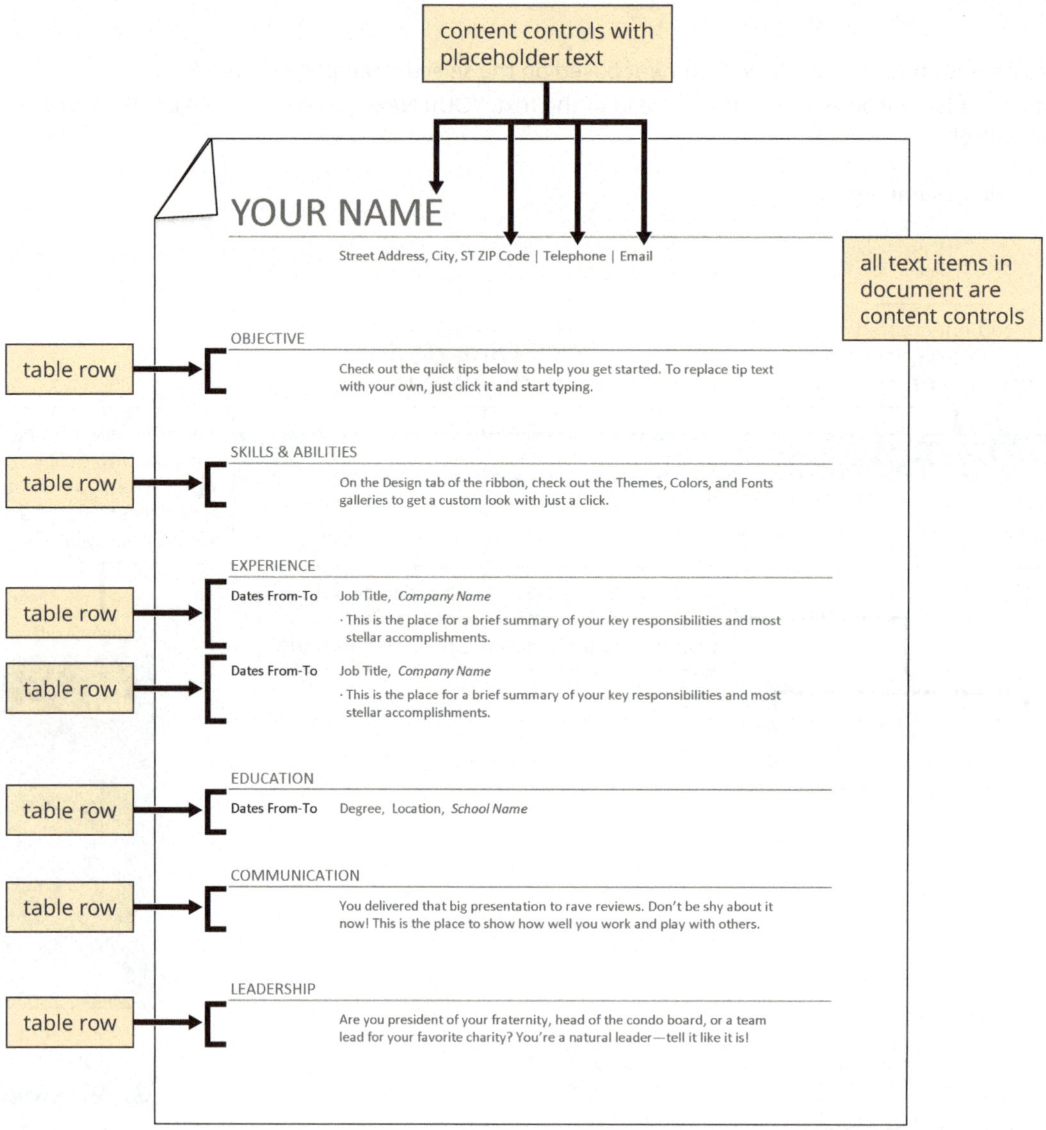

Figure 5–5

Consider This

How do you craft a successful resume?

Two types of resumes are the chronological resume and the functional resume. A chronological resume sequences information by time, with the most recent listed first. This type of resume highlights a jobseeker's job continuity and growth. A functional resume groups information by skills and accomplishments. This resume emphasizes a jobseeker's experience and qualifications in specialized areas. Some resumes use a combination of the two formats. For an entry-level job search, experts recommend a chronological resume or a combination of the two types of resumes.

When creating a resume, be sure to include necessary information and present it appropriately. Keep descriptions concise, using action words and bulleted lists.

- **Include necessary information.** Your resume should include contact information, a clearly written objective, educational background, and experience. Use your name and mailing address, along with your phone number, email address, and LinkedIn profile address, if you have one. Other sections you might consider including are memberships, skills, credentials, recognitions and awards, and/or community service. Do not include your Social Security number, marital status, age, height, weight, gender, physical appearance, health, citizenship, previous pay rates, reasons for leaving a prior job, current date, high school information (if you are a college graduate), and references. Employers assume you will provide references, if asked, and this information simply clutters a resume.
- **Present your resume appropriately.** For printed resumes, use a high-quality ink-jet or laser printer to print your resume on standard letter-sized white or ivory paper. Consider using paper that contains cotton fibers for a professional appearance.

Resume Template

The resume created from the template, shown in Figure 5–5, contains several content controls and a table. A content control is an object that contains sample text or instructions for filling in text and graphics. To select a content control, you click it or its tag, which (if one exists) is located in the upper-left corner of the content control. As soon as you begin typing in the selected content control, your typing replaces the text or instructions in the control. Thus, you do not need to delete the selected text or instructions before you begin typing. Depending on settings on your computer or mobile device, some content controls already may contain customized text, which you will change in this module.

Below the name in the document are several individual one- or two-row tables, some with headings above the table rows. The following pages personalize the resume created by the resume template using these general steps:

1. Change the name at the top of the resume.
2. Fill in the contact information below the name.
3. Fill in the Objective section.
4. Move the Education and Experience sections above the Skills & Abilities section.
5. Fill in the Experience section.
6. Add a row to the Education section and fill in this section.
7. Delete the Skills & Abilities section.
8. Change the heading, Communication, to Credentials and fill in this section.
9. Change the heading, Leadership, to Professional Skills, and fill in this section.

BTW
Word Help
At any time while using Word, you can find answers to questions and display information about various topics through Word Help. Used properly, this form of assistance can increase your productivity and reduce your frustrations by minimizing the time you spend learning how to use Word.

To Change Theme Colors

Word provides document themes, which contain a variety of color schemes and other effects. This resume uses the Green theme colors. The following steps change the theme colors.

1. Click Design on the ribbon to display the Design tab.
2. Click the Colors button (Design tab | Document Formatting group) to display the Colors gallery.
3. Scroll to and then click Green in the Colors gallery to change the theme colors to the selected theme.

BTW
Set Theme Settings as the Default
If you wanted to change the default theme, you would select the theme you want to be the default theme, or select the color scheme, font set, and theme effects that you would like to use as the default. Then, click the 'Set as Default' button (Design tab | Document Formatting group) (shown in Figure 5–9), which uses the current settings as the new default.

To Set Custom Margins

The resume template selected in this project uses .75-inch top and bottom margins and 1.1-inch left and right margins. You prefer 1-inch margins for the top, left, and right edges of the resume and a smaller bottom margin. **Why?** You want the margins to be even on the top edge and sides of the page and do not want the resume to spill to a second page. Because the margins you will use for the resume in this module are not predefined, you cannot use the predefined settings in the Margins gallery. Thus, the following steps set custom margins.

1

- Display the Layout tab.
- Click the Margins button (Layout tab | Page Setup group) to display the Margins gallery (Figure 5–6).

Q&A What is the difference between the Custom Margins setting and the Custom Margins command?
The Custom Margins setting applies the most recent custom margins to the current document, whereas the Custom Margins command displays the Page Setup dialog box so that you can specify new margin settings.

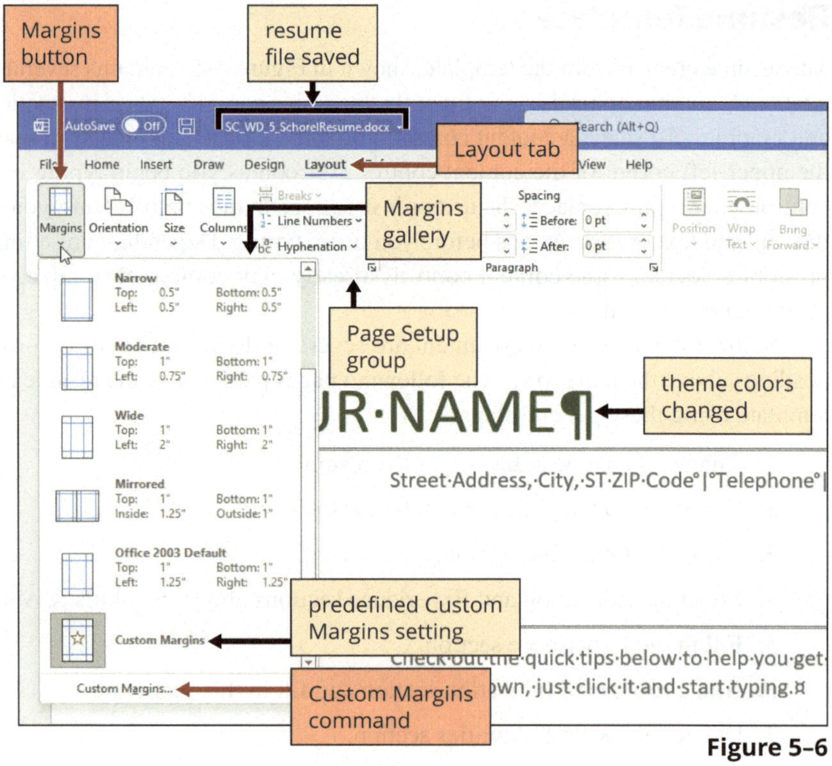

Figure 5–6

2

- Click Custom Margins at the bottom of the Margins gallery to display the Page Setup dialog box. If necessary, click the Margins tab (Page Setup dialog box) to display the Margins sheet.
- Type **1** in the Top box to change the top margin setting and then press TAB to position the insertion point in the Bottom box.
- Type **.5** in the Bottom box to change the bottom margin setting and then press TAB to position the insertion point in the Left box.
- Type **1** in the Left box to change the left margin setting and then press TAB to position the insertion point in the Right box.
- Type **1** in the Right box to change the right margin setting (Figure 5–7).

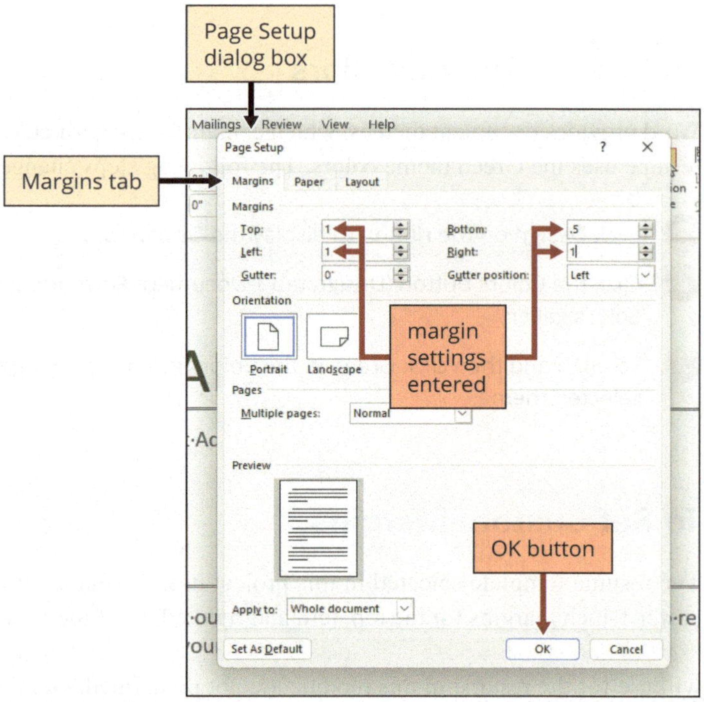

Figure 5–7

3

- Click OK to set the custom margins for this document.

Other Ways

1. Drag margin boundaries on ruler

To View Gridlines

When tables contain no borders, such as those in this resume, it can be difficult to see the individual cells in the table. To help identify the location of cells, you can display gridlines, which show cell outlines on the screen. The following steps show gridlines if they are not already displayed on your screen.

1. Click in any table cell (in this case, the cell containing the contact information).
2. Display the contextual Layout tab.
3. If it is not selected already, click the View Gridlines button (contextual Layout tab | Table group) to show gridlines in the table (Figure 5–8).

Q&A Is the contextual Layout tab different from the main Layout tab?
Yes, recall that the main Layout tab, which always appears on the ribbon, is used to change page setup, format paragraphs, and arrange objects in a document. The contextual Layout tab appears only when you are working in a table and is used to change the properties and organization of a table and its rows, columns, and cells.

BTW
The Ribbon and Screen Resolution
Word may change how the groups and buttons within the groups appear on the ribbon, depending on the screen resolution of your computer. Thus, your ribbon may appear different from the ones in this book if you are using a screen resolution other than 1366 × 768.

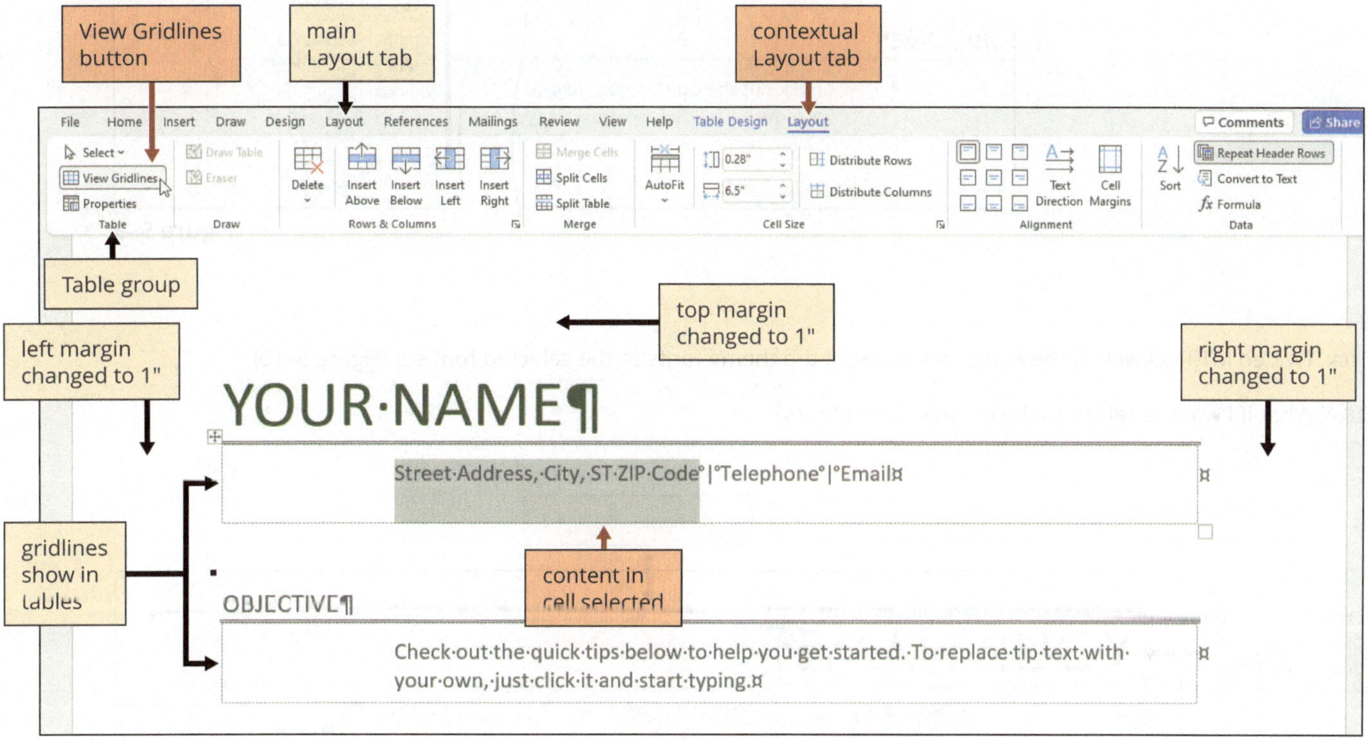

Figure 5–8

To Change Theme Fonts

The next step is to change the heading and body text fonts used in the resume. **Why?** You would prefer a bolder font for the headings. If text is entered using the headings and body text fonts, you easily can change the font in the entire document by changing the theme fonts, or font set. A **font set** is a format that defines one font for headings and another for body text. The default font set is Office, which uses the Calibri Light font for headings and the Calibri font for body text. In Word, you can select from more than 20 predefined, coordinated font sets to give the document's text a new appearance.

If you previously changed a font using buttons on the ribbon or Mini toolbar, Word will not alter those when you change the font set because changes to the font set are not applied to individually changed fonts. The following steps change the theme fonts to Tw Cen MT-Rockwell, which uses the Tw Cen MT font for headings and the Rockwell font for body text.

1

- Display the Design tab.
- Click the Fonts button (Design tab | Document Formatting group) to display the Fonts gallery.
- Scroll to display the 'Tw Cen MT-Rockwell' theme font in the gallery (Figure 5–9).

◦ **Experiment:** Point to various theme fonts in the Fonts gallery and watch the fonts of text in the document change.

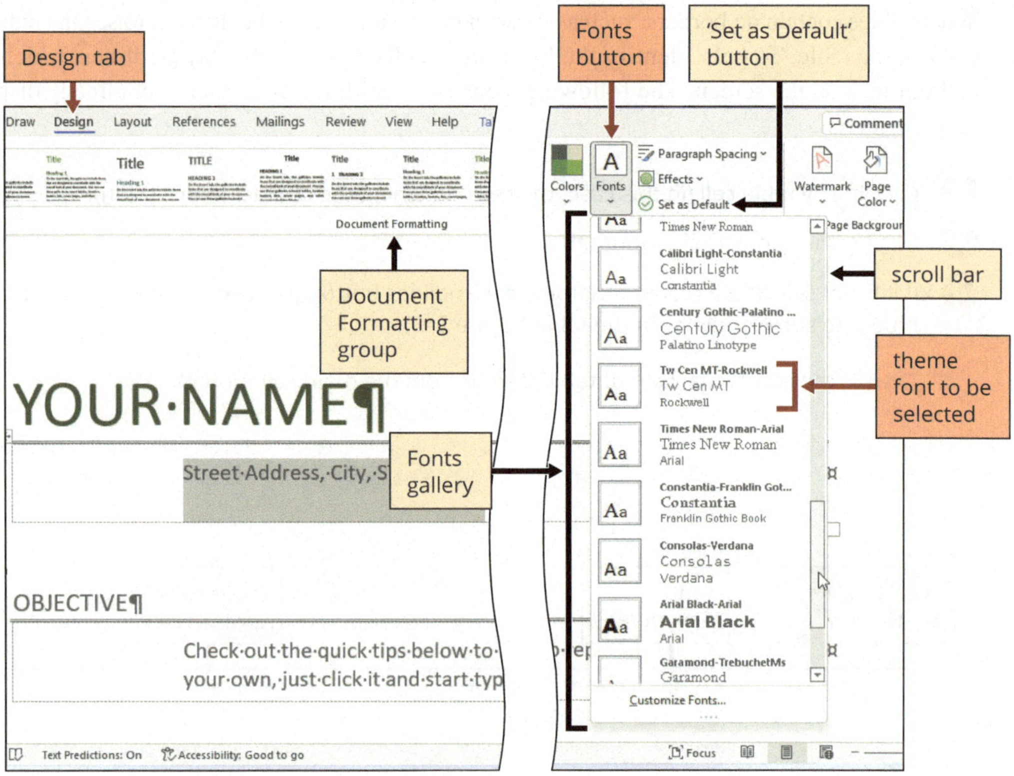

Figure 5–9

2

- Click 'Tw Cen MT-Rockwell' in the Fonts gallery to set the theme fonts to the selected font set (Figure 5–10).

Q&A What if I want to return to the default theme fonts?
You would click the Fonts button and then click Office in the Fonts gallery.

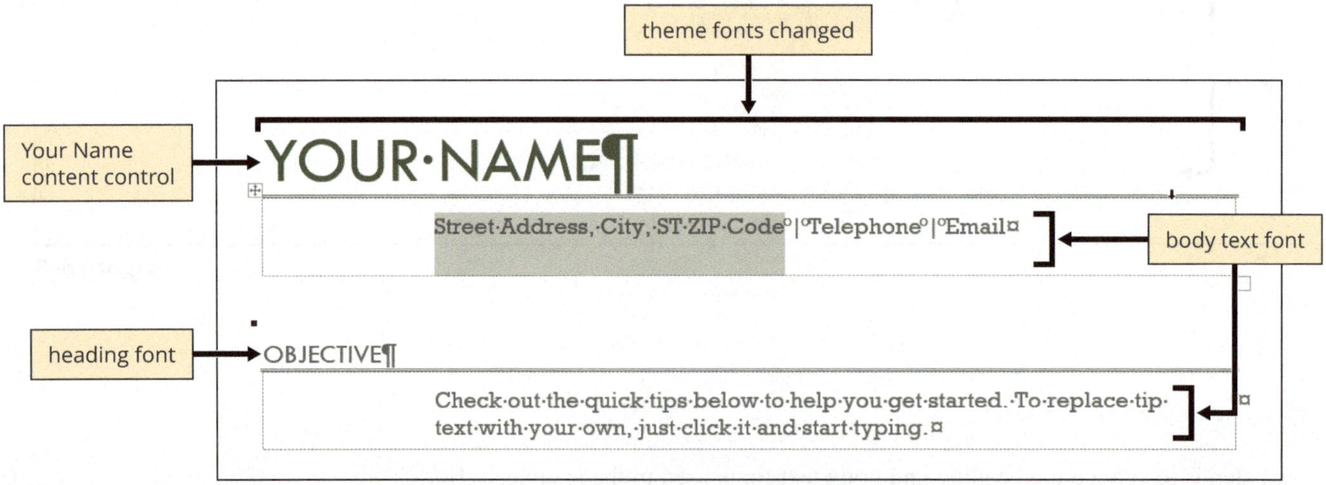

Figure 5–10

To Enter Text in a Content Control

The next step is to select the Your Name content control that the template inserted at the top of the resume and replace its placeholder text with the jobseeker's name. Word uses placeholder text to indicate where text can be typed. To replace placeholder text in a content control, you select the content control and then type.

The Your Name content control on your resume already may contain your name because Word may copy the user name from the Word Options dialog box and place it in the Your Name content control. Note that if your name appears instead of the text, YOUR NAME, the next set of steps may execute differently. The following steps enter text in a content control.

BTW
Touch Mode Differences
The Office and Windows interfaces may vary if you are using Touch mode. For this reason, you might notice that the function or appearance of your touch screen differs slightly from this module's presentation.

1. Click the content control to be modified (in this case, the Your Name content control) to select it.

   Q&A How can I tell if a content control is selected?
   The appearance of selected content controls varies. When you select some content controls, they are surrounded by a rectangle; others appear selected. Selected content controls also may have a name that is attached to the top and/or a tag that is attached to its upper-left corner. You can drag a tag to move a content control from one location to another.

2. Type **Turan Schorel** to replace the content control with the jobseeker's name (Figure 5–11).

   Q&A Why does all the text appear in uppercase letters even though I typed some letters in lowercase?
   This content control includes formatting that displays the text in uppercase letters.

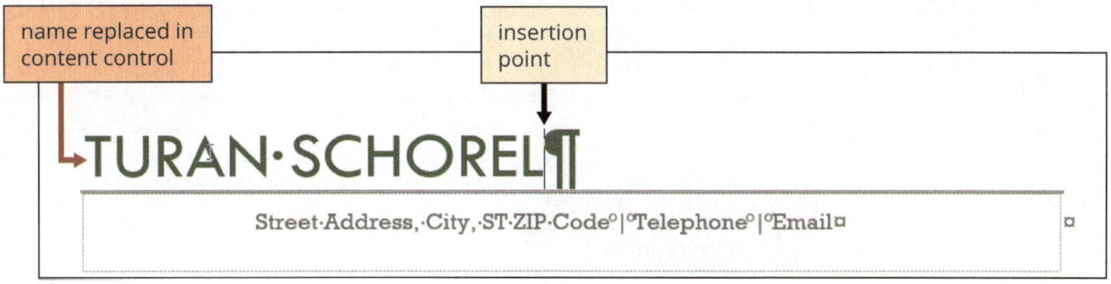

Figure 5–11

To Enter Text in More Content Controls

The next step is to select the contact information content controls in the resume and replace their placeholder text with personal information. The following steps replace the placeholder text in content controls.

1. Click the content control with the placeholder text of Street Address, City, ST ZIP Code to select it, and then type **8523 Vada Road, Bainbridge, GA 39817** as the mailing address information.
2. Click the Telephone content control to select it and then type **229-555-3698** as the phone number.
3. Press DELETE three times to delete the space, vertical bar, and space, and then press ENTER to move the Email content control to the next line.

4. Click the Email content control to select it and then type **tschorel05@cengage.net** as the email address. (If Word capitalizes the first letter in the email address, position the pointer in the capitalized text to display a small blue box below the capitalized letter T, point to the small blue box to display the AutoCorrect Options button, click the AutoCorrect Options button to display the AutoCorrect Options menu, and then click 'Undo Automatic Capitalization' on the AutoCorrect Options menu to undo the automatic correction.)

5. Press SPACEBAR, type a vertical bar (|), press SPACEBAR and then type **linkedin.com/in/turan-schorel-agent** as the LinkedIn profile address (Figure 5–12). (If the email address is formatted as a hyperlink, right-click the email address and then click Remove Hyperlink on the shortcut menu.)

Q&A What is a LinkedIn profile address and why include it?
A LinkedIn profile address is the web address for a LinkedIn profile page. On LinkedIn, you share professional interests, education, and employment history, enabling potential employers who review your profile to learn about your specific skills. Many employers post jobs using LinkedIn and consider information in your profile as your online resume.

Why do red wavy lines appear below the first and last names in the LinkedIn profile address?
Word flagged the names as potential spelling errors. You can select Ignore All when you check spelling to ignore the flagged text.

What are the small raised circles between content controls?
They are nonbreaking spaces, which are formatting marks. A nonbreaking space is a special space character that prevents two words from splitting if the first word falls at the end of a line. Similarly, a nonbreaking hyphen is a special type of hyphen that prevents two words separated by a hyphen from splitting at the end of a line. To insert a nonbreaking space, press CTRL+SHIFT+SPACEBAR (instead of SPACEBAR), and to insert a nonbreaking hyphen, press CTRL+SHIFT+HYPHEN (instead of HYPHEN). Or, click the Symbol button (Insert tab | Symbols group), click More Symbols, click the Special Characters tab (Symbol dialog box), click Nonbreaking Space or Nonbreaking Hyphen in the Character list, click the Insert button, and then click Close.

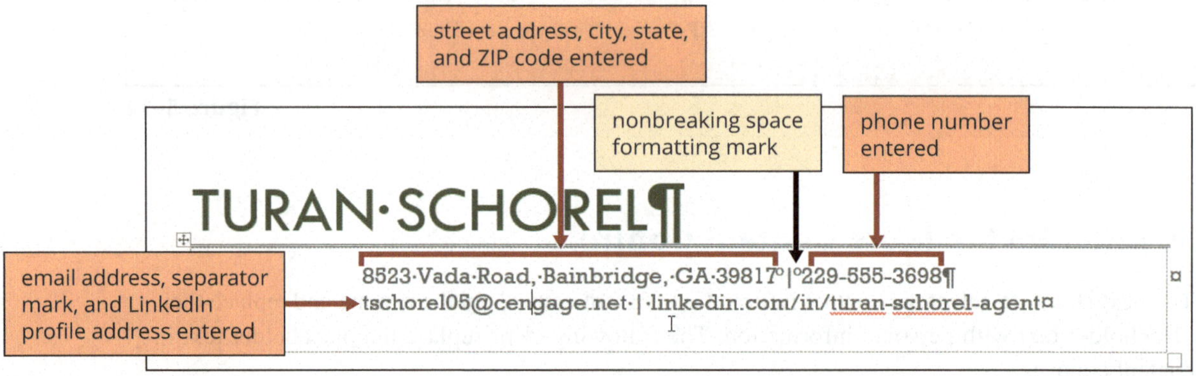

Figure 5–12

To Create Custom Theme Fonts

This resume currently uses the Tw Cen MT-Rockwell theme fonts, which specifies the Tw Cen MT font for the headings and the Rockwell font for body text. The resume in this module creates a custom theme font. **Why?** The Tw Cen MT font is a sans serif font, which is a font that does not include short decorative lines at the upper and lower ends of its characters. The Rockwell font is a serif font, which is a font that has short decorative lines at the upper and lower ends of its characters. You want the font used in the body text to be a sans serif font so that it is the same style as the headings. The following steps create a customized theme font set with the name, Resume Text, that changes the font for the body text in the resume to Franklin Gothic Medium Cond.

1

- If necessary, display the Design tab.
- Click the Fonts button (Design tab | Document Formatting group) to display the Fonts gallery (Figure 5–13).

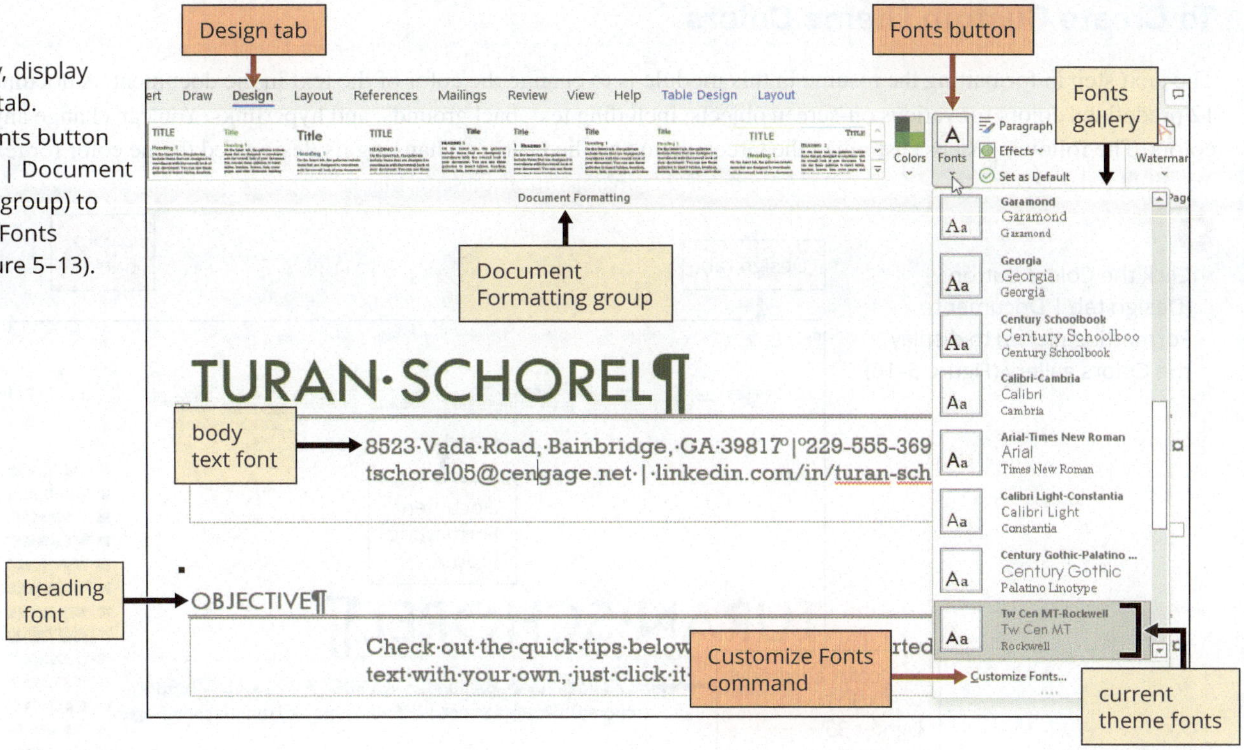

Figure 5–13

2

- Click Customize Fonts in the Fonts gallery to display the Create New Theme Fonts dialog box.
- Click the Body font arrow (Create New Theme Fonts dialog box); scroll to and then click 'Franklin Gothic Medium Cond' (or a similar font).
- If necessary, select any text in the Name text box and then type **Resume Text** as the name for the new theme font (Figure 5–14).

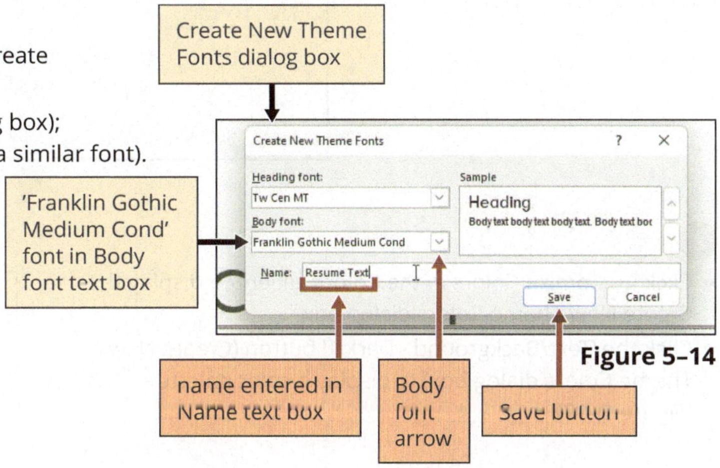

Figure 5–14

3

- Click the Save button (Create New Theme Fonts dialog box) to create the customized theme font with the entered name (Resume Text, in this case) and apply the new body text fonts to the current document (Figure 5–15).

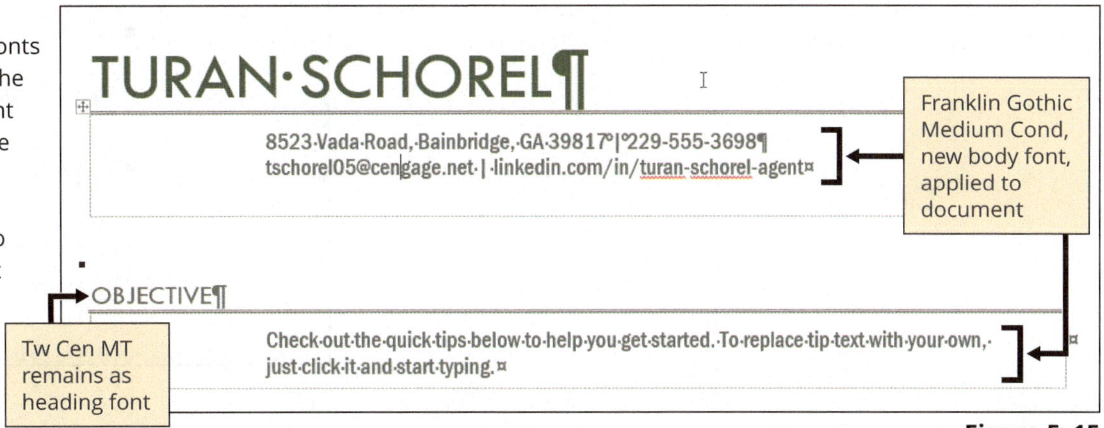

Figure 5–15

To Create Custom Theme Colors

The next step in formatting the resume in this module is to change the color of the text in the document. A document theme has 12 predefined colors for various on-screen objects, including text, backgrounds, and hyperlinks. You can change any of the theme colors. The following steps customize the Green theme applied earlier, changing its designated theme color for text. **Why?** You would like the text in the resume to be a shade of tan, instead of a shade of black.

1

- Click the Colors button (Design tab | Document Formatting group) to display the Colors gallery (Figure 5–16).

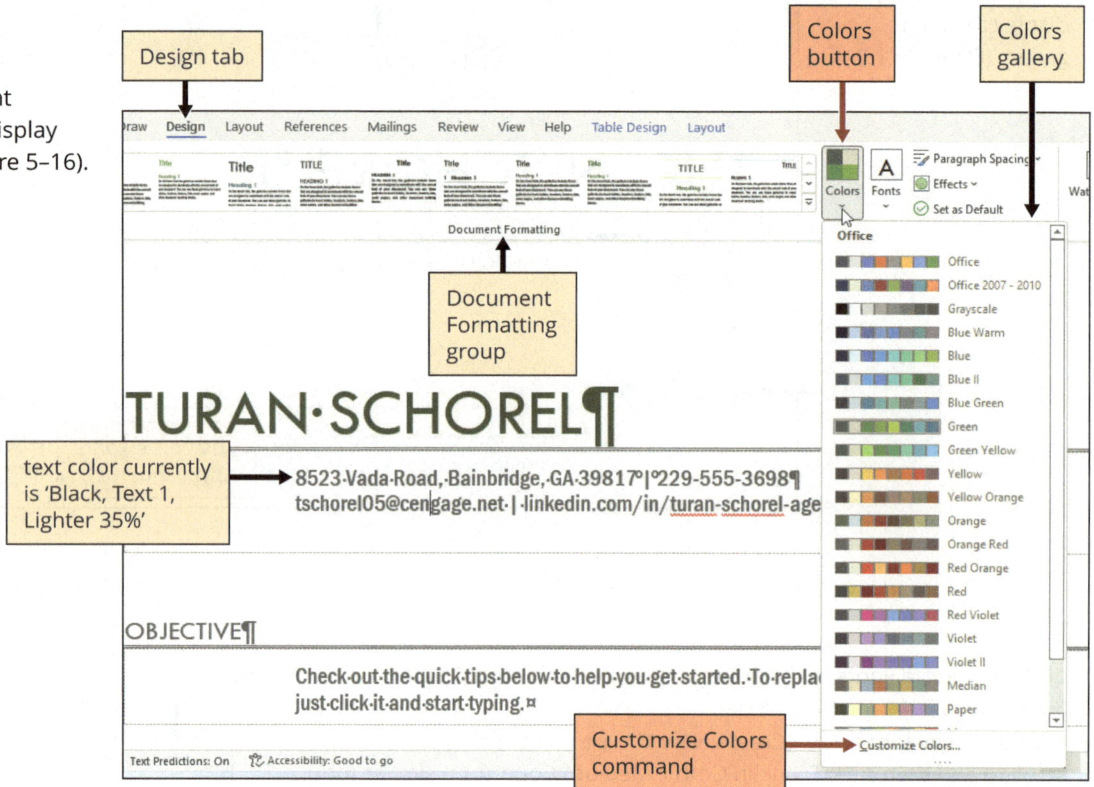

Figure 5–16

2

- Click Customize Colors in the Colors gallery to display the Create New Theme Colors dialog box.
- Click the 'Text/Background - Dark 1' button (Create New Theme Colors dialog box) to display a color palette (Figure 5–17).

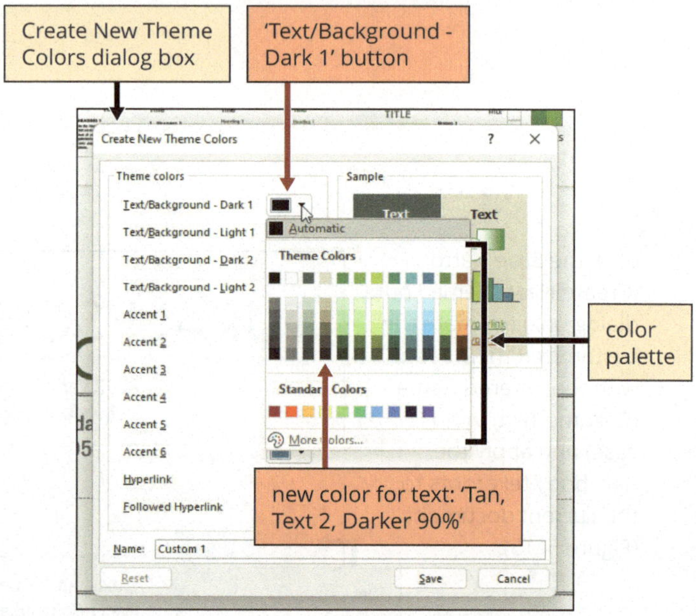

Figure 5–17

3

- Click 'Tan, Text 2, Darker 90%' (fourth color in last row) as the new text color.
- If necessary, select any text in the Name text box and then type **Resume Text** (Figure 5–18).

Q&A What if I wanted to reset all the original theme colors?
You would click the Reset button (Create New Theme Colors dialog box) before clicking the Save button.

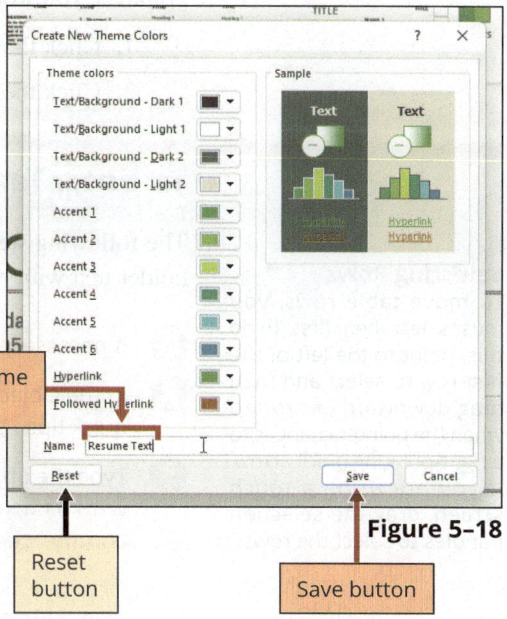

Figure 5–18

4

- Click the Save button (Create New Theme Colors dialog box) to save the modified color theme with the name, Resume Text, which will be positioned at the top of the Colors gallery for future access, and change the theme colors in the current document (Figure 5–19).

Q&A What if I do not enter a name for the modified theme?
Word assigns a name that begins with the letters, Custom, followed by a number (i.e., Custom8).

Figure 5–19

To Save Customized Themes

When you modify the theme colors, theme fonts, or theme effects, you can save the modified theme for future use. If you wanted to save a customized theme, you would perform the following steps.

1. Click the Themes button (Design tab | Document Formatting group) to display the Themes gallery.
2. Click 'Save Current Theme' in the Themes gallery.
3. Enter a theme name in the File name box (Save Current Theme dialog box).
4. Click the Save button to add the saved theme to the Themes gallery.

To Change Theme Effects If you wanted to change the look of graphics, such as SmartArt graphics, you would perform the following steps to change the theme effects.

1. Click the Effects button (Design tab | Document Formatting group).
2. Click the desired effect in the Effects gallery.

To Enter Text in a Content Control

BTW

Selecting Rows

To move table rows, you must select them first. To do this, point to the left of the first row to select and then drag downward or upward when the pointer changes to a right-pointing block arrow. If you are using a touch screen, drag the selection handles to select the rows.

The following steps select the Objective content control in the resume and then replace its placeholder text with personal information.

1. If necessary, scroll to display the Objective section of the resume in the document window.
2. In the Objective section of the resume, click the placeholder text that begins, 'Check out the quick tips...', in the Objective content control (shown in Figure 5–19) to select it.
3. Type the objective (shown in Figure 5–20): **To obtain a real estate agent position with a national real estate franchise that will allow me to grow in residential and commercial sales.**

To Move Table Rows Using Cut and Paste

In the resume, you would like the Education and Experience sections immediately below the Objective section, in that order. **Why?** You want to emphasize your educational background and experience. Thus, the next step is to move the Education section in the resume below the Objective section by selecting the table row and associated heading paragraph for the Education section, cutting the selected items, and then pasting them from the Office Clipboard to the appropriate location. Then, you will use the same process to move the Experience section so that it appears below the moved Education section. The following steps use cut and paste to move table rows and paragraphs.

1

- Click the Zoom Out button on the status bar as many times as necessary so that the resume is displayed at 80 percent zoom in the document window.
- Scroll so that the Objective, Experience, and Education sections appear in the document window at the same time.

2

- Select the row and heading paragraph to be moved by dragging through it, in this case, the Education section (Figure 5–20).

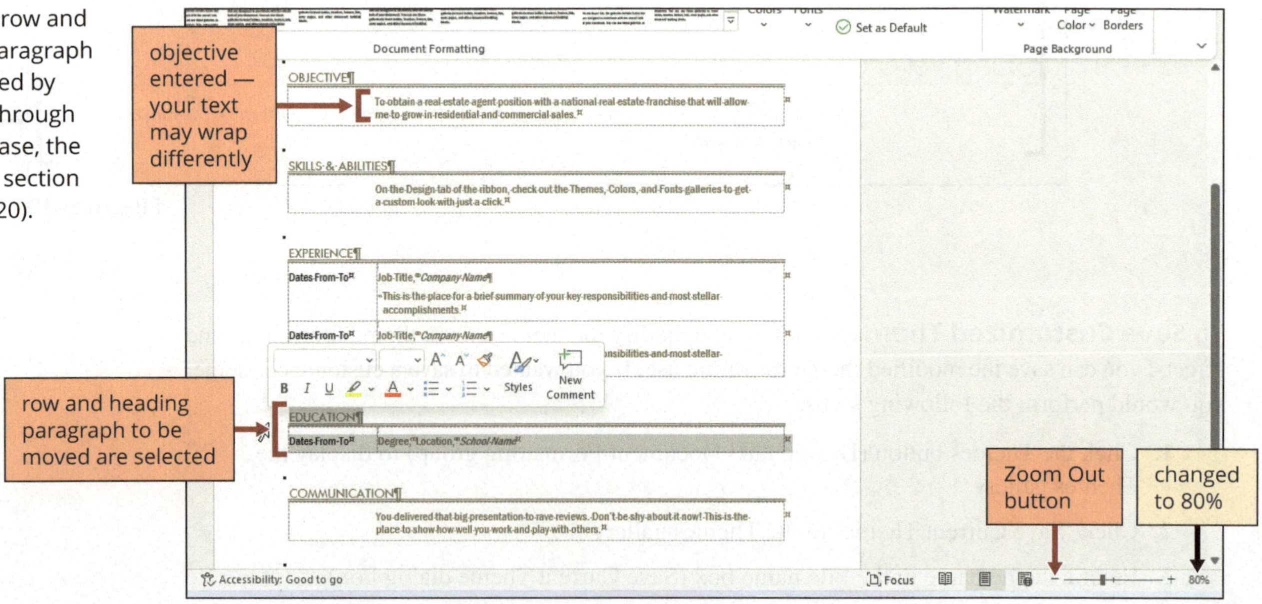

Figure 5–20

3

- Display the Home tab.
- Click the Cut button (Home tab | Clipboard group) to cut the selection and place it on the Office Clipboard.
- Position the insertion point at the location where the cut text is to be moved (pasted), in this case, to the left of the S in the Skills & Abilities heading (you may need to press the LEFT ARROW key after clicking Skills & Abilities to position the insertion point) (Figure 5–21).

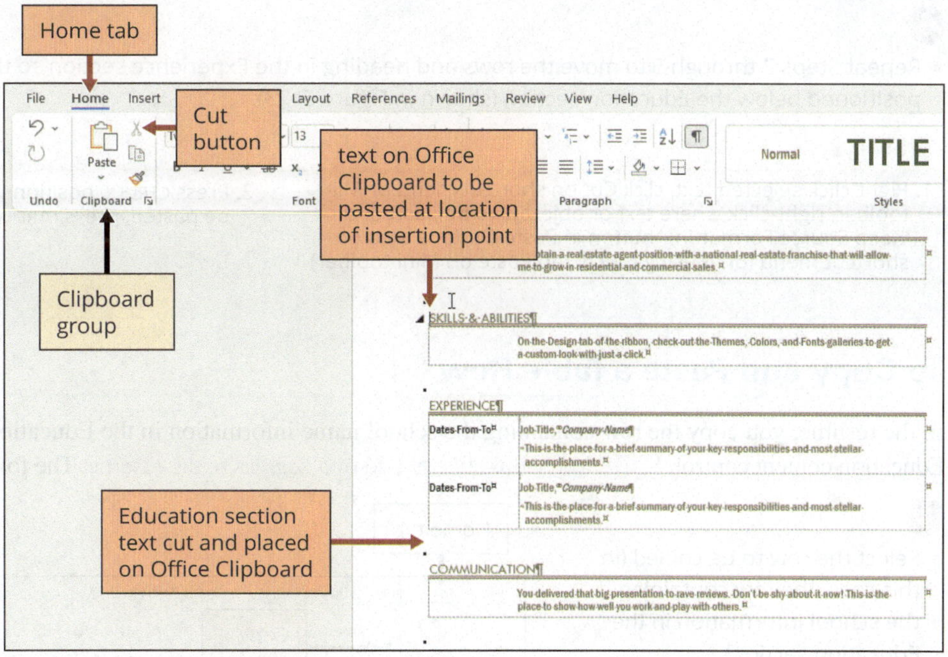

Figure 5–21

4

- Click the Paste arrow (Home tab | Clipboard group) to display the Paste menu.
- Point to the 'Keep Source Formatting' button on the Paste menu to display a Live Preview of that paste option applied to the selected content in the document (Figure 5–22).

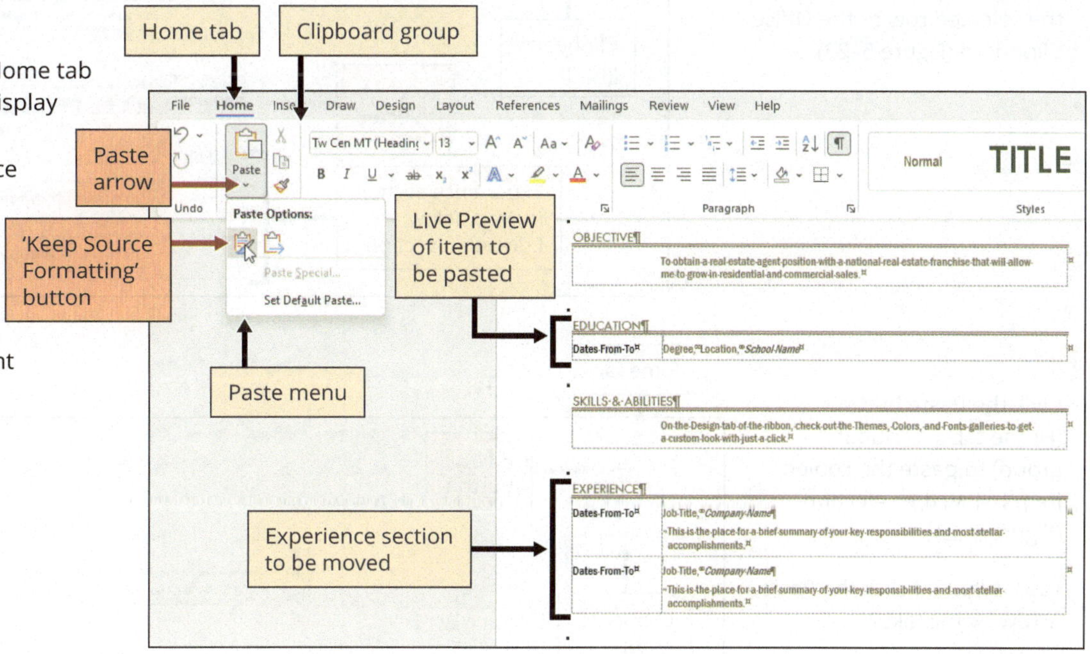

Figure 5–22

5

- **Experiment:** Point to each paste option button on the Paste menu and watch the Live Preview of the pasted item change.
- Click the 'Keep Source Formatting' button on the Paste menu to paste the content on the Office Clipboard using source formatting at the location of the insertion point.

Q&A Can I use this procedure to copy and paste an entire table with source formatting?

Yes, you would select the table to be copied, click Copy (Home tab | Clipboard group) to copy the table, position the insertion point at the location where you want to paste the table, click the Paste arrow (Home tab | Clipboard group), and then click the 'Keep Source Formatting' button on the Paste menu to paste the table with source formatting.

Can I use drag and drop instead of cut and paste to move the selected content?

Yes, but because the resume templates have many individual tables, it often is easier to use cut and paste.

6

- Repeat Steps 2 through 5 to move the rows and heading in the Experience section so that the Experience section is positioned below the Education section (shown in Figure 5–23).

Other Ways

1. Right-click selected text, click Cut on shortcut menu or Mini toolbar, right-click where text or object is to be pasted, click 'Keep Source Formatting' button in Paste Options area on shortcut menu (or, if using touch, tap Paste on Mini toolbar)
2. Press CTRL+X, position insertion point where text or object is to be pasted, press CTRL+V

To Copy and Paste a Table Row

In the resume, you copy the row containing the school name information in the Education section so that it appears twice in the Education content control. **Why?** You would like to add two degrees to the resume. The following steps copy and paste a table row.

1

- Select the row to be copied (in this case, the row containing the school information in the Education section).
- Click the Copy button (Home tab | Clipboard group) to copy the selected row to the Office Clipboard (Figure 5–23).

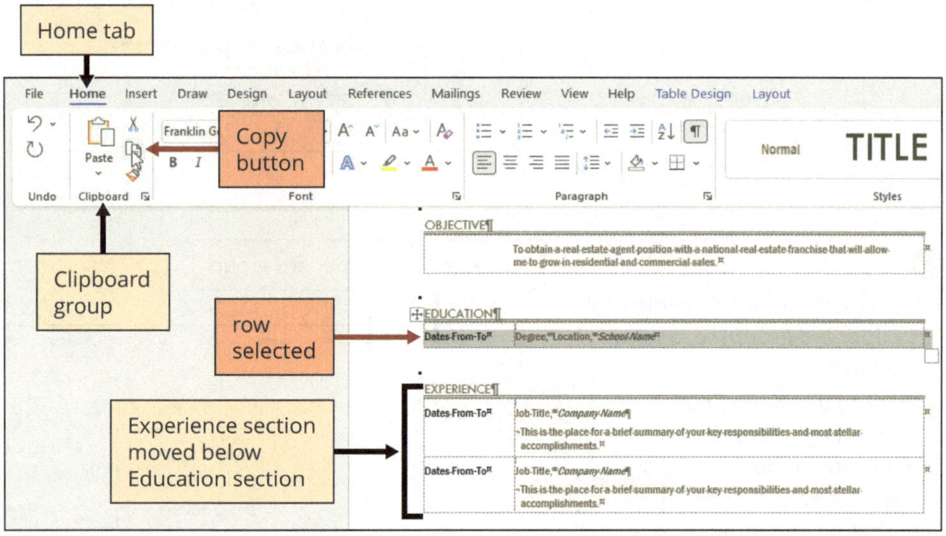

Figure 5–23

2

- Click the Paste button (Home tab | Clipboard group) to paste the copied item below the selection (Figure 5–24).

Q&A What if I click the Paste arrow by mistake?
Click the Paste arrow again to remove the Paste menu and repeat Step 2.

What if I wanted to paste in a different location in the document?
You would position the insertion point at the location where the copied item should be pasted and then click the Paste button (Home tab | Clipboard group).

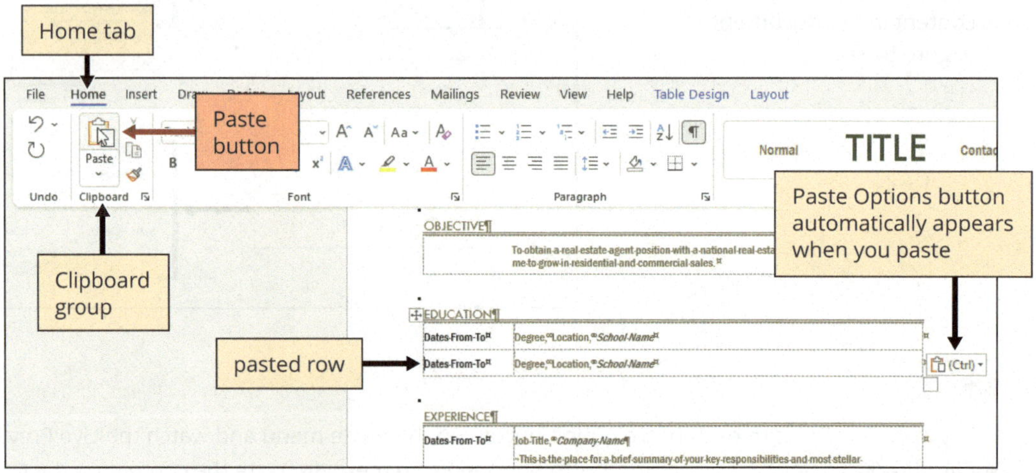

Figure 5–24

Other Ways

1. Click Copy on shortcut menu (or, if using touch, tap Copy on Mini toolbar), right-click where item is to be pasted, click 'Keep Source Formatting' button in Paste Options area on shortcut menu (or, if using touch, tap Paste on Mini toolbar)
2. Select item, press CTRL+C, position insertion point at paste location, press CTRL+V

To Delete a Row and Paragraph

Because you will not be using the Skills & Abilities section of the resume template, the next task is to delete this section. The following steps delete a row and a paragraph.

1 Select the Skills & Abilities paragraph heading and associated table row (Figure 5–25).

2 Press DELETE to delete the selected text because you do not need this section (shown in Figure 5–38) and you want to ensure the document has one page only.

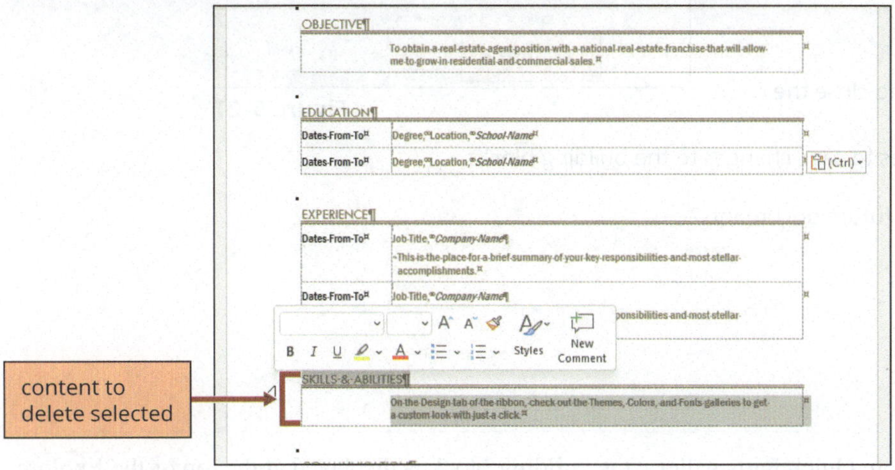

Figure 5–25

To Create a Building Block

If you use the same text or graphic frequently, you can store the text or graphic as a **building block**, which is a ready-made stored text element or graphic that you can insert in a document. That is, you can create the entry once as a building block and then insert the building block when you need it. In this way, you avoid entering text or graphics inconsistently or incorrectly in different locations throughout the same or multiple documents.

The following steps create a building block for the city name, Bainbridge. **Why?** You use the city name multiple times throughout the resume and want to use a building block to insert it instead of typing the city name repeatedly.

1

- Change the zoom to page width.
- Select the text to be a building block, in this case, Bainbridge, in the contact information at the top of the resume.
- Display the Insert tab.
- Click the 'Explore Quick Parts' button (Insert tab | Text group) to display the Explore Quick Parts gallery (Figure 5–26).

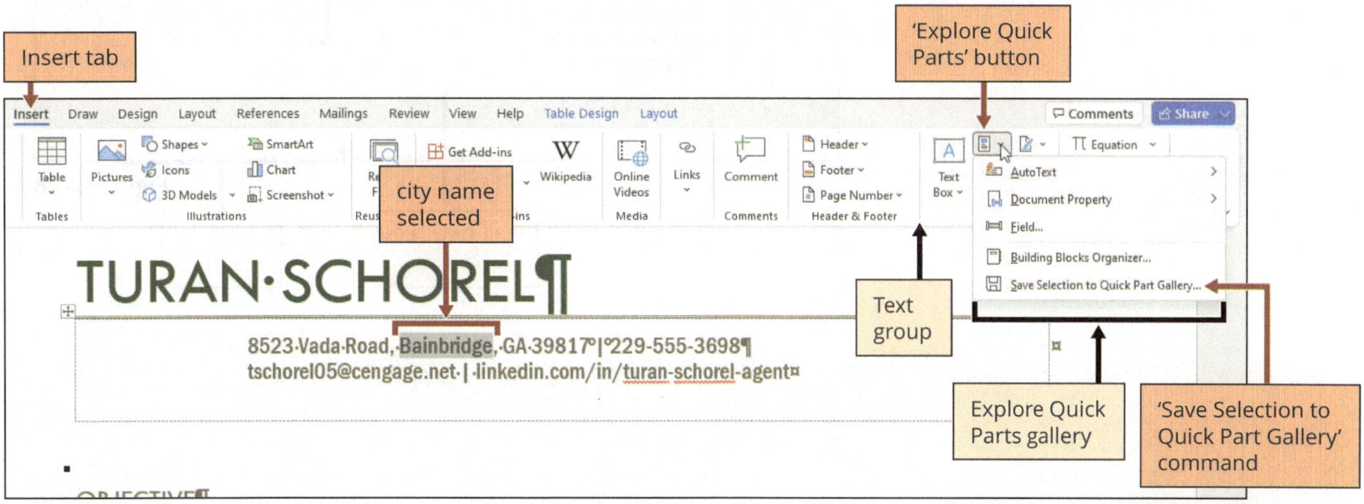

Figure 5–26

2

- Click 'Save Selection to Quick Part Gallery' in the Explore Quick Parts gallery to display the Create New Building Block dialog box.
- Type **bb** in the Name text box (Create New Building Block dialog box) to replace the proposed building block name (Bainbridge, in this case) with a shorter building block name (Figure 5–27).

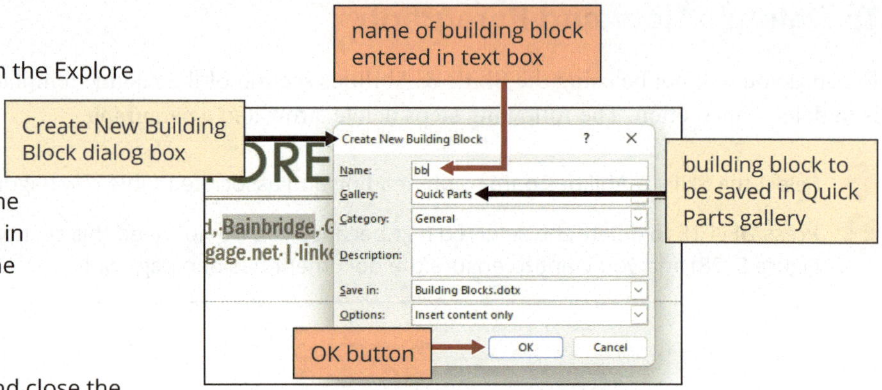

Figure 5–27

3

- Click OK to store the building block entry and close the dialog box.
- If Word displays another dialog box, click Yes to save changes to the building blocks.

Q&A Will this building block be available in future documents?
When you exit Word, a dialog box may appear asking if you want to save changes to the building blocks. Click Save if you want to use the new building block in future documents.

To Modify a Building Block

When you save a building block in the Explore Quick Parts gallery, the building block is displayed at the top of the Explore Quick Parts gallery. When you point to the building block in the Explore Quick Parts gallery, a ScreenTip displays the building block name. If you want to display more information when the user points to the building block, you can include a description in the ScreenTip.

The following steps modify a building block to include a description and change its category to AutoText. **Why?** Because you want to reuse this text, you place it in the AutoText gallery, which also is accessible through the Explore Quick Parts gallery.

1

- Click the 'Explore Quick Parts' button (Insert tab | Text group) to display the Explore Quick Parts gallery.
- Right-click the Bainbridge building block to display a shortcut menu (Figure 5–28).

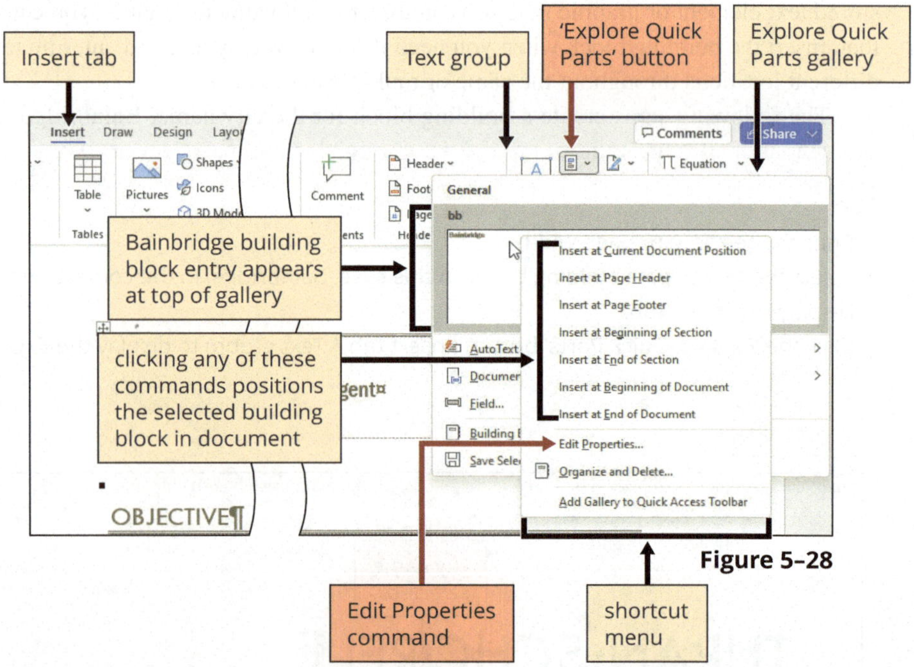

Figure 5–28

2

- Click Edit Properties on the shortcut menu to display the Modify Building Block dialog box, filled in with information related to the selected building block.
- Click the Gallery arrow (Modify Building Block dialog box) and then click AutoText to change the gallery in which the building block will be placed.
- Type **shortcut for entering the city name, Bainbridge** in the Description text box (Figure 5–29). (Note that depending on settings, your dialog box may not display the extension of .dotm after Normal in the Save in box.)

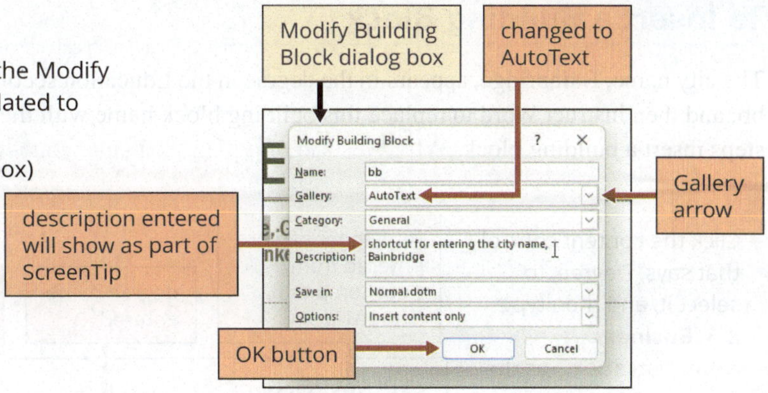

Figure 5–29

3

- Click OK to store the building block entry and close the dialog box.
- Click Yes when asked if you want to redefine the building block entry.

To Use AutoComplete

As you begin typing, Word may display a ScreenTip that presents a suggestion for the rest of the word or phrase you are typing. **Why?** With its AutoComplete feature, Word predicts the text, numbers, dates, or phrases you are typing and displays its prediction in a ScreenTip. If the AutoComplete prediction is correct, you can instruct Word to finish your typing with its prediction, or you can ignore Word's prediction. Word draws its AutoComplete suggestions from its dictionary and from AutoText entries you create and save in the Normal template.

The following steps use the AutoComplete feature as you type the graduation date in the Education section of the resume.

1

- If necessary, display the Education section of the document window. In the first row of the Education section of the resume, click the content control that says, Dates From, to select it, and then type **Sept** and notice the AutoComplete ScreenTip that appears on the screen (Figure 5–30).

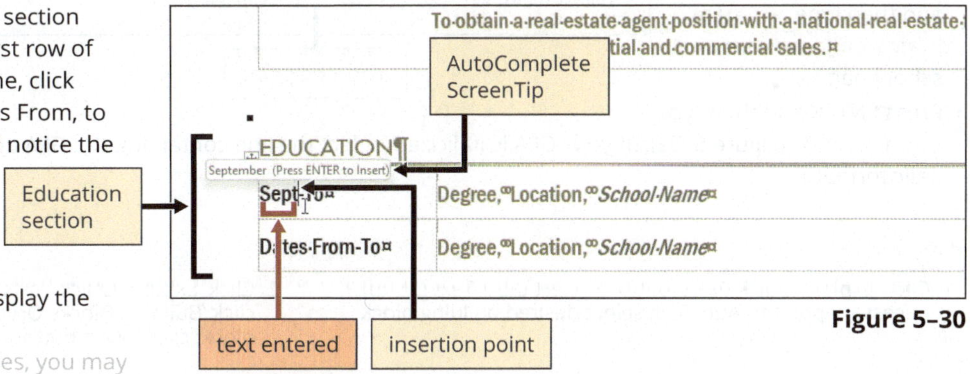

Figure 5–30

Q&A Why would my screen not display the AutoComplete ScreenTip?
Depending on previous Word entries, you may need to type more characters in order for Word to predict a particular word or phrase accurately. Or, you may need to turn on AutoComplete by clicking File on the ribbon to open Backstage view, clicking Options in Backstage view to display the Word Options dialog box, clicking Advanced in the left pane (Word Options dialog box), placing a check mark in the 'Show AutoComplete suggestions' check box in the Editing options section, and then clicking OK.

2

- Press ENTER to instruct Word to finish your typing with the word or phrase that appeared in the AutoComplete ScreenTip.

Q&A What if I do not want to use the text proposed in the AutoComplete ScreenTip?
Simply continue typing and the AutoComplete ScreenTip will disappear from the screen.

3

- Press SPACEBAR. Type **2027** and then click the content control that says, To, to select it. Type **May 2029** to enter the date (shown in Figure 5–31).

To Insert a Building Block

The city name, Bainbridge, appears in the degree in the Education section of the resume. You will type the building block name, bb, and then instruct Word to replace this building block name with the stored building block entry, Bainbridge. The following steps insert a building block. **Why?** Instead of typing the name, you will insert the stored building block.

1

- Click the content control that says, Degree, to select it, and then type **B.S. Business Administration** as the degree name.
- Click the content control that says, Location, to select it, and then type the building block name, **bb** (Figure 5–31).

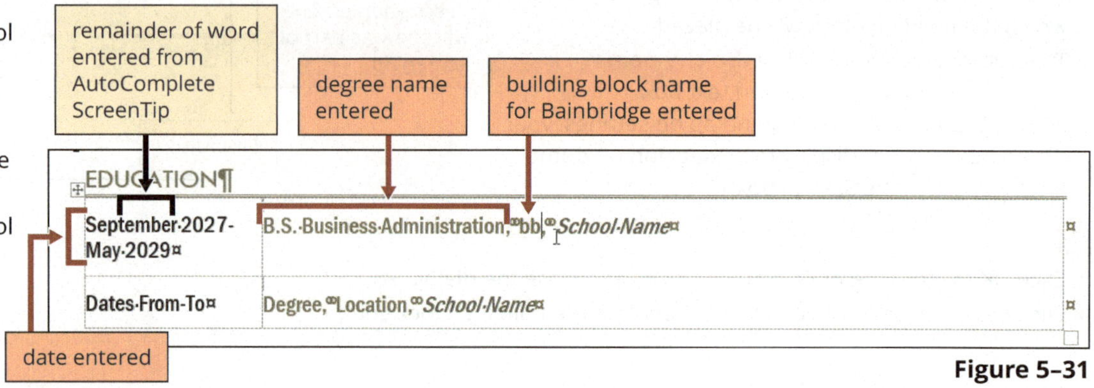

Figure 5–31

2

- Press F3 to instruct Word to replace the building block name (bb) with the stored building block entry (Bainbridge).
- Type **, GA** as the state.
- Click the content control that says, School Name, and then type **Coastal Plains College** as the school name.
- Press ENTER and then type **- GPA 3.7/4.0** (Figure 5–32). (If your GPA is italicized, select the line containing the GPA and then press CTRL+I to remove the italic format.)

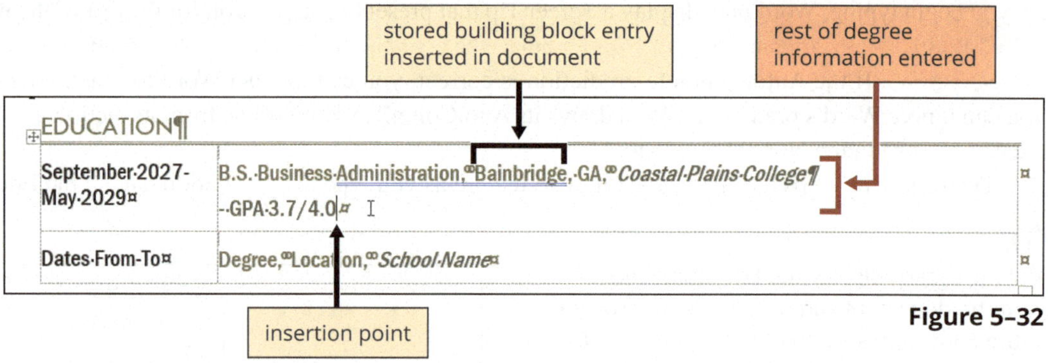

Figure 5–32

Other Ways

1. Click 'Explore Quick Parts' button (Insert tab | Text group), if necessary point to AutoText, select desired building block
2. Click 'Explore Quick Parts' button (Insert tab | Text group), click 'Building Blocks Organizer', select desired building block, click Insert button

Building Blocks versus AutoCorrect

The AutoCorrect feature enables you to insert and create AutoCorrect entries, similarly to how you created and inserted building blocks in this module. The difference between an AutoCorrect entry and a building block entry is that the AutoCorrect feature makes corrections for you automatically as soon as you press SPACEBAR or type a punctuation mark, whereas you must instruct Word to insert a building block. That is, you enter the building block name and then press F3, or click the Explore Quick Parts button (Insert tab | Text group) and then select the building block from one of the galleries or the Building Blocks Organizer.

To Enter Text in Content Controls

The next step is to enter the rest of the text in the Education section of the resume. The following steps enter text in content controls.

1. In the second row of the Education section of the resume, click the content control that says, Dates From, to select it and then type **September 2025** as the from date.
2. Click the content control that says, To, to select it and then type **May 2027** as the end date.
3. Click the content control that says, Degree, to select it, and then type **A.A. Real Estate Studies** as the degree name.
4. Click the content control that says, Location, to select it, and then type **bb** as the building block name. Press F3 to instruct Word to replace the building block name (bb) with the stored building block entry (Bainbridge).
5. Type **, GA** as the state.
6. Click the content control that says, School Name, and then type **Bass Capitol Community College** as the school name.
7. Press ENTER and then type **- GPA 3.8/4.0** (Figure 5–33). (If your GPA is italicized, select the line containing the GPA and then press CTRL+I to remove the italic format.)

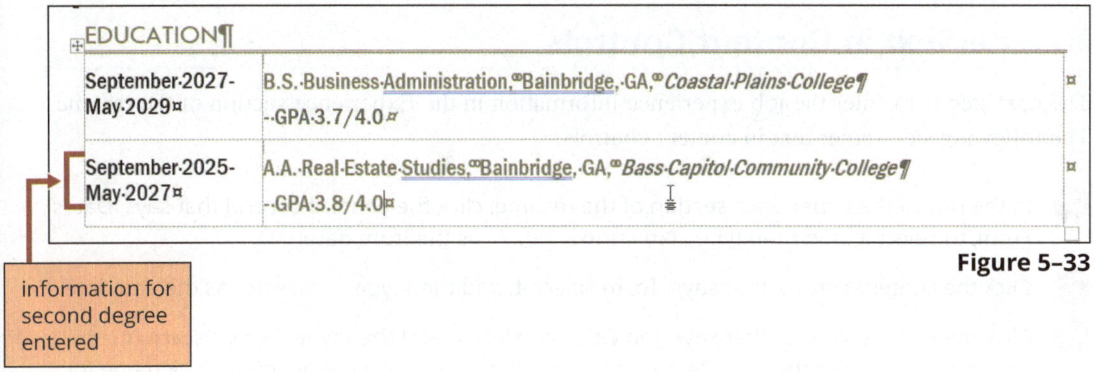

Figure 5–33

To Delete a Row

Because you have only one job to list in the Experience section, the next step is to delete the second row in the Experience section. The following steps delete a row.

1. Scroll to, if necessary, and then click somewhere in the second row of the Experience section, as shown in Figure 5–34.
2. Display the contextual Layout tab.
3. Click the Delete button (contextual Layout tab | Rows & Columns group) to display the Delete menu (Figure 5–34).
4. Click Delete Rows on the Delete menu to delete the current table row (in this case, the second row in the Experience section) (shown in Figure 5–35).

BTW

Building Blocks

If you wanted to make building blocks available in other documents and templates, instead of just the current document or template, you would save them in the Normal .dotm file instead of the Building Blocks.dotx file. To do this, click the 'Explore Quick Parts' button (Insert tab | Text group), click 'Building Blocks Organizer' in the Explore Quick Parts gallery, click the building block for which you want to change the save location, click the Edit Properties button (Building Blocks Organizer dialog box), click the Save in arrow (Modify Building Block dialog box), select Normal in the list, click OK (Modify Building Block dialog box), and then close the Building Blocks Organizer dialog box.

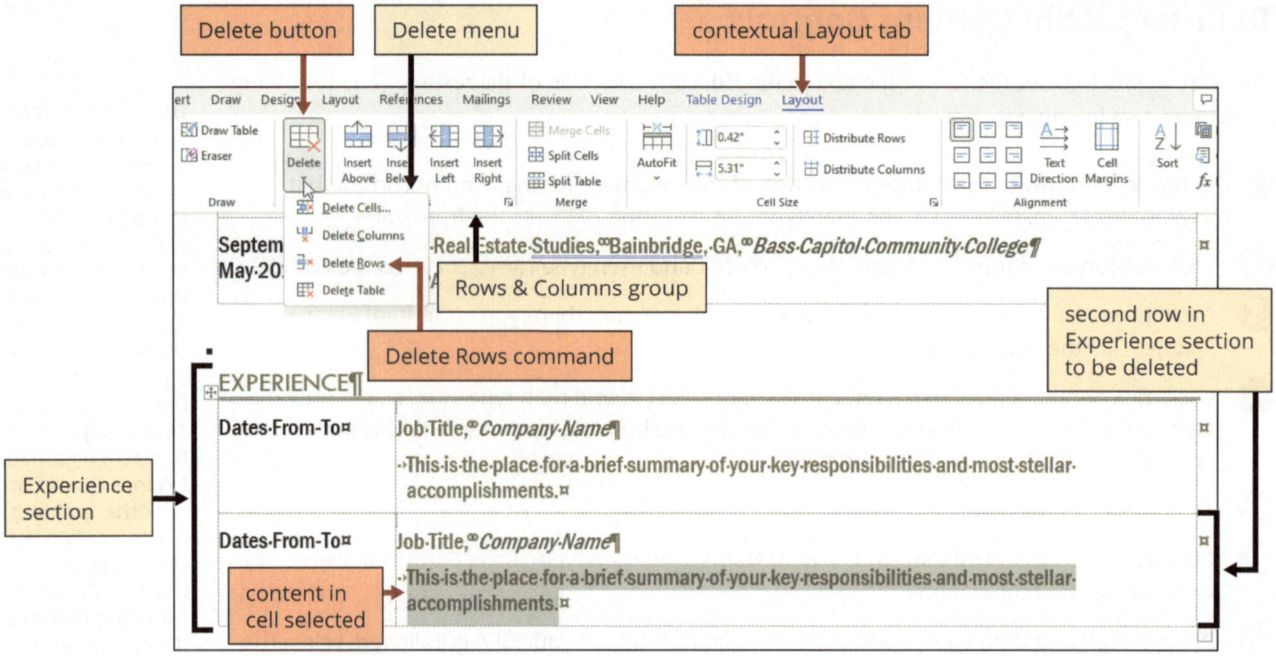

Figure 5–34

To Enter Text in Content Controls

The next step is to enter the job experience information in the Experience section of the resume. The following steps enter text in content controls.

1. In the row of the Experience section of the resume, click the content control that says, Dates From, to select it, and then type **November 2027** as the from date.
2. Click the content control that says, To, to select it, and then type **Present** as the end date.
3. Click the content control that says, Job Title, to select it, and then type **Real Estate Intern, Bainbridge, GA** for the job title, city, and state (be sure to use the building block name for the city name, Bainbridge).
4. Click the content control that says, Company Name, and then type **Piedmont Real Estate** as the company name.
5. Click the content control that begins, 'This is the place for ...', and then type **Show homes to prospective buyers, advise clients on current market trends, prepare purchase agreements, evaluate mortgage options with clients, assist with promoting active listings on social media platforms** (Figure 5–35).

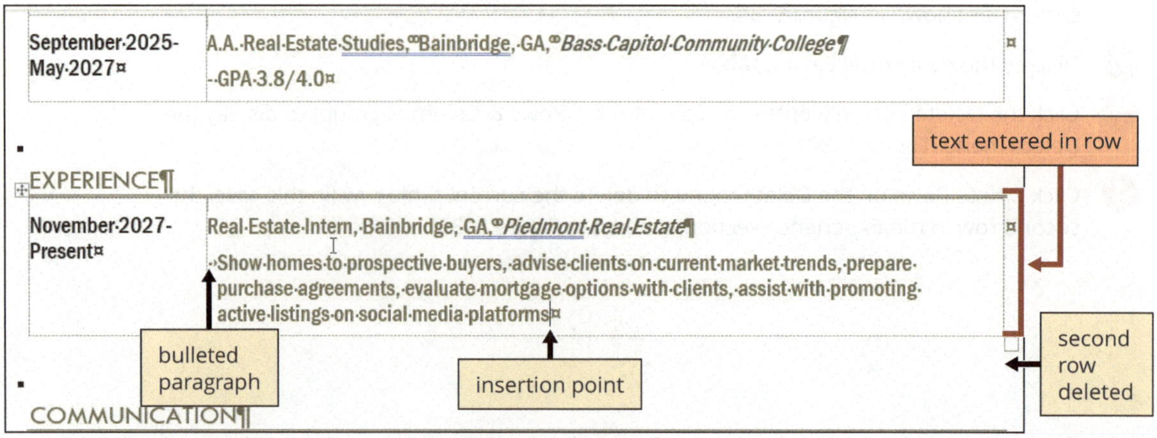

Figure 5–35

To Remove Bullets from a Paragraph

You do not want the experience entry to be a list. Thus, the following steps remove bullets from a list.

1. Display the Home tab.
2. With the insertion point in the bulleted paragraph, click the Bullets button (Home tab | Paragraph group) to remove the bullet from the paragraph (Figure 5–36).

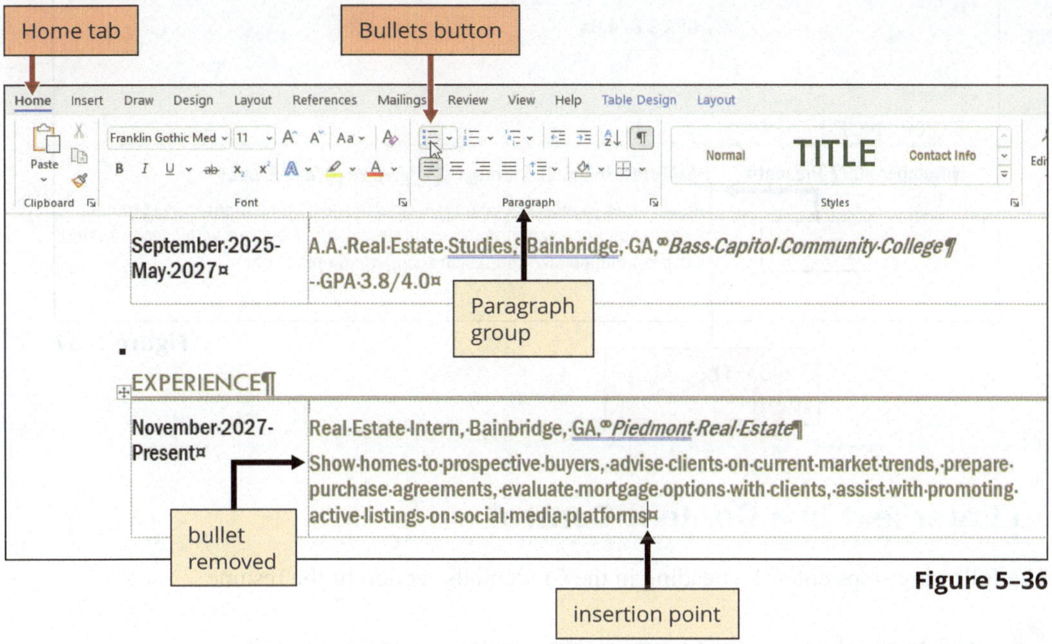

Figure 5–36

BTW
Working with Lists
In a numbered list, if you wanted to restart numbering, you would click the Numbering arrow (Home tab | Paragraph group), click 'Set Numbering Value' in the Numbering gallery to display the Set Numbering Value dialog box, if necessary, click to select the 'Start new list' option button (Set Numbering Value dialog box), and then click OK. To continue list numbering in a subsequent list, you would click the 'Continue from previous list' option button in the Set Numbering Value dialog box. You also can specify a starting number in a list by clicking the Numbering arrow, clicking 'Set Numbering Value' on the Numbering menu, and then entering the value in the 'Set value to' box (Set Numbering Value dialog box).

To Resize Table Columns

You do not want the dates to wrap in the Education and Experience sections of the resume. Thus, you will widen the columns containing these dates. The following steps resize table columns to make them wider.

1. Display the Education and Experience sections in the document window.
2. Position the pointer on the column boundary to the right of the column to adjust (in this case, to the right of the first column of dates in the Education section) so that the pointer changes to a double-headed arrow split by two vertical bars.
3. Drag the column boundary to the right so that Word adjusts the column width so that the from and to dates fit on a single line.
4. Position the pointer on the column boundary to the right of the column to adjust (in this case, to the right of the first column of dates in the Experience section) so that the pointer changes to a double-headed arrow split by two vertical bars.
5. Drag the column boundary to the right so that Word adjusts the column width so that the from and to dates fit on a single line and this column is the same width as the one containing dates in the Education section (Figure 5–37).

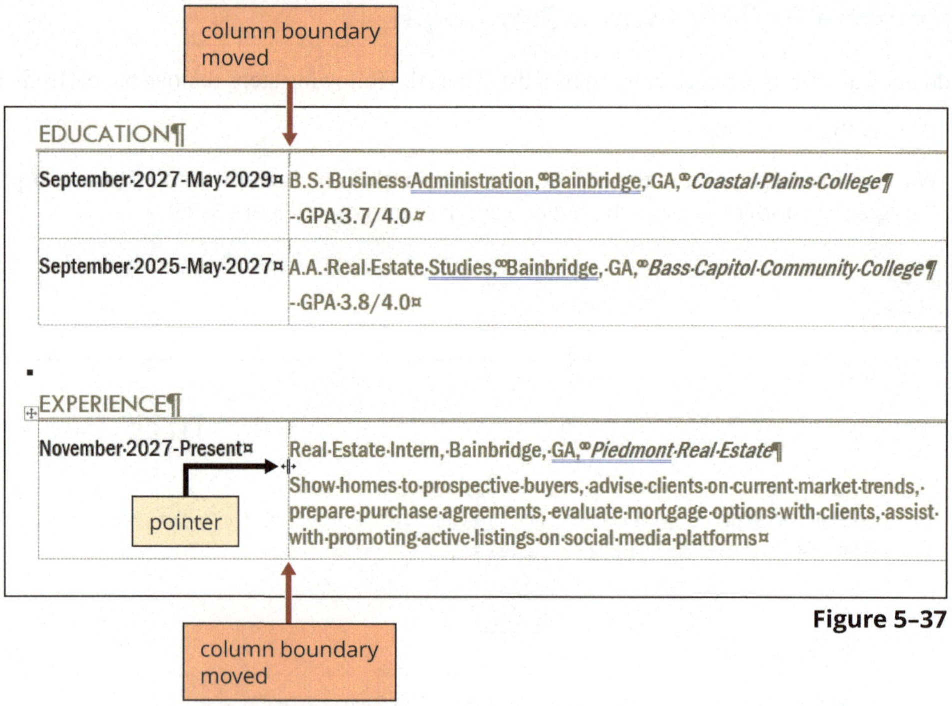

Figure 5–37

To Enter Text in a Content Control

The following steps enter the heading in the Credentials section of the resume.

1. Scroll to and then click the Communication content control to select it.
2. Type **Credentials** as the heading (shown in Figure 5–38).

To Enter a Line Break

The next step in personalizing the resume is to enter content in the Credentials section. The default paragraph spacing in the resume placed 5 points after each line. For the list of credentials, you do not want this extra space after paragraphs. Thus, you will not press ENTER between each line. Instead, you will create a line break. **Why?** A line break, which is created by pressing SHIFT+ENTER, inserts a nonprinting character that advances the insertion point to the beginning of the next physical line, ignoring any paragraph formatting. The following steps enter the list of credentials using a line break, instead of a paragraph break, between each line.

1

- In the Credentials section of the resume, click the content control that begins, 'You delivered that ...', to select it.
- Type **Licensed Real Estate Agent, GA** and then press SHIFT+ENTER to insert a line break character and move the insertion point to the beginning of the next physical line (Figure 5–38).

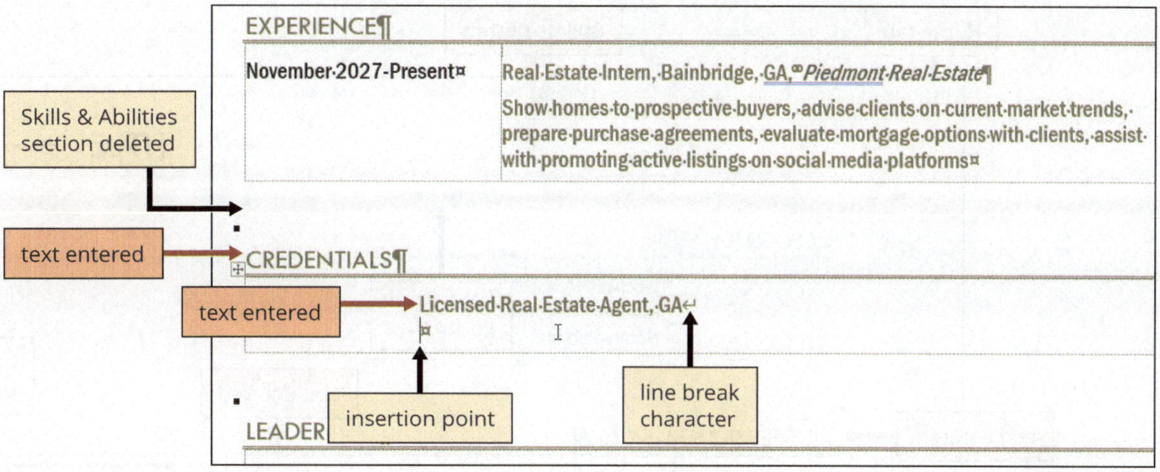

Figure 5–38

2

- Type **National Association of Realtors, member** and then press SHIFT+ENTER.
- Type **Notary Public** as the last entry. Do not press SHIFT+ENTER at the end of this line (Figure 5–39).

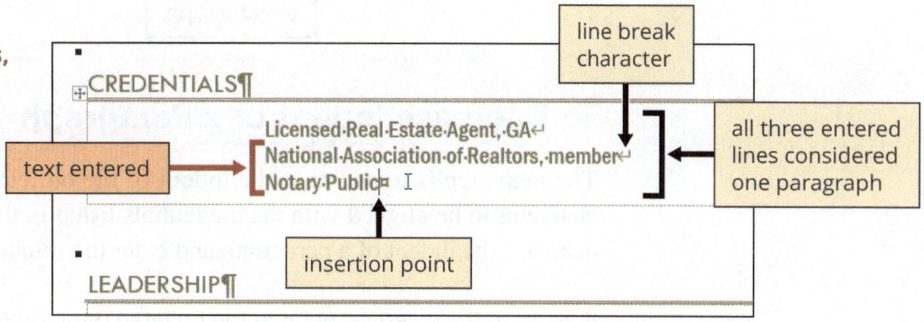

Figure 5–39

To Enter Text in Content Controls

The next step is to begin to enter content in the Professional Skills section of the resume. This should be a bulleted list. The following steps enter text in content controls.

1. Scroll to and then click the Leadership content control to select it.
2. Type **Professional Skills** as the heading (shown in Figure 5–40).
3. In the Professional Skills section of the resume, click the content control that begins, 'Are you president of ...', to select it.
4. Click the Bullets button (Home tab | Paragraph group) to format the current paragraph as a bulleted list item.
5. Type this text: **Excellent communication skills, including negotiations and presentations** (Figure 5–40).

BTW

Line Break Characters

A line break character is a formatting mark that indicates a line break at the end of the line. Like paragraph marks, tab characters, and other formatting marks, line break characters do not print.

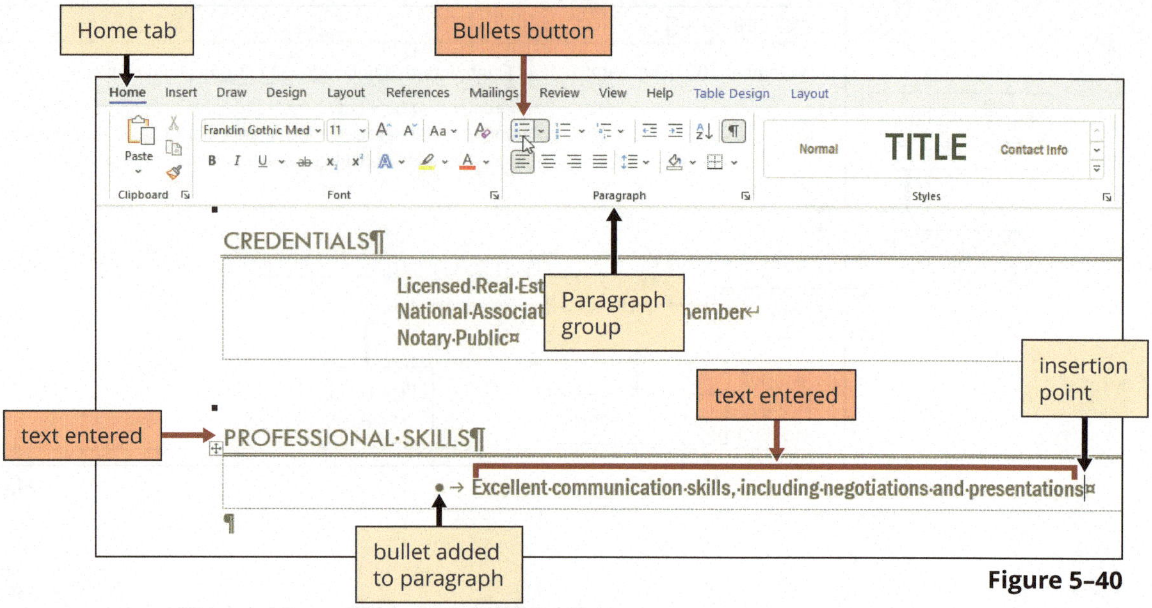

Figure 5–40

To Decrease Indent of a Paragraph

The next step is to decrease the indent of the bulleted paragraph because you want the bullet character to be aligned with the credentials listed in the Credentials section. The following steps decrease the indent of a paragraph and enter the remainder of the bulleted list items.

1. With the insertion point in the bulleted paragraph, as shown in Figure 5–40, click the Decrease Indent button (Home tab | Paragraph group) to decrease the indent of the bulleted list item.
2. Press ENTER and then type **Fluent in English, Spanish, and Persian languages** to enter the second professional skills item.
3. Press ENTER and then type **Proficient with MLS (multiple listing service) database** to enter the third professional skills item.
4. Press ENTER and then type **Extensive knowledge of market trend analysis techniques** to complete the bulleted list (Figure 5–41).

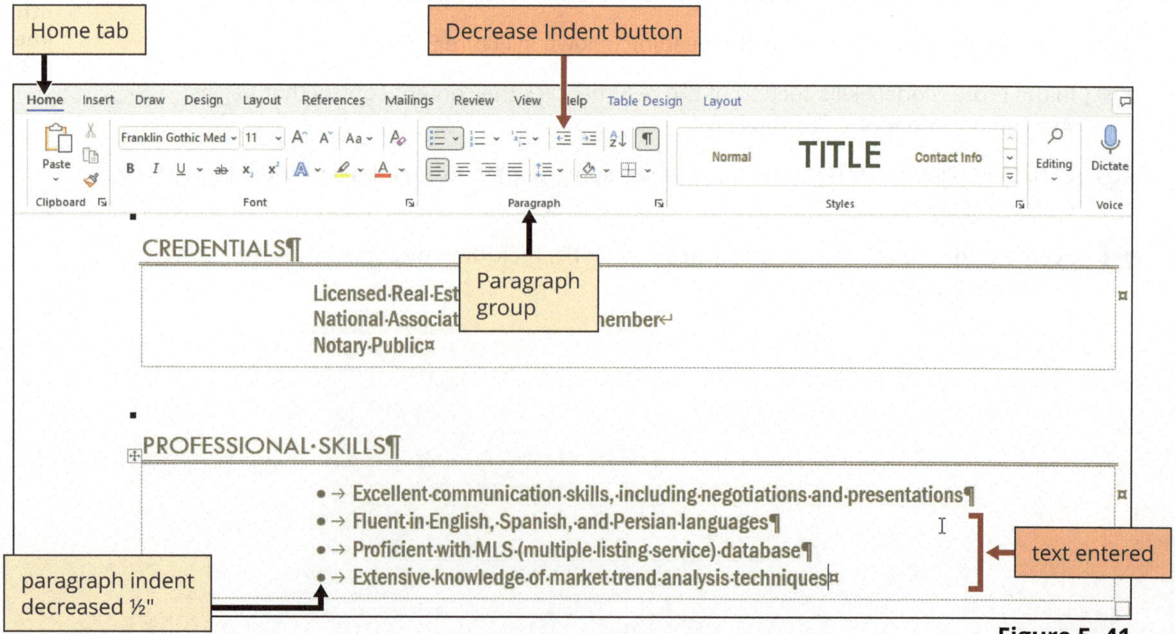

Figure 5–41

To Change a Bullet to a Predefined Symbol

The next step is to change the bullet character in the bulleted list in the Professional Skills section from a dot to a square. The following steps change a bullet character.

1. Select the bulleted list in the Professional Skills section.
2. Click the Bullets arrow (Home tab | Paragraph group) to display the Bullets gallery (Figure 5–42).
3. Click the desired bullet character in the Bullets gallery, in this case, the square, to change the bullet character in the selected bulleted list (shown in Figure 5–43).
4. Click anywhere to remove the selection from the text.
5. Save the resume again on the same storage location with the same file name.

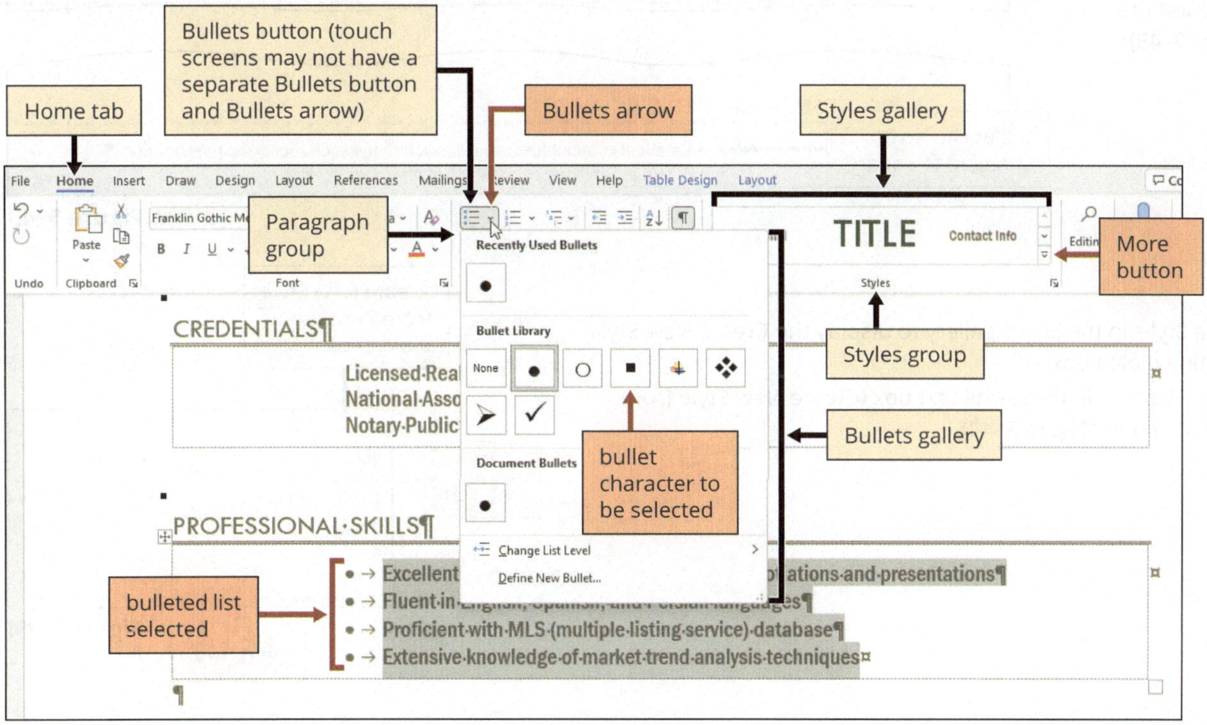

Figure 5–42

To Create a Paragraph Style

A style is a predefined set of formats that appears in the Styles gallery. In addition to using styles in the Styles gallery to apply formats to text and updating existing styles, you also can create your own styles.

The next task in this project is to create a style for the dates in the resume. **Why?** To illustrate creating a style, you will change the color of a date range in the resume and save the new format as a style. Then, you will apply the newly defined style to the remaining dates in the resume. The following steps format text and then create a style based on the formats in the selected text.

1

- Scroll to and then select the date range in the Experience section.
- Use the Font Color gallery to change the color of the selected text to 'Lime, Accent 2, Darker 50%' (sixth color in last row).
- With the date range selected, click the More button (shown in Figure 5–42) in the Styles gallery (Home tab | Styles group) to expand the gallery (Figure 5–43).

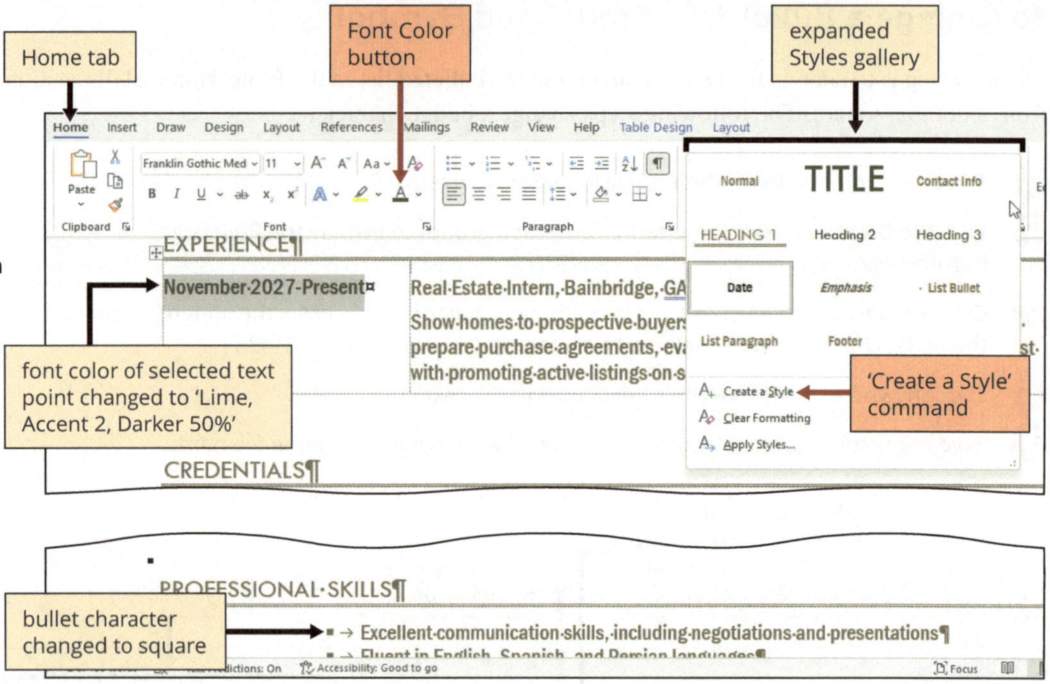

Figure 5–43

2

- Click 'Create a Style' in the Styles gallery to display the Create New Style from Formatting dialog box.
- Type **Resume Dates** in the Name text box (Create New Style from Formatting dialog box) (Figure 5–44).

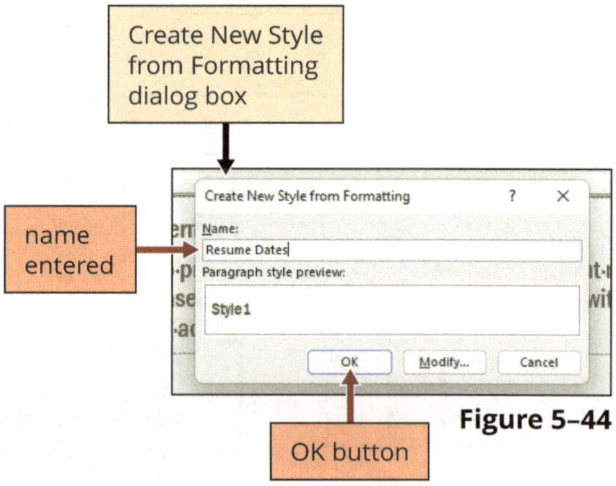

Figure 5–44

3

- Click OK to create the new style and add it to the Styles gallery (shown in Figure 5–45).

Q&A How can I view the style just created?
If the style name does not appear in the in-ribbon Styles gallery, click the More button in the Styles gallery (Home tab | Styles group) to display the expanded Styles gallery.

To Apply a Style

The next task is to apply the style just created to the other dates in the resume. The following steps apply a style.

1 If necessary, scroll to display the Education section of the resume in the document window.

2 One at a time, position the insertion point in each date in the Education section of the resume and then click Resume Dates in the Styles gallery to apply the selected style to each heading (shown in Figure 5–45).

Q&A Do I need to select the text first?
No, just position the insertion point in the text to be formatted and then apply the style.

To Reveal Formatting

Sometimes, you want to know which formats were applied to certain text items in a document. **Why?** For example, you may wonder which font, font size, font color, and other effects were applied to the dates in the resume. To display formatting applied to text, use the Reveal Formatting pane. The following steps open and then close the Reveal Formatting pane.

1

- Position the insertion point in the text for which you want to reveal formatting (in this case, the dates in the Education section).
- Press SHIFT+F1 to open the Reveal Formatting pane, which shows formatting applied to the location of the insertion point (Figure 5–45). (If necessary, drag the edge of the pane to widen or narrow it.)
- **Experiment:** Click the Font collapse button to hide the Font formats. Click the Font expand button to redisplay the Font formats.

Q&A Why do some of the formats in the Reveal Formatting pane appear as links?
Clicking a link in the Reveal Formatting pane displays an associated dialog box, allowing you to change the format of the current text. For example, clicking the FONT link in the Reveal Formatting pane would display the Font dialog box. If you made changes in the Font dialog box and then clicked OK, Word would change the format of the current text.

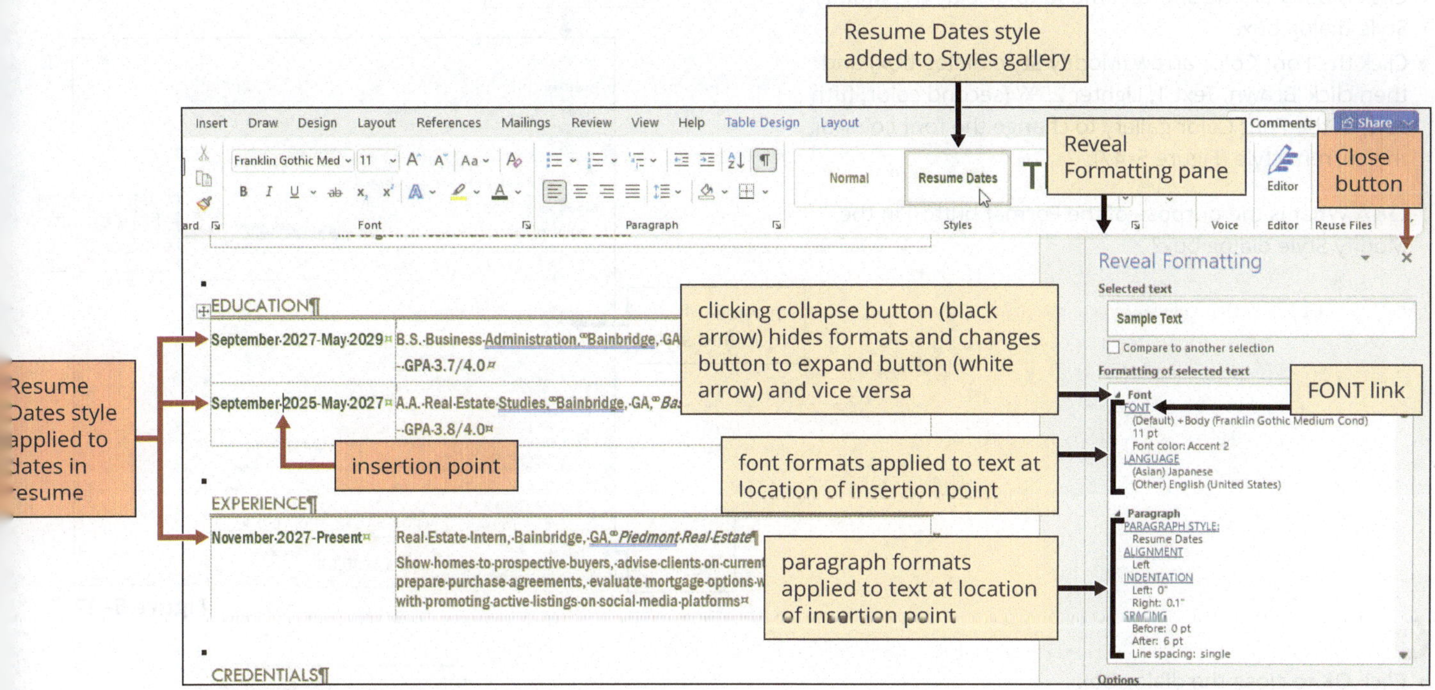

Figure 5–45

2

- Close the Reveal Formatting pane by clicking its Close button.

To Modify a Style Using the Styles Dialog Box

The next step is to modify the Normal style. **Why?** The tan text in the resume is a little light. You prefer that it be a bit darker. Thus, the following steps modify a style.

1

- Position the insertion point somewhere in text formatted with the Normal style (in this case, somewhere in the tan body text) and then right-click the style name to modify in the Styles gallery (Normal, in this case) (Home tab | Styles group) to display a shortcut menu (Figure 5–46).

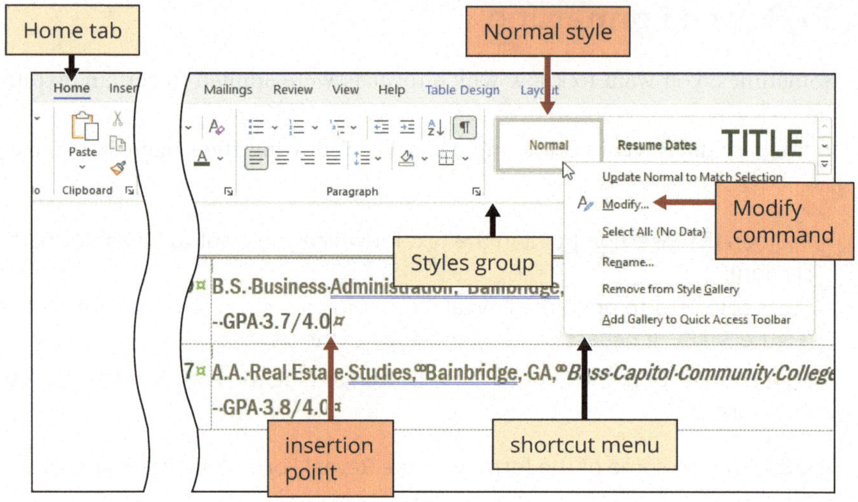

Figure 5–46

2

- Click Modify on the shortcut menu to display the Modify Style dialog box.
- Click the Font Color arrow (Modify Style dialog box) and then click 'Brown, Text 1, Lighter 25%' (second color, fifth row) in the Font Color gallery to change the font color of the current style (Figure 5–47).

Q&A What is the purpose of the Format button in the Modify Style dialog box?

If the formatting you wish to change for the style is not available in the Modify Style dialog box, you can click the Format button (Modify Style dialog box) to display the Format menu and then select the desired command on the Format menu to display a dialog box that contains additional formatting options.

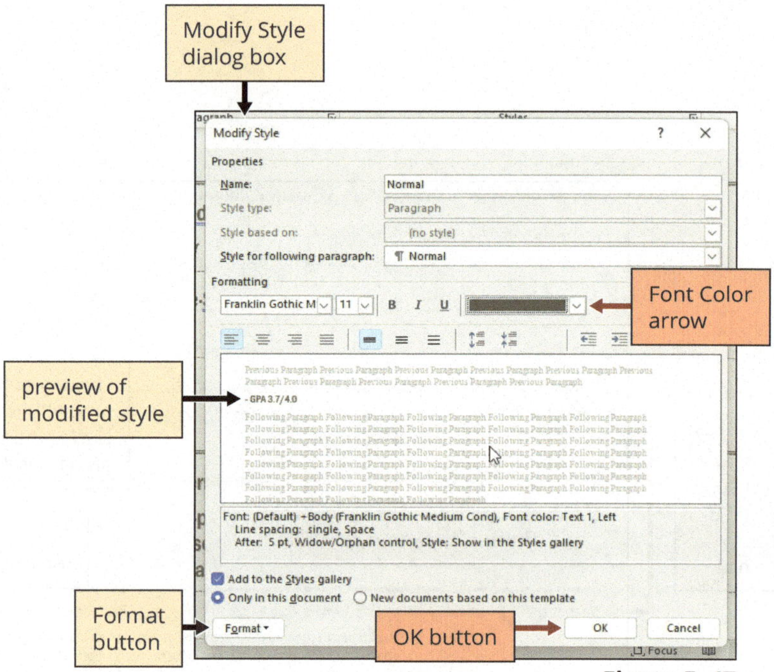

Figure 5–47

3

- Click OK to close the dialog box and apply the style changes to the paragraphs in the document (Figure 5–48).
- If the resume spills to two pages, adjust spacing above and below paragraphs so that the entire resume fits on a single page.

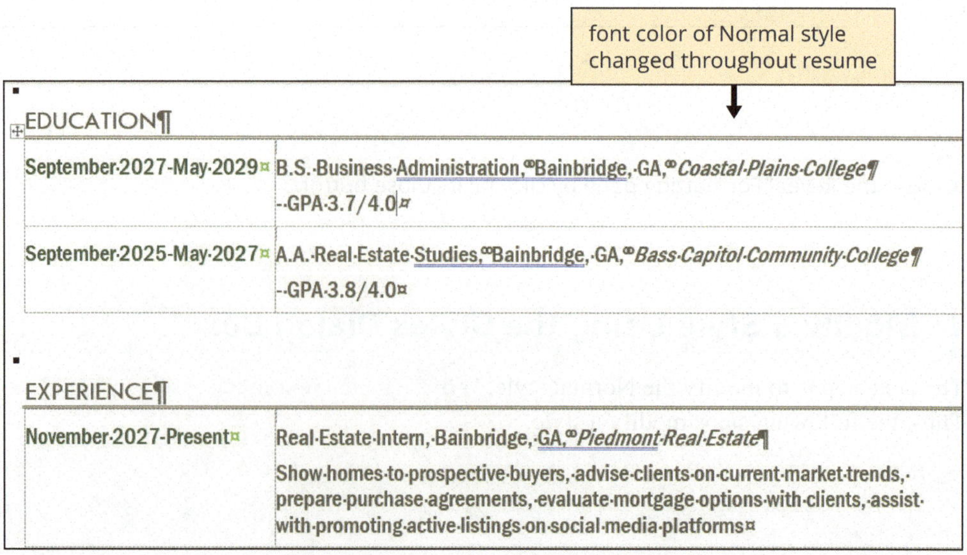

Figure 5–48

Other Ways

1. Click Styles Dialog Box Launcher (Home tab | Styles group), click arrow to right of style to modify, click Modify on menu, change settings (Modify Style dialog box), click OK
2. Click Styles Dialog Box Launcher, click Manage Styles button, scroll to style and then select it (Manage Styles dialog box), click Modify button, change settings (Modify Style dialog box), click OK in each dialog box

To Center Page Contents Vertically

In Word, you can center the page contents vertically. **Why?** This places the same amount of space at the top and bottom of the page. The following steps center resume page contents vertically.

1

- If necessary, click Layout on the ribbon to display the Layout tab.
- Click the Page Setup Dialog Box Launcher (Layout tab | Page Setup group) to display the Page Setup dialog box.
- Click the Layout tab (Page Setup dialog box) to display the Layout sheet.
- Click the Vertical alignment arrow (Page Setup dialog box) to display the list of alignment options and then click Center in the list (Figure 5–49).

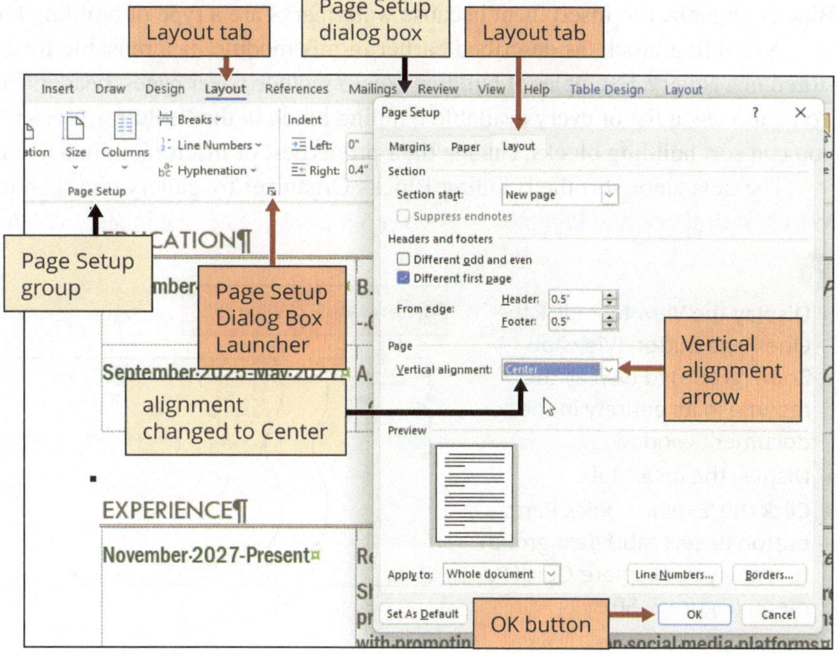

Figure 5–49

2

- Click OK to center the page contents vertically on the screen (shown in Figure 5–1 at the beginning of this module).

Q&A What if I wanted to change the alignment back?
You would select the Top vertical alignment from the Vertical alignment list in the Layout sheet (Page Setup dialog box).

- Save the resume again on the same storage location with the same file name.
- If requested by your instructor, print the finished resume (shown in Figure 5–1).

Break Point: If you want to take a break, this is a good place to do so. You can exit Word now. To resume later, start Word, open the file called SC_WD_5_SchorelResume.docx, and continue following the steps from this location forward.

BTW
Conserving Ink and Toner
If you want to conserve ink or toner, you can instruct Word to print draft quality documents by clicking File on the ribbon to open Backstage view, clicking Options in Backstage view to display the Word Options dialog box, clicking Advanced in the left pane (Word Options dialog box), scrolling to the Print area in the right pane, placing a check mark in the 'Use draft quality' check box, and then clicking OK. Then, use Backstage view to print the document as usual.

Sharing a Document with Others

You may want to share Word documents with others electronically, such as via email, USB flash drive, or cloud storage. To ensure that others can read and/or open the files successfully, Word provides a variety of formats and tools to assist with sharing documents. This section uses the Schorel Resume created in this module to present a variety of these formats and tools.

To Insert a Quick Part

You would like to place the text, DRAFT, as a watermark on the resume before you share it, so that others are aware you might be making additional changes to the document. While you can insert a watermark using the ribbon, you also can use the Building Blocks Organizer to insert them because watermarks are a type of building block.

A building block, as described earlier in this module, is a reusable formatted ready-made graphic or text element that is stored in a gallery. Examples of building blocks include cover pages, headers, footers, page numbers, watermarks, and text boxes. You can view a list of every available building block in the **Building Blocks Organizer**. From the Building Blocks Organizer, you can sort building blocks, change their properties, or insert them in a document.

The next steps sort the Building Blocks Organizer by gallery and then insert the Draft 1 building block in the document. **Why?** Sorting the building blocks by gallery makes it easier to locate the building blocks.

1

- Display the View tab. Click the One Page button (View tab | Zoom group) to display the resume in its entirety in the document window.
- Display the Insert tab.
- Click the 'Explore Quick Parts' button (Insert tab | Text group) to display the Explore Quick Parts menu (Figure 5–50).

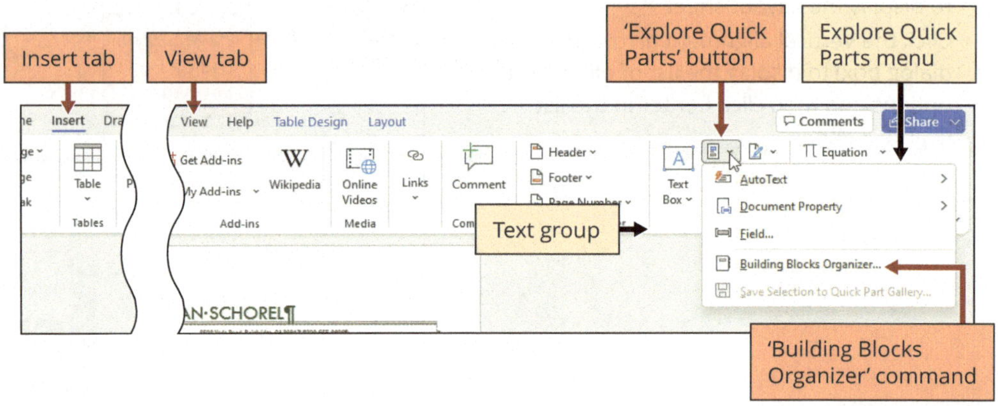

Figure 5–50

2

- Click 'Building Blocks Organizer' on the Explore Quick Parts menu to display the Building Blocks Organizer dialog box.
- **Experiment:** Drag the scroll bars in the Building Blocks Organizer so that you can view all the columns and rows in the dialog box.
- Click the Gallery heading (Building Blocks Organizer dialog box) in the building blocks list to sort the building blocks by gallery (Figure 5–51).
- **Experiment:** Click various names in the building blocks list and notice that a preview of the selected building block appears in the dialog box.

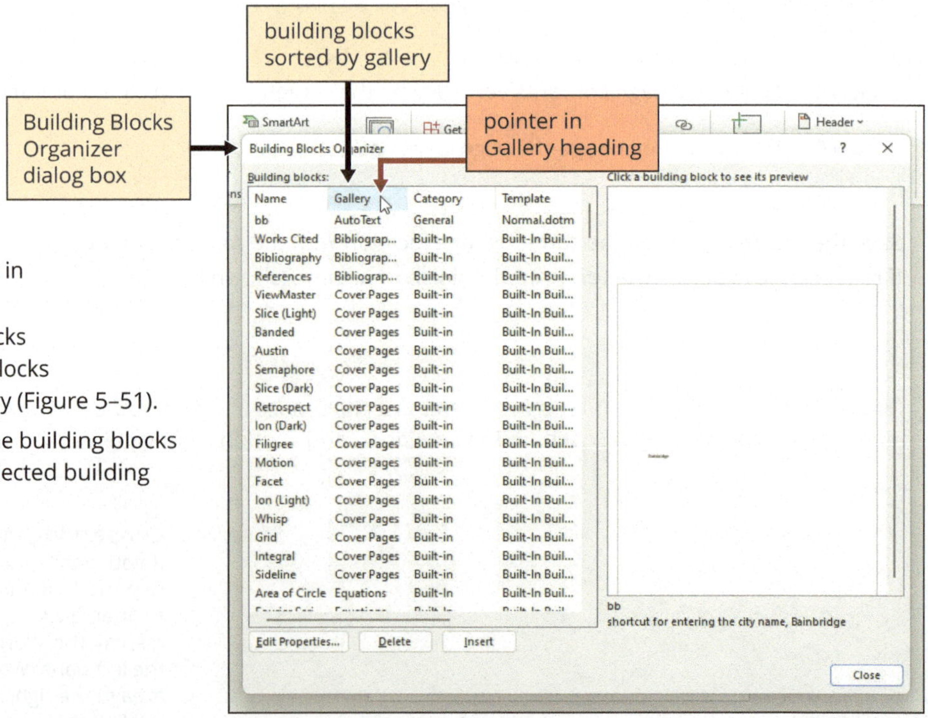

Figure 5–51

3

- Scroll through the building blocks list to the Watermarks group in the Gallery column and then click DRAFT 1 to select this building block (Figure 5–52).

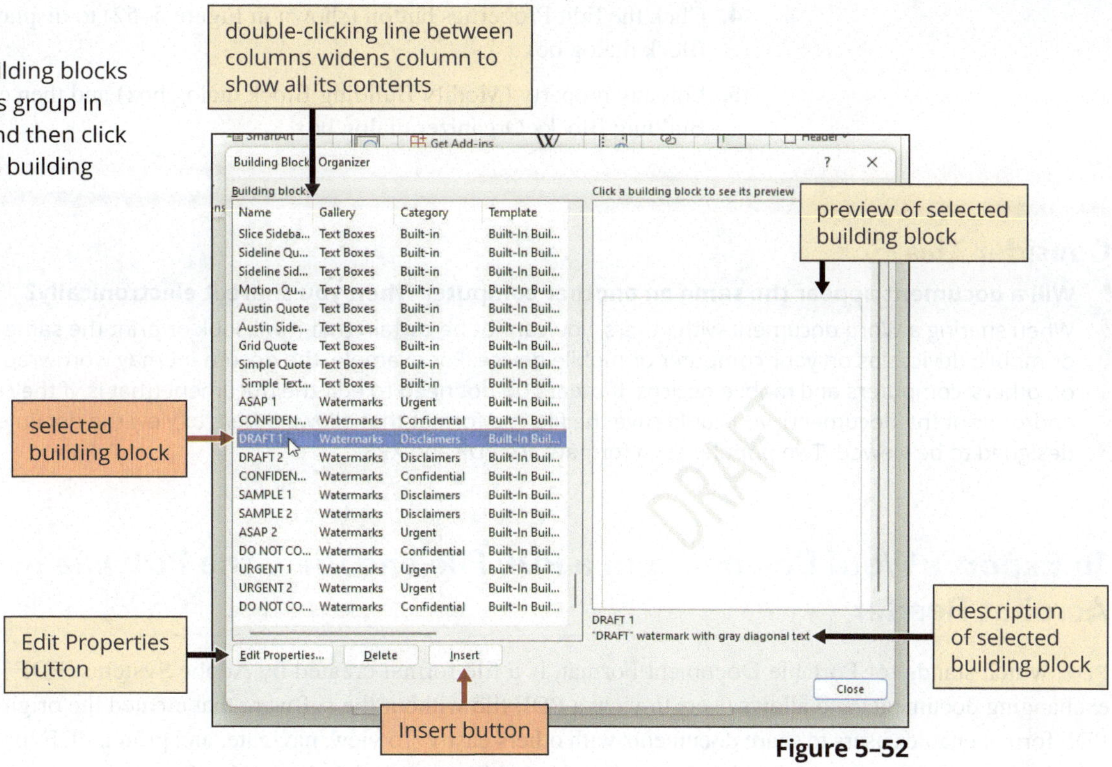

Figure 5–52

4

- Click the Insert button to insert the selected building block in the document (Figure 5–53).

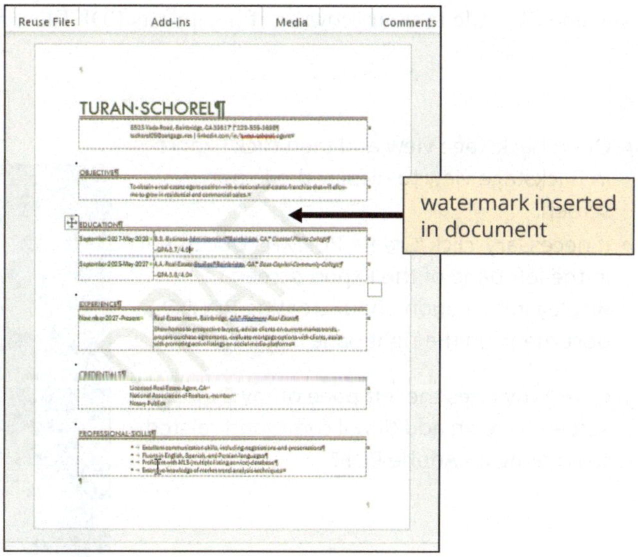

Figure 5–53

To Edit Properties of Building Block Elements (Quick Parts) Properties of a building block include its name, gallery, category, description, location where it is saved, and how it is inserted in the document. If you wanted to change any of these building block properties for a particular building block, you would perform these steps.

1. Click the 'Explore Quick Parts' button (Insert tab | Text group) to display the Explore Quick Parts menu.
2. Click 'Building Blocks Organizer' on the Explore Quick Parts menu to display the Building Blocks Organizer dialog box.
3. Select the building block you wish to edit (Building Blocks Organizer dialog box).

4. Click the Edit Properties button (shown in Figure 5–52) to display the Modify Building Block dialog box.

5. Edit any property (Modify Building Block dialog box) and then click OK. Close the Building Blocks Organizer dialog box.

Consider This

Will a document appear the same on another computer when you share it electronically?

When sharing a Word document with others, you cannot be certain that it will look or print the same on their computers or mobile devices as on your computer or mobile device. For example, the document may wordwrap text differently on others' computers and mobile devices. If others do not need to edit the document (that is, if they need only to view and/or print the document), you could save the file in a format that allows others to view the document the way it was designed to be viewed. Two popular such formats are PDF and XPS.

To Export a Word Document to a PDF File and View the PDF File in Adobe Acrobat Reader

PDF, which stands for Portable Document Format, is a file format created by Adobe Systems. PDF is a standard format for exchanging documents and allows users to view a PDF file without the software that created the original document. Thus, the PDF format enables users to share documents with others easily. To view, navigate, and print a PDF file, you use an application called **Adobe Acrobat Reader**, which can be downloaded free from Adobe's website. Some browsers also can display PDF files.

When you save a Word document as a PDF file, the original Word document remains intact; that is, Word creates a copy of the file in the PDF format. The following steps save the Schorel Resume Word document as a PDF file and then open the Schorel Resume PDF file in your browser, if it supports PDF files, or Adobe Acrobat Reader. **Why?** You want to share the resume with others but want to ensure it appears the same on their computer or mobile device as it does on yours.

1

- Open Backstage view and then click Export in Backstage view to display the Export screen.
- If necessary, click 'Create PDF/XPS Document' in the left pane of the Export screen to display information about creating PDF/XPS documents in the right pane (Figure 5–54).

Q&A Why does the left pane of my Export screen have an additional command related to creating an Adobe PDF?
Depending on your installation settings in Adobe, you may have an additional tab on your ribbon and/or additional commands in screens, etc., related to Adobe functionality.

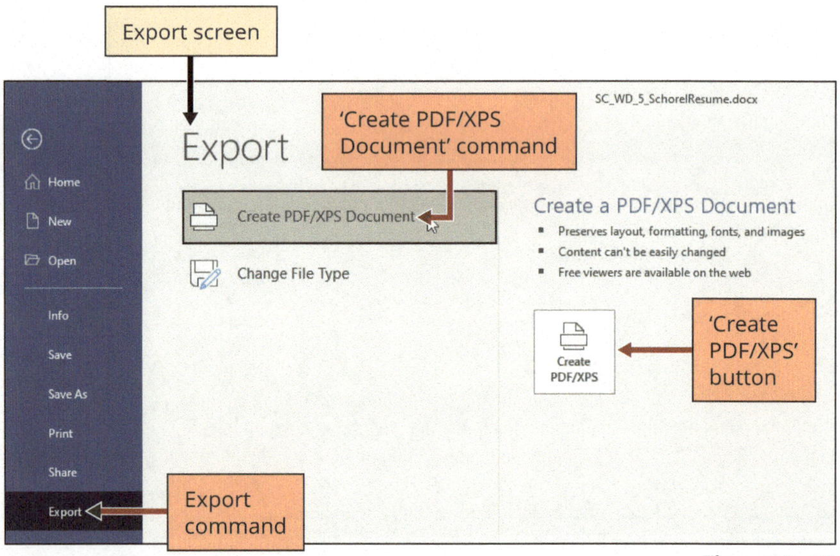

Figure 5–54

2

- Click the 'Create PDF/XPS' button in the right pane to display the Publish as PDF or XPS dialog box.
- Navigate to the desired save location (Publish as PDF or XPS dialog box).

Q&A Can the file name be the same for the Word document and the PDF file?
Yes. The file names can be the same because the file types (and the file extensions) are different: one is a Word document and the other is a PDF file.

- If necessary, click the 'Save as type' arrow and then click PDF.
- If necessary, place a check mark in the 'Open file after publishing' check box so that Word will display the resulting PDF file in a browser window or Adobe Acrobat Reader (Figure 5–55).

Q&A Why is my 'Open file after publishing' check box dimmed?
Your browser does not support PDF files and you do not have Adobe Acrobat Reader installed on your computer. Use a search engine, such as Google, to search for the text, get adobe acrobat reader. Then, click the link in the search results to download Adobe Acrobat Reader and follow the on-screen instructions to install the program. After installing Adobe Acrobat Reader, repeat these steps.

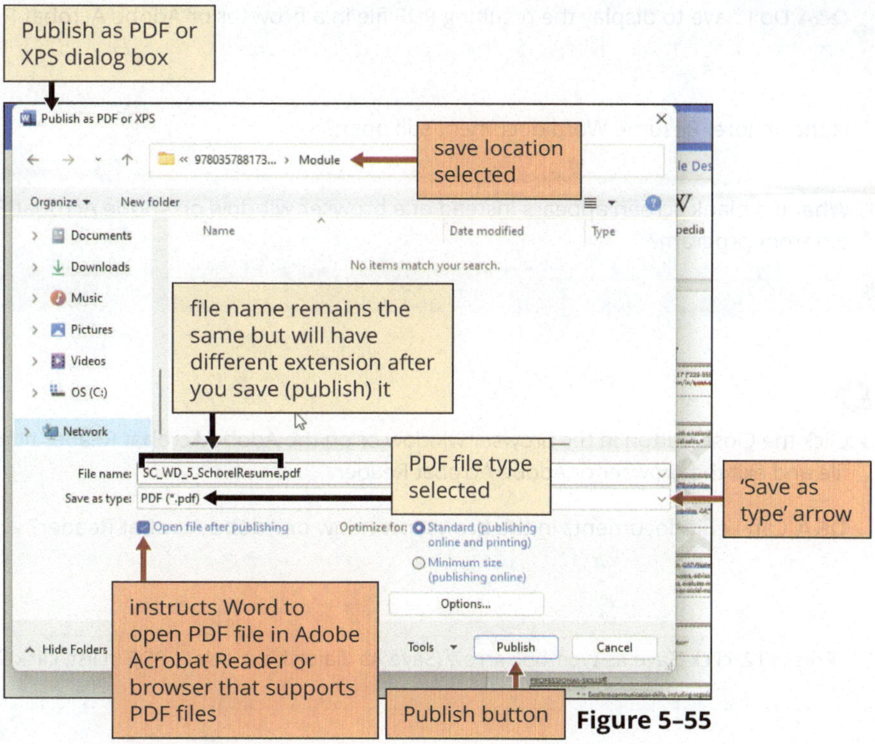

Figure 5–55

3

- Click the Publish button to create the PDF file from the Word document and then, because the check box was selected, open the resulting PDF file in a browser window, such as Microsoft Edge, or Adobe Acrobat Reader, depending on settings.
- If necessary, click the Maximize button in the browser window or Adobe Acrobat Reader window to maximize the window (Figure 5–56). Note that your screen may differ depending on your browser or Adobe Acrobat Reader.

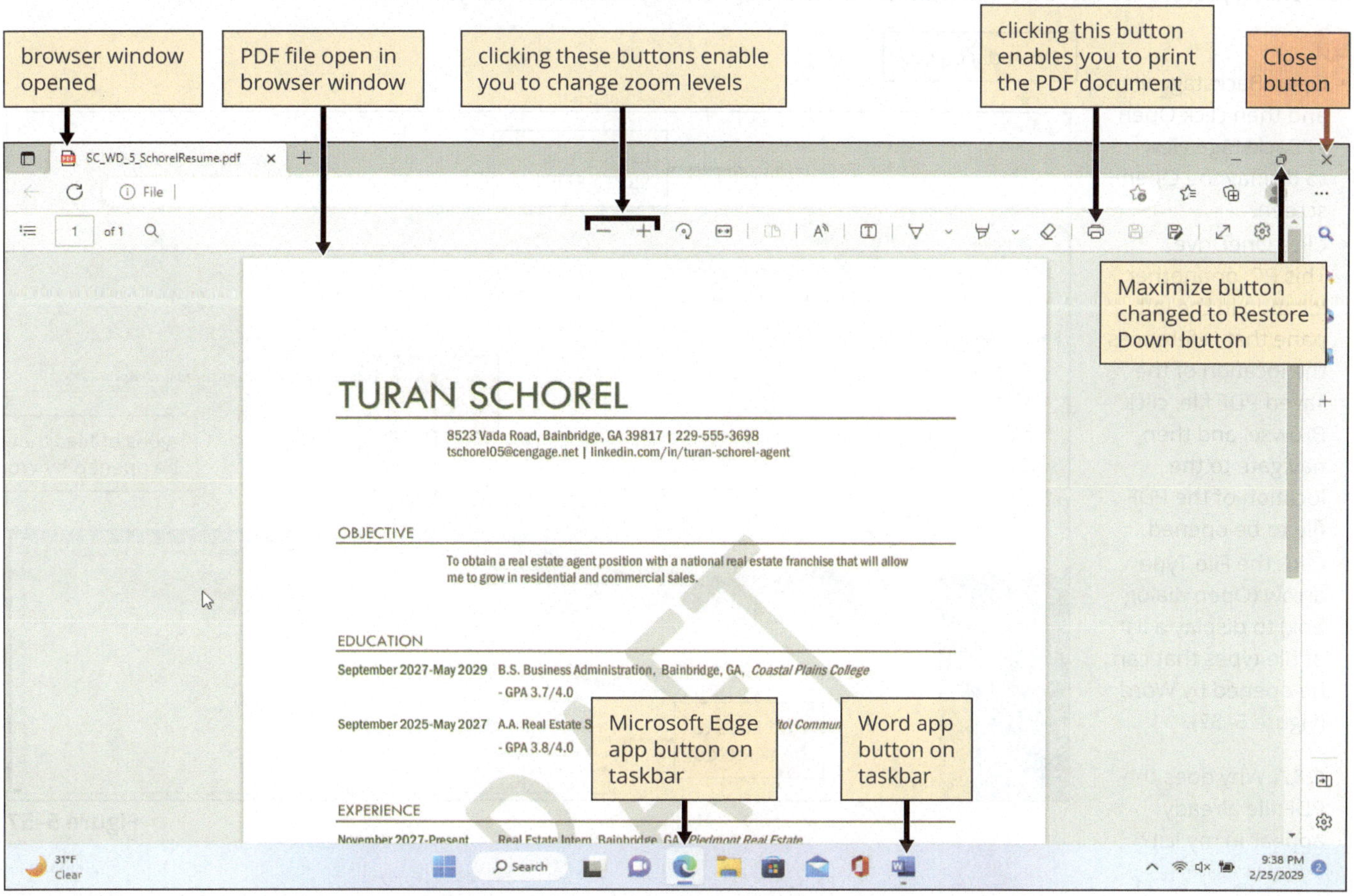

Figure 5–56

Q&A Do I have to display the resulting PDF file in a browser or Adobe Acrobat Reader?
No. If you do not want to display the document in a browser or Adobe Acrobat Reader, you would not place a check mark in the 'Open file after publishing' check box in the Publish as PDF or XPS dialog box (shown in Figure 5–55).

Is the Schorel Resume Word document still open?
Yes. Word still is running with the Schorel Resume document opened.

What if a blank screen appears instead of a browser window or Adobe Acrobat Reader or if the document appears in a different program?
Your browser may not support PDF files and you may not have Adobe Acrobat Reader installed. Press the Start key on the keyboard to redisplay the Start screen and then navigate back to Word, or close the program in which the document opened.

4

- Click the Close button in the browser window or on the Adobe Acrobat Reader title bar to close the SC_WD_5_SchorelResume.pdf file and exit the browser or Adobe Acrobat Reader.

Q&A Can I edit documents in the browser window or Adobe Acrobat Reader?
No, you need Adobe Acrobat Pro or some other program that enables editing of PDF files.

Other Ways

1. Press F12, click 'Save as type' box arrow (Save As dialog box), select PDF in list, click Save

To Open a PDF File from Word to Edit It

When you use Word to open a PDF file, Word converts it to an editable document. **Why?** You may want to change the contents of a PDF file. The editable PDF file that Word creates from the PDF file may appear slightly different from the PDF due to the conversion process. To illustrate this feature, the following steps open the PDF file just saved.

1

- Open Backstage view and then click Open in Backstage view to display the Open screen.
- Click OneDrive, This PC, or another location in the left pane that references the location of the saved PDF file, click Browse, and then navigate to the location of the PDF file to be opened.
- Click the File Type arrow (Open dialog box) to display a list of file types that can be opened by Word (Figure 5–57).

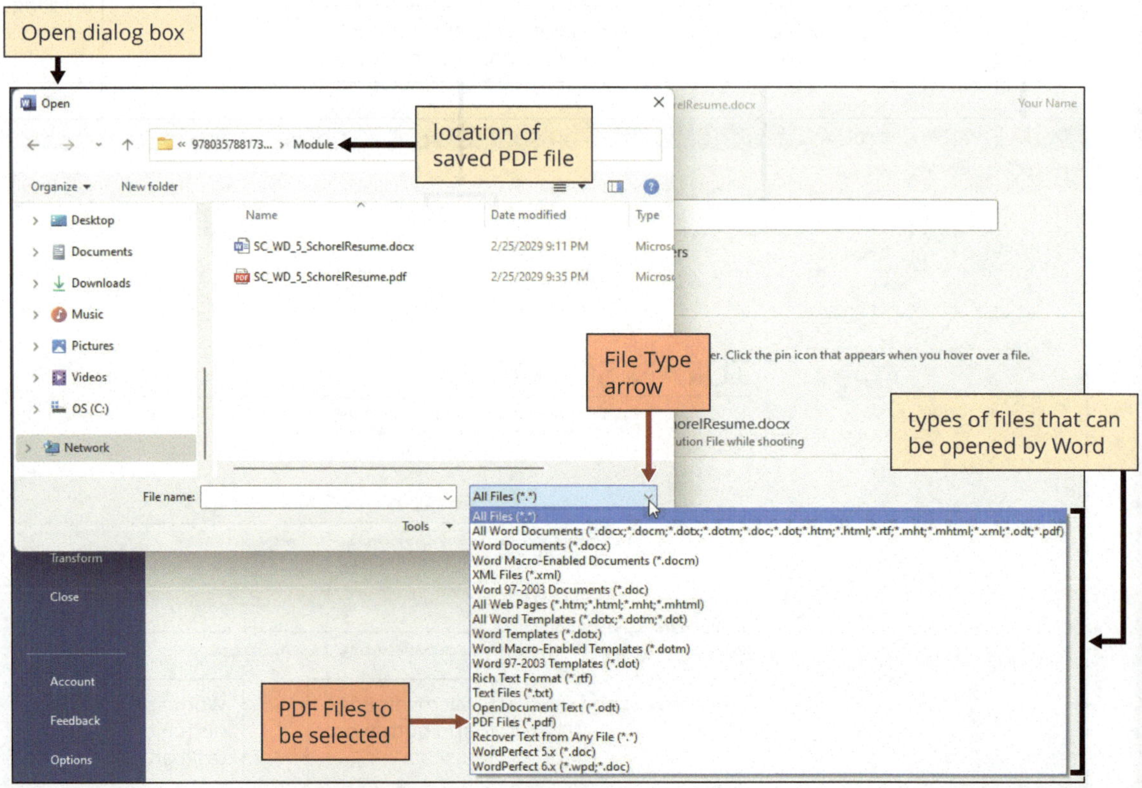

Figure 5–57

Q&A Why does the PDF file already appear in my list?
If the file type is All Word Documents, Word displays all file types that it can open in the file list.

2

- Click PDF Files in the File Type list, so that Word displays PDF file names in the dialog box.
- Click SC_WD_5_SchorelResume to select the PDF file to be opened (Figure 5–58). (Depending on settings, the file name box may not show the .pdf extension after the file name.)

3

- Click the Open button (Open dialog box) to open the selected file and display the opened document in the Word window.
- If Word displays a dialog box indicating it will begin converting the document, click OK.

4

- If necessary, click the Print Layout button on the status bar to switch to Print Layout view.
- **Experiment:** Scroll through the PDF that Word converted, noticing any differences between it and the original resume created in this module. Change a word in the document to practice editing it.
- Close the Word window and do not save this converted PDF file.

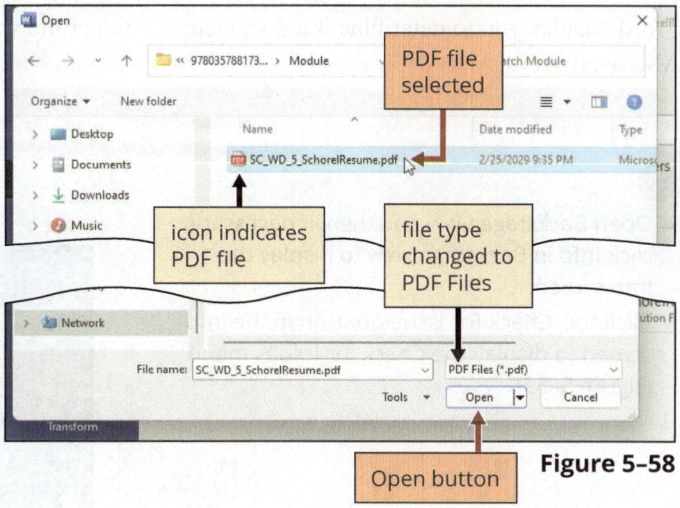

Figure 5–58

To Export a Word Document to an XPS Document **XPS**, which stands for XML Paper Specification, is a file format created by Microsoft that shows all elements of a printed document as an electronic image. As with the PDF format, users can view an XPS document without the software that created the original document. Thus, the XPS format also enables users to share documents with others easily. Windows includes an XPS Viewer, which enables you to view, navigate, and print XPS files.

When you save a Word document as an XPS document, the original Word document remains intact; that is, Word creates a copy of the file in the XPS format. If you wanted to save a Word document as an XPS document, you would perform the following steps.

1. Open Backstage view and then click Export in Backstage view to display the Export screen.
2. Click 'Create PDF/XPS Document' in the left pane of the Export screen to display information about PDF/XPS documents in the right pane and then click the 'Create PDF/XPS' button to display the Publish as PDF or XPS dialog box.
3. If necessary, navigate to the desired save location.
4. If necessary, click the 'Save as type' arrow and then click XPS Document.
5. Click the Publish or Save button to create the XPS document from the Word document and then, if the 'Open file after publishing' check box was selected, open the resulting XPS document in the XPS Viewer.

or

1. Press F12 to display the Save As dialog box.
2. If necessary, navigate to the desired save location.
3. If necessary, click the 'Save as type' arrow and then click XPS Document.
4. Click the Publish or Save button to create the XPS document from the Word document and then, if the 'Open file after publishing' check box was selected, open the resulting XPS document in the XPS Viewer.

Q&A What if I do not have an XPS Viewer?

The document will open in a browser window, if your browser supports XPS files. If it does not, you will need to download an XPS viewer.

5. If necessary, exit the XPS Viewer.

BTW

PDFs and Accessibility

If your document contains any potential accessibility issues, Word displays an Investigate Accessibility button when you select the 'Create PDF/XPS Document' button in the Export screen. When you click the Investigate Accessibility button, Word opens the Accessibility pane so that you can fix any identified accessibility issues before creating the PDF version of the document.

To Check Document Compatibility

Word enables you to determine if a document is compatible with (will work with) versions earlier than the current version of Microsoft Word. **Why?** If you would like to save a document, such as your resume, in the Word 97-2003 format so that it can be opened by users with earlier versions of Microsoft Word, you want to ensure that all its elements (such as building blocks, content controls, and graphics) are compatible with earlier versions of Word. The following steps run the compatibility checker.

1

- Open Backstage view and then, if necessary, click Info in Backstage view to display the Info screen.
- Click the 'Check for Issues' button in the Info screen to display the Check for Issues menu (Figure 5–59).

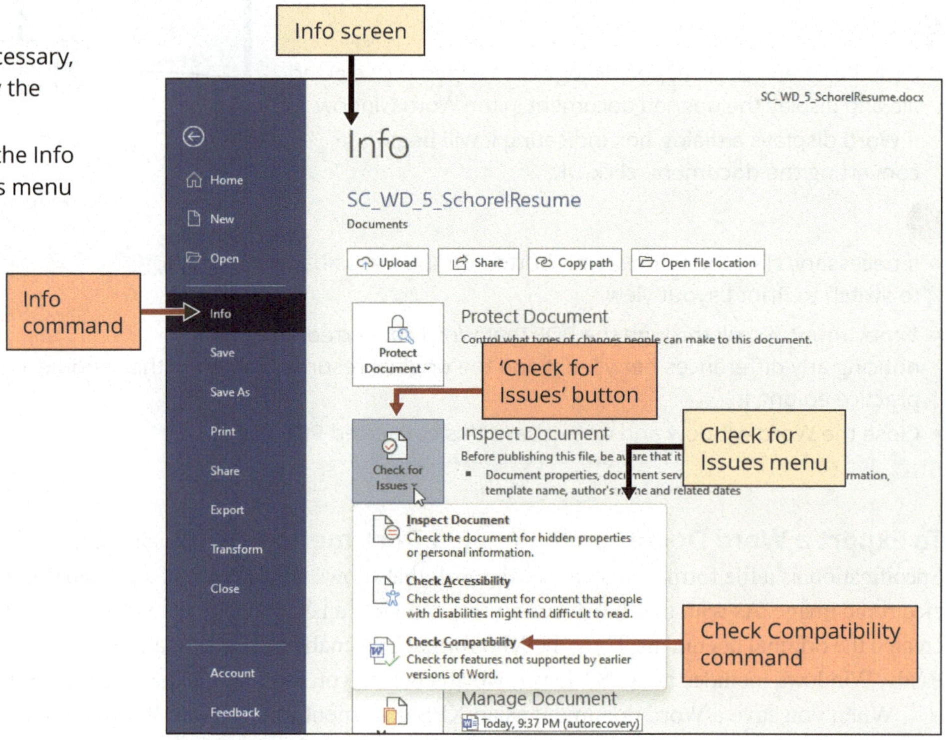

Figure 5–59

2

- Click Check Compatibility on the Check for Issues menu to display the Microsoft Word Compatibility Checker dialog box, which shows any content that may not be supported by earlier versions of Word (Figure 5–60).

3

- Click OK (Microsoft Word Compatibility Checker dialog box) to close the dialog box.

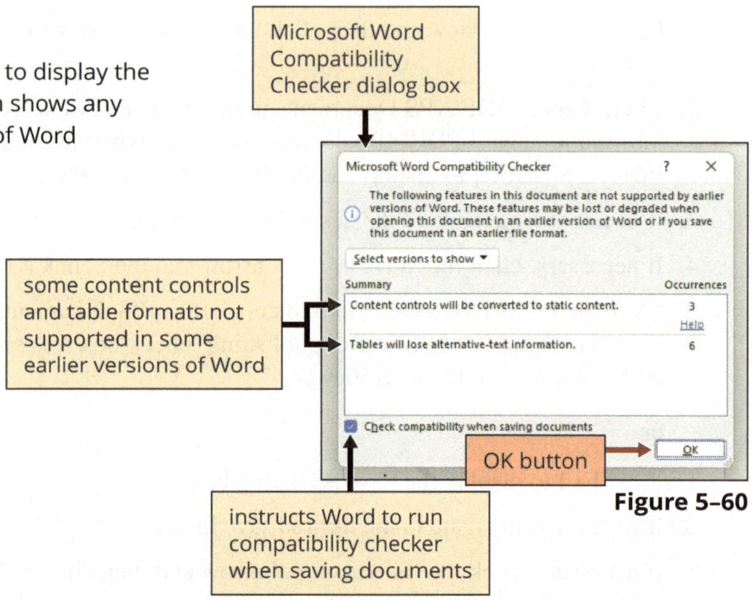

Figure 5–60

To Save a Word 365 Document in an Earlier Word Format

If you send a document created in Word 365 to users who have a version of Word earlier than Word 2007, they will not be able to open the Word 365 document. **Why?** Word 365 saves documents in a format that is not backward compatible with versions earlier than Word 2007. Word 365 documents have a file type of .docx, and versions prior to Word 2007 have a .doc file type. To ensure that all Word users can open your Word 365 document, you should save the document in a Word 97-2003 format. The following steps save the Word 365 format of the SC_WD_5_SchorelResume.docx document in the Word 97-2003 format.

1

- Open Backstage view and then click Export in Backstage view to display the Export screen.
- Click 'Change File Type' in the left pane of the Export screen to display information in the right pane about various Word file types.
- Click 'Word 97-2003 Document' in the right pane to specify the new file type (Figure 5–61).

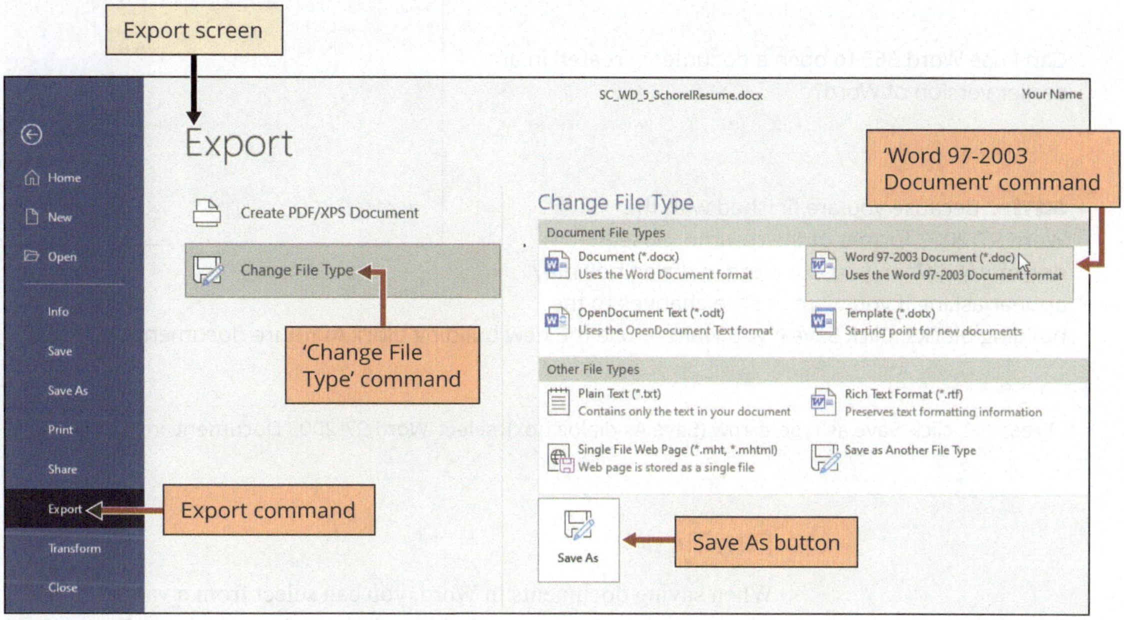

Figure 5–61

2

- Click the Save As button in the right pane to display the Save As dialog box.
- If necessary, navigate to the desired save location (Save As dialog box) (Figure 5–62).

Q&A Can the file name be the same for the Word 365 document and the Word 97-2003 document?

Yes. The file names can be the same because the file types (and file extensions) are different: one is a Word document with a .docx extension, and the other is a Word document with a .doc extension. The next section discusses file types and extensions.

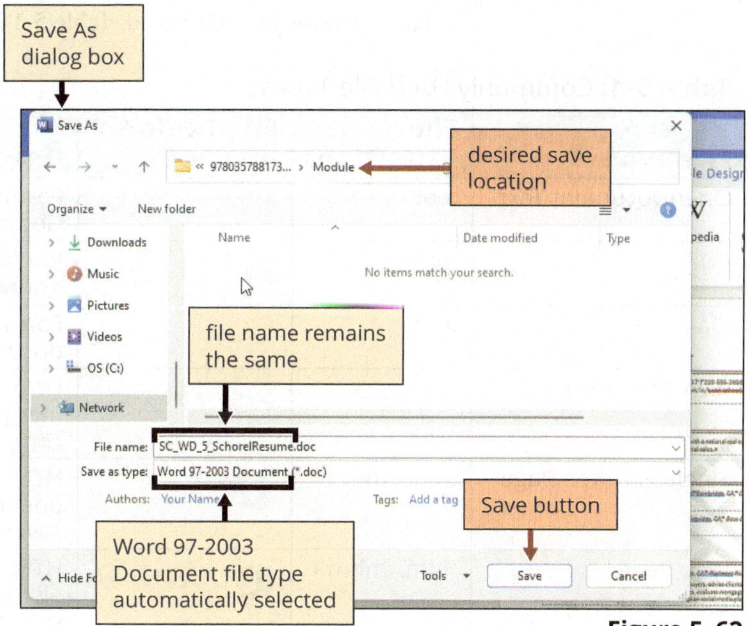

Figure 5–62

3

- Click Save (Save As dialog box), which may display the Microsoft Word Compatibility Checker dialog box before saving the document (shown in Figure 5–60).

Q&A My screen did not display the Microsoft Word Compatibility Checker dialog box. Why not?

If the 'Check compatibility when saving documents' check box is not selected (as shown in Figure 5–60), Word will not check compatibility when saving a document.

- If the Microsoft Word Compatibility Checker dialog box is displayed, click its Continue button to save the document on the selected drive with the current file name in the specified format (Figure 5–63).

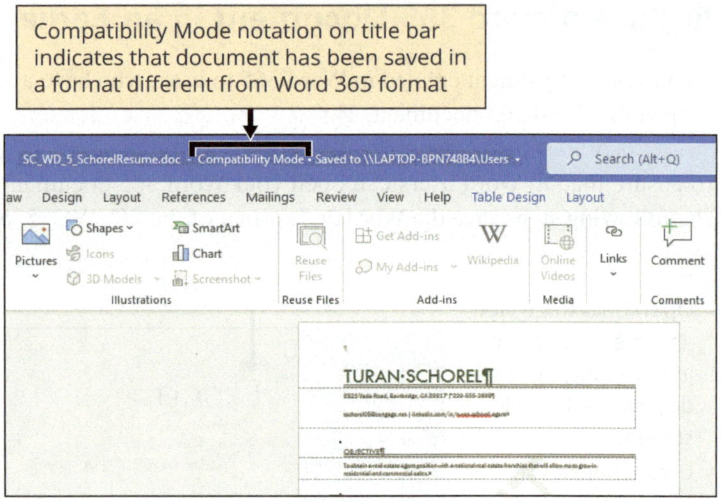

Figure 5–63

Q&A Is the Word 365 format of the SC_WD_5_SchorelResume.docx document still open?
No. Word closed the original document (the Word 365 format of the SC_WD_5_SchorelResume.docx).

Can I use Word 365 to open a document created in an earlier version of Word?
Yes, but you may notice that the appearance of the document differs when opened in Word 365.

- **sam** Because you are finished with the Word 97-2003 format of the resume, close the document. (When you exit Word, a dialog box may appear asking if you want to save changes to the building blocks. Click Save if you want to use the new building block in future documents.)

Other Ways

1. Press F12, click 'Save as type' arrow (Save As dialog box), select 'Word 97-2003 Document' in list, click Save

File Types

When saving documents in Word, you can select from a variety of file types that can be opened in Word using the Export screen in Backstage view (shown in Figure 5–61) or by clicking the 'Save as type' arrow in the Save As dialog box. To save in these varied formats, you follow the same basic steps as just illustrated. Table 5-1 identifies the more commonly used file types.

Table 5–1: Commonly Used File Types

File Type	File Extension	File Explorer Image	Description
OpenDocument Text	.odt		Format used by other word processing programs, such as Google Docs and OpenOffice.org
PDF	.pdf		Portable Document Format, which can be opened in Adobe Acrobat Reader
Plain Text	.txt		Format where all or most formatting is removed from the document
Rich Text Format	.rtf		Format designed to ensure file can be opened and read in many programs; some formatting may be lost to ensure compatibility
Single File Web Page	.mht, .mhtml		HTML (Hypertext Markup Language) format that can be opened in a browser; all elements of the webpage are saved in a single file
Web Page	.htm, .mhtml		HTML format that can be opened in a browser; various elements of the webpage, such as graphics, saved in separate files and folders
Word 97-2003 Document	.doc		Format used for documents created in versions of Word from Word 97 to Word 2003
Word 97-2003 Template	.dot		Format used for templates created in versions of Word from Word 97 and Word 2003
Word Document	.docx		Format used for Word 365, Word 2019, Word 2016, Word 2013, Word 2010, or Word 2007 documents
Word Template	.dotx		Format used for Word 365, Word 2019, Word 2016, Word 2013, Word 2010, or Word 2007 templates
XPS	.xps		XML (Extensible Markup Language) Paper Specification, which can be opened in the XPS Viewer

To Save a Word 365 Document as a Different File Type To save a Word 365 document as a different file type, you would follow these steps.

1. Open Backstage view and then click Export in Backstage view to display the Export screen.
2. Click 'Change File Type' in the Export screen to display information in the right pane about various file types that can be opened in Word.
3. Click the desired file type in the right pane and then click the Save As button to display the Save As dialog box.
4. Navigate to the desired save location (Save As dialog box) and then click Save in the dialog box.
5. If the Microsoft Word Compatibility Checker dialog box appears and you agree with the changes that will be made to the document, click the Continue button (Microsoft Word Compatibility Checker dialog box) to save the document on the selected drive with the current file name in the specified format.

BTW
AutoSave and AutoRecover
If you do not want Word to save files automatically on OneDrive, you can disable this option by doing the following: open Backstage view, click Options to display the Word Options dialog box, click Save in the left pane (Word Options dialog box), and then remove the check mark from the 'AutoSave files stored in the Cloud by default in Word' check box. If you wanted to change the frequency with which Word saves AutoRecover information, enter the number of minutes in the 'Save AutoRecover information every' box.

To Share a Document on OneDrive

If you have a OneDrive account, you can share a Word document saved on OneDrive with others through email message invitations. **Why?** Invited users can click a link in an email message that displays a webpage enabling them to view or edit the document on OneDrive. The following steps invite a user to view the resume. If you do not have a Microsoft account or an Internet connection, read these steps without performing them.

1

- If necessary, start Word. Open the Word 365 format of the SC_WD_5_SchorelResume.docx file and then save the resume document on OneDrive.

Q&A Why is the Word 365 format not in the Open dialog box?
You may need to change the file type from PDF to All Files.

- Click the Share button in the upper-right corner of the ribbon to display the Share menu (Figure 5–64).

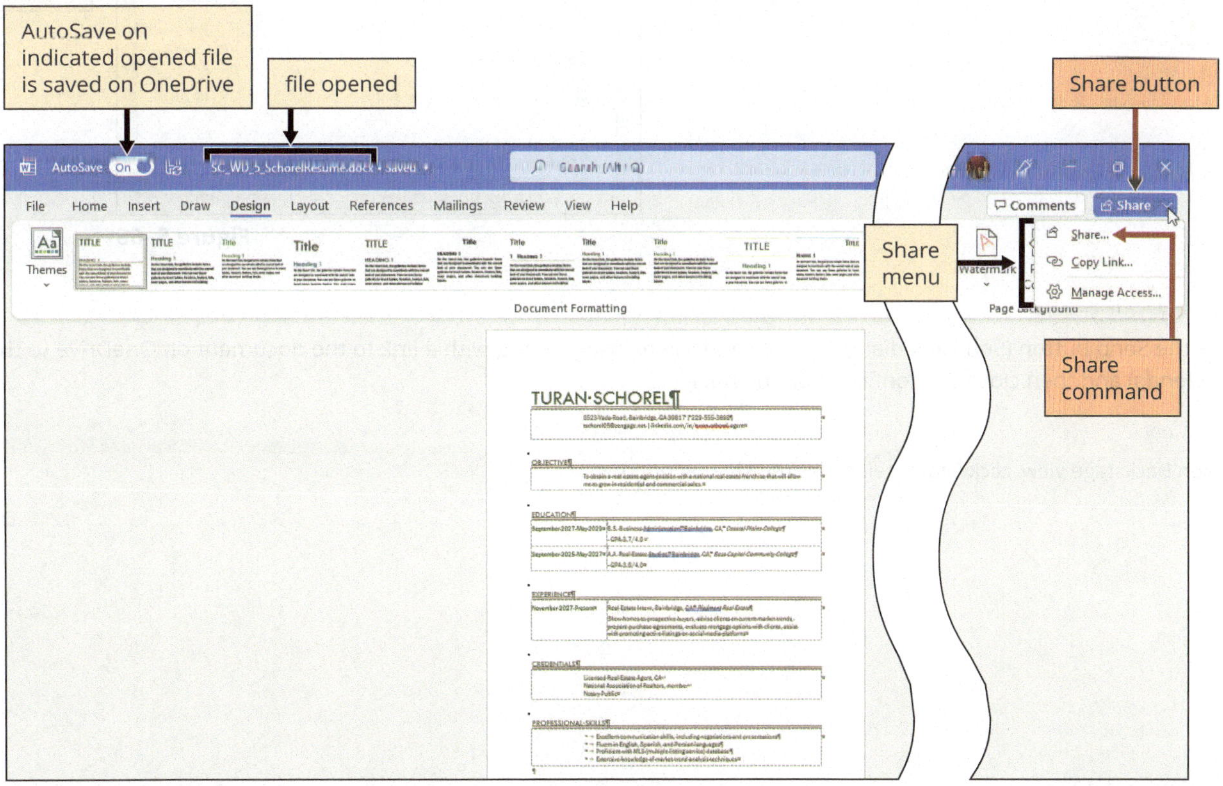

Figure 5–64

2

- Click Share on the Share menu to display the Send link dialog box (Figure 5–65).

Q&A Why does a Share dialog box appear instead of a Send link dialog box?
The document has not been saved on OneDrive and/or you are not signed in to your Microsoft account.

What if Word displayed the Send link dialog box instead of the Share menu?
Proceed to Step 3.

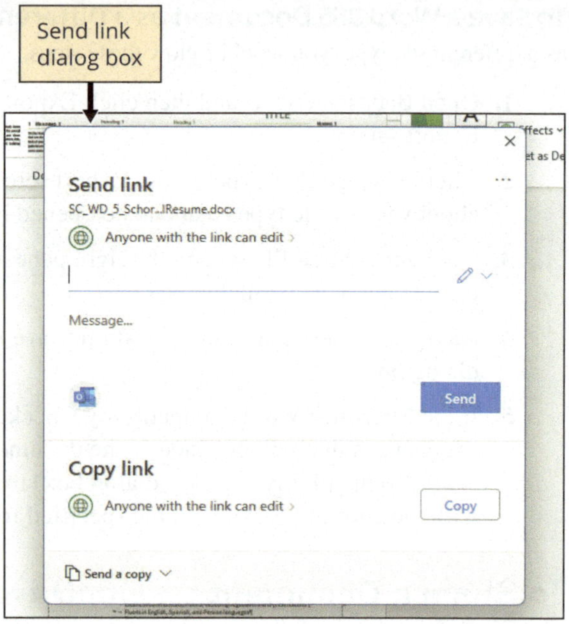

Figure 5–65

3

- In the Send link dialog box, type the email address(es) of the person(s) with whom you want to share the document, click the box arrow so that you can specify Can edit, if necessary, and then type a message to the recipient(s) (Figure 5–66).

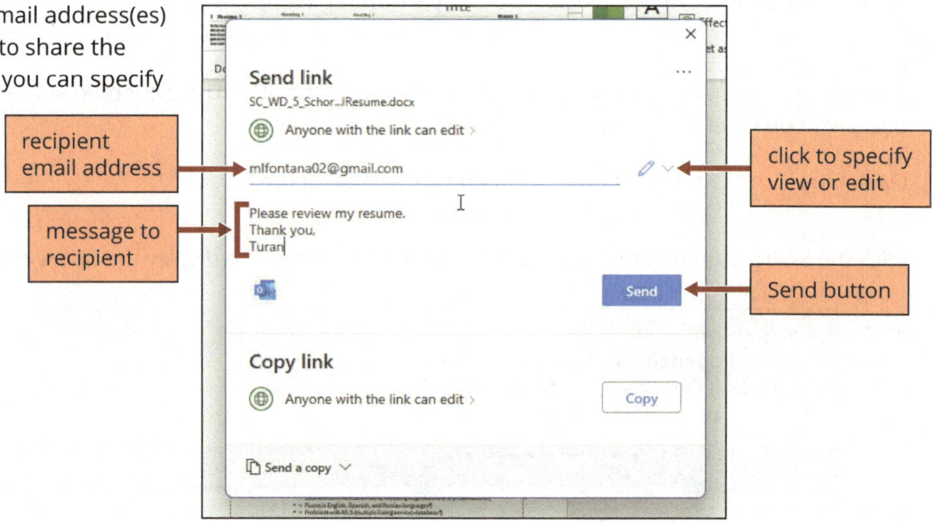

Figure 5–66

4

- Click the Send button (Send link dialog box) to send the message along with a link to the document on OneDrive to the listed recipient(s) and then close the confirmation message.

Other Ways

1. Open Backstage view, click Share, select desired sharing options

Consider This

How does a recipient access the shared document?

The recipient receives an email message that indicates it contains a link to a shared document (Figure 5–67). When the recipient clicks the link in the email message, the document opens in Word Online on OneDrive (Figure 5–68).

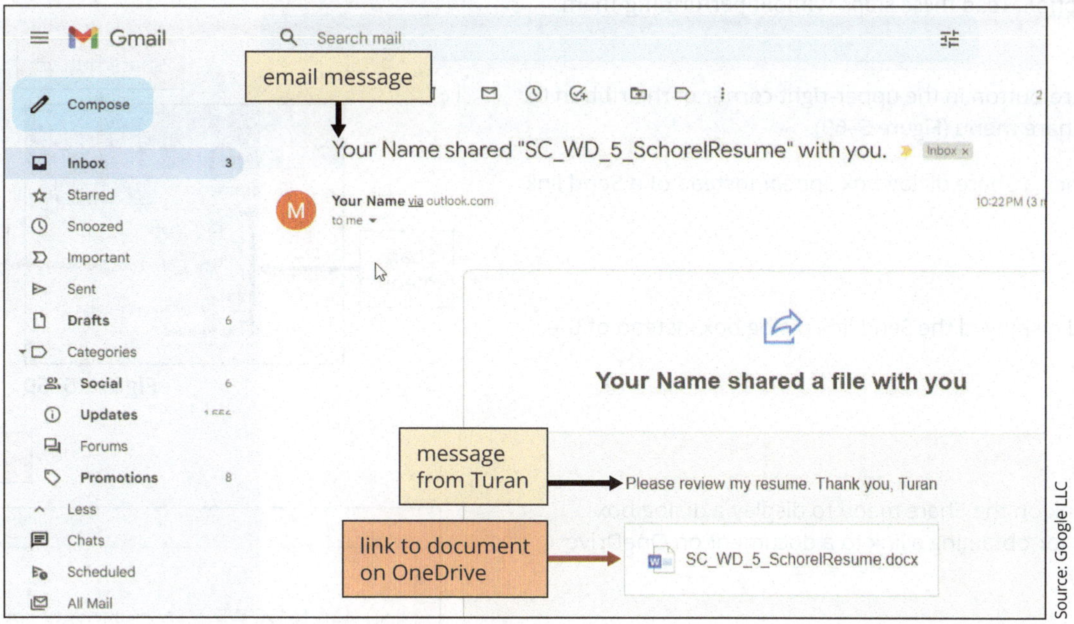

Figure 5–67

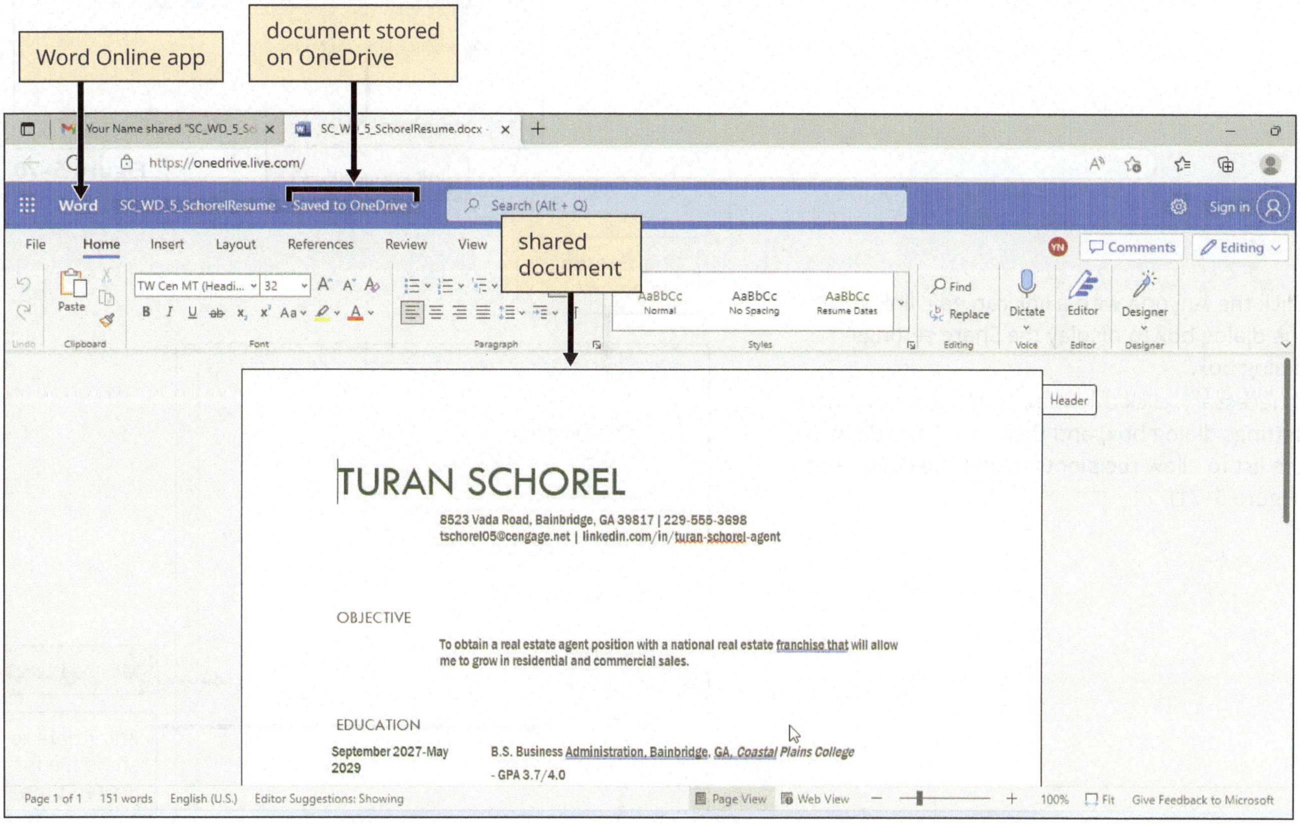

Figure 5–68

To Get a Sharing Link

Why share a link? Instead of inviting people to view or edit a document, you can create a link to the document's location on OneDrive and then send others the link via an email message or text message, post it on a website or online social network, or communicate it via some other means. The following steps get a sharing link. If you do not have a Microsoft account or an Internet connection, read these steps without performing them.

1

- Click the Share button in the upper-right corner of the ribbon to display the Share menu (Figure 5–69).

Q&A Why does a Share dialog box appear instead of a Send link dialog box?
The document has not been saved on OneDrive and/or you are not signed in to your Microsoft account.

What if Word displayed the Send link dialog box instead of the Share menu?
Proceed to Step 3.

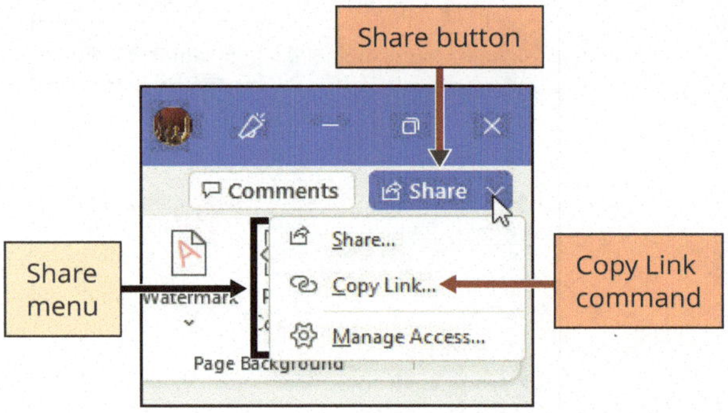

Figure 5–69

2

- Click Copy Link on the Share menu to display a dialog box with options for obtaining a link to a document on OneDrive (Figure 5–70).

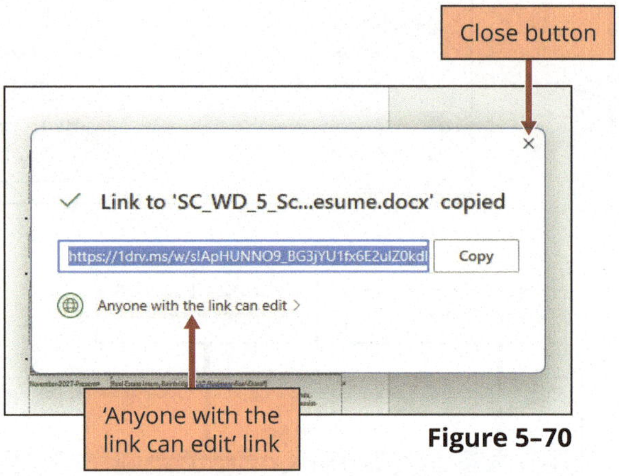

Figure 5–70

3

- Click the 'Anyone with a link can edit' link in the dialog box to display the Share settings dialog box.
- If necessary, click the More settings arrow (Share settings dialog box) and then click Can edit in the list to allow recipients to edit the document (Figure 5–71).

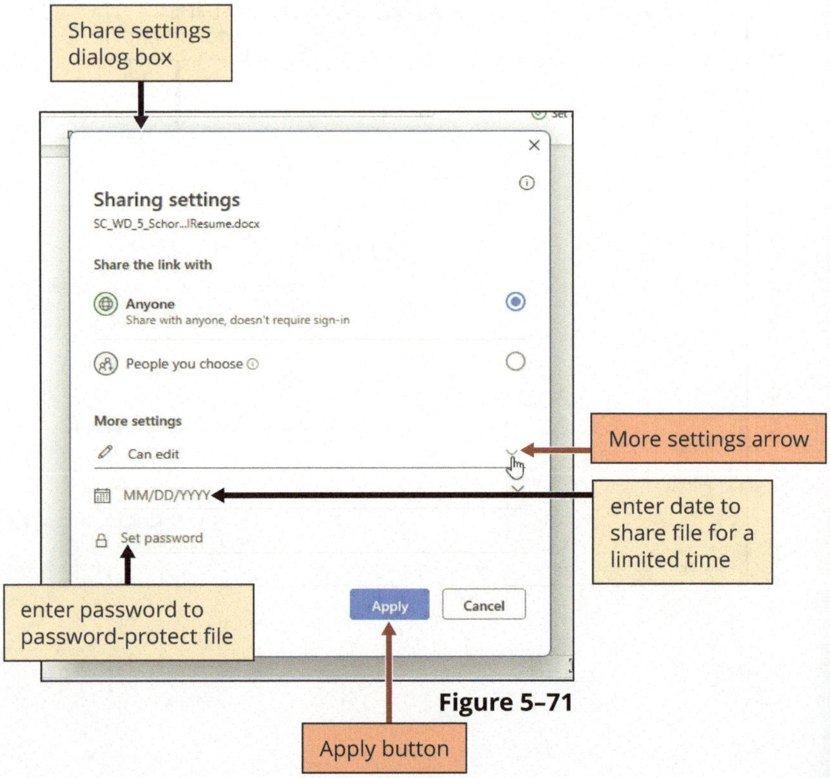

Figure 5–71

4

- Click the Apply button to create the link associated with the file on OneDrive.

Q&A What do I do with the link?
You can copy and paste the link in an email or text message, on a webpage, or some other location.

Could I skip Step 3 and use the link dialog box shown in Figure 5–70 if the settings were correct?
Yes.

5

- Click the Close button in the upper-right corner of the Share settings dialog box (shown in Figure 5–70) to close the dialog box.
- Because you are finished working with the resume on OneDrive, close the document. You also can sign out of your Microsoft account, if you wish to do so.

Other Ways

1. Open Backstage view, click Share, select desired sharing options

To Remove a Watermark

The following steps remove the DRAFT watermark from the resume in the document window, if it was saved with the document, because you now consider the document final and would like to distribute it to potential employers.

1. If necessary, start Word and open the SC_WD_5_SchorelResume.docx (Word 365 format). If your document contains the DRAFT watermark, perform Steps 2 through 5; otherwise, skip these steps.
2. Display the Design tab.
3. Click the Watermark button (Design tab | Page Background group) to display the Watermark gallery.
4. Click Remove Watermark in the Watermark gallery to remove the watermark.
5. Save the resume again with the same file name.

Consider This

What file type should you use when emailing documents?

If you email a document, such as your resume, consider that the recipient, such as a potential employer, may not have the same software you used to create the resume and, thus, may not be able to open the file. As an alternative, you could save the file in a format, such as a PDF or XPS, that can be viewed with a reader program. Many jobseekers also post their resumes on the web.

To Send a Document Using Email

In Word, you can include the current document as an attachment to an email message. An attachment is a file included with an email message. The following steps send the resume as an email attachment, assuming you use Outlook as your default email program. If you do not use Outlook, read these steps without performing them. **Why?** When you attach an email document from within Word, it automatically uses the default email program, which is Outlook in this case.

1

- Click the Share button in the upper-right corner of the ribbon and then click Share on the Share menu to display a Share dialog box (if your document is saved on local media) or the Send link dialog box (if your document is saved on OneDrive) (Figure 5–72).

Q&A What if the Send as link dialog box appears?
Click the 'Send a copy' button at the bottom of the dialog box and then click Word document.

What is the purpose of the PDF button?
Word converts the current document to the PDF format and then attaches the PDF to the email message.

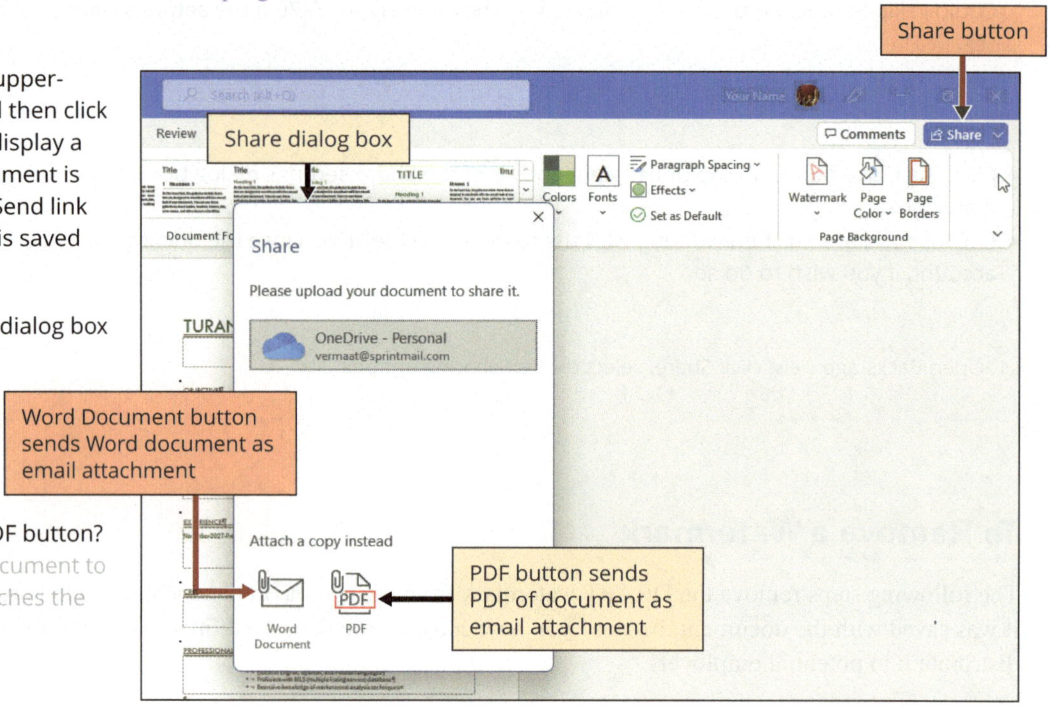

Figure 5–72

2

- Click the Word Document button (Share dialog box) to start your default email program (Outlook, in this case), which automatically attaches the active Word document to the email message (or click the 'Send a copy' link if your screen displays the Send link dialog box).
- Fill in the To text box with the recipient's email address.
- Fill in the message text (Figure 5–73).

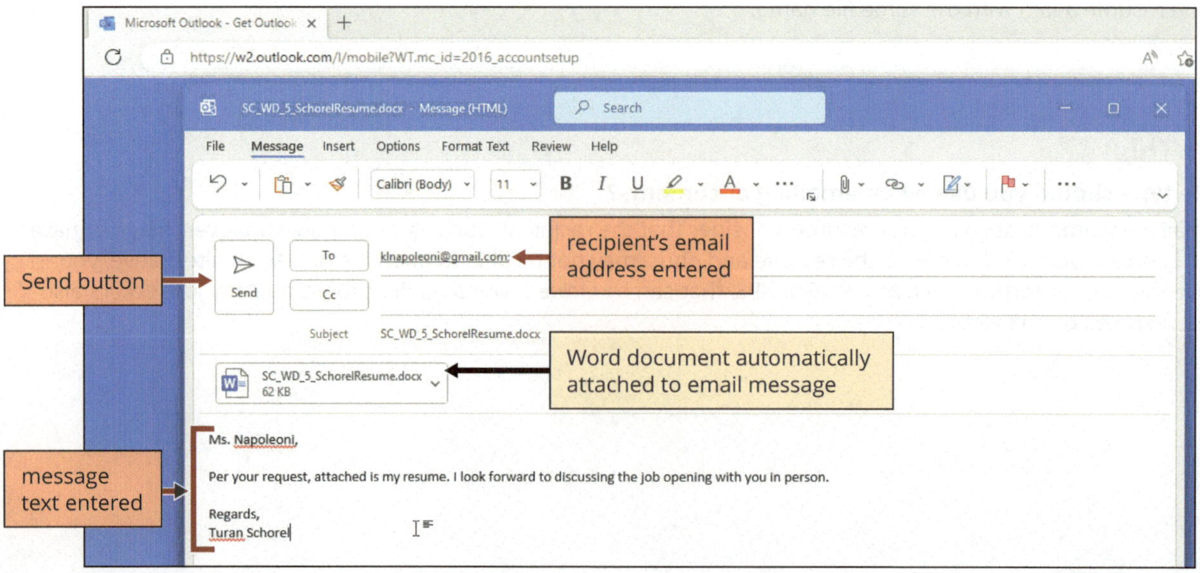

Figure 5–73

3

- Click the Send button to send the email message along with its attachment to the recipient named in the To text box and then close the email window.

To Customize How Word Opens Email Attachments When a user sends you an email message that contains a Word document as an attachment, Word may display the document in Read mode. This view is designed to increase the readability and legibility of an on-screen document. Read mode, however, does not represent how the document will appear when it is printed. For this reason, many users prefer working in Print Layout view to read documents. To exit Read mode, press ESC.

If you wanted to customize how Word opens email attachments, you would do the following.

1. Open Backstage view and then click Options in Backstage view to display the Word Options dialog box.
2. If necessary, click General in the left pane (Word Options dialog box).
3. If you want email attachments to open in Read mode, place a check mark in the 'Open e-mail attachments and other uneditable files in reading view' check box in the Start up options area; otherwise, remove the check mark to open email attachments in Print Layout view.
4. Click OK to close the dialog box.

Creating a Webpage from a Word Document

If you have created a document, such as a resume, using Word, you can save it in a format that can be opened by a browser, such as Microsoft Edge. When you save a file as a webpage, Word converts the contents of the document into **HTML** (Hypertext Markup Language), which is a special language that software developers use to create and format webpage elements. Some of Word's formatting features are not supported by webpages. Thus, your webpage may appear slightly different from the original Word document.

When saving a document as a webpage, Word provides you with three choices:

- The **single file web page format** saves all the components of the webpage in a single file that has a **.mht** extension. This format is particularly useful for sending documents via email in HTML format.
- The **web page format** saves some of the components of the webpage in a folder, separate from the webpage. This format is useful if you need access to the individual components, such as images, that make up the webpage.
- The **filtered web page format** saves the file in webpage format and then reduces the size of the file by removing specific Microsoft Office formats. This format is useful if you want to speed up the time it takes to download a webpage that contains graphics, video, audio, or animations.

The webpage created in this section uses the single file web page format.

To Save a Word Document as a Webpage

The following steps save the resume created earlier in this module as a webpage. **Why?** You intend to post your resume online.

1

- If necessary, open the Word 365 format of the resume file. Open Backstage view and then click Export in Backstage view to display the Export screen.
- Click 'Change File Type' in the left pane of the Export screen to display information in the right pane about various file types that are supported by Word.
- Click 'Single File Web Page' in the right pane to specify a new file type (Figure 5–74).

Q&A What if I wanted to save the document as a web page instead of a single file web page?
You would click 'Save as Another File Type' in the Change File Type area, click the Save As button, click the 'Save as type' arrow in the Save As dialog box, and then click Web Page in the Save as type list.

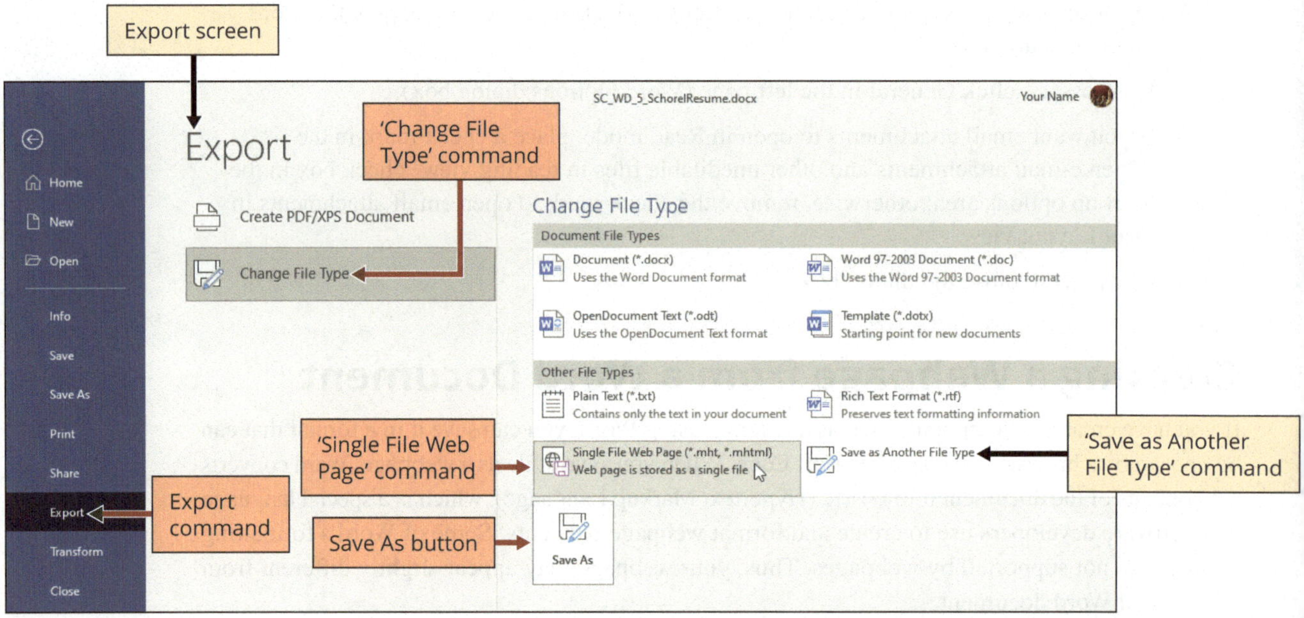

Figure 5–74

2

- Click the Save As button in the right pane to display the Save As dialog box.
- If necessary, navigate to the desired save location (Save As dialog box).
- If necessary, type **SC_WD_5_SchorelResume** in the File name box to change the file name.
- Click the Change Title button to display the Enter Text dialog box.
- Type **Schorel Resume** in the Page title text box (Enter Text dialog box) (Figure 5–75).

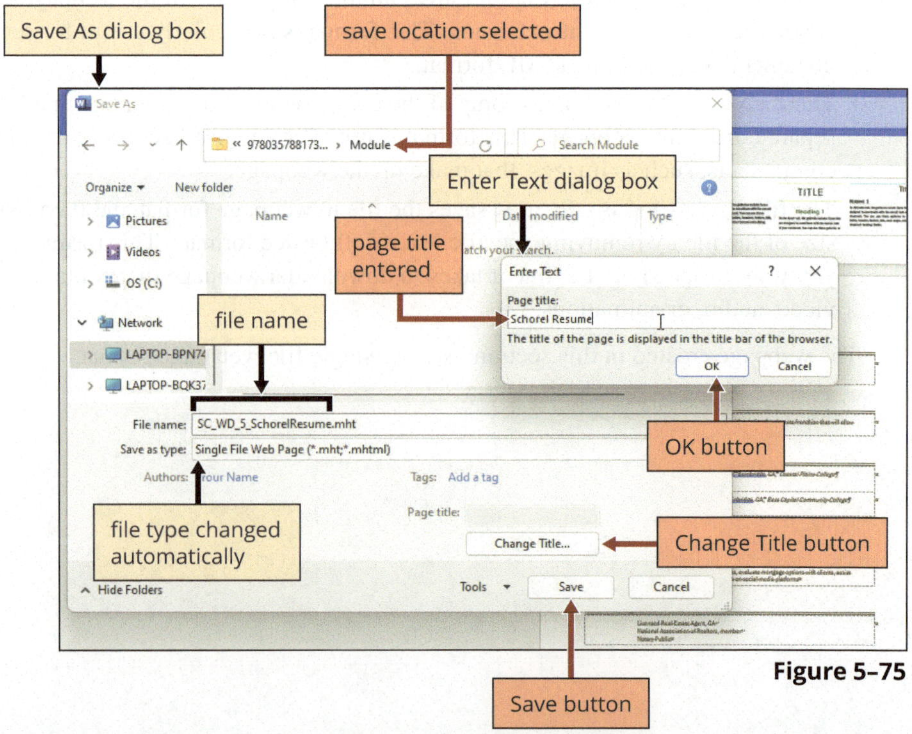

Figure 5–75

3

- Click OK (Enter Text dialog box) to close the dialog box.
- Click Save (Save As dialog box) to save the resume as a webpage and then display it in the document window in Web Layout view.
- If necessary, change the zoom to 100% (Figure 5–76).
- If the Microsoft Word Compatibility Checker dialog box appears, click its Continue button.

Q&A Can I switch to Web Layout view at any time by clicking the Web Layout button on the taskbar?
Yes.

Can I save the webpage to a web server?
If you have access to a web server, you can save the webpage from Word directly to the web server.

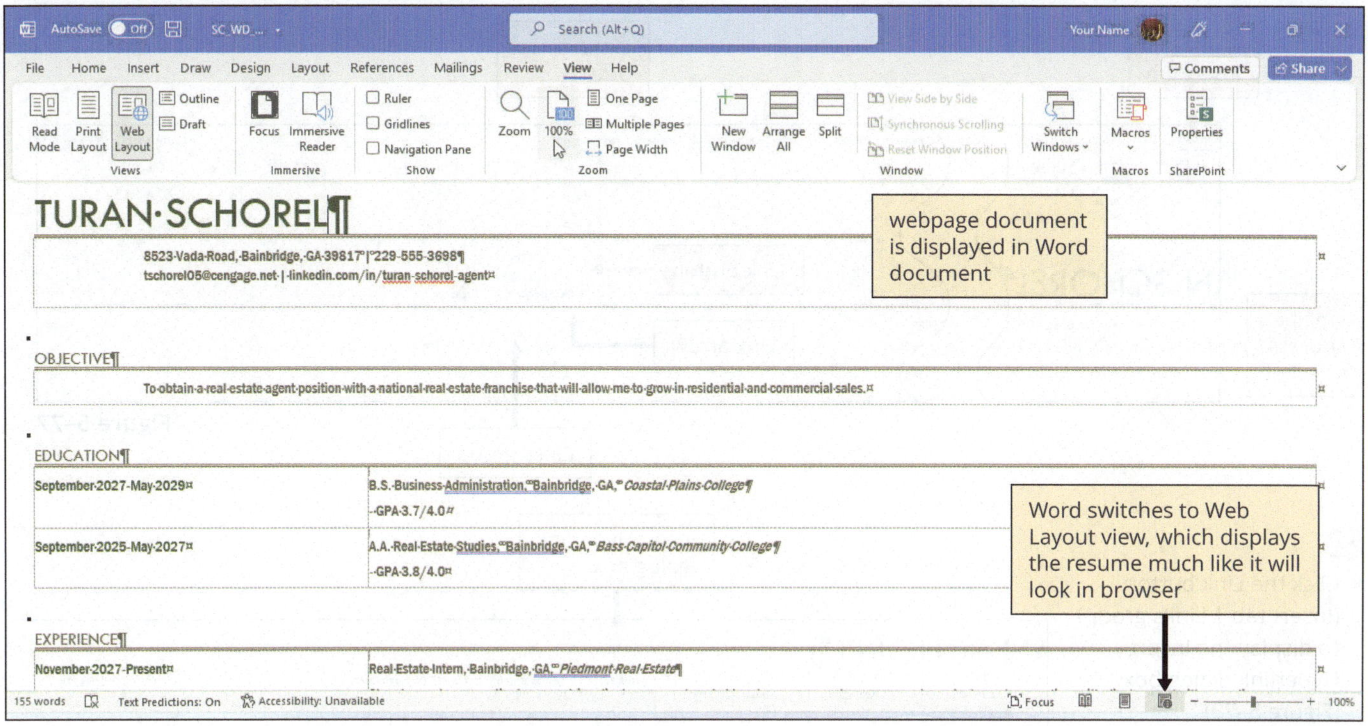

Figure 5–76

To Set a Default Save Location If you wanted to change the default location that Word uses when it saves a document, you would do the following.

1. Open Backstage view and then click Options in Backstage view to display the Word Options dialog box.
2. Click Save in the left pane (Word Options dialog box) to display options for saving documents in the right pane.
3. In the 'Default local file location' text box, type the new desired save location.
4. Click OK to close the dialog box.

To Format Text as a Hyperlink

The email address in the resume webpage should be formatted as a hyperlink. **Why?** When webpage visitors click the hyperlink-formatted email address, you want their email program to start automatically and open an email window with the email address already filled in. The following steps format the email address as a hyperlink.

1

- Select the email address in the resume webpage (tschorel05@cengage.net, in this case).
- Display the Insert tab.
- Click the Links group button (Insert tab) to display the Links group (Figure 5–77).

Q&A What if my screen shows a Links group instead of a Links group button?
Proceed to Step 2.

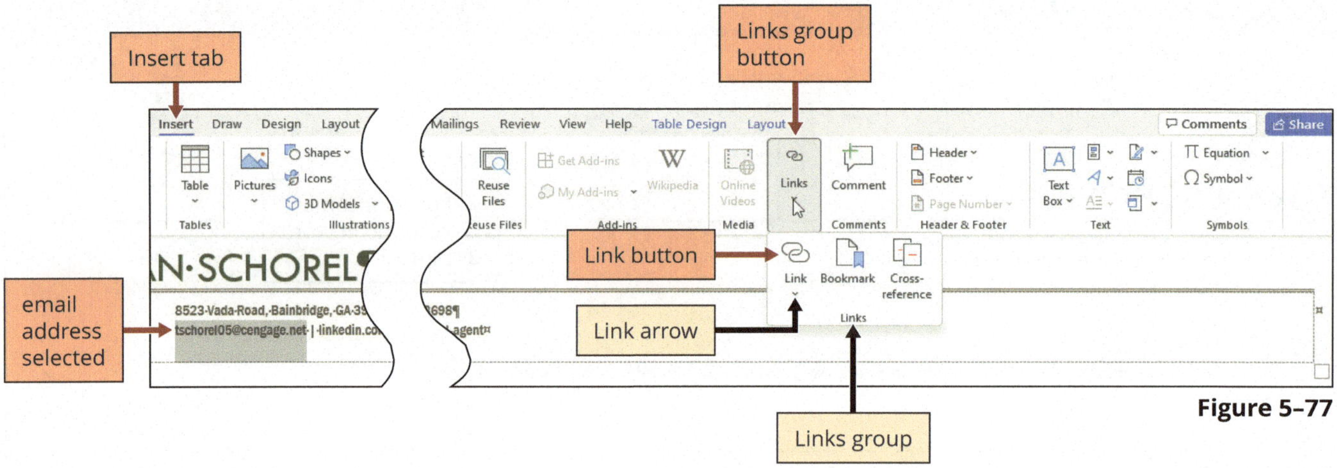

Figure 5–77

2

- Click the Link button (Insert tab | Links group) to display the Insert Hyperlink dialog box (Figure 5–78).

Q&A Why did my screen display a menu?
You clicked the Link arrow. Press ESC and repeat Step 2.

Why does my Address box have extra characters after the .net?
You included the space after the email address in your selection in the resume. Delete the extra characters after the .net.

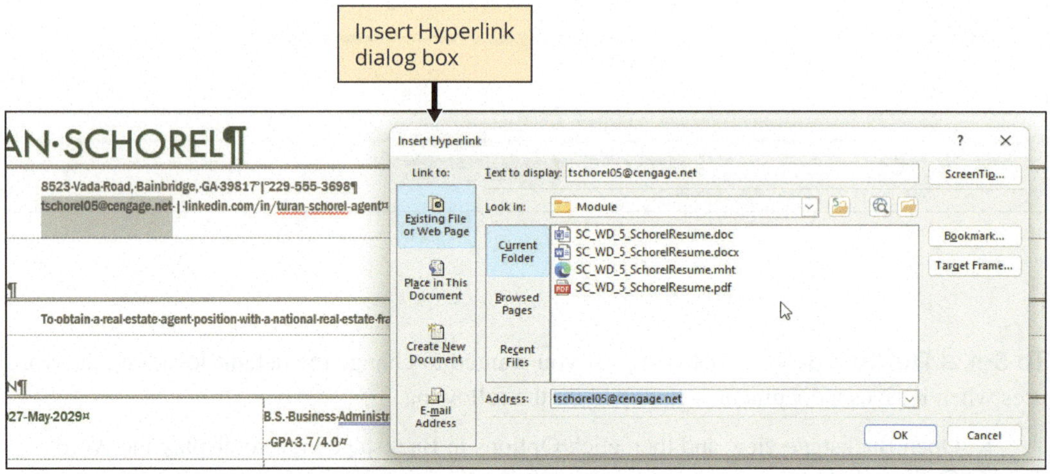

Figure 5–78

3

- Click E-mail Address in the Link to bar (Insert Hyperlink dialog box) so that the dialog box displays email address settings instead of webpage settings.
- In the E-mail address text box, type **tschorel05@cengage.net** to specify the email address that the browser uses when a user clicks the hyperlink.

Q&A Can I change the text that automatically appeared in the 'Text to display' text box?
Yes. Word assumes that the hyperlink text should be the same as the email address, so as soon as you enter the email address, the same text is entered in the 'Text to display' text box.

- If the email address in the 'Text to display' text box is preceded by the text, mailto:, delete this leading text because you want only the email address to appear in the document.
- Click the ScreenTip button to display the Set Hyperlink ScreenTip dialog box.
- Type **Send email message to Turan Schorel.** in the ScreenTip text text box (Set Hyperlink ScreenTip dialog box) to specify the text that will be displayed when a user points to the hyperlink (Figure 5–79).

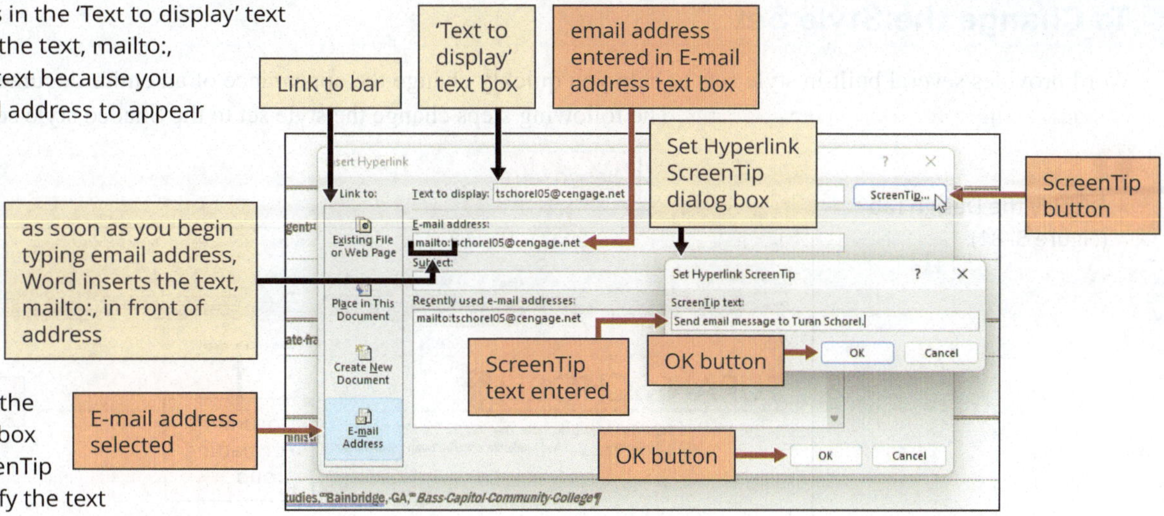

Figure 5–79

4

- Click OK in each dialog box to format the email address as a hyperlink (Figure 5–80).

Figure 5–80

Q&A How do I know if the hyperlink works?
In Word, you can test the hyperlink by holding down CTRL while clicking the hyperlink. In this case, CTRL+clicking the email address should open an email window.

Could I also format the LinkedIn profile address as a hyperlink?
Yes. For illustration purposes, only the email address is formatted as a hyperlink in this project.

Other Ways

1. Right-click selected text, click Link on shortcut menu
2. Select text, press CTRL+K

To Edit a Hyperlink If you needed to edit a hyperlink, for example, to change its ScreenTip or its link, you would follow these steps.

1. Position the insertion point in the hyperlink.
2. Click the Links group button (Home tab), if necessary, to display the Links group, click the Link button (Insert tab | Links group) or press CTRL+K to display the Edit Hyperlink dialog box.

or

1. Right-click the hyperlink to display a shortcut menu.
2. Click Edit Hyperlink on the shortcut menu to display the Edit Hyperlink dialog box.

BTW

Inserting Hyperlinks

In addition to inserting a hyperlink to an email address, you can insert a hyperlink to a webpage or to a file. To insert a hyperlink to a webpage, enter and select the text to be the hyperlink; click the Links group button (Home tab), if necessary, to display the Links group; click the Link button (Insert tab | Links group) to display the Insert Hyperlink dialog box; click 'Existing File or Web Page' in the Link to bar (Insert Hyperlink dialog box); be sure the web address is correct in the Address box, and then click OK. To insert a hyperlink to a file, follow the same steps except select the location of the file instead of entering a web address in the Address box.

To Change the Style Set

Word provides several built-in style sets to help you quickly change the appearance of an entire document. **Why?** A style set contains formats for fonts and paragraphs. The following steps change the style set to the Shaded style set.

1

- Display the Design tab (Figure 5–81).

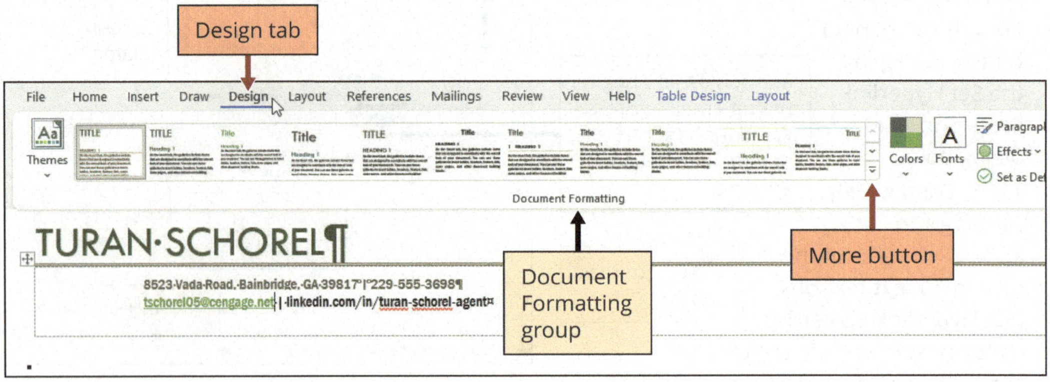

Figure 5–81

2

- Click the More button (Design tab | Document Formatting group) to display the expanded Style Set gallery.
- Point to Shaded in the Style Set gallery to display a Live Preview of the style set applied to the document (Figure 5–82).
- **Experiment:** Point to various style sets in the Style Set gallery and watch the font and paragraph formatting change in the document window.

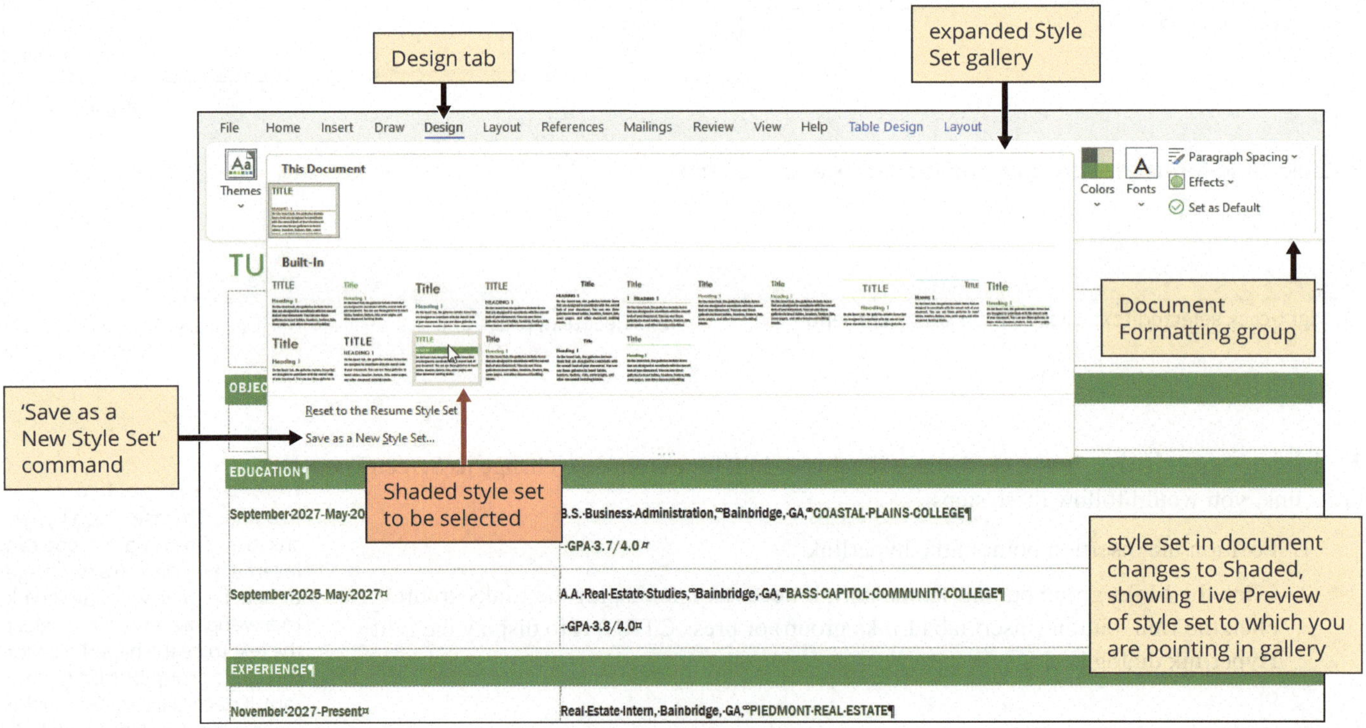

Figure 5–82

3

- Click Shaded to change the style set to the selected style set (shown in Figure 5–82).

Q&A Can I create my own style sets?

Yes. Modify the fonts and other formats as desired, click 'Save as a New Style Set' in the expanded Style Set gallery (shown in Figure 5–82), enter the name for the style set (Save as a New Style Set dialog box), and then click Save to create the custom style set. You then can access the custom style set through the Style Set gallery.

To Highlight Text

To emphasize text in an online document, you can highlight it. **Highlighting** alerts a reader to online text's importance, much like a highlighter pen does on a printed page. Word provides 15 colors you can use to highlight text, including the traditional yellow and green, as well as some nontraditional highlight colors, such as gray, dark blue, and dark red. The following steps highlight the job title being sought in the color yellow. **Why?** You want to emphasize this text on the resume.

1

- Select the text to be highlighted, which, in this case, is the text, real estate agent position.
- Display the Home tab.
- Click the 'Text Highlight Color' arrow (Home tab | Font group) to display the Text Highlight Color gallery (Figure 5–83).

Q&A The Text Highlight Color gallery did not appear. Why not?
You clicked the 'Text Highlight Color' button instead of the 'Text Highlight Color' arrow. Click the Undo button (Home tab | Undo group) and then repeat Step 1.

What if the icon on the 'Text Highlight Color' button already displays the color I want to use?
You can click the 'Text Highlight Color' button instead of the arrow.

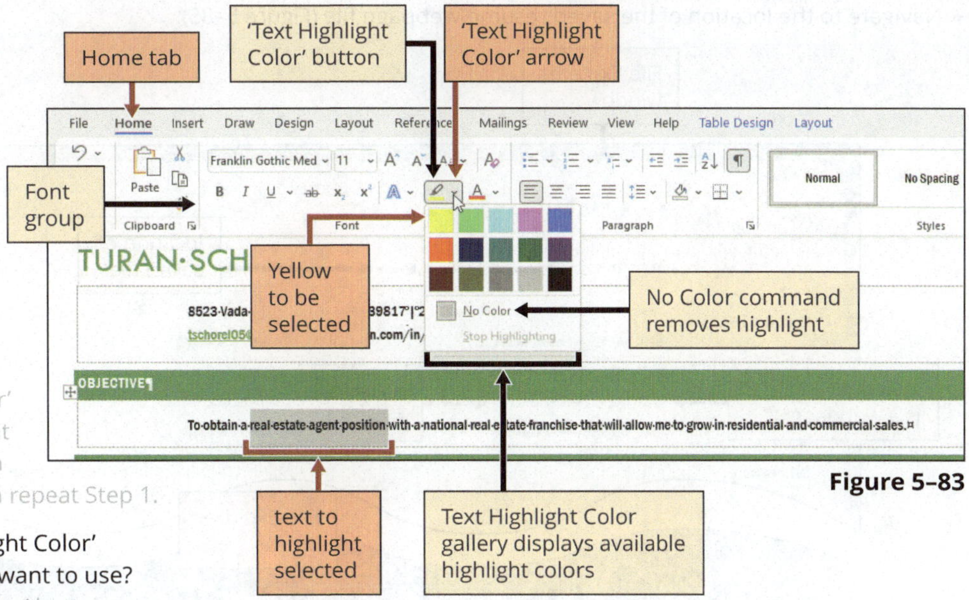

Figure 5–83

2

- **Experiment:** Point to various colors in the Text Highlight Color gallery and watch the highlight color on the selected text change.
- Click Yellow in the Text Highlight Color gallery to highlight the selected text in the selected highlight color (Figure 5–84).
- Save the resume webpage again on the same storage location with the same file name and then exit Word.

Q&A How would I remove a highlight from text?
Select the highlighted text, click the 'Text Highlight Color' arrow, and then click No Color in the Text Highlight Color gallery.

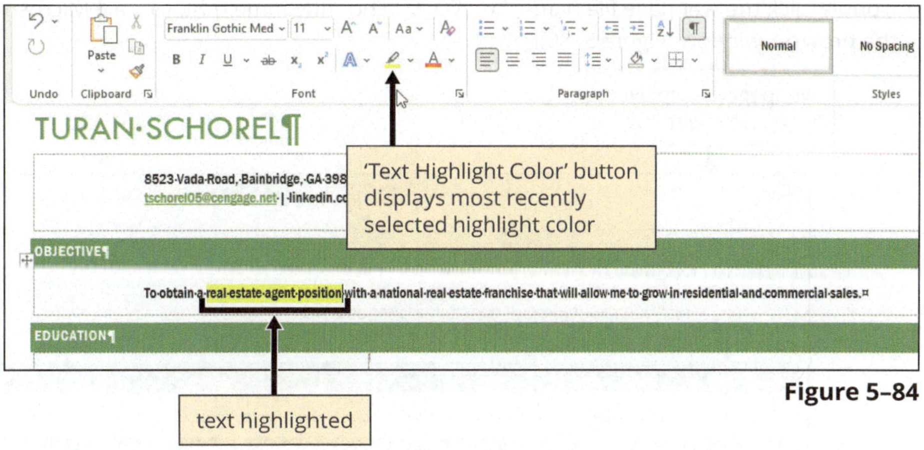

Figure 5–84

Other Ways

1. Click 'Text Highlight Color' arrow (Home tab | Font group), select desired color, select text to be highlighted in document, select any additional text to be highlighted, click 'Text Highlight Color' button to turn off highlighting

To Test a Webpage in a Browser

After creating and saving a webpage, you should test it in at least one browser. **Why?** You want to be sure it appears and works the way you intended. The following steps use File Explorer to display the resume webpage in the Microsoft Edge browser.

1

- Click the File Explorer button on the Windows taskbar to open the File Explorer window.
- Navigate to the location of the saved resume webpage file (Figure 5–85).

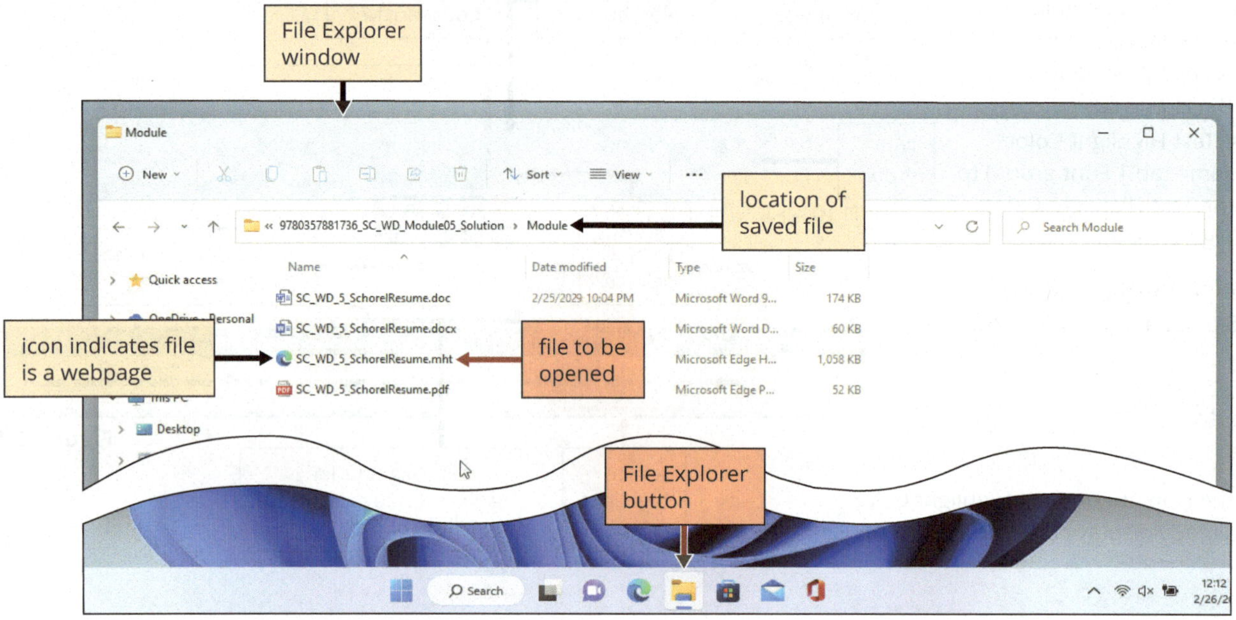

Figure 5–85

2

- Double-click the webpage file name, SC_WD_5_SchorelResume.mht, to start Microsoft Edge and display the webpage file in the browser window (Figure 5–86).

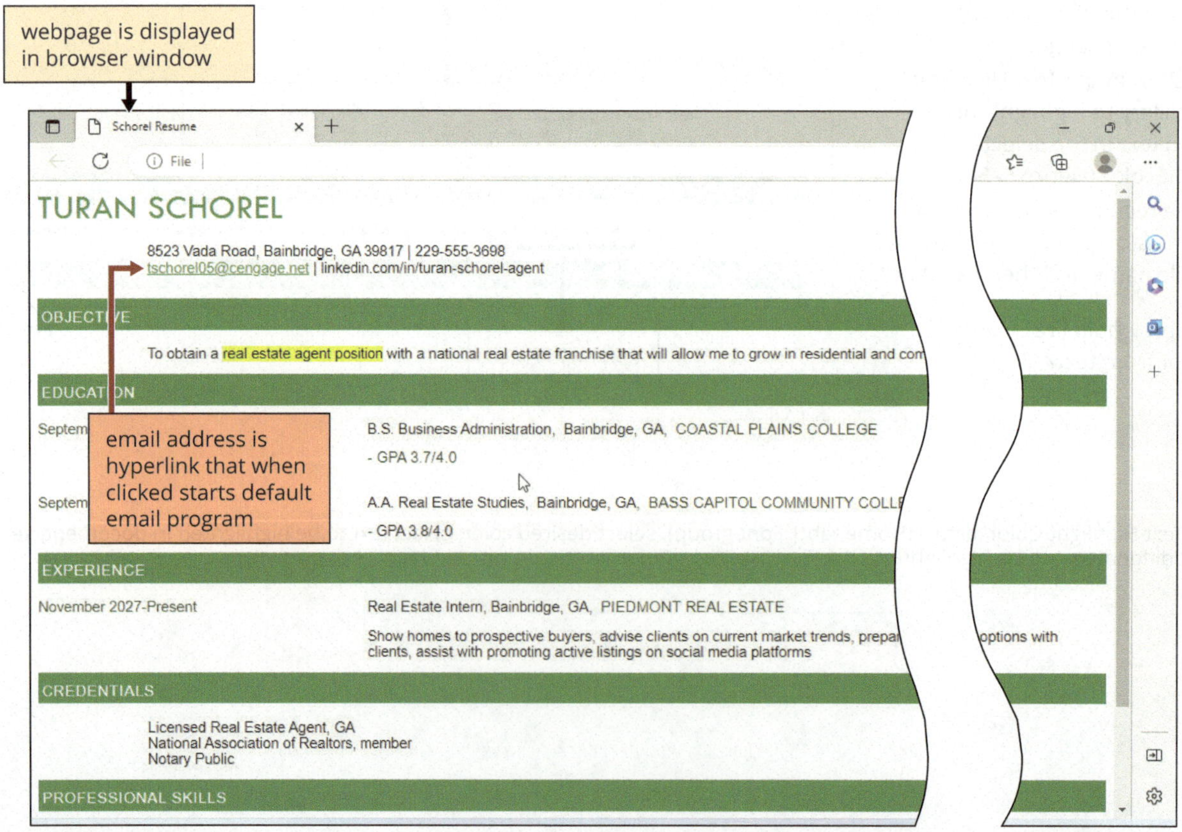

Figure 5–86

3

- With the webpage document displayed in the browser, click the email address link to start the email program with the email address displayed in the email window (Figure 5–87).
- If your browser displays a security dialog box, click its Allow button.

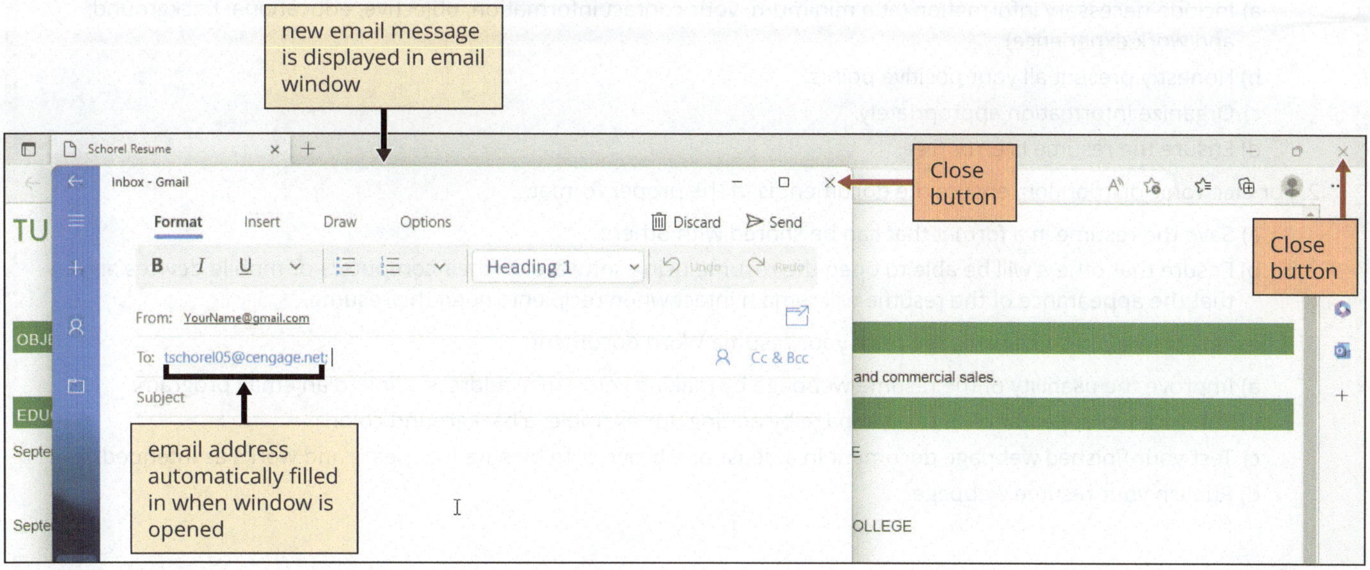

Figure 5–87

4

- Exit all running apps.

Consider This

How do you publish a webpage?

Once you have created a webpage, you can publish it. **Publishing** is the process of making a webpage available to others on a network, such as the Internet or a company's intranet. Many Internet service providers (ISPs) offer storage space on their web servers at no cost to their subscribers.

Summary

In this module, you learned how to use a Word template to create a document, set custom margins, personalize a document template, change and customize theme fonts, customize theme colors, work with building blocks, create a style, modify a style, save a Word document in a variety of formats, share a document on OneDrive, get a sharing link, send a document using email, create a webpage from a Word document, insert a hyperlink, change the style set, and highlight text.

Consider This: Plan Ahead

What decisions will you need to make when creating your next resume?

Use these guidelines as you complete the assignments in this module and create your own resumes outside of this class.

1. Craft a successful resume.
   a) Include necessary information (at a minimum, your contact information, objective, educational background, and work experience).
   b) Honestly present all your positive points.
   c) Organize information appropriately.
   d) Ensure the resume is error free.
2. For electronic distribution, ensure the document is in the proper format.
   a) Save the resume in a format that can be shared with others.
   b) Ensure that others will be able to open the resume using software on their computers or mobile devices and that the appearance of the resume will remain intact when recipients open the resume.
3. If desired, create a resume webpage from your resume Word document.
   a) Improve the usability of the resume webpage by making your email address a link to an email program.
   b) Enhance the appearance of the webpage by adding, for example, a background color.
   c) Test your finished webpage document in at least one browser to be sure it appears and works as intended.
   d) Publish your resume webpage.

Student Assignments

Apply Your Knowledge

Reinforce the skills and apply the concepts you learned in this module.

Saving a Word Document in a Variety of Formats

Note: To complete this assignment, you will be required to use the Data Files. Please contact your instructor for information about accessing the Data Files.

Instructions: Start Word. Open the document, SC_WD_5-1.docx, which is located in the Data Files. The document is a draft outlining tips to protect computers from malware. As assistant to the director of IT, you have been asked to modify and then distribute the document companywide. You are to change the theme fonts, create custom theme fonts, change theme effects (Figure 5–88), and then save the revised document as a single file web page, a PDF document, an XPS document, and in the Word 97-2003 format.

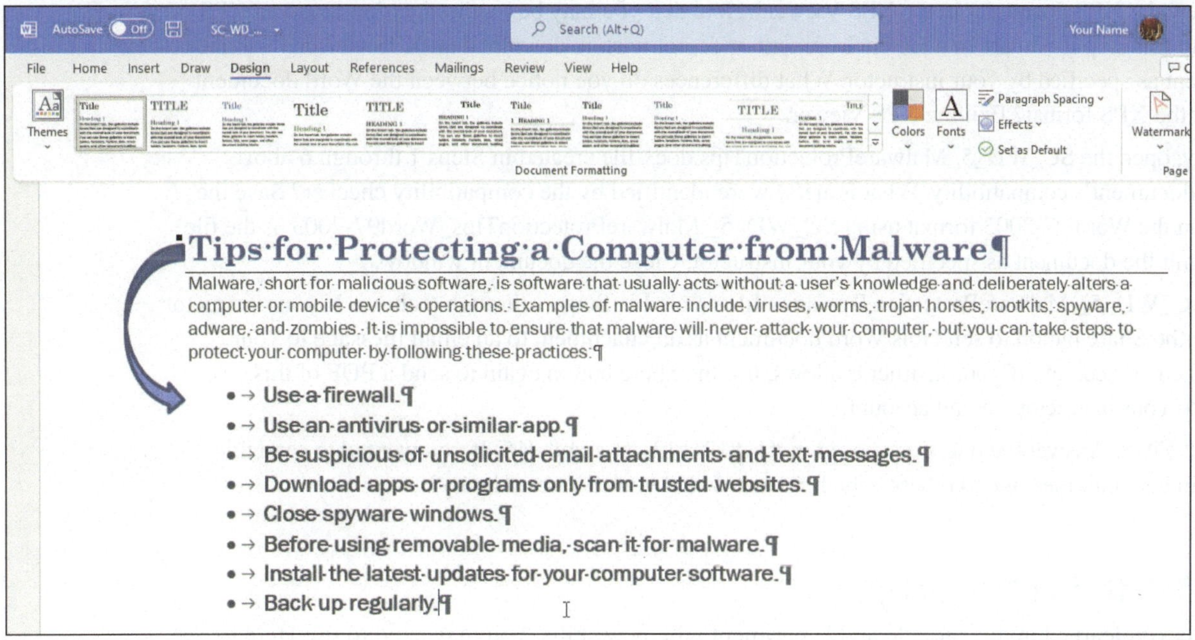

Figure 5–88

Perform the following tasks:

1. Click File on the ribbon and then click Save As and save the document using the new file name, SC_WD_5_MalwareProtectionTips.
2. Change the theme fonts to Century Schoolbook.
3. Create custom theme fonts to change the body font from Century Schoolbook to Franklin Gothic Book. Save the custom theme with the name, Malware Protection Tips.
4. Change the theme effects to Frosted Glass. What did the theme effects change in the document?
5. If requested by your instructor, add your name in parentheses immediately after the last bulleted item (on the same line).
6. Save the document again with the same file name (Figure 5–88).
7. Save the document as a single file web page using the file name, SC_WD_5_MalwareProtectionTips_Webpage. In the Save As dialog box, click the Change Title button and then change the webpage title to Malware Protection Tips. If necessary, change the view from Print Layout to Web Layout. If necessary, increase the zoom percentage so that the document is readable on your screen.
8. Delete the arrow shape from the document.
9. Change the style set to Minimalist.

Continued on next page

10. Highlight the text, protect your computer by following these practices, in the yellow highlight color.
11. Save the document again with the same file name.
12. Use Microsoft Edge or another browser to view the webpage. If requested by your instructor, print the webpage. What differences do you notice between the Word document format and the single file web page format? Exit the browser and then close the webpage document in Word.
13. Open the SC_WD_5_MalwareProtectionTips.docx file created in Steps 1 through 6 above. If necessary, change the view from Web Layout to Print Layout. Export the document to a PDF document using the file name, SC_WD_5_MalwareProtectionTips, ensuring you check the 'Open file after publishing' check box so that you can view the PDF document in your browser (if it supports PDF files) or Adobe Acrobat Reader. Submit the document as specified by your instructor. Exit your browser or Adobe Acrobat Reader, whichever one displayed the PDF file. From within Word, open the PDF document just created. What differences do you notice between the Word document format and the PDF format? Close the converted PDF document in Word without saving it.
14. If necessary, open the SC_WD_5_MalwareProtectionTips.docx file created in Steps 1 through 6 above. If requested by your instructor, export the document to an XPS Document using the file name, SC_WD_5_MalwareProtectionTips, ensuring you check the 'Open file after publishing' check box so that you can view the XPS document in the XPS Viewer. (Note that you may be required to download an XPS viewer. Skip this step if you are in a lab environment or do not wish to download an XPS viewer.) Submit the document as specified by your instructor. What differences do you notice between the Word document format and the XPS format? Exit the XPS Viewer.
15. If necessary, open the SC_WD_5_MalwareProtectionTips.docx file created in Steps 1 through 6 above. Check the document's compatibility. What issue(s) were identified by the compatibility checker? Save the document in the Word 97-2003 format using SC_WD_5_ MalwareProtectionTips_Word97-2003 as the file name. Submit the document as specified by your instructor. Close the document window.
16. Open the SC_WD_5_ MalwareProtectionTips.docx file created in Steps 1 through 6 above. If your instructor allows, use the Share button to send this Word document as an attachment to an email message to your instructor's email account. If your instructor allows, use the Share button again to send a PDF of this document to your instructor's email account.
17. **Consider This:** Answer the questions posed in #4, #12, #13, #14, and #15. If you wanted to send this document in an email message to others, which format would you choose and why?

Extend Your Knowledge

Extend the skills you learned in this module and experiment with new skills. You may need to use Help to complete the assignment.

Modifying and Editing a Resume Template and Creating a Multi-File Webpage

Note: To complete this assignment, you will be required to use the Data Files. Please contact your instructor for information about accessing the Data Files.

Instructions: Start Word. Open the document, SC_WD_5-2.docx, which is located in the Data Files. The document is a resume draft. As an upcoming graduate in business with a major in accounting, you have been using a resume template to compose your resume. You will modify and edit the resume template by working with content controls and table elements, hyperlinks, and building blocks, and you will save a Word document as a multi-file webpage and format it by inserting links, adding a pattern fill effect as the background, and applying highlights to text.

Perform the following tasks:

1. Use Help to learn more about creating links to webpages, saving as a webpage (not a single file web page), hyperlinks, and pattern fill effects.
2. Click File on the ribbon and then click Save As and save the document using the new file name, SC_WD_5_AccountantResume. If necessary, change the zoom to 120%.

3. If requested by your instructor, change the name on the resume to your name.
4. Enter the text, 602-555-9468, in the Telephone content control.
5. Enter the LinkedIn profile address, linkedin.com/in/mfontana, in the Website placeholder. (If Word capitalizes the l in linkedin, undo the automatic capitalization.) Delete the space after the LinkedIn profile address and press ENTER to place the phone number on a separate line. Use cut and paste or drag and drop to move the phone number above the LinkedIn profile address.
6. Insert a hyperlink to the LinkedIn profile address. (**Hint:** Click 'Existing File or Web Page' in the Link to bar (Insert Hyperlink dialog box).) In the Address box, use www.cengage.com as the LinkedIn profile address.
7. Insert a hyperlink to the email address. Add the following ScreenTip for the hyperlink: Send me an email message.
8. Edit the hyperlink to change the 07 in the email address to 06.
9. Create custom theme colors to change the Hyperlink color and Followed Hyperlink colors to colors that are easier to read (which also will remove the 'Hard-to-read text contrast' message from the Accessibility checker) (Figure 5–89). Save the custom theme colors with a meaningful name.

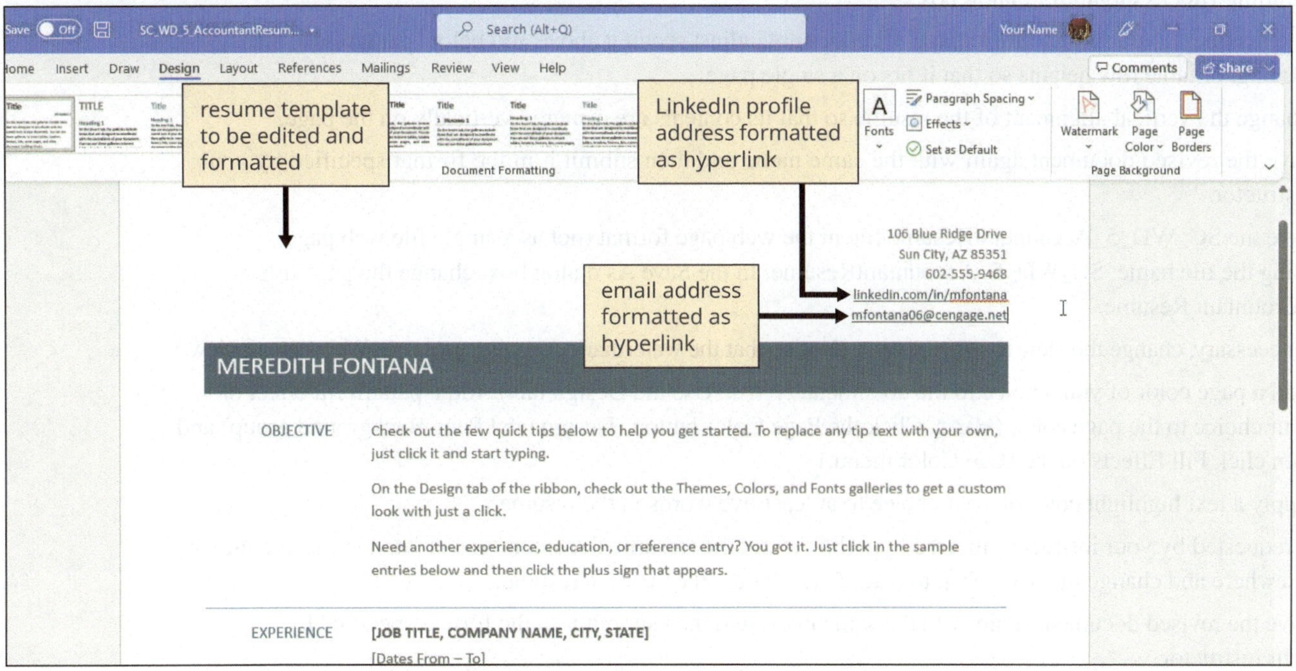

Figure 5–89

10. Test each of the hyperlinks to be sure they work as intended. Fix any errors.
11. The applicant would like to work at large corporation in an urban area. Click the text in the Objective section and then write an objective for the resume.
12. Create a building block (Quick Part) for the text, accounting, and save the building block with the name, ac. Insert the building block (Quick Part) whenever you have to enter the text, accounting.
13. Use copy and paste or drag and drop to move the row containing the Education section so that it appears above the Experience row.
14. Copy the Memberships row and then paste the row (with source formatting) so that the pasted row appears immediately below the Education section. Change the heading of the pasted row from Memberships to Awards. Change the text in the right column of the pasted row to the following, with each item on a separate line: Cengage Accounting Award of Excellence, CPA Society Accounting Tuition Scholarship, Dean's List (seven semesters), Outstanding Student Award.
15. In the Experience section of the resume, insert a content control so that you can enter two jobs. (**Hint:** Click the content control to the right of the Experience heading which contains job experience details, and then click the Insert Control button at the right of the control, or right-click the content control and then click the location to insert the content control on the shortcut menu.)

Continued on next page

16. Enter this job information for two jobs in the Experience section: Auditing Internship, Eureka Industries, Sun City, AZ, June 2028-Present; Accounting Internship, Sun City Hotel and Conference Center, Sun City, AZ, June 2027-May 2028.
17. Below the dates in the Auditing Internship job, add this description on a separate paragraph, indented: Assisted with financial duties, including auditing, credit checks, forecasting, and financial reporting.
18. Copy and paste with source formatting the paragraph you entered in #17 on a blank paragraph below the dates in the Accounting Internship job. Change the pasted text so that it reads: Assisted with financial duties, including payroll, inventory, receivables, invoicing, and reporting.
19. Change the format of the Objective heading in the resume to a format you feel is more noticeable. Create a paragraph style for the newly formatted Objective heading and name the format Resume Headings. (**Hint:** Use the More button in the Styles gallery.) Apply the Resume Headings style to the remaining headings in the resume.
20. Change the format of the bulleted lists in the resume to a bullet symbol of your choice.
21. Insert one of the SAMPLE watermarks using the Explore Quick Part button (Insert tab | Text group) and the Building Blocks Organizer dialog box.
22. The resume should fit on a single page. If it does not, adjust spacing above and below paragraphs, line spacing, or table row heights so that it fits on a single page.
23. Change the vertical alignment of the resume so that its contents are centered vertically on the page.
24. Save the revised document again with the same name and then submit it in the format specified by your instructor.
25. Save the SC_WD_5_AccountantResume file in the web page format (not as a single file web page) using the file name, SC_WD_5_AccountantResume. In the Save As dialog box, change the page title to Accountant Resume.
26. If necessary, change the view to Web Layout. (Notice that the watermark does not appear in Web Layout view.)
27. Add a page color of your choice to the document. (**Hint:** Use the Design tab.) Add a pattern fill effect of your choice to the page color. (**Hint:** Click the Page Color button (Design tab | Page Background group) and then click Fill Effects on the Page Color menu.)
28. Apply a text highlight color of your choice to at least five words in the resume.
29. If requested by your instructor, insert a hyperlink to another resume document you created in this module or elsewhere and change the ScreenTip to read: Click for another sample resume.
30. Save the revised document again with the same name and then submit it in the format specified by your instructor.
31. Test the webpage by double-clicking its file name in File Explorer. Test the LinkedIn profile address link and the email address link. Close the browser window.
32. Copy the entire resume table. Paste the table with source formatting in a new Word document window. Click the Paste Options button and point the various paste options to observe how they change the appearance of the pasted table. Close the Word window without saving the document.
33. **Consider This:** Why would you add a pattern fill effect to a background?

Expand Your World

Create a solution that uses cloud or web technologies by learning and investigating on your own from general guidance.

Sharing a Resume Online and Creating a Calendar

Notes:

- You will use OneDrive and a job search website account, which you can create at no cost, to complete this assignment. If you do not have these accounts and do not want to create them, read Steps 9 through 12 in this assignment without performing the instructions.

- To complete this assignment, you will be required to use the Data Files. Please contact your instructor for information about accessing the Data Files.

Instructions: You are a hospitality management graduate from Putnam College. You will make some final edits to your resume and then will share it with potential employers. You will save it on your OneDrive account, invite others to view it, get a sharing link, send it via email, and post it on a job search website (Figure 5–90). You also will use a calendar template to help organize your upcoming appointments and important dates.

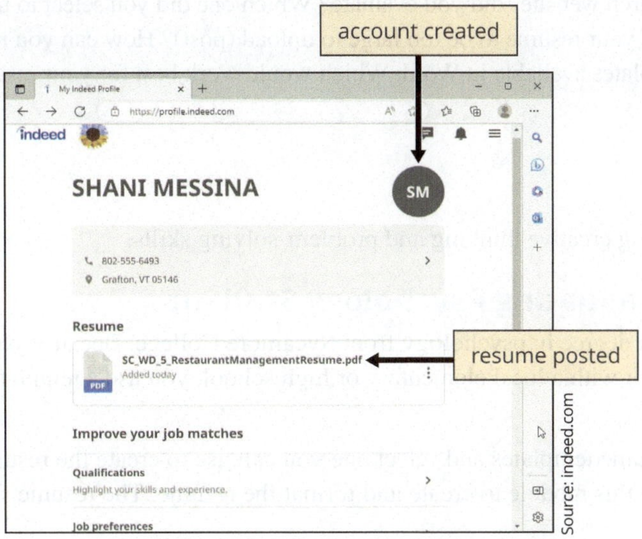

Figure 5–90

Perform the following tasks:

1. Start Word. Open the document, SC_WD_5-3.docx, which is located in the Data Files.
2. Click File on the ribbon and then click Save As and save the document using the new file name, SC_WD_5_RestaurantManagementResume.
3. If requested by your instructor, change the name at the top of the resume to your name.
4. Set custom margins to .75-inch top, bottom, left, and right. If the entire resume does not fit on a single page, adjust spacing above and below paragraphs, line spacing, or table row heights so that it fits on a single page.
5. Reveal formatting of a heading in the resume. Notice that the headings use the Accent 1 color for paragraph shading. Close the Reveal Formatting pane.
6. Create a custom theme color so that Accent 1 is a color different from 'Blue-Gray, Accent 1'. Save the custom theme with the name Restaurant Management Resume Headings.
7. If requested by your instructor, save the current theme settings as the default.
8. Save the revised document again with the same name and then submit it in the format specified by your instructor.
9. Save the SC_WD_5_RestaurantManagementResume resume on your OneDrive account so that you can share it.
10. Using the Share button in Word, invite at least one of your classmates to view your resume document. If requested, include your instructor in the invitation.
11. In Word, get a sharing link for the resume. Send the sharing link in an email message to at least one of your classmates. Submit the link in the format requested by your instructor.
12. Export the resume to a PDF file. Search for the text, post resume online, using a search engine. Visit several of the job search websites and determine on which one you would like to post a resume. If requested, create an account or profile, fill in the requested information, and then upload the PDF format of the resume (shown in Figure 5–90). Submit the posting in the format requested by your instructor. Delete the posted resume from the job search website.
13. Browse through Word's calendar templates, download an appropriate calendar template, change the theme colors to a color of your choice, change the theme fonts to a font set of your choice, and then enter the following appointments in the calendar for the month of December: December 3 – Job interview at Grafton

Continued on next page

Hotel and Conference Center at 11:00 a.m., December 6 – Job interview at Riverview Eateries at 2:00 p.m., December 7 – Alumni Association meeting at 1:00 p.m. in Campus Plaza Center, December 12 – Job Fair from noon to 4:00 p.m. in Blair Hall, December 13 – Dentist appointment at 10:30 a.m., December 18 – Lunch at 11:30 a.m. with Dr. Farnsworth at Cornerstone Café, December 27 – Eye doctor appointment at 2:30 p.m. Save the calendar using the file name, SC_WD_5_AppointmentCalendar and then submit it in the format specified by your instructor.

14. **Consider This:** Which job search websites did you evaluate? Which one did you select to use and why? What would cause the file size of your resume to be too large to upload (post)? How can you reduce the file size? Review all the resume templates available in Word. Which would work best for your resume? Why?

In the Lab

Design and implement a solution using creative thinking and problem-solving skills.

Create a Resume for a Graduating Psychology Student

Problem: You are graduating with a degree in psychology from Sycamore College. Because you soon will be seeking employment as a counselor with a local elementary or high school, you use a template to create a resume for your job search.

Part 1: Browse through Word's resume templates and select one you can use to create the resume. Use the concepts and techniques presented in this module to create and format the resume. The resume should contain the following content:

Name: Andile De Lang (if requested by your instructor, use your name).

Address: 6687 Pine Street, Apt. 3B, Attica, IN, 47918 (if requested by your instructor, use your address).

Phone: 765-555-2878 (if requested by your instructor, use your phone number).

Email: andile@cengage.net (if requested by your instructor, use your email address).

LinkedIn profile address: linkein.com/in/andile-counselor (if requested by your instructor, use your LinkedIn profile address if you have one).

Objective: To obtain a counselor position with a local elementary or high school.

Education: B.A. Psychology from Sycamore College in May 2029. GPA 3.8/4.0.

Awards received: Dean's List, every semester; Diversity Advocate Award; Human Development Concentration Award. Areas of concentration: Behavioral disorders, Cognitive science, Psychology of personality, Youth and child psychology. A.A. Health Sciences from Wilton Community College in May 2027. GPA 3.75/4.00.

Experience: Crisis Advocate at Attica Community Center from January 2027-Present. Work 15 hours a week at the crisis call center or local hospital offering emotional support, information, education, option identification, safety planning, and intervention to callers and clients.

Memberships: Psychology Club, secretary; Psi Chi National Honor Society; Student Government Association.

Community Service: Advisory Board Member at Attica School District After-School Program from October 2028-Present. Volunteer on the advisory board for youth programs; assist with planning, media relations, education, and community outreach.

When you are finished with the resume, be sure to check the spelling and grammar. Save it in a form suitable for sharing using the file name, SC_WD_5_SchoolCounselorResume. Also save the resume as a webpage and format the webpage appropriately. Submit your assignment documents and answers to the Part 2 critical thinking questions in the format specified by your instructor.

Part 2: **Consider This:** You made several decisions while creating the resume in this assignment: which template to use, where to position elements, how to format resume elements, in which format to save the document for sharing, and how to format the webpage elements. What was the rationale behind each of these decisions?

Using Mail Merge

Objectives

After completing this module, you will be able to:

- Explain the merge process
- Use the Mail Merge wizard
- Use a letter template as the starting document for a mail merge
- Arrange objects on a page
- Modify save settings
- Create and edit a recipient list in a data source
- Insert merge fields in a main document
- Insert a custom field in a main document
- Merge form letters
- Sort a recipient list
- Merge to mailing labels and envelopes
- Change page orientation
- Merge to a directory
- Convert text to a table
- Sort table data

Introduction

People are more likely to open and read a personalized letter than a letter addressed as Dear Sir, Dear Madam, or To Whom It May Concern. Creating individual personalized letters, though, can be a time-consuming task. Thus, Word provides the capability of creating a form letter, which is an easy way to generate mass mailings of personalized letters. The basic content of a group of form letters is similar. Items such as name and address, however, vary from one letter to the next. With Word, you easily can address and print mailing labels or envelopes for the form letters.

Project: Form Letters, Mailing Labels, and a Directory

Both businesses and individuals regularly use form letters to communicate with groups of people via the postal service or email. Types of form letter correspondence include announcements of sales to customers, notices of benefits to employees, and job application letters to potential employers.

The project in this module follows generally accepted guidelines for writing form letters and uses Word to create the form letters shown in Figure 6–1. The form letters inform potential employers of your interest in a job opening at their organization. Each form letter states the potential employer's name and address, available job position, and whether the available position is for full-time or part-time employment.

Figure 6–1(a): Main Document for the Form Letter

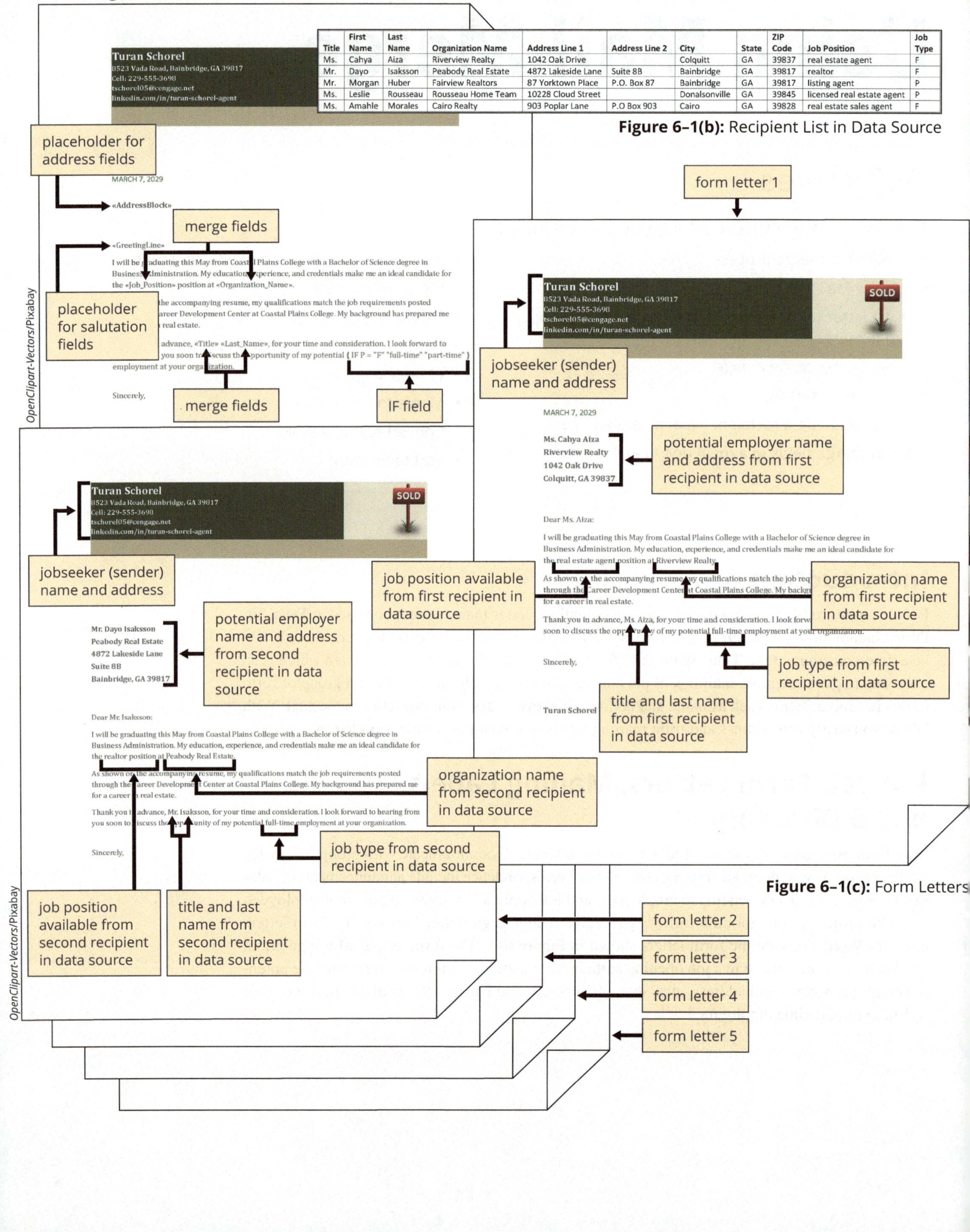

Title	First Name	Last Name	Organization Name	Address Line 1	Address Line 2	City	State	ZIP Code	Job Position	Job Type
Ms.	Cahya	Aiza	Riverview Realty	1042 Oak Drive		Colquitt	GA	39837	real estate agent	F
Mr.	Dayo	Isaksson	Peabody Real Estate	4872 Lakeside Lane	Suite 8B	Bainbridge	GA	39817	realtor	F
Mr.	Morgan	Huber	Fairview Realtors	87 Yorktown Place	P.O. Box 87	Bainbridge	GA	39817	listing agent	P
Ms.	Leslie	Rousseau	Rousseau Home Team	10228 Cloud Street		Donalsonville	GA	39845	licensed real estate agent	P
Ms.	Amahle	Morales	Cairo Realty	903 Poplar Lane	P.O Box 903	Cairo	GA	39828	real estate sales agent	F

Figure 6–1(b): Recipient List in Data Source

Figure 6–1(c): Form Letters

To generate form letters, such as the ones shown in Figure 6–1, you create a main document for the form letter (Figure 6–1a), create or specify a data source, which contains a recipient list (Figure 6–1b), and then **merge**, or combine, the main document with the recipient list in the data source to generate a series of individual letters (Figure 6–1c). In Figure 6–1a, the main document represents the portion of the form letter that is repeated from one merged letter to the next. In Figure 6–1b, the recipient list in the data source contains the organization's contact person, name, address, available job position, and job type for various potential employers. To personalize each letter, you merge the potential employer data in the recipient list in the data source with the main document for the form letter, which generates or prints an individual letter for each potential employer listed in the recipient list in the data source.

Word provides two methods of merging documents: the Mail Merge wizard and the Mailings tab on the ribbon. The Mail Merge wizard, which uses the Mail Merge pane, is a step-by-step progression that guides you through the merging process. The Mailings tab provides buttons and boxes you use to merge documents. This module illustrates both techniques.

In this module, you will learn how to create the form letters shown in Figure 6–1. You will perform the following general tasks as you progress through this module:

1. Identify the starting document for the form letters.
2. Create the recipient list for a data source.
3. Compose the main document for the form letters.
4. Merge the recipient list in the data source with the main document.
5. Address mailing labels.
6. Merge all recipients in a data source to a directory.

To Start Word and Specify Settings

The following steps start Word, display formatting marks, change the zoom to page width, and verify ruler and Mouse mode settings. If you are using a computer to step through the project in this module and you want your screens to match the figures in this book, you should change your screen's resolution to 1366 × 768.

1. **sam** Start Word and create a blank document in the Word window. If necessary, maximize the Word window.
2. If the Print Layout button on the status bar is not selected, click it so that your screen is in Print Layout view.
3. If the 'Show/Hide ¶' button (Home tab | Paragraph group) is not selected already, click it to display formatting marks on the screen.
4. To display the page the same width as the document window, if necessary, click the Page Width button (View tab | Zoom group).
5. Verify that the Ruler check box (View tab | Show group) is not selected. (If it is selected, click it to remove the check mark because you do not want the rulers to appear on the screen.)

BTW
Touch Mode Differences
The Office and Windows interfaces may vary if you are using Touch mode. For this reason, you might notice that the function or appearance of your touch screen differs slightly from this module's presentation.

6 If you are using a mouse and you want your screens to match the figures in the book, verify that you are using Mouse mode by doing the following: display the Quick Access Toolbar, if necessary, by clicking the 'Ribbon Display Options' button at the right edge of the ribbon and then clicking 'Show Quick Access Toolbar' on the menu; clicking the 'Touch/Mouse Mode' button on the Quick Access Toolbar and then, if necessary, clicking Mouse on the menu (if your Quick Access Toolbar does not display the 'Touch/Mouse Mode' button, click the 'Customize Quick Access Toolbar' button on the Quick Access Toolbar and then click Touch/Mouse Mode on the menu to add the button to the Quick Access Toolbar); then hide the Quick Access Toolbar by clicking the 'Ribbon Display Options' button at the right edge of the ribbon and then clicking 'Hide Quick Access Toolbar' on the menu.

Identifying the Starting Document for Form Letters

The first step in the mail merge process is to identify the type of document you are creating for the main document. Typical installations of Word support five types of main documents: letters, email messages, envelopes, labels, and a directory. In this section of the module, you create letters as the main document. Later in this module, you will specify labels and a directory as the main document.

Consider This

How should you create the letter for the main document?

When creating form letters, you either can type the letter for the main document from scratch in a blank document window or use a letter template. If you enter the contents of the main document from scratch, you can compose it according to the block, modified block, or semi-block letter style, formatted appropriately with business letter spacing. Alternatively, you can use a letter template to save time because Word prepares a letter with text and/or formatting common to all letters. Then, you customize the resulting letter by selecting and replacing prewritten text.

To Start the Mail Merge Wizard

This module uses a template for the main document for the form letter, where you select predefined content controls and placeholder text and replace them with personalized content, adjusting formats as necessary. **Why?** You can use the same or similar style that you use with a resume so that the two documents complement each other. The following steps use the Mail Merge wizard to identify the Timeless letter template as the starting document for a form letter.

1
- Click Mailings on the ribbon to display the Mailings tab.
- Click the 'Start Mail Merge' button (Mailings tab | Start Mail Merge group) to display the Start Mail Merge menu (Figure 6–2).

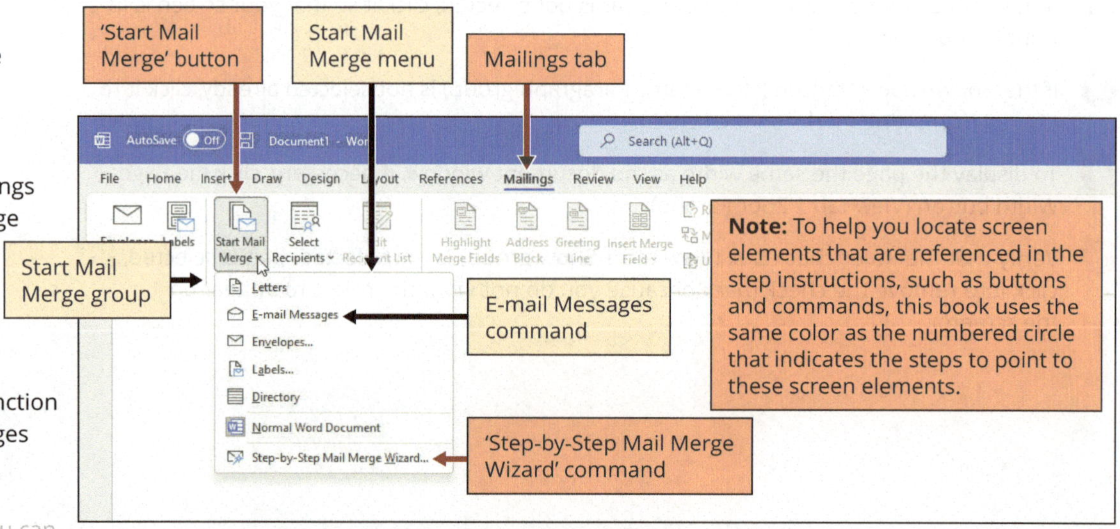

Figure 6–2

Q&A What is the function of the E-mail Messages command?
Instead of sending individual letters, you can send individual email messages using email addresses in the recipient list in the data source or using a Microsoft Outlook Contacts list as the data source.

2

- Click 'Step-by-Step Mail Merge Wizard' on the Start Mail Merge menu to display Step 1 of the Mail Merge wizard in the Mail Merge pane (Figure 6–3).

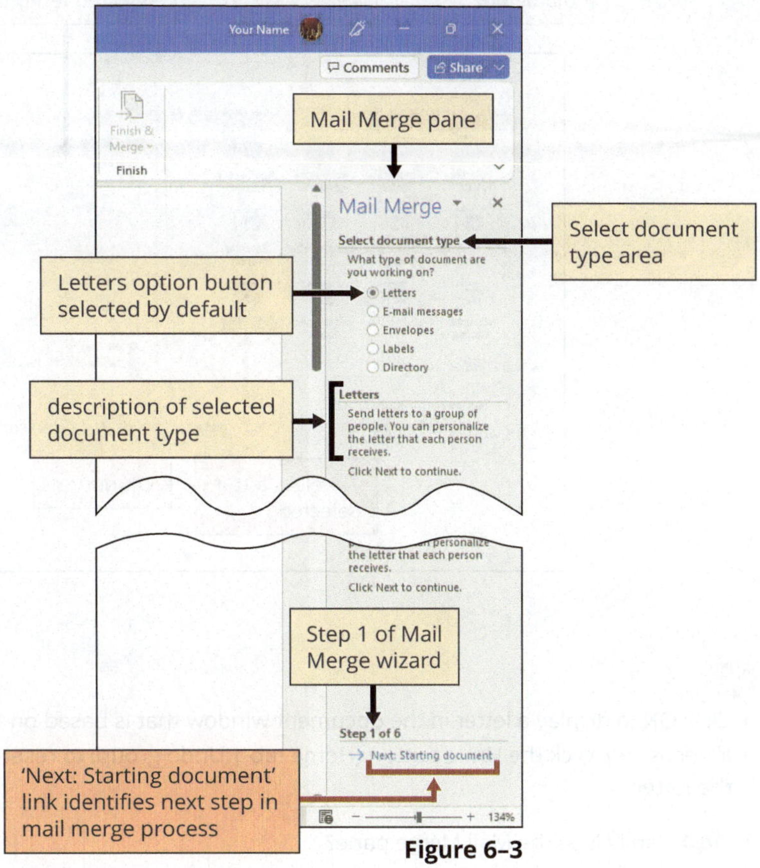

Figure 6–3

3

- Ensure that Letters is selected in the Select document type area and then click the 'Next: Starting document' link at the bottom of the Mail Merge pane to display Step 2 of the Mail Merge wizard, which requests that you select a starting document.
- Click 'Start from a template' in the Select starting document area and then click the Select template link to display the Select Template dialog box.
- Click the Letters tab (Select Template dialog box) to display the Letters sheet and then click Timeless letter, which displays a preview of the selected template in the Preview area (Figure 6–4).
- **Experiment:** Click various Letter templates in the Letters sheet and watch the preview change in the right pane of the dialog box. When you are finished experimenting, click the Timeless letter template to select it.

Q&A What if I cannot locate the Timeless letter template?

Click the Cancel button to close the Select Template dialog box, click the 'Start from existing document' option button in the Mail Merge pane to display options for opening a document in the pane, click the Open button that appears in the Mail Merge pane to display the Open dialog box, navigate to the location of the Support_WD_6_TimelessLetterTemplate.docx, click the file to select it, click the Open button (Open dialog box) to open the selected file, and then proceed to Step 5.

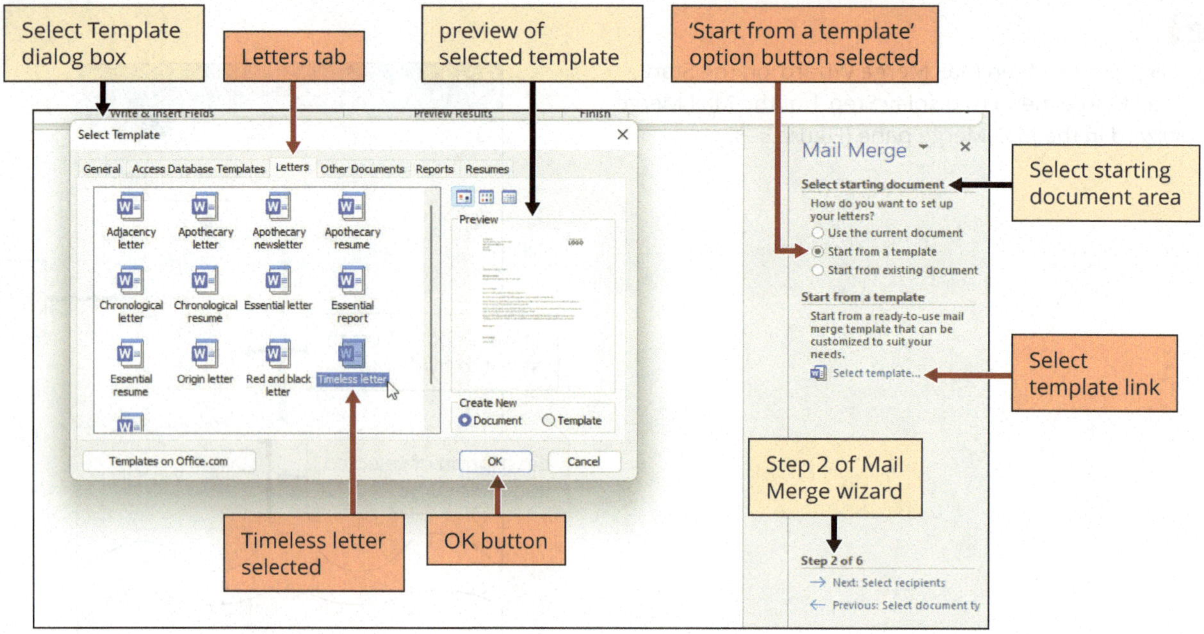

Figure 6–4

4

- Click OK to display a letter in the document window that is based on the Timeless letter template (Figure 6–5).
- If necessary, click the Undo button (Home tab | Undo group) to reset the Your Name content control at the bottom of the letter.

Q&A Can I close the Mail Merge pane?
Yes, you can close the Mail Merge pane at any time by clicking its Close button. When you want to continue with the merge process, repeat these steps and Word will resume the merge process at the correct step in the Mail Merge wizard.

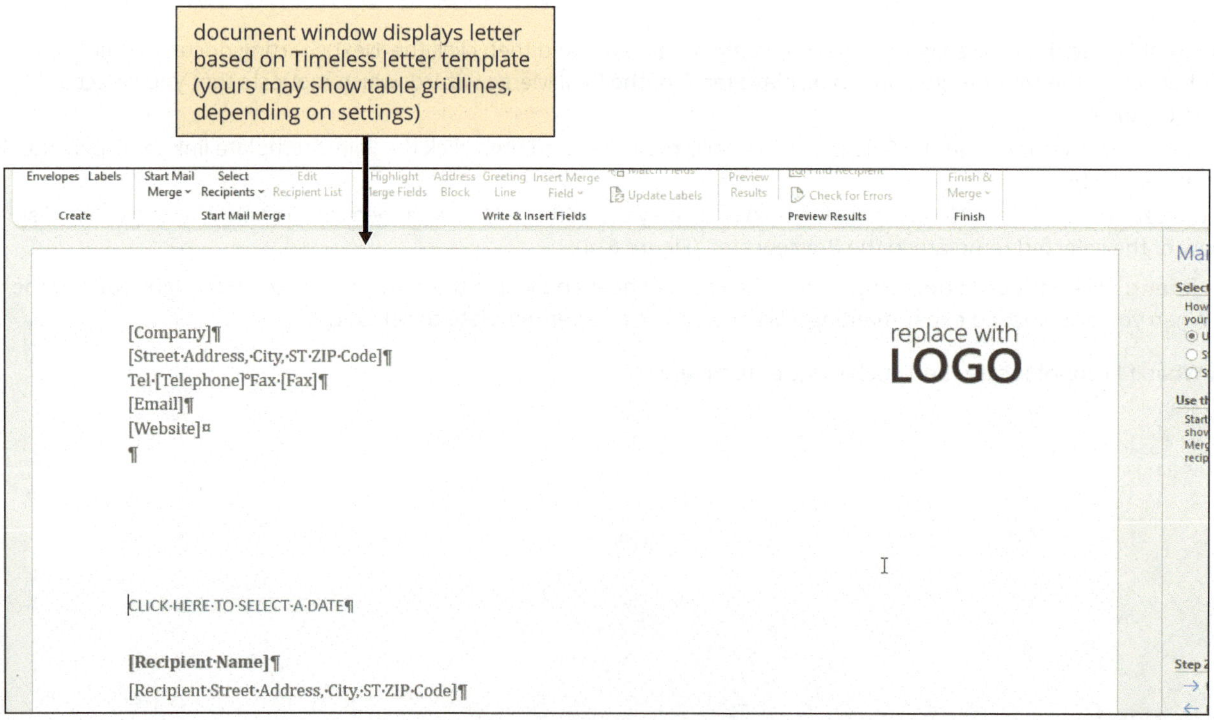

Figure 6–5

5

- Print the document shown on the screen so that you easily can view the entire letter contents (Figure 6–6).

Q&A What are the content controls in the document?
Recall that a content control contains placeholder text and instructions for filling in areas of the document. To select a content control, click it. Later in this module, you will personalize the placeholder text and content controls. You also will remove the content controls as you are finished adding text to them.

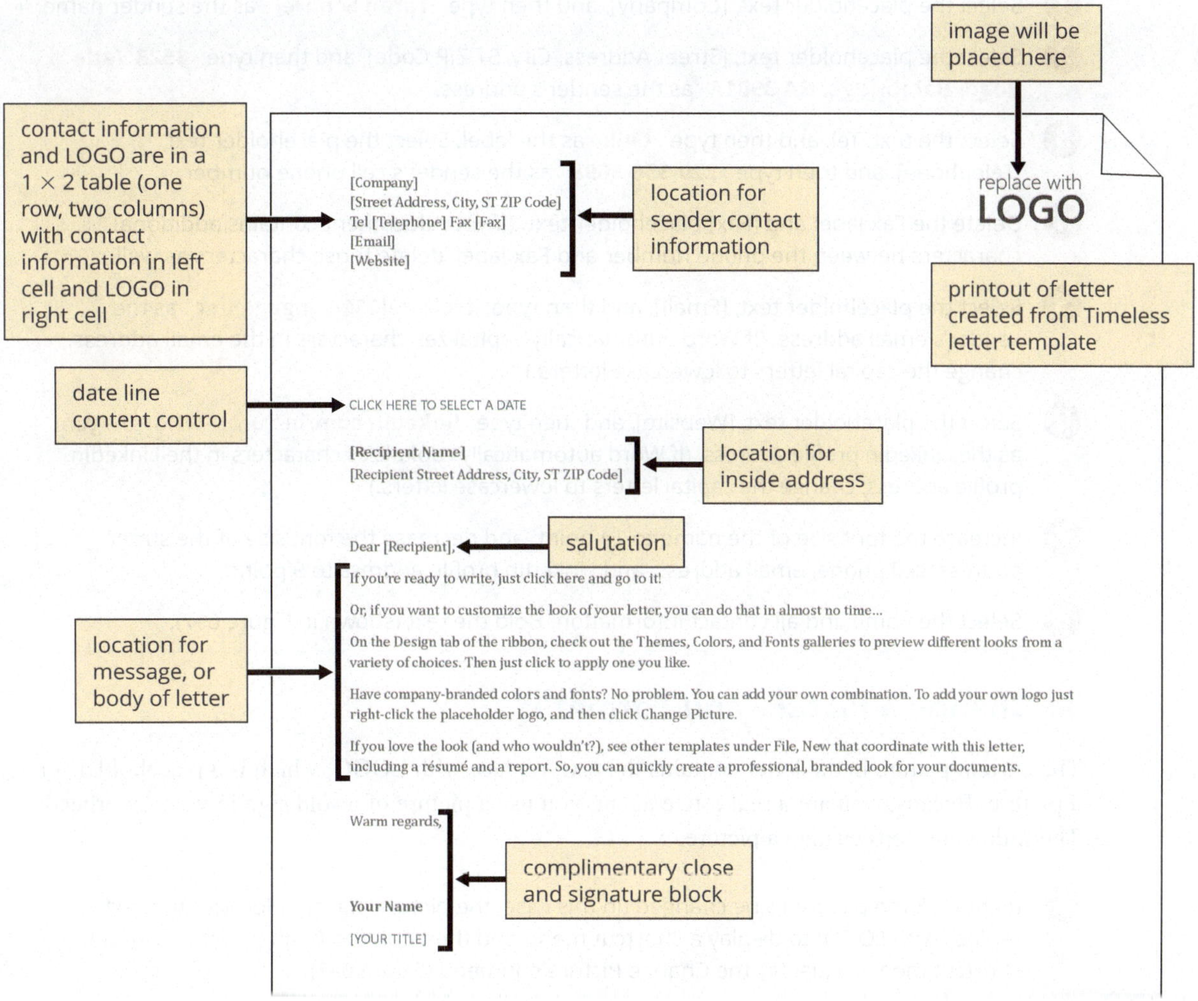

Figure 6–6

Other Ways

1. Open Backstage view, click New, type **letters** in 'Search for online templates' box, click Start searching button, click desired letter template, click Create button

To Change Theme Colors

Word provides document themes, which contain a variety of color schemes and other effects. This cover letter uses the Green theme colors to match the theme colors used in the associated resume. The following steps change the theme colors.

1. Click Design on the ribbon to display the Design tab.
2. Click the Colors button (Design tab | Document Formatting group) to display the Colors gallery.
3. Scroll to and then click Green in the Colors gallery to change the theme colors to the selected theme.

To Enter and Format the Sender Information

The next step is to enter the sender's contact information at the top of the letter. You will use the [Company] placeholder text for the sender's name. You will delete the [Fax] placeholder text because this sender does not have a fax. Then, you will format the text. The following steps enter and format the sender information.

1. Select the placeholder text, [Company], and then type **Turan Schorel** as the sender name.
2. Select the placeholder text, [Street Address, City, ST ZIP Code], and then type **8523 Vada Road, Bainbridge, GA 39817** as the sender's address.
3. Select the text, Tel, and then type **Cell:** as the label. Select the placeholder text, [Telephone], and then type **229-555-3698** as the sender's cell phone number.
4. Delete the Fax label and [Fax] placeholder text. (If your document contains additional characters between the phone number and Fax label, delete those characters as well.)
5. Select the placeholder text, [Email], and then type **tschorel05@cengage.net** as the sender's email address. (If Word automatically capitalizes characters in the email address, change the capital letters to lowercase letters.)
6. Select the placeholder text, [Website], and then type **linkedin.com/in/turan-schorel-agent** as the LinkedIn profile address. (If Word automatically capitalizes characters in the LinkedIn profile address, change the capital letters to lowercase letters.)
7. Increase the font size of the name to 14 point, and decrease the font size of the street address, cell phone, email address, and LinkedIn profile address to 9 point.
8. Select the name and all contact information. Bold the text (shown in Figure 6–7).

To Change a Picture and Format It

The current picture in the letter contains the text, replace with LOGO, which is a placeholder for a picture. Because you are a real estate agent, you use a picture of a sold sign in your letterhead. The following steps change a picture.

1. Right-click the picture to be changed (in this case, the picture placeholder with the text, replace with LOGO) to display a shortcut menu and then point to Change Picture on the shortcut menu to display the Change Picture submenu (Figure 6–7).
2. Click 'From Online Sources' on the Change Picture submenu to display the Online Pictures dialog box.

   Q&A Can I use the Change Picture button (Picture Format tab | Adjust group) instead of the shortcut menu to display the Online Pictures dialog box?
   Yes.

3. Type **sold sign** in the Search box (Online Pictures dialog box) and then press ENTER to display a list of images that matches the entered search text.
4. Scroll through the list of images to locate the one shown in Figure 6–8 (or a similar image), click the image to select it, and then click the Insert button (Online Pictures dialog box) to download the image, close the dialog box, and replace the selected placeholder with the new picture file (shown in Figure 6–8).

   Q&A What if I cannot locate the same image?
   Click Cancel and then repeat Step 1 above, click 'From a File' (or This Device, depending on settings) on the Change Picture submenu to display the Insert Picture dialog box, navigate to and select the Support_WD_6_SoldSign.png file in the Data Files (Insert Picture dialog box), and then click the Insert button to replace the selected placeholder with the new picture file.

5. Use the Shape Height and Shape Width boxes (Picture Format tab | Size group) to change the picture height to approximately 1" and width to .71". (Note: You might need to remove the check mark from the 'Lock aspect ratio' check box by clicking the Size Dialog Box Launcher (Picture Format tab | Size group) in order to size the image exactly.)

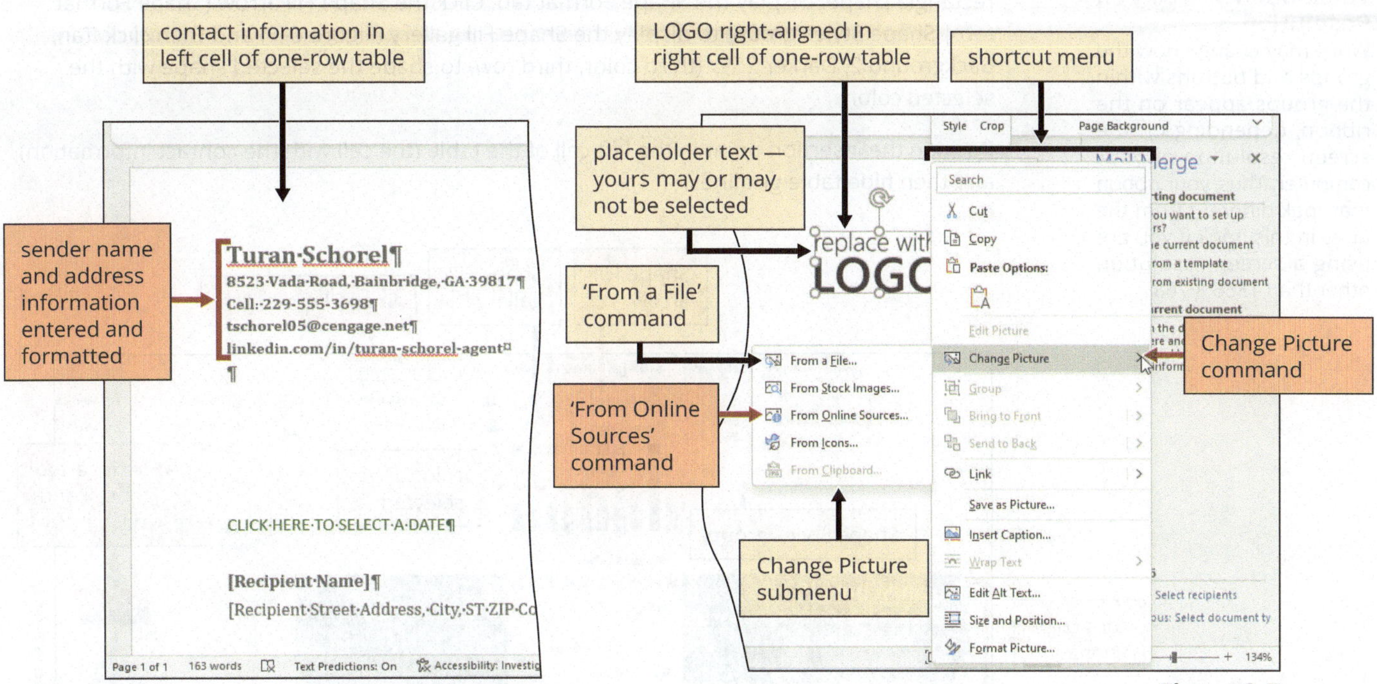

Figure 6–7

To Shade Cells and a Shape

In the letter in this module, the left and right cells of the table containing the contact information and picture are shaded different colors. These two cells are contained in a rectangular shape, which extends below these two cells. By shading the cells in the table and the rectangular shape each a separate color, you create a letterhead with three different colors. The following steps shade table cells and a shape.

1. Position the insertion point in the contact information (upper-left cell of table). Display the contextual Layout tab and then, if necessary, click the View Gridlines button (contextual Layout tab | Table group) to show table gridlines.

   Q&A Is the contextual Layout tab different from the main Layout tab?
   Yes. Recall that the main Layout tab, which always appears on the ribbon, is used to change page setup, format paragraphs, and arrange objects in a document. The contextual Layout tab appears only when you are working in a table and is used to change the properties and organization of a table and its rows, columns, and cells.

   Why display table gridlines?
   With table gridlines displayed, the cells are easier to identify.

2. Display the Table Design tab. With the insertion point in the left cell, click the Shading arrow (Table Design tab | Table Styles group) and then click 'Green, Accent 1, Darker 50%' (fifth color, last row) to shade the current cell with the selected color.

3. Select the contact information in the left cell and change its font color to 'White, Background 1' (first color, first row).

4. Position the insertion point in the cell with the picture, click the Shading arrow (Table Design tab | Table Styles group) and then click 'Tan, Background 2' (third color, first row) to shade the current cell with the selected color.

BTW
The Ribbon and Screen Resolution
Word may change how the groups and buttons within the groups appear on the ribbon, depending on the screen resolution of your computer. Thus, your ribbon may look different from the ones in this book if you are using a screen resolution other than 1366 × 768.

5. Position the insertion point on the paragraph mark below the shaded cell to select the rectangle shape. Display the Shape Format tab. Click the Shape Fill arrow (Shape Format tab | Shape Styles group) to display the Shape Fill gallery (Figure 6–8) and then click 'Tan, Background 2, Darker 25%' (third color, third row) to shade the selected shape with the selected color.

6. Position the insertion point in the left cell of the table (the cell with the contact information) and then hide table gridlines.

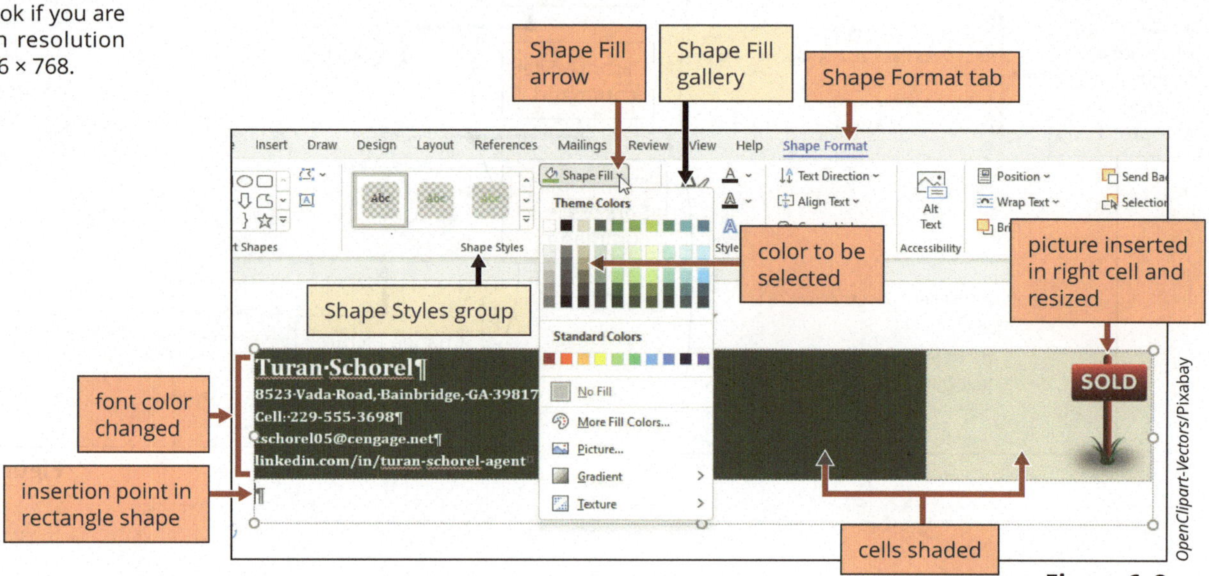

Figure 6–8

To Change Margin Settings

The Timeless letter template uses 1.9-inch top and .75-inch bottom, left, and right margins. You want the form letter to use 1-inch top and bottom margins and 1.25-inch left and right margins. The following steps change the margin settings.

1. Click the Date content control to deselect the table.

2. Display the Layout tab. Click the Margins button (Layout tab | Page Setup group) to display the Margins gallery and then click Custom Margins at the bottom of the gallery to display the Page Setup dialog box.

3. Change the values in the Top, Bottom, Left, and Right boxes (Page Setup dialog box) to 1", 1", 1.25", and 1.25", respectively (Figure 6–9).

4. Click OK to change the margin values.

Q&A Why is the top margin unchanged?
The template specifies that the rectangle shape be positioned a certain distance from the top of the page, regardless of margin settings. The next steps change the position (location) of the shape.

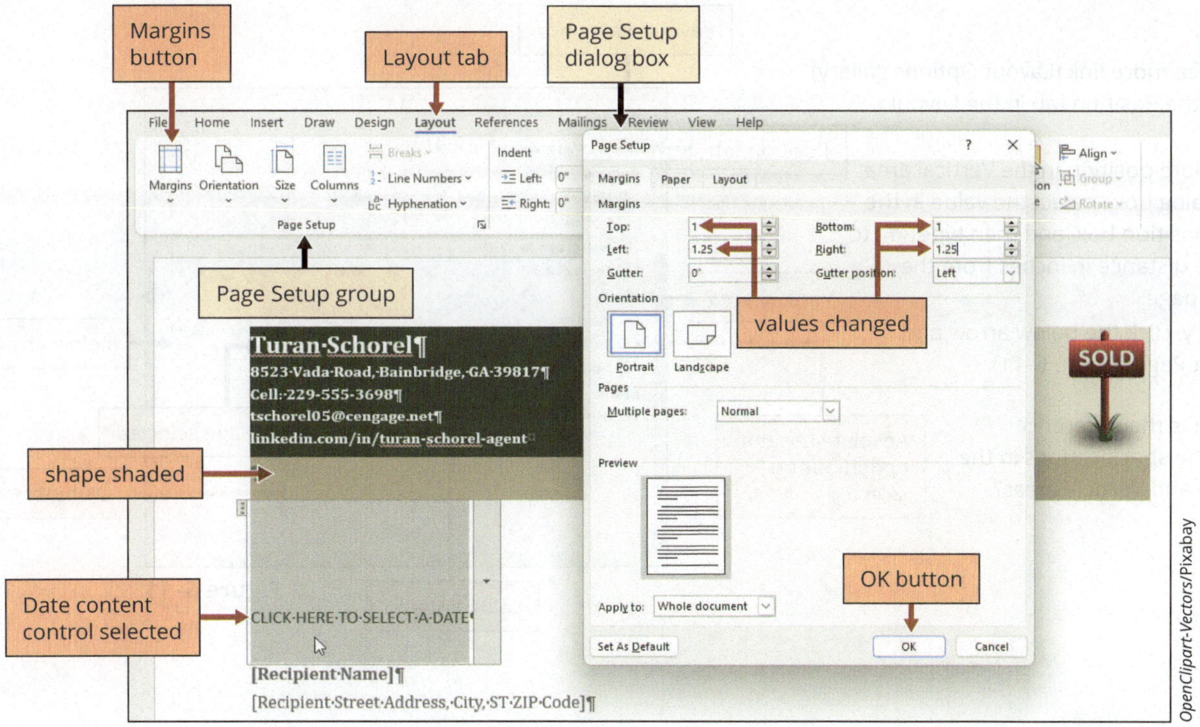

Figure 6–9

To Specify the Position of a Graphic

The next step is to change the distance between the shape and the top of the page. **Why?** You want a one-inch space above the shape. The following steps specify the position of a graphic.

1

- Click the rectangle shape to select it.
- Click the Layout Options button attached to the shape to display the Layout Options gallery (Figure 6–10).

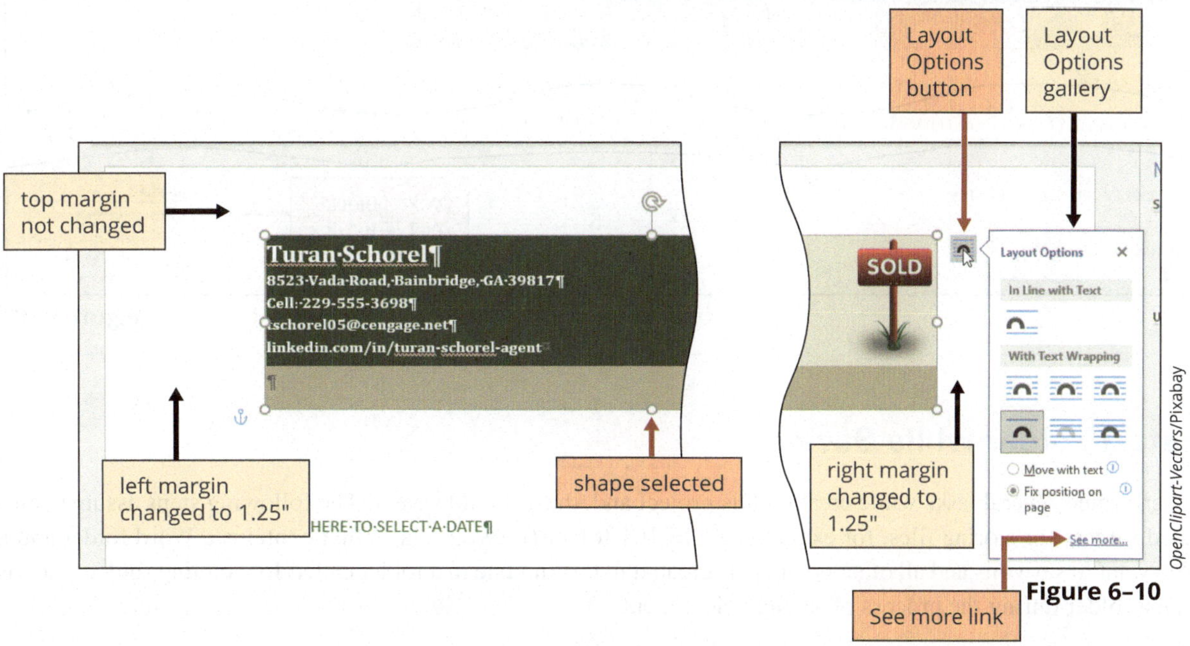

Figure 6–10

2

- Click the See more link (Layout Options gallery) to display the Position tab in the Layout dialog box.
- Click Absolute position in the Vertical area (Layout dialog box), select the value in the Absolute position box, and then type **1** to specify the distance in inches from the top of the page.
- If necessary, click the below arrow and then select Page (Figure 6–11).

Q&A What is the difference between the specifications in the Horizontal and Vertical areas?
Horizontal settings specify the graphic's position left to right on the page, whereas vertical settings specify the graphic's position top to bottom on the page.

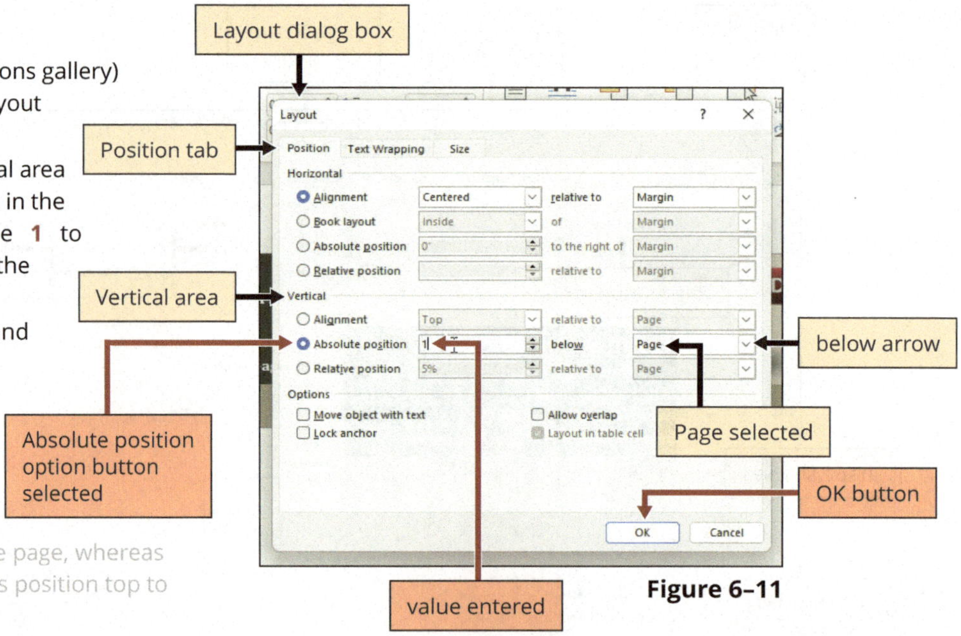

Figure 6–11

3

- Click OK to change the position of the selected graphic (Figure 6–12).

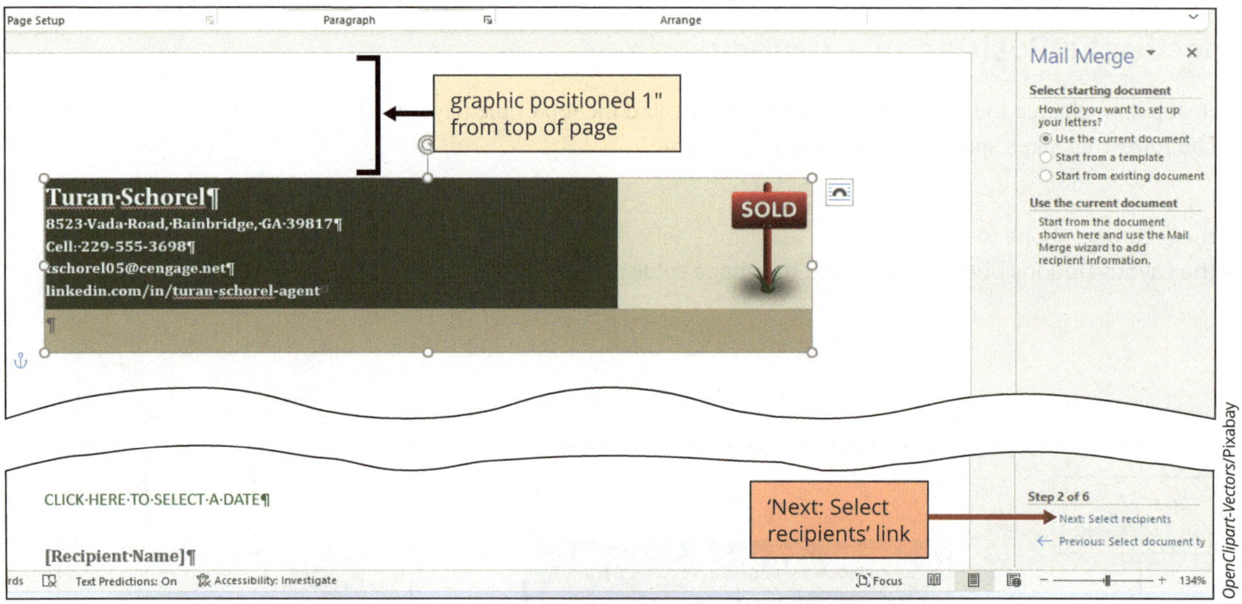

Figure 6–12

To Create a Folder while Saving

You have performed several tasks while creating this project and, thus, should save it. The following steps assume you already have created folders for storing files, for example, a CIS 101 folder (for your class) that contains a Word folder and module folders. You want to save this and all other documents created in this module in a folder called JobHunting folder. The following steps create a folder during the process of saving a document. **Why?** This folder does not exist, so you must create it. Rather than creating the folder in Windows, you can create folders in Word.

1

- Display the Save As dialog box associated with your desired save location, type **SC_WD_6_SchorelCoverLetter** as the file name, and navigate to the desired save location for the new folder.
- Click the New folder button (Save As dialog box) to display a new folder icon with the name, New folder, selected in the dialog box (Figure 6–13).

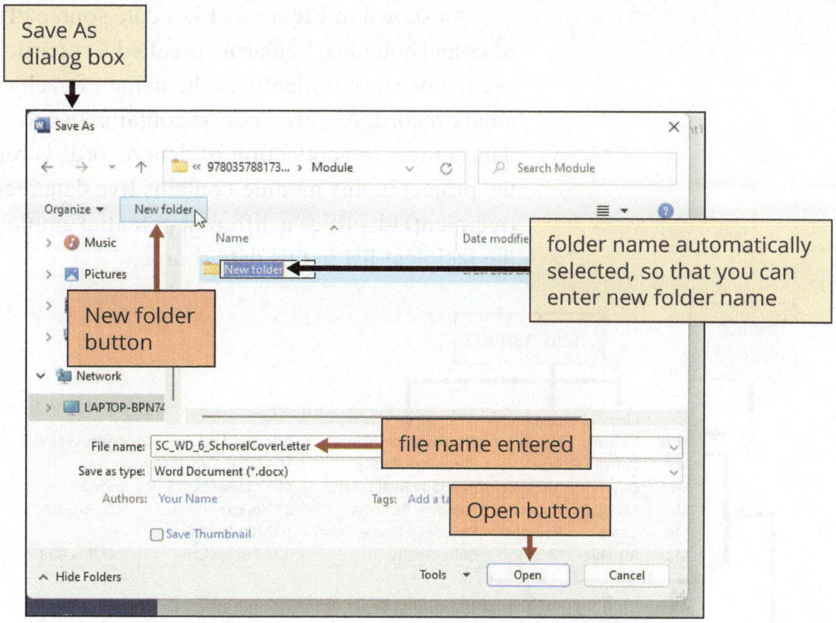

Figure 6–13

2

- Type **JobHunting** as the new folder name and then press ENTER to create the new folder.
- Click the Open button to open the selected folder, in this case, the JobHunting folder (Figure 6–14).

3

- Click Save (Save As dialog box) to save the current document in the selected folder on the selected drive.

Q&A Can I create a folder in any other dialog box?

Yes. Any dialog box that displays a File list, such as the Open and Insert File dialog boxes, also has the New folder button, allowing you to create a new folder in Word instead of using Windows for this task.

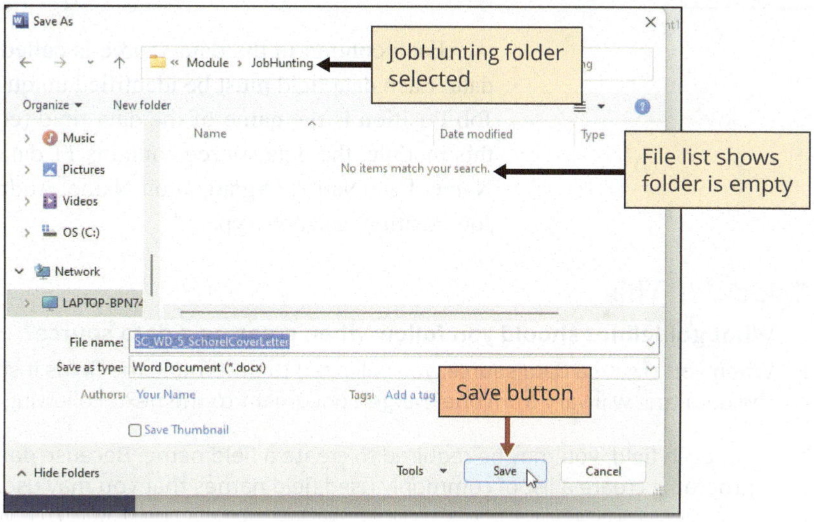

Figure 6–14

Creating a Data Source

The **data source** is a file that contains the variable, or changing, values from one merged document to the next. A data source can be an Access database table, an Outlook contacts list, or an Excel worksheet. If the necessary and properly organized data already exists in one of these Microsoft 365 programs, you can instruct Word to use the existing file as the data source for the mail merge. Otherwise, you can create a new data source using one of these programs.

BTW
Fields and Records
Field and record are terms that originate from the software development field. Do not be intimidated by these terms. A field is simply a column in a table, and a record is a row. Rather than using the term, field, some software developers identify a column of data as a variable or an attribute. All three terms (field, variable, and attribute) have the same meaning.

As shown in Figure 6–15, a data source often is shown as a table that consists of a series of rows and columns. Each row is called a **record**. The first row of a data source is called the **header record** because it identifies the name of each column. Each row below the header row is called a data record. A **data record** contains the complete set of related text for each recipient in the data source; the collection of data records is referred to as the recipient list. The data source for the project in this module contains five data records (recipients). In this project, each data record (recipient) identifies a different potential employer. Thus, five form letters will be generated from the recipient list in this data source.

header record

field names

data source

Title	First Name	Last Name	Organization Name	Address Line 1	Address Line 2	City	State	ZIP Code	Job Position	Job Type
Ms.	Cahya	Aiza	Riverview Realty	1042 Oak Drive		Colquitt	GA	39837	real estate agent	F
Mr.	Dayo	Isaksson	Peabody Real Estate	4872 Lakeside Lane	Suite 8B	Bainbridge	GA	39817	realtor	F
Mr.	Morgan	Huber	Fairview Realtors	87 Yorktown Place	P.O. Box 87	Bainbridge	GA	39817	listing agent	P
Ms.	Leslie	Rousseau	Rousseau Home Team	10228 Cloud Street		Donalsonville	GA	39845	licensed real estate agent	P
Ms.	Amahle	Morales	Cairo Realty	903 Poplar Lane	P.O Box 903	Cairo	GA	39828	real estate sales agent	F

data records (recipients)

data fields

Figure 6–15

Each column in the data source is called a **data field**, which represents a group of similar data. Each data field must be identified uniquely with a name, called a **field name**. For example, Job Position is the name of the data field (column) that contains the available job position. In this module, the data source contains 11 data fields with the following field names: Title, First Name, Last Name, Organization Name, Address Line 1, Address Line 2, City, State, ZIP Code, Job Position, and Job Type.

Consider This

What guidelines should you follow when creating a data source?

When you create a data source, you will need to determine the fields it should contain. That is, you will need to identify the data that will vary from one merged document to the next. Following are a few important points about fields:

- For each field, you may be required to create a field name. Because data sources often contain the same fields, some programs create a list of commonly used field names that you may use.
- Field names must be unique; that is, no two field names may be the same.
- Fields may be listed in any order in the data source. That is, the order of fields has no effect on the order in which they will print in the main document.
- Organize fields so that they are flexible. For example, separate the name into individual fields: title, first name, and last name. This arrangement allows you to print a person's title, first name, and last name (e.g., Ms. Cahya Aiza) in the inside address but only the title and last name in the salutation (Dear Ms. Aiza).

To Type a New Recipient List for a Data Source

Word provides a list of 13 commonly used field names. This project uses 9 of the 13 field names supplied by Word: Title, First Name, Last Name, Company Name, Address Line 1, Address Line 2, City, State, and ZIP Code. This project does not use the other four field names supplied by Word: Country or Region, Home Phone, Work Phone, and E-mail Address. Thus, you will delete these four field names. Then, you will change the Company Name field name to Organization Name. **Why?** The term, organization, better describes the potential employers in this project. You also will add two new field names (Job Position and Job Type) to the data source because you want to reference the available position, as well as the type of job (full time or part time), in the form letter. The next steps type a new recipient list for a data source for a mail merge.

1

- Click the 'Next: Select recipients' link at the bottom of the Mail Merge pane (shown in Figure 6–12) to display Step 3 of the Mail Merge wizard, which requests you select recipients.
- Click 'Type a new list' in the Select recipients area, which displays the Type a new list area.
- Click the Create link to display the New Address List dialog box (Figure 6–16).

Q&A When would I use the other two option buttons in the Select recipients area?
If a data source already was created, you would use the first option: Use an existing list. If you wanted to use your Outlook contacts list as the data source, you would choose the second option.

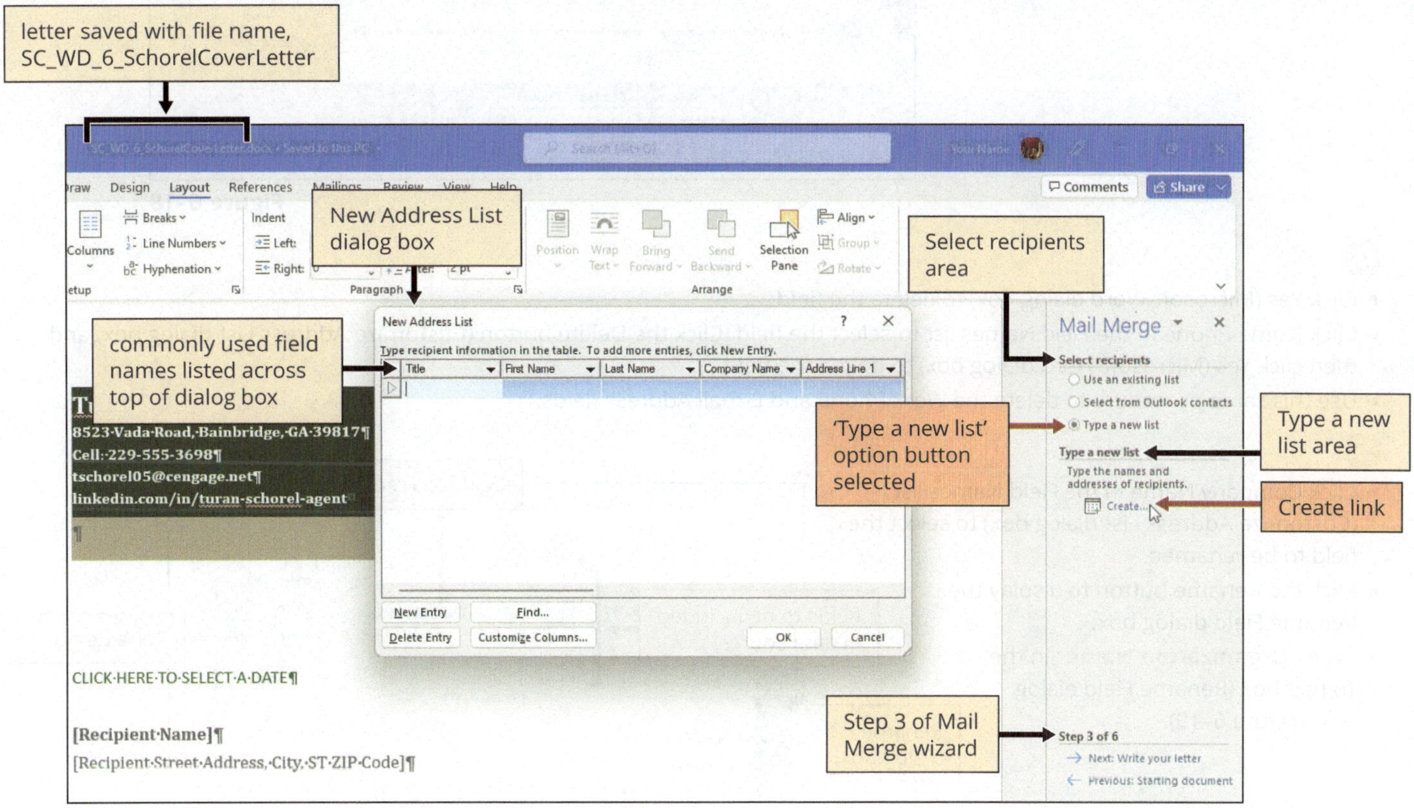

Figure 6–16

2

- Click the Customize Columns button (New Address List dialog box) to display the Customize Address List dialog box (Figure 6–17).

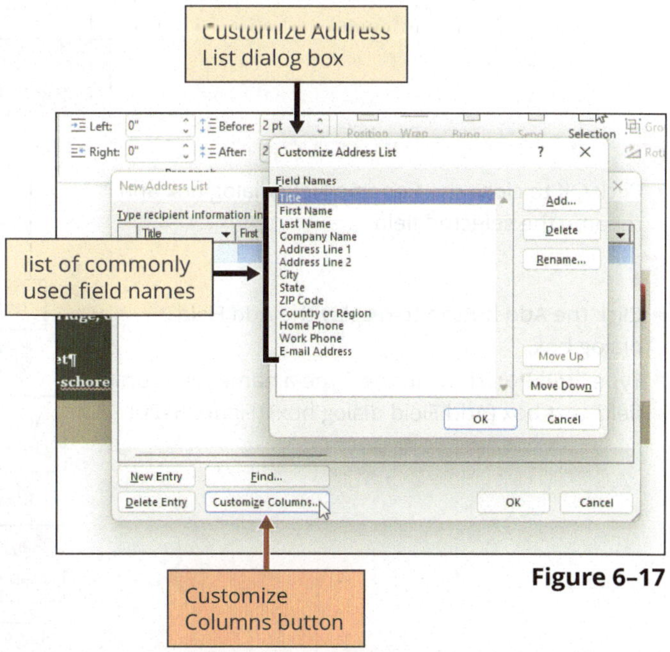

Figure 6–17

3

- Click 'Country or Region' in the Field Names list (Customize Address List dialog box) to select the field to be deleted and then click the Delete button to display a Microsoft Word dialog box asking if you are sure you want to delete the selected field (Figure 6–18).

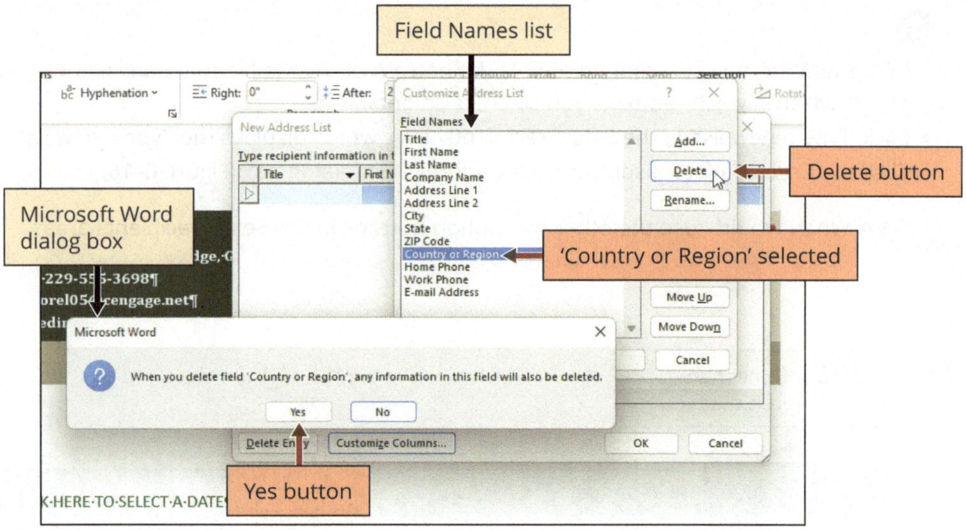

Figure 6–18

4

- Click Yes (Microsoft Word dialog box) to delete the field.
- Click Home Phone in the Field Names list to select the field. Click the Delete button (Customize Address List dialog box) and then click Yes (Microsoft Word dialog box) to delete the field.
- Use this same procedure to delete the Work Phone and E-mail Address fields.

5

- Click Company Name in the Field Names list (Customize Address List dialog box) to select the field to be renamed.
- Click the Rename button to display the Rename Field dialog box.
- Type **Organization Name** in the To text box (Rename Field dialog box) (Figure 6–19).

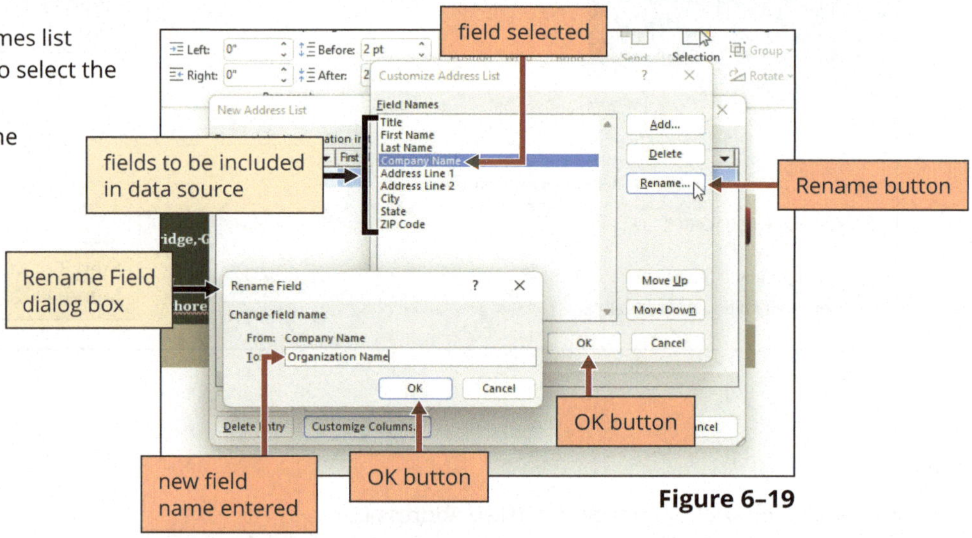

Figure 6–19

6

- Click OK to close the Rename Field dialog box and rename the selected field.

7

- Click the Add button to display the Add Field dialog box.
- Type **Job Position** in the 'Type a name for your field' text box (Add Field dialog box) (Figure 6–20).

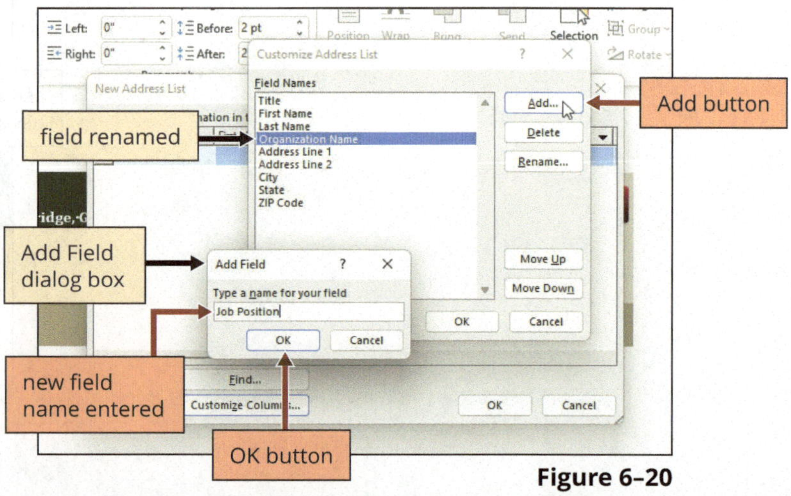

Figure 6–20

8

- Click OK to close the Add Field dialog box and add the Job Position field name to the Field Names list immediately below the selected field (Figure 6–21).

Q&A Can I change the order of the field names in the Field Names list?
Yes. Select the field name and then click the Move Up or Move Down button (Customize Address List dialog box) to move the selected field in the direction of the button name.

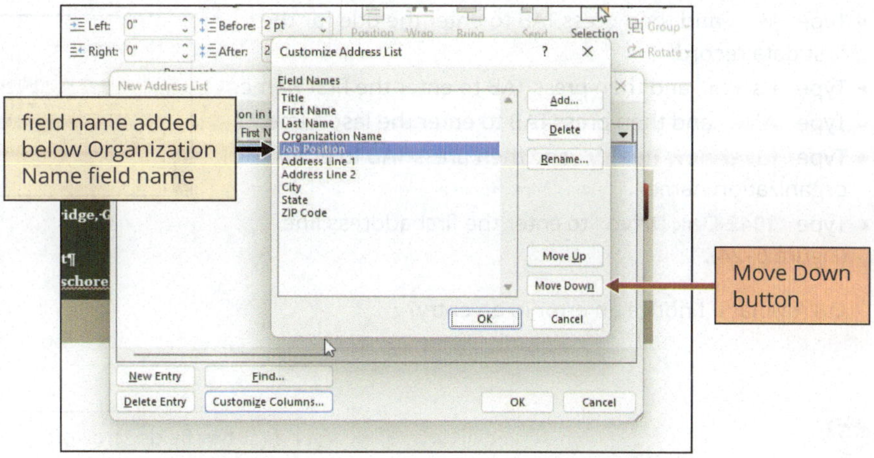

Figure 6–21

9

- With the Job Position field selected, click the Move Down button five times to position the selected field at the end of the Field Names list. (If the Job Position field is not at the bottom of the list, click the Move Down button to move it down as necessary.)
- Click the Add button to display the Add Field dialog box.
- Type **Job Type** (Add Field dialog box) in the 'Type a name for your field' text box and then click OK to close the Add Field dialog box and add the Job Type field name to the bottom of the Field Names list (Figure 6–22).

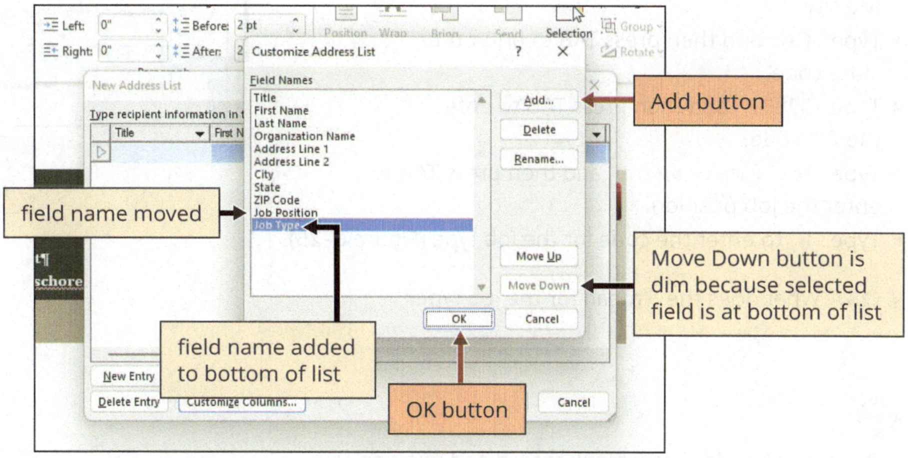

Figure 6–22

Q&A Could I add more field names to the list?
Yes. You would click the Add button for each field name you want to add.

10

- Click OK to close the Customize Address List dialog box, which positions the insertion point in the Title text box for the first data record (row or recipient) in the New Address List dialog box (Figure 6–23).

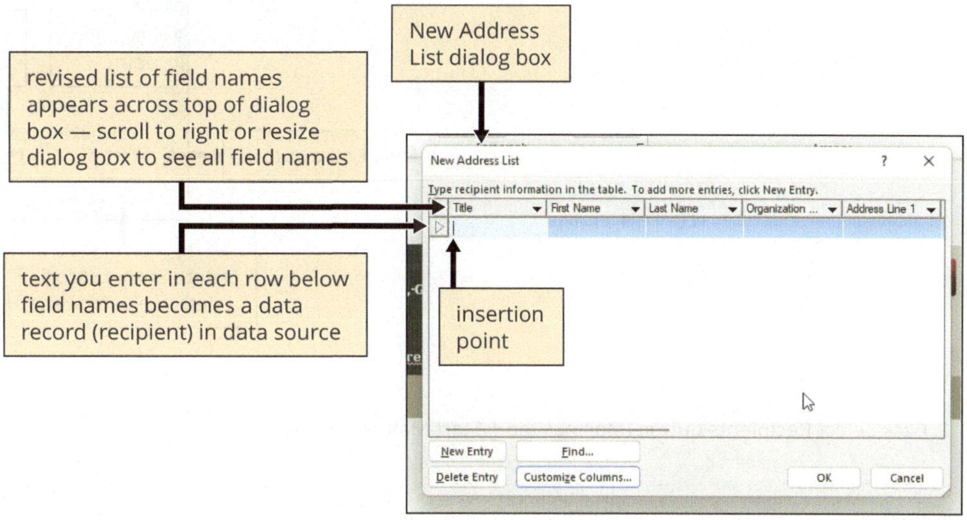

Figure 6–23

11

- Type **Ms.** and then press TAB to enter the title for the first data record.
- Type **Cahya** and then press TAB to enter the first name.
- Type **Aiza** and then press TAB to enter the last name.
- Type **Riverview Realty** and then press TAB to enter the organization name.
- Type **1042 Oak Drive** to enter the first address line (Figure 6–24).

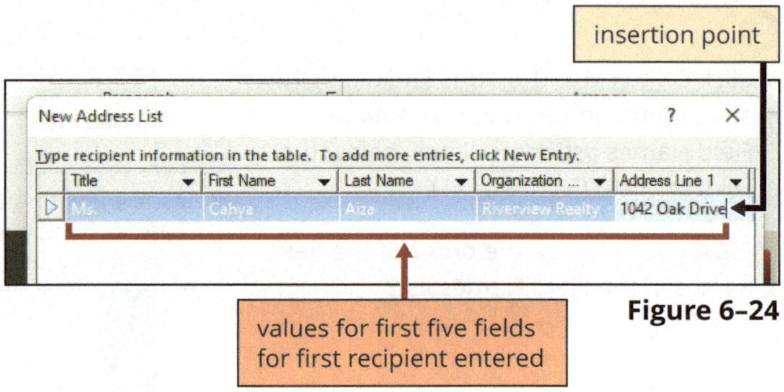

Figure 6–24

Q&A What if I notice an error in an entry?
Click the entry and then correct the error as you would in the document window.

12

- Press TAB twice to leave the second address line empty.
- Type **Colquitt** and then press TAB to enter the city.
- Type **GA** and then press TAB to enter the state code.
- Type **39837** and then press TAB to enter the ZIP code.
- Type **real estate agent** and then press TAB to enter the job position.
- Type **F** to enter the code for the job type (Figure 6–25).

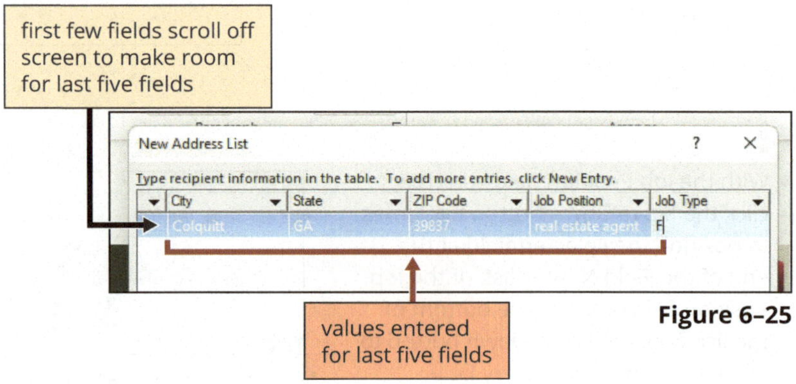

Figure 6–25

Q&A What does the F mean for the job type?
You decide to enter F for full-time and P for part-time to minimize the amount of redundant typing for these records.

13

- Press TAB to add a new blank record and position the insertion point in the Title field of the new record (Figure 6–26).

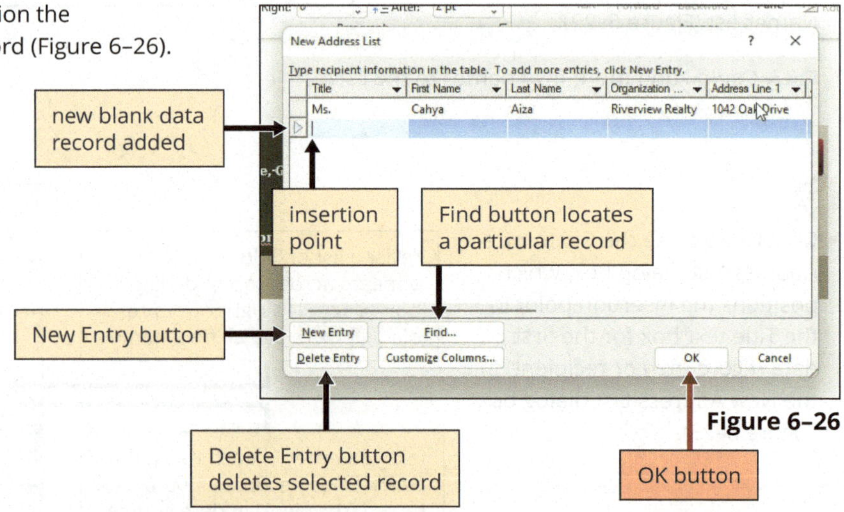

Figure 6–26

Other Ways

1. Click Select Recipients button (Mailings tab | Start Mail Merge group)

To Enter More Recipients

The following steps enter the remaining four data records (recipients) in the New Address List dialog box.

1 Type **Mr.** and then press TAB. Type **Dayo** and then press TAB. Type **Isaksson** and then press TAB. Type **Peabody Real Estate** and then press TAB.

Q&A What happened to the rest of the Organization Name entry?
It is stored in the field, but you cannot view the entire entry because it is longer than the display area.

2 Type **4872 Lakeside Lane** and then press TAB. Type **Suite 8B** and then press TAB.

3 Type **Bainbridge** and then press TAB. Type **GA** and then press TAB. Type **39817** and then press TAB.

4 Type **realtor** and then press TAB. Type **F** and then press TAB.

Q&A Instead of pressing TAB, can I click the New Entry button at the end of one row to add a new blank record?
Yes. Clicking the New Entry button at the end of a row has the same effect as pressing TAB.

5 Type **Mr.** and then press TAB. Type **Morgan** and then press TAB. Type **Huber** and then press TAB. Type **Fairview Realtors** and then press TAB.

6 Type **87 Yorktown Place** and then press TAB. Type **P.O. Box 87** and then press TAB.

7 Type **Bainbridge** and then press TAB. Type **GA** and then press TAB. Type **39817** and then press TAB.

8 Type **listing agent** and then press TAB. Type **P** and then press TAB.

9 Type **Ms.** and then press TAB. Type **Leslie** and then press TAB. Type **Rousseau** and then press TAB. Type **Rousseau Home Team** and then press TAB.

10 Type **10228 Cloud Street** and then press TAB twice. Type **Donalsonville** and then press TAB. Type **GA** and then press TAB. Type **39845** and then press TAB.

11 Type **licensed real estate agent** and then press TAB. Type **P** and then press TAB.

12 Type **Ms.** and then press TAB. Type **Amahle** and then press TAB. Type **Morales** and then press TAB. Type **Cairo Realty** and then press TAB.

13 Type **903 Poplar Lane** and then press TAB. Type **P.O. Box 903** and then press TAB.

14 Type **Cairo** and then press TAB. Type **GA** and then press TAB. Type **39828** and then press TAB.

15 Type **real estate sales agent** and then press TAB. Type **F** and then click OK (shown in Figure 6–26), which displays the Save Address List dialog box (shown in Figure 6–27).

BTW

Saving Data Sources

Word, by default, saves a data source in the My Data Sources folder on your computer or mobile device's default storage location. Likewise, when you open a data source, Word initially looks in the My Data Sources folder for the file. Because the data source files you create in Word are saved as Microsoft Access database file types, you can open and view these files in Access if you are familiar with Microsoft Access.

To Save a Data Source when Prompted by Word

When you click OK in the New Address List dialog box, Word displays the Save Address List dialog box. **Why?** Word prompts you to immediately save the data source so that you do not lose any entered information. By default, the save location is the My Data Sources folder on your computer's hard drive. In this module, you save the data source in the JobHunting folder created earlier in this module. The following steps save the data source.

1

- Type **SC_WD_6_SchorelProspectiveEmployers** in the File name box (Save Address List dialog box) as the name for the data source. Do not press ENTER after typing the file name because you do not want to close the dialog box at this time.
- Navigate to the desired save location for the data source (for example, the JobHunting folder) (Figure 6–27).

Q&A What is a Microsoft Office Address Lists file type?
It is a Microsoft Access database file. If you are familiar with Microsoft Access, you can open the SC_WD_6_SchorelProspectiveEmployers file in Access. You do not have to be familiar with Access or have Access installed on your computer, however, to continue with this mail merge process. Word stores a data source as an Access table simply because it is an efficient method of storing a data source.

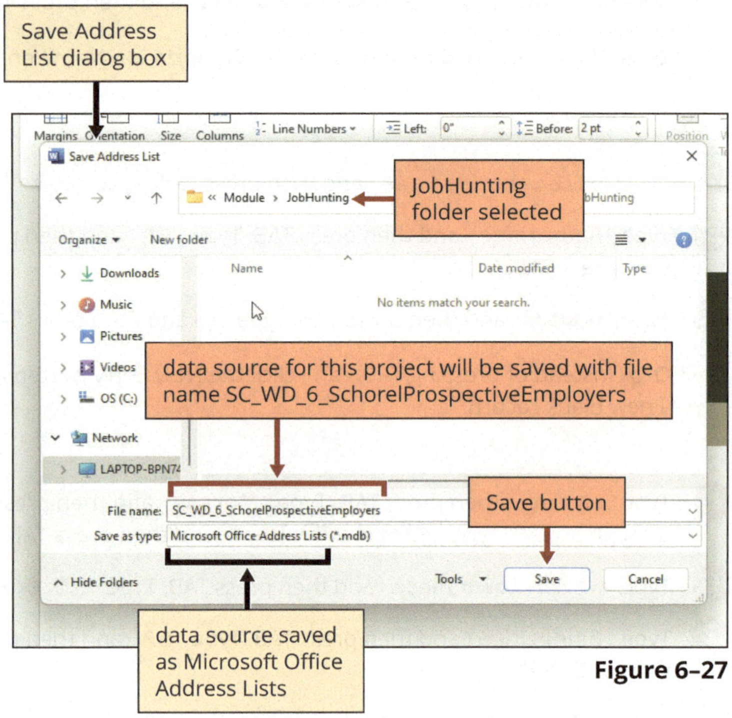

Figure 6–27

2

- Click Save (Save Address List dialog box) to save the data source in the selected folder using the entered file name and then display the Mail Merge Recipients dialog box (Figure 6–28).

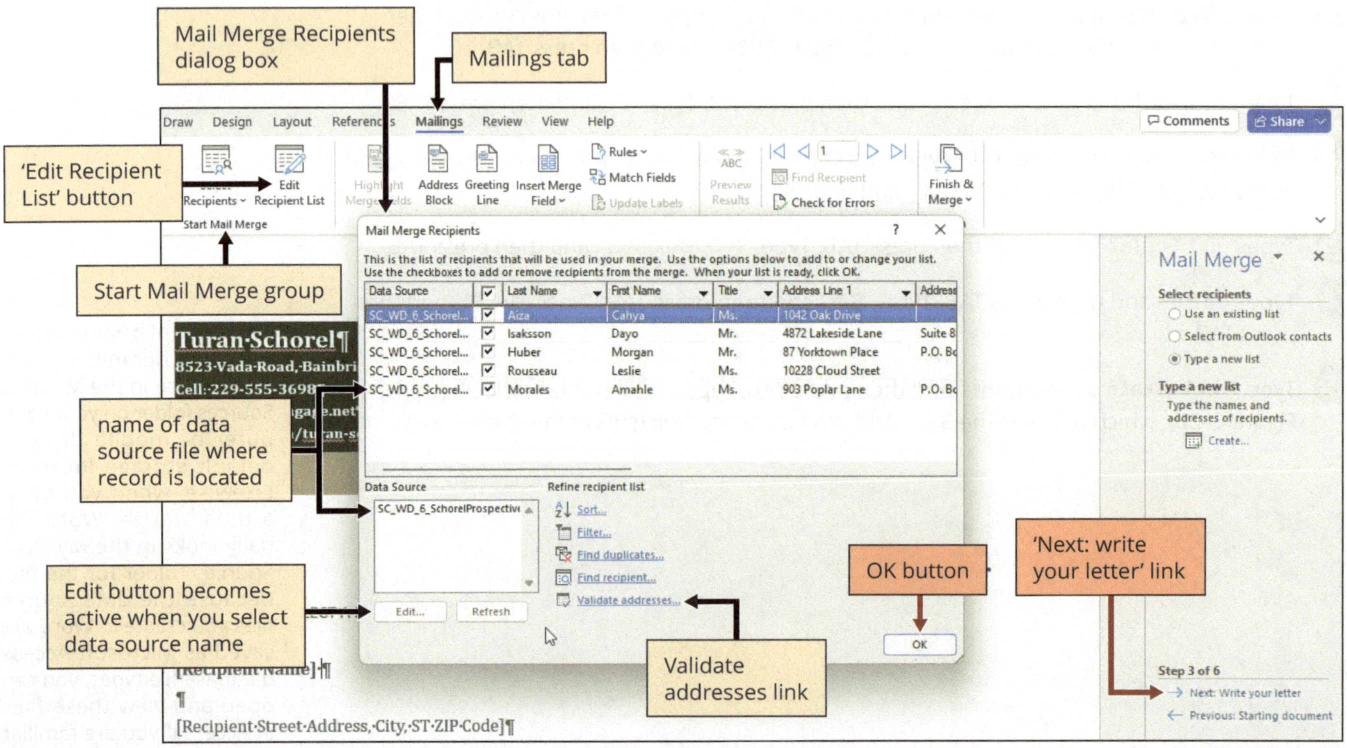

Figure 6–28

Q&A What if the fields in my Mail Merge Recipients list are in a different order?

The order of fields in the Mail Merge Recipients list has no effect on the mail merge process. If Word rearranges the order, you can leave them in the revised order.

3

- Click OK to close the Mail Merge Recipients dialog box.

Editing Data Records (Recipients) in the Data Source

All of the data records (recipients) have been entered in the data source and saved with the file name, SC_WD_6_SchorelProspectiveEmployers. To add or edit recipients in the data source, you would click the 'Edit Recipient List' button (Mailings tab | Start Mail Merge group) to display the Mail Merge Recipients dialog box (shown in Figure 6–28). Click the data source name in the Data Source list and then click the Edit button (Mail Merge Recipients dialog box) to display the data records in a dialog box similar to the one shown in Figure 6–26. Then, add or edit records as described in the previous steps. If you want to edit a particular record and the list of data records (recipients) is long, you can click the Find button to locate an item, such as a last name, quickly in the list.

To delete a record, select it using the same procedure described in the previous paragraph. Then, click the Delete Entry button in the dialog box (shown in Figure 6–26).

BTW

Validating Addresses

If you have installed address validation software, you can click the Validate addresses link (shown in Figure 6–28) in the Mail Merge Recipients dialog box to validate your recipients' addresses. If you have not yet installed address validation software and would like information about doing so, click the Validate addresses link in the Mail Merge Recipients dialog box and then click Yes in the Microsoft Word dialog box to display a related Microsoft webpage.

Using an Existing Data Source

Instead of creating a new data source, you can use an existing Microsoft Outlook Contacts list, an Access database table, or an Excel table as a data source in a mail merge. To use an existing data source, select the appropriate option in the Select recipients area in the Mail Merge pane or click the Select Recipients button (Mailings tab | Start Mail Merge group) and then click the desired option on the Select Recipients menu.

For a Microsoft Outlook Contacts list, click 'Select from Outlook contacts' in the Mail Merge pane or 'Choose from Outlook Contacts' on the Select Recipients menu to display the Select Contacts dialog box. Next, select the contact folder you wish to import (Select Contacts dialog box) and then click OK.

For other existing data source types, such as an Access database table or an Excel worksheet, click 'Use an existing list' in the Mail Merge pane or on the Select Recipients menu to display the Select Data Source dialog box. Next, select the file name of the data source you wish to use and then click the Open button (Select Data Source dialog box).

With Access, you can use any field in the database in the main document. (Later in this module you use an existing Access database table as the data source.) For the merge to work correctly with an Excel table, you must ensure data is arranged properly and that the table is the only element in the file. The first row of the table should contain unique field names, and the table cannot contain any blank rows.

Composing the Main Document for the Form Letters

The next step in this project is to enter and format the text and fields in the main document for the form letters (shown in Figure 6–1a at the beginning of this module). A **main document** contains the constant, or unchanging, text, punctuation, spaces, and graphics, as well as references to the data in the data source. You will follow these steps to compose the main document for the form letter.

1. Enter the date.
2. Enter the address block.
3. Enter the greeting line (salutation).
4. Enter text and insert a merge field.

5. Enter additional text and merge fields.
6. Insert an IF field.
7. Enter the remainder of the letter.
8. Merge the letters.

Consider This

What guidelines should you follow when composing the main document for a form letter?

The finished main document letter should look like a symmetrically framed picture with evenly spaced margins, all balanced below an attractive letterhead or return address. The content of the main document for the form letter should contain proper grammar, correct spelling, logically constructed sentences, flowing paragraphs, and sound ideas; it also should reference the data in the data source properly.

Be sure the main document for the form letter includes all essential business letter elements. All business letters should contain a date line, inside address, message, and signature block. Many business letters contain additional items, such as a special mailing notation(s), an attention line, a salutation, a subject line, a complimentary close, reference initials, and an enclosure notation. When finished, proofread your letter carefully.

To Display the Next Step in the Mail Merge Wizard

The following step displays the next step in the Mail Merge wizard, which is to write the letter.

1. Click the 'Next: Write your letter' link at the bottom of the Mail Merge pane (shown in Figure 6–28) to display Step 4 of the Mail Merge wizard in the Mail Merge pane (shown in Figure 6–29).

To Enter the Date from a Content Control

The next step is to enter the date in the letter. **Why?** All business letters should contain a date, which usually is positioned below the letterhead or return address. You can click the date content control and type the correct date, or you can click the arrow and select the date from a calendar. The following steps use the calendar to select the date.

1

- Click the Date content control to select it and then click its arrow to display a calendar.
- Scroll through the calendar months until the desired month appears, March 2029, in this case (Figure 6–29).

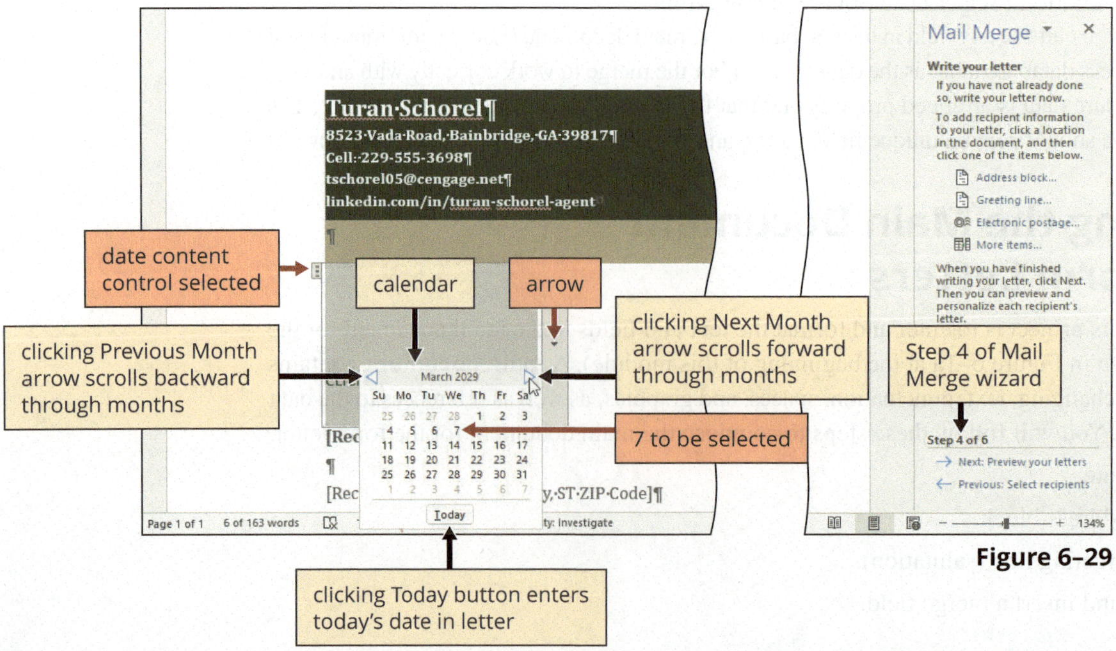

Figure 6–29

2

- Click 7 in the calendar to display the selected month, day, and year in the date line of the form letter (shown in Figure 6–30).
- Click outside the content control to deselect it.
- Right-click the date to display a shortcut menu and then click 'Remove Content Control' on the shortcut menu so that your text (the selected date) remains but the content control is deleted.

Q&A Why delete the content control?
You no longer need the content control because you already selected the date.

Other Ways

1. Type date in Date content control
2. Click 'Insert Date & Time' button (Insert tab | Text group)

Merge Fields

In this form letter, the inside address appears below the date line, and the salutation is placed below the inside address. The contents of the inside address and salutation are located in the data source. To link the data source to the main document, you insert the field names from the data source in the main document.

In the main document, field names linked to the data source are called **merge fields** because they merge, or combine, the main document with the contents of the data source; that is, merge fields indicate where the data from each data record (recipient) should be inserted when you perform a mail merge. When a merge field is inserted in the main document, Word surrounds the field name with **merge field characters**, which are chevrons (« ») that mark the beginning and ending of a merge field. Merge field characters are not on the keyboard; therefore, you cannot type them directly in the document. Word automatically displays them when a merge field is inserted in the main document.

Most letters contain an address and salutation. For this reason, Word provides an AddressBlock merge field and a GreetingLine merge field. The **AddressBlock merge field** contains several fields related to an address: Title, First Name, Middle Name, Last Name, Suffix, Company, Street Address 1, Street Address 2, City, State, and ZIP Code. When Word uses the AddressBlock merge field, it automatically looks for any fields in the associated data source that are related to an address and then formats the address block properly when you merge the data source with the main document. For example, if your inside address does not use a middle name, suffix, or company, Word omits these items from the inside address and adjusts the spacing so that the address prints correctly.

To Insert the AddressBlock Merge Field

The default format for the AddressBlock merge field is the first name and last name on one line, followed by the street address on the next line, and then the city, state, and postal code on the next line. In this letter, you want the potential employer's title (i.e., Ms.) to appear to the left of the first name. **Why?** *You want to address the potential employers formally.* You also want the organization name to appear above the street address, if it does not already. The following steps insert the AddressBlock merge field in this format.

1

- Scroll to, if necessary, and then delete the content control that contains placeholder text for the recipient's address, [Recipient Street Address, City, ST ZIP Code], and then, if necessary, press DELETE to delete the blank paragraph that followed the recipient's address.
- If a blank line appears below the [Recipient Name] placeholder text, delete the blank paragraph mark.
- Delete the [Recipient Name] placeholder text and any space that follows it but leave the paragraph mark; position the insertion point to the left of the paragraph mark because you will insert the AddressBlock merge field in that location.
- Click the Address block link in the Mail Merge pane to display the Insert Address Block dialog box.
- Scroll through the list of recipient name formats (Insert Address Block dialog box) and then, if necessary, click the format 'Mr. Joshua Randall Jr.' in this list to select it, because that format places the title to the left of the first name and last name.

- **Experiment:** Click various recipient name formats and watch the preview change in the dialog box. When finished experimenting, click 'Mr. Joshua Randall Jr.' for the format.

Q&A Why is the 'Insert company name' check box dimmed?

The data source does not have a match to the Company Name in the AddressBlock merge field so this check box will be dimmed. Recall that earlier in this project the Company Name field was renamed as Organization Name, which causes the fields to be unmatched. The next step matches these two fields. If the Organization Name already appears in your AddressBlock merge field, proceed to Step 4.

- Click the Match Fields button (Insert Address Block dialog box) to display the Match Fields dialog box (Figure 6–30).

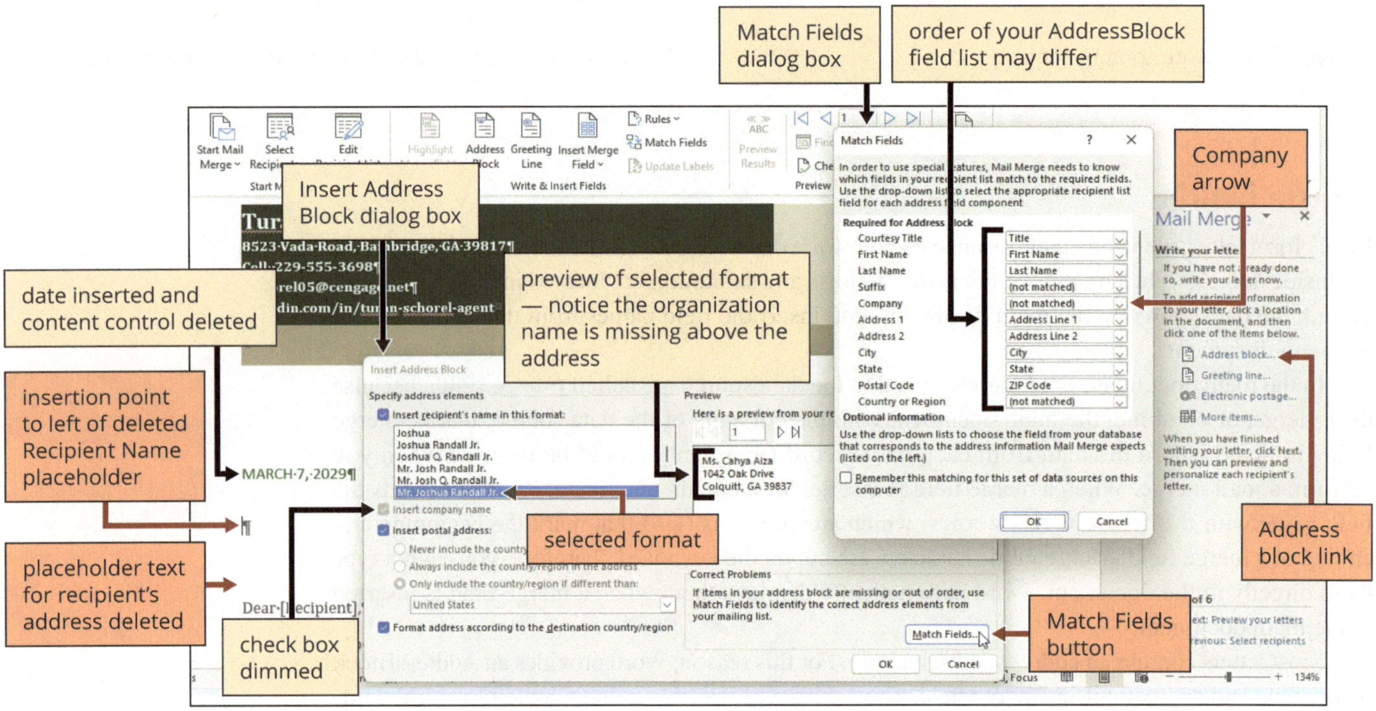

Figure 6–30

2

- Click the Company arrow (Match Fields dialog box) to display a list of fields in the data source and then click Organization Name to place that selected field as the match field (Figure 6–31).

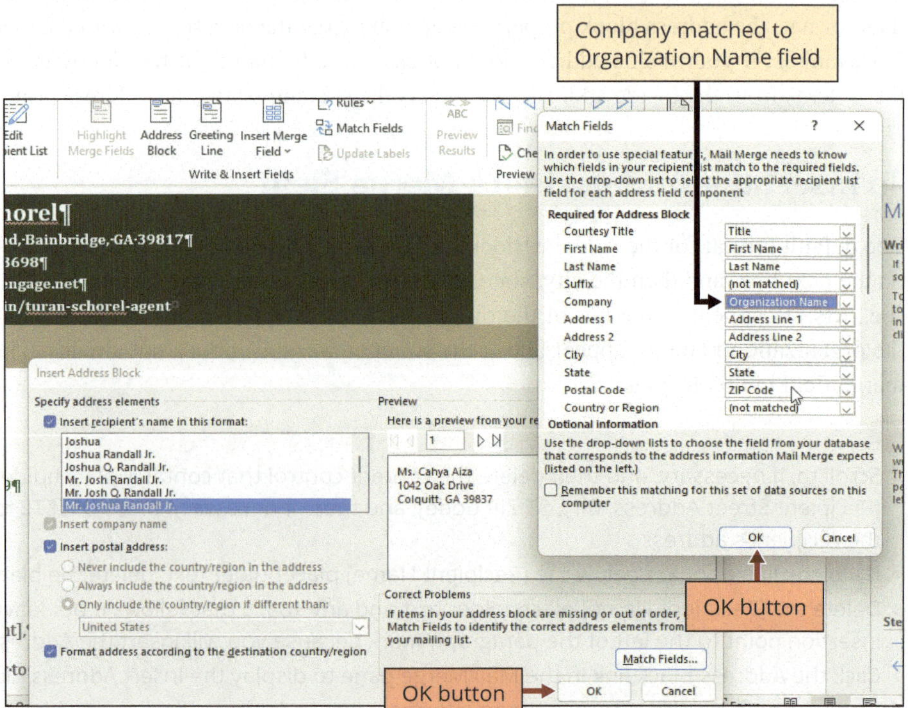

Figure 6–31

3

- Click OK (Match Fields dialog box) to close the dialog box, and notice the 'Insert company name' check box no longer is dimmed and the company name appears in the preview of the selected format (Insert Address Block dialog box) because the Company field now has a matched field in the data source.

4

- Click OK (Insert Address Block dialog box) to insert the AddressBlock merge field at the location of the insertion point (Figure 6–32).

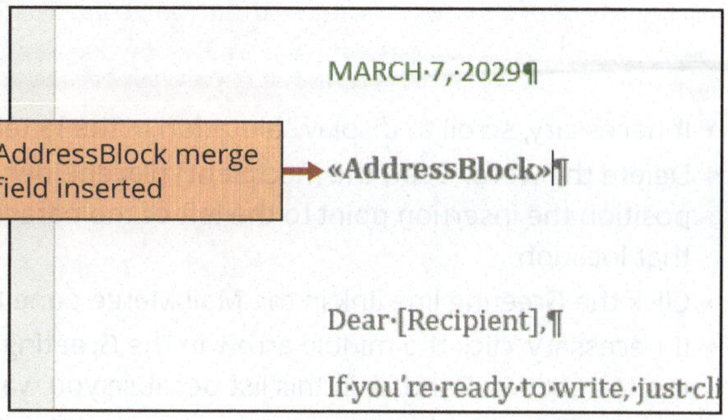

Figure 6–32

Other Ways

1. Click Address Block button (Mailings tab | Write & Insert Fields group), select options (Insert Address Block dialog box), click OK

To Edit the AddressBlock Merge Field If you wanted to change the format of or match fields in the AddressBlock merge field, you would perform the following steps.

1. Right-click the AddressBlock merge field to display a shortcut menu.
2. Click 'Edit Address Block' on the shortcut menu to display the Modify Address Block dialog box.
3. Make necessary changes and then click OK (Modify Address Block dialog box).

To Preview Results in the Main Document

Instead of displaying merge fields, you can display merged data. *Why? One way to view how fields, such as the AddressBlock fields, will look in the merged letter is to preview results.* The following step previews results.

1

- Click the Preview Results button (Mailings tab | Preview Results group) to display the values in the current data record, instead of the merge fields.
- Scroll up, if necessary, to view the address fields.
- If necessary, click to the right of the address field to deselect it (Figure 6–33).

Q&A How can I tell which record is displayed?

The current record number is displayed in the Preview Results group.

Why is the spacing in my address different from Figure 6–33?

You may have inserted the AddressBlock field on the line in the template that contained the recipient's address, instead of the line that contained the recipient's name. To fix the address spacing, select the entire address and then change the spacing before and after to 2 pt (Layout tab | Paragraph group).

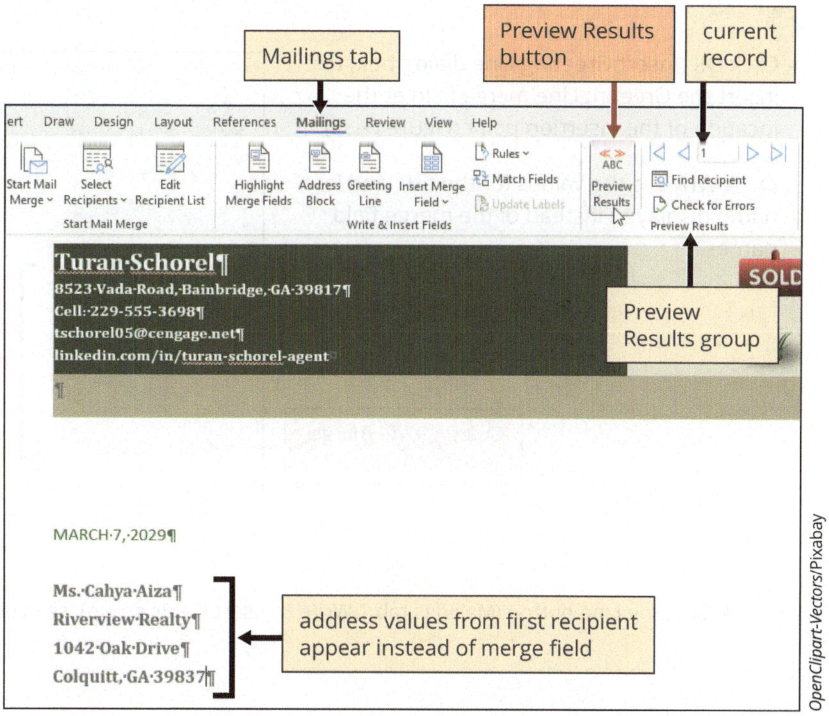

Figure 6–33

To Insert the GreetingLine Merge Field

The **GreetingLine merge field** contains text and fields related to a salutation. The default greeting for the salutation is in the format, Dear Cahya, followed by a comma. In this letter, you want the salutation to be followed by a colon. **Why?** Business letters often use a more formal salutation (Dear Ms. Aiza:). The following steps insert the GreetingLine merge field.

1

- If necessary, scroll to display salutation in the letter.
- Delete the word, Dear, the [Recipient] placeholder text, and the comma in the salutation but leave the paragraph mark; position the insertion point to the left of the paragraph mark because you will insert the GreetingLine merge field in that location.
- Click the Greeting line link in the Mail Merge pane to display the Insert Greeting Line dialog box.
- If necessary, click the middle arrow in the Greeting line format area (Insert Greeting Line dialog box); scroll to and then click the format, Mr. Randall, in this list because you want the title followed by the last name format.
- If necessary, click the rightmost arrow in the Greeting line format area and then click the colon (:) in the list (Figure 6–34).

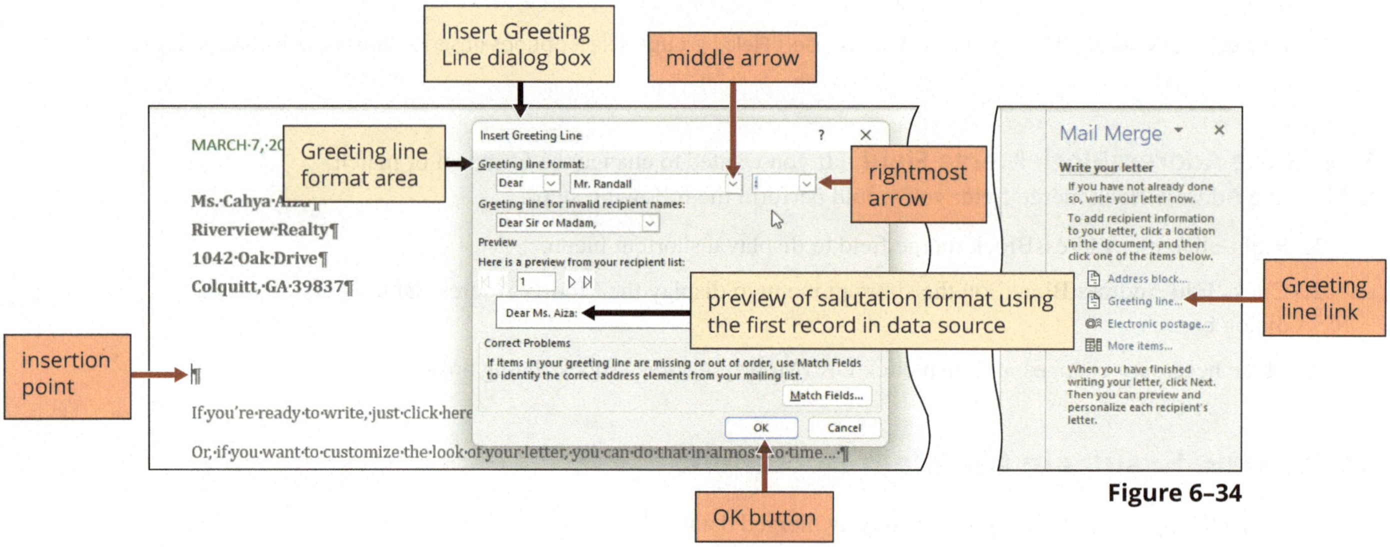

Figure 6–34

2

- Click OK (Insert Greeting Line dialog box) to insert the GreetingLine merge field at the location of the insertion point (Figure 6–35).

Q&A Why are the values for the title and last name displayed instead of the merge field names?

With the Preview Results button (Mailings tab | Preview Results group) still selected, the field values are displayed instead of the field names.

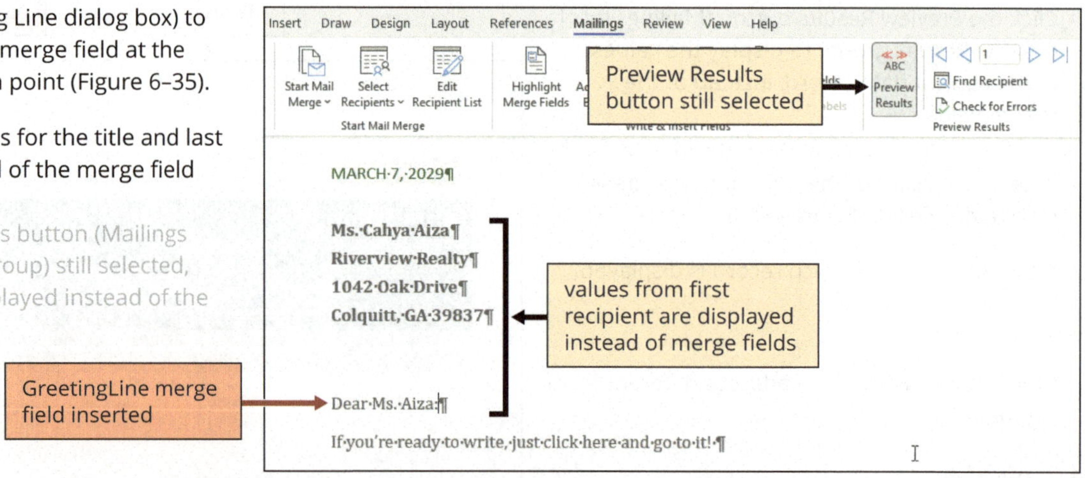

Figure 6–35

Other Ways

1. Click Greeting Line button (Mailings tab | Write & Insert Fields group), select options (Insert Greeting Line dialog box), click OK

To Edit the GreetingLine Merge Field If you wanted to change the format of or match fields in the GreetingLine merge field, you would perform the following steps.

1. Right-click the GreetingLine merge field to display a shortcut menu.
2. Click 'Edit Greeting Line' on the shortcut menu to display the Modify Greeting Line dialog box.
3. Make the necessary changes and then click OK (Modify Greeting Line dialog box).

To View Merge Fields in the Main Document

Because you will be entering merge fields in the document next, you wish to display the merge fields instead of the merged data. The following step views merge fields instead of merged data.

1. Click the Preview Results button (Mailings tab | Preview Results group) to display the merge fields instead of the values in the current data record (shown in Figure 6–36).

To Begin Typing the Body of the Form Letter

The next step is to begin typing the message, or body of the letter, which is located at the content control that begins with the placeholder text, If you're ready to write..., below the GreetingLine merge field. The following steps begin typing the letter at the location of the content control.

1. Click the body of the letter to select the content control (Figure 6–36).
2. With the content control selected, type **I will be graduating this May from Coastal Plains College with a Bachelor of Science degree in Business Administration. My education, experience, and credentials make me an ideal candidate for the** and then press SPACEBAR (shown in Figure 6–37).

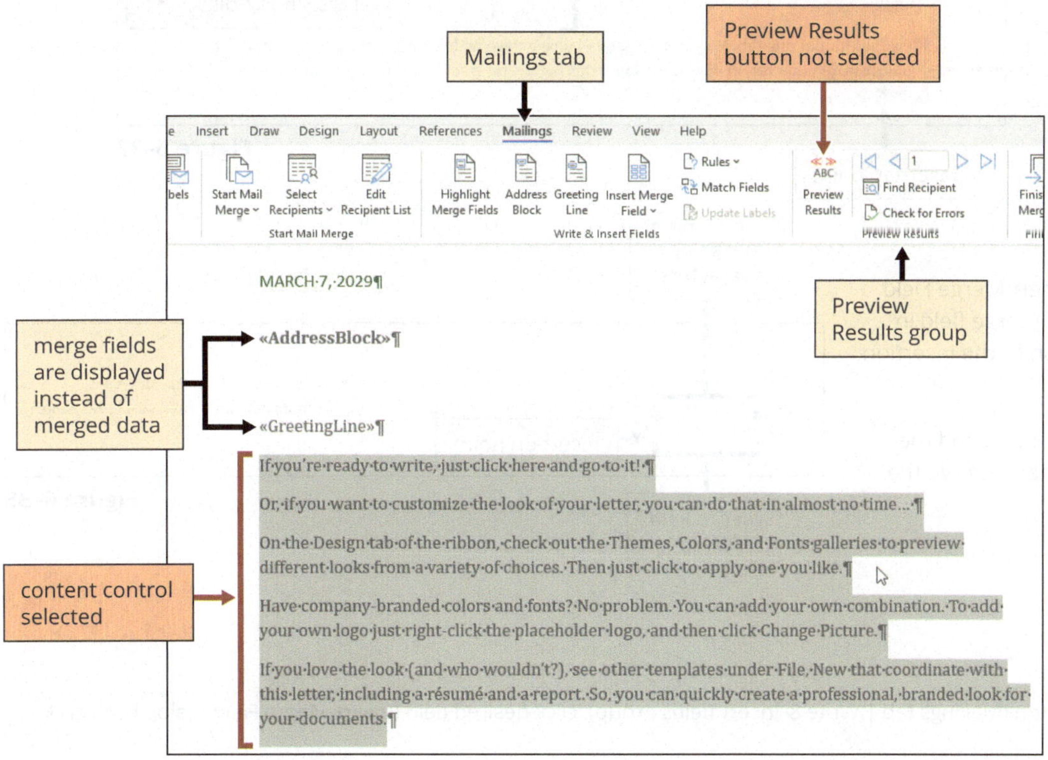

Figure 6–36

BTW
'Insert Merge Field' Button
If you click the 'Insert Merge Field' button instead of the 'Insert Merge Field' arrow (shown in Figure 6–37), Word displays the Insert Merge Field dialog box instead of the Insert Merge Field menu. To insert fields from the dialog box, click the field name and then click the Insert button. The dialog box remains open so that you can insert multiple fields, if necessary. When you have finished inserting fields, click Close in the dialog box.

To Insert a Merge Field in the Main Document

The next step is to insert the Job Position merge field into the main document. **Why?** The first sentence in the first paragraph of the letter identifies the advertised job position, which is a merge field. To instruct Word to use data fields from the data source, you insert merge fields in the main document for the form letter. The following steps insert a merge field at the location of the insertion point.

1

- Click the 'Insert Merge Field' arrow (Mailings tab | Write & Insert Fields group) to display the Insert Merge Field menu (Figure 6–37).

Q&A What if I accidentally click the 'Insert Merge Field' button instead of the arrow?
Click Cancel in the Insert Merge Field dialog box and repeat Step 1.

Why is the underscore character in some of the field names?
Word places an underscore character in place of the space in merge fields.

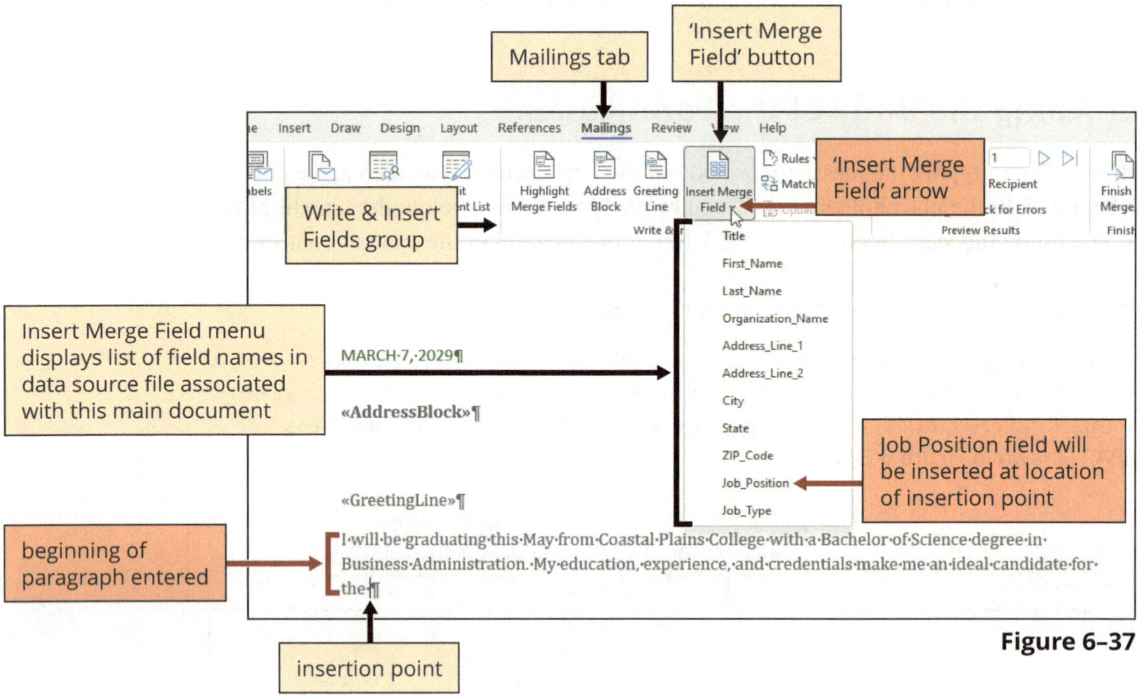

Figure 6–37

2

- Click Job_Position on the Insert Merge Field menu to insert the selected merge field in the document at the location of the insertion point (Figure 6–38).

Q&A Will the words, Job Position, and the chevron characters print when I merge the form letters?
No. When you merge the data source with the main document, the value in the Job Position field (e.g., real estate agent) will print at the location of the merge field, Job Position.

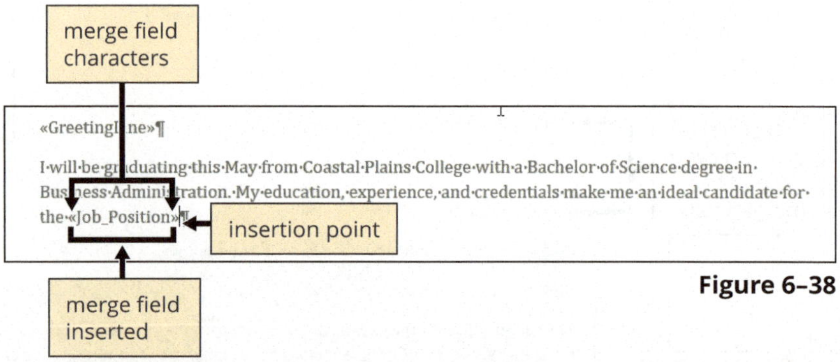

Figure 6–38

Other Ways

1. Click 'Insert Merge Field' button (Mailings tab | Write & Insert fields group), click desired field (Insert Merge Field dialog box), click Insert button, click Close

To Enter More Text and Merge Fields in the Main Document

The following steps enter more text and merge fields into the form letter.

1. With the insertion point at the location shown in Figure 6–38, press SPACEBAR, type **position at** and then press SPACEBAR again.

2. Click the 'Insert Merge Field' arrow (Mailings tab | Write & Insert Fields group) and then click Organization_Name on the Insert Merge Field menu to insert the selected merge field in the document. Press PERIOD.

3. Press ENTER. Type **As shown on the accompanying resume, my qualifications match the job requirements posted through the Career Development Center at Coastal Plains College. My background has prepared me for a career in real estate.** and then press ENTER.

4. Type **Thank you in advance,** and then press SPACEBAR. Insert the Title merge field, press SPACEBAR, and then insert the Last Name merge field. Type **, for your time and consideration. I look forward to hearing from you soon to discuss the opportunity of my potential** and then press SPACEBAR (shown in Figure 6–39).

BTW
Merge Fields
When you insert merge fields in a document, the displayed fields may be surrounded by braces instead of chevrons, and extra instructions may appear between the braces. If this occurs, then field codes have been turned on. To turn off field codes so that they are not displayed, press ALT+F9.

IF Fields

In addition to merge fields, you can insert Word fields that are designed specifically for a mail merge. An **IF field** is an example of a Word field used during a mail merge that tests whether a condition is true. One form of the IF field is called an **If...Then**: If a condition is true, then perform an action. For example, if Mary owns a house, then send her information about homeowner insurance. Another form of the IF field is called an **If...Then...Else**, where Word chooses between two options, depending on the contents of a particular field. If a condition is true, Word then performs an action; otherwise (else) Word performs a different action. For example, if John has an email address, then send him an email message; else send him the message via the postal service.

In this project, the form letter checks the job type and displays text associated with the job type. If the job type is F, then the form letter should print the text, full-time; else if the job type is P, then the form letter should print the text, part-time. Thus, you will use an If...Then...Else.

The phrase that appears after the word If is called a rule, or condition. A **condition** consists of an expression, followed by a comparison operator, followed by a final expression.

Expression The expression in a condition can be a merge field, a number, a series of characters, or a mathematical formula. Word surrounds a series of characters with quotation marks ("). To indicate an empty, or null, expression, Word places two quotation marks together ("").

Comparison Operator The comparison operator in a condition must be one of six characters: = (equal to or matches the text), <> (not equal to or does not match text), < (less than), <= (less than or equal to), > (greater than), or >= (greater than or equal to).

If the result of a condition is true, then Word evaluates the **true text**. If the result of the condition is false, Word evaluates the **false text** if it exists. In this project, the first expression in the condition is a merge field (Job_Type); the comparison operator is equal to (=); and the second expression is the text "F". The true text is "full-time". The false text is "part-time". The complete IF field is as follows:

IF Job_Type = "F"	"full-time"	"part-time"
condition	true text	false text

BTW
IF Fields
The phrase, IF field, originates from computer programming. Do not be intimidated by the terminology. An IF field simply specifies a decision. Some software developers refer to it as an IF statement. Complex IF statements include one or more nested IF fields. A nested IF field is a second IF field inside the true or false text of the first IF field.

To Insert an IF Field in the Main Document

The next step is to insert an IF field in the main document. **Why?** You want to indicate whether the job is for full-time or part-time employment in the letter. The following steps insert this IF field in the form letter: If the Job_Type is equal to F, then insert full-time, else insert part-time.

1

- With the insertion point positioned as shown in Figure 6–39, click the Rules button (Mailings tab | Write & Insert Fields group) to display the Rules menu (Figure 6–39).

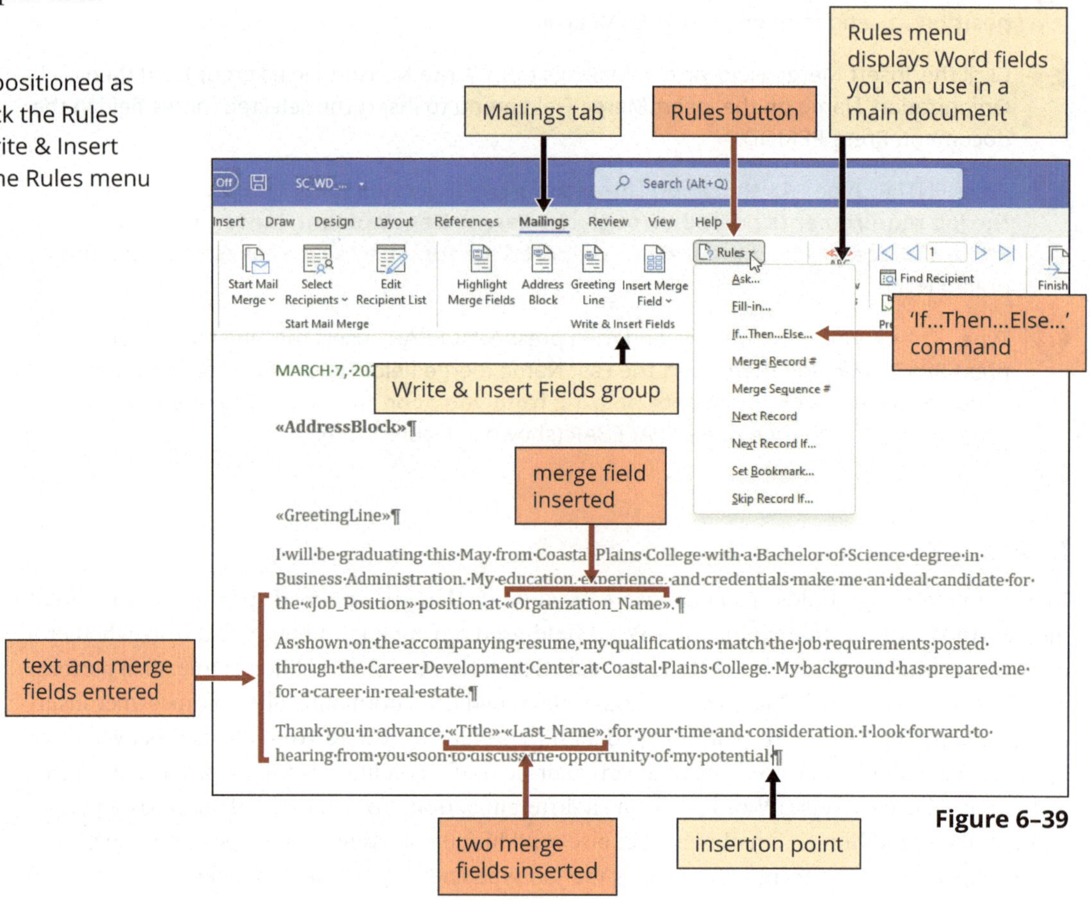

Figure 6–39

2

- Click 'If...Then...Else...' on the Rules menu to display the Insert Word Field: IF dialog box, which is where you enter the components of the IF field (Figure 6–40).

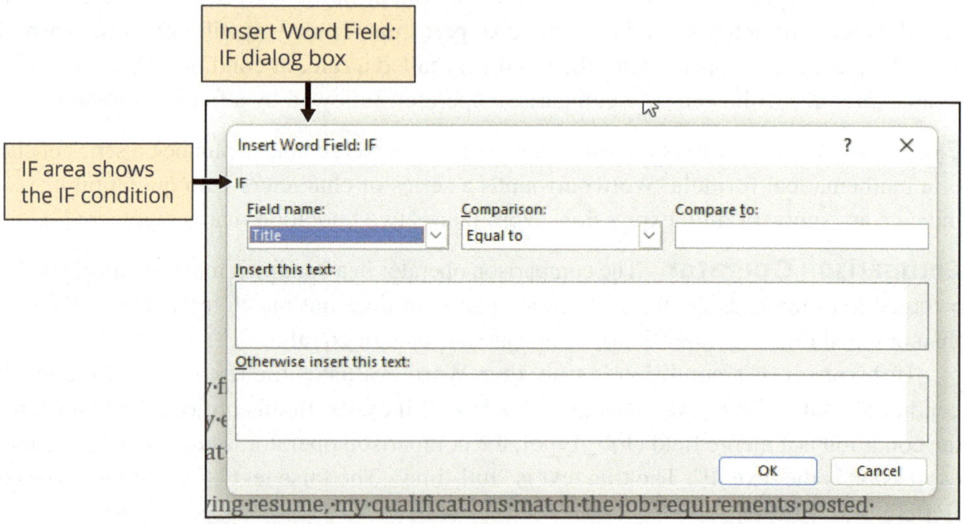

Figure 6–40

3

- Click the Field name arrow (Insert Word Field: IF dialog box) to display the list of fields in the data source.
- Scroll through the list of fields in the Field name list and then click Job_Type to select the field.
- Position the insertion point in the Compare to text box and then type **F** as the comparison text.
- Press TAB and then type **full-time** as the true text.
- Press TAB and then type **part-time** as the false text (Figure 6–41).

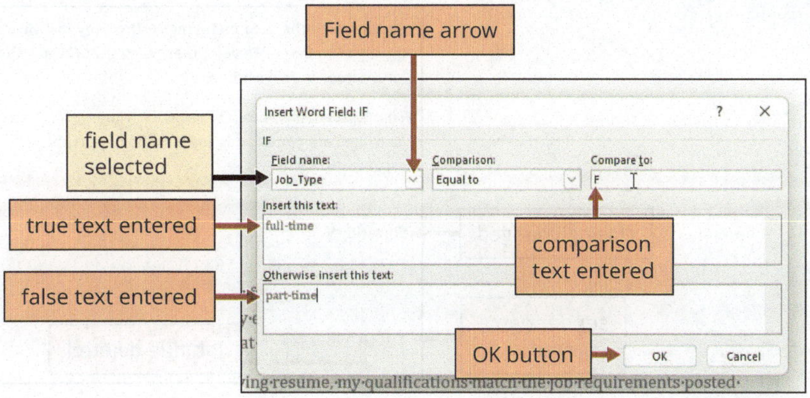

Figure 6–41

Q&A Does the capitalization matter in the comparison text?
Yes. The text, F, is different from the text, f, in a comparison. Be sure to enter the text exactly as you entered it in the data source.

4

- Click OK (Insert Word Field: IF dialog box) to insert the IF field at the location of the insertion point (Figure 6–42).

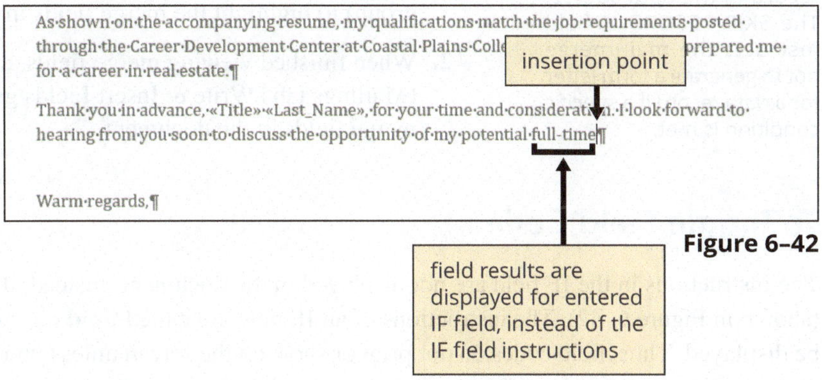

Figure 6–42

Q&A Why does the main document display the text, full-time, instead of the IF field instructions?
The text, full-time, is displayed because the first record in the data source has a job type equal to F. Word, by default, evaluates the IF field using the current record and displays the results, called the **field results**, in the main document instead of displaying the IF field instructions. Later in the module, you will view the IF field instructions.

To Enter the Remaining Text in the Main Document

The following steps enter the remainder of the text into the form letter.

1. Press SPACEBAR. Type **employment at your organization.**
2. Change the closing to the word, Sincerely.
3. Change the placeholder text in the Your Name content control to Turan Schorel. If necessary, delete the content control so that the name remains but the content control is deleted.
4. Delete the Your Title content control and the paragraph mark that follows it (Figure 6–43).
5. Make any additional adjustments to spacing, formats, etc., so that your main document looks like Figure 6–1 shown at the beginning of this module.

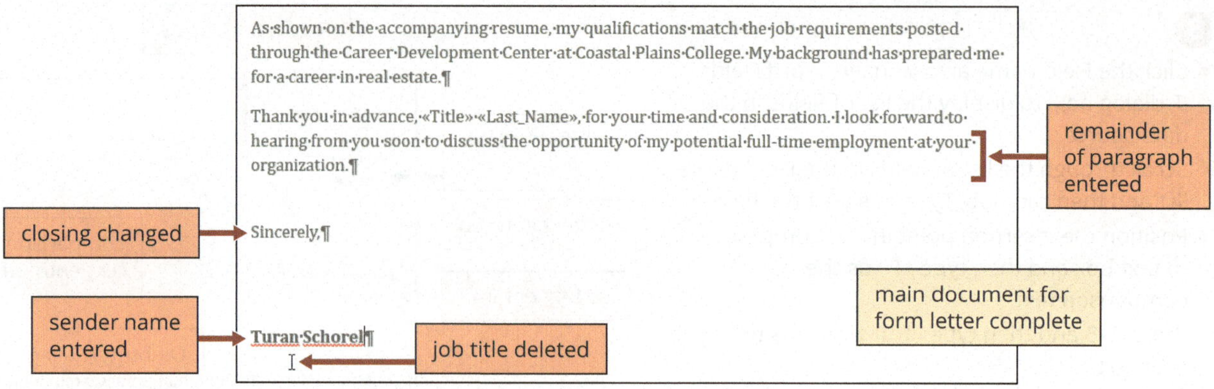

Figure 6–43

BTW
Word Fields
In addition to the IF field, Word provides other fields that may be used in form letters. For example, the ASK and FILLIN fields prompt the user to enter data for each record in the data source. The SKIP RECORD IF field instructs the mail merge not to generate a form letter for a data record if a specific condition is met.

To Highlight Merge Fields If you wanted to highlight all the merge fields in a document so that you could identify them quickly, you would perform the following steps.

1. Click the 'Highlight Merge Fields' button (Mailings tab | Write & Insert Fields group) to highlight the merge fields in the document.
2. When finished viewing merge fields, click the 'Highlight Merge Fields' button (Mailings tab | Write & Insert Fields group) again to remove the highlight from the merge fields in the document.

To Toggle Field Codes

The instructions in the IF field are not displayed in the document; instead, the field results are displayed for the current record (shown in Figure 6–42). The instructions of an IF field are called **field codes**, and the default for Word is for field codes not to be displayed. Thus, field codes do not print or show on the screen unless you turn them on. You use one procedure to show field codes on the screen and a different procedure to print them on a hard copy.

The following steps display a field code on the screen. **Why?** You might want to turn on a field code to verify its accuracy or to modify it. Field codes tend to clutter the screen. Thus, most Word users turn them off after viewing them.

1

- If necessary, scroll to display the last paragraph of the letter in the document window.
- Right-click the field results showing the text, full-time, to display a shortcut menu (Figure 6–44).

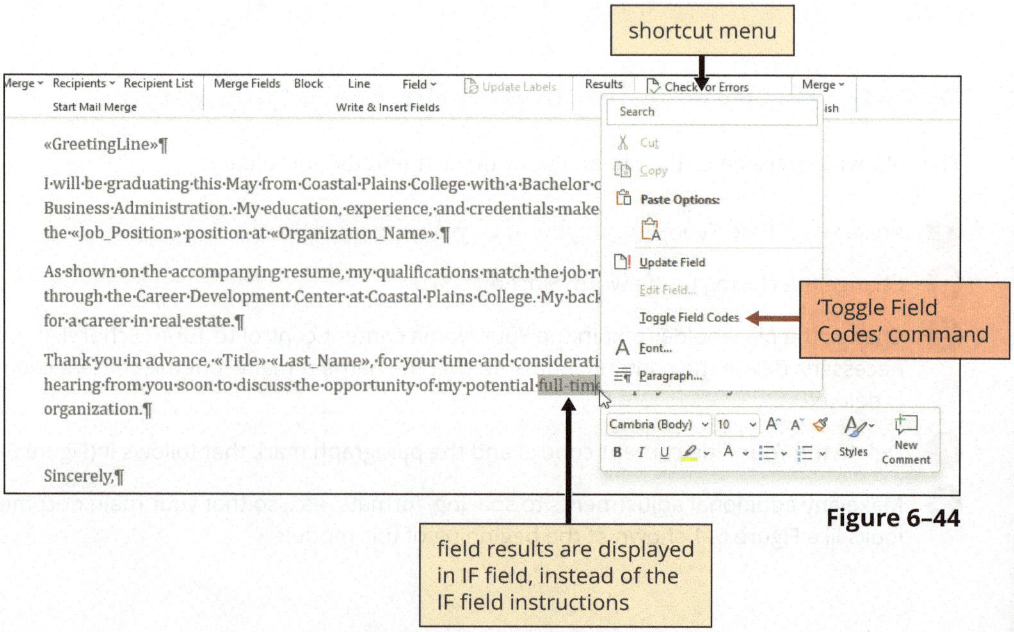

Figure 6–44

2

- Click 'Toggle Field Codes' on the shortcut menu to display the field codes instead of the field results for the IF field (Figure 6–45).

Q&A Will displaying field codes affect the merged documents?

No. Displaying field codes has no effect on the merge process.

What if I wanted to display all field codes in a document?

You would press ALT+F9. Then, to hide all the field codes, press ALT+F9 again.

Why does the IF field turn gray?

Word, by default, shades a field in gray when the field is selected. The shading appears on the screen to help you identify fields; the shading does not print on a hard copy.

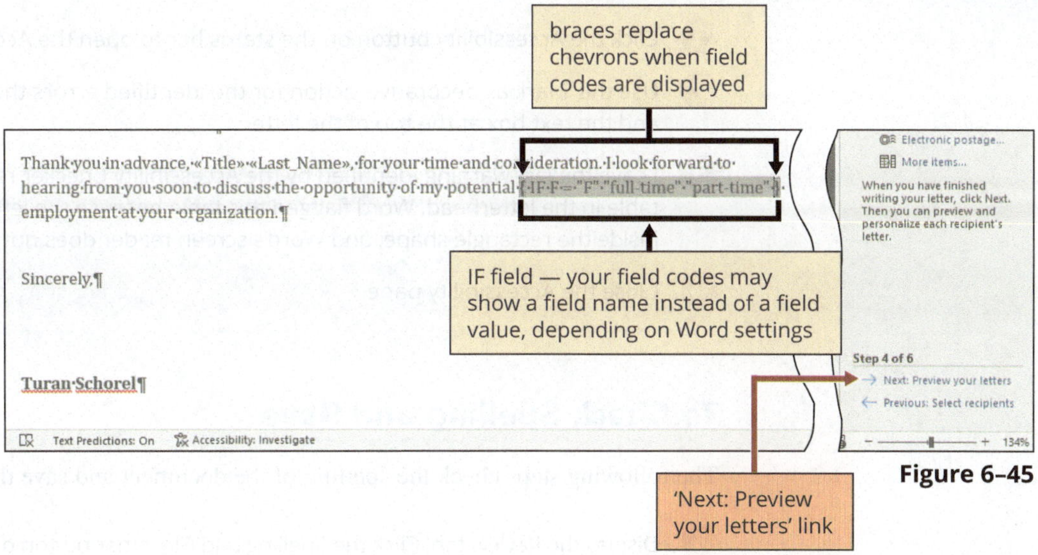

Figure 6–45

Other Ways

1. With insertion point in field, press ALT+F9

To Print Field Codes in the Main Document

When you merge or print a document, Word automatically converts field codes that are displayed on the screen to field results. You may want to print the field codes version of the form letter, however, so that you have a hard copy of the field codes for future reference. When you print field codes, you must remember to turn off the field codes option so that merged documents print field results instead of field codes. If you wanted to print the field codes in the main document, you would perform the following steps.

1. Open Backstage view and then click Options to display the Word Options dialog box.
2. Click Advanced in the left pane (Word Options dialog box) to display advanced options in the right pane and then scroll to the Print area in the right pane of the dialog box.
3. Place a check mark in the 'Print field codes instead of their values' check box.
4. Click OK to instruct Word to display field codes when the document prints.
5. Open Backstage view, click Print, and then click the Print button to print the document with all field codes visible.
6. Open Backstage view and then click Options to display the Word Options dialog box.
7. Click Advanced in the left pane (Word Options dialog box) to display advanced options in the right pane and then scroll to the Print area in the right pane of the dialog box.
8. Remove the check mark from the 'Print field codes instead of their values' check box.
9. Click OK to instruct Word to display field results the next time you print the document.

BTW

Locking Fields

If you wanted to lock a field so that its field results cannot be changed, click the field and then press CTRL+F11. To subsequently unlock a field so that it may be updated, click the field and then press CTRL+SHIFT+F11.

BTW

Printing Document Properties

To print document properties, click File on the ribbon to open Backstage view, click Print in Backstage view to display the Print screen, click the first button in the Settings area to display a list of options specifying what you can print, click Document Info in the list to specify you want to print the document properties instead of the actual document, and then click the Print button in the Print screen to print the document properties on the currently selected printer.

To Use the Accessibility Checker

Recall that Word includes an Accessibility Checker that identifies potential accessibility issues and presents suggestions to make your documents more inclusive. Notice that instead of the phrase, Good to go, the Accessibility button on the status bar displays the word, Investigate. The following steps use the Accessibility Checker.

1. Click the Accessibility button on the status bar to open the Accessibility pane.
2. Use the 'Mark as decorative' action for the identified errors that relate to the sold sign image and the text box at the top of the letter.
3. Leave the last warning identified by the Accessibility Checker related to reading order of the table in the letterhead. Word flagged this table because the letter template inserted the table inside the rectangle shape, and Word's screen reader does not read the content of shapes.
4. Close the Accessibility pane.

To Check Spelling and Save

The following steps check the spelling of the document and save the document.

1. Display the Review tab. Click the Spelling and Grammar button or Editor button (Review tab | Proofing group) to begin the spelling and grammar check. Correct any misspelled words. Ignore proper names. When finished checking spelling, if necessary, close the Editor pane.
2. sam Save the main document for the form letter again on the same storage location with the same file name.

Opening a Main Document

You open a main document the same as you open any other Word document (i.e., clicking Open in Backstage view). If Word displays a dialog box indicating it will run an SQL command, click Yes (Figure 6–46).

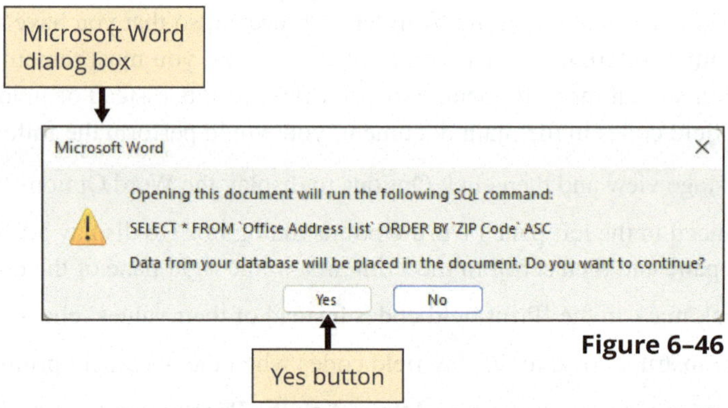

Figure 6–46

When you open a main document, Word attempts to open the associated data source file, too. If the data source is not in exactly the same location (i.e., drive and folder) as when it originally was saved, Word may display a dialog box indicating that it could not find the data source (Figure 6–47). When this occurs, click the 'Find Data Source' button to display the Open Data Source dialog box, which allows you to locate the data source file. (Word may display several messages or dialog boxes requiring you to click an OK (or similar) button until the one shown in Figure 6–47 appears.)

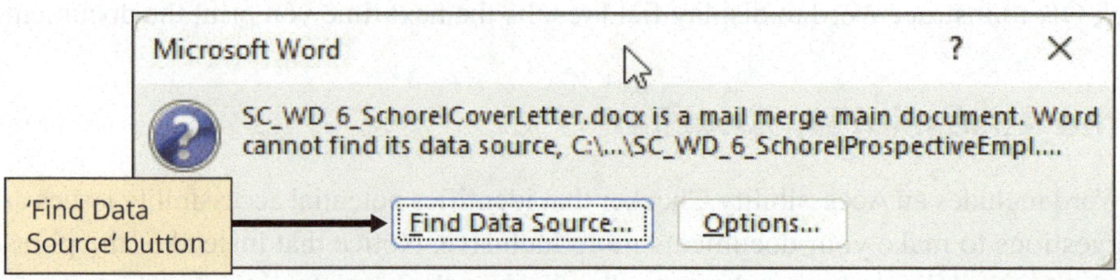

Figure 6–47

BTW
Data Source and Main Document Files
When you open a main document, if Word cannot locate the associated data source file or it does not display a dialog box with the 'Find Data Source' button, then the data source may not be associated with the main document. To associate the data source with the main document, click the Select Recipients button (Mailings tab | Start Mail Merge group), click 'Use an Existing List' on the Select Recipients menu, and then locate the data source file. When you save the main document, Word will associate the data source with the main document.

Break Point: If you want to take a break, this is a good place to do so. You can exit Word now. To resume later, start Word, open the file called SC_WD_6_SchorelCoverLetter.docx, and continue following the steps from this location forward.

Merging the Recipient List in the Data Source with the Main Document to Generate Form Letters

The next step in this project is to merge the recipient list in the data source with the main document to generate the form letters (shown in Figure 6–1c at the beginning of this module). **Merging** is the process of combining the contents of a data source with a main document.

You can merge the form letters to a new document, which you can edit, or you can merge the form letters directly to a printer. You also have the option of merging all data in a data source or merging just a portion of it. The following sections discuss various ways to merge.

To Preview a Mail Merge Using the Mail Merge Wizard

Earlier in this module, you previewed the data in the letters using a button on the ribbon. The following step uses the Mail Merge wizard to preview the letters. **Why?** The next wizard step previews the letters so that you can verify the content is accurate before performing the merge.

1

- Click the 'Next: Preview your letters' link at the bottom of the Mail Merge pane (shown in Figure 6–45) to display Step 5 of the Mail Merge wizard in the Mail Merge pane (Figure 6–48).
- **Experiment:** Click the forward and backward buttons in the Preview your letters area in the Mail Merge pane and watch the contents of the letter change to display various recipients in the data source. When you are finished experimenting, display recipient 1.

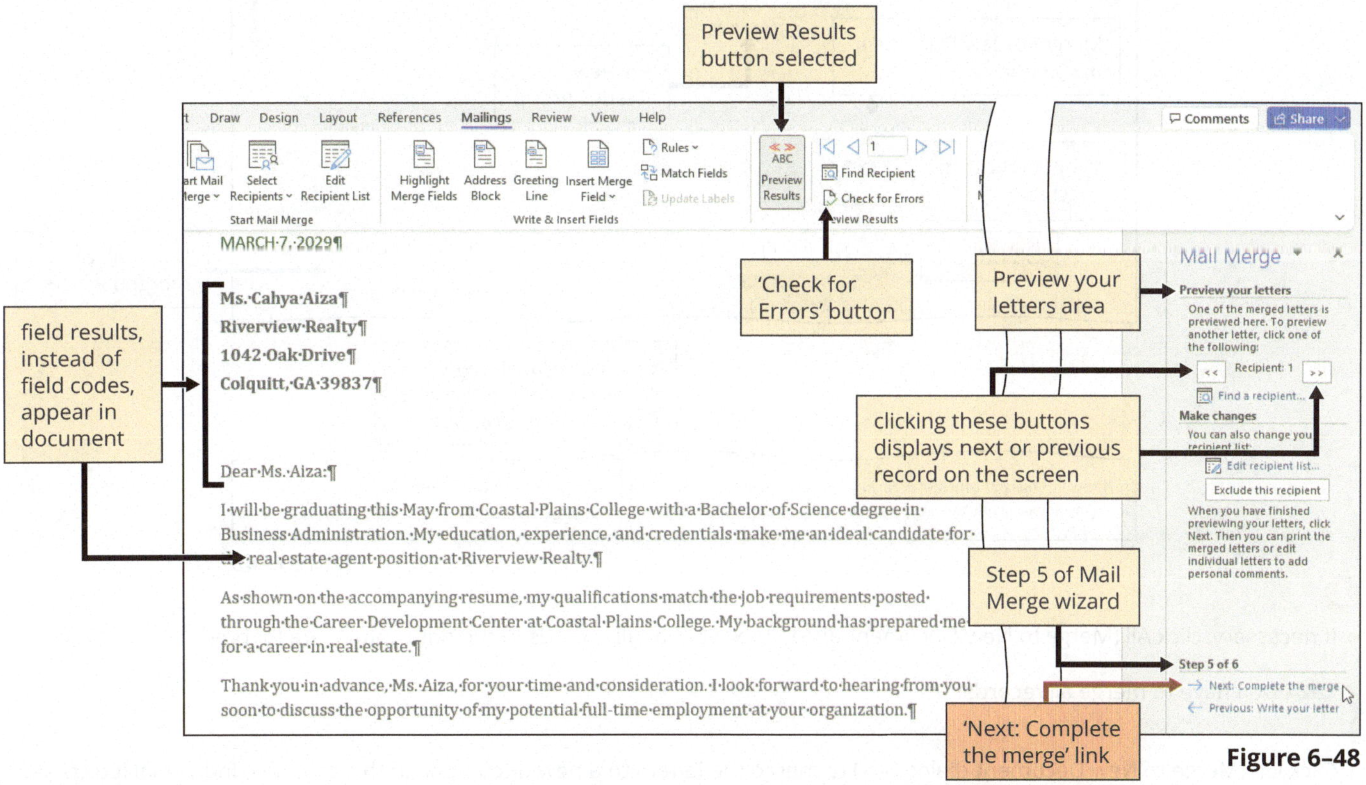

Figure 6–48

To Check for Errors Before merging documents, you can instruct Word to check for errors that might occur during the merge process. If you wanted to check for errors, you would perform the following steps.

1. Click the 'Check for Errors' button (Mailings tab | Preview Results group) (shown in Figure 6–48) or press ALT+SHIFT+K to display the Checking and Reporting Errors dialog box.
2. Select the desired option and then click OK.

To Merge the Form Letters to a New Document Using the Mail Merge Wizard

With the data source and main document for the form letter complete, the next step is to merge them to generate the individual form letters. You can merge the letters to the printer or to a new document. **Why?** If you merge the documents to a new document, you can save the merged documents in a file and then print them later, review the merged documents for accuracy and edit them as needed, or you can add personal messages to individual merged letters. The following steps merge the form letters to a new document.

1

- Click the 'Next: Complete the merge' link at the bottom of the Mail Merge pane (shown in Figure 6–48) to display Step 6 of the Mail Merge wizard in the Mail Merge pane.
- Click the 'Edit individual letters' link in the Mail Merge pane to display the Merge to New Document dialog box (Figure 6–49).

Q&A What if I wanted to print the merged letters immediately instead of reviewing them first in a new document window?
You would click the Print link instead of the 'Edit individual letters' link.

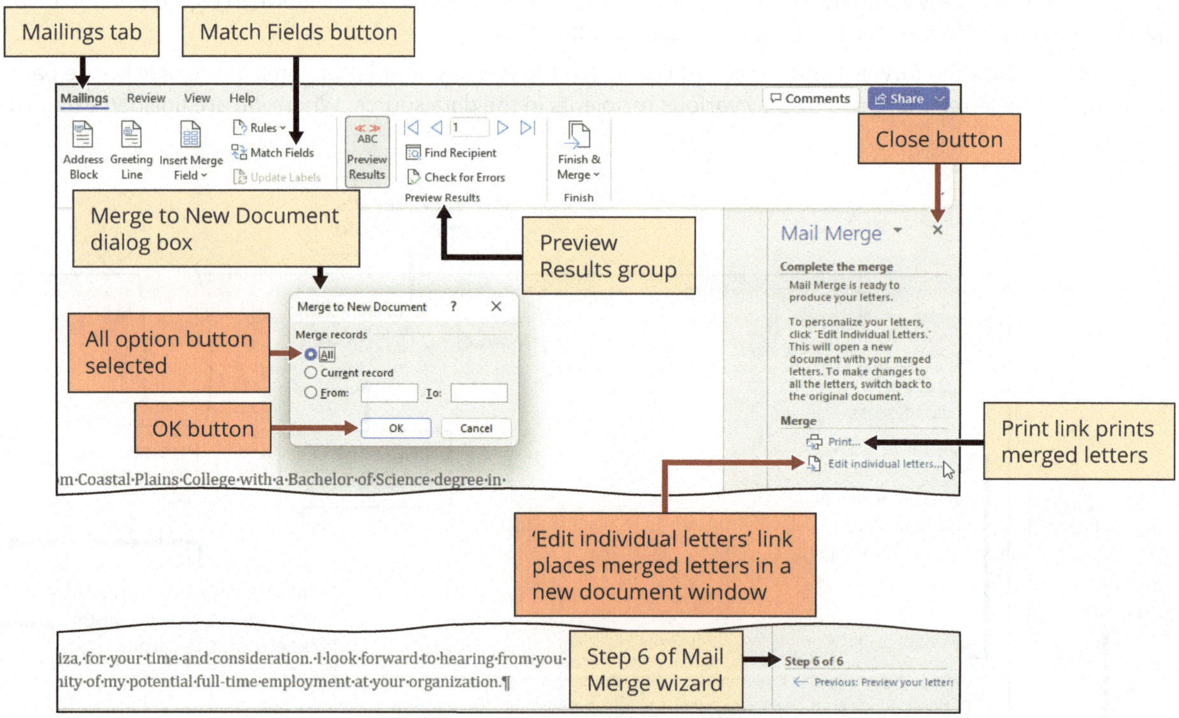

Figure 6–49

2

- If necessary, click All (Merge to New Document dialog box) so that all records in the data source are merged.

Q&A Do I have to merge all records?
No. Through this dialog box, you can merge the current record or a range of record numbers.

- Click OK (Merge to New Document dialog box) to merge the letters to a new document, in this case, five individual letters — one for each potential employer in the recipient list in the data source. (If Word displays a dialog box containing a message about locked fields, click OK.)

3

- Display the View tab and then click the Multiple Pages button (View tab | Zoom group) so that you can view miniature versions of all five letters in the document window at once (Figure 6–50). (You may need to change the zoom percentage to view all five letters at once on your screen.)

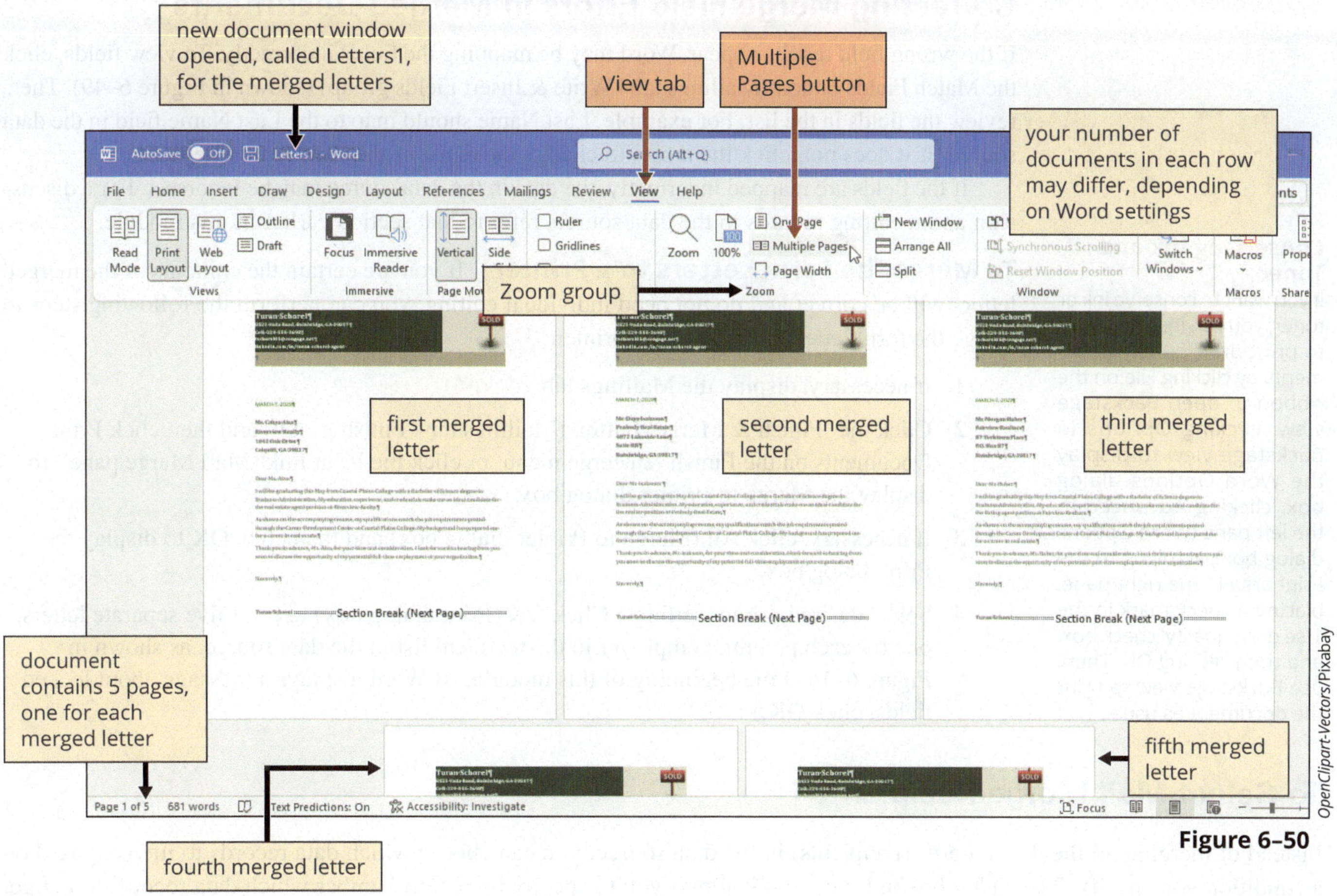

Figure 6–50

4

- Change the zoom back to page width.
- **Experiment:** Scroll through the merged documents so that you can read all five letters.

Q&A Why does my screen display an extra blank page at the end?
You might have a blank record in the recipient list in the data source, or the spacing may cause an overflow to a blank page.

Can I edit the merged letters?
Yes, you can edit the letters as you edit any other Word document. Always proofread the merged letters for accuracy before distributing them.

5

- Save the merged letters in the JobHunting folder on your hard drive, OneDrive, or other storage location using the file name, SC_WD_6_SchorelMergedCoverLetters. If requested by your instructor, print the merged letters. Close the document window containing the merged letters.

Q&A Do I have to save the document containing the merged letters?
No. You can close the document without saving it.

- If necessary, click the Close button on the Mail Merge pane title bar (shown in Figure 6–49) because you are finished with the Mail Merge wizard.
- If necessary, click the Preview Results button (Mailings tab | Preview Results group) to display field codes instead of merged data.

Other Ways

1. Click 'Finish & Merge' button (Mailings tab | Finish group), click 'Edit Individual Documents'

Correcting Merge Field Errors in Merged Documents

If the wrong field results appear, Word may be mapping the fields incorrectly. To view fields, click the Match Fields button (Mailings tab | Write & Insert Fields group) (shown in Figure 6–49). Then, review the fields in the list. For example, Last Name should map to the Last Name field in the data source. If it does not, click the arrow to change the name of the data source field.

If the fields are mapped incorrectly, the data in the data source may be incorrect. For a discussion about editing records in the data source, refer to that section earlier in this module.

BTW
Conserving Ink and Toner
If you want to conserve ink or toner, you can instruct Word to print draft quality documents by clicking File on the ribbon to open Backstage view, clicking Options in Backstage view to display the Word Options dialog box, clicking Advanced in the left pane (Word Options dialog box), scrolling to the Print area in the right pane, placing a check mark in the 'Use draft quality' check box, and then clicking OK. Then, use Backstage view to print the document as usual.

To Merge the Form Letters to a Printer If you are certain the contents of the merged letters will be correct and do not need individual editing, you can perform the following steps to merge the form letters directly to the printer.

1. If necessary, display the Mailings tab.
2. Click the 'Finish & Merge' button (Mailings tab | Finish group) and then click Print Documents on the Finish & Merge menu, or click the Print link (Mail Merge pane), to display the Merge to Printer dialog box.
3. If necessary, click All (Merge to Printer dialog box) and then click OK to display the Print dialog box.
4. Select desired printer settings. Click OK (Print dialog box) to print five separate letters, one for each potential employer in the recipient list in the data source, as shown in Figure 6–1c at the beginning of this module. (If Word displays a message about locked fields, click OK.)

To Select Mail Merge Recipients

Instead of merging all the data records (recipients) in the data source, you can choose which data records to merge, based on a condition you specify. The dialog box in Figure 6–49 allows you to specify by record number which data records to merge. Often, though, you want to merge based on the contents of a specific field. The following steps select data records (recipients) for a merge. **Why?** You want to merge just those potential employers who are advertising part-time employment.

1

- Click the 'Edit Recipient List' button (Mailings tab | Start Mail Merge group) to display the Mail Merge Recipients dialog box (Figure 6–51).

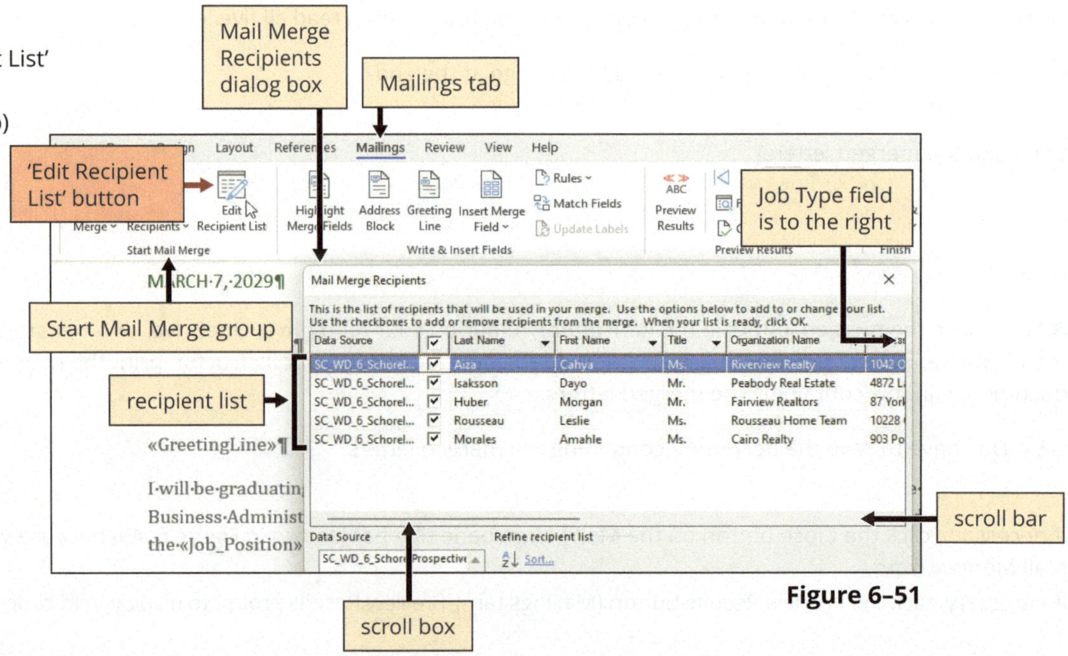

Figure 6–51

2

- Drag the scroll box to the right edge of the scroll bar (Mail Merge Recipients dialog box) so that the Job Type field appears in the dialog box.
- Click the arrow to the right of the field name, Job Type, to display sort and filter criteria for the selected field (Figure 6–52).

Q&A What are the filter criteria in the parentheses?
The (All) option clears any previously set filter criteria. The (Blanks) option selects records that contain blanks in that field, and the (Nonblanks) option selects records that do not contain blanks in that field. The (Advanced) option displays the Filter and Sort dialog box, which allows you to perform more advanced record selection operations.

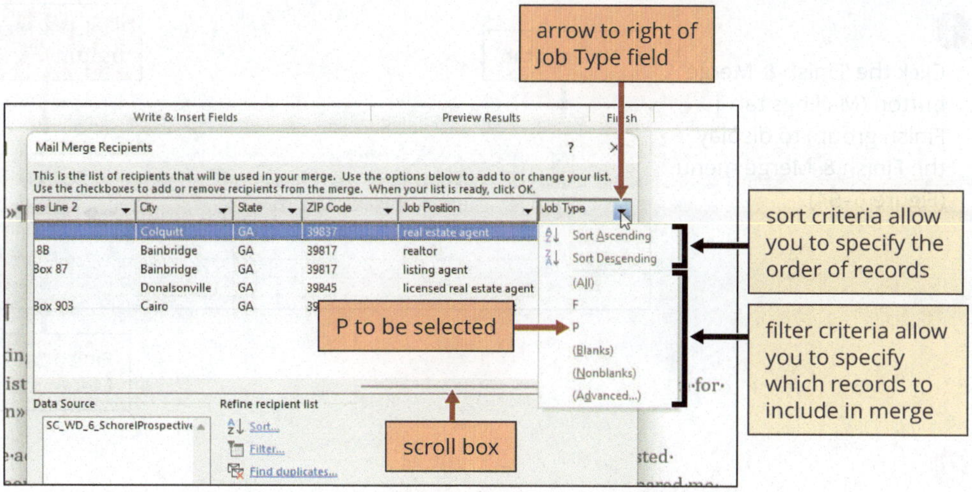

Figure 6–52

3

- Click P to reduce the number of data records displayed (Mail Merge Recipients dialog box) to two, because two potential employers are offering part-time employment (Figure 6–53).

Q&A What happened to the other three records that did not meet the criteria?
They still are part of the data source; they just are not appearing in the Mail Merge Recipients dialog box. When you clear the filter, all records will reappear.

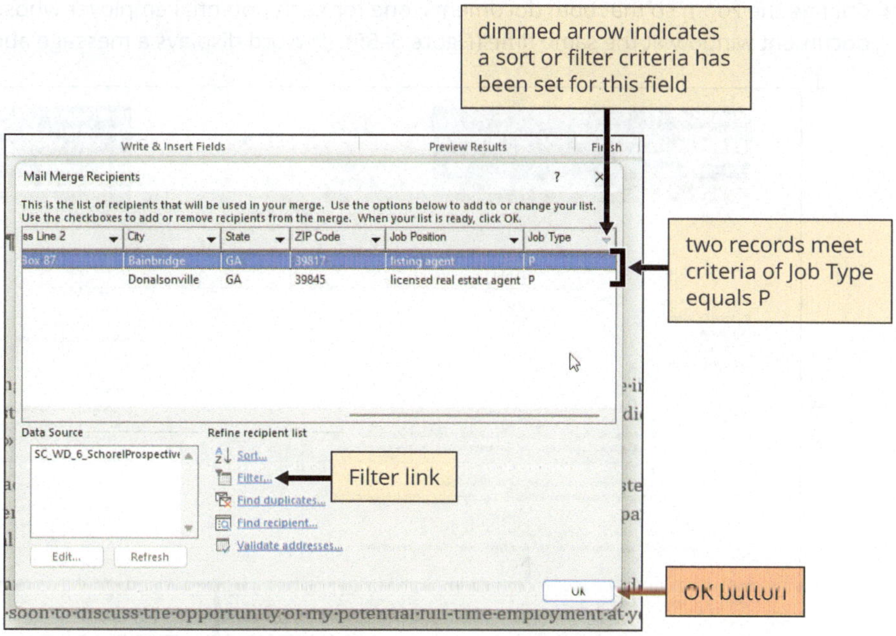

Figure 6–53

4

- Click OK to close the Mail Merge Recipients dialog box.

Other Ways

1. Click Filter link (Mail Merge Recipients dialog box), click Filter Records tab (Filter and Sort dialog box), enter filter criteria, click OK

To Merge the Form Letters to a New Document Using the Ribbon

The next step is to merge the selected records. To do this, you follow the same steps described earlier. The difference is that Word will merge only those records that meet the criteria specified, that is, just those with a job type equal to P (for part-time). **Why?** Word will merge only those data records that meet the specified filter criteria. The following steps merge the filtered data records (recipients) to a new document using the ribbon.

1

- Click the 'Finish & Merge' button (Mailings tab | Finish group) to display the Finish & Merge menu (Figure 6–54).

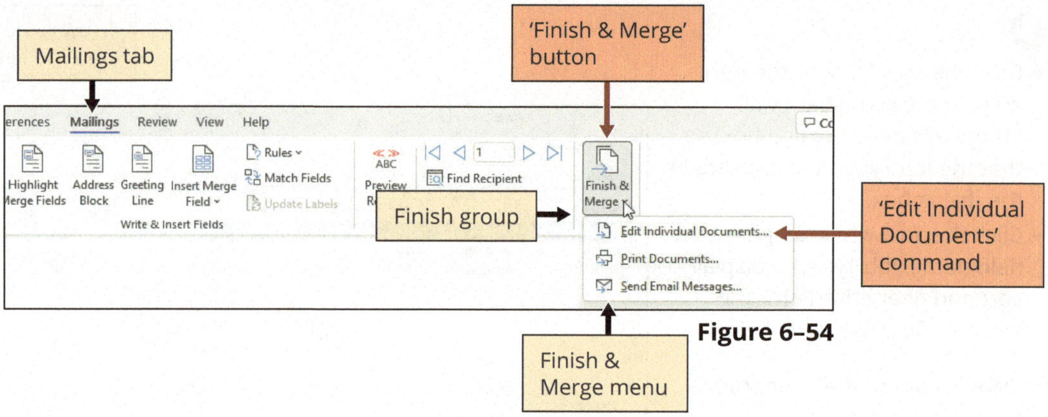

Figure 6–54

2

- Click 'Edit Individual Documents' on the Finish & Merge menu to display the Merge to New Document dialog box. If necessary, click All in the dialog box.
- Click OK (Merge to New Document dialog box) to display the merged documents in a new document window.

3

- Change the zoom so that both documents, one for each potential employer whose job type field equals P, appear in the document window at the same time (Figure 6–55). (If Word displays a message about locked fields, click OK.)

OpenClipart-Vectors/Pixabay

Figure 6–55

4

- Close the window. Do not save the merged documents.

To Remove a Merge Condition

The next step is to remove the merge condition. *Why? You do not want future merges to be restricted to potential employers with a job type equal to P.* The following steps remove a merge condition.

1

- Click the 'Edit Recipient List' button (Mailings tab | Start Mail Merge group) to display the Mail Merge Recipients dialog box.

2

- Click the Filter link (Mail Merge Recipients dialog box) to display the Filter and Sort dialog box.
- If necessary, click the Filter Records tab to display the Filter Records sheet (Figure 6–56).

Q&A Can I specify a merge condition in this dialog box instead of using the box arrow in the Mail Merge Recipients dialog box?

Yes.

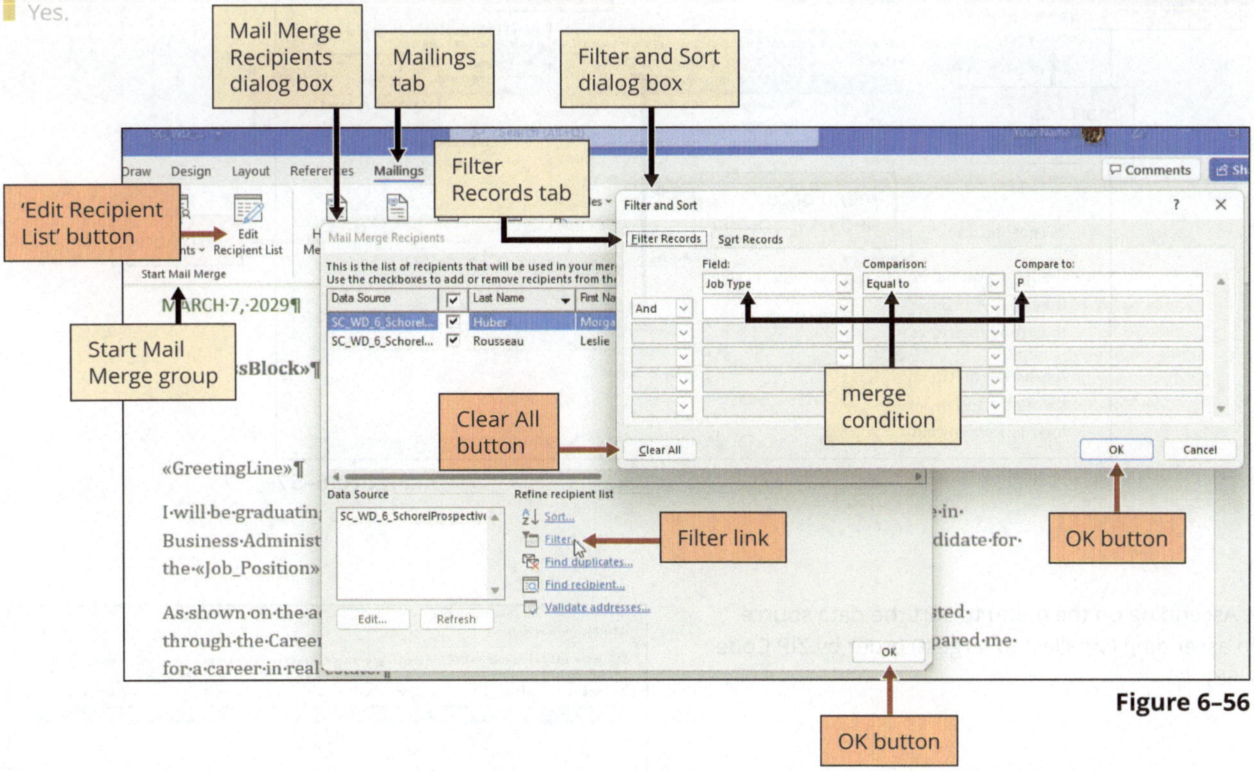

Figure 6–56

3

- Click the Clear All button (Filter and Sort dialog box) to remove the merge condition from the dialog box.
- Click OK in each of the two open dialog boxes to close the dialog boxes.

To Sort a Recipient List

The following steps sort the data records (recipient list) by ZIP code. **Why?** You may want the form letters printed in a certain order. For example, if you mail the form letters using the U.S. Postal Service's bulk rate mailing service, the post office requires that you sort and group the form letters by ZIP code.

1

- Click the 'Edit Recipient List' button (Mailings tab | Start Mail Merge group) to display the Mail Merge Recipients dialog box.
- Scroll to the right until the ZIP Code field shows in the dialog box.
- Click the arrow to the right of the field name, ZIP Code, to display a menu of sort and filter criteria (Figure 6–57).

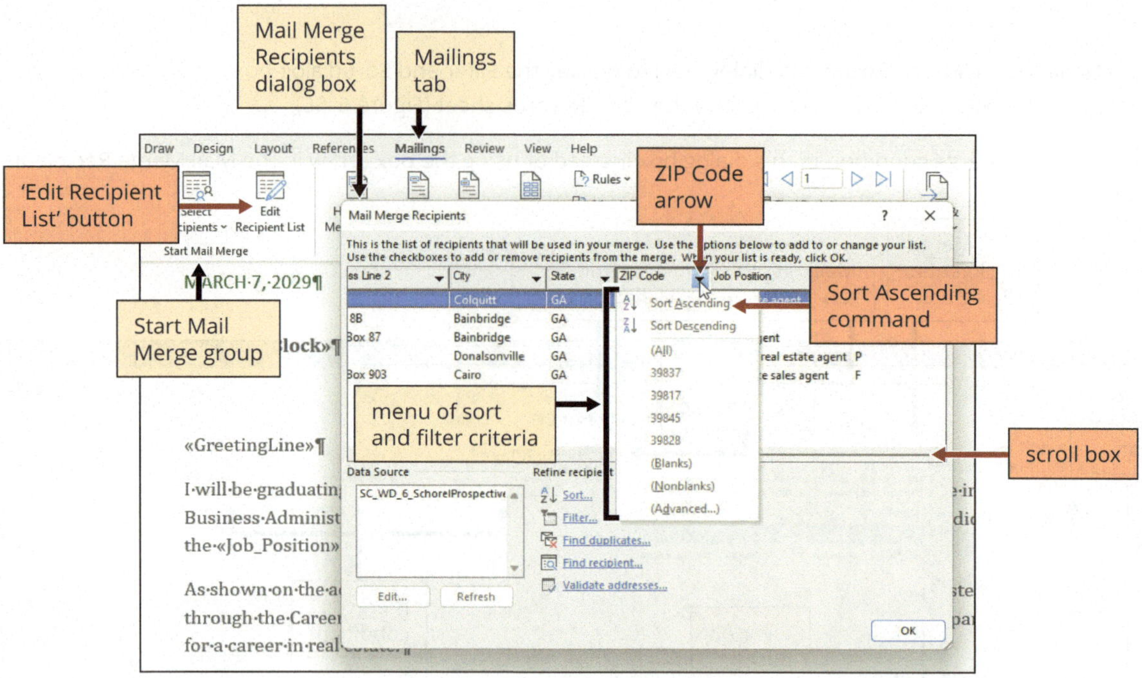

Figure 6–57

2

- Click Sort Ascending on the menu to sort the data source records in ascending (smallest to largest) order by ZIP Code (Figure 6–58).

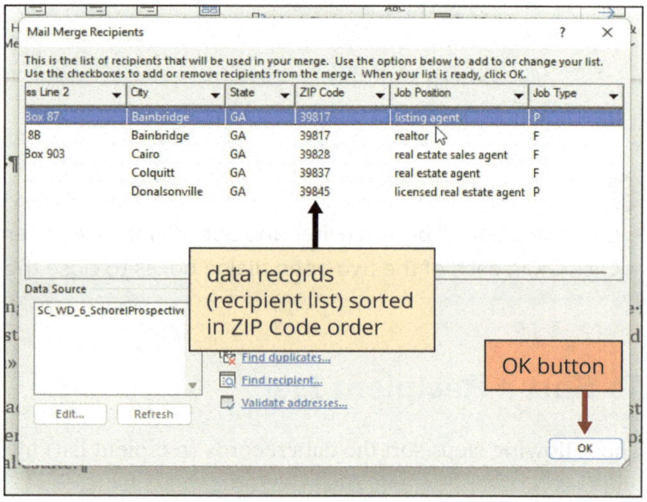

Figure 6–58

3

- Click OK to close the Mail Merge Recipients dialog box.

Q&A In what order would the form letters print if I merged them again now?

Word would merge them in ZIP code order; that is, the record with ZIP code 39817 would appear first, and the record with ZIP code 39845 would appear last.

Other Ways

1. Click Sort link (Mail Merge Recipients dialog box), enter sort criteria (Filter and Sort dialog box), click OK

To Find Mail Merge Recipients

Why? If you wanted to find a particular data record in the recipient list in the data source and display that recipient's data in the main document on the screen, you can search for a field value. The following steps find Rousseau, which is a last name in the recipient list in the data source, and display that recipient's values in the form letter currently displaying on the screen.

1

- If necessary, click the Preview Results button (Mailings tab | Preview Results group) to display field results instead of merged fields on the screen.
- Click the Find Recipient button (Mailings tab | Preview Results group) to display the Find Entry dialog box.

Q&A Why is my Find Recipient button dim?
The shape at the top of the letter is selected. Click outside the shape and then repeat Step 1.

- Type **Rousseau** in the Find text box (Find Entry dialog box) as the search text.
- Click the Find Next button to display the record containing the entered text (Figure 6–59).

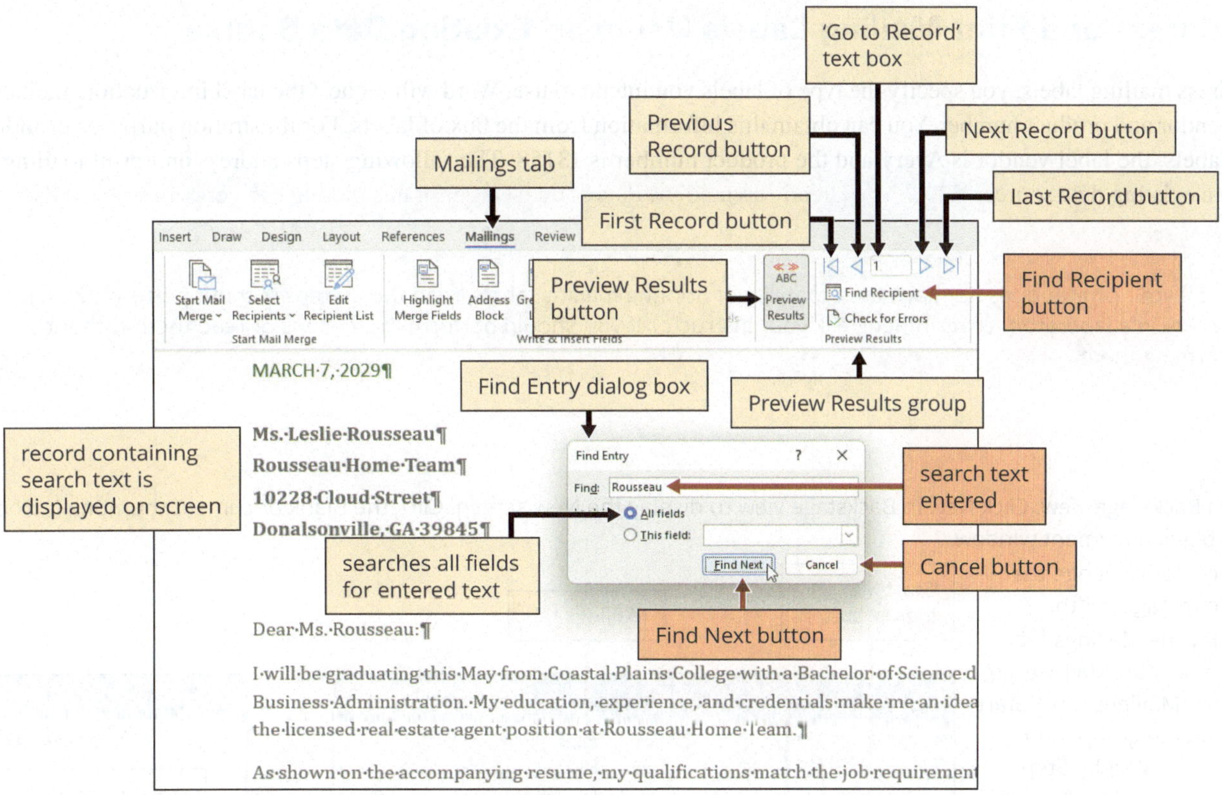

Figure 6–59

2

- Click Cancel (Find Entry dialog box) to close the dialog box.
- Close the open document. If a Microsoft Word dialog box is displayed, click Save to save the changes.

Displaying Mail Merge Recipients in the Main Document

When you are viewing merged data in the main document (shown in Figure 6–59) — that is, the Preview Results button (Mailings tab | Preview Results group) is selected — you can click buttons and boxes in the Preview Results group on the Mailings tab to display different results and values. For example, click the Last Record button to display the values from the last record in the data source, the First Record button to display the values in record one, the Next Record button to display the values in the next consecutive record number, or the Previous Record button to display the values from the previous record number. You also can display a specific record by clicking the 'Go to Record' text box, typing the record number you would like to be displayed in the main document, and then pressing ENTER.

BTW
Closing Main Document Files
Word always asks if you want to save changes when you close a main document, even if you just saved the document. If you are sure that no additional changes were made to the document, click Don't Save; otherwise, click Save — just to be safe.

Addressing Mailing Labels and Envelopes

Now that you have merged and printed the form letters, the next step is to print addresses on mailing labels to be affixed to envelopes for the form letters. The mailing labels will use the same data source as the form letter, SC_WD_6_SchorelProspectiveEmployers. The format and content of the mailing labels will be exactly the same as the inside address in the main document for the form letter. That is, the first line will contain the title and first name followed by the last name. The second line will contain the organization name, and so on. Thus, you will use the AddressBlock merge field in the mailing labels.

You follow the same basic steps to create the main document for the mailing labels as you did to create the main document for the form letters. That is, determine the appropriate data source, create the label main document, and then merge the main document with the data source to generate the mailing labels and envelopes. The major difference here is that the data source already exists because you created it earlier in this module.

To Address and Print Mailing Labels Using an Existing Data Source

To address mailing labels, you specify the type of labels you intend to use. Word will request the label information, including the label vendor and product number. You can obtain this information from the box of labels. For illustration purposes in addressing these labels, the label vendor is Avery and the product number is J8158. The following steps address and print mailing labels using an existing data source. **Why?** You already created the data source earlier in this module, so you will use that data source.

Note: If your printer does not have the capability of printing mailing labels, read these steps without performing them. If you are in a laboratory environment, ask your instructor if you should perform these steps or read them without performing them.

1

- Open Backstage view. Click New in Backstage view to display the New screen. Click the Blank document thumbnail to open a new blank document window.
- If necessary, change the zoom to page width.
- Display the Mailings tab. Click the 'Start Mail Merge' button (Mailings tab | Start Mail Merge group) and then click 'Step-by-Step Mail Merge Wizard' on the Start Mail Merge menu to display Step 1 of the Mail Merge wizard in the Mail Merge pane.
- Click Labels in the Select document type area to specify labels as the main document type (Figure 6–60).

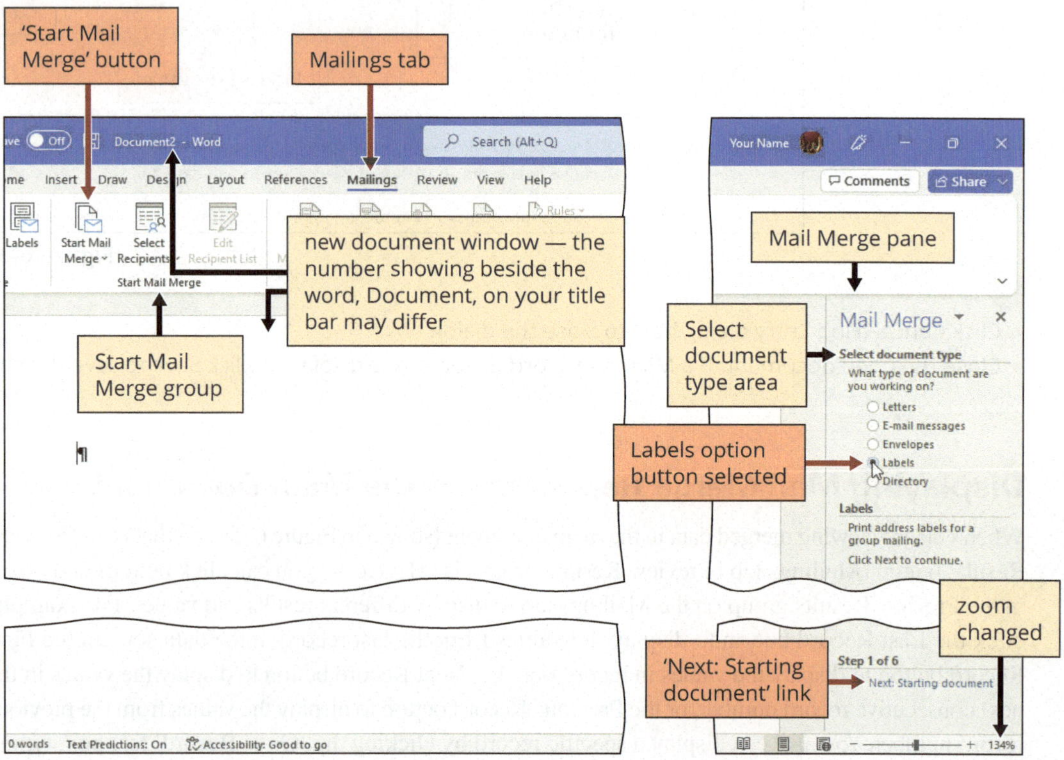

Figure 6–60

2

- Click the 'Next: Starting document' link at the bottom of the Mail Merge pane to display Step 2 of the Mail Merge wizard.
- In the Mail Merge pane, click the Label options link to display the Label Options dialog box.
- Select the label vendor and product number (in this case, Avery A4/A5 and J8158), as shown in Figure 6–61.

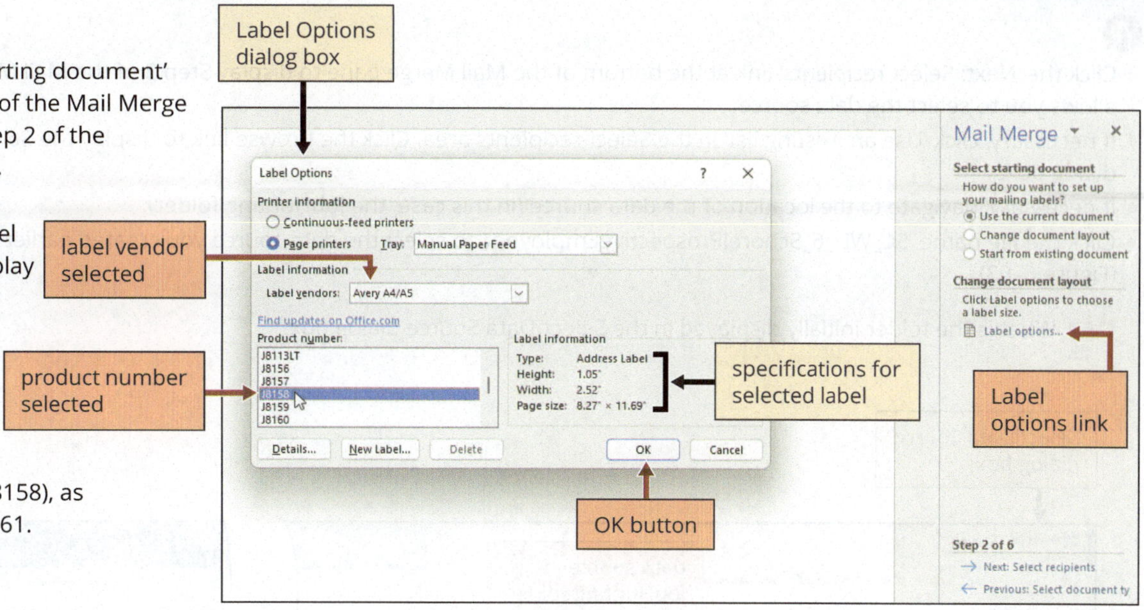

Figure 6–61

3

- Click OK (Label Options dialog box) to display the selected label layout as the main document (Figure 6–62).
- If gridlines are not displayed, click the View Gridlines button (contextual Layout tab | Table group) to display gridlines.

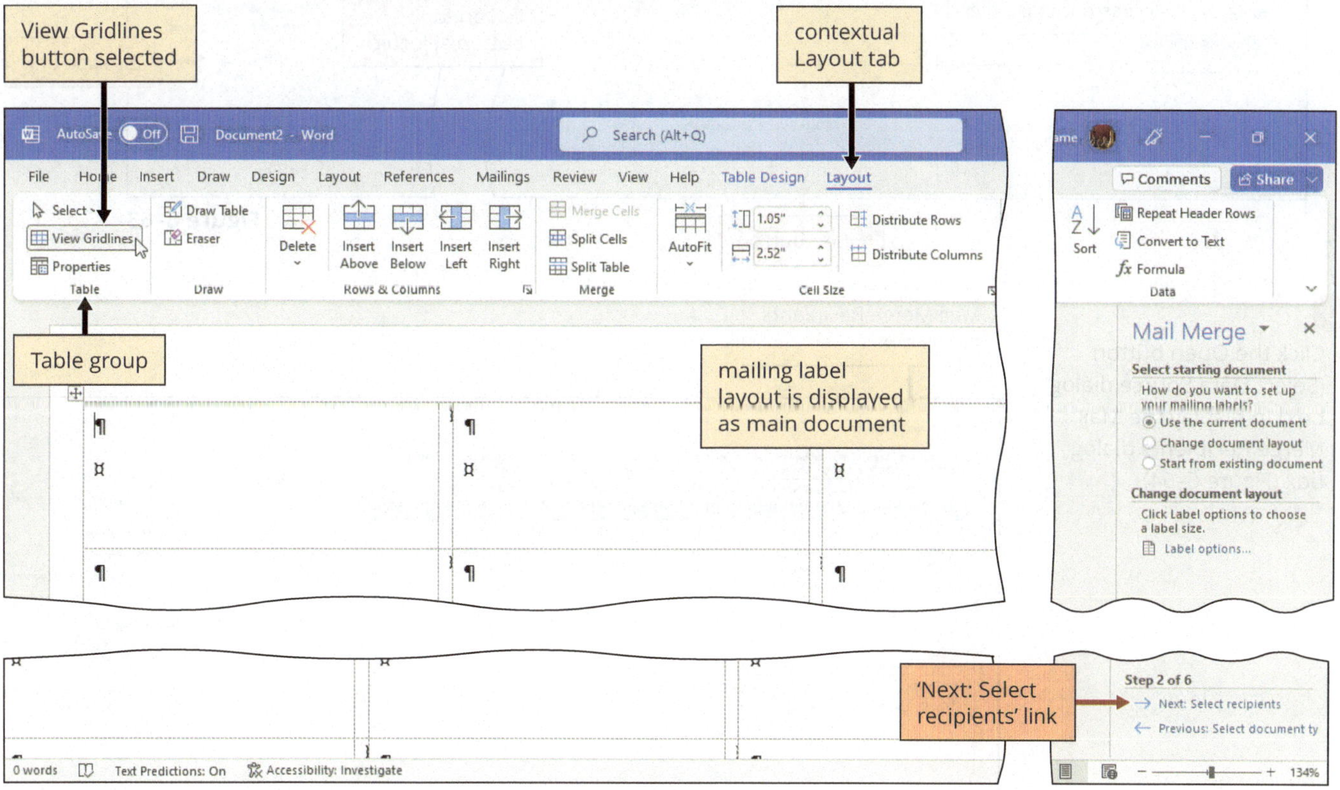

Figure 6–62

4

- Click the 'Next: Select recipients' link at the bottom of the Mail Merge pane to display Step 3 of the Mail Merge wizard, which allows you to select the data source.
- If necessary, click 'Use an existing list' in the Select recipients area. Click the Browse link to display the Select Data Source dialog box.
- If necessary, navigate to the location of the data source (in this case, the JobHunting folder).
- Click the file name, SC_WD_6_SchorelProspectiveEmployers, to select the data source you created earlier in the module (Figure 6–63).

Q&A What is the folder initially displayed in the Select Data Source dialog box?
It is the default folder for storing data source files. Word looks in that folder, by default, for an existing data source.

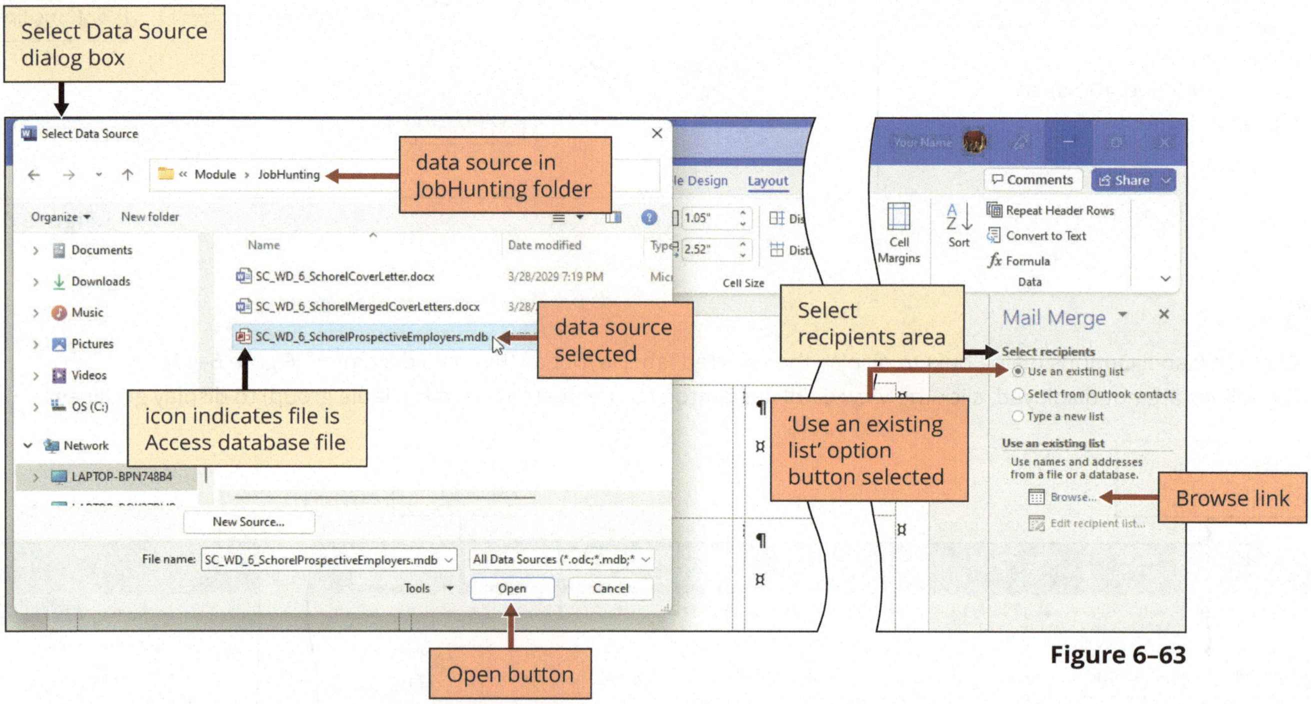

Figure 6–63

5

- Click the Open button (Select Data Source dialog box) to display the Mail Merge Recipients dialog box (Figure 6–64).

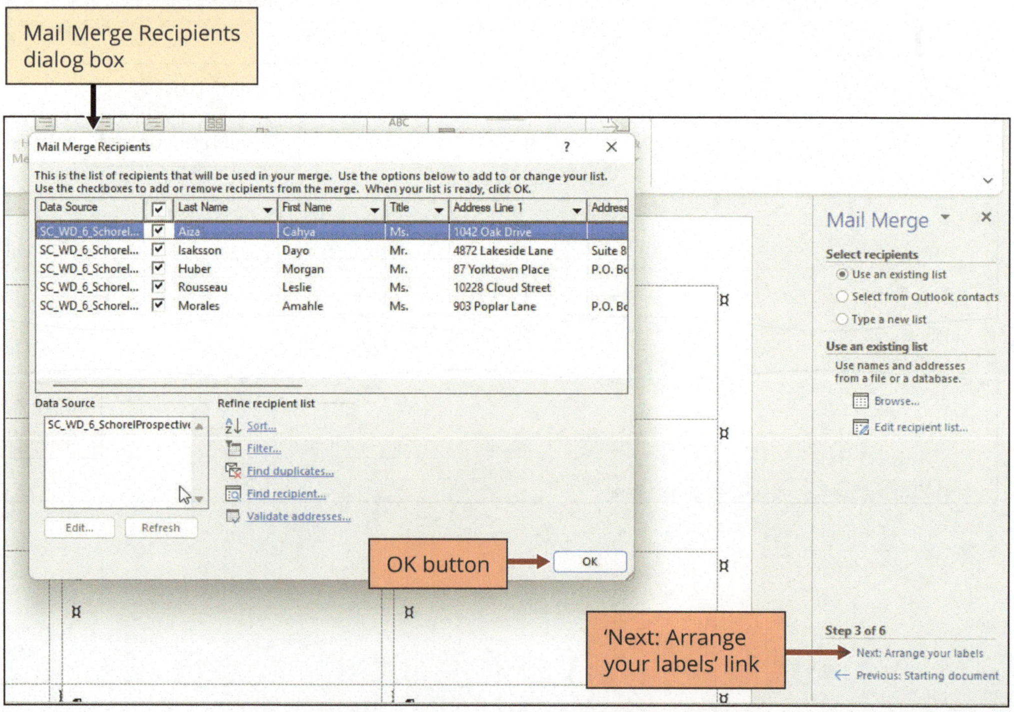

Figure 6–64

6

- Click OK (Mail Merge Recipients dialog box) to close the dialog box and insert the Next Record field in each label after the first (shown in Figure 6–66).
- At the bottom of the Mail Merge pane, click the 'Next: Arrange your labels' link to display Step 4 of the Mail Merge wizard in the Mail Merge pane.
- In the Mail Merge pane, click the Address block link to display the Insert Address Block dialog box.
- If necessary, match the company name to the Organization Name field by clicking the Match Fields button (Insert Address Block dialog box), clicking the Company box arrow (Match Fields dialog box), clicking Organization Name in the list, and then clicking OK (Match Fields dialog box) (Figure 6–65).

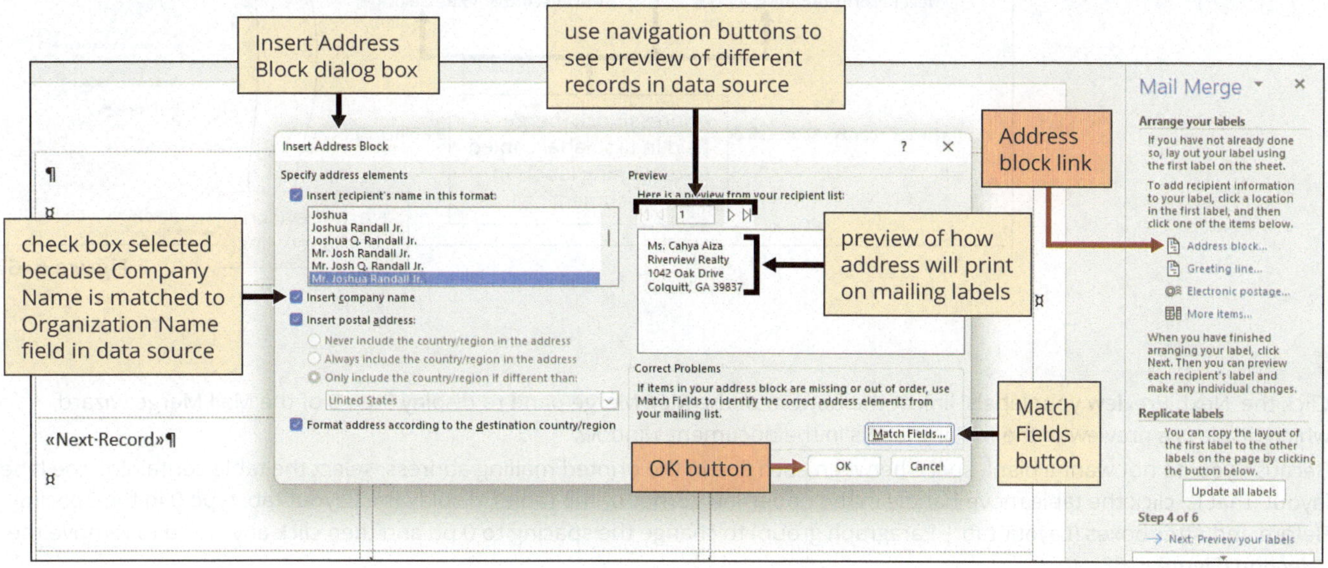

Figure 6–65

7

- Click OK to close the dialog box and insert the AddressBlock merge field in the first label of the main document (Figure 6–66).

Q&A Do I have to use the AddressBlock merge field?
No. You can click the Insert Merge Field button (Mailings tab | Write & Insert Fields group) and then select the preferred fields for the mailing labels, organizing the fields as desired.

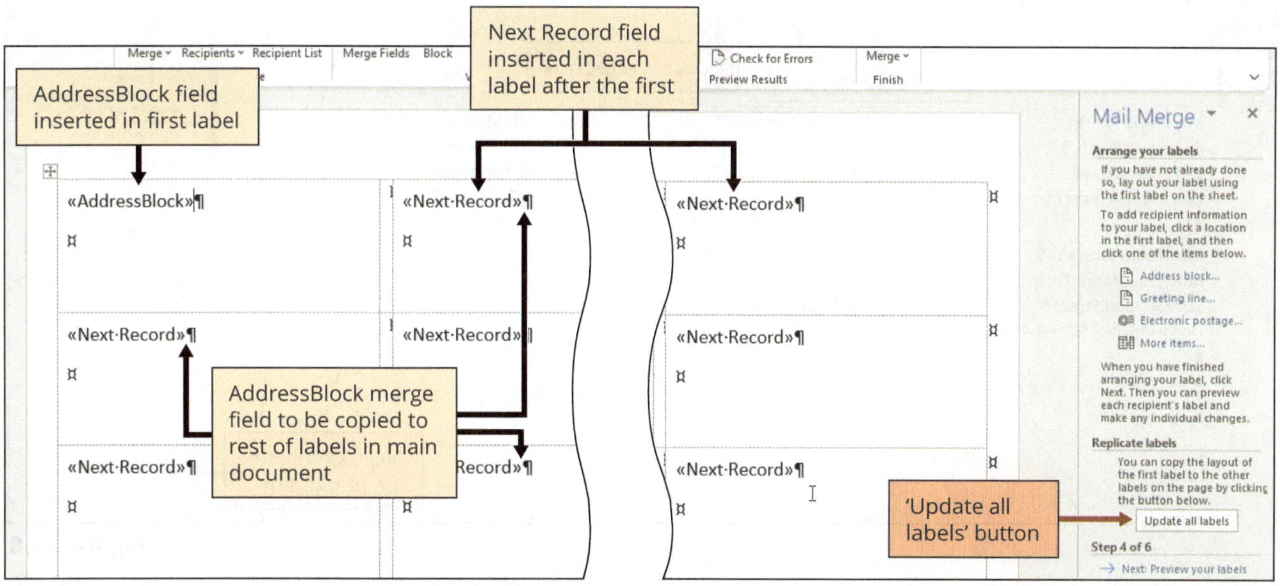

Figure 6–66

8

- Click the 'Update all labels' button in the Mail Merge pane to copy the layout of the first label to the remaining label layouts in the main document (Figure 6–67).

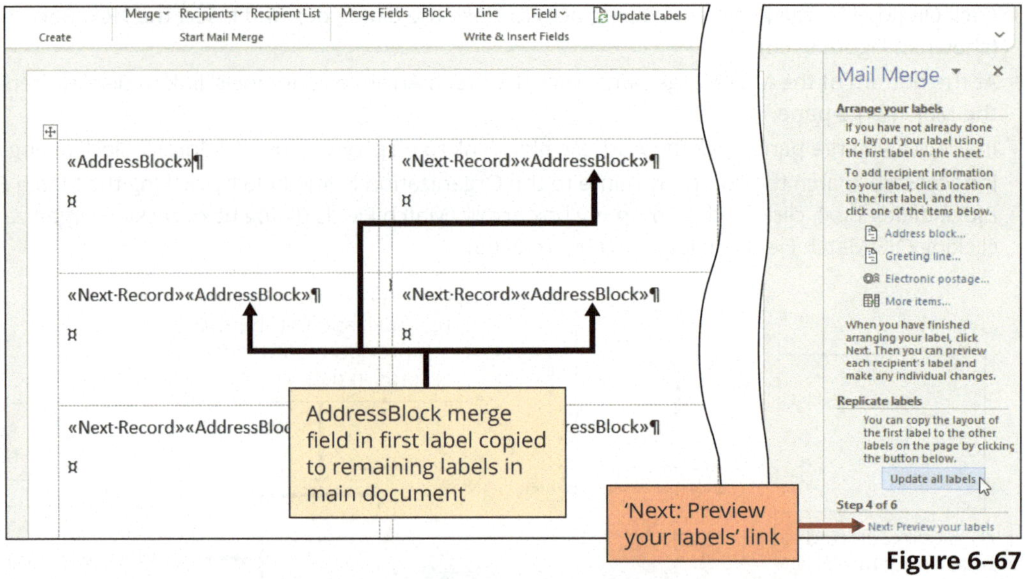

Figure 6–67

9

- Click the 'Next: Preview your labels' link at the bottom of the Mail Merge pane to display Step 5 of the Mail Merge wizard, which displays a preview of the mailing labels in the document window.
- Because you do not want a blank space between each line in the printed mailing address, select the table containing the label layout (that is, click the table move handle in the upper-left corner of the table), display the Layout tab, type 0 in the Spacing Before and After boxes (Layout tab | Paragraph group) to change the spacing to 0 pt, and then click anywhere to remove the selection (Figure 6–68).

Q&A What if the spacing does not change?

Drag through the labels and try changing the Spacing Before and After boxes to 0 again.

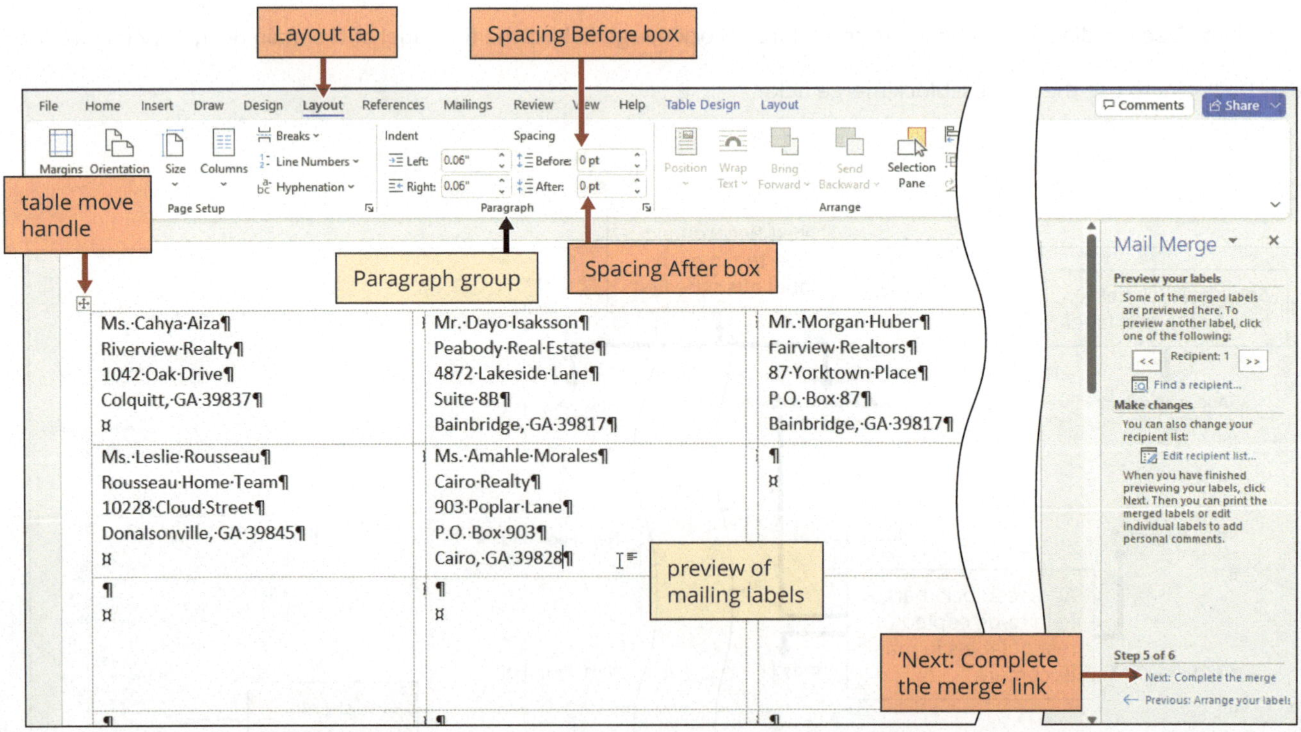

Figure 6–68

10

- Click the 'Next: Complete the merge' link at the bottom of the Mail Merge pane to display Step 6 of the Mail Merge wizard.
- Click the 'Edit individual labels' link to display the Merge to New Document dialog box.
- If necessary, click All (Merge to New Document dialog box) so that all records in the data source will be included in the merge (Figure 6–69).

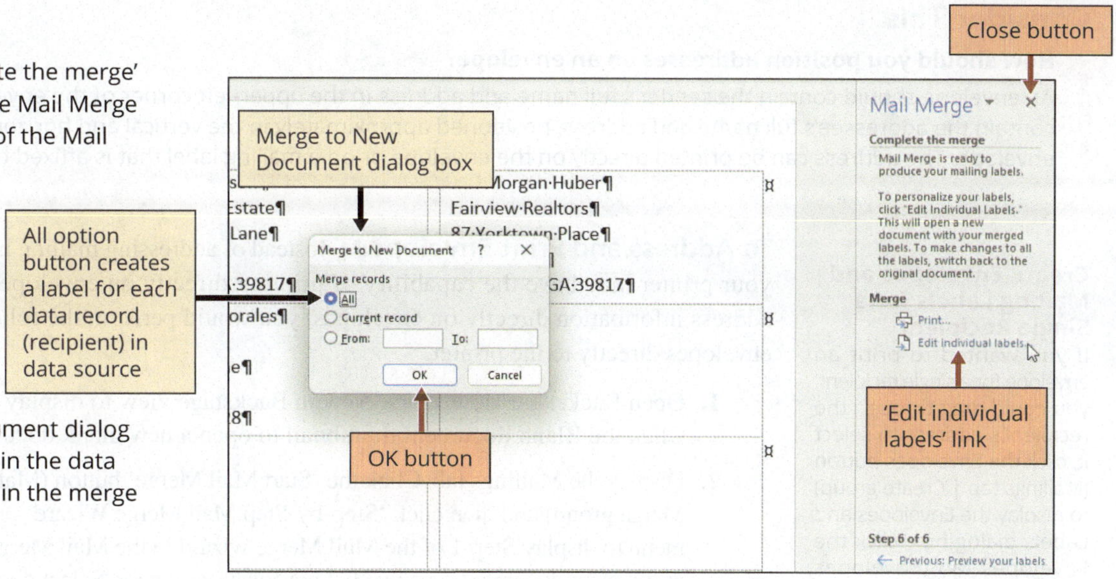

Figure 6–69

11

- Click OK (Merge to New Document dialog box) to merge the mailing labels to a new document.
- If necessary, insert a sheet of blank mailing labels in the printer.
- Save the merged mailing labels in the JobHunting folder on your hard drive, OneDrive, or other storage location using the file name, SC_WD_6_SchorelMergedMailingLabels. If requested by your instructor, print the merged labels (Figure 6–70).

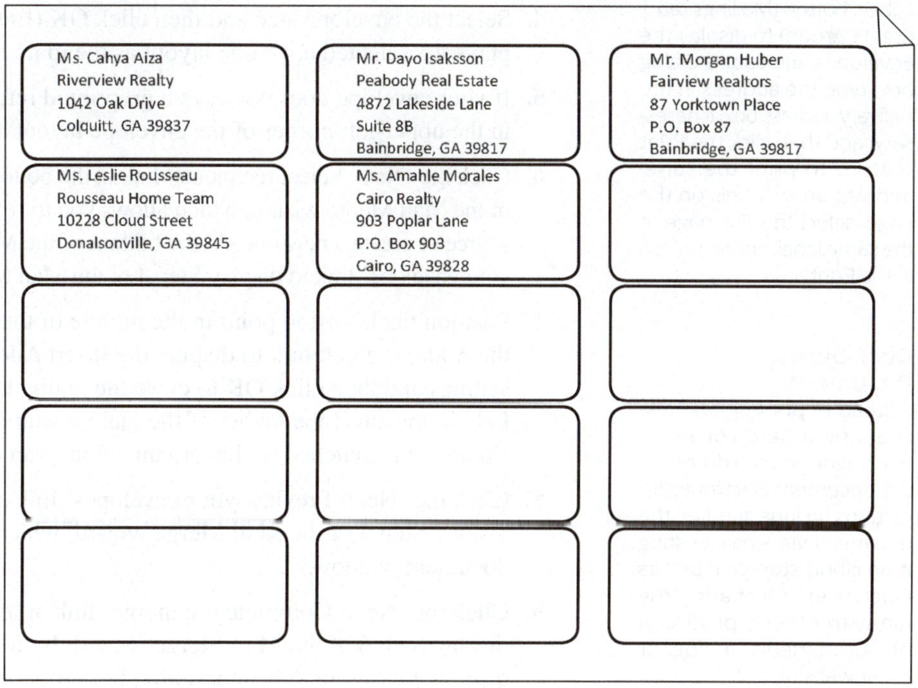

Figure 6–70

12

- Close the document window containing the merged labels.
- Click the Close button at the right edge of the Mail Merge pane (shown in Figure 6–69).
- Display the Mailings tab. Click the Preview Results button to display field codes instead of merged data on the labels.
- Save the mailing label main document in the JobHunting folder on your hard drive, OneDrive, or other storage location using the file name, SC_WD_6_SchorelMailingLabelLayout.
- Close the mailing label main document.

Consider This

How should you position addresses on an envelope?

An envelope should contain the sender's full name and address in the upper-left corner of the envelope. It also should contain the addressee's full name and address, positioned approximately in the vertical and horizontal center of the envelope. The address can be printed directly on the envelope or on a mailing label that is affixed to the envelope.

BTW

Create Envelopes and Mailing Labels for a Single Recipient

If you wanted to print an envelope for a single recipient, you could drag through the recipient's address to select it, click the Envelopes button (Mailings tab | Create group) to display the Envelopes and Labels dialog box, click the Envelopes tab (Envelopes and Labels dialog box), type the return address, and then click the Print button. To print a mailing label for a single recipient, click the Labels button (Mailings tab | Create group) to display the Envelopes and Labels dialog box, type the address in the Delivery address box, if necessary, and then click the Print button. To print the same address on all labels on the page, select the 'Full page of the same label' option button in the Print area.

BTW

Distributing a Document

Instead of printing and distributing a hard copy of a document, you can distribute the document electronically. Options include sending the document via email; posting it on cloud storage (such as OneDrive) and sharing the file with others; posting it on social media, a blog, or other website; and sharing a link associated with an online location of the document. You also can create and share a PDF or XPS image of the document, so that users can view the file in Acrobat Reader or XPS Viewer instead of in Word.

To Address and Print Envelopes Instead of addressing mailing labels to affix to envelopes, your printer may have the capability of printing directly on envelopes. If you wanted to print address information directly on envelopes, you would perform the following steps to merge the envelopes directly to the printer.

1. Open Backstage view. Click New in Backstage view to display the New screen. Click the Blank document thumbnail to open a new blank document window.
2. Display the Mailings tab. Click the 'Start Mail Merge' button (Mailings tab | Start Mail Merge group) and then click 'Step-by-Step Mail Merge Wizard' on the Start Mail Merge menu to display Step 1 of the Mail Merge wizard in the Mail Merge pane. Specify envelopes as the main document type by clicking Envelopes in the Select document type area.
3. Click the 'Next: Starting document' link at the bottom of the Mail Merge pane to display Step 2 of the Mail Merge wizard. In the Mail Merge pane, click the Envelope Options link to display the Envelope Options dialog box.
4. Select the envelope size and then click OK (Envelope Options dialog box), which displays the selected envelope layout as the main document.
5. If your envelope does not have a preprinted return address, position the insertion point in the upper-left corner of the envelope layout and then type a return address.
6. Click the 'Next: Select recipients' link at the bottom of the Mail Merge pane to display Step 3 of the Mail Merge wizard, which allows you to select the data source. Select an existing data source or create a new one. At the bottom of the Mail Merge pane, click the 'Next: Arrange your envelope' link to display Step 4 of the Mail Merge wizard in the Mail Merge pane.
7. Position the insertion point in the middle of the envelope. In the Mail Merge pane, click the Address block link to display the Insert Address Block dialog box. Select desired settings and then click OK to close the dialog box and insert the AddressBlock merge field in the envelope layout of the main document. If necessary, match fields so that the Company is matched to the Organization_Name field.
8. Click the 'Next: Preview your envelopes' link at the bottom of the Mail Merge pane to display Step 5 of the Mail Merge wizard, which shows a preview of an envelope in the document window.
9. Click the 'Next: Complete the merge' link at the bottom of the Mail Merge pane to display Step 6 of the Mail Merge wizard. In the Mail Merge pane, click the Print link to display the Merge to Printer dialog box. If necessary, click All (Merge to Printer dialog box) so that all records in the data source will be included in the merge.
10. If necessary, insert blank envelopes in the printer. Click OK to display the Print dialog box. Click OK (Print dialog box) to print the addresses on the envelopes. Close the Mail Merge pane.

Merging All Data Records to a Directory

You may want to print the data records (recipient list) in the data source. Recall that the data source is saved as a Microsoft Access database table. Thus, you cannot open the data source in Word. To view the data source, you click the 'Edit Recipient List' button (Mailings tab | Start Mail Merge group), which displays the Mail Merge Recipients dialog box. This dialog box, however, does not have a Print button.

One way to print the contents of the data source is to merge all data records in the data source into a single document, called a directory. A **directory** is a listing of data records (recipients) from the data source. A directory does not merge each data record to a separate document; instead, a directory lists all records together in a single document. When you merge to a directory, the default organization of a directory places each record one after the next, similar to the look of entries in a phone book.

To create a directory, follow the same process as for the form letters. That is, determine the appropriate data source, create the directory main document, and then merge the main document with the data source to create the directory.

The directory in this module is more organized with the rows and columns divided and field names placed above each column (shown in Figure 6–83). To accomplish this look, the following steps are required:

1. Change the page orientation from portrait to landscape, so that each record fits on a single row.
2. Create a directory layout, placing a separating character between each merge field.
3. Merge the directory to a new document, which creates a list of all data records (recipients) in the data source.
4. Convert the directory to a table, using the separator character as the identifier for each new column.
5. Format the table containing the directory.
6. Sort the table by organization name within city, so that it is easy to locate a particular record.

To Change Page Orientation

When a document is in **portrait orientation**, the short edge of the paper is the top of the document, and the document is taller than it is wide. You can instruct Word to lay out a document in **landscape orientation**, so that the long edge of the paper is the top of the document, and the document is wider than it is tall. The following steps change the orientation of the document from portrait to landscape. **Why?** You want an entire record to fit on a single line in the directory.

1

- sam If necessary, create a new blank document in the Word window and change the zoom to page width.
- Display the Layout tab.
- Click the Orientation button (Layout tab | Page Setup group) to display the Orientation gallery (Figure 6–71).

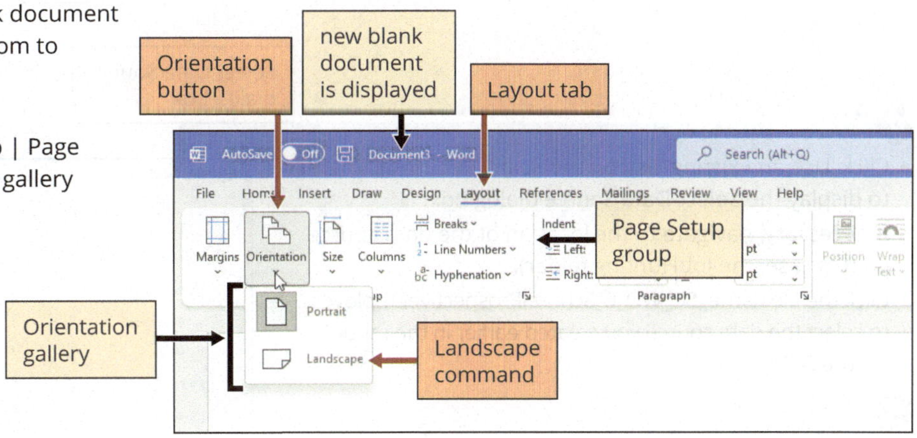

Figure 6–71

2

- Click Landscape in the Orientation gallery to change the page orientation to landscape.
- If necessary, change the zoom to page width again so that both the left and right edges of the page are visible in the document window.

To Merge to a Directory

The next steps merge the data records (recipients) in the data source to a directory. **Why?** You would like a listing of all data records (recipients) in the data source. For illustration purposes, the following steps use the buttons on the Mailings tab rather than using the Mail Merge wizard to merge to a directory.

1

- Display the Mailings tab.
- Click the 'Start Mail Merge' button (Mailings tab | Start Mail Merge group) to display the Start Mail Merge menu (Figure 6–72).

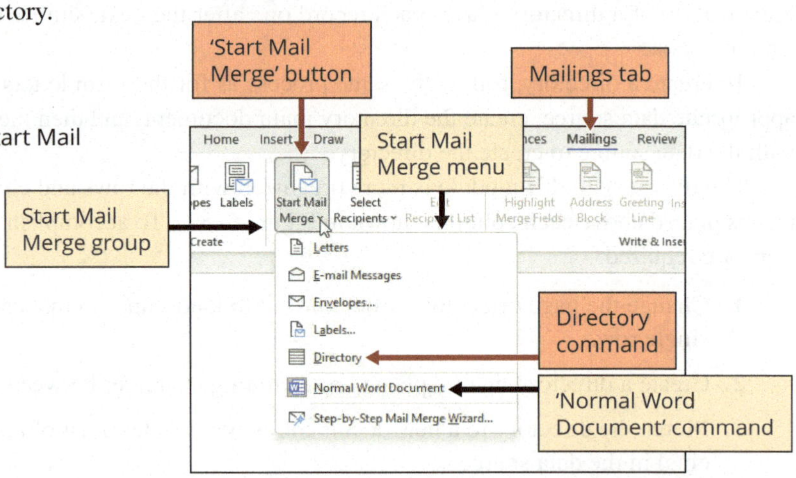

Figure 6–72

2

- Click Directory on the Start Mail Merge menu to select the main document type.

3

- Click the Select Recipients button (Mailings tab | Start Mail Merge group) to display the Select Recipients menu (Figure 6–73).

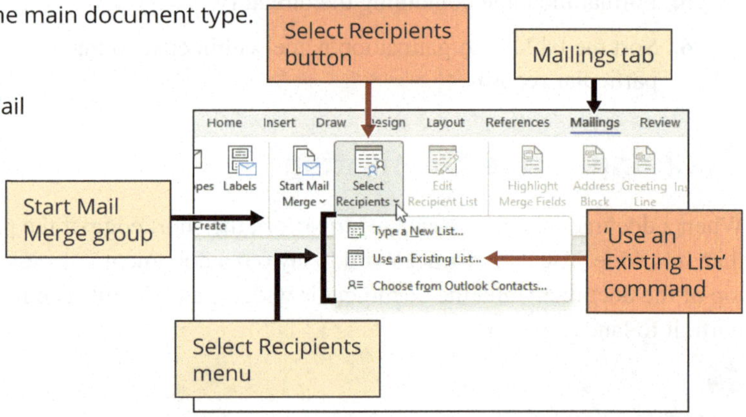

Figure 6–73

4

- Click 'Use an Existing List' on the Select Recipients menu to display the Select Data Source dialog box.
- If necessary, navigate to the location of the data source (in this case, the JobHunting folder).
- Click the file name, SC_WD_6_SchorelProspectiveEmployers, to select the data source you created earlier in the module (Figure 6–74).

5

- Click the Open button (Select Data Source dialog box) to associate the selected data source with the current main document.

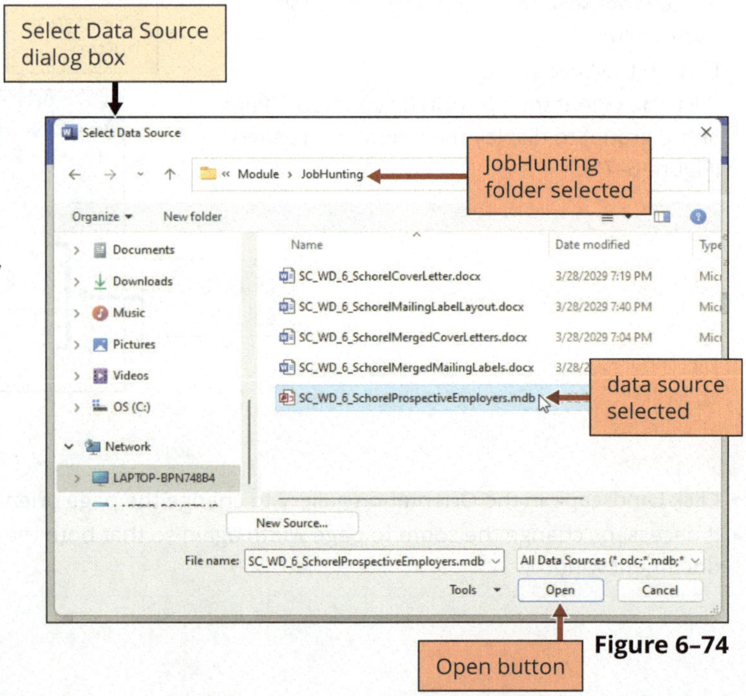

Figure 6–74

6

- Click the 'Insert Merge Field' arrow (Mailings tab | Write & Insert Fields group) to display the Insert Merge Field menu (Figure 6–75).

Q&A What if I accidentally click the 'Insert Merge Field' button instead of the arrow?
Click Cancel in the Insert Merge Field dialog box and repeat Step 6.

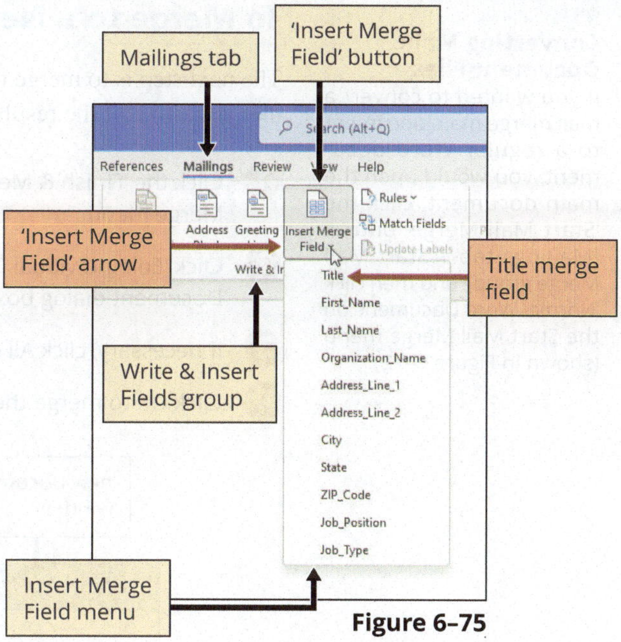

Figure 6–75

7

- Click Title on the Insert Merge Field menu to insert the selected merge field in the document.
- Press the COMMA (,) key to place a comma after the inserted merge field.

Q&A Why insert a comma after the merge field?
In the next steps, you will convert the entered merge fields to a table format with the records in rows and the fields in columns. To do this, Word divides the columns based on a character separating each field. In this case, you use the comma to separate the merge fields.

8

- Repeat Steps 6 and 7 for the First_Name, Last_Name, Organization_Name, Address_Line_1, Address_Line_2, City, State, and ZIP_Code fields on the Insert Merge Field menu, so that these fields in the data source appear in the main document separated by a comma, except do not type a comma after the last field (ZIP_Code).
- Press ENTER (Figure 6–76).

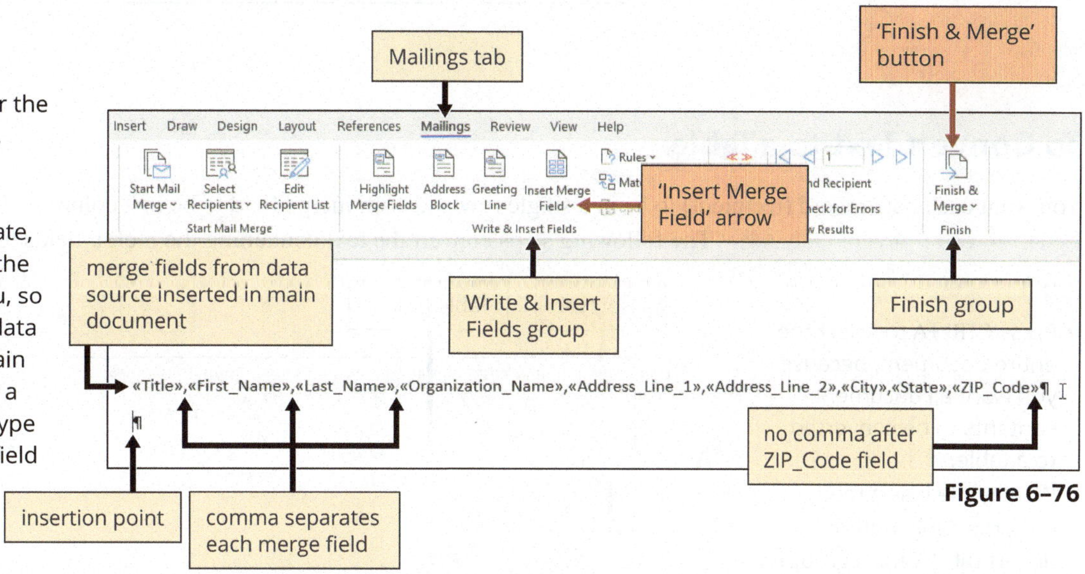

Figure 6–76

Q&A Why press ENTER after entering the merge fields names?
This will place the first field in each data record at the beginning of a new line.

Why are the Job_Position and Job_Type fields not included in the directory?
You just want the directory listing to display the contact information for each potential employer.

9

- **sam** Save the directory main document in the JobHunting folder on your hard drive, OneDrive, or other storage location using the file name, SC_WD_6_SchorelPotentialEmployerDirectoryLayout.

To Merge to a New Document

BTW
Converting Main Document Files
If you wanted to convert a mail merge main document to a regular Word document, you would open the main document, click the 'Start Mail Merge' button (Mailings tab | Start Mail Merge group), and then click 'Normal Word Document' on the Start Mail Merge menu (shown in Figure 6–72).

The next step is to merge the data source and the directory main document to a new document, so that you can edit the resulting document. The following steps merge to a new document.

1. Click the 'Finish & Merge' button (Mailings tab | Finish group) to display the Finish & Merge menu.
2. Click 'Edit Individual Documents' on the Finish & Merge menu to display the Merge to New Document dialog box.
3. If necessary, click All (Merge to New Document dialog box).
4. Click OK to merge the data records to a directory in a new document window (Figure 6–77).

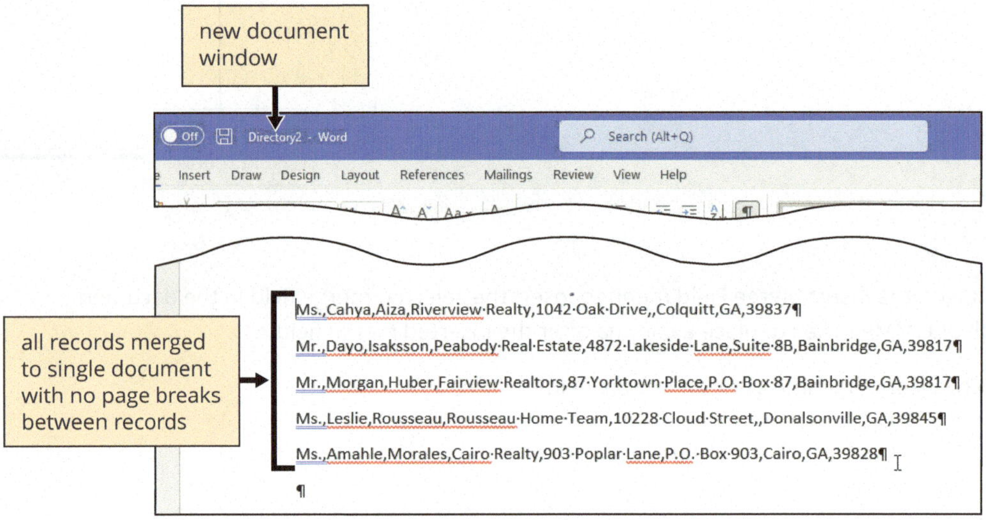

Figure 6–77

To Convert Text to a Table

You want each data record (recipient) to be in a single row and each merge field to be in a column. **Why?** The directory will be easier to read if it is in table form. The following steps convert the text containing the merge fields to a table.

1.
- Press CTRL+A to select the entire document, because you want all document contents to be converted to a table.
- Display the Insert tab.
- Click the Table button (Insert tab | Tables group) to display the Table gallery (Figure 6–78).

Q&A Can I convert a section of a document to a table?
Yes, simply select the characters, lines, or paragraphs to be converted before displaying the Convert Text to Table dialog box.

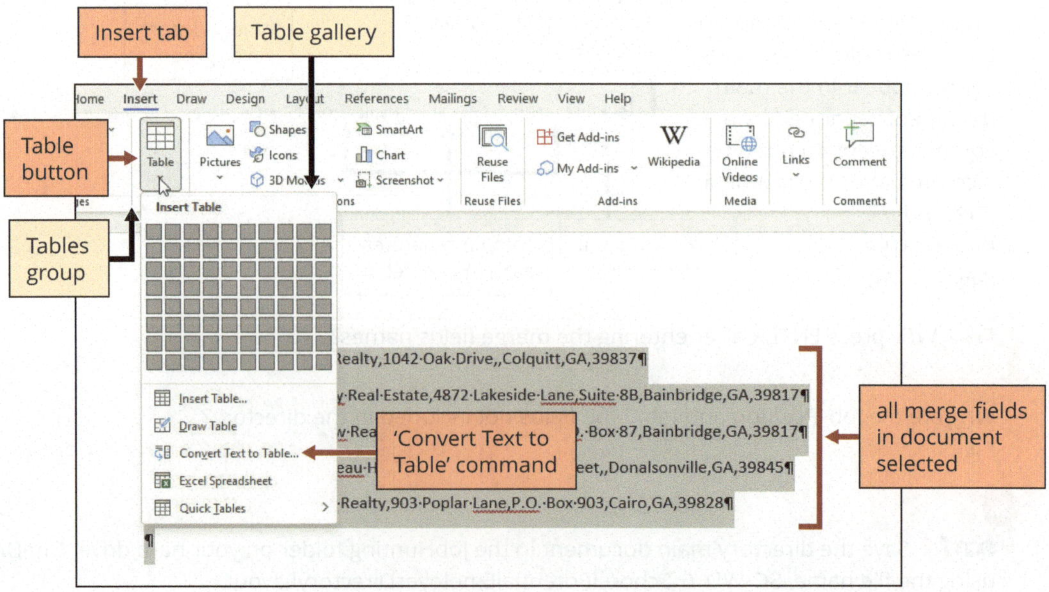

Figure 6–78

2

- Click 'Convert Text to Table' in the Table gallery to display the Convert Text to Table dialog box.
- If necessary, type **9** in the 'Number of columns' box (Convert Text to Table dialog box) to specify the number of columns for the resulting table.
- Click 'AutoFit to window', which instructs Word to fit the table and its contents to the width of the window.
- If necessary, click Commas to specify the character that separates the merge fields in the document (Figure 6–79).

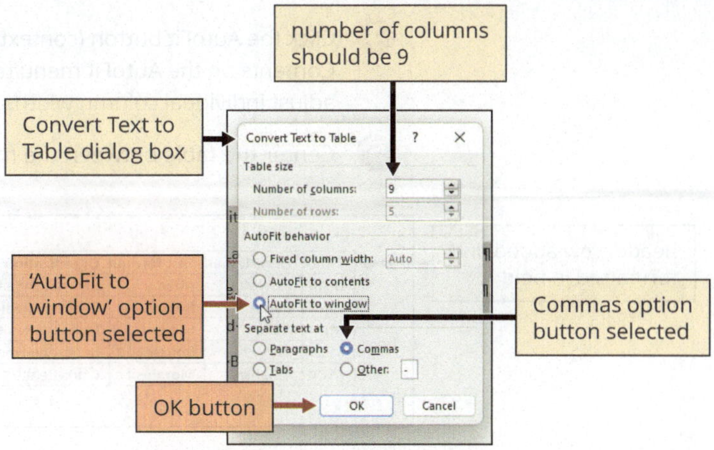

Figure 6–79

3

- Click OK to convert the selected text to a table and then, if necessary, click to remove the selection from the table (Figure 6–80).

Q&A Can I format the table?

Yes. You can position the insertion point in the table and then use any of the commands on the contextual Table Design and Layout tabs to change the look of the table.

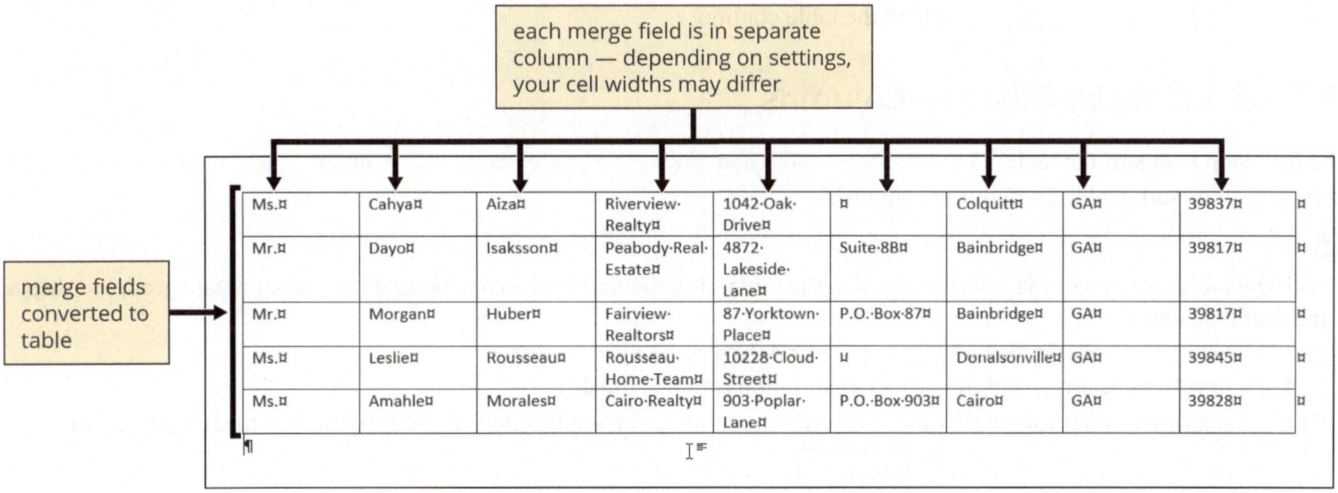

Ms.	Cahya	Aiza	Riverview Realty	1042 Oak Drive		Colquitt	GA	39837
Mr.	Dayo	Isaksson	Peabody Real Estate	4872 Lakeside Lane	Suite 8B	Bainbridge	GA	39817
Mr.	Morgan	Huber	Fairview Realtors	87 Yorktown Place	P.O. Box 87	Bainbridge	GA	39817
Ms.	Leslie	Rousseau	Rousseau Home Team	10228 Cloud Street		Donalsonville	GA	39845
Ms.	Amahle	Morales	Cairo Realty	903 Poplar Lane	P.O. Box 903	Cairo	GA	39828

Figure 6–80

To Modify and Format a Table

The table would be more descriptive if the field names were displayed in a row above the actual data. The following steps add a row to the top of a table and format the data in the new row.

1 Add a row to the top of the table by positioning the insertion point in the first row of the table, displaying the contextual Layout tab, and then clicking the Insert Above button (contextual Layout tab | Rows & Columns group).

2 Click in the first (leftmost) cell of the new row. Type **Title** and then press TAB. Type **First Name** and then press TAB. Type **Last Name** and then press TAB. Type **Organization Name** and then press TAB. Type **Address Line 1** and then press TAB. Type **Address Line 2** and then press TAB. Type **City** and then press TAB. Type **State** and then press TAB. Type **ZIP Code** as the last entry in the row.

3 Bold the contents of the first row.

4. Click the AutoFit button (contextual Layout tab | Cell Size group) and then click AutoFit Contents on the AutoFit menu to make all columns as wide as their contents. If necessary, adjust individual column widths so that the table looks like Figure 6–81.

5. Center the table between the margins (Figure 6–81).

Title	First Name	Last Name	Organization Name	Address Line 1	Address Line 2	City	State	ZIP Code
Ms.	Cahya	Aiza	Riverview Realty	1042 Oak Drive		Colquitt	GA	39837
Mr.	Dayo	Isaksson	Peabody Real Estate	4872 Lakeside Lane	Suite 8B	Bainbridge	GA	39817
Mr.	Morgan	Huber	Fairview Realtors	87 Yorktown Place	P.O. Box 87	Bainbridge	GA	39817
Ms.	Leslie	Rousseau	Rousseau Home Team	10228 Cloud Street		Donalsonville	GA	39845
Ms.	Amahle	Morales	Cairo Realty	903 Poplar Lane	P.O. Box 903	Cairo	GA	39828

Figure 6–81

To Repeat Header Rows If you had a table that exceeded a page in length and you wanted the header row (the first row) to appear at the top of the table on each continued page, you would perform the following steps.

1. Position the insertion point in the header row.
2. Click the 'Repeat Header Rows' button (contextual Layout tab | Data group) (shown in Figure 6–82) to repeat the row containing the insertion point at the top of every page on which the table continues.

To Sort a Table by Multiple Columns

The next step is to sort the table. **Why?** In this project, the table records are displayed by organization name within city. The following steps sort a table by multiple columns.

1.

- With the table selected or the insertion point in the table, click the Sort button (contextual Layout tab | Data group) to display the Sort dialog box.
- Click the Sort by arrow (Sort dialog box); scroll to and then click City in the list.
- Click the first Then by arrow and then click Organization Name in the list.
- If necessary, click Header row so that the first row remains in its current location when the table is sorted (Figure 6–82).

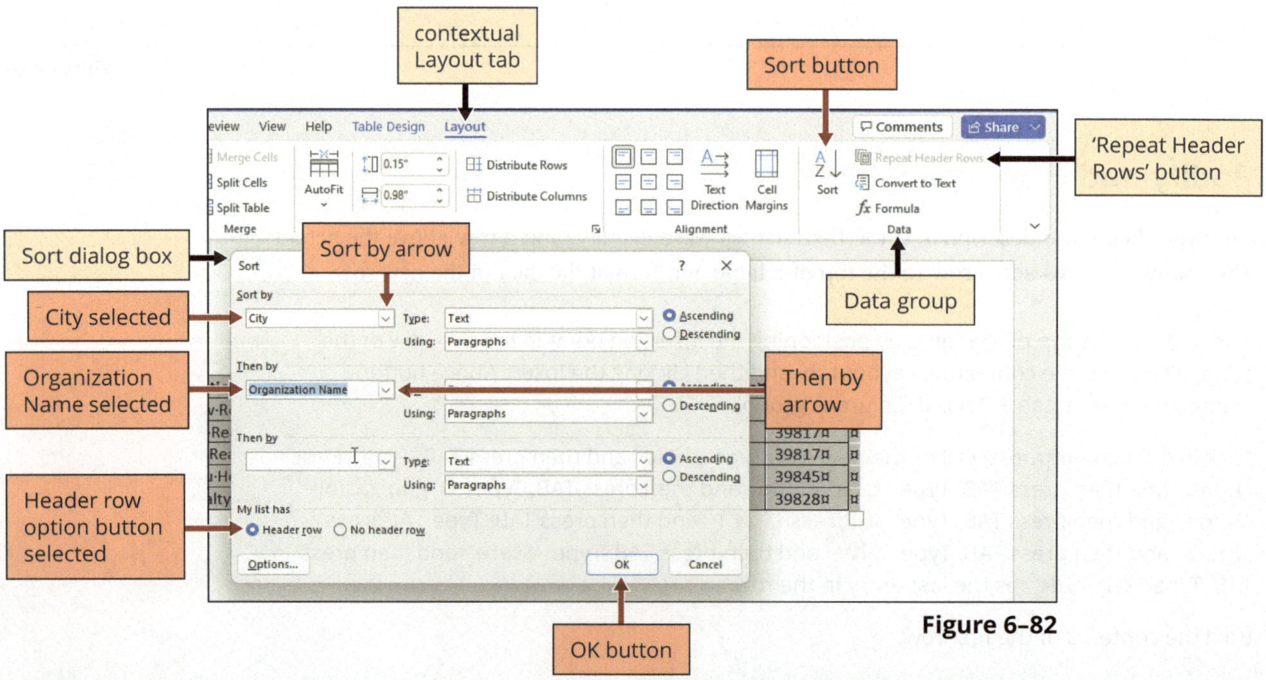

Figure 6–82

2

- Click OK (Sort dialog box) to sort the records in the table in ascending Organization Name order within ascending City order.
- If necessary, click to deselect the table (Figure 6–83).
- **sam** Save the merged directory in the JobHunting folder on your hard drive, OneDrive, or other storage location using the file name, SC_WD_6_SchorelMergedPotentialEmployerDirectory.
- If requested by your instructor, print the merged directory.

Q&A If Microsoft Access is installed on my computer, can I use that to print the data source?
As an alternative to merging to a directory and printing the results, if you are familiar with Microsoft Access and it is installed on your computer, you can open and print the data source in Access.

- Close all open files, if necessary, and then exit Word.

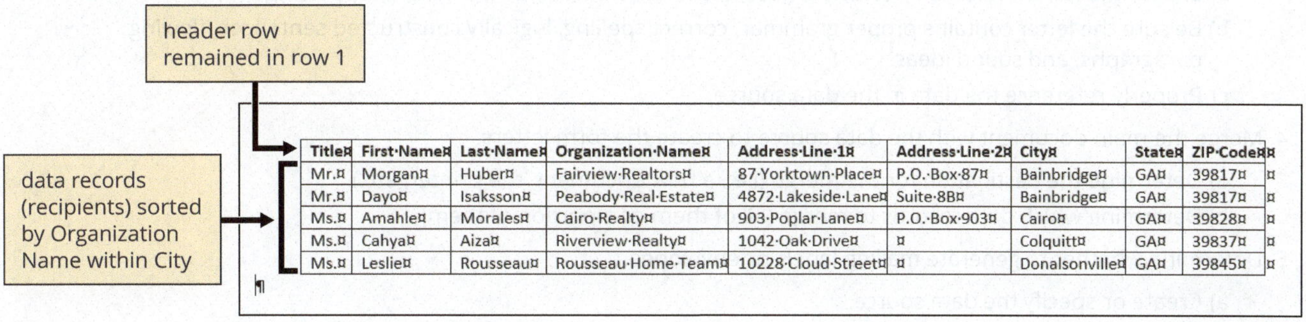

Title	First Name	Last Name	Organization Name	Address Line 1	Address Line 2	City	State	ZIP Code
Mr.	Morgan	Huber	Fairview Realtors	87 Yorktown Place	P.O. Box 87	Bainbridge	GA	39817
Mr.	Dayo	Isaksson	Peabody Real Estate	4872 Lakeside Lane	Suite 8B	Bainbridge	GA	39817
Ms.	Amahle	Morales	Cairo Realty	903 Poplar Lane	P.O. Box 903	Cairo	GA	39828
Ms.	Cahya	Aiza	Riverview Realty	1042 Oak Drive		Colquitt	GA	39837
Ms.	Leslie	Rousseau	Rousseau Home Team	10228 Cloud Street		Donalsonville	GA	39845

Figure 6–83

Summary

In this module, you learned how to create and print form letters, work with merge fields and an IF field, open a main document, create and edit a recipient list in a data source, address mailing labels and envelopes from a data source, change page orientation, merge to a directory, and convert text to a table.

Consider This: Plan Ahead

What decisions will you need to make when creating your next form letter?

Use these guidelines as you complete the assignments in this module and create your own form letters outside of this class.

1. Identify the starting document for the form letter.
   a) Determine whether to type the letter from scratch in a blank document window or use a letter template.
2. Create or specify the recipient list for the data source.
   a) Determine if the data exists already in an Access database table, an Outlook contacts list, or an Excel worksheet.
   b) If you cannot use an existing data source, create a new one using appropriate field names.
3. Compose the main document for the form letter.
   a) Ensure the letter contains all essential business letter elements and is visually appealing.
   b) Be sure the letter contains proper grammar, correct spelling, logically constructed sentences, flowing paragraphs, and sound ideas.
   c) Properly reference the data in the data source.
4. Merge the main document with the data source to create the form letters.
   a) Determine the destination for the merge (i.e., a new document, the printer, etc.).
   b) Determine which data records to merge (all of them or a portion of them).
5. Determine whether to generate mailing labels or envelopes.
   a) Create or specify the data source.
   b) Ensure the mailing label or envelope contains all necessary information.
6. Create a directory of the data source.
   a) Create or specify the data source.
   b) If necessary, format the directory appropriately.

Student Assignments

Apply Your Knowledge

Reinforce the skills and apply the concepts you learned in this module.

Editing, Printing, and Merging a Form Letter and Recipients in a Data Source

Note: To complete this assignment, you will be required to use the Data Files. Please contact your instructor for information about accessing the Data Files.

Instructions: Using a file manager, such as File Explorer in Windows, copy the file Support_WD_6_VersaillesNewStudentList in the Data Files to the location where you will save your documents in this assignment and then rename the copied file to SC_WD_6_VersaillesNewStudentList.

You will use this data source and the Mail Merge wizard to work with a main document for the form letters created by the admissions director at Versailles Community College to reach out to new students about the upcoming orientation (Figure 6–84). You will enter a date using the date content control, insert the AddressBlock and GreetingLine merge fields, insert additional merge fields, print the form letter, edit the recipients in the data source, and merge the form letters.

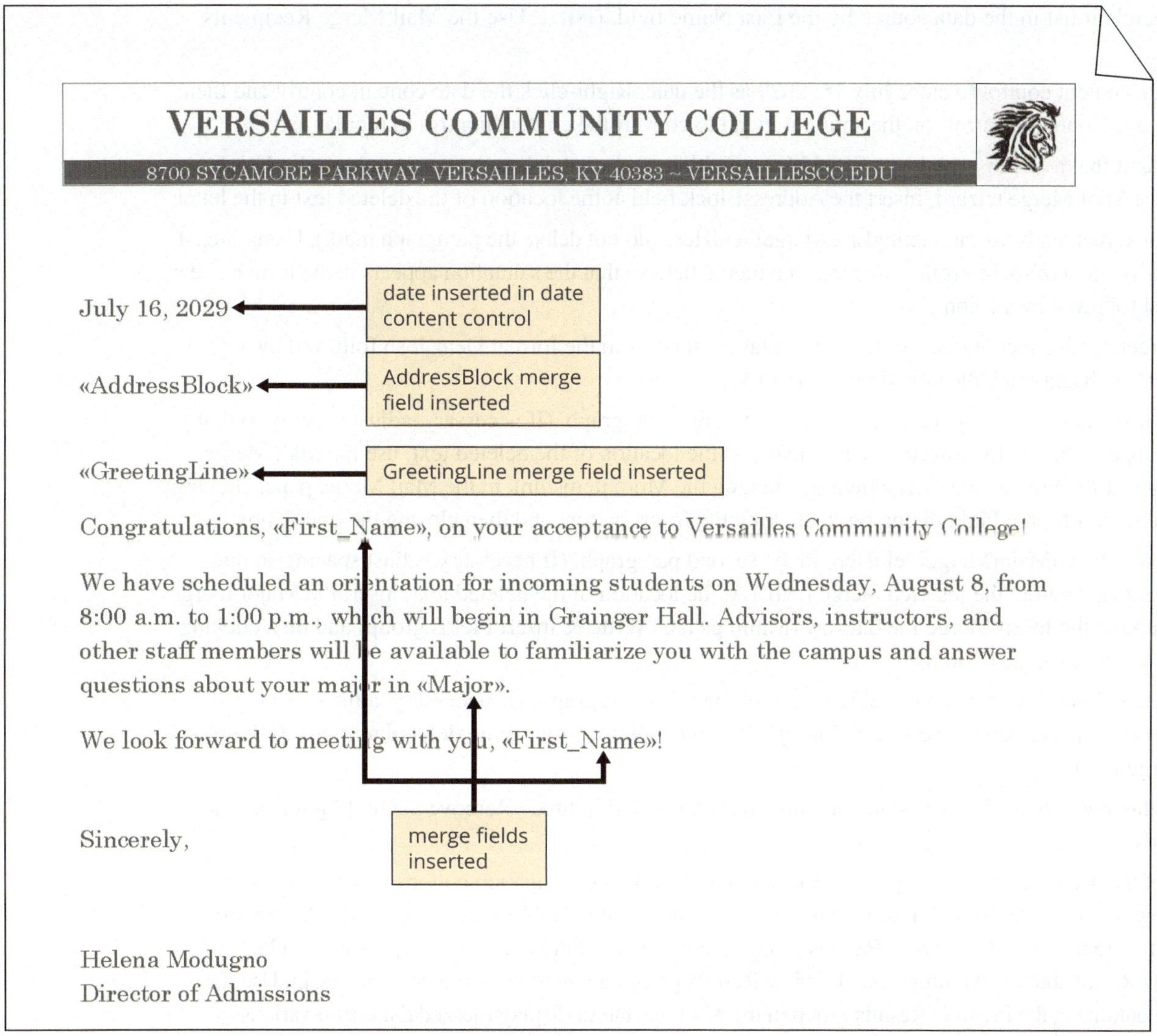
VERSAILLES COMMUNITY COLLEGE
8700 SYCAMORE PARKWAY, VERSAILLES, KY 40383 ~ VERSAILLESCC.EDU

July 16, 2029

«AddressBlock»

«GreetingLine»

Congratulations, «First_Name», on your acceptance to Versailles Community College!

We have scheduled an orientation for incoming students on Wednesday, August 8, from 8:00 a.m. to 1:00 p.m., which will begin in Grainger Hall. Advisors, instructors, and other staff members will be available to familiarize you with the campus and answer questions about your major in «Major».

We look forward to meeting with you, «First_Name»!

Sincerely,

Helena Modugno
Director of Admissions

Clker-Free-Vector-Images/Pixabay

Figure 6–84

Continued on next page

Perform the following tasks:

1. Start Word and create a new blank document and then start the Mail Merge wizard.
2. In Step 1 of the Mail Merge wizard, select Letters as the document type.
3. In Step 2 of the Mail Merge wizard, select 'Start from an existing document' as the starting document and then use the Open button in the Mail Merge pane to open the file called SC_WD_6-1.docx, which is located in the Data Files.
4. Save the document using SC_WD_6_NewStudentOrientationFormLetter as the file name.
5. In Step 3 of the Mail Merge wizard, select 'Use an existing list' and then use the Browse link to open the data source called SC_WD_6_VersaillesNewStudentList (the file you copied from the Data Files at the beginning of this assignment, which contains the new student recipient list). When the Mail Merge Recipients dialog box appears, click OK to close the dialog box.
6. If requested by your instructor, add a record to the data source that contains your personal information and lists your major in the Major field. (**Hint:** Use the 'Edit recipient list' link in the Mail Merge pane or the 'Edit Recipient List' button (Mailings tab | Start Mail Merge group) to display the Mail Merge Recipients dialog box, click the data source name in the Mail Merge Recipients dialog box, and click the Edit button to display the Edit Data Source dialog box.)
7. In the data source (recipient list), change Dana Abrahamsen's apartment number in the Address Line 2 field from 2A to 12A. (Refer to the Hint in Step 6 above.)
8. Sort the recipient list in the data source by the Last Name field. (**Hint:** Use the Mail Merge Recipients dialog box.)
9. Use the date content control to enter July 16, 2029 as the date. Right-click the date content control and then click 'Remove Content Control' on the shortcut menu to convert the content control to regular text.
10. Delete the text that reads InsertAddressBlockMergeFieldHere (do not delete the paragraph mark). Using Step 4 of the Mail Merge wizard, insert the AddressBlock field at the location of the deleted text in the letter.
11. Delete the text that reads InsertGreetingLineMergeFieldHere (do not delete the paragraph mark). Using Step 4 of the Mail Merge wizard, insert the GreetingLine merge field so that the salutation appears in the format, Dear Mr. Randall followed by a colon.
12. Edit the GreetingLine merge field so that the salutation appears in the format Dear Josh followed by a comma. (**Hint:** Right-click the GreetingLine field.)
13. Delete the text InsertFirstNameMergeFieldHere in the first paragraph. (If necessary, adjust spacing so that one space appears before the inserted merge field.) At the location of the deleted text, use the Mail Merge wizard to insert the First Name merge field by clicking the More items link in the Mail Merge pane, clicking First Name (Insert Merge Field dialog box), clicking the Insert button, and then closing the dialog box.
14. Delete the text InsertMajorMergeFieldHere in the second paragraph. (If necessary, adjust spacing so that one space appears before the inserted merge field.) At the location of the deleted text, insert the Major merge field by clicking the Insert Merge Field arrow (Mailings tab | Write & Insert Fields group) and then clicking Major in the Insert Merge Field list.
15. Delete the text InsertFirstNameMergeFieldHere in the third paragraph. (If necessary, adjust spacing so that one space appears before the inserted merge field.) At the location of the deleted text, insert the First Name merge field.
16. Highlight the merge fields in the document. How many were highlighted? Remove the highlight from the merge fields.
17. In Step 4 of the Mail Merge wizard, preview the mail merge. Use the navigation buttons in the Mail Merge pane to view merged data from various data records in the recipient list in the data source. Click the Preview Results button (Mailings tab | Preview Results group) to view merge fields (turn off the preview results). Click the Preview Results button (Mailings tab | Preview Results group) again to view merged data again. Use the navigation buttons in the Preview Results group in the Mailings tab to display merged data from various records in the data source. What is the last name shown in the first record? The third record? The fifth record?
18. Use the 'Find a recipient' link in the Mail Merge pane in Step 5 of the Mail Merge wizard or the Find Recipient button (Mailings tab | Preview Results group) to find the name, Bailey. In what city does Bailey live?

19. Print the main document for the form letter (shown in Figure 6–84). If requested by your instructor, save the main document as a PDF.
20. Save the main document for the form letter again.
21. In Step 6 of the Mail Merge wizard, merge the form letters to a new document using the 'Edit individual letters' link. Save the new document with the file name, SC_WD_6_NewStudentMergedLetters. Close the merged letters document.
22. If requested by your instructor, merge the form letters directly to the printer using the Print link in Step 6 of the Mail Merge wizard.
23. Close the Mail Merge pane.
24. Submit the saved documents in the format specified by your instructor.
25. **Consider This:** Answer the questions posed in #16, #17, and #18. If you did not want to use the AddressBlock and GreetingLine fields, how would you enter the address and salutation so that the letters printed the correct fields from each record?

Extend Your Knowledge

Extend the skills you learned in this module and experiment with new skills. You may need to use Help to complete the assignment.

Working with an IF Field and a Fill-In Field, and Merging Using Email

Note: To complete this assignment, you will be required to use the Data Files. Please contact your instructor for information about accessing the Data Files.

Instructions: Using your file manager, such as File Explorer in Windows, copy the SC_WD_6-2.docx and Support_WD_6_ArrowInsuranceClientList.mdb files in the Data Files to the location where you will save your documents in this assignment and then rename the copied files to SC_WD_6_ArrowInsuranceFormLetter.docx and SC_WD_6_ArrowInsuranceClientList.mdb, respectively.

Start Word. Open the document, SC_WD_6_ArrowInsuranceFormLetter. When you open the main document, if Word displays a dialog box about an SQL command, click the Yes button. If Word prompts for the name of the data source, navigate to and open the file you just copied and named SC_WD_6_ArrowInsuranceClientList. (If Word does not prompt for the data source name, change the data source to the file you just copied and named SC_WD_6_ArrowInsuranceClientList.)

The Word document is a main document for a form letter from a customer service manager with Arrow Insurance alerting customers of a new payment address (Figure 6–85). You will modify the letter, insert and modify an IF field, insert a Fill-in field, print field codes, create envelopes for records in the data source, use an Access database file as a data source, and merge to email addresses.

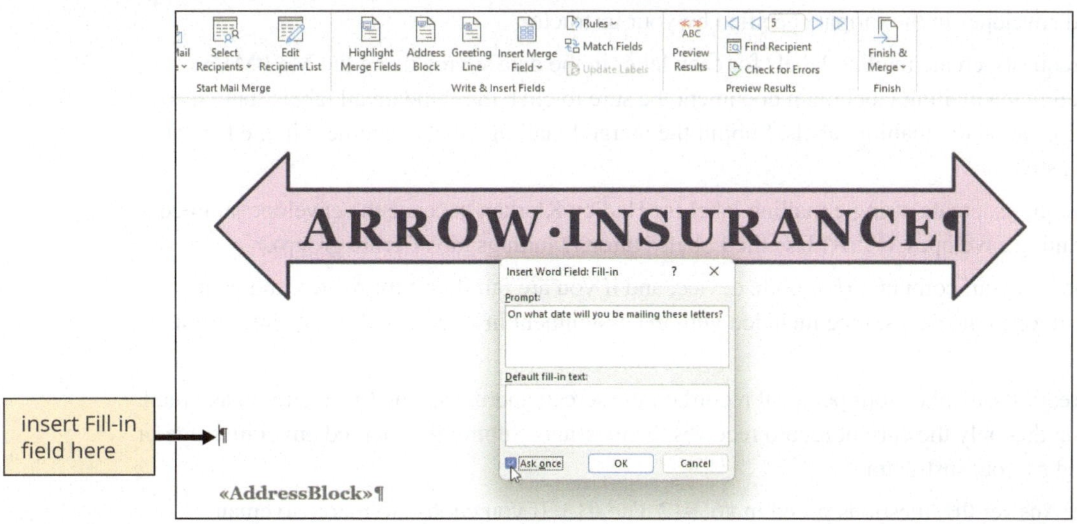

Figure 6–85

Continued on next page

Perform the following tasks:

1. Use Help to learn about mail merge, IF fields, Fill-in fields, and merging to email addresses.
2. Change the top margin to .75 inches, the bottom margin to 1 inch, and the left and right margins to 1.25 inches.
3. Specify the position of the arrow shape that contains the company name to .75 inch from the top of the page.
4. Position the insertion point on the blank paragraph mark below the text, Payment Processing Center, in the body of the letter. At this location, insert an IF field that tests the value in the Region Code field. If the value in the Region Code field is a W, then the text, P.O. Box 2902, should be displayed; otherwise, the text, P.O. Box 2904, should be displayed. View merged data and scroll through the data records to be sure the IF field works as intended.
5. When viewing merged data, you notice that post office box for the west region is incorrect: it should be 2903 instead of 2902. Edit the IF field so that the text displayed is P.O. Box 2903 if the value in the Region field is a W. (**Hint:** Use the 'Toggle Field Codes' command on the shortcut menu (right-click the IF field code in the document window) and edit the IF field directly in the document.) Note that you may need to right-click the field and then click Update Field on the shortcut menu for the update to be displayed on the screen.
6. On the blank paragraph mark above the AddressBlock merge field, insert a Fill-in field that asks this question (shown in Figure 6–85): On what date will you be mailing these letters? Select the Ask once check box so that the question is asked only once, instead of for each letter. When merging the letters, select any weekday that occurs during the month of August 2029. (Be sure to include the month, day, and year, and enter the date in an appropriate format for a letter.) What is the purpose of the Fill-in field?
7. Add a field to the data source called Insurance Type. Enter a value of your choice into this field for each data record in the recipient list (i.e., auto, homeowner, liability, etc.).
8. In the second sentence in the first paragraph, insert the new field called Insurance Type immediately to the left of the word, insurance. If necessary, add a space after the inserted field in the document.
9. If requested by your instructor, add a record to the data source that contains your personal information along with an insurance type of your choice.
10. Merge the letters to a new document. Save the merged letters using the file name, SC_WD_6_ArrowInsuranceMergedLetters. Close this document.
11. Print the main document for the form letter. If requested by your instructor, save the main document as a PDF.
12. Print the form letter with field codes visible; that is, print it with the 'Print field codes instead of their values' check box selected in the Word Options dialog box. Be sure to deselect this check box after printing the field codes version of the letter. How does this printout differ from the one printed in #11?
13. Filter the recipient list to display only those clients in the west region. How many are there? Clear the filter.
14. Submit the main document and merged letters in the format specified by your instructor.
15. If your instructor requests, create envelopes for each letter in the data source using the Mail Merge wizard. Submit the merged envelopes in the format specified by your instructor.
16. If your instructor requests, create mailing labels for each letter in the data source using the Mail Merge wizard. While creating the mailing label main document, be sure to click the 'Update all labels' button so that all recipients appear on the mailing labels. Submit the merged mailing labels document in the format specified by your instructor.
17. If your instructor requests, create a single mailing label for Hadley Klerken because the envelope jammed when you were printing envelopes. (**Hint:** Use the Labels button (Mailings tab | Create group).)
18. If Access is installed on your computer or mobile device, and if you are familiar with Access and your instructor requests it, open the data source included with the assignment in Access and then print it from within Access.
19. If your instructor requests, display your personal record on the screen and merge the form letter to an email message, specifying that only the current record receives the message. Submit the merged email message in the format specified by your instructor.
20. **Consider This:** Answer the questions posed in #6, #12, and #13. If you choose to merge to email addresses, what is the purpose of the various email formats?

Expand Your World

Create a solution that uses cloud or web technologies by learning and investigating on your own from general guidance.

Exploring Add-Ins for Microsoft 365 Apps

Instructions: You regularly use apps on your phone and tablet to look up a variety of information. In Microsoft 365 apps, you can use add-ins, which essentially are apps that work with Word (and the other Microsoft 365 apps). You would like to investigate some of the add-ins available for Word to determine which ones would be helpful for you to use.

Note: You will be required to use your Microsoft account to complete this assignment. If you do not have a Microsoft account and do not want to create one, read this assignment without performing the instructions.

Perform the following tasks:

1. Use Help to learn about add-ins. If necessary, sign in to your Windows account.
2. Start Word and create a new blank document. If you are not signed in already, sign in to your Microsoft Account in Word.
3. Click the Get Add-ins button (Insert tab | Add-ins group) to display the Office Add-ins dialog box. If necessary, click the STORE tab (Office Add-ins dialog box) to visit the online Office Store. (Note that if your Insert tab does not have a Get Add-ins button, search through Help for the location of the button in your version of Word that enables you to work with add-ins.)
4. Scroll through add-ins in the various categories (Figure 6–86). Locate a free add-in that you feel would be helpful to you while you use Word, click the Add button, and then follow the instructions to add the add-in to Word.

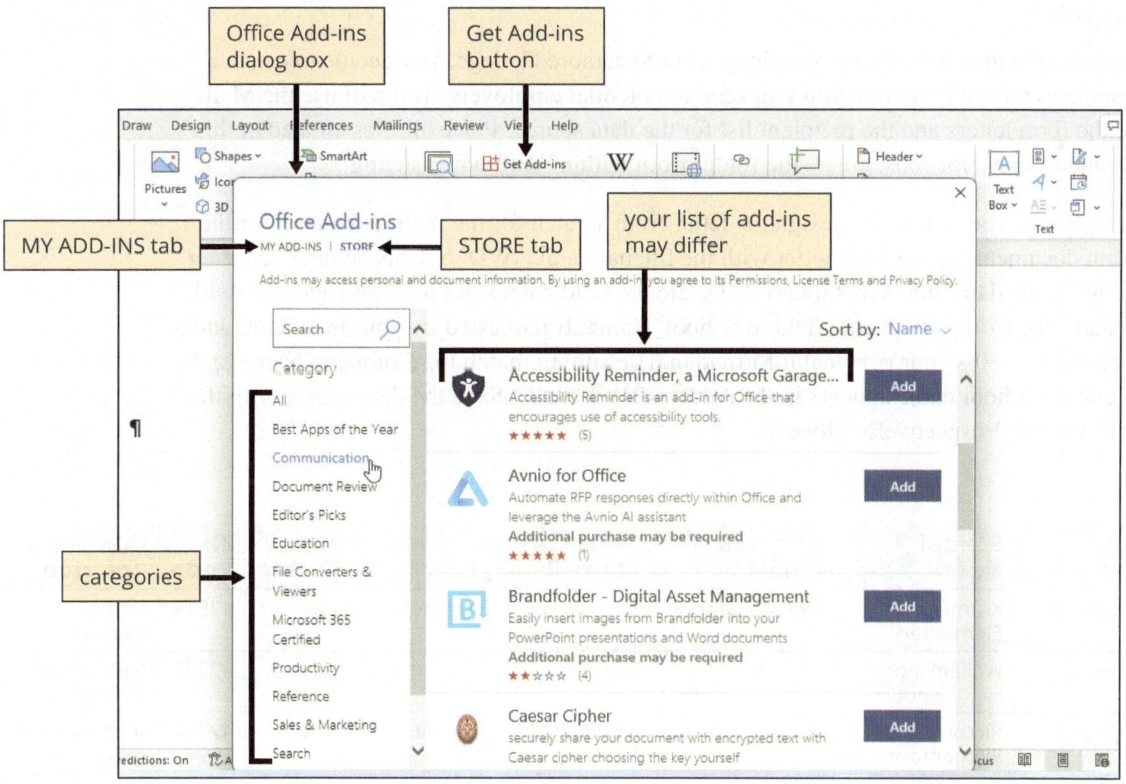

Figure 6–86

Continued on next page

5. In Word, click the My Add-ins button (Insert tab | Add-ins group) to display the MY ADD-INS tab in the Office Add-ins dialog box. Click the add-in you added and then click the Add button to use the add-in.
6. Practice using the add-in. Does the add-in work as you intended? Would you recommend the add-in to others? If you rated this add-in, what would your rating be? Why?
7. In Word, click the My Add-ins button (Insert tab | Add-ins group) to display the MY ADD-INS tab in the Office Add-ins dialog box. Click the 'Manage My Add-ins' link in the upper-right corner of the Office Add-ins dialog box to open the My Office and SharePoint add-ins window in a browser and display available add-ins. Note that if you want to cancel a paid subscription to an add-in, you would do it in this window. Close the My Office and SharePoint add-ins window.
8. To view add-ins included with Microsoft 365, open Backstage view, click Options to display the Word Options dialog box, and click Add-ins in the left pane (Word Options dialog box). To manage an add-in, select the desired add-in type in the Manage list at the bottom of the Word Options dialog box and then click the Go button. Close the Word Options dialog box.
9. In Word, click the My Add-ins button (Insert tab | Add-ins group) to display the MY ADD-INS tab in the Office Add-ins dialog box. Right-click the add-in you added in this assignment, click Remove on the shortcut menu, and then click the Remove button in the dialog box to remove the add-in from your Word app.
10. **Consider This:** Which add-ins, if any, were already on your computer or mobile device? Which add-in did you download and why? Answer the questions in #6.

In the Lab

Design and implement a solution using creative thinking and problem-solving skills.

Use Mail Merge to Create Cover Letters for a Graduating Psychology Student

Problem: You are graduating with a degree in psychology from Sycamore College. You decide to create a cover letter for your resume as a form letter that you will send to potential employers. You will use the Mail Merge wizard to create the form letters and the recipient list for the data source. Place all files created in this assignment in a folder called Counselor Jobs; create the folder from within Word when saving.

Part 1: Use a letter template of your choice or design the letter from scratch for the main document for the form letter. Save the main document for the form letter with the file name, SC_WD_6_CounselorCoverLetter. Type a new data source using the data shown in Table 6–1. Delete the field names not used and add one field name: Job Position. Rename the Company_Name field to School_Name. If requested by your instructor, add a record to the data source that contains your personal information. (Be sure to match the Company Name to the School_Name field so that the school name appears in the AddressBlock field.) Save the data source with the file name, SC_WD_6_CounselorProspectiveEmployers.

Table 6–1

Title	First Name	Last Name	School Name	Address Line 1	Address Line 2	City	State	ZIP Code	Job Position
Ms.	Nia	Huddleston	Kramer Elementary	998 Main Street		Kramer	IN	47918	school counselor
Ms.	Lydia	Ballerini	Williamsport High School	8031 Mill Street	P.O. Box 23	Williamsport	IN	47993	high school counselor
Mr.	Saule	Nogueira	Rictor Elementary	4093 Vine Street	Building C	Veedersburg	IN	47987	school-based counselor
Ms.	Malvina	Miyake	Newtown School District	819 Roberts Place	HR Department	West Lebanon	IN	47991	counselor
Mr.	Ramzan	Courtenay	Johnston Elementary School	6201 Boyer Street		Pine Village	IN	47975	guidance counselor

Use this information in the cover letter:

Name: Andile De Lang (if requested by your instructor, use your name).

Address: 6687 Pine Street, Apt. 3B, Attica, IN, 47918 (if requested by your instructor, use your address).

Phone: 765-555-2878 (if requested by your instructor, use your phone number).

Email: andile@cengage.net (if requested by your instructor, use your email address).

LinkedIn profile address: linkedin.com/in/andile-counselor (if requested by your instructor, use your LinkedIn profile address if you have one).

First paragraph in body of letter, inserting a merge field as indicated: I enjoyed meeting with you during the Sycamore College job fair this week. My resume is enclosed for your review. I am interested in the <InsertJobPositionMergeFieldHere> position at <InsertSchoolNameMergeFieldHere> that we discussed and am confident I am the ideal candidate for the job.

Second paragraph in body of letter: I will graduate in May with a Bachelor of Arts degree in Psychology. My education has been strengthened through my work experience, memberships, and community service.

Third paragraph in body of letter, inserting merge fields as indicated: Thank you in advance, <InsertTitleMergeFieldHere> <InsertLastNameMergeFieldHere>, for your time and consideration. I look forward to hearing from you soon to discuss my qualifications and the opportunity for my potential employment as a <InsertJobPositionMergeFieldHere> at <InsertSchoolNameMergeFieldHere>.

In the main document, include the AddressBlock and GreetingLine merge fields. Use the concepts and techniques presented in this module to create and format this form letter. Be sure to check the accessibility and spelling and grammar of the finished documents. Use the 'Check for Errors' button (Mailings tab | Preview Results group) to check if the main document contains merge errors and fix any errors identified. If requested by your instructor, save the main document as a PDF. Merge all records to a new document. Save the merged letters in a file called SC_WD_6_CounselorMergedCoverLetters.

In a new document window, create a directory of the recipient list in the data source. Begin by specifying the main document type as a directory. Change the page layout to landscape orientation. Change the margins to narrow. Insert all merge fields in the document, separating each with a comma. Save the directory layout with the file name, SC_WD_6_CounselorProspectiveEmployersDirectoryLayout. Merge the directory layout to a new document window. Convert the list of fields to a Word table (the table will have 10 columns). Add a row to the top of the table and insert field names in the empty cells. Format the table appropriately. Sort the table in the directory listing by the Last Name field. Save the merged directory with the file name, SC_WD_6_CounselorProspectiveEmployersMergedDirectoryListing.

Submit your assignment documents and answers to the Part 2 critical thinking questions in the format specified by your instructor.

Part 2: **Consider This:** You made several decisions while creating the form letter, data source, and directory in this assignment: whether to use a template or create the letter from scratch, layout of letter elements, how to format elements, how to set up the data source, and how to format the directory. What was the rationale behind each of these decisions?

Creating a Newsletter

Objectives

After completing this module, you will be able to:

- Create, edit, and format WordArt
- Set custom tab stops
- Add and format paragraph and page borders
- Format objects
- Arrange objects on a page
- Insert section and column breaks
- Format text in columns
- Justify a paragraph
- Insert text from an external file
- Hyphenate a document
- Format a character as a drop cap
- Insert and format a text box
- Copy and paste using a split Word window
- Modify and format a SmartArt graphic
- Copy and paste from one open document to another

Introduction

Professional-looking documents, such as newsletters and brochures, often are created using desktop publishing software. With desktop publishing software, you can divide a document in multiple columns, wrap text around diagrams and other graphical images, change fonts and font sizes, add color and lines, and so on, to create an attention-grabbing document. Desktop publishing software, such as Microsoft Publisher, Adobe InDesign, or QuarkXPress, enables you to open an existing word processing document and enhance it through formatting tools not provided in your word processing app. Word, however, provides many of the formatting features that you would find in a desktop publishing app. Thus, you can use Word to create eye-catching newsletters and brochures.

Project: Newsletter

A newsletter is a publication geared for a specific audience that is created on a recurring basis, such as weekly, monthly, or quarterly. The audience may be subscribers, employees, customers, patrons, students, etc.

The project in this module uses Word to produce the two-page newsletter shown in Figure 7–1. The newsletter is a monthly publication called *Healthy Habits* that is written by Hope Medical Center for staff, patients, and visitors. Each issue of *Healthy Habits* contains a feature article and announcements. This month's feature article discusses some health concerns of using technology. The feature article spans the first two columns of the first page of the newsletter and then continues on the second page. The announcements, which are located in the third column of the first page, inform readers about an upcoming webinar, encourage them to join the walking club, and announce the topic of the next issue's feature article.

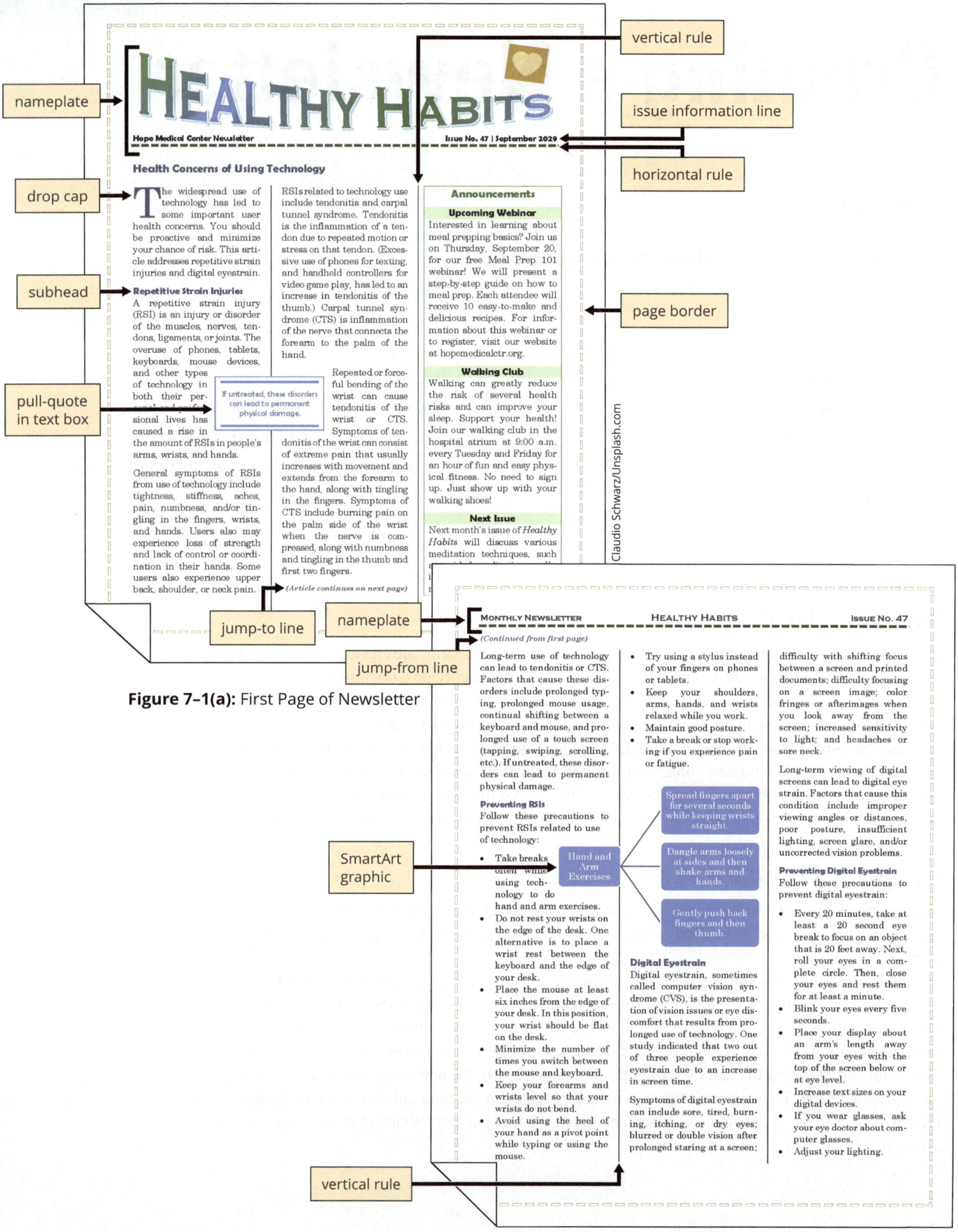

HEALTHY HABITS

Hope Medical Center Newsletter | Issue No. 47 | September 2029

Health Concerns of Using Technology

The widespread use of technology has led to some important user health concerns. You should be proactive and minimize your chance of risk. This article addresses repetitive strain injuries and digital eyestrain.

Repetitive Strain Injuries

A repetitive strain injury (RSI) is an injury or disorder of the muscles, nerves, tendons, ligaments, or joints. The overuse of phones, tablets, keyboards, mouse devices, and other types of technology in both their personal and professional lives has caused a rise in the amount of RSIs in people's arms, wrists, and hands.

If untreated, these disorders can lead to permanent physical damage.

General symptoms of RSIs from use of technology include tightness, stiffness, aches, pain, numbness, and/or tingling in the fingers, wrists, and hands. Users also may experience loss of strength and lack of control or coordination in their hands. Some users also experience upper back, shoulder, or neck pain.

RSIs related to technology use include tendonitis and carpal tunnel syndrome. Tendonitis is the inflammation of a tendon due to repeated motion or stress on that tendon. (Excessive use of phones for texting, and handheld controllers for video game play, has led to an increase in tendonitis of the thumb.) Carpal tunnel syndrome (CTS) is inflammation of the nerve that connects the forearm to the palm of the hand.

Repeated or forceful bending of the wrist can cause tendonitis of the wrist or CTS. Symptoms of tendonitis of the wrist can consist of extreme pain that usually increases with movement and extends from the forearm to the hand, along with tingling in the fingers. Symptoms of CTS include burning pain on the palm side of the wrist when the nerve is compressed, along with numbness and tingling in the thumb and first two fingers.

(Article continues on next page)

Announcements

Upcoming Webinar

Interested in learning about meal prepping basics? Join us on Thursday, September 20, for our free Meal Prep 101 webinar! We will present a step-by-step guide on how to meal prep. Each attendee will receive 10 easy-to-make and delicious recipes. For information about this webinar or to register, visit our website at hopemedicalctr.org.

Walking Club

Walking can greatly reduce the risk of several health risks and can improve your sleep. Support your health! Join our walking club in the hospital atrium at 9:00 a.m. every Tuesday and Friday for an hour of fun and easy physical fitness. No need to sign up. Just show up with your walking shoes!

Next Issue

Next month's issue of *Healthy Habits* will discuss various meditation techniques, such

MONTHLY NEWSLETTER | HEALTHY HABITS | ISSUE NO. 47

(Continued from first page)

Long-term use of technology can lead to tendonitis or CTS. Factors that cause these disorders include prolonged typing, prolonged mouse usage, continual shifting between a keyboard and mouse, and prolonged use of a touch screen (tapping, swiping, scrolling, etc.). If untreated, these disorders can lead to permanent physical damage.

Preventing RSIs

Follow these precautions to prevent RSIs related to use of technology:

- Take breaks often while using technology to do hand and arm exercises.
- Do not rest your wrists on the edge of the desk. One alternative is to place a wrist rest between the keyboard and the edge of your desk.
- Place the mouse at least six inches from the edge of your desk. In this position, your wrist should be flat on the desk.
- Minimize the number of times you switch between the mouse and keyboard.
- Keep your forearms and wrists level so that your wrists do not bend.
- Avoid using the heel of your hand as a pivot point while typing or using the mouse.
- Try using a stylus instead of your fingers on phones or tablets.
- Keep your shoulders, arms, hands, and wrists relaxed while you work.
- Maintain good posture.
- Take a break or stop working if you experience pain or fatigue.

Hand and Arm Exercises: Spread fingers apart for several seconds while keeping wrists straight. / Dangle arms loosely at sides and then shake arms and hands. / Gently push back fingers and then thumb.

Digital Eyestrain

Digital eyestrain, sometimes called computer vision syndrome (CVS), is the presentation of vision issues or eye discomfort that results from prolonged use of technology. One study indicated that two out of three people experience eyestrain due to an increase in screen time.

Symptoms of digital eyestrain can include sore, tired, burning, itching, or dry eyes; blurred or double vision after prolonged staring at a screen; difficulty with shifting focus between a screen and printed documents; difficulty focusing on a screen image; color fringes or afterimages when you look away from the screen; increased sensitivity to light; and headaches or sore neck.

Long-term viewing of digital screens can lead to digital eye strain. Factors that cause this condition include improper viewing angles or distances, poor posture, insufficient lighting, screen glare, and/or uncorrected vision problems.

Preventing Digital Eyestrain

Follow these precautions to prevent digital eyestrain:

- Every 20 minutes, take at least a 20 second eye break to focus on an object that is 20 feet away. Next, roll your eyes in a complete circle. Then, close your eyes and rest them for at least a minute.
- Blink your eyes every five seconds.
- Place your display about an arm's length away from your eyes with the top of the screen below or at eye level.
- Increase text sizes on your digital devices.
- If you wear glasses, ask your eye doctor about computer glasses.
- Adjust your lighting.

Figure 7–1(a): First Page of Newsletter

Figure 7–1(b): Second Page of Newsletter

The *Healthy Habits* newsletter in this module incorporates the desktop publishing features of Word. The body of each page of the newsletter is divided in three columns. A variety of fonts, font sizes, and colors add visual appeal to the document. The first page has text wrapped around a pull-quote, and the second page has text wrapped around a graphic. Horizontal and vertical lines separate distinct areas of the newsletter, including a page border around the perimeter of each page.

The project in this module involves several steps requiring you to drag and drop. If you drag to the wrong location, you may want to cancel an action. Remember that you always can click the Undo button (Home tab | Undo group) or press CTRL+Z to cancel your most recent action.

In this module, you will learn how to create the newsletter shown in Figure 7–1. You will perform the following general tasks as you progress through this module:

1. Create the nameplate for the first page of the newsletter.
2. Format the first page of the body of the newsletter.
3. Create a pull-quote on the first page of the newsletter.
4. Create the nameplate for the second page of the newsletter.
5. Format the second page of the body of the newsletter.
6. Add a page border to the newsletter.

Desktop Publishing Terminology

As you create professional-looking newsletters and brochures, you should be familiar with several desktop publishing terms. Figure 7–1 identifies these terms:

- A **nameplate**, or **banner**, is the portion of a newsletter that contains the title of the newsletter and usually an issue information line.
- The **issue information line** identifies the specific publication.
- A **ruling line**, usually identified by its direction as a **horizontal rule** or **vertical rule**, is a line that separates areas of the newsletter.
- A **subhead** is a heading within the body of the newsletter that is subordinate to a higher level heading.
- A **pull-quote** is a text box that contains a quote or excerpt from the document that is pulled, or copied, from the text of the document and given graphical emphasis when it is placed elsewhere in the document.

To Start Word and Specify Settings

If you are using a computer to step through the project in this module and you want your screens to match the figures in this book, you should change your screen's resolution to 1366 × 768. The following steps start Word, display formatting marks, change the zoom to page width, and verify ruler and Mouse mode settings.

1. sam Start Word and create a blank document in the Word window. If necessary, maximize the Word window.
2. If the Print Layout button on the status bar is not selected, click it so that your screen is in Print Layout view.
3. If the 'Show/Hide ¶' button (Home tab | Paragraph group) is not selected already, click it to display formatting marks on the screen.
4. To display the page the same width as the document window, if necessary, click the Page Width button (View tab | Zoom group).
5. Verify that the Ruler check box (View tab | Show group) is not selected. (If it is selected, click it to remove the check mark because you do not want the rulers to appear on the screen.)

6 If you are using a mouse and you want your screens to match the figures in the book, verify that you are using Mouse mode by doing the following: display the Quick Access Toolbar, if necessary, by clicking the 'Ribbon Display Options' button at the right edge of the ribbon and then clicking 'Show Quick Access Toolbar' on the menu; clicking the 'Touch/Mouse Mode' button on the Quick Access Toolbar and then, if necessary, clicking Mouse on the menu (if your Quick Access Toolbar does not display the 'Touch/Mouse Mode' button, click the 'Customize Quick Access Toolbar' button on the Quick Access Toolbar and then click Touch/Mouse Mode on the menu to add the button to the Quick Access Toolbar); then hide the Quick Access Toolbar by clicking the 'Ribbon Display Options' button at the right edge of the ribbon and then clicking 'Hide Quick Access Toolbar' on the menu.

To Adjust Margins

Word is preset to use standard 8.5-by-11-inch paper, with 1-inch top, bottom, left, and right margins. For the newsletter in this module, all margins (left, right, top, and bottom) are .75 inches, which is not a predefined setting in the Margins gallery. Thus, the following steps set custom margins.

1. Display the Layout tab.
2. Click the Margins button (Layout tab | Page Setup group) to display the Margins gallery and then click Custom Margins at the bottom of the Margins gallery to display the Page Setup dialog box.
3. If necessary, click the Margins tab and then change each value in the Top, Bottom, Left, and Right boxes (Page Setup dialog box) to .75 (Figure 7–2).
4. Click OK to change the margin values.

BTW
Touch Mode Differences
The Office and Windows interfaces may vary if you are using Touch mode. For this reason, you might notice that the function or appearance of your touch screen differs slightly from this module's presentation.

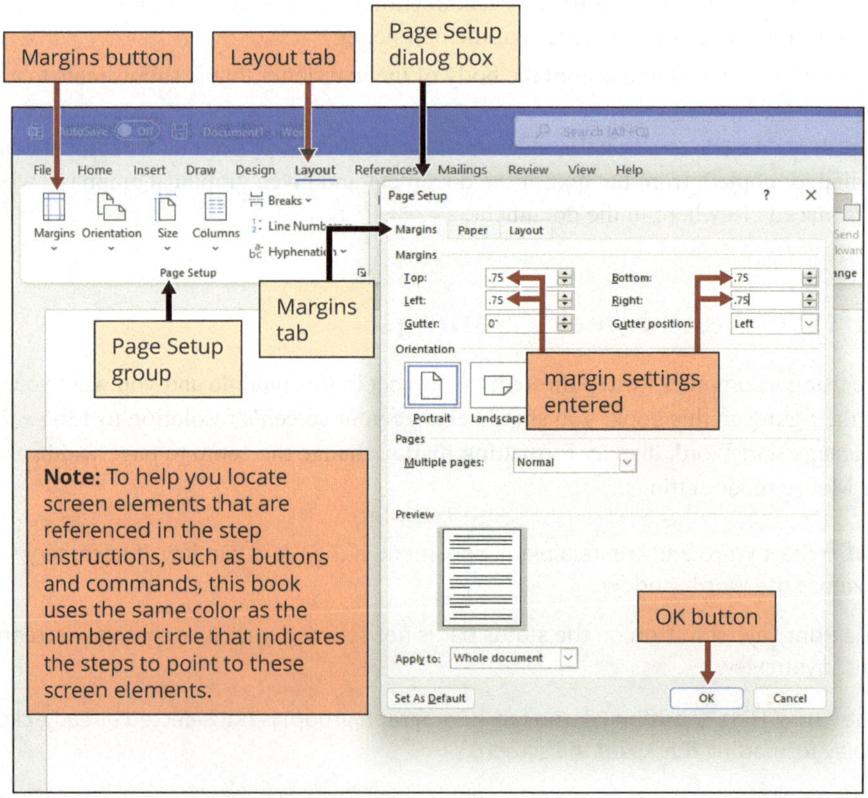

Figure 7–2

BTW
The Ribbon and Screen Resolution
Word may change how the groups and buttons within the groups appear on the ribbon, depending on the screen resolution of your computer. Thus, your ribbon may look different from the ones in this book if you are using a screen resolution other than 1366 × 768.

To Change Theme Fonts

The newsletter in this module uses a customized set of fonts. The following steps change the theme fonts.

1. Display the Design tab.
2. Click the Fonts button (Design tab | Document Formatting group) and then click Customize Fonts in the Fonts gallery to display the Create New Theme Fonts dialog box.
3. Select 'Berlin Sans FB Demi' as the Heading font and then select Century Schoolbook as the Body font (Create New Theme Fonts dialog box).
4. Type **Newsletter** in the Name text box to name the custom font and then click Save (Create New Theme Fonts dialog box).

Creating the Nameplate

The nameplate on the first page of this newsletter consists of the information above the multiple columns (shown in Figure 7–1a at the beginning of this module). In this project, the nameplate includes the newsletter title, Healthy Habits, an image of a medical heart, and the issue information line.

The following sections use the steps outlined below to create the nameplate for the first page of the newsletter in this module.

1. Enter and format the newsletter title using WordArt.
2. Set custom tab stops for the issue information line.
3. Enter text in the issue information line.
4. Add a horizontal rule below the issue information line.
5. Insert and format the image.

Consider This

How should you design a nameplate?

A nameplate visually identifies a newsletter. It should catch the attention of readers and pique their interest in reading a newsletter. Usually, the nameplate is positioned horizontally across the top of the newsletter, although some nameplates are vertical. The nameplate typically consists of the title of the newsletter and the issue information line. Some also include a subtitle, a slogan, and a graphical image or logo.

Guidelines for the newsletter title and other elements in the nameplate are as follows:

- Compose a title that is short, yet conveys the contents of the newsletter. In the newsletter title, eliminate unnecessary words and avoid the word, newsletter. Use a decorative font in as large a font size as possible so that the title stands out on the page.
- Other elements on the nameplate should not compete in size with the title. Use colors that complement the title. Select easy-to-read fonts.
- Arrange the elements of the nameplate so that it does not have a cluttered appearance. If necessary, use ruling lines to visually separate areas of the nameplate.

To Convert Text to WordArt

WordArt is a type of graphic that enables you to create decorative text in a text box or other shape with special effects, such as shadowed, rotated, stretched, skewed, and wavy effects. This project uses WordArt for the newsletter title, Healthy Habits. **Why?** A title created with WordArt is likely to draw the reader's attention. The following steps convert text to WordArt.

1

- Type **Healthy Habits** on the first line of the document and then select the entered text.
- Display the Insert tab.
- Click the Insert WordArt button (Insert tab | Text group) to display the WordArt gallery (Figure 7–3).

Q&A Once I select a WordArt style, can I customize its appearance?
Yes. The next steps customize the WordArt style selected here.

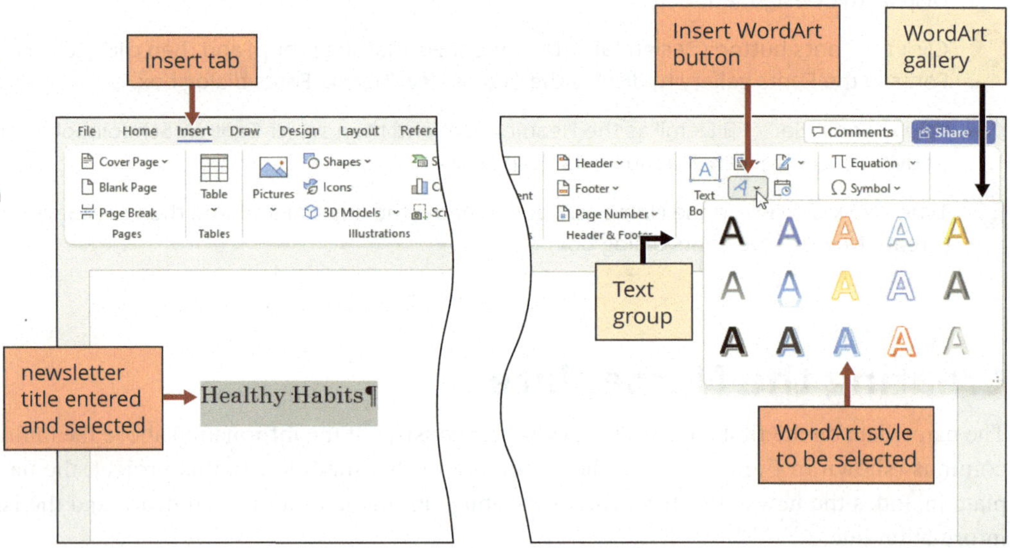

Figure 7–3

2

- Click 'Fill: Blue, Accent color 5; Outline: White, Background color 1; Hard Shadow: Blue, Accent color 5' in the WordArt gallery (third WordArt style in last row) to insert a WordArt object in the document that is formatted according to the selected style, which contains the selected text, Healthy Habits (Figure 7–4).

Q&A What if I do not select text before selecting a WordArt style?
WordArt initially contains the placeholder text, Your text here, which you can replace with your desired text.

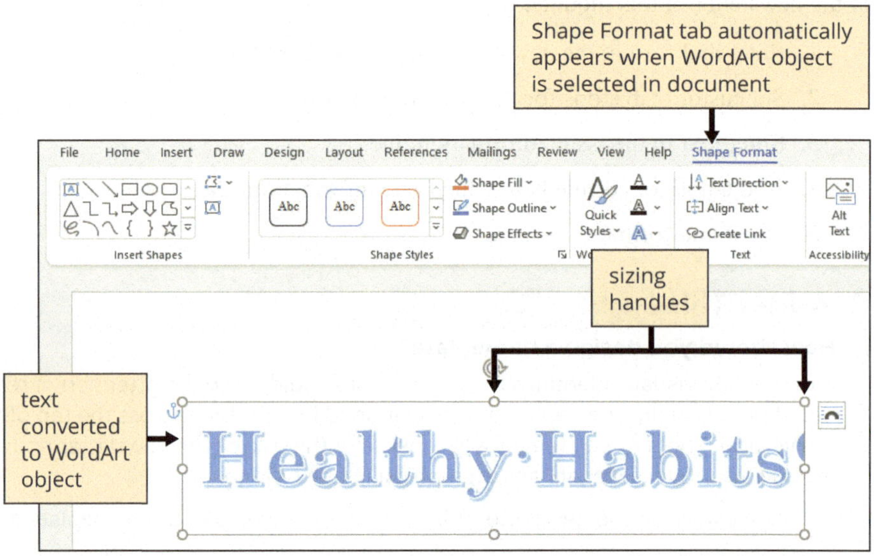

Figure 7–4

To Resize WordArt

You resize a WordArt object the same way you resize any other graphic. That is, you can drag its sizing handles or enter values in the Shape Height and Shape Width boxes. The next steps resize the WordArt object.

1 With the WordArt object selected, if necessary, display the Shape Format tab.

2 Change the value in the Shape Height box (Shape Format tab | Size group) to 1.44 and the value in the Shape Width box (Shape Format tab | Size group) to 7 (Figure 7–5). (Note that you may need to press ENTER after typing 7 in the Shape Width box for the change to take effect.)

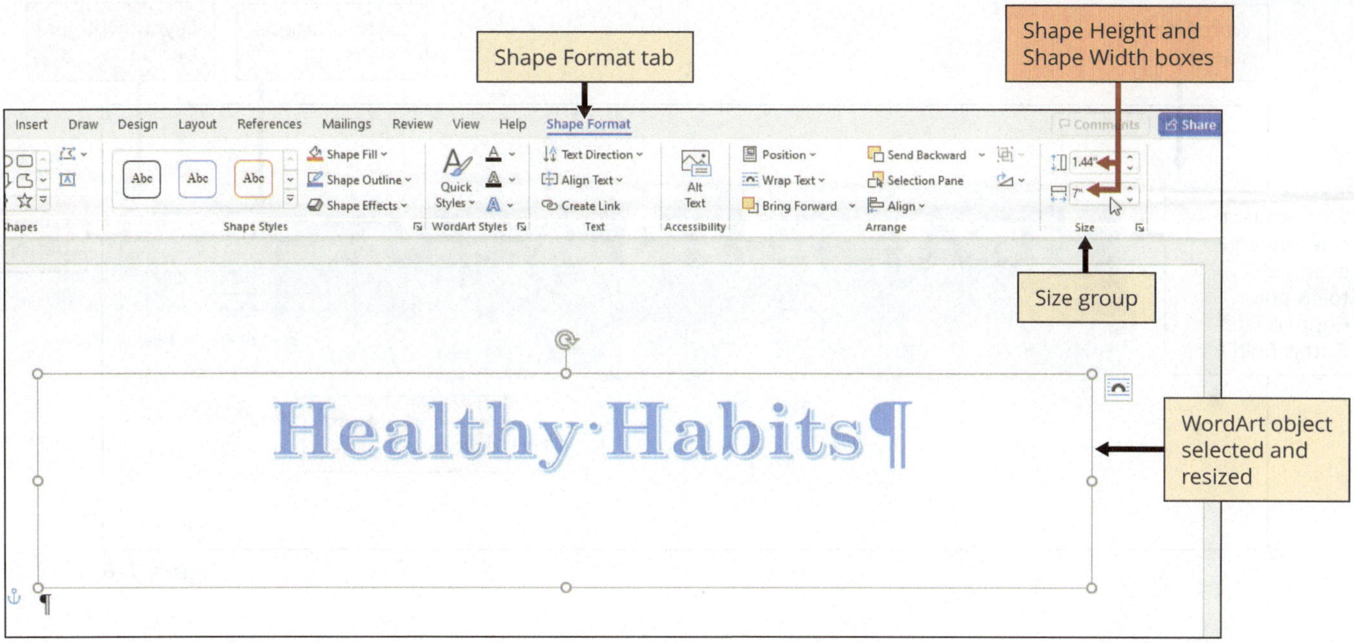

Figure 7-5

To Change the Font and Font Size of WordArt Text

You change the font and font size of WordArt text the same way you change the font and font size of any other text. That is, you select the text and then change its font and font size. The following steps change the font and font size of the WordArt text.

1. If necessary, select the text, Healthy Habits.
2. Change the font of the selected text to 'Copperplate Gothic Bold' (or a similar font).
3. Change the font size of the selected text to 48 point (shown in Figure 7–6).

To Change an Object's Text Wrapping

When you insert an object in a Word document, the default text wrapping is Square, which means text will wrap around the object in the shape of a square. Because you want the nameplate above the rest of the newsletter, you change the text wrapping for the shape to Top and Bottom. The following steps change an object's text wrapping.

1. With the WordArt object selected, click the Layout Options button that is attached to the WordArt object to display the Layout Options gallery.
2. Click 'Top and Bottom' in the Layout Options gallery so that the WordArt object will not cover the document text (Figure 7–6).
3. Close the Layout Options gallery.

Q&A What if my WordArt does not show a Layout Options button?
With the WordArt selected, click the Wrap Text button (Shape Format tab | Arrange group) to display the Wrap Text gallery and then click 'Top and Bottom' in the Wrap Text gallery.

BTW
Deleting WordArt
If you want to delete a WordArt object, right-click it and then click Cut on the shortcut menu, or select the WordArt object and then click the Cut button (Home tab | Clipboard group).

Figure 7–6

To Change the WordArt Text Fill Color

The next step is to change the color of the WordArt text so that it displays a green and blue gradient fill color. **Gradient** is a gradual progression of colors and shades, usually from one color to another color or from one shade to another shade of the same color. Word includes several built-in gradient fill colors, or you can customize one for use in objects. The following steps change the fill color of the WordArt text to a built-in gradient fill color and then customize the selected fill color. **Why?** Using a gradient fill color will add interest to the title.

1

- With the WordArt object selected, click the Text Fill arrow (Shape Format tab | WordArt Styles group) to display the Text Fill gallery.

Q&A The Text Fill gallery did not appear. Why not?
Be sure you click the Text Fill arrow, which is to the right of the Text Fill button. If you mistakenly click the Text Fill button, Word places a default fill in the selected WordArt instead of displaying the Text Fill gallery.

2

- Point to Gradient in the Text Fill gallery to display the Gradient gallery (Figure 7–7).

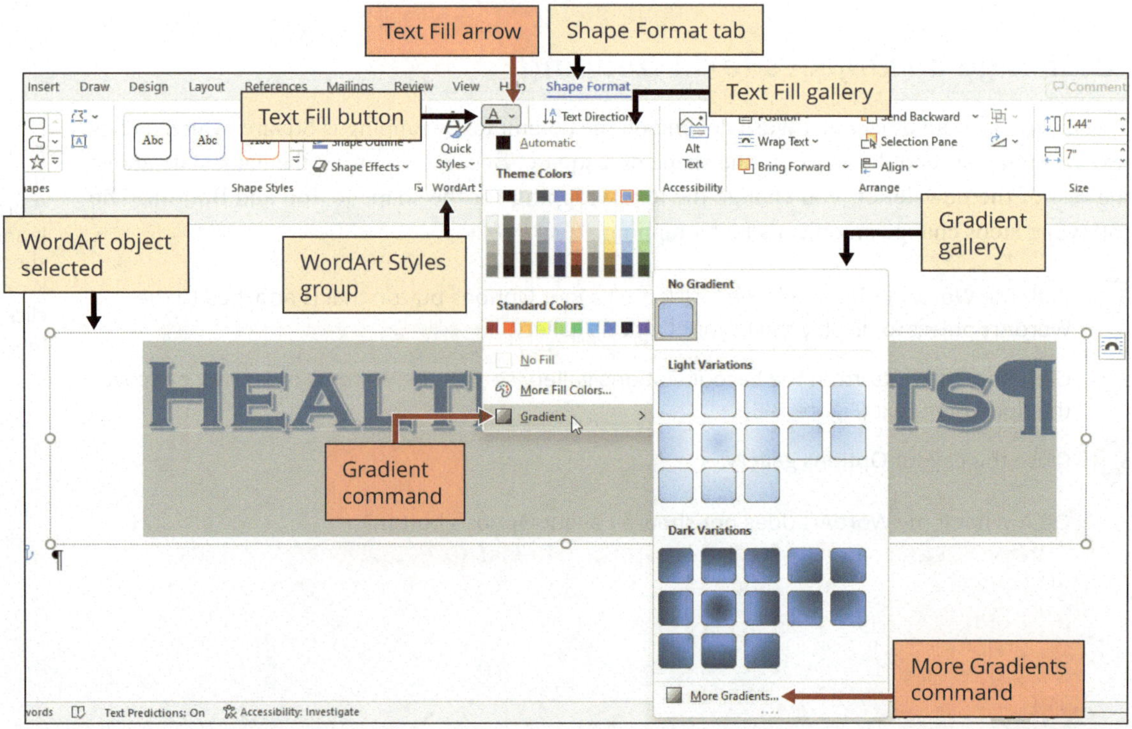

Figure 7–7

3

- Click More Gradients in the Gradient gallery to open the Format Shape pane. If necessary, click the Text Options tab in the Format Shape pane and then, if necessary, click the 'Text Fill & Outline' button. If necessary, expand the Text Fill section.
- Click Gradient fill in the Text Fill section to display options related to gradient colors in the pane (Figure 7–8).

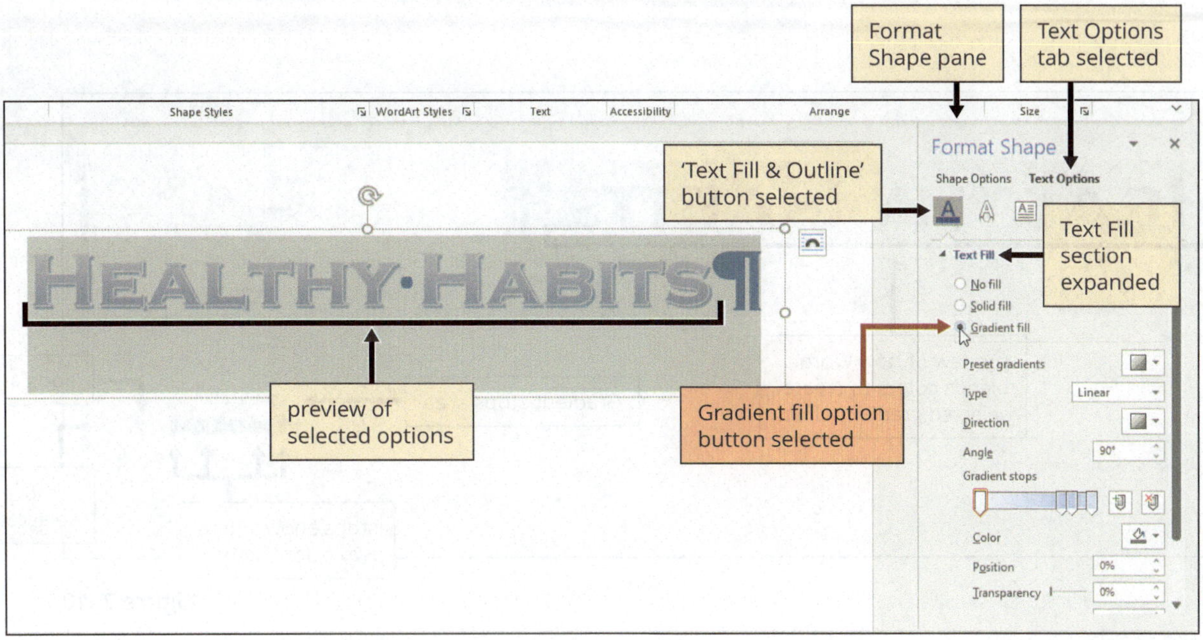

Figure 7–8

4

- Click the Preset gradients button in the Format Shape pane to display a palette of built-in gradient fill colors (Figure 7–9).

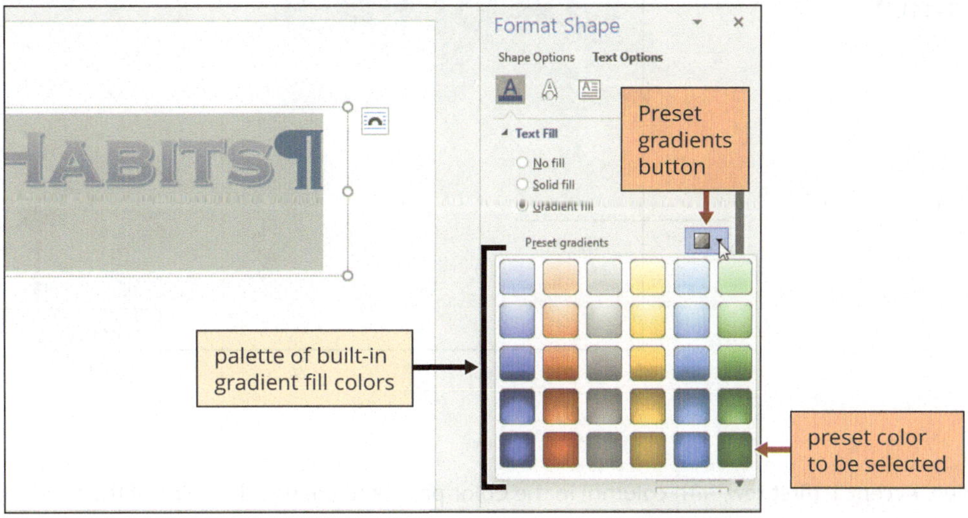

Figure 7–9

5

- Click 'Radial Gradient - Accent 6' (bottom row, sixth column) in the Preset gradients palette to select the built-in gradient color, which shows a preview in the Gradient stops area (Figure 7–10).

Q&A What is a gradient stop?
A gradient stop is the location where two colors blend. You can change the color of a stop so that Word changes the color of the blend. You also can add or delete stops, with a minimum of two stops and a maximum of ten stops per gradient fill color.

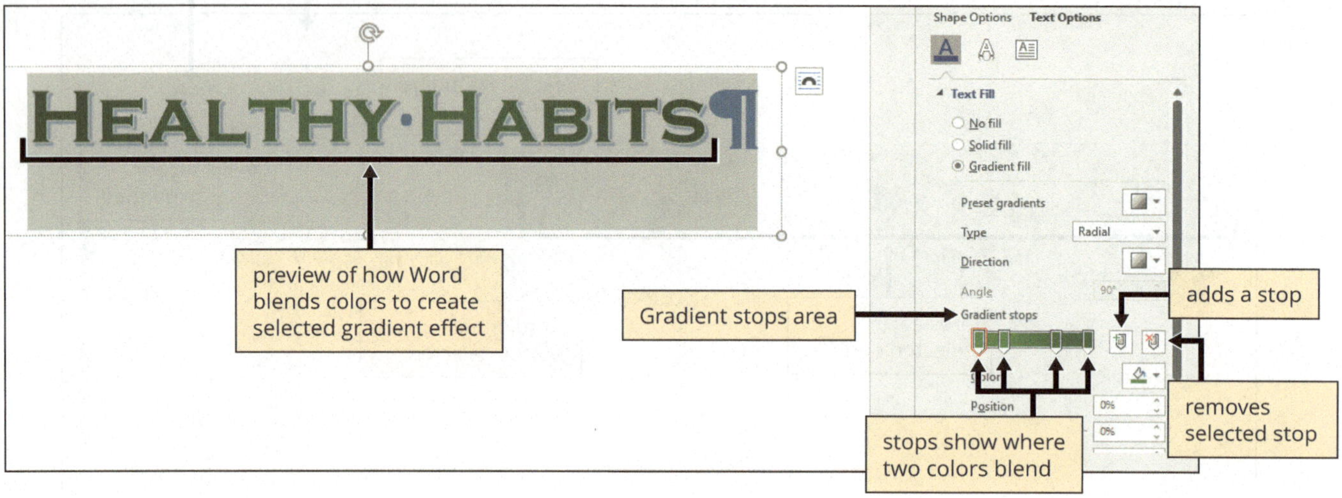

Figure 7–10

6

- Click the second gradient stop to select it and then click the Color button to display a Color palette, from which you can select a color for the selected stop (Figure 7–11).

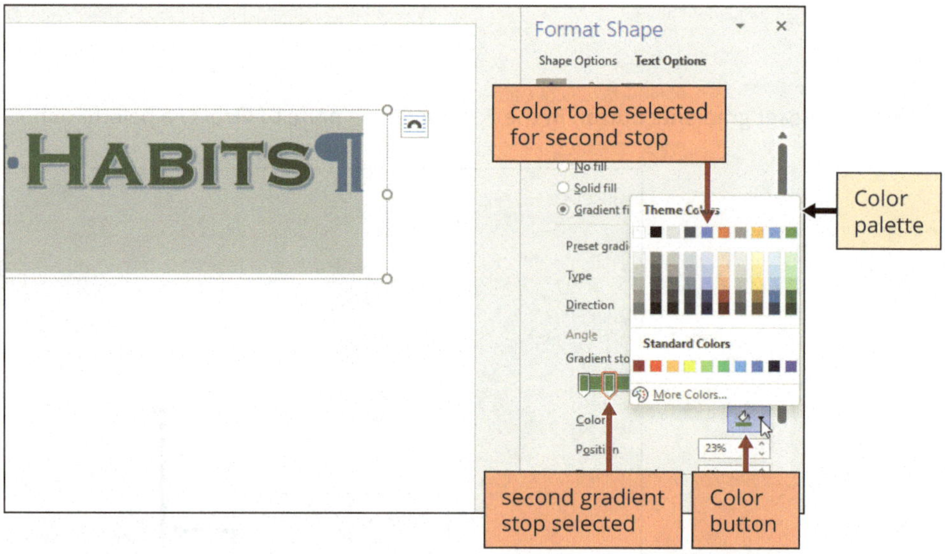

Figure 7–11

7

- Click 'Blue, Accent 1' (first row, fifth column) in the Color palette to change the color of the selected stop and the gradient between the selected stop and the next stop.
- Click the rightmost gradient stop to select it and then click the Color button again to display a Color palette. Click 'Blue, Accent 1' (first row, fifth column) in the Color palette to change the color of the selected stop and the gradient between the selected stop and the previous stop.

Q&A Can I move a gradient stop?
Yes. You can drag a stop to any location along the color bar. You also can adjust the position, brightness, and transparency of any selected stop.

8

- Click the Direction button to display a gallery that shows a variety of directions for the gradient colors (Figure 7–12).

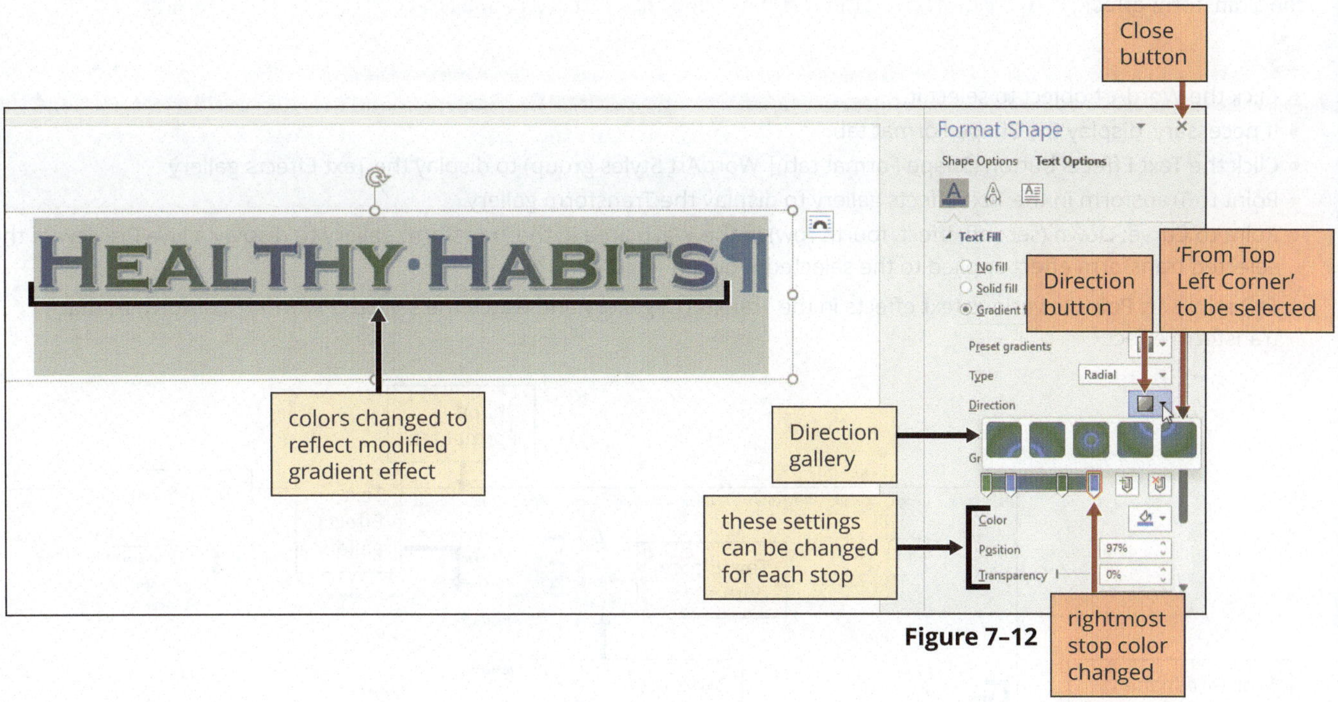

Figure 7–12

9

- Click 'From Top Left Corner' (rightmost option) in the Direction gallery to specify the direction to blend the colors.
- Click the Close button in the pane.
- Click the paragraph mark below the WordArt object to deselect the text so that you can see its gradient fill colors (Figure 7–13).

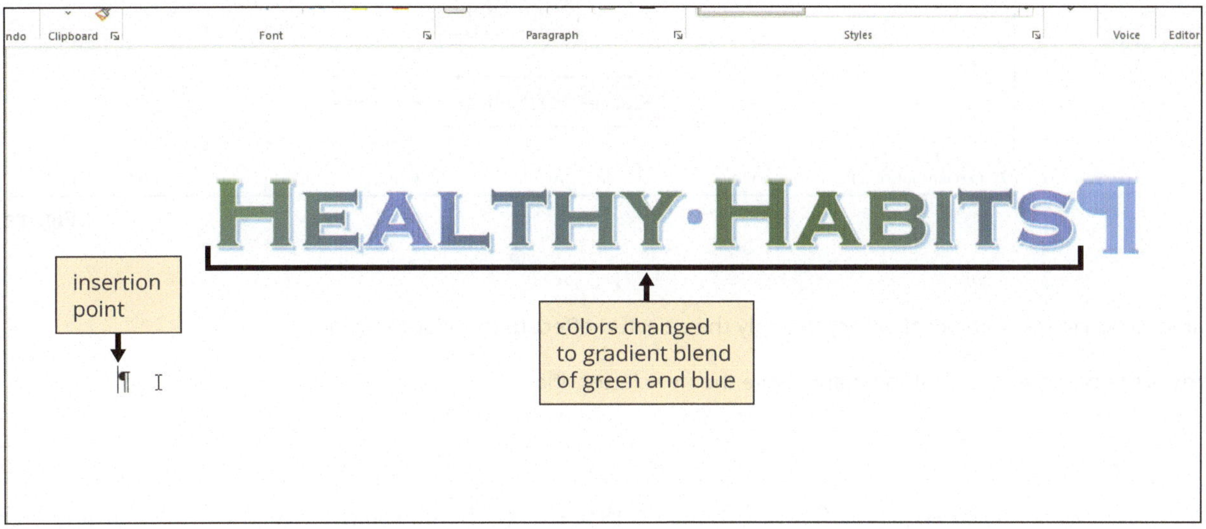

Figure 7–13

To Change the WordArt Shape Using the Transform Effect

Word provides a variety of effects to make your WordArt more interesting. The following steps change the WordArt shape using the Transform effect. **Why?** The WordArt in this newsletter has a curved appearance.

1

- Click the WordArt object to select it.
- If necessary, display the Shape Format tab.
- Click the Text Effects button (Shape Format tab | WordArt Styles group) to display the Text Effects gallery.
- Point to Transform in the Text Effects gallery to display the Transform gallery.
- Point to Curve: Down (second effect, fourth row) in the Warp area in the Transform gallery to display a Live Preview of the selected transform effect applied to the selected WordArt (Figure 7–14).

- **Experiment:** Point to various text effects in the Transform gallery and watch the selected WordArt conform to that transform effect.

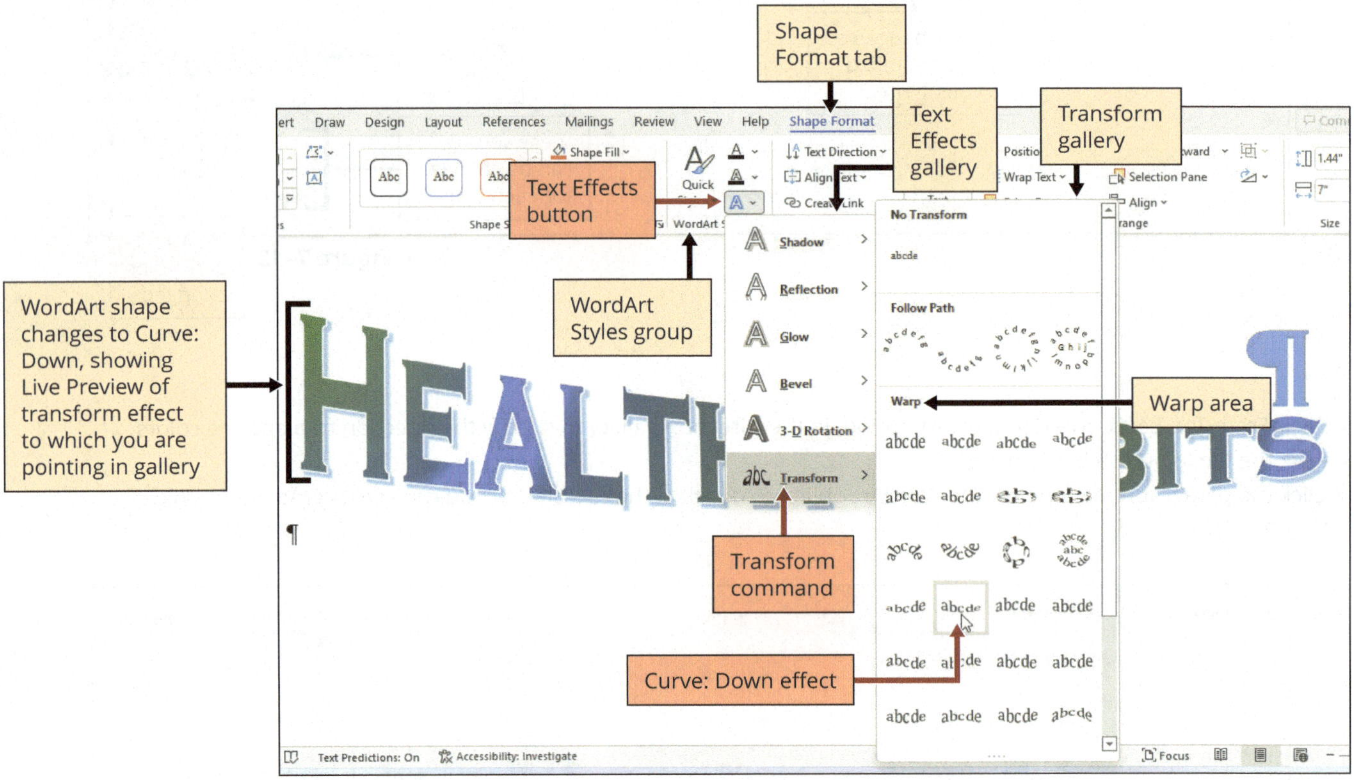

Figure 7–14

2

- Click Curve: Down in the Transform gallery to apply the selected effect to the WordArt object.

Q&A Why is the paragraph formatting mark above the newsletter title?
The formatting marks remain at the original location of the text before you applied the transform effect.

To Apply a Glow Effect to WordArt If you wanted to apply a glow effect to WordArt, you would perform the following steps:

1. Select the WordArt object.
2. Click the Text Effects button (Shape Format tab | WordArt Styles group) to display the Text Effects gallery.
3. Point to Glow in the Text Effects gallery and then click the desired glow effect in the Glow gallery.

To Apply a Shadow Effect to WordArt If you wanted to apply a shadow effect to WordArt, you would perform the following steps:

1. Select the WordArt object.
2. Click the Text Effects button (Shape Format tab | WordArt Styles group) to display the Text Effects gallery.
3. Point to Shadow in the Text Effects gallery and then click the desired shadow effect in the Shadow gallery.

To Set Custom Tab Stops Using the Tabs Dialog Box

The issue information line in this newsletter contains the text, Hope Medical Center Newsletter, at the left margin and the issue number and date at the right margin (shown in Figure 7–1a at the beginning of this module). In Word, a paragraph cannot be both left-aligned and right-aligned. **Why?** If you click the Align Right button (Home tab | Paragraph group), for example, all text will be right-aligned. To place text at the right margin of a left-aligned paragraph, you set a tab stop at the right margin.

One method of setting custom tab stops is to click the ruler at the desired location of the tab stop. You cannot click, however, at the right margin location. Thus, the following steps use the Tabs dialog box to set a custom tab stop.

1

- If necessary, display the Home tab.
- Position the insertion point on the paragraph mark below the WordArt object, which is the paragraph to be formatted with the custom tab stops.
- Click the Paragraph Dialog Box Launcher to display the Paragraph dialog box (Figure 7–15).

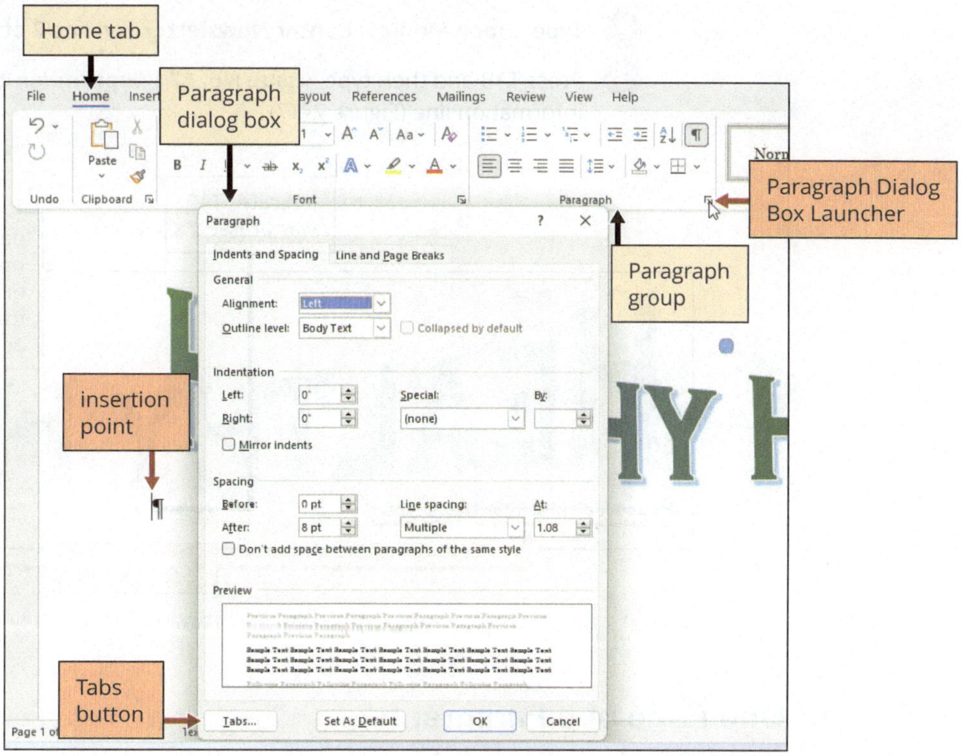

Figure 7–15

2

- Click the Tabs button (Paragraph dialog box) to display the Tabs dialog box.
- Type **7** in the 'Tab stop position' text box (Tabs dialog box).
- Click Right in the Alignment area to specify alignment for text at the tab stop (Figure 7–16).

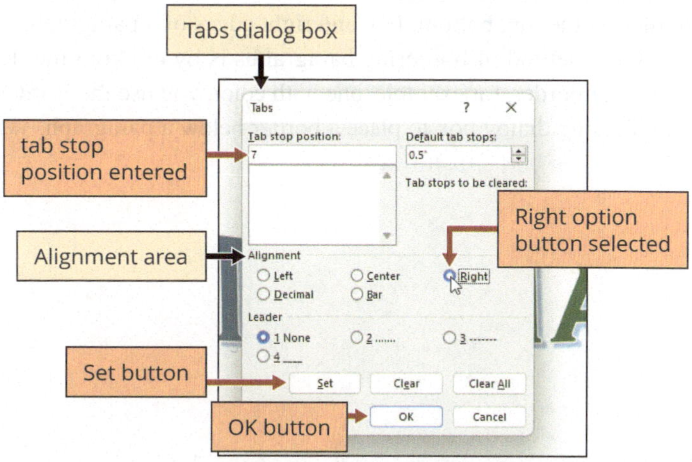

Figure 7–16

3

- Click the Set button (Tabs dialog box) to set a right-aligned custom tab stop at the specified position.
- Click OK to set the defined tab stops.

Other Ways

1. Click desired tab stop on ruler
2. Right-click paragraph (or, if using touch, tap 'Show Context Menu' button on Mini toolbar), click Paragraph on shortcut menu, click Tabs button (Paragraph dialog box), enter desired settings, click OK

To Enter Text

The following steps enter the issue information line text.

1. With the insertion point on the paragraph below the WordArt object, change the font to 'Berlin Sans FB Demi' (or a similar font) and the font size to 10 point.
2. Type **Hope Medical Center Newsletter** on line 2 of the newsletter.
3. Press TAB and then type **Issue No. 47 | September 2029** to complete the issue information line (Figure 7–17).

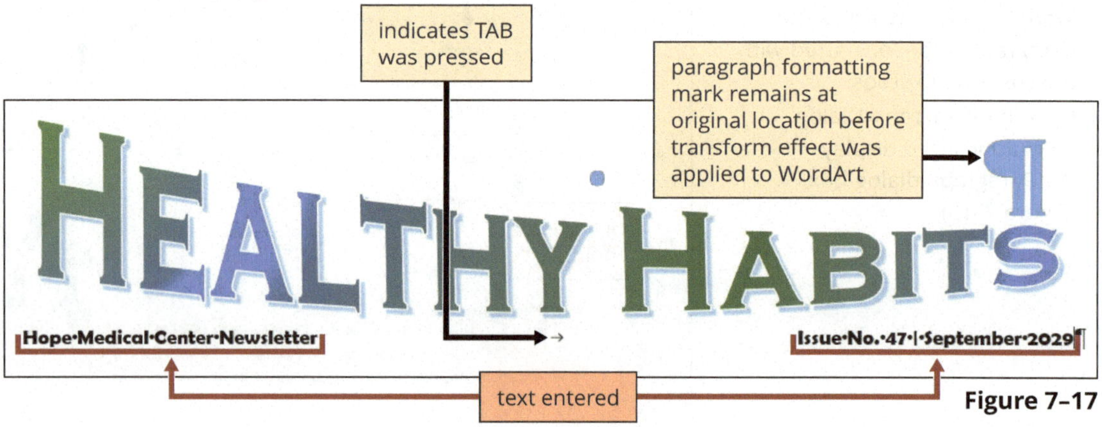

Figure 7–17

To Border One Edge of a Paragraph

In Word, you use borders to create ruling lines. Word can place borders on any edge of a paragraph; that is, Word can place a border on the top, bottom, left, and right edges of a paragraph.

One method of bordering paragraphs is by clicking the desired border in the Borders gallery. If you want to specify a particular border, for example, one with color, you use the Borders and Shading dialog box. The following steps use the Borders and Shading dialog box to place a border below a paragraph. **Why?** In this newsletter, the issue information line has a 3-point dashed green border below it.

1

- With the insertion point in the issue information line, click the Borders arrow (Home tab | Paragraph group) to display the Borders gallery (Figure 7–18).

Q&A Why did a border appear below the issue information line?
You clicked the Borders button instead of the Borders arrow. Click the Borders button again to remove the added border and then click the Borders arrow to display the Borders gallery.

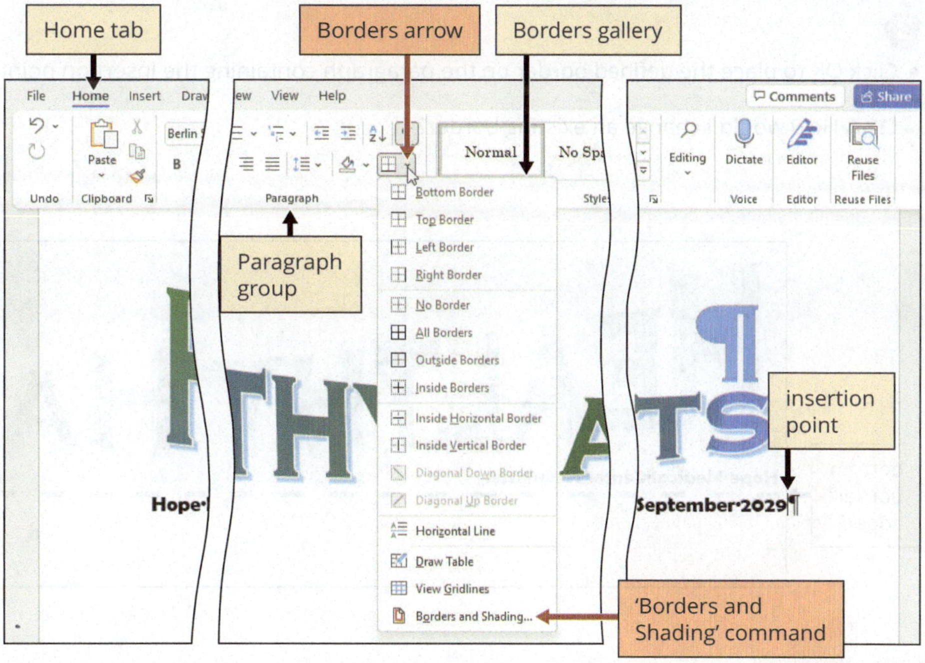

Figure 7–18

2

- Click 'Borders and Shading' in the Borders gallery to display the Borders and Shading dialog box.
- Click Custom in the Setting area (Borders and Shading dialog box) because you are setting just a bottom border.
- Click the style shown in Figure 7–19, which is dashed lines for the border.
- Click the Color button and then click 'Green, Accent 6, Darker 50%' (last column, bottom row) in the Color gallery.
- Click the Width button and then click 3 pt in the list.
- Click the Bottom Border button in the Preview area of the dialog box to show a preview of the selected border style (Figure 7–19).

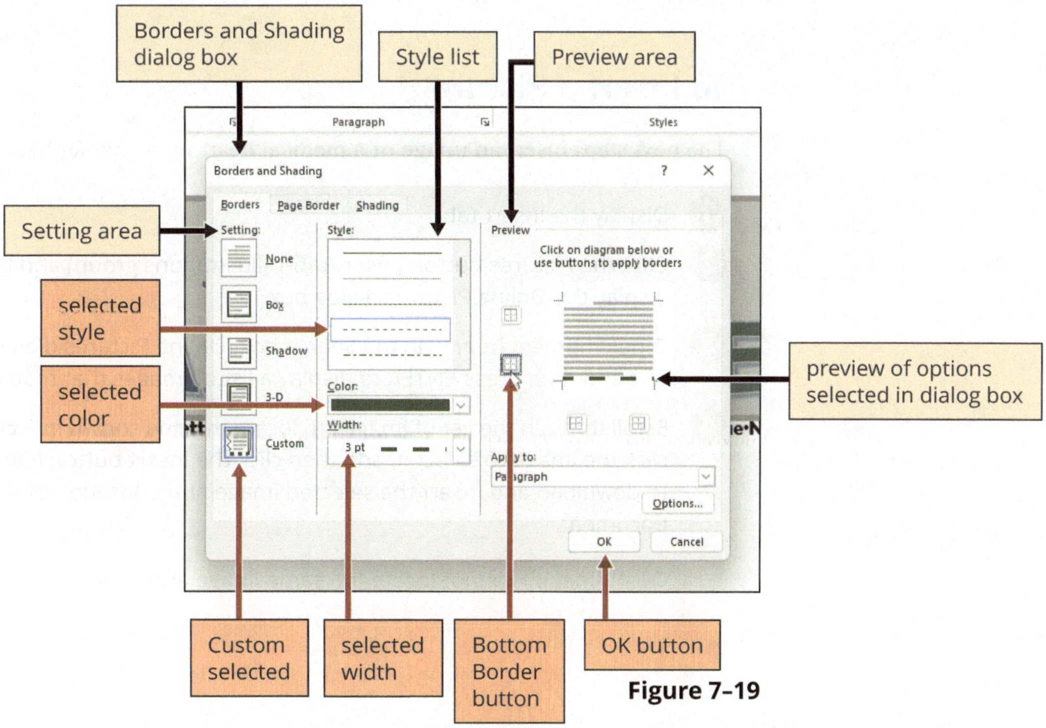

Figure 7–19

Q&A What is the purpose of the buttons in the Preview area?
They are toggles that display and remove the top, bottom, left, and right borders from the diagram in the Preview area.

3

- Click OK to place the defined border on the paragraph containing the insertion point (Figure 7–20).

Q&A How would I change an existing border?
You first remove the existing border by clicking the Borders arrow (Home tab | Paragraph group) and then clicking the border in the Borders gallery that identifies the border you wish to remove. Then, add a new border as described in these steps.

Figure 7–20

Other Ways

1. Click Page Borders button (Design tab | Page Background group), click Borders tab (Borders and Shading dialog box), select desired border, click OK

To Insert a Picture

The next steps insert an image of a medical heart in the nameplate.

1. Display the Insert tab.
2. Click the Pictures button (Insert tab | Illustrations group) and then click Online Pictures to display the Online Pictures dialog box.
3. Type **medical heart** in the Search box (Online Pictures dialog box) to specify the search text and then press ENTER to display a list of images that match the entered search text.
4. Scroll through the list of images to locate the one shown in Figure 7–21 (or a similar image), click the image to select it, and then click the Insert button (Online Pictures dialog box) to download and insert the selected image at the location of the insertion point in the document.

Q&A What if I cannot locate the same image as in Figure 7–21?
Click Cancel (Online Pictures dialog box) to close the dialog box, click the Pictures button (Insert tab | Illustrations group), click This Device to display the Insert Picture dialog box, navigate to and select the Support_WD_7_MedicalHeart.jpg file in the Data Files, and then click the Insert button (Insert Picture dialog box) to insert the picture.

What if my inserted image is not in the same location as in Figure 7–21?
The image may be in a different location, depending on the position of the insertion point when you inserted the image. In a later section, you will move the image to a different location.

To Crop a Graphic

The next step is to format the image just inserted. **Why?** In addition to the medical heart, the inserted image also contains a medical first aid symbol. You only want the medical heart to appear in the newsletter. Word allows you to **crop**, or trim away part of, a graphic. The following steps crop a graphic.

1

- With the graphic selected, click the Crop button (Picture Format tab | Size group), which places crop handles on the image in the document.

Q&A What if I mistakenly click the Crop arrow?
Click the Crop button.

- Position the pointer on the left-middle crop handle so that it looks like a sideways letter T (Figure 7–21).

Q&A What if the left-middle crop handle is not in the document window?
Scroll to display it in the document window and then position the pointer on the left-middle crop handle.

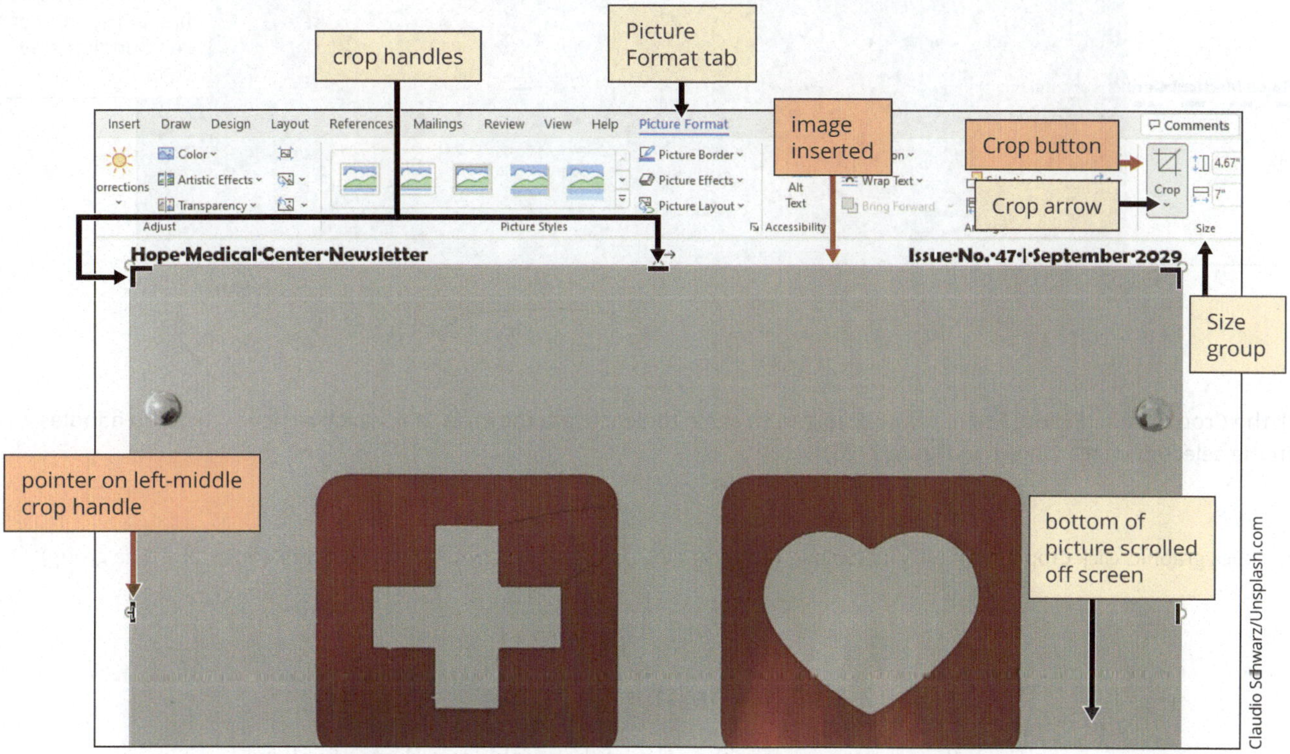

Figure 7–21

2

- Drag the left-middle crop handle inward to slightly past the left edge of the heart graphic to crop the medical first aid symbol from the image.
- Drag the right-middle crop handle inward to slightly past the right edge of the heart graphic to crop the blank space on the right side of the image.
- Drag the top-middle crop handle downward to slightly inside the top edge of the heart graphic to crop the blank space above the image.

- Drag the bottom-middle crop handle upward to slightly inside the bottom edge of the heart graphic to crop the blank space below the image (Figure 7–22). Drag the crop handles as necessary so they are positioned similarly to Figure 7–22.

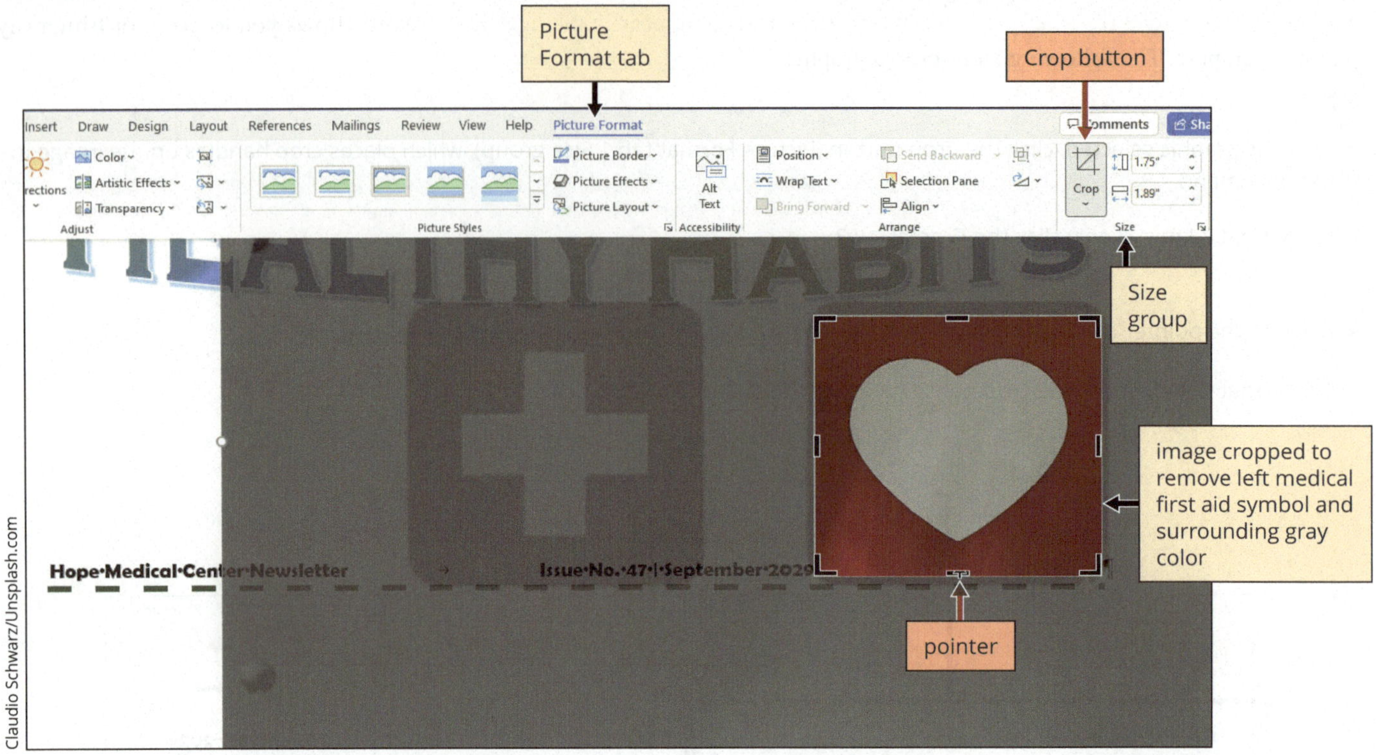

Figure 7–22

3

- Click the Crop button (Picture Format tab | Size group) again to deactivate the crop tool, which removes the crop handles from the selected image (shown in Figure 7–23).

Other Ways

1. Right-click graphic, click Crop button on Mini toolbar, drag cropping handles, click Crop button (Picture Format tab | Size group)

To Change the Color of a Graphic

The following steps change the color of the graphic to a shade of yellow.

1 With the graphic still selected, click the Color button (Picture Format tab | Adjust group) to display the Color gallery (Figure 7–23).

Q&A Why does the original graphic appear in the Color gallery?
Word retains the original graphic in case you want to revert to it at any time or adjust the crop handles again.

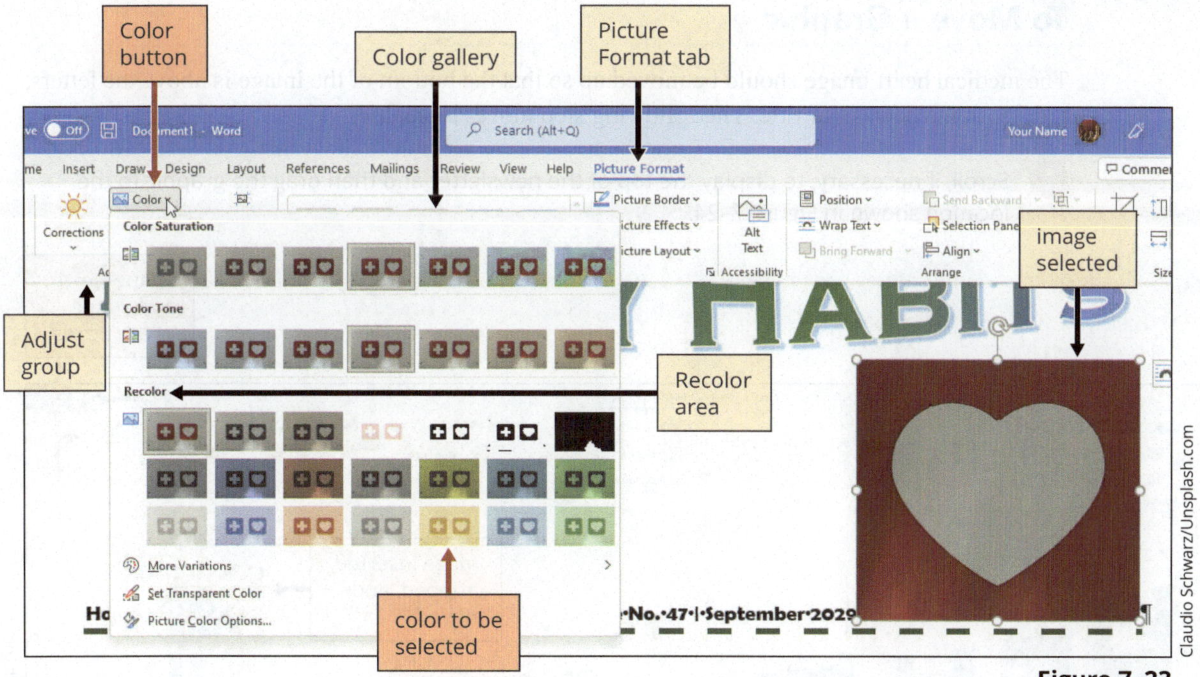

Figure 7–23

2. Click 'Gold, Accent color 4 Light' (fifth color, bottom row) in the Recolor area in the Color gallery to change the color of the selected graphic.

To Change an Object's Text Wrapping and Size

When you insert an object (image) in a Word document, the default text wrapping is In Line with Text, which means the object is part of the current paragraph. Because you want the medical heart image behind the newsletter title, you change the text wrapping for the image to Behind Text. The next steps change an object's text wrapping and its size.

1. With the medical heart graphic selected, click the Layout Options button attached to the graphic to display the Layout Options gallery.
2. Click Behind Text in the Layout Options gallery so that the image is positioned behind text in the document.
3. Close the Layout Options gallery.
4. If necessary, display the Picture Format tab. Change the values in the Shape Height and Shape Width boxes (Picture Format tab | Size group) to .59" and .64", respectively. If you are not able to resize the graphic exactly, click the Size Dialog Box Launcher (Picture Format tab | Size group), remove the check mark from the 'Lock aspect ratio' check box, and then try again.

To Move a Graphic

The medical heart image should be moved up so that the bottom of the image is above the letters, t and s, in the newsletter title. The following step moves a graphic.

1. Scroll, if necessary, to display the top of the newsletter and then drag the graphic to the location shown in Figure 7–24.

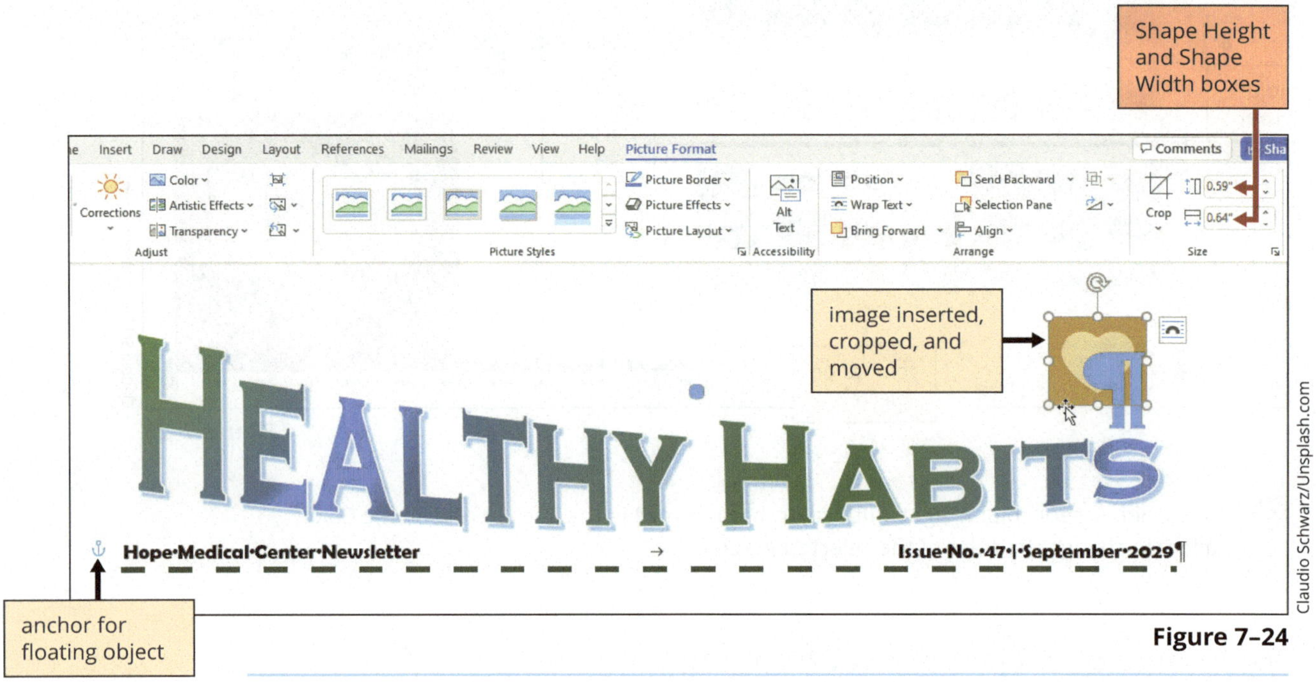

Figure 7–24

BTW

Anchors on Floating Objects

If you want to move an anchor on a floating object that is locked, you can unlock the anchor by selecting the object, clicking the Layout Options button attached to the object, clicking the See more link in the Layout Options gallery to display the Layout dialog box, clicking the Position tab, removing the check mark from the Lock anchor check box, and then clicking OK.

To Specify or Change the Absolute Position for a Floating Graphic If you wanted to move a floating graphic and specify its absolute position, you would perform the following steps.

1. Select the graphic to be moved.
2. Click the Layout Options button attached to the graphic to display the Layout Options gallery.
3. Click the See more link (Layout Options gallery) to display the Position tab in the Layout dialog box.
4. Click Absolute position in the Vertical area (Layout dialog box), select the value in the Absolute position box, and then type the desired value to specify the distance in inches from the top of the page.
5. If necessary, click the below arrow and then select Page.
6. Click OK to change the position of the selected graphic to the specified position.

To Use the Selection Pane

The next step is to rotate the medical heart image, but because it is positioned behind the text, it may be difficult to select it. The following step opens the Selection pane. **Why?** The Selection pane enables you easily to select items on the screen that are layered behind other objects.

1

- With the graphic selected, if necessary, display the Picture Format tab.
- Click the Selection Pane button (Picture Format tab | Arrange group) to open the Selection pane (Figure 7–25).

Q&A What if the Picture Format tab is not on the ribbon?
Display the Layout tab and then click the Selection Pane button (Layout tab | Arrange group).

- **Experiment:** Click 'Text Box 1' in the Selection pane to select the WordArt object. Click Picture 2 in the Selection pane to select the medical heart image.

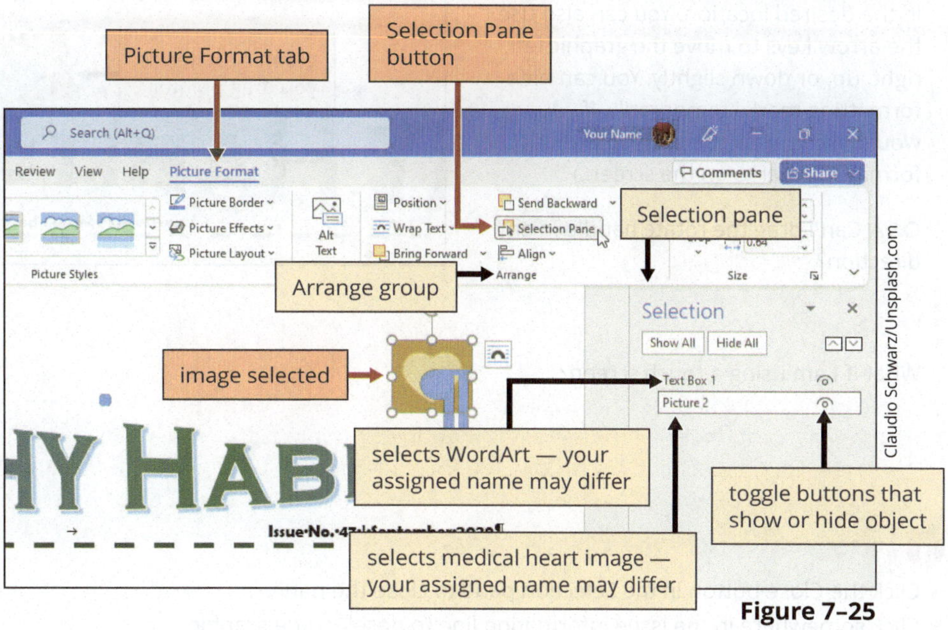

Figure 7–25

Q&A What are the displayed names in the Selection pane?
Word assigns names to each object in the document. The names displayed on your screen may differ.

Other Ways

1. Click Selection Pane button (Layout tab | Arrange group)
2. Click WordArt, click Selection Pane button (Shape Format tab | Arrange group)

To Rotate a Graphic

The following steps rotate a graphic. **Why?** You would like the medical heart image angled to the right a bit.

1

- If necessary, click Picture 2 in the Selection pane to select the medical heart image.
- Position the pointer on the graphic's rotate handle (Figure 7–26).

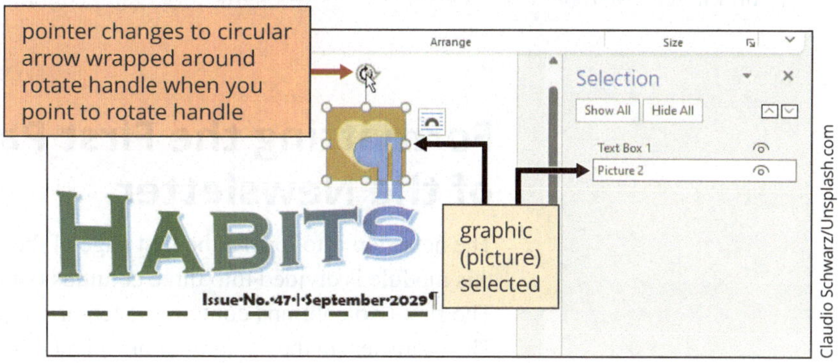

Figure 7–26

2

- Drag the rotate handle clockwise to rotate the graphic slightly as shown in Figure 7–27. (You may need to rotate the graphic a few times to position it in the desired location. You can also use the arrow keys to move the graphic left, right, up, or down slightly. You can hide formatting marks temporarily, if you would like to view the graphic without the formatting marks on the screen.)

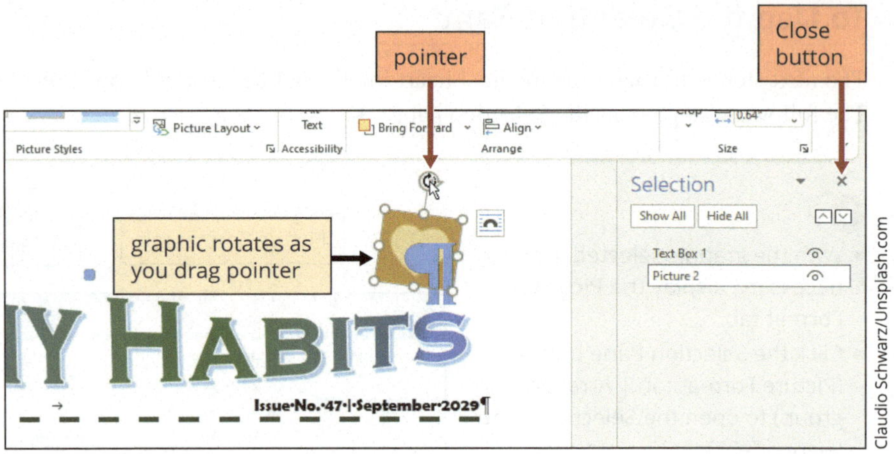

Figure 7–27

Q&A Can I drag the rotate handle in any direction?

You can drag the rotate handle clockwise or counterclockwise.

What if I am using a touch screen?

Because the rotate handle is not available on a touch screen, you enter the degree of rotation in the Size dialog box. Tap the Rotate Objects button (Picture Format tab | Arrange group) to display the Rotate Objects menu, tap 'More Rotation Options' on the Rotate Objects menu to display the Size sheet in the Layout dialog box, change the Rotation value to 8, and then tap OK.

3

- Click the Close button in the Selection pane to close the pane.
- Click somewhere in the issue information line to deselect the graphic.
- Save the newsletter on your hard drive, OneDrive, or other storage location using the file name, SC_WD_7_HealthyHabitsNewsletter.

Other Ways

1. Click Rotate Objects button (Picture Format tab | Arrange group), click 'More Rotation Options' on Rotate Objects menu, enter rotation value in Rotation box (Layout dialog box), click OK
2. Right-click object, click 'Size and Position' on shortcut menu, enter rotation value in Rotation box (Layout dialog box), click OK
3. Click Size Dialog Box Launcher (Picture Format tab | Size group), enter rotation value in Rotation box (Layout dialog box), click OK

Break Point: If you want to take a break, this is a good place to do so. You can exit Word now. To resume later, start Word, open the file called SC_WD_7_HealthyHabitsNewsletter.docx, and continue following the steps from this location forward.

Formatting the First Page of the Body of the Newsletter

The next step is to format the first page of the body of the newsletter. The body of the newsletter in this module is divided into three columns (shown in Figure 7–1a at the beginning of this module). The first two columns contain the feature article, and the third column contains announcements. The characters in the paragraphs are aligned on both the right and left edges — similar to newspaper columns. The first letter in the first paragraph is much larger than the rest of the characters in the paragraph. A vertical rule separates the columns. The steps in the following sections format the first page of the body of the newsletter using these desktop publishing features.

Consider This

What guidelines should you follow when creating the body of a newsletter?

While content and subject matter of newsletters may vary, the procedures used to create newsletters are similar:

- **Write the body copy.** Newsletters should contain articles of interest and relevance to readers. Some share information, while others promote a product or service. Use active voice in body copy, which is more engaging than passive voice. Proofread the body copy to be sure it is error free. Check all facts for accuracy.
- **Organize body copy in columns.** Most newsletters arrange body copy in columns. The body copy in columns, often called **snaking columns** or newspaper-style columns, flows from the bottom of one column to the top of the next column.
- **Format the body copy.** Begin the feature article on the first page of the newsletter. If the article spans multiple pages, use a continuation line, called a jump or jump line, to guide the reader to the remainder of the article. The message at the end of the article on the first page of the newsletter is called a **jump-to line**, and a **jump-from line** marks the beginning of the continuation, which is usually on a subsequent page.
- **Maintain consistency.** Be consistent with placement of body copy elements in newsletter editions. If the newsletter contains announcements, for example, position them in the same location in each edition so that readers easily can find them.
- **Maximize white space.** Allow plenty of space between lines, paragraphs, and columns. Tightly packed text is difficult to read. Separate the text adequately from graphics, borders, and headings.
- **Incorporate color.** Use colors that complement those in the nameplate. Be careful not to overuse color. Restrict color below the nameplate to drop caps, subheads, graphics, and ruling lines. If you do not have a color printer, still change the colors because the colors will print in shades of black and gray, which add variety to the newsletter.
- **Select and format subheads.** Develop subheads with as few words as possible. Readers should be able to identify content of the next topic by glancing at a subhead. Subheads should be emphasized in the newsletter but should not compete with text in the nameplate. Use a larger, bold, or otherwise contrasting font for subheads so that they stand apart from the body copy. Use this same format for all subheads for consistency. Leave a space above subheads to visually separate their content from the previous topic. Be consistent with spacing above and below subheads throughout the newsletter.
- **Divide sections with vertical rules.** Use vertical rules to guide the reader through the newsletter.
- **Enhance the document with visuals.** Add energy to the newsletter and emphasis to important points with graphics, pull-quotes, and other visuals, such as drop caps to mark beginning of an article. Use these elements sparingly, however, so that the newsletter does not have a crowded appearance. Fewer, large visuals are more effective than several smaller ones. If you use a graphic that you did not create, be sure to obtain permission to use it in the newsletter and give necessary credit to the creator of the graphic.

To Clear Formatting

The next step is to enter the title of the feature article below the horizontal rule. To do this, position the insertion point at the end of the issue information line (after the 9 in 2029) and then press ENTER. Recall that the issue information line has a bottom border. When you press ENTER in a bordered paragraph, Word carries forward any borders to the next paragraph. Thus, after you press ENTER, you should clear formatting to format the new paragraph as the Normal style. The following steps clear formatting.

1. Click at the end of line 2 (the issue information line) so that the insertion point is immediately after the 9 in 2029. Press ENTER to advance the insertion point to the next line, which also moves the border down one line.

2. If necessary, display the Home tab. Click the 'Clear All Formatting' button (Home tab | Font group) to apply the Normal style to the location of the insertion point, which in this case moves the new paragraph below the border on the issue information line.

To Format Text as a Heading Style, Modify a Heading Style, and Adjust Spacing before and after the Paragraph

Below the bottom border in the nameplate is the title of the feature article, Health Concerns of Using Technology. The following steps apply the Heading 1 style to this paragraph, modify the style, and adjust the paragraph spacing.

1. If necessary, display formatting marks.
2. With the insertion point on the paragraph mark below the border, click Heading 1 (Home tab | Styles group) to apply the Heading 1 style to the paragraph containing the insertion point.
3. Decrease the font size to 14 point. Update the Heading 1 style to reflect this change.
4. Type **Health Concerns of Using Technology** as the title of the feature article.
5. Display the Layout tab. Change the Spacing Before box to 18 pt and the Spacing After box to 12 pt (Figure 7–28).

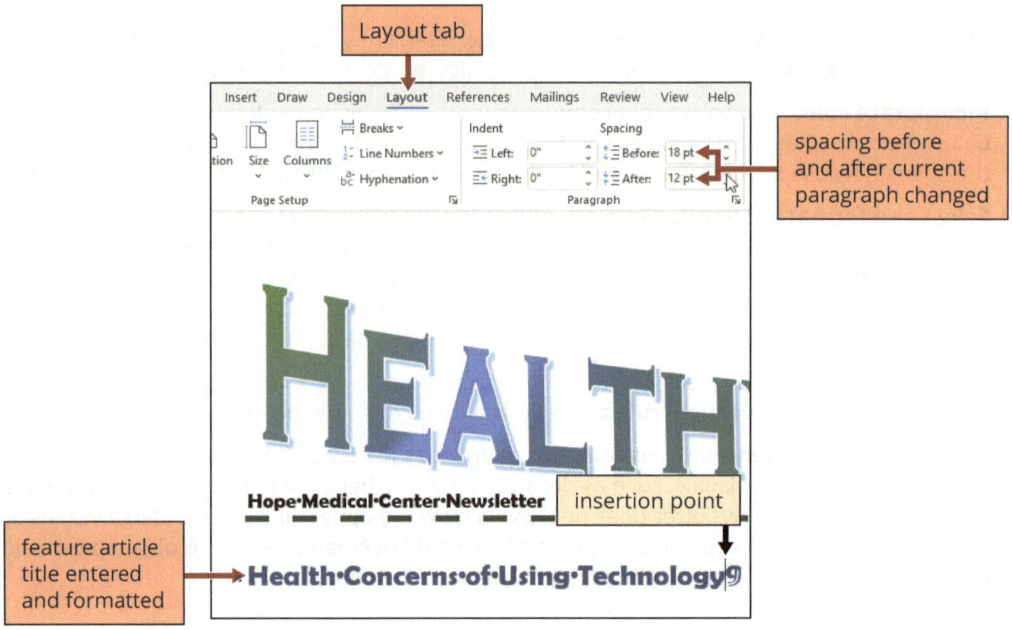

Figure 7–28

Columns

When you begin a document in Word, it has one column. You can divide a portion of a document or the entire document into multiple columns. Within each column, you can type, modify, or format text.

To divide a portion of a document into multiple columns, you use section breaks. Word requires that a new section be created each time you alter the number of columns in a document. Thus, if a document has a nameplate (one column) followed by an article of three columns followed by an article of two columns, the document would be divided into three separate sections.

Consider This

How should you organize the body copy in columns?

Be consistent from page to page with the number of columns. Narrow columns generally are easier to read than wide ones. Columns, however, can be too narrow. A two- or three-column layout generally is appealing and offers a flexible design. Try to have between five and fifteen words per line. To do this, you may need to adjust the column width, the font size, or the leading (line spacing). The font size of text in columns should be no larger than 12 point but not so small that readers must strain to read the text.

Sections

All Word documents have at least one section. A Word document can be divided into any number of sections. While creating a document, you create a new **section** if you need to change the top margin, bottom margin, page alignment, paper size, page orientation, page number position, columns, or contents or position of headers, footers, or footnotes in just a portion of the document.

BTW
Section Numbers
If you want to display the current section number on the status bar, right-click the status bar to display the Customize Status Bar menu and then click Section on the Customize Status Bar menu. The section number appears at the left edge of the status bar. To remove the section number from the status bar, perform the same steps.

To Insert a Continuous Section Break

The next step is to insert a continuous section break below the nameplate. Why? In this module, the nameplate is one column and the body of the newsletter is three columns. The term, continuous, means the new section should be on the same page as the previous section, which, in this case, means that the three columns of body copy will be positioned directly below the nameplate on the first page of the newsletter. The following steps insert a continuous section break.

1

- With the insertion point at the end of the feature article title (shown in Figure 7–28), press ENTER to position the insertion point below the article title.
- Click the Breaks button (Layout tab | Page Setup group) to display the Breaks gallery (Figure 7–29).

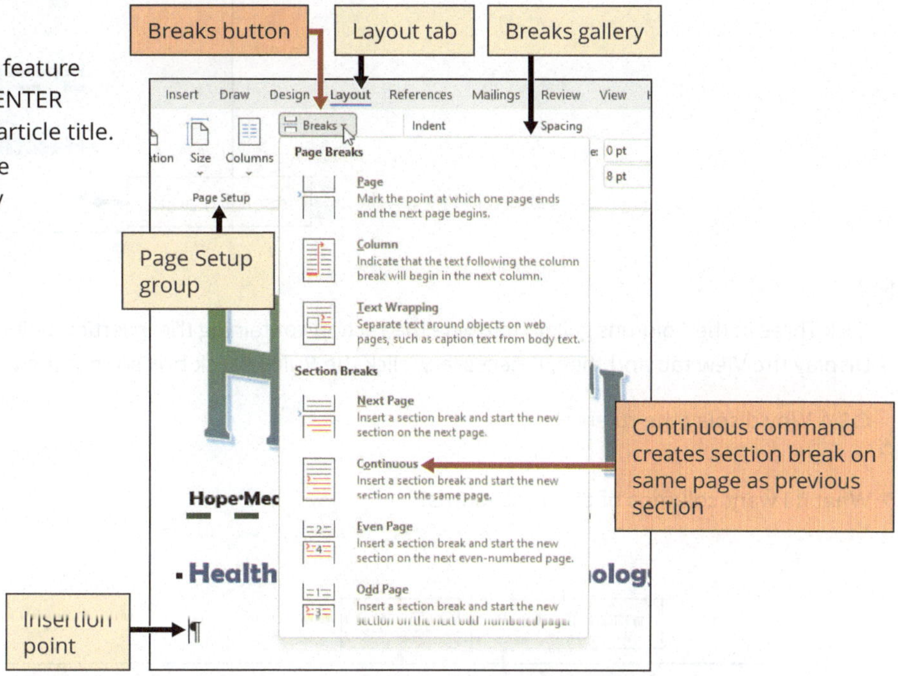

Figure 7–29

2

- Click Continuous in the Breaks gallery to insert a continuous section break above the insertion point (Figure 7–30).

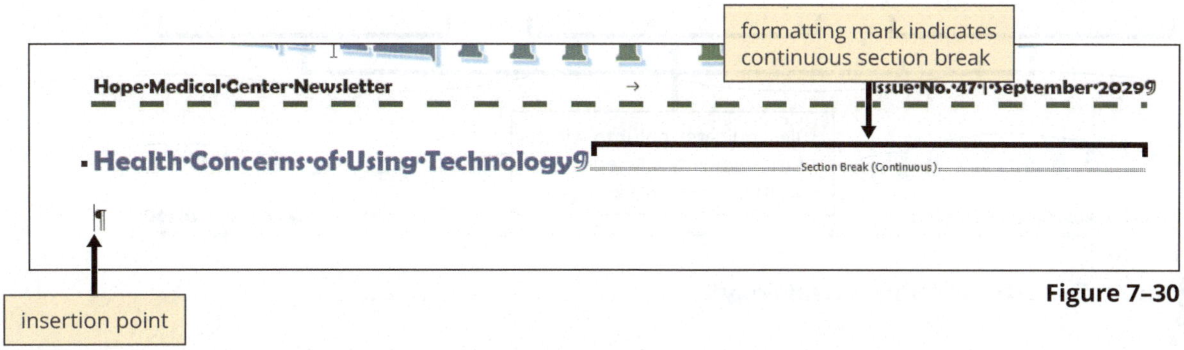

Figure 7–30

To Format Text in Columns

The document now has two sections. The nameplate is in the first section, and the insertion point is in the second section. The second section should be formatted into three columns. **Why?** The feature article and announcements appear in three columns that snake across the page. Thus, the following steps format the second section in the document as three columns.

1

- Click the Columns button (Layout tab | Page Setup group) to display the Columns gallery (Figure 7–31).

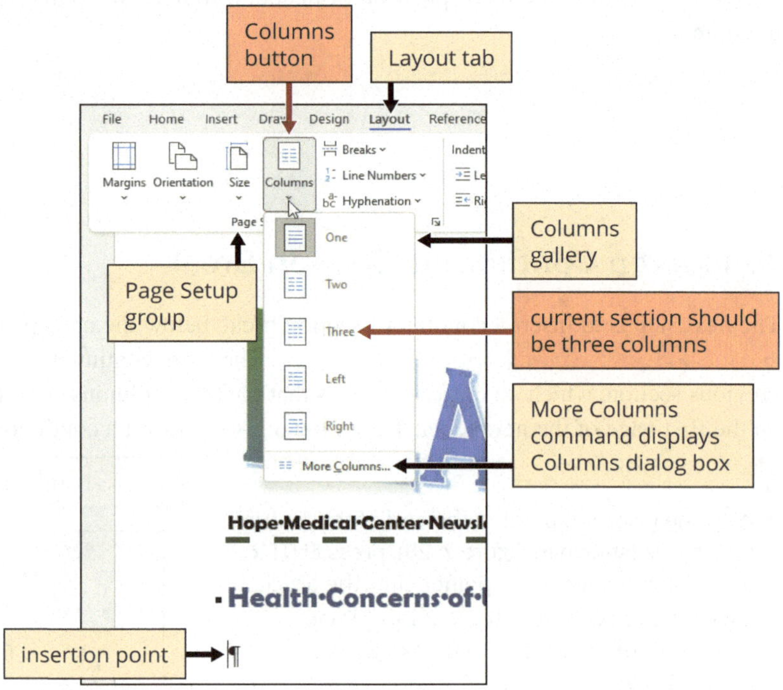

Figure 7–31

2

- Click Three in the Columns gallery to divide the section containing the insertion point into three evenly sized and spaced columns.
- Display the View tab and then, if necessary, click the Ruler check box so that the rulers appear on the screen (Figure 7–32).

Q&A Why display the rulers?

You want to see the column widths on the ruler.

What if I want columns of different widths?

You would click More Columns in the Columns gallery (shown in Figure 7–31), which displays the Columns dialog box. In this dialog box, you can specify varying column widths and spacing.

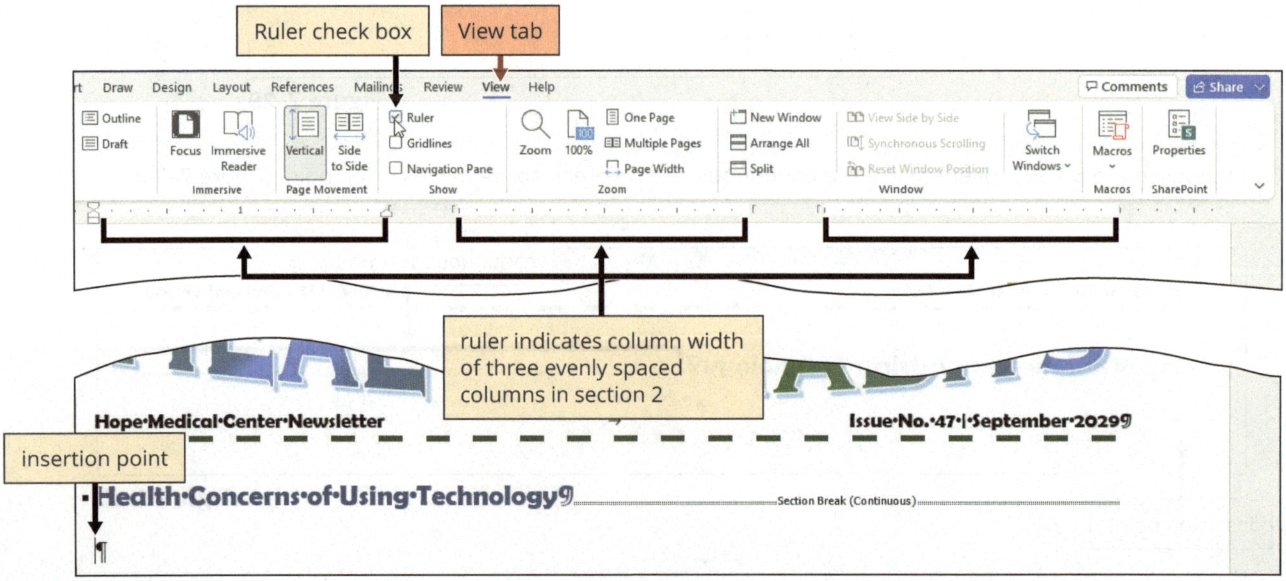

Figure 7–32

To Justify a Paragraph

The following step enters the first paragraph of the feature article using justified alignment. **Why?** The text in the paragraphs of the body of the newsletter is **justified**, which means that the left and right margins are aligned, like the edges of newspaper columns.

1

- Display the Home tab.
- Click the Justify button (Home tab | Paragraph group) so that Word aligns both the left and right margins of typed text.
- Type the first paragraph of the feature article (Figure 7–33): **The widespread use of technology has led to some important user health concerns. You should be proactive and minimize your chance of risk. This article addresses repetitive strain injuries and digital eyestrain.** and then press ENTER.

Q&A Why do some words have extra space between them?
When a paragraph is formatted to justified alignment, Word places extra space between words so that the left and right edges of the paragraph are aligned. To remedy big gaps, sometimes called rivers, you can add or rearrange words, change the column width, change the font size, and so on.

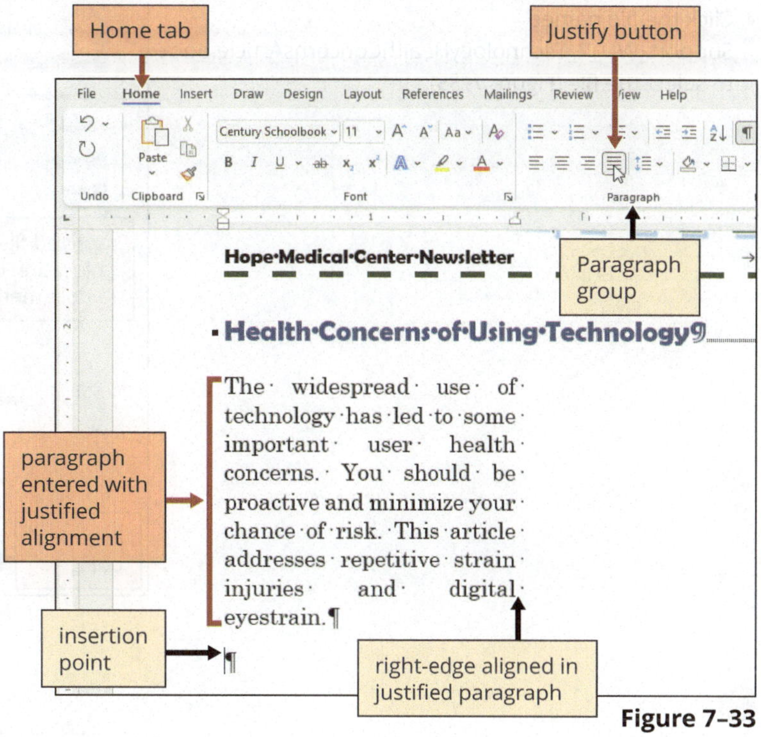

Figure 7–33

Other Ways

1. Right-click paragraph (or, if using touch, tap 'Show Context Menu' button on Mini toolbar), click Paragraph on shortcut menu, click 'Indents and Spacing' tab (Paragraph dialog box), click Alignment arrow, click Justified, click OK
2. Click Paragraph Dialog Box Launcher (Home tab or Layout tab | Paragraph group), click Indents and Spacing tab (Paragraph dialog box), click Alignment arrow, click Justified, click OK
3. Press CTRL+J

To Insert Text from a File into a Document

The next step is to insert a file named Support_WD_7_TechnologyHealthConcernsArticle.docx in the newsletter. **Why?** To save you time typing, the rest of the feature article is located in the Data Files. Please contact your instructor for information about accessing the Data Files. The following steps insert the Support_WD_7_TechnologyHealthConcernsArticle.docx file in a column of the newsletter.

1

- Display the Insert tab.
- With the insertion point positioned in the left column as shown in Figure 7–33, click the Object arrow (Insert tab | Text group) to display the Object menu (Figure 7–34).

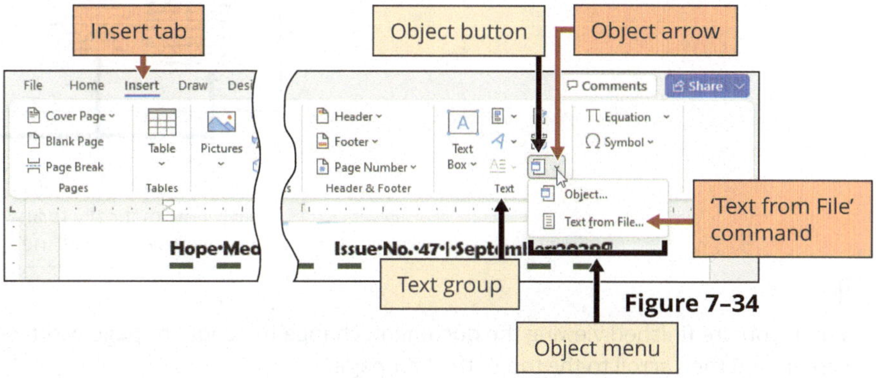

Figure 7–34

2

- Click 'Text from File' on the Object menu to display the Insert File dialog box.
- Navigate to the location of the file to be inserted.
- Click the file named Support_WD_7_TechnologyHealthConcernsArticle.docx to select the file (Figure 7–35).

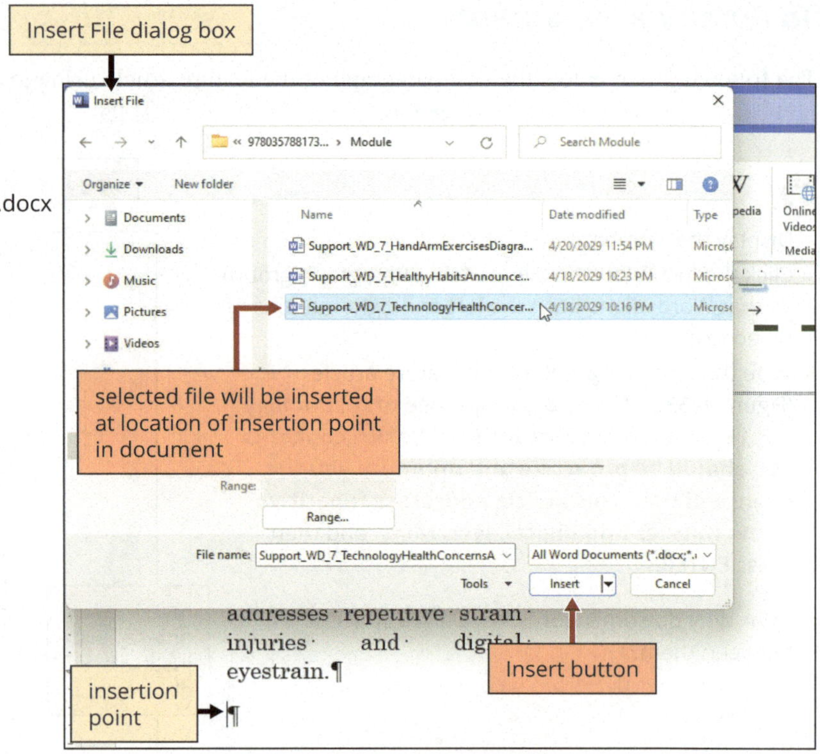

Figure 7–35

3

- Click the Insert button (Insert File dialog box) to insert the file, Support_WD_7_TechnologyHealthConcernsArticle.docx, in the current document at the location of the insertion point.
- So that you can review the entire inserted article, display multiple pages on the screen by clicking the Multiple Pages button (View tab | Zoom group) (Figure 7–36).

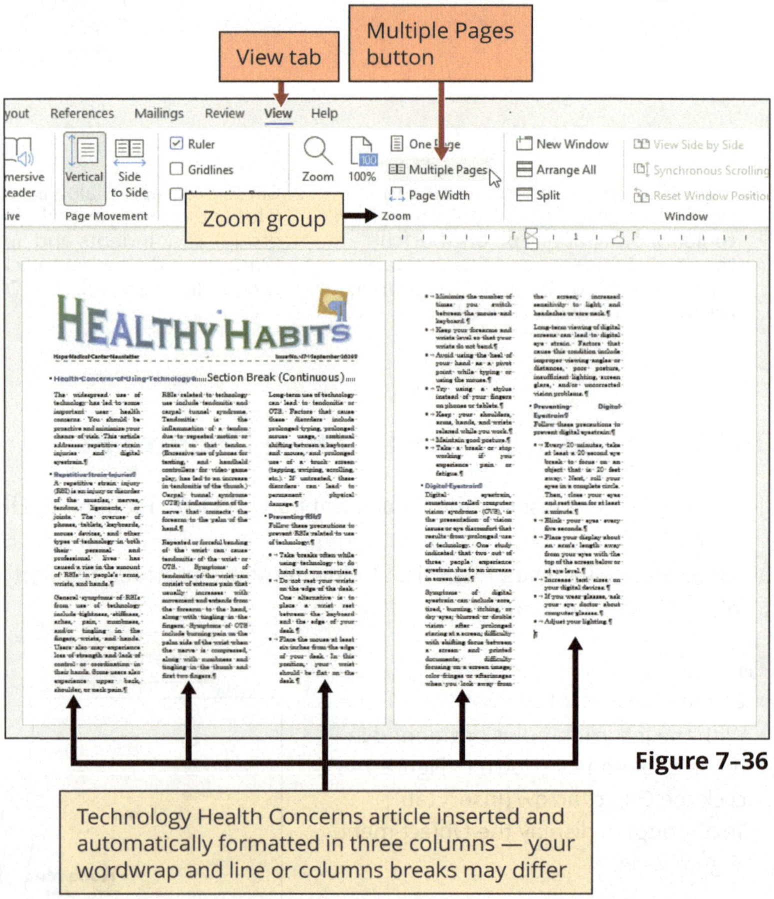

Figure 7–36

Claudio Schwarz/Unsplash.com

4

- When you are finished viewing the document, change the zoom to page width so that the newsletter content is larger on the screen and then scroll to the top of the first page.

To Adjust the Width of Columns and Place a Vertical Line between Columns

The columns in the newsletter currently contain many rivers. **Why?** The justified alignment in the narrow column width often causes large gaps, or rivers, between words. To eliminate some of the rivers, you increase the size of the columns slightly in this newsletter. In newsletters, you often see a vertical rule (line) separating columns. Through the Columns dialog box, you can change column width and add vertical lines. The following steps increase column widths and add vertical lines between columns.

1

- Position the insertion point somewhere in the feature article text.
- Display the Layout tab.
- Click the Columns button (Layout tab | Page Setup group) to display the Columns gallery (shown in Figure 7–31).

2

- Click More Columns in the Columns gallery to display the Columns dialog box.
- In the Width and spacing area (Columns dialog box), click the Width up arrow until the Width box reads 2.1". (Notice that as you change the width, the Spacing box automatically adjusts the spacing that will appear between columns.)

Q&A Why does my Spacing box show a value different from the figure?

Verify that your paper size is set to letter by clicking the Page Setup Dialog Box Launcher (Layout tab), clicking the Paper tab (Page Setup dialog box), ensuring that the paper size is set to Letter applied to the Whole document, and then clicking OK.

How would I make the columns different widths?

You would remove the check mark from the 'Equal column width' check box and then set the individual column widths in the dialog box.

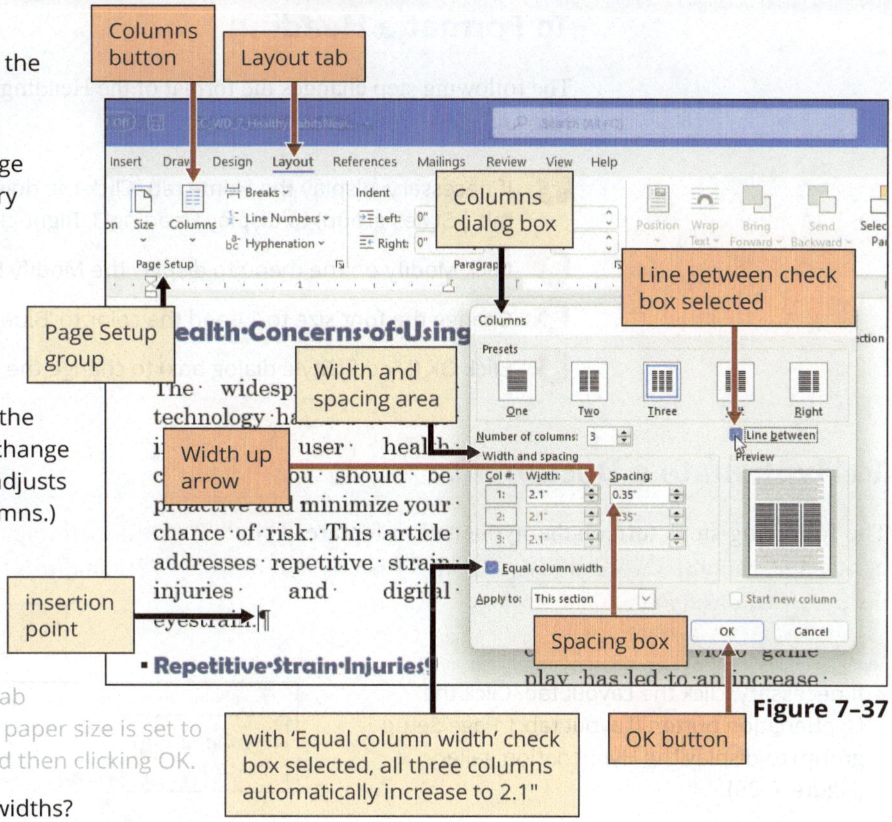

Figure 7–37

- Place a check mark in the Line between check box to select the check box (Figure 7–37).

3

- Click OK to make the columns slightly wider and place a line (vertical rule) between each column in the document (Figure 7–38).

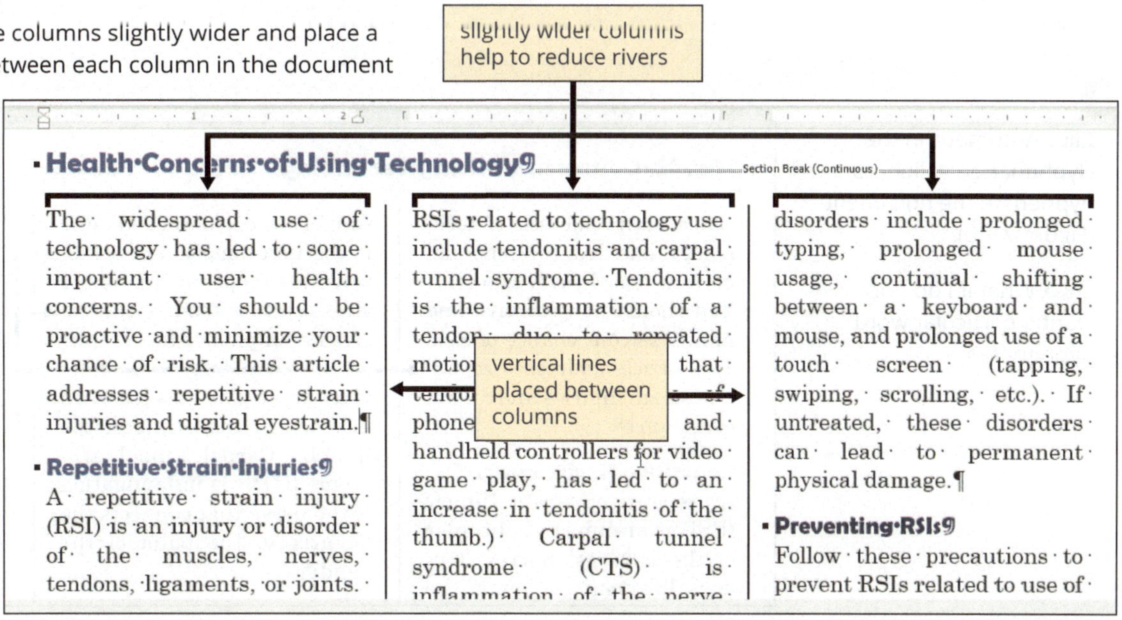

Figure 7–38

Other Ways

1. Double-click shaded space between columns on ruler, enter settings (Columns dialog box), click OK
2. To adjust column widths, drag column boundaries on ruler
3. To insert single rule, click Borders arrow (Home tab | Paragraph group)

To Format a Heading

The following step changes the format of the Heading 3 style so that these headings have a smaller font and a different color.

1. If necessary, display the Home tab. Click the down scroll arrow in the Styles gallery (Home tab | Styles group) to display Heading 3. Right-click Heading 3 to display the heading menu.
2. Click Modify on the menu to display the Modify Style dialog box.
3. Change the font size to 11 and the color to 'Blue, Accent 1, Darker 25%' (fifth color, fifth row).
4. Click OK (Modify Style dialog box) to change the heading to the selected formats.

To Hyphenate a Document

The following steps turn on the hyphenation feature. **Why?** To further eliminate some of the rivers in the columns of the newsletter, you turn on Word's hyphenation feature so that words with multiple syllables are hyphenated at the end of lines instead of wrapped in their entirety to the next line.

1

- If necessary, click the Layout tab. Click the Hyphenation button (Layout tab | Page Setup group) to display the Hyphenation gallery (Figure 7–39).

Q&A What is the difference between Automatic and Manual hyphenation?
Automatic hyphenation places hyphens wherever words can break at a syllable in the document. With manual hyphenation, Word displays a dialog box for each word it could hyphenate, enabling you to accept or reject the proposed hyphenation.

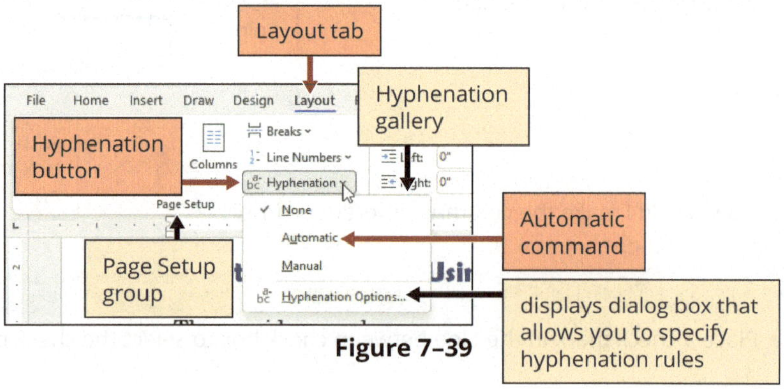

Figure 7–39

2

- Click Automatic in the Hyphenation gallery to hyphenate the document (Figure 7–40).

Q&A What if I do not want a particular word hyphenated?
You can reword text, and Word will redo the hyphenation automatically.

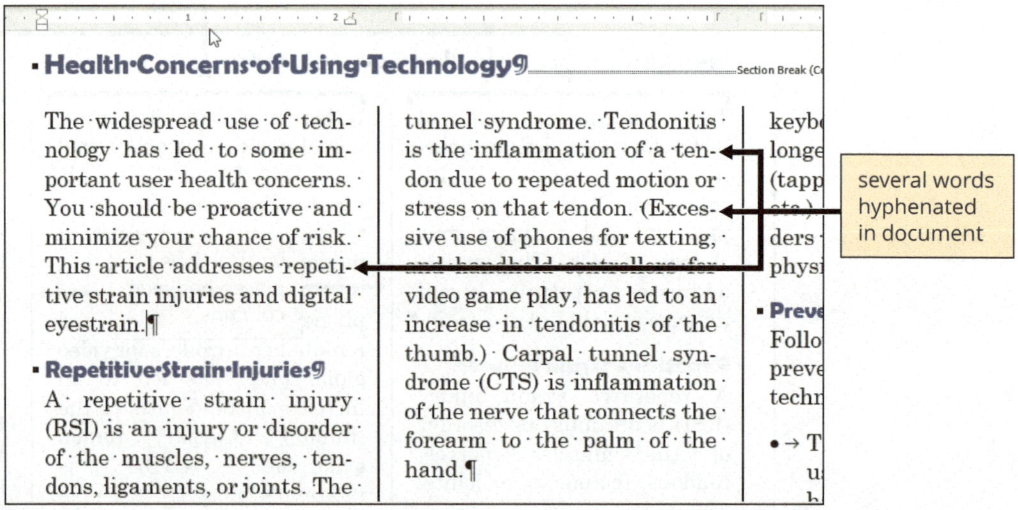

Figure 7–40

To Format a Character as a Drop Cap

The first character in the feature article in this newsletter — that is, the capital letter T — is formatted as a drop cap. **Why?** To add interest to an article, you often see a **drop cap**, which is a decorative, large, initial capital letter that extends below the other letters in the line. In Word, the drop cap can sink into the first few lines of text, or it can extend into the left margin, which often is called a stick-up cap. In this newsletter, the paragraph text wraps around the drop cap.

The following steps create a drop cap in the first paragraph of the feature article in the newsletter.

1

- Position the insertion point somewhere in the first paragraph of the feature article.
- Display the Insert tab.
- Click the 'Add a Drop Cap' button (Insert tab | Text group) to display the Add a Drop Cap gallery (Figure 7–41).
- **Experiment:** Point to various commands in the Add a Drop Cap gallery to see a Live Preview of the drop cap formats in the document.

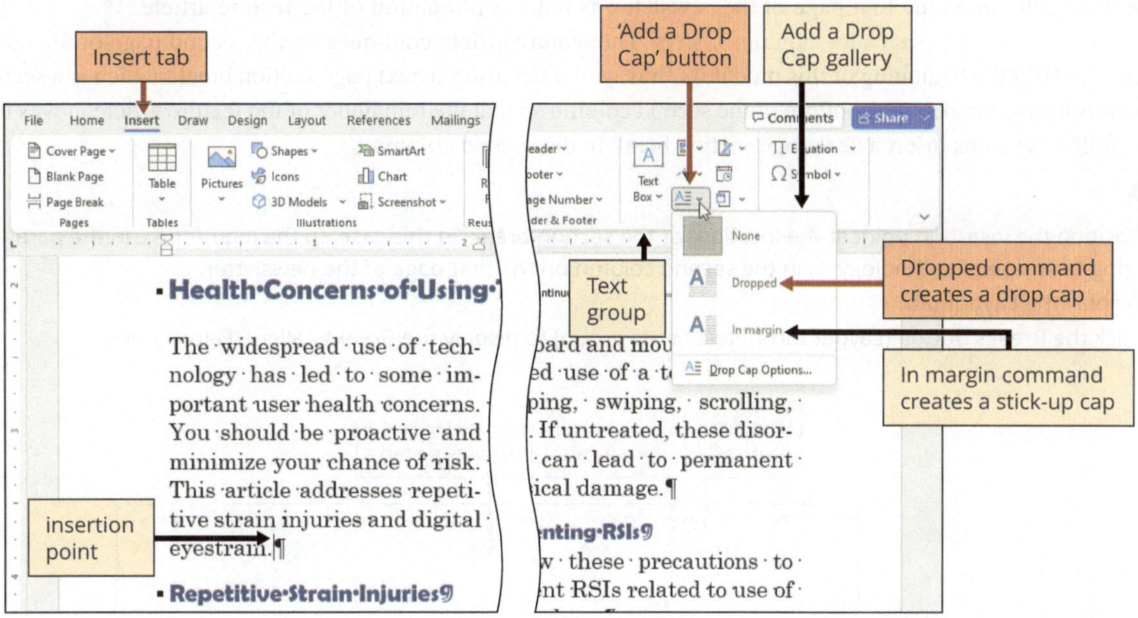

Figure 7–41

2

- Click Dropped in the Add a Drop Cap gallery to format the first letter in the paragraph containing the insertion point (the T in The, in this case) as a drop cap and wrap subsequent text in the paragraph around the drop cap (Figure 7–42).

Q&A What is the outline around the drop cap in the document?
When you format a letter as a drop cap, Word places a frame around it. A **frame** is a container for text that allows you to position the text anywhere on the page. Word formats a frame for the drop cap so that text wraps around it. The frame also contains a paragraph mark nonprinting character to the right of the drop cap, which may or may not be visible on your screen.

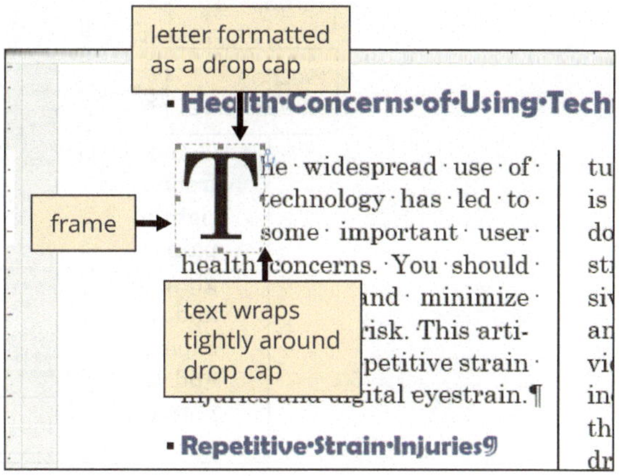

Figure 7–42

To Format the Drop Cap

The following step changes the font color of the drop cap.

1. With the drop cap selected, display the Home tab and then change the font color of the drop cap to 'Blue, Accent 1, Darker 25%' (fifth color, fifth row) in Font Color gallery (shown in Figure 7–1a at the beginning of this module).

Q&A What if my frame no longer is displayed?
Click the drop cap to select it. Then, click the selection rectangle to display the frame.

To Insert a Next Page Section Break

The third column on the first page of the newsletter is not a continuation of the feature article. **Why not?** The third column, instead, contains several reader announcements. The feature article continues on the second page of the newsletter (shown in Figure 7–1b at the beginning of this module). Thus, you must insert a next page section break, which is a section break that also contains a page break, at the bottom of the second column so that the remainder of the feature article moves to the second page. The following steps insert a next page section break in the second column.

1.

- Position the insertion point at the location for the section break, in this case, to the left of the L in the paragraph beginning, Long-term use of technology ..., in the second column on the first page of the newsletter.
- Display the Layout tab.
- Click the Breaks button (Layout tab | Page Setup group) to display the Breaks gallery (Figure 7–43).

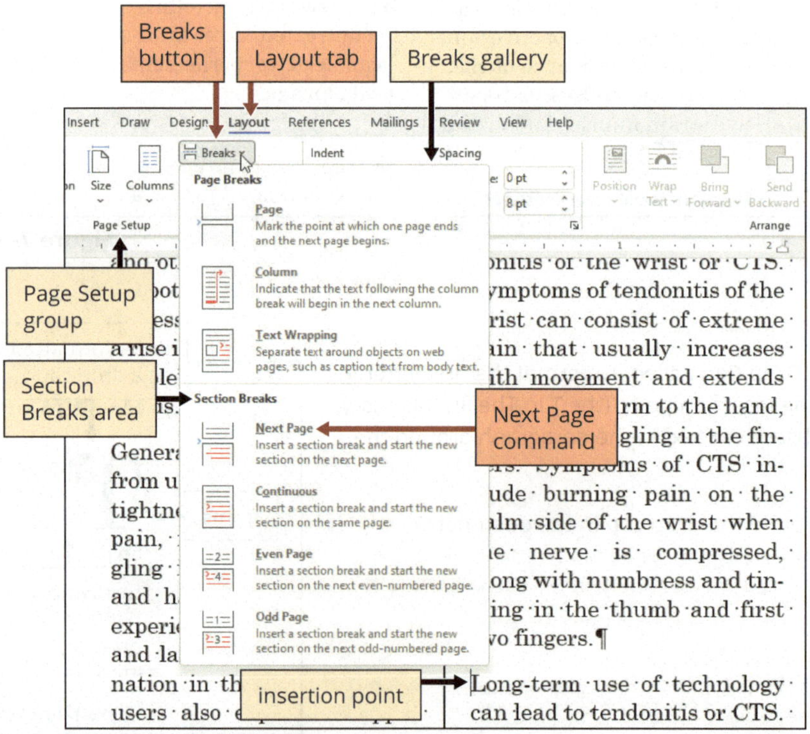

Figure 7–43

2

- In the Section Breaks area in the gallery, click Next Page to insert a next page section break, which positions the insertion point on the next page.
- If necessary, scroll to the bottom of the first page so that you can see the moved text (Figure 7–44).

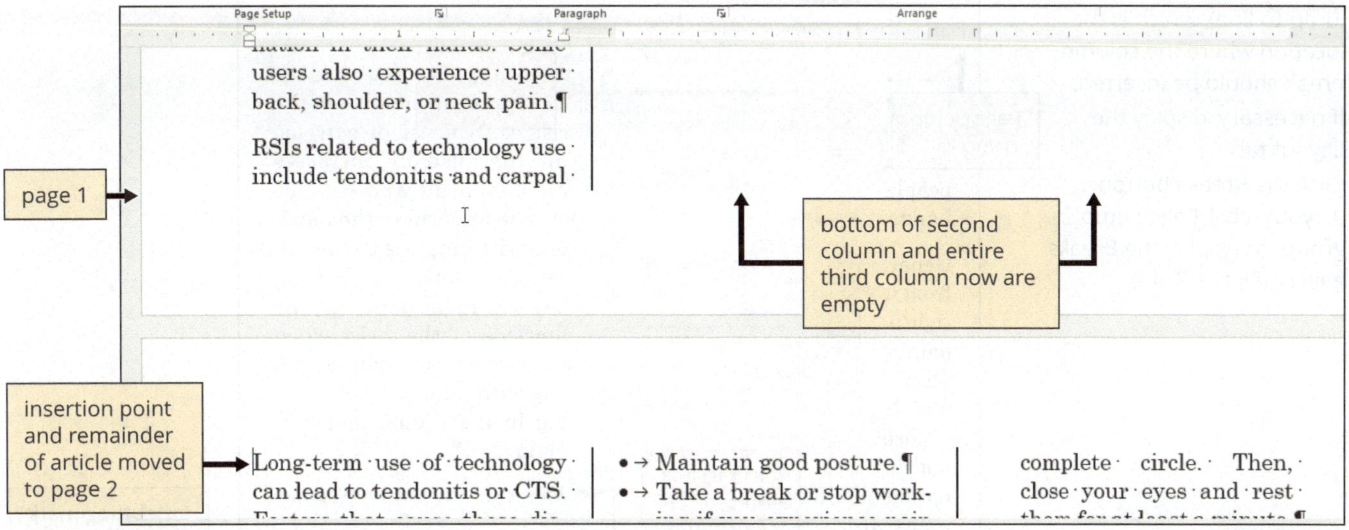

Figure 7–44

To Enter Text

The next step is to insert a jump-to line at the end of the second column, informing the reader where to look for the rest of the feature article. The following steps insert a jump-to line at the end of the text in the second column on the first page of the newsletter.

1. Scroll to display the end of the text in the second column of the first page of the newsletter and then position the insertion point to the left of the paragraph mark that is to the left of the next page section break notation.
2. Press ENTER twice to insert a blank line for the jump-to text above the section break notation.
3. Press the UP ARROW key to position the insertion point on the blank line.
4. Press CTRL+R to right align the paragraph mark. Decrease the font size to 9 point. Change the font color to 'Blue, Accent 1, Darker 25%' (fifth color, fifth row) in Font Color gallery. Press CTRL+B to turn on the bold format, and press CTRL+I to turn on the italic format. Type **(Article continues on next page)** as the jump-to text (shown in Figure 7–45) and then press CTRL+B and CTRL+I again to turn off the bold and italic formats.

To Insert a Column Break

In the *Healthy Habits* newsletters, for consistency, the reader announcements always begin at the top of the third column. If you insert the file containing the announcements at the current location of the insertion point, however, they will begin at the bottom of the second column. **Why?** The insertion point currently is at the bottom of the second column.

For the reader announcements to be displayed in the third column, you insert a **column break** at the bottom of the second column, which places the insertion point at the top of the next column. Thus, the following steps insert a column break at the bottom of the second column.

1

- Position the insertion point to the left of the paragraph mark on the line containing the next page section break (below the jump-to line), which is the location where the column break should be inserted.
- If necessary, display the Layout tab.
- Click the Breaks button (Layout tab | Page Setup group) to display the Breaks gallery (Figure 7–45).

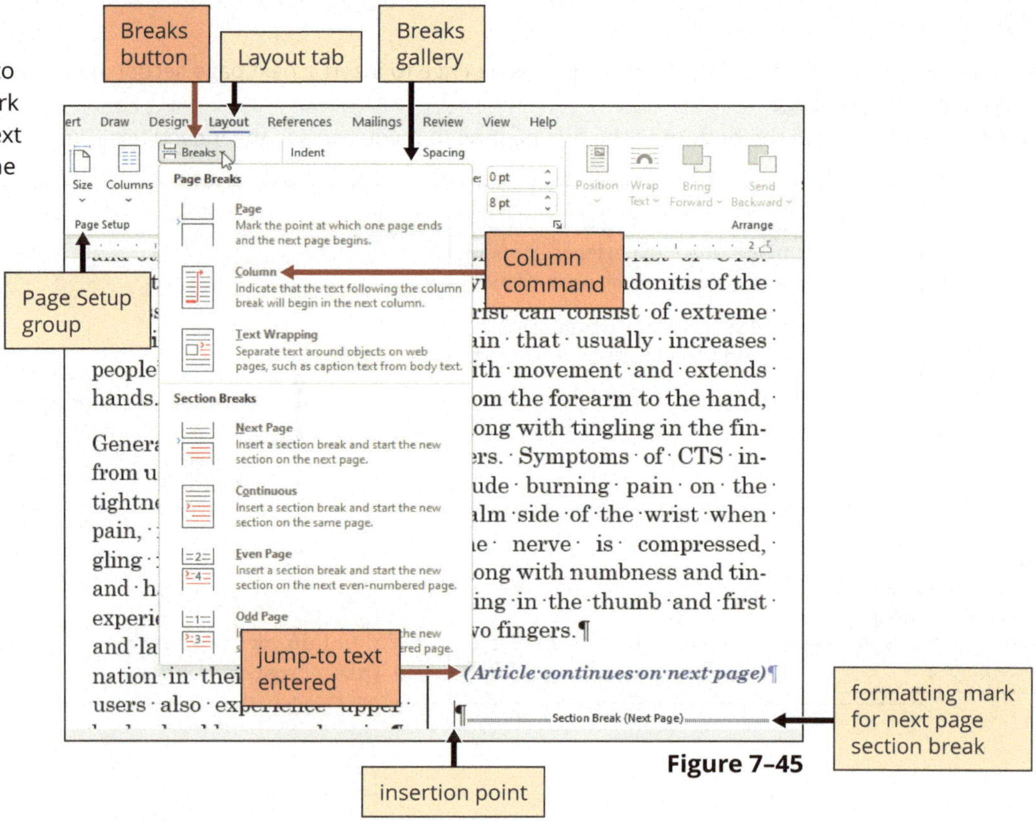

Figure 7–45

2

- Click Column in the Breaks gallery to insert a column break at the location of the insertion point and move the insertion point to the top of the next column (Figure 7–46).

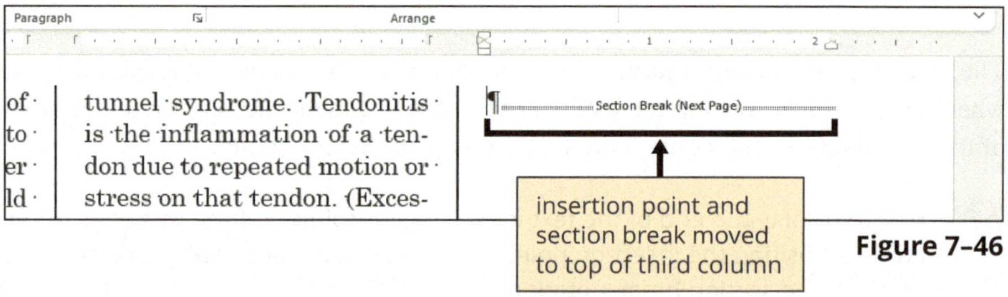

Figure 7–46

Q&A What if I wanted to remove a column break?

You would double-click it to select it and then click the Cut button (Home tab | Clipboard group) or press DELETE.

Other Ways

1. Press CTRL+SHIFT+ENTER

To Insert Text from a File into a Document

So that you do not have to enter the entire third column of announcements in the newsletter, the next step in the project is to insert the file named Support_WD_7_HealthyHabitsAnnouncements.docx in the third column of the newsletter. This file contains the three announcements: the first about an upcoming webinar, the second about the walking club, and the third about the topic of the next newsletter issue.

The Support_WD_7_HealthyHabitsAnnouncements.docx file is located in the Data Files. Please contact your instructor for information about accessing the Data Files. The following steps insert a file in a column of the newsletter.

1. With the insertion point at the top of the third column as shown in Figure 7–46, display the Insert tab.

2. Click the Object arrow (Insert tab | Text group) to display the Object menu and then click 'Text from File' on the Object menu to display the Insert File dialog box.

3. Navigate to the location of the file to be inserted (in this case, the Data Files folder).
4. Click Support_WD_7_HealthyHabitsAnnouncements.docx to select the file.
5. Click the Insert button (Insert File dialog box) to insert the file, Support_WD_7_HealthyHabitsAnnouncements.docx, in the document at the location of the insertion point.
6. If the insertion point is on a blank page, press DELETE or BACKSPACE to delete the blank paragraph and position the insertion point at the end of the third column.
7. Press SHIFT+F5 to return the insertion point to the last editing location, in this case, the top of the third column on the first page of the newsletter (Figure 7–47).
8. Save the newsletter again on the same storage location with the same file name.

BTW
Inserting Documents
When you insert a Word document in another Word document, the entire inserted document is placed at the location of the insertion point. If the insertion point is positioned in the middle of the open document when you insert another Word document, the open document continues after the last character of the inserted document; therefore, pay close attention to where the insertion point is positioned before inserting a document.

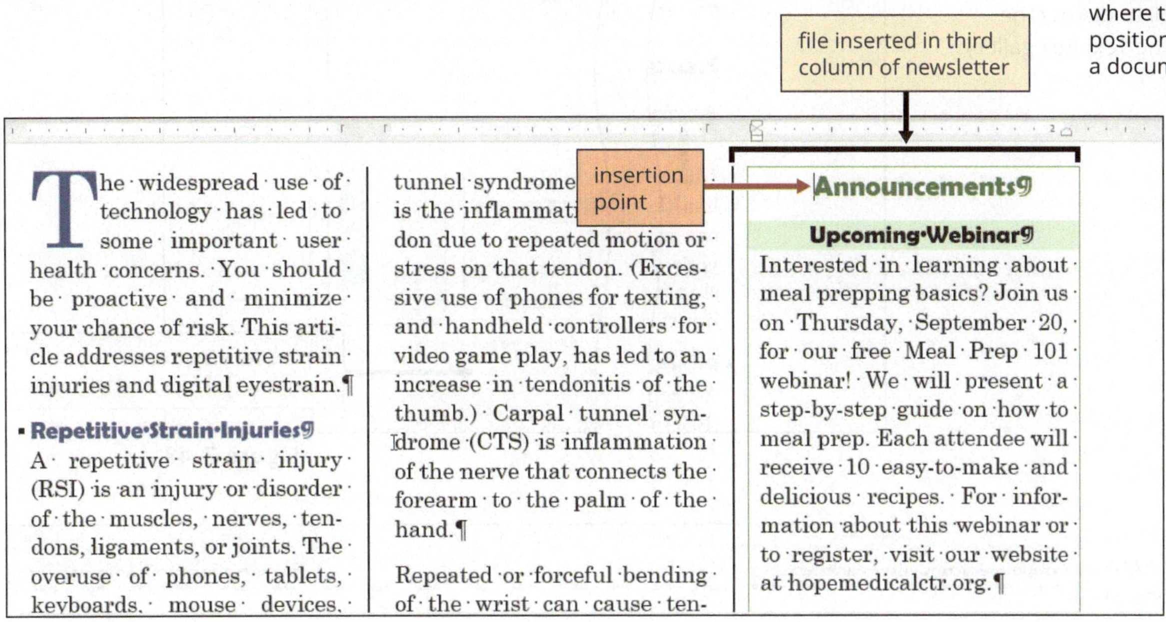

Figure 7–47

Creating a Pull-Quote

A pull-quote is text pulled, or copied, from the text of the document and given graphical emphasis so that it stands apart and commands the reader's attention. The newsletter in this project copies text from the second page of the newsletter and places it in a pull-quote, on the first page between the first and second columns (shown in Figure 7–1a at the beginning of this module).

Consider This

What guidelines should you follow when using pull-quotes?

Because of their bold emphasis, pull-quotes should be used sparingly in a newsletter. Pull-quotes are useful for breaking the monotony of long columns of text. Typically, quotation marks are used only if you are quoting someone directly. If you use quotation marks, use curly (or smart) quotation marks instead of straight quotation marks.

To create the pull-quote in this newsletter, follow this general procedure:

1. Create a **text box**, which is an object that contains text and that allows you to position the text anywhere on the page.
2. Copy the text from the existing document to the Office Clipboard and then paste the text from the Office Clipboard to the text box.
3. Resize and format the text box.
4. Move the text box to the desired location.

To Insert a Preformatted Text Box

The first step in creating the pull-quote is to insert a text box. A text box is like a frame; the difference is that a text box has more graphical formatting options than does a frame. The following steps insert a built-in text box. **Why?** Word provides a variety of built-in text boxes, saving you the time of formatting the text box.

1

- Click the Text Box button (Insert tab | Text group) to display the Text Box gallery.
- **Experiment:** Scroll through the Text Box gallery to see the variety of available text box styles.
- If necessary, scroll to display the Austin Quote in the Text Box gallery (Figure 7–48).

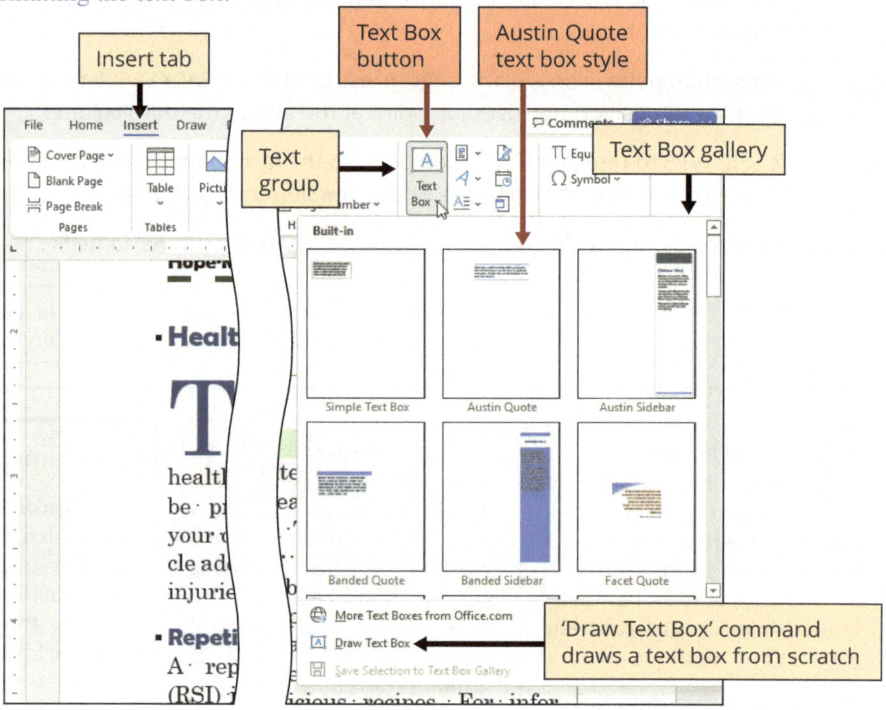

Figure 7–48

2

- Click Austin Quote in the Text Box gallery to insert that style of text box in the document.
- If necessary, drag the text box to the approximate location shown in Figure 7–49.

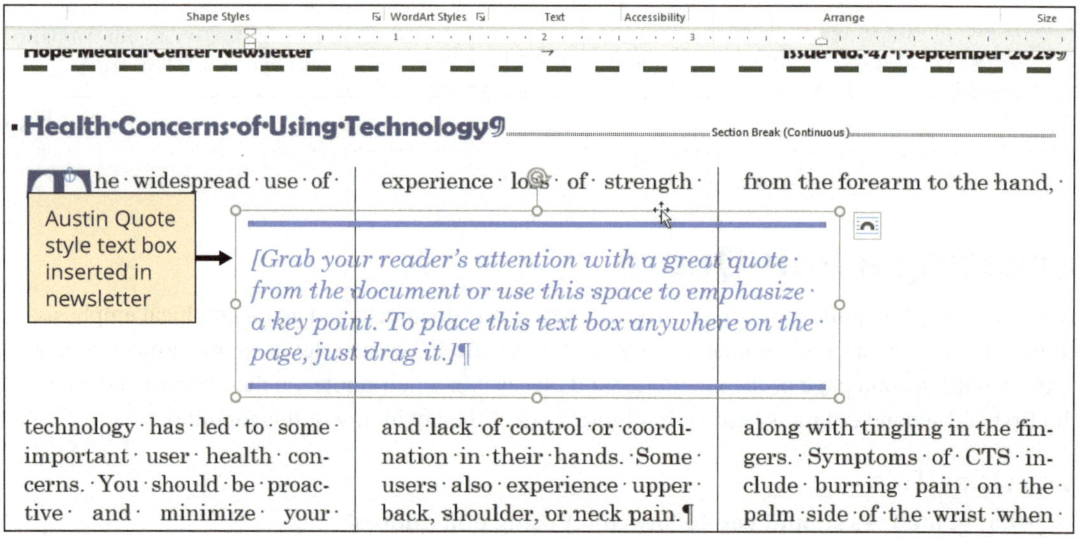

Figure 7–49

Q&A Does my text box need to be in the exact same location as in Figure 7–49?

No. You will move the text box later.

The layout of the first page is not correct because of the text box. What do I do?

You will enter text in the text box and then position it in the correct location. At that time, the layout of the first page will be fixed.

What if I did not want to insert a preformatted text box?

You would click 'Draw Text Box' at the bottom of the Text Box gallery (shown in Figure 7–48) and then draw the text box from scratch.

Other Ways

1. Click 'Explore Quick Parts' button (Insert tab | Text group), click 'Building Blocks Organizer' on Explore Quick Parts menu, select desired text box name in Building blocks list, click Insert button

To Split the Word Window

The text that you will copy for the pull-quote is in the left column of the second page on the newsletter and the pull-quote (text box) is near the top of the first page of the newsletter. Thus, the next step is to copy the pull-quote text from the second page and then paste it in the pull-quote at the top of the first page. You would like to view the pull-quote and the text to be copied on the screen at the same time. **Why?** Viewing both simultaneously will simplify the copying and pasting process.

Word allows you to split the window into two separate panes, each containing the current document and having its own scroll bar. This enables you to scroll to and view two different portions of the same document at the same time. The following step splits the Word window.

1

- Display the View tab.
- Click the Split button (View tab | Window group) to divide the document window into two separate panes — both the upper and lower panes display the current document (Figure 7–50).

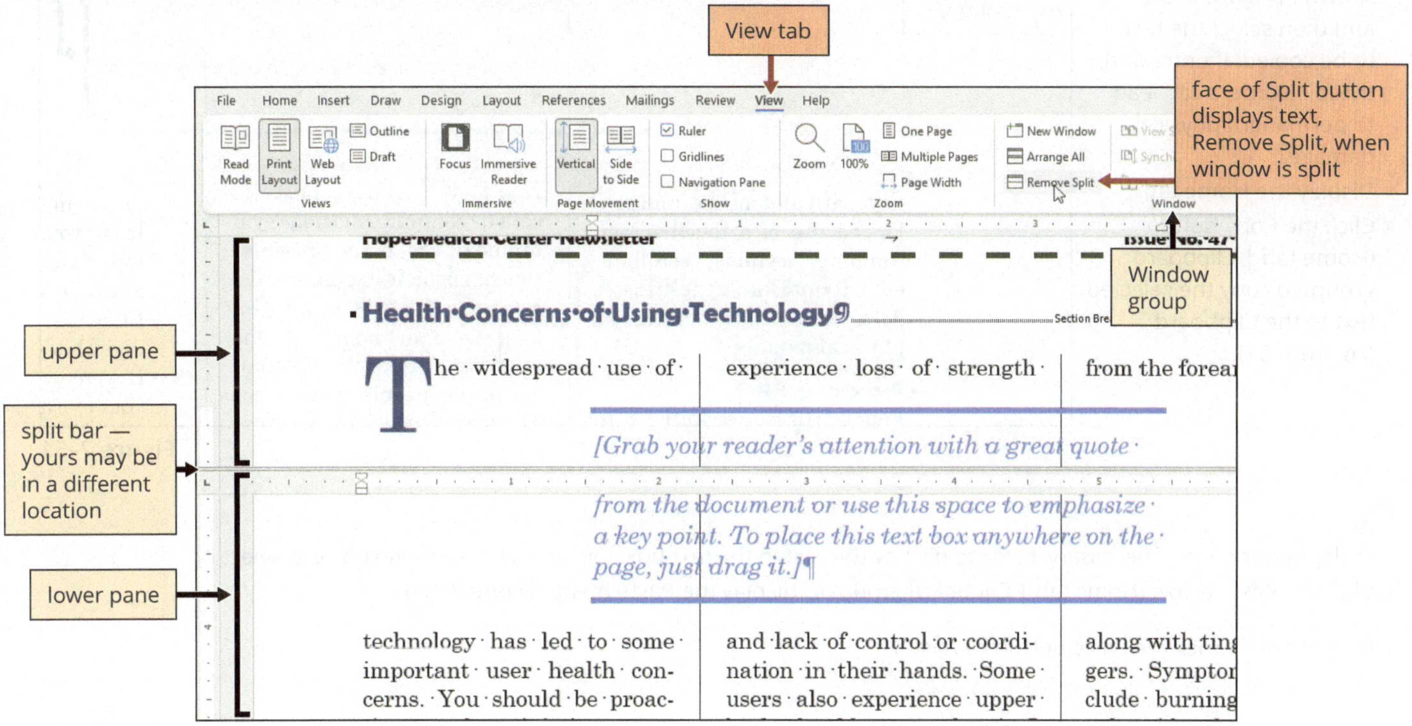

Figure 7–50

Other Ways

1. Press ALT+CTRL+S

To Arrange All Open Word Documents on the Screen If you have multiple Word documents open and want to view all of them at the same time on the screen, you can instruct Word to arrange all the open documents on the screen from top to bottom. If you wanted to arrange all open Word documents on the same screen, you would perform the following steps.

1. Click the Arrange All button (View tab | Window group) to display each open Word document on the screen.
2. To make one of the arranged documents fill the entire screen again, maximize the window by clicking its Maximize button or double-clicking its title bar.

To Copy and Paste Using Split Windows

The following steps copy text from the first column of the second page of the newsletter to the Clipboard (the source) and then paste the text into the text box (the destination) at the top of the newsletter. **Why?** The item being copied is called the **source**. The location to which you are pasting is called the **destination**.

1

- In the upper pane, scroll so that all placeholder text in the text box is visible, as shown in Figure 7–51.
- In the lower pane, scroll to page 3 to display the text to be copied, as shown in Figure 7–51, and then select the text to be copied: If untreated, these disorders can lead to permanent physical damage.
- Display the Home tab.
- Click the Copy button (Home tab | Clipboard group) to copy the selected text to the Clipboard (Figure 7–51).

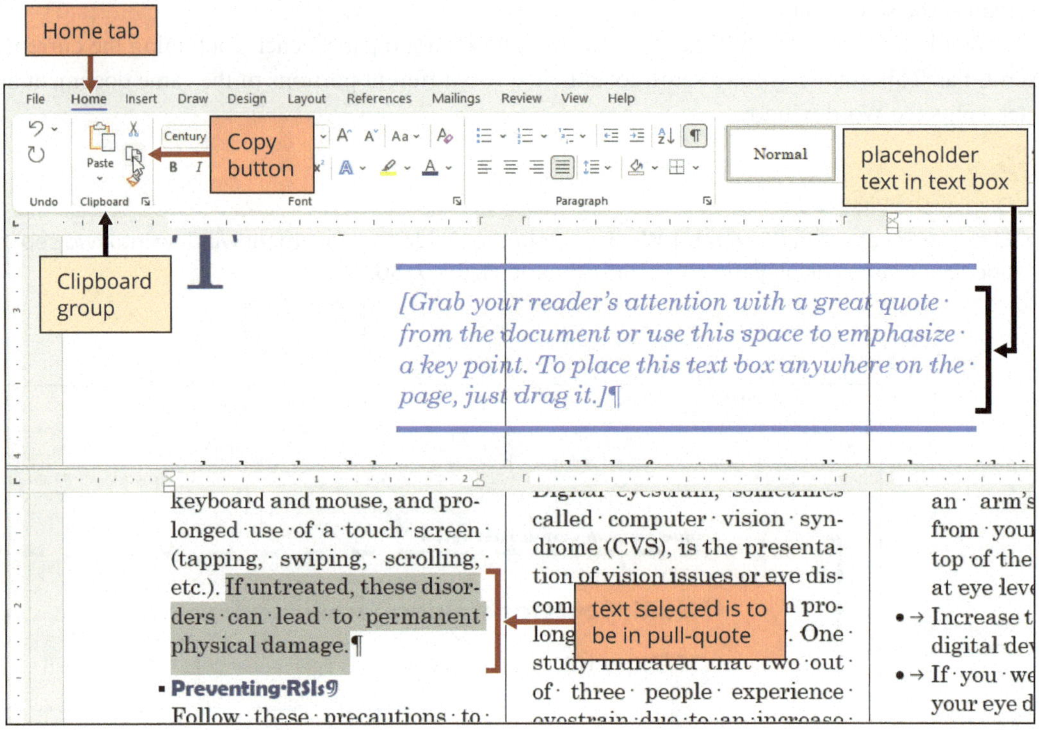

Figure 7–51

2

- In the upper pane, if necessary, scroll to display the text in the text box. Click the text in the text box to select it.
- Click the Paste arrow (Home tab | Clipboard group) to display the Paste menu (Figure 7–52).

Q&A What if I click the Paste button by mistake?
Click the Paste Options button to the right of the pasted text in the text box to display the Paste Options menu.

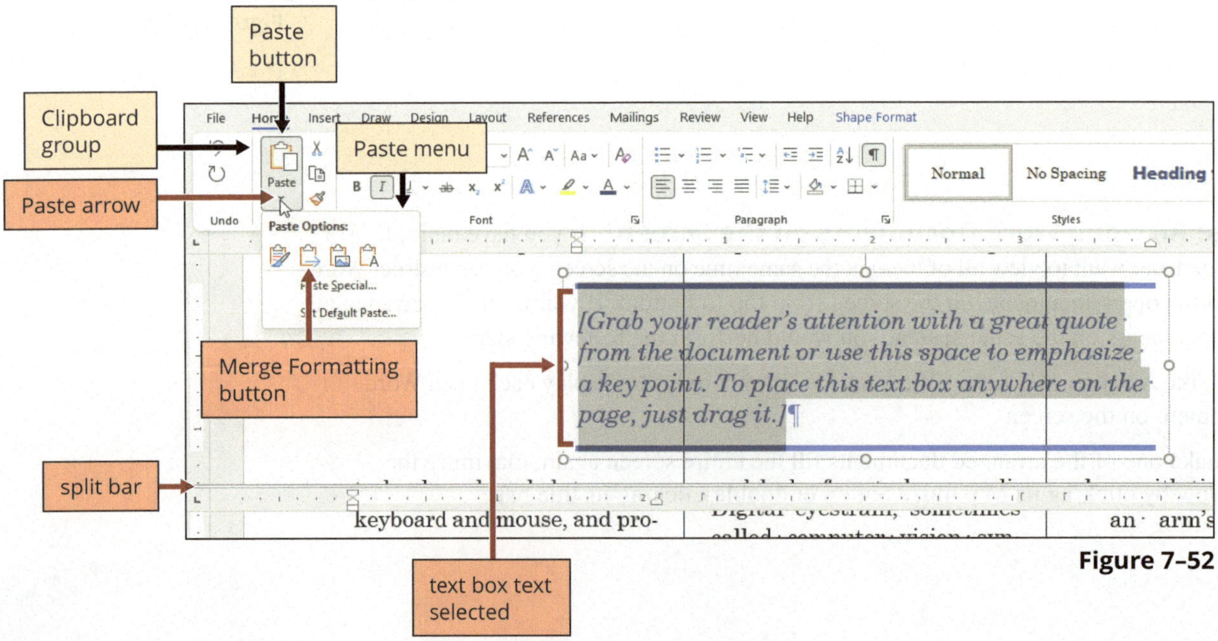

Figure 7–52

3

- Click the Merge Formatting button on the Paste menu to paste the copied text into the text box (shown in Figure 7–53).

Q&A Why select the Merge Formatting button on the Paste menu?
You want the pasted text to use the formats that were in the text box (the destination) instead of the formats of the copied text (the source).

Other Ways

1. Click copy on shortcut menu (or, if using touch, tap Copy on Mini toolbar), right-click where item is to be pasted, click Merge Formatting in Paste Options area on shortcut menu (or, if using touch, tap Paste on Mini toolbar)
2. Select text to copy, press CTRL+C; select destination for pasted text, press CTRL+V

To Remove a Split Window

The next step is to remove the split window so that you can position the pull-quote. The following step removes a split window.

1. Double-click the split bar (shown in Figure 7–52), or click the Remove Split button (View tab | Window group), or press ALT+SHIFT+C to remove the split window and return to a single Word window on the screen.

To Edit and Format Text in the Text Box

The next steps format text in the pull-quote.

1. If necessary, scroll to display the text box in the document window.
2. Select all the text in the text box, if necessary, change its font to 'Berlin Sans FB' (or a similar font), remove the italic format from the text, and change its font size to 10 point. Center the paragraph. If necessary, change font color to 'Blue, Accent 1' (fifth color, first row) in the Font Color gallery.
3. Click in the text box to deselect the text, but leave the text box selected (shown in Figure 7–53).
4. If the Selection pane is open, click its Close button to close the pane.

To Change the Text Wrapping and Size of a Text Box

The next step in formatting the pull-quote is to change its text wrapping to square and to resize the text box. You resize a text box the same way as any other object. That is, you drag its sizing handles or enter values in the height and width boxes through the Size button (Shape Format tab | Size group). The following steps change the text wrapping and resize the text box.

1. Drag the sizing handles so that the pull-quote looks about the same size as Figure 7–53.
2. Verify the pull-quote dimensions in the Shape Height and Shape Width boxes (Shape Format tab | Size group) and, if necessary, change the value in the Shape Height box to .91 and the Shape Width box to 1.8. (Note that depending on your printer and other settings, the text wrapping in your newsletter may not match the figure.)
3. With the text box selected, click the Layout Options button attached to the text box to display the Layout Options gallery.

BTW
Rotating Text Box Text
To rotate text in a text box, select the text box, click the Text Direction button (Shape Format tab | Text group), and then click the desired direction on the Text Direction menu.

4. Click Square in the Layout Options gallery so that the text wraps in a square around the text box (Figure 7–53).

5. Close the Layout Options gallery.

Q&A What if some of the words in a text box are hyphenated?
Insert line break characters to eliminate any hyphenated words in the text box; that is, position the insertion point to the left of the first letter in the hyphenated word and then press SHIFT+ENTER to insert a line break character, which places the entire word on the next line and removes the hyphen.

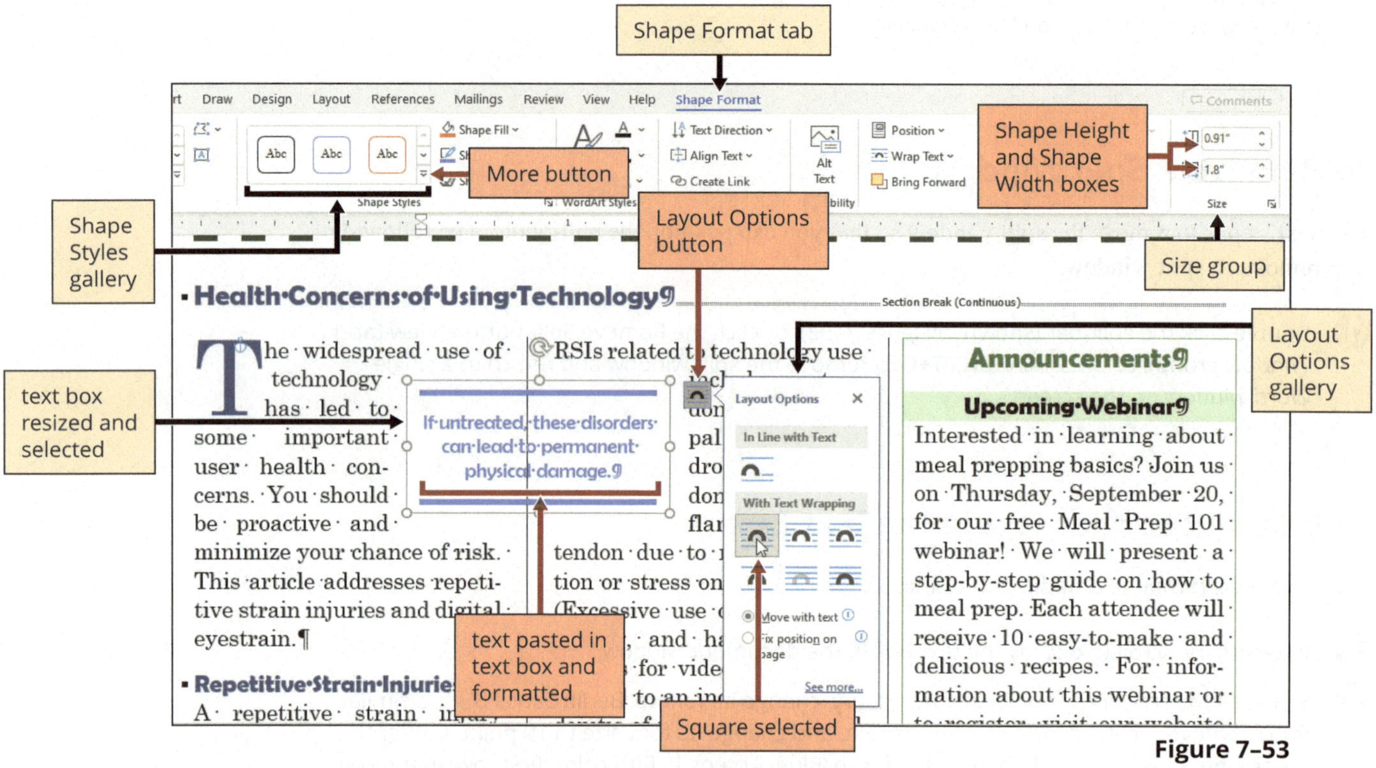

Figure 7–53

To Apply a Shape Style to a Text Box

BTW
Text Box Styles
Like other objects or pictures, text boxes can be formatted or have styles applied. You can change the fill in a text box by clicking the Shape Fill button or arrow (Shape Format tab | Shape Styles group), add an outline to a text box by clicking the Shape Outline button or arrow (Shape Format tab | Shape Styles group), and apply an effect, such as shadow or 3-D effects, by clicking the Shape Effects button (Shape Format tab | Shape Styles group).

The next step in formatting the pull-quote is to apply a shape style to the text box to coordinate its colors with the rest of the newsletter. The following steps apply a shape style to a text box.

1. With the text box still selected, click the More button (shown in Figure 7–53) in the Shape Styles gallery (Shape Format tab | Shape Styles group) to expand the gallery.

2. Point to 'Colored Outline - Blue, Accent 1' (second style, first row in Theme Styles area) in the Shape Styles gallery to display a Live Preview of that style applied to the text box (Figure 7–54).

3. Click 'Colored Outline - Blue, Accent 1' in the Shape Styles gallery to apply the selected style to the shape.

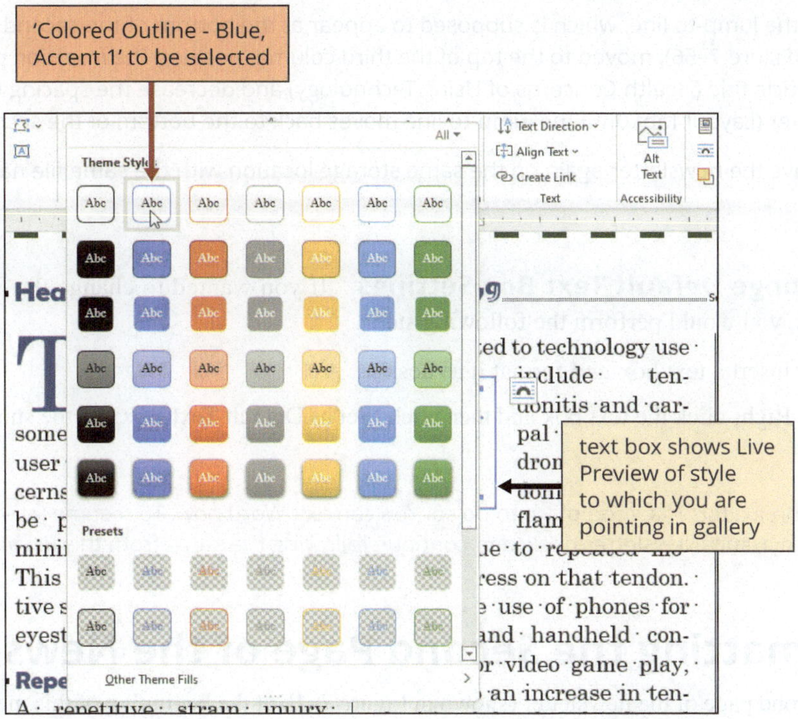

Figure 7–54

To Position a Text Box

The following steps move the text box to the desired location in the newsletter.

1. With the text box still selected, drag the text box to its new location (Figure 7–55). You may need to drag and/or resize the text box a couple of times so that it looks similar to this figure.

2. Click outside the text box to remove the selection.

Q&A Why does my text wrap differently around the text box?
Differences in wordwrap often relate to the printer used by your computer. Thus, your document may wordwrap around the text box differently.

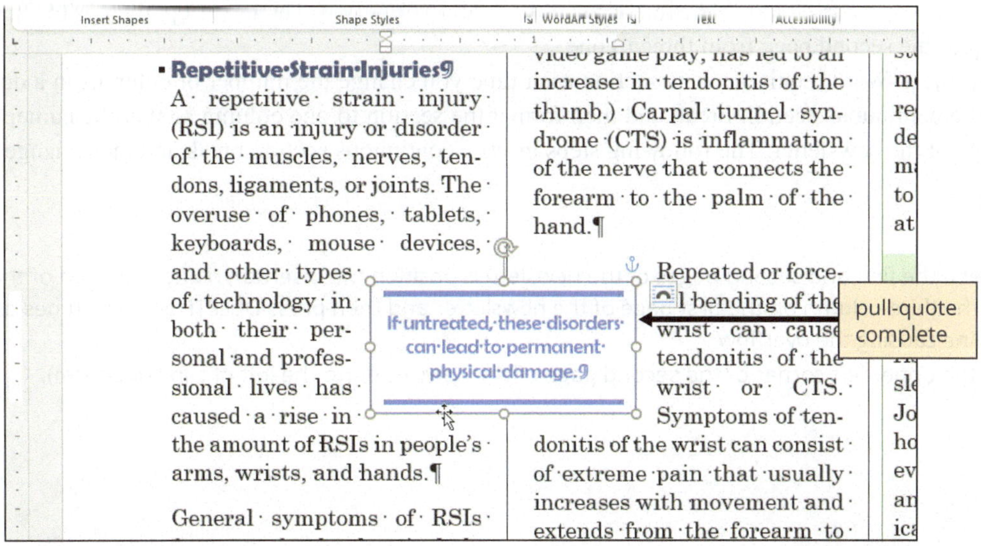

Figure 7–55

BTW
Moving Text Boxes
To move a text box using the keyboard, select the text box and then press the arrow keys on the keyboard. For example, each time you press the DOWN ARROW key, the selected text box moves down one space incrementally.

3. If the jump-to line, which is supposed to appear at the bottom of the second column (shown in Figure 7–56), moved to the top of the third column, position the insertion point in the article title (Health Concerns of Using Technology) and decrease the spacing before and after (Layout tab) until the jump-to line moves back to the bottom of the second column.

4. Save the newsletter again on the same storage location with the same file name.

To Change Default Text Box Settings If you wanted to change the default text box settings, you would perform the following steps.

1. Insert a text box and format it as desired.
2. Right-click the text box and then click 'Set as Default Text Box' on the shortcut menu.

Break Point: If you want to take a break, this is a good place to do so. You can exit Word now. To resume later, start Word, open the file called SC_WD_7_HealthyHabitsNewsletter.docx, and continue following the steps from this location forward.

Formatting the Second Page of the Newsletter

The second page of the newsletter (shown in Figure 7–1b at the beginning of this module) continues the feature article that began in the first two columns on the first page. The nameplate on the second page is less elaborate than the one on the first page of the newsletter. In addition to the text in the feature article, page two contains a graphic. The following sections format the second page of the newsletter in this project.

Consider This

How do you create a nameplate for inner pages of a newsletter?

The top of the inner pages of a newsletter may or may not have a nameplate. If you choose to create one for your inner pages, it should not be the same as, or compete with, the one on the first page. Inner page nameplates usually contain only a portion of the nameplate from the first page of a newsletter.

To Change Column Formatting

The document currently is formatted in three columns. The nameplate at the top of the second page, however, should be in a single column. **Why?** The nameplate should span across the top of the three columns below it. The next step, then, is to change the number of columns at the top of the second page from three to one.

As discussed earlier in this project, Word requires a new section each time you change the number of columns in a document. Thus, you first must insert a continuous section break and then format the section to one column so that the nameplate can be entered on the second page of the newsletter. The following steps insert a continuous section break and then change the column format.

1

- If you have a blank page between the first and second pages of the newsletter, position the insertion point to the left of the paragraph mark at the end of the third column on the first page of the newsletter and then press DELETE as many times as necessary to delete the blank line causing the overflow.
- Position the insertion point at the upper-left corner of the second page of the newsletter (to the left of L in Long-term).

- Display the Layout tab.
- Click the Breaks button (Layout tab | Page Setup group) to display the Breaks gallery (Figure 7–56).

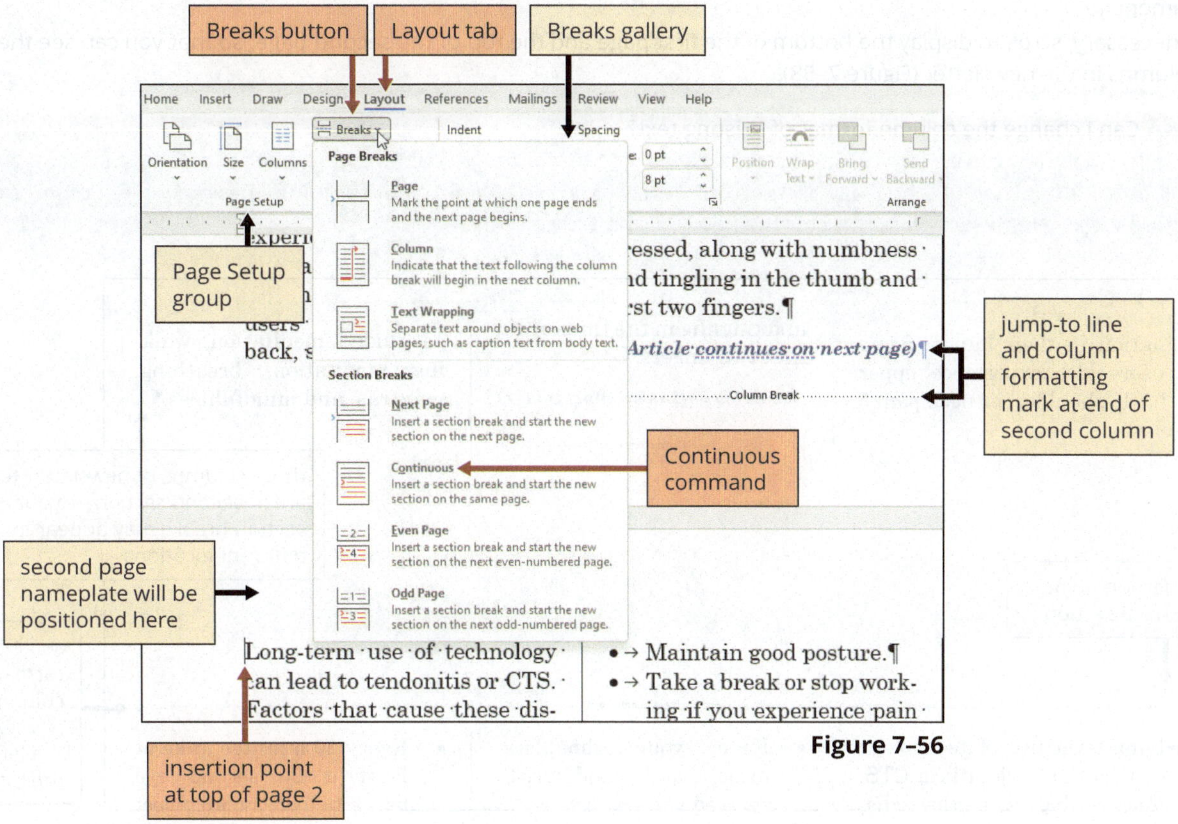

Figure 7–56

2

- Click Continuous in the Breaks gallery to insert a continuous section break above the insertion point.
- Press the UP ARROW key to position the insertion point to the left of the continuous section break just inserted.
- Click the Columns button (Layout tab | Page Setup group) to display the Columns gallery (Figure 7–57).

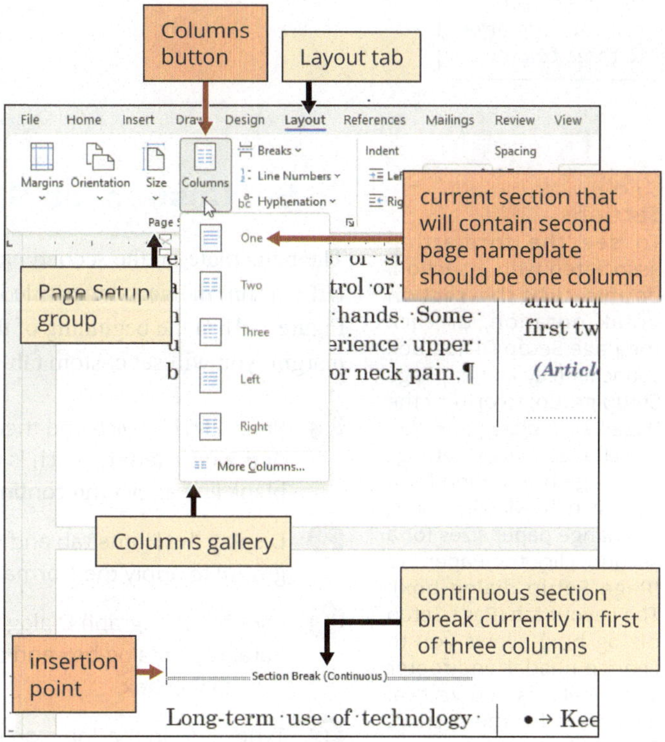

Figure 7–57

3

- Click One in the Columns gallery to format the current section to one column, which now is ready for the second page nameplate.
- If necessary, scroll to display the bottom of the first page and the top of the second page, so that you can see the varying columns in the newsletter (Figure 7–58).

Q&A Can I change the column format of existing text?
Yes. If you already have typed text and would like it to be formatted in a different number of columns, select the text, click the Columns button (Layout tab | Page Setup group), and then click the number of columns desired in the Columns gallery. Word automatically creates a new section for the newly formatted columns.

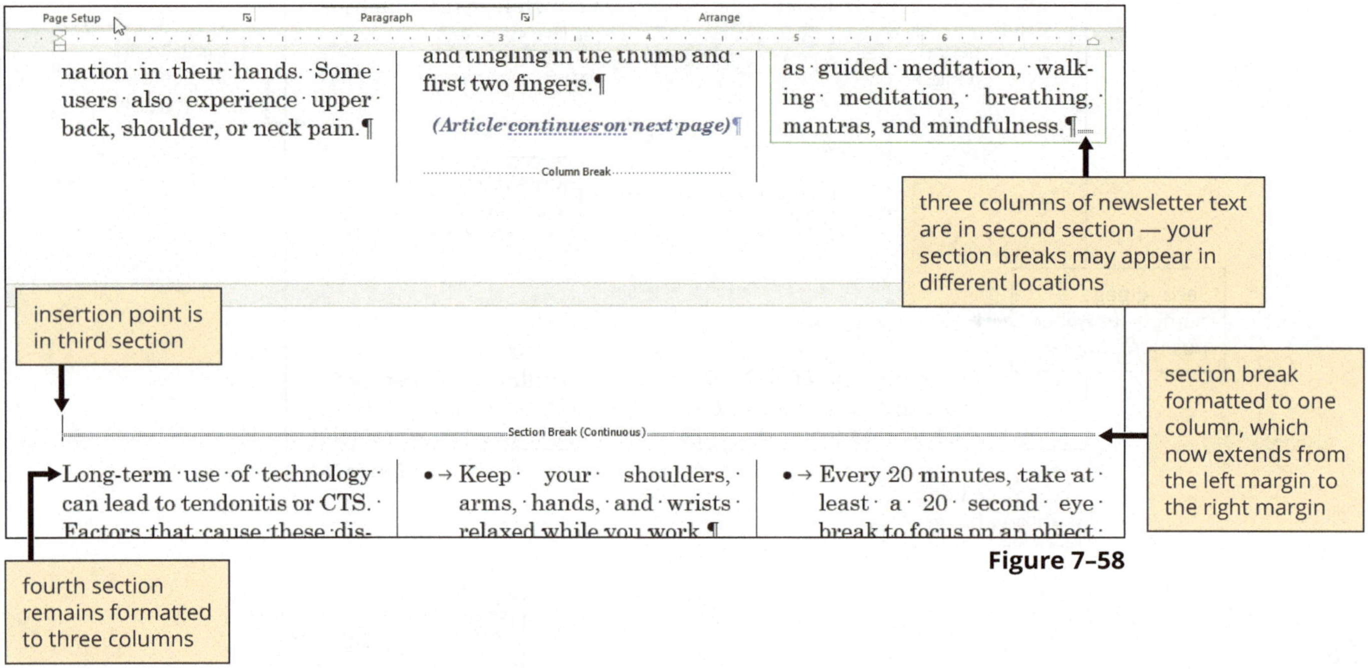

Figure 7–58

BTW
Sections
To see the formatting associated with a section, double-click the section break notation, or click the Page Setup Dialog Box Launcher (Layout tab | Page Setup group) to display the Page Setup dialog box. You can change margin settings and page orientation for a section in the Margins sheet. To change paper sizes for a section, click the Paper tab (Page Setup dialog box). The Layout tab (Page Setup dialog box) allows you to change header and footer specifications and vertical alignment for the section. To add a border to a section, click the Borders button in the Layout sheet.

To Set Custom Tab Stops Using the Tabs Dialog Box

The nameplate on the second page of the newsletter contains the text, Monthly Newsletter, at the left margin, the newsletter title in the center, and the issue number at the right margin (shown in Figure 7–1b at the beginning of this module). To properly align the text in the center and at the right margin, you will set custom tab stops at these locations. The following steps set custom tab stops.

1. Press ENTER twice and then position the insertion point on the first line of the second page of the newsletter, which is the paragraph to be formatted with the custom tab stops (the blank line above the continuous section break).
2. Display the Home tab and then click the 'Clear All Formatting' button (Home tab | Font group) to apply the Normal style to the first line on the second page of the newsletter.
3. Click the Paragraph Dialog Box Launcher (Home tab | Paragraph group) to display the Paragraph dialog box and then click the Tabs button (Paragraph dialog box) to display the Tabs dialog box.
4. Type **3.5** in the Tab stop position text box (Tabs dialog box), click Center in the Alignment area to specify the tab stop alignment, and then click the Set button to set the custom tab stop.

5. Type **7** in the Tab stop position text box (Tabs dialog box), click Right in the Alignment area to specify the tab stop alignment, and then click the Set button to set the custom tab stop (Figure 7–59).
6. Click OK to set custom tab stops using the specified alignments.

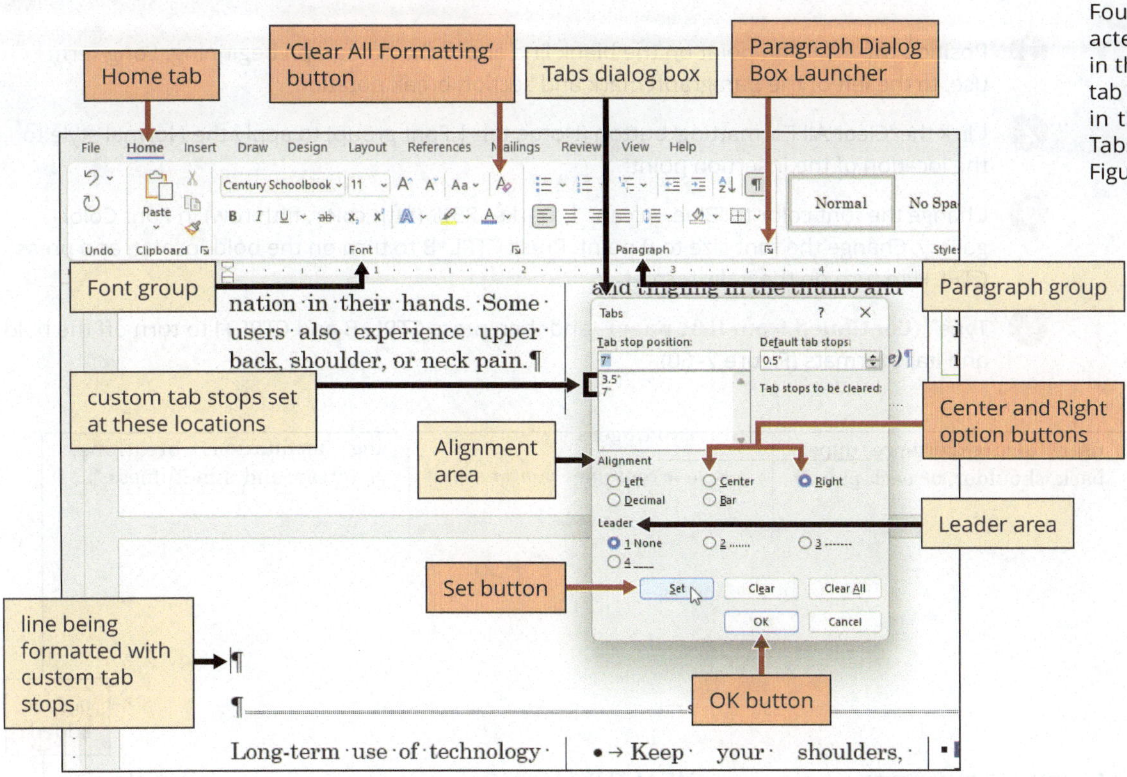

Figure 7–59

BTW
Leader Characters
Leader characters, such as a series of dots, often are used in a table of contents to precede page numbers. Four types of leader characters, which Word places in the space occupied by a tab character, are available in the Leader area of the Tabs dialog box (shown in Figure 7–59).

To Format and Enter Text and Add a Border

The following steps enter the newsletter title at the top of the second page in the third section.

1. With the insertion point on the first line of the second page of the newsletter, click the Font Color arrow and then change the font color of the current text to 'Blue, Accent 1, Darker 50%' (fifth column, bottom row). Change the font to 'Copperplate Gothic Bold' (or a similar font), the font size to 10 point, and type **Monthly Newsletter** at the left margin.
2. Press TAB to advance the insertion point to the centered tab stop. Increase the font size to 12 point and then type **Healthy Habits** at the centered tab stop.
3. Press TAB to advance the insertion point to the right-aligned tab stop. Reduce the font size to 10 point and then type **Issue No. 47** at the right-aligned tab stop.
4. Click the Borders button (Home tab | Paragraph group) to add a bottom border (shown in Figure 7–60).

Q&A Why is the border formatted already?
When you define a custom border, Word uses that custom border the next time you click the Borders button in the Borders gallery.

What if my border is not formatted the same as the one on the first page?
Follow the steps titled, To Border One Edge of a Paragraph, earlier in this module to add the same bottom border to the nameplate on the second page of the newsletter.

To Enter Text

The second page of the feature article on the second page of this newsletter begins with a jump-from line (the continued message) immediately below the nameplate. The next steps enter the jump-from line.

1. Position the insertion point on the blank line above the paragraph beginning, Long-term use, to the left of the paragraph mark and section break notation.
2. Click the 'Clear All Formatting' button (Home tab | Font group) to apply the Normal style to the location of the insertion point.
3. Change the font color to 'Blue, Accent 1, Darker 25%' (fifth color, fifth row) in Font Color gallery. Change the font size to 9 point. Press CTRL+B to turn on the bold format, and press CTRL+I to turn on the italic format.
4. Type **(Continued from first page)** and then press CTRL+B and CTRL+I to turn off the bold and italic formats (Figure 7–60).

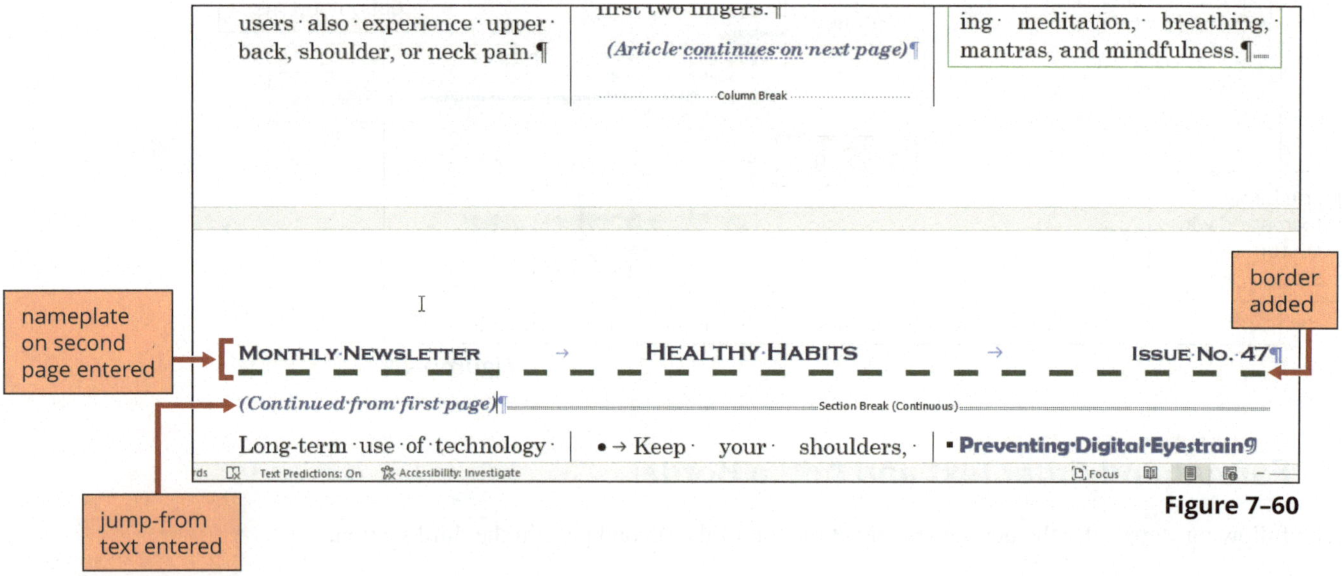

Figure 7–60

To Balance Columns

Currently, the text on the second page of the newsletter completely fills up the first and second columns and fills a portion of the third column. The text in the three columns should consume the same amount of vertical space. **Why?** Typically, the text in columns of a newsletter is balanced. To balance columns, you insert a continuous section break at the end of the text. The following steps balance columns.

1

- Scroll to the bottom of the text in the third column on the second page of the newsletter and then position the insertion point on the blank line below the end of the text.
- Display the Layout tab.

- Click the Breaks button (Layout tab | Page Setup group) to display the Breaks gallery (Figure 7–61).

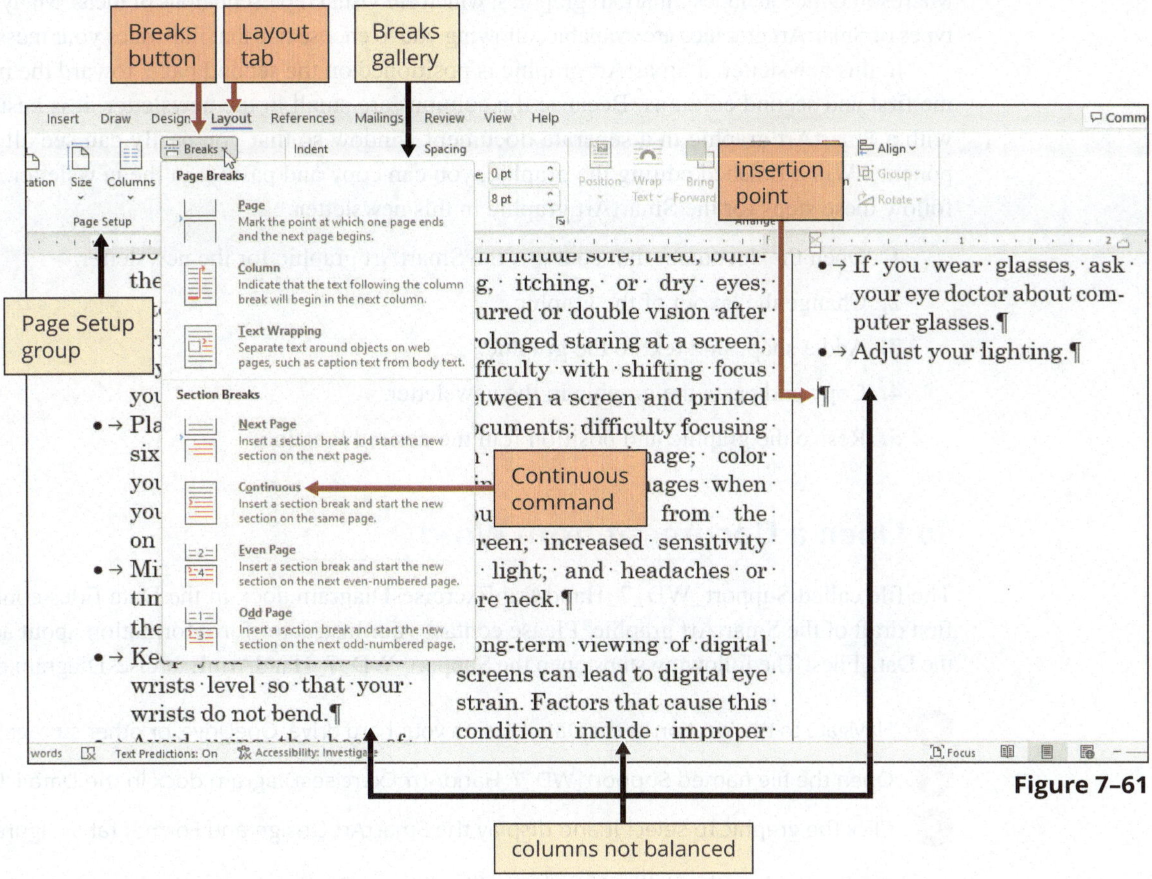

Figure 7–61

2

- Click Continuous in the Breaks gallery to insert a continuous section break, which balances the columns on the second page of the newsletter (Figure 7–62).
- Save the newsletter again on the same storage location with the same file name.

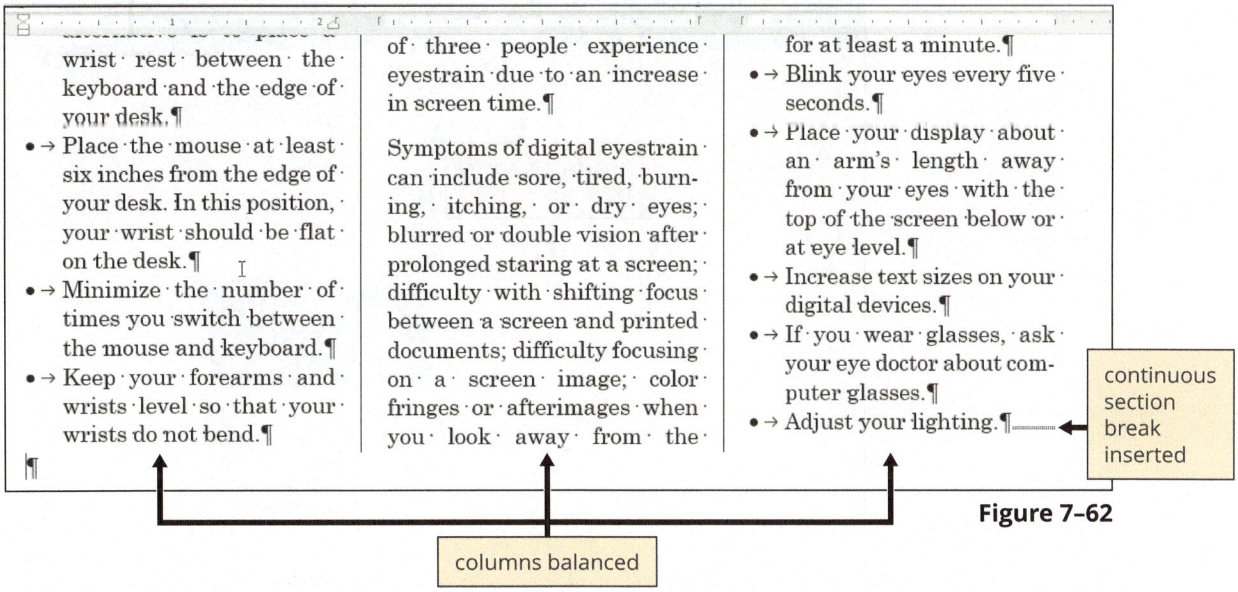

Figure 7–62

Modifying and Formatting a SmartArt Graphic

Microsoft Office includes SmartArt graphics, which are visual representations of ideas. Many different types of SmartArt graphics are available, allowing you to choose one that illustrates your message best.

In this newsletter, a SmartArt graphic is positioned on the second page, toward the middle of the first and second columns. Because the columns are small in the newsletter, it is best to work with a SmartArt graphic in a separate document window so that you easily can see all its components. When finished editing the graphic, you can copy and paste it in the newsletter. You will follow these steps for the SmartArt graphic in this newsletter:

1. Open the document that contains the SmartArt graphic for the newsletter.
2. Change the layout of the graphic.
3. Add a shape and text to the graphic.
4. Copy and paste the graphic in the newsletter.
5. Resize the graphic and position it in the desired location.

To Open a Document from Word

The file called Support_WD_7_HandArmExercisesDiagram.docx in the Data Files contains the first draft of the SmartArt graphic. Please contact your instructor for information about accessing the Data Files. The following steps open the Support_WD_7_HandArmExercisesDiagram.docx file.

1. Navigate to the location of the Data Files on your hard drive, OneDrive, or other storage location.
2. Open the file named Support_WD_7_HandArmExercisesDiagram.docx in the Data Files.
3. Click the graphic to select it and display the SmartArt Design and Format tabs (Figure 7-63).

Q&A Is the Healthy Habits Newsletter file still open?

Yes. Leave it open because you will copy the modified diagram to the second page of the newsletter.

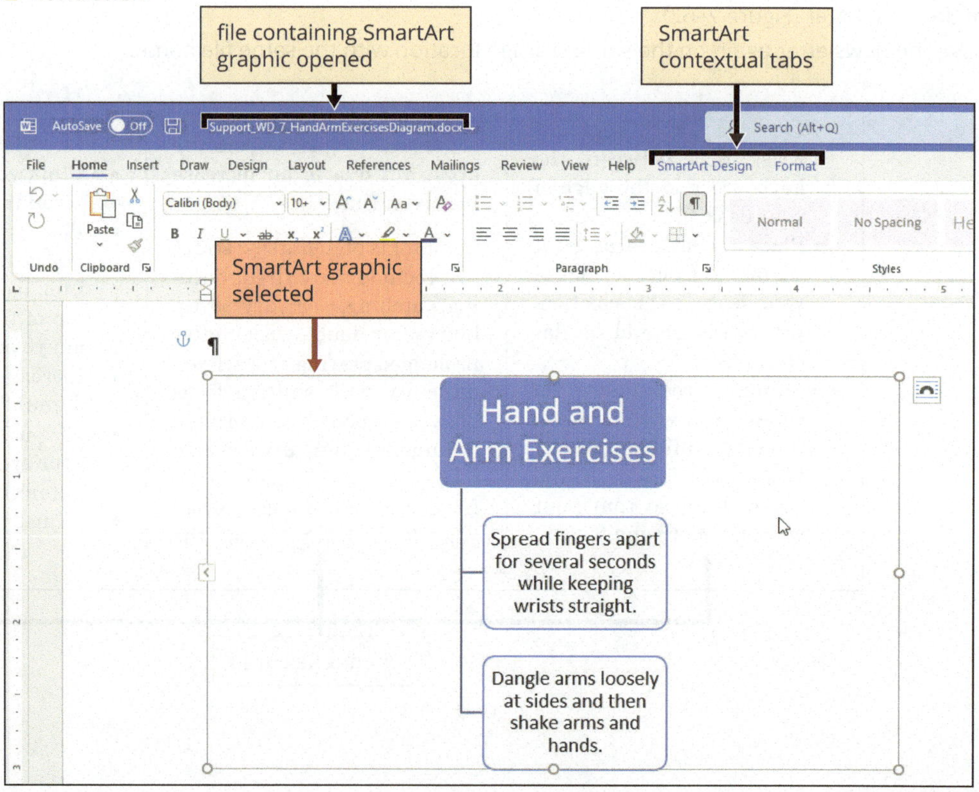

Figure 7-63

To Change the Layout of a SmartArt Graphic

The following step changes the layout of an existing SmartArt graphic. **Why?** The SmartArt graphic currently uses the Hierarchy List layout, and this newsletter uses the Horizontal Hierarchy layout.

1

- If necessary, display the SmartArt Design tab.
- If necessary, use the scroll arrows in the Layouts gallery (SmartArt Design tab | Layouts group) to scroll through the layouts until Horizontal Hierarchy appears and then click Horizontal Hierarchy to change the layout of the SmartArt graphic (Figure 7–64).

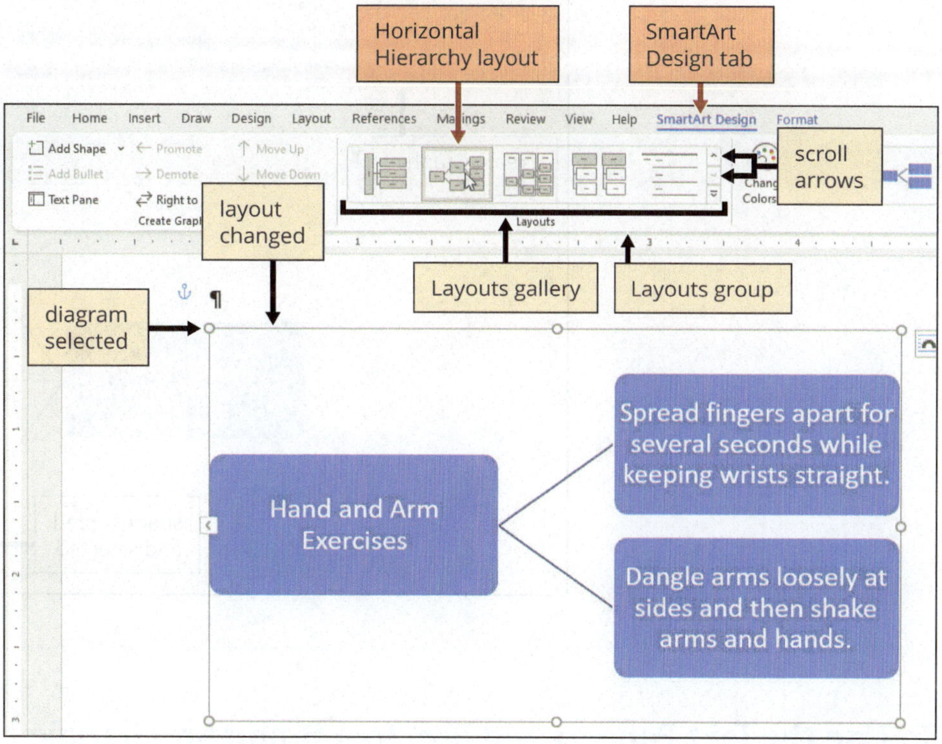

Figure 7–64

Other Ways

1. Right-click the selected graphic, click Layout button on Mini toolbar and select desired layout, or click Change Layout on shortcut menu, select desired layout, click OK

To Add a Shape to a SmartArt Graphic

The current SmartArt graphic has two perimeter shapes. This newsletter has a third shape. The following step adds a shape to a SmartArt graphic.

1 With the diagram selected, click the Add Shape button (SmartArt Design tab | Create Graphic group) to add a shape to the SmartArt graphic (Figure 7–65).

Q&A Why did my screen display a menu instead of adding a shape?
You clicked the Add Shape arrow instead of the Add Shape button. Clicking the Add Shape button adds the shape automatically; clicking the Add Shape arrow displays a menu allowing you to specify the location of the shape.

How do I delete a shape?
Select the shape by clicking it and then press DELETE, or right-click the shape and then click Cut on the Mini toolbar or shortcut menu.

How do I decrease the size of a SmartArt shape?
You drag the sizing handles or enter the desired value in the Height box (Format tab | Size group). You also can select the shape and then click the Smaller button (Format tab | Shapes group) to decrease the size of the selected shape. (Similarly, you can select the Larger button to increase the size of the selected shape.)

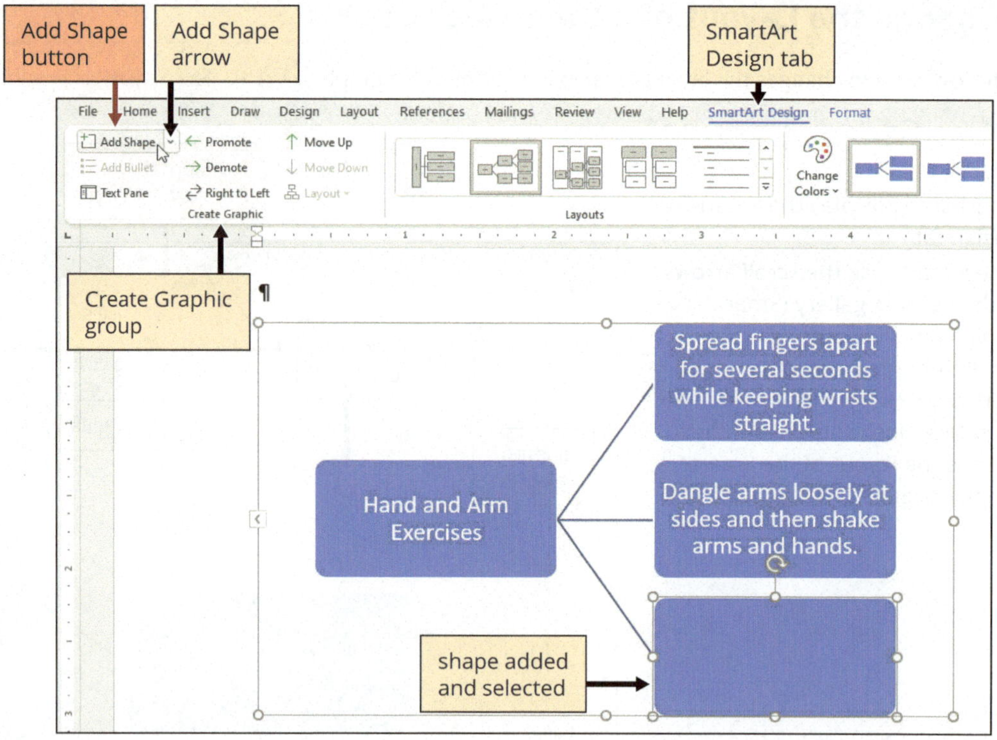

Figure 7–65

To Use the Text Pane to Add Text to a SmartArt Graphic

One way to add text to a SmartArt graphic is to add it directly to the shapes in a SmartArt graphic. In this project, however, you add text to a SmartArt graphic by entering the text through the Text Pane. **Why?** Some users prefer to enter text in the Text Pane instead of in the shape. The following steps use the Text Pane to add text to a shape.

1

- Click the Text Pane control, which is on the left side of the SmartArt graphic, to open the Text Pane to the left of the SmartArt graphic.

2

- In the Text Pane, if necessary, position the insertion point to the right of the bullet that has no text to its right.
- Type **Gently push back fingers and then thumb.** as the text for the shape (Figure 7–66).

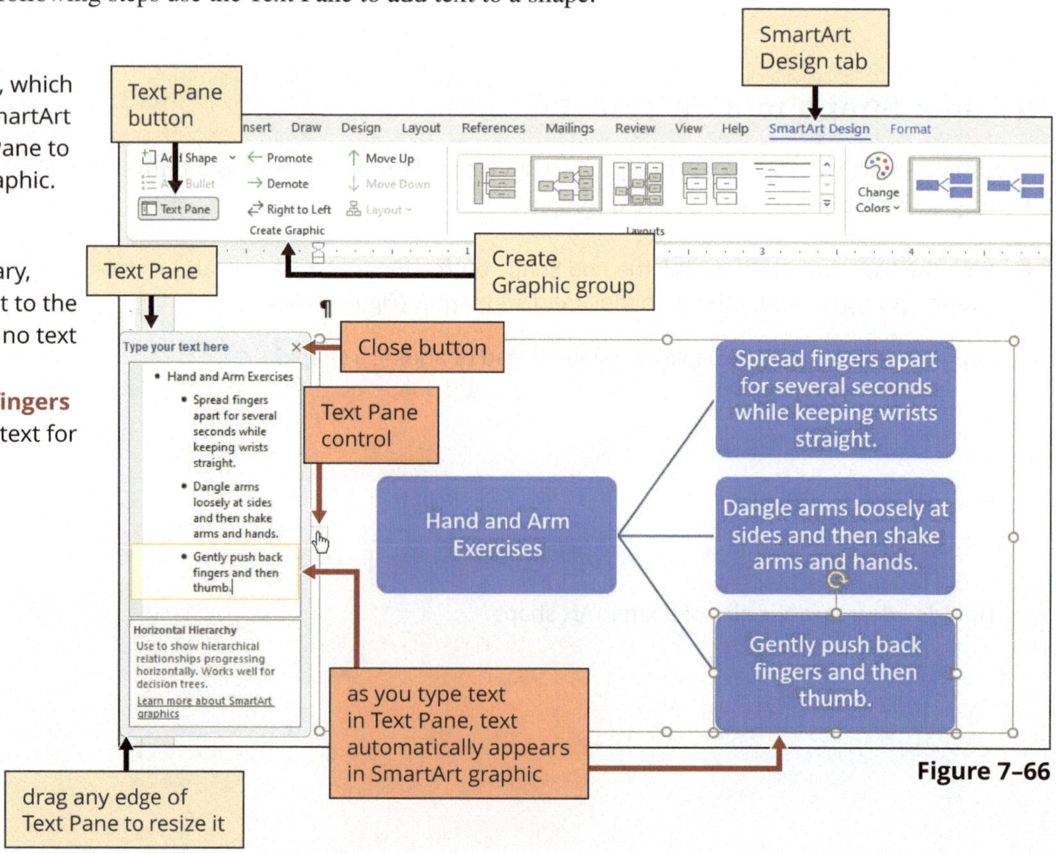

Figure 7–66

3

- Click the Close button in the Text Pane to close the Text Pane.

Q&A Can I instead close the Text Pane by clicking the Text Pane button (SmartArt Design tab | Create Graphic group)?
Yes.

- Save the file containing the SmartArt graphic with a new file name on your hard drive, OneDrive, or other storage location using SC_WD_7_HandArmExercisesDiagramModified as the file name.

Other Ways

1. Click Text Pane button (SmartArt Design tab | Create Graphic group)

To Change a SmartArt Shape If you wanted to change a SmartArt shape, you would perform the following steps.

1. Right-click the shape, point to Change Shape on the shortcut menu, and then select the desired shape in the Change Shape gallery.

or

1. Select the shape.
2. Click the Change Shape button (Format tab | Shapes group) and then select the desired shape in the Change Shape gallery.

To Add a Picture to a SmartArt Shape If you wanted to add a picture to a SmartArt shape, you would perform the following steps.

1. Select the shape.
2. Click the Shape Fill arrow (Format tab | Shapes group) and then click Picture in the Shape Fill gallery to display the Insert Pictures dialog box.
3. Click 'From a File' to locate a picture on your storage media or click Online Pictures to search for a picture online. After locating the desired picture, click the Insert button in the appropriate dialog box to add the selected picture to the selected shape.

BTW

Demoting Text Pane Text

Instead of pressing TAB in the Text Pane, you could click the Demote button (SmartArt Design tab | Create Graphic group) to increase (or move to the right) the indent for a bulleted item. You also can click the Promote button (SmartArt Design tab | Create Graphic group) to decrease (or move to the left) the indent for a bulleted item.

Copying and Pasting

The next step is to copy the SmartArt graphic from this document window and then paste it in the newsletter. To copy from one document and paste into another, you can use the Office Clipboard. Through the Office Clipboard, you can copy multiple items from any Office document and then paste them into the same or another Office document by following these general guidelines:

1. Items are copied from a **source document**. If the source document is not the active document, display it in the document window.
2. Open the Office Clipboard pane and then copy items from the source document to the Office Clipboard.
3. Items are copied to a **destination document**. If the destination document is not the active document, display the destination document in the document window.
4. Paste items from the Office Clipboard to the destination document.

To Copy a SmartArt Graphic Using the Office Clipboard

The following step copies the SmartArt graphic to the Office Clipboard. **Why?** Sometimes you want to copy multiple items to the Office Clipboard through the Clipboard pane and then paste them later.

1

- Display the Home tab.
- Click the Clipboard Dialog Box Launcher (Home tab | Clipboard group) to open the Clipboard pane.
- If the Office Clipboard in the Clipboard pane is not empty, click the Clear All button in the Clipboard pane.
- Select the SmartArt graphic in the document window and then click the Copy button (Home tab | Clipboard group) to copy the selected text to the Clipboard (Figure 7–67).

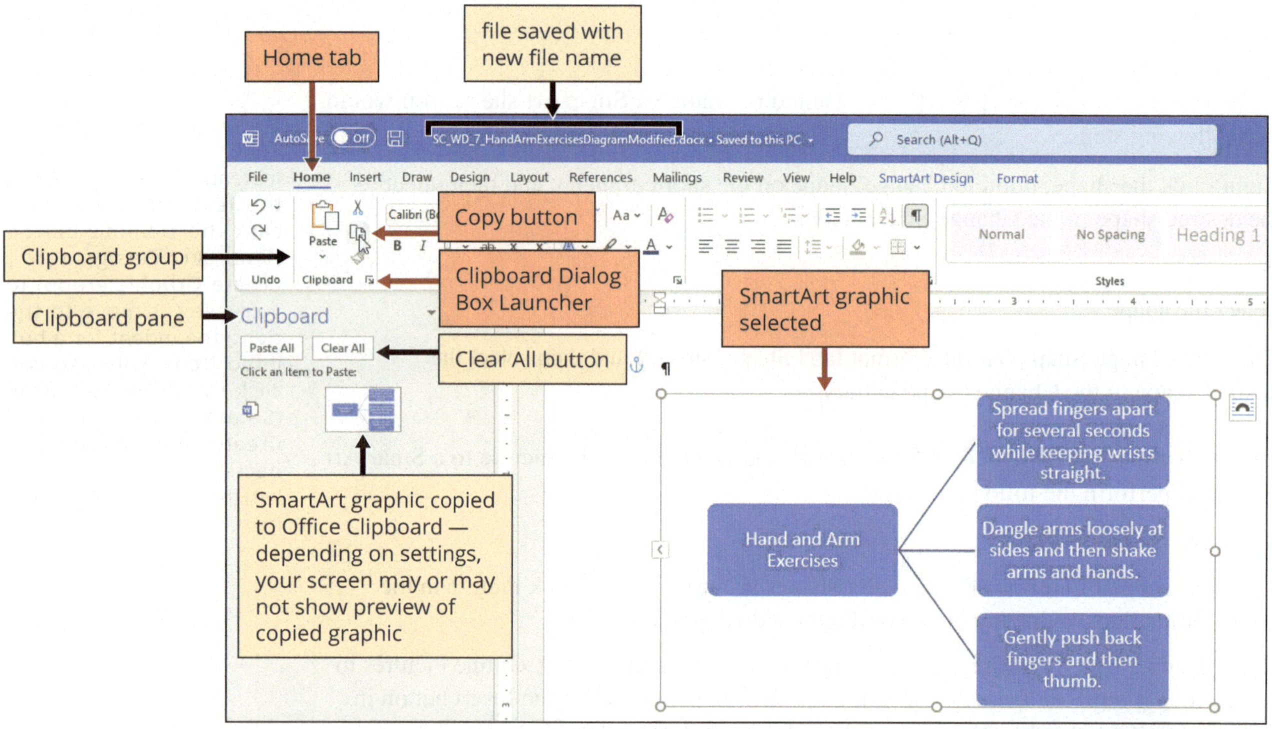

Figure 7–67

Other Ways

1. With Clipboard pane open, right-click selected item, click Copy on shortcut menu
2. With Clipboard pane open and item to copy selected, press CTRL+C

To Switch from One Open Document Window to Another

The following steps switch from the open SC_WD_7_HandArmExercisesDiagramModified.docx document (the source document) to the open SC_WD_7_HealthyHabitsNewsletter.docx document (the destination document). **Why?** You want to paste the copied diagram into the newsletter document.

1

- Point to the Word app button on the taskbar to display a Live Preview of the open documents or window titles of the open documents, depending on your computer's configuration (Figure 7–68).

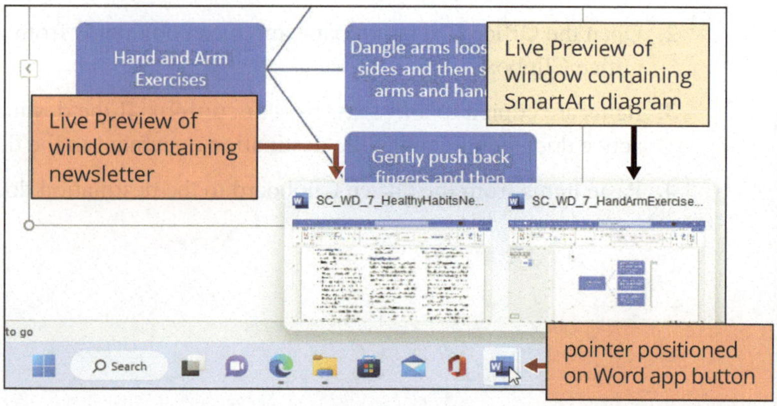

Figure 7–68

2

- Click the Live Preview of SC_WD_7_HealthyHabitsNewsletter.docx on the Windows taskbar to display the selected document in the document window (shown in Figure 7–69).

Other Ways

1. Click Switch Windows button (View tab | Window group), click document name
2. Press ALT+TAB

To Paste from the Office Clipboard

The following steps paste from the Office Clipboard. **Why?** *You want to paste the copied SmartArt graphic into the destination document, in this case, the newsletter document.*

1

- Position the insertion point at the end of the first paragraph below the Preventing RSIs paragraph in the first column on the second page of the newsletter.
- If the Clipboard pane is not open on the screen, display the Home tab and then click the Clipboard Dialog Box Launcher (Home tab | Clipboard group) to open the Clipboard pane.
- Click the SmartArt graphic entry in the Office Clipboard to paste it in the document at the location of the insertion point (Figure 7–69).

Q&A What if my pasted graphic is in a different location?
The location of your graphic may differ. You will move the graphic in the next steps.

Does the destination document have to be a different document?
No. The source and destination documents can be the same document.

What is the function of the Paste All button?
If you have multiple items on the Office Clipboard, it pastes all items in a row, without any characters between them, at the location of the insertion point or selection.

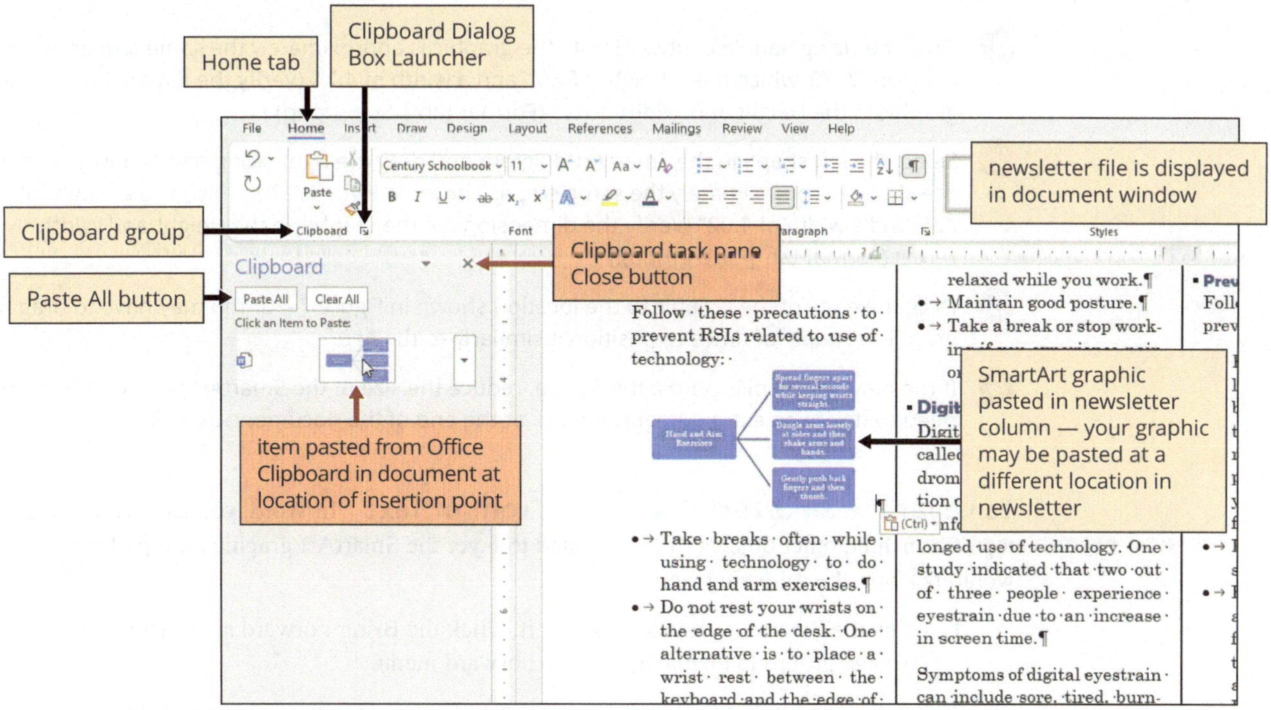

Figure 7–69

2

- Click the Close button in the Clipboard pane.

Other Ways

1. With Clipboard pane open, right-click selected item, click Paste on shortcut menu
2. With Clipboard pane open, press CTRL+V

BTW

Clipboard Pane and Icon

You can control when the Clipboard pane opens on the Word screen and the Office Clipboard icon appears in the notification area on the taskbar. To do this, first open the Clipboard pane by clicking the Clipboard Dialog Box Launcher on the Home tab. Next, click the Options button at the bottom of the Clipboard pane and then click the desired option on the menu. For example, if you want to be able to open the Clipboard pane by clicking the Office Clipboard icon on the Windows taskbar, click 'Show Office Clipboard Icon on Taskbar' on the Options menu.

To Format a Graphic as Floating

The text in the newsletter should wrap tightly around the graphic; that is, the text should conform to the graphic's shape. Thus, the next step is to change the graphic from inline to floating with a wrapping style of tight. The following steps format the graphic as floating with tight wrapping.

1. Click the SmartArt graphic to select it.
2. With the SmartArt graphic selected, click the Layout Options button that is attached to the graphic to display the Layout Options gallery.
3. Click Tight in the Layout Options gallery to change the graphic from inline to floating with tight wrapping.
4. Close the Layout Options gallery.

To Format, Resize, and Position the SmartArt Graphic

The next tasks are to increase the size of the graphic, decrease the size of a shape in the graphic, and then position it across the middle of the first and second columns on the second page. The following steps format and then position the graphic.

1. Drag the sizing handles outward until the graphic is approximately the same size as shown in Figure 7–70, which has a height of 2.7" and a width of 4.7". (Verify the dimensions of the graphic in the Height and Width boxes (Format tab | Size group).)
2. Select the left shape in the SmartArt diagram and drag the right sizing handle inward until the shape is approximately the same size as shown in Figure 7–70, which has a height of .69" and a width of 1.02" (Verify the dimensions of the graphic in the Height and Width boxes (Format tab | Size group).)
3. Drag the edge of the graphic to the location shown in Figure 7–70. You may have to drag the graphic a couple of times to position it similarly to the figure.
4. If the newsletter spills onto a third page, reduce the size of the SmartArt graphic. You may need to delete an extra paragraph mark at the end of the document, as well.

To Layer the SmartArt Graphic in Front of Text In Word, you can layer objects on top of or behind other objects. If you wanted to layer the SmartArt graphic on top of all text, you would perform the following steps.

1. Click the SmartArt graphic to select it. Click the Bring Forward arrow (Format tab | Arrange group) to display the Bring Forward menu.
2. Click 'Bring in Front of Text' on the Bring Forward menu to position the selected object on top of all text.

To Edit Wrap Points in an Object

In Word, you can change how text wraps around an object, called editing wrap points. The following steps edit the wrap points in the SmartArt diagram near the middle of the second page of the newsletter. **Why?** You want to ensure that text starts on a complete line below the bottom of the graphic.

1

- If necessary, click the SmartArt graphic to select it and then click the Format tab. If necessary, display the Arrange group (Format tab). Click the Wrap Text button (Format tab | Arrange group) to display the Wrap Text menu (Figure 7–70). (If your Format tab contains a Wrap Text button, click the button.)

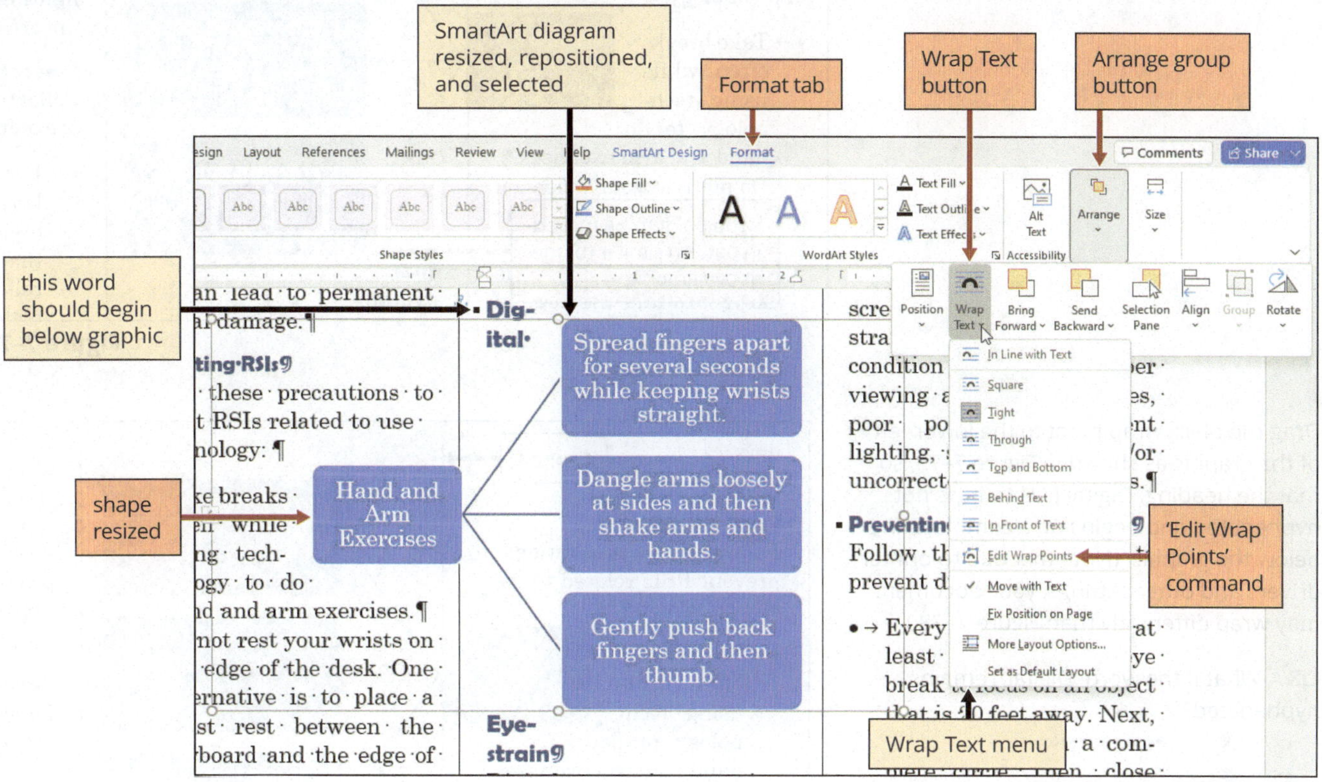

Figure 7–70

2

- Click 'Edit Wrap Points' on the Wrap Text menu to display wrap points around the graphic.
- Click the black wrap point to the upper-left of the top shape in the diagram, as shown in Figure 7–71, so that the pointer changes to a four-headed dot.

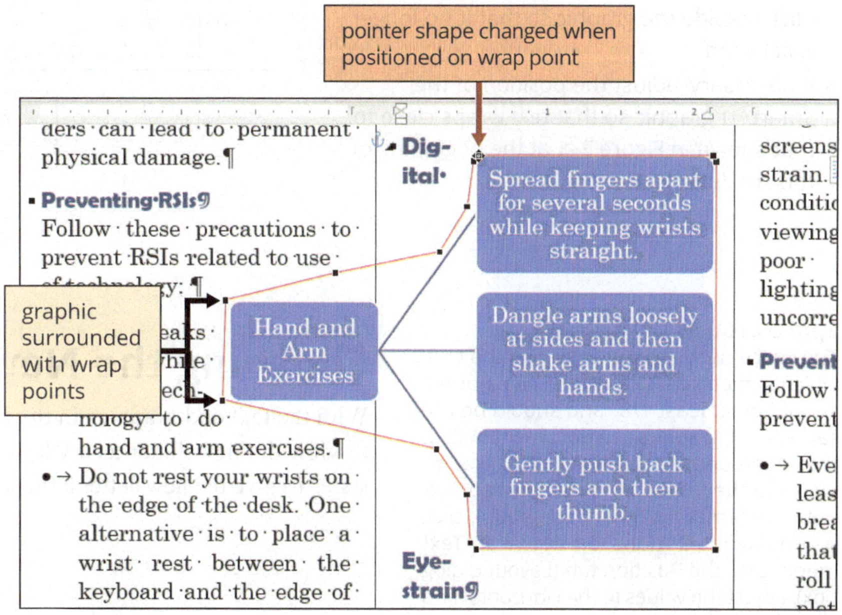

Figure 7–71

3

- Drag the black wrap point to the upper-left of the graphic as shown in Figure 7–72, so that the text (the first part of the word, Digital, in this case) will appear on a complete line below the SmartArt object.

Q&A What if the word, Digital, did not move below the SmartArt object?
Repeat Step 3 as necessary until the heading is below the SmartArt object.

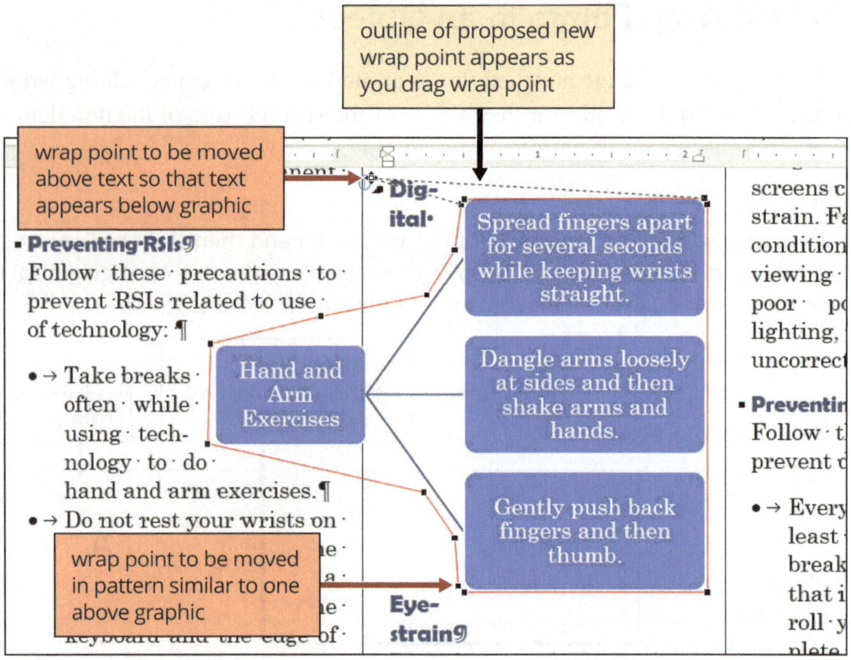

Figure 7–72

4

- Drag the black wrap point to the lower-left of the graphic as shown in Figure 7–73, so that the heading, Digital Eyestrain, is not hyphenated and begins on a complete line below the graphic. (Note that due to printer drivers and other settings, your document may wrap differently than Figure 7–73.)

Q&A What if the word, Digital, remains hyphenated?
Repeat Step 4 as necessary until the heading is on a single line below the SmartArt object.

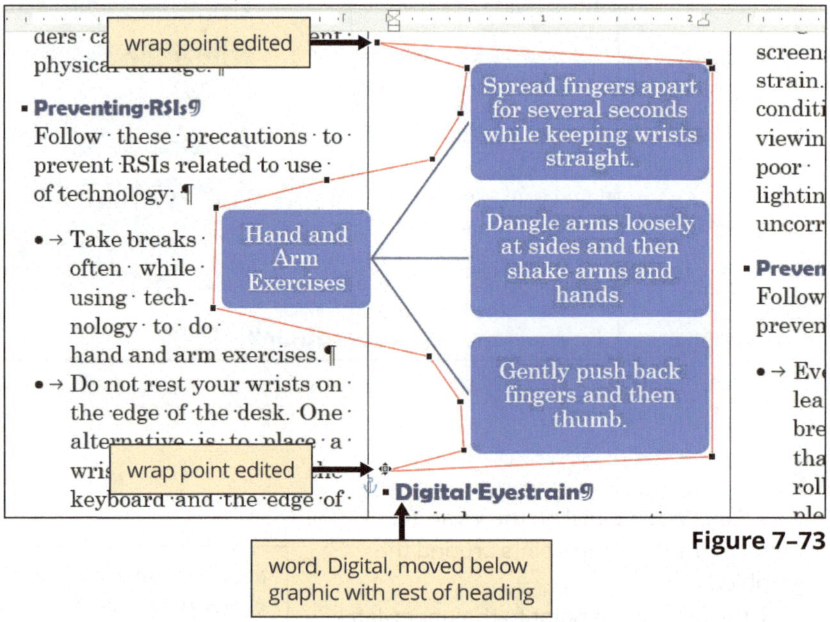

Figure 7–73

5

- Click outside the graphic so that it no longer is selected.
- If necessary, adjust the position of the SmartArt graphic so that text wraps close to that shown in Figure 7–1 at the beginning of this module.

BTW
Space around Graphics
The space between a graphic and the text, which sometimes is called the run-around, should be at least 1/8" and should be the same for all graphics in a document. Adjust the run-around of a selected floating graphic by doing the following: click the Wrap Text button (Format tab | Arrange group), click 'More Layout Options' on the Wrap Text menu, click the Position tab (Layout dialog box), adjust the values in the Horizontal and Vertical boxes, and then click OK.

Finishing the Newsletter

With the text and graphics in the newsletter entered and formatted, the next step is to view the newsletter as a whole and determine if it looks finished in its current state. To give the newsletter a finished appearance, you will add a border to its edges.

To Turn Off Formatting Marks and Zoom Multiple Pages

The last step in formatting the newsletter is to place a border around its edges. You turn off formatting marks to remove the clutter from the screen, and you place both pages in the document window at once so that you can see all the page borders applied. The following steps turn off formatting marks and zoom multiple pages.

1. If necessary, display the Home tab and then turn off formatting marks.
2. Display the View tab and then display multiple pages on the screen.

To Add an Art Page Border

The following steps add a page border around the pages of the newsletter. **Why?** This newsletter has a yellow art border around the perimeter of each page.

1

- Display the Design tab.
- Click the Page Borders button (Design tab | Page Background group) to display the Borders and Shading dialog box. If necessary, click the Page Border tab.

Q&A What if I cannot select the Page Borders button because it is dimmed?
Click somewhere in the newsletter to make the newsletter the active document and then repeat Step 1.

2

- Click Box in the Setting area (Borders and Shading dialog box) to specify a border on all four sides of the page.
- Click the Art arrow, scroll to and then click the art border shown in Figure 7–74.
- Click the Color arrow and then click 'Gold, Accent 4, Darker 25%' (fifth row, eighth column) on the palette (Figure 7–74).

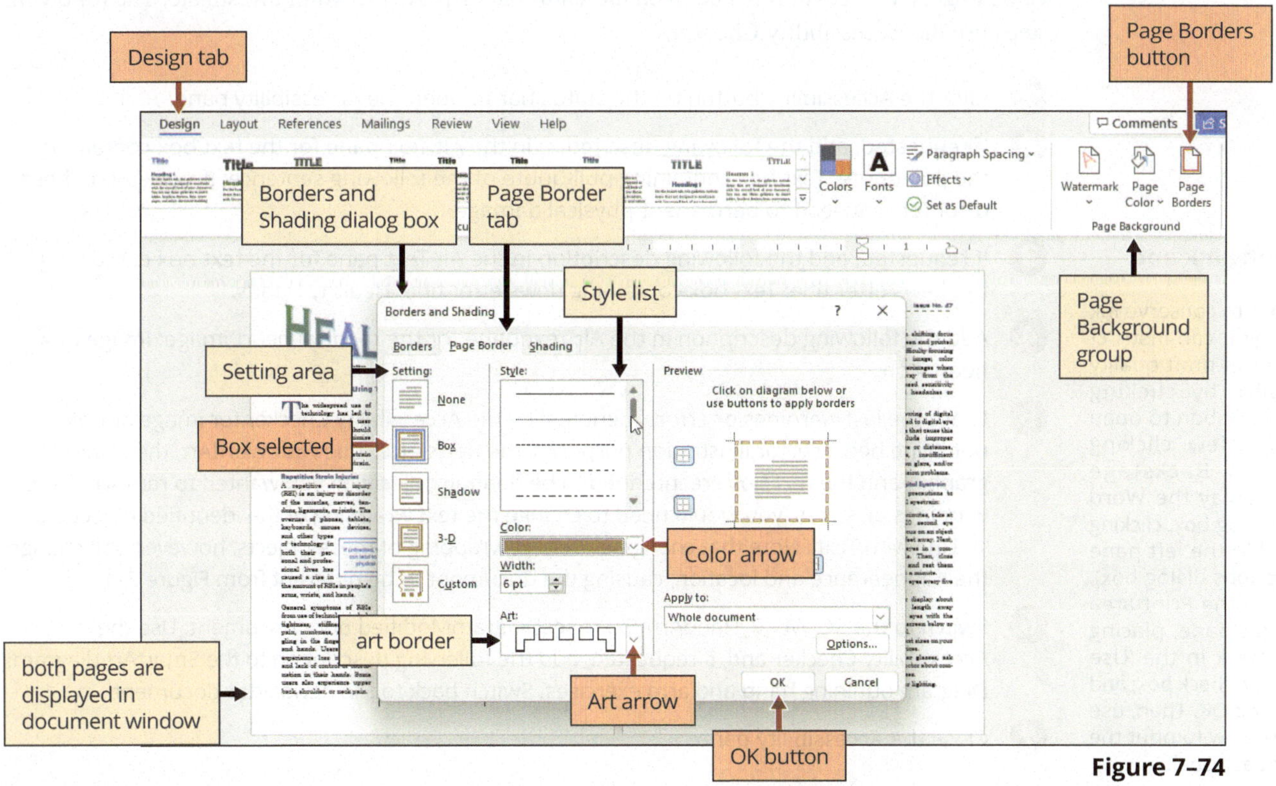

Figure 7–74

3

- Click OK to place the defined border on each page of the newsletter (Figure 7–75). (Note that depending on resolution, zoom, and other settings, the border in the document window may look different from how it appears on the printed document.)

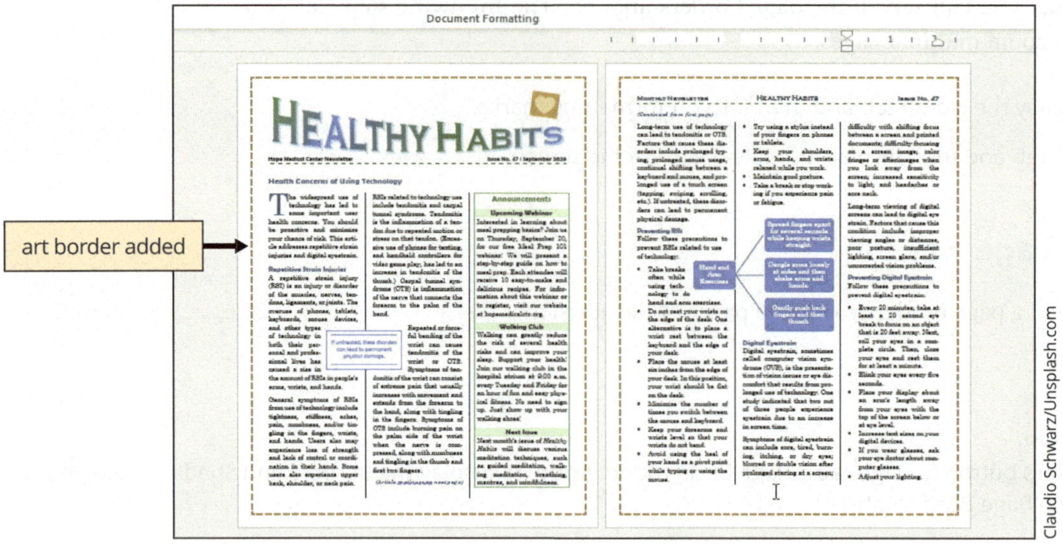

Figure 7–75

To Use the Accessibility Checker

Recall that Word includes an Accessibility Checker that identifies potential accessibility issues and presents suggestions to make your documents more inclusive. Notice that instead of the phrase, Good to go, the Accessibility button on the status bar displays the word, Investigate. The following steps use the Accessibility Checker.

1. Click the Accessibility button on the status bar to open the Accessibility pane.
2. If requested, add the following description in the Alt Text pane for the text box containing the pull-quote: Text box containing pull-quote of the following sentence: If untreated, these disorders can lead to permanent physical damage.
3. If requested, add the following description in the Alt Text pane for the text box containing the newsletter title: Text box containing newsletter title, Healthy Habits.
4. Add the following description in the Alt Text pane for the medical heart image: Image of a heart icon.
5. Leave the last warnings or errors identified by the Accessibility Checker for image or object not inline because, for illustration purposes, the newsletter title with WordArt, the rotated graphic, and the text box are intended to be floating objects. (If you wanted to remove these warnings or errors, you would need to change the text wrapping of the identified objects to 'In Line with Text'. Note that changing the text wrapping of these objects, however, will change their appearance and location, causing the document to be different from Figure 7–1.)
6. Switch to the SC_WD_7_HandArmExercisesDiagramModified.docx document. Use the Accessibility Checker and, if requested, add the following description to the SmartArt diagram: Diagram outlining hand and arm exercises. Switch back to the newsletter document.
7. Close the Accessibility pane.

BTW

Conserving Ink and Toner

If you want to conserve ink or toner, you can instruct Word to print draft quality documents by clicking File on the ribbon to open Backstage view, clicking Options in Backstage view to display the Word Options dialog box, clicking Advanced in the left pane (Word Options dialog box), scrolling to the Print area in the right pane, placing a check mark in the 'Use draft quality' check box, and then clicking OK. Then, use Backstage view to print the document as usual.

To Check Spelling, Save, and Print the Newsletter and then Exit Word

The newsletter now is complete. You should save the document, print it, and then exit Word.

1. Check and fix any spelling errors in the document.
2. sam Save the newsletter again on the same storage location with the same file name.
3. If desired, print the newsletter (shown in Figure 7–1 at the beginning of this module).

Q&A What if an error message appears about margins?
Depending on the printer you are using, you may need to set the margins differently for this project.

What if one or more of the borders do not print?
Click the Page Borders button (Design tab | Page Background group), click the Options button (Borders and Shading dialog box), click the Measure from arrow and click Text, change the four text boxes to 15 pt, and then click OK in each dialog box. Try printing the document again. If the borders still do not print, adjust the text boxes in the dialog box to a number smaller than 15 pt.

4. Exit Word, closing all open documents.

BTW
Distributing a Document
Instead of printing and distributing a hard copy of a document, you can distribute the document electronically. Options include sending the document via email; posting it on cloud storage (such as OneDrive) and sharing the file with others; posting it on social media, a blog, or other website; and sharing a link associated with an online location of the document. You also can create and share a PDF or XPS image of the document, so that users can view the file in Acrobat Reader or XPS Viewer instead of in Word.

Summary

In this module, you have learned how to create a professional-looking newsletter using Word's desktop publishing features, such as the following: inserting and modifying WordArt, organizing a document in columns, adding horizontal and vertical rules, inserting and formatting pull-quotes, inserting and formatting graphics, and adding an art page border.

Consider This: Plan Ahead

What decisions will you need to make when creating your next newsletter?

Use these guidelines as you complete the assignments in this module and create your own newsletters outside of this class.

1. Create the nameplate.
   a) Determine the location of the nameplate.
   b) Determine content, formats, and arrangement of text and graphics.
   c) If appropriate, use ruling lines.
2. Determine content for the body of the newsletter.
   a) Write the body copy.
   b) Organize the body copy in columns.
   c) Format the body copy and subheads.
   d) Incorporate color.
   e) Divide sections with vertical rules.
   f) Enhance with visuals.
3. Bind and distribute the newsletter.
   a) Determine if newsletters should be printed, posted on bulletin boards, sent as an email message, or posted on websites.
   b) For multipage newsletters that will be printed, determine the appropriate method of binding the pages.
   c) For online newsletters, select a format that most users will be able to open.

BTW
Printing Document Properties
To print document properties, click File on the ribbon to open Backstage view, click Print in Backstage view to display the Print screen, click the first button in the Settings area to display a list of options specifying what you can print, click Document Info in the list to specify you want to print the document properties instead of the actual document, and then click the Print button in the Print screen to print the document properties on the currently selected printer.

Student Assignments

Apply Your Knowledge

Reinforce the skills and apply the concepts you learned in this module.

Working with Desktop Publishing Elements of a Newsletter

Note: To complete this assignment, you will be required to use the Data Files. Please contact your instructor for information about accessing the Data Files.

Instructions: Start Word. Open the document, SC_WD_7-1.docx, which is located in the Data Files. The document contains a newsletter, called *Secure Insight*, written by the administrative assistant at Insight Insurance, that will be sent via email to clients and also placed on lobby tables at the agency. You are to modify the newsletter so that it appears as shown in Figure 7–76.

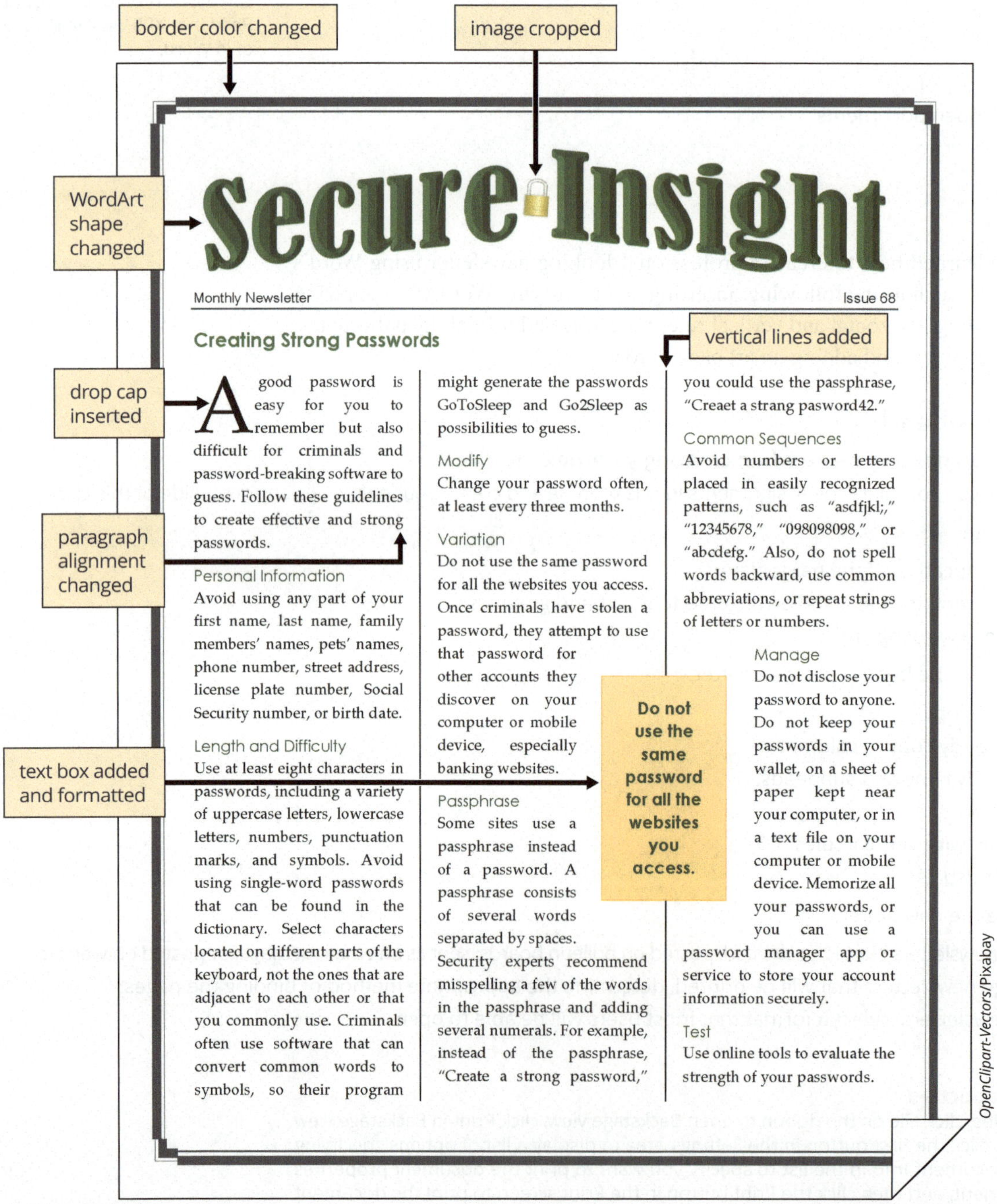

Secure Insight

Monthly Newsletter Issue 68

Creating Strong Passwords

A good password is easy for you to remember but also difficult for criminals and password-breaking software to guess. Follow these guidelines to create effective and strong passwords.

Personal Information
Avoid using any part of your first name, last name, family members' names, pets' names, phone number, street address, license plate number, Social Security number, or birth date.

Length and Difficulty
Use at least eight characters in passwords, including a variety of uppercase letters, lowercase letters, numbers, punctuation marks, and symbols. Avoid using single-word passwords that can be found in the dictionary. Select characters located on different parts of the keyboard, not the ones that are adjacent to each other or that you commonly use. Criminals often use software that can convert common words to symbols, so their program might generate the passwords GoToSleep and Go2Sleep as possibilities to guess.

Modify
Change your password often, at least every three months.

Variation
Do not use the same password for all the websites you access. Once criminals have stolen a password, they attempt to use that password for other accounts they discover on your computer or mobile device, especially banking websites.

Do not use the same password for all the websites you access.

Passphrase
Some sites use a passphrase instead of a password. A passphrase consists of several words separated by spaces. Security experts recommend misspelling a few of the words in the passphrase and adding several numerals. For example, instead of the passphrase, "Create a strong password," you could use the passphrase, "Creaet a strang pasword42."

Common Sequences
Avoid numbers or letters placed in easily recognized patterns, such as "asdfjkl;," "12345678," "098098098," or "abcdefg." Also, do not spell words backward, use common abbreviations, or repeat strings of letters or numbers.

Manage
Do not disclose your password to anyone. Do not keep your passwords in your wallet, on a sheet of paper kept near your computer, or in a text file on your computer or mobile device. Memorize all your passwords, or you can use a password manager app or service to store your account information securely.

Test
Use online tools to evaluate the strength of your passwords.

OpenClipart-Vectors/Pixabay

Figure 7–76

Perform the following tasks:

1. Click File on the ribbon and then click Save As and save the document using the new file name, SC_WD_7_SecureInsightNewsletter.
2. Resize the WordArt shape to a height and width of 1.44" and 7", respectively. (**Hint:** Select the WordArt object and then use the Shape Format tab.)
3. Change the text fill color of the WordArt text to 'Green, Accent 6, Darker 25%'. (**Hint:** Select the WordArt text and then use the Text Fill arrow (Shape Format tab | WordArt Styles group).)
4. Change the WordArt shape to Chevron: Up using the Transform Effect.
5. Crop the image of the locks so that only the leftmost lock shows. Crop the top so that the amount of space above the lock image is the same as the amount of space on the left, right, and bottom. Change the height and width of the cropped image to 0.42" and 0.29" (or as close as possible to these dimensions), respectively. Change the wrapping of the image to Behind Text and then move the image to the location shown in Figure 7–76.
6. Open the Selection pane. Practice selecting the items in the selection pane. Select the lock image using the Selection pane. Rotate the image slightly clockwise as shown in Figure 7–76. Close the Selection pane.
7. Turn off automatic hyphenation.
8. Change the column width of the columns in the body of the newsletter to 2.1".
9. Add a vertical line between each column.
10. Format the first paragraph with a drop cap.
11. Change the alignment of the paragraph containing the drop cap from left-aligned to justified.
12. Change the color of the page border to 'Blue-Gray, Text 2, Darker 25%'.
13. Insert a Whisp Quote preformatted text box into the newsletter near the top of the second column. Select the line in the lower-right corner of the text box that contains the placeholder text for citing a source and then delete the entire line.
14. Split the screen. Display the text box in the top screen and the Variation heading in the bottom screen. Copy the first sentence below the Variation heading and then paste the sentence into the placeholder text in the text box in the top screen using the destination theme. (**Hint:** Use the Merge Formatting button on the Paste Options menu.) Remove the split from the window.
15. Change the shape style of the pull-quote (text box text) to 'Subtle Effect - Gold, Accent 4' (Shape Format tab | Shape Styles group).
16. Change the height and width of the text box (pull-quote) to 2.17" and 1.24", respectively.
17. Select the text in the pull quote and format it to 12-point Century Gothic (or a similar font). Bold the text, center the text, and change its color to 'Green, Accent 6, Darker 50%'.
18. Move the pull-quote so that it is positioned similarly to the one in Figure 7–76. (You may need to change the zoom so that the entire newsletter appears in the document window.)
19. If requested by your instructor, add your name to the left of the text, Monthly Newsletter, in the issue information line.
20. If the newsletter flows to two pages, reduce the size of elements such as WordArt or pull-quote, or adjust spacing above or below paragraphs so that the newsletter fits on a single page. Make any other necessary adjustments to the newsletter.
21. Use the accessibility checker to add alt text with appropriate descriptions for the text boxes and the picture as requested (leave any warnings or errors identified by the Accessibility Checker for image or object not inline). Save the revised document again with the same name and then submit it in the format specified by your instructor.
22. **Consider This:** How many sections are in this newsletter? How many columns are in each section? If you wanted to add a second page to this newsletter, what type of section break would appear at the end of the first page?

Extend Your Knowledge

Extend the skills you learned in this module and experiment with new skills. You may need to use Help to complete the assignment.

Modifying and Enhancing a Newsletter

Note: To complete this assignment, you will be required to use the Data Files. Please contact your instructor for information about accessing the Data Files.

Instructions: Start Word. Open the document, SC_WD_7-2.docx, which is located in the Data Files. The document contains a draft of a newsletter, written by an administrative assistant to a government official at Oakwood Village Hall, that will be distributed to all community members. You will add and format WordArt, clear tabs, insert leader characters, add and format a drop cap, adjust the hyphenation rules, modify and format a SmartArt graphic, draw and format a text box, and move the page border closer to the text.

Perform the following tasks:

1. Use Help to learn more about WordArt options, hyphenation, tabs, SmartArt graphics, and art borders.
2. Click File on the ribbon and then click Save As and save the document using the new file name, SC_WD_7_OakwoodVillagerNewsletter.
3. Convert the text, Oakwood Villager, in the nameplate to WordArt using a WordArt style of your choice. Change the text wrapping of the WordArt shape to 'Top and Bottom'. Resize the WordArt object to approximately 1" × 7".
4. Change the WordArt shape using a transform effect of your choice, a glow effect of your choice, and a shadow effect of your choice.
5. Change the color of the WordArt text outline. Change the color of the WordArt text fill.
6. Add a shape fill color to the text box surrounding the WordArt object.
7. Clear the tabs in the issue information line in the nameplate. Use the Tabs dialog box to insert a right-aligned tab stop at the 7" mark. Fill the tab space with a leader character of your choice.
8. Add a border of your choice below the issue information line.
9. Select the oak tree picture in the middle of the newsletter. What object is attached to the picture's anchor? Unlock the anchor so that the anchor moves with the floating object. (**Hint:** Click the Layout Options button attached to the picture and then click the See more link in the Layout Options gallery.)
10. Move the oak tree picture up to the right of the Arbor Day heading by dragging it to an approximate location. Specify an absolute position of 1.7" to the right of the column and 2.1" below the top margin for the floating picture. (**Hint:** Click the Layout Options button and then click the See more link in the Layout Options gallery.) If necessary, adjust the absolute position as necessary to reposition the oak tree picture to your desired location on the newsletter.
11. Add a drop cap to the first paragraph in the body of the newsletter. Change the number of lines to drop from three to four. Change the distance from the text to 0.1". (**Hint:** Right-click the frame and then click Drop Cap on the shortcut menu.)
12. Apply automatic hyphenation to the document. Change the hyphenation rules to limit consecutive hyphens to two.
13. Save the document again using the same file name. Keep the document open for the next step.
14. Open the document, SC_WD_7-3.docx, which is located in the Data Files. This document contains a SmartArt graphic.
15. Click File on the ribbon and then click Save As and save the document using the new file name, SC_WD_7_ContactsDiagram.
16. Decrease the size of the Permit Department shape so it is the same size as the blank shape. (**Hint:** Use the Smaller button (Format tab | Shapes group).)
17. Change the layout of the SmartArt graphic to Hierarchy List.

18. Open the SmartArt Text Pane. Use the Text Pane to add the text, Public Works Department, to the empty shape in the SmartArt graphic. Close the SmartArt Text Pane. With the insertion point in the shape after the word, Department, press ENTER and add the text, 402-555-1020.
19. Add a shape below the Public Works Department shape. Add the text, Village Hall, in the added shape. Then, add the phone number, 402-555-1030.
20. Add the picture called Support_WD_7_ChatBubble.png to the Call shape (Figure 7–77). The picture is located in the Data Files. (**Hint:** Use the Shape Fill arrow (Format tab | Shape Styles group).) If necessary, decrease the size of the text for the word, Call, to fit in the chat bubble. Change the color of the chat bubble to a color of your choice. (**Hint:** Use the Picture Format tab.) If necessary, change the color of the text, Call.

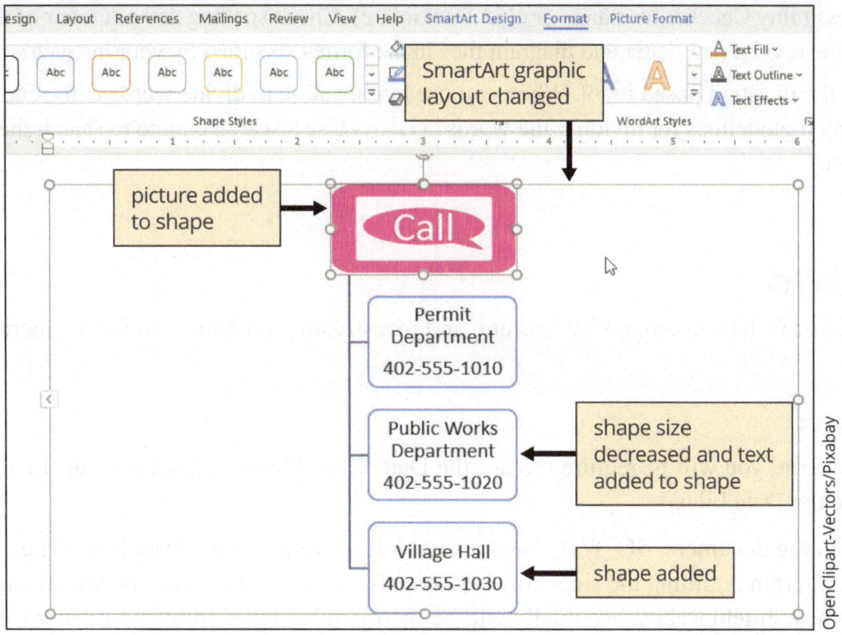

Figure 7–77

21. Change the shape of the Permit Department, Public Works Department, and Village Hall shapes to a shape of your choice. (**Hint:** Use the Change Shape button (Format tab | Shape Styles group).)
22. Check accessibility, adding alt text as requested (leave any warnings or errors identified by the Accessibility Checker for image or object not inline). Save the document again using the same file name. Keep the document open for the next step.
23. Open the Clipboard pane. Clear all items from the Clipboard pane. Copy the SmartArt graphic to the Clipboard. Switch document windows so that the SC_WD_7_OakwoodVillagerNewsletter.docx is displayed on the screen. Paste the SmartArt graphic from the Clipboard pane at the bottom of the third column in the newsletter below the Business Spotlight section.
24. Change the text wrapping of the SmartArt graphic in the third column of the newsletter to 'Top and Bottom'. Change the height and width of the SmartArt graphic in the third column of the newsletter to 3.3" and 2.1", respectively, or to a height and width of your choice.
25. Change the style of the SmartArt graphic in the newsletter to a style of your choice. Change the color of the SmartArt graphic in the newsletter to a color of your choice.
26. Draw a text box in the newsletter. Enter the text, Spring Is Here!, in the text box. Change the wrapping of the text box to Square. Format and position the text box appropriately. If requested by your instructor, change the default text box setting to the settings of this new text box.
27. If the newsletter flows to two pages, reduce the size of elements, such as WordArt or the text box or the graphic, or adjust spacing above or below paragraphs so that the newsletter fits on a single page. Make any other necessary adjustments to the newsletter.
28. Add an art page border of your choice to the newsletter. Change the page border so that the border is closer to the text. (**Hint:** Use the Options button in the Borders and Shading dialog box.)

Continued on next page

29. If requested by your instructor, add your name to the left of the text, Oakwood Village Newsletter, in the issue information line.
30. Save the newsletter with the same file name.
31. Copy the text box to the Clipboard. Create a new blank document. Practice using the Paste All button in the Clipboard to paste all its contents to the new document. Close the document without saving it. Close the Clipboard pane.
32. Arrange both Word documents (the newsletter and diagram) on the screen. Scroll through both open windows. Close the document containing the diagram.
33. Check accessibility, adding alt text as requested and fixing any identified contrast issues (leave any warnings or errors identified by the Accessibility Checker for image or object not inline). Check spelling and grammar of the finished newsletter. Submit the revised newsletter and diagram files in the format specified by your instructor.
34. **Consider This:** Answer the question posed in #9. When you use hyphenation to divide words at the end of a line, what are the accepted guidelines for dividing the words? (**Hint:** Use a search engine to search the text, end of line hyphenation.)

Expand Your World

Create a solution that uses cloud or web technologies by learning and investigating on your own from general guidance.

Inserting Online Videos

Note: To complete this assignment, you will be required to use the Data Files. Please contact your instructor for information about accessing the Data Files.

Instructions: Start Word. Open the document, SC_WD_7-4.docx, which is located in the Data Files. The document contains a SmartArt diagram outlining the steps involved to paint a room. This diagram, which was designed by a sales associate at Marshfield Realty, eventually will be incorporated in an online newsletter for distribution to clients. You will add online videos beside each step in the process for clients to view as they read the newsletter.

Perform the following tasks:

1. Use Help to learn about inserting online videos, noting their terms of use and privacy policies.
2. Click File on the ribbon and then click Save As and save the document using the new file name, SC_WD_7_PaintRoomDiagram.
3. Change the position of the SmartArt diagram to 'Position in Top Center with Square Text Wrapping'. (**Hint:** Use the Format tab.)
4. Start a browser and go to youtube.com or a video website that Word supports.
5. In the search box on the video website, type **choose a paint color** and then press ENTER to display a list of videos that match your search criteria.
6. Select a video and then copy the URL of the video webpage from the Address bar of your browser.
7. In Word, display the Insert tab and then click the Online Videos button (Insert tab | Media group) to display the Insert a video dialog box (Figure 7–78).
8. Paste the URL into the text box and then click Insert (Insert a video dialog box).
9. Change the wrapping of the video in the document to 'In Front of Text'. Resize the video in the document to approximately 0.44" × 0.59". Move the video in the document so that it is in the rounded rectangle shape to the left of Step 1 in the SmartArt diagram.
10. Repeat Steps 5 through 9 for each of the other steps in the SmartArt diagram, locating an online video appropriate to the content of the step.
11. Test each video by clicking it in the Word document to be sure it works as intended.

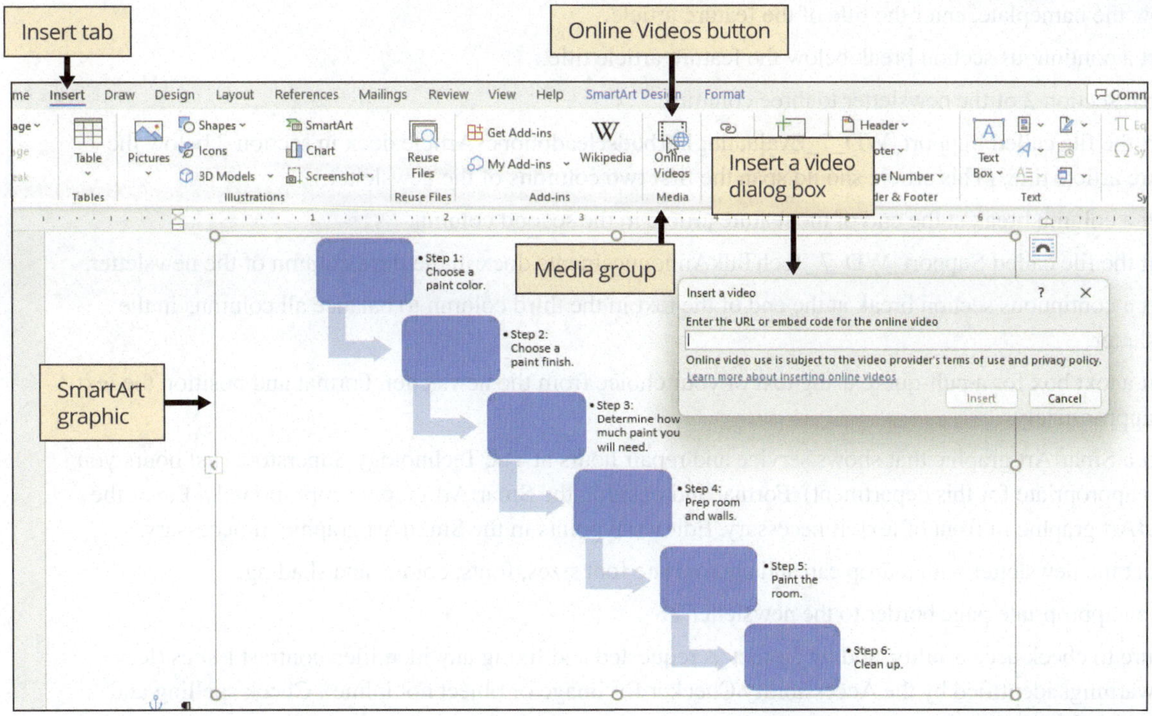

Figure 7–78

12. Check accessibility, adding alt text as requested (leave any warnings or errors identified by the Accessibility Checker for image or object not inline). Save the document with the same file name. Export it to a PDF using the file name, SC_WD_7_PaintRoomDiagram.
13. Access the SC_WD_7_PaintRoomDiagram.pdf file through File Explorer. Test the videos in the PDF.
14. Submit the documents in the format specified by your instructor.
15. **Consider This:** What options are available while you are watching a video from Word? What are some of the sources for the videos in the dialog box? Which videos did you insert in the form, and why? How do you play the videos inserted on the form?

In the Lab

Design and implement a solution using creative thinking and problem-solving skills.

Create a Newsletter for The Technology Superstore

Note: To complete this assignment, you will be required to use the Data Files. Please contact your instructor for information about accessing the Data Files.

Problem: As a service and repair agent for The Technology Superstore, you have been assigned the task of creating a newsletter called Tech Talk, which will be emailed to all customers and available in store on the service and repair counter.

Part 1: The feature article in Issue 32 of the Tech Talk newsletter covers evaluating earbuds and headphones in the first two columns. The rightmost column of the newsletter contains store announcements. The text for the feature article and announcements is in the Data Files. The newsletter should contain a SmartArt graphic and a pull-quote (text box). Enhance the newsletter with a drop cap, WordArt, color, ruling lines, and a page border. Be sure to use appropriate desktop publishing elements, including a nameplate, columns of text, balanced columns, and a variety of font sizes, font colors, and shading. Use the concepts and techniques presented in this module to create and format the newsletter. While creating the newsletter, be sure to do the following:

1. Change all margins as necessary.
2. Create a nameplate that contains the newsletter title and an issue information line. Insert WordArt for the newsletter title. Format the WordArt object as desired. Insert an appropriate picture or other image in the nameplate.

Continued on next page

3. Below the nameplate, enter the title of the feature article.
4. Insert a continuous section break below the feature article title.
5. Format section 2 of the newsletter to three columns.
6. Insert the file called Support_WD_7_EvaluatingEarbudsHeadphonesArticle.docx in section 2 below the feature article title. (This article should span the first two columns of the newsletter.)
7. Insert a column break at the end of the feature article in the second column.
8. Insert the file called Support_WD_7_TechTalkAnnouncements.docx in the third column of the newsletter.
9. Insert a continuous section break at the end of the text in the third column to balance all columns in the newsletter.
10. Insert a text box for a pull-quote using text of your choice from the newsletter. Format and position the text box appropriately.
11. Insert a SmartArt graphic that shows service and repair hours at The Technology Superstore (list hours you deem appropriate for this department). Format and position the SmartArt graphic appropriately. Layer the SmartArt graphic in front of text, if necessary. Edit wrap points in the SmartArt graphic, if necessary.
12. Format the newsletter with a drop cap and appropriate font sizes, fonts, colors, and shading.
13. Add an appropriate page border to the newsletter.
14. Be sure to check accessibility, adding alt text as requested and fixing any identified contrast issues (leave any warnings identified by the Accessibility Checker for image or object not inline). Check spelling and grammar of the finished newsletter.

When you are finished with the newsletter, save it with the file name, SC_WD_7_TechTalkNewsletter. Submit your assignment and answers to the Part 2 critical thinking questions in the format specified by your instructor.

Part 2: **Consider This:** You made several decisions while creating the newsletter in this assignment: how to organize and format the nameplate (location, content, formats, arrangement of text and graphics, ruling lines, etc.), how to organize and format the pull-quote (text box), how to organize and format the SmartArt graphic, and how to organize and format the body copy (columns, formats, headings and subheads, color, vertical rules, etc.). What was the rationale behind each of these decisions? When you proofread the document, what further revisions did you make and why?

Customizing Slide Masters and Presentations

Objectives

After completing this module, you will be able to:

- Apply slide and font themes and effects to a slide master
- Add a placeholder into a slide layout
- Change a slide master background
- Add a background style and graphic to a slide master
- Crop a picture to a shape
- Save a presentation as a template
- Use the Thesaurus
- Change the theme variant
- Change an individual slide background to a pattern, texture, or gradient fill
- Inspect a presentation
- Protect a presentation
- Annotate slides with highlights and a pen and pointer during a slide show
- Rehearse slide timings

Introduction

PowerPoint provides a variety of designs and layouts to meet most presenters' needs. At times, however, you may want a different set of colors, fonts, placeholders, or graphics to display throughout a presentation. PowerPoint allows you to customize the master layouts for slides, handouts, and speaker notes. These masters specify the precise locations and styles of placeholders, pictures, text boxes, and other slide and handout elements.

Once you determine your custom specifications in these masters, you can save the file as a template so that you can reuse these key elements as a starting point for multiple presentations. This unique **template** is a predesigned, preformatted Microsoft 365 file that contains default text formats, themes, placeholder text, headers and footers, and graphics that you can replace with your own information for hundreds of purposes, including budgets, flyers, and resumes; the PowerPoint template files have a slightly different file extension (.potx) than standard application files (.pptx). You use this set of special slides to create and then use similar presentations. A template consists of a general master slide layout that has elements common to all the slide layouts. One efficient way to create similar presentations is to create a template, save the template, open the template, and then save the slides as a different PowerPoint presentation each time a new presentation is required.

Templates help speed and simplify the process of creating a presentation, so many PowerPoint designers create a template for common presentations they develop frequently. Templates can have a variable number of slide layouts depending upon the complexity of the presentation. A simple presentation can have a few slide layouts; for example, the emergency preparedness presentation will have three slide layouts. A more complex template can have many slide masters and layouts.

Project: Presentation with Customized Slides

BTW

Masters Assure Universal Style

Masters are convenient because they allow you to make unique and uniform style changes to every slide in your presentation, including ones added later. Using slide masters saves time because you do not need to format every slide or type the same information repeatedly. You can customize the presentation theme and slide layouts, including the background, color, fonts, effects, and placeholder sizes and location.

In this module's project, you will follow proper design guidelines and learn to use PowerPoint to create the slides shown in Figures 4–1a through 4–1i. The objective is to produce a presentation for customers of the local credit union to inform them of strategies to save money, such as when they are shopping online or at the grocery store, dining out, and using electricity at home. All five slides are created by starting with an overall template, called the **slide master** (Figure 4–1a), that is formatted with a theme, customized title and text fonts, and other objects that appear on all slides in the presentation. The Title Slide Layout (Figure 4–1b) is used to create Slide 1 (Figure 4–1c), which introduces audiences to methods of reducing expenses. Similarly, the Master Comparison Layout (Figure 4–1d) is used for Slide 2 (Figure 4–1e), which describes strategies for saving money when shopping online, and Slide 5 (Figure 4–1f), which gives tips when shopping for groceries or dining at restaurants. The Master Title and Content Layout (Figure 4–1g) is used to develop the Slide 3 text (Figure 4–1h) describing money management techniques and reducing electricity on Slide 4 (Figure 4–1i).

In this module, you will learn how to create the slides shown in Figure 4–1. You will perform the following general tasks as you progress through this module:

1. Customize slide masters by changing theme fonts and colors.
2. Format and arrange slide master placeholders.
3. Rename and delete slide layouts.
4. Save a presentation as a template.
5. Change slide backgrounds.
6. Use presentation tools.
7. Inspect and protect a presentation.
8. Rehearse slide timings.

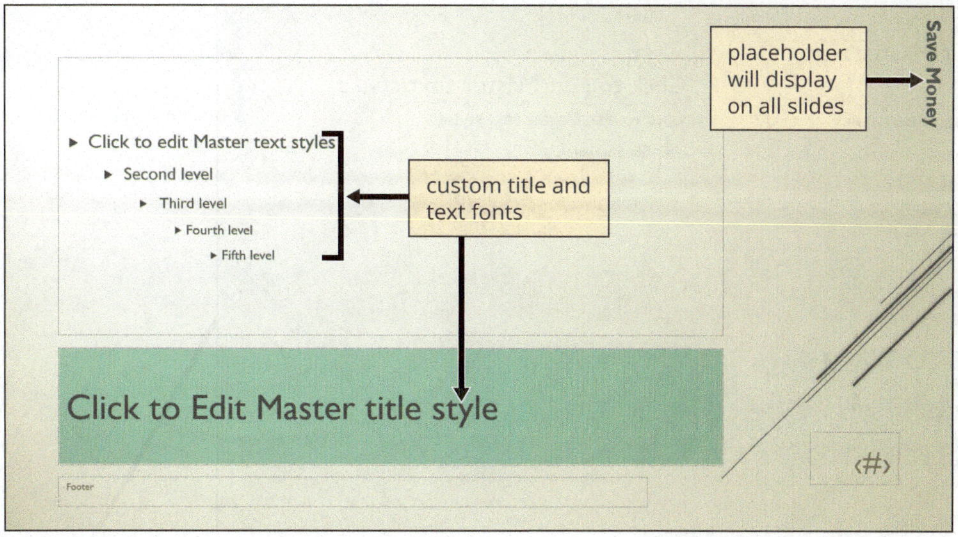

Figure 4–1(a): Slide Master

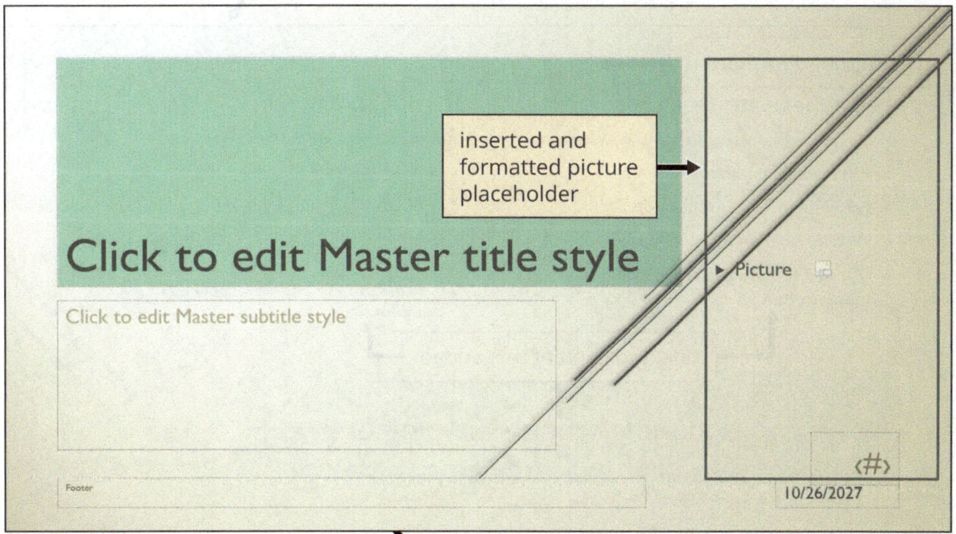

Figure 4–1(b): Master Title Slide Layout

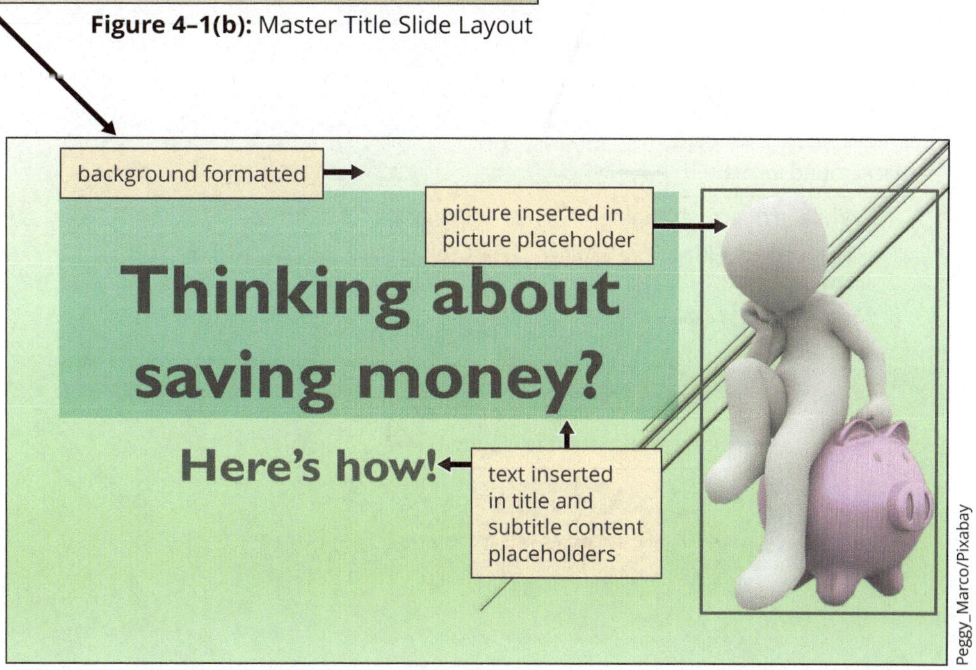

Figure 4–1(c): Slide 1

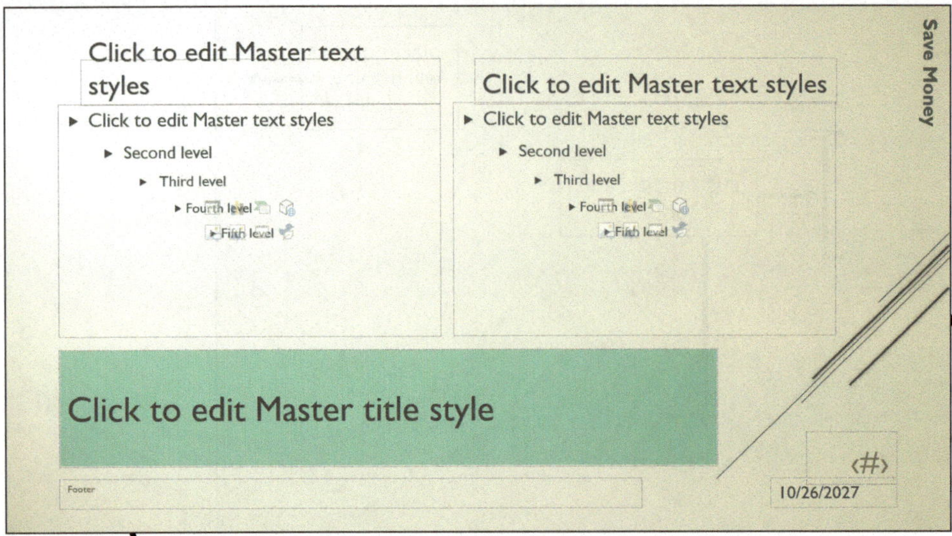

Figure 4–1(d): Master Comparison Layout

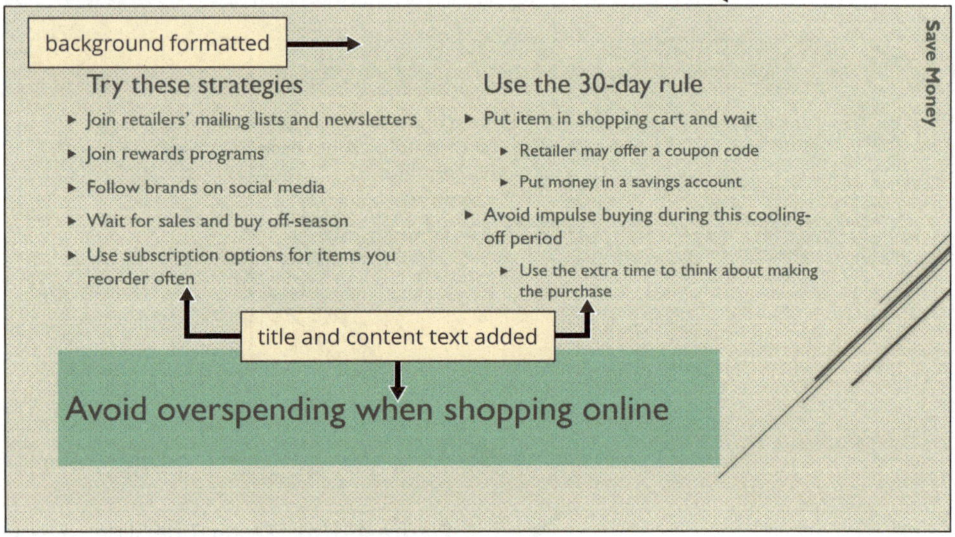

Figure 4–1(e): Slide 2

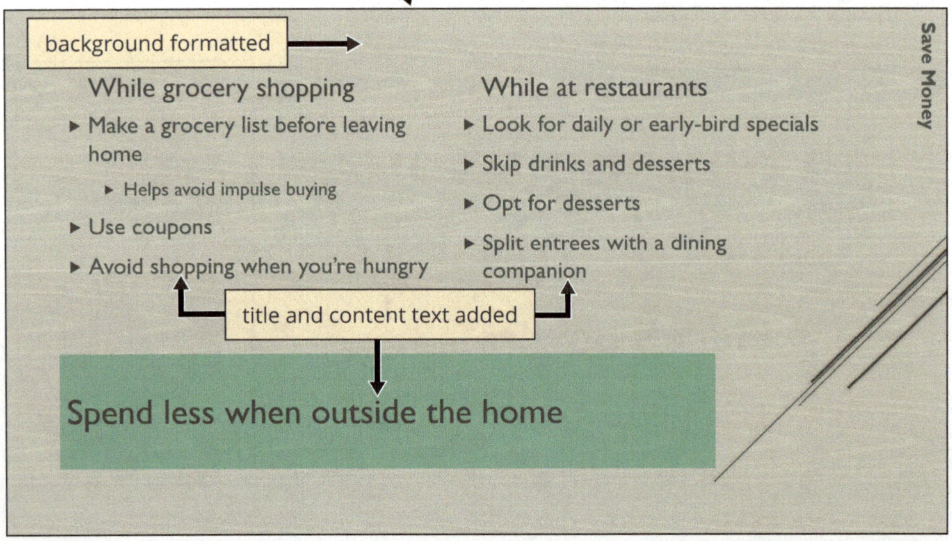

Figure 4–1(f): Slide 5

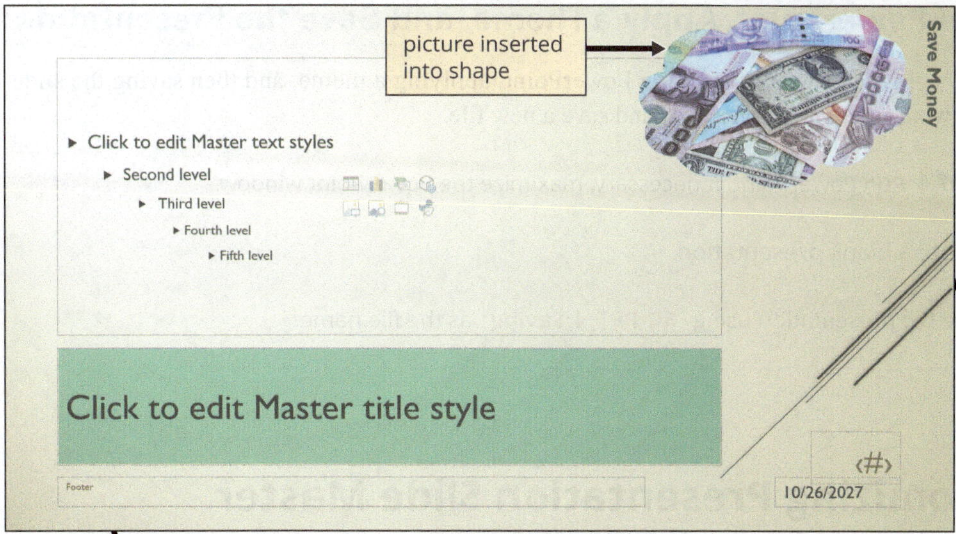

TheDigitalWay/Pixabay

Figure 4–1(g): Master Title and Content Layout

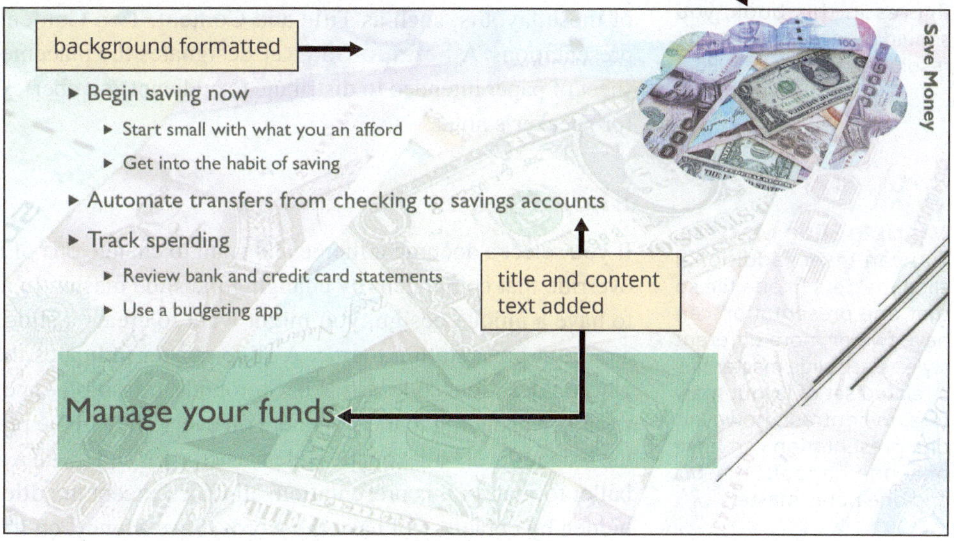

TheDig talWay/Pixabay

Figure 4–1(h): Slide 3

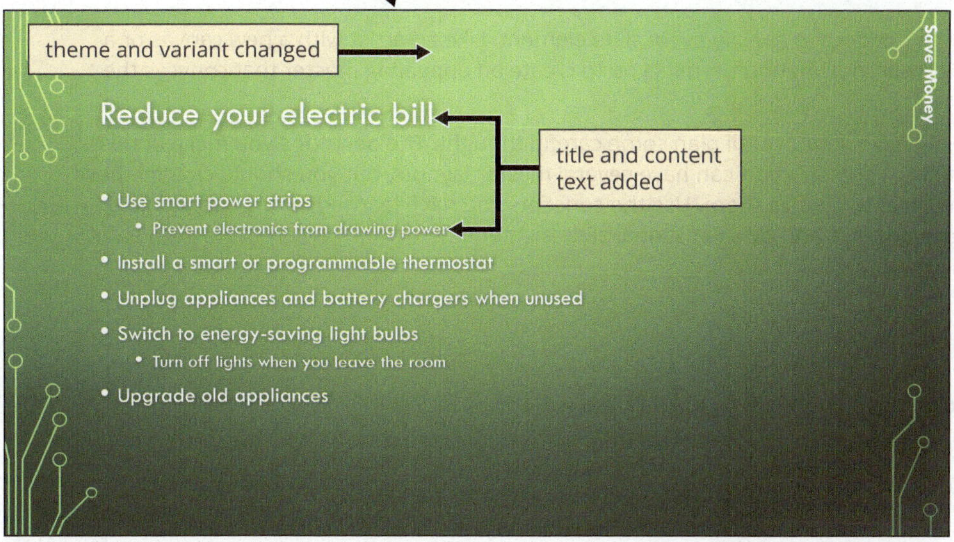

Figure 4–1(i): Slide 4

To Run PowerPoint, Apply a Theme, and Save the Presentation

You can begin the project by running PowerPoint, applying a theme, and then saving the slide. The following steps run PowerPoint and save a new file.

1. sam Run PowerPoint. If necessary, maximize the PowerPoint window.
2. Create a blank presentation.
3. Save the presentation using **SC_PPT_4_Saving** as the file name.

BTW
Screen Resolution
If you are using a computer to step through the project in this module and you want your screens to match the figures in this book, you should change your screen's resolution to 1920 × 1080.

Customizing Presentation Slide Master Backgrounds and Fonts

PowerPoint has many template files with the file extension .potx. Each template file has three masters: slide, handout, and notes. A slide master has at least one layout; you have used many of these layouts, such as Title and Content, Two Content, and Picture with Caption, to create presentations. A **handout master** designates the placement of text, such as page numbers, on a sheet of paper intended to distribute to audience members. A **notes master** defines the formatting for speaker's notes.

BTW
Multiple Slide Masters
You can insert additional slide masters in one file so that one presentation can have two or more different styles. Each slide master has a related set of layout masters. In contrast, however, one presentation can have only one handout master and one notes master.

Slide Master

If you select a document theme and want to change one of its components on every slide, you can override that component by changing the slide master. In addition, if you want your presentation to have a unique design, you might want to create a slide master rather than attempt to modify a current presentation theme. A slide master indicates the size and position of text and object placeholders, font styles, slide backgrounds, transitions, and effects. Any change to the slide master results in changing that component on every slide in the presentation. For example, if you change the second-level bullet on the slide master, each slide with a second-level bullet will display this new bullet format. In this presentation, all slides except the title slide, which has background graphics hidden by default, will have the words, Save Money, on the slide master.

Consider This

Plan the slide master.

Using a new slide master gives you the freedom to specify every slide element. Like an artist with a new canvas or a musician with a blank sheet of music, your imagination permits you to create an appealing master that conveys the overall look of your presentation.

Before you start developing the master, give your overall plan some careful thought. The decisions you make at this point should be reflected on every slide. A presentation can have several master layouts, but you should change these layouts only if you have a compelling need to change them. Use the concepts you have learned in this book to guide your decisions about fonts, colors, backgrounds, art, and other essential slide elements.

To Switch to Slide Master View

To begin developing the saving money slides, you need to display the slide master. **Why?** The slide master allows you to customize the slide components and create a unique design. The following steps switch to Slide Master view and display the slide master.

1

- Click View on the ribbon to display the View tab (Figure 4–2).

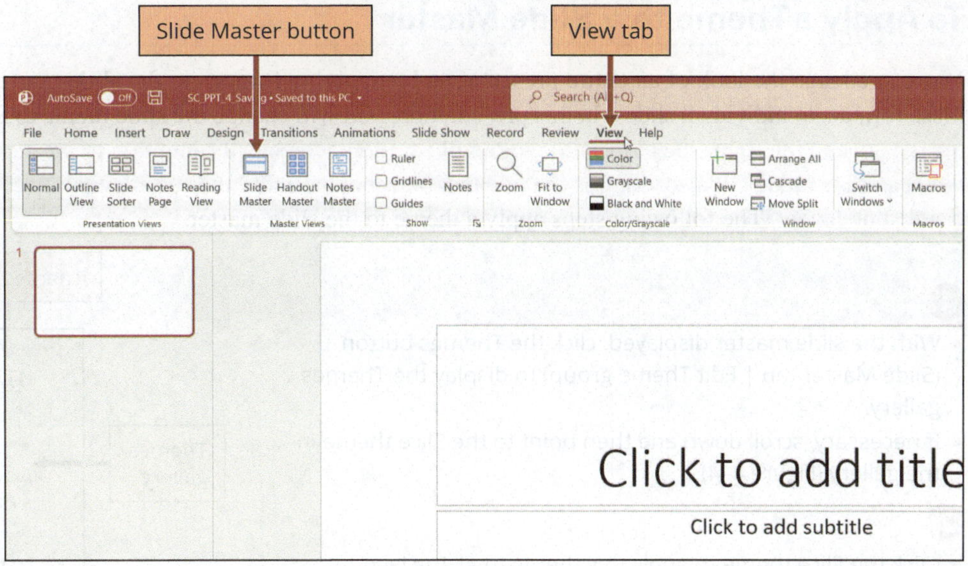

Figure 4–2

2

- Click the Slide Master button (View tab | Master Views group) to display the Slide Master tab and the slide thumbnails in the Slides tab.
- Scroll up and then click the Office Theme Slide Master layout (Figure 4–3).

Q&A What are all the other thumbnails below the slide master?

They are all the slide layouts associated with this slide master. You have used many of these layouts in the presentations you have developed in the exercises in this book.

Why is the layout given this name?

The slide layout names begin with the theme applied to the slides. In this case, the default Office Theme is applied. The first slide layout in the list is called the master because it controls the colors, fonts, and objects that are displayed on all the other slides in the presentation.

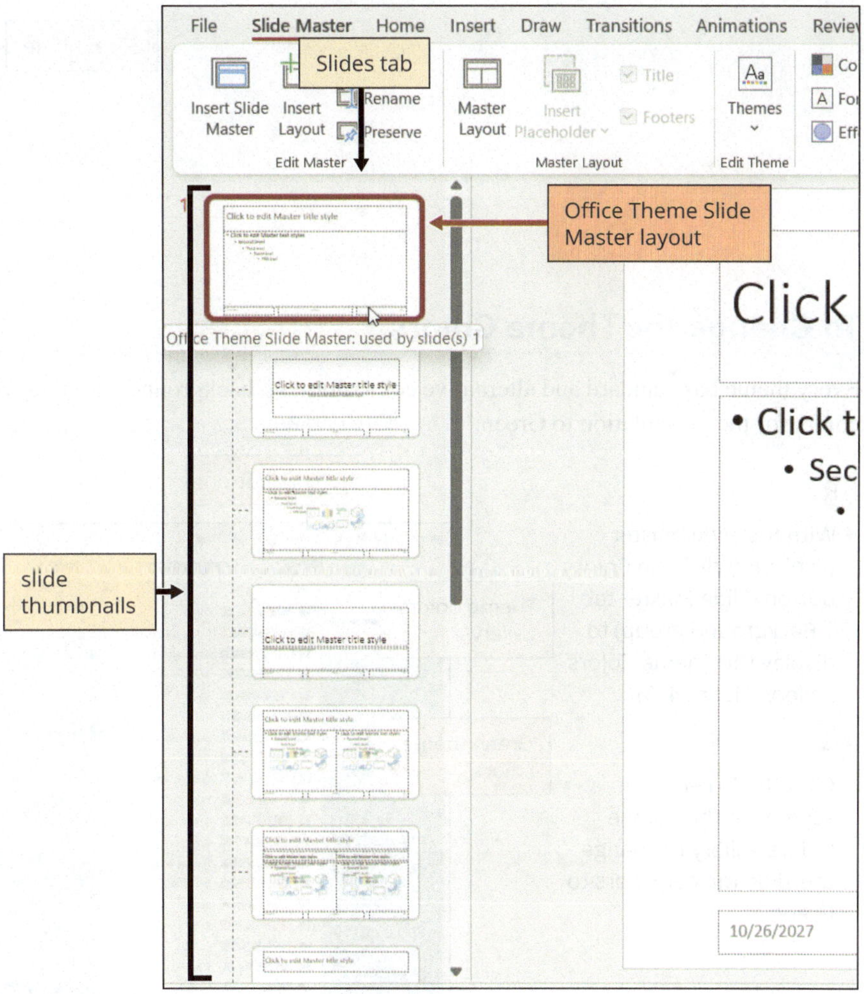

Figure 4–3

To Apply a Theme to a Slide Master

You can change the look of an entire presentation by applying formats to the slide master in the same manner that you apply these formats to individual slides. In this presentation, you will change the slide theme to Slice. **Why?** The Slice theme features a large area on the right side of the slide for an illustration, which calls attention to the subject matter of people wondering how they can save money. It also features the title text placeholder under the subtitle text placeholder, which is a departure from the usual slide layout. The following steps apply a theme to the slide master.

1

- With the slide master displayed, click the Themes button (Slide Master tab | Edit Theme group) to display the Themes gallery.
- If necessary, scroll down and then point to the Slice theme in the gallery (Figure 4–4).

2

- Click the Slice theme to apply this theme to all the layouts associated with the slide master.

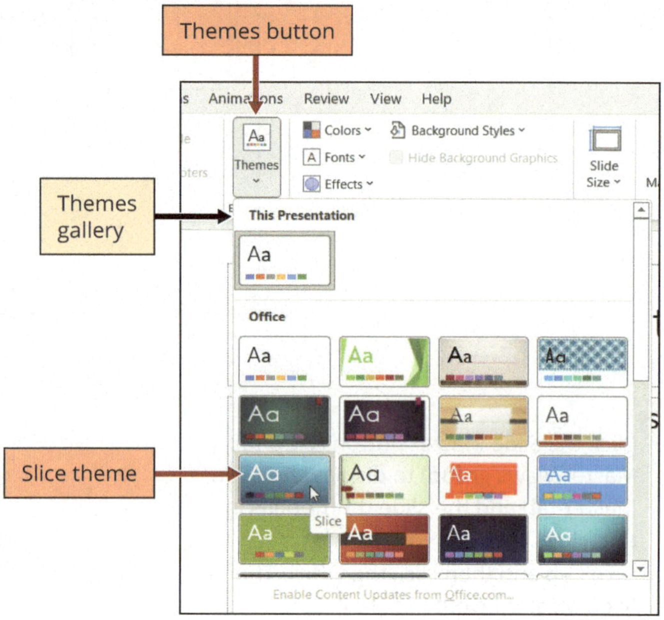

Figure 4–4

To Change the Theme Colors

Every theme has standard and alternative colors for text, backgrounds, accents, and hyperlinks. The following steps change the colors for the presentation to Green. **Why?** Green colors are associated with banking, money, and finances.

1

- With the slide master displayed, click the Colors button (Slide Master tab | Background group) to display the Theme Colors gallery (Figure 4–5).

2

- Click the Green color scheme in the Theme Colors gallery to change the slide master colors to Green.

Figure 4–5

To Create Custom Theme Colors

You can modify the colors associated with a particular theme by selecting specific colors and then see samples in the 'Create New Theme Colors' dialog box. Once you determine the specific colors you desire, you can save this combination in the Colors menu. **Why?** You can use this color scheme in other presentations. The following steps customize the colors for the Slice theme.

1

- Click Colors again to display the Theme Colors gallery (Figure 4–6).

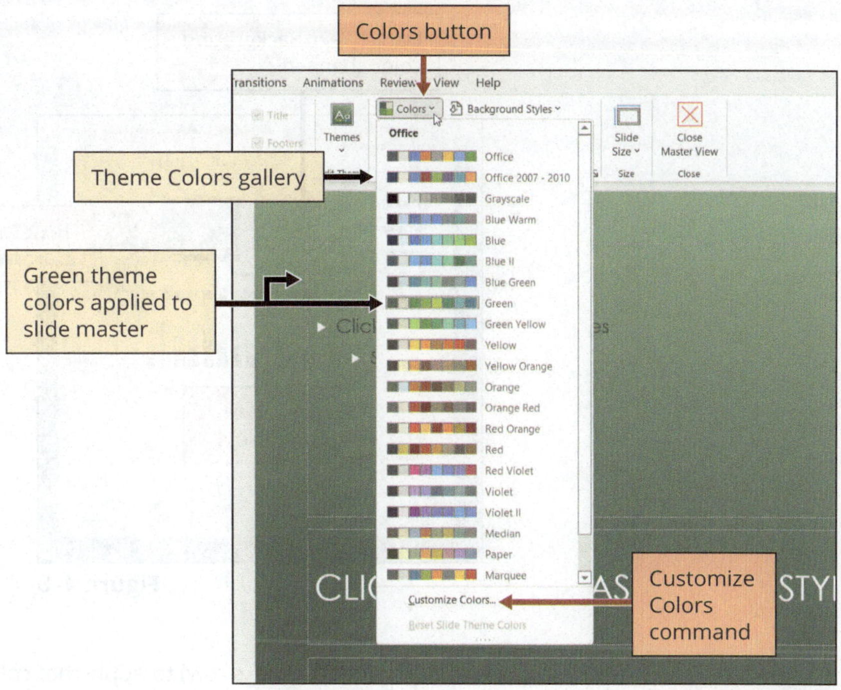

Figure 4–6

2

- Click Customize Colors in the Theme Colors gallery to display the Create New Theme Colors dialog box.
- Click the 'Text/Background-Light 1' arrow to display the Colors gallery (Figure 4–7).

Q&A Can I preview the colors to see how they are displayed on the slide master?
No preview is available when using the Create New Theme Colors dialog box. Once you select the color, however, PowerPoint will display text in the Sample box.

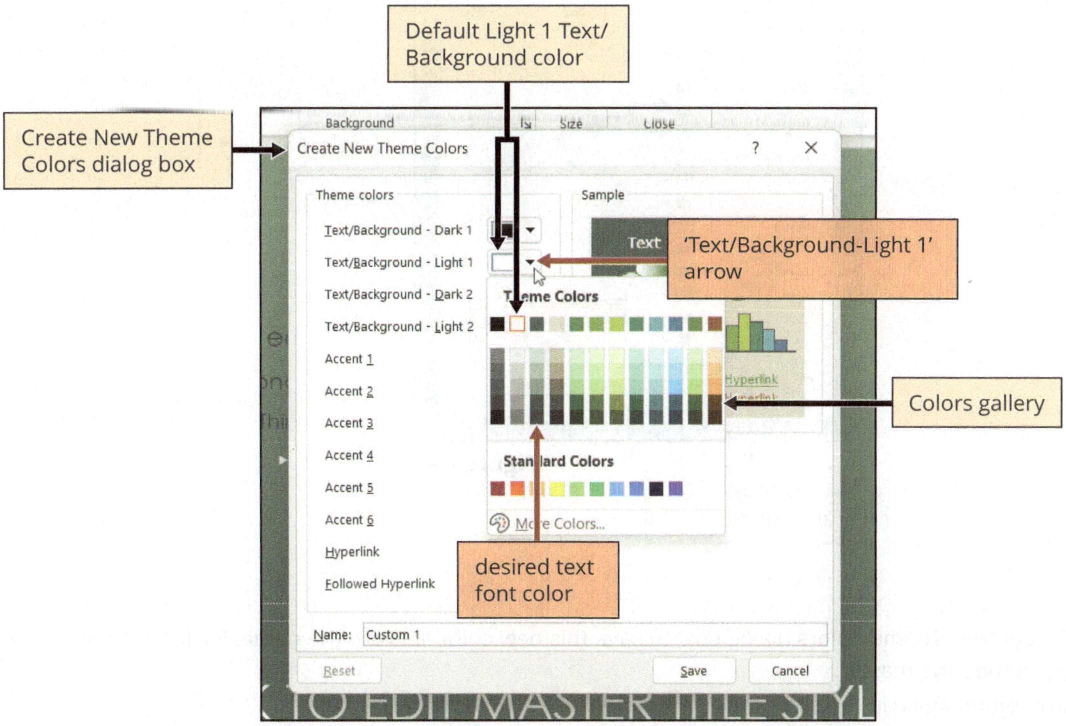

Figure 4–7

3

- Click 'Dark Green, Background 2, Darker 50%' (last color in the third Theme Colors column) to apply that color as the title text font color.
- Click the 'Text/Background-Dark 2' arrow to display the Colors gallery again (Figure 4–8).

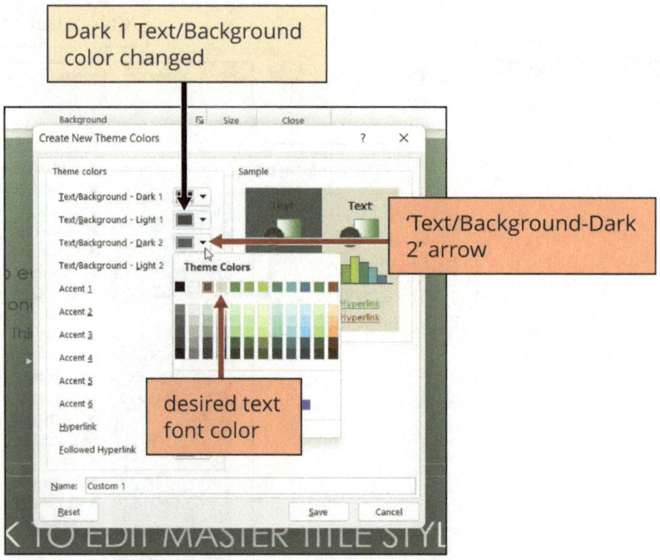

Figure 4–8

4

- Click 'Tan, Text 2' (fourth color in the first Theme Colors row) to apply that color as the background color.
- Select the text, Custom 1, in the Name text box (Create New Theme Colors dialog box) and then type **Saving** as the name of the new custom theme colors palette (Figure 4–9).

Q&A Must I name this custom color scheme I just created?

No. If you name the set, however, you easily will recognize this combination in your color set if you want to use it in new presentations. It will display in the Custom area of the Colors gallery.

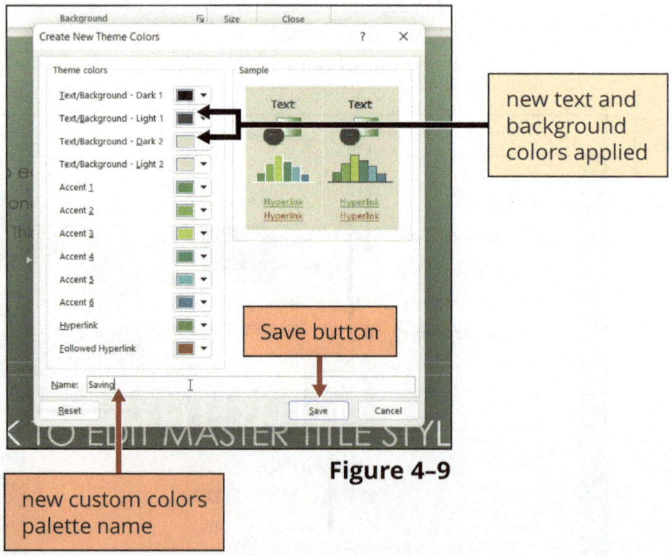

Figure 4–9

5

- Click Save (Create New Theme Colors dialog box) to save this new color set with the name, Saving, and to display the font color changes in the slide master.
- Save the presentation again in the same storage location with the same file name.

To Edit Master Text Styles

You can modify the text styles associated with a particular theme, such as changing from uppercase to sentence case. **Why?** You want to change from UPPERCASE (all caps) to Sentence case (initial cap only) because Sentence case is considered easier to read. The following steps edit the master title text style for the Slice theme.

1

- With the slide master displayed, click the label, 'CLICK TO EDIT MASTER TITLE STYLE' to select the title text placeholder.
- Display the Home tab and then click the Change Case button (Home tab | Font group) to display the Change Case gallery (Figure 4–10).
- **Experiment:** Point to various options in the Sentence case gallery and watch the words in the placeholder change case.

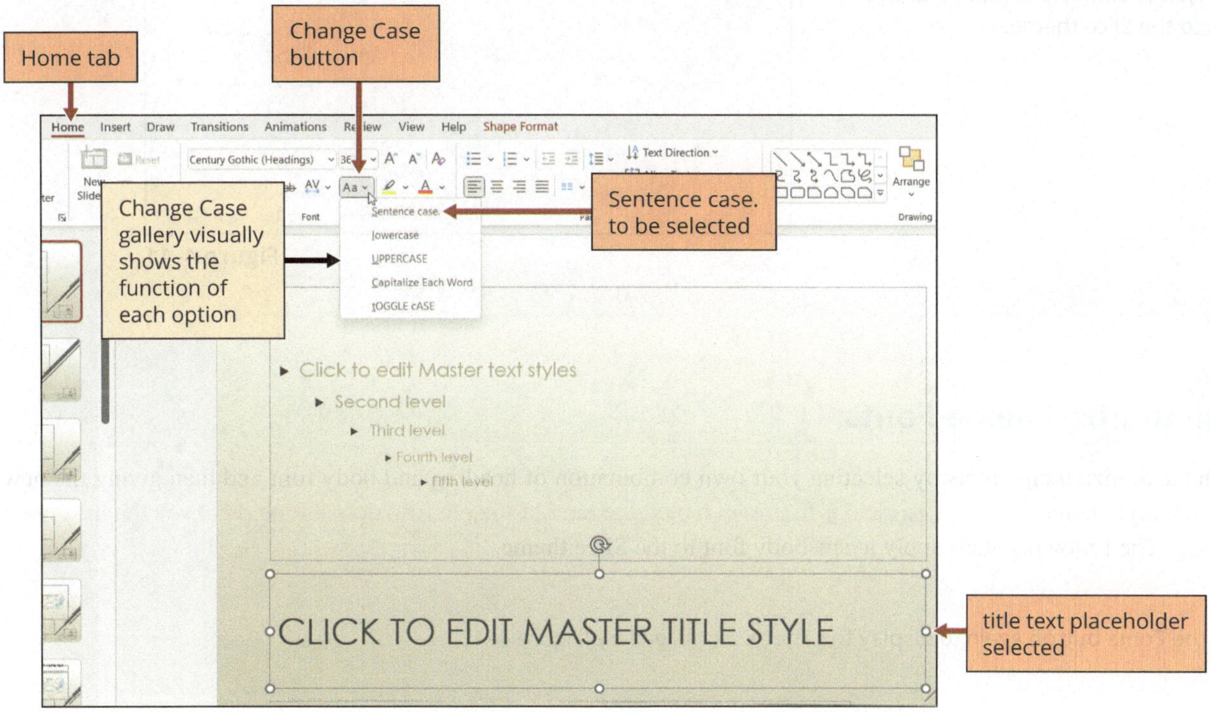

Figure 4–10

2

- Click Sentence case. in the Change Case gallery to change the case of the title text from UPPERCASE to Sentence case.

Other Ways

1. Press SHIFT+F3 repeatedly until text is desired case

To Change the Theme Fonts

Each theme has a heading font and a body font applied to it. At times both fonts are the same, and at other times, the heading font differs from the body font, but both fonts coordinate with each other. You can change the text in your slides by selecting one of the font sets. **Why?** This is a quick and easy method of changing all the text simultaneously. The following steps apply a new heading font and body font to the Slice theme.

1

- Display the Slide Master tab.
- With the slide master displayed, click the Fonts button (Slide Master tab | Background group) to display the Theme Fonts gallery.

- Scroll down and then point to the Calibri-Cambria font set (Figure 4–11).

Q&A How are the font sets arranged in the Theme Fonts gallery?
Calibri is the heading font, and Cambria is the body font. The fonts are previewed in the boxes on the left side of the gallery and in the text displaying their names.

2

- Click Calibri-Cambria to apply the two fonts to the Slice theme.

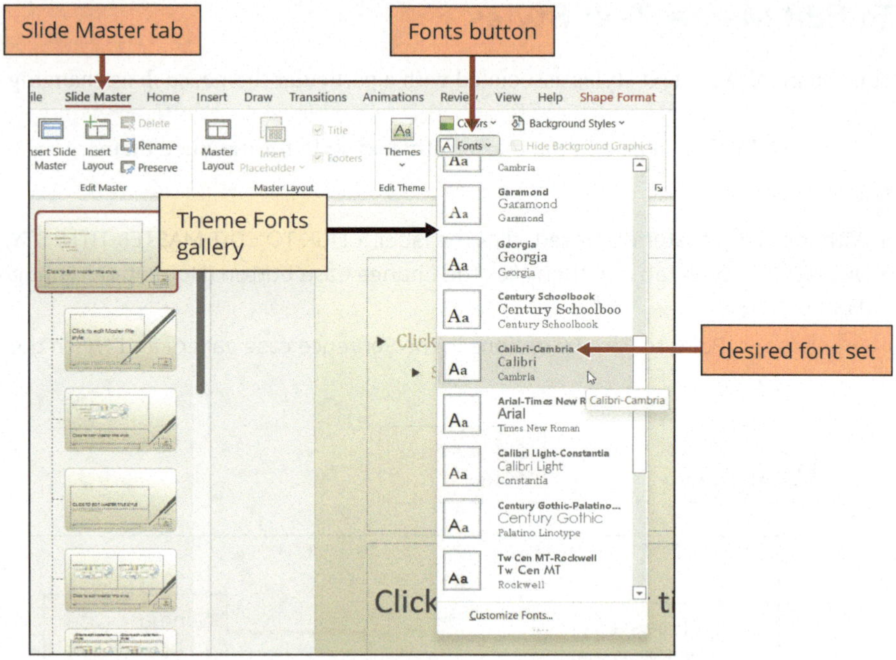

Figure 4–11

To Customize Theme Fonts

You can customize theme fonts by selecting your own combination of heading and body font and then giving the new theme font set a unique name. **Why?** A particular font may match the tone of the presentation and help convey the message you are presenting. The following steps apply a new body font to the Slice theme.

1

- Click the Fonts button again to display the Theme Fonts gallery (Figure 4–12).

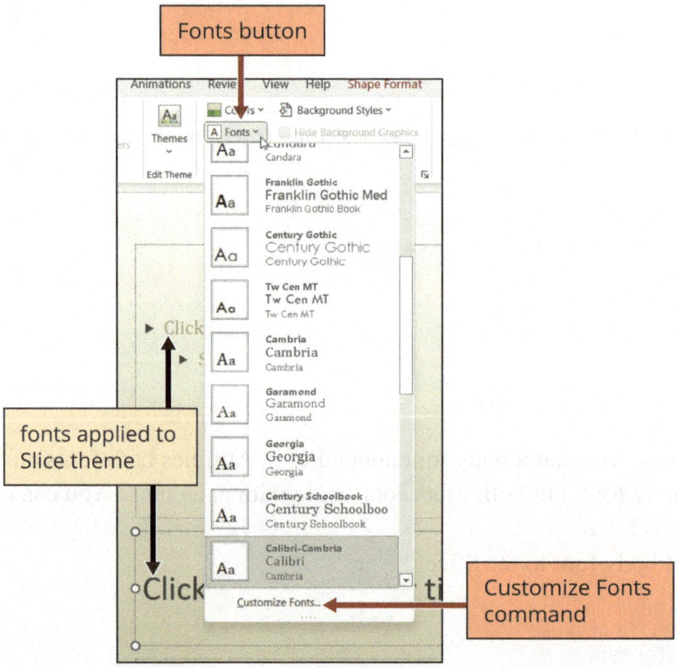

Figure 4–12

2

- Click Customize Fonts in the Theme Fonts gallery to display the Create New Theme Fonts dialog box.
- Click the Body font arrow and then scroll down and point to Gill Sans MT in the list (Figure 4–13).

Q&A Can I preview the fonts to see how they are displayed on the slide master?
No preview is available when using the Create New Theme Fonts dialog box. Once you select the font, however, PowerPoint will apply the font to the text in the Sample box.

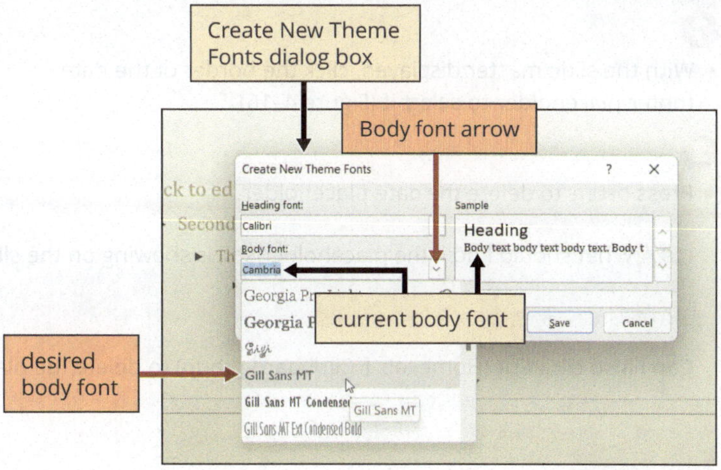

Figure 4–13

3

- Click Gill Sans MT to apply that font as the new body text font (Figure 4–14).

Q&A What if the Gill Sans MT font is not in my list of fonts?
Select a font that resembles the font shown in Figure 4–14.

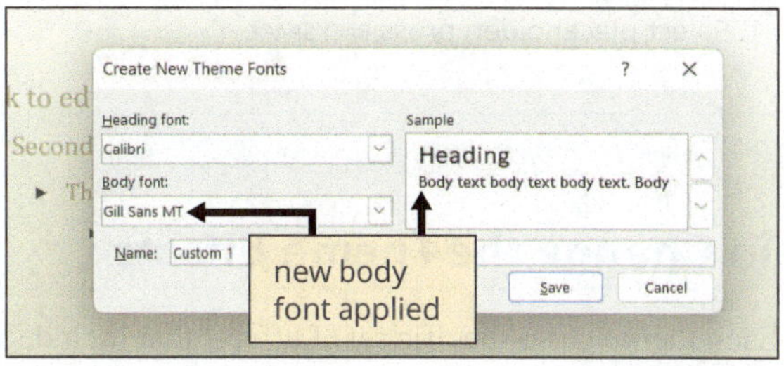

Figure 4–14

4

- Select the text, Custom 1, in the Name text box and then type **Saving** to name the new font set (Figure 4–15).

Q&A Must I name this font set I just created?
No. If you name the set, however, you easily will recognize this combination in your font set if you want to use it in new presentations. It will display in the Custom area of the Fonts gallery.

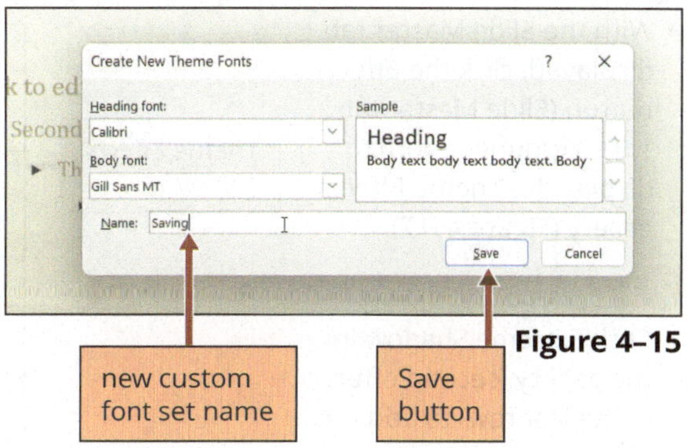

Figure 4–15

5

- Click Save (Create New Theme Fonts dialog box) to save this new font set with the name, Saving, and to display the font changes in the slide master.
- Save the presentation again in the same storage location with the same file name.

To Delete a Content Placeholder

When you run a slide show, empty placeholders do not display. At times, you may desire to delete these unused elements, such as a slide number, date and time, and footer placeholder, from a slide. **Why?** Empty placeholders can be a distraction when you are designing slide content because they interfere with other slide content or they use an area of the slide that can display other slide content. Or, you might not want to display information, such as a page number. The following steps delete the date placeholder on the slide master.

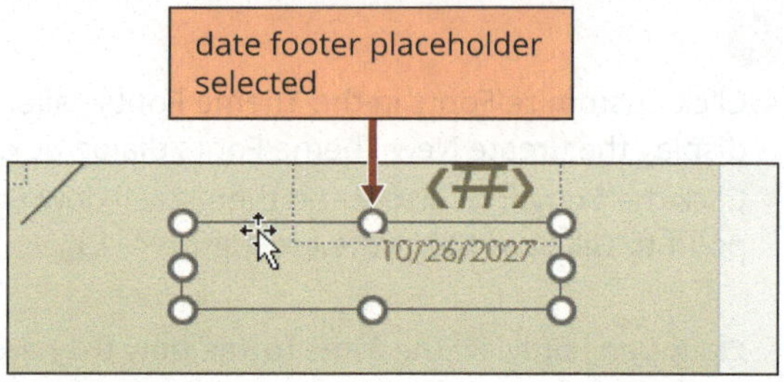

Figure 4–16

1

- With the slide master displayed, click the border of the date footer placeholder to select it (Figure 4–16).

2

- Press DELETE to delete the date placeholder.

Q&A What should I do if the placeholder still is showing on the slide?
Be certain you clicked the placeholder border and not just the text. The border must display as a solid line before you can delete it.

Can I also click Cut (Home tab | Clipboard group) to delete the placeholder?
Yes. Generally, however, Cut is used when you desire to remove a selected slide element, place it on the Clipboard, and then paste it in another area. DELETE is used when you do not want to reuse that particular slide element.

If I am using a touch screen, how do I delete the placeholder?
Press and hold on a border of the title text placeholder and then tap DELETE on the shortcut menu to remove the placeholder.

Other Ways

1. Select placeholder, press BACKSPACE

To Change the Theme Effects

Each theme has a specific set of effects that include such elements as shadows, reflections, lines, and fills. You cannot customize a set of theme effects, but you can change the effects associated with a particular theme. **Why?** A set of effects may fit the message you are giving in the presentation. The following steps change the theme effects.

1

- With the Slide Master tab displayed, click the Effects button (Slide Master tab | Background group) to display the Theme Effects gallery (Figure 4–17).

2

- Click Extreme Shadow in the gallery (second effect in the last row) to add this effect.

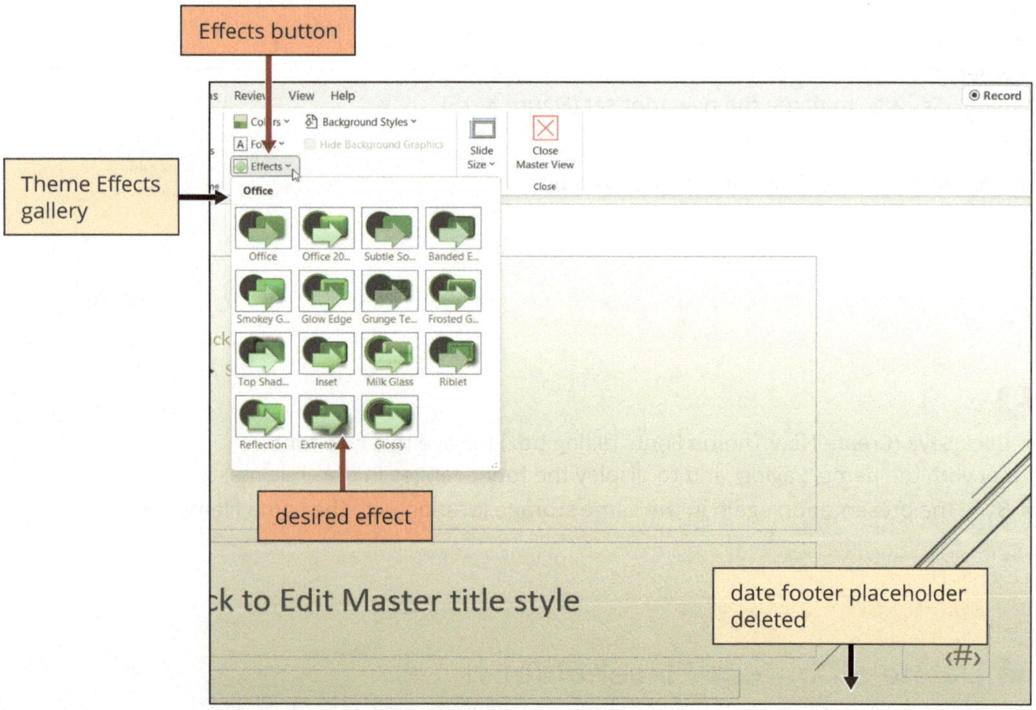

Figure 4–17

Adding and Formatting Placeholders

Each design theme determines where placeholders appear on individual layouts. The slide master has placeholders for bulleted lists, title text, pictures, and other graphical elements. At times, you may find that you need a specific placeholder for a design element not found on any of the slide master layouts. You can add a placeholder in Slide Master view for text, SmartArt, charts, tables, and other graphical elements.

To Insert a Placeholder into a Blank Layout

The words, Save Money, will appear in the title text on the title slide, but you may desire to add these words to every text slide. **Why?** Displaying this text in the same location on all slides helps emphasize the goal of the presentation and provides a consistent, uniform look. One efficient method of adding this text is to insert a placeholder, type the words, and, if necessary, format the characters. The following steps insert a text placeholder into the Blank Layout.

1

- In the Slides tab, scroll down and then click the Blank Layout to display this layout.
- Click the Insert Placeholder arrow (Slide Master tab | Master Layout group) to display the Insert Placeholder gallery (Figure 4–18).

Q&A Why does the Insert Placeholder button on my screen differ from the button shown in Figure 4–18?
The image on the button changes based on the type of placeholder content that was last inserted. A placeholder can hold any content, including text, pictures, and tables. If the last type of placeholder inserted was for a picture, for example, the Insert Placeholder button would display the Picture icon.

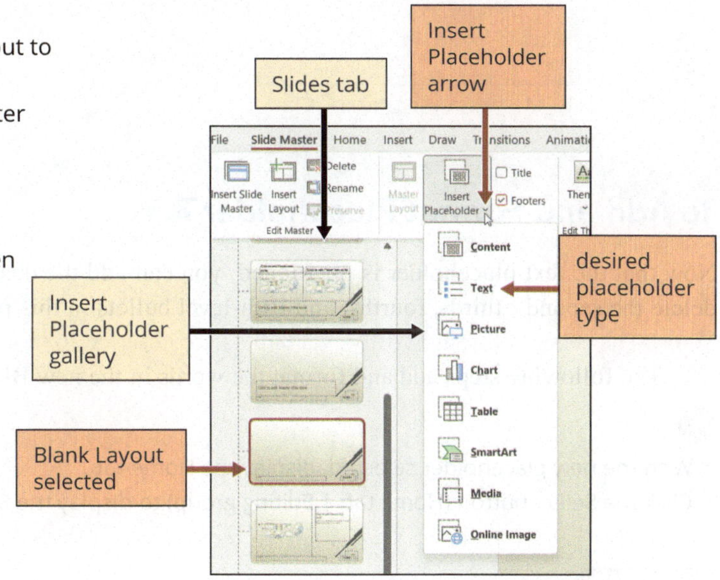

Figure 4–18

2

- Click Text in the gallery.

Q&A Could I have inserted a Content placeholder rather than a Text placeholder?
Yes. The Content placeholder is used for any of the seven types of slide content: text, table, chart, SmartArt, picture, clip art, or media. In this project, you will insert text in the placeholder. If you know the specific kind of content you want to place in the placeholder, it is best to select that placeholder type.

3

- Position the pointer, which is a crosshair, near the upper-right corner of the slide layout (Figure 4–19).

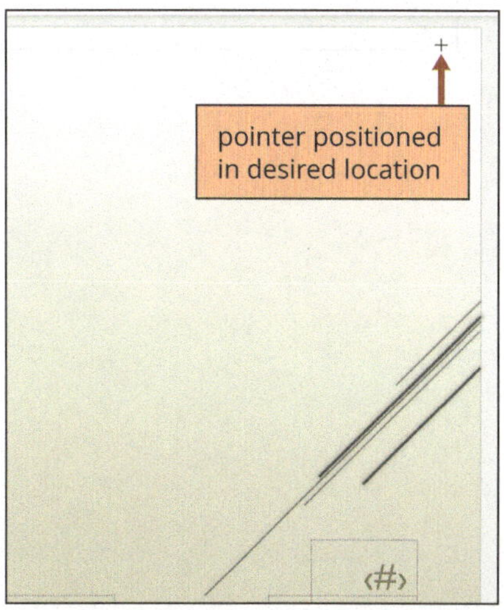

Figure 4–19

4

- Click to insert the new placeholder into the layout. Click inside the new placeholder (Figure 4–20).

Q&A Could I have inserted the Text placeholder anywhere on the slide rather than in the upper-right corner?
Yes. Because you are going to display that placeholder on every slide, however, it is best to make the necessary formatting changes and see how it is going to appear on your final product.

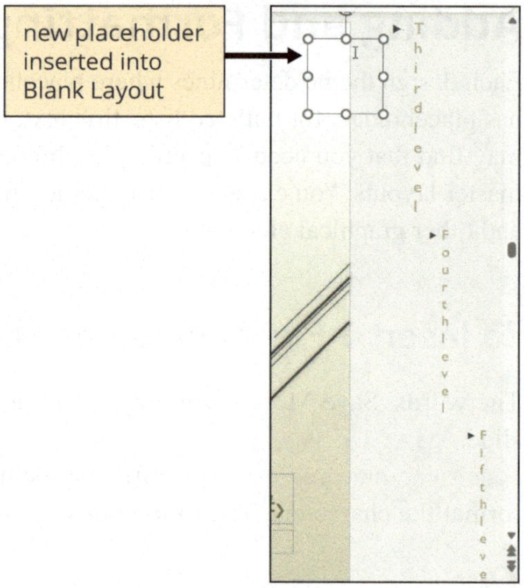

Figure 4–20

To Add and Format Placeholder Text

Now that the text placeholder is positioned, you can add the desired text and then format the characters. You will need to delete the second-, third-, fourth-, and fifth-level bullets in this placeholder and remove the bullet from the first-level text. **Why?** The second- through fifth-level bullets are not used in this presentation, and you do not want a bullet on your primary text. The following steps add and format the words in the new Blank Layout placeholder.

1

- With the new placeholder selected, display the Home tab.
- Click the Select button (Home tab | Editing group) to display the Select menu (Figure 4–21).

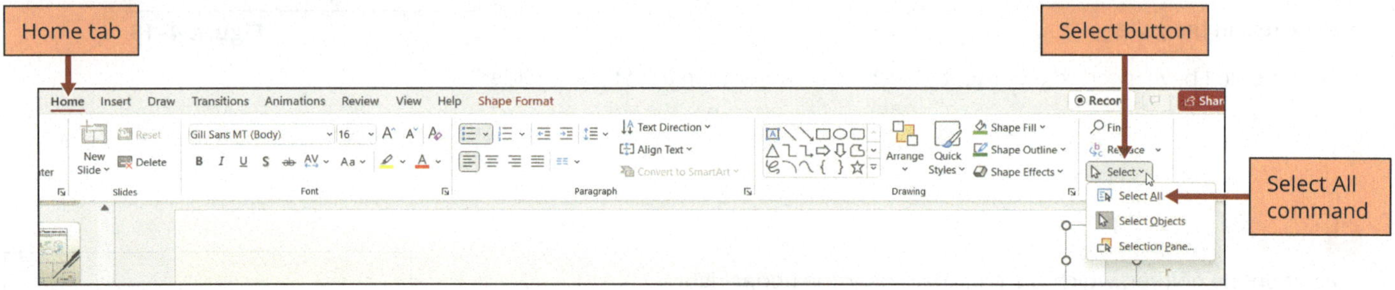

Figure 4–21

2

- Click Select All in the Select menu to select all the text in the placeholder (Figure 4–22).

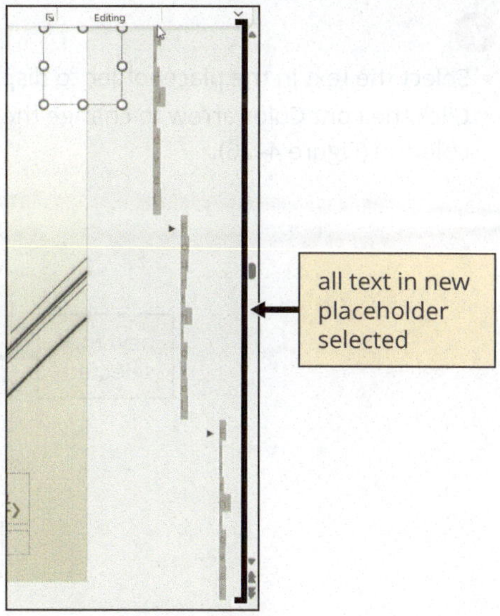

Figure 4–22

3

- Press DELETE to delete all the selected text in the placeholder.
- Click the Bullets button (Home tab | Paragraph group) to remove the bullet from the placeholder.
- Type **Save Money** in the placeholder (Figure 4–23).

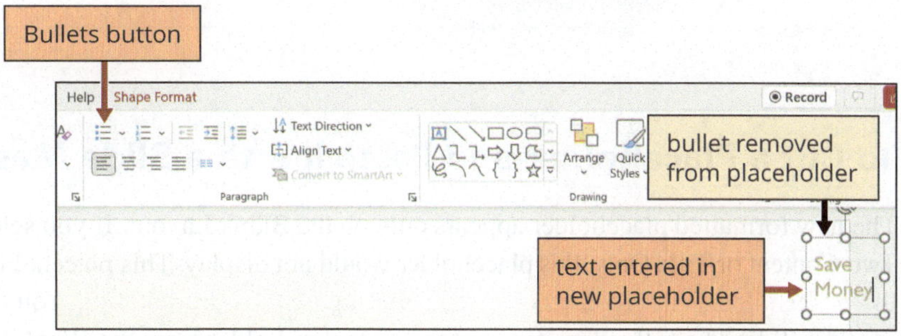

Figure 4–23

4

- Click the Shape Format tab and then change the height of the placeholder to 2" and the width to 0.5" (Figure 4–24).

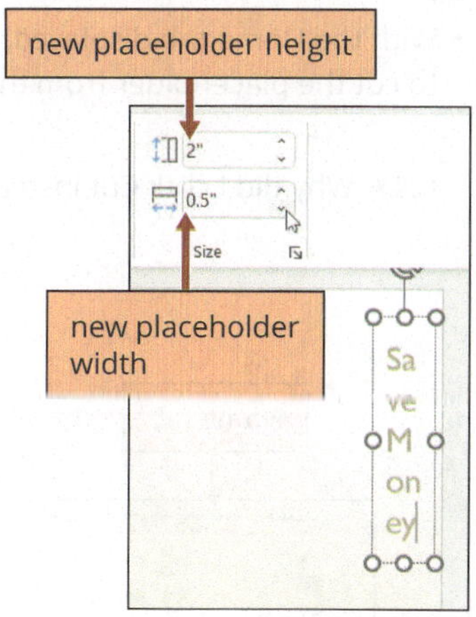

Figure 4–24

5

- Display the Home tab, select the new placeholder, and then click the Text Direction button (Home tab | Paragraph group) to display the Text Direction gallery (Figure 4–25).

◦ **Experiment:** Point to various directions in the Text Direction gallery and watch the words in the placeholder change direction on the layout.

6

- Click 'Rotate all text 90°' to turn the text so that it faces inward.

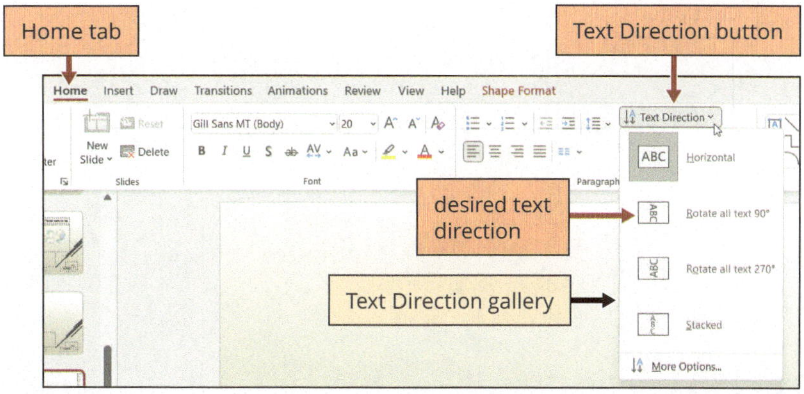

Figure 4–25

7

- Select the text in the placeholder to display the Mini toolbar and then click the Bold button to bold the text.
- Click the Font Color arrow to change the color to 'Dark Green, Text 1, Lighter 10%' (last color in the second Theme Colors column) (Figure 4–26).

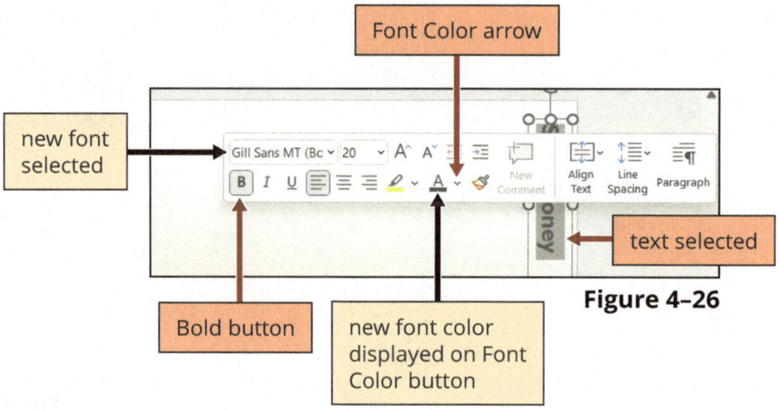

Figure 4–26

To Cut a Placeholder and Paste It into a Slide Master

The new formatted placeholder appears only on the Blank Layout. If you selected any other layout in your presentation, such as Two Content or Title Only, this placeholder would not display. This placeholder should appear on all text slides. **Why?** Repeating this placeholder will provide consistency throughout the presentation. You can paste a placeholder that you copied or cut from another slide. The following steps cut the new placeholder from the Blank Layout and paste it into the slide master.

1

- With the Home tab displayed, click the new placeholder border, and then click the Cut button (Home tab | Clipboard group) to cut the placeholder from the layout and copy it to the Clipboard (Figure 4–27).

Q&A Why did I click Cut instead of Copy?
Tapping or clicking Cut deletes the placeholder. Tapping or clicking Copy keeps the original placeholder on the slide, so if you paste the placeholder on the slide master, a second, identical placeholder would display on the Blank Layout.

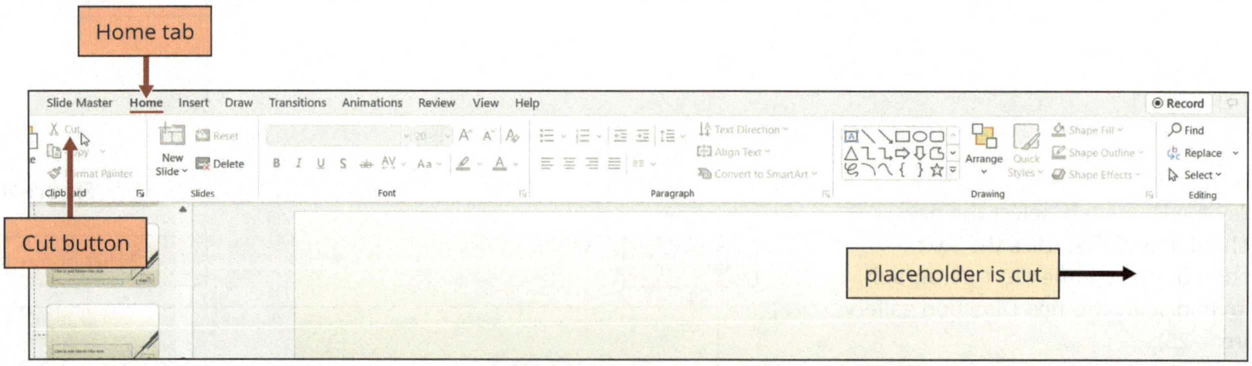

Figure 4–27

2

- Scroll up and then click the Slice Slide Master thumbnail in the Slides tab to display the slide master.
- Click the Paste button (Home tab | Clipboard group) to copy the placeholder from the Clipboard to the slide master.
- Use the smart guides to position the placeholder in the location shown in Figure 4–28.

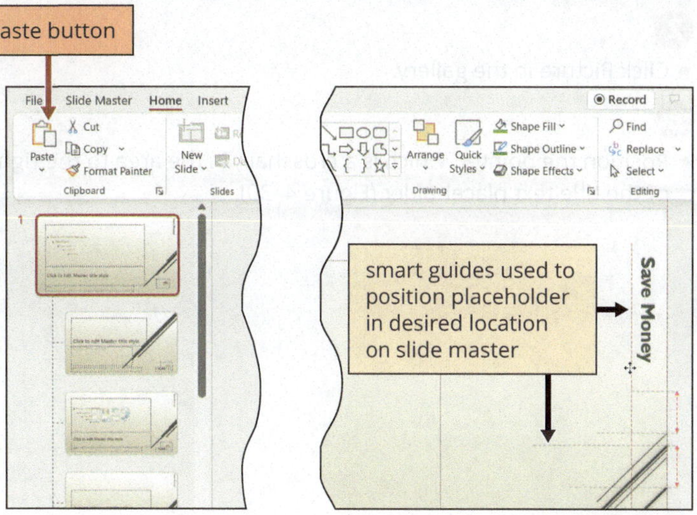

Figure 4–28

To Insert a Picture Placeholder

The right side of the Title Slide Layout contains a large area to the right of the title text placeholder. You can add a picture placeholder to this area of the slide in the slide master. **Why?** You can draw attention to your presentation's purpose if you add a picture to this slide layout. You add a picture placeholder in the same manner as you add a text placeholder. You then can size and format this placeholder by adding an outline, effect, or other enhancements. The following steps insert a picture placeholder into the Title Slide Layout.

1

- In the Slides tab, click the Title Slide Layout to display this layout.
- Display the Slide Master tab and then click the Insert Placeholder arrow (Slide Master tab | Master Layout group) to display the Insert Placeholder gallery (Figure 4–29).

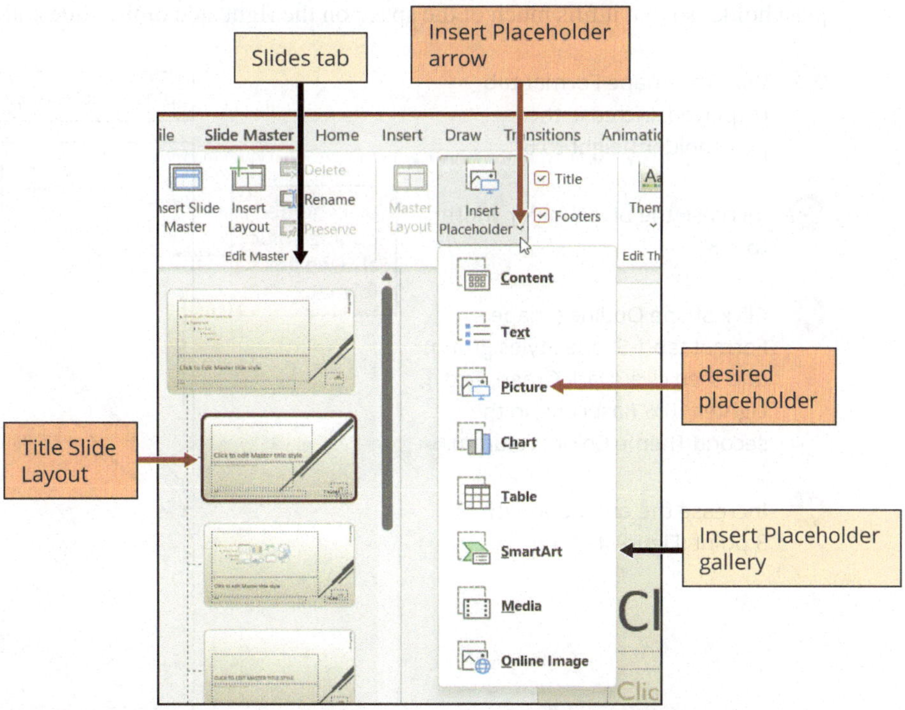

Figure 4–29

2
- Click Picture in the gallery.

3
- Position the pointer, which is a crosshair, in the area to the right of the title text placeholder (Figure 4–30).

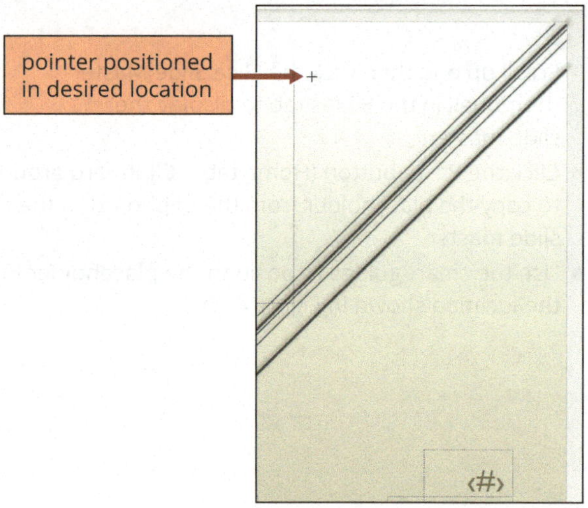

Figure 4–30

4
- Click to insert the new placeholder into the Title Slide Layout (Figure 4–31).

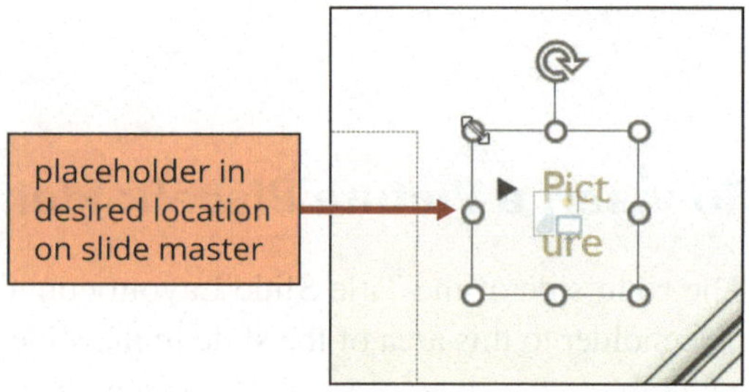

Figure 4–31

To Size and Format the Picture Content Layout

You can size the picture placeholder on the right side of the title slide. You also can add an outline to enhance the visual appeal of this element. The following steps increase the size of the picture placeholder so that it fills much of the space on the right side of the slide and then add an outline.

1. With the Shape Format tab displayed, increase the placeholder height to 6".
2. Increase the placeholder width to 3.3".
3. Click Shape Outline (Shape Format tab | Shape Styles group) and then click 'Dark Green, Text 1, Lighter 10%' (last color in the second Theme Colors column).
4. Increase the outline weight to 3 point (Figure 4–32).

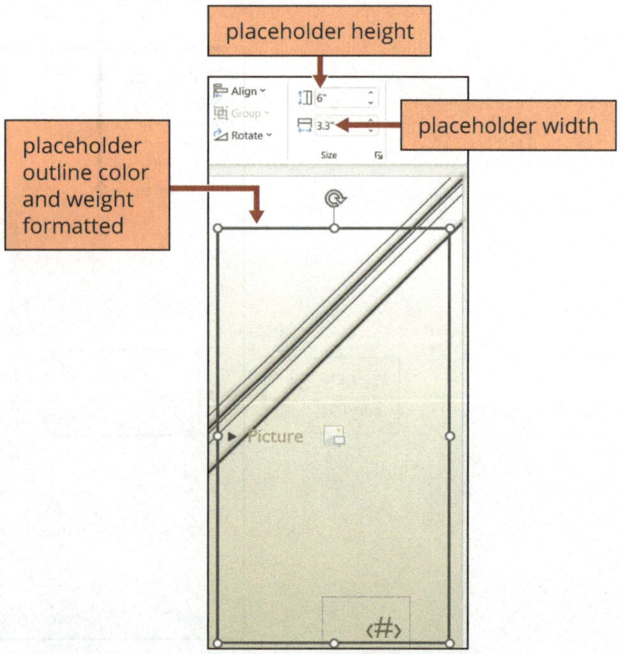

Figure 4–32

To Copy a Content Placeholder

At times you may want the same slide content to appear in another area of the slide or on another slide. To perform this action, you would copy the element, such as a placeholder, and then paste it. When you copy this element, it is stored on the **Clipboard**. You can copy a maximum of 24 items from Office documents and then paste them in the same or other documents. To copy a placeholder to another slide master, you would perform the following steps.

1. Select the item you want to copy.
2. Display the Home tab and then click Copy (Home tab | Clipboard group).
3. Place the insertion point where you want the item to display and then click Paste (Home tab | Clipboard group).

To Format a Slide Master Background, Apply a Quick Style, and Format Text

Once you have applied a theme to the slide master and determined the fonts for the presentation, you can further customize the slide master. **Why?** Adding a unique background and customizing the colors can give your presentation a unique look that matches the message you are conveying. The following steps format the slide master background, apply a Quick Style, and format the subtitle text.

1

- Display the Slice Slide Master and then, if necessary, display the Slide Master tab.
- Click the Background Styles button (Slide Master tab | Background group) to display the Background Styles gallery (Figure 4–33).

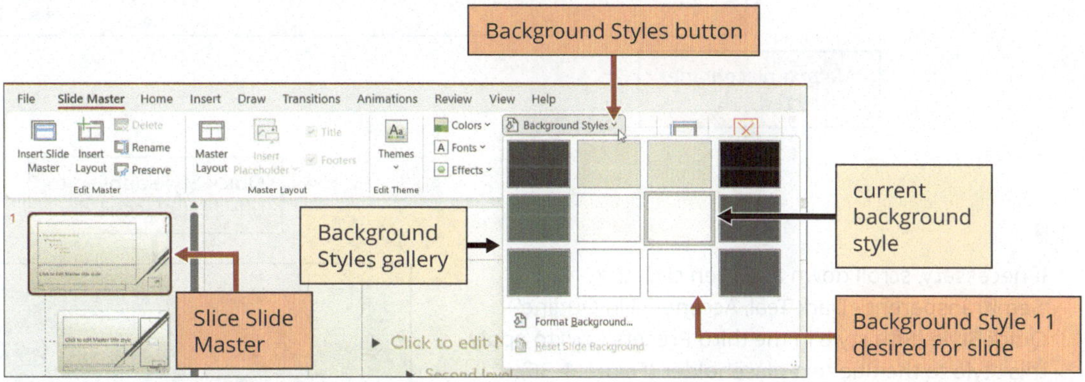

Figure 4–33

- **Experiment:** Point to various styles in the Background Styles gallery and watch the backgrounds change on the slide master.

2

- Click Style 11 (third style in the third row) to apply this background to the slide master (Figure 4–34).

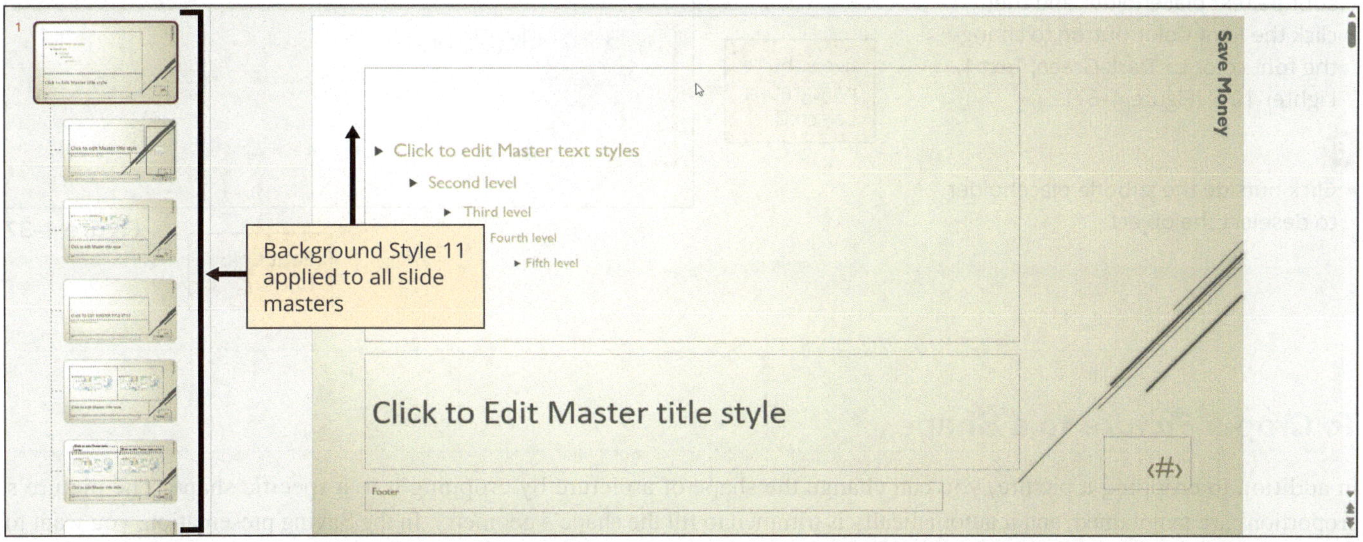

Figure 4–34

3

- Click the outer edge of the slide master title text placeholder to select it.
- Display the Home tab and then click the Quick Styles button (Home tab | Drawing group) to display the Shape Quick Styles gallery (Figure 4–35).
- **Experiment:** Point to various styles in the Quick Styles gallery and watch the background and borders change on the slide master title text placeholder.

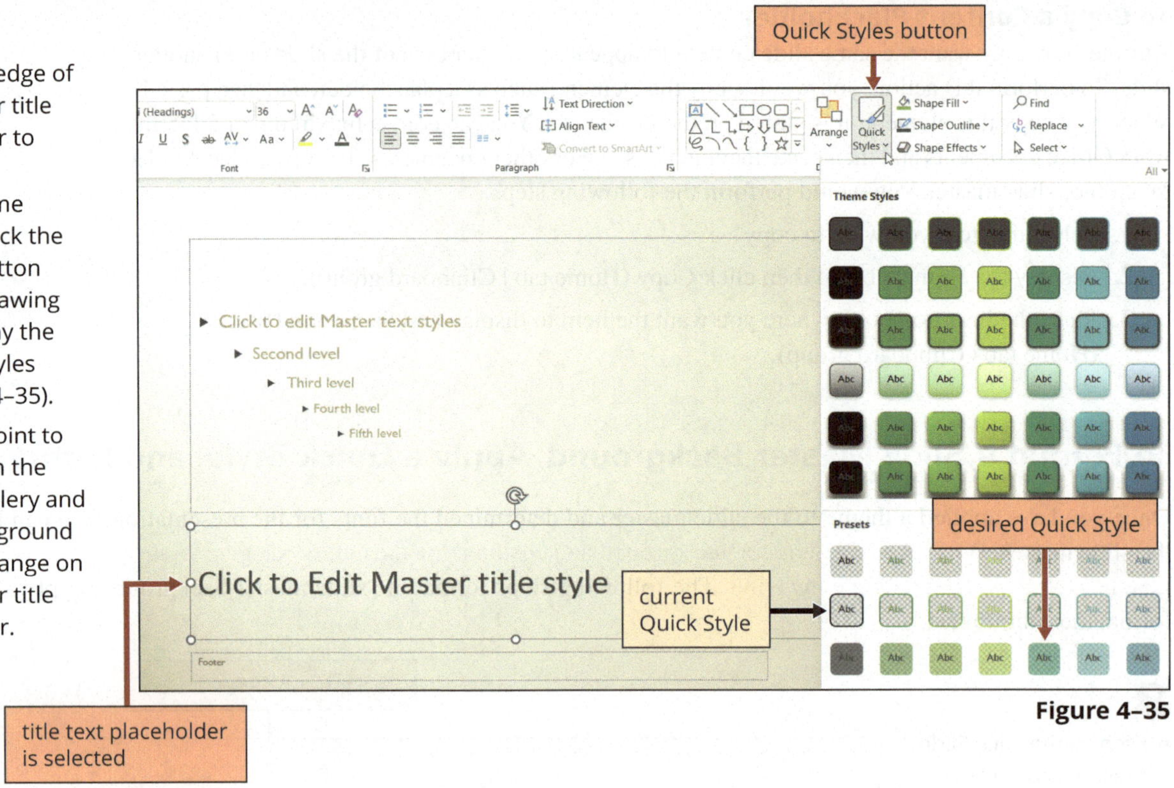

Figure 4–35

4

- If necessary, scroll down and then click the 'Semitransparent - Dark Teal, Accent 4, No Outline' Quick Style (fifth style in the third Presets row) to apply this style to the title text placeholder (Figure 4–36).

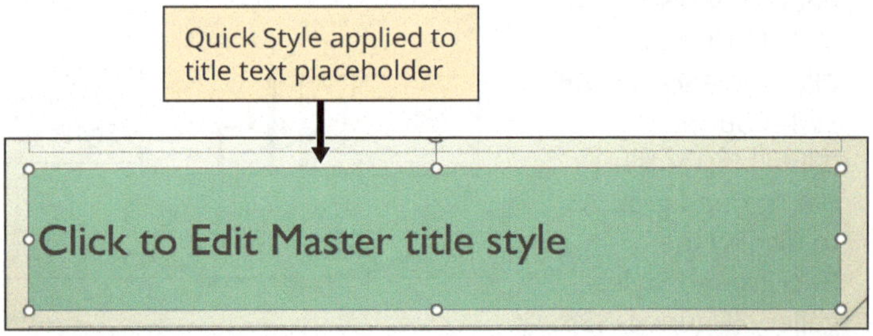

Figure 4–36

5

- Select all five-paragraphs in the subtitle text placeholder and then click the Font Color button to change the font color to 'Dark Green, Text 1, Lighter 10%' (Figure 4–37).

6

- Click outside the subtitle placeholder to deselect the object.

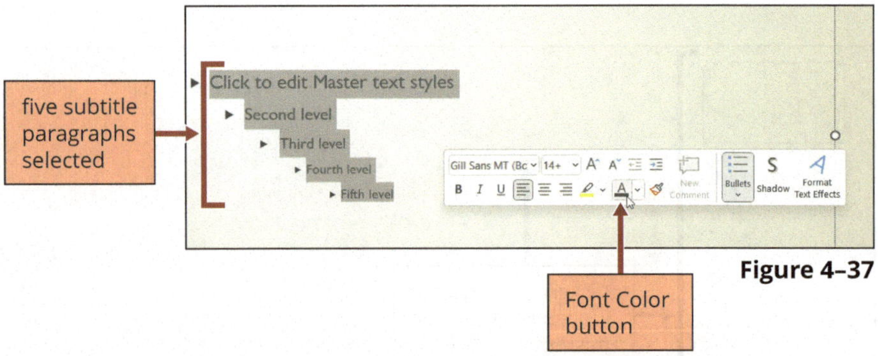

Figure 4–37

To Crop a Picture to a Shape

In addition to cropping a picture, you can change the shape of a picture by cropping it to a specific shape. The picture's proportions are maintained, and it automatically is trimmed to fill the shape's geometry. In the Saving presentation, you want to insert a picture of money cropped in a cloud shape on the Title and Content Layout. You will use the same picture as the Slide 3 background. **Why?** Displaying the same picture repeats the money topic, and the cloud shape reinforces the idea of thinking about money on the title slide. The following steps crop the money picture to a cloud shape.

1

- Display the Title and Content Layout and then display the Insert tab.
- Click the Pictures button, click This Device, and then insert the Support_PPT_4_Money.jpg file, which is located in the Data Files.

2

- Select the money picture and then click the Crop arrow (Picture Format Tab | Size group) to display the Crop menu.
- Point to 'Crop to Shape' to display the Shapes gallery (Figure 4–38).

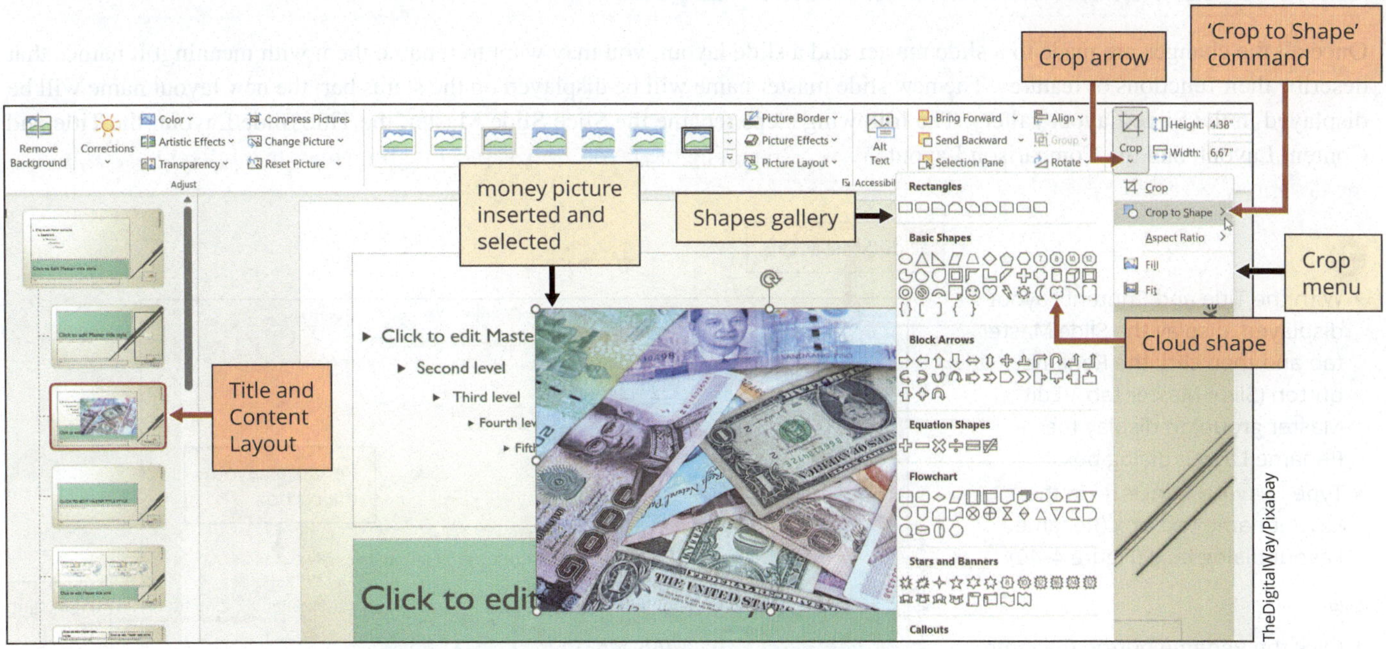

Figure 4–38

3

- Click the Cloud shape (tenth shape in the third Basic Shapes row) to crop the picture.
- Change the shape height to 2.5".
- Use the smart guides to move the picture to the upper-right area of the slide, as shown in Figure 4–39.

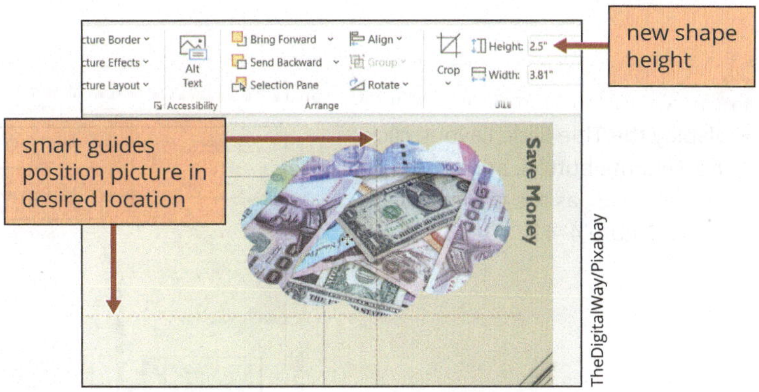

Figure 4–39

To Hide and Unhide Background Graphics

The placeholder, text box, pictures, and other graphical elements are displayed on some slide master layouts and are hidden on others. You have the ability to change the default setting by choosing to hide or unhide the background graphics. The Hide Background Graphics check box is a toggle that displays and conceals the graphics. To hide background graphics on a layout, you would perform the following steps.

1. Display the Slide Master tab, select the desired layout, and then click the Hide Background Graphics check box (Slide Master tab | Background group) to insert a check mark in it.
2. To unhide the graphics, click the same check box to make them appear.

To Rename a Slide Master and a Slide Layout

Once all the changes are made to a slide master and a slide layout, you may want to rename them with meaningful names that describe their functions or features. The new slide master name will be displayed on the status bar; the new layout name will be displayed in the Slide Layout gallery. The following steps rename the Slice Slide Master, the Title Slide Layout, the Title and Content Layout, and the Comparison Layout. **Why?** Renaming the layouts gives meaningful names that reflect the purpose of the design.

1

- With the Title and Content Layout displayed, display the Slide Master tab and then click the Rename button (Slide Master tab | Edit Master group) to display the Rename Layout dialog box.
- Type **Saving Content** in the Layout name text box (Rename Layout dialog box) (Figure 4–40).

2

- Click the Rename button (Rename Layout dialog box) to give the Title and Content Layout the new name, Saving Content Layout.

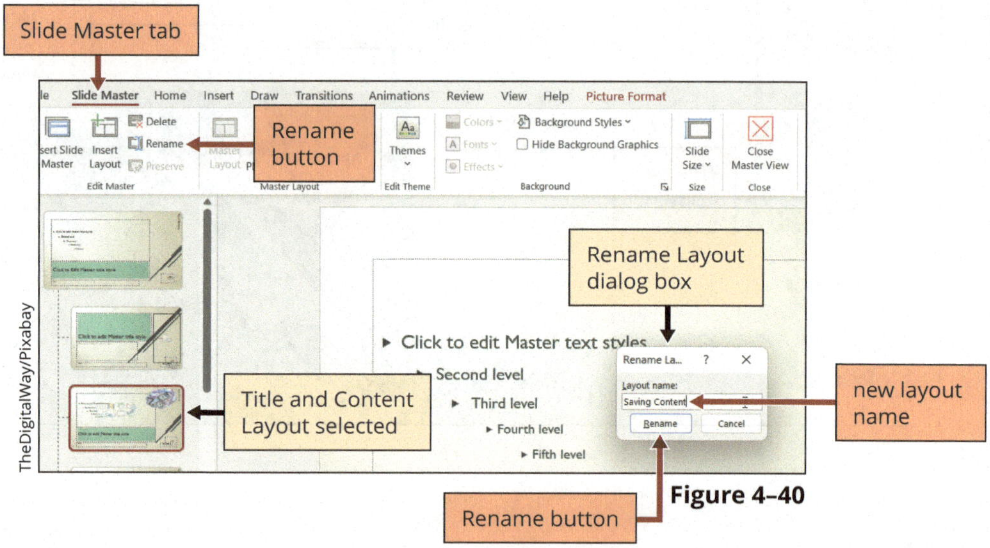

Figure 4–40

3

- Display the Title Slide Layout, click the Rename button, and then type **Saving Title** as the new layout name (Figure 4–41).

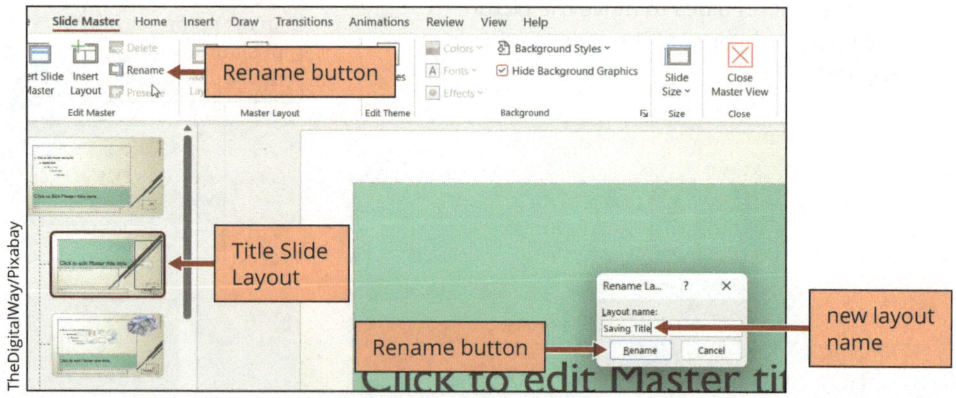

Figure 4–41

4

- Click the Rename button (Rename Layout dialog box) to rename the Title Slide Layout.
- Click the Slice Slide Master layout to display it, click the Rename button, and then type **Saving Master** as the new layout name (Figure 4–42).

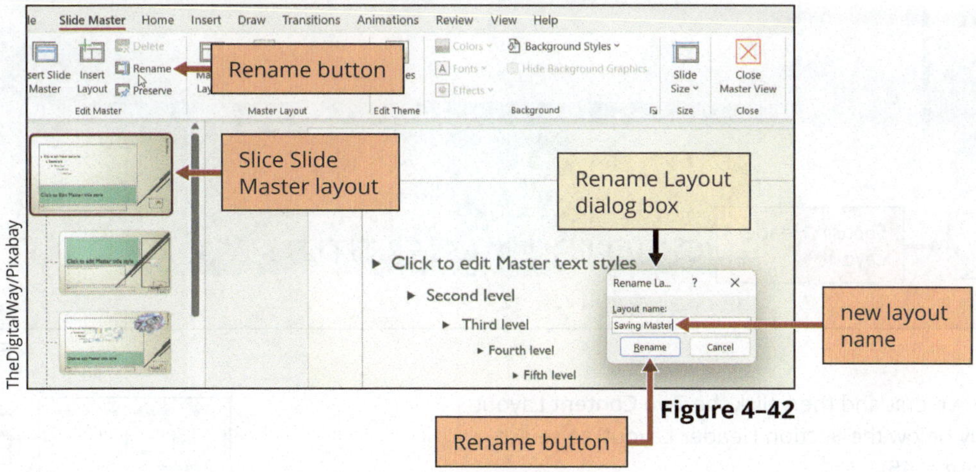

Figure 4–42

5

- Click the Rename button (Rename Layout dialog box).
- Scroll down and display the Comparison Layout, click the Rename button, and then type **Saving Compare** as the new layout name (Figure 4–43).
- Click the Rename button.

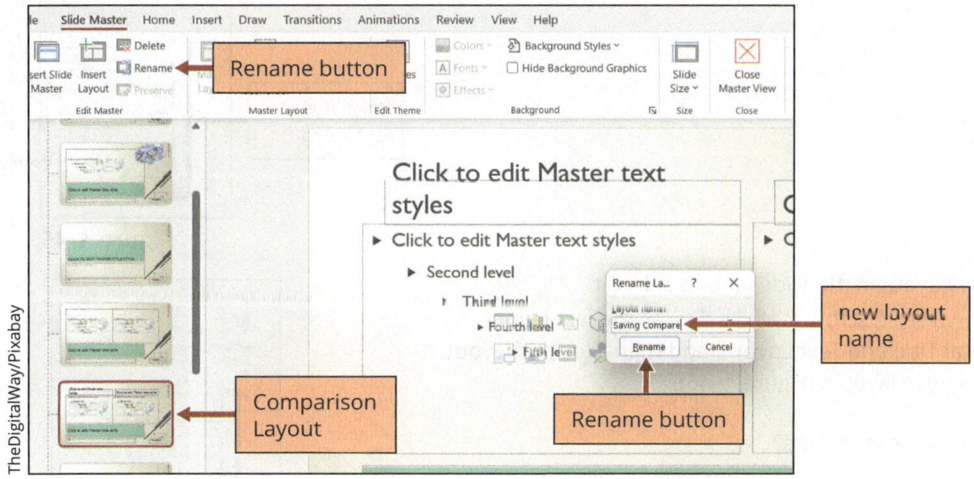

Figure 4–43

To Delete a Slide Layout

You have made many changes to the slide master and three slide layouts. You will use these layouts when you close Master view and then add text to the presentation in Normal view. You can delete the other layouts in the Slides tab. **Why?** You will not use them in this presentation. The following steps delete slide layouts that will not be used to create the presentation.

1

- Scroll up and then click the Section Header Layout in the Slides tab to select it (Figure 4–44).

Figure 4–44

2

- Press and hold down CTRL and then click the Two Content Layout (the layout directly below the Section Header Layout) to select both layouts (Figure 4–45).

3

- Click the Delete button (Slide Master tab | Edit Master group) to delete the two layouts.

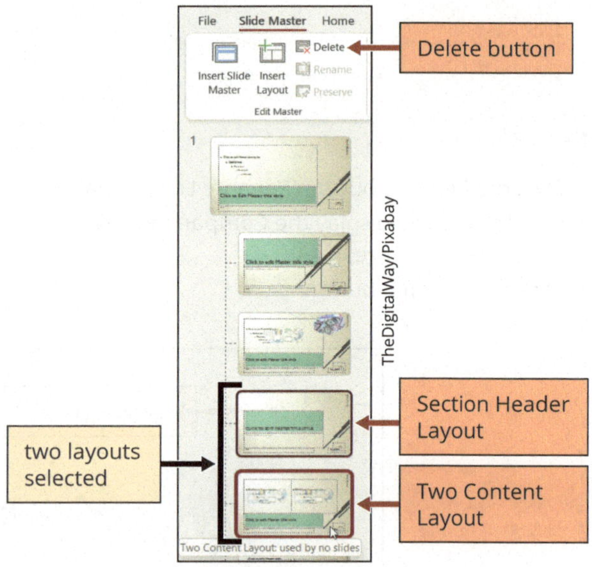

Figure 4–45

4

- Click the Title Only Layout in the Slides tab to select it.
- Press and hold down SHIFT, scroll down to display the last layout, which is the Vertical Title and Text Layout, and then click this layout to select 12 consecutive layouts (Figure 4–46).

Q&A Why did I select these layouts?
You will not use any of these layouts in your presentation.

Why did I hold down SHIFT instead of CTRL to select these layouts?
You press SHIFT to select a range of consecutive slides whereas you press CTRL to select specific slides that may or may not be consecutive.

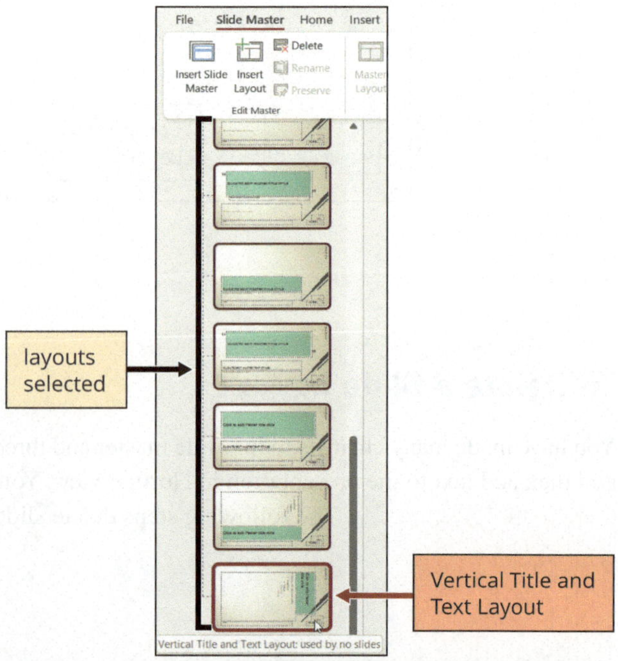

Figure 4–46

5

- Click the Delete button (Slide Master tab | Edit Master group) to delete the 12 layouts (Figure 4–47).

Q&A Now that I have created this slide master, can I ensure that it will not be changed when I create future presentations?

Yes. Normally a slide master is deleted when a new design template is selected. To keep the original master as part of your presentation, you can preserve it by selecting the thumbnail and then clicking Preserve in the Edit Master group. An icon in the shape of a pushpin is displayed below the slide number to indicate the master is preserved. If you decide to unpreserve a slide master, select this thumbnail and then click Preserve.

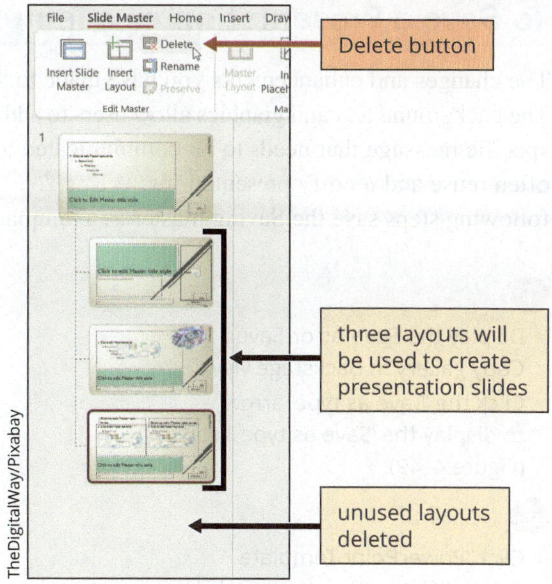

Figure 4–47

Other Ways

1. Click Delete (Home tab | Slides group)
2. Right-click selected slide, click Delete Layout on shortcut menu
3. Press DELETE on keyboard

To Add a New Slide Master Layout

The slide layouts included within each slide master are practical and varied. At times, however, you may desire to create a layout from scratch, especially if your design requires many placeholders and unique design elements. To add a new slide layout, you would perform the following steps.

1. Display the Slide Master tab and then click between the layout thumbnails in the Slides tab to place the pointer where you desire the new slide layout to appear.
2. Click Insert Layout to insert a new slide layout with the name, Custom Layout.
3. Click the Rename button (Slide Master tab | Edit Master group) and type a meaningful name for the new layout.

To Close Master View

You now can exit Master view and return to Normal view. **Why?** All the changes to the slide master are complete. The following steps close Master view.

1

- If necessary, display the Slide Master tab (Figure 4–48).

2

- Click the 'Close Master View' button (Slide Master tab | Close group) to exit Master view and return to Normal view.

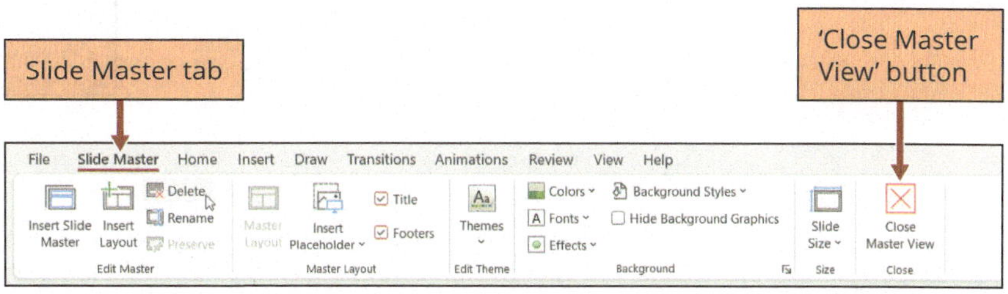

Figure 4–48

To Save a Presentation as a Template

The changes and enhancements you have made to the Saving slide master are excellent starting points for future presentations. The background text and graphics allow users to add text boxes, pictures, SmartArt, tables, and other elements depending upon the specific message that needs to be communicated to an audience. Saving a slide master as a template is convenient when you often reuse and modify presentations. **Why?** You can save your slide layouts as a template to use for a new presentation. The following steps save the Saving master as a template.

1

- Display the Save As or Save a Copy gallery in Backstage view.
- Click the 'Save as type' arrow to display the 'Save as type' list (Figure 4–49).

2

- Click 'PowerPoint Template (*.potx)' in the 'Save as type' list to change the save as type.

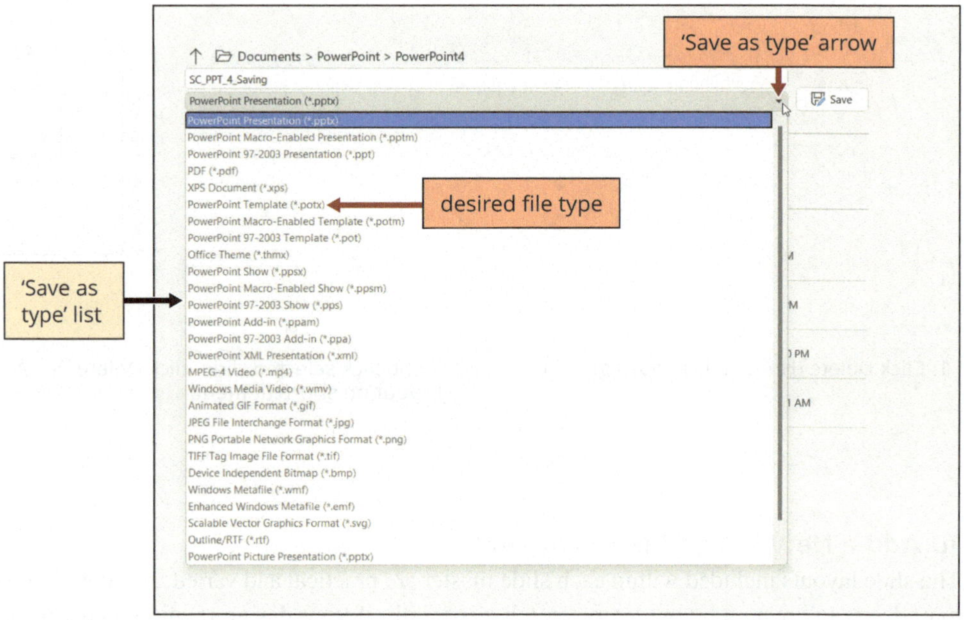

Figure 4–49

Q&A Why do the file name extensions, such as (*.potx), display after the file type in my 'Save as type' list?
These letters identify the file format or type. You can configure Windows to show or hide all common file extensions by opening File Explorer, displaying the View tab, clicking Options, clicking the View tab in the Folder Options dialog box, and then either checking or unchecking 'Hide extensions for known file types' in the Advanced settings area.

- Type **SC_PPT_4_Saving_Template** in the File name box and then navigate to the desired save location (Figure 4–50).

3

- Click Save (Save As or Save a Copy gallery) to save the Saving presentation as a template.

4

- Close the Saving Template file.

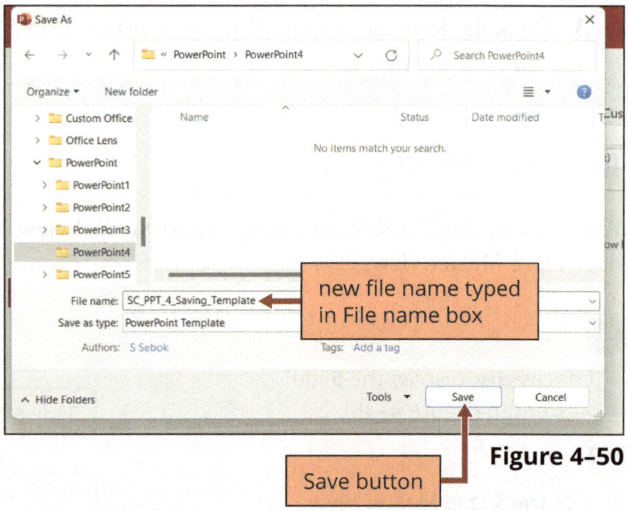

Figure 4–50

Break Point: If you wish to take a break, this is a good place to do so. Be sure the SC_PPT_4_Saving_Template file is saved and then you can exit PowerPoint. To resume later, start PowerPoint and continue following the steps from this location forward.

To Open a Template and Save a Presentation

The Saving Template file you created is a convenient start to a new presentation. The graphical elements and essential slide content are in place; you then can customize the layouts for a specific need, such as a new event or special program. Unless users specify a different location, PowerPoint saves templates they create in a folder called 'Custom Office Templates' in the Documents folder. The following steps open the Saving Template file and save the presentation with the Saving name.

1

- In Backstage view, click the Open tab to display the Open pane.
- If necessary, navigate to the save location, click the file name, SC_PPT_4_Saving_Template.potx, and then click Open (Open dialog box) to open the Saving Template file (Figure 4–51).

Q&A If I did not change the default save location, can I select SC_PPT_4_Saving_Template.potx from the list of Recent Presentations or by opening the Custom Office Templates folder?
Yes. Either technique will locate the desired template.

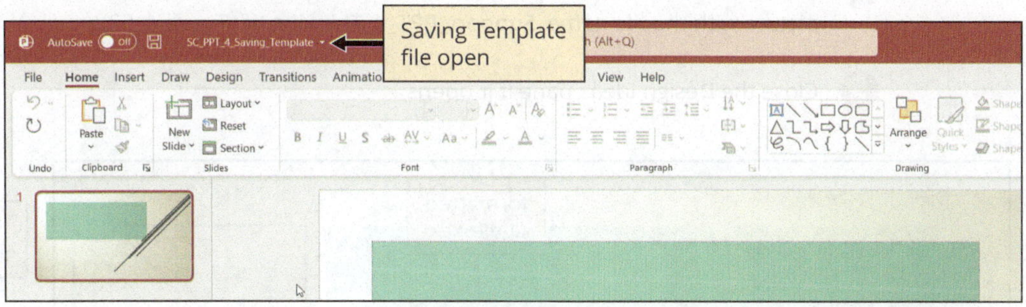

Figure 4–51

2

- In Backstage view, click the Save As or Save a Copy tab to display the Save As or Save a Copy pane.

Q&A Why do I see 'Save a Copy' instead of Save As?
PowerPoint automatically defaults to AutoSave when opening documents.

- Navigate to the location where your files are saved.
- Click the 'Save as type' arrow to display the 'Save as type' list, and then click PowerPoint Presentation (*.pptx) in the 'Save as type' list to change the save as type.
- Click SC_PPT_4_Saving in the Save As dialog box to select the file (Figure 4–52).

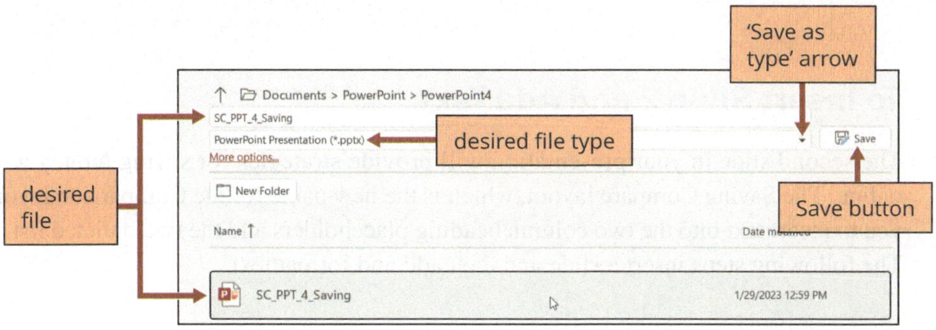

Figure 4–52

3

- Click Save (Save As dialog box) to display the Confirm Save As dialog box.
- Click OK to replace the file.

To Add Text to the Title Slide Layout

The Saving Title layout needs to be applied so that the picture placeholder is displayed on Slide 1. The following steps apply the Saving Title layout and then add text and a picture to the Slide 1 Saving Title layout.

1. Apply the Saving Title layout (Home tab | Slides group), type **Thinking about saving money?** as the title text, and then type **Here's how!** as the subtitle text.
2. Increase the title text font to 72 point and then center and bold this text.
3. Increase the subtitle text font to 48 point, bold and center this text, and then click the Font Color button to change the font color to 'Dark Green, Text 1, Lighter 10%' (last item in the second Theme Colors column).
4. Click the Pictures content placeholder on the right side of the slide and then insert the picture with the file name, Support_PPT_4_Thinking.tif (Figure 4–53).
5. Close the Design Ideas pane if it opens.

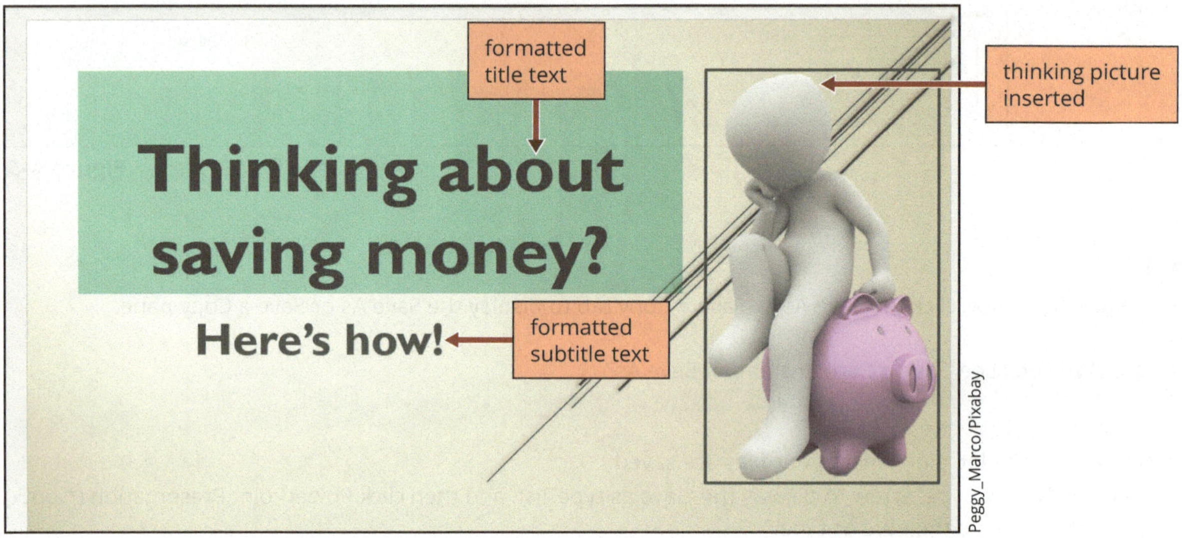

Figure 4–53

To Insert Slide 2 and Add Text

The second slide in your presentation will provide strategies for saving money when shopping online. The Saving Compare layout, which is the new name for the Comparison layout, will allow you to insert text into the two column heading placeholders and the two bulleted list placeholders. The following steps insert a slide and then add and format text.

1. Click the Home tab, insert a slide with the Saving Compare layout, and then type the column headings, bulleted paragraphs, and title text shown in Figure 4–54.

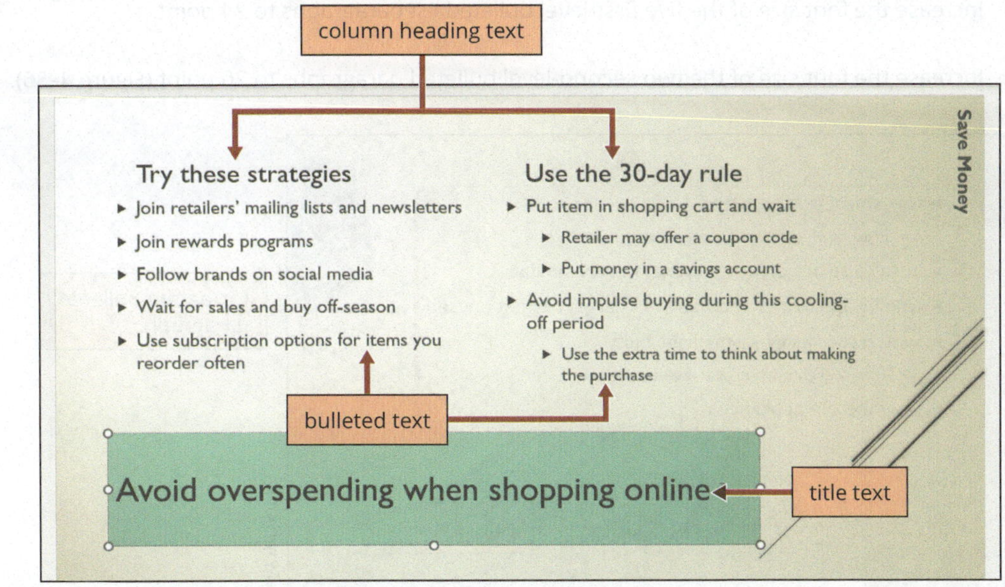

Figure 4–54

To Insert Slide 3 and Add Text

The third slide in your presentation will list details about handling funds and reviewing your spending. The Saving Content layout, which is the new name for the Title and Content Layout, is designed so that you can add variable slide content in the placeholder located next to the picture. The following steps insert a slide and then add and format text.

1. Insert a slide with the Saving Content layout and then type the text shown in Figure 4–55.
2. Increase the font size of the three first-level bulleted paragraphs to 24 point.
3. Increase the font size of the four second-level bulleted paragraphs to 20 point (Figure 4–55).

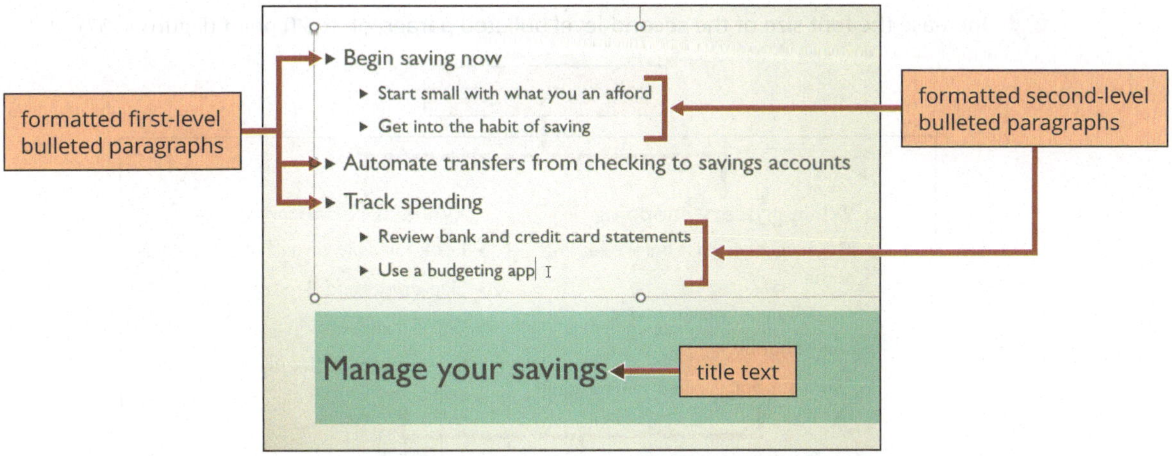

Figure 4–55

To Insert Slide 4 and Add Text

The fourth slide in your presentation will list steps to conserve electricity. This slide uses the Saving Content layout, which you used to create Slide 3. The following steps insert a slide and then add and format text.

1. Insert a slide with the Saving Content layout and then type the text shown in Figure 4–56.
2. Increase the font size of the five first-level bulleted list paragraphs to 24 point.
3. Increase the font size of the two second-level bulleted paragraphs to 20 point (Figure 4–56).

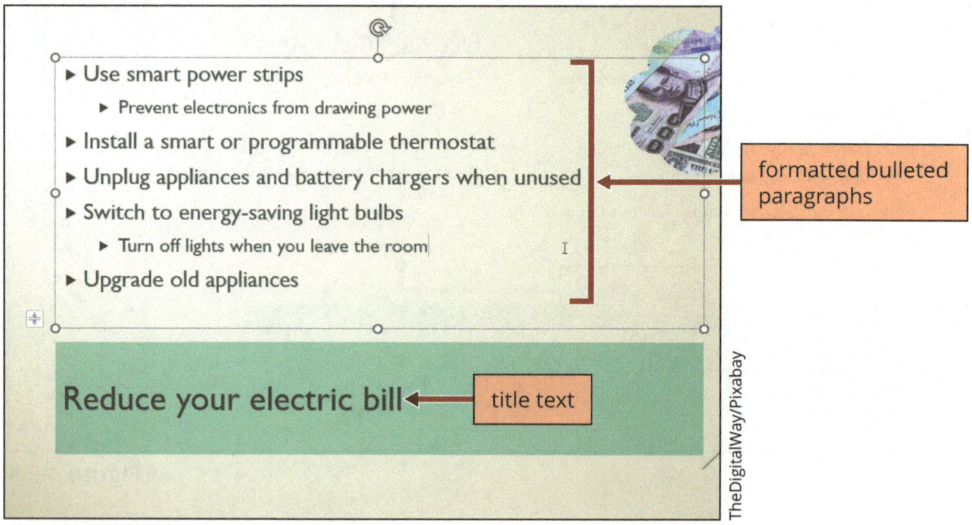

Figure 4–56

To Insert Slide 5 and Add Text

The last slide in your presentation gives advice on saving money when grocery shopping and dining at restaurants. It uses the Saving Compare layout, which is the layout you used for Slide 2. The following steps insert a slide and then add and format text.

1. Insert a slide with the Saving Compare layout and then type the text shown in Figure 4–57.
2. Increase the font size of the seven first-level bulleted paragraphs to 24 point.
3. Increase the font size of the second-level bulleted paragraph to 20 point (Figure 4–57).

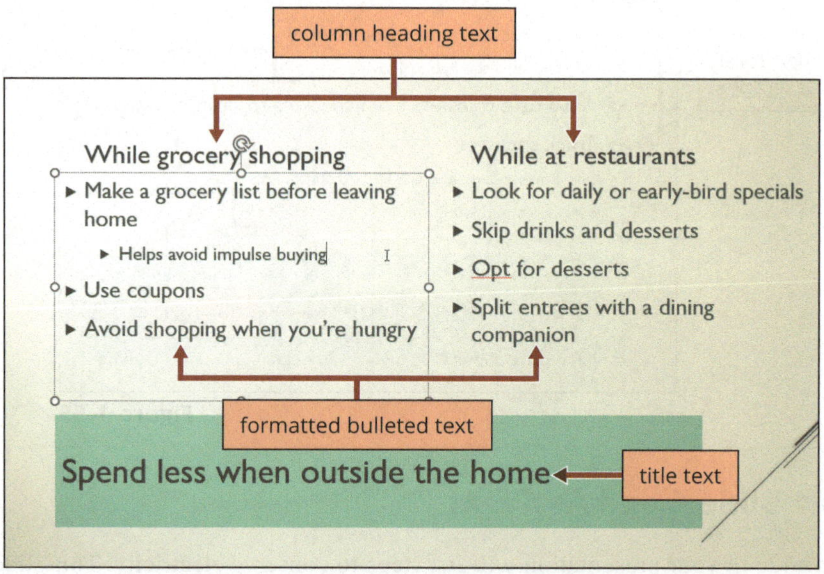

Figure 4–57

To Use the Thesaurus

Why? When reviewing your slide show, you may decide that a particular word does not express the exact usage you intended or that you used the same word on multiple slides. In these cases, you could find a **synonym**, or word similar in meaning, to replace the inappropriate or duplicate word. PowerPoint provides a **thesaurus**, which is a list of synonyms, to help you find a replacement word.

In this project, you want to find a synonym to replace the word, savings, on Slide 3 with the word, funds. The following steps locate an appropriate synonym and replace the word.

BTW

Touch Mode Differences

The Microsoft 365 and Windows interfaces may vary if you are using a touch screen. For this reason, you might notice that the function or appearance of your touch screen differs slightly from this module's presentation.

1

- Display Slide 3 and then place the insertion point in the word, savings, in the title text placeholder.

2

- Display the Review tab and then click the Thesaurus button (Review tab | Proofing group) to display the Thesaurus pane with synonyms for the word, savings (Figure 4–58).

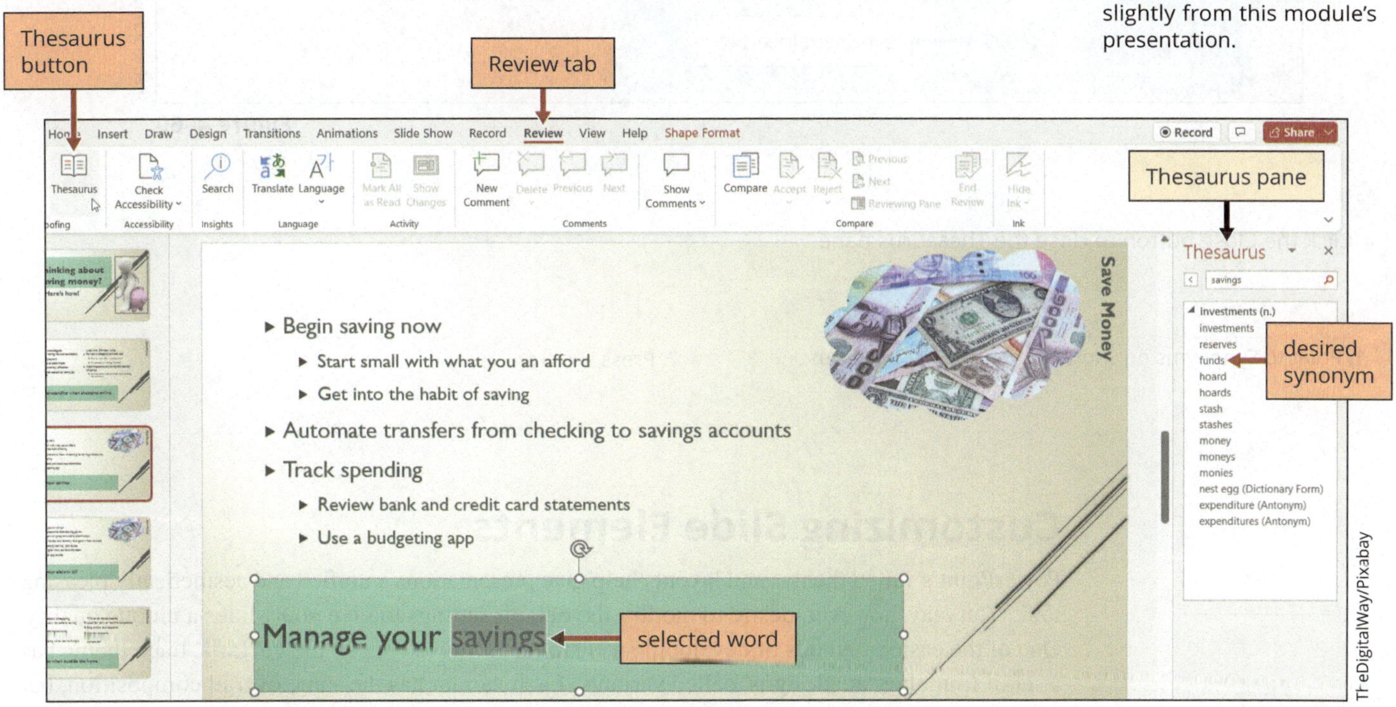

TI eDigitalWay/Pixabay

Figure 4–58

3

- Point to the synonym you want (funds) in the synonyms list and then click the arrow on the right side of that word to display the synonym menu (Figure 4–59).

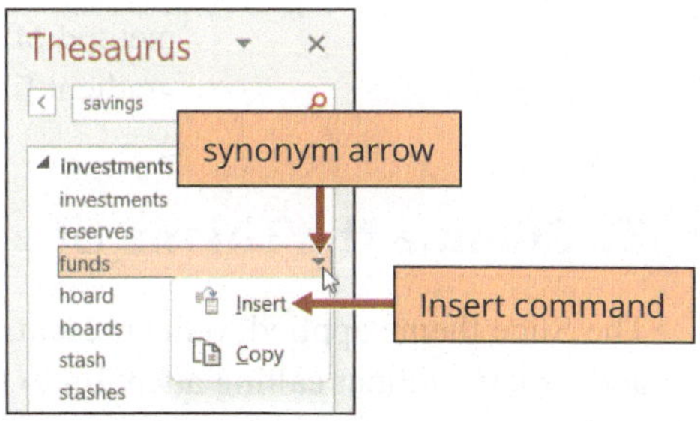

Figure 4–59

Q&A How do I locate a synonym for multiple words?

You need to select all the words and then right-click to display the shortcut menu.

If I am using a touch screen, how do I find a synonym?

Tap Thesaurus (Review tab | Proofing group) to display the Thesaurus pane for the selected word. Then, in the pane, tap the arrow next to the word to display a shortcut menu.

4

- Click Insert to replace the word, savings, with the word, funds (Figure 4–60).

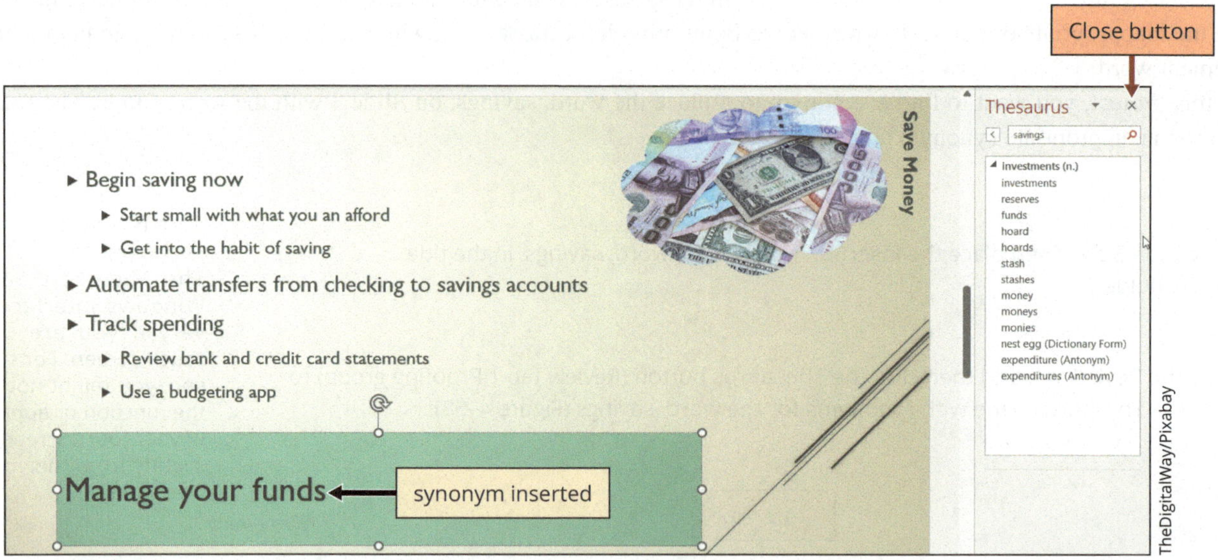

Figure 4–60

5

- Click the Close button to close the Thesaurus pane.

Other Ways

1. Point to Synonyms on shortcut menu, click Thesaurus
2. Press SHIFT+F7

Customizing Slide Elements

PowerPoint's varied themes and layouts help give presentations a unified and aesthetically pleasing look. You may, however, desire to modify the default settings to give your slides a unique quality. One of the easier methods of developing a custom show is to change the **variant**. Each theme has a set of four alternate designs, called variants. Each variant has the same overall composition, but the colors, fonts, and design elements differ. You can select a variant that best fits your overall design needs. If you later decide that another variant would better fit the presentation's general theme, you can change this element while you are developing slides.

You also can change the theme for one or more slides, not an entire presentation. One other method of altering your slides slightly is to change the backgrounds, including adding a picture, gradient fill, pattern, or texture.

To Change the Theme of a Single Slide

The Slice theme applied to the presentation is appropriate for this topic. The font and placeholder locations are simple and add variety without calling attention to the design elements. The following steps change the theme for Slide 5. **Why?** To call attention to the electricity content in the bulleted list on Slide 5, you can apply an equally effective theme that has a design element resembling a circuit board. You then can modify this new theme by changing the variant on one slide.

1

- Display Slide 4, click the Design tab, click the Themes More button, and then point to the Circuit theme to see a preview of that theme on Slide 4 (Figure 4–61).
- **Experiment:** Point to various document themes in the Themes gallery and watch the colors and fonts change on Slide 4.

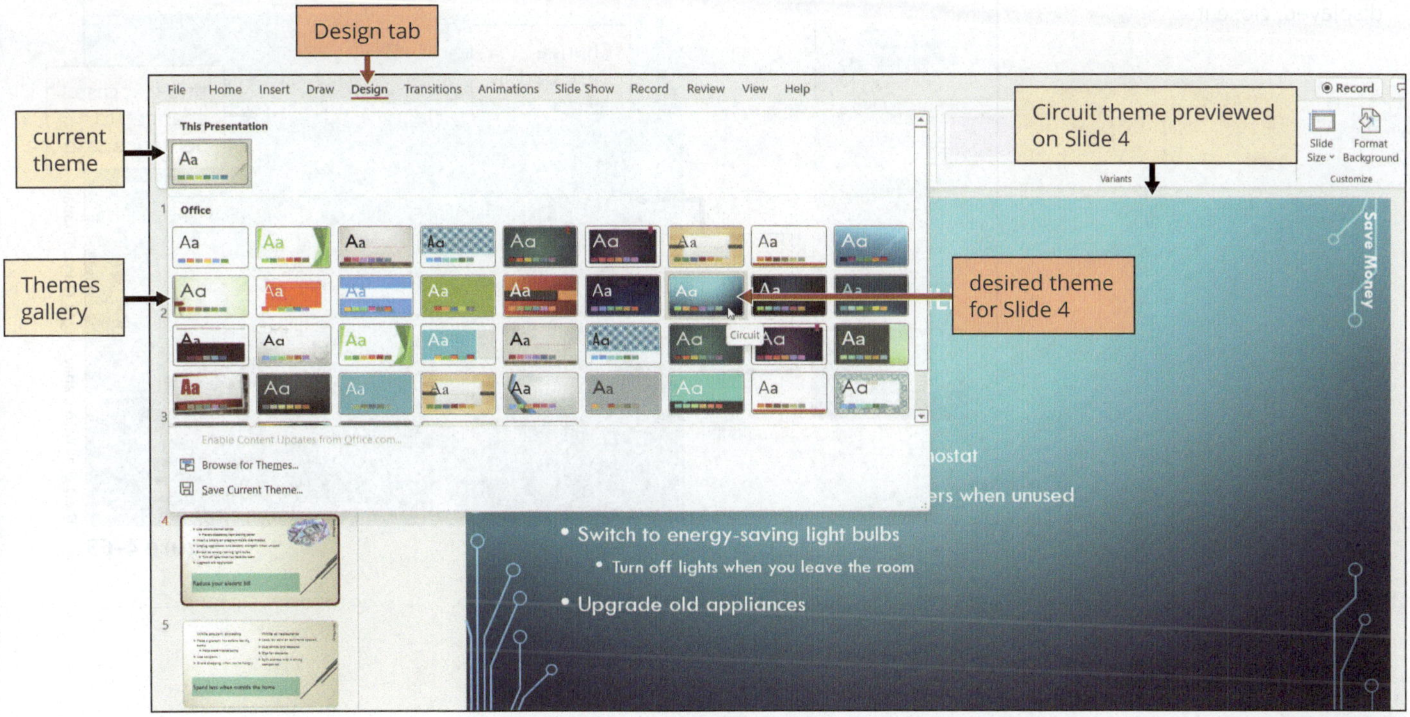

Figure 4–61

2

- Right-click the Circuit theme to display a shortcut menu (Figure 4–62).

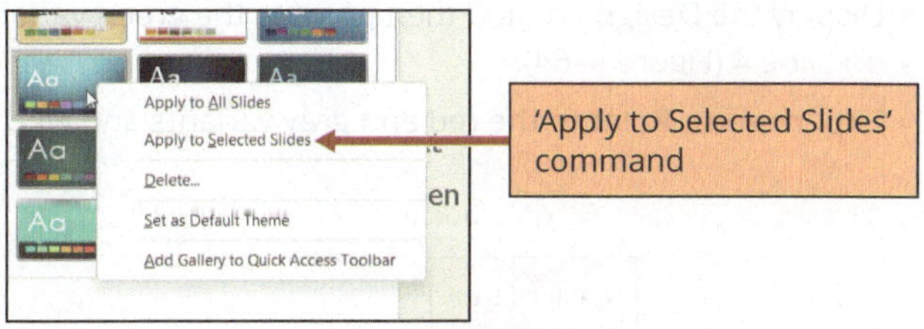

Figure 4–62

3

- Click 'Apply to Selected Slides' to apply the Circuit theme to Slide 4 only.

4

- Select the title text (REDUCE YOUR ELECTRIC BILL), display the Home tab, and then click the Change Case button.
- Click Sentence case. in the Change Case gallery to change the case of the title text.

5

- Click outside of the title text placeholder to deselect the object (Figure 4-63).
- If the Design Ideas pane is displayed, close it.

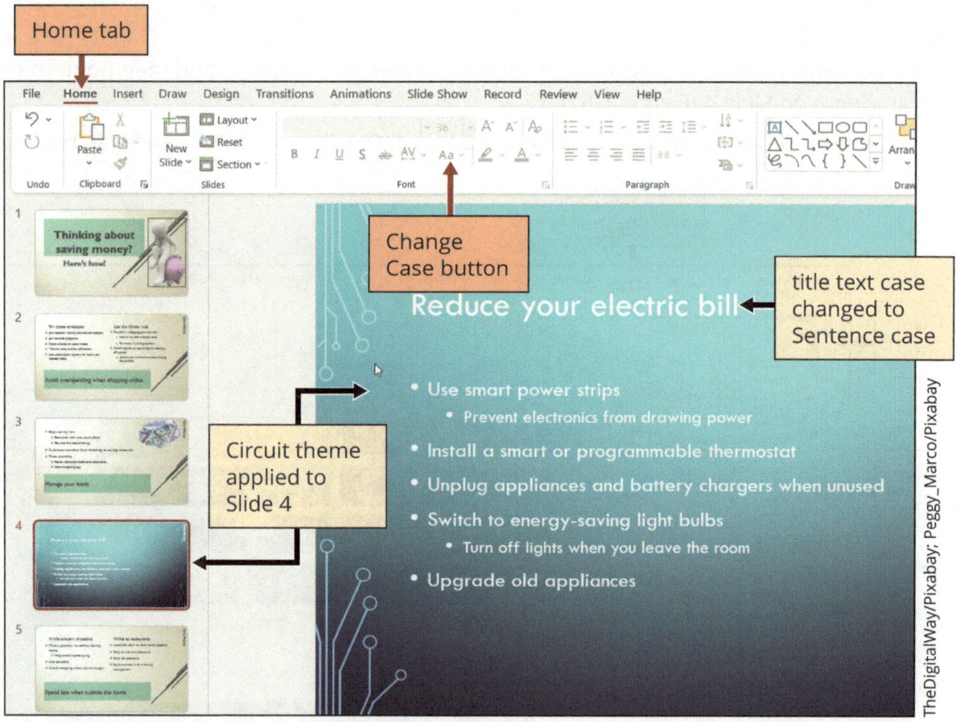

TheDigitalWay/Pixabay; Peggy_Marco/Pixabay

Figure 4–63

To Change the Theme Variant

The Circuit theme on Slide 4 has a default blue variant. You can change the color variant for this slide at any time for any theme, and you want to change the color to green **Why?** The theme colors are green, so this color on Slide 4 complements the presentation's color scheme. The following steps change the variant from blue to green.

1

- Display the Design tab and then point to the green variant (Design tab | Variants group) to see a preview of the green variant on Slide 4 (Figure 4–64).
- **Experiment:** Point to the red and gray variants and watch the colors change on the slide.

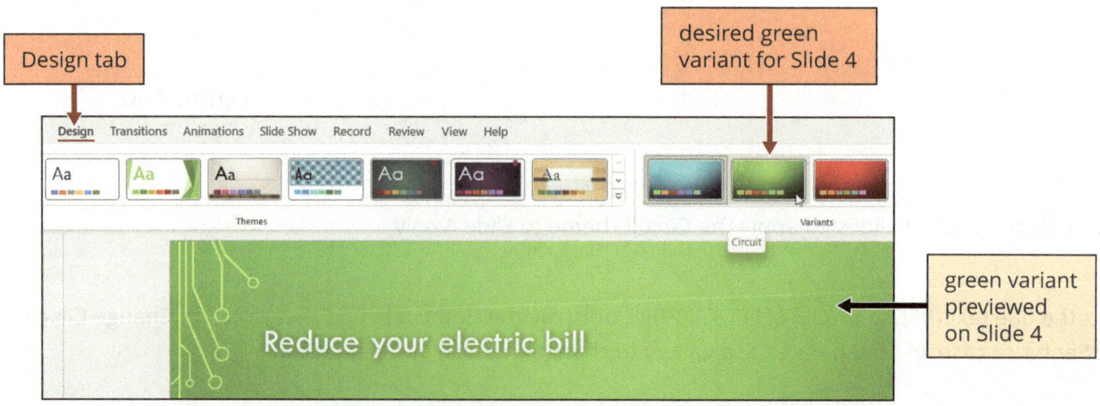

Figure 4–64

2

- Click the green variant to apply this color to Slide 4 (Figure 4–65).

Q&A If I decide at some future time that this color variation does not fit the theme of my presentation, can I apply a different variant?
Yes. You can repeat these steps at any time.

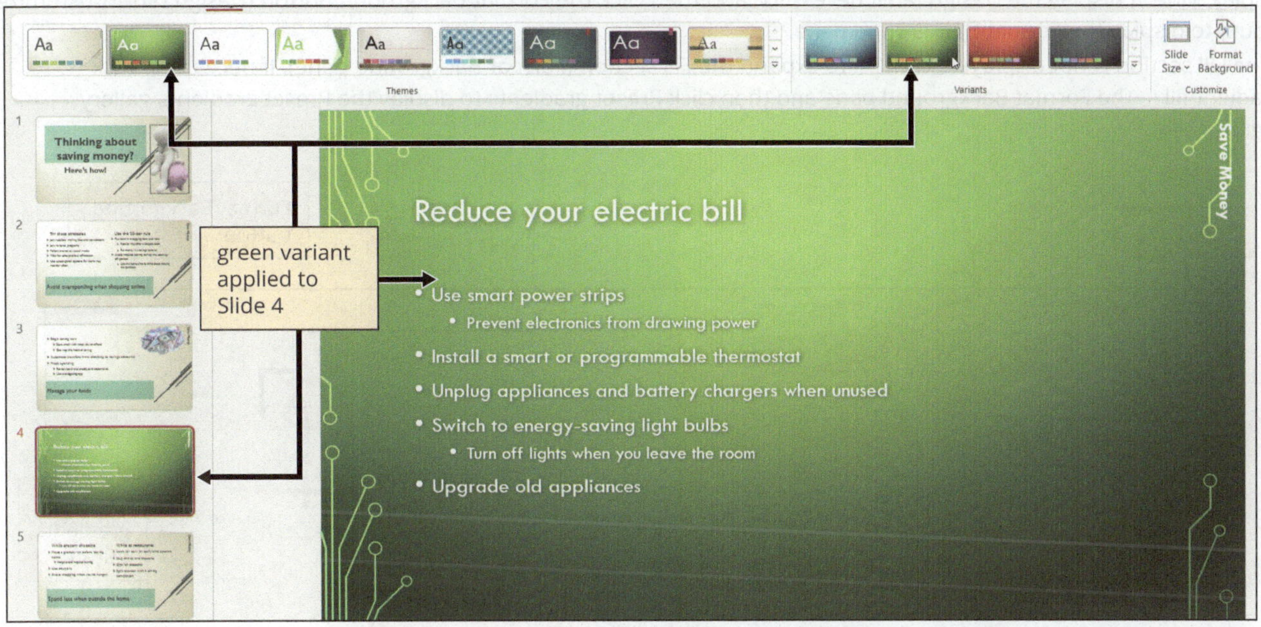

TheDigitalWay/Pixabay; Peggy_Marco/Pixabay

Figure 4–65

3

- If the Design Ideas pane is displayed, close it.

Formatting Slide Backgrounds

A slide's background is an integral part of a presentation because it can generate audience interest. Every slide can have the same background, or different backgrounds can be used in a presentation. This background is considered **fill**, which is the content that makes up the interior of a shape, line, or character. Four fills are available: solid, gradient, picture or texture, and pattern. **Solid fill** is one color used throughout the entire slide. **Gradient fill** is one color shade gradually progressing to another shade of the same color or one color progressing to another color. **Picture fill** uses a specific file or image to fill the background or shape. **Texture fill** uses a specific file or an image that simulates a material, such as cork, granite, marble, or canvas. **Pattern fill** adds designs, such as dots or dashes, which repeat in rows across the slide.

Once you add a fill, you can adjust its appearance. For example, you can adjust its **transparency**, or the opacity of an object, which allows you to see through the background, so that any text on the slide is visible. You also can select a color that is part of the theme or a custom color. You can use an **offset**, another background feature, to move the background away from the slide borders in varying distances by percentage. A **tiling option** repeats the background image many times vertically and horizontally on the slide; the smaller the tiling percentage, the greater the number of times the image is repeated.

To Change the Slide Background to a Gradient Fill

For each theme, PowerPoint provides 30 preset gradient fills with five designs for each of the six major theme colors. Each fill has one dark color shade that gradually lightens to either another shade of the same color or another color. You decide that a gradient fill would be suitable for Slide 1. **Why?** The current background is plain, so you want to add a minimal design element to enhance the overall slide. The following steps replace the background on Slide 1 to a preset gradient fill.

1

- Display Slide 1, display the Design tab if necessary, and then click the Format Background button (Design tab | Customize group) to display the Format Background pane.
- If the Fill section is not displayed, click Fill to expand the Fill section (Format Background pane). If necessary, click Gradient fill in the Format Background pane and then click Preset gradients to display the Preset gradients gallery (Figure 4–66).

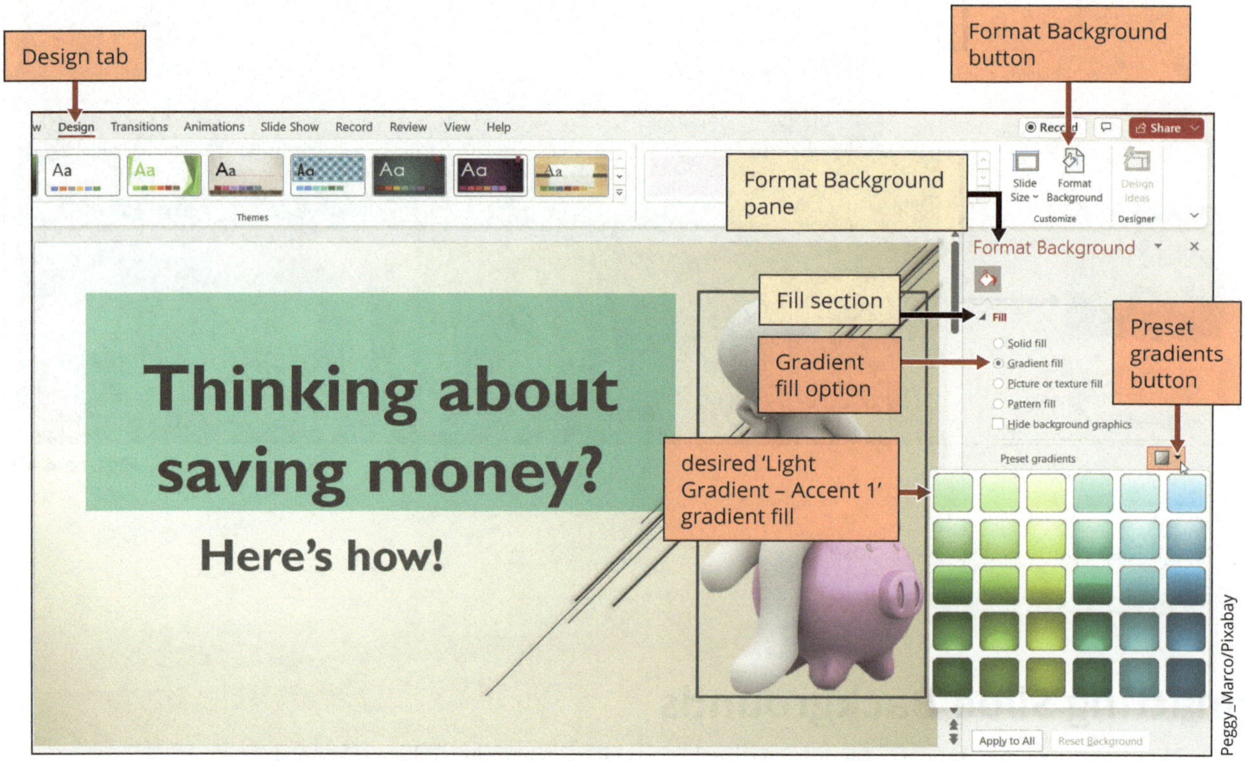

Figure 4–66

Q&A Are the backgrounds displayed in a specific order?
Yes. The first row has light colors at the top of the background; the middle rows have darker fills at the bottom; the bottom row has overall dark fills on all edges.

Is a live preview available to see the various gradients on this slide?
No. Live preview is not an option with the background textures and fills.

2

- Click 'Light Gradient – Accent 1' (first fill in the first row) to apply that style to Slide 1 (Figure 4–67).

Q&A If I decide later that this background gradient does not fit the theme of my presentation, can I apply a different background?
Yes. You can repeat these steps at any time while creating your presentation.

Peggy_Marco/Pixabay

Figure 4–67

Other Ways

1. Click Design tab, click Format Background (Customize group), select desired options (Format Background pane)
2. Right-click background, click Format Background on shortcut menu, select desired options (Format Background pane)

To Change the Slide Background to a Picture

Why? For variety and interest, you want to use a picture as the Slide 3 background. The picture can be the same picture inserted in the Saving Content slide master. PowerPoint will stretch the height and width of this picture to fill the slide area. The following steps insert the money picture as a background on Slide 3 only.

1

- Display Slide 3. With the Fill section displayed (Format Background pane), click 'Picture or texture fill', click Insert (Format Background pane), and then click From a File to display the Insert Picture dialog box. If necessary, navigate to the location where your Data Files are located.
- Click Support_PPT_4_Money to select the .jpg file (Figure 4–68).

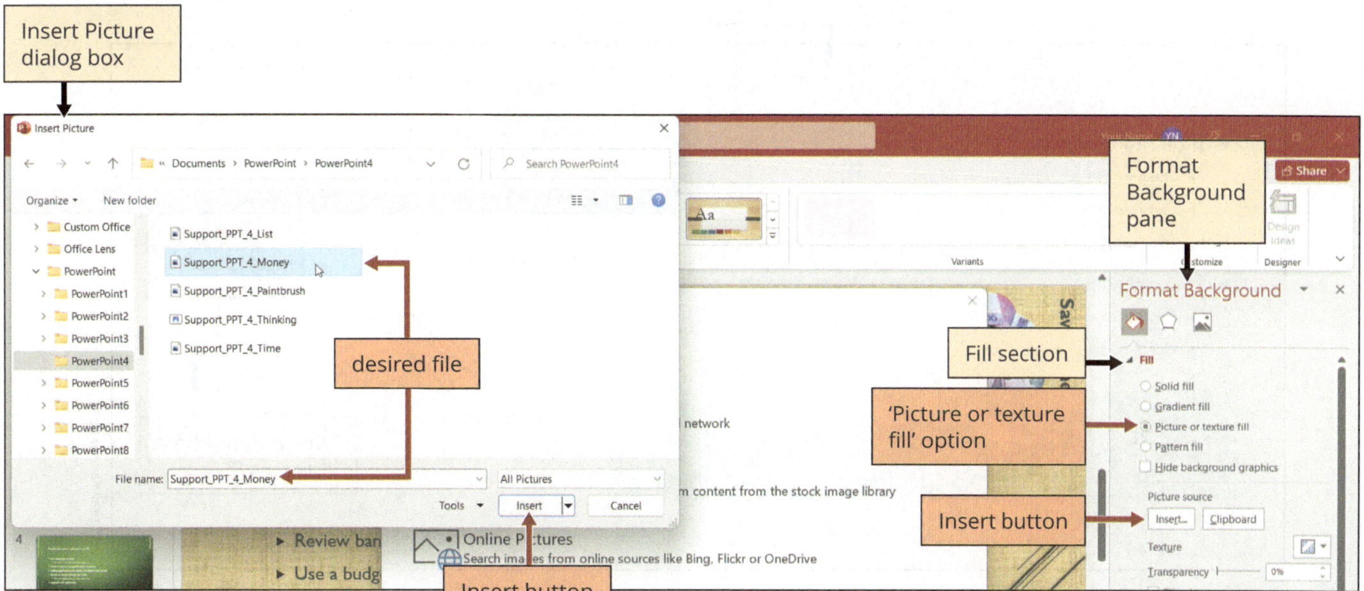

Figure 4–68

2

- Click the Insert button (Insert Picture dialog box) to insert the money picture as the Slide 2 background (Figure 4–69).

Q&A What if I do not want to use this picture?
Click Undo on the Home tab or click Reset Background at the bottom of the Format Background pane.

Figure 4–69

To Change the Transparency of a Slide Background

The **Transparency slider** lets you indicate the degree of an object's opaqueness. The default setting is 0, which is fully opaque. The opposite extreme is 100%, which is fully transparent. To change the transparency, you can move the Transparency slider or enter a number in the box next to the slider. The following step increases the Slide 3 background transparency to 85%. **Why?** The colorful money picture is obscuring the slide text.

1

- Click the Transparency slider in the Fill section (Format Background pane) and drag it to the right until 85% is displayed in the Transparency box (Figure 4–70).

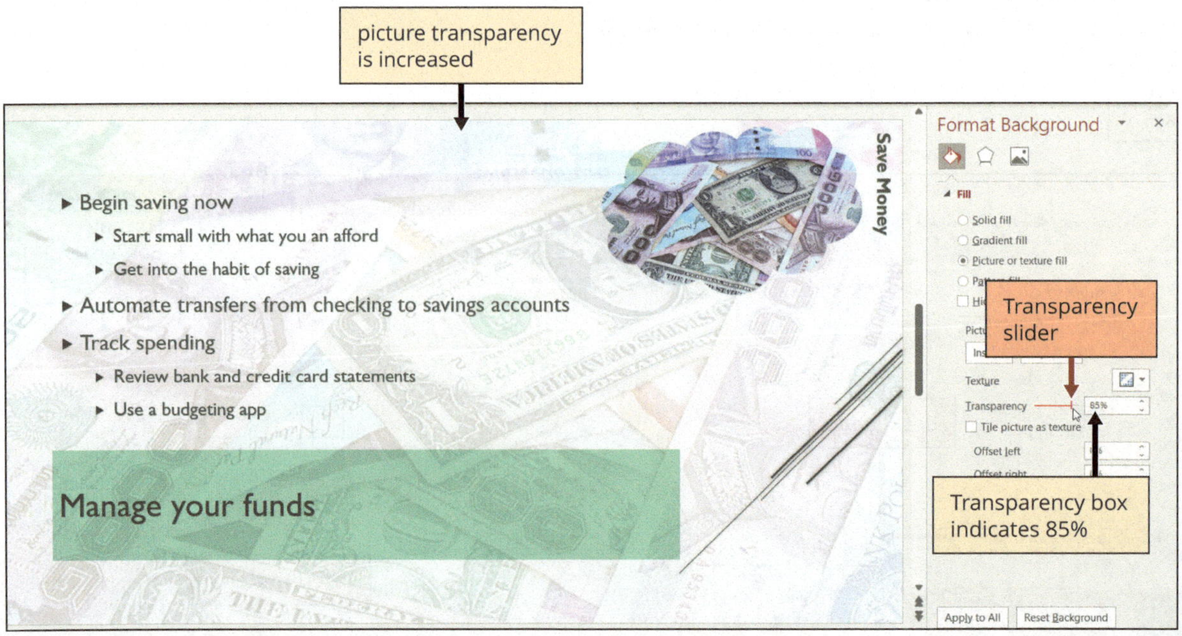

Figure 4–70

- **Experiment:** Drag the Transparency slider to the left and right and watch the text box background change.

Q&A Can I move the slider in small increments so that I can get a precise percentage easily?
Yes. Click the up or down arrows in the Transparency box to move the slider in 1% increments.

Other Ways

1. Enter percentage in Transparency text box
2. Click Transparency up or down arrow

To Change the Slide Background to a Pattern

You add variety to a slide by making a pattern fill. This design of repeating horizontal or vertical lines, dots, dashes, or stripes can enhance the visual appeal of one or more slides in the presentation. If you desire to change the colors in the pattern, PowerPoint allows you to select the fill foreground and background colors by clicking Color and then choosing the desired colors. The following steps apply a pattern to Slide 2. **Why?** The dots in this pattern are a subtle contrast to the Slice theme slide elements.

1

- Display Slide 2. With the Fill section displayed (Format Background pane), click Pattern fill to display the Pattern gallery and the Dotted: 5% pattern on Slide 2 (Figure 4–71).
- **Experiment:** Click various patterns in the Pattern gallery and watch the Slide 3 background change.

Q&A How can I delete a pattern if I decide not to apply one to my slide?
If the Format Background pane is displayed, click Reset Background. If you already have applied the pattern, you must click Undo on the Quick Access Toolbar.

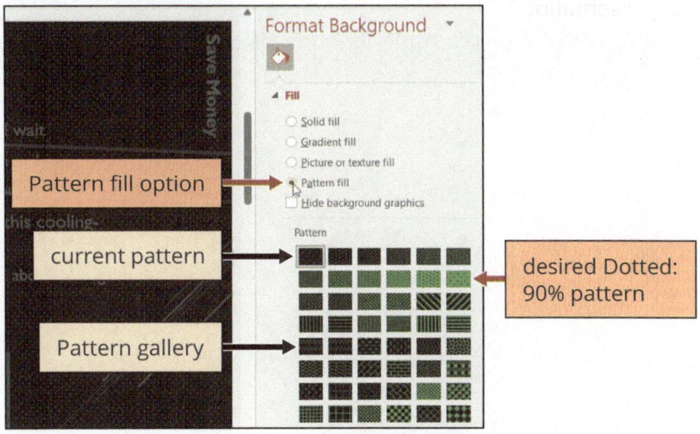

Figure 4–71

2

- Click Dotted: 90% (last pattern in the second row) to apply this pattern to the Slide 2 background (Figure 4–72).

Q&A Can I apply this pattern to all the slides in the presentation?
Yes. You would click 'Apply to All' in the Format Background pane.

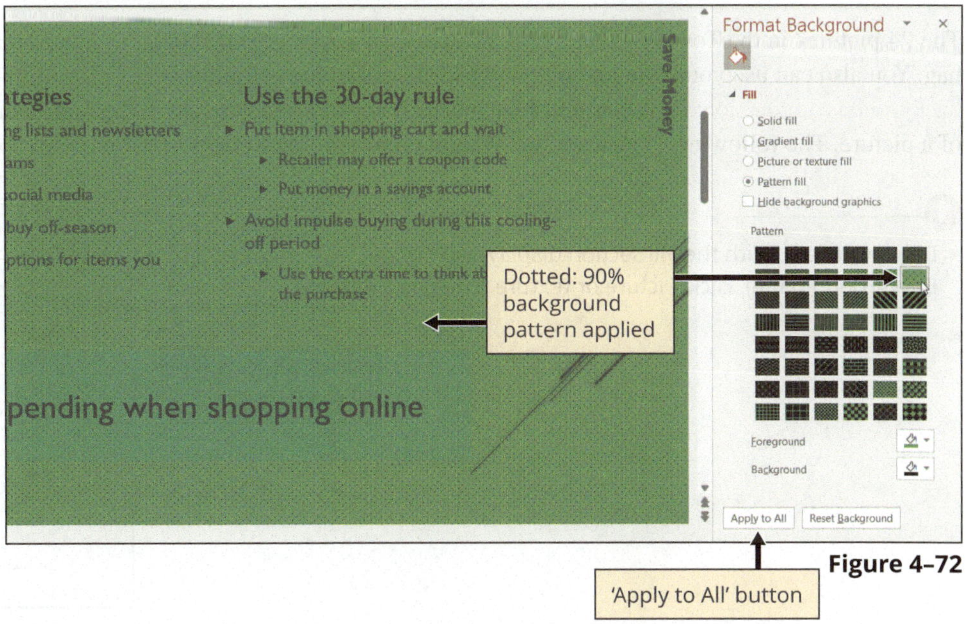

Figure 4–72

3

- Click the Foreground button (Format Background pane) to display the Colors gallery (Figure 4–73).

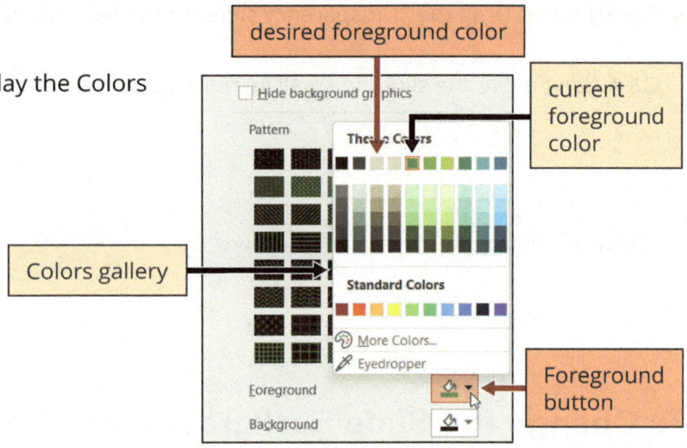

Figure 4–73

4

- Click 'Tan, Background 2' (third color in the first Theme Colors row) to change the foreground color (Figure 4–74).

Q&A Can I apply this pattern and color to all the slides in the presentation?
Yes. You would click 'Apply to All' in the Format Background pane.

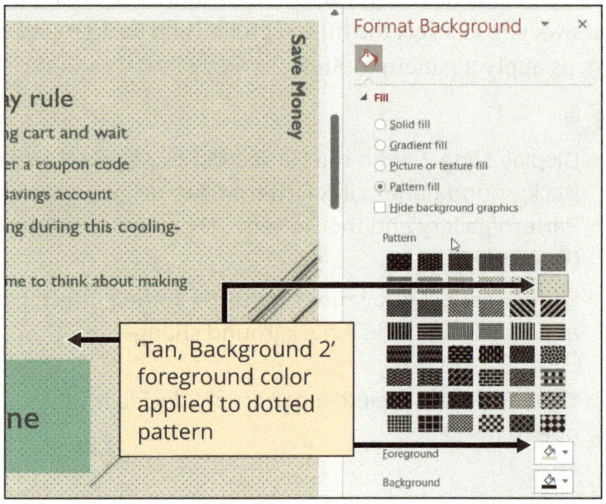

Figure 4–74

To Change the Slide Background to a Texture

The 24 pictures in the Texture gallery give the appearance of a physical object, such as marble, sand, tissue paper, and a paper bag. You also can use your own texture pictures for custom backgrounds. **Why?** Various texture fills are available to give your background a unique look. You can adjust the transparency of a slide texture in the same manner that you change the transparency of a picture. The following steps insert the Walnut texture fill on Slide 5 in the presentation and then change the transparency.

1

- Display Slide 5. With the Fill section displayed (Format Background pane), click 'Picture or texture fill' (Figure 4–75).

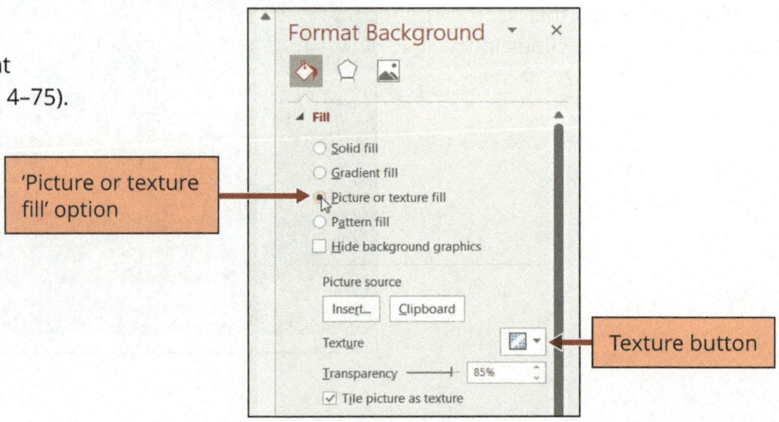

Figure 4–75

2

- Click the Texture button to display the Texture gallery (Figure 4–76).

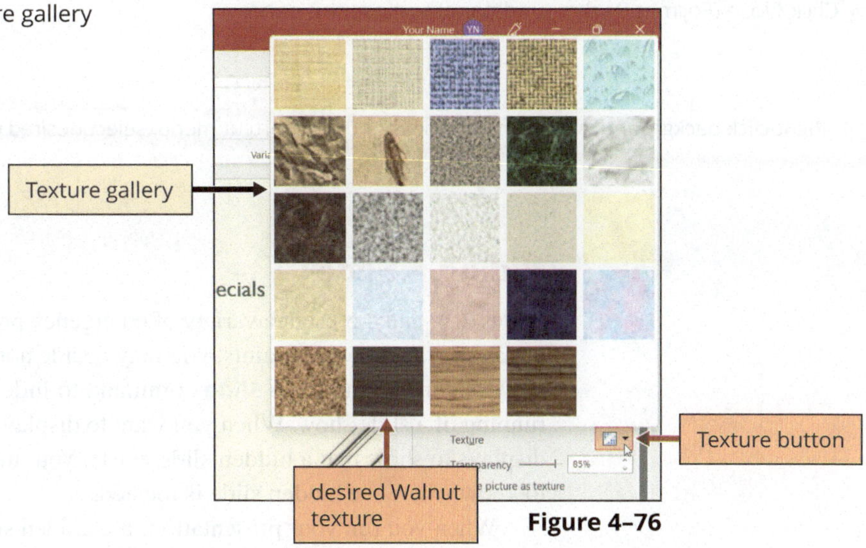

Figure 4–76

3

- Click the Walnut texture (second texture in the last row) to insert this texture fill as the background on Slide 5 (Figure 4–77).

Q&A Is a live preview available to see the various textures on this slide?

No. Live preview is not an option with the background textures and fills.

Why doesn't the Walnut texture appear dark brown as shown in the Texture gallery?

Because the transparency still is set to 85%.

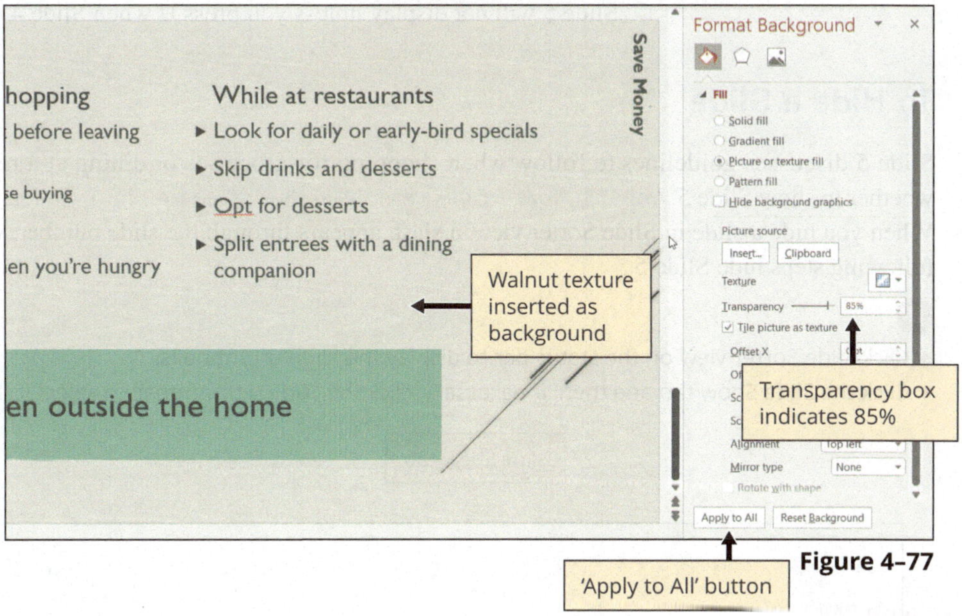

Figure 4–77

4

- Click the Transparency slider and drag it to the left until 75% is displayed in the Transparency box (Figure 4–78).
- **Experiment:** Drag the Transparency slider to the left and right and watch the slide background change.

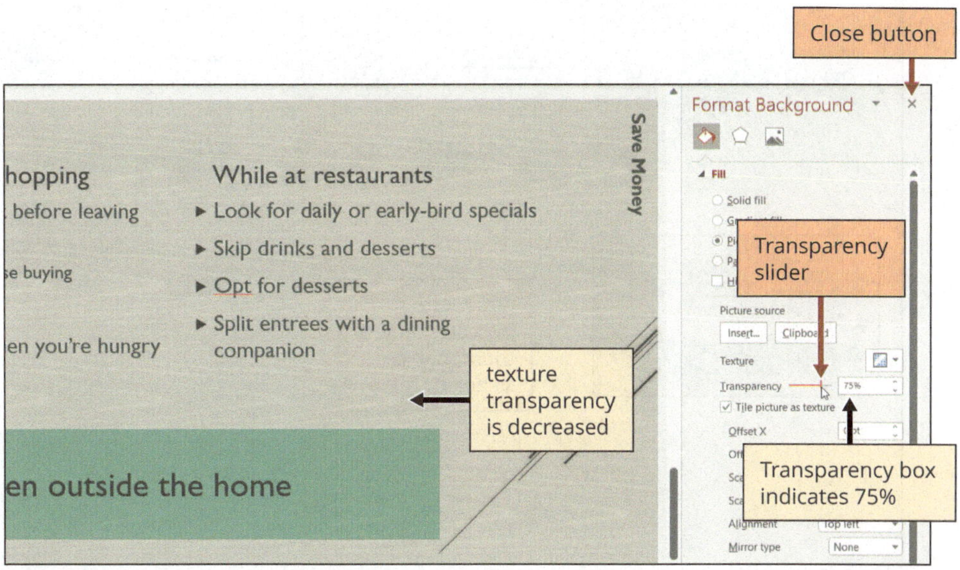

Figure 4–78

5

- Click Close (Format Background pane) to close the pane.

Other Ways

1. Right-click background, click Format Background on shortcut menu, select desired options (Format Background pane)

Hiding a Slide

Slides 2, 3, and 4 present a variety of emergency preparation advice. Depending on the audience's needs and the time constraints, you may decide not to display one or more of these slides. If need be, you can use the **Hide Slide** command to hide a slide from the audience during the normal running of a slide show. When you want to display the hidden slide, press H. No visible indicator displays to show that a hidden slide exists. You must be aware of the content of the presentation to know where the hidden slide is located.

When you run your presentation, the hidden slide does not display unless you press H when the slide preceding the hidden slide is displayed. For example, if you choose to hide Slide 5, then Slide 5 will not display unless you press H when Slide 4 displays in Slide Show view.

To Hide a Slide

Slide 5 discusses guidelines to follow when shopping for groceries or dining at a restaurant. As the presenter, you decide whether to show Slide 5. **Why?** If time permits, or if the audience requires information on this subject, you can display Slide 5. When you hide a slide in Slide Sorter view, a slash appears through the slide number, which indicates the slide is hidden. The following steps hide Slide 5.

1

- Click Slide Sorter view on the status bar to display the slide thumbnails.
- Click the Slide Show tab and then, if necessary, click the Slide 5 thumbnail to select it (Figure 4–79).

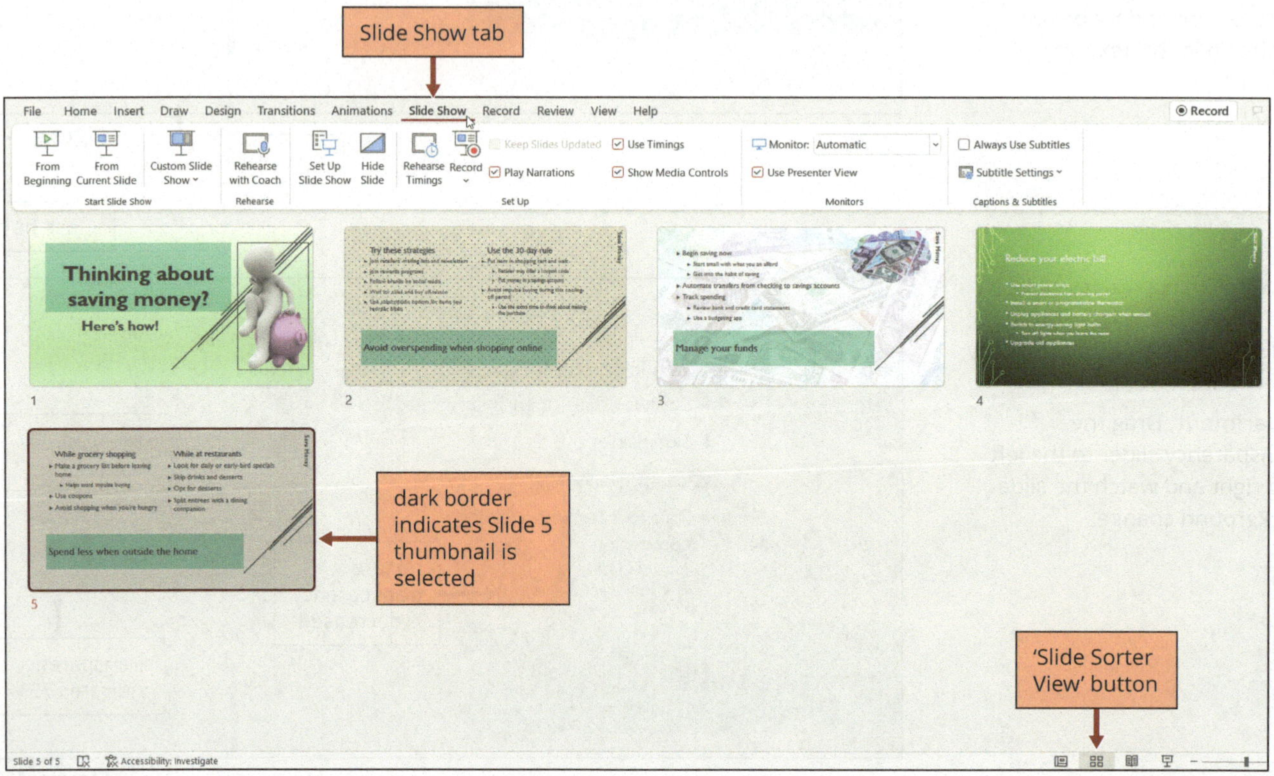

TheDigitalWay/Pixabay; Peggy_Marco/Pixabay

Figure 4–79

2

- Click the Hide Slide button (Slide Show tab | Set Up group) to hide Slide 5 (Figure 4–80).

Q&A How do I know that Slide 5 is hidden?

The slide number has a slash through it and the slide thumbnail is shaded to indicate Slide 5 is a hidden slide.

What if I decide I no longer want to hide a slide?

Repeat Step 2. The Hide Slide button is a toggle; it either hides or displays a slide.

3

- Click the Normal view button to display Slide 5.

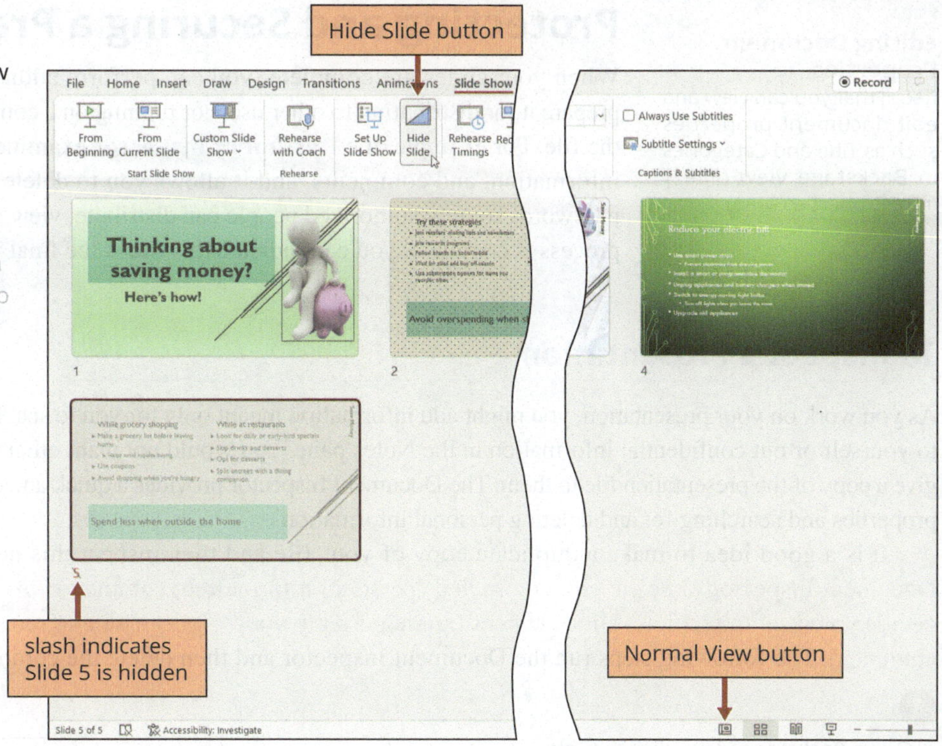

TheDigitalWay/Pixabay; Peggy_Marco/Pixabay

Figure 4–80

Other Ways

1. Right-click desired slide in Slide Sorter view or Normal view on Slides tab, click Hide Slide on shortcut menu

To Add a Slide Transition

A final enhancement you will make in this presentation is to apply the Cube transition to all slides and then change the transition speed and effect option. The following steps apply a transition and effect to the presentation.

1 Display the Transitions tab and then apply the Cube transition in the Exciting category.

2 Change the duration to 03.00 to all five slides in the presentation (Figure 4–81).

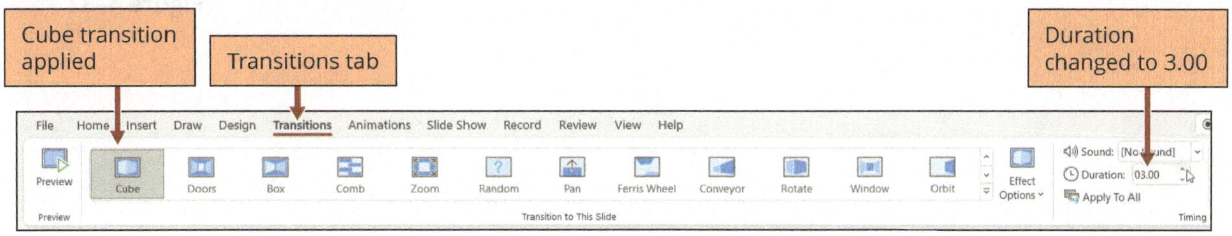

Figure 4–81

BTW
Editing Document Properties
Recall that you can view and edit document properties such as Title and Categories in Backstage view (File | Info, Properties area).

Protecting and Securing a Presentation

When your slides are complete, you can perform additional functions to finalize the file and prepare it for distributing to other users or running on a computer other than the one used to develop the file. For example, the **Document Inspector** examines a file for hidden properties, personal information, and comments, and it allows you to delete these slide elements. You also can set passwords so only authorized people can distribute, view, or modify your slides. When the review process is complete, you can indicate this file is the final version.

To Inspect a Presentation

As you work on your presentation, you might add information meant only for you to see. For example, you might write comments to yourself or put confidential information in the Notes pane. You would not want other people to access this information if you give a copy of the presentation file to them. The Document Inspector provides a quick and efficient method of viewing all document properties and searching for and deleting personal information.

It is a good idea to make a duplicate copy of your file and then inspect this new second copy. **Why?** If you tell the Document Inspector to delete content, such as personal information, comments, invisible slide content, or notes, and then decide you need to see those slide elements, quite possibly you will be unable to retrieve the information by using the Undo command. The following steps run the Document Inspector and then delete the comments.

1

- Open Backstage view, click the Info tab, and then click 'Check for Issues' to display the 'Check for Issues' menu (Figure 4–82).

2

- Click Inspect Document. If the Microsoft PowerPoint dialog box is displayed asking if you want to save your presentation, click Yes to save the file.
- Click Inspect to check the document and display the inspection results.

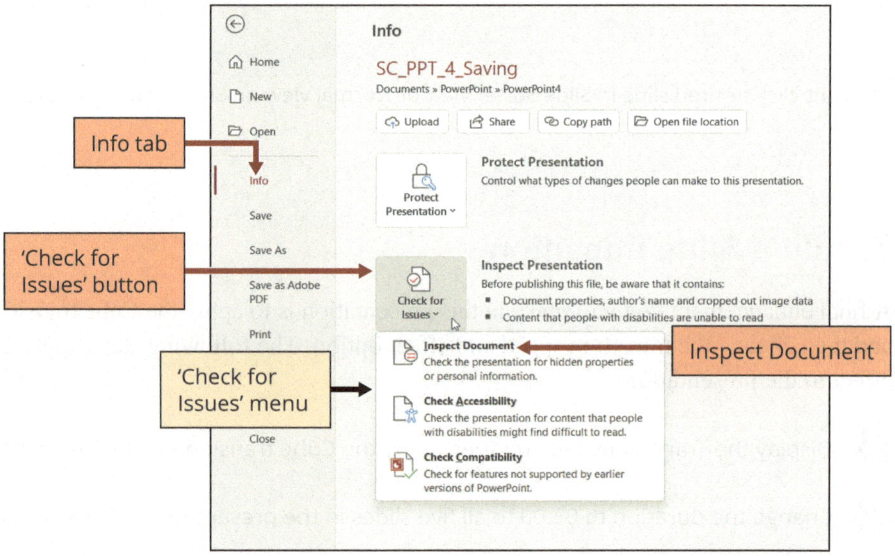

Figure 4–82

Q&A What information does the Document Inspector check?
This information includes text in the Info pane, such as your name and company. Other information includes details of when the file was last saved, objects formatted as invisible, graphics and text you dragged off a slide, presentation notes, and email headers.

3

- View the inspection results to see information that possibly could be removed (Figure 4–83).

Q&A What would happen if I click Remove All in the 'Document Properties and Personal Information' section of the inspection results?

You would delete all identifying information, such as your name, that is saved.

4

- Click the Close button (Document Inspector dialog box) to close the dialog box without removing any information.

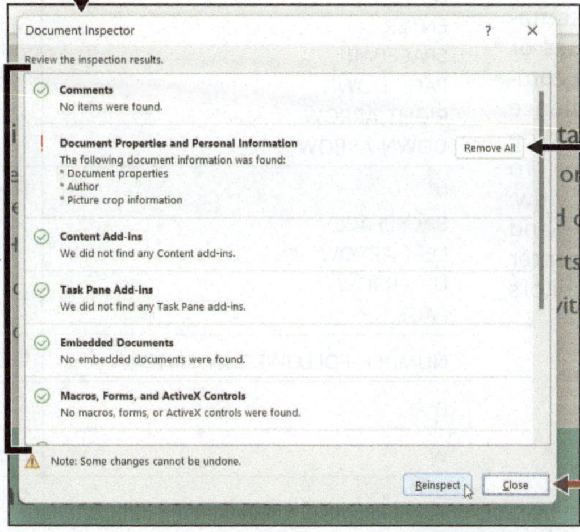

Figure 4–83

To Mark a Presentation as Final

When your slides are completed, you may want to prevent others or yourself from accidentally changing the slide content or features. If you use the **Mark as Final** command, the presentation becomes a read-only document. To mark the presentation as a final (read-only) document you would perform the following steps.

1. With Backstage view open and the Info tab displayed for the Saving file, click Protect Presentation to display the Protect Presentation menu.
2. Click 'Mark as Final' to display the Microsoft PowerPoint dialog box indicating that the presentation will be saved as a final document.
3. Click OK (Microsoft PowerPoint dialog box) to save the file and to display another Microsoft PowerPoint dialog box with information about a final version of a document and indicating that the presentation is final.

   Q&A Can I turn off this read-only status so that I can edit the file?

   Yes. Click Mark as Final in the Protect Presentation menu to toggle off the read-only status.

4. Click OK (Microsoft PowerPoint dialog box). If an Information bar is displayed above the slide, click Edit Anyway to allow changes to be made to the presentation.

BTW

Printing Document Properties

PowerPoint does not allow you to print document properties. This feature, however, is available in Microsoft 365 Word.

Navigating to a Slide During a Slide Show

When you display a particular slide and view the information, you may want to return to one of the other slides in the presentation. You **navigate** when you jump to other slides in a presentation. A set of keyboard shortcuts can help you navigate to various slides during the slide show. When running a slide show, you can press F1 to see a list of these keyboard controls. These navigational features are listed in Table 4–1.

BTW
Using Presenter View
If you have two monitors, you can switch to Presenter view to see the presentation with speaker notes or the next slide on one computer while your audience sees only the current slide on a second monitor. To switch to Presenter view, click the Slide Show tab and then click the 'Use Presenter View' button in the Monitors group.

Table 4–1: Slide Show Keyboard Shortcuts

Keyboard Shortcut	Purpose
N ENTER SPACEBAR PAGE DOWN RIGHT ARROW DOWN ARROW	Perform the next animation or advance to the next slide
P BACKSPACE LEFT ARROW UP ARROW PAGE UP	Perform the previous animation or return to the previous slide
NUMBER FOLLOWED BY ENTER	Go to a specific slide number
B	Display a blank black slide
W	Display a blank white slide
S	Stop or restart an automatic presentation
ESC	End a presentation
E	Erase on-screen annotations
H	Go to the next slide if the next slide is hidden
T	Set new timings while rehearsing
R	Rerecord slide narration and timing
CTRL+P	Change the pointer to a pen
CTRL+A	Change the pointer to an arrow
CTRL+E	Change the pointer to an eraser
CTRL+M	Show or hide ink markup

Navigating to a Slide Using the Control Bar

When you begin running a presentation and move the pointer, a control bar is displayed with buttons that allow you to navigate to the next slide or previous slide, mark up the current slide, display slide thumbnails, zoom, or change the current display. When you move the mouse, the control bar is displayed in the lower-left corner of the slide; it disappears after the mouse has not been moved for three seconds. Table 4–2 describes the buttons on the control bar.

Table 4–2: Slide Show Control Bar Buttons

Description	Image	Function
Previous		Go to previous slide or previous animated element on the slide
Next		Go to next slide or next animated element on the slide
Pen and laser pointer tools		Shortcut menu for laser pointer, pen, highlighter, and eraser
See all slides		View thumbnails of all slides in presentation
Zoom into the slide		Zoom in on specific slide area
Toggle Subtitles		Use the Subtitles feature to have PowerPoint transcribe your words as you present and display them on-screen as captions; also turns off the Subtitles feature.
Options		Shortcut menu for slide navigation and screen displays; also displays Presenter View on a single monitor

To Highlight Text

You click the arrows on the left side of the control bar to navigate backward or forward through the slide show. The 'Pen and laser pointer tools' button has a variety of functions, most often to emphasize aspects of slides or to make handwritten notes. The following steps highlight an item on a slide in Slide Show view. **Why?** You want to call attention to the presentation's emphasis on developing a plan.

1

- Display Slide 1 and then run the slide show.
- If the control bar is not visible in the lower-left corner of the slide, move the pointer on the slide.
- Click the 'Pen and laser pointer tools' icon on the control bar to display a menu (Figure 4–84).

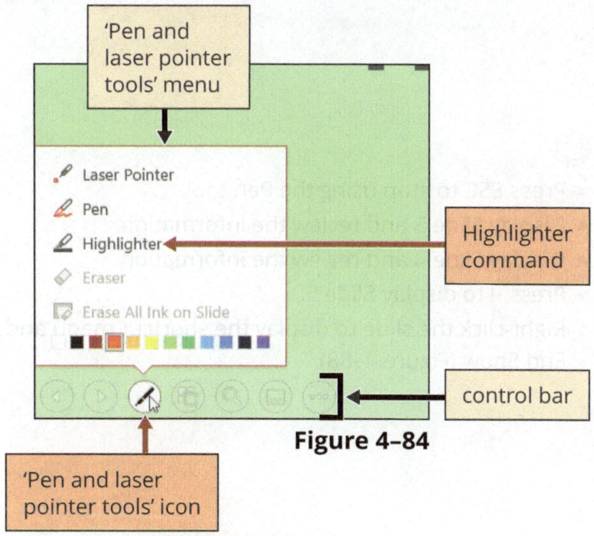

Figure 4–84

2

- Click the Highlighter icon on the control bar and then drag over the words, Here's how!, several times until all the letters are highlighted (Figure 4–85).

Figure 4–85

To Use Pen and Pointer Options During a Slide Show

Instead of Highlighter, you also can click Pen to draw or write notes on the slides. **Why?** The Pen tool is much thinner than the Highlighter, so you can write words or draw fine lines on the slides. When the presentation ends, PowerPoint will prompt you to keep or discard the ink annotations. The following steps change the pointer to a pen and then change the color of the ink during the presentation.

1

- Click Next on the control bar to display Slide 2. Click the 'Pen and laser pointer tools' icon on the control bar and then click Pen on the menu.
- Click 'Pen and laser pointer tools' on the control bar and then point to the color Dark Blue (Figure 4–86).

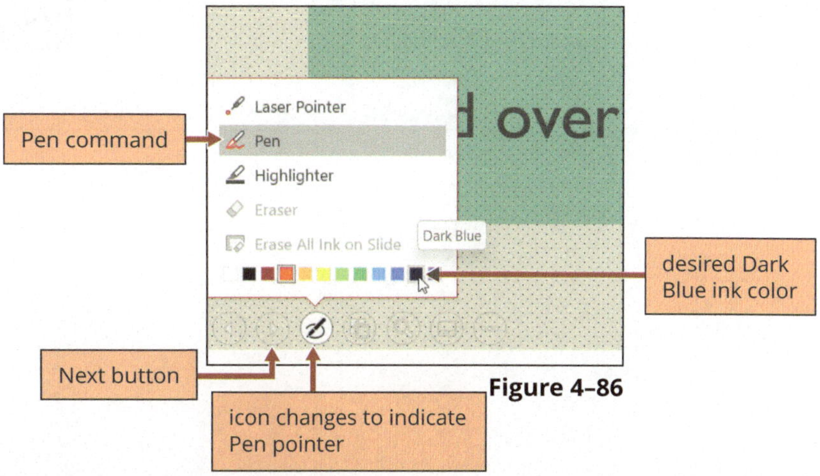

Figure 4–86

2

- Click the color Dark Blue.
- Drag the pointer around the title text words, Avoid overspending, to draw a circle around them (Figure 4–87).

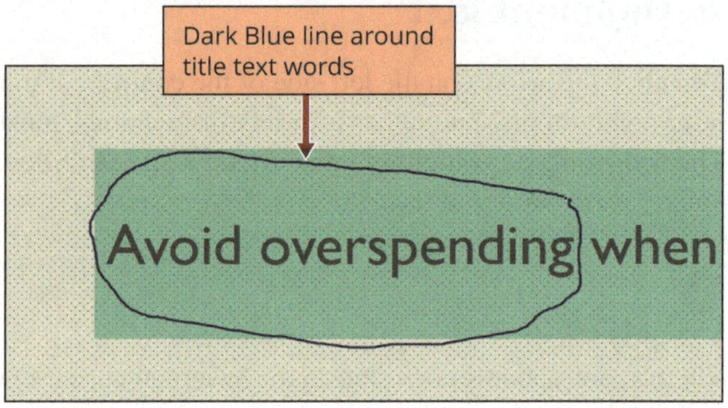

Figure 4–87

3

- Press ESC to stop using the Pen tool.
- Display Slide 3 and review the information.
- Display Slide 4 and review the information.
- Press H to display Slide 5.
- Right-click the slide to display the shortcut menu and then point to End Show (Figure 4–88).

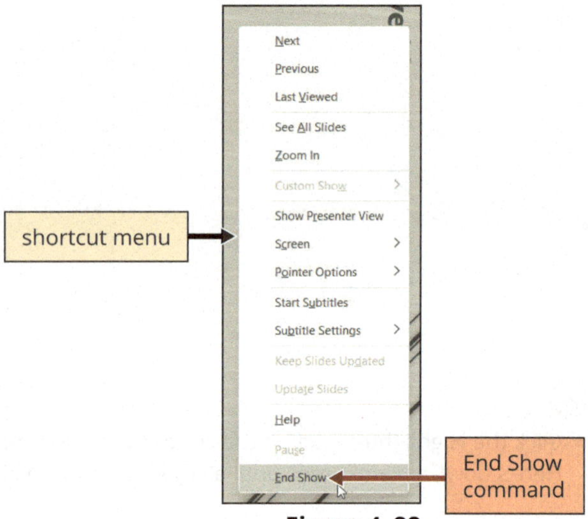

Figure 4–88

4

- Click End Show to display the Microsoft PowerPoint dialog box (Figure 4–89).

5

- Click the Discard button (Microsoft PowerPoint dialog box) to end the presentation without saving the ink annotations.

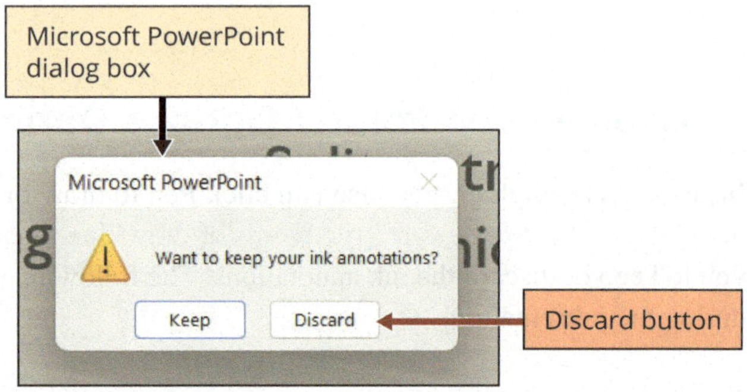

Figure 4–89

To Hide the Pointer and Slide Show Control Bar

To hide the pointer and the control bar during the slide show, you would perform the following step.

1. Click Options on the control bar, click Arrow Options, and then click Hidden.

To Constantly Display the Pointer and Slide Show Control Bar

By default, the pointer and control bar are set at Automatic, which means they are hidden after three seconds of no movement. After you hide the pointer and control bar, they remain hidden until you choose one of the other commands on the Options menu. They are displayed again when you move the mouse.

To keep the pointer and control bar displayed at all times during a slide show, you would perform the following step.

1. Click Options on the control bar, click Arrow Options, and then click Visible.

Rehearsing Slide Timings

In previous slide shows, you clicked to advance from one slide to the next. You also can set the time each slide is displayed on the screen. You can set these times in one of two ways. The first method is to specify each slide's display time manually. The second method is to use PowerPoint's **rehearsal feature**, which allows you to advance through the slides at your own pace, and the amount of time you view each slide is recorded. You will use the second technique in this module and then adjust the fourth slide's timing manually.

When you begin rehearsing a presentation, the Rehearsal toolbar is displayed. The **Rehearsal toolbar** contains buttons that allow you to start, pause, and repeat viewing the slides in the slide show and to view the times for each slide as well as the elapsed time. Table 4–3 describes the buttons on the Rehearsal toolbar.

BTW
Turn Off Slide Timings
PowerPoint gives you the option to turn slide timings off and then turn them back on without having to recreate them. Click the 'Set Up Slide Show' button (Slide Show tab | Set Up group) and then click Manually in the Advance slides area (Set Up Show dialog box). To turn the slide timings back on, click 'Using timings, if present' in the Advance slides area (Set Up Show dialog box).

Table 4–3: Rehearsal Toolbar Buttons

Button Name	Image	Description
Next	→	Displays the next slide or next animated element on the slide.
Pause Recording	❚❚	Stops the timer. Tap or click Next or Pause Recording to resume timing.
Slide Time	0:00:00	Indicates the length of time a slide has been displayed. You can enter a slide time directly in the Slide Time box.
Repeat	↶	Clears the Slide Time box and resets the timer to 0:00:00.
Elapsed Time	0:00:00	Indicates slide show total time.

Consider This

Give your audience sufficient time to view a slide.

The presentation in this module is designed to run continuously at a kiosk without a speaker's physical presence. Your audience, therefore, must read or view each slide and absorb the information without your help as a narrator. Be certain to give them time to read each slide and grasp the concept you are presenting. They will become frustrated if the slide changes before they have finished viewing and assimilating the material. As you set the slide timings, read each slide aloud and note the amount of time that elapses. Add a few seconds to this time and use this amount for the total time the slide is displayed.

To Rehearse Slide Timings

You need to determine the length of time each slide should be displayed. **Why?** Audience members need sufficient time to read the text and watch the animations. Table 4–4 indicates the desired timings for the five slides in the Saving presentation. Slide 1 is displayed and then the text appears for 10 seconds. Slides 2, 3, and 4 are displayed for 15 seconds. Slide 5 is displayed for 20 seconds.

Table 4–4: Slide Rehearsal Timings

Slide Number	Display Time	Elapsed Time
1	0:00	0:10
2	0:15	0:25
3	0:15	0:40
4	0:15	0:55
5	0:20	1:15

The following steps add slide timings to the slide show.

1

- Display Slide 1 and then click Slide Show on the ribbon to display the Slide Show tab (Figure 4–90).

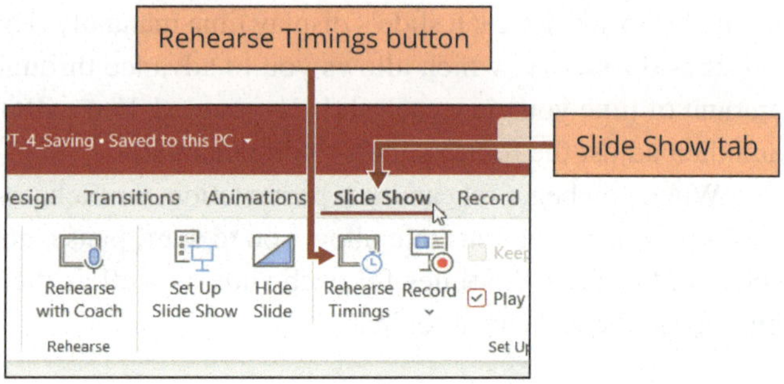

Figure 4–90

2

- Click the Rehearse Timings button (Slide Show tab | Set Up group) to start the slide show and the counter (Figure 4–91).
- If the 'Always Use Subtitles' pane is displayed, close it.

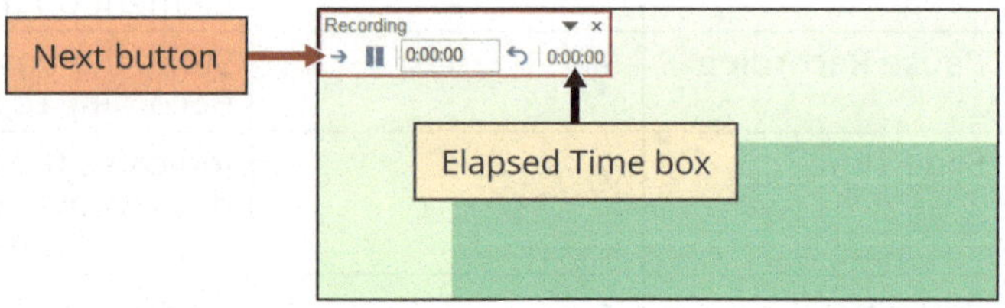

Figure 4–91

3

- When the Elapsed Time displays 00:10, click Next to display Slide 2.
- When the Elapsed Time displays 00:25, click Next to display Slide 3.
- When the Elapsed Time displays 00:40, click Next to display Slide 4.
- When the Elapsed Time displays 00:55, type H to display the hidden Slide 5.
- When the Elapsed Time displays 01:15, click Next to display the Microsoft PowerPoint dialog box (Figure 4–92).

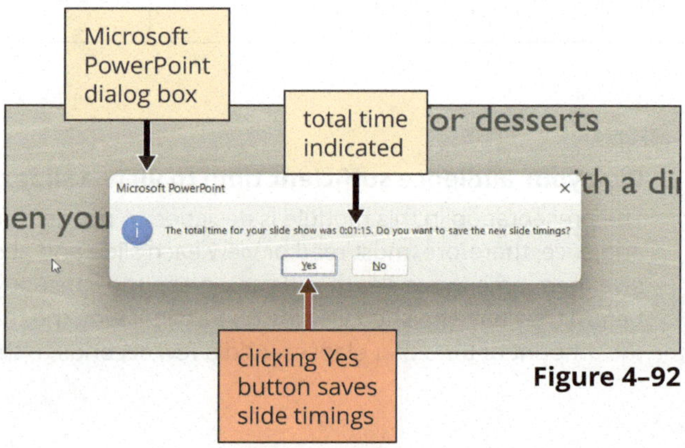

Figure 4–92

4

- Click Yes to keep the new slide timings with an elapsed time of 01:15.
- Click Slide Sorter view and then, if necessary, zoom the view to display all five thumbnails. Review the timings displayed in the lower-right corner of each slide (Figure 4–93).
- If the Always Use Subtitles pane opens, click Close to close it.

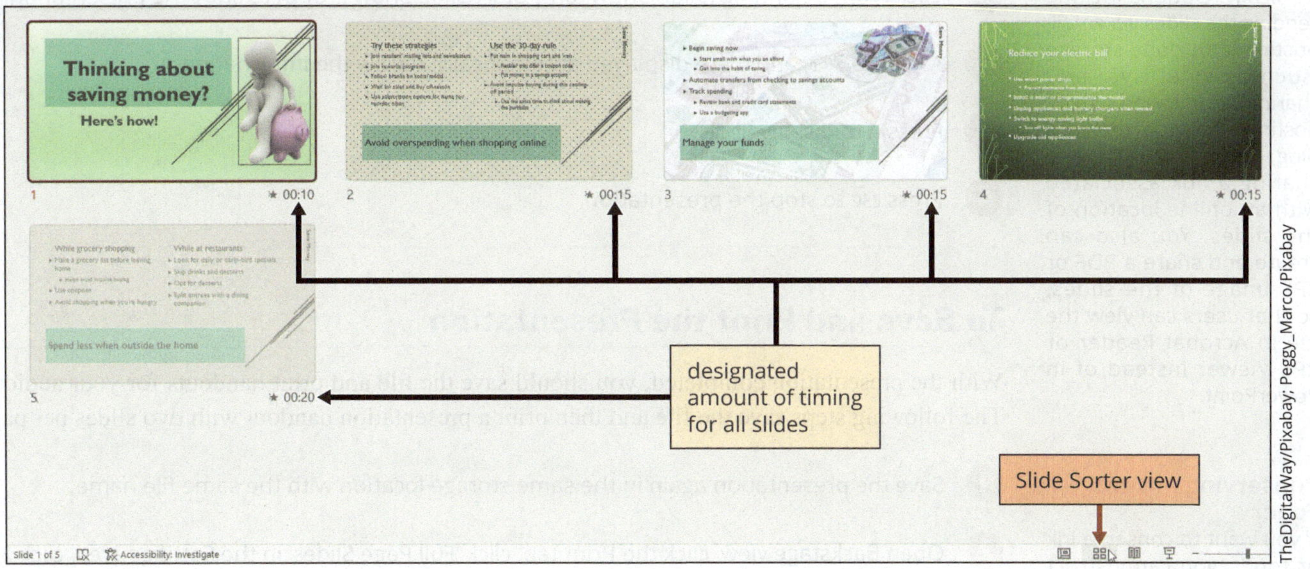

Figure 4–93

To Advance a Slide After a Specified Number of Seconds

Why? If the slide timings need adjustment, you manually can change the length of time each slide is displayed. In this presentation, you decide to display Slide 4 for 20 seconds instead of 15 seconds. The following step increases the Slide 4 timing.

1

- In Slide Sorter view, display the Transitions tab and then select Slide 4.
- Change the 'Advance Slide After' setting (Transitions tab | Timing group) to 00:20.00 (Figure 4–94).

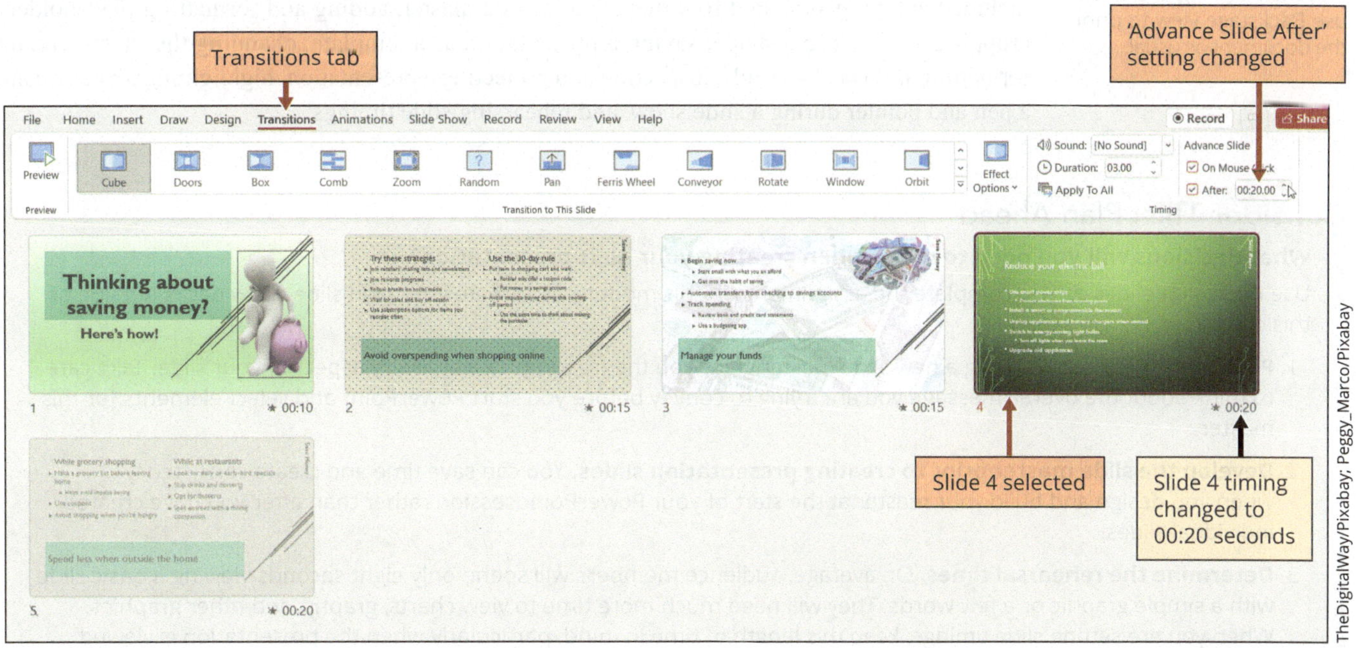

Figure 4–94

BTW
Distributing a Document
Instead of printing and distributing a hard copy of PowerPoint slides, you can distribute the slides electronically. Options include sending the slides via email; posting it on cloud storage (such as OneDrive) and sharing the link with others; posting it on social media, a blog, or other website; and sharing a link associated with an online location of the slides. You also can create and share a PDF or XPS image of the slides, so that users can view the file in Acrobat Reader or XPS Viewer instead of in PowerPoint.

BTW
Conserving Ink and Toner
If you want to conserve ink or toner, you can instruct PowerPoint to print draft quality documents by clicking File on the ribbon to open Backstage view, clicking Options in Backstage view to display the PowerPoint Options dialog box, clicking Advanced in the left pane (PowerPoint Options dialog box), scrolling to the Print area in the right pane, verifying there is no check mark in the High quality check box, and then clicking OK. Then, use Backstage view to print the document as usual.

To Run a Slide Show with Timings

All changes are complete. You now can view the presentation with timings. The following steps run the slide show.

1. Click From Beginning (Slide Show tab | Start Slide Show group) to start the presentation.
2. As Slides 2, 3, and 4 are displayed automatically, review the information.
3. Press H to display Slide 5.
4. Press ESC to stop the presentation.

To Save and Print the Presentation

With the presentation completed, you should save the file and print handouts for your audience. The following steps save the file and then print a presentation handout with two slides per page.

1. Save the presentation again in the same storage location with the same file name.
2. Open Backstage view, click the Print tab, click 'Full Page Slides' in the Settings area, click 2 Slides in the Handouts area to display a preview of the handout, and then click Print in the Print gallery to print the presentation.
3. sam Because the project now is complete, you can exit PowerPoint.

Summary

In this module, you learned how to customize slide masters and presentations. Topics covered included applying slide and font themes to a slide master, adding and formatting placeholders, cropping a picture to a shape, saving a presentation as a template, changing the theme variant, formatting slide backgrounds, inspecting and protecting a presentation, highlighting text and using a pen and pointer during a slide show, and rehearsing slide timings.

Consider This: Plan Ahead

What decisions will you need to make when creating your next presentation?

Use these guidelines as you complete the assignments in this module and create your own slide show decks outside of this class.

1. **Plan the slide master**. Using a new slide master gives you the freedom to plan every aspect of your slide. Take care to think about the overall message you are trying to convey before you start PowerPoint and select elements for this master.
2. **Develop the slide master prior to creating presentation slides.** You can save time and create consistency when you design and build your master at the start of your PowerPoint session rather than after you have created individual slides.
3. **Determine the rehearsal times.** On average, audience members will spend only eight seconds viewing a basic slide with a simple graphic or a few words. They will need much more time to view charts, graphs, and other graphics. When you are setting slide timings, keep this length of time in mind, particularly when the presentation is viewed without a speaker's physical presence.

Student Assignments

Apply Your Knowledge

Reinforce the skills and apply the concepts you learned in this module.

Creating and Formatting Slide Masters and a Template

Note: To complete this assignment, you will be required to use the Data Files. Please contact your instructor for information about accessing the Data Files.

Instructions: Start PowerPoint. Your school is promoting noncredit art classes for adults and teens, and the marketing department has asked you to help with the campaign. You decide to design a template that can be customized for sessions held throughout the year. Open the presentation called SC_PPT_4-1.pptx, which is located in the Data Files. You will delete and rename slide layouts, change slide backgrounds, save a slide master as a template, and then create the presentation shown in Figure 4–95.

Perform the following tasks:

1. Display Slide Master view. Delete all layouts except the Title Slide Layout and the Comparison Layout.
2. Display the Banded Slide Master. Delete the date footer placeholder. Change the title text case to Sentence case. Change the theme colors to Blue Warm. Customize the theme fonts by changing the heading font to Verdana and the body font to Times New Roman. Save the new font set with the name, **Art**.
3. On the Banded Slide Master, insert the picture Support_PPT_4_Paintbrush.jpg and then crop it to the Flowchart: Data shape (fourth shape in the first Flowchart area row). Click the More button in the Picture Format | Size group and uncheck the Lock aspect ratio box. Resize the paintbrush picture to a height of 2" and a width of 13" and then align it in the center and the top of the slide. Rename the Banded Slide Master as **Art**.
4. Display the Title Slide Layout, format the background texture fill to Purple mesh (fourth background in the fourth row), and then change the transparency to 15%. Close the Format Background pane.
5. To display the paintbrush picture on the Title Slide Layout (Figure 4–95a), click the 'Hide Background Graphics' check box (Slide Master tab | Background group) so that it no longer is checked. Rename this layout **Art Title**.
6. On the Art Title Layout, delete the date footer placeholder, insert a Text placeholder, and then change the height to 0.5" and the width to 4". Delete the default text and the bullet in the new placeholder and then type **Learn a new creative skill!** in the placeholder. Bold this text, increase the font size to 24 point, and then center it in the placeholder. Cut this placeholder from the layout and then paste it on the Art Slide Master layout. Position this placeholder by aligning it in the center and the bottom of the slide.
7. Display the Comparison Layout and then delete the title text placeholder. Change the slide background fill to the 'Radial Gradient – Accent 1' style (first fill in the last row), as shown in Figure 4–95b. Close the Format Background pane. Rename this layout **Art Comparison**.
8. Close Master view. Save the file as a template using the file name, **SC_PPT_4_Art_Template**.
9. On Slide 1, type **Programs for all ability levels** in the subtitle placeholder and then increase the font size to 48 point (Figure 4–95c).

   If requested by your instructor, replace the word, Spring, with the name of the first school you attended.
10. Insert a new slide as Slide 2 with the Art Comparison layout. Type the text shown in Figure 4–95d. Increase the font size of the two column headings to 32 point.
11. Apply the Page Curl transition in the Exciting category to both slides and then change the duration to 2.00 seconds.
12. View the presentation and then save the file as a PowerPoint presentation using the file name, **SC_PPT_4_Art**, and submit the revised presentation in the format specified by your instructor.

Continued on next page

13. **Consider This:** In this assignment, you created a new theme font in the Slide Master and named it Art. Are the fonts appropriate for this presentation? You also changed the theme colors to Blue Warm. Was this a good choice? Would another set of colors be a better complement for this topic? Why or why not?

Figure 4–95(a): Formatted Art Title Slide Master

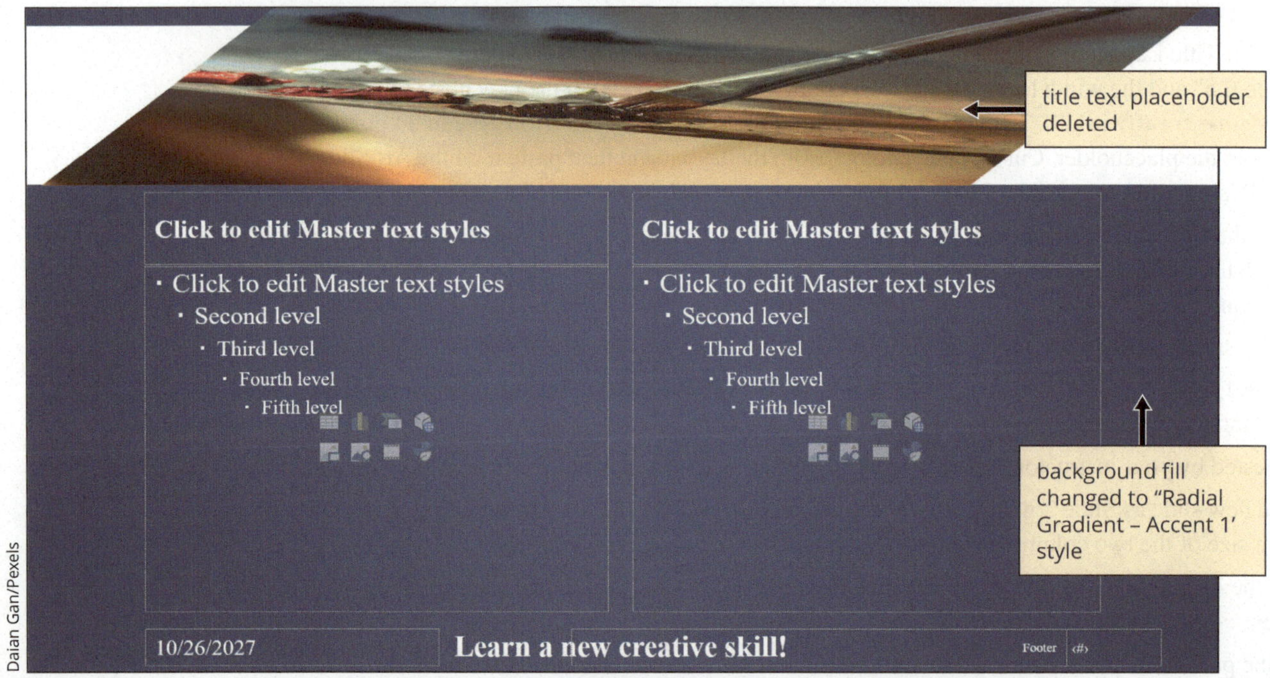

Figure 4–95(b): Formatted Art Comparison Slide Master

Figure 4–95(c): Slide 1

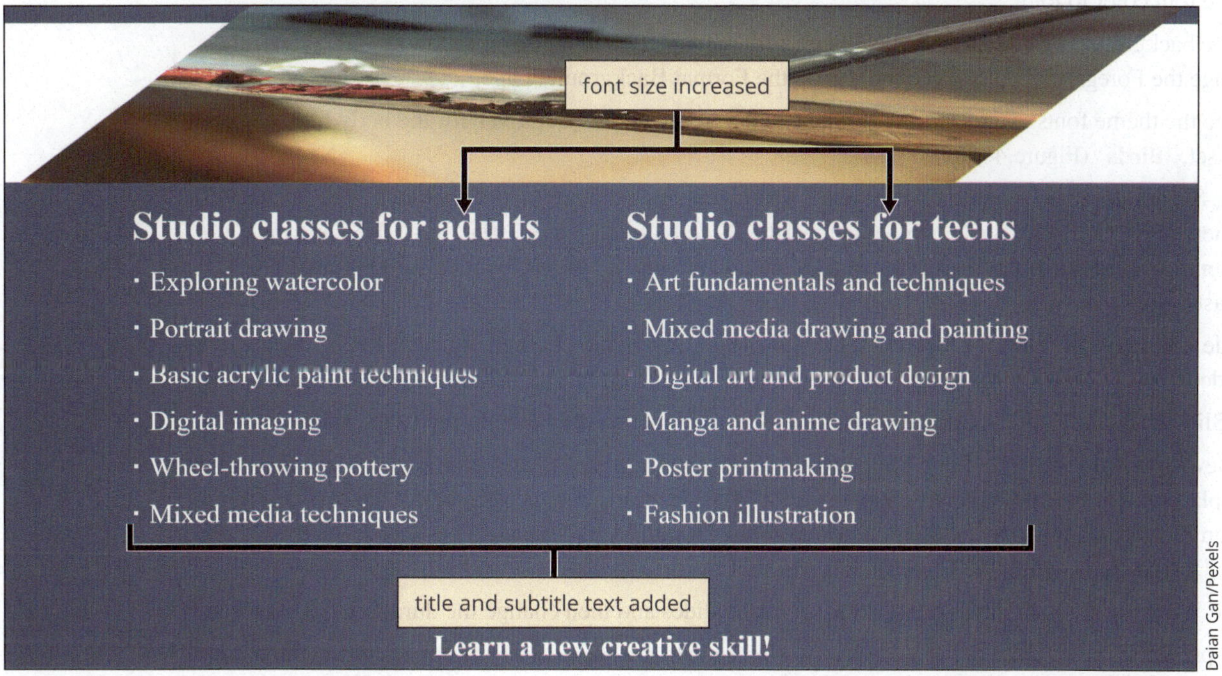

Figure 4–95(d): Slide 2

Extend Your Knowledge

Extend the skills you learned in the module and experiment with new skills. You may need to use Help to complete the assignment.

Using Design Ideas and Adjusting Footer Content

Note: To complete this assignment, you will be required to use the Data Files. Please contact your instructor for information about accessing the Data Files.

Instructions: Start PowerPoint. This semester you are interning at the Swallow Meadow Nature Center and are helping the naturalists develop fun and educational events and programs. One upcoming session will help area residents learn the basics about winter bird feeding, protecting birds in flight, and growing native plants. The naturalists have asked you to prepare slides to show at the Nature Center. They want you to create a PowerPoint template so they can change photographs for each program they have scheduled. Open the presentation called SC_PPT_4-2.pptx, which is located in the Data Files. You will use the Design Ideas pane to develop the title slide, adjust the footer content, and insert and rename a layout. The document you open is a partially formatted presentation. Slide 1 in the presentation has a title and three pictures. Slide 2 has a list of actions residents can take to help protect the birds. You will create the slide master layouts in Figure 4–96 and then add the slide content.

Perform the following tasks:

1. Display Slide Master view and then select the Office Theme Slide Master. Type the text, **Swallow Meadow Nature Center**, in the Footer text box and then apply the footer text box to all slides.

   If requested by your instructor, replace the word, Swallow, with the name of your high school mascot.
2. Align the Footer placeholder in the center and top of the slide and then increase font size to 20 point and change the font color to Red.
3. Format the background by adding the Divot pattern fill (first pattern in the seventh row) to all layouts and then change the Foreground color to Green. Close the Format Background pane.
4. Customize the theme fonts using Georgia for the heading font and Gill Sans MT for the body font. Name the new font set, **Birds** (Figure 4–96a).
5. Select the Section Header Layout and then delete this layout and all other layouts below it. Rename the Office Theme Slide Master, **Birds**. Rename the Title Slide Layout, **Birds Title Slide**. Rename the Title and Content Layout, **Birds Content**. Insert a layout and rename it, **Birds Final Slide** (Figure 4–96b). Close Master view.
6. With Slide 1 displayed (Figure 4–96c), click Design Ideas (Design tab | Designer group) to display the Design Ideas pane. Click the first design in the pane to apply that design to the title slide.
7. Display Slide 2 (Figure 4–96d). Click the first design in the pane to apply that design to the slide.
8. Insert a new slide with the Birds Final Slide layout. Type **Use binoculars and share your sightings** in the title text placeholder. Insert the picture, Support_PPT_4_Binoculars.jpg, and then select the first design in the Design Ideas pane. If, however, the first design in the Design Ideas pane does not match the other slides, scroll the Design Ideas to find the best match.
9. Apply the Wind transition in the Exciting category to all slides and then change the duration to 3.00 seconds.
10. View the presentation, save the file as a PowerPoint presentation using **SC_PPT_4_Birds** as the file name, and then submit the revised presentation in the format specified by your instructor.
11. **Consider This:** In this assignment, you created a new theme font in the Slide Master and named it Birds. Are the fonts appropriate for this presentation? Why or why not? How did the design ideas enhance the three slides?

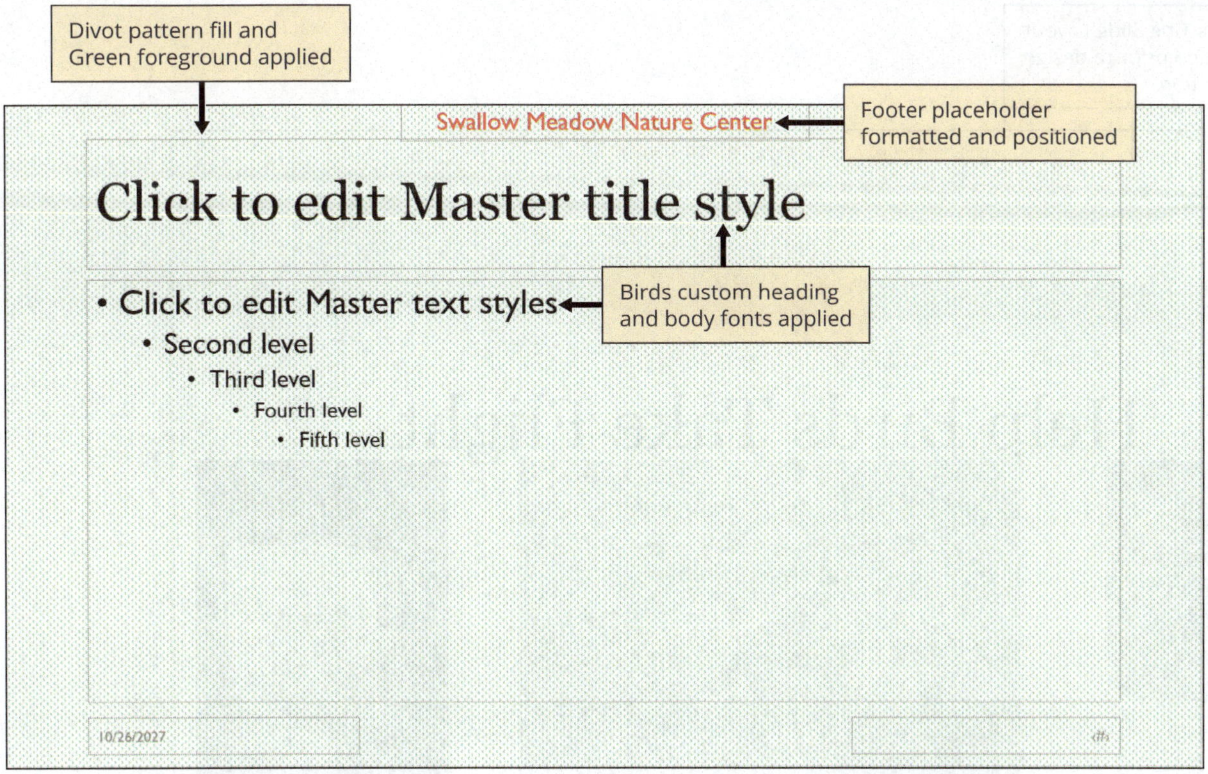

Figure 4–96(a): Birds Slide Master

Figure 4–96(b): Birds Final Slide Layout

Continued on next page

Birds Title Slide Layout applied prior to design selection

Rajesh S Balouria/Pexels; Büşranur Aydın/Pexels; Harrison Haines/Pexels

Figure 4–96(c): Slide 1

Birds Content Layout applied prior to design selection

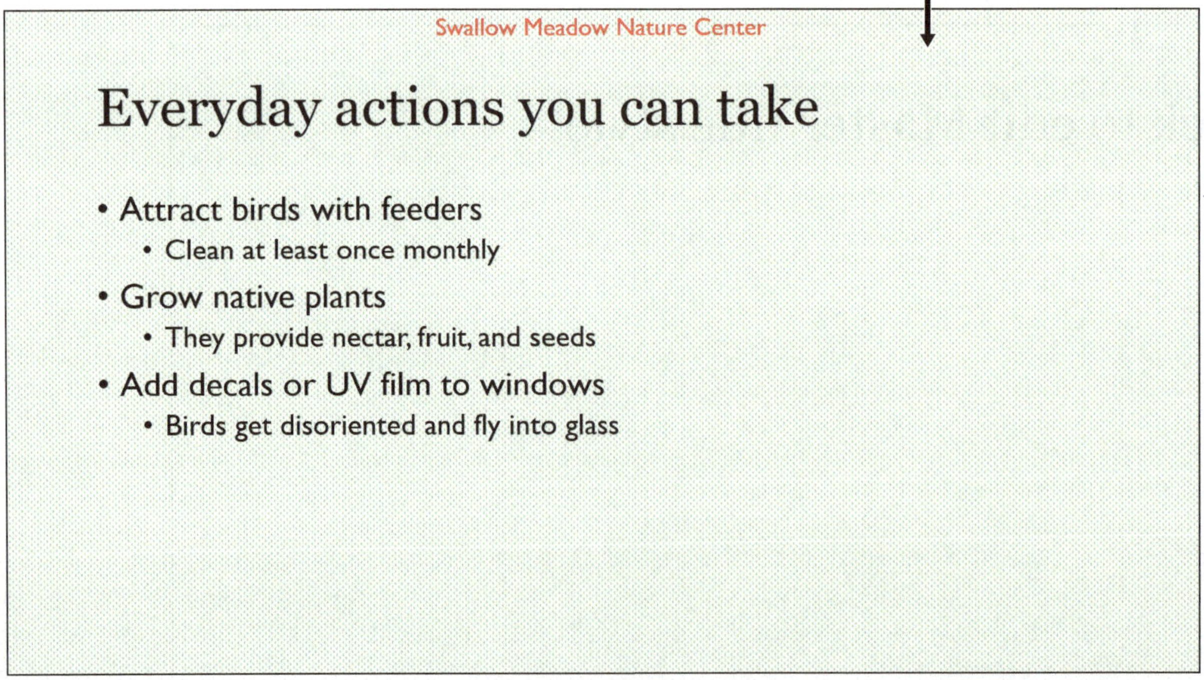

Figure 4–96(d): Slide 2

Expand Your World

Create a solution that uses cloud or web technologies by learning and investigating on your own from general guidance.

Exploring Add-ins

Instructions: You use apps on your phone and tablet to access information on the web. Similarly, when you are working with PowerPoint and other Microsoft 365 apps, you can use add-ins, which essentially are apps designed to increase your productivity. When you download an add-in from a reliable source, you enable it by clicking Enable Content on the Message Bar. You would like to investigate some of the add-ins available for PowerPoint to determine which ones would be helpful for you to use.

Note: You will be required to use your Microsoft account to complete this assignment. If you do not have a Microsoft account and do not want to create one, read this assignment without performing the instructions.

Perform the following tasks:

1. Use Help to learn about Office add-ins. If necessary, sign in to your Windows account and your Microsoft account in PowerPoint.
2. Display the Insert tab and then click Get Add-ins (Insert tab | Add-ins group) to display the Office Add-ins dialog box. (If a menu is displayed, click the 'See My Add-ins' link to display the Office Add-ins dialog box.) If necessary, click the STORE tab to visit the online Office Store (Figure 4–97).
3. Scroll through the add-ins in the various categories. Locate a free add-in that you feel would be helpful to you while you use PowerPoint, click this desired add-in, and then follow the instructions to add the add-in to PowerPoint.
4. In PowerPoint, click Get Add-ins to display the Office Add-ins dialog box. Click the MY ADD-INS tab to display the add-in you added, click this add-in, and then click Add (Office Add-ins dialog box) to use the add-in.
5. Practice using the add-in.
6. **Consider This:** Which add-in did you download and why? Does the add-in work as you intended? Would you recommend this add-in to others? Which add-ins, if any, were already on your computer?

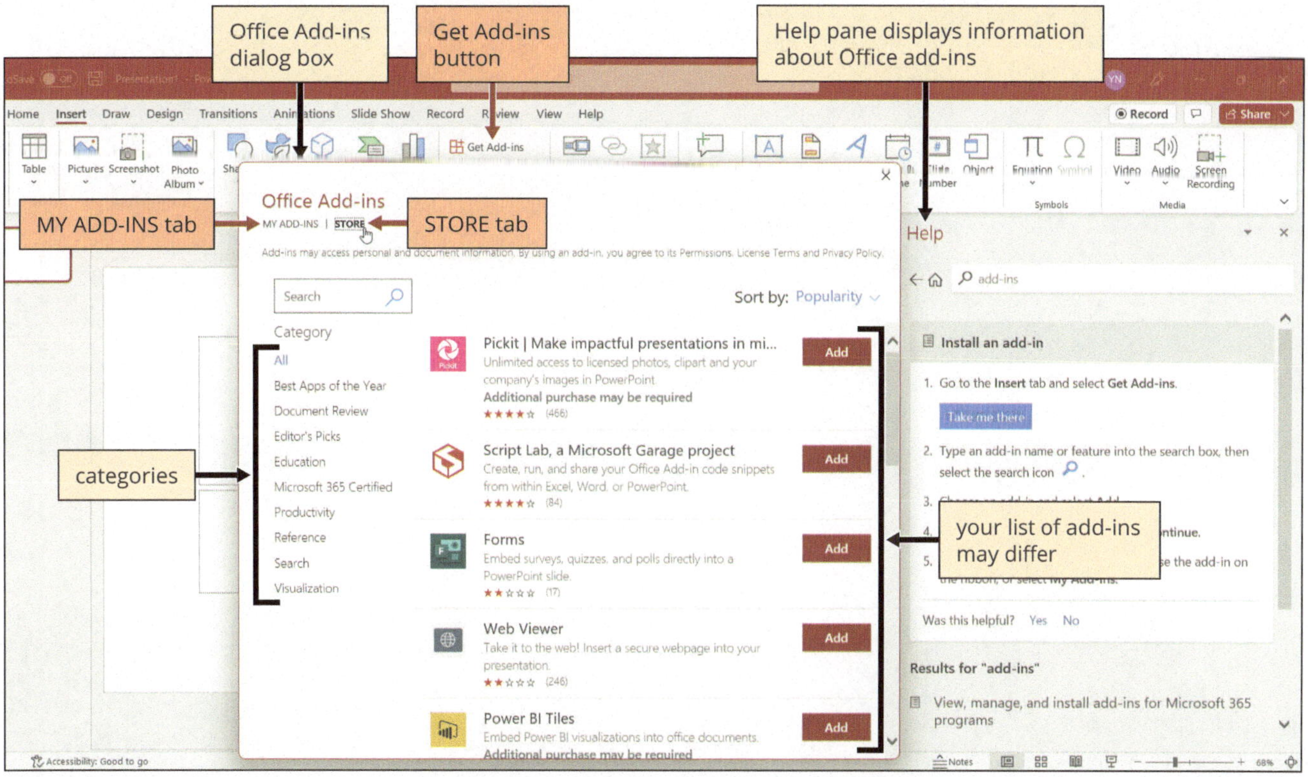

Figure 4–97

In the Lab

Apply your creative thinking and problem-solving skills to design and implement a solution.

Design and Create a Presentation about Increasing Productivity

Part 1: It may seem there are not enough hours in the day to complete all the items on your to-do list. One method of coping with the tasks at-hand is increasing productivity. You can implement several time-saving strategies to become more effective. For example, create a schedule with blocks of time for specific tasks. Eliminate visual distractions and social media notifications. Eat healthy snacks and get adequate sleep. You work in the counseling department at school and are helping to prepare a presentation for incoming students with advice on increasing productivity. Use the concepts and techniques presented in this module to prepare a presentation with a minimum of three slides with productivity tips. Review some websites to learn realistic methods of enhancing productivity at school. Use the pictures, Support_PPT_4_List.jpg and Support_PPT_4_Time.jpg, which are located in the Data Files. Develop at least two slide master layouts that include a picture and then rename these layouts. Delete the layouts you do not use. Change the theme colors. Customize the theme fonts. Modify a slide background. Add slide transitions. Rehearse the slide timings. Review and revise your presentation as needed and then save the file using the file name, **SC_PPT_4_Productive**. Submit your assignment in the format specified by your instructor.

Part 2: **Consider This:** You made several decisions while creating the presentation in this assignment: creating and formatting slide masters, changing theme colors and fonts, modifying a slide background, and rehearsing slide timings. What was the rationale behind each of these decisions? When you reviewed the document, what further revisions did you make and why? Where would you recommend showing this slide show?

Collaborating and Adding Animation

Objectives

After completing this module, you will be able to:

- Compare and merge presentations
- Accept and reject a reviewer's proposed changes
- Delete, reply to, and insert comments
- Change line and paragraph spacing
- Apply an artistic effect to a picture
- Change bullets to pictures and symbols
- Animate slide content
- Duplicate animations with the Animation Painter
- Apply the same formatting to objects with the Format Painter
- Add motion paths for animations
- Align content placeholders
- Control animation timing
- Create and manage sections

Introduction

Often presentations are enhanced when you collaborate with others to fine-tune text, visuals, and design elements on your slides. A **review cycle** occurs when a slide show designer shares a file with multiple reviewers so they can make comments and changes to their copies of the slides and then return the file to the designer. A **comment** is a note that an author or a reviewer adds to a document that normally does not display as part of the slide show. It can be used to clarify information that may be difficult to understand, to pose questions, or to communicate suggestions. The designer then can display the comments, add replies, ask the reviewers to again review the presentation, and continue this process until the slides are satisfactory. In addition, a presenter can use PowerPoint's variety of tools to run the show effectively and modify the presentation if needed.

BTW
Review Cycle Value
The review cycle plays an important role in developing an effective PowerPoint presentation. Your reviewers may raise issues and make comments about your material, and their concerns may help enhance your final slides. Terms and graphics that seem clear to you may raise questions among people viewing your material. Audience members may have diverse technical skills and educational levels, so it is important to understand how they may interpret your slides.

Project: Presentation with Comments and Animation

In this module's project, you will follow proper design guidelines and learn to use PowerPoint to create the slides shown in Figure 5–1a through 5–1e. The objective is to produce a presentation for a seminar at a car dealership in your town regarding strategies for driving safely. A variety of topics will be covered, including caring for tires, learning about available driver-assistance safety features, determining which vehicle has the right-of-way at a four-way intersection, and packing an emergency kit.

BTW
Pixels
Screen resolution specifies the amount of pixels displayed on your screen. The word, pixel, combines pix (for "pictures") and el (for "element").

All slides in the presentation were developed using an older version of PowerPoint. In the older version, the slides used a 4:3 width-to-height ratio, which was the standard proportion of computer monitors at that time. Today, however, most people use PowerPoint's default 16:9 ratio, which is the proportion of most widescreen monitors today. You will change the slide size in your presentation after all the slides are created.

When you are developing a presentation, it often is advantageous to ask a variety of people to review your work in progress. These individuals can evaluate the wording, art, and design, and experts in the subject can check the slides for accuracy. They can add comments to the slides in specific areas, such as a paragraph, a graphic, or a table. You then can review their comments and use them to modify and enhance your work. You also can insert slides from other presentations into your presentation.

In this module, you will learn how to create the slides shown in Figure 5–1. You will perform the following general tasks as you progress through this module:

1. Collaborate on a presentation by using comments.
2. Format and manage text spacing and bullets.
3. Format pictures with effects.
4. Modify bullets.
5. Animate paragraphs and objects.
6. Create and manage sections.
7. Use zoom links.

BTW
Reviewers' Technology Limitations
People who receive copies of your presentation to review may not be able to open a PowerPoint file saved in the default .pptx format because they have a previous version of this software or may not have Internet access available readily. For these reasons, you need to know their software and hardware limitations and distribute your file or handouts accordingly.

Collaborating on a Presentation

PowerPoint provides several methods to collaborate with friends or coworkers who can view your slide show and then provide feedback. When you **collaborate**, you work together on a presentation with other PowerPoint users who are cooperating jointly and assisting willingly with the endeavor. You can distribute your slide show physically to others by exchanging a flash drive or other portable storage media. You also can share your presentation through the Internet by sending the file as an email attachment or saving the file to a storage location, such as Microsoft OneDrive.

Consider This

What are some tips for collaborating successfully?

Working with others can yield numerous benefits. Your peers can assist in brainstorming, developing key ideas, revising your project, and keeping you on track so that your presentation meets the assignment goals.

The first step when collaborating with peers is to define success. What, ultimately, is the goal? For example, are you developing a persuasive presentation to school administrators in an effort to fund a new club? Next, you can set short-term and long-term goals that help lead you to completing the project successfully. These goals can be weekly tasks to accomplish, such as interviewing content experts, conducting online research, or compiling an annotated bibliography. After that, you can develop a plan to finish the project by outlining subtasks that each member must accomplish. Each collaborator should inform the group members when the task is complete or if problems are delaying progress. When collaborators meet, whether in person or online, they should establish an agenda and have one member keep notes of topics discussed.

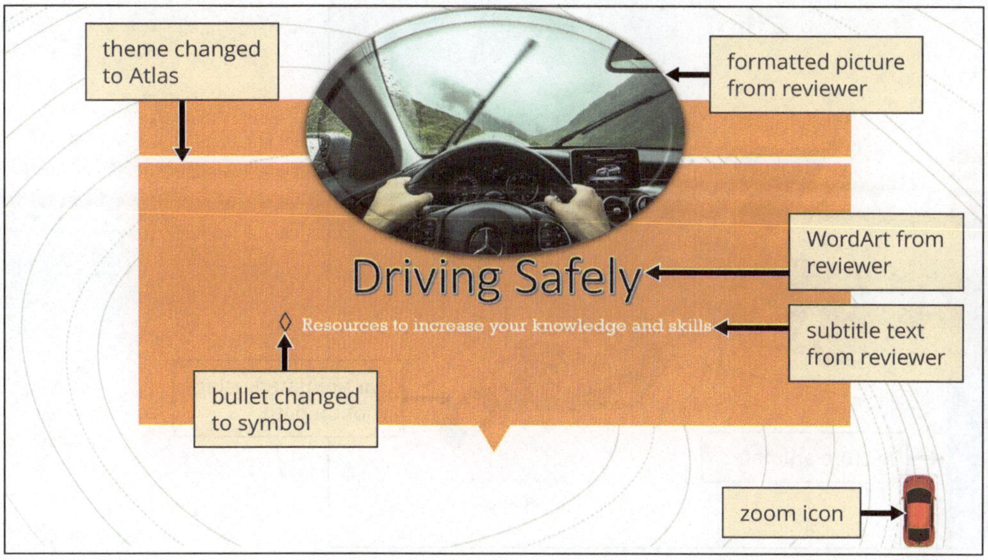

StockSnap/27551 images/Pixabay; OpenClipart-Vectors/27376 images/Pixabay

Figure 5–1(a): Slide 1 (Title Slide Enhanced from Reviewer)

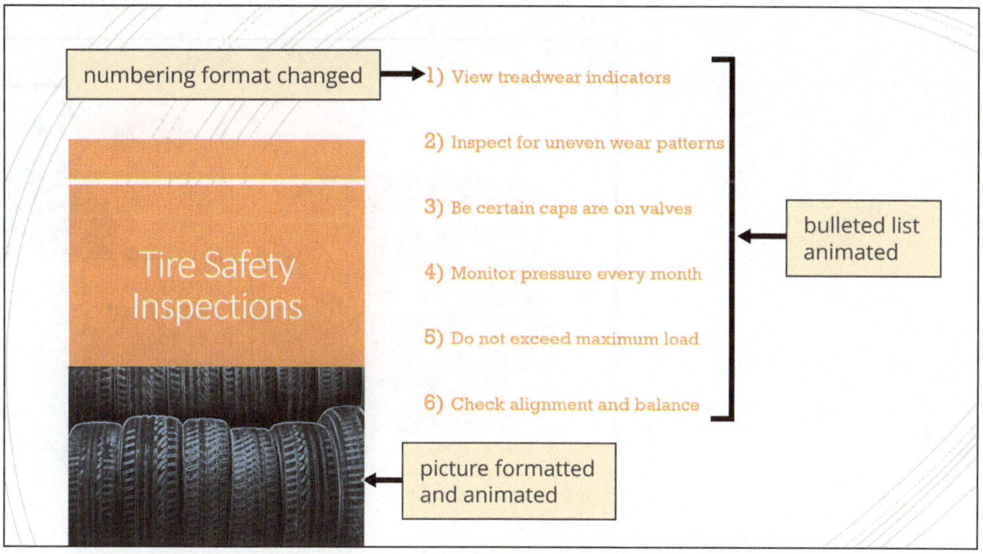

FlenderFunways/4 images/Pixabay

Figure 5–1(b): Slide 2 (Redesigned from Reviewer)

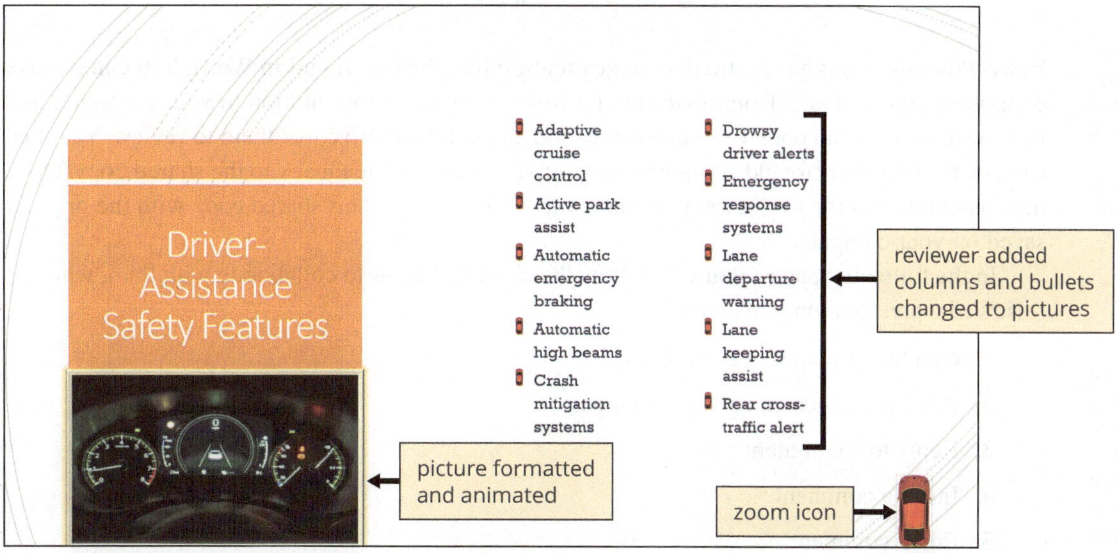

Nick Fewings/Unsplash.com; OpenClipart-Vectors/27376 images/Pixabay

Figure 5–1(c): Slide 3 (Enhanced from Reviewer)

OpenClipart-Vectors/27376 images/Pixabay; CopyrightFreePictures/202 images/Pixabay; ElasticComputeFarm/39 images/Pixabay; Clker-Free-Vector-Images/29538 images/Pixabay

Figure 5–1(d): Slide 4 (Animation Added to Reviewer's Slide)

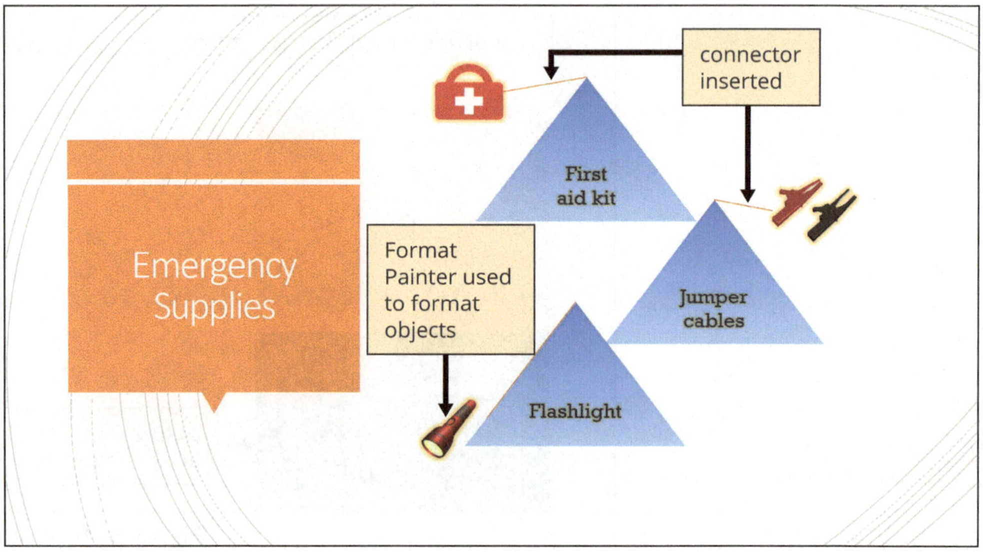

OpenClipart-Vectors/27376 images/Pixabay; OpenClipart-Vectors/27376 images/Pixabay; OpenClipart-Vectors/27376 images/Pixabay

Figure 5–1(e): Slide 5 (Enhanced from Reviewer)

BTW

Screen Resolution

If you are using a computer to step through the project in this module and you want your screens to match the figures in this book, you should change your screen's resolution to 1920 × 1080.

BTW

Touch Mode Differences

The Microsoft 365 and Windows interfaces may vary if you are using a touch screen. For this reason, you might notice that the function or appearance of your touch screen differs slightly from this module's presentation.

PowerPoint does not have a track changes feature like the one found in Word. You can receive comments and feedback from reviewers by first saving your presentation to your computer and then posting a second copy to a shared location, such as OneDrive, for them to review. You then can ask the reviewers to add comments to your slides and add feedback to the shared copy. Once they have finished their reviews, you can compare and merge their shared copy with the original saved on your computer.

In the following pages, you will follow these general steps to collaborate with Sam, who has reviewed a presentation you created:

1. Combine (merge) presentations.
2. Review and accept or reject changes.
3. Reply to a comment.
4. Insert a comment.
5. Edit a comment.
6. Delete a comment.

To Merge a Presentation

Sam's changes to the initial presentation include adding a subtitle, converting the Slide 1 title text to WordArt, and changing the Slide 3 bulleted list into columns. A transition is added to all slides, the theme is changed, and a slide is added. **Why?** Sam reviewed your Driving presentation and made several comments, so you want to combine (merge) his changes with your file to see if they improve the original design and slide content. The following steps merge this reviewer's file with your Driving Final presentation.

1

- sam Run PowerPoint. If necessary, maximize the PowerPoint window.
- Open the presentation, SC_PPT_5_Driving, from the Data Files. If a yellow Protected View message is displayed above Slide 1, click the Enable Editing button in the message.
- Save the presentation using **SC_PPT_5_Driving_Final** as the file name.
- Display the Review tab (Figure 5–2).

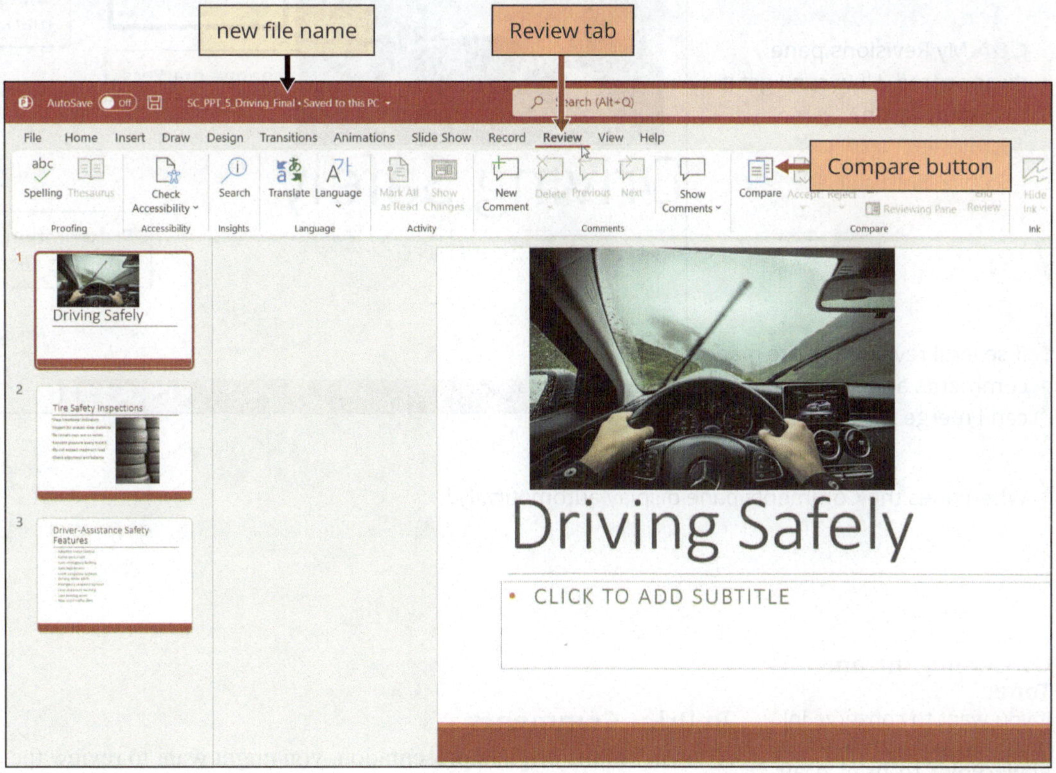

StockSnap/27551 images/Pixabay

Figure 5–2

Q&A Why do the slides have a different size than the slides I have seen in previous presentations?
The slides in the Driving presentation use a 4:3 ratio, which was the default setting in PowerPoint versions prior to PowerPoint 2013.

2

- Click the Compare button (Review tab | Compare group) to display the 'Choose File to Merge with Current Presentation' dialog box.
- With the list of your Data Files displayed, click SC_PPT_5_Driving - Sam to select the PowerPoint file (Figure 5–3).

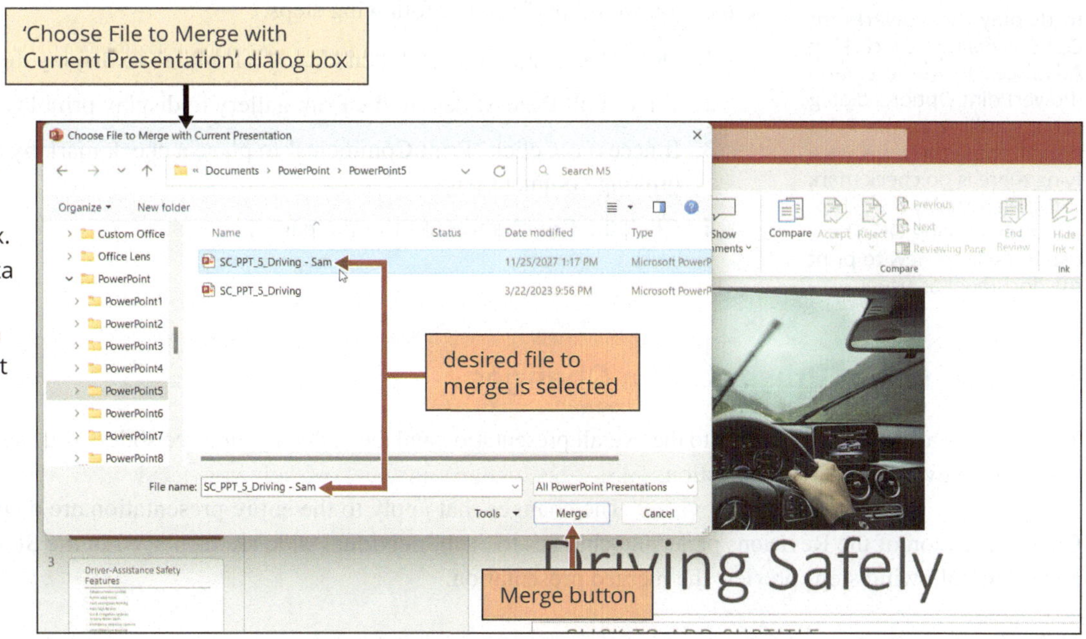

StockSnap/27551 images/Pixabay

Figure 5–3

3

- Click the Merge button (Choose File to Merge with Current Presentation dialog box) to merge Sam's presentation with the Driving_Final presentation and to display the Revisions pane (Figure 5–4).

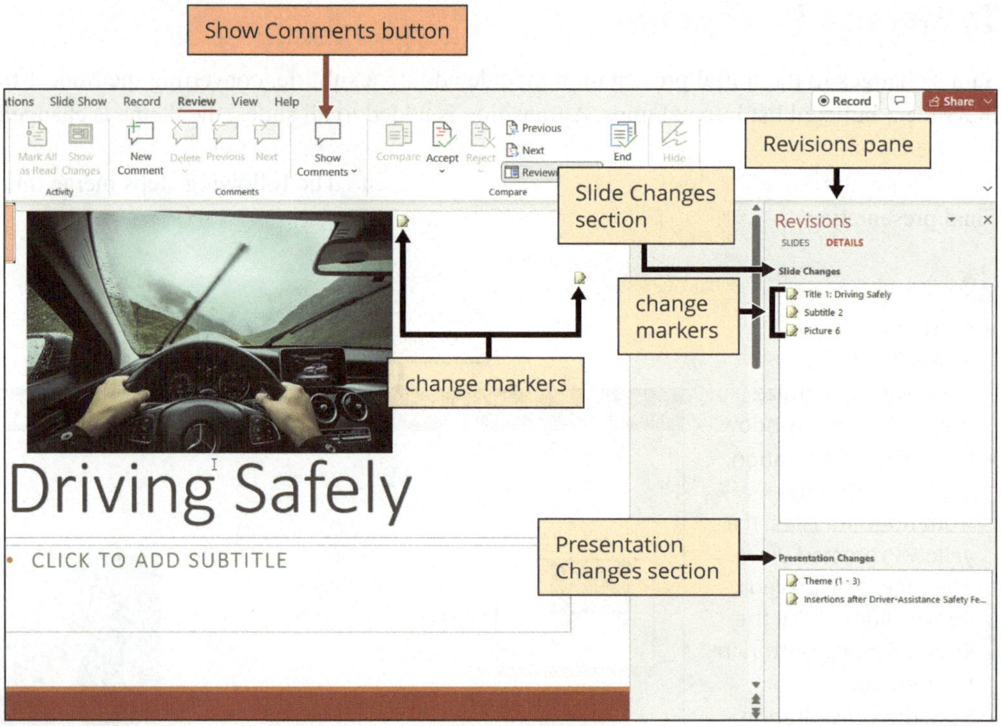

StockSnap/27551 images/Pixabay

Figure 5–4

Q&A My Revisions pane disappeared. How can I get it to display again?
Click Reviewing Pane (Review tab | Compare group) or click the Revisions button to the right of the Comments pane to display the Revisions pane instead of the Comments pane.

If several reviewers have made comments and suggestions, can I merge their files, too?
Yes. Repeat Steps 1, 2, and 3.

When does the Comments pane display automatically?
It displays if it was left open during a previous PowerPoint session. Clicking Show Comments or Comments on the ribbon displays or hides the Comments pane.

BTW
Conserving Ink and Toner
If you want to conserve ink or toner, you can instruct PowerPoint to print draft quality documents by clicking File on the ribbon to open Backstage view, clicking Options in Backstage view to display the PowerPoint Options dialog box, clicking Advanced in the left pane (PowerPoint Options dialog box), scrolling to the Print area in the right pane, verifying there is no check mark in the High quality check box, and then clicking OK. Then, use Backstage view to print the document as usual.

To Print Comments

As owner of the original presentation, you might want to review the comments and modifications on a hard copy before making decisions about whether to accept these suggestions. You can print each slide and the comments a reviewer has made before you begin to accept and reject each suggestion. PowerPoint can print these slides and comments on individual pages. To perform this action, you would perform the following steps.

1. Open Backstage view and then click the Print tab to display the Print gallery.
2. Click 'Full Page Slides' in the Print gallery to display print layouts.
3. If necessary, click 'Print Comments' to place a check mark by this option and turn on printing comment pages.
4. Click the Print button to print the pages.

To Preview the Presentation Changes

The reviewer made several changes to the overall presentation and then edited your three slides. You can preview the modifications to obtain an overview of the suggestions. **Why?** Seeing the edits now can help you decide later whether to accept or reject each change as you step through each revision. The changes that apply to the entire presentation are displayed in the Presentation Changes section of the Revisions pane, and changes to each individual slide are displayed in the Slide Changes section of this pane. The following steps preview the merged presentation.

1

- With the Review tab and Slide 1 displayed, click the SLIDES tab in the Revisions pane to display a thumbnail of merged Slide 1.
- Click the Sam check box above the Slide 1 thumbnail (Revisions pane) to view the proposed changes in the main slide pane (Figure 5–5).

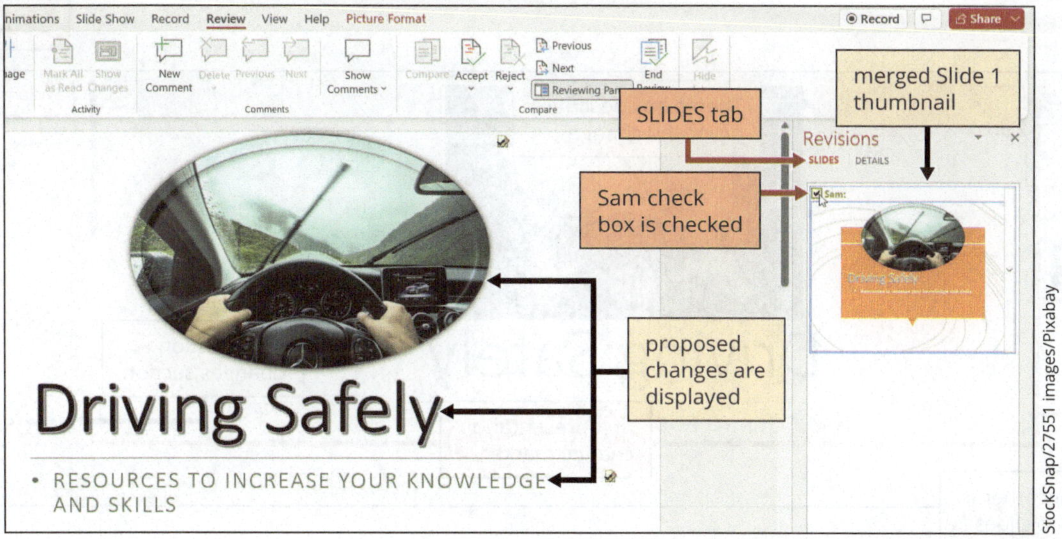

Figure 5–5

2

- Click the Sam check box again to remove the check mark and undo the changes.

Q&A Can I make some, but not all, of the reviewer's changes on Slide 1?
Yes. PowerPoint allows you to view each proposed change individually and then either accept or reject the modification.

Consider This

How do I accept and evaluate criticism positively?

Receiving feedback from others ultimately should enhance your presentation. If several of your reviewers make similar comments, such as too much text appears on one slide or that a chart would help present your concept, then you should heed their criticism and modify your slides. Criticism from a variety of people, particularly if they are from different cultures or vary in age, gives a wide range of viewpoints. Some reviewers might focus on the font size, some on color and design choices, while others might single out the overall message. These individuals should evaluate and comment on your work, such as saying that the overall presentation is good or that a particular paragraph is confusing, and then give specific information about what elements are effective or how you can edit the paragraph.

When you receive these comments, do not get defensive. Ask yourself why your reviewers would have made these comments. Perhaps they lack a background in the subject matter. Or they may have a particular interest in this topic and can add their expertise.

To Review, Accept, and Reject Presentation Changes

Changes that affect the entire presentation are indicated in the Presentation Changes section of the Revisions pane. These changes can include transitions, color schemes, fonts, and backgrounds. They also can include slide insertions. Sam added three slides in his review, so you can insert these slides in your presentation and then accept or reject each one. The following steps display and accept the reviewer's three slides and then delete one of the inserted slides. **Why?** You want to see all the slides and then evaluate how they add value to the presentation. One of the slides has a topic you want to use in another presentation, so you want to delete that slide.

1

- Click the DETAILS tab in the Revisions pane.
- In the Presentation Changes section of the Revisions pane, click the first presentation change marker, Theme (1 - 3) to display the Theme box with an explanation of the proposed change for all slides in the presentation (Figure 5–6).

StockSnap/27551 images/Pixabay; FlenderFunways/4 images/Pixabay

Figure 5–6

2

- Click the Theme check box to view the new Atlas theme on all slides (Figure 5–7).

StockSnap/27551 images/Pixabay; FlenderFunways/4 images/Pixabay

Figure 5–7

Q&A Can I also apply the change by tapping or clicking the Accept button (Review tab | Compare group)?

Yes. Either method applies the Atlas theme.

If I decide not to apply the new theme, can I reverse this change?

Yes. Click Reject (Review tab | Compare group) or click the check box to remove the check and reject the reviewer's theme modification.

3

- Click the second presentation change marker, 'Insertions after Driver-Assistance Safety Fe...' in the Presentation Changes section to display an insertion box with a list of the three proposed new slides to insert into the presentation (Intersection Right-of-Way, Distracted Driving, and Emergency Supplies) (Figure 5–8).

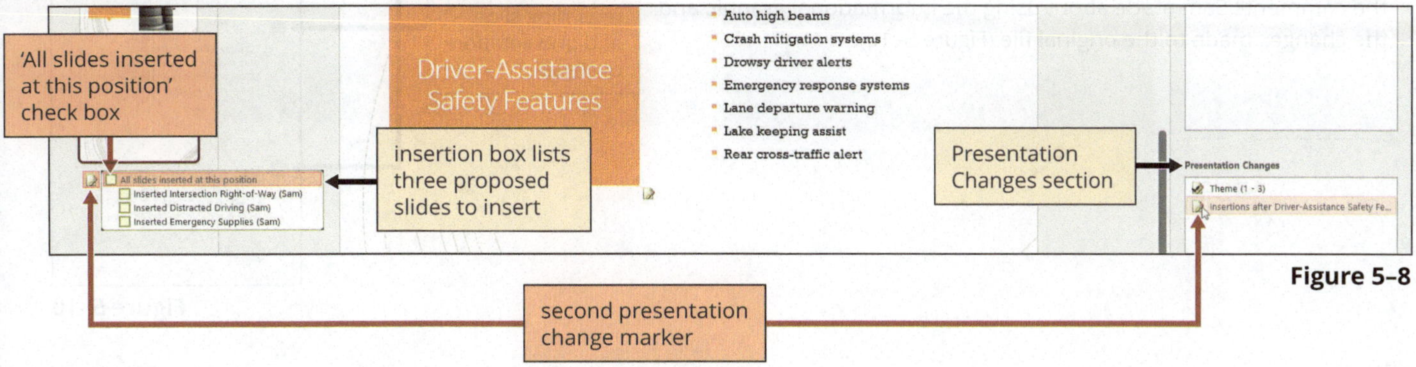

Figure 5–8

Q&A What is the significance of the check boxes in the insertion box?
You can click the first check box to insert all three slides in your presentation. You can elect to insert one or two slides by clicking the check mark to the left of each slide title.

4

- Click the 'All slides inserted at this position' check box to insert the three new slides (Figure 5–9).

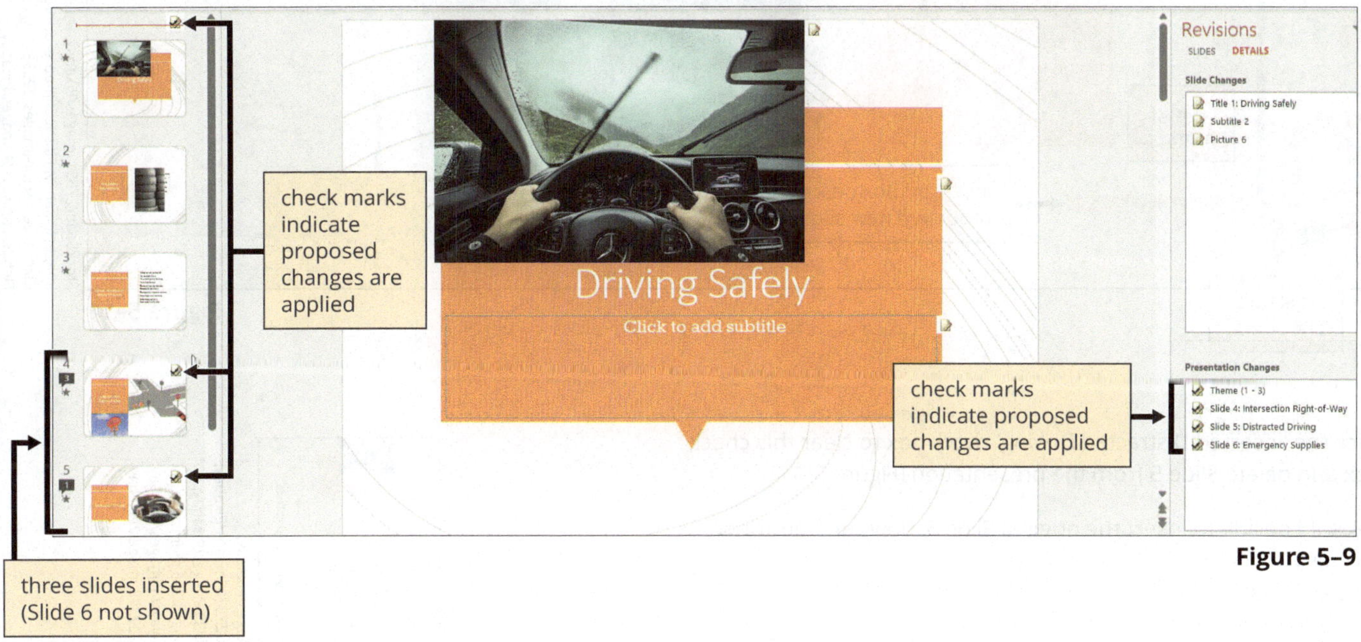

Figure 5–9

StockSnap/27551 images/Pixabay; OpenClipart-Vectors/27376 images/Pixabay; ElasticComputeFarm/39 images/Pixabay; Clker-Free-Vector-Images/29538 images/Pixabay; FlenderFunways/4 images/Pixabay

Q&A Why do check marks appear in the Slides 4, 5, and 6 thumbnails in the Slides tab and in the Presentation Changes section?
The check marks indicate you have applied the proposed changes.

5

- Display Slide 4 and review the slide contents. Then, display Slide 5 and review the information.
- Display Slide 4 again. If necessary, click the Show Comments button (Review tab | Comments group) to display comments, and then read the comments Sam made about using the informational graphic and the changes made to the original file (Figure 5–10).

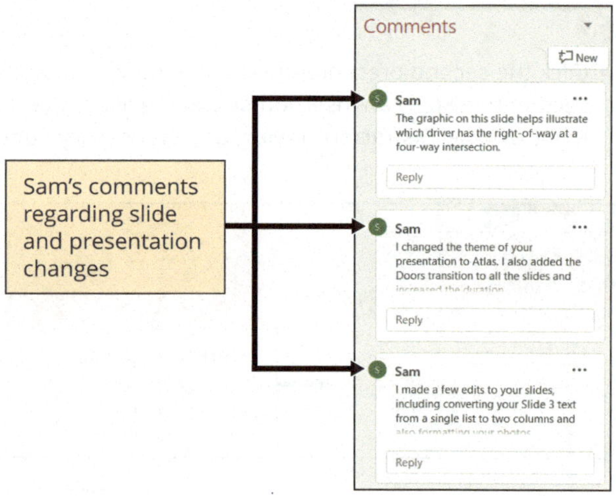

Figure 5–10

6

- Display Slide 5, read Sam's comment, and then click the change marker on the Slide 5 thumbnail to display the insertion box (Figure 5–11).

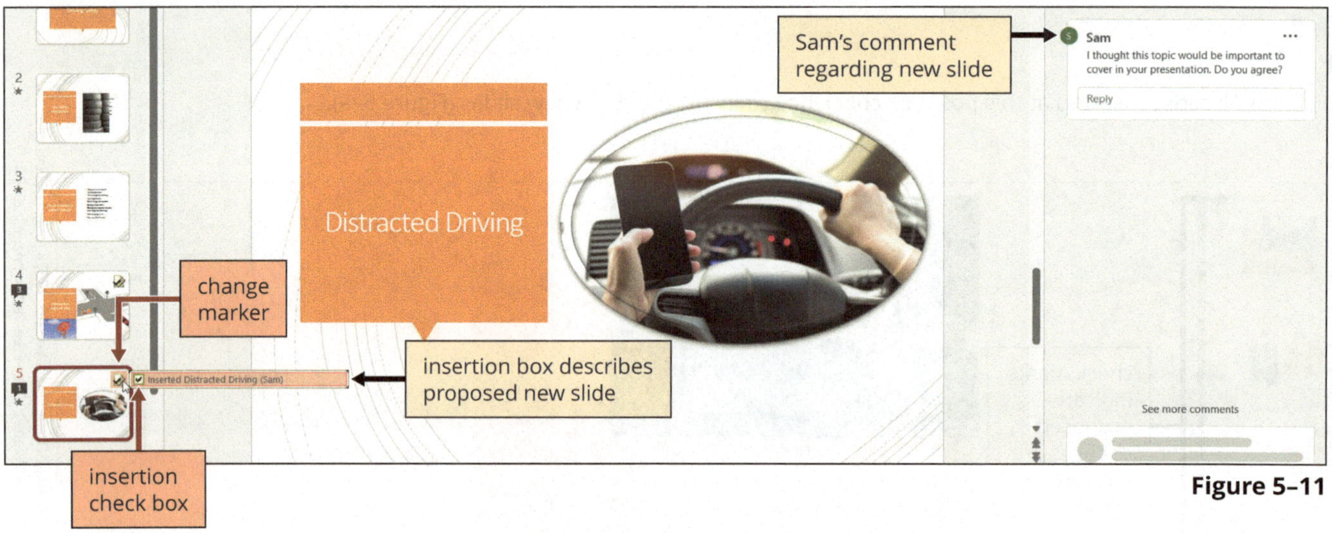

Figure 5–11

StockSnap/27551 images/Pixabay; OpenClipart-Vectors/27376 images/Pixabay; ElasticComputeFarm/39 images/Pixabay; Clker-Free-Vector-Images/29538 images/Pixabay; FlenderFunways/4 images/Pixabay

7

- Click the 'Inserted Distracted Driving' check box to clear this check box and delete Slide 5 from the presentation (Figure 5–12).

Q&A If I decide to insert the original Slide 5, how can I perform this task?

Click the change marker above the current Slide 5 to insert the slide you deleted.

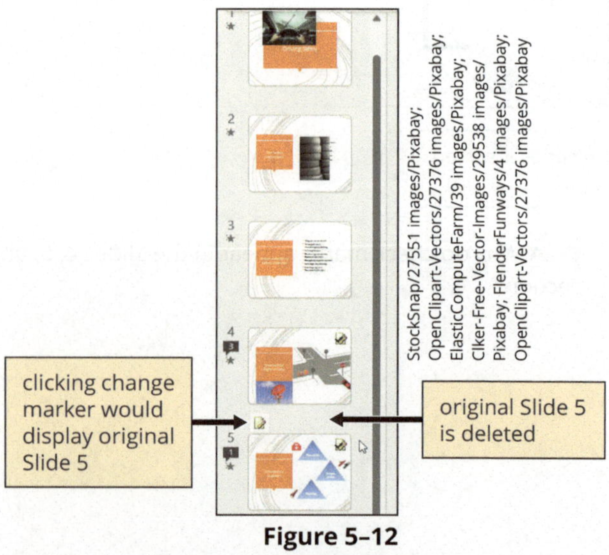

Figure 5–12

StockSnap/27551 images/Pixabay; OpenClipart-Vectors/27376 images/Pixabay; ElasticComputeFarm/39 images/Pixabay; Clker-Free-Vector-Images/29538 images/Pixabay; FlenderFunways/4 images/Pixabay; OpenClipart-Vectors/27376 images/Pixabay

Other Ways

1. Click Next or Previous (Review tab | Compare group), click Accept or Reject button
2. Right-click proposed change, click Accept Change or Reject Change on shortcut menu

To Review, Accept, and Reject Slide Changes

Changes that affect only the displayed slide are indicated in the Slide Changes section of the DETAILS tab on the Revisions pane. A reviewer can modify many aspects of the slide, such as adding and deleting pictures and clips, editing text, and moving placeholders. The following steps display and accept the reviewer's revisions to Slide 1. **Why?** You agree with most of the changes Sam suggested because they enhance your slides.

1

- Display Slide 1, if necessary display the Revisions pane, and then click the slide change 'Title 1: Driving Safely' in the Slide Changes section of the Revisions pane to display the Title 1 box with Sam's two proposed changes for the Driving Safely text in the rectangle (Figure 5–13).

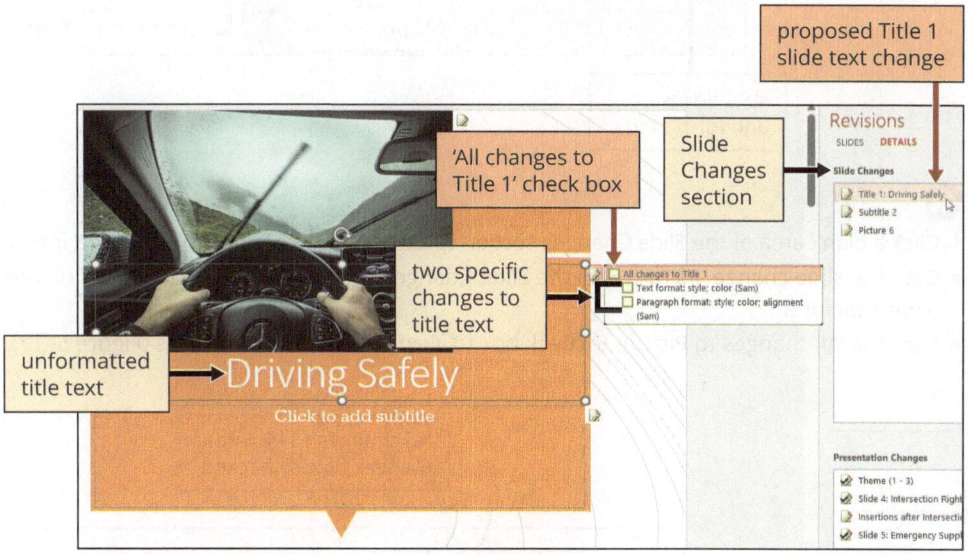

Figure 5–13

2

- Click the 'All changes to Title 1' check box to preview all proposed changes to the Driving Safely text (Figure 5–14).

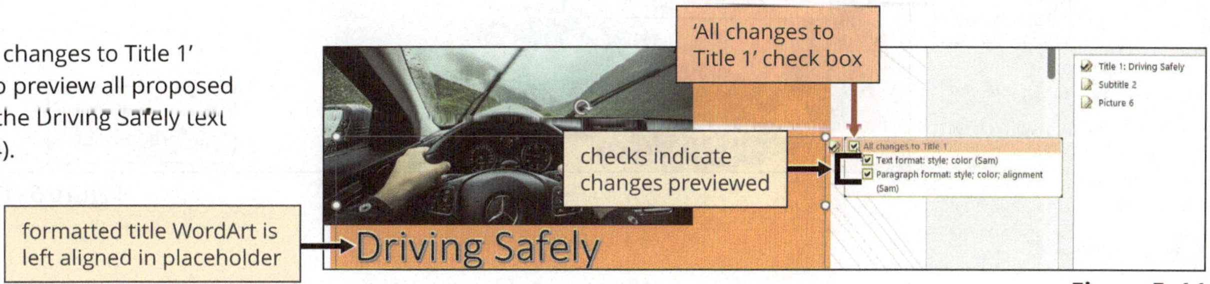

Figure 5–14

3

- Click the Paragraph format check box to uncheck it and preview only the other change to the title text, not the alignment of the title WordArt paragraph (Figure 5–15).

Figure 5–15

Q&A Can I select any combination of the check boxes to modify the text in the rectangle?
Yes. You can click the individual check boxes to preview the reviewer's modifications.

4

- Click a blank area of the Slide Changes section to close the 'All changes to Title 1' insertion box.
- Click the slide change, Subtitle 2, in the Slide Changes section to display the insertion box showing the changes to the Slide 1 subtitle.
- Click the 'All changes to Subtitle 2' check box to view the proposed changes (Figure 5–16).

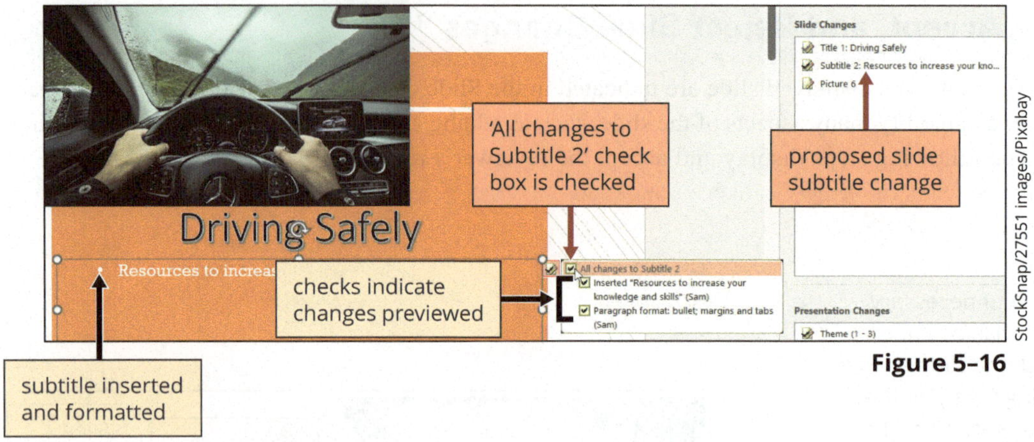

Figure 5–16

5

- Click a blank area of the Slide Changes section to close the 'All changes to Subtitle 2' insertion box.
- Click the slide change, Picture 6, in the Slide Changes section to display the insertion box showing the changes to the Slide 1 picture.
- Click the 'All changes to Picture 6' check box to view the proposed changes (Figure 5–17).

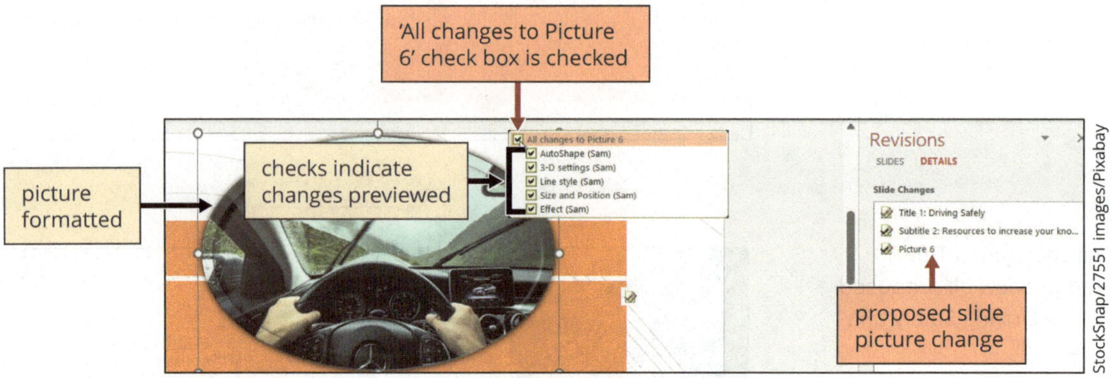

Figure 5–17

6

- Click a blank area of the Slide Changes section to close the 'All changes to Picture 6' insertion box.

Other Ways

1. Click Next or Previous (Review tab | Compare group), click Accept or Reject
2. Right-click proposed change, click Accept Change or Reject Change on shortcut menu

To Review and Accept Slide Changes on the Remaining Slides

You have accepted most of Sam's presentation and Slide 1 changes. He also made changes to slides 2 and 3. The following steps accept his modifications.

1

- Display Slide 2 and then click the SLIDES tab in the Revisions pane to show a thumbnail of Slide 2.

2

- Click the Sam check box above the Slide 2 thumbnail (Revisions pane) to display a preview of and accept the Slide 2 revisions (Figure 5–18).

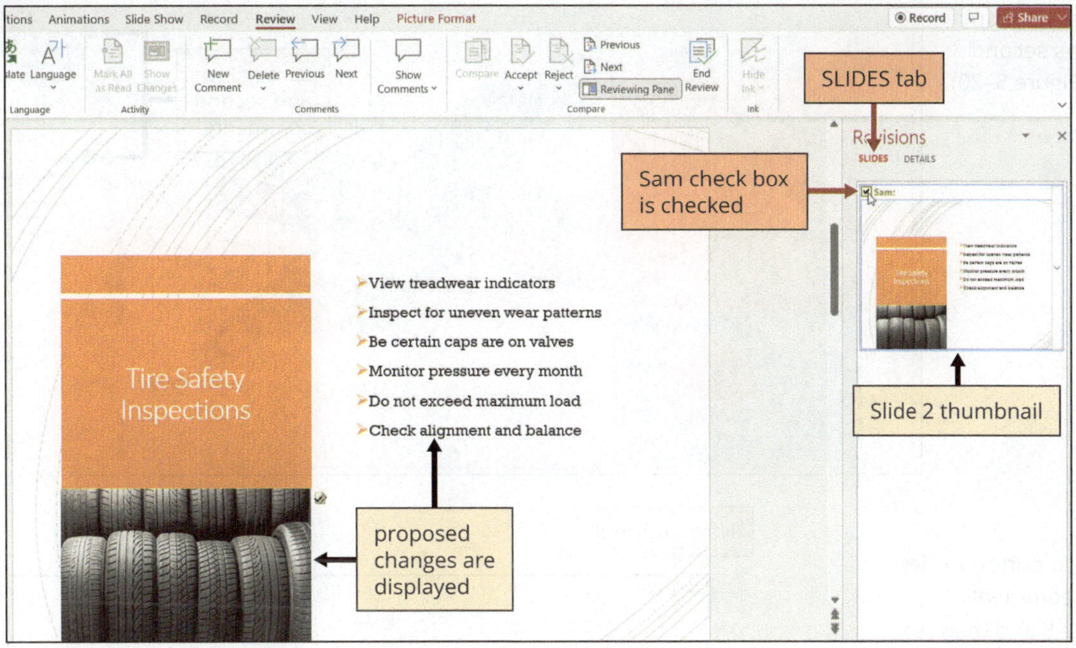

FlenderFunways/4 images/Pixabay

Figure 5–18

3

- Display Slide 3 and then click the Sam check box above the Slide 3 thumbnail (Revisions pane) to display a preview of and accept the Slide 3 revisions (Figure 5–19).

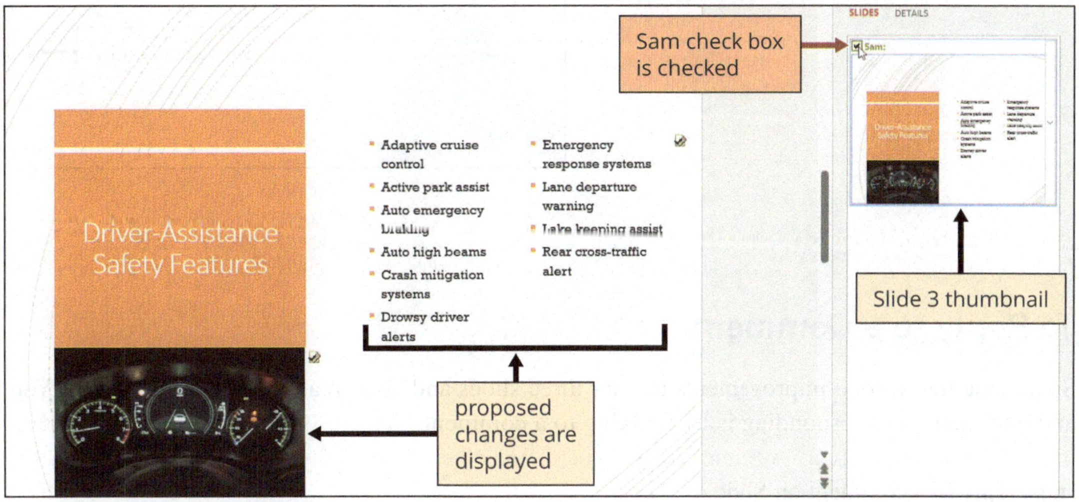

Nick Fewings/Unsplash.com

Figure 5–19

To Review Comments

The Comments pane displays the reviewer's name above each comment, and an associated comment marker is displayed on the slide. The following steps review comments for Slide 4. **Why?** You want to look at each comment before deciding to accept or reject the changes.

1

- Display Slide 4 and then click the Next button (Review tab | Comments group) to read Sam's first comment.
- Click the Next button to view Sam's second comment (Figure 5–20).

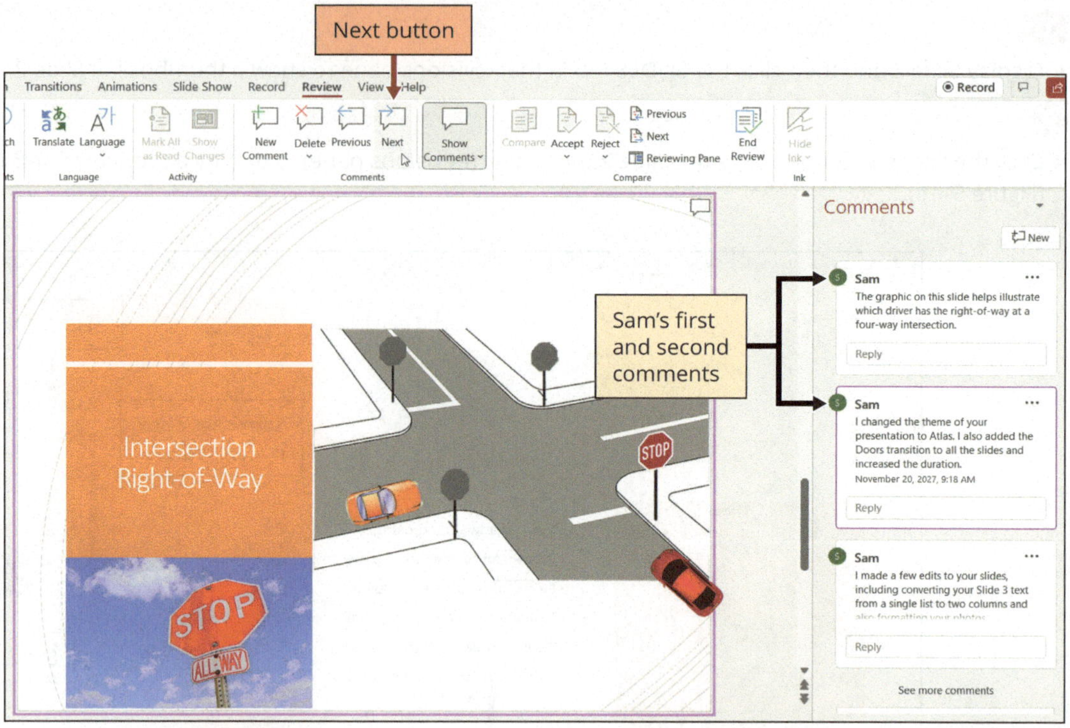

OpenClipart-Vectors/27376 images/Pixabay; CopyrightFreePictures/202 images/Pixabay; ElasticComputeFarm/39 images/Pixabay; Clker-Free-Vector-Images/29538 images/Pixabay

Figure 5–20

2

- Click the Next button to view Sam's third comment.
- Display Slide 5 and then read Sam's comment (Figure 5–21).

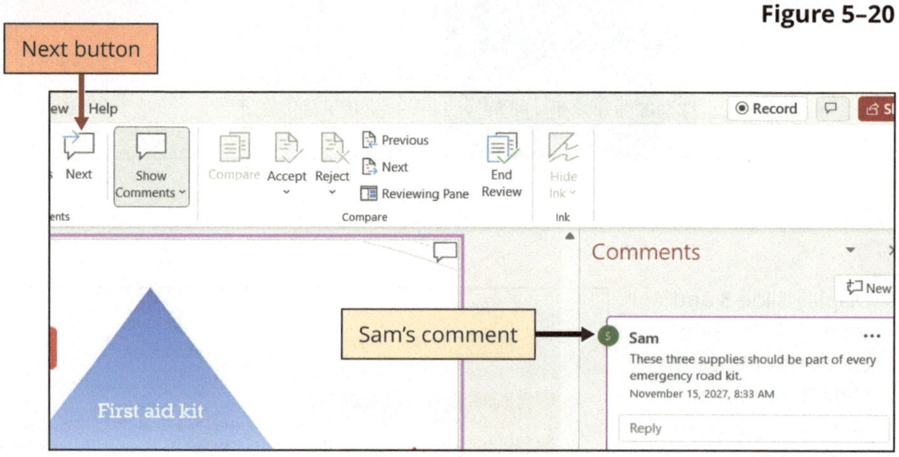

Figure 5–21

To Reply to a Comment

Sam made many good improvements to your three slides and also created some useful slides. You want to provide feedback, and one method of responding is by replying to a comment. **Why?** Giving feedback helps reviewers realize their efforts in improving the presentation were useful and encourages them to continue to participate in collaboration efforts. The following steps reply to a comment on Slide 4.

1

- Display Slide 4 and then select the first comment.
- Click the Reply box to place the insertion point in that box (Figure 5–22).

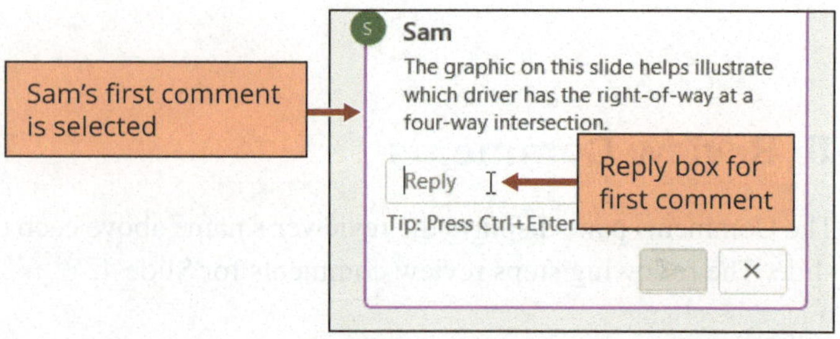

Figure 5–22

2

- Type **This graphic is great!** in the Reply box (Figure 5–23).

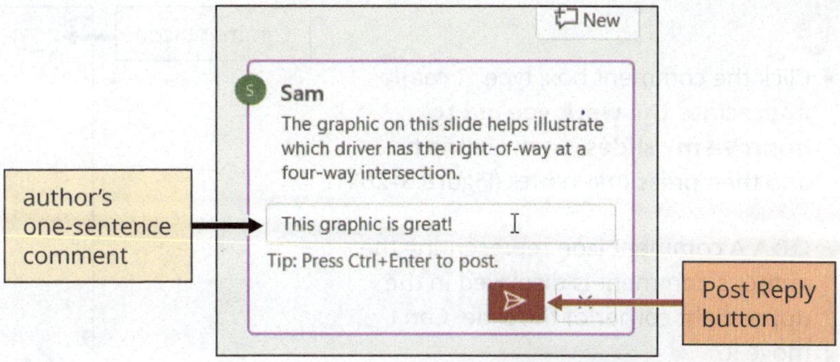

Figure 5–23

3

- Click the Post Reply button to post the comment (Figure 5–24).

Q&A Why does my name differ from that shown in the figure, which is Your Name?
The name reflects the information that was entered when Microsoft 365 was installed on your computer.

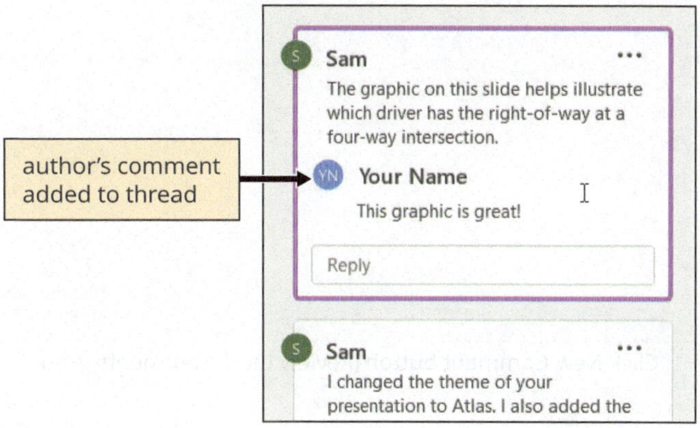

Figure 5–24

Other Ways

1. Press CTRL+ENTER

To Insert a Comment

Sam's comments and changes greatly enhanced your slide show, and you would like to thank him for taking the time to review your original slides. **Why?** He will be able to see what modifications you accepted. The following steps insert a comment on Slide 5.

1

- Display Slide 5 and then click the New button (Comments pane) to open a comment box in the Comments pane (Figure 5–25).

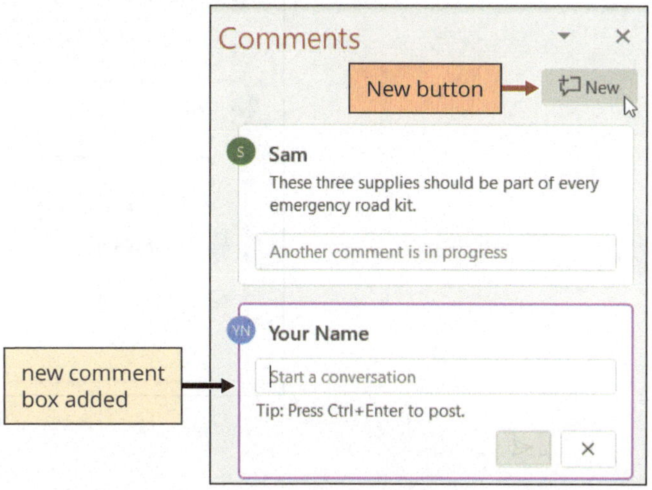

Figure 5–25

2

- Click the comment box, type **I really appreciate the work you did to improve my slides, Sam.** in the box, and then press CTRL+ENTER (Figure 5–26).

Q&A A comment icon representing the author's comment is displayed in the upper-right corner of the slide. Can I move it?
Yes. Select the comment icon on the slide and then drag it to another location on the slide.

Figure 5–26

Other Ways

1. Click New Comment button (Review tab | Comments group)

To Edit a Comment

Once you have reviewed comments, you may decide to change a comment you made to a reviewer. The following steps edit your comment to add another sentence. **Why?** You want to give Sam additional information about how you are going to modify one of the slides.

1

- Display Slide 4, click the first comment in the Comments pane to select it, and then point to your comment to display the Edit comment and 'More comment actions' buttons (Figure 5–27).

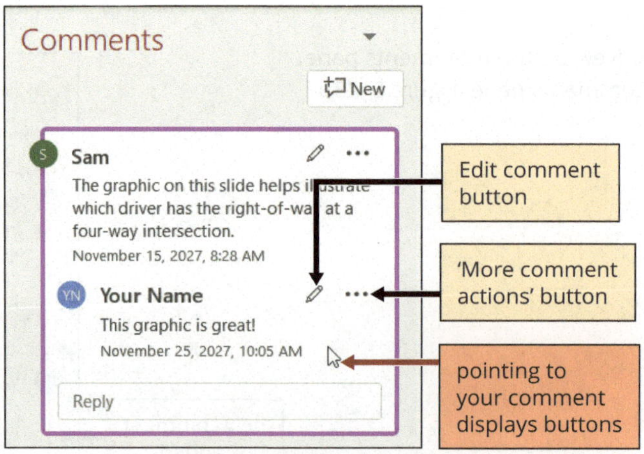

Figure 5–27

- Click the Edit comment button, place the insertion point after the exclamation point in your sentence, press SPACEBAR, type **I'm going to add some animation to illustrate which driver has the right-of-way in this intersection.** in the box, and then press CTRL+ENTER (Figure 5–28).

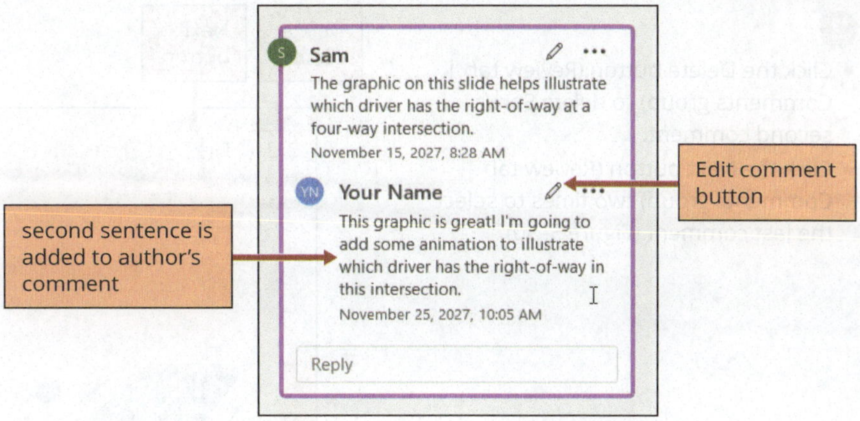

Figure 5–28

To Delete a Comment

Once you have reviewed comments, you may no longer want them to be a part of your slides. You can delete comments that you have read and considered as you are preparing your slides. The following steps delete three of Sam's comments. **Why?** They are not necessary now because you have incorporated the changes into your initial presentation.

1

- With Slide 4 displayed, click Sam's second comment in the Comments pane to select it (Figure 5–29).

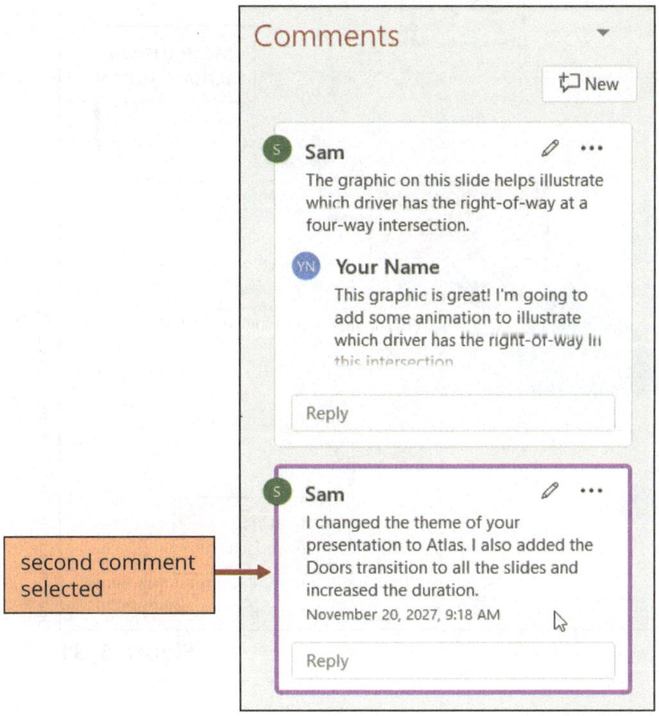

Figure 5–29

2

- Click the Delete button (Review tab | Comments group) to delete Sam's second comment.
- Click the Next button (Review tab | Comments group) two times to select the last comment (Figure 5–30).

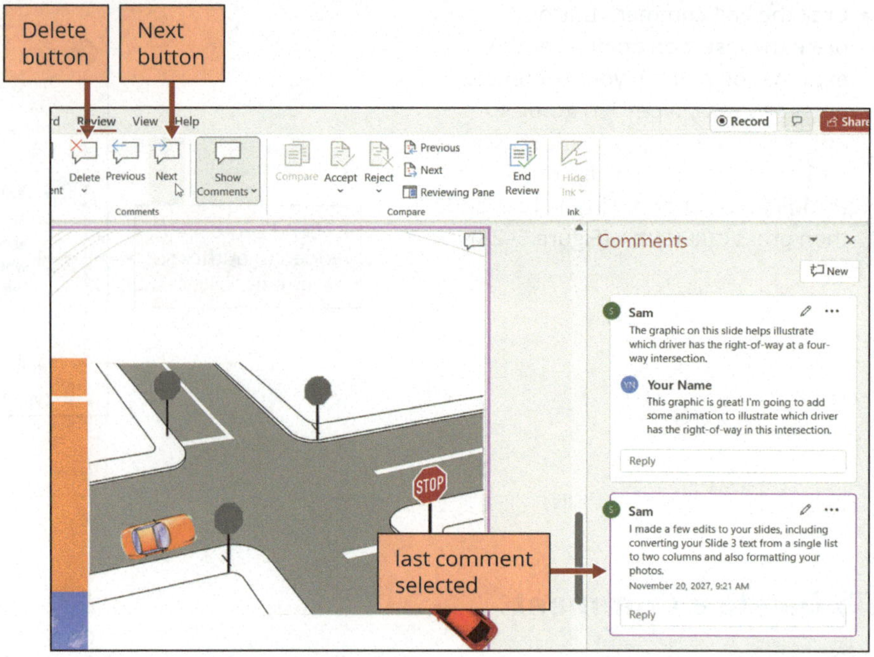

OpenClipart-Vectors/27376 images/Pixabay; CopyrightFreePictures/202 images/Pixabay; Clker-Free-Vector-Images/29538 images/Pixabay; ElasticComputeFarm/39 images/Pixabay

Figure 5–30

3

- Delete the selected comment and then click the Next button two times to select the first comment on Slide 5 (Figure 5–31).

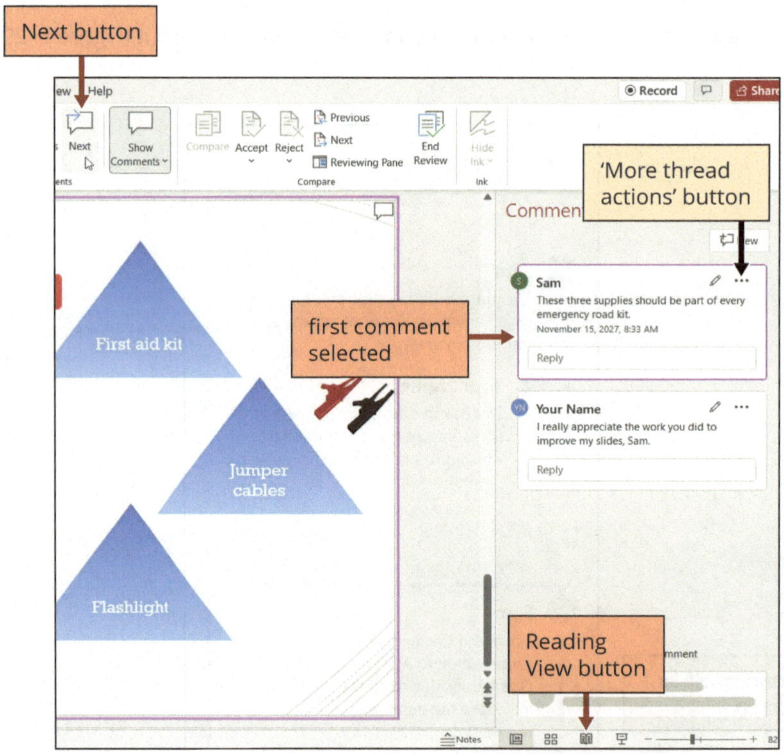

OpenClipart-Vectors/27376 images/Pixabay

Figure 5–31

4

- Delete the selected comment.
- Skip the last comment.

Other Ways

1. Click 'More thread actions' button (Comments pane), click Delete thread

To Run the Revised Presentation in Reading View

Sam's changes modified the original presentation substantially, so it is a good idea to review the new presentation. The following steps review the slides in Reading view. **Why?** This view helps you see large images of the slides so you can evaluate their content without needing to start Slide Show view.

1

- Display Slide 1 and then click the Reading View button on the status bar (shown in Figure 5–31) to display Slide 1 in this view (Figure 5–32).

Figure 5–32

2

- Click the Next and Previous buttons to advance the slides and review the changes on each slide.
- Click the black 'End of slide show' screen to end the slide show and return to Normal view.

Other Ways

1. Click Reading View button (View tab | Presentation Views group)

Consider This

How should I give constructive criticism when I am reviewing a presentation?

If you are asked to critique a presentation, begin and end with positive comments. Give specific details about a few key areas that can be improved. Be honest, but be tactful. Avoid using the word, you. For example, instead of writing, "You need to give some statistics to support your viewpoint," write "I had difficulty understanding which departments' sales have increased in the past six months. Perhaps a chart with specific figures would help depict how dramatically revenues have improved."

To End the Review and Hide Markup

You have analyzed all of the reviewer's proposed changes, so your review of the merged presentation is complete. You now can accept and apply all the changes and hide the comments that are present on slides 4 and 5. **Why?** You do not need to see the comments when you are developing the remainder of the presentation, so you can hide them. The following steps end the review of the merged slides.

BTW

Removing Comments

If you want to remove comments on slides before saving your presentation, inspect your presentation. To perform this action, open Backstage view, click the 'Check for issues' button in the Info tab, click Inspect Document, and then click the Inspect button.

1

- With the Review tab displayed, click the End Review button (Review tab | Compare group) to display the Microsoft PowerPoint dialog box (Figure 5–33).

2

- Click Yes (Microsoft PowerPoint dialog box) to apply the changes you accepted and discard the changes you rejected.

Q&A Which changes are discarded?
You did not apply the aligned WordArt on Slide 1 and did not insert Sam's proposed Slide 5.

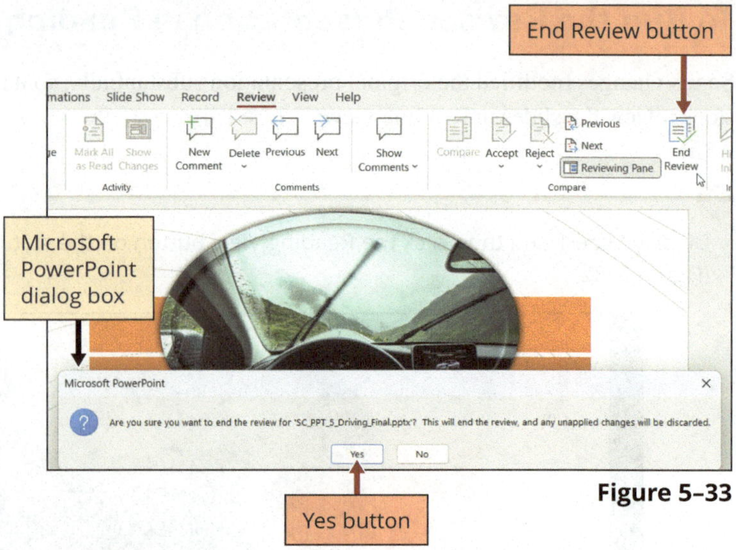

StockSnap/27551 images/Pixabay

Figure 5–33

- Click the Show Comments arrow (Review tab | Comments group) to display the Show Comments menu (Figure 5–34).
- If Comments Pane is checked in the menu, click it to remove the check mark.

3

- Click Show Markup in the menu to remove the check mark and hide comments on the slide.

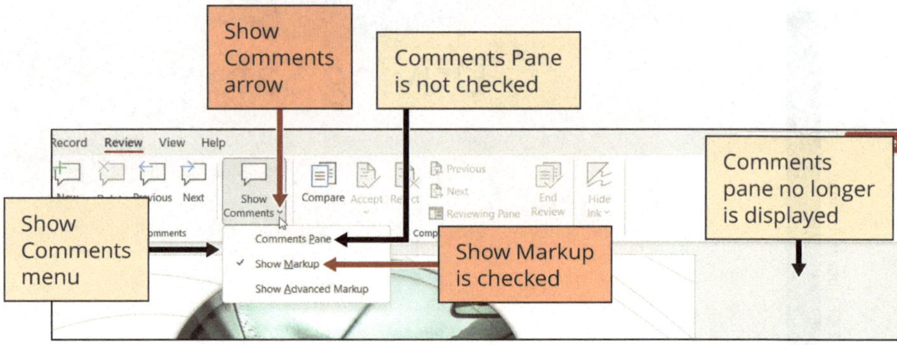

StockSnap/27551 images/Pixabay

Figure 5–34

To Resize Slides

Prior to PowerPoint 2013, PowerPoint set slides in a 4:3 aspect ratio, commonly known as the fullscreen or widescreen aspect ratio. This format was the first standard for monitors and televisions. Many videos were recorded in this configuration, which is the ratio between the width and height of the display. The higher the first number compared to the second number, the wider the screen will be compared to the height. If you know your presentation will be viewed on a widescreen display, you can change the slide size to optimize the proportions. The following steps change the default setting to 16:9. **Why?** This 16:9 dimension is the proportion of most widescreen displays.

1

- Display the Design tab and then click the Slide Size button (Design tab | Customize group) to display the Slide Size gallery (Figure 5–35).

StockSnap/27551 images/Pixabay

Figure 5–35

2

- Click Widescreen (16:9) to change the slide size setting.

To Align Pictures

You have accepted most of Sam's presentation and Slide 1 changes. He also made changes to other slides. The following steps change the picture sizes and alignments to better correspond to the Widescreen slide size.

1. Display Slide 2, change the tires picture width to 2.5", and then center the picture under the Tire Safety Inspections placeholder. If necessary, change the font size of the title text to 40 point, the font size of the six content paragraphs to 18 point, and the title text placeholder width to 3.83".
2. Display Slide 3, change the dashboard picture width to 4", and then center the picture under the Driver-Assistance Safety Features placeholder. If necessary, change the font size of the title text to 40 point, the font size of the content paragraphs in the two columns to 16 point, and the title text placeholder width to 3.83".
3. Display Slide 4, change the stop sign photo width to 4", and then center the picture under the Intersection Right-of-Way placeholder (Figure 5–36). If necessary, change the font size of the title text to 40 point and the title text placeholder width to 3.83".
4. Display Slide 5 and, if necessary, change the font size of the title text to 40 point.
5. Display Slide 1 and, if necessary, change the font size of the title text to 54 point.
6. If the Comments pane is displayed, close it.

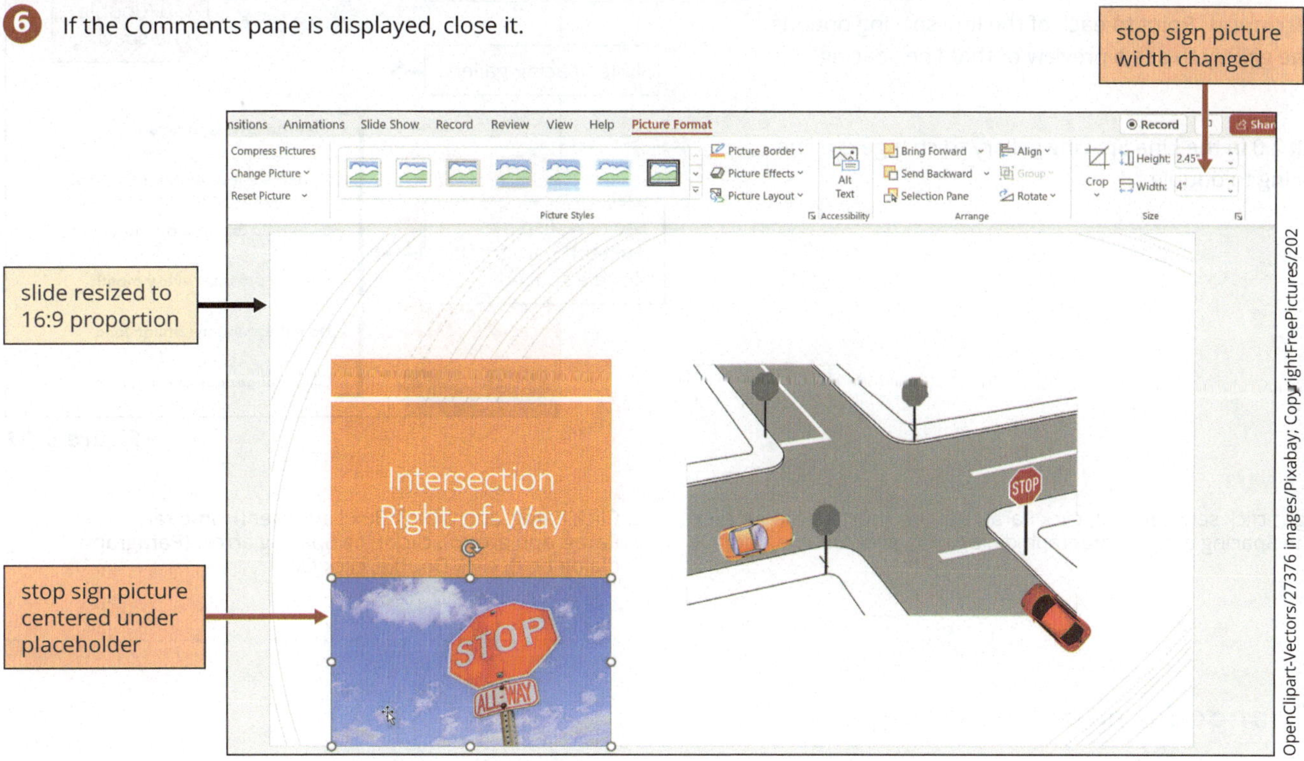

OpenClipart-Vectors/27376 images/Pixabay; CopyrightFreePictures/202 images/Pixabay; ElasticComputeFarm/39 images/Pixabay; Clker-Free-Vector-Images/29538 images/Pixabay

Figure 5–36

Break Point: If you wish to take a break, this is a good place to do so. Be sure the Driving Final file is saved and then you can exit PowerPoint. To resume later, start PowerPoint, open the file called SC_PPT_5_Driving_Final, and continue following the steps from this location forward.

Formatting and Managing Text

Design templates determine formatting characteristics, such as fonts, font styles, effects, colors, paragraph alignment, indentation, and spacing. The design theme also determines the amount of spacing around the sides of the placeholder and between the lines of text. An internal **margin** provides a cushion of space between text and the top, bottom, left, and right sides of the placeholder. **Line spacing** is the amount of vertical space between the lines of text in a paragraph, and **paragraph spacing** is the amount of space above and below a paragraph.

To Change Line Spacing

PowerPoint adjusts the amount of line spacing based on font size. Default line spacing is 1.0, which is considered single spacing. Other preset options are 1.5, 2.0 (double spacing), 2.5, and 3.0 (triple spacing). You can specify precise line spacing intervals between, before, and after paragraphs in the Indents and Spacing tab of the Paragraph dialog box. The following steps increase the line spacing of the content paragraphs from single (1.0) to double (2.0) on Slide 2. **Why?** The additional space helps fill some of the area on the slide and helps your audience read the paragraph text more easily.

1

- Display Slide 2 and then, if necessary, display the Home tab. Select the six content paragraphs.
- Click the Line Spacing button (Home tab | Paragraph group) to display the Line Spacing gallery.
- Point to 2.0 in the Line Spacing gallery to display a live preview of this line spacing (Figure 5–37).
- **Experiment:** Point to each of the line spacing options in the gallery to see a preview of that line spacing.

2

- Click 2.0 in the Line Spacing gallery to change the line spacing to double.

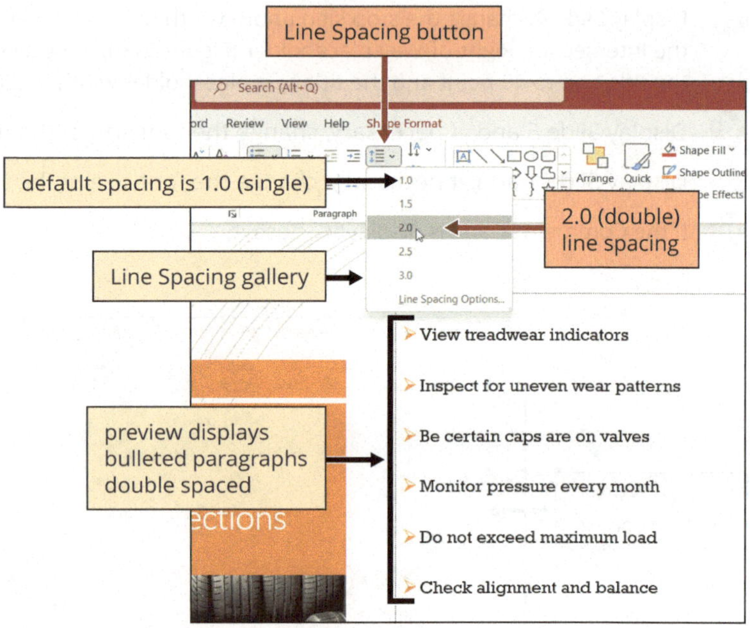

FlenderFunways/4 images/Pixabay

Figure 5–37

Other Ways

1. Right-click selected text, click Paragraph on shortcut menu, click Line Spacing arrow (Paragraph dialog box), click Double, click OK
2. Click Paragraph Dialog Box Launcher (Home tab | Paragraph group), click Line Spacing arrow (Paragraph dialog box), click Double, click OK

To Change Paragraph Spacing

PowerPoint adjusts the paragraph spacing above and below a paragraph automatically to accommodate various font sizes within the placeholder. The following steps change the paragraph spacing to add more space after each paragraph on Slide 2. **Why?** The additional space helps fill some of the area on the slide and also helps your audience read the paragraph text more easily.

1

- With the six content paragraphs selected, click the Line Spacing button (Home tab | Paragraph group) to display the Line Spacing gallery again (Figure 5–38).

2

- Click 'Line Spacing Options' to display the Paragraph dialog box.

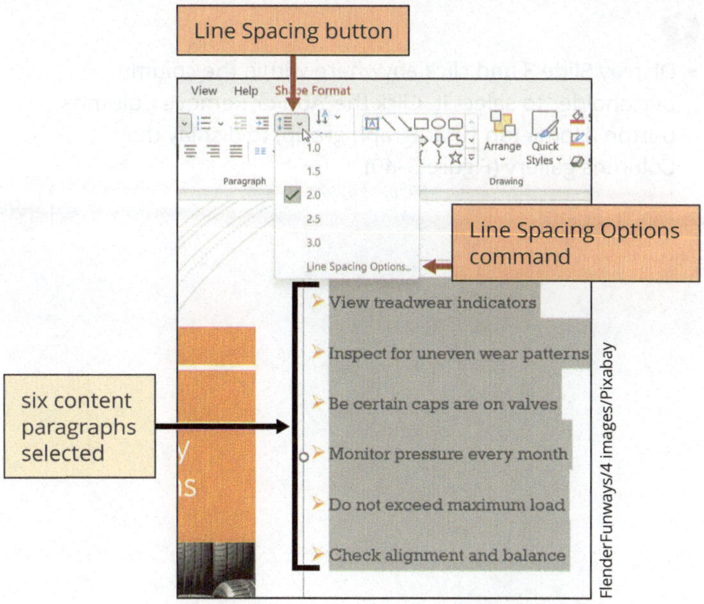

Figure 5–38

3

- Click the Spacing After up arrow twice to increase the spacing to 12 pt (Figure 5–39).

4

- Click OK to close the Paragraph dialog box and apply the new paragraph spacing setting.

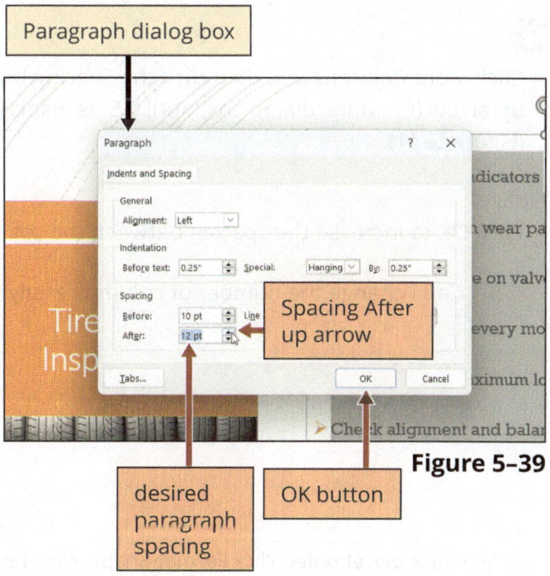

Figure 5–39

Other Ways

1. Right-click selected text, click Paragraph on shortcut menu, click Before or After Spacing arrows (Paragraph dialog box), click OK
2. Click Paragraph Dialog Box Launcher (Home tab | Paragraph group), click Before or After Spacing arrows (Paragraph dialog box), click OK

To Change Column Spacing

The following steps increase the spacing between the columns on Slide 3. **Why?** You wish to increase the space between the columns in the placeholder to fill the width of the placeholder.

1

- Display Slide 3 and click anywhere within the column placeholder to select it. Click the 'Add or Remove Columns' button (Home tab | Paragraph group) to display the Columns gallery (Figure 5–40).

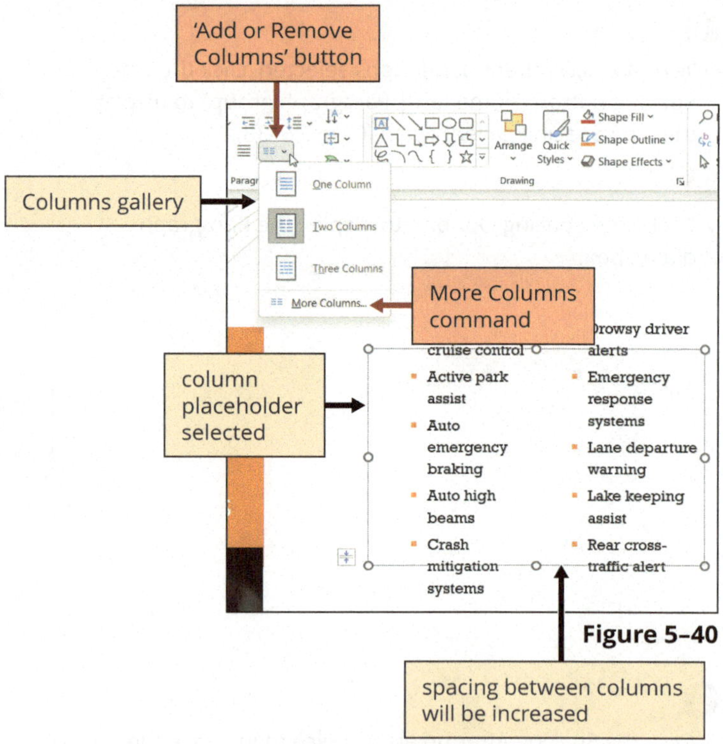

Figure 5–40

2

- Click More Columns and then click the Spacing box up arrow (Columns dialog box) until 0.5" is displayed (Figure 5–41).

3

- Click OK to increase the spacing between the columns.

Q&A Can I change the number of columns easily?
Yes. Click Columns and then click the number of columns you desire.

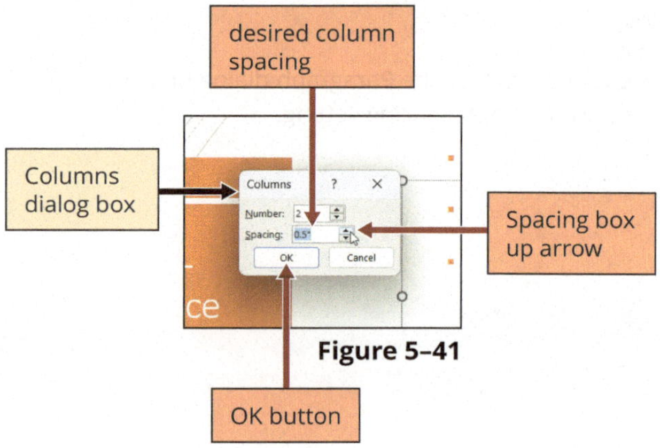

Figure 5–41

Other Ways

1. Right-click placeholder, click Format Shape, click Text Options (Format Shape pane), click Textbox, click Columns button, enter space between columns in Spacing box

To Format Text in Columns

You can add formatting characteristics to the column text to add interest. The following steps change the font color of the column text.

1 Select the text in the Slide 3 placeholder and then change the font color to Dark Blue (ninth color in the Standard Colors row).

2 Click a blank area of the slide to deselect the column text (Figure 5–42).

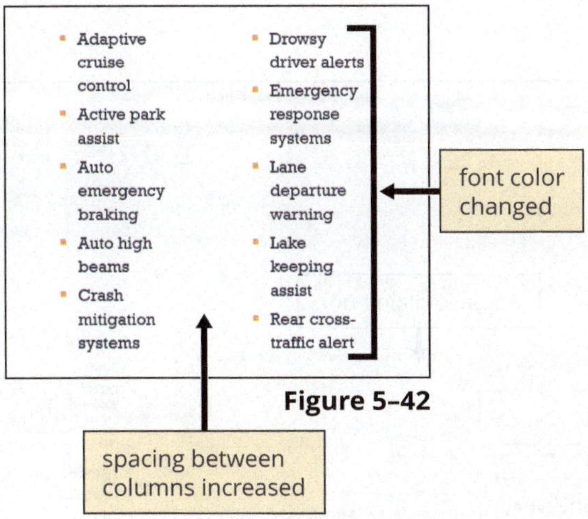

Figure 5–42

To Find Text

You can have PowerPoint locate specific text on any slide in your presentation and in the Notes pane. **Why?** This feature allows you to find particular text quickly and efficiently. It is especially useful when your presentation has many slides. The following steps find the word, Safety, which is found on two slides.

1

- With the Home tab selected, click the Find button (Home tab | Editing group) to display the Find dialog box.
- Type **Safety** in the Find what box (Figure 5–43).

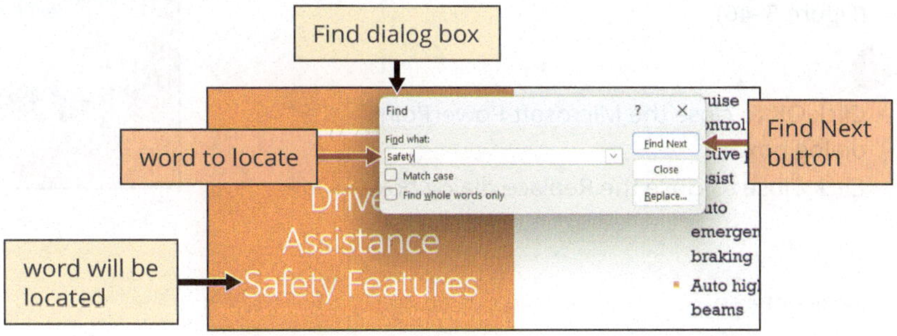

Figure 5–43

2

- Click the Find Next button to display the word, Safety, highlighted on Slide 3.
- Click the Find Next button to display the next occurrence of the word, Safety, on Slide 2 (Figure 5–44).

3

- Click Close to close the Find dialog box.

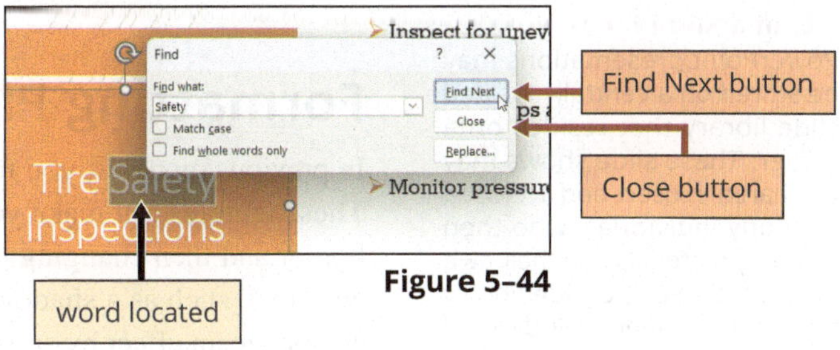

Figure 5–44

Other Ways

1. Press CTRL+F

To Find and Replace Text

If your presentation has many slides and you need to replace a word or phrase, use Find and Replace to efficiently modify the text. You can search for a word or phrase and then replace it with another word or phrase. To change the highlighted text, click the Replace button. To change wherever this text is found in your slides, click the Replace All button. To cancel a search in progress, press ESC. The following steps search for the word, Auto, and replace it with the word, Automatic. **Why?** You want to use the full word instead of a shortened form.

1

- With the Home tab displayed, click the Replace button (Home tab | Editing group) to display the Replace dialog box.
- Type **Auto** in the Find what box.
- Type **Automatic** in the Replace with box.
- Click the Find Next button to display the first occurrence of the word, Auto, on Slide 3 (Figure 5–45).

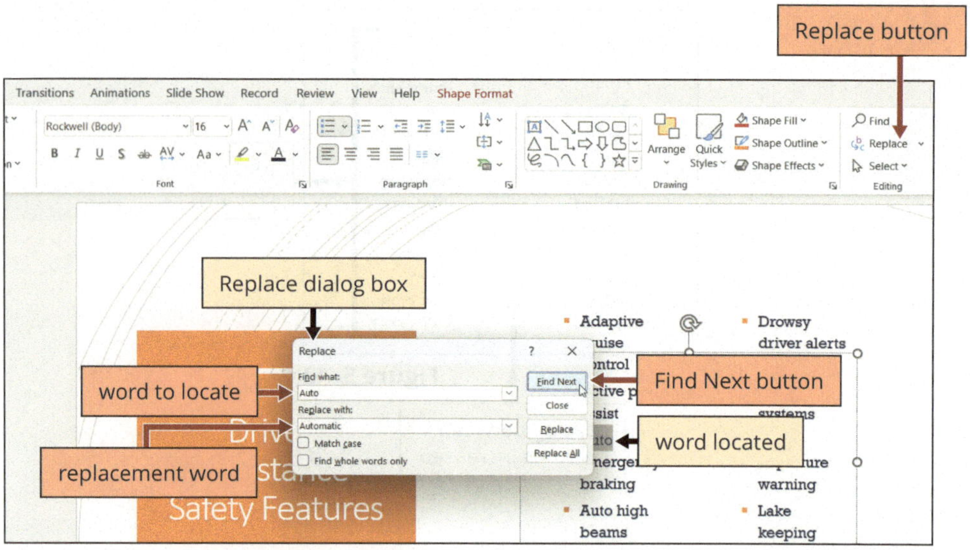

Figure 5–45

2

- Click the Replace button to change the highlighted word, Auto, to Automatic.
- Click the Replace button to change the second occurrence of the word, Auto, to Automatic (Figure 5–46).

3

- Click OK to close the Microsoft PowerPoint dialog box.
- Click Close to close the Replace dialog box.

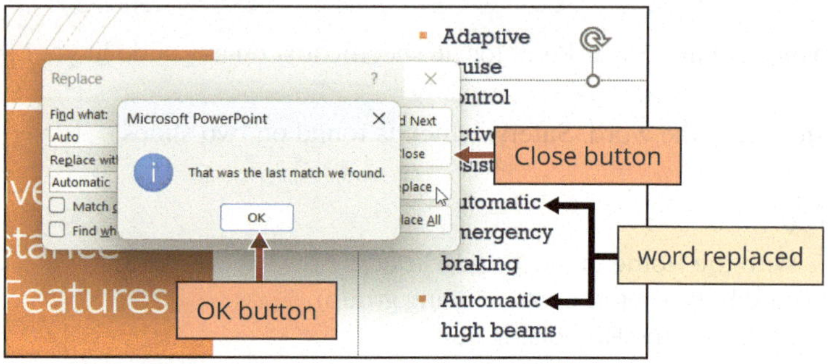

Figure 5–46

Other Ways

1. Press CTRL+H

BTW

Using a Slide Library

PowerPoint presentations may be stored on a centrally located slide library that resides on a server. These slide shows may be shared, reused, and accessed by many individuals who then can copy materials into their own presentations. The slide library time stamps when an individual has borrowed a particular slide or presentation and then time stamps the slide or presentation when it is returned. If a particular slide in the library has been updated, anyone who has borrowed that slide is notified that the content has changed. In this way, people creating PowerPoint presentations can track changes to presentations, locate the latest versions of slides, and check for slide updates.

Formatting Pictures

In previous modules, you formatted pictures by adding artistic effects and adjusting colors. These features can make your slides expressive and unique. One enhancement is adding a border and then changing the color, width, and line style of the shape. Another is creating an effect, such as a shadow, glow, reflection, soft edges, bevels, or 3-D rotation. You can customize an effect by selecting variations in the Format Picture pane.

PowerPoint includes accessibility features, including **alternative text**, also called **alt text**, which is descriptive text added to an object such as a picture, shape, text box, SmartArt graphic, or chart. Alt text helps people understand the content of graphics. When a screen reader is used to view a slide, alt text is displayed or read aloud when you move the pointer over an object. Alt text is a primary element of good design. The biggest advantage of having accurate and comprehensive alt text is that it makes digital assets more accessible. When giving a presentation, whether you are presenting it in person or sharing it on the web, having alt text is key to enhancing your information.

To Add an Artistic Effect to a Picture

In Module 3 you added an artistic effect to the Slide 1 picture. You similarly want to add an artistic effect to the Slide 2 picture in this presentation. The following steps add the Glow Edges artistic effect to the tires picture.

1. Display Slide 2 and then select the tires picture.
2. Click the Picture Format tab and then click the Artistic Effects button (Picture Format tab | Adjust group) to display the Artistic Effects gallery.
3. Point to Glow Edges (last thumbnail in the last row) to display a live preview of this effect on the picture.
4. Click Glow Edges to apply this artistic effect to the picture (Figure 5–47).

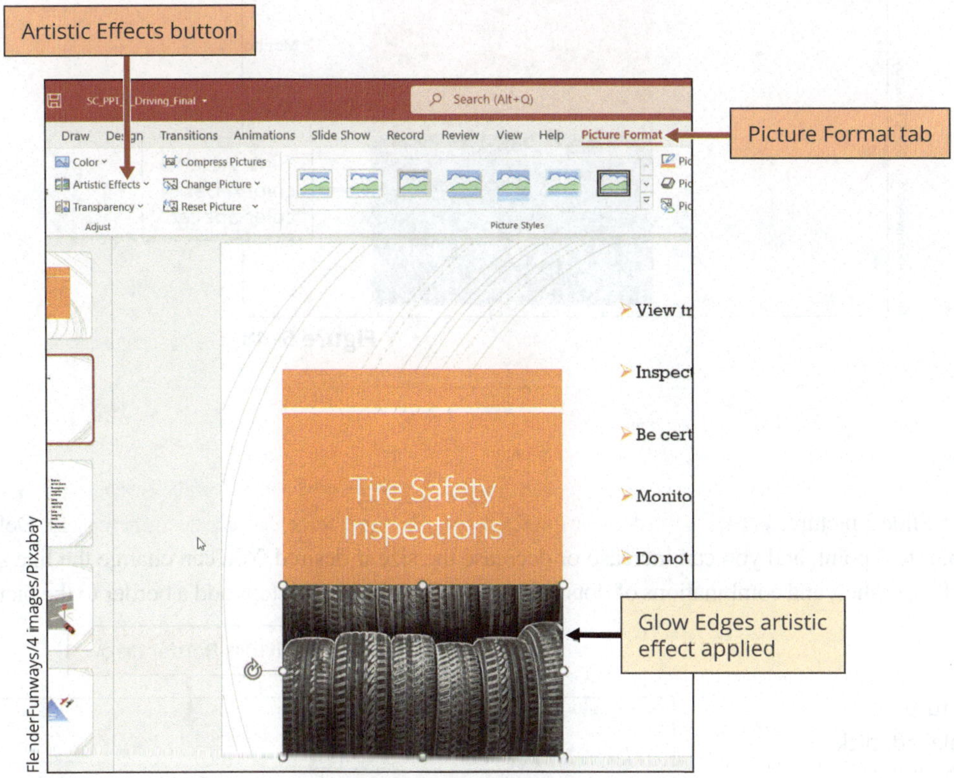

Figure 5–47

To Recolor a Picture

The Atlas theme is appropriate for this presentation on the subject of driving safely, and you have enhanced a slide with dark blue text. The following steps recolor the Slide 2 picture to further coordinate with the blue hues found in the presentation.

1. With the tires picture still selected, click the Color button (Picture Format tab | Adjust group) to display the Color gallery.
2. Point to 'Blue, Accent color 4 Dark' (fifth thumbnail in the second Recolor row) to display a live preview of this adjustment on the picture.

3. Click 'Blue, Accent color 4 Dark' to apply this recolor to the tires picture (Figure 5–48).

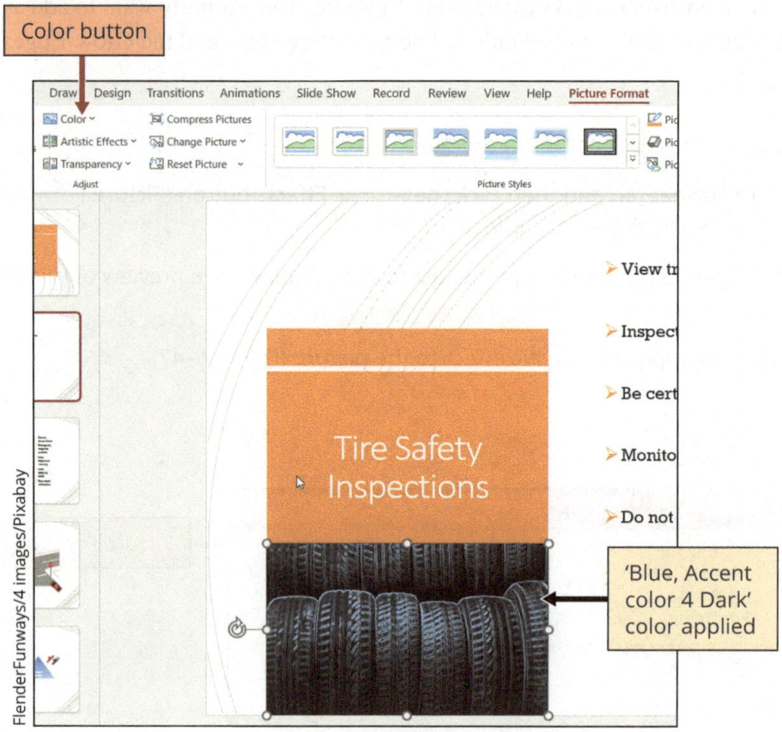

Figure 5–48

To Add a Picture Border

The next step is to add a border to the Slide 3 picture. **Why?** A border completes the picture and adds a subtle design element. Default borders range from a width of ¼ point to 6 point, and you can increase or decrease the size if desired. You can change the line style from a solid line to round or square dots, dashes, and combinations of dots and dashes. The following steps add a border to the picture.

1.
- Display Slide 3 and select the picture.
- With the Picture Format tab displayed, click the Picture Border arrow (Picture Format tab | Picture Styles group) to display the Picture Border gallery.

2.
- Point to Weight on the Picture Border gallery to display the Weight gallery.
- Point to 6 pt to display a live preview of this line weight on the picture (Figure 5–49).

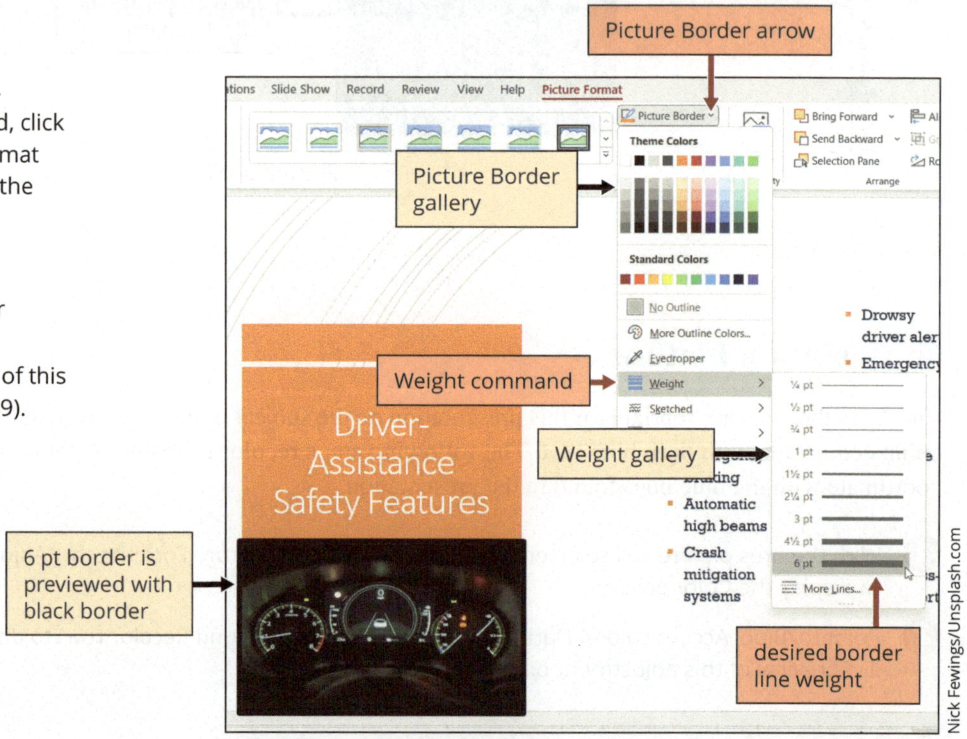

Figure 5–49

Q&A How can I make the line width more than 6 pt?
Click More Lines, click Solid line in the Line section of the Format Picture pane, and then increase the amount in the Width box.

- **Experiment:** Point to various line weights in the Weight gallery and watch the line thickness change.

3

- Click 6 pt to add this line weight to the picture.

To Change a Picture Border Color

The default color for the border you added to the Slide 3 picture is black, but you will change the border color to orange. **Why?** This color coordinates with the orange elements on the slide. The following steps change the Slide 3 picture border color.

1

- With the Slide 3 picture still selected, click the Picture Border arrow (Picture Format tab | Picture Styles group) to display the Picture Border gallery again.

2

- Point to 'Orange, Accent 1, Lighter 80%' (fifth color in the second Theme Colors row) in the Picture Border gallery to display a live preview of that border color on the picture (Figure 5–50).
- **Experiment:** Point to various colors in the Picture Border gallery and watch the border on the picture change on the slide.

3

- Click 'Orange, Accent 1, Lighter 80%' in the Picture Border gallery to change the picture border color.

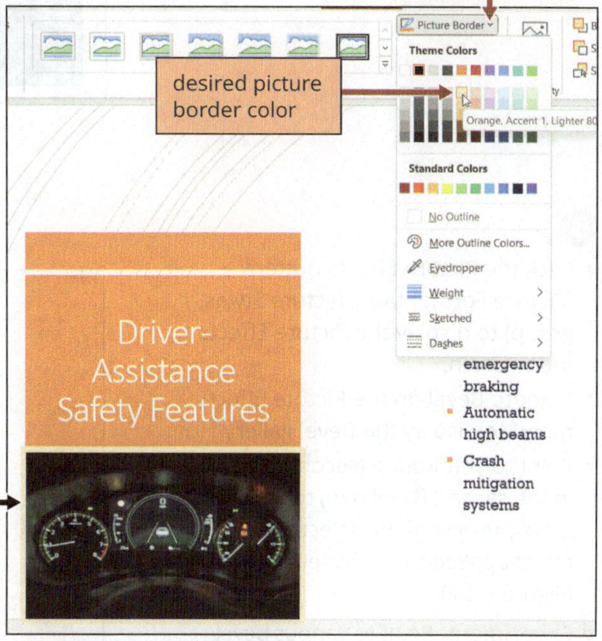

Figure 5–50

To Apply a Picture Effect

PowerPoint provides a variety of picture effects, including shadows, reflections, glow, soft edges, bevel, and 3-D rotation. **Why?** Picture effects allow you to further customize a picture. The difference between the effects and the styles is that each effect has several options, providing you with more control over the exact look of the image.

In this presentation, the picture on Slide 3 has an orange glow effect and a bevel applied to its edges. The following steps apply picture effects to the selected picture.

BTW
Compressing Pictures
Click the Compress Pictures button (Picture Format tab | Adjust group) to reduce the presentation file size. Determine the optimum resolution by selecting where or how you will show the slides, such as on the web or via printed handouts.

1

- With the Slide 3 picture still selected, click Picture Effects (Picture Format tab | Picture Styles group) to display the Picture Effects menu.

Q&A What if the Picture Format tab no longer is displayed on my ribbon?
Click the picture to display the Picture Format tab.

- Point to Glow on the Picture Effects menu to display the Glow gallery.
- Point to 'Glow: 8 point; Orange, Accent color 1' in the Glow Variations area (first glow in the second row) to display a live preview of the selected glow effect applied to the picture in the document window (Figure 5–51).
- **Experiment:** Point to various glow effects in the Glow gallery and watch the picture change in the document window.

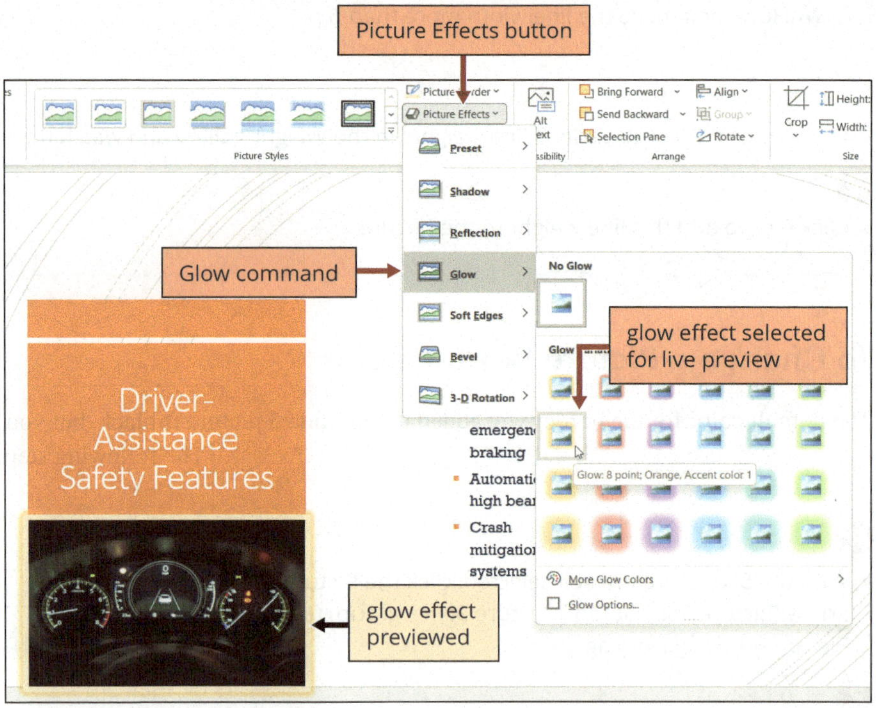

Nick Fewings/Unsplash.com

Figure 5–51

2

- Click 'Glow: 8 point; Orange, Accent color 1' in the Glow gallery to apply the selected picture effect.

3

- Click the Picture Effects button (Picture Format tab | Picture Styles group) to display the Picture Effects menu again.
- Point to Bevel on the Picture Effects menu to display the Bevel gallery.
- Point to Soft Round (second bevel in the second Bevel row) to display a live preview of the selected bevel effect applied to the Slide 3 picture (Figure 5–52).
- **Experiment:** Point to various bevel effects in the Bevel gallery and watch the picture change on the slide.

4

- Click Soft Round in the Bevel gallery to apply the selected picture effect.

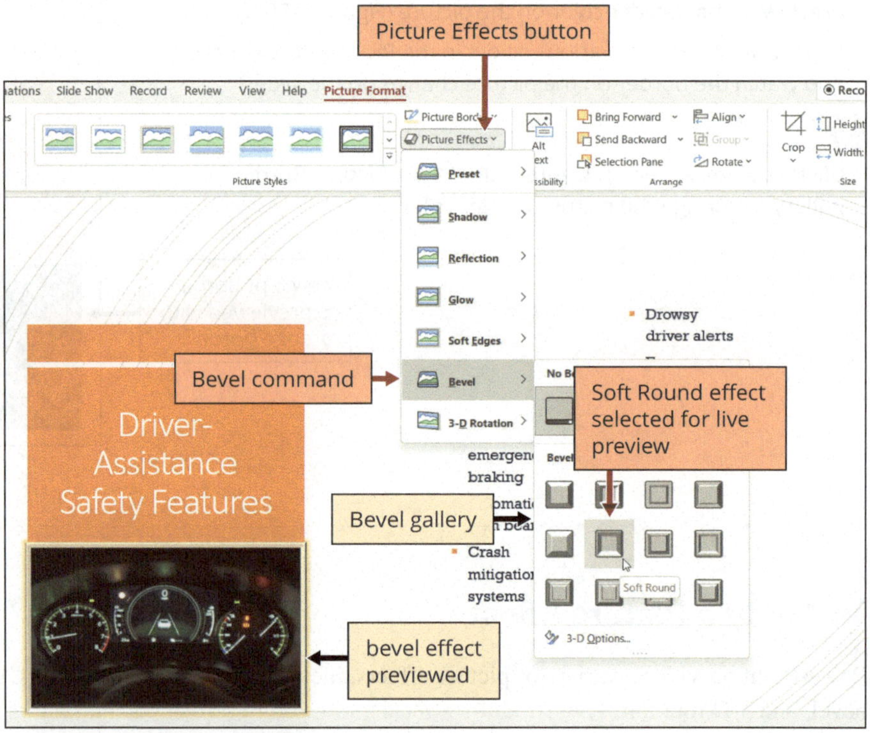

Nick Fewings/Unsplash.com

Figure 5–52

Other Ways

1. Right-click picture, click Format Picture on shortcut menu, select desired options (Format Picture pane), click Close
2. Click Format Picture dialog box launcher (Picture Format tab | Picture Styles group), select desired options (Format Picture pane), click Close

To Add Alt Text

The Slide 3 picture alt text has a general description of the dashboard. The following steps modify this text. **Why?** You want to add detail to the Alt text picture description.

1

- With the Slide 3 picture selected, click the Alt Text button (Picture Format tab | Accessibility group) to display the Alt Text pane.

2

- Click the Alt Text text box, delete any text in the box, and then type **Vehicle dashboard showing the tachometer, speedometer, and safety features** as the descriptive text (Figure 5–53).

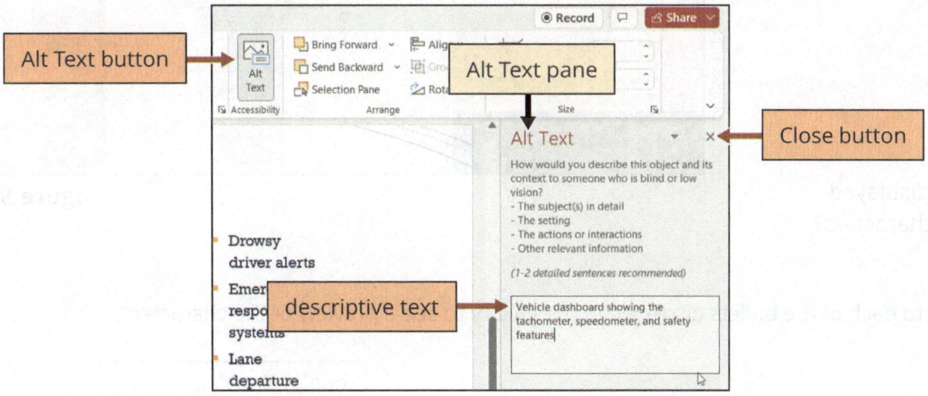

Figure 5–53

3

- Close the Alt Text pane.

Modifying Bullets and Adding Effects

PowerPoint allows you to change the default appearance of bullets in a slide show. The document themes determine the bullet character. A **bullet character** is a small graphic symbol, traditionally a closed circle, that sets off items in a list. It can be a predefined style, a variety of fonts and characters displayed in the Symbol gallery, or a picture from a file, from Online Pictures, or from the Microsoft icon collection. You may want to change a bullet character to add visual interest and variety. Once you change the bullet character, you also can change its size and color.

If desired, you can change every bullet in a presentation to a unique character. If your presentation has many bulleted slides, however, you can create a consistent look on all slides by making the bullets a similar color and size.

To customize your presentation, you can change the default slide layout bullets to numbers by changing the bulleted list to a numbered list. PowerPoint provides a variety of numbering options, including Arabic and Roman numerals. These numbers can be sized and recolored, and the starting number can be something other than 1 or I. In addition, PowerPoint's numbering options include uppercase and lowercase letters.

To Change a Bullet Character to a Picture

One method of modifying these bullets is to use a relevant picture. The following steps change the first paragraph bullet character to the red car picture, which is located in the Data Files. **Why?** The plain bullet characters for the Atlas document theme do not add much visual interest and do not relate to the topic of driving.

1

- With Slide 3 displayed, select all 10 paragraphs in the two columns.
- Click the Bullets arrow (Home tab | Paragraph group) to display the Bullets gallery (Figure 5–54).

Q&A What should I do if I clicked the Bullets button instead of the Bullets arrow?
If the paragraphs are bulleted, clicking the Bullets button removes the bullets. Click the Bullets button again to display the bullets.

Why is a gray box displayed around the three characters?
They are the default first-level bullet characters for the Atlas document theme.

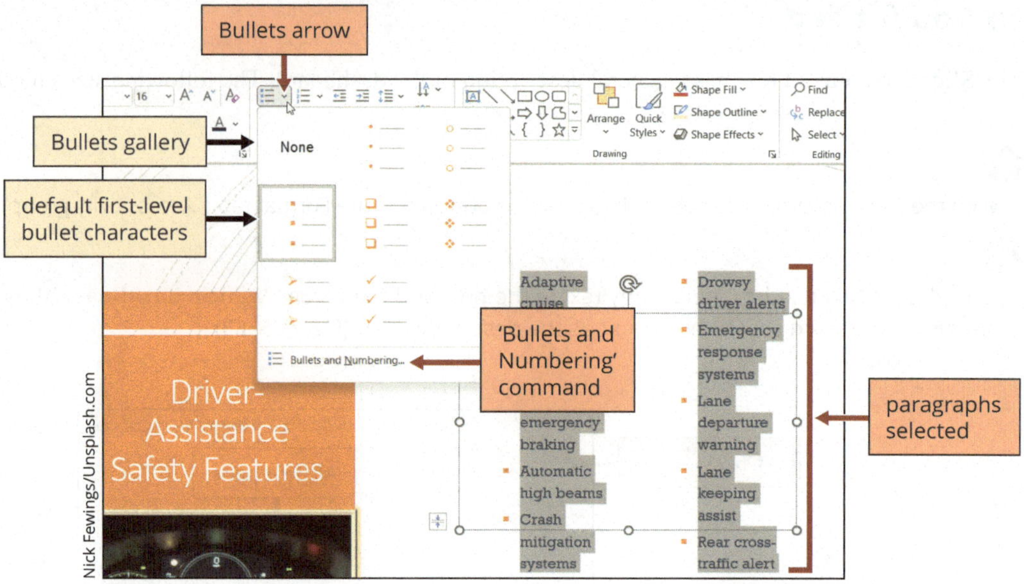

Figure 5–54

- **Experiment:** Point to each of the bullets displayed in the gallery to see a preview of the characters.

2

- Click 'Bullets and Numbering' to display the Bullets and Numbering dialog box (Figure 5–55).

Q&A Why are my bullets different from those displayed in Figure 5–55?
The bullets most recently inserted are displayed as the first items in the dialog box.

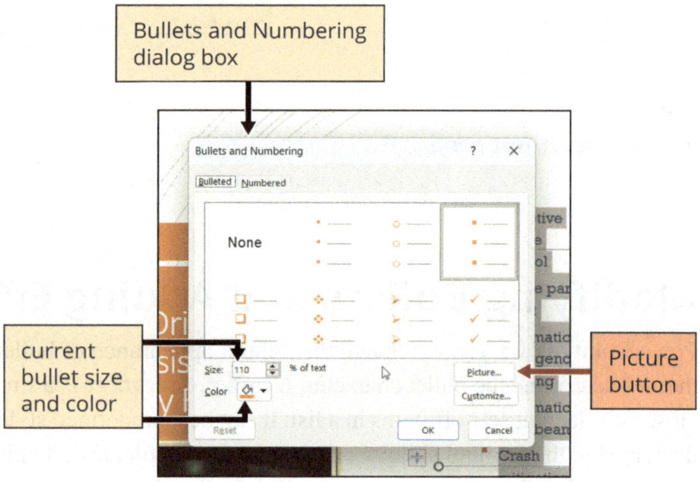

Figure 5–55

3

- Click the Picture button (Bullets and Numbering dialog box) to display the Insert Pictures dialog box (Figure 5–56).

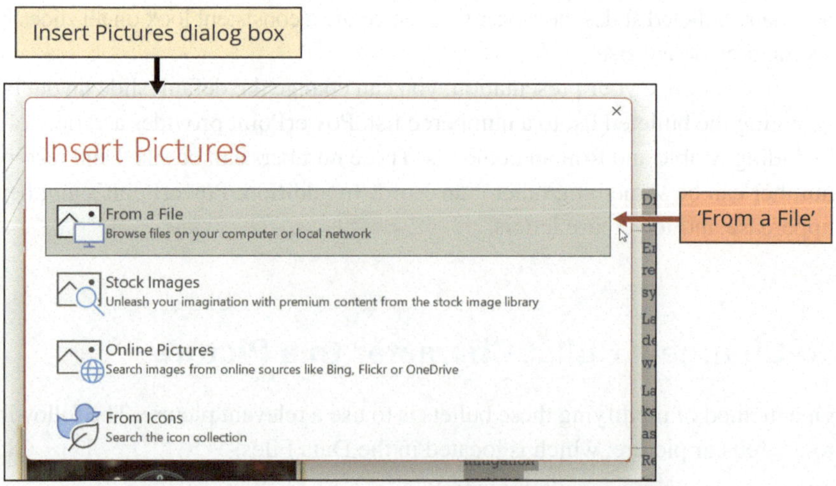

Figure 5–56

4

- Click 'From a File' (Insert Pictures dialog box) to display the Insert Picture dialog box.
- If necessary, navigate to the location of the Data Files.
- Click **Support_PPT_5_Red_Car** to select the .png file (Figure 5–57).

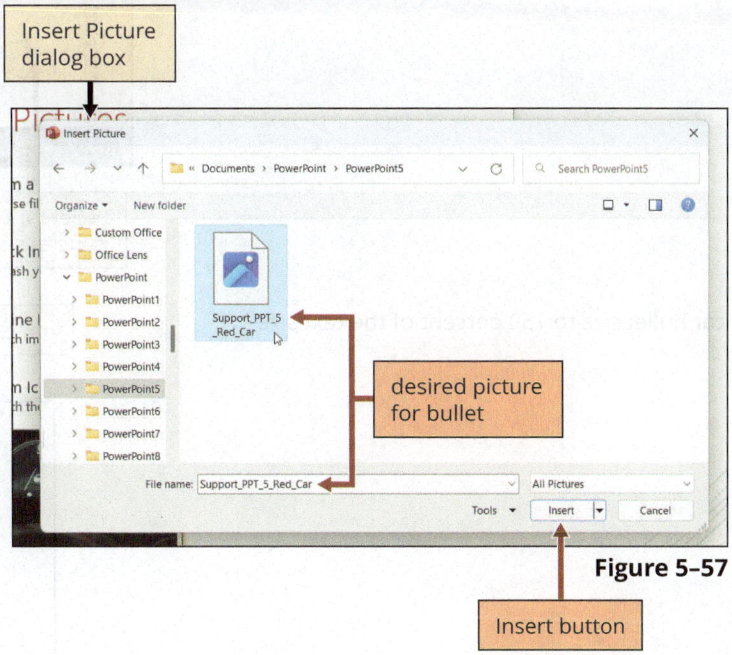

Figure 5–57

5

- Click the Insert button (Insert Picture dialog box) to insert the red car picture as the paragraph bullet character (Figure 5–58).

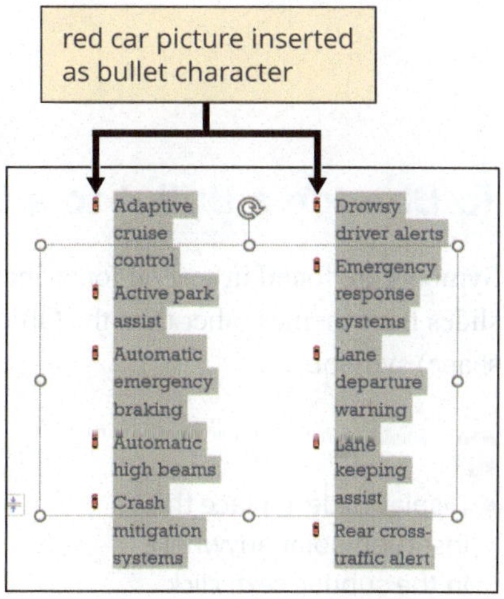

Figure 5–58

Other Ways

1. Right-click paragraph, point to Bullets on shortcut menu, click 'Bullets and Numbering'

To Change Bullet Size

Bullets have a default size determined by the document theme. **Bullet size** is measured as a percentage of the text size and can range from 25 to 400 percent. The following steps change the red car picture size. **Why?** It is difficult to see the picture, so increasing its size draws attention to the visual element and increases readability.

1

- With the Slide 3 paragraphs still selected, click the Bullets arrow (Home tab | Paragraph group) and then click 'Bullets and Numbering' in the Bullets gallery to display the Bullets and Numbering dialog box.
- Click the Size up arrow until 150 is displayed in the '% of text' Size box (Figure 5–59).

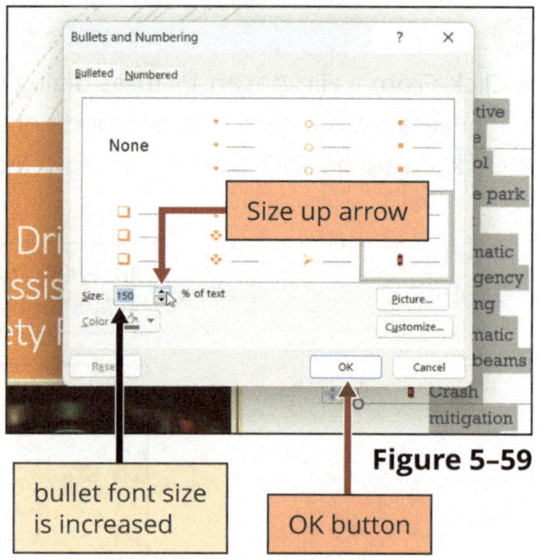

Figure 5–59

2

- Click OK to increase the red car bullet size to 150 percent of the text size (Figure 5–60).

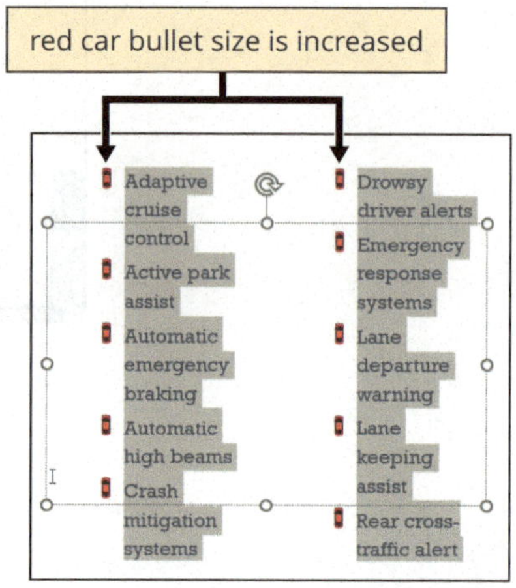

Figure 5–60

To Change a Bullet to a Symbol

Symbols are found in several fonts, including Webdings, Wingdings, Wingdings 2, and Wingdings 3. These fonts are available when slides have themes other than the Office theme. The following steps change the bullet character on Slide 1 to a Lozenge (diamond shape) symbol. **Why?** For variety and to add a unique characteristic to the presentation, you can insert a symbol as the character.

1

- Display Slide 1, place the insertion point anywhere in the subtitle text, click the Bullets arrow (Home tab | Paragraph group), and then click 'Bullets and Numbering' to display the Bullets and Numbering dialog box (Figure 5–61).

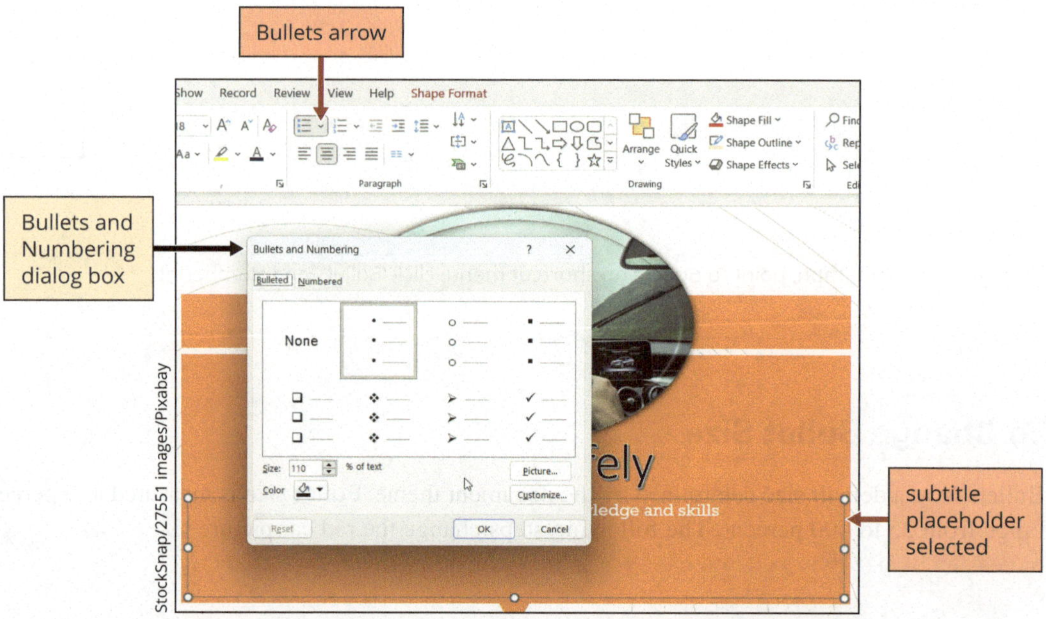

Figure 5–61

2

- Click the Customize button (Bullets and Numbering dialog box) to display the Symbol dialog box (Figure 5–62).

Q&A Why is a symbol selected?
That symbol is the default bullet for the first-level paragraphs in the Atlas document theme.

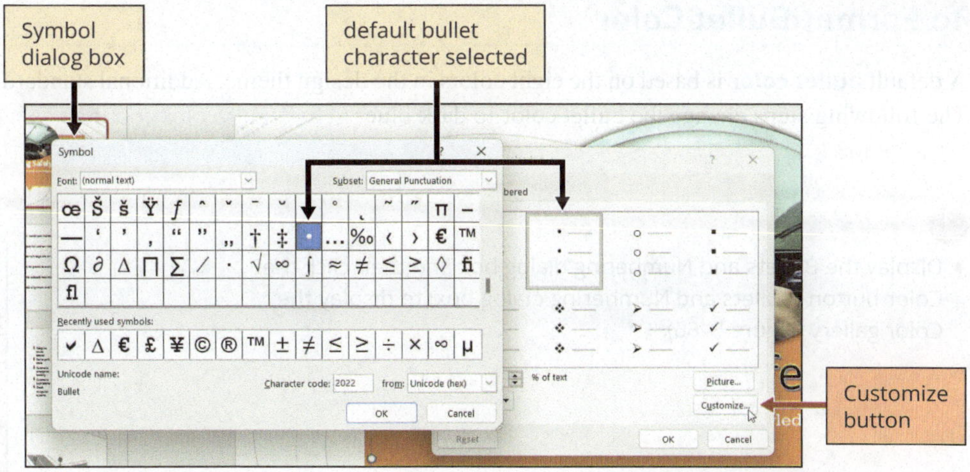

Figure 5–62

3

- Locate the Lozenge symbol (◊); scroll if necessary to find it.
- Click the Lozenge symbol to select it. The Unicode name and character code (25CA) appear at the bottom of the dialog box (Figure 5–63).

Q&A Why does my dialog box have more rows of symbols and different fonts from which to choose?
The rows and fonts displayed depend upon how PowerPoint was installed on your system and the screen you are viewing.

What is the character code that is displayed in the Symbol dialog box?
Each character in each font has a unique code. If you know the character code, you can type the number in the Character code box to display that symbol. The character code for the Lozenge symbol is 25CA.

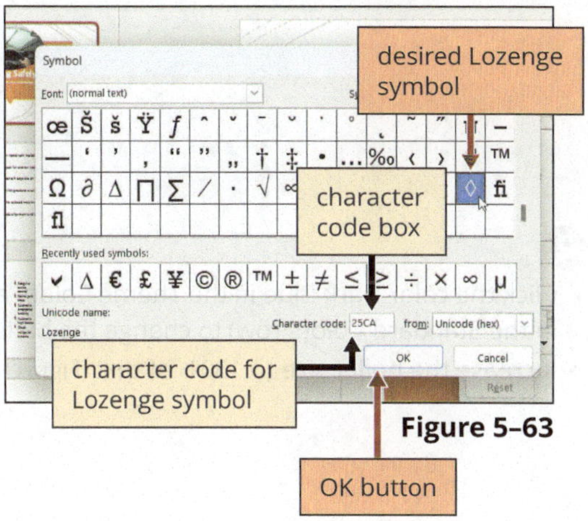

Figure 5–63

4

- Click OK (Symbol dialog box) to display the Lozenge bullet in the Bullets and Numbering dialog box (Figure 5–64).

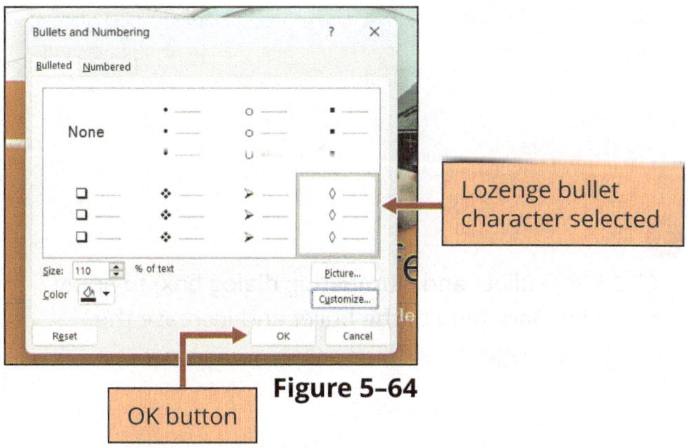

Figure 5–64

5

- Click OK (Bullets and Numbering dialog box) to insert the Lozenge symbol as the paragraph bullet (Figure 5–65).

Figure 5–65

To Format Bullet Color

A default **bullet color** is based on the eight colors in the design theme. Additional standard and custom colors also are available. The following steps change the bullet color to dark blue. **Why?** This color coordinates with other dark blue colors used in the presentation.

1

- Display the Bullets and Numbering dialog box and then click the Color button (Bullets and Numbering dialog box) to display the Color gallery (Figure 5–66).

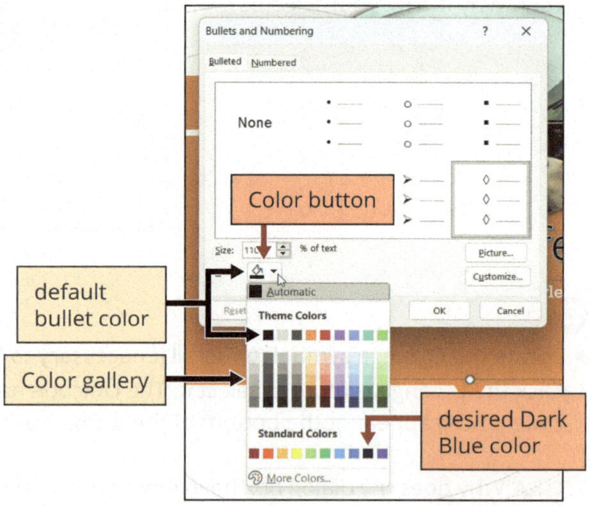

Figure 5–66

2

- Click the color Dark Blue in the Theme Colors area (ninth color in the Standard Colors row) to change the bullet color.
- Increase the bullet size to 150% of text (Figure 5–67).

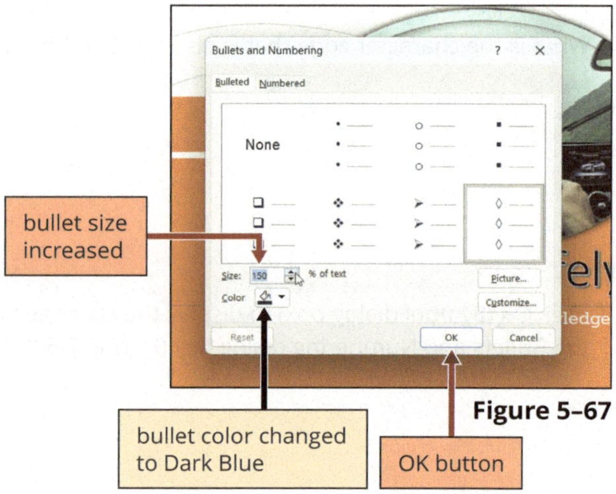

Figure 5–67

3

- Click OK (Bullets and Numbering dialog box) to apply the color Dark Blue to the bullet and increase the bullet size (Figure 5–68).

Figure 5–68

Other Ways

1. Right-click paragraph, point to Bullets on shortcut menu, click Bullets and Numbering, select color

To Change a Bullet Character to a Number

PowerPoint allows you to change the default bullets to numbers. The following steps change the first-level paragraph bullet characters on Slide 2 to numbers. **Why?** Numbers help to show steps in a sequence and also help guide a speaker during the presentation when referring to specific information in the paragraphs.

1

- Display Slide 2 and then select all six paragraphs in the content placeholder.
- With the Home tab displayed, click the Numbering arrow (Home tab | Paragraph group) to display the Numbering gallery.
- Point to the 1) 2) 3) numbering option in the Numbering gallery to display a live preview of these numbers (Figure 5–69).

  - **Experiment:** Point to each of the numbers in the Numbering gallery to watch the numbers change on Slide 2.

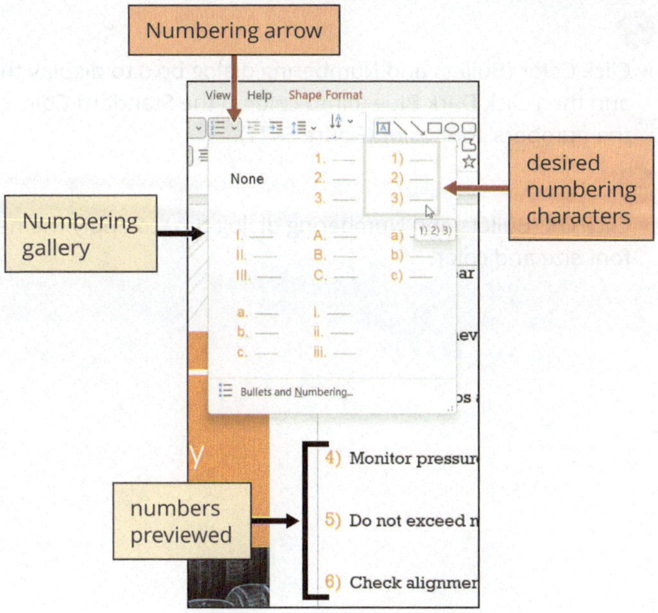

Figure 5–69

2

- Click the 1) 2) 3) numbering option to insert these numbers as the first-level paragraph characters (Figure 5–70).

Q&A How do I change the first number in the list?
Click 'Bullets and Numbering' at the bottom of the Numbering gallery and then click the up or down arrow in the Start at box to change the number.

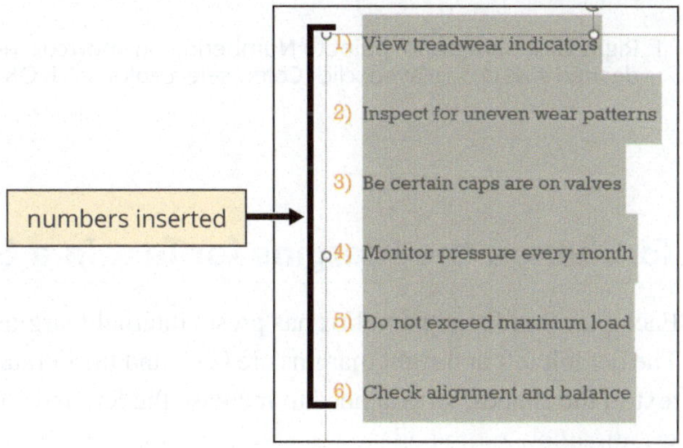

Figure 5–70

Other Ways

1. Right-click paragraph, point to Numbering on shortcut menu, select numbering characters

To Change the List Numbering Style

As with bullets, numbering characters are measured as a percentage of the text size and can range from 25 to 400 percent. The color of these numbers also can change. The following steps change the numbering color to dark blue and the size to 125 percent. **Why?** To add emphasis, you choose to increase the size of the new numbers inserted in Slide 2, and the color coordinates with other dark blue elements in the presentation.

1

- With the Slide 2 content placeholder paragraphs still selected, click the Numbering arrow (Home tab | Paragraph group) to display the Numbering gallery and then click 'Bullets and Numbering' to display the Bullets and Numbering dialog box again.
- Click the Size up arrow until 125 is displayed in the '% of text' Size text box.

2

- Click Color (Bullets and Numbering dialog box) to display the Color gallery and then click Dark Blue (ninth color in the Standard Colors row) to change the numbers' font color (Figure 5–71).

3

- Click OK (Bullets and Numbering dialog box) to apply the new numbers' font size and color.

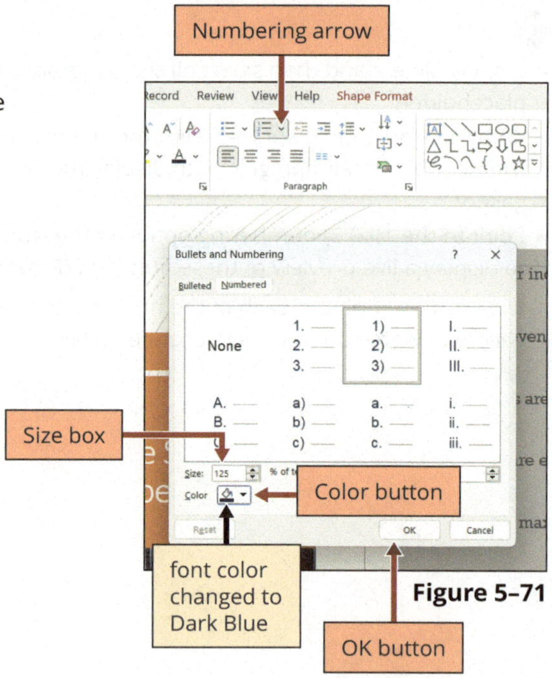

Figure 5–71

Other Ways

1. Right-click paragraph, point to Numbering on shortcut menu, click 'Bullets and Numbering', click up or down Size arrow until desired size is displayed, click Color, select color, click OK

To Change the Margins for Text in a Shape

Each placeholder and text box has preset internal margins, which are the spaces between the border and the contents of the box. The default left and right margins are 0.1", and the default top and bottom margins are 0.05". In this project, you will format the text in the shapes, so you need to increase the left and right margins and then decrease the top and bottom margins. **Why?** You want to allow room and sufficient white space for these design elements. The following steps change all three shape margins.

1

- Display Slide 5 and then right-click the First aid kit shape to display the shortcut menu (Figure 5–72).

2

- Click Format Shape to display the Format Shape pane and then click the 'Size & Properties' Shape Options button.

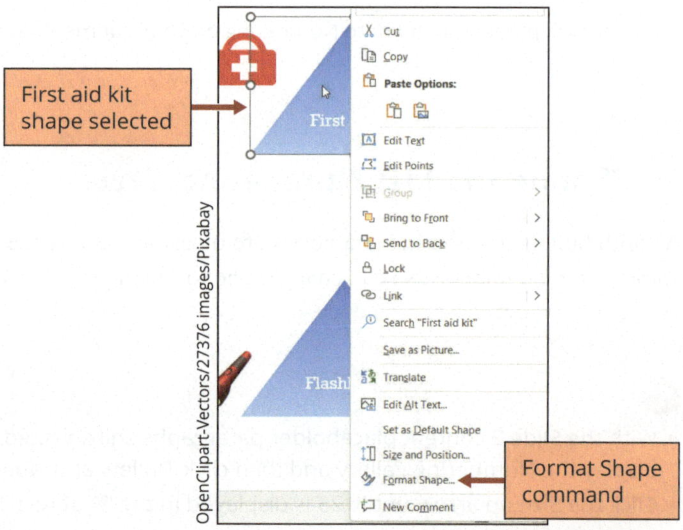

Figure 5–72

- If necessary, click Text Box to display the Text Box section (Figure 5–73).

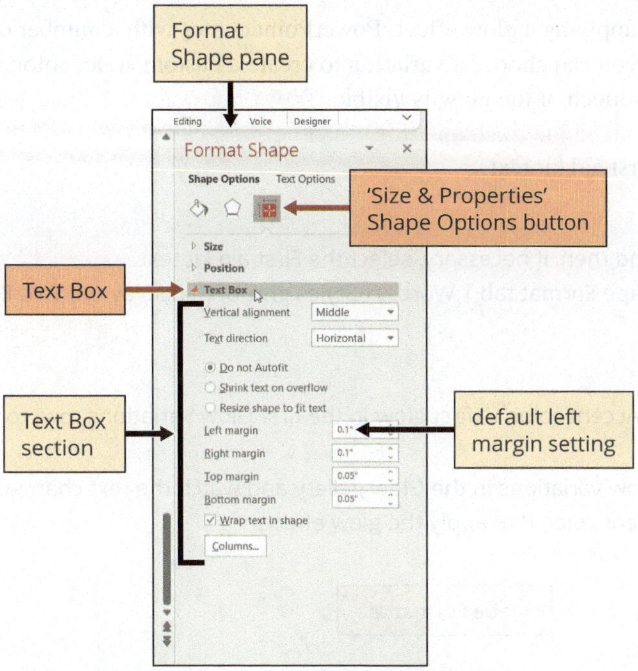

Figure 5–73

3

- If necessary, scroll down to display the entire Text box section and then increase the Left margin setting to 0.3".
- Increase the Right margin setting to 0.3".
- Decrease the Top margin setting to 0".
- Decrease the Bottom margin setting to 0" (Figure 5–74).

Q&A Must I change all the margins?

No. You can change one, two, three, or all four internal margins depending upon the placeholder shape and the amount of text entered.

4

- Click the Close button (Format Shape pane).

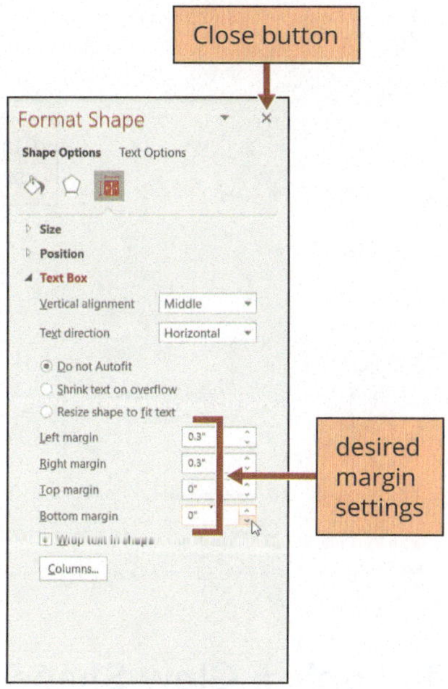

Figure 5–74

To Format Shape Text

Sufficient space exists in the shape to increase the font size. In addition, changing the font color adds a custom design element to the final slide in the presentation. The following steps format the First aid kit shape text.

1 Change the font size to 20 point.

2 Change the font color to Dark Blue (ninth color in the Standard Colors row).

To Apply a Glow Text Effect

You can add dimension to text by applying a glow effect. PowerPoint comes with a number of common preset glow variations. Once you have added this effect, you can choose a variation to create a custom style, color, and size. You also can change the transparency, which specifies how much of the glow is visible. **Why?** You want to emphasize items that drivers should have in their vehicles to deal with problems on the road, and this effect helps to call attention to the text in the shape. The following steps apply a glow effect to the First aid kit text.

1

- Display the Shape Format tab and then, if necessary, select the First aid kit text.
- Click the Text Effects button (Shape Format tab | WordArt Styles group) to display the Text Effects menu and then point to Glow to display the Glow gallery.

2

- Point to 'Glow: 5 point; Orange, Accent color 1' (first glow in the first Glow Variations row) to display a live preview of the glow effect (Figure 5–75).
- **Experiment:** Point to various glow variations in the Glow gallery and watch the text change in the shape.
- Click 'Glow: 5 point; Orange, Accent color 1' to apply the glow effect.

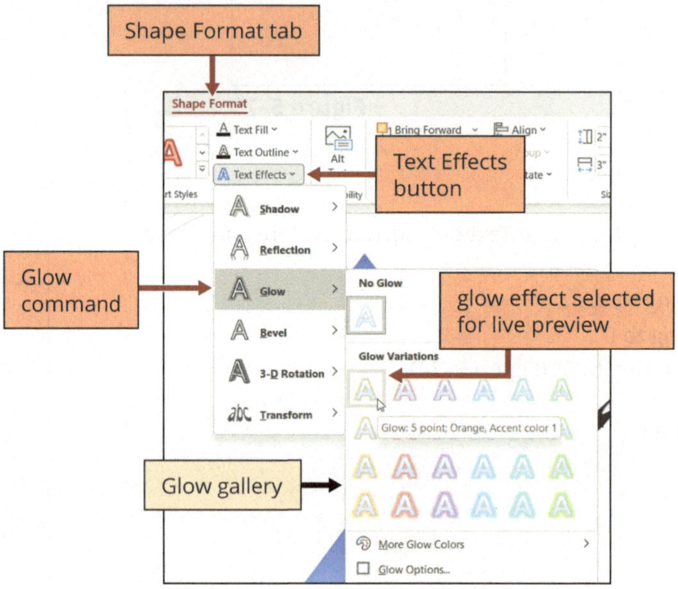

Figure 5–75

To Apply a Glow Shape Effect

You can apply glow effects to shapes and other objects. As with the glow text effect, the glow shape effect has several preset variations. The color, size, and transparency also can be changed. **Why?** You want to coordinate the text and icon design elements. The following steps apply a glow effect to the First aid kit icon.

1

- Select the First aid kit icon and then display the Picture Format tab.
- Click the Picture Effects button (Picture Format tab | Picture Styles group) to display the Picture Effects menu and then point to Glow to display the Glow gallery.

2

- Point to 'Glow: 5 point; Orange, Accent color 1' (first glow in the first Glow Variations row) to display a live preview of the glow effect (Figure 5–76).
- **Experiment:** Point to various glow variations in the Glow gallery and watch the image change in the shape.
- Click 'Glow: 5 point; Orange, Accent color 1' to apply the glow effect.

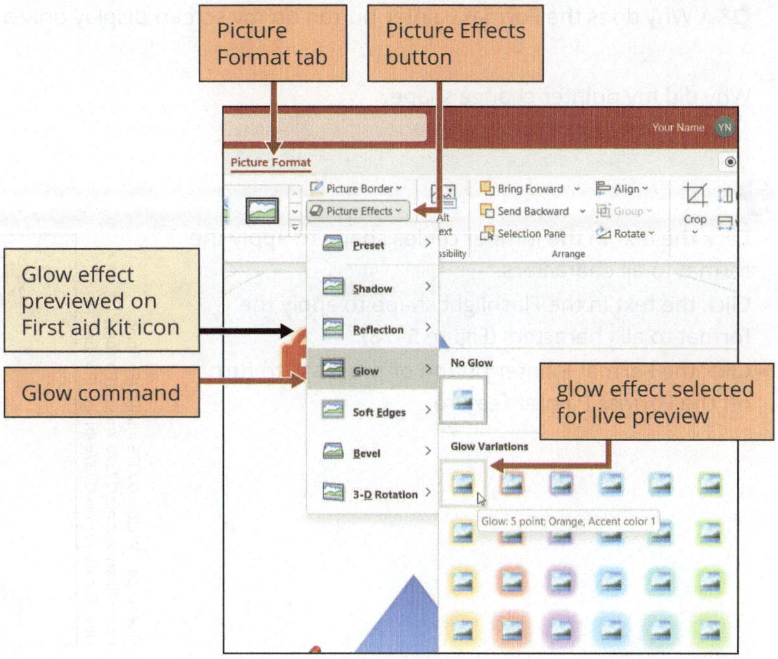

Figure 5–76

Format Painter

To save time and avoid formatting errors, you can use the **Format Painter** to copy custom formatting to other places in your presentation quickly and easily. You can use this feature in three ways:

- To copy only character attributes, such as font and font effects, select text that has these qualities.
- To copy both character attributes and paragraph attributes, such as alignment and indentation, select the entire paragraph.
- To apply the same formatting to multiple words, phrases, or paragraphs, double-click the Format Painter button and then select each item you want to format. You then can press ESC or click the Format Painter button to turn off this feature.

To Use the Format Painter with Text

The following steps use the Format Painter to copy formatting features. **Why?** To save time and duplicated effort, you quickly can use the Format Painter to copy formatting attributes from the First aid kit shape text and apply them to the two other shapes.

1

- Display the Home tab, select the First aid kit text, and then double-click the Format Painter button (Home tab | Clipboard group).
- Move the pointer off the ribbon (Figure 5–77).

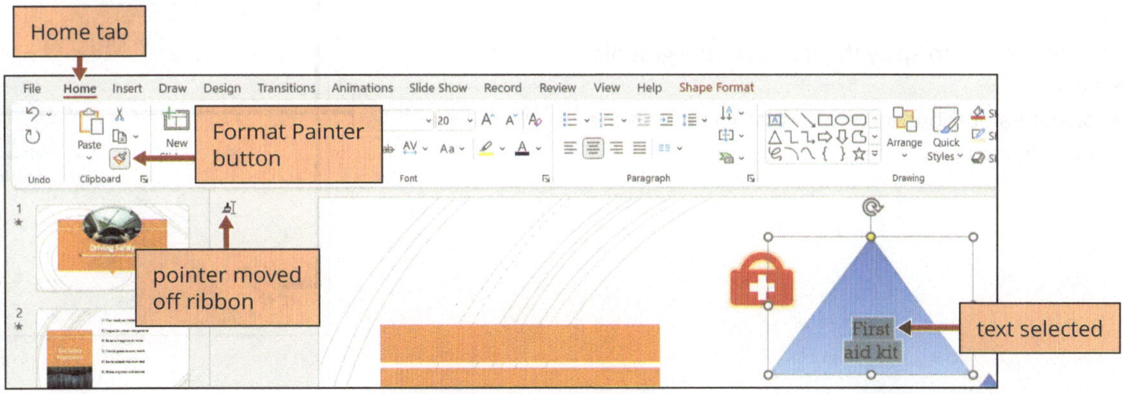

Figure 5–77

Q&A Why does the Format Painter button on my screen display only a paintbrush and not the words, Format Painter?
Monitor dimensions and resolution affect how buttons display on the ribbon.

Why did my pointer change shape?
The pointer changed shape by adding a paintbrush to indicate that the Format Painter function is active.

2

- Click the text in the Jumper cables shape to apply the format to all characters.
- Click the text in the Flashlight shape to apply the format to all characters (Figure 5–78).
- Click the Format Painter button or press ESC to turn off the Format Painter feature.

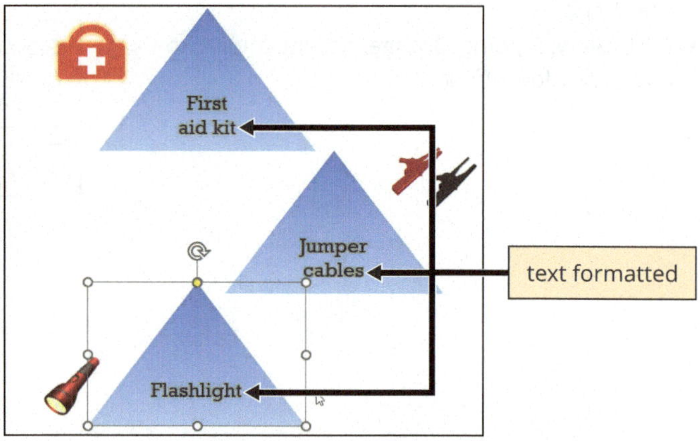

OpenClipart-Vectors/27376 images/Pixabay; OpenClipart-Vectors/27376 images/Pixabay; OpenClipart-Vectors/27376 images/Pixabay

Figure 5–78

Other Ways

1. Select text, double-click Format Painter button on Mini toolbar

To Use the Format Painter with Objects

The following steps use the Format Painter to copy an object's formatting features. **Why?** To save time and duplicated effort, you quickly can use the Format Painter to copy formatting attributes from the First aid kit icon and apply them to Jumper cables and Flashlight icons.

1

- Select the First aid kit icon and then double-click the Format Painter button (Home tab | Clipboard group).
- Move the pointer off the ribbon (Figure 5–79).

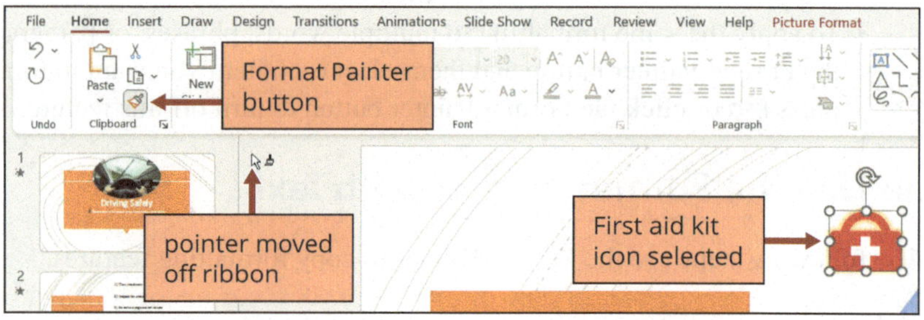

OpenClipart-Vectors/27376 images/Pixabay; StockSnap/27551 images/Pixabay

Figure 5–79

2

- Click the Jumper cables icon to apply the format to the graphic.
- Click the Flashlight icon to apply the format to the graphic (Figure 5–80).
- Click the Format Painter button or press ESC to turn off the Format Painter feature.

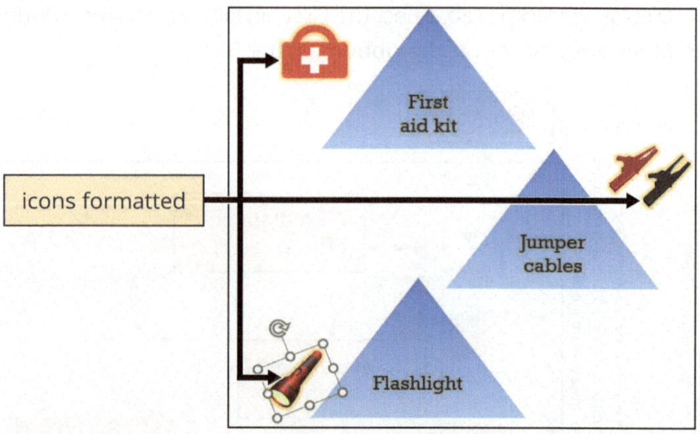

OpenClipart-Vectors/27376 images/Pixabay; OpenClipart-Vectors/27376 images/Pixabay; OpenClipart-Vectors/27376 images/Pixabay

Figure 5–80

Break Point: If you wish to take a break, this is a good place to do so. Be sure the Driving Final file is saved and then you can exit PowerPoint. To resume later, start PowerPoint, open the file called SC_PPT_5_Driving_Final, and continue following the steps from this location forward.

Animating Slide Content

If you need to move objects on a slide once they are displayed, you can define a **motion path**. This predefined movement determines where an object will be displayed and then travel. Motion paths are grouped into the Basic, Lines & Curves, and Special categories. You can draw a custom path if none of the predefined paths meets your needs.

Slide 2 contains several animation effects. When this slide is displayed, the tires automatically will float up under the title text after a brief delay. Next, the first content paragraph will display and then fade as the second paragraph displays. This animation sequence will continue until the sixth paragraph is displayed. Finally, the tires picture will pulse slightly. To create this animation on the slide, you will use entrance and emphasis effects.

BTW
Adding a Sound to an Animation
Once you have added an animation effect to text or an object, you then can add a sound. To do so, display the Animation Pane and then click the down arrow to the right of the effect. Click Effect Options in the menu, click the Sound arrow in the Enhancements area to display the Sound list, and then choose a sound. If none of the default sounds seems appropriate to accompany an animation, you can add your own. Click the Sound arrow to display the sound list, scroll down, click Other Sound, and then locate the sound you want to use from your storage medium.

To Animate a Picture Using an Entrance Effect

In Module 3 you animated a WordArt object using an entrance effect, changed its direction, and then changed the start option so that it displayed automatically. Similarly, you can animate a picture and change the animation effects. The tires picture you modified in Slide 2 will enter the slide from the lower edge and then continue moving upward until it is under the title text. The following steps apply an entrance effect to the tires picture.

1. Display Slide 2 and then click the tires picture to select it.
2. Display the Animations tab and then click the Float In animation in the Animation gallery (Animation group) to apply and preview this entrance animation for the tires picture.
3. Change the Start animation timing option to With Previous (Figure 5–81).

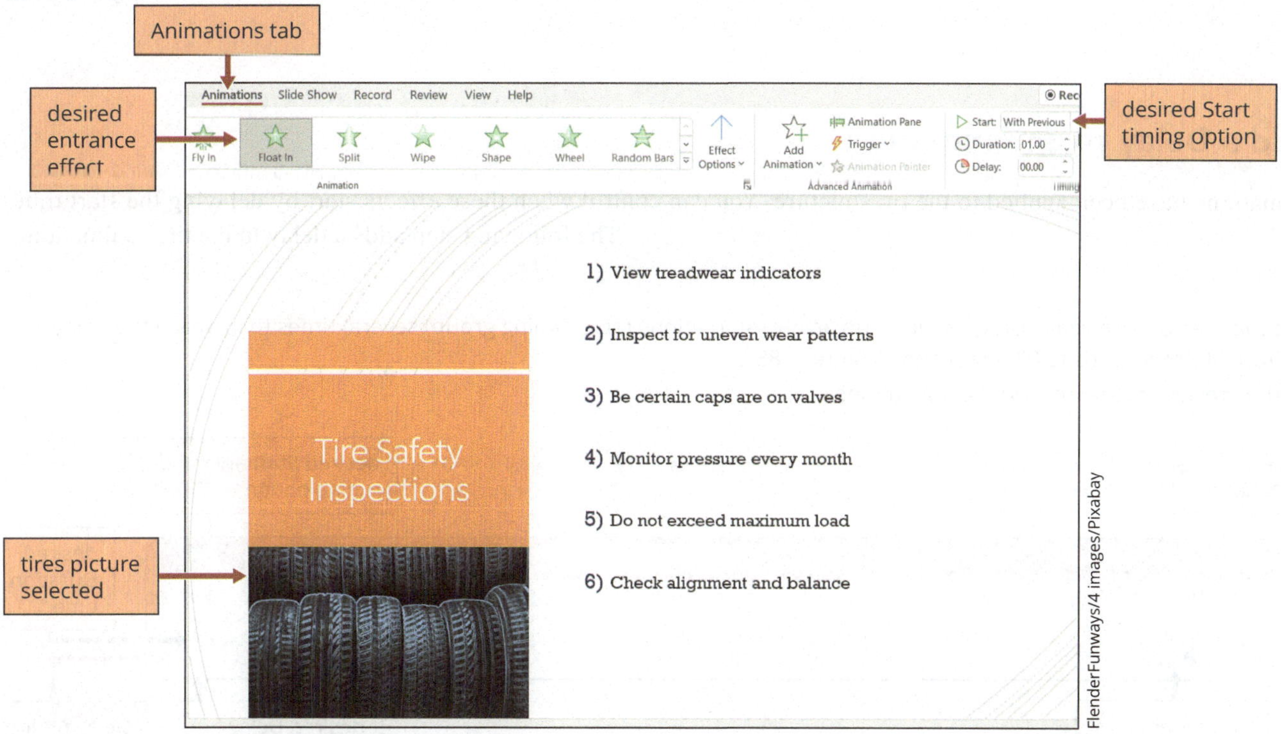

Figure 5–81

To Add an Emphasis Effect Animation

Once the tires picture has entered the slide, you want it to fade out and in, or pulse, slightly. PowerPoint provides several effects that you can apply to a picture once it appears on a slide. These movements are categorized as emphasis effects, and they are colored yellow in the Animation gallery. You already have applied an entrance effect to the tires picture, so you want to add another animation to this picture. **Why?** You want to call attention to this object as a subtle reminder of the need to inspect tires periodically. The following steps apply an emphasis effect to the tires picture after the entrance effect.

1

- Select the tires picture again and then click the Add Animation button (Animations tab | Advanced Animation group) to expand the Animation gallery (Figure 5–82).

2

- Click Pulse in the Emphasis section (first animation in the first row) to apply this effect to the tires picture.
- Change the Start animation timing option to With Previous.
- Change the Duration time to 02.00 seconds.

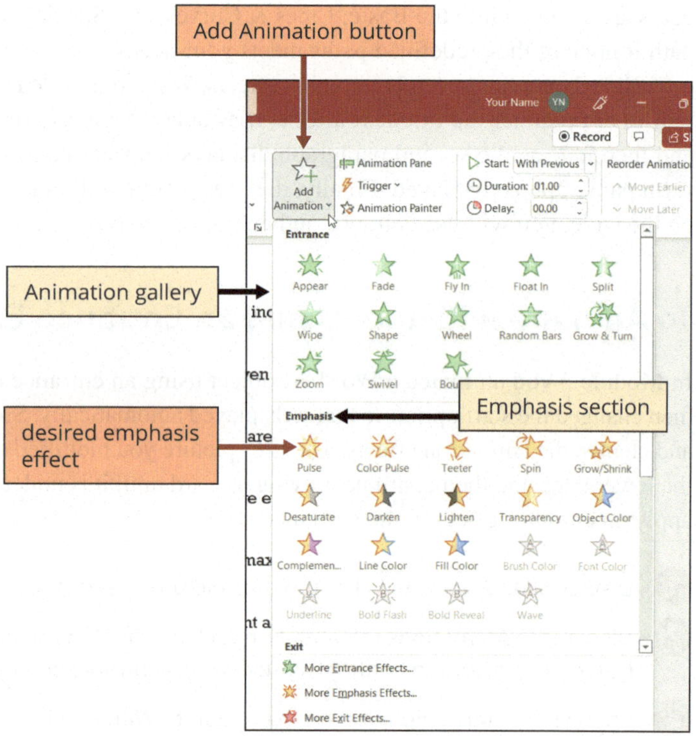

Figure 5–82

To Add a Delay to an Animation

All animations have been applied to the tires picture. You can control when these effects start by delaying the start time. **Why?** You want several seconds to pass before the animation runs. The following step adds a delay to the tires animations.

1

- Select the tires picture again, click the Delay up arrow (Animations tab | Timing group) several times to increase the delay time from 00.00 seconds to 03.00 seconds (Figure 5–83).
- Click the Preview button to view the animations.

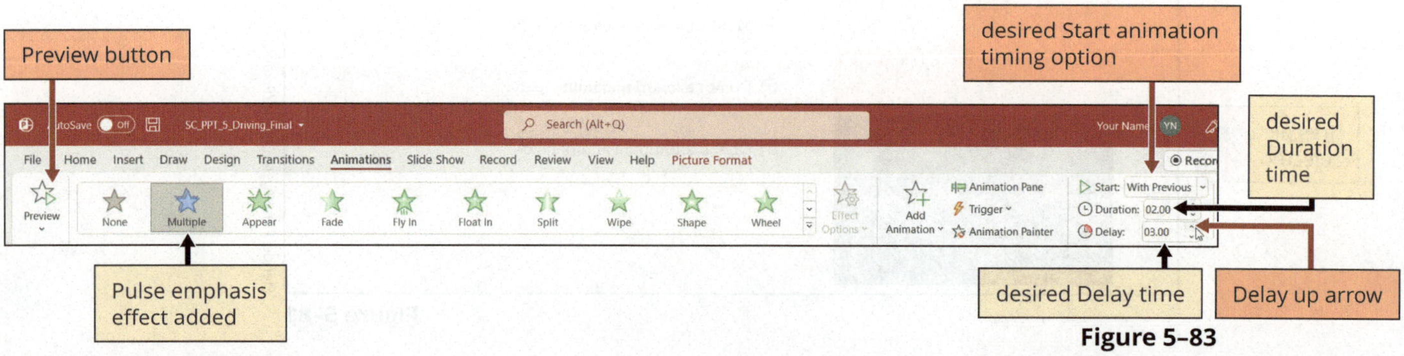

Figure 5–83

Q&A Can I type the time in the Delay box instead of click the arrow to adjust the time?
Yes. Typing the numbers allows you to set a precise timing.

Can I adjust the delay time I just set?
Yes. Click the Delay up or down arrows and run the slide show to display Slide 2 until you find the time that best fits your presentation.

To Animate Text

You can animate the six numbered paragraphs in the Slide 2 content placeholder. The following steps animate the numbered list paragraphs.

1. Click any numbered list paragraph in the Slide 2 content placeholder to select the placeholder and then click a placeholder border so that it displays as a solid line.
2. Click the Fade entrance effect in the Animation gallery to add and preview this animation.
3. Change the Start animation timing option to After Previous.
4. Change the Duration time to 02.00 seconds (Figure 5–84).
5. Click the Preview button to view the animations.

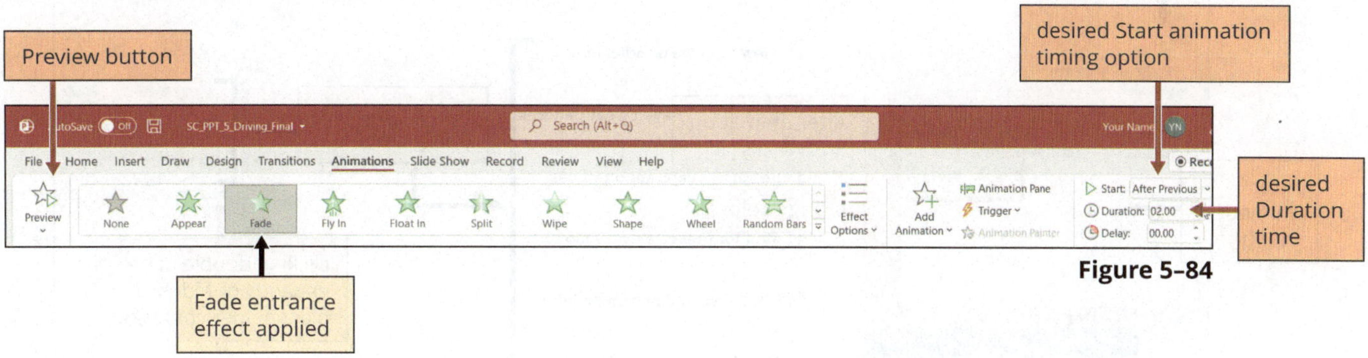

Figure 5–84

Consider This

Select colors for dimming text.
After paragraphs of text are displayed, you can change the color, or dim the text, to direct the audience's attention to another area of the slide. Choose the dimming colors carefully. Be certain the color you choose can be seen against the background. In addition, use a maximum of three colors unless you have a compelling need to present more variety.

To Dim Text after Animation

As each item in the list is displayed, you may desire to have the previous item removed from the screen or to have the font color change or **dim**. PowerPoint provides several options for you to alter this text by specifying an After Animation effect. The following steps dim each paragraph in the content placeholder by changing the font color to orange. **Why?** That color is found in many of the design elements throughout the presentation.

1

- With Slide 2 displayed, click the Animation Pane button (Animation tab | Advanced Animation group) to display the Animation Pane. Click the double arrow in the gray bar below the content placeholder to expand the contents showing the six placeholder paragraphs.

BTW
Turning Off Animations
You cannot remove all animations from an entire presentation in one step, but you can disable all animations in your presentation. To do this, click the 'Set Up Slide Show' button (Slide Show tab | Set Up group) to display the 'Set Up Show' dialog box and then click 'Show without animation' in the Show options area.

- Right-click the first paragraph in the list (View treadw...) to display the Animation Order menu (Figure 5–85).

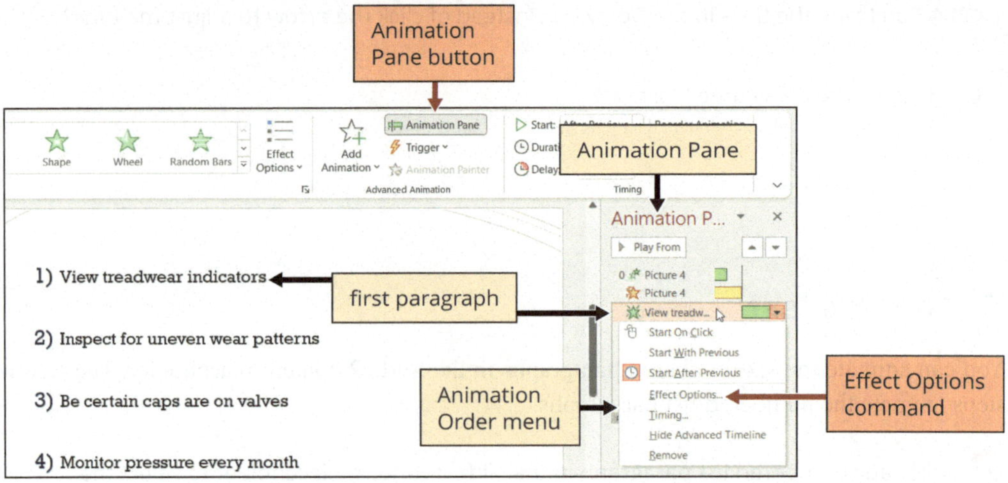

Figure 5–85

2

- Click Effect Options in the Animation Order menu to display the Fade dialog box.
- Click the After animation arrow to display the After animation menu (Figure 5–86).

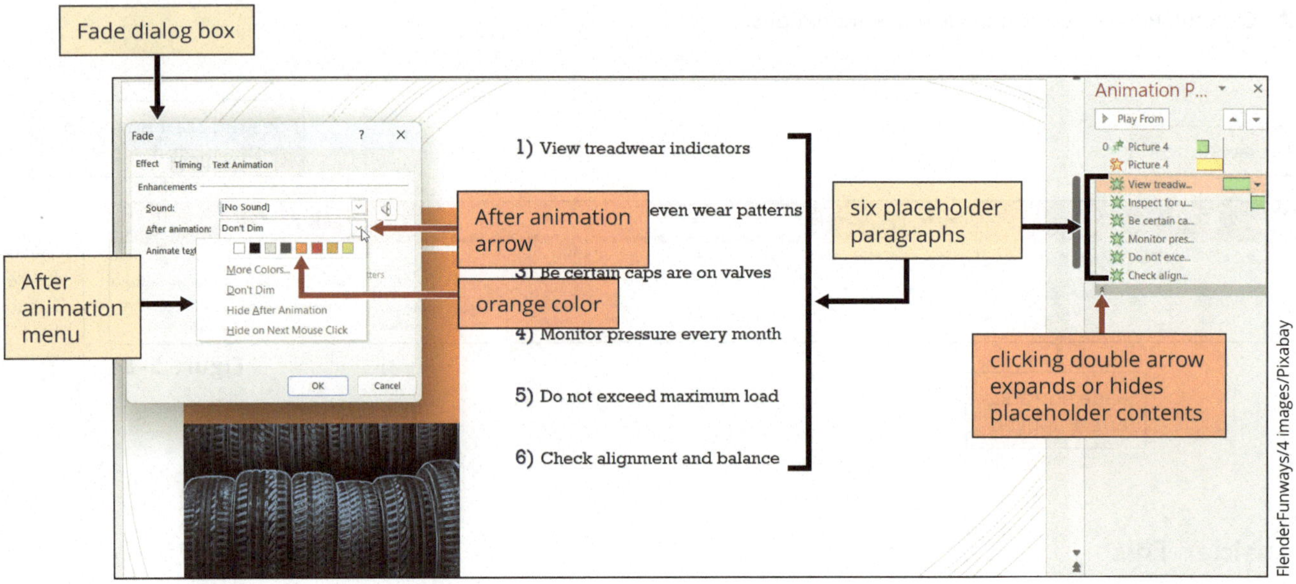

Figure 5–86

3

- Click the orange color (fifth color in the row of colors) to select this color for the dim effect (Figure 5–87).

4

- Click OK (Fade dialog box) to apply the dim effect to the first item in the content placeholder on Slide 2 and preview the animations.

5

- Repeat Steps 1 to 4 for each of the remaining five paragraphs in the list to apply and preview the dim After animation effect.

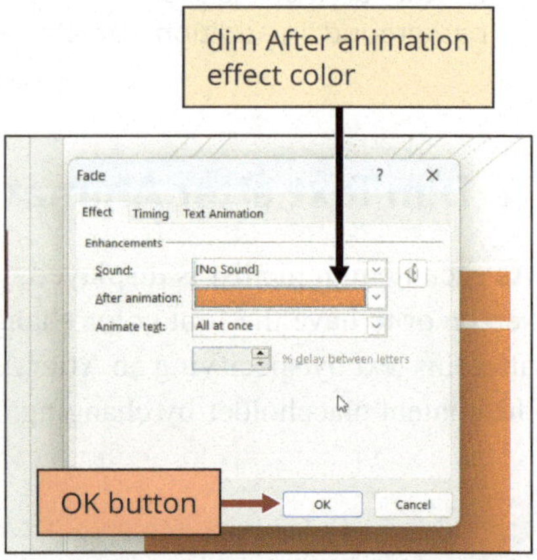

Figure 5–87

Q&A Could I select all six paragraphs and then apply the dim effect to them simultaneously?

Yes. This method is efficient and ensures consistency if you are applying the same effect to all the paragraphs.

To Reorder Animations on a Slide

By default, the tires picture's entrance and emphasis effects occur sequentially. You can modify this order by moving each animation earlier or later in the animation list. The following steps change the sequence for the Slide 2 animations so the tires picture is displayed when Slide 2 is shown, but the Pulse animation effect will occur after the six bulleted paragraphs are displayed. **Why?** You will direct the audience's attention to the picture after they have learned about factors to consider when inspecting tires.

1

- Click the Picture 4 Pulse Emphasis animation (with the yellow star) in the Animation Pane to select it (Figure 5–88).

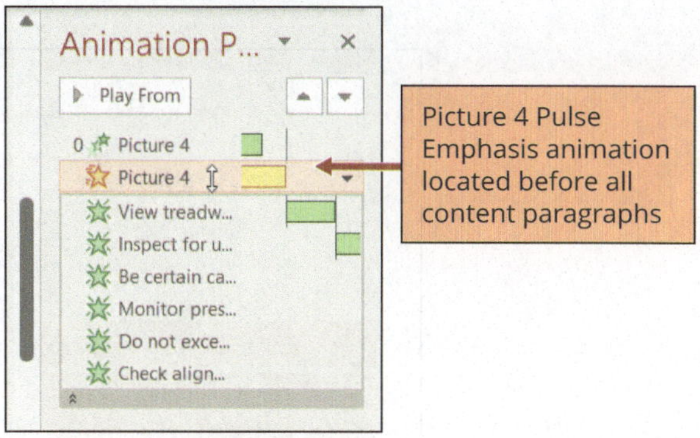

Figure 5–88

2

- Click the Move Later button (Animations tab | Timing group) six times to move the Pulse animation after all the content paragraphs.

Q&A Can I click the Move Later button in the Animation Pane instead of the button on the Animations tab to reorder the animation?
Yes. Either button performs the same action.

Would I click the Move Earlier button on the Animations tab if I wanted the animation to occur earlier in the sequence?
Yes. You also could click the Move Earlier button in the Animation Pane.

- Change the Start animation timing option to After Previous.
- Change the Delay time to 02.00 seconds (Figure 5–89).

3

- Preview the animations.

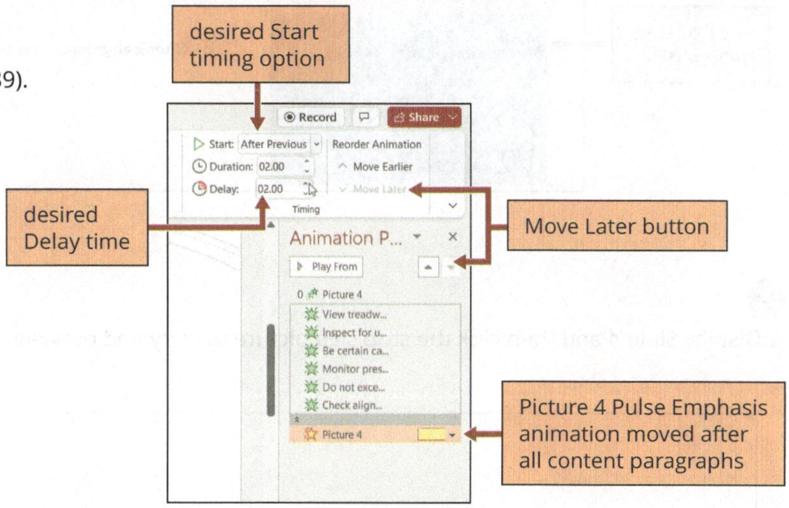

Figure 5–89

To Remove an Animation

You can remove an animation effect that has been applied to text or an object. To remove an animation, you would perform the following steps.

1. Display the Animations tab and then click the Animation Pane button.
2. Click the animated object that has the effect you want to remove.
3. In the Animation Pane, click the effect to remove, click the down arrow, and then click Remove.

BTW
Removing Multiple Animation Effects
To remove more than one animation effect from text or an object, in the Animation Pane, press CTRL, click each animation effect that you want to remove, and then press DELETE. To remove all animation effects from text or an object, click the object that you want to stop animating and then click None in the gallery of animation effects (Animations tab | Animation group).

To Use the Animation Painter

At times, you may desire to apply the same animation effects to several objects in a presentation. On Slide 4, for example, you want to animate the stop sign picture with the identical entrance and emphasis effects you applied to the Slide 2 tires picture. As with the Format Painter that is used to duplicate formatting attributes, the **Animation Painter** copies animations from one object to another. Using the Animation Painter can save time. **Why?** It duplicates numerous animation effects and characteristics uniformly to other objects with one click. The following steps use the Animation Painter to copy the animations from Slide 2 to Slide 4.

1

- Click the tires picture to select it.
- Click the Animation Painter button (Animations tab | Advanced Animation group).
- Move the pointer off the ribbon (Figure 5–90).

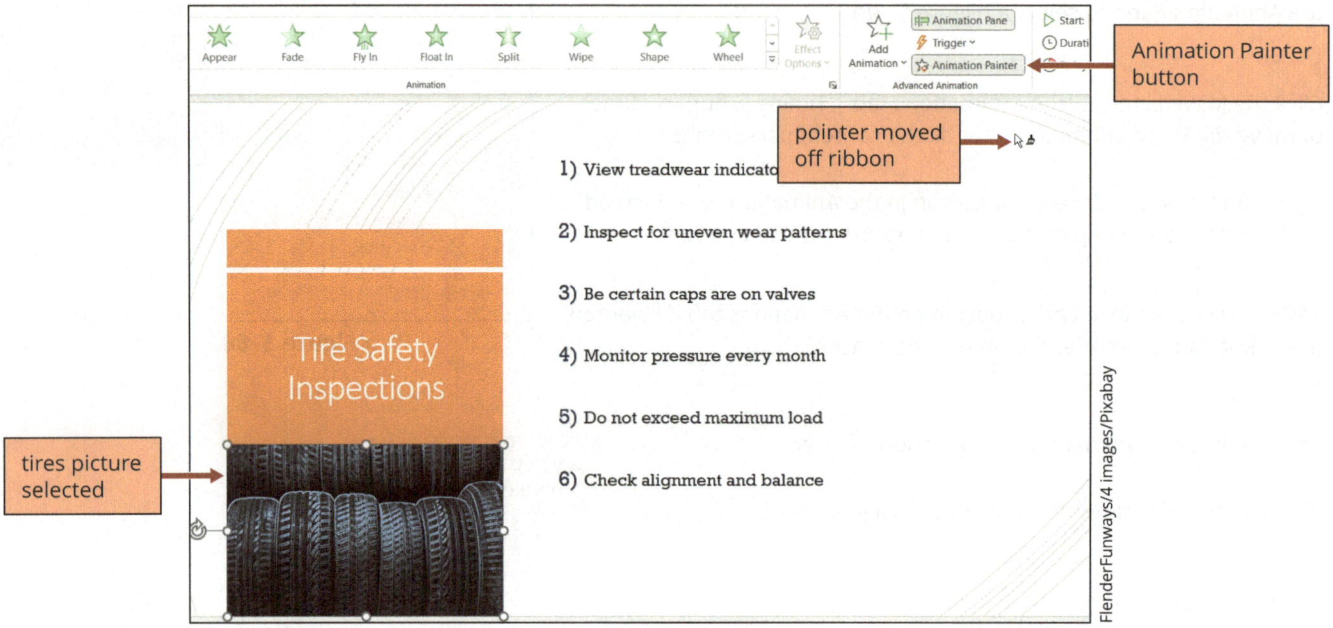

Figure 5–90

2

- Display Slide 4 and then click the stop sign picture to copy and preview the animations from Slide 2 (Figure 5–91).

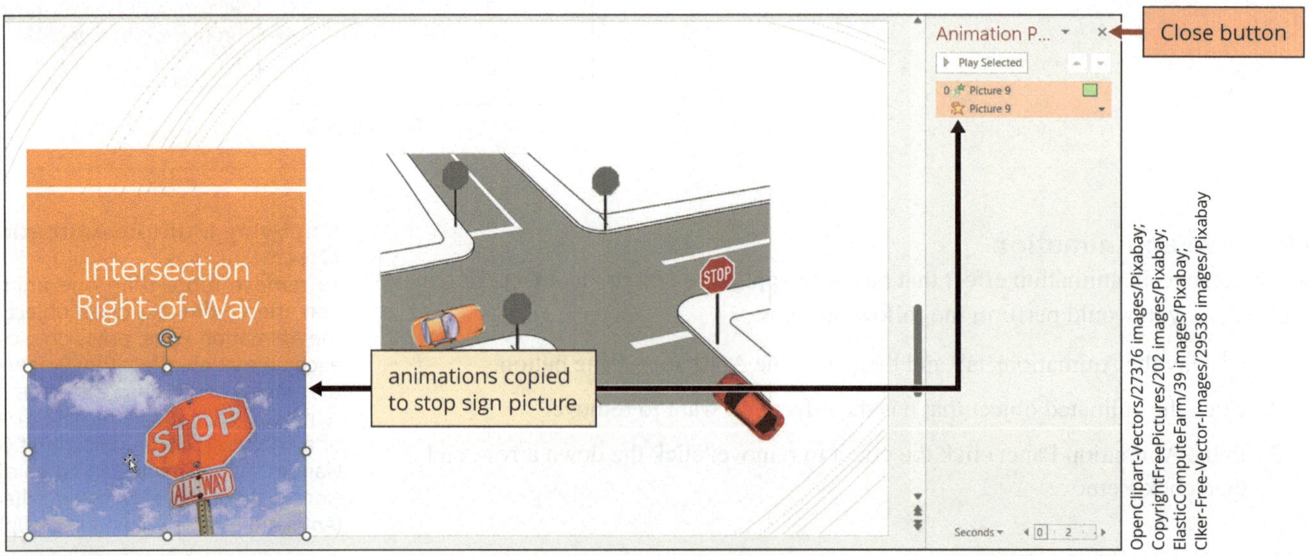

Figure 5–91

3

- If the Comments pane is displayed, close it. Close the Animation Pane.

Q&A My Animation Pane is not displayed. What should I do?
Click the Animation Pane icon to open it, and then you will be able to close it.

Other Ways

1. Press ALT+SHIFT+C

To Animate an Object Using a Preset Motion Path

Slide 3 has a picture you want to animate using a motion path. You will add the Loops motion path, which is one of the six options displayed in the Motion Paths section of the Animation gallery. **Why?** Most newer vehicles have driver-assistance safety features, and icons for many of them are displayed on the dashboard. You want to call attention to viewing them on a dashboard. In addition, many additional motion paths are available when you click More Motion Paths in the lower area of the Animation gallery. The following steps animate the picture using the Loops motion path.

1

- Display Slide 3 and select the dashboard picture.
- With the Animations tab selected, click the Add Animation button (Animations tab | Advanced Animation group) to display the Animation gallery.
- Scroll down until the Motion Paths section is visible (Figure 5–92).

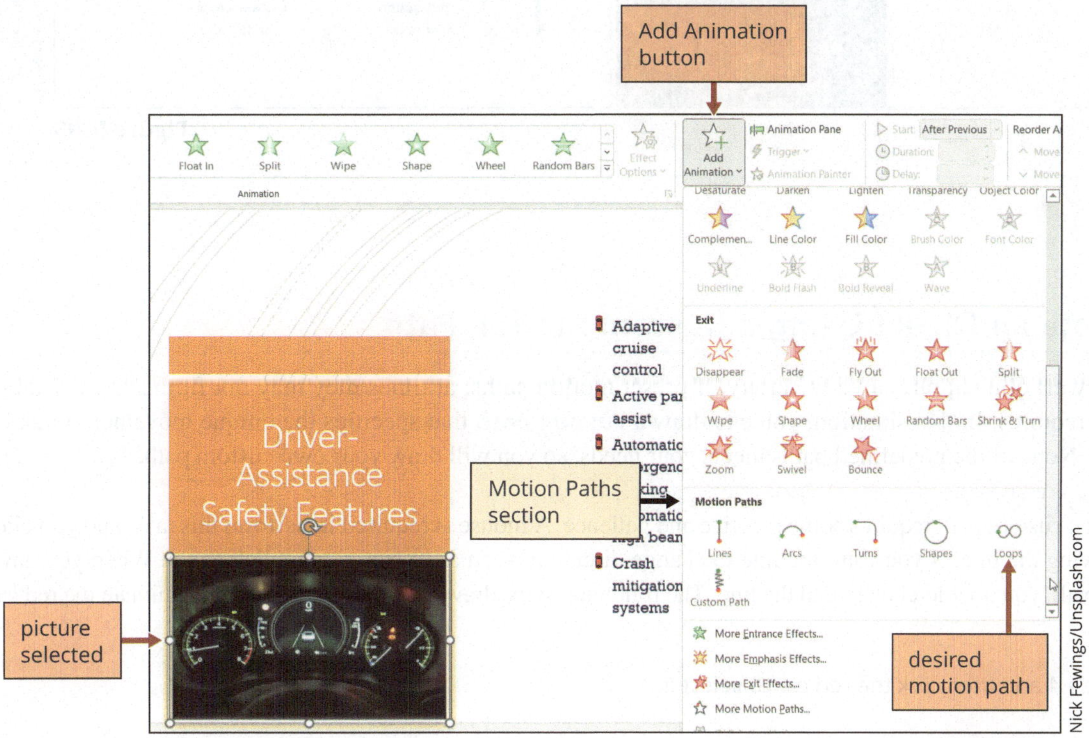

Figure 5–92

2

- Click the Loops motion path to apply the animation to the picture and preview the animation.
- Change the Duration to 05.00 seconds (Figure 5–93) and then preview the animation.

Q&A Are more motion paths available in addition to those shown in the Animation gallery?
Yes. To see additional motion paths, click More Motion Paths in the lower portion of the Animation gallery. The motion paths are arranged in the Basic, Lines & Curves, and Special categories.

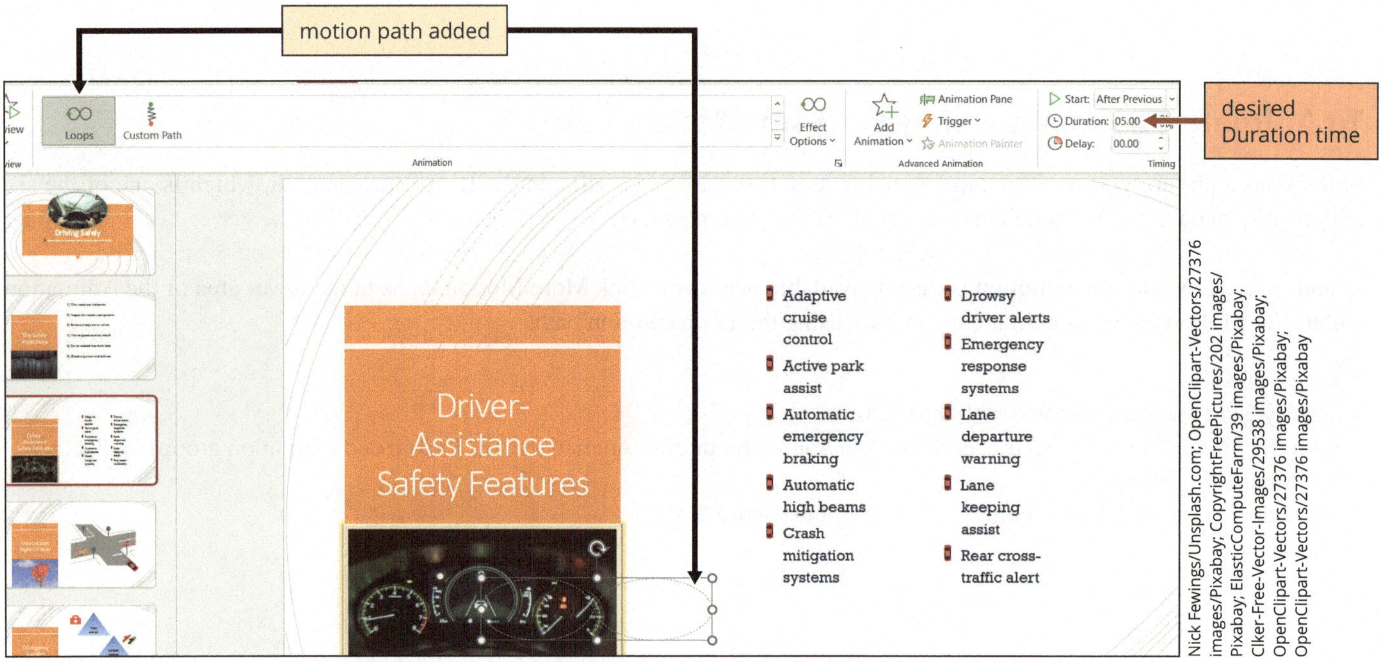

Nick Fewings/Unsplash.com; OpenClipart-Vectors/27376 images/Pixabay; CopyrightFreePictures/202 images/Pixabay; ElasticComputeFarm/39 images/Pixabay; Clker-Free-Vector-Images/29538 images/Pixabay; OpenClipart-Vectors/27376 images/Pixabay; OpenClipart-Vectors/27376 images/Pixabay

Figure 5–93

To Animate an Object Using a Custom Motion Path

Although PowerPoint supplies a wide variety of preset motion paths, at times they may not fit the precise animations your presentation requires. In that situation, you can draw a **custom path** that specifies the unique movement your slide element should make. None of the predefined paths meets your needs, so you will draw your own custom path. **Why?** You want to show a vehicle entering and traveling through an intersection.

Drawing a custom path requires some practice and patience. A mouse is required to perform this task, and you click the mouse to begin drawing the line. If you want the line to change direction, such as to curve, you click again. When you have completed drawing the path, you double-click to end the line. The following steps draw a custom motion path to animate the red car on Slide 4.

1

- Display Slide 4 and then click the red car to select it.

- With the Animations tab selected, click the Add Animation button and then scroll down until the entire Motion Paths section is visible (Figure 5–94).

Q&A Can I draw a custom motion path when using a touch screen?

No. You must use a mouse to perform this task.

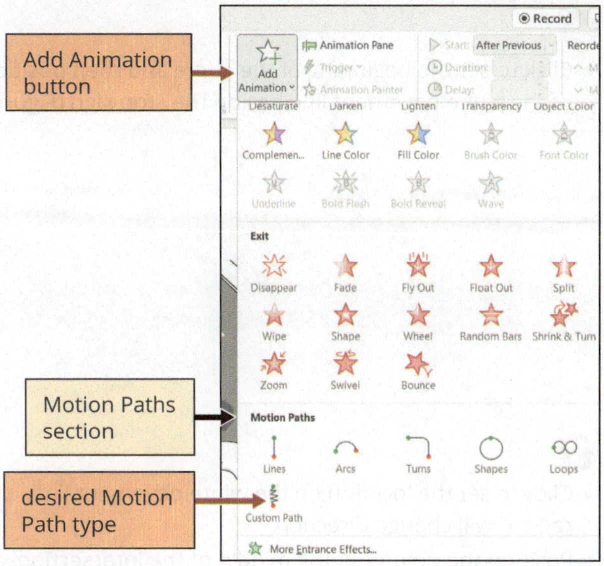

Figure 5–94

2

- Click Custom Path in the Motion Paths section to add this animation.
- Click the Effect Options button (Animations tab | Animation group) to display the Type gallery (Figure 5–95).

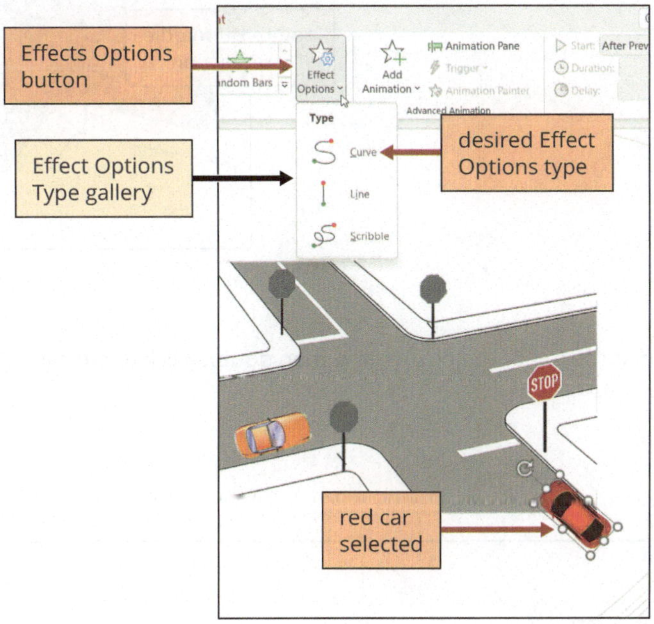

Figure 5–95

OpenClipart-Vectors/27376 images/Pixabay; CopyrightFreePictures/202 images/Pixabay; ElasticComputeFarm/39 images/Pixabay; Clker-Free-Vector-Images/29538 images/Pixabay

3

- Click Curve in the Type gallery and then position the pointer on the sizing handle in the middle of the red car's front bumper (Figure 5–96).

Q&A Why did I need to select Curve rather than Scribble or Line?

Your custom motion path will select particular locations on the slide, and the Curve type will create rounded edges to connect the lines you draw. The Scribble and Line options would draw only straight lines, so the arrow would not have smooth turns as it moves through the intersection.

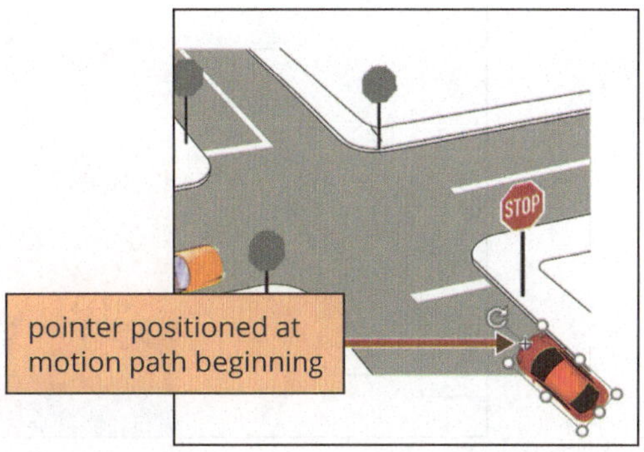

Figure 5–96

OpenClipart-Vectors/27376 images/Pixabay; CopyrightFreePictures/202 images/Pixabay; ElasticComputeFarm/39 images/Pixabay; Clker-Free-Vector-Images/29538 images/Pixabay

4

- Click to set the beginning of the curve and then position the pointer on the center of the white pavement line beside the stop sign (Figure 5–97).

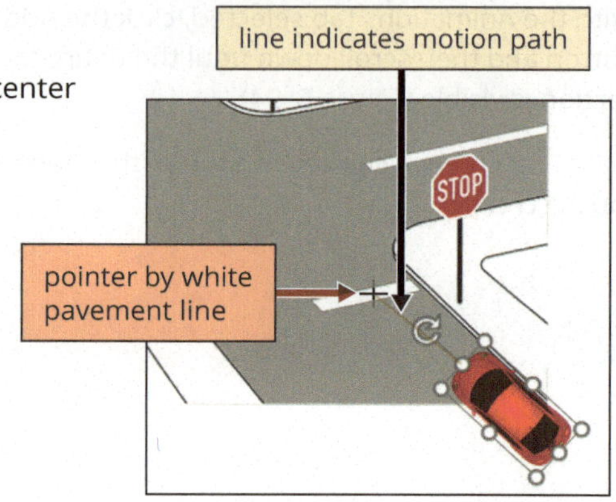

OpenClipart-Vectors/27376 images/Pixabay; CopyrightFreePictures/202 images/Pixabay; ElasticComputeFarm/39 images/Pixabay

Figure 5–97

5

- Click to set the location on the white pavement line, which is where the red car will change direction.
- Position the pointer in the middle of the intersection, as shown in Figure 5–98, and then click to set the top of the curve in this direction of travel.

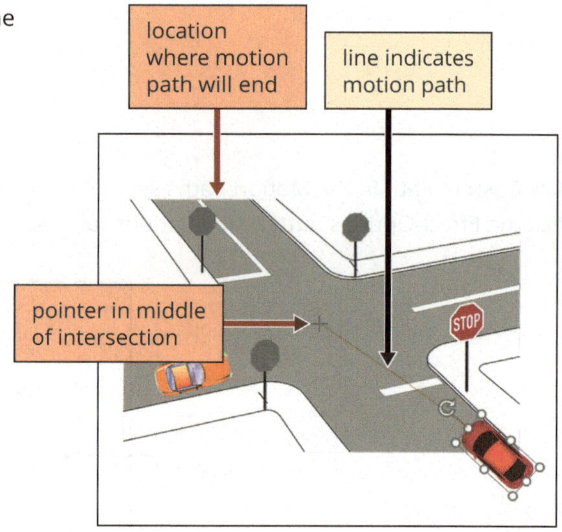

OpenClipart-Vectors/27376 images/Pixabay; CopyrightFreePictures/202 images/Pixabay; ElasticComputeFarm/39 images/Pixabay; Clker-Free-Vector-Images/29538 images/Pixabay

Figure 5–98

6

- Position the pointer at the end of the road at the top of the picture and then double-click to indicate the end of the motion path and preview this animation (Figure 5–99).

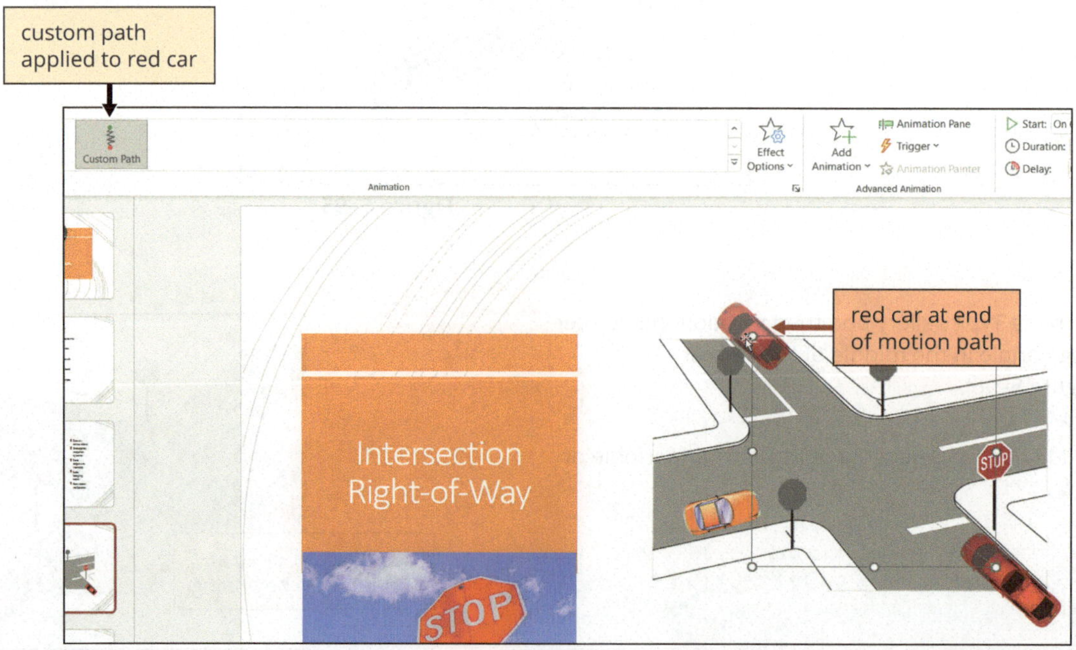

OpenClipart-Vectors/27376 images/Pixabay; CopyrightFreePictures/202 images/Pixabay; ElasticComputeFarm/39 images/Pixabay; Clker-Free-Vector-Images/29538 images/Pixabay

Figure 5–99

- Change the Duration setting to 07.00 seconds (Figure 5–100).

Q&A If my curve is not correct, can I delete it?
Yes. Select the motion path, press DELETE, and then repeat the previous steps.

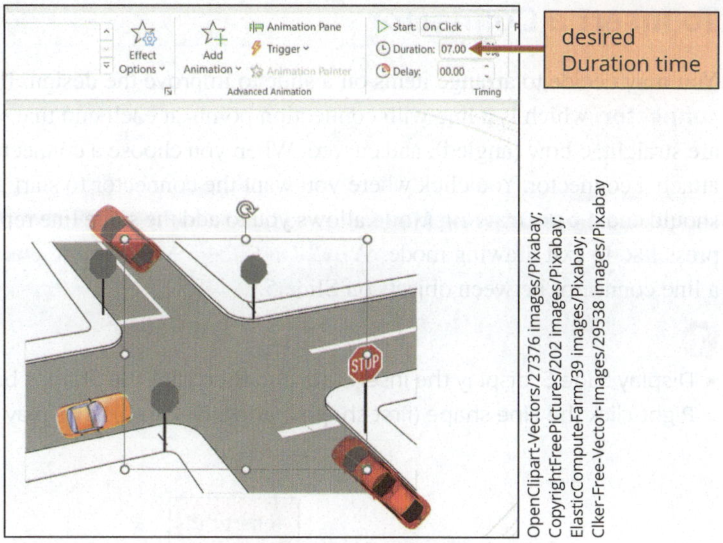

OpenClipart-Vectors/27376 images/Pixabay; CopyrightFreePictures/202 images/Pixabay; ElasticComputeFarm/39 images/Pixabay; Clker-Free-Vector-Images/29538 images/Pixabay

Figure 5–100

To Trigger an Animation Effect

If you select the On Click Start animation timing option and run the slide show, PowerPoint starts the animation when you click any part of the slide or press SPACEBAR. You may, however, want the option to play an animation in a particular circumstance. **Why?** You may have an animated sequence ready to show if time permits or if you believe your audience needs time to understand a process and would understand the concept more readily if you revealed one part of a slide element at a time. A **trigger** specifies when an animation or other action should occur. It is linked to a particular component of a slide so that the action occurs only when you click this slide element. For example, you can trigger an animation effect to start when you click a shape or other object that has the animation applied, or you can trigger an animation effect to begin playing at the start of, or sometime during, an audio or video clip. If you click any other part of the slide, PowerPoint will display the next slide in the presentation. The following steps set clicking the red car on Slide 4 as the trigger to move that vehicle.

1

- Click the red car, click the Trigger button (Animations tab | Advanced Animation group) to display the Trigger menu, and then point to 'On Click of' to display the list of Slide 4 elements (Figure 5–101).

2

- Click Picture 5, which is the red car, as the object that will trigger the animation when clicked.

Q&A How do I know the trigger animation has been added to the red car?
The Animation Pane displays 'Trigger: Picture 5'.

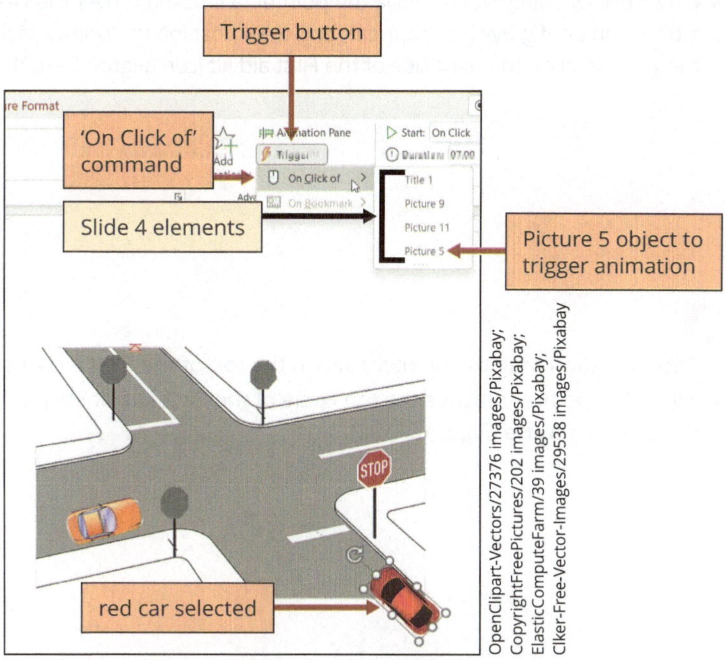

OpenClipart-Vectors/27376 images/Pixabay; CopyrightFreePictures/202 images/Pixabay; ElasticComputeFarm/39 images/Pixabay; Clker-Free-Vector-Images/29538 images/Pixabay

Figure 5–101

To Insert a Connector

You may decide to arrange items on a slide to improve the design. If some slide elements are related to each other, you can use a **connector**, which is a line with connection points at each end that stay attached to related shapes. The three types of connectors are straight, elbow (angled), and curved. When you choose a connector, dots appear on the shape outline to indicate where you can attach a connector. You click where you want the connector to start and then drag the pointer to the location where the connector should end. **Lock Drawing Mode** allows you to add the same line repeatedly. When you have completed adding the connector, you press ESC to exit drawing mode. *Why? On Slide 5, you want to connect each icon to its related shape.* The following steps insert a line connector between objects on Slide 5.

1

- Display Slide 5, display the Insert tab, and then click the Shapes button to display the Shapes gallery.
- Right-click the Line shape (first shape in the Lines area) to display the Drawing Mode menu (Figure 5–102).

StockSnap/27551 images/Pixabay

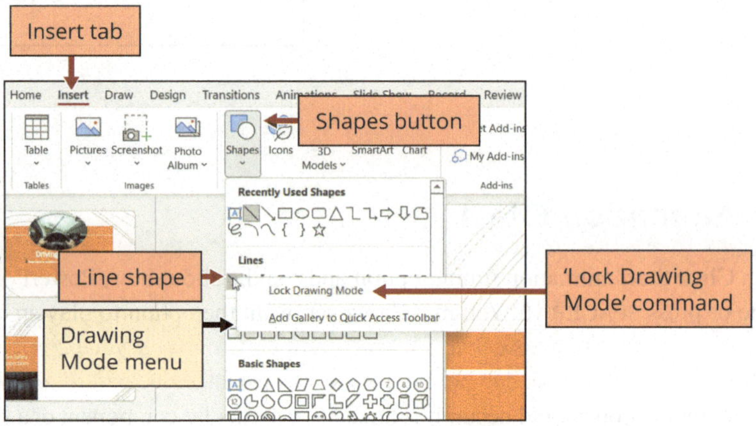

Figure 5–102

2

- Click 'Lock Drawing Mode', move the pointer (a crosshair) over the First aid kit icon until gray circles appear, and then position the pointer over the gray circle on the right side of the First aid kit icon (Figure 5–103).

OpenClipart-Vectors/27376 images/Pixabay

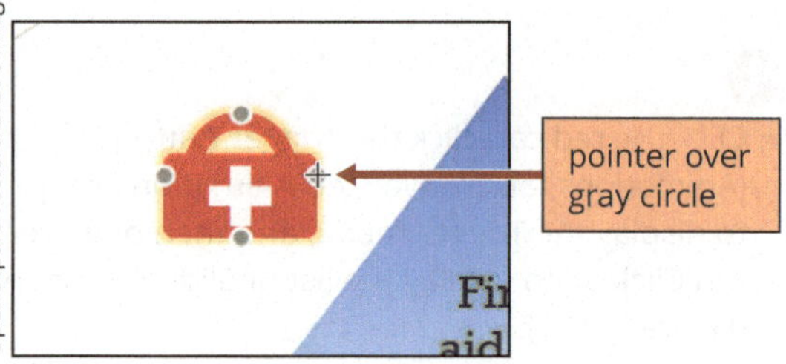

Figure 5–103

3

- Click and then drag the pointer toward the top of the First aid kit shape.
- When the pointer reaches the top circle of the First aid kit shape, release the mouse (Figure 5–104).

OpenClipart-Vectors/27376 images/Pixabay

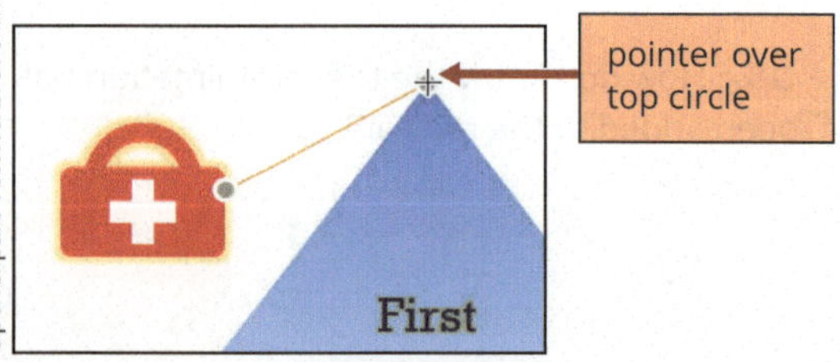

Figure 5–104

4

- Position the pointer over the gray circle on left side of the Jumper cables icon and then click and drag the pointer to the top circle of the Jumper cables shape.
- Position the pointer over the top gray circle on the right side of the Flashlight icon and then click and drag the pointer to the top circle of the Flashlight shape (Figure 5–105).

5

- Press ESC to exit Drawing Mode.

Q&A How do I know I have exited Drawing Mode?
The gray dots no longer are displayed.

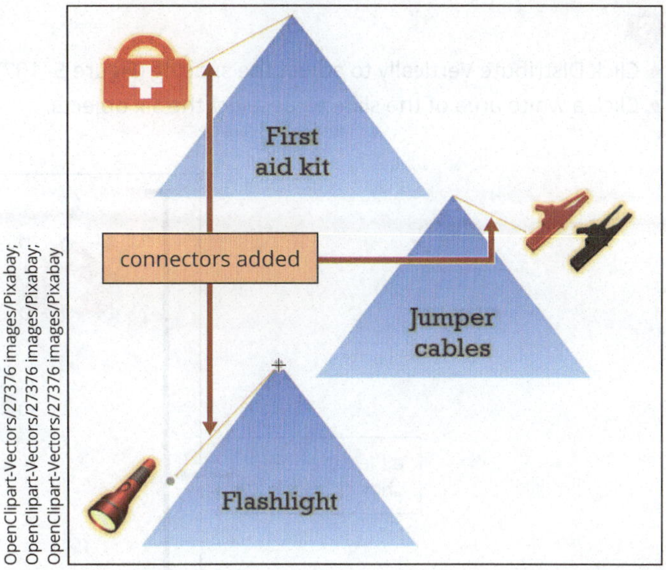

Figure 5–105

To Align Content Placeholders

You can have PowerPoint place the same amount of space between the three sets of icons and shapes on Slide 5. You have two distribution options: 'Align to Slide' spaces all the selected objects evenly across the entire width of the slide; 'Align Selected Objects' spaces the objects between the fixed right and left objects. The following steps use the 'Align Selected Objects' option. **Why?** This option will distribute the Slide 5 pictures and shapes vertically to evenly fill space in the middle of the slide.

1

- Select the six Slide 5 icons and shapes, display the Shape Format tab, and then click the Align button (Shape Format tab | Arrange group) to display the Align Objects menu.

2

- If necessary, click 'Align Selected Objects' so that PowerPoint will adjust the spacing of the pictures evenly and then click the Align button to display the Align menu again (Figure 5–106).

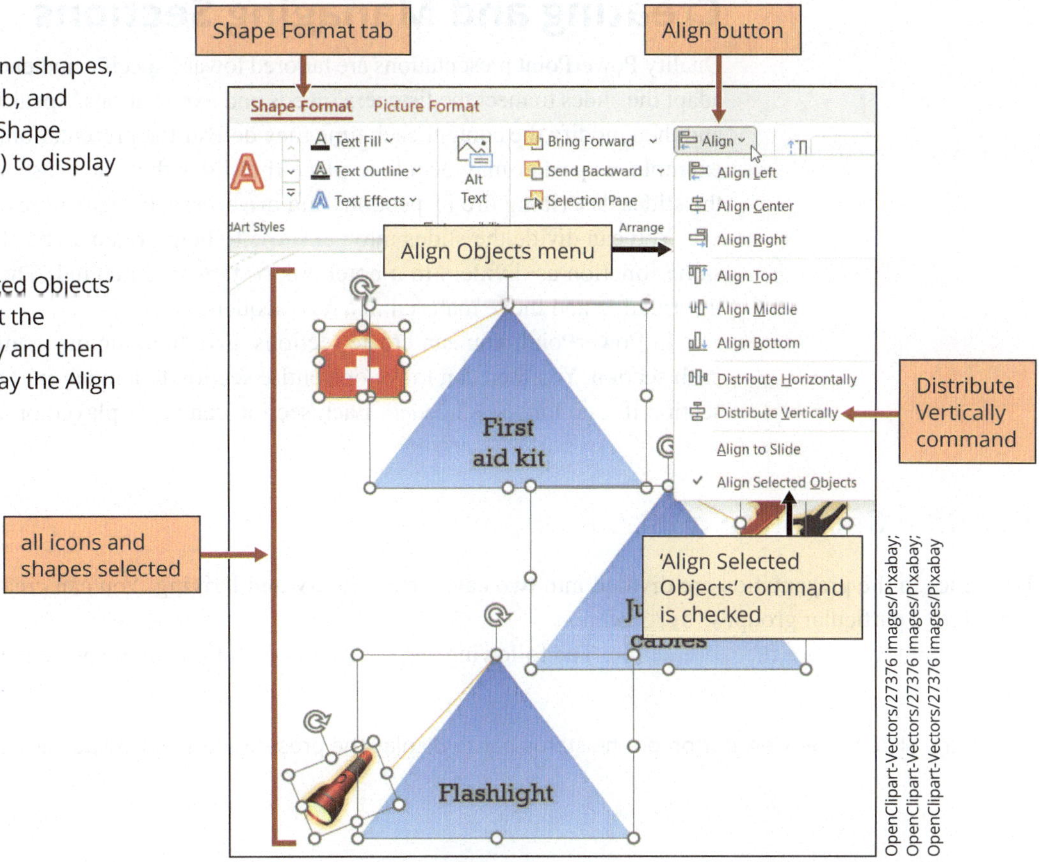

Figure 5–106

3

- Click Distribute Vertically to adjust the spacing (Figure 5–107).
- Click a white area of the slide to deselect the six objects.

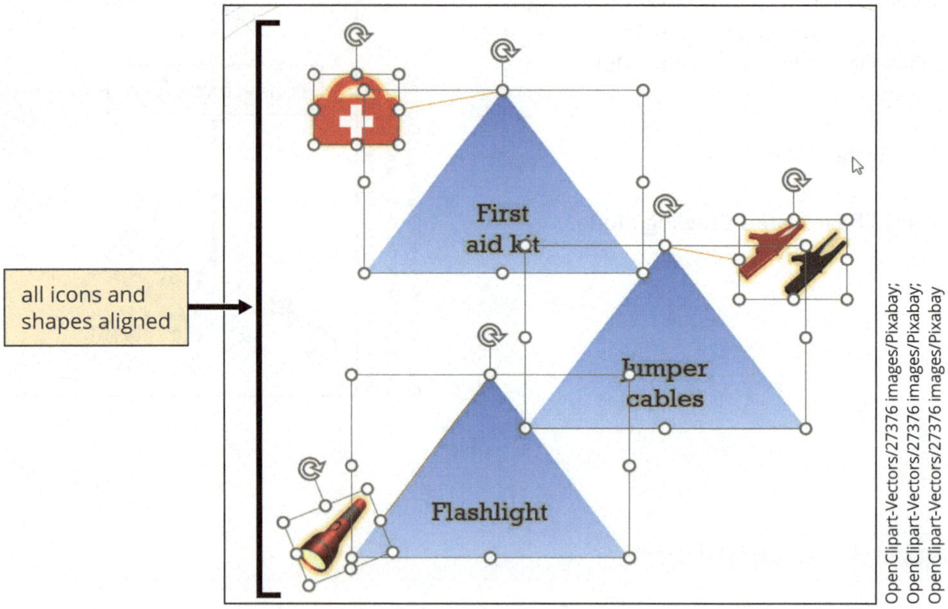

Figure 5–107

Creating and Managing Sections

Quality PowerPoint presentations are tailored toward specific audiences, and experienced presenters adapt the slides to meet the listeners' needs and expectations. Speakers can develop one slide show and then modify the content each time they deliver the presentation. In the Driving slide show, for example, a speaker may decide to place the slides that showcase safe driving techniques before the slides describing tire inspections and driver-assistance features.

You can divide the slides into **sections** to help organize the slides. These sections serve the same function as dividers in a notebook or tabs in a manual: They help the user find required information and move material in a new sequence.

In PowerPoint, you can create sections, give them unique names, and then move slides into each section. You then can move one entire section to another part of the slide show or delete the section if it no longer is needed. Each section can be displayed or printed individually.

To Add a Section to a Presentation

The slides in the presentation are divided into two categories: Safety and Driving. You can create a section break to organize slides into a particular group. **Why?** At times, you may want to display slides from one particular category or move a section of slides to another part of the presentation. The following steps create two sections in the presentation.

1

- Click the Slide Sorter view button on the status bar to display the presentation in Slide Sorter view.

- Position the pointer between Slide 3 and Slide 4 and then click once to display the vertical bar (Figure 5–108).

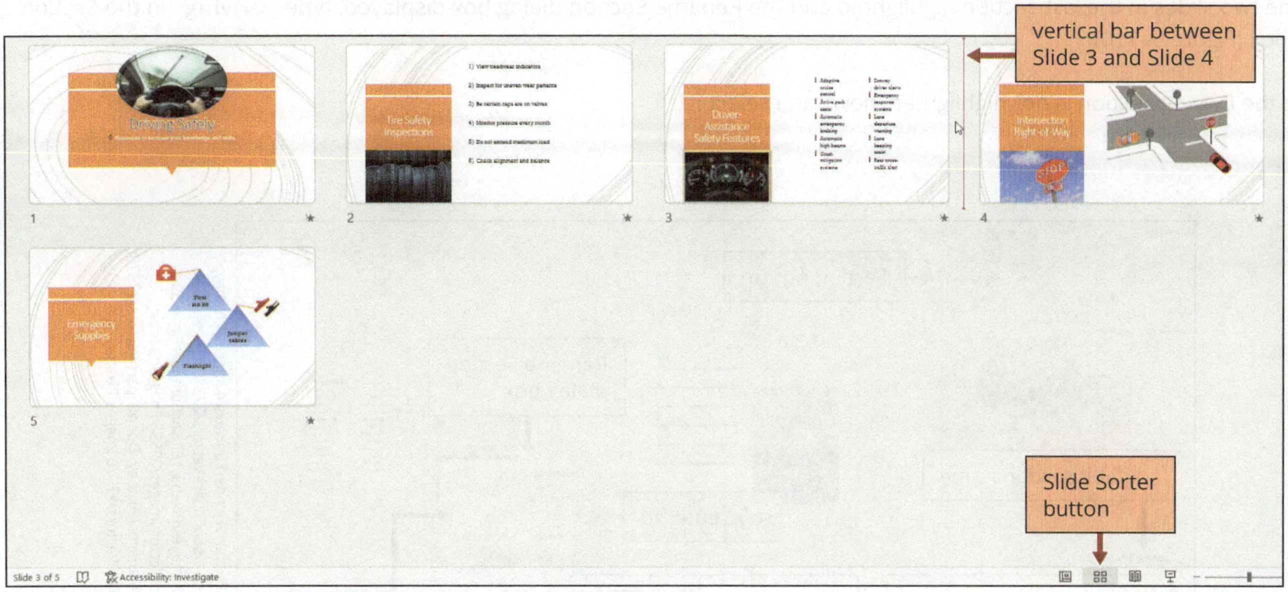

StockSnap/27551 images/Pixabay; FlenderFunways/4 images/Pixabay; Nick Fewings/Unsplash.com; OpenClipart-Vectors/27376 images/Pixabay; CopyrightFreePictures/202 images/Pixabay; ElasticComputeFarm/39 images/Pixabay; Clker-Free-Vector-Images/29538 images/Pixabay; OpenClipart-Vectors/27376 images/Pixabay; OpenClipart-Vectors/27376 images/Pixabay; OpenClipart-Vectors/27376 images/Pixabay

Figure 5–108

Q&A I am using a touch screen. When I tap between the slides to display the vertical bar, a shortcut menu also displays with an Add Section button. Can I just tap that button instead of using the Home tab Section button?
Yes.

2
- With the Home tab displayed, click the Section button (Home tab | Slides group) to display the Section menu (Figure 5–109).

3
- Click Add Section in the menu to create a section with the name, Untitled Section.

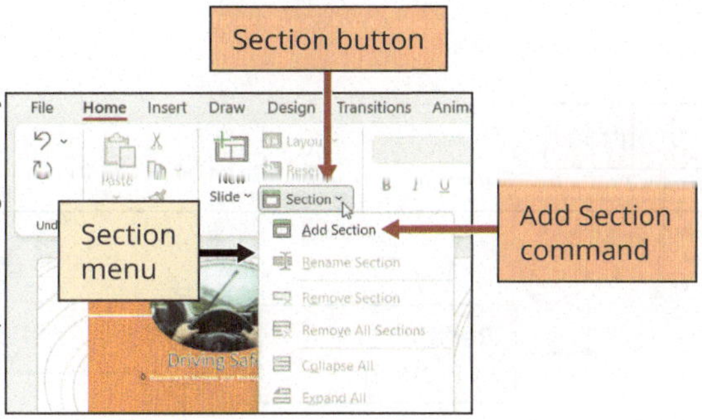

StockSnap/27551 images. Pixabay

Figure 5–109

To Rename a Section

The default section names, Default and Untitled, do not identify the content of the slides in the group. The following steps rename each of the two sections in the presentation. **Why?** Giving each section a unique name helps to categorize the slides easily.

1

- With the two slides in the last section highlighted and the Rename Section dialog box displayed, type **Driving** in the Section name box (Figure 5–110).

Q&A If the Driving section is not highlighted, how can I select it?

Click the divider between the sections. You will know the section is selected when the thumbnails have a colored border and the text and slide numbers have a colored font color.

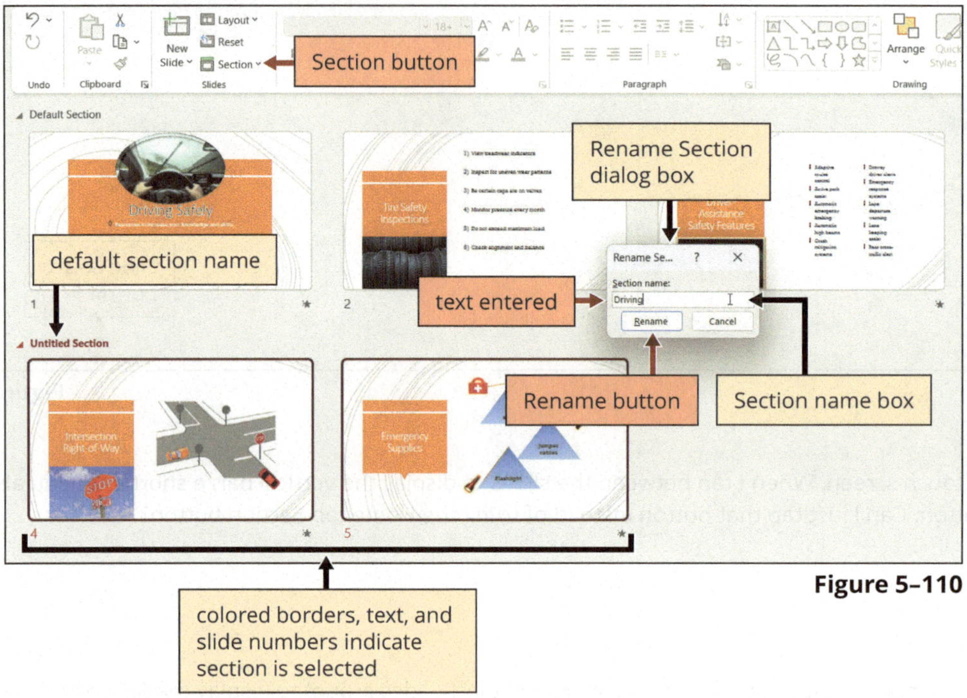

StockSnap/27551 images/Pixabay; FlenderFunways/4 images/Pixabay; Nick Fewings/Unsplash.com; OpenClipart-Vectors/27376 images/Pixabay; CopyrightFreePictures/202 images/Pixabay; ElasticComputeFarm/39 images/Pixabay; Clker-Free-Vector-Images/29538 images/Pixabay; OpenClipart-Vectors/27376 images/Pixabay; OpenClipart-Vectors/27376 images/Pixabay; OpenClipart-Vectors/27376 images/Pixabay

Figure 5–110

2

- Click the Rename button (Rename Section dialog box) to change the section name to Driving.
- Click the Default Section divider for Slides 1, 2, and 3 to select it and then click the Section button to display the Section menu (Figure 5–111).

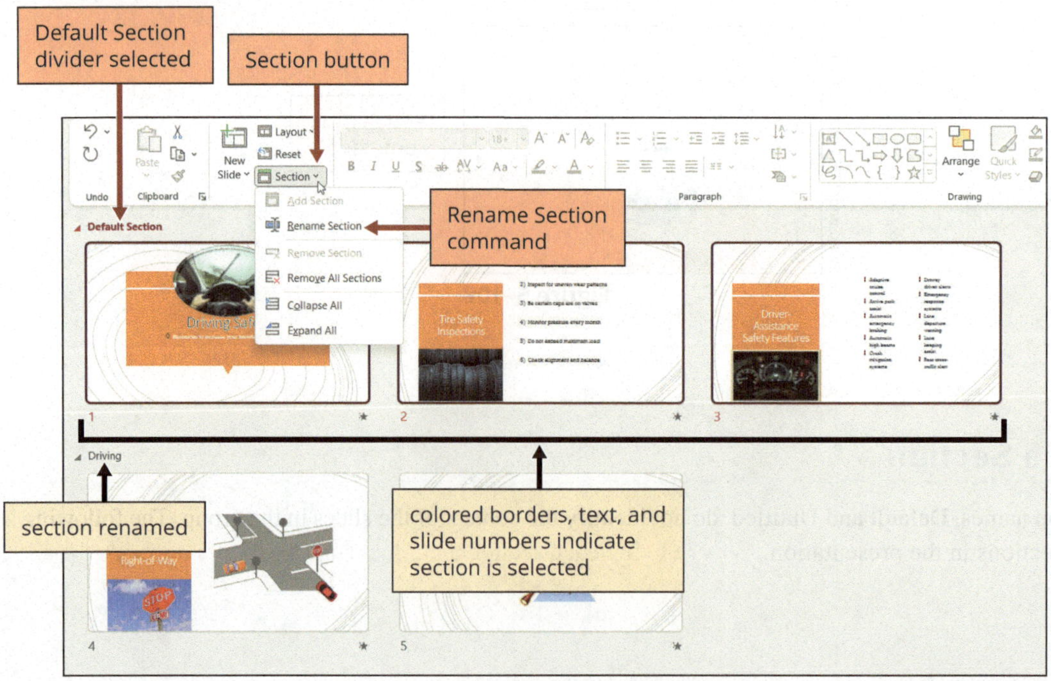

StockSnap/27551 images/Pixabay; FlenderFunways/4 images/Pixabay; Nick Fewings/Unsplash.com; OpenClipart-Vectors/27376 images/Pixabay; CopyrightFreePictures/202 images/Pixabay; ElasticComputeFarm/39 images/Pixabay; Clker-Free-Vector-Images/29538 images/Pixabay; OpenClipart-Vectors/27376 images/Pixabay; OpenClipart-Vectors/27376 images/Pixabay; OpenClipart-Vectors/27376 images/Pixabay

Figure 5–111

3

- Click Rename Section to display the Rename Section dialog box, type **Safety** in the Section name box, and then click the Rename button to change the section name (Figure 5–112).

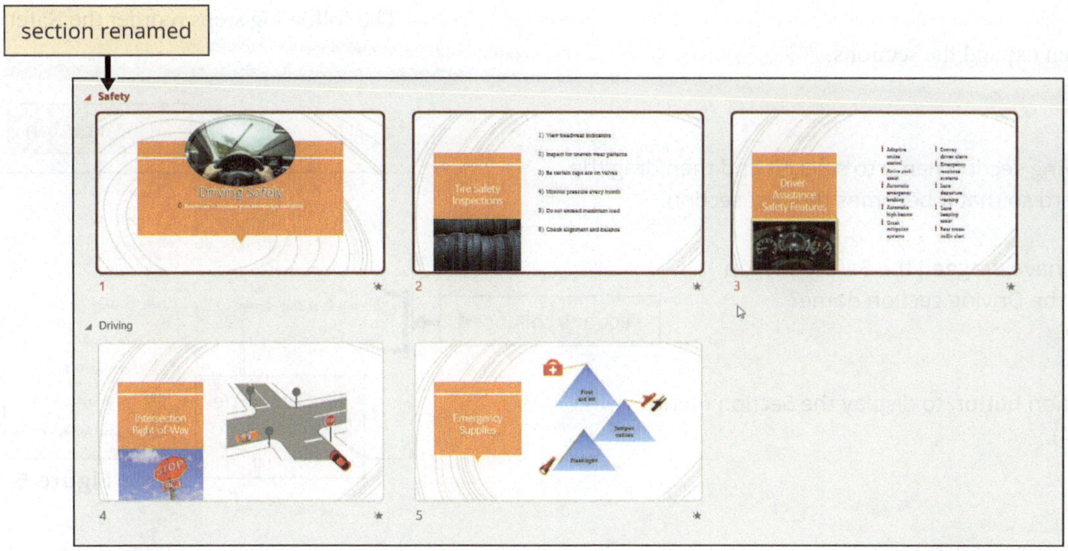

Figure 5–112

Other Ways

1. Right-click section divider, click Rename Section on shortcut menu

To Collapse Sections

You can collapse the sections so that only the two section titles are displayed. **Why?** It is convenient to view the names when the sections are displayed in a list. The following steps collapse the sections.

1

- With the first section, Safety, selected and the Home tab displayed, click the Section button (Figure 5–113).

Q&A Can I remove a section?

Yes. To delete one section, select the section title and then click Remove Section in the Section menu. To remove all sections, display the Section menu and then click 'Remove All Sections'.

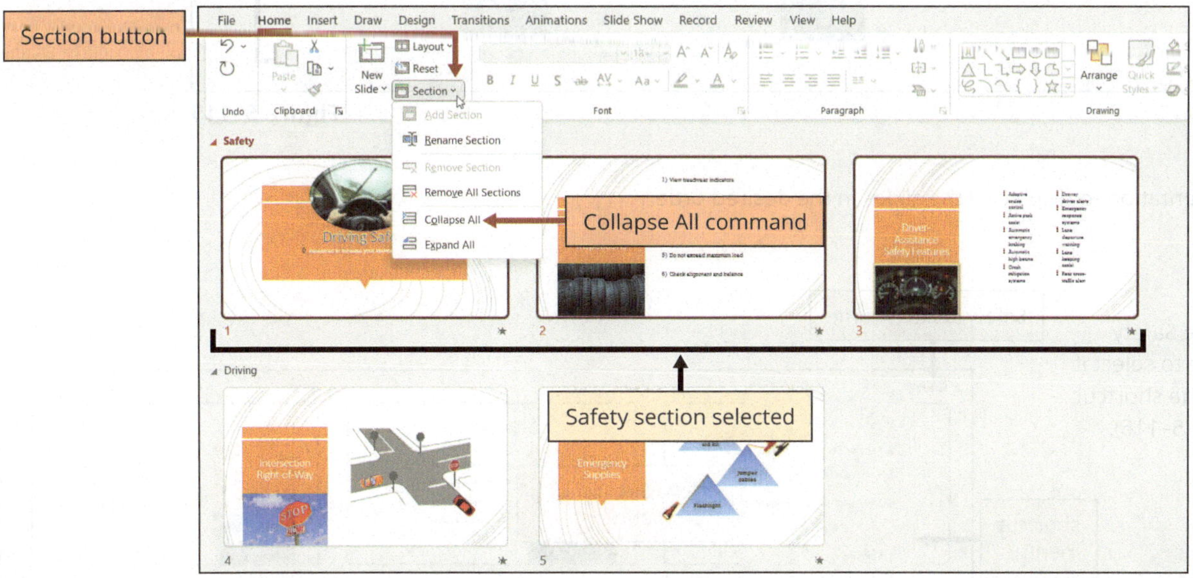

Figure 5–113

2

- Click Collapse All in the Section menu to display only the section names.

To Reorder Sections

When the slide sections are collapsed, it is easy to change the order in which the sections display. **Why?** You want to emphasize safe driving techniques before describing tires and driver safety features, so you want to present this information at the beginning of your talk and change the order of the two sets of slides in your presentation. The following steps reorder the Safety and Driving sections and then expand the sections.

1

- Click the Driving section name to select it and then drag the section upward so that it becomes the first section.

Q&A Could I have dragged the Safety section name below the Driving section name?
Yes. Either method would arrange the sections.

- Click the Section button to display the Section menu (Figure 5–114).

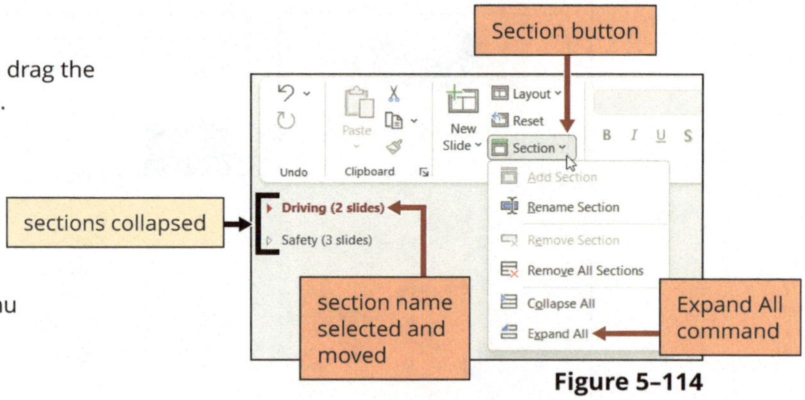

Figure 5–114

2

- Click Expand All to display all the slides in their corresponding sections (Figure 5–115).

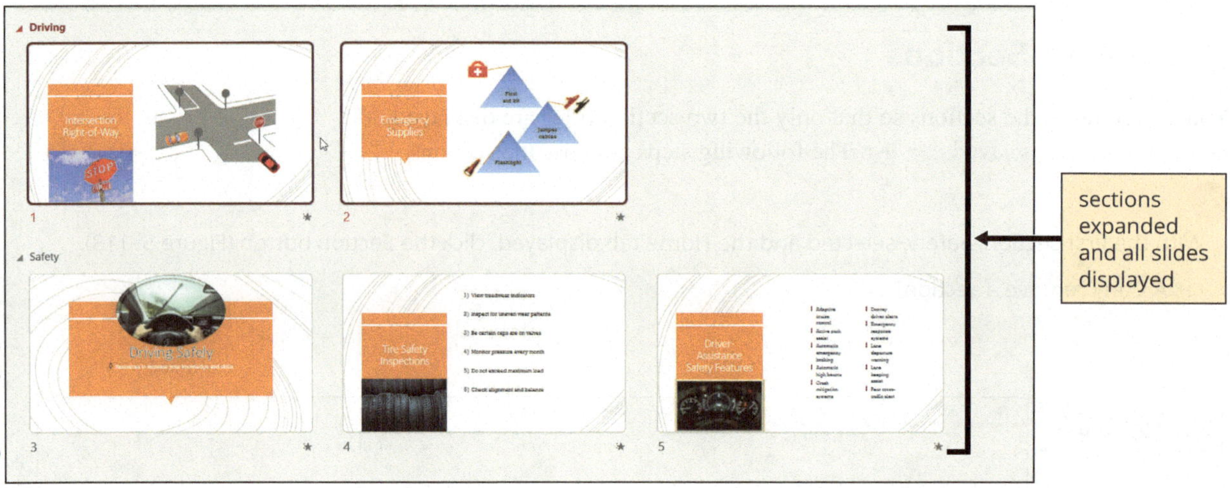

Figure 5–115

3

- Run the presentation to display all the slides in the desired order.

4

- Right-click the Safety section name to select it and display the shortcut menu (Figure 5–116).

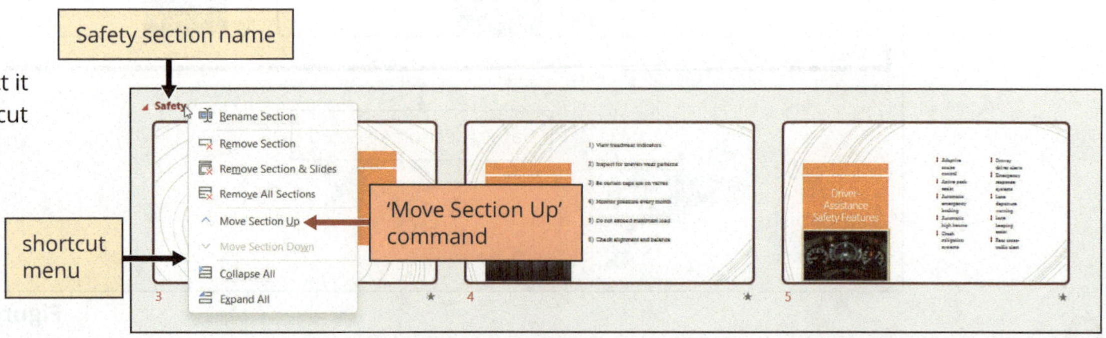

Figure 5–116

5

- Click 'Move Section Up' to position the Safety section as the first section in the presentation.

Other Ways

1. Right-click section name, click Move Section Up, Move Section Down, Collapse All, or Expand All on shortcut menu

Zoom Links

A **zoom link** is a dynamic feature that allows you to present your content creatively in a nonlinear way. When you create a zoom link, you can jump to and from specific slides, sections, and portions of your presentation in an order you decide when you are presenting. You can jump to specific slides and sections with slide zoom and section zoom. If your presentation has several sections, you can use a **section zoom** to return to sections you want to emphasize or highlight. To show only selected slides, you can use **slide zoom** to show a small version of a slide on another slide that you can click to display the slide in Slide Show view, which is useful when a shorter presentation does not have many sections. In addition, you can create an interactive table of contents with **summary zoom**, which is a slide that contains section zooms, usually for all of the sections in the presentation. When you are presenting your slide show, you click the section zoom or slide zoom to jump to the linked section. If you use the section zoom, PowerPoint will display the slides in a section and then automatically return to the original slide.

To Insert Section Zoom Links and Slide Zoom Links

The zoom link feature can be useful when presenting your Safe Driving slides if your audience expresses interest in a particular section or you need to jump to a particular slide to review or display information. When you are displaying the title slide, for example, you can click a section zoom link and then jump to the Driving section, starting with Slide 4. After Slide 5 is displayed, PowerPoint returns to Slide 1. In another example, you can click the slide zoom link on Slide 3 to skip to Slide 5. Once Slide 5 is displayed, the presentation ends. Why? You may decide to modify the slide order while you are speaking based on the audience's interest and background knowledge. The following steps insert section and slide zoom links.

1

- Click the Normal view button on the status toolbar.
- With Slide 1 displayed, click the Insert tab and then click the Zoom button (Insert tab | Links group) to display the Zoom menu (Figure 5–117).

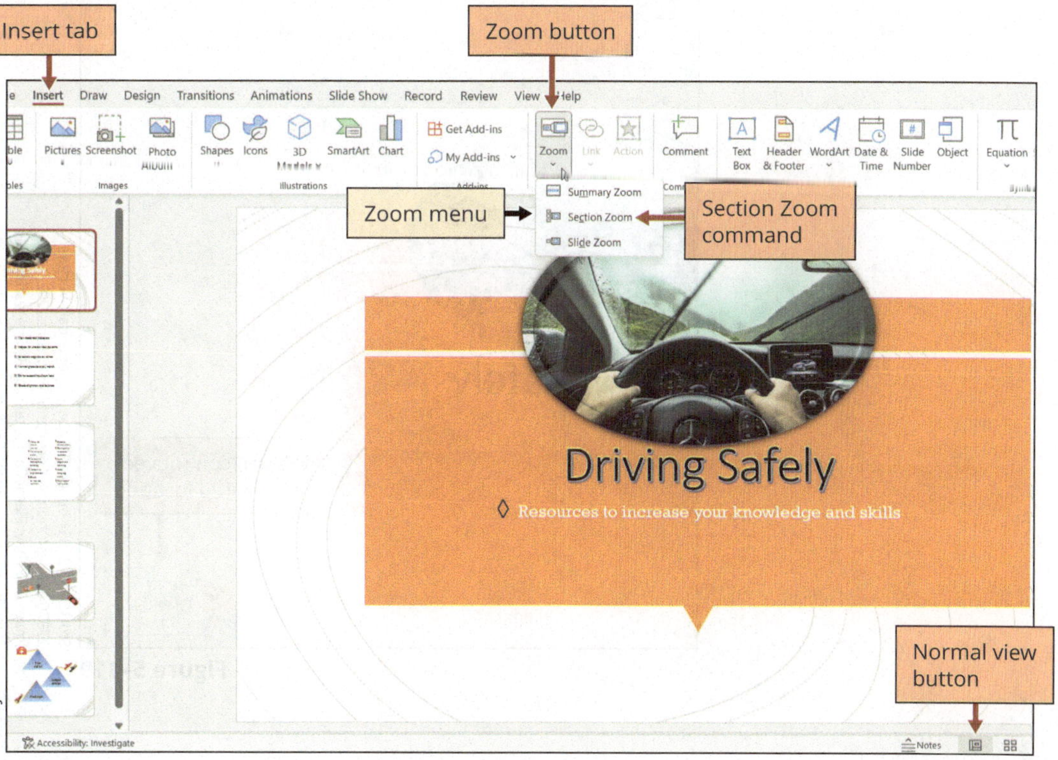

Figure 5–117

2

- Click Section Zoom and then click the 'Section 2: Driving' box to select that section (Figure 5–118).

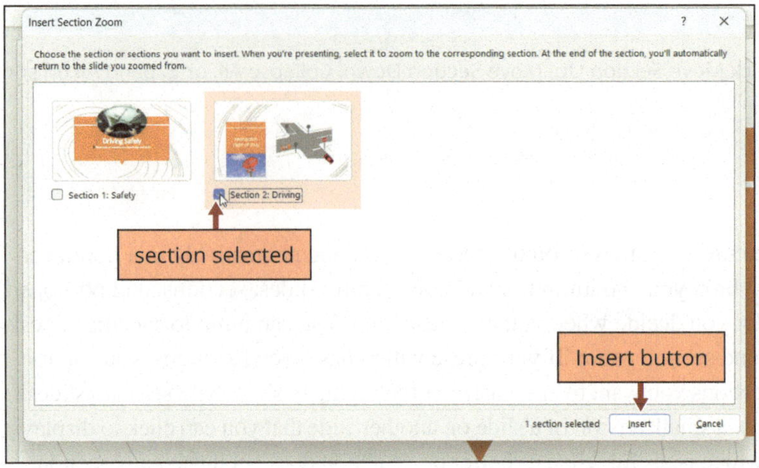

StockSnap/27551 images/Pixabay; OpenClipart-Vectors/27376 images/Pixabay; CopyrightFreePictures/202 images/Pixabay; ElasticComputeFarm/39 images/Pixabay; Clker-Free-Vector-Images/29538 images/Pixabay

Figure 5–118

3

- Click the Insert button ('Insert Section Zoom' dialog box) to create the Section Zoom.
- If a Round Trip box is displayed, click the Got it button to close the box.

4

- Click the Zoom tab and then resize the Section Zoom icon height to 1".
- Move the icon to the lower-right corner of the slide (Figure 5–119).

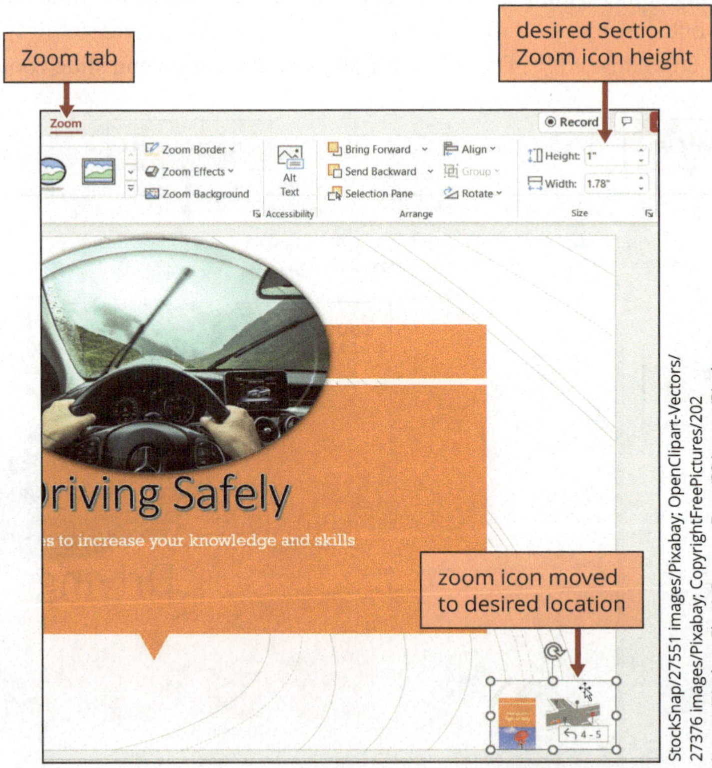

StockSnap/27551 images/Pixabay; OpenClipart-Vectors/27376 images/Pixabay; CopyrightFreePictures/202 images/Pixabay; ElasticComputeFarm/39 images/Pixabay; Clker-Free-Vector-Images/29538 images/Pixabay

Figure 5–119

5

- Display Slide 3. Click the Insert tab and then click the Zoom button to display the Zoom menu.
- Click Slide Zoom and then click the '5. Emergency Supplies' box to select this slide (Figure 5–120).

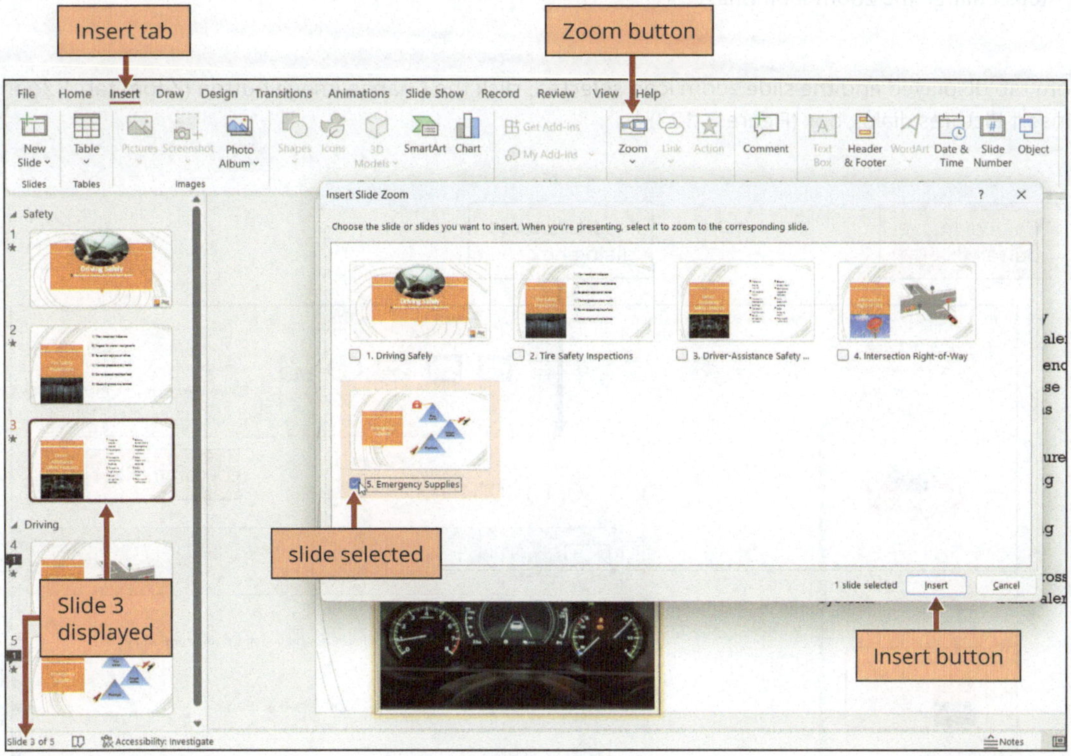

Figure 5–120

StockSnap/27551 images/Pixabay; FlenderFunways/4 images/Pixabay; Nick Fewings/Unsplash.com; OpenClipart-Vectors/27376 images/Pixabay; CopyrightFreePictures/202 images/Pixabay; ElasticComputerFarm/39 images/Pixabay; Clker-Free-Vector-Images/29538 images/Pixabay; OpenClipart-Vectors/27376 images/Pixabay; OpenClipart-Vectors/27376 images/Pixabay; OpenClipart-Vectors/27376 images/Pixabay

6

- Click the Insert button to create the Slide Zoom.
- If a 'Transitions with zip' box is displayed, click the Got it button to close the box.
- Click the Zoom tab and then resize the Slide Zoom icon height to 1".
- Move the icon to the lower-right corner of the slide (Figure 5–121).

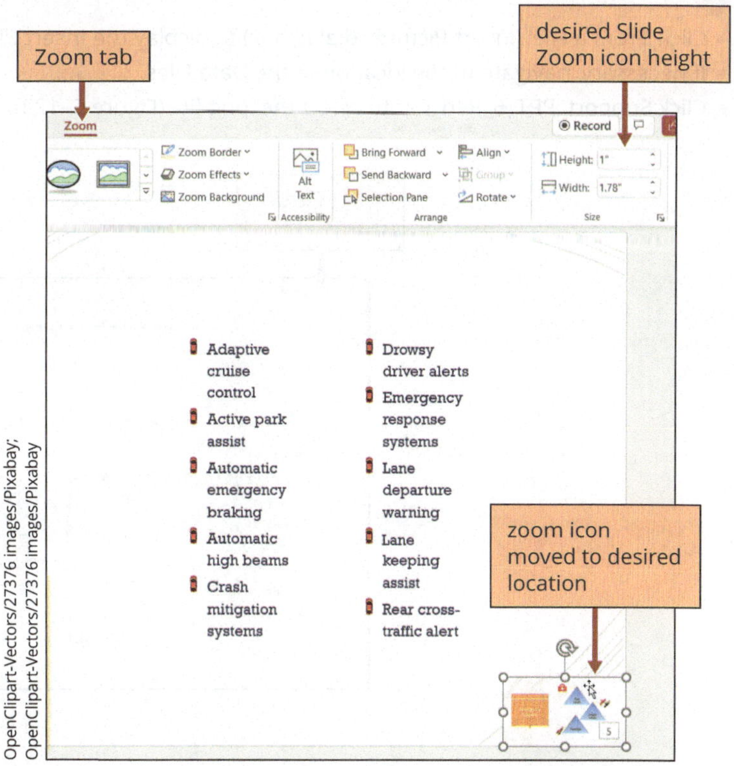

OpenClipart-Vectors/27376 images/Pixabay; OpenClipart-Vectors/27376 images/Pixabay; OpenClipart-Vectors/27376 images/Pixabay

Figure 5–121

To Change the Zoom Icon Image

As a default, PowerPoint uses a miniature copy of the slide as the zoom image. You can change this image and add styles, a border, effects, and a background. **Why?** The red car picture is the Slide 3 bullet, so the image is repeated throughout the slides. The following steps change the zoom icon image.

1

- With the Zoom tab displayed and the slide zoom icon selected, click the Change Image button (Zoom tab | Zoom Options) to display the Insert Pictures dialog box (Figure 5–122).

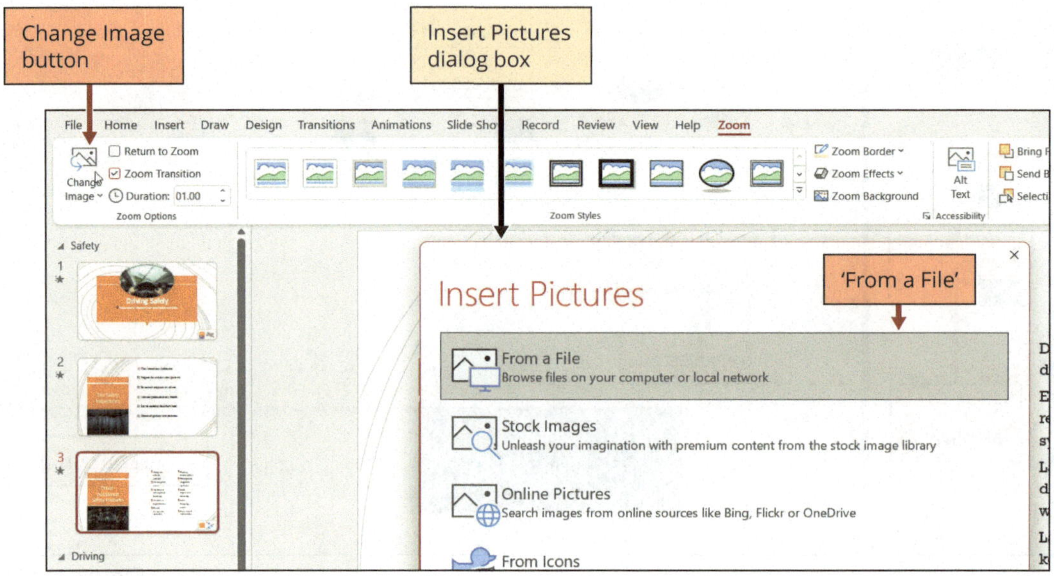

StockSnap/27551 images/Pixabay; FlenderFunways/4 images/Pixabay

Figure 5–122

2

- Click 'From a File' (Insert Pictures dialog box) to display the Insert Picture dialog box.
- If necessary, navigate to the location of the Data Files.
- Click Support_PPT_5_Red_Car to select the .png file (Figure 5–123).

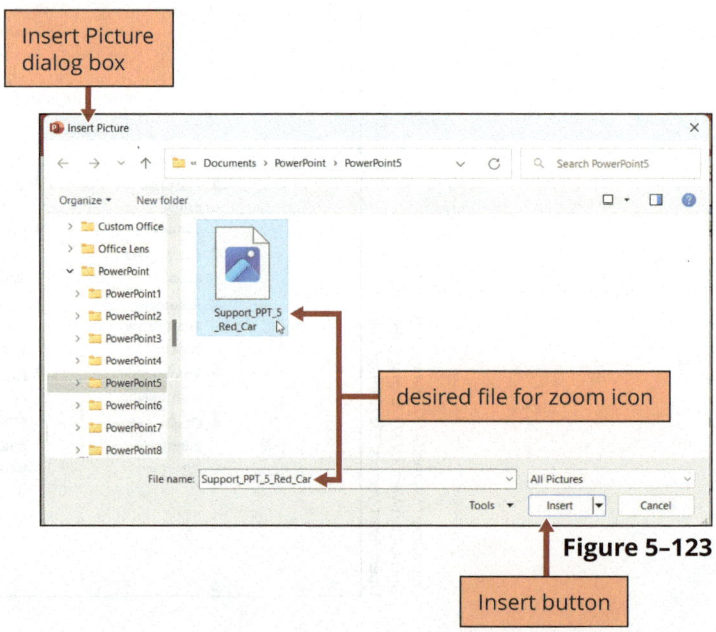

Figure 5–123

3

- Click the Insert button (Insert Picture dialog box) to insert the red car picture as the zoom icon.
- Display Slide 1 and then repeat Steps 1 and 2 above to change the section zoom icon to the red car picture (Figure 5-124).

Figure 5-124

To Run a Presentation with Section Zoom Links and Slide Zoom Links

All changes are complete. You now can view the presentation with animations and zoom links. The following steps run the slide show.

1. Display Slide 1 and then run the presentation.
2. Click the red car icon on Slide 1 to zoom to the 'Intersection Right-of-Way' Slide 4 and then click the red car to trigger the animation.
3. Click to display Slide 5 and then click to display Slides 1, 2, and 3.
4. When Slide 3 is displayed, click the red car zoom icon to zoom to the 'Emergency Supplies' slide.
5. Click twice to end the presentation.

BTW
Printing Document Properties
PowerPoint does not allow you to print document properties. This feature, however, is available in Microsoft 365 Word.

To Save and Print the Presentation

With the presentation completed, you should save the file and print handouts for your audience. The following steps save the file and then print a presentation handout.

1. Save the presentation again in the same storage location with the same file name.
2. Open Backstage view, click the Print tab, click 'Full Page Slides' in the Settings area, click '6 Slides Horizontal' in the Handouts area to display a preview of the handout, and then click Print in the Print gallery to print the presentation.
3. sam Because the project now is complete, you can exit PowerPoint.

BTW
Distributing a Document
Instead of printing and distributing a hard copy of PowerPoint slides, you can distribute the slides electronically. Options include sending the slides via email; posting it on cloud storage (such as OneDrive) and sharing the link with others; posting it on social media, a blog, or other website; and sharing a link associated with an online location of the slides. You also can create and share a PDF or XPS image of the slides, so that users can view the file in Acrobat Reader or XPS Viewer instead of in PowerPoint.

Summary

In this module, you learned how to merge presentations, evaluate a reviewer's comments, and then review, accept, and reject proposed changes, as well as reply to and insert comments. You managed text in columns and shapes, formatted a picture by adding a border and glow effect, changed bullets to a picture and a symbol, added animation, created and managed sections, and added zoom links.

Consider This: Plan Ahead

What decisions will you need to make when creating your next presentation?

Use these guidelines as you complete the assignments in this module and create your own slide show decks outside of this class.

1. Develop a collaboration plan for group members to follow.
    a) Set an overall group goal.
    b) Set long-term and short-term goals.
    c) Identify subtasks that must be completed.
    d) Set a schedule.
2. Accept both positive and negative feedback.
    a) Realize that this criticism helps you to improve yourself and your work.
    b) Oral and written comments from others can help reinforce positive aspects and identify flaws.
    c) Seek comments from a variety of people who genuinely want to help you develop an effective presentation.
3. Give constructive criticism when asked to critique a presentation.
    a) Begin and end with positive comments.
    b) Give specific details about a few areas that can be improved.
    c) Be honest, but be tactful.

Student Assignments

Apply Your Knowledge

Reinforce the skills and apply the concepts you learned in this module.

Inserting and Deleting Comments, Changing Bullets, and Adding Animations

Note: To complete this assignment, you will be required to use the Data Files. Please contact your instructor for information about accessing the Data Files.

Instructions: Start PowerPoint. Open the presentation called SC_PPT_5-1.pptx, which is located in the Data Files.

The slides in the presentation present information about a seminar for first-time home buyers. The document you open is a partially formatted presentation. You are to change the slide size, insert and reply to comments, add animations, change bullets, and change line spacing. Your presentation should look like Figure 5–125.

Perform the following tasks:

1. Change the slide size to Widescreen (16:9).
2. On Slide 1 (Figure 5–125a), insert a comment and then type **How about adding the word, "Free", to the title?** as the text. In the Reply box, type **That's a great idea! I'll change the title text.** as a reply to the comment.
3. Change the title text to **Free seminar for first-time home buyers** and then change the font size to 44 point.
4. On Slide 2 (Figure 5–125b), select the bulleted list, insert a new comment, and then type **Perhaps you can change the bullets to an image that's related to the presentation.** as the text. In the Reply box, type **I agree. I'll insert a picture of a key.** as a reply to the comment.
5. Edit the house picture's Alt Text to use **A picture of a small red and white house, a key, and a key ring** as the new description.
6. On Slide 2, change the bulleted paragraphs' line spacing to 1.5.
7. Change the bullets to the Support_PPT_5_Key.png picture. Increase the size to 125% of text.
8. Animate the bulleted paragraphs using the Fly In entrance effect. Use the After Previous Start option and change the Duration time to 03.00 seconds. Have each paragraph dim after it is displayed to the color red (the seventh color).
9. On Slide 2, add the Lines motion path to the picture of the house. Add a trigger to this picture (On Click of Picture 5).

   If requested by your instructor, add your current or previous pet's name in the Alt Text text box.
10. Save the presentation using the file name, **SC_PPT_5_House**.
11. Submit the presentation in the format specified by your instructor.
12. **Consider This:** In Step 7, you changed the bullets, and in Step 8 you animated the bulleted paragraphs. Did these changes improve the presentation? Why or why not?

Continued on next page

Figure 5–125(a): Slide 1

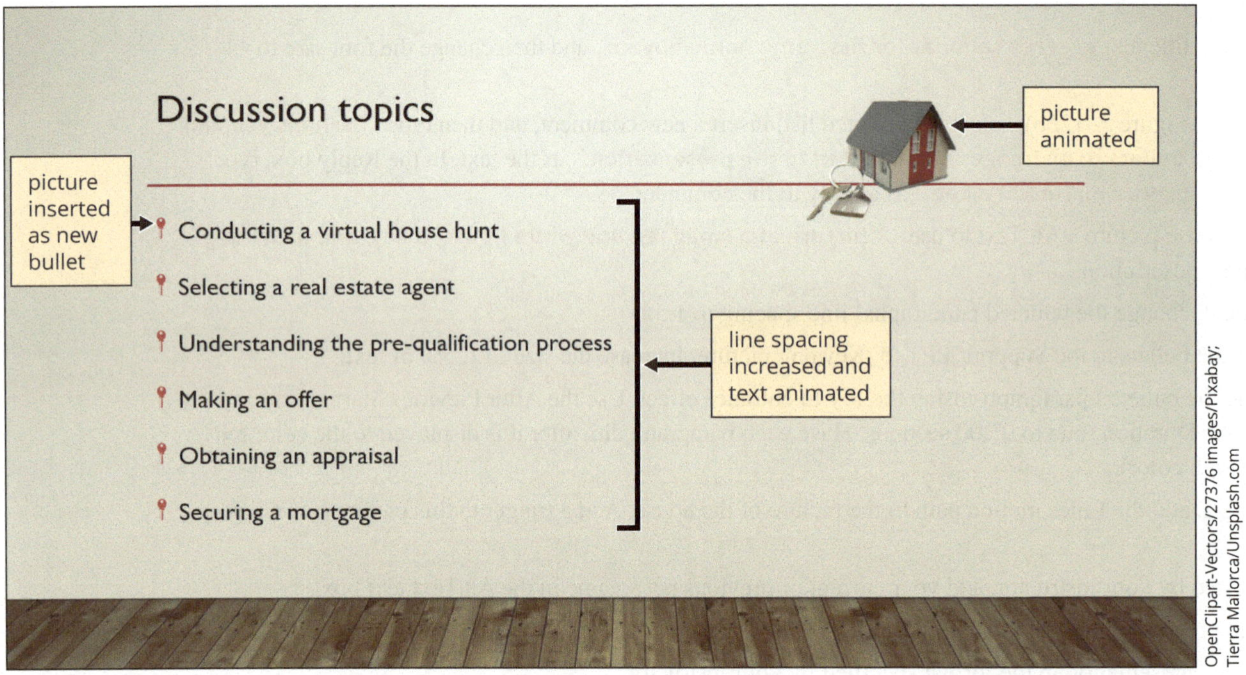

Figure 5–125(b): Slide 2

Extend Your Knowledge

Extend the skills you learned in this module and experiment with new skills. You may need to use Help to complete the assignment.

Creating Credits and Adding a Sound

Note: To complete this assignment, you will be required to use the Data Files. Please contact your instructor for information about accessing the Data Files.

Instructions: Start PowerPoint. Open the presentation called SC_PPT_5-2.pptx, which is located in the Data Files. You will display text as ascending credits on the slide. You then will add a sound to the animation (Figure 5–126).

Perform the following tasks:

1. Click the placeholder with the five paragraphs to select it.
2. Display the Animation gallery and then click 'More Entrance Effects' to display the Change Entrance Effect dialog box.
3. Scroll down to display the Exciting section.
4. Click the Credits entrance animation effect in the Exciting section to see a preview of the animation effect.
5. Click OK ('Change Entrance Effect' dialog box) to apply the effect.
6. Click the Effect Options button (Animations tab | Animation group) and then click By Paragraph to see a preview of the new animation effect.

   If requested by your instructor, replace the word, Naomi, in the footer with your high school mascot's name.
7. Change the Start animation timing option to After Previous and the Duration to 10.00 seconds.
8. To add a sound to the animation, display the Animation Pane and then click the down arrow to the right of the TextBox 3 animation. Click Effect Options in the menu to display the Credits dialog box. In the Enhancements area, click the Sound arrow to display the Sound list and then click Click.
9. Run the presentation and then save it using the file name, **SC_PPT_5_Ads**.
10. Submit the revised document in the format specified by your instructor.
11. **Consider This:** In this assignment, you added credits and a sound. Did these changes enhance the slide? Why or why not? Which sound other than Click could be used?

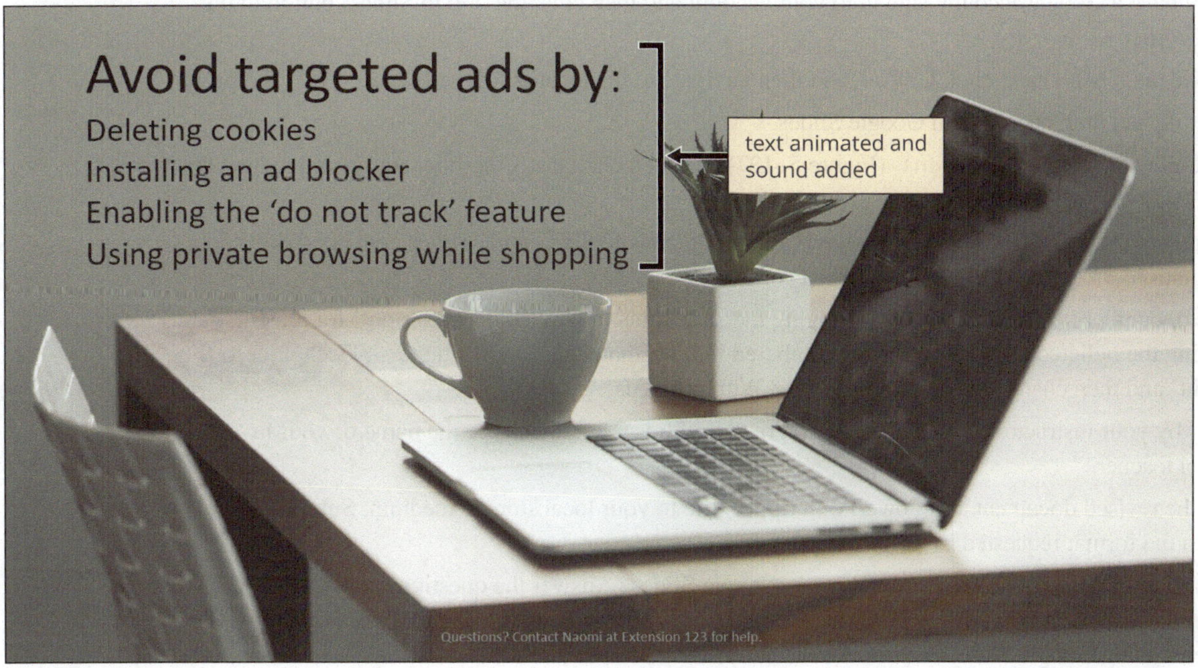

Life Of Pix/Pexels

Figure 5–126

Expand Your World

Create a solution that uses cloud or web technologies by learning and investigating on your own from general guidance.

Using Google Slides to Upload and Edit a File

Instructions: The project manager of the insurance company where you work has asked you to create a presentation to inform your clients about methods of driving in difficult conditions, including rain and snow. You began working on the slides at the office but did not have time to finish the slides there and need to complete the slide deck at home. Although you do not have PowerPoint on your home computer, you have an Internet connection and a Google account. You uploaded your PowerPoint presentation to Google Drive so you can view and edit it later from home.

Note: You will use a Google account, which you can create at no cost, to complete this assignment. If you do not have a Google account and do not want to create one, read this assignment without performing the instructions.

To complete this assignment, you will be required to use the Data Files. Please contact your instructor for information about accessing the Data Files.

Perform the following tasks:

1. Start PowerPoint. Open the presentation called SC_PPT_5-3.pptx, which is located in the Data Files. Review the slides so that you are familiar with their contents and formats. If desired, print the slides so that you easily can compare them to the Google Slides converted file. Close the presentation.
2. Run a browser. Search for the text, Google Slides, using a search engine. Visit several websites to learn about Google Slides and Google Drive. Navigate to the Google Slides website. If you do not have a Google account and you want to create one, click the 'Sign up for free' link and follow the instructions. If you do not have a Google account and do not want to create one, read the remaining instructions without performing them. If you have a Google account, sign in to your account and then click the 'Go to Slides' button in the upper-right corner.
3. Click the File tab, click Open, click Upload, and then navigate to the location of the file, SC_PPT_5-3.pptx.
4. Upload the file and then open it with Google Slides.
5. Rename the file **SC_PPT_5_Conditions** (Figure 5–127) and then click the Slideshow button and review the slides.
6. What differences do you see between the PowerPoint document and the Google Slides converted document? Which animations are shown? How do you add a comment?
7. Modify the document in Google Slides by changing the slide transition to 'Slide from right' for all slides and then changing the bulleted list on Slide 3 to a numbered list. Animate the Slide 1 title text placeholder to 'Fly in from right' and then change the Start condition to With previous.

   If requested by your instructor, add a bulleted paragraph on Slide 2 and then type the name of your favorite grade school teacher.
8. Download the revised document as a PowerPoint (.pptx) file to your local storage medium. Submit the document in the format requested by your instructor.
9. **Consider This:** What is Google Drive? What is Google Slides? Answer the questions posed in Step 6. If you have an Android smartphone, download the Google Slides app and edit the SC_PPT_5_Conditions file. Do you prefer using Google Slides or PowerPoint? Why?

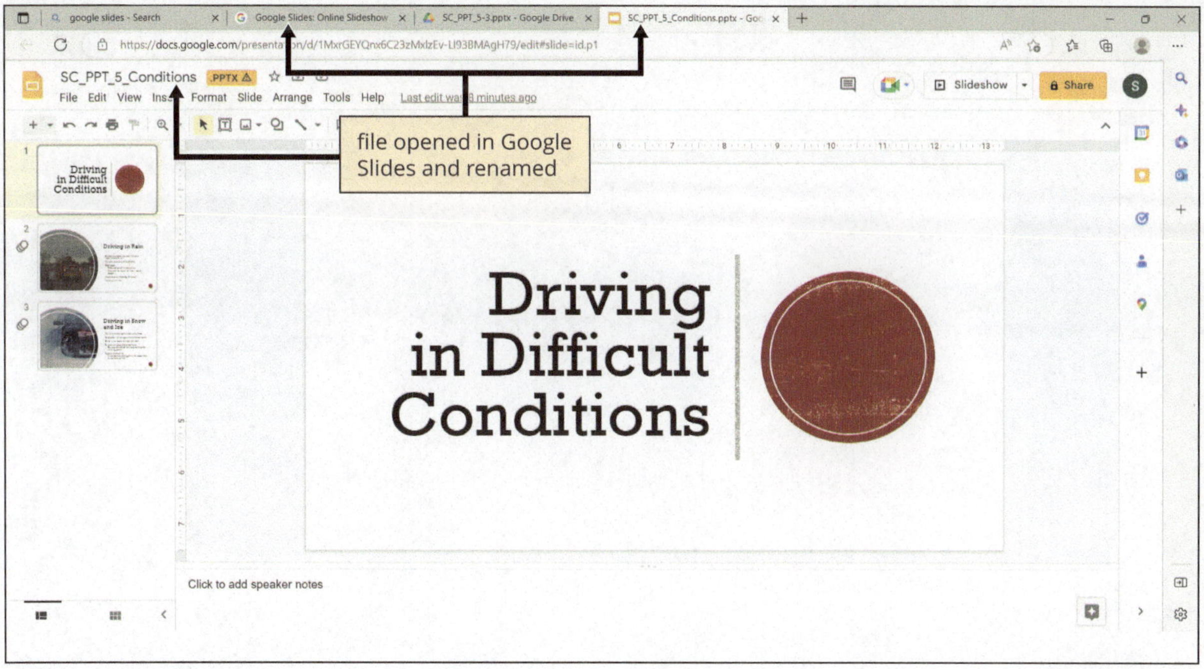

Valeria Miller/Pexels; Geni Hoka/Pexels

Figure 5–127

In the Lab

Apply your creative thinking and problem-solving skills to design and implement a solution.

Design and Create a Presentation about Getting a Car Loan

Part 1: The credit union near your school is planning a seminar for recent college graduates on the topic of car loans. The branch managers have begun developing content for PowerPoint slides and have located some pictures they would like to use in the presentation. They want to provide information about how graduates should prepare to obtain a loan and some of the terms they will encounter during the application process. Part of the loan process involves preparation, including budgeting, checking their credit report, securing required documents, and determining the best interest rates. Applicants will encounter many financial terms in the loan agreement, such as the annual percentage rate, the required down payment, and how much they will pay over the course of the loan. You agree to help them complete the project by developing slides. Perform some research about the process of obtaining a car loan and then create slides with animation. At least two of the slides should have bulleted lists with customized bullets and animation. Create the animation for one slide and then use the Animation Painter to copy these effects to another slide. Provide alt text when necessary. Change the line spacing for the bulleted lists. The Data Files folder contains pictures you could use. Add a comment asking for the branch managers' approval of your work. Review and revise your presentation as needed and then save the file using the file name, **SC_PPT_5_Loan**. Submit your assignment in the format specified by your instructor.

Part 2: **Consider This:** You made several decisions while creating the presentation in this assignment: what content to include, how to format the bulleted list, what text or pictures to animate, and which styles and effects to apply. What was the rationale behind each of these decisions? Where would you recommend showing this slide show? When you reviewed the document, what changes did you make?

Formatting Tables and Charts

Objectives

After completing this module, you will be able to:

- Insert slides from an outline
- Edit an embedded file
- Insert an object from a file
- Draw a table
- Format a table
- Resize, split, and distribute table columns and rows
- Insert and edit a linked Excel worksheet
- Switch chart rows and columns
- Change a chart type and layout
- Apply effects to chart elements
- Edit chart data
- Update linked objects
- Add a link to a file
- Navigate between slides in Reading and Outline views

Introduction

Adding visuals to a presentation can help audience members remember the important facts you want to share. Researchers have found that adding graphics such as tables, charts, graphs, and maps increases retention by more than 50 percent. Audiences also believe that speakers who include visuals in their presentations are more qualified and believable than speakers who do not have accompanying visuals. In addition, studies have shown that meeting times are reduced and decisions are reached more quickly when group members have seen visuals that help them reach a consensus.

PowerPoint has many features that allow you to insert visuals and then modify them directly on the slide. For example, you can embed a Word document and then edit its text or replace its graphics. You can link an Excel worksheet with a PowerPoint slide so that when numbers are modified in the slide, the corresponding numbers on the worksheet also are updated. These tools help you work productively and generate slides with graphics that help your audience comprehend and remember your message.

BTW
Using Tables and Charts
Charts and tables help audiences understand abstract concepts and the relationships between sets of data. These tools can give meaning to the figures and facts you want to emphasize in your presentation. Present only one main idea in a chart or table. Overloading your slides with data may confuse your audience and defeat the purpose of these graphical elements.

Project: Presentation with Embedded and Linked Files and Formatted Table and Chart

Fun runs are popular in many communities because they are enjoyable, stress-free events that bring families, friends, and co-workers together. The goal is for participants of all fitness levels to have fun while getting some exercise. The course distance often varies so that beginners easily can cross the finish line while experienced runners can challenge their times and speeds. Prizes can be awarded for first-place finishers, and people share a sense of accomplishment to cross

BTW

Checking for Accessibility Issues

As you develop tables and other slide elements, you may want to check the presentation for content that people with disabilities may be unable to read. To identify possible accessibility problems, display the Info tab in Backstage view and notice if the message, 'Content that people with disabilities are unable to read', is displayed next to the 'Check for Issues' button. If so, click the 'Check for Issues' button and then click Check Accessibility in the menu. The Accessibility Checker pane will display issues you can address.

the finish line and join the festivities awaiting them. Many fun runs are organized by charitable organizations, and the small entry fee and merchandise sales help raise funds for worthy causes.

In this module's project, you will follow proper design guidelines and learn to use PowerPoint to create the slides shown in Figure 6–1a through 6–1h. The objective is to produce a presentation that will be shown at fitness centers and sporting equipment stores in the city and suburbs to promote the Fun Run scheduled for June 21. You begin by importing a Word outline with the slide titles. On Slide 1 (Figure 6–1a), you insert and edit a flyer with graphics and text (Figure 6–1b) created in Word. You decide that the word, Fun, should be changed from multiple font colors to one color, so you edit this word directly on the slide.

The Fun Run promoters have used Excel to record data on the number of t-shirts and sweatshirts people have ordered. Slide 2 (Figure 6–1c) shows this Excel chart (Figure 6–1d), which you copy and then format. You obtain updated sales data, so you update the worksheet data that generated the chart, which, in turn, modifies the chart automatically.

The third slide (Figure 6–1e) includes a table that you draw and enhance using PowerPoint's tools and graphical features. The table shows the five course distances, start times, and prizes for the first-place finishers. If you click the title text when running the presentation, a linked Adobe PDF file displays showing the certificate all participants will receive (Figure 6–1f).

People have been registering for the past five months. The event promoters have tracked each month whether the participants are living in the city or the suburbs in a chart shown on Slide 4 (Figure 6–1g). This chart is inserted from an Excel worksheet (Figure 6–1h). Projected registrations also are included in the spreadsheet, and you will update these figures based on inquiries made via text and social media. The spreadsheet is linked to Slide 4, so once the numbers change in the spreadsheet, the updated numbers change on the slide.

Azmeyart-Design/Pixabay

Figure 6–1(a): Slide 1 (Title Slide)

Azmeyart-Design/Pixabay

Figure 6–1(b): Original Word Document

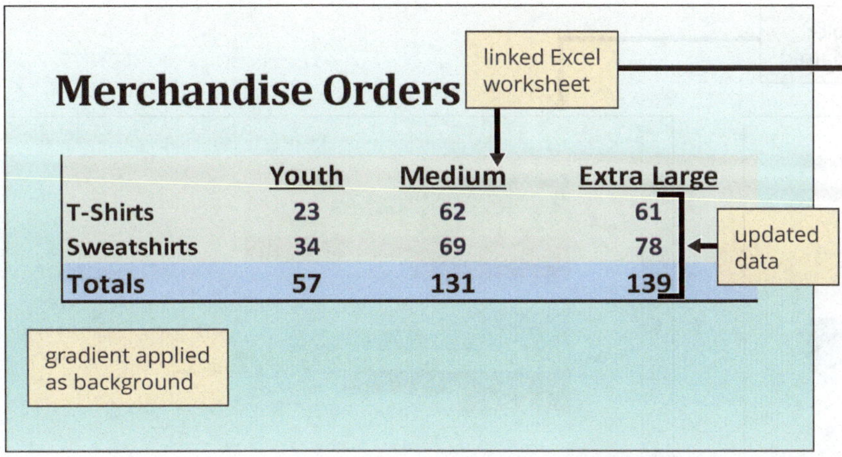

Figure 6–1(c): Slide 2

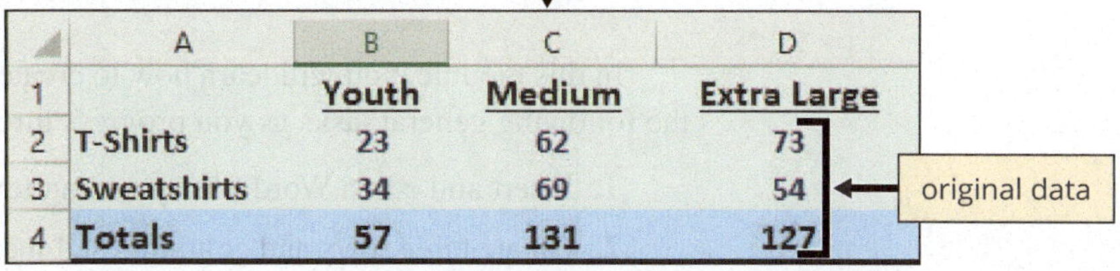

	A	B	C	D
1		Youth	Medium	Extra Large
2	T-Shirts	23	62	73
3	Sweatshirts	34	69	54
4	Totals	57	131	127

Figure 6–1(d): Original Excel Worksheet

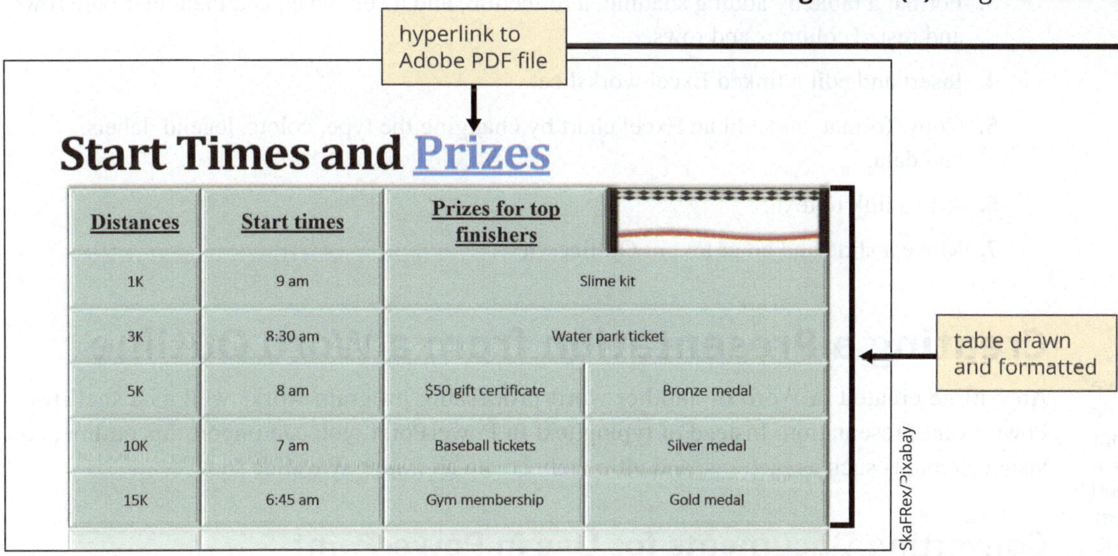

Figure 6–1(e): Slide 3

Figure 6–1(f): Hyperlinked Adobe PDF File

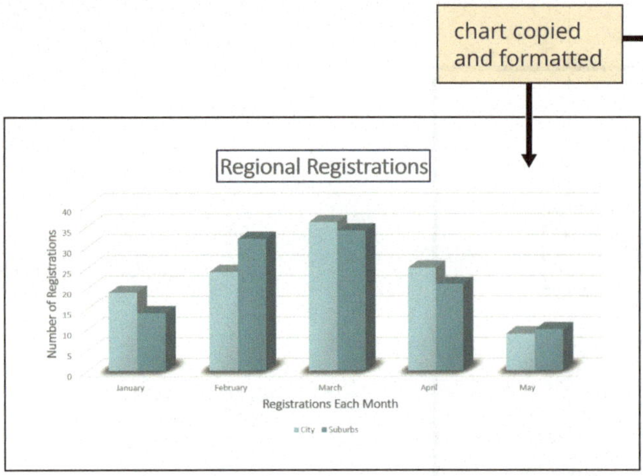

Figure 6–1(g): Slide 4

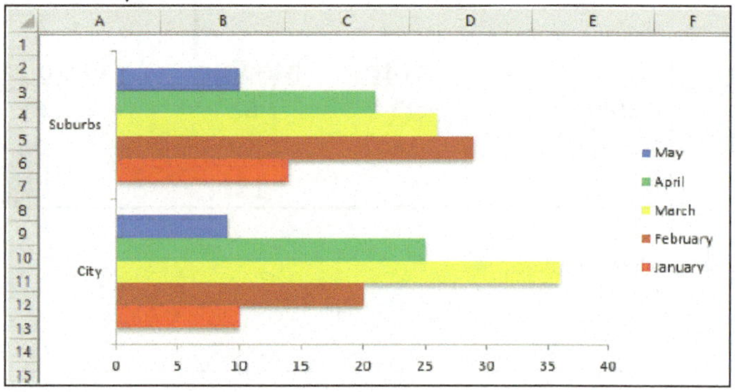

Figure 6–1(h): Original Excel Chart

In this module, you will learn how to create the slides shown in Figure 6–1. You will perform the following general tasks as you progress through this module:

1. Insert and edit a Word file by adding text.
2. Create table rows and columns, and then erase lines and split columns and rows.
3. Format a table by adding shading, a reflection, and a cell bevel, and then distribute rows and resize columns and rows.
4. Insert and edit a linked Excel worksheet.
5. Copy, format, and edit an Excel chart by changing the type, colors, legend, labels, and data.
6. Add a link to text.
7. Move a slide and enter text in Outline view.

Creating a Presentation from a Word Outline

An outline created in Word or another word-processing program works well as a shell for a PowerPoint presentation. Instead of typing text in PowerPoint, you can import this outline, add visual elements such as pictures, and ultimately create an impressive slide show.

BTW
Defining Outline Levels
Imported outlines can have a maximum of nine outline levels, whereas PowerPoint outlines are limited to six levels (one for the title text and five for body paragraph text). When you import an outline, all text in outline levels six through nine is treated as a fifth-level paragraph.

Converting Documents for Use in PowerPoint

PowerPoint can produce slides based on an outline created in Word, another word-processing program, or a webpage if the text was saved in a format that PowerPoint can recognize. Word files use the **.docx** file extension in their file names. Text originating in other word-processing programs for later use with PowerPoint should be saved in Rich Text Format (.rtf) or plain text (.txt). Webpage documents that use an HTML extension (.htm or .html) also can be imported.

PowerPoint automatically opens Microsoft 365 files, and many other types of files, in the PowerPoint format. When you insert a Word document into a presentation, PowerPoint creates an outline structure based on heading styles in the document. A Heading 1 in a source document becomes a slide title in PowerPoint, a Heading 2 becomes the first level of content text on the slide, a Heading 3 becomes the second level of text on the slide, and so on.

If the original document contains no heading styles, PowerPoint creates an outline based on paragraphs. For example, in a .docx or .rtf file, for several lines of text styled as Normal and broken into paragraphs, PowerPoint turns each paragraph into a slide title.

BTW
Ribbon and Screen Resolution
PowerPoint may change how the groups and buttons within the groups appear on the ribbon, depending on the screen resolution of your computer. Thus, your ribbon may look different from the ones in this book if you are using a screen resolution other than 1920 × 1080.

To Insert Slides from an Outline

The title text for the Run presentation is contained in a Word file. The following steps open this Word outline located in the Data Files as a presentation in PowerPoint. **Why?** Instead of typing text for each of the four PowerPoint slides, you can open a Word outline and have PowerPoint create the slides automatically.

1

- sam Run PowerPoint, create a blank presentation, and then apply the Metropolitan theme. If necessary, maximize the PowerPoint window. If the Design Ideas pane opens, close it.
- Save the presentation using the file name, **SC_PPT_6_Run**.

2

- Display the Home tab and then click the New Slide arrow (Home tab | Slides group) to display the New Slide gallery (Figure 6–2).

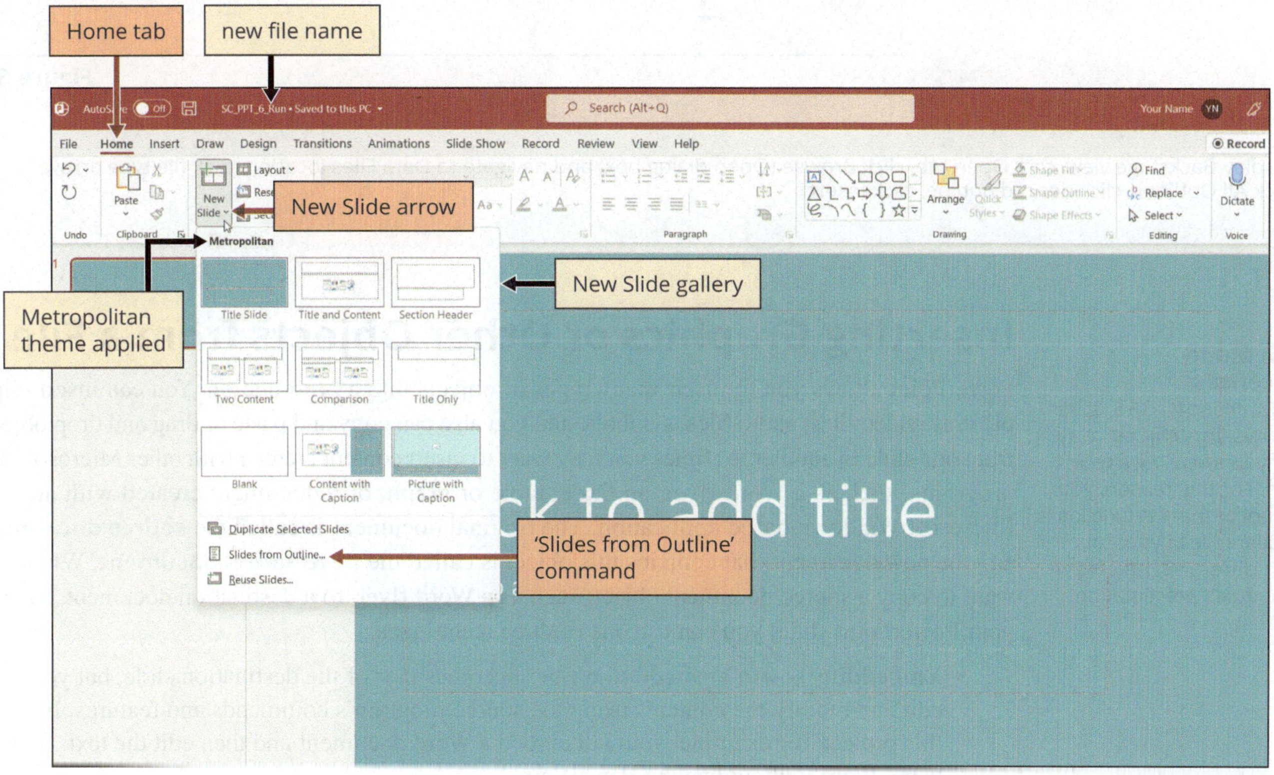

Figure 6–2

3

- Click 'Slides from Outline' to display the Insert Outline dialog box.
- Navigate to the location of the Data Files and then click Support_PPT_6_Run_Outline.docx to select the file (Figure 6–3).

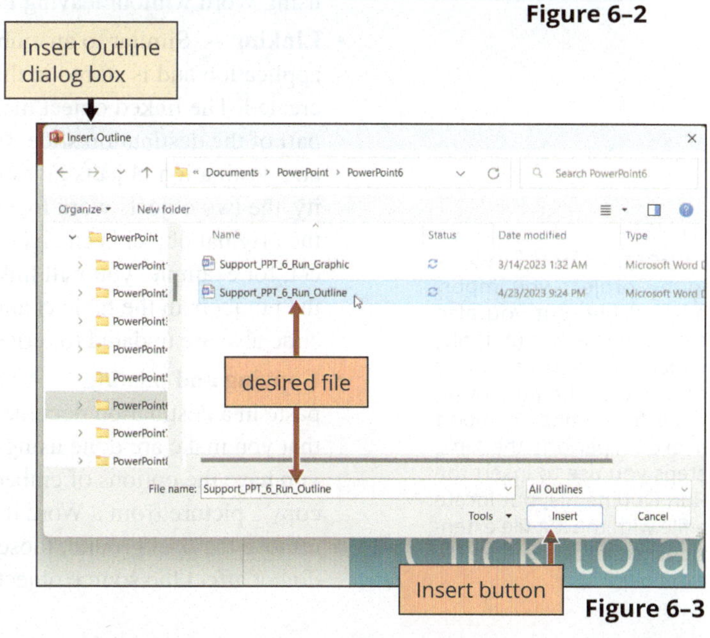

Figure 6–3

4

- Click the Insert button (Insert Outline dialog box) to add three slides based on your outline to your presentation (Figure 6–4).

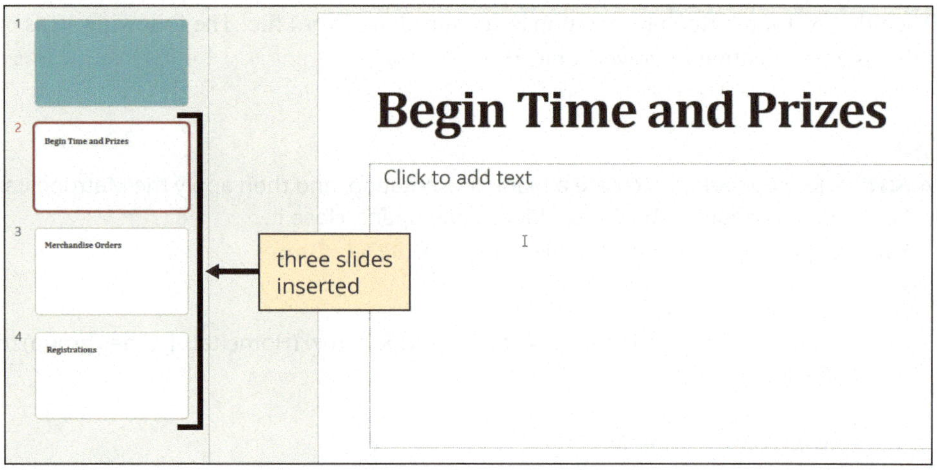

Figure 6–4

Other Ways

1. Display Backstage view, click Open tab, click Browse (Open dialog box) and navigate to Data Files location, click file type arrow, click All Outlines, click desired outline, click Insert

BTW
Touch Mode Differences
The Microsoft 365 and Windows interfaces may vary if you are using a touch screen. For this reason, you might notice that the function or appearance of your touch screen differs slightly from this module's presentation.

Inserting Graphics or Other Objects from a File

PowerPoint allows you to insert many types of objects into a presentation. You can insert clips, pictures, video files, audio files, symbols, and you also can copy and paste or drag and drop objects from one slide to another. At times you may want to insert content created with other Microsoft 365 programs, such as a Word flyer, an Excel table or graph, or a document created with another Microsoft Windows-based application. The original document is called the **source document**, and the new document that contains this object is called the **destination document**. When you want to copy a source document object, such as a Word flyer, to a destination document, such as your PowerPoint slide, you can use one of three techniques.

- **Embedding** — An **embedded object** becomes part of the destination slide, but you edit and modify the contents using the source program's commands and features. In this project, for example, you will embed a Word document and then edit the text using Word without leaving PowerPoint.
- **Linking** — Similar to an embedded object, a **linked object** also is created in another application and is stored in the **source file**, the original file in which the object was created. The linked object maintains a connection to its source and does not become part of the destination slide. Instead, a connection, or link, made between the source and destination objects gives the appearance that the objects are independent. In reality, the two objects work together so that when one is edited, the other is updated. If the original object is changed, the linked object on the slide also changes. In this project, for example, you will link an Excel table and then edit the data using Excel. As the numbers in the table change, the numbers in the linked table on the PowerPoint slide also are updated to reflect those changes.
- **Copying and pasting** — An object that you copy from a source document and then paste in a destination document becomes part of the destination program. Any edits that you make are done using the destination software. When you paste the object, you have the options of embedding or linking the document. For example, if you copy a picture from a Word document, embed it into your slide, and then recolor or remove the background, those changes are made using PowerPoint's commands and do not affect the source object.

BTW
Importing Text Files
In this project, you import a Word file, but you also can import a text (.txt) file, which has alphanumeric characters with little or no visual formatting. To import a text file, perform the same steps you use to insert the Run Outline file, but locate a file with the .txt file extension instead of the .docx file extension.

The first two techniques described above are termed **object linking and embedding** (**OLE**, pronounced o-lay). This means of sharing material developed in various sources and then updating the files within a destination program is useful when you deliver presentations frequently that display current data that changes constantly. For example, your PowerPoint presentation may contain a chart reflecting current registration statistics, or you may include a table with merchandise ordered totals for the event.

The first object you will add to your presentation is a graphical flyer created in Word. This flyer contains artwork and text developed as part of a promotion for the Fun Run. You desire to use this document in your slide show because the image and text fit the topic of your presentation.

To Delete a Placeholder

When you run a slide show, empty placeholders do not display. You may desire to delete unused placeholders from a slide. **Why?** By deleting them, they will not be a distraction when you are designing slide content. The title and subtitle text placeholders on Slide 1 are not required for this presentation, so you can remove them. The following steps remove the Slide 1 title and subtitle text placeholders.

1

- Display Slide 1 and then click a border of the title text placeholder so that it displays as a solid or finely dotted line (Figure 6–5).

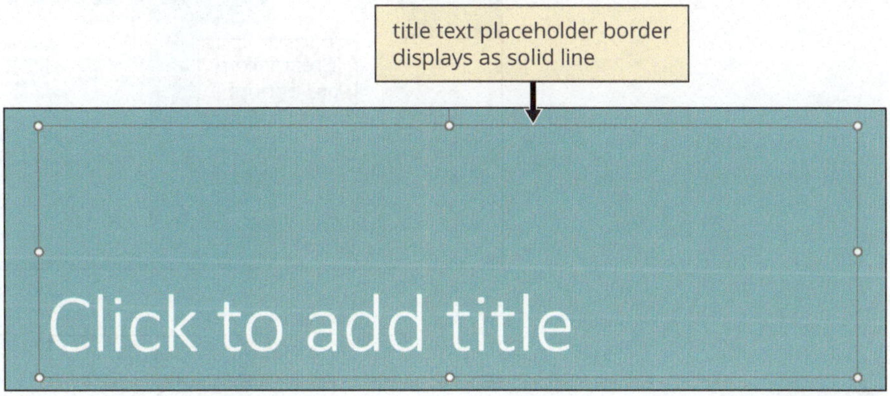

Figure 6–5

2

- Press DELETE to remove the title text placeholder.

Q&A Can I also click the Cut button to delete the placeholder?
Yes. Generally, however, the Cut button is used when you desire to remove a selected slide element, place it on the Clipboard, and then paste it in another area. The DELETE key is used when you do not want to reuse that particular slide element.

3

- Click a border of the subtitle text placeholder to select it (Figure 6–6).

4

- Press DELETE to remove the subtitle placeholder.

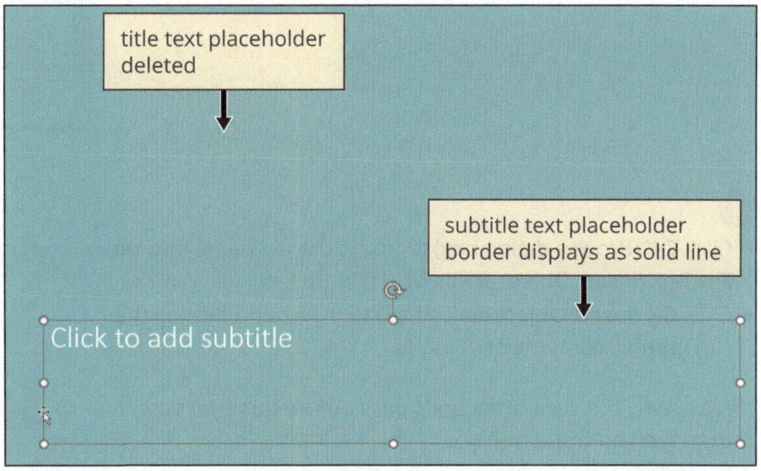

Figure 6–6

Other Ways

1. Select placeholder, press BACKSPACE
2. Right-click placeholder border, click Cut on shortcut menu

To Embed an Object from Another App

The first object you will add to your presentation is the artwork that was created for a graphical flyer being created in Word. This flyer eventually will be completed by promotions committee volunteers, and it contains a colorful graphic and text that should generate interest in the Fun Run. You desire to use this document in your slide show. **Why?** The flyer will be distributed to community members when they arrive at fitness centers and shop at sporting equipment stores. It will contain pertinent information about the Fun Run date, times, distances, and prizes. The following steps insert a Word file with a graphic and text.

1

- Display the Insert tab and then click the Object button (Insert tab | Text group) to display the Insert Object dialog box (Figure 6–7).

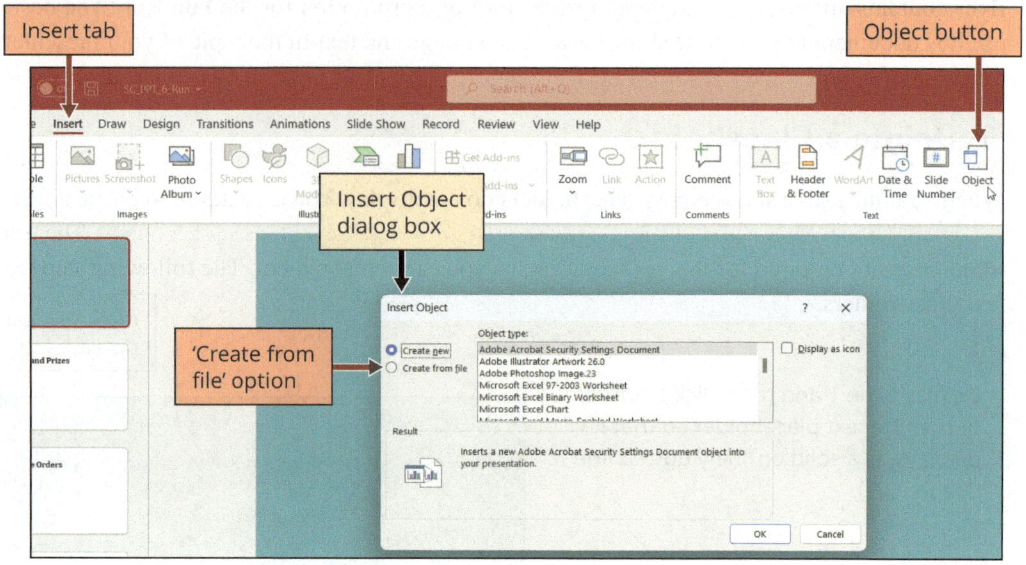

Figure 6–7

2

- Click 'Create from file' (Insert Object dialog box) to display the File box.
- Click the Browse button and then navigate to the location of the Data Files.
- Click Support_PPT_6_Run_Graphic.docx to select the Word file (Figure 6–8).

Q&A What is the difference between the 'Create new' and the 'Create from file' options?

The 'Create new' option opens an application and allows you to develop an original object. In contrast, the 'Create from file' option prompts you to locate a file that already is created and saved so you can modify the object using the program that was used to create it.

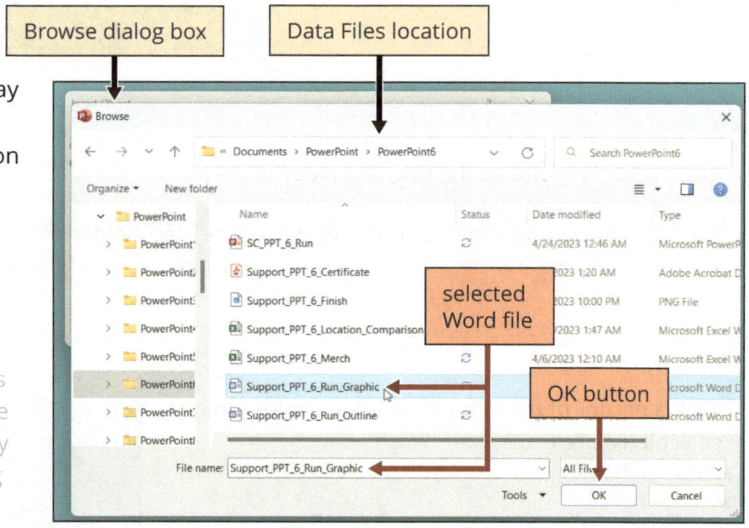

Figure 6–8

3

- Click OK (Browse dialog box) to insert the file name into the File box (Insert Object dialog box) (Figure 6–9).
- Click OK (Insert Object dialog box) to insert and display the run graphic contents on Slide 1.

Q&A Why did several seconds pass before this flyer was displayed on the slide?

PowerPoint takes more time to insert embedded and linked inserted objects than it takes to perform an ordinary cut-and-paste or copy-and-paste action. You must be patient while PowerPoint is inserting the object.

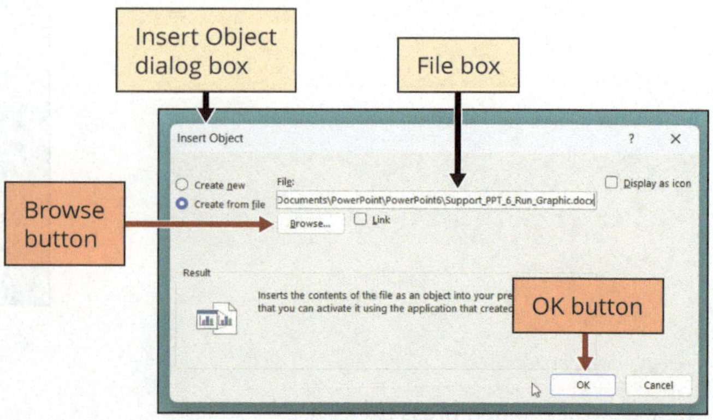

Figure 6–9

4

- Display the Shape Format tab and then click the Height up arrow to increase the height of the run graphic to 6".
- Click the Align button (Shape Format tab | Arrange group) to display the Align menu (Figure 6–10).

5

- Click Align Center to position the run graphic in the center of the slide.
- Click the Align button again and then click Align Middle to position the run graphic in the middle of the slide.

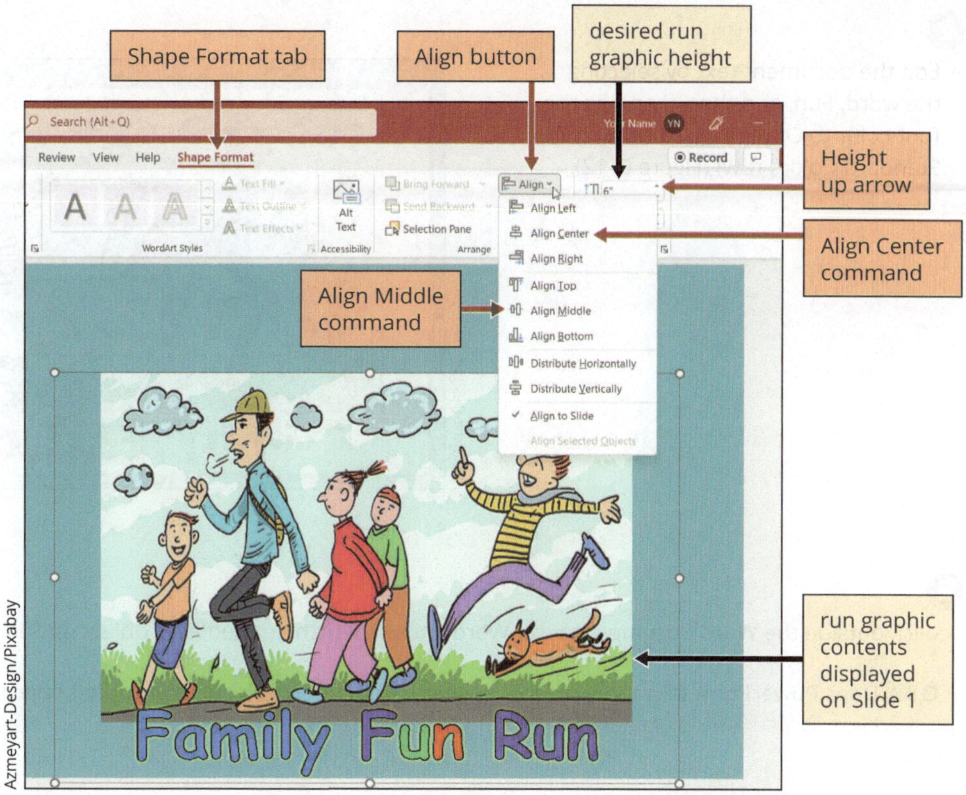

Figure 6–10

To Edit an Embedded File

The run graphic provides an excellent image and text to use on Slide 1, but you want to edit the text by changing the multiple colors in the word, Fun, to one color, orange. Why? You want to call attention to the fun aspect of the event, and the orange color is bright and vibrant. PowerPoint allows you to edit an embedded file easily by opening the source program, which in this case is Word. The following steps edit the Word text.

1

- Double-click the embedded run graphic to run Word and open the document on Slide 1 (Figure 6–11).

Figure 6–11

2

- Edit the document text by selecting the word, Fun, and then changing the font color to Orange (third color in the Standard Colors row) (Figure 6–12).

Figure 6–12

3

- Click outside the Word document to exit Word and display the edited flyer object on Slide 1.

Q&A Does PowerPoint take more time to position embedded objects than copied objects?
Yes, you must be patient while PowerPoint responds to your touch, mouse, or arrow key movements.

Other Ways

1. Right-click Word object, click Document Object on shortcut menu, click Edit

Drawing and Formatting a Table

Tables are useful graphical elements to present data organized in descriptive rows and columns. Each cell created from the intersection of a row and column has a unique location name and contains numeric or textual data that you can edit.

In the following steps, you will perform these tasks on Slide 2:

1. Draw a table.
2. Draw table rows and columns.
3. Erase a table border and enter text in a table.
4. Split a table cell.
5. Add bevel and shadow effects.
6. Distribute table rows.
7. Align data in cells.
8. Center the table and format table data.

Consider This

Develop tables that are clear and meaningful.

Use a table to present complex material, but be certain the information makes useful comparisons. Tables generally are used to show relationships between sets of data. For example, they may show prices for grades of gasoline in three states, the number of in-state and out-of-state students who have applied for admission to various college programs, or the rushing and passing records among quarterbacks in a particular league. The units of measurement, such as dollars, specific majors, or yards, should be expressed clearly on the slides. The data in the rows and columns should be aligned uniformly. Also, the table labels should be meaningful and easily read.

To Draw a Table

PowerPoint allows you to insert a table in several ways. You can click the Table button on the Insert tab (Tables group) and click the Insert Table command. You also can click the Insert Table button in a content placeholder. Another method that allows flexibility is to draw the entire table. However, you must use a mouse or other pointing device to use the Draw Table command. The following steps draw a table on Slide 2. **Why?** This method allows flexibility to draw the outer edges and then add the columns and rows.

1

- Display Slide 2, click a border of the content placeholder, and then press DELETE to remove this placeholder.

2

- Display the View tab and then, if necessary, select the Ruler check box (View tab | Show group) to display the horizontal and vertical rulers (Figure 6–13).

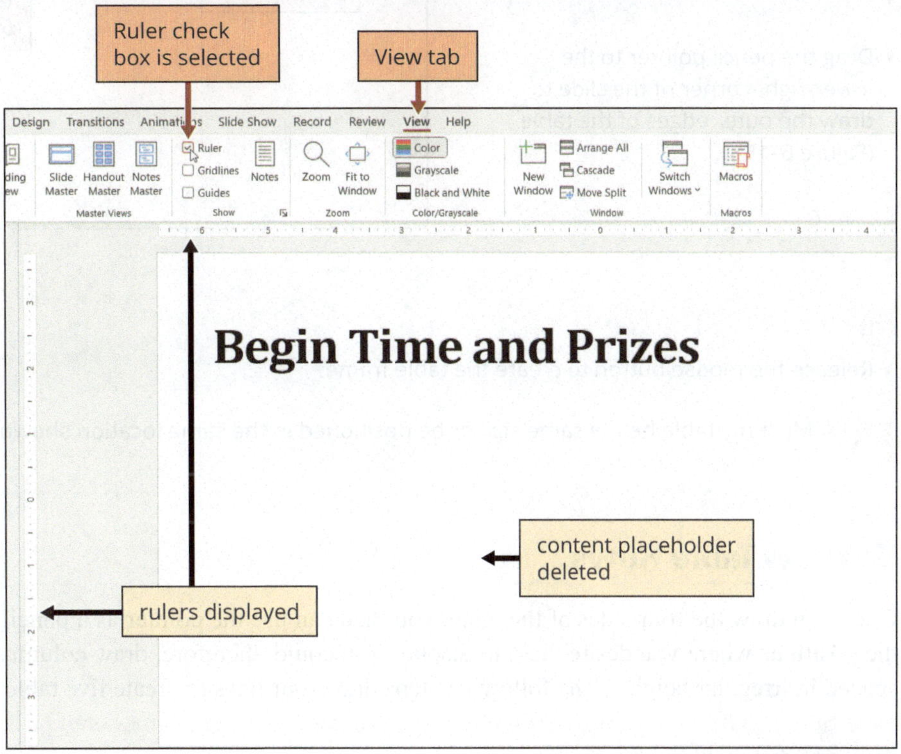

Figure 6–13

3

- Display the Insert tab and then click the Table button (Insert tab | Tables group) to display the Insert Table gallery (Figure 6–14).

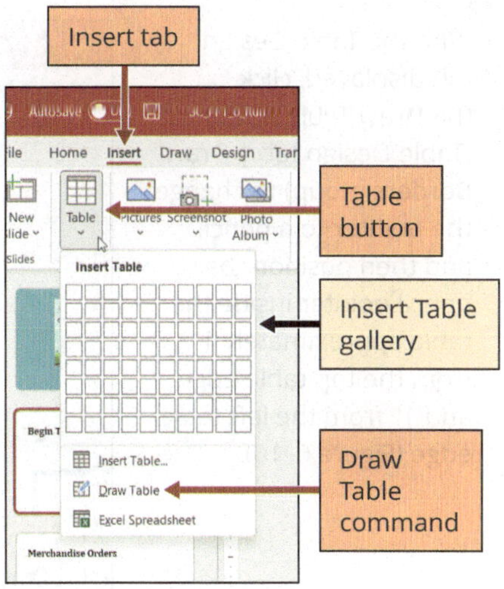

Figure 6–14

4

- Click Draw Table and then position the pointer, which has the shape of a pencil, under the word, Begin, in the upper-left area of the slide.

Q&A If I decide I do not want to draw a table, how can I change the pointer to the block arrow?
Press ESC.

- Drag the pencil pointer to the lower-right corner of the slide to draw the outer edges of the table (Figure 6–15).

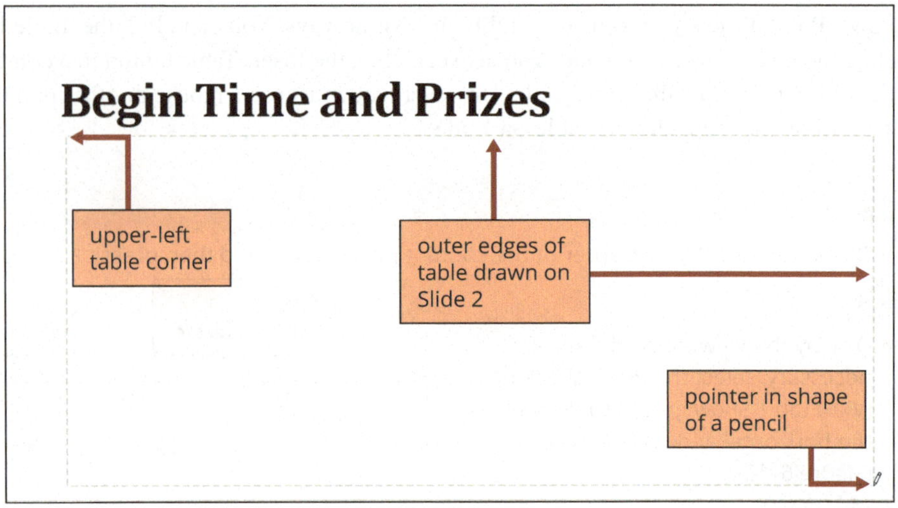

Figure 6–15

5

- Release the mouse button to create the table frame.

Q&A Must my table be the same size or be positioned in the same location shown in the figure?
No. You will resize and reposition the table later in this project.

To Draw Table Rows

Once you draw the four sides of the table, you then can use the pointer as a pencil to draw lines for the columns and rows in the positions where you desire them to display. You could, therefore, draw columns having different widths and rows that are spaced in irregular heights. The following steps draw four lines to create five table rows. **Why?** The first row will contain the table title, and the remaining rows will list specific distances, start times, and prizes. You must use a mouse or other pointing device to draw table rows.

1

- With the Table Design tab displayed, click the Draw Table button (Table Design tab | Draw Borders group) to change the pointer to a pencil and then position the pencil pointer inside the table approximately 1" from the top table edge and 1" from the left table edge (Figure 6–16).

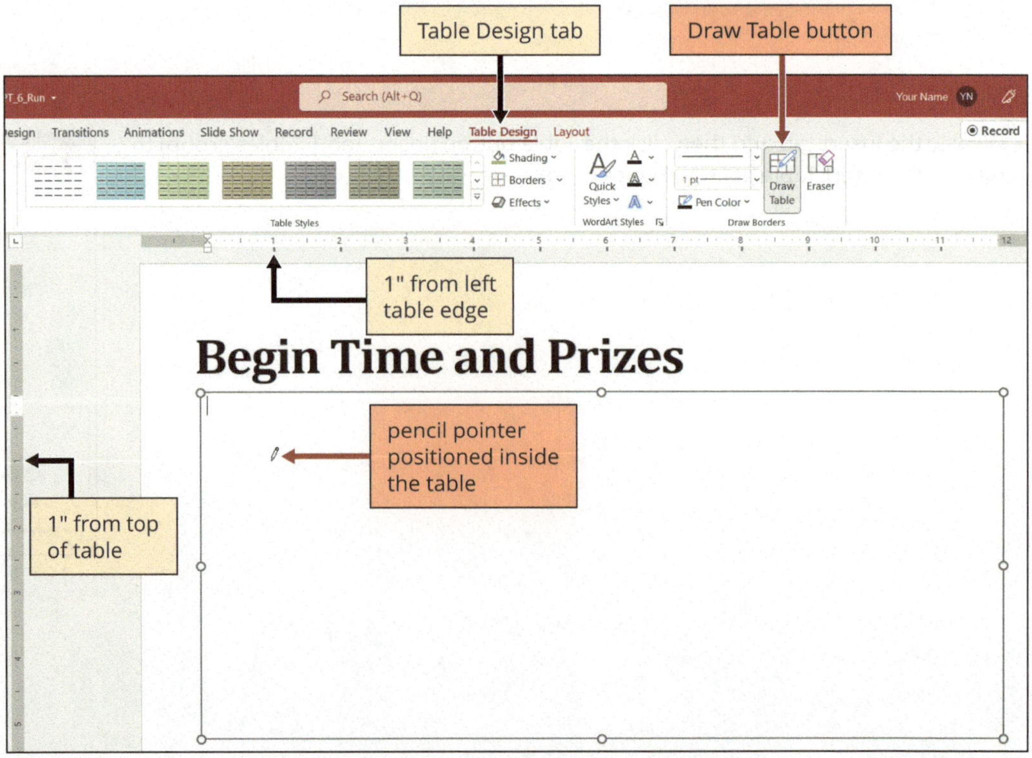

Figure 6–16

2

- Drag the pencil pointer to the right to draw a horizontal line across the entire table and divide it into two cells (Figure 6–17).

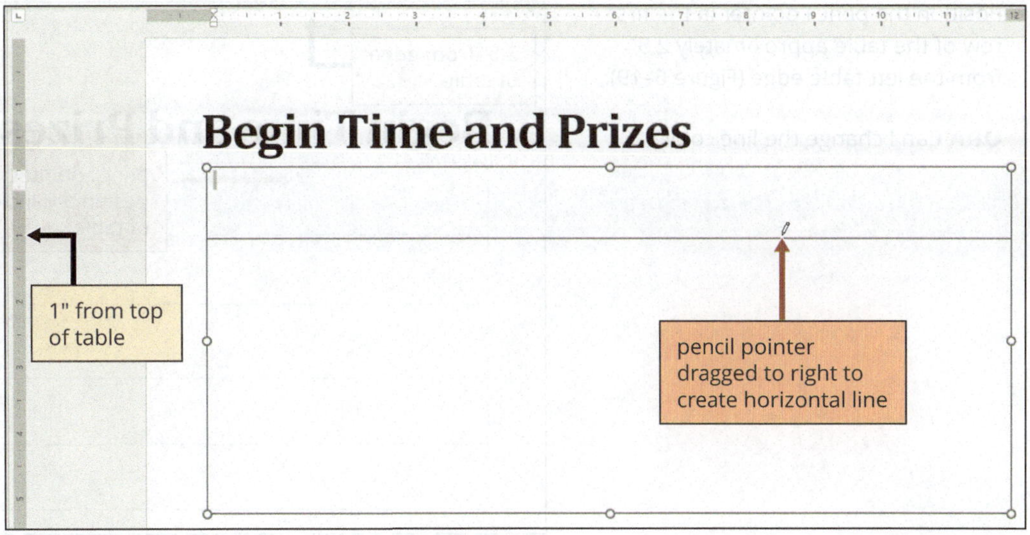

Figure 6–17

Q&A Should I drag the pencil pointer to the right edge of the table?
No. PowerPoint will draw a complete line when you begin to move the pencil pointer in one direction.

If I drew the line in an incorrect location, how can I erase it?
Press CTRL+Z, click the Undo button on the Quick Access Toolbar, or click the Eraser button (Table Design tab | Draw Borders group) and then click the line.

3

- Draw three additional horizontal lines, as shown in Figure 6–18. When you start drawing the lines, place your pencil pointer at a location away from the table border, not at a border, to prevent creating a new table.

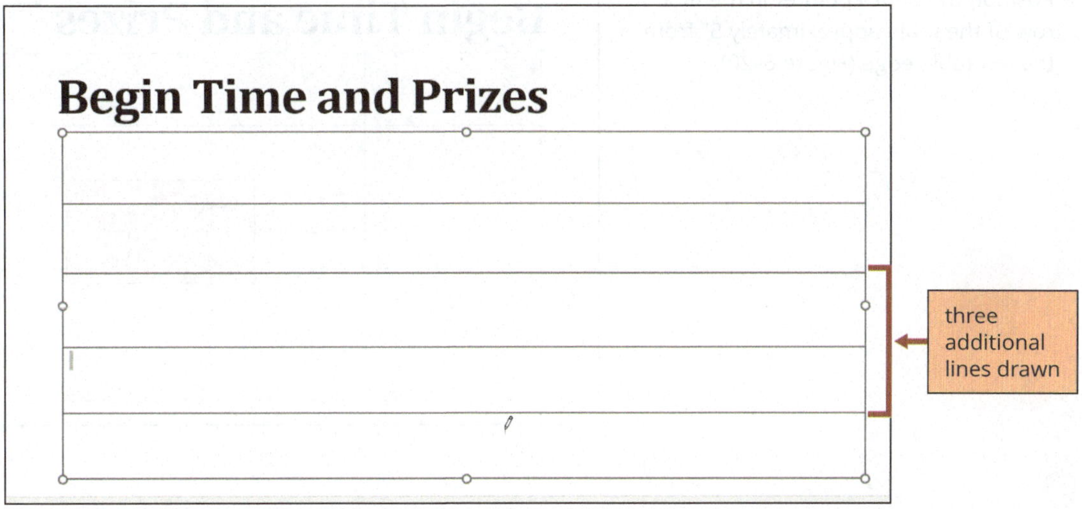

Figure 6–18

Q&A How can I get my pencil pointer to reappear if it no longer is displayed?
Click the Draw Table button again.

Do I need to align the lines in the precise positions shown?
No. You will create evenly spaced rows later in this project.

To Draw Table Columns

The pencil pointer is useful to draw table columns with varying widths. Each distance row has one start time and either one or two prizes. The title row will be subdivided. **Why?** You want to add interest to the slide, so you will insert a picture in the upper-right table cell. The following steps draw three vertical lines to create columns. You must use a mouse or other pointing device to draw table columns.

1

- Position the pencil pointer in the first row of the table approximately 2.5" from the left table edge (Figure 6–19).

Q&A Can I change the line color?
Yes. Click the Pen Color button (Table Design tab | Draw Borders group) and then select a different color.

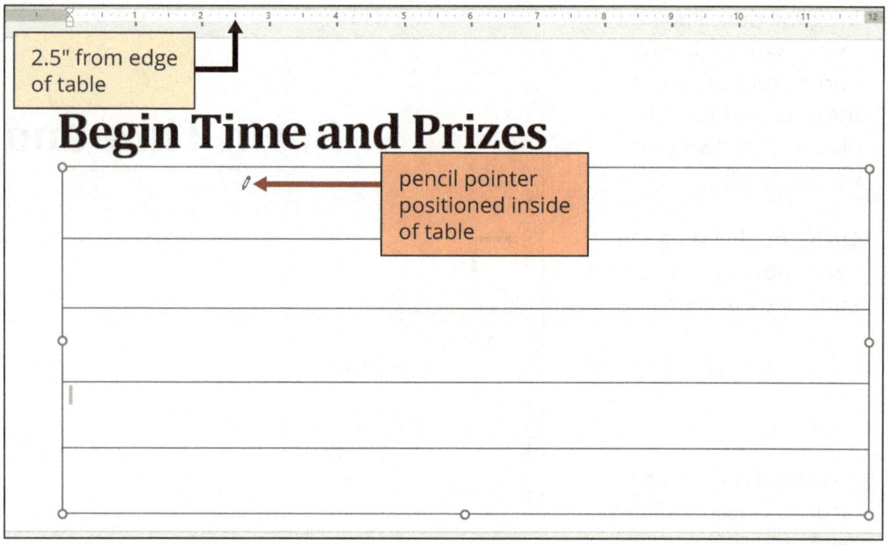

Figure 6–19

2

- Drag the pencil pointer down through all the horizontal lines to draw a vertical line that divides the table into 10 cells.
- Position the pencil pointer in the first row of the table approximately 5" from the left table edge (Figure 6–20).

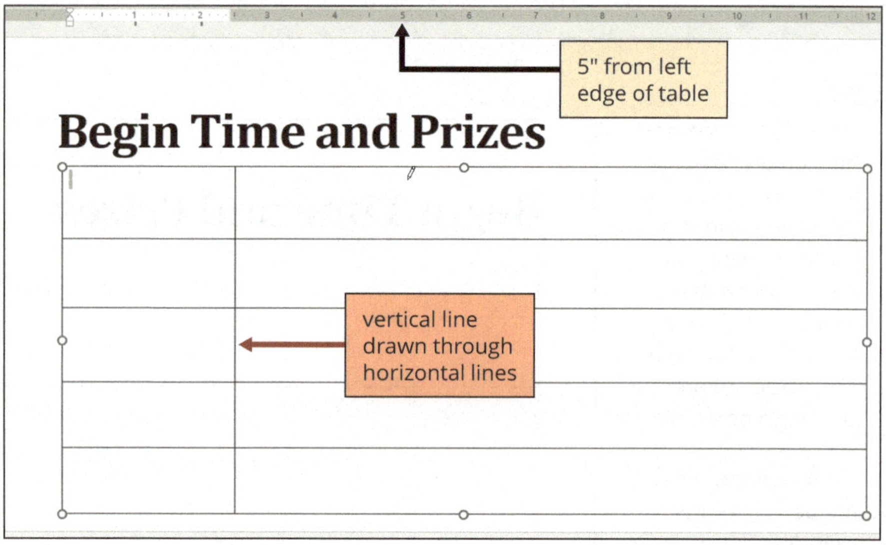

Figure 6–20

3

- Drag the pencil pointer down through all the horizontal lines to draw a vertical line that divides the table now into 15 cells.
- Position the pencil pointer in the middle of the right (last) cell in the second row and then drag down to the bottom edge of the table to draw a vertical line in second, third, fourth, and fifth rows (Figure 6–21).

Q&A Are vertical and horizontal lines the only types of lines I can draw?
No. You also can draw a diagonal line from one corner of a cell to another corner.

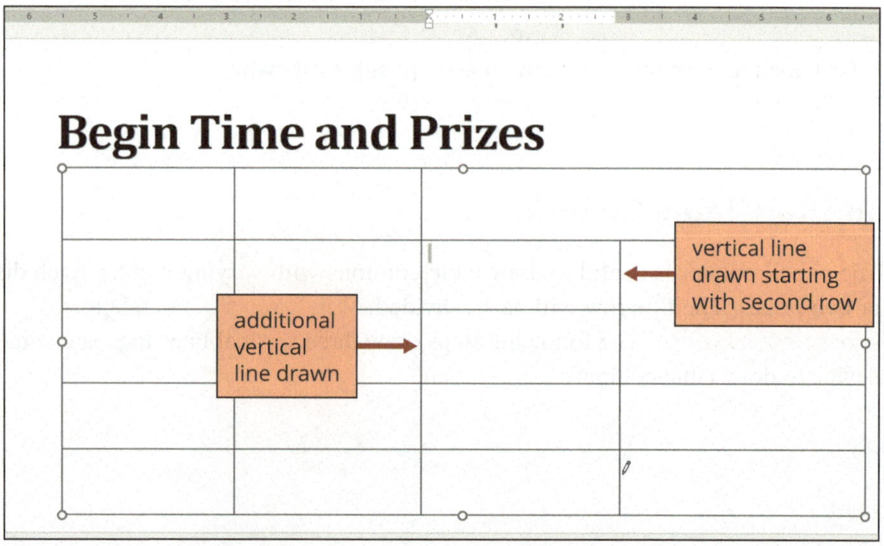

Figure 6–21

To Erase a Table Border

PowerPoint supplies an eraser tool that allows you to delete vertical and horizontal lines in a table. This eraser is useful to delete unnecessary column lines. You must use a mouse or other pointing device to use this tool. The following steps use the eraser to delete one vertical line in the second row. **Why?** You want to erase the vertical line because you need only three columns in this row, not four.

1

- Click the Eraser button (Table Design tab | Draw Borders group).
- Position the pointer, which has the shape of an eraser, over the rightmost vertical line in the second row (Figure 6–22).

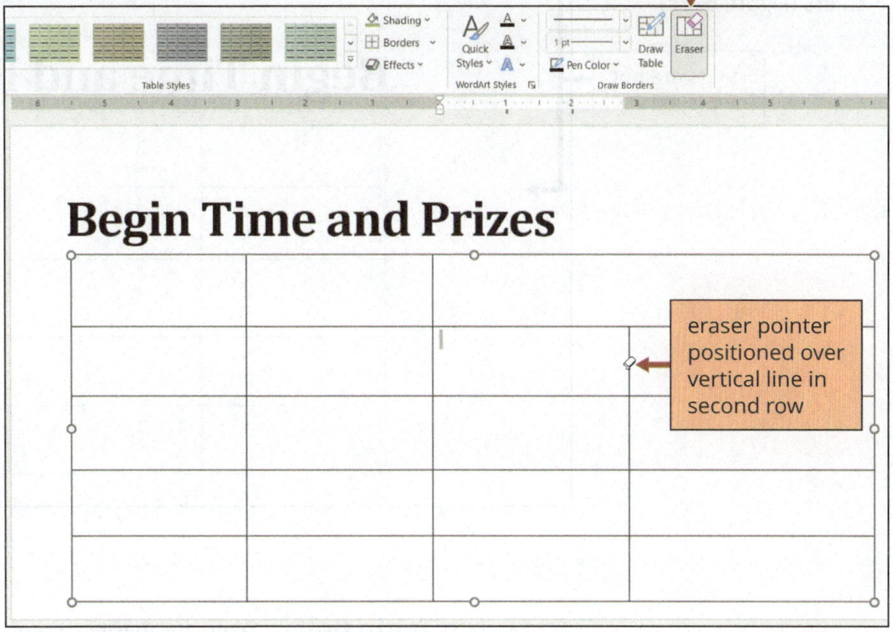

Figure 6–22

2

- Click the vertical line to erase it.
- Press ESC and then click inside the cell to change the pointer to the I-beam and display the insertion point (Figure 6–23).

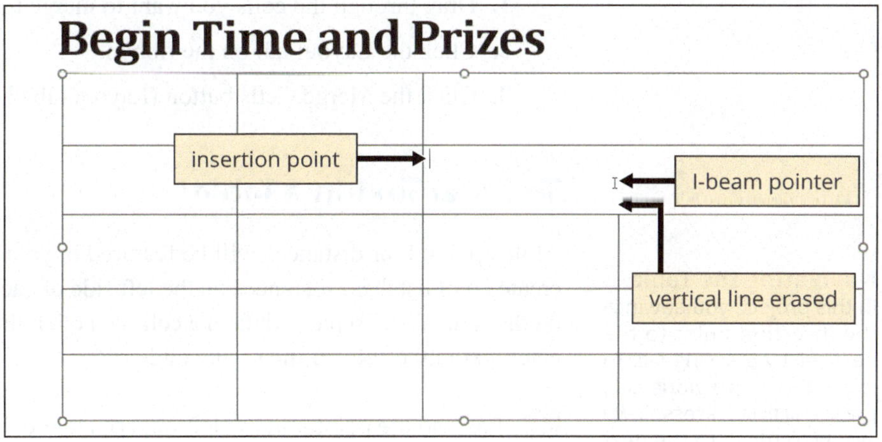

Figure 6–23

3

- Display the View tab and then click the Ruler check box (View tab | Show group) to uncheck the box and hide the horizontal and vertical rulers (Figure 6–24).

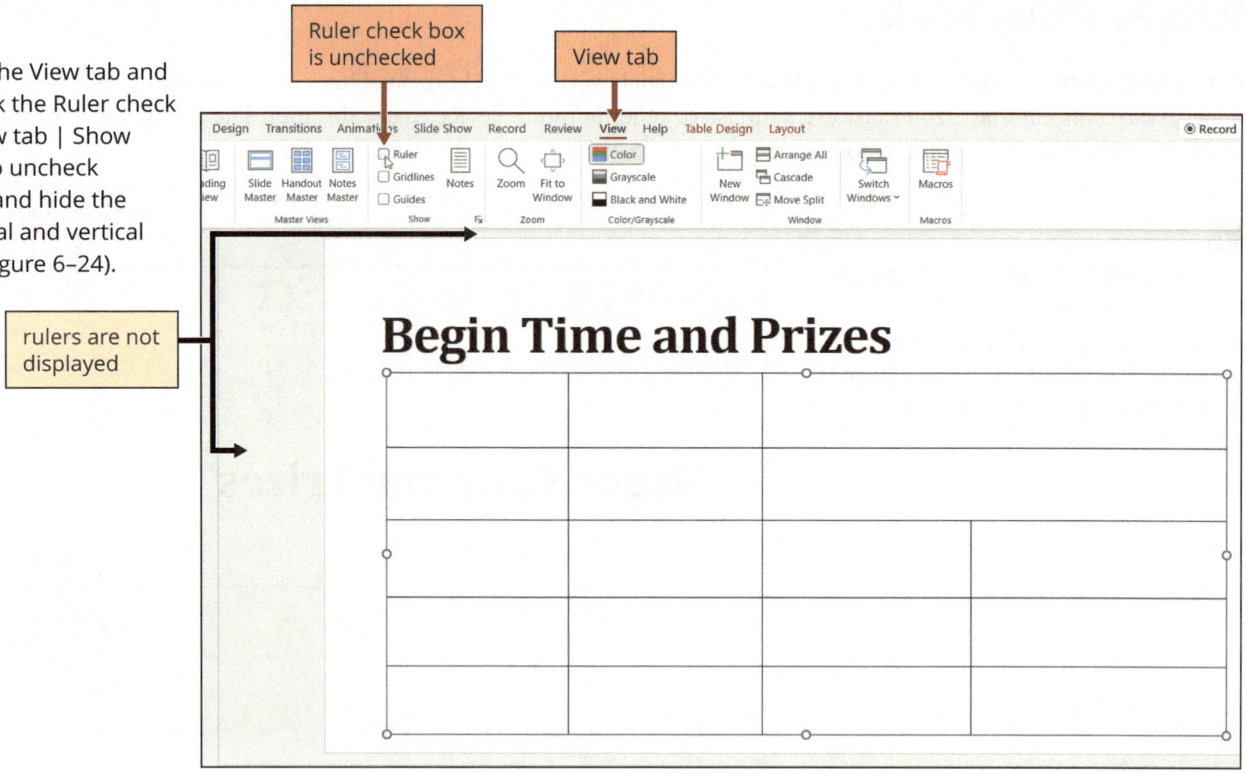

Figure 6–24

To Merge Table Cells You can merge two or more cells to create one large cell, making room for text or graphics. If you wanted to merge two or more cells in a table row or column into a single cell, you would perform the following steps. You may see a warning about an accessibility issue when you merge the table cells.

1. Drag through the cells you want to merge to select them.
2. Click the Layout tab on the ribbon.
3. Click the Merge Cells button (Layout tab | Merge group) to merge the cells into one cell.

To Enter Text in a Table

At this point, four distances will be featured in your table: 1K, 5K, 10K, and 15K. The table you created will list these distances on the left side of each row and give specific start times and prizes on the right side. To place data in a cell, you click the cell and then type text. The following steps enter text in the cells of the empty table.

BTW
Navigating the Table
In this project, you advance the insertion point to the next cell by pressing TAB. To move to the previous cell, press SHIFT+TAB. Press DOWN ARROW to move to the next row and UP ARROW to move up one row.

1 Position the pointer in the leftmost cell in the first row, click, and then type **Distances** in the cell. Press TAB to advance the insertion point to the second cell in the first row, type **Start times**, and then press TAB. Type **Prizes for top finishers** in the rightmost cell and then press TAB to advance the insertion point to the second row.

2 In the second row, type **1K** in the first cell, **9 am** in the second cell, and **Slime kit** in the third cell. Press TAB to advance the insertion point to the first cell in the third row.

3 In the third row, type **5K** in the first cell, **8 am** in the second cell, **$50 gift certificate** in the third cell, and **Bronze medal** in the last cell. Advance the insertion point to the first column of the fourth row.

4 In the fourth row, type **10K** in the first cell, **7 am** in the second cell, **Baseball tickets** in the third cell, and **Silver medal** in the last cell. Advance the insertion point to the first column of the last row.

5 In the last row, type **15K** in the first cell, **6:45 am** in the second cell, **Gym membership** in the third cell, and **Gold medal** in the last cell (Figure 6–25).

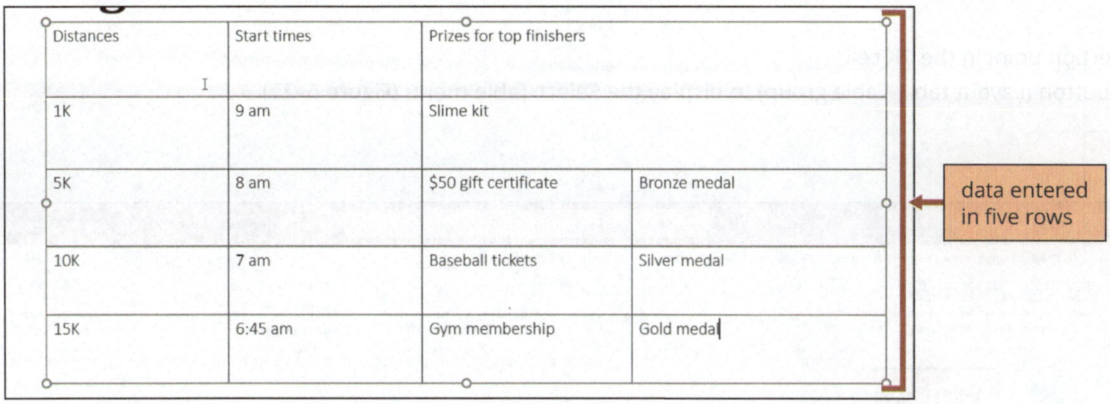

Figure 6–25

To Change the Direction of Text in a Table Cell By default, the text in a cell displays horizontally. You can, however, change the direction to rotate the text 90 degrees or 270 degrees, or you can stack the letters vertically. If you wanted to change the direction, you would perform the following steps.

1. Select the text you want to change and then click the Text Direction button (Layout tab | Alignment group) to display the Text Direction gallery.
2. Click the desired direction ('Rotate all text 90', 'Rotate all text 270', or Stacked) in the Text Direction gallery.

To Split Table Cells

You easily can create additional table columns and rows by dividing current cells and rows. The following steps use the Split Cells feature to divide a cell into two columns and to add a row. **Why?** You want to add a cell for a picture in the first row and add another distance category below the 1K row. You may see a warning about an accessibility issue when you split the table cells.

1

- Position the insertion point in the Prizes for top finishers cell.
- Click Layout on the ribbon to display the Layout tab and then click the Split Cells button (Layout tab | Merge group) to display the Split Cells dialog box (Figure 6–26).

Q&A Are the default numbers in the dialog box always 2 columns and 1 row?

Yes, but you can increase the numbers if you need to divide the cell into more than two halves or need to create two or more rows within one cell.

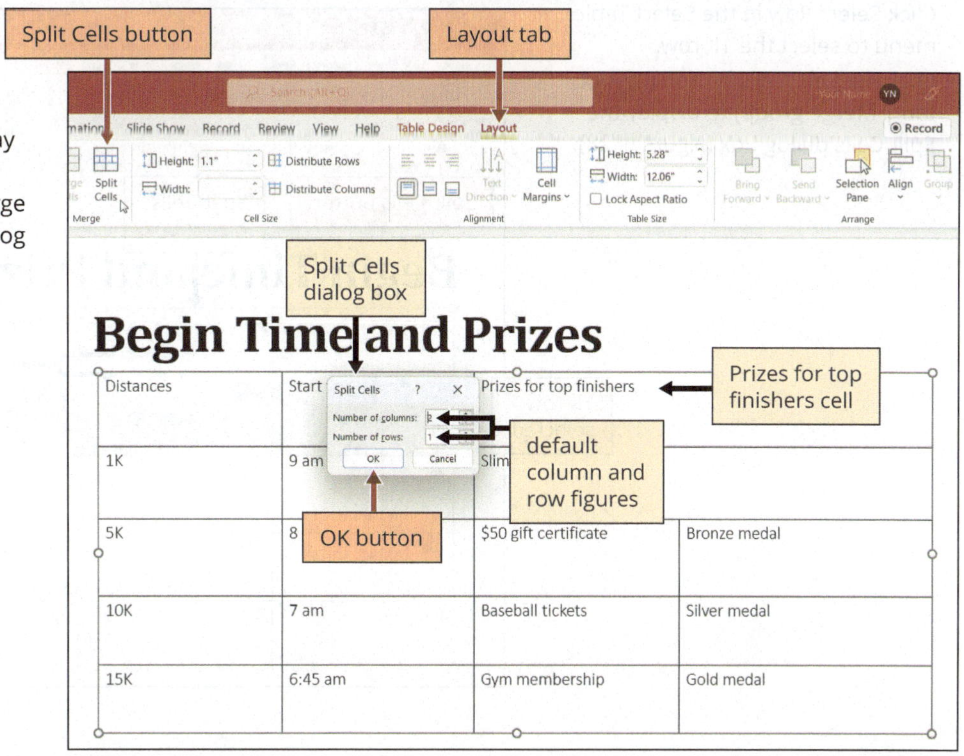

Figure 6–26

2

- Click OK (Split Cells dialog box) to create a fourth cell in the first row.

3

- Position the insertion point in the 1K cell.
- Click the Select button (Layout tab | Table group) to display the Select Table menu (Figure 6–27).

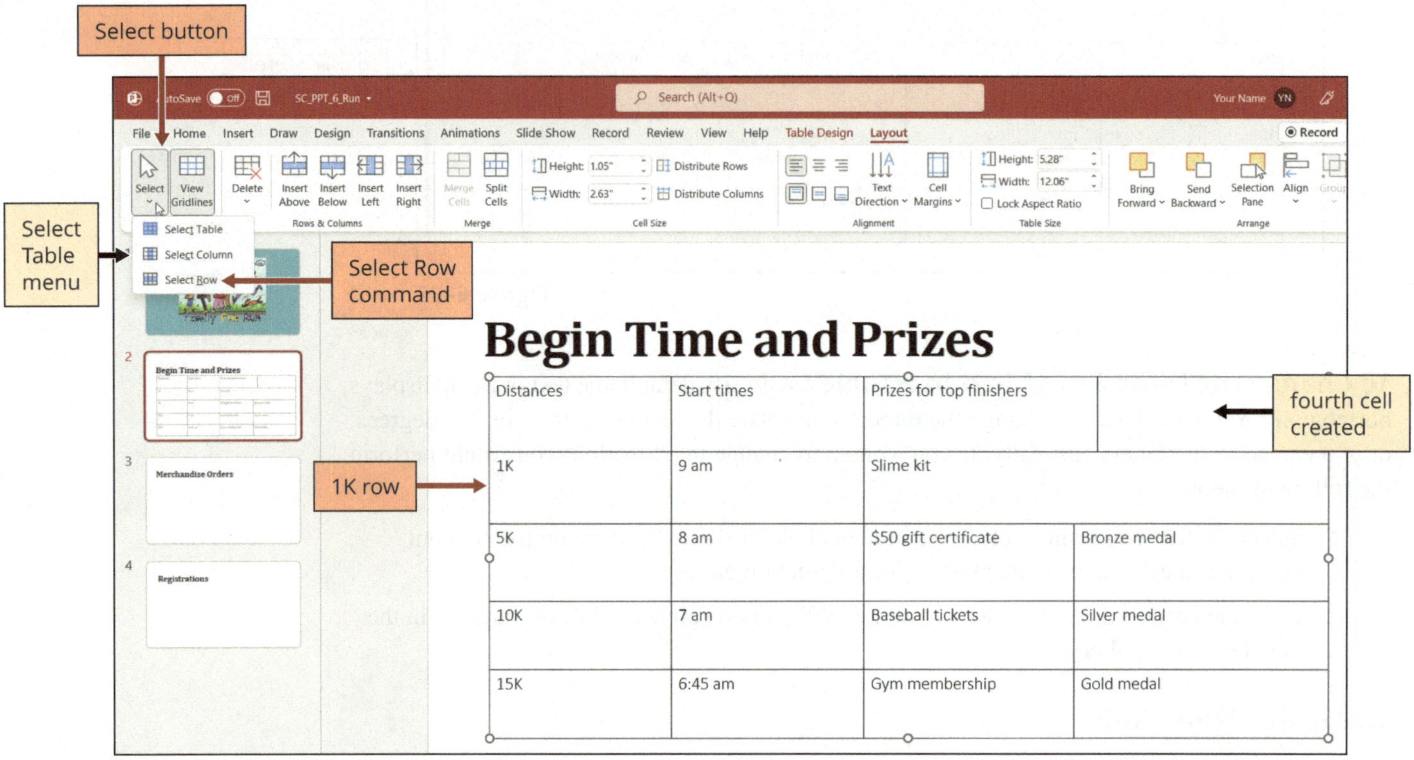

Figure 6–27

4

- Click Select Row in the Select Table menu to select the 1K row.
- Click the Split Cells button (Layout tab | Merge group) to display the Split Cells dialog box (Figure 6–28).

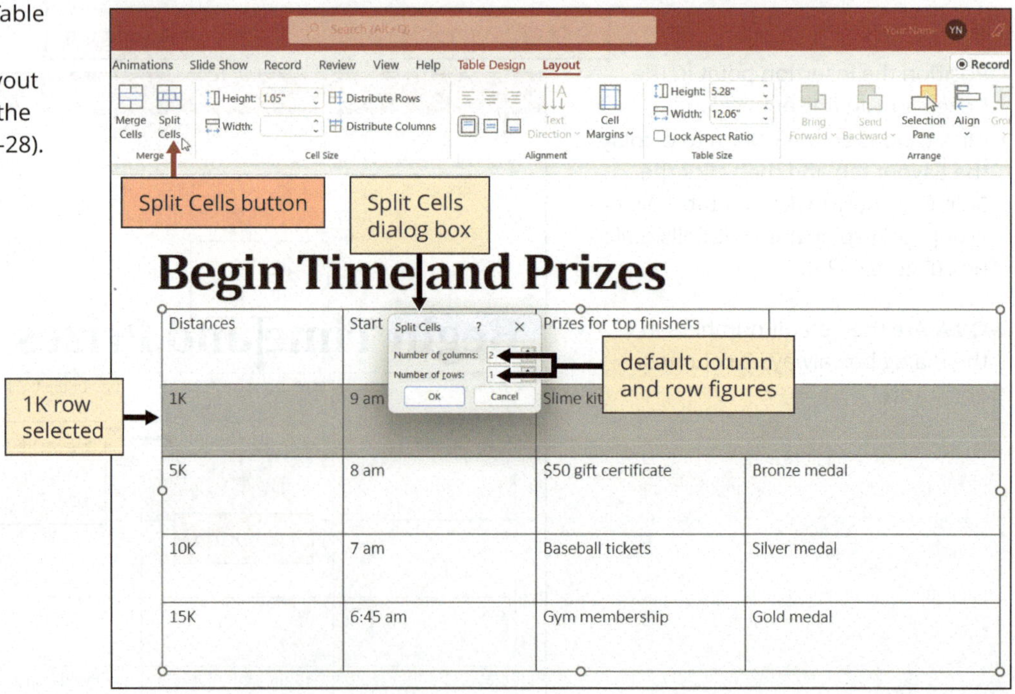

Figure 6–28

5

- Click the 'Number of columns' down arrow once to decrease the number of columns from 2 to 1.
- Click the 'Number of rows' up arrow once to increase the number of rows from 1 to 2 (Figure 6–29).

Q&A How many rows and columns can I create by splitting the cells?
The maximum number varies depending upon the width and height of the selected cell.

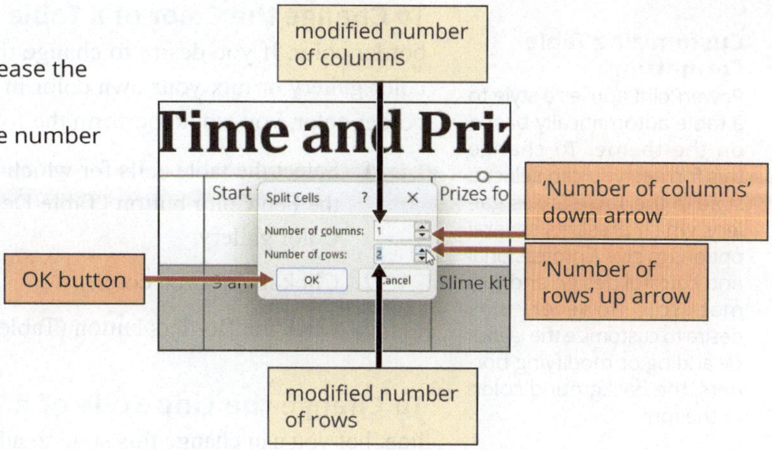

Figure 6–29

6

- Click OK (Split Cells dialog box) to create a row below the 1K row.

Other Ways

1. Right-click table, click Split Cells on shortcut menu, enter number of columns and rows, click OK

To Enter Additional Text in a Table

With the additional row added to the table, you now can add the 3K information in the inserted row. The following steps enter text in the new cells.

1 Position the insertion point in the first cell of the new row and then type **3K** in the cell. Advance the insertion point to the adjacent right column cell and then type **8:30 am** in the second cell and **Water park ticket** in the last cell in this row (Figure 6–30).

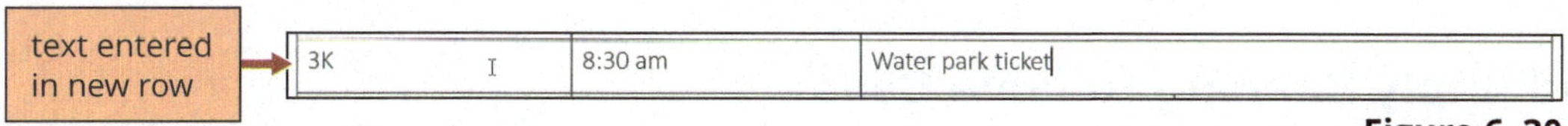

Figure 6–30

Consider This

Use appropriate colors when formatting graphics you want people to remember.
Studies have shown that men and women differ slightly in their recall of graphics formatted with various colors. Men remembered objects colored with shades of violet, dark blue, olive green, and yellow. Women recalled objects they had seen with dark blue, olive green, yellow, and red hues.

To Add a Table Border You can give your table some dimension and add to its visual appeal by adding borders. These lines can be applied around the entire table; between the cells; to the top, bottom, left, or right edges; or a combination of these areas. To add a table border, you would perform the following steps.

1. Select the table cells that you want to have a border and then click the Borders arrow (Table Design tab | Table Styles group) to display the Borders gallery.
2. Click the desired border in the Borders gallery.

BTW
Customizing Table Formatting
PowerPoint applies a style to a table automatically based on the theme. To change this format, you can select a style in the Table Styles gallery, which presents several options to give a professional and colorful design and format. You, however, may desire to customize the layout by adding or modifying borders, the background color, or the font.

To Change the Color of a Table Border The design theme determines the default table border color. If you desire to change this color, you can select a theme or standard color in the color gallery or mix your own color in the Custom tab (Colors dialog box). To change the table border color, you would perform the following steps.

1. Select the table cells for which you want to change the border color and then click the Pen Color button (Table Design tab | Draw Borders group) to display the Pen Color gallery.
2. Click the desired color.
3. Click the Borders button (Table Design tab | Table Styles group).

To Change the Line Style of a Table Border The default border line style is a solid line, but you can change this style to add a custom design element to this element. To change the table border line style, you would perform the following steps.

1. Select the table cells for which you want to change the border line style and then click the Pen Style button (Table Design tab | Draw Borders group) to display the Pen Style gallery.
2. Click the desired line style.
3. Click the Borders button (Table Design tab | Table Styles group).

To Change the Weight of a Table Border You can change the default 1 point border weight to a width ranging from ¼ point to 6 point. To change the table border weight, you would perform the following steps.

1. Select the table cells for which you want to change the weight and then click the Pen Weight arrow (Table Design tab | Draw Borders group) to display the Pen Weight gallery.
2. Click the desired line weight.
3. Click the Borders button (Table Design tab | Table Styles group).

To Select a Table and Apply Shading to Table Cells

You can format the table in several ways, including adding shading to color the background. The following steps add shading to the table. **Why?** Shading makes the table more visually appealing and helps distinguish each cell.

1

- With the Layout tab displayed, click the Select button to display the Select Table menu (Figure 6–31).

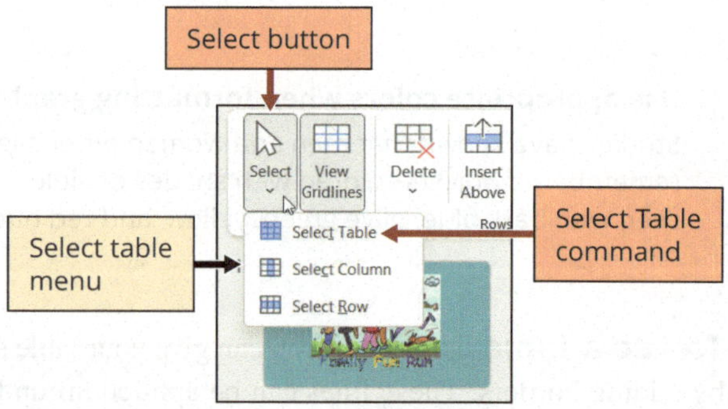

Azmeyart-Design/Pixabay

Figure 6–31

2

- Click Select Table in the Select Table menu to select the entire table.
- Click the Table Design tab and then click the Shading arrow (Table Design tab | Table Styles group) to display the Shading gallery.
- Point to 'Aqua, Accent 1, Lighter 80%' (fifth color in the second Theme Colors row) in the Shading gallery to display a live preview of that color applied to the table in the slide (Figure 6–32).

◦ **Experiment:** Point to various colors in the Shading gallery and watch the background of the table change.

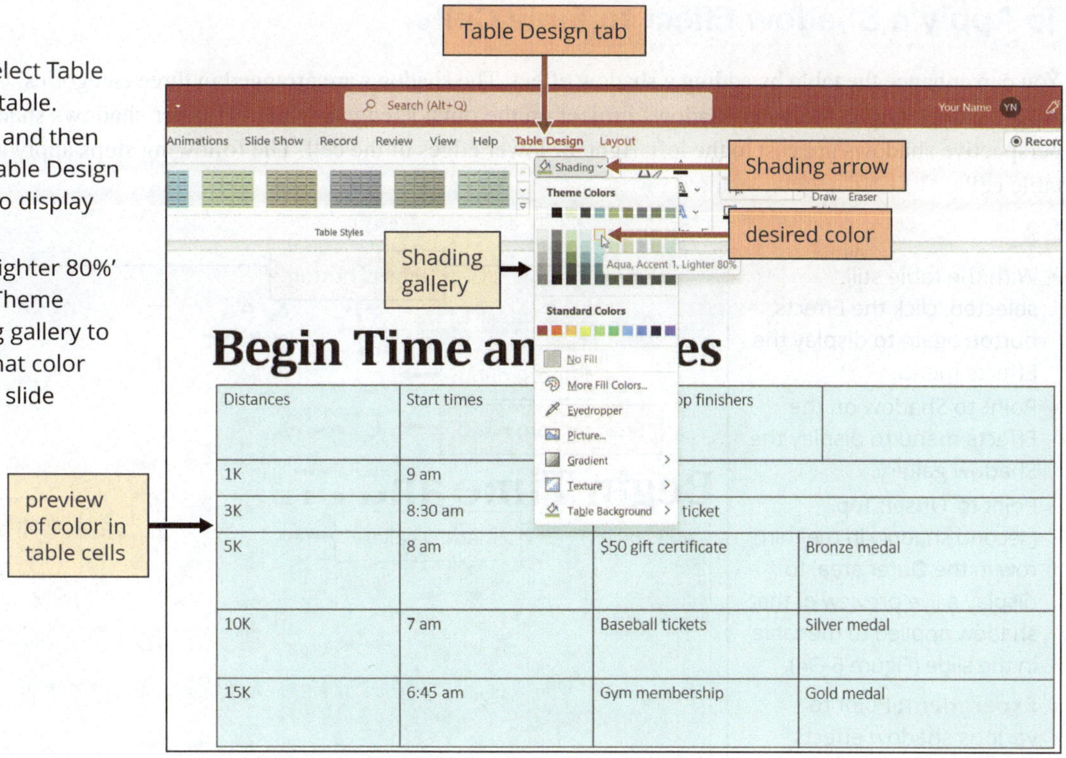

Figure 6–32

3

- Click 'Aqua, Accent 1, Lighter 80%' in the Shading gallery to apply the selected color to the table.

To Apply a Bevel Effect to Table Cells

Bevels modify the cell edges to give a 3-D effect. Some bevels give the appearance that the cell is protruding from the table, while others give the effect that the cell is depressed into the table. The following steps apply a bevel effect to the table cells. **Why?** You desire to make the individual table cells stand out.

1

- With the table still selected, click the Effects button (Table Design tab | Table Styles group) to display the Effects menu.
- Point to Cell Bevel on the Effects menu to display the Cell Bevel gallery.
- Point to Divot (first bevel in the third Bevel row) to display a live preview of that bevel applied to the table in the slide (Figure 6–33).

◦ **Experiment:** Point to various bevel effects in the Bevel gallery and watch the table cells change.

2

- Click Divot in the Bevel gallery to apply the selected bevel effect to the table.

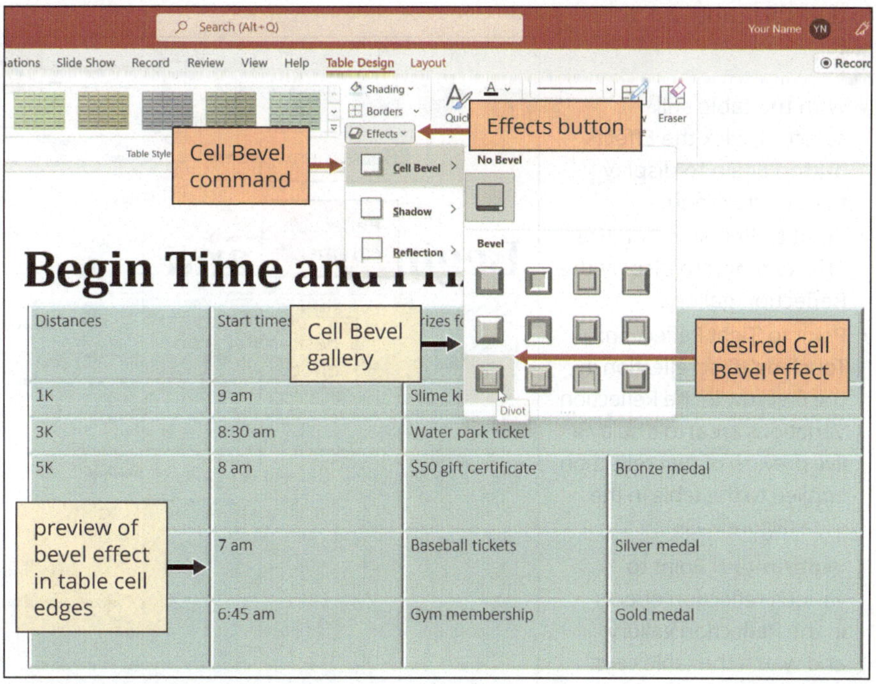

Figure 6–33

To Apply a Shadow Effect to Table Cells

You can enhance the table by adding a shadow effect. The shadows are arranged in three categories: Outer, Inner, and Perspective. As the names imply, the outer shadows project on the outside edges, while the inner shadows shade the inside edges. The five perspective shadows are cast to the left, right, or lower edges of the cell. The following steps apply an outer shadow effect to the table cells. **Why?** The outer shadow gives an effect that a light source is present on the lower edge of the slide.

1

- With the table still selected, click the Effects button again to display the Effects menu.
- Point to Shadow on the Effects menu to display the Shadow gallery.
- Point to 'Offset: Top' (second shadow in the third row in the Outer area) to display a live preview of that shadow applied to the table in the slide (Figure 6–34).
- **Experiment:** Point to various shadow effects in the Shadow gallery and watch the table cells change.

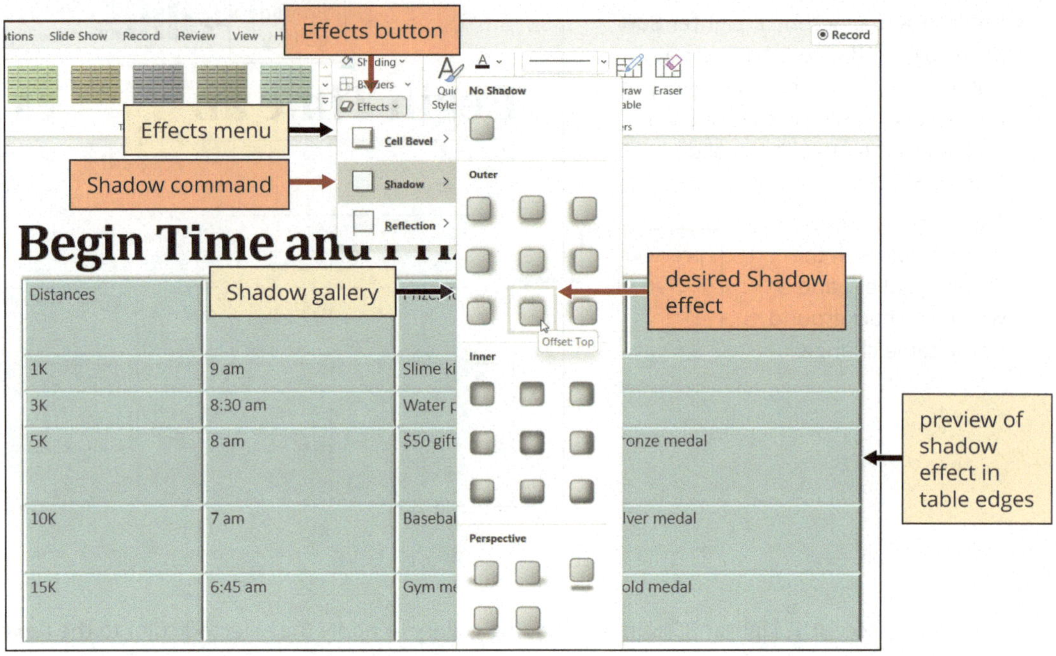

Figure 6–34

2

- Click 'Offset: Top' in the Shadow gallery to apply the selected shadow effect to the table.

To Apply a Reflection Effect to Table Cells

Reflections add a subtle effect by repeating the image beneath the slide. The various options in the Reflection gallery modify the distance and transparency. **Why?** Adding a reflection repeats the last table row. The following steps apply a reflection effect to the table cells.

1

- With the table still selected, click the Effects button again to display the Effects menu.
- Point to Reflection on the Effects menu to display the Reflection gallery.
- Point to 'Tight Reflection: Touching' (first reflection in the first row in the Reflection Variations area) to display a live preview of that reflection applied to the table in the slide (Figure 6–35).
- **Experiment:** Point to various reflection effects in the Reflection gallery and watch the table cells change.

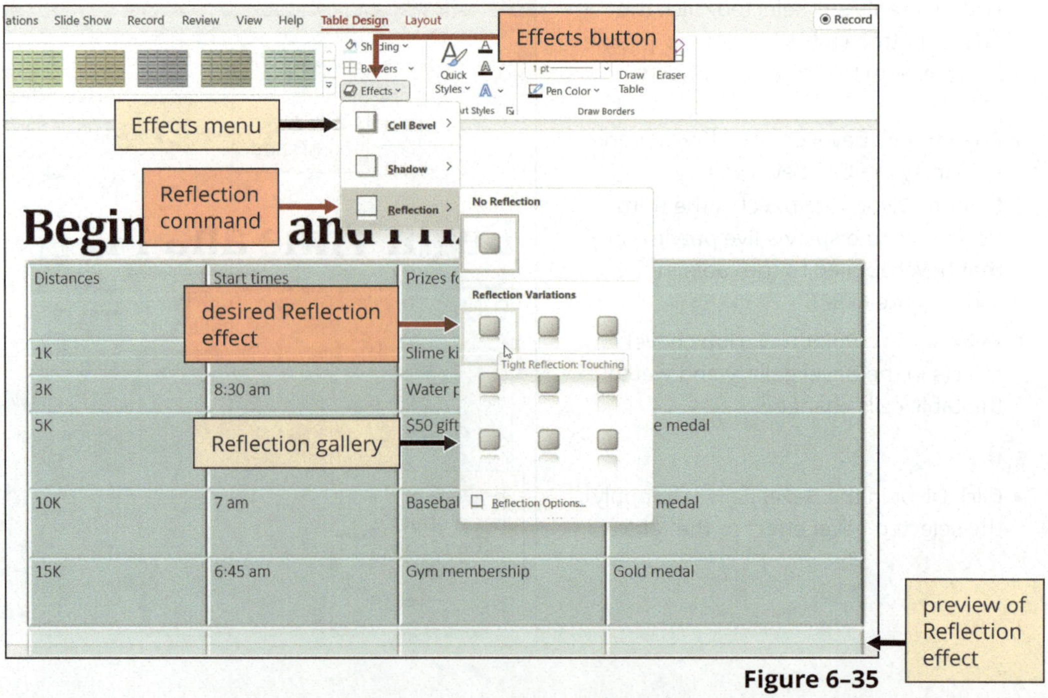

Figure 6–35

2

- Click 'Tight Reflection: Touching' in the Reflection gallery to apply the selected reflection effect to the table.

To Include a Total Row in a Table Many PowerPoint table styles emphasize particular rows by shading them a darker color. In many cases, the first row, called the header row, is highlighted. If you want to emphasize the last row, called the total row, in a table, you can apply a table style to this row. To include a total row, you would perform the following step.

1. Display the Table Design tab and then click the Total Row box (Table Design tab | Table Style Options) to select it and style the total row in the table.

To Add an Image to a Table Cell

A table enhancement you can make is to add a photo or illustration to a table cell. The following steps add a picture of a finish line to the upper-right table cell. **Why?** This illustration is another graphical element that reinforces the purpose of the table.

1

- Right-click the last cell in the first row to display the shortcut menu and Mini toolbar (Figure 6–36).

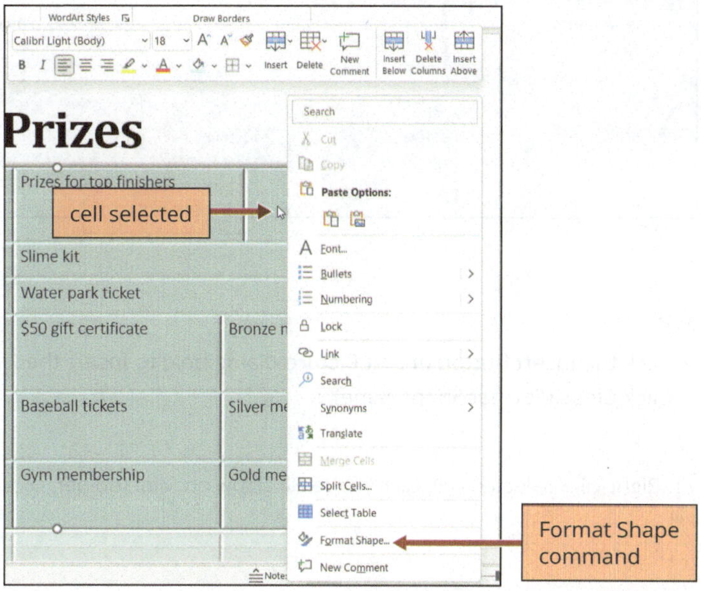

Figure 6–36

2

- Click Format Shape to display the Format Shape pane and then, if necessary, click Fill to expand the Fill section.
- Click 'Picture or texture fill' to select this option (Figure 6–37).

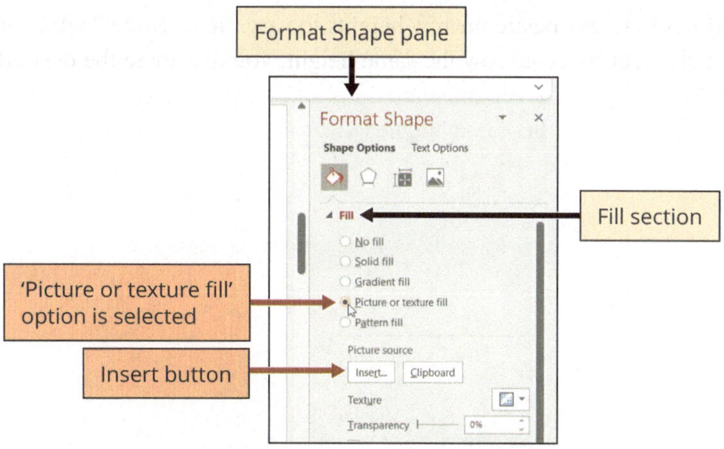

Figure 6–37

3

- Click the Insert button to display the Insert Pictures dialog box.
- Click From a File to display the Insert Picture dialog box.
- Navigate to the location of your Data Files and then click the Support_PPT_6_Finish picture to select this picture (Figure 6–38).

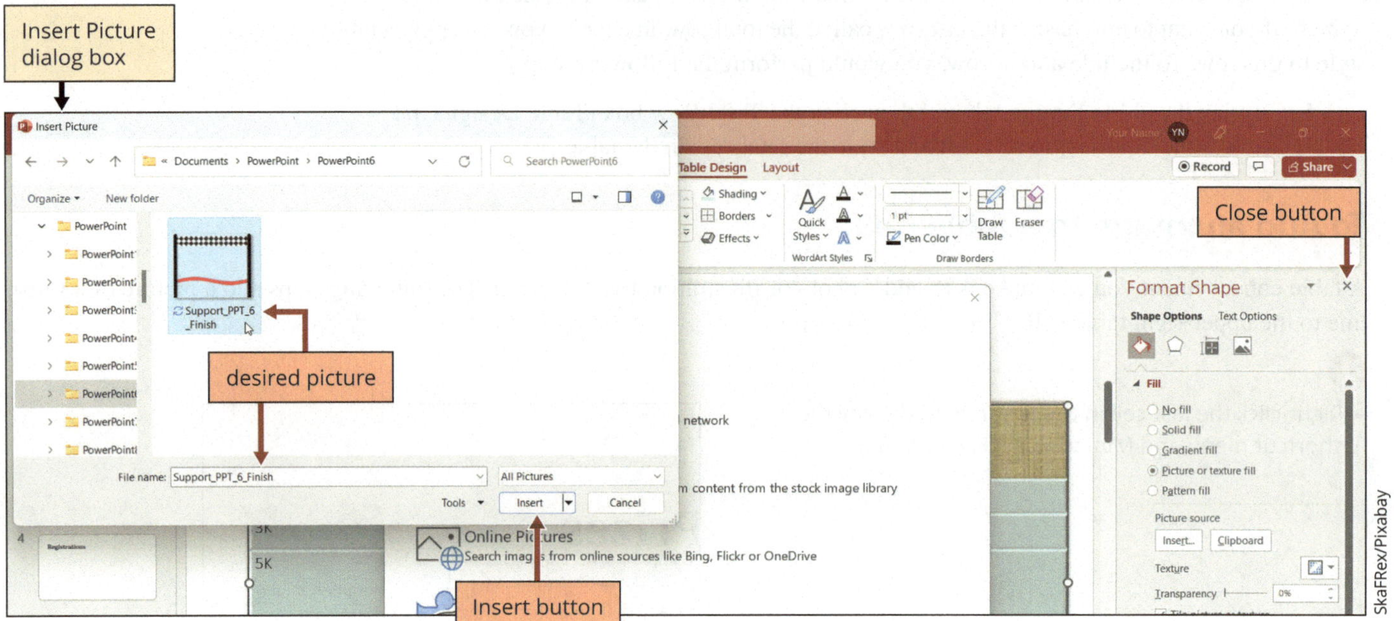

Figure 6–38

4

- Click the Insert button (Insert Picture dialog box) to insert the Finish picture into the table cell.
- Click Close (Format Shape pane).

Other Ways

1. Right-click selected cell, click Shape Fill arrow on Mini toolbar, click Picture

To Distribute Table Rows

At times you may desire the row heights to vary. In the Slide 2 table, however, you desire the heights of the rows to be uniform. To make each selected row the same height, you distribute the desired rows. The following steps distribute table rows. **Why?** The horizontal lines you drew are not spaced equidistant from each other, and distributing the rows is an efficient manner of creating rows with the same height.

1

- With the table still selected, display the Layout tab and then select the cells in the second, third, fourth, fifth, and sixth rows (all rows except the first row) (Figure 6–39).

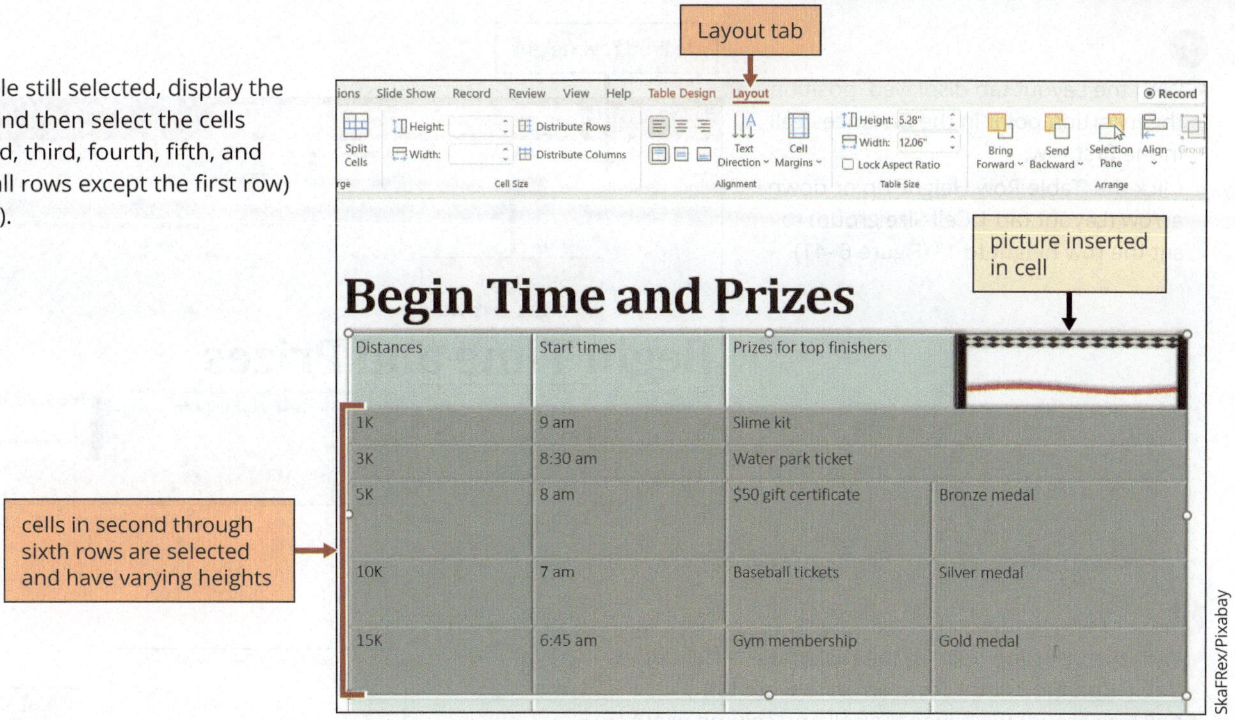

Figure 6–39

2

- Click the Distribute Rows button (Layout tab | Cell Size group) to equally space these five rows vertically (Figure 6–40).

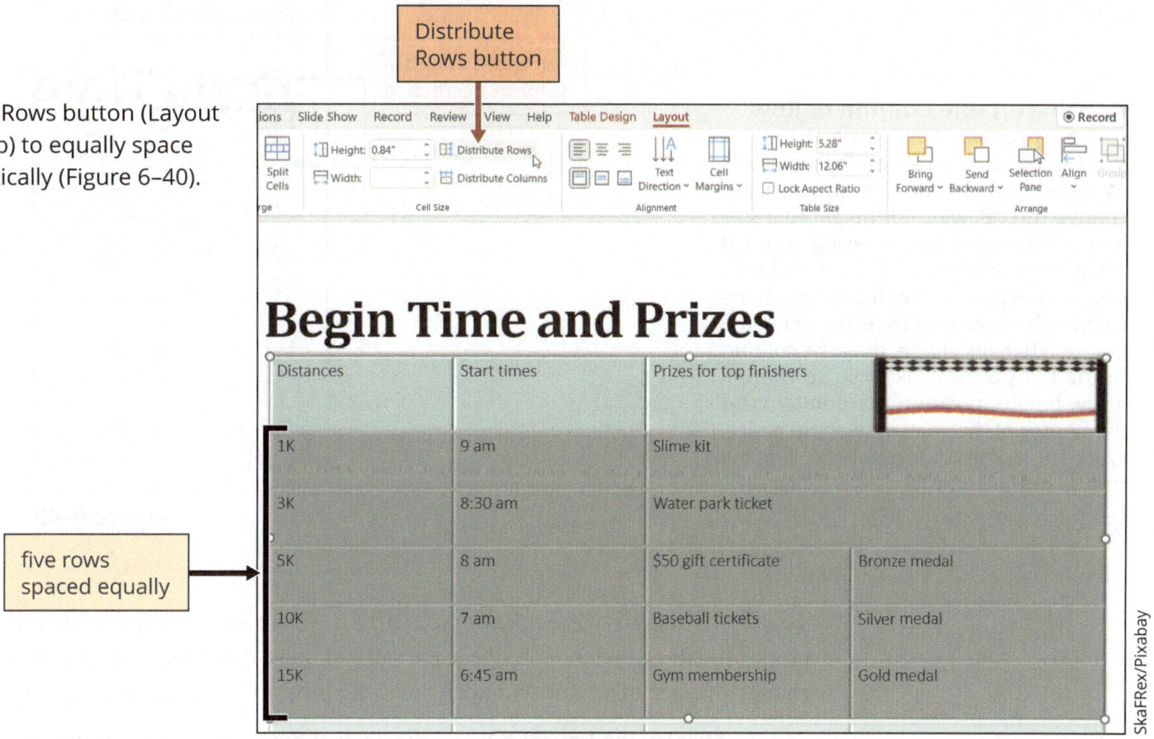

Figure 6–40

To Resize a Table Column and Row

The first table row should have a height taller than the rows beneath it. In addition, the cell width can be changed. **Why?** You can eliminate the extra space in the cells and allow sufficient room for all letters. The following steps resize the table columns and rows.

1

- With the Layout tab displayed, position the insertion point in the Distances cell in the first row.
- Click the 'Table Row Height' up or down arrow (Layout tab | Cell Size group) to set the row height to 1" (Figure 6–41).

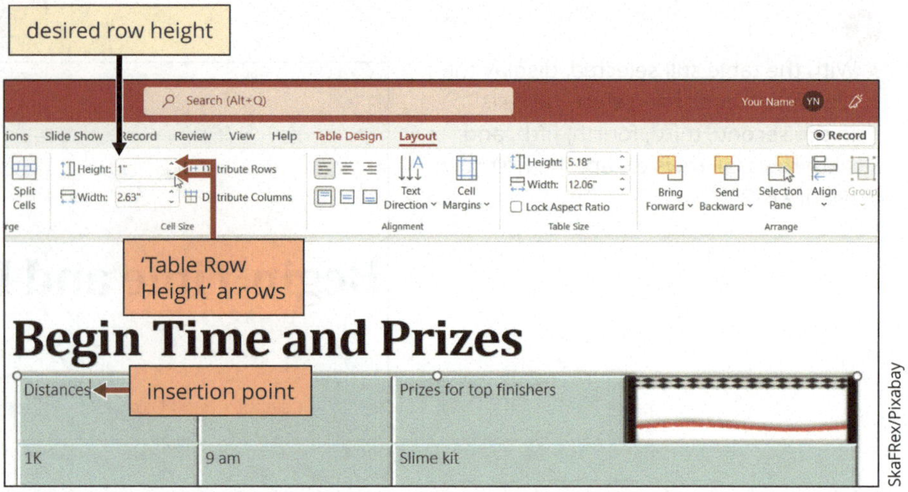

Figure 6–41

2

- With the insertion point in the Distances cell, click the 'Table Column Width' down arrow (Layout tab | Cell Size group) to change the cell and column width to 2" (Figure 6–42).

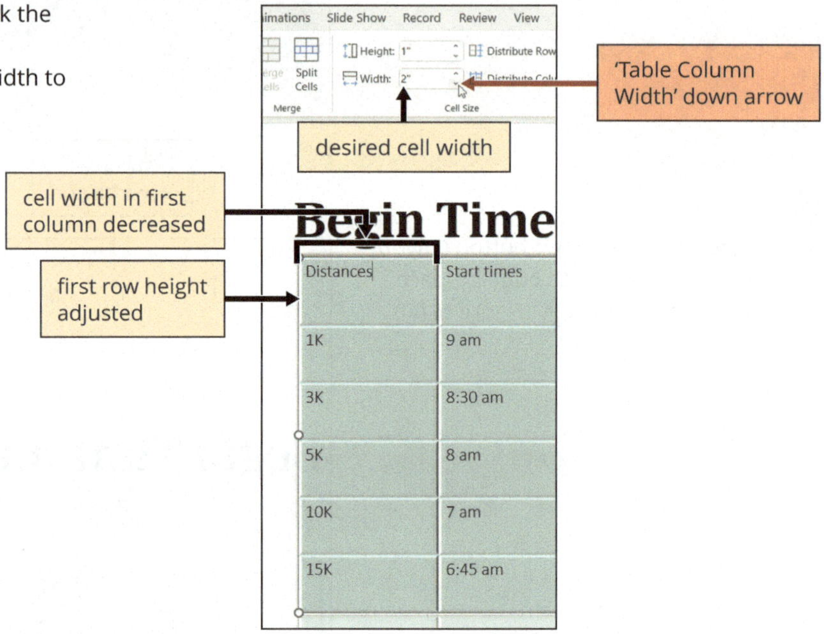

Figure 6–42

BTW
Resizing a Table Column or Row to an Approximate Value
In this module, you resized the table cells by entering a specific size. You also can change the cell width or height to a size that looks aesthetically pleasing to you. If you want to change the width of a column, position the pointer over the border of the column that you want to resize. When the pointer changes shape, drag the column to the right or left. Likewise, to change a row height, position the pointer over the border of the row you want to resize. When the pointer changes shape, drag the row up or down.

To Resize a Table Proportionally When you change the height and width of a table proportionally, you maintain the same ratio of these dimensions. If you want to enlarge, reduce, or change the size of a table and keep the same proportions, you would perform the following steps.

1. Display the Layout tab and then select the 'Lock Aspect Ratio' check box (Layout tab | Table Size group) to check the box.
2. Click the Height or Width up or down arrow to change the table dimensions.

To Align Data in a Table Cell

The data in each cell can be aligned horizontally and vertically. You change the horizontal alignment of each cell in a similar manner as you center, left-align, or right-align text in a placeholder. You also can change the vertical alignment so that the data displays at the top, middle, or bottom of each cell. The following steps center the text both horizontally and vertically in each table cell. **Why?** Having the text centered vertically and horizontally helps balance the cells by distributing the empty space evenly around the cell contents.

1

- Click the Select button to display the Select menu and then click Select Table to select the entire table.
- Click the Center button (Layout tab | Alignment group) to center the text between the left and right borders of each cell in the table (Figure 6–43).

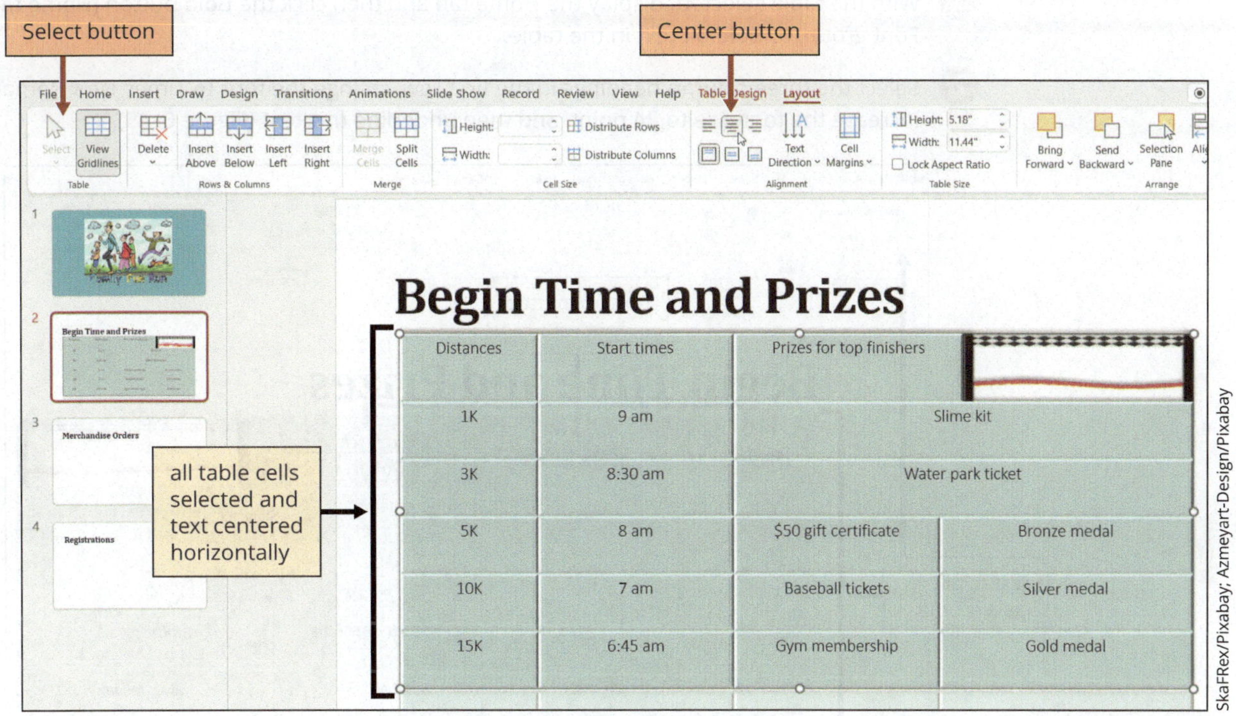

Figure 6–43

2

- Click the Center Vertically button (Layout tab | Alignment group) to center the text between the top and bottom borders of each cell in the table (Figure 6–44).

Q&A Must I center all the table cells, or can I center only specific cells?

You can center as many cells as you desire at one time by selecting one or more cells.

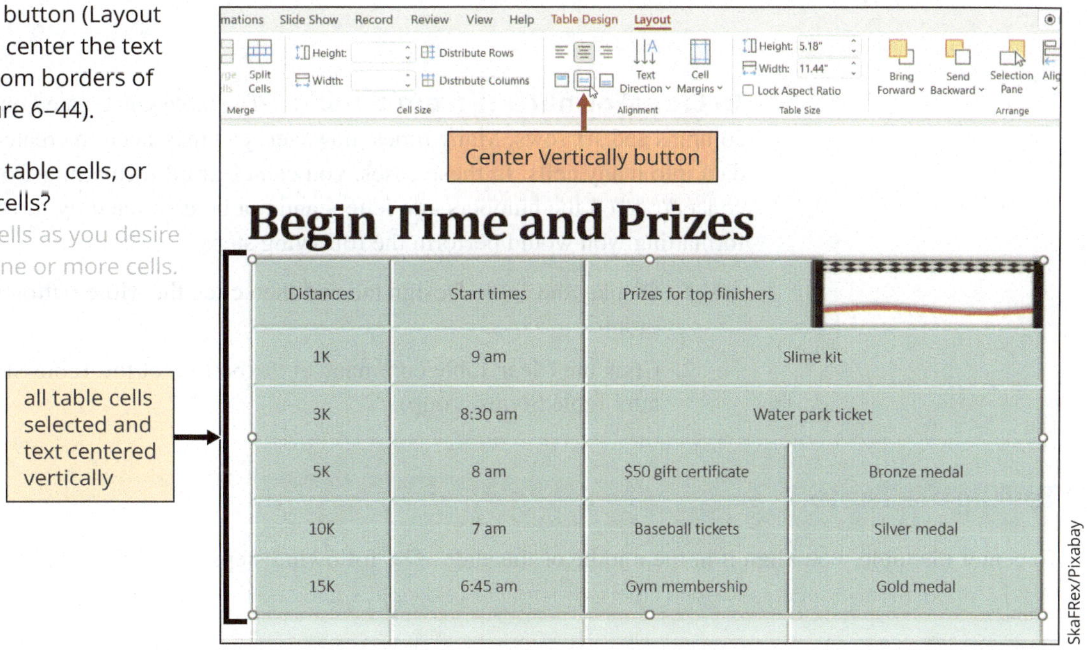

Figure 6–44

Other Ways

1. Right-click selected cells, click Format Shape on shortcut menu, click Text Options tab, click Textbox icon, click Vertical alignment arrow

To Format Table Data

The final table enhancement is to bold the text in all cells and format the column headings. The entire table is selected, so you can bold all text simultaneously. The following steps format the data.

1. With the table selected, display the Home tab and then click the Bold button (Home tab | Font group) to bold all text in the table.

2. Select the three column headings in the first row, change the font to Times New Roman, increase the font size to 24 point, and then underline this text (Figure 6–45).

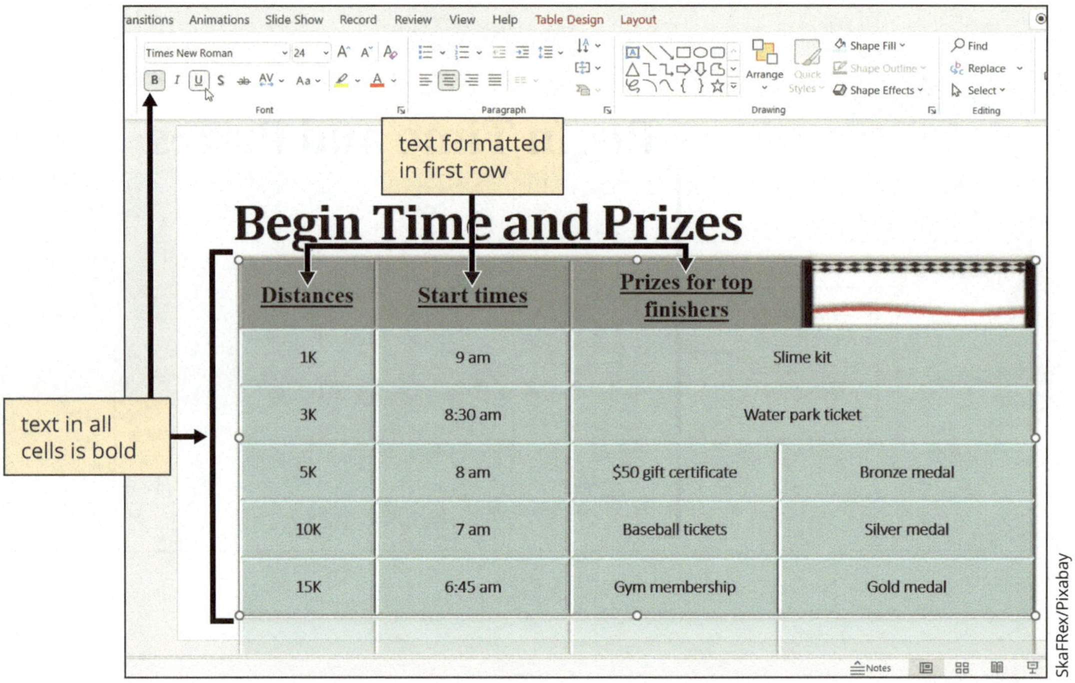

Figure 6–45

To Clear Formatting from a Table The table you created on the current Slide 2 has four columns and six rows. Many times, however, you may need to create larger tables and then enter data into many cells. In these cases, you can clear all formatting from the table so that you can concentrate on the numbers and letters and not be distracted by the colors and borders. To clear formatting, you would perform the following steps.

1. Display the Table Design tab and then click the More button in the Table Styles group.
2. Click the Clear Table command at the bottom of the Table Styles gallery (Table Design tab | Table Styles group).

To Align a Table

To center the table, you align it in the middle of the slide. The following steps center the table horizontally. **Why?** The table should be positioned an equal distance between the left and right slide edges to balance this object in the slide.

1

- With the table selected, display the Layout tab and then click the Align button (Layout tab | Arrange group) to display the Align Objects menu (Figure 6–46).

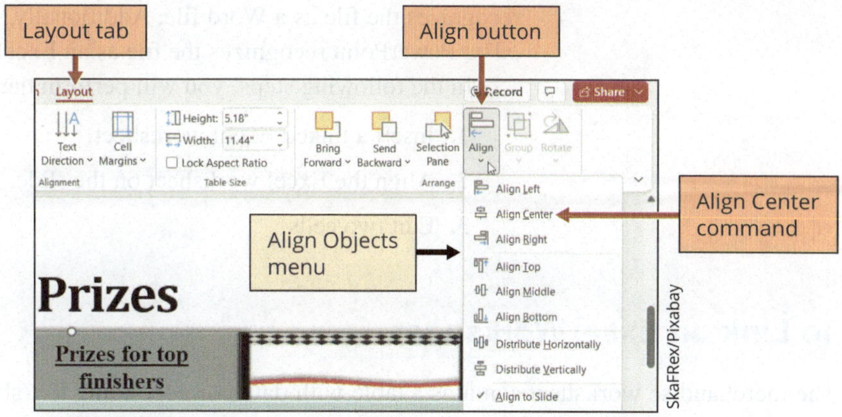

SkaFRex/Pixabay

Figure 6–46

2

- Click Align Center on the Align Objects menu, so PowerPoint adjusts the position of the table evenly between the left and right sides of the slide (Figure 6–47).

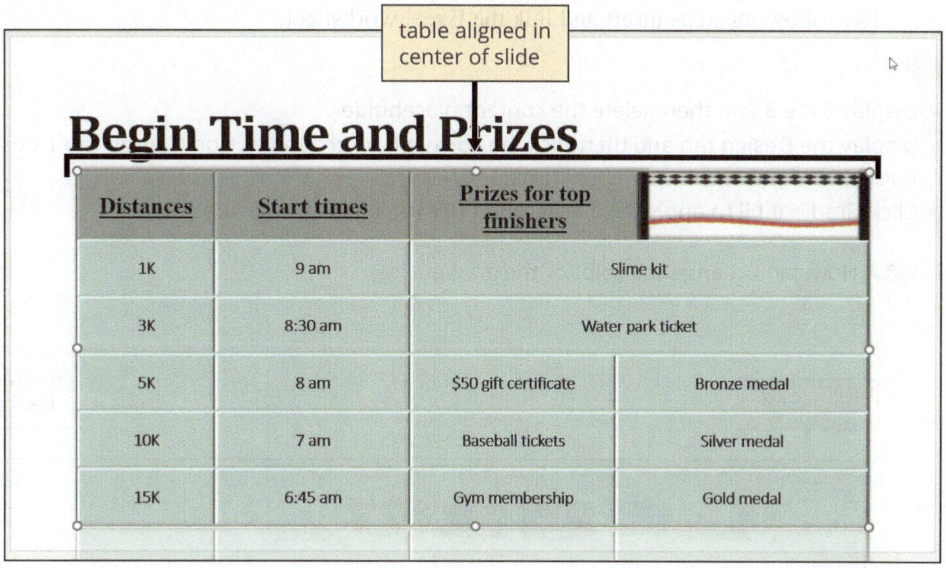

SkaFRex/Pixabay

Figure 6–47

Break Point: If you wish to take a break, this is a good place to do so. Be sure the Run file is saved and then you can exit PowerPoint. To resume later, start PowerPoint, open the file called SC_PPT_6_Run, and continue following the steps from this location forward. Note: PowerPoint will prompt you to update any files you modified.

Inserting a Linked Excel Worksheet

Linked files maintain a connection between the source file and the destination file. When you select the **Link check box** in the Insert Object dialog box, the object is inserted as a linked object instead of an embedded object. Your PowerPoint presentation stores a representation of the original file and information about its location. If you later move or delete the source file, the link is broken, and the object will not be available. Consequently, if you make a presentation on a computer other than the one on which the presentation was created, and the presentation contains linked objects, be certain to include a copy of the source files. The source files must be stored in the exact location as originally specified when you linked them to your presentation.

PowerPoint associates a linked file with a specific application, which PowerPoint bases on the file extension. For example, if you select a source file with the file extension .docx, PowerPoint

BTW
File Sizes
Files with embedded objects typically have larger file sizes than those with linked objects because the source data is stored in the presentation. To keep file sizes manageable, Microsoft recommends inserting a linked object rather than an embedded object when the source file is large or complex.

recognizes the file as a Word file. Additionally, if you select a source file with the file extension .xlsx, PowerPoint recognizes the file as an Excel file.

In the following steps, you will perform these tasks on Slide 3:

1. Insert a linked Excel worksheet.
2. Align the Excel worksheet on the slide.
3. Edit two cells.

To Link an Excel Worksheet

The merchandise worksheet contains a table with data corresponding to t-shirt and sweatshirt sales for three sizes and total sales for each of these items. You will update this table by editing the number of extra-large t-shirt and sweatshirt orders. These figures will update the original Excel worksheet. When you insert the merchandise table, you can specify that it is linked from the PowerPoint slide to the Excel worksheet. **Why?** Any edits made to specific cells are reflected in both the source and destination files. The following steps insert and link the Excel worksheet.

1

- Display Slide 3 and then delete the content placeholder.
- Display the Design tab and then click the Format Background button (Design tab | Customize group) to display the Format Background pane.
- Click Gradient fill to apply this background to the slide (Figure 6–48).

Q&A How can I change the color of the gradient?
Click the Color button in the Fill area of the Format Background pane and then choose the desired color.

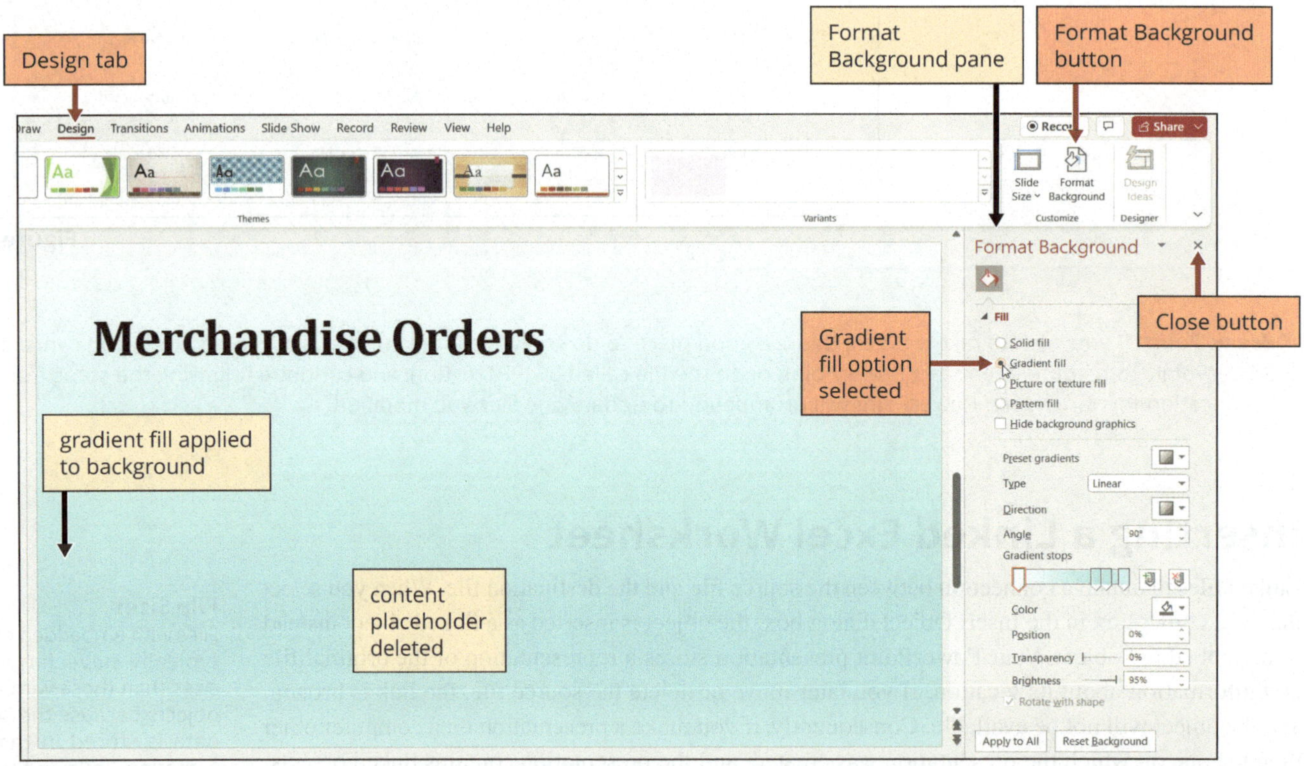

Figure 6–48

2

- Close the Format Background pane.
- Display the Insert tab and then click the Object button (Insert tab | Text group) to display the Insert Object dialog box.
- Click 'Create from file' (Insert Object dialog box) to display the File box (Figure 6–49).

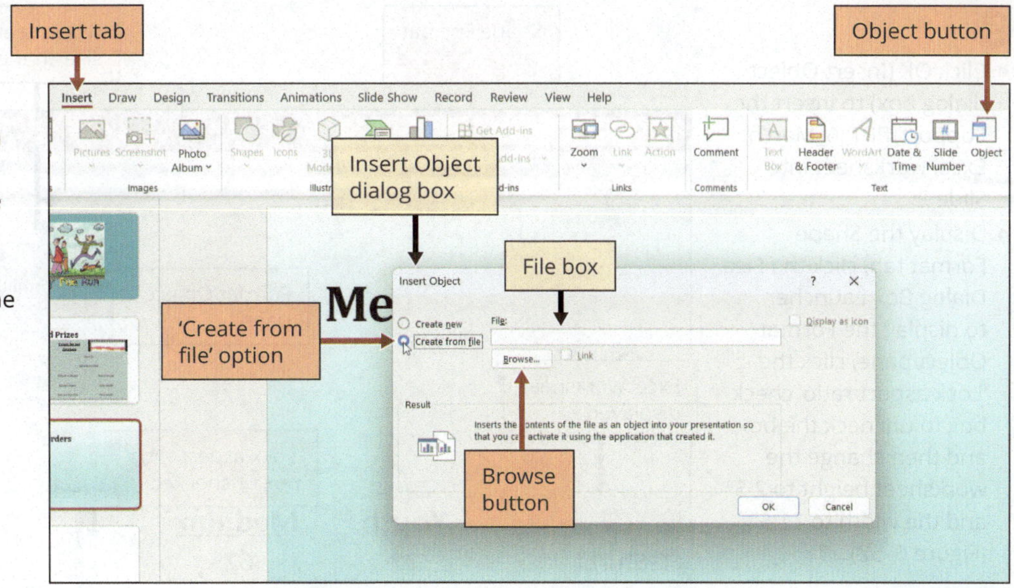

SkaFRex/Pixabay; Azmeyart-Design/Pixabay

Figure 6–49

3

- Click the Browse button to display the Browse dialog box, navigate to the location of your Data Files, and then click Support_PPT_6_Merch to select the Excel file name (Figure 6–50).

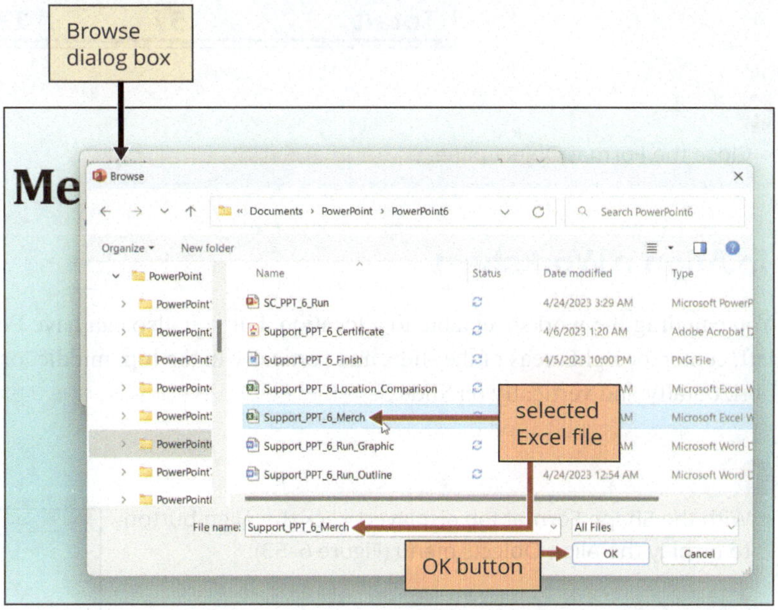

Figure 6–50

4

- Click OK (Browse dialog box) to insert the file name into the File box (Insert Object dialog box).
- Click the Link check box (Insert Object dialog box) to select the check box (Figure 6–51).

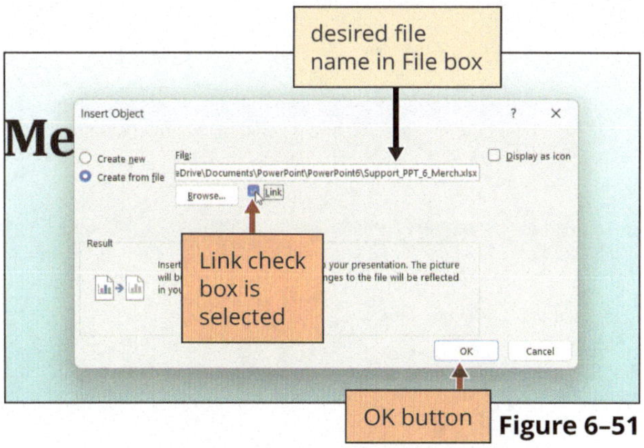

Figure 6–51

5

- Click OK (Insert Object dialog box) to insert the Support_PPT_6_Merch Excel worksheet into Slide 3.
- Display the Shape Format tab, click the Size Dialog Box Launcher to display the Format Object pane, click the 'Lock aspect ratio' check box to uncheck the box, and then change the worksheet height to 2.5" and the width to 11.5" (Figure 6–52).

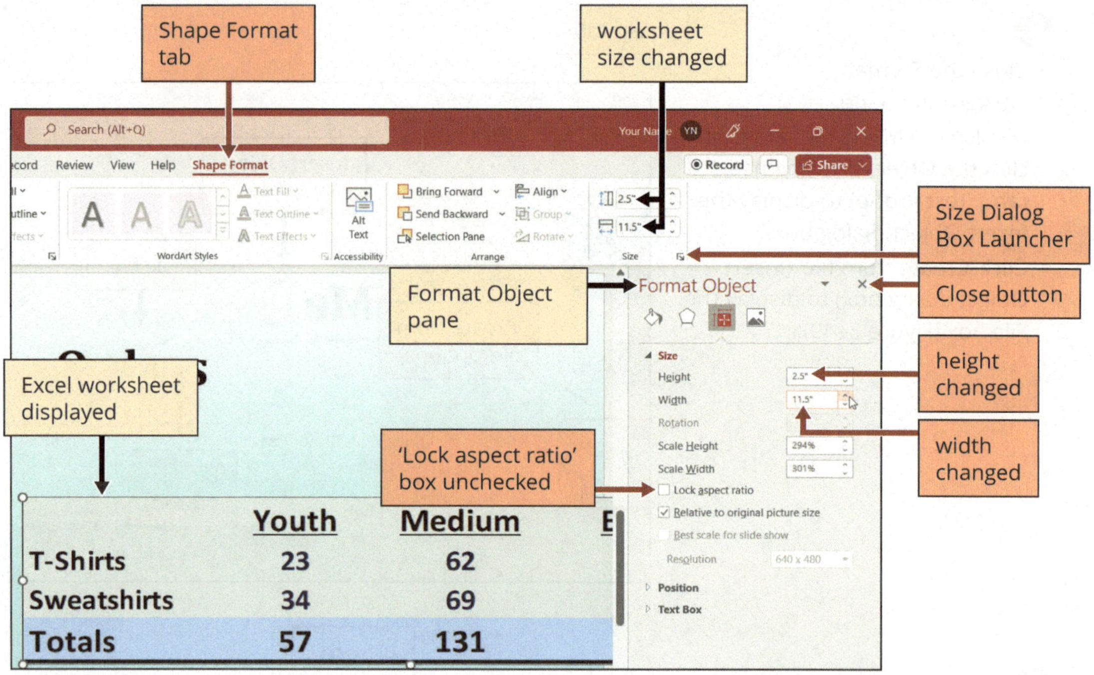

Figure 6–52

6

- Close the Format Object pane.

To Align a Worksheet

You can drag the worksheet table to a location, but you also can have PowerPoint precisely align the object horizontally in the left, center, or right areas of the slide, and vertically in the top, middle, or bottom of the slide. The following steps align the table horizontally and vertically on Slide 3. **Why?** PowerPoint inserts the table on Slide 3 in a location that is not visually appealing, so you want to center it on the slide.

1

- With the Shape Format tab displayed, click the Align button to display the Align Objects menu (Figure 6–53).

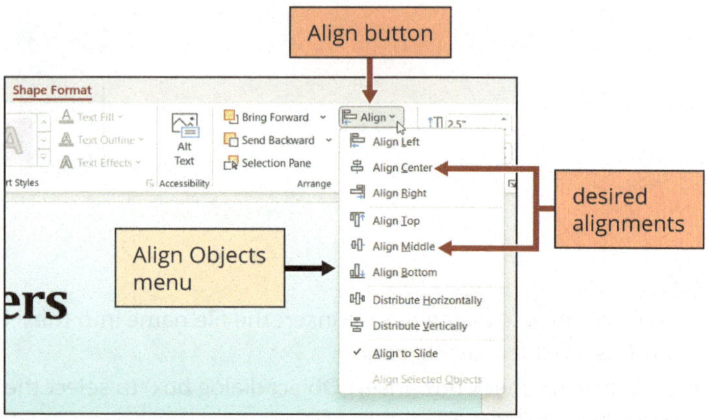

Figure 6–53

2

- Click Align Center on the Align Objects menu to position the worksheet evenly between the left and right edges of the slide.
- Click the Align button again to display the Align Objects menu and then click Align Middle to position the worksheet in the center of the slide (Figure 6–54).

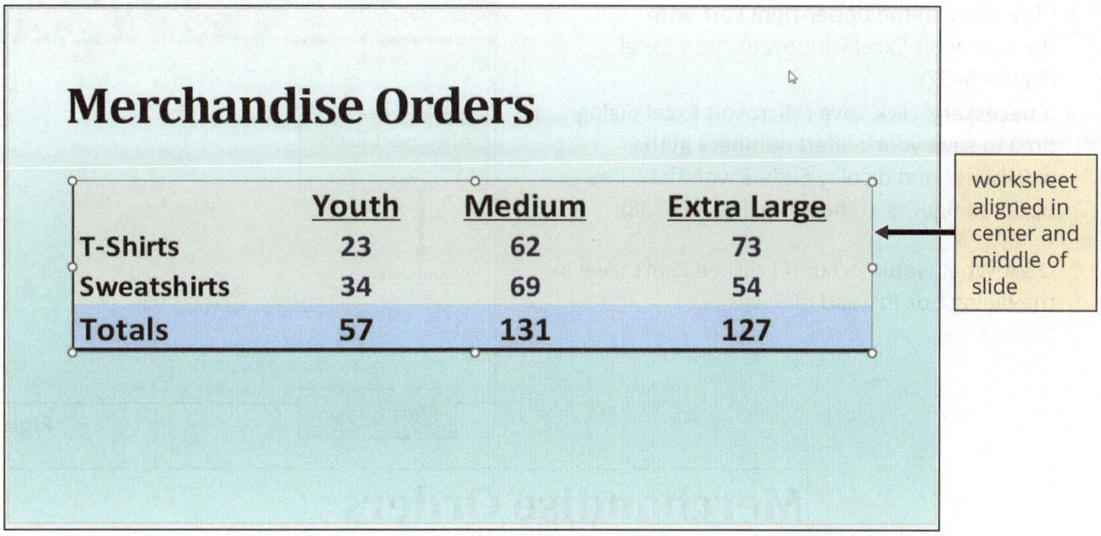

Figure 6–54

To Update a Linked Worksheet

Each table or worksheet cell is identified by a unique address, or **cell reference**, representing the intersection of a column and row. The column letter is first and is followed by the row number. For example, cell D2 is located at the intersection of the fourth column, D, and the second row. Two cells need updating. **Why?** You have received orders today for extra-large t-shirts and sweatshirts. The following steps edit cells in the linked table.

1

- Double-click the worksheet to run Excel and display the worksheet.
- Click the number 73 underneath the Extra Large column heading to make cell D2 the active cell (Figure 6–55).

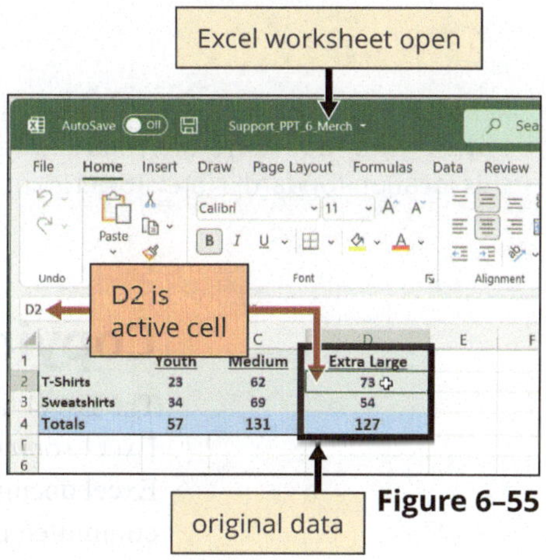

Figure 6–55

2

- Type **61** as the new Extra Large t-shirts number and then press ENTER to complete the entry and make cell D3 the active cell.
- Type **78** as the new Extra Large sweatshirts number and then press ENTER to complete the entry and make cell D4 the active cell (Figure 6–56).

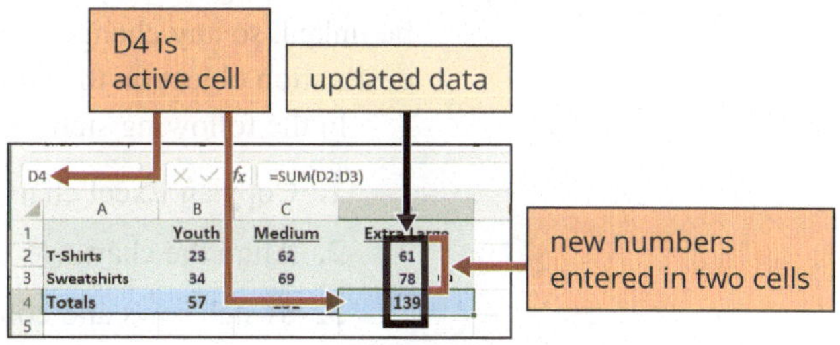

Figure 6–56

3

- Click Close in the upper-right corner of the Microsoft Excel window to close Excel (Figure 6–57).
- If necessary, click Save (Microsoft Excel dialog box) to save your edited numbers in the worksheet and display Slide 3 with the three updated figures in the table (Figure 6–58).

Q&A What would occur if I clicked Don't Save in the dialog box instead of Save?

The new figures in cells B3 and B4 would not be updated in the Excel spreadsheet.

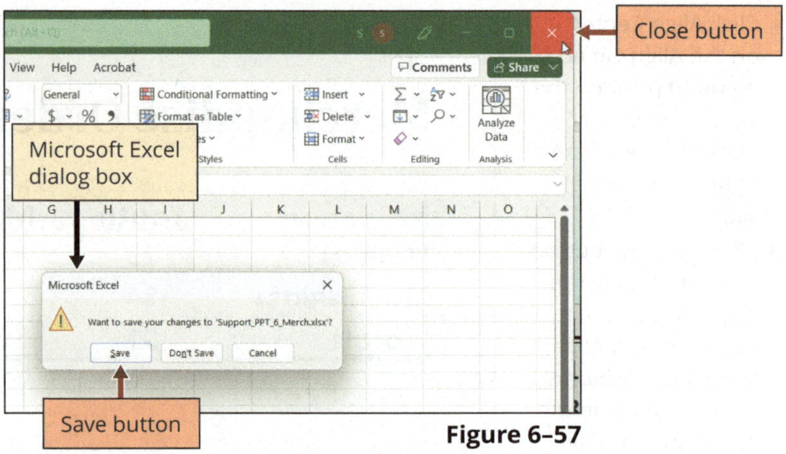

Figure 6–57

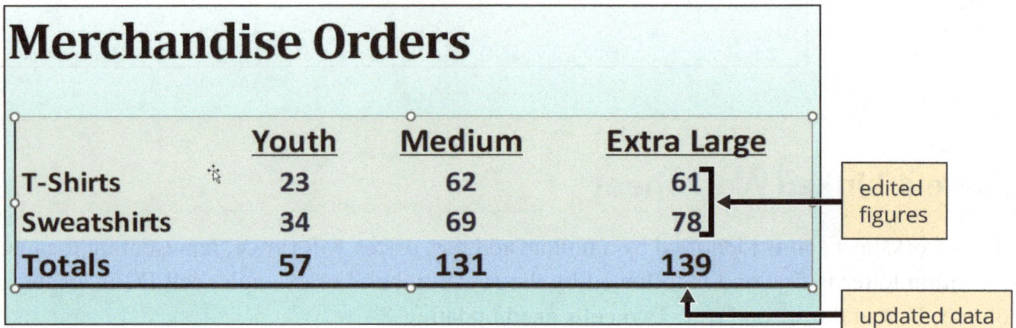

Figure 6–58

Break Point: If you wish to take a break, this is a good place to do so. Be sure the Run file is saved and then you can exit PowerPoint. To resume later, start PowerPoint, open the file called SC_PPT_6_Run, and continue following the steps from this location forward. Note: PowerPoint will prompt you to update any files you modified.

Copying and Modifying a Linked Excel Chart

The Excel table you inserted into Slide 3 is a linked object. You added data to the table using the Excel source program, and that change is reflected on the PowerPoint slide and in the original Excel document. Now you will insert and then modify an Excel chart on Slide 4. The registration committee members tracked the number of people living in the city and suburbs who have registered during the past five months and have used this data to develop this chart. This object will be linked, so any changes you make to the layout, legend, or background will be reflected in the destination object on the slide and in the original Excel worksheet.

In the following steps, you will perform these tasks on Slide 4:

1. Copy an Excel chart.
2. Align the chart.
3. Switch rows and columns.
4. Change the chart type.
5. Apply a style.
6. Add and format axis titles.
7. Add a chart title.
8. Edit data.

To Copy an Excel Chart

The chart you want to insert into your slide show was created in Excel. The file consists of two sheets: one for the chart and another for the numbers used to create the chart. The chart is on the sheet labeled Chart. One method of placing this chart into a PowerPoint presentation is to copy this object from the Excel worksheet and then paste it into a slide. The following steps copy and link a chart from the Chart sheet of the Excel file using the source formatting. **Why?** Copying and linking allows you to modify the chart content easily. You want to use the source formatting so that the chart uses the Office 2007-2010 theme colors and styles.

1

- Display Slide 4, delete the title text (Registrations), and then delete the title and content placeholders.

2

- Click the File Explorer app button (folder icon) on the taskbar to make the File Explorer window the active window. Navigate to the location where your Data Files are stored and then point to the Support_PPT_6_Location_Comparison Excel file in the Name list (Figure 6–59).

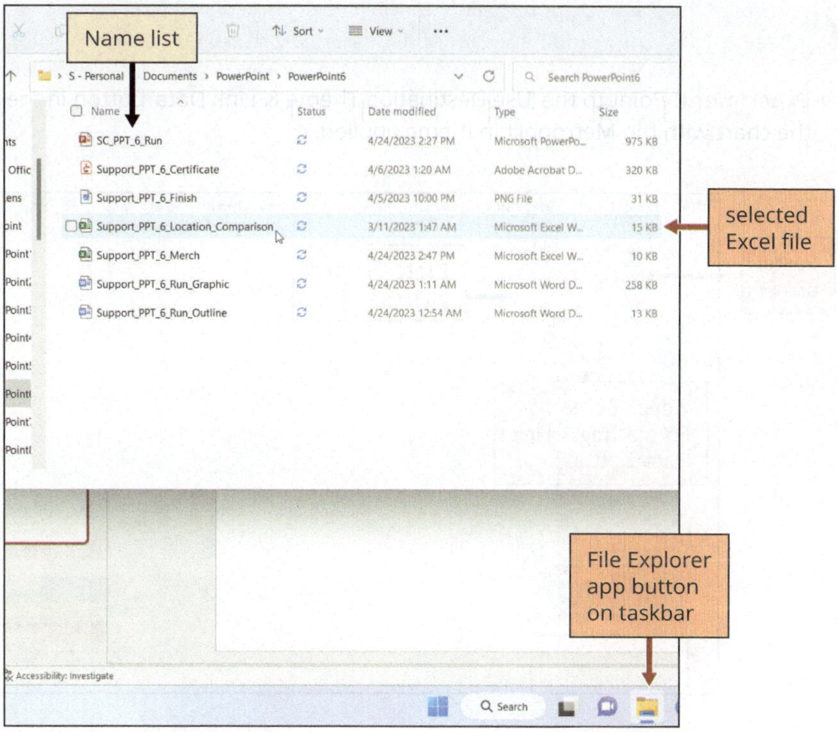

Figure 6–59

3

- Double-click the Support_PPT_6_Location_Comparison file to run Excel. If necessary, display the chart on the Chart sheet.
- Click a blank area above the chart legend in the Chart Area to select the entire chart.
- Click the Copy button (Home tab | Clipboard group) to copy the chart to the Office Clipboard (Figure 6–60).

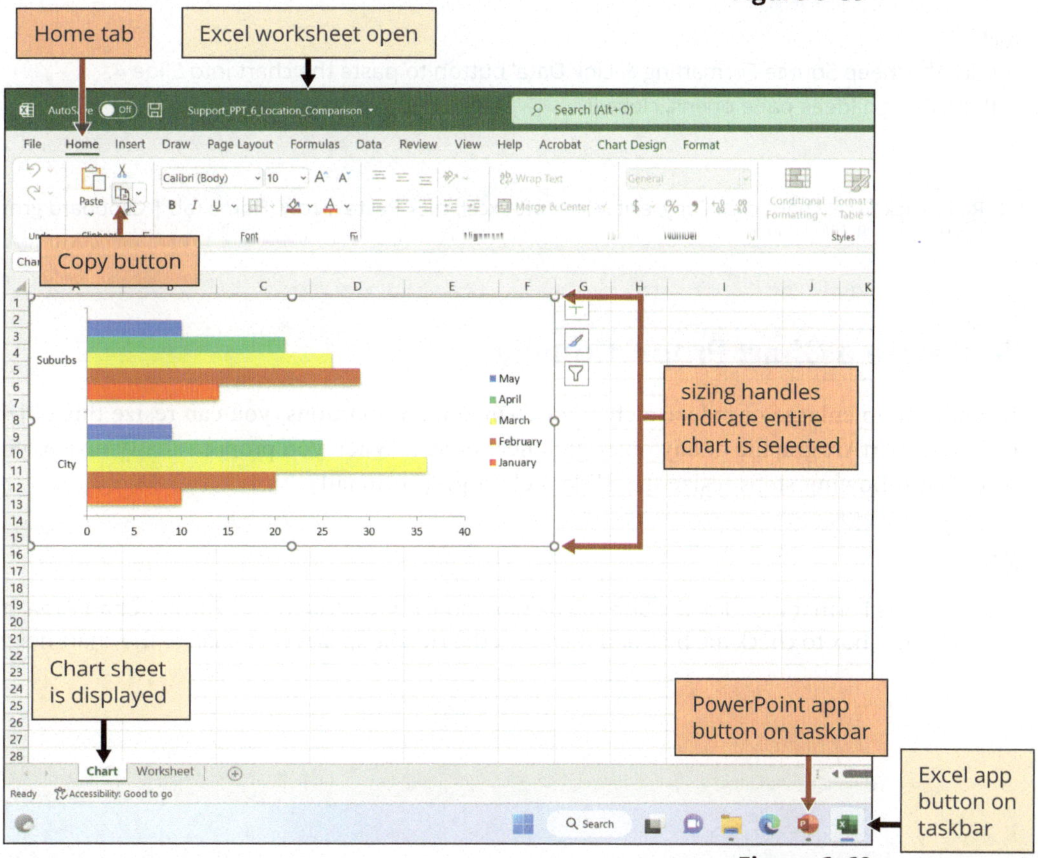

Figure 6–60

4

- Click the PowerPoint app button on the taskbar to make the PowerPoint window the active window. With Slide 4 and the Home tab displayed, click the Paste arrow (Home tab | Clipboard group) to display the Paste Options gallery.
- Point to the 'Keep Source Formatting & Link Data' button to display a live preview of the chart in the slide (Figure 6–61).

Q&A Why did I click the Paste arrow instead of the Paste button?
You want to use the colors and style of the chart on the Chart sheet of the Excel workbook (the source theme), so you need to display the Paste Options gallery to make that choice and to link the chart to the original Excel file. If you had clicked the Paste button, you would have embedded the chart using PowerPoint's Metropolitan theme (the destination theme).

- **Experiment:** Point to the 'Use Destination Theme & Link Data' button in the Paste Options gallery to display a live preview of the chart with the Metropolitan theme applied.

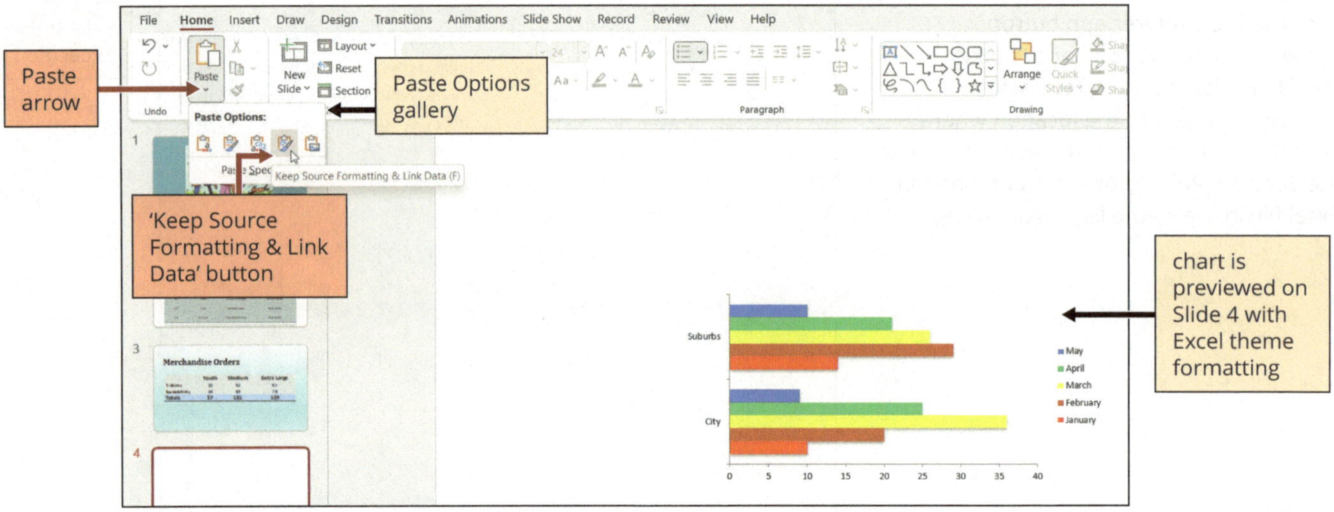

Figure 6–61

5

- Click the 'Keep Source Formatting & Link Data' button to paste the chart into Slide 4.
- If the Design Ideas pane opens, close it.

Other Ways

1. Right-click Excel chart, click Copy, exit Microsoft Excel, click Paste arrow (Home tab | Clipboard group), click 'Keep Source Formatting & Link Data'

To Resize a Chart Proportionally

If you want to enlarge or reduce a chart, or change its proportions, you can resize this object in the same manner that you resize a SmartArt graphic or any other graphical object. When you proportionally resize, you select the Lock Aspect Ratio box. The following steps resize the Slide 4 chart proportionally. **Why?** You want to maintain the same ratio between the height and width.

1

- Display the Format tab, click the Size Dialog Box Launcher to display the 'Format Chart Area' pane, select the 'Lock aspect ratio' check box to check the box, and then click the Height up arrow to change the chart height to 5.5" (Figure 6–62).

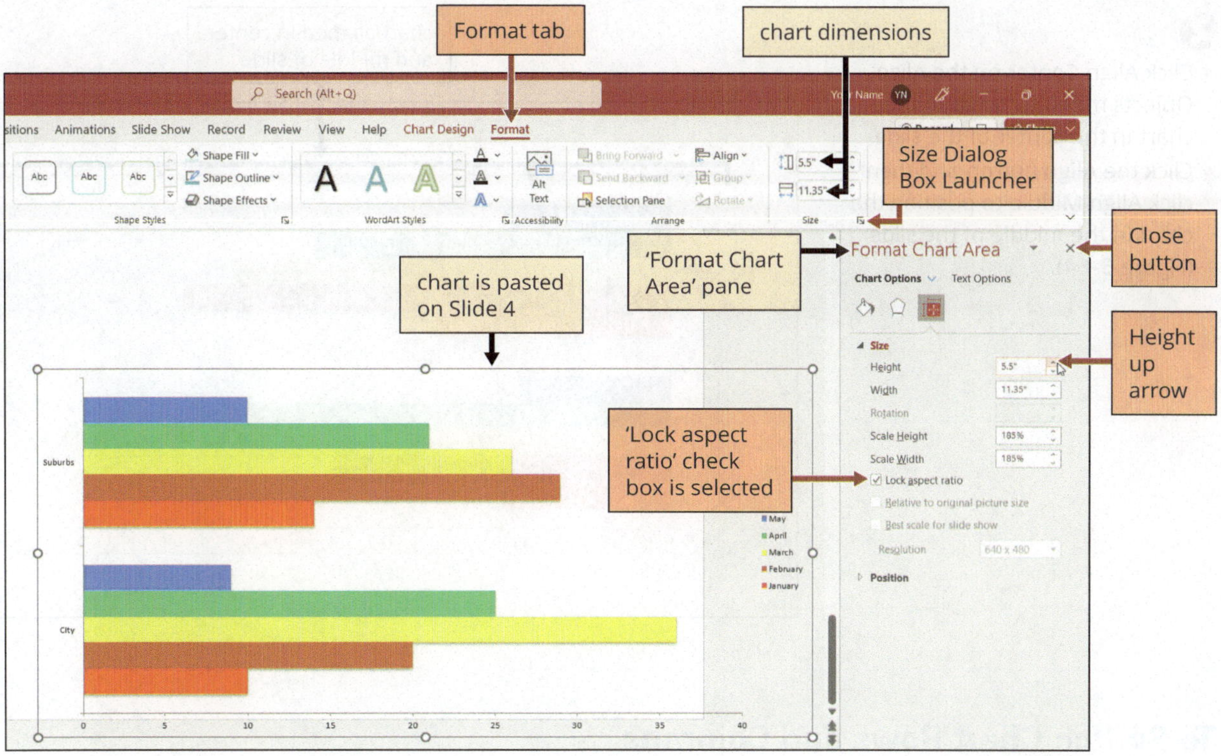

Figure 6–62

2

- Close the Format Chart Area pane.

To Align a Chart

Although you can drag the chart on the slide to realign it manually, you also can use PowerPoint commands to align the object horizontally in the left, center, or right areas of the slide, and vertically in the top, middle, or bottom of the slide. The following steps align the chart horizontally and vertically on Slide 4. **Why?** You aligned the table on Slide 3 horizontally and vertically. Likewise, you want to align the chart on Slide 4 so that it is displayed in an appropriate location on the slide.

1

- With the chart selected and the Format tab displayed, click the Align button to display the Align Objects menu (Figure 6–63).

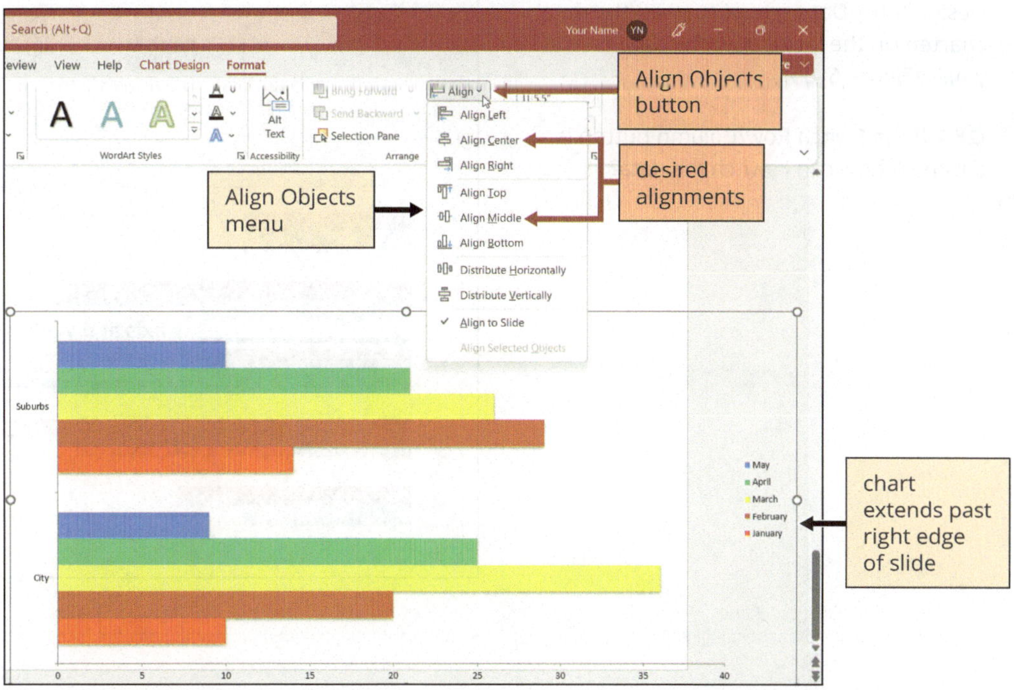

Figure 6–63

2

- Click Align Center on the Align Objects menu to position the chart in the center of the slide.
- Click the Align button and then click Align Middle to position the chart in the middle of the slide (Figure 6–64).

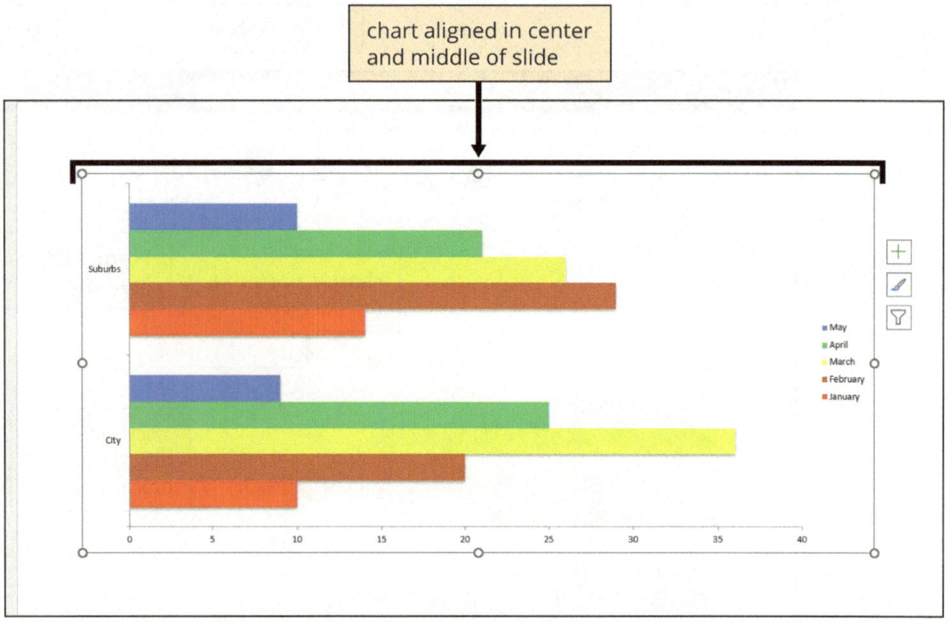

Figure 6–64

To Switch Chart Rows and Columns

Excel created the chart on Slide 4 (the Chart sheet in the Excel file) based on the values in the worksheet on the Worksheet sheet of the Excel file. The scale is based on the values in the **y-axis**, which also is called the **vertical axis** or **value axis**. The titles along the **x-axis**, also referred to as the **horizontal axis** or **category axis**, are derived from the top row of the Worksheet sheet and are displayed along the left edge of the chart. Each bar in the chart has a specific color to represent one of the five months—January, February, March, April, and May—grouped by city and suburbs. You can switch the data in the chart so that the city and suburbs totals display together in each month. **Why?** Audience members may be interested in comparing variations between the city and suburbs registrations during each month. The following step switches the rows and columns in the chart.

1

- Display the Chart Design tab on the ribbon.
- Click the Switch Row/Column button (Chart Design tab | Data group) to swap the data charted on the x-axis with the data on the y-axis (Figure 6–65).

Q&A If the Switch Row/Column button is dimmed, how can I switch the data?
Be certain the Excel worksheet is open. The button is active only when the worksheet is open.

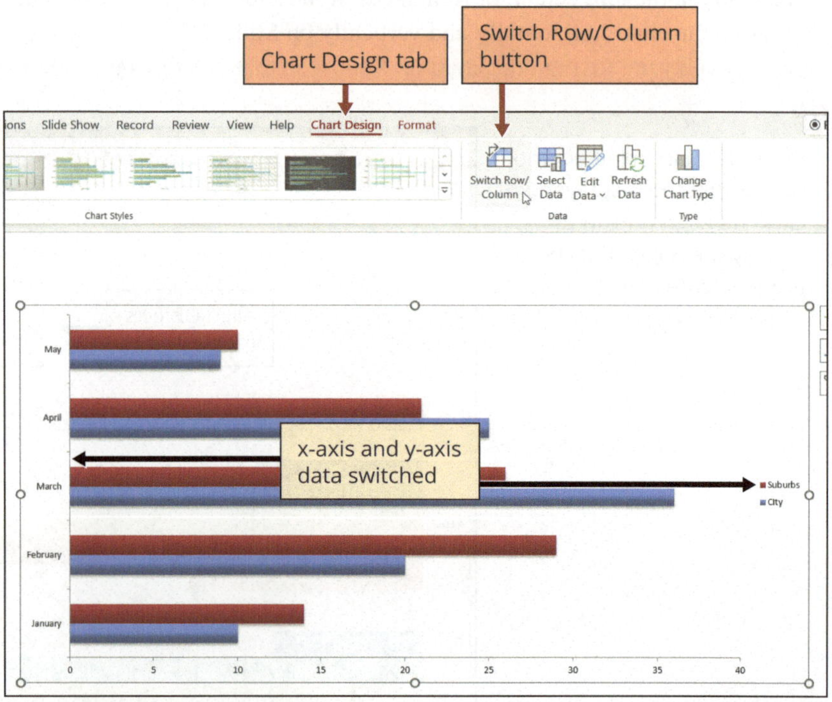

Figure 6–65

To Change the Chart Type

The bar chart represents data horizontally for each of five months. You can change the chart appearance by selecting another type in the Change Chart Type dialog box. The sample charts are divided into a variety of categories, including column, line, pie, and bar. The clustered column type that you want to use in the presentation is located in the Column area, which has seven layouts. The following steps change the chart to a 3-D Clustered Column chart type. **Why?** The vertical bars show the registrations during each month, and the 3-D effect adds an interesting visual element.

1

- Click the 'Change Chart Type' button (Chart Design tab | Type group) to display the 'Change Chart Type' dialog box.
- Click Column in the left pane ('Change Chart Type' dialog box) to display a Clustered Column thumbnail (Figure 6–66).

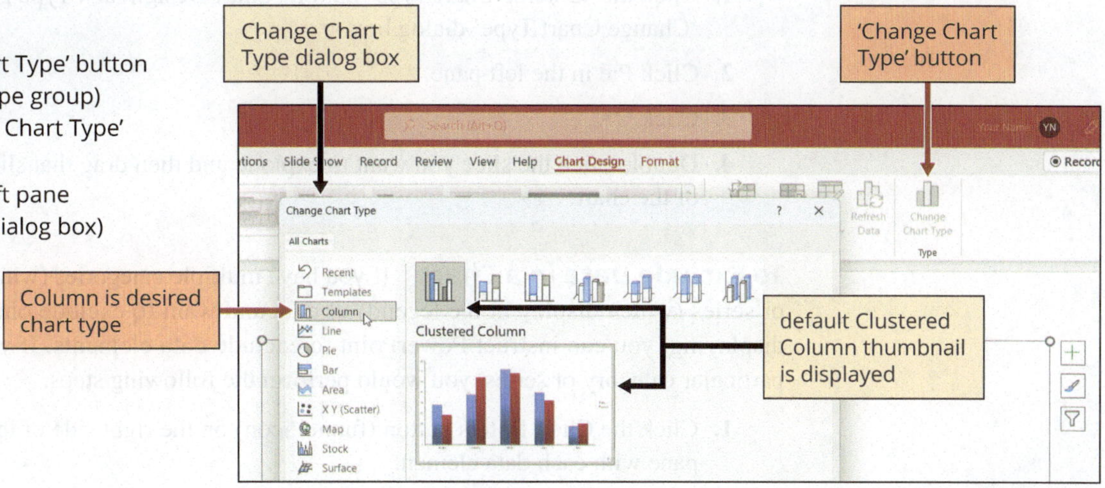

Figure 6–66

2

- Click the '3-D Clustered Column' chart (fourth chart) to select this chart type and display a thumbnail with a 3-D effect (Figure 6–67).

Q&A Can I see a larger preview of the chart?
Yes. You can point to the chart to enlarge the preview.

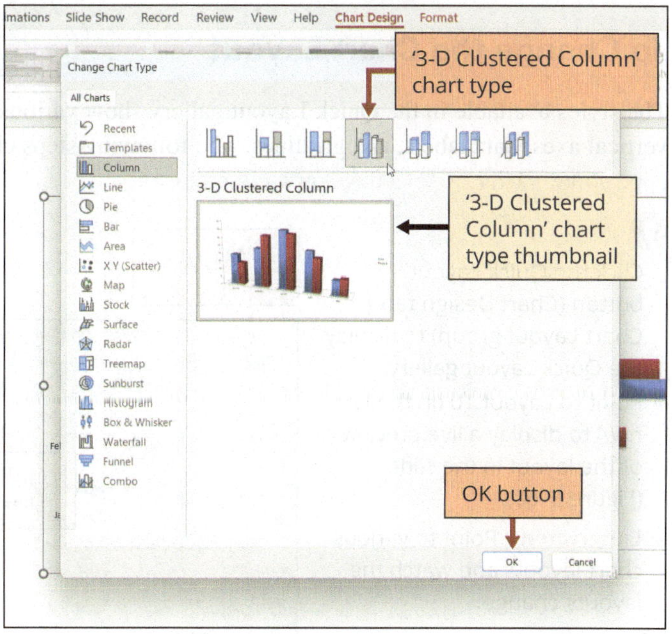

Figure 6–67

3

- Click OK ('Change Chart Type' dialog box) to change the chart type to 3-D Clustered Column.

BTW
Displaying Gridlines
Gridlines can help you align charts, shapes, and other objects on slides. To show the gridlines, display the View tab and then select the Gridlines check box (View tab | Show group).

To Change the Chart Type to Pie and Explode a Pie Chart Slice Pie charts are a popular method of showing how individual amounts contribute to a total amount. Each pie slice represents the size or percentage of that slice relative to the entire pie. You can emphasize an individual slice of the pie by moving, or exploding, it outward. If you wanted to change the 3-D Clustered Column chart on your slide to a pie chart and then explode a particular slice, you would perform the following steps.

1. Click the 'Change Chart Type' button (Chart Design tab | Type group) to display the 'Change Chart Type' dialog box.
2. Click Pie in the left pane.
3. Click OK.
4. Double-click the slice you want to explode and then drag that slice away from the center of the chart.

To Exclude Data in a Chart If you have multiple categories (which display in the x-axis) or series (which display in the legend) of data and want to exclude one or more of them from displaying, you can instruct PowerPoint to exclude data elements. If you wanted to exclude a particular category or series, you would perform the following steps.

1. Click the Chart Filters button (funnel icon) on the right side of the chart to display a pane with each data element.
2. Clear the check boxes of the elements you want to exclude in the chart.
3. To display an excluded data element, select the check box.

To Change the Chart Layout

The styles available in the Quick Layout gallery show various chart elements, including the chart title, legend, horizontal and vertical axes, data labels, and gridlines. The following steps change the layout of the chart. **Why?** You can modify the chart's appearance easily by selecting a predefined layout.

1

- Click the Quick Layout button (Chart Design tab | Chart Layout group) to display the Quick Layout gallery.
- Point to Layout 10 (in the last row) to display a live preview of the layout in the slide (Figure 6–68).
- **Experiment:** Point to various chart layouts and watch the layouts change.

2

- Click Layout 10 in the Quick Layout gallery to apply the layout to the chart.

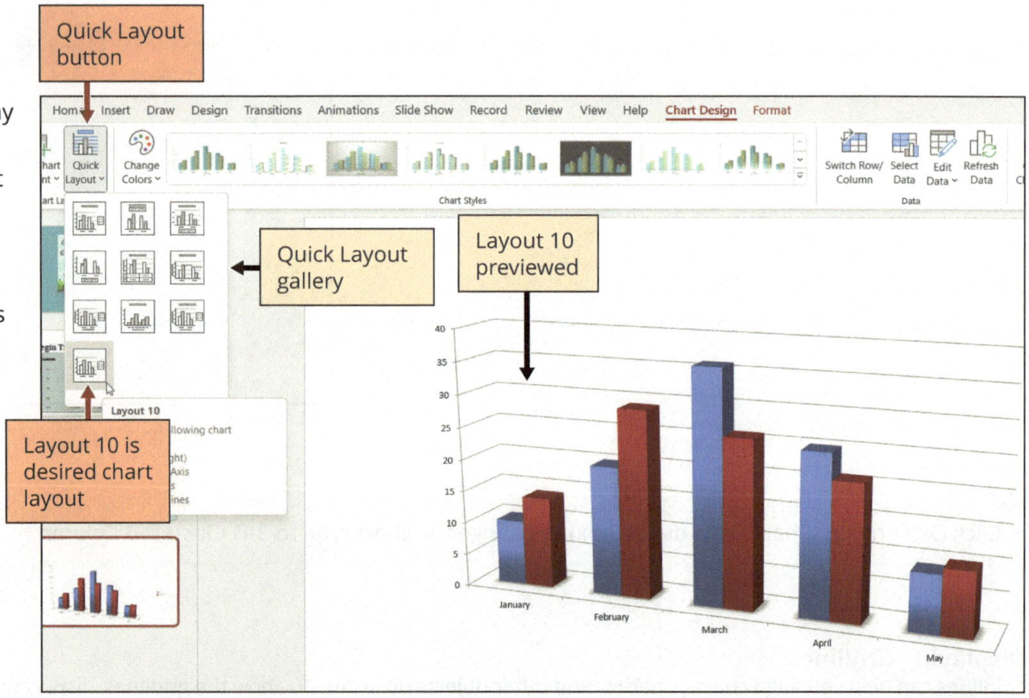

Figure 6–68

To Apply a Style to a Chart

The styles available in the Chart Styles gallery have a variety of colors and backgrounds and display in both 2-D and 3-D. The following steps apply a style to the chart. **Why?** You can modify the chart's appearance easily by selecting a predefined style.

1

- Click the Chart Styles button (paintbrush icon) on the right side of the chart area to display the Chart Styles gallery with the Style tab displayed.
- Scroll down until Style 11 (last style) is displayed in the Chart Styles gallery and then point to this style to see a live preview on Slide 4 (Figure 6–69).
- **Experiment:** Point to various chart styles and watch the layouts change.

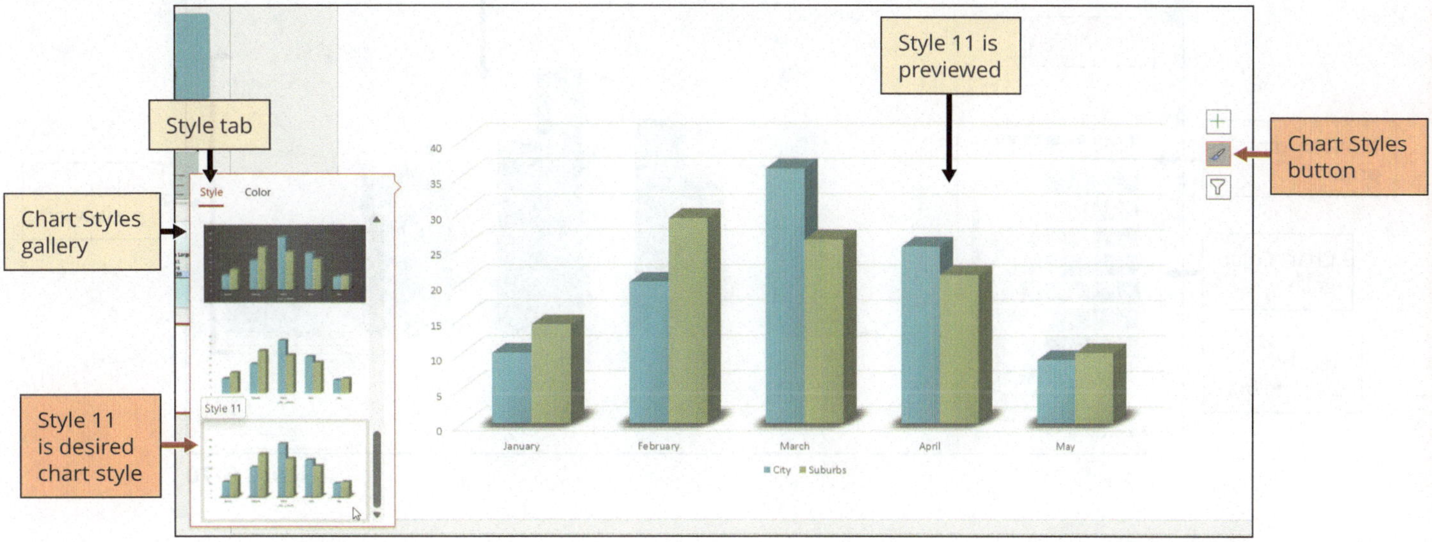

Figure 6–69

2

- Click Style 11 in the Chart Styles gallery to apply the chart style to the chart.

To Change Chart Colors

You can modify a chart's colors easily by selecting one of the color groups available in the Chart Color gallery. These colors are grouped into two categories: Colorful and Monochromatic. For a unique look, PowerPoint also allows you to create a custom color combination. The following steps change the chart colors. **Why?** The two columns' blue colors will coordinate with the blue hues displayed on the other slides in the presentation.

1

- With the Chart Styles gallery still displayed, click the Color tab at the top of the pane to display the Chart Color gallery.
- Scroll down and then point to 'Monochromatic Palette 8' (eighth row in the Monochromatic area) to display a live preview of the layout in the slide (Figure 6–70).
- **Experiment:** Point to various color groups and watch the chart colors change.

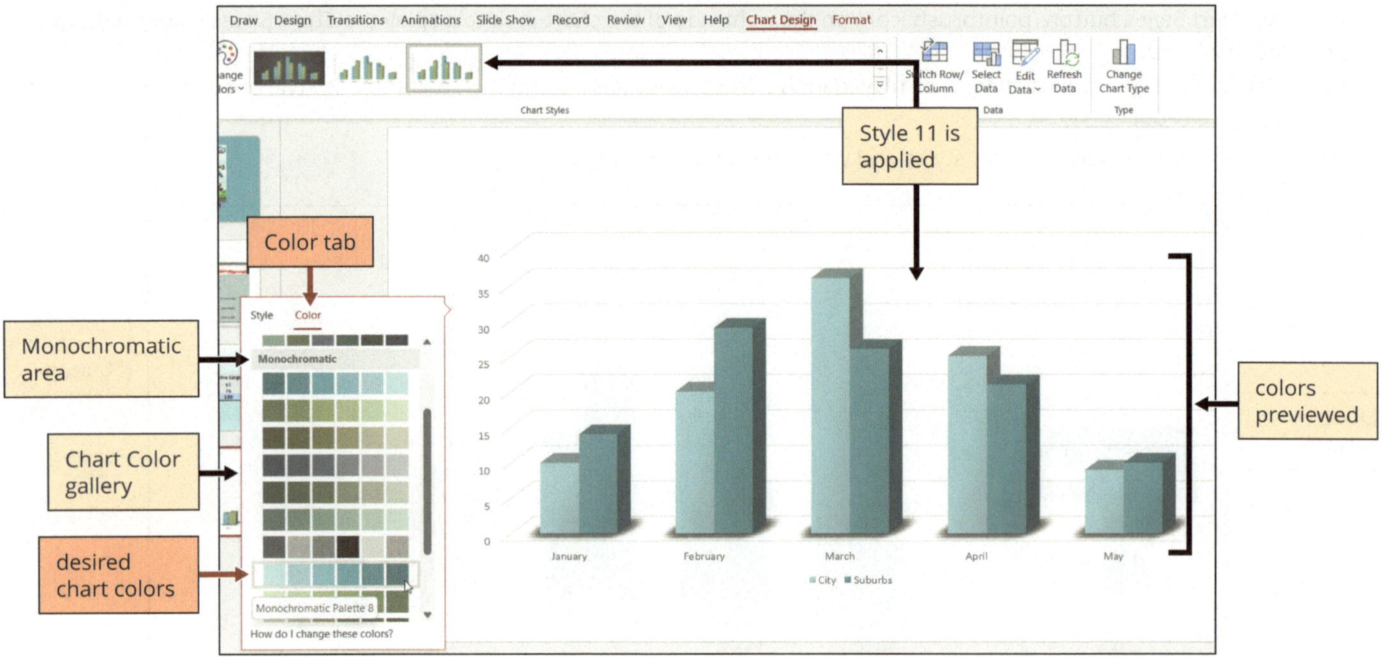

Figure 6–70

2

- Click 'Monochromatic Palette 8' to apply these colors to the chart.

Other Ways

1. Click Change Colors button (Chart Design tab | Chart Styles group)

To Add an Axis to a Chart

The legend below the chart identifies the colors assigned to each of the bars. You can modify the default legend in a variety of ways, including moving its location, changing the fill and outline, adding an effect, and changing the font. The Chart Elements button on the right side of the chart area allows you to display or hide a chart element. When you click this button, the Chart Elements pane is displayed. A check mark appears in the check box for each chart element that is displayed. You can check and uncheck each chart element to display or hide axes, the chart title, labels, gridlines, and the legend. The following steps display the axis titles and then format the text. **Why?** You want your audience to recognize that the y-axis represents the number of registrations and the x-axis represents each month.

1

- Click the Chart Elements button (plus sign icon) on the right side of the chart area to display the Chart Elements pane.
- Select the Axis Titles check box to display the two default titles for the x and y axes (Figure 6–71).

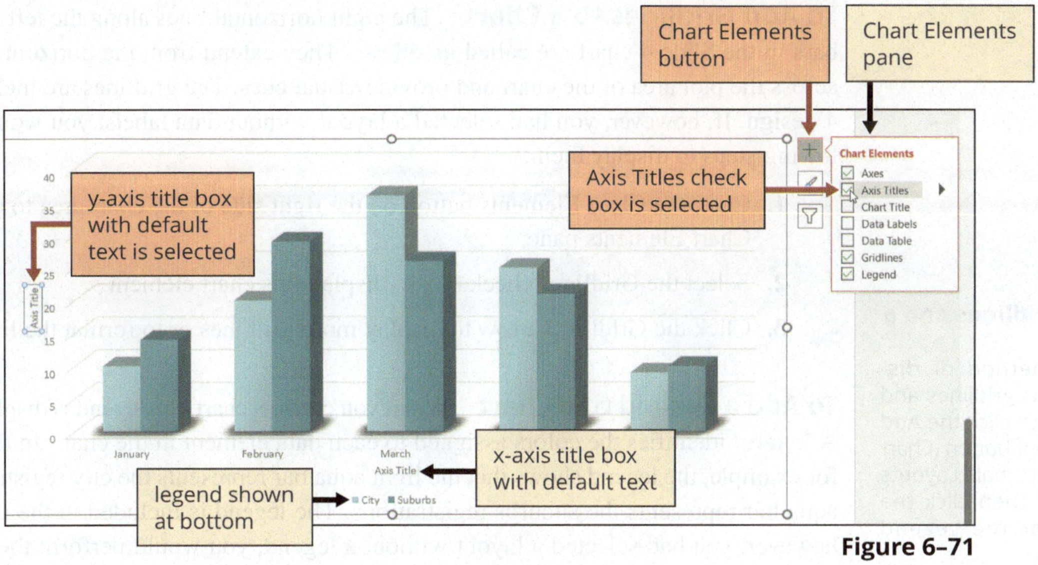

Figure 6–71

2

- With the default y-axis title box selected, type **Number of Registrations** in the text box.
- Select the text and then increase the font size to 18 point and bold the text.

3

- Click the x-axis title to select it and then type **Registrations Each Month** as the replacement text.
- Select the text and then increase the font size to 18 point and bold the text (Figure 6–72).

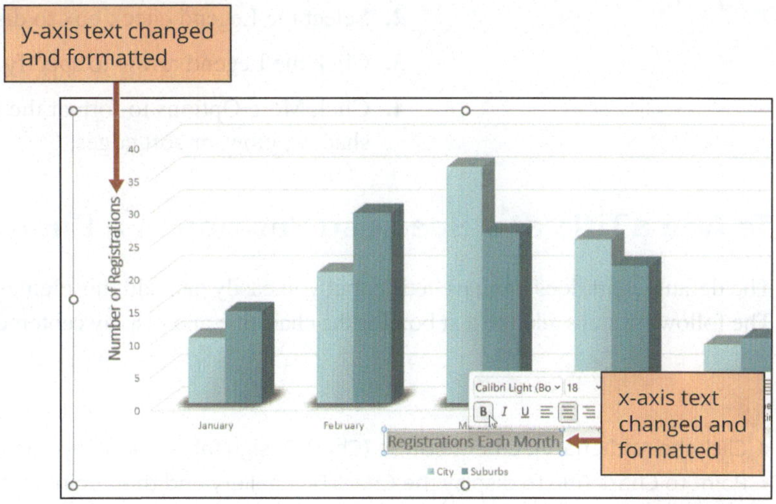

Figure 6–72

Other Ways

1. Click Add Chart Element button (Chart Design tab | Chart Layouts group), click Axis Titles

To Add Data Labels to a Chart The figures at the top of each bar in the Slide 4 chart are called **data labels**. They show the exact amount of average minutes the groups have exerted in each exercise Location. Data labels help audience members understand a chart's content by showing details about the data series. The data labels are included in the Layout 4 design. If, however, you had selected a layout without data labels, you would perform the following steps to display them.

1. Click the Chart Elements button on the right side of the chart area to display the Chart Elements pane.
2. Select the Data Labels check box to display the labels.
3. Click the Data Labels arrow to display more details or to format the labels.

Other Ways

1. Click Add Chart Element button (Chart Design tab | Chart Layouts group), click Data Labels

BTW

Embedding Fonts

If you plan to show your presentation using a computer other than yours, consider embedding the fonts to ensure that the fonts on your slides will be available. To embed the fonts, display the Save As dialog box, click the Tools button, click Save Options, select the 'Embed fonts in the file' check box in the 'Preserve fidelity when sharing this presentation' area (PowerPoint Options dialog box), and then click the OK and Save buttons.

To Add Gridlines to a Chart The eight horizontal lines along the left side and behind the bars in the Slide 4 chart are called **gridlines**. They extend from the horizontal and vertical axes across the plot area of the chart and provide visual cues. The gridlines are included in the Layout 4 design. If, however, you had selected a layout without data labels, you would perform the following steps to display them.

1. Click the Chart Elements button on the right side of the chart area to display the Chart Elements pane.
2. Select the Gridlines check box to display this chart element.
3. Click the Gridlines arrow to display more gridlines or to format the lines.

BTW

Adding Gridlines and a Legend

Another method of displaying chart gridlines and a legend is to click the Add Chart Element button (Chart Design tab | Chart Layouts group) and then click the Gridlines or the Legend button.

To Add a Legend to a Chart When you create a chart, the legend is displayed automatically. A **legend** identifies the colors assigned to each data element in the chart. In the chart on Slide 4, for example, the legend shows that the light aqua bar represents the city registrations and the dark aqua bar represents the suburbs registrations. The legend is included in the Layout 4 design. If, however, you had selected a layout without a legend, you would perform the following steps to display this chart element.

1. Click the Chart Elements button on the right side of the chart area to display the Chart Elements pane.
2. Select the Legend check box to display this chart element.
3. Click the Legend arrow to specify where the legend should appear.
4. Click More Options to format the legend by adding borders; a fill; and effects such as a shadow, glow, or soft edges.

To Add a Title at a Specified Position in a Chart

The default chart does not have a title, but you easily can add this element and specify where you want it to appear on the slide. The following steps add the text box for the chart title and display centered above the March registrations. Why? A title on Slide 4 would help audience members recognize the purpose of presenting this information.

1

- Click the Add Chart Element button (Chart Design tab | Chart Layouts group) to display the Add Chart Element menu.
- Point to Chart Title to display the Chart Title gallery and then point to Above Chart in the gallery (Figure 6–73).

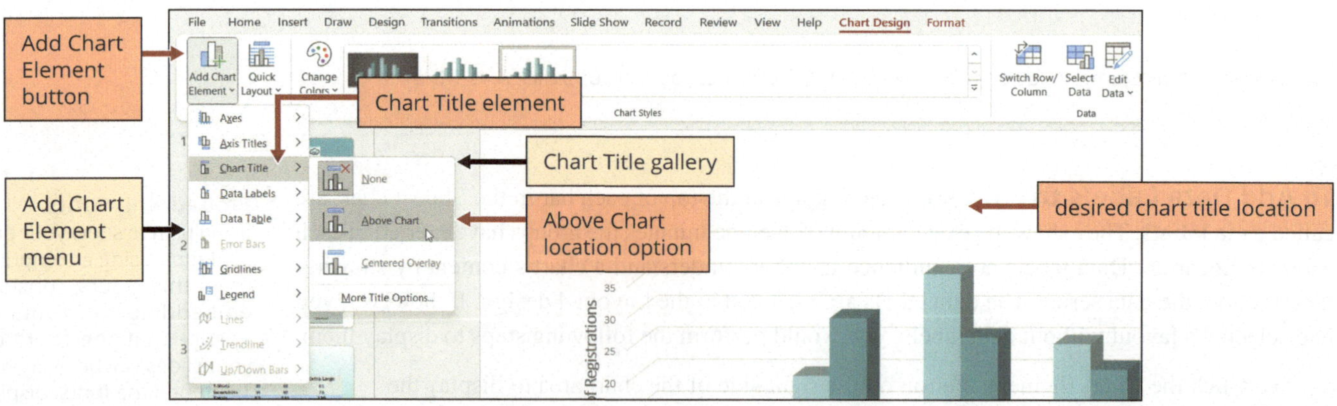

Figure 6–73

2

- Click Above Chart to display the default chart title.
- Type **Regional Registrations** as the chart title replacement text.
- Select the text and then increase the font size to 32 point (Figure 6–74).

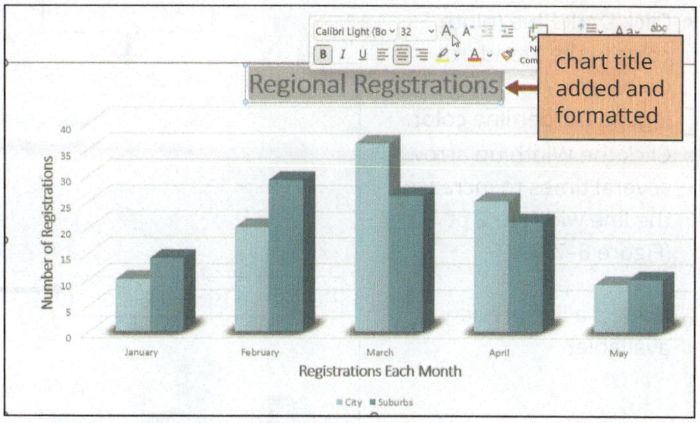

Figure 6–74

Other Ways

1. Click Chart Elements button on right side of chart, click Chart Title check box to select it, click Chart Title arrow

To Add a Border to a Chart Element

You can modify chart elements in a variety of ways, including adding borders and changing the border color. The following steps add a border to the chart title and then change the color and width. **Why?** Adding a border will call attention to the title text and help audience members understand the chart's purpose.

1

- With the chart title still selected, right-click to display the shortcut menu (Figure 6–75).

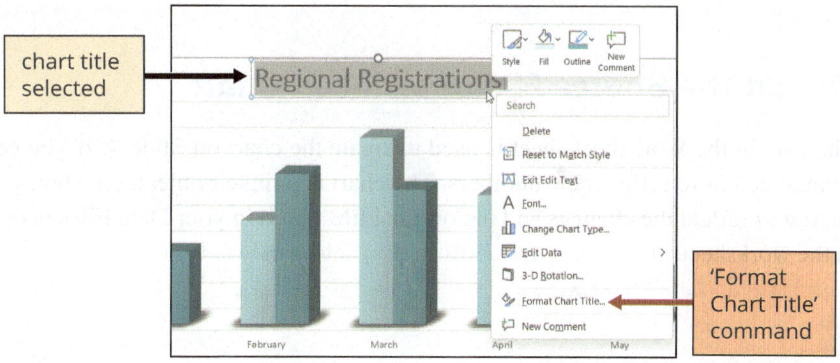

Figure 6–75

2

- Click 'Format Chart Title' to display the 'Format Chart Title' pane. If necessary, click the 'Fill & Line' button and then, if necessary, click Border to display the Border area. Scroll down to display the entire Border area.
- Click Solid line and then click the Color button to display the Color gallery (Figure 6–76).

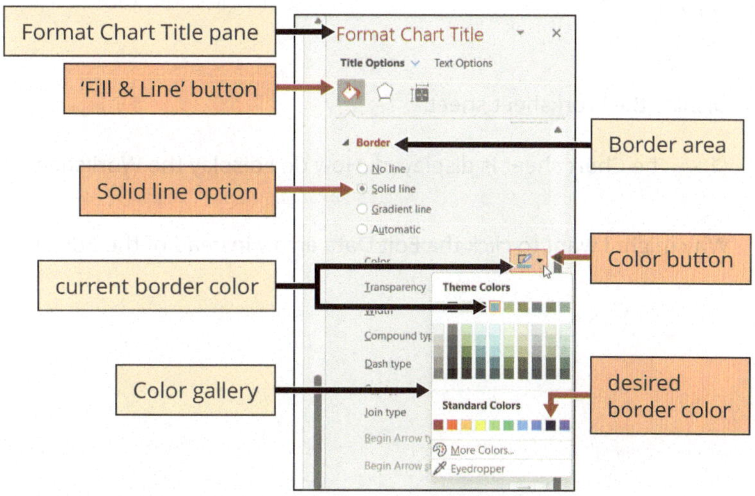

Figure 6–76

3

- Click Dark Blue (ninth color in the Standard Colors row) to change the legend border line color.
- Click the Width up arrow several times to increase the line width to 2 pt (Figure 6–77).

Q&A Is a live preview available?

No, this feature is not offered.

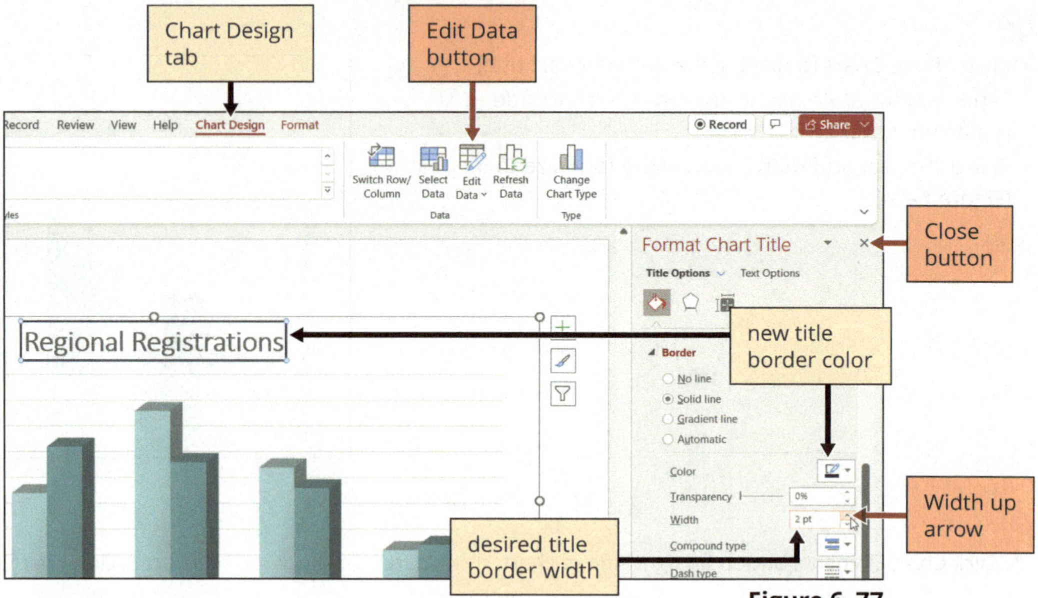

Figure 6–77

4

- Click Close ('Format Chart Title' pane).

Other Ways

1. Click Chart Elements button on right side of chart, click Chart Title, click Chart Title arrow, click More Options, click Solid Line, choose color

To Edit the Source File of a Linked Chart

The data in the Worksheet sheet is used to create the chart on Slide 4. If you edit this data, the corresponding bars in the chart change height to reflect new numbers. The chart is a linked object, so when you modify the data and close the worksheet, the chart will reflect the changes and the original file stored in your Data Files also will change. The following steps edit three cells in the worksheet. **Why?** Fun Run registrations have increased since the last time the worksheet was saved, so you need to update your chart and the Excel worksheet with this information.

1

- With the Chart Design tab displayed, click the Edit Data button (Chart Design tab | Data group) (shown in Figure 6–77) to display Excel.

Q&A I see a message that the data wasn't available because the worksheet was open in another application. What should I do?

Save and close the Excel worksheet and try again.

- Display the Worksheet sheet.

Q&A The Chart sheet is displayed. How do I display the Worksheet sheet?

Click the Worksheet tab at the bottom of the worksheet.

Why might I want to click the Edit Data arrow instead of the Edit Data button?

You would be given the option to run Microsoft Excel and then edit the worksheet using that app. More options would be available using Excel. If you simply need to edit data, you can perform that task easily using PowerPoint.

2

- Click cell B2 (city registrations in January) to make cell B2 the active cell (Figure 6–78).

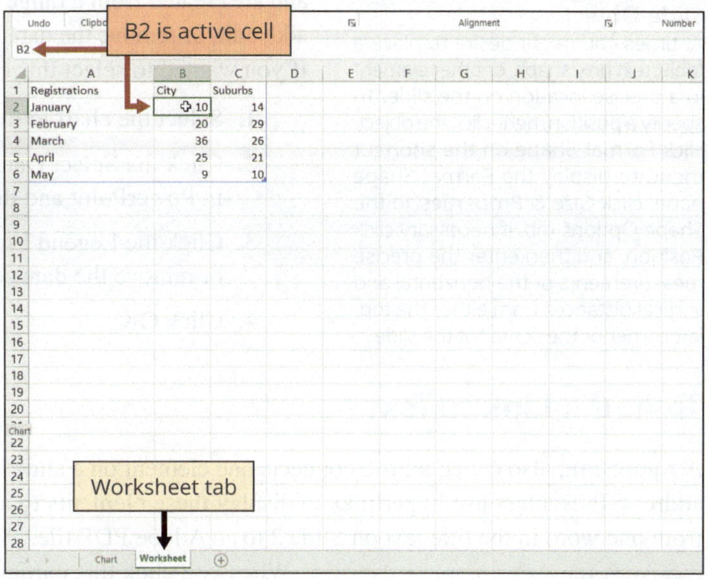

Figure 6–78

3

- Type **19** as the replacement number and then press DOWN ARROW to make cell B3 (city registrations in February) the active cell.
- Type **24** as the replacement number and then press RIGHT ARROW to make cell C3 (suburbs registrations in February) the active cell.
- Type **32** as the replacement number and then press DOWN ARROW to make cell C4 (suburbs registrations in March) the active cell.
- Type **34** as the replacement number and then press ENTER (Figure 6–79).

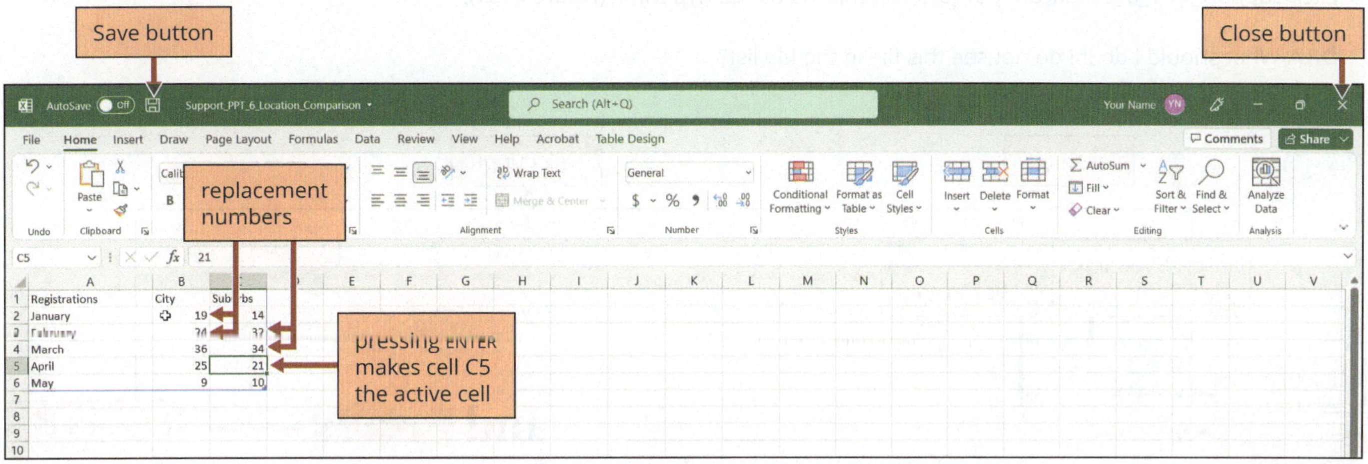

Figure 6–79

4

- If necessary, click Save on the spreadsheet toolbar to save the data to the Excel spreadsheet.
- Click Close on the spreadsheet to close the window and view the updated PowerPoint chart (Figure 6–80).

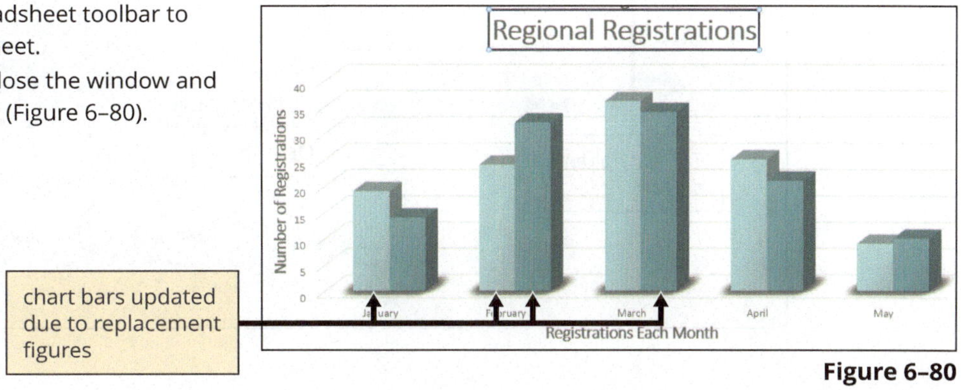

Figure 6–80

BTW

Positioning a Chart or Other Slide Object

At times you might desire to place a table, text box, shape, or other element in a precise location on the slide. To specify a position, right-click the object, click Format Shape on the shortcut menu to display the Format Shape pane, click 'Size & Properties' in the Shape Options tab, if necessary click Position, and then enter the precise measurements of the horizontal and vertical distances from either the top-left corner or the center of the slide.

To Select Chart Data Charts always are associated with an Excel-based worksheet and are created from a range of data in a row or column, called a data series. If you want to add, edit, or remove the data used to develop the chart, you need to select a new data series. If you wanted to select this chart data, you would perform the following steps.

1. Select the chart to display the Chart Design tab.
2. Click the Select Data button (Chart Design tab | Data group) to display the chart in PowerPoint and display the 'Select Data Source' dialog box.
3. Click the Legend Entries or the Horizontal Axis Labels check boxes to add, edit, or remove the data series in the chart.
4. Click OK.

To Add a Link to Text

A **hyperlink**, also called a **link**, connects one element on a slide to another slide, presentation, picture, file, webpage, or email address. Presenters use hyperlinks to display these elements to an audience. In this presentation, you will create a hyperlink from one word in the title text on Slide 2 to an Adobe PDF file. **Why?** You want to show your audience the certificate they will receive when they complete their run. When you click this particular word during a slide show, Adobe Acrobat starts and then opens this PDF file. The following steps hyperlink title text to a PDF file.

1

- Display Slide 2 and then select the word, Prizes, in the title.
- Display the Insert tab and then click the Link button (Insert tab | Links group) to display the Insert Hyperlink dialog box.
- If necessary, click the 'Existing File or Web Page' button in the Link to area.
- If necessary, click the Current Folder button in the Look in area and navigate to the location where your Data Files are stored.
- Click Support_PPT_6_Certificate.pdf to select this file as the hyperlink (Figure 6–81).

Q&A What should I do if I do not see this file in the file list?

Click the file type arrow ('Link to File' dialog box) to display the file types and then click 'All Files (*.*)' in the list.

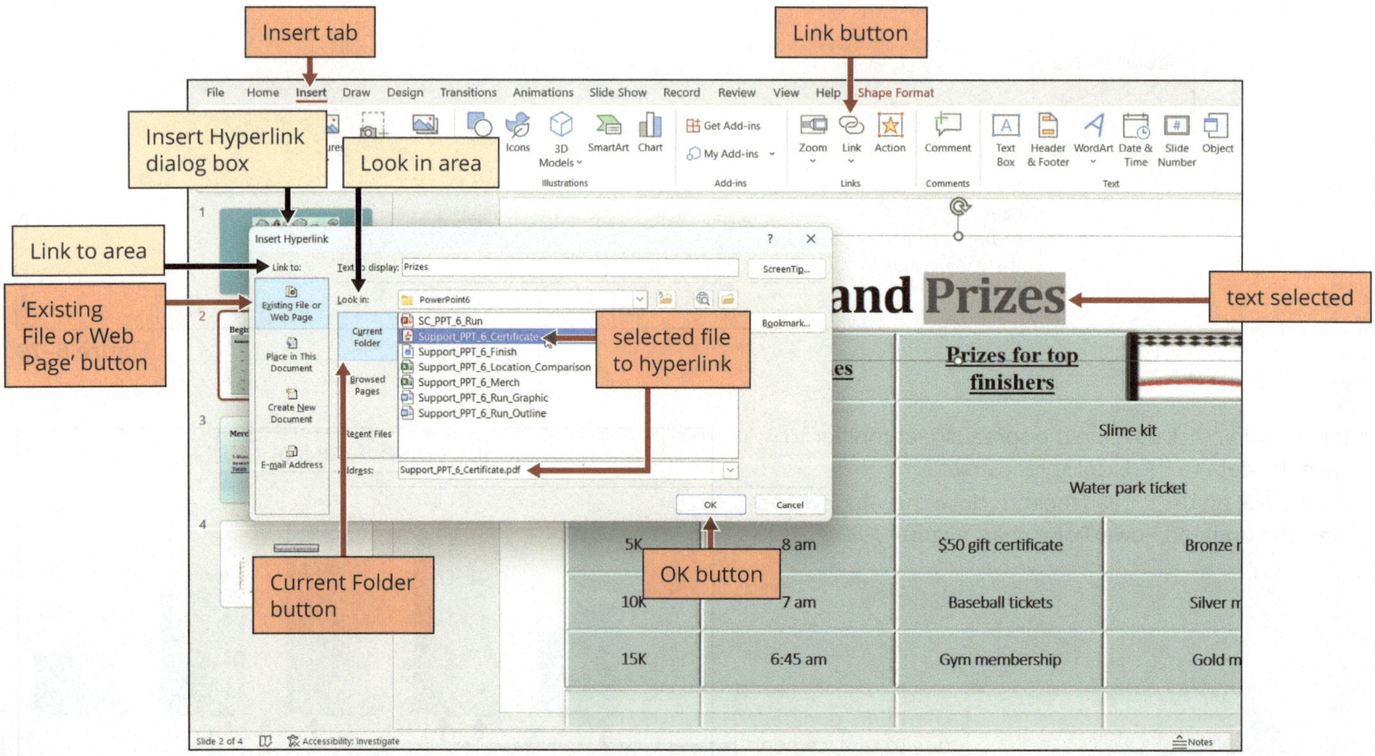

Figure 6–81

2

- Click OK (Insert Hyperlink dialog box) to insert the hyperlink.

Q&A How do I remove a hyperlink?
Select the text, click the Hyperlink button (Insert tab | Links group), and then click Remove Link (Edit Hyperlink dialog box).

Changing Views

You have been using Normal view to create and edit your slides. Once you completed your slides in projects for previous modules, you reviewed the final products by displaying each slide in Slide Show view, which occupies the full computer screen. You were able to view how the transitions, graphics, and effects will display in an actual presentation before an audience.

PowerPoint has other views to help review a presentation for content, organization, and overall appearance. **Reading view** is similar to Slide Show view because each slide displays individually, but the slides do not fill the entire screen. Using this view, you easily can progress through the slides forward or backward with simple controls at the bottom of the window. Switching between Slide Sorter, Reading, and Normal views helps you review your presentation, assess whether the slides have an attractive design and adequate content, and make sure they are organized for the most impact. After reviewing the slides, you can change the view to Normal so that you may continue working on the presentation.

You also can display your presentation in **Outline view** to show the titles and main text from each slide. Each title is displayed on the left side of the pane along with a slide icon and slide number. A slide without a title has no text displayed on the right side of the slide number. You can create a presentation in Outline view by typing or copying text.

To Navigate between Slides in Reading View

The following steps change the view from Normal view to Reading view and back to Normal view. **Why?** You want to use Reading view to display all the slides in the presentation in a full screen.

1

- Display Slide 1 and then click the Reading View button on the status bar to display Slide 1 of the presentation in Reading view (Figure 6–82).

Figure 6–82

2

- Click the Next button three times to advance through the presentation.
- Click the Previous button three times to display Slide 3, Slide 2, and then Slide 1.
- Click the Menu button to display commonly used commands (Figure 6–83).

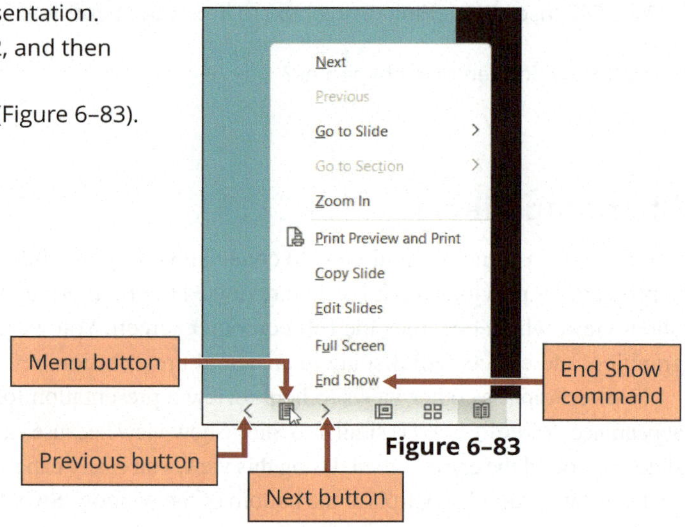

Figure 6–83

3

- Click End Show to return to Normal view, which is the view you were using before Reading view.

To Switch to Outline View

The following step changes the view from Normal view to Outline view. **Why?** You can review the text on your slides without seeing any graphical items.

1

- With Slide 1 displayed, click the View tab and then click the Outline View button (View tab | Presentation Views group) (Figure 6–84).
- If you see a Microsoft PowerPoint dialog box stating, 'Real-time editing is not supported in outline view', click OK to close the dialog box.

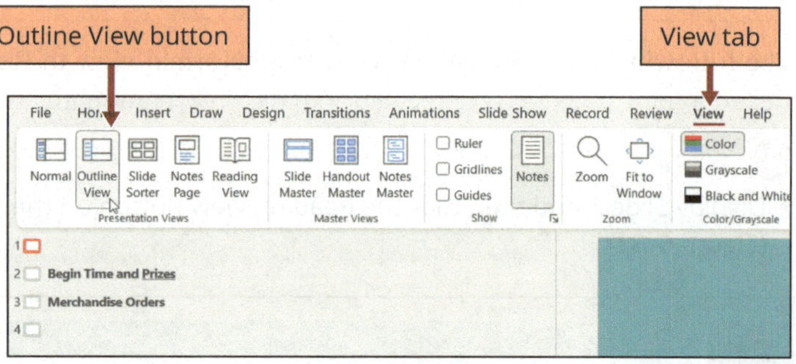

Figure 6–84

To Navigate between Slides in Outline View

The following steps display all four slides in Outline view. **Why?** Using Outline view, you can click a slide icon to display any slide.

1

- Click the Slide 2 icon to select that slide (Figure 6–85).

2

- Press DOWN ARROW to navigate to Slide 3.
- Press DOWN ARROW again to navigate to Slide 4.

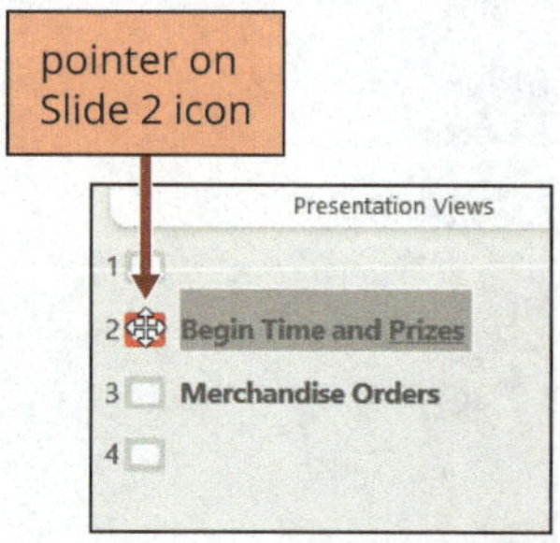

Figure 6–85

To Move a Slide in Outline View

The following steps reverse the order of Slides 2 and 3. **Why?** You desire to change the slide order, which you can do easily in Outline view by dragging the slide icon to the desired location.

1

- Click the Slide 2 icon and then drag the pointer downward between the Slides 3 and 4 icons (Figure 6–86).

2

- Release the mouse to move Slide 2 so that it becomes the new Slide 3.

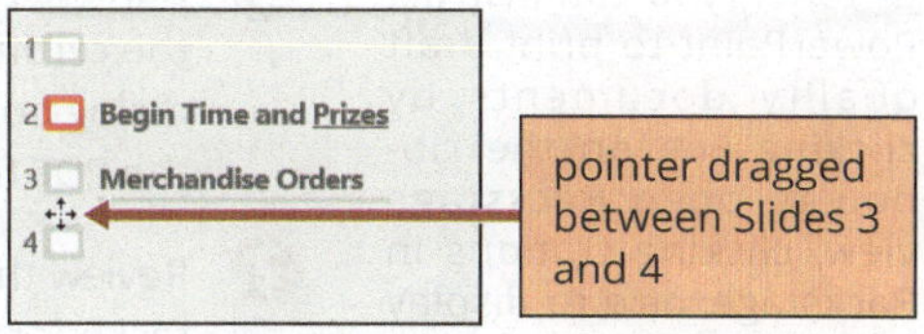

Figure 6–86

To Enter Text in Outline View

The following steps edit the Slide 3 title text in Outline view. **Why?** You decide that the words, Start Times, rather than Begin Time should match the second column title text in the table.

1

- With Slide 3 displayed in Outline view, select the words, Begin Time, and then type **Start Times** as the replacement text (Figure 6–87).

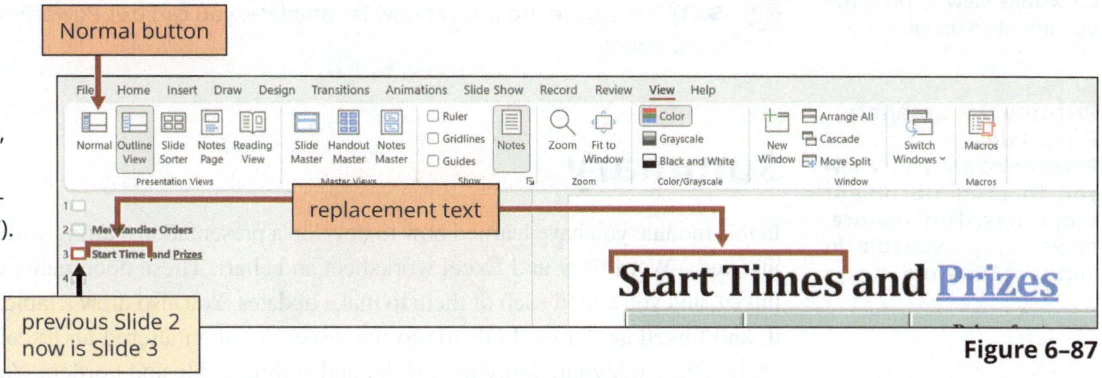

Figure 6–87

2

- Click the Normal button (View tab | Presentation Views group) (shown in Figure 6–87) to display the slides in Normal view.

Other Ways

1. Click Normal view button on status bar

To Add a Transition between Slides

The final enhancements you will make in this presentation are to apply a transition, change the transition effect option, and change the transition speed. The following steps apply these transition effects to the presentation.

1. Apply the Clock transition in the Exciting category to all slides.
2. Change the effect option to Wedge.
3. Change the transition duration to 03.00 seconds.

BTW

Distributing a Document

Instead of printing and distributing a hard copy of PowerPoint slides, you can distribute the slides electronically. Options include sending the slides via email; posting it on cloud storage (such as OneDrive) and sharing the link with others; posting it on social media, a blog, or other website; and sharing a link associated with an online location of the slides. You also can create and share a PDF or XPS image of the slides, so that users can view the file in Acrobat Reader or XPS Viewer instead of in PowerPoint.

To Run, Print, Save, and Exit PowerPoint

The presentation now is complete. You should run the presentation, view the hyperlinked file, print the slides, save the presentation, and then exit PowerPoint.

1. Run the Run presentation. When Slide 3 is displayed, click Prizes in the title text to display the certificate document as the hyperlinked file. If the Microsoft PowerPoint Security Notice dialog box is displayed, click Yes, then click OK in the Microsoft Office dialog box, to open the PDF file.
2. Review the contents of the certificate document. Point to the PowerPoint app button on the taskbar to see the PowerPoint window and a live preview of Slide 3.
3. Click the thumbnail of Slide 3 to display that slide and then display Slide 4.
4. End the slide show. Close the certificate document.
5. Print the Run presentation as a handout with two slides per page.
6. Save the Run presentation again with the same file name.
7. Because the project now is complete, you can exit PowerPoint, closing all open documents.

BTW
Conserving Ink and Toner
If you want to conserve ink or toner, you can instruct PowerPoint to print draft quality documents by clicking File on the ribbon to open Backstage view, clicking Options in Backstage view to display the PowerPoint Options dialog box, clicking Advanced in the left pane (PowerPoint Options dialog box), scrolling to the Print area in the right pane, verifying there is no check mark in the High quality check box, and then clicking OK. Then, use Backstage view to print the document as usual.

BTW
Printing Document Properties
PowerPoint does not allow you to print document properties. This feature, however, is available in Microsoft 365 Word.

Summary

In this module you have learned how to develop a presentation starting with a Word outline. You then inserted a Word flyer and Excel worksheet and chart. These documents were either embedded or linked, and you edited each of them to make updates. You also drew a table, enhanced and formatted it, and linked an Adobe PDF file to the table. You then altered an Excel object by changing the chart type and layout, applying a style, and adding a title and borders. You reviewed the slides by changing views and then moved a slide and edited text in Outline view.

Consider This: Plan Ahead

What decisions will you need to make when creating your next presentation?

Use these guidelines as you complete the assignments in this module and create your own slide show decks outside of this class.

1. **Use powerful words to accompany the text on your slides.** The slides are meant to enhance your talk by clarifying main points and calling attention to key ideas. Your speech should use words that explain and substantiate your visuals.
2. **Develop tables that are clear and meaningful.** Tables are extremely useful vehicles for presenting complex relationships. Their design plays an important part in successfully conveying the information to the audience.
3. **Use appropriate colors when formatting graphics you want people to remember.** Numerous studies have shown that appropriate graphics help audiences comprehend and remember the information presented during a speech. Color has been shown to increase retention by as much as 80 percent. When choosing colors for your graphics, use hues that fit the tone and objective of your message.

Student Assignments

Apply Your Knowledge

Reinforce the skills and apply the concepts you learned in this module.

Inserting Slides from an Outline, Adding a Link, and Inserting and Formatting a Table and Chart

Note: To complete this assignment, you will be required to use the Data Files. Please contact your instructor for information about accessing the Data Files.

Instructions: Start PowerPoint and create a blank presentation.

The nature center in your town has a birding club with more than 100 members. The club promotes birding through many activities, including nature walks, bird counts, and various contests. Community residents often contact club members to ask about which feeders are appropriate to attract particular types of birds, so the club president is preparing a presentation to describe various types of feeders and also to display the results of a recent bird count event. In addition, the club wants to promote its birdhouse building event. The president has given you a Word document with topics to cover in the presentation and has supplied an Excel file that includes a chart showing the number of four common birds that visited feeders during a recent weekend. You also have a PDF file promoting the Birdhouse Building Challenge event. You will create the three slides shown in Figure 6–88.

Perform the following tasks:

1. Apply the Frame theme and then use the Slides from Outline feature to insert slides from the Word outline, Support_PPT_6_Feeder_Outline.docx, which is located in the Data Files. Delete Slide 1.
2. Change the new Slide 1 layout to Title Slide and then increase the title text font size to 72 point and the subtitle text font size to 40 point.
3. Add a link from the subtitle text to the file named Support_PPT_6_Challenge.pdf, which is located in the Data Files. Change the subtitle text color to Purple (last color in the Standard Colors row).
4. Insert the picture Support_PPT_6_Birdhouse.png, change the height to 7.5", and then move the photo to the right side of the slide, as shown in Figure 6–88a.

   If requested by your instructor, change the words, Your Yard, in the title text placeholder to the city where you were born.
5. Display Slide 2, delete the content placeholder, and then draw the table shown in Figure 6–88b. Size the table with a height of 6" and a width of 9" and then move it to the right of the title text placeholder. Merge or split cells as necessary and add the table text as shown in Figure 6–88b.
6. Apply the 'Medium Style 4 – Accent 1' table style (second style in the fourth Medium row). Apply the 'Linear Diagonal – Bottom Right to Top Left' shading gradient (last gradient in the third Variations row). Apply the 'Perspective: Lower Left' shadow effect (first shadow in the last Perspective row). Add borders to all table cells.
7. Increase the font size of the table column headings (Bird and Type of Feeder) to 32 point and then, if necessary, bold this text and change the font color to Purple. Increase the font size of the four bird rows to 28 point.
8. Align all the table text in the center of the table cells. Distribute the table rows. Align the table to the right and the middle of the slide.
9. Display Slide 3 and then delete the content placeholder. Open the Excel file called Support_PPT_6_Feeder_Counts.xlsx, which is located in the Data Files, and then copy the bar chart located on the Chart sheet. Paste the chart onto Slide 3 with the 'Use Destination Theme & Link Data' option and then resize the chart height to 6" and the width to 9.5". Align the chart in the right and the middle of the slide.
10. Close Excel.

Continued on next page

11. Change the chart style to Style 16.
12. Click the Edit Data button (Chart Design tab | Data group) to display Excel and then, if necessary, click the Worksheet tab to display the worksheet. Change the House Finch figure in cell B2 from 38 to 67, as shown in Figure 6–88c. Save and close the worksheet.
13. Save the presentation using the file name, **SC_PPT_6_Birding**.
14. Submit the presentation in the format specified by your instructor.
15. **Consider This:** Did the formatting and effects enhance the Slide 2 table? What other enhancements could you have made to improve the table? In Step 11, you changed the chart style to Style 16. Was this style a good choice? Why or why not?

Clker-Free-Vector-Images/Pixabay

Figure 6–88(a): Slide 1

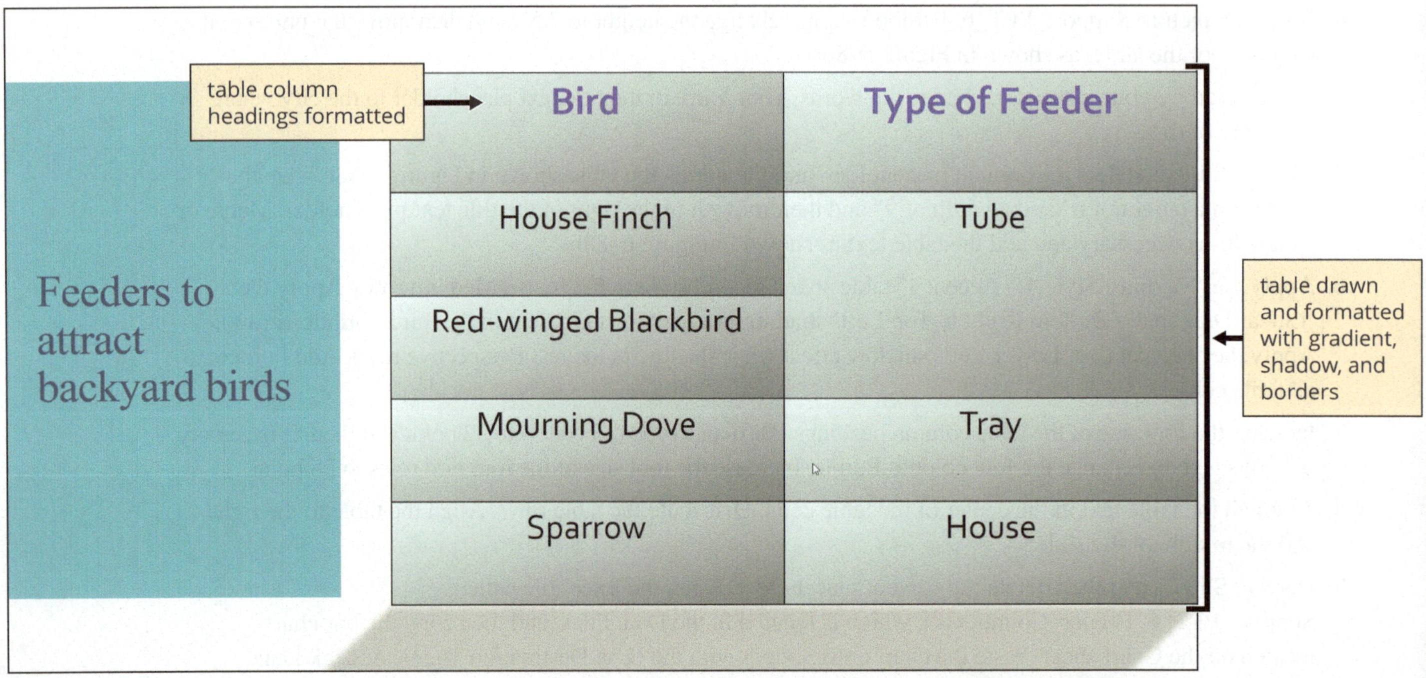

Figure 6–88(b): Slide 2

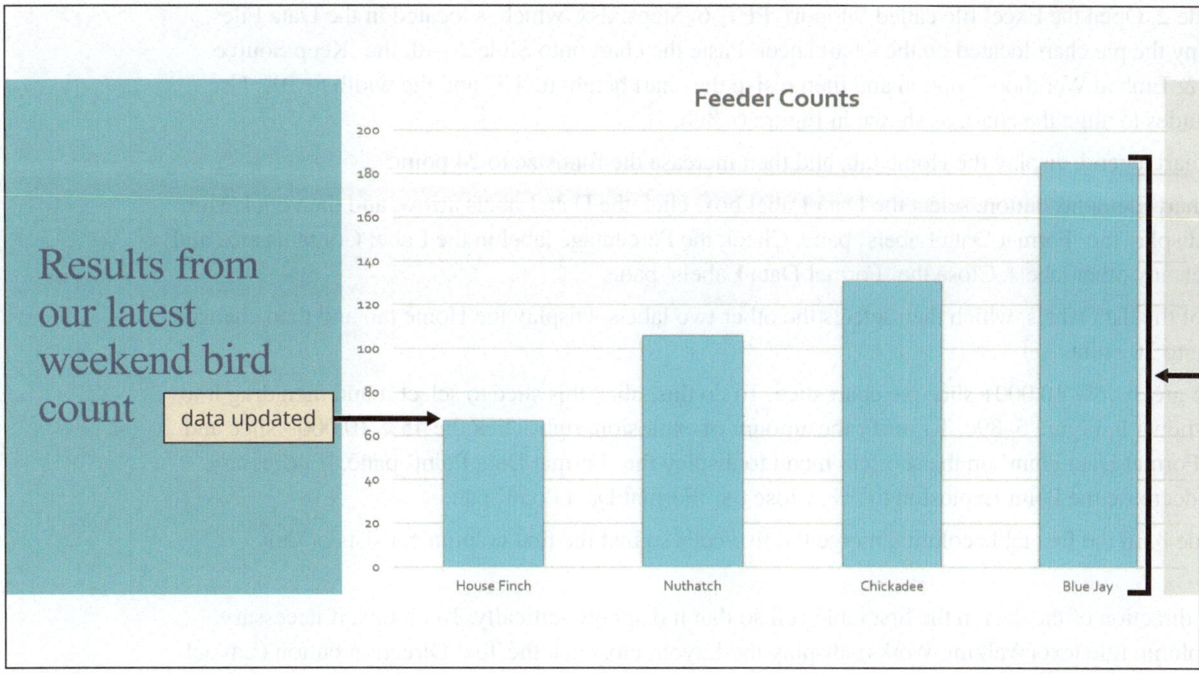

Figure 6–88(c): Slide 3

Extend Your Knowledge

Extend the skills you learned in this module and experiment with new skills. You may need to use Help to complete the assignment.

Modifying a Word Document, Excel Pie Chart, and Table

Note: To complete this assignment, you will be required to use the Data Files. Please contact your instructor for information about accessing the Data Files.

Instructions: Start PowerPoint. Open the presentation called SC_PPT_6-1.pptx, which is located in the Data Files.

Going for a walk is one of the most beneficial activities people can take. This form of exercise improves fitness and well-being, and its many health benefits include working arm, leg, and shoulder muscles, easing stress, and strengthening the heart and lungs. Studies indicate that walking in nature is particularly effective. Students at your school participate in a walking group, and they encourage members to log their steps, often exceeding 10,000 steps per outing. These facts are applied in the slides you will create in this assignment. You will insert and format a Word object, copy and modify an Excel pie chart, and format a table.

Perform the following tasks:

1. On Slide 1, display the Design tab and then click the Format Background button (Design tab | Customize group) to display the Format Background pane.
2. Click Gradient fill and then click the Color button in the Fill area to display the Color gallery. Click Light Blue (seventh color in Standard Colors row) to change the gradient color.
3. In the Position box, located below the Color button, change the Position setting to 30%. Close the Format Background pane.
4. Insert the Word object, Support_PPT_6_Walk.docx, which is located in the Data Files. Display the Shape Format tab and then click the Size Dialog Box Launcher to display the Format Object pane. Click the 'Lock aspect ratio' check box to uncheck it and then increase the Word object size height to 6" and the width to 13".
5. Change the text, Let's Walk, to Let's Take a Walk in the title. (You may need to scroll up in the Word object to display the title text.)
6. Click outside the Word object and then close the Format Object pane. Align the object in the center and middle of the slide (Figure 6–89a).

Continued on next page

7. Display Slide 2. Open the Excel file called Support_PPT_6_Steps.xlsx, which is located in the Data Files, and then copy the pie chart located on the Chart sheet. Paste the chart onto Slide 2 with the 'Keep Source Formatting & Embed Workbook' option and then resize the chart height to 5.5" and the width to 10". Use the smart guides to align the chart, as shown in Figure 6–89b.
8. Select the chart legend, display the Home tab, and then increase the font size to 24 point.
9. Click the Chart Elements button, select the Data Label box, click the Data Labels arrow, and then click More Options to display the 'Format Data Labels' pane. Check the Percentage label in the Label Contains area and then uncheck any other labels. Close the 'Format Data Labels' pane.
10. Select one of the data labels, which then selects the other two labels. Display the Home tab and then change the font size to 20 point.
11. Explode the green 45% 10,000+ slice pie chart slice. To do this, click this slice to select it and then drag it to the left, as shown in Figure 6–89c. To verify the amount of explosion, right-click the 45% 10,000+ slice and then click 'Format Data Point' on the shortcut menu to display the 'Format Data Point' pane. If necessary, increase or decrease the Point Explosion to 5%. Close the 'Format Data Point' pane.
12. Display Slide 3. In the first table column, merge the five cells so that the first column consists of only one cell.
13. Change the direction of the data in the first table cell so that it displays vertically. To do this, if necessary, select the column title text (Walking Works), display the Layout tab, click the Text Direction button (Layout tab | Alignment group) to display the Text Direction gallery, and then click 'Rotate all text 270°' to rotate the text in the cell. Change the font size to 28 point and then center this text.
14. Change the first column cell size width to 1.5" and the second column cell size width to 2". Change the table height to 4" and the table width to 10.5" and then align the table in the center and middle of the slide (Figure 6–89d).

    If requested by your instructor, add the name of your high school mascot in the first column.
15. Save the presentation using the file name, **SC_PPT_6_Walk**.
16. Submit the revised document in the format specified by your instructor.
17. **Consider This:** In this assignment, you modified the gradient and edited a Word document. You also exploded a pie chart slice. Did these changes enhance the slides and increase the audience's understanding of the benefits of walking? Why or why not?

Figure 6–89(a): Slide 1

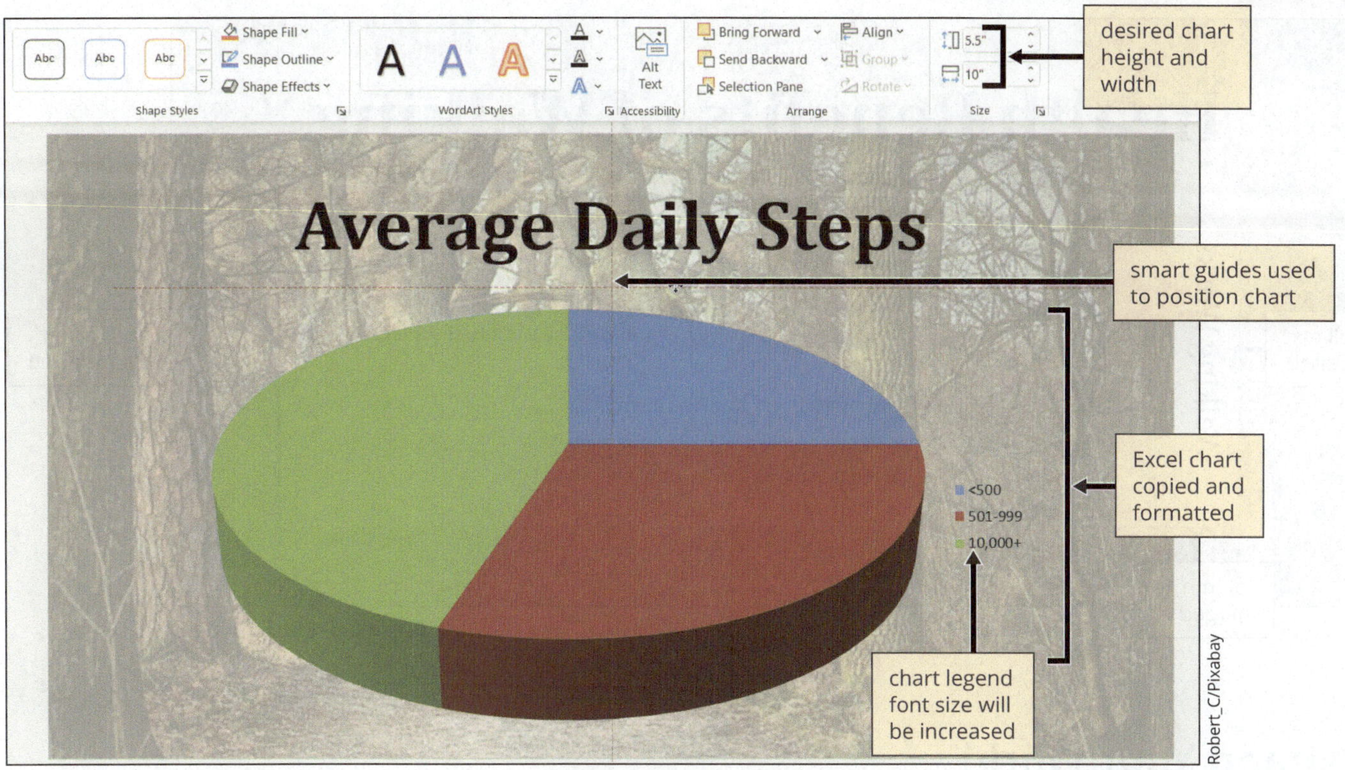

Figure 6–89(b): Slide 2 Chart Positioned with Smart Guides

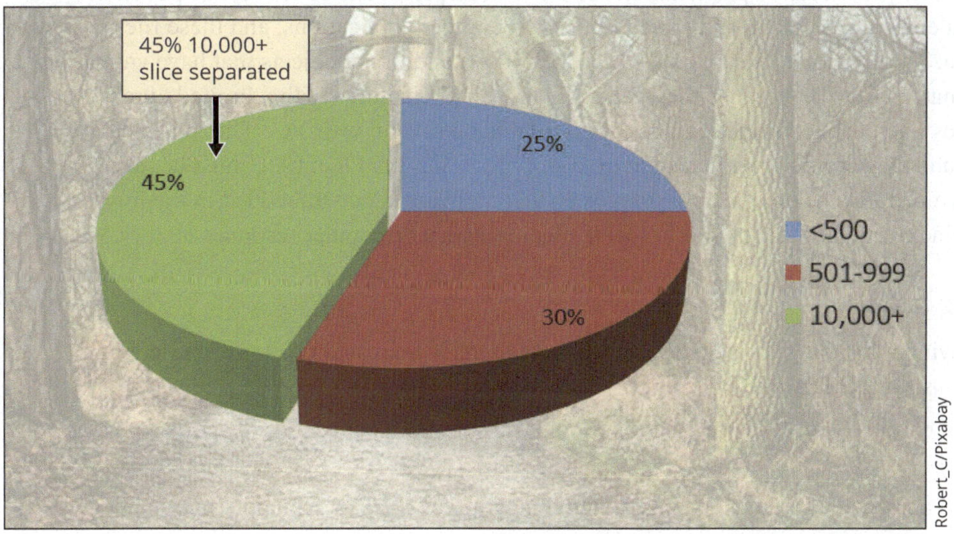

Figure 6–89(c): Slide 2 Pie Slice Exploded

Continued on next page

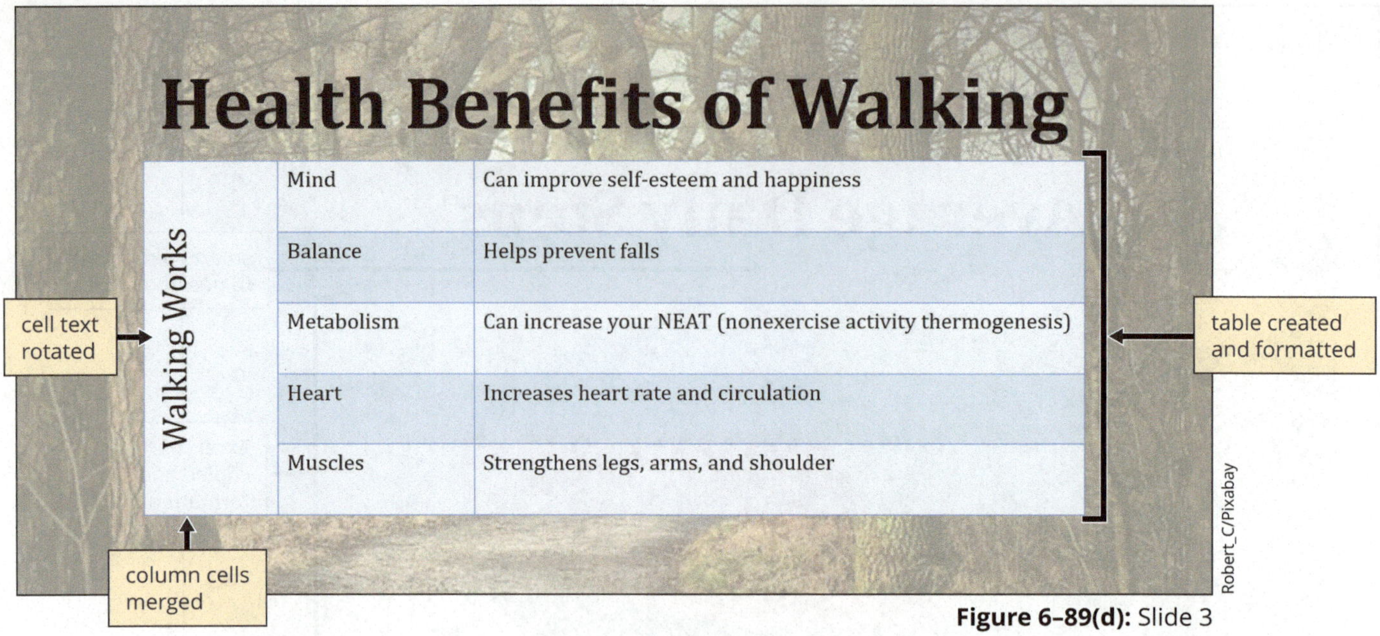

Figure 6–89(d): Slide 3

Expand Your World

Create a solution that uses cloud or web technologies by learning and investigating on your own from general guidance.

Locating and Inserting Animated GIF Files

Instructions: In this module, you created a presentation for the fun run promoters to encourage people to register for the event. You embedded, linked, and edited objects from other applications, and these files greatly enhanced the presentation. The promoters now would like you to insert additional objects that have animation. You decide to locate animated GIF files because they generally are simple pictures with a limited number of colors. GIF, or Graphics Interchange Format, images are available on several websites. The images may or may not be animated, and they can be downloaded at no cost or for a minimal fee. Care must be taken, however, to visit and download files from reputable sources so that malware is not embedded in the images. You can use a search engine or another search tool to locate recommended or popular resources.

Perform the following tasks:

1. Visit one of the following websites or locate other websites that contain animated GIFs: pixabay.com/gifs, gifs.cc, BestAnimations.com, GIFanimations.com, or Giphy.com.
2. Locate files that could enhance your Run presentation. Some websites have collections of sports activities that could be useful.
3. Download at least two animated GIFs and then insert them into your SC_PPT_6_Run.pptx presentation.

   If requested to do so by your instructor, change the word, Water, in the Slide 3 table to the town where you were born.
4. Save the presentation using the file name, **SC_PPT_6_Run_GIF**.
5. Submit the assignment in the format specified by your instructor.
6. **Consider This:** Why did you select these particular images for your slides? Do the animated GIF images enhance or detract from your presentation? Where might you use GIF files other than in PowerPoint slides?

In the Lab

Apply your creative thinking and problem-solving skills to design and implement a solution.

Design and Create a Presentation about Gardening

Part 1: Students at your school have established a community garden in a one-acre plot on campus. While the vegetables and fruit provide nutritious produce, the garden also provides health benefits for the students who tend to the area. When these gardeners pull weeds, haul buckets of water, and rake the soil, they are stretching, bending, and twisting, which adds to their flexibility and strength. They are connecting with nature, increasing their exposure to Vitamin D, improving their self-esteem, and reducing their stress levels.

The students also have planted flowers and shrubs to support monarch butterflies and hummingbirds. The monarchs depend on milkweed and also favor purple coneflowers, asters, meadow blazing stars, and prairie phlox. The hummingbirds are attracted to columbine, milkweed, wild bergamot, spotted jewelweed, and cardinal flower. The students want to promote interest in their community garden, and you have been tasked with creating a PowerPoint presentation to accompany a webinar on this topic.

Perform some research about the benefits of gardening and the plants that attract butterflies and hummingbirds. Begin by creating a Word outline with the information for each slide and then insert the slides from this outline. Also create a Word document flyer promoting the community garden and showing the plants community members can purchase to provide a feeding station for butterflies and hummingbirds. Link this document to one of your PowerPoint slides. The Data Files folder contains pictures you could use. Review and revise your presentation as needed and then save the file using the file name, **SC_PPT_6_Garden**. Submit your assignment in the format specified by your instructor.

Part 2: **Consider This:** You made several decisions while creating the presentation in this assignment: what content to include, how to format the Word documents, where to insert the link to the Word flyer, and which styles and effects to apply. What was the rationale behind each of these decisions? Where would you recommend showing this slide show? When you reviewed the document, what changes did you make?

Adding Media and Enhancing SmartArt

Objectives

After completing this module, you will be able to:

- Insert a SmartArt graphic
- Convert a picture to SmartArt
- Add pictures into a SmartArt shape
- Change the SmartArt color
- Rearrange SmartArt shape locations
- Promote and demote SmartArt shapes
- Remove a picture background
- Change picture brightness, contrast, and color saturation
- Insert and edit a video clip
- Insert and edit an audio clip
- Compress a video
- Insert a hyperlink
- Add a hyperlink action
- Insert an action button

Introduction

Well-produced slides are enhanced with a variety of visual content. PowerPoint's themes determine the default characteristics of slide objects, but colors, fills, effects, and other formatting options can give the slides a unique character. Graphics, such as SmartArt, have individual layouts, styles, and color schemes. If a SmartArt design does not meet the specific needs of your slide content, you can modify it by adding shapes, reordering the current shapes, and changing the color and effects.

Audio and video clips can emphasize slide content and focus the audience's attention on the material, particularly when they present a concept that a picture or graphic cannot depict. A simple, uncluttered picture can help audience members comprehend and retain important facts, and removing a picture's background can direct the audience's attention to the material being presented. You can save your presentation as a PDF (Portable Document Format) file, which is an electronic image file format by Adobe® that mirrors the appearance of the original document and allows you to present and exchange your presentation independent of software, hardware, or operating system.

BTW
PDF Option Settings
Your PDF file can include comments, ink notations, handouts, outlines, and non-printing information such as document properties. You can choose the number of slides to include and specify whether the order is horizontal or vertical.

Project: Presentation with Audio and Video Clips, SmartArt, and Hyperlinks

People begin a fitness program for many reasons. Some may train to look better, manage stress, or simply feel better. Whatever the goal, total body fitness should become part of an overall lifetime health habit. Elements include cardio and strength exercises, recovery activities such as yoga, and

BTW
Ribbon and Screen Resolution
PowerPoint may change how the groups and buttons within the groups appear on the ribbon, depending on the screen resolution of your computer. Thus, your ribbon may look different from the ones in this book if you are using a screen resolution other than 1920 × 1080.

proper nutrition. To reduce injury and promote recovery, warmup and cooldown exercises provide benefits well beyond the actual exercise session.

In this module's project, you will follow proper design guidelines and learn to use PowerPoint to create the slides shown in Figure 7–1a through 7–1f. You also will create a PDF file of the presentation, shown in Figure 7–1g. The objective is to produce a presentation for health professionals to use during their seminars held for individuals considering beginning a fitness program. You begin by opening a file and then changing the image on Slide 1 (Figure 7–1a). You will insert a screen clipping from another PowerPoint presentation and then later edit a video and an audio clip.

The second slide (Figure 7–1b) includes SmartArt that you will create and enhance. The slide shows a picture of various fitness elements and four aspects of a complete healthy regimen.

On Slide 3 (Figure 7–1c), you will add a video poster frame that covers the first frame of a video that you will insert on that slide. When the slide is displayed, the poster frame uncovers the video that plays full screen (Figure 7–1d).

The final slide (Figure 7–1e) shows three steps people can take to begin a fitness program. The slide contains another SmartArt graphic that you will format by moving the shapes. The picture on this slide has a background that you will remove, and then you will change the contrast and color saturation and flip the image. The slide contains a hyperlink from the words, Getting Started, to a slide in another PowerPoint presentation showing warmup benefits and exercises (Figure 7–1f). That slide contains an action button that will return the presenter to Slide 4 in the original presentation.

The final steps in the project create and save a PDF file (Figure 7–1g) from the presentation.

BTW
Distributing a Document
Instead of printing and distributing a hard copy of PowerPoint slides, you can distribute the slides electronically. Options include sending the slides via email; posting it on cloud storage (such as OneDrive) and sharing the link with others; posting it on social media, a blog, or other website; and sharing a link associated with an online location of the slides. You also can create and share a PDF or XPS image of the slides, so that users can view the file in Acrobat Reader or XPS Viewer instead of in PowerPoint.

In this module, you will learn how to create the slides shown in Figure 7–1. You will perform the following general tasks as you progress through this module:

1. Change a picture.
2. Create, format, and modify a SmartArt graphic by inserting pictures, changing colors and effects, and moving shapes.
3. Format a picture by removing the background, changing the contrast and color saturation, and flipping the image.
4. Insert and trim a video and an audio clip.
5. Add a video poster frame.
6. Insert a link to a second PowerPoint presentation.
7. Save the presentation as a PDF.

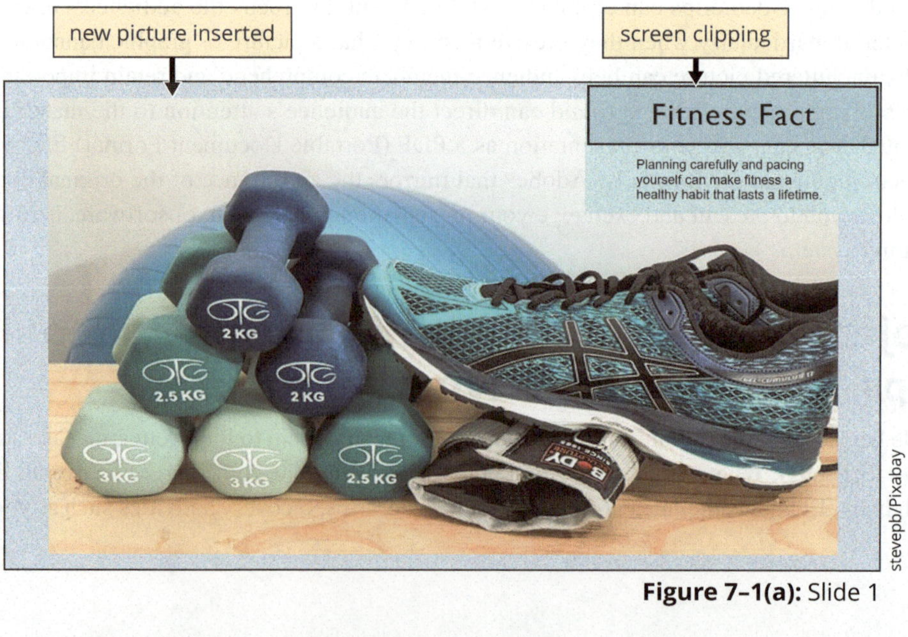

Figure 7–1(a): Slide 1

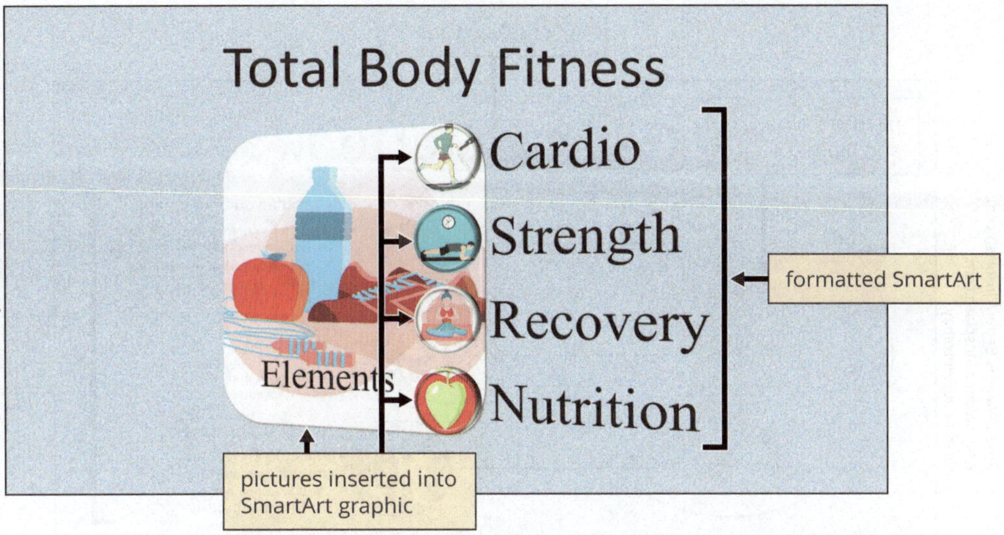

TotalShape/Pixabay; Bill_Bowler/Pixabay; Mohamed_hassan/Pixabay; TotalShape/Pixabay; Merio/Pixabay

Figure 7–1(b): Slide 2 (SmartArt Enhanced with Pictures)

Greg Rosenke/Unsplash.com

Figure 7–1(c): Slide 3 (Video Poster Frame)

freefitnessmedia/Pixabay

Figure 7–1(d): Slide 3 (Video Clip)

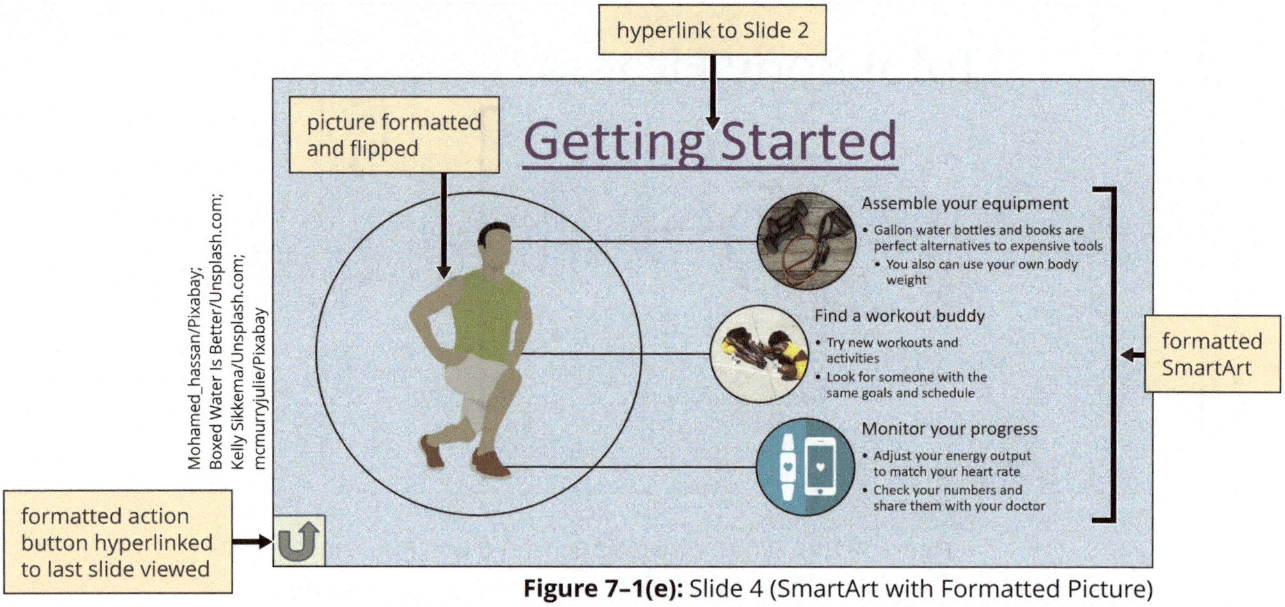

Figure 7–1(e): Slide 4 (SmartArt with Formatted Picture)

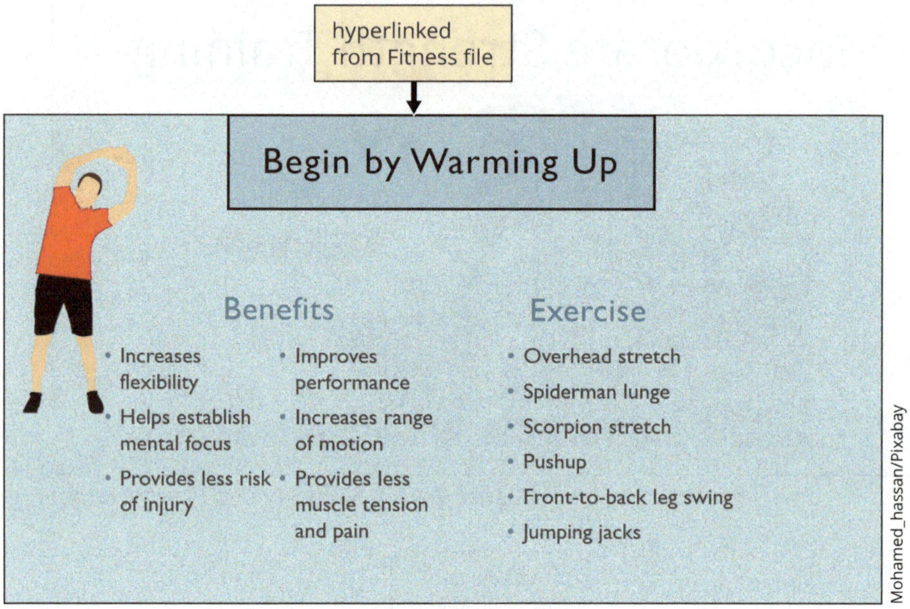

Figure 7–1(f): Slide 2 (Hyperlinked from First Presentation)

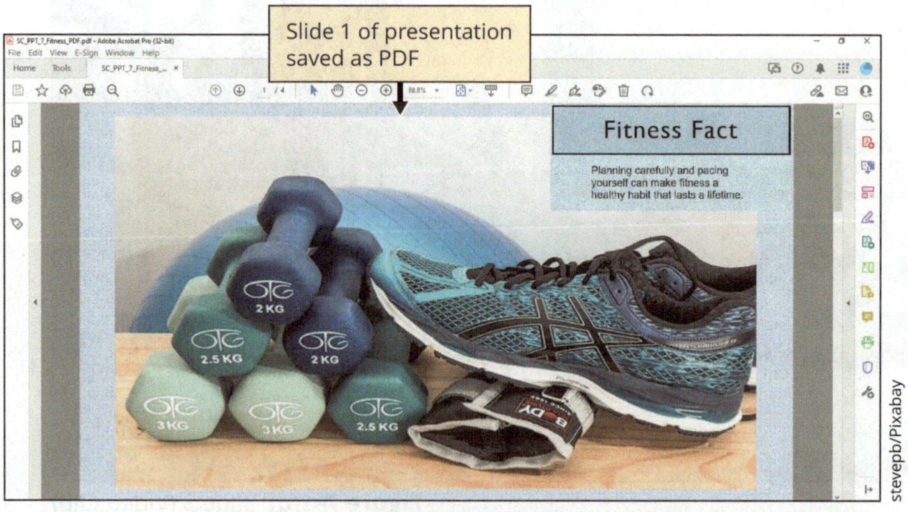

Figure 7–1(g): Slide 1 of PDF file

Modifying a Slide by Changing a Picture and Inserting a Screen Clipping

You begin this module by opening a file containing four partially completed slides. You then change, resize, and align the picture on the first slide, open a second file, and insert a screen clipping from the last slide in the second presentation.

In the following pages, you will perform these tasks:

1. Change and resize the picture on Slide 1.
2. Insert a screen clipping.

BTW
Touch Mode Differences
The Microsoft 365 and Windows interfaces may vary if you are using a touch screen. For this reason, you might notice that the function or appearance of your touch screen differs slightly from this module's presentation.

To Open and Save a Presentation

The following steps open the starting file and then save it with a new file name.

1. sam Run PowerPoint. If necessary, maximize the PowerPoint window.
2. Open the presentation, SC_PPT_7_Starting.pptx, from the Data Files.
3. Save the presentation using **SC_PPT_7_Fitness** as the file name.

To Change a Picture

The starting file has a picture on Slide 1 of a person running on a treadmill. You want to change that picture to one of the pictures in the Data Files showing a variety of fitness equipment. **Why?** The health professionals who will present this slide show want to introduce audience members to the overall theme of the presentation instead of focusing on the cardio aspect of total body fitness. The following steps change the Slide 1 picture to the Equipment picture, which is located in the Data Files folder.

1.
- Click the Slide 1 picture to select it and then display the Picture Format tab.
- Click the Change Picture button (Picture Format tab | Adjust group) to display the Change Picture menu (Figure 7-2).

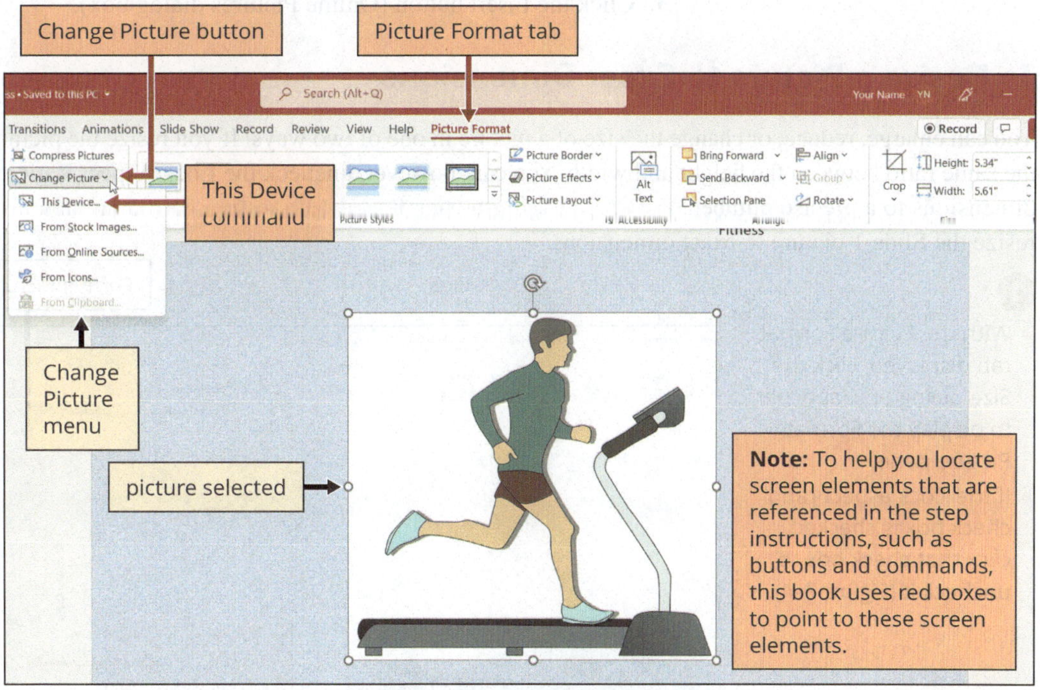

Bill_Bowler/Pixabay

Figure 7-2

2

- Click 'This Device' or 'From a File' to display the Insert Picture dialog box.
- If necessary, navigate to the location where the Data Files are located and then click Support_PPT_7_Equipment to select the .jpg file (Figure 7–3).

3

- Click the Insert button (Insert Picture dialog box) to insert the picture into Slide 1 and change the original picture.
- If the Design Ideas pane is displayed, close it.

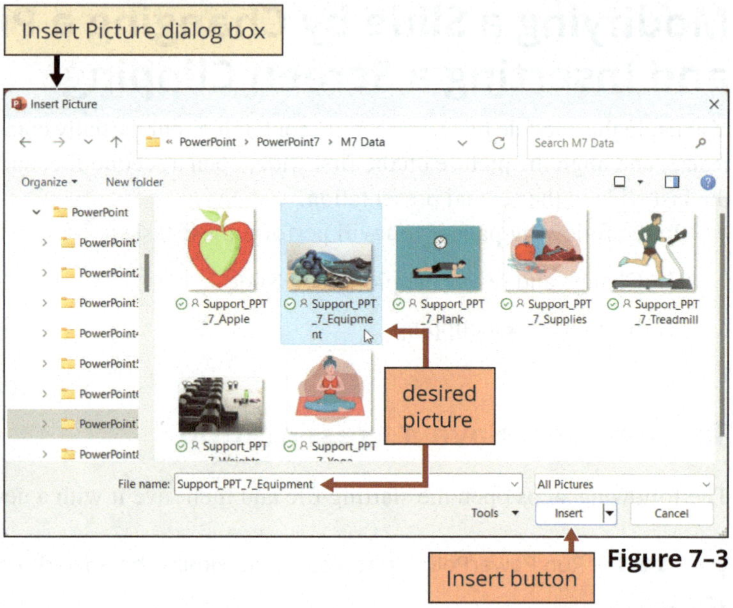

stevepb/Pixabay; TotalShape/Pixabay; Bill_Bowler/Pixabay; Greg Rosenke/Unsplash.com; Mohamed_hassan/Pixabay; Merio/Pixabay; TotalShape/Pixabay

Figure 7–3

Other Ways

1. Right-click picture, click Change Picture on shortcut menu, click 'From a File'

To Insert an Online Picture without Using a Content Placeholder If you wanted to change or insert an online picture into a slide that does not have a content placeholder, you would perform the following steps.

1. Display the Insert tab, click the Pictures button (Insert tab | Images group), and then click Online Pictures to display the Online Pictures dialog box.
2. Select a category and then select the desired picture.
3. Click the Insert button (Online Pictures dialog box).

To Resize a Picture to Exact Dimensions

You can enlarge, reduce, or change the size of a picture in one of two ways. If you resize the picture proportionally, you maintain the same ratio between the height and width. You can, however, uncheck the Lock Aspect Ratio check box and then change the dimensions to a precise number. **Why?** You want the height or width to fit a particular area of the slide. The following steps resize the Slide 1 picture to exact dimensions.

1

- With the Picture Format tab displayed, click the Size dialog box launcher to display the Format Picture pane.
- If the 'Lock aspect ratio' check box is checked, click that check box to uncheck it (Figure 7–4).

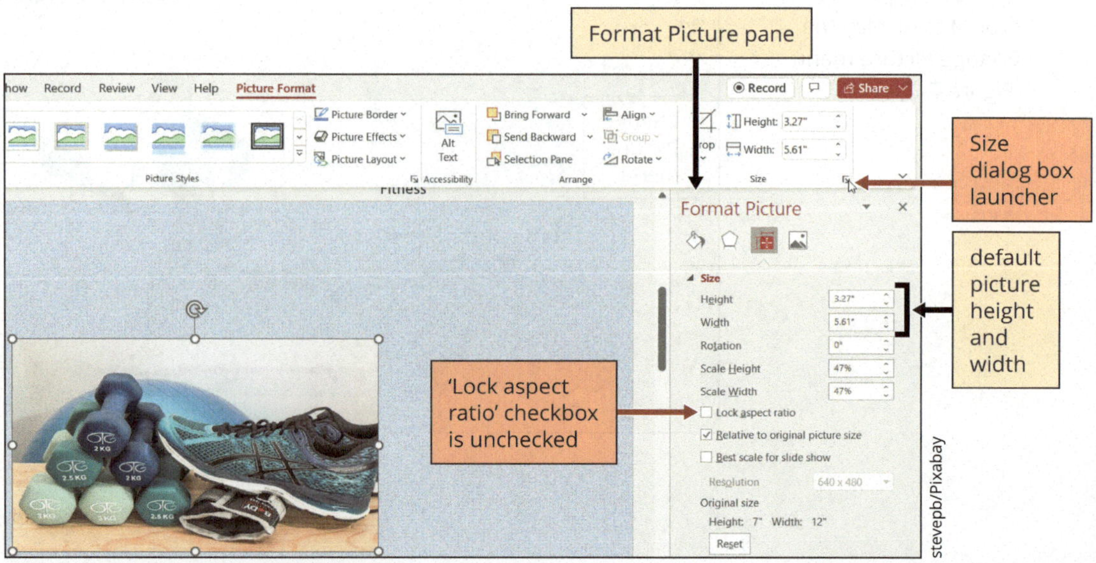

stevepb/Pixabay

Figure 7–4

2

- Click the Height up arrow several times to change the picture height to 7".
- Click the Width up arrow several times to change the picture width to 12" (Figure 7–5).

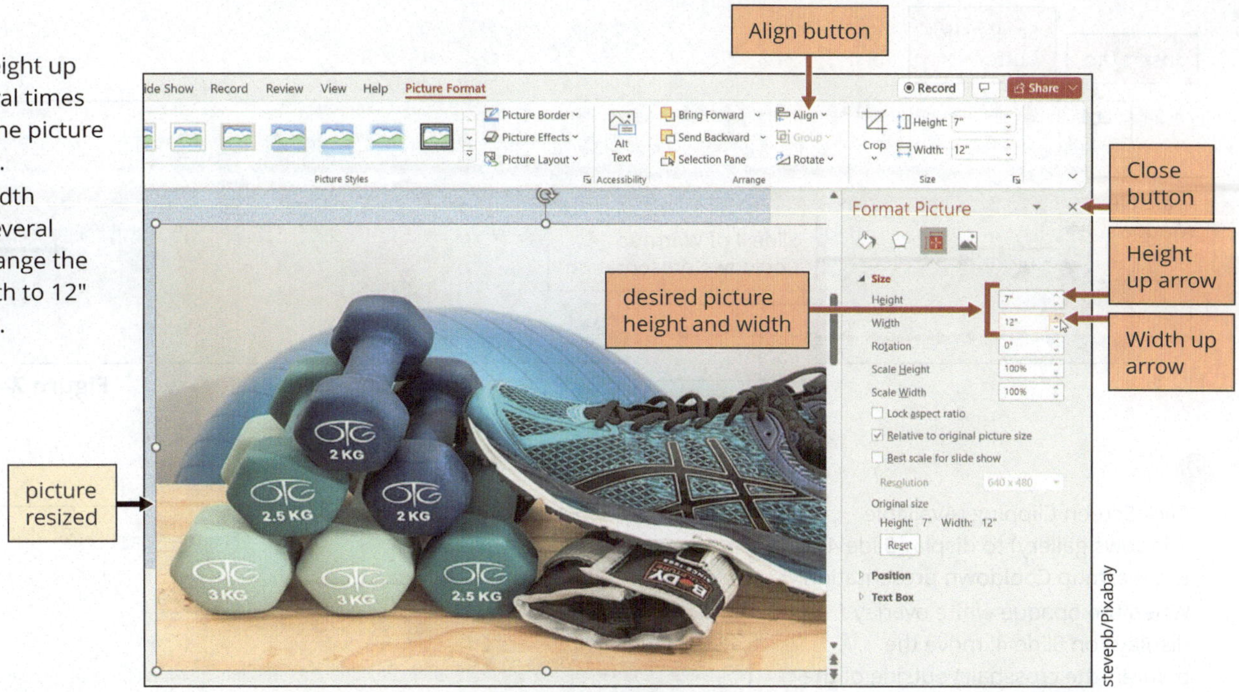

Figure 7–5

3

- Close the Format Picture pane.
- Click the Align button (Picture Format tab | Arrange group) and then click the Align Center button.
- Click the Align button again and then click the Align Middle button.
- Click an area outside the picture so that it no longer is selected.

To Insert a Screen Clipping

At times you may be developing a presentation and need a portion of a clip or picture from another presentation. You can capture all or part of a slide in another presentation that is open. PowerPoint refers to this presentation as being open or available. Open program windows are displayed as thumbnails in the Available Windows gallery. A **screenshot** is a snapshot of a program or window that is open. A **screen clipping** is a screen capture of part of an open window. When you click the Screen Clipping tool, your window becomes opaque. After you select the part of the window that you desire to capture, your selection is displayed through this opaqueness. The following steps clip part of an image on Slide 4 of another presentation that is available in the Data Files and then paste this selection on Slide 1 of your Fitness presentation. Why? On the first slide, you want to focus on how proper planning and execution can lead to a lifetime of healthy habits.

1

- Open the Support_PPT_7_Warmup.pptx file from your Data Files and then save it in the same location as your Fitness file using **SC_PPT_7_Warmup_Cooldown** as the file name.
- Display Slide 4 of that presentation.
- Display Slide 1 of the Fitness presentation.
- Display the Insert tab and then click the Screenshot button (Insert tab | Images group) to display the Available Windows gallery (Figure 7–6).

Q&A What if more than one available window is displayed?
Select the window showing Slide 4 of the Warmup Cooldown presentation and then continue with the steps.

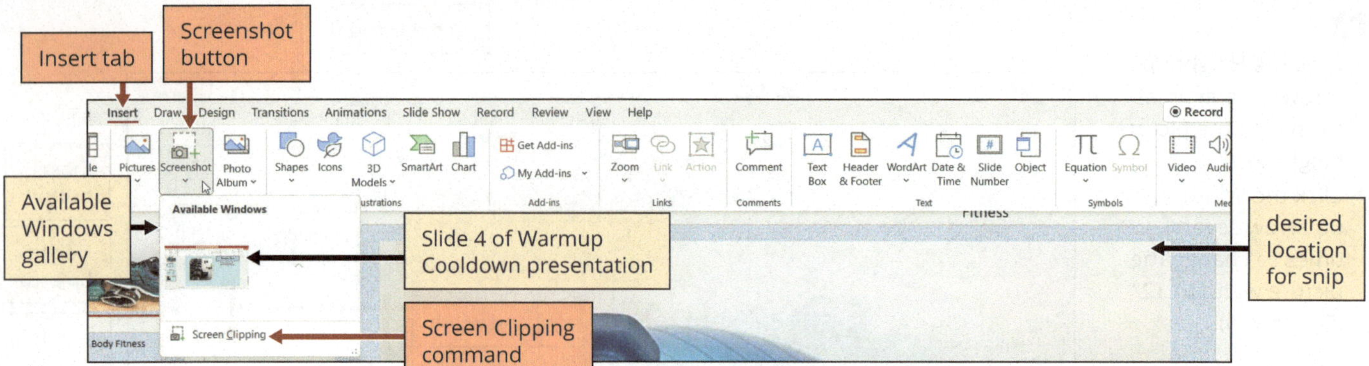

stevepb/Pixabay

Figure 7–6

2

- Click Screen Clipping (Available Windows gallery) to display Slide 4 of the Warmup Cooldown presentation.
- When the opaque white overlay displays on Slide 4, move the pointer (the crosshair) outside of the upper-left corner of the Fitness Fact text box, as shown in Figure 7–7.
- Press and hold the left mouse button and drag diagonally downward to the right to select the text box and the entire text paragraph. Do not release the mouse button (Figure 7–8).

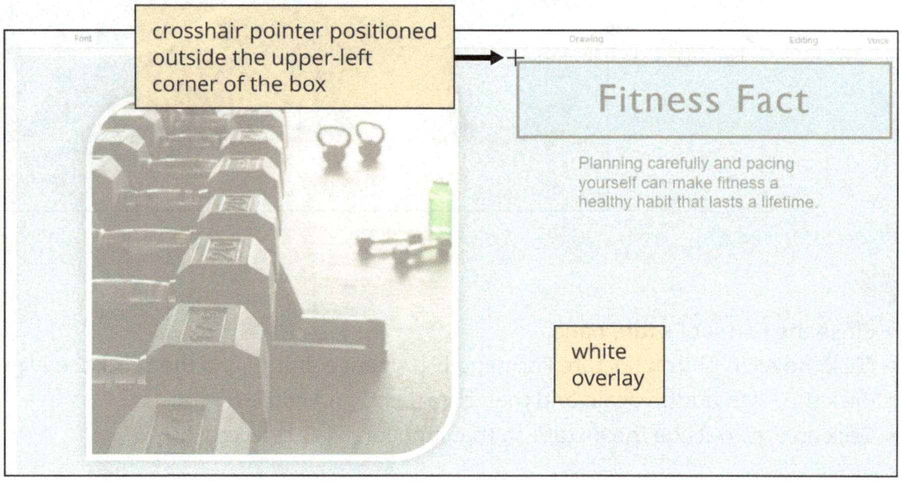

Greg Rosenke/Unsplash.com

Figure 7–7

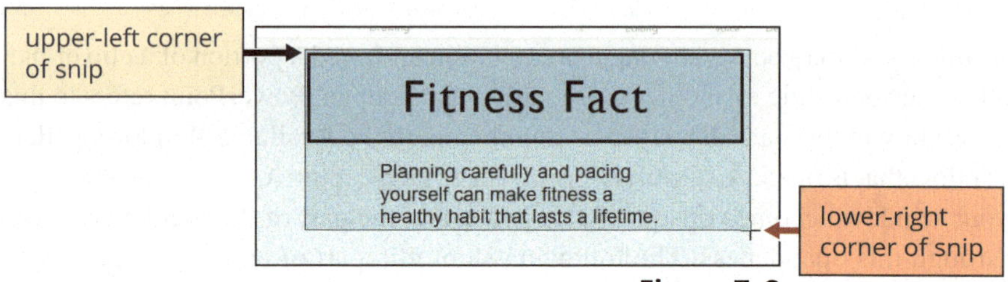

Figure 7–8

3

- Release the mouse button.
- When the clip displays on Slide 1 of the Fitness presentation, resize it to a height of 2".
- Drag the clip to the upper-right corner of the slide (Figure 7–9).

4

- Close the Warmup Cooldown presentation.

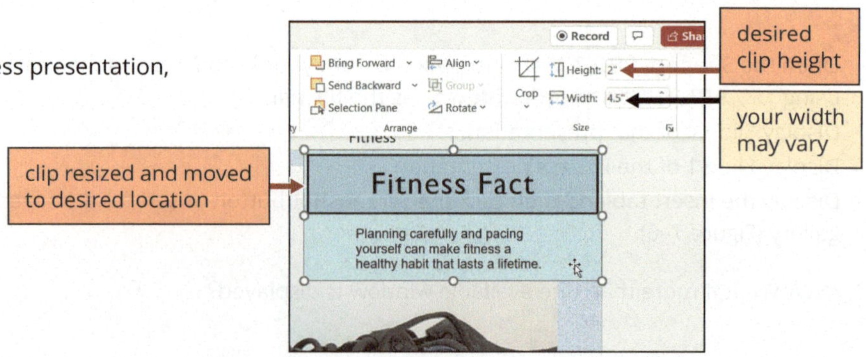

Figure 7–9

To Insert a Screenshot To insert a screenshot, you would perform the following steps.

1. Click the slide where you want to insert the screenshot.
2. Display the Insert tab and then click the Screenshot button (Insert tab | Images group).
3. Click the thumbnail of the desired window in the Available Windows gallery.

To Insert an Equation The Microsoft 365 apps have built-in equations for common calculations, such as the area of a circle and the Pythagorean Theorem. You can include one of these equations in your slide. If you need a different equation, you can edit, change the existing equation, or insert math symbols to develop your own equation. If you wanted to insert a built-in equation in a slide, you would perform the following steps.

1. Display the Insert tab and then click the Equation button (Insert tab | Symbols group) to display the Equation tab.
2. Choose the equation you want from the gallery.
3. If needed, add symbols and structures available on the Equation tab.

BTW
Creating Equations with Touch Screens
If you are using a touch screen, use your finger or stylus to write the numbers and symbols, being certain the Math Input Control box understands your handwriting.

Creating and Formatting a SmartArt Graphic

The predefined SmartArt graphics are visual representations of information to help convey information to your audience. The variety of shapes, arrows, and lines correspond to the major points you want your audience to remember. You can create a SmartArt graphic and then customize the content and design.

In the following pages, you will perform these tasks:

1. Insert a SmartArt graphic.
2. Enter and format text.
3. Add pictures.
4. Add and move SmartArt shapes.
5. Promote and demote SmartArt shapes.

To Insert SmartArt Using a Content Placeholder

Several SmartArt layouts have placeholders for one or more pictures, and they are grouped in the Picture category. The Accented Picture graphic is appropriate for this presentation. Why? It has one large area for a picture and three other areas for smaller pictures. These images help generate an understanding that total body fitness involves more than just exercising or eating healthy foods. The following steps insert the Accented Picture SmartArt graphic on Slide 2.

1

- Display Slide 2 and then point to the 'Insert a SmartArt Graphic' icon in the content placeholder (Figure 7–10).

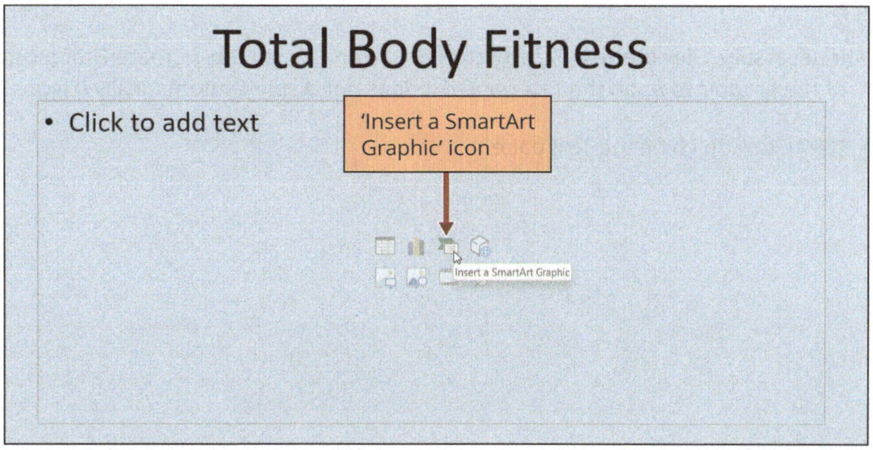

Figure 7–10

2

- Click the 'Insert a SmartArt Graphic' icon to display the 'Choose a SmartArt Graphic' dialog box.
- Click Picture in the left pane to display the Picture gallery.
- Click the Accented Picture graphic (first graphic in the first row) to display a preview of this layout in the right pane (Figure 7–11).
- **Experiment:** Click various categories and graphics in the SmartArt Styles gallery and view the various layouts.

3

- Click OK to insert this SmartArt layout into Slide 2.

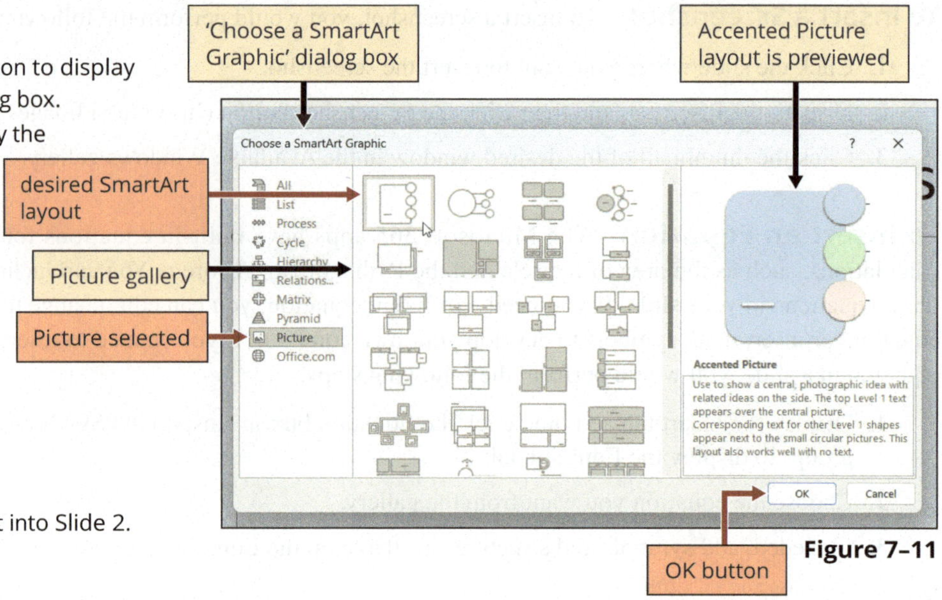

Figure 7–11

Other Ways

1. Click SmartArt button (Insert tab | Illustrations group)

To Convert a Picture to SmartArt You quickly can convert a picture on your slide into a SmartArt graphic. PowerPoint automatically places the picture into a shape and arranges it based on the layout you choose. If you wanted to convert a picture to SmartArt, you would perform the following steps.

1. Select the picture you want to convert and then display the Picture Format tab.
2. Click the Picture Layout button (Picture Format tab | Picture Styles group) to display the Picture Layout gallery.
3. Click the desired layout.

To Show or Hide the SmartArt Text Pane

You can show the Text pane to add or edit text in the SmartArt graphic, or you can hide it to see more of your slide when you are developing the graphic. If you are entering a large amount of text, consider showing the Text pane. **Why?** The bullets in the top portion of the pane function as an outline. You can create new lines of bulleted text and then indent and demote these lines. You also can check spelling. The following step shows the Text pane on Slide 2.

1

- If necessary, click the Text Pane button (SmartArt Design tab | Create Graphic group) or the arrow icon in the center-left edge of the graphic to open the Text pane if it does not display automatically (Figure 7–12).

Q&A How do I hide the Text pane?

Click the Close button in the upper-right corner of the Text pane or click the Text Pane button again.

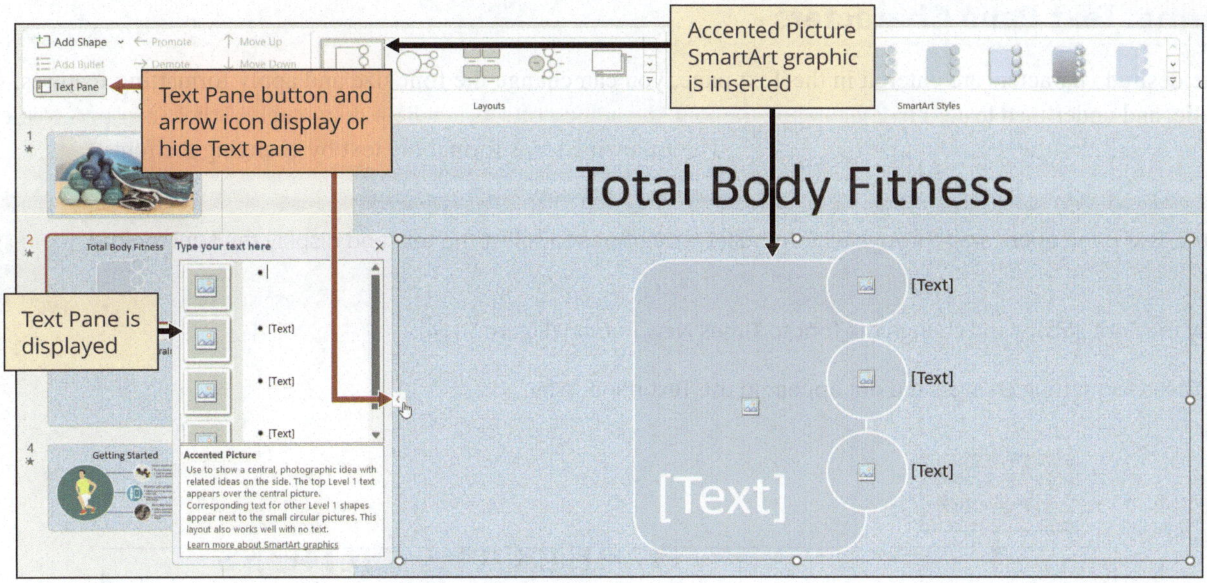

stevepb/Pixabay; Mohamed_hassan/Pixabay; Boxed Water Is Better/Unsplash.com; mcmurryjulie/Pixabay; Kelly Sikkema/Unsplash.com

Figure 7–12

To Enter Text in SmartArt

The Accented Picture graphic has placeholders for text that can supplement the visuals. The following steps insert four lines of text in the Text pane and in the corresponding SmartArt shapes on Slide 2.

1. If necessary, position the insertion point beside the first bullet in the Text pane. Type **Elements** in the first bullet paragraph and then click the second bullet line or press DOWN ARROW to move the insertion point to the second bullet paragraph.
2. Type **Cardio** in the second bullet paragraph and then click the third bullet line or press DOWN ARROW to move the insertion point to the third bullet paragraph.
3. Type **Strength** in the third bullet paragraph and then click the fourth bullet line or press DOWN ARROW to move the insertion point to the fourth bullet paragraph.
4. Type **Nutrition** in the fourth bullet paragraph. Do not press DOWN ARROW or ENTER (Figure 7–13).

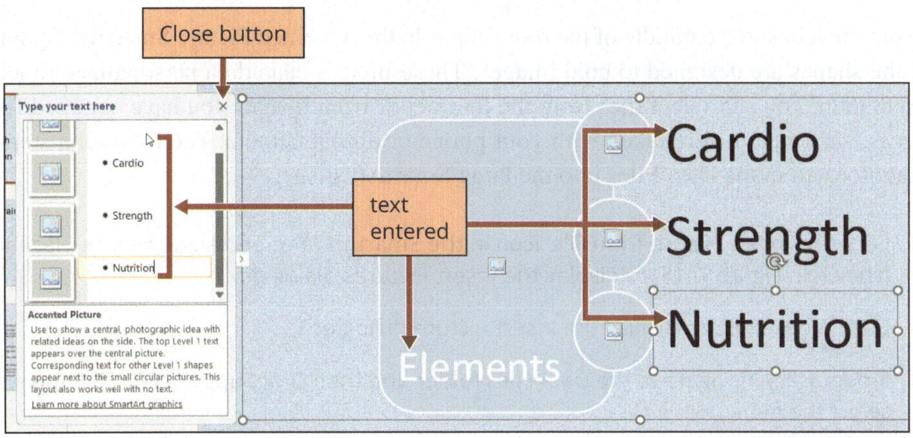

Figure 7–13

Other Ways

1. Enter text directly in SmartArt text boxes

To Format Text Pane Characters

Once the desired characters are entered in the Text pane, you can change the font size and apply formatting features, such as bold, italic, and underlined text. **Why?** Changing the font and adding effects can help draw the audience members to the varied slide content and coordinate with the visual content. The following steps format the text by changing the font.

1

- With the Text pane open, drag through all four bullet paragraphs to select the text and display the Mini toolbar.

2

- Display the Font gallery and change the font to Times New Roman (Figure 7–14).

Q&A These formatting changes did not appear in the Text pane. Why?
Not all the formatting changes are evident in the Text pane, but they appear in the corresponding shape.

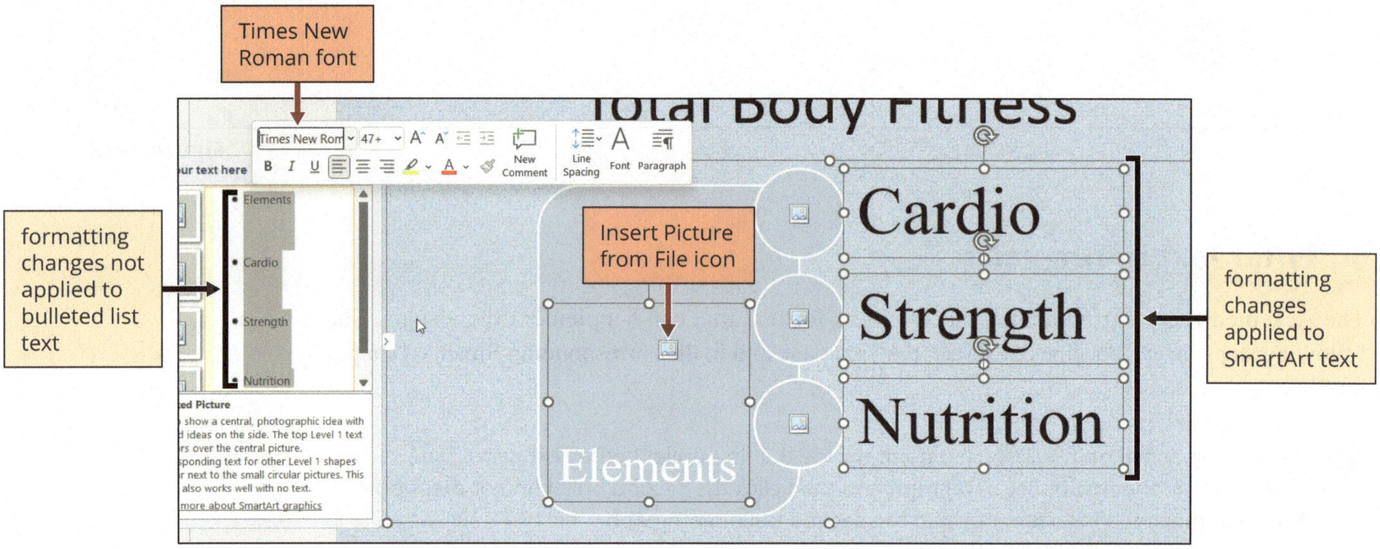

Figure 7–14

3

- Click the SmartArt Text pane Close button (shown in Figure 7–13) so that the pane no longer is displayed.

To Add a Picture to SmartArt

The picture icons in the middle of the four shapes in the Accented Picture SmartArt layout indicate that the shapes are designed to hold images. These images can add a personalized touch to your presentation. You can select files from the Internet or from images you have obtained from other sources, such as a picture taken with your phone or digital camera. The following steps insert a picture located in the Data Files into the large SmartArt shape.

1. Click the 'Insert Picture from File' icon in the SmartArt large rectangle picture placeholder (shown in Figure 7–15) to display the Insert Pictures dialog box.
2. Click 'From a File' to display the Insert Picture dialog box.
3. If necessary, navigate to the Data Files folder and then click Support_PPT_7_Supplies.png to select the file.
4. Click the Insert button (Insert Picture dialog box) to insert the Supplies picture into the SmartArt large rectangle picture placeholder.

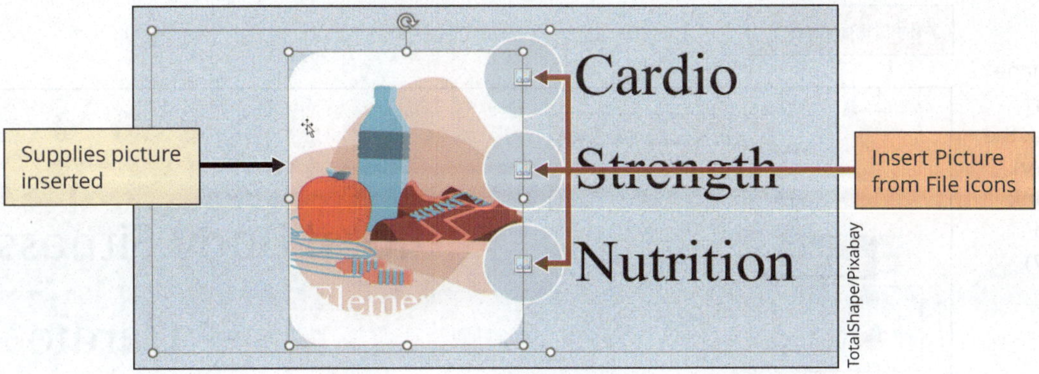

Figure 7–15

To Insert a Picture into a SmartArt Shape

The Supplies picture fills the left shape in the SmartArt graphic, and you want to insert additional fitness pictures in the three circles in the right portion of the graphic. These images are located in the Data Files. The following steps insert pictures into the three smaller SmartArt graphic circles.

1. Click the 'Insert Picture from File' icon in the top circle to the left of the word, Cardio, to display the Insert Pictures dialog box.
2. Click 'From a File', click Support_PPT_7_Treadmill.png in the list of picture files, and then click the Insert button (Insert Picture dialog box) to insert the picture into the top-right SmartArt circle picture placeholder.
3. Click the center 'Insert Picture from File' icon to the left of the word, Strength, click 'From a File', and then insert the picture with the file name, Support_PPT_7_Plank.png, into the placeholder.
4. Click the bottom 'Insert Picture from File' icon to the left of the word, Nutrition, and then insert the picture with the file name, Support_PPT_7_Apple.jpg, into the placeholder (Figure 7–16).

Figure 7–16

To Add a SmartArt Shape

You can add a new SmartArt shape to the layout if you need to display additional information. PowerPoint gives you the option of adding this shape above or below a selected shape or to the left or the right side of the shape. *Why? You want to display another element of providing total body fitness.* The following steps add a SmartArt shape.

1

- With the Apple picture shape selected and the SmartArt Design tab displayed, click the Add Shape arrow (SmartArt Design tab | Create Graphic group) to display the Add Shape menu (Figure 7–17).

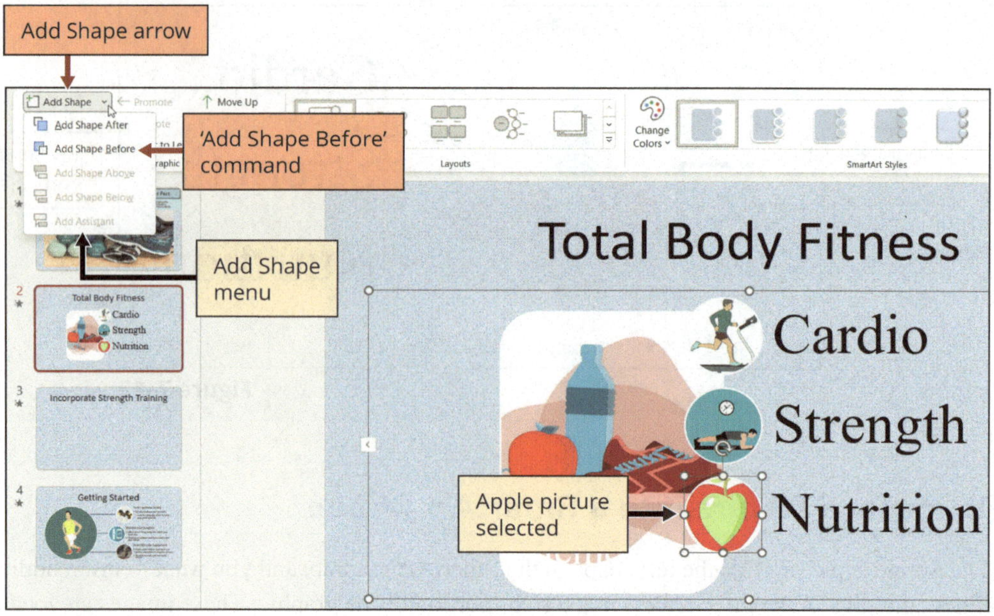

TotalShape/Pixabay; Merio/Pixabay; Bill_Bowler/Pixabay; Mohamed_hassan/Pixabay

Figure 7–17

2

- Click 'Add Shape Before' to create a new shape above the Nutrition shape.
- Type **Recovery** as the new shape text and then change the font to Times New Roman.
- Insert the Support_PPT_7_Yoga.jpg file into the placeholder (Figure 7–18).

Q&A What happens if I click the Add Shape button instead of the Add Shape arrow?

A shape would be added below the selected shape by default.

TotalShape/Pixabay; Merio/Pixabay; Bill_Bowler/Pixabay; Mohamed_hassan/Pixabay

Figure 7–18

To Apply 3-D Effects to SmartArt

You can change the look of your SmartArt graphic easily by applying a SmartArt style. **Why?** These professionally designed effects customize the appearance of your presentation with a variety of shape fills, edges, shadows, line styles, gradients, and dimensions. The following steps add the Metallic Scene 3-D effect to the SmartArt.

1

- Select the entire SmartArt graphic by clicking an outer edge of the graphic and then, if necessary, display the SmartArt Design tab (Figure 7–19).

Q&A How will I know the entire graphic is selected?

You will see the Text pane control and sizing handles around the outer edge of the SmartArt.

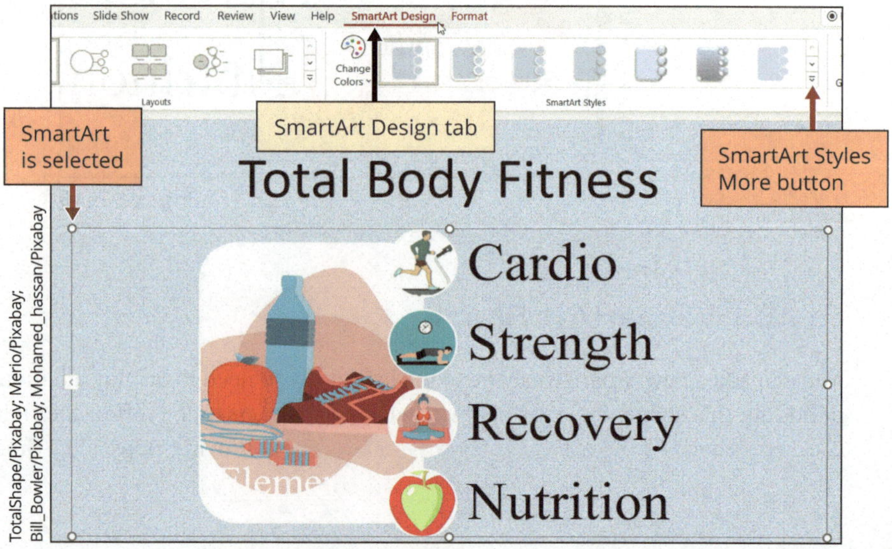

TotalShape/Pixabay; Merio/Pixabay; Bill_Bowler/Pixabay; Mohamed_hassan/Pixabay

Figure 7–19

2

- Click the SmartArt Styles More button (SmartArt Design tab | SmartArt Styles group) (shown in Figure 7–19) to expand the SmartArt Styles gallery (Figure 7–20).

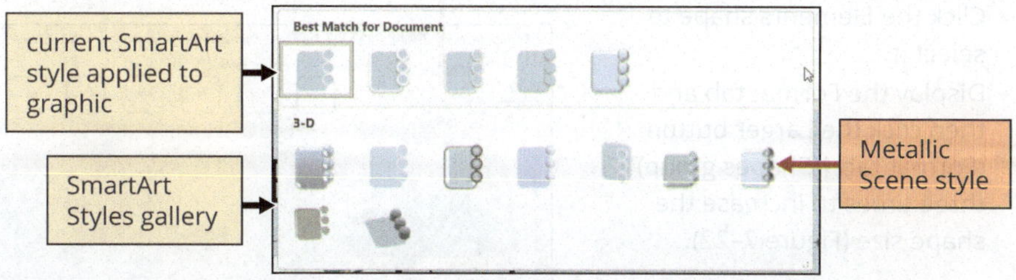

Figure 7–20

3

- Point to the Metallic Scene style in the 3-D area (seventh style in the first 3-D row) in the SmartArt Styles gallery to display a live preview of this style (Figure 7–21).
- **Experiment:** Point to various styles in the SmartArt Styles gallery and watch the Accented Picture graphic change styles.

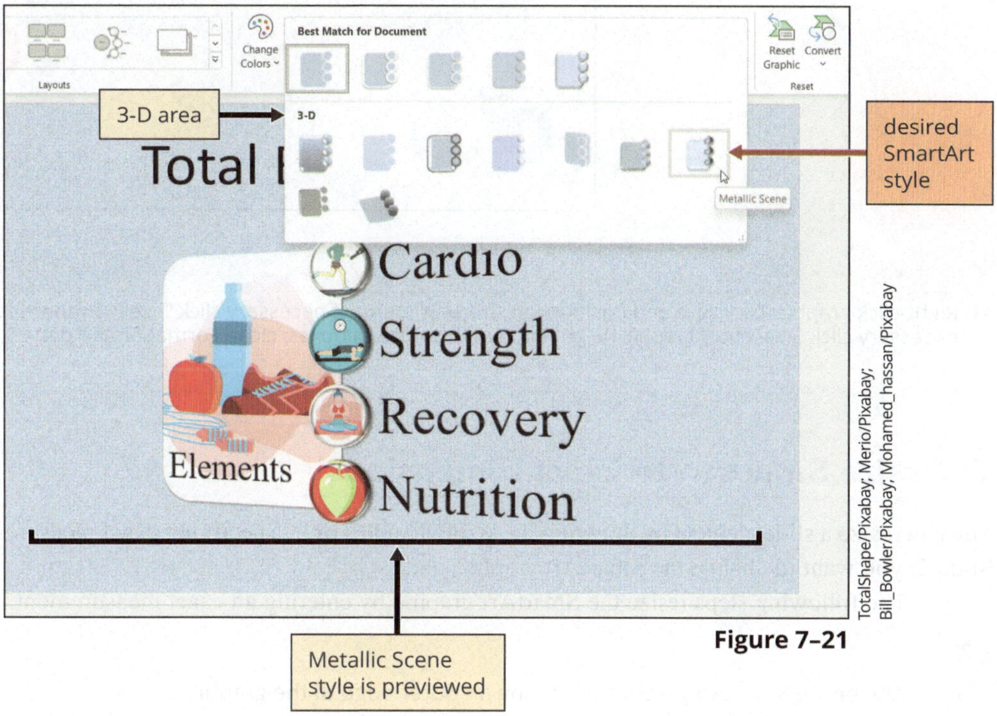

TotalShape/Pixabay; Merio/Pixabay; Bill_Bowler/Pixabay; Mohamed_hassan/Pixabay

Figure 7–21

4

- Click Metallic Scene to apply this style to the graphic.

Other Ways

1. Right-click SmartArt graphic in an area other than a picture, click Style button

To Increase the Size of a SmartArt Shape

When you view the completed graphic, you may decide that individual shapes or the entire piece of art needs to be enlarged or reduced. All the shapes will enlarge proportionally when you adjust the graphic's height and width to maintain proportions. Likewise, the font size may change in all the shapes if you increase or decrease the font size of one shape. On Slide 2, you want to change the SmartArt graphic size. **Why?** A larger graphic size will fill the empty space on the slide and add readability. The following step resizes one SmartArt graphic shape.

1

- Click the Elements shape to select it.
- Display the Format tab and then click the Larger button (Format tab | Shapes group) three times to increase the shape size (Figure 7–22).

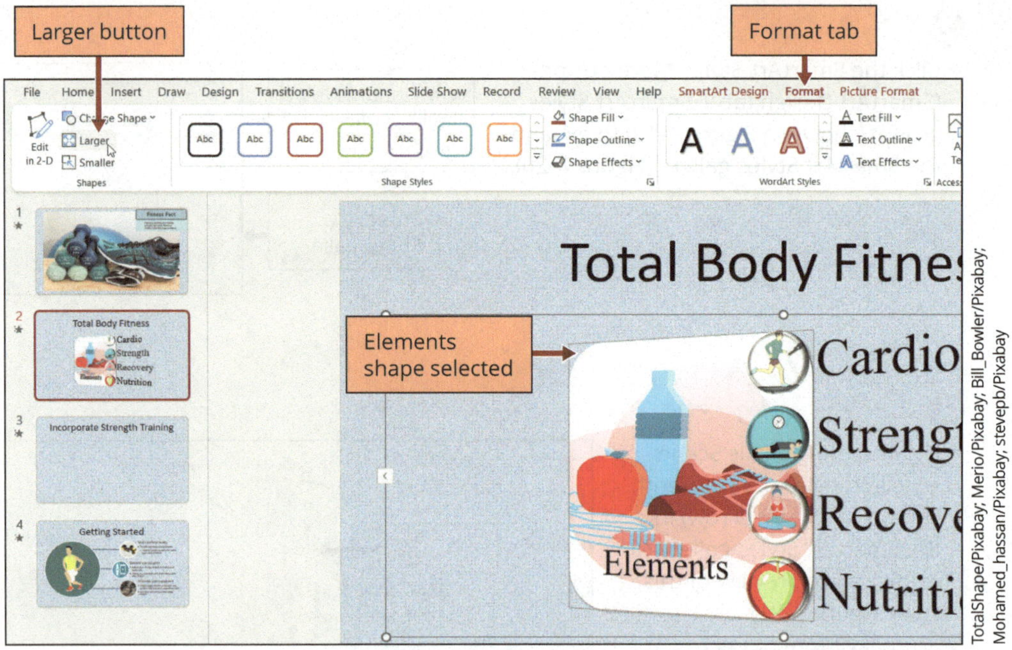

Figure 7–22

Other Ways

1. Right-click graphic, click 'Size and Position' on shortcut menu, if necessary click 'Size & Properties' icon (Format Shape pane), if necessary click Size, enter graphic height and width values in boxes, close Format Shape pane

To Resize SmartArt to Exact Dimensions

You can resize a slide element by dragging the sizing handles or by specifying exact measurements for the height and width. On Slide 2, you want to change the SmartArt graphic size. **Why?** Adequate space exists on the slide to increase all the SmartArt shapes. The following steps resize the SmartArt graphic by entering an exact measurement.

1

- Select the entire SmartArt graphic by clicking an outer edge of the graphic.
- With the Format tab displayed, change the Height measurement to 5.3" and the Width measurement to 13" (Figure 7–23).

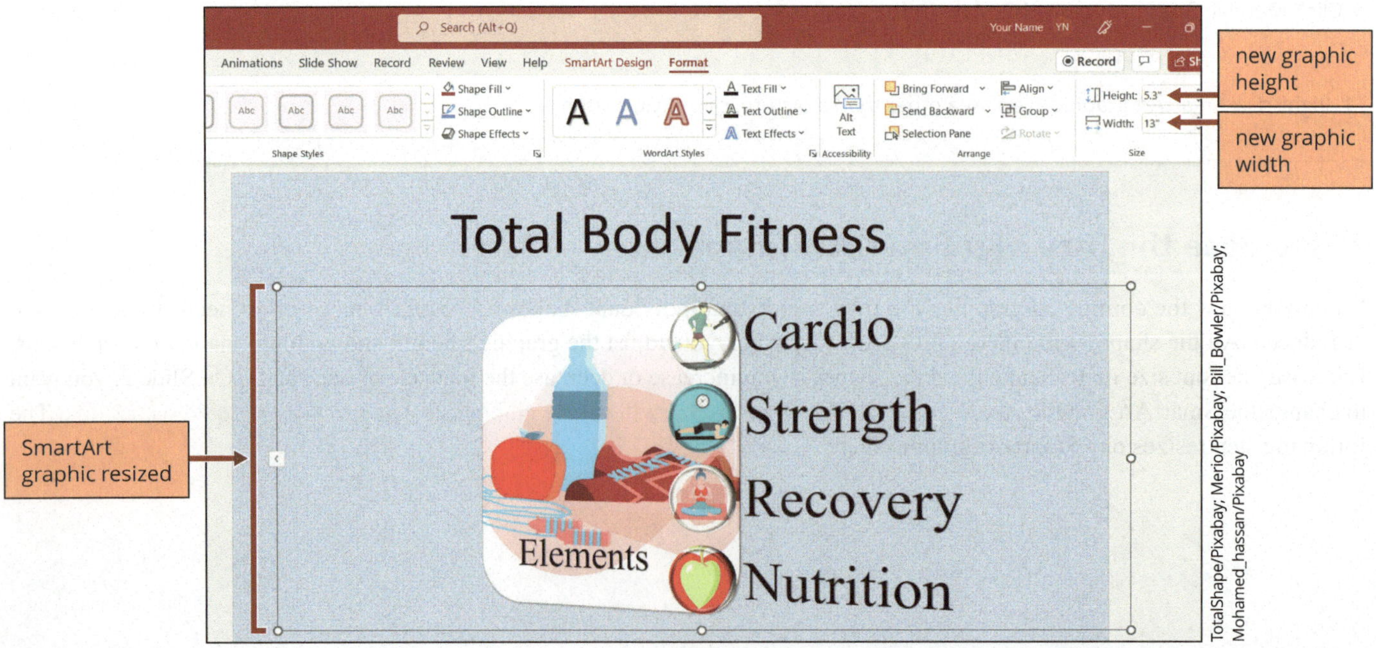

Figure 7–23

3

- Use the smart guides to align the SmartArt object, as shown in Figure 7–24.

TotalShape/Pixabay; Merio/Pixabay; Bill_Bowler/Pixabay; Mohamed_hassan/Pixabay

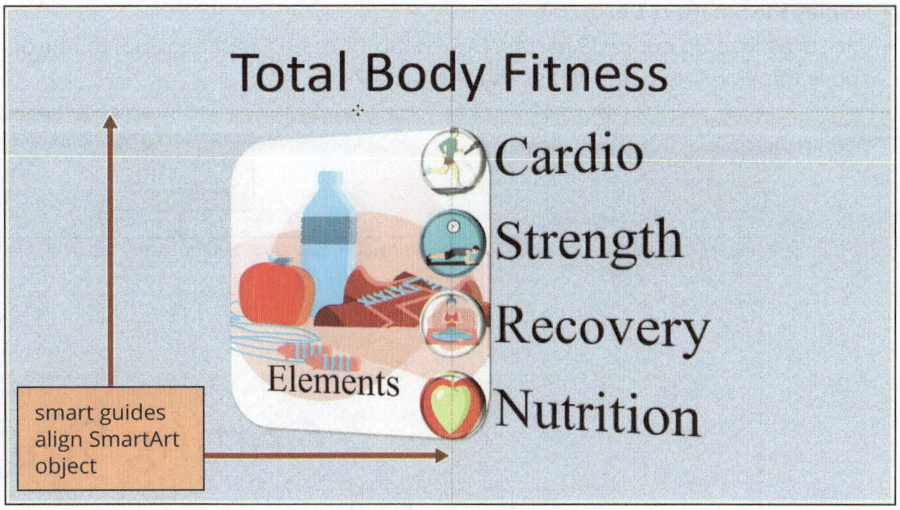

Figure 7–24

Other Ways

1. Right-click graphic, click 'Size and Position' on shortcut menu, if necessary click 'Size & Properties' icon (Format Shape pane), if necessary click Size, enter graphic height and width values in boxes, close Format Shape pane

To Move a SmartArt Shape Up

One modification that you can make to a SmartArt layout is to change the order of the shapes. Slide 4 contains SmartArt with information about beginning a fitness program. You decide that two items in the graphic should be displayed in a different order. **Why?** Audience members may be concerned about the equipment they will need to obtain when beginning their fitness routines, so you want to display this information more prominently in the graphic. A workout buddy helps with accountability and motivation, and you want to emphasize that fact, too. PowerPoint provides tools to move shapes and paragraphs in a vertical layout up or down. The following steps move the Assemble your equipment shape up in the graphic.

1

- Display Slide 4.
- Position the pointer in the words, Assemble your equipment, and then click to select it and the bulleted paragraphs (Figure 7–25).

Q&A Is all the text selected in the Assemble your equipment shape?

Yes. The words, Assemble your equipment, are in a first-level paragraph, and the bulleted second-level paragraphs are associated with it. When a shape is selected, all related paragraphs are selected with it.

Mohamed_hassan/Pixabay; Boxed Water Is Better/Unsplash.com; mcmurryjulie/Pixabay; Kelly Sikkema/Unsplash.com

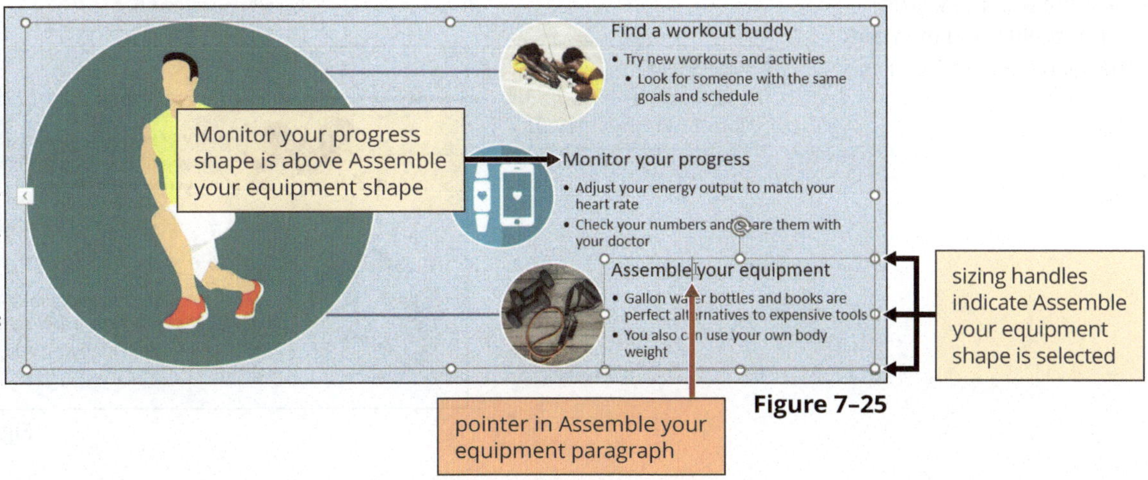

Figure 7–25

2

- Display the SmartArt Design tab.
- Click the Move Up button (SmartArt Design tab | Create Graphic group) to reorder the Assemble your equipment shape above the Monitor your progress shape (Figure 7–26).

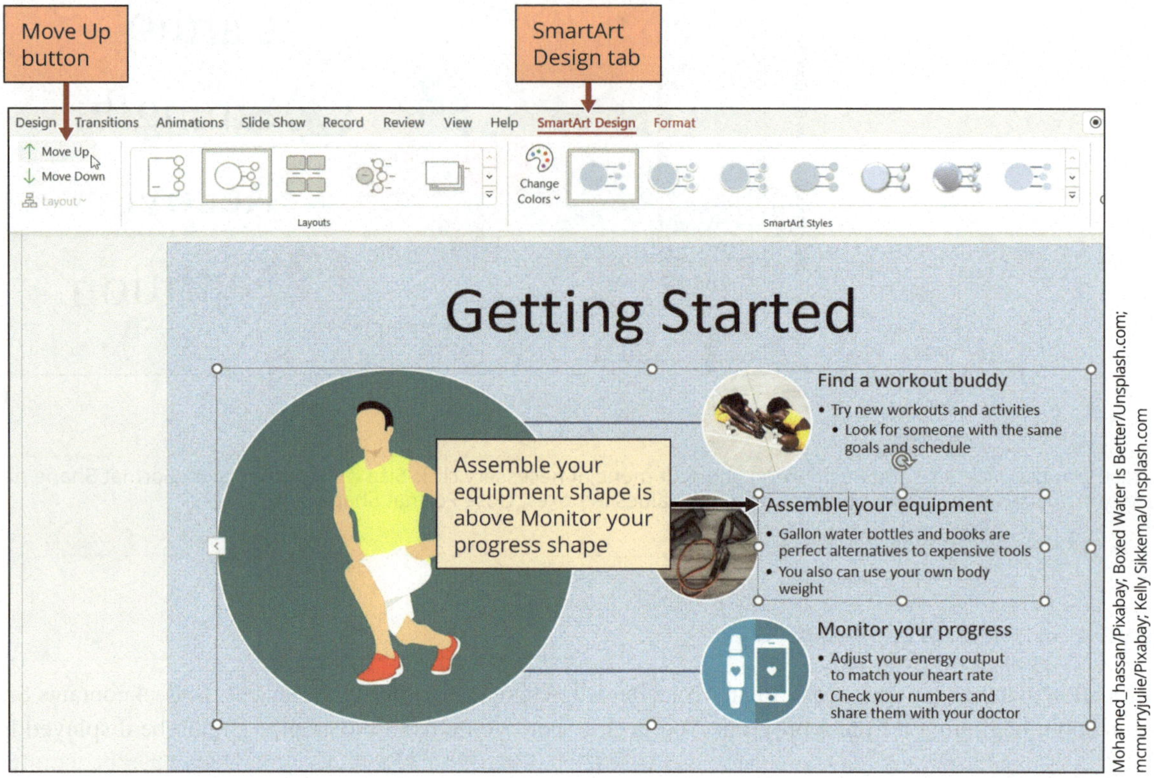

Figure 7–26

To Move a SmartArt Shape Down

You can move shapes down in a SmartArt graphic in a similar manner that you move a shape up. You desire to move the Find a workout buddy shape down. **Why?** While a workout partner and a fitness monitor are important aspects of a successful fitness program, having proper equipment is key to achieving goals and preventing injuries. The Assemble your equipment shape, therefore, should be at the top of the graphic so that your audience members remember this information. The following steps move the Find a workout buddy shape down in the graphic.

1

- Position the pointer in the words, Find a workout buddy, and then click to select the shape (Figure 7–27).

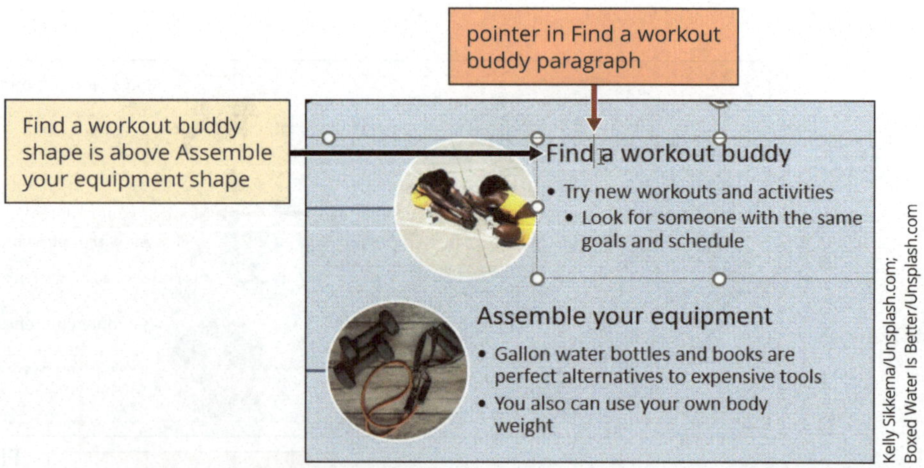

Figure 7–27

2

- Click the Move Down button (SmartArt Design tab | Create Graphic group) to reorder the Find a workout buddy shape below the Assemble your equipment shape (Figure 7–28).

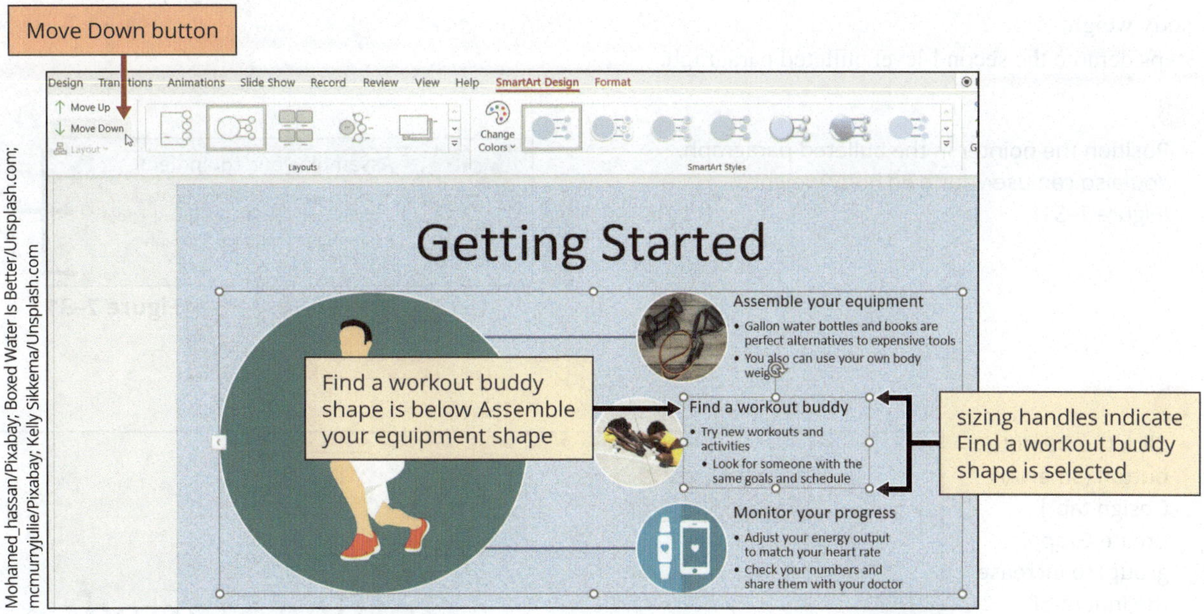

Mohamed_hassan/Pixabay; Boxed Water Is Better/Unsplash.com; mcmurryjulie/Pixabay; Kelly Sikkema/Unsplash.com

Figure 7–28

To Promote SmartArt Text

PowerPoint provides tools that allow you to promote and demote bulleted text to change the indents for these elements. In the Find a workout buddy shape, you want to promote the bulleted paragraph, Look for someone with the same goals and schedule, to the same level as the bullet above it. **Why?** Both these elements are equally important in encouraging people to find a suitable workout partner. The following steps promote the second bullet in the Find a workout buddy shape.

1

- Position the pointer in the bulleted paragraph, Look for someone with the same goals and schedule (Figure 7–29).

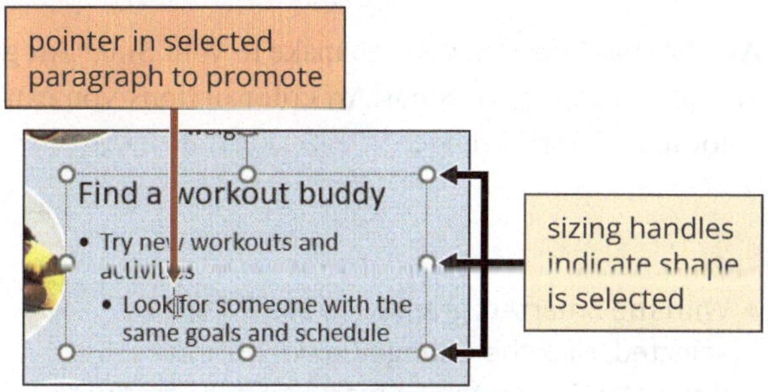

Figure 7–29

2

- Click the Promote button (SmartArt Design tab | Create Graphic group) to decrease the indent of the bulleted paragraph (Figure 7–30).

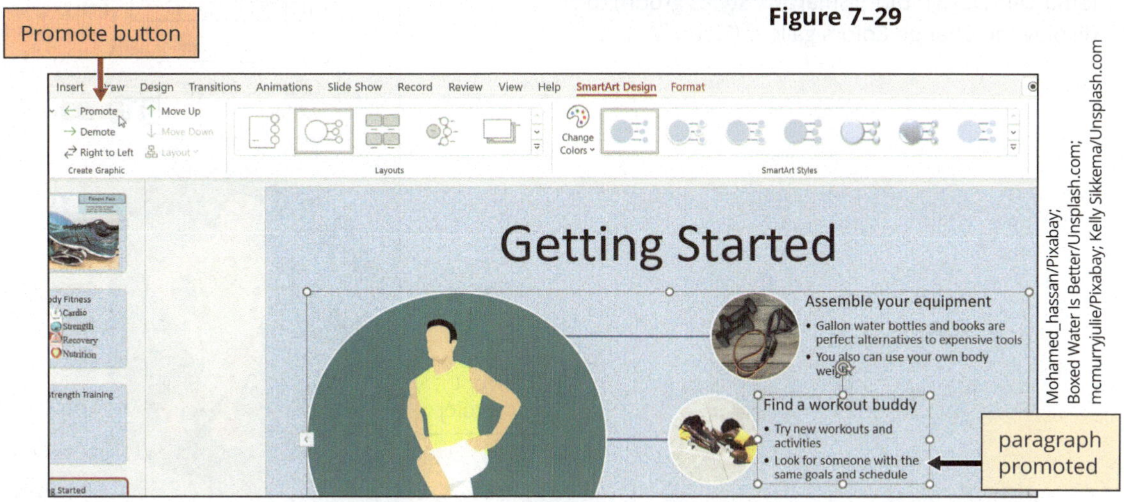

Mohamed_hassan/Pixabay; Boxed Water Is Better/Unsplash.com; mcmurryjulie/Pixabay; Kelly Sikkema/Unsplash.com

Figure 7–30

To Demote SmartArt Text

Another change you want to make on Slide 4 is to demote a paragraph in the Assemble your equipment shape. The bulleted items in this shape are second-level paragraphs, but you decide to demote the second paragraph, You also can use your own body weight. **Why?** People can realize that they do not need to purchase weights to achieve their strength goals. The following steps demote the second-level bulleted paragraph.

1

- Position the pointer in the bulleted paragraph, You also can use your own body weight (Figure 7–31).

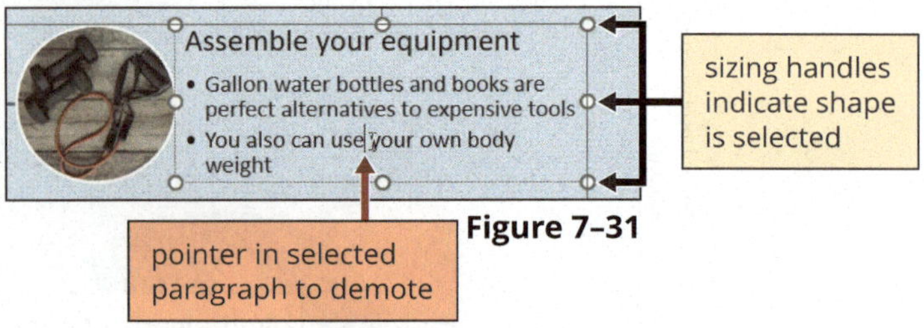

Kelly Sikkema/Unsplash.com

Figure 7–31

2

- Click the Demote button (SmartArt Design tab | Create Graphic group) to increase the indent of the bulleted paragraph (Figure 7–32).

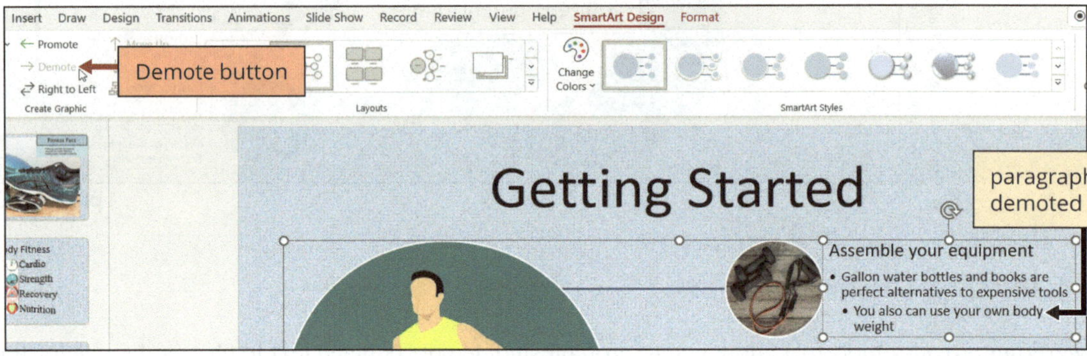

Kelly Sikkema/Unsplash.com; Mohamed_hassan/Pixabay

Figure 7–32

To Change the Color of SmartArt

Another modification you can make to your SmartArt graphic is to change its color. As with the WordArt Style gallery, PowerPoint provides a gallery of SmartArt color options you can preview and evaluate. The following steps change the SmartArt graphic color to a Colorful range. **Why?** The slide background and the line colors are blue. Also, the lines around the circles are white. You want these SmartArt line elements to change to black so they are more visible against the blue background.

1

- With the SmartArt graphic on Slide 4 still selected, click the Change Colors button (SmartArt Design tab | SmartArt Styles group) to display the Change Colors gallery (Figure 7–33).

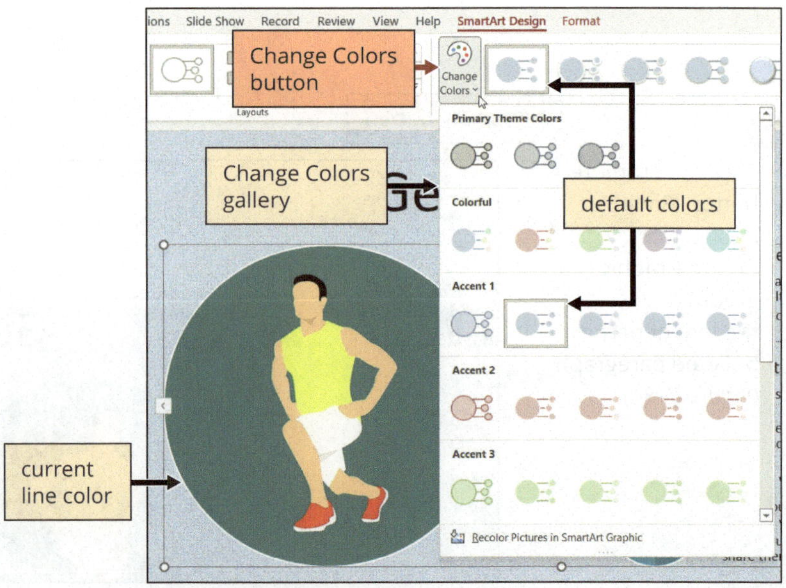

Mohamed_hassan/Pixabay

Figure 7–33

2

- Point to 'Dark 1 Outline' (first theme) in the Primary Theme Colors area to display a live preview of these colors (Figure 7–34).
- **Experiment:** Point to various colors in the Change Colors gallery and watch the shapes change colors.

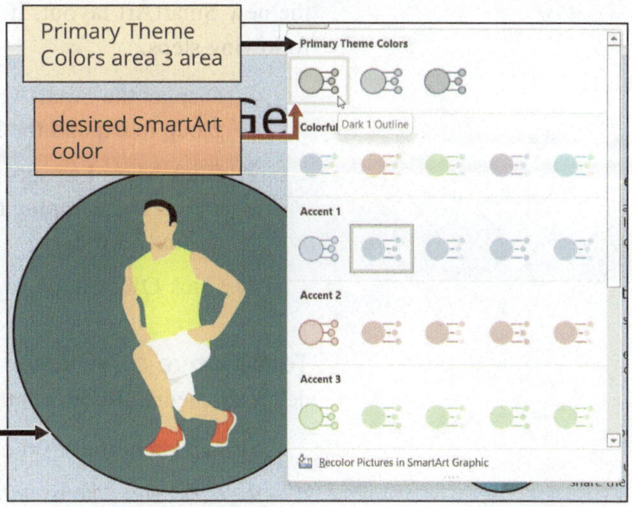

Mohamed_hassan/Pixabay

Figure 7–34

3

- Click 'Dark 1 Outline' to apply this color variation to the graphic (Figure 7–35).

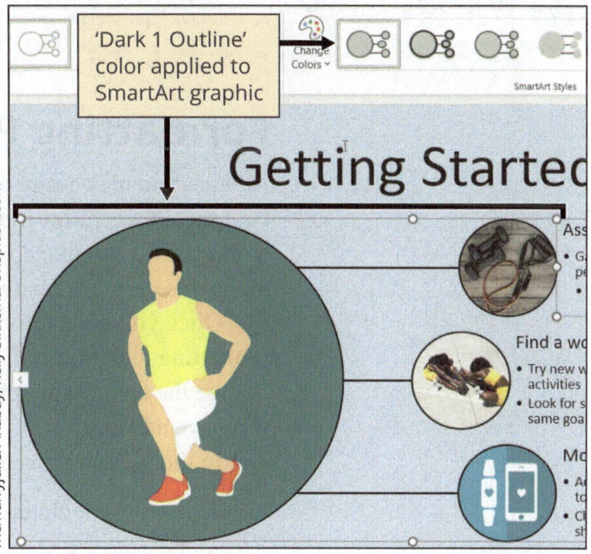

Mohamed_hassan/Pixabay; Boxed Water Is Better/Unsplash.com; mcmurryjulie/Pixabay; Kelly Sikkema/Unsplash.com

Figure 7–35

Other Ways

1. Right-click SmartArt graphic in an area other than a picture, click Color button

To Add a Bullet to a SmartArt Shape If you need to add information to a SmartArt shape, you can create a new bulleted paragraph. This text would display below the last bulleted paragraph in the shape. If you wanted to add a SmartArt bullet, you would perform the following steps.

1. Select the SmartArt graphic shape where you want to insert the bulleted paragraph.
2. Click the Add Bullet button (SmartArt Design tab | Create Graphic group) to insert a new bulleted paragraph below any bulleted text.

To Change the SmartArt Layout Once you begin formatting a SmartArt shape, you may decide that another layout better conveys the message you are communicating to an audience. PowerPoint allows you to change the layout easily. Any graphical changes that were made to the original SmartArt, such as moving shapes or promoting and demoting paragraphs, are applied to the new SmartArt layout. If you wanted to change the SmartArt layout, you would perform the following steps.

1. Display the SmartArt Design tab and then click the More button in the Layouts group to expand the Layouts gallery.
2. Click More Layouts at the bottom of the Layouts gallery to display the Choose a SmartArt Graphic dialog box, click the desired category, and then click the desired layout.
3. Click OK (Choose a SmartArt Graphic dialog box).

To Remove a SmartArt Shape One change you can make to a SmartArt graphic is to delete elements. If you wanted to remove a shape, you would perform the following steps.

1. Click a border of the SmartArt shape you wish to delete to select the entire shape.
2. Press DELETE to delete the shape.

Break Point: If you wish to take a break, this is a good place to do so. Be sure the Fitness file is saved and then you can quit PowerPoint. To resume at a later time, start PowerPoint, open the file called Fitness, and continue following the steps from this location forward.

Formatting Pictures

At times you may desire to emphasize one section of a picture and eliminate distracting background content. PowerPoint includes formatting tools that allow you to edit pictures. The **Remove Background** command isolates the foreground from the background. Once you format the picture to include only the desired content, you can **compress** the image to reduce the file size.

Once you have removed the background, you may want to enhance the image with another formatting tool. You can, for example, improve the picture's brightness and contrast. You also can change the color to match other content on the slide based on the design theme or other elements you have added.

In the following pages, you will perform these tasks:

1. Remove a picture's background.
2. Change a picture's contrast and brightness.
3. Compress pictures.

To Remove a Picture Background

Slide 4 in the Fitness presentation has a picture of a person on the left side of the SmartArt graphic. You want to eliminate the green background from the image. Why? The green circle is a large element on the slide and detracts from the message being presented. The person can display prominently if it is the only element within the circle border. The PowerPoint Background Removal feature makes it easy to eliminate unwanted background aspects. When you click the Remove Background button, PowerPoint attempts to select the foreground of the picture and overlay a magenta marquee selection on this area. You then can adjust the marquee shape and size to contain all foreground picture components you want to keep. The following steps remove the background from the picture.

1

- With Slide 4 displayed, click the large circle picture with the green background to select it and then click the Picture Format tab (Figure 7–36).

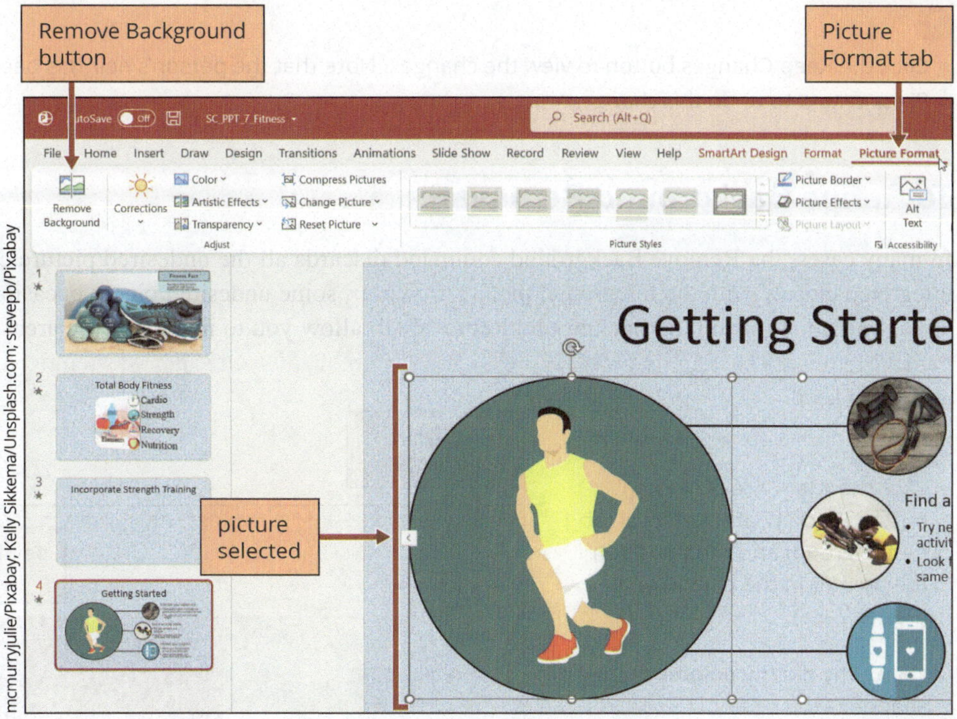

Mohamed_hassan/Pixabay; Boxed Water Is Better/Unsplash.com; mcmurryjulie/Pixabay; Kelly Sikkema/Unsplash.com; stevepb/Pixabay

Figure 7–36

2

- Zoom the slide to 140%. If necessary, use the vertical and horizontal scroll bars to adjust the slide so the entire picture of the person is visible.
- Click the Remove Background button (Picture Format tab | Adjust group) to display the Background Removal tab and a marquee selection area (Figure 7–37).

Q&A How does PowerPoint determine the area to display within the marquee?

Microsoft Research software engineers developed the algorithms that determine the portions of the picture in the foreground.

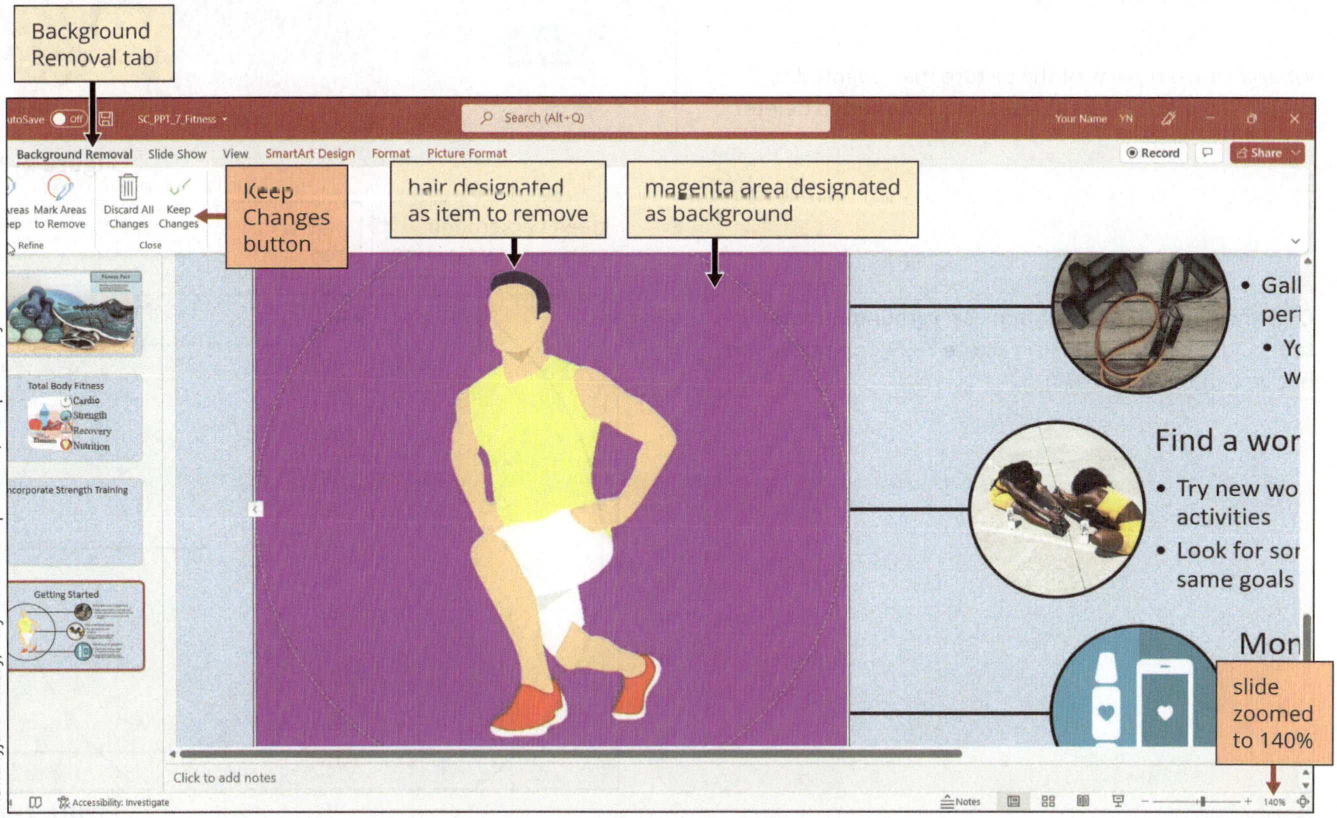

Mohamed_hassan/Pixabay; Boxed Water Is Better/Unsplash.com; mcmurryjulie/Pixabay; Kelly Sikkema/Unsplash.com; stevepb/Pixabay

Figure 7–37

3

- Click the Keep Changes button to view the changes. Note that the person's hair has been removed.
- Press CTRL+Z to undo this change.

To Refine Background Removal

In many cases, the Remove Background command discards all the undesired picture components. When the background is integrated closely with the foreground picture, however, some undesired pieces occasionally remain and other desired pieces are discarded. Tools on the Background Removal tab allow you to mark specific areas to remove and to keep. **Why?** In the picture, the green background was removed. In addition, the person's hair was removed. The following steps mark the hair as an area to keep.

1

- Click the 'Mark Areas to Keep' button (Background Removal tab | Refine group) and then position the pointer in the person's hair (Figure 7–38).

Q&A Why did my pointer change shape?
The pointer changed to a pencil to indicate you are about to draw on a precise area of the picture.

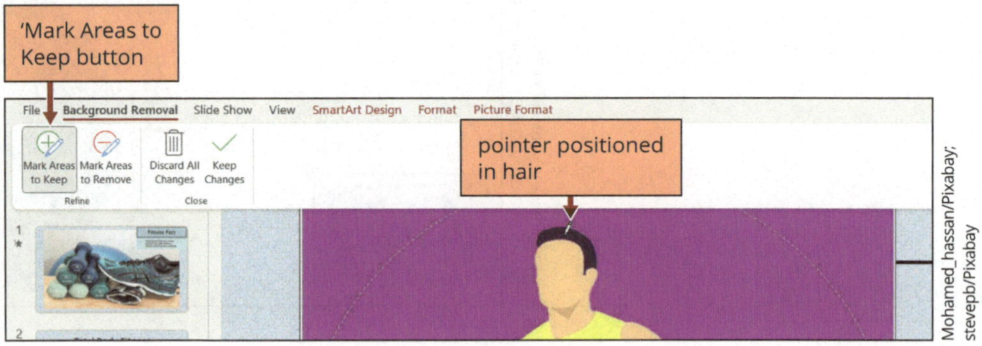

Figure 7–38

2

- Click and then drag the pointer in the person's hair to indicate the portion of the picture to keep (Figure 7–39).

Q&A If I marked an area that I want to delete, can I reverse my action?
Yes. Press CTRL+Z immediately after you click the area.

What if I erased parts of the picture that I wanted to keep or I did not select all the areas I wanted to delete?
You may need to make several passes to keep part of the picture.

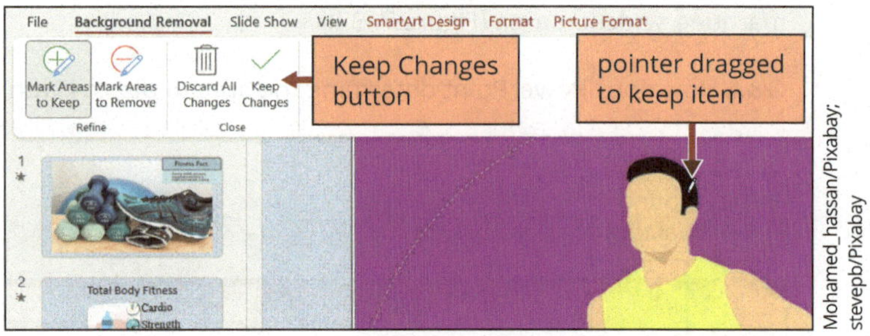

Figure 7–39

3

- Click the Keep Changes button (Background Removal tab | Close group) (shown in Figure 7–39) to remove the background (Figure 7–40).

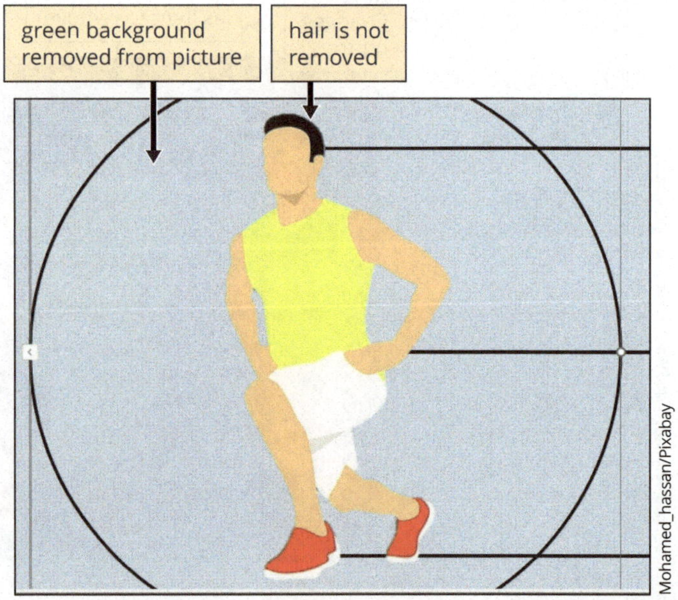

Figure 7–40

To Mark Areas to Remove If you wanted to remove areas of a picture, you would perform the following steps.

1. Click the 'Mark Areas to Remove button (Background Removal tab | Refine group) and then position the pointer in the desired area.
2. Click and then drag the pointer across the area to remove.
3. Click the Keep Changes button (Background Removal tab | Close group).

To Flip a Picture

You can flip the picture so that the person is pointed in the opposite direction. **Why?** The person's knees will point inward toward the graphic's content and help direct the audience's attention to the three getting started measures. The following steps flip the picture horizontally.

1

- With the picture selected and the Picture Format tab displayed, click the Rotate button (Picture Format tab | Arrange group) to display the Rotate Objects menu.
- Point to Flip Horizontal in the list to see a preview of the flipped picture (Figure 7–41).

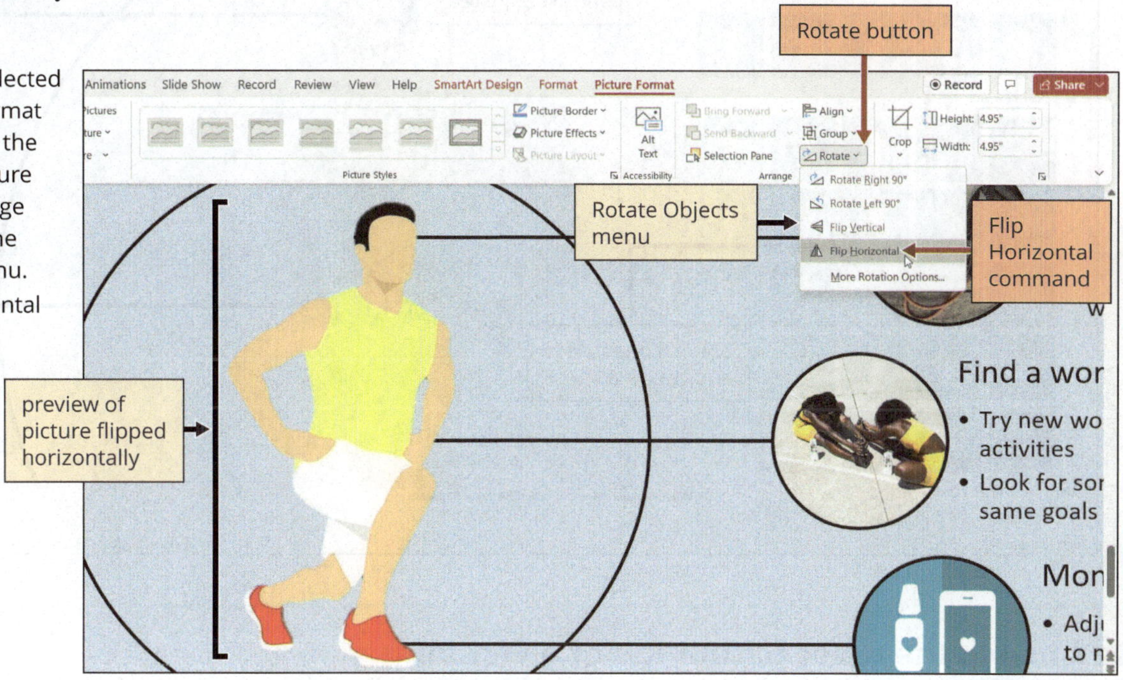

Mohamed_hassan/Pixabay; Boxed Water Is Better/Unsplash.com; mcmurryjulie/Pixabay; Kelly Sikkema/Unsplash.com

Figure 7–41

2

- Click Flip Horizontal in the Rotate Objects menu to flip the picture.

To Change the Brightness and Contrast of a Picture

A picture's brightness and contrast can be altered in predefined percentage increments. The overall lightness or darkness of the entire image is determined by the brightness setting, and the difference between the darkest and lightest areas of the image is determined by the contrast setting. **Why?** The person's bright yellow shirt displays prominently on the slide. Decreasing the contrast will help direct the audience's attention to the other slide elements. The following step decreases the contrast and brightness.

1

- Zoom the slide to 200%.

2

- With the picture still selected, click the Corrections button (Picture Format tab | Adjust group) to display the Corrections gallery.
- Point to 'Brightness: -20% Contrast: -20%' (second picture in the second Brightness/Contrast row) to display a live preview of this correction on the picture (Figure 7–42).
- **Experiment:** Point to various brightness and contrast variations in the gallery and watch the colors change in the picture.
- Click 'Brightness: -20% Contrast: -20%' to apply this correction.

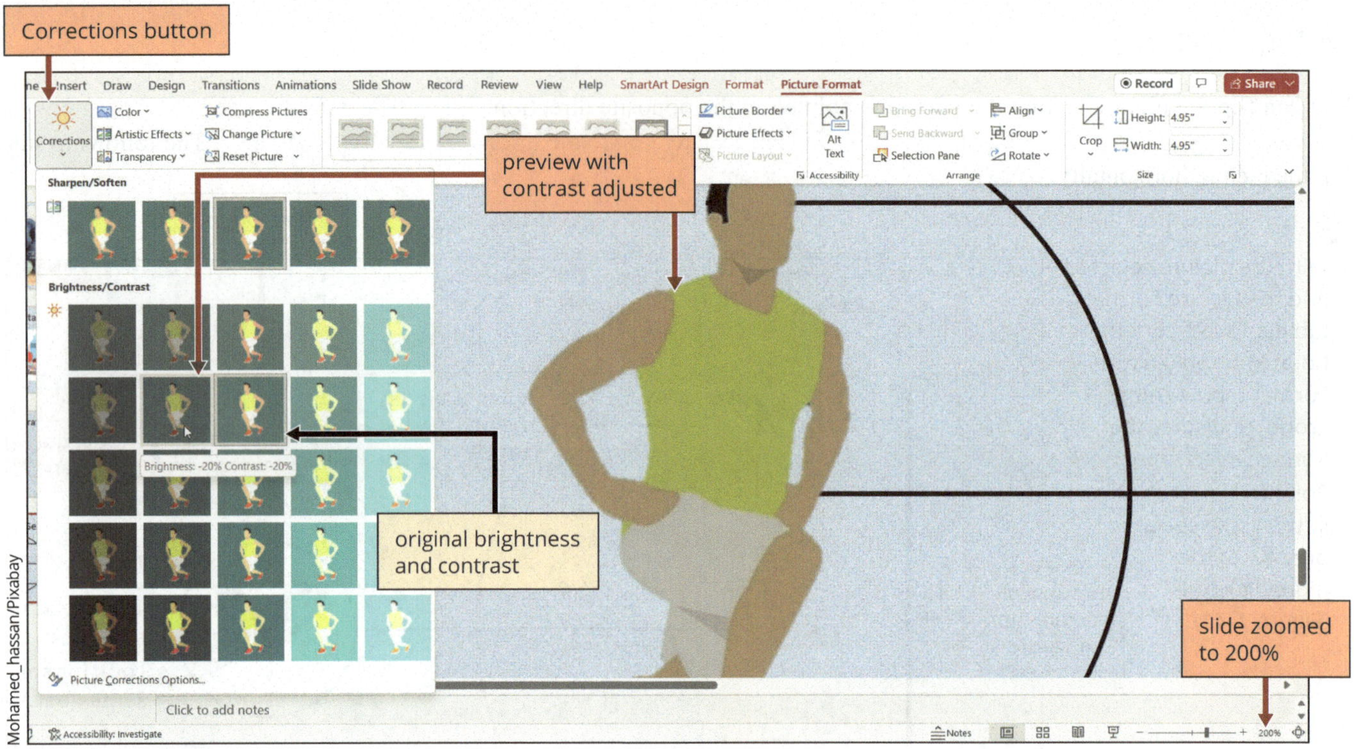

Figure 7–42

To Change the Color Saturation of a Picture

The Color gallery has a wide variety of preset formatting combinations that allow you to match or add contrast to slide elements. High color saturation produces vivid colors, and low saturation produces gray tones. The following steps change the color saturation of the Slide 4 picture. **Why?** You want to make the shirt's yellow color less vivid.

1

- With the picture still selected, click the Color button (Picture Format tab | Adjust group) to display the Color gallery (Figure 7–43).

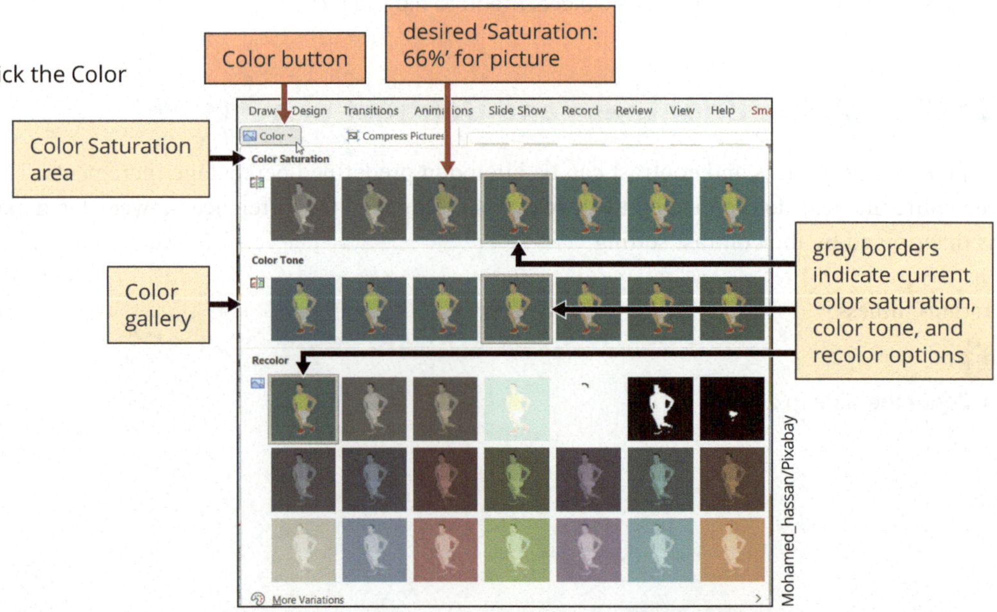

Figure 7–43

2

- Point to 'Saturation: 66%' (third thumbnail in the Color Saturation row) to display a live preview of this adjustment on the picture (Figure 7–44).
- **Experiment:** Point to various saturation variations in the gallery and watch the colors change in the picture.
- Click 'Saturation: 66%' to apply this saturation to the picture.

3

- Zoom the slide to 80%.

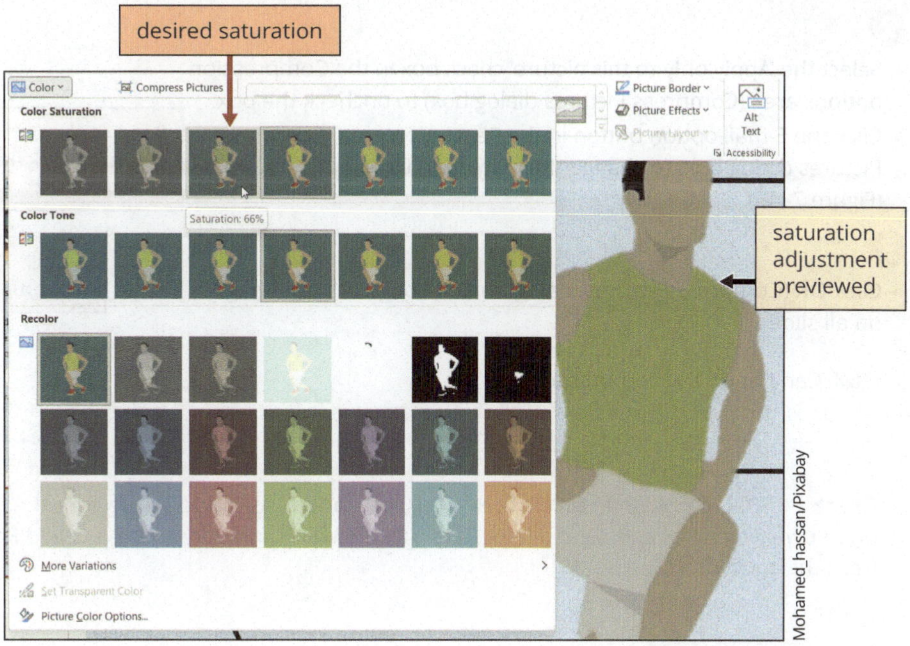

Figure 7–44

To Reset a Picture To remove all effects from a picture, you would perform the following step.

1. Click the Reset Picture button (Picture Format tab | Adjust group).

To Compress a Picture

Photos inserted into slides greatly increase the total PowerPoint file size. PowerPoint automatically compresses picture files inserted into slides by eliminating details, generally with no visible loss of quality. You can increase the compression and, in turn, decrease the file size if you instruct PowerPoint to compress a picture you have modified or cropped so you can save space on a storage medium such as a solid-state drive, memory card, or USB flash drive. Although these storage devices generally have a large storage capacity, you might want to reduce the file size. **Why?** A smaller size reduces the download time from a server or website. Also, some Internet service providers restrict an attachment's file size.

The background of the picture on Slide 4 has been removed. You will not need any of the invisible portions of the picture, so you can delete them permanently and reduce the picture file size. The following steps compress the size of the Slide 4 picture.

1

- With the picture selected, click the Compress Pictures button (Picture Format tab | Adjust group) to display the Compress Pictures dialog box (Figure 7–45).

Q&A If I want to add an artistic effect, should I apply the effect prior to or after compressing a picture?

Compress a picture and then apply the artistic effect.

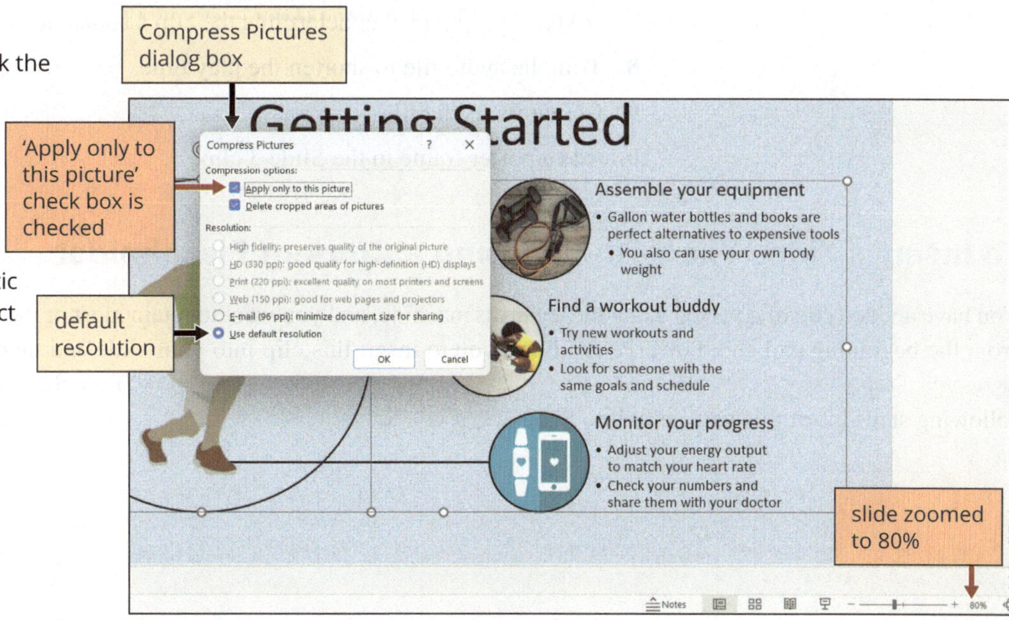

Mohamed_hassan/Pixabay; Boxed Water Is Better/Unsplash.com; mcmurryjulie/Pixabay; Kelly Sikkema/Unsplash.com

Figure 7–45

2

- Select the 'Apply only to this picture' check box in the Compression options area (Compress Pictures dialog box) to uncheck the box.
- Click the E-mail option button in the Resolution area (Compress Pictures dialog box) to change the resolution to 96 ppi (Figure 7–46).

3

- Click OK (Compress Pictures dialog box) to compress the images on all slides.

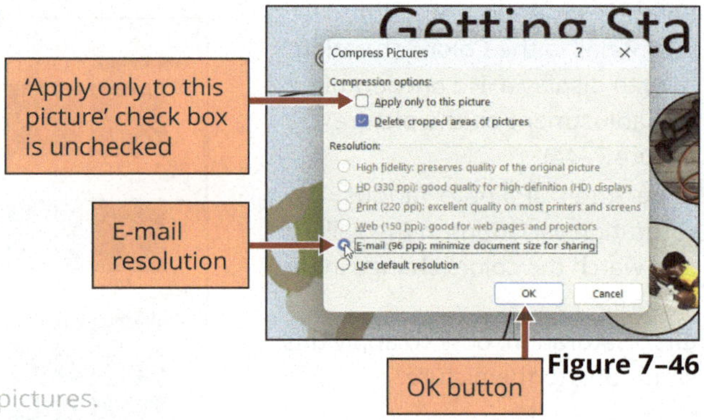

Figure 7–46

Mohamed_hassan/Pixabay; Boxed Water Is Better/Unsplash.com; mcmurryjulie/Pixabay; Kelly Sikkema/Unsplash.com

Q&A Can I undo the compression?
Yes, as long as you have not saved the file after compressing the pictures.

Break Point: If you wish to take a break, this is a good place to do so. Be sure the Fitness file is saved and then you can quit PowerPoint. To resume at a later time, start PowerPoint, open the file called Fitness, and continue following the steps from this location forward.

BTW
Play Options for Online Videos
Play options are not available for online videos, such as YouTube videos. They are available only for videos inserted from your computer, network, or OneDrive.

Inserting a Video and an Audio Clip

Strength is an important element of total body fitness, as shown by the SmartArt on Slide 2. On Slide 3 you want to emphasize that regular strength exercises can help develop strong bones, increase metabolism, contribute to better balance, and protect joints from injury. You can enhance this presentation's content by adding a video clip on Slide 3 demonstrating one strength training technique: leg presses. The clip does not have audio, so you will add an audio clip of upbeat music.

In the following pages, you will perform these tasks:

1. Insert a video file into Slide 3.
2. Trim the video file to shorten the play time.
3. Add video options that determine the clip's appearance and playback.
4. Resize the Slide 3 video clip.
5. Add a video style to the Slide 3 clip.
6. Insert an audio file into Slide 3.
7. Add audio options that determine the clip's appearance and playback.
8. Trim the audio file to shorten the play time.
9. Compress media files.
10. Add a poster frame to the Slide 3 clip.

To Insert a Video File without Using a Content Placeholder

You have a video clip of a person using the leg press machine, and you want to retain most of the clip but eliminate a few seconds from the beginning and end. PowerPoint allows you to insert this clip into your slide and then trim the file. **Why?** You want to play just a portion of the video when you preview the clip or run the slide show. This clip is available in the Data Files. The following steps insert this video clip into Slide 3.

1

- Display Slide 3 and then display the Insert tab.
- Click the Video button (Insert tab | Media group) to display the Insert Video menu (Figure 7–47).

Figure 7–47

2

- Click This Device on the Insert Video From menu to display the Insert Video dialog box.
- If necessary, navigate to the location where the Data Files are located and then click Support_PPT_7_Leg_Press to select the .mp4 file (Figure 7–48).

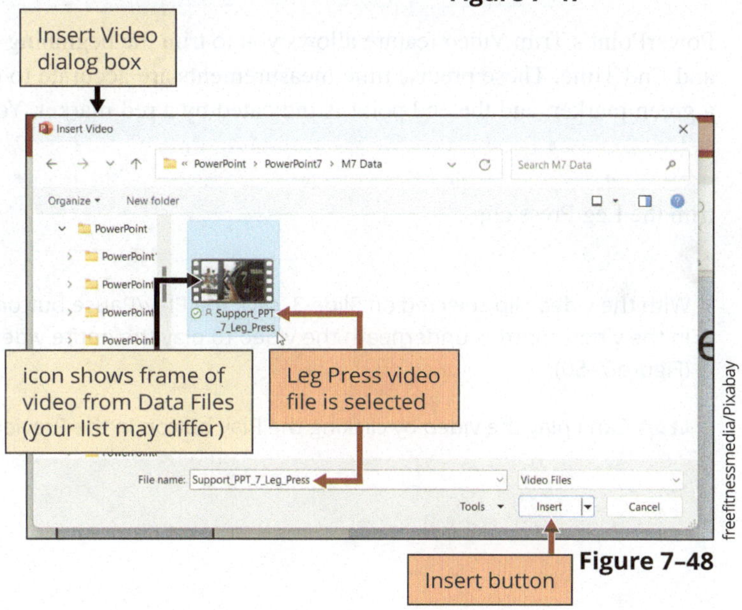

Figure 7–48

3

- Click the Insert button (Insert Video dialog box) to insert the Leg Press video clip into Slide 3 (Figure 7–49).
- If the Design Ideas pane opens, close it.

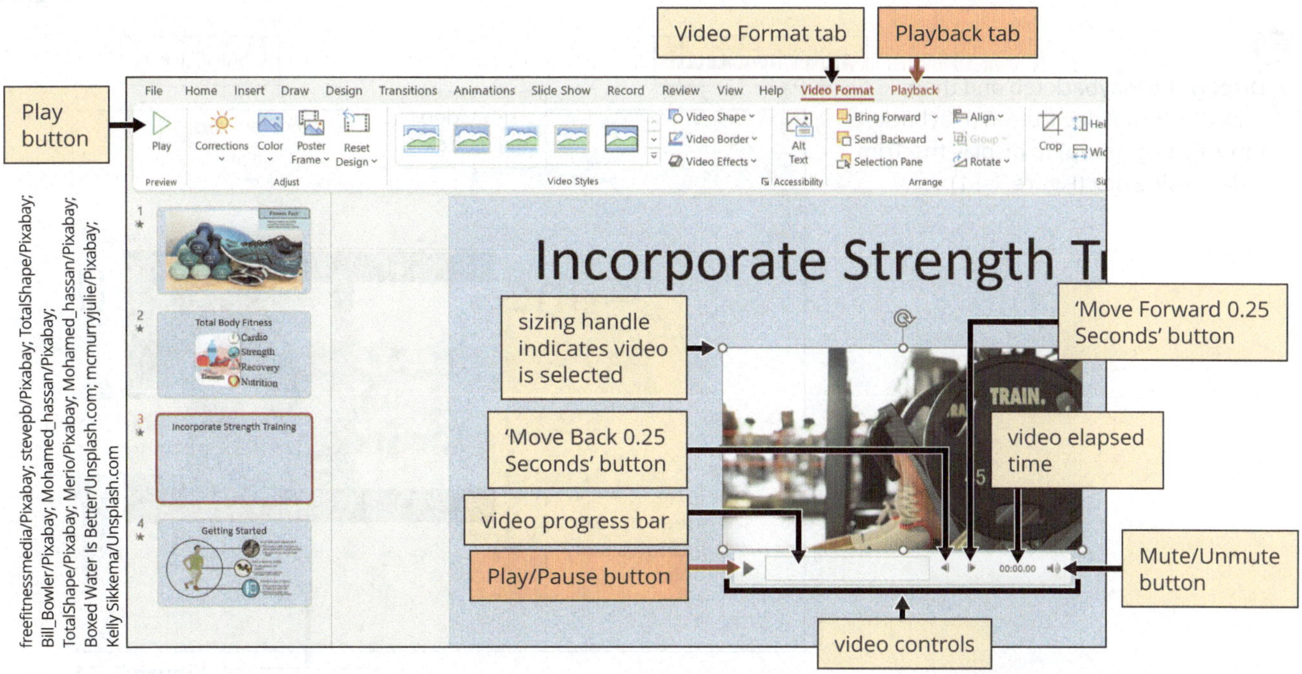

Figure 7–49

To Insert an Online Video PowerPoint allows you to insert or link to an online video, such as those found on YouTube, and then play this file during your presentation. These videos are stored on and played from the website, so you must be connected to the Internet when you play these files. To insert an online video, you would perform the following steps.

1. Display the Insert tab and then click the Video button (Insert tab | Media group) to display the Video menu.
2. Click Online Video to display the Insert Video dialog box.
3. In the search box, enter the web address of a video from a supported video provider to insert a video from a website.
4. Click the Insert button to insert the video clip into the slide.

To Trim a Video File

PowerPoint's Trim Video feature allows you to trim the beginning and end of your clip by designating your desired Start Time and End Time. These precise time measurements are accurate to one-thousandth of a second. The start point is indicated by a green marker, and the end point is indicated by a red marker. You want to shorten the duration of the Leg Press video clip. **Why?** The Leg Press video file has a running time of almost 12 seconds. Much of the video is the same view of the person exercising, so you decide to delete a few seconds from the beginning and the end to shorten the duration. The following steps trim the Leg Press clip.

1

- With the video clip selected on Slide 3, click the Play/Pause button in the video controls underneath the video to play the entire video (Figure 7–50).

Q&A Can I play the video by clicking the Play button in the Preview group?
Yes. This Play button plays the entire clip. You may prefer to click the Play/Pause button displayed in the video controls to stop the video and examine one of the frames.

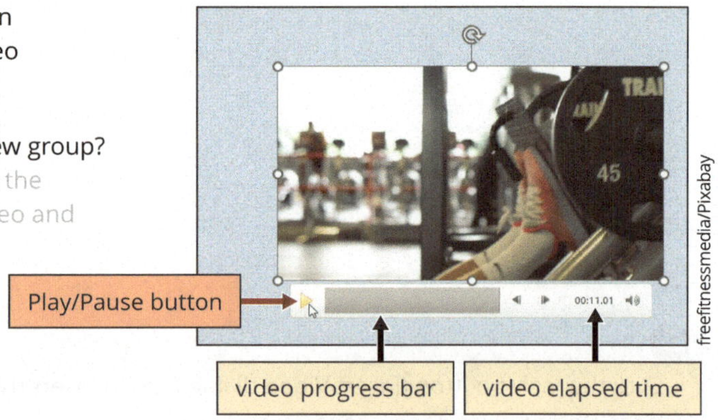

Figure 7–50

2

- Display the Playback tab and then click the Trim Video button (Playback tab | Editing group) to display the Trim Video dialog box (Figure 7–51).

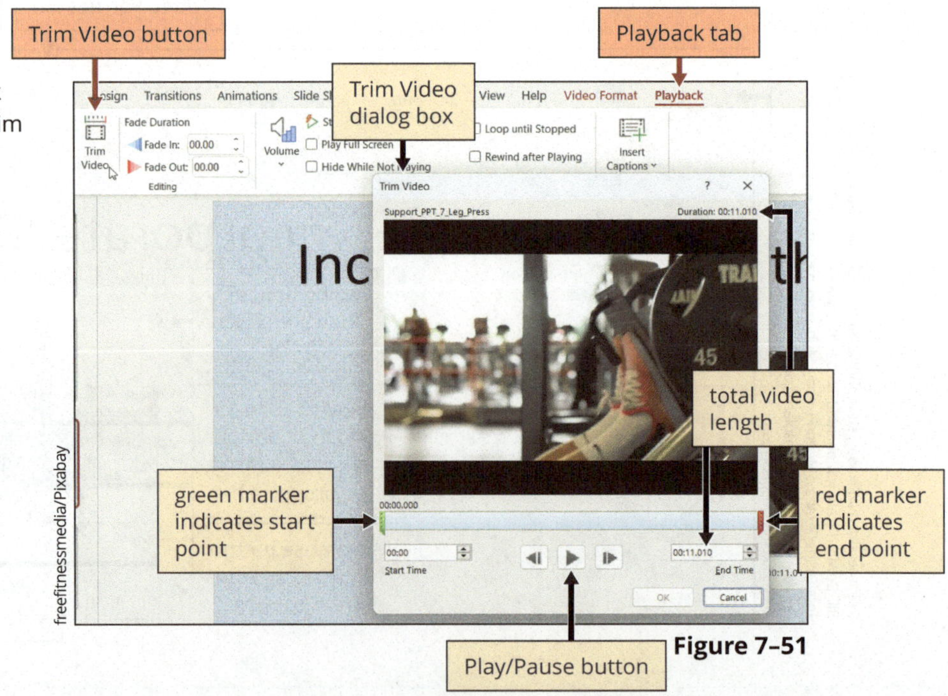

Figure 7–51

3

- Click the Start Time up arrow several times until 00:01.353 is displayed (Figure 7–52).

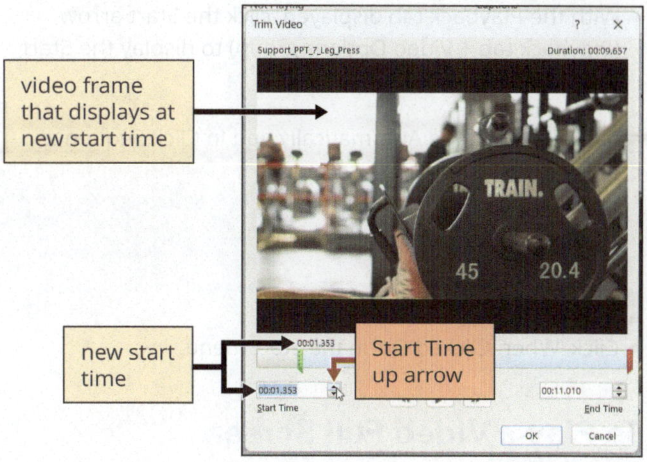

freefitnessmedia/Pixabay

Figure 7–52

4

- Click the End Time down arrow several times until 00:10.263 is displayed (Figure 7–53).

Q&A Can I specify the start or end times by dragging the markers?
Yes. You can drag the green marker to determine the start time and the red marker to determine the end time. You also can click the Next Frame and Previous Frame buttons or enter the time in the Start Time or End Time boxes (Trim Video dialog box).

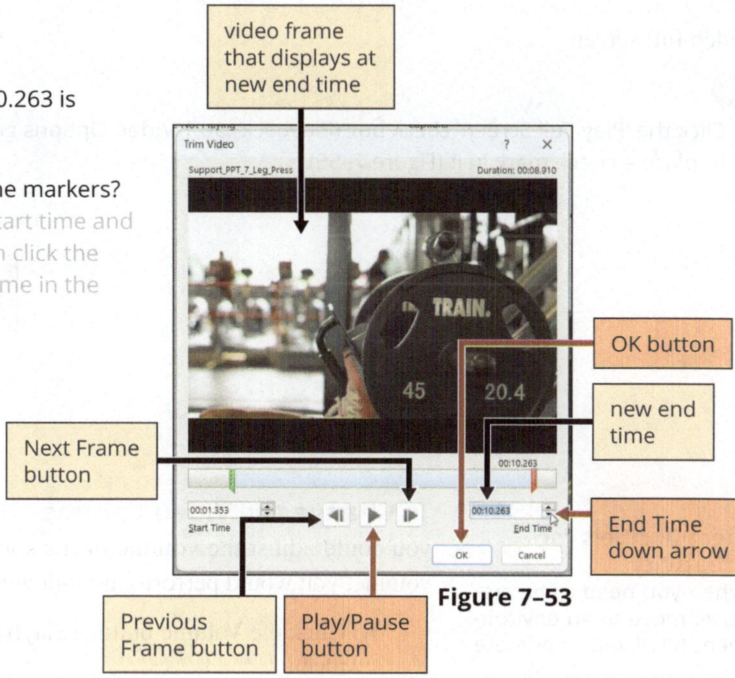

freefitnessmedia/Pixabay

Figure 7–53

5

- Click the Play/Pause button (Trim Video dialog box) to review the shortened video clip.
- Click OK (Trim Video dialog box) to set the Start Time and End Time and to close the Trim Video dialog box.

Other Ways

1. Right-click clip, click Trim on Mini toolbar
2. In Trim Video dialog box, press ALT+S and ALT+E

To Change the Video Start Option

Once the video clip is inserted into Slide 3, you can specify that the video plays when the presenter clicks the area of the slide with the video after the slide is displayed. Other options are to run the video immediately when the slide is displayed or in a click sequence. **Why?** When you are giving your presentation, you want to discuss the slide topic and then click the mouse to start the video. The following steps add the option of playing the video when a frame is clicked.

1

- With the Playback tab displayed, click the Start arrow (Playback tab | Video Options group) to display the Start menu (Figure 7–54).

Q&A What do the Automatically and In Click Sequence options do?
The video clip would begin playing immediately when a slide is displayed during the slide show.

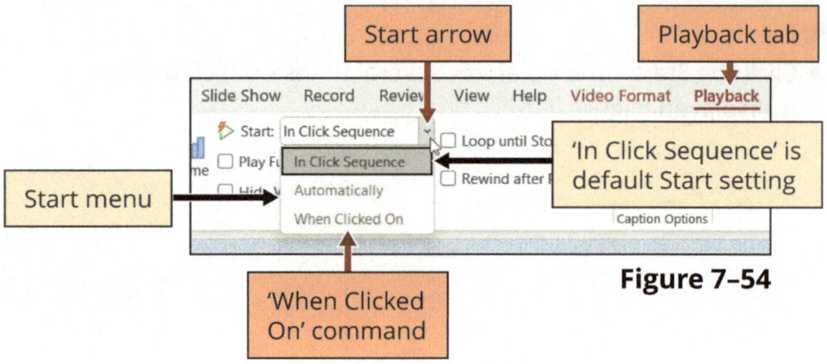

Figure 7–54

2

- Click 'When Clicked On' in the Start menu.

To Play a Video Full Screen

Once the video clip is inserted into Slide 3, you can specify that the video fills the entire screen when the video plays. **Why?** You want your audience to see the details of using the leg press machine. The following step adds the option of playing the video full screen.

1

- Click the 'Play Full Screen' check box (Playback tab | Video Options group) to place a check mark in it (Figure 7–55).

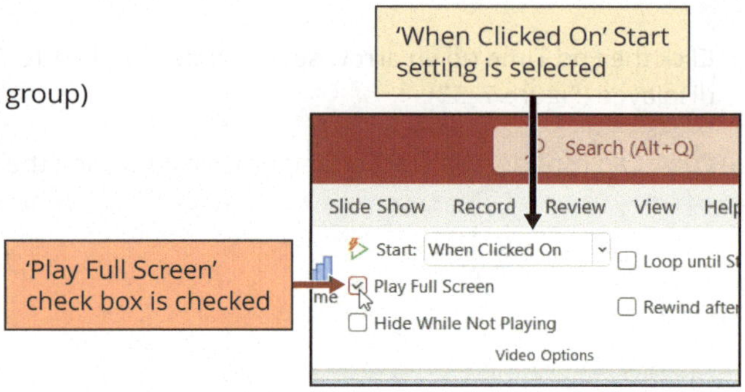

Figure 7–55

BTW
Ideal Decibels for Creativity
When you need to be creative, move to an environment filled with moderate background noise, such as a coffee shop. Researchers at the University of British Columbia state that a noise level of approximately 70 decibels, which is the sound of a quiet conversation or highway noise from afar, fosters original ideas. Anything louder than this ambient noise level decreases the thought process.

To Change the Video Volume The Leg Press video does not have audio. If it did, however, you could adjust the volume of the sound. The default video volume is High. To decrease the volume, you would perform the following steps.

1. Click the Volume button (Playback tab | Video Options group) to display the Volume menu.
2. Click Medium or Low on the Volume menu to set the audio volume or click Mute if you do not want your audience to hear any recorded sounds.

To Rewind a Video after Playing To rewind your video clip after playing during your presentation, you would perform the following step.

1. Click the 'Rewind after Playing' check box (Playback tab | Video Options group) to place a check mark in it.

To Resize a Video Proportionally

The default Leg Press video frame size can be changed. You resize a video clip in the same manner that you resize pictures. The following steps increase the Leg Press video frame using a sizing handle. **Why?** You want to fit the video near the center of the slide.

1

- With the video still selected, click Video Format on the ribbon to display the Video Format tab (Figure 7–56).

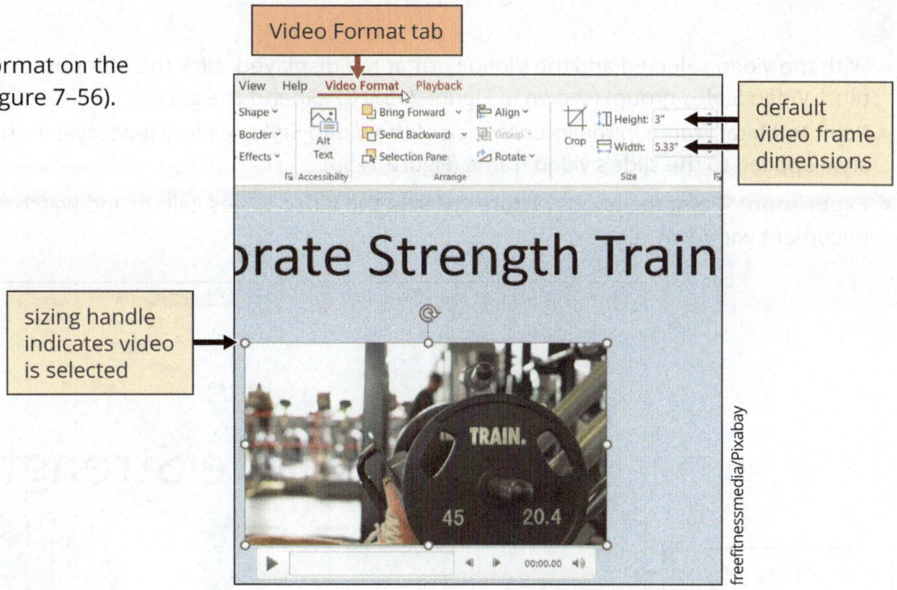

Figure 7–56

2

- Drag any corner sizing handle diagonally outward until the frame is resized to approximately 5.6" × 9.96".
- Use the smart guides to position the clip, as shown in Figure 7–57.

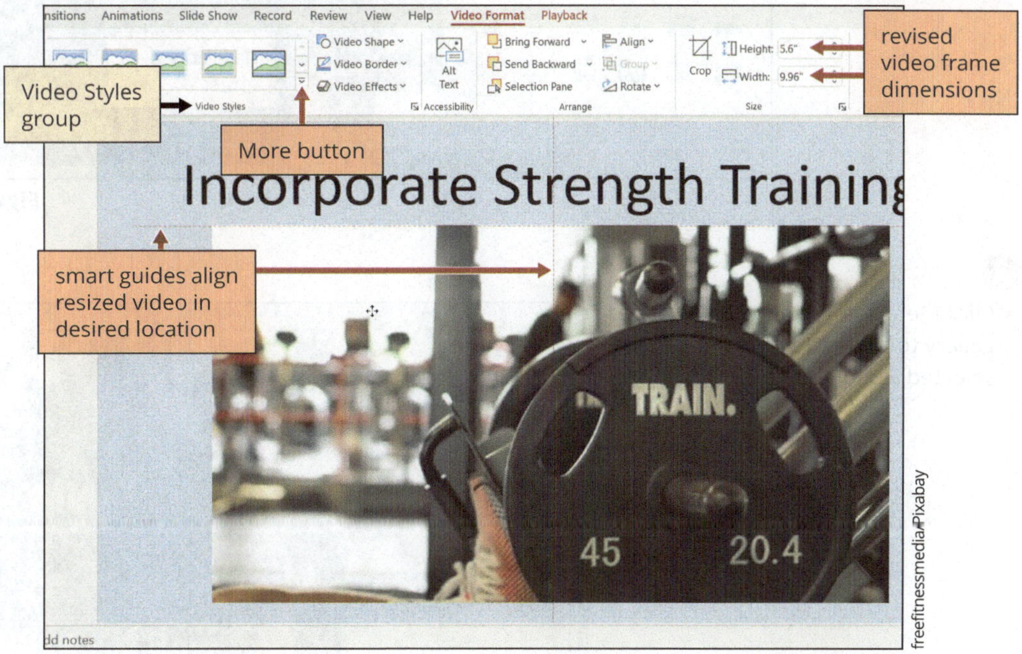

Figure 7–57

To Apply a Video Style

The video styles are similar to the picture styles you applied in previous modules and include various shapes, angles, borders, and reflections. The following steps apply a video style to the Leg Press video clip on Slide 3. **Why?** The Leg Press video clip on Slide 3 displays full screen when it is playing, but you decide to increase the visual appeal of the clip when it is not playing by applying a video style.

1

- With the video selected and the Video Format tab displayed, click the More button in the Video Styles gallery (Video Format tab | Video Styles group) (shown in Figure 7–57) to expand the gallery.
- Point to Metal Frame in the Intense area of the Video Styles gallery (last style in the last row) to display a live preview of that style applied to the slide's video frame (Figure 7–58).
- **Experiment:** Point to various picture styles in the Video Styles gallery and watch the style of the video frame change in the document window.

Figure 7–58

2

- Click Metal Frame in the Video Styles gallery to apply the style to the selected video (Figure 7–59).

Figure 7–59

To Add a Video Poster Frame

A **poster frame** is the frame that appears on a video object when the video is not playing. This preview image of your video helps an audience anticipate the content of the video. This frame can be a picture or one frame from the video you are going to play. In this module, you will use a picture from the Data Files. **Why?** You used this Weights picture as part of the SmartArt graphic on Slide 2, so your audience will be familiar with this image. The following steps apply a poster frame to the Leg Press video clip.

1

- With the video clip selected, click the Poster Frame button (Video Format tab | Adjust group) to display the Poster Frame menu (Figure 7–60).

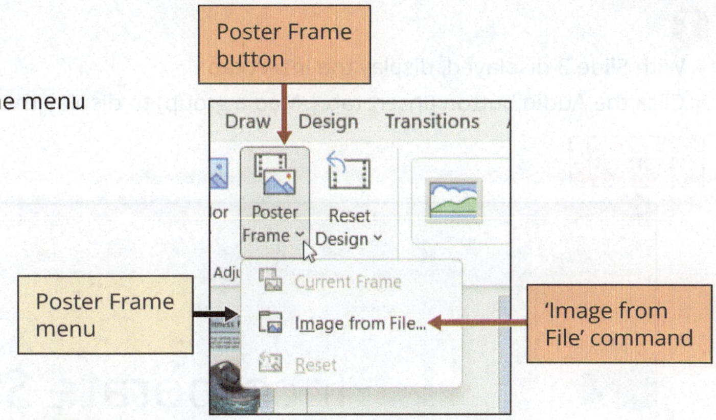

Figure 7–60

stevepb/Pixabay

2

- Click 'Image from File' to display the Insert Pictures dialog box.
- Click 'From a File' to display the Insert Picture dialog box.
- If necessary, navigate to the location where the Data Files are located and then click Support_PPT_7_Weights.png to select the file (Figure 7–61).

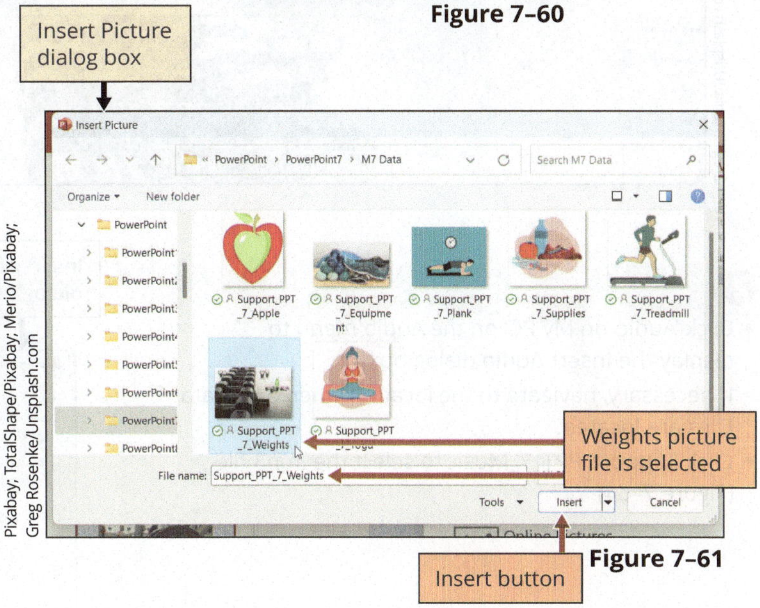

Figure 7–61

stevepb/Pixabay; TotalShape/Pixabay; Bill_Bowler/Pixabay; Mohamed_hassan/Pixabay; TotalShape/Pixabay; Merio/Pixabay; Greg Rosenke/Unsplash.com

3

- Click the Insert button (Insert Picture dialog box) to insert this picture into Slide 3 as a poster frame (Figure 7–62).

Figure 7–62

Greg Rosenke/Unsplash.com

To Insert an Audio Clip from a File

If your computer has a microphone, you can enable it and record audio for your presentation. In addition, if you have an app on your smartphone or mobile device or a digital audio recorder, you can record sounds to insert into your presentation. You also can locate audio files on a variety of websites. The following steps insert an audio clip into Slide 3. **Why?** The video clip does not have any sound, so you want to add an audio clip of upbeat music to add interest when Slide 3 is displayed.

1

- With Slide 3 displayed, display the Insert tab.
- Click the Audio button (Insert tab | Media group) to display the Audio menu (Figure 7–63).

Figure 7–63

Greg Rosenke/Unsplash.com

2

- Click 'Audio on My PC' on the Audio menu to display the Insert Audio dialog box.
- If necessary, navigate to the location where the Data Files are located.
- Click Support_PPT_7_Music to select the .mp3 file (Figure 7–64).

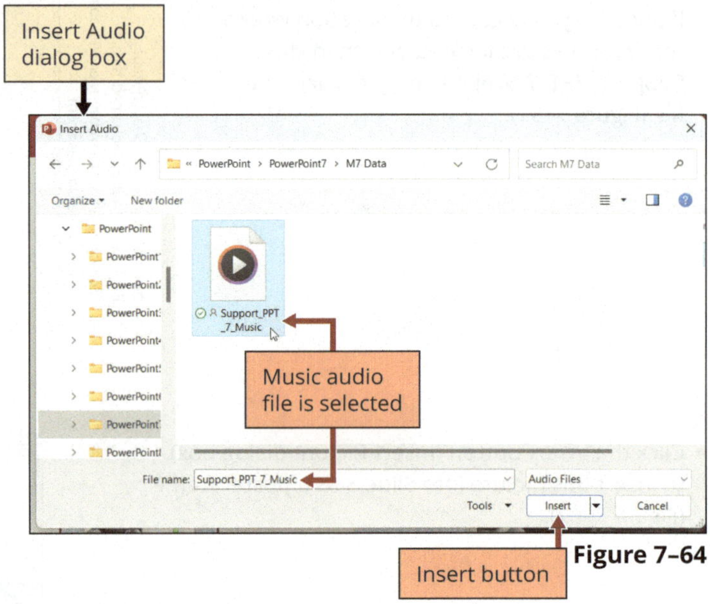

Figure 7–64

3

- Click the Insert button (Insert Audio dialog box) to insert the audio clip into Slide 3 (Figure 7–65).

Q&A Why does a sound icon display on the slide?

The icon indicates an audio file is inserted.

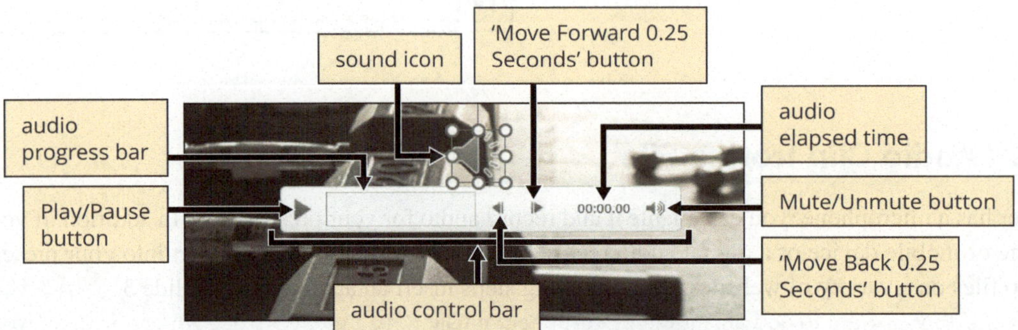

Figure 7–65

Greg Rosenke/Unsplash.com

4

- Drag the sound icon and the audio control bar near the lower-left corner of the slide (Figure 7–66).

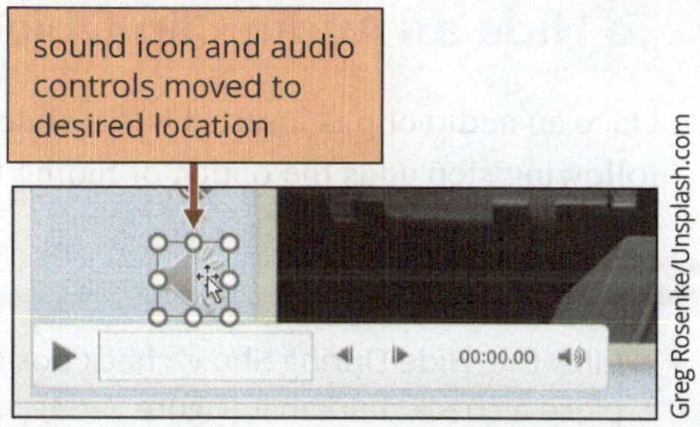

Figure 7–66

Q&A Must I move the icon on the slide?
No. Although your audience will not see the icon when you run the slide show, it is easier for you to see the audio controls in this area of this slide.

Can I preview the audio clip?
Yes. Click the Play button on the ribbon (Preview group) or the Play/Pause button on the audio controls.

To Change the Audio Clip Start Option

Once an audio clip is inserted into a slide, you can specify options that control playback and appearance. The audio clip can play either automatically or when clicked. The following steps add the option of starting automatically. **Why?** You do not want to click the screen to start the sound.

1

- With the Playback tab displayed, click the Start arrow (Playback tab | Audio Options group) to display the Start menu (Figure 7–67).

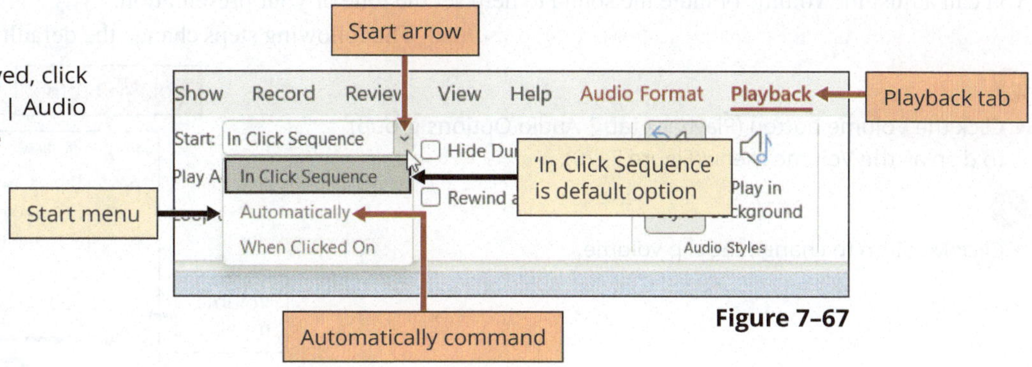

Figure 7–67

2

- Click Automatically in the Start menu.

Q&A How do the 'In Click Sequence' and the 'When Clicked On' options function?
If you were to select either of these options, the sound would begin playing only after the presenter clicks Slide 3 during a presentation.

To Loop an Audio Clip

Once an audio clip is inserted into a slide, you can specify that it can repeat while a particular slide is displayed. The following step adds the option of playing until the slide no longer is displayed. **Why?** You want the music to repeat while the slide is displayed to coordinate with the picture prominently shown and to keep the audience's attention focused on the video.

1

- Click the 'Loop until Stopped' check box (Playback tab | Audio Options group) to place a check mark in it (Figure 7–68).

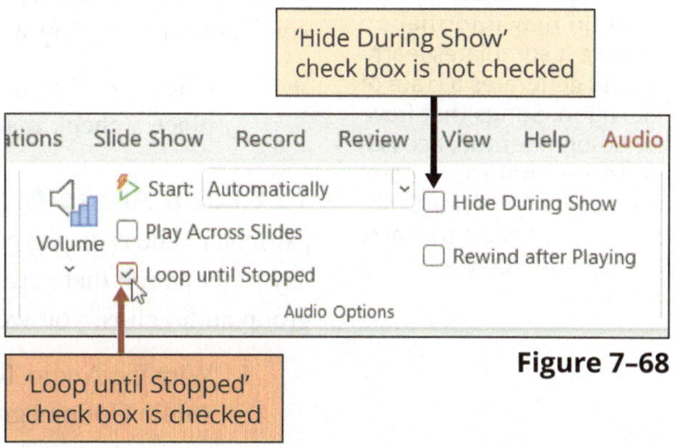

Figure 7–68

Q&A What is the difference between the 'Loop until Stopped' option and the 'Play Across Slides' option?
The audio clip in the 'Loop until Stopped' option repeats for as long as one slide is displayed. In contrast, the 'Play Across Slides' option would play the clip only once, but it would continue to play while other slides in the presentation are displayed. Once the end of the clip is reached, the sound would end and not repeat.

To Hide an Audio Clip Object during a Slide Show

Once an audio clip is inserted into a slide, you can specify that the icon does not display when the presentation is running. The following step adds the option of hiding the sound icon on the slide. **Why?** You will not click the screen to start the sound, so you do not need to see the icon.

1

- Click the 'Hide During Show' check box (Playback tab | Audio Options group) to place a check mark in it (Figure 7–69).

Q&A Why would I want the icon to display during the show?
If you had selected the On Click option, you would need to find this icon on the slide and click it to start playing the clip.

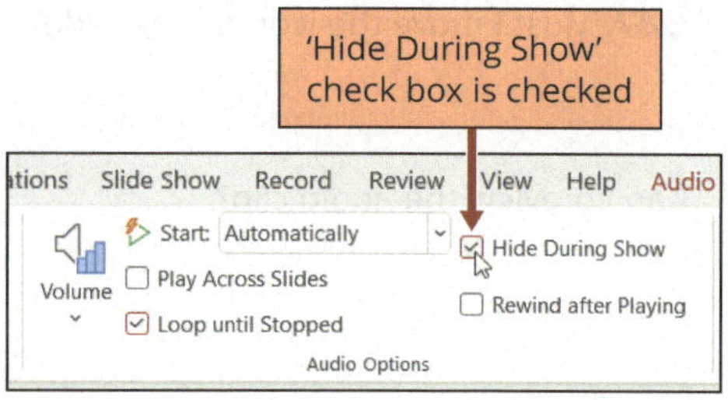

Figure 7–69

To Change the Volume of an Audio Clip

You can adjust the volume or mute the sound to help set the tone of your presentation. **Why?** The default High sound level may be too loud and distract from the content being presented. The following steps change the default volume from High to Medium.

1

- Click the Volume button (Playback tab | Audio Options group) to display the Volume menu (Figure 7–70).

2

- Click Medium to change the clip volume.

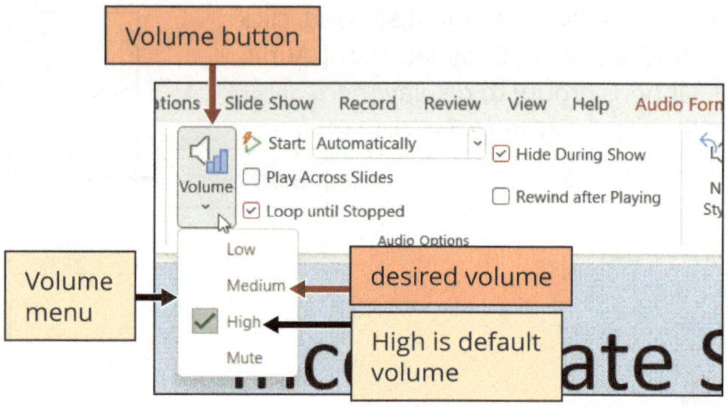

Figure 7–70

Other Ways

1. Click Mute/Unmute button on Media Controls bar, adjust volume slider

BTW
Ideal Beats Per Minute
Keep your mind alert, but calm, by listening to music that has 60 beats per minute (bpm). According to brain-research.us, this rate allows you to keep focused and to retain new information because it stimulates learning and generates a state of relaxation. Songs that have the 60-bpm tempo, according to bpmdatabase.com, are "Lover" by Taylor Swift, "Sign of the Times" by Harry Styles, and "Daylight" by Maroon 5.

To Play an Audio Clip across Slides If you wanted the audio clip to play during the entire presentation, you would perform the following step.

1. Click the 'Play Across Slides' check box (Playback tab | Audio Options group) to place a check mark in it.

To Rewind an Audio Clip after Playing To rewind your audio clip after playing during your presentation, you would perform the following step.

1. Click the 'Rewind after Playing' check box (Playback tab | Audio Options group) to place a check mark in it.

To Group Audio Clips You may desire to play several audio clips in sequence while a particular slide is displayed. If so, you can specify that they begin by clicking the slide or performing any other action that activates the next action on the slide, such as pressing the RIGHT ARROW. To group audio clips, you would perform the following steps.

1. With the Audio Tools Playback tab displayed, click the Start arrow (Playback tab | Audio Options group) to display the Start menu.
2. Click 'In Click Sequence' in the Start menu.

To Trim an Audio Clip

The audio control buttons have the same functions as the video control buttons that were displayed when you inserted the Leg Press video clip. They include playing and pausing the sound, moving back or forward 0.25 seconds, audio progress, elapsed time, and muting or unmuting the sound.

As with the video clip you inserted on this slide, PowerPoint's Trim Audio feature allows you to set the beginning and end of a clip. You select the desired sound to play by designating a Start Time and End Time, which are accurate to one-thousandth of a second. The Start Time is indicated by a green marker and the End Time is indicated by a red marker. The following steps trim the music file. **Why?** The audio clip is too long and you want a shorter clip.

1

- Click the Play/Pause button in the audio controls to play the entire clip.

Q&A Can I play the clip by clicking the Play button in the Preview group?
Yes. This Play button plays the entire clip. You may prefer to click the Play/Pause button displayed in the audio controls to pause and play the audio.

- With the Playback tab displayed, click the Trim Audio button (Playback tab | Editing group) to display the Trim Audio dialog box.
- Click and hold the Start Time up arrow or drag the green marker to the right until 00:08.000 is displayed (Figure 7–71).

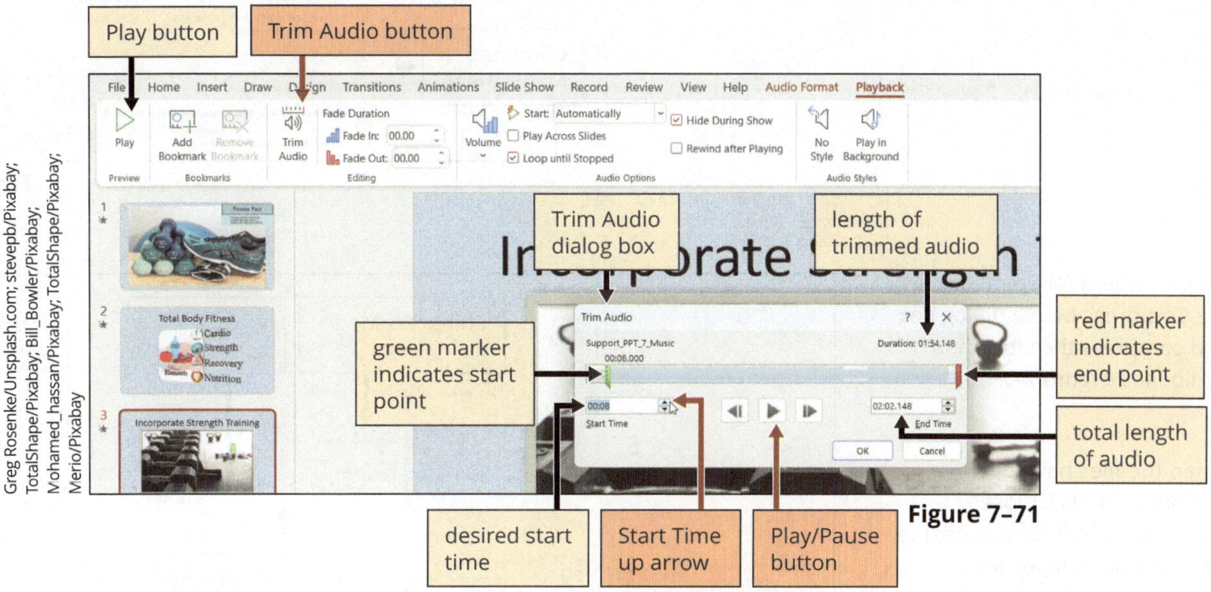

Figure 7–71

2

- Click and hold the End Time down arrow or drag the red marker to the left until 00:15.500 is displayed.
- Click the Play/Pause button (Trim Audio dialog box) to review the shortened audio clip (Figure 7–72).

Q&A Can I specify the start or end times by entering the time in the Start Time and End Time boxes (Trim Audio dialog box)?
Yes. You also can click the Next Frame and Previous Frame buttons.

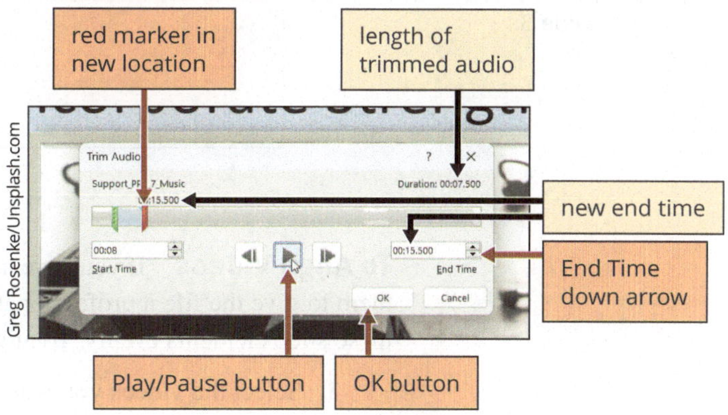

Figure 7–72

3

- Click OK to set the Start Time and End Time and to close the Trim Audio dialog box.

Other Ways

1. Right-click clip, click Trim on Mini toolbar
2. In Trim Audio dialog box, press ALT+S and ALT+E

To Compress a Video and an Audio File

PowerPoint includes a feature that will compress your audio and video files to reduce their size. Media files can be quite large, which can pose a problem if you want to email a presentation or if the space on your storage device is small. You can specify one of three compression qualities: Full HD, HD, or Standard. **Why?** You want to decrease the file size of the audio and video files you have inserted so you can email the presentation if desired. The following steps compress the media files.

1

- With the audio clip selected on Slide 3, click the File tab to display Backstage view and then click the Info tab.
- Click the Compress Media button (Info tab | Media Size and Performance section) to display the Compress Media menu (Figure 7–73).

Q&A Why am I seeing an error message stating that the media could not be compressed?
Graphics cards have acceleration capabilities that allow video, animation, transitions, and other graphics to display smoothly. Your PowerPoint file may have too many graphics that are consuming the resources of your graphics card. If so, you may need to disable hardware graphics acceleration. These settings are found in the Display section of the PowerPoint Options Advanced tab.

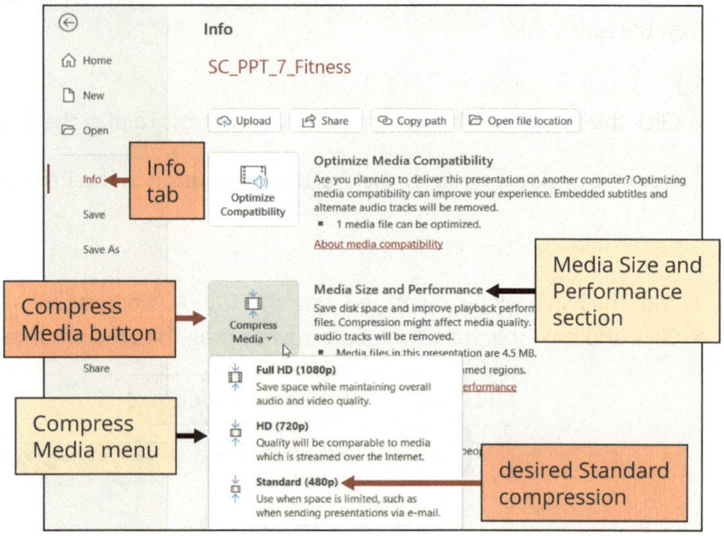

Figure 7–73

2

- Click Standard (480p) to display the Compress Media dialog box and compress the video and audio files (Figure 7–74).

3

- When the files have been compressed, click Close (Compress Media dialog box) to return to Backstage view.
- Click the Back button (Info tab) to return to Slide 3.

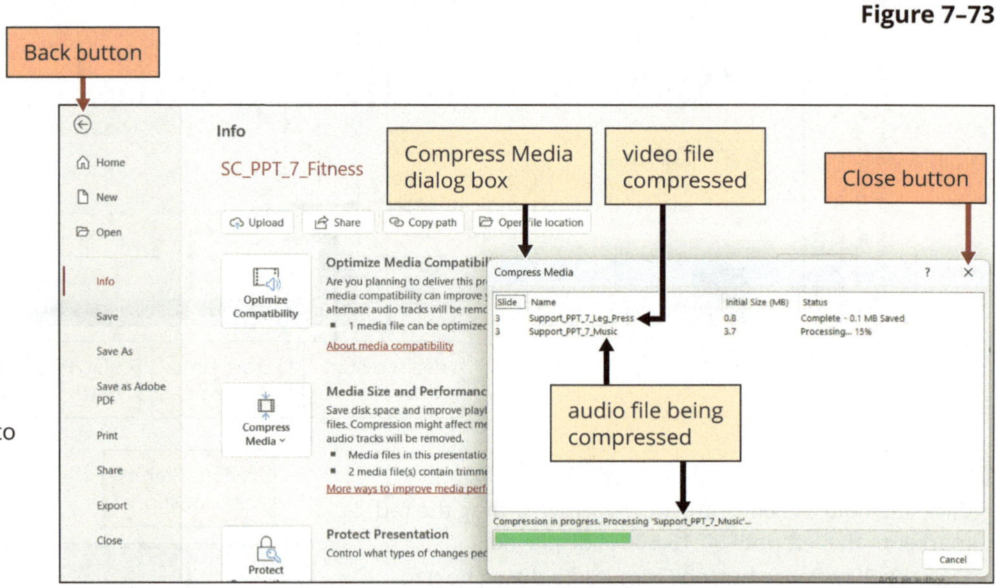

Figure 7–74

To Align Videos If you have multiple videos displayed on one slide, you may desire to arrange them to give the file a professional appearance. PowerPoint includes a feature to help you space these slide elements evenly. To align videos, you would perform the following steps.

1. Select the videos you want to align by pressing SHIFT and clicking each object.
2. Display the Video Format tab, click the Align button (Arrange group), and then click one of the align or distribute options in the Align menu.

Break Point: If you wish to take a break, this is a good place to do so. Be sure the Fitness file is saved and then you can quit PowerPoint. To resume at a later time, start PowerPoint, open the file called Fitness, and continue following the steps from this location forward.

Consider This

Choose outstanding hyperlink images or text.

Good speakers are aware of their audiences and know their speech material well. They have rehearsed their presentations and know where the hypertext is displayed on the slides. During a presentation, however, they sometimes need to divert from their planned material. Audience members may interrupt with questions, the room may not have optimal acoustics or lighting, or the timing may be short or long. It is helpful, therefore, to make the slide hyperlinks as large and noticeable to speakers as possible. The presenters can glance at the slide and receive a visual cue that it contains a hyperlink. They then can decide whether to click the hyperlink to display a webpage or other link.

Adding Hyperlinks and Action Buttons

When presenting the Fitness slide show, you may want to jump nonsequentially to omit some material or to display one or more slides in another presentation in response to audience needs or timing issues. To skip to particular slides, you can click a hyperlink or an action button on a slide. The hyperlink, or link, can be any element of a slide, such as a single letter, a word, a paragraph, or any graphical image such as a picture, shape, or graph. The link connects one slide to another slide, another PowerPoint presentation, a webpage, an email address, or a file.

To Insert a Hyperlink to a Place in the Current Presentation

When you point to a hyperlink, the pointer becomes the shape of a hand to indicate the text or object contains a hyperlink. When you click this hyperlink, PowerPoint connects to the specified slide or other designated area. **Why?** In the Fitness presentation, the Equipment picture on Slide 1 will link to the next slide in the same presentation. The following steps create the first hyperlink for the Equipment picture on Slide 1.

1

- Display Slide 1, select the Equipment picture, and then display the Insert tab.
- Click the Link button (Insert tab | Links group) to display the Insert Hyperlink dialog box.
- Click the 'Place in This Document' button in the Link to area.
- Click '2. Total Body Fitness' in the 'Select a place in this document' area (Insert Hyperlink dialog box) to select and display a preview of this slide (Figure 7–75).

Q&A Could I also have selected the Next Slide link in the 'Select a place in this document' area?
Yes. Either action would create the hyperlink to Slide 2.

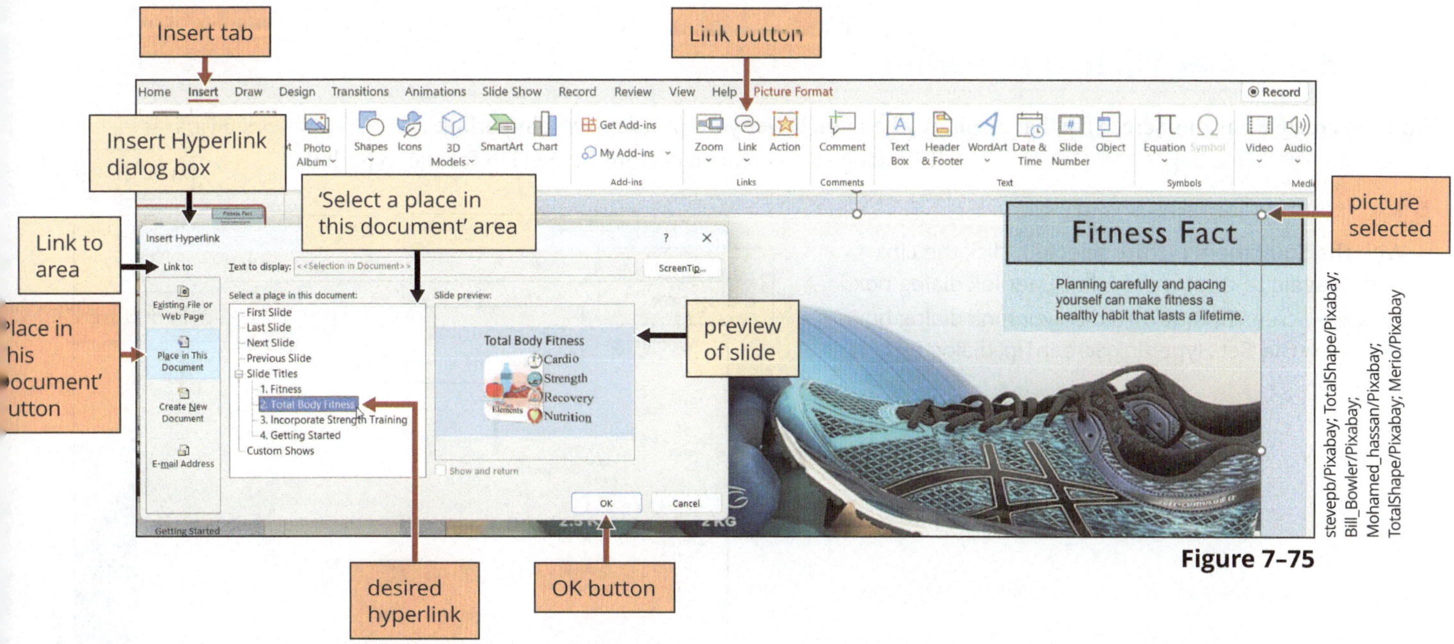

Figure 7–75

2

- Click OK (Insert Hyperlink dialog box) to insert the hyperlink.

Q&A I clicked the Equipment picture, but Slide 2 did not display. Why?
Hyperlinks are active only when you run the presentation or are in Reading view, not when you are creating a presentation in Normal or Slide Sorter view.

Other Ways

1. Right-click text or object, click Link, select slide, click OK
2. Select text or object, press CTRL+K, select slide, press ENTER

To Edit a Hyperlink

Once you have created the hyperlink, you may decide to change the specified action. In the Fitness presentation, you want to hyperlink to Slide 4 instead of Slide 2. **Why?** You decide that audience members may be eager to begin their healthy programs rather than learn about the components of total body fitness. The following steps edit the hyperlink on Slide 1.

1

- With the Equipment picture still selected, click the Link button again to display the Edit Hyperlink dialog box.
- Click '4. Getting Started' in the 'Select a place in this document' area to select and display a preview of this slide (Figure 7–76).

Q&A Could I also have selected the Last Slide link in the 'Select a place in this document' area?
Yes. Either action would create the hyperlink to Slide 4.

2

- Click OK (Edit Hyperlink dialog box) to change the hyperlink.

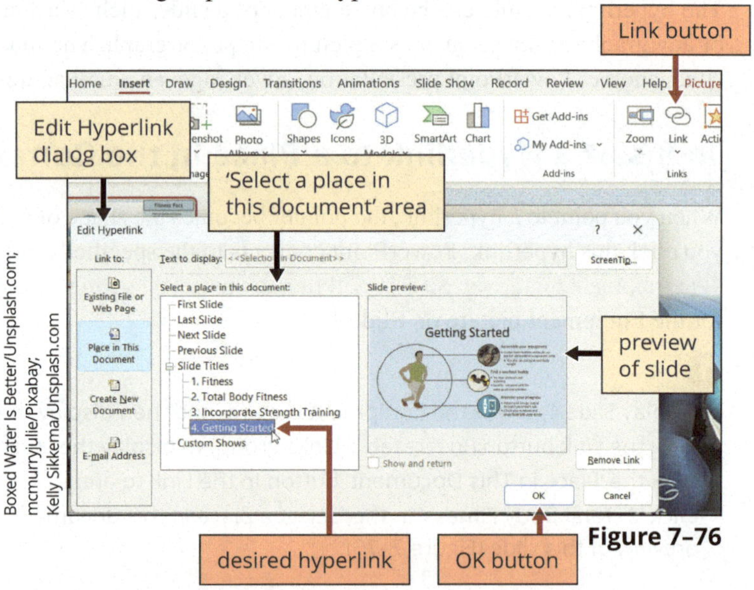

Figure 7–76

Other Ways

1. Right-click text or object, click Edit Link, select slide, click OK
2. Select text or object, press CTRL+K, select slide, press ENTER

To Add a ScreenTip to a Hyperlink

You can create a custom ScreenTip that displays when you hover your mouse over a hyperlink. **Why?** This ScreenTip is a visual cue of the action the hyperlink will take. The following steps create a custom ScreenTip for the hyperlink.

1

- With the Equipment picture selected, click the Link button again to display the Edit Hyperlink dialog box.
- Click the ScreenTip button (Edit Hyperlink dialog box) to display the 'Set Hyperlink ScreenTip' dialog box (Figure 7–77).

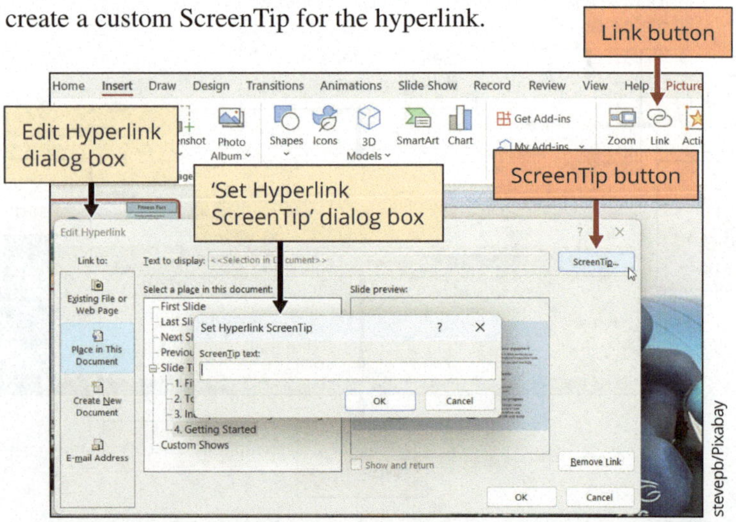

Figure 7–77

2

- Type **Getting Started** in the 'ScreenTip text' box (Figure 7–78).

3

- Click OK ('Set Hyperlink ScreenTip' dialog box).
- Click OK (Edit Hyperlink dialog box).

4

- Click outside the image to deselect it.
- Hover the mouse over the image until the ScreenTip and 'Ctrl+Click to follow link' are displayed.
- Press CTRL+CLICK to test the link.

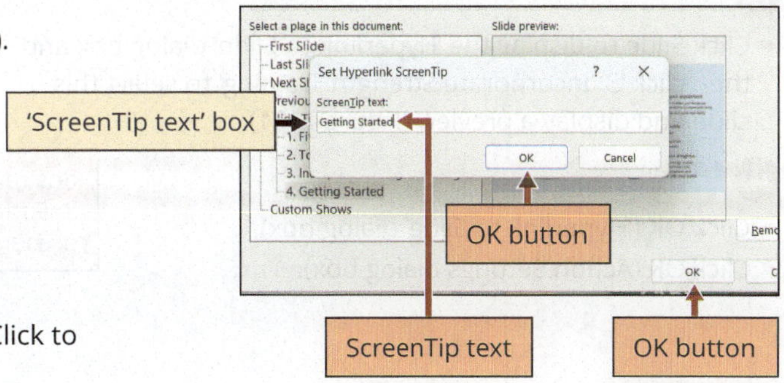

Figure 7–78

To Add a Hyperlink Action Setting to a Picture

You also can use an Action to create a link to another slide or object. In the Fitness presentation, you used the Plank picture in the SmartArt and the Weights picture as the poster frame. You can create a hyperlink between these two elements. *Why? When you are discussing the four components of total body fitness shown in the Slide 2 SmartArt graphic, you can mention the importance of strength training and then quickly jump to the leg press video.* The following steps create a hyperlink from the Plank picture in the Slide 2 SmartArt to Slide 3.

1

- Display Slide 2 and then click the Plank picture to select it.
- Click the Action button (Insert tab | Links group) to display the Action Settings dialog box (Figure 7–79).

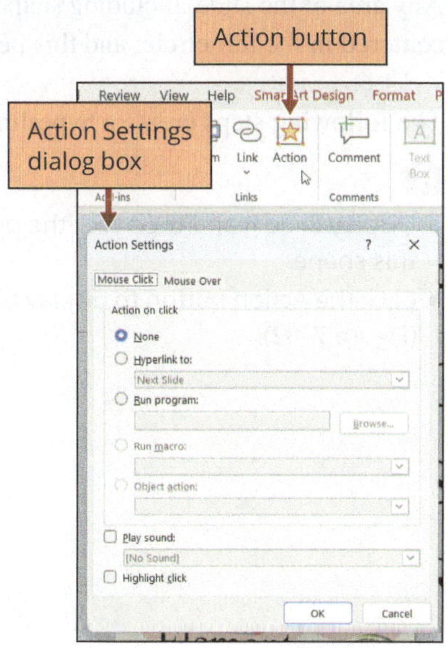

Figure 7–79

2

- Click Hyperlink to, click the Hyperlink to arrow in the 'Action on click' area to display the Hyperlink to menu, and then point to Slide (Figure 7–80).

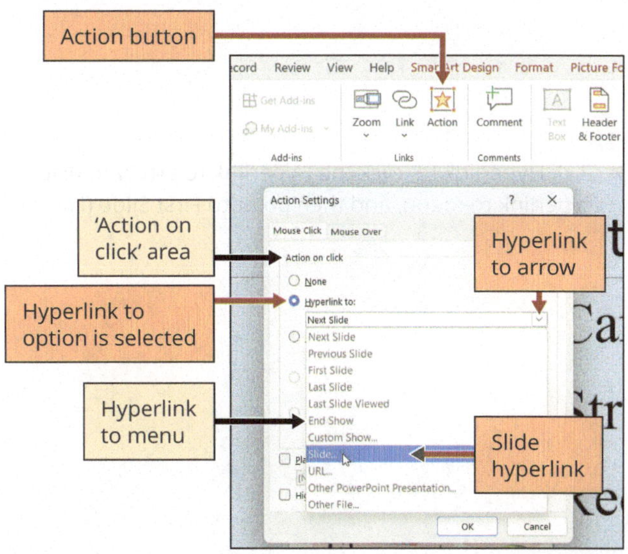

Figure 7–80

3

- Click Slide to display the 'Hyperlink to Slide' dialog box and then click '3. Incorporate Strength Training' to select this slide and display a preview (Figure 7–81).

4

- Click OK ('Hyperlink to Slide' dialog box).
- Click OK (Action Settings dialog box).

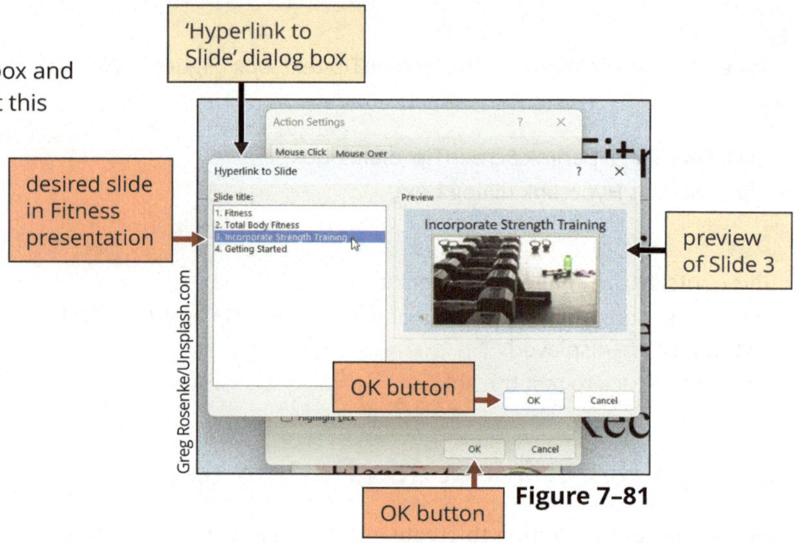

Figure 7–81

To Add a Hyperlink Action Setting to a Shape

Any area of the slide, including shapes, can be designated as a hyperlink element. The SmartArt graphic on Slide 4 has a person centered in the left circle, and this person can serve as the hyperlink. **Why?** The person is a large component of the slide, so it would be relatively easy for a presenter to locate this graphic and then click to jump to another slide or presentation element. The following steps create a hyperlink for the person in the SmartArt shape.

1

- Display Slide 4 and then click the person in the left circle to select this shape.
- Click the Action button to display the Action Settings dialog box (Figure 7–82).

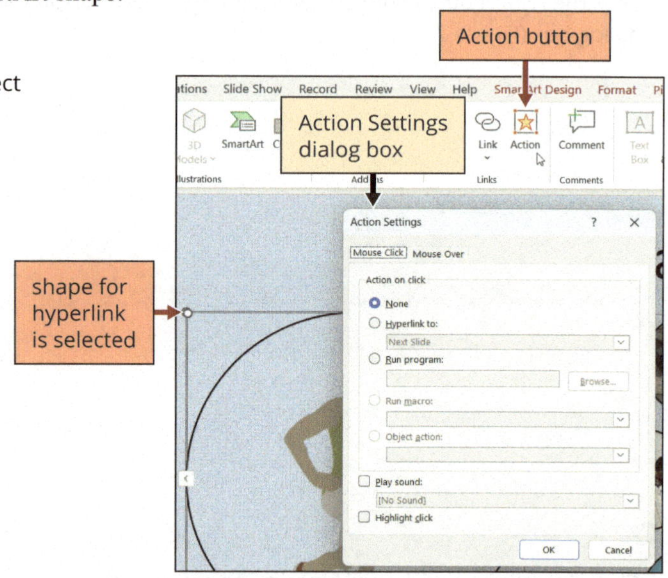

Figure 7–82

2

- Click Hyperlink to, click the Hyperlink to arrow to display the Hyperlink to menu, and then point to First Slide (Figure 7–83).

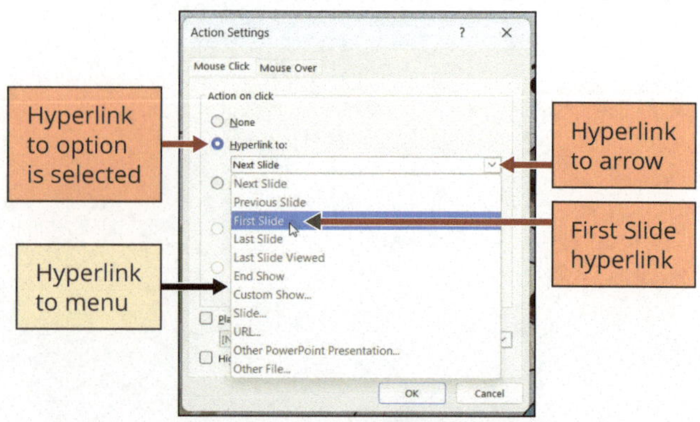

Figure 7–83

3

- Click First Slide to select this slide as the hyperlink (Figure 7–84).

4

- Click OK (Action Settings dialog box).

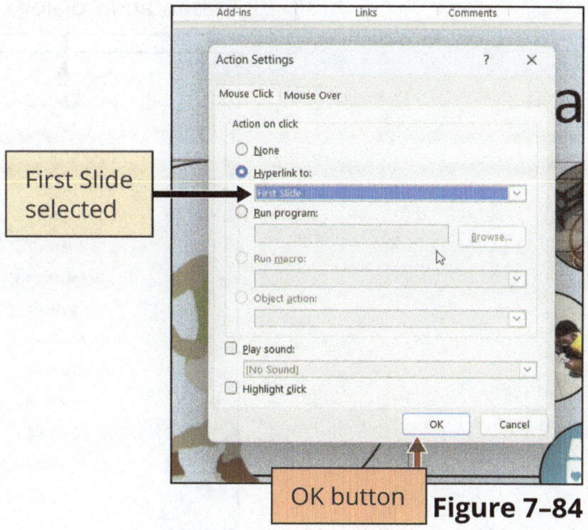

Figure 7–84

To Insert a Hyperlink to a Slide in Another Presentation

While hyperlinks are convenient tools to navigate through the current PowerPoint presentation, they also allow you to open a second PowerPoint presentation and display a particular slide in that file. A hyperlink offers a convenient method of moving from one presentation to another. A speaker has the discretion to use the hyperlink depending on the audience's interest in the topic and time considerations. The following steps hyperlink the words, Getting Started, on Slide 4 to the second slide in the Warmup Cooldown presentation. **Why?** You want to emphasize that the warmup phase is important to prepare your muscles and joints for the exercise session and to reduce the likelihood of injuries.

1

- With Slide 4 displayed, select the words, Getting Started, in the title text placeholder.
- Click the Action button, click Hyperlink to, and then click the Hyperlink to arrow to display the Hyperlink to menu (Figure 7–85).

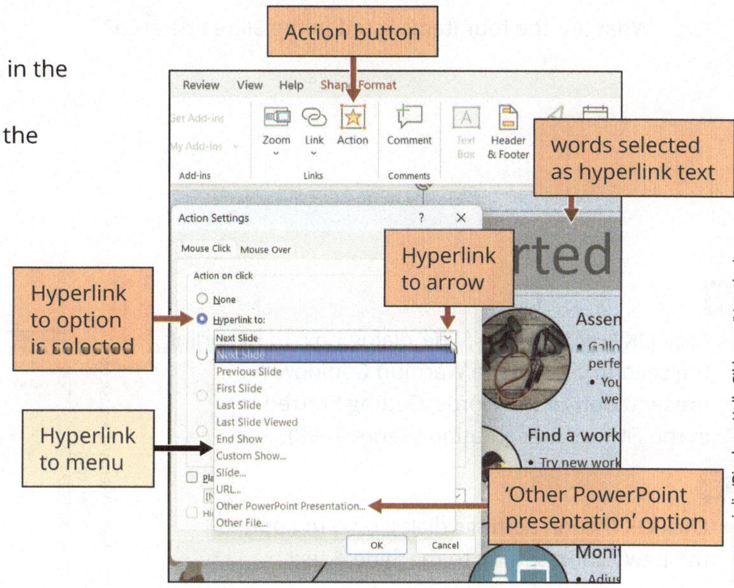

Figure 7–85

mcmurryjulie/Pixabay; Kelly Sikkema/Unsplash.com; Boxed Water Is Better/Unsplash.com

2

- Scroll down and then click 'Other PowerPoint Presentation' to display the 'Hyperlink to Other PowerPoint Presentation' dialog box.
- If necessary, navigate to the location where you saved the Warmup Cooldown file.
- Click SC_PPT_7_Warmup_Cooldown to select this .pptx file as the hyperlinked presentation (Figure 7–86).

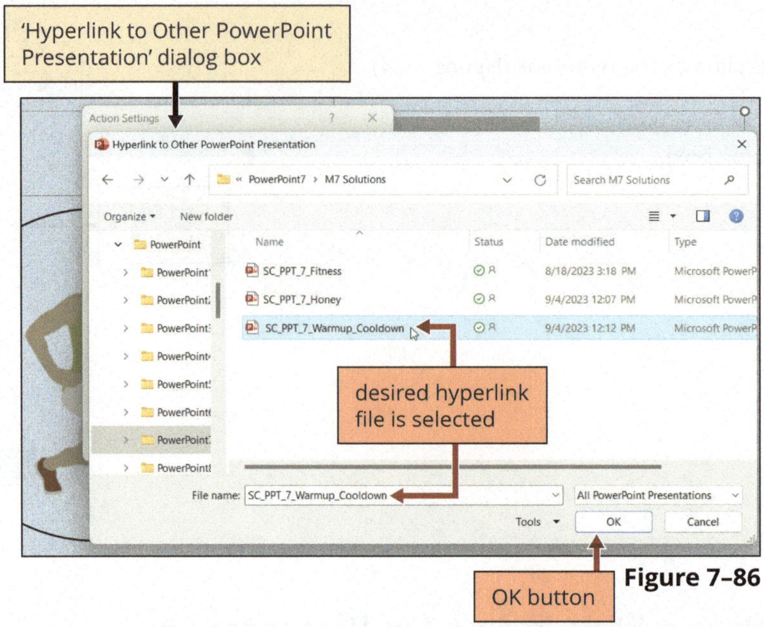

Figure 7–86

3

- Click OK ('Hyperlink to Other PowerPoint Presentation' dialog box) to display the 'Hyperlink to Slide' dialog box.
- Click '2. Begin by Warming Up' ('Hyperlink to Slide' dialog box) to hyperlink the second slide in the Warmup Cooldown presentation to the words, Getting Started, in the Fitness presentation (Figure 7–87).

Q&A What are the four items listed in the Slide title area?
They are the title text of the four slides in the Warmup Cooldown presentation.

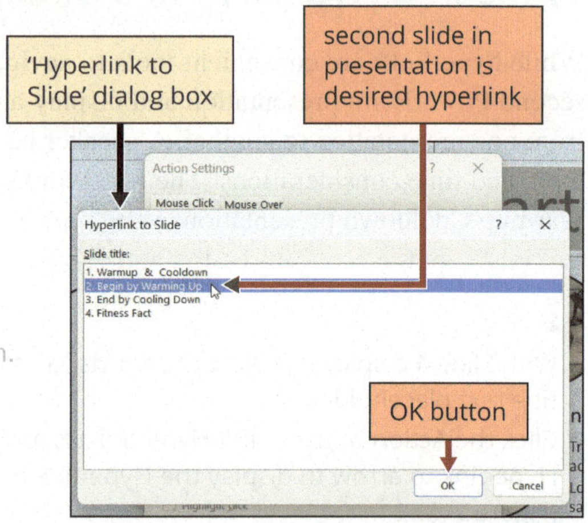

Figure 7–87

4

- Click OK ('Hyperlink to Slide' dialog box) to hyperlink the second slide in the Warmup Cooldown presentation to the words, Getting Started, in the Fitness presentation (Figure 7–88).

5

- Click OK (Action Settings dialog box) to apply the new action setting to the Slide 4 text.

mcmurryjulie/Pixabay; Kelly Sikkema/Unsplash.com; Boxed Water Is Better/Unsplash.com

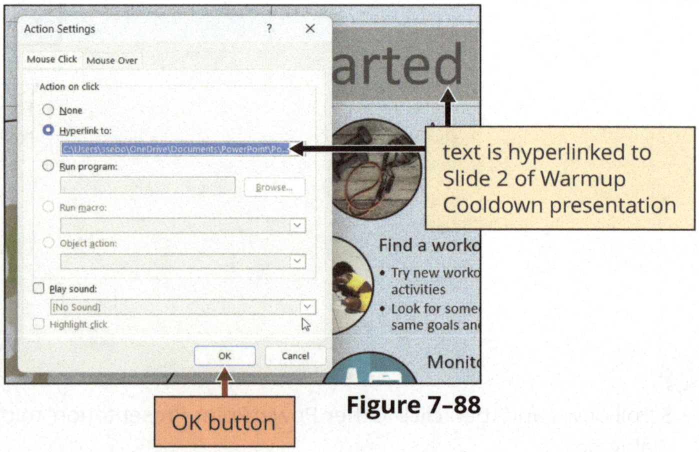

Figure 7–88

Other Ways

1. Select picture, click Hyperlink button (Insert menu | Links group), click 'Existing File or Web Page' (Link to: area), browse to and select desired file, click OK
2. Right-click picture, click Hyperlink on shortcut menu, click 'Existing File or Web Page' (Link to: area), browse to and select desired file, click OK

To Remove a Hyperlink If you wanted to remove a hyperlink, you would perform the following steps.

1. Select the text or object from which you want to remove the hyperlink.
2. Display the Insert tab and then click the Hyperlink button (Insert tab | Links group) to display the Edit Hyperlink dialog box.
3. Click the Remove Link button (Edit Hyperlink dialog box).

BTW

Using Action Buttons

The action buttons have images representing their functions, such as a right-pointing arrow representing moving forward to the next slide. These buttons are useful when using a touch screen or when a keyboard is not present, such as when a presentation is run at a kiosk. Slide designers also type specific years or descriptive words, such as True or False, on action buttons that link to slides with corresponding information. Be imaginative when developing your own presentations and creating buttons that have a specific meaning for your intended audience.

Action Buttons

PowerPoint provides 12 built-in action buttons. An **action button** is an interactive button you click in Slide Show view to perform an activity, such as advancing to the next slide. This particular type of hyperlink can activate a hyperlink that allows users to jump to a specific slide in the presentation. The picture on the action button indicates the type of function it performs. For example, the button with the house icon represents the home slide, or Slide 1. To achieve a personalized look, you can customize an action button with a picture, graph, piece of clip art, logo, text, or any graphic you desire. Table 7–1 describes each of the built-in action buttons.

Table 7–1: Built-In Action Buttons

Button Name	Image	Description
Back or Previous		Returns to the previous slide displayed in the same presentation.
Forward or Next		Jumps to the next slide in the presentation.
Beginning		Jumps to Slide 1. This button performs the same function as the Home button.
End		Jumps to the last slide in the presentation.
Home		Jumps to Slide 1. This button performs the same function as the Beginning button.
Information		Does not have any predefined function. Use it to direct a user to a slide with details or facts.
Return		Returns to the previous slide displayed in any presentation. For example, you can place it on a hidden slide or on a slide in a custom slide show and then return to the previous slide.
Movie		Does not have any predefined function. You generally would use this button to jump to a slide with an inserted video clip.
Document		Opens a program other than PowerPoint. For example, you can open Word or Excel and display a page or worksheet.
Sound		Does not have any predefined function. You generally would use this button to jump to a slide with an inserted audio clip.
Help		Does not have any predefined function. Use it to direct a user to a slide with instructions or contact information.
Custom		Does not have any predefined function. You can add a clip, picture, graphic, or text and then specify a unique purpose.

Consider This

Customize action buttons for a unique look.

PowerPoint's built-in action buttons have icons that give the presenter an indication of their function. Designers frequently customize these buttons with images related to the presentation. For example, in a grocery store presentation, the action buttons may have images of a coupon, dollar sign, and question mark to indicate links to in-store coupons, sale items, and the customer service counter. Be creative when you develop your own presentations and attempt to develop buttons that have specific meanings for your intended audience.

To Insert an Action Button

In the Fitness slide show, you will insert an action button shape in Slide 4 and then create a link to the previous slide displayed. **Why?** After your audience members learn how to begin their exercise program, you may want to emphasize that when they incorporate a variety of exercises and eat well, they can establish a lifetime of healthy habits. The following steps insert an action button on Slide 4 of the Warmup Cooldown presentation and link it to the previous slide displayed.

1

- With Slide 4 and the Insert tab displayed, click the Shapes button (Insert tab | Illustrations group) to display the Shapes gallery.
- Scroll down and then point to the 'Action Button: Return' shape in the Action Buttons area (seventh image) (Figure 7–89).

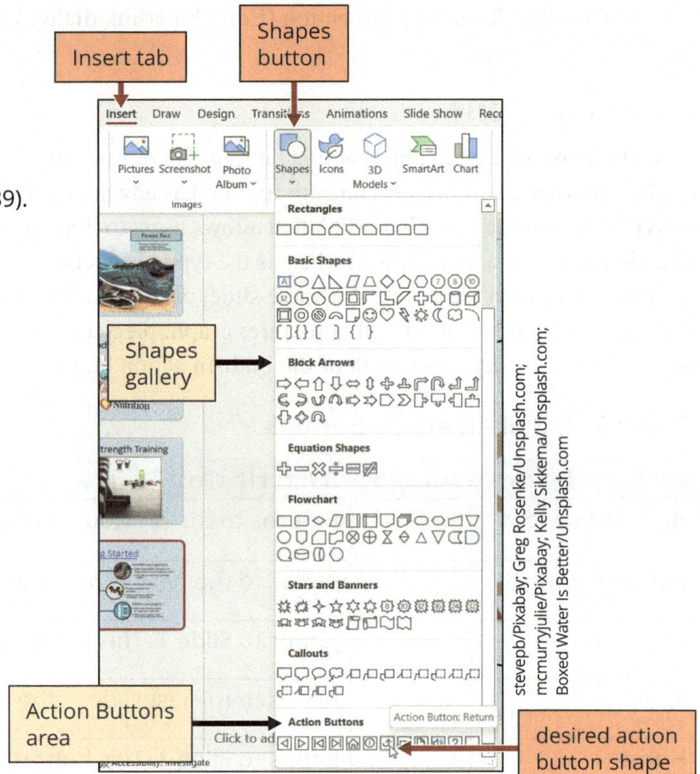

Figure 7–89

2

- Click the 'Action Button: Return' shape.
- Click the lower-left corner of the slide to insert the action button and to display the Action Settings dialog box.
- If necessary, click the Mouse Click tab (Action Settings dialog box) (Figure 7–90).

Q&A Why is 'Last Slide Viewed' the default hyperlink setting?
The 'Action Button: Return' shape establishes a hyperlink to the previous slide displayed in any presentation.

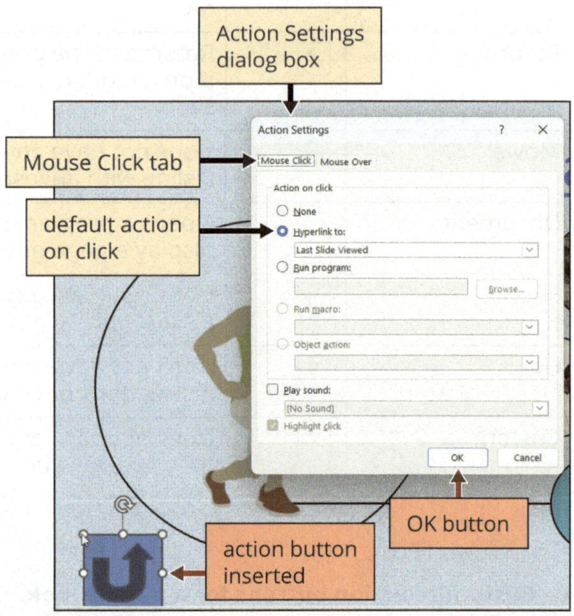

Figure 7–90

3

- Click OK (Action Settings dialog box) to apply the hyperlink setting.

To Size an Action Button

The Return action button size can be decreased to make it less obvious on the slide. The following step resizes the selected action button.

1. With the action button still selected and the Shape Format tab displayed, size the action button so that the height and width are 0.8". If necessary, move the action button to the lower-left corner of the slide (Figure 7–91).

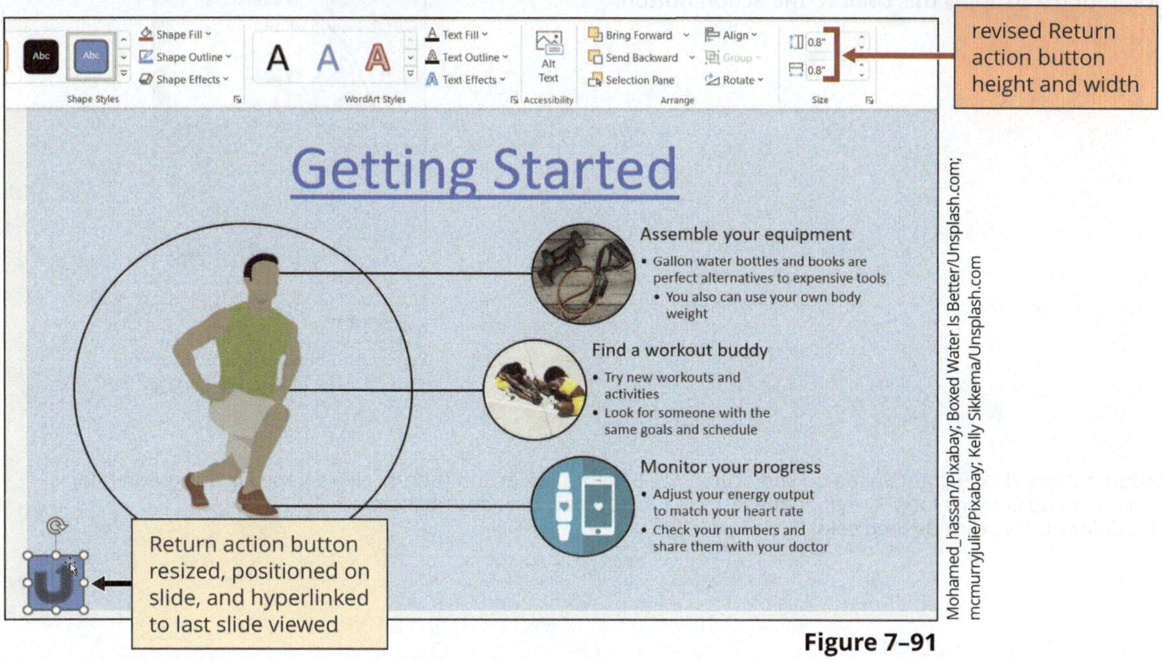

Figure 7–91

To Change an Action Button Fill Color

You can select a new action button fill color to coordinate with slide elements. The following steps change the fill color to tan. **Why?** The action button's blue color is prominent and the tan color would be more subtle.

1.
- With the action button still selected, click the Shape Fill arrow (Shape Format tab | Shape Styles gallery) to display the Shape Fill gallery (Figure 7–92).

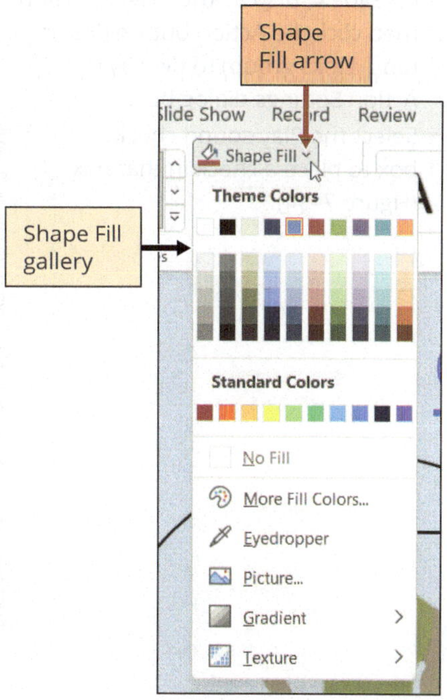

Figure 7–92

2

- Point to Tan, Background 2 (third color in the first Theme Colors row) to display a live preview of that fill color on the action button (Figure 7–93).
- **Experiment:** Point to various colors in the Shape Fill gallery and watch the fill color change in the action button.

3

- Click Tan, Background 2 to apply this color to the action button.

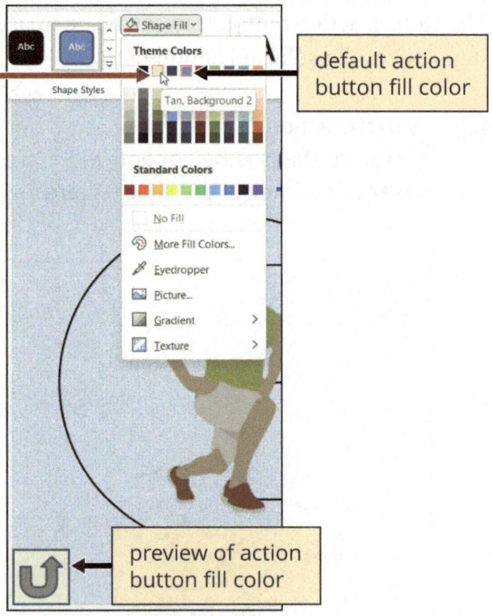

Figure 7–93

Other Ways

1. Right-click action button, click Format Shape on shortcut menu, click Fill on Shape Options tab (Format Shape pane), click Fill Color button, click desired color
2. Right-click action button, click Shape Fill button on Mini toolbar, click desired color

To Add Sound to an Action

To emphasize a hyperlink, you can add a sound. PowerPoint includes a variety of sounds that you can use. The following steps edit the Slide 4 hyperlink by adding a sound. **Why?** For variety, you want a sound to play when the action button is clicked.

1

- With the action button still selected on Slide 4, display the Insert tab and then click the Action button (Insert tab | Links group) to display the Action Settings dialog box.
- Select the Play sound check box to place a check in that box (Figure 7–94).

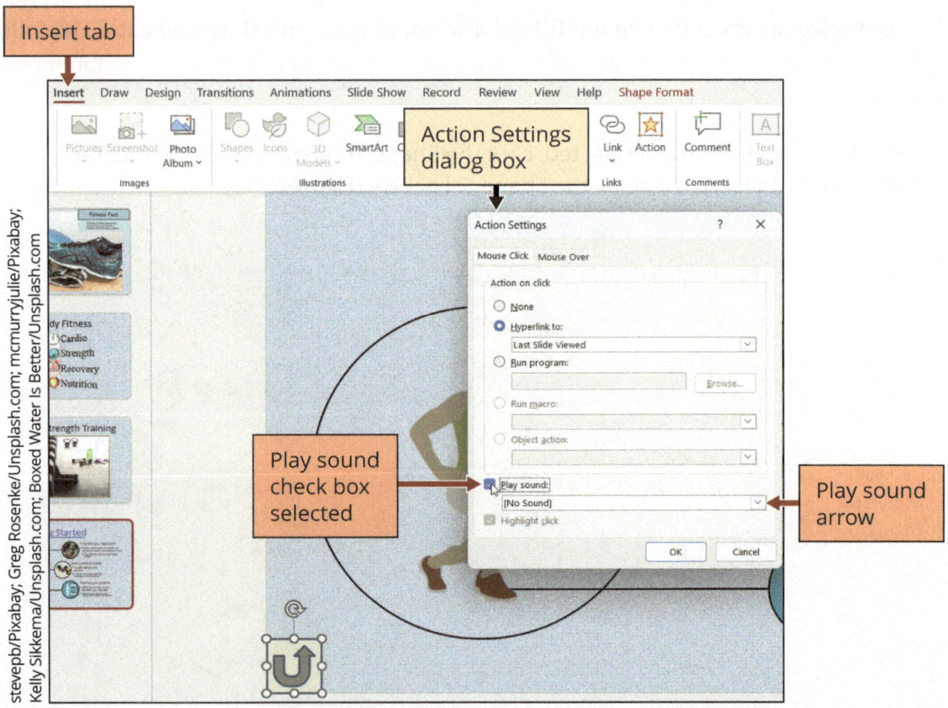

Figure 7–94

stevepb/Pixabay; Greg Rosenke/Unsplash.com; mcmurryjulie/Pixabay; Kelly Sikkema/Unsplash.com; Boxed Water Is Better/Unsplash.com

2

- Click the Play sound arrow to display the Play sound list (Figure 7–95).

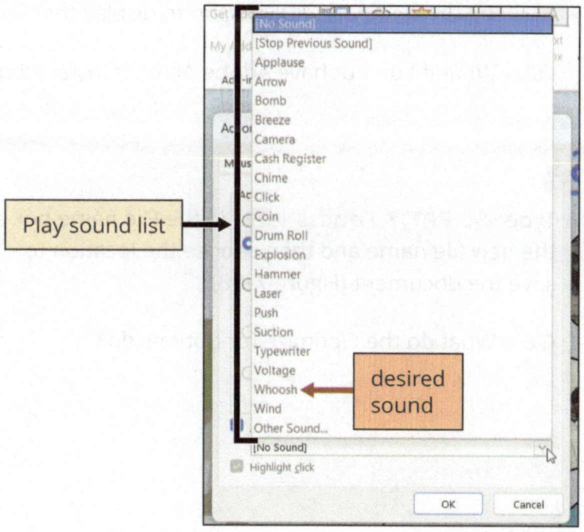

Figure 7–95

3

- Click Whoosh in the Play sound list to select that sound to play when the action button is clicked (Figure 7–96).

Q&A I did not hear the sound when I selected it. Why not?
The Whoosh sound will play when you run the slide show and click the action button.

4

- Click OK to apply the sound to the action button and to close the Action Settings dialog box.
- If necessary, save the Fitness presentation using the same file name.

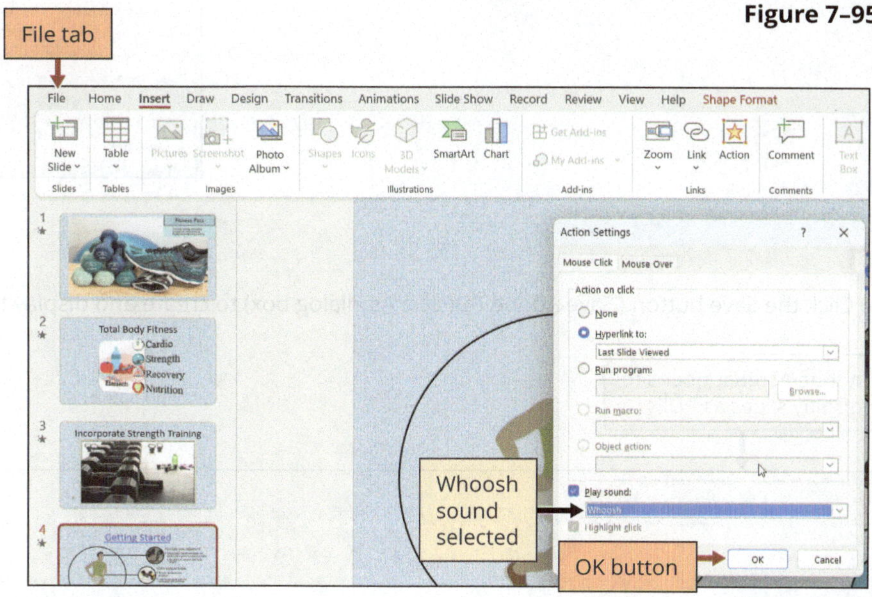

Figure 7–96

stevepb/Pixabay; Greg Rosenke/Unsplash.com; mcmurryjulie/Pixabay; Kelly Sikkema/Unsplash.com; Boxed Water Is Better/Unsplash.com

To Save the Presentation as a PDF

When you save your presentation as a PDF file, the formatting and layouts cannot be changed. This file format is convenient when you want to distribute your document online. **Why?** People who do not have PowerPoint can view the slides, but they cannot make changes to the file. The following steps save the Fitness presentation as a PDF.

1

- With the Fitness presentation displayed, click the File tab (shown in Figure 7–96) and then click the Export tab to open the Export panel (Figure 7–97).

Q&A Could I select the 'Save as Adobe PDF' tab instead of the Export tab?
Yes, if you see that option.

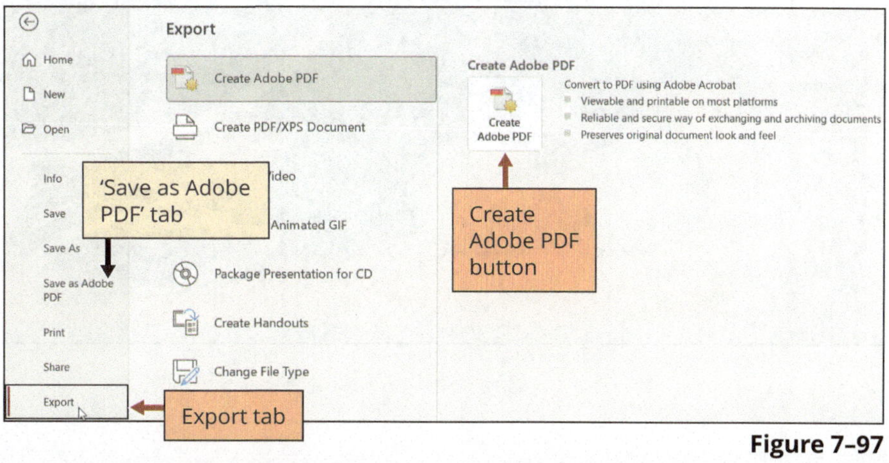

Figure 7–97

2

- Click the Create Adobe PDF button to display the 'Save Adobe PDF File As' dialog box.

Q&A What if I do not have Adobe Acrobat installed on my computer?
You can choose Create PDF/XPS Document instead.

3

- Type **SC_PPT_7_Fitness_PDF** in the File name box as the new file name and then choose the location to save the document (Figure 7–98).

Q&A What do the Optimize for options do?
Standard saves the file in high quality, which is good for printing. Minimum size reduces the file size and is preferable if you plan to send the file as an email attachment.

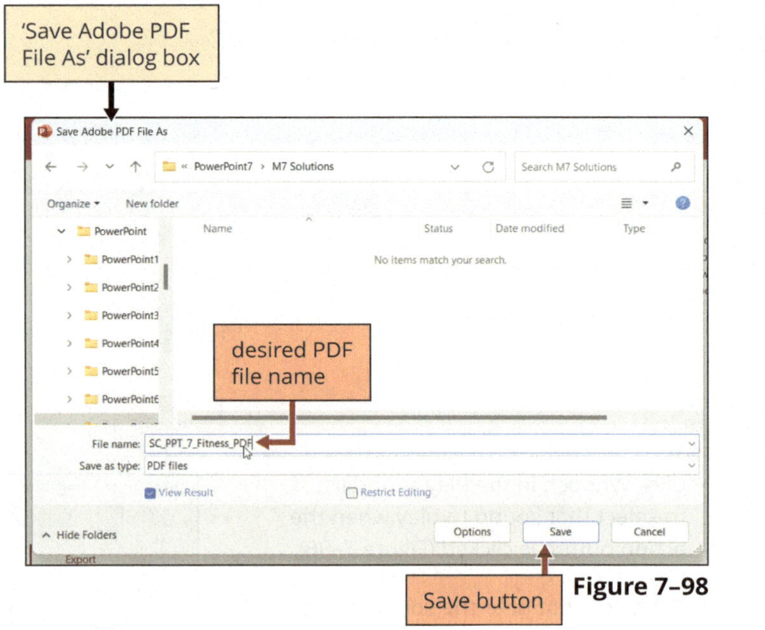

Figure 7–98

4

- Click the Save button ('Save Adobe PDF File As' dialog box) to create and display the PDF (Figure 7–99).

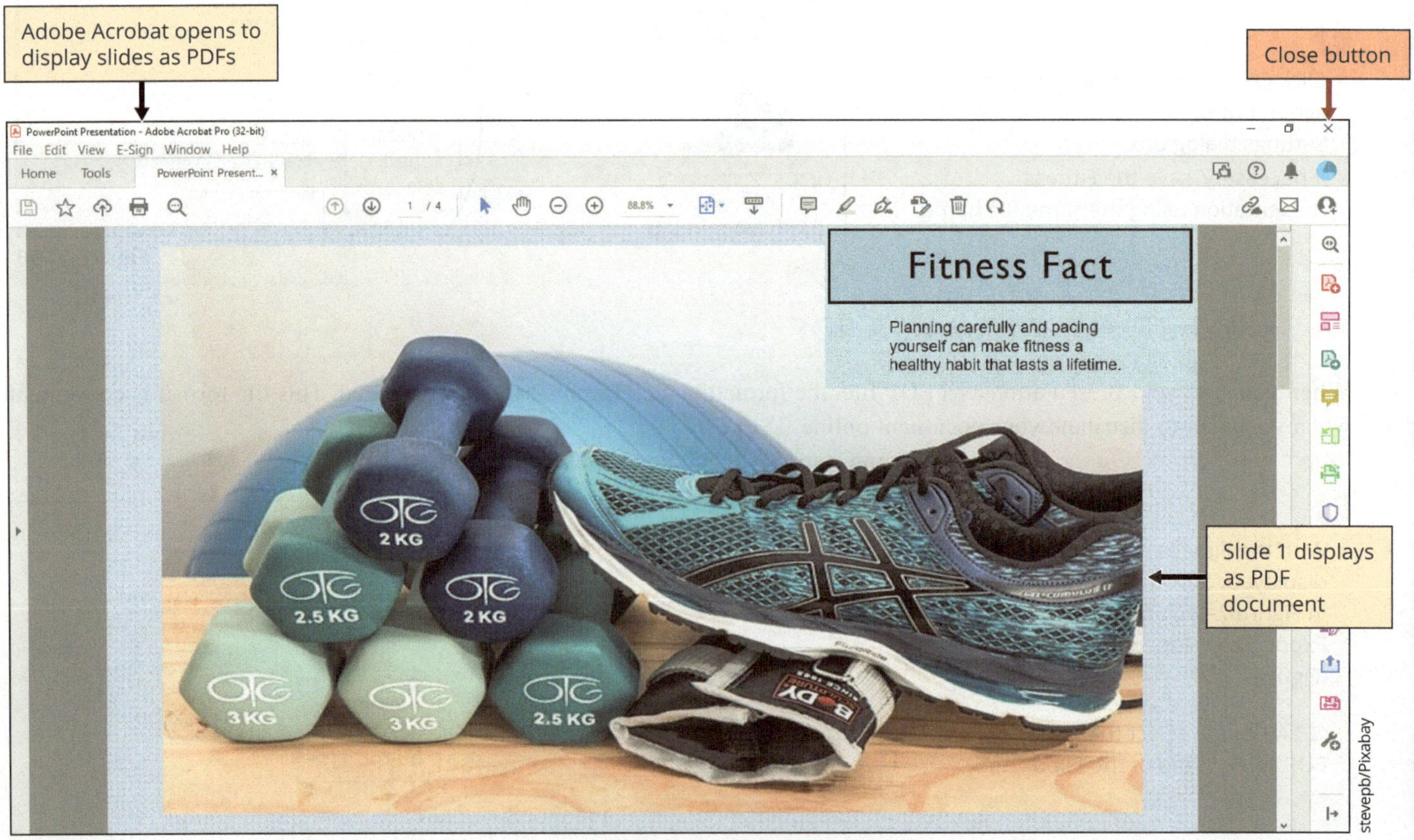

Figure 7–99

5

- Click Close ('PowerPoint Presentation – Adobe Acrobat' dialog box).

Q&A What if my PDF displays in a different program?
Depending on your computer settings and available software, the PDF may display in Adobe Acrobat, Word, OneDrive, or a different program.

Other Ways

1. Click File tab, click Save As, click Save as type arrow, click PDF (*.pdf), click Save

To Run, Save, and Exit PowerPoint

The presentation now is complete. You should run the presentation, view the hyperlinks, save the presentation, and then exit PowerPoint.

1. Run the Fitness presentation. Click the Equipment picture on Slide 1 to display Slide 4.
2. Click the Return button on Slide 4 to hear the Whoosh sound and return to Slide 1.
3. Display Slide 2 and then click the Plank picture on Slide 2 to display Slide 3. When the audio begins to play, click the Weights picture to view the video.
4. When the video is complete, display Slide 4.
5. Click the words, Getting Started, in the Slide 4 title text to open the Warmup Cooldown file and display its Slide 2. If the Microsoft PowerPoint Security Notice is displayed, click the Yes button to proceed.
6. View the Slide 2 contents and then display Slide 3 and Slide 4.
7. End the Warmup Cooldown slide show.
8. End the Fitness slide show.
9. sam Because the project now is complete, you can exit PowerPoint, closing all open documents.

BTW
Conserving Ink and Toner
If you want to conserve ink or toner, you can instruct PowerPoint to print draft quality documents by clicking File on the ribbon to open Backstage view, clicking Options in Backstage view to display the PowerPoint Options dialog box, clicking Advanced in the left pane (PowerPoint Options dialog box), scrolling to the Print area in the right pane, verifying there is no check mark in the High quality check box, and then clicking OK. Then, use Backstage view to print the document as usual.

BTW
Printing Document Properties
PowerPoint does not allow you to print document properties. This feature, however, is available in Microsoft 365 Word.

Summary

In this module, you have learned how to develop a presentation with SmartArt, digital media, and hyperlinks. You started by changing a picture and inserting a screen clip. You then inserted, edited, and enhanced a SmartArt graphic. You also removed a picture background and enhanced a picture by changing the contrast and color saturation. You inserted and edited video and audio clips and then compressed media to reduce the overall PowerPoint file size. Next, you inserted hyperlinks and an action button. Finally, you saved a presentation as a PDF file.

Consider This: Plan Ahead

What decisions will you need to make when creating your next presentation?

Use these guidelines as you complete the assignments in this module and create your own slide show decks outside of this class.

1. **Choose outstanding hyperlink images or text.** Format hypertext graphics or words that are easy to find on the slide. Make the hypertext graphics or letters large so a speaker is prompted to click them easily during a speaking engagement.
2. **Customize action buttons.** Create a unique look for your action buttons by adding pictures and other graphical elements to add interest or to make the buttons less obvious to your viewers.

Student Assignments

Apply Your Knowledge

Reinforce the skills and apply the concepts you learned in this module.

Adding Media and Enhancing SmartArt

Note: To complete this assignment, you will be required to use the Data Files. Please contact your instructor for information about accessing the Data Files.

Instructions: Start PowerPoint. Open the presentation called SC_PPT_7-1.pptx, which is located in the Data Files.

Vendors at the farmers' market in your town offer a variety of items, including local produce, flowers, and honey. You talked to the apiarists, who are the people caring for and raising bees and then extracting honey from the hives. They are planning a presentation at the local library about bees and the practice of beekeeping, and they have asked you to help develop slide content. You have received a PowerPoint presentation, video and audio files, and a picture, and you need to format the slides. You will create the three slides shown in Figure 7–100.

Perform the following tasks:

1. On Slide 1, change the color saturation to 33% (second Color Saturation picture) and then change the brightness and contrast setting to 'Brightness: +20% Contrast: -20' (fourth picture in the second Brightness/Contrast row) (Figure 7–100a).
2. On Slide 2, insert the video file named Support_PPT_7_Hive.mp4, which is located in the Data Files. Start the video clip to play automatically and to play full screen. Trim the video clip to a Start Time at 00:06 seconds and an End Time at 00.27 seconds. Resize the video height to 6" and then align the video in the center and the middle of the slide.
3. Add a poster video frame using the picture named Support_PPT_7_Apiary.jpg, which is located in the Data Files. Apply the 'Snip Diagonal Corner, White' video style (last style in the first Moderate row) (Figure 7–100b).
4. On Slide 3, delete the blue background from the bee picture in the upper-left corner of the slide. Flip the picture horizontally. Delete the dark blue background from the beekeeper picture in the upper-right corner of the slide. You may want to zoom the slide to simplify the background removal process. Resize the height of the bee picture to 3" and the beekeeper picture to 3" and then move them to the upper-left and upper-right corners of the slide.
5. Convert the bulleted list to a SmartArt graphic by right-clicking anywhere in the content placeholder, pointing to 'Convert to SmartArt' in the shortcut menu, and then clicking 'More SmartArt Graphics'. Display the List gallery and then select the 'Varying Width List' graphic (last graphic in the second row).
6. Move the Average hive shape up so that it is the first shape in the SmartArt graphic.
7. Insert the equation shown in Figure 7–100c. To insert the equation, position the pointer after the word, tall, in the last paragraph and then press ENTER. Display the Insert tab and then click the Equation button (Insert tab | Symbols group). Type **Beehive volume** in the 'Type equation here' box, click the Equal symbol (Equation tab | Symbols group) to insert that symbol, type **Length**, click the Multiplication Sign symbol, type **Width** in the box, click the Multiplication Sign, and then type **Height**, as shown in Figure 7–100c. Click an area other than the equation to close the 'Type equation here' box.
8. Select the entire SmartArt graphic, resize the height to 4" and width to 11", and then align it in the center and middle of the slide.
9. Change the SmartArt colors to 'Colored Outline – Accent 2' (first color in the Accent 2 area).

   If requested by your instructor, insert your grandmother's first name after the word, queen, in the first SmartArt shape.

10. Insert the audio file named Support_PPT_7_Buzzing.mp3, which is located in the Data Files. Start the audio clip to play Automatically and then change the volume to Medium. Hide the sound icon during the show. Trim the audio clip to a Start Time at 00:07 seconds and an End Time at 00:30 seconds (Figure 7–100d).
11. Insert a hyperlink from the Slide 3 title text (Busy Beekeepers) to Slide 2.
12. Compress the media in the presentation using the Standard setting.
13. Run the presentation and then save it using the file name, **SC_PPT_7_Honey**.
14. Submit the presentation in the format specified by your instructor.
15. **Consider This:** Did the color and corrections formatting changes enhance the Slide 1 picture? Why would you click the Slide 3 hyperlink? Were the revised lengths of the video and audio clips sufficient? In Step 5 you converted the bulleted list to the 'Varying Width List' SmartArt graphic. Was this layout a good choice? Why or why not? In Step 9, you changed the SmartArt colors. Was the Colored Outline a good choice? Why or why not?

picture color saturation, brightness, and contrast changed

Figure 7–100(a): Slide 1

poster video frame picture inserted and video style applied

Figure 7–100(b): Slide 2 (Video Poster Frame)

Continued on next page

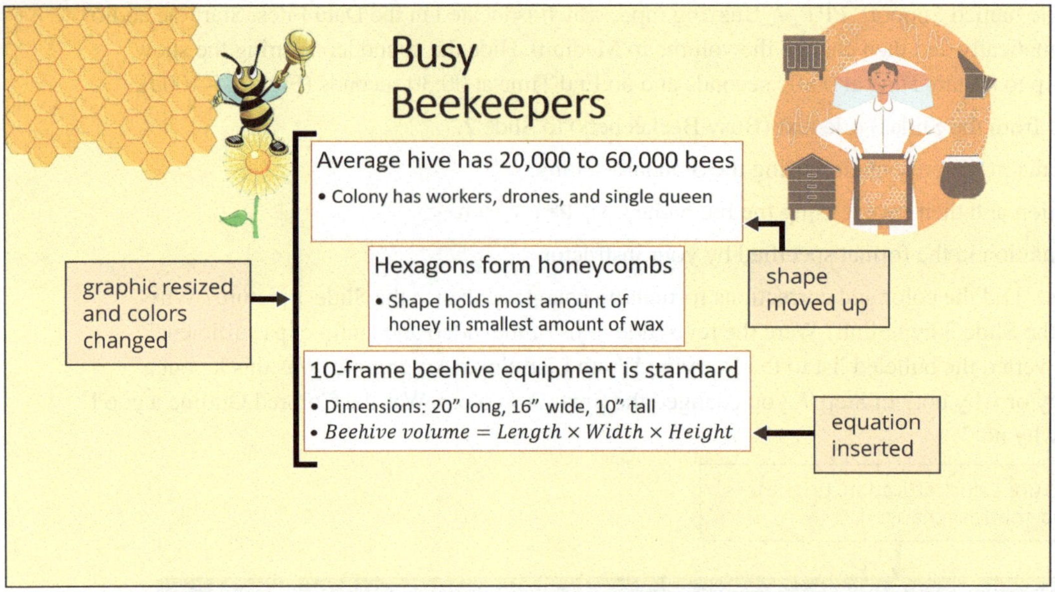

Elf-Moondance/Pixabay; Mohamed_hassan/Pixabay

Figure 7–100(c): Slide 3

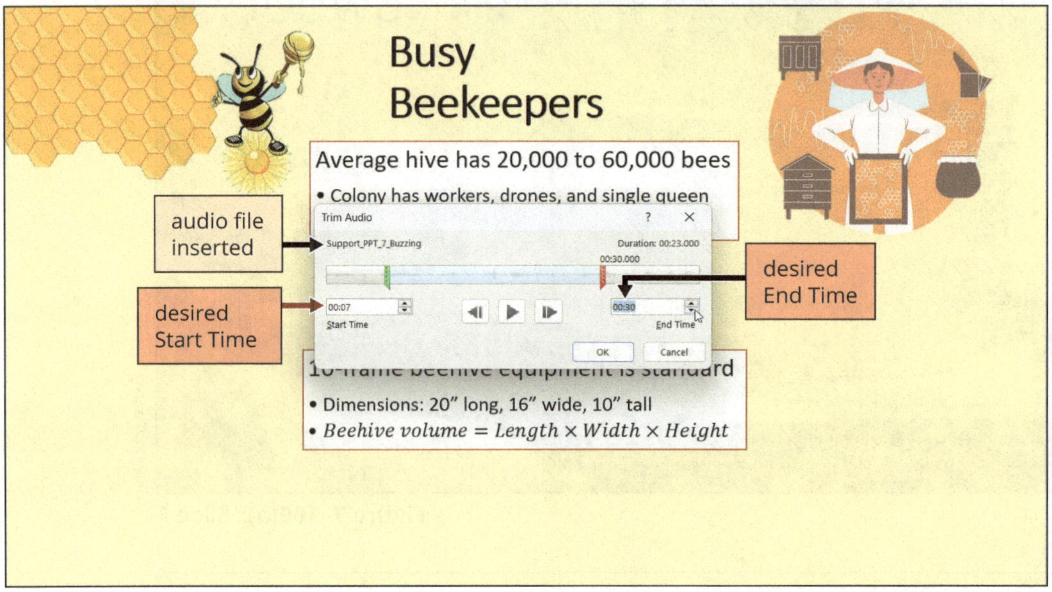

Elf-Moondance/Pixabay; Mohamed_hassan/Pixabay

Figure 7–100(d): Slide 3 (Trim Audio Dialog Box)

Extend Your Knowledge

Extend the skills you learned in this module and experiment with new skills. You may need to use Help to complete the assignment.

Creating and Modifying SmartArt

Note: To complete this assignment, you will be required to use the Data Files. Please contact your instructor for information about accessing the Data Files.

Instructions: Start PowerPoint. Open the presentation called SC_PPT_7-2.pptx, which is located in the Data Files.

Social media sites offer convenient methods of purchasing items, but influencers sometimes urge users to buy quickly, which can lead to overspending and sometimes fraudulent sites. To make wise purchases, check online reviews, use a VPN when shopping, and use browser extensions to compare prices. This information is listed in the slides you will create for this assignment. On Slide 1, you will convert WordArt to a SmartArt graphic. You then will duplicate Slide 2 and convert the SmartArt graphic on Slide 2 to text and the SmartArt graphic on Slide 3 to a shape. Finally, you will copy the Slide 3 graphic to Slide 4 and delete Slide 3.

Perform the following tasks:

1. On Slide 1, right-click anywhere in the WordArt bulleted list paragraphs to display the shortcut menu.
2. Point to 'Convert to SmartArt' to display the SmartArt gallery.
3. Click 'More SmartArt Graphics' to display the 'Choose a SmartArt Graphic' dialog box.
4. Click List in the list of graphic categories and then click 'Vertical Bullet List' (first graphic in the second row). Click OK to convert the SmartArt.
5. With the entire SmartArt graphic selected, resize the graphic height to 5" and width to 10" and then align the graphic in the center and bottom of the slide (Figure 7–101a).
6. Display Slide 2 and then duplicate this slide. On Slide 2, select the entire SmartArt graphic. Click the Convert button (SmartArt Design tab | Reset group) and then click 'Convert to Text' to display the four bulleted list paragraphs.
7. Change the font size of the bulleted list paragraphs to 44 point. Increase the list level of the second paragraph, Open another browser to check, to a second-level paragraph. Align the content placeholder in the center and bottom of the slide (Figure 7–101b).
8. Display Slide 3. Select the entire SmartArt graphic and then click the Convert button. Click 'Convert to Shapes' to change the graphic to a shape.
9. Copy the SmartArt shape to Slide 4. Resize the shape height to 5" and the width to 10". Align the shape in the center and the bottom of the slide (Figure 7–101c).
10. Delete Slide 3.

    If requested by your instructor, change the words, a public area, on Slide 1 to the city where you attended first grade.
11. Run the presentation and then save it using the file name, **SC_PPT_7_Shopper.**
12. Submit the revised document in the format specified by your instructor.
13. **Consider This:** In this assignment, you changed WordArt to SmartArt and then changed a SmartArt graphic to text and a shape. Was the original Slide 1 with WordArt easier or more difficult to comprehend than the revised Slide 1 with SmartArt? Was the Vertical Bullet List a good layout choice? Is Slide 2 or Slide 3 the better choice to display the 'Resist the urge to purchase instantly' information? What are the advantages and disadvantages of converting a SmartArt graphic to a shape?

Figure 7–101(a): Slide 1 (WordArt Converted to SmartArt)

Continued on next page

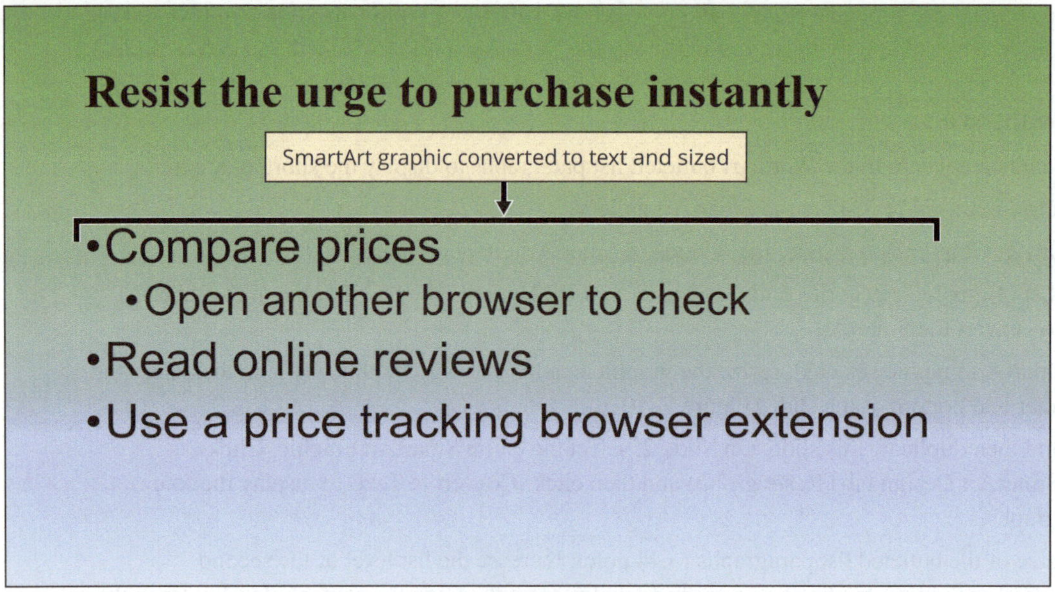

Figure 7–101(b): Slide 2 (Smart Art Converted to Text)

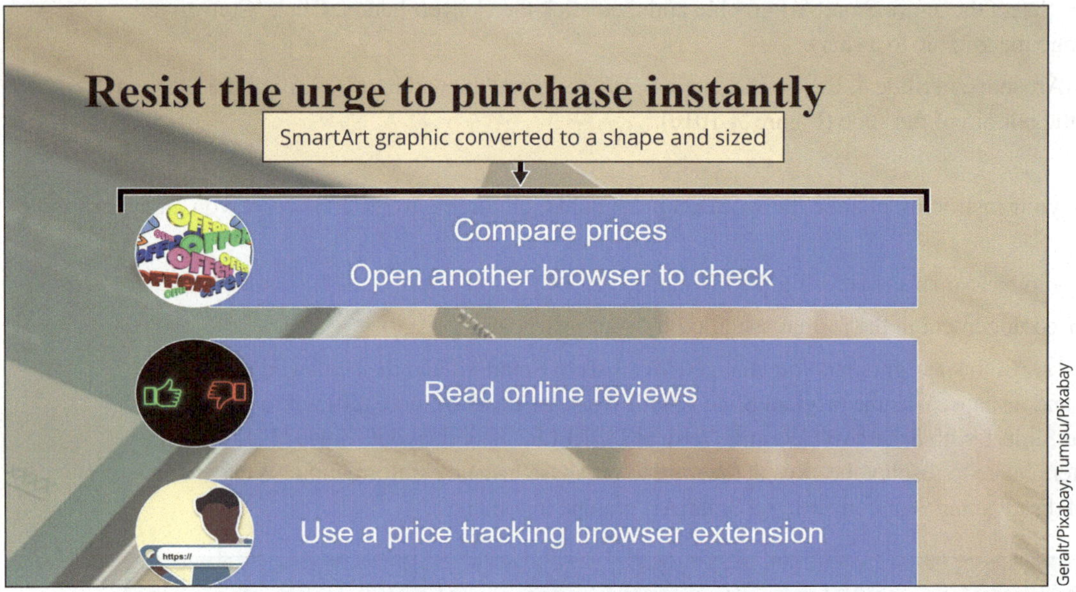

Figure 7–101(c): Slide 3 (SmartArt Converted to a Shape)

Expand Your World

Create a solution that uses cloud or web technologies by learning and investigating on your own from general guidance.

Reviewing Google Images SmartArt

Note: To complete this assignment, you will be required to use the Data Files. Please contact your instructor for information about accessing the Data Files.

Instructions: You want to add SmartArt to a presentation you have created to accompany the Fitness presentation you developed in this module. The counselors at your school have added meditation sessions at the Wellness Center to help students find methods to reduce stress and anxiety. The counselors want a second presentation to use at their seminars to promote the sessions. You have developed four slides, but you want to add graphical interest and decide to browse Google Images for SmartArt ideas.

Perform the following tasks:

1. Start PowerPoint. Open the presentation called SC_PPT_7-3.pptx, which is located in the Data Files.
2. Open your browser and navigate to Google.com. Click Images at the top of the screen to display the Google Images webpage. Click the Google Images search box, type **creative smartart design** as the search text, and then click the Search button (the magnifying glass) or press ENTER.
3. View several SmartArt images with designs that would be appropriate for the material on all slides and then use these design ideas as inspiration to convert the SmartArt on these slides. Do not click or download any files; simply use them as suggestions for design concepts. Recall that to change the SmartArt design you would select the SmartArt, click the More button (SmartArt Design tab | Layouts gallery), click More Layouts, and then select the desired category and layout.
4. If desired, you can change the SmartArt styles and colors and also arrange the slide elements.

   If requested to do so by your instructor, change the word, Wellness, on the title slide to the make of your first car.
5. Save the presentation using the file name, **SC_PPT_7_Meditation_SmartArt**.
6. Submit the assignment in the format specified by your instructor.
7. **Consider This:** Which SmartArt images on the Google Images webpage did you use for your presentation? Why did you select these particular examples? Did you change any SmartArt styles and colors or arrange the slide elements? Why or why not?

In the Lab

Apply your creative thinking and problem-solving skills to design and implement a solution.

Design and Create a Presentation about Teaching Children to Use Debit and Credit Cards

Part 1: One of the best methods of teaching children how to use financial products, including debit and credit cards, is to talk to them at an early age. Even preschoolers can learn skills that will give them a foundation for becoming financially responsible adults. Parents can introduce tweens and teens to debit cards and prepaid credit cards and opening a checking account. The New Account managers at the bank where you work are developing materials to distribute to parents of tweens and teens at a financial literacy program they are planning. They have asked you to create a PowerPoint presentation giving advice on teaching children to use debit and credit cards responsibly.

Your bank has a debit card specifically for children, and it has parental controls for setting spending limits. In addition, your bank allows children to open a secured credit card that is backed by a cash deposit used as collateral. When children use this card, they will be building a credit history because your bank reports payments and other account activity to the three major credit bureaus. Parents should give their children the freedom to spend, but rules should be established limiting where the card can be used. Parents also should monitor due dates and monthly balances, explaining that penalties and interest will be incurred for late and partial payments.

Perform some research to learn additional methods of educating children about sensibly using debit and credit cards. Then create slides with this information. The Data Files folder contains pictures you could use, and change the color saturation, brightness, or contrast on at least one of these images. Create at least one slide with SmartArt. Review and revise your presentation as needed and then save the file using the file name, **SC_PPT_7_Credit**. Submit your assignment in the format specified by your instructor.

Part 2: **Consider This:** You made several decisions while creating the presentation in this assignment: what content to include, how to format the slides and pictures, and which styles and effects to apply. What was the rationale behind each of these decisions? Where would you recommend showing this slide show? When you reviewed the document, what changes did you make?

Financial Functions, Data Tables, and Amortization Schedules

Objectives

After completing this module, you will be able to:

- Assign a name to a cell and refer to the cell in a formula using the assigned name
- Determine the monthly payment of a loan using the financial function PMT
- Describe the financial functions PV (present value) and FV (future value)
- Create a data table to analyze data in a worksheet
- Create an amortization schedule
- Control the color and thickness of outlines and borders
- Add a pointer to a data table
- Analyze worksheet data by changing values
- Use range names and print sections of a worksheet
- Set print options
- Protect and unprotect cells in a worksheet
- Hide and unhide worksheets and workbooks
- Use the formula checking features of Excel

Introduction

Two of the more powerful aspects of Excel are its wide array of functions and its capability of organizing answers to what-if questions. In this module, you will learn about financial functions such as the PMT function, which allows you to determine a monthly payment for a loan, and the PV function, which allows you to determine the present value of an investment.

In earlier modules, you learned how to analyze data by using the Excel recalculation feature and goal seeking. This module introduces an additional what-if analysis tool, called a data table. A **data table** is a range of cells that shows the resulting values when one or more input values are varied in a formula. You use a data table to automate data analyses and organize the results returned by Excel. Another important loan analysis tool is an amortization schedule. An **amortization schedule** is a schedule that shows loan balances and the payment amounts applied to the principal and interest for each payment period.

In previous modules, you learned how to print in a variety of ways. In this module, you will learn additional methods of printing using range names and a print area.

Finally, this module introduces you to cell protection, hiding and unhiding worksheets and workbooks, and formula checking. **Cell protection** ensures that users do not inadvertently change values that are critical to the worksheet. Hiding portions of a workbook lets you show only the parts of the workbook that the user needs to see. The **formula checker** examines the formulas in a workbook in a manner similar to the way the spelling checker examines a workbook for misspelled words.

Project: Mortgage Payment Calculator

The project in this module uses Excel to create a mortgage payment calculator as shown in Figure 4–1. Windshore Bank provides mortgages (loans) for homes and other types of properties. The president of the bank has asked for an interactive worksheet that will be displayed on the bank website. The worksheet will allow customers to calculate potential mortgage payment information, review an amortization schedule, and compare varying interest rates. To ensure customers will not delete any formulas in the worksheet, certain cells will need to be protected to prevent any changes, so that the mortgage calculator functions properly.

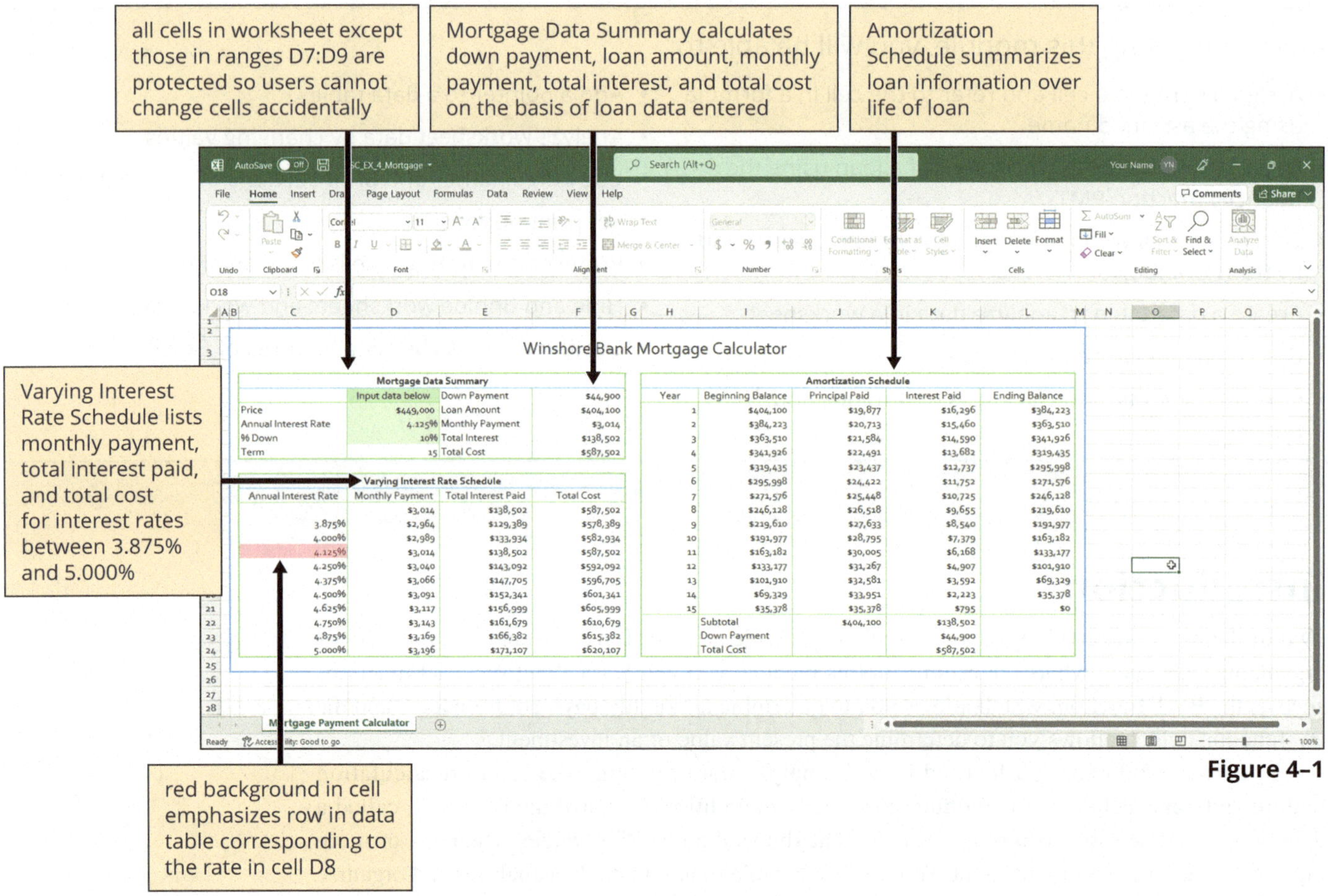

Figure 4–1

The requirements document for the Windshore Bank Mortgage Calculator worksheet is shown in Figure 4–2. It includes the needs, source of data, summary of calculations, and special requirements.

Worksheet Title	**Windshore Bank Mortgage Calculator**
Needs	An easy-to-read worksheet that: 1. Determines the down payment, loan amount, monthly payment, total interest, and total cost for a mortgage. 2. Shows a data table that answers what-if questions based on changing interest rates. 3. Highlights the rate in the data table that matches the actual interest rate. 4. Shows an amortization schedule that lists annual summaries of beginning balance, principal paid, interest paid, and the ending balance.
Source of Data	Data supplied by the bank is the term of mortgage. Data supplied by the customer includes the price, interest rate, and percentage of down payment. All other data is calculated or created in Excel.
Calculations	1. The following calculations must be made for each mortgage: a. Mortgage Amount = Price − Down Payment b. Monthly Payment = PMT function c. Total Interest = 12 × Term × Monthly Payment − Loan Amount d. Total Cost = 12 × Term × Monthly Payment + Down Payment 2. The Amortization Schedule involves the following calculations: a. Beginning Balance = Loan Amount b. Principal Paid = Beginning Balance − Ending Balance c. Interest Paid = 12 × Monthly Payment − Principal Paid or 0 d. Ending Balance = PV function or zero e. Paid on Principal Subtotal = SUM function f. Interest Paid Subtotal = SUM function
Special Requirements	1. Assign names to the ranges of the three major worksheet components separately and together to allow the worksheet components to be printed separately or together easily. 2. Use locked cells and worksheet protection to prevent loan officers and customers from inadvertently making changes to formulas and functions contained in the worksheet.

Figure 4–2

In addition, using a sketch of the worksheet can help you visualize its design. The sketch of the worksheet consists of titles, column and cell headings, the location of data values, and a general idea of the desired formatting (Figure 4–3).

BTW
Good Worksheet Design
Consider creating worksheets with an eye toward reusing them in the future. Carefully design worksheets as if they will be displayed for and evaluated by your fellow workers. Smart worksheet design starts with visualizing the results you need. A well-designed worksheet often is used for many years.

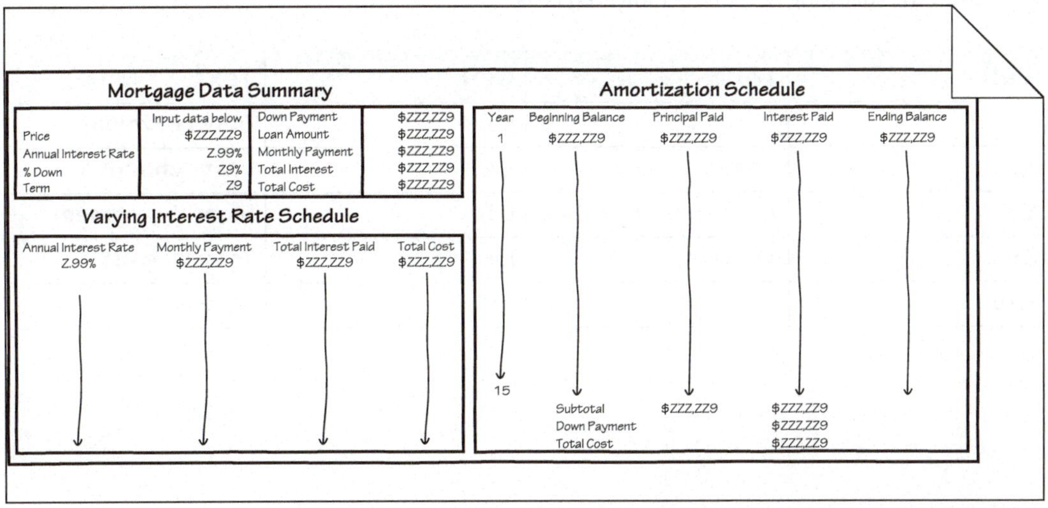

Figure 4–3

BTW
Ribbon and Screen Resolution
Excel may change how the groups and buttons within the groups appear on the ribbon, depending on the screen resolution of your computer. Thus, your ribbon may look different from the ones in this book if you are using a screen resolution other than 1920 × 1080.

As shown in the worksheet sketch in Figure 4–3, the three basic sections of the worksheet are the Mortgage Data Summary on the upper-left side, the Varying Interest Rate Schedule data table on the lower-left side, and the Amortization Schedule on the right side. The worksheet will be created in this order.

With a good understanding of the requirements document, an understanding of the necessary decisions, and a sketch of the worksheet, the next step is to use Excel to create the worksheet.

In this module, you will learn how to create and use the workbook shown in Figure 4–1.

To Apply a Theme to the Worksheet

The following steps apply the Parallax theme to the workbook.

1. sam Start Excel and create a blank workbook in the Excel window.
2. Apply the Parallax theme to the workbook.

BTW
Global Formatting
To assign formats to all the cells in all the worksheets in a workbook, click the Select All button, right-click a sheet tab, and click 'Select All Sheets' on the shortcut menu. Next, assign the formats. To deselect the worksheets, hold down SHIFT and click the Sheet1 tab or select Ungroup sheets on the shortcut menu. You also can select a cell or a range of cells and then select all worksheets to assign formats to that cell or a range of cells on all worksheets in a workbook.

To Enter the Section and Row Titles and System Date

The next step is to enter the Mortgage Data Summary section title and row titles. The Mortgage Data Summary section title also will be changed to a Heading cell style and vertically middle-aligned. The following steps enter the section title and row titles.

1. Select cell C5 and then enter **Mortgage Data Summary** as the section title.

   Q&A Why did I not begin creating the worksheet in cell A1?
   Two rows at the top of the worksheet and two columns on the left of the worksheet will be left blank to provide a border around the worksheet. Two more rows at the top will be left blank to leave space for the worksheet title.

2. Select the range C5:F5 and then click the 'Merge & Center' button (Home tab | Alignment group) to merge and center the section title in the selected range.
3. Click the Cell Styles button (Home tab | Styles group) and then click the Heading 3 cell style in the Cell Styles gallery to apply the selected style to the active cell.
4. Click the Middle Align button (Home tab | Alignment group) to vertically center the text in the selected cell.
5. Enter the following text in the indicated cells:

Cell	Text	Cell	Text
		E6	**Down Payment**
C7	**Price**	E7	**Loan Amount**
C8	**Annual Interest Rate**	E8	**Monthly Payment**
C9	**% Down**	E9	**Total Interest**
C10	**Term**	E10	**Total Cost**

BTW
Touch Mode Differences
The Office and Windows interfaces may vary if you are using Touch Mode. For this reason, you might notice that the function or appearance of your touch screen differs slightly from this module's presentation.

BTW
Touch and Pointers
Remember that if you are using your finger on a touch screen, you will not see the pointer.

To Adjust the Column Widths and Row Heights

To make the worksheet easier to read, the width of columns A and B will be decreased and used as a separator between the left edge of the worksheet and the row headings. Using a column(s) as a separator between sections on a worksheet is a technique used by spreadsheet specialists. The width of columns C through L, excluding column G, will be increased so that the intended values fit. The height of row 3, which contains the title, will be increased so that it stands out. The height of rows 1 and 2 will be decreased to act as visual separators for the top of the calculator. The following steps adjust the column widths and row heights.

1. Click column heading A and then drag through column heading B to select both columns. Position the pointer on the right boundary of column heading B and then drag to the left until the ScreenTip indicates Width: 1.00 to change the width of both columns.

Q&A What if I am unable to drag to set the exact column widths and row heights specified? Depending on your display settings, you may be unable to set the exact column widths and row heights by dragging. In this case, right-click the column or row heading to resize, click Column Width (for columns) or Row Height (for rows) to display the Column Width or Row Height dialog box, type the exact column width or row height, and then click OK.

2. Position the pointer on the right boundary of column heading C and then drag to the right until the ScreenTip indicates Width: 19.75 to change the column width.

3. Click column heading D to select it and then drag through column headings E and F to select multiple columns. Position the pointer on the right boundary of column heading F and then drag until the ScreenTip indicates Width: 17.00 to change multiple column widths.

4. Click row heading 1 to select it and then drag through row heading 2 to select both rows. Position the pointer on the bottom boundary of row heading 2 and then drag until the ScreenTip indicates Height: 9.00.

5. Select an empty cell to deselect the selected rows (Figure 4–4).

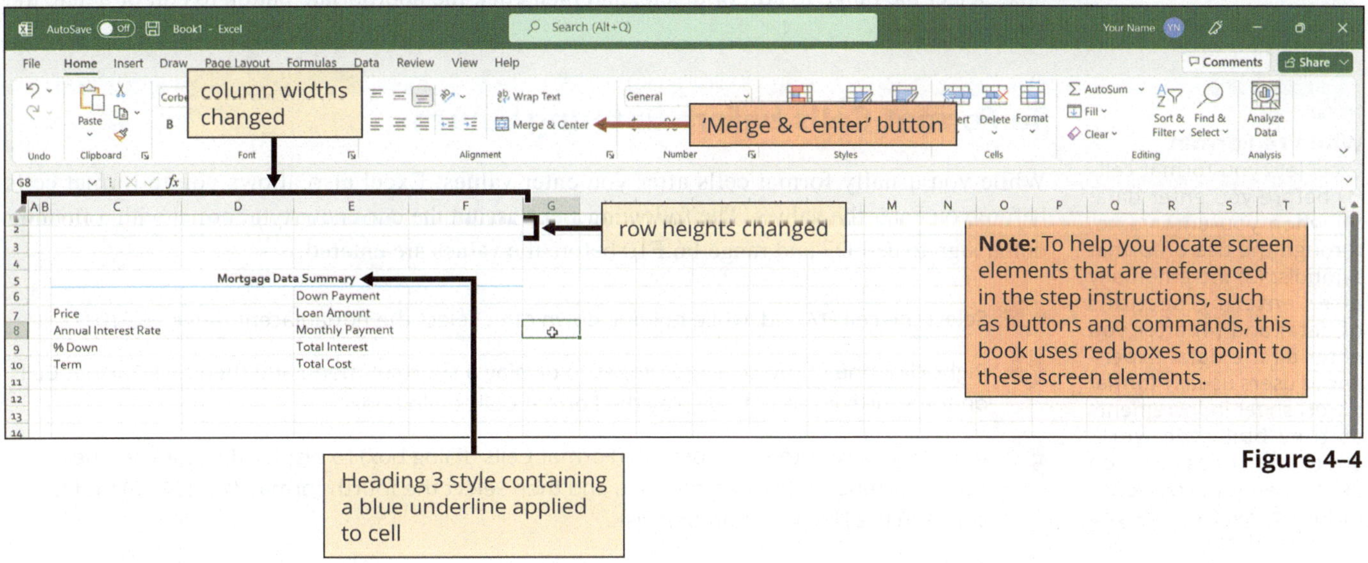

Figure 4–4

To Change the Sheet Tab Name

The following steps change the Sheet1 sheet tab name to a descriptive name and then save the workbook.

1. Double-click the Sheet1 tab and then enter **Mortgage Payment Calculator** as the sheet tab name.
2. Save the workbook on your hard drive, OneDrive, or location that is most appropriate to your situation using **SC_EX_4_Mortgage** as the file name.

Q&A Why should I save the workbook at this time?
You have performed many tasks while creating this workbook and do not want to risk losing work completed thus far.

BTW
Cell References in Formulas
Are you tired of writing formulas that are difficult to decipher because of cell references? The Name Manager can help add clarity to your formulas by allowing you to assign names to cells. You can then use the name, such as Rate, rather than the cell reference, such as D2, in the formulas you create. To access the Name Manager, click the Name Manager button (Formulas tab | Defined Names group).

Creating Cell Names

A **cell name** is a name you assign to a cell or range. You can then use that name in formulas in place of the cell or range address. Using names instead of addresses makes formulas easier to understand. Using names also lets you build formulas more quickly because you can select them quickly using the Name box (shown in Figure 4–7). Clicking the name will select the corresponding cell or range and highlight the cell or range on the worksheet. Names are global to the workbook. That is, a name assigned to a cell or cell range on one worksheet in a workbook can be used on other worksheets in the same workbook to reference the named cell or range. You can assign names to cells, ranges, formulas, and constants.

To assign names to selected cells, you can use the Define Name button (Formulas tab | Defined Names group). But worksheets often have column titles at the top of each column and row titles to the left of each row that describe the data within the worksheet, and you can use these titles to create names. If you make a mistake while creating a name, click the Name Manager button (Formulas tab | Defined Names group) to display the Name Manager dialog box. Select the range to edit or delete, and then click the appropriate button to edit or delete the selected range.

BTW
When to Format
Excel lets you format cells (1) before you enter data; (2) when you enter data, through the use of format symbols; (3) incrementally after entering sections of data; and (4) after you enter all the data. Experienced users usually format a worksheet in increments as they build the worksheet, but occasions do exist when it makes sense to format cells before you enter any data.

To Format Cells before Entering Values

While you usually format cells after you enter values, Excel also allows you to format cells before you enter the values. The following steps assign the currency style format with a floating dollar sign to cell D7 and range F6:F10 before the values are entered.

1. Select the cell D7 and, while holding down CTRL, select the nonadjacent range F6:F10.
2. Right-click one of the selected ranges to display a shortcut menu and then click Format Cells on the shortcut menu to display the Format Cells dialog box.
3. If necessary, click the Number tab (Format Cells dialog box) to display the Number sheet, select Currency in the Category list, and then select the fourth format, ($1,234.10) (red font color), in the Negative numbers list.
4. To adjust the number of decimal places from 2 to 0, click the down arrow twice next to Decimal Places.
5. Click OK (Format Cells dialog box) to assign the currency style format with a floating dollar sign to the selected cell and range, D7 and F6:F10.

Q&A What will happen when I enter values in these cells?
As you enter numbers into these cells, Excel will display the numbers using the currency style format. The currency style format has no impact on text in a cell.

To Enter the Loan Data

As shown in the Source of data section of the requirements document in Figure 4–2, four items make up the loan data in the worksheet: the price of the item, the interest rate, the percentage of total price for the down payment, and the term (number of years) over which the loan is paid back. The following steps enter the loan data.

1. Select cell D7 and then enter **449,000** for the price of the house.
2. Select cell D8 and then enter **4.125%** for the annual interest rate.
3. Select cell D8, if necessary, and then click the Increase Decimal button (Home tab | Number group) once to increase the number of decimal places to three.

Q&A How can I decrease the number of decimal places?

You can click the Decrease Decimal button (Home tab | Number group) to decrease the number of decimal places.

4. Select cell D9 and then enter **10%** for the percentage of total price for the down payment.
5. Select cell D10 and then enter **15** for the number of years in the term (Figure 4–5).

Q&A Why are the entered values already formatted?

The value in cell D7 in Figure 4–5 is formatted using the currency style because you assigned this format to the cell prior to entering the values. Because you typed the percent sign (%) after typing 4.125 in cell D8, Excel formatted the interest rate using the percentage style with two decimal places (you may have noticed that the value originally appeared as 4.13). Using the Increase Decimal button increased the number of visible decimal places to three.

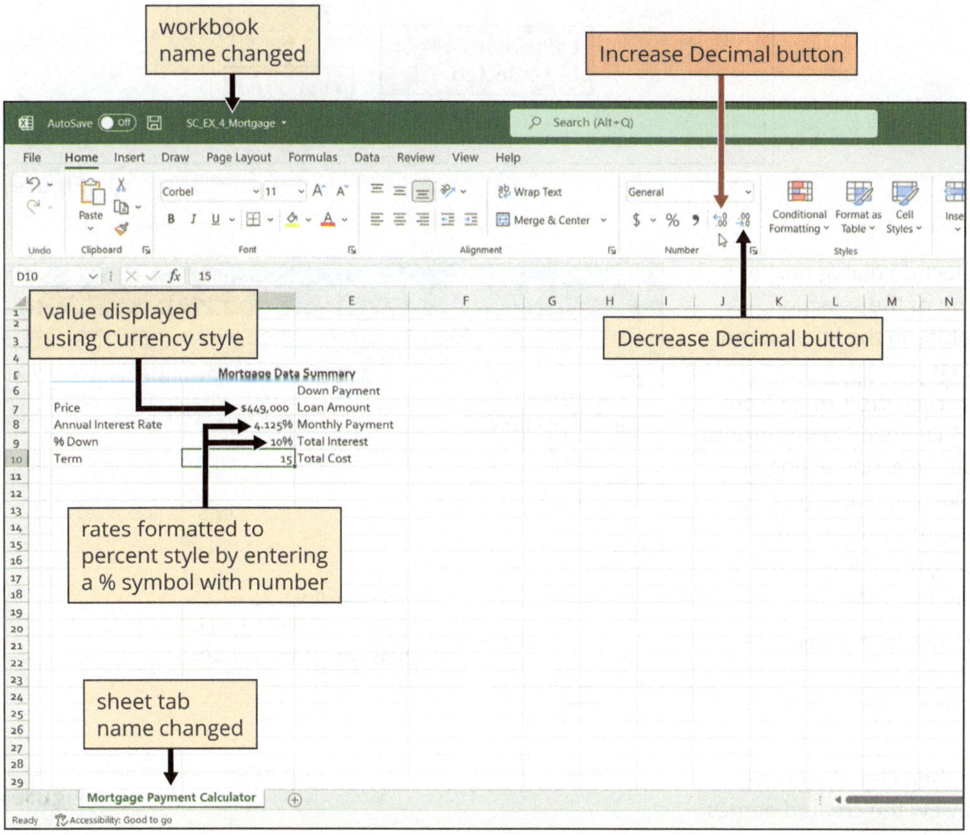

Figure 4–5

BTW
Entering Percentages

When you format a cell to display percentages, Excel assumes that whatever you enter into that cell in the future will be a percentage. Thus, if you enter the number .5, Excel translates the value as 50%. A potential problem arises, however, when you start to enter numbers greater than or equal to one. For instance, if you enter the number 25, do you mean 25% or 2500%? If you want Excel to treat the number 25 as 25% and Excel interprets the number 25 as 2500%, click Options in Backstage view. When the Excel Options dialog box appears, click Advanced in the left pane, and make sure the 'Enable automatic percent entry' check box in the right pane is selected.

BTW
Entering Interest Rates

An alternative to requiring the user to enter an interest rate as a percentage, such as 4.125%, is to allow the user to enter the interest rate as a number without a percent sign (4.125) and then divide the interest rate by 1,000, rather than 10.

To Create Names Based on Row Titles

Why? Naming a cell that you plan to reference in a formula helps make the formula easier to read and remember. For example, the down payment amount in cell F6 is equal to the price in cell D7 times the percentage down (the percentage of the down payment paid) in cell D9. According to what you learned in earlier modules, you can enter the down payment amount formula in cell F6 as =D7 * D9. By naming cells D7 and D9 using the corresponding row titles in cells C7 and C9, however, you can enter the loan amount formula as =Price * Down, which is clearer and easier to understand than =D7 * D9. In addition to assigning a name to a single cell, you can follow the same steps to assign a name to a range of cells. The following steps assign the row titles in the range C7:C10 to their adjacent cell in column D and assign the row titles in the range E6:E10 to their adjacent cell in column F.

1

- Select the range C7:D10.
- Display the Formulas tab.
- Click the 'Create from Selection' button (Formulas tab | Defined Names group) to display the Create Names from Selection dialog box (Figure 4–6).

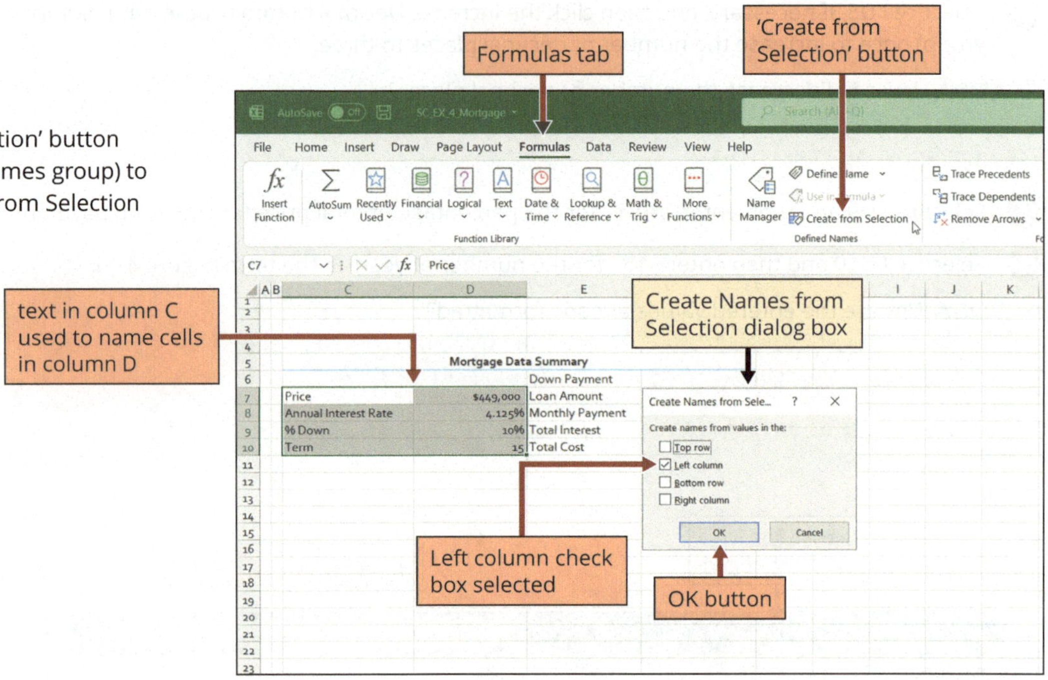

Figure 4–6

2

- Click OK (Create Names from Selection dialog box) to name the cells in the right column of the selection, D7:D10 in this case, using the values in the left column of the selection, C7:C10 in this case.
- Select the range E6:F10 and then click the 'Create from Selection' button (Formulas tab | Defined Names group) to display the Create Names from Selection dialog box.
- Click OK (Create Names from Selection dialog box) to assign names to the cells in the right column of the selection, F6:F10 in this case, using the values in the left column of the selection, E6:E10 in this case.

Q&A Are names absolute or relative cell references?
Names are absolute cell references. This is important to remember if you plan to copy formulas that contain names rather than cell references.

- Deselect the selected range and then click the Name box arrow in the formula bar to view the created names (Figure 4–7).

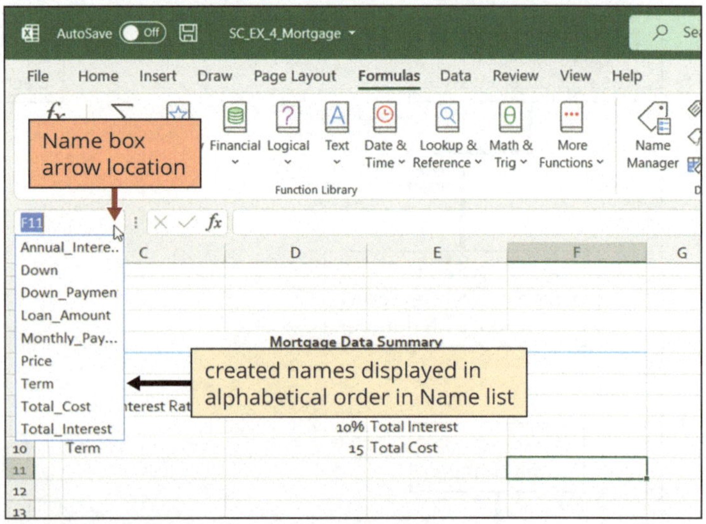

Figure 4–7

Q&A Are there any limitations on cell names? Can they contain punctuation?
Names may not be longer than 255 characters. They may contain periods and underscore characters. However, a cell name may not begin with a period or an underscore. Notice D9 is named Down, instead of % Down, like the cell reference C9. This is due to the percent character not being allowed as part of a cell name.

Other Ways

1. Select cell or range, type name in Name box, press ENTER
2. Select cell or range, click Define Name button (Formulas tab | Defined Names group), type name, click OK (New Name dialog box)
3. Select cell or range, click Name Manager button (Formulas tab | Defined Names group), click New (Name Manager dialog box), type name, click OK (New Name dialog box), click Close button (Name Manager dialog box)
4. Select range, press CTRL+SHIFT+F3

Consider This

What do you do if a cell you want to name does not have a text item in an adjacent cell?

If you want to assign a name that does not appear as a text item in an adjacent cell, use the Define Name button (Formulas tab | Defined Names group) or select the cell or range and then enter the name in the Name box in the formula bar.

Consider This

What do I need to consider when naming cells, and how can I use named cells?

You can use the assigned names in formulas to reference cells in the ranges D7:D10 or F6:F10. Excel is not case sensitive with respect to names of cells. You can enter the cell names in formulas in either uppercase or lowercase letters. To use a name that consists of two or more words in a formula, you should replace any space with the underscore character (_), as this is a commonly used standard for creating cell names. For example the name, Down Payment, can be written as down_payment or Down_Payment when you want to reference the adjacent cell F6. The Name Manager dialog box appears when you click the Name Manager button. The Name Manager dialog box allows you to create new names and edit or delete existing names.

To Enter the Down Payment Amount Formula Using Names

Why? Once you have created names, you can use them instead of cell references in formulas because they are easier to remember. To determine the down payment amount, enter the formula =Price * Down in cell F6. Excel makes this easier by including any cell names you have assigned in the list of functions. The following steps enter the formula using names.

1

- Select cell F6.
- Type **=p** and then scroll down the Formula AutoComplete list until you see the Price entry (Figure 4–8).

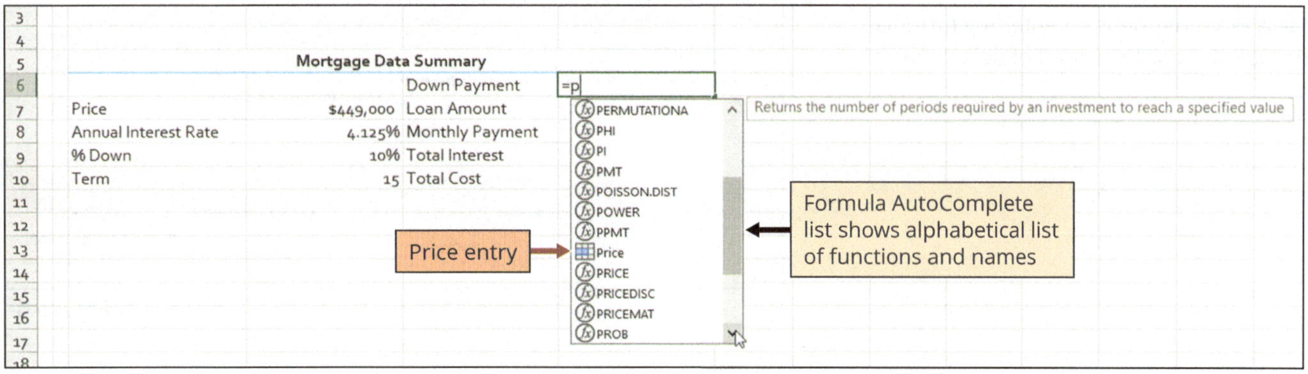

Figure 4–8

2

- Double-click Price to enter it in cell F6.
- Type ***d**.
- Scroll down to and double-click Down in the Formula AutoComplete list to select it and display the formula in both cell F6 and the formula bar using the cell names instead of the cell references (Figure 4–9).

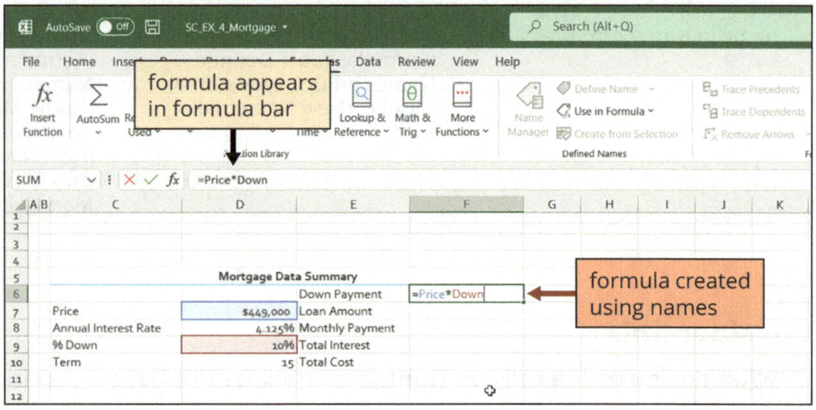

Figure 4–9

3

- Click the Enter button to assign the formula =Price * Down to the selected cell, F6 (Figure 4–10).

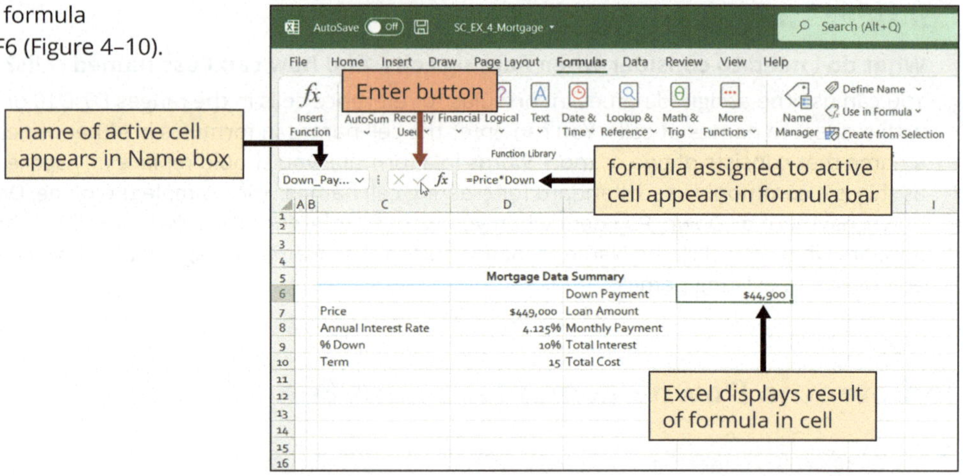

Figure 4–10

4

- Repeat the process for Loan Amount in cell F7 to assign the formula =Price−Down_Payment using assigned names (Figure 4–11).

Q&A What happens if I enter my formula using Point mode instead of using names?
If you enter a formula using Point mode and click a cell that has an assigned name, Excel will insert the name of the cell rather than the cell reference.

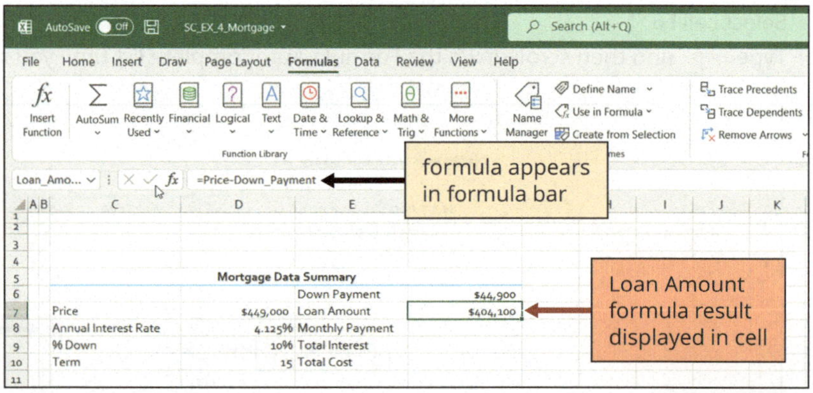

Figure 4–11

The PMT Function

You can use the Excel PMT function to determine the monthly payment. The **PMT function** is a financial function that calculates the payment schedule required to repay a loan based on constant payments and a constant interest rate. The PMT function has three arguments: rate, periods, and loan amount. Its general form is as follows:

=PMT(rate, periods, loan amount)

where rate is the interest rate per payment period, periods is the number of payments over the life of the loan, and loan amount is the amount of the loan.

In the worksheet shown in Figure 4–11, Excel displays the annual interest rate in cell D8. Financial institutions, however, usually calculate interest on a monthly basis. The rate value in the PMT function is, therefore, Annual_Interest_Rate / 12 (cell D8 divided by 12), rather than just Annual_Interest_Rate (cell D8). The periods (or number of payments) in the PMT function is 12 * Term (12 times cell D10) because each year includes 12 months, or 12 payments.

Excel considers the value returned by the PMT function to be a debit and, therefore, returns a negative number as the monthly payment. To display the monthly payment as a positive number, begin the function with a negative sign instead of an equal sign. The PMT function for cell F8 is:

=–PMT(Annual_Interest_Rate/12, 12*Term, Loan_Amount)

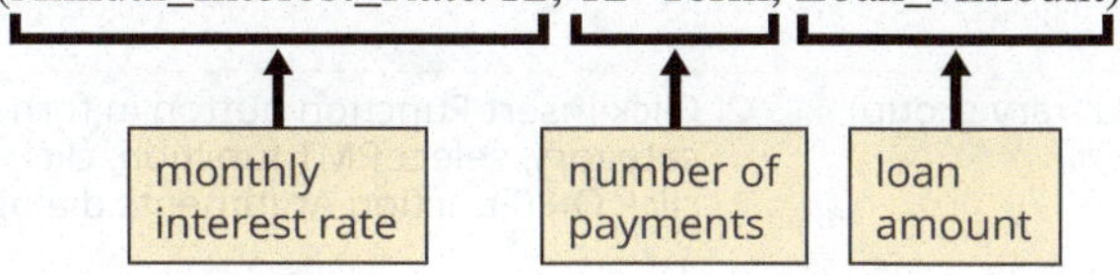

To Enter the PMT Function

Why? The next step in building the mortgage payment calculator is to determine the monthly payment for the mortgage. The following steps use the keyboard, rather than Point mode or the Insert Function dialog box, to enter the PMT function to determine the monthly payment in cell F8.

1

- Select cell F8.
- Type the function **=-pmt(Annual_Interest_Rate/12,12*Term,Loan_Amount** in cell F8, which also displays in the formula bar (Figure 4–12).

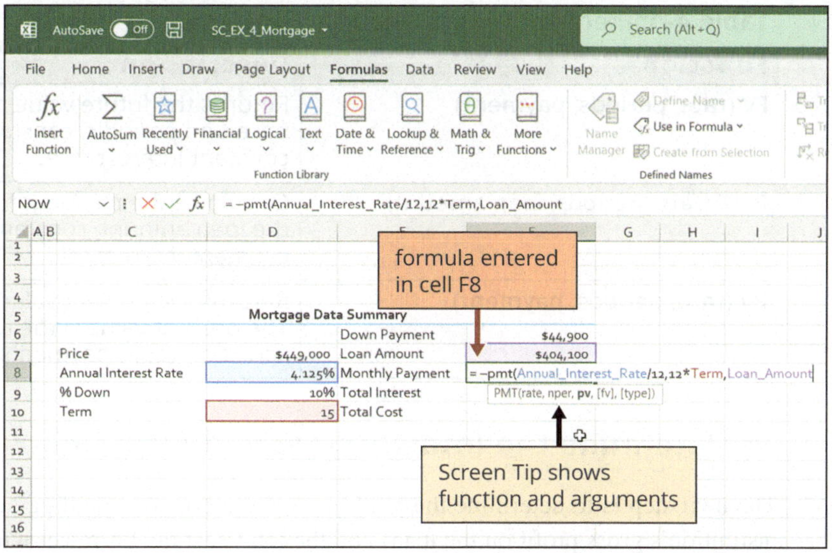

Figure 4–12

2

- Click the Enter button in the formula bar to complete the function (Figure 4–13).

Q&A What happens as I begin to enter the function?

The ScreenTip shows the general form of the PMT function (after you type the opening parenthesis). The arguments in brackets in the ScreenTip are optional and not required for the computation required in this project. The Formula AutoComplete list (Figure 4–8) shows functions and cell names that match the letters that you type on the keyboard. You can type the complete cell name, such as Loan_Amount, or double-click the cell name in the list. When you have completed entering the function and click the Enter button or press ENTER, Excel will add the closing parenthesis to the function. Excel also may scroll the worksheet to the right in order to accommodate the ScreenTip.

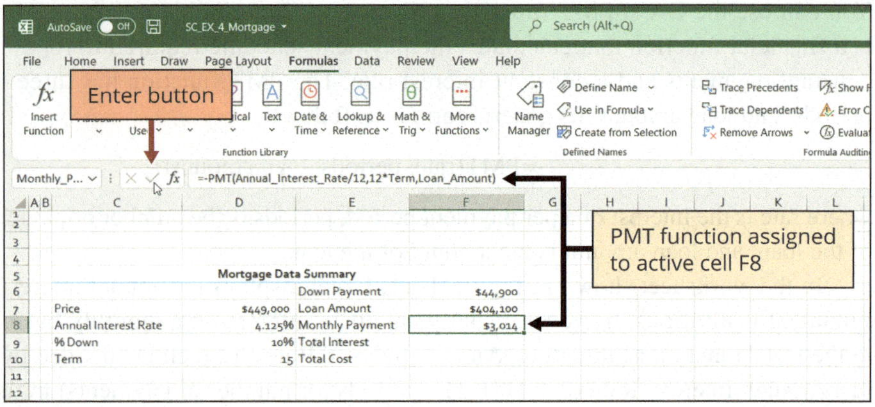

Figure 4–13

Other Ways

1. Click Financial button (Formulas tab | Function Library group), select PMT function, enter arguments, click OK
2. Click Insert Function button in formula bar, select Financial category, select PMT function, click OK, enter arguments, click OK (Function Arguments dialog box)

Other Financial Functions

In addition to the PMT function, Excel provides more than 50 financial functions to help you solve the most complex finance problems. These functions save you from entering long, complicated formulas to obtain needed results. For example, the **FV function** returns the future value of an investment based on scheduled payments and an unchanging interest rate. The FV function requires the following arguments: the interest rate per period, the number of periods, and the payment made each period (which cannot change). For instance, if you want to invest $100 per month for five years at an annual interest rate of 4.5%, the FV function will calculate how much money you will have at the end of five years. Table 4–1 summarizes three of the more frequently used financial functions.

Table 4–1: Frequently Used Financial Functions

Function	Description
FV (rate, periods, payment)	Returns the future value of an investment based on periodic, constant payments and a constant interest rate.
PMT (rate, periods, loan amount)	Calculates the payment for a loan based on the loan amount, constant payments, and a constant interest rate.
PV (rate, periods, payment)	Returns the present value of an investment. The present value is the total amount that a series of future payments now is worth.

To Determine the Total Interest and Total Cost

The next step is to determine the total interest the borrower will pay on the loan (the lending institution's gross profit on the loan) and the total cost the borrower will pay for the item being purchased. The total interest (cell F9) is equal to the number of payments times the monthly payment, minus the loan amount:

=12*Term*Monthly_Payment–Loan_Amount

The total cost of the item to be purchased (cell F10) is equal to the price plus the total interest:

=Price+Total_Interest

The following steps enter formulas to determine the total interest and total cost using names.

1. Select cell F9, use the keyboard to enter the formula **=12*term*Monthly_Payment-Loan_Amount** to determine the total interest (selecting names in the AutoComplete list where appropriate can speed entry), and then click the Enter button.
2. Select cell F10 and then use the keyboard to enter the formula **=Price+Total_Interest** to determine the total cost.
3. Select an empty cell to deselect cell F10.
4. Save the workbook again in the same storage location with the same file name (Figure 4–14).

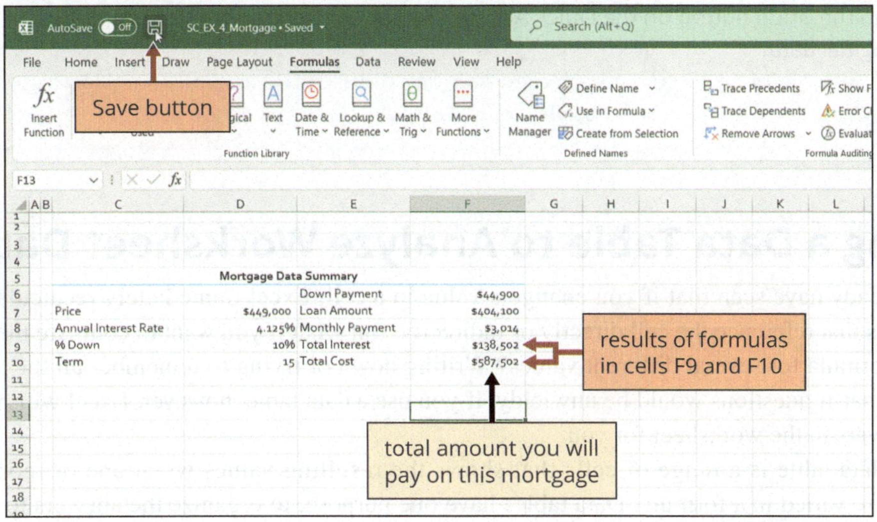

Figure 4–14

BTW
Range Finder
Remember to check all your formulas carefully. You can double-click a cell containing a formula and Excel will use Range Finder to highlight the cells that provide data for that formula. While Range Finder is active, you can drag the outlines from one cell to another to change the cells referenced in the formula, provided the cells have not been named.

BTW
Testing a Worksheet
It is good practice to test the formulas in a worksheet repeatedly until you are confident they are correct. Use data that tests the limits of the formulas. For example, you should enter negative numbers, zero, and large positive numbers when testing formulas.

To Enter New Loan Data

Assume a customer wants to purchase a condominium for $275,000. The customer plans to pay 12% down and wants the loan for a term of 10 years. Windshore Bank currently is charging 5.250% interest for a 10-year loan. The following steps enter the new loan data.

1. Enter **275000** in cell D7.
2. Enter **5.250%** in cell D8.
3. Enter **12%** in cell D9.
4. Enter **10** in cell D10 and then select an empty cell to deselect cell D10 (Figure 4–15).

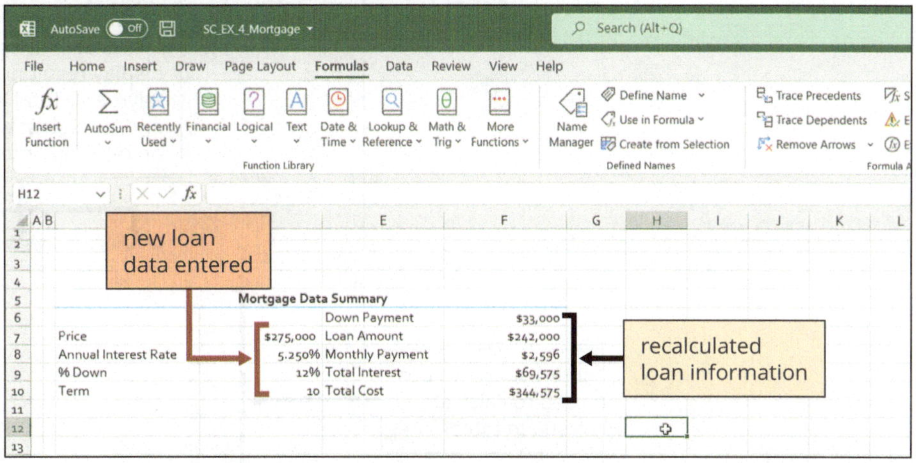

Figure 4–15

To Enter the Original Loan Data

The following steps reenter the original loan data.

1. Enter **449000** in cell D7.
2. Enter **4.125%** in cell D8.
3. Enter **10%** in cell D9.
4. Enter **15** in cell D10 to complete the entry of the original loan data.

Q&A What is happening on the worksheet as I enter the original data?
Excel instantaneously recalculates all formulas in the worksheet each time you enter a value. Once you have re-entered all the initial data, Excel displays the original loan information, as shown in Figure 4–14.

Can the Undo button on the Quick Access Toolbar be used to change back to the original data?
Yes. The Undo button must be clicked four times, once for each data item. You also can click the Undo arrow and drag through the first four entries in the Undo list.

BTW
Expanding Data Tables
The data table created in this module is relatively small. You can continue the series of percentages to the bottom of the worksheet and insert additional formulas in columns to create as large a data table as you want.

Using a Data Table to Analyze Worksheet Data

You already have seen that if you change a value in a cell, Excel immediately recalculates any formulas that reference the cell directly or indirectly. But what if you want to compare the results of the formula for several different values? Writing down or trying to remember all the answers to the what-if questions would be unwieldy. If you use a data table, however, Excel will organize the answers in the worksheet for you.

A data table is a range of cells that shows the resulting values when one or more input values are varied in a formula. Data tables have one purpose: to organize the answers to what-if questions. Data tables must be built in an unused area of the worksheet (in this case, the range C12:F24). Figure 4–16a illustrates the content needed for the Data Table command. A **one-input data table** (also called a **one-variable data table**) is a range of cells that shows resulting values when one input value in a formula is changed (in this worksheet, cell D8, the interest rate). Excel then calculates the results of one or more formulas and fills the data table with the results. Figure 4–16b shows the completed one-input data table.

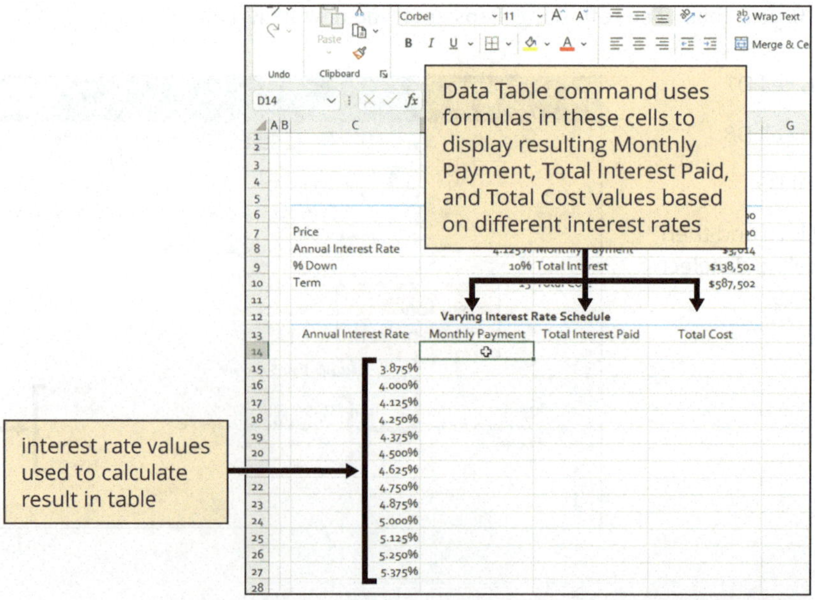

Figure 4–16(a)

The interest rates that will be used to analyze the loan formulas in this project range from 3.875% to 5.000, increasing in increments of 0.125%. The one-input data table shown in Figure 4–16b illustrates the impact of varying the interest rate on three formulas: the monthly payment (cell F8), total interest paid (cell F9), and the total cost of the item to be purchased (cell F10). The series of interest rates in column C are called input values.

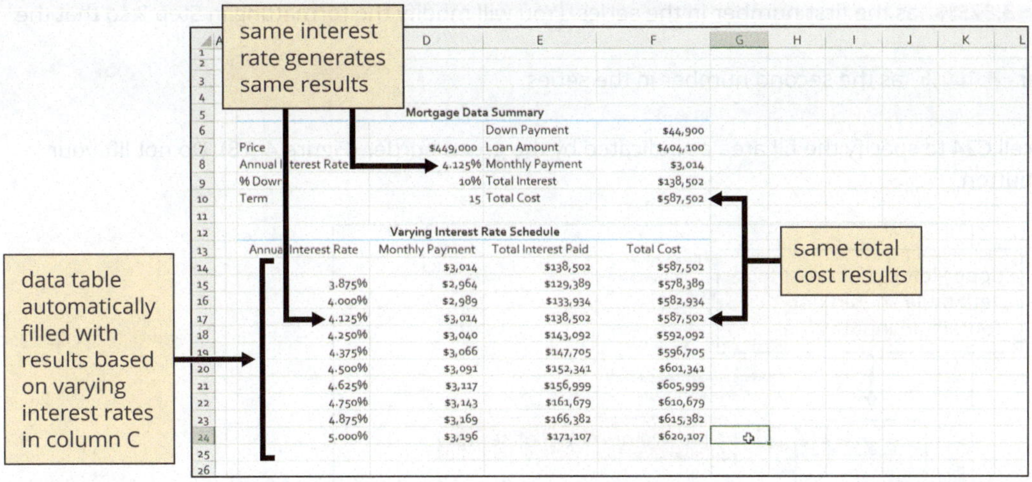

Figure 4–16(b)

To Enter the Data Table Title and Column Titles

The first step in constructing the data table shown in Figure 4–16b is to enter the data table section title and column titles in the range C12:F13. The following steps enter the data table and column titles.

1. Select cell C12 and then enter **Varying Interest Rate Schedule** as the data table section title.
2. Select cell C5 and then click the Format Painter button (Home tab | Clipboard group) to copy the format of the cell. Click cell C12 to apply the copied Heading 3 format, including its blue underlining, to the cell.
3. Type **Annual Interest Rate** in cell C13, **Monthly Payment** in cell D13, **Total Interest Paid** in cell E13, and **Total Cost** in cell F13 to create headers for the data table. Select the range C13:F13 and center-align the column titles.
4. Click cell C15 to deselect the range C13:F13 (Figure 4–17).

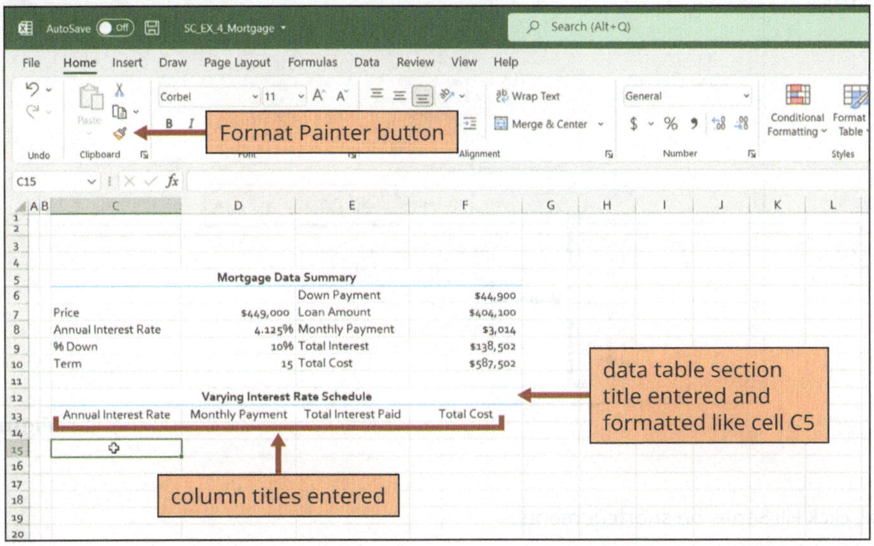

Figure 4–17

To Create a Percentage Series Using the Fill Handle

Why? These percentages will serve as the input data for the data table. The following steps create the percentage series in column C using the fill handle.

1

- With cell C15 selected, enter **3.875%** as the first number in the series. (You will modify the formatting in Step 2 so that the exact value is displayed.)
- Select cell C16 and then enter **4.000%** as the second number in the series.
- Select the range C15:C16.
- Drag the fill handle through cell C24 to specify the fill area as indicated by the green border (Figure 4–18). Do not lift your finger or release the mouse button.

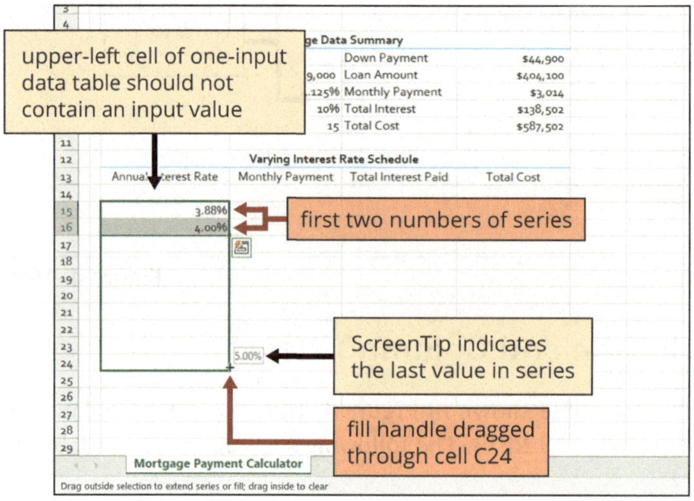

Figure 4–18

2

- Lift your finger or release the mouse button to generate the percentage series, in this case from 3.88% to 5.00%.
- Click the Increase Decimal button (Home tab | Number group) to increase the number of decimal places shown to 3.
- Click cell D14 to deselect the selected range, C15:C24 in this case (Figure 4–19).

Q&A What is the purpose of the percentages in column C?

The percentages in column C represent different annual interest rates, which will be used when calculating the data table. The series begins in cell C15, not cell C14, because the cell immediately to the upper left of the formulas in a one-input data table should not include an input value.

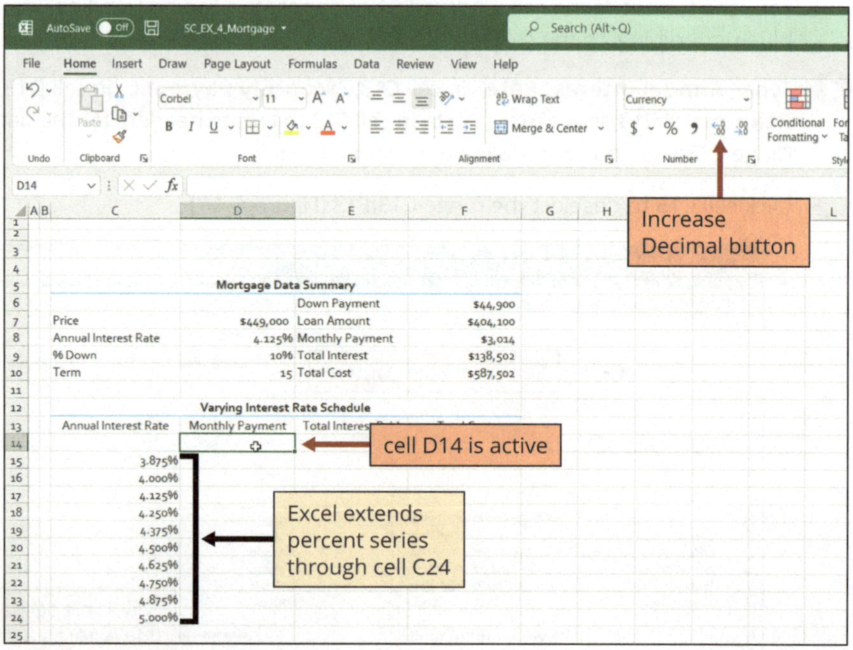

Figure 4–19

Other Ways

1. Right-drag fill handle in direction to fill, click Fill Series on shortcut menu

To Enter the Formulas in the Data Table

The next step in creating the data table is to enter the three formulas at the top of the table in cells D14, E14, and F14. The three formulas are the same as the monthly payment formula in cell F8, the total interest formula in cell F9, and the total cost formula in cell F10. The number of formulas you place at the top of a one-input data table depends on the purpose of the table. Some one-input data tables will have only one formula, while others might have several. In this case, three formulas are affected when the interest rate changes.

Excel provides four ways to enter these formulas in the data table: (1) retype the formulas in cells D14, E14, and F14; (2) copy cells F8, F9, and F10 to cells D14, E14, and F14, respectively; (3) enter the formulas **=monthly_payment** in cell D14, **=total_interest** in cell E14, and **=total_cost** in cell F14; or (4) enter the formulas **=f6** in cell D14, **=f7** in cell E14, and **=f8** in cell F14.

The best alternative to define the formulas in the data table is the fourth alternative, which involves using the cell references preceded by an equal sign. This method is best because (1) it is easier to enter; (2) if you change any of the formulas in the range F8:F10, the formulas at the top of the data table are immediately updated; and (3) Excel automatically will assign the format of the cell reference (currency style format) to the cell. Using the third alternative, which involves using cell names, is nearly as good an alternative, but Excel will not assign formatting to the cells when you use cell names. The following steps enter the formulas of the data table in row 14.

1. With cell D14 active, type **=f8** and then press the RIGHT ARROW key to enter the first parameter of the function to be used in the data table.
2. Type **=f9** in cell E14 and then press the RIGHT ARROW key.
3. Type **=f10** in cell F14 and then click the Enter button to assign the formulas and apply the Currency style format (Figure 4–20).

Q&A Why are these cells assigned the values of cells in the Mortgage Payment Calculator area of the worksheet?

It is important to understand that the entries in the top row of the data table (row 14) refer to the formulas that the loan officer and customer want to evaluate using the series of percentages in column C. Furthermore, recall that when you assign a formula to a cell, Excel applies the format of the first cell reference in the formula to the cell. Thus, Excel applies the currency style format to cells D14, E14, and F14 because that is the format of cells F8, F9, and F10.

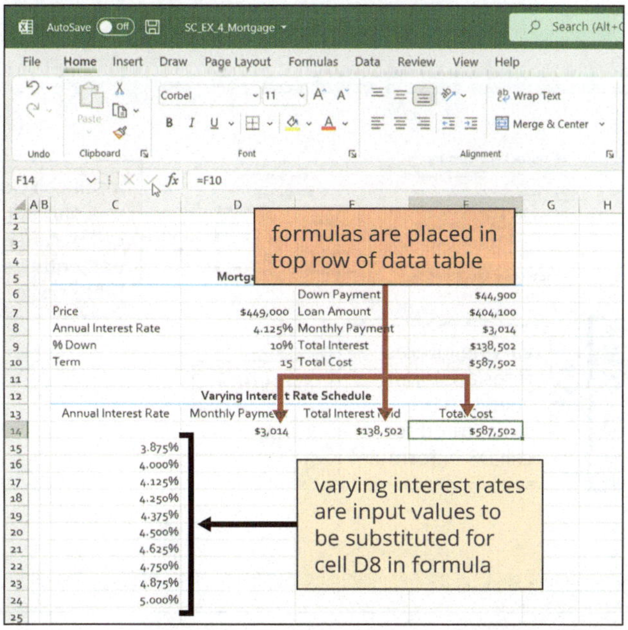

Figure 4–20

To Define a Range as a Data Table

After creating the interest rate series in column C and entering the formulas in row 14, the next step is to define the range C14:F24 as a data table. Cell D8 is the input cell for the data table, which means cell D8 is the cell in which values from column C in the data table are substituted in the formulas in row 14. **Why?** You want Excel to generate the monthly payment, monthly interest, and total cost for the various interest rates. The following steps define the range of the Varying Interest Rate Schedule as a data table.

1

- Select the range C14:F24 as the range in which to create the data table.
- Display the Data tab and then click the 'What-If Analysis' button (Data tab | Forecast group) to display the What-If Analysis menu (Figure 4–21).

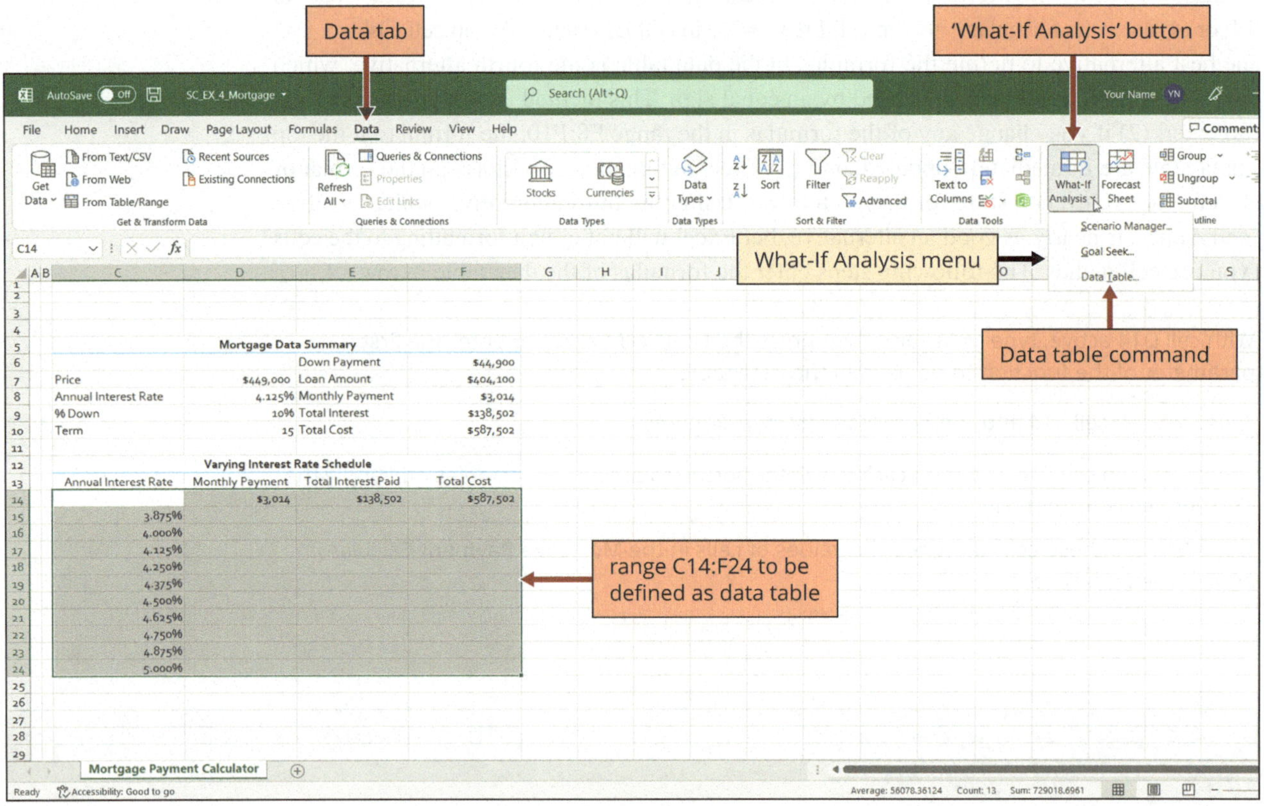

Figure 4–21

2

- Click Data Table on the What-If Analysis menu to display the Data Table dialog box.
- Click the 'Column input cell' box (Data Table dialog box) and then click cell D8 in the Mortgage Data Summary section of the spreadsheet to select the input cell for the data table (Figure 4–22).

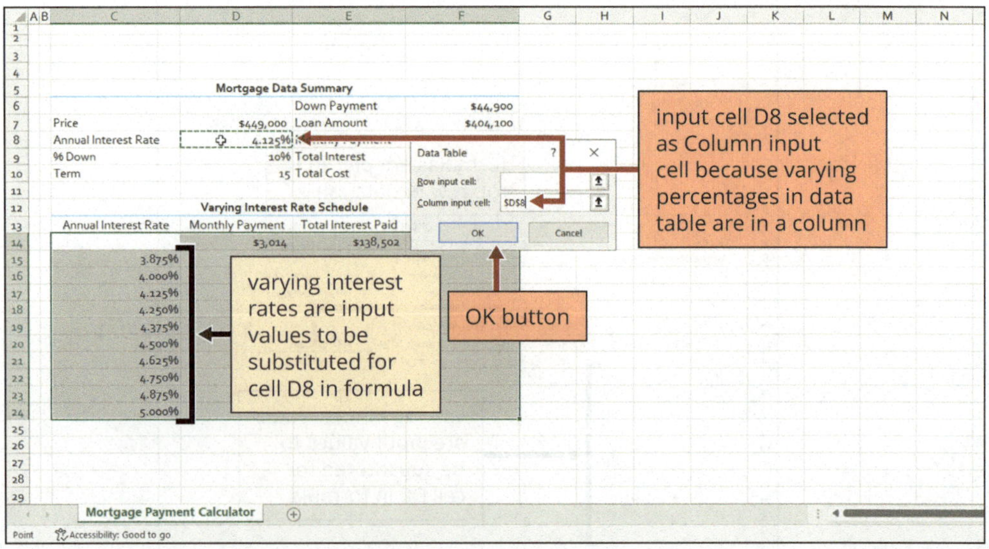

Figure 4–22

Q&A What is the purpose of clicking cell D8?

The purpose of clicking cell D8 is to select it for the Column input cell. A marquee surrounds the selected cell D8, indicating it will be the input cell in which values from column C in the data table are substituted in the formulas in row 14. $D$8 now appears in the 'Column input cell' box in the Data Table dialog box.

3

- Click OK (Data Table dialog box) to create the data table.
- Select cell range D14:F14 and click the Format Painter button (Home tab | Clipboard group) to copy the format of the cell range. Select cell range D15:F24 to apply the copied format to the cells.
- Deselect the selected range, D15:F24 in this case (Figure 4–23).

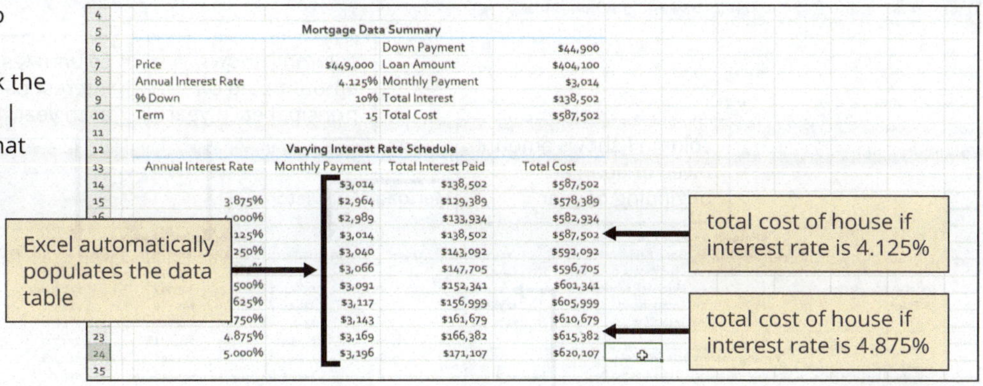

Figure 4–23

Q&A How does Excel create the data table?
Excel calculates the results of the three formulas in row 14 for each interest rate in column C and immediately fills columns D, E, and F of the data table. The resulting values for each interest rate are displayed in the corresponding rows.

More about Data Tables

The following list details important points you should know about data tables:

1. The formula(s) you are analyzing must include a cell reference to the input cell.
2. You can have as many active data tables in a worksheet as you want.
3. While only one value can vary in a one-input data table, the data table can analyze as many formulas as you want.
4. To include additional formulas in a one-input data table, enter them in adjacent cells in the same row as the current formulas (row 14 in Figure 4–23) and then define the entire new range as a data table by using the Data Table command on the What-If Analysis menu.
5. You delete a data table as you would delete any other item on a worksheet. That is, select the data table and then press DELETE.
6. An alternative to a one-input table is a two-input data table. A **two-input data table** allows you to vary the value in two cells and then see the recalculated results. For example, you can use a two-input data table to see how your monthly mortgage payment will be affected by changing both the interest rate and the term of the loan.

Break Point: If you want to take a break, this is a good place to do so. Be sure to save the SC_EX_4_Mortgage file again, and then you can exit Excel. To resume later, start Excel, open the file called SC_EX_4_Mortgage.xlsx, and continue following the steps from this location forward.

Creating an Amortization Schedule

The next step in this project is to create the Amortization Schedule section on the right side of Figure 4–24. An amortization schedule shows the beginning and ending balances of a loan and the amount of payment that applies to the principal and interest for each year over the life of the loan. For example, if a customer wanted to pay off the loan after six years, the Amortization Schedule section would tell the loan officer what the payoff would be (cell L12 in Figure 4–24). The Amortization Schedule section shown in Figure 4–24 will work only for loans of up to 15 years; however, you could extend the table to any number of years. The Amortization Schedule section also contains summaries in rows 22, 23, and 24. These summaries should agree exactly with the corresponding amounts in the Mortgage Data Summary section in cells F9, F6, and F10.

BTW
Amortization Schedules
Hundreds of websites offer amortization schedules. To find these websites, use a search engine, such as Google, and search using the keywords, amortization schedule.

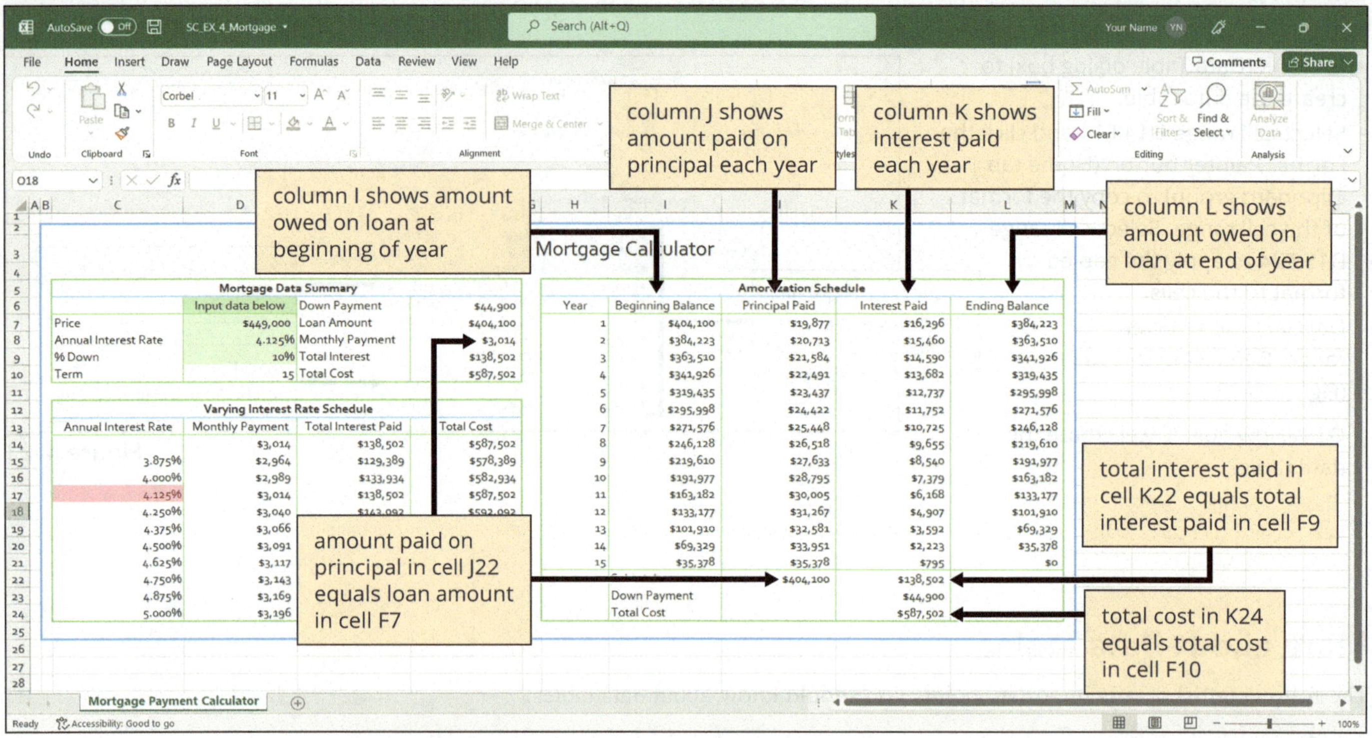

Figure 4–24

BTW

Column Borders

In this module, columns A, B, and G are used as column borders to divide sections of the worksheet from one another, as well as dividing the row headings. A column border is an unused column with a significantly reduced width. You also can use row borders to separate sections of a worksheet.

To Enter Titles and Change Column Widths

The first step in creating the Amortization Schedule section is to enter the section title and column titles and adjust the column widths. **Why?** After entering the titles, you can format the column widths to adjust the Amortization Schedule formatting to match your initial design. The following steps adjust column widths and enter column titles for the Amortization Schedule section.

1. Select cell H5. Type **Amortization Schedule** and then press ENTER to enter the section title.
2. Select cell C5, click the Format Painter button (Home tab | Clipboard group) to activate the format painter, and then click cell H5 to copy the format of cell C5.
3. Click the 'Merge & Center' button (Home tab | Alignment group) to split the selected cell, cell H5 in this case. Select the range H5:L5 and then click the 'Merge & Center' button (Home tab | Alignment group) to merge and center the section title over the selected range. If necessary, reapply the Heading 3 Cell Style (Home tab | Styles Group) to the merged cells.
4. Enter the following column headings in row 6: **Year** in cell H6, **Beginning Balance** in cell I6, **Principal Paid** in cell J6, **Interest Paid** in cell K6, and **Ending Balance** in cell L6.
5. Position the pointer on the right boundary of column heading G and then drag to the left until the ScreenTip shows Width: 2.22 to change the column width.
6. Position the pointer on the right boundary of column heading H and then drag to the right until the ScreenTip shows Width: 10.00 to change the column width.
7. Drag through column headings I through L to select them. Position the pointer on the right boundary of column heading L, and then drag to the right until the ScreenTip shows Width: 17.00 to change the column widths.

8. Select the range H6:L6 and then click the Center button (Home tab | Alignment group) to center the column headings.

9. Select cell H7 to display the centered section title and column headings (Figure 4–25).

Q&A Why was cell H5 split, or unmerged, in Step 3?
After using the format painter, Excel attempted to merge and center the text in cell H5 because the source of the format, cell C5, is merged and centered across four columns. The Amortization Schedule section, however, includes five columns. Splitting cell H5 changed cell H5 back to being one column instead of including four columns. Next, the section heading was merged and centered across five columns as required by the design of the worksheet.

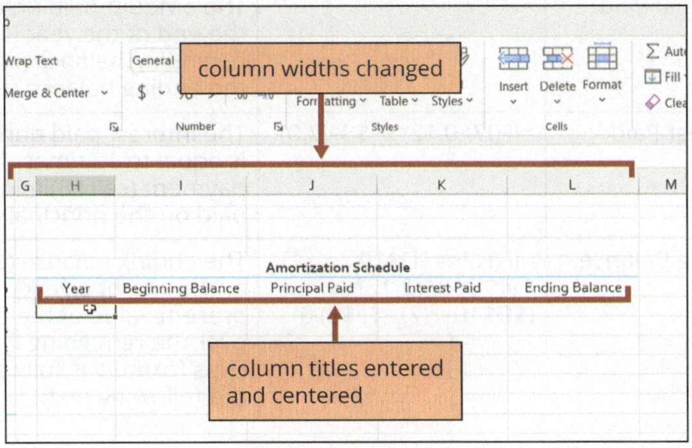

Figure 4–25

To Create a Series of Integers Using the Fill Handle

The next step is to use the fill handle to create a series of numbers that represent the years during the life of the loan. The series begins with 1 (year 1) and ends with 15 (year 15). The following steps create a series of years in the range H7:H21.

1. With cell H7 active, enter **1** as the initial year. Select cell H8 and then enter **2** to represent the next year.

2. Select the range H7:H8 and then drag the fill handle through cell H21 to complete the creation of a series of integers, 1 through 15 in the range H7:H21 in this case (Figure 4–26).

3. Release the mouse button.

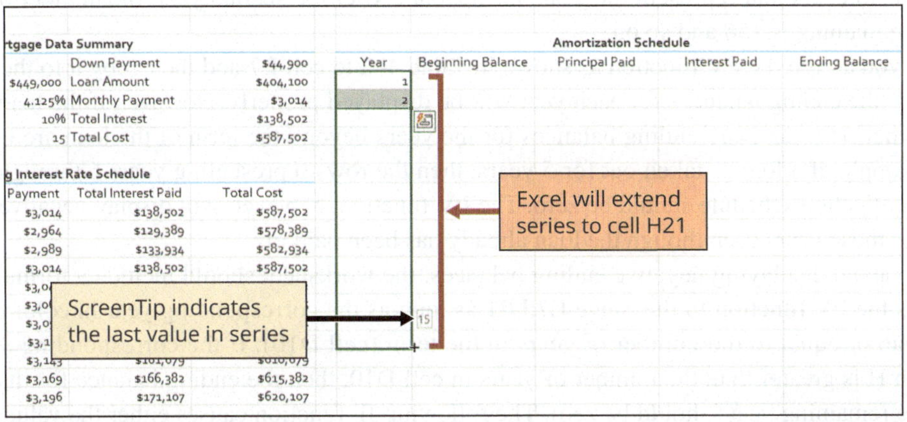

Figure 4–26

Formulas in the Amortization Schedule

Four formulas form the basis of the amortization schedule. You will enter these formulas in row 7. Later, you will copy these formulas through row 21. The formulas are summarized in Table 4–2.

Table 4–2: Formulas for the Amortization Schedule

Cell	Column Heading	Formula	Example
I7	Beginning Balance	=F7	The beginning balance (the balance at the end of a year) is the initial loan amount in cell F7.
J7	Principal Paid	=I7-L7	The amount paid on the principal at the end of the year is equal to the beginning balance (cell I7) minus the ending balance (cell L7).
K7	Interest Paid	=IF(I7>0,12*$F$8–J7,0)	The interest paid during the year is equal to 12 times the monthly payment (cell F8) minus the amount paid on the principal (cell J7).
L7	Ending Balance	=IF(H7<=$D$10, PV($D$8/12,12*($D$10–H7),–$F$8),0)	The ending balance (the balance at the end of a year) is equal to the present value of the payments paid over the remaining life of the loan. (This formula is fully explained in the following text.)

Of the four formulas in Table 4–2, perhaps the most difficult to understand is the PV function that will be entered in cell L7. The **PV function** returns the present value of an annuity. An **annuity** is a series of fixed payments (such as the monthly payment in cell F8) made at the end of each of a fixed number of periods (months) at a fixed interest rate. You can use the PV function to determine the amount the borrower still owes on the loan at the end of each year. The PV function has three arguments: rate, number of periods, and payment amount per period. Its general form is as follows:

=PV(rate, period, payment)

where rate is the interest rate per payment period, period is the number of payments remaining in the life of the loan, and payment is the amount of the monthly payment.

The PV function is used to determine the ending balance after the first year (cell L7) by using a term equal to the number of months for which the borrower still must make payments. For example, if the loan is for 15 years (180 months), then the borrower still owes 168 payments after the first year (180 months–12 months). The number of payments outstanding can be determined from the formula 12*($D$10–H7) or 12*(15–1), which equals 168. Recall that column H contains integers that represent the years of the loan. After the second year, the number of payments remaining is 156 and so on.

If you assign the PV function as shown in Table 4–2 to cell L7 and then copy it to the range L8:L21, the ending balances for each year will be displayed properly. However, if the loan is for fewer than 15 years, any ending balances for the years beyond the term of the loan are invalid. For example, if a loan is taken out for 5 years, then the rows representing years 6 through 15 in the amortization schedule should be zero. The PV function, however, will display negative numbers for those years even though the loan already has been paid off.

To avoid displaying negative ending balances, the worksheet should include a formula that assigns the PV function to the range L7:L21 as long as the corresponding year in column H is less than or equal to the number of years in the term (cell D10). If the corresponding year in column H is greater than the number of years in cell D10, then the ending balance for that year and the remaining years should be zero. The following IF function causes either the value of the PV function or zero to be displayed in cell L7, depending on whether the corresponding value in column H is greater than—or less than or equal to—the number of years in cell D10. Recall that the dollar signs within the cell references indicate the cell references are absolute and, therefore, will not change as you copy the function downward.

=IF(H7<=$D$10,PV($D$8/12,12*($D$10–H7),–$F$8),0)

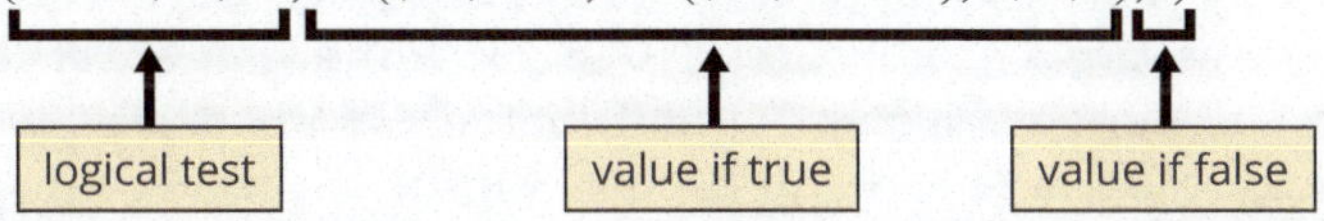

In the preceding formula, the logical test determines if the year in column H is less than or equal to the term of the loan in cell D10. If the logical test is true, then the IF function assigns the PV function to the cell. If the logical test is false, then the IF function assigns zero (0) to the cell. You also could use two double-quote symbols ("") to indicate to Excel to leave the cell blank if the logical test is false.

The PV function in the IF function includes absolute cell references (cell references with dollar signs) to ensure that the references to cells in columns D and F do not change when the IF function is later copied down the column.

To Enter the Formulas in the Amortization Schedule

Why? Creating an amortization schedule allows you to see the costs of a mortgage and the balance still owed for any year in the term of the loan. This information can be very helpful when making financial decisions. The following steps enter the four formulas shown in Table 4–2 into row 7. Row 7 represents year 1 of the loan.

1

- Select cell I7 and then enter **=f7** as the beginning balance of the loan.
- Select cell J7. Enter the formula **=i7-l7,** and then press the RIGHT ARROW key to complete the entry and select cell K7.

Q&A Why is Principal Paid equal to Beginning Balance?
The formula for Principal Paid uses the Ending Balance, which we have not yet calculated. Excel is evaluating the empty Ending Balance cell as having a value of zero.

- Type the formula **=if(i7>0,12*f8-j7,0)** in cell K7 (Figure 4–27).

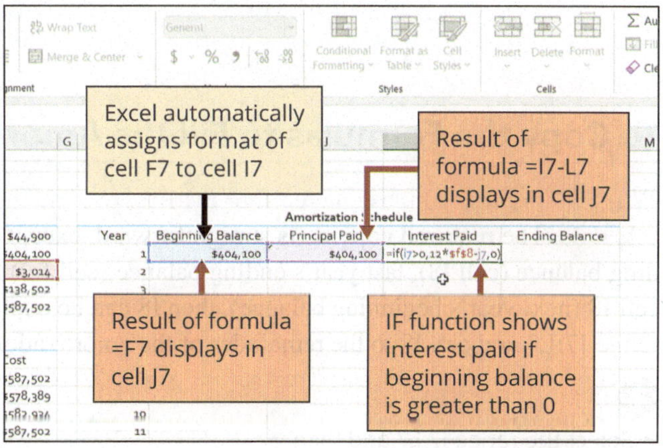

Figure 4–27

2

- Click the Enter button in the formula bar to insert the formula in the selected cell.

Q&A What happens when the Enter button is clicked?
Excel evaluates the IF function in cell K7 and displays the result of the PV function (367926.5401), because the value in cell H7 (1) is less than the term of the loan in cell D10 (15). With cell K7 active, Excel also displays the formula in the formula bar. If the borrower wanted to pay off the loan after one year, the cost would be $367,926.54.

- Select cell L7 and then enter **=if(h7<=d10,pv(d8/12,12*(d10-h7),-f8),0)** as the entry (Figure 4–28).

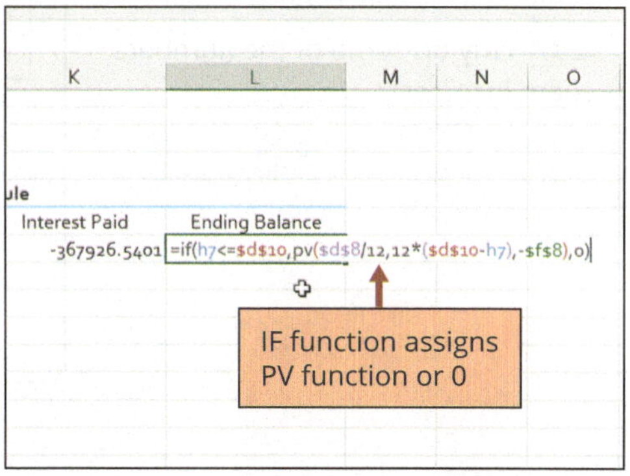

Figure 4–28

3

- Click the Enter button in the formula bar to complete the entry of the formula (Figure 4–29).

Q&A Why are some of the cells in the range I7:L7 not formatted?

When you enter a formula in a cell, Excel assigns the cell the same format as the first cell reference in the formula. For example, when you enter =F7 in cell I7, Excel assigns the format in cell F7 to cell I7. The same applies to cell J7. Although this method of formatting also works for most functions, it does not work for the IF function. Thus, the results of the IF functions in cells K7 and L7 are formatted using the general style format, which is the default format when you open a new workbook.

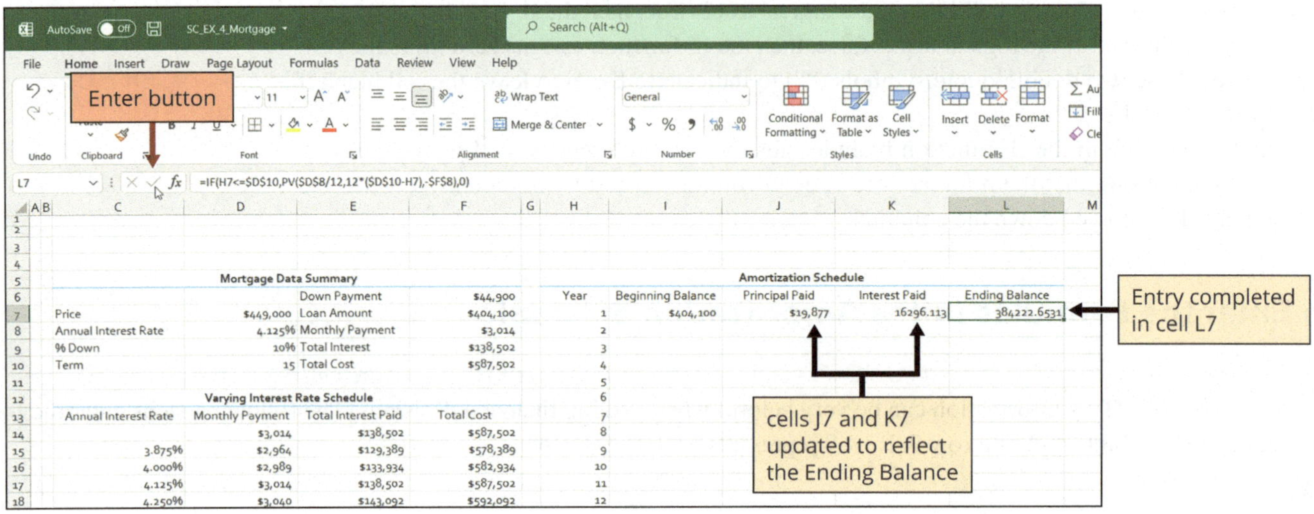

Figure 4–29

To Copy the Formulas to Fill the Amortization Schedule

Why? With the formulas entered into the first row, the next step is to copy them to the remaining rows in the amortization schedule. The required copying is straightforward, except for the beginning balance column. To obtain the next year's beginning balance (cell I8), last year's ending balance (cell L7) must be used. After cell L7 (last year's ending balance) is copied to cell I8 (next year's beginning balance), then I8 can be copied to the range I8:I21. The following steps copy the formulas in the range J7:L7 and cell I8 to the remainder of the amortization schedule.

1

- Select the range J7:L7 and then drag the fill handle down through row 21 to copy the formulas through the amortization schedule, J8:L21 in this case (Figure 4–30).

Q&A Why do some of the numbers seem incorrect?

Many of the numbers are incorrect because the cells in column I, except for cell I7, do not yet contain values.

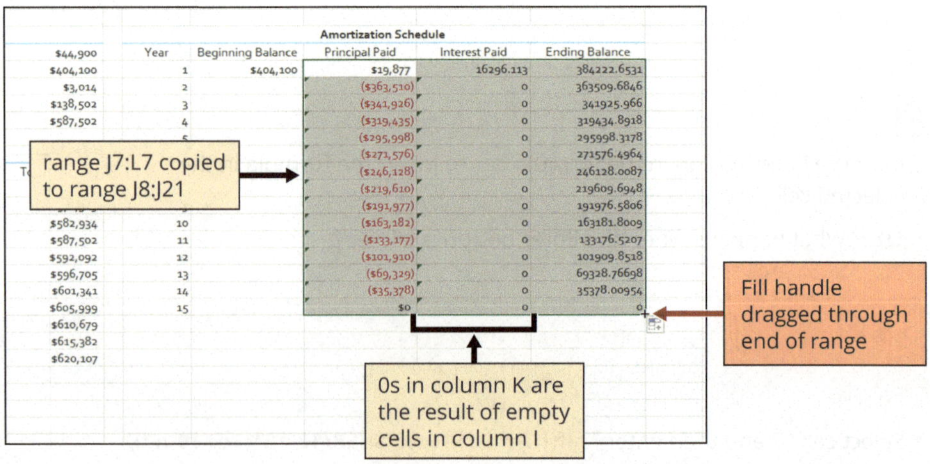

Figure 4–30

2

- Select cell I8, type **=l7** (note that this is an L, not the number 1) as the cell entry, and then click the Enter button in the formula bar to display the ending balance 384222.6531 for year 1 as the beginning balance for year 2 (Figure 4–31).

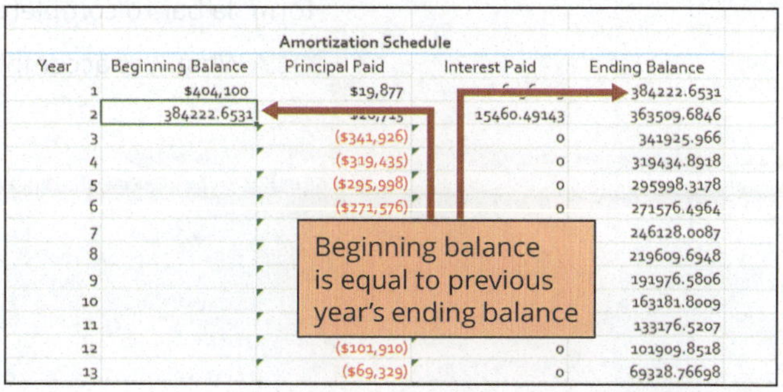

Figure 4–31

3

- With cell I8 active, drag the fill handle down through row 21 to copy the formula in cell I8 (=L7) to the range I9:I21 (Figure 4–32).

Q&A What happens after the fill operation is complete?

Because the cell reference L7 is relative, Excel adjusts the row portion of the cell reference as it is copied downward. Thus, each new beginning balance in column I is equal to the ending balance of the previous year.

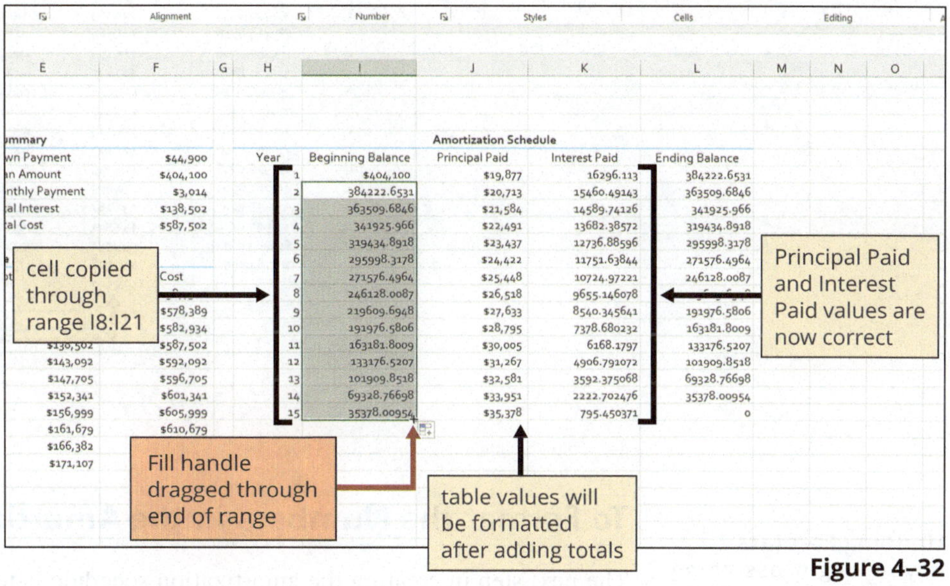

Figure 4–32

Other Ways

1. Select cells containing formulas to copy, click Copy (Home tab | Clipboard group), select destination cell or range, click Paste (Home tab | Clipboard group)

To Enter the Total Formulas in the Amortization Schedule

The next step is to determine the amortization schedule totals, which will appear in rows 22 through 24. These totals should agree with the corresponding totals in the Mortgage Data Summary section (range F9:F10). The following steps enter the total formulas in the amortization schedule.

1. Select cell I22 and then enter **Subtotal** as the row title.
2. Select the range J22:K22 and then click the AutoSum button (Home tab | Editing group) to sum the selected range.
3. Select cell I23 and then enter **Down Payment** as the row title.
4. Select cell K23 and then enter **=f6** to copy the down payment to the selected cell.
5. Select cell I24 and then enter **Total Cost** as the row title.

6. Select cell K24, type **=j22+k22+k23** as the total cost, and then click the Enter button in the formula bar to complete the amortization schedule totals (Figure 4–33).

Q&A What was accomplished in the previous steps?
The formula assigned to cell K24 (=J22+K22+K23) sums the total amount of principal paid (cell J22), the total interest paid (cell K22), and the down payment (cell K23). Excel assigns cell J22 the same format as cell J7 because cell J7 is the first cell reference in =SUM(J7:J21). Furthermore, because cell J22 was selected first when the range J22:K22 was selected to determine the sum, Excel assigned cell K22 the same format it assigned to cell J22. Finally, cell K23 was assigned the currency style format because cell K23 was assigned the formula =f6, and cell F6 has a currency style format. For the same reason, the value in cell K24 appears with the currency style format.

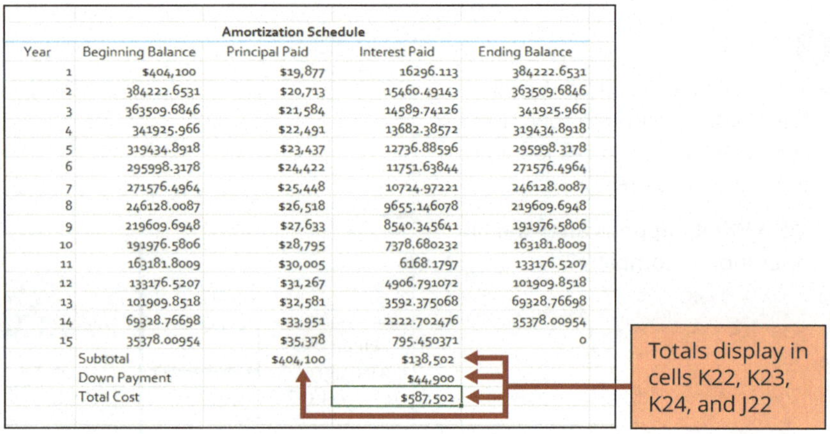

Amortization Schedule

Year	Beginning Balance	Principal Paid	Interest Paid	Ending Balance
1	$404,100	$19,877	16296.113	384222.6531
2	384222.6531	$20,713	15460.49143	363509.6846
3	363509.6846	$21,584	14589.74126	341925.966
4	341925.966	$22,491	13682.38572	319434.8918
5	319434.8918	$23,437	12736.88596	295998.3178
6	295998.3178	$24,422	11751.63844	271576.4964
7	271576.4964	$25,448	10724.97221	246128.0087
8	246128.0087	$26,518	9655.146078	219609.6948
9	219609.6948	$27,633	8540.345641	191976.5806
10	191976.5806	$28,795	7378.680232	163181.8009
11	163181.8009	$30,005	6168.1797	133176.5207
12	133176.5207	$31,267	4906.791072	101909.8518
13	101909.8518	$32,581	3592.375068	69328.76698
14	69328.76698	$33,951	2222.702476	35378.00954
15	35378.00954	$35,378	795.450371	0
	Subtotal	$404,100	$138,502	
	Down Payment		$44,900	
	Total Cost		$587,502	

Figure 4–33

To Format the Numbers in the Amortization Schedule

BTW
Undoing Formats
If you begin assigning formats to a range and then realize you made a mistake and want to start over, select the range, click the Cell Styles button (Home tab | Styles group), and then click Normal in the Cell Styles gallery.

The next step in creating the amortization schedule is to format it so that it is easier to read. When the beginning balance formula (=f7) was entered earlier into cell I7, Excel copied the currency style format along with the value from cell F7 to cell I7. The following steps copy the currency style format from cell I7 to the range K7:L7. The comma style format then will be assigned to the range I8:L21.

1. Select cell I7 and then click the Format Painter button (Home tab | Clipboard group) to turn on the format painter. Drag through the range K7:L7 to assign the currency style format to the cells.
2. Select the range I8:L21 and then right-click the selected range to display a shortcut menu. Click Format Cells on the shortcut menu to display the Format Cells dialog box and then, if necessary, click the Number tab (Format Cells dialog box) to display the Number sheet.
3. Select Currency in the Category list to select a currency format and then click the fourth format, ($1,234.10), in the Negative numbers list to create a currency format.
4. Select the 2 in the Decimal places box and change it to 0.
5. Click OK (Format Cells dialog box) to apply the currency format to the selected range.
6. Deselect the range I8:L21 and display the numbers in the amortization schedule, as shown in Figure 4–34.

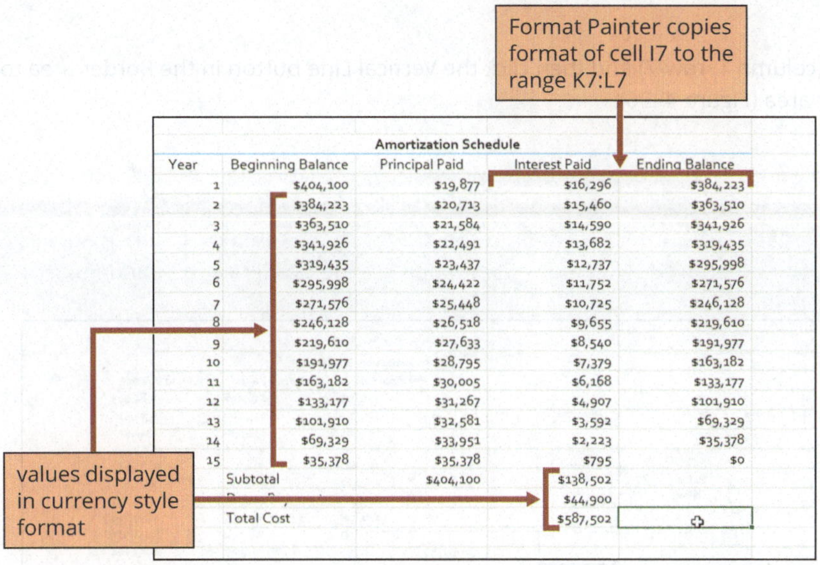

Figure 4–34

Formatting the Worksheet

Previous modules introduced you to outlining a range using cell borders or cell background colors to differentiate portions of a worksheet. The Borders button (Home tab | Font group), however, offers only a limited selection of border thicknesses. To control the color and thickness, Excel requires that you use the Border sheet in the Format Cells dialog box.

To Add Custom Borders to a Range

Why? Borders can be used to distinguish the different functional parts of a worksheet. The following steps add a medium green border to the Mortgage Data Summary section. To subdivide the row titles and numbers further, light borders also are added within the section, as shown in Figure 4–1.

1

- Select the range C5:F10 and then right-click to display a shortcut menu and mini toolbar. Click Format Cells on the shortcut menu to display the Format Cells dialog box and then click the Border tab (Format Cells dialog box) to display the Border sheet.
- Click the Color arrow to display the Colors palette and then select the Lime, Accent 2 color (column 6, row 1) in the Theme Colors area.
- Click the medium border in the Style area (column 2, row 5) to select the line style for the border.
- Click the Outline button in the Presets area to preview the outline border in the Border area (Figure 4–35).

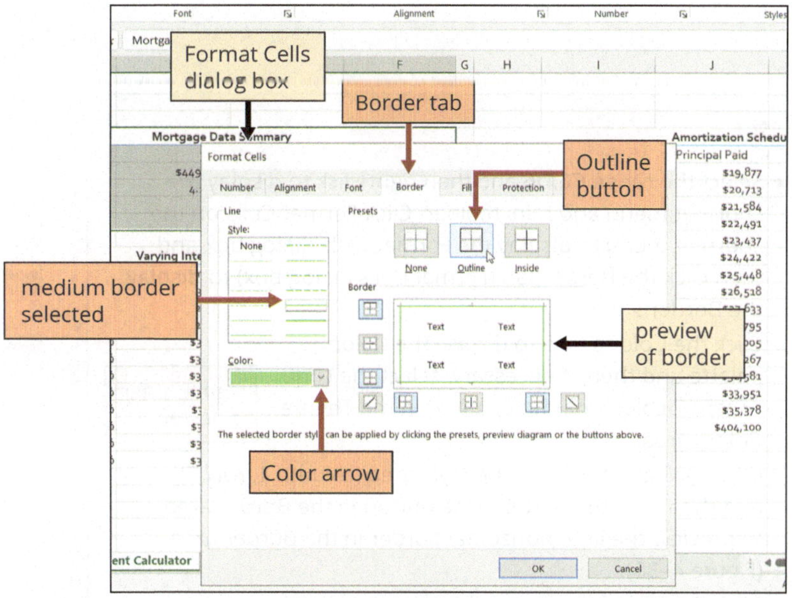

Figure 4–35

2

- Click the light border in the Style area (column 1, row 7) and then click the Vertical Line button in the Border area to preview the green vertical border in the Border area (Figure 4–36).

Q&A How do I create a border?

As shown in Figure 4–37, you can add a variety of borders with different colors to a cell or range of cells. It is important that you select border characteristics in the order specified in the steps, that is, (1) choose the border color, (2) choose the border line style, and then (3) choose the border type. This order first defines the border characteristics and then applies those characteristics. If you do these steps in any other order, you may not end up with the borders you intended.

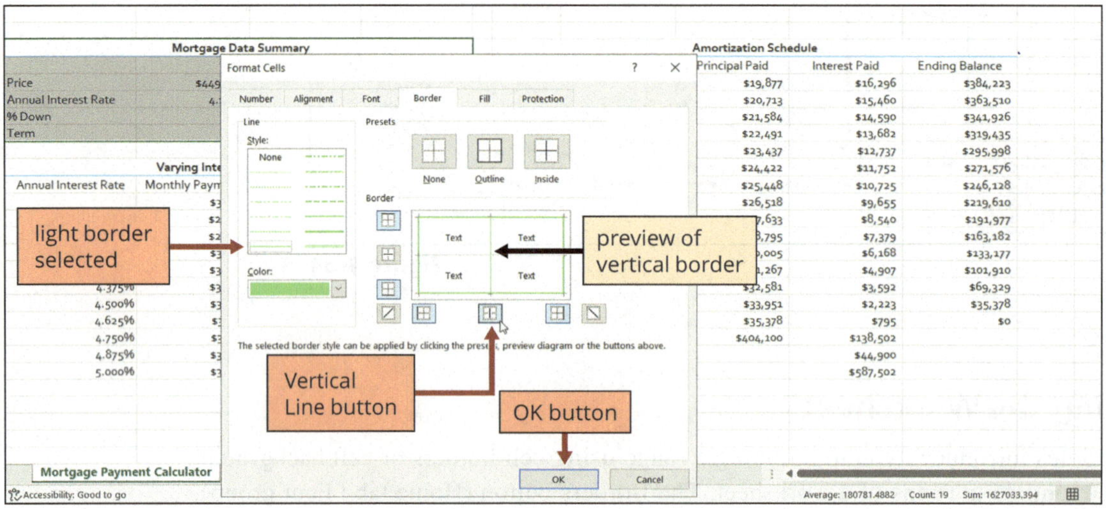

Figure 4–36

3

- Click OK to add a green outline with vertical borders to the right side of each column in the selected range, C5:F10 in this case. Click cell C6 to deselect the range (Figure 4–37).

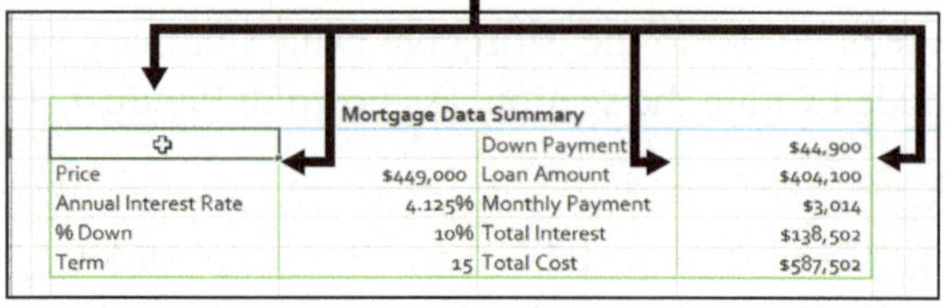

Figure 4–37

4

- Select the range C6:D6 and then right-click to display a shortcut menu and mini toolbar. Click Format Cells on the shortcut menu to display the Format Cells dialog box and then click the Border tab (Format Cells dialog box) to display the Border sheet.
- Click the Color arrow to display the Colors palette and then, if necessary, select the Lime, Accent 2 color (column 6, row 1) in the Theme Colors area.
- Click the light border in the Style area (column 1, row 7) and then click the Bottom Line button in the Border area to preview the lime horizontal border in the Border area (Figure 4–38).
- Click OK to add the lime, light horizontal border.

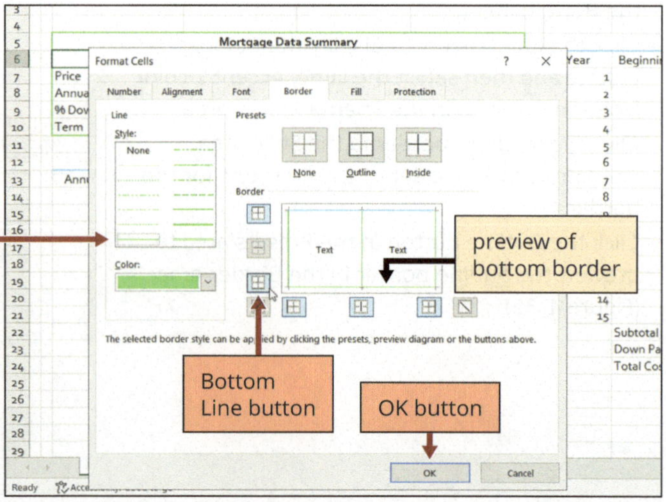

Figure 4–38

Q&A How else can I add custom borders?

If you want to specify exactly where borders should be drawn in your worksheet, you can draw the borders manually. To draw borders, click the Border button arrow (Home tab | Font group), click Draw Border, and then click the cell borders where you want to draw a border.

Other Ways

1. Click Borders arrow (Home tab | Font group), click More Borders, select border options
2. Click Format button (Home tab | Cells group), click Format Cells, click Border tab, select border options, click OK

To Add Borders to the Varying Interest Rate Schedule

The following steps add the same borders you applied to the Mortgage Data Summary to the Varying Interest Rate Schedule. **Why?** By applying similar formatting to different section of the Mortgage Calculator, you are creating a more cohesive end product.

1. Select the range C12:F24. Right-click the selected range to display a shortcut menu and then click Format Cells on the shortcut menu to display the Format Cells dialog box.
2. If necessary, click the Border tab (Format Cells dialog box) to display the Border sheet. Click the Color arrow to display the Colors palette and then click Lime, Accent 2 (column 6, row 1) in the Theme Colors area to select the border color.
3. Click the medium border in the Style area (column 2, row 5). Click the Outline button in the Presets area to preview the border in the Border area.
4. Click the light border in the Style area (column 1, row 7). Click the Vertical Line button in the Border area to preview the border in the Border area.
5. Click OK (Format Cells dialog box) to apply custom borders to the selected range.
6. Select the range C13:F13 and then use the Format Cells dialog box to apply a lime, light bottom border to the selected range.
7. Deselect the range to display the worksheet, as shown in Figure 4–39.

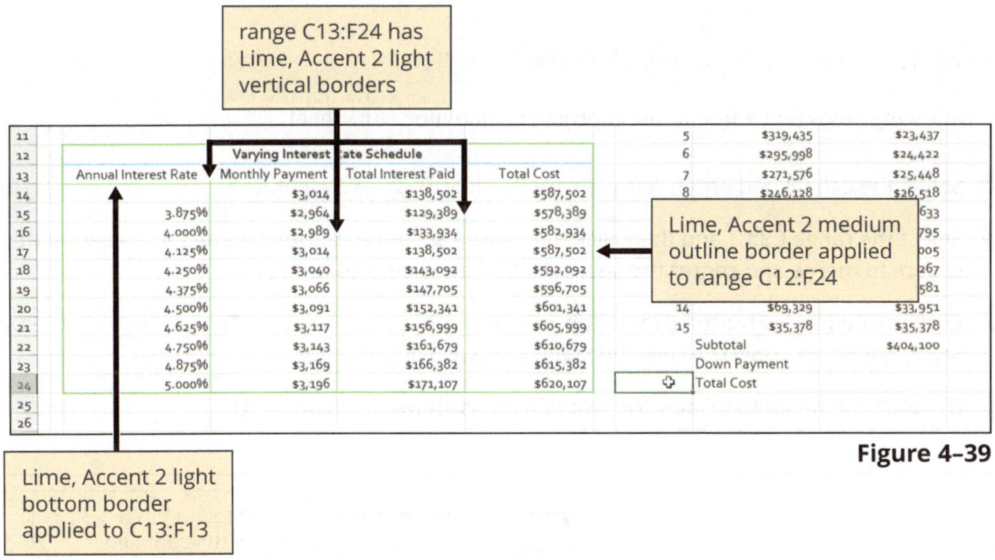

Figure 4–39

To Add Borders to the Amortization Schedule

The following steps add the borders to the Amortization Schedule.

1. Select the range H5:L24, and then display the Format Cells dialog box.
2. Apply a Lime, Accent 2, medium (column 2, row 5) border style using the Outline preset.
3. Click OK to apply custom borders to the selected range.
4. Select the range H6:L6 and then use the Format Cells dialog box to apply a lime, light (column 1, row 7) bottom border.
5. Select the range H6:L24 and then use the Format Cells dialog box to apply a lime, light vertical border to the selected range.
6. Select the range H22:L22 and then use the Format Cells dialog box to apply a lime, light upper border to the selected range.
7. Deselect the range to display the worksheet, as shown in Figure 4–40.

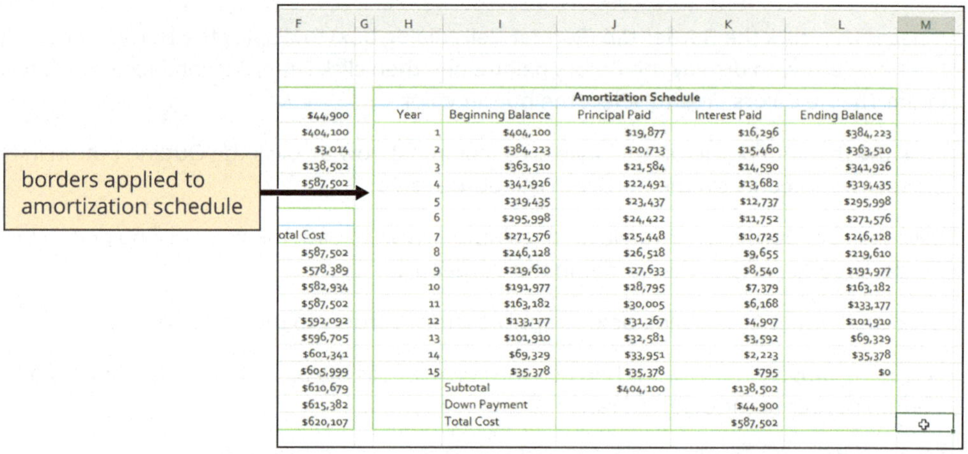

Figure 4–40

To Add a Title to the Worksheet

The following steps add a title to the mortgage calculator worksheet.

1. Select the cell C3 and enter **Windshore Bank Mortgage Calculator**.
2. Select the range C3:L3 and then click the 'Merge & Center' button (Home tab | Alignment group) to merge and center the section title in the selected range.
3. Click the Cell Styles button (Home tab | Styles group) and then click Title cell style in the Cell Styles gallery to apply the selected style to the active cell.
4. Deselect the range to display the worksheet, as shown in Figure 4–41.

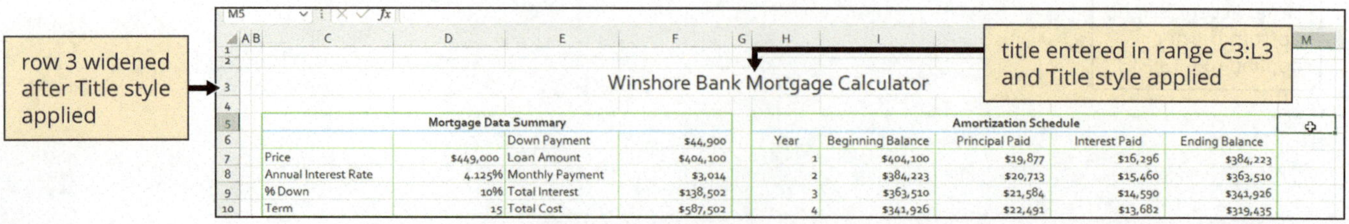

Figure 4–41

To Use Borders and Fill Color to Visually Define and Group the Financial Tools

The following steps add a border and fill color to the entire group of financial tools on the worksheet.

1. Change the height of row 25 to 15.00.
2. Change the width of column M to 1.00.
3. Select the range B2:M25.
4. Add a Blue, Accent 1, (column 5, row 1) heavy style (column 2, row 6) Outline border to the selected range.
5. With the range B2:M25 still selected, click the Fill Color arrow (Home tab | Font group) and apply a fill color of White, Background 1 (column 1, row 1) to the selected range. Deselect the range.
6. Select cell D6 and then enter **Input data below**. Center align the text in the cell.
7. With cell D6 still selected, click the Fill Color arrow (Home tab | Font group) and apply a fill color of Lime, Accent 2, Lighter 60% (column 6, row 3) to the selected range. Deselect the cell.
8. Select the range D7:D9, click the Fill Color arrow (Home tab | Font group), and then apply a fill color of Lime, Accent 2, Lighter 80% (column 6, row 2) to the selected range. Deselect the range.
9. Save the workbook again in the same storage location with the same file name (Figure 4–42).

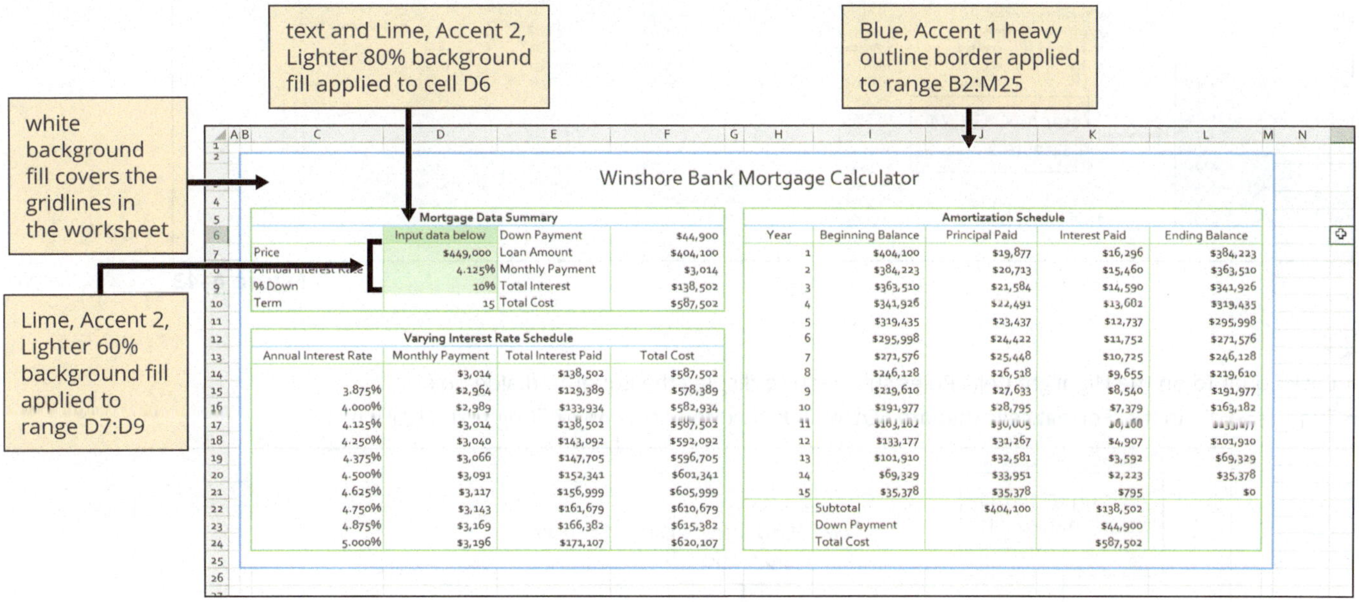

Figure 4–42

Highlighting Cells in the Data Table Using Conditional Formatting

If the interest rate in cell D8 is between 3.875% and 5.000% and its decimal portion is a multiple of 0.125 (such as 4.625%), then one of the rows in the data table agrees exactly with the monthly payment, interest paid, and total cost in the range F8:F10. For example, in Figure 4–42, row 17 (4.125%) in the data table agrees with the results in the range F8:F10, because the interest rate in cell C17 is the same as the interest rate in cell D8. Analysts often look for the row in the data table that agrees with the input cell results. You can use conditional formatting to highlight a row, or a single cell in the row.

BTW

Conditional Formatting

You can add as many conditional formats to a range as you like. After adding the first condition, click the Conditional Formatting button (Home tab | Styles group) and then click New Rule to add more conditions. If more than one condition is true for a cell, then Excel applies the formats of each condition, beginning with the first.

To Add a Pointer to the Data Table Using Conditional Formatting

Why? To make the row with the active interest rate stand out, you can add formatting that serves as a pointer to that row. To add a pointer, you can use conditional formatting to highlight the cell in column C that agrees with the input cell (cell D8). The following steps apply conditional formatting to column C in the data table.

1

- Select the range C15:C24 and then click the Conditional Formatting button (Home tab | Styles group) to display the Conditional Formatting menu.
- Point to 'Highlight Cells Rules' to display the submenu (Figure 4–43).

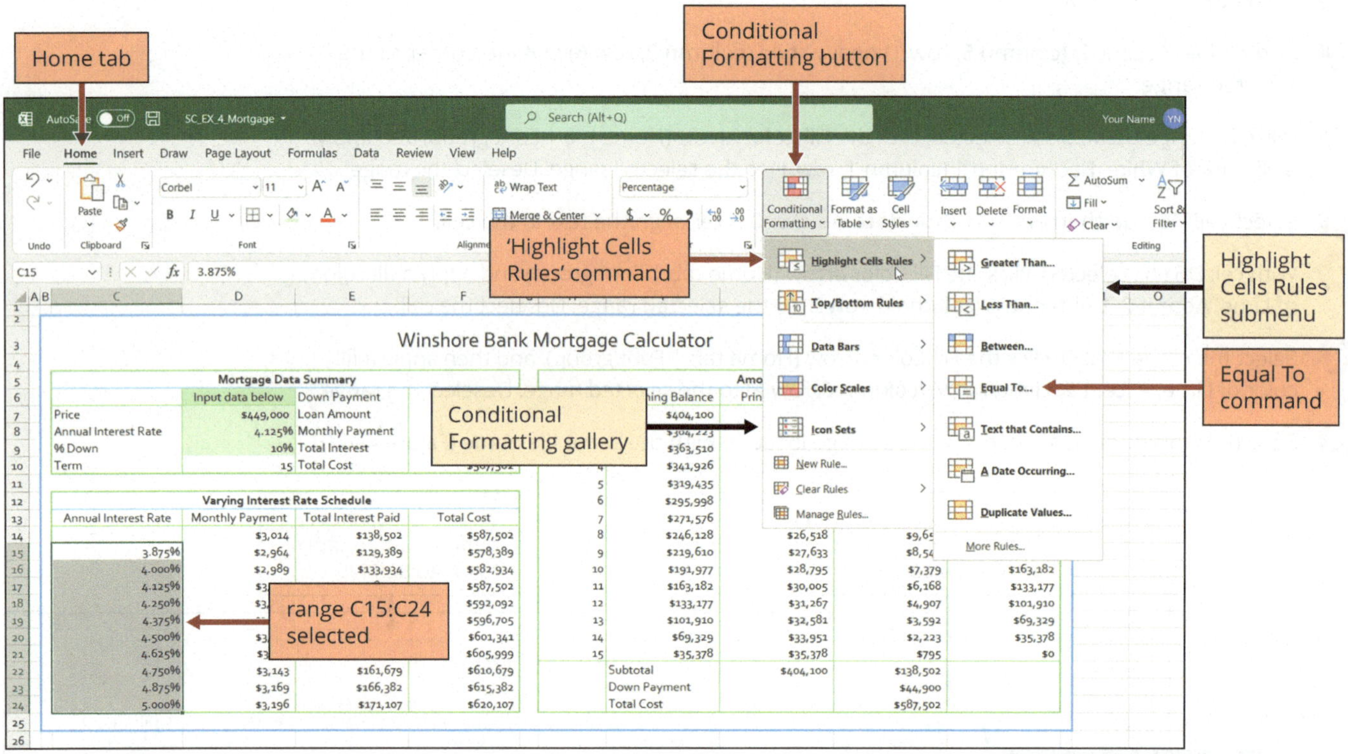

Figure 4–43

2

- Click Equal To on the Highlight Cells Rules submenu to display the Equal To dialog box.
- Type **=d8** in the 'Format cells that are EQUAL TO:' box, replacing any exiting text (Figure 4–44).

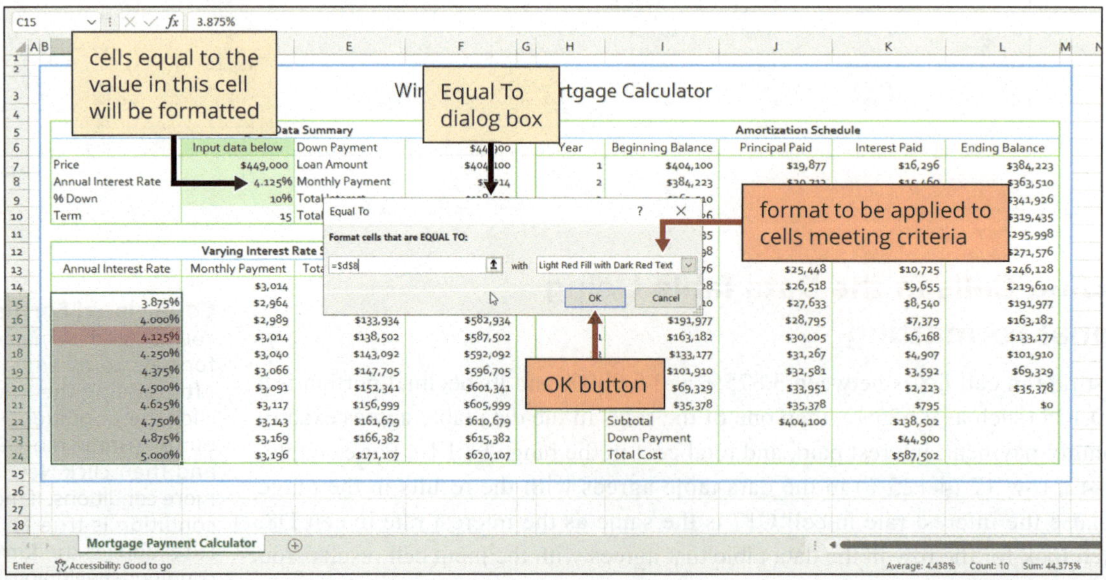

Figure 4–44

3

- Click OK to apply the conditional formatting rule.
- Deselect the range (Figure 4–45).

Q&A How does Excel apply the conditional formatting?
Cell C17 in the data table, which contains the value, 4.125%, appears with a red background and dark red text, because the value 4.125% is the same as the interest rate value in cell D8.

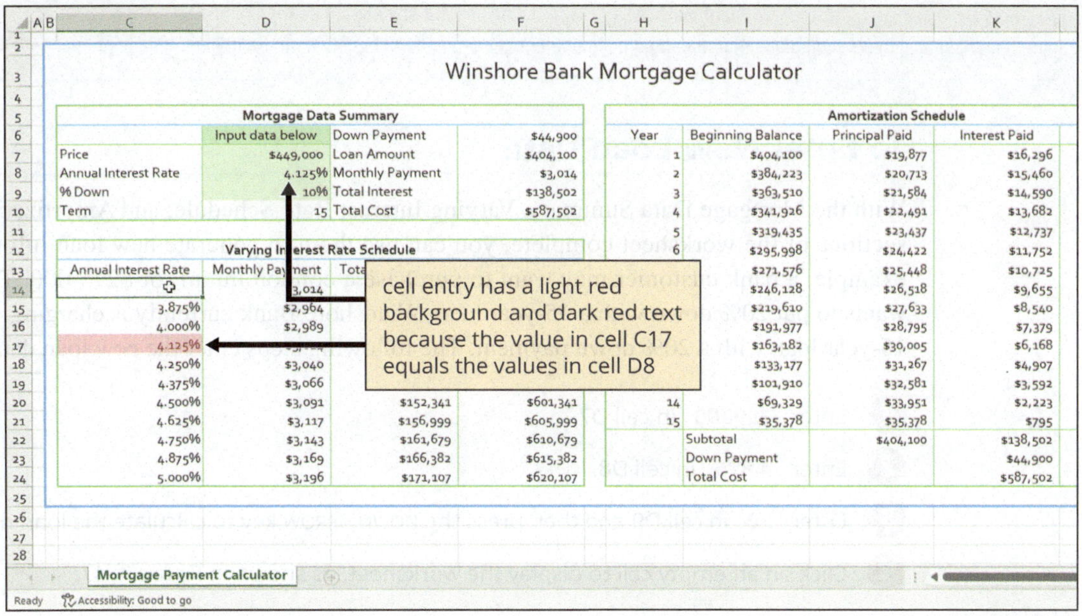

Figure 4–45

4

- Select cell D8 and then enter **4.625** as the interest rate (Figure 4–46).

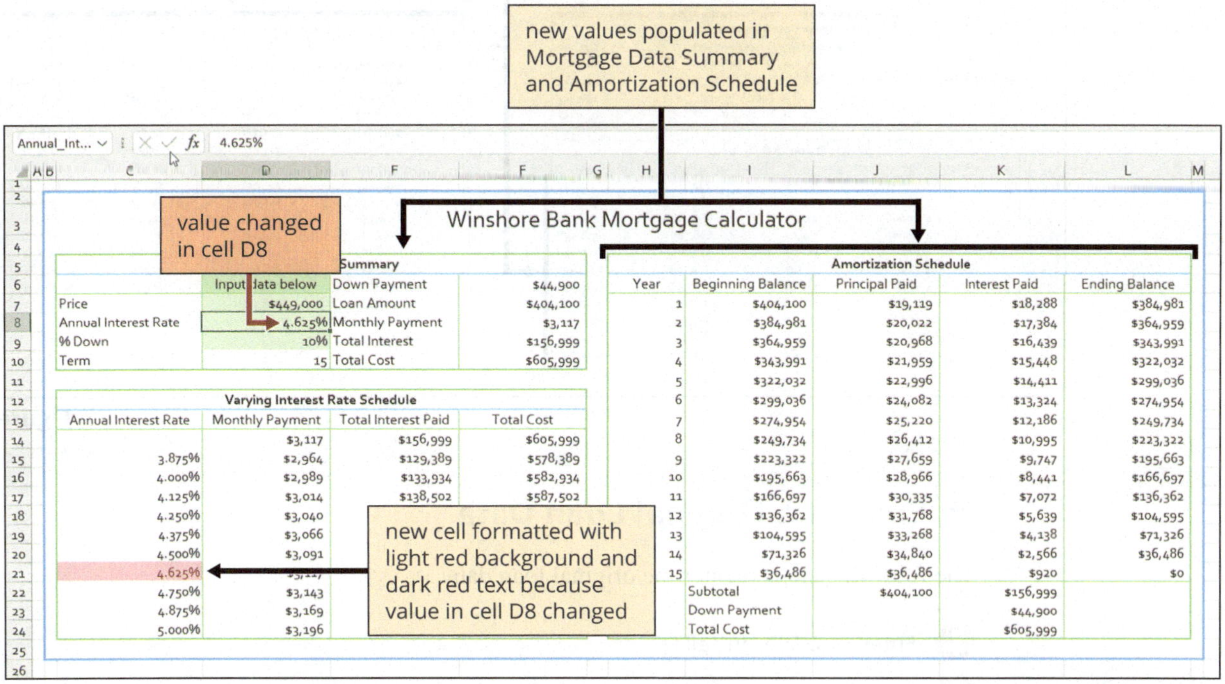

Figure 4–46

5

- Enter **4.125** in cell D8 to return the Mortgage Payment Calculator, Varying Interest Rate Schedule, and Amortization Schedule sections to their original states.

Q&A What happened when I changed the interest rate from 4.125% to 4.625%?
The cell containing the new rate received a red background and dark red text, while the original cell (cell C17) reverted to its original formatting (Figure 4–42). The red background and dark red text serve as a pointer in the data table to indicate which row agrees with the input cell (cell D8). When the loan officer using this worksheet enters a new percentage in cell D8, the pointer will move or disappear. The formatting will disappear if the interest rate in cell D8 falls outside the range of the data table or does not appear in the data table, for example, if the interest rate is 3.875% or 5.100%.

To Enter New Loan Data

With the Mortgage Data Summary, Varying Interest Rate Schedule, and Amortization Schedule sections of the worksheet complete, you can use them to generate new loan information. For example, a bank customer may want to purchase a condominium for $275,000. The customer wants to put 20% down with a 15-year loan. Windshore Bank currently is charging 4.875% for a 15-year loan with a 20% down payment. The following steps enter the new loan data.

1. Enter **250000** in cell D7.
2. Enter **4.875** in cell D8.
3. Enter **20** in cell D9 and then press the DOWN ARROW key to calculate the loan data.
4. Click on an empty cell to display the worksheet, as shown in Figure 4–47.

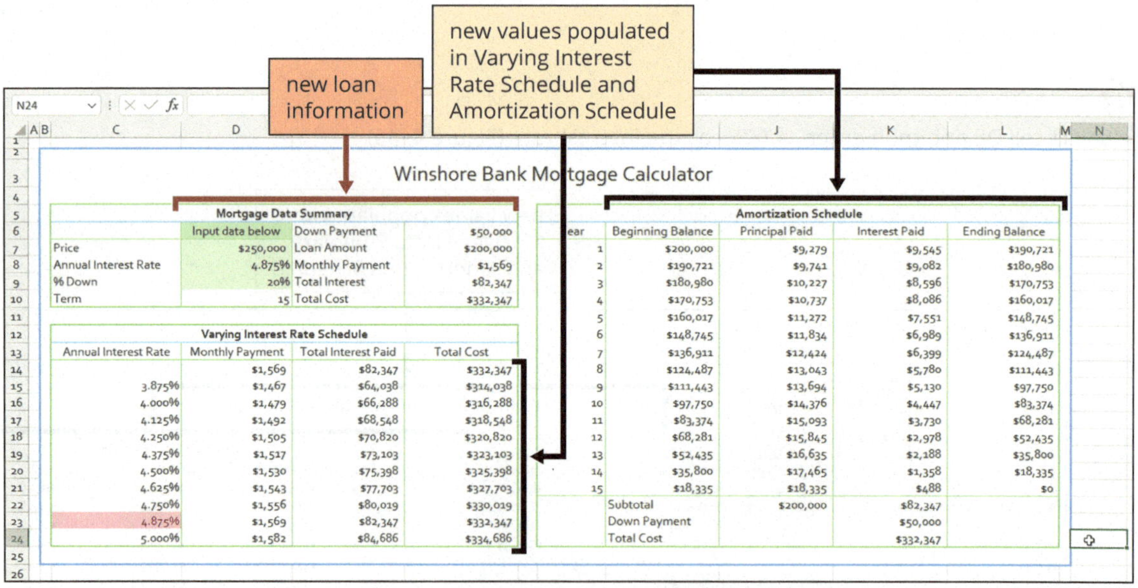

Figure 4–47

To Enter the Original Loan Data

The following steps reenter the original loan data.

1. Enter **449000** in cell D7.
2. Enter **4.125** in cell D8.
3. Enter **10** in cell D9 and then press the DOWN ARROW key to calculate the loan data.

Printing Sections of the Worksheet

In Module 2, you learned how to print a section of a worksheet by first selecting it and then using the Selection option in the Print dialog box. If you find yourself continually selecting the same range in a worksheet to print, you can set a specific range to print each time you print the worksheet. When you set a range to print, Excel will continue to print only that range until you clear it.

To Set Up a Worksheet to Print

Why? Specifying print options allows you to conserve paper and toner and to customize the layout of your worksheet on the printed page. This section describes print options available in the Page and Sheet tabs in the Page Setup dialog box (Figure 4–48). These print options affect the way the worksheet will appear in the printed copy or when previewed. One important print option is the capability of printing in black and white, even when your printer is a color printer. Printing in black and white not only speeds up the printing process but also saves ink. The following steps ensure any printed copy fits on one page and prints in black and white.

1

- Display the Page Layout tab and then click the Page Setup Dialog Box Launcher to display the Page Setup dialog box.
- If necessary, click the Page tab (Page Setup dialog box) to display the Page sheet and then click the Fit to option button in the Scaling area to set the worksheet to print on one page (Figure 4–48).

Q&A How can I specify the printed height and width?
Instead of using Backstage view, you can display the Page Layout tab and in the Scale to Fit group, use the Width and Height boxes to specify the number of pages for each direction.

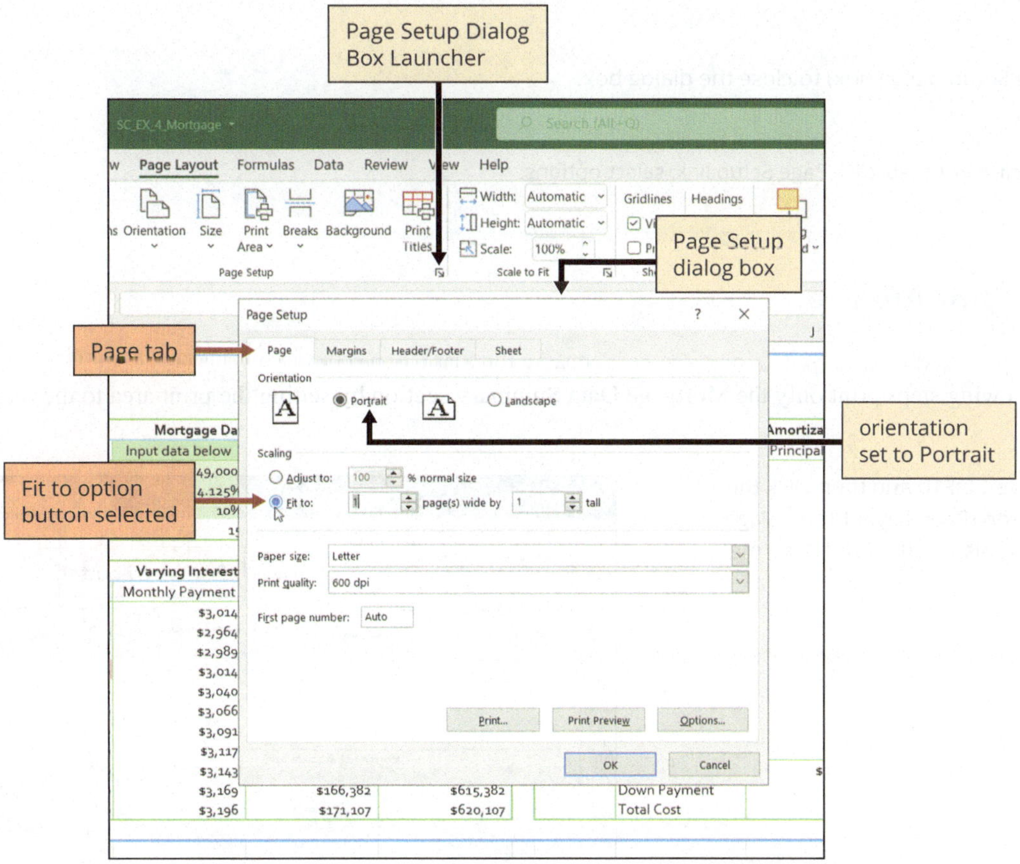

Figure 4–48

2

- Click the Sheet tab (Page Setup dialog box) and then click 'Black and white' in the Print area to select the check box (Figure 4–49).

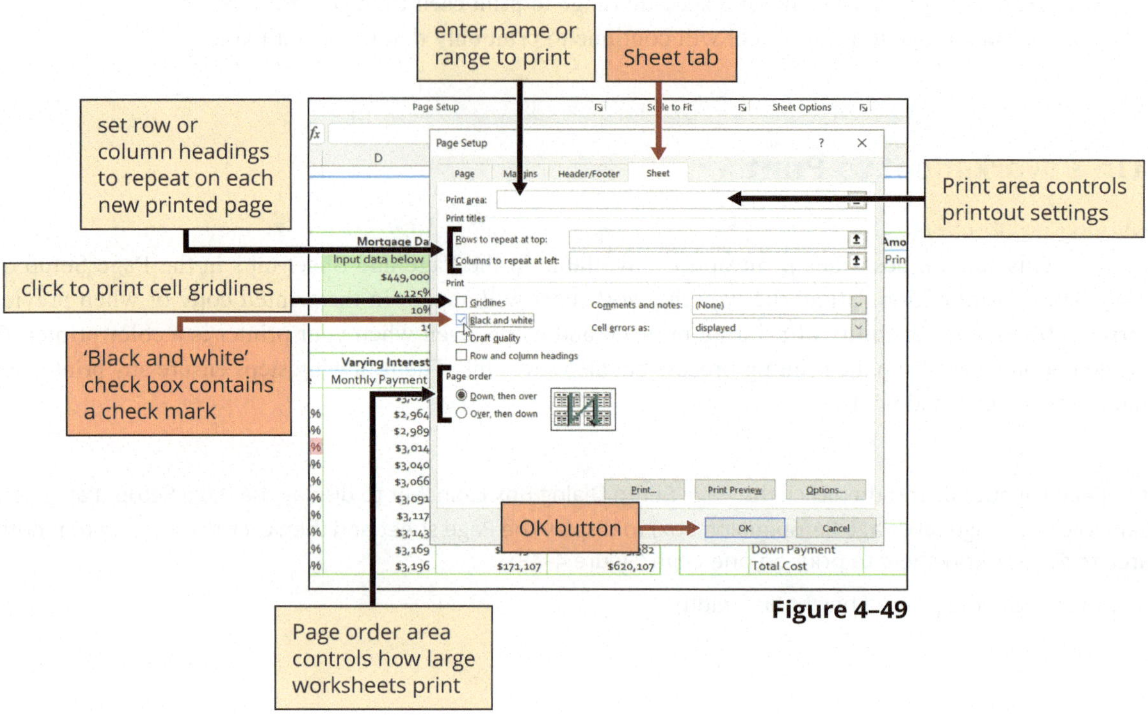

Figure 4–49

3

- Click OK (Page Setup dialog box) to close the dialog box.

Other Ways

1. Click File tab, click Print tab, click Page Setup link, select options.

To Set the Print Area

Why? *If you do not need to print the entire worksheet, setting the print area allows you to easily specify the section you want to print.* The following steps print only the Mortgage Data Summary section by setting the print area to the range C5:F10.

1

- Select the range C5:F10 and then click the Print Area button (Page Layout tab | Page Setup group) to display the Print Area menu (Figure 4–50).

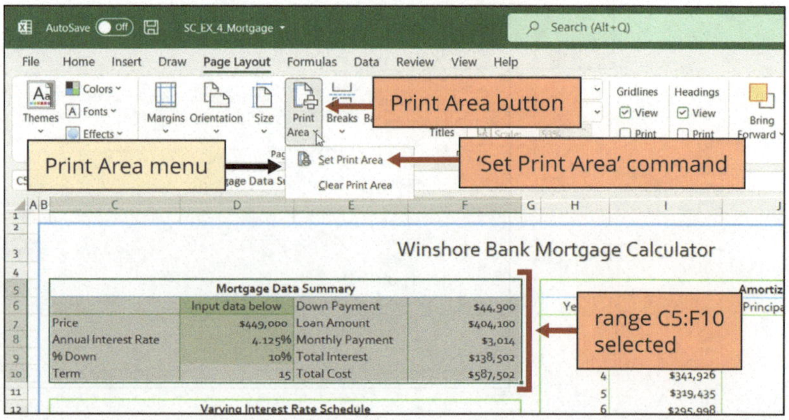

Figure 4–50

2

- Click 'Set Print Area' on the Print Area menu to set the range of the worksheet that Excel should print.
- Click File on the ribbon to open Backstage view and then click Print to display the Print screen.
- Verify that the preview displays the print area you specified, then click the Print button on the Print screen to print the selected area or, if you want to conserve paper, click the Back button (Figure 4-51).

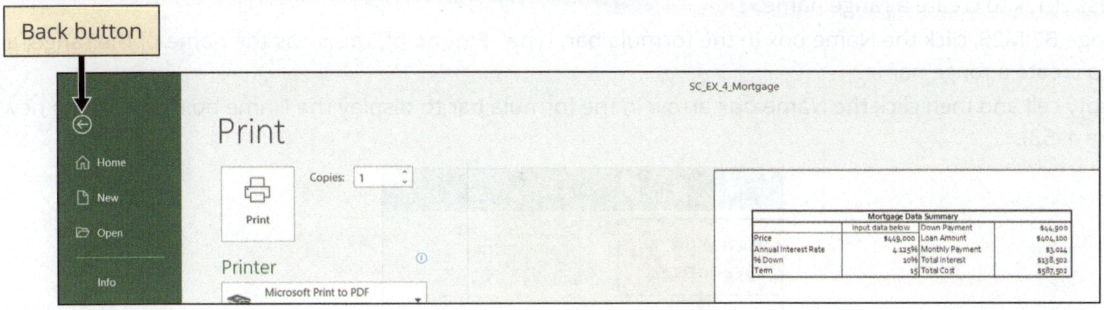

Figure 4-51

3

- Click the Print Area button (Page Layout tab | Page Setup group) to display the Print Area menu and then click the 'Clear Print Area' command to reset the print area to the entire worksheet.

Q&A What happens when I set a print area?
When you set a print area, Excel will print the specified range rather than the entire worksheet. If you save the workbook with the print area set, then Excel will remember the settings the next time you open the workbook and continue to print only the specified range. Clicking 'Clear Print Area' on the Print Area menu, as described in Step 3, will revert the settings so that the entire workbook will print.

To Name and Print Sections of a Worksheet

Why? If you regularly are going to print a particular section of a worksheet, naming the section allows you to specify that section whenever you need to print it. In some situations, you will want to print several different areas of a worksheet. Rather than using the 'Set Print Area' command or manually selecting the range each time you want to print, you can name the ranges using the Name box in the formula bar. You then can use one of the names to select an area before using the 'Set Print Area' command or Print Selection option.

If a worksheet spans multiple pages and you want to print only certain pages, you can enter the page numbers in the Pages text boxes on the Print screen. If you print a worksheet with multiple pages, you can specify print titles that will automatically repeat one or more rows or one or more columns on each page. To specify the rows or columns to repeat, click the Print Titles button (Page Layout tab | Page Setup group) and enter the desired row(s) and/or column(s) in the 'Rows to repeat at top' or 'Columns to repeat at left' text boxes. The following steps name the Mortgage Data Summary, the Varying Interest Rate Schedule, the Amortization Schedule sections, as well as the entire worksheet, and then print each section.

1

- Click the Page Setup Dialog Box Launcher to display the Page Setup dialog box, click the Sheet tab, and then click 'Black and white' to remove the check mark and ensure that Excel prints in color on color printers.
- Click OK to close the Page Setup dialog box.
- If necessary, select the range C5:F10, click the Name box in the formula bar, and then enter **Mortgage_Summary** to name the range (Figure 4-52). **Hint:** Remember to include the underscore between Mortgage and Summary.

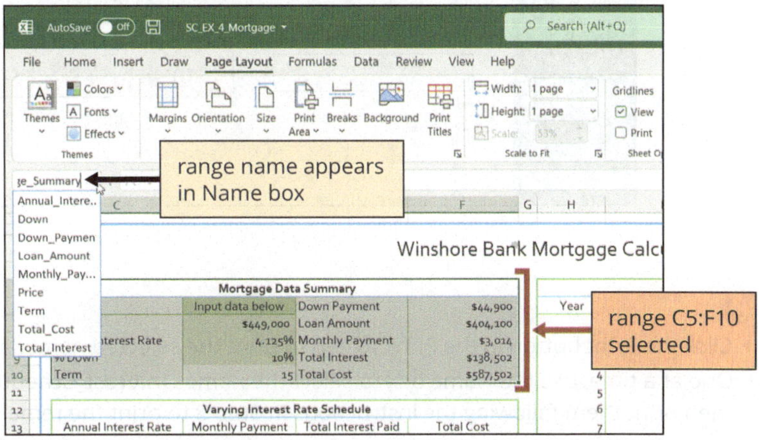

Figure 4-52

2

- Press ENTER to create the range name.
- Select the range C12:F24, click the Name box in the formula bar, type **Interest_Schedule** as the name of the range, and then press ENTER to create a range name.
- Select the range H5:L24, click the Name box in the formula bar, type **Amortization_Schedule** as the name of the range, and then press ENTER to create a range name.
- Select the range B2:M25, click the Name box in the formula bar, type **Financial_Tools** as the name of the range, and then press ENTER to create a range name.
- Select an empty cell and then click the Name box arrow in the formula bar to display the Name box list with the new range names (Figure 4–53).

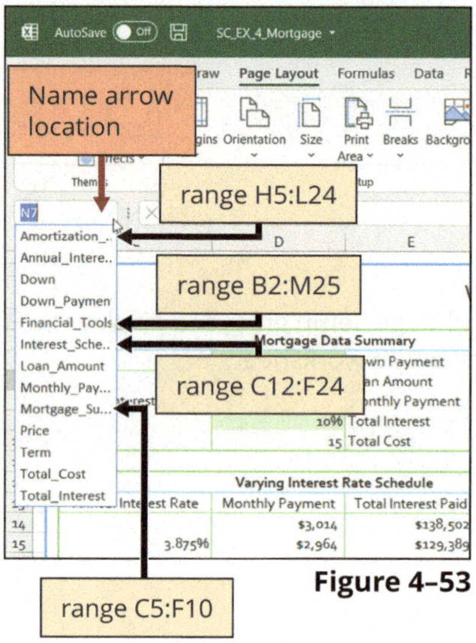

Figure 4–53

3

- Click Mortgage_Summary in the Name list to select the range associated with the name, C5:F10 in this case.
- Click File on the ribbon to open Backstage view and then click Print to display the Print screen.
- Click the 'Print Active Sheets' button in the Settings area and then click Print Selection to select the desired item to print (Figure 4–54).

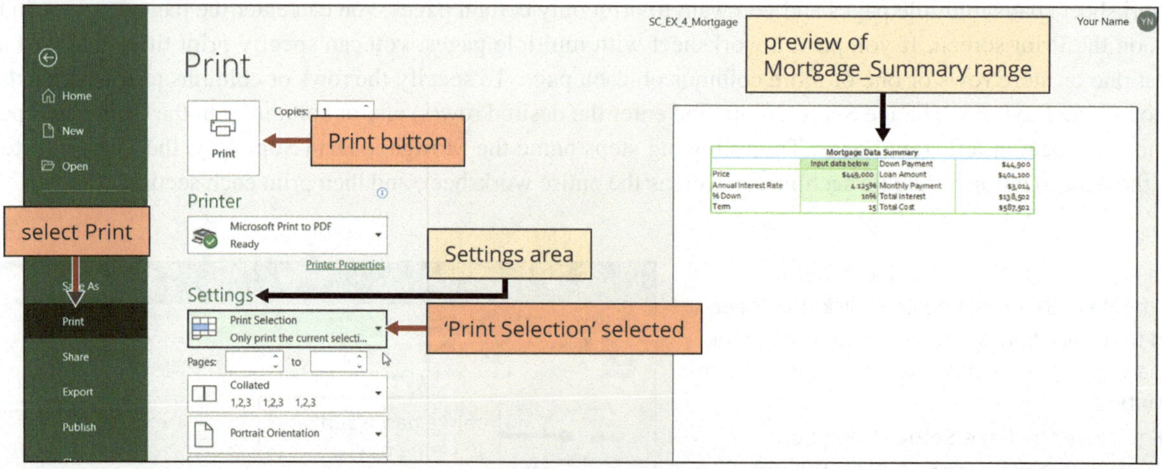

Figure 4–54

4

- Click the Print button in the Print screen to print the selected named range, Mortgage_Summary in this case.
- One at a time, use the Name box to select the names Interest_Schedule, Amortization_Schedule, and Financial_Tools, and then print them following the instructions in Step 3 to print the remaining named ranges (Figure 4–55).

5

- Save the workbook again in the same storage location with the same file name.

Mortgage Data Summary			
	Input data below	Down Payment	$44,900
Price	$449,000	Loan Amount	$404,100
Annual Interest Rate	4.125%	Monthly Payment	$3,014
% Down	10%	Total Interest	$138,502
Term	15	Total Cost	$587,502

Figure 4–55(a)

Varying Interest Rate Schedule			
Annual Interest Rate	Monthly Payment	Total Interest Paid	Total Cost
	$3,014	$138,502	$587,502
3.875%	$2,964	$129,389	$578,389
4.000%	$2,989	$133,934	$582,934
4.125%	$3,014	$138,502	$587,502
4.250%	$3,040	$143,092	$592,092
4.375%	$3,066	$147,705	$596,705
4.500%	$3,091	$152,341	$601,341
4.625%	$3,117	$156,999	$605,999
4.750%	$3,143	$161,679	$610,679
4.875%	$3,169	$166,382	$615,382
5.000%	$3,196	$171,107	$620,107

Figure 4–55(b)

Amortization Schedule				
Year	Beginning Balance	Principal Paid	Interest Paid	Ending Balance
1	$404,100	$19,877	$16,296	$384,223
2	$384,223	$20,713	$15,460	$363,510
3	$363,510	$21,584	$14,590	$341,926
4	$341,926	$22,491	$13,682	$319,435
5	$319,435	$23,437	$12,737	$295,998
6	$295,998	$24,422	$11,752	$271,576
7	$271,576	$25,448	$10,725	$246,128
8	$246,128	$26,518	$9,655	$219,610
9	$219,610	$27,633	$8,540	$191,977
10	$191,977	$28,795	$7,379	$163,182
11	$163,182	$30,005	$6,168	$133,177
12	$133,177	$31,267	$4,907	$101,910
13	$101,910	$32,581	$3,592	$69,329
14	$69,329	$33,951	$2,223	$35,378
15	$35,378	$35,378	$795	$0
	Subtotal	$404,100	$138,502	
	Down Payment		$44,900	
	Total Cost		$587,502	

Figure 4–55(c)

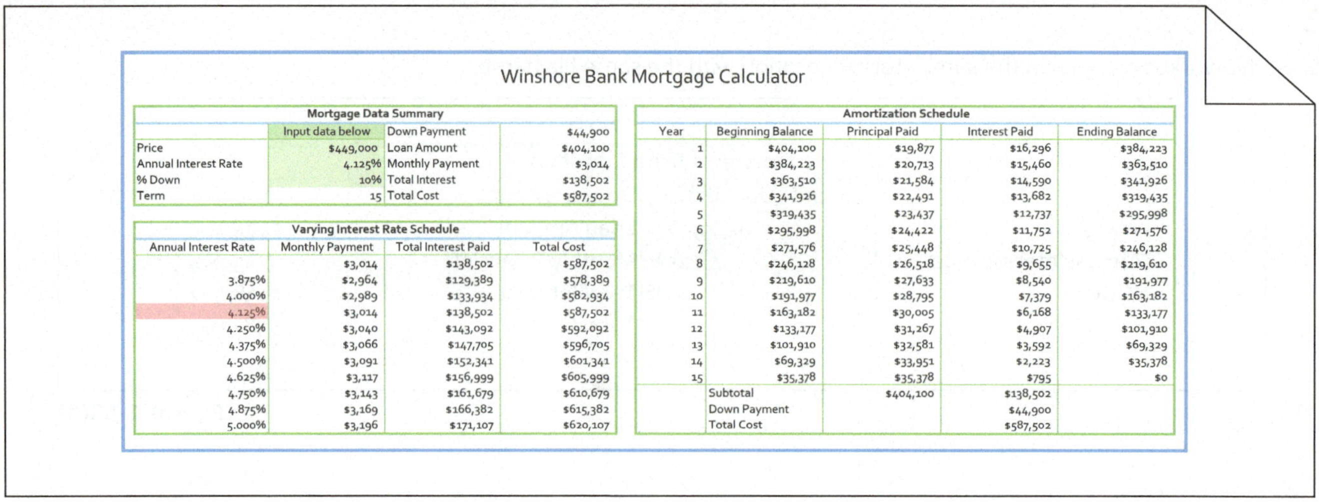

Winshore Bank Mortgage Calculator

Mortgage Data Summary			
	Input data below	Down Payment	$44,900
Price	$449,000	Loan Amount	$404,100
Annual Interest Rate	4.125%	Monthly Payment	$3,014
% Down	10%	Total Interest	$138,502
Term	15	Total Cost	$587,502

Varying Interest Rate Schedule			
Annual Interest Rate	Monthly Payment	Total Interest Paid	Total Cost
	$3,014	$138,502	$587,502
3.875%	$2,964	$129,389	$578,389
4.000%	$2,989	$133,934	$582,934
4.125%	$3,014	$138,502	$587,502
4.250%	$3,040	$143,092	$592,092
4.375%	$3,066	$147,705	$596,705
4.500%	$3,091	$152,341	$601,341
4.625%	$3,117	$156,999	$605,999
4.750%	$3,143	$161,679	$610,679
4.875%	$3,169	$166,382	$615,382
5.000%	$3,196	$171,107	$620,107

Amortization Schedule				
Year	Beginning Balance	Principal Paid	Interest Paid	Ending Balance
1	$404,100	$19,877	$16,296	$384,223
2	$384,223	$20,713	$15,460	$363,510
3	$363,510	$21,584	$14,590	$341,926
4	$341,926	$22,491	$13,682	$319,435
5	$319,435	$23,437	$12,737	$295,998
6	$295,998	$24,422	$11,752	$271,576
7	$271,576	$25,448	$10,725	$246,128
8	$246,128	$26,518	$9,655	$219,610
9	$219,610	$27,633	$8,540	$191,977
10	$191,977	$28,795	$7,379	$163,182
11	$163,182	$30,005	$6,168	$133,177
12	$133,177	$31,267	$4,907	$101,910
13	$101,910	$32,581	$3,592	$69,329
14	$69,329	$33,951	$2,223	$35,378
15	$35,378	$35,378	$795	$0
	Subtotal	$404,100	$138,502	
	Down Payment		$44,900	
	Total Cost		$587,502	

Figure 4–55(d)

Q&A Why does the Financial_Tools range print on one page?

Recall that you selected the Fit to option earlier (Figure 4–48). This selection ensures that each of the printouts fits across the page in portrait orientation.

Creating Formulas with Defined Names

Just as you can apply a name to a range of cells for printing, you can also use names to refer to ranges of cells in formulas. Naming a range of cells might make it easier for you to reference those cells as opposed to remembering the cell addresses corresponding to the range.

To Define a Name for a Range of Cells If you choose to define a name for a range of cells to use in a formula, you would follow these steps.

1. Select the cell or range of cells to name.
2. Click the Define Name button (Formulas tab | Defined Names group).
3. Type the desired name in the Name text box.
4. Click OK.

Once you have defined a name for a cell or range of cells, you can use the name in one or more formulas. You can also use table names in formulas; you will learn more about table names in Module 6.

To Use a Defined Name in a Formula If you choose to use a defined name in a formula, you would follow these steps.

1. Start typing the formula in the desired cell.
2. When you are ready to reference the cell or range of cells by its defined name, click the 'Use in Formula' button (Formulas tab | Defined Names group) to display a list of defined names.
3. Click the desired defined name to insert it into the formula.
4. Finish typing the formula.

Break Point: If you want to take a break, this is a good place to do so. You can exit Excel now. To resume later, start Excel, open the file called SC_EX_4_Mortgage, and continue following the steps from this location forward.

Protecting and Hiding Worksheets and Workbooks

When building a worksheet for novice users, you should protect the cells in the worksheet that you do not want changed, such as cells that contain text or formulas which are considered structural to the worksheet. Protecting cells prevents users from changing or deleting them.

When you create a new worksheet, all the cells are assigned a locked status, but the lock is not engaged, which leaves cells unprotected. **Unprotected cells** are cells whose values you can change at any time. **Protected cells** are cells that you cannot change. To protect a workbook so that structural changes cannot be made, click the Protect Workbook button (Review tab | Protect group). If desired, enter a password in the Password (optional) text box, verify the Structure check box contains a check mark, and then click OK.

Consider This

How do you determine which cells to protect in a worksheet?

Deciding which cells to protect often depends upon the audience for your worksheet. In general, the highest level of security would be to protect all cells except those that require an entry by the user of the worksheet. This level of protection might be recommended for novice users, clients, or customers. A lesser safeguard would be to protect any cells containing formulas, so that users of the worksheet cannot modify the formulas. Finally, if you are creating a worksheet for your boss or a trusted team member, you might want to leave the cells unprotected, in case they need to edit the worksheet. In any case, you should protect cells only after the worksheet has been tested fully and the correct results appear. Protecting a worksheet is a two-step process:

1. Select the cells you want to leave unprotected and then change their cell protection settings to an unlocked status.
2. Protect the entire worksheet.

At first glance, these steps may appear to be backward. However, once you protect the entire worksheet, you cannot change anything, including the locked status of individual cells.

To Protect a Worksheet

Why? Protecting a worksheet allows you to determine which cells a user can modify. In the Mortgage Payment Calculator worksheet, the user should be able to make changes to only three cells: the price in cell D7, the annual interest rate in cell D8, and the percent down in cell D9 (Figure 4–56). These cells must remain unprotected so that the user can enter data for the mortgage they are considering. The remaining cells in the worksheet can be protected so that the user cannot change them. The following steps protect the Mortgage Calculator worksheet.

1

- Select the range D7:D9 and right-click the range to display a shortcut menu and mini toolbar (Figure 4–56).

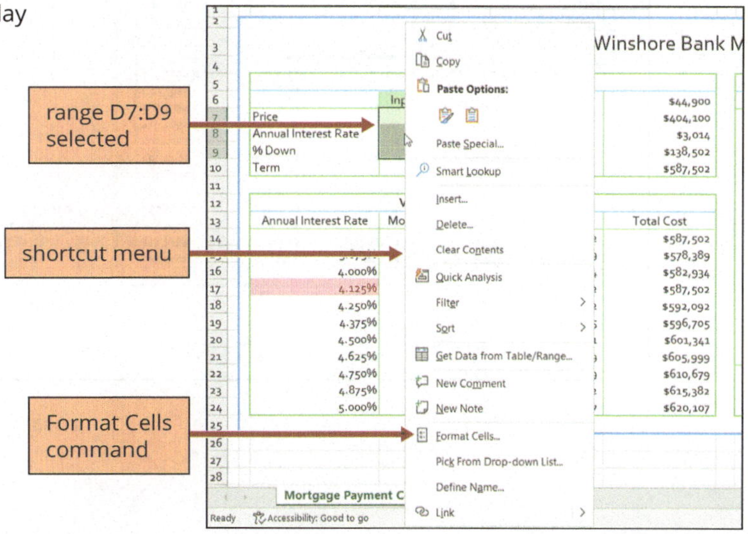

Figure 4–56

2

- Click Format Cells on the shortcut menu to display the Format Cells dialog box.
- Click the Protection tab (Format Cells dialog box) and then click Locked to remove the check mark (Figure 4–57).

Q&A What happens when I remove the check mark from the Locked check box?
Removing the check mark from the Locked check box allows users to modify the selected cells (D7:D9) after you use the Protect Sheet command.

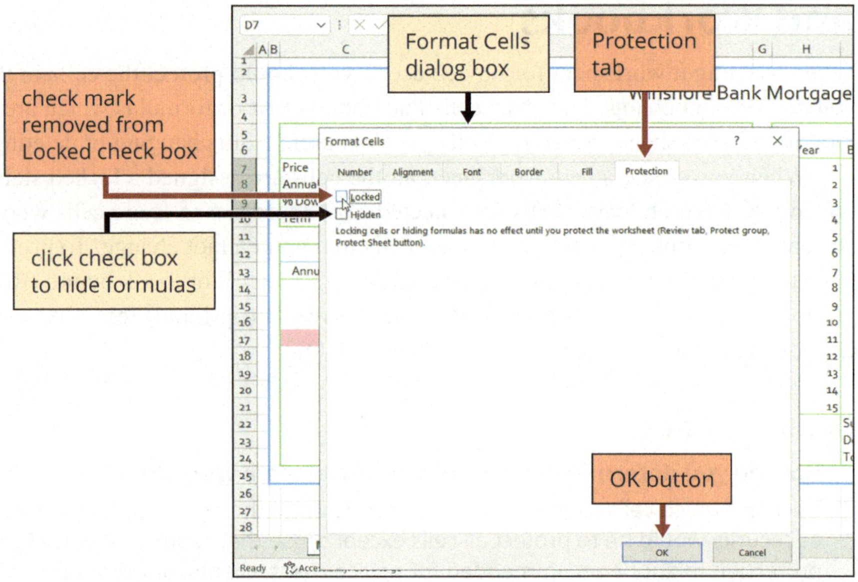

Figure 4–57

3

- Click OK to close the Format Cells dialog box.
- Deselect the range and display the Review tab (Figure 4–58).

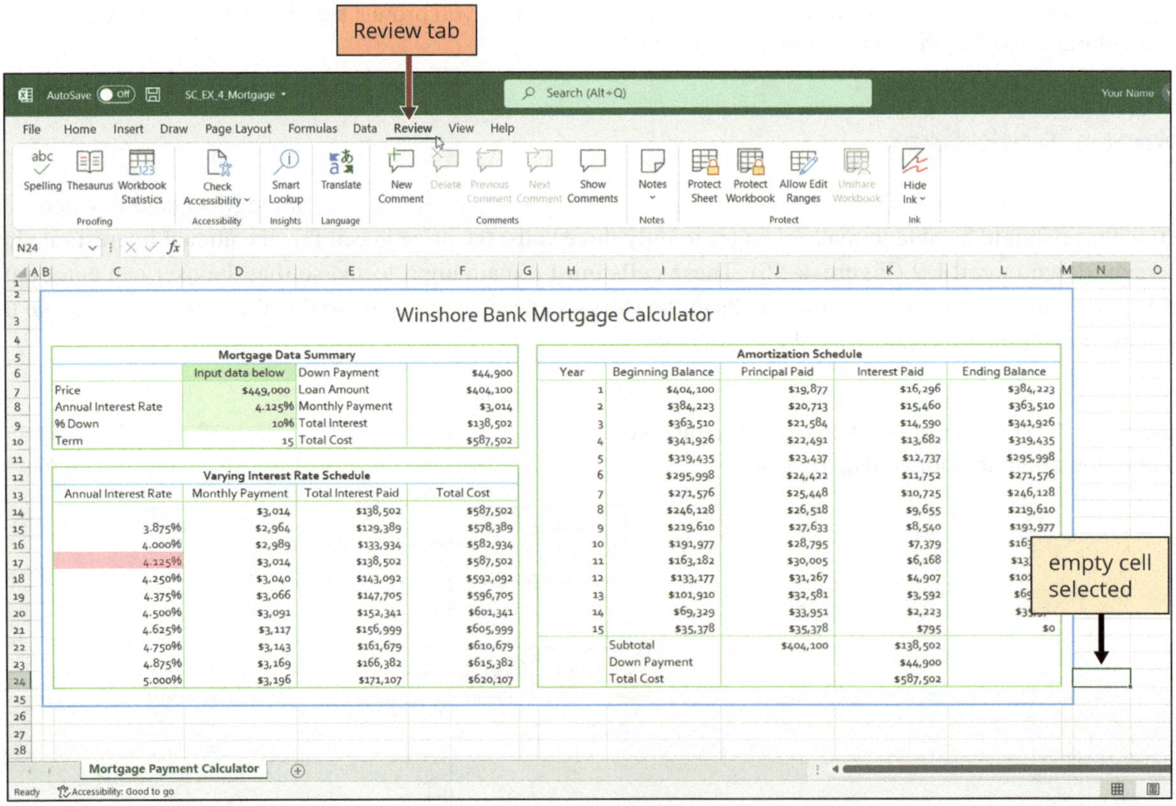

Figure 4–58

4

- Click the Protect Sheet button (Review tab | Protect group) to display the Protect Sheet dialog box.
- Verify that the 'Protect worksheet and contents of locked cells' check box (at the top of the Protect Sheet dialog box) and the first two check boxes in the list contain check marks so that the user of the worksheet can select both locked and unlocked cells (Figure 4–59).

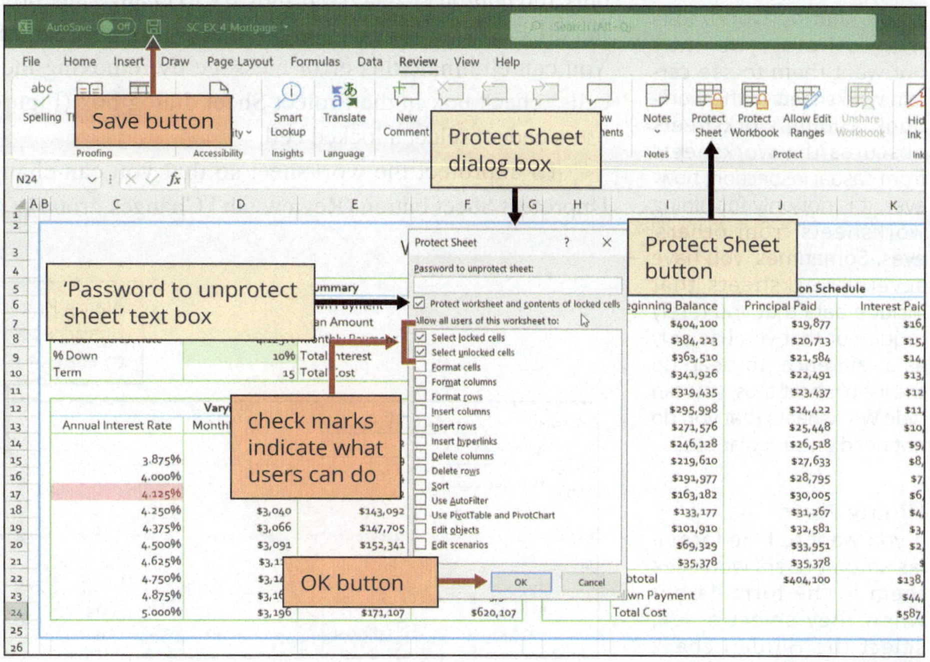

Figure 4–59

Q&A What do the three checked settings mean?

With all three check boxes selected, the worksheet (except for the cells left unlocked) is protected from modification. The two check boxes in the list allow users to select any cell on the worksheet, but they only can change unlocked cells.

What is the purpose of the 'Password to unprotect sheet' text box?

If you want to protect one or more cells from changes and do not want others to easily unprotect the sheet, you can assign a password that will be required when someone attempts to unprotect the sheet. If you do assign a password, however, make sure you keep a record of what it is, for future reference.

5

- Click OK (Protect Sheet dialog box) to close the Protect Sheet dialog box.
- Save the workbook again in the same storage location with the same file name.

Other Ways

1. Click Format Cells Dialog Box Launcher (Home tab | Font, Alignment, or Number group), click Protection tab, remove check mark from Locked check box, click OK
2. Click File tab, click Info tab, click Protect Workbook, click Protect Current Sheet, select options, click OK

More about Worksheet Protection

Now all of the cells in the worksheet, except for the range D7:D9, are protected. But the protection is not strong, because any user can remove the protection using the Unprotect Sheet button on the Review tab. The 'Password to Unprotect Sheet' text box in the Protect Sheet dialog box, shown in Figure 4–59, enables you to strengthen this protection by requiring a password. You can create a password when you want to prevent others from changing the worksheet from protected to unprotected. The additional settings in the list in the Protect Sheet dialog box also give you the option to modify the protection so that the user can make certain changes, such as formatting cells or inserting hyperlinks.

If you want to protect more than one worksheet in a workbook, either select each worksheet before you begin the protection process or click the Protect Workbook button, shown in Figure 4–59. If you want to unlock cells for specific users, you can use the 'Allow Edit Ranges' button (Review tab | Protect group).

BTW
Using Protected Worksheets
You can move from one unprotected cell to another unprotected cell in a worksheet by using TAB and SHIFT+TAB. This is especially useful when the cells are not adjacent to one another.

BTW
Hiding Worksheets
When sharing workbooks with others, you may not want them to see certain worksheets in the workbook. Hiding worksheets obscures the worksheets from casual inspection; however, it is not only for hiding worksheets from others' eyes. Sometimes, you have several worksheets that include data that you rarely require or that you use only as a reference. To clean up the list of sheet tabs, you can hide worksheets that you do not need on a regular basis.

BTW
Hiding Formulas
If you want to hide formulas so that users won't see them in the formula bar when they select a cell, select the Hidden check box in the Format Cells dialog box and then select Protect Sheet in the Protect group on the Review tab.

When this protected worksheet is made available to users, they will be able to enter data in only the unprotected cells. If they try to change any protected cell, such as the monthly payment in cell F8, Excel will display a dialog box with an error message, as shown in Figure 4–60. You can eliminate this error message by removing the check mark from the 'Select unlocked cells' check box in the Protect Sheet dialog box (Figure 4–59). With the check mark removed, users cannot select a locked cell.

To unprotect the worksheet so that you can change all cells in the worksheet, click the Unprotect Sheet button (Review tab | Changes group).

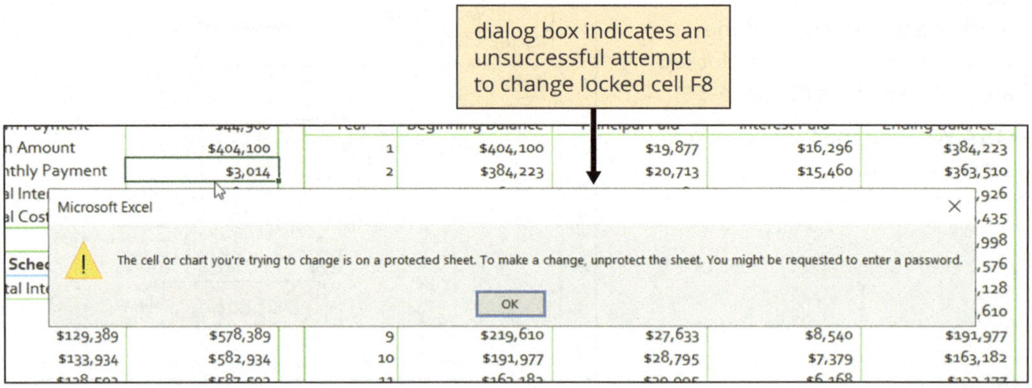

Figure 4–60

To Hide and Unhide a Worksheet

Why? You may want to hide worksheets that contain sensitive data. Afterwards, when you need to access these hidden worksheets, you can unhide them. If you do not think you will need the worksheet in the future, you may choose to delete the worksheet instead of hiding it. To delete a worksheet, right-click the desired worksheet tab and then click Delete on the shortcut menu. The following steps hide and then unhide a worksheet.

1

- Click the New sheet button to insert a new worksheet in the workbook.
- Right-click the Mortgage Payment Calculator sheet tab to display a shortcut menu (Figure 4–61).

Q&A Why insert a new worksheet?
Workbooks must contain at least one visible worksheet. In order to hide the Mortgage Payment Calculator worksheet, there must be another visible worksheet in the workbook.

Why does the Unhide command on the shortcut menu appear dimmed?
The Unhide command appears dimmed when it is unavailable; because no worksheets are hidden, the command is unavailable.

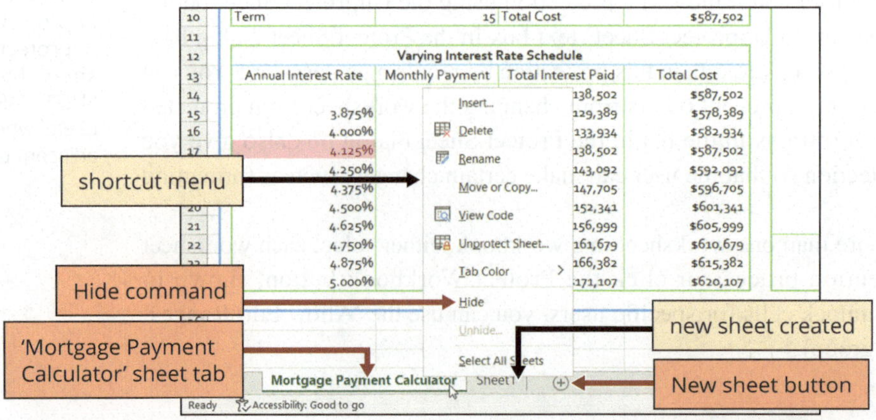

Figure 4–61

2

- Click Hide on the shortcut menu to hide the Mortgage Payment Calculator worksheet.
- Right-click the sheet tab to display a shortcut menu.
- Click Unhide on the shortcut menu to display the Unhide dialog box.
- If necessary, click Mortgage Payment Calculator in the Unhide sheet list (Unhide dialog box) to select the worksheet to unhide (Figure 4–62).

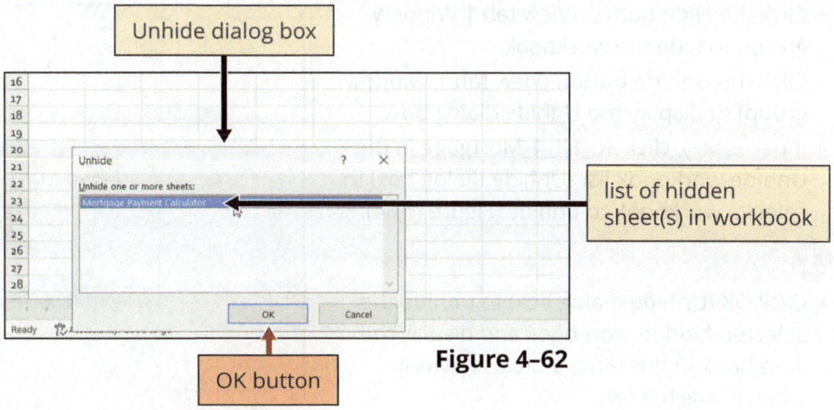

Figure 4–62

Q&A Why should I hide a worksheet?

Hiding worksheets in a workbook is a common approach when working with complex workbooks that contain one worksheet with the results users need to see and one or more worksheets with essential data that, while important to the functionality of the workbook, is unimportant to users of the workbook. Thus, these data worksheets often are hidden from view. Although the worksheets are hidden, the data and formulas on the hidden worksheets remain available for use by other worksheets in the workbook.

3

- Click OK (Unhide dialog box) to reveal the hidden worksheet.

To Hide and Unhide a Workbook

In addition to hiding worksheets, you also can hide an entire workbook. **Why?** This feature is useful when you have several workbooks open simultaneously and want the user to be able to view only one of them. Also, some users hide the entire workbook when the computer is unattended and they do not want others to be able to see the workbook. The following steps hide and unhide a workbook.

1

- Display the View tab (Figure 4–63).

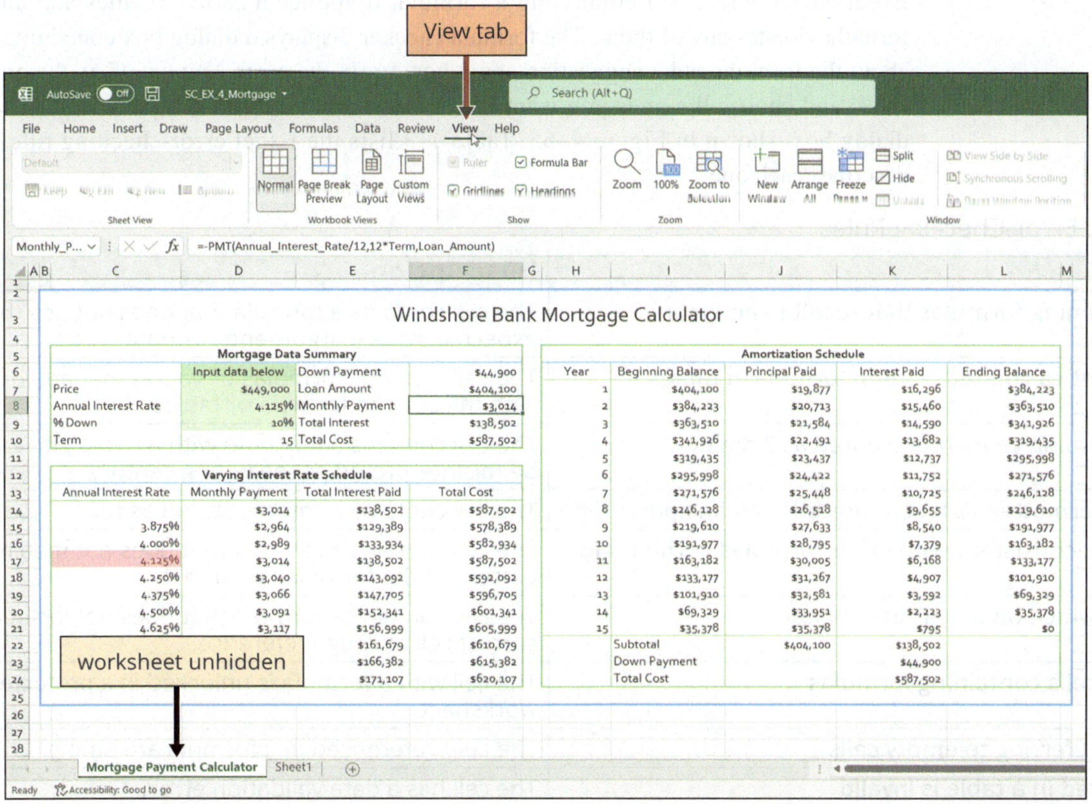

Figure 4–63

2

- Click the Hide button (View tab | Window group) to hide the workbook.
- Click the Unhide button (View tab | Window group) to display the Unhide dialog box.
- If necessary, click SC_EX_4_Mortgage in the Unhide workbook list (Unhide dialog box) to select a workbook to unhide (Figure 4–64).

3

- Click OK (Unhide dialog box) to unhide the selected hidden workbook and display the workbook in the same state as it was in when it was hidden.

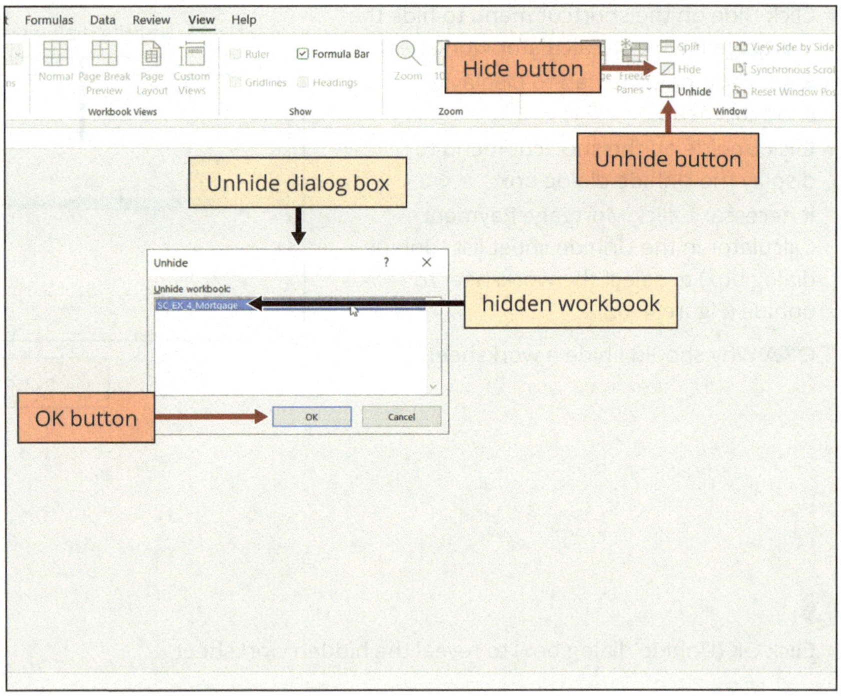

Figure 4–64

Checking Formulas

Before you submit a workbook to a customer, client, or supervisor, you should check it for formula errors, just as you would check any document for spelling errors. Excel has a formula checker that checks all the formulas in a worksheet and alerts you to any problems. Each time Excel encounters a cell containing a formula, it applies a series of rules and alerts you if a formula violates any of them. The formula checker displays a dialog box containing information about the formula and a suggestion about how to fix the error. You can view the error-checking rules, and choose the ones you want Excel to use, in the Formulas pane in the Excel Options dialog box, shown in Figure 4–65. Table 4–3 lists the Excel error-checking rules and briefly describes each one.

Table 4–3: Error-Checking Rules

Rule	Description
Cells containing formulas that result in an error	The cell contains a formula that does not use the expected syntax, arguments, or data types.
Inconsistent calculated column formula in tables	The cell contains formulas or values that are inconsistent with the column formula or tables.
Cells containing years represented as 2 digits	The cell contains a text date with a two-digit year that can be misinterpreted as the wrong century.
Numbers formatted as text or preceded by an apostrophe	The cell contains numbers stored as text.
Formulas inconsistent with other formulas in the region	The cell contains a formula that does not match the pattern of the formulas around it.
Formulas which omit cells in a region	The cell contains a formula that does not include a correct cell or range reference.
Unlocked cells containing formulas	The cell with a formula is unlocked in a protected worksheet.
Formulas referring to empty cells	The cells referenced in a formula are empty.
Data entered in a table is invalid	The cell has a data validation error.

To Enable Background Formula Checking

While you can run the formula checker at any time using the Formulas tab | Error Checking command, you may want Excel to automatically check your formulas and alert you to errors as you work. This is called working "in the background." Through the Excel Options dialog box, you can enable background formula checking. **Why?** You want Excel to continually review the workbook for errors in formulas as you create or manipulate data, formulas, and functions. The following steps enable background formula checking.

1

- Click File on the ribbon to open Backstage view and then click Options to display the Excel Options dialog box.
- Click Formulas in the left pane (Excel Options dialog box) to display options related to formula calculation, performance, and error handling in the right pane.
- If necessary, click any check box in the 'Error checking rules' area that does not contain a check mark so that all error checking rules are enabled (Figure 4–65). As you add check marks, click the 'Reset Ignored Errors' button in the Error Checking section to reset error checking.

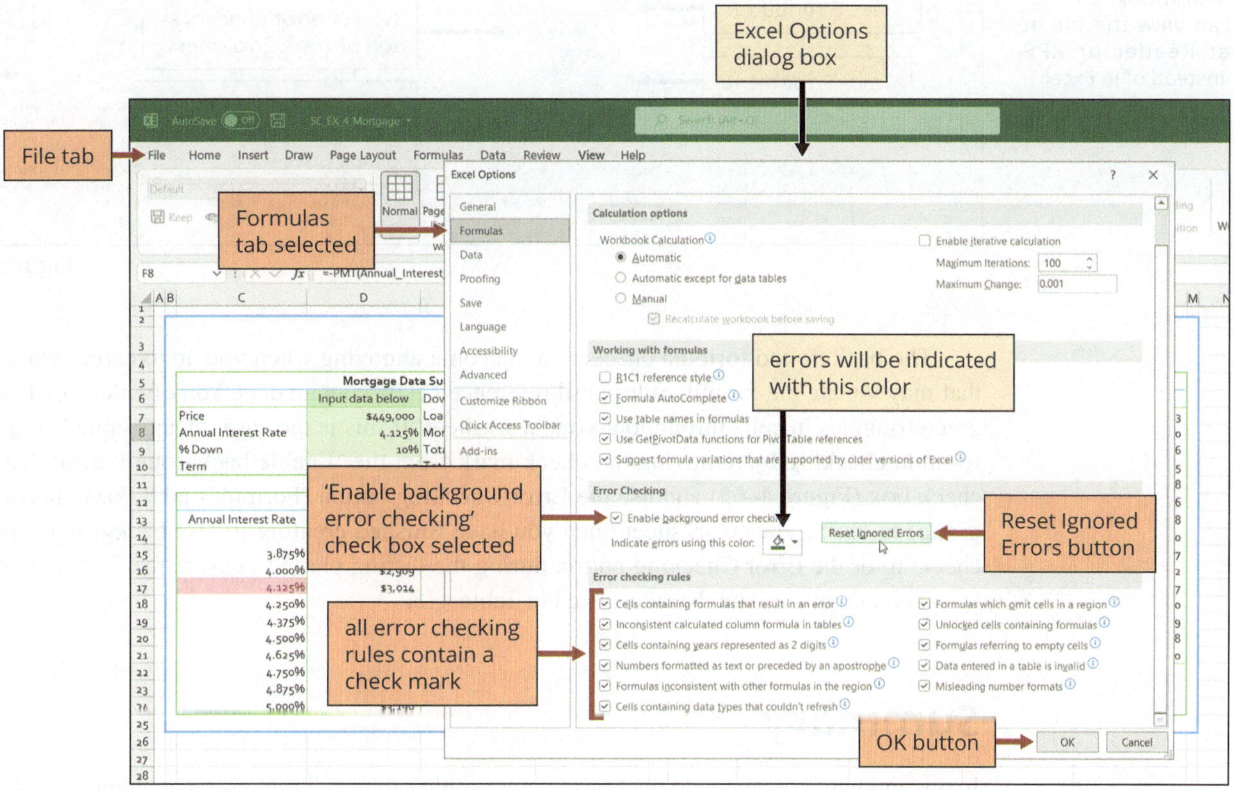

Figure 4–65

2

- Click OK (Excel Options dialog box) to close the Excel Options dialog box.
- If desired, sign out of your Microsoft account.
- sam Exit Excel.

More about Background Formula Checking

When background formula checking is enabled and a formula fails to pass one of the rules, Excel adds a small green triangle to the upper-left corner of the cell.

Assume, for example, that background formula checking is enabled and that cell F8, which contains the PMT function in the Mortgage Calculator workbook, is unlocked. Because one of

BTW
Distributing a Workbook
Instead of printing and distributing a hard copy of a workbook, you can distribute the workbook electronically. Options include sending the workbook via email; posting it on cloud storage (such as OneDrive) and sharing the file with others; posting it on social media, a blog, or other website; and sharing a link associated with an online location of the workbook. You also can create and share a PDF or XPS image of the workbook, so that users can view the file in Acrobat Reader or XPS Viewer instead of in Excel.

the error checking rules, shown in Table 4–3, stipulates that a cell containing a formula must be locked, Excel displays a green triangle in the upper-left corner of cell F8.

When you select the cell with the green triangle, a Trace Error button appears next to the cell. If you click the Trace Error button, Excel displays the Trace Error menu (Figure 4–66). The first item in the menu identifies the error (Unprotected Formula). The remainder of the menu lists commands from which you can choose. The first command locks the cell. Selecting the Lock Cell command fixes the problem so that the formula no longer violates the rule. Selecting the 'Error Checking Options' command displays the Excel Options dialog box with the Formulas tab active, as shown in Figure 4–66.

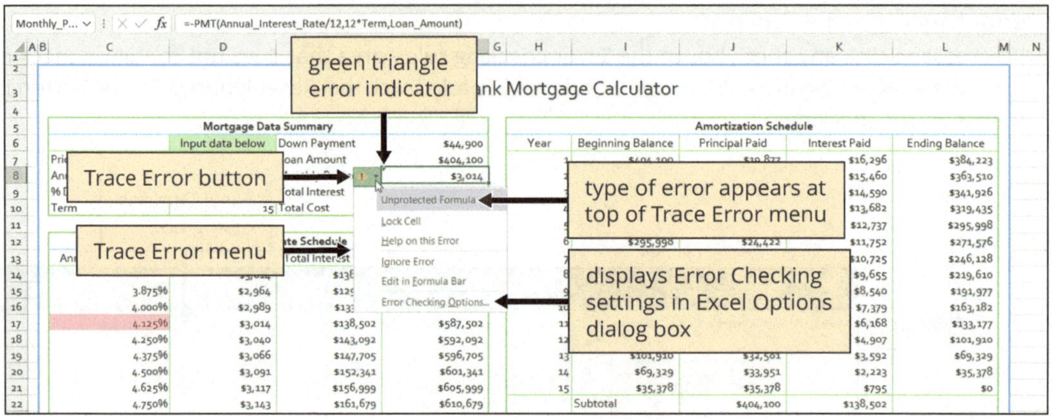

Figure 4–66

The background formula checker can become annoying when you are creating worksheets that may violate the formula rules until referenced cells contain data. You often can end up with green triangles in cells throughout your worksheet. If this is the case, then disable background formula checking by removing the check mark from the 'Enable background error checking' check box (Figure 4–65) and use the Error Checking button (Formulas tab | Formula Auditing group) to check your worksheet once you have finished creating it. Use background formula checking or the Error Checking button during the testing phase to ensure the formulas in your workbook do not violate the rules listed in Table 4–3.

Summary

In this module, you learned how to use names, rather than cell references, to enter formulas; use financial functions, such as the PMT and PV functions; analyze data by creating a data table and amortization schedule; set print options and print sections of a worksheet using names and the Set Print Area command; protect a worksheet or workbook; hide and unhide worksheets and workbooks; and check for errors.

Consider This: Plan Ahead

What decisions will you need to make when creating your next financial decision-making worksheet?

Use these guidelines as you complete the assignments in this module and create your own worksheets for evaluating financial scenarios.

1. Determine the worksheet structure.
   a) Determine the data you will need.
   b) Determine the layout of your data.
   c) Determine the layout of the financial calculator.
   d) Determine the layout of any data tables.
2. Create the worksheet.
   a) Enter titles, subtitles, and headings.
   b) Enter data, functions, and formulas.
   c) Assign names to cells and cell ranges.
   d) Create data tables.
3. Format the worksheet.
   a) Format the titles, subtitles, and headings.
   b) Format the numbers as necessary.
   c) Format the text.
4. Perform what-if analyses.
   a) Adjust values in the assumptions table to review scenarios of interest.
5. Secure the cell contents.
   a) Lock and unlock cells as necessary.
   b) Protect the worksheet.

Student Assignments

Apply Your Knowledge

Reinforce the skills and apply the concepts you learned in this module.

Calculating Loan Payments

Note: To complete this assignment, you will be required to use the Data Files. Please contact your instructor for information about accessing the Data Files.

Instructions: Start Excel. Open the workbook, SC_EX_4-1.xlsx, which is located in the Data Files. The workbook you open contains loan information from which you will create a data table. You are to create the loan payment calculator pictured in Figure 4–67. You will be instructed to print several times in this assignment. If requested or allowed by your instructor, consider saving paper by printing to a PDF file.

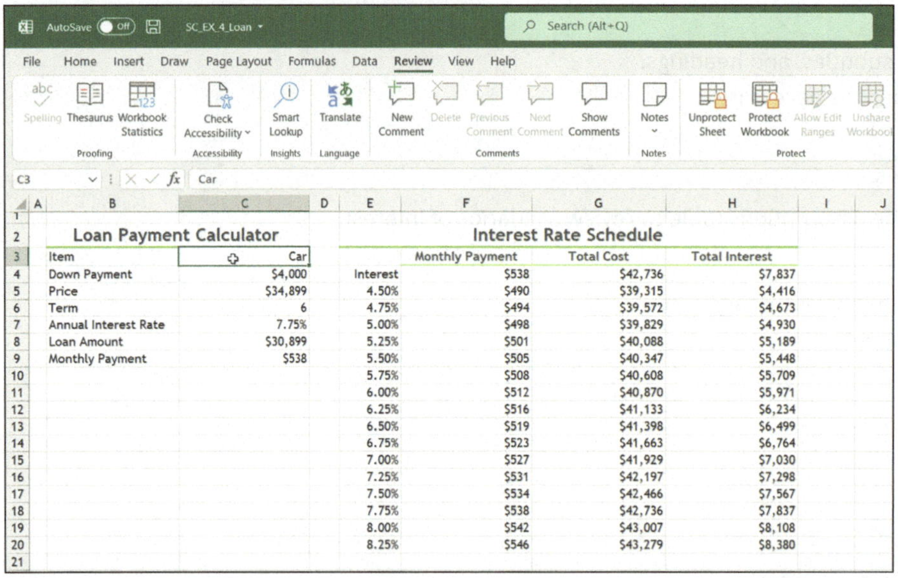

Figure 4–67

Perform the following tasks:

1. Save the workbook with the file name, SC_EX_4_Loan.
2. Select the range B4:C9. Use the 'Create from Selection' button (Formulas tab | Defined Names group) to create names for cells in the range C4:C9 using the names in the left column of the range B4:B9.
3. Enter the formulas shown in Table 4–4.

Table 4–4: Loan Payment Calculator and Interest Rate Schedule Formulas

Cell	Formula
C8	=Price-Down_Payment
C9	=-PMT(Annual_Interest_Rate/12,12*Term,Loan_Amount)
F4	=Monthly_Payment
G4	=12*Monthly_Payment*Term+Down_Payment
H4	=G4-Price

4. Use the Data Table button in the What-If Analysis menu (Data tab | Forecast group) to define the range E4:H20 as a one-input data table. Use the Interest Rate in the Loan Payment Calculator as the column input cell.
5. Format all cells showing currency to match the formatting to the cells in range C4:C5.
6. Use the Page sheet in the Page Setup dialog box to select the 'Fit to' 1 page by 1 page option, and the Sheet sheet to select the 'Black and white' option. Select the range B2:C9 and then use the 'Set Print Area' command to set a print area. Use the Print button on the Print screen in Backstage view to print the worksheet. Use the 'Clear Print Area' command to clear the print area.
7. Use the Name box on the formula bar to name the following ranges: B2:C9 as **Loan_Calculator**; E2:H20 as **Rate_Schedule**; and B2:H20 as **All_Sections**. Print each range by selecting the name in the Name box and using the Print Selection option on the Print screen in Backstage view.
8. Use a command in the Format Cells dialog box to unlock the range C3:C7. Protect the worksheet so that the user can select only unlocked cells.
9. Press CTRL+` and then print the formulas view of the worksheet in landscape orientation. Press CTRL+` again to return to the values view.
10. Hide and then unhide the Loan Payment Calculator worksheet. Hide and then unhide the workbook. Delete the extra worksheet you made so that you could hide the Loan Payment Calculator worksheet. Unprotect the worksheet and then hide columns E through H. Select columns D and I and reveal the hidden columns. Hide rows 11 through 19. Print the worksheet. Select rows 10 and 20 and unhide rows 11 through 19. Protect the worksheet so that the user can select only unlocked cells.
11. Determine the monthly payment and print the worksheet for each data set: (a) Item = **Motorcycle**; Down Payment = **$2500**; Price = **$22,000**; Term = **4**; Interest Rate = **6.75%**; (b) Item = **Debt Consolidation Loan**; Down Payment = **$0.00**; Price = **$45,000**; Term = **5**; Interest Rate = **8.00%**. Set the values in cells C3:C7 back to the Car values shown in Figure 4–67 after completing the above calculations.
12. If requested by your instructor, add your initials to cell E3. You will need to unprotect the worksheet and unlock the cell to do so. Make sure to lock the cell and protect the worksheet after adding your initials.
13. Submit the revised workbook (as shown in Figure 4–67) in the format specified by your instructor, and then exit Excel.
14. **Consider This:** How would you revise the Interest Rate Schedule to be more informative to the user?

Extend Your Knowledge

Extend the skills you learned in this module and experiment with new skills. You may need to use Help to complete the assignment.

Planning Retirement

Note: To complete this assignment, you will be required to use the Data Files. Please contact your instructor for information about accessing the Data Files.

Instructions: Start Excel. Open the workbook SC_EX_4-2.xlsx, which is located in the Data Files. The workbook you open contains a financial calculator for a 403(b) retirement plan. You are to create a two-input data table that will help employees understand the impact that the amount they invest and the rate of return will have on their retirement earnings (Figure 4–68). Recall from the module that a two-input data table allows for two variables (amount invested and rate of return, in this case) in a formula.

Continued on next page

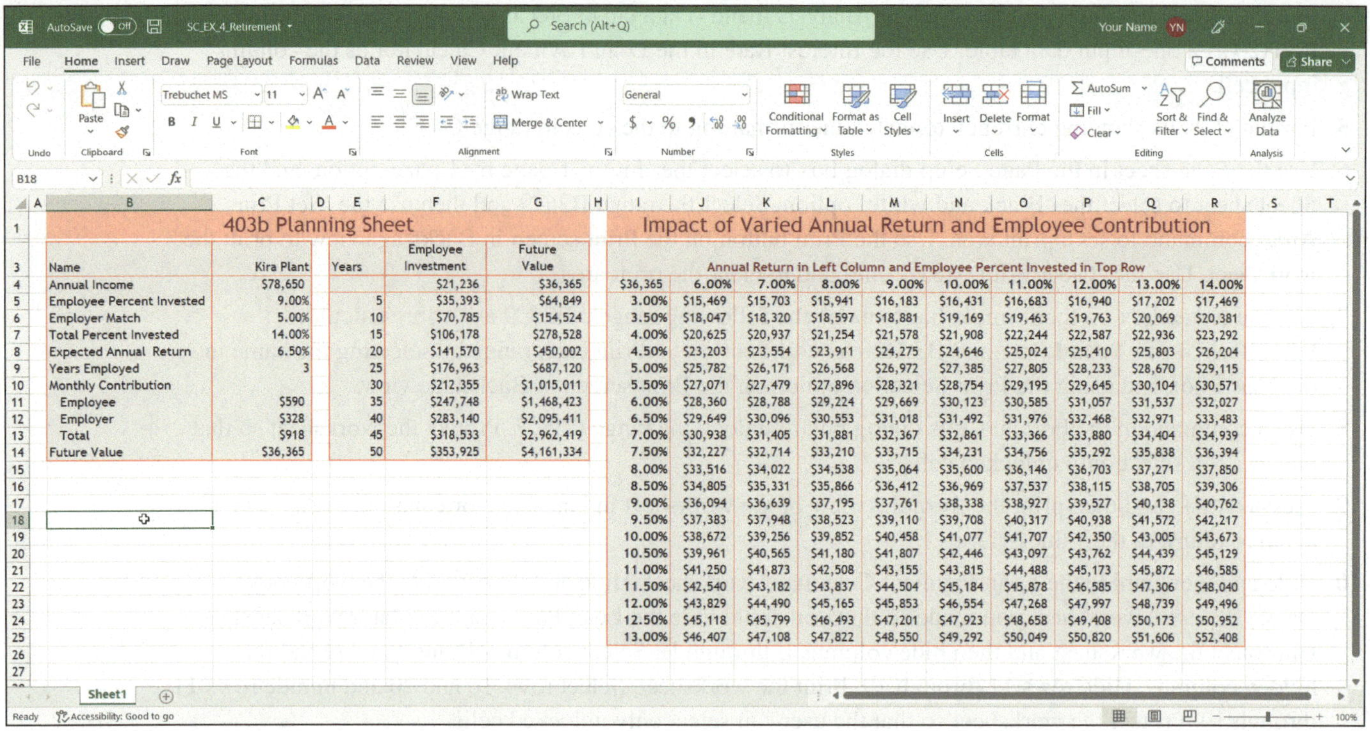

Figure 4–68

Perform the following tasks:

1. Save the workbook using the file name, SC_EX_4_Retirement.
2. Enter **Impact of Varied Annual Return and Employee Contribution** in cell I1. Enter **Annual Return in Left Column and Employee Percent Invested in Top Row** in cell I3.
3. Change the width of column H to 2.2. Merge and center the titles in cells I1 and I3 over columns I through R. Format the titles using the Title cell style for the title (in cell I1) and Heading 4 for the subtitle (in cell I3). Change the column widths of columns I through R to 9.22. Format cell I1 to match the fill color in cell B1, and format cell I3 to match the fill color used in cells B3:C14 (Light Gray, Background 2).
4. For a two-input data table, the formula you are analyzing must be assigned to the upper-left cell in the range of the data table. Because cell C14 contains the future value formula to be analyzed, enter **=c14** in cell I4.
5. Use the fill handle to create two lists of percentages: (a) 3.00% through 13.00% in increments of 0.50% in the range I5:I25, and (b) 6.00% through 14.00% in increments of 1.00% in the range J4:R4.
6. Use the Data Table button on the What-If Analysis menu (Data tab | Forecast group) to define the range I4:R25 as a two-input data table. Enter **C8** in the 'Row input cell' box and **C5** in the 'Column input cell' box (Data Table dialog box). Click OK to populate the table.
7. Format the two-input data table using the font and fill colors used in cells B1 and cells B3:C14. Bold ranges J4:R4 and I5:I25. Format cells J5:R25 to match the number format used in cells F5:G14. Place a medium style border (row 5, column 2) around the range I3:R25, matching the color of the border around B3:C14 (Rose, Accent 6). Place a light style border (row 6, column 1) between columns in I4:R25, and a light style top and bottom border on cell I4:R4 in the same border color.
8. Unlock cells C3:C6 and C8:C9, and then protect the worksheet so that the user can select only unlocked cells.
9. If necessary, change the print orientation to landscape. Print the worksheet using the Fit to option. Print the formulas version of the worksheet.

   If requested by your instructor, change the name in cell C3 to your name.
10. Save the file with the same filename and submit the revised workbook in the format specified by your instructor.
11. **Consider This:** How could you improve the design of the worksheet to make the impact of various combinations of Employee Contribution and Expected Annual Return easier to identify?

Expand Your World

Create a solution that uses cloud or web technologies by learning and investigating on your own from general guidance.

Down Payment Options for a Home

Note: To complete this assignment, you will be required to use the Data Files. Please contact your instructor for information about accessing the Data Files.

Instructions: You are planning to buy a home as soon as you can save enough to make a 10% down payment. Your task is to create a calculator that you can use to determine possible savings options, and to share this calculator with family using OneDrive. Start Excel. Open the workbook called SC_EX_4-3.xlsx, which is located in the Data Files. This workbook contains a basic structure to use in creating a down payment calculator. You are to create a two-input data table to help determine the future value of savings.

Perform the following tasks:

1. Save the file using the file name SC_EX_4_Calculator.
2. Identify a home for sale in your local housing market that you would consider buying. Use the asking price for that home as the current value of the property or use an online tool such as Zillow.com to find the current estimated value of the home. Enter this value in cell C3 of your Down Payment Calculator and calculate the needed down payment.
3. Determine the amount you consider reasonable as a monthly savings toward a down payment and enter this in your down payment calculator.
4. Use the Future Value function to calculate how much you could save, using the rate of return and years to save provided in the worksheet. Remember to use a minus sign before the function so that the calculation will appear positive, and make sure that the rate of return and the number of periods are calculated using the same time period, such as months.
5. Create a two-input data table that calculates the future value of savings. You can decide which two inputs you would like to use for your data table. For instance, you might want to calculate how long you'll need to save for based on the rate of return on your savings.
6. Format the worksheet using techniques you have learned to present the worksheet content in a visually appealing form. Figure 4–69 is an example of a possible solution, your solution should contain unique numbers and formatting (Figure 4–69).

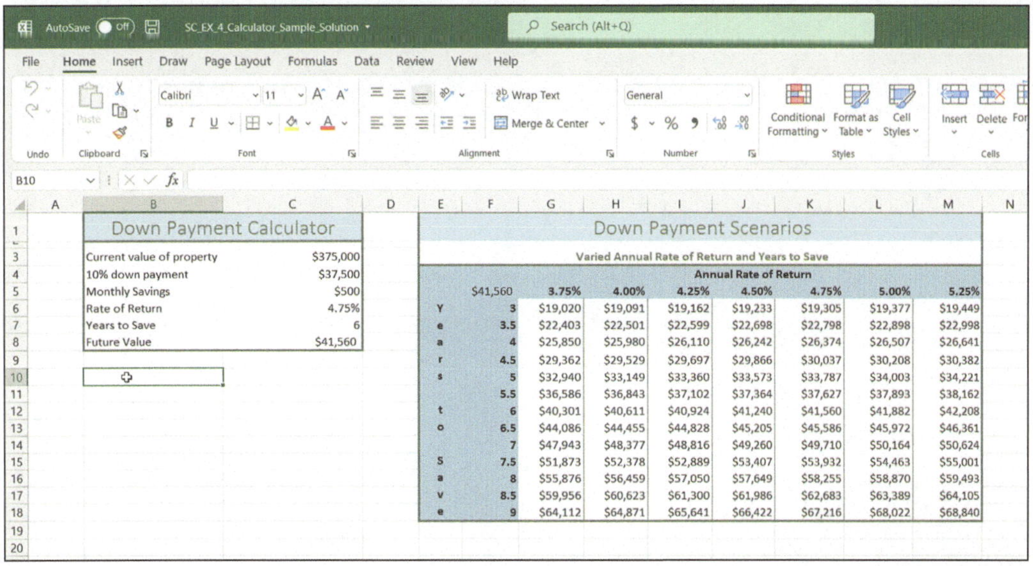

Down Payment Calculator	
Current value of property	$375,000
10% down payment	$37,500
Monthly Savings	$500
Rate of Return	4.75%
Years to Save	6
Future Value	$41,560

$41,560	3.75%	4.00%	4.25%	4.50%	4.75%	5.00%	5.25%
3	$19,020	$19,091	$19,162	$19,233	$19,305	$19,377	$19,449
3.5	$22,403	$22,501	$22,599	$22,698	$22,798	$22,898	$22,998
4	$25,850	$25,980	$26,110	$26,242	$26,374	$26,507	$26,641
4.5	$29,362	$29,529	$29,697	$29,866	$30,037	$30,208	$30,382
5	$32,940	$33,149	$33,360	$33,573	$33,787	$34,003	$34,221
5.5	$36,586	$36,843	$37,102	$37,364	$37,627	$37,893	$38,162
6	$40,301	$40,611	$40,924	$41,240	$41,560	$41,882	$42,208
6.5	$44,086	$44,455	$44,828	$45,205	$45,586	$45,972	$46,361
7	$47,943	$48,377	$48,816	$49,260	$49,710	$50,164	$50,624
7.5	$51,873	$52,378	$52,889	$53,407	$53,932	$54,463	$55,001
8	$55,876	$56,459	$57,050	$57,649	$58,255	$58,870	$59,493
8.5	$59,956	$60,623	$61,300	$61,986	$62,683	$63,389	$64,105
9	$64,112	$64,871	$65,641	$66,422	$67,216	$68,022	$68,840

Figure 4–69

Continued on next page

7. If requested by your instructor, save the file on OneDrive.
8. Submit the workbook as specified by your instructor.
9. **Consider This:** Why did you select the two inputs used in your data table? How useful are they for evaluating down payment savings options?

In the Lab

Design and implement a solution using creative thinking and problem-solving skills.

Determine the Break-Even Point

Problem: You have been hired by Maria Ortega, owner of a small start-up company, to create a data table that analyzes the break-even point for a new product she is developing. She would like you to analyze the break-even point for prices ranging from $5.99 to $19.99 per unit, in $1.00 increments. You can calculate the number of units she must sell to break even (the break-even point) if you know the fixed expenses, the price per unit, and the expense (cost) per unit. The following formula determines the break-even point:

Break-Even Point = Fixed Expenses/(Price per Unit – Expense per Unit)

Assume Fixed Expenses = $7,500; Price per Unit = $14.99; and Expense per Unit = $6.00

Perform the following tasks:

Part 1: Create a one-input data table using the information above. The data table should be able to calculate the number of units Maria would need to sell to break even at each individual price point. Use the concepts and techniques presented in this module to determine the break-even point. Use the Price per Unit as the input cell and the break-even value as the result. After creating the data table, protect the worksheet so that only cells with data can be selected. Submit your assignment in the format specified by your instructor.

Part 2: **Consider This:** You made several decisions while creating the worksheet for this assignment. How did you set up the worksheet? How did you decide how to create the data table? What was the rationale behind each of these decisions?

Working with Multiple Worksheets and Workbooks

Objectives

After completing this module, you will be able to:

- Format a consolidated worksheet
- Fill using a linear series
- Use date, time, and rounding functions
- Apply a custom format code
- Copy a worksheet
- Drill to add data to multiple worksheets at the same time
- Select and deselect sheet combinations
- Enter formulas that use 3-D cell references
- Use the Paste gallery
- Format a 3-D pie chart with an exploded slice and leader lines
- Save individual worksheets as separate workbook files
- View and hide multiple workbooks
- Consolidate data by linking separate workbooks

Introduction

Typically, a business will need to store data unique to various areas, departments, locations, or regions. If you enter each location's data, for example, on a different worksheet in a single workbook, you can use the sheet tabs at the bottom of the Excel window to move from worksheet to worksheet, or location to location. Note, however, that many business applications require data from several worksheets to be summarized on one worksheet. To facilitate this summarization, you can create a cumulative worksheet, entering formulas and functions that reference cells from the other worksheets. The process of combining data on multiple worksheets and displaying the result on another worksheet is called **consolidation**.

Another important concept presented in this module is the use of custom format codes. Custom format codes allow you to specify, in detail, how a cell entry will appear. For example, you can create a custom format code to indicate how positive numbers, negative numbers, zeros, and text are displayed in a cell.

As you learn how to work with multiple worksheets and workbooks, you also will learn about the many Excel formatting features for pie charts, such as exploding slices and adding leader lines.

Project: Consolidated Property Manager Worksheet

The project in the module follows proper design guidelines and uses Excel to create the worksheets shown in Figure 5–1. Blue Village Rental Properties manages four different rental properties. The property manager wants to project consolidated income and expenses for the next three years, along with separate worksheets for each property. Four individual rental property worksheets will each show income and expenses for one property for 2028, along with the projected percentage change, and the resulting income and expenses for 2029, 2030, and 2031. The consolidated worksheet will combine projected 2029 expenses for all four properties. This consolidated information will be highlighted in a 3-D pie chart.

Blue Village Rental Properties
River North Property Manager Worksheet
24-Aug-29

	Projected % Change	2028	Projected 2029	Projected 2030	Projected 2031	Total Projected Change
Income	3.00%	$1,266,208.98	$1,304,195.25	$1,343,321.11	$1,383,620.74	$117,411.76
Expenses						
Advertising	(2.00%)	$4,879.54	$4,781.95	$4,686.31	$4,592.58	($286.96)
Cleaning	2.00%	$12,987.56	$13,247.31	$13,512.26	$13,782.51	$794.95
Commissions	2.50%	$6,887.00	$7,059.18	$7,235.66	$7,416.55	$529.55
Insurance	1.50%	$15,002.37	$15,227.41	$15,455.82	$15,687.66	$685.29
Management	3.50%	$75,750.00	$78,401.25	$81,145.29	$83,985.38	$8,235.38
Repairs	(1.00%)	$40,270.03	$39,867.33	$39,468.66	$39,073.97	($1,196.06)
Taxes	2.20%	$35,020.56	$35,791.01	$36,578.41	$37,383.14	$2,362.58
Utilities	2.00%	$8,992.21	$9,172.05	$9,355.49	$9,542.60	$550.39
		$1,066,419.71	$1,100,647.76	$1,135,883.21	$1,172,156.35	$105,736.64

Blue Village Rental Properties
River West Property Manager Worksheet
24-Aug-29

	Projected % Change	2028	Projected 2029	Projected 2030	Projected 2031	Total Projected Change
Income	3.00%	$1,366,804.73	$1,407,808.87	$1,450,043.14	$1,493,544.43	$126,739.70
Expenses						
Advertising	(2.00%)	$4,340.35	$4,253.54	$4,168.47	$4,085.10	($255.25)
Cleaning	2.00%	$14,934.06	$15,232.74	$15,537.39	$15,848.14	$914.08
Commissions	2.50%	$7,887.00	$8,084.18	$8,286.28	$8,493.44	$606.44
Insurance	1.50%	$14,100.34	$14,311.85	$14,526.53	$14,744.43	$644.09
Management	3.50%	$70,750.00	$73,226.25	$75,789.17	$78,441.79	$7,691.79
Repairs	(1.00%)	$38,745.87	$38,358.41	$37,974.83	$37,595.08	($1,150.79)
Taxes	2.20%	$30,100.15	$30,762.35	$31,439.12	$32,130.78	$2,030.63
Utilities	2.00%	$8,952.09	$9,131.13	$9,313.75	$9,500.03	$547.94
		$1,176,994.87	$1,214,448.42	$1,253,007.60	$1,292,705.64	$115,710.77

data consolidated to one worksheet

Blue Village Rental Properties
Consolidated Property Manager Worksheet
24-Aug-29

	Projected % Change	2028	Projected 2029	Projected 2030	Projected 2031	Total Projected Change
Income	3.00%	$5,178,441.26	$5,333,794.50	$5,493,808.34	$5,658,622.59	$480,181.33
Expenses						
Advertising	(2.00%)	$19,923.57	$19,525.10	$19,134.60	$18,751.91	($1,171.66)
Cleaning	2.00%	$52,945.62	$54,004.53	$55,084.62	$56,186.31	$3,240.69
Commissions	2.50%	$35,528.00	$36,416.20	$37,326.61	$38,259.78	$2,731.78
Insurance	1.50%	$50,336.39	$51,091.44	$51,857.81	$52,635.68	$2,299.29
Management	3.50%	$289,800.00	$299,943.00	$310,441.01	$321,306.45	$31,506.45
Repairs	(1.00%)	$145,398.43	$143,944.45	$142,505.01	$141,079.96	($4,318.47)
Taxes	2.20%	$130,525.79	$133,397.36	$136,332.10	$139,331.41	$8,805.62
Utilities	2.00%	$37,677.70	$38,431.25	$39,199.88	$39,983.88	$2,306.18
		$4,416,305.76	$4,557,041.17	$4,701,926.70	$4,851,087.21	$434,781.45

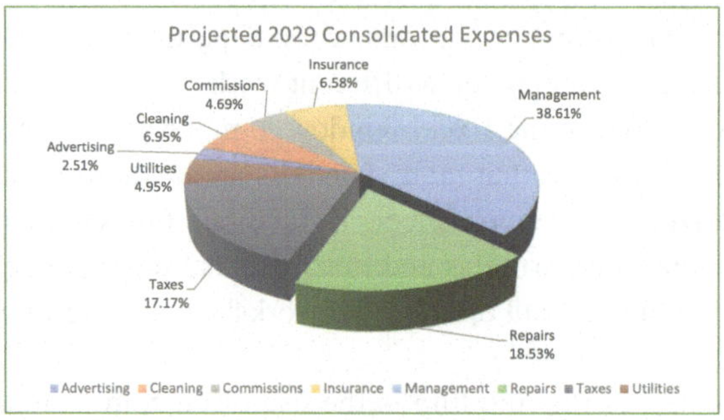

3-D pie chart

Blue Village Rental Properties
River East Property Manager Worksheet
24-Aug-29

	Projected % Change	2028	Projected 2029	Projected 2030	Projected 2031	Total Projected Change
Income	3.00%	$1,342,988.90	$1,383,278.57	$1,424,776.93	$1,467,520.24	$124,531.34
Expenses						
Advertising	(2.00%)	$5,883.23	$5,765.57	$5,650.26	$5,537.25	($345.98)
Cleaning	2.00%	$12,739.54	$12,994.33	$13,254.22	$13,519.30	$779.76
Commissions	2.50%	$9,324.00	$9,557.10	$9,796.03	$10,040.93	$716.93
Insurance	1.50%	$11,930.78	$12,109.74	$12,291.39	$12,475.76	$544.98
Management	3.50%	$72,350.00	$74,882.25	$77,503.13	$80,215.74	$7,865.74
Repairs	(1.00%)	$30,400.20	$30,096.20	$29,795.24	$29,497.29	($902.91)
Taxes	2.20%	$35,102.90	$35,875.16	$36,664.41	$37,471.03	$2,368.13
Utilities	2.00%	$10,540.68	$10,751.49	$10,966.52	$11,185.85	$645.17
		$1,154,717.57	$1,191,246.73	$1,228,855.73	$1,267,577.09	$112,859.52

Blue Village Rental Properties
River South Property Manager Worksheet
24-Aug-29

	Projected % Change	2028	Projected 2029	Projected 2030	Projected 2031	Total Projected Change
Income	3.00%	$1,202,438.65	$1,238,511.81	$1,275,667.16	$1,313,937.17	$111,498.52
Expenses						
Advertising	(2.00%)	$4,820.45	$4,724.04	$4,629.56	$4,536.97	($283.48)
Cleaning	2.00%	$12,284.46	$12,530.15	$12,780.75	$13,036.37	$751.91
Commissions	2.50%	$11,430.00	$11,715.75	$12,008.64	$12,308.86	$878.86
Insurance	1.50%	$9,302.90	$9,442.44	$9,584.08	$9,727.84	$424.94
Management	3.50%	$70,950.00	$73,433.25	$76,003.41	$78,663.53	$7,713.53
Repairs	(1.00%)	$35,982.33	$35,622.51	$35,266.28	$34,913.62	($1,068.71)
Taxes	2.20%	$30,302.18	$30,968.83	$31,650.14	$32,346.44	$2,044.26
Utilities	2.00%	$9,192.72	$9,376.57	$9,564.10	$9,755.38	$562.66
		$1,018,173.61	$1,050,698.27	$1,084,180.20	$1,118,648.16	$100,474.55

Figure 5–1

The requirements document for the Blue Village Rental Properties Consolidated Property Manager Workbook is shown in Table 5–1. It includes the needs, source of data, summary of calculations, and other facts about its development.

Table 5–1: Requirements Document

Worksheet Title	Blue Village Rental Properties
Needs	The needs are as follows: 1. Create a workbook containing four worksheets (one for each of the four properties), one worksheet to consolidate the expenses, and a pie chart. 2. Each worksheet should be identical in structure and allow for display of the current expenses and projected income and expenses for the next three years. 3. The worksheets should print with a common header and footer. 4. The chart should show the 2029 projected consolidated expenses and draw attention to the largest expense after management.
Source of Data	Blue Village Rental Properties will provide the data for each of the four properties. Projection assumptions also will be provided by Blue Village Rental Properties.
Calculations	The following formulas should be included: a. Projected 2029 Cost =2028 Cost * (Projected % Change + 1) b. Projected 2030 Cost =Projected 2029 Cost * (Projected % Change + 1) c. Projected 2031 Cost =Projected 2030 Cost *(Projected % Change + 1) d. Projected Change =Projected 2031 Cost − 2028 Cost e. Use the SUM function to determine totals Note: Use dummy data in the consolidated worksheet to verify the formulas. Round the percentages. Format other numbers with a custom accounting format.
Other Tasks	Investigate a method the company can use to consolidate data from multiple workbooks into a new workbook.

In addition, using a sketch of the worksheet can help you visualize its design. The sketch of the consolidated worksheet (the first of the five worksheets in this workbook) consists of titles, column and row headings, the location of data values, and a general idea of the desired formatting, as shown in Figure 5–2.

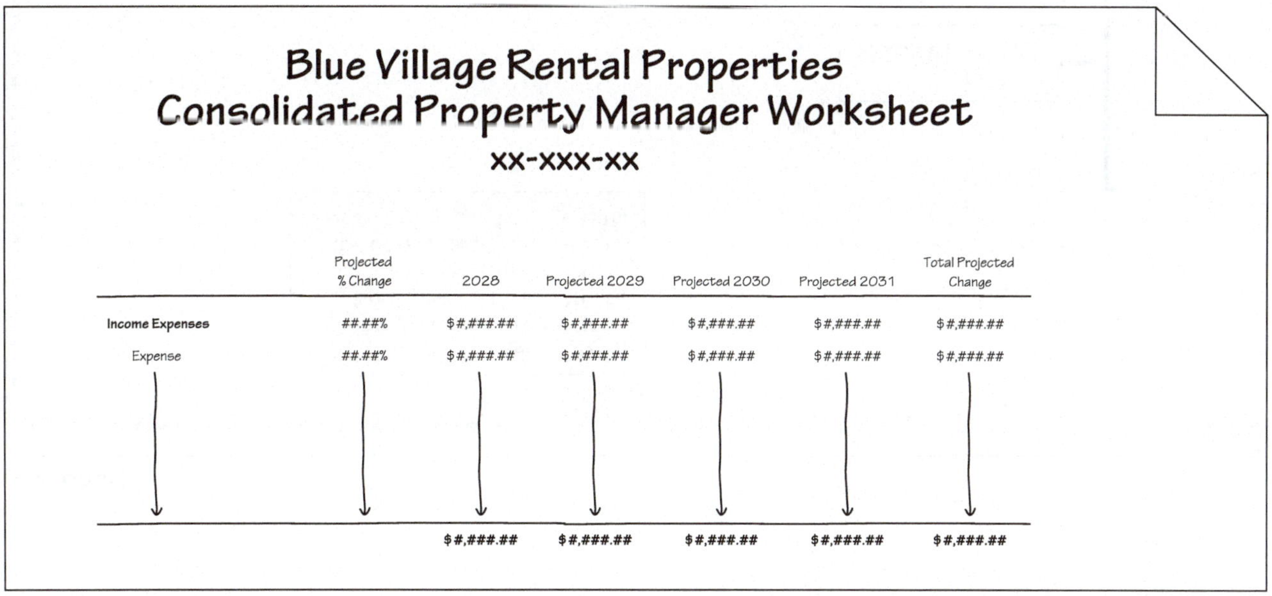

Figure 5–2

BTW
Ribbon and Screen Resolution
Excel may change how the groups and buttons within the groups appear on the ribbon, depending on the screen resolution of your computer. Thus, your ribbon may look different from the ones in this book if you are using a screen resolution other than 1920 × 1080.

Creating the Consolidated Worksheet

The first step in creating the workbook is to create the consolidated property management worksheet shown in Figure 5–1. This worksheet eventually will contain consolidated data with titles, column and row headings, formulas, and formatting. It also represents the format used on each of the individual locations, which will be copied to the four other worksheets. You will create sample data first, to verify formats and formulas.

To Enter the Title and Headings

The following steps enter the Title and Headings in the consolidated worksheet.

1. sam Start Excel and create a blank workbook in the Excel window.
2. Save the workbook on your hard drive, OneDrive, or location that is most appropriate to your situation using **SC_EX_5_Rental** as the file name.
3. Enter **Blue Village Rental Properties** in cell A1.
4. Enter **Consolidated Property Manager Worksheet** in cell A2.
5. Enter **Income** in cell A6, enter **Expenses** in cell A7, enter **Advertising** in cell A8, enter **Cleaning** in cell A9, enter **Commissions** in cell A10, enter **Insurance** in cell A11, enter **Management** in cell A12, enter **Repairs** in cell A13, enter **Taxes** in cell A14, and then enter **Utilities** in cell A15 (Figure 5–3).

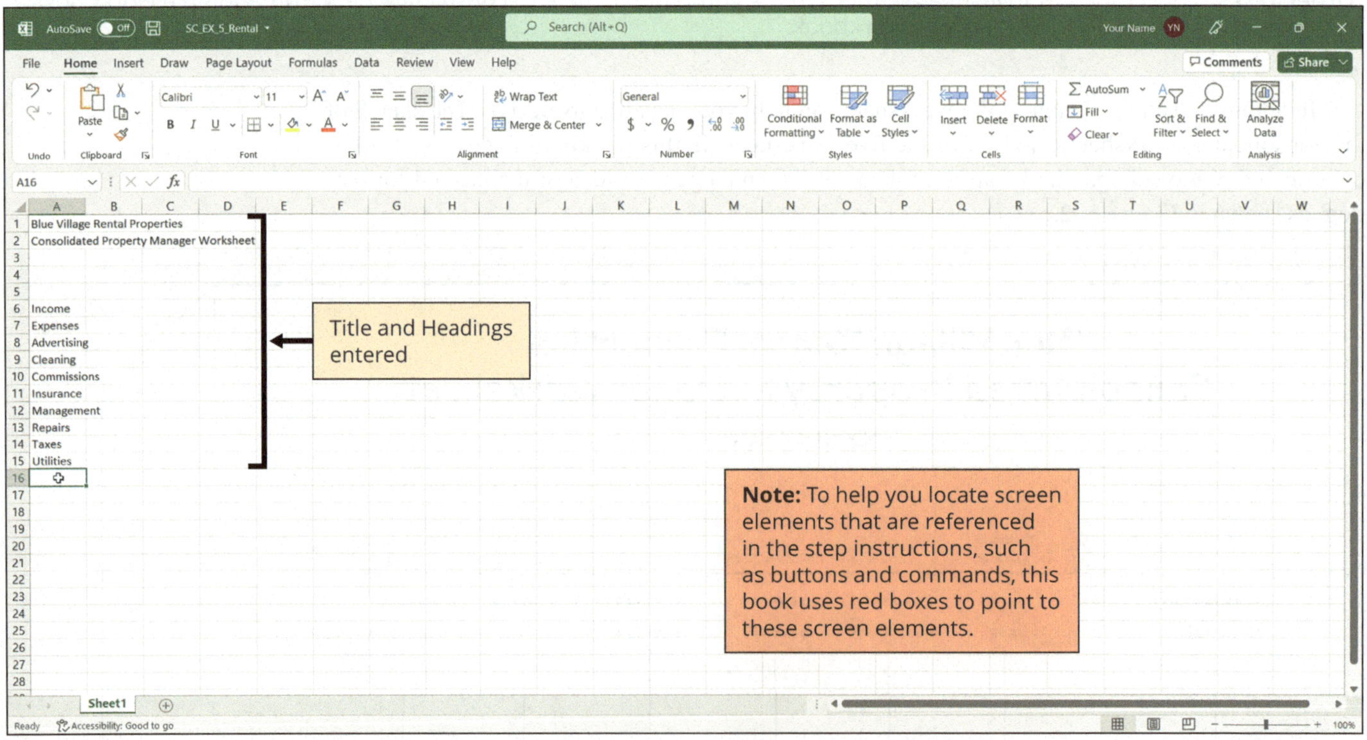

Figure 5–3

To Format the Worksheet

The following steps format the cells in the consolidated worksheet. The row heights and column widths need to be changed to accommodate the data in the worksheet.

1. Drag the bottom boundary of row 5 down until the row height is 37.8 to change the row height.
2. Drag the right boundary of column heading A to the right until the column width is 15.0 to change the column width.
3. Click the heading for column B and then SHIFT+CLICK the heading for column G to select all the columns in the range.
4. Drag the right boundary of column heading G to 14.67 to change the width of multiple columns.
5. Click cell A1 to deselect the columns (Figure 5–4).

BTW

Row Height and Column Width

If you are unable to match the exact row heights and column widths as instructed, it might be because of your display settings. In that case, choose a row height and column width as close as possible to the specified values. If you prefer, use the Row Height and Column Width dialog boxes (Home tab | Cells group) to make these changes.

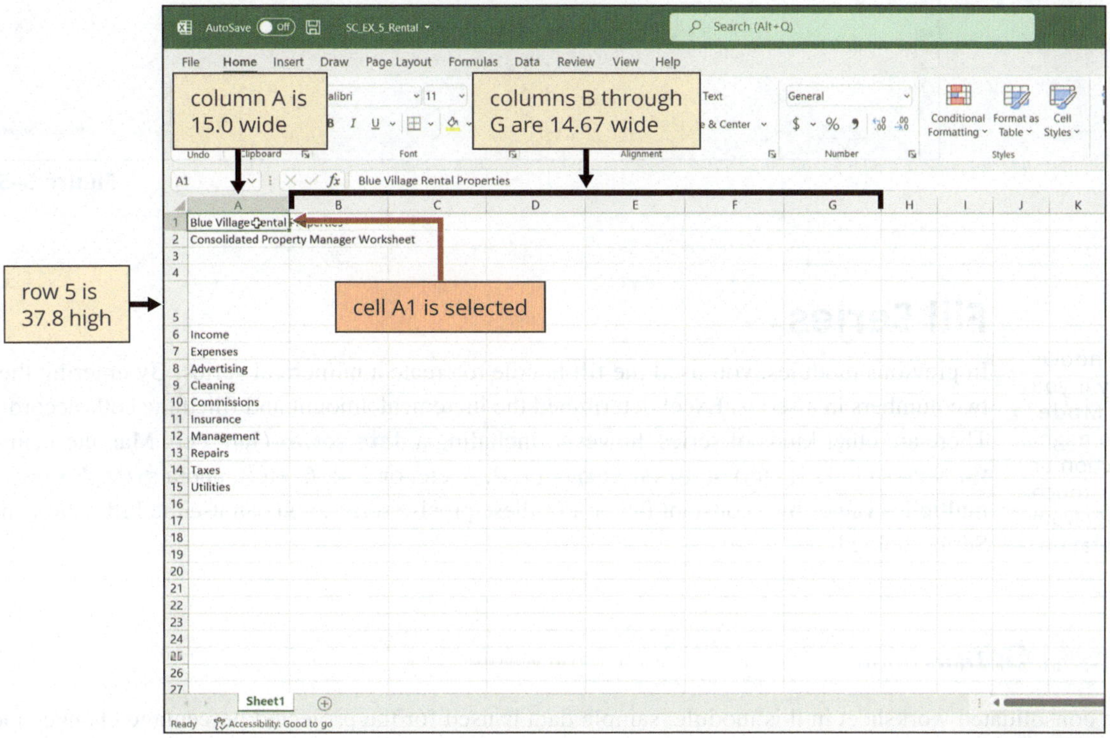

Figure 5–4

To Enter Column Titles

The following steps enter the column titles in row 5. Remember that multi-line titles are created by pressing ALT+ENTER to move to a new line within a cell.

1. Select cell B5. Type **Projected % Change** pressing ALT+ENTER to move to a new line after the word Projected, and then select cell C5 to enter the column heading.
2. Enter the following column titles beginning in cell C5, as shown in Figure 5–5: **2028**, **Projected 2029**, **Projected 2030**, **Projected 2031**, **Total Projected Change**. For the final title, remember to press ALT+ENTER to move to a new line after the word Projected.

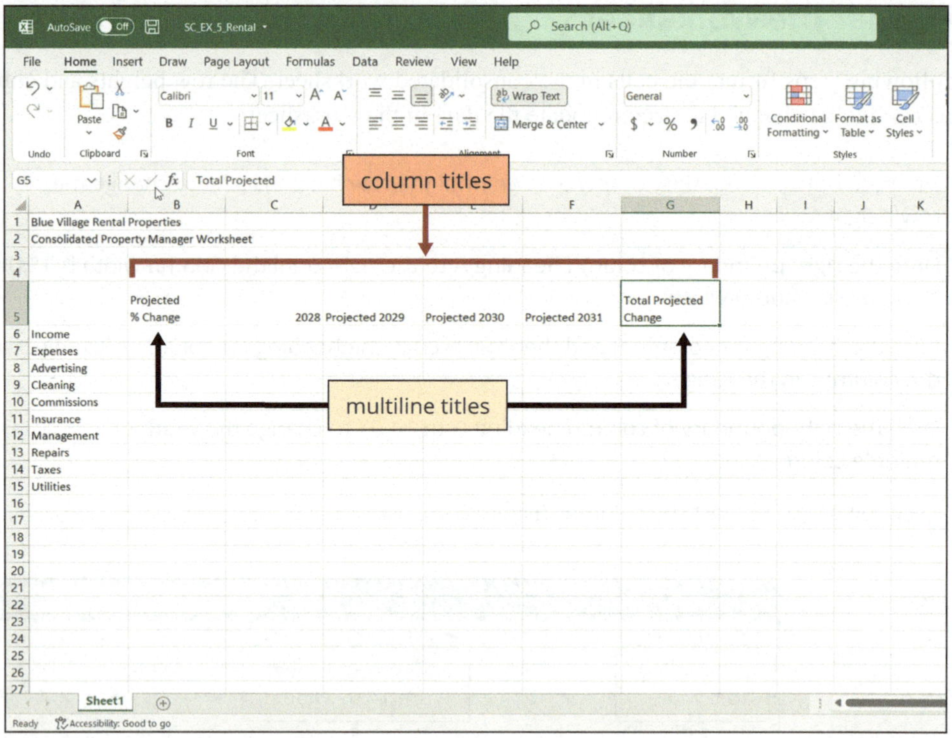

Figure 5–5

BTW

Touch Mode Differences

The Office and Windows interfaces may vary if you are using Touch Mode. For this reason, you might notice that the function or appearance of your touch screen differs slightly from this module's presentation.

Fill Series

In previous modules, you used the fill handle to create a numerical series. By entering the first two numbers in a series, Excel determined the increment amount and filled the cells accordingly. There are other kinds of series, however, including a **date series** (Jan, Feb, Mar, etc.), an **auto fill series** (1, 1, 1, etc.), a **linear series** (1, 2, 3, etc. or 2, 4, 6, etc.), and a **growth series** that multiplies values by a constant factor. For these precise series, you can use the Fill button and the Series dialog box.

To Create Linear Series

While creating the consolidated worksheet in this module, sample data is used for the projected percentage change, and the 2028 costs. **Why?** Entering sample data creates placeholder content and assists in the layout of the consolidated worksheet.

You will use the fill handle to create a series of integers in column B. Normally you would enter the first two numbers in a series so that Excel can determine the increment amount; however, if your series is incremented by 1, you do not have to enter two numbers. You can CTRL+drag the fill handle to increment by 1 across cells.

If you want to increment by a different value, you can use the Series dialog box. In the Series dialog box, you can choose to increment by any step value, including positive and negative decimals, again by entering only a single value. The following steps create sample data in the consolidated worksheet.

1

- Select cell B6.
- Type **2%** and then click the Enter button in the formula bar to enter the first value in the series.
- Select the range B6:B15 and then click the Fill button (Home tab | Editing group) to display the Fill gallery (Figure 5–6).

Q&A How are the directional commands in the Fill gallery used?

Those commands are alternatives to using the fill handle. Select an empty cell or cells adjacent to the cell that contains the data that you want to use. You then can fill the selection using the Fill button and the appropriate directional command.

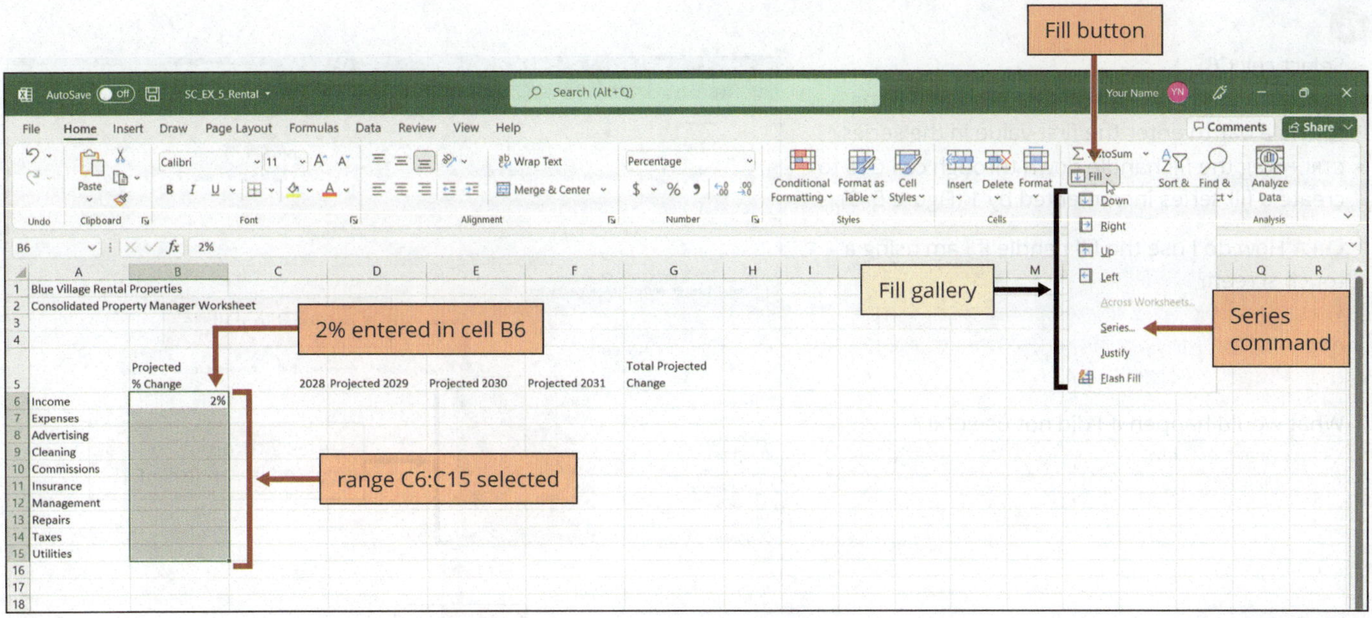

Figure 5–6

2

- Click Series to display the Series dialog box.
- Type **.024** in the Step value box to increment by a decimal number (Figure 5–7).

Q&A Why am I using an increment of .024?
You are generating random placeholder numbers. You can use any increment step; however, since this column will eventually be percentages, a decimal may be appropriate.

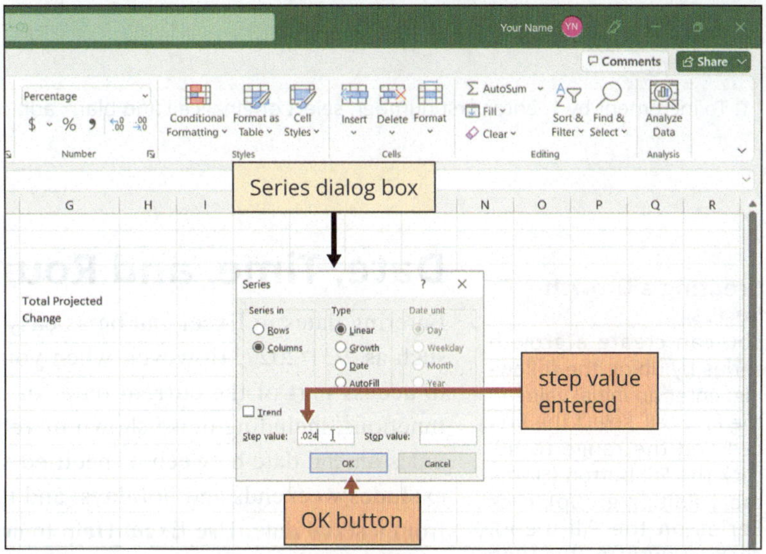

Figure 5–7

3

- Click OK (Series dialog box) to fill the series.
- Click the Increase Decimal button (Home tab | Number group) twice to display two decimal places (Figure 5–8).

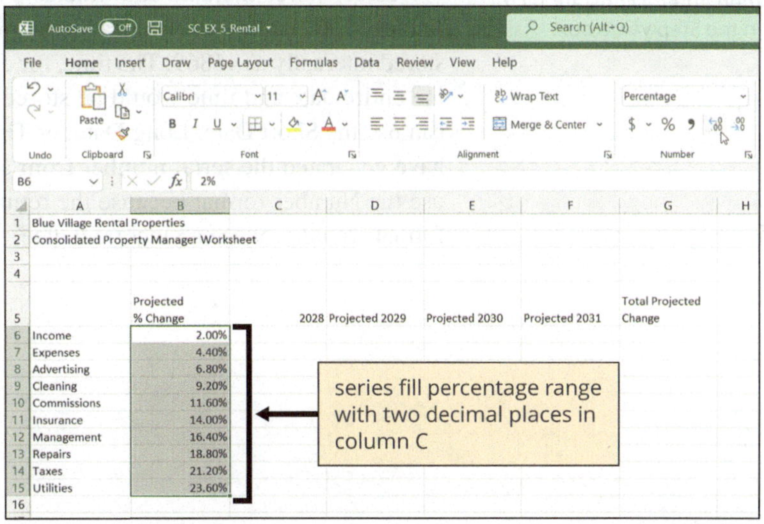

Figure 5–8

4

- Select cell C6.
- Type **1** and then click the Enter button in the formula bar to enter the first value in the series.
- CTRL+drag the fill handle down through cell C15 to create a fill series incremented by 1 (Figure 5–9).

Q&A How do I use the fill handle if I am using a touch screen?

Press and hold the selected cell to display the mini toolbar, tap AutoFill on the mini toolbar, and then drag the AutoFill icon.

What would happen if I did not use CTRL?

If you dragged without CTRL, the cells would be filled with the number, 1.

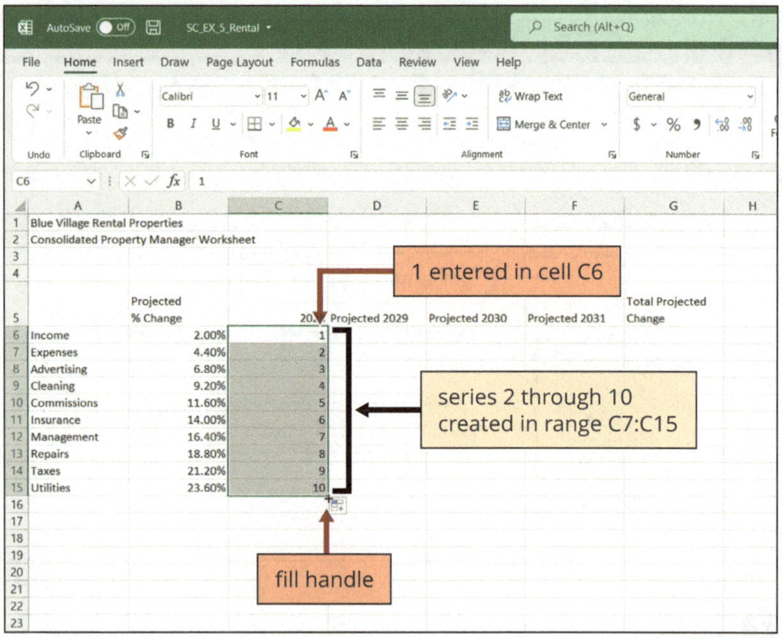

Figure 5–9

Other Ways

1. To increment by 1, enter first number; select original cell and blank adjacent cell, drag fill handle through range

BTW

Creating a Growth Series

You can create a growth series by doing the following: enter an initial value in the first cell, select the first cell and the range to fill, click the Fill button (Home tab | Editing group), click Series on the Fill menu, click Growth in the Type area (Series dialog box), and then enter a constant factor in the Step value box.

Date, Time, and Round Functions

Entering dates in Excel can be as easy as typing the parts of the date separated by slashes, such as 7/31/2027. However, when you want a date that automatically updates, or you want to access part of the current date for a variety of reasons, Excel has many date and time functions, including those shown in Table 5–2. For example, the **WORKDAY function** provides an end date between a specified start date and a specified number of workdays, which excludes weekends and holidays, and the **WEEKDAY function** returns the day of the week from a serial date. Use Excel Help to search for more information about these and other date and time functions.

Excel stores the date and time as a **serial number** representing the number of days since January 1900, followed by a fractional portion of a 24-hour day. For example, July 31, 2025, is stored internally as 45869. The time, for example 3:00 p.m., is stored internally as .625. Therefore the entire date and time would be stored as 45869.625. When you format a serial number, you can use the Short Date, Long Date, or Time formats (Format Cells dialog box). If, however, you have generated the serial number from a function such as MONTH, DAY, or YEAR, you must use the Number format because the return value is an integer; formatting it with a date or time format would produce an incorrect date.

Table 5–2: Functions Related to Date and Time

Category	Function	Definition	Syntax	Example	Sample Result
Date Functions	DATE	Returns the formatted date based on the month, day, and year	DATE(year, month, day)	=DATE(126,7,31)	7/31/2025
	DATEVALUE	Converts a date that is stored as text to a serial number for calculations	DATEVALUE(date_text)	=DATEVALUE ("7/31/2027")	46599
	DAY	Returns the day value from a serial date	DAY(serial_number)	=DAY(45869)	31
	MONTH	Returns the month value from a serial date	MONTH(serial_number)	=MONTH(45869)	7
	TODAY	Returns the current date	TODAY()	=TODAY()	7/31/2025
	WEEKDAY	Returns the day of the week from a serial date, with a second option for starting the week on Sunday (1) or Monday (2)	WEEKDAY(serial_number,return_type)	=WEEKDAY(45869,1)	5 (Thursday)
	YEAR	Returns the year value from a serial date	YEAR(serial_number)	=YEAR(45869)	2025
	WORKDAY	Returns the end date after a start date and specified number of workdays, which excludes weekends and holidays. The results of this function should be formatted as a date.	WORKDAY(start_date,days,holidays)	=WORKDAY (A1,100,A2:A4) (start date is formatted as a date in cell A1, and dates for holidays are formatted as dates in the range A2:A4)	12/23/2025
Time Functions	HOUR	Returns the hour value from a serial date	HOUR(serial_number)	=HOUR(0.33605324)	8
	MINUTE	Returns the minute value from a serial date	MINUTES(serial_number)	=MINUTE(0.33605324)	3
	SECOND	Returns the second value from a serial date	SECOND(serial_number)	=SECOND(0.33605324)	55
	TIME	Returns the formatted date based on the hour, minute, and second	TIME(hour, minute, second)	=TIME(8,3,55)	8:03 AM
	TIMEVALUE	Converts a time that is stored as text to a serial number for calculations	TIMEVALUE(time_text)	=TIMEVALUE("8:03:55 am")	0.336053241
Other Functions	NOW	Returns both date and time	NOW()	=NOW()	7/31/2025 8:03

If you are performing math with dates and times, your answer will result in a serial number. For example, if you wanted to calculate elapsed time from 9:00 a.m. to 3:30 p.m., subtraction would result in a serial number, 0.2708. You then would need to format the number with the TIME format (h:mm), which would result in 6:30 or 6 hours and 30 minutes (Figure 5–10).

BTW

Updating the TODAY function

If the TODAY function does not update the date when you expect it to, you might need to change the settings that control when the worksheet recalculates. On the File tab, click Options, and then in the Formulas category under Calculation options, make sure that Automatic is selected.

BTW
Copying
To copy the contents of a cell to the cell directly below it, click in the target cell and press CTRL+D.

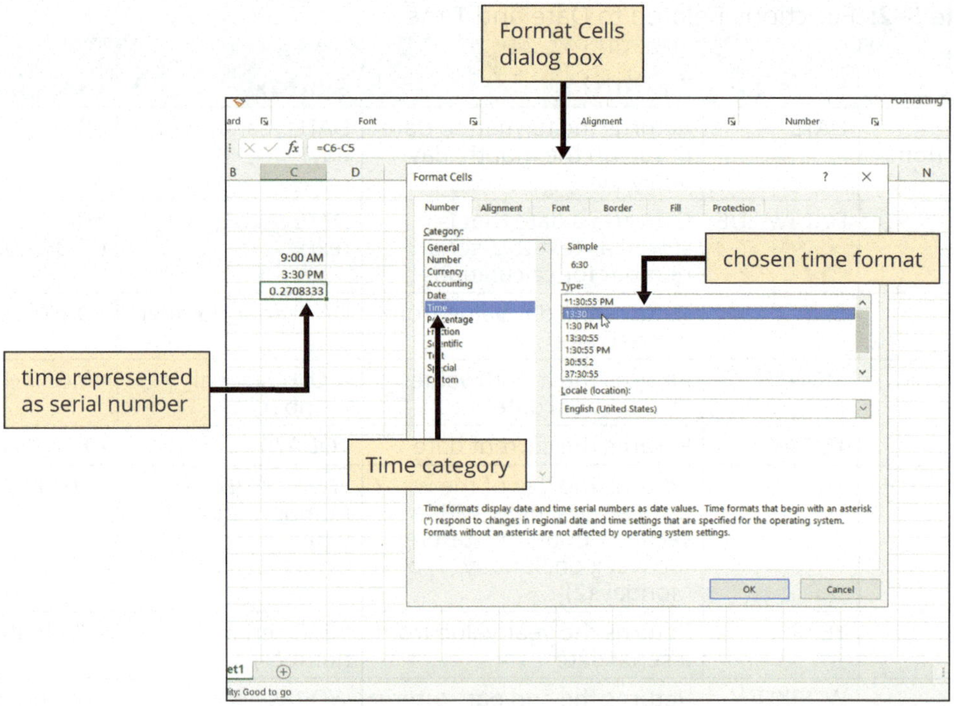

Figure 5–10

Another set of useful functions have to do with rounding. Rounding numbers, especially for dollars and cents, prevents formulas from creating awkward answers with long decimal notations. Table 5–3 displays some of the more popular round functions.

Table 5–3: Rounding Functions

Function	Definition	Syntax	Example	Sample Result
ROUND	Rounds a number to a specified number of decimal places	ROUND(number,num_digits)	=ROUND(833.77,0)	834
ROUNDDOWN	Rounds a number down, toward zero	ROUNDDOWN(number, num_digits)	=ROUNDDOWN(833.77,0)	833
ROUNDUP	Rounds a number up, away from zero	ROUNDUP(number,num_digits)	=ROUNDUP(833.77,0)	834
MROUND	Returns a number rounded to the desired multiple	MROUND(number,multiple)	=MROUND(833.77,5)	835

Consider This

When should you use the ROUND function?

When you multiply or divide decimal numbers, the answer may contain more decimal places than the format allows. If this happens, you run the risk of the column totals being off by a penny or so; resulting values of calculations could include fractions of a penny beyond the two decimal places that currency formats usually display.

To Use the TODAY Function

Recall that you have used the NOW function to access the system date and time. You also can use the **TODAY function**, which returns only the date. Both functions are designed to update each time the worksheet is opened. The function takes no arguments but accesses the internal clock on your computer and displays the current date. As with the NOW function, you can format the date in a variety of styles.

The TODAY function also is useful for calculating intervals. For example, if you want to calculate an age, you can subtract the birth year from the TODAY function to find that person's age as of this year's birthday. The following steps use the TODAY function to enter the system date into the worksheet. **Why?** The TODAY function will update each time the worksheet is opened.

1

- Select cell D3, type **=today()**, and then click the Enter button to enter the system date (Figure 5–11).

Q&A Should I use lowercase or uppercase on functions?

Either one will work. To delineate functions in the text passages of this book, they are displayed in all caps.

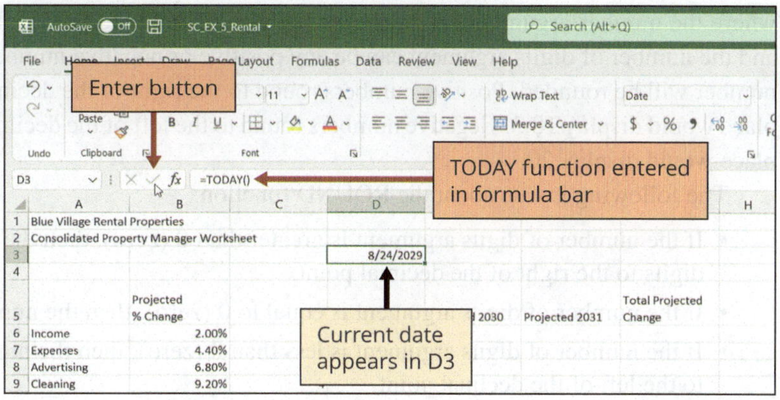

Figure 5–11

2

- Right-click cell D3 and then click Format Cells on the shortcut menu.
- If necessary, click the Number tab and then click Date in the Category list (Format Cells dialog box).
- Click the first instance of 14-Mar-12 in the Type list to format the date (Figure 5–12).

Q&A Why change the format of the date?

The date might be displayed as a series of number signs if the date, as initially formatted by Excel, does not fit in the width of the cell.

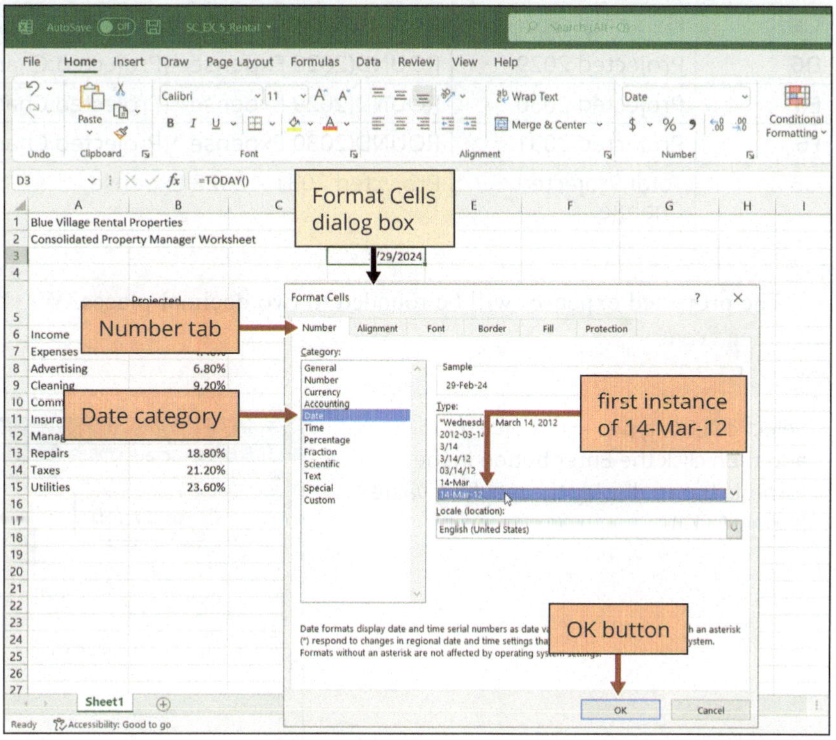

Figure 5–12

3

- Click OK (Format Cells dialog box) to close the dialog box.
- Click an empty cell to deselect the previous cell.

Other Ways

1. Select cell, click Date & Time button (Formulas tab | Function Library group), click TODAY, click OK (Function Arguments dialog box)

To Enter Formulas Using the ROUND Function

The **ROUND function** in Excel is used to round numbers to a specified number of decimal places. The general form of the ROUND function is

=ROUND(number, number of digits)

where the number argument can be a number, a cell reference that contains a number, or a formula that results in a number; and the number of digits argument can be any positive or negative number used to determine the number of places to which the number will be rounded. Positive numbers round to the right of the decimal point; for example, 18.257 formatted for 1 decimal place would display 18.3. Negative numbers round to the left of the decimal point; for example, 18.257 formatted for –1 decimal place would display 20.

The following is true about the ROUND function:

- If the number of digits argument is greater than 0 (zero), then the number is rounded to the specified number of digits to the right of the decimal point.
- If the number of digits argument is equal to 0 (zero), then the number is rounded to the nearest integer.
- If the number of digits argument is less than 0 (zero), then the number is rounded to the specified number of digits to the left of the decimal point.

The following steps enter the formulas for the first row, Income in cells D6, E6, F6, and G6. (Refer to Table 5–4.)

Table 5–4: Formulas for cells D6, E6, F6, and G6

Cell	Description	Formula	Entry
D6	Projected 2029	ROUND(2028 Expense *(Projected Change % + 1), 2)	=ROUND(C6*($B6+1),2)
E6	Projected 2030	ROUND(2029 Expense *(Projected Change % + 1), 2)	=ROUND(D6*($B6+1),2)
F6	Projected 2031	ROUND(2030 Expense *(Projected Change % + 1), 2)	=ROUND(E6*($B6+1),2)
G6	Total Projected Change	Projected 2031 – 2028 Expense	=F6-C6

The projected expenses will be rounded to two decimal places. **Why?** The projected expenses are represented using dollars and cents.

1

- Select cell D6, type **=round(c6*($b6+1),2)** and then click the Enter button in the formula bar to display the resulting value (Figure 5–13).

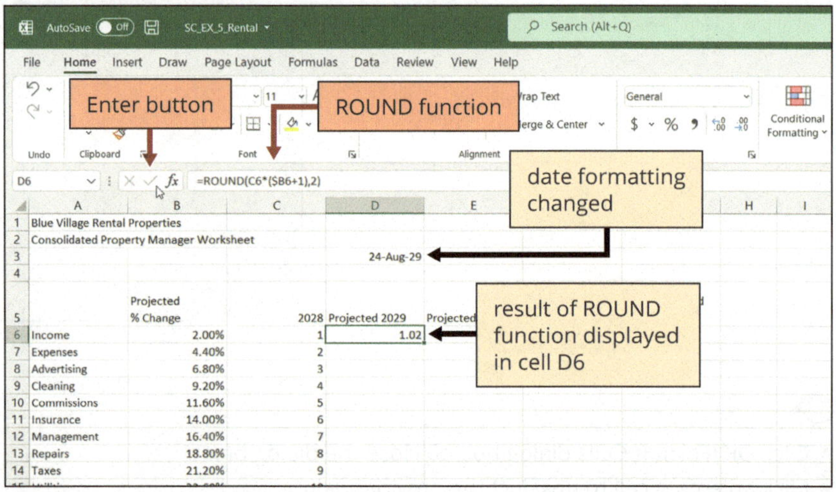

Figure 5–13

2

- Drag the fill handle on cell D6 across to copy the formula to cells E6:F6 (Figure 5–14).

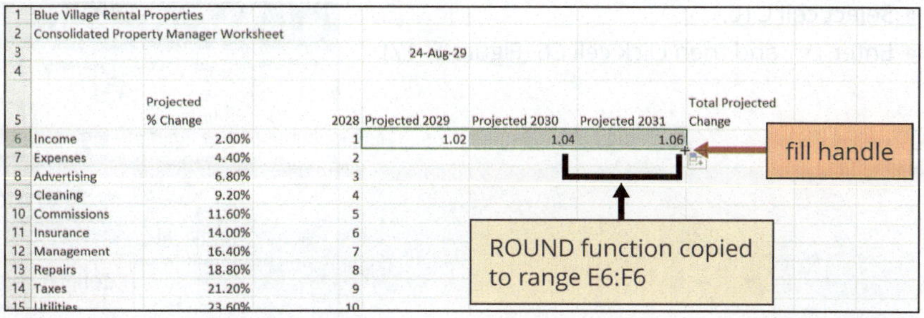

Figure 5–14

3

- Drag the fill handle on cell D6:F6 down to copy the formula to cells D7:F15 (Figure 5–15).

Q&A Do I need to use two sets of parentheses in the function?

Yes; the outer set of parentheses are for the function, and the inner set is to force Excel to add the two values before multiplying to calculate the projection. Recall that Excel follows the order of operations and performs multiplication and division before addition and subtraction, unless you use parentheses.

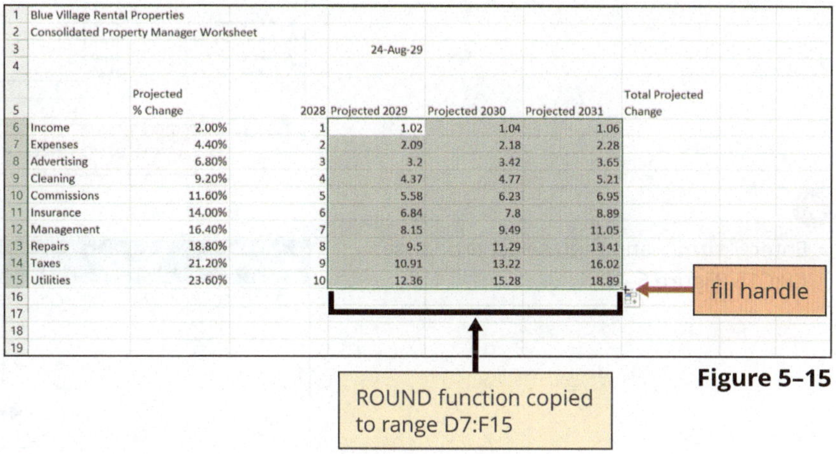

Figure 5–15

4

- Select cell G6.
- Enter **=f6-c6** and then click the Enter button in the formula bar to display the resulting value.
- Drag the fill handle on cell G6 down to copy the formula to cells G7:G15 (Figure 5–16).

5

- Select cells B7:G7 and delete their values.

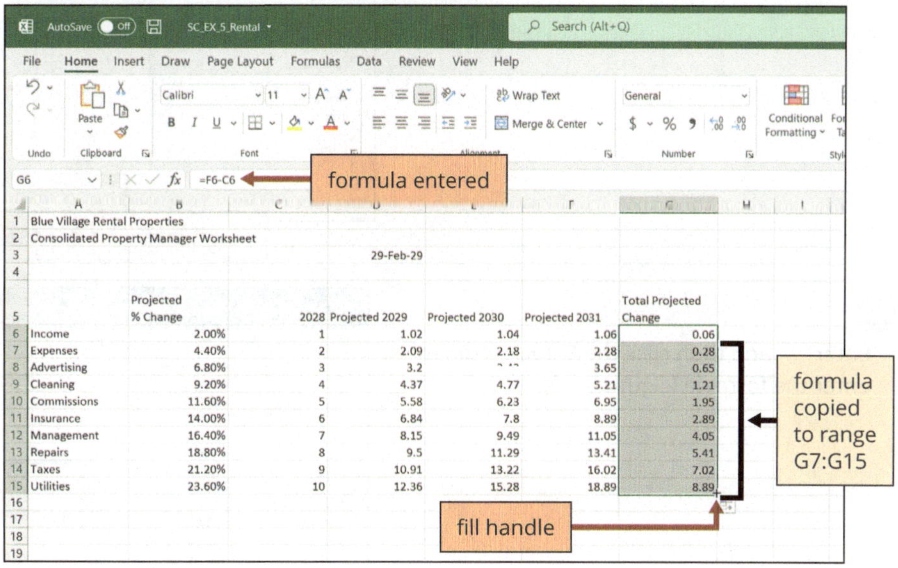

Figure 5–16

Q&A Why did we delete the values in cells B7:G7?

Recall from the sketch of the worksheet (Figure 5–2) that row 7 only contains the category name "Expenses" for each of the expenses listed underneath, in rows 8–15. There are no values to be calculated in row 7. It is easier to fill formulas and series including row 7, instead of omitting row 7 to begin with. Since the series we created in columns B and C are placeholder values, deleting one row of the series does not impact the overall worksheet.

6

- Select cell C16.
- Enter **=** and then click cell C6 (Figure 5–17).

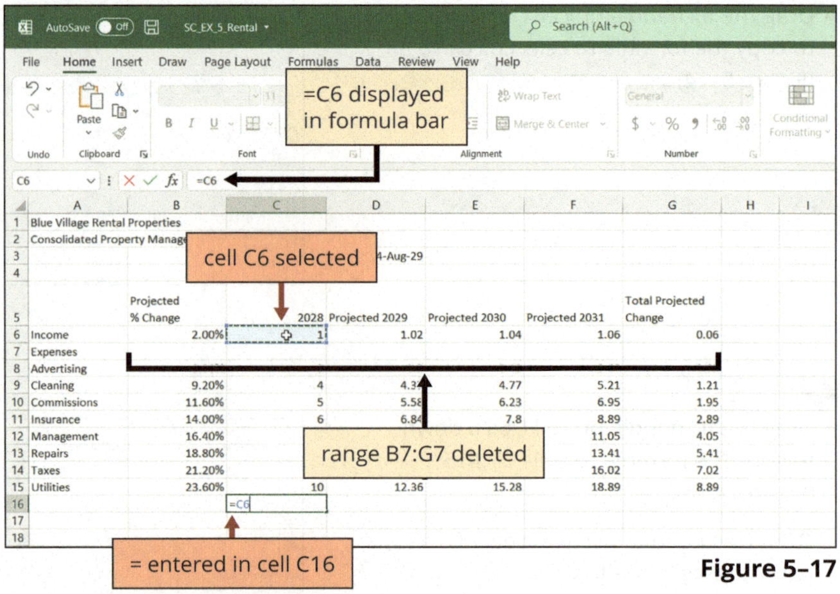

Figure 5–17

7

- Enter **-sum(** and then select the range C8:C15 (Figure 5–18).

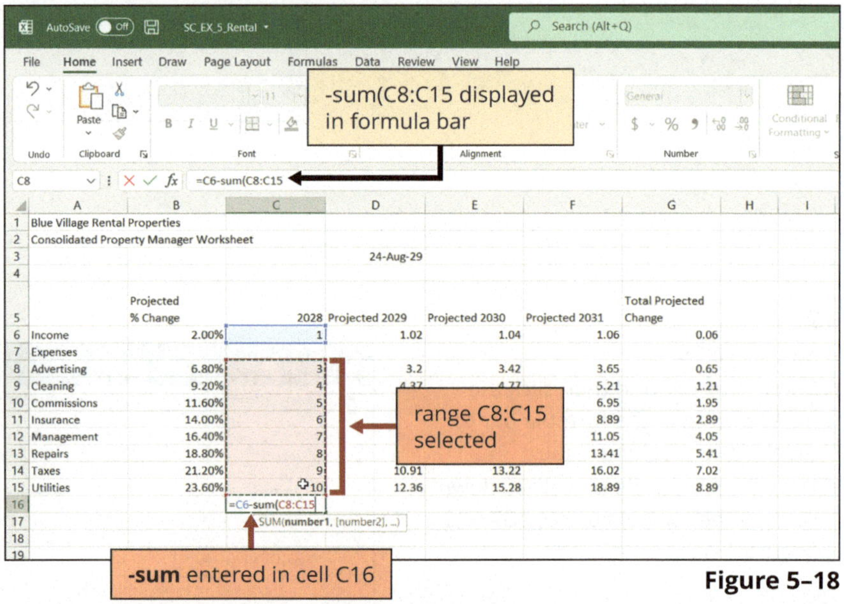

Figure 5–18

8

- Enter **)** and then click the Enter button to enter the formula (Figure 5–19).

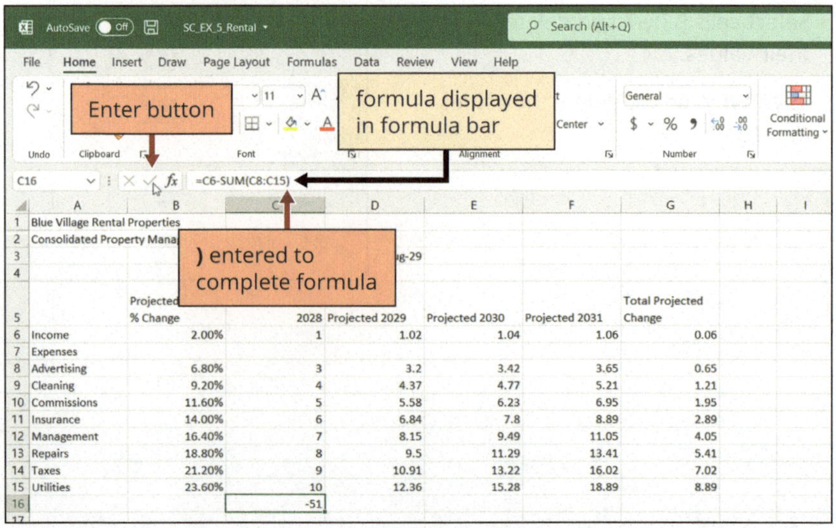

Figure 5–19

9

- Drag the fill handle on cell C16 across to copy the formula to cells D16:G16 (Figure 5–20).

10

- Save the workbook.

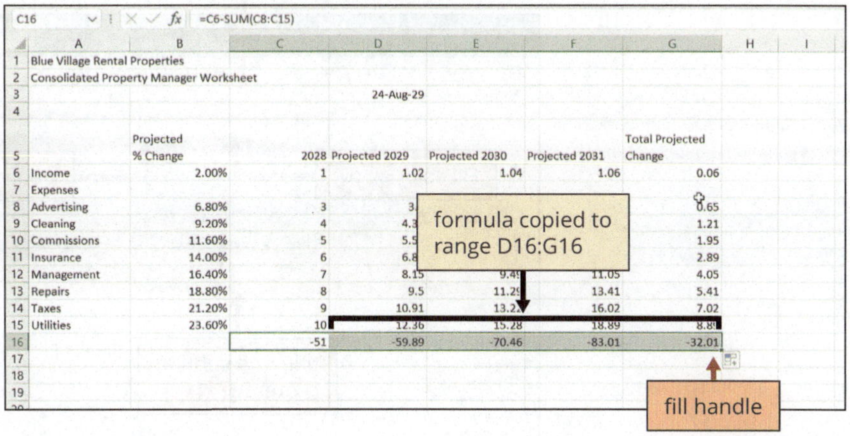

Figure 5–20

Other Ways

1. Select cell, click Math & Trig button (Formulas tab | Function Library group), click ROUND, enter formula in Number box (Formula Arguments dialog box), enter number of digits in Num_digits box, click OK

Break Point: If you want to take a break, this is a good place to do so. You can exit Excel now. To resume later, start Excel, open the file called SC_EX_5_Rental, and continue following the steps from this location forward.

To Format the Title, Subtitle, and Date

The following steps format the worksheet title, subtitle and date. You will change the font size, center both titles across columns A through G, and change the background color.

1. Select the range A1:A2, click the Cell Styles button (Home tab | Styles group), and then click the Title style to apply the style to the range.
2. Select cell A1 and change the font size to 22.
3. Select the range A1:G1 and then click the 'Merge & Center' button (Home tab | Alignment group) to merge and center the text in the selected range.
4. Select cell A2 and change the font size to 14.
5. Select the range A2:G2 and then click the 'Merge & Center' button (Home tab | Alignment group) to merge and center the text in the selected range.
6. Select cell D3, click the Cell Styles button (Home tab | Styles group), and then click the Heading 4 style to apply the style to the cell.
7. Click the Center button (Home tab | Alignment group) to center the text in cell D3.
8. Select the range A1:G3, click the Fill Color arrow (Home tab | Font group), and then click 'Gold, Accent 4, Lighter 60%' in the Fill Color gallery to change the fill color.
9. Click an empty cell to deselect the range (Figure 5–21).

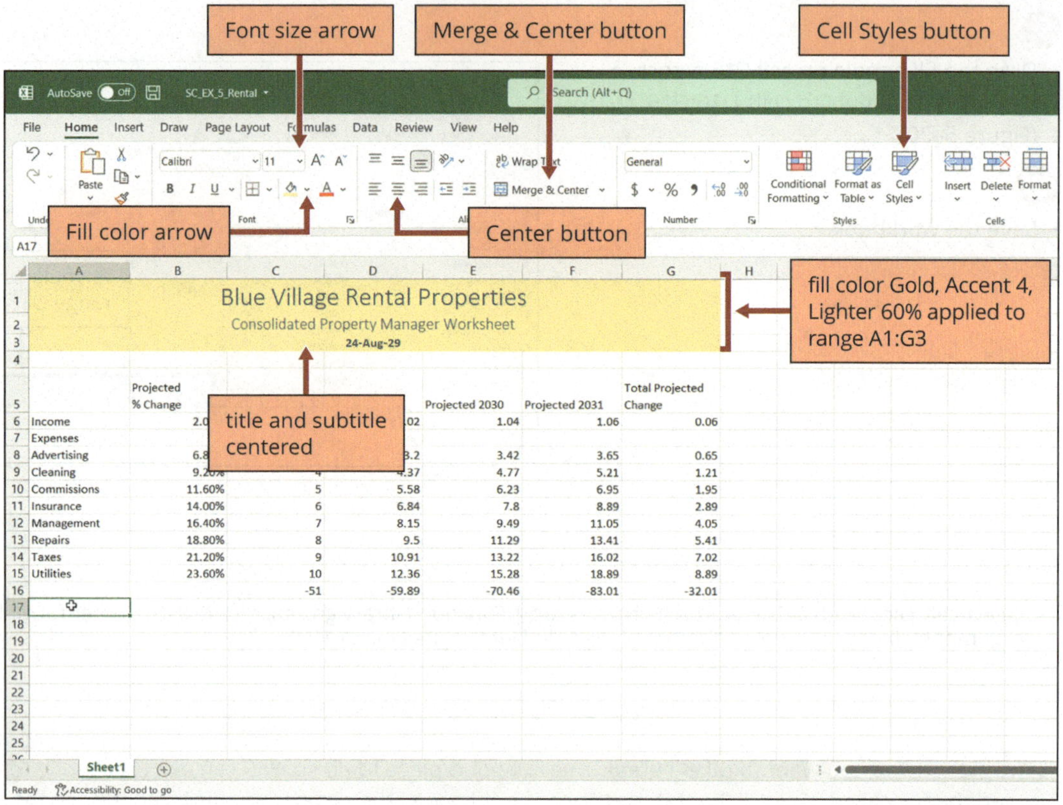

Figure 5–21

To Format the Column and Row Titles and Total Row

The following steps center and underline the column titles, bold and indent the row titles, and create borders on the total row.

1. Select the range B5:G5, and then click the Center button (Home tab | Alignment group) to center the text in the cells.
2. CTRL+click cell A5 to add it to the selected range, and then use the Cell Styles button (Home tab | Styles group) to apply the Heading 3 cell style.
3. Select the range A6:A7 and click the Bold button (Home tab | Font group) to bold the text in the cells.
4. Select the range A8:A15 and click the Increase indent button (Home tab | Alignment group) to indent the text in the cells.
5. Select the range A16:G16 and then assign the Total cell style to the range.
6. Click an empty cell to deselect the range (Figure 5–22).

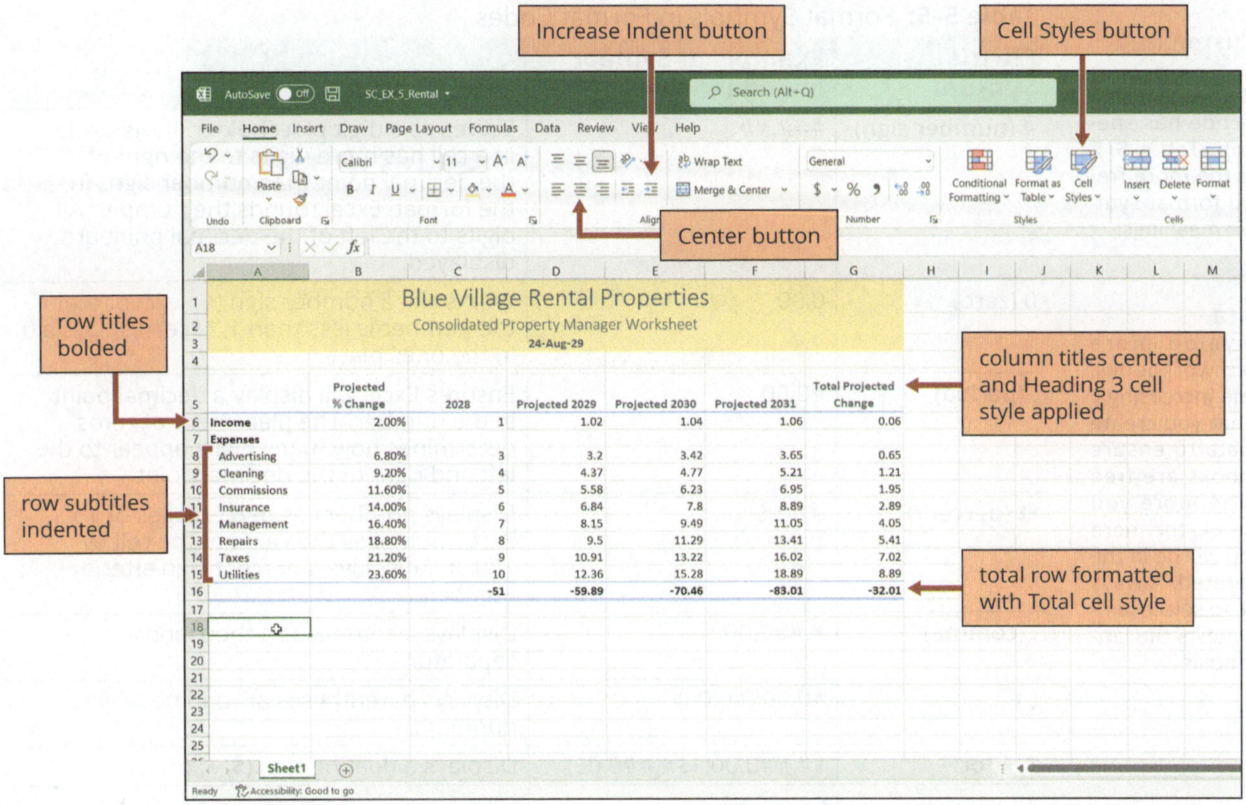

Figure 5–22

Format Codes

Excel assigns an internal **format code** to every format style listed in the Format Cells dialog box. These format codes do not print, but act as a template, with placeholders to define how you want to apply unique formatting.

Before you create custom format codes or modify existing codes, you should understand their makeup. A format code can have up to four sections: the desired format for positive numbers, the desired format for negative numbers, how zeros should be treated, and any desired format for text. Each section is separated by a semicolon. For example, the following format code would produce results similar to the sample values shown.

$* #,##0.00; [Magenta]$(#,##0.00); * -??; "The answer is "@

$ 15.75 | $(1,238.99) | – | The answer is yes

A format code need not have all four sections. For most applications, a format code will have a positive section and possibly a negative section. If you omit the zero formatting section, zero values will use the positive number formatting.

Table 5–5 provides a list of some of the format code symbols and how they can be combined into a new format code. To view the entire list of format codes that are provided with Excel, select Custom in the Category list (Format Cells dialog box).

BTW

Selecting a Range of Cells

You can select any range of cells with entries surrounded by blank cells by clicking a cell in the range and pressing CTRL+SHIFT+* (asterisk).

BTW

Summing a Row or Column

You can reference an entire column or an entire row in a function argument by listing only the column or only the row. For example, =sum(a:a) sums the values in all the cells in column A, and =sum(1:1) sums the values in all the cells in row 1. You can verify this by entering **=sum(a:a)** in cell C1 of a blank worksheet and then begin entering numbers in a few of the cells in column A. Excel will respond by showing the sum of the numbers in cell C1. The SUM function will return a circular reference if the cell it is entered in is included in the function. For instance, **=sum(a1:a4)** will return a circular reference if placed in any cell from A1:A4.

BTW
Creating Customized Formats
Each format symbol within the format code has special meaning. Table 5-2 summarizes the more frequently used format symbols and their meanings.

BTW
Sample Data
As you develop more sophisticated workbooks, it will become increasingly important that you create good test data to ensure your workbooks are free of errors. The more you test a workbook, the more confident you will be in the results generated. Always take the time to select sample data that tests the limits of the formulas.

Table 5-5: Format Symbols in Format Codes

Format Symbol	Example of Symbol in Code	Description
# (number sign)	###.##	Serves as a digit placeholder. If the value in a cell has more digits to the right of the decimal point than number signs in the format, Excel rounds the number. All digits to the left of the decimal point are displayed.
0 (zero)	0.00	Works like a number sign (#), except that if the number is less than 1, Excel displays a 0 in the ones place.
. (period)	#0.00	Ensures Excel will display a decimal point in the number. The placement of zeros determines how many digits appear to the left and right of the decimal point.
% (percent)	0.00%	Displays numbers as percentages of 100. Excel multiplies the value of the cell by 100 and displays a percent sign after the number.
, (comma)	#,##0.00	Displays a comma as a thousands separator.
( )	#0.00;(#0.00)	Displays parentheses around negative numbers.
$, +, or –	$#,##0.00; ($#,##0.00)	Displays a floating sign ($, +, or –).
* (asterisk)	$*##0.00	Displays a fixed sign ($, +, or –) to the left, followed by spaces until the first significant digit.
[color]	#.##;[Red]#.##	Displays the characters in the cell in the designated color. In the example, positive numbers appear in the default color, and negative numbers appear in red.
" " (quotation marks)	$0.00 "Surplus"; $-0.00 "Shortage"	Displays text along with numbers entered in a cell.
_ (underscore)	#,##0.00_)	Adds a space. When followed by a parenthesis, positive numbers will align correctly with parenthetical negative numbers.

To Create a Custom Format Code

The following steps create and assign custom format codes to apply to dollar amounts and percentages. **Why?** A workbook may call for a visual presentation of data that cannot be accomplished with the existing Excel format codes. The first format code you set will display dollar amounts with two decimal places to the right of the decimal point and also negative dollar amounts in blue with parentheses. The second format code you set will display percentages with two decimal places to the right of the decimal point and also negative percentages in blue with parentheses.

1

- CTRL+drag to select the ranges C6:G6 and C8:G16. Right-click any of the selected ranges to display the shortcut menu, and then click Format Cells to display the Format Cells dialog box.
- If necessary, click the Number tab (Format Cells dialog box) and then click Custom in the Category list.
- Delete the text in the Type box (Format Cells dialog box), and then type **$#,##0.00;[Blue]($#,##0.00)** to enter a custom format code (Figure 5-23).

Q&A What does the custom format mean?
The custom format has been modified to show dollar amounts with two decimal places and to show negative dollar amounts with two decimal places with parentheses. In the Sample area, Excel displays a sample of the custom format assigned to the first number in the selected ranges.

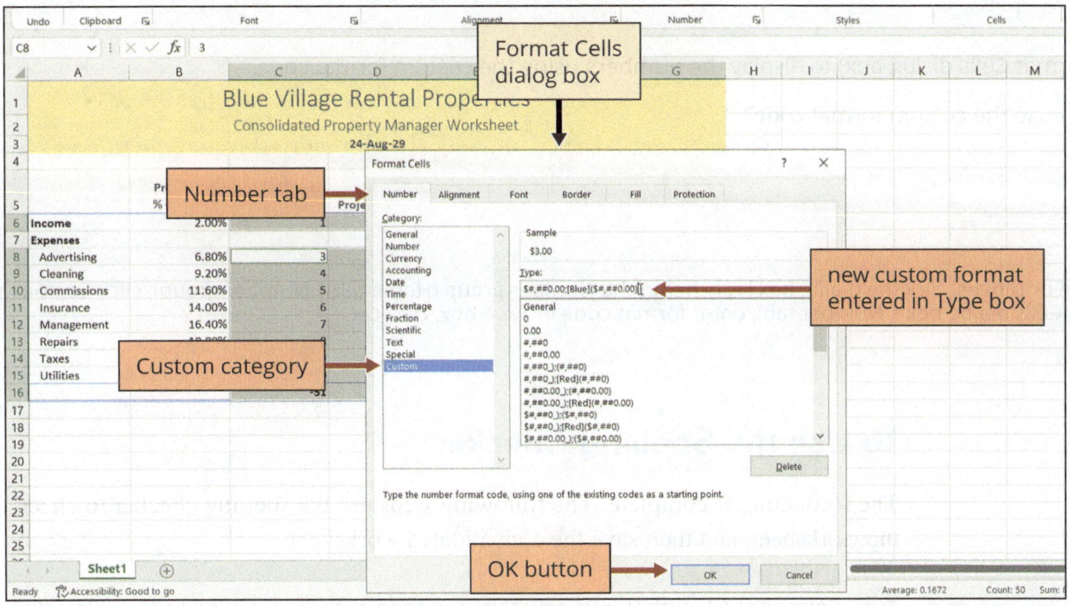

Figure 5–23

2

- Click OK (Format Cells dialog box) to display the numbers using the custom format code (Figure 5–24).

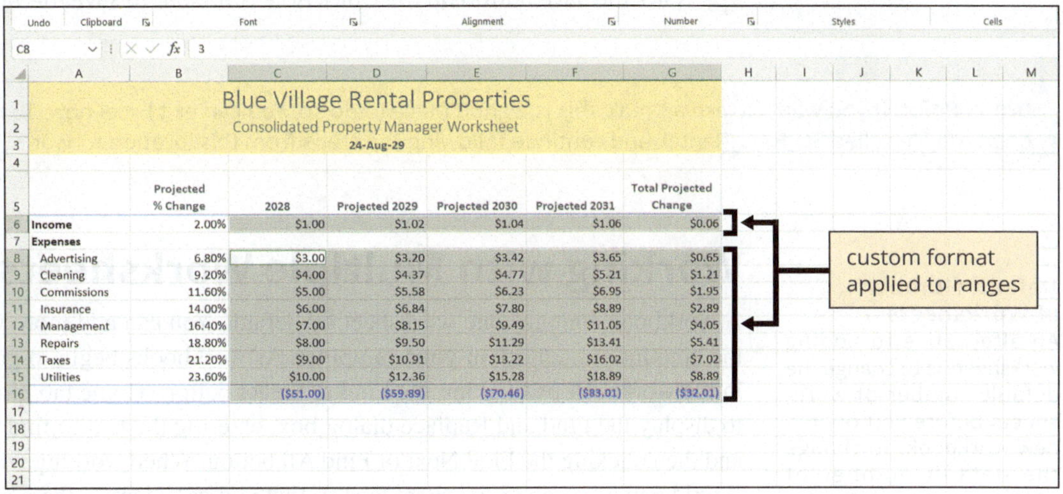

Figure 5–24

3

- Deselect the ranges C6:G6 and C8:G16.
- CTRL+drag to select the cell B6 and range B8:B15. Right-click any of the selected ranges to display the shortcut menu, and then click Format Cells to display the Format Cells dialog box.
- If necessary, click the Number tab (Format Cells dialog box) and then click Custom in the Category list.
- Delete the text in the Type box (Format Cells dialog box) and then type **0.00%;[Blue](0.00%)** to enter a custom format code (Figure 5–25).

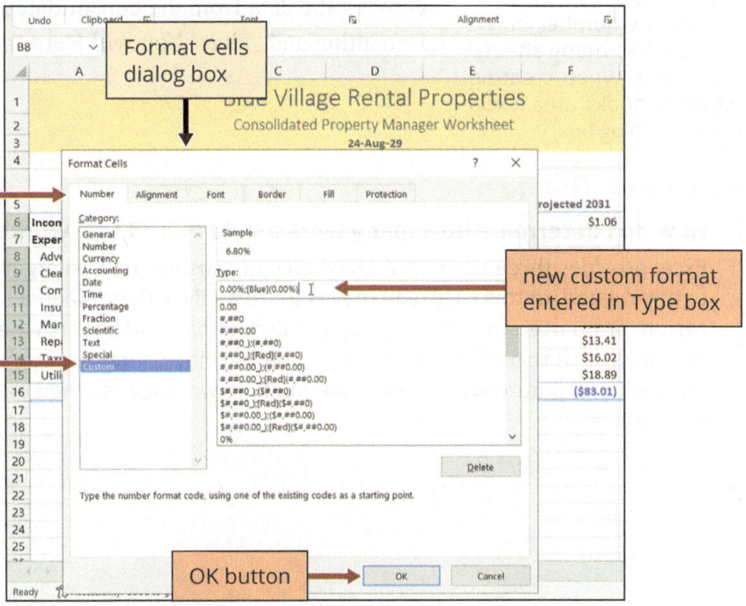

Figure 5–25

4

- Click OK (Format Cells dialog box) to display the numbers using the custom format code.

Q&A Can I reuse the custom format code?
Yes. When you create a new custom format code, Excel adds it to the bottom of the Type list on the Number sheet (Format Cells dialog box) to make it available for future use.

Other Ways

1. Select range or ranges, click the dialog box launcher in the Number group (Home tab | Number group), click Custom in Category list (Format Cells dialog box | Number tab), enter format code in Type box, click OK

To Use the Spelling Checker

The formatting is complete. The following steps use the spelling checker to check the spelling in the worksheet, and then save the consolidated worksheet.

1. Select cell A1, click the Review tab, and then click the Spelling button (Review tab | Proofing group) to check the spelling in the workbook. Correct any misspelled words.
2. Click the Save button on the Quick Access Toolbar to save the workbook.

Break Point: If you want to take a break, this is a good place to do so. You can exit Excel now. To resume later, start Excel, open the file called SC_EX_5_Rental, and continue following the steps from this location forward.

Working with Multiple Worksheets

A workbook contains one worksheet by default. You can add more worksheets, limited only by the amount of memory in your computer. As workbooks begin to grow, you can search for text in the workbook by clicking the Find & Select button (Home tab | Editing group), clicking Find to display the Find and Replace dialog box, entering the text to find in the 'Find what text' box, and then clicking the Find Next or Find All button. When working with multiple worksheets, you should name and color the sheet tabs so that you can identify them easily. With the consolidated worksheet complete, the next steps are to insert and populate worksheets in the workbook by copying the data from the consolidated worksheet to the location worksheets, and adjusting the formatting and values. You will learn three different ways to copy data across worksheets.

BTW
Default Number of Worksheets
An alternative to adding worksheets is to change the default number of worksheets before you open a new workbook. To change the default number of worksheets in a blank workbook, click Options in the Backstage view and then change the number in the 'Include this many sheets' box in the 'When creating new workbooks' area (Excel Options dialog box).

Consider This

How do I determine how many worksheets to add to a workbook?

Excel provides three basic choices when you consider how to organize data. Use a single worksheet when the data is tightly related. In this case, you may want to analyze the data in a table and use columnar data, such as department, region, or quarter, to identify groups. Use multiple worksheets when data is related but can stand alone on its own. For example, each region, department, or quarter may contain enough detailed information that you may want to analyze the data in separate worksheets. Use multiple workbooks when data is loosely coupled or when it comes from multiple sources.

To Add a Worksheet to a Workbook

In a previous module, you learned that you could add a worksheet to a workbook by clicking the New sheet button at the bottom of the workbook. The Blue Village Rental Properties Consolidated Property Manager Worksheet workbook requires five worksheets—one for each of the four properties and one for the consolidated totals. The following step adds the first new worksheet.

1 Click the New sheet button at the bottom of the window to add a new worksheet to the workbook.

To Copy and Paste from One Worksheet to Another

With two worksheets in the workbook, the next step is to copy the contents of Sheet1 to Sheet2. **Why?** When the desired content of the new worksheet mirrors or closely follows that of an existing worksheet, copying the existing content minimizes the chances of introducing errors. Sheet1 eventually will be used as the Consolidated worksheet with consolidated data. Sheet2 will be used for one of the four property worksheets.

In the process of copying, you must first select the populated cells. You can press CTRL+A to select a rectangular range that contains all populated cells, you can press CTRL+A twice to select all cells in the worksheet, you can drag to select the desired cells, or you can click the Select All button located just below the Name box at the intersection of the row and column headings. The method you use depends on where you are in the worksheet and your personal preference of using the mouse versus the keyboard. The following steps copy the content of one worksheet to another using the Select All button.

1

- Click the Sheet1 sheet tab to display the worksheet.
- Click the Select All button to select the entire worksheet.
- Click the Copy button (Home tab | Clipboard group) to copy the contents of the worksheet (Figure 5–26).

Q&A Can I use the shortcut keys, CTRL+C and CTRL+V, to copy and paste?

Yes. In addition, you can use the shortcut menu to copy and paste.

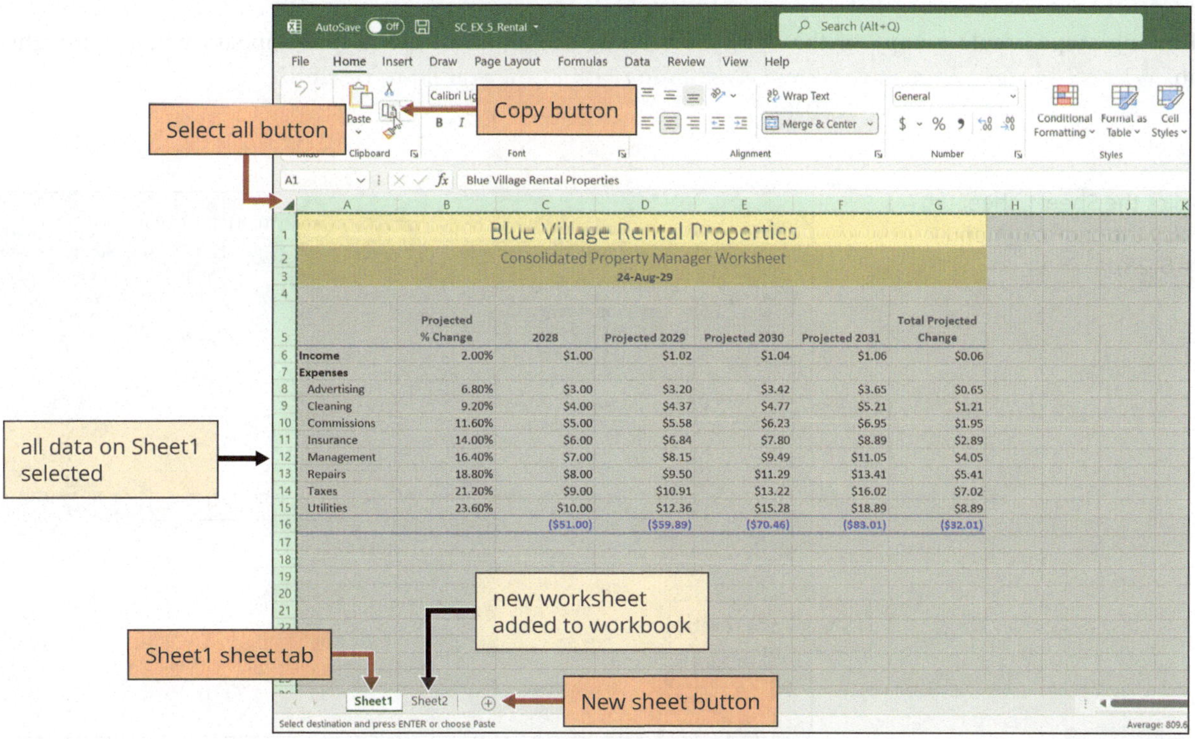

Figure 5–26

2

- Click the Sheet2 sheet tab at the bottom of the worksheet to display Sheet2.
- Press ENTER to copy the data from the Office Clipboard to the selected sheet (Figure 5–27).

Q&A Can I use the Paste button (Home tab | Clipboard group) to paste the data?
Yes. Recall that if you complete a paste operation using ENTER, however, the marquee disappears and the Office Clipboard is cleared, as it no longer contains the copied data following the action.

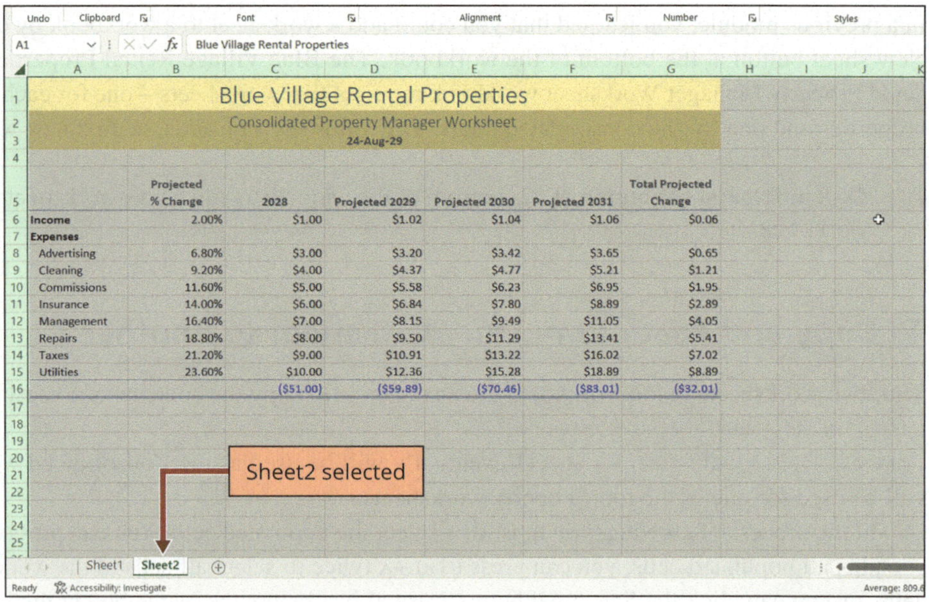

Figure 5–27

Other Ways

1. Select cells, press CTRL+C, select destination cell, press CTRL+V
2. Select cells, press CTRL+C, select destination cell, press ENTER
3. Right-click selected cells, click Copy, right-click destination cell, click appropriate Paste button

To Copy a Worksheet Using a Shortcut Menu

The following steps create a copy of the worksheet using the shortcut menu that appears when you right-click a sheet tab. **Why?** The shortcut menu and resulting dialog box allow you more flexibility in exactly where and how to move and copy.

1

- Right-click the Sheet1 sheet tab to display the shortcut menu (Figure 5–28).

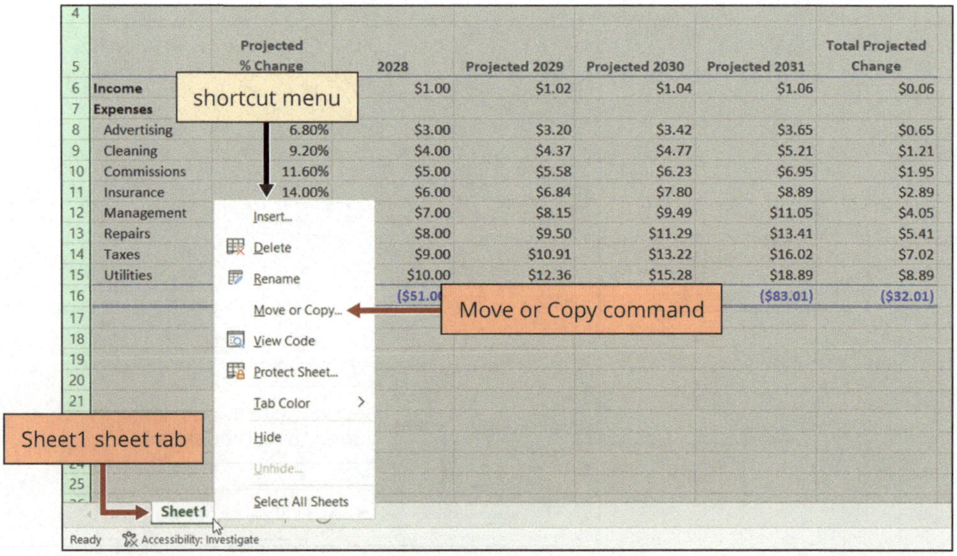

Figure 5–28

2

- Click 'Move or Copy' to display the Move or Copy dialog box.
- In the Before sheet list (Move or Copy dialog box), click '(move to end)' and then click to place a check mark in the 'Create a copy' check box (Figure 5–29).

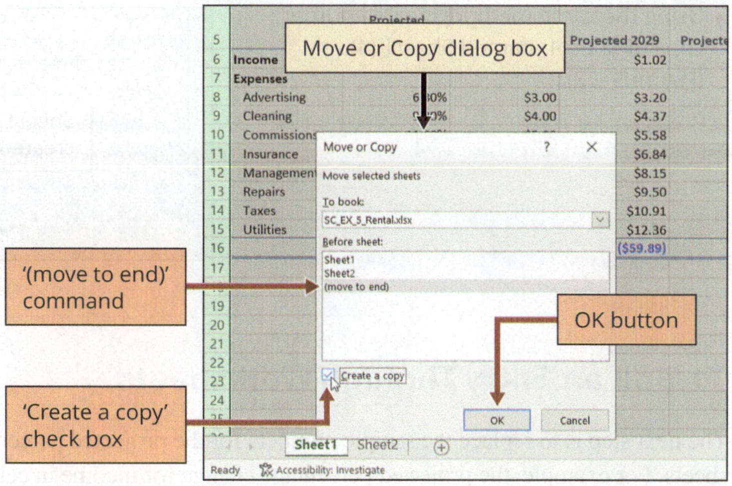

Figure 5–29

3

- Click OK to add a copy of the Sheet1 worksheet to the workbook (Figure 5–30).

Q&A Why is it named Sheet1 (2) instead of Sheet3?

Although this is the third sheet in the workbook, the name indicates that it is a copy of Sheet1.

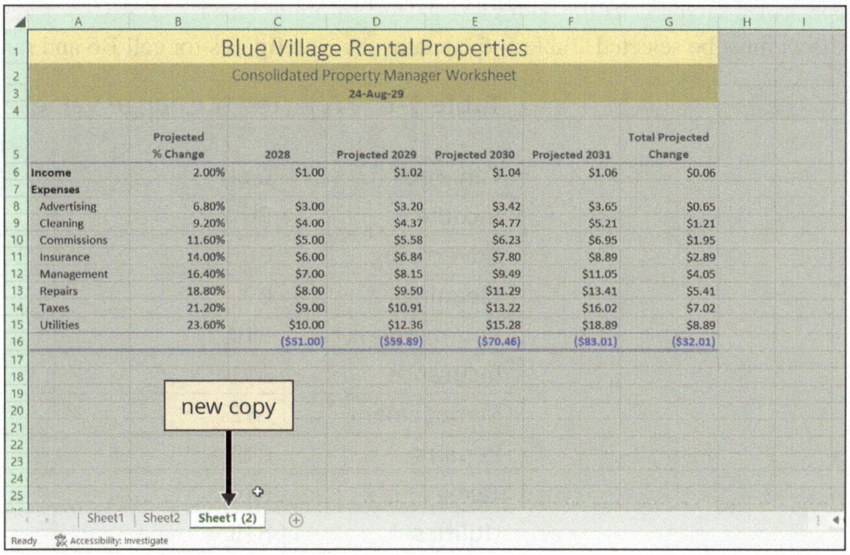

Figure 5–30

To Copy a Worksheet Using CTRL

Another way to create a copy of a worksheet is by pressing CTRL while you drag the sheet tab. *Why? Using CTRL is faster than selecting and copying, then pasting.* As you drag, Excel will display a small triangular arrow to show the destination location of your copy. The following steps create a third copy, for a total of four worksheets in the workbook.

1

- Select Sheet1.
- CTRL+drag the Sheet1 sheet tab to a location to the right of the other sheet tabs. Do not release the drag (Figure 5–31).

2

- Release the drag to create the worksheet copy named Sheet1 (3).

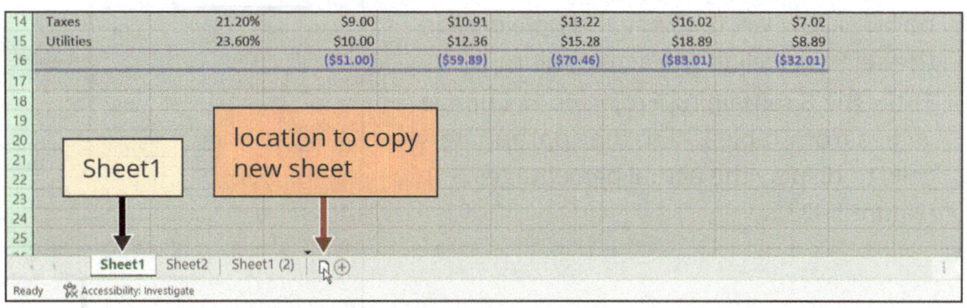

Figure 5–31

3

- Using the same method, create another copy of Sheet1, named Sheet1 (4) (Figure 5–32).

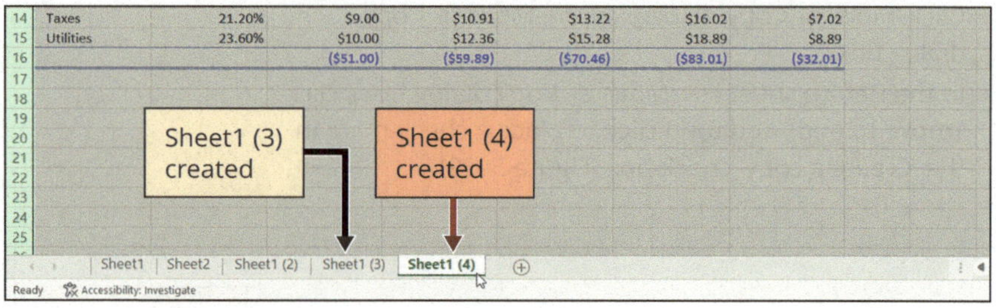

Figure 5–32

To Drill an Entry Through Worksheets

The next step is to replace the sample numbers for the projected percentage change. The percentage changes are identical on all five sheets. For example, the projected percentage change for income in cell B6 will be changed to 3.00 percent on all five sheets.

To speed data entry, Excel allows you to enter a number in the same cell through all selected worksheets. This technique is referred to as **drilling an entry**. Why? In cases where multiple worksheets have the same layout and the same calculations performed on data, drilling entries of data or formulas ensures consistency across the worksheets. When you drill, all affected sheets must be selected. Table 5–6 contains the new figures for cell B6 and range B8:B15.

Table 5–6: Projected % Change Values

Category	Cell	Projected % Change
Income	B6	3
Advertising	B8	–2
Cleaning	B9	2
Commissions	B10	2.5
Insurance	B11	1.5
Management	B12	3.5
Repairs	B13	–1
Taxes	B14	2.2
Utilities	B15	2

The following steps group all sheets, drill the projected percentage change entries from Table 5–6 through all five worksheets, and then ungroup the sheets.

1

- Right-click Sheet1 and then click 'Select All Sheets' on the shortcut menu to group the sheets.
- Select cell B6. Type **3** and then press the DOWN ARROW key to change sample data in the selected cell to the actual value.
- Enter the 8 remaining Projected % Change values from Table 5–6 to the appropriate cells to display the actual percentages (Figure 5–33).

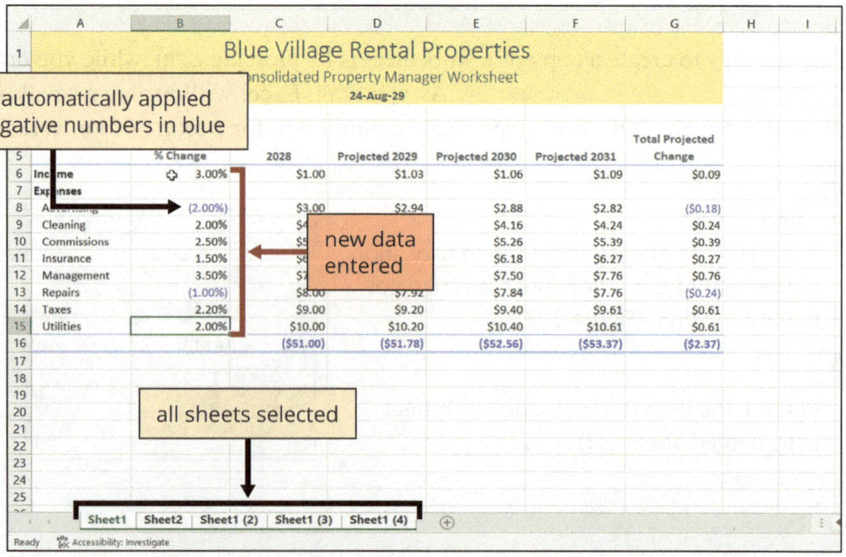

Figure 5–33

Q&A What is the benefit of drilling data through worksheets?
In these steps, 9 new numbers were entered on one worksheet. By drilling the entries through the other worksheets, 45 new numbers now appear, 9 on each of the worksheets. The Excel capability of drilling data through selected worksheets is an efficient way to enter data that is common among worksheets.

BTW
Selecting Multiple Worksheets
When multiple worksheets are selected, the Excel title bar reflects the selection by adding the notation, [Group]. All of the sheet tabs also are highlighted.

2
- Right-click Sheet1 and then click Ungroup Sheets on the shortcut menu.
- **Experiment:** One at a time, click the Sheet2 sheet tab, the Sheet1 (2) sheet tab, Sheet1 (3) sheet tab, and Sheet1 (4) sheet tab to verify that all five worksheets are identical.

Selecting and Deselecting Sheets Beginning Excel users sometimes have difficulty trying to select and deselect sheets. Table 5–7 summarizes how to select (group) and deselect (ungroup) multiple sheets using a mouse and keyboard.

BTW
Deleting Worksheets
Recall from Module 4 that you can delete a worksheet by right-clicking the sheet tab of the worksheet you want to delete, and then clicking Delete on the shortcut menu.

Table 5–7: Summary of How to Select and Deselect Sheets

Task	How to Carry Out the Task
Select individual sheet	Click sheet tab.
Select all sheets	Right-click any sheet tab, click 'Select All Sheets' on shortcut menu.
Select adjacent sheets	Select the first sheet by clicking its tab, and then hold down SHIFT and click the sheet tab at the other end of the list of adjacent sheet tabs.
Select nonadjacent sheets	Select the first sheet by clicking its tab, then hold down CTRL and click the sheet tabs of the remaining sheets you want to select.
Deselect all sheets	Right-click any sheet tab, click Ungroup Sheets on shortcut menu or click the individual sheet tab that you wish to select.
Deselect one of many sheets	CTRL+click the sheet tab you want to deselect.

Customizing the Individual Worksheets With the outline of the Blue Village Rental Properties Consolidated Property Manager workbook created, you will modify the individual worksheets by changing the worksheet name, sheet tab color, and worksheet subtitle. You also will change the color of the title and calculation area and enter the 2028 Income and Expenses in column B.

BTW
Opening Workbooks in New Windows
If you want to open a copy of the existing workbook in a new window, click the New Window button (View tab | Window group).

To Modify the River North Worksheet

The following steps modify the River North worksheet (Sheet2).

1. Double-click the Sheet2 sheet tab to select it. Type **River North** and then press ENTER to change the worksheet name.
2. Right-click the River North sheet tab, point to Tab Color on the shortcut menu, and then click 'Gray, Accent 3' in the Theme Colors area to change the sheet tab color.
3. Double-click cell A2. Drag through the word, Consolidated, to select the text, and then type **River North** to change the worksheet subtitle.
4. Select the range A1:G3. Click the Fill Color arrow (Home tab | Font group) and then click 'Gray, Accent 3, Lighter 60%' in the Theme Colors area (Fill Color gallery) to change the fill color of the selected range.

5. Select the range A4:G16. Click the Fill Color arrow (Home tab | Font group) and then click 'Gray, Accent 3, Lighter 80%' in the Theme Colors area (Fill Color gallery) to change the fill color of the selected range.

6. Enter the following data in the indicated cells:

Cell	Data for River North	Cell	Data for River North
C6	1266208.98	C12	75750.00
C8	4879.54	C13	40270.03
C9	12987.56	C14	35020.56
C10	6887	C15	8992.21
C11	15002.37		

7. Click an empty cell to deselect the previous cell (Figure 5–34).

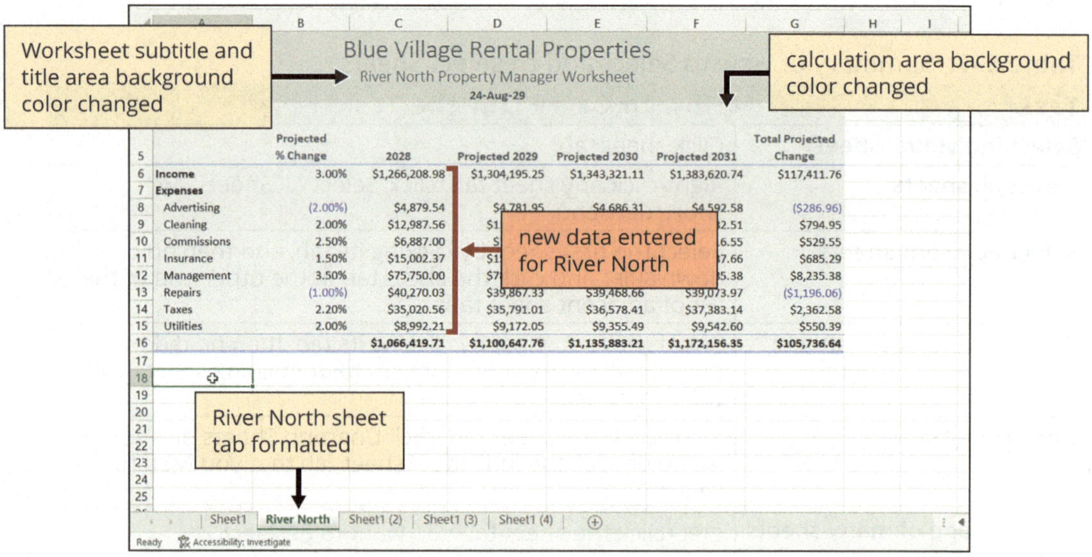

Figure 5–34

To Modify the River West Worksheet

The following steps modify the River West worksheet (Sheet1 (2)).

1. Double-click the Sheet1 (2) sheet tab to select it. Type **River West** and then press ENTER to change the worksheet name.

2. Right-click the River West sheet tab, point to Tab Color on the shortcut menu, and then click 'Orange, Accent 2, Lighter 60%' in the Theme Colors area to change the sheet tab color.

3. Double-click cell A2. Drag through the word, Consolidated, to select the text, and then type **River West** to change the worksheet subtitle.

4. Select the range A1:G3. Click the Fill Color arrow (Home tab | Font group) and then click 'Orange, Accent 2, Lighter 60%' in the Theme Colors area (Fill Color gallery) to change the fill color of the selected range.

5. Select the range A4:G16. Click the Fill Color arrow (Home tab | Font group) and then click 'Orange, Accent 2, Lighter 80%' in the Theme Colors area (Fill Color gallery) to change the fill color of the selected range.

6 Enter the following data in the indicated cells:

Cell	Data for River West	Cell	Data for River West
C6	1366804.73	C12	70750.00
C8	4340.35	C13	38745.87
C9	14934.06	C14	30100.15
C10	7887.00	C15	8952.09
C11	14100.34		

7 Click an empty cell to deselect the previous cell (Figure 5–35).

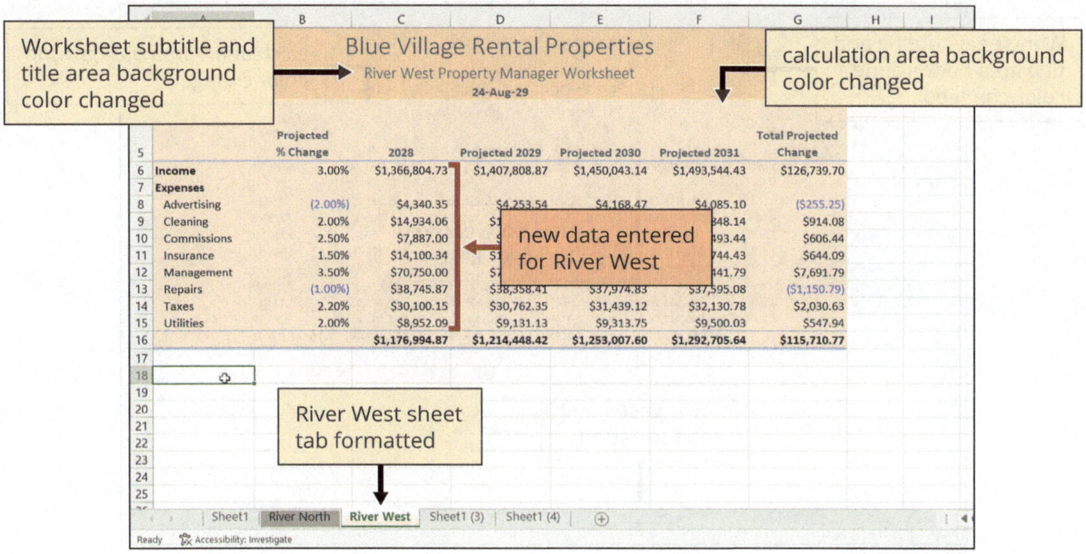

Figure 5–35

To Modify the River East Worksheet

The following steps modify the River East worksheet (Sheet1 (3)).

1 Double-click the Sheet1 (3) sheet tab to select it. Type **River East** and then press ENTER to change the worksheet name.

2 Right-click the River East sheet tab, point to Tab Color on the shortcut menu, and then click 'Blue, Accent 5, Lighter 60%' in the Theme Colors area to change the sheet tab color.

3 Double-click cell A2. Drag through the word, Consolidated, to select the text, and then type **River East** to change the worksheet subtitle.

4 Select the range A1:G3. Click the Fill Color arrow (Home tab | Font group) and then click 'Blue, Accent 5, Lighter 60%' in the Theme Colors area (Fill Color gallery) to change the fill color of the selected range.

5 Select the range A4:G16. Click the Fill Color arrow (Home tab | Font group) and then click 'Blue, Accent 5, Lighter 80%' in the Theme Colors area (Fill Color gallery) to change the fill color of the selected range.

6 Enter the following data in the indicated cells:

Cell	Data for River East	Cell	Data for River East
C6	1342988.90	C12	72350.00
C8	5883.23	C13	30400.20
C9	12739.54	C14	35102.90
C10	9324.00	C15	10540.68
C11	11930.78		

7 Click an empty cell to deselect the previous cell (Figure 5–36).

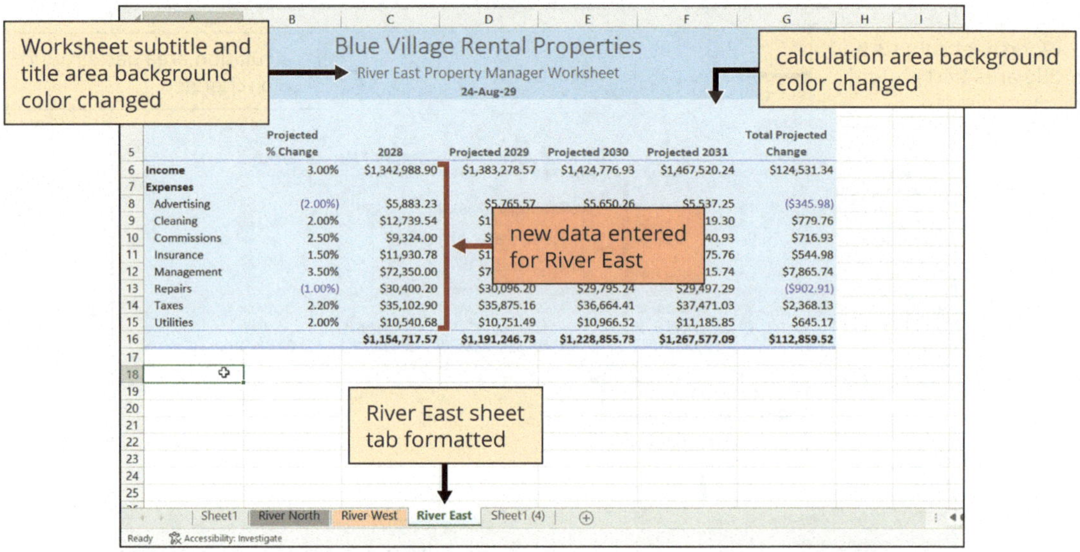

Figure 5–36

To Modify the River South Worksheet

The following steps modify the River South worksheet (Sheet1 (4)).

1. Double-click the Sheet1 (4) sheet tab to select it. Type **River South** and then press ENTER to change the worksheet name.
2. Right-click the River South sheet tab, point to Tab Color on the shortcut menu, and then click 'Green, Accent 6, Lighter 60%' in the Theme Colors area to change the sheet tab color.
3. Double-click cell A2. Drag through the word, Consolidated, to select the text, and then type **River South** to change the worksheet subtitle.
4. Select the range A1:G3. Click the Fill Color arrow (Home tab | Font group) and then click 'Green, Accent 6, Lighter 60%' in the Theme Colors area (Fill Color gallery) to change the fill color of the selected range.
5. Select the range A4:G16. Click the Fill Color arrow (Home tab | Font group) and then click 'Green, Accent 6, Lighter 80%' in the Theme Colors area (Fill Color gallery) to change the fill color of the selected range.

6 Enter the following data in the indicated cells:

Cell	Data for River South	Cell	Data for River South
C6	1202438.65	C12	70950.00
C8	4820.45	C13	35982.33
C9	12284.46	C14	30302.18
C10	11430.00	C15	9192.72
C11	9302.90		

7 Click an empty cell to deselect the previous cell (Figure 5–37).

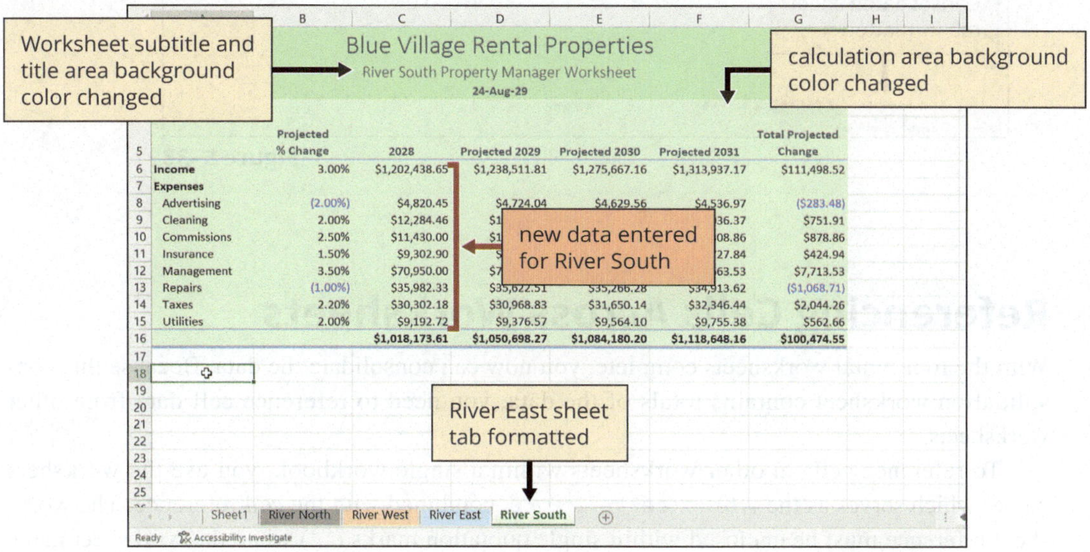

Figure 5–37

To Modify the Consolidated Worksheet

The following steps change the worksheet name from Sheet1 to Consolidated, add fill color to the calculation area, and color the sheet tab.

1 Double-click the Sheet1 sheet tab. Type **Consolidated** and then press ENTER to rename the tab.

2 Right-click the Consolidated sheet tab, point to Tab Color on the shortcut menu, and then click 'Gold, Accent 4, Lighter 60%' (row 3, column 8) in the Theme Colors area to change the sheet tab color.

3 Select the range A4:G16. Click the Fill Color arrow (Home tab | Font group) and then click 'White, Background 1' in the Theme Colors area (Fill Color gallery) to change the fill color of the selected range.

4 Deselect the range (Figure 5–38).

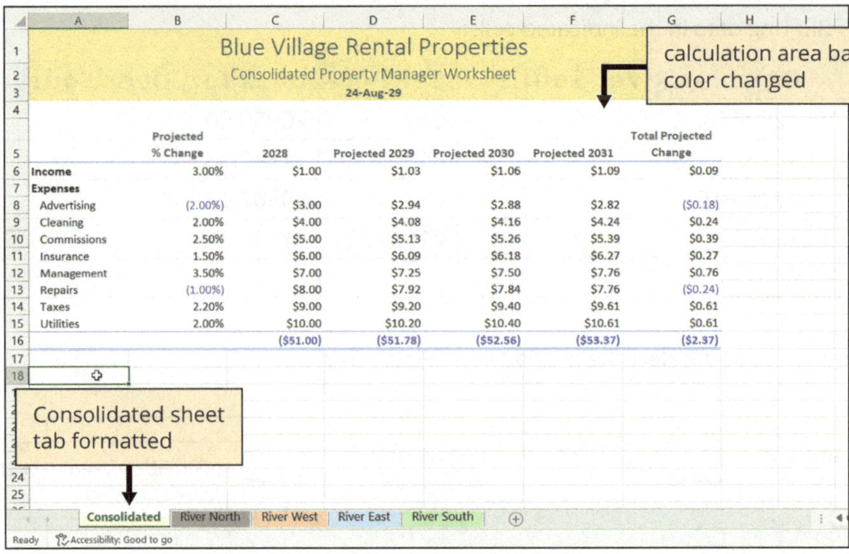

Figure 5–38

BTW
Drilling an Entry
Besides drilling a number down through a workbook, you can drill a format, a function, or a formula down through a workbook.

BTW
Importing Data
Expenses, such as those entered into the range C8:C15, often are maintained in another workbook, file, or database. If the expenses are maintained elsewhere, ways exist to link to a workbook or to import data from a file or database into a workbook. Linking to a workbook is discussed later in this module. To access a list of typical sources of outside data, click the 'Get Data' button (Data tab | Get & Transform Data group).

BTW
3-D References
If you are summing numbers on noncontiguous sheets, hold down CTRL rather than SHIFT when selecting the sheets.

Referencing Cells Across Worksheets

With the four rental worksheets complete, you now can consolidate the data. Because this consolidation worksheet contains totals of the data, you need to reference cell data from other worksheets.

To reference cells in other worksheets within a single workbook, you use the worksheet name, which serves as the **worksheet reference**, combined with the cell reference. The worksheet reference must be enclosed within single quotation marks (' ') when the worksheet name contains a nonalphabetical character such as a space. Excel requires an exclamation point (!) as a delimiter between the worksheet reference and the cell reference. Therefore, the reference to cell B6 on the River North worksheet would be entered as

='River North'!B6

These worksheet and cell references can be used in formulas, such as

='River North'!B6 + 'River West'!B6 + 'River West'!B6 + 'River South'!B6

A worksheet reference such as 'River North' always is absolute, meaning that the worksheet reference remains constant if you copy the formula to other locations.

Worksheet references also can be used in functions and range references such as

=SUM('River North:River South'!B6)

The SUM argument ('River North:River South'!B6) instructs Excel to sum cell B6 on each of the four worksheets (River North, River West, River East, and River South). The colon (:) delimiter between the first worksheet name and the last worksheet name instructs Excel to include these worksheets and all worksheets in between, just as it does with a range of cells on a worksheet. A range that spans two or more worksheets in a workbook, such as 'River North:River South'!B6, is called a **3-D range**. The reference to this range is a **3-D reference**. A 3-D reference is also absolute. You can paste the 3-D reference to other cells on the worksheet.

To Enter a 3-D Reference

To consolidate the payroll expenses, the following steps create 3-D references in cells C6 and C8:C15 on the Consolidated worksheet. **Why?** Using 3-D references is the most efficient method of referencing cells that reside in the same location on different worksheets. You can enter a worksheet reference in a cell by typing the worksheet reference or by clicking the appropriate sheet tab while in Point mode. When you click the sheet tab, Excel activates the worksheet and automatically adds the worksheet name and an exclamation point after the insertion point in the formula bar. Then, click the desired cell or drag through the cells you want to reference on the sheet.

If the range of cells to be referenced is located on several worksheets (as when selecting a 3-D range), click the first sheet tab and then select the cell(s). Finally, SHIFT+click the last sheet tab you want to reference. Excel will include the cell(s) on the first worksheet, the last worksheet, and any worksheets in between.

1

- Select cell C6 and then click the AutoSum button (Home tab | Editing group) to display the SUM function (Figure 5–39).

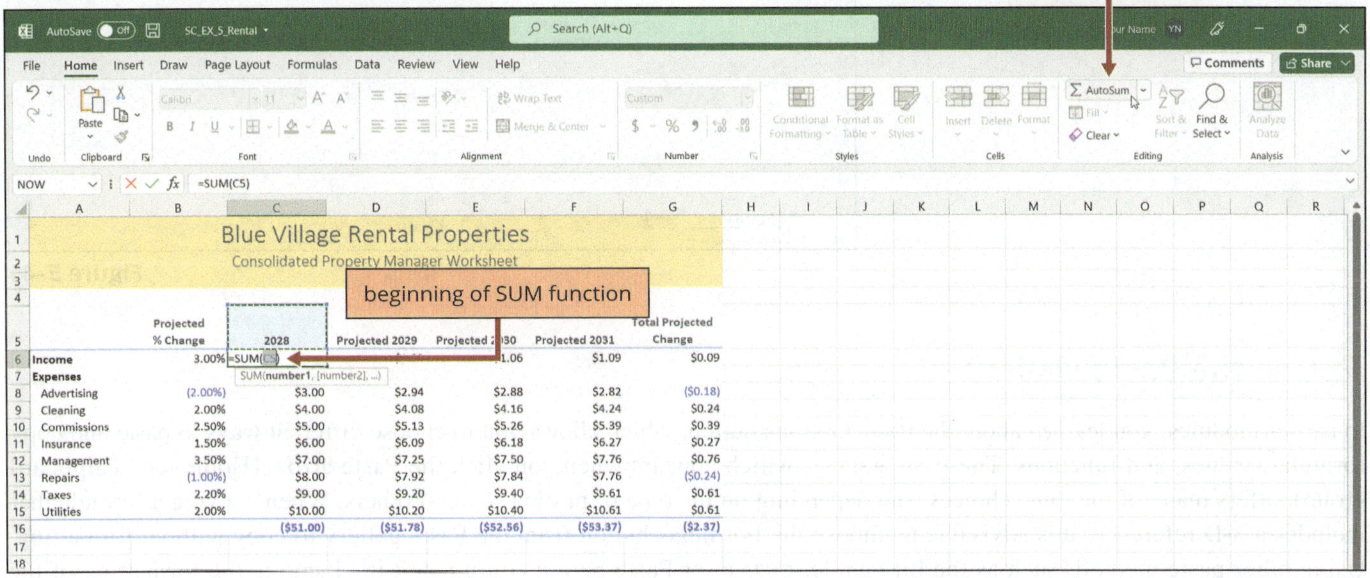

Figure 5–39

2

- Click the River North tab and then click cell C6 to select the first portion of the argument for the SUM function.
- SHIFT+click the River South tab to select the ending range of the argument for the SUM function (Figure 5–40).

Q&A Could I just type the 3-D reference?
Yes, however the Point mode is used in this step, which prevents any errors in typing the reference.

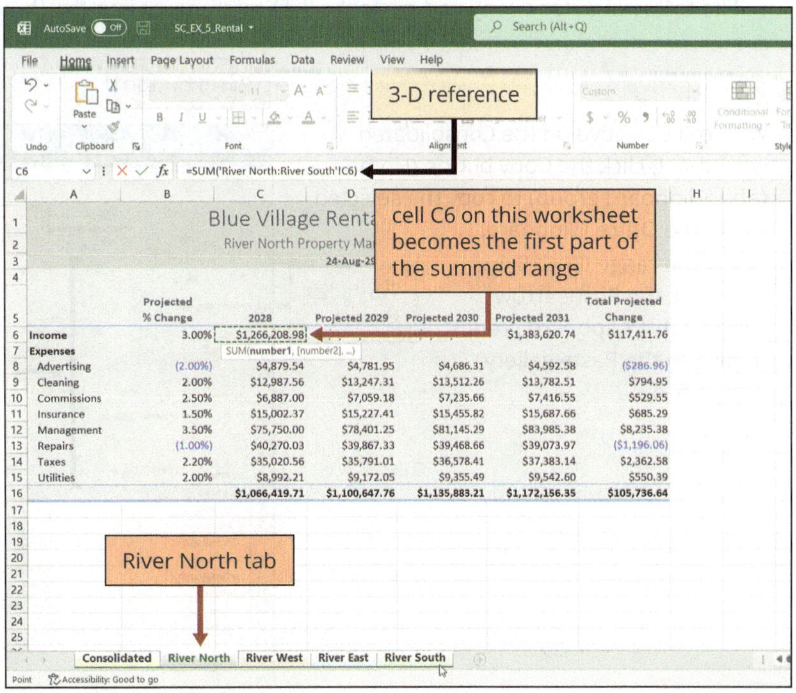

Figure 5–40

3

- Click the Enter button in the formula bar to enter the SUM function with the 3-D references in the selected cell, in this case =SUM('River North:River South'!C6) (Figure 5–41).

Q&A Should each worksheet name in the function have individual sets of single quotes?

No, in a 3-D reference that uses a range, Excel requires a single quote before the first worksheet name in the range and an ending single quote after the last worksheet name.

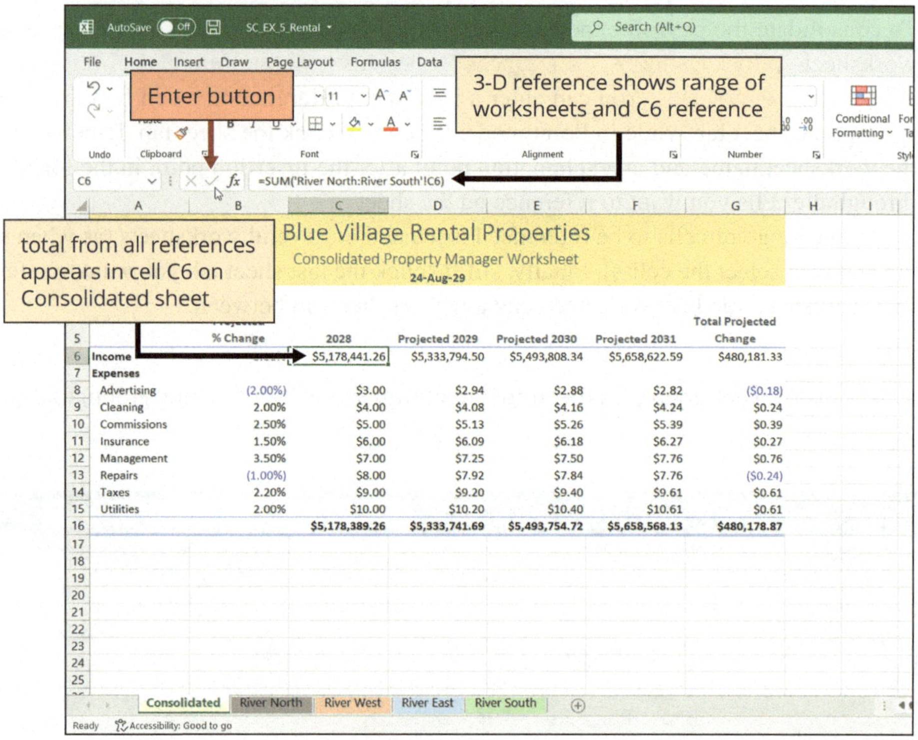

Figure 5–41

To Use the Paste Gallery

In earlier modules, you learned about the Paste Options button, which allows you to choose different ways to paste and copy formulas, values, and functions. The Paste gallery, which appears when you click the Paste arrow (Home tab | Clipboard group), offers many of the same choices, and depending on the type of pasting, several others. When copying a formula that includes a 3-D reference, it is advisable to choose the Formulas button from the Paste gallery to copy without formatting. Using other paste methods such as the fill handle, ENTER, or Paste button could result in changing the formatting of the destination cells.

The following steps copy and paste the 3-D reference using the Paste gallery. **Why?** Using the Paste gallery will enable you to maintain the destination formatting.

1

- With cell C6 active on the Consolidated worksheet, click the Copy button (Home tab | Clipboard group) to copy the selected cell to the Office Clipboard.
- Select the range C8:C15 and then click the Paste arrow (Home tab | Clipboard group) to display the Paste gallery (Figure 5–42).

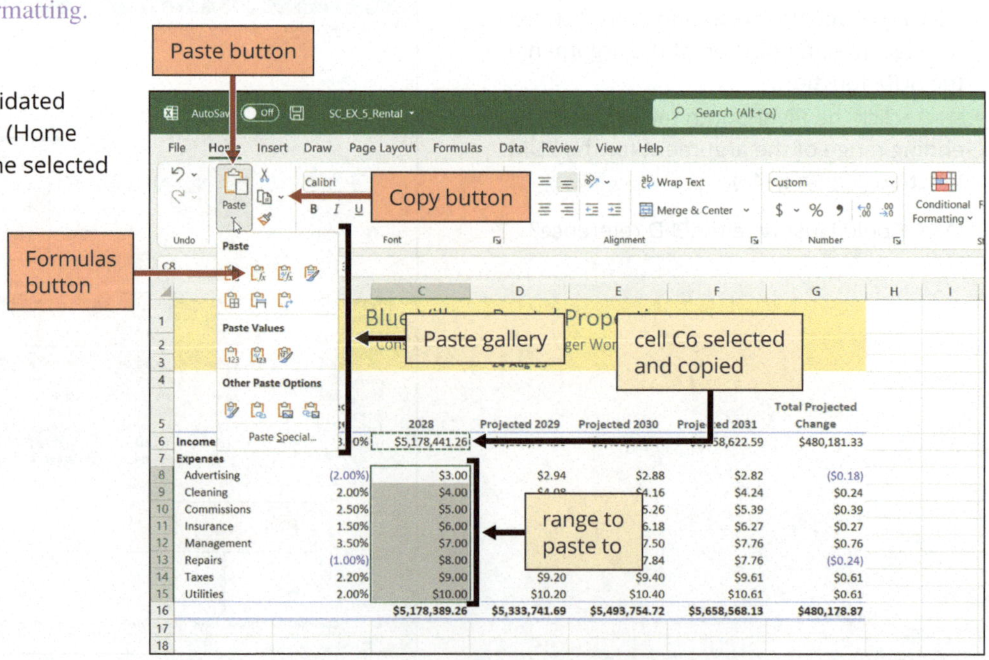

Figure 5–42

2

- Click the Formulas button (column 2, row 1) in the Paste gallery to copy the SUM function to the desired range, replicating the 3-D references.
- Press ESC to clear the marquee.
- Deselect the previous range (Figure 5–43).
- Click the Save button on the Quick Access Toolbar to save the workbook.

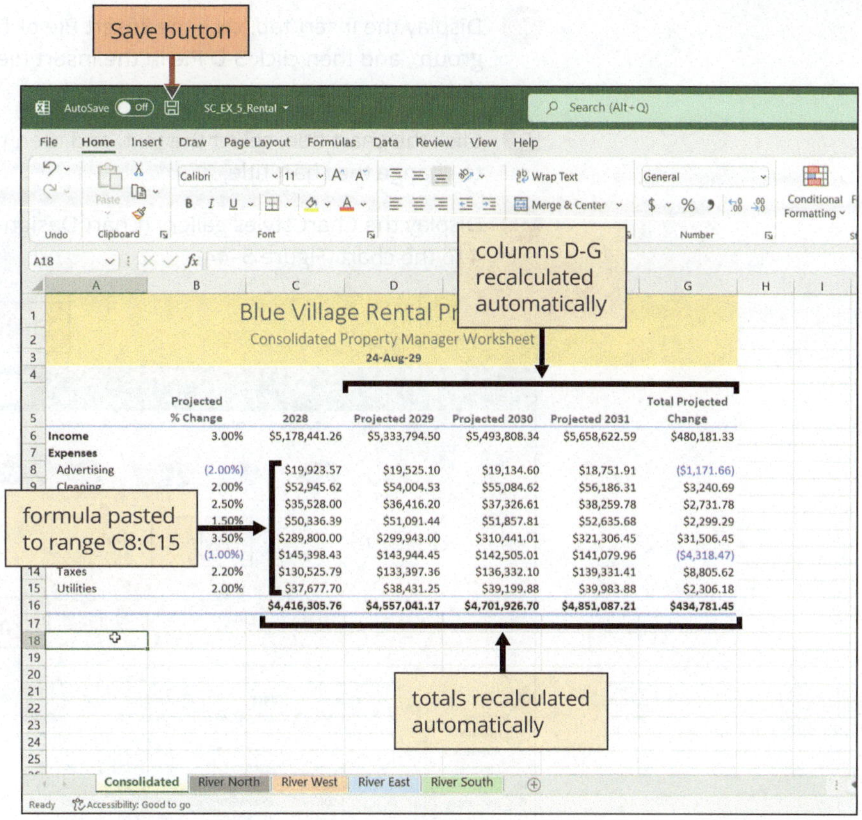

Figure 5–43

Other Ways

1. Right-click selected cell(s), click Copy, right-click destination cell(s), click appropriate Paste button

Break Point: If you want to take a break, this is a good place to do so. You can exit Excel now. To resume later, start Excel, open the file called SC_EX_5_Rental, and continue following the steps from this location forward.

Formatting Pie Charts

In Module 1, you created a pie chart. Pie charts show the contribution of each piece of data to the whole, or total, of the data. You can format a pie chart in many ways including resizing, moving, rotating, adding data labels and leader lines, adding a decorative background, and exploding a slice. In addition, if your chart displays numeric data labels, you can format the data by clicking a data label and then entering the desired formatting options and format code in the Number area of the Format Data Labels pane.

As outlined in the requirements document in Table 5–1, the worksheet should include a pie chart to represent graphically the Projected 2029 expenses totals for all four properties. The pie chart should reside at the bottom of the consolidated worksheet.

BTW

Y-Rotation and Perspective

The Y-Rotation arrows tilt the chart toward the back or front, allowing you to control the elevation of the chart. You can tilt the chart toward or away from you to enhance the view of the chart. The Perspective value makes close slices appear larger and those further away appear smaller.

To Insert a 3-D Pie Chart on a Worksheet

The following steps insert the 3-D pie chart on the Consolidated worksheet.

1 Select the range A8:A15, then press CTRL and select the range D8:D15 to identify the category names and data for the pie chart.

2. Display the Insert tab, click the 'Insert Pie or Doughnut Chart' button (Insert tab | Charts group), and then click 3-D Pie in the Insert Pie or Doughnut Chart gallery to create the desired chart type.

3. Click the chart title, select the text, and then type **Projected 2029 Consolidated Expenses** to change the chart title.

4. Display the Chart styles gallery (Chart Design tab | Chart Styles group), and then apply Style 4 to the chart (Figure 5–44).

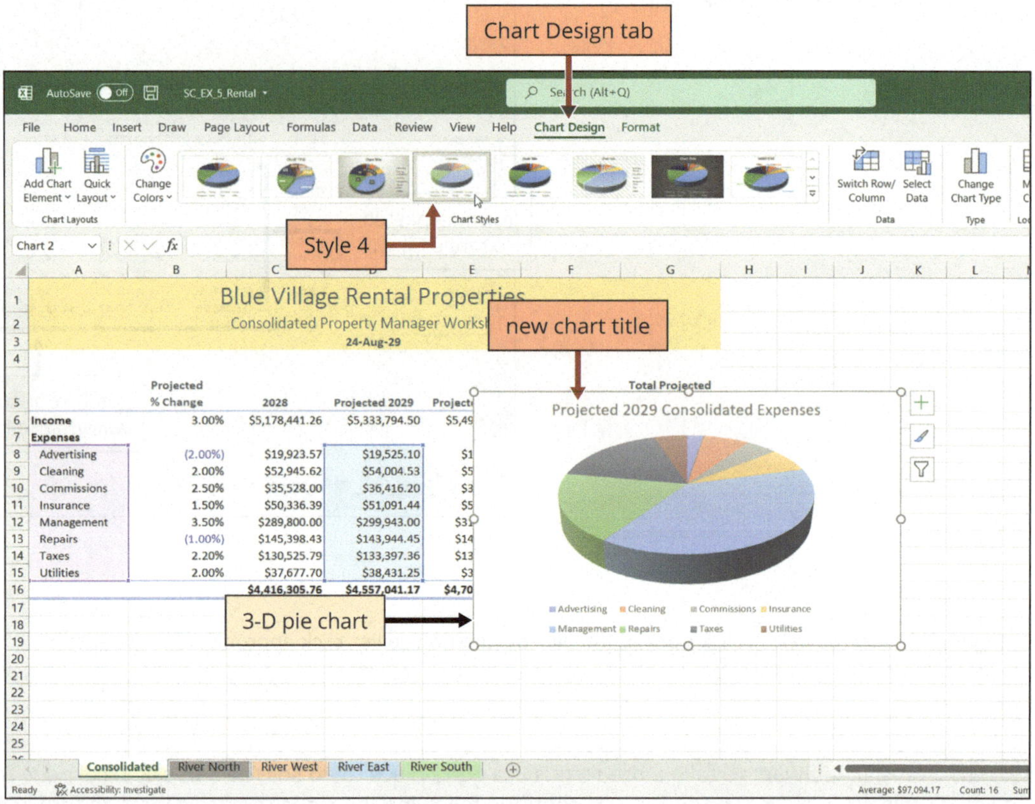

Figure 5–44

To Move a Chart on the Same Worksheet

As you learned in an earlier module, you can move a chart to a new worksheet or move a chart on the same worksheet. If you want move a chart to a different worksheet, select the chart and then select the Move Chart button (Chart Design tab | Location group). Then, select the New sheet option button, type the name of the new sheet in the corresponding text box, and click OK. The following step moves the chart on the same worksheet to the space below the data that was used to create the chart. **Why?** By default, Excel places charts in the center of the worksheet. You need to move it out of the way of the data on the worksheet.

1

- Point to the border of the chart. When the pointer changes to a four-headed arrow, drag the chart to the desired location (in this case, approximately cell B18) (Figure 5–45).
- **Experiment:** Point to each of the styles in the Chart Styles group (Chart Design tab) and notice the changes in the chart to reflect each style.

Q&A Could I use the Move Chart button (Chart Design tab | Location group) to move the chart?

No. That button moves the chart from sheet to sheet rather than to a new location on the same worksheet.

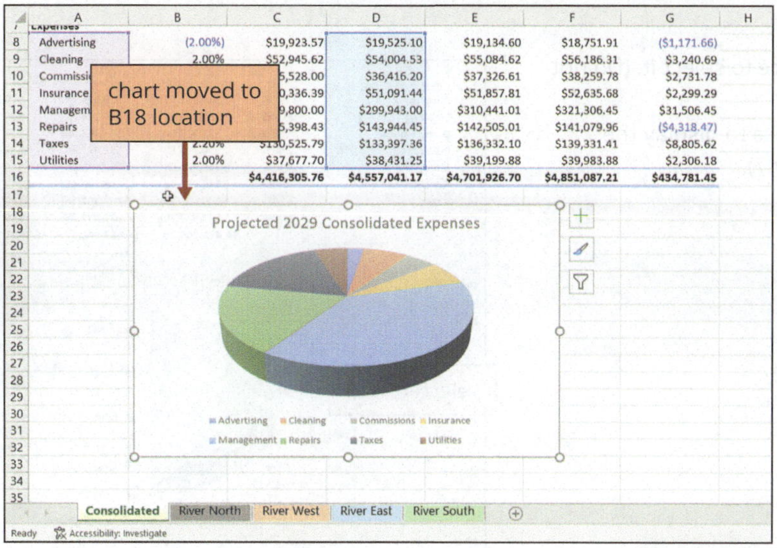

Figure 5–45

To Resize a Chart

If you want to resize a chart, you either can do so by dragging the sizing handles until the chart is the desired size, or you can resize the chart to exact dimensions. To resize a chart to exact dimensions, click to select the chart, click the Format tab on the Ribbon, and then enter the desired height and width in the Size group. The following step resizes the chart proportionally by dragging to make it larger and more legible. To resize a chart nonproportionally, do not hold SHIFT while dragging the sizing handles. **Why?** The chart as created by Excel may not be the optimal size for your worksheet needs.

1

- If necessary, scroll down until you can see both the bottom of the chart and row 34.
- Drag the lower-right sizing handle of the chart until the chart is the desired size (in this case, approximately to the bottom right corner of cell F34).
- If necessary, zoom out until you can observe the entire chart (Figure 5–46).

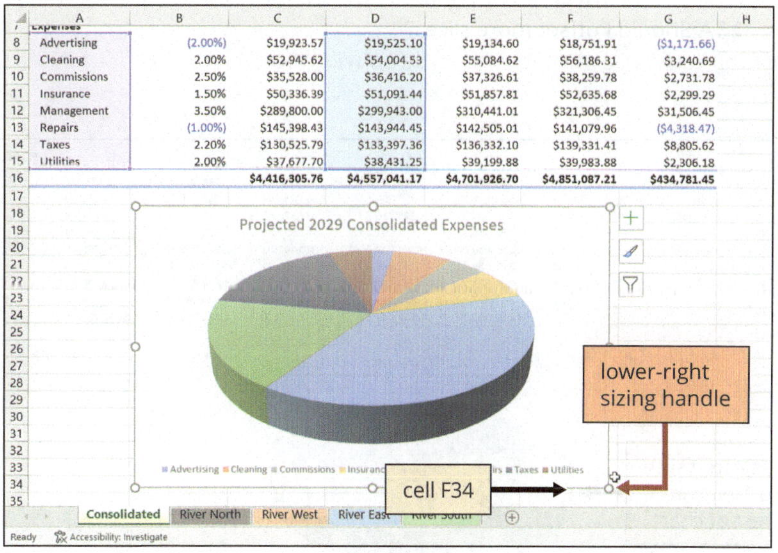

Figure 5–46

To Explode a Slice

In this chart, the Management slice dominates because it is so large. The following steps explode the next-largest slice of the 3-D pie chart to draw attention to the second-largest contributing expense. **Why?** Exploding, or offsetting, a slice in a chart emphasizes it.

1

- Click the Repairs slice twice to select it. (Do not double-click.)
- Right-click the selected slice to display the shortcut menu (Figure 5–47).

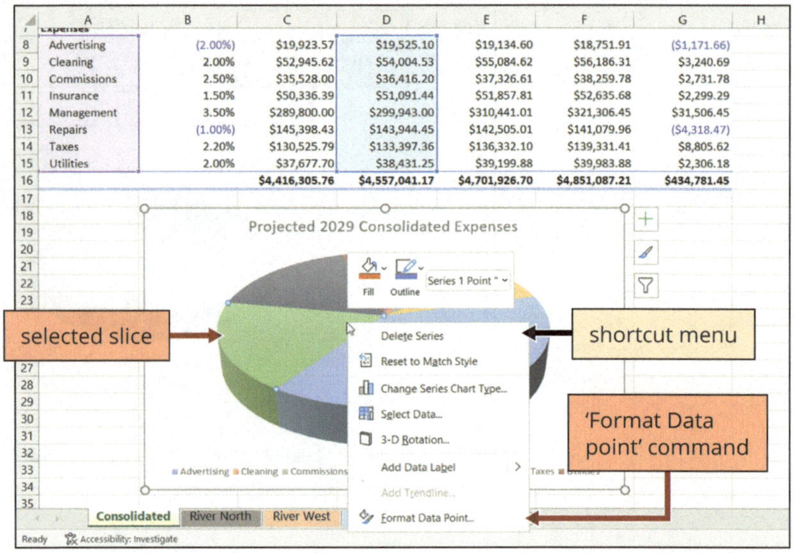

Figure 5–47

2

- Click 'Format Data Point' on the shortcut menu to open the Format Data Point pane.
- Drag the Point Explosion slider to the right until the Point Explosion box reads 20% to edit the offset distance for the slice (Figure 5–48).

◦ **Experiment:** Select different slices and use the Point Explosion slider to offset additional slices and note how the size of the chart changes as you offset additional slices. When done, reset the slices so that the Repairs slice is the only slice offset, set to 15%.

Q&A Should I offset more slices?
You can offset as many slices as you want; however, remember that the reason for offsetting a slice is to emphasize it. Offsetting multiple slices tends to reduce the intended impact and it reduces the overall size of the pie chart.

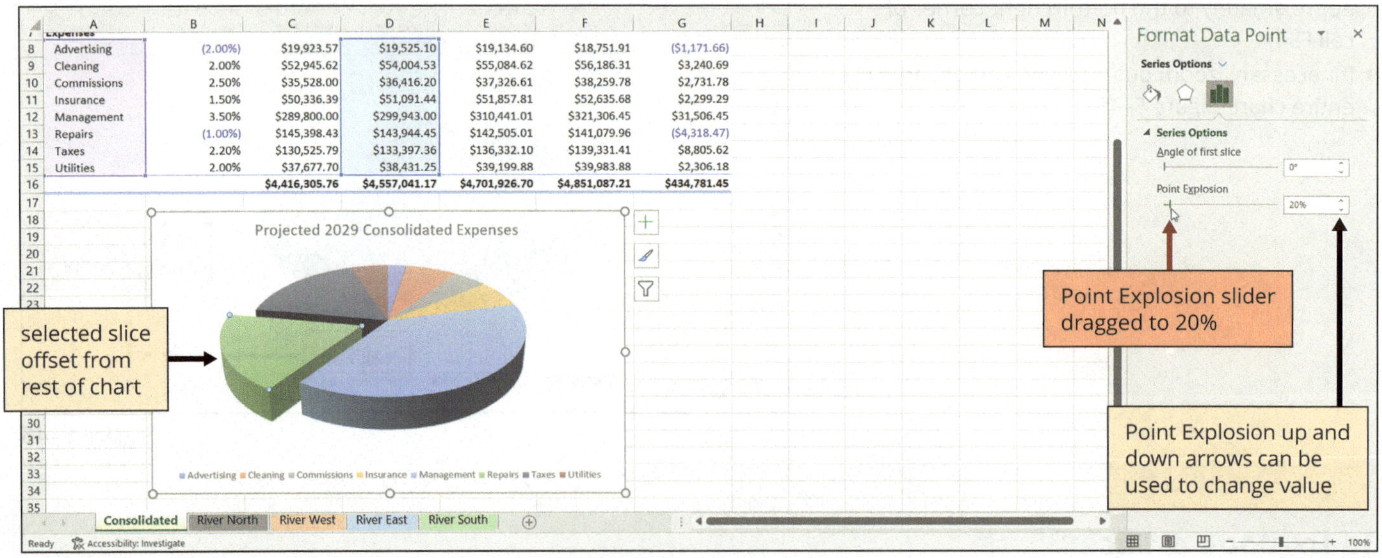

Figure 5–48

Other Ways

1. Click slice twice, drag away from other slices

To Rotate the 3-D Pie Chart

When Excel initially draws a pie chart, it always positions the chart so that one of the dividing lines between two slices is a straight line pointing to 12 o'clock (or 0°). As shown in Figure 5–48 that line currently divides the Advertising and Utilities slices. This line defines the rotation angle of the 3-D pie chart. Excel allows you to control the rotation angle, elevation, perspective, height, and angle of the axes. The following steps rotate the 3-D pie chart. **Why?** With a three-dimensional chart, you can change the view to better show the section of the chart you are trying to emphasize.

1

- Right-click the chart to display the shortcut menu, and then click '3-D Rotation' on the shortcut menu to open the Format Chart Area pane.
- In the X Rotation box (Format Chart Area pane), type **280** to rotate the chart (Figure 5–49).

Q&A What happens if I click the X Rotation up arrow?
Excel will rotate the chart 10° in a clockwise direction each time you click the X Rotation up arrow.

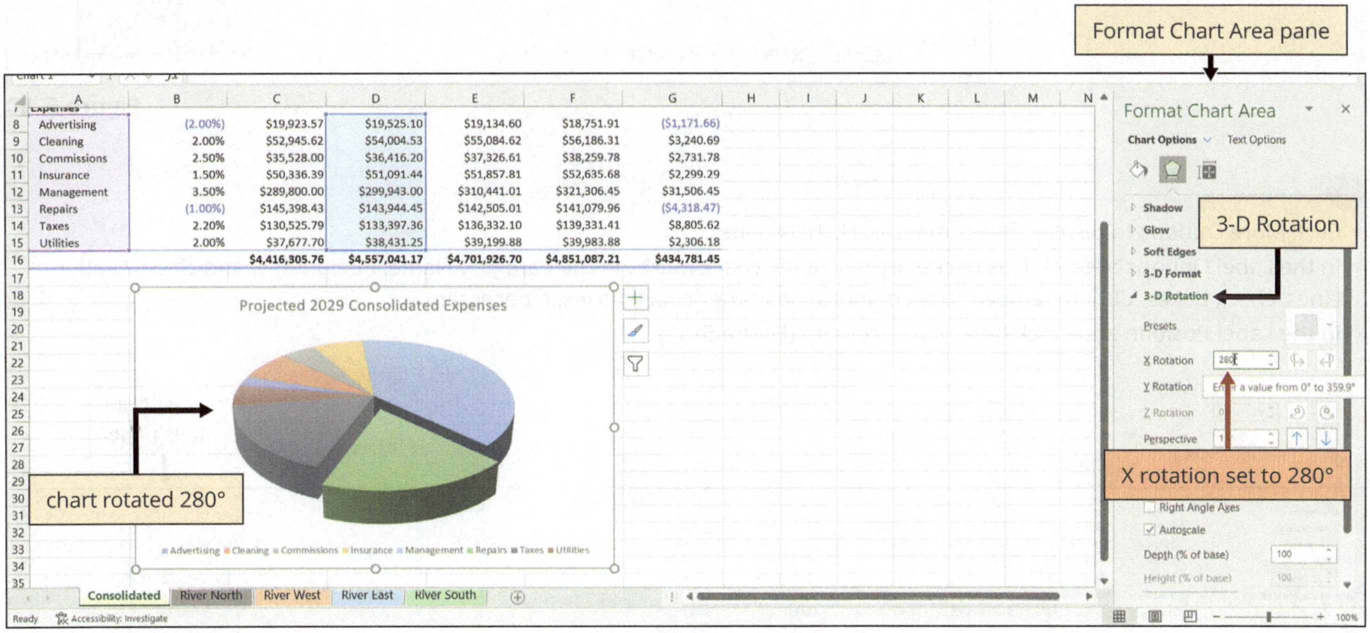

Figure 5–49

2

- Click the Close button (Format Chart Area pane) to close the pane.

To Format Data Labels

The following steps format the data labels using the Format Data Labels pane. You will choose the elements to include in the data label, set the position, choose number formatting, and create leader lines. **Why?** A **leader line** connects a data label with its data point helping you identify individual slices.

1

- Click the Chart Elements button to display the Chart Elements gallery. Point to Data Labels and then click the Data Labels arrow to display the Data Labels submenu (Figure 5–50).

Q&A How does the Legend check box affect the pie chart?
If you uncheck the Legend check box, Excel will remove the legend from the chart. If you point to Legend, an arrow will appear. Clicking the arrow displays a list for legend placement.

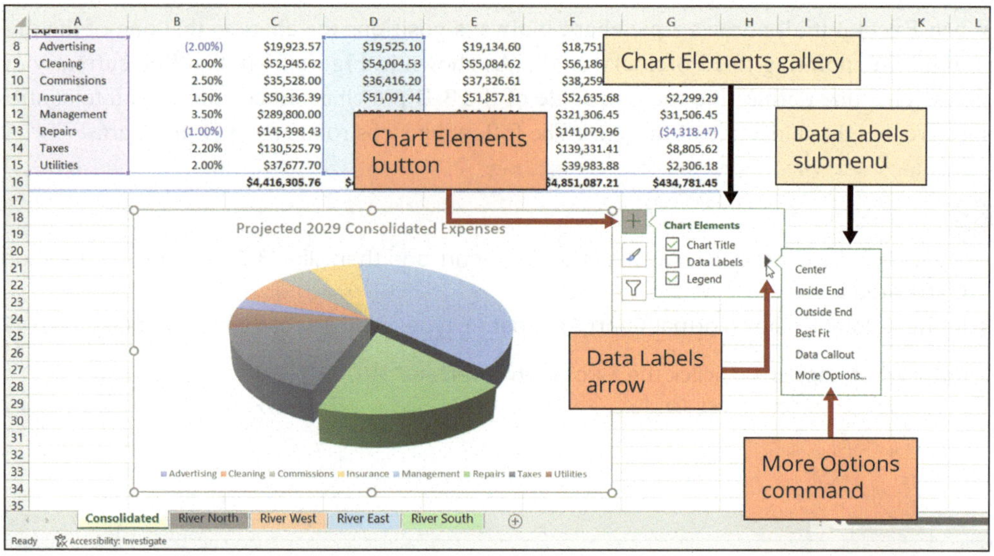

Figure 5–50

2

- Click More Options to display the Format Data Labels pane.
- In the Label Options area, click as necessary to display check marks in the Category Name, Percentage, and 'Show Leader Lines' check boxes. Click to remove check marks in any other check boxes, if necessary.
- In the Label Position area, click Best Fit if necessary (Figure 5–51).

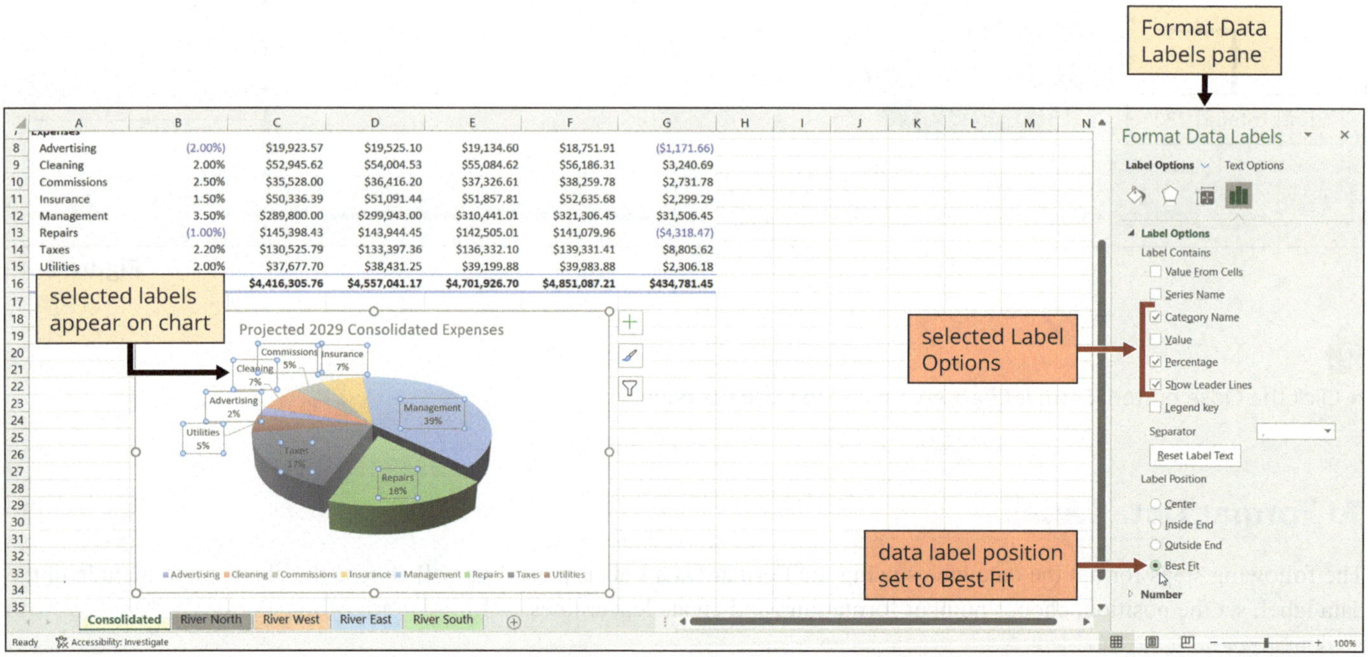

Figure 5–51

3

- Scroll down in the pane and click the Number arrow to display the Number settings.
- Scroll as necessary to click the Category button and then click Percentage to choose the number style.
- If necessary, select any text in the Decimal places text box and then type **2** to format the percentage with two decimal places (Figure 5–52).

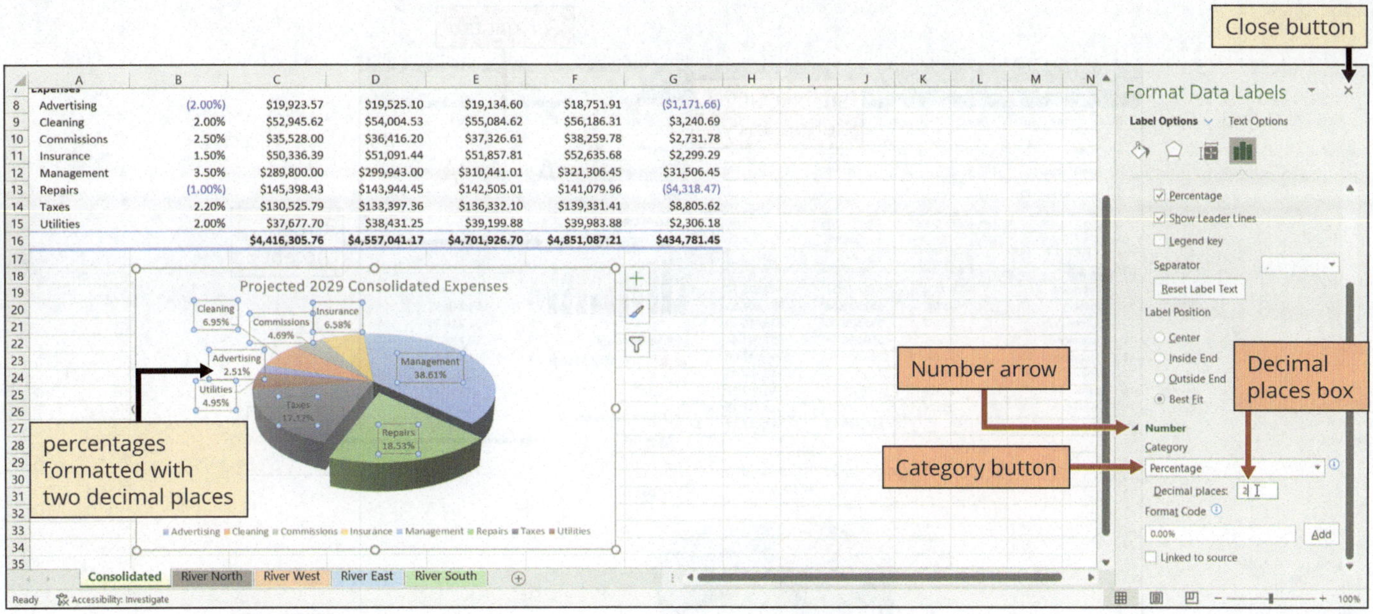

Figure 5–52

4

- Click the Close button on the Format Data Labels pane to close it.
- One at a time, using Figure 5–53 as a guide, drag each data label out slightly from the chart, far enough to make each leader line visible.

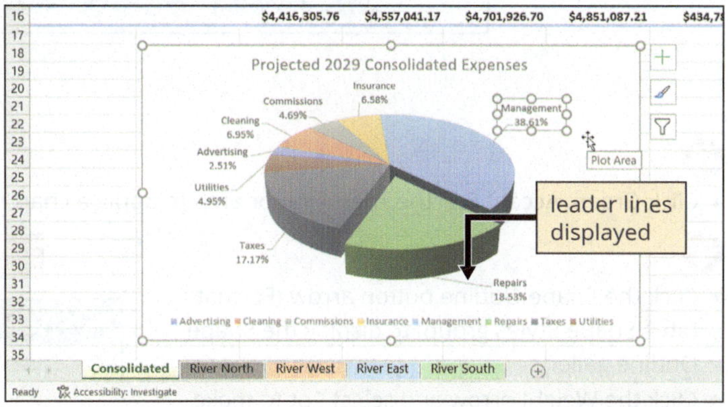

Figure 5–53

To Add a Chart Border

The following steps add a border to the Projected 2029 Consolidated Expenses chart. In addition to adding a border to a chart, you can add a border to a chart element using these same steps. Instead of selecting the entire chart before adding the border, first select the element to which you want to add the border. **Why?** Adding a chart border helps to separate the chart from the other worksheet contents.

1

- If necessary, click to select the chart.
- Click Format on the ribbon to display the Format tab.
- Click the Shape Outline arrow (Format tab | Shape Styles group) to display the Shape Outline gallery (Figure 5–54).

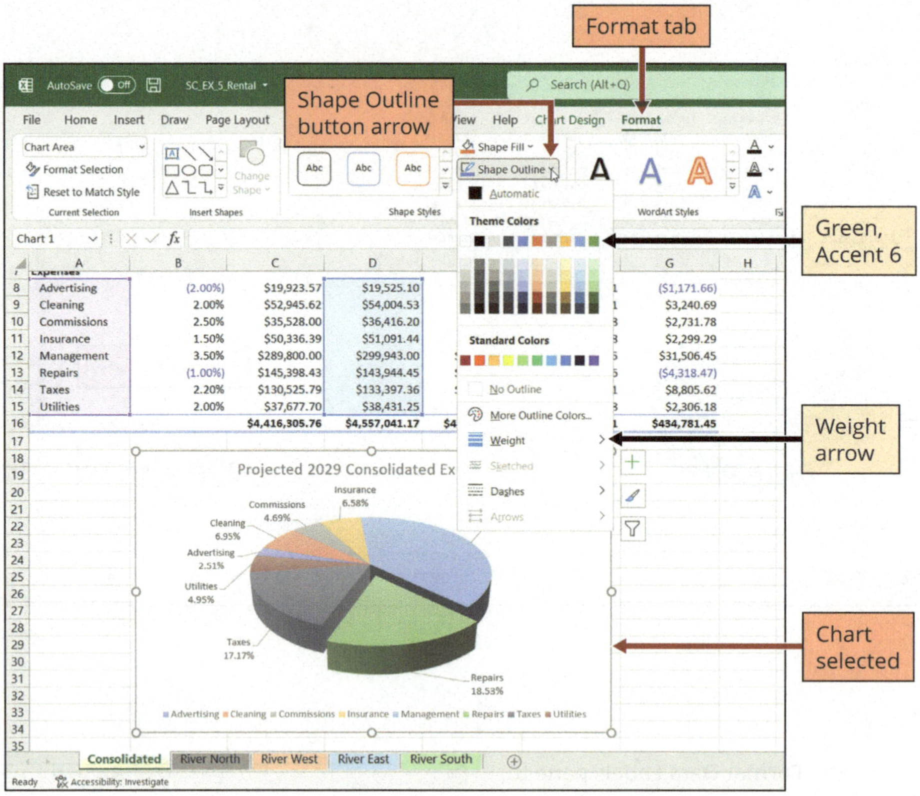

Figure 5–54

2

- Click Green, Accent 6 in the Theme Color area to apply a chart border.

3

- Click the Shape Outline button arrow (Format tab | Shape Styles group) to display the Shape Outline gallery.
- Click the Weight arrow and select 1pt to make the border thicker.
- Click an empty cell on the worksheet to display the chart border (Figure 5–55).
- Click Save on the Quick Access Toolbar to save the workbook.

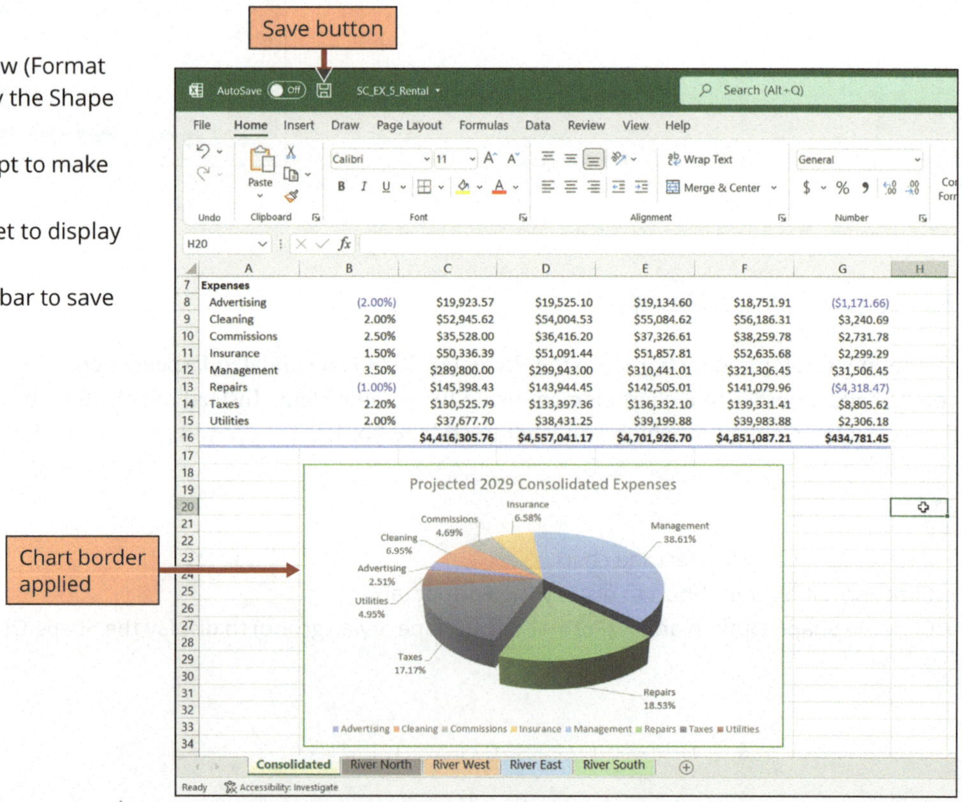

Figure 5–55

To Use the Accessibility Checker

In module 3 you learned to use the Accessibility Checker to identify issues that could prove difficult for people with disabilities to read, either alone or with adaptive tools, such as screen readers. The following steps use the Accessibility Checker to identity and fix an accessibility issue.

1

- Click the Review tab and then click the 'Check Accessibility' arrow (Review tab | Accessibility group) to display the Accessibility menu.

2

- Click Check Accessibility to display the Accessibility pane with a list of Errors or Warnings in the Inspection Results box.
- Click the Missing alternative text (1) direction arrow to display the object affected by the issue (Figure 5–56).

Q&A Why do my Inspection Results look different?
If you have a different version of Microsoft 365, your version may display different accessibility warnings. Additional accessibility warnings are listed for all accessibility errors made in forming the worksheet.

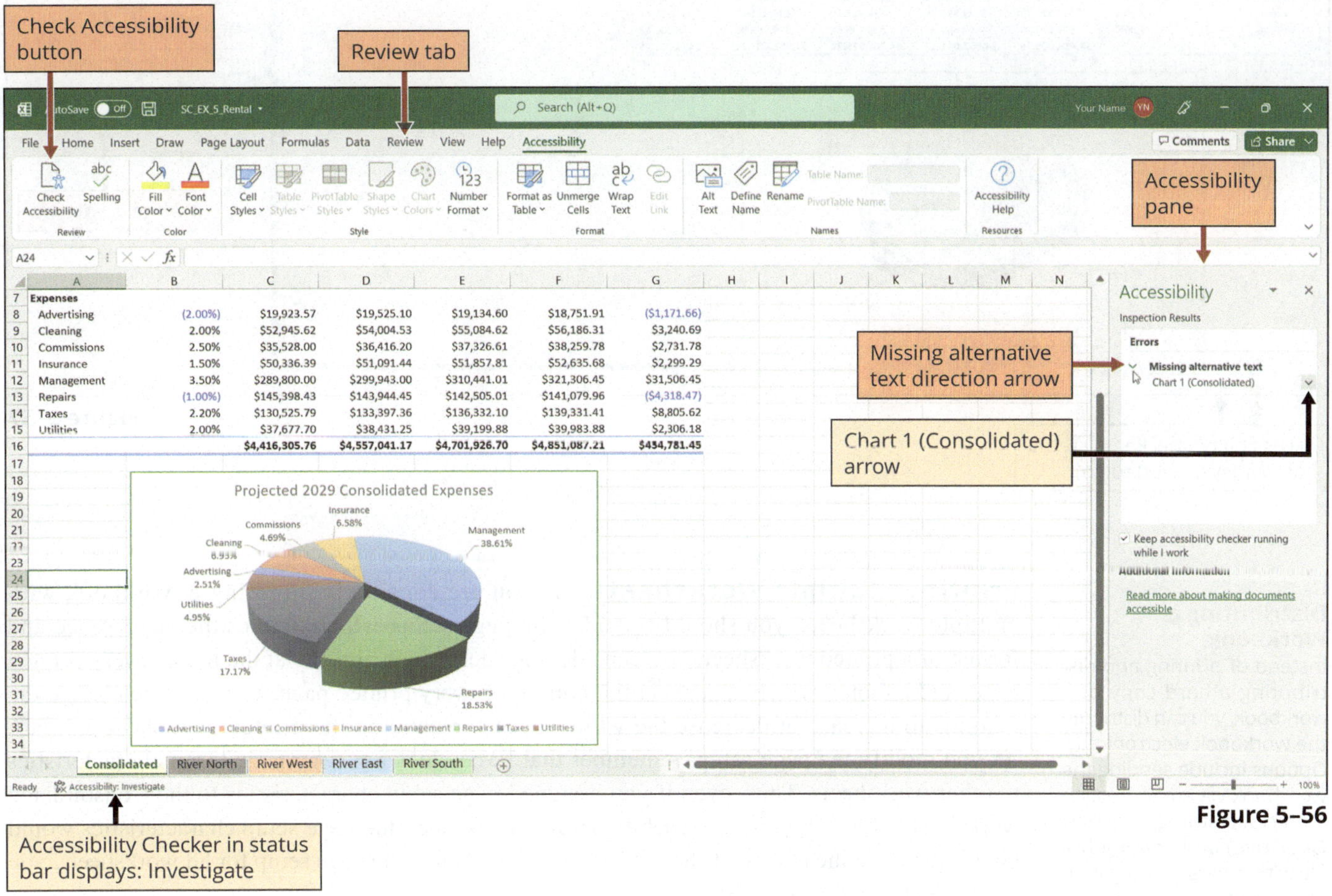

Figure 5–56

3

- Click the Chart 1 (Consolidated) arrow in the Accessibility pane to display the Recommended Actions list.

4

- Click Add a description to display the Alt Text pane.

5

- Enter the following alt text description in the text box: **3-D pie chart showing the Projected 2029 Consolidated Expenses. The Repairs category is being emphasized. The categories shown are Advertising, Cleaning, Commissions, Insurance, Management, Repairs, Taxes, and Utilities.** (Figure 5–57).

6

- Click the close button on the Alt text pane to enter the alt text and close the pane. The Accessibility pane is now updated to show no accessibility issues in the worksheet.

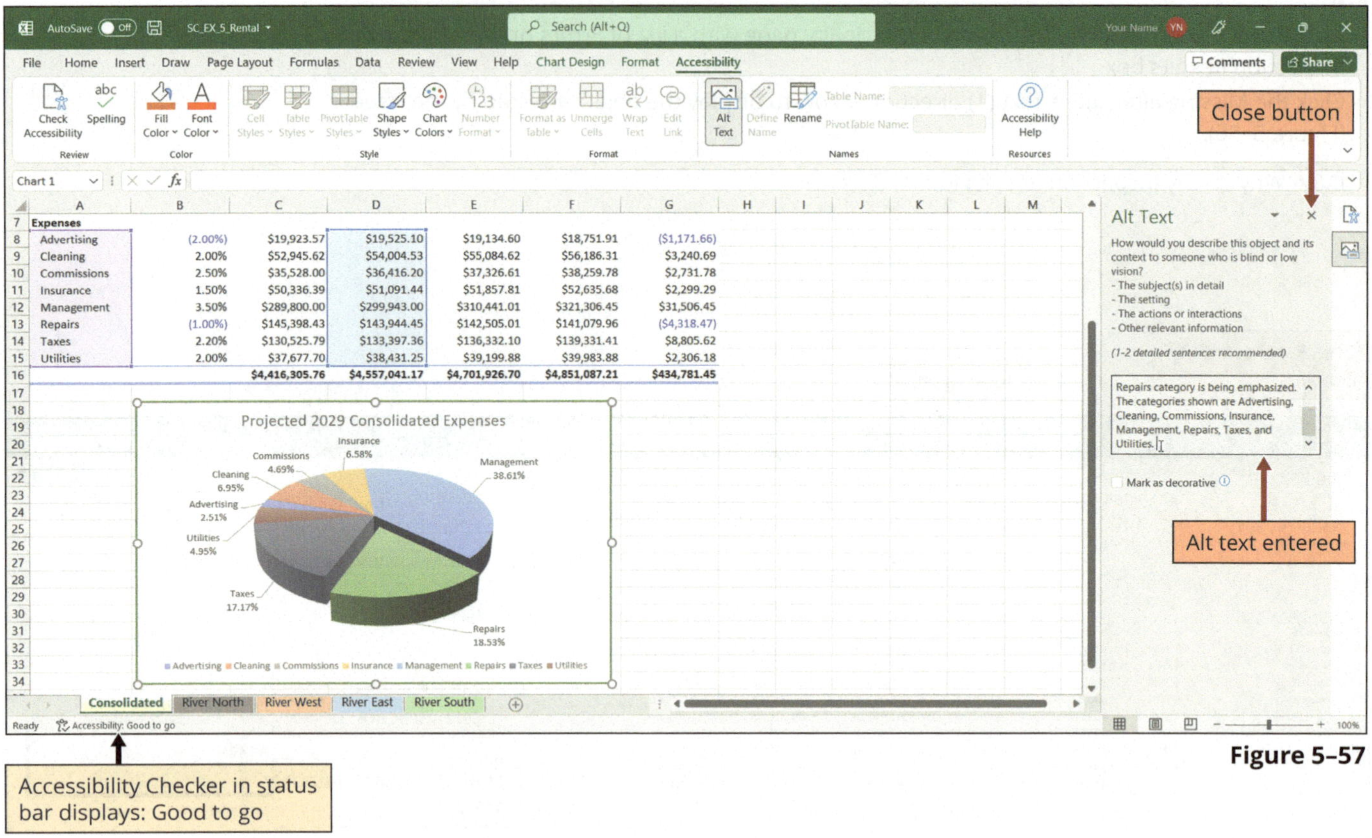

Figure 5–57

Distributing a Workbook
Instead of printing and distributing a hard copy of a workbook, you can distribute the workbook electronically. Options include sending the workbook via email; posting it on cloud storage (such as OneDrive) and sharing the file with others; posting it on social media, a blog, or other website; and sharing a link associated with an online location of the workbook. You also can create and share a PDF or XPS image of the workbook, so that users can view the file in Acrobat Reader or XPS Viewer instead of in Excel.

Printing Multiple Worksheets If you are considering printing a workbook with multiple worksheets, you should consider the page setup, which defines the appearance and format of a printed worksheet. You can add a header, which appears at the top of every printed page, and a footer, which appears at the bottom of every printed page. You also can change the margins to increase or decrease the white space surrounding the printed worksheet or chart. As you modify the page setup, remember that Excel does not copy page setup characteristics to other worksheets. Thus, even if you assigned page setup characteristics to the Consolidated worksheet before copying it to each location's worksheet, the page setup characteristics would not be copied to the new worksheet. If you want to change the page setup for all worksheets, you must select all worksheets first.

To Change Margins and Center the Printout Horizontally

The following steps select all of the worksheets and then use the Page Setup dialog box to change the margins and center the printout of each location's worksheet horizontally.

1. Right-click the Consolidated sheet tab and then click Select All Sheets on the shortcut menu.
2. Display the Page Layout tab and then click the Page Setup Dialog Box Launcher to display the Page Setup dialog box.
3. If necessary, click the Page tab (Page Setup dialog box) and then click Landscape to set the page orientation to landscape.
4. Click the Margins tab. Enter **.5** in both the Left box and Right box to change the left and right margins.
5. Click the Horizontally check box in the Center on page area to center the worksheet on the printed page horizontally (Figure 5–58).
6. Click OK (Page Setup dialog box) to close the Page Setup dialog box.

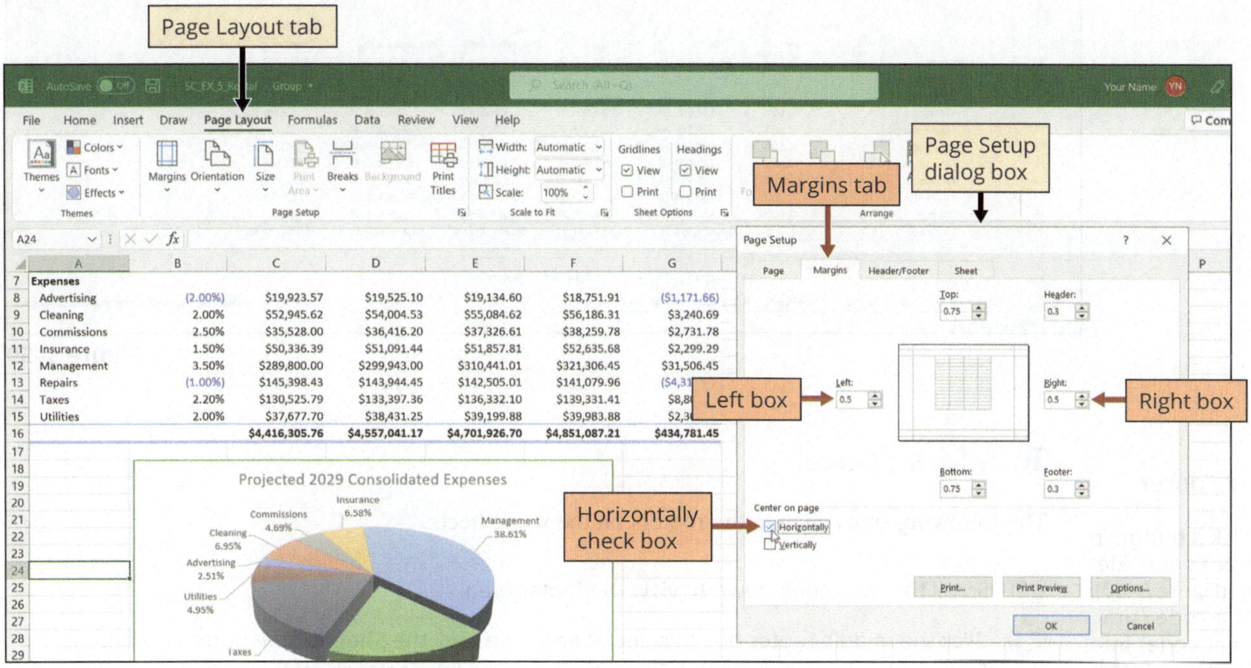

Figure 5–58

To Add a Header

The following steps use Page Layout view to change the headers on the worksheets.

1. With all of the worksheets still selected, click the Page Layout button on the status bar to display the first worksheet in Page Layout view.
2. If necessary, scroll the worksheet up until the Header area appears. Click the left header box and then type **Shelly Cashman** (or your name) to enter a page header in the left header box. If requested by your instructor, add your student ID number to the left header box, below the name entry.
3. Click the center header box and then type **Property Manager Worksheet** to enter the title (Figure 5–59).

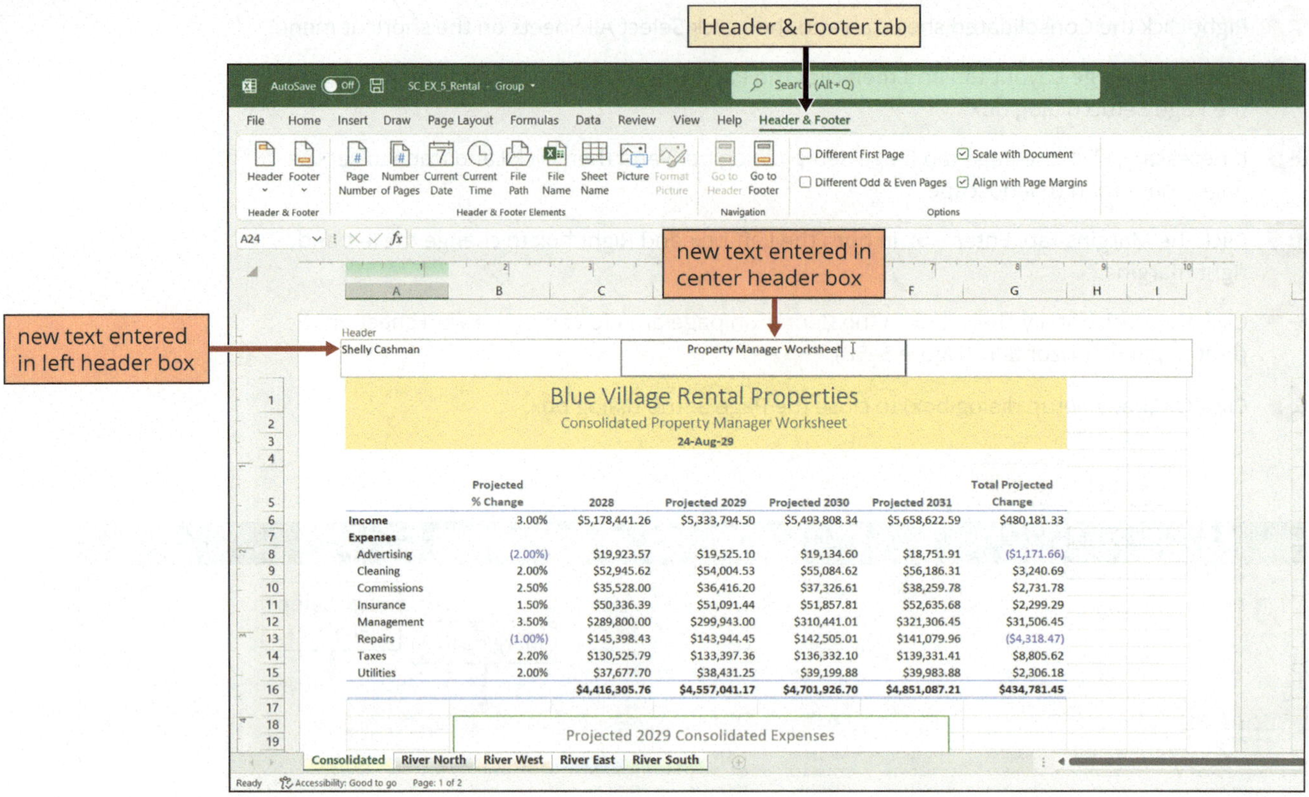

Figure 5–59

BTW
Header and Footer Codes
When you click a button in the Header & Footer Elements group (Figure 5–60), Excel enters a code (similar to a format code) into the active header or footer section. A code such as &[Page] instructs Excel to insert the page number. When you click outside of the footer box that contains the code, the results of the code are visible.

To Add a Footer

The following steps change the footers on the worksheets.

1. Scroll the workbook down to view the footer area.
2. Click the middle footer box to select it and then click the Sheet Name button (Header & Footer tab | Header & Footer Elements group) to insert the sheet name that appears on the sheet tab as part of the footer. Press SPACEBAR to add a space.
3. While in the same box, type **Page** as text. Press SPACEBAR and then click the Page Number button (Header & Footer tab | Header & Footer Elements group) to insert the page number in the footer (Figure 5–60).
4. Click anywhere on the worksheet to deselect the page footer.
5. Click the Normal button on the status bar to return to Normal view.

- **Experiment:** Click the left footer box, and then click other buttons in the Header & Footer Elements group on the Header & Footer tab. When finished, delete the contents of the left footer box.

Q&A My chart spills on to a second page. Is this a problem?
If your chart spills on to a section page while editing the header or footer, it is due to the default printer settings for your printer. This will not affect our distribution of the worksheet, but keep in mind you can always edit the print settings to fix this problem if it arises.

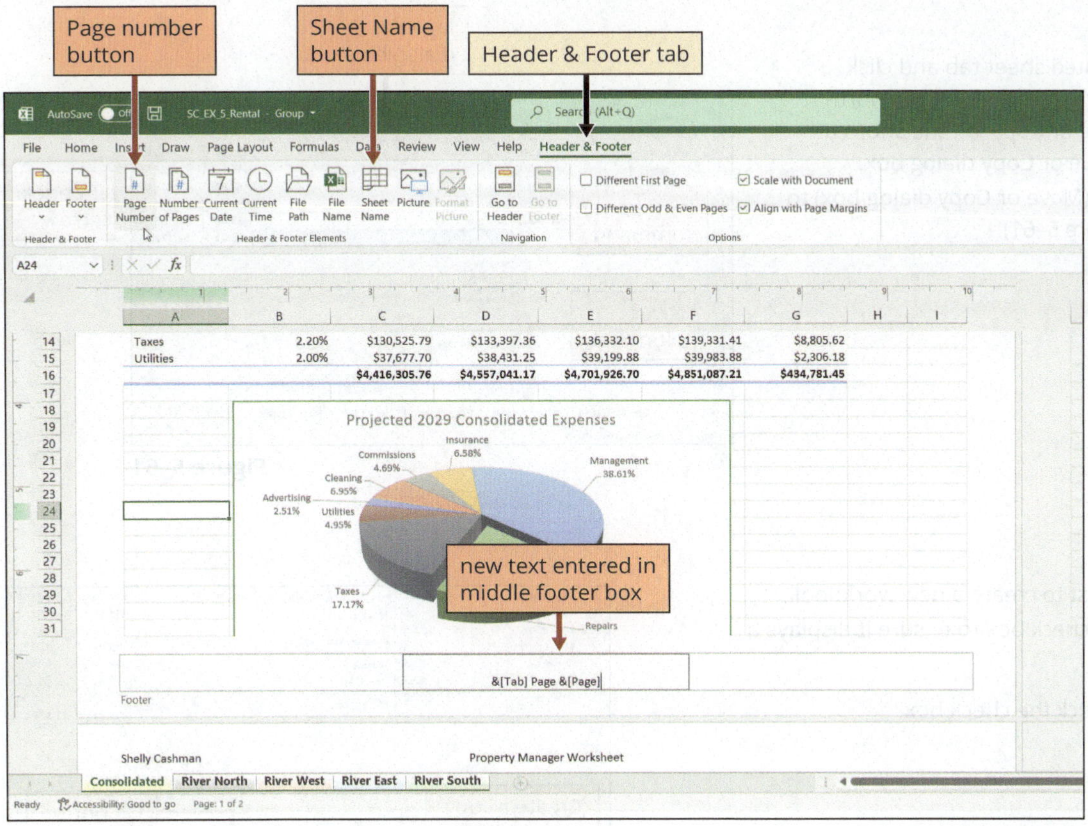

Figure 5–60

To Print Nonadjacent Sheets in a Workbook If you wanted to print nonadjacent sheets in a workbook, you would perform the following steps.

1. With the first sheet active, hold down CTRL, and then click the nonadjacent sheet tab.
2. Display the Print gallery in the Backstage view and then click the Print button to print the nonadjacent worksheets.
3. SHIFT+click the first sheet tab to deselect the nonadjacent sheet.

Creating Separate Files from Worksheets

Sometimes you may want to save individual worksheets as their own separate workbooks. For example, you may want to reveal only the data in an individual worksheet to certain customers or clients, or individual departments or franchises may want a copy of their own data. Keep in mind that any 3-D references will not work in the newly saved workbook. Saving, moving, or copying a worksheet to a new workbook sometimes is called splitting or breaking out the worksheets.

To Create a Separate File from a Worksheet

The following steps create a new workbook from each location worksheet. **Why?** Each individual rental property would like to receive a file with its own projections for the next three years. None of the four property worksheets contains a 3-D reference.

1

- Right-click the Consolidated sheet tab and click Ungroup Sheets. Then, right-click the River North sheet tab and click 'Move or Copy' on the shortcut menu to display the Move or Copy dialog box.
- Click the To book arrow (Move or Copy dialog box) to display the choices (Figure 5–61).

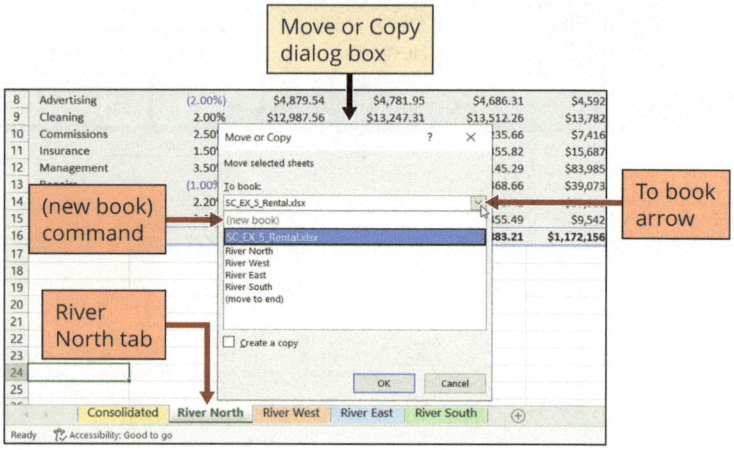

Figure 5–61

2

- Click (new book) in the list to create a new workbook.
- Click the 'Create a copy' check box to ensure it displays a check mark (Figure 5–62).

Q&A What if I do not check the check box?
In that case, Excel would remove the worksheet from the current workbook in a move function. The Consolidated sheet no longer would display values from the moved worksheet, breaking the 3-D reference.

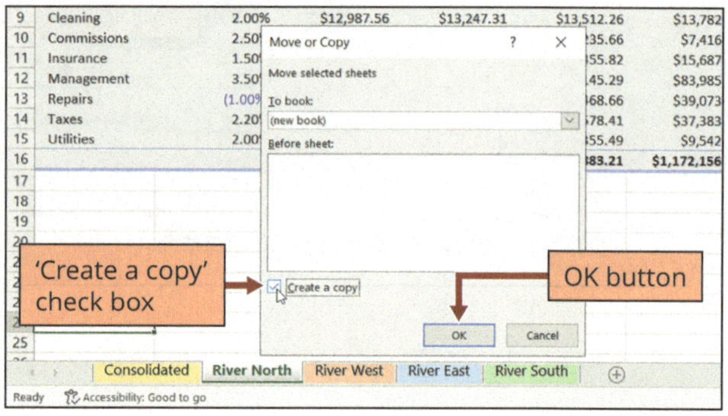

Figure 5–62

3

- Click OK to create the new workbook.
- Save the new file with the name **SC_EX_5_RiverNorth** in the same folder as the SC_EX_5_Rental file.

4

- Repeat Steps 1 through 3 to save the River West, River East and River South worksheets as separate workbooks in the same location. Use the new file names, **SC_EX_5_RiverWest**, **SC_EX_5_RiverEast** and **SC_EX_5_RiverSouth**.
- Save and close each workbook, including the SC_EX_5_Rental workbook.

BTW
Consolidation
You also can consolidate data across different workbooks using the Consolidate button (Data tab | Data Tools group), rather than by entering formulas. For more information on the consolidate button, type **Consolidate data** in the Search box.

Consolidating Data by Linking Separate Workbooks

Earlier in this module, the data from four worksheets was consolidated into a fifth worksheet in the same workbook using 3-D references; however, sometimes the data you need is not in the same workbook. In those cases, it is necessary to consolidate data from separate workbooks, which is also referred to as **linking**. A **link** is a reference to a cell, or range of cells, in another workbook. The consolidated main workbook that contains the links to the separate workbooks is called the **dependent workbook**. The separate, individual workbooks from which you need data are called the **source workbooks**.

You can create a link using the point mode if both the source workbook and dependent workbook(s) are open. If the source workbook is not open, you have to type the entire drive path, folder, worksheet name, and cell reference into the formula bar. This is known as an **absolute path**. You must include single quotes (‘’) surrounding the drive, folder, workbook name, and worksheet name. You must surround the workbook name with brackets ([ ]). You must include an exclamation point (!) as a delimiter between the sheet name and cell reference. The exclamation point is called an **external reference indicator** and is used in a formula to indicate that a referenced cell is outside the active sheet. For example, you might type the following:

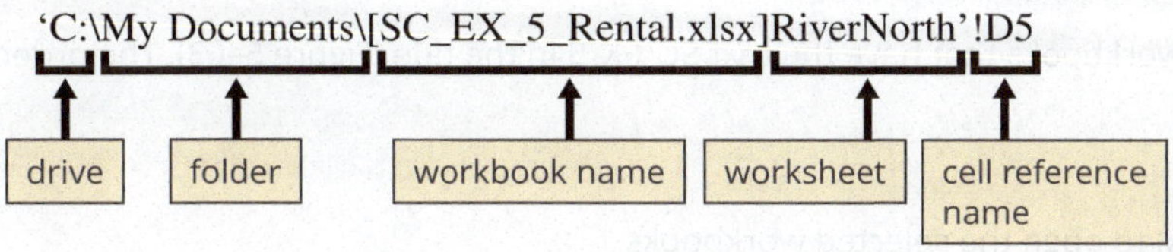

BTW

Circular References

A circular reference is a formula that depends on its own value. The most common type is a formula that contains a reference to the same cell in which the formula resides.

Moving Linked Workbooks Special care should be taken when moving linked workbooks. You should move all of the workbooks together. If you move the dependent workbook without the source workbook(s), all links become absolute—even if you used the point mode to reference them. In addition, if you happen to move the dependent workbook to another computer, without the source workbook(s), the link is broken.

Excel may offer to update or enable your links when you open the dependent workbook independent of the source workbook(s). After moving workbooks, it is best to open the source workbooks first.

The remainder of this module demonstrates how to search for workbooks and how to link separate workbooks, creating a Projected 2029 Consolidated Expenses Worksheet.

Consider This

What happens if I update data in one or more of the linked workbooks?

If the source workbooks are open, Excel automatically reads the data in the source workbooks and recalculates formulas in the dependent workbook. Any value changes in the open source workbooks will update in the dependent workbook.

If the source workbooks are not open, then Excel displays a security warning in a pane below the ribbon. If you click the Enable Content button in the warning pane, Excel reads the data in the source workbooks and recalculates the formulas in the dependent workbook, but it does not open the source workbooks.

To Open a Data File and Save It to a New Location

The SC_EX_5-1 workbook is located in the Data Files. Please contact your instructor for information about accessing the Data Files. The file contains headings and formatting and is ready for linking. In the following steps, you will open the workbook and save it to the same location as the files created in the previous steps. If the Data Files are saved in the same location as your previously saved solution files, you can omit these steps.

1. Start Excel, if necessary, and then open the file named SC_EX_5-1.
2. Go to Backstage view, click Save As, and then click Browse to open the Save As dialog box.
3. Navigate to the location of your previously saved files, and then save the workbook with the name, SC_EX_5-1, to save a copy of the file in the new location.
4. Close the file without exiting Excel.

To Search for and Open Workbooks

Excel has a powerful search tool that you can use to locate workbooks (or any file) stored on the hard drive, using the Search box in the Open dialog box. **Why?** The search tool can be used when you cannot remember exactly the name of the file or its location. In this example, the search text will be used to locate the necessary workbooks. The following steps locate and open the six workbooks of interest.

1

- Go to Backstage view and then click Open to display the Open screen.
- Click Browse in the left pane and then navigate to the location of your previously saved solution files.
- Type **SC_EX_5** in the Search box as the search text and then click the arrow button to display the files associated with this module.
- One at a time, CTRL+click each of the 6 workbooks that have the text SC_EX_5 in the title (Figure 5–63). The order and layout of your files may vary.

2

- Click the Open button (Open dialog box) to open the selected workbooks.

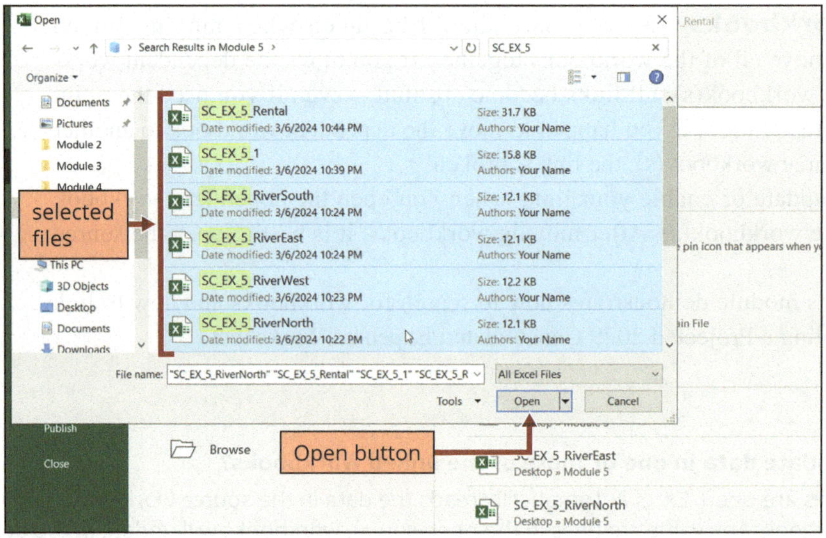

Figure 5–63

To Switch to a Different Open Workbook

The following steps switch to a different open workbook. **Why?** You may want to change quickly to another workbook to verify data.

1

- Display the View tab and then click the Switch Windows button (View tab | Window group) to display the names of the open workbooks (Figure 5–64). The order of your files may differ. However, if you do not see all six workbooks in your list, open the necessary file or files.

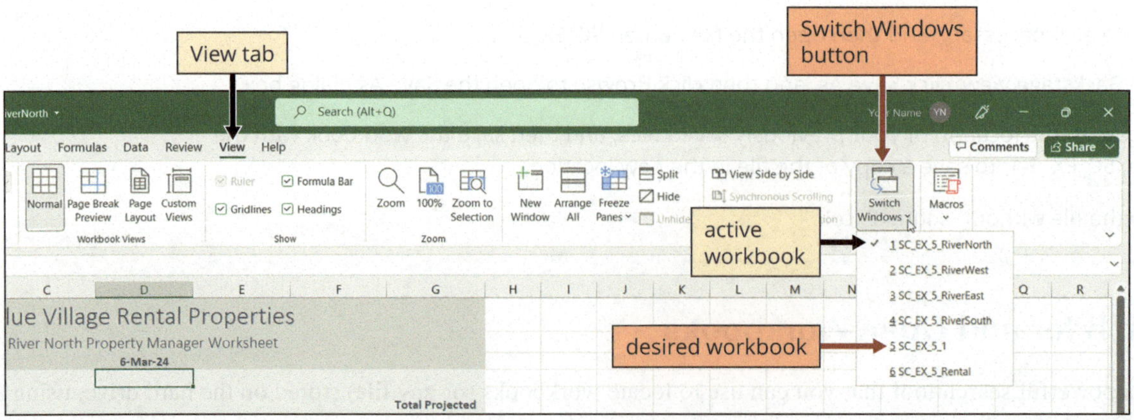

Figure 5–64

2

- Click the name of the SC_EX_5-1 workbook (Figure 5–65).

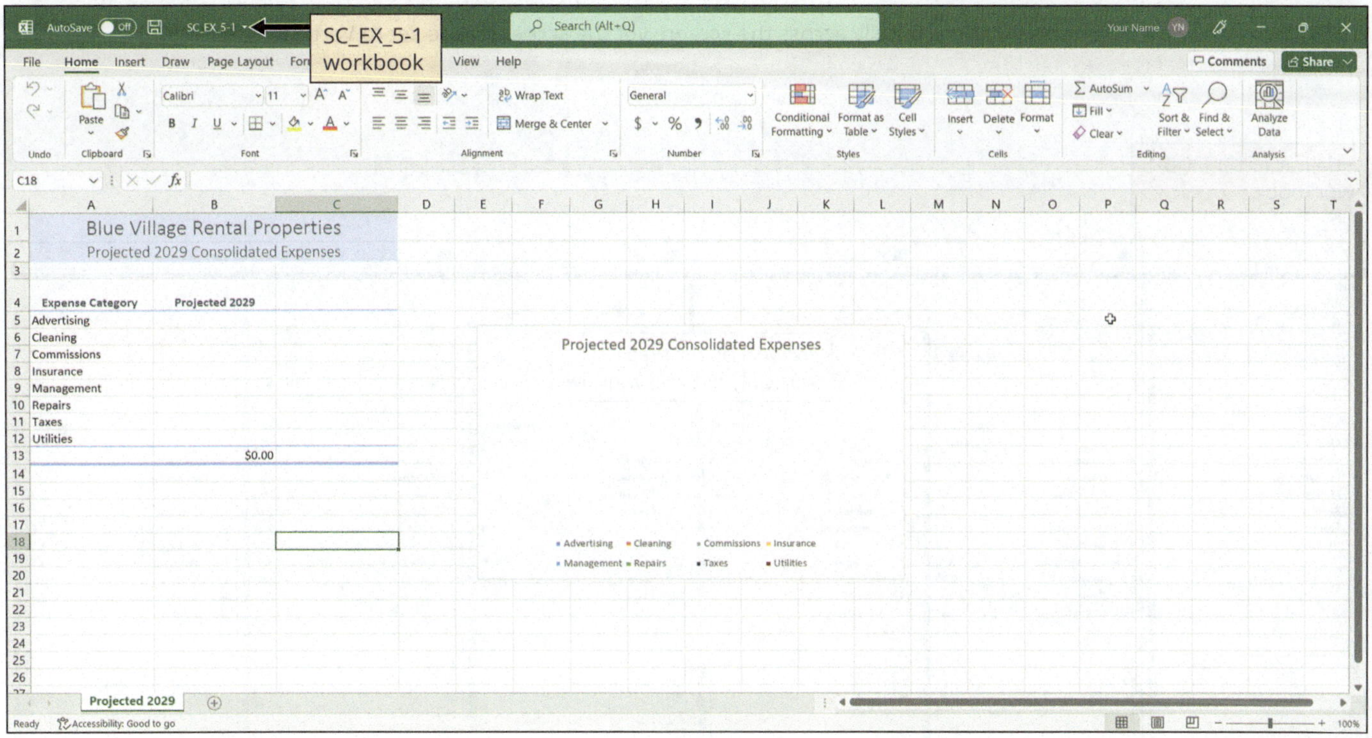

Figure 5–65

To Arrange Multiple Workbooks

The following steps arrange the multiple open workbooks on the screen so that each one appears in its own window. **Why?** Viewing multiple workbooks gives you a chance to check for related data and verify formats.

1

- Click the Arrange All button (View tab | Window group) to display the Arrange Windows dialog box.
- Click Vertical (Arrange Windows dialog box) to arrange the windows vertically, and then, if necessary, click the 'Windows of active workbook' check box to clear it (Figure 5–66).

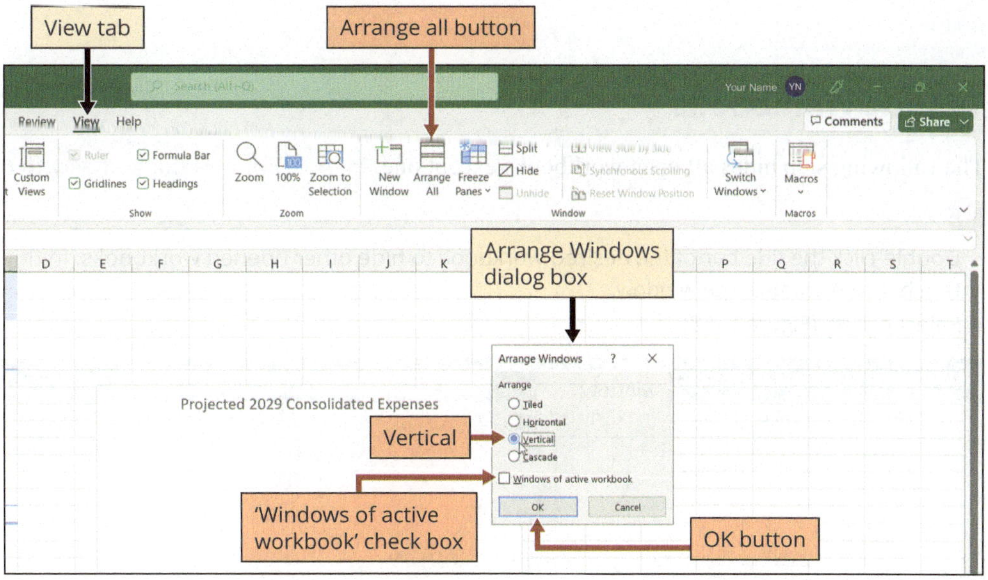

Figure 5–66

Q&A How can I arrange workbooks in the Excel window?

Multiple opened workbooks can be arranged in four ways as shown in the Arrange Windows dialog box. You can modify any of the arranged workbooks after first clicking within its window to activate it. To return to showing one workbook, double-click its title bar.

2

- Click OK (Arrange Windows dialog box) to display the opened workbooks arranged vertically (Figure 5–67). The order of your workbooks might vary; this is not a problem.

Q&A Why do the windows display horizontally across the screen, yet the screens were set to Vertical?
The chosen effect determines the change on an individual window, not the group of windows. When you select Vertical, each individual window appears vertically as tall as possible. If you choose Horizontal, the windows appear as wide as possible.

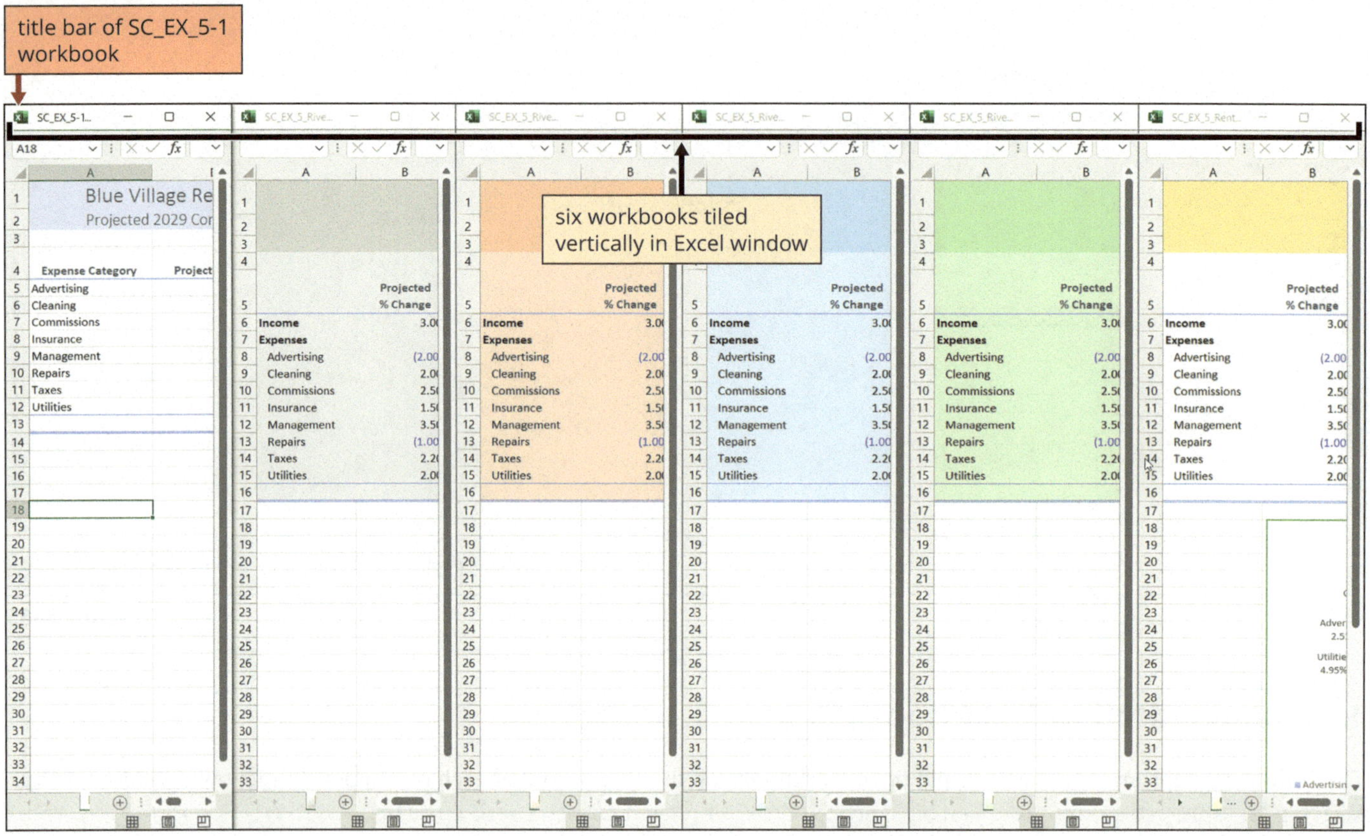

Figure 5–67

To Hide Workbooks

The following step hides all open workbooks except one. **Why?** Hiding is the best way to remove any tiling or arrangement.

1

- Double-click the title bar of the desired workbook to hide other opened workbooks. In this case, double-click the SC_EX_5-1 title bar to maximize the window.
- Select cell B5 (Figure 5–68).

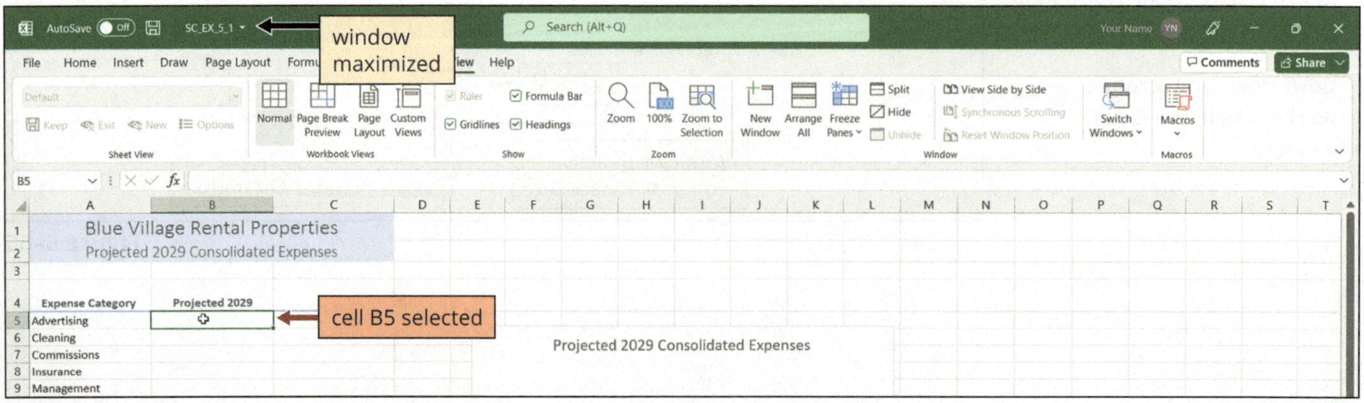

Figure 5–68

To Consolidate Data by Linking Workbooks

The following steps consolidate the data from the four location workbooks into the SC_EX_5-1 workbook. **Why?** When set up correctly, linking workbooks provides the user with a simple method of consolidating and updating linked data in the original workbook and any workbook with links to the updated data.

1

- Click the AutoSum button (Home tab | Editing group) to begin a SUM function entry in cell B5.
- Display the View tab and then click the Switch Windows button (View tab | Window group) to display the Switch Windows menu (Figure 5–69).

Q&A Does the workbook have to be open to link to it?

Yes, the workbook needs to be open if you want to use point mode. Otherwise, you would have to type the absolute or relative link.

Could I drill cell references in the formula?

No, drilling only applies to selected worksheets within a single workbook, not multiple open workbooks.

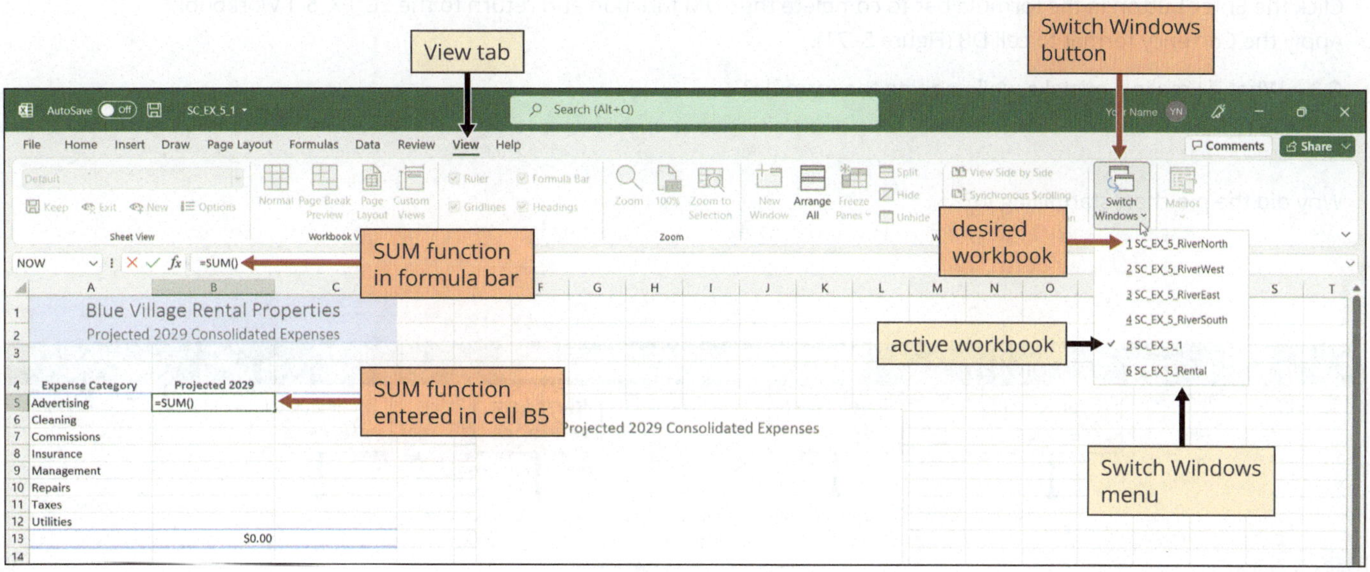

Figure 5–69

2

- Click the SC_EX_5_RiverNorth workbook name on the Switch Windows menu to select the workbook. Maximize the workbook window.
- Click cell D8 to select it.
- In the formula bar, delete the dollar signs ($) so that the cell reference is not absolute.
- In the formula bar, click immediately after D8 and then press COMMA (Figure 5–70).

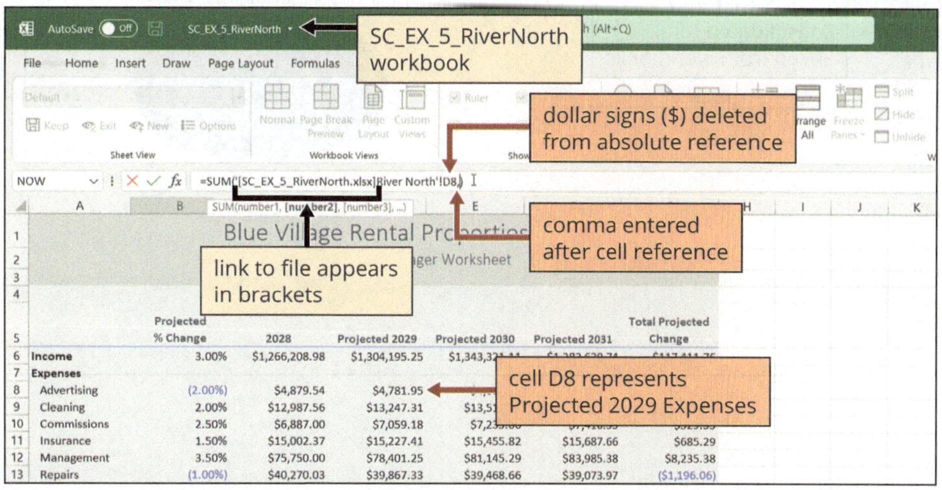

Figure 5–70

Q&A Why do I have to remove the dollar signs ($)?

Linked cell references are absolute ($D$8). You must edit the formula and change these to relative cell references because you plan to copy the SUM function in a later step. If the cell references were left as absolute, then the copied function always would refer to cell B5 in the three workbooks no matter where you copy the SUM function.

3

- Click the Switch Windows button (View tab | Window group) and then click the SC_EX_5_RiverWest workbook to display the workbook. Maximize the workbook window.
- Select cell D8 as the next argument in the SUM function.
- If necessary, click the Expand Formula Bar arrow (Formula bar) to display the entire formula. Delete the dollar signs ($) in the reference. Click immediately after D8 in the formula bar and then press COMMA.
- Click the Switch Windows button (View tab | Window group), and then click the SC_EX_5_RiverEast workbook. Maximize the workbook window.
- Select cell D8 as the next argument in the SUM function.
- If necessary, click the Expand Formula Bar arrow (Formula bar) to display the entire formula. Delete the dollar signs ($) in the reference. Click immediately after D8 in the formula bar and then press COMMA.
- Click the Switch Windows button (View tab | Window group), and then click the SC_EX_5_RiverSouth workbook. Maximize the workbook window.
- Select cell D8 as the final argument in the SUM function.
- In the formula bar, delete the dollar signs ($) in the reference.
- Click the Enter button in the formula bar to complete the SUM function and return to the SC_EX_5-1 workbook.
- Apply the Currency format to cell D8 (Figure 5–71).

Q&A What if I make a mistake while editing the formula?

If you are still editing, click the Cancel button in the formula bar, and start again. If you have entered the formula already, click the Undo button. Note that Excel formula error messages do not always indicate the exact location of the error.

Why did the pie chart start filling in?

Excel offers a live preview called **cell animation** that updates as you insert new data. The data file had the pie chart set up to reference the appropriate cells in column B.

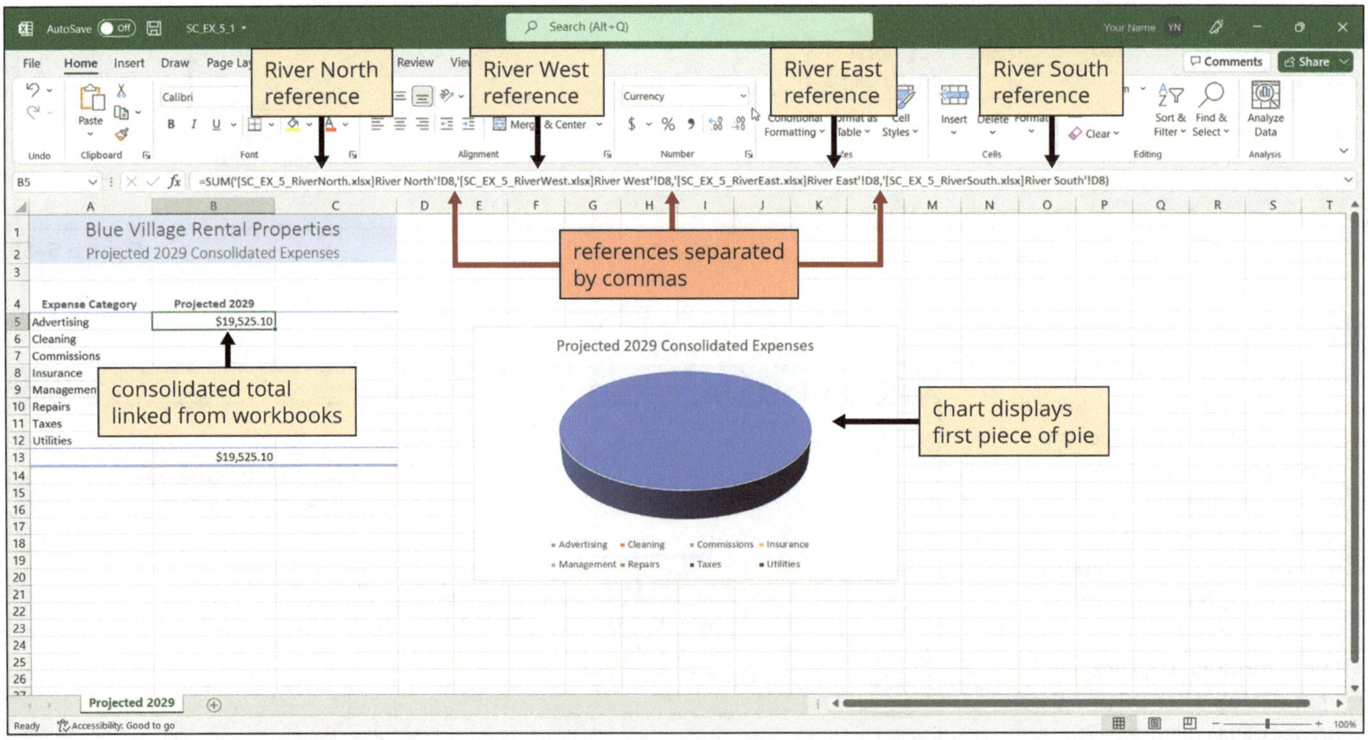

Figure 5–71

4

- With cell B5 active in the SC_EX_5-1 workbook, drag the cell's fill handle down through cell B12 to copy the formula to the range.
- Apply the Comma Style format (Home tab | Number group) to cells B6:B12 to remove the floating dollar signs.
- Format the chart as necessary, exploding the Repairs slice, adding percentages (with two decimal places), and adding leader lines as shown in Figure 5–72.

Q&A I cannot access the Chart Elements button. What should I do?
Click the Chart Elements arrow (Format tab | Current Selection group) and then choose the area you wish to format. Click the Format Selection button (Format tab | Current Selection group). The same dialog box or pane will open.

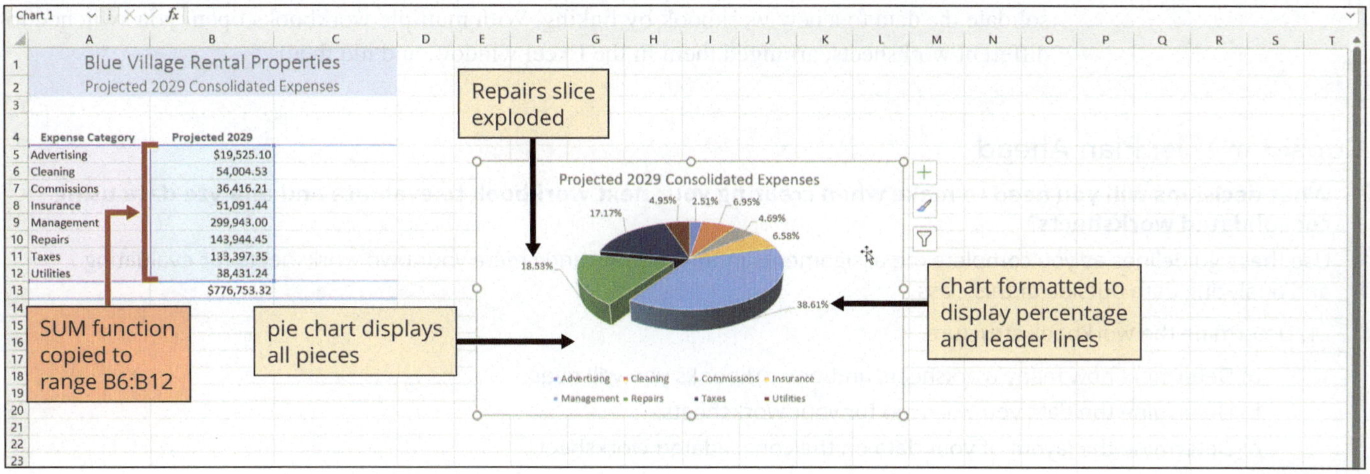

Figure 5–72

5

- Save the workbook using **SC_EX_5_Projected2029Expenses** as the filename.
- If Excel displays a dialog box, click OK (Microsoft Excel dialog box) to save the workbook.

To Close All Workbooks at One Time

To close all five workbooks at one time and exit Excel, complete the following steps.

1 **sam** Right-click the Excel app button on the taskbar and then click 'Close all windows' on the shortcut menu to close all open workbooks and exit Excel.

2 If a dialog box appears, click the Save button to save any changes made to the files since the last save.

3 The workbooks, SC_EX_5_Projected2029Expenses and SC_EX_5_Rental, are the workbooks you will submit for this module.

BTW
Recovering Unsaved Changes
If you have to recover an unsaved workbook in Excel, you may be able to do so by clicking File on the Ribbon, clicking Info, clicking Manage Workbook, and then clicking Recover Unsaved Workbooks.

Summary

In this module, you learned how to create and use a consolidated worksheet. After using the Fill button to create a series, you used the TODAY and ROUND functions to format data. You created a custom format code that used specialized percentage styles for both positive and negative numbers. You learned how to work with multiple worksheets including several ways to copy worksheet data to a new worksheet and drill an entry through those new worksheets. As you created the consolidated worksheet, you entered a 3-D reference and used the Paste gallery to replicate that reference. You added a pie chart to the consolidated worksheet complete with an exploded slice and formatted data labels with leader lines. You printed the multiple worksheets. Finally, you learned how to break out or split the worksheets into separate workbooks and consolidate the data to a new workbook by linking. With multiple workbooks open, you switched to different worksheets, arranged them in the Excel window, and hid them.

Consider This: Plan Ahead

What decisions will you need to make when creating your next workbook to evaluate and analyze data using consolidated worksheets?

Use these guidelines as you complete the assignments in this module and create your own worksheets for evaluating and analyzing data outside of this class.

1. Determine the workbook structure.
   a) Determine how many worksheets and/or workbooks you will need.
   b) Determine the data you will need for your worksheets.
   c) Determine the layout of your data on the consolidated worksheet.
2. Create and format the consolidated worksheet.
   a) Enter titles, subtitles, and headings.
   b) Enter placeholder data, functions, and formulas.
3. Format the worksheet.
   a) Format the titles, subtitles, and headings.
   b) Format the numbers as necessary.
   c) Create and use custom format codes and styles.
4. Create the additional worksheets.
   a) Determine the best method for adding additional worksheets, based on the data in the consolidated worksheet.
   b) Add the new worksheets to the workbook.
   c) Add data and formatting to the new worksheets.
   d) Create 3-D references where necessary to replace placeholders in the consolidated sheet with calculated values.
5. Create and use charts.
   a) Select the data to chart.
   b) Select a chart type for selected data.
   c) Format the chart elements.
6. Consolidate workbooks.
   a) Create separate workbooks from worksheets if necessary.
   b) Link multiple workbooks to facilitate easy updating of data across workbooks.

Student Assignments

Apply Your Knowledge

Reinforce the skills and apply the concepts you learned in this module.

Consolidating Payroll Worksheets

Note: To complete this assignment, you will be required to use the Data Files. Please contact your instructor for information about accessing the Data Files.

Instructions: Start Excel. Open the workbook SC_EX_5-2.xlsx, which is located in the Data Files. The workbook you open contains budget information for three locations of a Restaurant Management company over the period of six months. You are to consolidate the budgetary figures. At the conclusion of the instructions, the Consolidated sheet should resemble the worksheet shown in Figure 5–73.

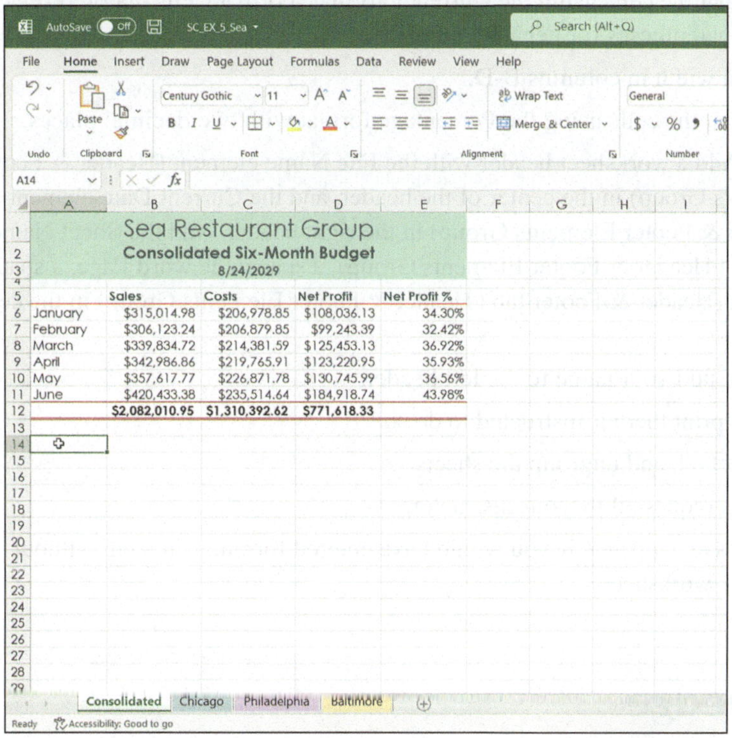

Figure 5–73

Perform the following tasks:

1. Save the workbook with the file name, SC_EX_5_Sea.
2. One by one, click each of the tabs and review the individual cities monthly sales and costs. Change each tab color to match the background color of cell A1 on the corresponding worksheet for all four worksheets.
3. To consolidate the worksheets, first click the Consolidated sheet tab to select only the Consolidated worksheet. To create a SUM function with a 3-D reference, select cell B6, and then click the AutoSum button (Home tab | Editing group). Click the Chicago sheet tab to display the worksheet, and then click cell B6 to select the first portion of the argument for the SUM function. SHIFT+click the Baltimore sheet tab to select the ending range of the argument for the SUM function. Click the Enter button in the formula bar to enter the SUM function with the 3-D references in the selected cell.

Continued on next page

4. On the Consolidated sheet, copy the formula in cell B6. Paste the formula into the ranges B7:B11 and C6:C11 using the Formulas button in the Paste gallery.
5. Right-click the Consolidated tab and then click Select All Sheets on the shortcut menu to group them. Perform the following steps.
   a. Select cell D6. Calculate the net profit by subtracting the January costs from the January sales.
   b. Use the fill handle to copy the formula to cells D7:D11.
   c. Select cell E6. Use the ROUND function with four decimal places to calculate the net profit % by dividing the net profit by sales.
   d. Use the fill handle to replicate the function to cells E7:E11.
   e. Format the range A12:E12 with the Total cell style.
   f. Use the SUM function to total the data in columns B, C, and D.
   g. Insert the date in cell C3 using the TODAY function, apply the Heading 4 cell style, and center the text in the cell.
   h. Select the range B6:D12. Format the cells using the Currency format (Format Cells dialog box) with a floating dollar sign and black parentheses for negative numbers.
   i. If necessary, adjust the column width in columns B-D.
   j. Select the range E6:E11. Format the cells using the Percentage format with two decimal places.
   k. Switch to Page Layout view. Add a worksheet header with the File Name element (Header & Footer tab | Header & Footer Elements Group) in the center of the header, and the Current Date element (Header & Footer tab | Header & Footer Elements Group) in the right header. Add the Sheet Name element (Header & Footer tab | Header & Footer Elements Group), a space, the word Page, a space, and the Page Number element (Header & Footer tab | Header & Footer Elements Group) in the center of the footer.
   l. If requested by your instructor, add your name to the left header.
6. Preview the four worksheets and print them if instructed to do so.
7. Right-click the Consolidated sheet tab and ungroup the sheets.
8. Save the workbook and submit as requested by your instructor.
9. **Consider This:** What would have happened if you would have entered formulas in a tab without drilling the data through the other worksheets?

Extend Your Knowledge

Extend the skills you learned in this module and experiment with new skills. You may need to use Help to complete the assignment.

Creating and Editing Custom 3-D Charts

Note: To complete this assignment, you will be required to use the Data Files. Please contact your instructor for information about accessing the Data Files.

Instructions: Start Excel. Open the workbook called SC_EX_5-3.xlsx, which is located in the Data Files and shown in Figure 5–74. This workbook you open contains sales data, for which you will create a custom format code, and then turn into a 3-D graph.

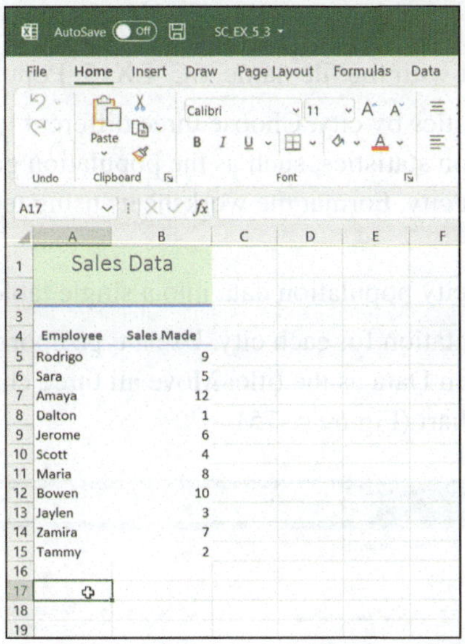

Figure 5–74

Perform the following tasks:

1. Save the workbook as SC_EX_5_SalesData.
2. Select cell A2. Enter a formula to display today's date. Change the format to mm/dd/yy.
3. Insert a 3-D pie chart for the data.
   a. Change the title to **Monthly Sales Made**.
   b. Change the chart style to Style 8, and format the Data Labels to display values in addition to category names.
   c. Emphasize the three highest performing sales associates by exploding the three corresponding slices by 15%.
   d. Change the X Rotation to 50° and the Y Rotation to 40°.
4. Using the Accessibility Checker, add the alt text description to the pie chart: **3-D pie chart showing the Monthly Sales Made. Amaya, Bowen, and Rodrigo are being emphasized for having the highest performance.**
5. Move the chart if necessary so the left edge of the chart aligns with the left edge of column D and the top aligns with the top of row 2.
6. Add a header to the worksheet that contains the file name in the center section.
7. If requested by your instructor, enter your name in the right header section.
8. Set the print orientation to Landscape.
9. Save your changes to the workbook and submit the revised workbook as specified by your instructor, printing if required by your instructor.
10. **Consider This:** Are there any other chart modifications you would have made? Does exploding three pie slices work in this context, or would you have chosen a different amount of slices to explode?

Expand Your World

Create a solution that uses cloud and web technologies by learning and investigating on your own from general guidance.

Consolidating and Charting Census Data in a Workbook

Instructions: Start Excel. You are to gather and analyze census data from four cities for a group social studies project. You decide to use Excel to create the charts and store the data.

Continued on next page

Perform the following tasks:

1. Start Excel. Open a blank workbook, and save it with the file name, SC_EX_5_Population.
2. Navigate to data.census.gov for population statistics by city. Choose three different locations or use ones suggested by your instructor. Copy the population statistics, such as the population groups by age, to your workbook. Create a separate worksheet for each city. Format the worksheets using techniques you have used in this module.
3. Create a master worksheet that consolidates all city population data into a single table.
4. For each city, create a chart depicting the precipitation for each city. Use a type appropriate to your data. Use the City Name and Senior Citizen Population Data as the title. Move all three charts to a single new worksheet. Enter alt text descriptions for each chart (Figure 5–75).

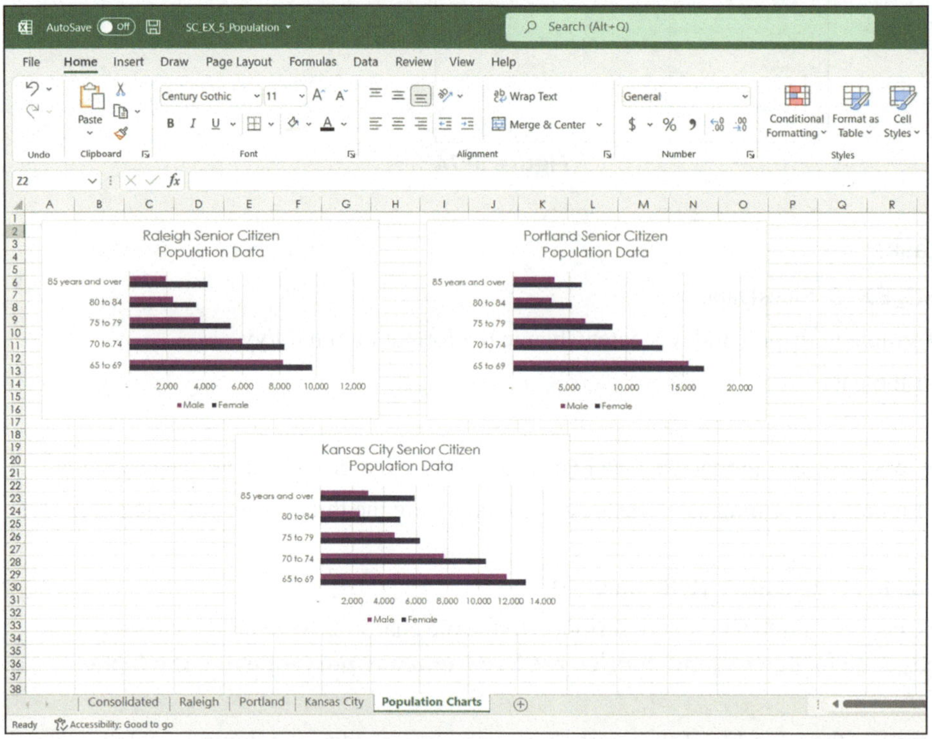

Figure 5–75

5. Save the workbook and submit it as specified by your instructor.
6. **Consider This:** How did you choose your chart type? How could you make the charts more meaningful? What kind of chart would you use for the consolidated worksheet?

In the Lab

Design and implement a solution using creative thinking and problem-solving skills.

Tracking Phone Usage Data

Problem: You have decided to try and cut back on time spent on your phone. You decide to track the times you spend on some of your favorite mobile apps. You decide to use Excel to track information about the amount of time spent on each app, and the frequency of usage on each, divided into different categories. For instance, you might choose to track your time spent on your favorite gaming apps, social media apps, video media apps, messaging apps, and so on. You plan to record the time spent on every app in each category you select, giving each category its own sheet, and track daily usage for seven days. You then plan to consolidate the data so that you can track and review both individual usage and overall usage time by category for these apps.

Perform the following tasks:

Part 1: Use the concepts and techniques presented in this module to create a workbook for tracking the time you spend on mobile apps. You want to create a workbook that contains multiple worksheets to allow you to review daily data, as well as consolidated data. Use your knowledge of consolidation to design a workbook that will allow you to analyze your progress. You should have at least one computed field, such as average time spent per application, in your worksheets. You should include at least one chart presenting mobile app usage data. Submit your assignment in the format specified by the instructor.

Part 2: **Consider This:** This exercise had you create a chart presenting mobile app usage data. List one type of chart you used to display your mobile app usage. Why did you use this type of chart?

Creating, Sorting, and Querying a Table

Objectives

After completing this module, you will be able to:

- Create and manipulate a table
- Delete duplicate records
- Use the VLOOKUP and XLOOKUP functions to look up a value in a table
- Add calculated columns to a table with structured references
- Use icon sets with conditional formatting
- Insert a total row
- Sort a table on one field or multiple fields
- Sort, query, and search a table using AutoFilter
- Remove filters
- Create criteria and extract ranges
- Evaluate table data with the DAVERAGE and DCOUNT database functions
- Apply the SUMIF and COUNTIF statistical functions
- Display automatic subtotals
- Use outline features to group, hide, and unhide data
- Create a treemap chart

Introduction

A **table**, also called a **database**, is an organized collection of rows and columns of similarly structured data on a worksheet. For example, a list of friends, a group of students registered for a class, an inventory list, a club membership roster, or an instructor's grade book—all can be arranged as tables on a worksheet. In these cases, the data related to each person or item is called a **record**, and the individual data items that make up a record are called **fields**. For example, in a table of clients, each client would make up a separate record; each record might include several fields, such as name, address, phone number, current balance, billing rate, and status. A record also can include fields that contain references, formulas, and functions.

You can use a worksheet's row-and-column structure to organize and store a table. Each row of a worksheet can store a record, and each column can store one field for each record. Additionally, a row of column headings at the top of the worksheet can store field names that identify each field.

After you enter a table onto a worksheet, you can use Excel to (1) add and delete records, (2) change the values of fields in records, (3) sort the records so that Excel presents them in a different order, (4) determine subtotals for numeric fields, (5) display records that meet comparison criteria, and (6) analyze data using database functions. This module illustrates all six of these table capabilities.

Project: Analyzing Coffee Company Invoices

The project in this module follows proper design guidelines and uses Excel to create the worksheet shown in Figures 6–1a and 6–1b, and the chart (Figure 6–1c). A direct-to-consumer online coffee company has been collecting invoices and plans to analyze their marketing strategies using the information collected. One strategy involved introducing a promotional code to be used in the month of March. Unfortunately, the promo code was not correctly coded for use on the website; consequently, all orders that were placed in March using the promo code were incorrectly charged to reflect the full price. The marketing team has produced a monthly workbook that lists invoice numbers, dates, and amounts, as well as shipping destination, sale origin and promo code usage. The marketing team will need to assess the invoices and determine which orders require a refund to properly reflect their promo code usage. The data in the workbook should be easy to summarize, sort, edit, and query.

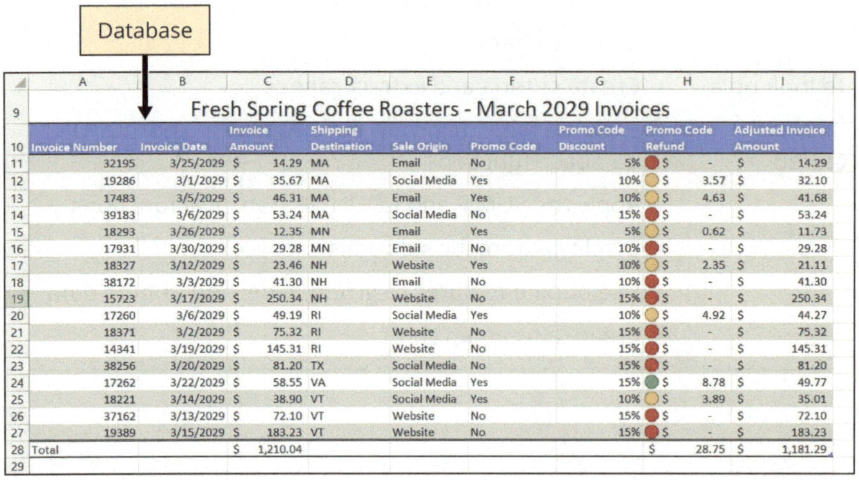

Fresh Spring Coffee Roasters - March 2029 Invoices

Invoice Number	Invoice Date	Invoice Amount	Shipping Destination	Sale Origin	Promo Code	Promo Code Discount	Promo Code Refund	Adjusted Invoice Amount
32195	3/25/2029	$ 14.29	MA	Email	No	5%	$ -	$ 14.29
19286	3/1/2029	$ 35.67	MA	Social Media	Yes	10%	$ 3.57	$ 32.10
17483	3/5/2029	$ 46.31	MA	Email	Yes	10%	$ 4.63	$ 41.68
39183	3/6/2029	$ 53.24	MA	Social Media	No	15%	$ -	$ 53.24
18293	3/26/2029	$ 12.35	MN	Email	Yes	5%	$ 0.62	$ 11.73
17931	3/30/2029	$ 29.28	MN	Email	No	10%	$ -	$ 29.28
18327	3/12/2029	$ 23.46	NH	Website	Yes	10%	$ 2.35	$ 21.11
38172	3/3/2029	$ 41.30	NH	Email	No	10%	$ -	$ 41.30
15723	3/17/2029	$ 250.34	NH	Website	No	15%	$ -	$ 250.34
17260	3/6/2029	$ 49.19	RI	Social Media	Yes	10%	$ 4.92	$ 44.27
18371	3/2/2029	$ 75.32	RI	Website	No	15%	$ -	$ 75.32
14341	3/19/2029	$ 145.31	RI	Website	No	15%	$ -	$ 145.31
38256	3/20/2029	$ 81.20	TX	Social Media	No	15%	$ -	$ 81.20
17262	3/22/2029	$ 58.55	VA	Social Media	Yes	15%	$ 8.78	$ 49.77
18221	3/14/2029	$ 38.90	VT	Social Media	Yes	10%	$ 3.89	$ 35.01
37162	3/13/2029	$ 72.10	VT	Website	No	15%	$ -	$ 72.10
19389	3/15/2029	$ 183.23	VT	Website	No	15%	$ -	$ 183.23
Total		$ 1,210.04					$ 28.75	$ 1,181.29

Figure 6–1a

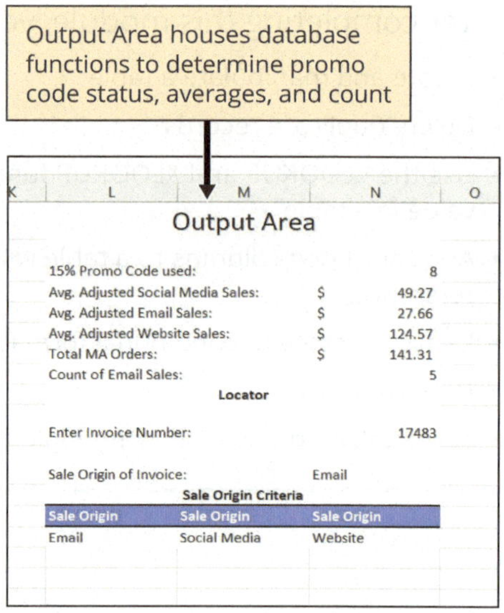

Output Area

15% Promo Code used:		8
Avg. Adjusted Social Media Sales:	$	49.27
Avg. Adjusted Email Sales:	$	27.66
Avg. Adjusted Website Sales:	$	124.57
Total MA Orders:	$	141.31
Count of Email Sales:		5

Locator

Enter Invoice Number:		17483
Sale Origin of Invoice:	Email	

Sale Origin Criteria

Sale Origin	Sale Origin	Sale Origin
Email	Social Media	Website

Figure 6–1b

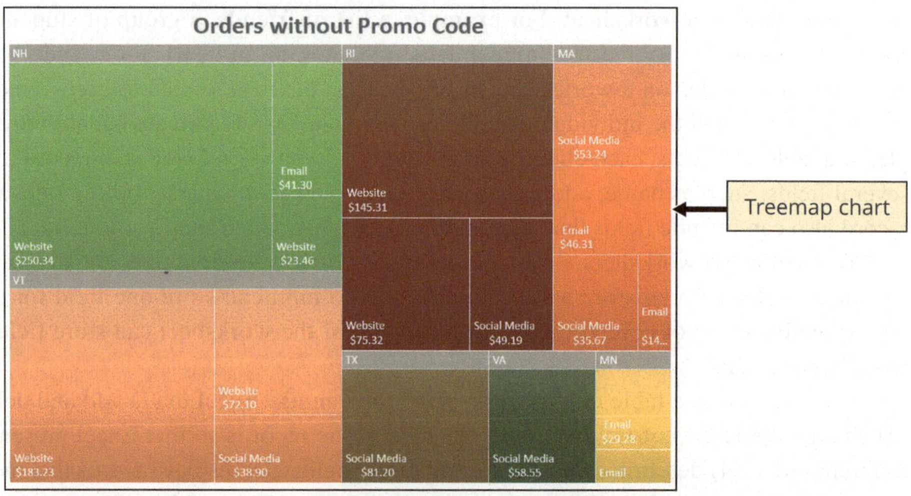

Figure 6–1c

Figure 6–2 shows a sample requirements document for the Fresh Spring Coffee Roasters Invoice Table. It includes the needs, source of data, calculations, special requirements, and other facts about its development.

Worksheet Title	Fresh Spring Coffee Roasters Invoice Table
Needs	• A worksheet table that lists the invoice number, invoice date, invoice, product code, sale origin, shipping destination, and if a promotional code was used at checkout. • The worksheet also should assign the promo code percentage based on the invoice amount. • The worksheet should calculate the amount of money to be refunded to the customer based on the promo code percentage, and the adjusted invoice amount after the refund. • The worksheet should be easy for management to sort, search, filter, and total.
Source of Data	Data supplied by the coffee company includes the information listed in the first Needs bullet above and detailed in Table 6–1 below. Remaining numbers on the worksheet are based on calculations.

Calculations	The following calculations are needed:
	• Promo Code Refund = Invoice Amount * Promo Code Discount (IF function)
	• Adjusted Invoice Amount = Invoice Amount − Promo Code Refund
	• Promo Code Discount that is determined as follows:
	  • 15% if Invoice Amount is more than $50
	  • 10% if Invoice Amount is between $20 and $50
	  • 5% if Invoice Amount is less than $20
	• Average Adjusted Sales for each sale origin (DAVERAGE function)
	• Count of 15% promo code used (DCOUNT function)
	• Total Massachusetts orders (SUMIF function)
	• Total count of email sales (COUNTIF function)

Other Requirements	• Provide a way to search, sort, and select data based on certain criteria. • Provide an area to ascertain statistics about the invoices, such as averages, counts, and totals based on specific factors. • A criteria area will be created above the table to store criteria for use in a query. An extract area will be created below the table to display records that meet the criteria. • Provide a hierarchical and visual chart to display all of the orders without promo codes, the type of order, and the order amounts.

Figure 6–2

Table 6–1 describes the field names, columns, types of data, and descriptions that you can refer to when creating the table.

Table 6–1: Column Information for Fresh Spring Coffee Roasters Invoice Table

Column Heading (Field Names)	Column in Worksheet	Type of Data	Description
Invoice Number	A	Numeric	5-digit whole number
Invoice Date	B	Numeric	Date of sale
Invoice Amount	C	Numeric	Dollar value of sale
Shipping Destination	D	Text	Destination of the product shipped, designed by two letter state code
Sale Origin	E	Text	Categorizes where the sale originated from, either social media, email, or the company website
Promo Code	F	Text	Confirms with a yes or no whether a promo code was entered at checkout
Promo Code Discount	G	Numeric calculation (XLOOKUP function)	Percentage of 5, 10, or 15 categorized by invoice amount
Promo Code Refund	H	Numeric calculation (IF function with invoice amount * promo code discount)	Dollar amount
Adjusted Invoice Amount	I	Numeric calculation (Invoice Amount − Promo Code Refund)	Dollar amount

Using a sketch of the worksheet can help you visualize its design. The sketch of the table consists of the title, column headings, location of data values, and an idea of the desired formatting, as well as promo code table (Figure 6–3a). (The sketch does not show the criteria area above the table or the extract area below the table.) The general layout of the output area, and required statistics and query are shown in Figure 6–3b.

Fresh Spring Coffee Roasters - March 2029 Invoices

Invoice Number	Invoice Date	Invoice Amount	Shipping Destination	Sale Origin	Promo Code	Promo Code Discount	Promo Code Refund	Adjusted Invoice Amount
XXXXX	X/XX/XXX	$99.99	XX	XXXXX	XXX	XX%	$99.99	$99.99

Promo Code Table

Spend ($)	Promo Code Discount
50	15%
20	10%
0	5%

Figure 6–3a

Output Area		
15% Promo Code used:		8
Avg. Adjusted Social Media Sales:	$	49.27
Avg. Adjusted Email Sales:	$	27.66
Avg. Adjusted Website Sales:	$	124.57
Total MA Orders:	$	141.31
Count of Email Sales:		5
Locator		
Enter Invoice Number:		17483
Sale Origin of Invoice:	Email	
Sale Origin Criteria		

Figure 6–3b

To Open and Save a File

The following steps open a file and save it with a new name. To complete these steps, you will be required to use the Data Files. Please contact your instructor for information about accessing the Data Files.

1. **sam** Start Excel and open the Data File named SC_EX_6-1.xlsx.
2. If the Excel window is not maximized, click the Maximize button on its title bar to maximize the window.

3. Save the workbook on your hard drive, OneDrive, or a location that is most appropriate to your situation, using **SC_EX_6_Invoices** as the file name.
4. If necessary, click cell A1 (Figure 6–4).

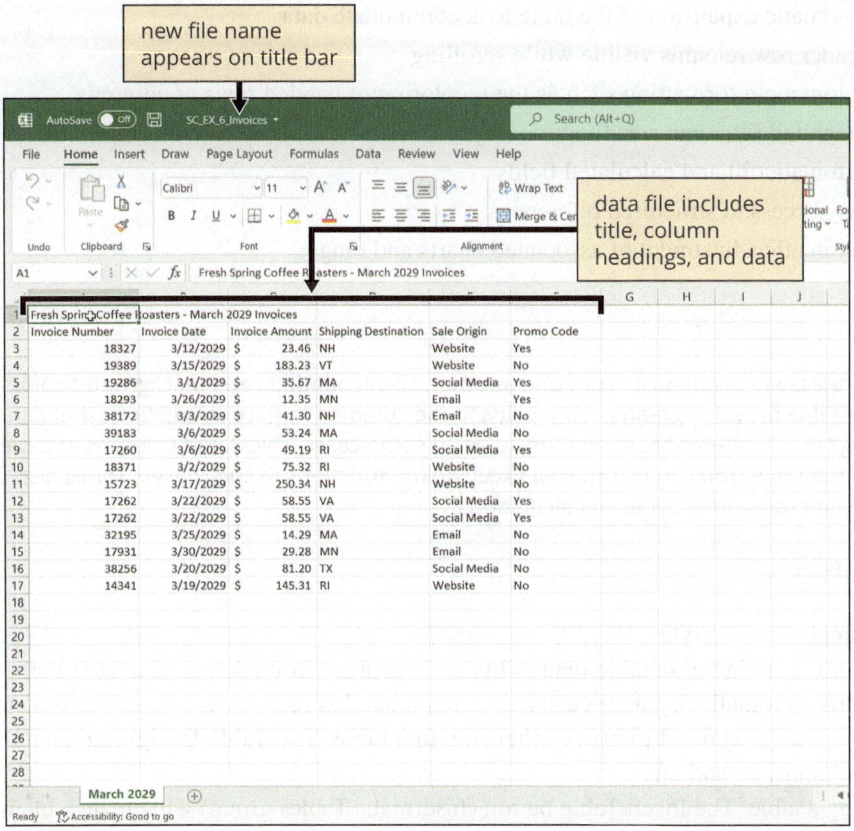

Figure 6–4

Table Guidelines

When you create a table in Excel, you should follow some basic guidelines, as listed in Table 6–2.

Table 6–2: Guidelines for Creating a Table in Excel

Table Size and Workbook Location
1. Do not enter more than one table per worksheet.
2. Maintain at least one blank row between a table and other worksheet entries.
3. A table can have a maximum of 16,384 fields and 1,048,576 records on a worksheet.
Column Headings (Field Names)
1. Place column headings (field names) in the first row of the table.
2. Do not use blank rows or rows with repeating characters, such as dashes or underscores, to separate the column headings from the data.
3. Apply a different format to the column headings than to the data. For example, bold the column headings and format the data below the column headings using a regular style. Most table styles follow these guidelines.
4. While column headings can be up to 32,767 characters in length, it is advisable to keep them short so more information can fit on the screen. The column headings should be meaningful.
Contents of Table
1. Each cell in any given column should have similarly structured data. For example, each Shipping Destination entry should use a two-letter state abbreviation. Do not use the full state name for some records and the state abbreviation for others.
2. Format the data to improve readability, but do not vary the format of individual cells within a column, other than the column's title cell.

BTW

Ribbon and Screen Resolution

Excel may change how the groups and buttons within the groups appear on the ribbon, depending on the screen resolution of your computer. Thus, your ribbon may look different from the ones in this book if you are using a screen resolution other than 1920 × 1080.

BTW
Touch Mode Differences
The Office and Windows interfaces may vary if you are using Touch Mode. For this reason, you might notice that the function or appearance of your touch screen differs slightly from this module's presentation.

Creating a Table

When you create a table in Excel, you can manage and analyze the data in that table independently from the rest of the data on the worksheet. The advantages of creating a table include:

- Automatic expansion of the table to accommodate data
- Header row remains visible while scrolling
- Automatic reformatting such as the recoloring of banded rows or columns
- Integrated filter and sort functionality
- Automatic fill and calculated fields
- Easy access to structured references
- Automatic adjustment of associated charts and ranges

Consider This

How should you format a table?

Format a table so that the records are easy to distinguish from one another. Using banded rows (background colors varying between rows) to format the table provides greater readability. Some columns require calculations that can be created by using the column headings or cell references within formulas. In some cases, calculated columns in tables require looking up values outside of the table. You can use special Excel lookup functions in such cases. Totals also can be added to the table for averages, sums, and other types of calculations.

To Format a Range as a Table

The easiest way to create a table is to apply a table style. **Why?** Excel automatically creates the table when you apply a table style to a range. Table styles are a quick way to increase table readability and usability. You can create a table before or after entering column headings and data. Most automatically-applied styles contain banded rows. A **banded row** is a row that is highlighted or delineated in some way, usually applied to every other row in a table. The Table Design tab contains check boxes to turn banded rows or banded columns, on and off.

You also have the option of inserting a table. The Insert Table button (Insert tab | Tables group) will create a blank table in a specified range, using the default color scheme. The following steps format a range as a table.

1

- Select the range A2:F17, which includes the column headings.
- Click the 'Format as Table' button (Home tab | Styles group) to display the Format as Table gallery (Figure 6–5).

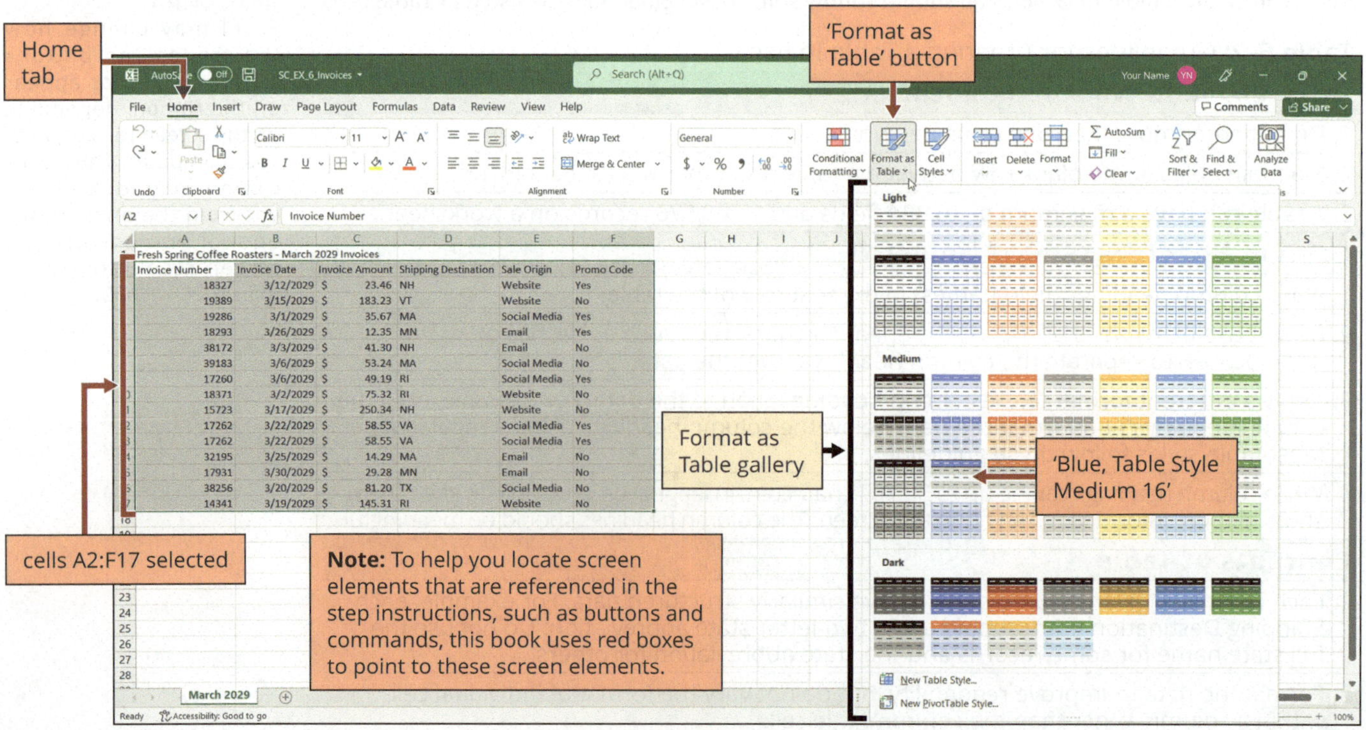

Figure 6–5

2

- Click 'Blue, Table Style Medium 16' in the Format as Table gallery to display the Create Table dialog box.
- If necessary, click the 'My table has headers' check box to select the option to format the table with headers (Figure 6–6).

Q&A What is a header?
A table header is the column heading that appears above the data. In this case, you want to create the table and include the column headings.

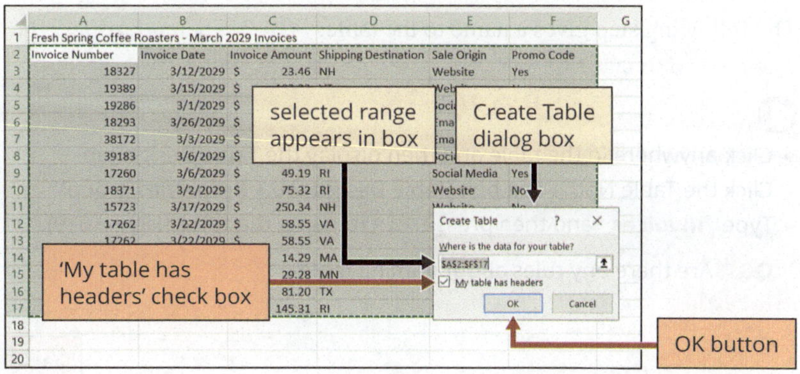

Figure 6–6

3

- Click OK (Create Table dialog box) to create a table from the selected range.
- Click outside the table to deselect it (Figure 6–7).

Q&A What are the buttons with the arrows beside the column headings?
The buttons are part of the AutoFilter that you will learn about later in the module.

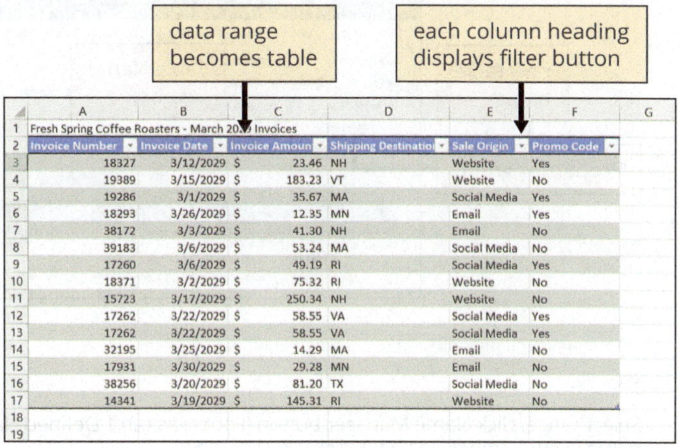

Figure 6–7

Other Ways

1. Select range, click Table button (Insert tab | Tables group), click OK, choose table style
2. Select range, press CTRL+T, click OK (Create Table dialog box), choose table style

To Wrap Text

The following steps wrap the text in cells C2 and D2 to make the headings easier to read.

1 Change the width of columns C and D to 12. Change the height of row 2 to 27.

2 Select cells C2 and D2, and then click the Wrap Text button (Home tab | Alignment group) (Figure 6–8).

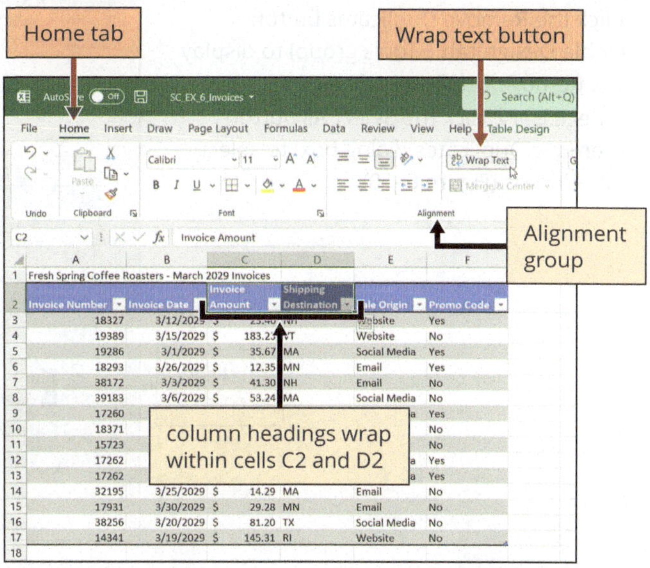

Figure 6–8

BTW
Ranges to Tables
If you select a range before clicking the 'Format as Table' button (Home tab | Styles group), Excel will fill in a suggested range for you in the Format As Table dialog box.

To Name the Table

The following step gives a name to the table. **Why?** When referring to the table in formulas, referring to it by name rather than by range reference will save time.

1

- Click anywhere in the table and then display the Table Design tab.
- Click the Table Name text box (Table Design tab | Properties group).
- Type **Invoices** and then press ENTER to name the table (Figure 6–9).

Q&A Are there any rules about naming tables?
Excel does not allow spaces in table names. Excel also requires that table names begin with a letter or underscore.

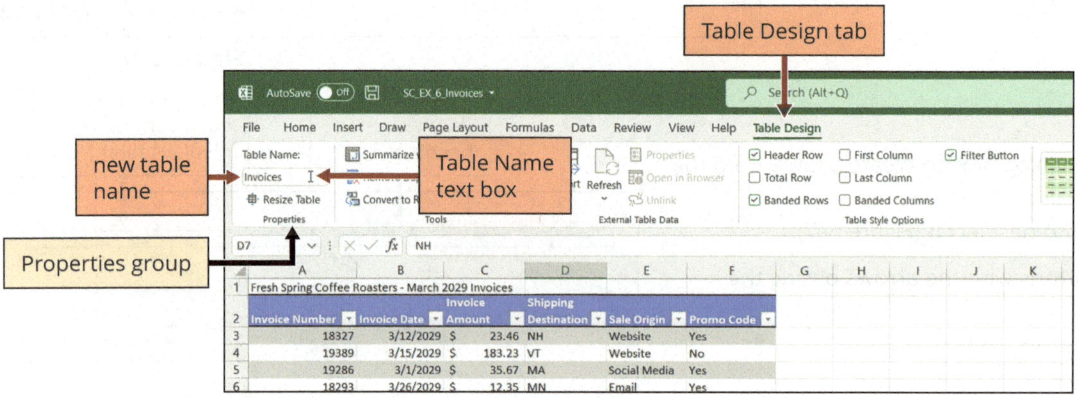

Figure 6–9

Other Ways

1. Select range, click Name Manager button (Formulas tab | Defined Names group), click New button (Name Manager dialog box), enter name (New Name dialog box), click OK, click Close

To Remove Duplicates

The following steps locate and remove any duplicate records in the table. **Why?** Duplicates can occur when data is entered incorrectly, by more than one person, or from more than one source. In this particular table, the Invoice Number 17262 was entered twice by mistake.

1

- Click anywhere in the table.
- Click the Remove Duplicates button (Table Design tab | Tools group) to display the Remove Duplicates dialog box.
- If necessary, click the Select All button (Remove Duplicates dialog box) to select all columns (Figure 6–10).

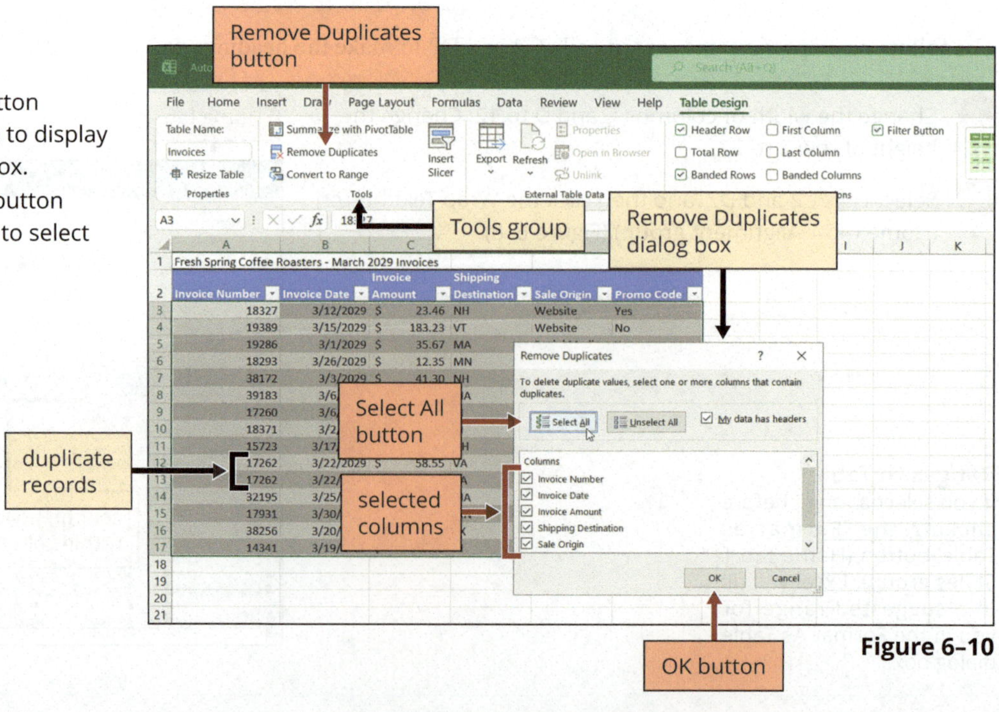

Figure 6–10

2

- Click OK (Remove Duplicates dialog box) to remove duplicate records from the table (Figure 6–11).

Q&A Did Excel reformat the table?

Yes. The Banded Rows check box (Table Design tab | Table Style Options group) was checked automatically when you selected the table format. **Row banding** causes adjacent rows to have different formatting, even if you delete a row; each row in the table is distinguishable from surrounding rows.

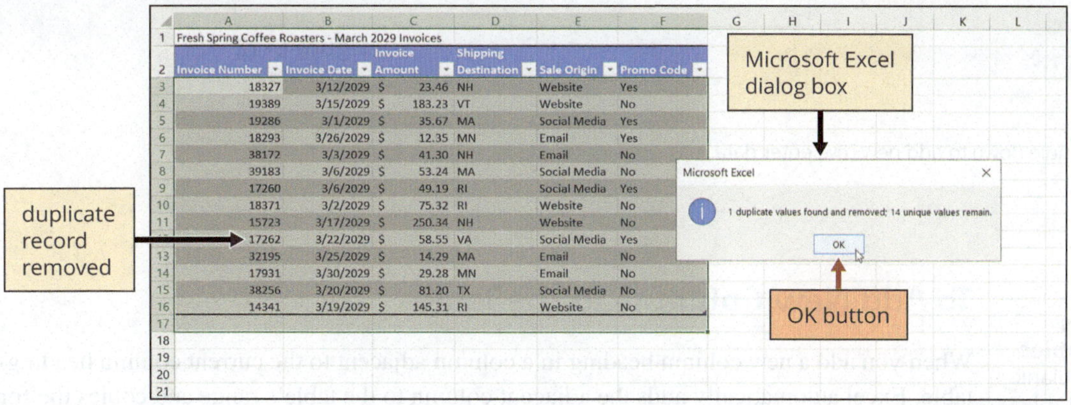

Figure 6–11

3

- Click OK (Microsoft Excel dialog box) to finish the process.
- **Experiment:** Examine the table to verify removal of the duplicate record for Invoice Number 17262.

Other Ways

1. Select range, click Remove Duplicates button (Data tab | Data Tools group)

To Enter New Rows and Records into a Table

The following step enters new invoices into the table. You will insert the information just below the table. **Why?** Data entered in rows or columns adjacent to the table becomes part of the table. Excel will format the new table data automatically.

1

- Select cell A17.
- Type the new entries below.
- **Experiment:** As you enter the data, notice that Excel tries to complete your fields based on previous common entries. You can press TAB to move between cells.

17483	3/5/2029	46.31	MA	Email	Yes
37162	3/13/2029	72.10	VT	Website	No
18221	3/14/2029	38.90	VT	Social Media	Yes

- Click the Home tab. If necessary, click outside the table to deselect it (Figure 6–12).

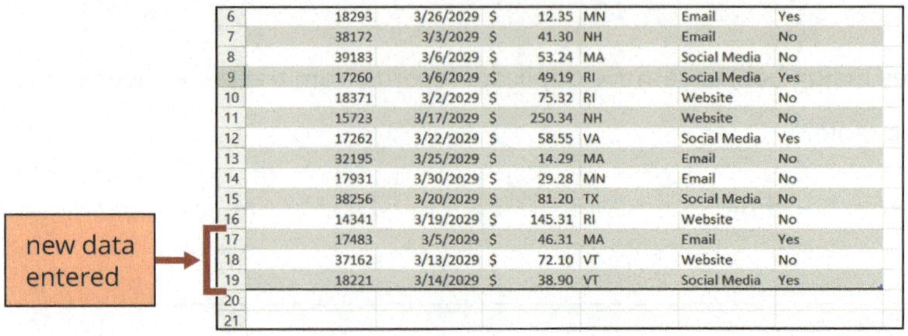

Figure 6–12

Other Ways

1. Drag table sizing handle down to add new row, enter data

BTW
Adding Blank Rows and Columns to Tables
If you want to add a blank row or column to a table, the easiest way is to right-click a cell within the table. Then, on the shortcut menu, click Insert. Excel displays options for columns and rows, above and below the selected cell.

To Add New Columns to the Table

When you add a new column heading in a column adjacent to the current column headings in the table, Excel automatically adds the adjacent column to the table's range and copies the format of the existing table heading to the new column heading. The following steps insert column headings for three new columns in the table.

1. Change the column width of column G to 13.00. Click cell G2. Type **Promo Code Discount** and then click the Enter button to enter the heading. Click the Wrap Text button (Home tab | Alignment group) to wrap the text.

2. Change the column width of column H to 13.00. Click cell H2. Type **Promo Code Refund** and then click the Enter button to enter the heading. Wrap the text in the cell.

3. Change the column width of column I to 15.00. Click cell I2. Type **Adjusted Invoice Amount** and then click the Enter button to enter the heading. Wrap the text in the cell (Figure 6–13).

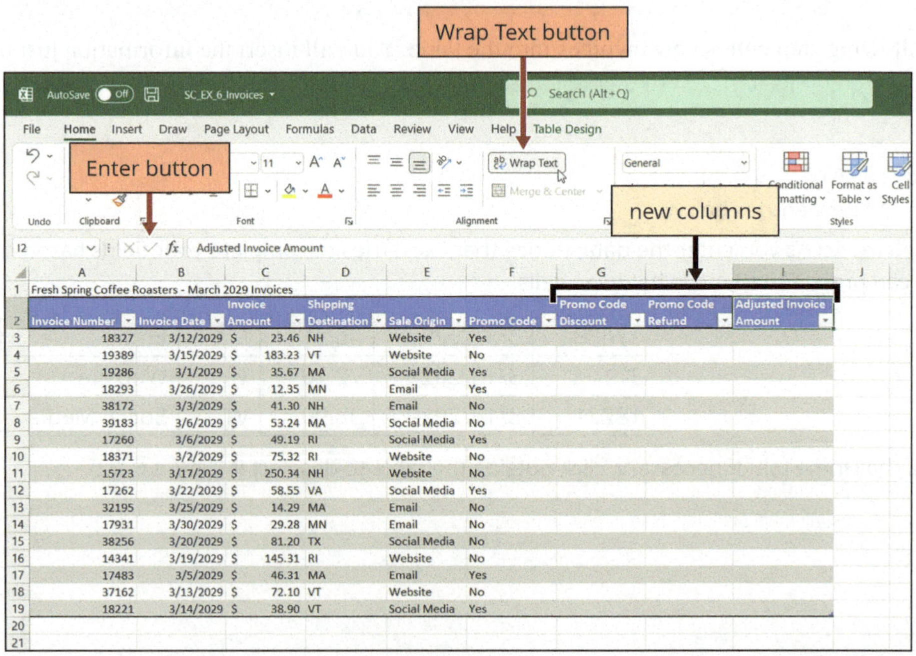

Figure 6–13

To Center Across a Selection

The following steps center the title in cell A1 across a selection using the Format Cells dialog box. In earlier modules, recall you used the 'Merge & Center' button (Home tab | Alignment group) to center text across a range. **Why?** This earlier technique centered the title, but it removed access to individual cells, because the cells were merged. The Center Across Selection format centers text across multiple cells but does not merge the selected cell range into one cell.

1

- Select the range A1:I1. Right-click the selected range to display the shortcut menu (Figure 6–14).

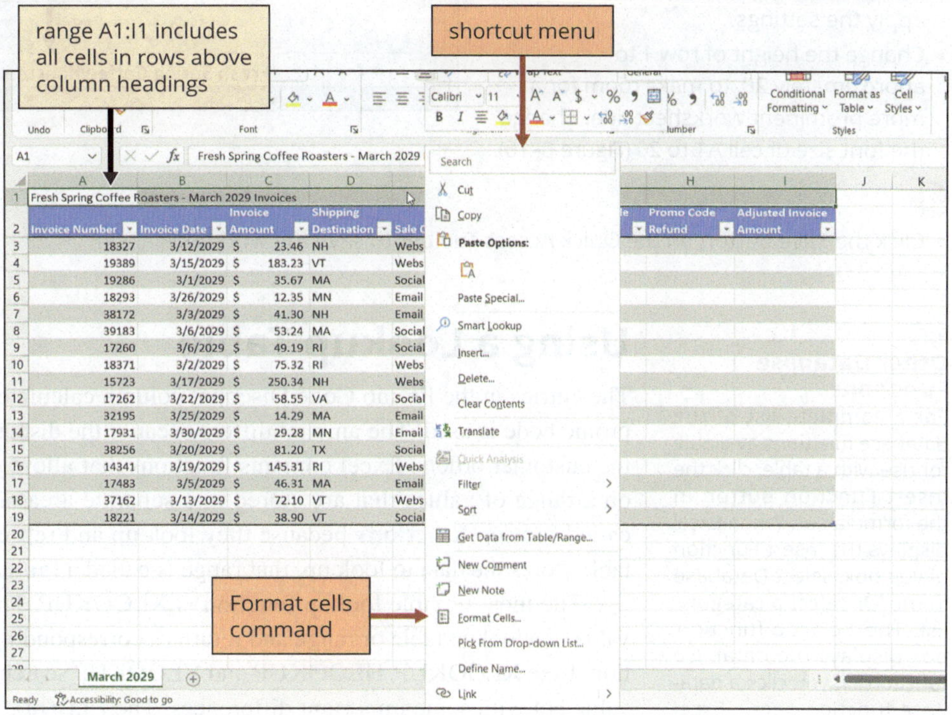

Figure 6–14

2

- Click Format Cells on the shortcut menu to display the Format Cells dialog box.
- Click the Alignment tab (Format Cells dialog box) and then click the Horizontal button in the Text alignment area to display a list of horizontal alignments (Figure 6–15).

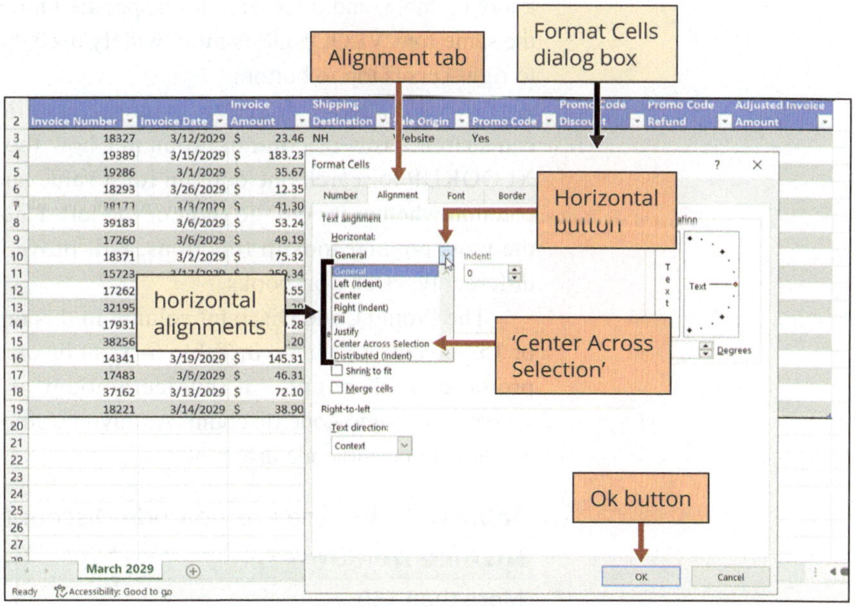

Figure 6–15

3

- Click 'Center Across Selection' in the Horizontal list (Format Cells dialog box) to select the option to center the title across the selection.
- Click OK (Format Cells dialog box) to apply the settings.
- Change the height of row 1 to approximately 28, to make room for a more prominent worksheet title. Change the font size of cell A1 to 20 (Figure 6–16).

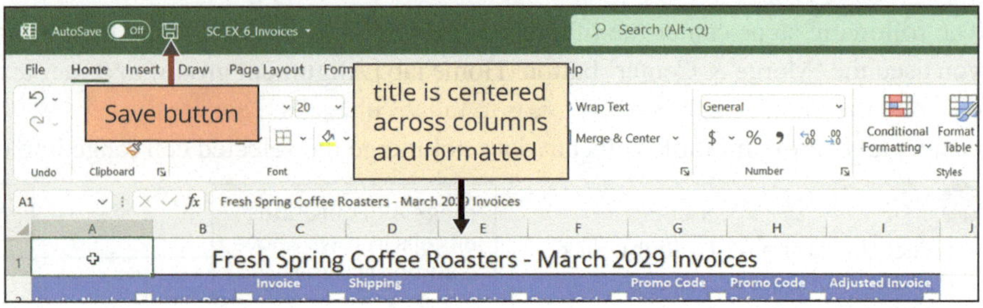

Figure 6–16

4

- Click the Save button on the Quick Access Toolbar to save the workbook again.

BTW
Other Database Functions
For a complete list of the database functions available for use with a table, click the Insert Function button in the formula bar. When Excel displays the Insert Function dialog box, select Database in the 'Or select a category' list. The 'Select a function' box displays the database functions. If you click a database function name, Excel displays a description of the function.

Using a Lookup Table

The entries in the Promo Code Discount column calculate the discount for each order when the promo code is used. The amount differs because the discount percentage is based on the amount the customer orders. Excel contains functions that allow you to assign these percentages based on a range of values that are stored in a separate area on the worksheet. These functions are called **lookup functions** because they look up and retrieve a value from a table or range. If a table stores the data to look up, that range is called a **lookup table**.

The most flexible lookup function is XLOOKUP. The **XLOOKUP function** searches for a value in a lookup table or range and returns a corresponding value to the cell containing the function. Like XLOOKUP, HLOOKUP and VLOOKUP search for values and return a corresponding value but with some important differences. The **HLOOKUP function** searches for a value in the top row of a lookup table, and then searches down a specified number of rows to return a corresponding value in the same column. The **VLOOKUP function** searches for a value in a column of a lookup table, and then searches a specified number of columns to the right to return a value in the same row. VLOOKUP is more widely used than HLOOKUP as most tables are read from left to right versus top to bottom.

The XLOOKUP function is more versatile than HLOOKUP or VLOOKUP because it can search a row or column no matter how the data is organized. For example, you can use XLOOKUP to search one column for a value and return a result from the same row in another column, whether it is to the right or the left. Knowing how to use XLOOKUP and VLOOKUP, the most popular lookup functions, will prove helpful in creating, and analyzing, numerous different types of workbooks.

The Promo Code Discount column in this table provides each invoice with a value of 5, 10, or 15 percent. As shown in Table 6–3, an invoice amount of at least $50 receives a 15 percent promo code discount. An invoice amount of at least $20 (but less than $50) receives a 10 percent promo code discount. An invoice amount of any amount (but less than $20) receives a 5 percent promo code discount.

Table 6–3: How the Promo Code Discounts Are Determined

Invoice Amount	Promo Code Discount
More than $50	15%
$20 to $50	10%
Less than $20	5%

To facilitate the calculation of each promo code discount, you will use the XLOOKUP function. The general form of the XLOOKUP function is

=XLOOKUP(lookup_value, lookup_array, return_array)

The three arguments of the XLOOKUP function represent the data that the function needs to do its job. The first argument is the **lookup value**, which is the data, or the location of the data, that you want to look up. In the case of the Invoices table, that data is located in column C, the Invoice Amount. You only need to enter the first occurrence of the data, cell C3.

The second argument, lookup_array, is the location of the data to search. In this case, the lookup_array will be located away from the main table, in the range A24:A26. In this project, the values to search are 0, 20, and 50—the lowest value in each rating.

The third argument, return_array, is the location of the return values. The **return value** is the answer you want to appear as a result of the XLOOKUP function. In the Invoices table, the return value will be 5, 10, or 15 percent. In the spreadsheet, the return values will be located away from the main table, in the range B24:B26.

XLOOKUP has three optional arguments. The first, if_not_found, is text to return in case the lookup value is not found, such as "Rating not found." Use the second optional argument, match_mode, to specify the type of match you want, such as an exact match. Use the third optional argument, search_mode, to specify how to search, such as from bottom to top. In this project, you only need to specify a match_mode argument of −1 to look for an exact match in a range of values or return the next smaller number (the lowest value for each promo code discount).

To Create an Area for Lookup and Return Arrays

The following steps create the arrays and headings in the range A22:B26. **Why?** Before using the XLOOKUP function, you must create the lookup and return arrays so that you can build the formula. Cells A22:B26 do not contain other data but are near the main table, and serve as a good location for the arrays.

1. Click cell A22. Type **Promo Code Table** as the table array title and then click the Enter button in the formula bar.
2. Change the font size in cell A22 to 14.
3. Select the range A22:B22. Right-click the selection and then click Format Cells on the shortcut menu to display the Format Cells dialog box. On the Alignment tab (Format Cells dialog box), click the Horizontal button, and then click 'Center Across Selection'. Click OK to apply the settings.
4. In cell A23, type **Spend ($)** to enter the column heading.
5. In cell B23, type **Promo Code Discount** to enter the column heading.
6. Select cell A2. Click the Format Painter button (Home tab | Clipboard group) and then drag through cells A23:B23 to copy the format of the selected cell to the column headings.
7. Wrap the text in cell B23 and change the height of row 23 to 27.
8. Enter the data shown below (Figure 6–17).

Cell	Data	Cell	Data
A24	50	B24	15%
A25	20	B25	10%
A26	0	B26	5%

Q&A Why does the lookup_array contain single digits instead of a range?
You need to enter only the lowest value for each rating. Excel will evaluate all values in the range.

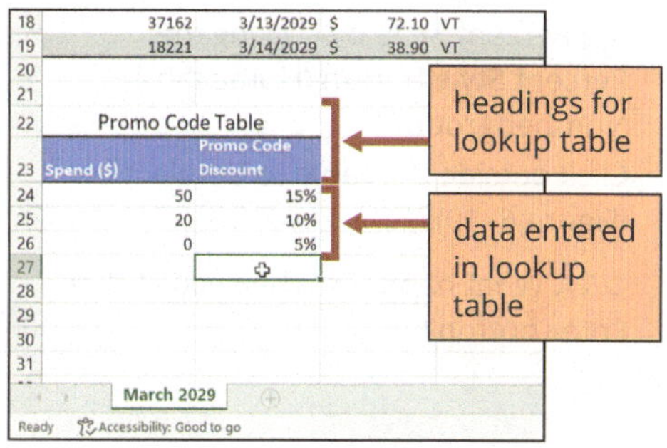

Figure 6–17

To Use the XLOOKUP Function

The following steps use the XLOOKUP function and the lookup and return arrays to determine the promo code discount for each invoice. **Why?** Using the XLOOKUP function with a table allows Excel to display the discounts, rather than the user typing them in individually.

1

- Scroll up until cell A2 is at the top of the workspace.
- Click cell G3. Type **=xlookup(c3,a24:a26,b24:b26,,-1)** as the cell entry (Figure 6–18).

Q&A Why should I use absolute cell references in the function?
You need to use absolute cell references, indicated by the dollar signs, so that Excel will not adjust the table array location when it creates the calculated column in the next step. If Excel adjusted the cell references, you would notice incorrect results in the other cells in column G.

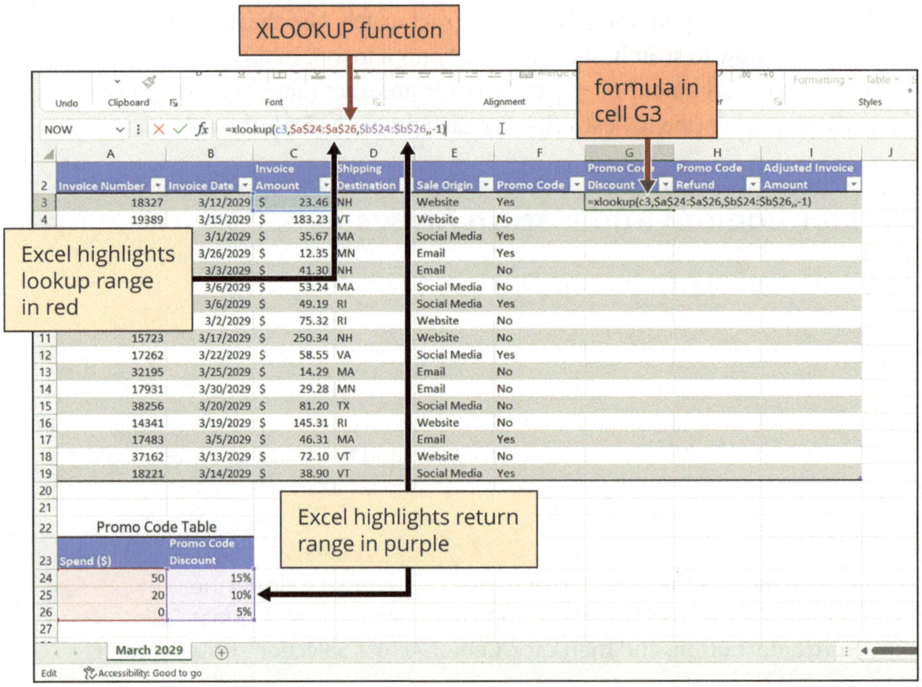

Figure 6–18

2

- Click the Enter button to create a calculated column for the selected field, the Promo Code Discount field in this case.
- Select range G3:G19, and then apply the Percent Style by clicking the Percent Style button (Home tab | Number group).
- Click outside the table to deselect it (Figure 6–19).

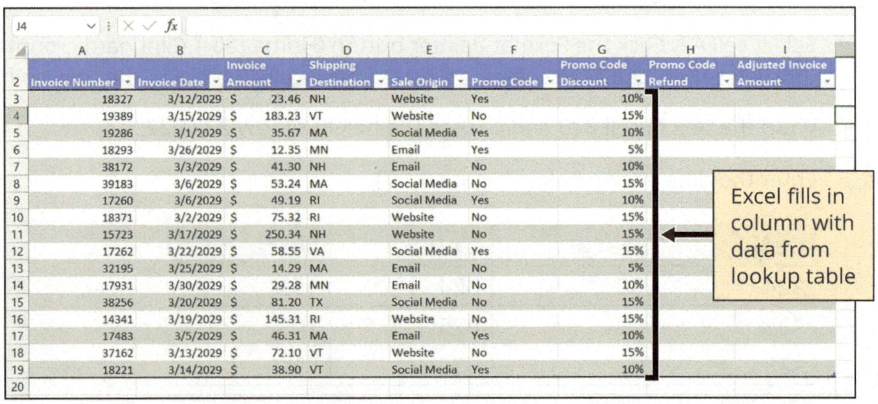

Figure 6–19

Q&A What happens when you click the Enter button?
Because cell G3 is the first record in a table, Excel continues the calculated column by replicating the XLOOKUP function through row 19.

How does the XLOOKUP function determine the ratings?
The match_mode argument of –1 means the XLOOKUP function looks for an exact match; if it does not find one, it looks for the closest match less than the lookup value (which in this case is 1), and then returns the corresponding value from column M.

Other Ways

1. Click Insert Function box in formula bar, click 'Or select a category', click 'Lookup & Reference', click XLOOKUP in 'Select a function' list, click OK, enter arguments
2. Click 'Lookup & Reference' button (Formulas tab | Function Library group), click XLOOKUP, enter arguments

Adding Calculated Fields to the Table

A **calculated field** or **computational field** is a field (column) in a table that contains a formula, function, cell reference, structured reference, or condition. When you create a calculated field, Excel automatically fills in the column without the use of a fill or copy command; you do not have to use the fill handle to replicate formulas in a calculated field.

Table 6–4 describes the three calculated fields used in this project. You created the first one in the previous steps.

Table 6–4: Calculated Fields

Column Heading	Column	Calculated Field
Promo Code Discount	G	Uses the XLOOKUP function to determine a promo code discount based upon the Invoice Amount (column C).
Promo Code Refund	H	Uses the IF function to evaluate the Promo Code column. If the customer used a promo code and the cell value is Yes, multiply the Invoice Amount by the Promo Code Discount. If it is No, the amount will be 0.
Adjusted Invoice Amount	I	Calculates the Adjusted Invoice Amount by subtracting the Promo Code Refund from the Invoice Amount.

To Create Calculated Fields

When you type formulas in a calculated field, Excel allows you to enter structured references rather than using normal cell references. A **structured reference** is a reference that allows table formulas to refer to table columns by names that are automatically generated when the table is created. A structured reference uses some combination of the table name (such as Promo Code Discount), the column heading (such as Invoice Number), or any named or special rows, rather than the usual column letter and row number references (such as E10). If you use a named row in a structured reference, you must use a # sign before the row name (such as #Totals). If a column heading used in a structured reference contains any spaces between words, its name must be enclosed in brackets (such as [Invoice Amount]).

Using structured references has several advantages. **Why?** Excel updates structured references automatically when any column heading changes or when you add new data to the table. Using this notation also makes formulas easier to read. If you have multiple tables, you can include the table name in the structured reference, making it easier to locate data in large workbooks.

In this calculated field, you also will use an IF function. Recall that an IF function has three parts: the condition, the result if the condition is true, and the result if the condition is false. The result can be a value, a reference, or in this case, a calculated field with a structured reference.

The following steps enter structured references for the last two columns of data in the table.

1

- Click cell H3 to select it. Click the 'Accounting Number Format' button (Home tab | Number group) so that data in the selected column is displayed as a dollar amount with two decimal places.
- Type **=if([** to display the list of available fields in the table (Figure 6–20).

Q&A What is the purpose of the [(left bracket)?

The [begins a structured reference and causes Excel to display the list of table fields (column headings).

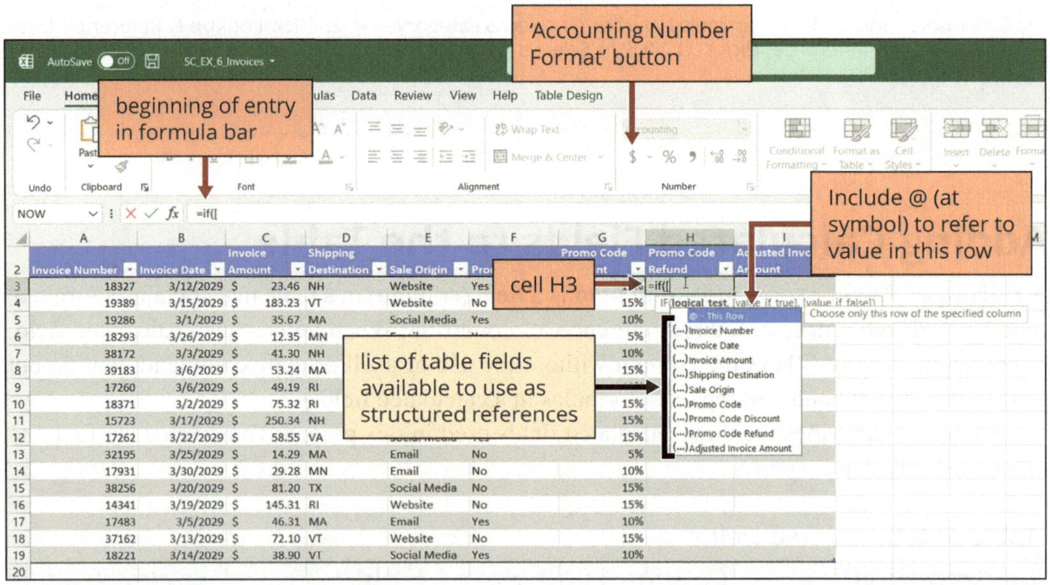

Figure 6–20

2

- Type **@** to refer to the value in this row.
- Double-click Promo Code in the drop-down list to select the field to use for the IF function.
- Type **]="Yes",[@[Invoice Amount]]*[@[Promo Code Discount]],0)** to complete the structured reference, and then click the Enter button to create the calculated column (Figure 6–21).

Q&A Do I have to set the formatting before I enter the structured reference formula?

No, you do not have to; however, applying formatting before entering the formula prompts Excel to generate the calculated column with your desired formatting. Otherwise, you would have to format the column manually after it generates.

Why do the structured references use a second set of brackets?

You insert an @ (at sign) and a field name within one set of brackets. If the field name includes a space, you also add brackets around the field name, as in [@[Promo Code].

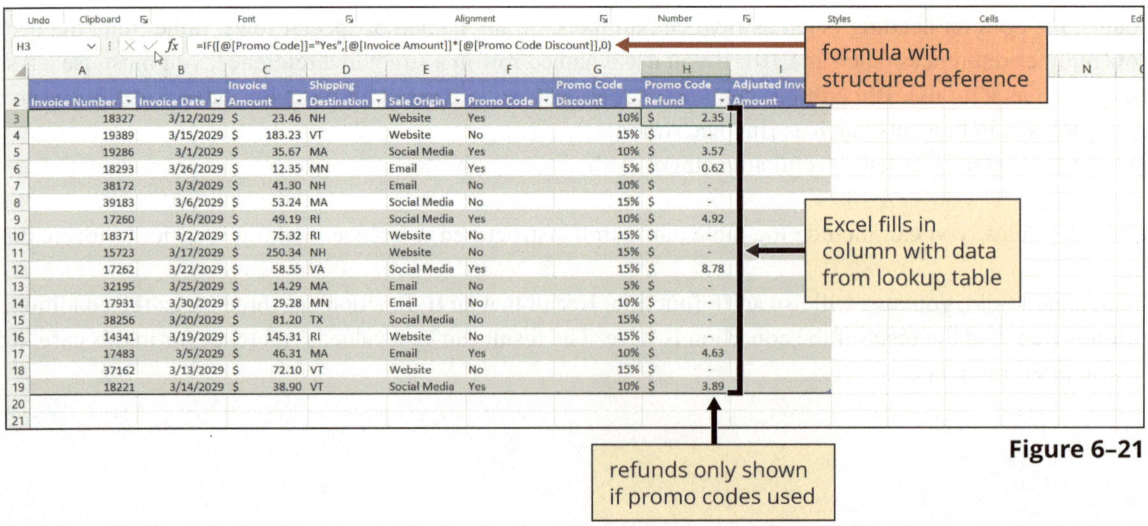

Figure 6–21

3

- Click cell I3 to select it.
- Click the 'Accounting Number Format' button (Home tab | Number group).
- Type **=[@** and double-click Invoice Amount to select the field for use, type **]-[@** and double-click Promo Code Refund to select the field for use, type **]** and then click the Enter button to create a calculated column (Figure 6–22).
- Click the Save button on the Quick Access Toolbar to save the workbook again.

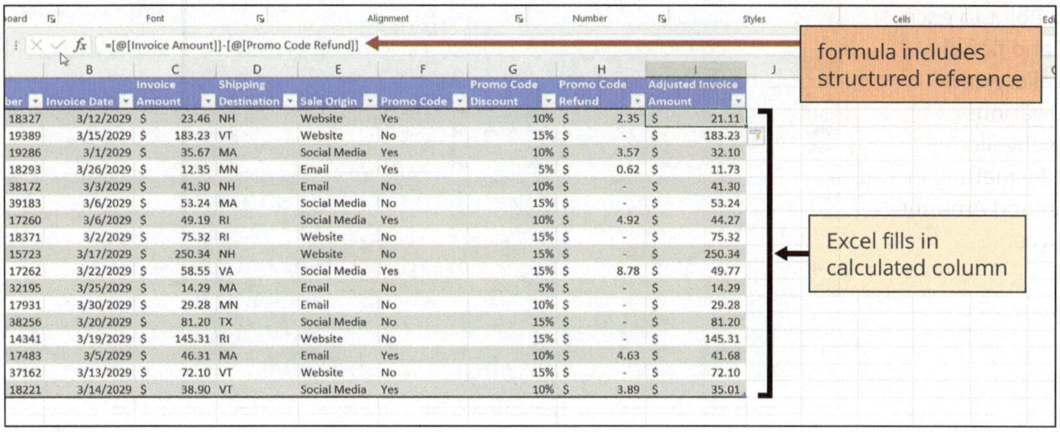

Figure 6–22

Conditional Formatting

Conditional formatting allows you to create rules that change the formatting of a cell based on its value. For example, you might want negative values to appear highlighted in red. Excel includes five preset types of conditional formats: highlight, top and bottom rules, data bars, color scales, and icon sets, as well as the ability to create your own conditional formats. You can combine different types of formats on any cell or range. For example, based on a cell's value, you can format it to include both an icon and a specific background color.

The Conditional Formatting Rules Manager dialog box allows you to view all of the rules for the current selection or for an entire worksheet and change the order in which the rules are applied to a cell or range. In addition, you can stop applying subsequent rules after one rule is found to be true. For example, if the first rule specifies that a negative value should appear in red, then you may not want to apply any other conditional formats to the cell.

To Add a Conditional Formatting Rule with an Icon Set

In the Invoices table, the Promo Code Refund field informs the user about the amount of refund to issue the customer after the correct promo code is applied. In addition to the numerical information, it can be helpful to visually group the refund amounts so that a user can quickly determine which are large, which are smaller, and which do not require a refund at all. You can do this quickly by displaying an icon in the Promo Code Refund cells. Conditional formatting provides a variety of icons, including traffic signals, circles, flags, bars, and arrows. Icon sets include sets of three, four, or five icons. **Why?** You choose an icon set depending on how many ways you want to group your data. In the case of the promo code refunds, you will use three different icons. Once you choose an icon set, you define rules for each of the conditions. The following steps add a conditional format to the Promo Code Refund field in the Invoices table.

1

- Select the range H3:H19, and then click the Conditional Formatting button (Home tab | Styles group) to display the Conditional Formatting gallery (Figure 6–23).
- **Experiment:** Point to each item in the Conditional Formatting gallery and then point to various items in the subgalleries to notice the formatting in the Promo Refund Amount column changes.

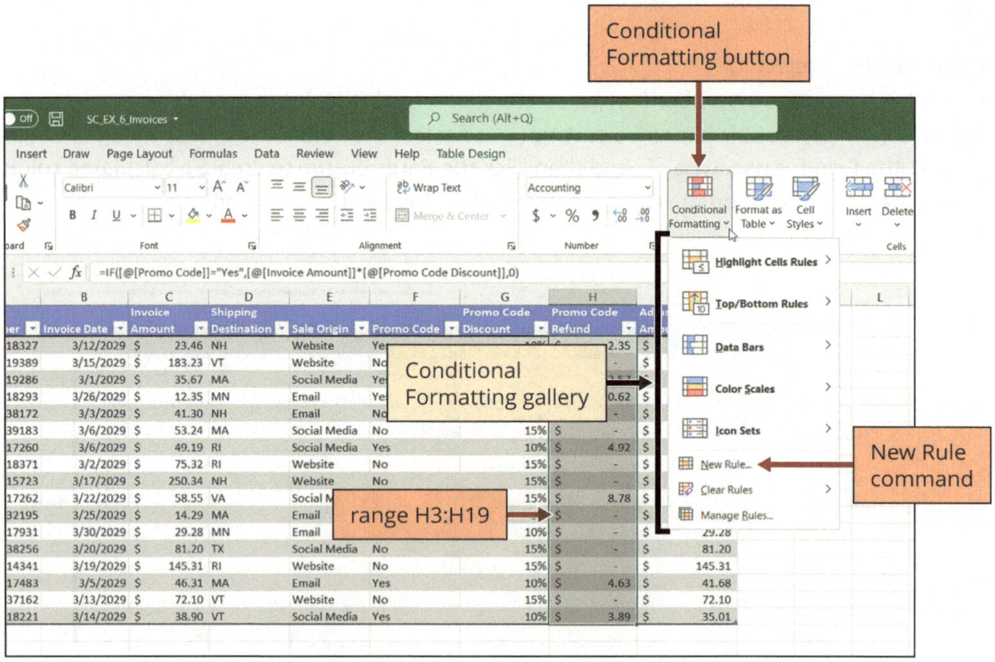

Figure 6–23

2

- Click New Rule in the Conditional Formatting gallery to display the New Formatting Rule dialog box.
- Click the Format Style button (New Formatting Rule dialog box) to display the Format Style list (Figure 6–24).

Q&A What do the color scale formats do?

You can choose between two or three values and apply different color backgrounds. Excel graduates the shading from one value to the next.

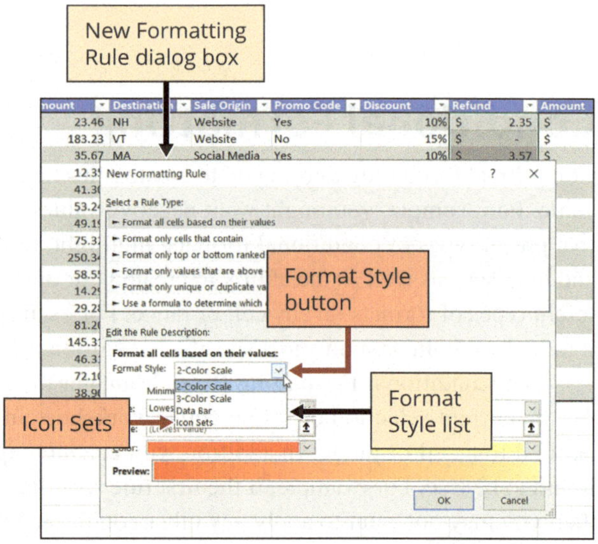

Figure 6–24

3

- Click Icon Sets in the Format Style list (New Formatting Rule dialog box) to display the Icon Style area.
- Click the Icon Style arrow to display the Icon Style list and then scroll as necessary to display the '3 Traffic Lights (Unrimmed)' icon style in the list (Figure 6–25).
- **Experiment:** Click a variety of icon styles in the Icon Styles list to view the options for each style.

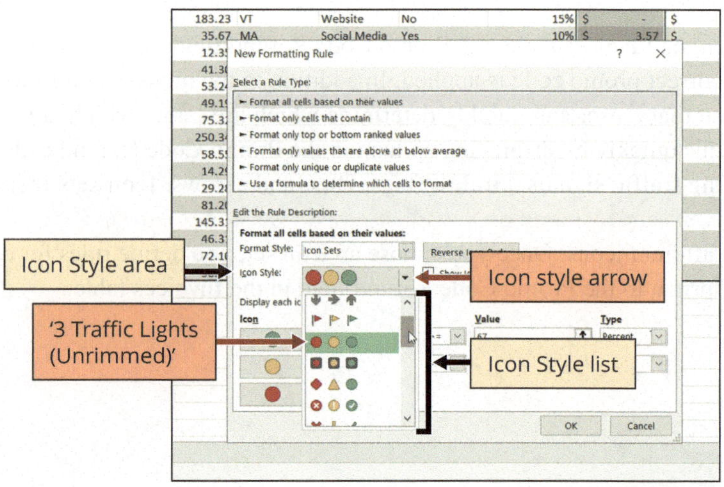

Figure 6–25

4

- Click the '3 Traffic Lights (Unrimmed)' icon style in the Icon Style list (New Formatting Rule dialog box) again to select this icon style.
- Click the first Type list arrow and then click Number in the list to select a numeric value.
- Click the second Type list arrow and then click Number in the list.
- Click the second inequality list arrow and then click the Greater than symbol to select it.
- Type **5** in the first Value field. Type **0** in the second Value field if necessary, and then press TAB to complete the conditions (Figure 6–26).

Q&A Why do the numbers next to each icon change as I type?
Excel automatically updates this area as you change the conditions. Use this area as an easy-to-read status of the conditions that you are creating.

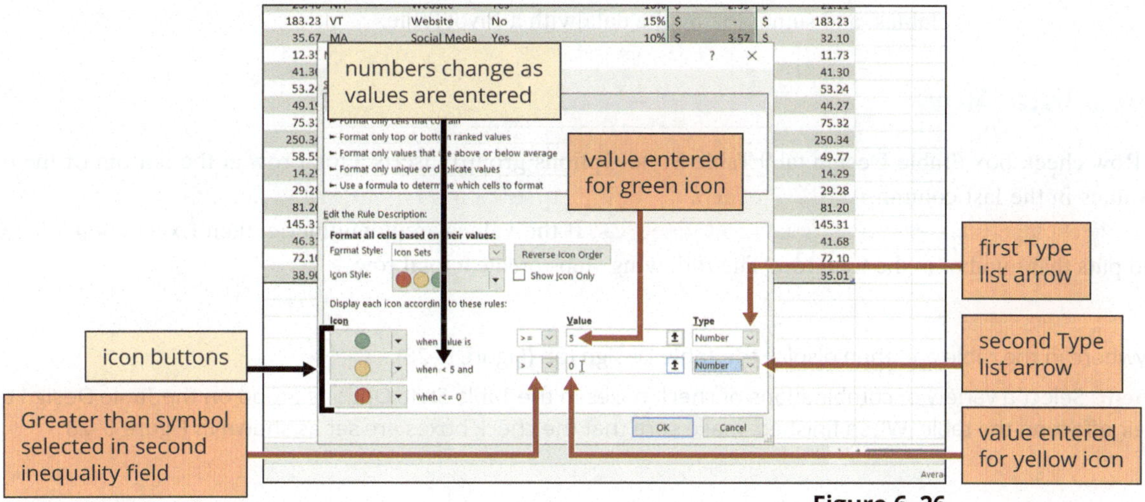

Figure 6–26

5

- Click OK (New Formatting Rule dialog box) to display icons in each row of the table in the Promo Code Refund field (Figure 6–27).

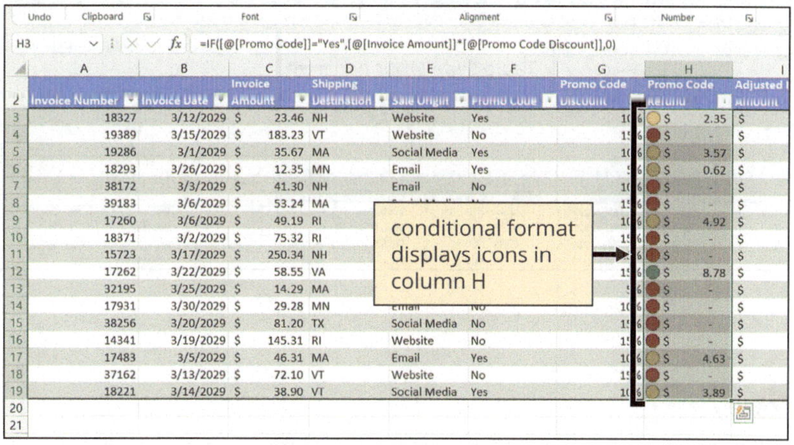

Figure 6–27

Finding Duplicates with Conditional Formatting

As you will learn later in the module, you can find duplicate values or records with a filter; however, conditional formatting also can pinpoint duplicates easily. To use the feature for this purpose, click the Conditional Formatting button (Home tab | Styles group), and then click New Rule. When Excel displays the New Formatting Rule dialog box, click 'Format only unique or duplicate values' in the Select a Rule Type area (refer to Figure 6–26). You then can choose a highlight, style, or other format for duplicate values.

Data Bars

Another popular conditional formatting option is data bars. Chosen from the Conditional Formatting gallery (refer to Figure 6–23), **data bars** display as colored, horizontal rectangles in the cell. The larger the number, the wider the data bar. Excel allows you to choose between solid and gradient colors, and select the direction of the rectangle, among other settings.

Working with Tables in Excel

When a table is active, the Table Design tab on the ribbon provides powerful commands that allow you to alter the appearance and contents of a table quickly. For example, you can add and remove header and total rows in a table quickly. You also can change the style of the first or last column. Other commands that you will learn in later modules include inserting slicers, exporting tables, and summarizing the data with a PivotTable.

To Insert a Total Row

The Total Row check box (Table Design tab | Table Style Options group) inserts a total row at the bottom of the table, summing the values in the last column. **Why?** The default setting creates a total in the last column; however, total rows display a button beside each cell to create other totals and functions. If the values are nonnumeric, then Excel counts the number of records and puts that number in the total row. The following steps create a total row.

1

- Click anywhere in the table and then display the Table Design tab (Figure 6–28).
- **Experiment:** Select a variety of combinations of check boxes in the Table Style Options group on the Table Design tab to learn their effect on the table. When finished, make sure that the check boxes are set as shown in Figure 6–28.

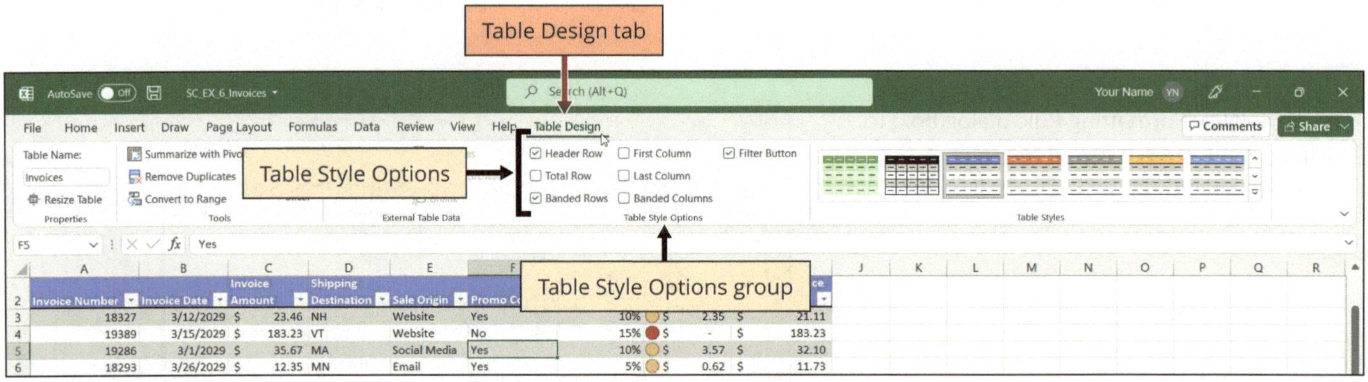

Figure 6–28

2

- If necessary, click the Total Row check box (Table Design tab | Table Style Options group) to display the total row and display the sum in the last column of the table, cell I20 in this case.
- Select cell H20 in the total row and then click the arrow on the right side of the cell to display a list of available functions (Figure 6–29).

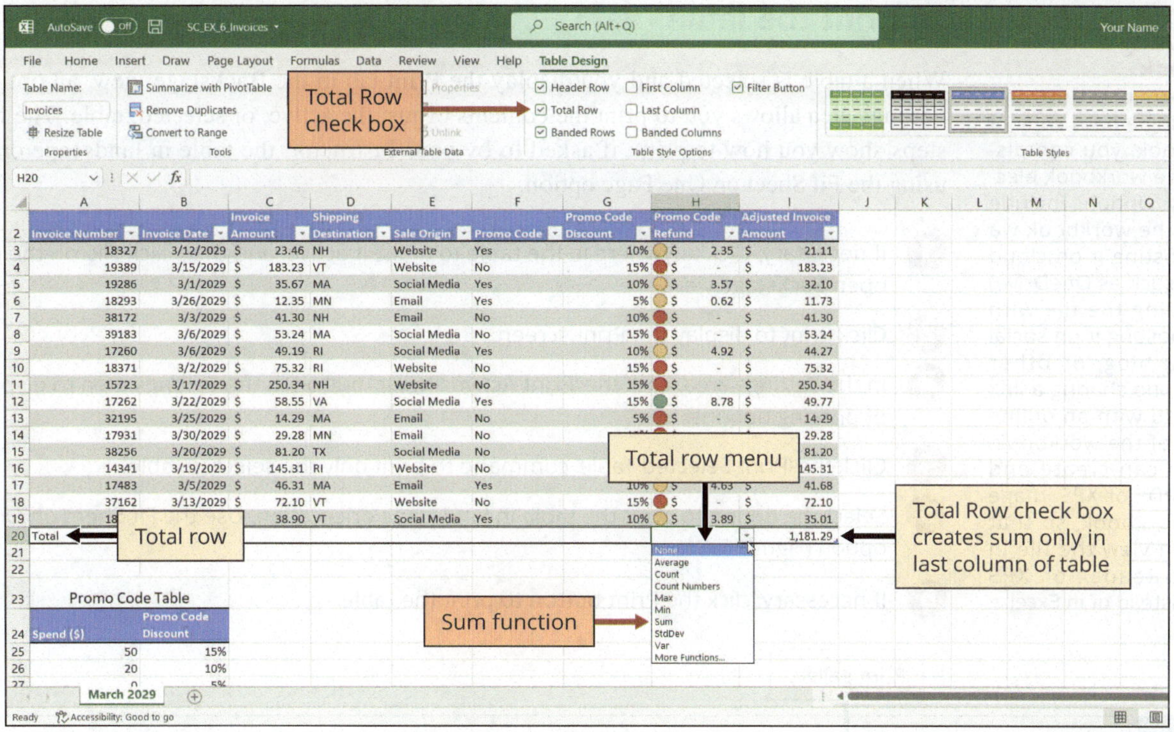

Figure 6–29

3

- Click Sum in the list to select the Sum function for the selected cell in the total row, thus totaling the promo code refund amounts.
- Repeat the process to create a sum in cell C20 (Invoice Amount) (Figure 6–30).
- **Experiment:** Choose cells in the total row and experiment with the different kinds of statistical functions, such as using the MAX function in cell C20 or the AVERAGE function in cell H20. After experimenting, make sure to delete any changes made while experimenting.

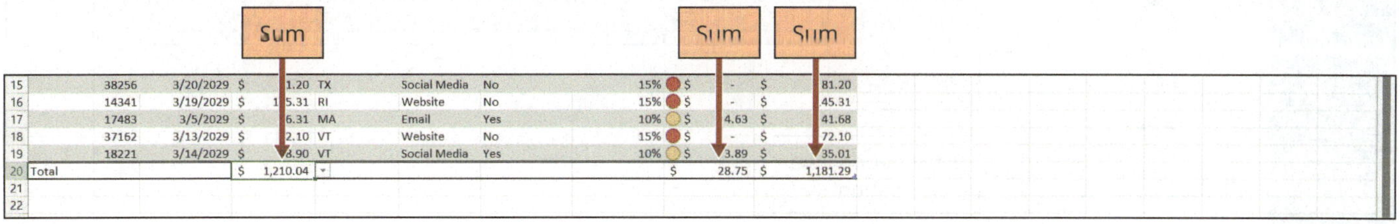

Figure 6–30

4

- Click the Save button on the Quick Access Toolbar to save the workbook again.

Other Ways

1. Right-click table, point to Table on shortcut menu, click Totals Row on submenu

Break Point: If you want to take a break, this is a good place to do so. You can exit Excel now. To resume later, start Excel, open the file called SC_EX_6_Invoices, and continue following the steps from this location forward.

BTW
Distributing a Workbook
Instead of printing and distributing a hard copy of a workbook, you can distribute the workbook electronically. Options include sending the workbook via email; posting it on cloud storage (such as OneDrive) and sharing the file with others; posting it on social media, a blog, or other website; and sharing a link associated with an online location of the workbook. You also can create and share a PDF or XPS image of the workbook, so that users can view the file in Acrobat Reader or XPS Viewer instead of in Excel.

To Print the Table

When a table is selected and you display the Print tab in the Backstage view, an option in the Settings area allows you to print the contents of just the active, or selected, table. The following steps show you how to print, if asked to by your Instructor, the table in landscape orientation using the Fit Sheet on One Page option.

1. If necessary, click anywhere in the table to make it active, and then click File on the ribbon to open Backstage view.
2. Click Print to display the Print screen.
3. In the Settings area, click the 'Print Active Sheets' button in the Settings area to display a list of printing options.
4. Click the 'Print Selected Table' command to print only the selected table.
5. Select the option to print the table in landscape orientation. Use the Fit Sheet on One Page option (Figure 6-31).
6. If necessary, click the Print button to print the table.

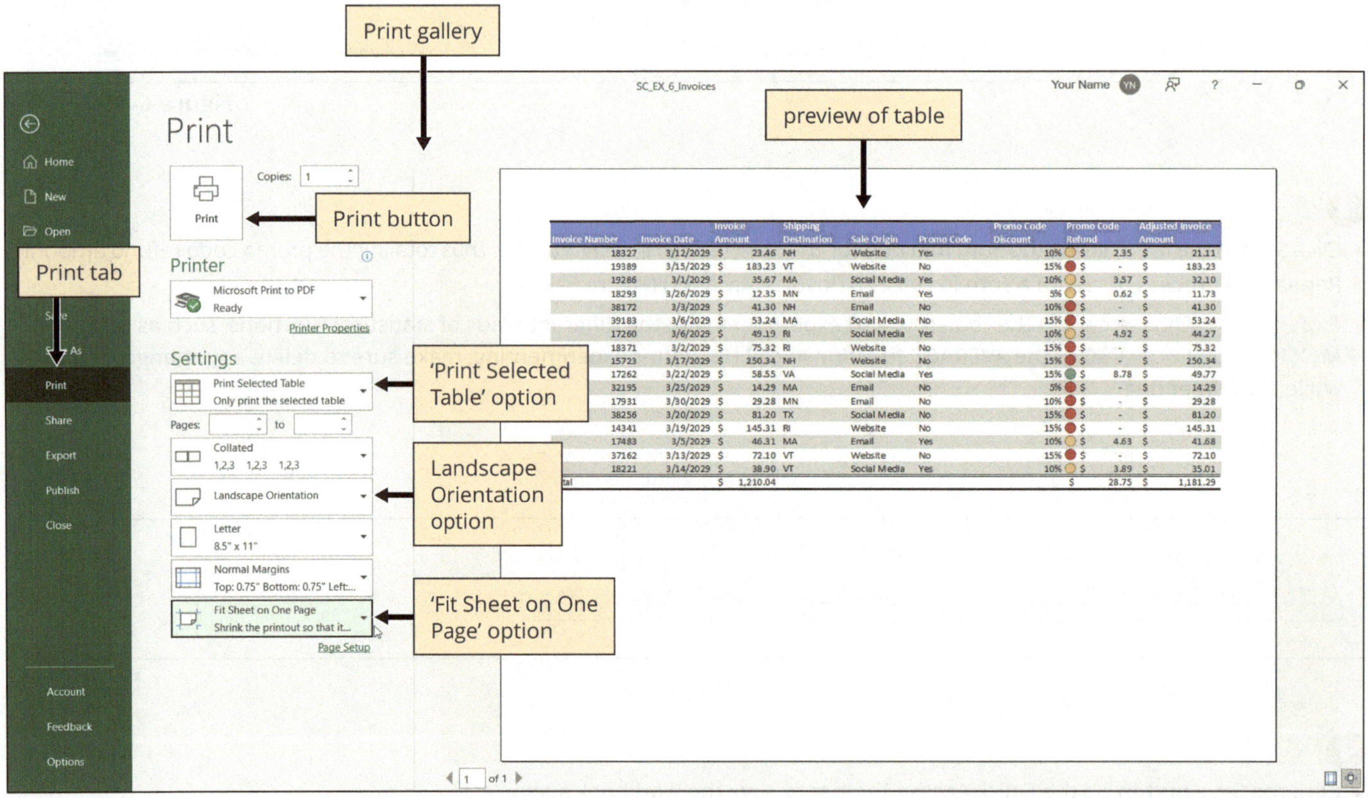

Figure 6-31

BTW
Sorting Non-Table Data
If the data you wish to sort is not in a table, highlight the data first, then click the Sort & Filter button (Home tab | Editing group).

Sorting a Table

The data in a table is easier to work with and more meaningful if records appear sequentially based on one or more fields. Arranging records in a specific sequence is called **sorting**. Data is in **ascending order** if it is sorted from lowest to highest, earliest to most recent, or alphabetically from A to Z. Data is in **descending order** if it is sorted from highest to lowest, most recent to earliest, or alphabetically from Z to A. The field or fields you select to sort are called **sort keys**.

When you sort a table, all the records in each row move together, so even if the selected cell is in the last name column of a table, for example, the first name and all data in the row will be moved when the table is sorted by last name. It is always a good idea to save a copy of your worksheet before applying sorts.

You can sort data in a table by using one of the following techniques:

- Select a cell in the field on which to sort, click the 'Sort & Filter' button (Home tab | Editing group), and then click one of the sorting options on the Sort & Filter menu.
- With the table active, click the filter button in the column on which to sort and then click one of the sorting options on the menu.
- Use the Sort button (Data tab | Sort & Filter group).
- Use the 'Sort A to Z' or 'Sort Z to A' button (Data tab | Sort & Filter group).
- Right-click anywhere in a table and then point to Sort on the shortcut menu to display the Sort submenu.

BTW
Sorting Dates
When you use AutoFilter to sort date fields, the filter menu will list commands such as 'Sort Newest to Oldest' and 'Sort Oldest to Newest.'

Consider This

Which field is best for sorting?

Ideally, the user of the worksheet should be able to sort the table on any field using a variety of methods and sort using multiple fields at the same time. Depending on what you want to show, you may sort by a name field or list value, by a numeric field, or by date. You also can sort a table in ascending or descending order.

To Sort Ascending

The following steps sort the table in ascending, earliest to most recent, order by the Invoice Date field using the 'Sort & Filter' button (Home tab | Editing group). **Why?** Dates commonly display in ascending order.

1

- Scroll to display the entire table and top of worksheet, including row 1. If necessary, display the Home tab.
- Click cell B3 and then click the 'Sort & Filter' button (Home tab | Editing group) to display the Sort & Filter menu (Figure 6–32).

Q&A What if the column I choose includes numeric or alphabetical data?

If the column you choose includes numeric data, then the Sort & Filter menu shows the 'Sort Smallest to Largest' and 'Sort Largest to Smallest' commands. If the column you choose includes alphabetical data, then the Sort & Filter menu shows the 'Sort A to Z' and 'Sort Z to A' commands.

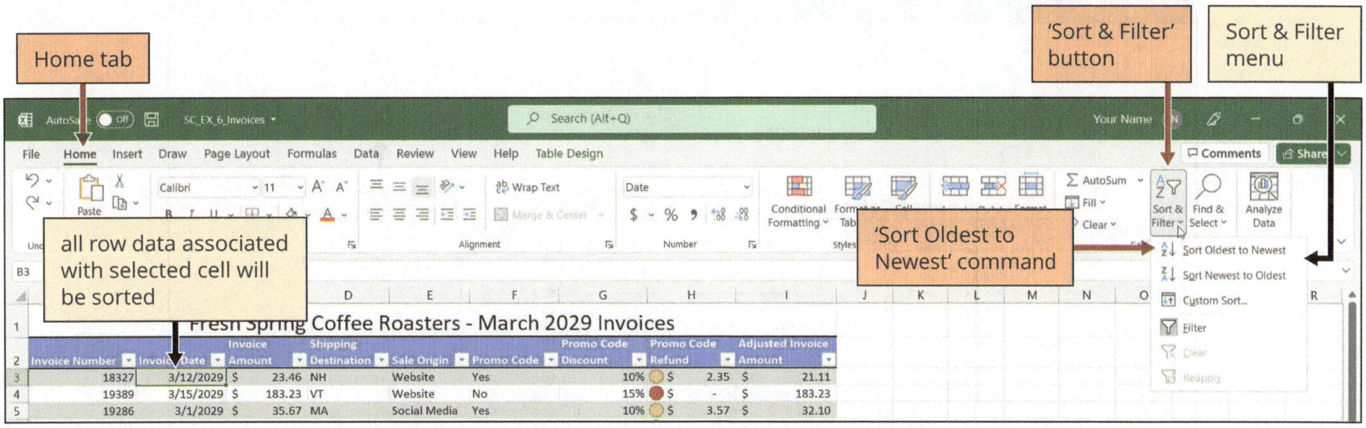

Figure 6–32

2

- Click 'Sort Oldest to Newest' to sort the table in ascending order by the selected field, Name in this case (Figure 6–33).
- **Experiment:** Select other fields in the table and use the same procedure to sort on the fields you choose. When you are finished, remove any sorting, select cell B2, and repeat the two steps above.

Q&A Can I undo the sort?

Yes, you can click the Undo button (Quick Access Toolbar) or press CTRL+Z; however, if you close your file, the original order will be lost. If you want to undo a sort, it is a good practice to do so before continuing with other commands.

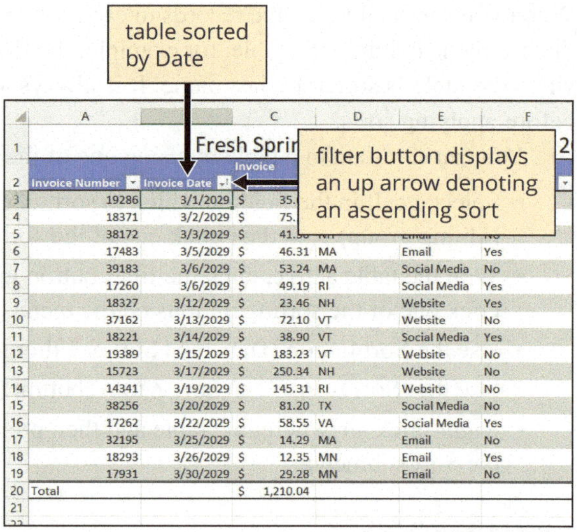

Figure 6–33

Other Ways

1. Select field in table, click 'Sort A to Z' button (Data tab | Sort & Filter group)
2. Click filter button of field on which to sort, click 'Sort A to Z'
3. Right-click column to sort, point to Sort on shortcut menu, click 'Sort A to Z'

To Sort Descending

The following step sorts the records in descending order by Invoice Amount using the 'Sort Largest to Smallest' button on the Data tab. **Why?** Sometimes it is more convenient to use the Data tab and sort with a single click.

1

- Click cell C3 to position the sort in the Invoice Amount column.
- Display the Data tab.
- Click the 'Sort Largest to Smallest' button (Data tab | Sort & Filter group) to sort the table in descending sequence by the selected field, Invoice Amount, in this case (Figure 6–34).

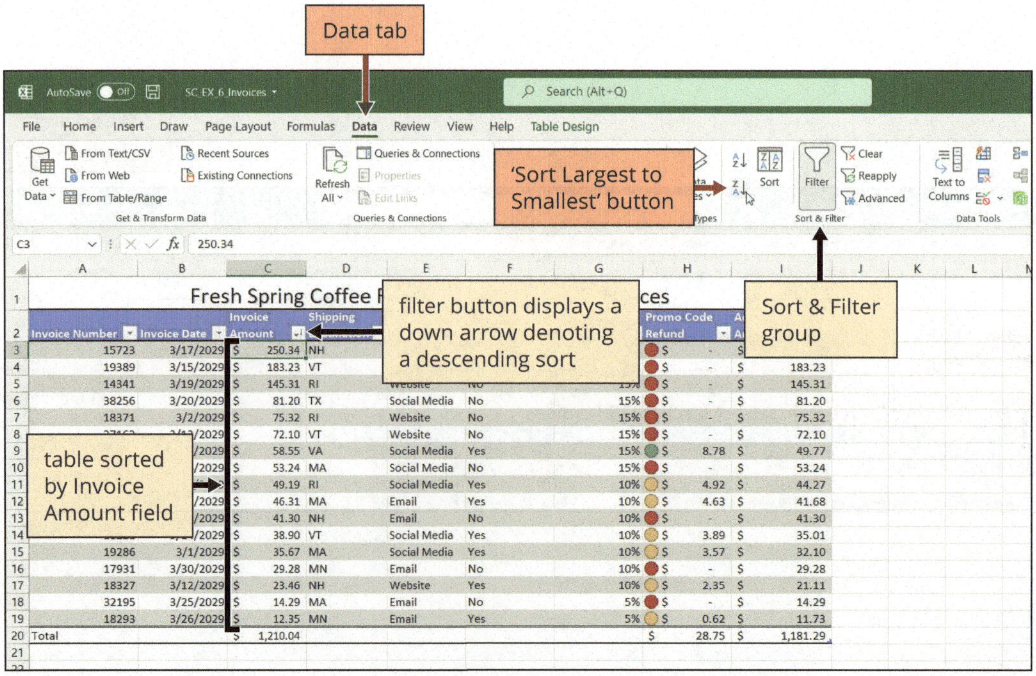

Figure 6–34

Other Ways

1. Select field in table, click 'Sort and Filter' button (Home tab | Editing group), click 'Sort Largest to Smallest'
2. Click filter button of field on which to sort, click 'Sort Largest to Smallest'
3. Right-click column to sort, point to Sort on shortcut menu, click 'Sort Largest to Smallest'

To Custom Sort

While Excel allows you to sort on up to 256 fields in a single custom sort operation, in these steps you will use the Custom Sort command to sort the Invoices table using three fields. **Why?** Sorting on three fields enables you to customize the sort sufficiently so that records appear in a logical order. You will sort by Promo Code Discount within Shipping Destination within Sale Origin. That phrase means that the records within the table first are arranged by Sale Origin (Email, Social Media, and Website). Then, within Sale Origin, the records are arranged alphabetically by Shipping Destination. Finally, within Promo Code Discount, the records are arranged from largest to smallest by the Promo Code Discount number. In this case, Sale Origin is the major sort key, Shipping Destination is the intermediate sort key, and Promo Code Discount is the minor sort key. You can sort any field in ascending or descending order, depending on how you want the data to look. The following steps sort the Invoices table on multiple fields.

1

- Display the Home tab.
- With a cell in the table active, click the 'Sort & Filter' button (Home tab | Editing group) to display the Sort & Filter menu.
- Click Custom Sort on the Sort & Filter menu to display the Sort dialog box.
- Click the 'Column Sort by' button (Sort dialog box) to display the field names in the table (Figure 6–35).

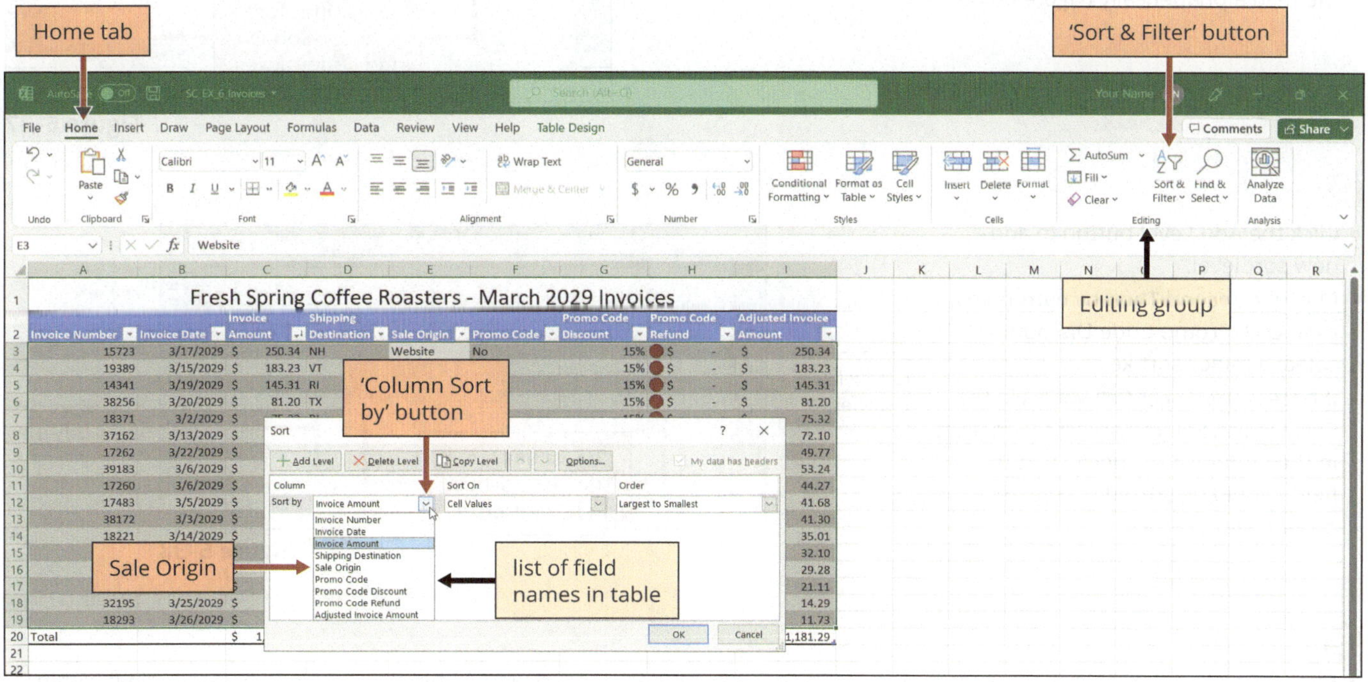

Figure 6–35

2

- Click Sale Origin to select the first sort level, or major sort key.
- If necessary, click the Sort on button (Sort dialog box) and then click Cell Values in the Sort On list.
- If necessary, click the Order button and then click 'A to Z' to sort the field alphabetically (Figure 6–36).

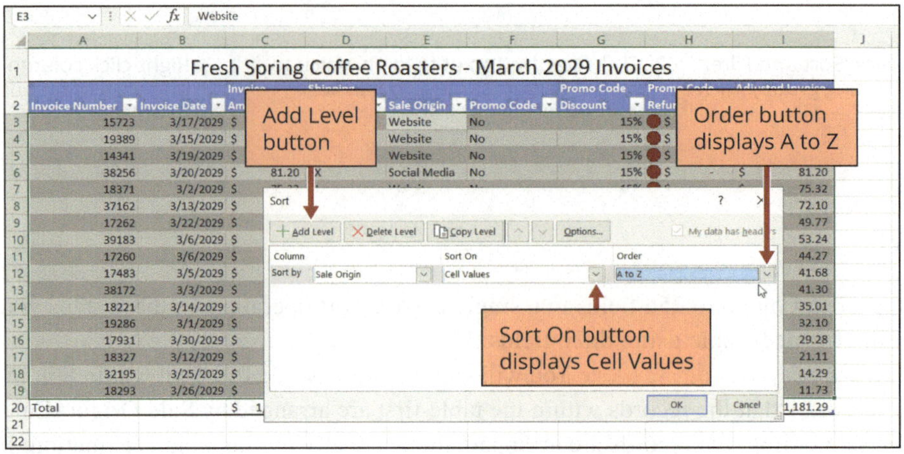

Figure 6–36

3

- Click the Add Level button (Sort dialog box) to add a second sort level.
- Click the Then by button, and then click Shipping Destination in the Then by list to select an intermediate sort key.
- If necessary, select Cell Values in the Sort On list.
- If necessary, select 'A to Z' in the Order list to sort the field alphabetically (Figure 6–37).

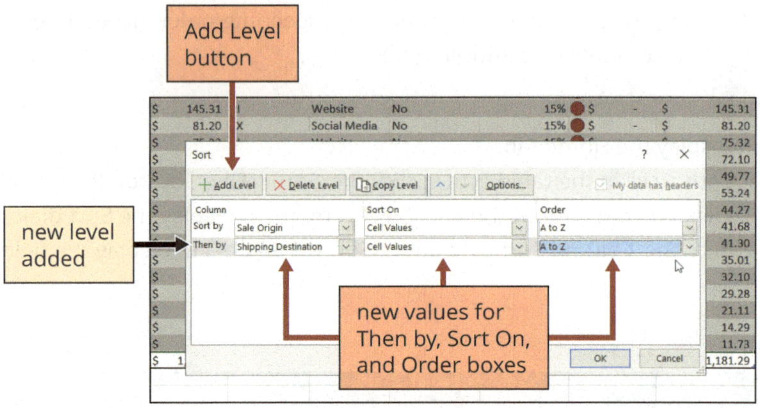

Figure 6–37

4

- Click the Add Level button to add a new sort level.
- Click the second Then by button and then click Promo Code Discount to select a minor sort key.
- If necessary, select Cell Values in the Sort On list. Select 'Largest to Smallest' in the Order list to specify that the field should be sorted in reverse order (Figure 6–38).

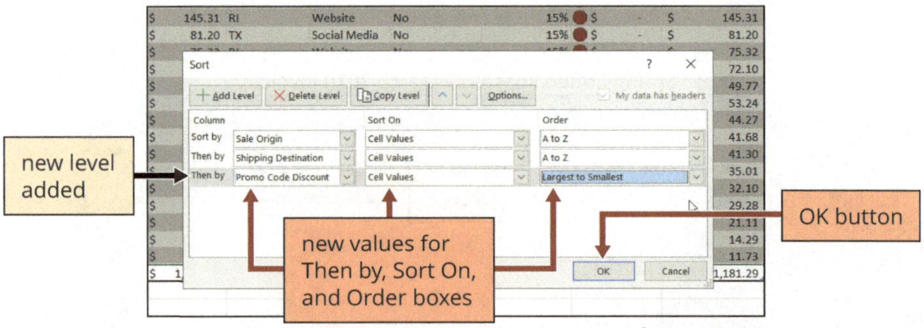

Figure 6–38

5

- Click OK to sort the table, in this case by Promo Code Discount (descending) within Shipping Destination (ascending) within Sale Origin (ascending) (Figure 6–39).

Q&A What should I do if I make a sorting error?

If you make a mistake in a sort operation, you can return the records to their previous order by clicking the Undo button on the Quick Access Toolbar or by pressing CTRL+Z. You can undo all steps back to when you originally opened the file—even if you have saved multiple times. Once you close the file however, you cannot undo a sorting error, and you would have to perform another sort.

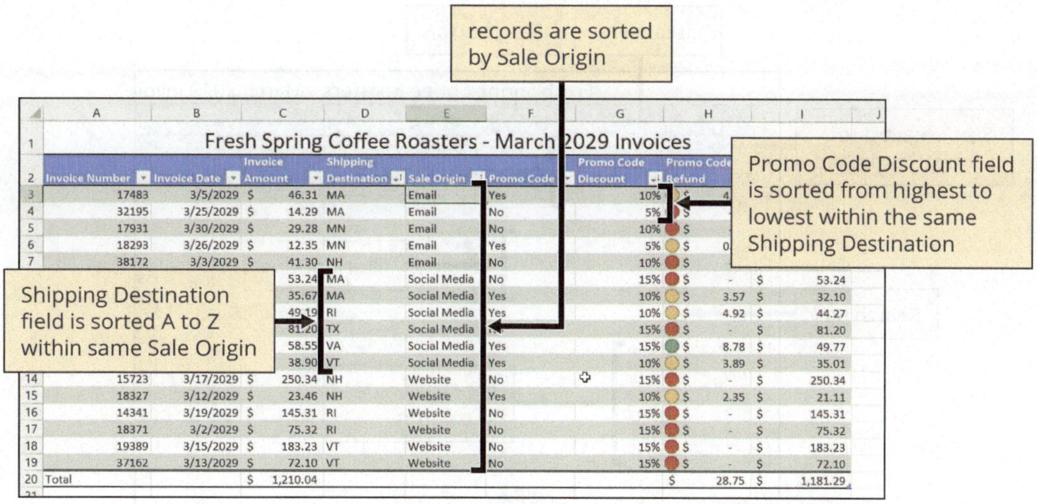

Figure 6–39

Querying a Table Using AutoFilter

When you first create a table, Excel automatically enables AutoFilter, a tool used to sort, query, and filter the records in a table. While using AutoFilter, the filter buttons appear to the right of the column headings. Clicking a button displays the filter menu for the column with various commands and a list of all items in the field (shown in Figure 6–40).

The sort commands work the same way as the sort buttons that you learned about earlier. The filter commands let you choose to display only those records that meet specified criteria such as color, number, or text. In this context, **criteria** means a logical rule by which data is tested and chosen. For example, you can filter the table to display a specific name or item by typing it in a Search box. The name you selected acts as the criterion for filtering the table, which results in Excel displaying only those records that match the criterion. Alternately, the selected check boxes indicate which items will appear in the table. By default, all of the items are selected. If you deselect an item from the filter menu, it is removed from the filter criterion. Excel will not display any record that contains the unchecked item.

As with the previous sort techniques, you can include more than one column when you filter by clicking a second filter button and making choices. The process of filtering records based on one or more filter criteria is called a **query**. After you filter data, you can copy, find, edit, format, chart, or print the filtered data without rearranging or moving it.

BTW
Scrolling Tables
When you scroll down in a table to display more rows, the column headings remain on the screen in a manner similar to using the Freeze Panes command (View tab | Window group).

To Sort a Table Using AutoFilter

The following steps sort the table by Invoice Amount using the 'Sort Smallest to Largest' command on the filter menu. Why? Using the filter menu sometimes is easier than other sort methods; you do not have to leave the table area and move to the ribbon to perform the sort.

1

- Click the filter button in the Invoice Amount column to display the filter menu (Figure 6–40).
- **Experiment:** Click filter buttons for other fields. Notice that the filter menu is context sensitive, which means it changes depending on what you are trying to filter. When you are finished, again click the Filter button in the Invoice Amount column.

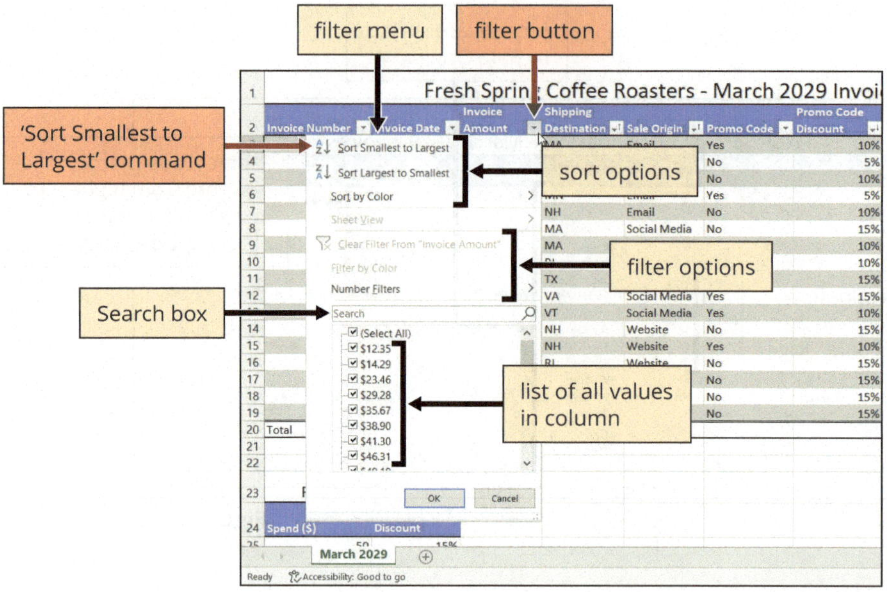

Figure 6–40

2

- Click 'Sort Smallest to Largest' on the filter menu to sort the table in ascending sequence by the selected field (Figure 6–41).

Q&A Does performing a new sort overwrite the previous sort?

Yes. A new sort undoes the previous sort, even if it is a custom sort or a sort based on multiple sort keys.

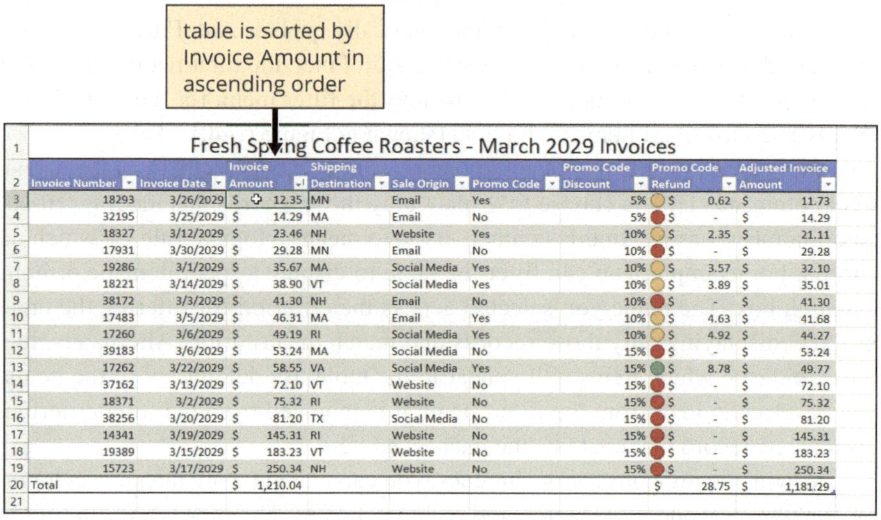

Fresh Spring Coffee Roasters - March 2029 Invoices

	Invoice Number	Invoice Date	Invoice Amount	Shipping Destination	Sale Origin	Promo Code	Promo Code Discount	Promo Code Refund	Adjusted Invoice Amount
3	18293	3/26/2029	$ 12.35	MN	Email	Yes	5%	$ 0.62	$ 11.73
4	32195	3/25/2029	$ 14.29	MA	Email	No	5%	$ -	$ 14.29
5	18327	3/12/2029	$ 23.46	NH	Website	Yes	10%	$ 2.35	$ 21.11
6	17931	3/30/2029	$ 29.28	MN	Email	No	10%	$ -	$ 29.28
7	19286	3/1/2029	$ 35.67	MA	Social Media	Yes	10%	$ 3.57	$ 32.10
8	18221	3/14/2029	$ 38.90	VT	Social Media	Yes	10%	$ 3.89	$ 35.01
9	38172	3/3/2029	$ 41.30	NH	Email	No	10%	$ -	$ 41.30
10	17483	3/5/2029	$ 46.31	MA	Email	Yes	10%	$ 4.63	$ 41.68
11	17260	3/6/2029	$ 49.19	RI	Social Media	Yes	10%	$ 4.92	$ 44.27
12	39183	3/6/2029	$ 53.24	MA	Social Media	No	15%	$ -	$ 53.24
13	17262	3/22/2029	$ 58.55	VA	Social Media	Yes	15%	$ 8.78	$ 49.77
14	37162	3/13/2029	$ 72.10	VT	Website	No	15%	$ -	$ 72.10
15	18371	3/2/2029	$ 75.32	RI	Website	No	15%	$ -	$ 75.32
16	38256	3/20/2029	$ 81.20	TX	Social Media	No	15%	$ -	$ 81.20
17	14341	3/19/2029	$ 145.31	RI	Website	No	15%	$ -	$ 145.31
18	19389	3/15/2029	$ 183.23	VT	Website	No	15%	$ -	$ 183.23
19	15723	3/17/2029	$ 250.34	NH	Website	No	15%	$ -	$ 250.34
20	Total		$ 1,210.04					$ 28.75	$ 1,181.29

Figure 6–41

To Query a Table Using AutoFilter

The following steps query the Invoices table using AutoFilter. **Why?** *The AutoFilter will cause the table to display only specific records, which may be helpful in very large tables.* In this case, using the check boxes on the filter menu, you will choose those invoices with a shipping destination other Texas with a Sale Origin of Social Media.

1

- Click the filter button in cell D2 to display the filter menu for the Shipping Destination column.
- Click TX in the filter menu to remove the checkmark and cause Excel to hide rows for all invoices shipping to Texas (Figure 6–42).

Q&A What else appears on the filter menu?

Below the Text Filters command is a list of all of the values that occur in the selected column. A check mark in the top item, (Select All), indicates that all values for this field are displayed in the table.

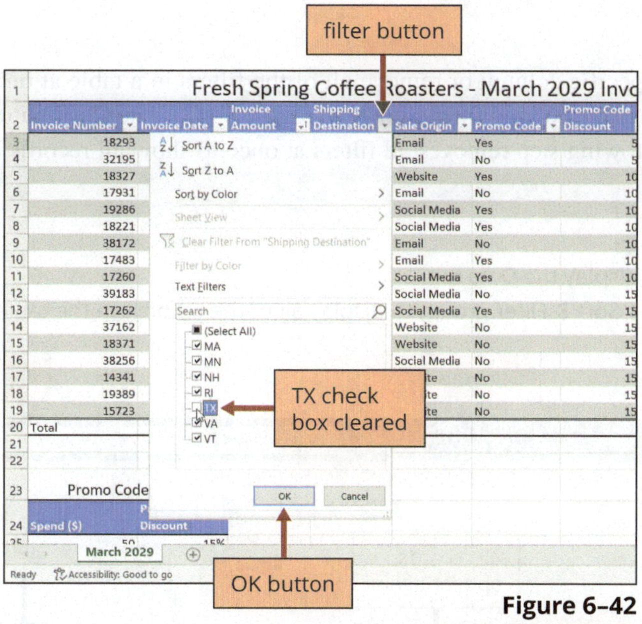

Figure 6–42

2

- Click OK to apply the AutoFilter criterion and display the records for all specialties except Texas.
- Click the filter button in cell E2 to display the filter menu for the Sale Origin column.
- Click to remove the check marks beside Email and Website, so that only the Social Media check box contains a check mark (Figure 6–43).

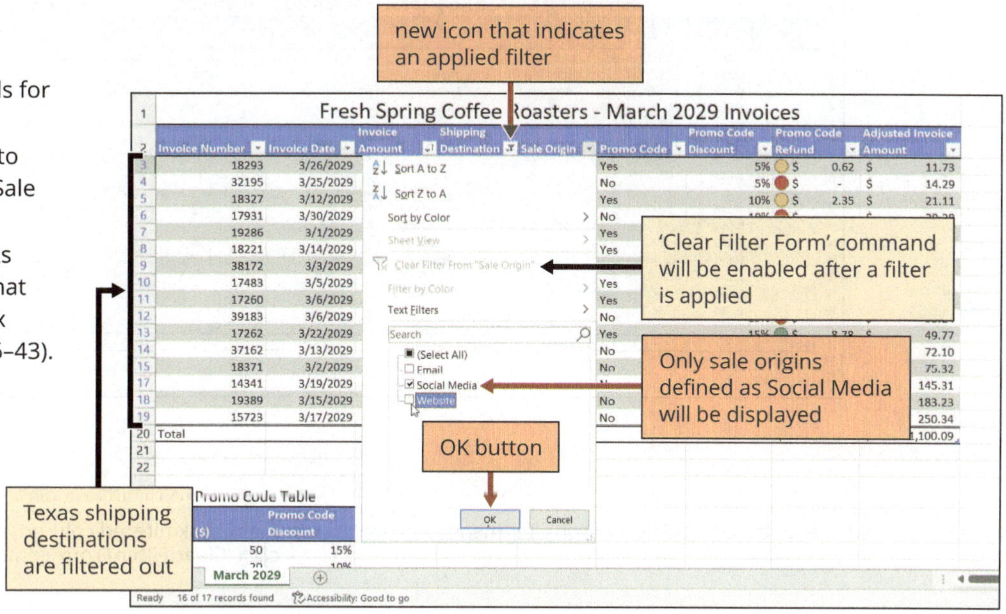

Figure 6–43

3

- Click OK to apply the AutoFilter criterion (Figure 6–44).

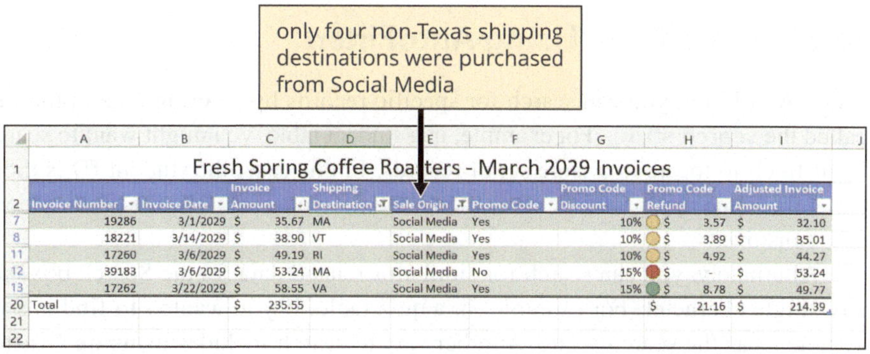

Figure 6–44

Q&A Are both filters now applied to the table?

Yes. When you select a second filter criterion, Excel adds it to the first; hence, each record must pass two tests to appear as part of the final subset of the table.

Did the filter remove the previous sort?

No. Notice in Figure 6–44 that the records still are sorted in ascending order by Invoice Amount.

Other Ways

1. Click filter button, enter desired data in Search box (filter menu), click OK

To Remove Filters

You can remove a filter from a specific column or remove all of the filters in a table at once. Each filter menu has a 'Clear Filter From' command that removes the column filter (shown in Figure 6–43). The Clear button (Data tab | Sort & Filter group) removes all of the filters. The following step removes all filters at once to show all records in the table. **Why?** The filters, or query, hid some of the records in the previous steps.

1

- Click anywhere in the table and display the Data tab.
- Click the Clear button (Data tab | Sort & Filter group) to display all of the records in the table (Figure 6–45).

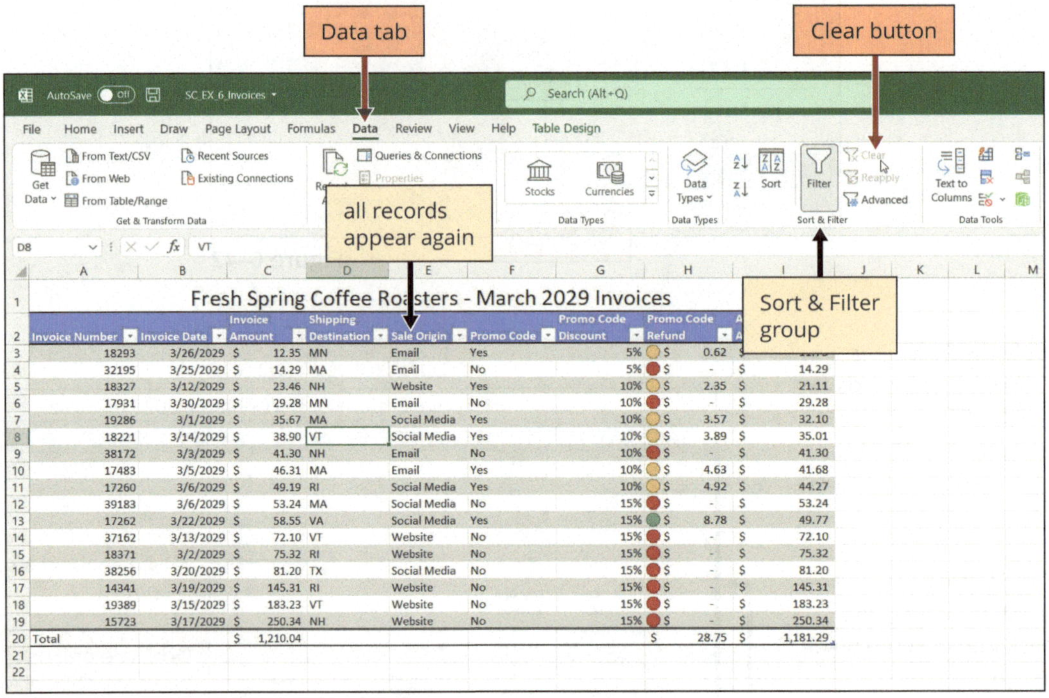

Figure 6–45

Other Ways

1. Click desired filter button, click (Select All) on filter menu
2. Right-click filtered column, point to Filter on shortcut menu, click 'Clear Filter From' command

To Search a Table Using AutoFilter

Using AutoFilter, you can search for specific records by entering data in the Search box. The sequence of data you enter is called the **search string**. For example, in a student table, you might want to search for a specific student ID number that might be difficult to locate in a large set of records. In this case, the student ID is the search string. If an exact match exists in the table, the value appears in the filter menu; then, if you click OK, the entire record appears in the table. Table searches are not case sensitive.

Alternately, you can search for similar or related data. In the Search box, you can type **?** (question mark) to represent any single character. For example, in a quiz table, if you wanted to find answer1, answer2, and answer3, you could type **answer?** as the search string. Another way to search includes using an * (asterisk) to represent a series of characters. For example, in an inventory table, to find all of the items that relate to drive, you could type ***drive*** in the Search box. The filter would display results such as flash drives, CD-R drive, and drivers. The ? and * are called **wildcard characters**.

The following steps search for a specific record in a table using the filter menu. **Why?** When tables are large, searching for individual records using the filter menu is quick and easy.

1

- Click the filter button in the Invoice Date column to display the filter menu.
- Click the Search box, and then type **22** as the search string (Figure 6–46).

Q&A Is this search the same as using the Find command?

No. This command searches for data within the table only and then displays all records that match the search string. Two records matching the search appear in Figure 6–47. The Find command looks over the entire worksheet and highlights one cell.

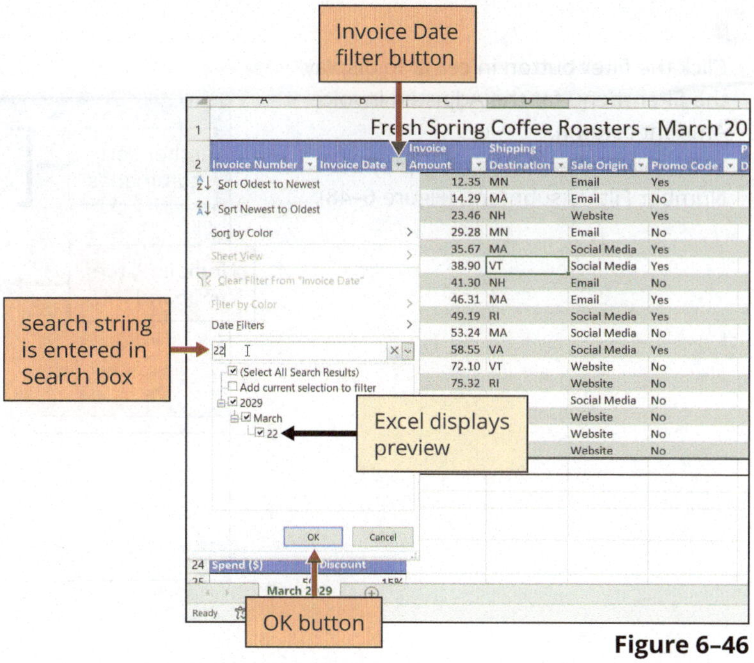

Figure 6–46

2

- Click OK to perform the search (Figure 6–47).
- **Experiment:** Search other columns for different kinds of data. Note that the total row reflects only the records displayed by the filter.

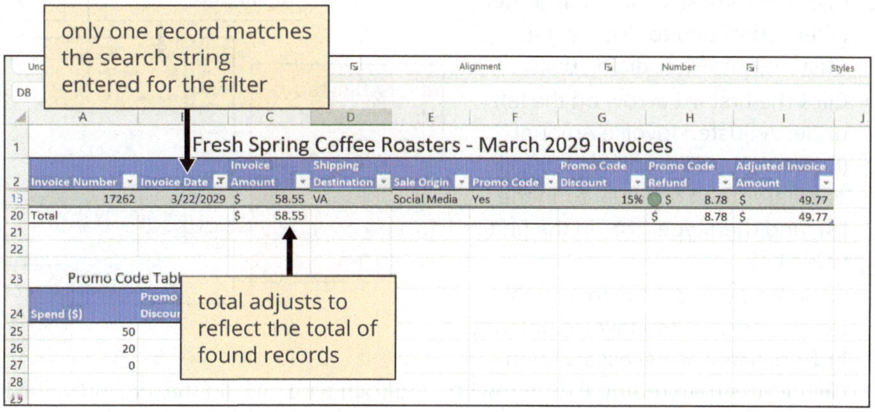

Figure 6–47

3

- Click the Clear button (Data tab | Sort & Filter group) to display all of the records in the table.

To Enter Custom Criteria Using AutoFilter

Another way to query a table is to use the Custom Filter command. The Custom Filter command allows you to enter custom criteria, such as multiple options or ranges of numbers. **Why?** Not all queries are exact numbers; many times, a range of numbers is required. The following steps enter custom criteria to display records that represent invoices whose Adjusted Invoice Amount is between \$10 and \$45, inclusive; that is, the number is greater than or equal to \$10 and less than or equal to \$45 (\$10 ≤ Adjusted Invoice Amount ≤ \$45).

1

- Click the filter button in cell I2 to display the filter menu for the Adjusted Invoice Amount column.
- Point to Number Filters to display the Number Filters submenu (Figure 6–48).

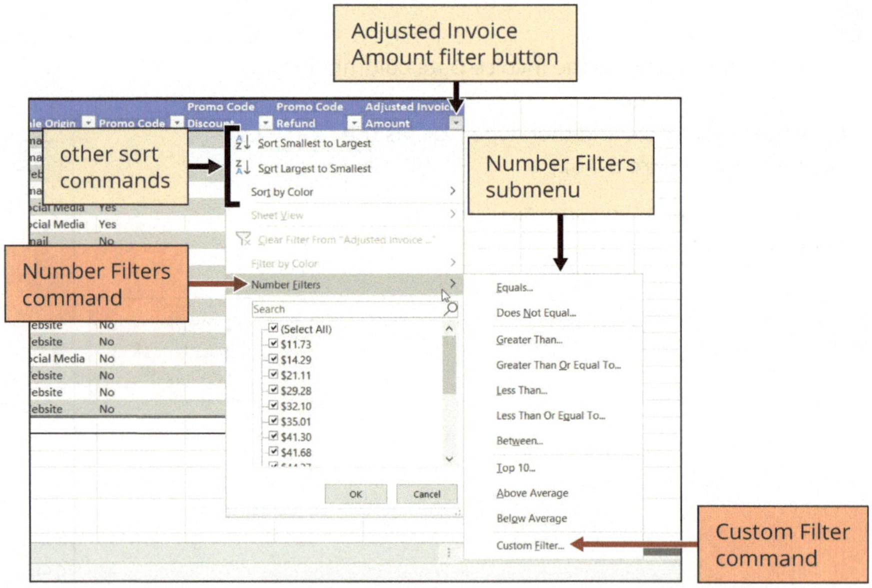

Figure 6–48

2

- Click Custom Filter on the Number Filters submenu to display the Custom AutoFilter dialog box.
- Click the first list arrow on the left under Adjusted Invoice Amount (Custom AutoFilter dialog box), click 'is greater than or equal to' in the list, and then type **10** in the first value box.
- Click the second list arrow on the left under Adjusted Invoice Amount button. Scroll as necessary, then click 'is less than or equal to' in the list, and then type **45** in the second value box (Figure 6–49).

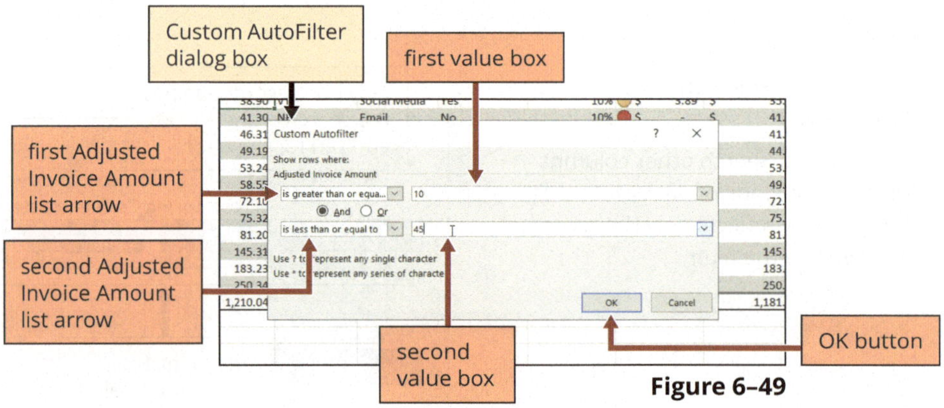

Figure 6–49

Q&A How are the And and Or option buttons used?

You can click option buttons to select the appropriate operator. The AND operator indicates that both parts of the criteria must be true; the OR operator indicates that only one of the two must be true.

3

- Click OK (Custom AutoFilter dialog box) to display records in the table that match the custom AutoFilter criteria, in this case, invoices in which the Adjusted Invoice Amount number is between $10 and $45, inclusive (Figure 6–50).

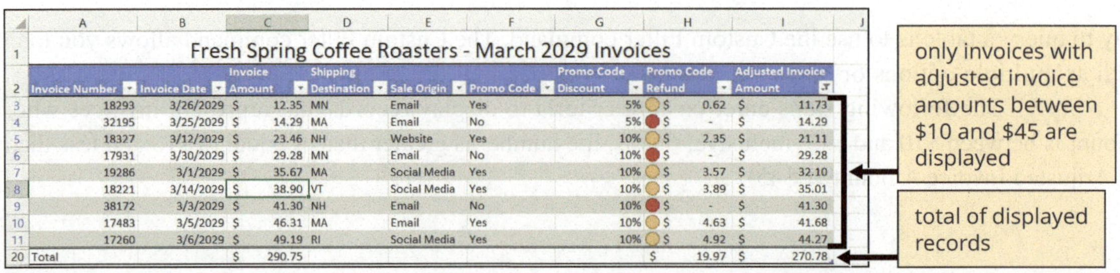

Figure 6–50

4

- Click the Clear button (Data tab | Sort & Filter group) to display all of the records in the table.

More about AutoFilters Other important points regarding AutoFilter include the following:

- When you query a table to display some records and hide others, Excel displays a filter icon on the filter buttons used to establish the filter.
- Excel does not sort hidden records.
- If the filter buttons do not appear, then you must manually enable AutoFilter by clicking the Filter button (Data tab | Sort & Filter group).
- To remove a filter criterion for a single piece of data in a field, click the Select All check box on the filter menu for that field.
- When you create a formula in the total row of a table, the formula automatically recalculates the values even when you filter the list. For example, the results shown in the Total row in Figure 6–50 update automatically if you apply a filter to the table.
- You can filter and sort a column by color or conditional formatting using the 'Sort by Color' and 'Filter by Color' commands on the filter menu (shown in Figure 6–48).
- To reapply a filter or sort, click the Sort & Filter button (Home tab | Editing group), and then click Reapply.

To Turn Off AutoFilter

The following steps turn the AutoFilter feature off and on by hiding and then showing the filter buttons. Why? Sometimes you may want to view the table without the distraction of the buttons. The following steps hide and then redisplay the AutoFilter.

1

- Click the Filter button (Data tab | Sort & Filter group) to hide the filter buttons in the table (Figure 6–51).

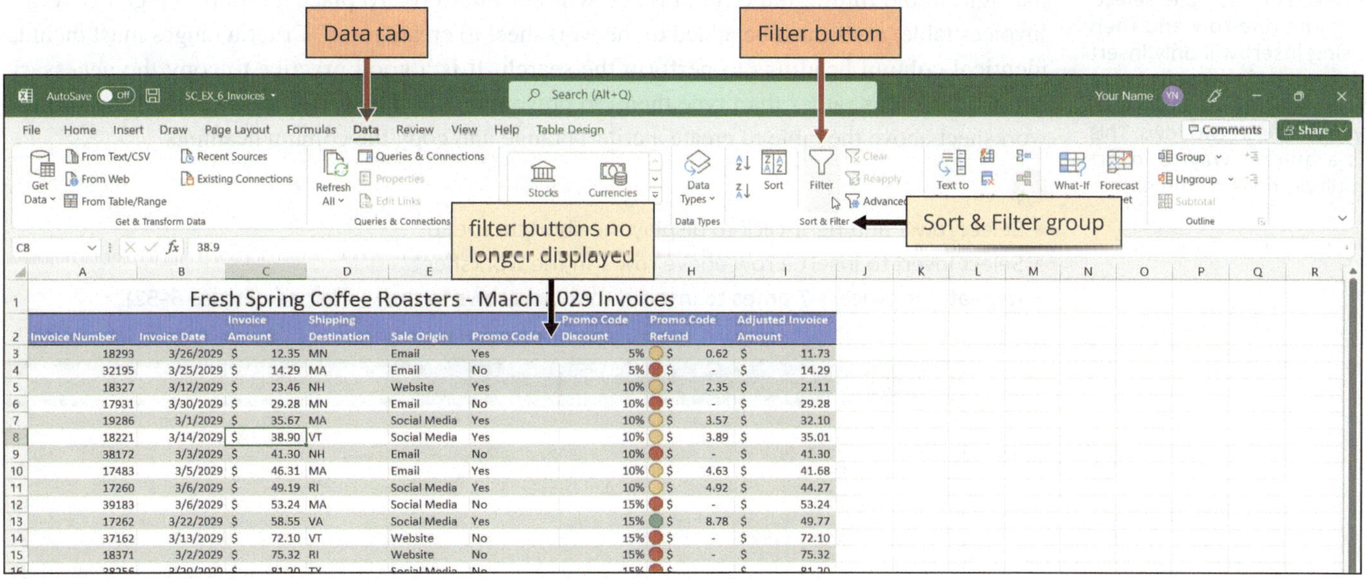

Figure 6–51

2

- Click the Filter button (Data tab | Sort & Filter group) again to display the filter buttons in the table.

3

- Click the Save button on the Quick Access Toolbar to save the workbook.

Other Ways

1. Click 'Sort & Filter' button (Home tab | Editing group), click Filter command in 'Sort & Filter' list
2. CTRL+SHIFT+L

Using Criteria and Extract Ranges

Another advanced filter technique called a criteria range manipulates records that pass comparison criteria. A **criteria range** is a location separate from the table used to list specific search specifications. Like a custom filter, a criteria range compares entered data with a list or table, based on column headings. Using a criteria range is sometimes faster than entering criteria through the AutoFilter system because once the range is established, you do not have to access any menus or dialog boxes to perform the query. You also can create an **extract range** in which Excel copies the records that meet the comparison criteria in the criteria range to another part of the worksheet.

Consider This

Does Excel provide another way to pull data out of a table?

Yes. You can create a criteria area and extract area on the worksheet. The criteria area can be used to enter rules regarding which records to extract, without having to change the AutoFilter settings. For example, the criteria area might ask for all full-time students with a grade of A from the table. The extract area can be used to store the records that meet the criteria. Extracting records allows you to pull data from a table so that you can analyze or manipulate the data further. For example, you may want to know which customers are delinquent on their payments. Extracting records that meet this criterion allows you then to use the records to create a mailing to such customers.

BTW

Inserting Rows

You can insert rows more quickly by selecting the number of rows you want to insert. For example, selecting just one row and then using Insert will only insert one row. If you select two rows and then use Insert, you will insert two rows. This is a quicker way to insert multiple rows at a time.

To Create a Criteria Range

When creating a criteria range, it is important to place it away from the table itself. Commonly, criteria ranges are located directly above the table. That way, if the table grows downward or to the right in the future, the criteria range will not interfere. To place a criteria range above the Invoices table, rows must be added to the worksheet to create room. Criteria ranges must include identical column headings to perform the search. It is a good practice to copy the necessary column headings rather than type them, to prevent errors. The following steps add rows to the worksheet above the table to create a criteria range and copy the column headings.

1

- Select row 1 and right-click to display the shortcut menu.
- Select Insert to insert a row above row 1 in the worksheet.
- Repeat this process 7 times to insert 8 total new rows to the worksheet (Figure 6–52).

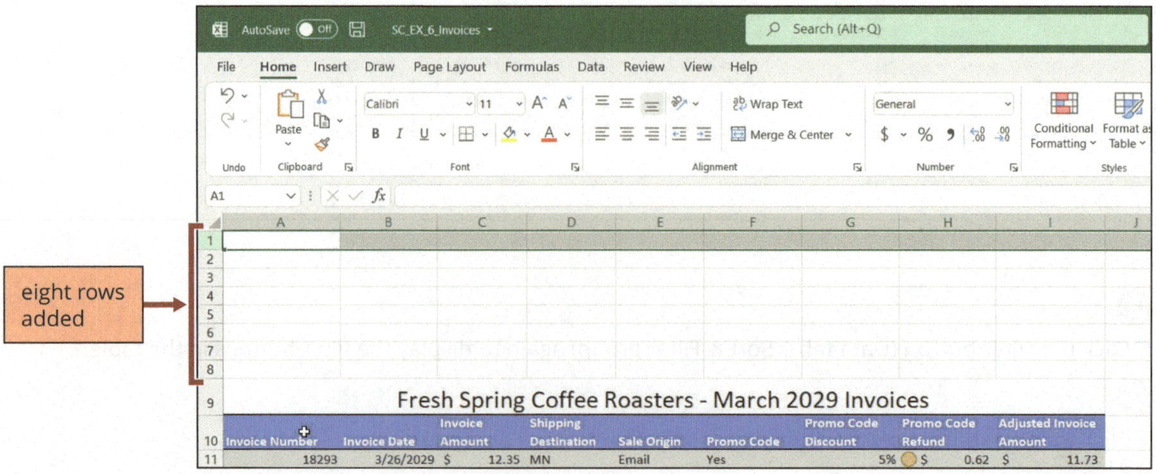

Figure 6–52

2

- Select the range A9:I10 and then press CTRL+C to copy the range.
- Select cell A1 and then press ENTER to paste the Clipboard contents.
- Change the title to **Criteria Range** in cell A1.
- If necessary, use the format painter to copy the formatting from row 10 to row 2.
- Select the range A2:I3, click the Name box, type **Criteria** as the range name, and then press ENTER (Figure 6–53).

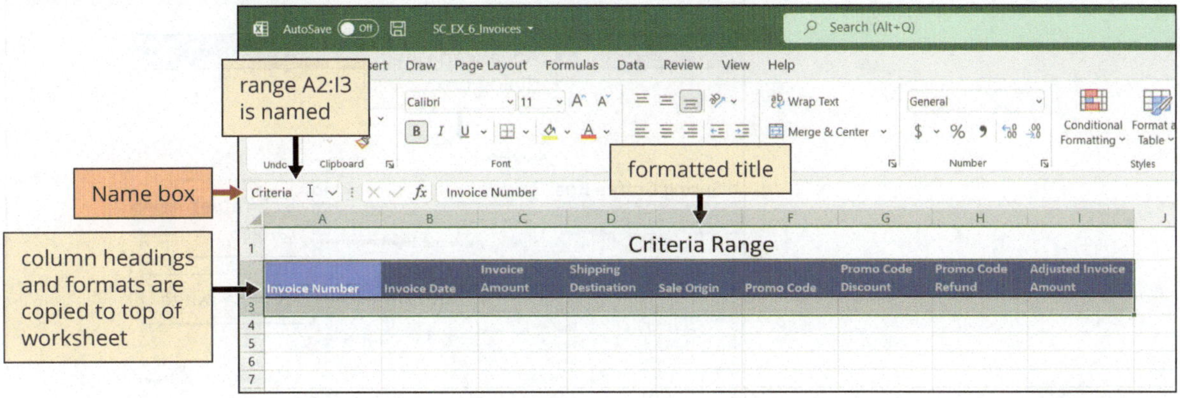

Figure 6–53

To Query Using a Criteria Range

The following steps use the criteria range and the Advanced Filter dialog box to query the table and display only the records that pass the test: Sale Origin = Social Media AND Adjusted Invoice Amount > 25. The criteria data is entered directly below the criteria range headings. **Why?** Because the Advanced Filter dialog box searches for a match using column headings and adjacent rows.

1

- In cell E3 enter the criteria **Social Media**, and in cell I3 type **>25** (Figure 6–54).
- If your filter buttons are turned off, click the Filter button (Data tab | Sort & Filter group) to toggle them on.

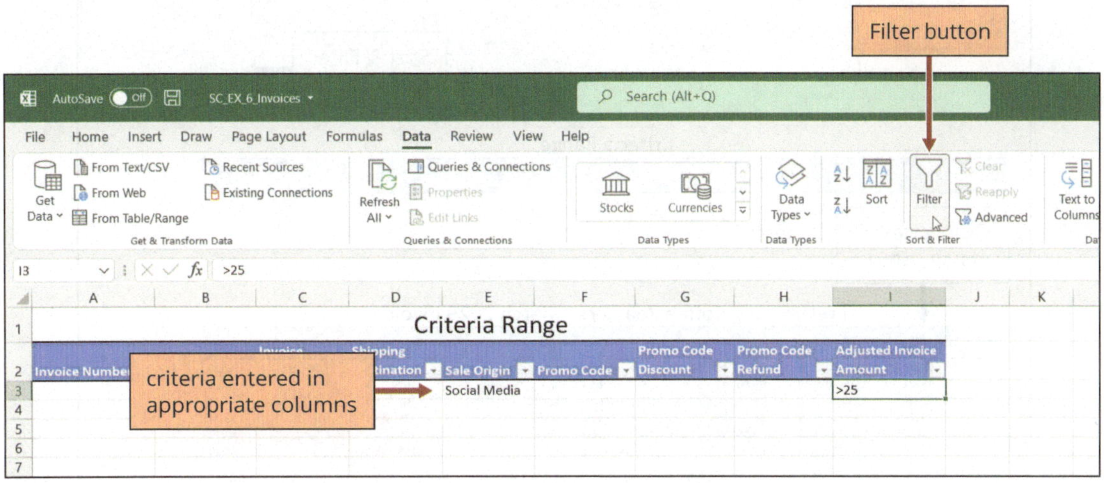

Figure 6–54

2

- Click the Invoices table to make it active.
- Click the Advanced button (Data tab | Sort & Filter group) to display the Advanced Filter dialog box.
- If necessary, type **a10:i28** in the List range box (Figure 6–55).

Q&A My values in the Advanced Filter dialog box are different. Did I do something wrong?
If your values are different, type $A$10:$I$28 in the List range box. Excel selects the criteria range ($A$2:$I$3) in the Criteria range box, because you assigned the name Criteria to the range A2:I3 earlier.

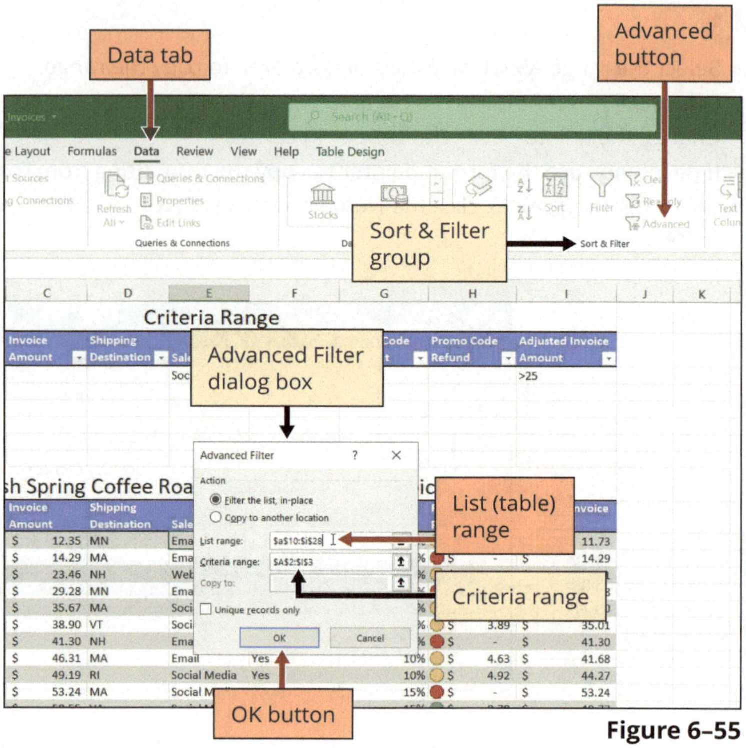

Figure 6–55

3

- Click OK (Advanced Filter dialog box) to hide all records that do not meet the comparison criteria (Figure 6–56).

Q&A What is the main difference between using the AutoFilter query technique and using the Advanced Filter dialog box with a criteria range?
Like the AutoFilter query technique, the Advanced Filter command displays a subset of the table. The primary difference between the two is that the Advanced Filter command allows you to create more complex comparison criteria, because the criteria range can be as many rows long as necessary, allowing for many sets of comparison criteria.

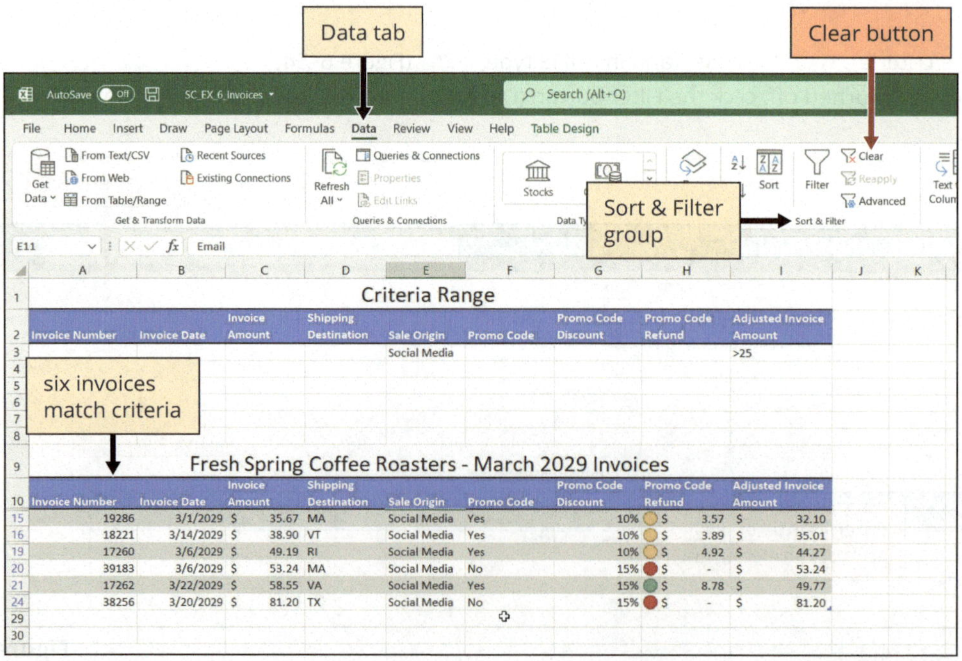

Figure 6–56

4

- Click the Clear button (Data tab | Sort & Filter group) to show all records. If your banded rows no longer display correctly, click the 'Blue, Table Style Medium 16' button (Table Design tab | Table Styles group).

To Create an Extract Range

In the previous steps, you filtered data in place within the table itself; however, you can copy the records that meet the criteria to another part of the worksheet, rather than displaying them as a subset of the table. **Why?** Extracting the filtered data to another location leaves the table intact; and, it allows you to compare the data more easily. The following steps create an extract range below the table.

1. Select the range A9:I10 and then press CTRL+C to copy the range.
2. Select cell A38 and then press ENTER to paste the contents.
3. Change the title in cell A38 to **Extract Area**.
4. If necessary, use the format painter to copy the formatting from row 10 to row 39.
5. Select the range A39:I58, click the Name box, type **Extract** as the range name, and then press ENTER (Figure 6–57).

Q&A Why am I including so many rows in the extraction range?
The table has many records; you want to make sure you have enough room for any search that the company might desire.

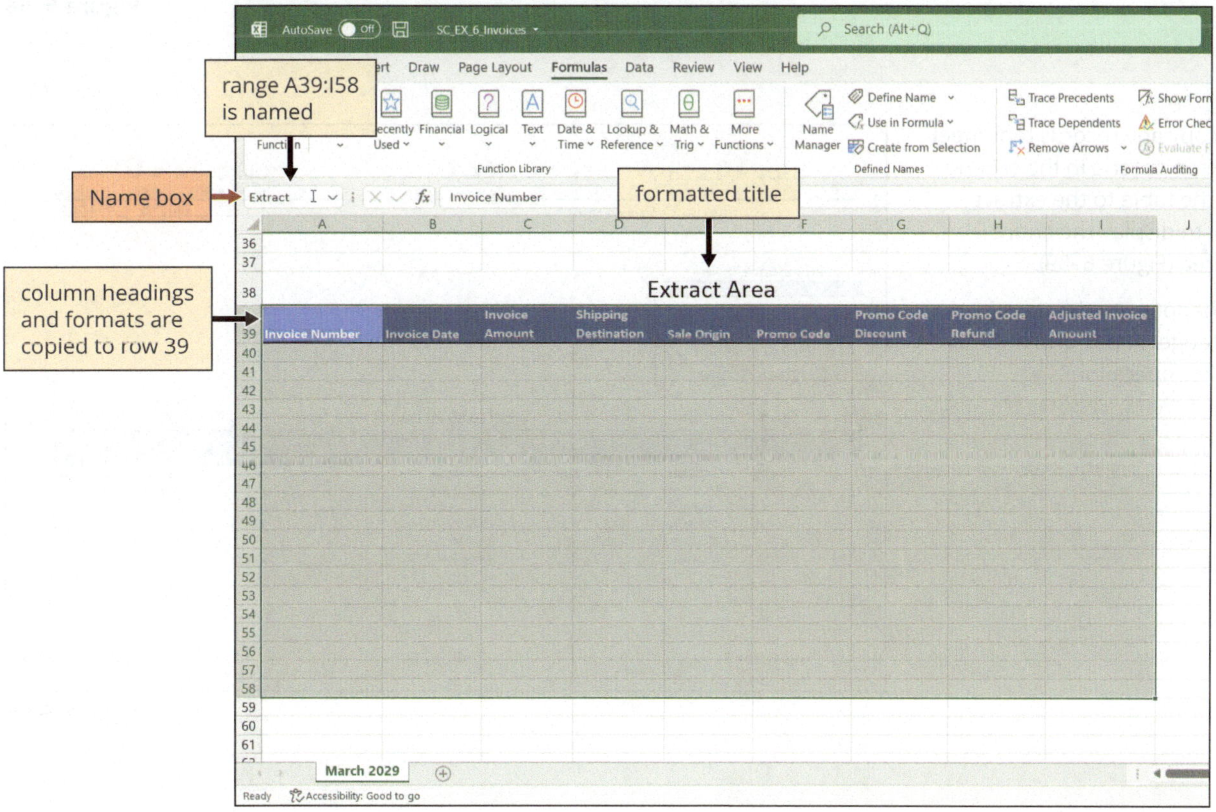

Figure 6–57

BTW
AND and OR Queries
If you want to create a query that displays records that meet the criteria for two pieces of data, you enter the data across the same row in the criteria range. If you want to create a query that displays records that meet the criteria for either one piece of data OR another, enter the second piece of data on the next row.

To Extract Records

The following steps extract records that meet the previous criteria, using the Advanced Filter dialog box. **Why?** The Advanced Filter dialog box allows you to use the complex criteria from a criteria range on the worksheet and send the results to a third location, leaving the table undisturbed.

1

- Scroll up and click the Invoices table to make it active.
- Click the Advanced button (Data tab | Sort & Filter group) to display the Advanced Filter dialog box.
- Click the 'Copy to another location' option button in the Action area (Advanced Filter dialog box) to cause the records that meet the criteria to be copied to a different location on the worksheet (Figure 6–58).

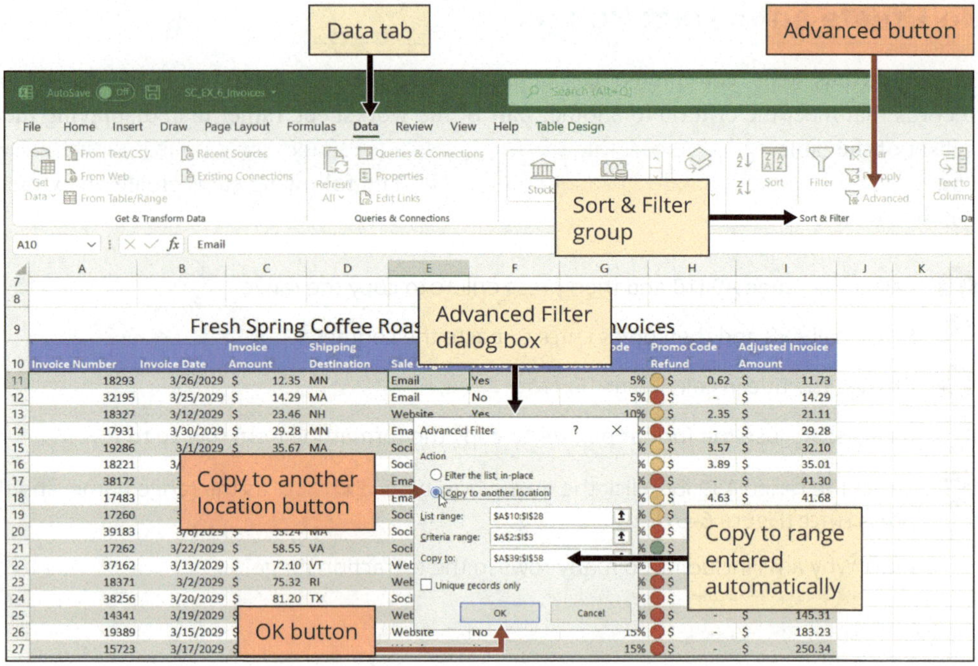

Figure 6–58

2

- Click OK to copy any records that meet the comparison criteria in the criteria range from the table to the extract range. Scroll to display the entire extraction area (Figure 6–59).

Q&A What happens to the rows in the extract range if I perform another advanced filter operation?

Each time you use the Advanced Filter dialog box with the 'Copy to another location' option, Excel clears cells below the field names in the extract range before it copies a new set of records that pass the new test.

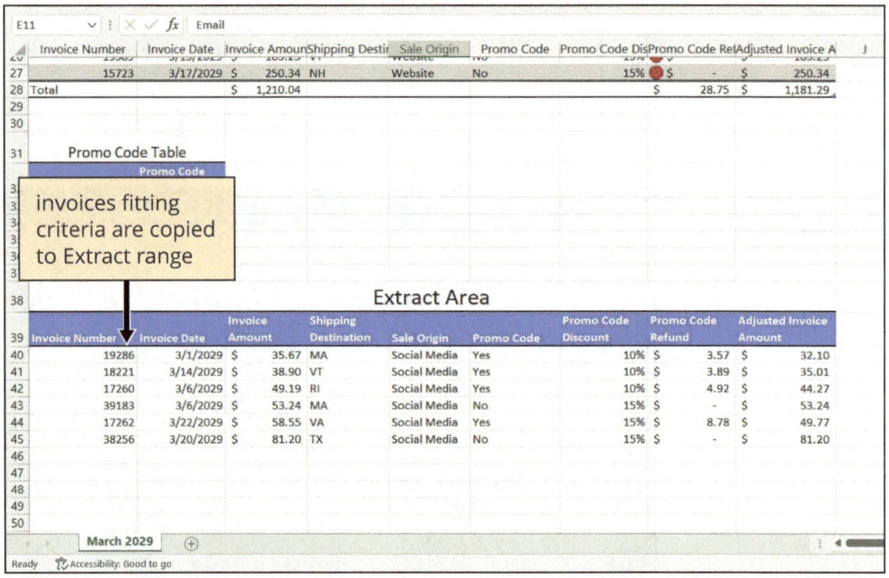

Figure 6–59

3

- Click the Save button on the Quick Access Toolbar to save the workbook again.

Break Point: If you want to take a break, this is a good place to do so. You can exit Excel now. To resume later, start Excel, open the file called SC_EX_6_Invoices, and continue following the steps from this location forward.

More about the Criteria Range

The comparison criteria in the criteria range determine the records that will pass the test when the Advanced Filter dialog box is used. As you have likely noticed, multiple entries in a single data row of the criteria range create an AND condition. The following examples describe different comparison criteria.

- If the criteria range contains a blank row, it means that no comparison criteria have been defined. Thus, all records in the table pass the test and will be displayed.
- If you want an OR operator in the same field, your criteria range must contain two (or more) data rows. Enter the criteria data on separate rows. Records that pass either (or any) comparison criterion will be displayed.
- If you want an AND operator in the same field name, you must add a column in the criteria range and duplicate the column heading.
- If you want an OR operator on two different fields, your criteria range must contain two (or more) data rows. Enter the criteria for each field on a separate row. Records will display that pass either (or any) comparison criterion.
- When the comparison criteria below different field names are in the same row, then records pass the test only if they pass all the comparison criteria, an AND condition. If the comparison criteria for the field names are in different rows, then the records must pass only one of the tests, an OR condition.

BTW
Keeping Data in Order
If you want to perform various sorts but need to have a way to return to the original order, you might consider adding a column that numbers the entries before sorting. Then, you can always sort on this field to restore the original order of the entries.

Using Database Functions

Excel includes 12 database functions that allow you to evaluate numeric data in a table. These functions each begin with the letter D for data table, to differentiate them from their worksheet counterparts. As the name implies, the **DAVERAGE function** calculates the average of numbers in a table field that pass a test. The general form of the DAVERAGE function is

=DAVERAGE(table range, "field name", criteria range)

Another often-used table function is the DCOUNT function. The **DCOUNT function** counts the number of numeric entries in a table field that pass a test. The general form of the DCOUNT function is

=DCOUNT(table range, "field name", criteria range)

In both functions, table range is the location of the table, field name is the name of the field in the table, and criteria range is the comparison criteria or test to pass. The criteria range must include a column heading with the data. Note that Excel requires that you surround field names with quotation marks unless you previously named the field.

Other database functions that are similar to the functions described in previous modules include the DMAX, DMIN, and DSUM functions. Refer to Excel Help for a complete list of database functions.

BTW
The DGET Function
The DGET function extracts a single value from a column of a list or database that matches conditions that you specify. The three arguments include database, column number, and criteria.

BTW
Functions and Ranges
When using a function such as DAVERAGE or DCOUNT, Excel automatically adjusts the first argument if the table grows or shrinks. With functions such as SUMIF and COUNTIF, you must correct the function argument to reflect the new range if the range grows or shrinks.

To Create an Output Area

In order to demonstrate the database functions and other functions, the following steps set up an output area in preparation for entering functions.

1. Change the width of columns L, M, and N to 16.00.
2. Select cell L1 and then type **Output Area** to enter a criteria area title. Center the title across the selection L1:N1 and change the font size to 20.

3 Enter other labels as shown below. Bold the title cells L8 and L11, and center them across columns L through N. Select range L1:N13 and apply the fill color White, Background 1. Use the format painter to copy the formatting from cell I10 to cells L12:N12. If necessary, ensure that cell L2 matches the formatting of cell L3; if not, use the format painter to copy the formatting from cell L3 to cell L2 (Figure 6–60).

Cell	Text
L2	15% Promo Code used:
L3	Avg. Adjusted Social Media Sales:
L4	Avg. Adjusted Email Sales:
L5	Avg. Adjusted Website Sales:
L6	Total MA Orders:
L7	Count of Email Sales:
L8	Locator
L9	Enter Invoice Number:
L10	Sale Origin of Invoice:
L11	Sale Origin Criteria
L12	Sale Origin
L13	Email
M12	Sale Origin
M13	Social Media
N12	Sale Origin
N13	Website

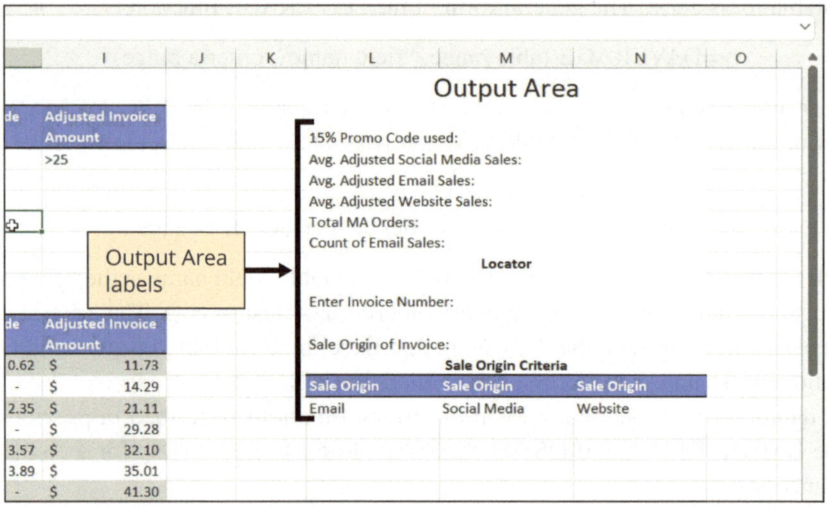

Figure 6–60

To Use the DAVERAGE and DCOUNT Database Functions

The following steps use the DCOUNT function to count the number of 15% promo codes used. You will use the DAVERAGE function to find the average adjusted invoice amounts from each sale origin. **Why?** The DAVERAGE and DCOUNT functions allow you to enter a range to average, and criteria with which to filter the table. The DAVERAGE function requires a numeric field from the table range; therefore, you will use "Promo Code Discount" as the second argument. Field names used as numeric arguments in these functions should be surrounded with quotation marks unless previously named.

1

- Select cell N2 and then type **=dcount(a10:i28,"Promo Code Discount",b32:b33)** to enter the database function (Figure 6–61).

Q&A My function wraps. Did I do something wrong?

No, it depends on how far to the right you are scrolled. If there is not enough room on the screen, Excel will wrap long cell entries.

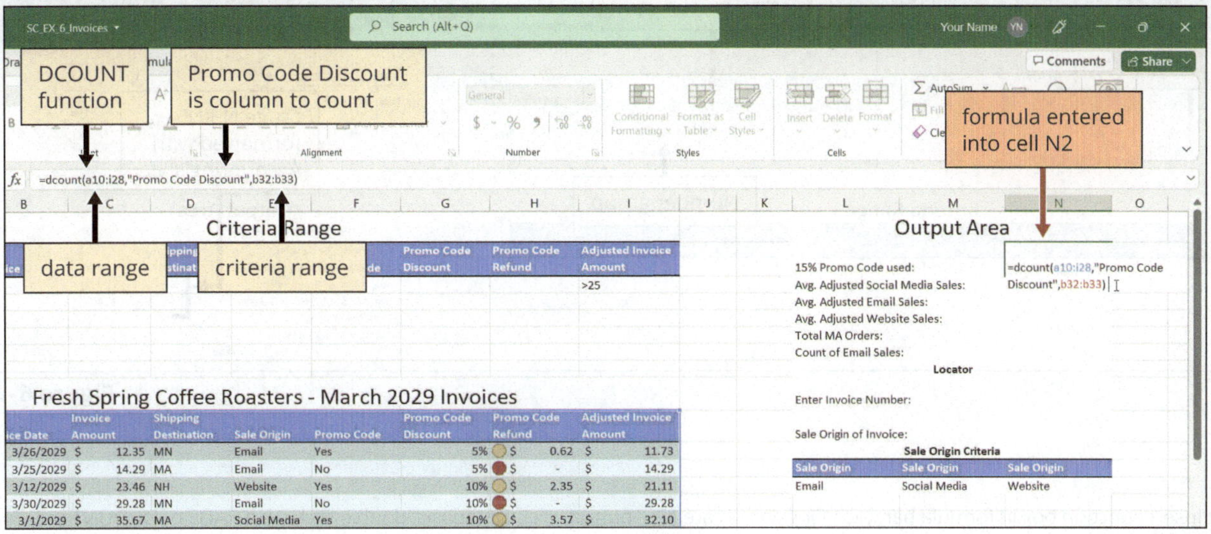

Figure 6–61

2

- Click the Enter button to finish the function and display the answer.
- Select cell N3 and then type **=daverage(a10:i28,"Adjusted Invoice Amount",m12:m13)**
- Select cell N4 and then type **=daverage(a10:i28,"Adjusted Invoice Amount",l12:l13)**
- Select cell N5 and then type **=daverage(a10:i28,"Adjusted Invoice Amount",n12:n13)** (Figure 6–62).

Q&A What is the DCOUNT function actually counting?

The DCOUNT function is counting the number of 15% promo code discounts in the table, as referenced by the B32:B33 criteria.

Why do the three DAVERAGE functions, which use the Adjusted Invoice Amount, generate different answers?

The criteria range differentiates the entries. The range M12:M13 averages the Adjusted Invoice Amount results for Social Media sales. The range L12:L13 averages Email sales. The range N12:N13 averages Website sales.

Could I use the table name instead of the range, A10:I28, as the first argument in the function?

To use a table name, you would have to enter a structured reference such as Invoices[#All] to reference the entire table.

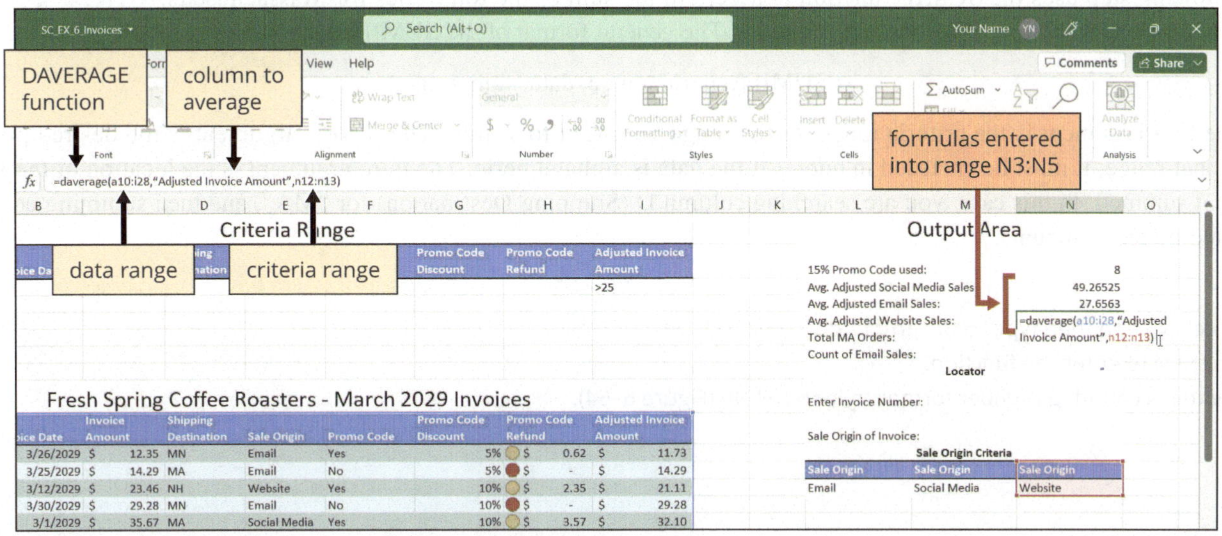

Figure 6–62

3

- Click the Enter button to finish the function.
- Format cells N3:N5 with the Accounting format (Figure 6–63).

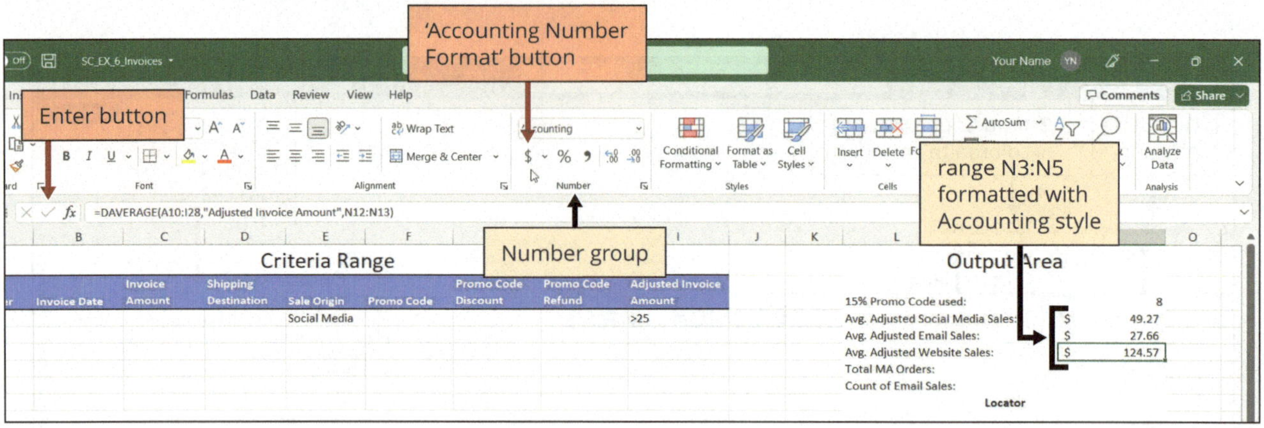

Figure 6–63

Other Ways

1. Click Insert Function box in formula bar, click 'Or select a category' button, click 'Database', double-click DAVERAGE or DCOUNT in 'Select a function' list, enter arguments

BTW

Using Quotation Marks

Many of the database functions require a field name as one of the arguments. If your field name is text, rather than a cell reference, number, or range, the argument must be enclosed in quotation marks.

Using the SUMIF and COUNTIF Functions

Two other functions are useful when querying a table and analyzing its data. The SUMIF and COUNTIF functions sum values in a range, or count values in a range, only if they meet a criteria. These functions combine the SUM and COUNT functions with the IF function and allow us to sum or count a range based on certain criteria.

To Use the SUMIF Function

The following step uses the SUMIF function to ascertain the sum of the total sales for Massachusetts. **Why?** The SUMIF function allows you to sum a range based on criteria. The general format of the SUMIF function is

=SUMIF(criteria_range, data, sum_range)

The first argument is the criteria range, or the range you want to search. The second argument is the desired piece of data in that range; it must be enclosed in quotes if the data is alphanumeric. The third argument is the location of the values you want summed. In this case, you are searching column D (Shipping Destination) for "MA", and then summing column I (Adjusted Invoice Amount).

1

- Click cell N6 and then type **=sumif(d11:d27,"MA",i11:i27)**
- Press ENTER to enter the function.
- Apply the accounting number format style to cell N6 (Figure 6–64).

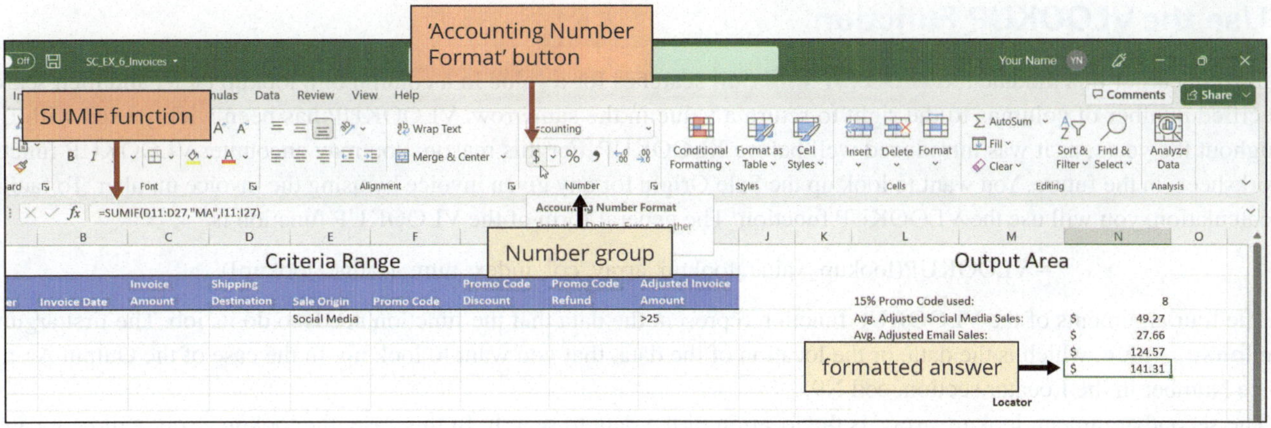

Figure 6–64

Other Ways

1. Click Insert Function box in formula bar, click 'Or select a category' button, click 'Math & Trig', double-click SUMIF in 'Select a function' list, enter arguments
2. Click 'Math & Trig' button (Formulas tab | Function Library group), click SUMIF, enter arguments

To Use the COUNTIF Function

The following step uses the COUNTIF function to ascertain the number of email sales. **Why?** In large tables, counting the number of records that match certain conditions provides useful data for analysis. The general format of the COUNTIF function is

=COUNTIF(count_range, data)

The first argument is the range containing the cells with which to compare the data in the second argument. Again, if the data is text rather than numbers, the data must be enclosed in quotes. In this case, you are counting the number of "Email" in Column E.

1

- In cell N7, type **=countif(e11:e27,"Email")** and then click the Enter button to enter the function (Figure 6–65).

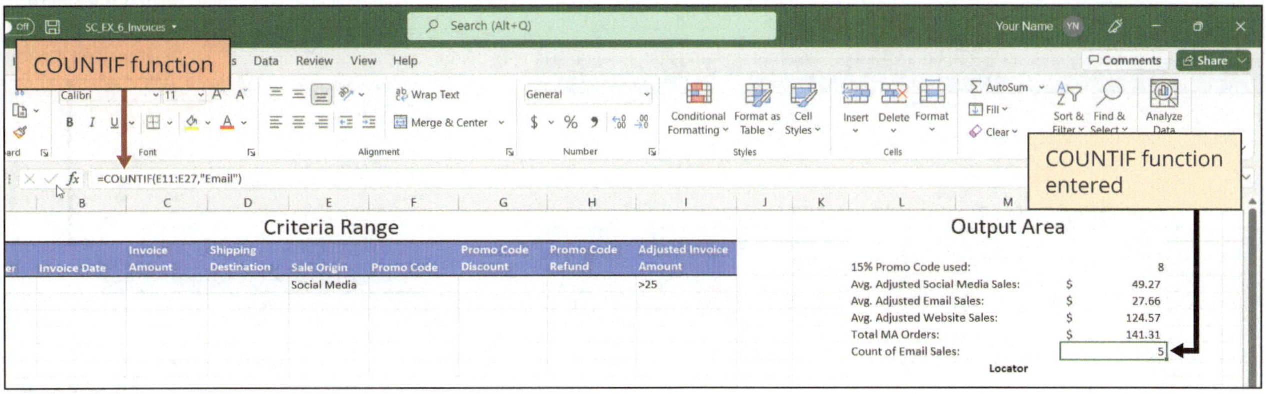

Figure 6–65

Other Ways

1. Click Insert Function box in formula bar, click 'Or select a category' button, click 'Statistical', double-click COUNTIF in 'Select a function' list, enter arguments
2. Click 'More Functions' button (Formulas tab | Function Library group), point to 'Statistical', click COUNTIF, enter arguments

To Use the VLOOKUP Function

Recall from earlier this module the **VLOOKUP function** searches for a value in a column of a lookup table, and then searches a specified number of columns to the right to return a value in the same row. VLOOKUP has been widely used with Excel throughout the years, as it was introduced well before XLOOKUP. For this reason, you may encounter VLOOKUP functions in worksheets in the future. You want to look up the Sale Origin for any given invoice by using the invoice number. To facilitate this calculation, you will use the VLOOKUP function. The general form of the VLOOKUP function is

=VLOOKUP(lookup_value, lookup_array, col_index_num, [range_lookup])

The four arguments of the VLOOKUP function represent the data that the function needs to do its job. The first argument is the **lookup value**, which is the data, or the location of the data, that you want to look up. In the case of the Output Area, the Invoice Number in the Locator section, cell N9.

The second argument, lookup_array, is the location of the data to search. In this case, the lookup_array will be located in the Invoices table, the range A11:I27.

The third argument, col_index_num is the column location of the return values. The **return value** is the answer you want to appear as a result of the VLOOKUP function. In the Invoices table, the return value will come from the Sale Origin column, which is column number 5, counted left to right, in the table. Column A would be number 1, column B would be number 2, etc.

The fourth argument, [range_lookup], is an optional parameter for the function. By default, the VLOOKUP function will return an approximate match, which is designated by TRUE or 1. If you want an exact match, enter FALSE or 0. In this project, you only need to use an argument of 0 or FALSE, to look for an exact match for the invoice number.

The following steps assume you want to look up the Sale Origin for any given invoice by using the invoice number. **Why?** The table is not sorted by Invoice Number; this method makes it easier for the company to find the sale origin for a specific invoice number.

1

- Click cell N9 and then type **17483** to enter a lookup value.
- In cell N10, type **=vlookup(n9,a11:i27,5,false)** and then press ENTER to enter the function (Figure 6–66).

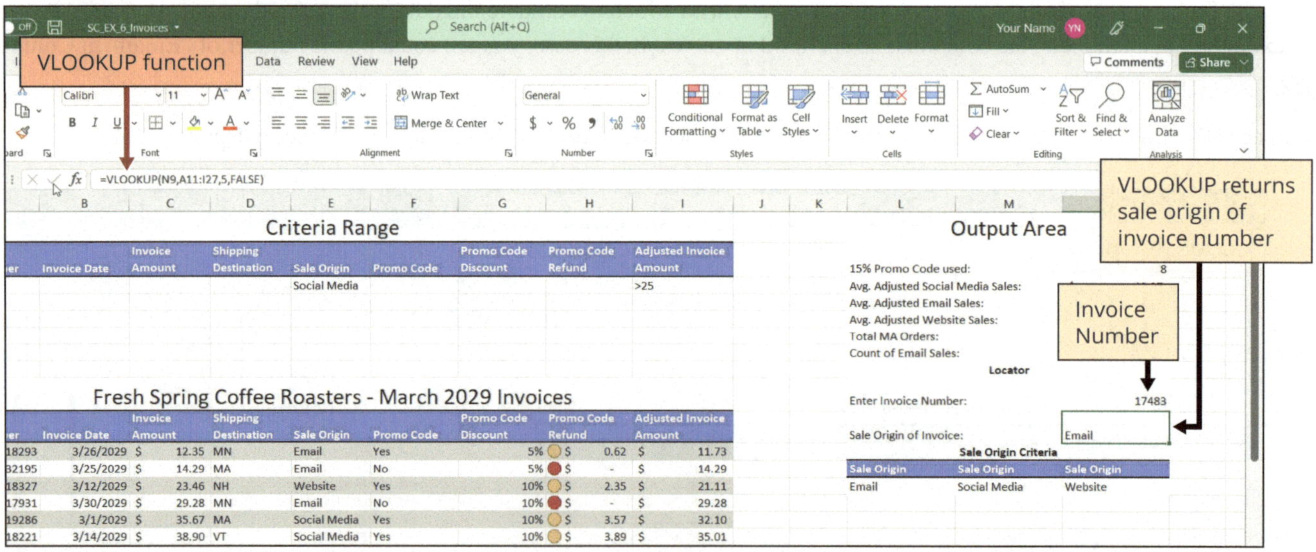

Figure 6–66

2

- Click the Save button on the Quick Access Toolbar to save the workbook again.

Other Functions

You have learned that logical operators help you compare cells and ranges. You used the IF function to evaluate a logical test containing a comparison operator. The IF function returns a value or reference if true and a different value or reference if false. Four logical functions are similar to their operator counterparts as they use function keywords with two or more logical comparisons as arguments. The **AND function** returns the word TRUE if both arguments are true. The **OR function** returns TRUE if either part of the condition is true. A rarely used **XOR function** returns TRUE if either argument is true and returns FALSE if both are true or false. Finally, the **NOT function** uses a single argument and returns TRUE if the condition is false. Table 6–5 displays examples of the four logical functions.

Table 6–5: Examples of Logical Functions

Function	Description	Example	Explanation
AND	Returns TRUE if all of the arguments are TRUE	=AND(A1="Yes", B2<5)	Returns TRUE if cell A1 is equal to "Yes" and B2 is less than 5. Otherwise, it returns FALSE.
OR	Returns TRUE if either argument is TRUE	=OR(A1="Yes", B2<5)	Returns TRUE if either cell A1 is equal to "Yes" or B2 is less than 5. If neither of the conditions is met, it returns FALSE.
XOR	Returns a logical Exclusive Or of all arguments	=XOR(A1="Yes", B2<5)	Returns TRUE if either cell A1 is equal to "Yes" or B2 is less than 5. If neither of the conditions is met or both conditions are met, it returns FALSE.
NOT	Returns the reversed logical value of its argument; if the argument is FALSE, then it returns TRUE, and vice versa	=NOT(A1="Yes")	Returns TRUE if cell A1 is anything other than "Yes."

In a previous module, you learned about the Transpose paste option, which returns a vertical range of cells as a horizontal range, or vice versa. The **TRANSPOSE function** works in a similar manner. For example, if you have the values 100, 200, and 300 in a column running down (cells A1, A2, and A3), you could change them to display in a row running across. To do so, select the first cell in the destination location and then type

=TRANSPOSE(A1:A3)

The **AVERAGEIF function** returns the average of values within a range that meet a given criteria. The function takes two arguments: range and criteria. For example, you could find the average A-level test score in a named range using

=AVERAGEIF(scores, >=90)

An optional third argument allows the criteria to be measured against the first range, while averaging a different range.

Summarizing Data

Another way to summarize data is by using subtotals. A subtotal is the sum of a subset of data while a grand total sums all of the data in a row or column. You can create subtotals automatically, as long as the data is sorted. For subtotals, the field on which you sort is called the **control field**. For example, if you choose the Sale Origin field as your control field, all of the Email, Social Media, and Website entries will be grouped together within the data range. You then might request subtotals for the Promo Code Refund and Adjusted Invoice Amount field. Excel calculates and displays the subtotal each time the Sale Origin field changes. A grand total displays at the bottom of the range. The most common subtotal uses the SUM function, although you can use other functions. If you change the control field, Excel updates the subtotal automatically. Note that the subtotal feature cannot be used with the table feature, only with normal ranges of data.

The Subtotal command displays outline symbols beside the rows or above the columns of the data you wish to group. The **outline symbols** include plus and minus signs for showing and hiding grouped portions of the worksheet, as well as brackets identifying the groups. For example, you might want to minimize the display of promo code discounts of 5% and only display the discounts at 10% or 15%. Outlining is extremely useful for making large tables more manageable in size and appearance.

To Sort the Data

The following step sorts the table by Sale Origin. **Why?** Subtotals can only be performed on sorted data, or where data is entered in such a way that all identical entries for a column are grouped together.

1. Scroll down to display the table. Click any cell within the table. If necessary, click the Filter button (Data tab | Sort & Filter group) to display the filter arrows. Click the filter button in cell E10 and then click the 'Sort A to Z' command to sort the data by Sale Origin.

To Convert a Table to a Range

In preparation for creating subtotals, the following steps convert the table back to a range. **Why?** The Subtotal command is not available for tables.

1

- Right-click anywhere in the table and then point to Table on the shortcut menu to display the Table submenu (Figure 6–67).

2

- Click 'Convert to Range' (Table submenu) to display a Microsoft Excel dialog box.
- Click Yes (Microsoft Excel dialog box) to convert the table to a range.

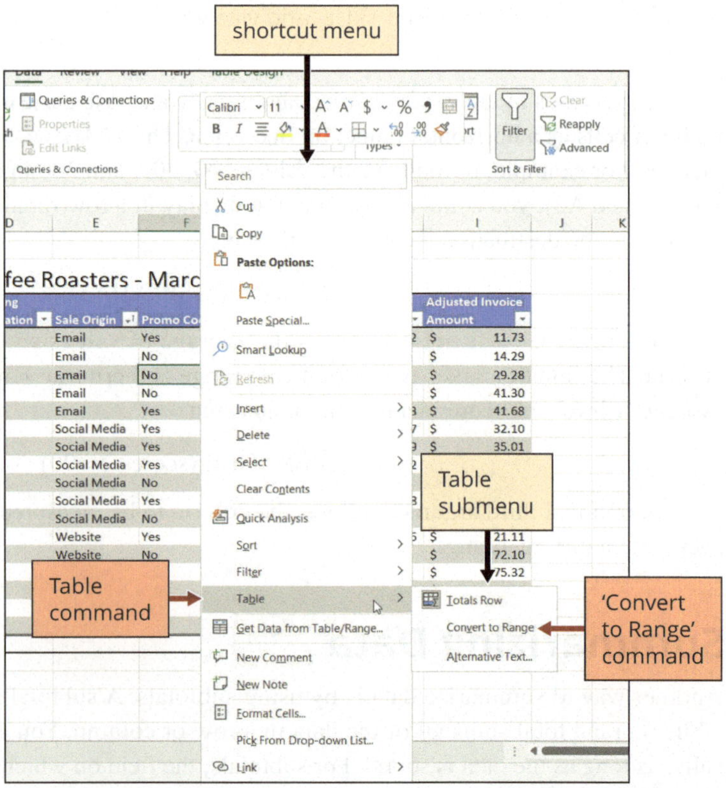

Figure 6–67

Other Ways

1. Click 'Convert to Range' button (Table Design tab | Tools group), click Yes (Microsoft Excel dialog box)

To Display Subtotals

The following steps display subtotals for the Adjusted Invoice Amount based on Sale Origin. **Why?** Subtotals are useful pieces of data for comparisons and analysis.

1

- Click in one of the numeric fields you wish to subtotal (in this case, any numeric field in column I).
- Click the Subtotal button (Data tab | Outline group) to display the Subtotal dialog box.
- Click the 'At each change in' list arrow (Subtotal dialog box) and then click Sale Origin to select the control field.
- If necessary, click the Use function button and then select Sum in the Use function list.
- In the 'Add subtotal to' list (Subtotal dialog box), click Adjusted Invoice Amount, if necessary, to select values to subtotal. Clear any other check boxes (you may need to scroll to view all check boxes) (Figure 6–68).

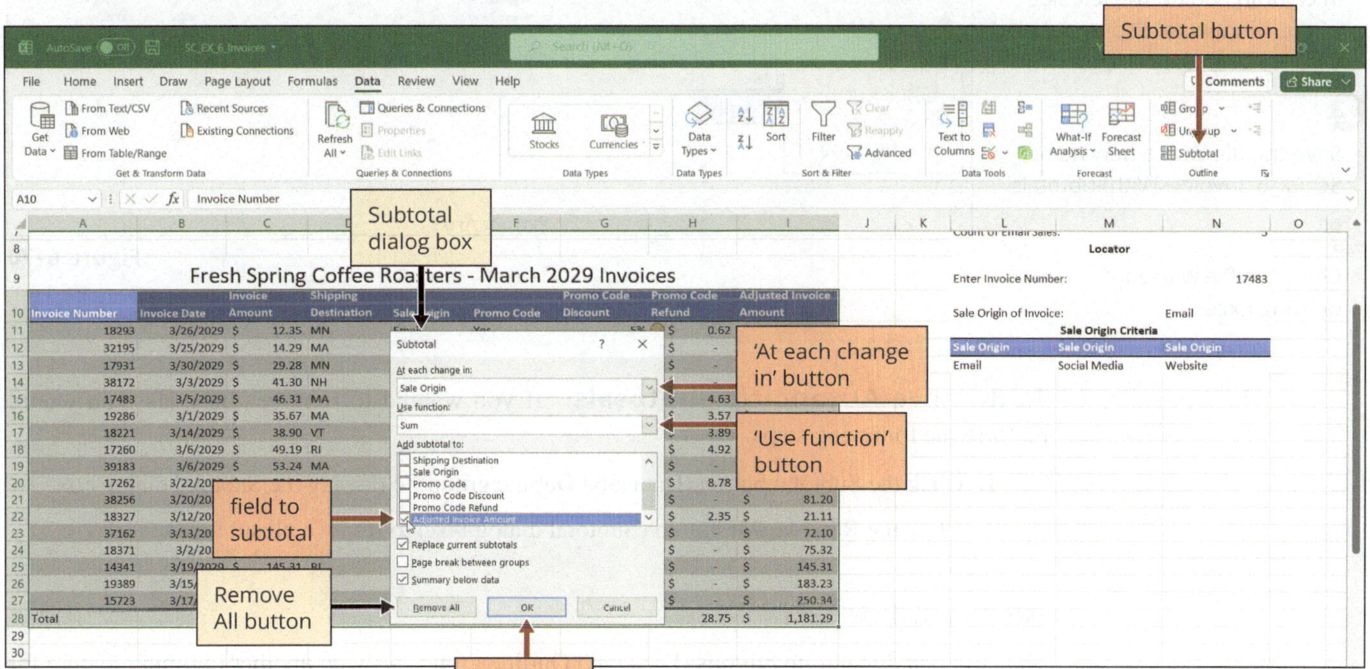

Figure 6–68

2

- Click OK (Subtotal dialog box) to add subtotals to the range. Deselect the range, if necessary.
- Scroll as necessary to display the entire subtotal and outline area (Figure 6–69).

Q&A What changes does Excel make to the worksheet?

Excel adds three subtotal rows—one subtotal for each different Sale Origin—and one grand total row for the entire table. The names for each subtotal row come from the sorted control field and appear in bold. Thus, the text, Email Total, in cell E16 identifies the row that contains the subtotal for Adjusted Invoice Amount for the Email sales. Excel also displays the outlining feature to the left of the row numbers.

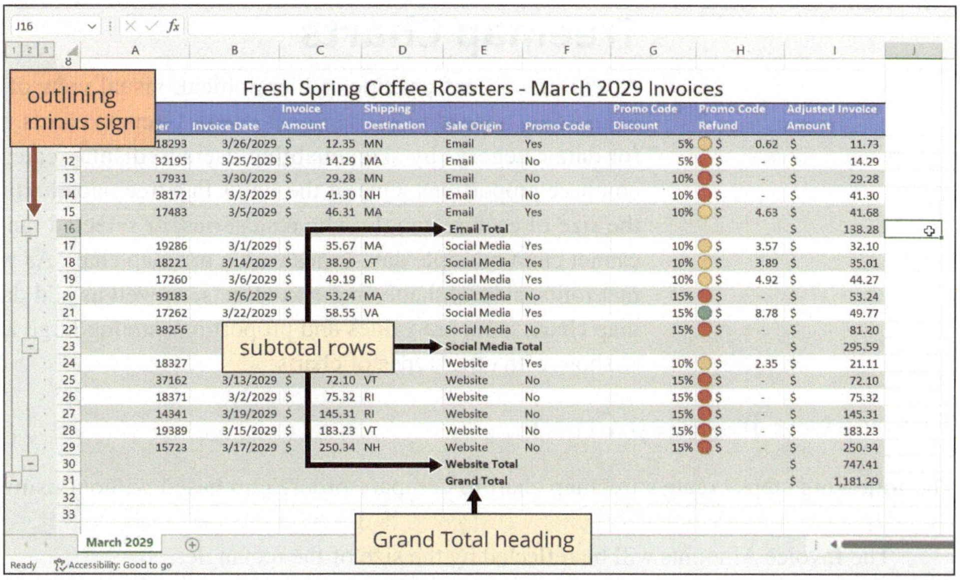

Figure 6–69

To Use the Outline Feature

Excel turns on the outline feature automatically when you create subtotals. The following steps use the outline feature of Excel. **Why?** The outline feature allows you to hide and show data and totals.

1

- Click the second outlining column header to collapse the outline and hide the data (Figure 6–70).
- **Experiment:** One at a time, click each of the plus signs (+) in column two on the left side of the window to display detailed data for each Sale Origin.

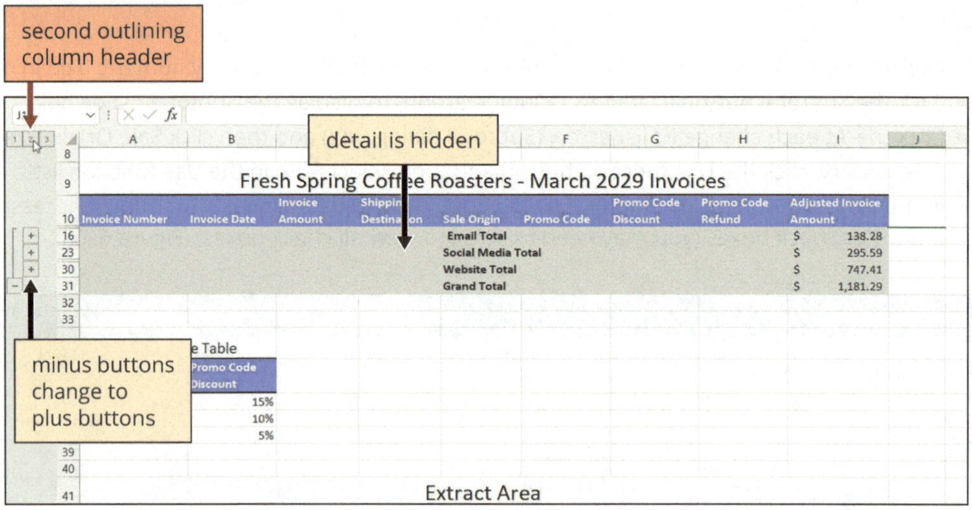

Figure 6–70

2

- Save the file with a new name, SC_EX_6_InvoicesWithSubtotals.

3

- Close the file without quitting Excel.

To Remove Automatic Subtotals If you wanted to remove subtotals, you would perform the following steps.

1. Click the Subtotal button (Data tab | Outline group) to display the Subtotal dialog box.
2. Click the Remove All button (Subtotal dialog box) to remove all subtotals.

Auto Outline

The Group and Ungroup buttons (Data tab | Outline group) provide another outlining feature for larger amounts of data. When you click the Auto Outline command on the Group button menu, Excel displays only the header column or columns, and various numeric fields, including any totals. Outlining headers display above the data and can be collapsed or expanded just as you did with the subtotals.

Treemap Charts

A **treemap chart** provides a hierarchical, visual view of data, making it easy to spot patterns and trends. Instead of hierarchical levels, treemap charts use rectangles to represent sale origin (or data category) by size, enabling users to display categories by color and proximity, and to compare proportions. One of the fields in a treemap chart must be numeric, in order to generate the size of each rectangle. The data series, or selected range of data, must be contiguous—you cannot chart multiple data series with a treemap chart. As with other types of charts, you can format fonts, colors, shape, and text effects, as well as add data fields and adjust data labels. Treemap charts compare values and proportions among large amounts of data that might be difficult to show with other types of charts.

To Create a Treemap Chart

The following steps create a treemap chart to compare orders purchased without using a promo code. **Why?** The company would like to know the amount spent by customers in different locations and via different sale origins without using a promo code. The Invoice Amounts will be reflected by the size of the rectangles.

1

- Open the file named SC_EX_6_Invoices. Scroll as necessary to display the table.
- Click any cell in the table. If necessary, click the Filter button (Data tab | Sort & Filter group) to display the filter buttons. Sort the data in ascending order by Shipping Destination. Click the Filter button in cell F10, click Yes to remove the check mark, and click OK.
- Drag to select cells C10:E27.
- Display the Insert tab and then click the 'Insert Hierarchy Chart' button (Insert tab | Charts group) to display the gallery (Figure 6–71).

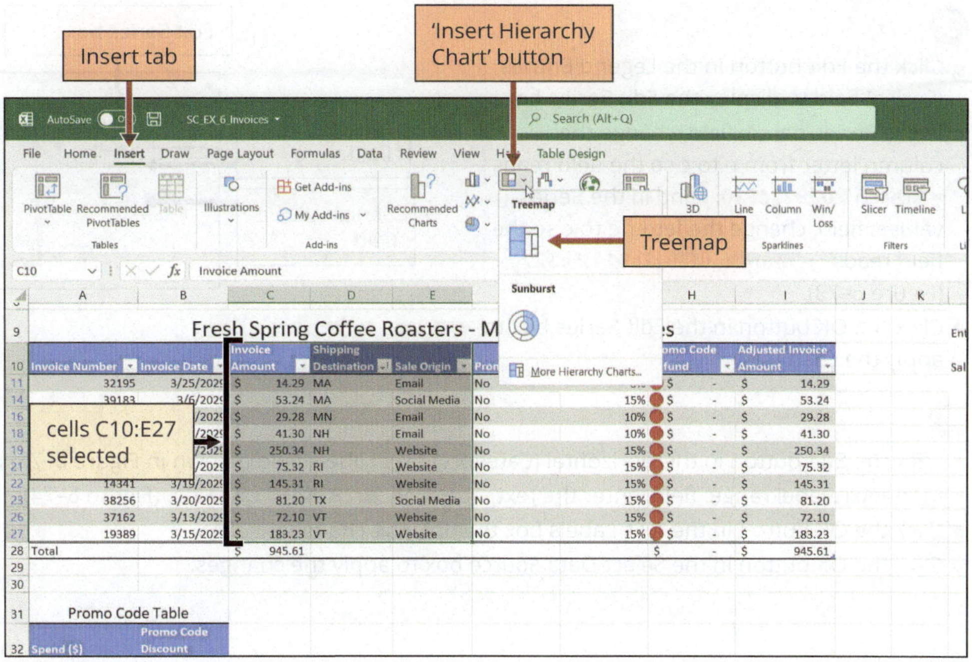

Figure 6–71

Q&A Do I have to use the table file rather than the file with subtotals?
Recall that you removed the table formatting in the file with subtotals. It is easier to start with the data stored as a table.

2

- Click Treemap (Insert Hierarchy Chart gallery) to insert the chart.
- Click Select Data (Chart Design | Data Group) to display the Select Data Source box (Figure 6–72).

Q&A Why does my Treemap data look different?
Depending on your version of Excel, your data source entries may look different. This will not impact your project, as we will edit the data in the following steps.

Why are we selecting this data for the Treemap?
The three columns selected are the data we want to use for the Treemap. However, we will need to alter the data selection to make the Treemap display the data in a way that is useful.

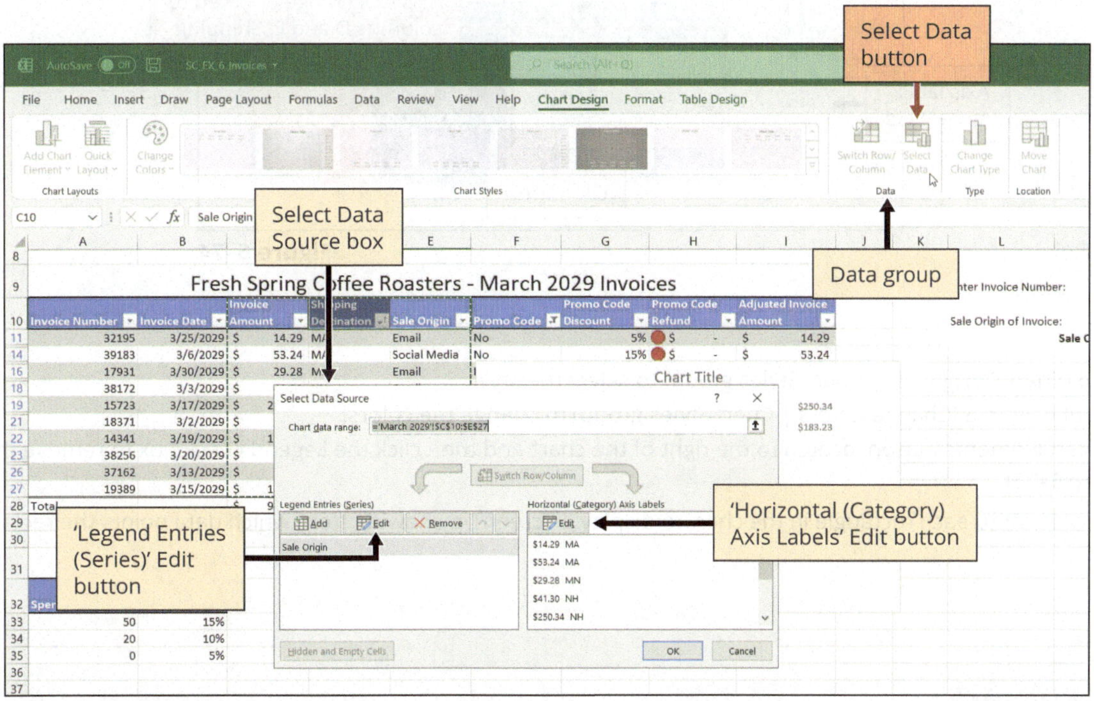

Figure 6–72

3

- Click the Edit button in the Legend Entries (Series) field to display the Edit Series box.
- In the Series name: field, change the column letter from e to c so the field reads **='March 2029'!c10**, and in the Series values: field, change the letter e to c so the field reads **='March 2029'!c11:c27** (Figure 6–73).
- Click the OK button in the Edit Series box to apply the changes.

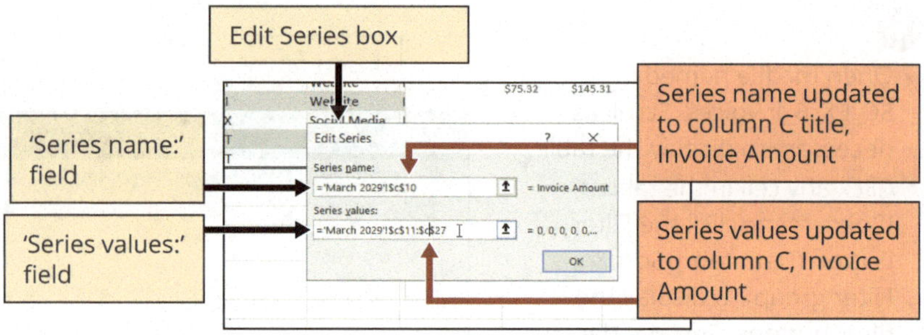

Figure 6–73

4

- Click the Edit button in the Horizontal (Category) Axis Labels field (shown in Figure 6–72) to display the Axis Labels box.
- In the Axis label range: field, enter the text **='March 2029'!d11:e27** (Figure 6–74).
- Click the OK button in the Axis Labels box to apply the changes.
- Click the OK button in the Select Data Source box to apply the changes.

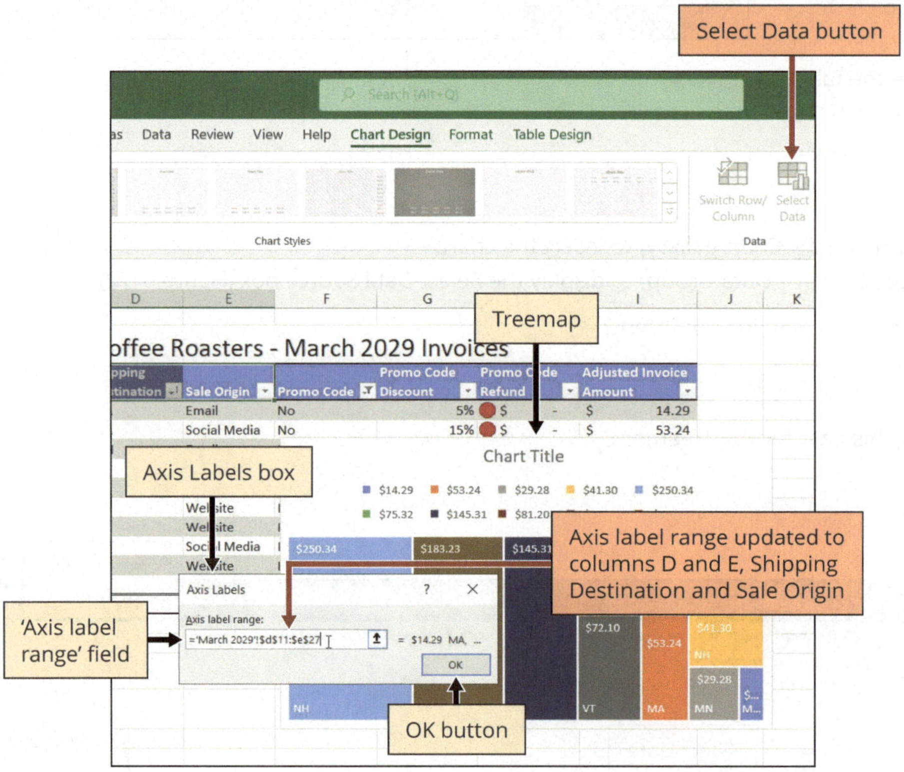

Figure 6–74

5

- Click Style 4 (Chart Design tab | Chart Styles group) to select the style.
- Click Colorful Palette 3 (Change Colors | Chart Styles group) to change the colors.
- Click the Chart Elements button located to the right of the chart and then click the Legend check box to remove the check mark (Figure 6–75).
- **Experiment:** Point to each rectangle in the chart to display a ScreenTip showing from which data points the rectangle was created.

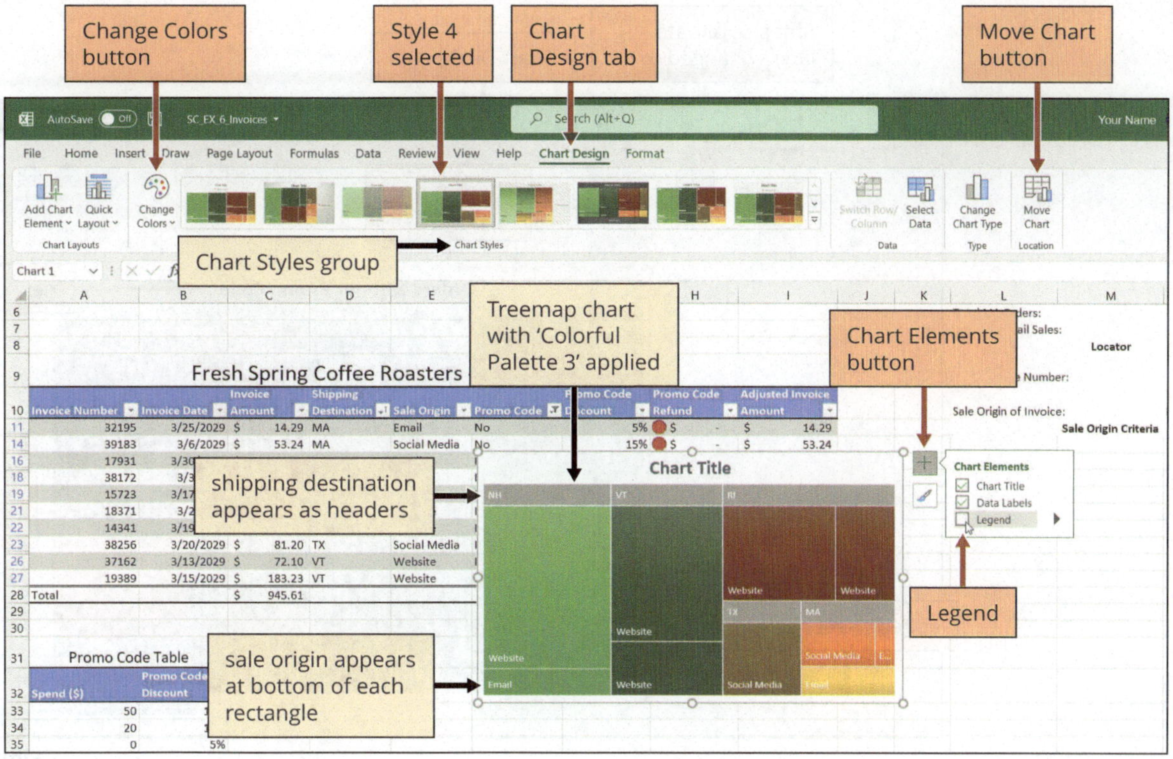

Figure 6–75

Other Ways

1. Select data, click the Recommended Charts button (Insert tab | Charts group), click All Charts tab (Insert Chart dialog box), click Treemap, click OK

To Move the Chart and Edit Fonts

The following steps move the chart to its own named worksheet and then edit the chart title and data label fonts.

1. Click the Move Chart button (Chart Design tab | Location group) and then click New sheet in the Move Chart dialog box.
2. Type **Treemap** in the New sheet text box (Move Chart dialog box) and then click OK.
3. Right-click the Chart Title and then click Edit Text on the shortcut menu. On the Home tab, change the font size to 25. Type **Orders without Promo Code** to change the title.
4. Click any of the data labels in the chart. Change the font size to 12 (Figure 6–76).

Q&A How is the data presented in this chart?

The treemap allows you to compare each shipping destination to the other shipping destinations: the size of the invoice amount (size of color block) and sale origins (number of subdivisions within each color block).

BTW

Removing Data Series in Charts

Treemaps and other kinds of charts may contain multiple data series. If you want to delete a data series, click the Select Data button (Chart Design tab | Data Group). Excel displays the Select Data Source dialog box. Select the series and then click the Remove button.

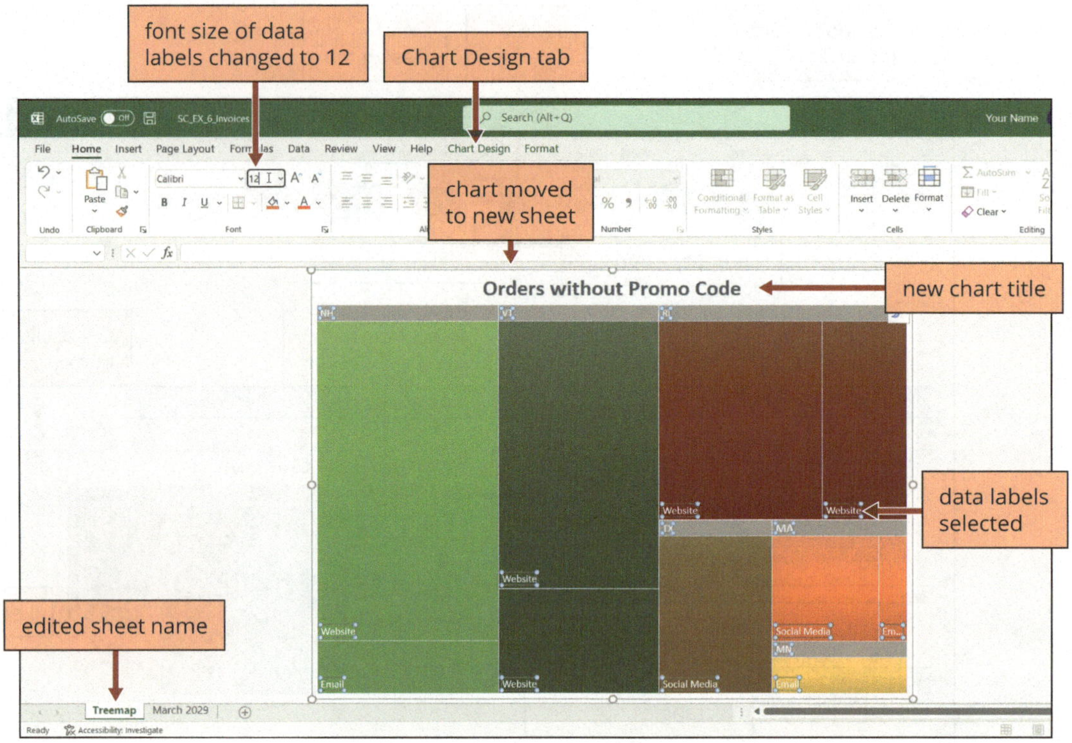

Figure 6–76

To Edit Treemap Settings

The following steps format the chart with settings that are unique to treemaps. **Why?** Changing some of the settings will add invoice amounts and make the chart more informative.

1

- Right-click any of the data labels to display the shortcut menu. Do not right-click a rectangle (Figure 6–77).

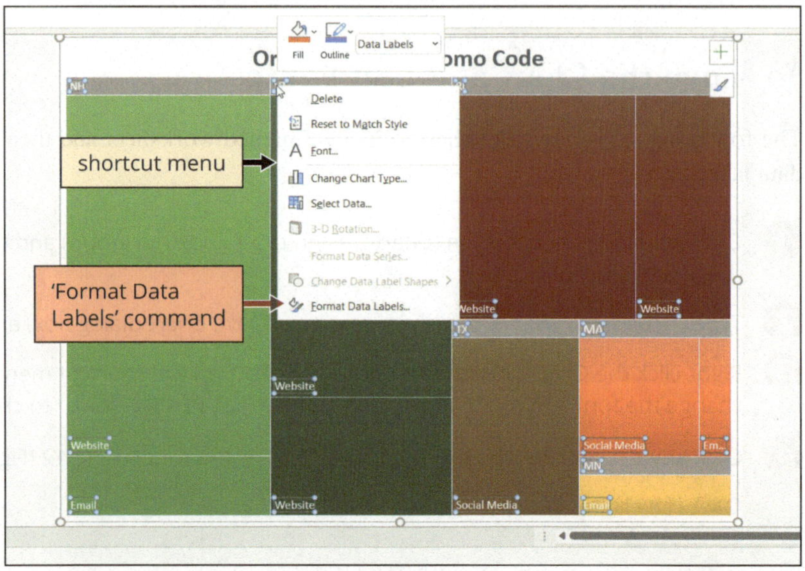

Figure 6–77

2

- Click 'Format Data Labels' on the shortcut menu to display the Format Data Labels pane.
- Click to display a check mark in the Value check box. The Category Name check box should contain a check mark already.
- Click the Separator arrow and then click (New Line) in the list to display each value on a new line under its category name (Figure 6–78).

Q&A What other choices can I make in the Format Data Series pane?

In the Effects section, you can add shadows, a glow, or other special effects. In the Fill & Line section, you can change the color of the fill and the borders for each rectangle.

- **Experiment:** Click various combinations of the check marks and observe the changes to the chart. When you are finished experimenting, select only Category Name and Value.

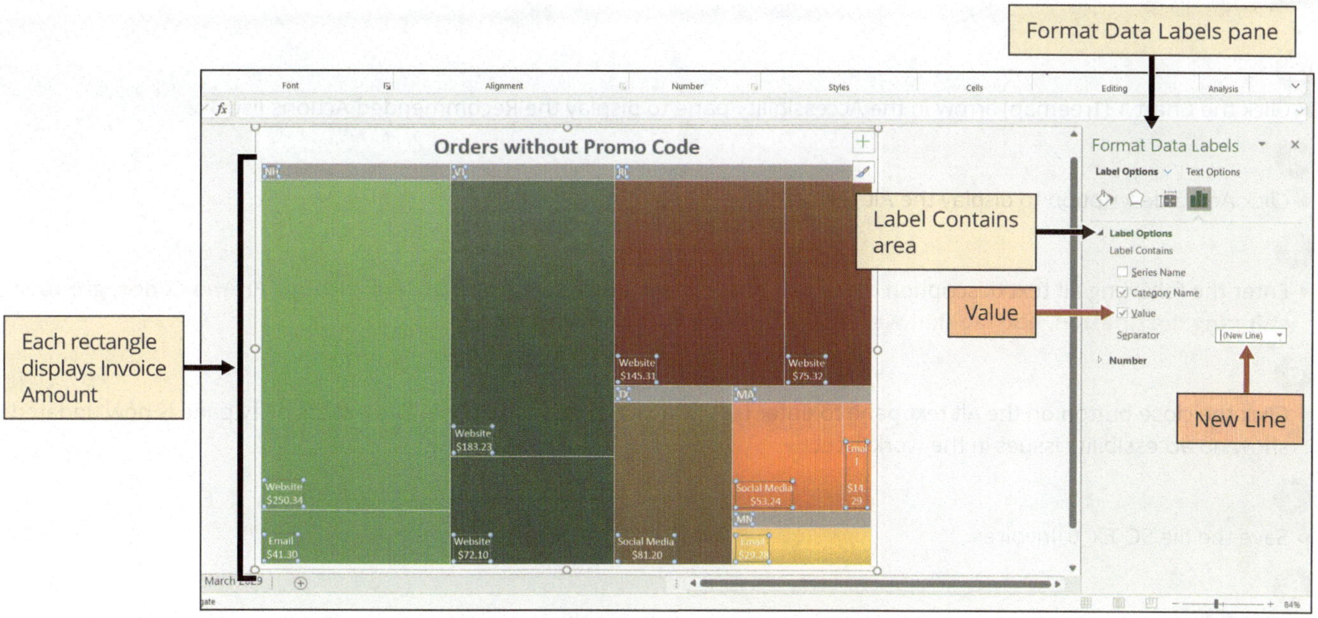

Figure 6–78

To Use the Accessibility Checker

The following steps use the Accessibility Checker to identify and fix an accessibility issue.

1

- Click the Review tab and then click the 'Check Accessibility' arrow (Review tab | Accessibility group) to display the Accessibility menu.

2

- Click Check Accessibility to display the Accessibility pane with a list of Errors or Warnings in the Inspection Results box.
- Click the Missing alternative text (1) direction arrow to display the object affected by the issue (Figure 6–79).

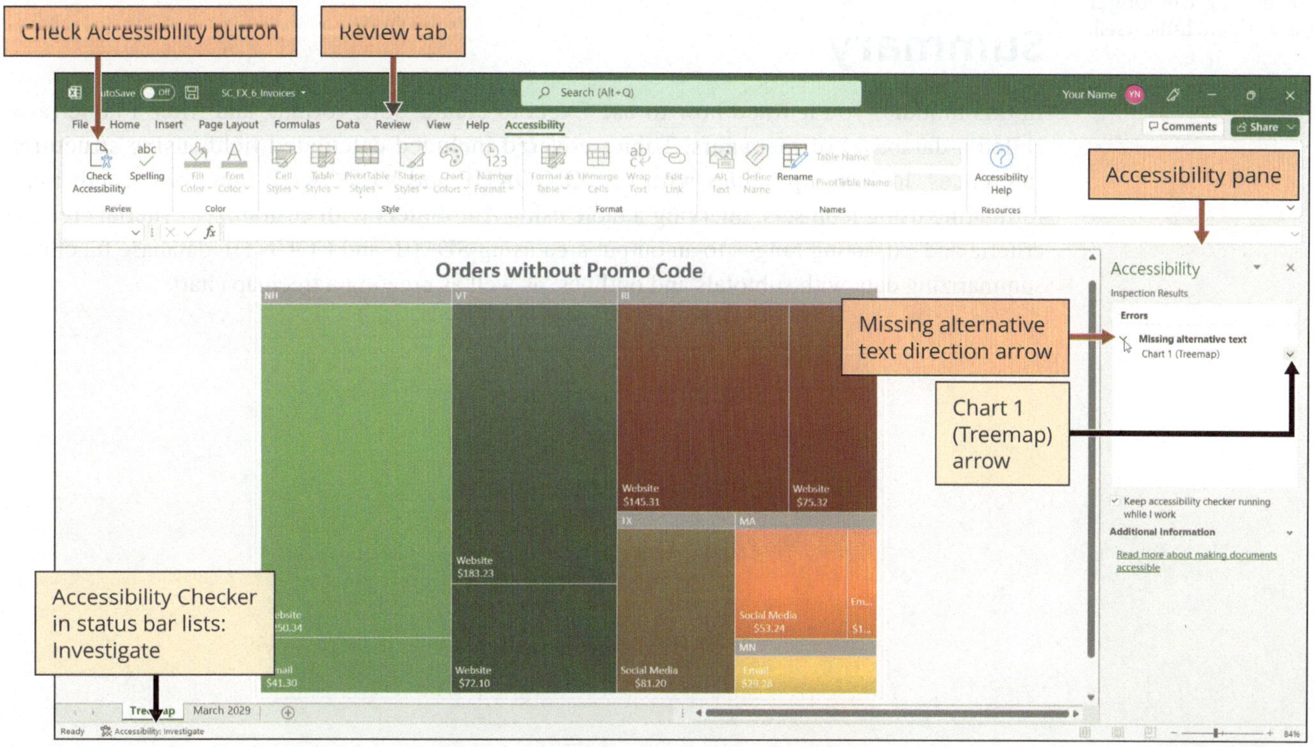

Figure 6–79

Q&A Why do my Inspection Results look different?
If you have a different version of Microsoft 365, your version may display different accessibility warnings. Additional accessibility warnings are listed for all accessibility errors made in forming the worksheet.

3
- Click the Chart 1 (Treemap) arrow in the Accessibility pane to display the Recommended Actions list.

4
- Click Add a description to display the Alt Text pane.

5
- Enter the following alt text description in the text box: **Treemap showing the Orders without Promo Codes, grouped by shipping destination, and labeled with sale origin and invoice amount.**

6
- Click the close button on the Alt text pane to enter the alt text and close the pane. The Accessibility pane is now updated to show no accessibility issues in the worksheet.

7
- Save the file SC_EX_6_Invoices.

8
- **sam** Click the Close button on the right side of the title bar to close the file and close Excel.

BTW
Large Labels in a Treemap
When you have large numbers and labels in small boxes, you sometimes will have to get creative. Your options include reducing the font size, removing the decimal places or dollar signs, limiting the data further, or editing the longer labels in the data table itself.

More about Data Series

Treemaps and other kinds of charts may illustrate multiple data series. If you want to delete a data series, click the Select Data button (Chart Design tab | Data Group). Excel displays the Select Data Source dialog box. Select the series and then click the Remove button.

If you want to change the color of an individual data series or category, select the series on the chart, click the Shape Fill button (Format tab | Shape Styles group) and then click the desired style.

Summary

In this module, you learned how to use Excel to create, sort, format, and filter a table (also called a database) of managers. Topics covered included calculated fields using structured references, looking up values with the XLOOKUP and VLOOKUP functions, conditional formatting using icon sets, querying a table using AutoFilters with customized criteria, creating criteria and extracting ranges to an output area using SUMIF and COUNTIF database functions, summarizing data with subtotals and outlines, as well as creating a treemap chart.

Consider This: Plan Ahead

What decisions will you need to make when creating your next worksheet with a table to create, sort, and query?

Use these guidelines as you complete the assignments in this module and create your own worksheets for evaluating and analyzing data outside of this class.

1. Enter data for the table.
   a) Use columns for fields of data.
   b) Put each record on a separate row.
   c) Create user-friendly column headings.
   d) Format the range as a table.
   e) Format individual columns as necessary.
2. Create other fields.
   a) Use calculated fields with structured references.
   b) To apply rankings or settings, use a lookup table.
   c) To apply conditional formatting, consider icon sets or color groupings.
   d) Use total rows.
3. Sort the table.
   a) Sort ascending, descending, or combinations using tools on the Home tab and the Data tab.
4. Employ table AutoFilters for quick searches and sorts.
5. Create criteria and extract ranges to simplify queries.
6. Use functions.
   a) Use DAVERAGE and DCOUNT for database functions analyzing table data.
   b) Use SUMIF, COUNTIF, MATCH, and INDEX to find answers based on conditions.
7. Summarize data with subtotals and use outlining.
8. Create a treemap chart.

Student Assignments

Apply Your Knowledge

Reinforce the skills and apply the concepts you learned in this module.

Creating a Table with Conditional Formatting

Note: To complete this assignment, you will be required to use the Data Files. Please contact your instructor for information about accessing the Data Files.

Instructions: Start Excel. Open the workbook called SC_EX_6-2.xlsx, which is located in the Data Files. The spreadsheet you open contains a list from Blue Acre Recruiting, including log numbers, field assignments, the quarter in which the recruitment was logged, and recruiter identification numbers. You are to create a table to include the name of the recruiter based on a lookup table as shown in Figure 6–80. The conditional formatting is based on the quarter of the year the recruiting took place.

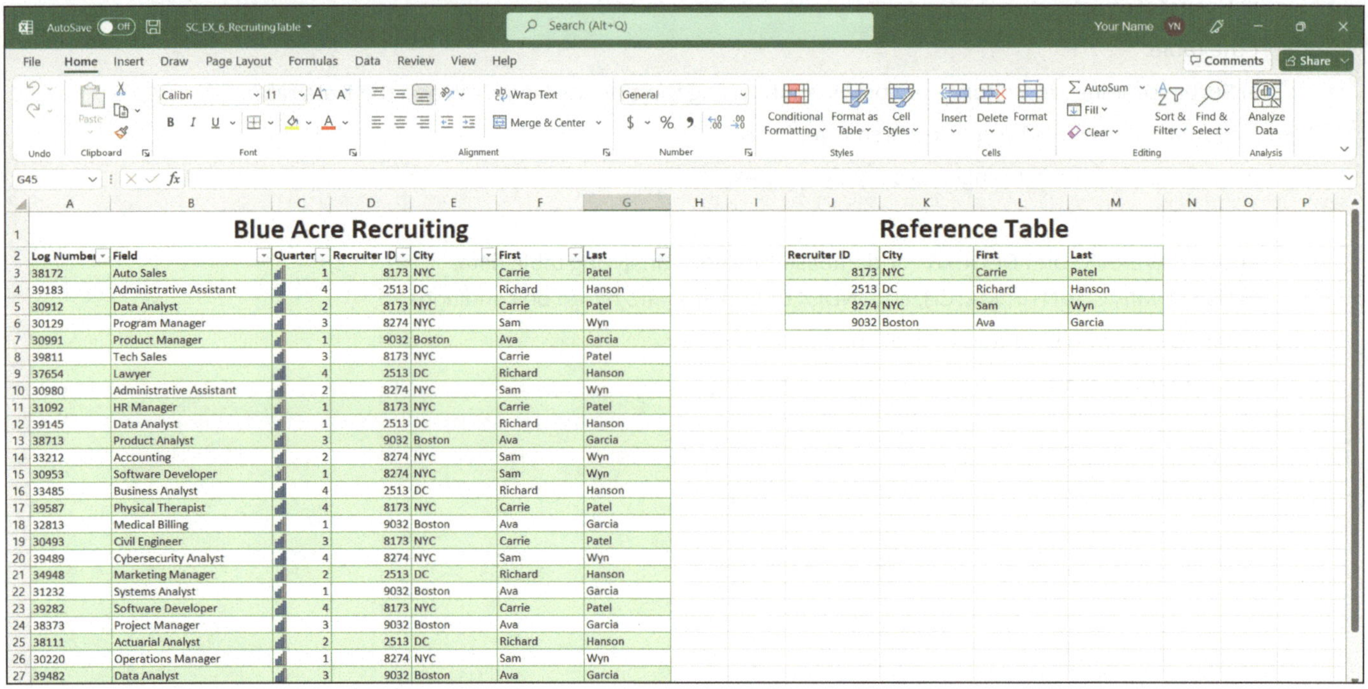

Blue Acre Recruiting

Log Number	Field	Quarter	Recruiter ID	City	First	Last
38172	Auto Sales	1	8173	NYC	Carrie	Patel
39183	Administrative Assistant	4	2513	DC	Richard	Hanson
30912	Data Analyst	2	8173	NYC	Carrie	Patel
30129	Program Manager	3	8274	NYC	Sam	Wyn
30991	Product Manager	1	9032	Boston	Ava	Garcia
39811	Tech Sales	3	8173	NYC	Carrie	Patel
37654	Lawyer	4	2513	DC	Richard	Hanson
30980	Administrative Assistant	2	8274	NYC	Sam	Wyn
31092	HR Manager	1	8173	NYC	Carrie	Patel
39145	Data Analyst	1	2513	DC	Richard	Hanson
38713	Product Analyst	3	9032	Boston	Ava	Garcia
33212	Accounting	2	8274	NYC	Sam	Wyn
30953	Software Developer	1	8274	NYC	Sam	Wyn
33485	Business Analyst	4	2513	DC	Richard	Hanson
39587	Physical Therapist	4	8173	NYC	Carrie	Patel
32813	Medical Billing	1	9032	Boston	Ava	Garcia
30493	Civil Engineer	3	8173	NYC	Carrie	Patel
39489	Cybersecurity Analyst	4	8274	NYC	Sam	Wyn
34948	Marketing Manager	2	2513	DC	Richard	Hanson
31232	Systems Analyst	1	9032	Boston	Ava	Garcia
39282	Software Developer	4	8173	NYC	Carrie	Patel
38373	Project Manager	3	9032	Boston	Ava	Garcia
38111	Actuarial Analyst	2	2513	DC	Richard	Hanson
30220	Operations Manager	1	8274	NYC	Sam	Wyn
39482	Data Analyst	3	9032	Boston	Ava	Garcia

Reference Table

Recruiter ID	City	First	Last
8173	NYC	Carrie	Patel
2513	DC	Richard	Hanson
8274	NYC	Sam	Wyn
9032	Boston	Ava	Garcia

Figure 6–80

Perform the following tasks:

1. Save the file with the name, SC_EX_6_RecruitingTable.
2. Select the range, A2:D31. Click the 'Format as Table' button (Home tab | Styles group) and then click 'Light Green, Table Style Light 21' in the Format as Table gallery. When Excel displays the Create Table dialog box, if necessary, click the 'My table has headers' check box to select the option to format the table with headers and then click OK.
3. Name the table, Recruiting, by using the Table Name text box (Table Design tab | Properties group).
4. Remove duplicates in the table by clicking the Remove Duplicates button (Table Design tab | Tools group). When Excel displays the Remove Duplicates dialog box, click the Select All button and then click OK.
5. Insert a new column in the table (column E), with the column heading, City.
6. Insert a new column in the table (column F), with the column heading, First.

7. Insert a new column in the table (column G), with the column heading, Last. Change all three column widths to 13.
8. Change the row height of row 1 to 30. Click cell A1. Apply a bold style and a font size of 24. Center the title across the selection, A1:G1, using the Format Cells dialog box and the 'Center Across Selection' command.

Table 6–6: Recruiter Table

Reference Table			
Recruiter ID	**City**	**First**	**Last**
8173	NYC	Carrie	Patel
2513	DC	Richard	Hanson
8274	NYC	Sam	Wyn
9032	Boston	Ava	Garcia

9. To create the lookup table, enter the data from Table 6–6, beginning with the text, Reference Table, in cell J1.
10. Use the format painter to copy the format from cells A1:G1 to cells J1:M1. Copy the format of the headings and cells from cells D2:G6 to cells J2:M6. Change the column width of columns J, K, L, and M to 14.
11. In cell E3, type **=xlookup(d3,j3:j6,k3:k6)** to enter the City column in the main table. Repeat the process to enter a function for the First in cell F3, and again to enter a function for Last in cell G3. (**Hint:** The return_array argument of the function will be absolute references to the values in the range J3:M6.)
12. To apply conditional formatting:
    a. Select the range C3:C30, click the Conditional Formatting button (Home tab | Styles group), and then click New Rule to display the New Formatting Rule dialog box.
    b. Click the Format Style list arrow (New Formatting Rule dialog box) to display the Format Style list.
    c. Click Icon Sets in the Format Style list (New Formatting Rule dialog box) to display the Icon area.
    d. Click the Icon Style arrow and then click 4 Ratings in the Icon Style list (New Formatting Rule dialog box) to select an icon style that includes four different bar charts.
    e. Click the first Type list arrow and then click Number in the list to select a numeric value. Repeat the process for the other two Type list arrows.
    f. Type **3** in the first Value box, type **2** in the second Value box, and type **1** in the third Value box.
    g. Change the first, second, and third inequality boxes to greater than. Press TAB to complete the conditions.
    h. Click OK (New Formatting Rule dialog box) to display icons in each row of the table.
13. Save the file.
14. Use the Sort Ascending button on the Data tab to sort the table in ascending order by log number.
15. Use the 'Sort & Filter' button on the Home tab to sort in descending order by quarter.
16. Use the Sort button on the Data tab to create a custom sort first by Recruiter ID in ascending order, and then within that, by Field in descending order.
17. Change the name of the sheet tab to Recruiting.
18. Save the file, submit the workbook in the format specified by your instructor, and then exit Excel.
19. **Consider This:** What other kind of criteria, filter, or output might be helpful if the table were larger? When might you use some of the database and statistical functions on this kind of data? Why?

Extend Your Knowledge

Extend the skills you learned in this module and experiment with new skills. You may need to use Help to complete the assignment.

Using Functions

Note: To complete this assignment, you will be required to use the Data Files. Please contact your instructor for information about accessing the Data Files.

Instructions: Start Excel. Open the workbook called SC_EX_6-3, which is located in the Data Files. The workbook you open contains a list of food truck data, including employees, the type of truck they staff, and their position. You are to summarize the data in a variety of ways as shown in Figure 6–81.

F	G	H	I	J
	Output Area			
	Total count of BDT Employees		7	
	Total count of BDP Employees		6	
	Avg Employment of BDT Employee		1.79	
	Avg Employment of BDP Employee		2.92	
	Total years of Employment of Chefs		6	
	General Manager Name		Perett, Chani	

Figure 6–81

Perform the following tasks:

1. Save the workbook using the file name, SC_EX_6_FoodTruckTable.
2. Beside the table, starting in column G, create summary title and row headings as shown in Figure 6–81. Center the title across the range G1:I1 using 'Center Across Selection' command. Change the column widths of columns G, H, and I to 15. Apply the formatting from cells A1:C1 to cells G1:I1 using the format painter.
3. Use the COUNTIF function to obtain a total count for BDT and BDP employees. Use the AVERAGEIF function for the average employment length. (**Hint:** Use Help to learn about the AVERAGEIF function.) Round off the averages to two decimal places.
4. Use the SUMIF function to find the total years of employment for all Chefs in the table.
5. Use the XLOOKUP, as you did in the module, to find the name of the General Manager. Right-align the cell contents.
6. Save the file again and submit the assignment as requested by your instructor.
7. **Consider This:** What else could you have looked up in the Output Area? What function(s) would you have used?

Expand Your World

Create a solution that uses cloud and web technologies by learning and investigating on your own from general guidance.

Converting Files

You would like to place your Excel table on the web in a user-friendly format. You decide to investigate an online tool that will help you convert your table into various file formats.

Instructions: Start Excel. Open any completed exercise from this module.

Perform the following tasks:

1. Drag through the column headings and table rows to select them. Press CTRL+C to copy the table cells.
2. Start a browser and navigate to https://tableconvert.com/ (Figure 6–82).

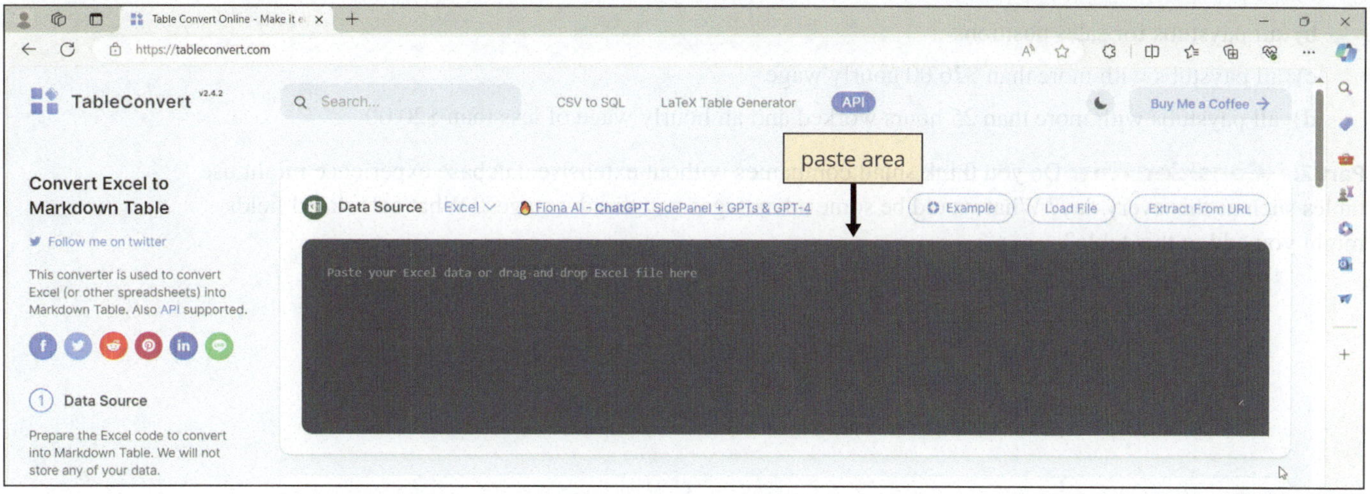

Figure 6–82

3. Click inside the dark blue area, and then press CTRL+V to paste the cells.
4. Scroll down to the Table Generator and select a file format, such as SQL or HTML. Select a different format, such as CSV, and observe the differences.
5. To create an HTML page, choose the HTML format, and then copy the HTML code generated by the table converter into a text editor such as Notepad. Save the Notepad file with the file name, SC_EX_6_TableConvert.html. Display the file in a browser.
6. **Consider This:** Many websites use tables to compare products, services, and pricing plans. Research HTML tables and web accessibility. What kinds of issues do screen readers have with HTML tables? Is it the best way to present information on the web?

In the Lab

Design and implement a solution using creative thinking and problem-solving skills.

Create and Query Payroll Data

Problem: A local company would like to be able to search their payroll data in an easy manner. They have given you sample data shown in Table 6–7.

Table 6–7: Weekly Payroll Data

Paystub Number	Location	Hours Worked	Hourly Wage
1484	Warehouse	48	$24.00
1523	Sales	40	$18.50
1634	Sales	24	$17.50
1345	Accounting	40	$32.00
1543	Warehouse	42	$25.50
1422	Warehouse	50	$27.00
1564	Sales	24	$19.00
1372	Warehouse	18	$26.50
1360	Accounting	32	$30.50

Continued on next page

Perform the following tasks:

Part 1: Create the criteria range, the table, and the extract range with formatted headings and data.

Save the workbook. Perform the following extractions.

a) all paystubs with less than 30 hours worked

b) all paystubs for sales positions

c) all paystubs with more than $26.00 hourly wage

d) all paystubs with more than 25 hours worked and an hourly wage of less than $20.00

Part 2: **Consider This:** Do you think small companies without extensive database experience might use tables such as this every day? What would be some advantages and disadvantages? What calculated fields might you add to this table?

Creating Templates, Importing Data, and Working with SmartArt, Images, and Screenshots

Objectives

After completing this module, you will be able to:

- Create and use a template
- Import data from a text file, an Access database, a webpage, and a Word document
- Use text functions
- Paste values and paste text
- Transpose data while pasting it
- Convert text to columns
- Replicate formulas
- Use the Quick Analysis gallery
- Create and format a shape
- Insert and format a bar chart
- Insert and modify a SmartArt graphic
- Add pictures to a SmartArt Graphic
- Apply text effects
- Use alt text
- Differentiate ways to link and embed
- Include a hyperlinked screenshot

Introduction

In today's business environment, you often find that you need to create multiple worksheets or workbooks that follow the same basic format. A **template** is a special-purpose workbook you can create and use as a pattern for new, similar workbooks, and can contain one or more worksheets. A template usually includes content and formatting (such as worksheet title, column and row titles, and numeric formatting) as well as worksheets. Templates can be saved to a common storage location so that everyone in a company can use them to create standardized documents.

Another important concept to understand is the Excel capability to use and analyze data from a wide variety of sources. In this module, you will learn how to **import**, or bring in, data from various external sources into an Excel worksheet and then analyze that data. Excel allows you to import data from a number of types of sources, including text files, webpages, database tables, data stored in Word documents, and XML files.

Finally, a chart, graphic, image, icon, or screenshot often conveys information or an idea better than words or numbers. You can insert and modify graphics, images, and screenshots to enhance the visual appeal of an Excel workbook and illustrate its contents. Many of the skills you learn when working with graphics in Excel will be similar when working in other Office programs, such as Word, Publisher, or PowerPoint.

Project: Cosmic Cosmetology

Cosmic Cosmetology (CC) is a retail outlet for cosmetology products and supplies. The company owner has requested an analysis of in-store and curbside pickup sales results for the last two years among its four store locations. One of the locations provides the requested data in a plain text format (Figure 7–1a) rather than in an Excel workbook. To make use of that data in Excel, the data must be imported before it can be formatted and manipulated. The same is true of formats in which the other locations store data, such as Microsoft Access tables (Figure 7–1b), webpages (Figure 7–1c), or Microsoft Word documents (Figure 7–1d). Excel provides the tools necessary to import and manipulate the data from these sources into a single worksheet that compares the sales for each store for the past two years (Figure 7–1e). Using the data from the worksheet, you will create a bar chart to summarize total sales by category for 2029 (Figure 7–1f). Finally, you will add SmartArt graphics that include images (Figure 7–1g) and a hyperlinked screenshot to support your work (Figure 7–1h).

Figure 7–2 illustrates the requirements document for the CC Sales Analysis workbook. It includes the needs, sources of data, calculations, charts, and other facts about the workbook's development.

In addition, using a sketch of the main worksheet can help you visualize its design. The sketch of the worksheet consists of titles, column and cell headings, the location of data values, and a general idea of the desired formatting in the worksheet. The data will include 2028 and 2029 data, with a summary on the right (Figure 7–3a). Figure 7–3b displays a basic sketch of the requested graph, a bar chart, showing the 2029 totals by category.

With a good understanding of the requirements document, an understanding of the necessary decisions, and a sketch of the worksheet and graph, the next step is to use Excel to create the workbook.

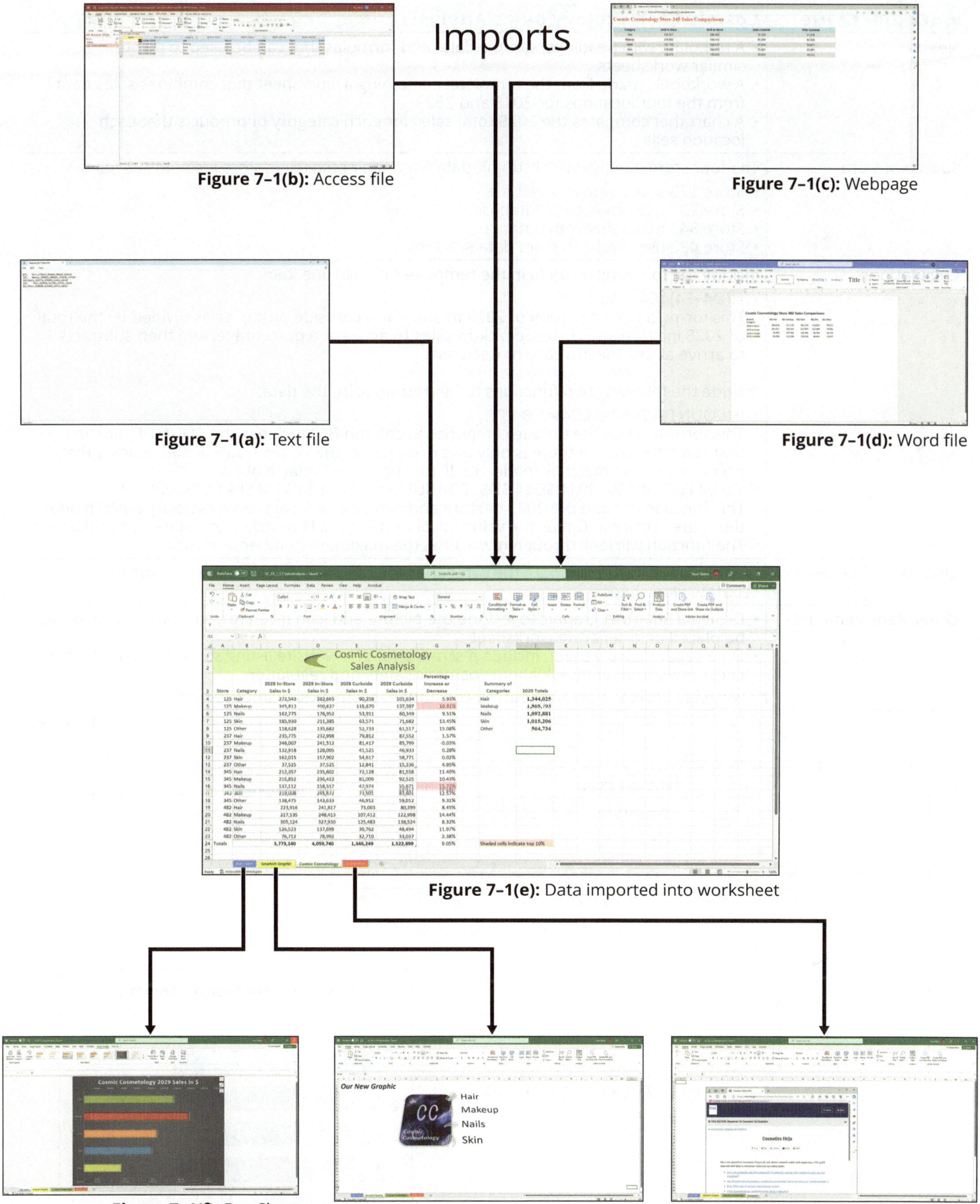

Figure 7–1(b): Access file

Figure 7–1(c): Webpage

Figure 7–1(a): Text file

Figure 7–1(d): Word file

Figure 7–1(e): Data imported into worksheet

Figure 7–1(f): Bar Chart

Figure 7–1(g): SmartArt with Images

Figure 7–1(h): Screenshot in Worksheet

Worksheet Title	Cosmic Cosmetology Sales Analysis
Needs	• A template with headings, sample data, and formulas that can be used to create similar worksheets • A workbook, made from the template, containing a worksheet that combines sales data from the four locations for 2028 and 2029 • A chart that compares the 2029 total sales for each category of products that each location sells
Source of Data	The four store managers will submit data from their respective store locations as follows: • Store 125 saves data in a text file. • Store 237 uses an Access database. • Store 345 maintains Web data. • Store 482 uses Word to store data in a table.
Calculations	Include the following formula in the template for each line item: • =((D4+F4)/(C4+E4))-1 This formula takes the total of 2029 in-store and curbside pickup sales divided by the total of 2028 in-store and curbside pickup sales to arrive at a percentage, and then subtracts 1 to arrive at just the increase or decrease. Include the following two functions to help summarize the data: • IF(COUNTIF($B$4:B4,B4)=1,B4,"") This formula finds the unique categories in column B. It includes the COUNTIF function that will return true if there is only one occurrence; the IF function will then display that occurrence. If no match is made, the IF function will display a blank. • =SUMIF($B$4:$B$100,I4,$D$4:$D$100)+SUMIF($B$4:$B$100,I4,$F$4:$F$100) This function will add the 2029 in-store and curbside pick sales on a category basis. It adds the value in column D plus the value in column F, if cell I4 matches the value from column B. The function will look through row 100 as the maximum number of records.
Chart Requirements	Create a bar chart to compare the categories for sales in 2029. Include the chart on a separate worksheet.
Other Requirements	• Design a SmartArt graphic to include the picture and icon given to you by the company, to be placed on a separate worksheet • On a separate worksheet, include a screenshot of a website listing some of the questions consumers frequently ask about cosmetic safety and regulation: www.fda.gov/cosmetics/resources-consumers-cosmetics/cosmetics-faqs

Figure 7–2

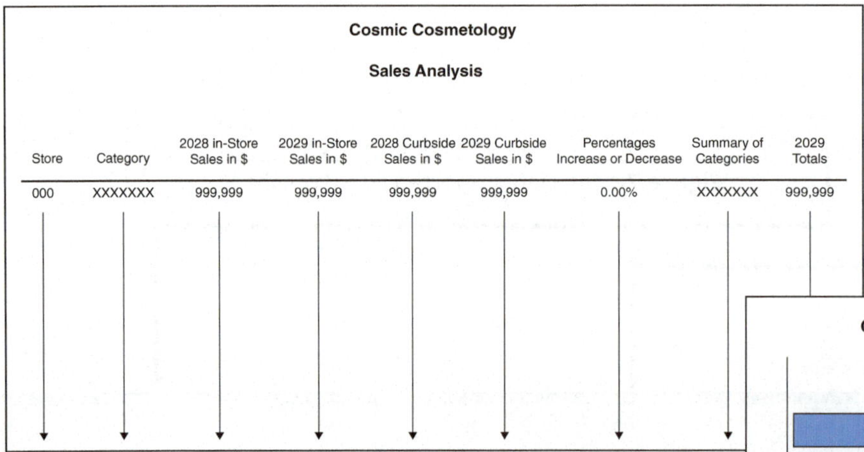

Figure 7–3(a): Sketch of worksheet

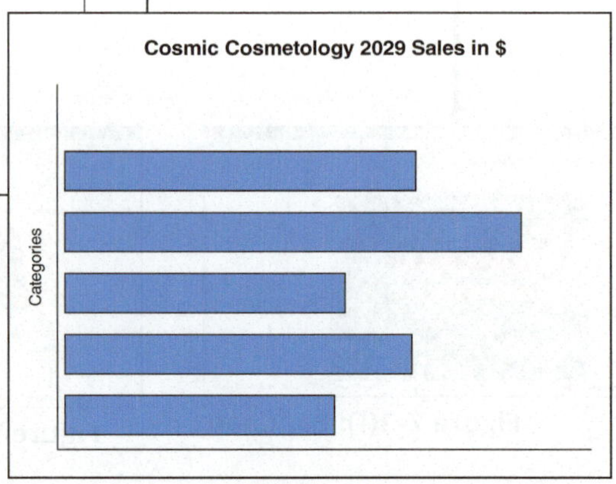

Figure 7–3(b): Sketch of chart

Creating Templates

The first step in building the project in this module is to create and save a template that contains the titles, column and row headings, formulas, and formats. After the template is saved, it can be used every time a similar workbook is developed. Because templates help speed and simplify their work, many Excel users create a template for each project on which they work. Templates can be simple—possibly using a special font or worksheet title; or they can be more complex—perhaps using specific labels, formulas, and format styles, such as the template for the CC Sales Analysis workbook.

Consider This

What factors should you keep in mind when building a template?

A template usually contains data and formatting that will appear in every workbook created from that template. Because the template will be used to create a number of other worksheets, make sure you consider the layout, cell formatting, and contents of the workbook as you design the template. Set row heights and column widths. Use placeholders for data when possible and use sample data to verify formulas. Format the cells in the template.

Creating a template, such as the one shown in Figure 7–4, follows the same basic steps used to create a workbook. The main difference between developing a workbook and a template is the file type used when saving the template.

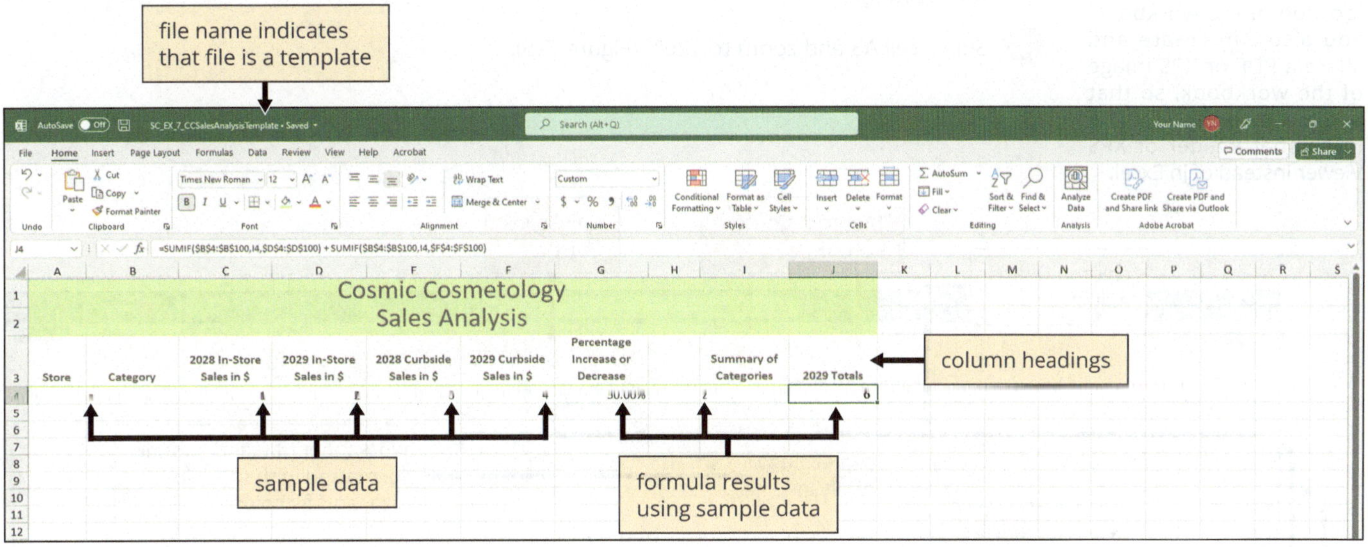

Figure 7–4

To Open a Blank Workbook and Format the Rows and Columns

The following steps open a blank workbook and set the row height and column widths.

1. sam Start Excel.
2. Click the Blank workbook thumbnail on the Excel start screen to create a blank workbook and display it in the Excel window.
3. If the Excel window is not maximized, click the Maximize button on its title bar to maximize the window.
4. Change the row height of rows 1 and 2 to 25. Change the height of row 3 to 45.

BTW

Ribbon and Screen Resolution

Excel may change how the groups and buttons within the groups appear on the ribbon, depending on the screen resolution of your computer. Thus, your ribbon may look different from the ones in this book if you are using a screen resolution other than 1920 × 1080.

BTW
Touch Mode Differences
The Office and Windows interfaces may vary if you are using Touch Mode. For this reason, you might notice that the function or appearance of your touch screen differs slightly from this module's presentation.

BTW
Distributing a Document
Instead of printing and distributing a hard copy of a workbook, you can distribute the workbook electronically. Options include sending the workbook via email; posting it on cloud storage (such as OneDrive) and sharing the file with others; posting it on social media, a blog, or other website; and sharing a link associated with an online location of the workbook. You also can create and share a PDF or XPS image of the workbook, so that users can open the file in Acrobat Reader or XPS Viewer instead of in Excel.

To Enter Titles in the Template

The following steps enter and format the titles in cells A1 and A2.

1. In cell A1, enter **Cosmic Cosmetology** as the worksheet title.
2. In cell A2, enter **Sales Analysis** as the worksheet subtitle.
3. Display the Page Layout tab. Click the Themes button (Page Layout tab | Themes group) and then click Basis in the gallery to apply the Basis theme to the worksheet.
4. Click the Fonts button (Page Layout tab | Themes group), and then click Calibri in the Fonts gallery to apply the Calibri font to the worksheet.
5. Set the column widths as follows: A = 9.00, B through G = 15.00, H = 8.00, I and J = 14.00.
6. Select the range A1:A2. Click the Cell Styles button (Home tab | Styles group) and then apply the Title cell style to the range. Change the font size to 24.
7. Select the range A1:J1. Click the 'Merge & Center' button (Home tab | Alignment group) to merge and center the selected cells.
8. Repeat Step 7 to merge and center the range A2:J2.
9. Select the range A1:A2, click the Fill Color arrow (Home tab | Font group), and then click 'Green, Accent 1, Lighter 60%' (column 5, row 3) in the Fill Color gallery to set the fill color for the range.
10. Select cell A3 and zoom to 120% (Figure 7–5).

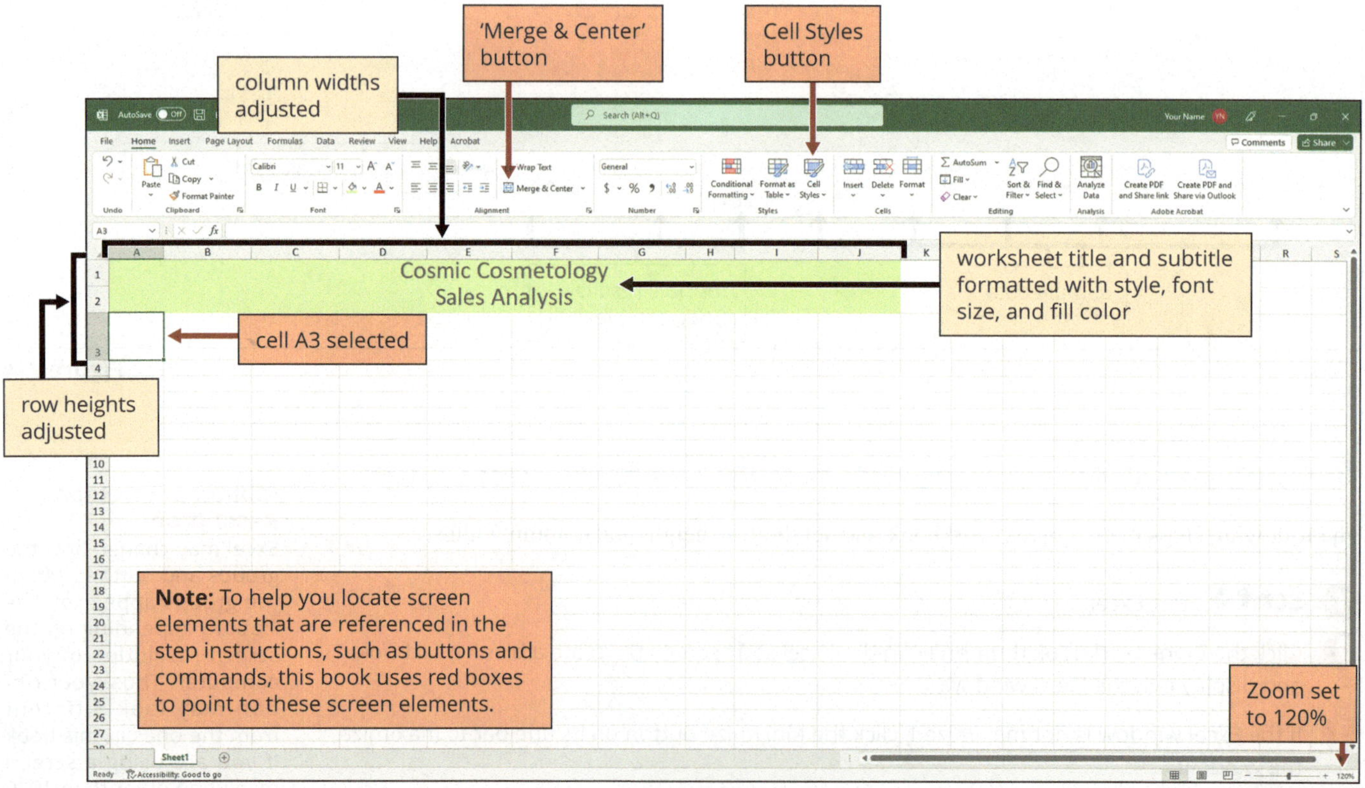

Figure 7–5

To Enter Column Titles in the Template

The following steps enter and format the column titles in row 3.

1. Select cells A3:J3 and then click the Wrap Text button (Home tab | Alignment group) to apply the formatting. Click the Center button (Home tab | Alignment group) and then apply the Heading 3 cell style to the range.

2. Type the following column titles into the appropriate cells (Figure 7–6). Do not enter any text in cell H3.

A3	Store
B3	Category
C3	2028 In-Store Sales in $
D3	2029 In-Store Sales in $
E3	2028 Curbside Sales in $
F3	2029 Curbside Sales in $
G3	Percentage Increase or Decrease
H3	<blank>
I3	Summary of Categories
J3	2029 Totals

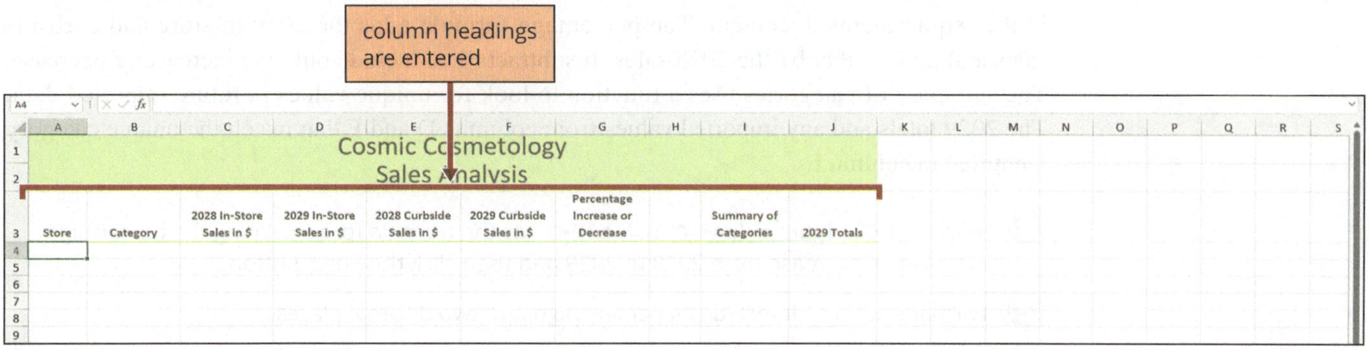

Figure 7–6

To Enter Sample Data in the Template

When you create a template, it is good practice to use sample data in place of actual data to verify the formulas in the template. Entering simple text, such as a, b, or c, and numbers, such as 1, 2, or 3, allows you to check quickly to know if the formulas are generating the proper results. In templates with more complex formulas, you may want to use numbers that test the extreme boundaries of valid data, such as the lowest or highest possible number, or a maximum number of records.

In preparation for entering formulas, the following steps enter sample data in the template.

1. Select cell B4. Type **z** to enter the first piece of sample data.
2. Select cell C4. Type **1** to enter the first number in the series.
3. Enter the other sample data as shown in Figure 7–7.
4. Select the range C4:F4. Apply the comma style with no decimal places to the selected range.

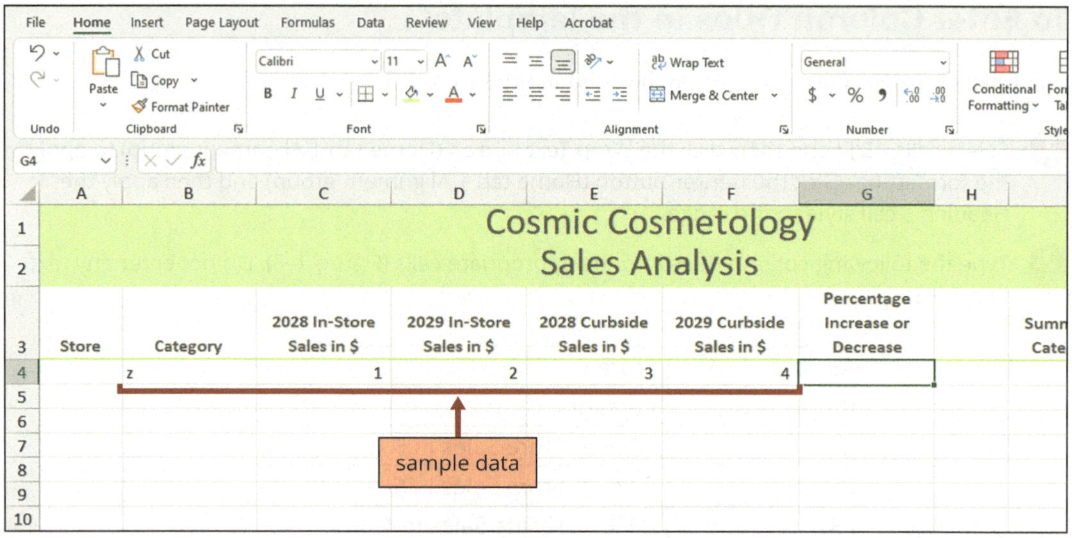

Figure 7–7

To Enter Formulas and Functions in the Template

The following steps enter formulas and functions to summarize data in the template, as described in the requirements document. The percentage formula adds the 2029 in-store and curbside sales and divides that by the 2028 sales. It subtracts 1 to include only the increase or decrease. The summary of categories uses a function to look for unique values in future imported data. The 2029 totals add any imported values from columns D and F that match the unique category identified in column I.

1. Select cell G4. Type **=((d4+f4)/(c4+e4))–1** as the formula for calculating the percentage increase or decrease from 2028 to 2029 and then click the Enter button.
2. Format cell G4 so it includes a percent sign and two decimal places.
3. Select cell I4. Type **=if(countif(b4:b4,b4)=1,b4,"")** to enter a function that displays a value from the Category list if it is unique. Click the Enter button.
4. Select cell J4. Type **=sumif(b4:b100,i4,d4:d100)+sumif(b4:b100,i4, f4:f100)** to enter a function that adds columns d and f, if the value returned in cell I4 matches the data in the Category list in column B. The function will look through row 100 as the maximum number of records. Click the Enter button.

   Q&A What if a warning triangle shows indicating the formula refers to empty cells?
   If after entering the formula in step #4 and pressing Enter, if you receive a warning triangle indicating the formula refers to empty cells, do not be concerned. Since the cells from row 5 through 100 are currently empty, this warning is just letting you know that no data is currently present in those cells.

5. Format cell J4 with a comma and no decimal places.
6. Change the sheet tab name to read, Cosmic Cosmetology, to provide a descriptive name for the worksheet.
7. Change the sheet tab color to Green, Accent 1 to format the tab (Figure 7–8).

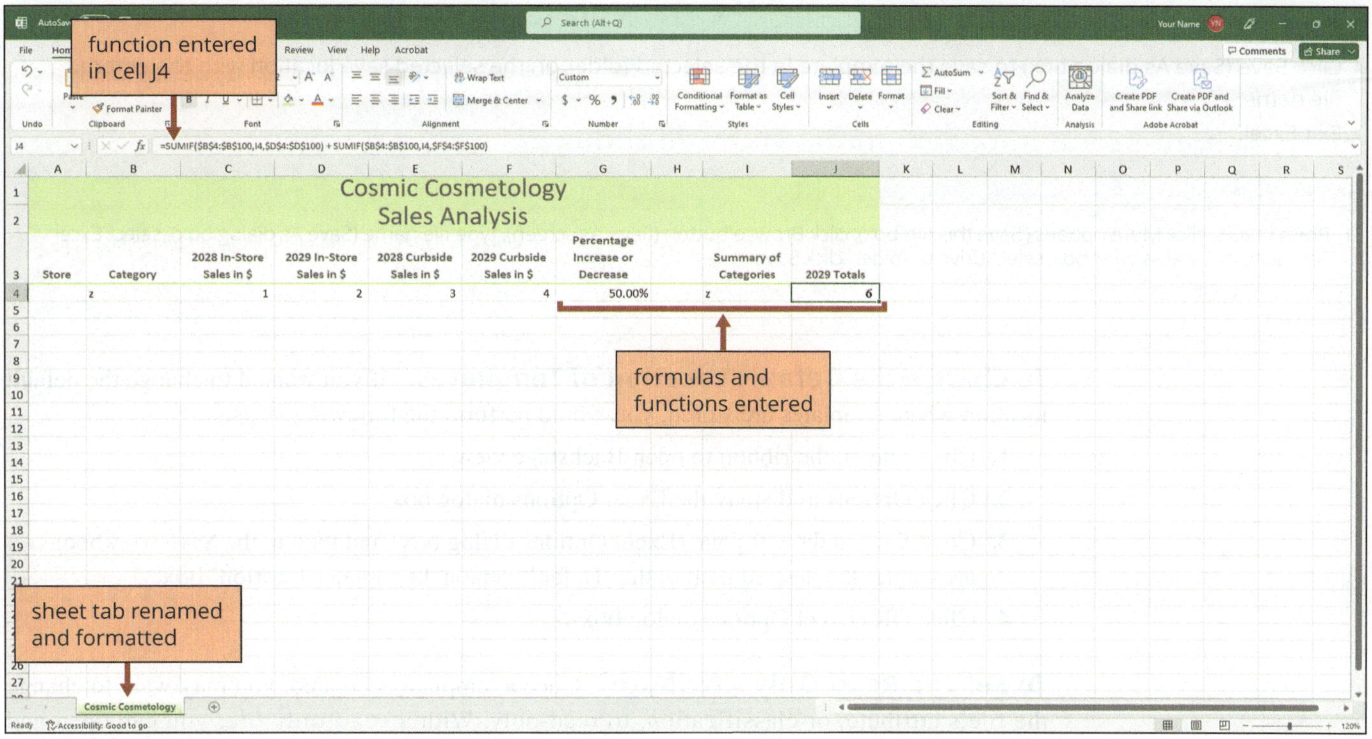

Figure 7–8

To Save the Template

Saving a template is similar to saving a workbook, except that the file type, Excel Template, is selected in the 'Save as type' box (Save As dialog box). Excel saves the file with the extension, .xltx, to denote its template status. Saving in that format prevents users from accidentally saving over the template file, and causes Excel to open new workbooks based on the template with the proper format. In business situations, it is a good idea to save the template in the default Templates folder location. **Why?** Company templates saved in the Templates folder appear with other templates when users need to find them. In lab situations, however, you should save templates on your personal storage device. The following steps save the template using the file name, SC_EX_7_CCSalesAnalysisTemplate.xltx, on your storage device.

1

- Click cell A4 to position the current cell.
- Click the File tab, click Save As to display the Save As screen, and then click the Browse button to display the Save As dialog box.
- Type **SC_EX_7_CCSalesAnalysisTemplate** in the File name box to enter a name for the file.
- Click the 'Save as type' arrow and then click Excel Template (or Excel Template (*.xltx)) in the list to specify that this workbook should be saved as a template.
- Navigate to your storage device and desired folder, if any (Figure 7–9).

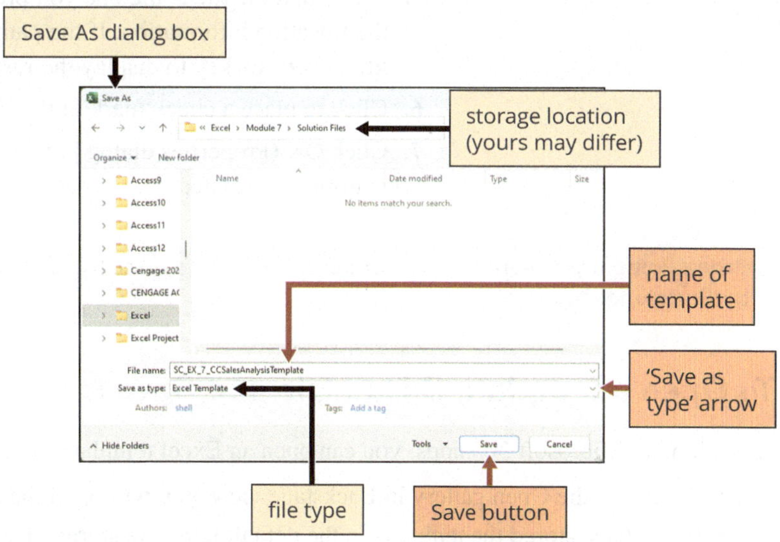

Figure 7–9

Q&A Why does Excel change the folder location when the Excel Template file type is chosen?
When the Excel Template file type is chosen in the 'Save as type' box, Excel automatically changes the location to the Templates folder created when Microsoft 365 was installed. In a production environment—that is, when you are creating a template for a business, a school, or an application—the template typically would be saved in the Templates folder, not on your personal storage device.

2

- Click Save (Save As dialog box) to save the template in the selected folder on the selected save location with the entered file name.
- Exit Excel.

Other Ways

1. Press CTRL+S, click More options ('Save this file' box), click Browse button (Save As screen), type file name (Save As dialog box), select Excel Template in 'Save as type' box, select drive or folder, click Save

To Change the Default Location of Templates If you wanted to change the default location where templates are stored, you would perform the following steps.

1. Click File on the ribbon to open Backstage view.
2. Click Options to display the Excel Options dialog box.
3. Click Save in the left pane (Excel Options dialog box) and then in the Save workbooks area, enter the desired path in the 'Default personal templates location' box.
4. Click OK (Excel Options dialog box).

To Set the Read-Only Attribute Once a template is created, you may want to change the file's attribute, or classification, to read-only. With a **read-only file**, you can open and access the file normally, but you cannot make permanent changes to it. That way, users will be forced to save changes to the template with a new file name, keeping the original template intact and unchanged for the next user.

While you can open system properties in Excel, you cannot change the read-only attribute from within Excel. Setting the read-only attribute is a function of the operating system. If you wanted to set the read-only property of the template, you would perform the following steps.

1. Click the File Explorer app button on the taskbar. Navigate to your storage location.
2. Right-click the template file name to display the shortcut menu.
3. Click Properties on the shortcut menu to display the Properties dialog box.
4. If necessary, click the General tab (Properties dialog box) to display the General sheet.
5. Verify that the file is the one you previously saved on your storage device by checking the Location information. If the path is long, click in the path and then press the RIGHT-ARROW key to display the rest of the path.
6. Click to place a check mark in the Read-only check box in the Attributes area.
7. Click OK (Properties dialog box) to close the dialog box and apply the read-only attribute.

Break Point: If you want to take a break, this is a good place to do so. To resume later, continue following the steps from this location forward.

To Open a Template-Based File and Save It as a Workbook

As with other Microsoft 365 apps, you can open an Excel template in one of several ways:

- If you use the Open gallery in Backstage view, you will open the template file itself for editing.
- If you have stored the template in the default template storage location, you can click the New tab in Backstage view and then click Personal. Clicking the template file in the Personal gallery will open a new file based on the template.
- If you stored the template in another location, you must double-click the file in the File Explorer window to create a new file based on the template.

When you open a file based on a template, Excel names the new workbook using the template name with an appended digit 1 (e.g., Monthly Budget Template1). **Why?** Adding a 1 to the file name delineates it from the template; it is similar to what Excel does when you first run Excel and it assigns the name Book1 to the new workbook. You can save the file with a new file name if you want.

The following steps open a file based on the template. You then will save it in the .xlsx format with a new file name in order to proceed with data entry.

1

- Click the File Explorer button on the taskbar to open a File Explorer window.
- Navigate to your Data File storage location (Figure 7–10).

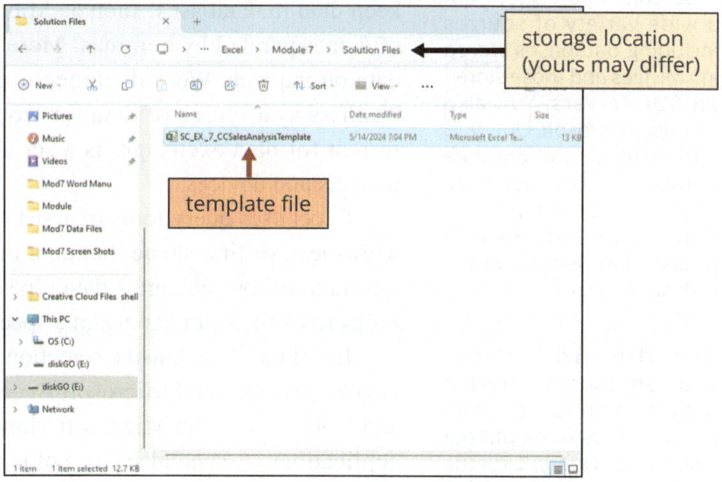

Figure 7–10

2

- Double-click the file named SC_EX_7_CCSalesAnalysisTemplate.xltx to open a new file based on the template (Figure 7–11).

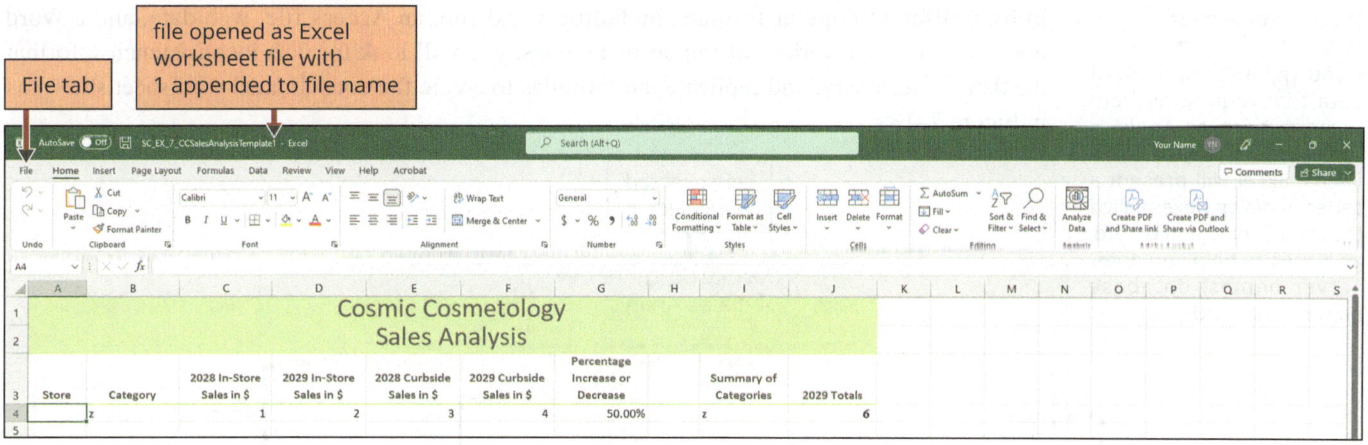

Figure 7–11

3

- Click the File tab and then click Save As to display the Save As screen in Backstage view.
- Click Browse to display the Save As dialog box.
- Type **SC_EX_7_CCSalesAnalysis** in the File name box (Save As dialog box) and then navigate to your storage location (Figure 7–12).

Q&A Should I change the file type?

No. Excel automatically selects Excel Workbook as the file type when you attempt to save a file based on a template.

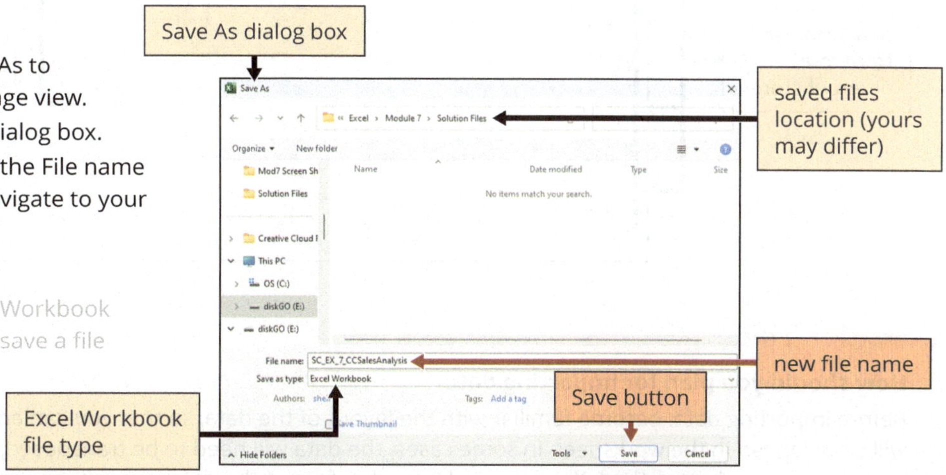

Figure 7–12

4

- Click Save (Save As dialog box) to save the file with the new file name.

BTW

Importing from Databases

Excel can import data from a wide variety of sources including databases stored in XML files and those stored on SQL servers. You also can use Microsoft Query to retrieve data from corporate databases. The Get Data button (Data tab | Get & Transform Data group) presents an extensive list with submenus.

BTW

Importing Azure Data

You can import different data from an Azure cloud-based service to be utilized with Power Query. Click the Get Data button (Data tab | Get & Transform Data group) and then click From Azure to display a complete list.

BTW

Data Connection Wizard

If you import some kinds of data that require authentication, such as Analysis Services or OData Data Feeds, Excel will present a series of dialog boxes called the Data Connection Wizard, as it tries to help you enter server names, database names, passwords, etc.

Importing Data

Data may come from a variety of sources and in a range of formats. Even though many users keep data in databases, such as Microsoft Access, it is common to receive text files with fields of data separated by commas. More and more companies are creating HTML files and posting data on the web. Word documents, especially those including tables of data, often are used in business as a source of data for workbooks. **XML (Extensible Markup Language)**, a popular format for data exchange, is a set of encoding rules that formats data to be readable by both humans and devices.

Excel uses query tools to assist you in importing data. You can load the data directly to your worksheet, or first shape that data in ways that meet your needs. For example, you can remove a column or row, change a data type, or merge data before moving it into your worksheet. Excel keeps track of your changes in a special pane.

Excel has an extensive selection of file formats. You can import data from databases such as Oracle, MySQL, and Microsoft Access; from online services such as Salesforce and Sharepoint; and from **Azure**, the Microsoft cloud service, which allows you to build, manage, and deploy applications. A special From Folder command even imports data about the files in a folder to which you are connected. These and many more forms of data are listed when you click the Get Data button (Data tab | Get & Transform Data group). Importing data into Excel can create a link that can be used to update data whenever the original file changes.

In the following sections, you will import data from four different store locations and in four different popular formats, including a text file, an Access file, web data, and a Word document. Using a variety of import techniques, you will look for data inconsistencies, format the data as necessary, and replicate the formulas to create the consolidated worksheet shown as in Figure 7–13.

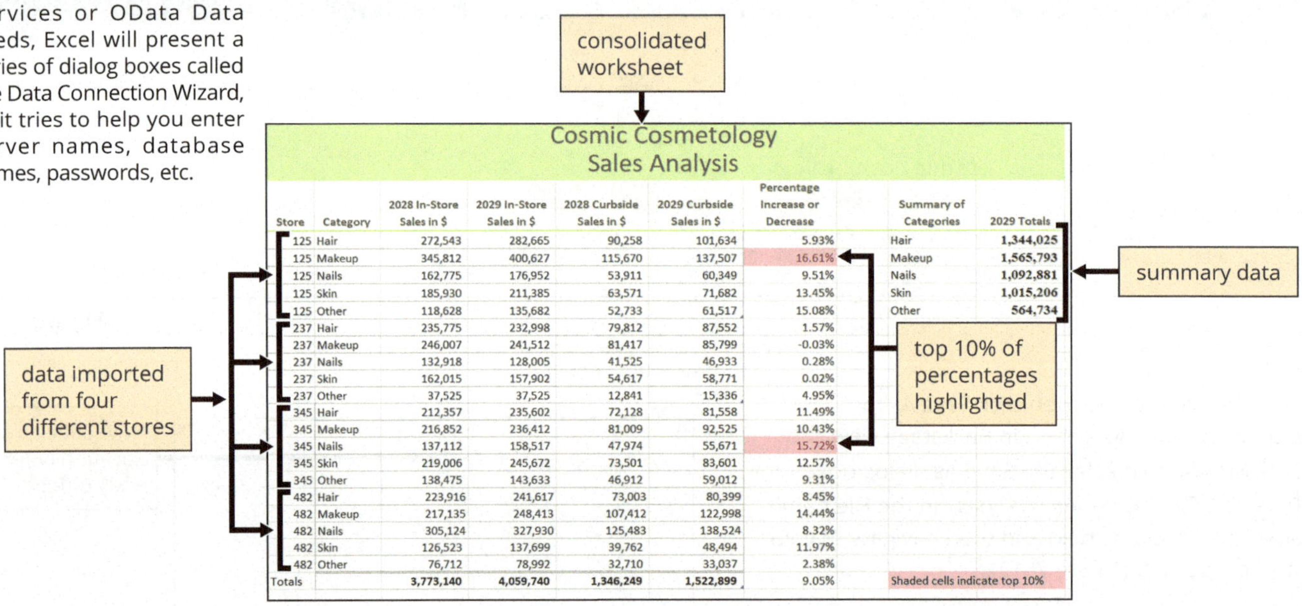

Store	Category	2028 In-Store Sales in $	2029 In-Store Sales in $	2028 Curbside Sales in $	2029 Curbside Sales in $	Percentage Increase or Decrease	Summary of Categories	2029 Totals
125	Hair	272,543	282,665	90,258	101,634	5.93%	Hair	1,344,025
125	Makeup	345,812	400,627	115,670	137,507	16.61%	Makeup	1,565,793
125	Nails	162,775	176,952	53,911	60,349	9.51%	Nails	1,092,881
125	Skin	185,930	211,385	63,571	71,682	13.45%	Skin	1,015,206
125	Other	118,628	135,682	52,733	61,517	15.08%	Other	564,734
237	Hair	235,775	232,998	79,812	87,552	1.57%		
237	Makeup	246,007	241,512	81,417	85,799	-0.03%		
237	Nails	132,918	128,005	41,525	46,933	0.28%		
237	Skin	162,015	157,902	54,617	58,771	0.02%		
237	Other	37,525	37,525	12,841	15,336	4.95%		
345	Hair	212,357	235,602	72,128	81,558	11.49%		
345	Makeup	216,852	236,412	81,009	92,525	10.43%		
345	Nails	137,112	158,517	47,974	55,671	15.72%		
345	Skin	219,006	245,672	73,501	83,601	12.57%		
345	Other	138,475	143,633	46,912	59,012	9.31%		
482	Hair	223,916	241,617	73,003	80,399	8.45%		
482	Makeup	217,135	248,413	107,412	122,998	14.44%		
482	Nails	305,124	327,930	125,483	138,524	8.32%		
482	Skin	126,523	137,699	39,762	48,494	11.97%		
482	Other	76,712	78,992	32,710	33,037	2.38%		
Totals		3,773,140	4,059,740	1,346,249	1,522,899	9.05%	Shaded cells indicate top 10%	

Figure 7–13

Consider This

How should you plan for importing data?

Before importing data, become familiar with the layout of the data, so that you can anticipate how each data element will be arranged in the worksheet. In some cases, the data will need to be transposed, meaning that the rows and columns need to be switched. You also might need to format the data, move it, or convert it from or to a table.

Text Files

A **text file** contains data with little or no formatting. Many programs, including Excel, offer an option to import data from a text file. Text files may have a file extension such as .txt, .csv, .asc, or .cdl, among others. Companies sometimes generate these text files from input fields via proprietary business applications.

In text files, commas, tabs, or other characters often separate the fields. Alternatively, the text file may have fields of equal length in columnar format. Each record usually exists on a separate line. A **delimited file** is a file in which each record is on a separate line and the fields are separated by a special character, called a **delimiter**. A delimited file in which the data is separated by commas is called a **comma-delimited text file**. A **fixed-width file** contains data fields of equal length with spaces between the fields. In the case of a fixed-width file, a special character need not separate the data fields. During the import process, Excel provides a preview to help identify the type of text file being imported.

To Import Data from a Text File

The following steps import a comma-delimited text file into the CC Sales Analysis workbook using the Load To command. **Why?** The Load To command imports data as a table, directly into the current worksheet. Alternatively, the Load command imports data into a new sheet within the workbook. The text file contains data about sales for Store #125 (shown in Figure 7–1a). To complete these steps, you will be required to use the Data Files. Please contact your instructor for information about accessing the Data Files.

1

- With the Cosmic Cosmetology worksheet active, select cell A5.
- Click Data on the ribbon to display the Data tab.
- Click the 'From Text/CSV' button (Data tab | Get & Transform Data group) to display the Import Data dialog box.
- If necessary, navigate to the location of the Data Files to display the files (Figure 7–14).

Q&A Should I import data to cell A4?

No. The import process will not overwrite current data, as in cell B4. You will delete the sample data later in the module.

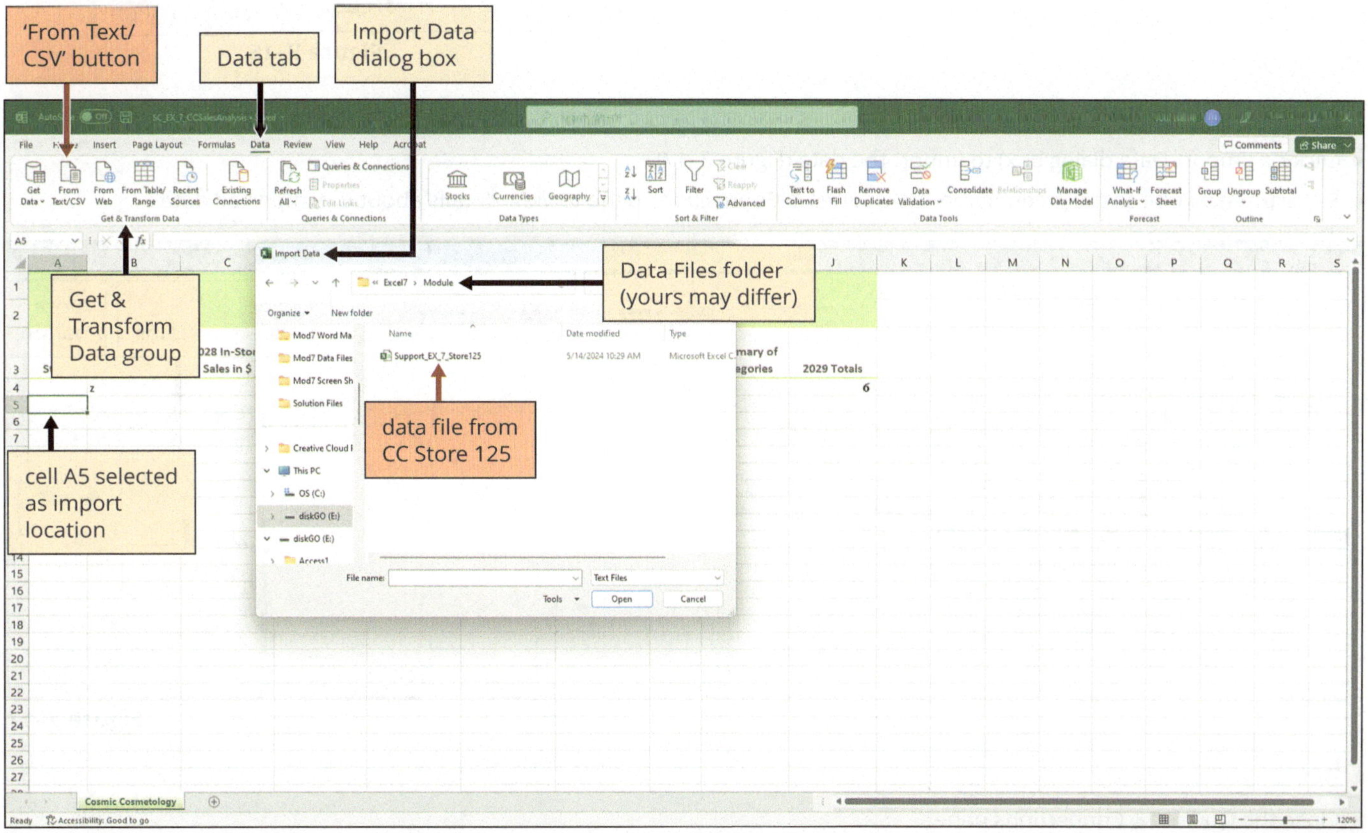

Figure 7–14

2

- Double-click the file name 'Support_EX_7_Store125.csv' to display the preview window.
- Click the Load arrow (Figure 7–15).

Q&A What happened to the Text Import Wizard?
The Text Import Wizard has been replaced by the query functions. If you want to use the wizard, click File, click Options, and then click Data (Excel Options dialog box). Click to display a checkmark in the 'From Text (Legacy)' check box. Click the OK button. A Legacy Wizards option will be added to the Get Data list.

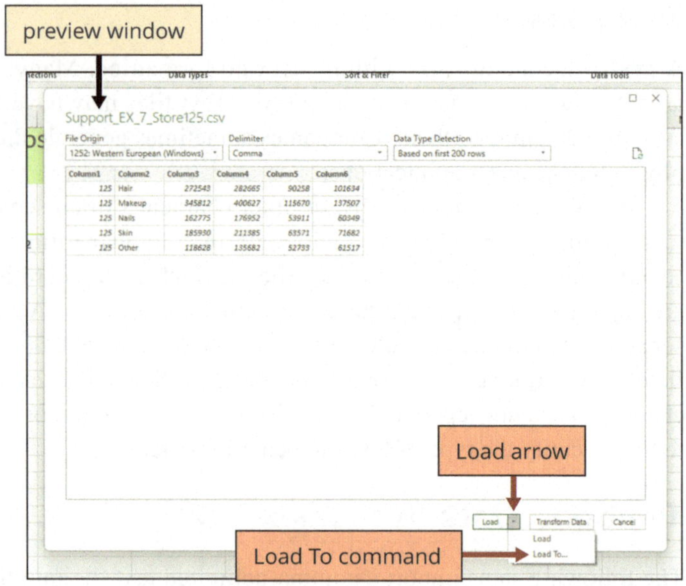

Figure 7–15

3

- Click Load To to display the Import Data dialog box.
- Click the Existing worksheet option button to place the data in the current worksheet rather than on a new sheet (Figure 7–16).

Q&A What is shown in the Import Data dialog box when importing from a text file?
The Import Data dialog box allows you to choose whether to import the data into a table, a PivotTable Report, a PivotChart, or only create a connection to the data. You also can choose to import the data to an existing worksheet or a new worksheet.

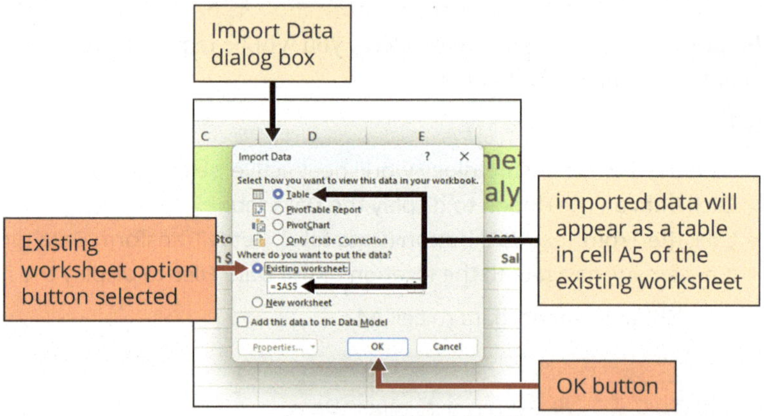

Figure 7–16

4

- Click OK (Import Data dialog box) to import the data (Figure 7–17).
- **Experiment:** Point to the green bar in the Queries & Connections pane to view details about the imported data.

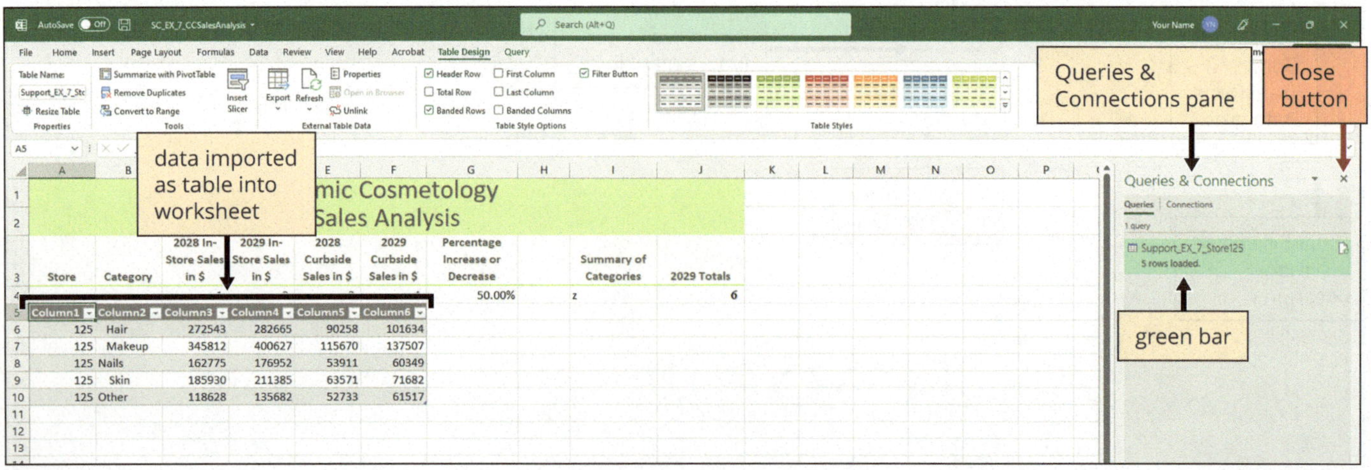

Figure 7–17

5

- Close the Queries & Connections pane.

To Format the CSV Data

When Excel imports text or CSV data, it comes in as a table; thus, you will need to remove features specific to tables, such as banded rows and a header row. **Why?** Removing those table features will format the data to match the worksheet.

1

- Display the Table Design tab, if necessary.
- Click to remove the checkmark in the Banded Rows check box (Table Design tab | Table Style Options group).
- Click to remove the checkmark in the Header Row check box (Table Design tab | Table Style Options group) to display a Microsoft Excel dialog box (Figure 7–18).

Q&A What is the small, blue corner indicator in cell F10?
That indicator is a table corner. You can drag it to add more rows or columns to the table if adjacent cells are empty. If the dialog box is covering the table corner, you may drag the dialog box to the right until you are no longer covering the table corner.

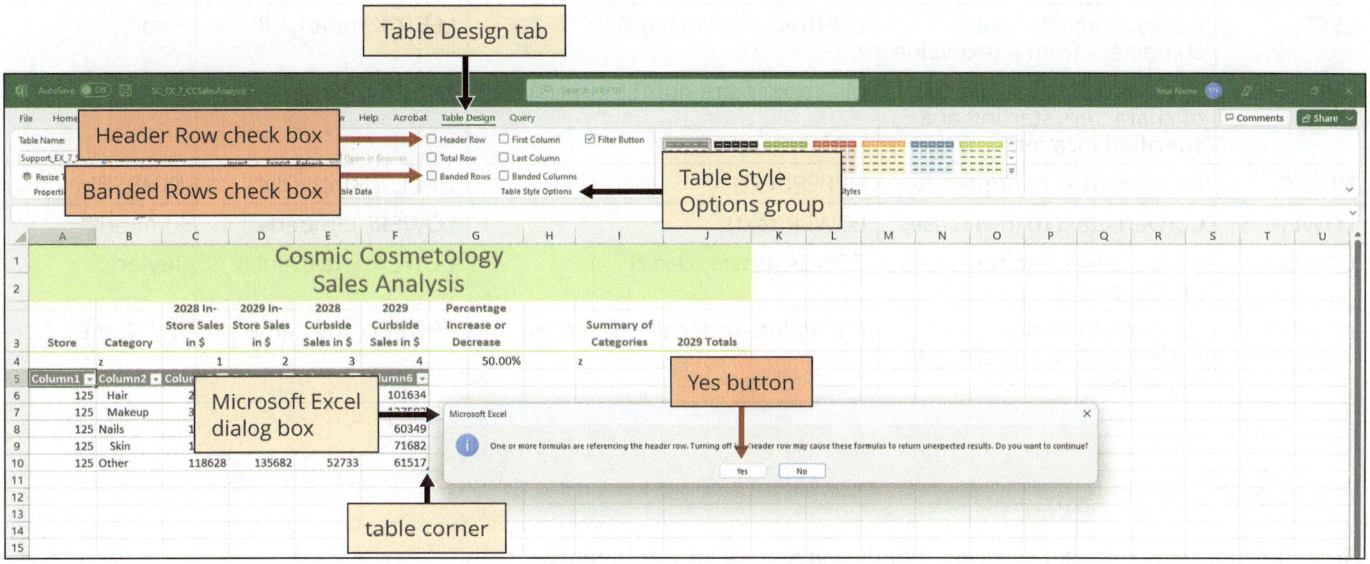

Figure 7–18

2

- Click the Yes button to remove the header row.
- Delete row 5.
- Because the import changed the column widths, select columns B:G and change the column width back to 15.

Text Formatting

Sometimes imported data will have some input inconsistencies and will need to be reformatted. It is important to check imported data closely and make corrections as necessary, without changing any values. Excel has a series of text functions to help you convert numbers to text, correct inconsistencies in capitalization, and trim off excess spaces, as well as functions to retain only parts of a cell's contents or join pieces of text together.

For example, the **CONCAT function** (which stands for "concatenate," or join) joins two or more text data items into a single expression. The **LEFT function** displays a specified number of characters from the beginning of a specified text string, and the **RIGHT function** displays a specified number of characters from the end of a specified text string The **PROPER function** converts the first letter of each word in a text string to uppercase, similar to title case in word processing.

Table 7–1 displays some of the available text functions.

Table 7–1: Text Functions

Function	Purpose	Syntax	Example	Result
TEXT	Converts a numeric value to text and lets you specify the display formatting by using special format strings (Once converted, you cannot use it in calculations)	TEXT(value, format, text)	TEXT(23.5, "$0.00")	$23.50
TRIM	Removes all spaces from text except for single spaces between words	TRIM(text)	TRIM(" Bob E. Wilson ")	Bob E. Wilson
RIGHT	Returns the rightmost characters from a text value	RIGHT(text,[num_chars])	RIGHT("Kimberly",1)	y
LEFT	Returns the leftmost characters from a text value	LEFT(text,[num_chars])	LEFT("Kimberly",3)	Kim
MID	Returns a specific number of characters starting at a specified location	MID(text,[start_num],[num_chars])	MID("Kimberly",4,3)	ber
UPPER	Converts text to uppercase	UPPER(text)	UPPER("Kimberly")	KIMBERLY
LOWER	Converts text to lowercase	LOWER(text)	LOWER("Kimberly")	kimberly
CONCAT	Joins several text items into one text item	CONCAT(text1,[text2], ...)	CONCAT("Tay","lor")	Taylor
PROPER	Converts the first letter of each word in a text string to uppercase	PROPER(text or cell reference)	PROPER("my name")	My Name

To Use the Trim Function

The following steps trim extra spaces from the category data you imported. **Why?** The data was stored with extra spaces, making it impossible to align the words in the column. In a separate part of the workspace, you will use the TRIM function to remove all spaces from text except for single spaces between words. You then will paste the trimmed values to replace the originals.

1

- Select cell B11, type **=trim(b5)** and then click the Enter button to trim the spaces from the data in cell B5 and display it in cell B11 (Figure 7–19).

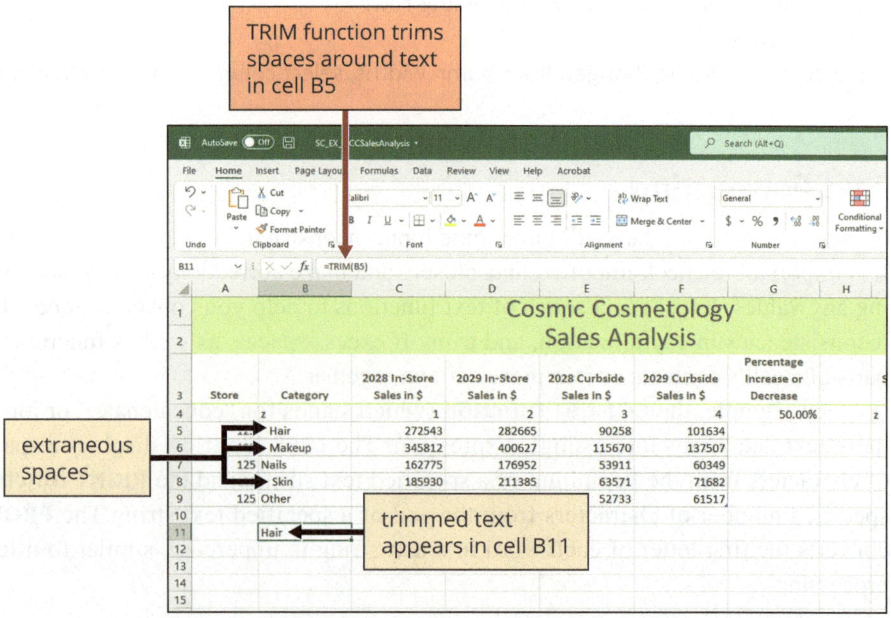

Figure 7–19

2

- Drag the fill handle of cell B11 down through cell B15 to display the trimmed data for all categories.
- Do not deselect the data (Figure 7–20).

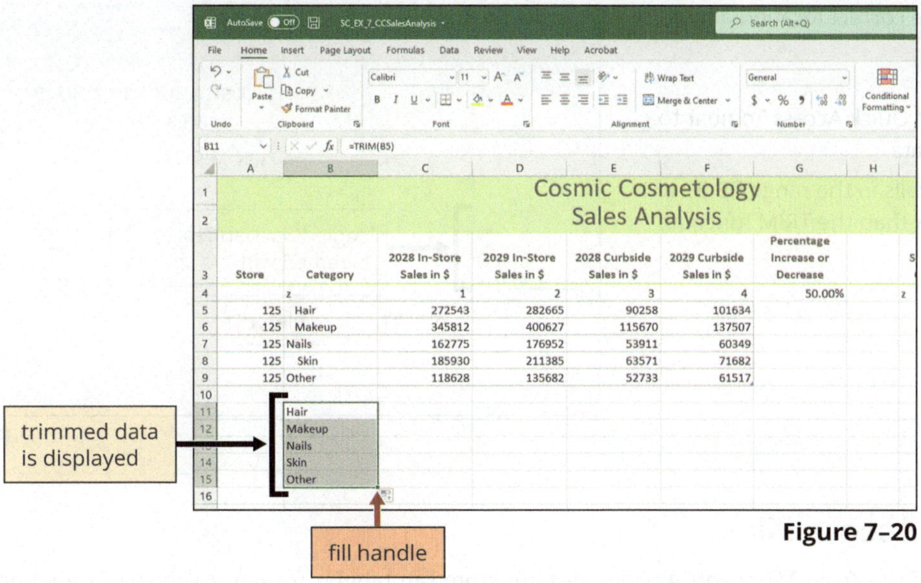

Figure 7–20

To Paste Values Only

The following steps cut the data from cells B11 through B15 and paste only the trimmed values back to cells B5 through B9. *Why? If you simply paste the contents of the clipboard using CTRL+V, you will retain the trim function notation. You want only the trimmed values.* To paste values, you will use Paste Options.

1

- With the range B11:B15 still selected, press CTRL+C to copy the data.
- Right-click cell B5 to display the shortcut menu (Figure 7–21).

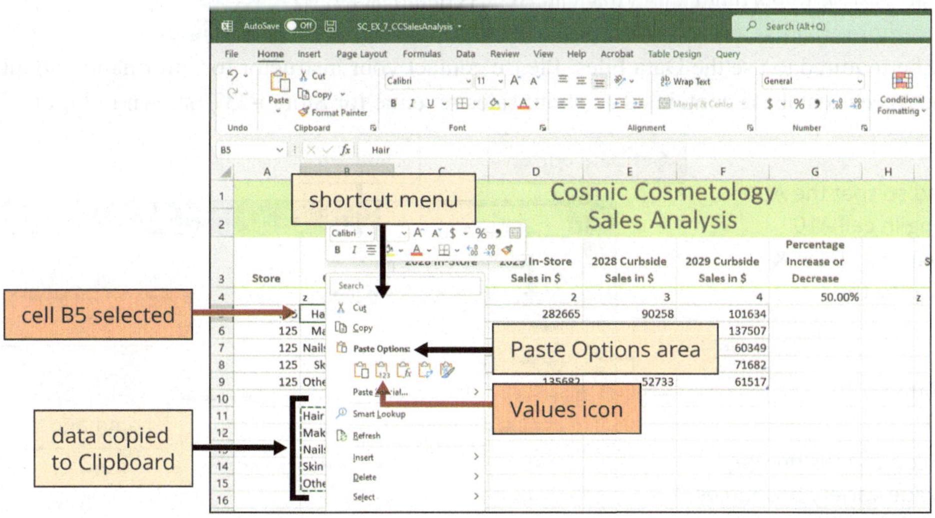

Figure 7–21

2

- In the Paste Options area, click the Values icon to paste only the values.
- Delete the data in the range B11:B15 because you have already pasted it to the correct location and no longer need it.
- Select cell A10 (Figure 7–22).
- Click the Save button on the Quick Access Toolbar to save the file with the new data.
- **Experiment:** Click various cells in the range B5:B9 to verify that the values, rather than the TRIM function, were pasted.

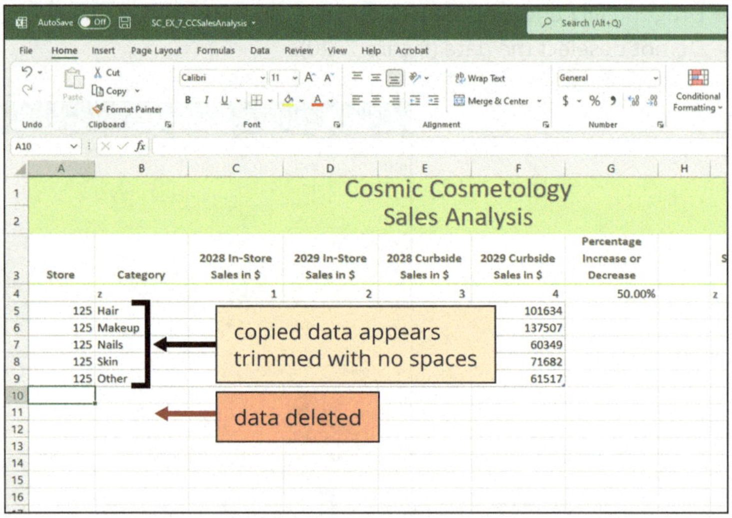

Figure 7–22

Access Files

Data from Microsoft Access files are stored in tabular format. Each row is a record; columns represent fields. When you import Access files, you usually import an entire table, which includes column headings and sometimes extra data. Excel will display a preview. If you need to edit the data before completing the import, Excel uses **Power Query**, a tool that allows you to perform advanced editing or querying of the database before committing it to your worksheet.

There are advantages to editing the data this way. Power Query has many tools to help you make changes easily, and if the Access file is updated in the future, you will not have to redo the edits. The changes are brought into Excel automatically the next time you open the file.

You will learn more about Power Query in a future module.

To Import Data from an Access Table

The following steps begin the process of importing a table from an Access database. **Why?** Access is used by many businesses, and importing an Access file is representative of how you would work with many other different kinds of database files. To complete these steps, you will be required to use the Data Files. Please contact your instructor for information about accessing the Data Files. The table in the Access database contains data about sales revenue for Store #237 (shown in Figure 7–1b).

1

- Verify that cell A10 is selected so that the Access table will be imported starting in cell A10.
- Click the Get Data button (Data tab | Get & Transform Data group) to display the Get Data menu.
- Point to the From Database command to display the submenu (Figure 7–23).
- **Experiment:** Point to other commands on the Get Data menu, noting the wide variety of sources that Excel will accept. When you are finished, point to the From Database command again.

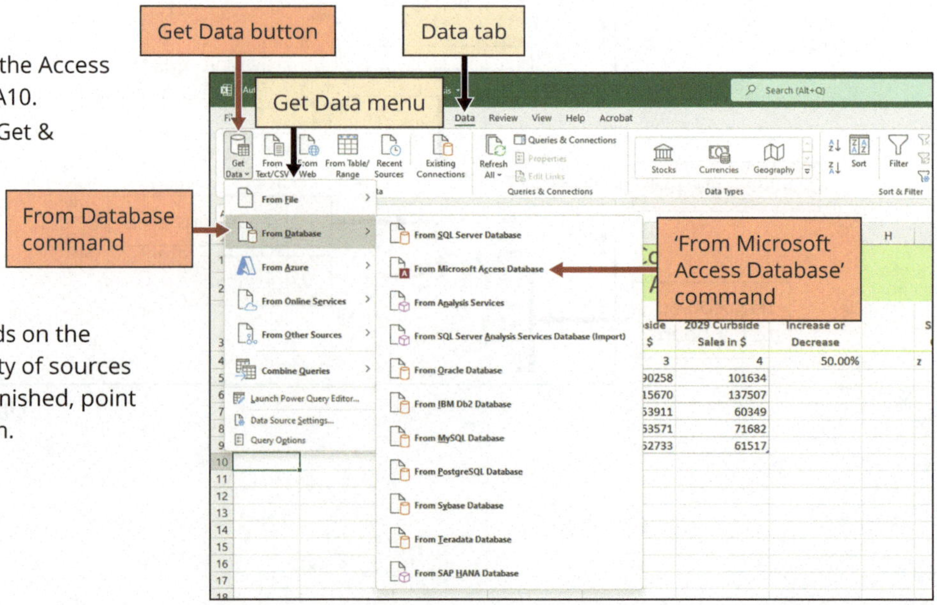

Figure 7–23

2

- Click 'From Microsoft Access Database' to display the Import Data dialog box.
- If necessary, navigate to the location of the Data Files (Figure 7–24).

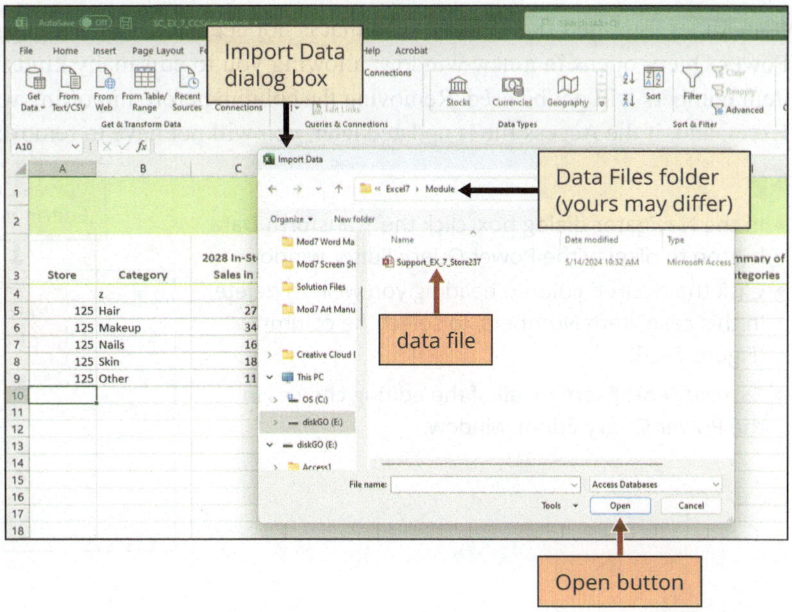

Figure 7–24

3

- Double-click the file, Support_EX_7_Store237.accdb, to display the Navigator dialog box.
- Click the name of the table, 'CC Store 237 Sales,' to display the preview (Figure 7–25).

Q&A What if the database contains more than one table?
The Navigator dialog box will display all available tables. You can import only one table at a time.

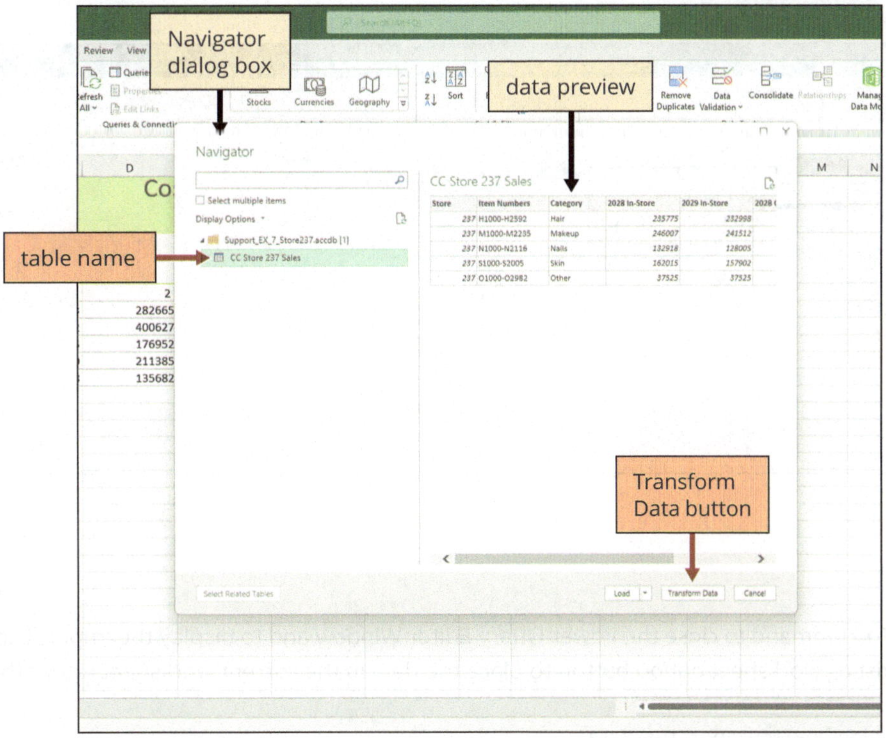

Figure 7–25

To Delete a Column Using Power Query

Sometimes imported files contain data that is not needed, such as total rows, extra columns, or undesired records. The Excel Power Query opens in a new window, allowing you to edit many kinds of imported data. In this database, one column with item numbers will not be used. Removing the column before importing will cause only the appropriate data to be transferred to Excel, and, if the Access file is updated later, you will not have to remove the extra column again.

1

- In the Navigator dialog box, click the Transform Data button to display the Power Query Editor window.
- Click the desired column heading you wish to delete, in this case, Item Numbers, to select the column (Figure 7–26).
- **Experiment:** Examine all of the editing choices in the Power Query Editor window.

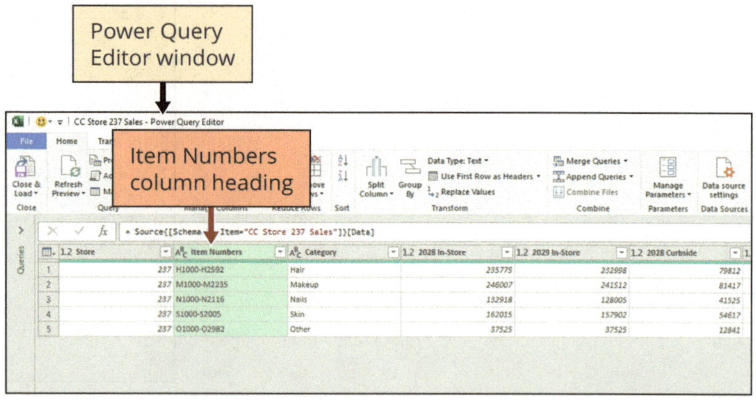

Figure 7–26

2

- Click the Remove Columns button (Power Query Editor Home tab | Manage Columns group) to remove the column from the import.
- Click the 'Close & Load' arrow (Power Query Editor Home tab | Close group) to display the 'Close & Load' menu (Figure 7–27).

Q&A What is the purpose of the APPLIED STEPS area?

The APPLIED STEPS area allows you to track edits to the data and undo them if necessary.

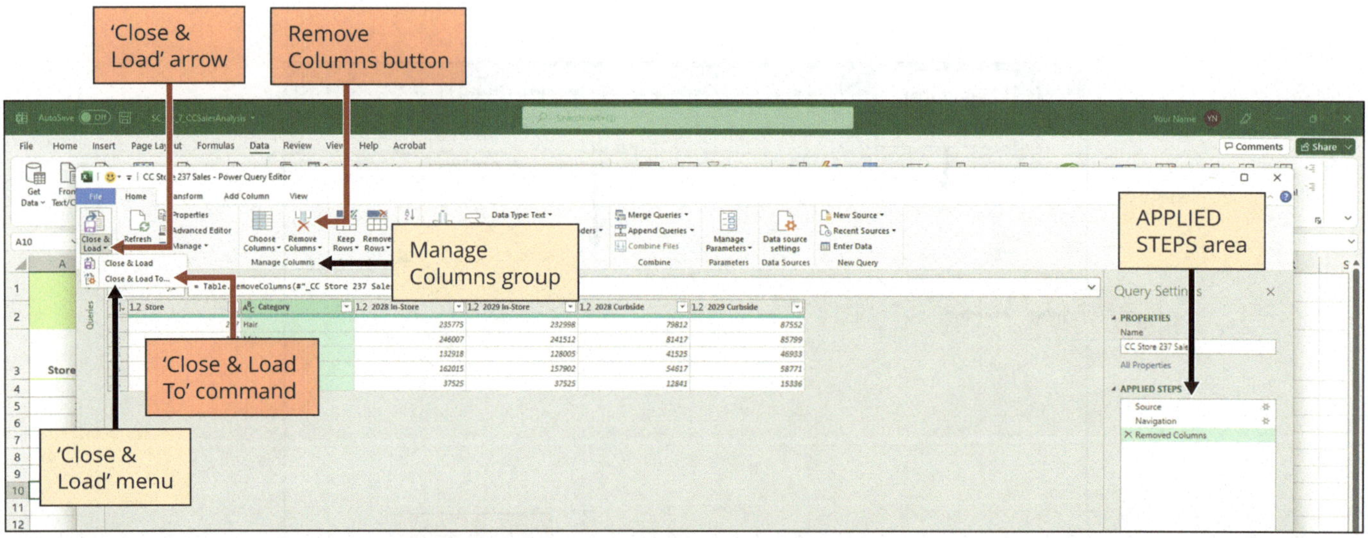

Figure 7–27

3

- Click the 'Close & Load To' command to close the Power Query Editor Window and to display the Import Data dialog box.
- If necessary, click the Existing worksheet option button to place the data in the current worksheet rather than on a new sheet (Figure 7–28).
- Click OK (Import Data dialog box) to import the data.

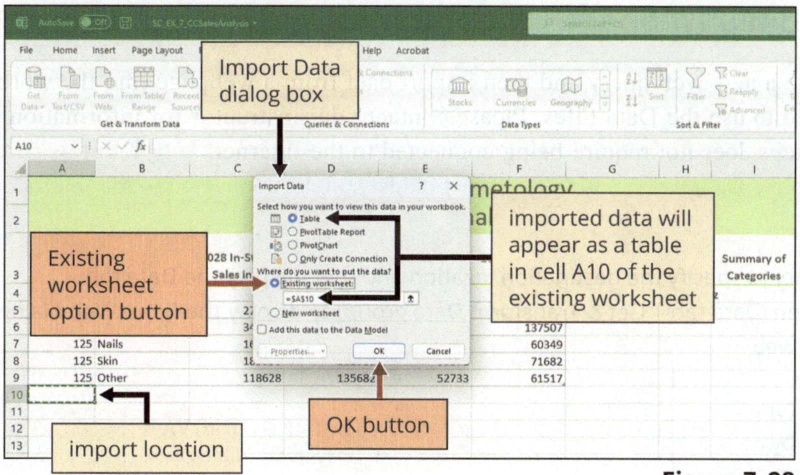

Figure 7–28

To Format the Access Data

The following steps format the Access data.

1. With cell A10 selected, click the Banded Rows check box (Table Design tab | Table Style options) to remove its checkmark.
2. Click the Header Row check box (Table Design tab | Table Style options) to remove its check mark. When Excel displays a dialog box, click the Yes button.
3. Delete row 10 to move the data up.
4. Click the Save button on the Quick Access Toolbar to save the file.
5. Close the Queries & Connections pane, and then click on cell A15 (Figure 7–29).

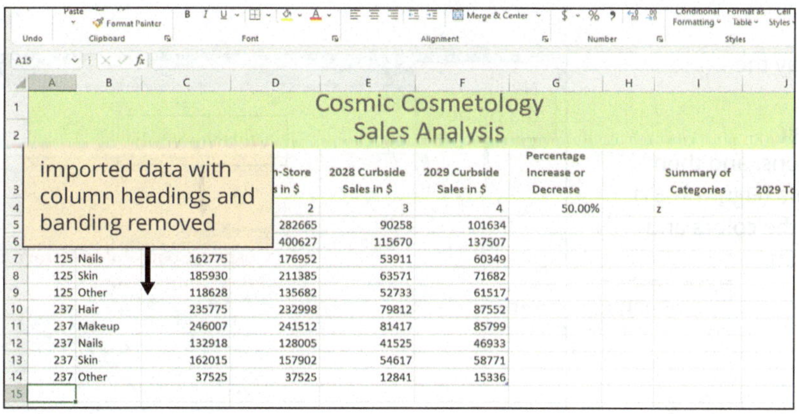

Figure 7–29

Web Data

Webpages use a file format called HTML. **HTML** stands for **Hypertext Markup Language**, which is a special language that software developers use to create and format webpage elements and that browsers can interpret. Excel can import data from a webpage into preformatted areas of the worksheet using a web query. A **web query** selects data from the Internet or from an HTML file to add to the Excel worksheet. The New Web Query dialog box includes options to specify which parts of the webpage to import and how much of the HTML formatting to keep.

Using a web query has advantages over other methods of importing data from a webpage. For example, copying data from webpages to the Office Clipboard and then pasting it into Excel does not maintain all of the webpage formatting. In addition, copying only the desired data from a webpage can be tedious.

To Import Data from a Webpage

The following steps create a new web query and then import data from a webpage into the worksheet. To complete these steps, you will be required to use the Data Files. Please contact your instructor for information about accessing the Data Files. Performing these steps does not require being connected to the Internet. **Why?** In this case, the webpage (shown in Figure 7–1c) is stored with the Data Files; normally you would have to be connected to the Internet.

1

- Select cell A15 if necessary to specify the destination location and then display the Data tab.
- Click the From Web button (Data tab | Get & Transform Data group) to display the From Web dialog box.
- In the URL box, type the web address, in this case, the location of the data file: Type the drive letter followed by a COLON (:), the path location of the Data Files, followed by the name of the desired file, in this case, Support_EX_7_Store345.html. Separate the name of each folder with a BACKSLASH (\). For example, type **c:\users\username\documents\cis 101\data files\Support_EX_7_Store345.html** to insert the file name. Your file path will differ (Figure 7–30).

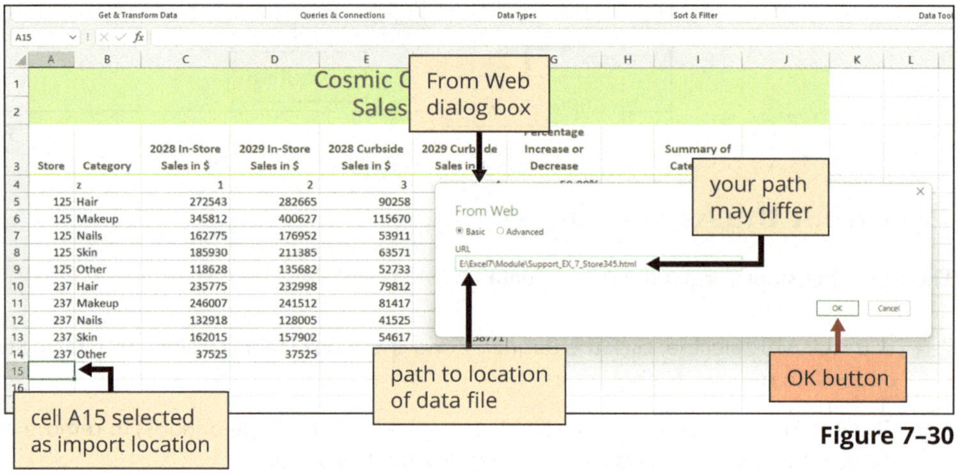

Figure 7–30

Q&A Could I navigate to the file and double-click?
No, double-clicking the file would open it in a browser, rather than creating a query. You must type in the location, just as you would for a URL. Contact your instructor for the exact path and location.

2

- Click OK (From Web dialog box) to display the Navigator dialog box.
- If necessary, click the table name, Cosmic Cosmetology Store 345 Sales Comparisons, and then click the Web View tab to display the data (Figure 7–31). Depending on your computer settings, the colors and text wrapping of the data might vary from the data in the figure; this does not affect the data itself.

Q&A Can I accept the data as is?
No. The data is not right-aligned, and the first column is Category, not the store number.

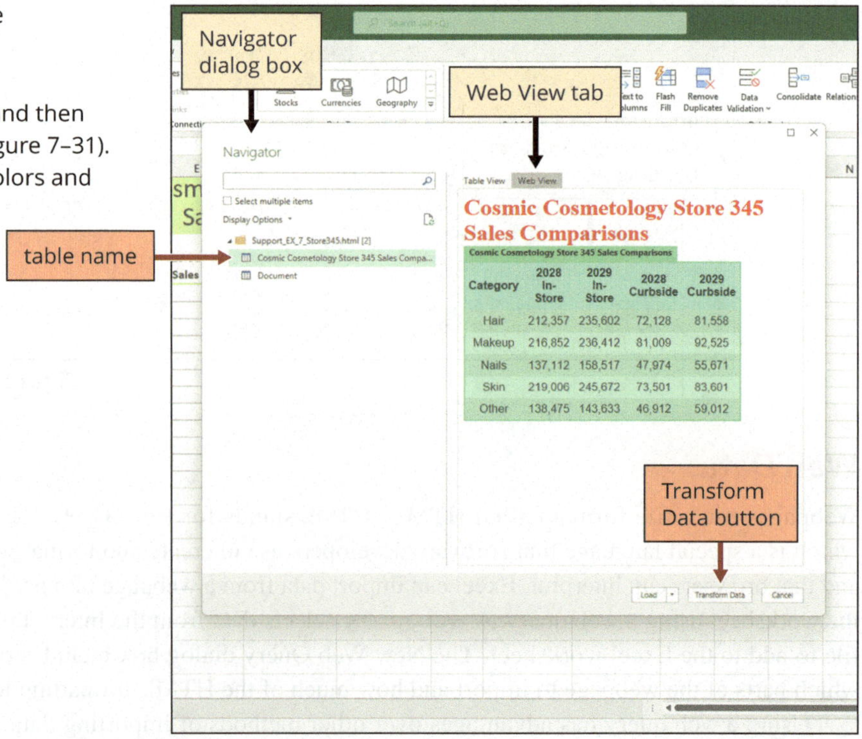

Figure 7–31

3

- Click the Transform Data button to display the Power Query Editor window.
- Click the column heading in the second column, 2028 In-Store, then SHIFT+click the column heading in the 2029 Curbside column to select all of the numeric data.
- Click the 'Data Type:Decimal Number' arrow (PowerQuery Editor Home tab | Transform group) to display its menu (Figure 7–32).

Q&A What should I do if my button is named 'Data Type: Whole Number'?

You can follow the same steps, clicking the arrow and then performing Step 4, without affecting the data.

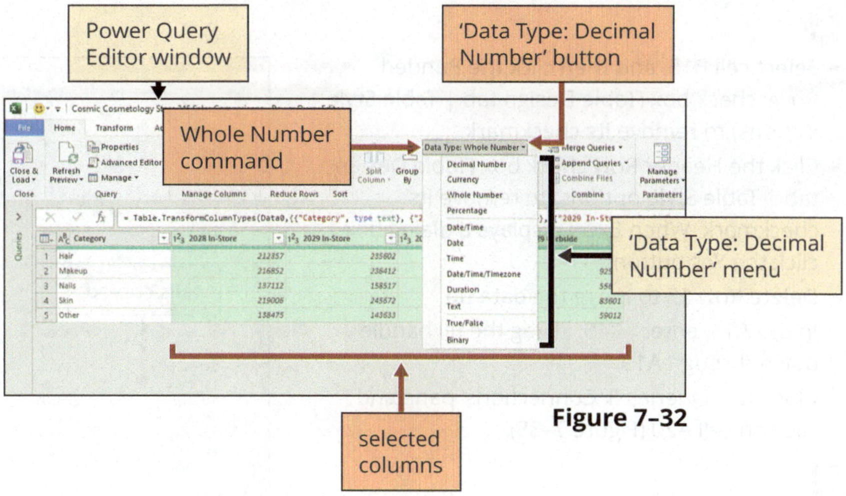

Figure 7–32

4

- Click Whole Number to convert the data to numbers and right-align them. If the Change Column Type dialog box is displayed, click the Replace Current button (Figure 7–33).

Q&A Should I try to insert the missing Store column?

No. You can add that directly to the worksheet.

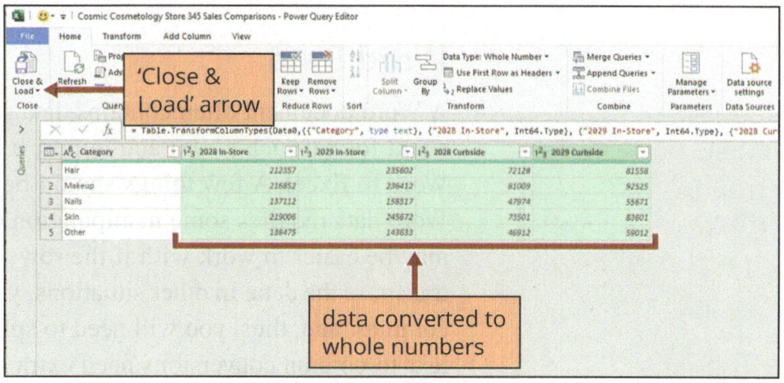

Figure 7–33

5

- Click the 'Close & Load' arrow (Power Query Editor Home tab | Close group) and then click the 'Close & Load To' command to close the Power Query Editor Window.
- When Excel displays the Import Data dialog box, click the Existing worksheet option button. Because there is no Store data in the imported file, change the location of the import to **=$B$15** (Figure 7–34).
- Click the OK button (Import Data dialog box) to import the data.

Q&A Why should I use a web query instead of copying and pasting from a webpage?

Using a web query has advantages over other methods of importing data from a webpage. For example, copying data from webpages to the Office Clipboard and then pasting it into Excel does not maintain all of the webpage formatting. In addition, copying only the desired data from a webpage can be tedious. Finally, copying and pasting does not create a link to the webpage for future updating.

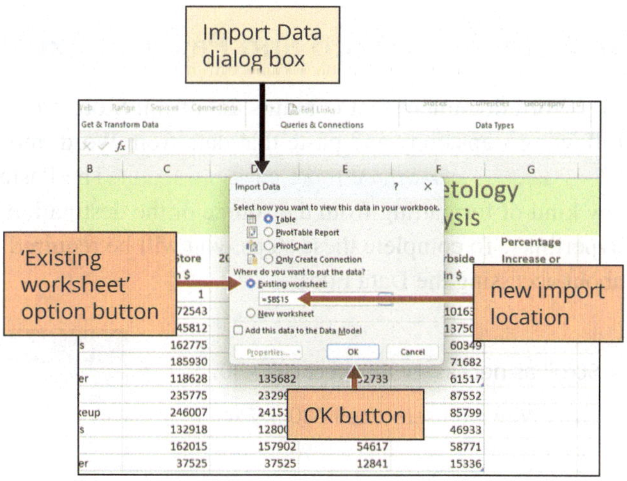

Figure 7–34

6

- Select cell B15, and then click the Banded Rows check box (Table Design tab | Table Style options) to remove its checkmark.
- Click the Header Row check box (Table Design tab | Table Style options) to remove its checkmark. When Excel displays a dialog box, click the Yes button.
- Delete Row 15 to move the data up.
- In cell A15, enter **345**. Drag the fill handle down through A19.
- Close the 'Queries & Connections' pane and click on cell A20 (Figure 7–35).

7

- Click the Save button on the Quick Access Toolbar to save the file.

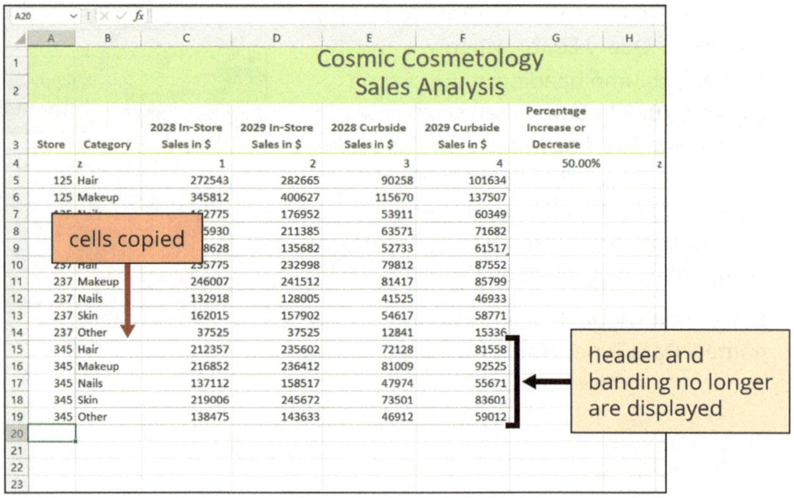

Figure 7–35

Word Data

A Word document often contains data stored in a table. While you could save your Word data in a text format such as .txt and import it as you did earlier, you can copy and paste directly from Word to Excel. A few things should be taken into consideration, however. On some occasions, Word data requires some manipulation once you paste it into Excel. For example, the Word data may be easier to work with if the rows and columns were switched, and, thus, you will need to transpose the data. In other situations, you may find that Excel did not paste the data into separate columns, and, thus, you will need to split the data or convert the text into columns. Finally, some text-to-column conversions need extra space or columns when the data is split, requiring you to move other data out of the way. An example of each will occur in the following sections, as you copy, paste, transpose, move, and split data from Word to Excel.

To Copy from Word and Paste to Excel

The Word document that contains data from Store #482 (Figure 7–1d) includes a Word table with rows and columns. The following steps copy and paste that data from Word into Excel. **Why?** The manipulations that you will need to make to the Word data are performed more easily in Excel. The Paste Special command allows you to choose to paste text only without any kind of formatting from the source or the destination locations; it also provides options for pasting HTML, pictures, and hyperlinks. To complete these steps, you will be required to use the Data Files. Please contact your instructor for information about accessing the Data Files.

1

- Scroll as necessary to select cell A30.

Q&A Why did I select cell A30 in Excel?
You will paste the data to that location, out of the way, in order to manipulate it.

- Start Word and then open the Word document named, Support_EX_7_Store482.docx, from the Data Files.
- In the Word document, drag through all of the cells in columns 2 through 6 in the table to select the table cells without selecting the row headings in column 1.
- Press CTRL+C to copy the contents of those columns to the Office Clipboard (Figure 7–36).

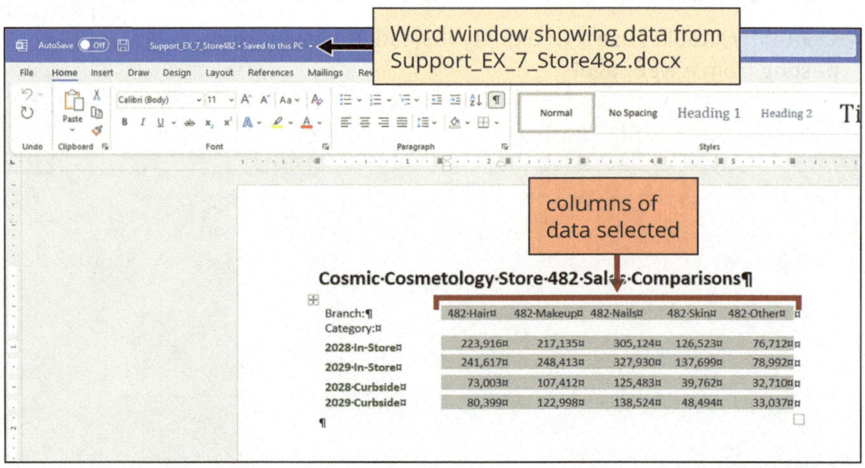

Figure 7–36

2

- Close Word and, if necessary, click the Excel app button on the taskbar to make Excel the active window.
- With cell A30 still selected, press CTRL+V to paste the data.
- Scroll as necessary to display the data, but do not select any other cells (Figure 7–37).

Q&A What if the line breaks in my pasted data differ from those shown in the figure?
Based on your screen size and resolution, the imported data may fit on one line within each column or break into two lines. This will not cause a problem with later steps.

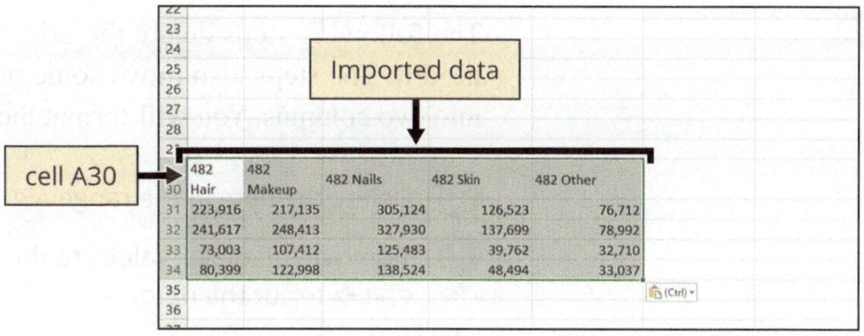

Figure 7–37

To Transpose Columns and Rows

Recall that the Paste gallery may display many different kinds of paste options, depending upon the data on the Office Clipboard and the paste location. When you copy and paste within Excel (rather than across apps), the Paste gallery displays many more options for pasting, such as pasting only the formulas, pasting only the values, pasting as a picture, and pasting transposed data, among others. The Transpose option in the Paste gallery automatically flips the rows and columns during the paste. In other words, the row headings become column headings or vice versa. All pasted data is switched as well. The following steps copy the data and paste it, transposed. **Why?** The original Word data had category titles across the top; the spreadsheet template expects titles down the left side.

1

- With the range A30:E34 still selected, press CTRL+C to copy the selection to the Office Clipboard.
- Scroll as necessary, and then select cell A20 to prepare for pasting the data to that location.
- Click the Paste arrow (Home tab | Clipboard group) to display the Paste gallery (Figure 7–38).
- **Experiment:** Using live preview, point to each of the paste options in the Paste gallery to display how each pasted format changes.

Q&A Why do I have to copy the data to the clipboard again?
The Transpose paste command is available only when Excel recognizes the cell format. You cannot transpose directly from copied Word tables.

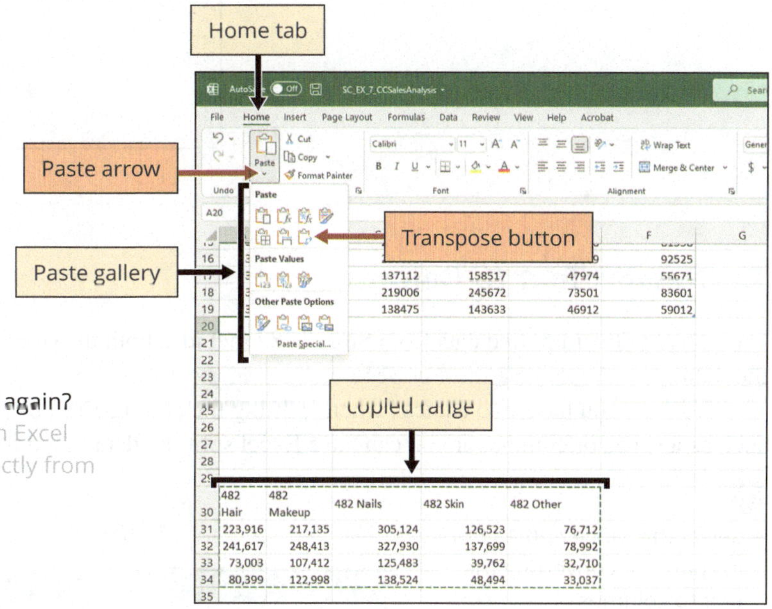

Figure 7–38

2

- Click the Transpose button in the Paste gallery to transpose and paste the copied cells to the range beginning with cell A20.
- If necessary, select cells A20:A24, and then click the Wrap Text button (Home tab | Alignment group) to turn off text wrapping (Figure 7–39).

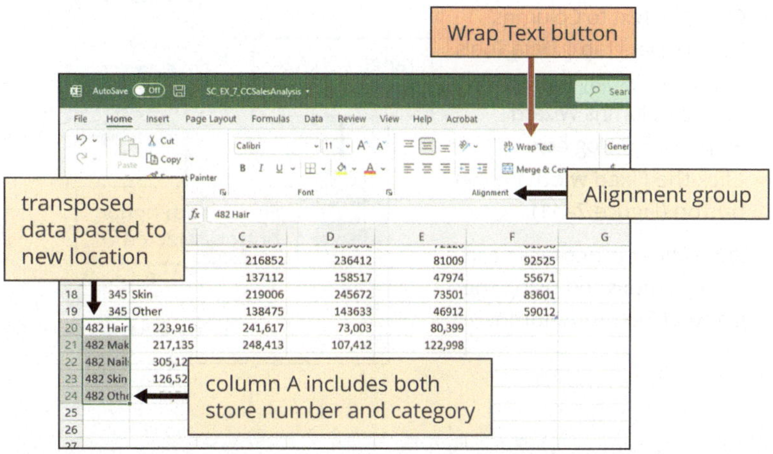

Figure 7–39

To Delete, Cut, and Paste Data

The following steps delete the original Word data from range A30:E34 because you no longer need it. The steps also move some of the transposed data to make room for splitting column A into two columns. You will format the data later in this module.

1. Delete the data in the range A30:E34.
2. To move the dollar values to the correct columns, select the range B20:E24 and then press CTRL+X to cut the data.
3. Select cell C20 and then press CTRL+V to paste the data (Figure 7–40).

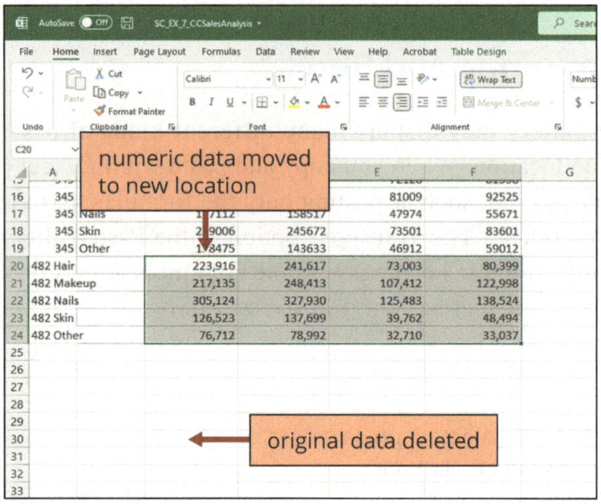

Figure 7–40

To Convert Text to Columns

Column A of the imported data from Store #482 includes both the store and category in the same cell. The following steps split the data. **Why?** The data must be separated using the Excel 'Text to Columns' command so that the category information is in column B. You have two choices when splitting the column. You can have Excel split the data based on a specific character, such as a space or comma, or you can have Excel split the data based on a certain number of characters or fixed width.

1.
- Select the range A20:A24 to prepare for converting the text to columns.
- Display the Data tab.
- Click the 'Text to Columns' button (Data tab | Data Tools group) to display the Convert Text to Columns Wizard - Step 1 of 3 dialog box.
- Click the Fixed width option button (Figure 7–41).

Q&A What other tasks can be accomplished using the Convert Text to Columns Wizard?

With the Delimited option, you can split the data into separate columns by specifying a break at a specific character.

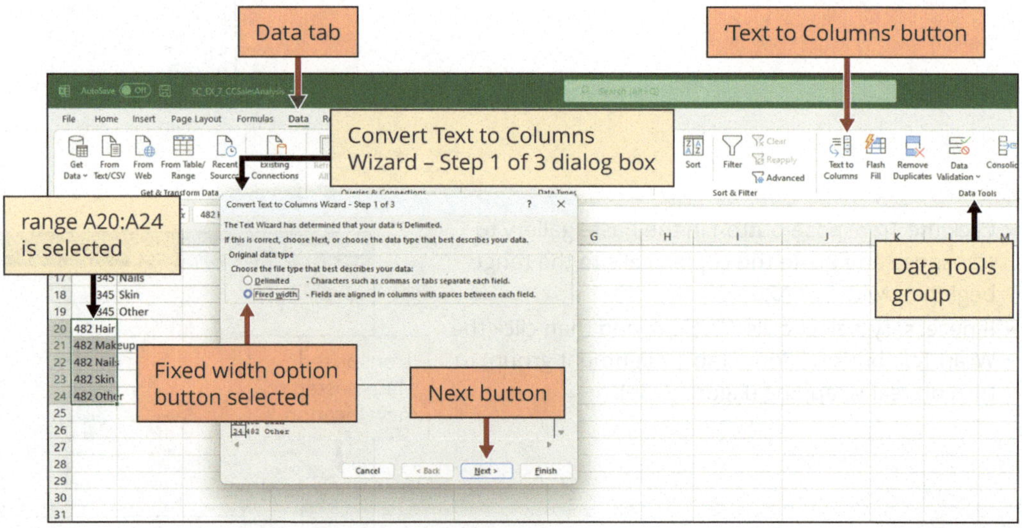

Figure 7–41

2

- Click the Next button (Convert Text to Columns Wizard - Step 1 of 3 dialog box) to accept a fixed width column and to display the Convert Text to Columns Wizard - Step 2 of 3 dialog box (Figure 7–42).
- **Experiment:** Click the Next button to view options related to formatting or skipping parts of the data before splitting it. Do not make any changes.

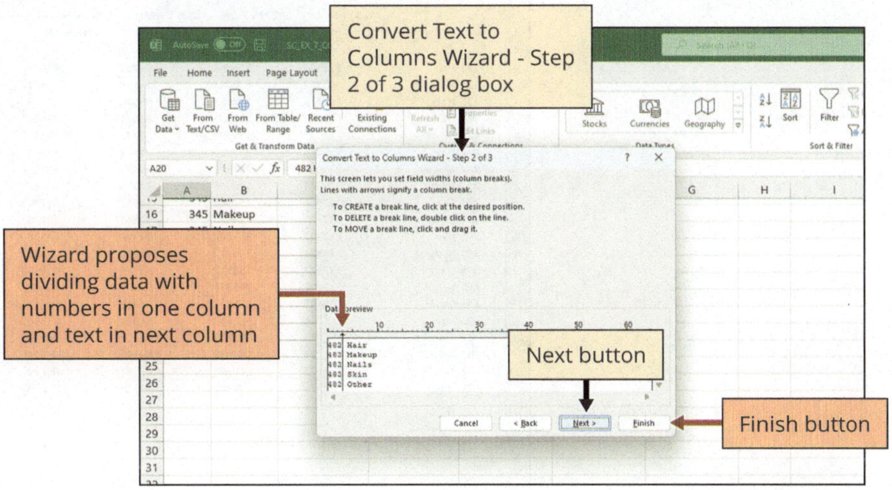

Figure 7–42

3

- Click the Finish button (Convert Text to Columns Wizard - Step 2 of 3 dialog box) to close the dialog box. If Excel displays a dialog box, click the Yes button to separate the data in column A into two columns (Figure 7–43).
- If necessary, adjust column widths approximately match those shown in the figure.

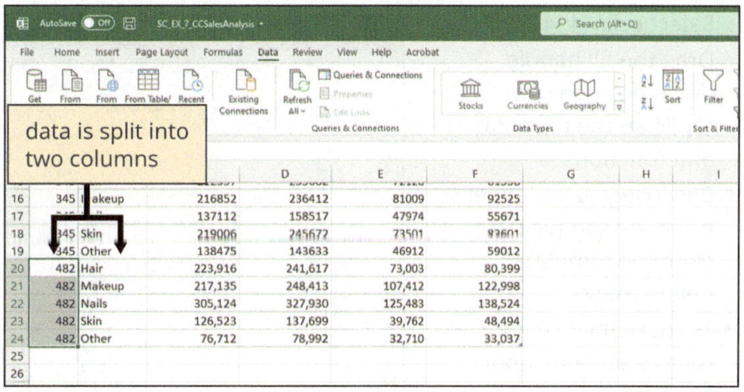

Figure 7–43

To Replicate Formulas

When you opened the workbook derived from the template, it contained a worksheet title, headings for each column, and a formula to calculate the percentage increase or decrease from 2028 to 2029. The formula and functions in cells G4, I4, and J4 must be copied or filled to complete the calculations. Some spreadsheet specialists refer to copying formulas as **replication**. You often replicate formulas after completing an import. **Why?** Usually, the total number of records to be imported is unknown when you first begin a workbook.

The following steps use the fill handle to replicate the formulas. You also will perform some final formatting edits.

1

- Select the location of the formula you wish to replicate (in this case, cell G4).
- Drag the fill handle down through the end of the data (in this case, row 24) to replicate the formula (Figure 7–44).

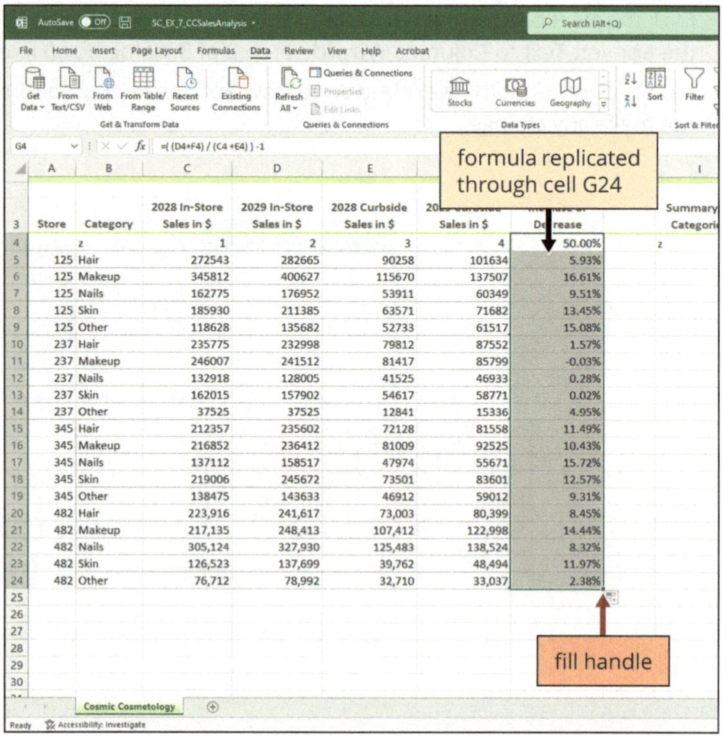

Figure 7–44

2

- Select cells I4:J4.
- Drag the fill handle down through row 9 to replicate the formulas and functions.
- Because you no longer need the sample data from the template, delete row 4.
- To make the category totals stand out, apply the Times New Roman font to cells J4:J8 and bold the values, and then click on cell J10 (Figure 7–45).

Q&A Why did I stop the replication of the summary at row 9?

Only five categories are used for the stores; however, you can replicate further if more categories are added.

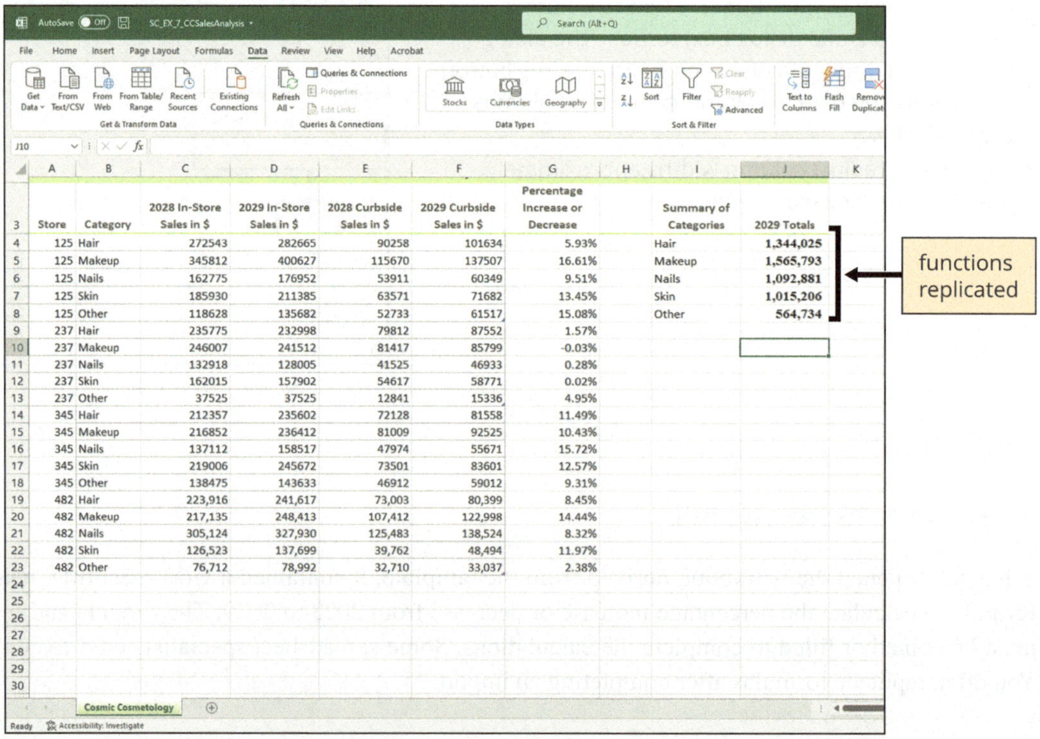

Figure 7–45

3

- Click the Save button (Quick Access Toolbar) to save the workbook with the same name in the same location.

Break Point: If you want to take a break, this is a good place to do so. You can exit Excel now. To resume later, start Excel, open the file called SC_EX_7_CCSalesAnalysis, and continue following the steps from this location forward.

Using the Quick Analysis Gallery

Recall that in a previous module you used the status bar to produce a basic analysis of selected data. Another tool for analyzing data quickly is the Quick Analysis gallery. Quick Analysis first appears as a button below and to the right of selected data. When you click the button, Excel displays the Quick Analysis gallery (Figure 7–46).

Each tab at the top of the gallery displays its own set of buttons to help you complete a task easily. For example, notice in Figure 7–46 that the Formatting tab displays conditional formatting options. The tabs always apply to the selected area of the worksheet. In addition, the Quick Analysis gallery uses live preview—in other words, you can preview how the feature will affect your data by pointing to the button in the gallery.

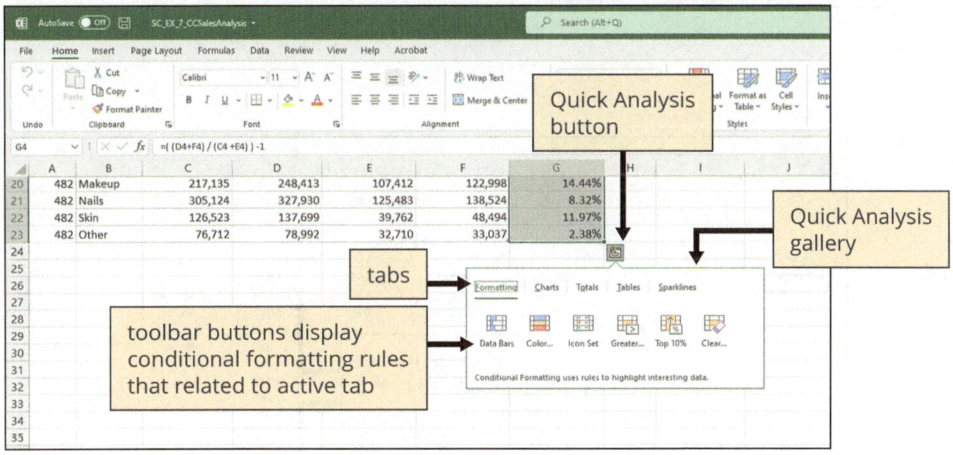

Figure 7–46

The Totals tab in the Quick Analysis toolbar can be used to create totals quickly, as long as none of the data is in tables. When you click Totals, Excel displays a variety of formulas and functions as thumbnails, including SUM, AVERAGE, and COUNT. Pointing to any thumbnail gives you a live preview of the answer. Clicking the thumbnail inserts the formula into the worksheet.

To Format Using the Quick Analysis Gallery

The following steps use the Quick Analysis gallery to format the top 10% of column G, the percentage increase or decrease in sales. **Why?** The company executives want to know the stores and categories with the highest increase in sales. Formatting using the Quick Analysis gallery is much faster than using the ribbon to apply conditional formatting.

1

- Select the range you want to analyze, in this case, G4:G23.
- Click the Quick Analysis button to display the Quick Analysis gallery.
- If necessary, click the Formatting tab to display the Quick Analysis gallery formatting options (Figure 7–47).
- **Experiment:** Point to each of the buttons on the Quick Analysis gallery to display a live preview.

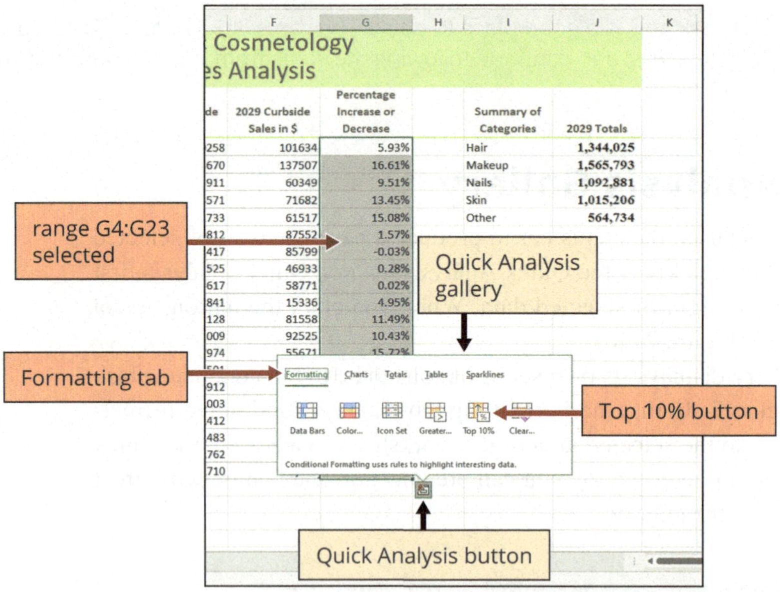

Figure 7–47

2

- Click the Top 10% button (Quick Analysis gallery).
- Click outside the selection and scroll as necessary to display the cells highlighted by the conditional formatting (Figure 7–48).

Q&A Why did Excel highlight the numbers in light red?

The default value for conditional formatting is light red.

- **Experiment:** Scroll through the list to display the other options.

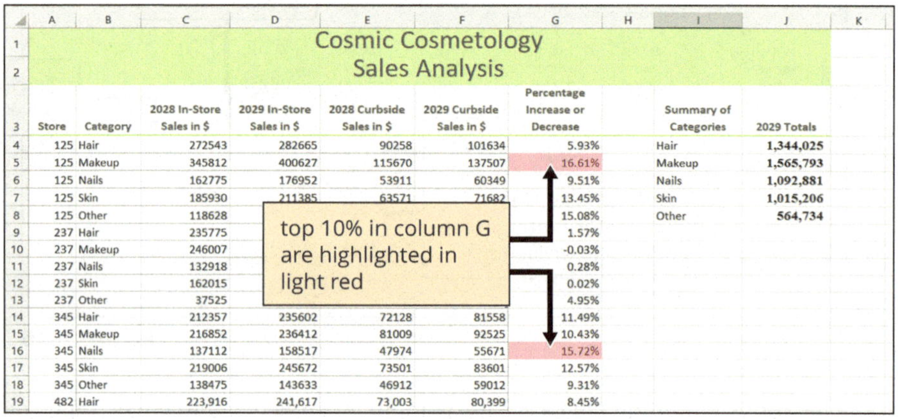

Figure 7–48

3

- Click cell I24. Type **Shaded cells indicate top 10%** and then press ENTER to create a legend for the formatting.
- Drag through cells I24:J24 and display the Home tab.
- Click the Fill Color arrow (Home tab | Font Group) and then choose More Colors from the menu. In the Colors dialog box, click the Custom tab, if not already selected. Set the Red, Green, and Blue values to the following: Red: 255, Green: 199, and Blue: 206. The Hex value will then be #FFC7CE. Click OK to accept the value and close the Colors dialog box. This custom fill color will match the Light Red color of the top 10% values highlighted.
- Click outside the selection to view the formatting (Figure 7–49).

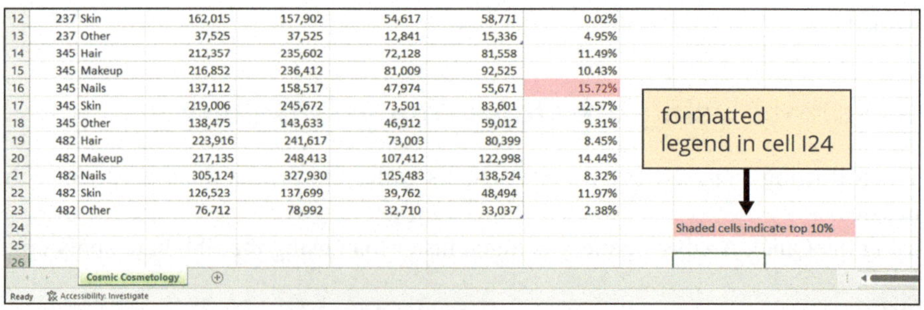

Figure 7–49

To Total Data

The following steps total the sales data from the four stores. **Why?** When analyzing sales, companies routinely want to examine grand totals for all locations.

1

- Click cell C24. Type **=sum(c4:c23)** and then click the ENTER button.
- Drag the fill handle to the right, to replicate the totals for columns D through F (Figure 7–50).

Q&A Could I use the Quick Analysis Gallery to create the totals?

No. The Quick Analysis button will not appear because the data crosses multiple table imports.

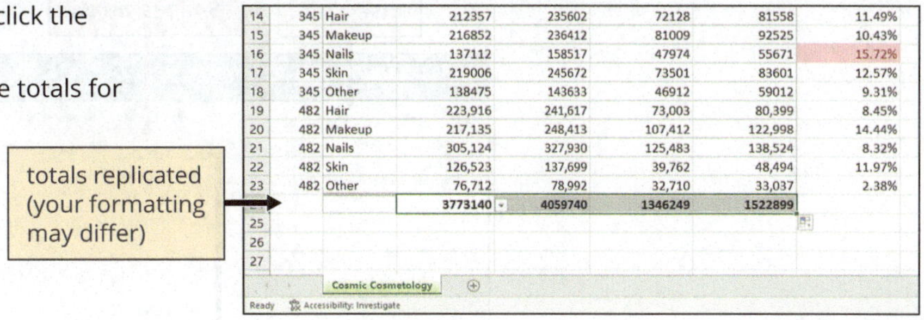

Figure 7–50

2

- Select cell A24 and then type **Totals** to enter a row heading.
- Replicate cell G23 down to G24 to indicate the total percentage increase or decrease.

3

- Add the Comma Style formatting with no decimal places to the sales figures in columns C:F (Figure 7–51).

Q&A What if the pasted Word values don't align exactly with the other worksheet values?

You can clear the formatting from the pasted Word values using the Clear Formats button (Home tab | Editing group | Clear arrow) and reapply the Comma Style.

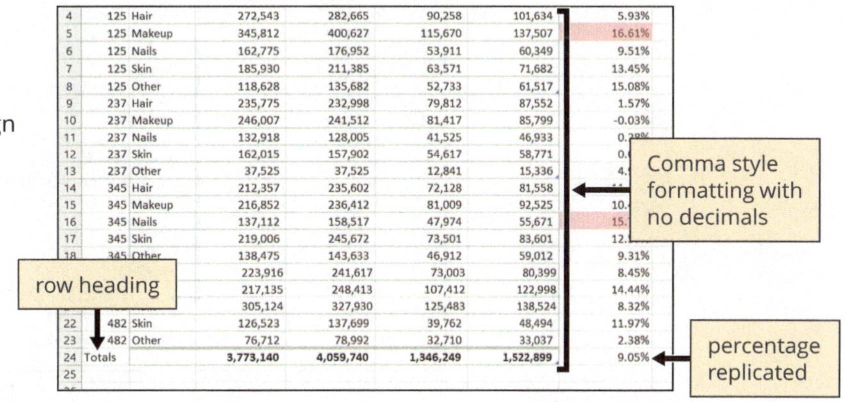

Figure 7–51

Creating and Formatting a Shape

Excel includes more than 150 shapes that you can use to create, graphics, banners, illustrations, logos, and other ornamental objects. A **shape** is a drawing object, such as a rectangle, oval, triangle, line, or block arrow. You can change the color and weight of shape outlines and can apply fill effects, shadows, reflections, glows, pictures, and other special effects to shapes. Adding text, bullets, or numbering to shapes increases the graphic possibilities. You even can edit points, which creates sizing handles along the edge to convert your shape into something new and unique.

To Add a Shape to a Worksheet

The following steps add a shape to the worksheet. In this case, you will add the shape of a moon to the heading of the worksheet, just to the left of the Cosmic Cosmetology Sales Analysis heading in column D occupying rows 1 and 2. **Why?** Cosmic Cosmetology often uses space-related imagery in its advertising, so adding a moon shape to the spreadsheet supports a sense of continuity across the company's materials.

1

- Display the Insert tab.
- Click the 'Shapes' button arrow (Insert tab | Illustrations group) to display the Shapes menu listing all of the available shapes (Figure 7–52).

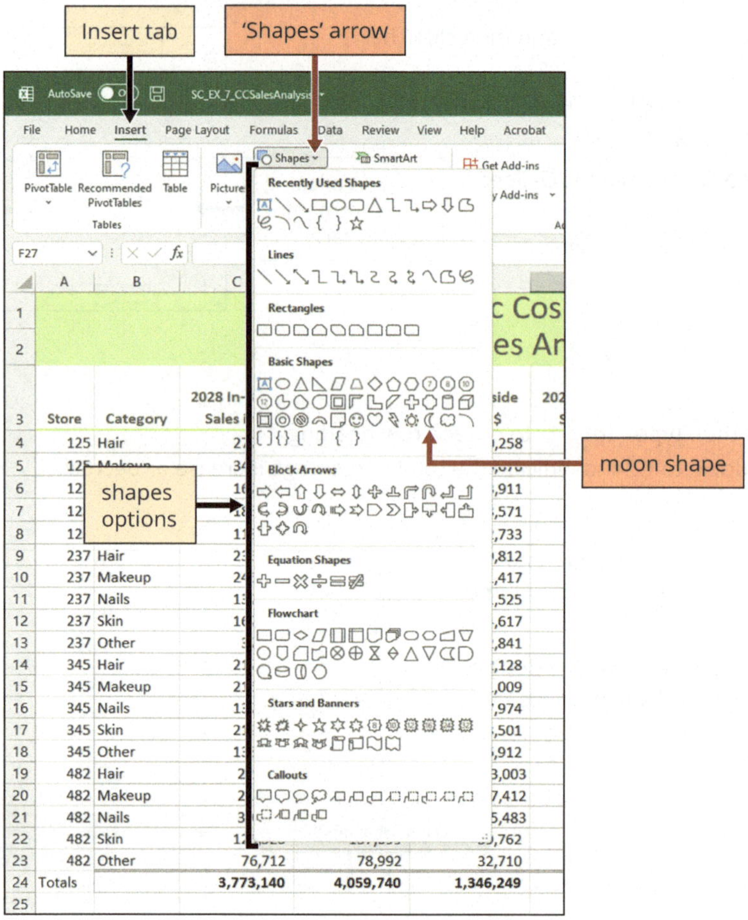

Figure 7–52

2

- Click on the Moon shape located in the Basic Shapes section. Notice that your cursor changes to a thin crosshair pointer.
- Move the cursor near the top left of cell D1 (Figure 7–53), and then click and drag to near the bottom right of cell D2, without infringing upon the Cosmic Cosmetology worksheet title.

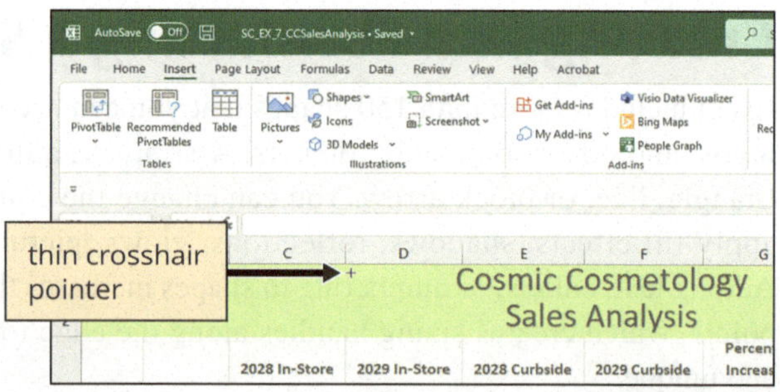

Figure 7–53

Q&A What if the moon shape overlaps with the heading?
Should the moon shape overlap with the heading, simply decrease the size of the Moon shape by dragging the bottom right handle to the left until it no longer overlaps with the heading.

What if the shape is a different color than the one pictured?
Should the moon color be different than the one pictured, with the shape still selected, click 'Colored Fill - Green, Accent 1' in the Quick Styles gallery (Shape Format tab | Shapes Style group).

How to Format a Shape

Once a shape has been added to the spreadsheet, you can format the shape by setting various attributes. You will now format the moon shape. **Why?** Making formatting changes allows you to fine-tune the look of a shape.

1

- With the moon shape selected, right-click the shape to display the shortcut menu (Figure 7–54).

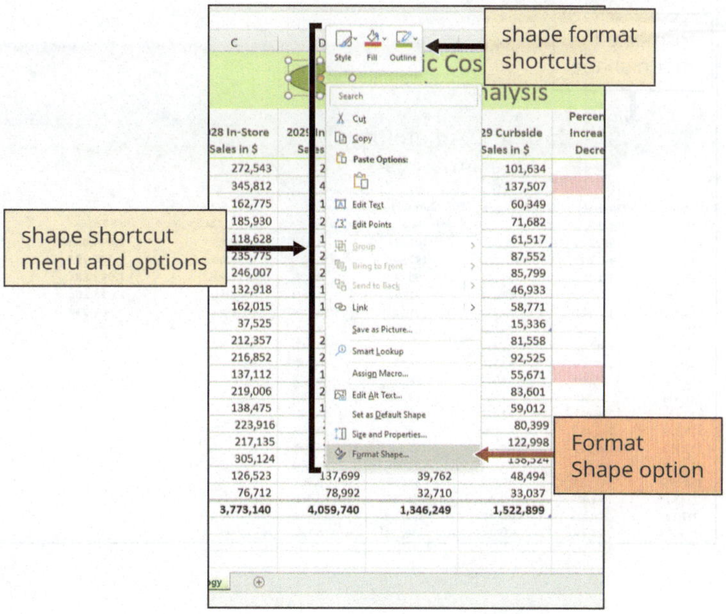

Figure 7–54

2

- Click the Format Shape option from the shortcut menu. The Format Shape task pane appears on the right side of the window, displaying Shape Options. The three icons below the Shape Options heading display three sheets: Fill & Line on the left, Effects in the middle, and Size & Properties on the right.
- If necessary, click the Fill & Line button to display the Fill & Line sheet, then click to expand both the Fill and Line options.
- In the expanded Line options, click Gradient line. Notice that the outline of the moon shape is now changed from a solid line to one containing a gradient (Figure 7–55).

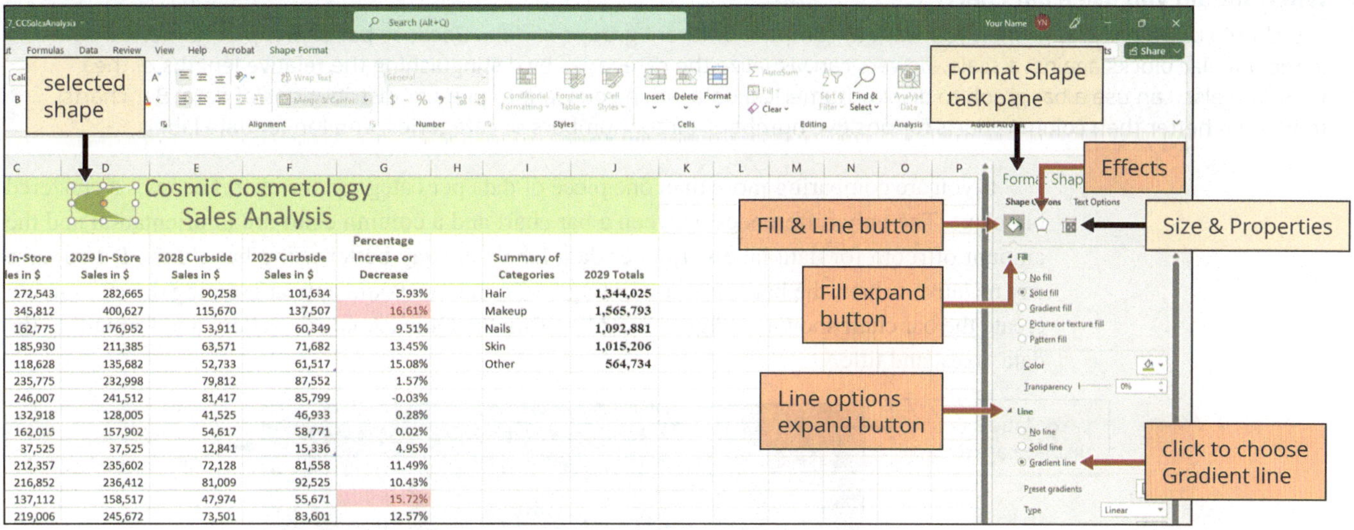

Figure 7–55

3

- Click the Effects button, just to the right of the Fill & Line button. Click to expand the Shadow options. These options allow you to set the color of the shadow, the degree of transparency, the size, and so on. You can also choose a Preset, which is a pre-designed combination of shadow settings.
- Click the Presets arrow to display the available presets, scroll to the Inner area, then click the Inside: Top Left button to add an inside top left shadow effect to the moon shape (Figure 7–56).
- Close the Format Shape task pane and then click in an empty cell to deselect the moon shape.
- Click the Save button (Quick Access Toolbar) to save the workbook with the same name in the same location.

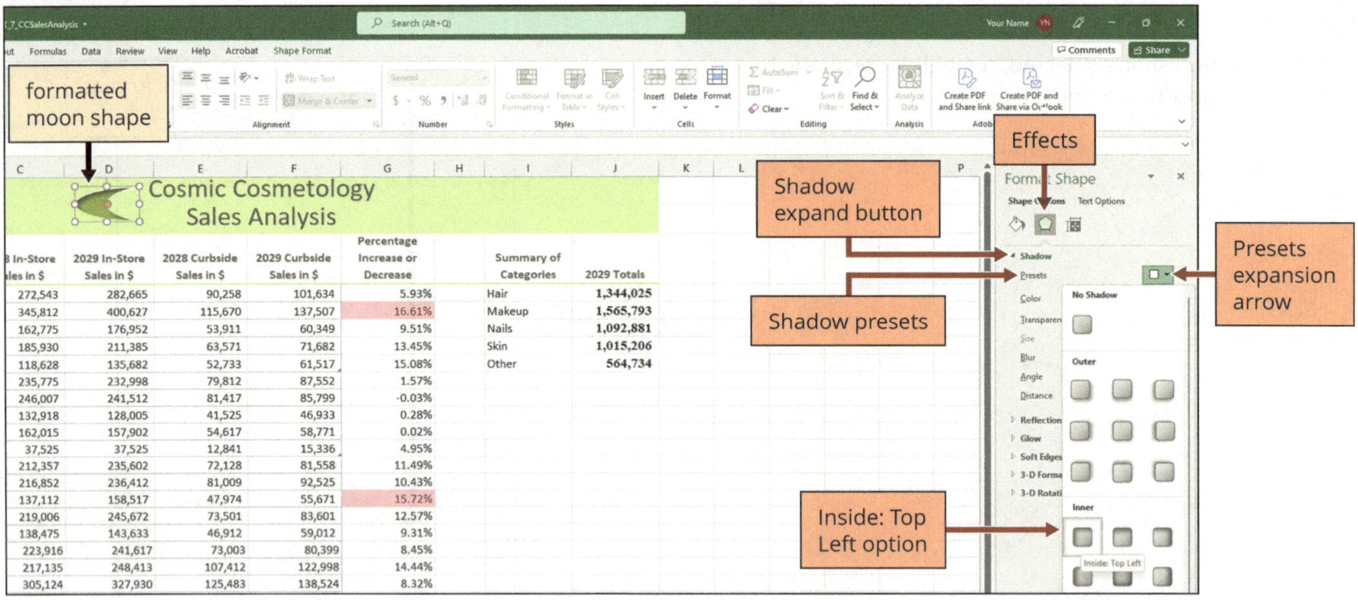

Figure 7–56

Inserting a Bar Chart

The requirements document shown in Figure 7–2 specifies that the workbook should include a bar chart, sometimes called a bar graph. A bar chart uses parallel, horizontal bars of varying lengths to measure and compare categories of data or amounts, such as sales, counts, or rates. The bars can be all one color, or each bar may be a different color.

Consider This

When should you use a bar chart?

You should use a bar graph when you want to compare different groups of data. Because bar charts plot numerical data in rectangular blocks against a scale, viewers can visualize the categories by distinguishing the relative lengths of the bars. You also can use a bar graph to display numerical data when you want to present distributions of data. Bar charts tend to be better than column charts for positive numbers, larger numbers of categories, and longer data labels.

If you are comparing more than one piece of data per category, the chart becomes a clustered bar chart. The only differences between a bar chart and a column chart are in orientation and the amount of room for data labels. Longer data labels display better using bar charts. If you have any negative values, the bars appear pointing left; columns would appear pointing down. You will create the bar chart shown in Figure 7–57 by using the Quick Analysis gallery and formatting the data, axes, and title.

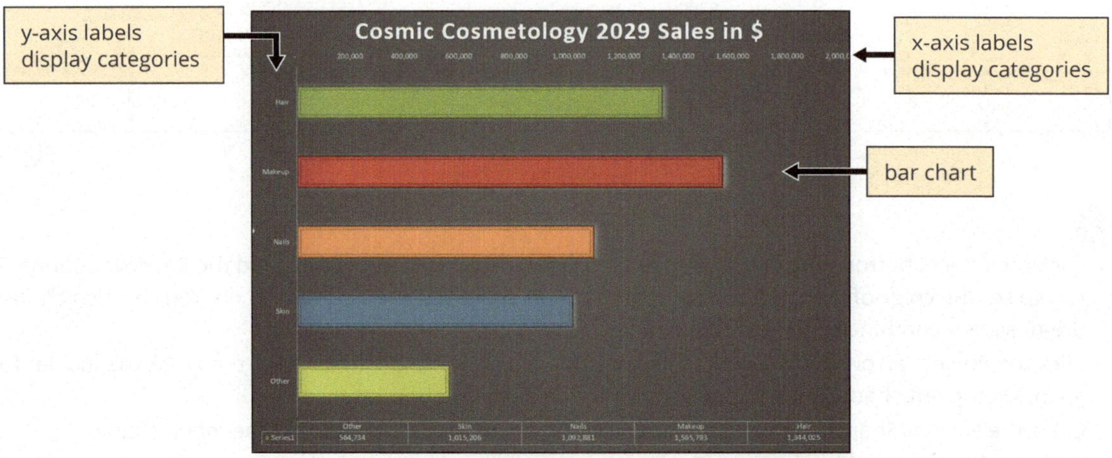

Figure 7–57

To Insert a Chart Using the Quick Analysis Gallery

The following steps insert a chart using the Quick Analysis gallery. **Why?** The Quick Analysis gallery is near the data and provides an easy way to access charts. The Quick Analysis gallery recommends charts that match the data.

1

- Select the range I4:J8 to select the data to include in the chart.
- Click the Quick Analysis button to display the Quick Analysis gallery.
- Click the Charts tab to display the buttons related to working with charts in the gallery (Figure 7–58).

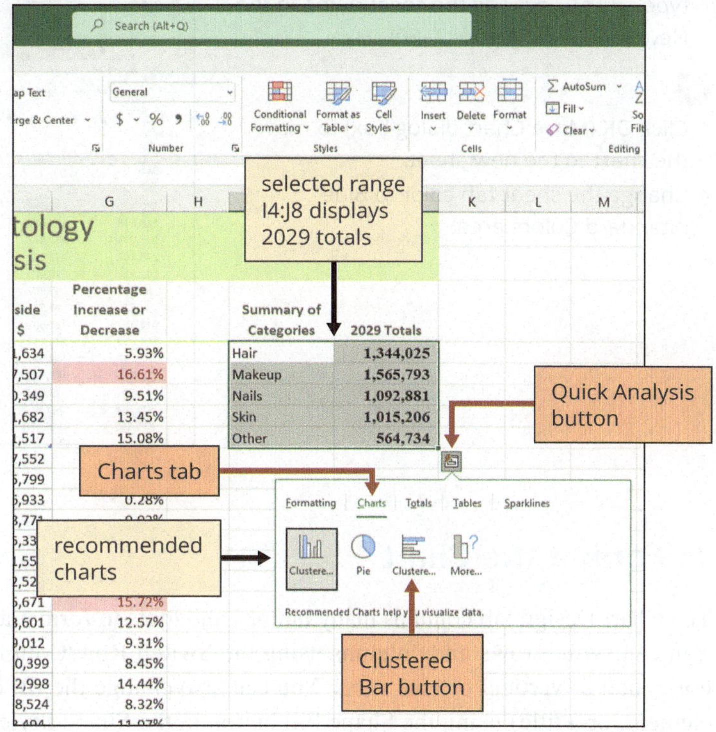

Figure 7–58

2

- Click the Clustered Bar button (Quick Analysis gallery) to insert the chart (Figure 7–59).

Q&A Why are only three charts displayed?
Excel lists the charts that it recommends for your data. You can click the More Charts button (Quick Analysis gallery) to open the Insert Chart dialog box and choose another chart style.

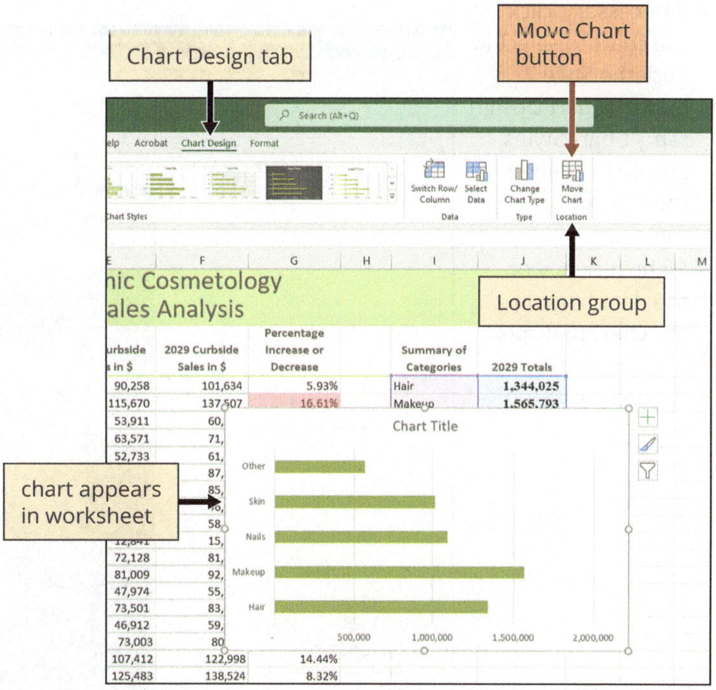

Figure 7–59

3

- Click the Move Chart button (Chart Design tab | Location group) to display the Move Chart dialog box.
- Click the New sheet option button and then type **Bar Chart** as the sheet name in the New sheet box (Figure 7–60).

4

- Click OK (Move Chart dialog box) to move the chart to the new sheet.
- Change the sheet tab color to Blue (Standard Colors area).

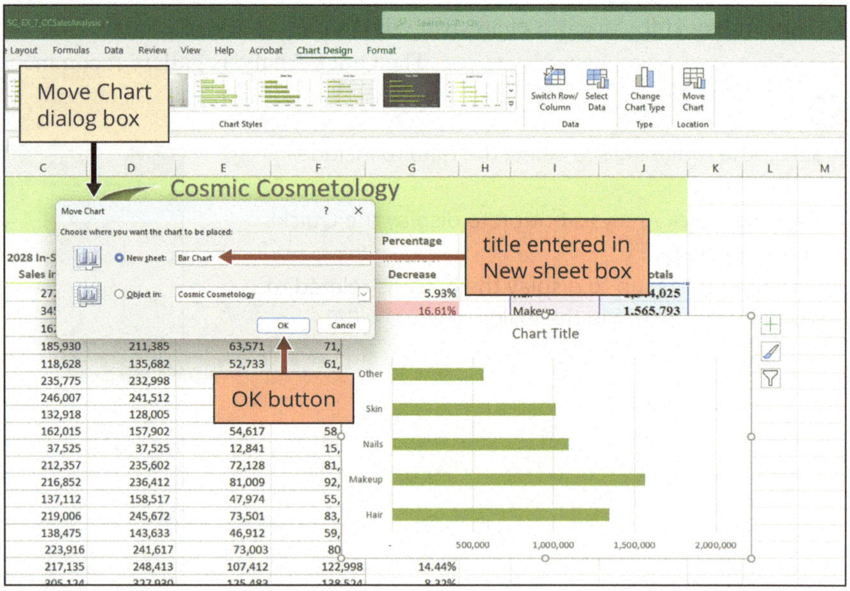

Figure 7–60

To Format the Chart

The Chart Design tab contains many buttons and tools to format a chart, including legends, styles, outlines, and the data bars. You can switch rows and columns using the Switch Row/Column button in the Data group, which changes the bars from horizontal to vertical or vice versa. You can also change the fill of any chart element (such as its background, a data series element, or a title) using the Shape Fill button in the Shape Styles group. The fill can be a color or a picture. The following steps change the style of the chart, as well as the color, bevel, and shadow of all the category bars, using the Format Data Series command on the shortcut menu. **Why?** You always should customize a chart with formatting that helps emphasize the data and the concept you are trying to portray.

1

- If necessary, click the chart to select it. Click the Style 7 option (Chart Design tab | Chart Styles group) to change the style of the chart.
- Right-click any of the data bars on the chart to display the shortcut menu (Figure 7–61).

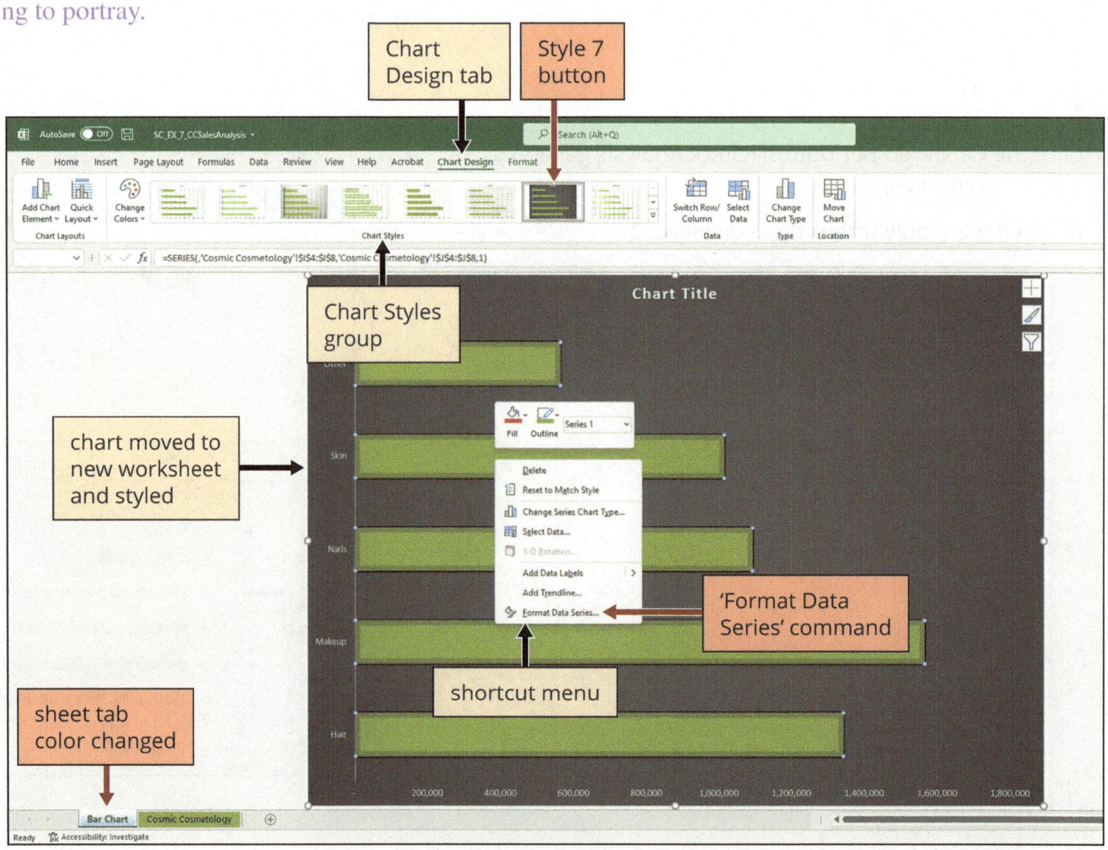

Figure 7–61

2

- Click 'Format Data Series' on the shortcut menu to display the Format Data Series pane.
- Click the 'Fill & Line' button (Format Data Series pane) to display the Fill & Line sheet.
- If necessary, display the Fill settings and then click the 'Vary colors by point' check box to display the bars in various colors (Figure 7–62).

- **Experiment:** Click the Series Options button (Format Data Series pane) to display the settings. Notice that you can set the Series Overlap (for clustered charts) and the Gap Width (the interval between bars).

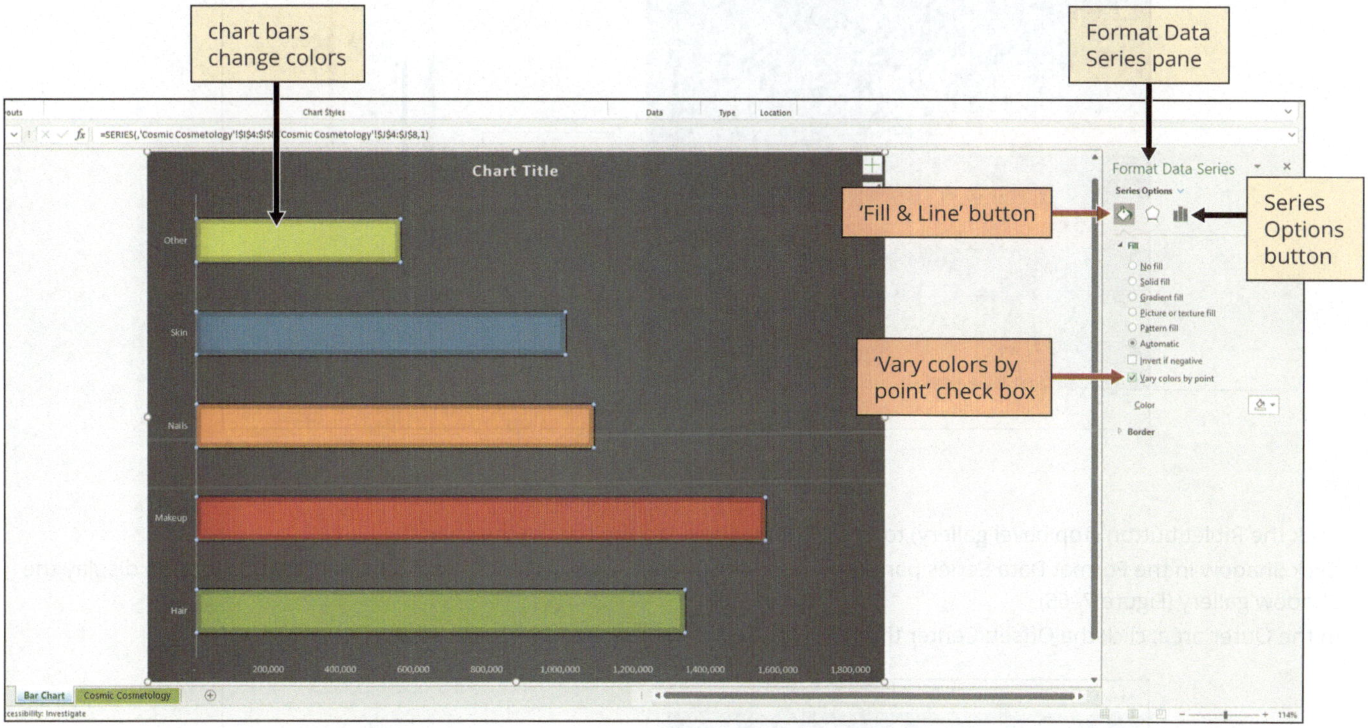

Figure 7–62

3

- Click the Effects button to display the Effects sheet. If necessary, display the 3-D Format settings (Figure 7–63).

Q&A What kinds of effects can I change on the Effects sheet?

You can change the shadow, glow, edges, bevel, and 3-D format of the bars.

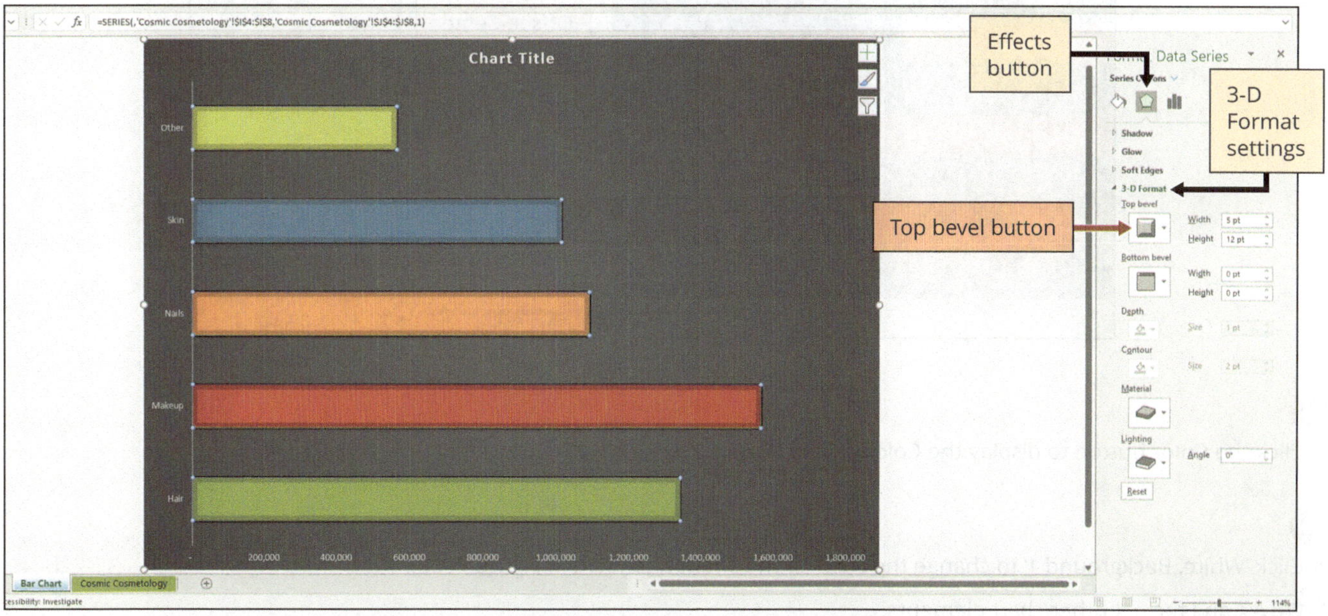

Figure 7–63

4

- Click the Top bevel button to display the Top bevel gallery (Figure 7–64).

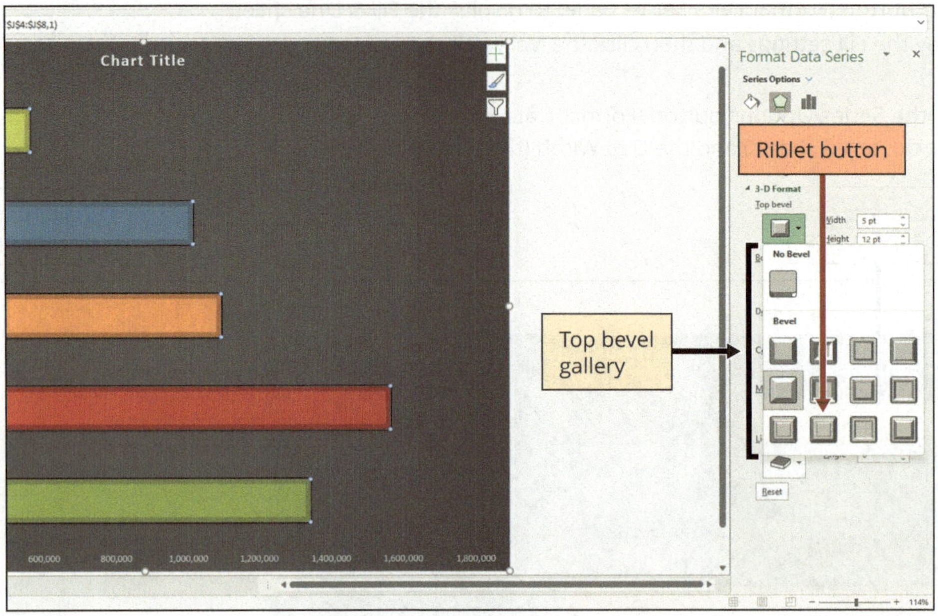

Figure 7–64

5

- Click the Riblet button (Top bevel gallery) to apply a Riblet bevel to the bars in the chart.
- Click Shadow in the Format Data Series pane to expand the Shadow options, and then click the Presets button to display the Shadow gallery (Figure 7–65).
- In the Outer area, click the Offset: Center thumbnail to select a placement for the shadow.

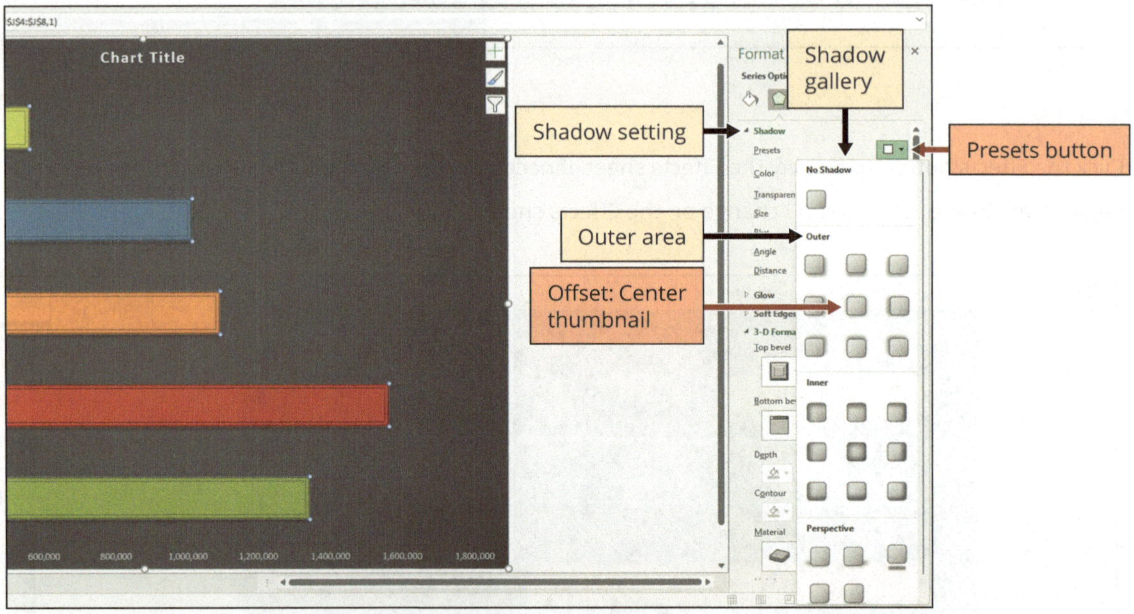

Figure 7–65

6

- Click the Color button to display the Color gallery (Figure 7–66).

7

- Click 'White, Background 1' to change the color of the shadow (shown in Figure 7–67).

Q&A Can I format other chart elements?
Yes, select the chart element and then use the Format tab to apply shape styles or WordArt styles.

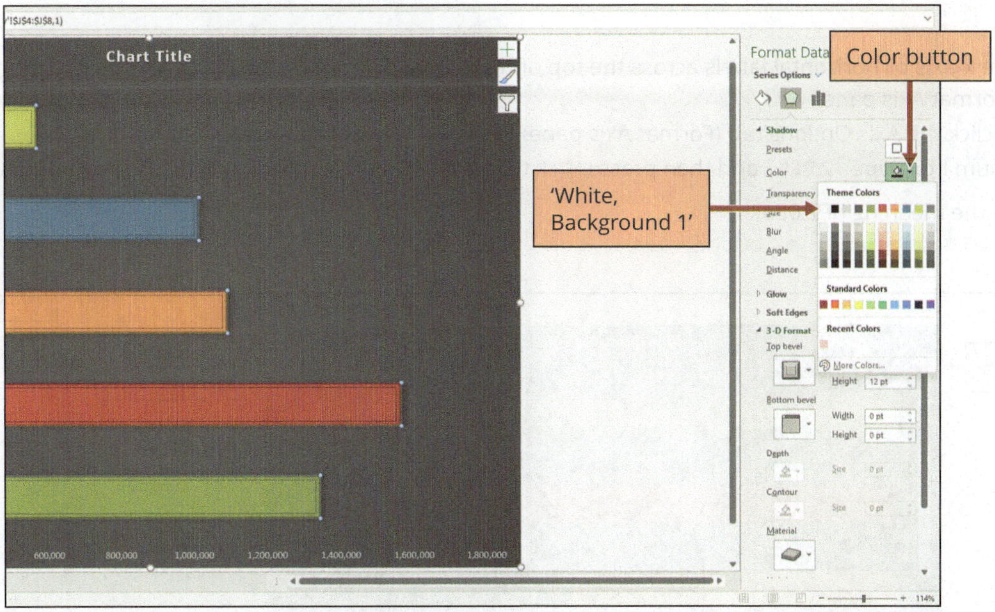

Figure 7–66

To Format Axis Options

The following steps format the y-axis and x-axis of the clustered bar chart. You also will change the order of the categories. **Why?** Changing the order will put the minor category of Other at the bottom of the chart. You also will lengthen the bars by changing the maximum value on the x-axis.

1

- Right-click the y-axis or vertical category labels and then click Format Axis on the shortcut menu to display the Format Axis pane.
- If necessary, click the Axis Options button (Format Axis pane) to display the sheet.
- In the Axis position area, click the 'Categories in reverse order' check box (Figure 7–67).

Q&A What other options can I set using the Format Axis pane?

You can change how tick marks, labels, and numbers display. On the Size & Properties tab, you can set the alignment, text direction, and margins of the axes. The Fill & Line tab and the Effects tab are similar to the Format Data Series pane that you used earlier.

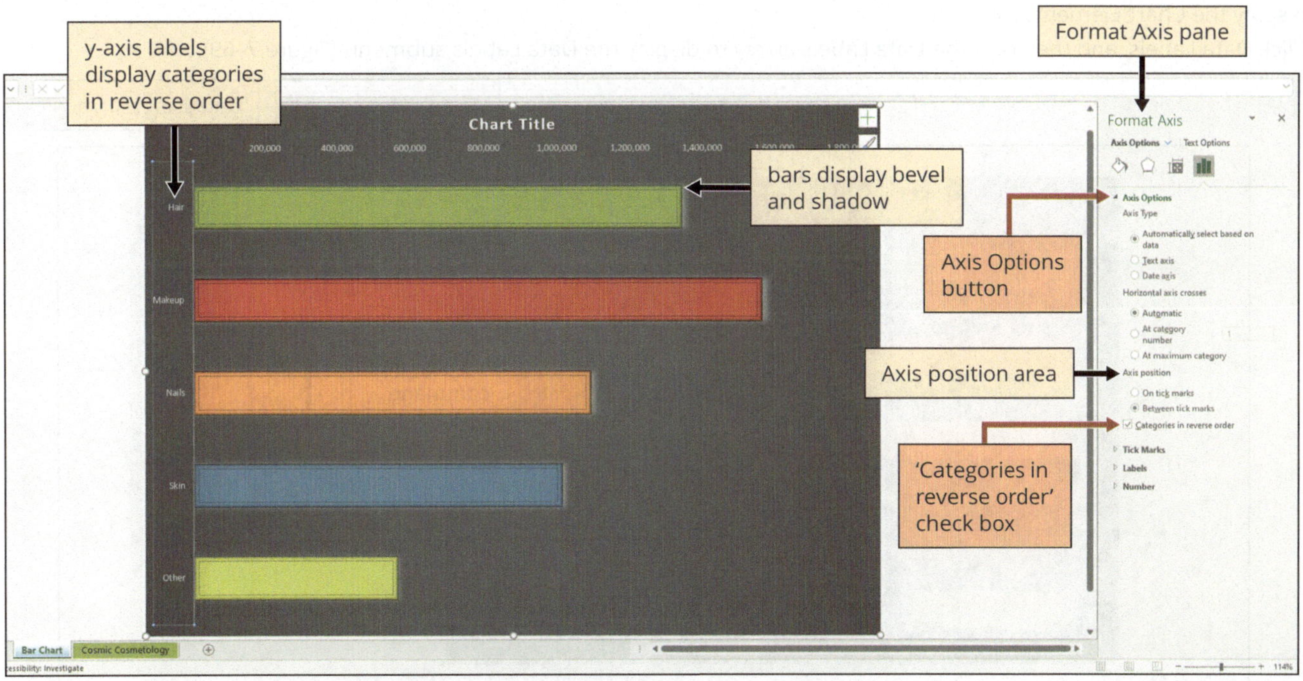

Figure 7–67

2

- Right-click the x-axis or horizontal labels across the top of the chart and then click Format Axis on the shortcut menu to display the Format Axis pane.
- If necessary, click the Axis Options tab (Format Axis pane) to display the Bounds area.
- In the Maximum box, type **2.0E6** and then press ENTER to indicate that two million will be the maximum value (Figure 7–68).

Q&A What is the meaning of 2.0E6?

The entry 2.0E6 is the scientific notation for two million.

Figure 7–68

To Add Data Labels

The following steps add data labels to the bars. **Why?** Data labels will show viewers the exact value for each category, rather than having them estimate based on the x-axis.

1

- Click the Chart Elements button, which displays as a plus sign when you point to the upper-right corner of the chart, to display the Chart Elements list.
- Click Data Labels, and then click the Data Labels arrow to display the Data Labels submenu (Figure 7–69).

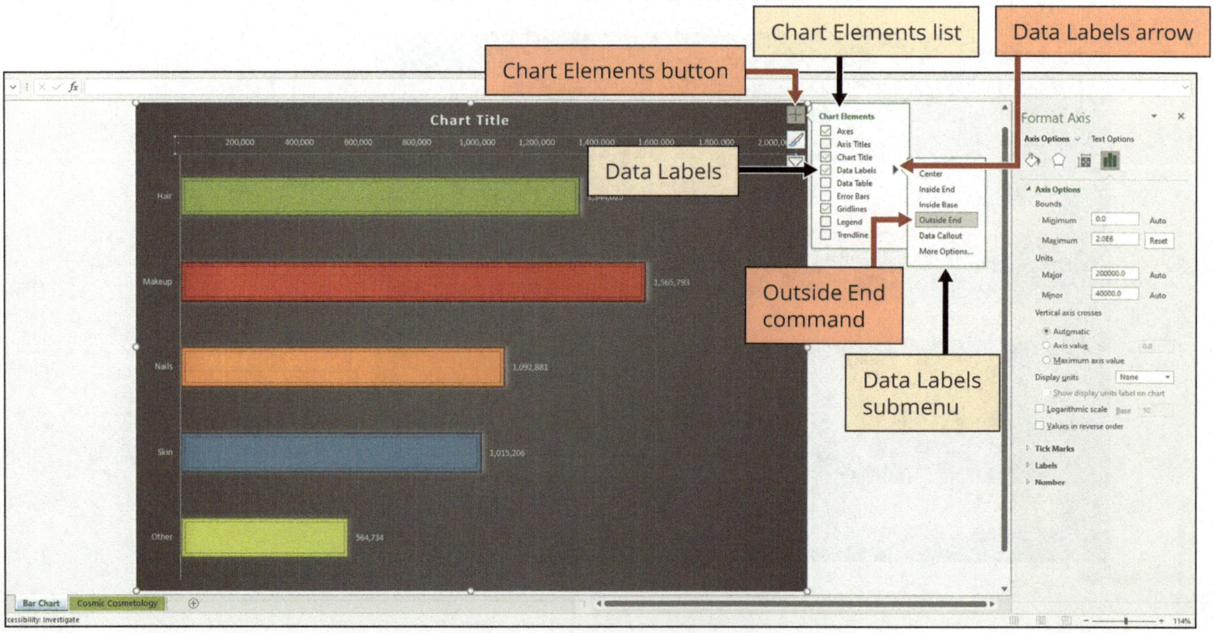

Figure 7–69

2

- Click Outside End (Figure 7–70).

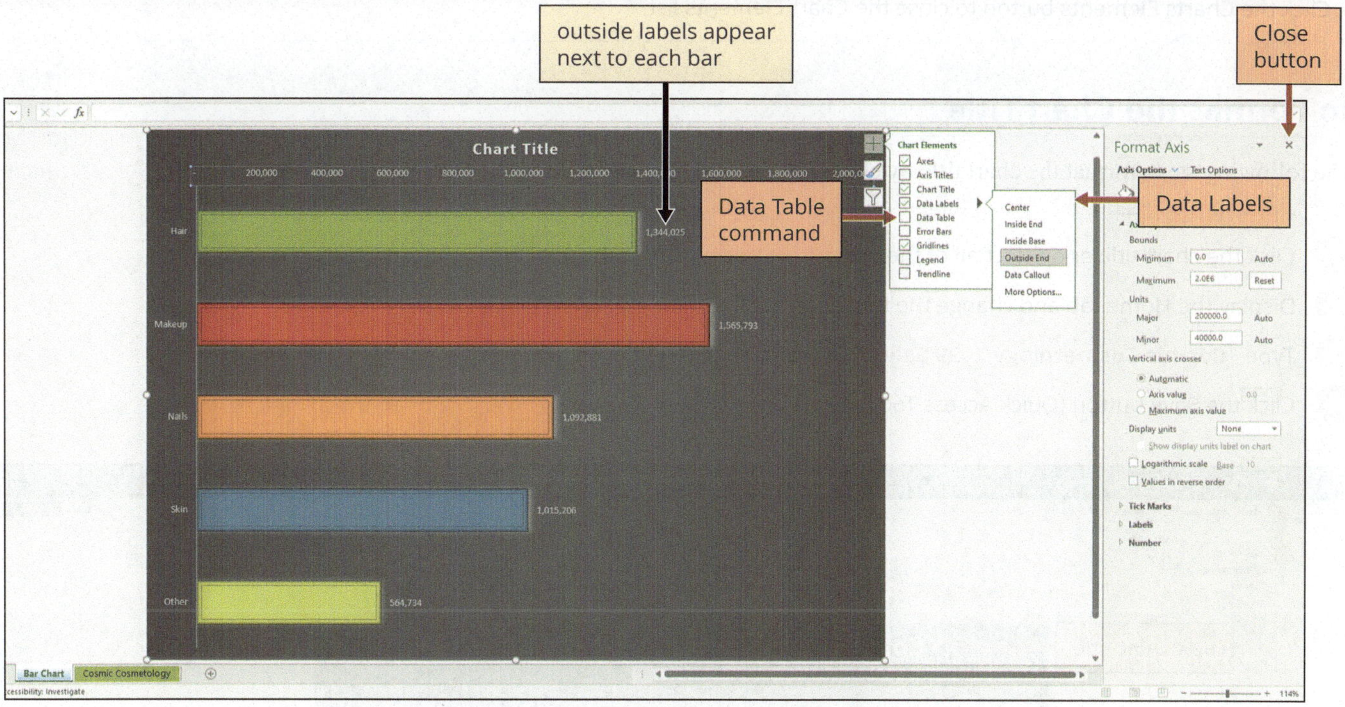

Figure 7–70

To Display a Data Table

In Excel, you can add a data table to a chart. A **data table** is a chart element that displays the data as a grid below the chart itself. Data tables are available for line charts, area charts, column charts, or bar charts. You can format a data table using fills, borders, legends, and other text effects. In the following step, you will turn off data labels and display a data table. Why? Displaying the data both ways is repetitive and therefore unnecessary.

1

- In the Chart Elements list, click Data Labels again to turn off the feature.
- Click Data Table to display the data table below the chart (Figure 7–71).

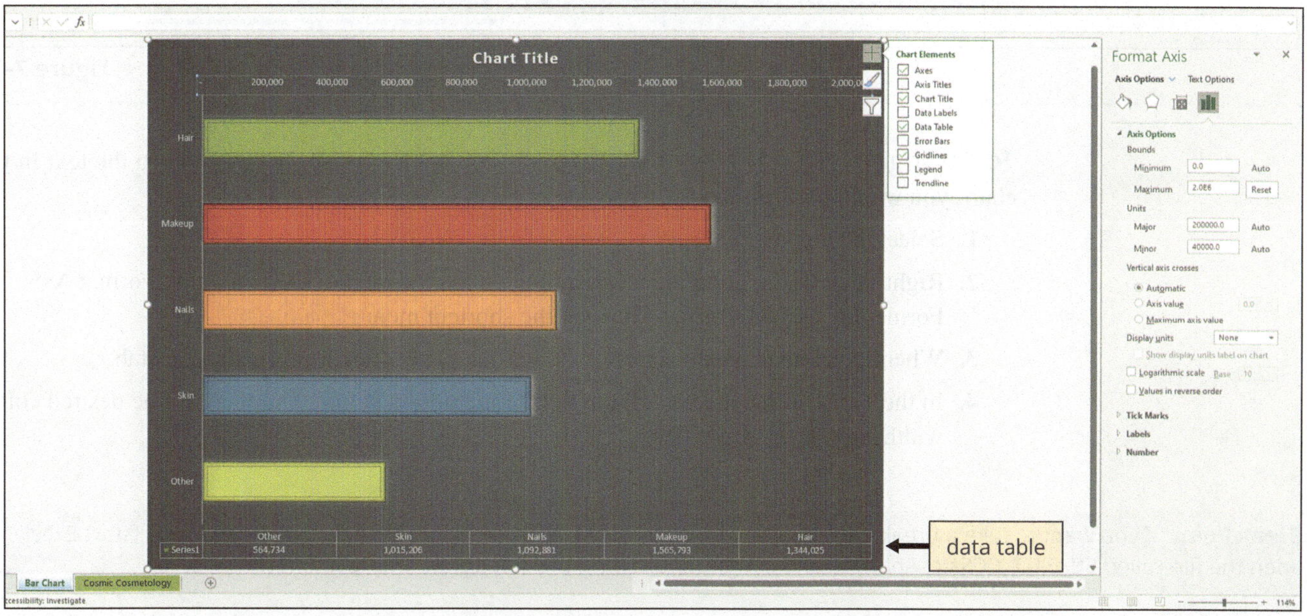

Figure 7–71

2

- Close the Format Axis pane.
- Click the Charts Elements button to close the Chart Elements list.

To Format the Chart Title

The following steps format the chart title by changing the font size and editing the text. **Why?** Adding a meaningful, prominent title will help readers quickly grasp the purpose of the chart.

1. Click the chart title and select all of the text.
2. Display the Home tab and change the font size to 28.
3. Type **Cosmic Cosmetology 2029 Sales in $** to change the title (Figure 7–72).
4. Click the Save button (Quick Access Toolbar).

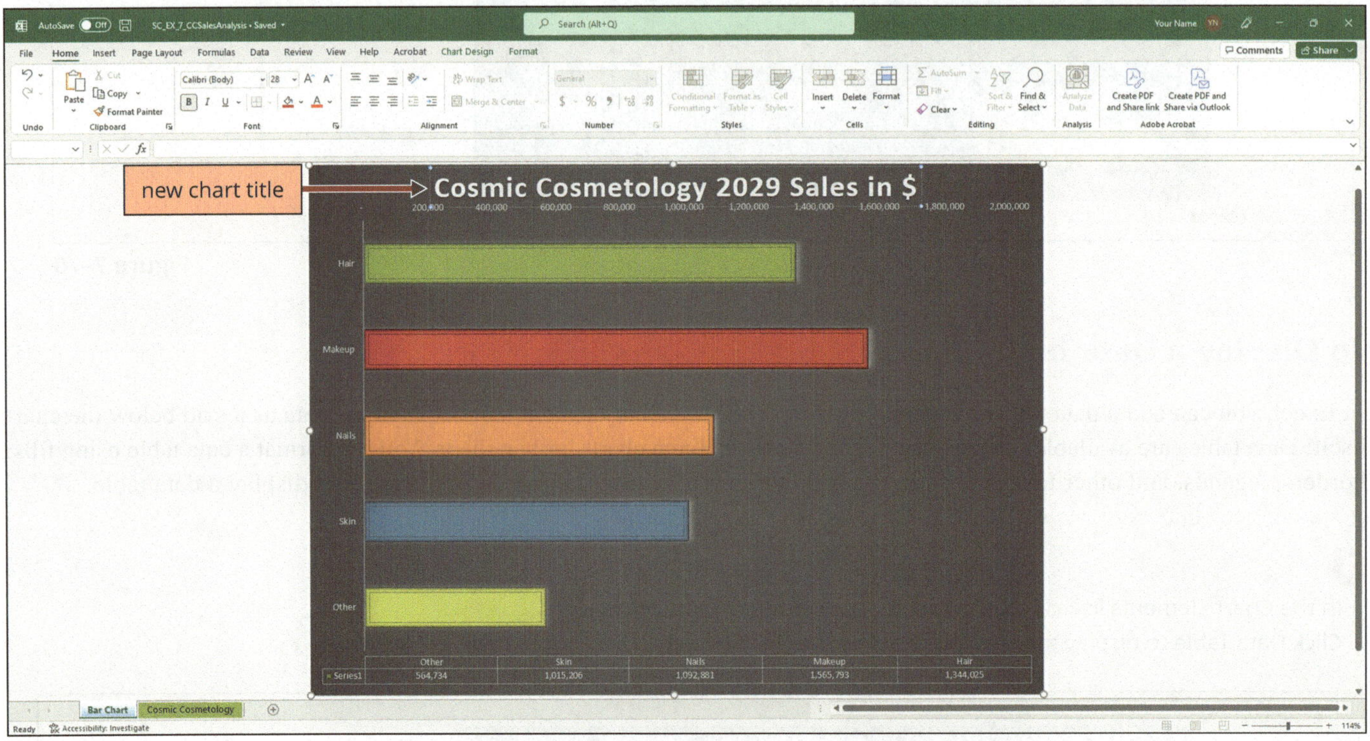

Figure 7–72

To Change the Chart Text Online If you wanted to apply outlining to the text in the chart, you would perform the following steps.

1. Select the text on the chart.
2. Right-click the text and then, depending on the location of the text, click Format Axis, Format Legend, or Format Chart on the shortcut menu.
3. When Excel displays the appropriate Format pane, click the Text Options tab.
4. In the Text Outline area, click the Solid Line option button, and then set the desired color, width, and other formatting.

Break Point: If you want to take a break, this is a good place to do so. You can exit Excel now. To resume later, start Excel, open the file called SC_EX_7_CCSalesAnalysis, and continue following the steps from this location forward.

Working with SmartArt Graphics

A **SmartArt graphic** is a customizable diagram that you use to pictorially present lists, processes, and relationships. For example, you can use a SmartArt graphic to illustrate the manufacturing process to produce an item. Excel includes nine SmartArt categories: List, Process, Cycle, Hierarchy, Relationship, Matrix, Pyramid, Picture, and Office.com, which includes additional layouts available from Office.com. Each type of graphic includes several layouts, or templates, from which to choose. After selecting a SmartArt graphic type and layout, you customize the graphic to meet your needs and present your information and ideas in a compelling manner.

In the following sections, you will create a SmartArt graphic with shapes, pictures, and text. You then will add a style to the SmartArt graphic.

Consider This

How do you choose the type of SmartArt graphics to add?

Consider what you want to illustrate in the SmartArt graphic. For example, if you are showing nonsequential or grouped blocks of information, select a SmartArt graphic in the List category. To show progression or sequential steps in a process or task, select a Process diagram. After inserting a SmartArt graphic, increase its visual appeal by formatting the graphic, for example, with 3-D effects and coordinated colors.

To Create a New Sheet

In preparation for inserting a SmartArt graphic, the following steps create a new sheet and hide gridlines.

1. Click the New sheet button to create a third sheet in the workbook.
2. Rename the worksheet **SmartArt Graphic** to provide a descriptive name for the worksheet.
3. Change the color of the tab to Yellow (Standard Colors area) to distinguish it from other sheets.
4. Click View on the ribbon to display the View tab.
5. Click the Gridlines check box (View tab | Show group) to turn off the gridlines.
6. If necessary, select cell A1 (Figure 7–73).

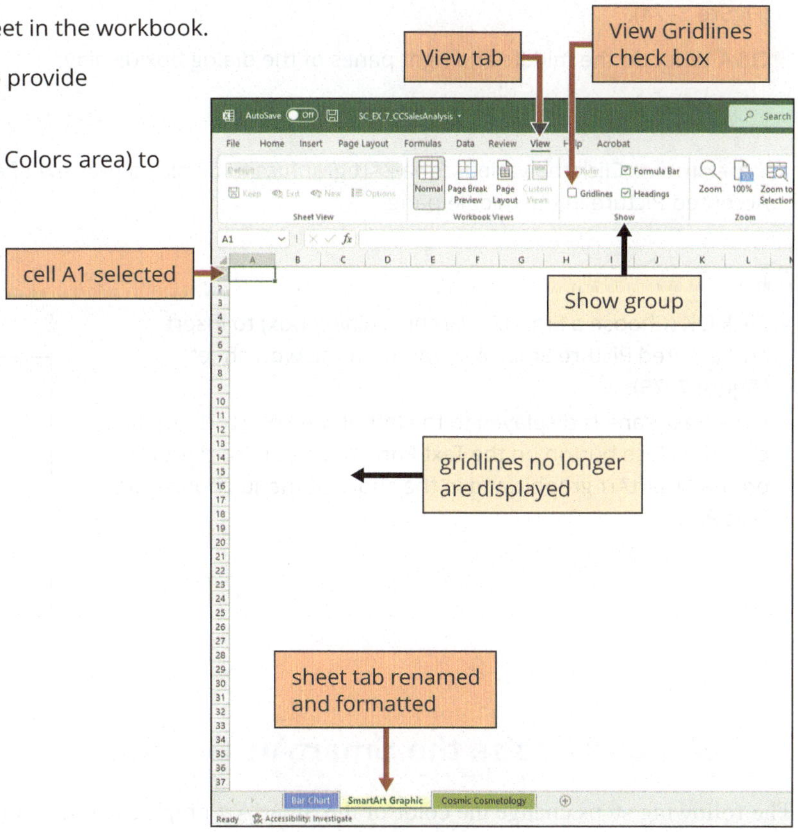

Figure 7–73

To Insert a SmartArt Graphic

To illustrate the categories of products sold by CC, you decide to use a SmartArt graphic. **Why?** A SmartArt graphic with pictures can be used in marketing and promotional material for the company. The following steps insert a SmartArt graphic named Accented Picture.

1

- Display the Insert tab.
- Click the SmartArt button (Insert tab | Illustrations group) to display the Choose a SmartArt Graphic dialog box.
- Click the desired type of SmartArt in the left pane; in this case, click Picture to display the available SmartArt Picture layouts in the middle pane (Choose a SmartArt Graphic dialog box).
- Click the desired layout, in this case, the Accented Picture layout, to display a preview of the chart in the preview area (Figure 7–74).

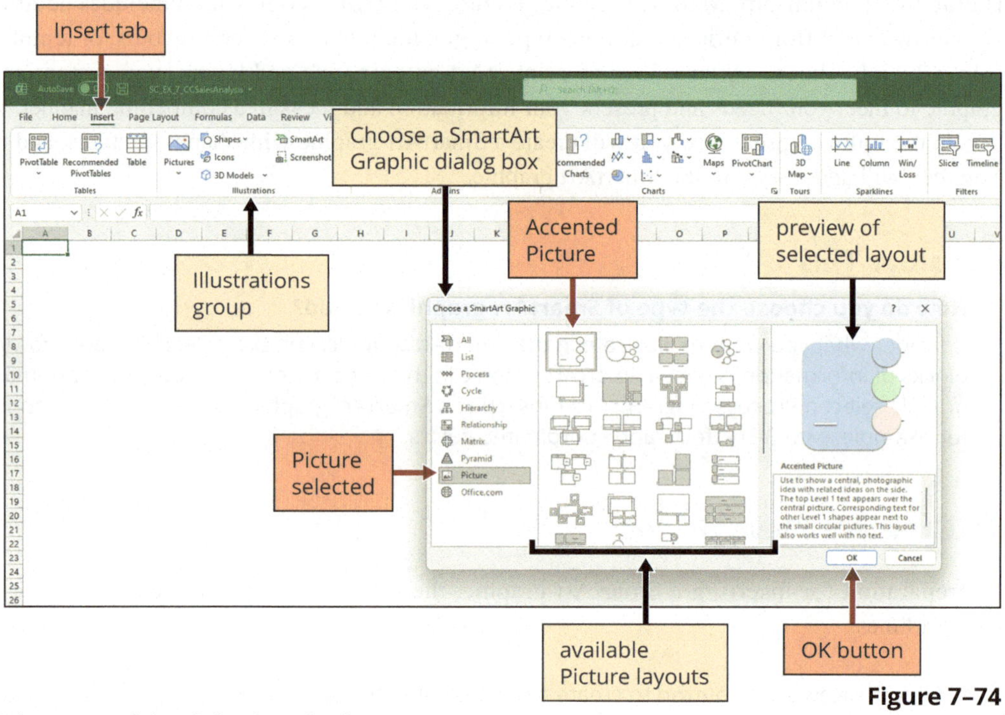

Figure 7–74

Q&A What do the middle and right panes of the dialog box display?
The middle pane of the dialog box (the layout gallery) displays available SmartArt graphics in the currently selected category, and the right pane (the preview area) displays a preview of the currently selected SmartArt graphic.

- **Experiment:** Click the various SmartArt graphics to display a preview of each in the preview area. When you are finished, click Accented Picture in the middle pane.

2

- Click OK (Choose a SmartArt Graphic dialog box) to insert an Accented Picture SmartArt graphic in the worksheet (Figure 7–75).
- If the Text Pane is displayed to the left of the SmartArt graphic, click the close button on the Text Pane to close it, or right-click on the SmartArt graphic and in the shortcut menu choose Hide Text Pane.

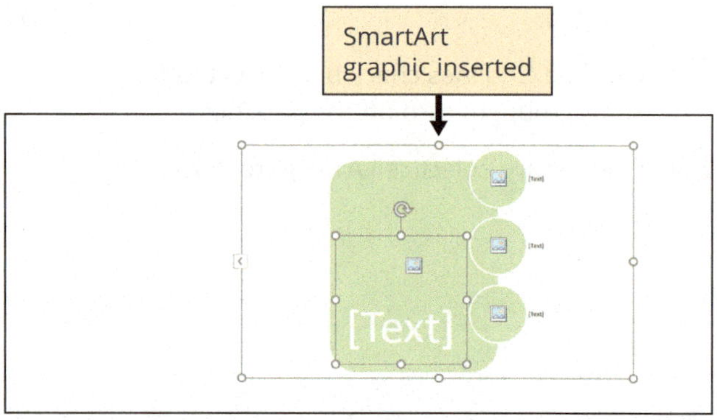

Figure 7–75

To Color and Resize the SmartArt Graphic

The following steps change the color of the SmartArt graphic and then resize it. **Why?** You want the color to coordinate with an image you plan to include and you want it to be as large as possible in the given space.

1

- Click the Change Colors button (SmartArt Design tab | SmartArt Styles group) to display the Change Colors gallery and use the scroll bar to scroll down to the Accent 6 section (Figure 7–76).

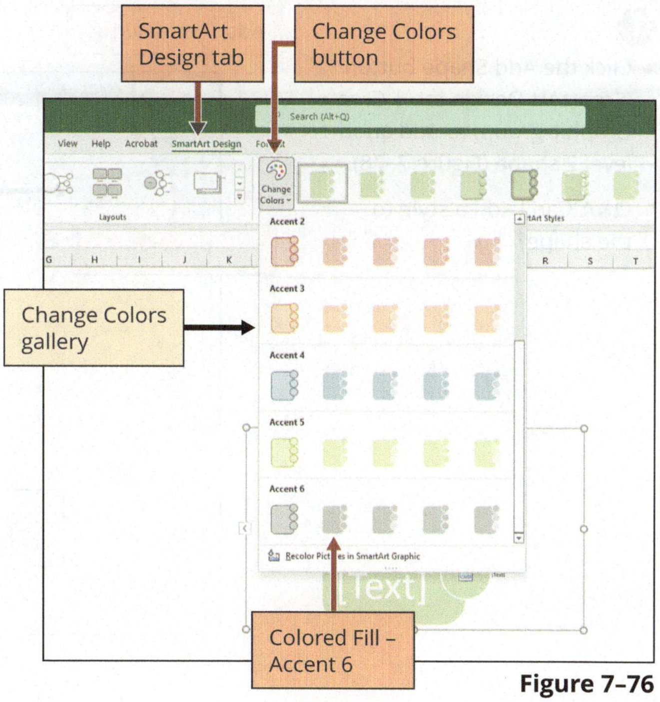

Figure 7–76

2

- Click 'Colored Fill - Accent 6' in the gallery to change the color.
- Drag the sizing handles to resize the SmartArt graphic to fill the range F1:Q23 (Figure 7–77).
- **Experiment:** Click the Format tab and look at the various groups, buttons, and galleries available to format SmartArt graphics.

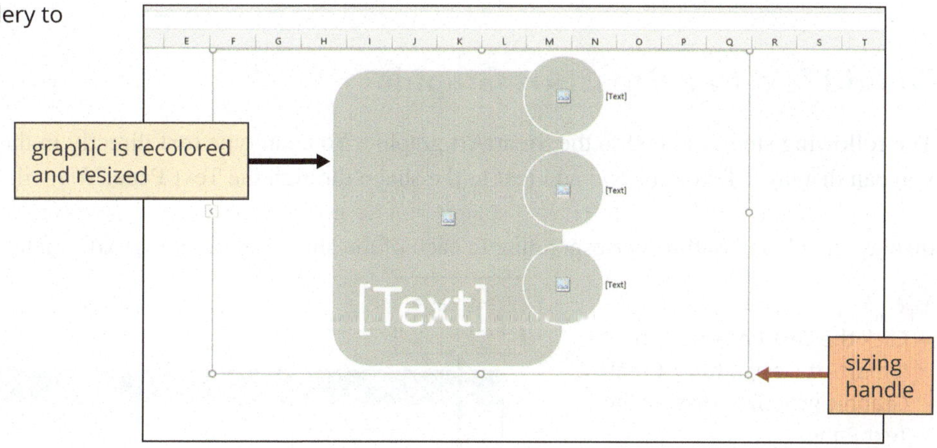

Figure 7–77

To Add a Shape to a SmartArt Graphic

Many SmartArt graphics include more than one shape, such as a picture, text box, or combinations, grouped in levels. Level 1 is considered the largest object or main level. Level 2 is a sublevel and may display one to three shapes when first created. You can add a shape or text box to each level. You also can **demote** or **promote** a shape, which means you can move the shape to a lower level or an upper level, respectively.

The default Accented Picture SmartArt graphic layout includes a large shape for level 1 and three smaller shapes for level 2. The following step adds a new shape to level 2 in the SmartArt graphic. **Why?** You want to show four categories in the SmartArt graphic.

1

- Click the Add Shape button (SmartArt Design tab | Create Graphic group) to add another level 2 shape (Figure 7–78).

Q&A Can I add a style to the shape?
Yes. To do so, select the shape, and then click the More button (Format tab | Shape Styles group). Excel displays a gallery with many Theme Styles and Presets.

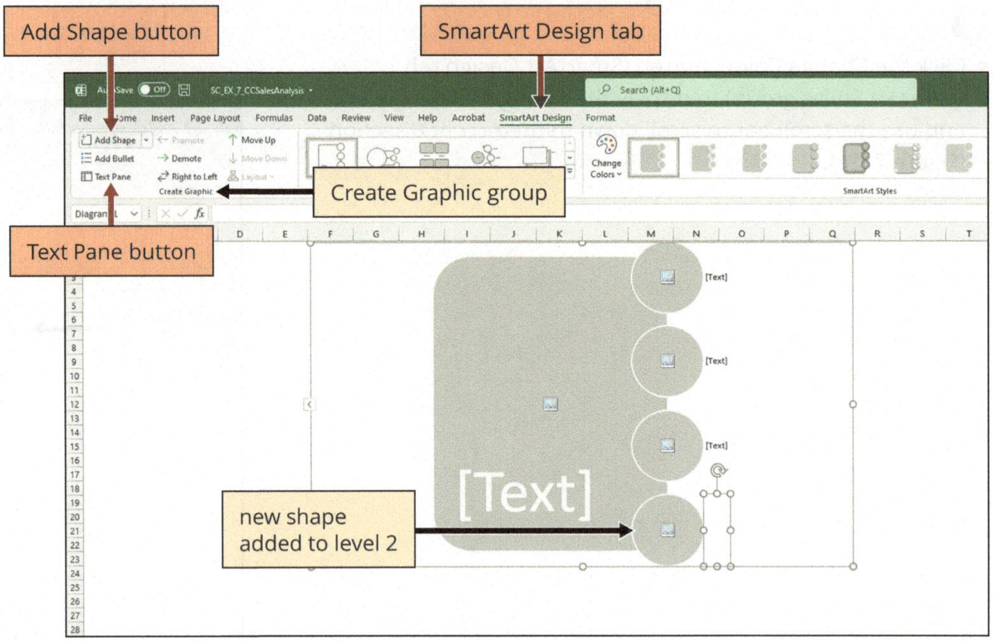

Figure 7–78

Other Ways

1. Right-click SmartArt graphic, point to Add Shape on shortcut menu, click 'Add Shape After' or 'Add Shape Before' on Add Shape submenu

To Add Text to a SmartArt Graphic

The following steps add text to the SmartArt graphic. You can type text directly in the text boxes of the SmartArt graphic, or you can display a Text Pane and add text to the shape through the Text Pane. You will use the Text Pane. **Why?** You may find it easier to enter text in the Text Pane because you do not have to select any object to replace the default text. The Text Pane displays a bulleted outline corresponding to each of the shapes in the SmartArt graphic.

1

- Click the Text Pane button (SmartArt Design tab | Create Graphic group) to display the Text Pane.
- Click the first bulleted item in the Text Pane and then type **Cosmic Cosmetology** to replace the default text (Figure 7–79).

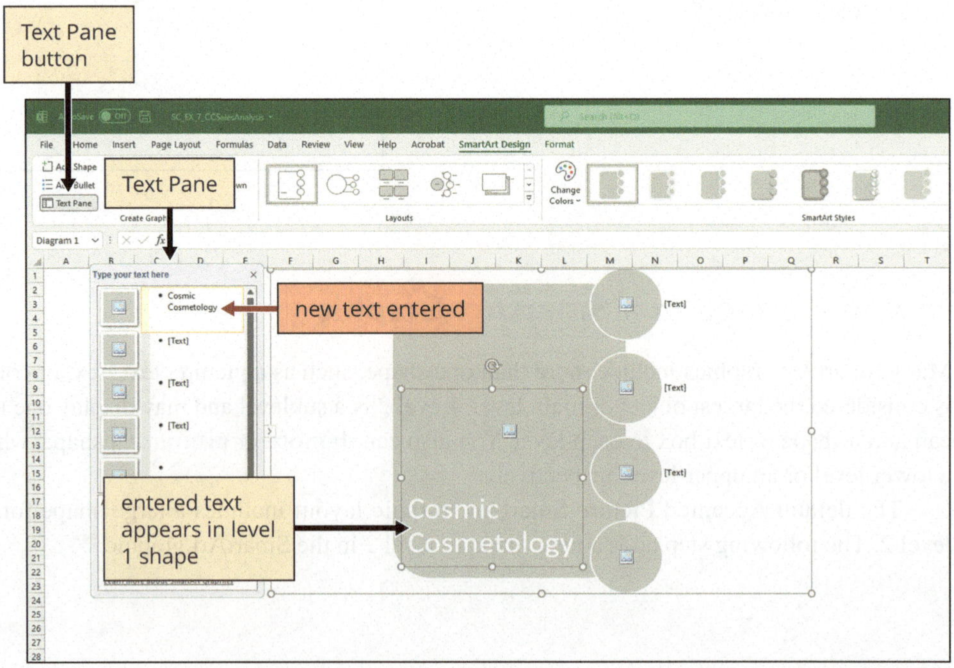

Figure 7–79

2

- Enter text in the other Text Pane boxes as shown in Figure 7–80. Note you are adding the text, Hair, Makeup, Nails, and Skin, in the text boxes from first to fourth vertically.

Q&A Did Excel resize my font?
Yes. Excel resizes all of the level 2 fonts to autofit the text in the graphic.

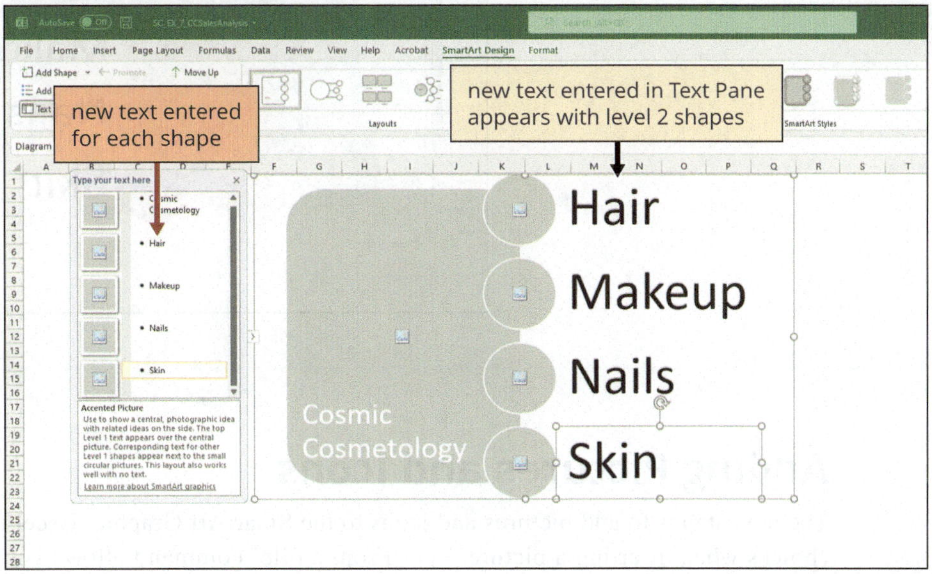

Figure 7–80

Other Ways

1. Click left arrow on edge of SmartArt graphic border to open Text Pane, type text
2. Click individual text box in SmartArt graphic, type text

To Add a Style to a SmartArt Graphic

Excel allows you to change the style of a SmartArt graphic. The following steps change the style of the Cosmic Cosmetology SmartArt graphic. **Why?** Choosing a different style creates different special effects for added emphasis or flair.

1

- If necessary, display the SmartArt Design tab.
- Click the More button (SmartArt Design tab | SmartArt Styles group) to display the SmartArt Styles gallery (Figure 7–81).
- **Experiment:** Point to each of the SmartArt styles in the gallery to display a live preview of the effect on the worksheet.

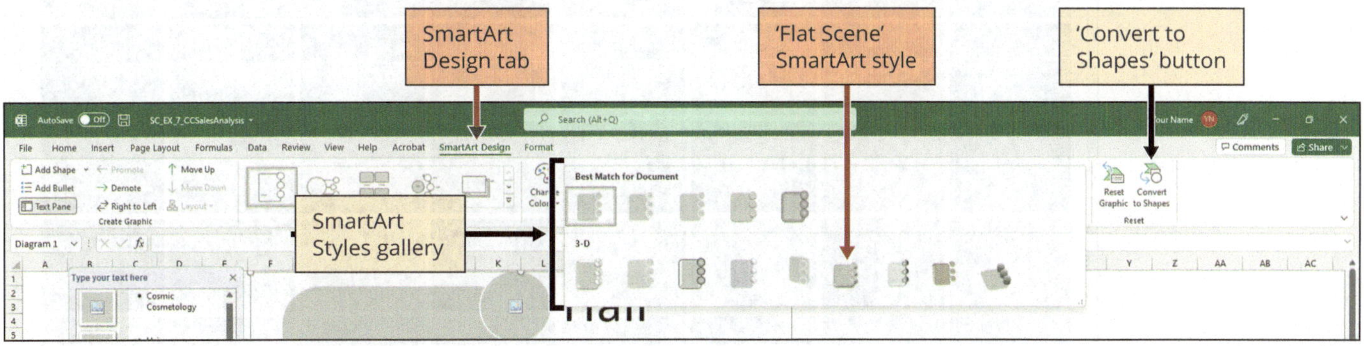

Figure 7–81

2

- Click the 'Flat Scene' style to apply it to the SmartArt graphic (Figure 7–82).

Q&A What does the 'Convert to Shapes' button do?
Clicking the 'Convert to Shapes' button (SmartArt Design tab | Reset group) converts the SmartArt graphic to individual shapes that can be resized, moved, or deleted independently of the others.

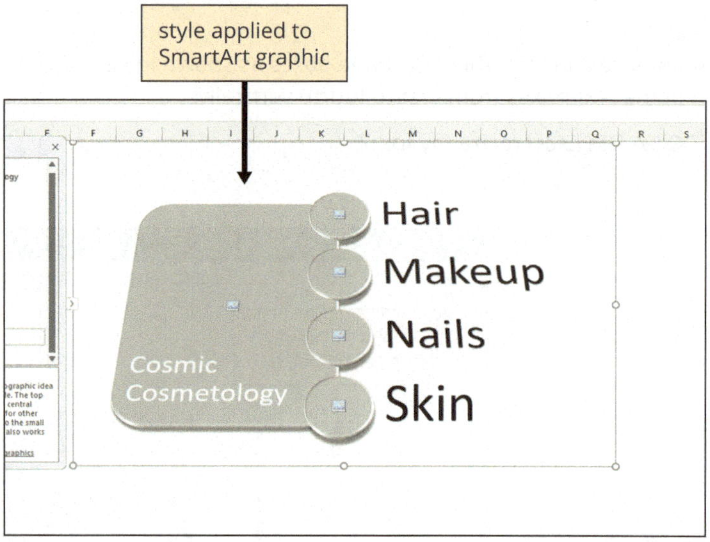

Figure 7–82

Adding Pictures and Icons

The next step is to add pictures and icons to the SmartArt Graphic. Excel offers four different choices when inserting a picture. The 'From a File' command allows you to choose a digital picture of almost any file type that is stored on an accessible storage device. Stock Images allow you to search premium content from a stock image gallery. If you choose Online Pictures, Excel opens a Bing search window organized into various categories (Figure 7–83). You can search one of the categories or enter a keyword. The fourth command, From Icons, lets you choose an icon from an online collection. An **icon** is usually a graphic representation of a picture, idea, or process. Excel includes a large number of icons, which can be formatted once they are added to the worksheet.

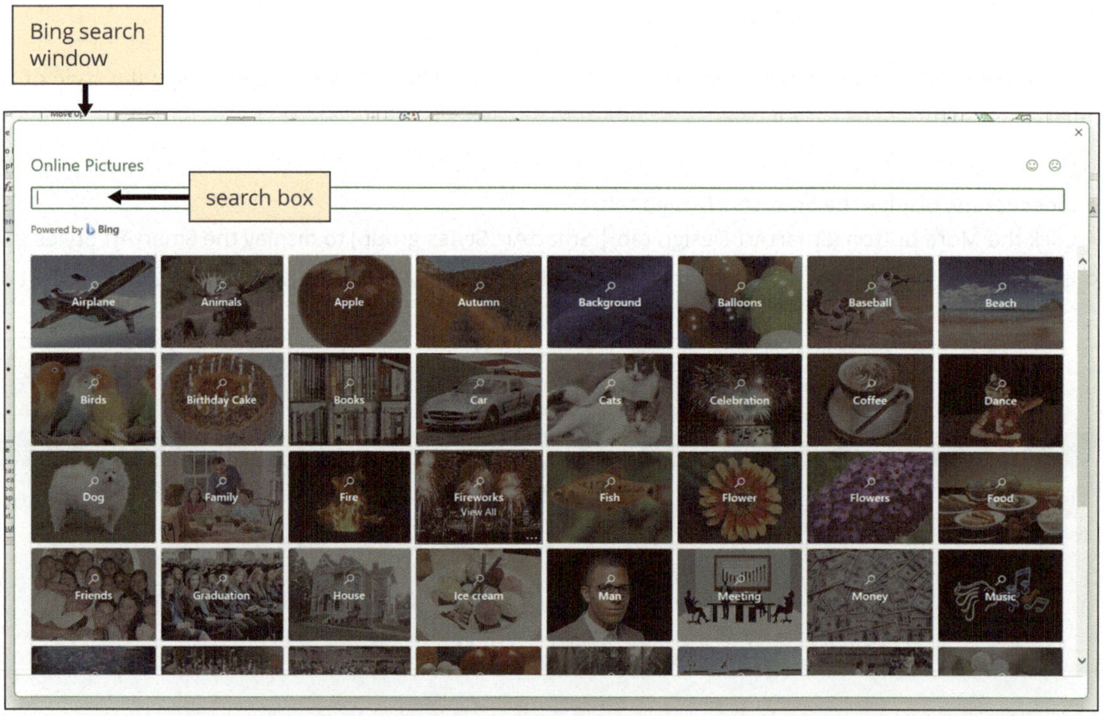

Figure 7–83

Consider This

How do I locate a picture to use in a worksheet?

To use a picture in an Excel worksheet, the image must be stored digitally in a file. Files containing pictures are available from a variety of sources:

- The web has pictures available, some of which are free, while others require a fee.
- You can take a picture with a digital camera or smartphone and **download** it, which is the process of copying the picture (or other file) from the camera or phone to your computer.
- With a scanner, you can convert a printed picture, drawing, diagram, or other object to a digital file.

If you receive a picture from a source other than yourself, do not use the file until you are certain it does not contain a virus. A **virus** is a computer program designed to copy itself into other programs with the intention of causing mischief, harm, or damage to files, programs, and apps on your computer, usually without your knowledge or permission. Use an **antivirus program** or app to locate and destroy viruses or other malware before they infect a device.

In the following sections, you will insert a picture from a file for the Level 1 part of the SmartArt graphic. The Level 2 graphics will be icons.

To Add a Picture to a SmartArt Graphic

The following steps add a picture to the SmartArt graphic. **Why?** The CEO wants to highlight a popular CC logo graphic created by his daughter. Other times, you may want to locate stock images categorized by image type, or images or clip art from the web, also called online pictures. Excel uses the Bing search engine to help you locate images licensed under Creative Commons. **Creative Commons** is a nonprofit organization that makes it easy for content creators to license and share their work by supplying easy-to-understand copyright licenses; the creator chooses the conditions under which the work can be used. The resulting images may or may not be royalty and copyright-free. You must read the specific license for any image you plan to use, even for educational purposes. In this module, you will add pictures from the Data Files. Please contact your instructor for information about accessing the Data Files.

1

- In the Text Pane, click the first Insert Picture icon (next to Cosmic Cosmetology) to display the Insert Pictures dialog box (Figure 7–84).

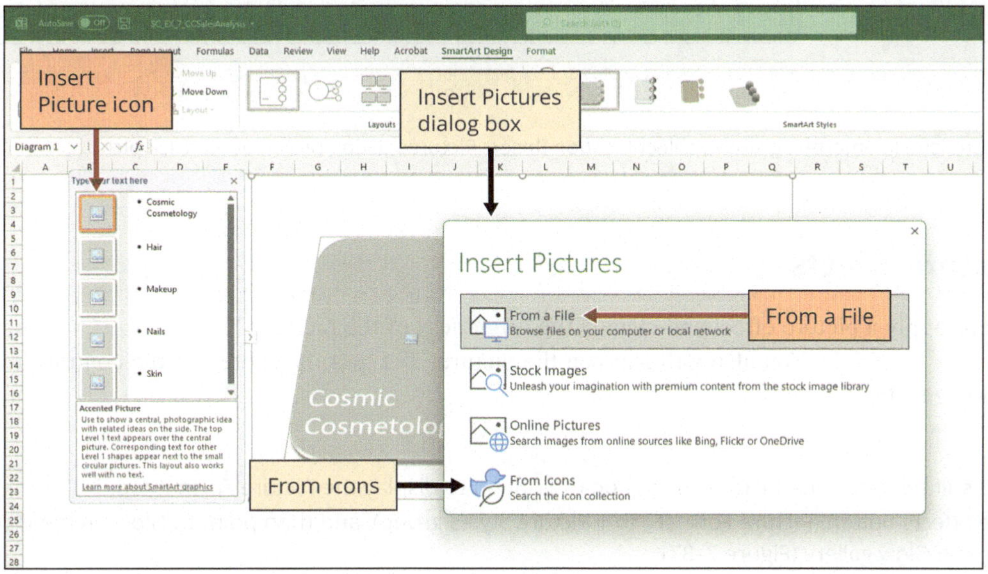

Figure 7–84

2

- Click the 'From a File' button to display the Insert Picture dialog box and then browse to the Data Files (Figure 7–85).

Q&A Why do the files in my dialog box appear differently?
Your system may display a different view. If you want to match the display in Figure 7–85, click the 'Change your view' arrow, and then click Large icons.

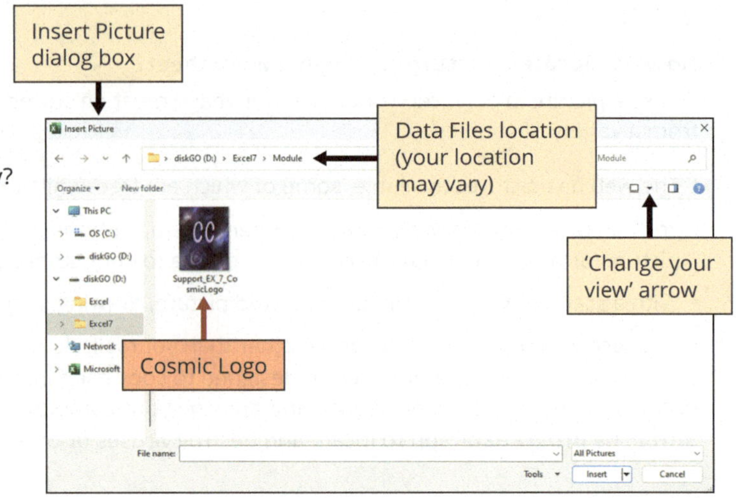

Figure 7–85

3

- Double-click the file named Support_EX_7_CosmicLogo.jpg Cosmic Cosmetology Logo to place it in the SmartArt graphic (Figure 7–86).

Q&A Do I need to use a special type of picture file or format?
Excel accepts a wide variety of formats including .png, .gif, .bmp, .jpg, and .tif, among others. Excel will resize the graphic as necessary to fit the space in the SmartArt graphic.

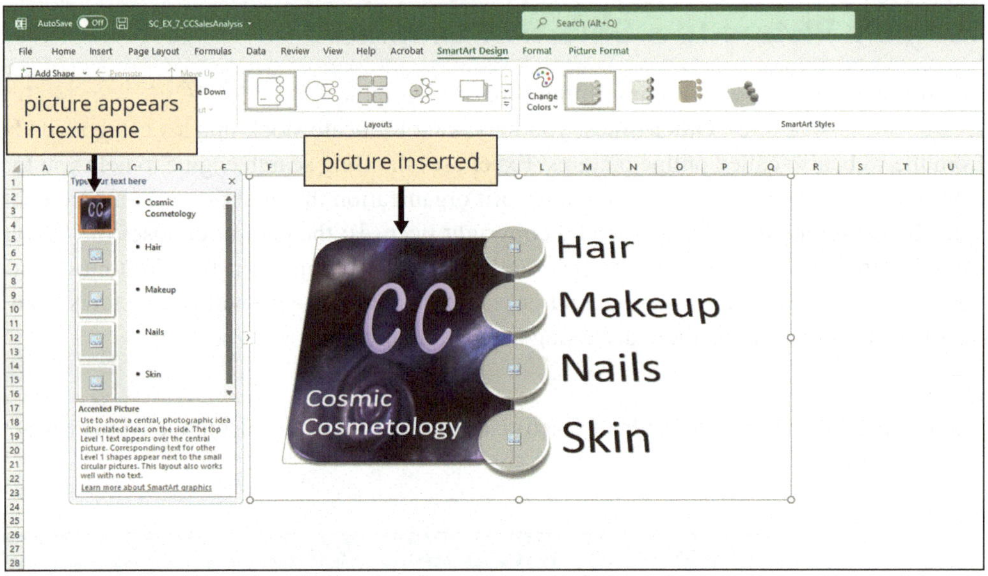

Figure 7–86

Other Ways

1. Click Insert Picture icon in SmartArt graphic, select location (Insert Pictures dialog box), double-click picture.

To Apply Picture Effects

The following steps apply a picture effect and change the brightness of the picture. **Why?** You want to make the SmartArt graphic as attractive as possible. You also will sharpen the picture. **Sharpening** increases the contrast at color changes to emulate a more defined edge.

1

- With the picture still selected, click Picture Format on the ribbon to display the Picture Format tab.
- Click the Picture Effects button (Picture Format tab | Picture Styles group), and then point to Glow on the Picture Effects menu to display the Glow gallery (Figure 7–87).
- **Experiment:** Point to each item on the Picture Effects menu to view the galleries. When you are finished, point to Glow again.

Q&A What does the Glow Options command do?
Each of the Picture Effects menu's Options commands opens the Format Picture pane. The Glow Options include controls to manipulate the color, size, and transparency.

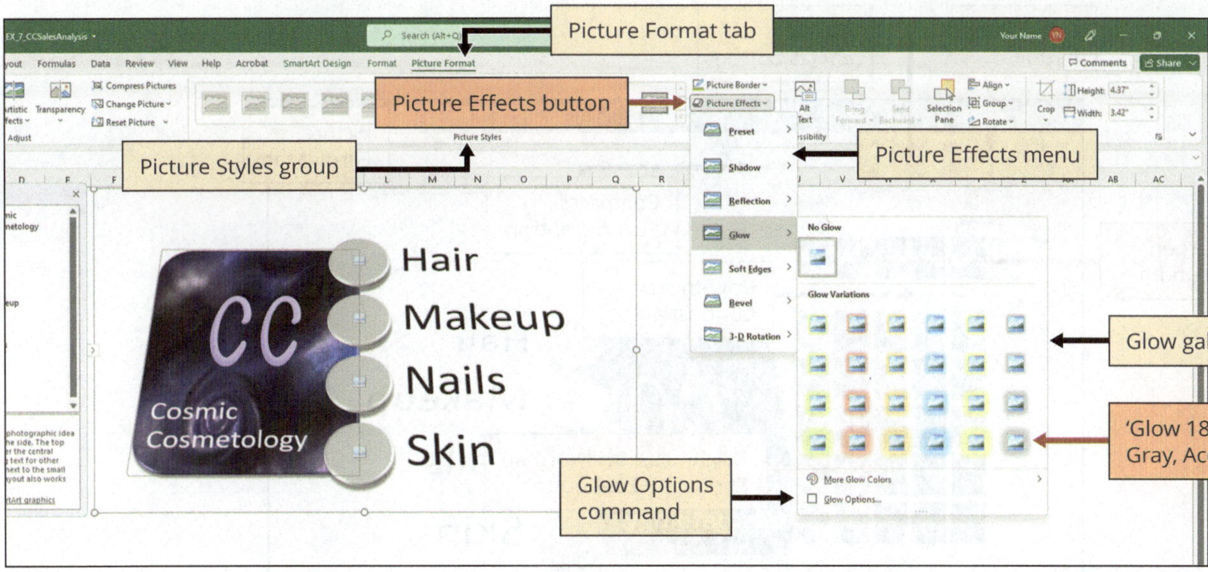

Figure 7–87

2

- In the Glow Variations area (Glow gallery), click 'Glow 18 point; Gray, Accent color 6' to select a gray glow.
- Click the Corrections button (Picture Format tab | Adjust group) to display the Corrections gallery (Figure 7–88).

◦ **Experiment:** Point to each preview in the Corrections gallery to preview its effect on the picture.

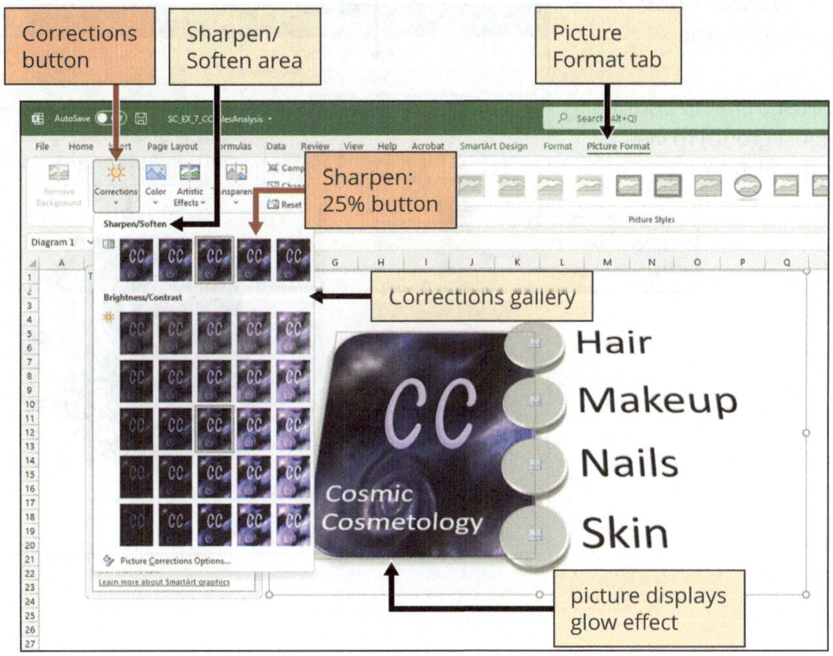

Figure 7–88

3

- In the Sharpen/Soften area, click the Sharpen: 25% button to sharpen the picture.
- Click the Corrections button (Picture Format tab | Adjust group) again to display the Corrections gallery (Figure 7–89).

Q&A What does the Compress Pictures command do?

The Compress Pictures command reduces the size of the pictures by deleting any cropped areas and flattening any grouped objects.

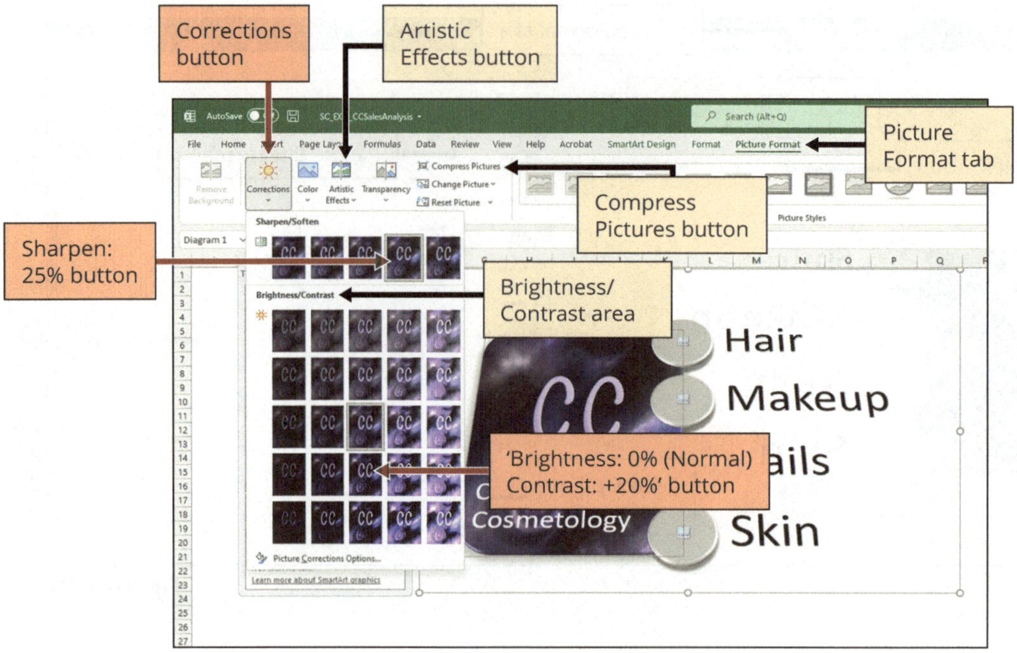

Figure 7–89

4

- In the Brightness/Contrast area, click the 'Brightness: 0% (Normal) Contrast: +20%' button to increase the contrast in the picture (Figure 7–90).
- **Experiment:** Click the Artistic Effects button (Picture Format tab | Adjust group) to view the available effects for the picture.

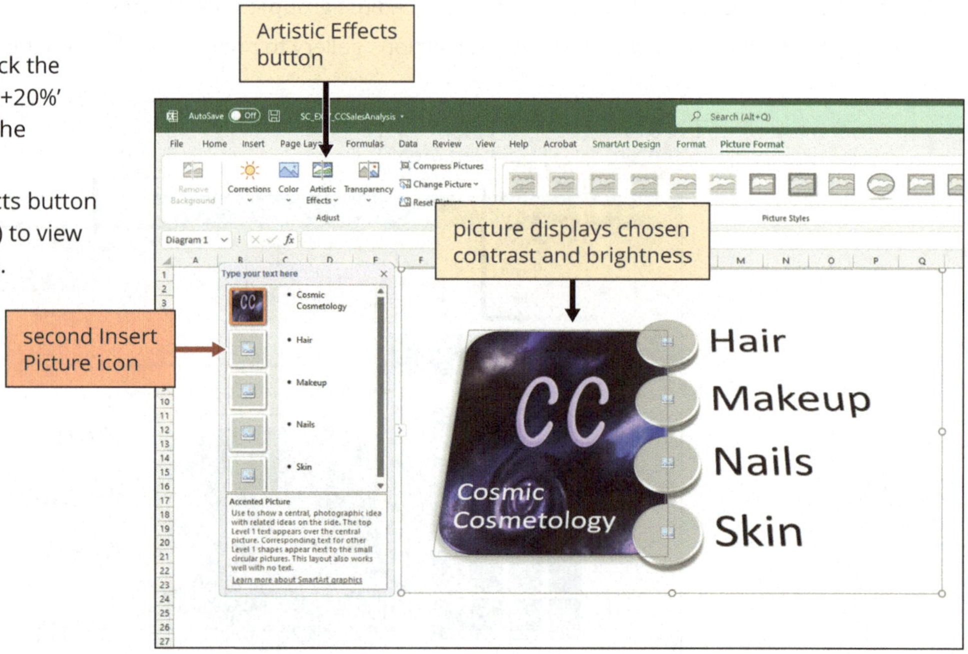

Figure 7–90

To Insert Icons

Excel includes a library of icons you can use in your worksheets. The following steps insert icons for the four Level 2 graphics. **Why?** Icons will represent the kinds of products sold by the company.

1

- In the Text Pane, click the second Insert Picture icon (next to Hair) to display the Insert Pictures dialog box.
- Click From Icons (shown in Figure 7–84) to display the Insert Icons dialog box.
- At the top of the dialog box, enter 'comb' into the search box and press Enter. Click on the right figure (the lighter comb) as shown in Figure 7–91.
- **Experiment:** Scroll through the Insert Icons dialog box to check out the categories and varieties of icons.

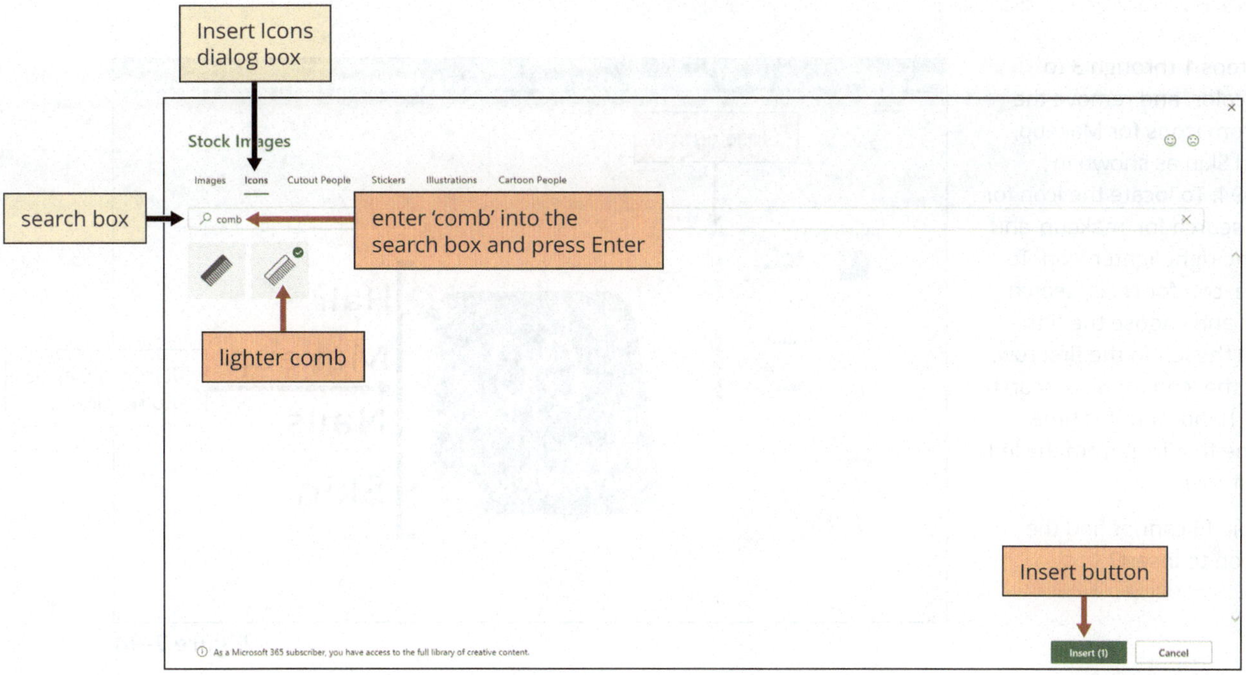

Figure 7–91

2

- Click Insert (1) (Insert Icons dialog box) to insert the icon.
- Click the Graphics Format tab on the ribbon to display the tab.
- Click the Graphics Fill button (Graphics Format tab | Graphics Styles group) to display the Graphics Fill gallery (Figure 7–92).

Q&A Why did Excel change the color when the icon was inserted?

Excel matched the color to the chosen color scheme of the SmartArt graphic.

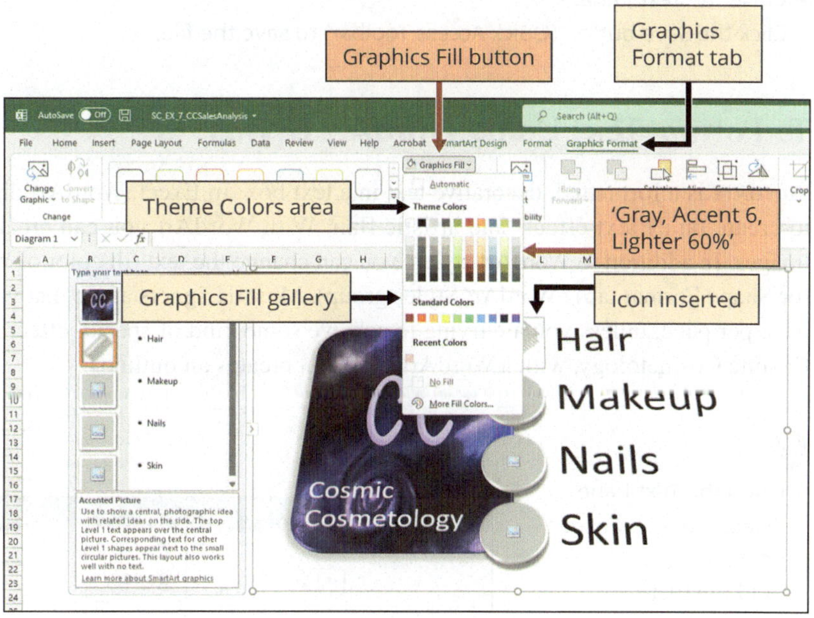

Figure 7–92

3

- Click 'Gray, Accent 6, Lighter 60%' in the Theme Colors area (Graphics Fill gallery) to recolor the icon.
- With the icon still selected, click the Graphics Outline button in the Graphics Styles group, and, if it is not already selected, select No Outline (Figure 7–93).

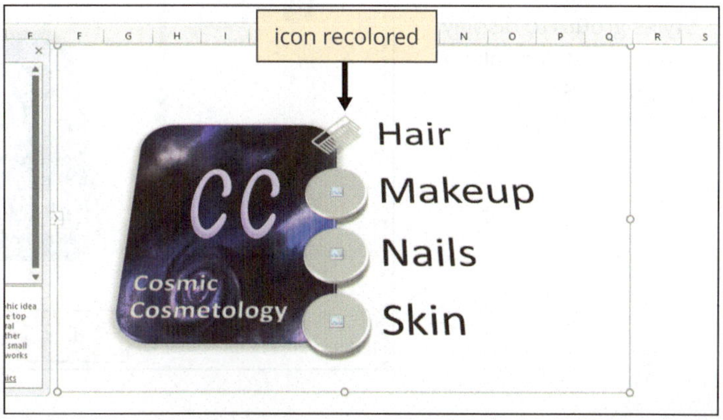

Figure 7–93

4

- Repeat Steps 1 through 3 to insert, recolor, and remove the outline from icons for Makeup, Nails, and Skin as shown in Figure 7–94. To locate the icon for Makeup, search for 'makeup' and choose the right lighter icon. To locate the icon for Nails, search for 'hand' and choose the fifth icon from the left in the first row. To locate the icon for Skin, search again for 'hand' and this time choose the first icon from the left in the first row.

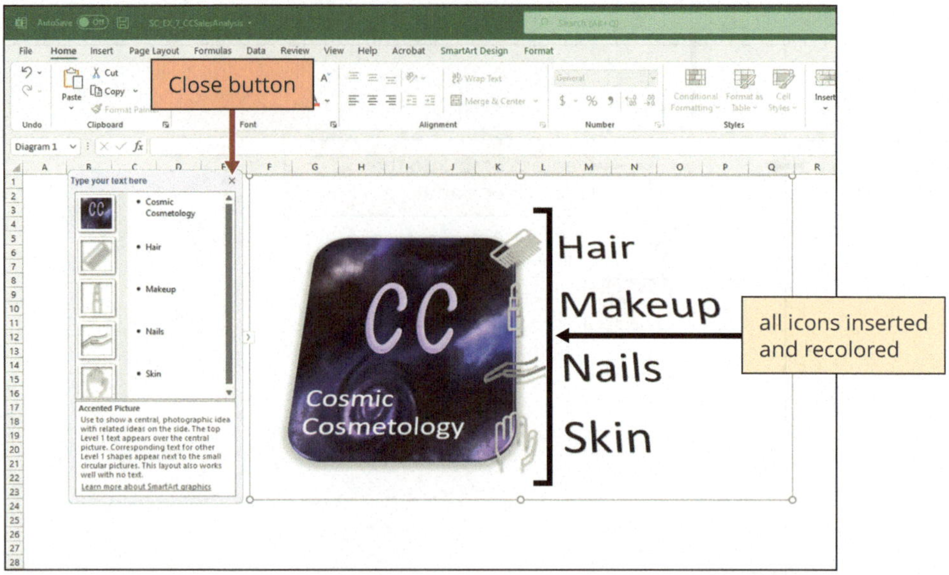

Figure 7–94

Q&A What if I cannot find the correct icon to insert?
If you want to search for an icon, enter the search text in the Search box (shown in Figure 7–91) to display search results matching the text you entered.

- Close the Text Pane.
- Click the Save button (Quick Access Toolbar) to save the file.

To Format Text Using WordArt Styles

WordArt is a formatted, decorative text in a text box. In Excel, WordArt displays a gallery of text styles that work with Excel to create fancy text effects and artistic flair. With WordArt you can create eye-catching headlines, banners, or watermark images. In addition to WordArt styles, you can change the text fill color of WordArt by clicking the Text Fill arrow (Format tab (or Shape Format tab) | WordArt Styles group). Most designers agree that you should use WordArt sparingly and, at most, only once per page, unless you are trying to achieve some kind of special effect or illustration. The following steps format the text, Cosmic Cosmetology, with a WordArt style that creates an outline. **Why?** Outlining, also called stroking the letters, will make them easier to read against the logo background.

1

- Open the Text Pane.
- Select the text, Cosmic Cosmetology.
- Bold the text.
- Display the Format tab.
- Click the More button (Format tab | WordArt Styles group) to display the Quick Styles gallery (Figure 7–95).

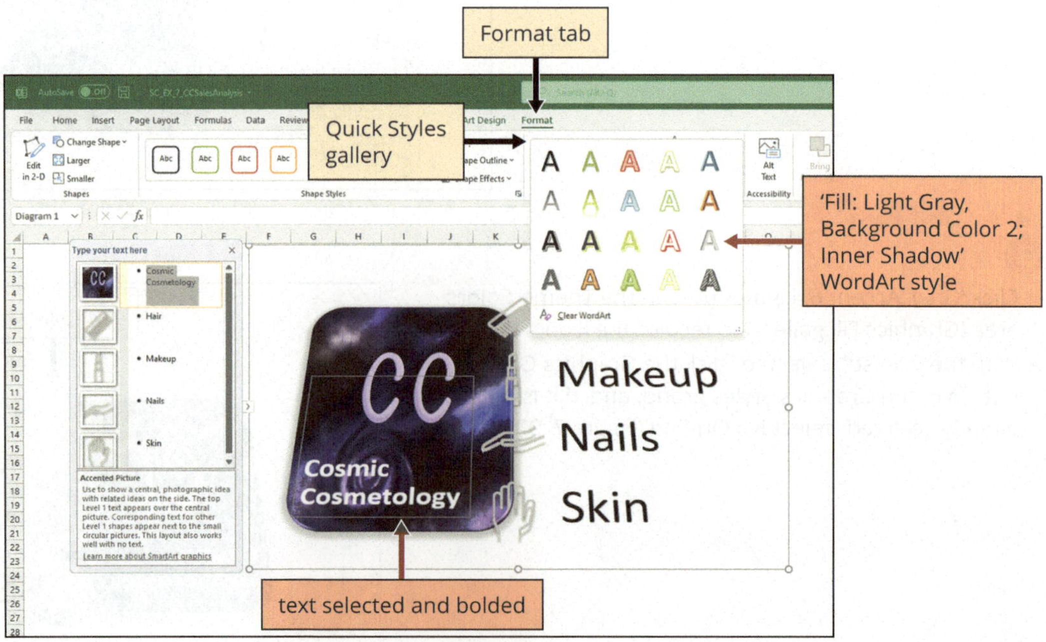

Figure 7–95

2

- Click 'Fill: Light Gray, Background color 2; Inner Shadow' in the WordArt Quick Style gallery to add this style to the text.
- Click outside of the SmartArt graphic to remove the selection and display the formatting (Figure 7–96).
- Close the Text Pane, if necessary.

3

- Save the workbook.

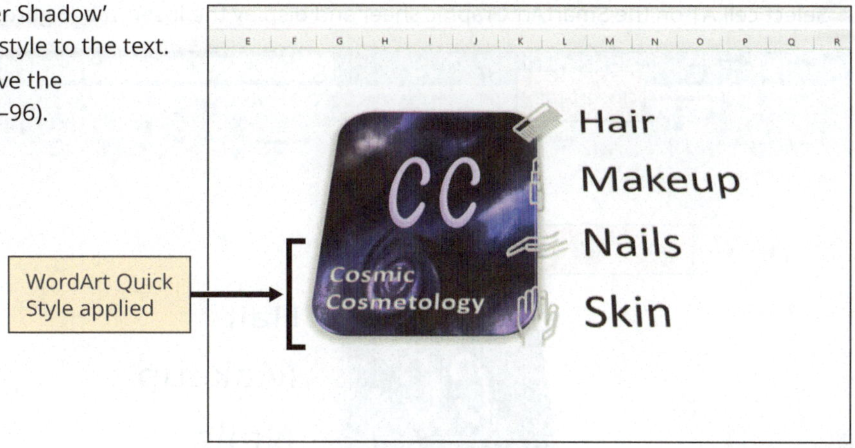

Figure 7–96

To Insert an Individual Image into a Workbook If you wanted to insert an individual image into your workbook, you would perform the following steps.

1. Select the cell at which you wish the image to display.
2. Display the Insert tab.
3. Click the Pictures button (Insert tab | Illustrations group), and then click This Device to display the Insert Picture dialog box.
4. Navigate to the location of the picture to insert and then double-click the file to insert the picture in the worksheet.
5. Resize the picture as necessary.
6. To format the picture, display the Picture Format tab.
7. Click the Quick Styles More button (Picture Format tab | Picture Styles group) to display the Picture Styles gallery.
8. Click the desired picture style to apply the style to the image.

Break Point: If you want to take a break, this is a good place to do so. You can exit Excel. To resume later, start Excel, open the file called SC_EX_7_CCSalesAnalysis, and continue following the steps from this location forward.

Working with Text Boxes

To add text to a workbook that is separate from the text in cells, chart titles, or labels, you can insert a text box. You then can enter the text that you want. Text boxes can be static, presenting read-only information, or they can be bound or linked to a cell by typing an equal sign (=) in the formula bar and then a cell reference, formula, or function. The text inside the box is easily formatted. You can edit the shape of the text box by using the Edit Shapes button (Shape Format tab | Insert Shapes group).

To Draw a Text Box

The following steps draw a text box to create a decorative heading for the SmartArt graphic. **Why?** The advantage of using a text box is that you can move the text box and resize it; it floats freely in the worksheet and is independent of row and column boundaries, preserving the layout of the data on the worksheet.

1

- Select cell A1 on the SmartArt Graphic sheet and display the Insert tab (Figure 7–97).

Figure 7–97

2

- Click the Text Box button and then move the pointer into the worksheet.
- Drag to create a text box in the upper-left corner of the worksheet, approximately 6 columns wide and 8 rows tall.
- Type **Our New Graphic** to enter the text (Figure 7–98).

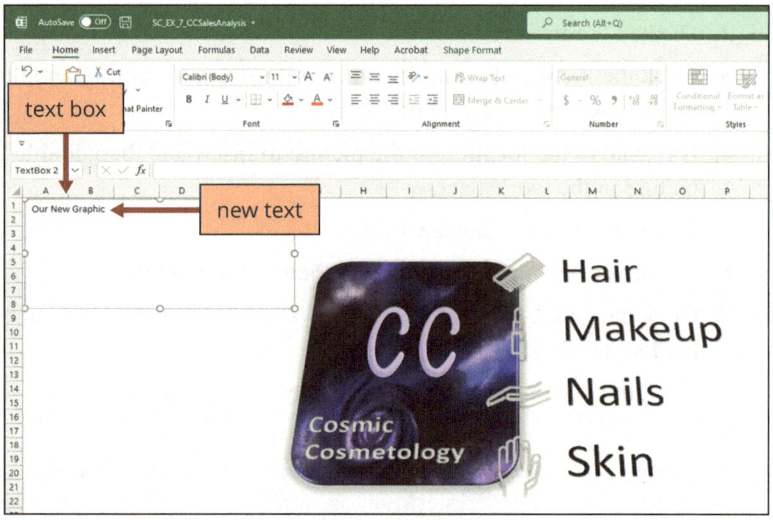

Figure 7–98

3

- Select the text and then change the font size to 36. Bold and italicize the text.
- Click the Shape Outline button (Shape Format tab | Shape Styles group) and then click No Outline to remove the border of the text box.
- Click away from the text box to view it without selection (Figure 7–99).

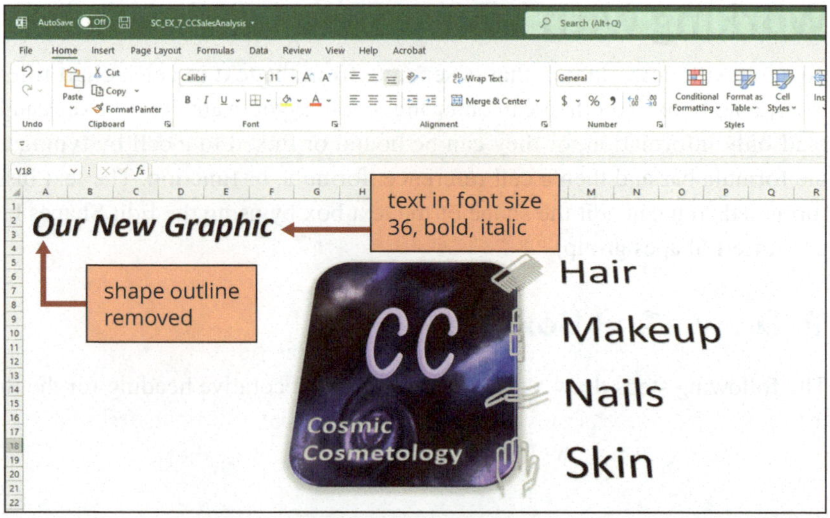

Figure 7–99

Adding Alternative Text

An important consideration when using graphics is accessibility. Screen readers that read worksheets and webpages for people who are blind or visually impaired can provide feedback about pictures, but only if the picture has alternative text. **Alternative text**, also called **alt text** or an **ALT tag**, is descriptive text that appears as an alternative to a graphic image. Screen readers read the alternative text aloud. Graphics without alternative text are not usable by screen readers, so people with disabilities will not hear picture descriptions. Browsers may display alternative text while graphics are loading or when graphics are missing.

To Add Alt Text

The following steps insert alternative text for the SmartArt graphic, and other items within the workbook. **Why?** You want the worksheet to be accessible to screen readers.

1

- Right-click the border of the SmartArt graphic to display the shortcut menu (Figure 7–100).

Q&A Are there rules about appropriate alternative text?

Sources vary on appropriate alternative text; however, most users agree that alternative text should not be redundant of other text, and should convey the meaning or purpose.

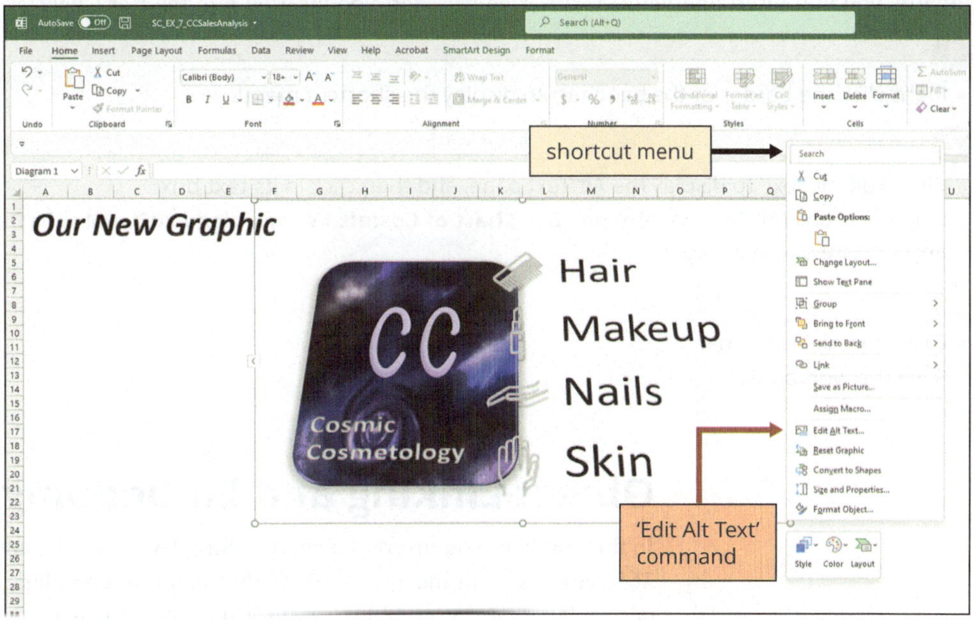

Figure 7–100

2

- Click 'Edit Alt Text' to display the Alt Text pane and click in its text box
- In the text box (Alt Text pane), type **Cosmic Cosmetology SmartArt graphic representing the types of available categories** to enter appropriate alternative text (Figure 7–101).

Q&A Some of my text has a red underline. Is that a problem?

Make sure your words are spelled correctly. A red underline indicates a misspelled word, or a word that is not in the Excel dictionary. Many names are not in the dictionary.

What if my shortcut menu reads "View Alt Text" instead of "Edit Alt Text?"

This is not an issue. Select 'View Alt Text' from the menu.

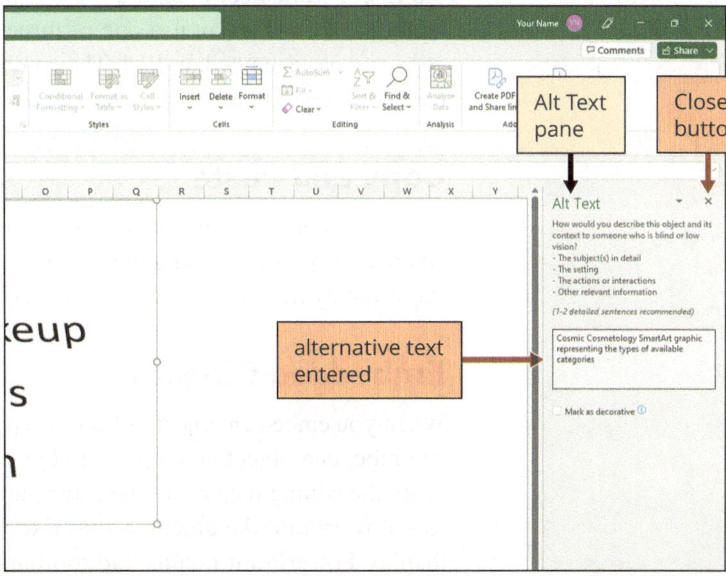

Figure 7–101

3

- Close the Alt Text pane.

Next, you will insert alternative text for the moon shape you inserted into the Cosmic Cosmetology tab of the workbook previously.

1

- Right-click the border of the moon shape to display the shortcut menu.

2

- Click 'Edit Alt Text' to display the Alt Text pane, and then click in its text box
- In the text box (Alt Text pane), type **Moon Shape Graphic Logo** to enter appropriate alternative text.

3

- Close the Alt Text pane.

Finally, you will insert alternative text for the bar chart you inserted into the Bar Chart tab of the workbook previously.

1

- Right-click the border of the bar chart to display the shortcut menu.

2

- Click 'Edit Alt Text' to display the Alt Text pane, and then click in its text box
- In the text box (Alt Text pane), type **Bar Chart of Cosmic Cosmetology 2029 Sales in Dollars by Category** to enter appropriate alternative text.

3

- Close the Alt Text pane.
- Save the workbook.

Object Linking and Embedding

In this module, you inserted a chart, a SmartArt graphic, and a SmartArt shape. With Microsoft 365, you also can insert an **object** that is an independent element on a worksheet (such as a document, chart, or graphic)—even if that object was created in another app. For example, you could insert a PowerPoint slide into an Excel worksheet. In this case, the PowerPoint slide (the object) is called the **source document** (the document from which items are being copied) and the Excel worksheet is called the **destination document** (the document to which items are being pasted). You can use one of three techniques to insert objects from one app to another: copy and paste, embed, or link. The combining of objects and data from two or more applications using linking or embedding is known as **integration**.

Copy and Paste

When you copy an object from another application, the source object appears in Excel. You then edit a **pasted object**, using the features of Excel. For example, earlier you edited the data from a Word file by transposing the rows and columns in Excel.

Embedded Objects

When you embed an object, it becomes part of the destination document. The difference between an embedded object and a pasted object is that you edit the contents of an **embedded object** using the editing features of the source app. For example, an embedded PowerPoint slide appears as a PowerPoint document within Excel. To edit the slide, double-click the slide. Excel will display PowerPoint menus and toolbars within the worksheet. When you edit an embedded object, the original PowerPoint slide (file) is unchanged.

To Embed an Object from Another App If you wanted to embed an object, you would perform the following steps.

1. Select the cell at which location you wish to begin embedding the object.
2. Click the Text button (Insert tab | Text group), and then click the Object button to display the Object dialog box.
3. Click the 'Create from File' tab and then click the Browse button. Navigate to the location of your object and double-click the file.
4. Ensure that the Link checkbox does *not* display a checkmark.
5. Click the OK button (Object dialog box) to embed the object.

Linked Objects

A **linked object**, by contrast, does not become a part of the destination document, even though it appears to be a part of it. Rather, a connection is established between the source and destination documents so that when you open the destination document, the linked object displays as part of it. When you edit a linked object, the source app starts and opens the source document that contains the linked object. For example, a linked PowerPoint slide remains as a PowerPoint slide. To edit the slide from Excel, double-click the slide to start PowerPoint and display the slide in a PowerPoint window. Unlike an embedded object, if you edit the PowerPoint slide by opening it from PowerPoint, the linked object will be updated in the Excel worksheet.

You would use linking when the contents of an object are likely to change and when you want to ensure that the most current version of the object appears in the source document. Another reason to link an object is if the object is large, such as a video clip or a sound clip.

To Link an Object from Another App If you wanted to link an object, you would perform the following steps.

1. Select the location in which you want to locate the linked object.
2. Click the Text button (Insert tab | Text group), and then click the Object button to display the Object dialog box.
3. Click the 'Create from File' tab and then click the Browse button. Navigate to the location of your object and double-click the file.
4. Click the Link to file checkbox so that it displays a checkmark.
5. Click the OK button (Object dialog box) to link the object.

If you wanted to link or embed Excel data into another app, you would perform the same techniques, but starting in the other app. For example, to link worksheet data to a Word document, you would open Word, click the Object button (Insert tab | Text group) and proceed to link the worksheet.

To Edit the Link to a File To edit the link to a file, you would perform the following steps.

1. Open the file containing the link.
2. Click File to open Backstage View. On the Info screen, click the 'Edit Links to Files' button to display the Edit Links dialog box.
3. Click the Change Source button (Edit Links dialog box).
4. Edit the location in the Change Links dialog box.
5. Click OK (Change Links dialog box).
6. Click Close (Edit Links dialog box).

To Create a New Object Integration tools also let you create a new object in Excel based on another app. For example, you can create a WordPad document to include further text information or create a PowerPoint slide to illustrate an example. The command opens the app associated with the new object. Once created, the new object is embedded and can be edited as described above. To create a new object, perform the following steps.

1. Choose the location where you want to create the new object.
2. Click the Text button (Insert tab | Text group), and then click the Object button to display the Object dialog box.
3. Click the 'Create New' tab.
4. In the Browse box, scroll as necessary to choose the type of embedded object you wish to create.
5. Click OK (Object dialog box) to embed the object.
6. While the tools of the source app are visible, insert content or formatting as necessary.
7. Click outside the object to redisplay the tools of the destination app.

To Break an External Link Sometimes you may want to break an external link between Excel and another app, so that the destination object will no longer update when the source object is modified. To do so, perform the following steps. When Excel breaks the link, the object becomes an Excel picture or shape, depending on the source app.

1. Click the Edit Links button (Data tab | 'Queries & Connections' group) to display the Edit Links dialog box.
2. In the Source area, select the desired file.
3. Click the Break Link button (Edit Links dialog box).
4. When Excel displays a dialog box, click the Break Links button.
5. Click Close (Edit Links dialog box).

To Update a Linked Object from Another App When you open an Excel file that contains linked objects (as opposed to embedded objects), Excel checks for changes and offers you the chance to update the linked object. To update a linked object from another app, you would perform the following steps.

1. Start the app that created the linked object (e.g., Word).
2. Edit the file as necessary, save, and then close the app.
3. Open the corresponding Excel worksheet.
4. When Excel displays the Microsoft Excel dialog box, click Update.
5. If Excel displays a dialog box about trusting the file, click OK.

Using Screenshots on a Worksheet

Excel allows you to take a screenshot of any open window and add it to a worksheet. Using the screenshot feature, you can capture whole windows or only part of a window. For example, if your company has a webpage, you can take a screenshot of the page and insert it into a worksheet before presenting the workbook at a meeting. In addition, you can capture a screen clipping. A **screen clipping** is a portion of a screen, usually of one object or a section of a window. You first will create a new worksheet in the workbook to hold the screenshot and then insert a screenshot of a webpage.

To Create Another New Sheet

In preparation for inserting the screenshot, the following steps create another new sheet.

1. Click the New sheet button to create a fourth sheet in the workbook. If necessary, drag the sheet tab to the right of the other tabs.
2. Rename the worksheet **Screenshot** to provide a descriptive name for the sheet.
3. Change the color of the tab to Red (Standard Colors area) and hide the gridlines on the sheet.
4. If necessary, click cell A1 to make it the active cell (Figure 7–102).

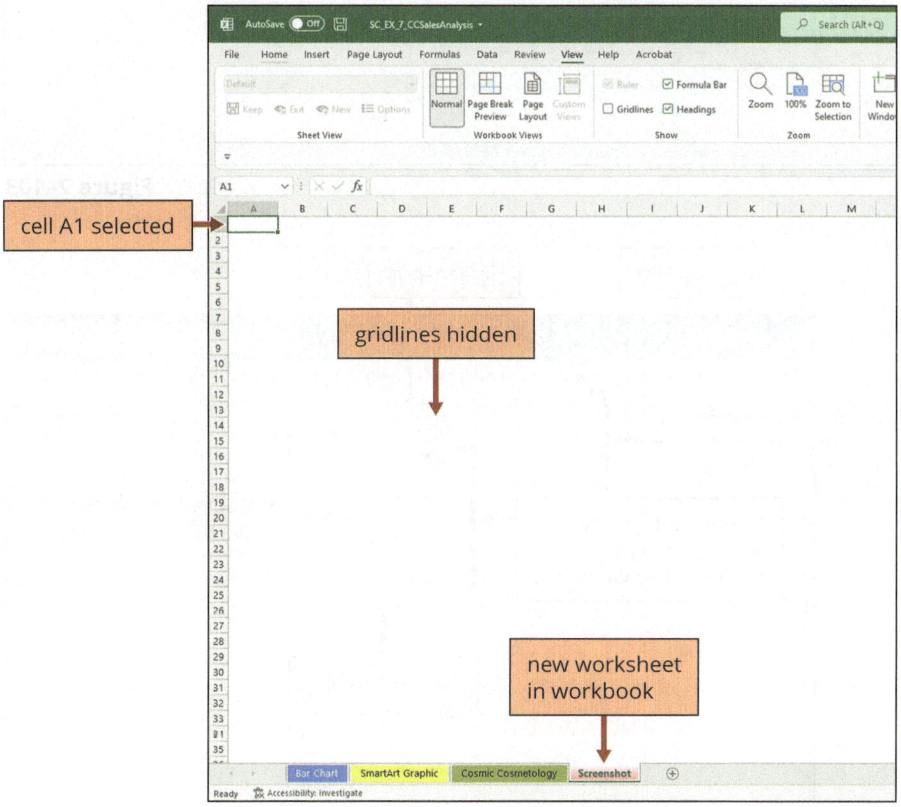

Figure 7–102

To Insert a Screenshot on a Worksheet

The staff at Cosmic Cosmetology often shares helpful cosmetology websites with customers. The following steps add a screenshot to a worksheet and then add a hyperlink to the inserted screenshot. **Why?** In anticipation of an upcoming meeting where the sales analysis will be reviewed, the CEO requests a screenshot of a popular website that answers typical cosmetology questions. Adding a hyperlink to the screenshot will enable users to click the screenshot to open the site in their web browser.

1

- Start Microsoft Edge or a similar browser.
- Type **www.fda.gov/cosmetics/resources-consumers-cosmetics/cosmetics-faqs** in the address bar, and then press ENTER to display the webpage (Figure 7–103).

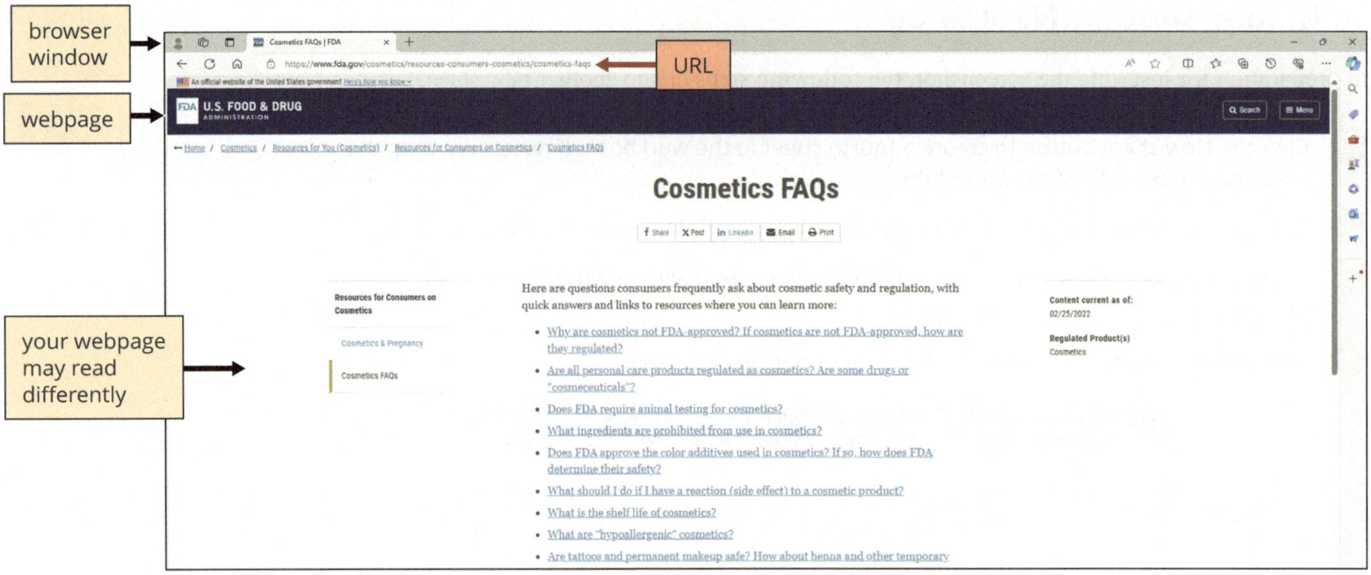

Figure 7–103

2

- Click the Excel app button on the taskbar to return to Excel.
- Display the Insert tab.
- Click the Screenshot button (Insert tab | Illustrations group) to display the Screenshot gallery (Figure 7–104).

Q&A My browser window is not displayed in the gallery. Did I do something wrong?
If Excel cannot link to your browser, you may have to insert a screen clipping instead of a screenshot. To do so, click Screen Clipping (Take a Screenshot gallery), navigate to the desired window, and then draw a rectangle over the portion of the screen you want to insert into the Excel workbook.

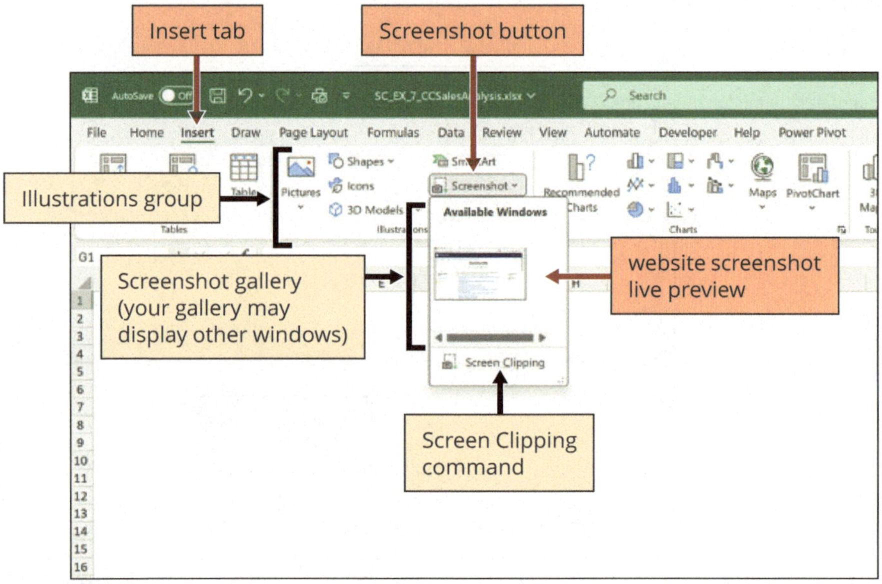

Figure 7–104

3

- Click the live preview of the FDA Cosmetics web page to insert the screenshot.

4

- Right-click the screenshot, and in the shortcut menu point to the Link arrow to display the Link submenu.
- Click Insert Link from the submenu to display the Insert Hyperlink dialog box.
- In the Link To options in the left column (Insert Hyperlink dialog box), click Existing File or Webpage, if it is not already selected.
- Enter the URL of the FDA Cosmetics web page into the Address box (Figure 7–105).

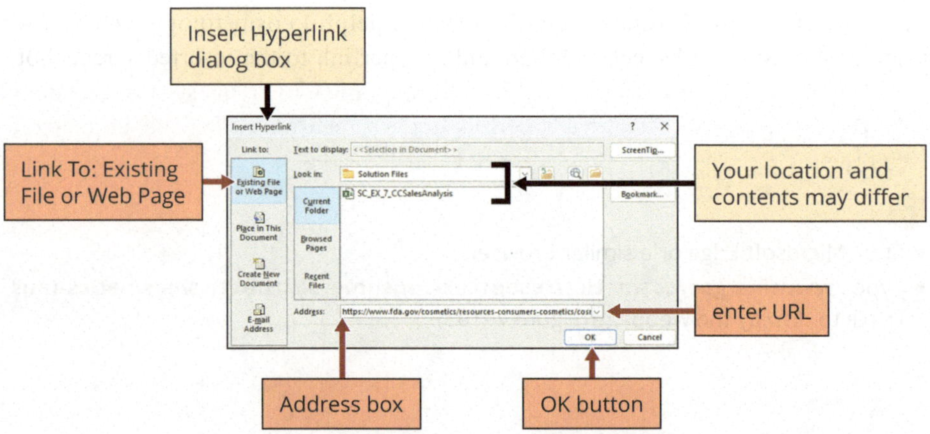

Figure 7–105

5

- Click the OK button of the Insert Hyperlink dialog box to add the hyperlink to the screenshot. (Figure 7–106).
- **Experiment:** Scroll to display the entire screenshot. Note that the screenshot displays only the part of the webpage displayed in the browser.

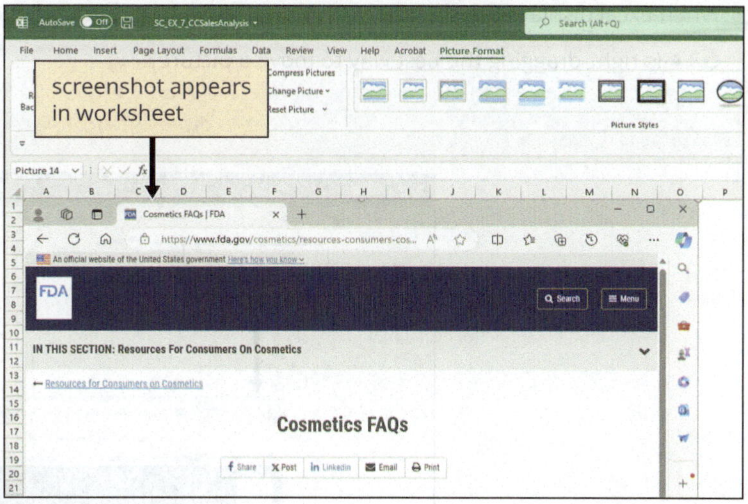

Figure 7–106

6

- Right-click the browser app button on the taskbar and then click Close window on the shortcut menu to exit the browser.

Now that the screenshot has been inserted, you will insert alternative text for the screenshot.

1

- Right-click the border of the screenshot to display the shortcut menu.

2

- Click 'Edit Alt Text' to display the Alt Text pane and click in its text box
- In the text box (Alt Text pane), type **Screenshot of the FDA Cosmetics FAQs website** to enter an appropriate alternative text.

3

- Close the Alt Text pane.

To Move an Object

The following steps move the screenshot.

1

- Right-drag the screenshot to a location near cell D3 (Figure 7–107).

Q&A Can you drag the screenshot to a new location without holding down the right mouse button?
No. Because the screenshot is now a hyperlink, clicking it opens the linked website. If you do not have the ability to right-drag, you would have to click the Selection Pane button (Page Layout tab | Arrange group) and then select the screenshot in the Selection pane. Once selected, you could move it in the normal way.

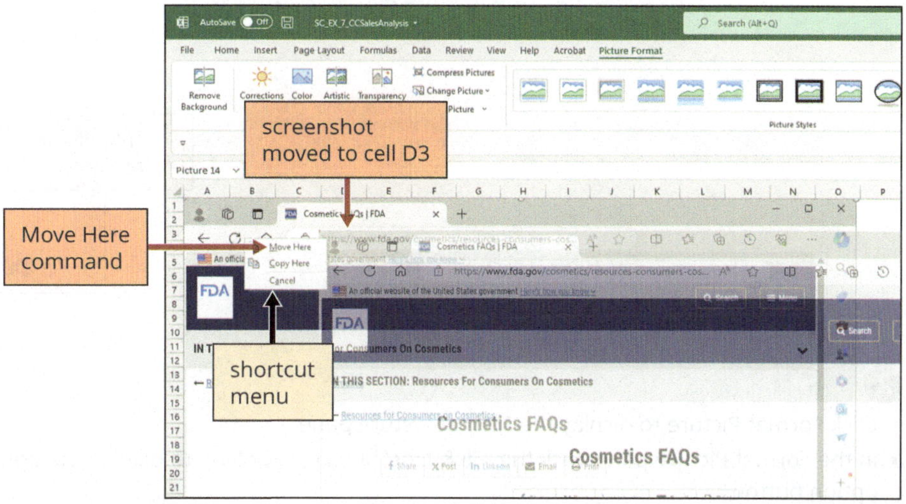

Figure 7–107

2

- When Excel displays the shortcut menu, click Move Here to move the screen shot (Figure 7–108).

Q&A Is right-dragging the best way to move a picture?

If the picture is a hyperlink, yes. If the picture is not a hyperlink, you can simply drag it to a new location on the same worksheet. If you need to move the picture to a different worksheet, you should cut and paste.

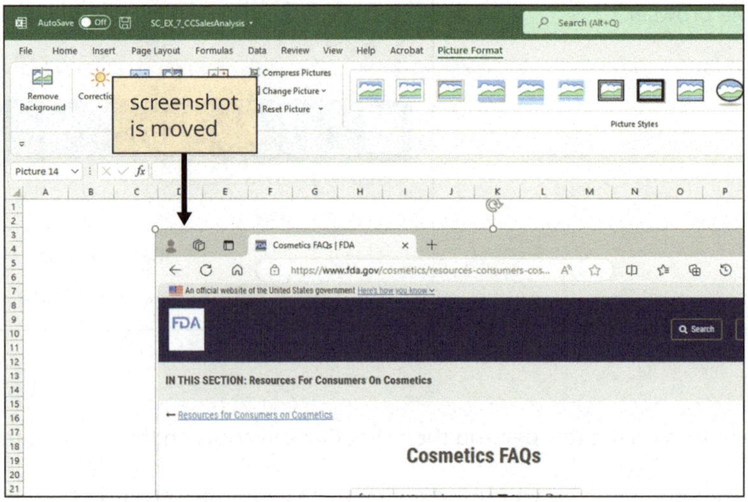

Figure 7–108

To Add a Picture Border

The following steps add a border to the screenshot. **Why?** A border helps to delineate the edges of the screenshot from the worksheet itself.

1

- Right-click the screenshot to display the shortcut menu (Figure 7–109).

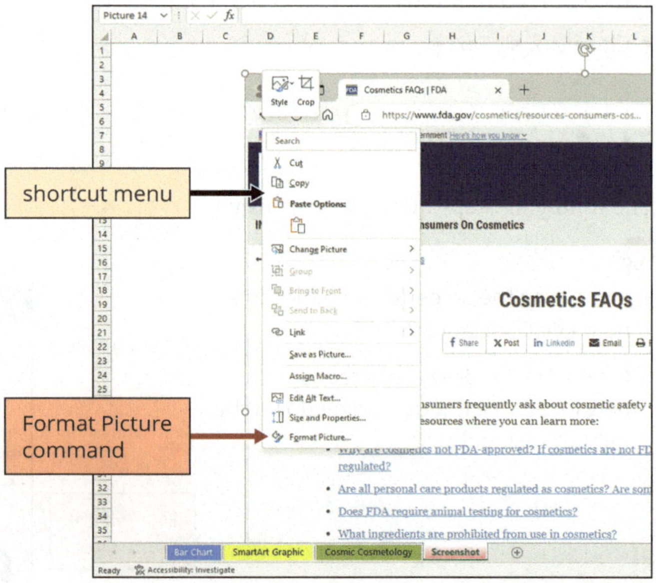

Figure 7–109

2

- Click Format Picture to display the Format Picture pane.
- In the Format Picture pane, click the 'Fill & Line' button, click Line to display the options, then click the Solid Line option button.
- Click the Color button to display the Color gallery (Figure 7–110).

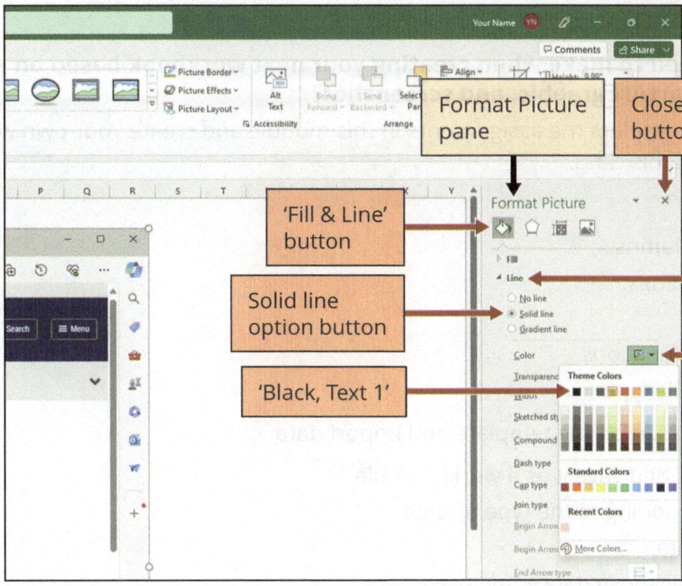

Figure 7–110

3

- Click 'Black, Text 1' to apply a border.
- Close the Format Picture pane and click cell A1 to deselect the picture and display the border (Figure 7–111).

Q&A Is there a different method to apply borders to pictures than on screenshots?

No, you apply borders the same way.

- In Excel, click the Save button on the Quick Access Toolbar.
- **sam** Click the Close button in the upper-right corner of the title bar to exit Excel.

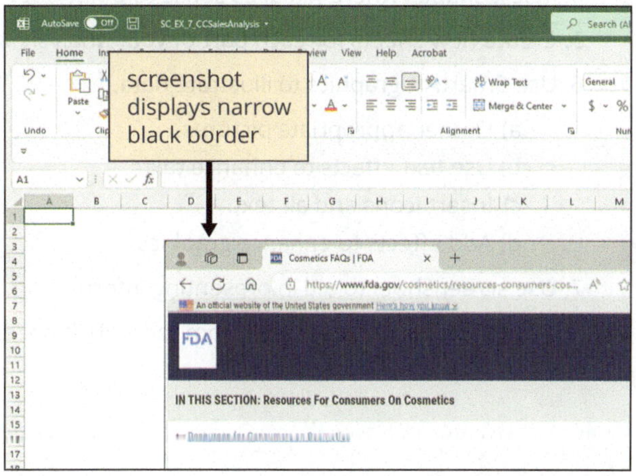

Figure 7–111

Summary

In this module, you learned how to create a template that can be used every time a similar workbook is developed. Starting from the template, you gathered external data by importing a text file, an Access database, a Word document, and a website. You formatted the data and transposed it when necessary. You replicated the formulas and functions and then used Quick Analysis to display specific formatting. You created and formatted a shape to illustrate data in the workbook. Then, you created a bar chart, formatting the bars with a style, color, and level. After reversing the order of the categories, you edited the number format of the horizontal labels. While creating a SmartArt graphic, you inserted pictures relevant to the worksheet and formatted the SmartArt with text, styles, and ALT text. You learned about object linking and embedding and inserted a hyperlinked screenshot, which you also moved and formatted.

Consider This: Plan Ahead

What decisions will you need to make when creating your next workbook based on a template to analyze data including a chart, SmartArt graphic, and screenshot?

Use these guidelines as you complete the assignments in this module and create your own worksheets for evaluating and analyzing data outside of this class.

1. Create a template.
    a) Format rows and columns.
    b) Enter titles and headings.
    c) Enter sample data.
    d) Enter formulas and functions.
    e) Save as a template file type.
2. Create a new workbook based on the template and import data.
    a) Open a template file and save it as a workbook file.
    b) Import data corresponding to the type of data.
    c) Format imported data.
    d) Paste special and transpose data when necessary.
3. Format using the Quick Analysis gallery.
    a) Apply formatting or totals using the Quick Analysis gallery.
4. Insert shapes where it makes sense to point out data.
5. Create new sheets for each part of your analysis workbook.
6. Use SmartArt graphics to illustrate data.
    a) Gather appropriate pictures.
    b) Use text effects to enhance text.
    c) Insert icons and alt text.
    d) Add effects to enhance graphics.
7. Use screenshots to aid in presenting information.
    a) Hyperlink screenshots from the web, if necessary.

Student Assignments

Apply Your Knowledge

Reinforce the skills and apply the concepts you learned in this module.

Using a Template to Create a Consolidated Workbook

Note: To complete this assignment, you will be required to use the Data Files. Please contact your instructor for information about accessing the Data Files.

Instructions: You are to create the consolidated workbook and SmartArt graphic for the Lunch Wagon mobile eatery shown in Figure 7–112. Lunch Wagon has four mobile units that serve the tri-county area and are available for special event catering. The owners would like an analysis of their sales for the months of June, July, and August.

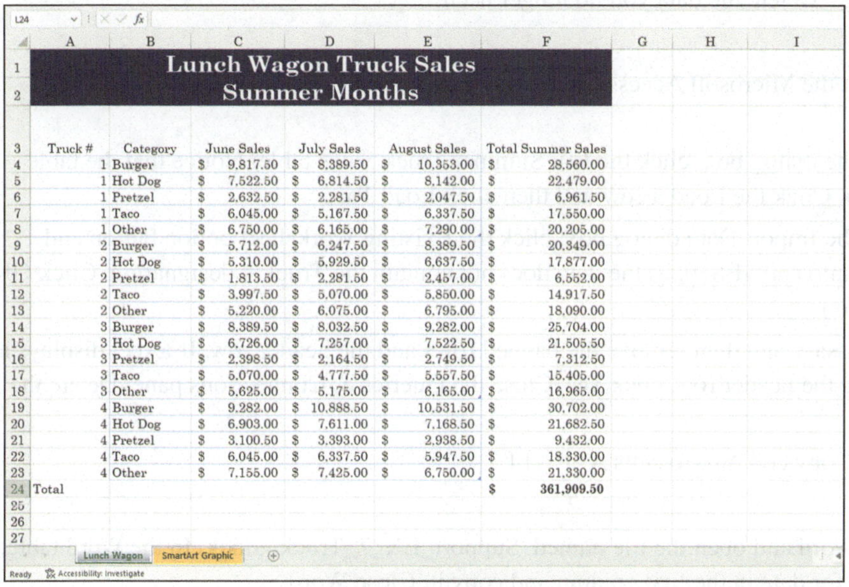

Lunch Wagon Truck Sales
Summer Months

Truck #	Category	June Sales	July Sales	August Sales	Total Summer Sales
1	Burger	$ 9,817.50	$ 8,389.50	$ 10,353.00	$ 28,560.00
1	Hot Dog	$ 7,522.50	$ 6,814.50	$ 8,142.00	$ 22,479.00
1	Pretzel	$ 2,632.50	$ 2,281.50	$ 2,047.50	$ 6,961.50
1	Taco	$ 6,045.00	$ 5,167.50	$ 6,337.50	$ 17,550.00
1	Other	$ 6,750.00	$ 6,165.00	$ 7,290.00	$ 20,205.00
2	Burger	$ 5,712.00	$ 6,247.50	$ 8,389.50	$ 20,349.00
2	Hot Dog	$ 5,310.00	$ 5,929.50	$ 6,637.50	$ 17,877.00
2	Pretzel	$ 1,813.50	$ 2,281.50	$ 2,457.00	$ 6,552.00
2	Taco	$ 3,997.50	$ 5,070.00	$ 5,850.00	$ 14,917.50
2	Other	$ 5,220.00	$ 6,075.00	$ 6,795.00	$ 18,090.00
3	Burger	$ 8,389.50	$ 8,032.50	$ 9,282.00	$ 25,704.00
3	Hot Dog	$ 6,726.00	$ 7,257.00	$ 7,522.50	$ 21,505.50
3	Pretzel	$ 2,398.50	$ 2,164.50	$ 2,749.50	$ 7,312.50
3	Taco	$ 5,070.00	$ 4,777.50	$ 5,557.50	$ 15,405.00
3	Other	$ 5,625.00	$ 5,175.00	$ 6,165.00	$ 16,965.00
4	Burger	$ 9,282.00	$ 10,888.50	$ 10,531.50	$ 30,702.00
4	Hot Dog	$ 6,903.00	$ 7,611.00	$ 7,168.50	$ 21,682.50
4	Pretzel	$ 3,100.50	$ 3,393.00	$ 2,938.50	$ 9,432.00
4	Taco	$ 6,045.00	$ 6,337.50	$ 5,947.50	$ 18,330.00
4	Other	$ 7,155.00	$ 7,425.00	$ 6,750.00	$ 21,330.00
Total					**$ 361,909.50**

Figure 7–112(a): Imported Data in Worksheet

Figure 7–112(b): SmartArt Graphic

Perform the following tasks:

1. Open a File Explorer window and double-click the file named SC_EX_7-1.xlsx from the Data Files. Save the file with the file name, SC_EX_7_LunchWagonAnalysis.
2. Add a second sheet to the workbook, named, SmartArt Graphic. Color the tab orange (Standard Colors area).

Continued on next page

3. To import a text file:
   a. Make the Lunch Wagon worksheet active, and then select cell A5. Use the Data tab to import the text file named, Support_EX_7_Truck1.csv, from the Data Files.
   b. When Excel displays the dialog box, click the Load arrow and then click Load To.
   c. When Excel displays the Import Data dialog box, click the Existing Worksheet option button to select it. Click OK (Import Data dialog box) to put the data in cell $A$5.
   d. If necessary, click the new table to select it, and then use the Table Design tab to remove the banded rows and the header row. If Excel displays a dialog box, referencing the header row, click Yes. Close the Queries & Connections pane.
   e. Select cells A5:E5. Right-click the selection and then click Delete on the shortcut menu. When Excel displays the Delete dialog box, click the 'Shift cells up' option button, if necessary. Click OK (Delete dialog box).
   f. Use a separate area of the worksheet to trim the extra spaces from cells B5:B9. Copy the trimmed values back to the range. Delete the data you no longer need.
4. To import an Access table:
   a. Select cell A10. Import the Microsoft Access file named, Support_EX_7_Truck2.accdb, from the Data Files.
   b. When Excel displays the dialog box, click the LW Summer Truck Sales table. Notice that the table has no Truck # column. Click the Load arrow and then click Load To.
   c. When Excel displays the Import Data dialog box, click the Existing Worksheet option button and then choose to import into cell $B$10, as the data does not contain the Truck # designation. Click OK (Import Data dialog box).
   d. Select the table if necessary and then remove the banded rows and the header row. If Excel displays a dialog box, referencing the header row, click Yes. Close the Queries & Connections pane. Delete the resulting empty row.
   e. Type **2** in cell A10. Copy cell A10 to cells A11:A14.
5. To paste data from Word:
   a. Select cell A22. Start Word and open the file named, Support_EX_7_Truck3.docx. In the Word table, select all of the except for data in the first column and copy it. Close Word.
   b. Return to Excel and use the Paste Special command to paste the data as Text (Paste Special dialog box) in cell A22.
   c. Copy the Excel range A22:E25. Click cell A15 and transpose the data while pasting it.
   d. Delete the original imported data in cells A22:E25.
   e. Cut the data in cells B15:D19 and paste it to cell C15 to move the data one column to the right.
   f. Select cells A15:A19. Click the 'Text to Columns' button (Data tab | Data Tools group). In the Convert Text to Columns Wizard dialog box, choose the Fixed Width option button, and then click Finish.
6. To import Web data:
   a. Select cell A20. Click the From Web button (Data tab | Get & Transform Data group). In the URL box, enter the location of the HTML data file, such as c:\users\username\documents\cis 101\data files\Support_EX_7_Truck4.html, and then press ENTER.
   b. When Excel displays the Navigator dialog box, click the name of the table, Lunch Wagon Truck Sales -- Summer Months, and click the Web View tab. Click the Transform Data button (Navigator dialog box) to open the Power Query Editor window.
   c. Remove the Truck # column. Click the 'Close & Load' arrow (Power Query Editor Home tab | Close group) and then click the 'Close & Load To' command to close the Power Query Editor Window.
   d. When Excel displays the Import Data dialog box, if necessary, click the Existing worksheet option button, choose cell B20, and then click OK.

e. Remove the banded rows and the header row. If Excel displays a dialog box, referencing the header row, click Yes.

f. Delete the blank row. Enter **4** in cell A20, and replicate the value in cells A21:A24.

g. Close the Queries & Connections pane.

7. Use the fill handle to replicate cell F4 to F5:F24.
8. Copy the formatting from C4:F4 to C5:F24.
9. Delete row 4.
10. Select cells F4:F23. Click the Quick Analysis button and create a total in cell F24. In cell A24, type the word, **Total**. Adjust column widths as necessary.
11. If directed by your instructor, insert your name and course number in cell A25.
12. Go to the SmartArt Graphic sheet. Click the Gridlines check box (View tab | Show group) to hide gridlines.
13. Display the Insert tab. Click the SmartArt button (Insert tab | Illustrations group). Click List in the left pane (Choose a SmartArt Graphic dialog box) and then click Picture Caption List in the middle pane. Click the OK button to insert the graphic.
14. One at a time, using the Text Pane (SmartArt Design tab | Create Graphic group), replace the word, Text, with the words, Burger, Hot Dog, Taco, and Pretzel, respectively.
15. Change the SmartArt style to Polished.
16. One at a time, click the picture icon in each part of the graphic, and search the Stock Images for images similar to those shown in Figure 7–112(b), to illustrate each of the four text labels.
17. Resize and move the graphic to fill the area D1:L24.
18. Add alternative text to the SmartArt graphic added. Use the following for the alternative text: **Graphical Images of the Items the Lunch Wagon sells, including a Burger, Hot Dog, Taco, and Pretzel.**
19. Save the file and submit the revised workbook in the format specified by your instructor.
20. **Consider This:** In what format do you think most companies submit data? Why? If the data changes, how do consolidated workbooks adjust? Do all the formats lend themselves to recalculating? Why or why not?

Extend Your Knowledge

Extend the skills you learned in this module and experiment with new skills. You may need to use Help to complete the assignment.

Inserting a SmartArt Organization Chart and Image on a Worksheet

Note: To complete this assignment, you will be required to use the Data Files. Please contact your instructor for information about accessing the Data Files.

Instructions: Start Excel. Open the workbook named SC_EX_7-2, which is located in the Data Files. You are to add a SmartArt graphic and an image to the workbook and then format both graphics.

Perform the following tasks:

1. Save the file with the file name SC_EX_7_HillValley.
2. Insert a SmartArt graphic on the Medical Team sheet using the Hierarchy type and the Name and Title Organization Chart layout.
3. Select the top shape in the first row of the SmartArt graphic. Confirm that only the top shape is selected, remembering that selection handles around an object indicate it is selected, then then press Delete. This removes that shape and you are left with one shape in the top row and three shapes in the second row below.

Continued on next page

4. Select the first shape in the second row. Right-click on the shape and choose Add Shape from the shortcut menu. In the expanded menu, select Add Shape Below. This creates a shape in a third row connected to the first shape in the second row.
5. Repeat step #4 to add a second shape below the first shape in the second row.
6. Select the second shape in the second row. Right-click on the shape and choose Add Shape from the shortcut menu. In the expanded menu, select Add Shape Below. This creates a third shape in the third row connected to the second shape in the second row.
7. Select the third shape in the second row. Right-click on the shape and choose Add Shape from the shortcut menu. In the expanded menu, select Add Shape Below. This creates a fourth shape in the third row connected to the third shape in the second row.
8. Repeat step #7 to add a second shape below the third shape in the second row.
9. Display the Text Pane and drag its border to the right side of the chart. Use copying and pasting techniques to insert the names and positions from columns A through B into the SmartArt, as shown in Figure 7–113. Insert your name in place of one of the employees of your choosing.

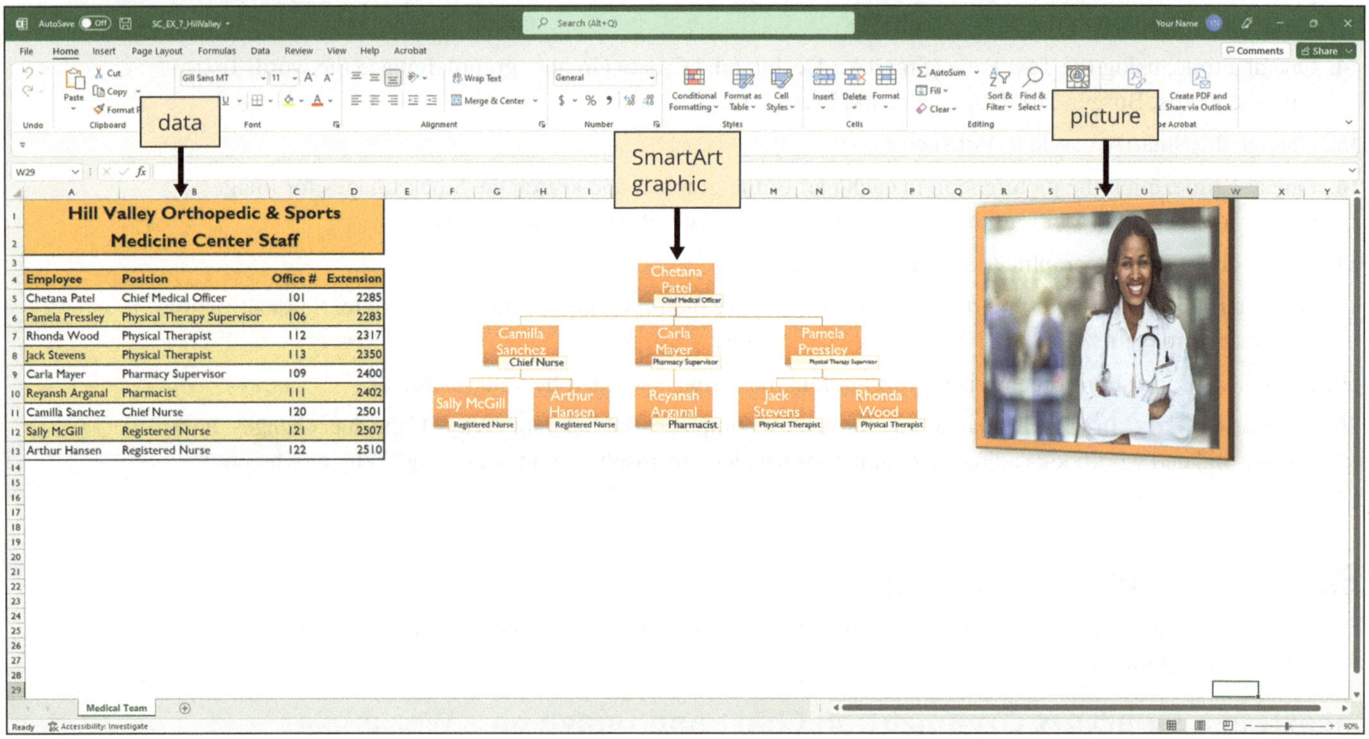

Figure 7–113

10. Change the color scheme of the hierarchy chart to 'Colored Fill – Accent 1' in the Change Colors gallery if necessary.
11. Use the SmartArt Styles gallery to change the style to Intense Effect.
12. Move the SmartArt Graphic as necessary so it is positioned to the right of the data.
13. Add the following alternative text to the SmartArt graphic: **Hierarchy Chart of the Hill Valley Medical Team.**
14. Use Help to read about formatting pictures. Insert a stock picture related to the search term, nurse (you may wish to choose the image shown in Figure 7–113, or another image of a nurse). Place the picture to the right of the SmartArt graphic. Format the picture using the Metal Frame picture style (Picture Format tab | Picture Styles group).
15. Change the picture border to 'Orange, Accent 1'.
16. Add a Picture Effect (Picture Format tab | Picture Styles group) using the 3-D Rotation named 'Perspective: Left'.

17. Delete any existing alternative text and enter **Picture of a Hill Valley Medical Team Member.**
18. Move and resize the picture so that it fits beside the SmartArt graphic, approximately covering cells Q1 to W13 (as shown in Figure 7–113).
19. Add your name and course number to the worksheet if instructed to do so by your instructor.
20. Save the file and submit the revised workbook in the format specified by your instructor.
21. **Consider This:** When do you think a company would use a spreadsheet like this? What formatting and changes might make it even more useful?

Expand Your World

Create a solution that uses cloud and web technologies by learning and investigating on your own from general guidance.

Using Web Data

Note: To complete this assignment, you will be required to use the Data Files. Please contact your instructor for information about accessing the Data Files.

Instructions: You would like to import some web statistics about your state. You decide to retrieve U.S. census data from the web pertaining to Households & Families in your state (Figure 7–114).

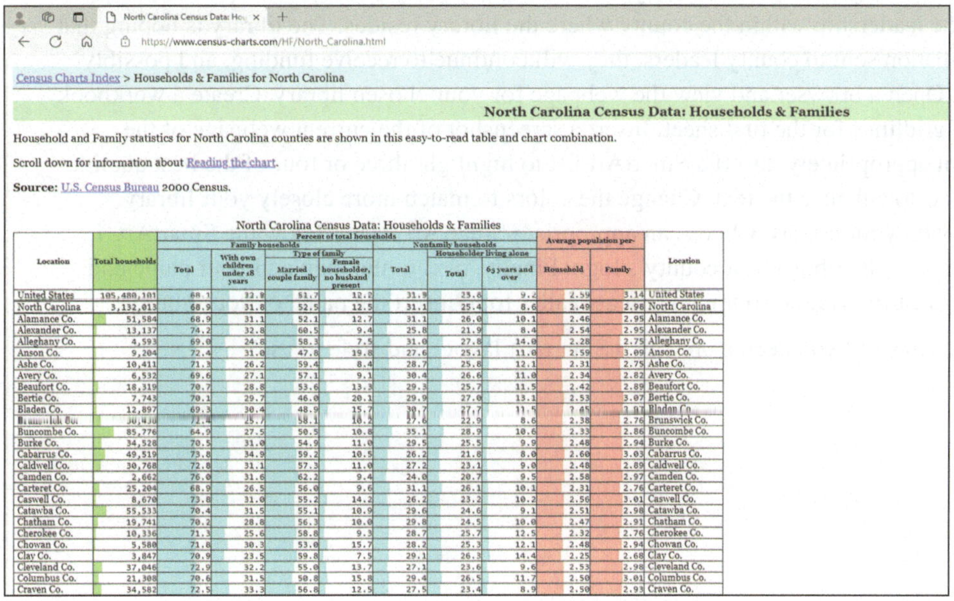

Location	Total households	Percent of total households: Family households: Total	Family households: With own children under 18 years	Type of family: Married couple family	Type of family: Female householder, no husband present	Nonfamily households: Total	Householder living alone: Total	Householder living alone: 65 years and over	Average population per-: Household	Average population per-: Family	Location
United States	105,480,101	68.1	32.9	51.7	12.2	31.9	25.8	9.2	2.59	3.14	United States
North Carolina	3,132,013	68.9	31.8	52.5	12.5	31.1	25.4	8.6	2.49	2.98	North Carolina
Alamance Co.	51,584	68.9	31.1	52.1	12.7	31.1	26.0	10.1	2.46	2.95	Alamance Co.
Alexander Co.	13,137	74.2	32.8	60.5	9.4	25.8	21.9	8.4	2.54	2.95	Alexander Co.
Alleghany Co.	4,593	69.0	24.8	58.3	7.5	31.0	27.8	14.0	2.28	2.75	Alleghany Co.
Anson Co.	9,204	72.4	31.0	47.8	19.8	27.6	25.1	11.0	2.59	3.09	Anson Co.
Ashe Co.	10,411	71.3	26.2	59.4	8.4	28.7	25.8	12.1	2.31	2.75	Ashe Co.
Avery Co.	6,532	69.6	27.1	57.1	9.1	30.4	26.6	11.0	2.34	2.82	Avery Co.
Beaufort Co.	18,319	70.7	28.8	53.6	13.3	29.3	25.7	11.5	2.42	2.89	Beaufort Co.
Bertie Co.	7,743	70.1	29.7	46.0	20.1	29.9	27.0	13.1	2.53	3.07	Bertie Co.
Bladen Co.	12,897	69.3	30.4	48.9	15.7	30.7	27.7	11.5	2.45	3.07	Bladen Co.
[illegible]	[illegible]	72.4	25.7	58.1	10.2	27.6	22.9	8.6	2.38	2.76	Brunswick Co.
Buncombe Co.	85,776	64.9	27.5	50.5	10.8	35.1	28.9	10.6	2.33	2.86	Buncombe Co.
Burke Co.	34,528	70.5	31.0	54.9	11.0	29.5	25.5	9.9	2.48	2.94	Burke Co.
Cabarrus Co.	49,519	73.8	34.9	59.2	10.5	26.2	21.8	8.0	2.60	3.03	Cabarrus Co.
Caldwell Co.	30,768	72.8	31.1	57.3	11.0	27.2	23.1	9.0	2.48	2.89	Caldwell Co.
Camden Co.	2,662	76.0	31.6	62.2	9.4	24.0	20.7	9.5	2.58	2.97	Camden Co.
Carteret Co.	25,204	68.9	26.5	56.0	9.6	31.1	26.1	10.1	2.31	2.76	Carteret Co.
Caswell Co.	8,670	73.8	31.0	55.2	14.2	26.2	23.2	10.2	2.56	3.01	Caswell Co.
Catawba Co.	55,533	70.4	31.5	55.1	10.9	29.6	24.6	9.1	2.51	2.98	Catawba Co.
Chatham Co.	19,741	70.2	28.8	56.3	10.0	29.8	24.5	10.0	2.47	2.91	Chatham Co.
Cherokee Co.	10,336	71.3	25.6	58.8	9.3	28.7	25.7	12.5	2.32	2.76	Cherokee Co.
Chowan Co.	5,580	71.8	30.3	53.0	15.7	28.2	25.3	12.1	2.48	2.94	Chowan Co.
Clay Co.	3,847	70.9	23.5	59.8	7.5	29.1	26.3	14.4	2.25	2.68	Clay Co.
Cleveland Co.	37,046	72.9	32.2	55.0	13.7	27.1	23.6	9.6	2.53	2.98	Cleveland Co.
Columbus Co.	21,308	70.6	31.5	50.8	15.8	29.4	26.5	11.7	2.50	3.01	Columbus Co.
Craven Co.	34,582	72.5	33.3	56.8	12.5	27.5	23.4	8.9	2.50	2.93	Craven Co.

Figure 7–114

Perform the following tasks:

1. Start a browser and navigate to https://www.census-charts.com/.
2. In the Data by State and County area, click 'Households & Families,' and then click your state.
3. When the website presents the data, copy the URL address.
4. Start Excel and open a blank workbook.
5. Hide the gridlines and rename the sheet, Screenshot. Use the Screenshot button (Insert tab | Illustrations group) to insert a screenshot of your data, or if necessary, use screen clipping. Insert a hyperlink for the screenshot using the URL is step #3. Close the browser.
6. Add a new sheet to the workbook, named Web Data.
7. Select cell B3. Click the 'From Web' button (Data tab | Get & Transform Data group). Paste the URL into the address text box in the From Web dialog box. Click the OK button (From Web dialog box).

Continued on next page

8. If Excel displays the Access Web content dialog box, click the Connect button.
9. When Excel displays the Navigator dialog box, click your chosen state table and then click the Transform Data button.
10. When Excel displays the Power Query Editor window, use the 'Close and Load To' command to load the data to the existing worksheet. Close the Queries & Connections pane.
11. When Excel displays the data, add and format a title, and adjust column widths, if necessary.
12. Add the following alt text to the screenshot: **Households & Families Census Data from the U.S. Census Bureau for an Individual State.**
13. Save the file as SC_EX_07_WebData, and submit the revised workbook in the format specified by your instructor.
14. **Consider This:** What kinds of analysis could you perform in Excel on the data you downloaded from the census website? What would make the data more meaningful and useful? Why?

In the Lab

Design and implement a solution using creative thinking and problem-solving skills.

Create a Cover Sheet

Part 1: You are competing to design a cover sheet for your local library to include in their workbooks when they send out statistics to the leadership within the county where the library resides. The library is hoping that by having up-to-date information sent to county leaders, they will continue to receive funding, and possibly receive additional funding. Open a browser and view the webpage for your chosen library. Create a workbook and turn off the viewing of gridlines for the first sheet. Insert a screenshot of the current webpage of the library, and move and size it appropriately. Insert a SmartArt list to highlight three or four of the best qualities of the library. Use text effects to enhance the text. Change the colors to match more closely your library colors, or those associated with your county. Choose an appropriate SmartArt style. Below the SmartArt graphic, add a screen clipping of the library's or county's logo. Finally, next to the logo add your name and format it so that it appears as a title. Below your name, in a smaller font, insert the name of your library.

Part 2: **Consider This:** How did you decide on which SmartArt layout and style to use?

Creating Reports and Forms

Objectives

After completing this module, you will be able to:

- Organize data in a report by grouping and sorting
- Include calculated controls in a report or form
- Format a control
- Filter records in a report
- Create a report from multiple tables
- Create a report using Layout view
- Describe options to apply a theme to a report or form
- Create a summary report
- Create a form using the Form Wizard
- Apply a control layout
- Include special items on a report or form to enhance its design
- Move a control
- Add a field to a report or form
- Use the Advanced filter/sort tool
- Prepare mailing labels

Introduction

One of the advantages to maintaining data in a database is the ability to present the data in attractive reports and forms that highlight certain information. Reports present data in an organized format that is usually printed. The data can come from one or more tables. On the other hand, you usually view forms on the screen, although you can print them. In addition to viewing data, you can also use forms to update data. That is, you can use forms to add records, delete records, or change records. Like reports, the data in the form can come from one or more tables.

This module shows how to create reports and forms by creating two reports and a form. There are several ways to create both reports and forms. One approach is to use the Report or Form Wizard. You can also use either Layout view or Design view to create or modify a report or form. In this module, you will use Layout view for this purpose. In later modules, you will learn how to use Design view. You will also use the Label Wizard to produce mailing labels.

Project: Reports and Forms

The paralegals at Partners Law Firm are now able to better keep track of their closings information and to target the needs of the practice by using its database. Partners paralegals hope to improve their closing preparation processes further by using custom reports that meet the practice's specific needs. They also need to create some reports in response to requests from the Accounting Department. Figure 4–1 shows the Closings and Properties report, which is a modified version of an existing report. The report features grouping. That is, the report shown in Figure 4–1 groups records by state. There are two separate groups, one each for the two states, Pennsylvania and New York, where properties are located. The appropriate state name appears above each group. The total of the Payoff Amount field just for the properties within each group (called a **subtotal**) appears below the group. Further below, at the end of the report, is the grand total of the same field for all the properties. This report contains conditional formatting.

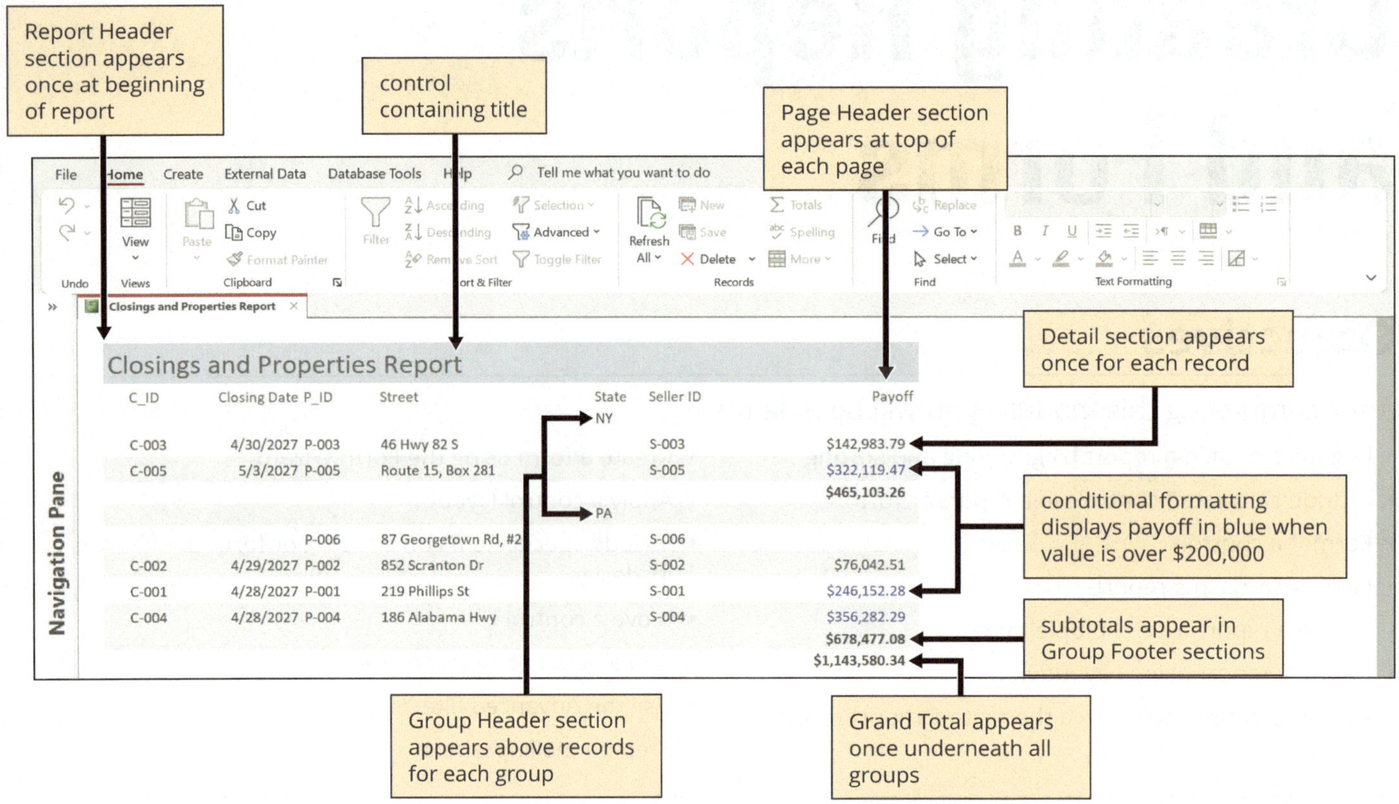

Figure 4–1a Closings and Properties Report

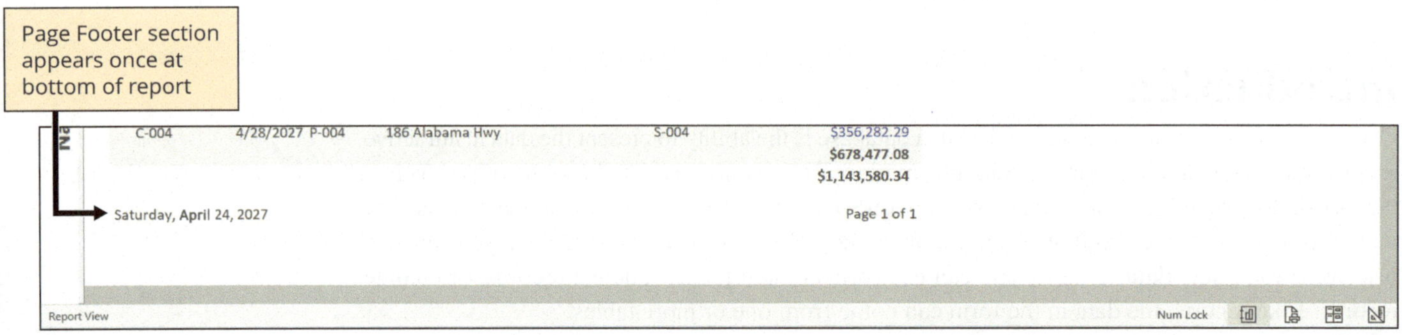

Figure 4–1b Closings and Properties Report

BTW
Consider Your Audience
Always design reports and forms with your audience in mind. Make your reports and forms accessible to individuals who may have problems with colorblindness or reduced vision.

Figure 4–2 shows the second report. This report encompasses data from the Sellers, Properties, Closings, and Closing Fees tables. Like the report in Figure 4–1, the data is grouped, although this time it is grouped by the month of the closing date. Not only does the closing date appear in each group, but each group's subtotal of agent commissions appears as well.

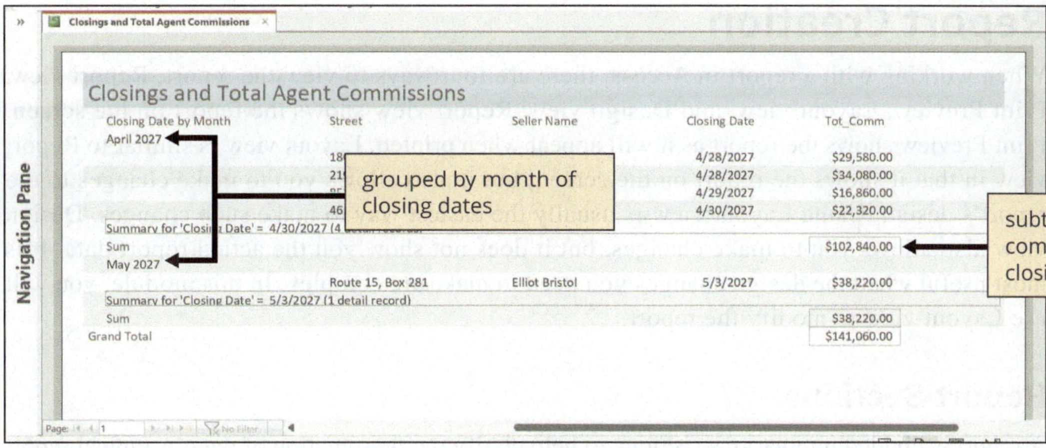

Figure 4–2

Partners paralegals also want to improve the process of updating data by using a custom form, as shown in Figure 4–3. The form has a title, but unlike the form you can create by clicking the Form button, this form does not contain all the fields in the Mortgage Companies table. In addition, the fields are in a different order than in the table. For this form, Partners paralegals like the appearance of including the fields in a stacked layout.

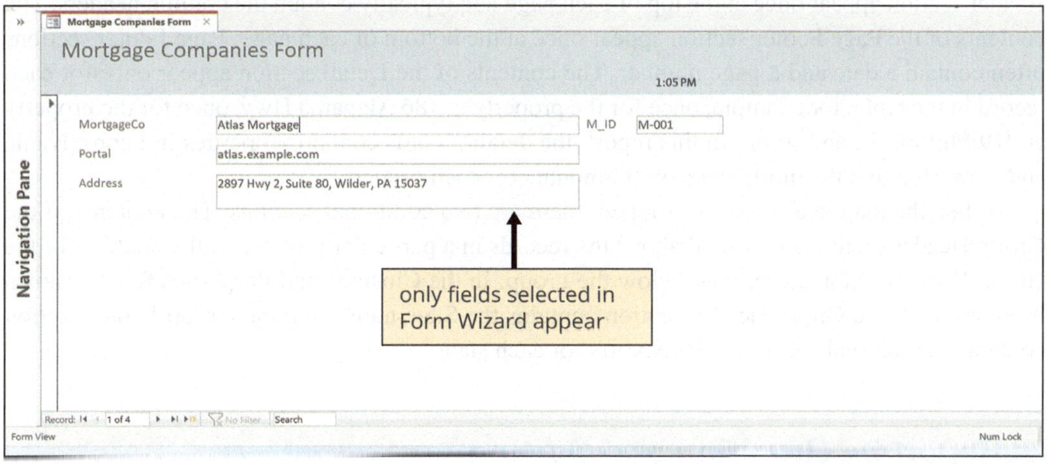

Figure 4–3

Partners also wants to be able to produce mailing labels for new property owners. These labels must align correctly with the particular labels Partners uses and must be sorted by postal code (Figure 4–4).

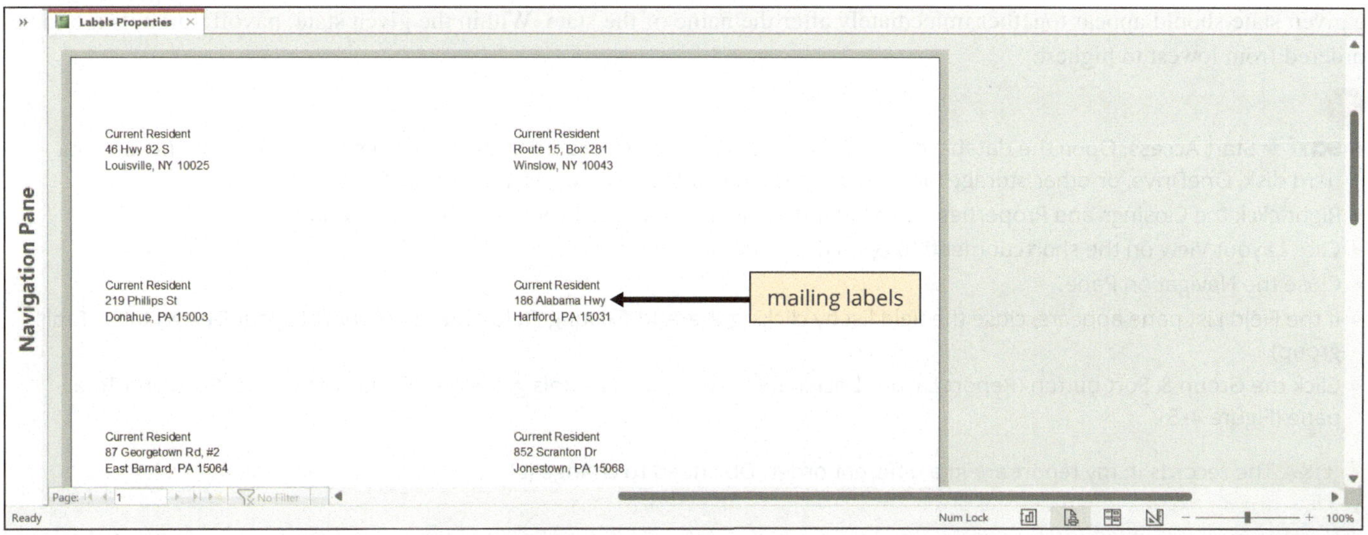

Figure 4–4

BTW
The Ribbon and Screen Resolution
Access may change how the groups and buttons within the groups appear on the ribbon, depending on the computer or mobile device's screen resolution. Thus, your ribbon may look different from the ones in this course if you are using a screen resolution other than 1920 x 1080.

BTW
Touch Screen Differences
The Office and Windows interfaces may vary if you are using a touch screen. For this reason, you might notice that the function or appearance of your touch screen differs slightly from this module's presentation.

BTW
Enabling the Content
For each of the databases you use in this module, you will need to enable the content.

Report Creation

When working with a report in Access, there are four ways to view the report: Report view, Print Preview, Layout view, and Design view. Report view shows the report on the screen. Print Preview shows the report as it will appear when printed. Layout view is similar to Report view in that it shows the report on the screen, but it also allows you to make changes to the report's design. Using Layout view is usually the easiest way to make such changes. Design view also allows you to make changes, but it does not show you the actual report data. It is most useful when the design changes you need to make are complex. In this module, you will use Layout view to modify the report.

Report Sections

A report is divided into various sections to help clarify the presentation of data. A typical report consists of a Report Header section, Page Header section, Detail section, Page Footer section, and Report Footer section, as shown earlier in Figure 4–1.

The contents of the Report Header section appear once at the beginning of the report. In the Closings and Properties Report, the report title is in the Report Header section. The contents of the Report Footer section appear once at the end of the report. In the Closings and Properties Report, the Report Footer section contains the grand totals of Payoff amounts. The contents of the Page Header section appear once at the top of each page and typically contain the column headers. The contents of the Page Footer section appear once at the bottom of each page; Page Footer sections often contain a date and a page number. The contents of the Detail section appear once for each record in the table; for example, once for the property at 186 Alabama Hwy, once for the property at 219 Phillips St, and so on. In this report, the detail records contain properties in Pennsylvania and New York and the mortgage payoff amounts for each property.

When the data in a report is grouped, there are two additional sections. The contents of the Group Header section are printed above the records in a particular group, and the contents of the Group Footer section are printed below the group. In the Closings and Properties Report shown in Figure 4–1, the Group Header section contains the State name, and the Group Footer section contains the subtotals of mortgage payoffs for each state.

To Organize Data in a Report by Grouping and Sorting

In Layout view of the report, you can specify both grouping and sorting by using the Group & Sort button on the Design tab. The following steps open the Closings and Properties Report in Layout view and then specify both grouping and sorting in the report. **Why?** Partners paralegals have determined that the records in the report should be grouped by state and sorted by payoff amount to produce a report requested by the Accounting department. That is, all the mortgage payoff amounts for properties in a given state should appear together immediately after the name of the state. Within the given state, payoff amounts are to be ordered from lowest to highest.

1

- **sam** Start Access. Open the database, SC_AC_04-1.accdb, which is located in the Data Files folder. Save the file on your hard disk, OneDrive, or other storage location using the file name, **SC_AC_04_Partners**. Enable the content.
- Right-click the Closings and Properties Report in the Navigation Pane to produce a shortcut menu.
- Click Layout View on the shortcut menu to open the report in Layout view.
- Close the Navigation Pane.
- If the Field List pane appears, close the field list by clicking the 'Add Existing Fields' button (Report Layout Design tab | Tools group).
- Click the Group & Sort button (Report Layout Design tab | Grouping & Totals group) to display the Group, Sort, and Total pane (Figure 4–5).

Q&A The records in my report are in a different order. Do I need to change it?
No. You will change the order of the records in the following steps.

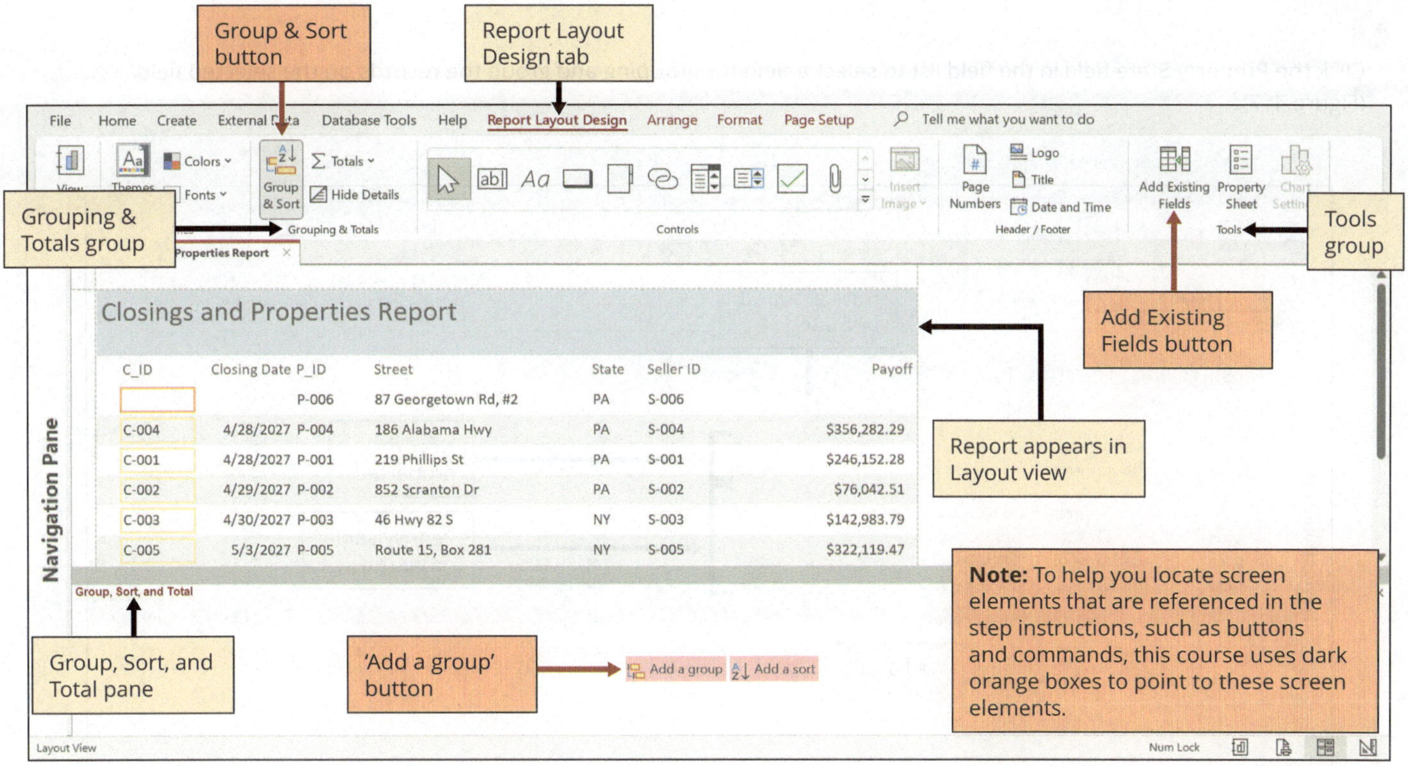

Figure 4–5

2

- Click the 'Add a group' button to add a group and display a field list (Figure 4–6).

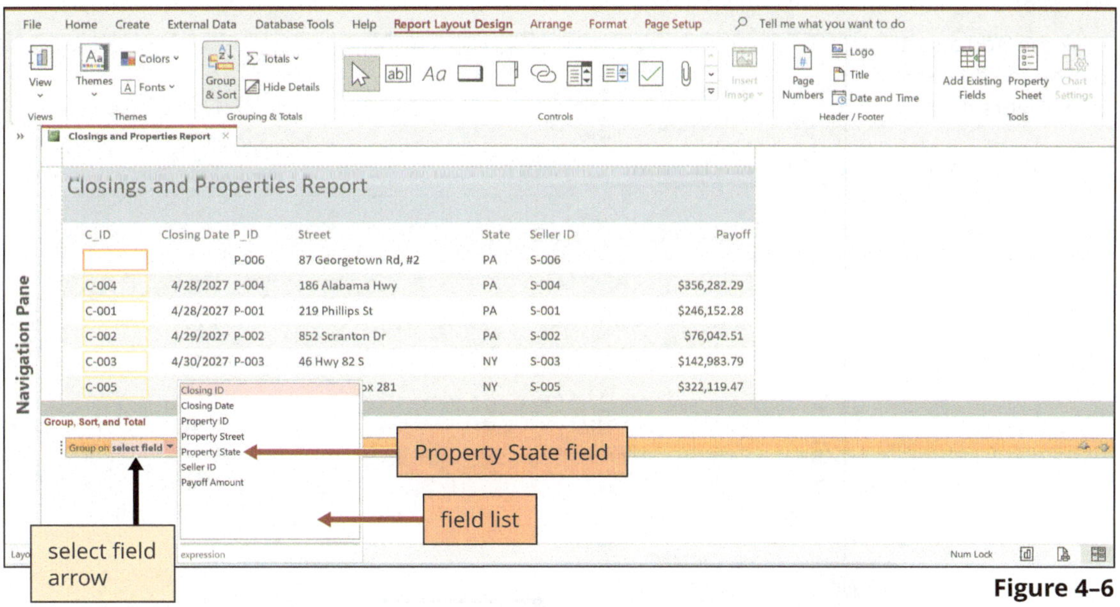

Figure 4–6

3

- Click the Property State field in the field list to select a field for grouping and group the records on the selected field (Figure 4–7).

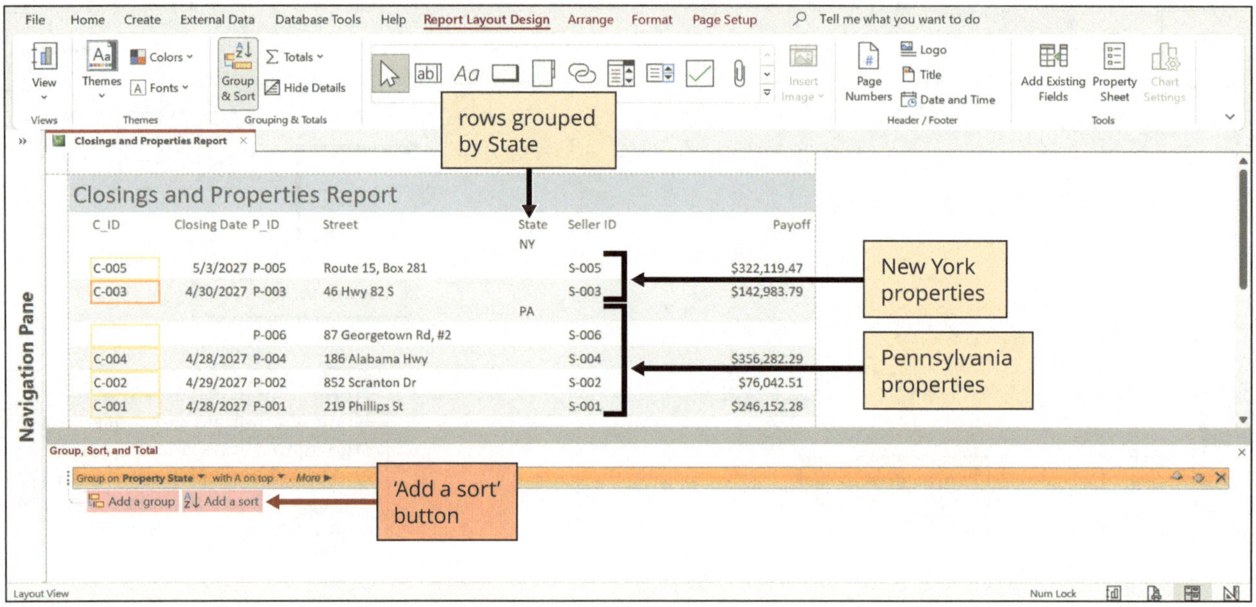

Figure 4–7

4

Click the 'Add a sort' button to add a sort level (Figure 4–8).

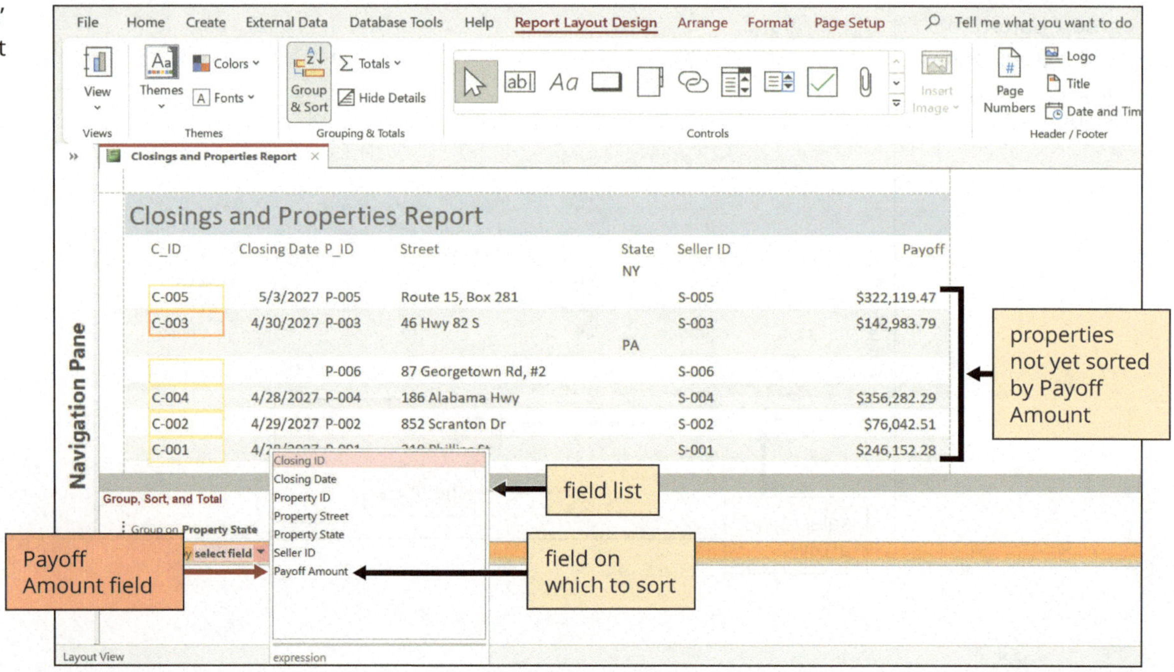

Figure 4–8

5

- Click the Payoff Amount field in the field list to specify the field on which the records in each group will be sorted (Figure 4–9).

Q&A I thought the report would be sorted by State, because I chose to group on that field. What is the effect of choosing to sort by Payoff Amount?

This second sort takes place within groups. You are specifying that within the list of the same State, the rows will be ordered by Payoff Amount.

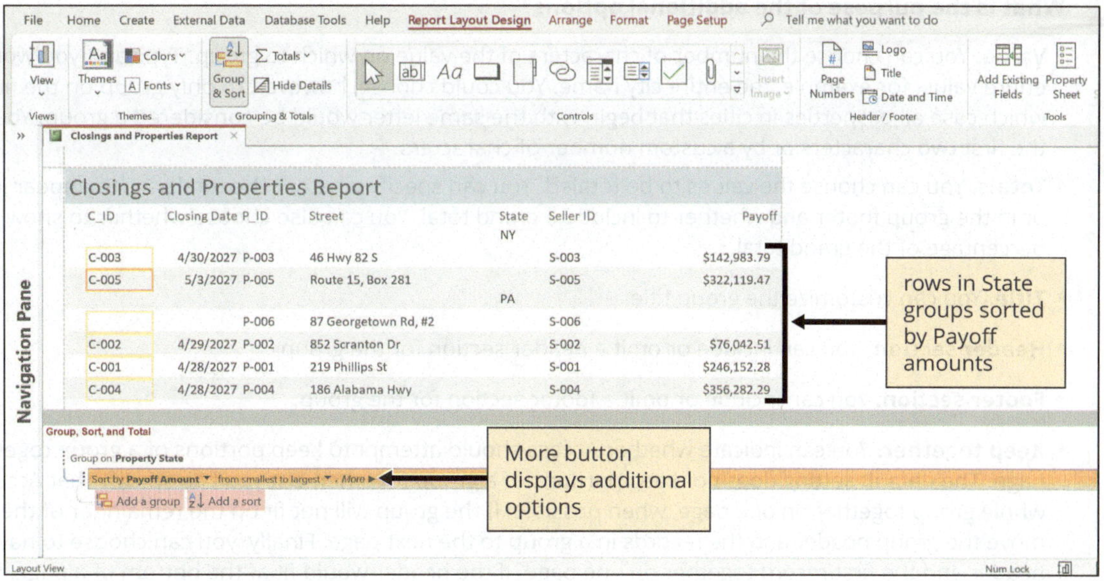

Figure 4–9

Other Ways

1. Right-click column header for field, click Group On (field name) to add grouping

Grouping and Sorting Options

For both grouping and sorting, you can click the More button to specify additional options (Figure 4–10).

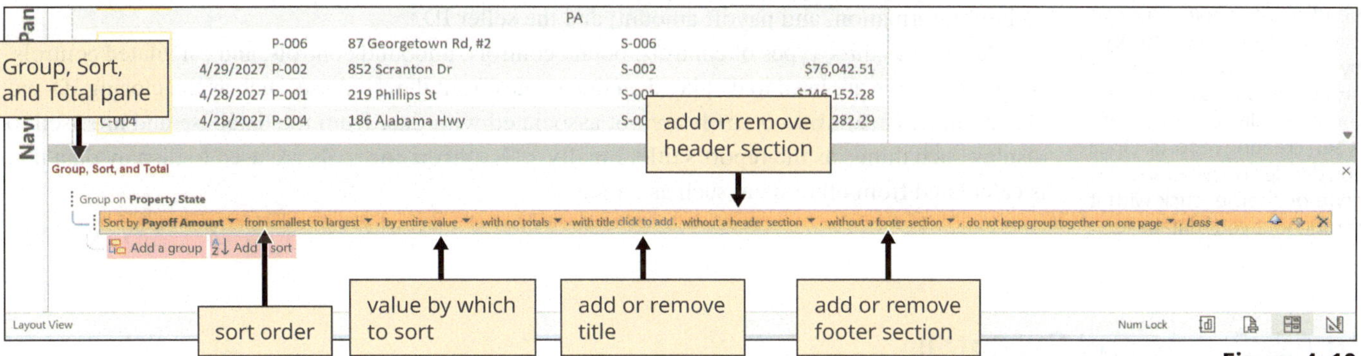

Figure 4–10

Consider This

What is the purpose of the additional options?

- **Value.** You can choose the number of characters of the value on which to group. Typically, you would group by the entire value, for example, the entire city name. You could choose, however, to only group on the first character, in which case all properties in cities that begin with the same letter would be considered a group. You could also group by the first two characters or by a custom number of characters.
- **Totals.** You can choose the values to be totaled. You can specify whether the totals are to appear in the group header or in the group footer and whether to include a grand total. You can also choose whether to show group totals as a percentage of the grand total.
- **Title.** You can customize the group title.
- **Header section.** You can include or omit a header section for the group.
- **Footer section.** You can include or omit a footer section for the group.
- **Keep together.** You can indicate whether Access should attempt to keep portions of a group together on the same page. The default setting does not keep portions of a group together, but you can specify that Access should keep a whole group together on one page, when possible. If the group will not fit on the remainder of the page, Access will move the group header and the records in a group to the next page. Finally, you can choose to have Access keep the header and the first record together on one page. If the header would fit at the bottom of a page, but there would not be room for the first record, Access will move the header to the next page.

BTW
Grouping
You should allow sufficient white space between groups. If you feel the amount is insufficient, you can add more space by enlarging the group header or group footer.

BTW
Report Design Considerations
The purpose of any report is to present specific information. Make sure the meaning of the row and column headings is clear. You can use different fonts and sizes by changing the appropriate properties, but do not overuse them. Finally, be consistent when creating reports. Once you decide on a general report style or theme, stick with it throughout your database.

Report Controls

The various objects on a report are called **controls**. You can manipulate these controls to modify their location and appearance. The report title, column headers, contents of various fields, subtotals, and so on are all contained in controls. When working in Layout view, as you will do in this module, Access handles details concerning placement, sizing, and format of these controls for you automatically. When working in Design view, you will see and manipulate the controls. Even when working in Layout view, however, it is useful to understand the concepts of controls.

The report shown in Figure 4–1 has a control containing the title, Closings and Properties Report. The report also includes controls containing each column header (C_ID, Closing Date, P_ID, Street, State, Seller ID, and Payoff). A control in the Group Header section displays the state name.

In the finished report, there are two controls in the Group Footer section: One control displays the subtotal of Payoff Amounts and a second displays the total of Payoff Amounts for all the groups. The Detail section has controls containing the closing ID and date; the property ID, address information, and payoff amount; and the seller ID.

Access has three types of controls: bound controls, unbound controls, and calculated controls. **Bound controls** are used to display data that comes from the database, such as the closing ID and closing date. **Unbound controls** are not associated with data from the database and are used to display such things as the report's title. Finally, **calculated controls** are used to display data that is calculated from other data, such as a total.

To Add Totals and Subtotals

To add totals or other statistics, use the Totals button on the Design tab. You then select from a menu of aggregate functions, which are functions that perform some mathematical function against a group of records. The available aggregate functions, or calculations, are Sum (total), Average, Count Records, Count Values, Max (largest value), Min (smallest value), Standard Deviation, and Variance. Because the report is grouped, each group will have a subtotal, that is, a total for just the records in the group. At the end of the report, there will be a **grand total**, that is, a total for all records.

The following steps specify totals for the Payoff Amount field. **Why?** Along with grouping data in this report, Partners accountants have also requested that subtotals and a grand total of the Payoff Amount field be included in the report.

1

- Click any record in the Payoff field, and then click the Totals button (Report Layout Design tab | Grouping & Totals group) to display the list of available calculations (Figure 4–11).

Q&A Can I click the column header?

Yes, you can try to click the column header, but if you are unable to select the field, click the Payoff field on any record. If you click the column header and the Totals button does not become available, you will need to click a Payoff field in a record.

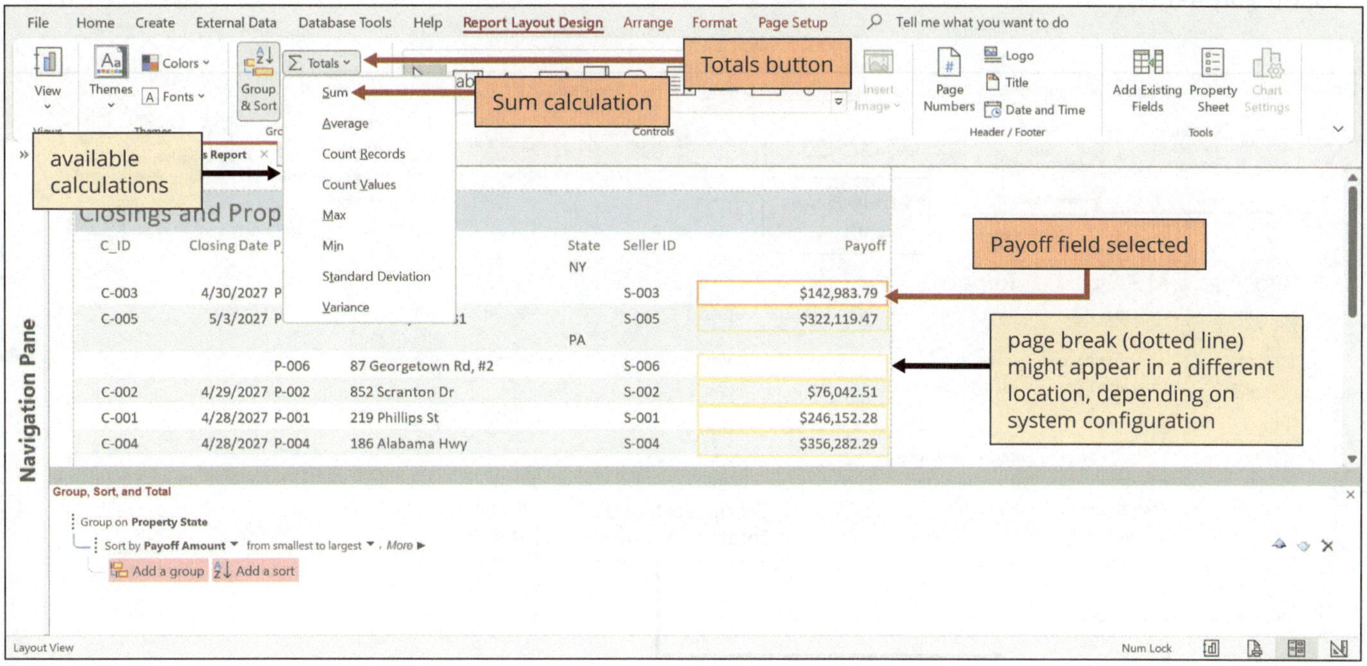

Figure 4–11

2

- Click Sum to calculate the sum of the Payoff values.
- If the subtotal does not appear completely, click the subtotal control and then drag the lower boundary of the control to the approximate position shown in Figure 4–12.

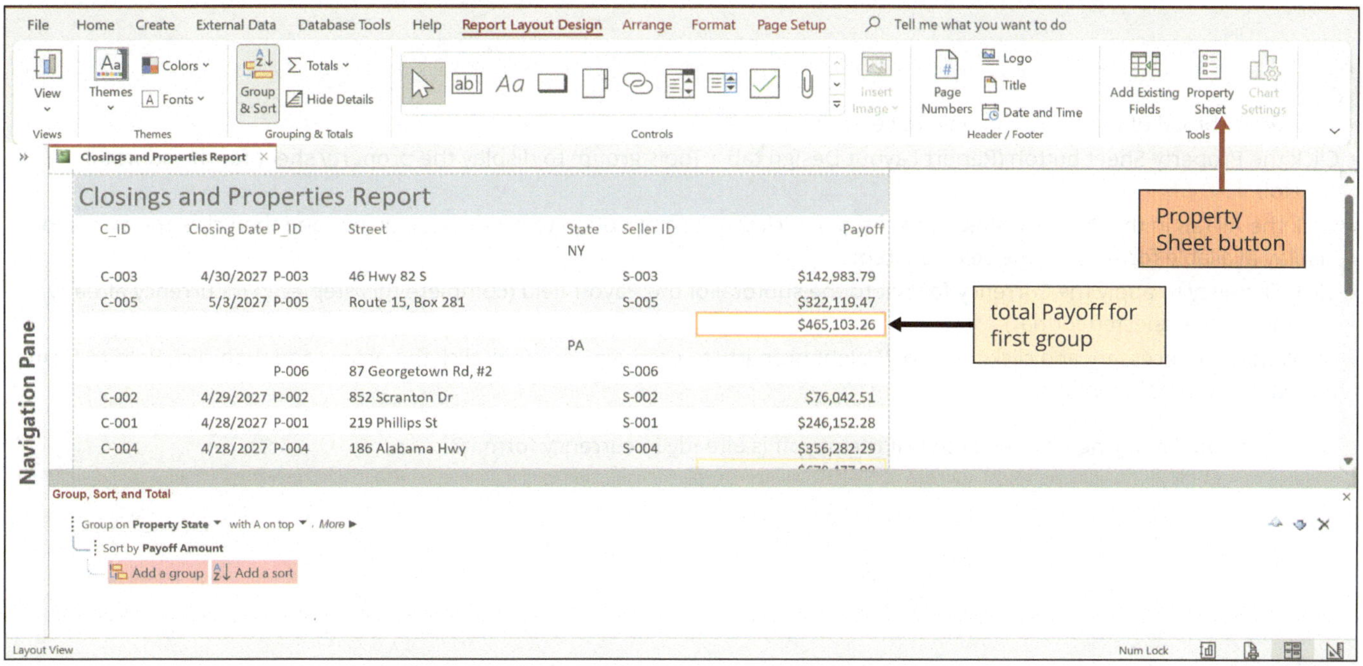

Figure 4–12

Q&A I moved the control rather than resizing it. What did I do wrong?

You dragged the control rather than dragging its lower boundary. Click the Undo button (Home tab | Undo group) to undo your change and then drag again, making sure you are pointing to the control's lower boundary.

3

- Click the Group & Sort button (Report Layout Design tab | Grouping & Totals group) to remove the Group, Sort, and Total pane (Figure 4–13).

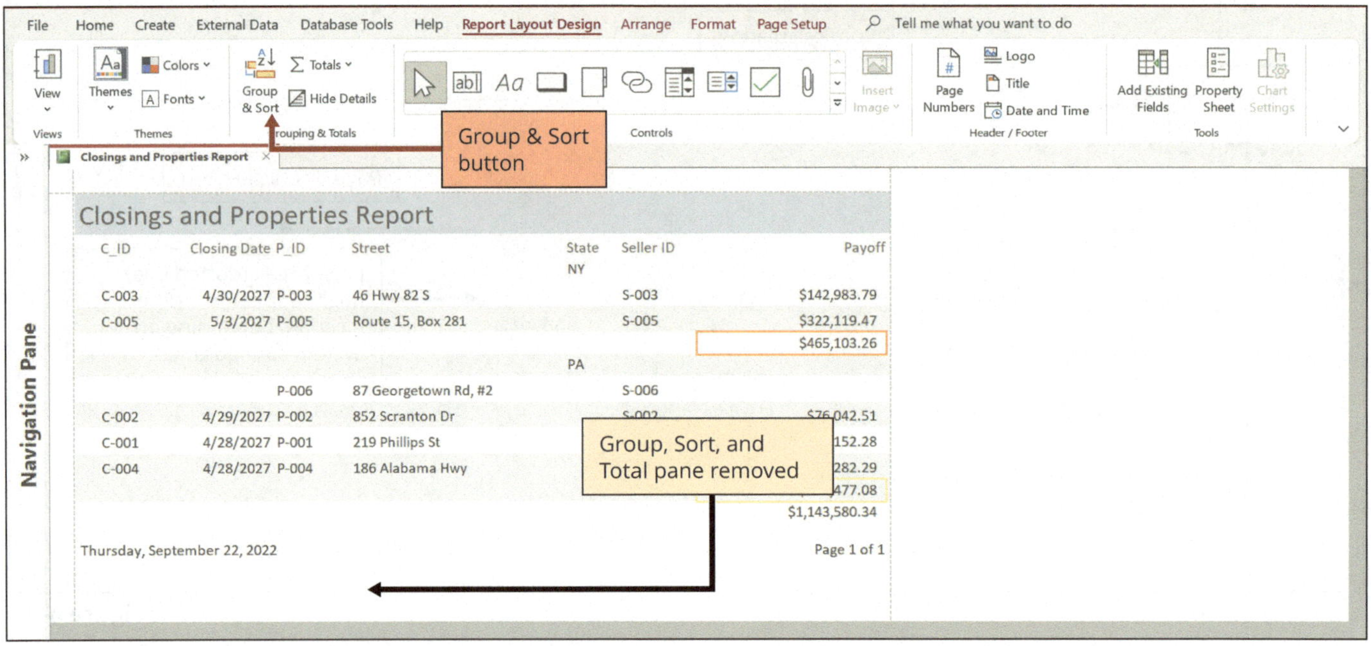

Figure 4–13

Q&A Do I need to remove the Group, Sort, and Total pane?

No. Doing so provides more room on the screen for the report, however. You can easily display the pane whenever you need it by clicking the Group & Sort button again.

4

- Click the subtotal of the NY Payoff field to select it.
- Click the Property Sheet button (Report Layout Design tab | Tools group) to display the property sheet for the subtotal control.
- Click the All tab in the Property Sheet if necessary, click the Format option to produce an arrow, and then click the arrow to display available formats for the selected item.
- Click Currency to apply the Currency format to the subtotal of the Payoff field (complete this step even if Currency already appears as the selected format).
- Scroll down if necessary and click the Font Weight property to produce an arrow, click the arrow, and then click Bold to format the Payoff with bold font (Figure 4–14)

Q&A Why am I applying a currency style if the payoff is already in currency format?

Access contains many options for currency. Confirming and applying the correct format will ensure the format is correct even if you make other changes to the report.

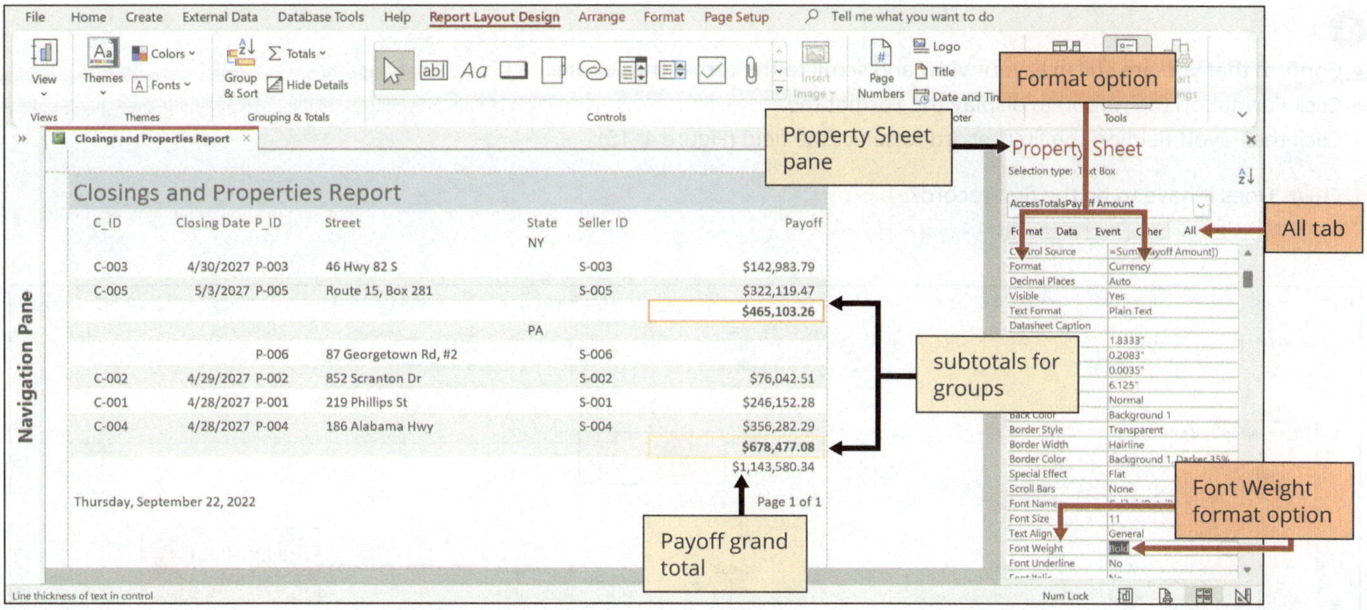

Figure 4–14

5

- Scroll to the bottom of the report and use the same technique to change the format for the grand total of Payoff to Currency and Bold.
- If necessary, drag the grand total control's lower boundary so the numbers are completely visible.
- Click the Property Sheet button (Report Layout Design tab | Tools group) to close the property sheet.
- Click Save to save your changes to the report.

Other Ways

1. Click 'Close Grouping Dialog Box' button in upper-right corner of Group, Sort, and Total pane to close pane

Consider This

How do you determine the organization of the report or form?

Determine various details concerning how the data in your report or form is to be organized.

Determine sort order. Is there a special order in which the records should appear?

Determine grouping. Should the records be grouped in some fashion? If so, what should appear before the records in a group? If, for example, records are grouped by city, the name of the city should probably appear before the group. What should appear after the group? For example, does the report include some fields for which subtotals should be calculated? If so, the subtotals would come after the group. Determine whether you need multiple levels of grouping.

To Conditionally Format Controls

Conditional formatting is special formatting that is applied to values that satisfy some criterion. Partners paralegals have decided to apply conditional formatting to the Payoff field. **Why?** They would like to emphasize values in the Payoff field that are greater than or equal to $200,000.00 by changing the font color to blue. By emphasizing the payoff amounts are equal to or higher in cost than $200,000, they can review the higher payoff amounts that may carry additional tax implications. The following steps conditionally format the Payoff field by specifying a **rule** stating that if the values in the field are greater than or equal to $200,000.00, such values will be formatted in blue.

1

- Confirm that you are still in Layout View and scroll to the top of the report.
- Click Format on the ribbon to display the Format tab.
- Click the Payoff field on the first record to select the field (Figure 4–15).

Q&A Does it have to be the first record?
No. You could click the Payoff field on any record.

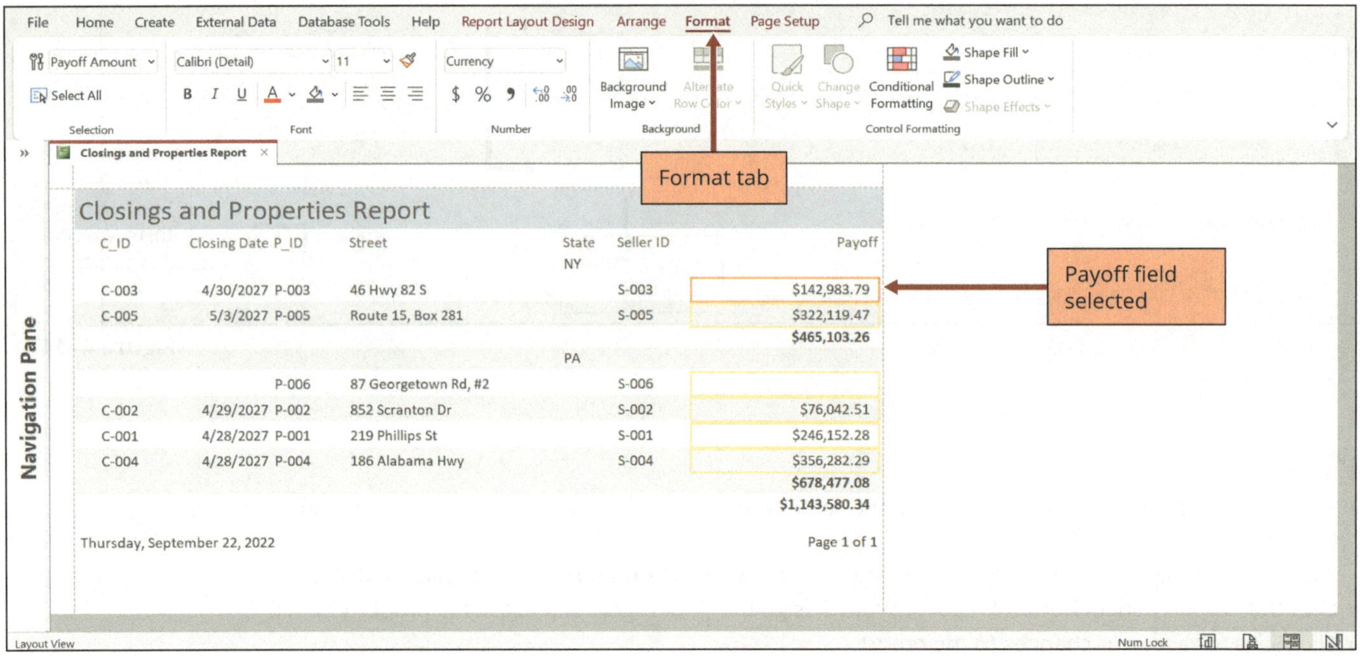

Figure 4–15

2

- Click the Conditional Formatting button (Format tab | Control Formatting group) to display the Conditional Formatting Rules Manager dialog box (Figure 4–16).

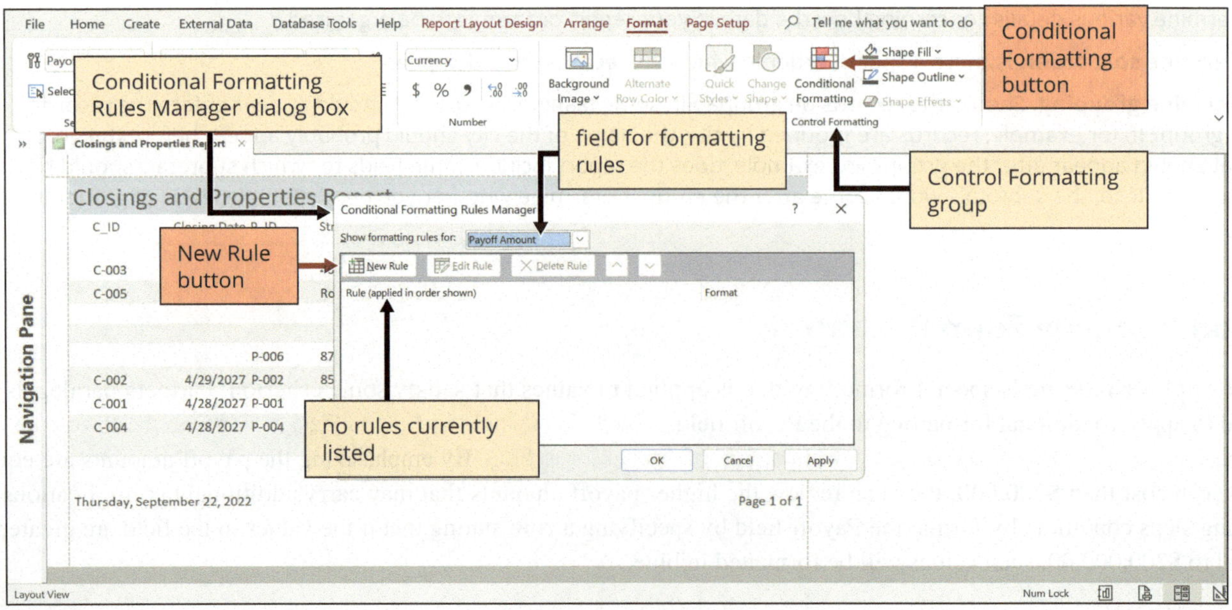

Figure 4–16

3

- Click the New Rule button (Conditional Formatting Rules Manager dialog box) to display the New Formatting Rule dialog box (Figure 4–17).

Q&A I see there are two boxes to enter numbers. I only have one number to enter, 200000. Am I on the right screen?
Yes. Next, you will change the comparison operator from "between" to "greater than or equal to." Once you have done so, Access will display only one box for entering a number.

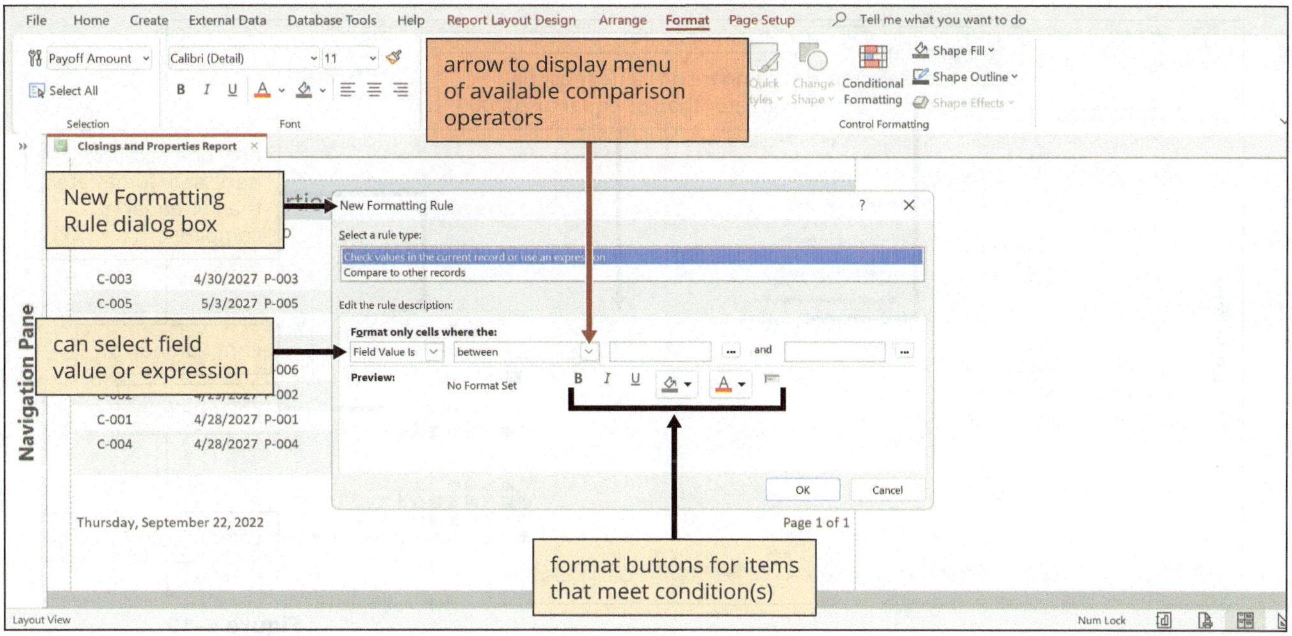

Figure 4–17

4

- Click the arrow to display the list of available comparison operators (New Formatting Rule dialog box) (Figure 4–18).

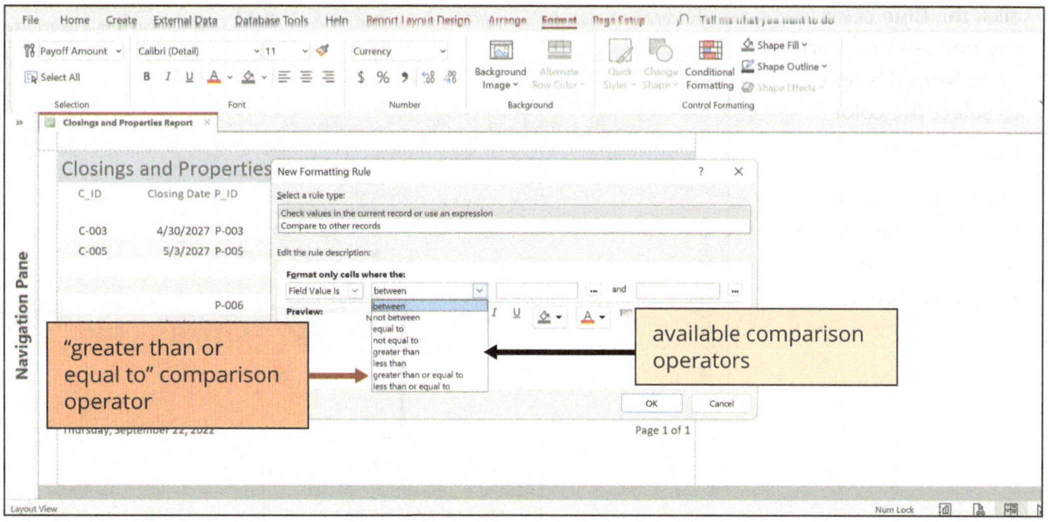

Figure 4–18

5

- Click "greater than or equal to" to select the comparison operator.
- Click the box for the comparison value, and then type **200000** as the comparison value.
- Click the Font Color arrow (New Formatting Rule dialog box) to display a color palette (Figure 4–19).

Q&A What is the effect of selecting this comparison operator and entering this number?
Values in the field that are greater than or equal to 200000 satisfy this rule. Any formatting that you now specify will apply to those values and no others.

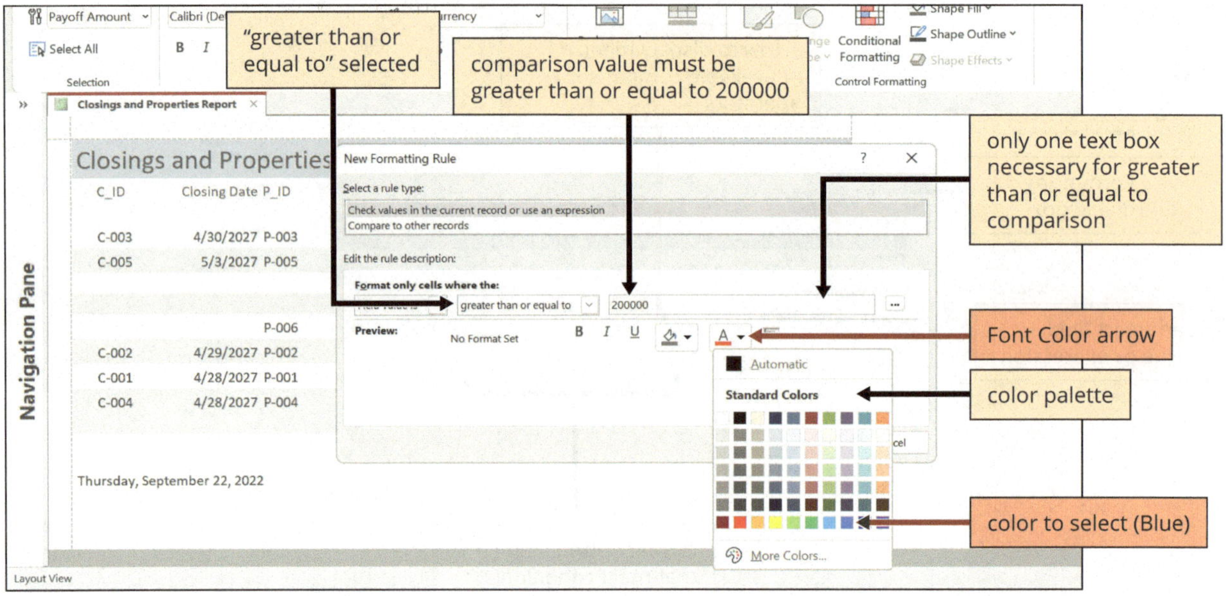

Figure 4–19

6

- On the color palette, click the Blue color in the bottom row, third color from the right to select the color (Figure 4–20).

Q&A What other changes could I specify for those values that satisfy the rule?
You could specify that the value is bold, italic, and/or underlined. You could also specify a background color.

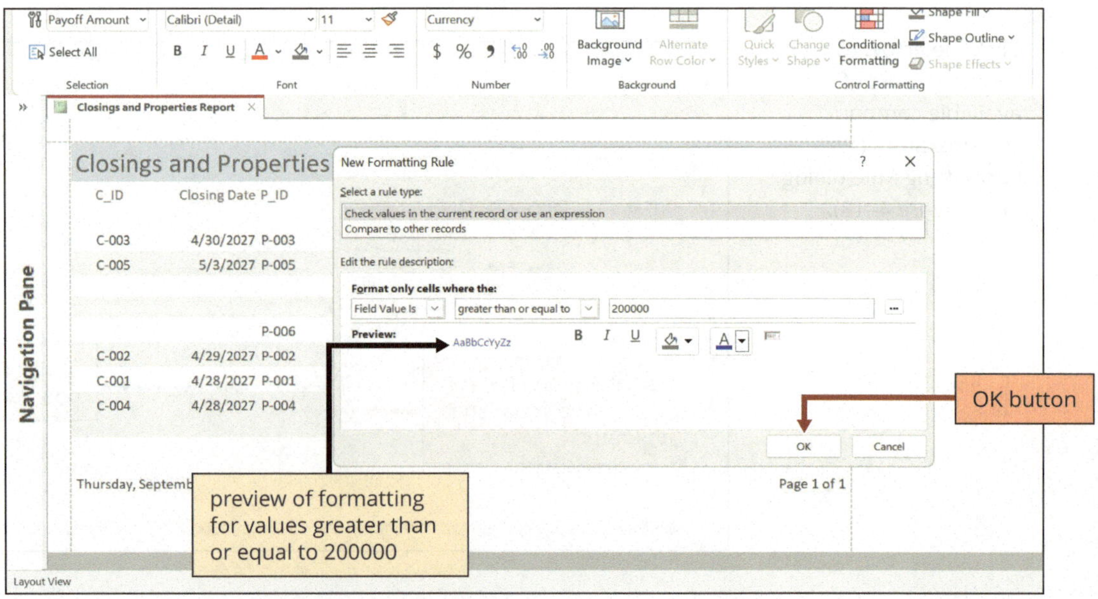

Figure 4–20

7

- Click OK (New Formatting Rule dialog box) to enter the rule (Figure 4–21).

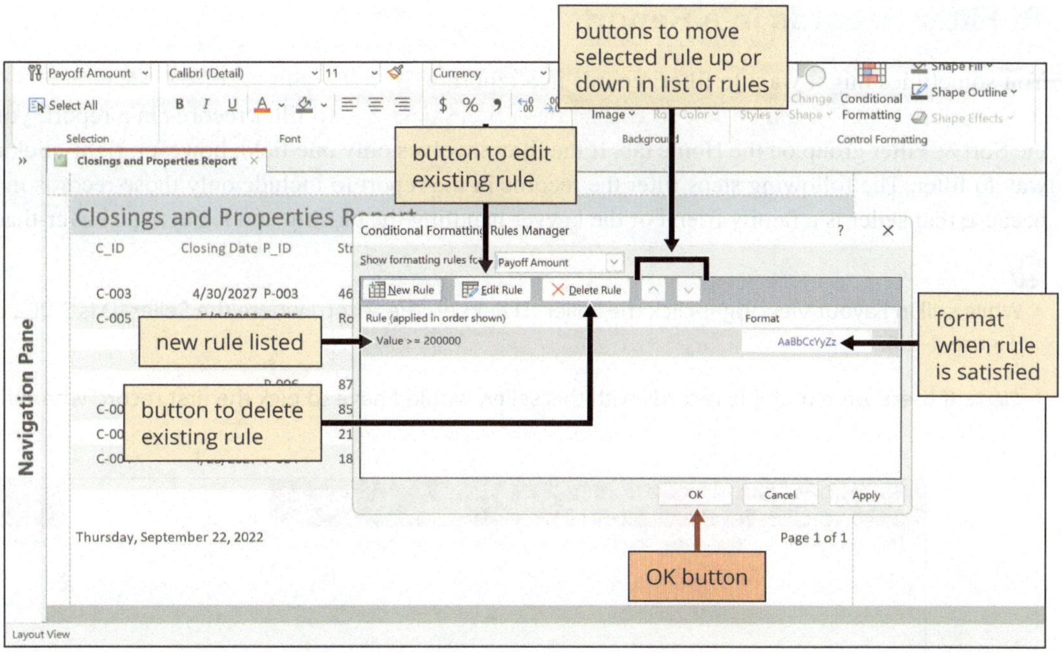

Figure 4–21

Q&A What if I have more than one rule?

The rules are applied in the order in which they appear in the dialog box. If a value satisfies the first rule, the specified formatting will apply, and no further rules will be tested. If not, the value will be tested against the second rule. If it satisfies the rule, the formatting for the second rule would apply. If not, the value would be tested against the third rule, and so on.

Can I change this conditional formatting later?

Yes. Select the field for which you had applied conditional formatting on any record, click the Conditional Formatting button (Format tab | Control Formatting group), click the rule you want to change, click the Edit Rule button, and then make the necessary changes. You can also delete the selected rule by clicking the Delete Rule button, or move the selected rule by clicking the Move Up or Move Down buttons.

8

- Click OK (Conditional Formatting Rules Manager dialog box) to complete the entry of the conditional formatting rules and apply the rule (Figure 4–22).

9

- Click Save on the Quick Access Toolbar to save your changes to the report.
- **Experiment:** After saving your changes, experiment with different rules. Add a second rule that changes the format for any current due amount that is greater than or equal to $350,000 to a different color to see the effect of multiple rules. Change the order of rules to see the effect of a different order. When you have finished, delete any additional rules you have added so the report contains only the one rule you created earlier.

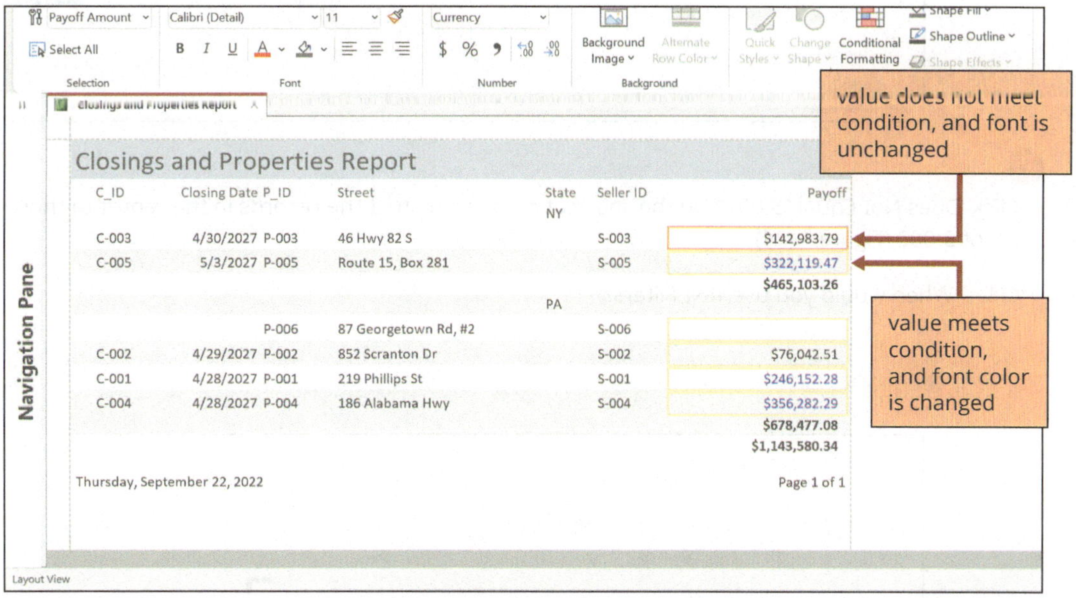

Figure 4–22

To Filter Records in a Report

You sometimes might want to filter records in a report. **Why?** You might want to include in a report only those records that satisfy some criterion and be able to change that criterion easily. To filter records in a report, you can use the filter buttons in the Sort & Filter group on the Home tab. If the filter involves only one field, however, right-clicking the field provides a simple way to filter. The following steps filter the records in the report to include only those records in which the seller is not S-002 because that seller is a family friend of the lawyer handling the closing and is paying a lower-than-standard fee.

1

- While still in Layout View, right-click the Seller ID field on the record where the Seller ID is S-002 to display a shortcut menu (Figure 4–23).

Q&A If there were multiple records with this seller, would I have to pick the first record where the value is S-002?
No. You could pick any record on which the Seller ID value is S-002.

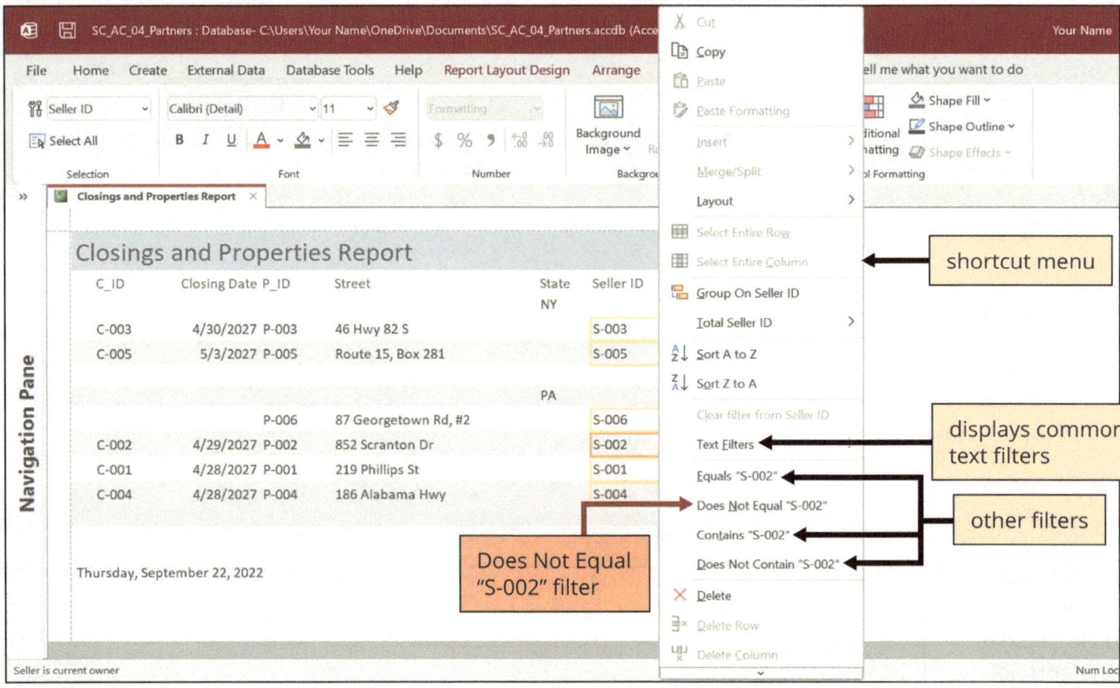

Figure 4–23

2

- Click 'Does Not Equal "S-002"' on the shortcut menu to restrict the records in the report to those on which the Seller ID value is not S-002 (Figure 4–24).

Q&A When would you use Text Filters?
You would use Text Filters if you need filters that are not on the main shortcut menu or if you need the ability to enter specific values other than the ones shown on the shortcut menu. If those filters are insufficient for your needs, you can use Advanced Filter/Sort, which is accessible through the Advanced button (Home tab | Sort & Filter group).

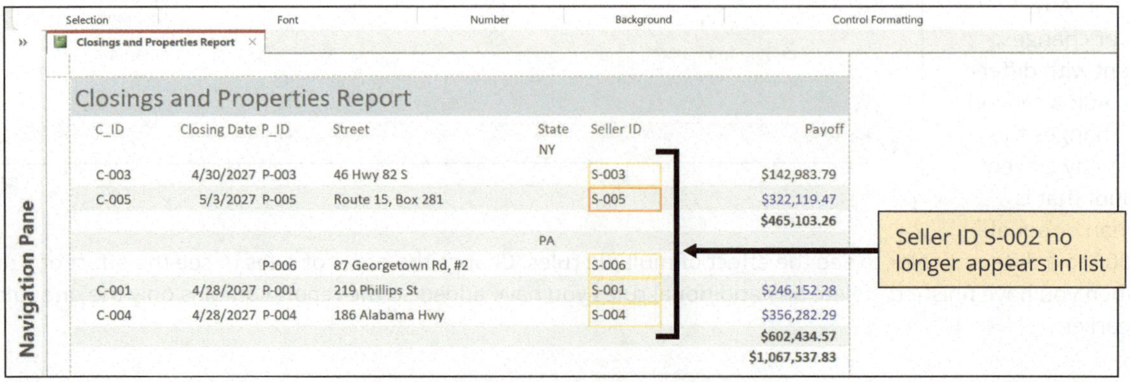

Figure 4–24

Other Ways

1. Click Selection button (Home tab | Sort & Filter group) to apply filter

To Clear a Report Filter

The following steps clear the filter on the Seller ID field. **Why?** When you no longer want the records to be filtered, you clear the filter so all records are again included.

1

- On the first record, right-click the Seller ID field to display a shortcut menu (Figure 4–25).

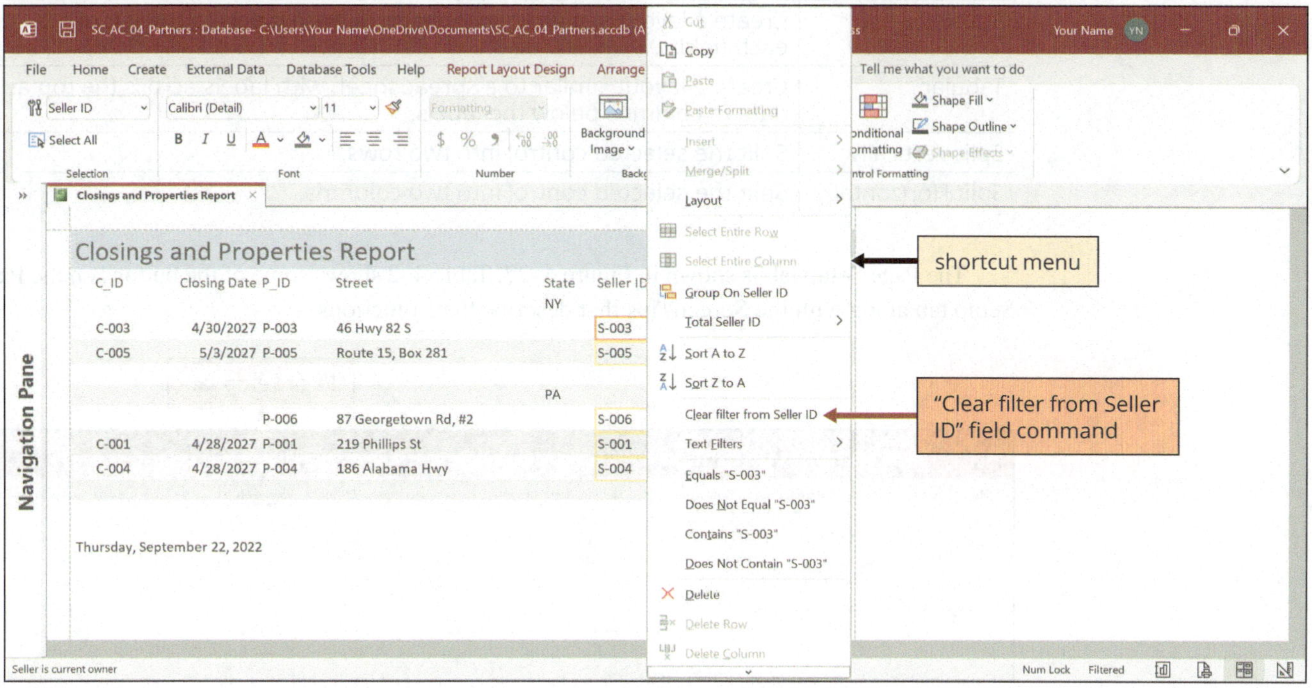

Figure 4–25

Q&A Did I have to pick the first record?

No. You could pick the Seller ID field on any record.

- Click 'Clear filter from Seller ID' on the shortcut menu to clear the filter and redisplay all records.
- **Experiment:** Try other filters on the shortcut menu for the Seller ID field to see their effect. When you are done with each, clear the filter.
- Save your work.
- Close the Closings and Properties Report.

Other Ways

1. Click Advanced button (Home tab | Sort & Filter group) to clear filter.

The Arrange and Page Setup Tabs

When working on a report in Layout view, you can make additional layout changes by using the Arrange and/or Page Setup tabs. The Arrange tab is shown in Figure 4–26. Table 4–1 shows some of the buttons on the Arrange tab along with the ScreenTips that describe their functions.

BTW

Using the Arrange Tab

Because the commands located on the Arrange tab are actions associated with previously selected controls, be sure to select the desired control or controls first.

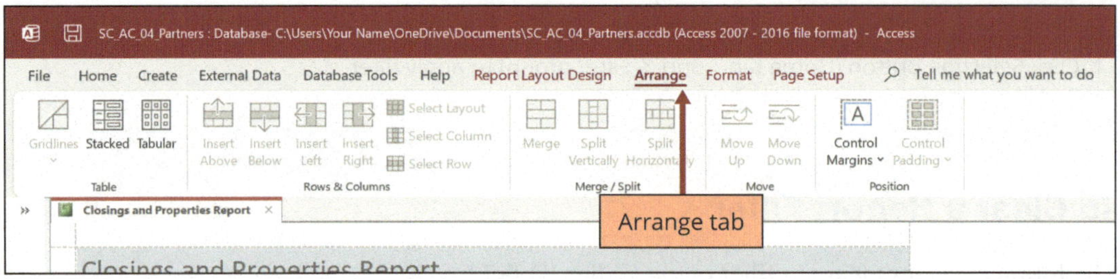

Figure 4–26

Table 4–1 Arrange Tab

Button	ScreenTip
Stacked	Create a layout similar to a paper form, with labels to the left of each field.
Tabular	Create a layout similar to a spreadsheet, with labels across the top and data in columns below the labels.
Split Vertically	Split the selected control into two rows.
Split Horizontally	Split the selected control into two columns.

The Page Setup tab is shown in Figure 4–27. Table 4–2 shows some of the buttons on the Page Setup tab along with the ScreenTips that describe their functions.

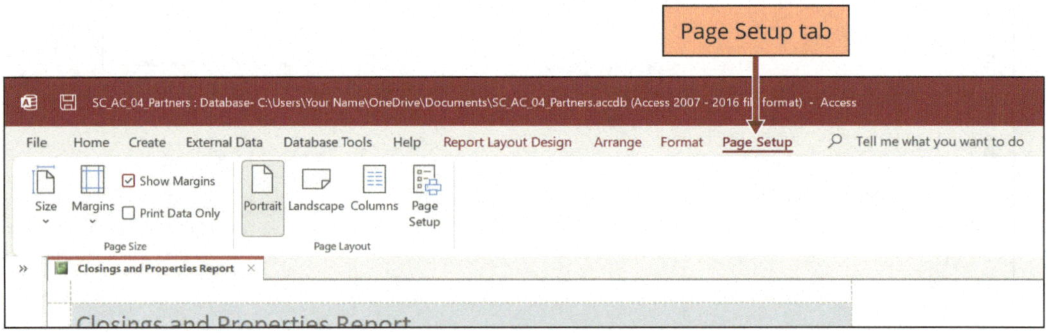

Figure 4–27

Table 4–2 Page Setup Tab

Button	ScreenTip
Size	Choose a paper size for your document.
Margins	Set the margin sizes for the entire document or the current section. Choose from several commonly-used margin formats, or customize your own.
Portrait	Change to portrait orientation.
Landscape	Change to landscape orientation.
Page Setup	Don't see what you're looking for? Check out the full set of page formatting options.

BTW
Distributing a Document
Instead of printing and distributing a hard copy of a document, you can distribute the document electronically. Options include sending the document via email; posting it on cloud storage (such as OneDrive) and sharing the file with others; posting it on a social networking site, blog, or other website; and sharing a link associated with an online location of the document. You can also create and share a PDF or XPS image of the document, so that users can view the file in Acrobat Reader or XPS Viewer instead of in Access.

To Print a Report

If you wanted to print your report, you would use the following steps.

1. With the report selected in the Navigation Pane, click File on the ribbon to open the Backstage view.
2. Click Print tab in Backstage view to display the Print gallery.
3. Click the Quick Print button to print the report.

Q&A How can I print multiple copies of my report?

Click File on the ribbon to open Backstage view. Click the Print tab, click Print in the Print gallery to display the Print dialog box, increase the number in the Number of Copies box, and then click OK (Print dialog box).

Break Point: If you wish to take a break, this is a good place to do so. You can quit Access now. To resume at a later time, start Access, open the database called SC_AC_04_Partners.accdb, and continue following the steps from this location forward.

BTW

Searching for Records in a Report

You can use the Find button to search for records in a report. To do so, open the report in Report view or Layout view and select the field in the report on which to search. Click the Find button (Home tab | Find group) to display the Find dialog box. Type the desired value on which to search in the Find What text box (Find dialog box), and then click the Find Next button.

Multiple-Table Reports

Sometimes you will create reports that require data from more than one table. You can use the Report Wizard to create a report based on multiple tables just as you can use it to create reports based on single tables or queries. The following steps use the Report Wizard to create a report that includes fields from the Sellers, Properties, Closings, and Closing Fees tables.

To Create a Report that Involves Multiple Tables

Currently, there are two existing relationships, one between the Closings table and Mortgage Companies table and another between the Closings table and the Properties table. To produce the report currently needed by the managers, you will need to add relationships for the Sellers and Closing Fees tables. **Why?** Partners paralegals need a report that shows detailed agent commission information and that includes the Property Street, Seller Name, Closing Date, and Total Agent Commission information from existing tables.

Before starting to create reports from multiple tables, it is always a good idea to check the current relationships between tables and add any necessary relationships to the tables. The Closings table will be the basis for much of the information in the report needed by Partners paralegals. The following steps review the existing relationships and add the necessary tables to the Relationships window.

1

- Click the Database Tools tab, and then click the Relationships button to open the Relationships window (Figure 4–28).

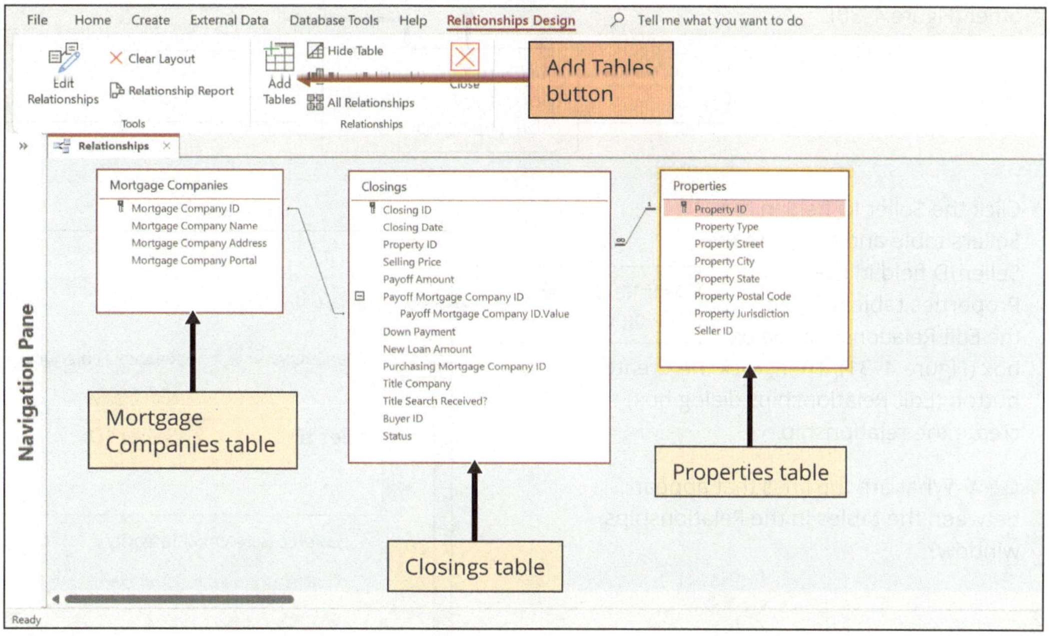

Figure 4–28

2

- Click the Add Tables button to view available tables in the Add Tables pane.
- Click the Sellers table and then click the Add Selected Tables button to add this table to the Relationships window (Figure 4–29).

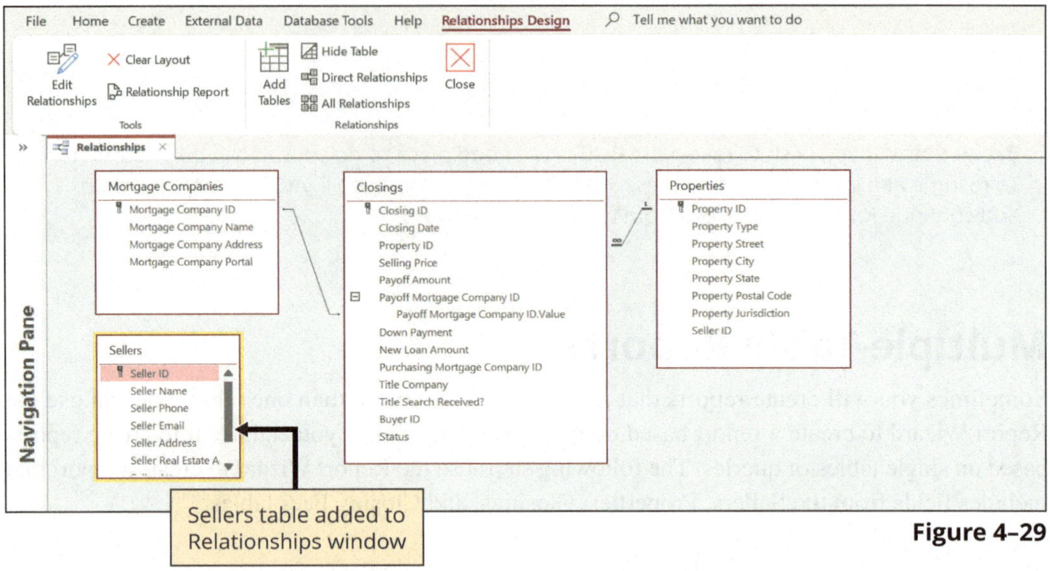

Figure 4–29

3

- Adjust the positions and sizes of the tables so you can see the Seller ID field in the Sellers table and the Seller ID field in the Properties table. It might also be easier to create the relationship if the Sellers and Properties tables are positioned next to each other (Figure 4–30).

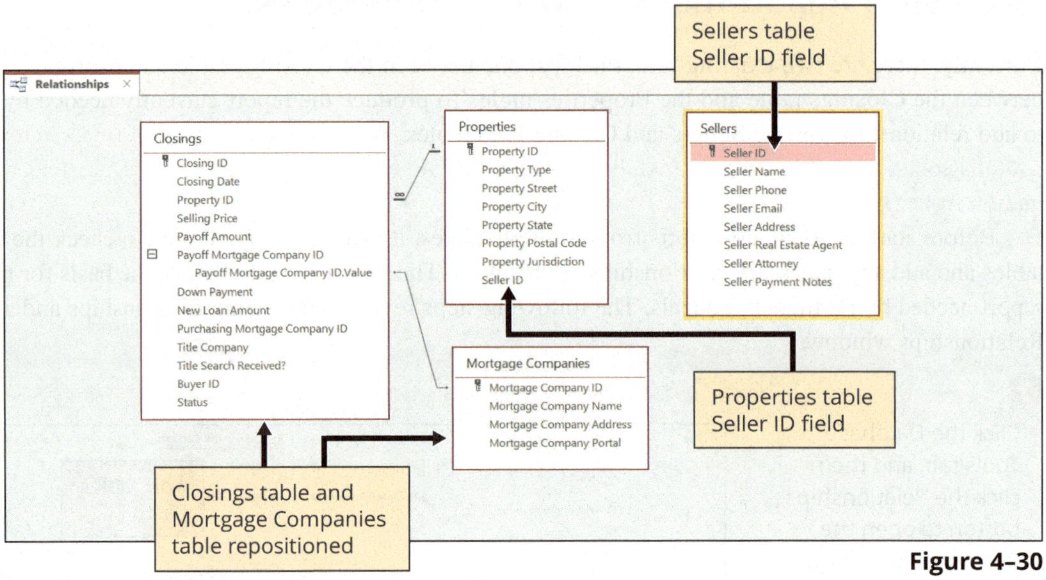

Figure 4–30

- Click the Seller ID field in the Sellers table and drag it to the Seller ID field in the Properties table to open the Edit Relationships dialog box (Figure 4–31). Then, click the Create button (Edit Relationships dialog box) to create the relationship.

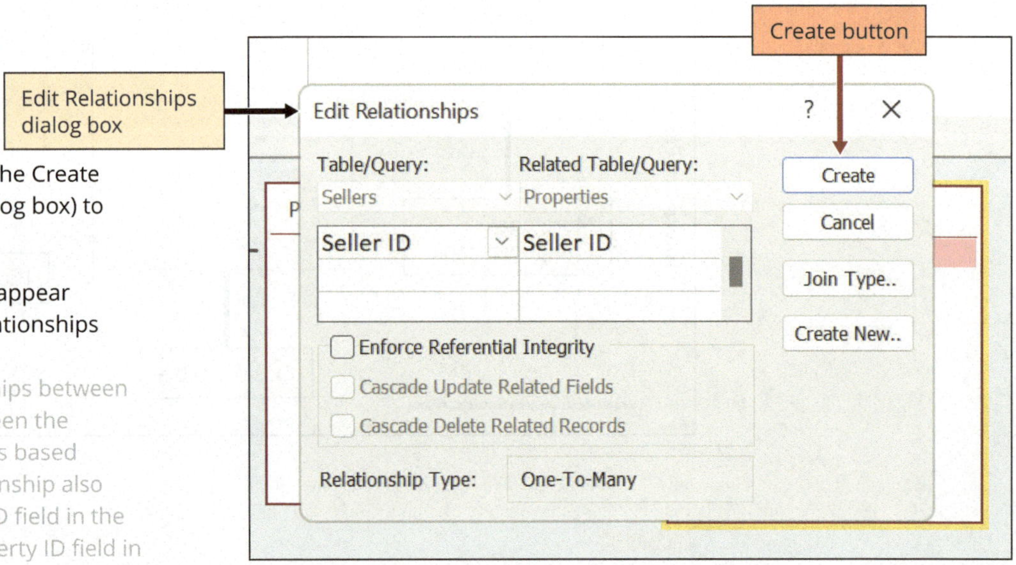

Figure 4–31

Q&A What are the lines that appear between the tables in the Relationships window?

The lines depict the relationships between tables. The relationship between the Properties and Sellers tables is based on the Seller ID field. A relationship also exists between the Property ID field in the Properties table and the Property ID field in the Closings table.

4

- Click the Closing Fees table in the Add Tables pane, and click the Add Selected Tables button to add the table to the Relationship window. Resize and reposition the tables as desired so the Closing Fees table is positioned near the Closings table (Figure 4–32).
- Click the Closing ID field in the Closing Fees table and drag it to the Closing ID field in the Closings table to open the Edit Relationships dialog box. Click the Create button to create the relationship, which will enable you to view fees in the report.

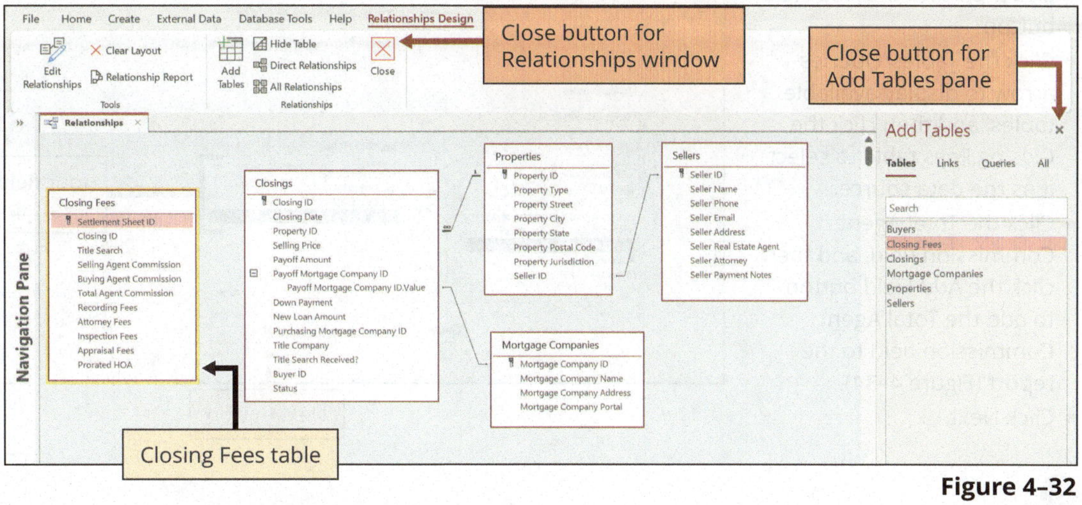

Figure 4–32

Q&A How does Access relate the Closings and Mortgage Companies tables?

Access recognizes there is a relationship between the Payoff Mortgage Company ID.Value field in the Closings table and the Mortgage Company ID field in the Mortgage Companies table. Mortgage Company ID and Payoff Mortgage Company ID.Value are displayed on two lines in the Closings table for the same field because this field was previously updated to a multivalued lookup field that displays the field on multiple lines.

5

- Click Save on the Quick Access Toolbar to save your changes.
- Click the Close button on the Add Tables pane.
- Click the Close button (Relationships Design tab | Relationships group) to close the Relationships window.

6

- Open the Navigation Pane if it is currently closed, and then select the Properties table.
- Click Create on the ribbon to display the Create tab.
- Click the Report Wizard button (Create tab | Reports group) to open the Report Wizard.
- Click the Property Street field, and then click the Add Field button to add the street information to the report (Figure 4–33).

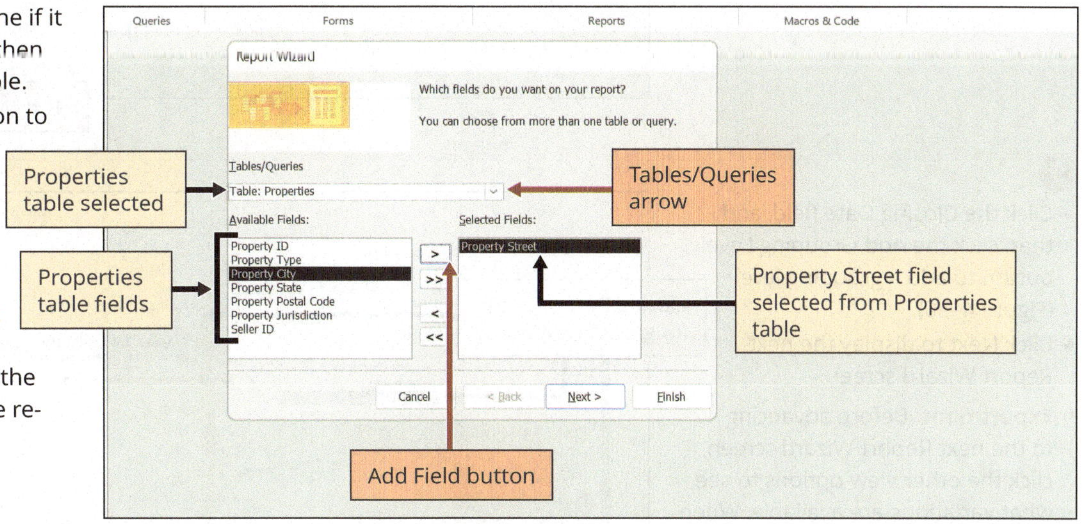

Figure 4–33

7

- Click the Tables/Queries arrow to display available tables and then click Table: Sellers to select the Sellers table as the data source.
- Click the Seller Name field and then click the Add Field button.
- Click the Tables/Queries arrow to display available tables, and then click the Closings table to select it as the data source.

- Click the Closing Date field, and then click the Add Field button
- Click the Tables/Queries arrow to display available tables, and then click the Closing Fees table to select it as the data source.
- Click the Total Agent Commission field, and then click the Add Field button to add the Total Agent Commission field to the report (Figure 4–34).
- Click Next.

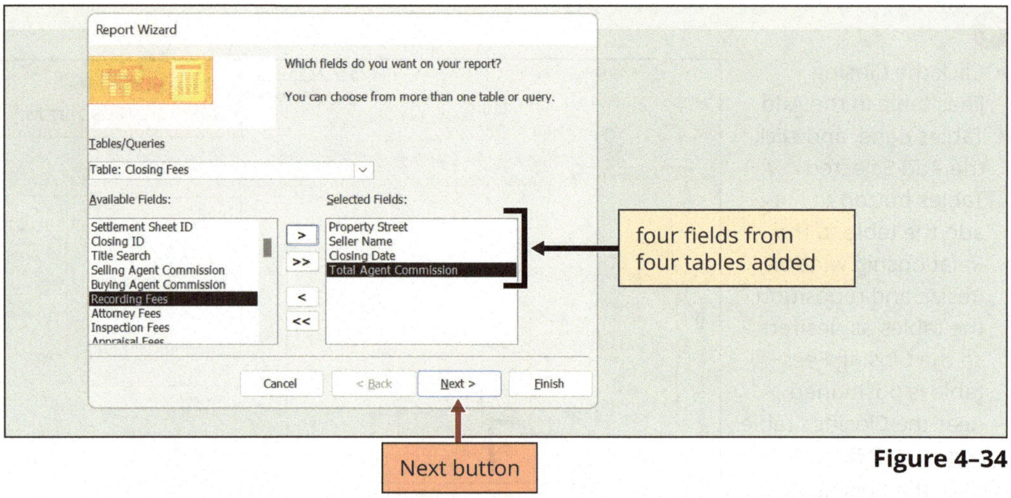

Figure 4–34

8

- For the most efficient layout of the included information, click the 'by Closing Fees' option (Figure 4–35).
- Click Next.

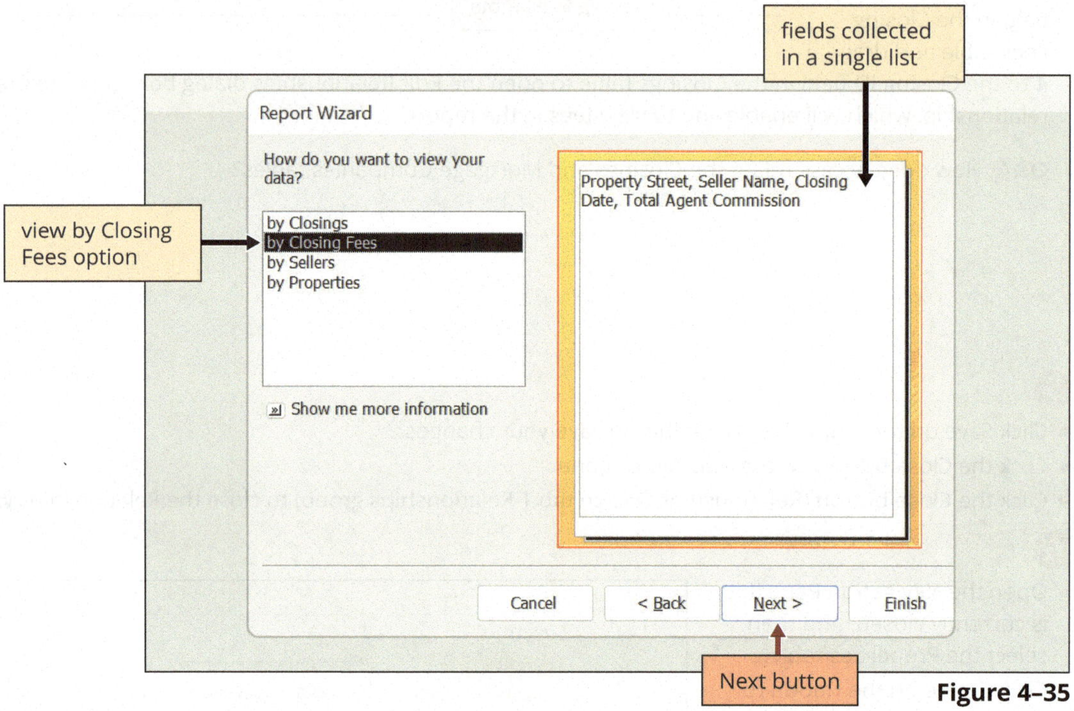

Figure 4–35

9

- Click the Closing Date field, and then click the Add Grouping Level button to add a grouping level (Figure 4–36).
- Click Next to display the next Report Wizard screen.
- **Experiment:** Before advancing to the next Report Wizard screen, click the other view options to see what variations are available. When you're ready, again select the 'by Closing Fees' option.

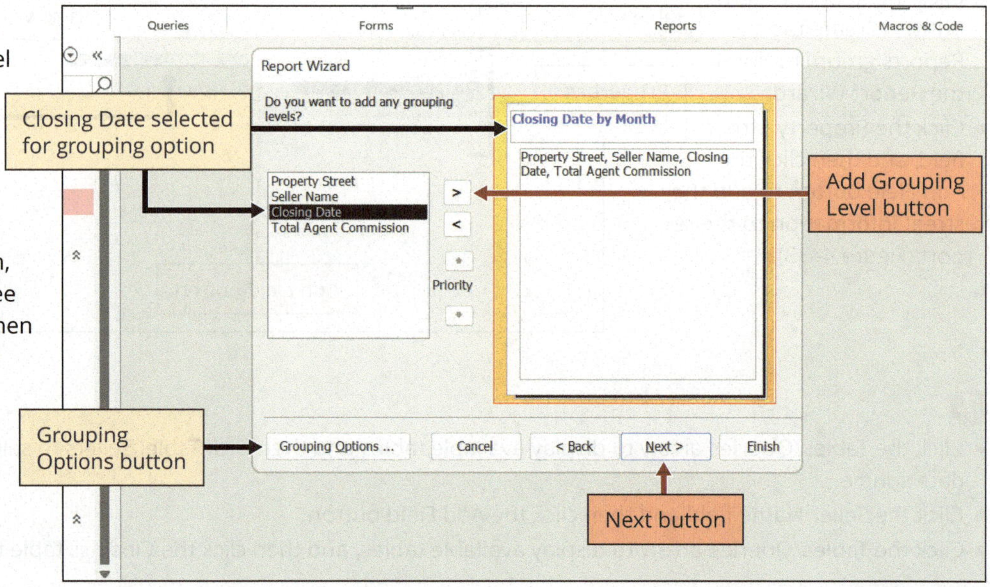

Figure 4–36

10

- Click the Summary Options button to display the Summary Options dialog box.
- Click the Sum check box to calculate the sum of Total Agent Commissions.
- If necessary, click the Detail and Summary option button to select it (Figure 4–37).
- Click OK (Summary Options dialog box) to close the Summary Options dialog box.
- Click Next to display the next Report Wizard screen.

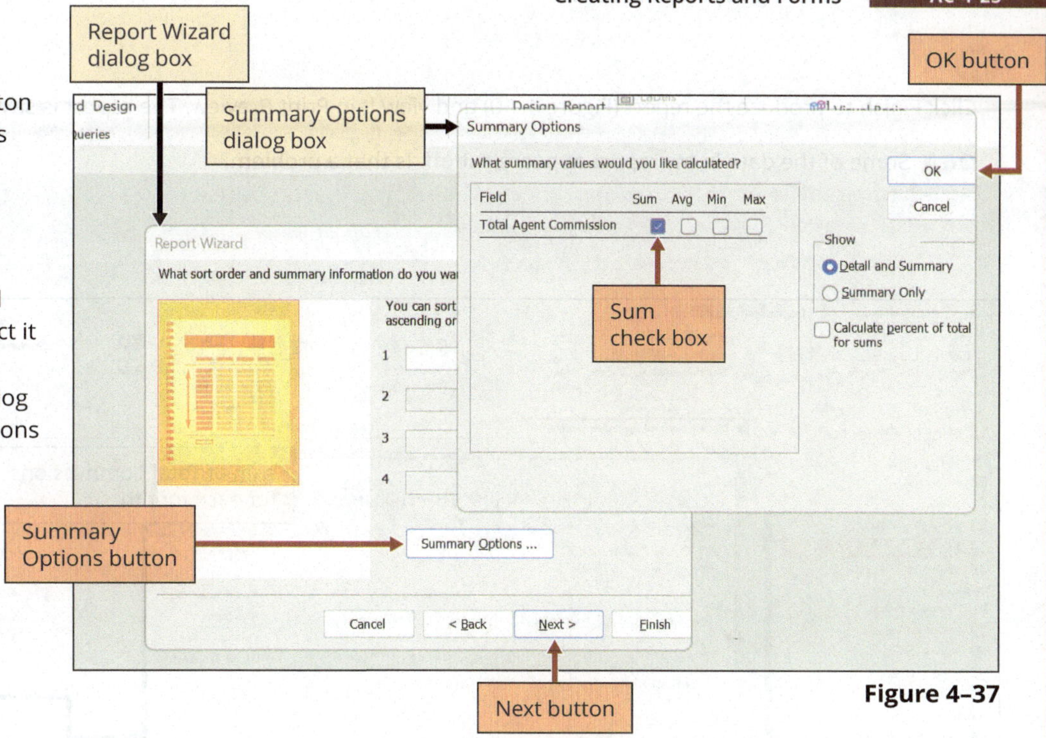

Figure 4–37

11

- Confirm that Stepped layout is selected, and then click the Landscape option button to select landscape orientation (Figure 4–38).
- Click Next to display the next Report Wizard screen.

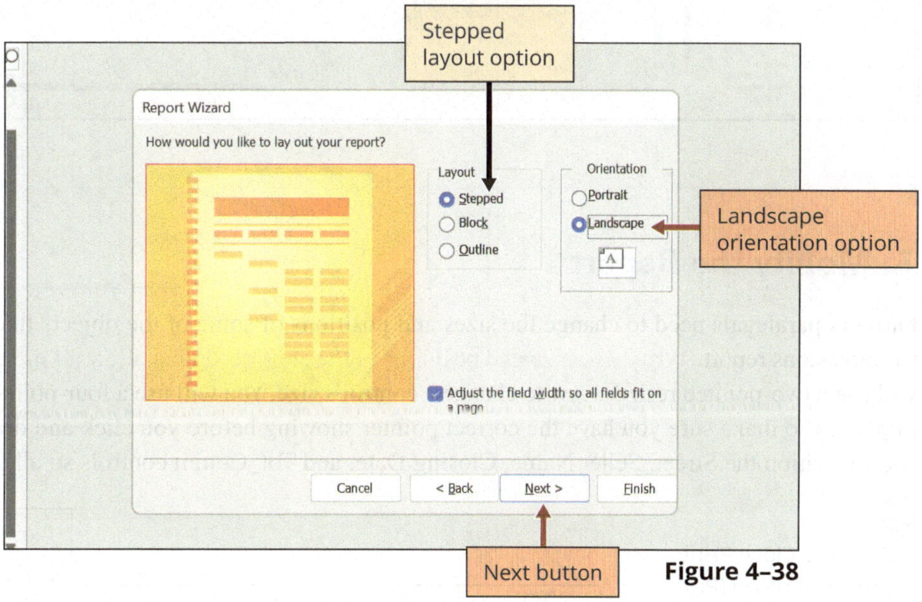

Figure 4–38

12

- Click the text box for the title, delete any existing text, and then type **Closings and Total Agent Commissions** as the title (Figure 4–39).

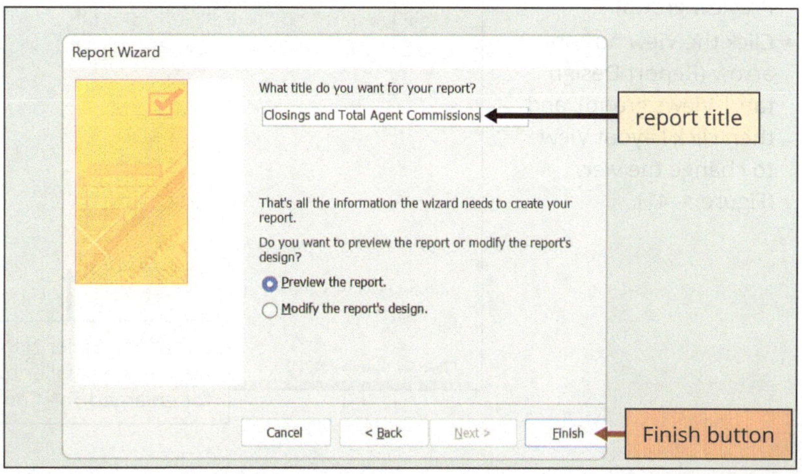

Figure 4–39

13

- Click Finish to produce the report (Figure 4–40) and view it in Print Preview. The report is saved automatically.

Q&A Some of the data in my report appears cut off. Is that a problem?
No. It's common for some data to appear cut off when you first produce a report. You will resolve this issue when you modify the report.

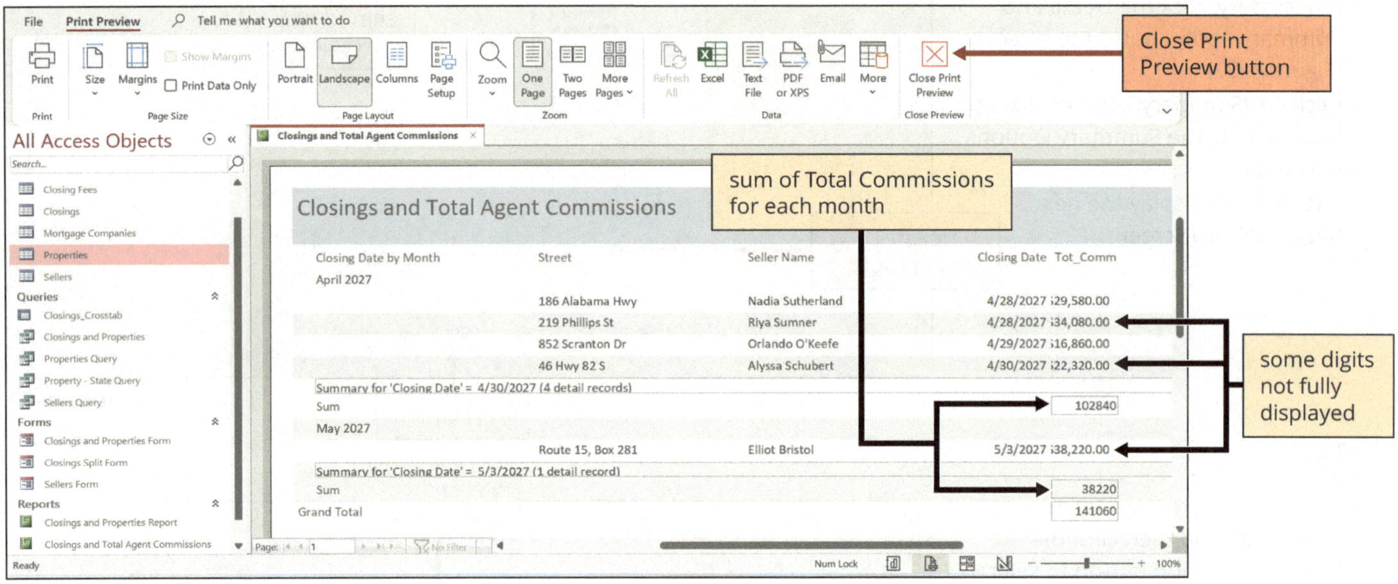

Figure 4–40

To Modify the Report

Partners paralegals need to change the sizes and positions of some of the objects that appear in the Closings and Total Agent Commissions report. **Why?** The size and positions of the controls do not allow all the data to appear in some of the controls. You will use a two-pointed resize arrow to change a control's size. You will use a four-pointed move arrow to reposition a control. It's important to make sure you have the correct pointer showing before you click and drag the pointer. The following steps resize and reposition the Street, Seller Name, Closing Date, and Tot_Comm controls so all the data is visible.

1

- Click the Close Print Preview button (Print Preview tab | Close Preview group).
- Click the View button arrow (Report Design tab | Views group), and then click Layout View to change the view (Figure 4–41).

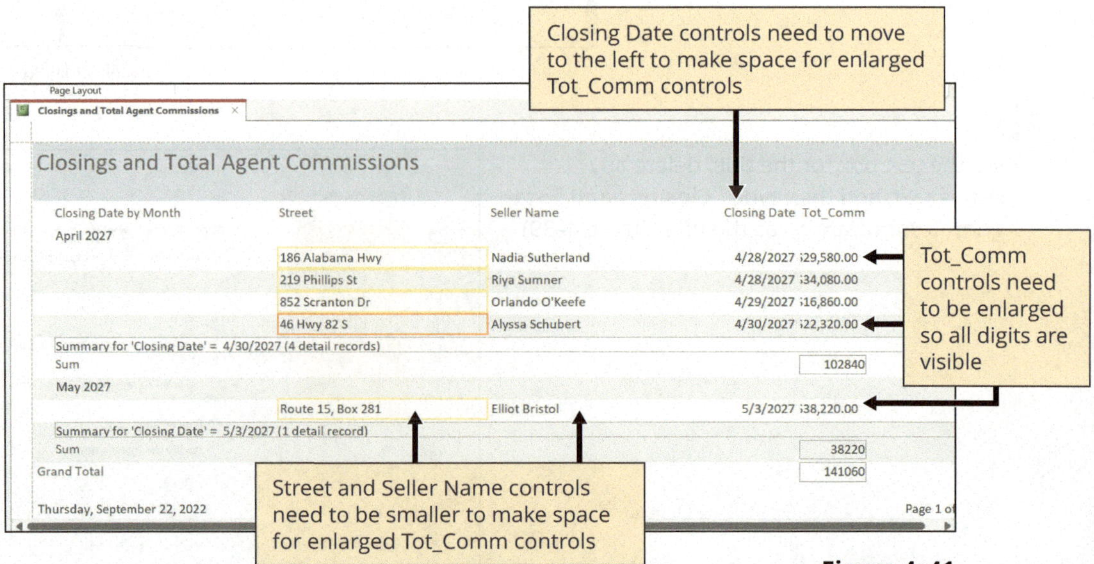

Figure 4–41

2

- Click the Street control under the Street heading to select it.
- Point to the right border of the Street control until the pointer becomes a double-pointed arrow (Figure 4–42). Then, drag the pointer to the left to make the control smaller.

3

- Using the process you followed in Step 2, decrease the size of the Seller Name control.

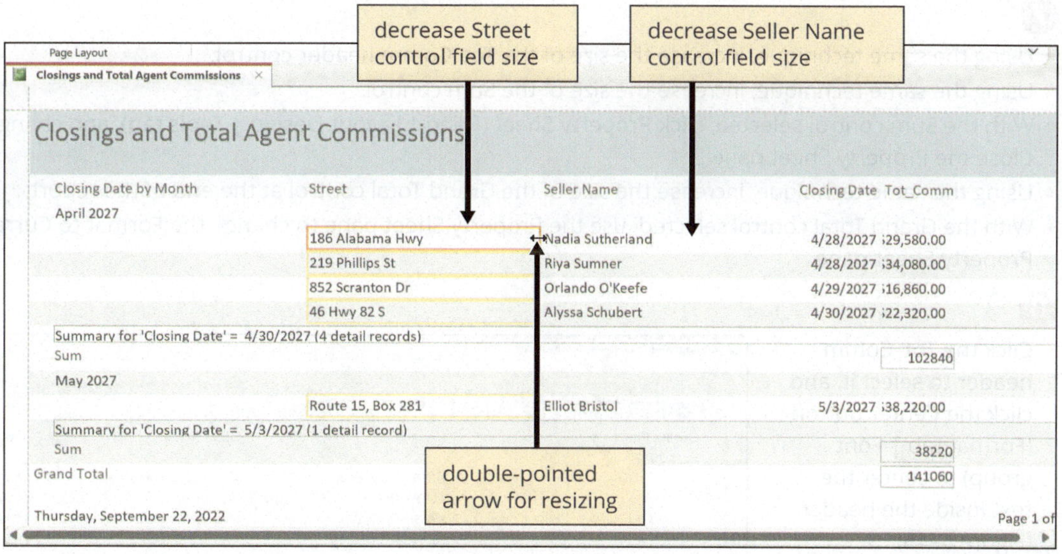

Figure 4–42

4

- Click the Seller Name heading. While holding SHIFT on your keyboard, click the Seller Name control to select both the heading and the data field controls at the same time.
- Point to the Seller Name control until the pointer becomes a four-pointed arrow (Figure 4–43). Then, drag the pointer to the left to move the Seller Name column closer to the Street column.

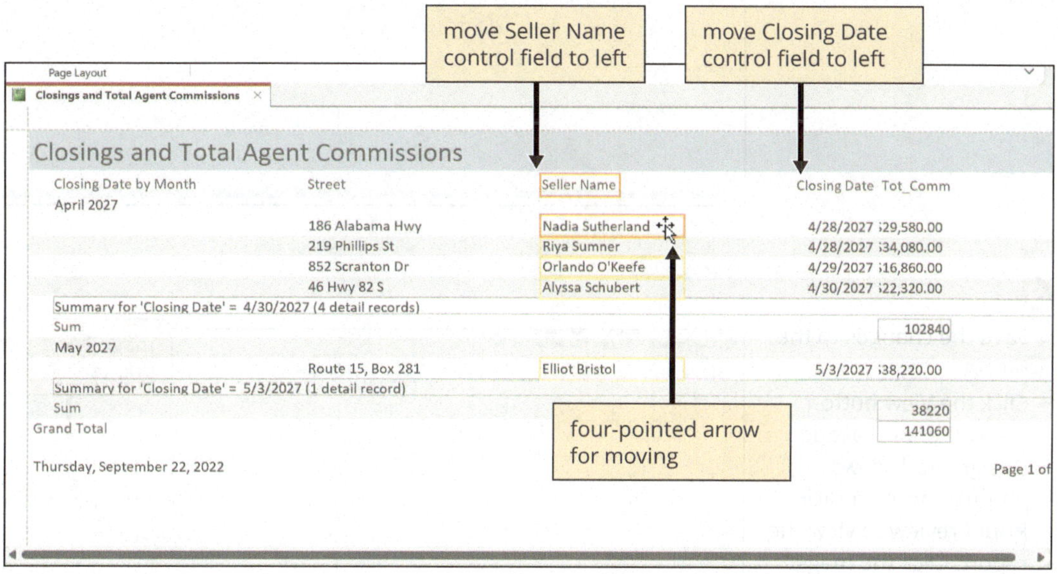

Figure 4–43

5

- Using the process you followed in Step 4, move the Closing Date control closer to the Seller Name control.

6

- Click the Tot_Comm control, point to the left border of the control until you see the two-pointed arrow, and then drag the border to the left to increase the control's size so all the digits are displayed (see Figure 4–44).

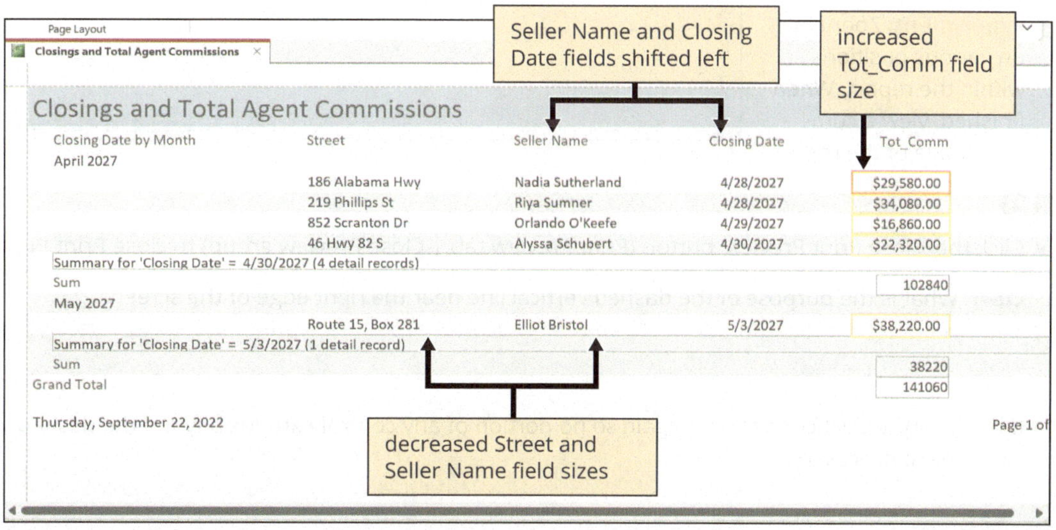

Figure 4–44

7

- Using the same technique, increase the size of the Tot_Comm header control.
- Using the same technique, increase the size of the Sum control.
- With the Sum control selected, click Property Sheet (Report Layout Design | Tools tab), and change the Format to Currency. Close the Property Sheet pane.
- Using the same technique, increase the size of the Grand Total control at the end of the report.
- With the Grand Total control selected, use the Property Sheet pane to change the Format to Currency, and then close the Property Sheet pane.

8

- Click the Tot_Comm header to select it, and click the Center button (Format tab | Font group) to center the text inside the header (Figure 4–45).

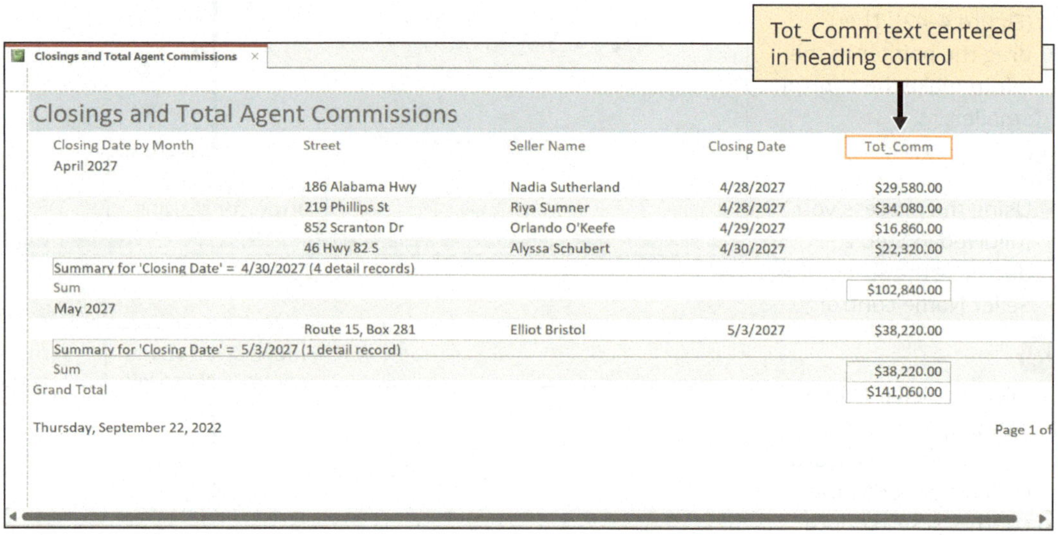

Figure 4–45

9

- Save the changes to the report.
- Click the View button arrow (Report Layout Design tab | Views group), and then click Print Preview to view the report. Click the magnifying glass pointer to view more of the report (Figure 4–46).
- **Experiment:** Zoom in on various positions within the report. When finished, view a complete page of the report.

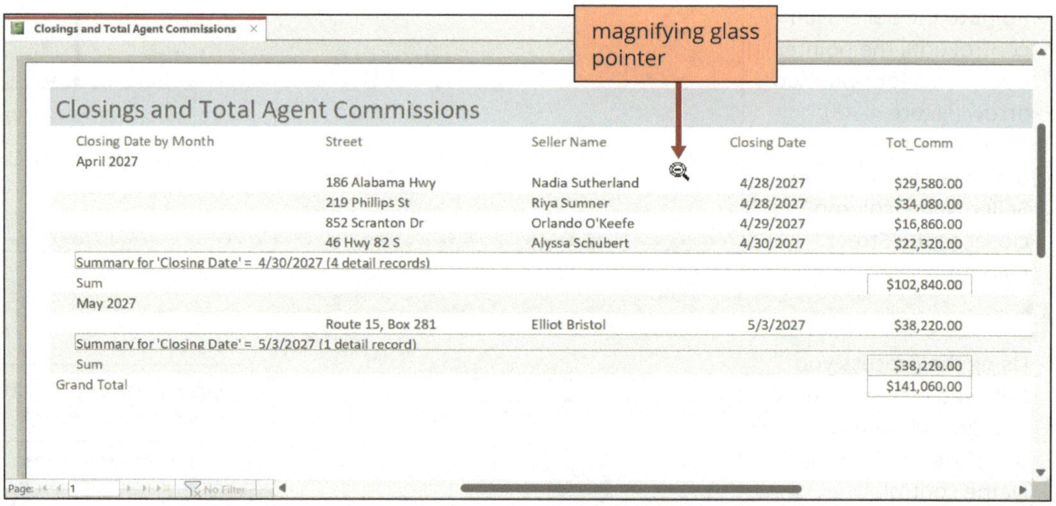

Figure 4–46

10

- Click the 'Close Print Preview' button (Print Preview tab | Close Preview group) to close Print Preview.

Q&A What is the purpose of the dashed vertical line near the right edge of the screen?
The line shows the right border of the amount of the report that will print on one page. If any portion of the report extends beyond the line, the report might not print correctly.

- If necessary, adjust control sizes again so no portion of any control extends beyond the dashed vertical line. Close the Field List pane, if necessary.

Q&A Do I have to resize all the controls that begin with the word, Summary, individually?
No. When you resize one of them, the others will all be resized the same amount automatically.

- Ensure the Page Number control is visible in the lower-right corner of the report. Click the Page Number control to select it, and then drag it to the left, if necessary, so no portion of the control extends beyond the dashed line. For more precise repositioning, with the Page Number control selected, use the arrow keys on your keyboard.
- Save your work and close the report.

Consider This

How do you determine the tables and fields that contain the data needed for the report?

First, you need to know the requirements for the report. Precisely what data is the report intended to convey? Once you understand those requirements, follow these guidelines:

- **Examine the requirements for the report to determine the tables.** Do the requirements only relate to data in a single table, or does the data come from multiple tables? What is the relationship between the tables?
- **Examine the requirements for the report to determine the fields necessary.** Look for all the data items specified for the report. Each should correspond to a field in a table or be able to be computed from fields in a table. This information gives you the list of fields to include.
- **Determine the order of the fields.** Examine the requirements to determine the order in which the fields should appear. Be logical and consistent in your ordering. For example, in an address, the city should come before the state and the state should come before the postal code, unless there is some compelling reason for another order.

Creating a Report in Layout View

You can use the Report button to create a report that automatically contains all the fields in a table. You then can delete the unwanted fields so the resulting report contains only the desired fields. At that point, you can use Layout view to modify the report and produce the report you want.

You can also use Layout view to create single- or multiple-table reports from scratch. To do so, you first create a blank report and display a field list for the table containing the first fields you want to include on the report.

There are times when you might want to create a report that has multiple columns. For example, a phone list with employee names and phone numbers could be printed in multiple columns. To do so, create the report using Layout view or Design view and then click the Page Setup tab, click the Columns button, enter the number of columns, select the desired column layout, and then click OK.

Next you would drag any fields you want from the table onto the report in the order you want them to appear. You would then change the size of the controls as you did previously by clicking the control, pointing to the edge of the selected control, and dragging to the desired size.

If the report involves a second table, you display the fields from the second table in the field list and then drag the fields from the second table onto the report in the desired order.

When you create a report in Layout view, the report does not automatically contain a title, but you can add one by clicking the Title button (Report Layout Design tab | Header / Footer group).

Once you have added the title, you can type whatever title you want for the report.

BTW
Adding a Second Table to a Report
If the report involves a second table, display the fields in the second table, and then drag the fields from the second table onto the report in the desired order.

To Create a Report in Layout View by Creating a Blank Report

Partners paralegals need an additional report that shows information related to closings and their fees. The paralegals want to create the report in Layout view. **Why?** Layout view works best when you need to change the look and feel of a report because you can rearrange fields and change their sizes. The following steps create a report in Layout view.

1

- Click Create on the ribbon to display the Create tab.
- Click the Blank Report button (Create tab | Reports group) to create a blank report. If necessary, close the Navigation Pane.
- If the Field List pane does not appear, display it by clicking the 'Add Existing Fields' button (Report Layout Design tab | Tools group) (Figure 4–47).

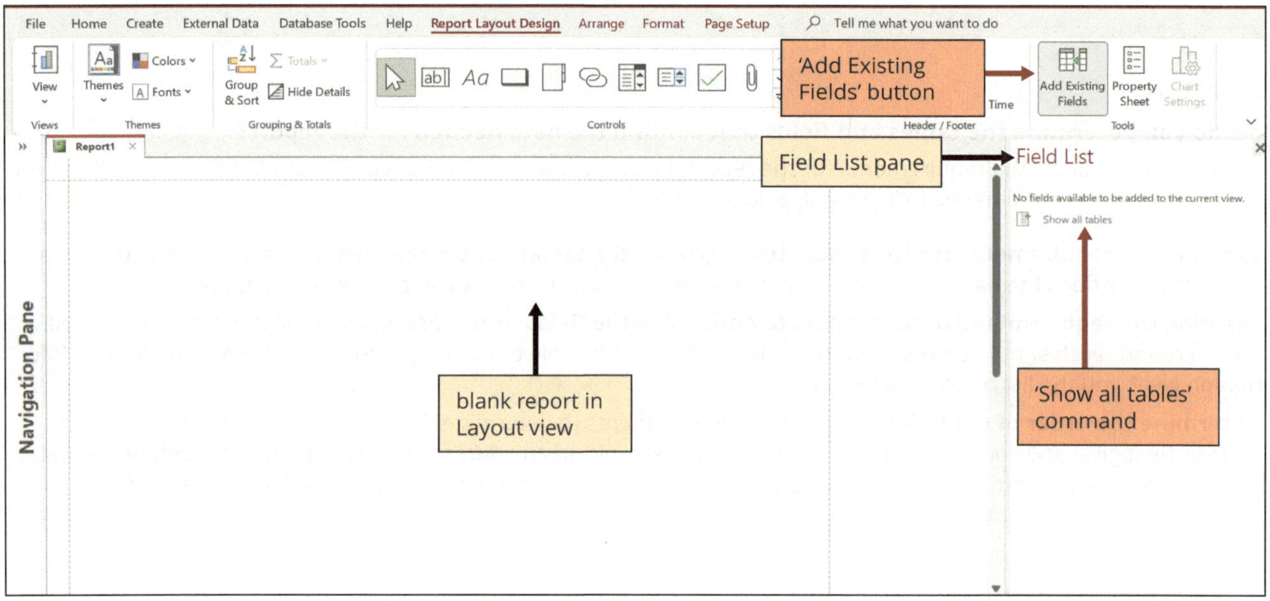

Figure 4–47

2

- If the tables do not appear in the field list, click 'Show all tables.'
- Click the plus sign (+) next to the Closing Fees table name to display its fields in the Field List pane (Figure 4–48).
- Drag the Closing ID, Title Search, Total Agent Commission, Recording Fees, Attorney Fees, Inspection Fees, Appraisal Fees, and Prorated HOA fields from the Field List pane to the report, positioning the fields as shown in Figure 4–49.

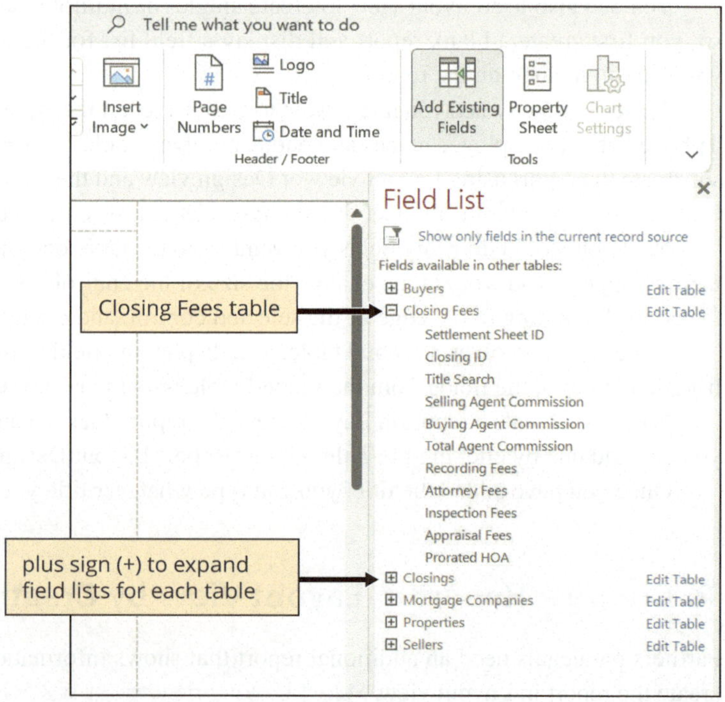

Figure 4–48

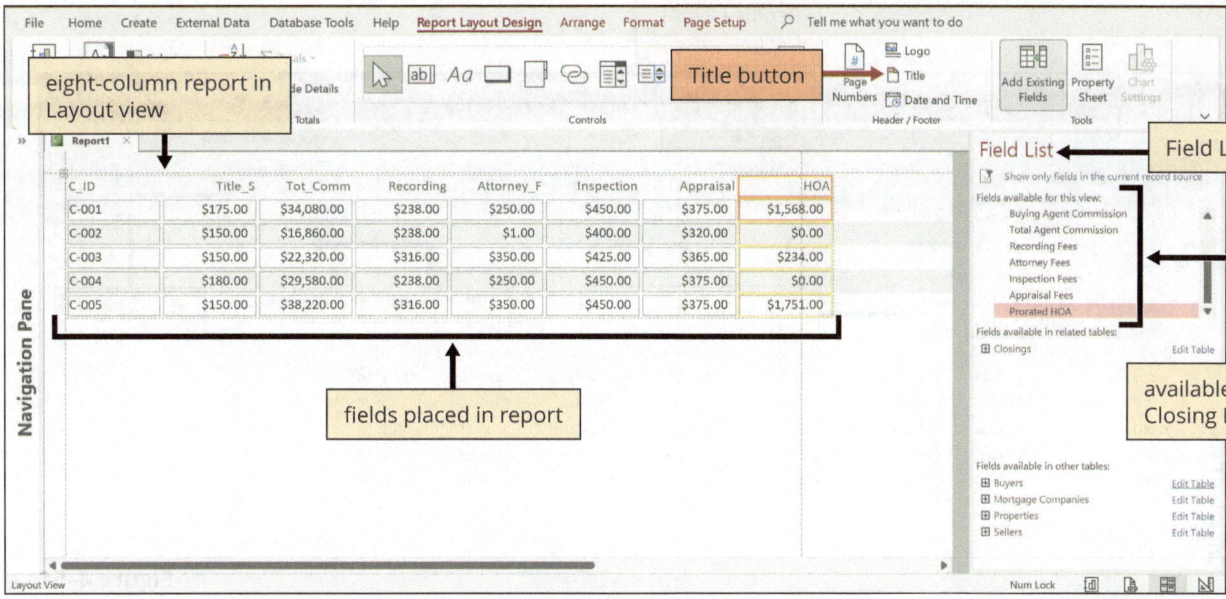

Figure 4–49

3

- Close the Field List pane.
- To fit all the columns on the same page, click the Landscape button (Page Setup tab | Page Layout group), which sets a wider page orientation (Figure 4–50).

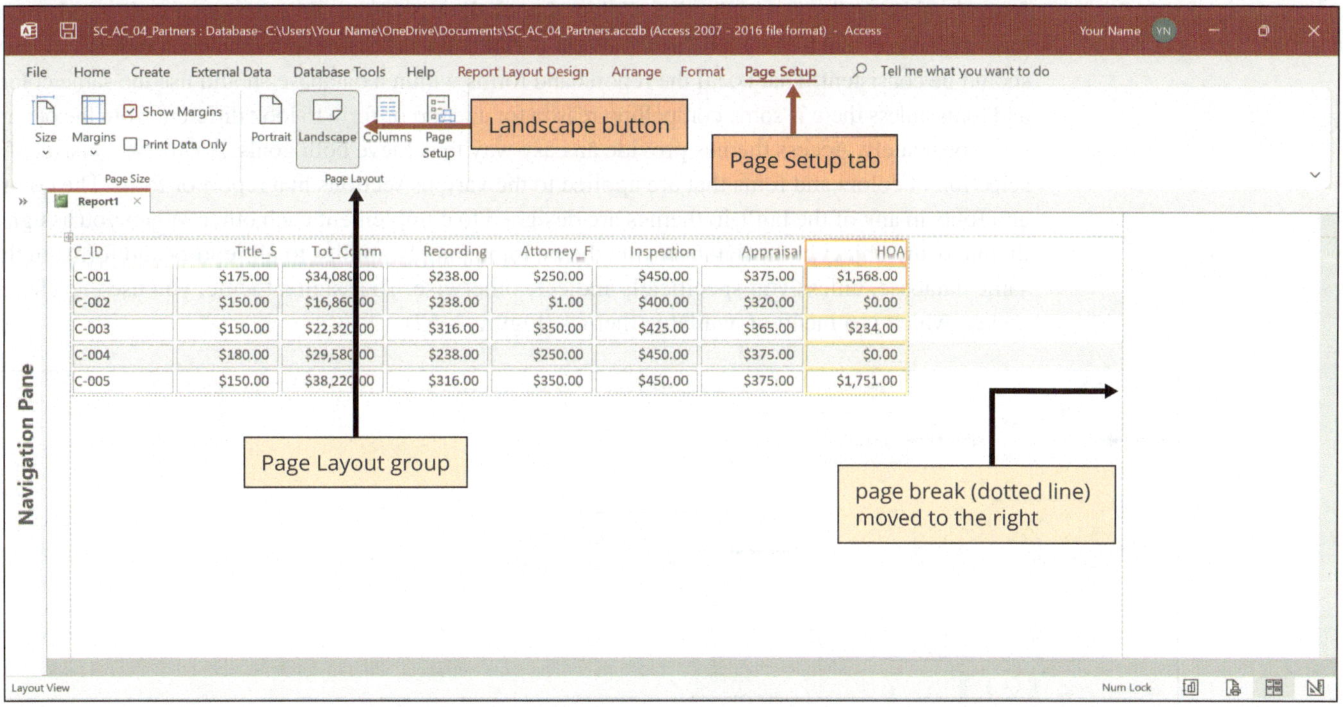

Figure 4–50

4

- To add a report title, click the Title button (Report Layout Design tab | Header / Footer group) and then type **Closing Fees Report** (Figure 4–51).
- Save the report as **Closing Fees Report**, and then close the report.

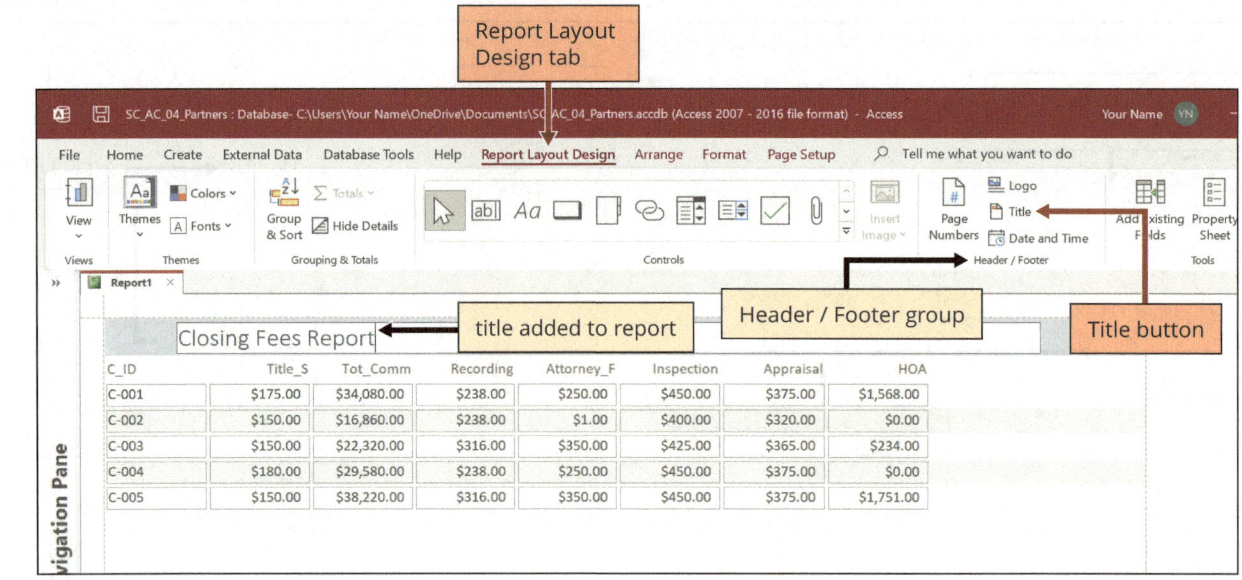

Figure 4–51

Using Themes

The most important characteristic of a report or form is that it presents the desired data in a useful arrangement. Another important characteristic, however, is the general appearance of the form. The colors and fonts that you use in the various sections of a report or form contribute to this look. You should keep in mind two important goals when assigning colors and fonts. First, the various colors and fonts should complement each other. Colors that clash or two fonts that do not go well together can produce a report that looks unprofessional or is difficult to read. Second, the choice of colors and fonts should be consistent. That is, all the reports and forms within a database should use the same colors and fonts unless there is some compelling reason for a report or form to look different from the others.

Fortunately, Access themes provide an easy way to achieve both goals. A **theme** consists of a selection of colors and fonts that are applied to the various sections in a report or form. The colors and fonts in any of the built-in themes are designed to complement each other. When you assign a theme to any object in the database, the theme immediately applies to all reports and forms in the same database, unless you specifically indicate otherwise. To assign a theme, you use the Theme picker, which is a menu of available themes (Figure 4–52).

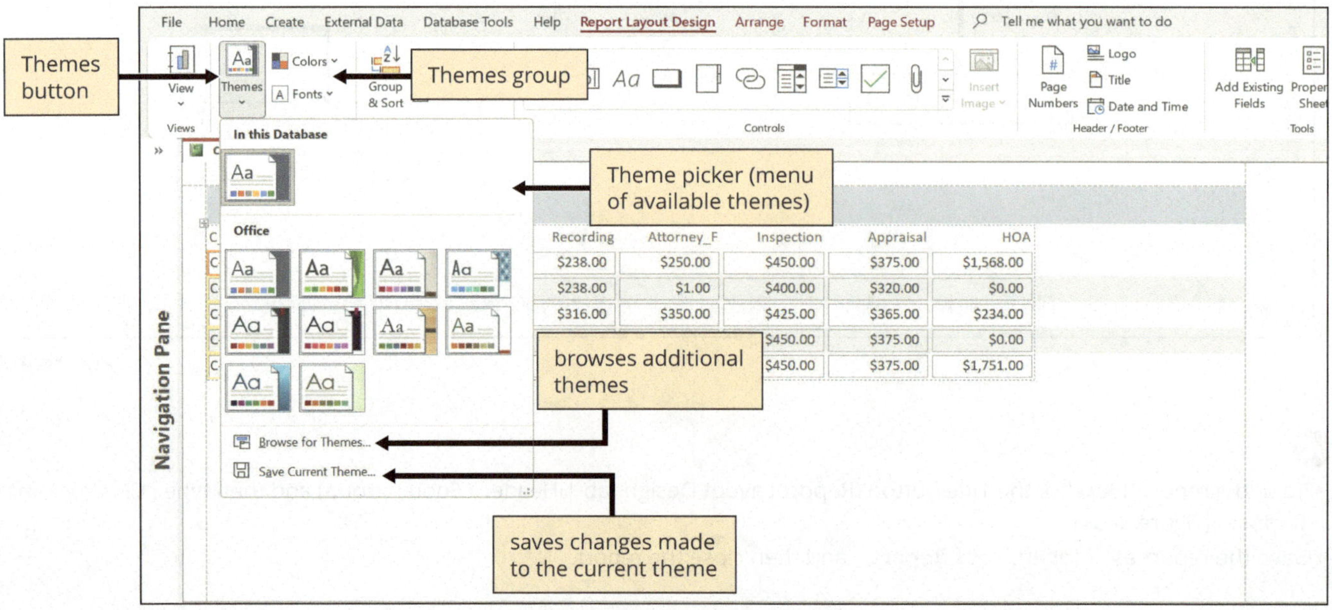

Figure 4–52

If you point to any theme in the Theme picker, you will see a ScreenTip giving the name of the theme. When you select a theme, the colors and fonts represented by that theme will immediately be applied to all reports and forms. If you later decide that you would prefer a different theme, you can change the theme for all the objects in the database by repeating the process with a different theme.

You can also use the Browse for Themes command to browse for themes that are not listed as part of a standard Access installation but are available for download. You can also create your own customized theme by specifying a combination of fonts and colors and using the Save Current Theme command to save your combination. If, after selecting a theme using the Themes button, you do not like the colors in the current theme, you can change the theme's colors. Click the Colors button (Report Layout Design tab | Themes group) (Figure 4–53), and then select an alternative color scheme.

BTW
Using Themes
Office themes are designed to enhance an organization's brand identity. Many organizations consistently use themes, styles, and color schemes to visually assist in identifying their products and/or services.

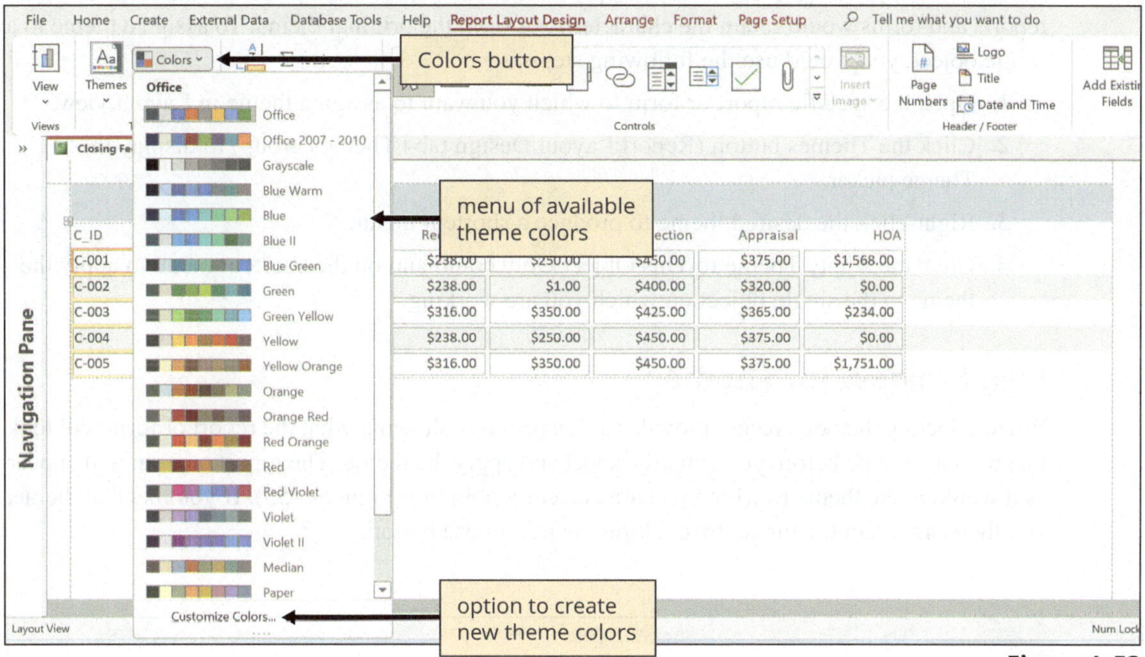

Figure 4–53

Similarly, if you do not like the fonts in the current theme, you can click the Fonts button (Report Layout Design tab | Themes group) (Figure 4–54). You then can select an alternative font for the theme.

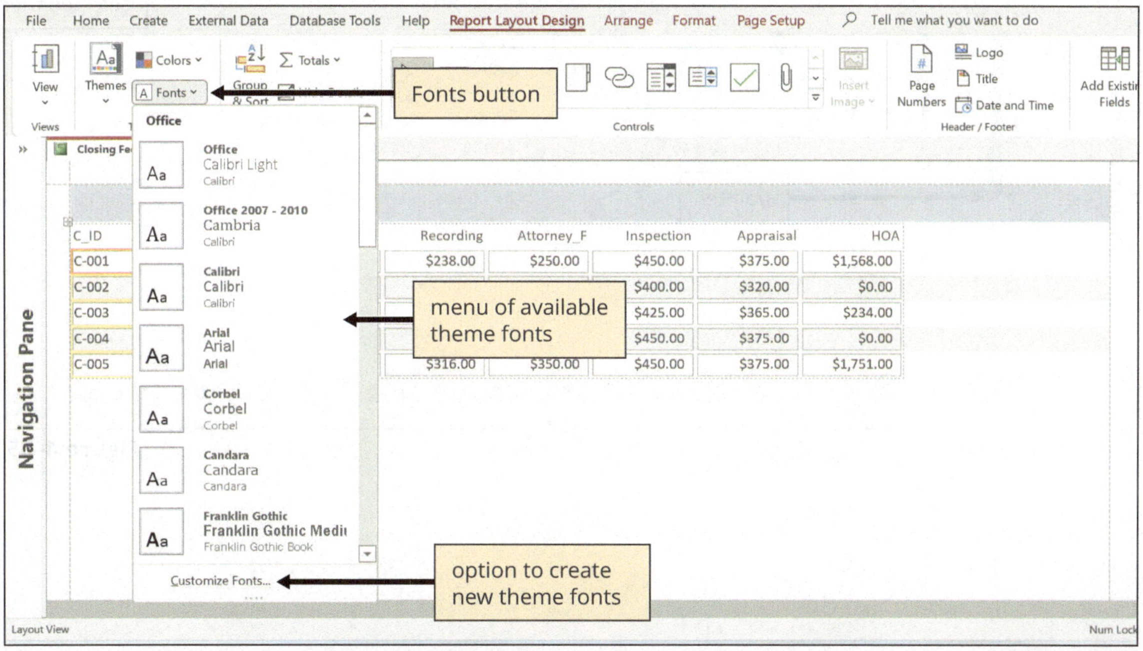

Figure 4–54

To Assign a Theme to All Objects

To assign a theme, it is easiest to use Layout view. You can use Design view as well, but it is easier to see the result of picking a theme when you are viewing the report or form in Layout view. To assign a theme to all reports and forms, you would use the following steps.

1. Open any report or form in Layout view.
2. Click the Themes button (Report Layout Design tab | Themes group) to display the Theme picker.
3. Click the desired theme.

To Assign a Theme to a Single Object

In some cases, you might only want to apply a theme to the current report or form, while all other reports and forms would retain the characteristics from the original theme. To assign a theme to a single object, you would use the following steps.

1. Open the specific report or form to which you want to assign a theme in Layout view.
2. Click the Themes button (Report Layout Design tab | Themes group) to display the Theme picker.
3. Right-click the desired theme to produce a shortcut menu.
4. Click the Apply Theme to This Object Only command on the shortcut menu to apply the theme to the single object on which you are working.

Live Preview for Themes

When selecting themes, Access provides a **live preview** showing what the report or form will look like with the theme before you actually select and apply the theme. The report or form will appear as it would in the theme to which you are currently pointing (Figure 4–55). If you like that theme, you then can select the theme by clicking the left mouse button.

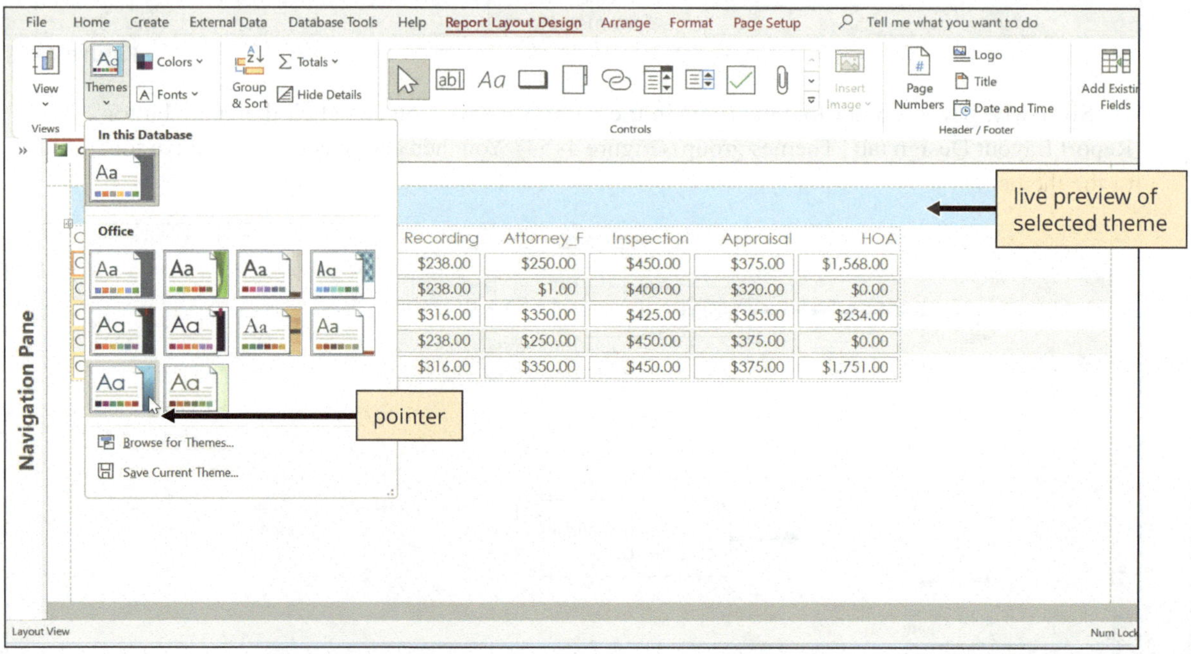

Figure 4–55

To Create a Summary Report

A report that includes group calculations such as subtotals, but does not include the individual detail lines, is called a **summary report**. **Why?** You might need a report that only shows the overall group calculations, but not all the records. The following steps hide the detail lines in the Closings and Properties Report, thus creating a summary report.

1

- Open the Navigation Pane, open the Closings and Properties Report in Layout view, and then close the Navigation Pane.
- Click the Hide Details button (Report Layout Design tab | Grouping & Totals group) to hide the details in the report (Figure 4–56).

Q&A How can I see the details once I have hidden them?
Click the Hide Details button a second time.

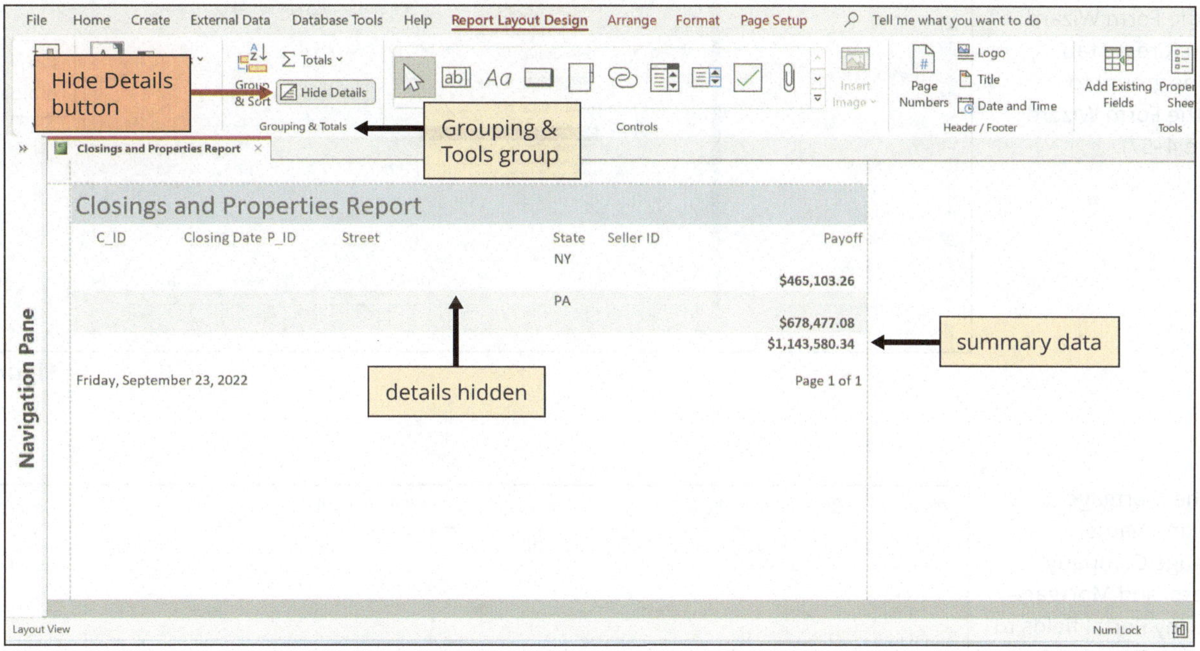

Figure 4–56

- Close the report without saving your changes.

Q&A What would happen if I saved the report?
The next time you viewed the report, the details would still be hidden. If that happened and you wanted to show all the details, you would click the Hide Details button a second time.

Break Point: If you wish to take a break, this is a good place to do so. You can quit Access now. To resume at a later time, start Access, open the database called SC_AC_04_Partners.accdb, and continue following the steps from this location forward.

Form Creation

You can create a simple form consisting of all the fields in the Mortgage Companies table using the Form button (Create tab | Forms group). To create more customized forms, you can use the Form Wizard. Once you have used the Form Wizard to create a form, you can modify that form in either Layout view or Design view.

BTW
Summary Reports
You can create a summary report in either Layout view or Design view.

To Use the Form Wizard to Create a Form

The following steps use the Form Wizard to create an initial version of the Mortgage Companies Form. **Why?** Using the Form Wizard is the easiest way to create this form. The initial version will contain the Mortgage Company Name, Address, and Portal fields.

1

- Open the Navigation Pane and select the Mortgage Companies table.
- Click Create on the ribbon to display the Create tab.
- Click the Form Wizard button (Create tab | Forms group) to start the Form Wizard (Figure 4–57).

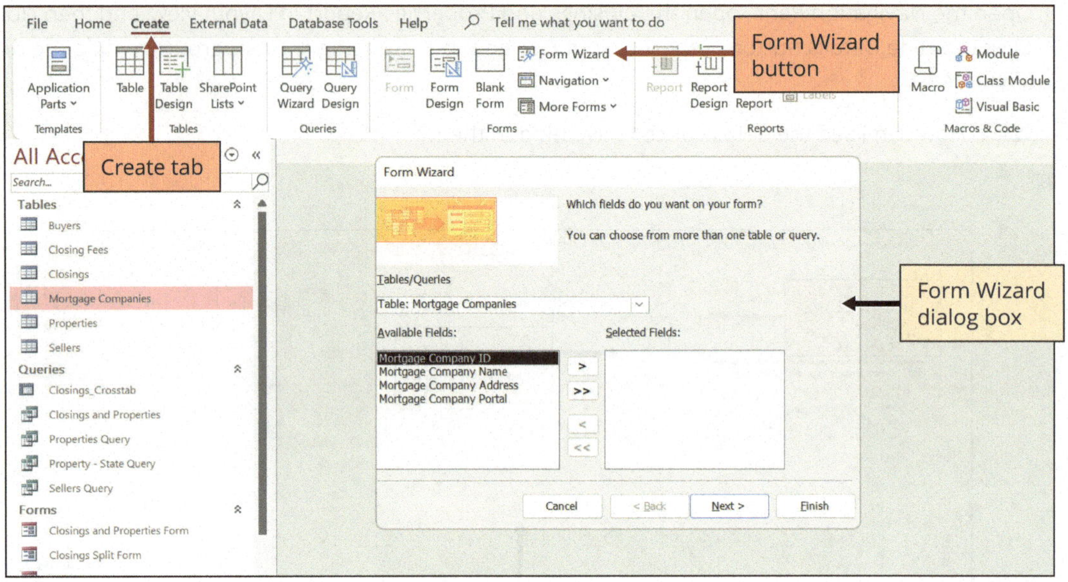

Figure 4–57

2

- Add the Mortgage Company Name, Mortgage Company Address, and Mortgage Company Portal fields to the form (Figure 4–58).

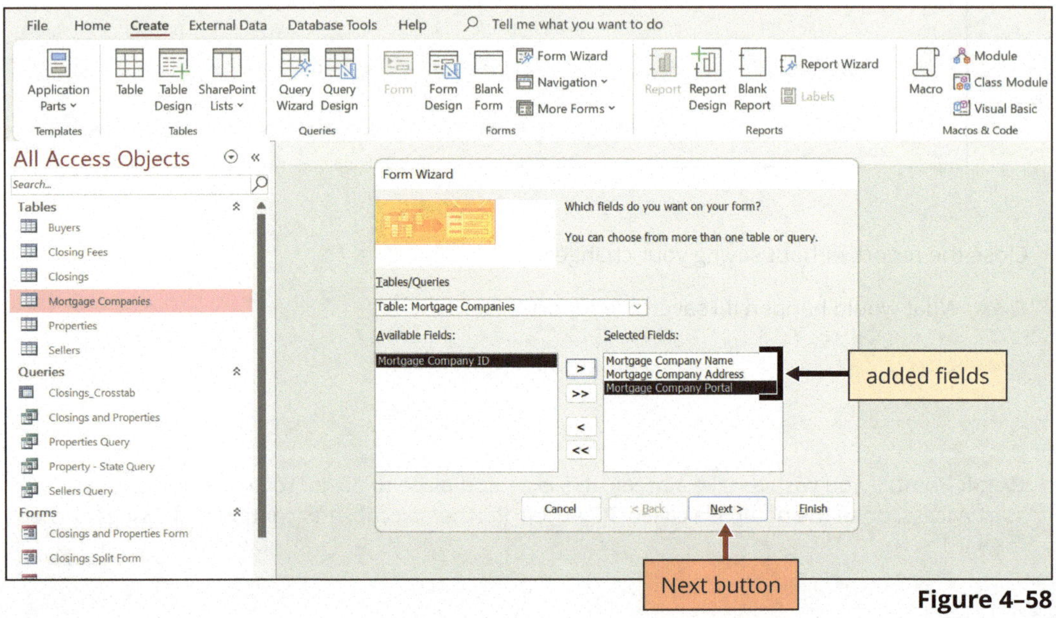

Figure 4–58

3

- Click Next to display the next Form Wizard screen (Figure 4–59).
- Be sure the Columnar layout is selected, and then click Next to display the next Form Wizard screen.

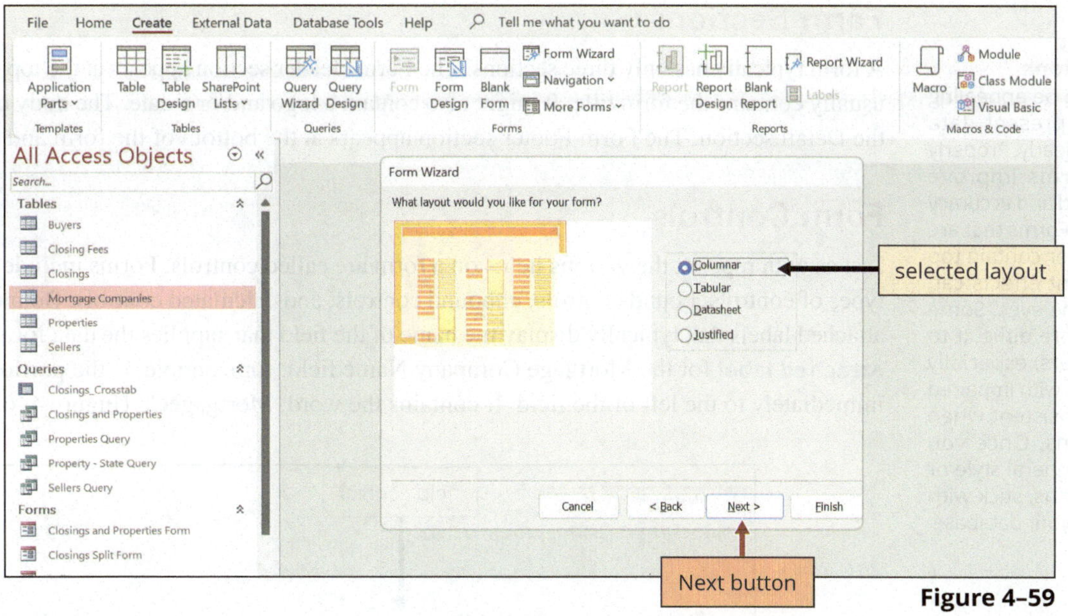

Figure 4–59

4

- Click in the Title text box at the end of the existing text and type **Form** so the title reads, Mortgage Companies Form (Figure 4–60).

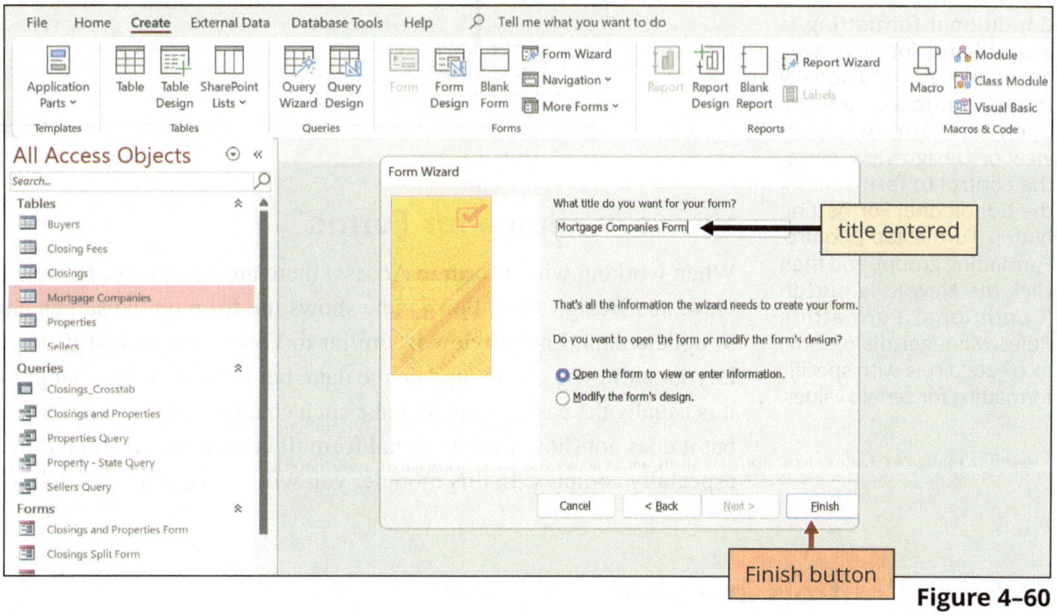

Figure 4–60

5

- Click Finish to complete and display the form (Figure 4–61).
- Click the form's Close button to close the Mortgage Companies Form.

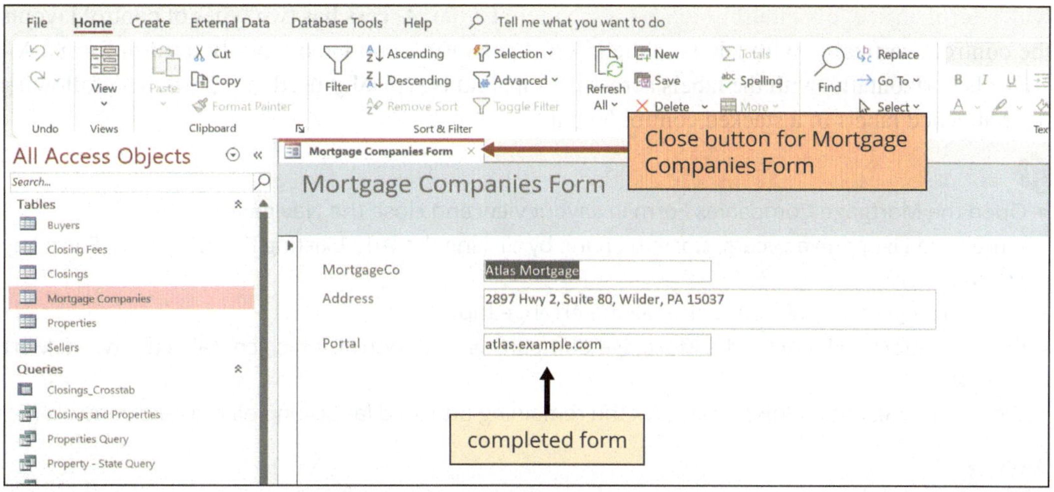

Figure 4–61

BTW
Form Design Considerations
Forms should be appealing visually and present data logically and clearly. Properly designed forms improve both the speed and accuracy of data entry. Forms that are too cluttered or contain too many different effects can be hard on the eyes. Some colors are more difficult to see than others, especially for individuals with impaired vision. Be consistent when creating forms. Once you decide on a general style or theme for forms, stick with it throughout your database.

BTW
Conditional Formatting
Conditional formatting is available for forms as well as reports. To conditionally format controls on a form, open the Form in Layout view or Design view, select the control to format, click the Conditional Formatting button (Format tab | Control Formatting group), and then click the New Rule button (Conditional Formatting Rules Manager dialog box) to create a rule with specific formatting for certain values.

Form Sections

A form typically has only three sections. The Form Header section appears at the top of the form and usually contains the form title. It might also contain a logo and/or a date. The body of the form is in the Detail section. The Form Footer section appears at the bottom of the form and is often empty.

Form Controls

Just as with reports, the various items on a form are called controls. Forms include the same three types of controls: bound controls, unbound controls, and calculated controls. Bound controls have attached labels that typically display the name of the field that supplies the data for the control. The **attached label** for the Mortgage Company Name field, for example, is the portion of the screen immediately to the left of the field. It contains the word, MortgageCo (Figure 4–62).

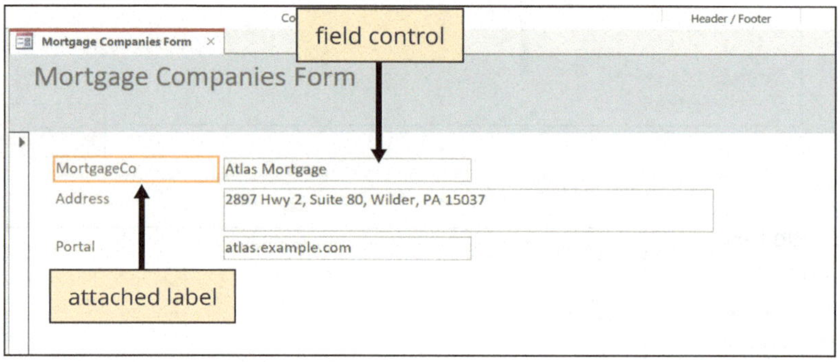

Figure 4–62

Views Available for Forms

When working with a form in Access, there are three ways to view the form: Form view, Layout view, and Design view. Form view shows the form on the screen and allows you to use the form to update data. Layout view is similar to Form view in that it shows the form on the screen. In Layout view, you cannot update the data, but you can make changes to the layout of the form, and it is usually the easiest way to make such changes. Design view also allows you to make changes, but it does not show you the actual form. It is most useful when the changes you need to make are especially complex. In this module, you will use Layout view to modify the form.

To Place Controls in a Control Layout

A **control layout** is a guide that aligns the controls to give the form or report a uniform appearance. **Why?** To use Layout view with a form, the controls must be placed in a control layout. Access has two types of control layouts. A **stacked layout** arranges the controls vertically, with labels to the left of the control, and is commonly used in forms. A **tabular layout** arranges the controls horizontally, with the labels across the top, and is typically used in reports. The following steps place the controls and their attached labels in a stacked control layout.

1

- Open the Mortgage Companies Form in Layout view and close the Navigation Pane.
- If the Field List pane appears, close the pane by clicking the 'Add Existing Fields' button (Form Layout Design tab | Tools group).
- Click Arrange on the ribbon to display the Arrange tab.
- Click the attached label for the Mortgage Company Name control, which contains the word, MortgageCo, to select the control.
- While pressing and holding SHIFT, click the remaining attached labels and all the field controls (Figure 4–63).

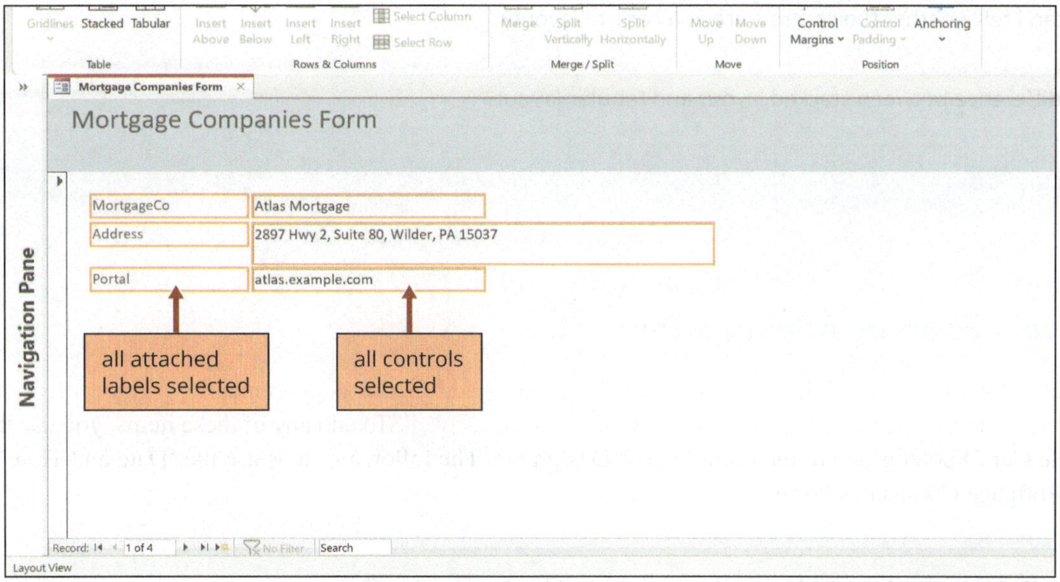

Figure 4–63

Q&A Why did I have to hold SHIFT when I clicked the remaining labels and controls?

If you did not hold SHIFT, you would only select one control at a time. The other controls no longer would be selected. Holding SHIFT allows you to select multiple labels and controls at one time.

Did I have to select the attached labels and controls in a particular order?

No. As long as you selected all controls, the order in which you selected them does not matter.

When I clicked some of the controls, they moved so they are no longer aligned as well as they are in the figure. What should I do?

You do not have to worry about it. Once you complete the next step, they will once again be aligned properly.

Is there a faster way to select all the attached labels and controls?

Yes. You could instead press CTRL + A to select all the items, and then hold SHIFT while clicking the title control in the header to deselect it.

2

- Click the Stacked button (Arrange tab | Table group) to place the controls in a stacked layout (Figure 4–64).

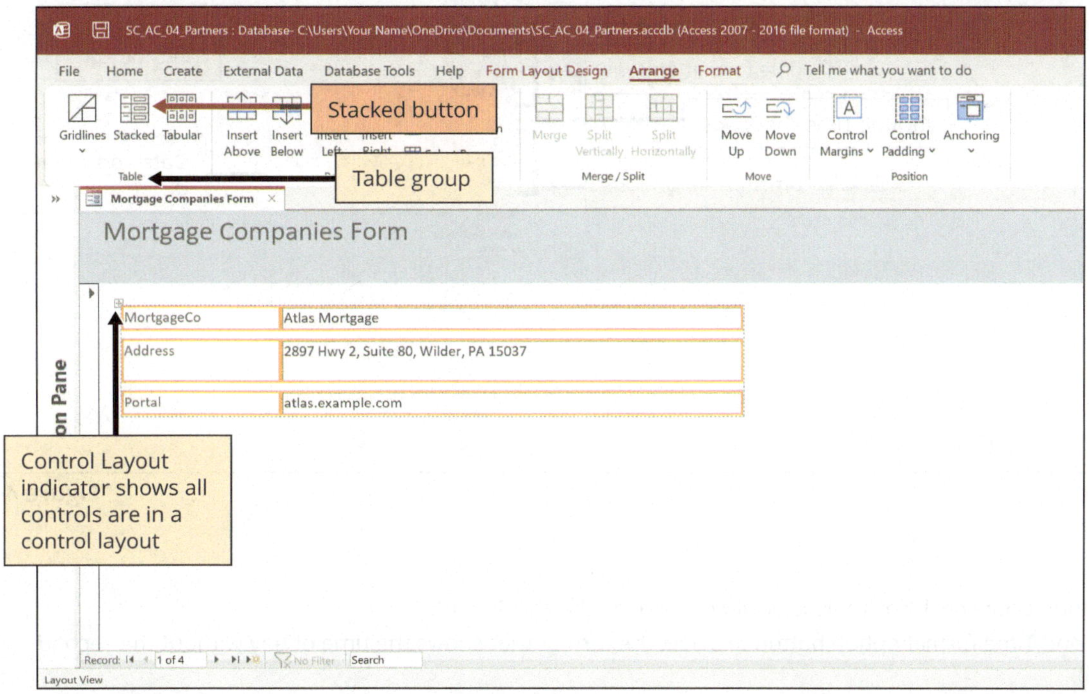

Figure 4–64

Q&A How can I tell whether the controls are in a control layout?
Look for the Control Layout indicator in the upper-left corner of the control layout.

What is the difference between stacked layout and tabular layout?
In a stacked layout, which is more often used in forms, the controls are placed vertically with the labels to the left of the controls. In a tabular layout, which is more often used in reports, the controls are placed horizontally with the labels above the controls.

To Enhance a Form by Adding a Date

Why? To enhance the look or usability of a report or form, you can add special items, such as a logo or title. You can also add the date and time. In the case of reports, you can add a page number as well. To add any of these items, you use the appropriate button in the Header / Footer group of the Form Layout Design tab. The following steps use the 'Date and Time' button to add a time to the Mortgage Companies Form.

1

- Click Form Layout Design on the ribbon to display the Form Layout Design tab.
- Click the 'Date and Time' button (Form Layout Design tab | Header / Footer group) to display the Date and Time dialog box (Figure 4–65).

Q&A What is the purpose of the various check boxes and option buttons?
If the Include Date check box is checked, you must pick a date format from the three options underneath the check box. If it is not checked, the options will be dimmed. If the Include Time check box is checked, you must pick a time format from the three options underneath the check box. If it is not checked, the options will be dimmed.

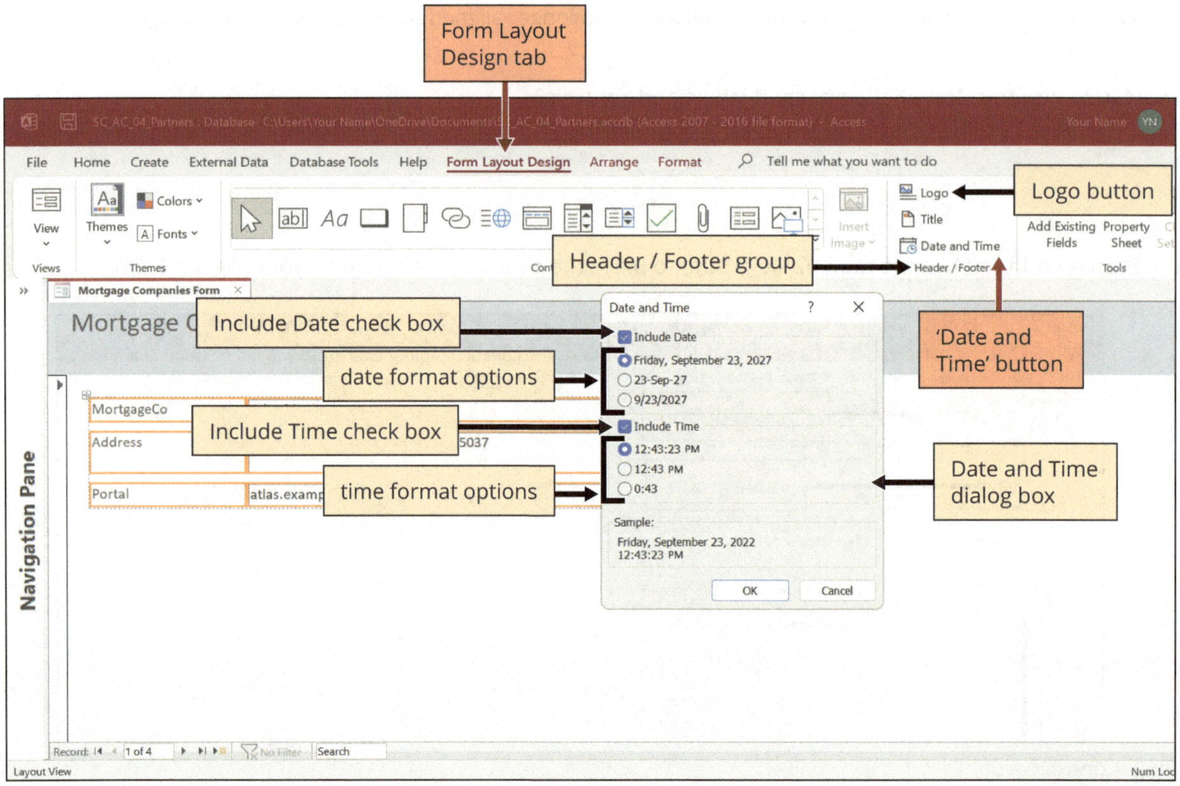

Figure 4–65

2

- Click the Include Date check box to deselect it and remove the check mark.
- Click the second Time format option button to select the format that shows the time of day without the seconds (Figure 4–66).

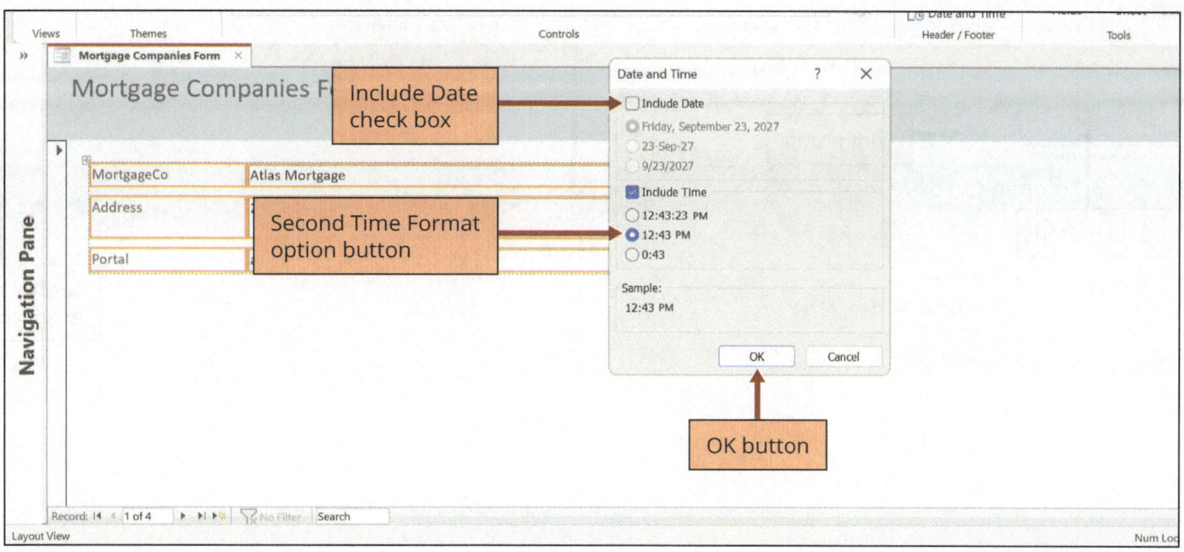

Figure 4–66

3

- Click OK (Date and Time dialog box) to add the time to the form (Figure 4–67).

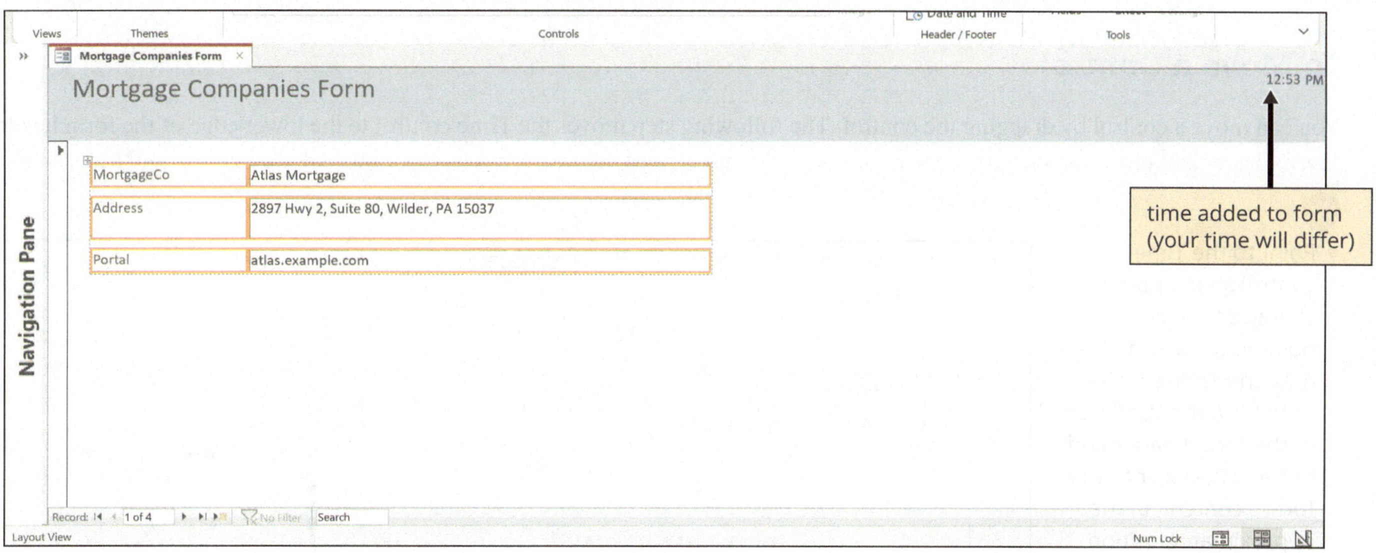

Figure 4–67

To Change the Format of a Control

You can change the format of a control by clicking the control and then clicking the appropriate button on the Format tab. The following step uses this technique to bold the time. **Why?** Formatting controls on a form lets you visually emphasize certain controls.

1

- Click the Time control to select it.
- Click Format on the ribbon to display the Format tab.
- Click the Bold button (Format tab | Font group) to bold the time (Figure 4–68).

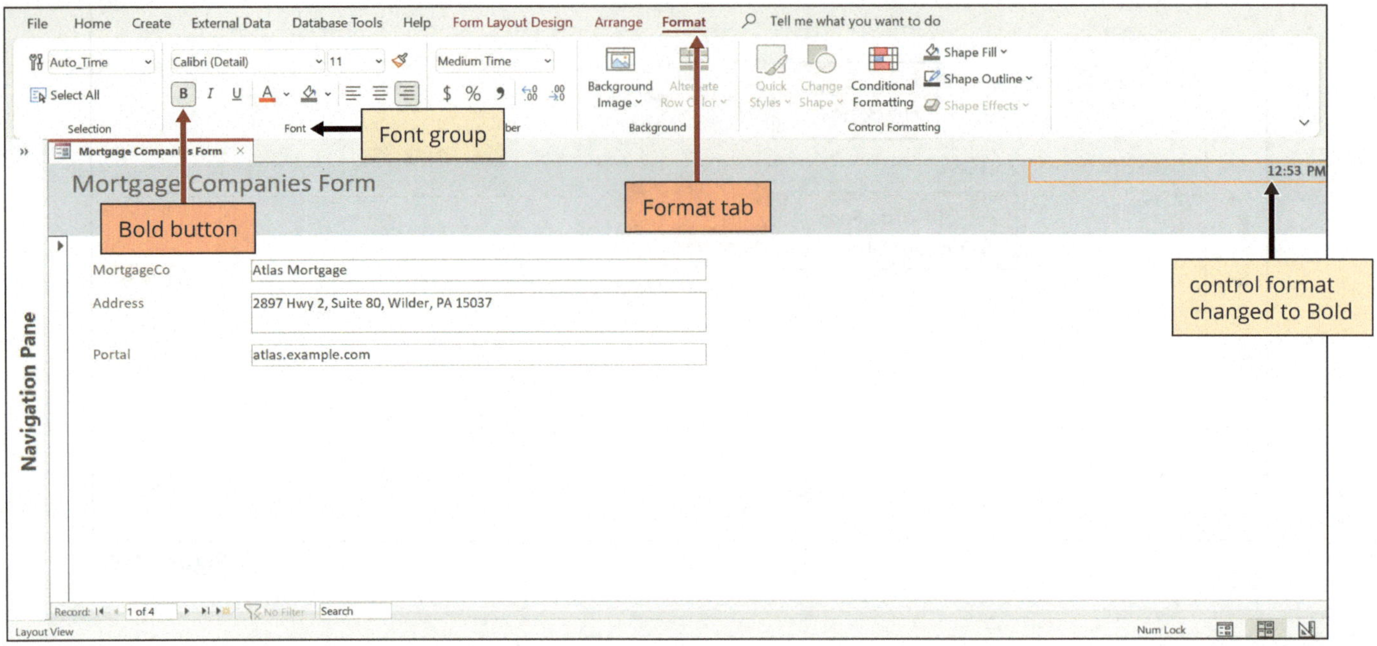

Figure 4–68

To Move a Control

You can move a control by dragging the control. The following step moves the Time control to the lower edge of the form header. **Why?** The default location of some controls might not be ideal; moving controls lets you adjust the design to your specifications.

1

- Point to the Time control so the pointer changes to a four-pointed arrow, and then drag the Time control to the lower boundary of the form header and to the left, closer to the form's content, in the approximate position shown in Figure 4–69.
- Save your changes to the form. Do not close it yet.

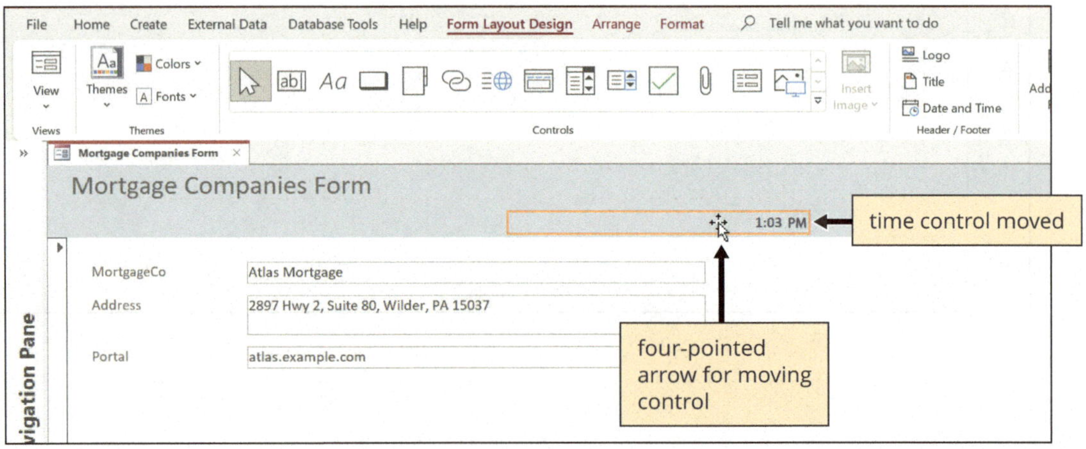

Figure 4–69

Q&A I moved my pointer a little bit and it became a two-pointed arrow. Can I still drag the pointer?

If you drag when the pointer is a two-pointed arrow, you will resize the control. To move the control, it must be a four-pointed arrow.

Could I drag other objects as well? For example, could I drag the title to the center of the form header?

Yes. Be sure you are pointing at the object and the pointer is a four-pointed arrow. You then can drag the object to the desired location.

To Move Controls in a Control Layout

Just as you moved the Time control in the previous section, you can move any control within a control layout by dragging the control to the location you want. As you move it, a line will indicate the position where the control will be placed when you release the mouse button or your finger. You can move more than one control in the same operation by selecting multiple controls prior to moving them.

The following steps move a control in the Mortgage Companies Form. These steps will move the Mortgage Company Portal field so it follows the Mortgage Company Name field. **Why?** The web portal is the primary means used to interact with mortgage company documents and resources, and this field would be quicker to access when listed directly below the Mortgage Company Name, which is called MortgageCo in the form.

1

- With the Mortgage Companies Form in Layout view, click the label for the Portal field to select it.
- While holding SHIFT, click the control for the Portal field to select both the field and its label (Figure 4–70).

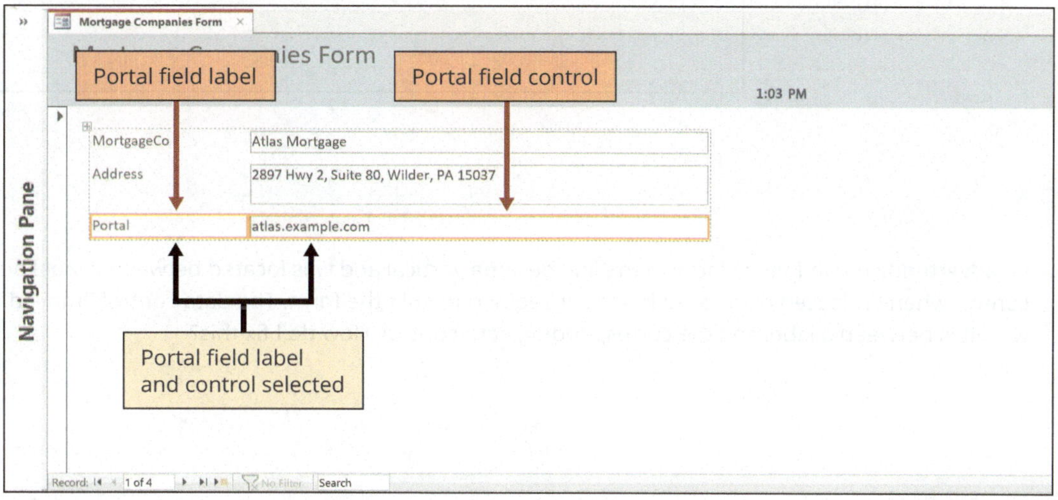

Figure 4–70

2

- Using the four-pointed, move arrow, drag the field straight up to the position of the red line shown in Figure 4–71; the red line appears as you move the field to its new location.

Q&A What is the purpose of the line by the pointer?
It shows you where the field will be positioned once you release it.

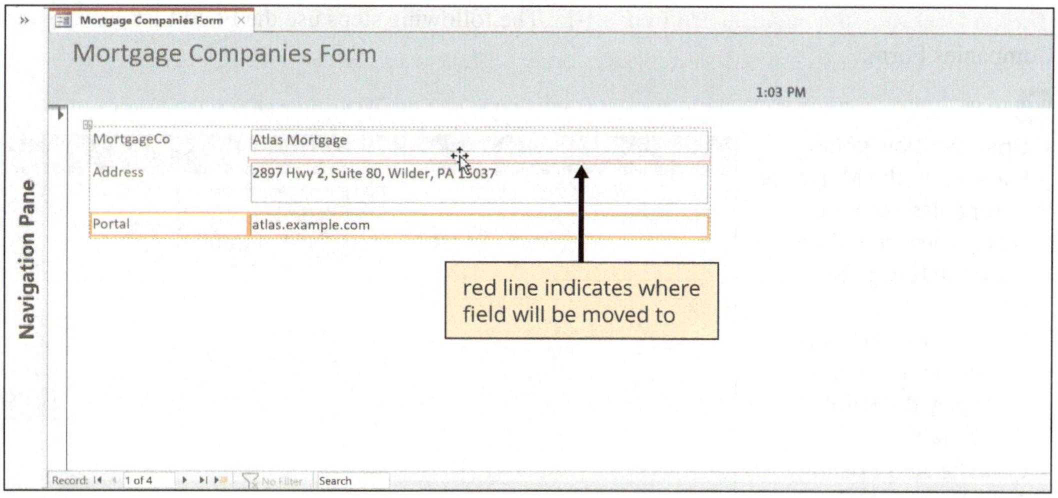

Figure 4–71

3

- Release the mouse button or your finger to complete the movement of the field (Figure 4–72).
- Save and close the Mortgage Companies Form.

Q&A I inadvertently dragged the label instead of the data control and dropped it under the MortgageCo data control. The label I moved is now in the data controls column, and the data control I moved is in a new column to the right. How do I fix this?

You can try to move it back where it was, but that can be tricky. The easiest way is to use the Undo button (Home tab | Undo group) to undo your change, or press CTRL + Z to undo. Then, try again, making sure to release the mouse button only when the red line is correctly positioned.

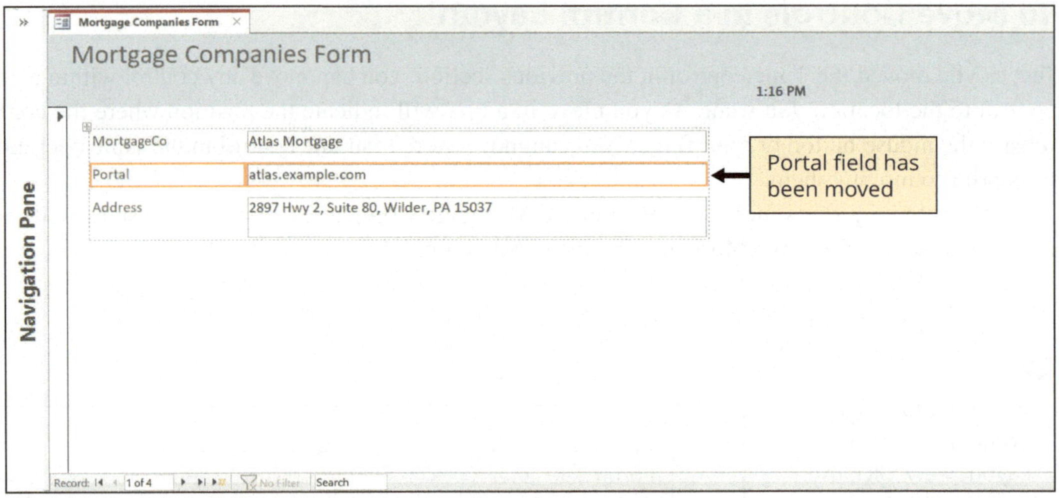

Figure 4–72

I inadvertently moved my pointer so the line became vertical and was located between a label and the corresponding data control when I released the mouse button. It seemed to split the form. The data control I moved appears right where the line was. It is between a label and the corresponding data control. How do I fix this?

Use the Undo button (Home tab | Undo group) to undo your change, or press CTRL + Z to undo. Then, try again, making sure to release the mouse button only when the red line is correctly positioned.

To Add a Field

After reviewing the Mortgage Companies Form, management decided that ID fields would help keep information straight between multiple tables, forms, and reports. **Why?** Just as with a report, once you have created an initial form, you might decide that the form should contain an additional field. The following steps use the Field List pane to add the ID field to the Mortgage Companies Form.

1

- Open the Navigation Pane, open the Mortgage Companies Form in Design view, and then close the Navigation Pane.
- If necessary, click Form Design on the ribbon to display the Form Design tab.
- Click the 'Add Existing Fields' button (Form Design tab | Tools group) to display the Field List pane (Figure 4–73).

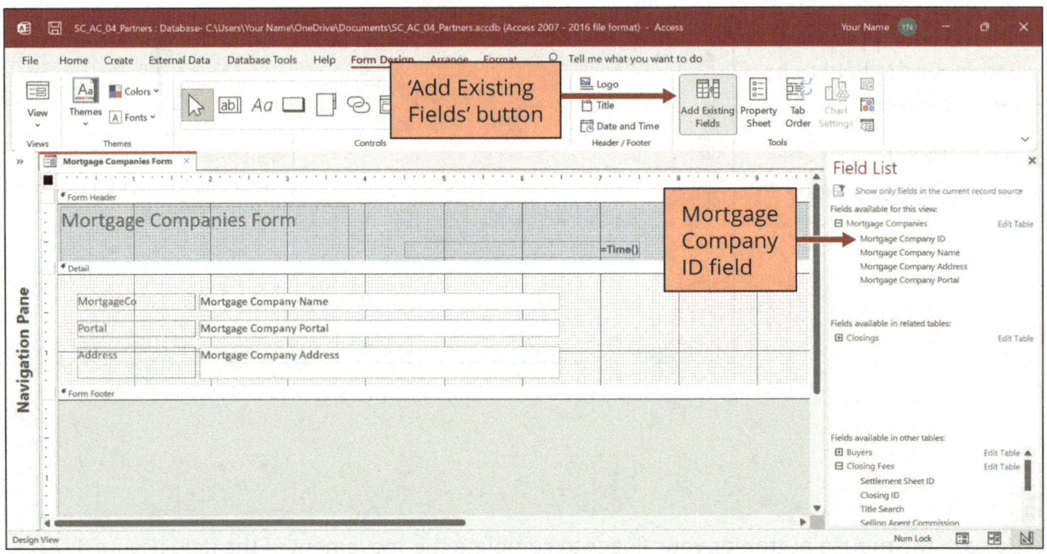

Figure 4–73

2

- Point to the Mortgage Company ID field in the field list, and then drag the pointer to the position shown in Figure 4–74.

Q&A Does the position of the ID field have to be exact?

The exact position is not critical at this time as long as the field is in the general position shown in the figure.

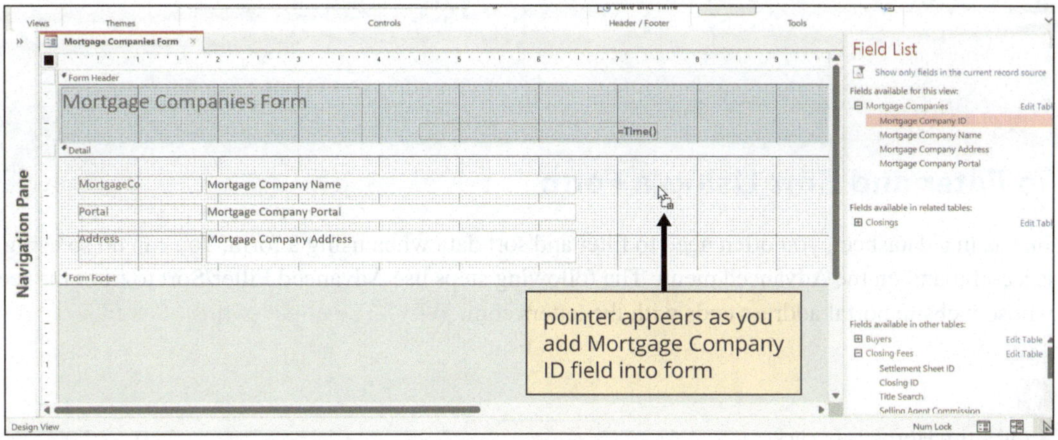

Figure 4–74

3

- Release the mouse button or your finger to place the field (Figure 4–75).

Q&A What if I make a mistake?

Just as when you are modifying a report, you can delete the field by clicking the field and then pressing DEL and then try again. Alternatively, you can move the field by dragging it to the correct position.

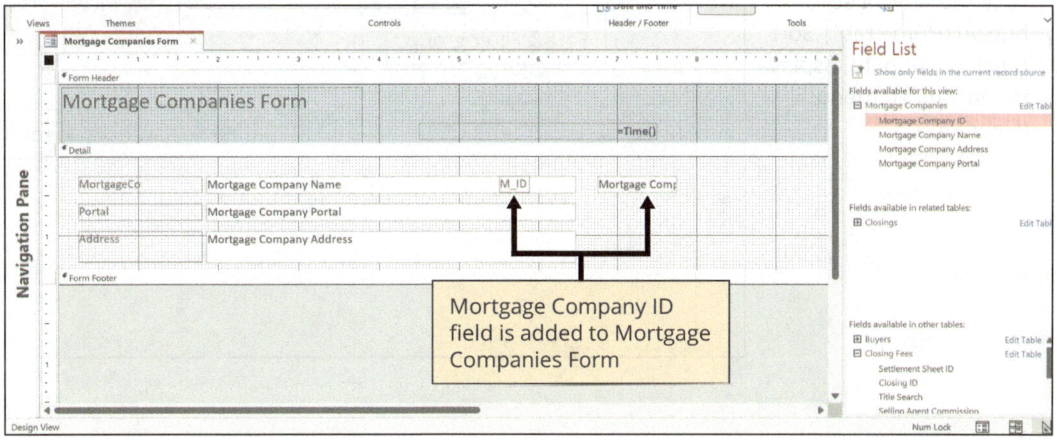

Figure 4–75

4

- Click the 'Add Existing Fields' button (Form Design tab | Tools group) to remove the Field List pane.
- Click the Mortgage Company Name field to select it.
- Use the two-pointed, resize arrow to reduce the size of the column holding the other controls so the Mortgage Company Name control does not overlap the M_ID label (Figure 4–76). This will give you sufficient space to position both the Mortgage Company Name field and the M_ID field on the same page, even though you cannot see the page borders at this time. Resize and reposition the Mortgage Company ID control as needed to fit the space as shown in Figure 4-76.
- Save your changes to the form. Do not close it yet.

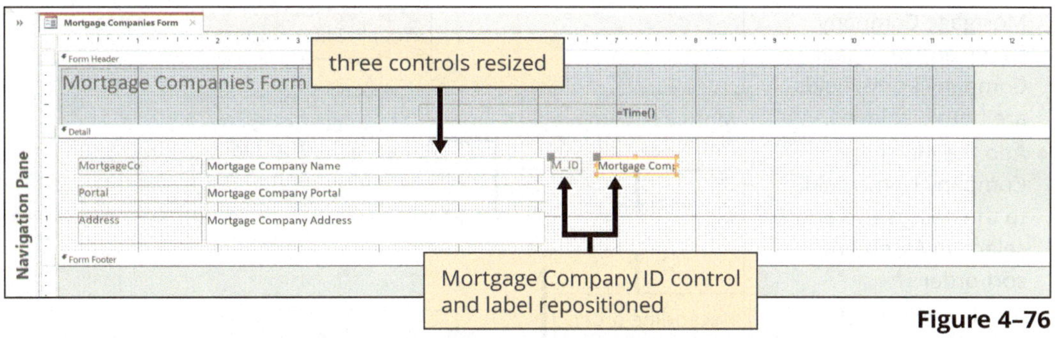

Figure 4–76

Q&A In the figure, it looks like the M_ID label is closer to the Mortgage Company ID control than it is on my screen. How do I match my screen to the figure?

When you select the Mortgage Company ID control or its label, gray boxes appear over each component. You can drag one of these gray boxes to change the distance between the control and its label.

To Filter and Sort Using a Form

Just as in a datasheet, you often need to filter and sort data when using a form. You can do so using Advanced Filter/Sort, which is a command on the Advanced menu. The following steps use Advanced Filter/Sort to filter the records to mortgage companies whose website portal address ends with the letters com. **Why?** The effect of this filter and sort is that you use the form to view only those mortgage companies using a .com website.

1

- Click the Home tab, click the View button arrow, and then select Layout View to change the view.
- Click the Advanced button (Home tab | Sort & Filter group) to display the Advanced menu (Figure 4–77).

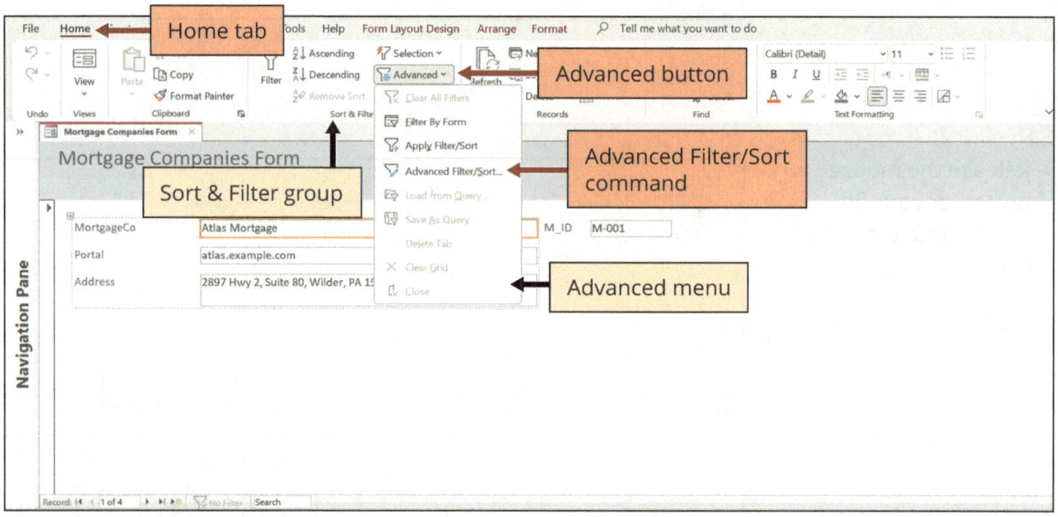

Figure 4–77

2

- Click Advanced Filter/Sort on the Advanced menu.
- If necessary, resize the field list so the Mortgage Company Name and Mortgage Company Portal fields are both displayed.
- Add the Mortgage Company Name field to the design grid and select an Ascending sort order.
- Add the Mortgage Company Portal field and type ***com** as the criterion for the Mortgage Company Portal field (Figure 4–78).

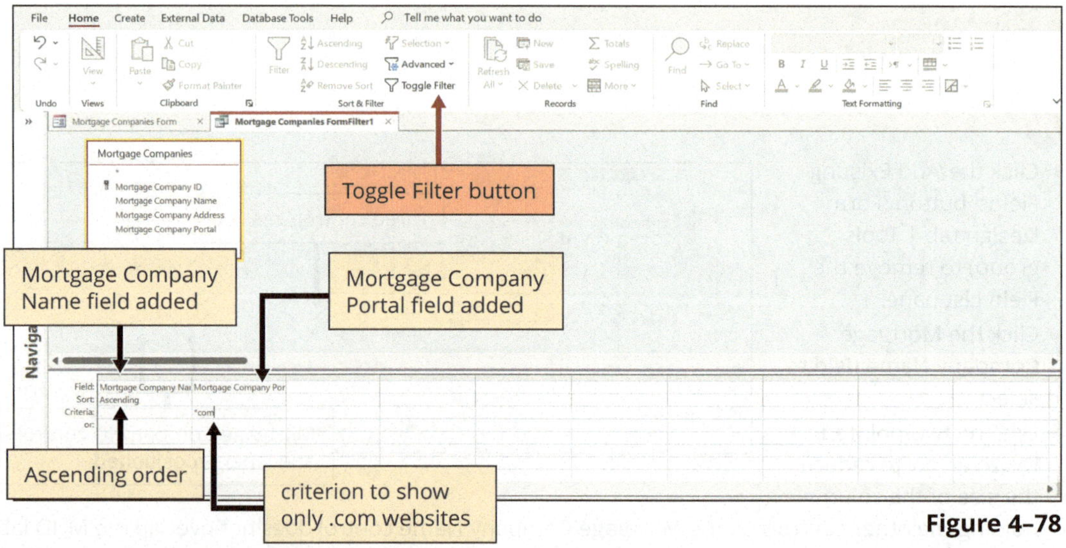

Figure 4–78

3

- Click the Toggle Filter button (Home tab | Sort & Filter group) to filter the records (Figure 4–79).

Q&A I can only see one record at a time in the form. How can I see which records are included?
You need to scroll through the records using the arrows in the Navigation bar.

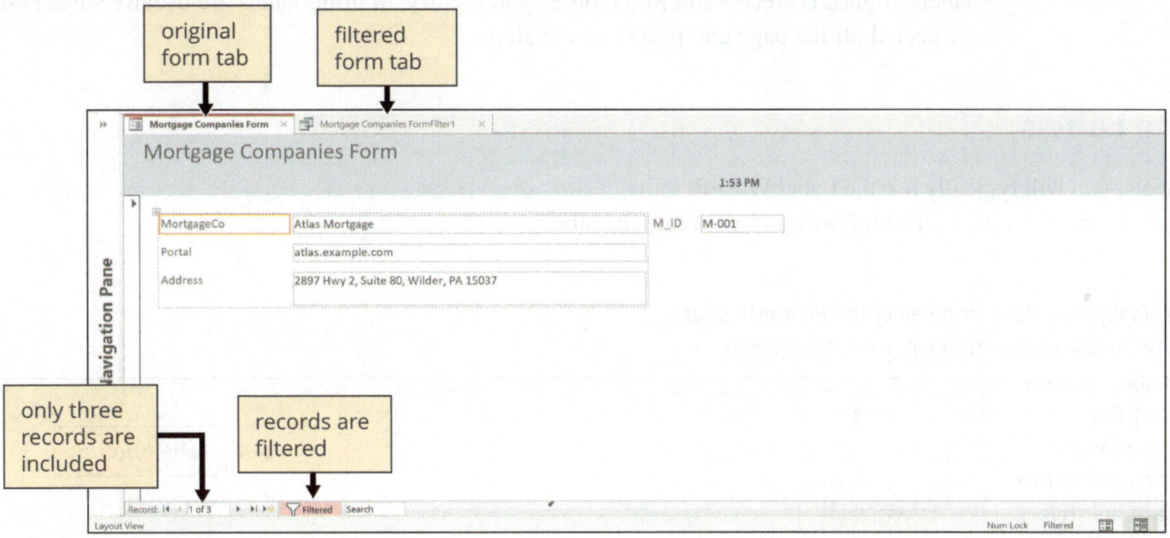

Figure 4–79

To Clear a Form Filter

When you no longer want the records to be filtered, you clear the filter. The following steps clear the current filter for the Mortgage Companies Form.

1

- Click the Advanced button (Home tab | Sort & Filter group) to display the Advanced menu.
- Click Clear All Filters on the Advanced menu to clear the filter.

2

- Save your work and close the form.

The Arrange Tab

Forms, like reports, have an Arrange tab that you can use to modify the form's layout. However, the Page Setup tab is not available for forms. The buttons on the Arrange tab and the functions of those buttons are just like the ones described in Table 4–1.

BTW
Printing Forms
To change the page setup and page layout options for a form, such as adjusting margins and changing the orientation, use the Print Preview window. To open the Print Preview window for a form, click File on the ribbon, click Print, and then click Print Preview.

To Print a Form

You can print all records, a range of records, or a selected record of a form by selecting the appropriate print range. To print the selected record, the form must be open. To print all records or a range of records, you can simply highlight the form in the Navigation Pane. To print a specific record in a form, you would use the following steps.

1. Be sure the desired form is open and the desired record is selected.
2. Click File on the ribbon to open Backstage view.
3. Click the Print tab in Backstage view to display the Print gallery.
4. Click the Print button to display the Print dialog box.
5. Click the Selected Record(s) option button in the Print Range section, and then click OK.

Mailing Labels

Organizations need to send all kinds of correspondence—such as invoices, letters, reports, and surveys—to accounts, customers, and other business partners on a regular basis. Using preprinted mailing labels eliminates much of the manual labor involved in preparing mailings. In Access, mailing labels are a special type of report. When this report prints, the data appears on the mailing labels aligned correctly and in the order you specify. Mailing labels are usually stickers that can be peeled off the page and pasted on envelopes.

To Create Labels

To create labels, you will typically use the Label Wizard. **Why?** Using the wizard, you can specify the type and dimensions, the font, and the content of the label. The following steps create the labels.

1

- Open the Navigation Pane and select the Properties table.
- Click Create on the ribbon to display the Create tab.
- Click the Labels button (Create tab | Reports group) to display the Label Wizard dialog box.
- Ensure that English is selected as the Unit of Measure and that Avery is selected in the Filter by manufacturer box.
- If necessary, scroll through the product numbers until C2163 appears, and then click C2163 in the Product number list to select the specific type of labels (Figure 4–80).

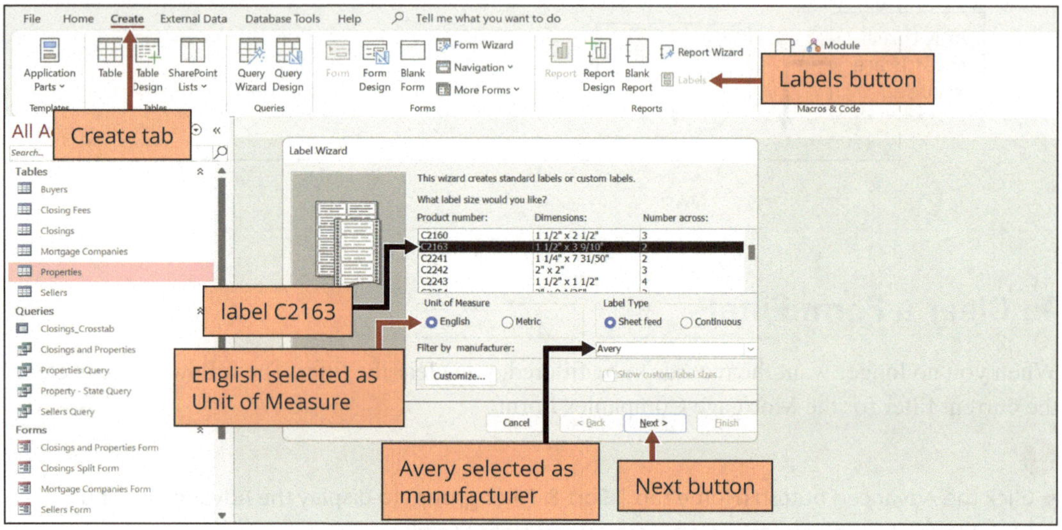

Figure 4–80

2

- Click Next (Figure 4–81).

Q&A What font characteristics could I change with this screen?
You could change the font, the font size, the font weight, and/or the font color. You could also specify italic or underline.

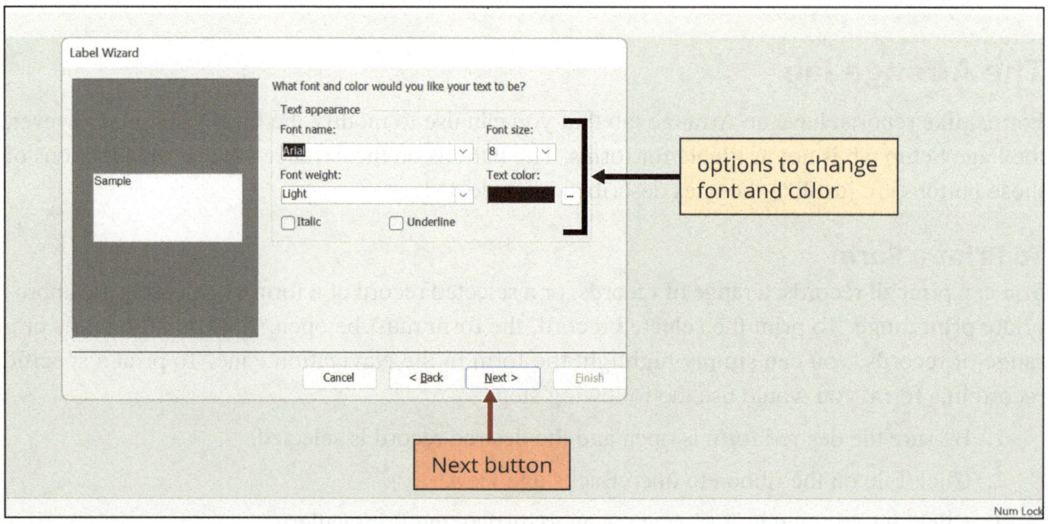

Figure 4–81

3

- Click Next to accept the default font and color settings.
- In the Prototype label section, type **Current Resident** on the first line (Figure 4–82).

Q&A What should I do if I make a mistake?
You can erase the contents of any line in the label by clicking in the line to produce an insertion point and then using DEL or BACKSPACE to erase the current contents. You then can add the correct text by typing or the correct field by clicking the field and then clicking the Add Field button.

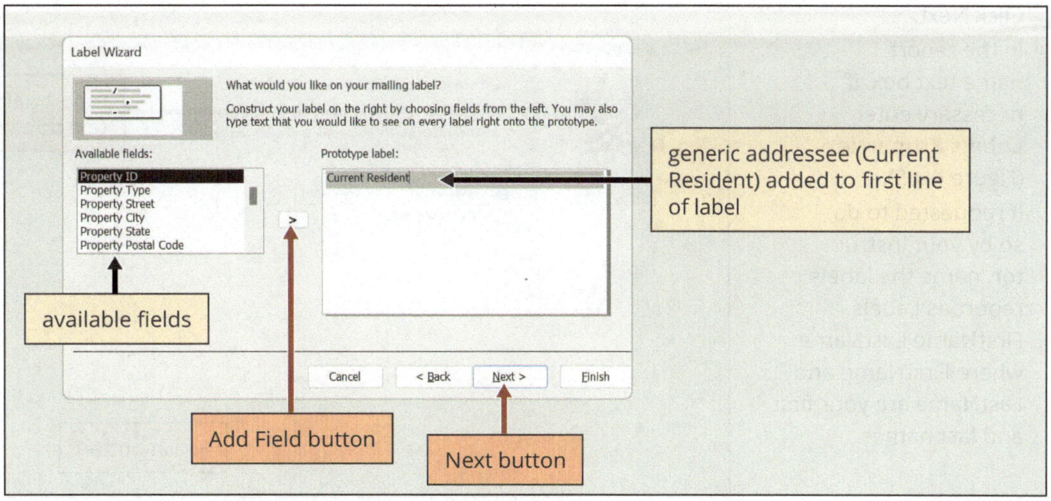

Figure 4–82

4

- Click the second line of the label, click the Property Street field, and then click the Add Field button.
- Click the third line of the label.
- Add the Property City field, type a comma (**,**), press the SPACEBAR, add the Property State field, press the SPACEBAR, and then add the Property Postal Code field (Figure 4–83).

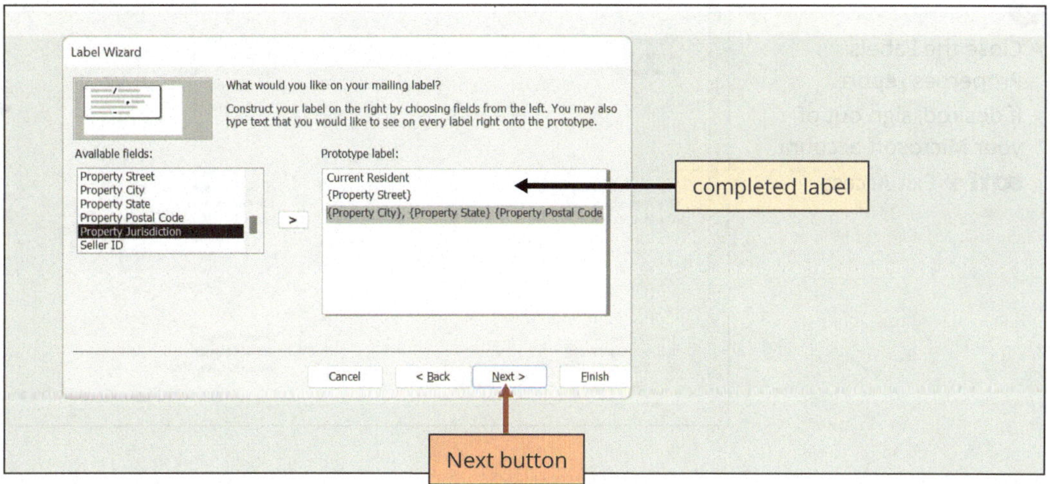

Figure 4–83

5

- Because you have now added all the necessary fields to the label, click Next.
- Select the Property Postal Code field as the field to sort by, and then click the Add Field button (Figure 4–84).

Q&A Why am I sorting by postal code?
When you need to do a bulk mailing, that is, send a large number of items using a special postage rate, businesses that provide mailing services often require that the mail be sorted in postal code order.

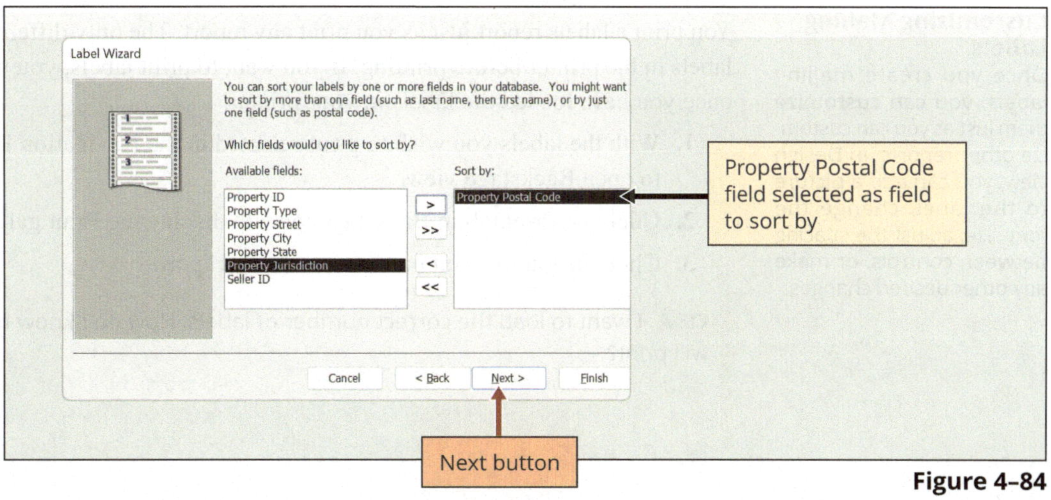

Figure 4–84

6

- Click Next.
- In the report name text box, if necessary enter **Labels Properties** (Figure 4–85).

  If requested to do so by your instructor, name the labels report as Labels FirstName LastName where FirstName and LastName are your first and last names.

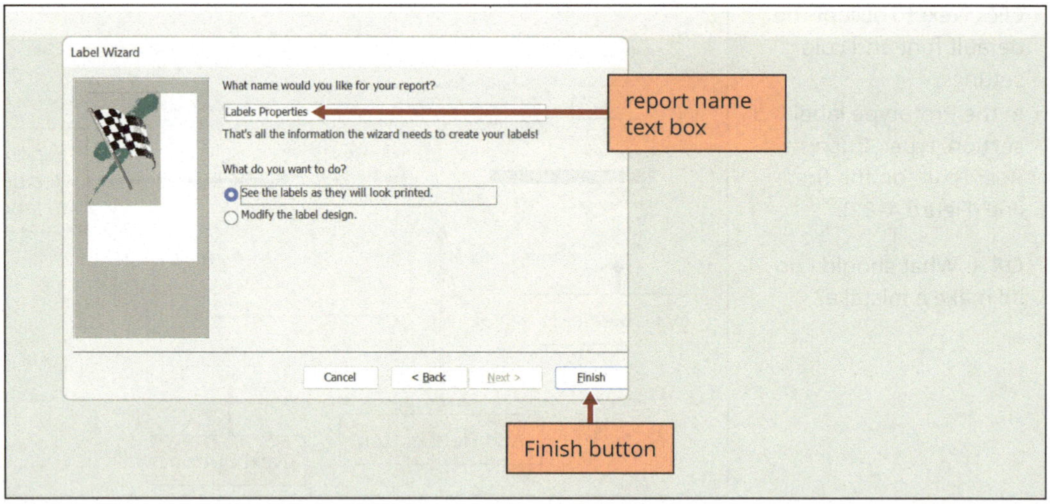

Figure 4–85

7

- Click Finish to complete the labels (Figure 4–86).

8

- Close the Labels Properties report.
- If desired, sign out of your Microsoft account.
- sam Exit Access.

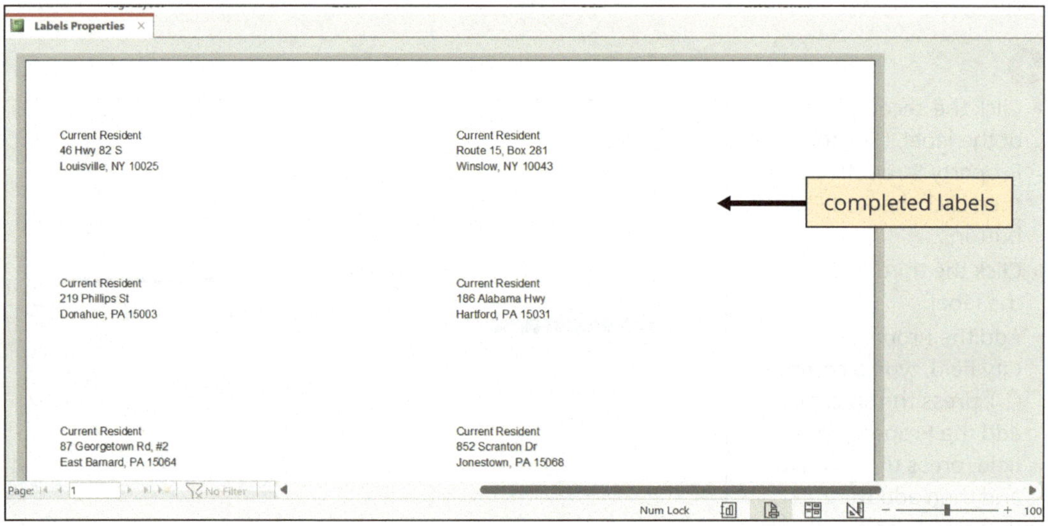

Figure 4–86

BTW

Customizing Mailing Labels

Once you create mailing labels, you can customize them just as you can customize other reports. In Design view, you can add a picture to the label, change the font size, adjust the spacing between controls, or make any other desired changes.

To Print Labels

You print a labels report just as you print any report. The only difference is that you must load the labels in the printer before printing. If you want to print labels, you would use the following steps once you have loaded the labels in your printer.

1. With the labels you wish to print selected in the Navigation Pane, click File on the ribbon to open Backstage view.
2. Click the Print tab in Backstage view to display the Print gallery.
3. Click the Quick Print button to print the report.

Q&A I want to load the correct number of labels. How do I know how many pages of labels will print?

If you are unsure how many pages of labels will print, open the label report in Print Preview first. Use the Navigation buttons in the status bar of the Print Preview window to determine how many pages of labels will print.

Summary

In this module you have learned to use wizards to create reports and forms, modify the layout of reports and forms using Layout view, group and sort in a report, add totals to a report, conditionally format controls, filter records in reports and forms, resize and move controls, add fields to reports and forms, create a stacked layout for a form, add a date/time, move controls in a control layout, apply themes, and create mailing labels.

Consider This: Plan Ahead

What decisions will you need to make when creating your own reports and forms?

Use these guidelines as you complete the assignments in this module and create your own reports and forms outside of this class.

1. Determine whether the data should be presented in a report or a form.
   a. Do you intend to print the data? If so, a report would be the appropriate choice.
   b. Do you intend to view the data on the screen, or will the user update data? If so, a form would be the appropriate choice.
2. Determine the intended audience for the report or form.
   a. Who will use the report or form?
   b. Will the report or form be used by individuals external to the organization? For example, many government agencies require reports from organizations. If so, government regulations will dictate the report requirements. If the report is for internal use, the user will have specific requirements based on the intended use.
   c. Adding unnecessary data to a report or form can make the form or report unreadable. Include only data necessary for the intended use.
   d. What level of detail should the report or form contain? Reports used in day-to-day operations need more detail than weekly or monthly reports requested by management.
3. Determine the tables that contain the data needed for the report or form.
   a. Is all the data found in a single table?
   b. Does the data come from multiple related tables?
4. Determine the fields that should appear on the report or form.
5. Determine the organization of the report or form.
   a. In what order should the fields appear?
   b. How should they be arranged?
   c. Should the records in a report be grouped in some way?
   d. Are any calculations required?
   e. Should the report be used to simply summarize data?
   f. Should the data for the report or form be filtered in some way?
6. Determine the format of the report or form.
   a. What information should be in the report or form header?
   b. Do you want a title and date?
   c. Do you want a logo?
   d. What information should be in the body of the report or form?
   e. Is any conditional formatting required?
   f. What style should be applied to the report or form? In other words, determine the visual characteristics that the various portions of the report or form should have.
   g. Is it appropriate to apply a theme to the reports, forms, and other objects in the database?
7. Review the report or form after it has been in operation to determine whether any changes are necessary.
   a. Is the order of the fields still appropriate?
   b. Are any additional fields required?

8. For mailing labels, determine the contents, order, and type of label.
    a. What fields should appear on the label?
    b. How should the fields be arranged?
    c. Is there a certain order (for example, by postal code) in which the labels should be printed?
    d. Who is the manufacturer of the labels and what is the style number for the labels?
    e. What are the dimensions for each label?
    f. How many labels print across a page?

Consider This

How should you submit solutions to critical thinking questions in the assignments?

Every assignment in this course contains one or more critical thinking questions. These questions require you to think beyond the assigned database. Present your responses to the questions in the format required by your instructor. Possible formats may include one or more of these options: write the answer; create a document that contains the answer; present your answer to the class; discuss your answer in a group; record the answer as audio or video using a webcam, smartphone, or portable media player; or post answers on a blog, wiki, or website.

Student Assignments

Apply Your Knowledge

Reinforce the skills and apply the concepts you learned in this module.

Creating Two Reports and a Form

Note: To complete this assignment, you will be required to use the Data Files. Please contact your instructor for information about accessing the Data Files.

Instructions: Start Access. Open the database, SC_AC_04-2.accdb, which is located in the Data Files folder. Enable the content.

Perform the following tasks:

1. Save the database using the file name, SC_AC_04_Construction. Enable the content.
2. Use the Report Wizard to create a report from the Accounting table that shows how much money is due to subcontractors. Group the report by Job Site number and sort the report by Current Due in Ascending order. Add subtotals and a total to the Current Due field. Save the report as Subcontractors with Current Due Amounts. Adjust control sizes, positions, and text alignment as needed so all data is visible. Your finished report should look like Figure 4–87.

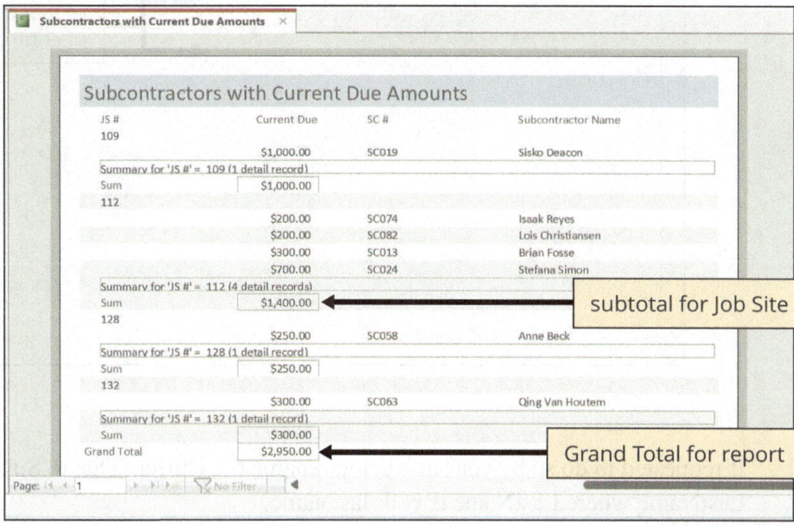

Figure 4–87

3. Create a report that counts the number of subcontractors for each Job Site. Group the report by Job Site Number and use the title Count of Subcontractors by Job Site. Modify the design to include a count of the subcontractors within each job site. Adjust control sizes and positions as needed so your finished report looks like Figure 4–88. Save the report.

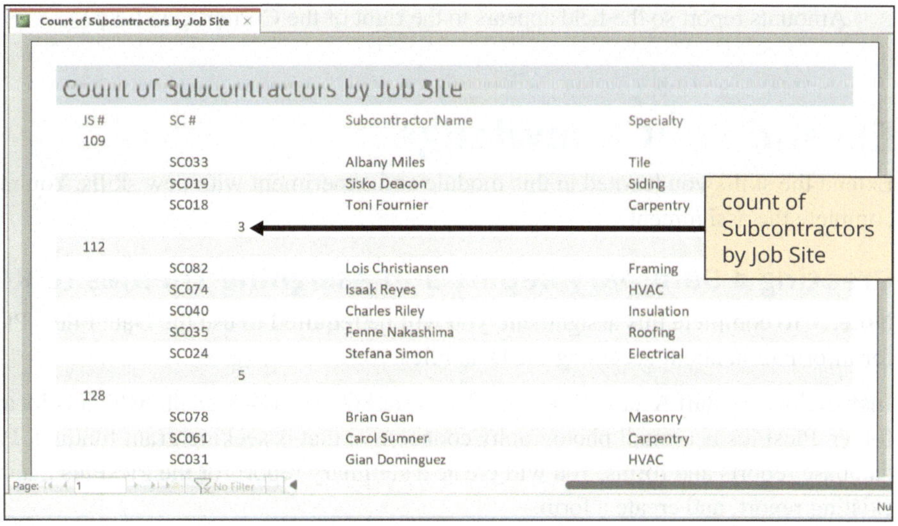

Figure 4–88

Continued on next page

4. Use the Form Wizard to create the Current Due to Subcontractor form shown in Figure 4–89. The form has a columnar layout and includes the current date. Bold the date control, change the Alignment to Align Left, and reposition the date control as shown in Figure 4–89. Decrease the size of the SC# and Subcontractor Name controls so they reflect the appropriate size for these fields. Use Figure 4–89 for reference. Save the form.

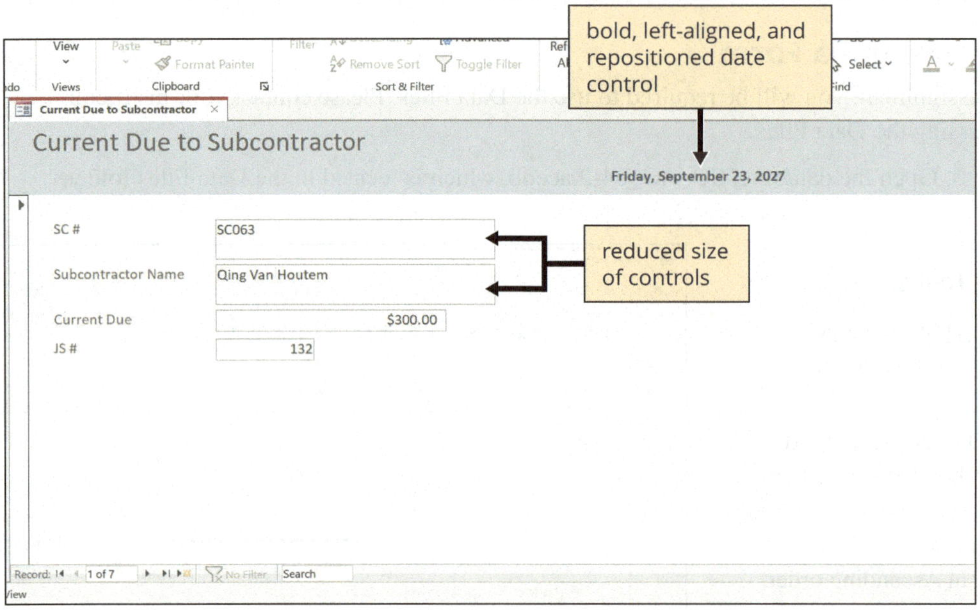

Figure 4–89

If requested to do so by your instructor, rename the Current Due to Subcontractor form as Current Due with LastName where LastName is your last name.

5. Submit the revised database in the format specified by your instructor.

6. **Consider This:** How would you add the Amount Paid field to the Subcontractors with Current Due Amounts report so the field appears to the right of the Current Due field?

Extend Your Knowledge

Extend the skills you learned in this module and experiment with new skills. You may need to use Help to complete the assignment.

Creating a Summary Report and Assigning Themes to Reports and Forms

Note: To complete this assignment, you will be required to use the Data Files. Please contact your instructor for information about accessing the Data Files.

Instructions: Start Access. Open the database, SC_AC_04-3.accdb, which is located in the Data Files folder. PicsPlus is a small photography cooperative that is seeking grant funding. PicsPlus needs to update its database reports and forms. You will create a summary report for the PicsPlus database, assign a theme to an existing report, and create a form.

Perform the following tasks:

1. Save the database using the file name, SC_AC_04_PicsPlus. Enable the content.

2. Use the Report Wizard to create the summary report shown in Figure 4–90. View the data by Photographer and sort by Client Name. Sum the Balance Due field for the Summary option. Save your report as Photographer Balances Summary Report. Apply the Gallery theme and resave it.

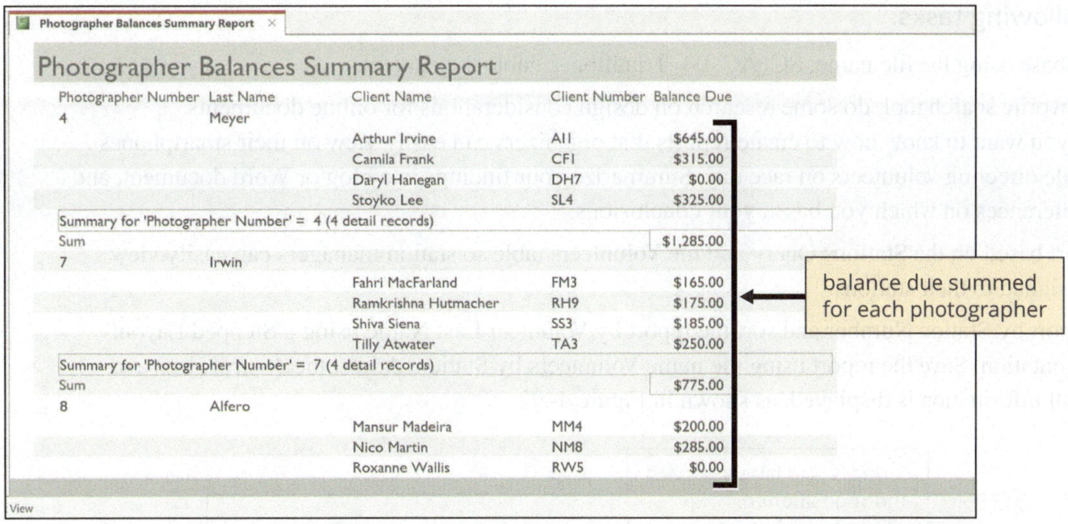

Figure 4–90

3. Create the Photographer Form shown in Figure 4–91, taking note of the included fields and the order they're listed. The form has a Columnar control layout. Use the Property Sheet to change the Caption of the Photographer Number label. Apply the Slice theme to this object only. Save the changes to the form.

Figure 4–91

If requested to do so by your instructor, open the Photographer Form in Form view and change the first name and last name for Tech# 7 to your first and last names.

4. Submit the revised database in the format specified by your instructor.
5. **Consider This:** How would you change the theme font for the Photographer Form to Arial?

Expand Your World

Create a solution, which uses cloud and web technologies, by learning and investigating on your own from general guidance.

Note: To complete this assignment, you will be required to use the Data Files. Please contact your instructor for information about accessing the Data Files.

Instructions: Start Access. Open the database, SC_AC_04-4.accdb, which is located in the Data Files folder, and enable the content. Organizers for a fundraising triathlon need to provide a list to all stations showing which volunteers are assigned where. The organizers have asked you to create a report that documents these relationships. Organizers need to view this report during their final planning meeting and on the morning of the event as volunteers arrive and check in.

Continued on next page

Perform the following tasks:

1. Save the database using the file name, SC_AC_04_Triathlon. Enable the content.
2. Using your favorite search tool, do some research on design considerations for online documents. Specifically, you want to know how to create reports that organizers can easily view on their smartphones or tablets while directing volunteers on race day. Summarize your findings in a blog or Word document, and include the references on which you based your conclusions.
3. Create a report based on the Stations Query and the Volunteers table so station managers can easily view volunteers assigned to their stations.
4. Group the report by Station Number and sort the report by Volunteer Last Name using a Stepped Layout in Portrait orientation. Save the report using the name Volunteers by Station. Adjust the control sizes and positions so all information is displayed, as shown in Figure 4–92.

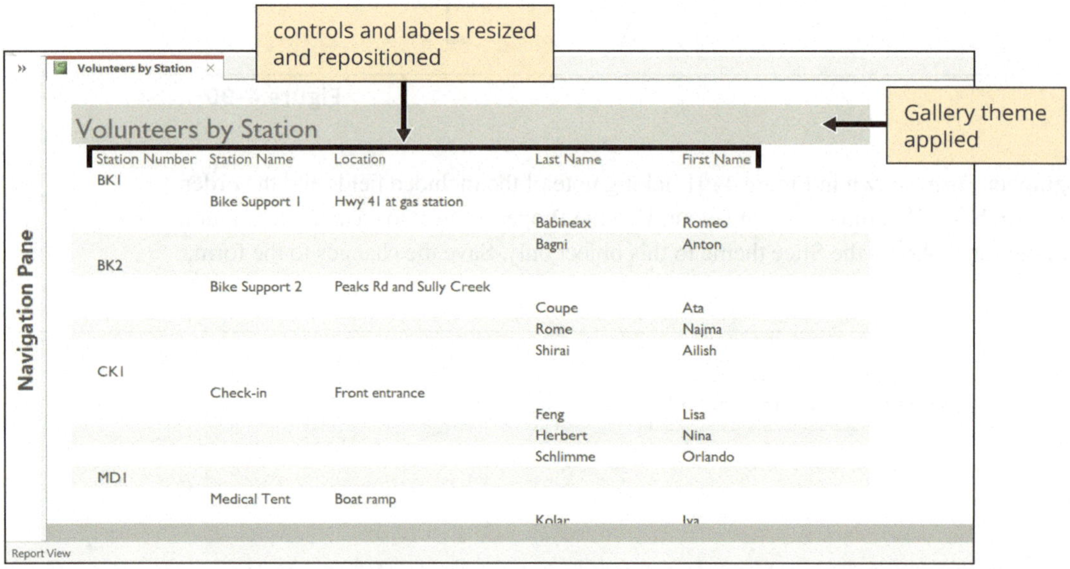

Figure 4–92

5. Add the Gallery theme to the Volunteers by Station report. Remove the Date field from the report and save the revised report with the new changes.
6. After completing the report, submit the revised database and the blog Word document you created in Step 2. Submit the files in the format specified by your instructor.
7. **Consider This:** After researching design considerations for reports, what changes to the Volunteers by Station report design would you suggest? Why do you think these changes would make the report more user friendly for station managers on race day?

In the Lab

Design and implement a solution using creative thinking and problem-solving skills.

Lab: Updating Reports and Forms in the Homegrown Nurse Staffing Agency Database

Note: To complete this assignment, you will be required to use the Data Files. Please contact your instructor for information about accessing the Data Files.

Problem: Homegrown Nurse Staffing Agency is growing and needs some data from its database to help attract more nursing professionals willing to travel. Your task is to create one report showing relevant information about recent assignments and another report with housing information for placing travelers with upcoming assignments. You also need to create a form that shows travelers who are available now for assignments.

Perform the following tasks:

Part 1: Open the SC_AC_04-5.accdb database from the Data Files folder. Save the file with the name, SC_AC_04_Travel-Nurses, and enable the content. Use the concepts and techniques presented in this module to create reports and forms so the data is easily viewed and understood.

a. The office manager wants to see assignment ID number, specialty, and term for all travel assignments. She also wants to be able to quickly see which assignments offer bill rates of $40,000 or more and an overall average of all assignment bill rates. Using a Tabular layout, create a report called Assignment Bill Rates that does not contain grouping. Include sorting, formatting, and a calculation that will produce a report similar to that shown in Figure 4–93.

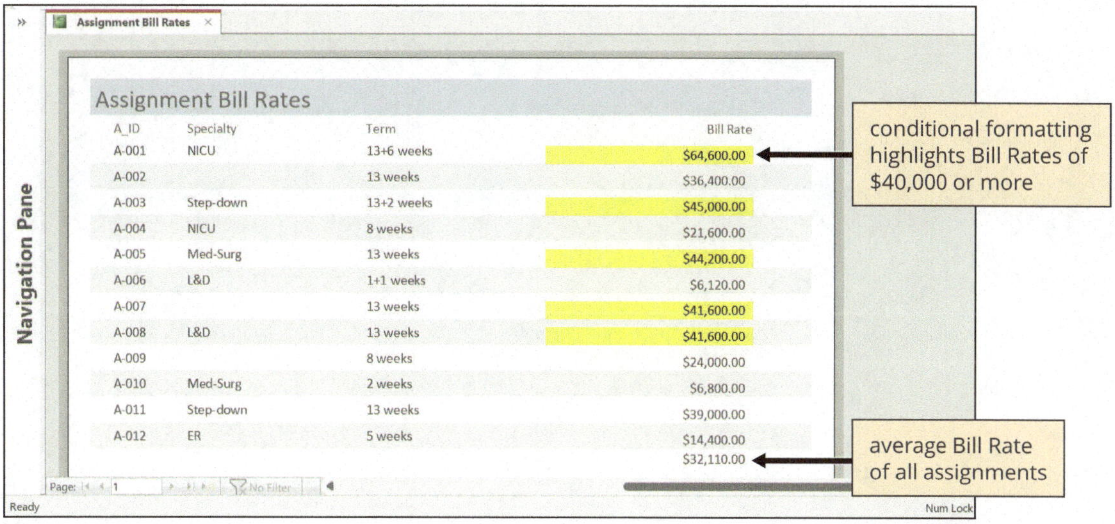

Figure 4–93

b. Create a one-page report that includes all fields in the Housing table. Apply grouping and sorting as shown in Figure 4–94. Adjust the size and position of the controls as necessary.

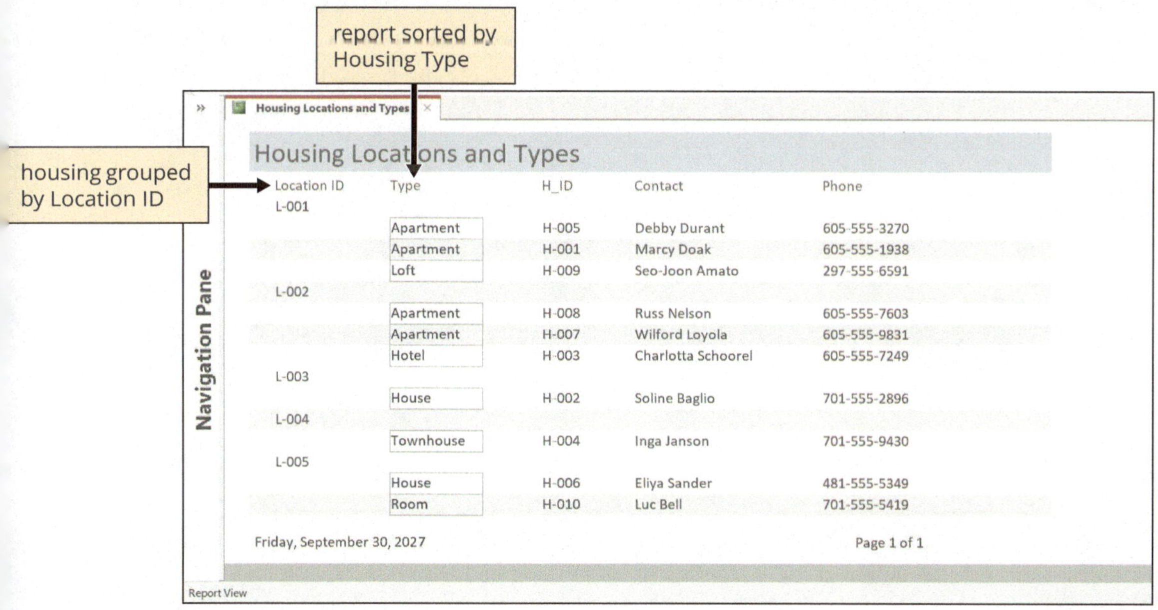

Figure 4–94

Continued on next page

c. Create a form for the Travelers table that includes each travel nurse's name, ID, license, phone number, and availability. While using this form to update traveler availability, office staff occasionally need to apply a filter to display all travelers who are currently available (that is, listed as available at any time) and sort the results in descending order by Traveler ID. Save the form as Filtered Traveler Availability. Reopen the form and confirm that your saved filter can be applied using the Toggle Filter button.

Submit your assignment in the format specified by your instructor.

Part 2: Consider This: You made several decisions while creating these reports and forms, including conditionally formatting values and applying grouping, sorting, and filtering. What was the rationale behind your decisions? How did you apply the filter and sort to the Filtered Traveler Availability Form? Why? What other options are available?

Multiple-Table Forms

Objectives

After completing this module, you will be able to:

- Use Yes/No, Long Text, and Attachment fields in a form
- Apply an input mask
- Enter data of various types
- Enter a file in an attachment field
- Create a form using Design view
- Create a form with a subform
- Modify subform and form design
- Modify a label in a form
- Enhance the appearance of a form title
- Set the tab stop sequence in a form
- Use a form to view data and attachments
- View object dependencies
- Use Date/Time, Long Text, and Yes/No fields in a query
- Explain how to include a datasheet on a form
- Explain how to create a multiple-table form

Introduction

When creating a form, you often need to incorporate data from more than one table. To accomplish this, it's important that the tables have an existing relationship that indicates the field connecting the tables and the type of relationship, such as one-to-many. This type of relationship identifies the table on the "one" side of the relationship and the table on the "many" side of the relationship. On the "one" side, a single record in the table relates to many records in the table on the "many" side. You might also need to add fields that can contain special data types, such as photos or other graphics, documents, or other attachments. These fields, then, can appear in queries that draw information from the relevant tables.

Project: Multiple-Table Forms

Clearnet uses its database to keep records about carriers and loads. The owners are in the process of contracting with some specialty carriers to handle complicated loads. The increase in complexity means that Clearnet needs to maintain additional data on its carriers. With this data, the team can promote the new carrier capabilities. They also want to include each carrier's available truck types as well as photos of the drivers. Additionally, Clearnet wants to connect the new carriers' online resources, such as a payment portal, and other documentation from the carriers, such as a bill of lading template. A bill of lading is required for each load, and sometimes carriers provide this documentation for their loads. These files are separate from the database; some are maintained in Word and others as PDFs. Clearnet would like a way to attach these files to the corresponding carrier's record in the database. Finally, Clearnet wants to adjust the Phone Number field in the Carriers table. Users should type only the digits in the phone number and then have Access format

BTW

Touch Screen Differences

The Office and Windows interfaces may vary if you are using a touch screen. For this reason, you might notice that the function or appearance of your touch screen differs slightly from this module's presentation.

BTW
Touch and Pointers
Remember that if you are using your finger on a touch screen, you will not see the pointer.

the number appropriately. For example, if the user enters 8255553455, Access will format the number as (825) 555–3455.

After the proposed fields have been added to the database, Clearnet wants users to be able to use a form that incorporates the Carriers and Loads tables and includes the newly added fields as well as some of the existing fields in the Carriers table. The form should also include the Carrier ID, the Carrier name, contact person, phone number, and list of drivers. Clearnet would like to see multiple loads for each carrier on the screen at the same time (Figure 5–1). The database should allow users to scroll through all the loads and see the start date, end date, rate confirmation, mileage, and truck type. At any time, the carrier's documentation can be opened for viewing. Finally, Clearnet will need queries that use the new fields and provide easy access to the data held in the new attachment fields.

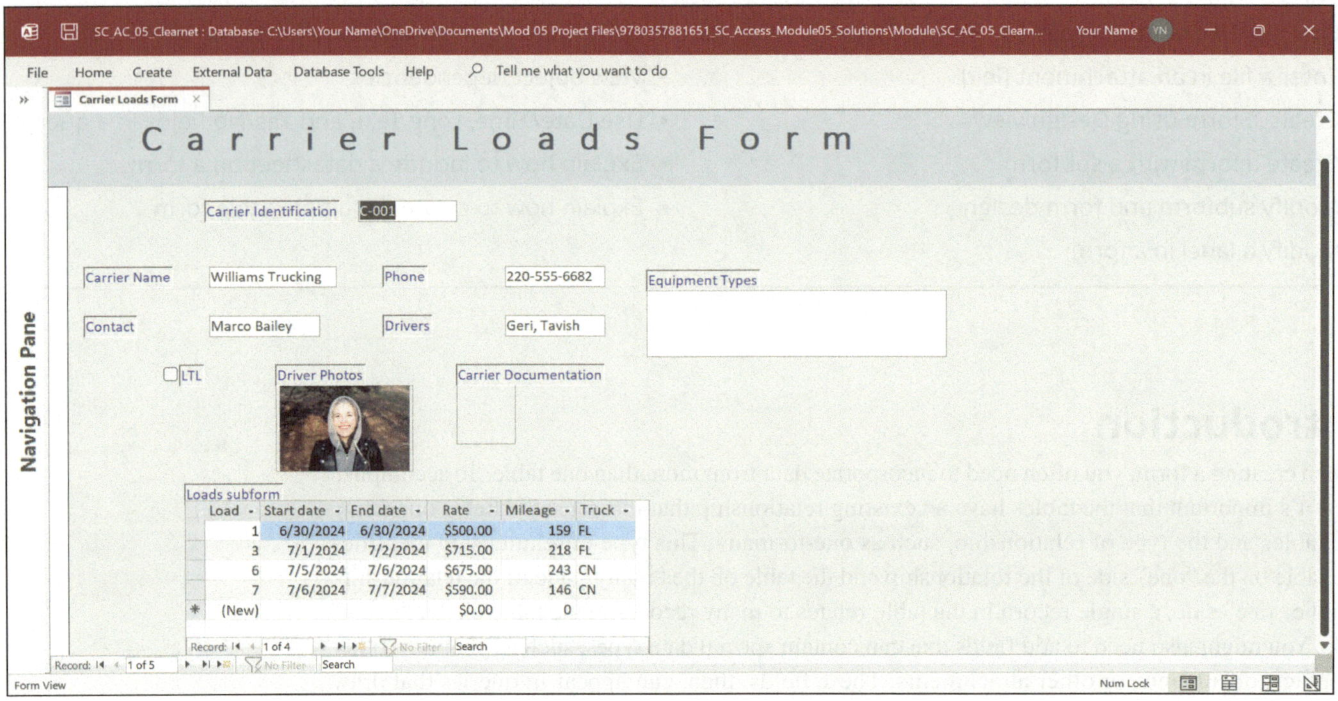

Marivi Pazos/Unsplash

Figure 5–1

BTW
The Ribbon and Screen Resolution
Access may change how the groups and buttons within the groups appear on the ribbon, depending on the computer's screen resolution. Thus, your ribbon might look different from the ones in this course if you are using a screen resolution other than 1920 × 1080.

BTW
OLE Object Fields
OLE Object fields can store video clips, sound, and other objects from Windows-based apps.

Adding Special Fields

Having analyzed its requirements, Clearnet management has identified a need for some new fields for the Carriers table. They need an LTL (Less than a Load) field, which indicates whether a carrier handles shipments that are less than a full truckload; this field's data type will be Yes/No. They need an Equipment Type field that identifies each carrier's available truck types, which will be a Long Text field. The Carrier Documentation field, which must be able to contain multiple attachments for each carrier, will be an Attachment field. The Driver Photos field is the only field whose data type is uncertain—the data type could be either OLE Object, which can contain objects created by a variety of applications, or Attachment. An OLE Object (Object Linking and Embedding Object) creates a bitmap of the image file, which can result in very large files, so Clearnet has decided to use the Attachment data type for greater efficiency.

Clearnet wants to assist users in entering the correct format for a phone number, so the field will use an input mask. An **input mask** specifies how data is to be entered and how it will appear. For example, an input mask can indicate that a phone number has parentheses around the first three digits and a hyphen between the sixth and seventh digits.

The form shown in Figure 5–1 contains two attachment fields, the Driver Photos field and the Carrier Documentation field. When viewed as a table, these both appear as paper clips, not as the actual attachment. However, when the table's attachment fields are displayed in a form, you can view the photo itself and an icon of the document, in this case, a Word file.

BTW
Long Text Fields
Long Text fields can store up to a gigabyte of text. If you need to keep a historical record of changes to a Long Text field, set the value for the Append Only property to Yes. To use formatting such as bold and underline in a Long Text field, set the value for the Text Format property to Rich Text.

To Add Fields with New Data Types to a Table

You add the new fields to the Carriers table by modifying the design of the table and inserting the fields at the appropriate position in the table structure. The following steps add the LTL (Less than a Load), Equipment Types, Driver Photos, and Carrier Documentation fields to the Carriers table. **Why?** These new fields will track required information as the business continues to grow.

1

- **sam** Start Access. Open the database, SC_AC_05-1.accdb, which is located in the Data Files folder. Save the file on your hard disk, OneDrive, or other storage location using the file name, **SC_AC_05_Clearnet**. Enable the content and open the Navigation Pane, if necessary.
- Right-click the Carriers table to display a shortcut menu (Figure 5–2).

BTW
Adding Captions to Attachment Fields
You can add a caption to an Attachment field. To add a caption in Design view, use the Caption property box.

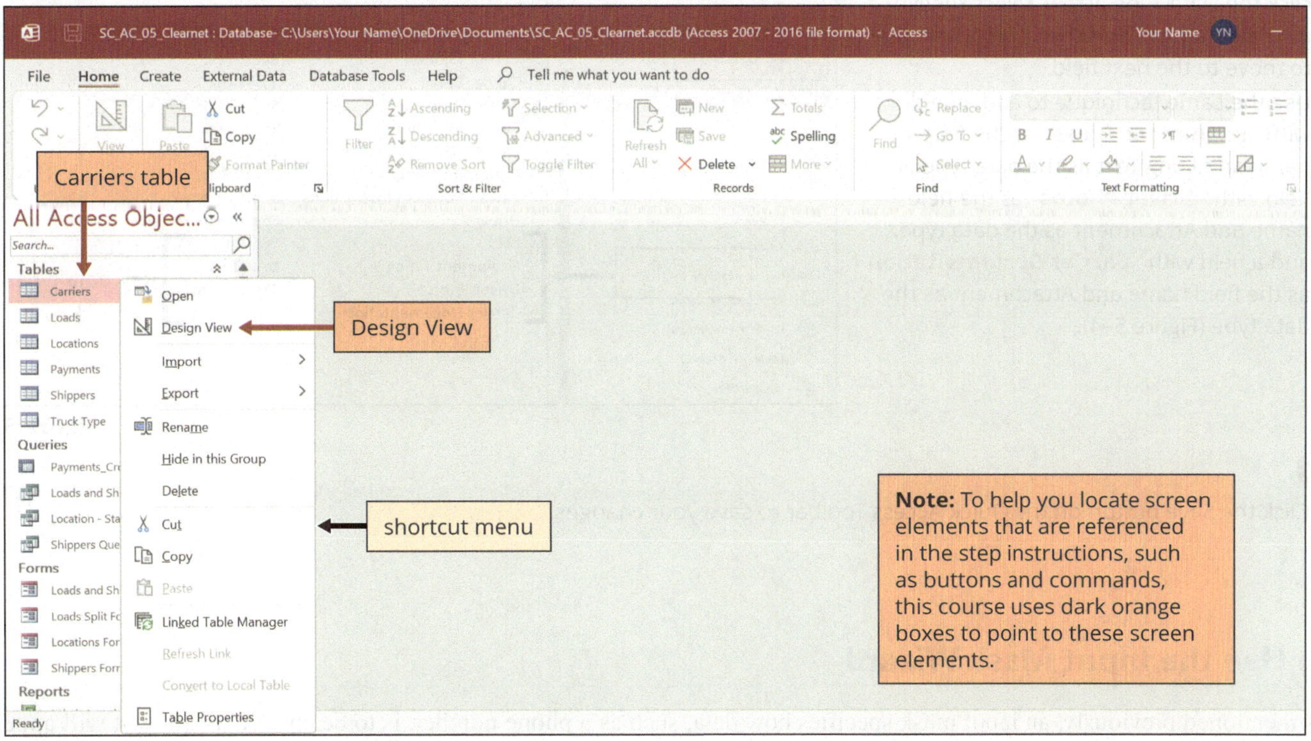

Figure 5–2

2

- Click Design View on the shortcut menu to open the table in Design view (Figure 5–3).

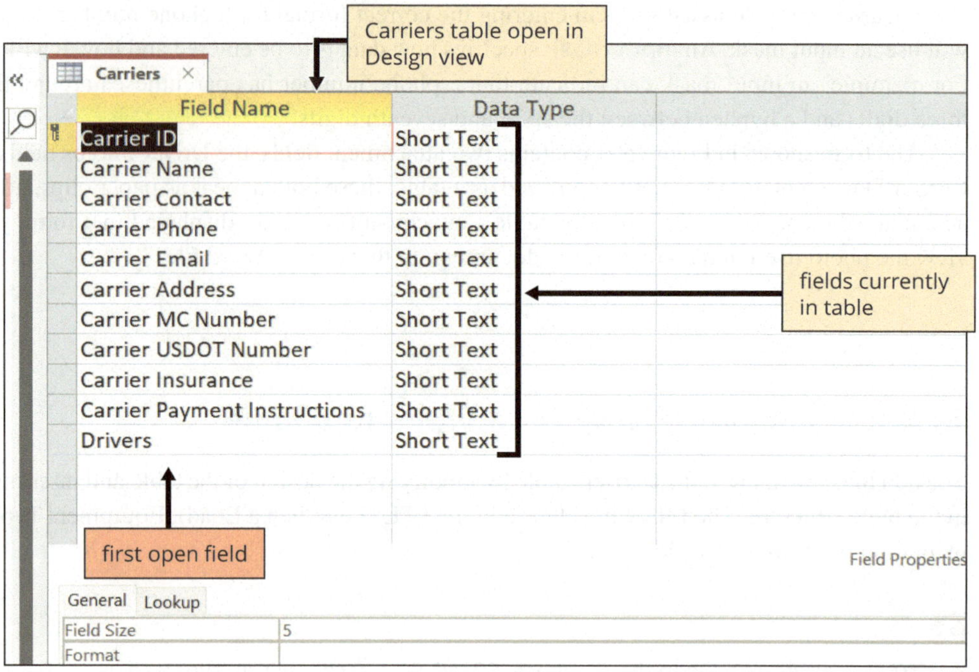

Figure 5–3

3

- Click the first open field to select the position for the first additional field.
- Type **LTL** as the field name, press TAB, click the Data Type arrow, select Yes/No as the data type, and then press TAB twice to move to the next field.
- Use the same technique to add a field with **Equipment Types** as the field name and Long Text as the data type, a field with **Driver Photos** as the field name and Attachment as the data type, and a field with **Carrier Documentation** as the field name and Attachment as the data type (Figure 5–4).

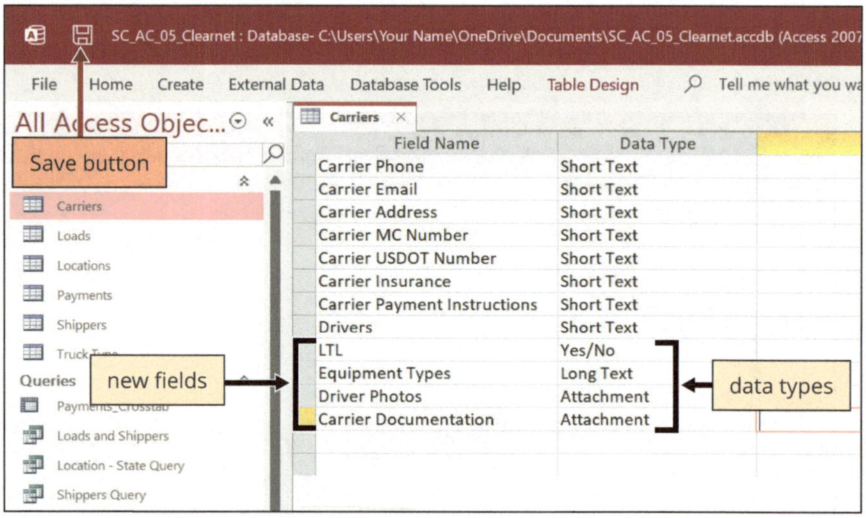

Figure 5–4

4

- Click the Save button on the Quick Access Toolbar to save your changes.

To Use the Input Mask Wizard

As mentioned previously, an input mask specifies how data, such as a phone number, is to be entered and how it will appear. You can enter an input mask directly, but you will use the Input Mask Wizard. **Why?** The wizard assists you in the creation of the input mask by allowing you to select from a list of the most frequently used input masks.

To use the Input Mask Wizard, select the Input Mask property in the field's property sheet and then select the Build button. The following steps use the Input Mask Wizard to specify how the carriers' phone numbers are to appear.

1

- Click the Carrier Phone field.
- Click the Input Mask property box (Figure 5–5).

Q&A Do I need to change the data type?
No. Short Text is the appropriate data type for a Phone Number field.

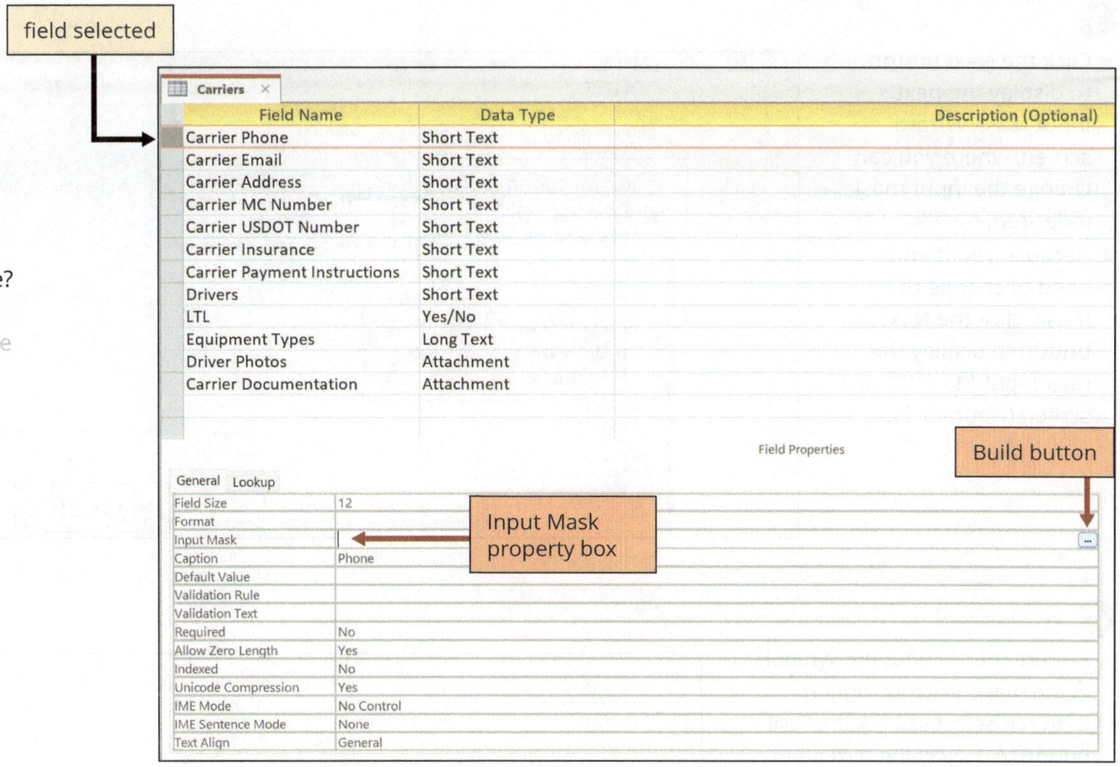

Figure 5–5

2

- Click the Build button to use a wizard to enter the input mask.
- If a dialog box appears asking you to save the table, click Yes. (If a dialog box displays a message that the Input Mask Wizard is not installed, check with your instructor before proceeding with the following steps.)
- Ensure that Phone Number is selected (Figure 5–6).

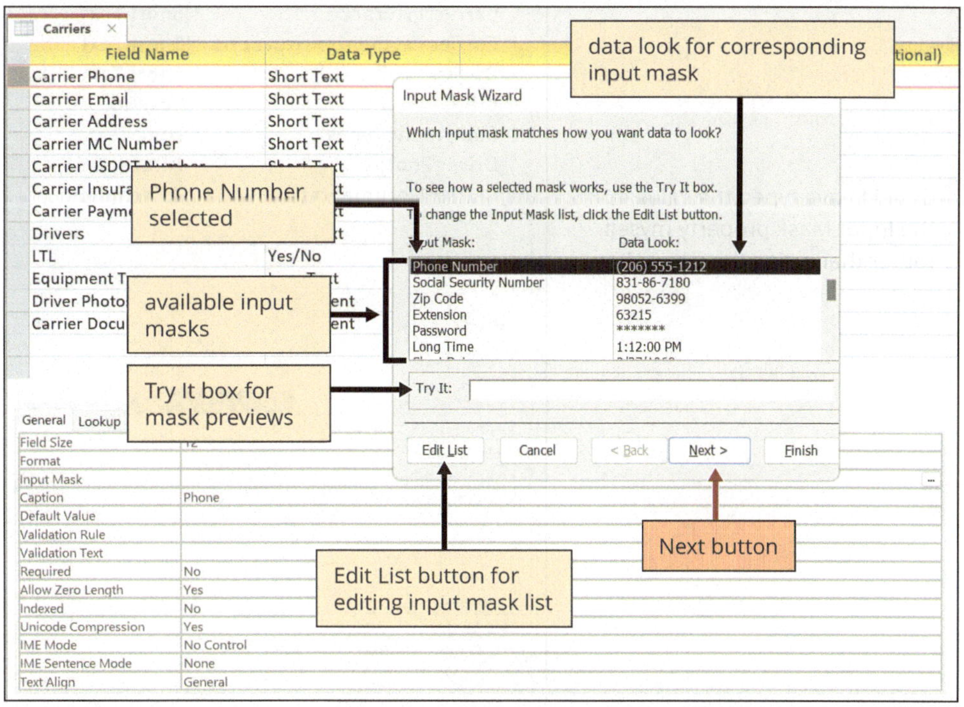

Figure 5–6

- **Experiment:** Click different input masks and enter data in the Try It text box to see the effect of the selected mask. When you are done, click the Phone Number input mask.

3

- Click the Next button to display the next Input Mask Wizard screen, where you can change the input mask, if desired.
- Because you do not need to change the mask, click the Next button to display the next Input Mask Wizard screen (Figure 5–7).

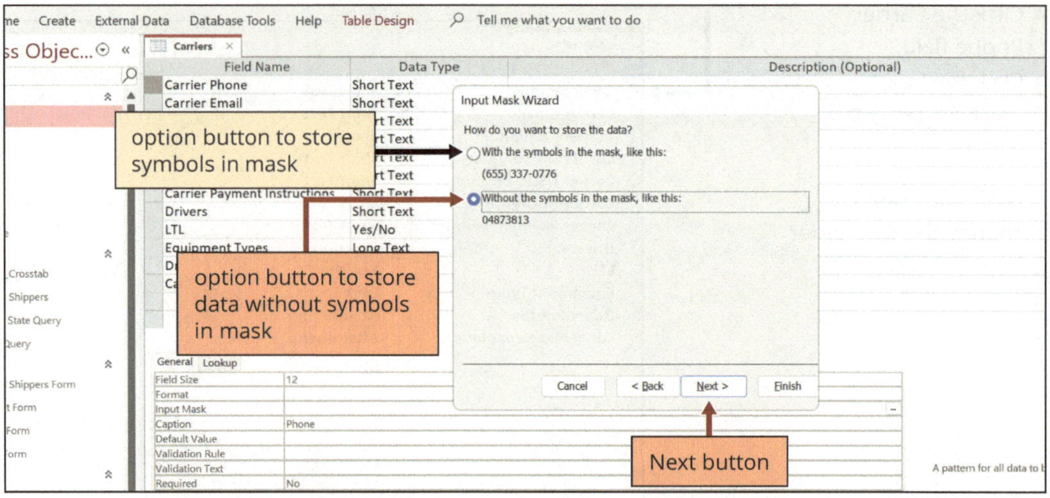

Figure 5–7

4

- Be sure the 'Without the symbols in the mask, like this:' option button is selected, click the Next button to display the next Input Mask Wizard screen, and then click the Finish button (Figure 5–8).

Q&A Why does the data type not change to Input Mask?

The data type of the Phone Number field is still Short Text. The only thing that changed is one of the field properties, the Input Mask property.

Could I have typed the value in the Input Mask property myself, rather than using the wizard?

Yes. Input masks can be complex, however, so it is usually easier and safer to use the wizard.

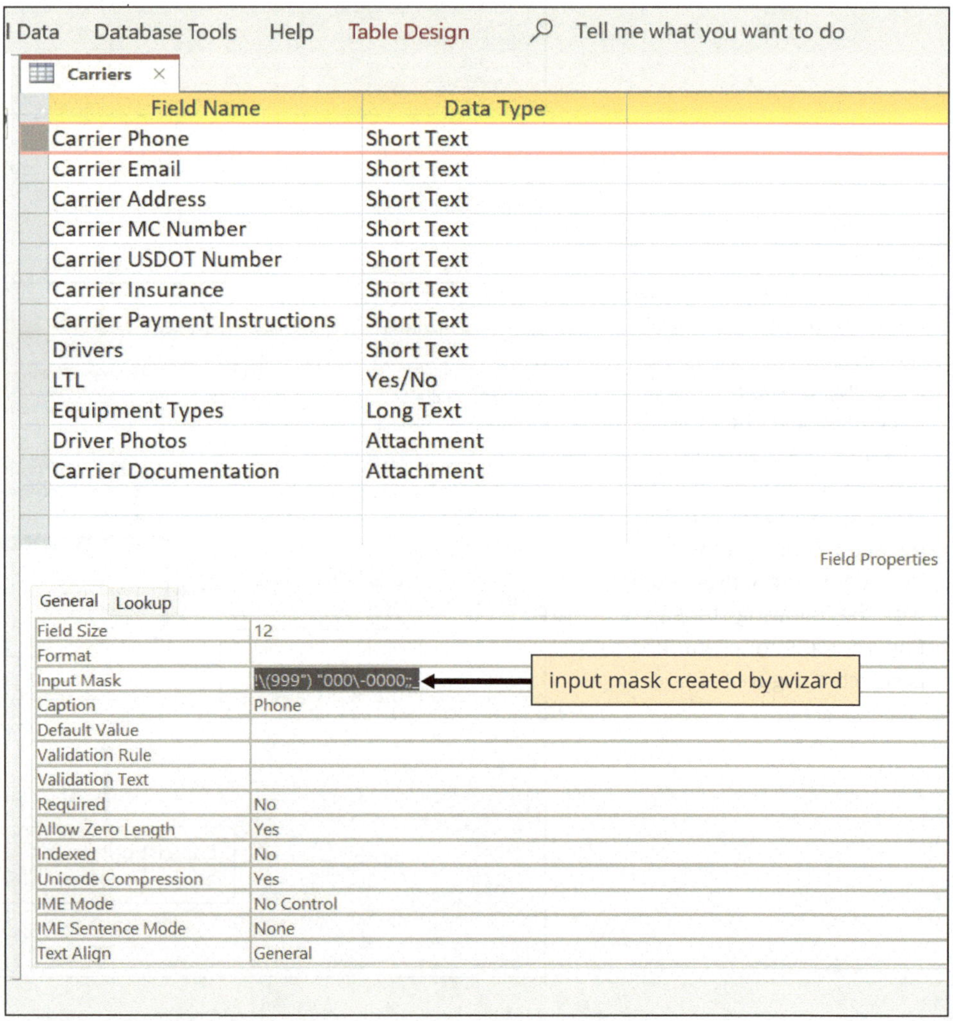

Figure 5–8

5

- Save the Carriers table.

Adding Fields in Datasheet View

Previously you added fields to a table using Design view. You can also add fields in Datasheet view. One way to do so is to use the Add & Delete group on the Table Fields tab (Figure 5–9). Select the field that precedes the position where you want to add the new field, and then click the appropriate button. You can click the Short Text button to add a Short Text field, the Number button to add a Number field, the Currency button to add a Currency field, and so on. Alternatively, you can click the More Fields button to display the Data Type gallery. You then can click a data type in the gallery to add a field with that type.

The gallery provides more options for ways to display various types of data. For example, if you click the Check Box version of a Yes/No field, the field will be displayed as a check box, which is the common way to display such a field. If instead you click the Yes/No version of a Yes/No field, the value in the field will be displayed as either the word, Yes, or the word, No.

If you scroll down in the Data Type gallery, you will find a Quick Start section. The commands in this section give you quick ways of adding some common types of fields. For example, clicking Address in the Quick Start section immediately adds several fields: Address, City, State Province, ZIP Postal, and Country Region. Clicking Start and End Dates immediately adds both a Start Date field and an End Date field.

In Datasheet view, you can rename fields by right-clicking the field name, clicking Rename Field on the shortcut menu, and then typing the new name. Delete a field by clicking the field and then clicking the Delete button (Table Fields tab | Add & Delete group). Move a field from one location to another by dragging the field.

BTW

Input Mask Characters

When you create an input mask, Access adds several characters. These characters control the literal values that appear when you enter data. For example, the first backslash in the input mask in Figure 5–8 displays the opening parenthesis. The double quotation marks direct Access to display the closing parenthesis and a space. The second backslash directs Access to display the hyphen that separates the first and second part of the phone number.

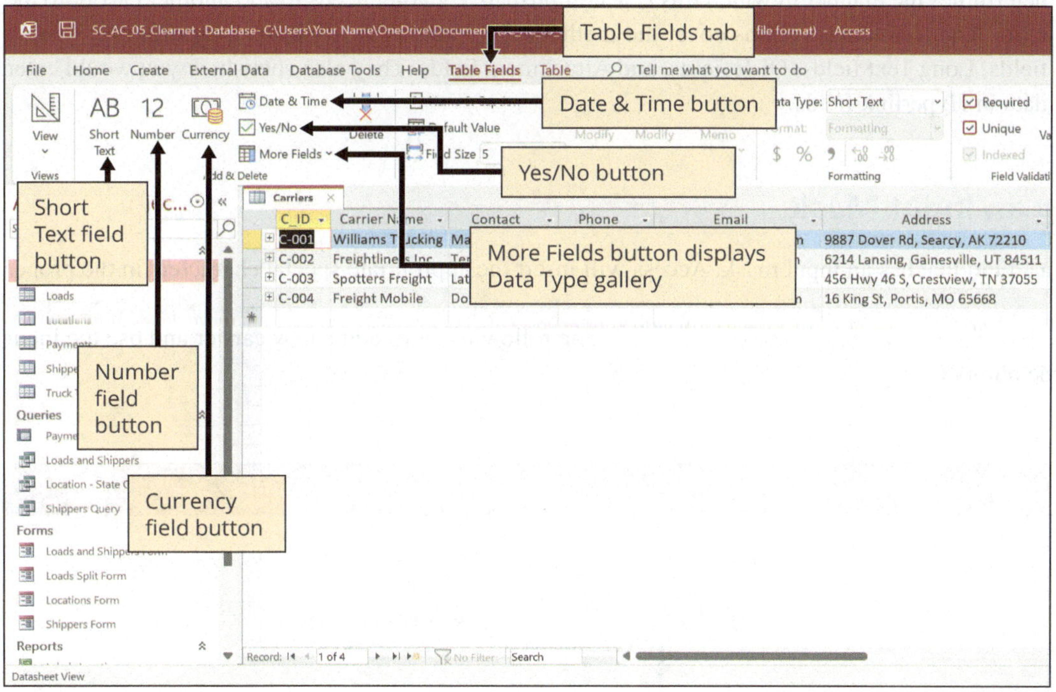

Figure 5–9

Consider This

How do you determine if fields need special data types or an input mask?

- **Determine whether an input mask is appropriate.** Sometimes the data in the field should be displayed in a special way, for example, with parentheses and a hyphen like a phone number, or separated into three groups of digits like a Social Security number. If so, should Access assist the user in entering the data in the right format? For example, by including an input mask in a field, Access can automatically insert the parentheses and a hyphen when a user enters phone number digits.

- **Determine whether the Yes/No data type is appropriate.** A field is a good candidate for the Yes/No data type if the only possible field values are Yes or No, True or False, or On or Off.
- **Determine whether the Long Text data type is appropriate.** A field that contains text that is variable in length and potentially very long is an appropriate use of the Long Text data type. If you want to use special text effects, such as bold and italic, you can assign the field the Long Text data type and change the value of the field's Text Format property from Plain Text to Rich Text. You can also collect history on the changes to a Long Text field by changing the value of the field's Append Only property from No to Yes. If you do so, when you right-click the field and click Show Column History on the shortcut menu, you will see a record of all changes made to the field.
- **Determine whether the Attachment data type or the OLE Object data type is appropriate for an image, such as a photo or artwork.** Does the field contain an image? Does it contain an object created by other applications that support **OLE (Object Linking and Embedding)**? Is your storage space limited? If storage space is limited, you should use the Attachment data type.
- **Determine whether the Attachment data type is appropriate for documents.** Will the field contain one or more attachments that were created in other applications? If so, the Attachment data type is appropriate. It allows you to store multiple attachments on each record. You can view and manipulate these attachments in their original application.
- **Determine whether the Hyperlink data type is appropriate.** A field with the hyperlink data type contains a hyperlink, that is, a link to another location such as a webpage or a file. Will the field contain an email address, links to other Office documents, or links to webpages? If so, Hyperlink is appropriate.

Updating the New Fields

After adding the new fields to the table, the next task is to enter data into the fields. The data type determines the manner in which this is accomplished. Clearnet needs to add another carrier to the table. The following sections cover the methods for updating fields with an input mask, Yes/No fields, Long Text fields, OLE fields, and Attachment fields. They also show how you would enter data in Hyperlink fields.

To Enter Data Using an Input Mask

When you are entering data in a field that has an input mask, Access will insert the appropriate special characters in the proper positions. **Why?** The input mask directs Access to automatically insert the parentheses around the area code, the space following the second parenthesis, and the hyphen in the Phone Number field. The following steps add a new carrier and use the input mask to add the carrier's phone number.

1

- Change the Carriers table to Datasheet view, and close the Navigation Pane.
- Click on the first blank row in the C_ID field and type **C-005**.
- Press TAB to move to the next field. Enter **Truck-n-Go Inc.** for the Carrier Name and **Filipa Martinez** for the Contact.
- Press TAB to move to the beginning of the Phone field on the new record and display an insertion point in the field (Figure 5–10).

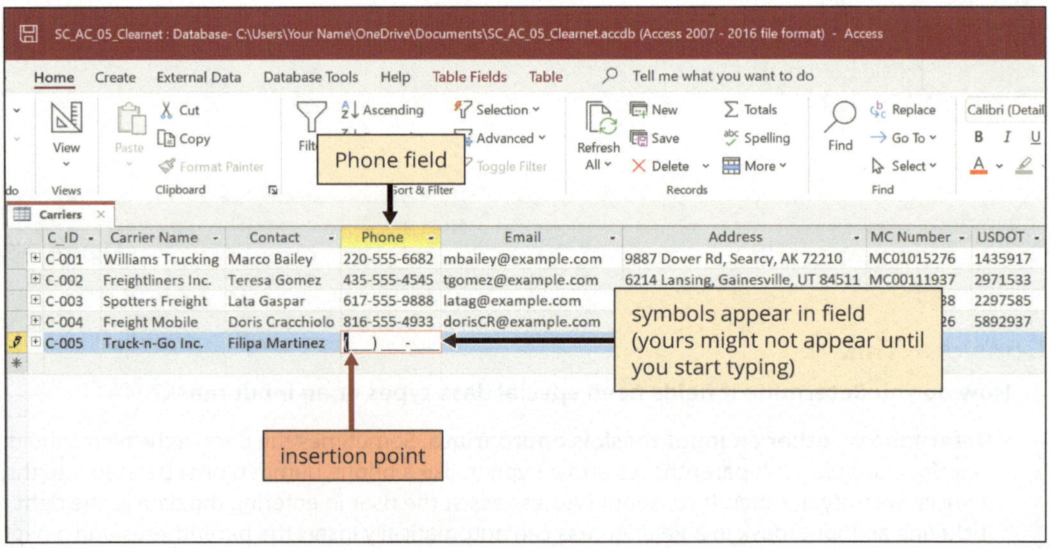

Figure 5–10

Q&A Do I need to click at the beginning of the field for the phone numbers?

Yes. If you do not, the data will not be entered correctly.

I do not see the parentheses and hyphen as shown in the figure. Did I do something wrong?

You might not see the symbols upon entering the field. Regardless, as soon as you start typing in the field, the symbols should appear.

2

- Type **8165552442** as the phone number (Figure 5–11).

BTW

Input Mask on New Records

When you place an input mask on a field with existing data, only new records added from this point on will adhere to that input mask.

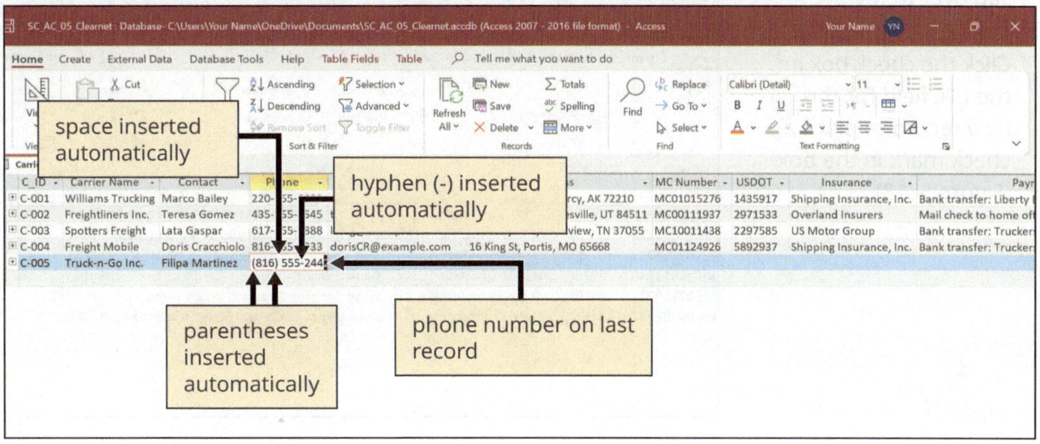

Figure 5–11

3

- Using TAB, enter the information provided in Table 5–1 for the next several fields (Figure 5–12).

Table 5–1 Data for New Record in Carriers Table

Field Name	Data
Email	**filipam@example.com**
Address	**Rt 59, Box 8822, Empire, MO 63044**
MC Number	**MC00102942**
USDOT	**3448229**
Insurance	**Overland Insurers**
Payment Instructions	**Bank transfer: Central State, account #2283-573-14**
Drivers	**Erika**

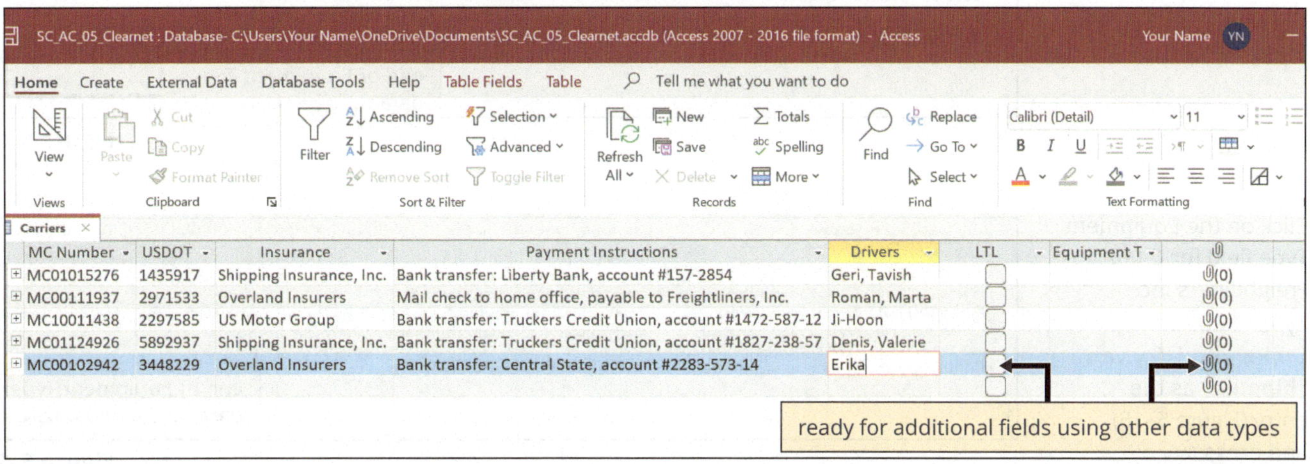

Figure 5–12

To Enter Data in Yes/No Fields

Fields that are Yes/No fields contain check boxes. To set the value to Yes, place a check mark in the check box. **Why?** A check mark indicates the value is Yes, or True. To set a value to No (False), leave the check box blank. The following step sets the value of the LTL field, a Yes/No field, to Yes for the new carrier. The other carriers do not accept LTL loads.

1

- Tab over to the LTL field.
- Click the check box in the LTL field for this new record to place a check mark in the box (Figure 5–13).

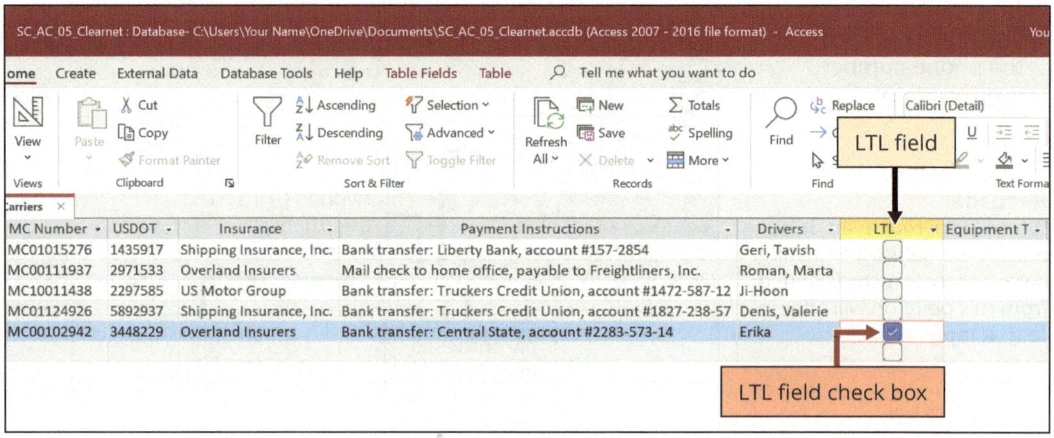

Figure 5–13

To Enter Data in Long Text Fields

To update a long text field, simply type the data in the field. You will later change the spacing to allow more room for the text. **Why?** With the current row and column spacing on the screen, only a small portion of the text will appear. The following steps enter the new carrier's available equipment types and similar information for another carrier.

1

- Press TAB to move to the Equipment Type field.
- For the new record, type **Container, reefer, and dry van shipping** as the entry (Figure 5–14), and press TAB. Recall that in shipping, reefer means refrigerated.

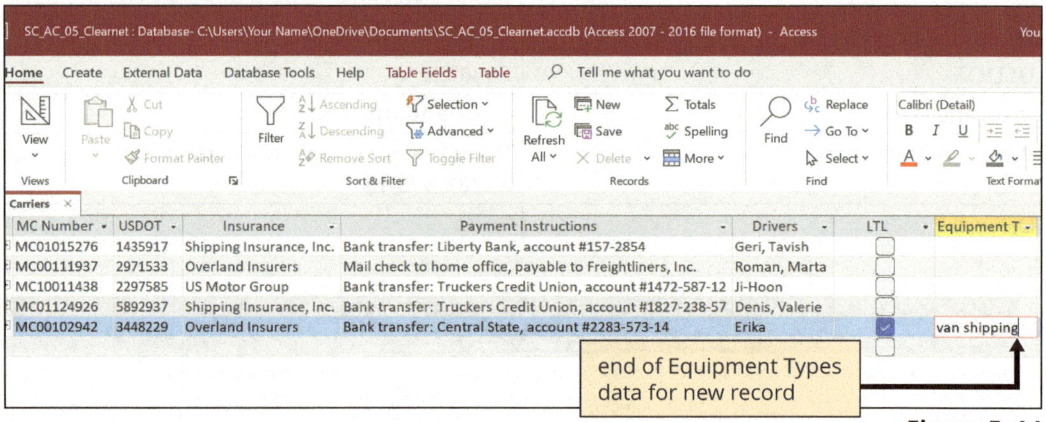

Figure 5–14

2

- Click on the Equipment Type field for C-002, Freightliners Inc.
- Type **Reefer, tanker, and dry van shipping** as the entry (Figure 5–15), and press TAB.

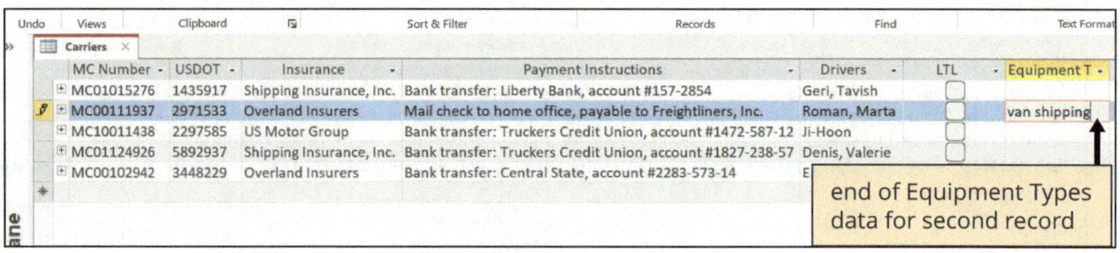

Figure 5–15

To Change the Row and Column Size

Only a small portion of the Equipment Type data appears in the datasheet. To allow more of the information to appear, you can expand the size of the rows and the columns. You can change the size of a column by using the field selector. The **field selector** is the bar containing the field name. To change the size of a row, you use a record's record selector.

The following steps resize the column containing the Equipment Type field, the reformatted Phone field, and the rows of the table. **Why?** Resizing the columns and the rows allows all data in these fields to appear.

1

- Double-click the right border of the Phone field's selector when you see the resize arrow, to autofit the column width (Figure 5–16).

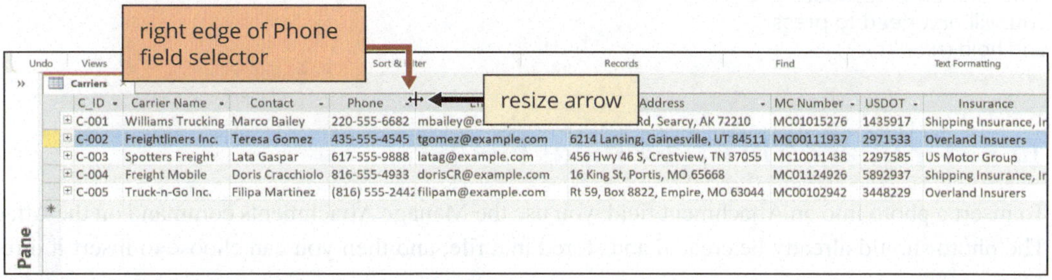

Figure 5–16

2

- Scroll a little past the Equipment Type field, and then drag the right edge of the field selector for the Equipment Type field to the right to resize the column to the approximate size shown in Figure 5–17.

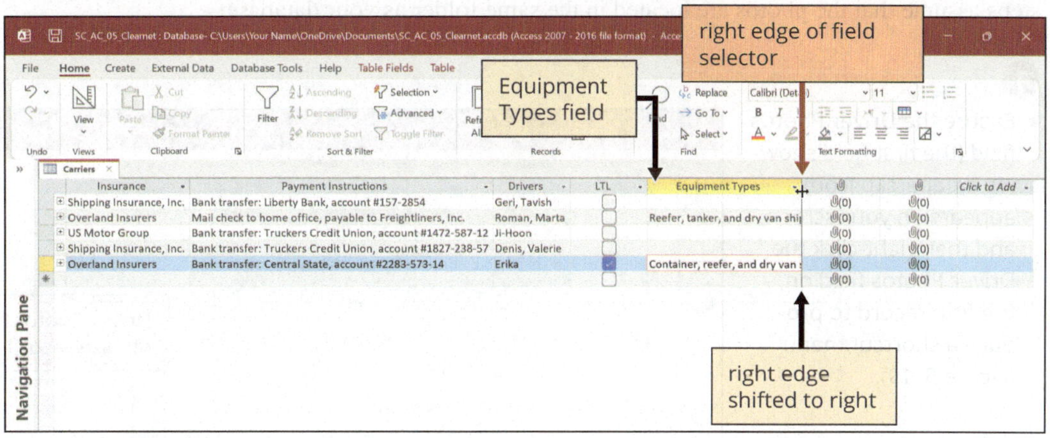

Figure 5–17

3

- Drag the lower edge of any record selector to approximately the position shown in Figure 5–18.

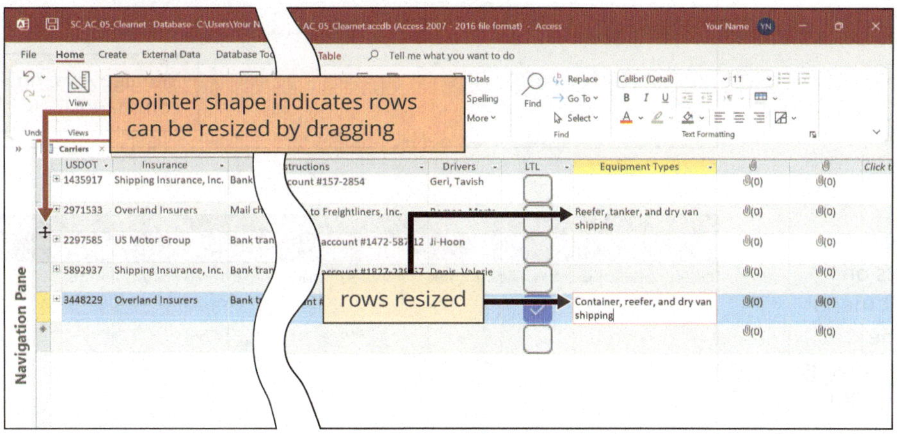

Figure 5–18

Q&A Can rows be different sizes?

No. Access formats all rows in a table to be the same size.

Other Ways

1. Right-click record selector, click Row Height to change row spacing
2. Right-click field selector, click Field Width to change column size

BTW
Entering Data in Long Text Fields
You also can enter data in a long text field using the Zoom dialog box. To do so, click the long text field and then press SHIFT+F2 to open the Zoom dialog box. Note that, on some keyboards, you will first need to press and hold FN.

Undoing Changes to Row Height and Column Width

If you later find that the changes you made to the row height or the column width are no longer appropriate, you can undo them. To undo changes to the row height, right-click the row selector, click Row Height on the shortcut menu, and then click the Standard Height check box (Row Height dialog box). To undo changes to the column width, right-click the field selector, click Field Width on the shortcut menu, and then click the Standard Width check box (Column Width dialog box).

To Enter Images in Attachment Fields

To insert a photo into an Attachment field, you use the Manage Attachments command on the Attachment field's shortcut menu. The photo should already be created and stored in a file, and then you can choose to insert it directly from the file. **Why?** The Manage Attachments command makes it easy to attach a photo to a field rather than using an OLE object field. The OLE object field requires Access to open a compatible application before you can view the photo.

The following steps insert photos into the Driver Photos field. The photos will appear as paper clips in the datasheet. The steps assume that the photos are located in the same folder as your database.

1

- Ensure the Driver Photos field (the first field showing a paperclip icon) appears on your screen, and then right-click the Driver Photos field on the fifth record to produce a shortcut menu (Figure 5–19).

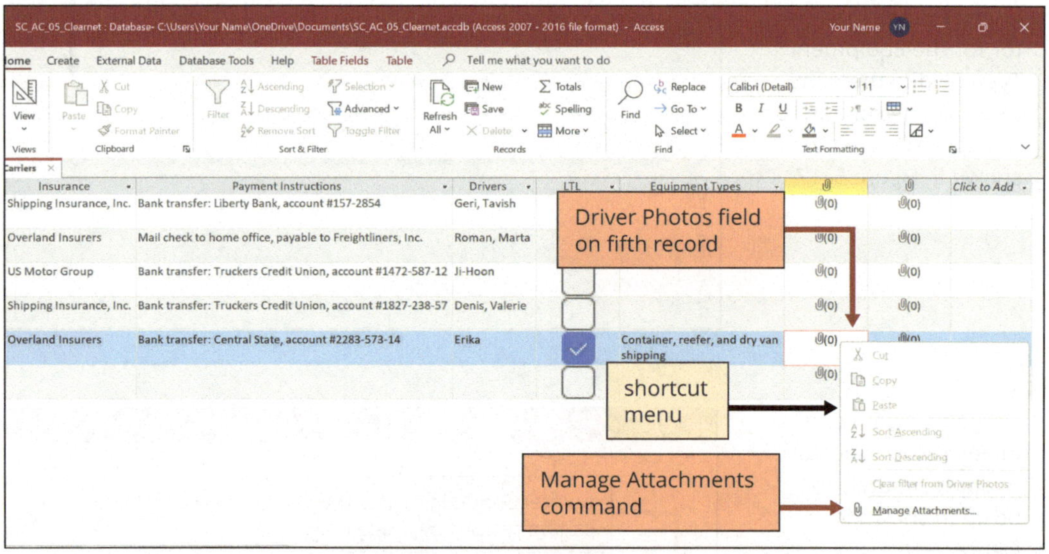

Figure 5–19

2

- Click Manage Attachments on the shortcut menu to display the Attachments dialog box (Figure 5–20).

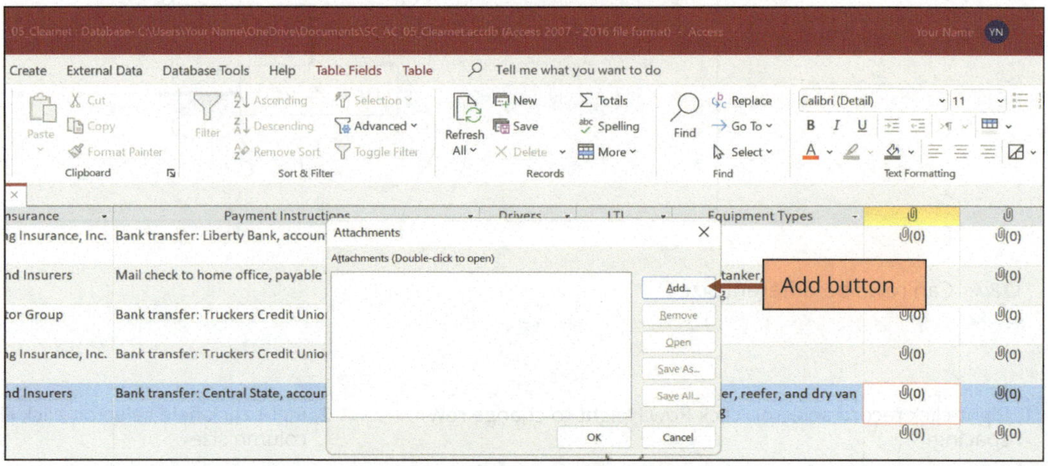

Figure 5–20

3

- Click the Add button.

Q&A Unlike the figure, my window is maximized. Does that make a difference?
No. The same steps will work in either case.

- Navigate to the photo file for Erika, Support_AC_05_Erika.jpg, click to select it, and then click Open (Figure 5–21).

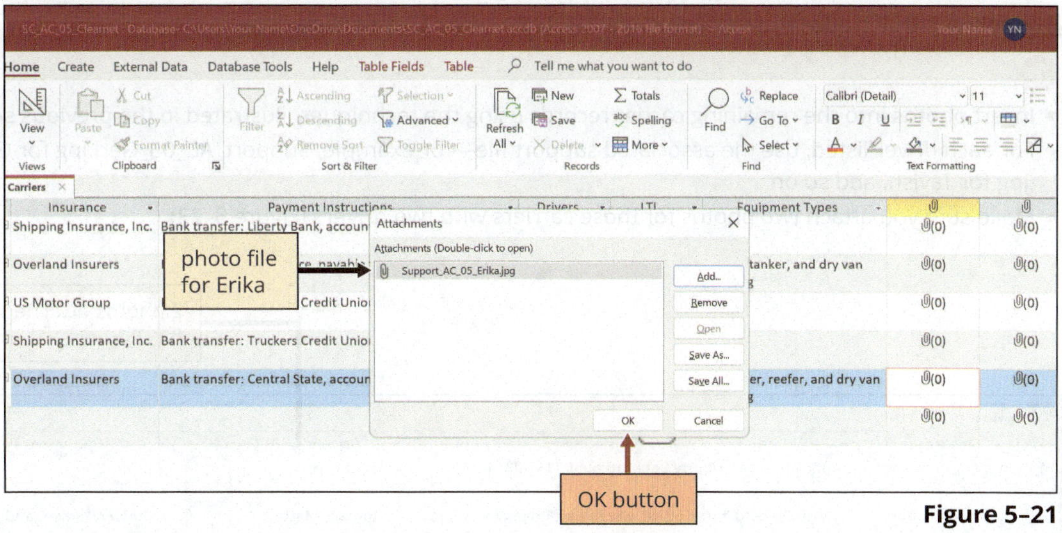

Figure 5–21

4

- Click the OK button to attach the photo (Figure 5–22).

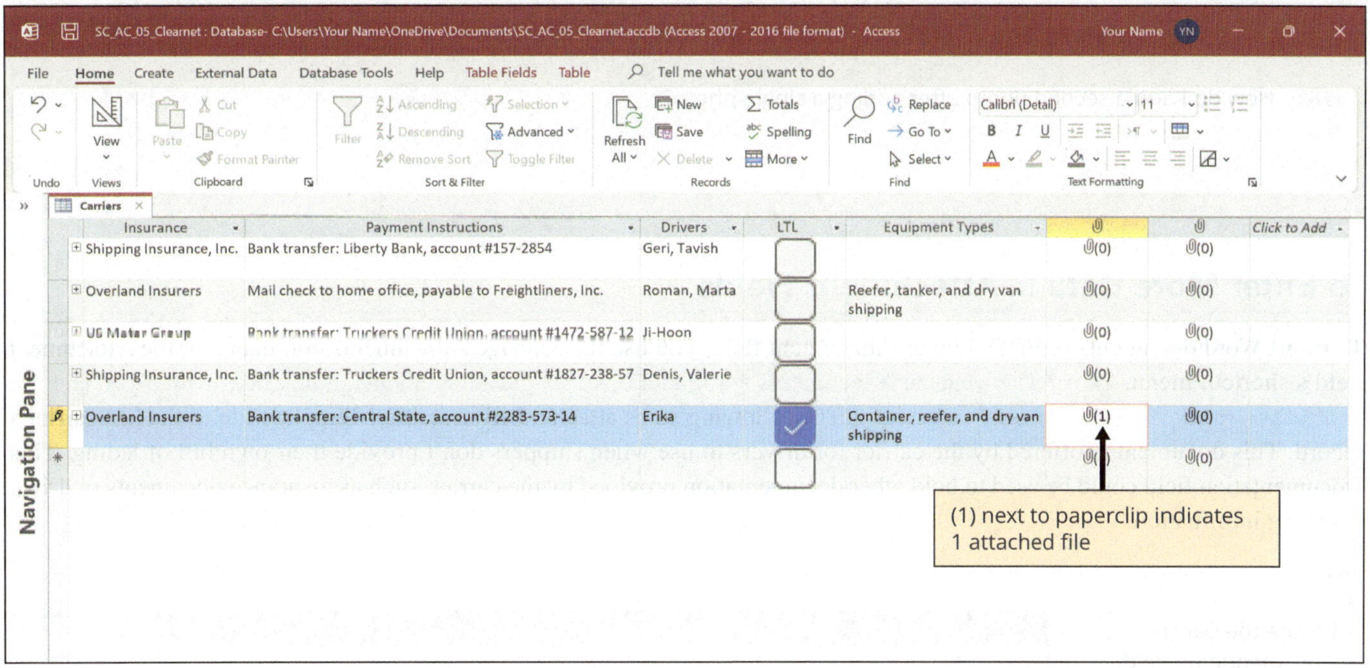

Figure 5–22

Q&A I do not see the photo. I just see the paper clip. Is that correct?
Yes. You will see the actual photo when you use this field in a form.

To Insert the Remaining Photos

The following step adds the remaining photos to the other Carrier records.

1

- Insert photos into the remaining carrier records using the techniques illustrated in the previous set of steps.
- For each driver listed, use the associated support file—for example, Support_AC_05_Geri.jpg for Geri, Support_AC_05_Tavish .jpg for Tavish, and so on.
- Make sure you attach two photos for those carriers with two drivers (Figure 5–23).

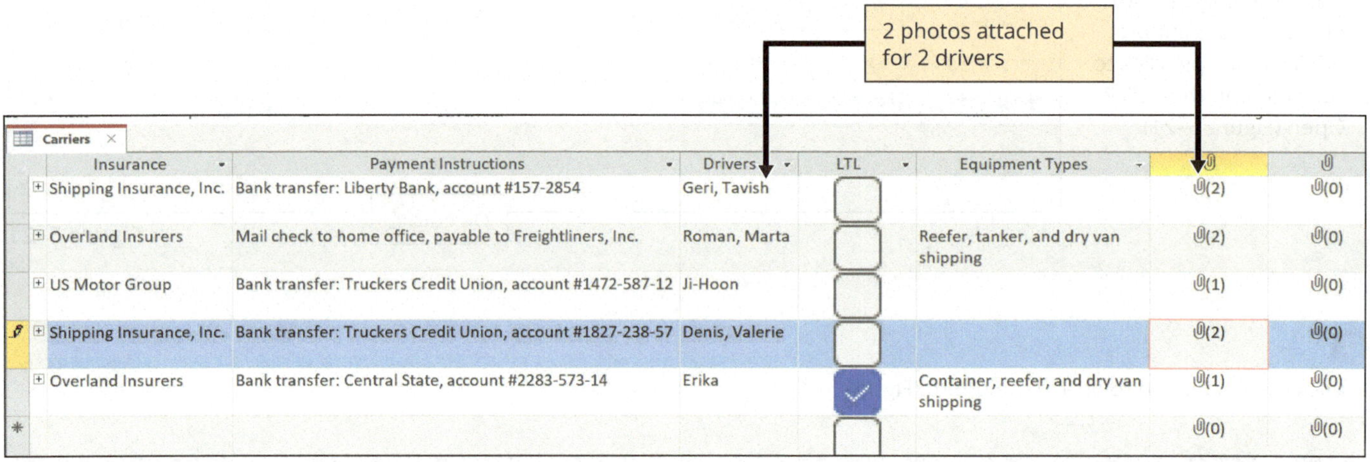

Figure 5–23

Q&A How do I add a second photo after adding a single photo?
Before closing the Attachments dialog box for that record, click the Add button again. Choose the second photo, and then click the Open button (Choose File dialog box). After the second photo is added, click the OK button (Attachments dialog box).

To Enter More Data in Attachment Fields

To insert Word documents or PDFs into an Attachment field, you use the Manage Attachments command on the Attachment field's shortcut menu. **Why?** The Manage Attachments command displays the Attachments dialog box, which you can use to attach as many files as necessary to the field. The following steps attach a Bill of Lading Template file to the last carrier's record. This document is offered by the carrier for drivers to use when shippers don't provide their own bill of lading. This Documentation field could be used to hold other documentation provided by the carrier, such as insurance documents or driver licensing information.

1

- Ensure the Carrier Documentation field, the second field that displays a paper clip in the field selector, appears on your screen, and then right-click the Carrier Documentation field on the fifth carrier record to produce a shortcut menu (Figure 5–24).

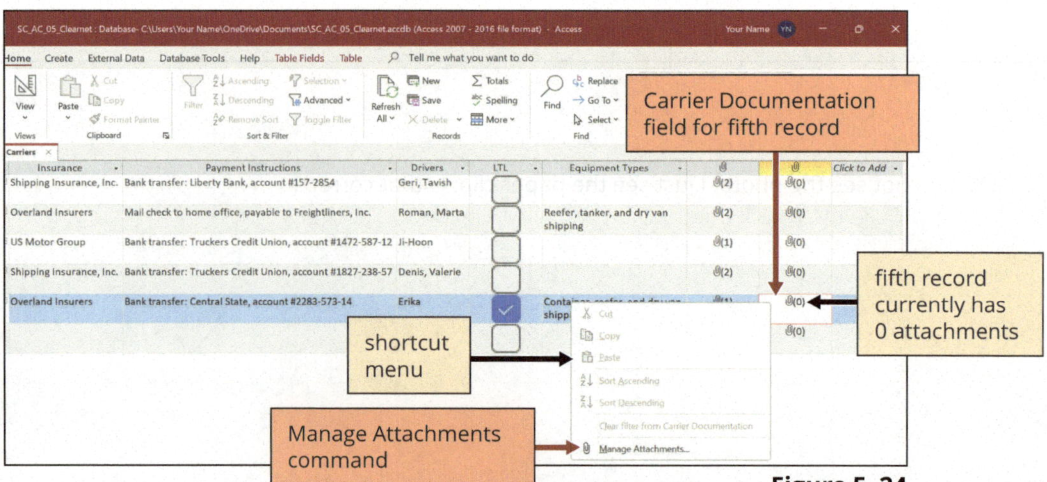

Figure 5–24

2

- Click Manage Attachments on the shortcut menu to display the Attachments dialog box (Figure 5–25).

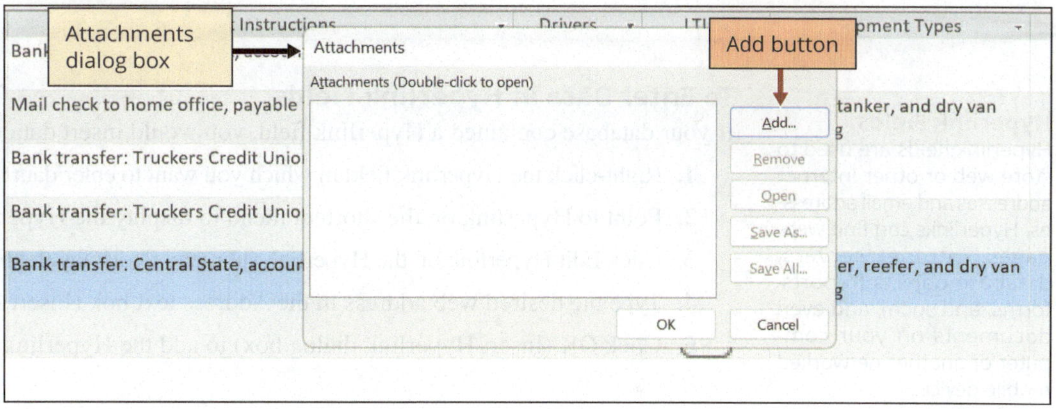

Figure 5–25

3

- Click Add (Attachments dialog box) to display the Choose File dialog box, where you can add an attachment.
- Navigate to the location containing your attachment files.
- Click Support_AC_05_Bill-of-Lading-Template.docx, which is a Word file, and then click the Open button (Choose File dialog box) to attach the file (Figure 5–26).

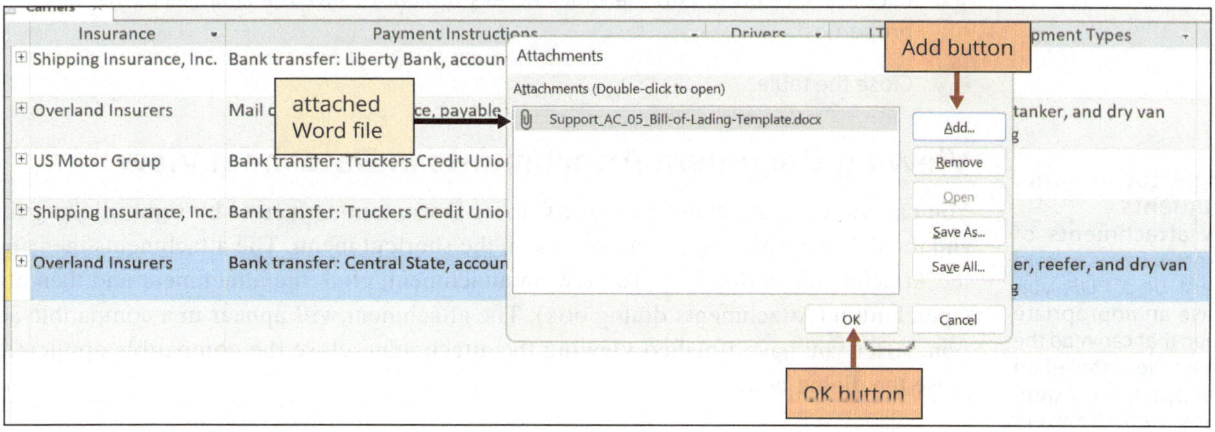

Figure 5–26

4

- Click OK (Attachments dialog box) to close the Attachments dialog box (Figure 5–27). The other carriers have no new attachments at this time.

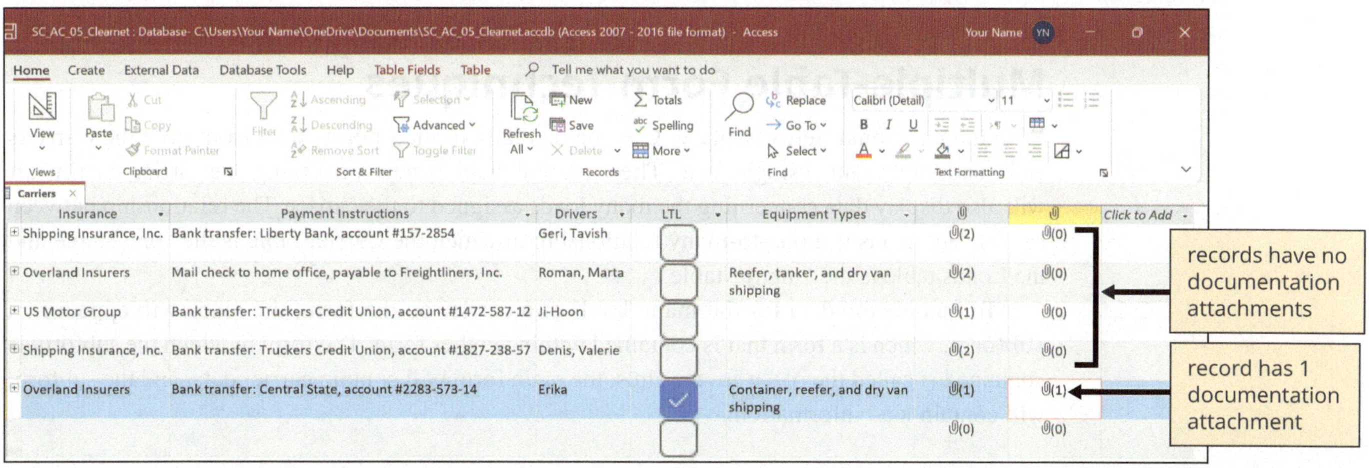

Figure 5–27

Q&A If I had more than one document to add to a load's record, could I attach multiple files in this one Attachment field?
Yes, you can attach multiple files to a single Attachment field.

BTW
Hyperlink Fields
Hyperlink fields are used to store web or other Internet addresses and email addresses. Hyperlinks can find webpages, intranet servers, database objects (reports, forms, and such), and even documents on your computer or another networked mobile device.

To Enter Data in Hyperlink Fields

If your database contained a Hyperlink field, you would insert data using the following steps.

1. Right-click the Hyperlink field in which you want to enter data to display a shortcut menu.
2. Point to Hyperlink on the shortcut menu to display the Hyperlink submenu.
3. Click Edit Hyperlink on the Hyperlink submenu to display the Insert Hyperlink dialog box.
4. Type the desired web address in the Address text box (Insert Hyperlink dialog box).
5. Click OK (Insert Hyperlink dialog box) to add the Hyperlink.

To Save the Properties

The row and column spacing are table properties. When changing any table properties, the changes apply only as long as the table is active *unless they are saved*. Once you have saved them, they will apply every time you open the table.

The following steps first save the properties and then close the table.

1. Click the Save button on the Quick Access Toolbar to save the changes to the table properties.
2. Close the table.

BTW
Viewing Attachments of Documents
To view attachments of documents, such as a Word document or a PDF, you must have an appropriate application that can read the attachment file installed on your computer. For example, many web browsers can open and read PDF files.

Viewing Document Attachments in Datasheet View

You can view the attachments in the Carrier Documentation field by right-clicking the field and then clicking Manage Attachments on the shortcut menu. The attachments then appear in the Attachments dialog box. To view an attachment, click the attachment and then click the Open button (Attachments dialog box). The attachment will appear in a compatible application. After you have finished viewing the attachment, close the compatible application and close the dialog box.

Break Point: If you wish to take a break, this is a good place to do so. You can quit Access now. To resume at a later time, start Access, open the database called SC_AC_05_Clearnet.accdb, and continue following the steps from this location forward.

Multiple-Table Form Techniques

With the additional fields in place, Clearnet is ready to incorporate data from both the Carriers and Loads tables into a single form. The form will display data concerning one carrier at a time. It will also display data concerning the many loads assigned to the carrier. The relationship between carriers and loads is a one-to-many relationship in which the Carrier table is the "one" table and the Loads table is the "many" table.

To include the data for the many loads of a carrier on the form, the loads will appear in a **subform**, which is a form that is contained within another form. The form in which the subform is contained is called the **main form**. Thus, the main form will contain carrier data, and the subform will contain load information.

Consider This

When a form includes data from multiple tables, how do you relate the tables?
Once you determine that you need data from more than one table, you need to determine the main table and its relationship to any other table.

- **Determine the main table the form is intended to view and/or update.** You need to identify the purpose of the form and the table it is mainly intended to show, which is the *main* table.
- **Determine how the additional table should fit into the form.** If the additional table is the "many" part of the relationship, the data should probably be in a subform or datasheet. If the additional table is the "one" part of the relationship, the data should probably simply appear as fields on the form.

To Create a Form in Design View

You can create a form in Design view. **Why?** Design view gives you increased flexibility in laying out a form by using a blank design on which you place objects in the precise locations you want. The following steps create a form in Design view.

1

- Open the Navigation Pane and be sure the Carriers table is selected.
- Click Create on the ribbon to display the Create tab (Figure 5–28).

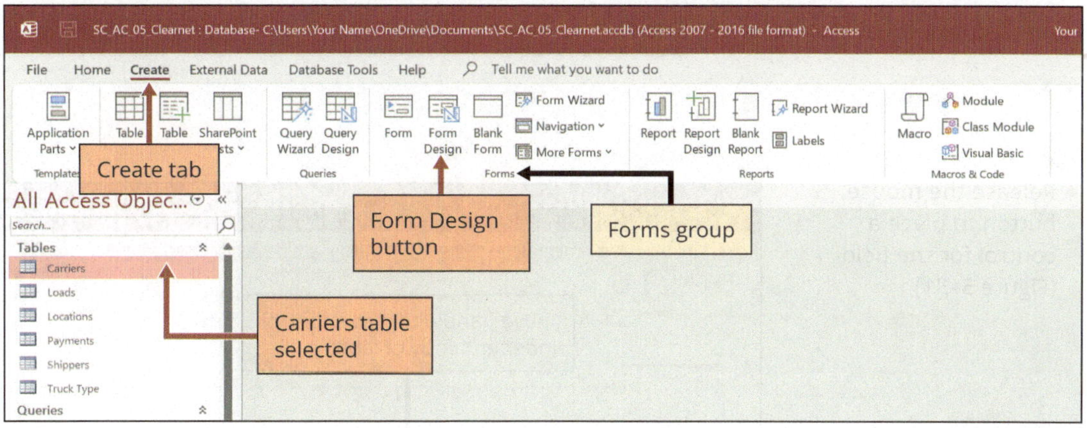

Figure 5–28

2

- Click the Form Design button (Create tab | Forms group) to create a new form in Design view.
- Close the Navigation Pane.
- If necessary, click the 'Add Existing Fields' button (Form Design tab | Tools group) to display the Field List pane (Figure 5–29). If you do not see the tables listed, click 'Show all tables'. (Your list might show all fields in the Carriers table.)

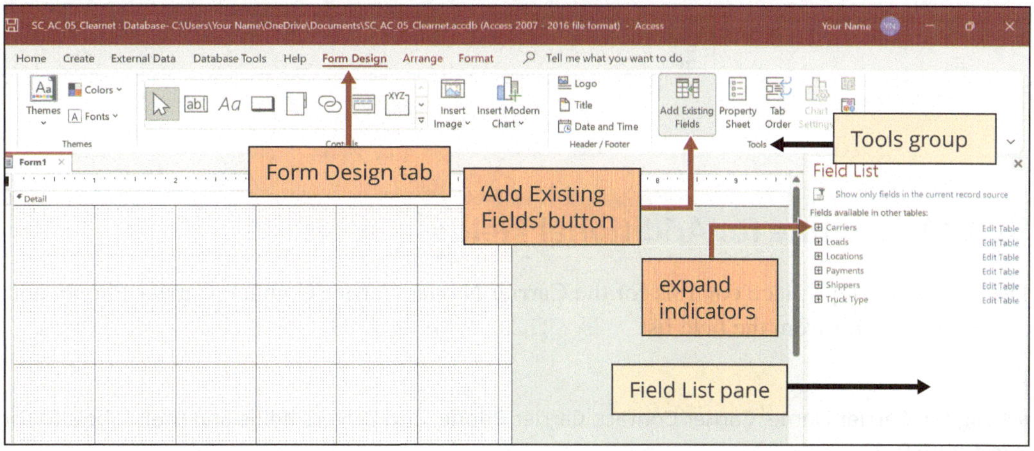

Figure 5–29

To Add a Control for a Field to the Form

To place a control for a field on a form, drag the field from the field list to the desired position. The following steps place the Carrier ID field on the form. **Why?** Dragging is the easiest way to place a field on a form.

1

- If necessary, click the expand indicator for the Carriers table to display the fields in the table. Drag the Carrier ID field in the field list for the Carriers table to the approximate position shown in Figure 5–30.

Q&A Do I have to be exact?

No. Just be sure you are in the same general location.

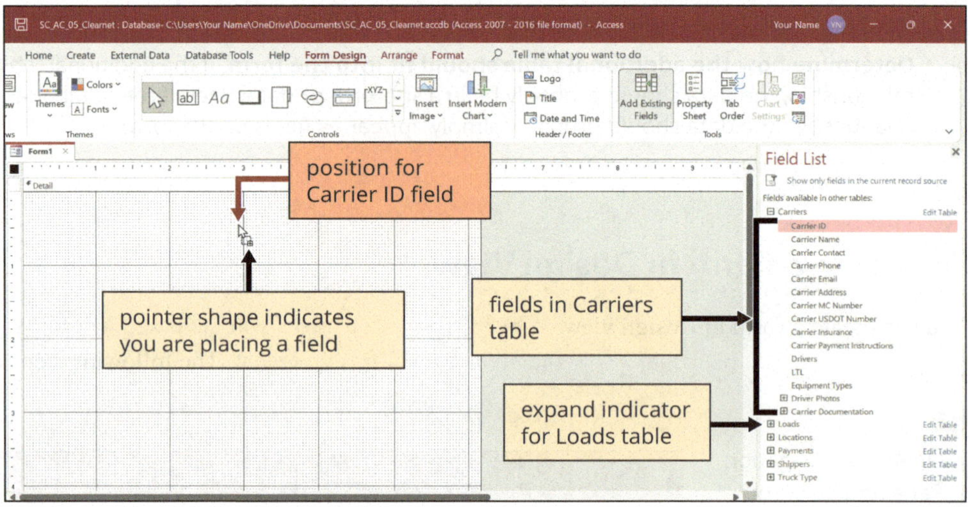

Figure 5–30

2

- Release the mouse button to place a control for the field (Figure 5–31).

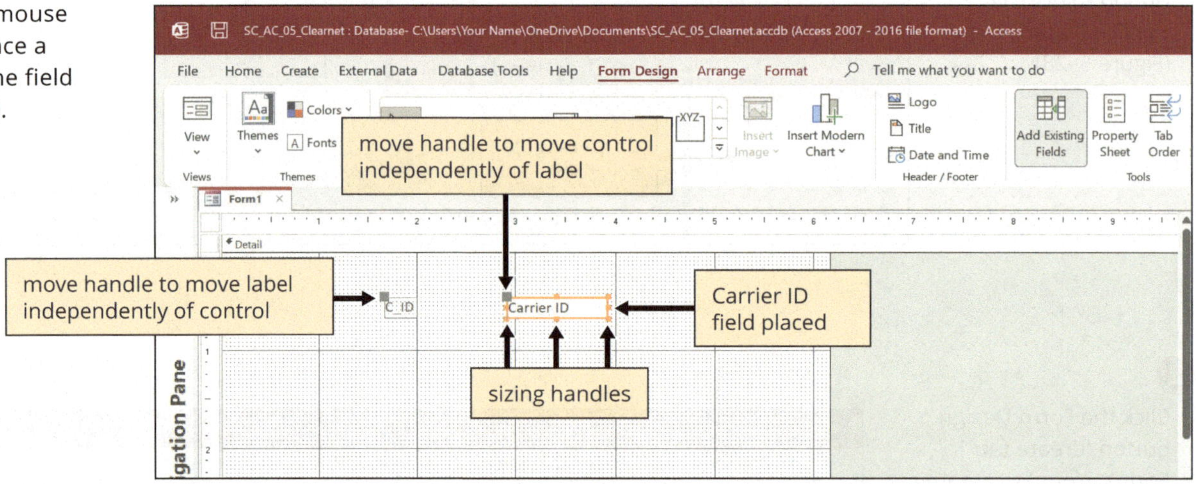

Figure 5–31

To Add Controls for Additional Fields

The following steps place controls for the Carrier Name, Carrier Contact, Carrier Phone, and Drivers fields on the form by dragging the fields from the field list. **Why?** These fields all need to be included in the form.

1

- Drag the Carrier Name, Carrier Contact, Carrier Phone, and Drivers fields and their labels to the approximate positions shown in Figure 5–32.

Q&A Do I have to align them precisely?

You can, but you do not need to. In the next steps, you will instruct Access to align the fields properly.

What if I drag the wrong field from the field list? Can I delete the control?

Yes. With the control selected, press DEL.

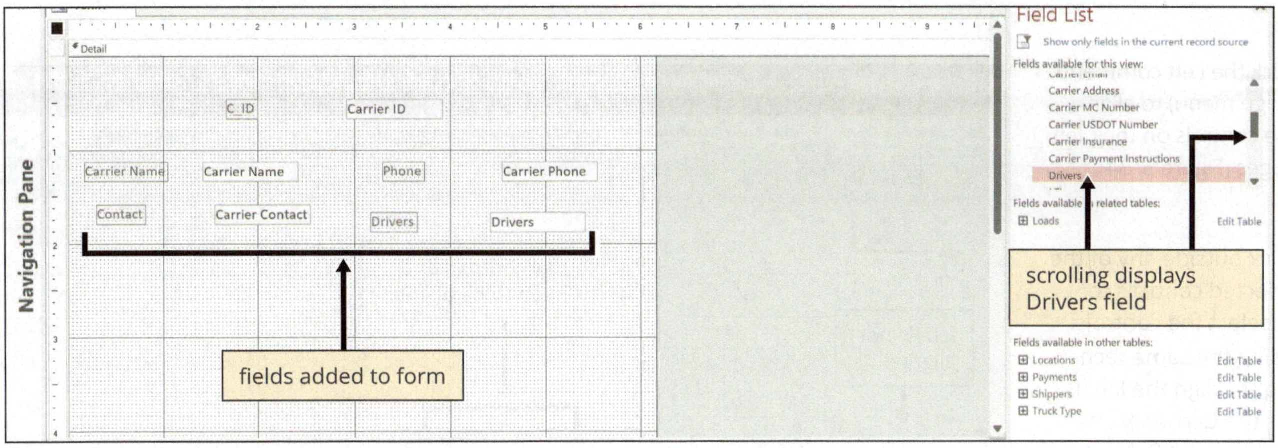

Figure 5–32

To Align Controls on the Left

To ensure that a group of controls is aligned properly with each other, select all the affected controls, and then use the appropriate alignment button on the Arrange tab. **Why?** Often, you will want form controls to be aligned in some fashion. For example, the controls might be aligned so their right edges are even with each other. In another case, controls might be aligned so their top edges are even.

You can use one of two methods to select multiple controls. One way is to use a ruler. If you click a position on the horizontal ruler, you will select all the controls for which a portion of the control is under that position on the ruler. Similarly, if you click a position on the vertical ruler, you will select all the controls for which a portion of the control is to the right of that position on the ruler.

The second way to select multiple controls is to select the first control by clicking it. Then, select all the other controls by holding down SHIFT while clicking each additional control.

The following steps select the Carrier Name, Carrier Contact, Carrier Phone, and Drivers controls and then align them so their left edges line up.

1

- Click the Carrier Name control (the one with the white box, not the label that shows the dotted background in the box) to select the control.
- Press and hold SHIFT and click the Carrier Contact control to select an additional control.

Q&A I selected the wrong collection of fields. How can I start over?
Simply begin the process again by clicking outside all controls to deselect fields, and then make sure you do not hold SHIFT down when you select the first field.

- Click Arrange on the ribbon to display the Arrange tab.
- Click the Align button (Arrange tab | Sizing & Ordering group) to display the Align menu (Figure 5–33).

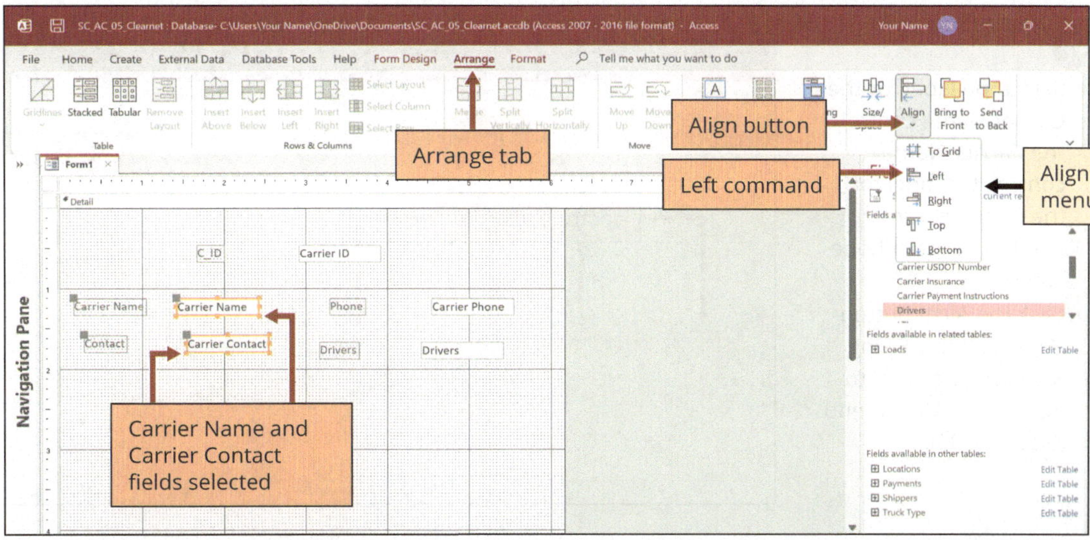

Figure 5–33

2

- Click the Left command (Align menu) to align the controls on their left edges (Figure 5–34).

3

- Click outside any of the selected controls to deselect the controls.
- Using the same technique, align the labels for the Carrier Name and Contact fields on their left edges.
- Using the same technique, align the Carrier Phone and Drivers fields on their left edges.
- Using the same technique, align the labels for the Phone and Drivers fields on their left edges.

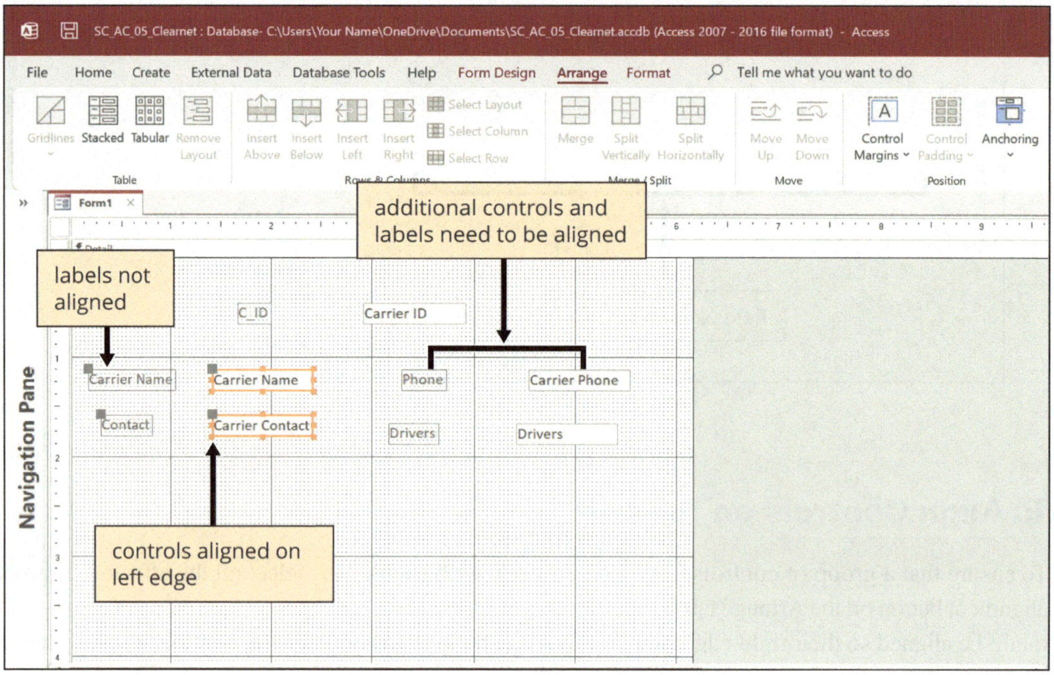

Figure 5–34

Q&A When I try to align the controls, some of them overlap others and aren't spaced out well. How can I fix this?
Before automatically aligning the controls, make sure they're spaced far enough apart that they will not overlap once they are aligned. You can also reposition each field control separately from its label control by using the gray move handle before performing the automatic alignment.

Other Ways

1. Right-click selected controls, point to Align, and choose an alignment to align controls

To Align Controls on the Top and Adjust Vertical Spacing

The following steps align each row of controls so they are aligned on their top edges. Once these controls are aligned, you adjust the vertical spacing so the same amount of space separates each row of controls. **Why?** Aligning the top edges of controls improves the neatness and appearance of a form. In addition, you might want the vertical spacing between controls to be the same.

1

- Select the label for the Carrier Name control, the Carrier Name control, the label for the Phone control, and the Carrier Phone control.
- Click the Align button (Arrange tab | Sizing & Ordering group) to display the Align menu (Figure 5–35).

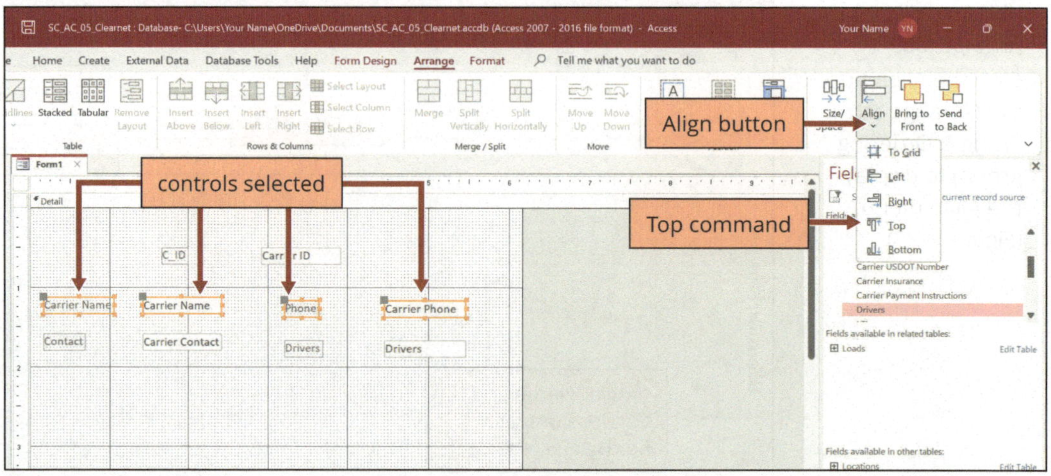

Figure 5–35

2

- Click the Top command on the Align menu to align the controls on the top.
- Select the Carrier Contact and Drivers fields and their labels, and then align the controls to the top.
- Click outside any of the selected controls to deselect the controls.
- Select the four fields, Carrier Name, Carrier Contact, Carrier Phone, and Drivers.
- Click the Size/Space button (Arrange tab | Sizing & Ordering group) to display the Size/Space menu (Figure 5–36).

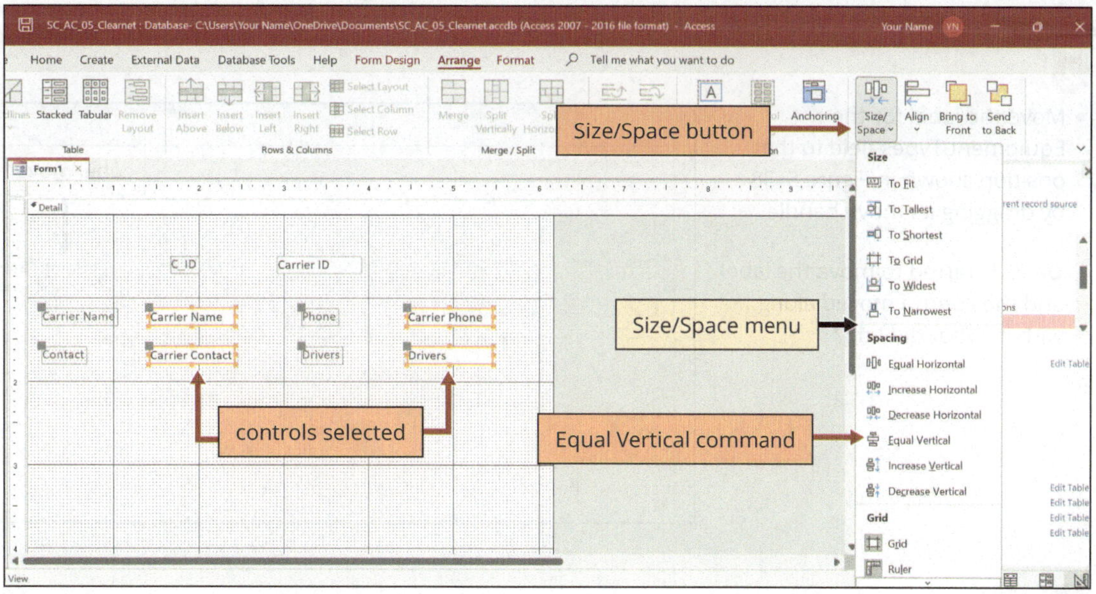

Figure 5–36

Q&A Do I need to select the labels too?

No. If you select the control and adjust its vertical spacing, its label's vertical position will also be adjusted.

3

- Click Equal Vertical (Size/Space menu) to specify the spacing.

Q&A What is the purpose of the other commands on the Size/Space menu?

You can adjust the spacing to fit the available space. You can adjust the space to match the tallest, shortest, widest, or narrowest section. You can adjust the space to match the closest grid points. You can specify equal horizontal spacing. Finally, you can increase or decrease either the vertical or the horizontal spacing.

- Click outside the controls to deselect the controls.
- Because it is a good idea to save the form before continuing, click the Save button on the Quick Access Toolbar.
- Type **Carrier Loads Form** as the name of the form, and then click OK to save the form.

To Add Controls for the Remaining Fields

The following steps place the attached labels and controls for the LTL, Equipment Types, Driver Photos, and Documentation fields in the desired positions. **Why?** Controls for these fields are to be included in the completed form.

1

- Drag the controls for the LTL and Equipment Types fields from the field list to the approximate positions shown in Figure 5–37.

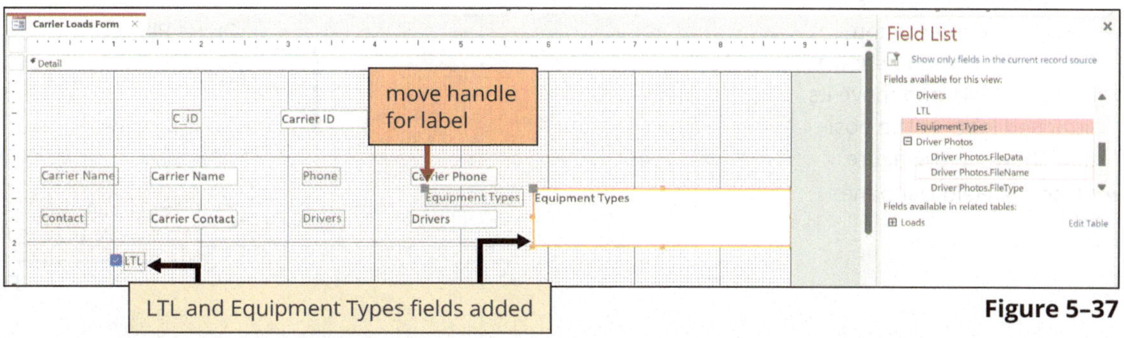

Figure 5–37

Q&A Is there enough space on the form to add the Equipment Types field?
Yes. The size of the form will expand as you drag the field to the form.

2

- Move the label for the Equipment Types field to the position shown in Figure 5–38 by dragging its move handle.

Q&A I started to move the label and the control moved along with it. What did I do?
You were not pointing at the handle to move the label independently of the control. Make sure you are pointing to the little box in the upper-left corner of the label.

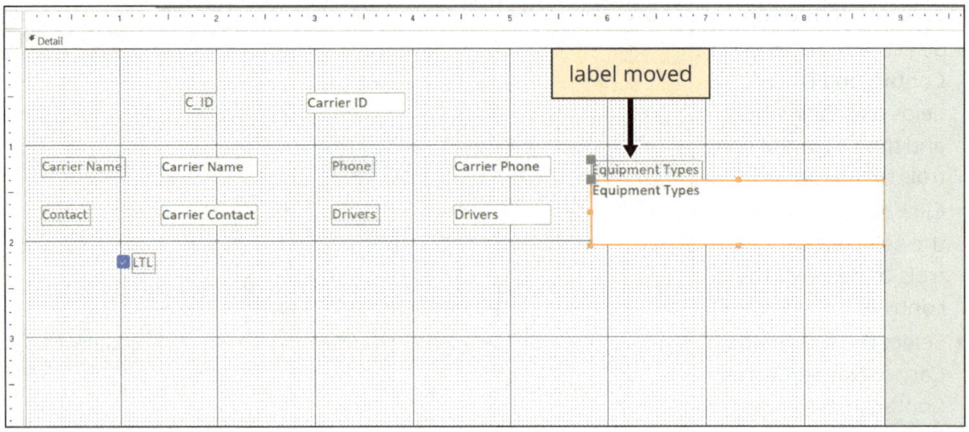

Figure 5–38

3

- Using the same techniques, add the control for the Driver Photos field to the approximate position shown in Figure 5–39, and move and resize its label to match the size and position shown in the figure.

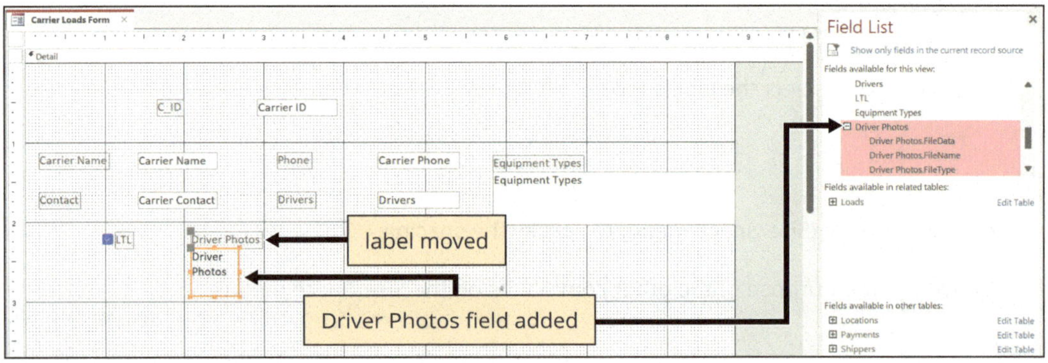

Figure 5–39

Q&A My Driver Photos label is next to the field, not above it as shown in the figure. Is that a problem?
You can use the move handle in the upper-left corner of the Driver Photos label to move it. Its position does not have to be precise. You will further rearrange the labels later in the module.

4

- Click the control for the Driver Photos field and drag the lower-right corner to the approximate position shown in Figure 5–40 to resize the control.
- Add the control for the Carrier Documentation field in the position shown in Figure 5–41 and move its attached label to the position shown in the figure.
- Close the Field List pane.

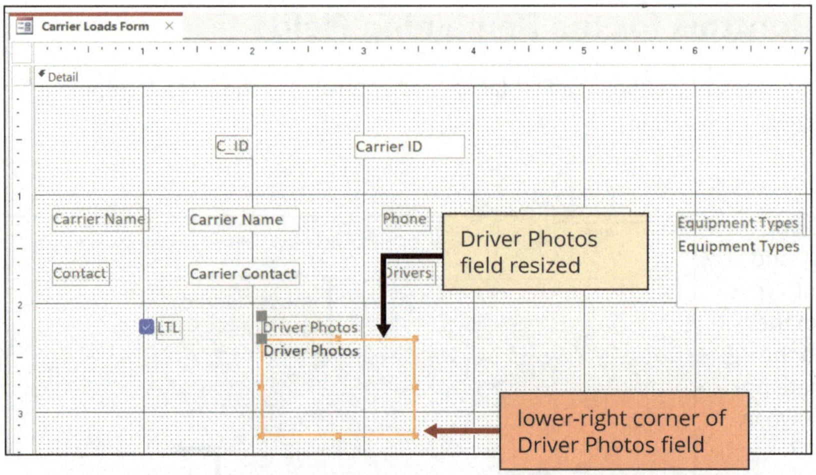

Figure 5–40

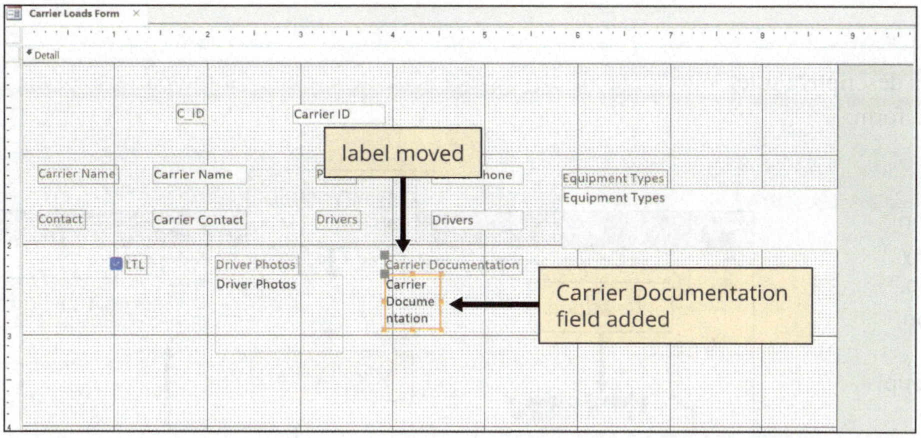

Figure 5–41

To Use a Shortcut Menu to Change the Fill/Back Color

You can use the Background Color button on the Format tab to change the background color of a form. You can also use a shortcut menu. The following steps use a shortcut menu to change the background color of the form to gray. **Why?** Using a shortcut menu is a simple way to change the background color.

1

- Right-click in the approximate position shown in Figure 5–42 to produce a shortcut menu.

Q&A Does it matter where I right-click?
You can right-click anywhere on the form as long as your pointer is not on or inside any controls.

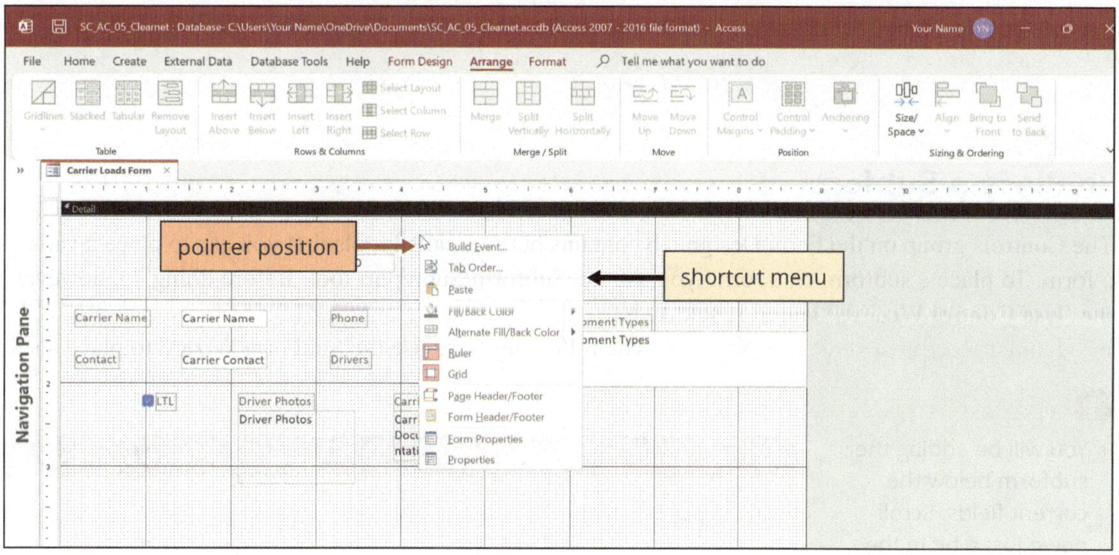

Figure 5–42

2

- Point to the Fill/Back Color arrow on the shortcut menu to display a color palette (Figure 5–43).

3

- Click the light gray color (row 2, column 1) shown in Figure 5–43 to change the fill/back color to light gray.

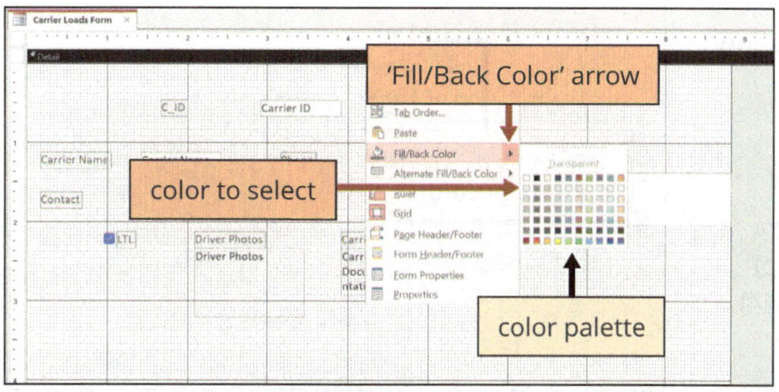

Figure 5–43

To Add a Title

A form should have a descriptive title. **Why?** The title gives a concise description of the purpose of the form. The following step adds a title to the form.

1

- Click Form Design on the ribbon to display the Form Design tab.
- Click the Title button (Form Design tab | Header / Footer group) to add a title to the form (Figure 5–44).

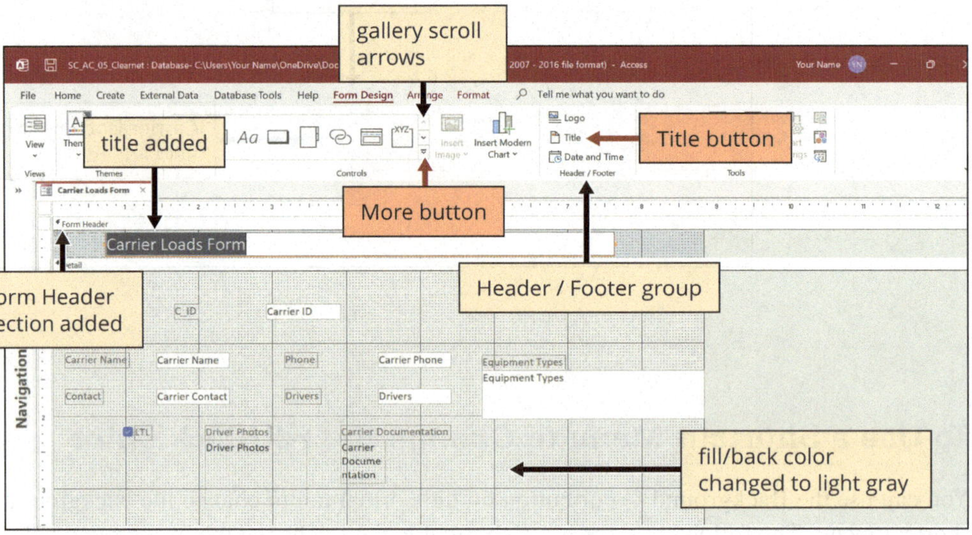

Figure 5–44

Q&A Can I change this title if I want something different?
Yes. You can change it as you would any other text. For the purposes of this project, however, you will leave the title as it is.

Why is there a new section?
The form title belongs in the Form Header section. When you clicked the Title button, Access added the Form Header section automatically and placed the title control in it.

Could I add a Form Header section without having to click the Title button?
Yes. Right-click anywhere on the form background and click Form Header/Footer on the shortcut menu.

To Place a Subform

The Controls group on the Form Design tab contains buttons called tools that you use to place a variety of types of controls on a form. To place a subform on a form, you use the Subform/Subreport tool. Before doing so, however, you should ensure that the 'Use Control Wizards' button is selected. **Why?** If the 'Use Control Wizards' button is selected, a wizard will guide you through the process of adding the subform. The following steps use the SubForm Wizard to place a subform.

1

- You will be adding the subform below the current fields. Scroll down just a bit in the form so you have space below the Driver Photos and Carrier Documentation controls.

2

- Click the More button (Form Design tab | Controls group) (shown in Figure 5–44) to display a gallery of available tools (Figure 5–45).

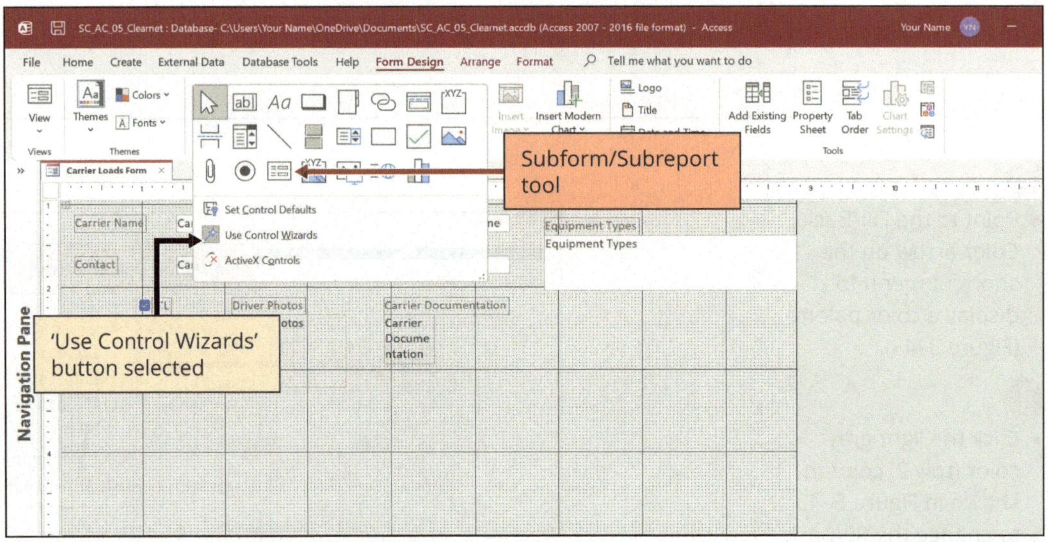

Figure 5–45

3

- Be sure the 'Use Control Wizards' button is selected, click the Subform/Subreport tool on the Form Design tab, and then move the pointer to the approximate position shown in Figure 5–46.

Q&A How can I tell whether the 'Use Control Wizards' button is selected?

The icon for the 'Use Control Wizards' button will be highlighted, as shown in Figure 5–45. If it is not, click the 'Use Control Wizards' button to select it, and then click the More button again and click the Subform/Subreport tool.

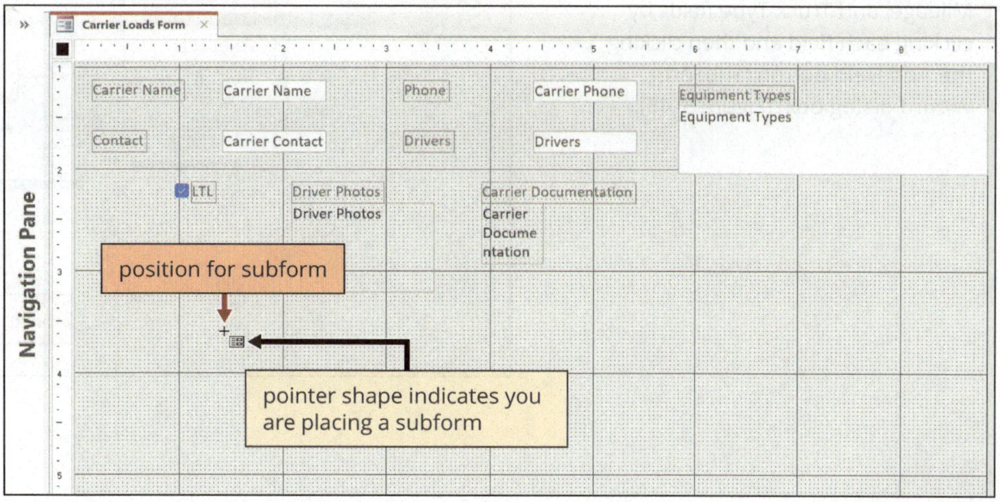

Figure 5–46

4

- Click the position shown in Figure 5–46 to place the subform and open the SubForm Wizard.
- Ensure the 'Use existing Tables and Queries' option button is selected (SubForm Wizard dialog box) (Figure 5–47).

Q&A My control is placed on the screen, but no wizard appeared. What should I do?

Press DEL to delete the control you placed. Ensure the 'Use Control Wizards' button is selected, as described previously, and then try Steps 3 and 4 again.

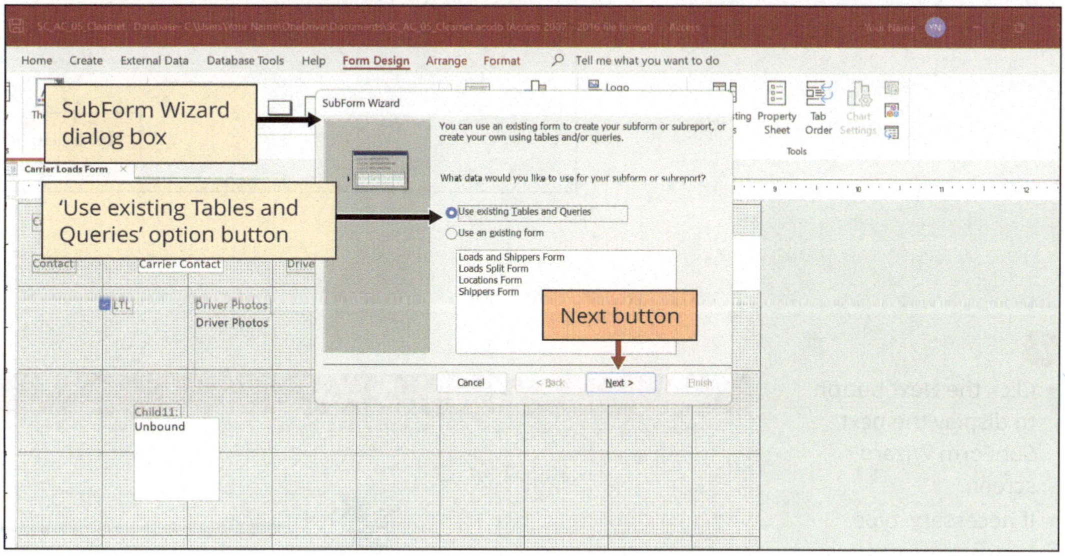

Figure 5–47

5

- Click the Next button to display the next SubForm Wizard screen.
- If the Loads table is not already selected, click the Tables/Queries arrow, and then click Table: Loads to select it as the table that contains the fields for the subform.

- Add the Load ID, Pickup Date, Dropoff Date, Rate Confirmation, Mileage, and Truck Type fields by clicking each field and then clicking the Add Field button (SubForm Wizard dialog box) (Figure 5–48).

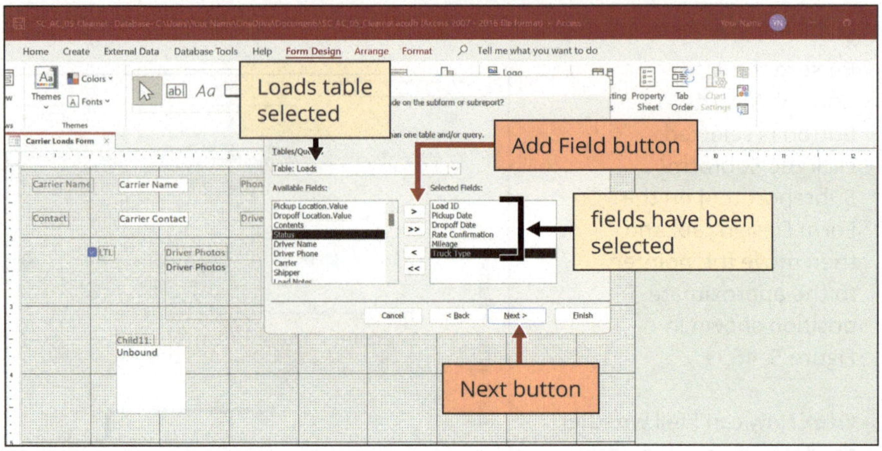

Figure 5–48

6

- Click Next to display the next SubForm Wizard screen.
- Be sure the 'Choose from a list.' option button is selected (Figure 5–49).

Q&A Why do I use this option?
Most of the time, Access will have determined the appropriate fields to link the subform and the main form and placed an entry specifying those fields in the list. By choosing from the list, you can take advantage of the information that Access has created for you. The other option is to define your own, in which case you would need to specify the appropriate fields.

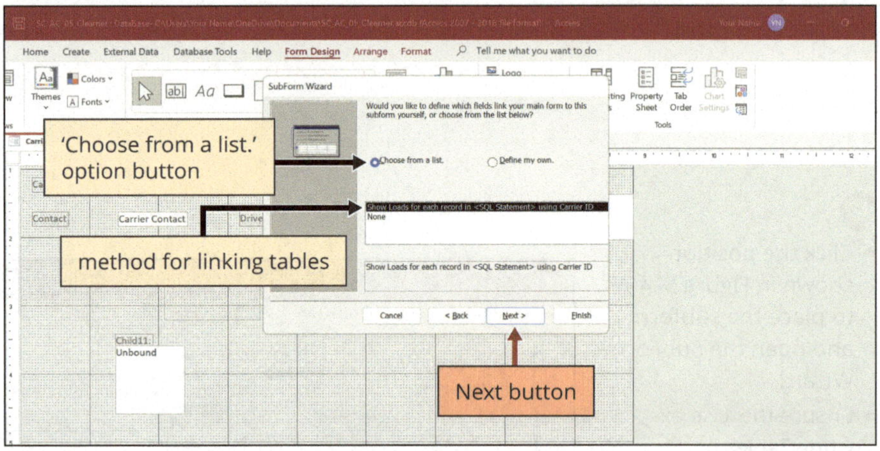

Figure 5–49

7

- Click the Next button to display the next SubForm Wizard screen.
- If necessary, type **Loads subform** as the name of the subform (Figure 5–50).

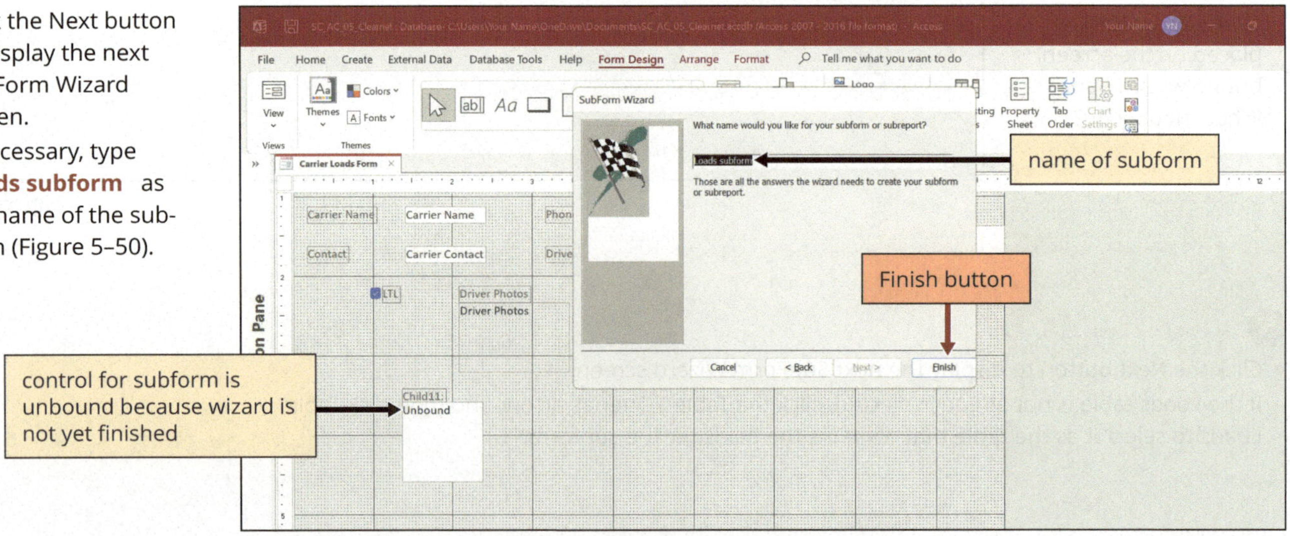

Figure 5–50

8

- Click the Finish button to place the subform.
- If necessary, shift the subform control and nearby controls to best use the space without any overlapping of controls and so subform fits above the Form Footer section (Figure 5–51).

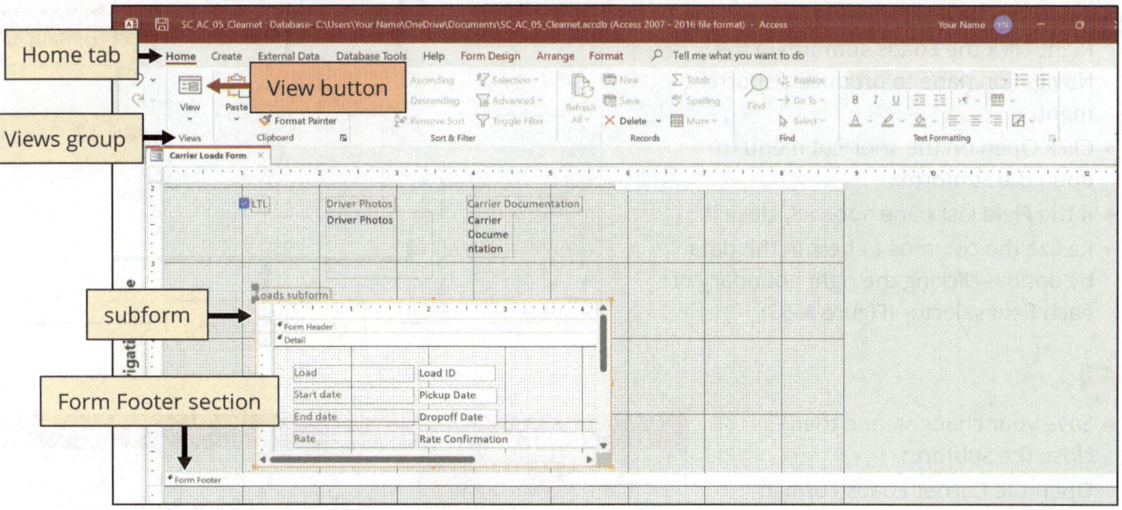

Figure 5–51

9

- Click the View button (Home tab | Views group) to choose Form view, and then navigate to the fifth record (Figure 5–52).

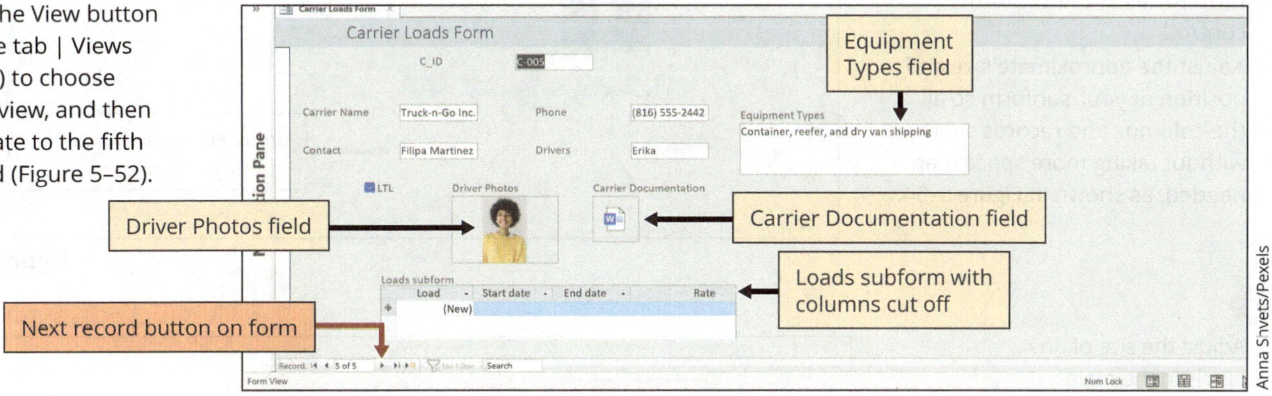

Figure 5–52

Q&A Everything looks good except the subform. I do not see all the fields I should see. What should I do?
You need to modify the subform, which you will do in the upcoming steps.

10

- Save and then close the form.

Break Point: If you wish to take a break, this is a good place to do so. You can quit Access now. To resume at a later time, start Access, open the database called SC_AC_05_Clearnet.accdb, and continue following the steps from this location forward.

To Modify a Subform and Move the Picture

The next task is to resize the columns in the subform, which appear on the form in Datasheet view. The subform exists as a separate object in the database; it is stored independently of the main form. The following steps open the subform and then resize the columns. Why? The column sizes need to be adjusted so the data is displayed correctly. The steps then view the form and, finally, move and resize the picture.

1

- Open the Navigation Pane.
- Right-click the Loads subform in the Navigation pane to produce a shortcut menu.
- Click Open on the shortcut menu to open the subform.
- If the Field List pane appears, close it.
- Resize the columns to best fit the data by double-clicking the right boundary of each field selector (Figure 5–53).

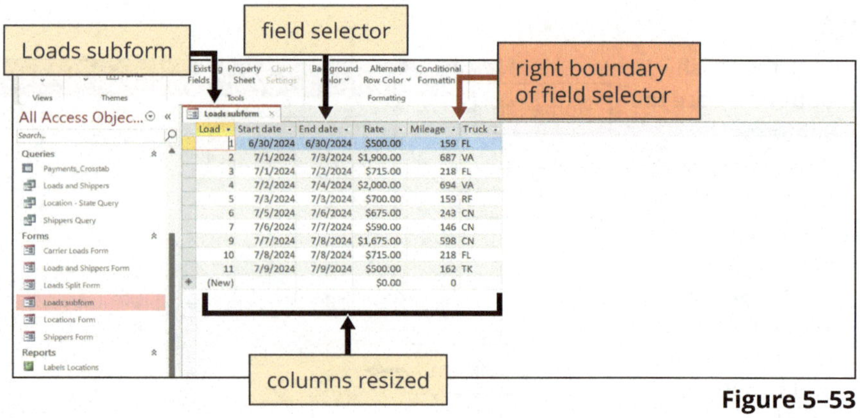

Figure 5–53

2

- Save your changes, and then close the subform.
- Open the Carrier Loads Form in Layout view, and then close the Navigation Pane.
- Click any boundary of the subform to select the subform control.
- Adjust the approximate size and position of your subform so all the columns and records show without taking more space than needed, as shown in Figure 5–54.

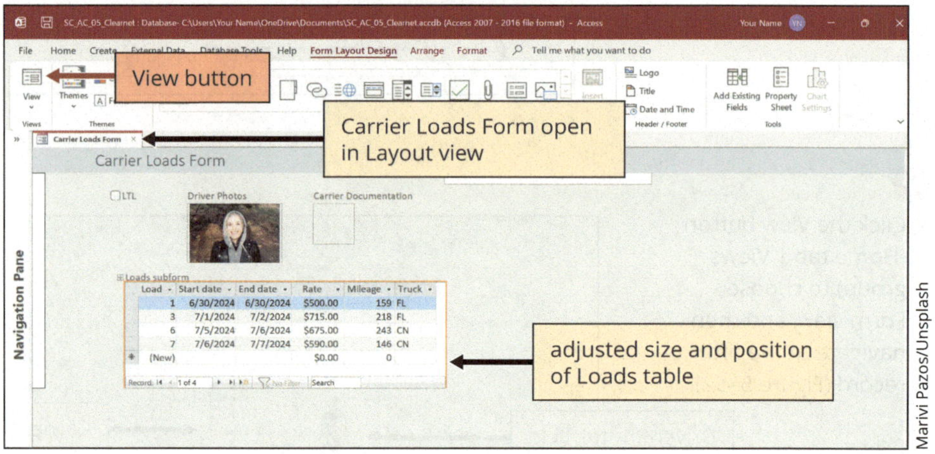

Figure 5–54

3

- Adjust the size of any labels in the main form whose names are obscured, such as increasing the width of the Carrier Name control. Navigate through the other carrier records to confirm the field controls are big enough for all data in all records.
- Click the View button (Form Layout Design tab | Views group) to view the form in Form view (Figure 5–55).

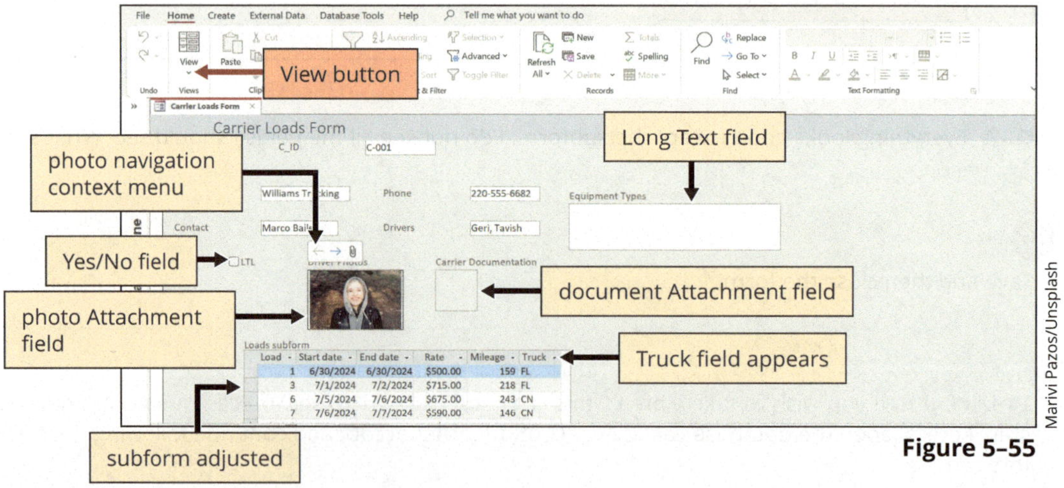

Figure 5–55

Q&A Could I have clicked the View arrow and then clicked Form View?

Yes. You can always use the arrow to see all view options. If the icon for the view you want appears on the face of the View button, however, you can just click the button.

The photo seems to be a slightly different size from the one in Figure 5–55. How do I fix this?

You can move and also resize the photo.

I know many of these carrier records contain more than one driver photo, but I only see one driver's photo on each record. How can I see the other photos?

You can toggle between all the photos for each carrier. Click the Driver Photos control to select it. A context menu appears above the photo (Figure 5–55). Click the blue navigation buttons to scroll to the right or left and see other photos, if available.

How can I tell if the new size and location are correct for the photo and for other controls?

View the form. If you are not satisfied with the size or location of any control, return to Design view or Layout view and make the necessary adjustments. Repeat the process until you are satisfied. You may have to allow a small amount of white on the borders of the photo. You will learn about some options you can use to adjust the specific look of the photo later in this module.

Consider This

Is there any way to determine the way images fit within the control?

Yes. Access determines the portion of an image that appears as well as the way it appears using the **size mode** property. The three size modes are as follows:

Clip: This size mode displays only a portion of the image that will fit in the space allocated to it.

Stretch: This size mode expands or shrinks the image to fit the precise space allocated on the screen. For photographs, usually this is not a good choice because fitting a photograph to the allocated space can distort the image, giving it a stretched appearance.

Zoom: This size mode does the best job of fitting the image to the allocated space without changing the look of the image. The entire image will appear and be proportioned correctly. Some white space may be visible either above or to the right of the image, however.

To Change a Label

Labels can be changed in a form to be more descriptive. **Why?** The form has enough room to display more than the entire field name, so adding extra information adds clarity. The following steps change the contents of the label from C_ID to Carrier Identification.

1

- Switch to Design view.
- Click the C_ID label to select it.
- Click the label a second time to produce an insertion point.
- Delete the existing text (C_ID), and then type **Carrier Identification** as the new label (Figure 5–56).

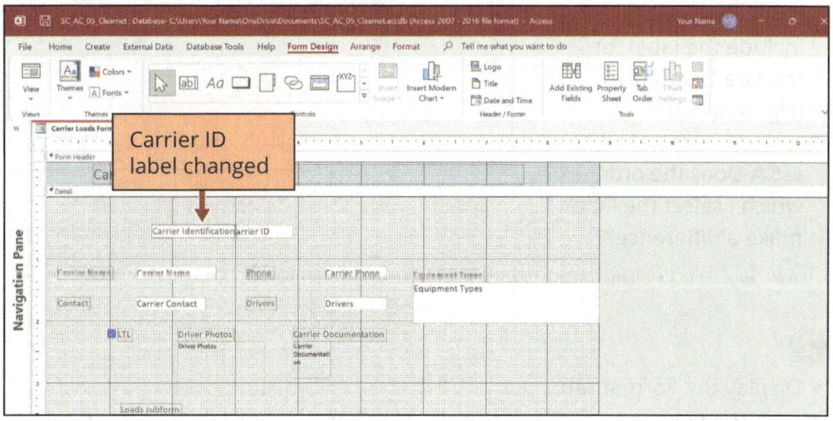

Figure 5–56

2

- Click outside the label to deselect it.
- Click the label to select it.
- Drag the move handle in the upper-left corner of the label control to move the label to the approximate position shown in Figure 5–57.

Q&A Why did I need to deselect the label and then select it again?

With the insertion point appearing in the label, you could not move the label. By deselecting it and then selecting it again, the label will be selected, but there will be no insertion point.

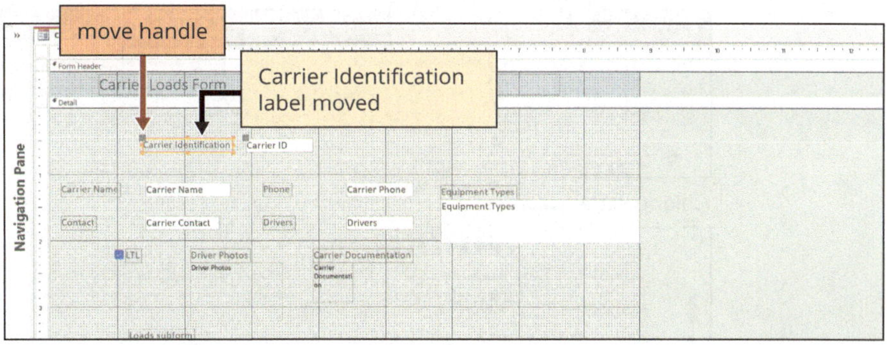

Figure 5–57

3

- Save your changes.

BTW
Moving Controls
When you are dragging a label or control, you might need to make very small movements. You can use the arrow keys on the keyboard to make fine adjustments to control placement.

To Change the Size Mode

Currently, the size mode for the Driver Photos should be Zoom, which is appropriate. If it were not and you wanted to change it, you would use the following steps.

1. Click the control containing the picture, and then click the Property Sheet button (Form Design tab | Tools group) to display the control's property sheet.
2. Click the Picture Size Mode property, and then click the Picture Size Mode property arrow.
3. Click Zoom, and then close the property sheet by clicking its Close button.

To Change Label Effects and Colors

Access allows you to change many of the characteristics of the labels in the form. You can change the border style and color, the background color, the font, and the font size. You can also apply special label effects, such as raised or sunken. The following steps change the font color of the labels and add special effects. **Why?** Modifying the appearance of the labels improves the appearance of the form.

1

- Click the Carrier Identification label to select it, if necessary.
- Select each of the remaining labels by holding down SHIFT while clicking each label. Be sure to include the label for the Loads subform (Figure 5–58).

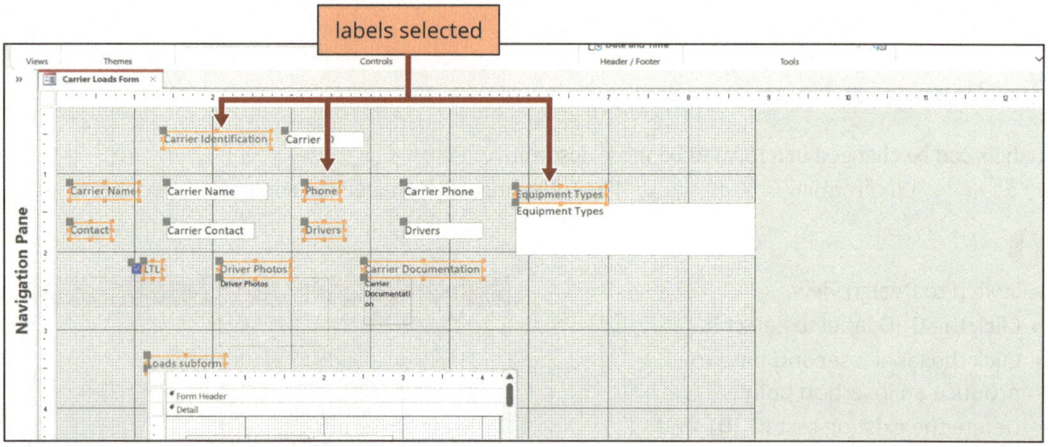

Figure 5–58

Q&A Does the order in which I select the labels make a difference?
No. The only thing that is important is that all label controls are selected when you are done.

2

- Display the Format tab.
- Click the Font Color arrow (Format tab | Font group) to display a color palette (Figure 5–59).

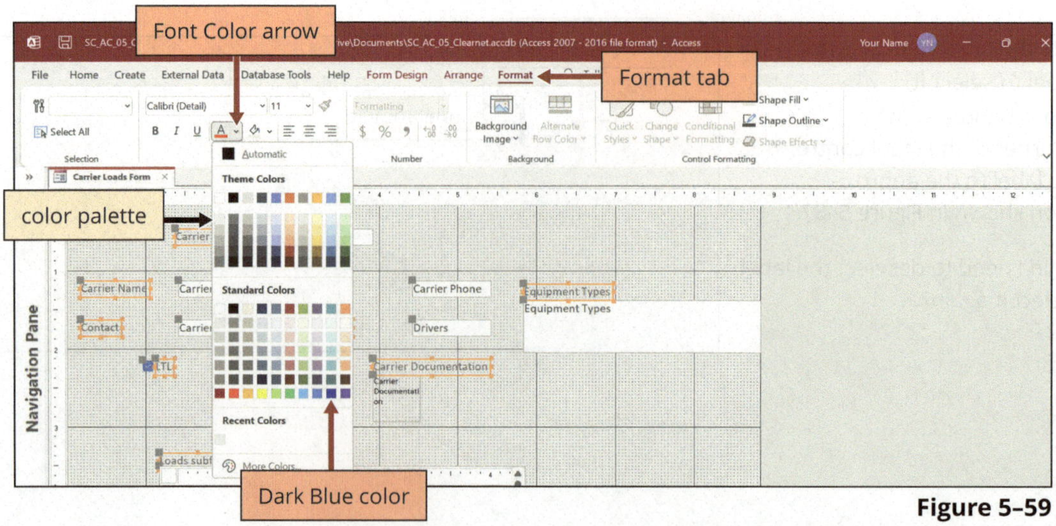

Figure 5–59

3

- In the Standard Colors section, click Dark Blue (bottom row, second position from the right) to change the font color for the labels.
- **Experiment:** Try other colors by clicking the Font Color arrow and then clicking other colors to see which colors you think would be good choices for the font. View the form to see the effect of your choice, and then return to Design view. When done, select the Dark Blue color.
- Display the Form Design tab.
- Click the Property Sheet button (Form Design tab | Tools group) to display the property sheet for the selected labels. Make sure the All tab is selected.
- Click the Border Style property box to display the Border Style property arrow, and then click the arrow to display a menu of border styles (Figure 5–60).

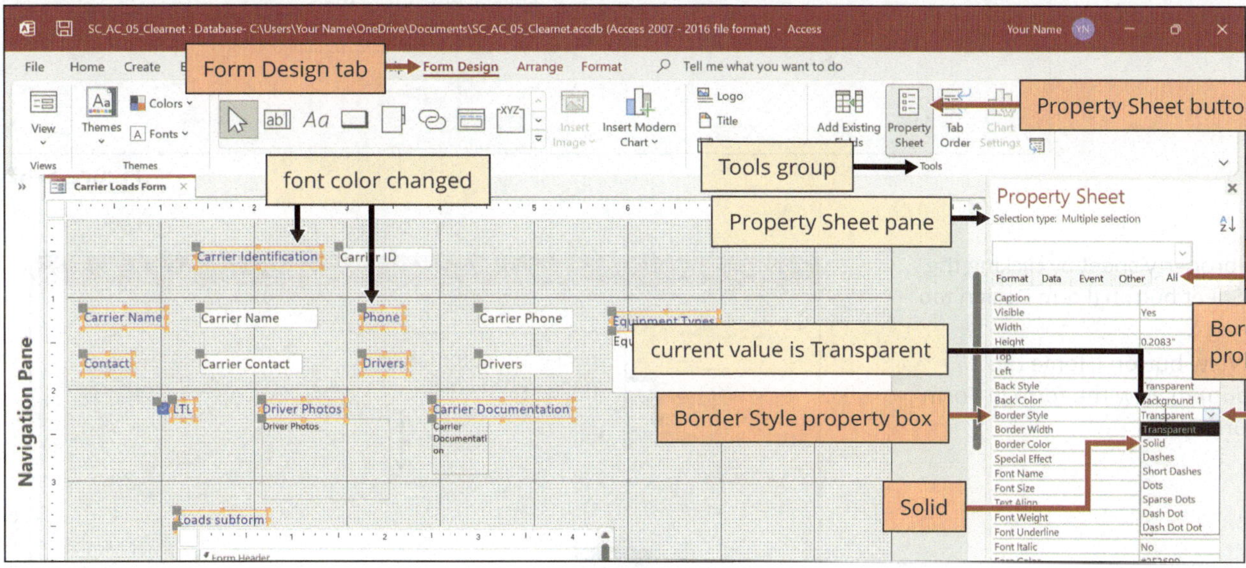

Figure 5–60

Q&A The Property Sheet pane is too small to display the property arrow. Can I change the size of the pane?
Yes. Point to the left border of the Property Sheet pane so that the pointer changes to a two-pointed arrow. You then can drag to adjust the size.

4

- Click Solid in the menu of border styles to select a border style.
- Click the Border Width property box to display the Border Width property arrow, and then click the arrow to display a menu of border widths.
- Click 3 pt to change the border width to 3 points.
- Click the Special Effect property box to display the Special Effect property arrow, and then click the arrow to display a menu of special effects (Figure 5–61).

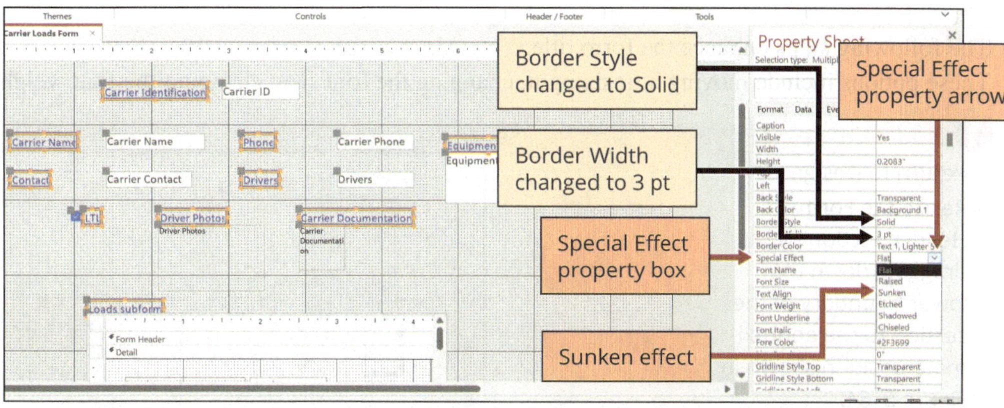

Figure 5–61

5

- Click Sunken in the menu of special effects to select this special effect (Figure 5–62).
- **Experiment:** Try other special effects. In each case, view the form to see the special effect you selected, and then return to Design view. When you are done, select Sunken for the Special Effect property.

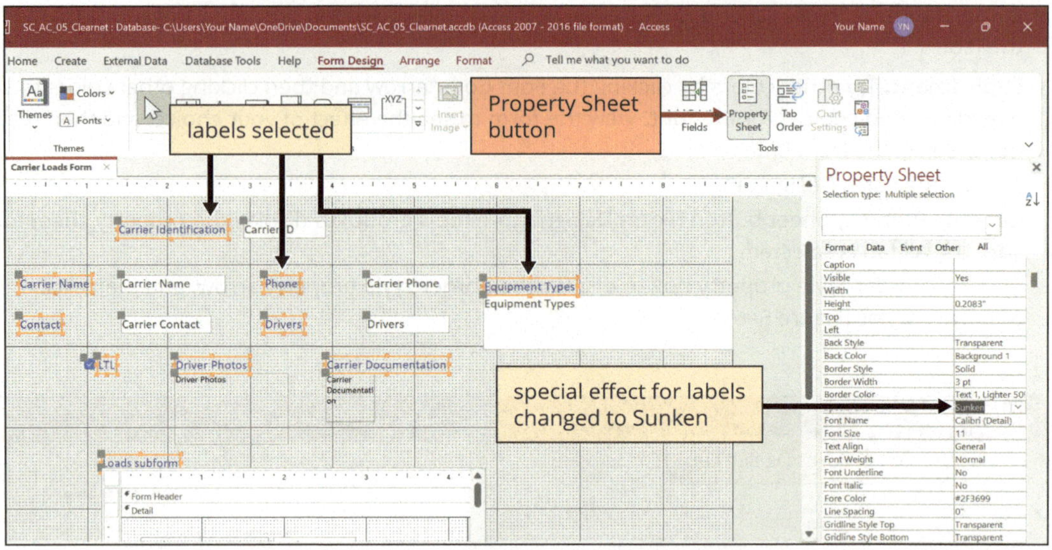

Figure 5–62

6

- Close the property sheet by clicking the Property Sheet button (Form Design tab | Tools group).
- Click the View button (Home tab | Views group) to view the form in Form view (Figure 5–63).

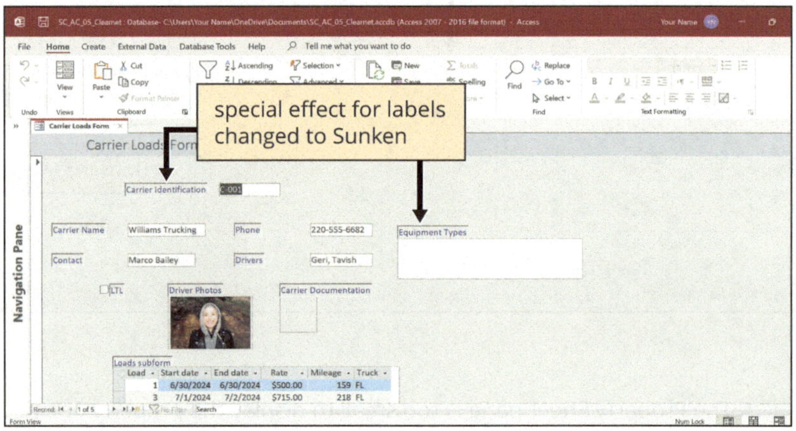

Marivi Pazos/Unsplash

Figure 5–63

To Modify the Appearance of a Form Title

The following steps enhance the form title. **Why?** You can enhance the title in a variety of ways by changing its appearance. These options include moving it, resizing it, changing the font size, changing the font weight, and changing the alignment.

1

- Return to Design view.
- Resize the Form Header section by dragging down the lower boundary of the section to the approximate position shown in Figure 5–64.

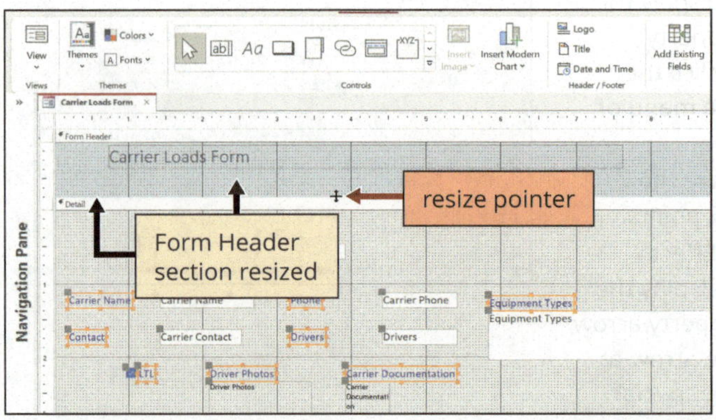

Figure 5–64

2

- Click the control containing the form title to select it.
- Drag the lower-right sizing handle to resize the control to the approximate size shown in Figure 5–65.

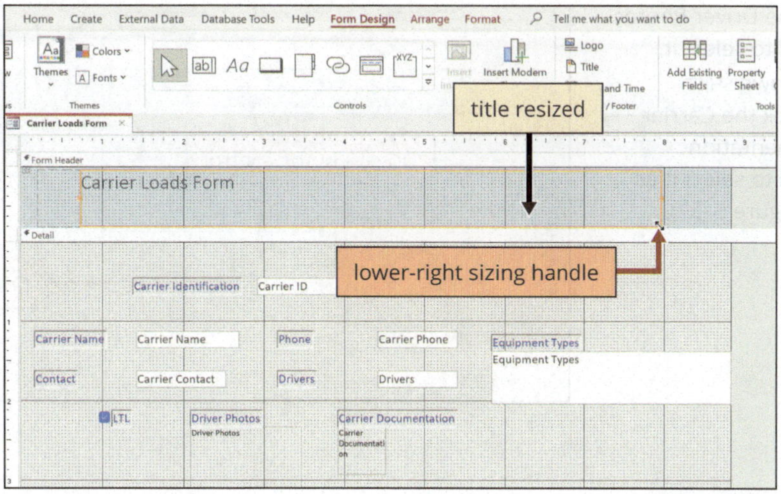

Figure 5–65

3

- Click the Property Sheet button (Form Design tab | Tools group) to display the control's property sheet.
- Click the Font Size property box, click the Font Size property arrow, and then click 28 to change the font size.
- In a similar fashion, change the Text Align property value to Distribute and the Font Weight property value to Semi-bold (Figure 5–66).

4

- Close the property sheet.

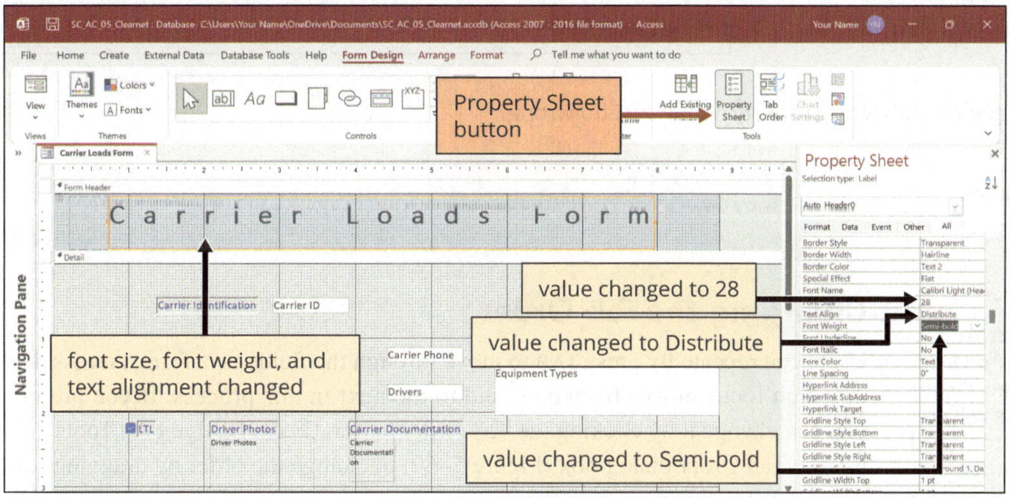

Figure 5–66

Other Ways

1. Enter font size value in Font Size box to set font size

To Change a Tab Stop

Users can repeatedly press TAB to move through the controls on the form; however, they should bypass the Driver Photos and Documentation controls because users do not enter data into these fields. To omit these controls from the tab stop sequence, the following steps change the value of the Tab Stop property for the controls from Yes to No. **Why?** Changing the Tab Stop property for these fields to No removes them from the Tab Stop sequence.

1

- Click the Driver Photos control to select it.
- Hold down SHIFT and click the Carrier Documentation control to select it as well (Figure 5–67).

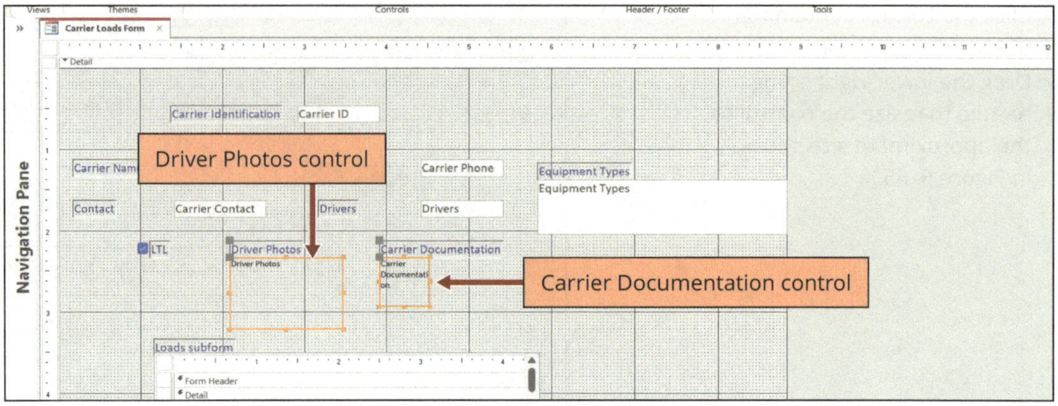

Figure 5–67

2

- Click the Property Sheet button (Form Design tab | Tools group) to display the property sheet.
- Make sure the All tab (Property Sheet) is selected, scroll down until the Tab Stop property appears, click the Tab Stop property, click the Tab Stop property arrow, and then click No to instruct Access to skip the Driver Photos and Carrier Documentation fields in the tab sequence (Figure 5–68).
- Close the property sheet.

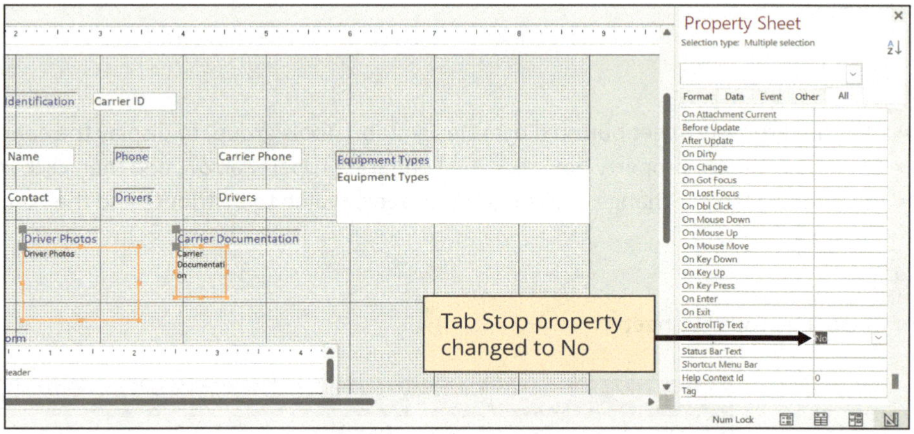

Figure 5–68

Q&A I do not see the Tab Stop property. What did I do wrong?

You clicked the controls for the labels, not the field controls.

- Save your changes.

BTW

Auto Order Button

If you click the Auto Order button in the Tab Order dialog box, Access will create a top-to-bottom and left-to-right tab order.

Changing the Tab Order

Users can repeatedly press TAB to move through the fields on a form. Access determines the order in which focus moves from one field to the next in this process. If you prefer a different order, you can change it by clicking the Tab Order button (Form Design tab | Tools group). You then can use the Tab Order dialog box (Figure 5–69) to change the order by dragging rows (fields) to their desired order as indicated in the dialog box.

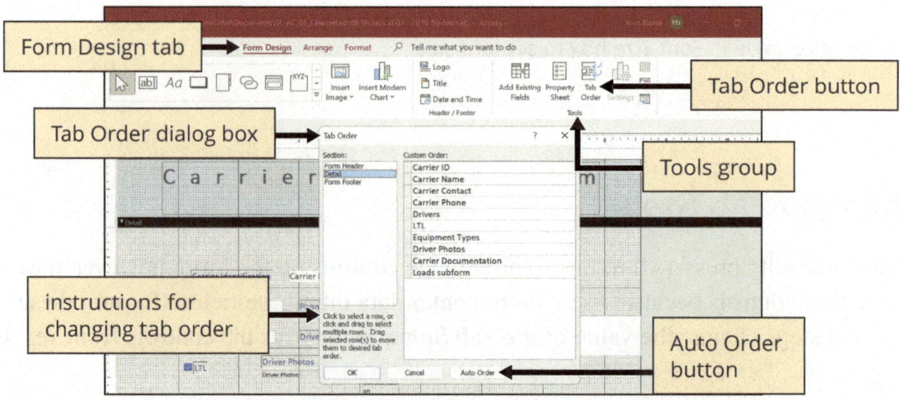

Figure 5–69

To Use the Form

The form gives you flexibility in selecting both carriers and their loads. **Why?** You can use the Navigation buttons at the bottom of the screen to move among carriers. You can use the Navigation buttons in the subform to move among the loads currently shown on the screen. The following steps use the form to display the desired data.

1

- Click the View button (Form Design tab | Views group) to view the form in Form view.
- In the form, navigate to the fifth record, Truck-n-Go Inc.
- Right-click the Carrier Documentation field to display a shortcut menu (Figure 5–70).

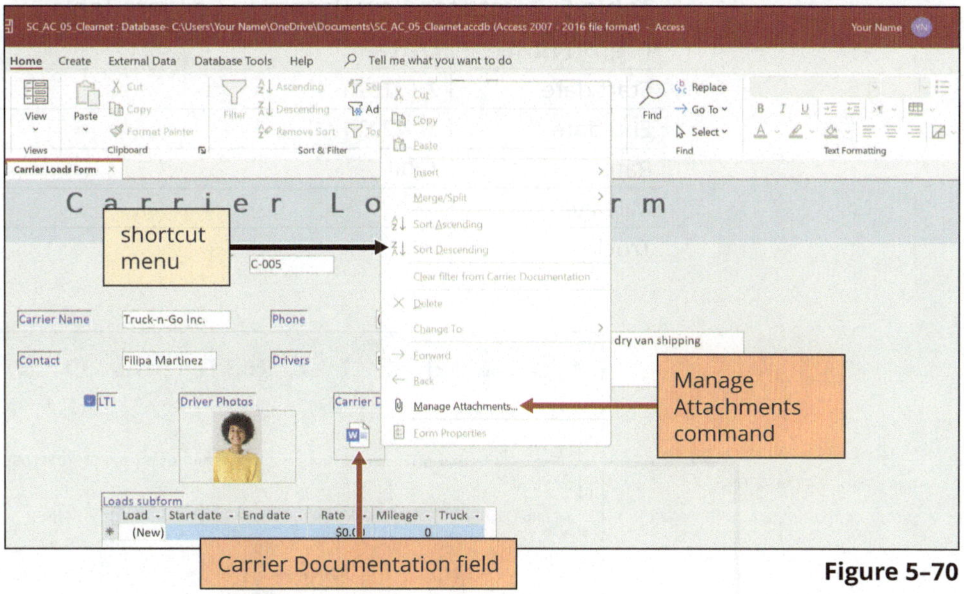

Figure 5–70

2

- Click the Manage Attachments command on the shortcut menu to display the Attachments dialog box (Figure 5–71).

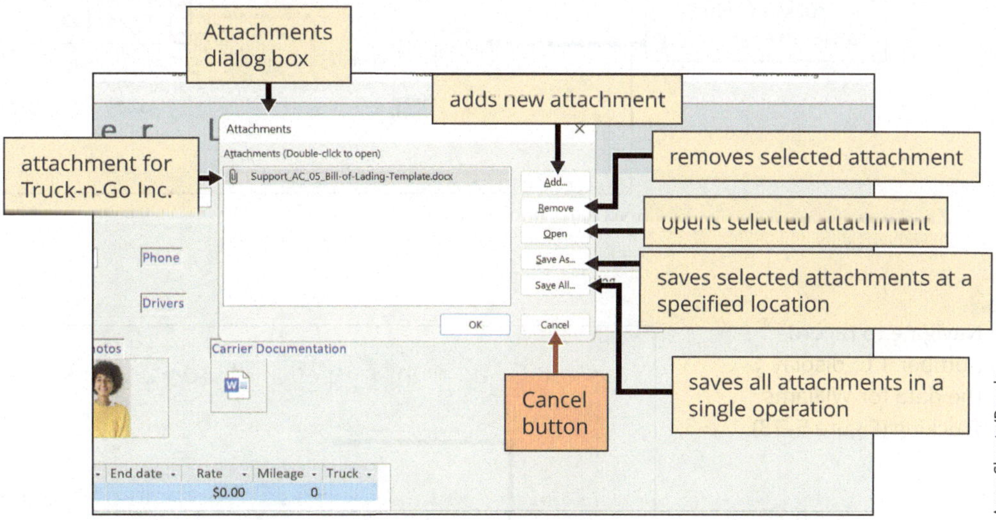

Figure 5–71

Q&A How do I use this dialog box?

Select an attachment and click the Open button to view the attachment in a compatible application. Click the Add button to add a new attachment or the Remove button to remove the selected attachment. By clicking the Save As button, you can save the selected attachment as a file in whatever location you specify. You can save all attachments at once by clicking the Save All button.

- **Experiment:** If you have a compatible application, such as Microsoft Word, Word Online, Google Docs, or Apple Pages, click the Open button to open and view the attachment. When finished, close the compatible application.

Other Ways

1. Double-click Attachments control to open an attachment

3

- Click the Cancel button to close the Attachments dialog box.
- In the Loads subform, click the Start date field next to the word, "(New)", to enter a new load.
- Enter the data listed in Table 5–2, pressing TAB to move from column to column (Figure 5–72). After completing the record, press TAB once to move to the next row.

Table 5–2 Data for New Record in Carriers Table

Field Name	Data
Start date	**7/9/2024**
End date	**7/9/2024**
Rate	**1200**
Mileage	**371**
Truck	**RF**

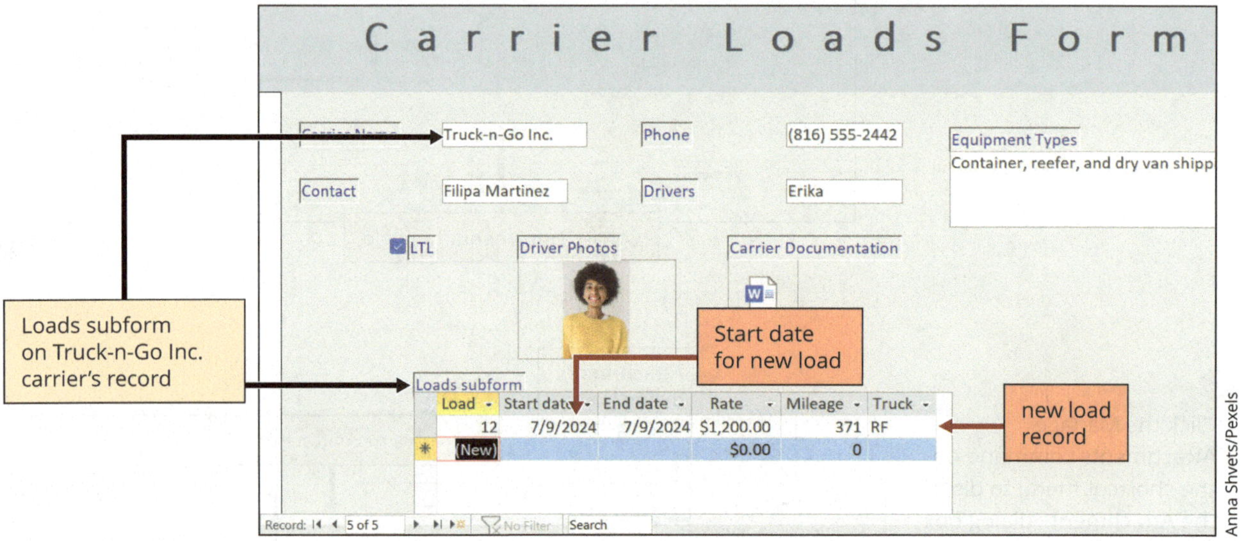

Figure 5–72

4

- Navigate to record number 1 to display the data for Williams Trucking (Figure 5–73).

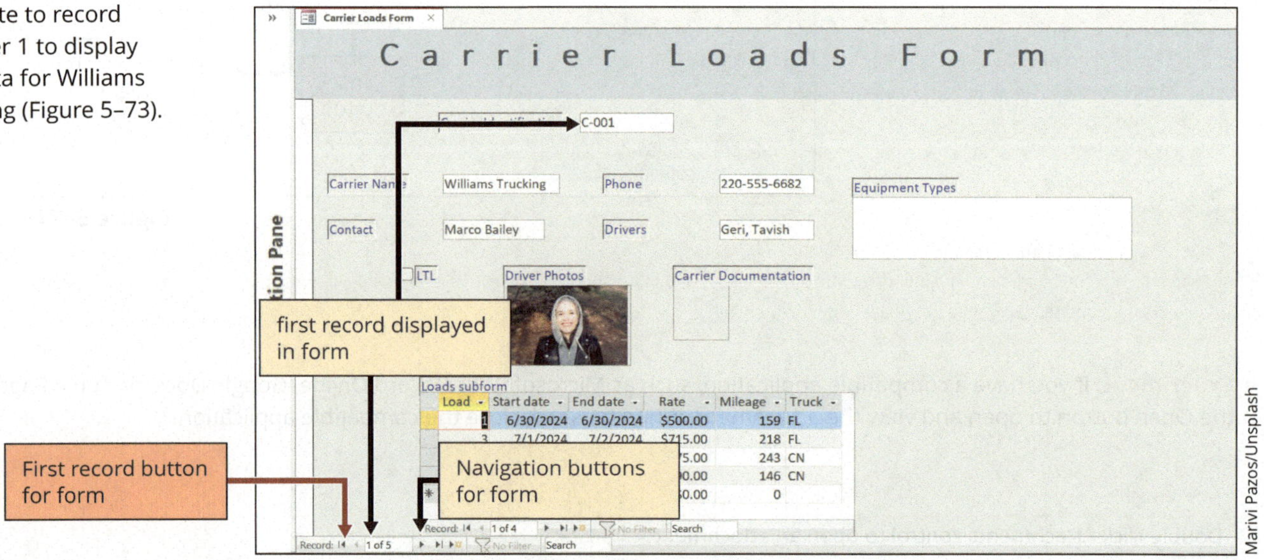

Figure 5–73

5

- Click the subform's Next record button once to highlight the carrier's load on 7/1/2024 (Figure 5–74).

6

- Close the form. If you are prompted to save your changes, click Yes.

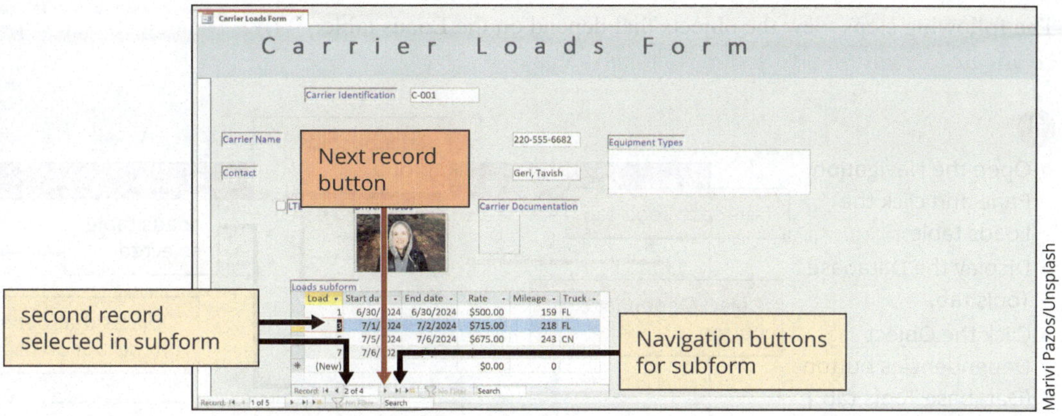

Figure 5–74

Navigation in the Form

The previous steps illustrated ways you work with a main form and subform. Clicking the Navigation buttons for the main form moves to a different carrier. Clicking the Navigation buttons for the subform moves to different loads of the carrier that currently appears in the main form. The following are other navigation actions you can take within the form:

1. To move from the last field in the main form to the first field in the subform, press TAB. To move back to the last field in the main form, press SHIFT+TAB.
2. To move from any field in the subform to the first field in the next record's main form, press CTRL+TAB.
3. To switch from the main form to the subform using touch or the mouse, click anywhere in the subform. To switch back to the main form, click any control in the main form. Clicking the background of the main form will not cause the switch to occur.

BTW
Navigation
To go to a specific record in the main form, enter the record number in the Current Record box for the main form. To go to a specific record in the subform, enter the record number in the Current Record box for the subform.

Break Point: If you wish to take a break, this is a good place to do so. You can quit Access now. To resume at a later time, start Access, open the database called SC_AC_05_Clearnet.accdb, and continue following the steps from this location forward.

Object Dependencies

In Access, some objects depend on other objects. For example, a report depends on the table or query on which it is based. That is, a change to the structure of the table or query could affect the report, so in that sense the report depends on the table or query. If you delete a field from the table, for instance, any report based on that table that uses the deleted field would no longer be valid.

You can view information on dependencies between database objects. Viewing a list of objects that depend on a specific object helps in the maintenance of a database and avoids errors when changes are made to the objects involved in the dependency. For example, many items, such as queries and forms, use data from the Loads table and thus depend on the Loads table. By clicking the Object Dependencies button, you can see what items are based on the object. You also can see the items on which the object depends.

If you are unfamiliar with a database, viewing object dependencies can help you better understand the structure of the database. Viewing object dependencies is especially useful after you have made changes to the structure of tables. If you know which reports, forms, and queries depend on a table, you will be better able to make changes to a table without negatively affecting the related database objects.

To View Object Dependencies

The following steps view the objects that depend on the Loads table. **Why?** The objects that depend on the Loads table might be affected by any change you make to this table.

1

- Open the Navigation Pane and click the Loads table.
- Display the Database Tools tab.
- Click the Object Dependencies button (Database Tools tab | Relationships group) to display the Object Dependencies pane.

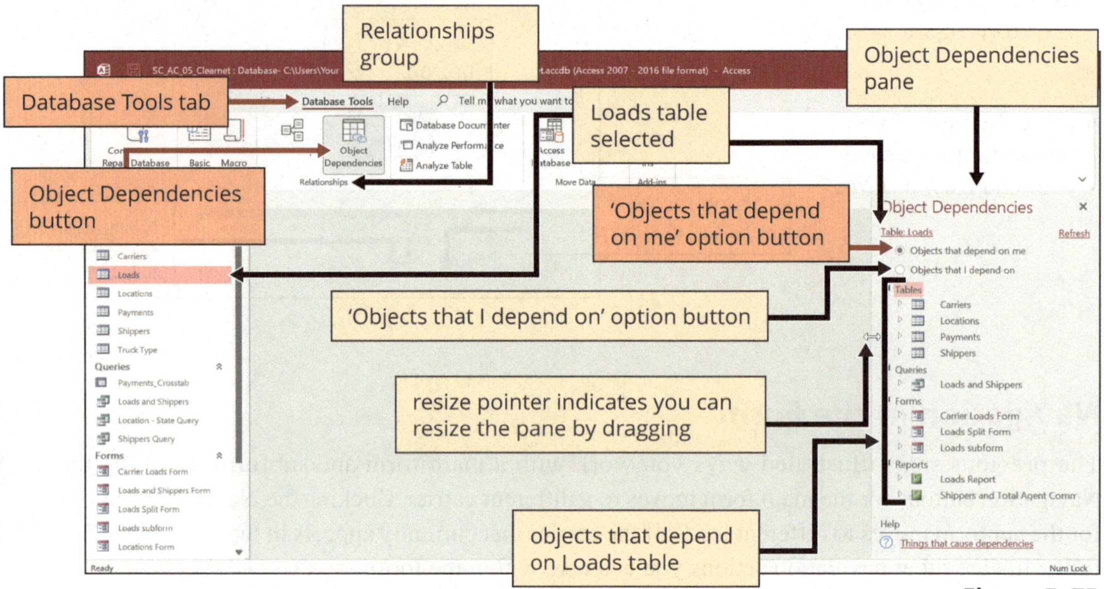

Figure 5–75

Q&A The Object Dependencies pane is squished on the side of my screen. How do I make it bigger?

Point to the left edge of the Object Dependencies pane until you see a two-pointed resize arrow. Press and drag the resize pointer to the left to enlarge the pane.

- If necessary, click the 'Objects that depend on me' option button to select it (Figure 5–75). The 'me' in this case is the selected object, the Loads table.
- **Experiment:** Click the 'Objects that I depend on' option button to see the objects on which the Loads table depends. Then try both options for other objects in the database.

2

- Close the Object Dependencies pane by clicking the Object Dependencies button (Database Tools tab | Relationships group) a second time.

BTW

Date Fields in Queries

To test for the current date in a query, type Date() in the Criteria row of the appropriate column. Typing <Date() in the Criteria row for the Dropoff Date, for example, finds those carriers who are scheduled to drop off a load today.

BTW

Long Text Fields in Queries

When you query long text fields, consider alternative spellings and phrases. For example, Computer Science also can be referenced as CS.

Date/Time, Long Text, and Yes/No Fields in Queries

By specifying load dates using Date/Time fields, Clearnet can run queries to find carriers' loads before or after a certain date. Similarly, management can search for carriers with specific equipment by adding Long Text and Yes/No fields.

To use Date/Time fields in queries, you simply type the dates, including the slashes. To search for records with a specific date, you must type the date. You also can use comparison operators. To find all the appointments whose date is after June 1, 2024, for example, you would type >6/1/2024 as the criterion.

You can also use Long Text fields in queries by searching for records that contain a specific word or phrase in the Long Text field. To do so, you use wildcards. For example, to find all the carriers who have the word, reefer, somewhere in the Equipment Types field, you type *reefer* as the criterion. The asterisk at the beginning indicates that any characters can appear before the word, reefer. The asterisk at the end indicates that any characters can appear after the word, reefer.

To use Yes/No fields in queries, type the word, Yes, or the word, No, as the criterion. The following steps create and run queries that use Date/Time, Long Text, and Yes/No fields.

To Use Date/Time, Long Text, and Yes/No Fields in a Query

The following steps use Date/Time, Long Text, and Yes/No fields in queries to search for carriers and loads that meet specific criteria. **Why?** Clearnet wants to find carrier loads dropped off after 7/3/2024; who have the word, reefer, in their equipment type field; or who accept LTL loads.

1

- Create a query for the Carriers and Loads tables and include the Carrier Name, Dropoff Date, Equipment Types, and LTL fields in the query (Figure 5–76).

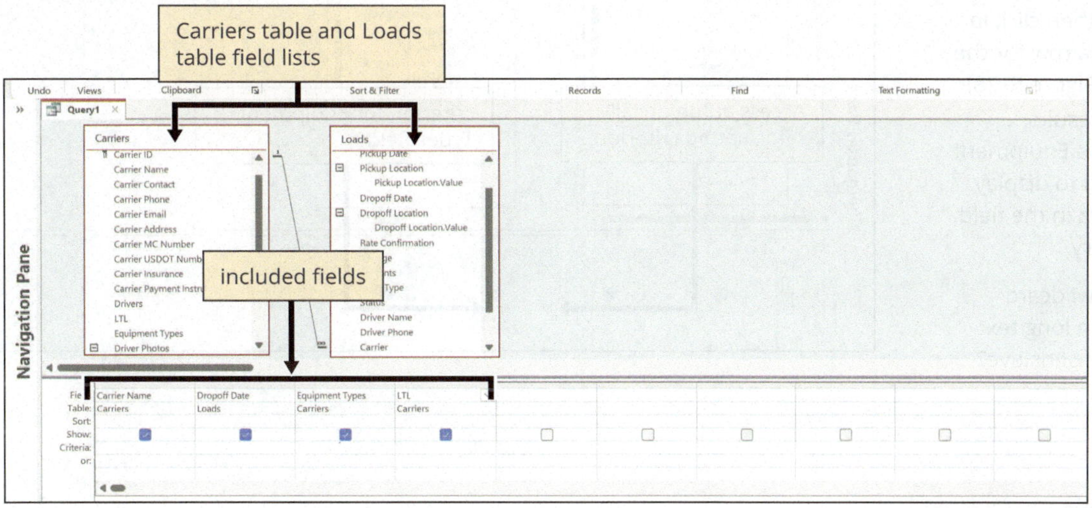

Figure 5–76

2

- Click the Criteria row under the Dropoff Date field, type **>7/3/2024** as the criterion, and then click in the Criteria row for the Equipment Types field (Figure 5–77).
- View the results.

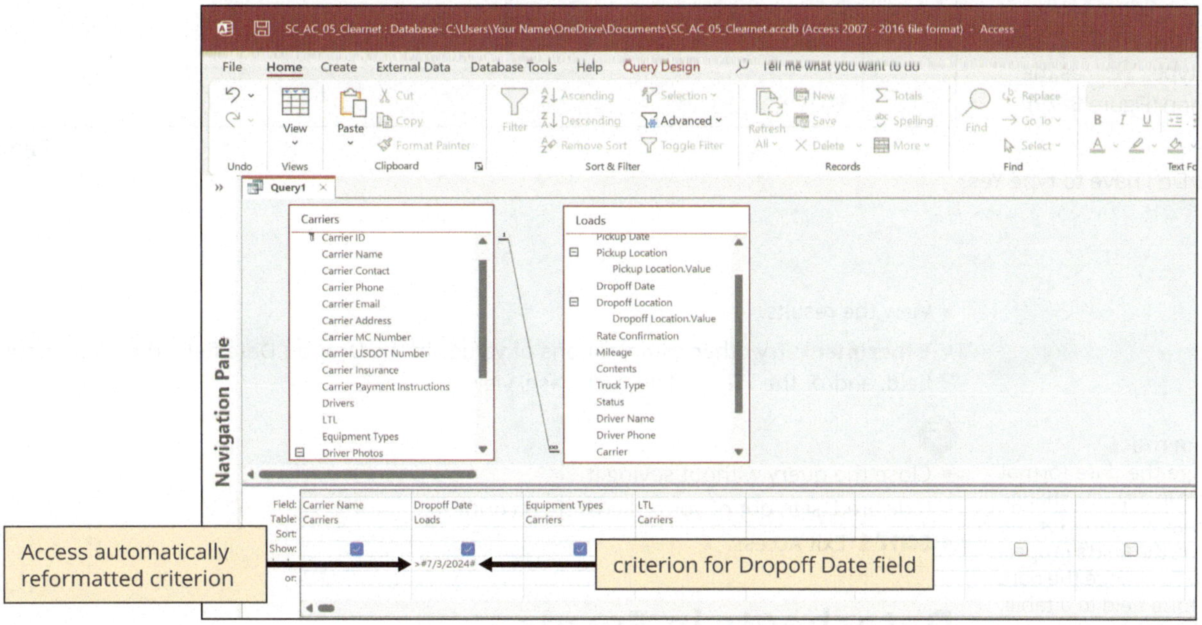

Figure 5–77

Q&A Why does the date have hash signs (#) around it?

This is the date format in Access. Access reformats the date appropriately when you click another Criteria cell.

3

- Click the View button to return to Design view.
- Erase the criterion in the Dropoff Date field.
- Click the Criteria row under the Equipment Types field, type ***reefer*** as the criterion, and then click in the Criteria row for the LTL field (Figure 5–78).
- View the results. Expand the Equipment Types field to display all the data in the field, if necessary.

Q&A Are wildcard searches in long text fields case-sensitive?
No.

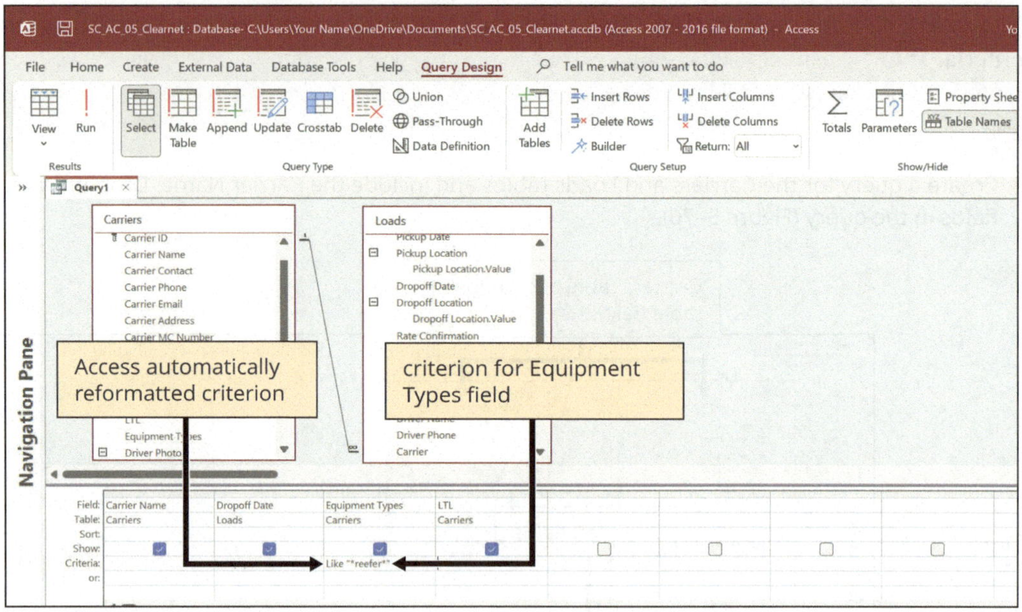

Figure 5–78

4

- Click the View button to return to Design view.
- Erase the criterion in the Equipment Types field.
- Click the Criteria row under the LTL field, and then type **Yes** as the criterion (Figure 5–79).

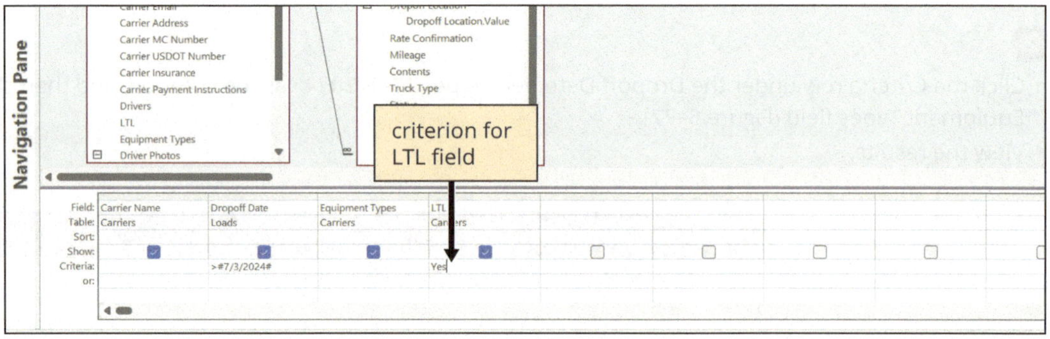

Figure 5–79

Q&A Do I have to type Yes?
You could also type True.

- View the results.
- **Experiment:** Try other combinations of values in the Dropoff Date field, the Equipment Types field, and/or the LTL field. In each case, view the results.

5

- Close the query without saving it.
- If desired, sign out of your Microsoft account.
- sam Exit Access.

BTW
Date Formats
To change the date format for a date in a query, change the format property for the field using the field's property sheet. To change the date format for a field in a table, open the table in Design view and change the format property for the field.

Datasheets in Forms

Subforms are not available in forms created in Layout view, but you can achieve similar functionality to subforms by including datasheets. Like subforms, datasheets contain data for the "many" table in the relationship.

Creating a Simple Form with a Datasheet

If you create a simple form for a table that is the "one" table in a one-to-many relationship, Access automatically includes the "many" table in a datasheet within the form. If you create a simple form for the Carriers table, for example, Access will include the Loads table in a datasheet within the form, as in Figure 5–80. The loads in the datasheet will be the loads of the carrier currently on the screen, in this case, Williams Trucking.

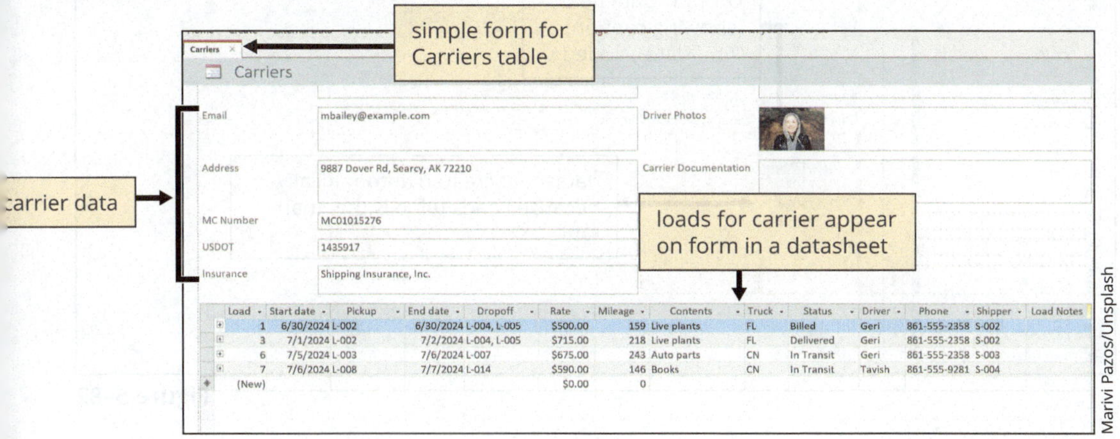

Figure 5–80

To Create a Simple Form with a Datasheet

To create a simple form with a datasheet, you would use the following steps.

1. Select the table in the Navigation Pane that is the "one" part of a one-to-many relationship.
2. Display the Create tab.
3. Click the Form button (Create tab | Forms group).

Creating a Form with a Datasheet in Layout View

You can create a form with a datasheet in Layout view. To create a form based on the Carriers table that includes the loads records, which are stored in the Loads table, you would first use the field list to add the required fields from the "one" table. In Figure 5–81, fields from the Carriers table have been added to the form.

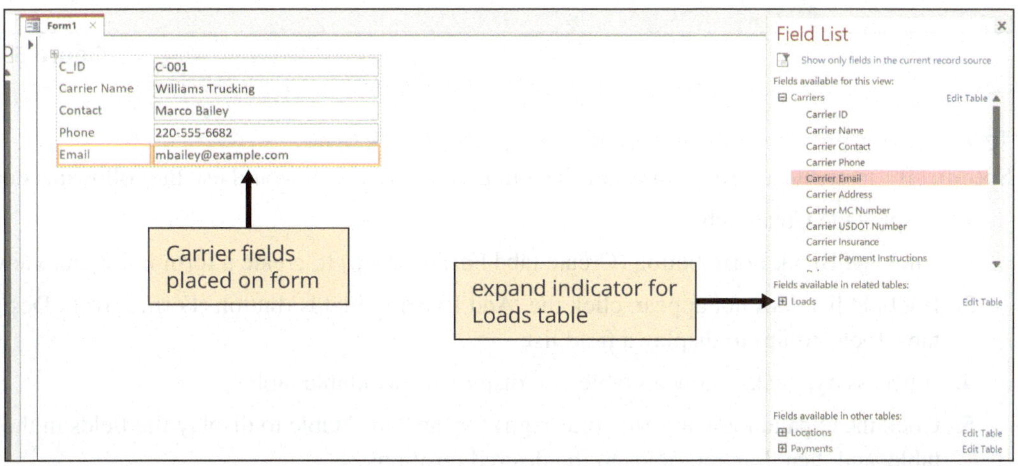

Figure 5–81

BTW

Distributing a Document

Instead of printing and distributing a hard copy of a document, you can distribute the document electronically. Options include sending the document via email; posting it on cloud storage (such as OneDrive) and sharing the file with others; posting it on a social networking site, blog, or other website; and sharing a link associated with an online location of the document. You also can create and share a PDF or XPS image of the document, so that users can view the file in Acrobat Reader or XPS Viewer instead of in Access.

BTW

Placing Fields on a Datasheet

Be sure to select the datasheet before adding additional fields to it. When dragging a field from the field list to the datasheet, drag the field to the right boundary of the previous field. The pointer will change to show that you are placing a control and you will see a vertical line.

Next, you would use the field list to add a single field from the "many" table, as shown in Figure 5–82, in which the Dropoff Date field has been added. Access will automatically create a datasheet containing this field.

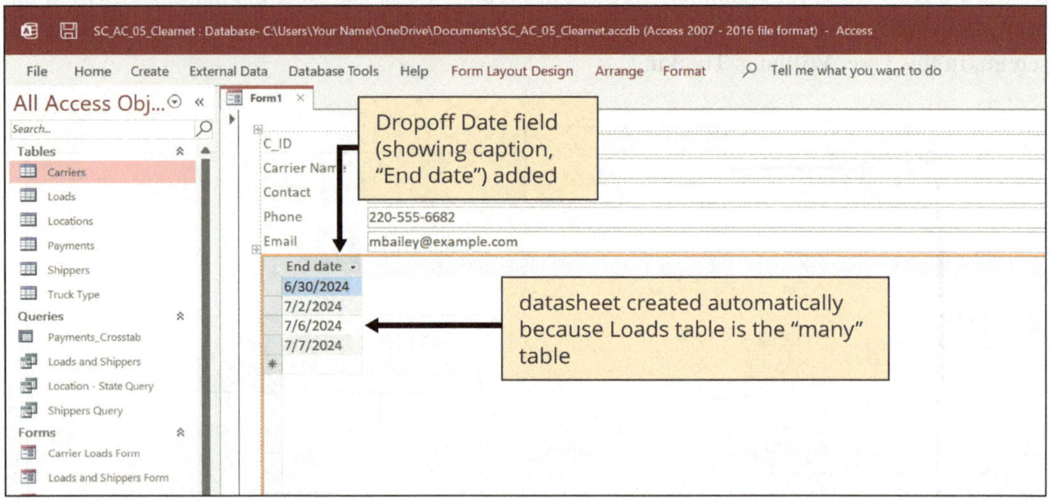

Figure 5–82

Finally, you would click the datasheet to select it and then use the field list to add the other fields from the "many" table that you want to include in the form, as shown in Figure 5–83.

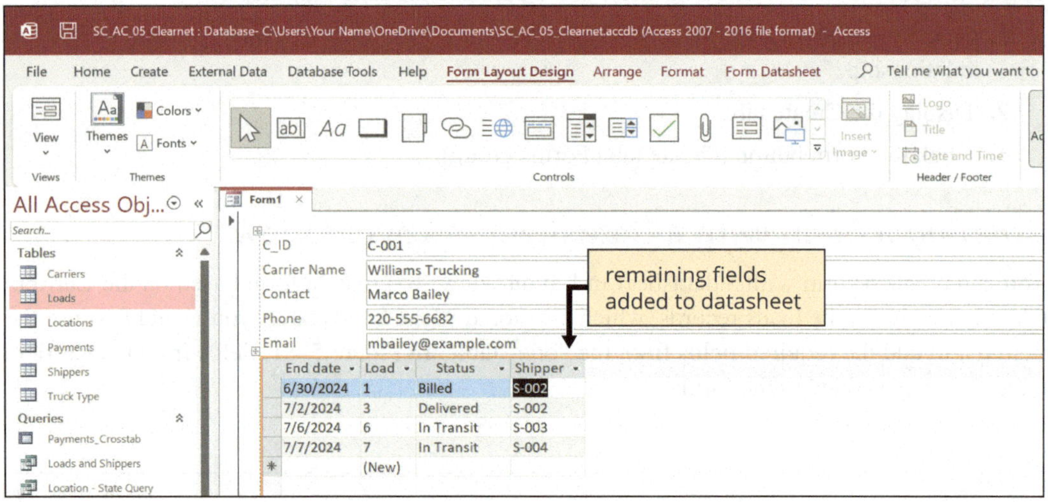

Figure 5–83

To Create a Form with a Datasheet in Layout View

Specifically, to create a form with a datasheet in Layout view, you would use the following steps.

1. Display the Create tab.
2. Click the Blank Form button (Create tab | Forms group) to create a form in Layout view.
3. If a field list does not appear, click the 'Add Existing Fields' button (Form Layout Design tab | Tools group) to display a field list.
4. If necessary, click 'Show all tables' to display the available tables.
5. Click the expand indicator (the plus sign) for the "one" table to display the fields in the table, and then drag the fields to the desired positions.

6. Click the expand indicator for the "many" table and drag the first field for the datasheet onto the form to create the datasheet.
7. Select the datasheet and drag the remaining fields for the datasheet from the field list to the desired locations in the datasheet.

Consider This

Can you modify the form so the complete labels for the carrier fields appear?

Yes. Click any of the labels for the carrier fields to select the label, and then click the Select Column button (Arrange tab | Rows & Columns group) to select all the labels. You can then drag the right boundary of any of the labels to resize all the labels simultaneously.

Creating a Multiple-Table Form Based on the Many Table

All the forms discussed so far in this module were based on the "one" table, in this case, the Carriers table. The records from the "many" table were included in a subform. You can also create a multiple-table form based on the "many" table, in this case, the Loads table. Such a form is shown in Figure 5–84.

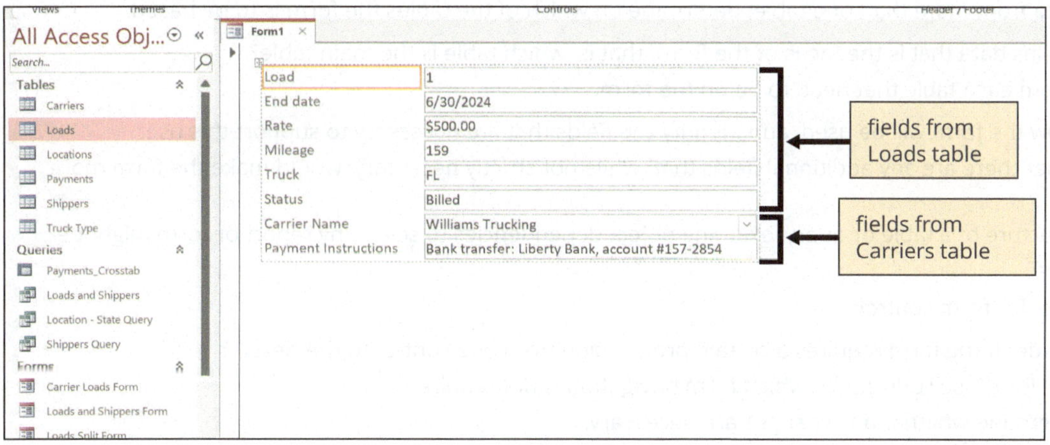

Figure 5–84

In this form, the Load, End date, Rate, Mileage, Truck, and Status fields are from the Loads table. The Carrier Name and Payment Instructions fields are found in the Carriers table and are included in the form to help identify the carrier whose load is appearing in the upper fields.

To Create a Multiple-Table Form Based on the Many Table

To create a multiple-table form based on the "many" table, you would use the following steps.

1. Click the Blank Form button (Create tab | Forms group) to create a form in Layout view.
2. If a field list does not appear, click the 'Add Existing Fields' button on the Design tab to display a field list.
3. Drag the fields for the "many" table to the desired positions.
4. Drag the fields for the "one" table to the desired positions.

Summary

In this module you have learned to use Yes/No, Long Text, and Attachment data types; create and use an input mask; create a form and add a subform; enhance the look of the controls on a form; change tab order and stops; use a form with a subform; create queries involving Yes/No, Date/Time, and Long Text fields; view object dependencies; and create forms containing datasheets in Layout view.

Consider This: Plan Ahead

What decisions will you need to make when creating your own forms?

Use these guidelines as you complete the assignments in this module and create your own forms outside of this class.

1. Determine the purpose of the fields to see if they need special data types.
    a. If the field only contains values such as Yes and No or True and False, it should have Yes/No as the data type.
    b. If the field contains an extended description, it should have Long Text as the data type.
    c. If the field contains a picture and you need to conserve storage space, its data type should be Attachment.
    d. If the field contains attached files, its data type should be Attachment.
2. Determine whether the form requires data from more than one table.
3. If the form requires data from more than one table, determine the relationship between the tables.
    a. Identify one-to-many relationships.
    b. For each relationship, identify the "one" table and the "many" table.
4. If the form requires data from more than one table, determine on which of the tables the form is to be based.
    a. Which table contains data that is the focus of the form, that is, which table is the main table?
5. Determine the fields from each table that need to be on the form.
    a. Decide exactly how the form will be used, and identify the fields that are necessary to support this use.
    b. Determine whether there are any additional fields that, while not strictly necessary, would make the form more functional.
6. When changing the structure of a table or query, examine object dependencies to see if any report or form might be impacted by the change.
7. Determine the tab order for form controls.
    a. Change the tab order if the form requires a certain progression from one control to the next.
    b. Remove tab stops for those controls for which form navigation is not required.
8. Review the form to determine whether any changes are necessary.
    a. Are there visual changes, such as different colors or a larger font, that would make the form easier to use?
    b. Does the form have a similar look to other forms in the database?
    c. Does the form conform to the organization's standards?

Consider This

How should you submit solutions to critical thinking questions in the assignments?

Every assignment in this course contains one or more critical thinking questions. These questions require you to think beyond the assigned database. Present your responses to the questions in the format required by your instructor. Possible formats may include one or more of these options: write the answer; create a document that contains the answer; present your answer to the class; discuss your answer in a group; record the answer as audio or video using a webcam, smartphone, or portable media player; or post answers on a blog, wiki, or website.

Student Assignments

Apply Your Knowledge

Reinforce the skills and apply the concepts you learned in this module.

Adding Phone Number, Yes/No, Long Text, and Picture Attachment Fields, Using an Input Mask Wizard, and Querying Long Text Fields

Note: To complete this assignment, you will be required to use the Data Files. Please contact your instructor for information about accessing the Data Files.

Instructions: Start Access. Open the database, SC_AC_05-2.accdb, which is located in the Data Files folder. Enable the content.

Perform the following tasks:

1. Save the database using the file name, SC_AC_05_City-Tutoring. Enable the content. Open the Counselors table in Design view.
2. Add the Phone Number, CPR Certification, Other Skills, and Photo fields to the Counselors table structure, as shown in Figure 5–85. Create an input mask for the new Phone Number field. When building the mask, instruct Access to store the phone number data without symbols. CPR Certification is a field that indicates whether the counselor has completed a CPR (Cardiopulmonary Resuscitation) and first aid training course and passed the course exam.

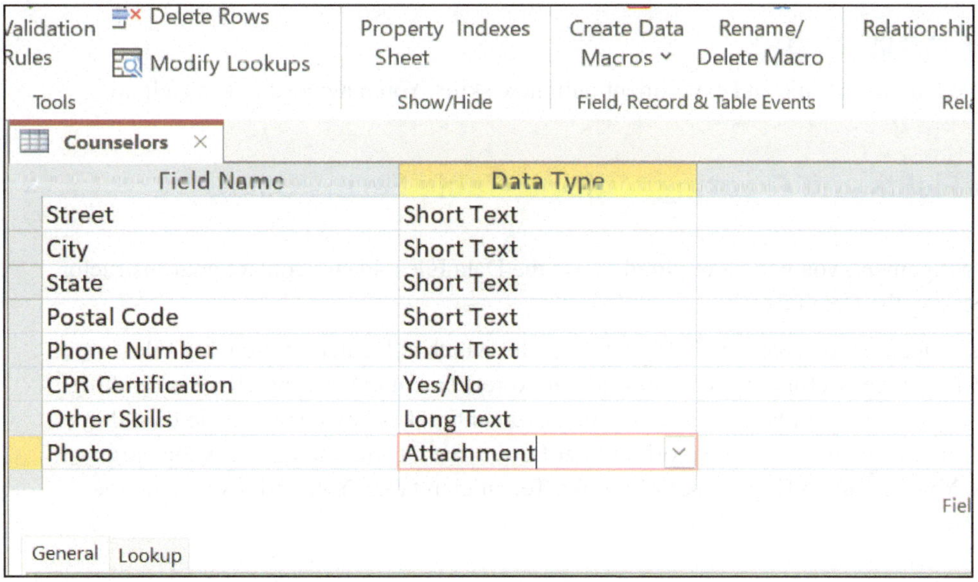

Figure 5–85

Continued on next page

3. Add the data shown in Table 5–3 to the Counselors table. Adjust the row and column spacing to best fit the data. Save the changes to the layout of the table.

Table 5–3 Data for Counselors Table

Counselor Number	Phone Number	CPR Certification	Other Skills	Photo
103	(615) 555-4648	Yes	Taught high school math for 10 years	Support_AC_05_Enrique.jpg
110	(931) 555-9105	Yes	Has a bachelor's degree in biology	Support_AC_05_Rachel.jpg
114	(423) 555-8589	No	Worked as an accountant for 4 years	Support_AC_05_Chou.jpg
120	(931) 555-5498	No	Working on a bachelor's degree in English	Support_AC_05_Chris.jpg

4. If requested to do so by your instructor, change the phone number for counselor number 103 to your phone number.
5. Query the Counselors table to find all counselors who have CPR Certification. Include the Counselor Number, Last Name, First Name, and Phone Number fields in the query result. Save the query as Apply 5 Step 5 Query.
6. Query the Counselors table to find all counselors with a bachelor's degree or pursuing a bachelor's degree who have completed the CPR Certification. Also include the Counselor Number, Last Name, and First Name fields in the query result. Save the query as Apply 5 Step 6 Query.
7. Submit the revised database in the format specified by your instructor.
8. **Consider This:** What value did you enter in the criteria row for the CPR Certification field in the query in Step 5 above? Could you have entered the criteria differently? If yes, then how else could you enter the criteria to find the information?

Extend Your Knowledge

Extend the skills you learned in this module and experiment with new skills. You may need to use Help to complete the assignment.

Adding Hyperlink Fields and Creating Multiple-Table Forms Using Layout View

Note: To complete this assignment, you will be required to use the Data Files. Please contact your instructor for information about accessing the Data Files.

Instructions: Start Access. Open the database, SC_AC_05-3.accdb, which is located in the Data Files folder. Feel Better, a physical therapy clinic, is being closed due to retirements. A nearby clinic is thinking of buying the practice to expand its client base. Before the management makes any decisions on this, they need more information about the technicians who work at Feel Better. Each technician has a webpage about their qualifications. You will add a Hyperlink field to the Technician table. You will also create the form shown in Figure 5–86.

Perform the following tasks:

1. Save the database using the file name, SC_AC_05_Physical-Therapists. Enable the content. Open the Technician table in Design view and add a field with the Hyperlink data type. Insert the field after the Earnings YTD field. Use Website as the name of the field.
2. Switch to Datasheet view and add data for the Website field to the first record. Use your school's URL as the data. If necessary, resize the column so the complete URL is displayed. Close the table.
3. If requested to do so by your instructor, enter your name as the technician name for the first record of the Technician table.

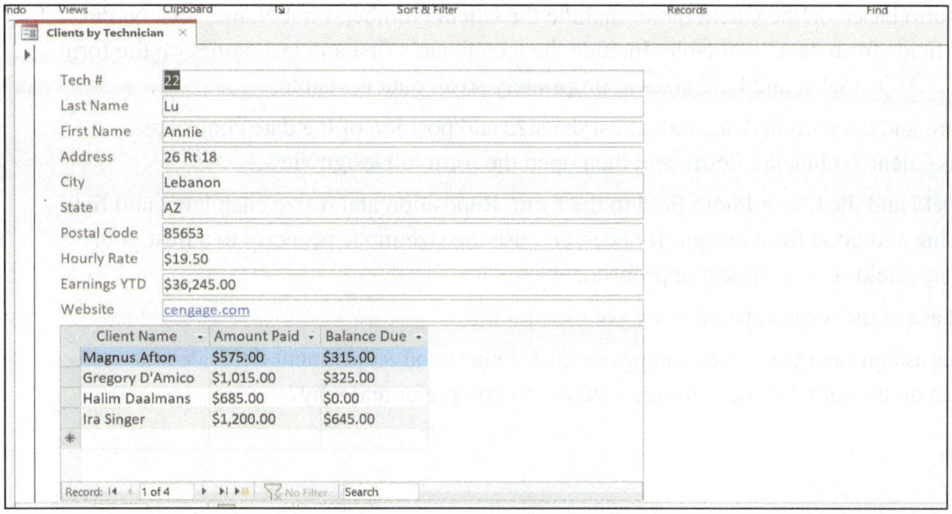

Figure 5–86

4. Use Layout view to create the new multiple-table form shown in Figure 5–86. The Client table appears as a subform in the form. The Technician table is the "one" table in the form. Use Clients by Technician as the form name.
5. Submit the revised database in the format specified by your instructor.
6. **Consider This:** How would you add a required field for an email address to the Technician table?

Expand Your World

Create a solution, which uses cloud and web technologies, by learning and investigating on your own from general guidance.

Note: To complete this assignment, you will be required to use the Data Files. Please contact your instructor for information about accessing the Data Files.

Instructions: Start Access. Open the database, SC_AC_05-4.accdb, which is located in the Data Files folder, and enable the content. This file is a database of clients and technicians. To understand the difference between Attachment and OLE Object data types, you will add one of each of these fields to the Clients table. Then, you will insert images that you download from the Internet. Finally, you will create a multiple-table form for the database.

Perform the following tasks:

1. Access any website containing royalty-free images and search the images to find four different photos of computers and related devices. As a suggestion, you might choose a desktop, laptop, printer, and gaming device.
2. Save these images to a storage location of your choice.
3. Save the database using the file name, SC_AC_05_Solutions-IT-Support. Enable the content. Open the Client table in Design view. Add a Device Image field with an OLE Object data type. Add a Client Photo field with an Attachment data type. Assign the caption, Photo, to the Client Photo field. The fields should appear after the Technician Number field.
4. Use the techniques shown in the module to add the photos of computers and other devices to the Device Image field. Reuse the 4 images as needed throughout the records. Add photos of yourself, your friends, or family members as attachments to the Client Photo field.

Continued on next page

5. Create a multiple-table form based on the Client table. Include the Client Number, First Name, Last Name, and Technician Number fields from the Client table. Include the technician's first and last names on the form from the Technician table. Adjust label and field sizes appropriately so all data is visible.
6. Include a title for the form and the current date, and adjust the size and position of the date control as needed. Save the form as Client Technician Form, and then open the form in Design view.
7. Add the Device Image field and the Client Photo field to the form. Reposition and resize each label and field as needed for clean spacing and good form design. If necessary, use the size mode property to adjust your images in the Device Image field so they appear appropriately.
8. Submit the revised database in the format specified by your instructor.
9. **Consider This:** In this assignment you stored images as OLE Object and Attachment fields. What differences did you notice on the form? Which storage method do you prefer and why?

In the Lab

Design and implement a solution using creative thinking and problem-solving skills.

Lab: Adding Fields and Creating Multiple-Table Forms for the Great Outdoors Database

Note: To complete this assignment, you will be required to use the Data Files. Please contact your instructor for information about accessing the Data Files.

Problem: The Great Outdoors staff would like you to add some fields to the Counselors table. They would also like to create a form for the Cabins table that shows the counselor assigned to each cabin and the camper enrollments for each cabin.

Perform the following tasks:

Part 1: Open the SC_AC_05-5.accdb database from the Data Files folder. Save the file with the name, SC_AC_05_Great-Outdoors, and enable the content. Use the concepts and techniques presented in this module to perform each of the following tasks.

a. For the Counselors table, add a photo field using the Attachment data type and a notes field using the Long Text data type.
b. For the counselor pictures, use your own photos. For the notes field, add the notes shown in Table 5–4. Make sure all data appears in the datasheet.

Table 5–4 Data for Counselors Table

Counselor ID	Notes
17893	Plays high school basketball
18797	Working on bachelor's in P.E.
18798	Camp counselor for 3 years
18990	Coached Little League baseball
78797	Ran track in high school
78979	Chess champion
79798	Camp alumnus
79879	Camp alumnus
82374	Plays high school volleyball
83329	Plays high school football
83648	Mother of a camper
85114	Played in college band
86718	Competitive video gamer

c. Form a relationship between the Enrollments table and the Cabins table on the field containing the cabin identification number in each table. Enforce referential integrity, and cascade updates. Form a relationship between the Cabins table and the Counselors table on the Cabin ID and Cabin fields, respectively. Enforce referential integrity, and cascade updates.

d. Create a Cabin Counselor Form for the Cabins table that is similar in design to the form shown in Figure 5–1. On the form, include the CabinID, CabinName, Min Campers, and Max Campers from the Cabins table, and include the First Name, Last Name, Photo, and Notes fields from the Counselors table. The subform should display the ID, Camper ID, and Camper First Name fields from the Enrollments table. Customize the form by adding special effects to controls and labels and by changing the background color of the form. Add a title and the current date to the form header.

e. Create a query that lists all cabin IDs and cabin names where the cabin offers a minimum of at least 5 campers and an assigned counselor has been involved in high school sports. Name the query Lab 5 Query 1.

Submit your assignment in the format specified by your instructor.

Part 2: **Consider This:** You made several decisions while adding the fields and creating the form and query for this assignment. What was the rationale behind your decisions? For example, how did you decide on layout details for the fields on the form? And how did you choose the criteria for the query? As you consider the functionality of the Counselors table, what additional fields would you add to this table to best reflect counselor experience levels and their preferences for the type and number of students they host in their cabins?

Advanced Report Techniques

Objectives

After completing this module, you will be able to:

- Import data to a table
- Enforce referential integrity in a table relationship
- Identify a query as a report's record source
- Use the Expression Builder
- Create a report using Design view
- Modify a label in a report
- Add a text box to a report
- Check a report's design using Print Preview
- Modify grouping of a report's controls
- Update multiple report controls
- Include a subreport in a report
- Modify section properties in a report
- Modify content and design of a report header or footer
- Include a calculation in a report
- Modify a report's page setup characteristics

Introduction

Previously you created forms and reports in Layout view for simpler designs, and you created forms in Design view for more complex configuration options. Design view offers extensive options for formatting, layout, functionality, and built-in logic. As you will see in this module, in Design view, you can set a control to expand its size automatically when the data held in that control needs more space. You can also group controls in sections according to the type of data being displayed and how much detail is required, or according to the type of calculations you want performed.

In this module, you will create two reports in Design view. Both reports feature grouping and sorting. The first report contains a subreport, which is a report that is contained within another report. The subreport contains data from a query and is related to data in the main report. The second report uses aggregate functions to calculate subtotals and totals. It also uses a function to calculate a value where the actual calculation will vary from record to record depending on whether a given criterion is true.

Project: Creating Detailed Reports

Partners Law Firm paralegals want a summary list of properties and the buyers for each property. This list should be available as an Access report and will have the name Buyers and Account Information Summary List. For each buyer, the report will include buyer, property, and closing information, even if the firm's client was instead the seller. In addition to offering its closing services, Partners offers workshops designed to educate buyers on various aspects of retirement planning. Data on workshop participation is stored in the database. To help Partners gauge the effectiveness of these workshops, the report should also list any workshops the buyers are enrolled in.

The Buyers and Account Information Summary List report is shown in Figure 6–1a. The report is organized by Buyer ID, with the data for each Buyer ID beginning on a new page. The buyer data includes the Buyer ID, buyer name, street address, attorney, closing date, property jurisdiction, and property location. For each workshop the buyer is taking, the report lists the workshop code, description, total hours the workshop requires, hours already spent, and hours remaining.

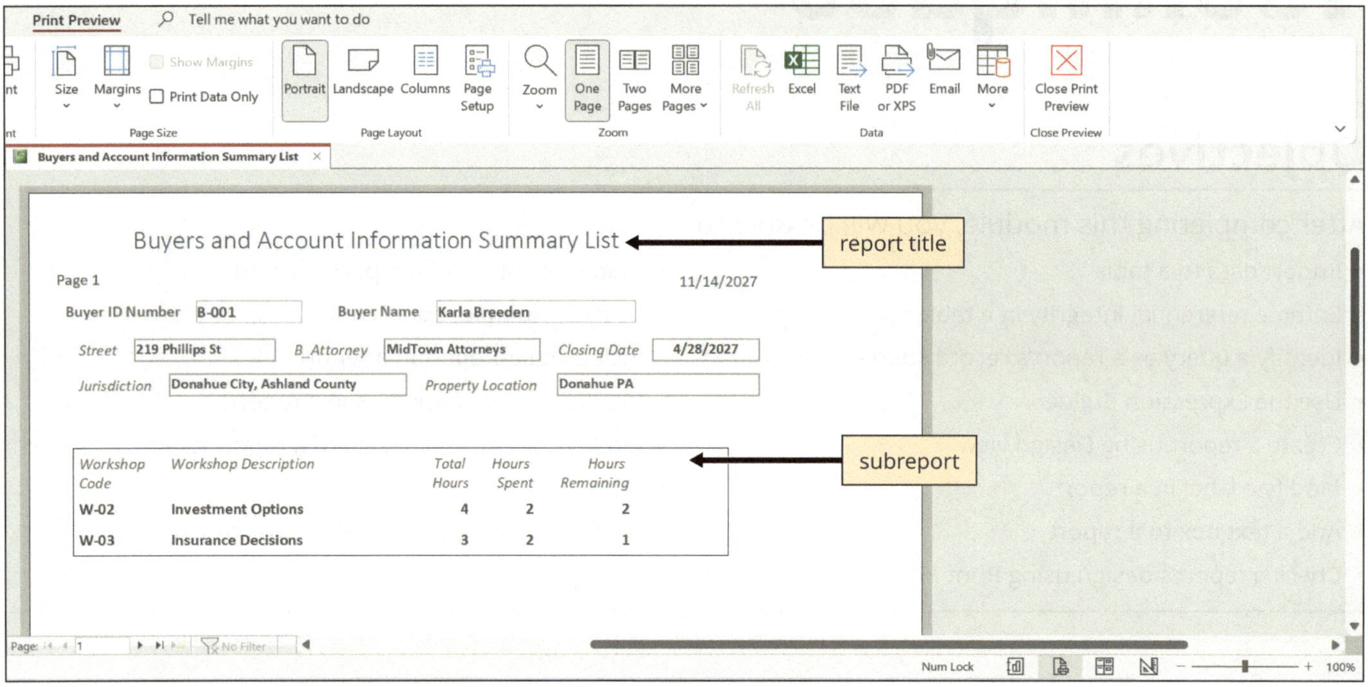

Figure 6–1a

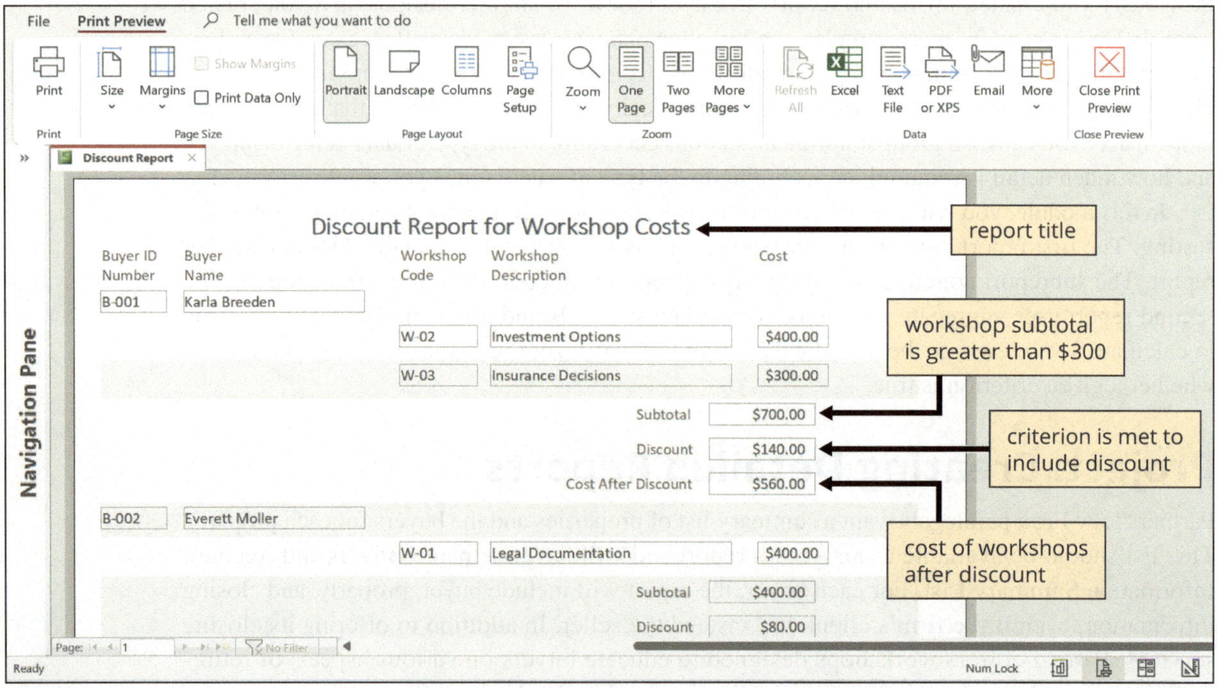

Figure 6–1b

To attract new clients and reward current clients, Partners Law Firm is considering offering a discount to clients who spend more than a certain amount on workshops. To assist in determining the discount, Partners paralegals need a report like the one shown in Figure 6–1b. The report groups clients by Buyer ID. It includes a subtotal of the workshop costs for that client. In addition, the report includes a discounted cost for the workshops, if the total workshop cost for that client is more than $300. Finally, it shows the cost of the workshops less the discount amount.

BTW
The Ribbon and Screen Resolution
Access may change how the groups and buttons within the groups appear on the ribbon, depending on the computer's screen resolution. Thus, your ribbon may look different from the ones in this course if you are using a screen resolution other than 1920 x 1080.

Additional Tables

Partners has recently teamed up with other local businesses, such as an insurance agency and an investment agency, to present workshops on various aspects of retirement planning. Partners paralegals would like to incorporate this workshop data into the Partners database.

Before creating the reports, you need to create two additional tables for the Partners database. The first table, Workshops, is shown in Table 6–1a. As described in Table 6–1a, each workshop has a code and a description. The table also includes the duration of the workshop in total hours and in increments, or standard time blocks in which the workshop is scheduled. Table 6–1b contains the specific workshops that Partners and the other workshop team members offer to their clients. The first row, for example, indicates that workshop W-01 is called Legal Documentation. It is typically offered in four total hours, organized into two-hour increments.

BTW
Touch Screen Differences
The Office and Windows interfaces may vary if you are using a touch screen. For this reason, you might notice the function or appearance of your touch screen differs slightly from this module's presentation.

BTW
Touch and Pointers
Remember that if you are using your finger on a touch screen, you will not see the pointer.

Table 6–1a Structure of Workshops Table

Field Name	Data Type	Field Size	Description
Workshop Code	Short Text	4	Primary Key
Workshop Description	Short Text	50	
Hours	Number	Integer	
Increments	Number	Integer	
Cost	Currency	n/a	

Table 6–1b Workshops Table

Workshop Code	Workshop Description	Hours	Increments	Cost
W-01	Legal Documentation	4	2	$400
W-02	Investment Options	4	2	$400
W-03	Insurance Decisions	3	1	$300
W-04	Budgeting For and In Retirement	3	1	$300
W-05	End-of-Life Decisions	2	1	$200

The second table, Workshop Enrollments, is described in Table 6–2a and contains a buyer ID, a workshop code, the total number of hours the workshop is scheduled for the buyer, and the number of hours already spent by the buyer in the workshop. Because each combination of Buyer and Workshop needs to be a uniquely identified record, you will create a combined primary key for this table. Shortly you will see why a combined primary key is a more effective approach for this table than if you instead used a single ID field as the primary key.

BTW
Enabling the Content
For each of the databases you use in this module, you will need to enable the content.

Table 6–2a Structure of Workshop Enrollments Table

Field Name	Data Type	Field Size	Description
Buyer ID	Short Text	5	Part of Primary Key
Workshop Code	Short Text	4	Part of Primary Key
Total Hours	Number	Integer	
Hours Spent	Number	Integer	

BTW
AutoNumber Field as Primary Key
When you create a table in Datasheet view, Access automatically creates an ID field with the AutoNumber data type as the primary key field. As you add records to the table, Access increments the ID field so each record will have a unique value in the field. AutoNumber fields are useful when there is no data field in a table that is a suitable primary key.

Table 6–2b gives the data for the Workshop Enrollments table. For example, the first record shows that Buyer ID B-001 is currently scheduled for the workshop W-02 (Investment Options). The workshop includes four hours of instructional time, and the buyer has so far spent two hours in class.

Table 6–2b Workshop Enrollments Table

Buyer ID	Workshop Code	Total Hours	Hours Spent
B-001	W-02	4	2
B-001	W-03	3	2
B-002	W-01	4	1
B-003	W-02	4	1
B-005	W-03	3	1
B-004	W-04	3	2
B-002	W-02	4	0

If you examine the data in Table 6–2b, you see the Buyer ID field cannot be the primary key for the Workshop Enrollments table. The first and second records, for example, both have a Buyer ID of B-001. The Workshop Code field also cannot be the primary key. The first, fourth, and seventh records have the same workshop code. This is why a combined primary key is needed for this table. Buyer IDs can be duplicated as buyers enroll in multiple workshops, and Workshop Codes can be duplicated as multiple buyers enroll in the same workshop. However, the combination of a single buyer with a single workshop creates a unique record. Therefore, the combination of the Buyer ID and the Workshop Code can, together, represent a unique enrollment.

To Create the New Tables

You will use Design view to create the new tables. The steps to create the new tables are similar to the steps you used previously to add fields to an existing table and to define primary keys. The only difference is the way you specify a primary key. Why? In the Workshop Enrollments table, the primary key consists of more than one field, which requires a slightly different process. To specify a primary key containing more than one field, you must select both fields that make up the primary key by clicking the row selector for the first field, and then press and hold CTRL while clicking the row selector for the second field. Once the fields are selected, you can use the Primary Key button to indicate the primary key consists of both fields. The following steps create the tables in Design view.

1

- sam Start Access. Open the database, SC_AC_06-1.accdb, which is located in the Data Files folder. Save the file to your hard disk, OneDrive, or other storage location using the file name, **SC_AC_06_Partners**. Enable the content.
- If necessary, close the Navigation Pane.
- Display the Create tab (Figure 6–2).

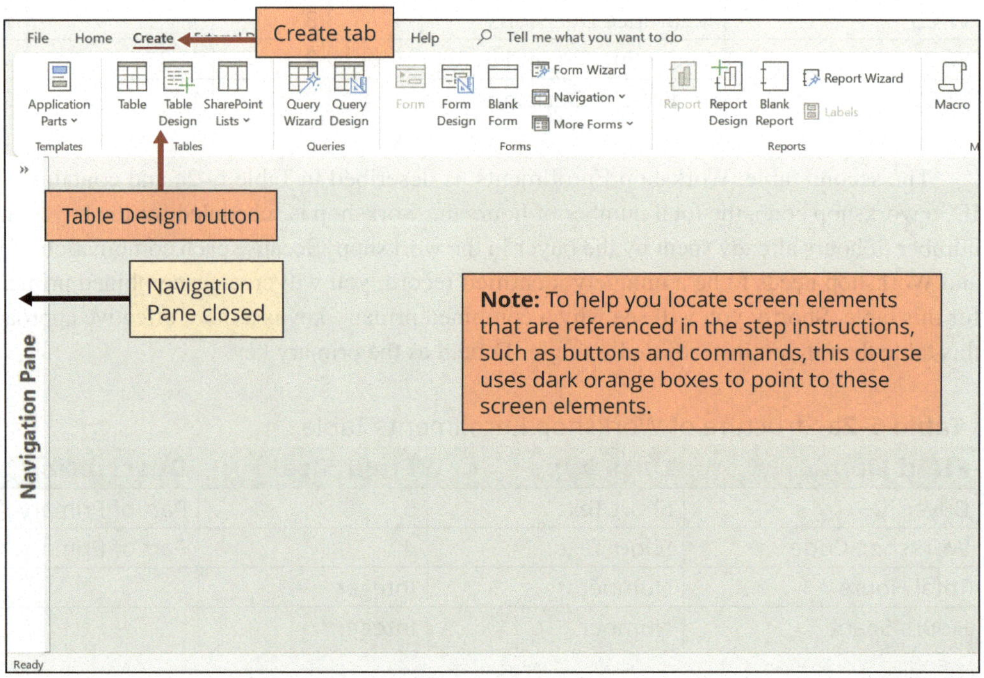

Figure 6–2

2

- Click the Table Design button (Create tab | Tables group) to create a table in Design view.
- Enter the information for the fields in the Workshop table as indicated in Table 6–1a, making Workshop Code the primary key, and specifying the indicated field sizes.
- Save the table using the name **Workshops** and close the table.

3

- Display the Create tab and then click the Table Design button (Create tab | Tables group) to create a second table in Design view.
- Enter the information for the fields in the Workshop Enrollments table as indicated in Table 6–2a. You will designate the primary key in Step 4.

4

- Click the row selector for the Buyer ID field.
- Hold down CTRL and then click the row selector for the Workshop Code field so both fields are selected.
- Click the Primary Key button (Table Design tab | Tools group) to select the combination of the two fields as the primary key (Figure 6–3).

5

- Save the table using the name **Workshop Enrollments** and close the table.

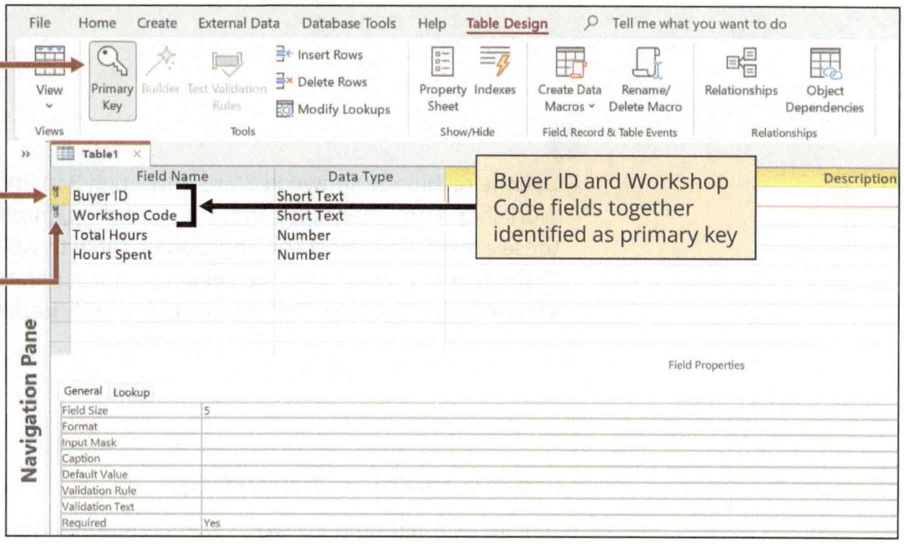

Figure 6–3

Q&A I realized I designated the wrong fields as the primary key. How can I correct the primary key?
Click any field that currently participates in the primary key, and then click the Primary Key button to remove the primary key designation. You then can specify the correct primary key.

To Import the Data

Now that the tables have been created, you need to add data to them. You could enter the data manually, or, if the data is already in electronic form, you could import the data. The data for the Workshops and Workshop Enrollments tables is included in the Data Files. The files are text files formatted as delimited files. The Workshops data is in a tab-delimited text (.txt) file, and the Workshop Enrollments data is in a comma-separated values (.csv) file, which is also a delimited text file. The following steps import the data for both tables.

1

- With the Partners database open, click the External Data tab, click the New Data Source button (External Data tab | Import & Link group), point to From File, and then click Text File to display the Get External Data – Text File dialog box.

2

- Click the Browse button (Get External Data – Text File dialog box), and then navigate to the location containing the text file for the Workshops table as specified by your instructor.

BTW
Copying the Structure of a Table
If you want to create a table that has a structure similar to that of an existing table, you can copy the structure of the table only. Select the table in the Navigation Pane and click Copy, and then click Paste. In the Paste Table As dialog box, type the new table name and click the Structure Only option button. Then click the OK button. To modify the new table, open it in Design view.

- Click the file, Support_AC_06_Workshops.txt, and then click Open.
- If necessary, click the 'Append a copy of the records to the table' option button, select the Workshops table from the list, and then click OK.

3

- With the Delimited option button selected, click Next.
- With the Tab option button selected, click the 'First Row Contains Field Names' check box, click Next, and then click Finish.
- Click the Close button to close the Get External Data – Text File dialog box without saving the import steps.

Q&A I got an error message after I clicked the Finish button that indicated there were errors. The data was not imported. What should I do?

First, click the Cancel button to terminate the process. Then, review the structure of the table in Design view to ensure the field names are all spelled correctly and the data types are correct. Correct any errors you find, save your work, and then repeat the steps to import the data.

4

- Use the technique shown in Steps 1 through 3 to import the text file, Support_AC_06_Workshop-Enrollments.csv, into the Workshop Enrollments table. Select the same options with these exceptions: select the appropriate table to which to append a copy of the file, select the Comma option button for the delimiter that separates your fields, and add a check mark if necessary in the 'First Row Contains Field Names' check box.

Linking versus Importing

When an external table or worksheet is imported into an Access database, a copy of the data is placed in a table in the database. The original data still exists, just as it did before, but no further connection exists between the source file and the data in the database. Changes to the original data do not affect the data in the database. Likewise, changes in the database do not affect the original data.

It is also possible to link data stored in a variety of formats to Access databases. To do so, you would select the 'Link to the data source by creating a linked table' option button when importing data, rather than the 'Import the source data into a new table in the current database' or 'Append a copy of the records to the table' option buttons. With linking, the connection is maintained; changes made to the data in the external table or worksheet affect the Access table.

To identify that a table is linked to other data, Access displays an arrow in front of the table in the Navigation Pane. In addition, an icon is displayed in front of the name that indicates the type of file to which the data is linked. For example, an Excel icon in front of the name indicates the table is linked to an Excel worksheet.

BTW
Linking
Two of the primary reasons to link data from another program to Access are to use the query and report features of Access. When you link an Access database to data in another application, all changes to the data must be made in the source application. For example, if you link an Excel workbook to an Access database, you cannot edit the linked table in Access. You must make all changes to the data in Excel.

To Modify Linked Tables

After you link tables between a worksheet and a database or between two databases, you can modify many of the linked table's features. To rename the linked table, set view properties, and set links between tables in queries, you would use the following steps.

1. Click the 'Linked Table Manager' button (External Data tab | Import & Link group) to update the links.
2. Select the linked table for which you want to update the links.
3. Click the OK button.

To Relate the New Tables

The following steps relate, or create a relationship between, the tables. **Why?** The new tables need to be related to the existing tables in the Partners database. The Buyers and Workshop Enrollments tables are related through the Buyer ID field that exists in both tables. The Workshops and Workshop Enrollments tables are related through the Workshop Code fields in both tables.

1

- Display the Database Tools tab.
- Click the Relationships button (Database Tools tab | Relationships group) to open the Relationships window (Figure 6–4).

Q&A I only see one table; did I do something wrong?

Click the All Relationships button to display all the tables in relationships.

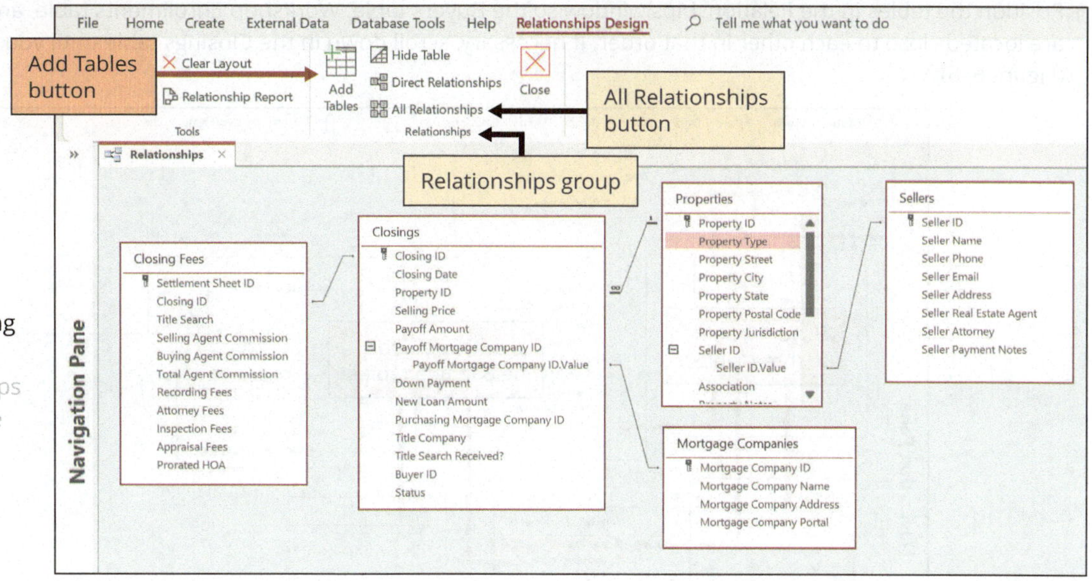

Figure 6–4

2

- Click the Add Tables button (Relationships Design tab | Relationships group) to display the Add Tables pane (Figure 6–5).

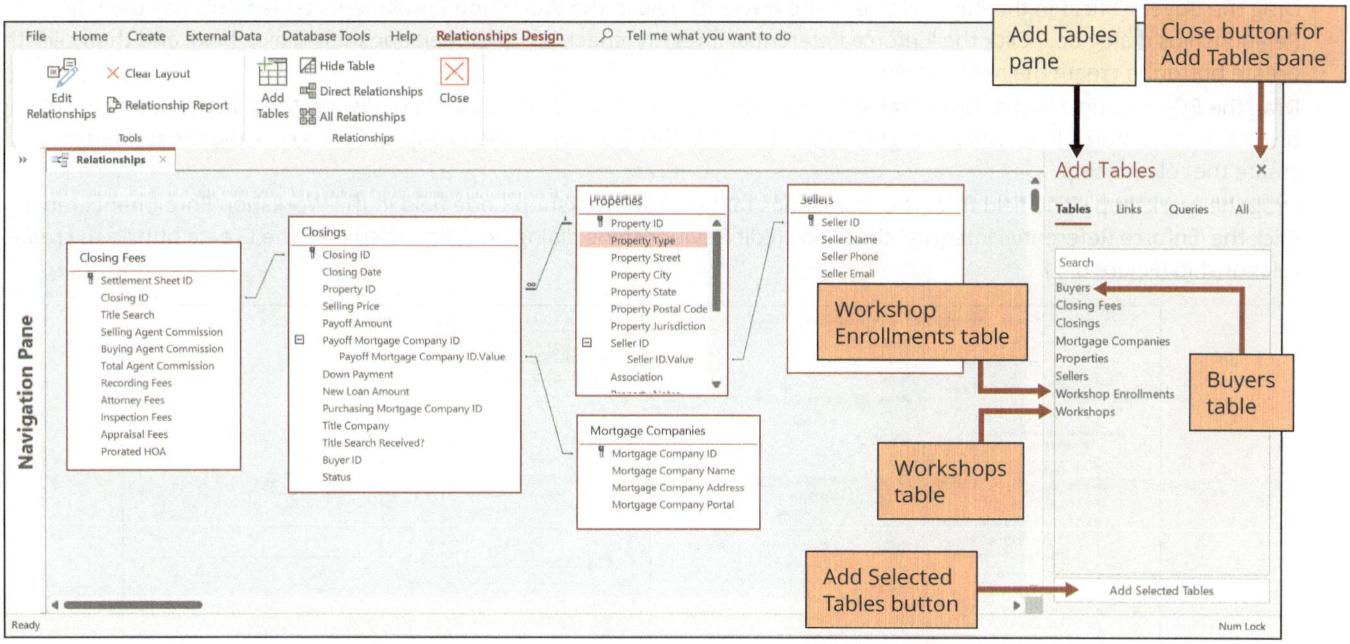

Figure 6–5

3

- Click the Workshop Enrollments table, press and hold CTRL, click the Workshops table, and then click the Buyers table to select all three tables. Click the Add Selected Tables button (Add Tables pane) to add the three tables to the Relationships window.
- Click Close to close the Add Tables pane.

Q&A I cannot see all the tables in the Relationships window; some are obscured.
Drag the tables to other locations in the Relationships window for easier viewing.

I cannot see the Workshop Enrollments table. Should I repeat the step?
If you cannot see the table, it likely is behind the Add Tables pane. You do not need to repeat the step.

4

- Position the tables in the Relationships window so the Buyers table, Workshop Enrollments table, and Workshops table are located close to each other in that order. If necessary, scroll down in the Closings table until you see the Buyer ID field (Figure 6–6).

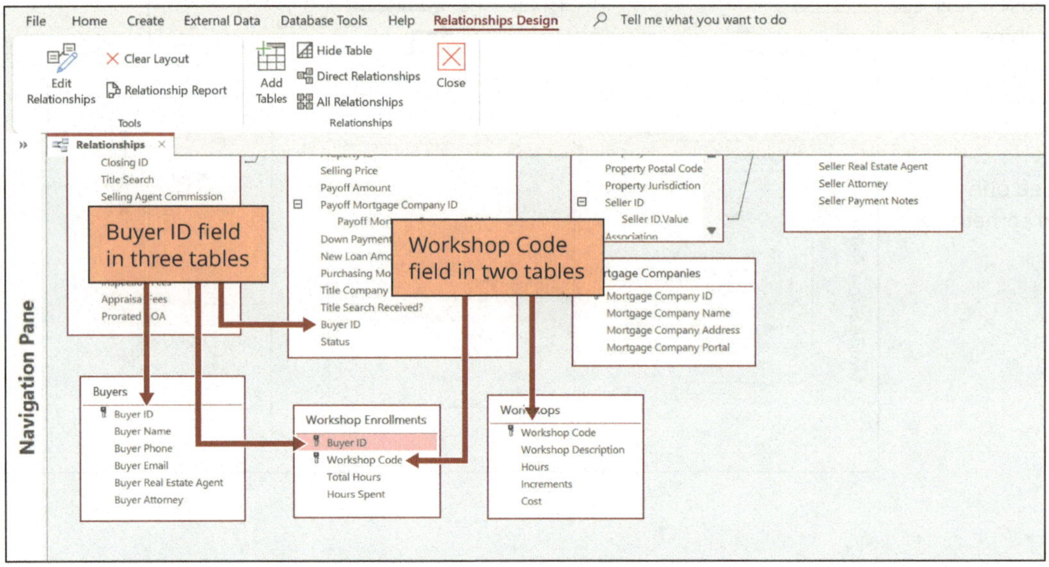

Figure 6–6

- Drag the Buyer ID field in the Buyers table to the Buyer ID field in the Workshop Enrollments table to display the Edit Relationships dialog box. Click the 'Enforce Referential Integrity' check box (Edit Relationships dialog box), and then click the Create button to create the relationship.
- Drag the Buyer ID in the Buyers table to the Buyer ID field in the Closings table to display the Edit Relationships dialog box. Click the 'Enforce Referential Integrity' check box (Edit Relationships dialog box), and then click the Create button to create the relationship.
- Drag the Workshop Code field from the Workshops table to the Workshop Code field in the Workshop Enrollments table. Click the 'Enforce Referential Integrity' check box (Edit Relationships dialog box), and then click the Create button to create the relationship (Figure 6–7).

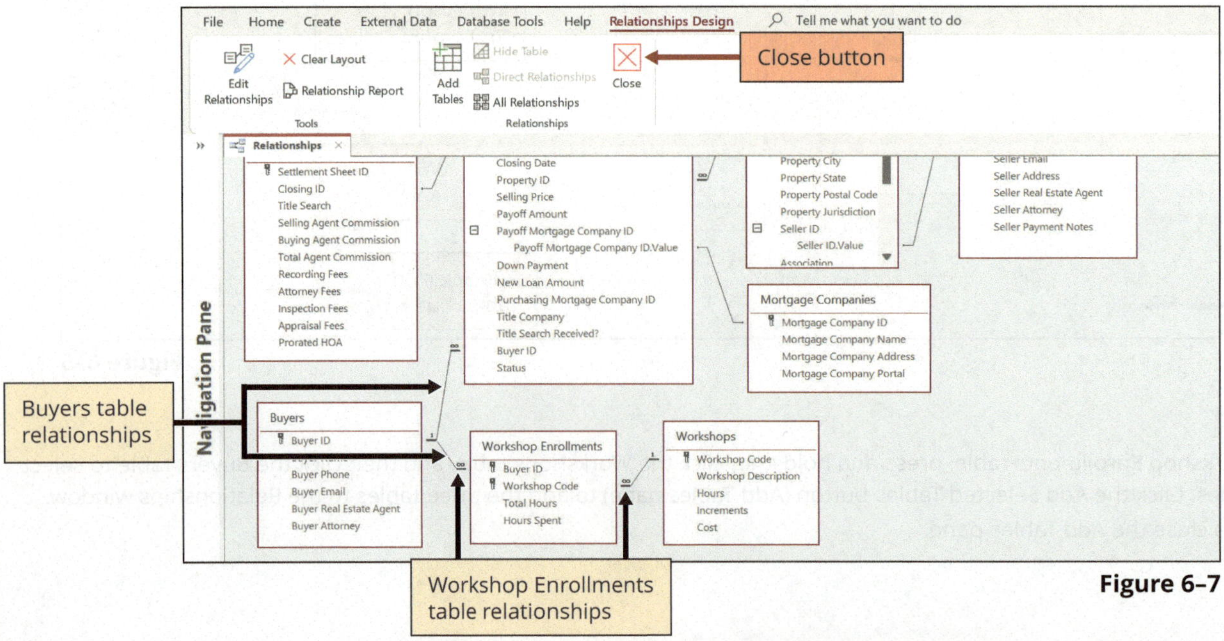

Figure 6–7

5

- Save the changes and then click the Close button (Relationships Design tab | Relationships group).

Creating Reports in Design View

Previously, you have used both Layout view and the Report Wizard to create reports. However, you can create a report in Design view. You can also use Design view to modify a report you previously created. When you create a report in Design view, you must place all the fields in the desired locations. You must also specify any sorting or grouping that is required.

Whether you use the wizard or simply use Design view to create a report, you must determine on which table or query to base the report. If you decide to base the report on a query, you must first create the query, unless it already exists.

BTW
Invalid Relationships
If Access will not allow you to create a relationship and enforce referential integrity, it could be because the two matching fields do not have the same data type. Open the tables in Design view and check the data types and field sizes. You should also check to be sure you do not have a foreign key value in the "many" table that does not match the primary key value in the "one" table. To do this, create a Find Unmatched Query using the Query Wizard to find the unmatched records in the "many" table.

BTW
Many-to-Many Relationships
There is a many-to-many relationship between the Buyers table and the Workshops table. To implement a many-to-many relationship in a relational database management system such as Access, you create a third table, often called a junction or intersection table, that has as its primary key the combination of the primary keys of each of the tables involved in the many-to-many relationship. The primary key of the Workshop Enrollments table is the combination of the Buyer ID and the Workshop Code fields.

To Create a Query for the Report

To create the two reports needed by Partners paralegals, it is more convenient to build each report from a query because each report will need to pull data from multiple tables. These two queries for the two reports do not yet exist, so you will need to create them. The first query relates buyers and their account information. The buyer account information consists of closing dates, properties purchased, property jurisdictions, and closing attorneys. The second query relates workshops and workshop enrollments. The following steps create the Buyers and Account Information query.

1

- Display the Create tab, and then click the Query Design button (Create tab | Queries group) to create a new query.

2

- Click the Buyers table (Add Tables pane).
- While holding CTRL, click the Closings table, and then click the Properties table.
- Release CTRL and click the Add Selected Tables button (Add Tables pane).
- Close the Add Tables pane by clicking its Close button, reposition the field lists as desired, and resize the field lists to display as many fields as possible.

Q&A Why must I use CTRL here instead of SHIFT to select the tables?
Holding SHIFT selects the first table clicked, the next table clicked, and all tables appearing in the list between them. Holding CTRL selects exactly the tables clicked and no other tables.

3

- In the Buyers table, double-click the Buyer ID, Buyer Name, and Buyer Attorney fields to display them in the design grid.
- In the Closings table, double-click the Closing Date field to display it in the design grid.
- In the Properties table, double-click the Property Street, Property City, Property State, and Property Jurisdiction fields to display them in the design grid.
- Select Sort in Ascending Order on the Closing Date field.

4

- Run the query to view the results.
- Scroll through the fields to make sure you have included all the necessary fields. If you have omitted a field, return to Design view and add it (Figure 6–8).

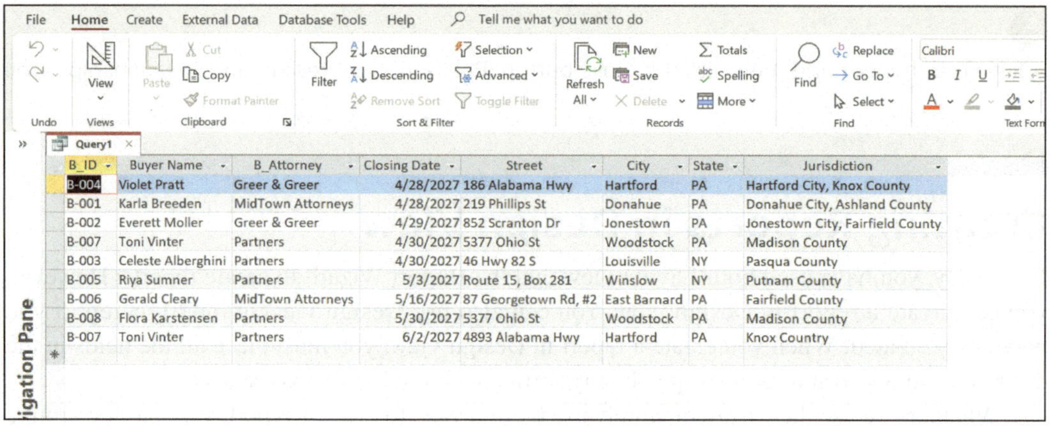

Figure 6–8

5

- Click the Save button on the Quick Access Toolbar to save the query, type **Buyers and Account Information** as the name of the query, and then click OK.
- Close the query.

To Create an Additional Query for the Report Using Expression Builder

The following steps create the Workshop Enrollments and Workshops query, which includes a calculated field for hours remaining in each buyer's current workshops, that is, the total number of hours minus the hours the buyer has spent in each offering. **Why?** Partners paralegals need to include in the Buyers and Account Information Summary List report the number of hours that remain in a workshop offering.

1

- Display the Create tab and then click the Query Design button (Create tab | Queries group) to create a new query.
- Use CTRL to select the Buyers table, Workshop Enrollments table, and Workshops table.
- Click the Add Selected Tables button, and then close the Add Tables pane.

2

- In the Buyers table, double-click the Buyer ID and Buyer Name fields to add the fields to the design grid.
- In the Workshop Enrollments table, double-click the Workshop Code field to add the field to the design grid.
- In the Workshops table, double-click the Workshop Description and Cost fields to add the fields to the design grid.
- In the Workshop Enrollments table, double-click the Total Hours and Hours Spent fields to add the fields to the design grid.

3

- Click in the top cell in the Field row of the first open column in the design grid to select it.
- Click the Builder button (Query Design tab | Query Setup group) to display the Expression Builder dialog box (Figure 6–9).

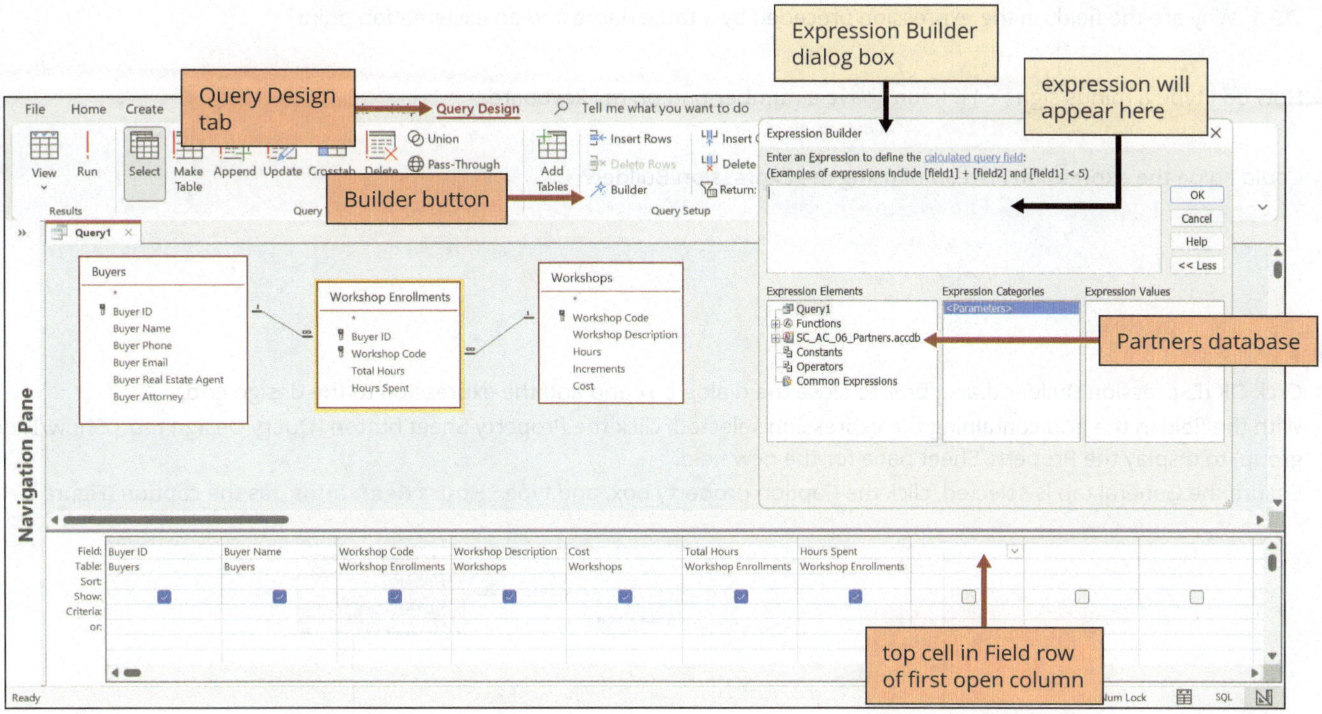

Figure 6–9

Other Ways

1. Right-click field in grid, click Build to open Expression Builder

4

- Double-click the Partners database in the Expression Elements section to display the categories of objects within the Partners database, and then double-click Tables to display a list of tables.
- Click the Workshop Enrollments table to select it.
- Double-click the Total Hours field to add it to the expression.
- Type a minus sign (–) to add it to the expression.
- Double-click the Hours Spent field to add it to the expression (Figure 6–10).

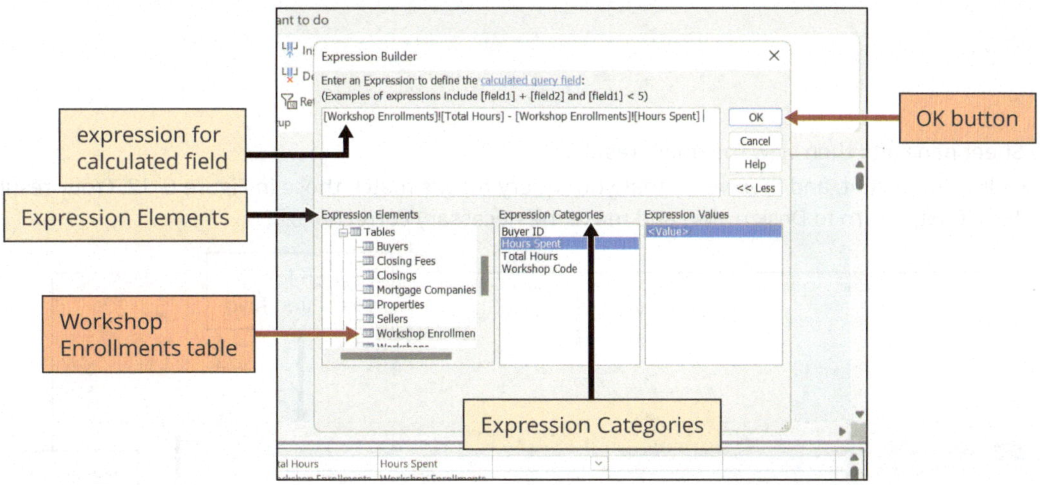

Figure 6–10

Q&A Why are the fields in the expression preceded by a table name and an exclamation point?
This notation qualifies the field; that is, it indicates to which table the field belongs.

How do I type a minus sign (−) if I don't have a number pad on my keyboard?
You can type a hyphen instead, which Access will interpret as a minus sign.

Could I type the expression instead of using the Expression Builder?
Yes. You could type it directly into the design grid. You could also right-click the column and click Zoom to allow you to type the expression in the Zoom dialog box. Finally, you could use the Expression Builder, but simply type the expression rather than clicking any buttons. Use whichever method you find most convenient.

5

- Click OK (Expression Builder dialog box) to close the dialog box and add the expression to the design grid.
- With the field in the grid containing the expression selected, click the Property Sheet button (Query Design tab | Show/Hide group) to display the Property Sheet pane for the new field.
- Ensure the General tab is selected, click the Caption property box, and type **Hours Remaining** as the caption (Figure 6–11).

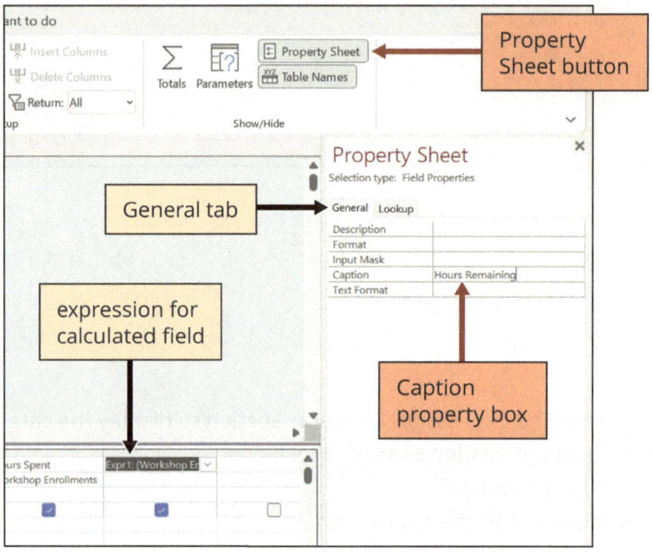

Figure 6–11

Q&A I do not have a Caption property in my property sheet. What went wrong? What should I do?
You either inadvertently clicked a different location in the grid, or you have not yet completed entering the expression. The easiest way to ensure you have done both is to click any other column in the grid and then click the column with the expression.

6

- Close the Property Sheet pane and then view the query results.
- Adjust the column widths for best fit, and then verify that your query results match those in Figure 6–12. (Your results might be in a different order.) If not, return to Design view and make the necessary corrections.

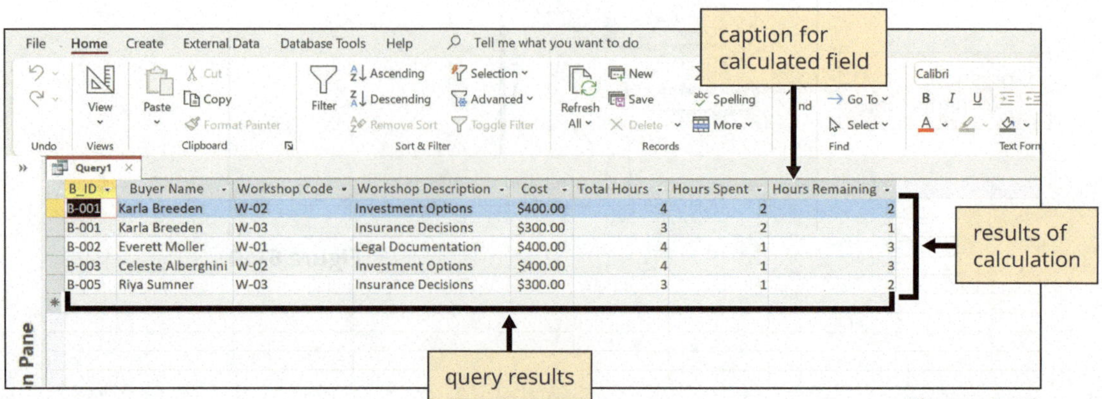

Figure 6–12

7
- Save the query as **Workshop Enrollments and Workshops**.
- Close the query.

Consider This

How do you determine the tables and fields for the report?

If you determine that data should be presented as a report, you then need to determine which tables and fields contain the data for the report.

- **Examine the requirements for the report in general to determine the tables.** Do the requirements only relate to data in a single table, or does the data come from multiple tables? Is the data in a query, or could you create a query that contains some or all the fields necessary for the report?
- **Examine the specific requirements for the report to determine the fields necessary.** Look for all the data items that are specified for the report. Each item should correspond to a field in a table, or it should be able to be computed from a field or fields in a table. This information gives you the list of fields to include in the query.
- **Determine the order of the fields.** Examine the requirements to determine the order in which the fields should appear. Be logical and consistent in your ordering. For example, in an address, the city should come before the state, and the state should come before the postal code, unless there is some compelling reason for another order.

What decisions do you make in determining the organization of the report?

- **Determine sort order.** Is there a special order in which the records should appear?
- **Determine grouping.** Should the records be grouped in some fashion? If so, what information should appear before the records in a group? If, for example, buyers are grouped by property ID number, the ID number of the property should probably appear before the group. Should the property address also appear? What should appear after the group? For example, are there some fields for which subtotals should be calculated? If so, the subtotals would come after the group.
- **Determine whether to include a subreport.** Rather than use grouping, you can include a subreport, as shown in the Buyers and Account Information Summary List in Figure 6–1a. The data concerning workshop enrollments for the buyers could have been presented by grouping the workshop enrollments' data by Buyer ID. The headings currently in the subreport would have appeared in the group header. Instead, it is presented in a subreport. Subreports, which are reports in their own right, offer more flexibility in formatting than using group headers and footers. More importantly, in the Buyers and Account Information Summary List, some buyers do not have any workshop enrollments. If this information were presented using grouping, the group header would still appear for these buyers, cluttering the report. With a subreport, buyers that have no workshop enrollments do not appear.

To Create an Initial Report in Design View

Creating from scratch the report shown in Figure 6–1a involves creating the initial report in Design view, adding the subreport, modifying the subreport separately from the main report, and then making the final modifications to the main report. When you want to create a report from scratch, you use Design view rather than the Report Wizard. Why? The Report Wizard is suitable for simple, customized reports. Using the Report Design screen, you can make advanced design changes, such as adding subreports. The following steps create the initial version of the Buyers and Account Information Summary List and select the **record source** for the report, that is, the table or query that will furnish the data for the report. The steps then specify sorting and grouping for the report.

1
- Display the Create tab.
- Click the Report Design button (Create tab | Reports group) to create a report in Design view.
- Ensure the selector for the entire report, the box in the upper-left corner of the report, contains a black square, which indicates the report is selected (Figure 6–13).

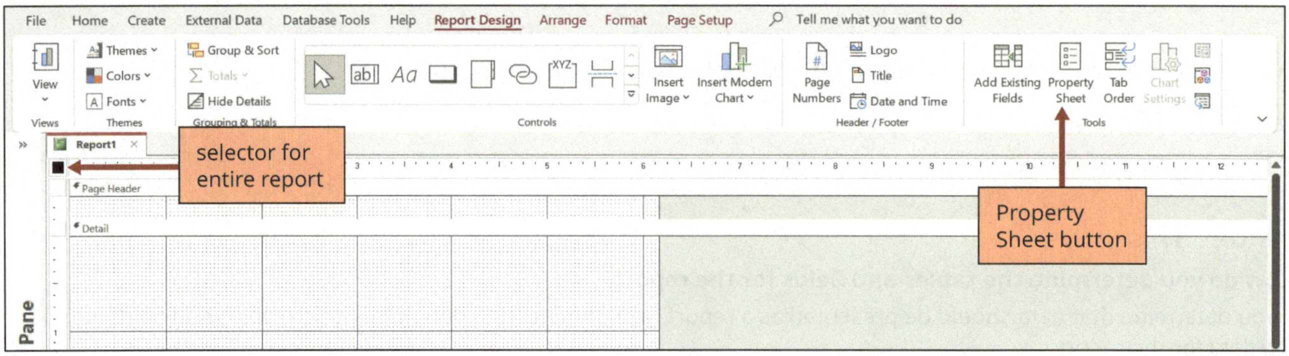

Figure 6–13

- Click the Property Sheet button (Report Design tab | Tools group) to display the Property Sheet pane.
- Drag the left border of the Property Sheet pane to increase its width.
- With the All tab (Property Sheet pane) selected, click the Record Source property box arrow to display the list of available tables and queries (Figure 6–14).

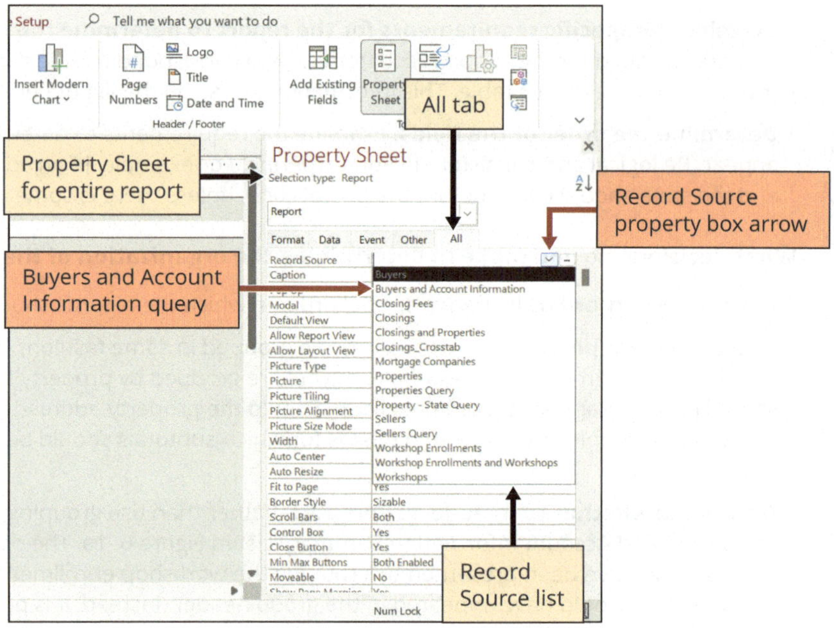

Figure 6–14

Q&A Can I move the Property Sheet pane?
Yes, you can move the Property Sheet pane by dragging its title bar. If you want to place the Property Sheet pane back in its original position, drag the pane to the right edge of your screen so it pops back into place.

Can I increase the size of the Record Sources list?
Yes, you can change the width of the portion of the pane used for the Record Source list by dragging the dividing line between the property names and the property boxes.

2

- Click the Buyers and Account Information query to select the query as the record source for the report.
- Close the Property Sheet pane.

To Group and Sort

In Design view of the report, you can specify both grouping and sorting by using the Group & Sort button on the Report Design tab, just as you did in Layout view. The following steps specify both grouping and sorting in the report. **Why?** Partners paralegals have determined the records in the report should be grouped by Buyer ID. That is, all the information of a given buyer should appear together. Within the account information of a given buyer, they have determined that closings are to be ordered by closing date.

1

- Click the Group & Sort button (Report Design tab | Grouping & Totals group) to display the Group, Sort, and Total pane (Figure 6–15).

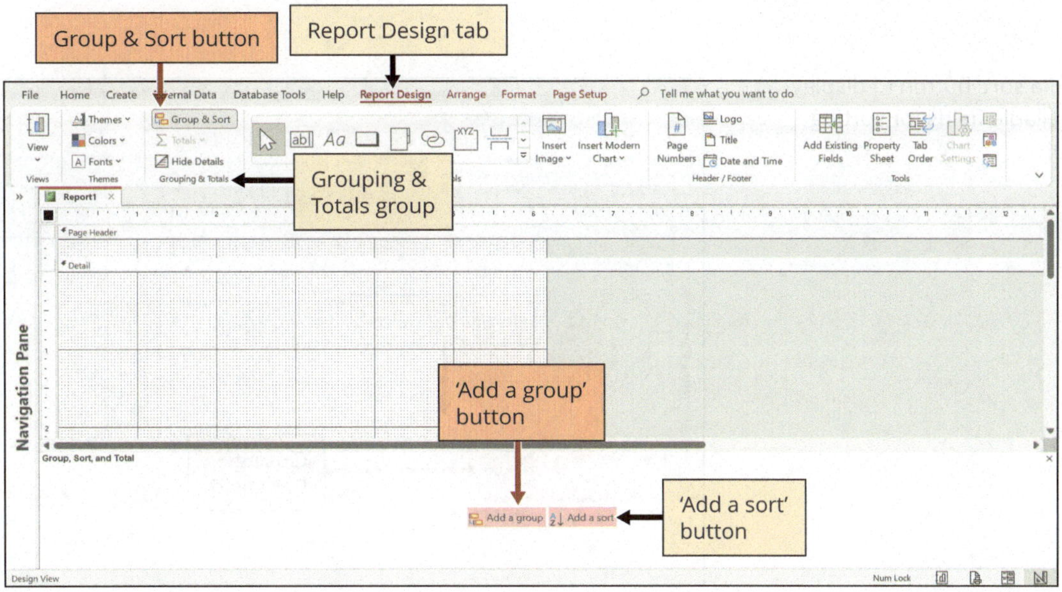

Figure 6–15

Other Ways

1. Right-click any open area of report, click Sorting & Grouping to open Group, Sort, and Total pane

2

- Click the 'Add a group' button to display the list of available fields for grouping (Figure 6–16).

Q&A The list of fields disappeared before I had a chance to select a field. What should I do?

Click the 'select field' arrow to once again display the list of fields.

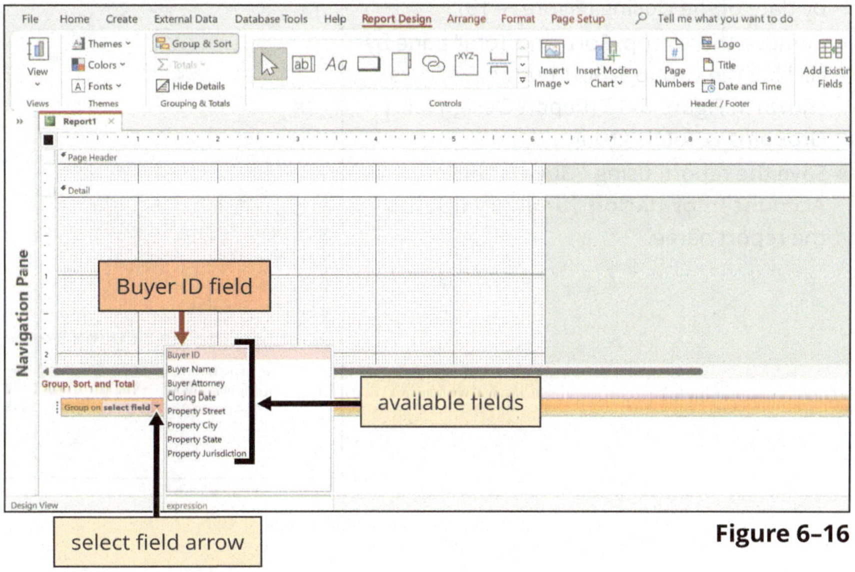

Figure 6–16

3

- Click the Buyer ID field to group by buyer ID number (Figure 6–17).

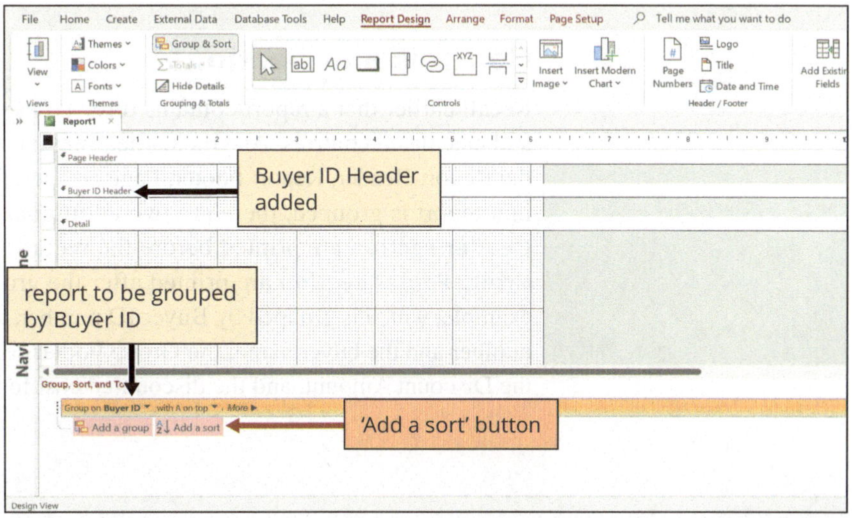

Figure 6–17

4

- Click the 'Add a sort' button to display the list of available fields for sorting (Figure 6–18).

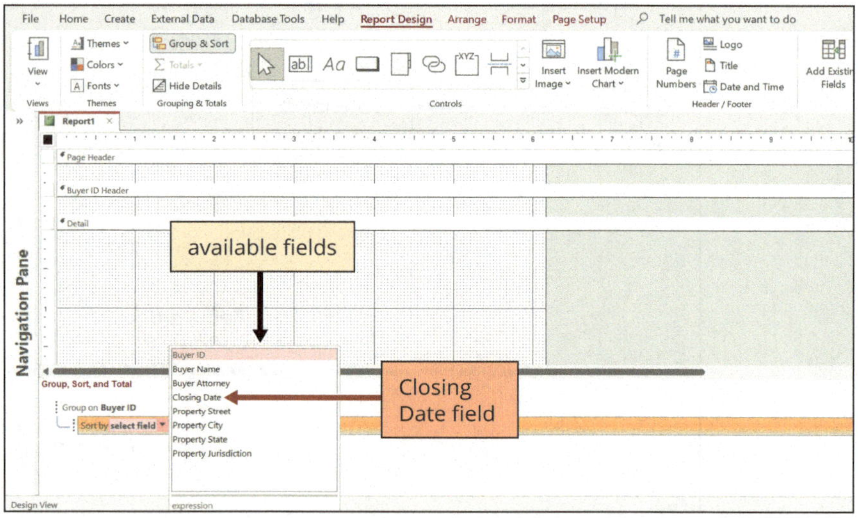

Figure 6–18

5

- Click the Closing Date field to sort closings by date of the closing (Figure 6–19).
- Remove the 'Group, Sort, and Total' pane by clicking the Group & Sort button, which is shown in Figure 6–15 (Report Design tab | Grouping & Totals group).
- Save the report, using **Buyers and Account Information Summary List** as the report name.

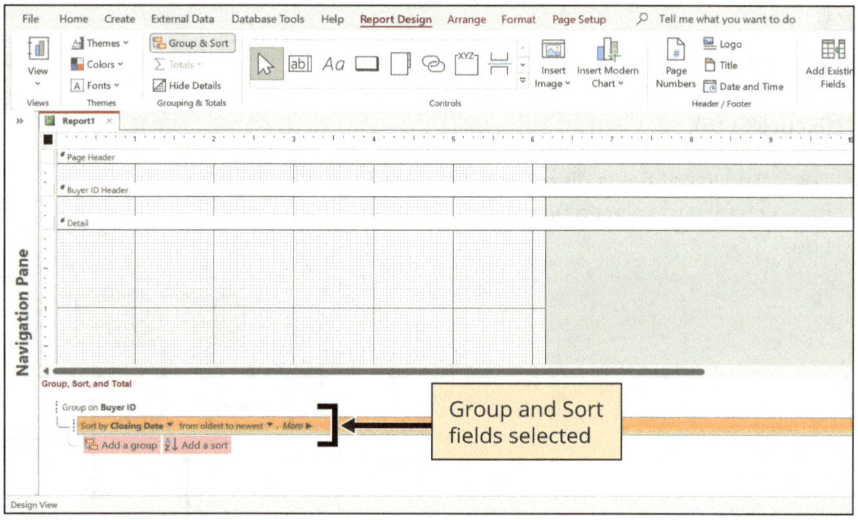

Figure 6–19

Controls and Sections

Recall earlier that a report contains three types of controls: bound controls, unbound controls, and calculated controls. As you learned previously, reports contain standard sections, including the Report Header, Report Footer, Page Header, Page Footer, and Detail sections. When the data in a report is grouped, there are two additional possible sections. The contents of the **Group Header section** are printed before the records in a particular group, and the contents of the **Group Footer section** are printed after the group. In the Discount Report (Figure 6–1b), for example, which is grouped by Buyer ID number, the Group Header section contains the Buyer ID number and the buyer name; the Group Footer section contains subtotals of the Workshop Costs, the Discount Amount, and the discounted cost for all workshops for that buyer.

To Add Fields to the Report in Design View

Why? Once you have determined the fields that are necessary for the report, you need to add them to the report design. You can add the fields to the report by dragging them from the field list to the appropriate position on the report. The following steps add the fields to the report.

1

- Click the 'Add Existing Fields' button (Report Design tab | Tools group) to display a field list.
- Drag the Buyer ID field to the approximate position shown in Figure 6–20. (The pointer shape appears as an arrow with a plus sign as you drag a field.)

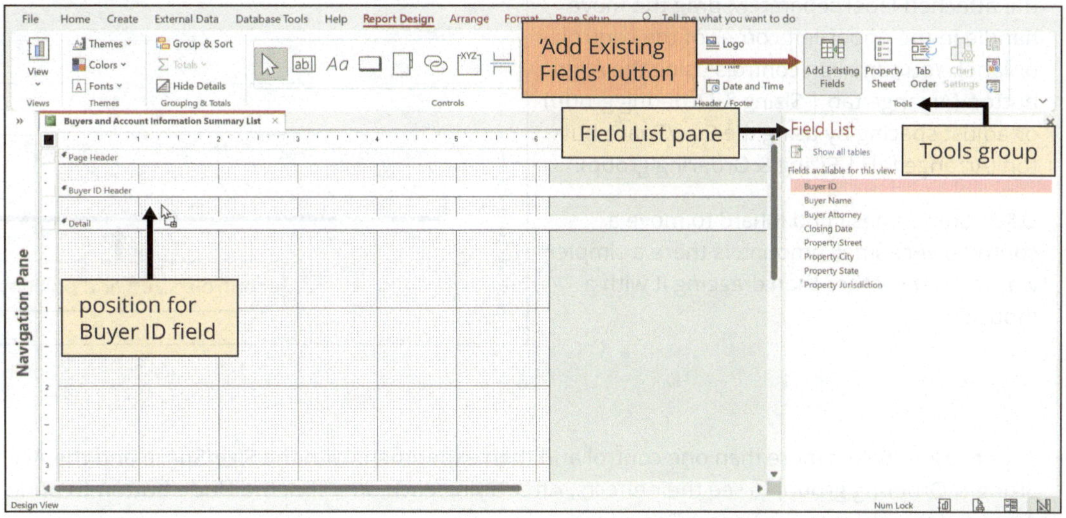

Figure 6–20

Q&A My field list does not look like the one in the figure. It has several tables listed, and at the top it has 'Show only fields in the current record source.' The figure has 'Show all tables.' What should I do?
Click the 'Show only fields in the current record source' link. Your field list should then match the one in the figure.

2

- Release the mouse button to place the field.
- Using the same technique, drag the Buyer Name field to the Buyer ID Header section.
- Place additional fields in the report Details section (Figure 6–21).

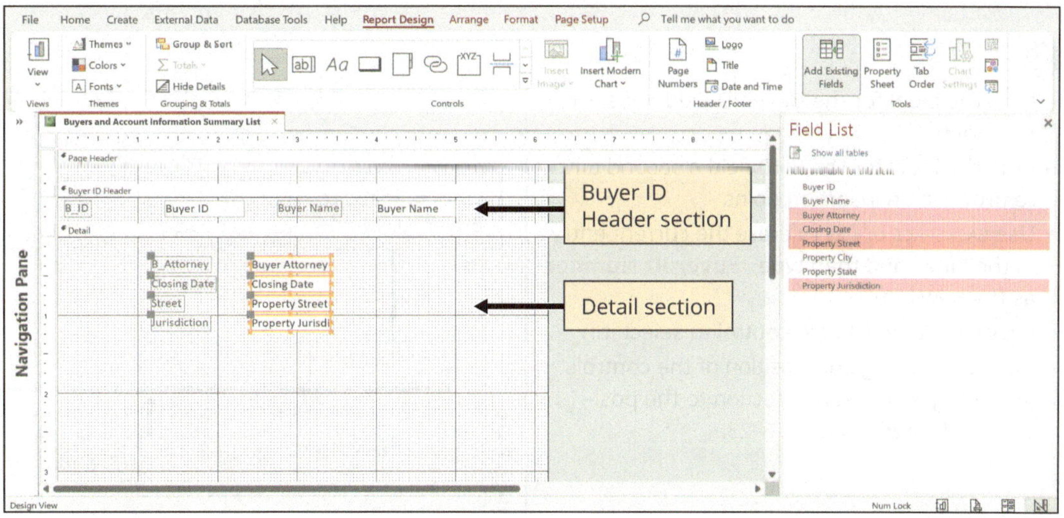

Figure 6–21

Q&A Could I drag several fields from the field list at once?
Yes. You can select multiple fields by selecting the first field, holding down the CTRL key, and selecting the additional fields. Once you have selected multiple fields, you can drag them all at once. How you choose to select fields and drag them onto the report is a matter of personal preference.

3

- Close the Field List pane.
- Adjust the positions and sizes of the labels and controls to those shown in Figure 6–22. If any field is not in the correct position, drag it to its correct location. To move the control or the attached label separately, drag the move handle in the upper-left corner of the control or label. You can align controls using the Align button (Arrange tab | Sizing & Ordering group) or adjust spacing by using the Size/Space button (Arrange tab | Sizing & Ordering group).

Q&A Sometimes I find it hard to move a control a very small amount. Is there a simpler way to do this other than dragging it with a mouse?

Yes. Once you have selected the control, you can use the arrow keys to move the control a very small amount in the desired direction.

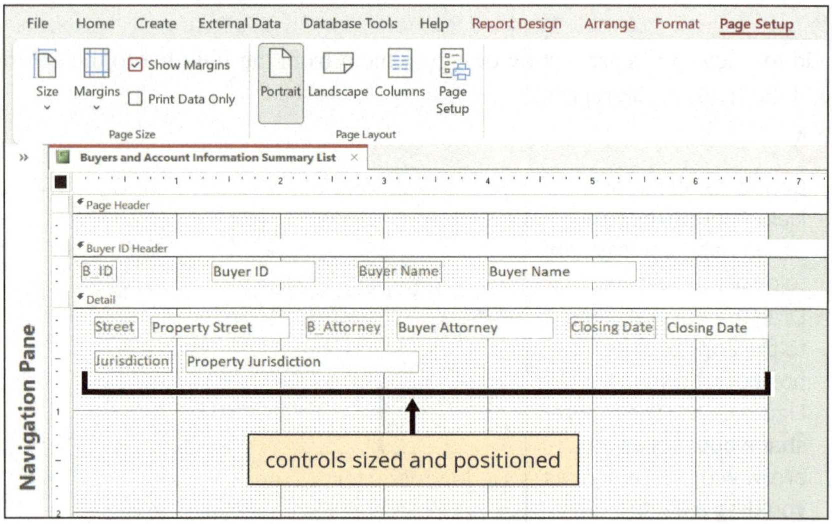

Figure 6–22

- **Experiment:** Select more than one control and then experiment with the Size/Space and the Align buttons (Arrange tab | Sizing & Ordering group) to see their effects. After trying each one, click the Undo button to undo the change. If you used the Arrange tab, return to the Report Design tab.

To Change Labels

The label for the Buyer ID field currently contains the caption B_ID for that field. The following step changes the contents of the label for the Buyer ID field from B_ID to Buyer ID Number. **Why?** Because there is plenty of room on the report to display a longer name for the field, you can make the report more descriptive by changing the label.

1

- Click the label for the Buyer ID field to select the label.
- Click the label for the B_ID field a second time to produce an insertion point.
- Use BACKSPACE or DEL to erase the current entry in the label, and then type **Buyer ID Number** as the new entry.
- Click the Buyer ID field control to select it.
- Adjust the sizing and position of the controls in the Buyer ID Header section to the positions indicated in Figure 6–23.

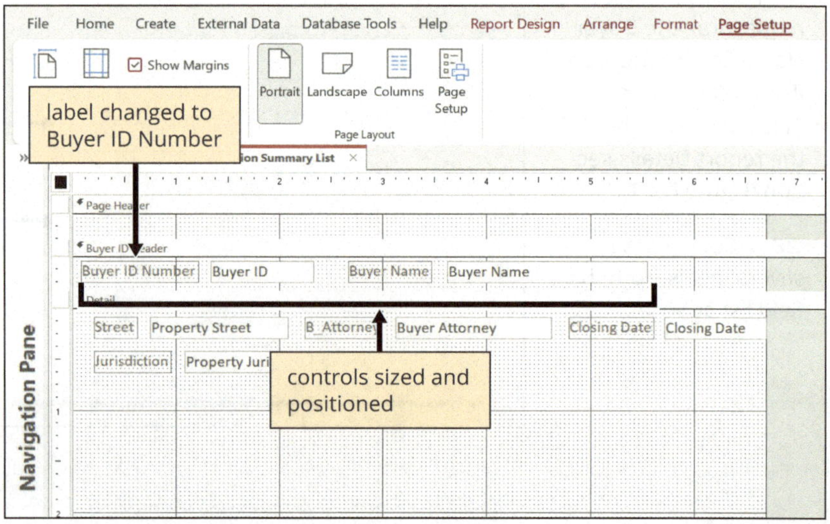

Figure 6–23

Using Other Tools in the Controls Group

Previously, you used the Subform/Subreport tool within the Controls group on the Design tab to place special controls on a form. The Controls group has additional tools available that can be used with forms and reports. A description of the additional tools appears in Table 6–3.

Table 6–3 Additional Tools in the Controls Group

Tool	Description
Select	Select to be able to size, move, or edit existing controls. If you click another tool and want to cancel the effect of the tool before using it, you can click the Select tool.
Text Box	Create a text box for entering, editing, and displaying data. You can also bind the text box to a field in the underlying table or query.
Label	Create a label, which is a box containing text that cannot be edited and is independent of other controls, such as a title.
Button	Create a command button.
Tab Control	Create a tab control, which contains a series of tabbed pages. Each tabbed page can contain its own controls.
Link	Insert a hyperlink to an existing file, web page, database object, or email address.
Option Group	Create an option group, which is a rectangle containing a collection of option buttons. To select an option, you click the corresponding option button.
Insert or Remove Page Break	Insert or remove a physical page break (typically in a report).
Combo Box	Create a combo box, which is a combination of a text box and a list box.
Line	Draw a line on a form or report.
Toggle Button	Add a toggle button. With a toggle button, a user can make a Yes/No selection by clicking the button. The button either appears to be pressed (for Yes) or not pressed (for No).
List Box	Create a list box, a box that allows the user to select from a list of options.
Rectangle	Create a rectangle.
Check Box	Insert a check box. With a check box a user can make multiple Yes/No selections.
Unbound Object Frame	Insert an OLE object (for example, a graph, picture, sound file, or video) that is not contained in a field in a table within the database.
Attachment	Insert a field to hold attached files, such as images, documents, or presentation slides.
Option Button	Insert an option button. With an option button, a user can make a single Yes/No selection from among a collection of at least two choices.
Subform/Subreport	Create a subform (a form contained within another form) or a subreport (a report contained within another report).
Bound Object Frame	Insert an OLE object (for example, a graph, picture, sound file, or video) that is contained in a field in a table within the database.
Image	Insert a frame into which you can insert a graphic. The graphic will be the same for all records.
Chart	Create a chart.

To Add Text Boxes

You can place a text box in a report or form by using the Text Box tool in the Controls group on the Design tab. The text box consists of a control that is initially unbound and an attached label. The next step is to update the **control source**, which is the source of data for the control. You can do so by entering the expression in the text box or by updating the Control Source property in the property sheet with the expression.

Once you have updated the control source property with the expression, the control becomes a calculated control. If the expression is just a single field (for example, =[Cost]), the control would be a bound control. Why? The control is bound (tied) to the corresponding field. The process of converting an unbound control to a bound control is called **binding**. Expressions can also be arithmetic operations: for example, calculating the sum of Cost and Current Due. Many times, you need to **concatenate**, or combine, two or more text data items into a single expression; the process is called **concatenation**. To concatenate text data, you use the **ampersand (&) operator**. For example, the expression =[Property City] & ' ' & [Property State] indicates the concatenation of a city name, a single blank space, and a state name.

BTW

Drop Down Controls

Drop-down boxes can be combo boxes or list boxes. To add a combo box to a report, click the Combo Box tool from the Controls gallery (Report Design tab | Controls group), move the pointer to the desired location, and click the position to place the combo box. Follow the directions in the Combo Box Wizard dialog box to specify the options and values for the combo box. To add a list box to a report, click the List Box tool from the Controls gallery (Report Design tab | Controls group) and follow the steps described above for a combo box.

The following steps add text boxes and create calculated controls. Remember that controls can be resized by clicking the control to select it and then dragging the edge of the control to the desired size.

1

- Click the Text Box tool (Report Design tab | Controls group) and move the pointer to the approximate position shown in Figure 6–24 in the Detail section.

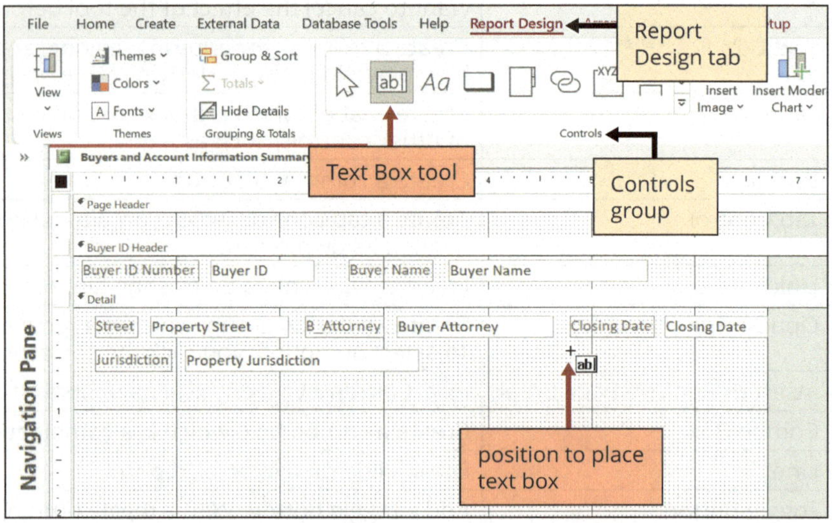

Figure 6–24

BTW

Default Names for Controls

Because each control has properties associated with it, Access assigns a default name to each new control. The default name includes a control identifier and a number. For example, if you create a text box on a report, the default name could be Text32. You should change the default name to something meaningful to make it easier to remember the purpose of the control.

2

- Click the position shown in Figure 6–24 to place a text box on the report (Figure 6–25). Reposition it if necessary so neither the text box nor its label overlap other controls.

Q&A My text box overlaps an object already on the screen. Is that a problem?

You can move and/or resize your text box to the desired location and size. You also can continue to make adjustments to the text box's size and position as other changes are made to the report.

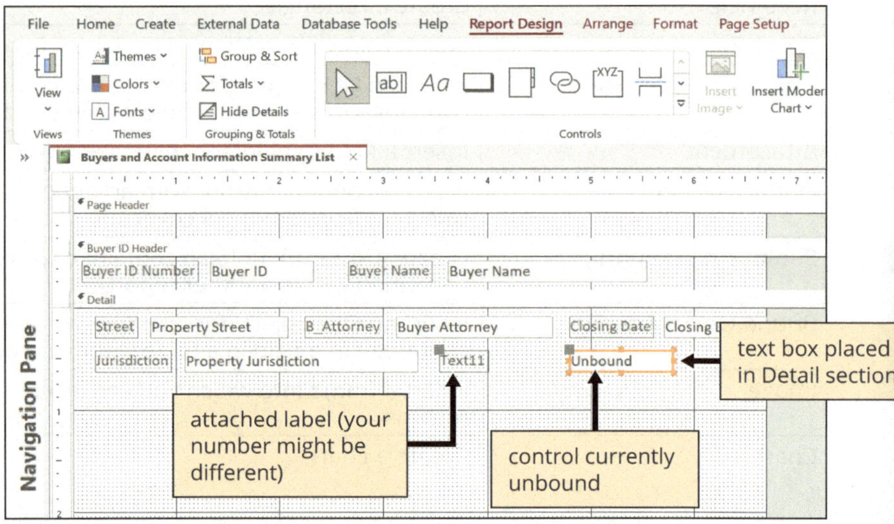

Figure 6–25

3

- Click in the text box to produce an insertion point (Figure 6–26).

Q&A I inadvertently clicked somewhere else, so the text box was no longer selected. When I clicked the text box a second time, it was selected, but there was no insertion point. What should I do?

Click the text box again to produce the insertion point.

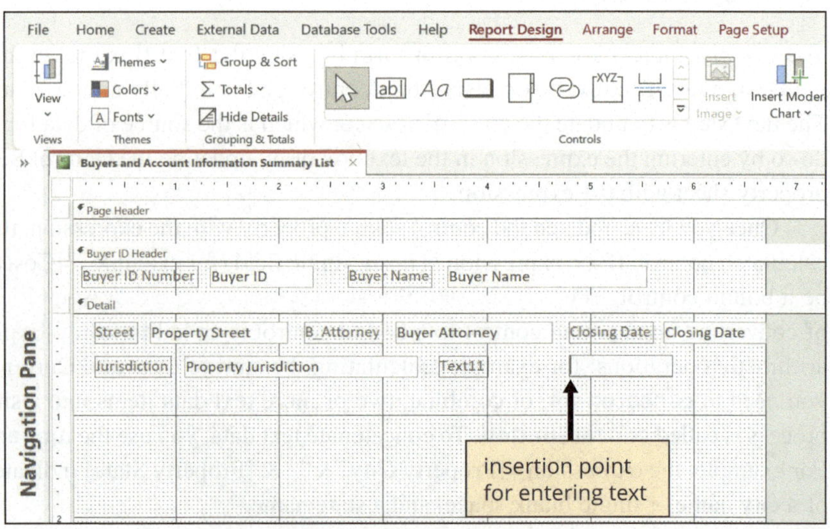

Figure 6–26

4

- In the text box, type **=[Property City] & ' ' & [Property State]** to display the name of the property city, followed by a space, and then the name of the property state.

Q&A Could I use the Expression Builder instead of typing the expression?

Yes. Click the Property Sheet button and then click the Build button, which contains three dots, next to the Control Source property.

Do I need to use single quotes (')?

No. You could also use double quotes (").

- Click in the text box label to select the label, and then click the label a second time to produce an insertion point (Figure 6–27).

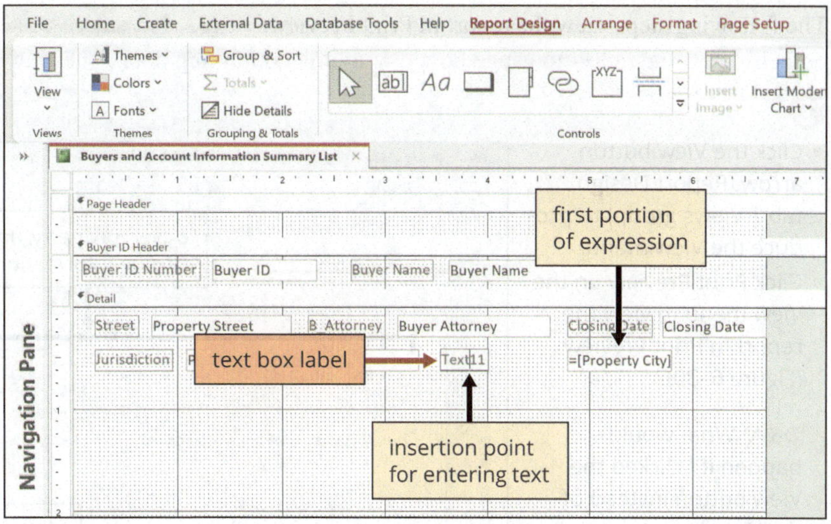

Figure 6–27

5

- Use BACKSPACE or DEL to erase the current entry in the label, and then type **Property Location** as the new entry.
- Click outside the label to deselect it, and then drag the label to the position shown in the figure by dragging the Move handle in the upper-left corner of the label (Figure 6–28).

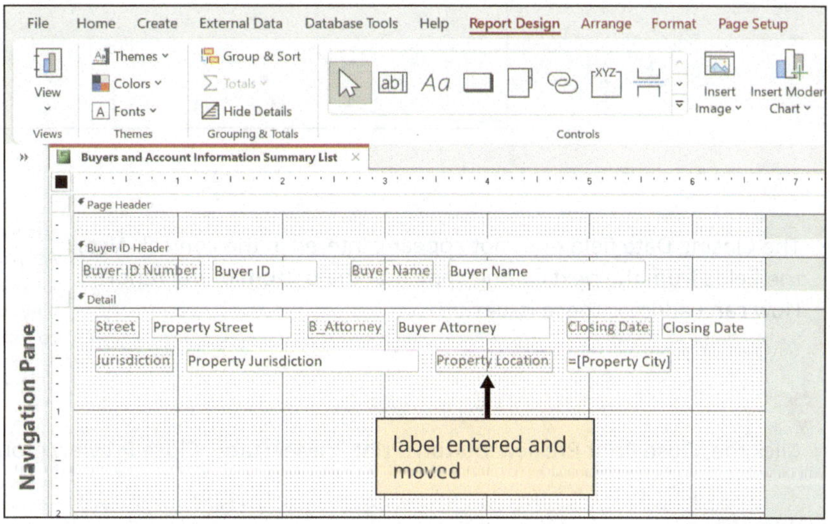

Figure 6–28

6

- Resize the text box control to display more of the expression (Figure 6–29).

7

- Save the report.

Q&A My label is not in the correct position. What should I do?

Click outside the label to deselect it, click the label to select it, and then use its move handle to drag it to the desired position.

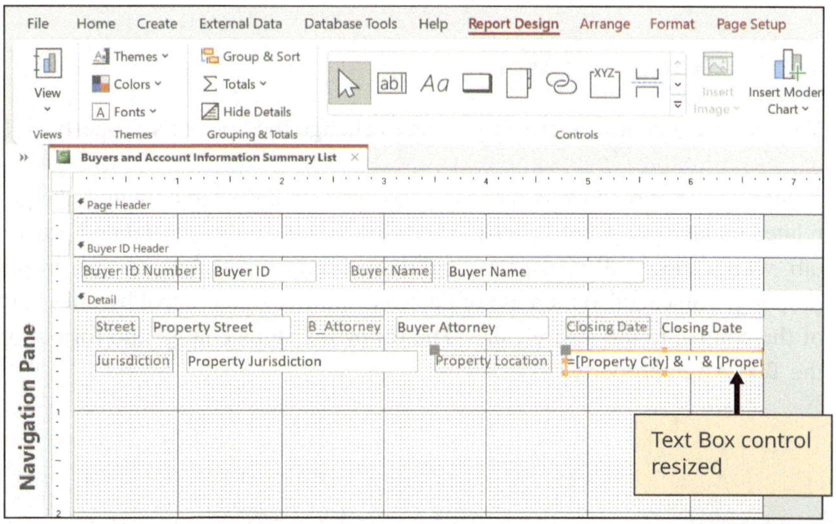

Figure 6–29

To View the Report in Print Preview

The following steps view the report in Print Preview. **Why?** As you are working on a report in Design view, it is useful to periodically view the report to gauge how it will look containing data. One way to do so is to use Print Preview.

1

- Click the View button arrow (Report Design tab | Views group) to produce the View menu.
- Click Print Preview on the View menu to view the report in Print Preview (Figure 6–30).

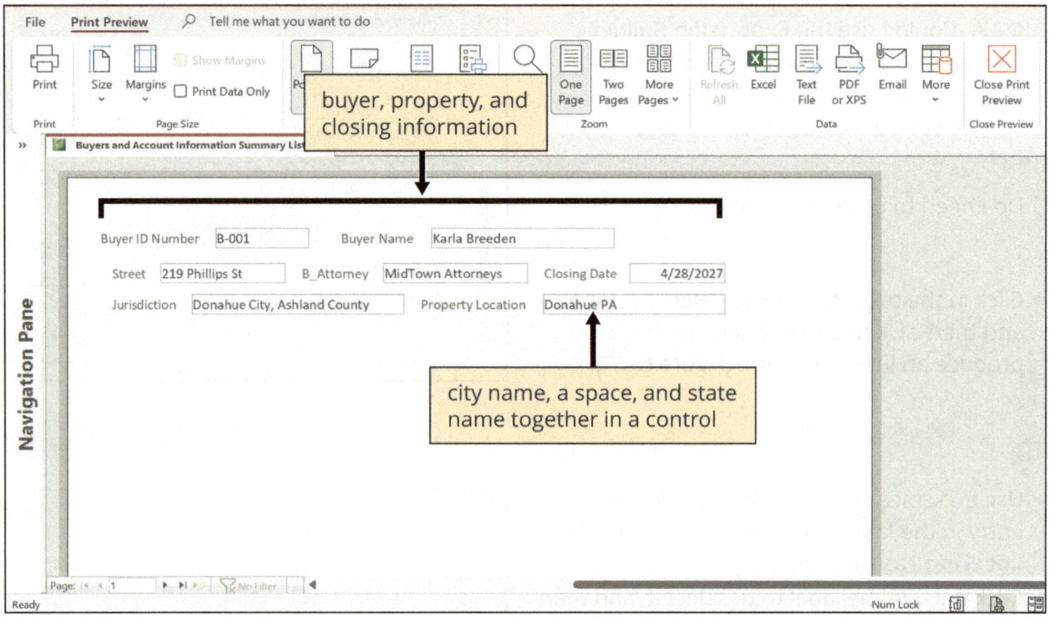

Figure 6–30

Q&A What would happen if I clicked the View button instead of the View button arrow?
The icon on the View button is the icon for Report View, so you would view the results in Report view. This is another useful way to view a report, but compared with Print Preview, Report view does not give as accurate a picture of how the final, printed report will look.

The Closing Date field does not appear centered in the control. Also, the fields from the next closing appear at the bottom of the report. How can I address these issues?
You will address these issues in the next sections.

BTW
Viewing Report Modifications
As you work through this module, switch between Design view and either Report view or Print Preview frequently to view your changes. An easy way to switch back and forth is to use the different view buttons on the status bar.

2

- Click the 'Close Print Preview' button (Print Preview tab | Close Preview group) to return to Design view.

Other Ways

1. Click Print Preview button on status bar to open Print Preview

To Format a Control

You can use a control's property sheet to change the control's property. **Why?** When you add controls to a report, you often need to format the control, for example, to add a bold or an alignment format. If a property does not appear in the control's property sheet, you have two choices. You can click the tab on which the property is located. For example, if it were a control related to data, you would click the Data tab to show only data-related properties. Many people, however, prefer to click the All tab, which shows all properties, and then simply scroll through the properties, if necessary, until locating the appropriate property. You can also increase or decrease the size of a control by clicking the control to select it and then dragging the edge of the control to the desired size. The following steps change the format of the Closing Date control to Center by changing the Text Align property.

1

- Click the Closing Date control to select it, and then click the Property Sheet button (Report Design tab | Tools group) to display the Property Sheet pane.
- If necessary, click the All tab (Figure 6–31).

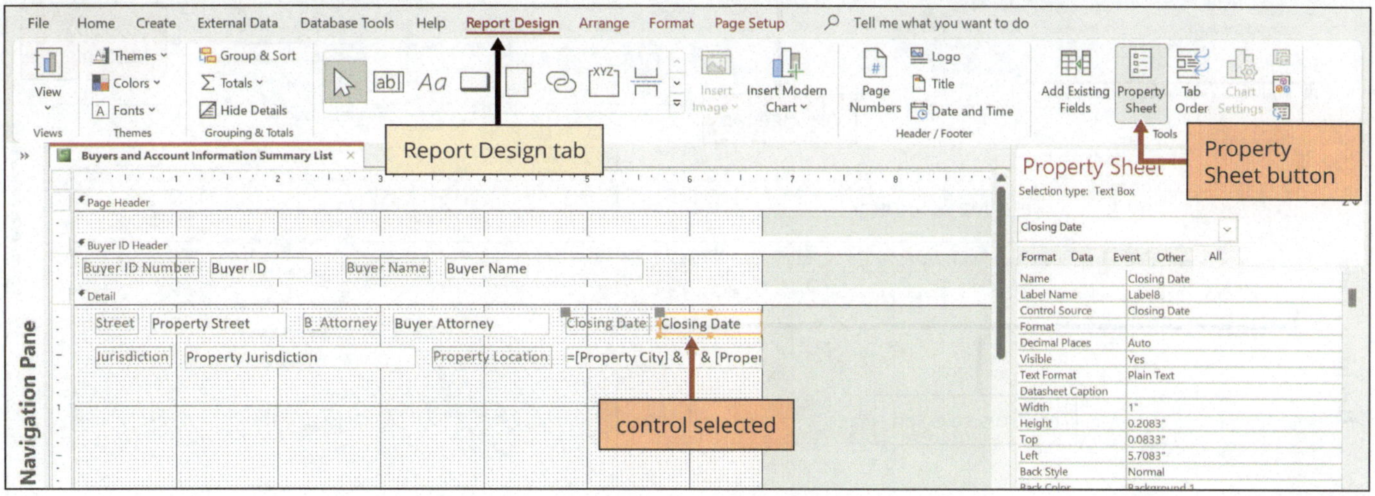

Figure 6–31

Other Ways

1. Right-click control, click Properties to open Property Sheet pane

- **Experiment:** Click the other tabs in the property sheet to see the types of properties on each tab. When finished, once again click the All tab.

2

- Click the Text Align property box (Property Sheet pane), click the arrow that appears, and then click Center to select Center as the control's alignment.
- Close the Property Sheet pane.
- Preview the report using Print Preview to see the effect of the property changes.
- Click the 'Close Print Preview' button (Print Preview tab | Close Preview group) to return to Design view.

To Group Controls

The following steps group the controls within the Detail section. **Why?** If your report contains a collection of controls that you will frequently want to format in the same way, you can simplify the process of selecting all the controls by grouping them. Once they are grouped, selecting any control in the group automatically selects all the controls in the group. You can then apply the desired change to all the controls.

1

- Click the Property Street control to select it.

Q&A Do I click the field control with the white background or the label control with the transparent background?
Click the field control with the white background.

- While holding SHIFT, click all the other field controls (not the label controls) in the Detail section to select them.

Q&A Does it matter in which order I select the other field controls?
No. It is only important that you select all the field controls in the Detail section, but do not select the label controls.

- Display the Arrange tab.
- Click the Size/Space button (Arrange tab | Sizing & Ordering group) to display the Size/Space menu, and then scroll to the bottom of that menu (Figure 6–32).

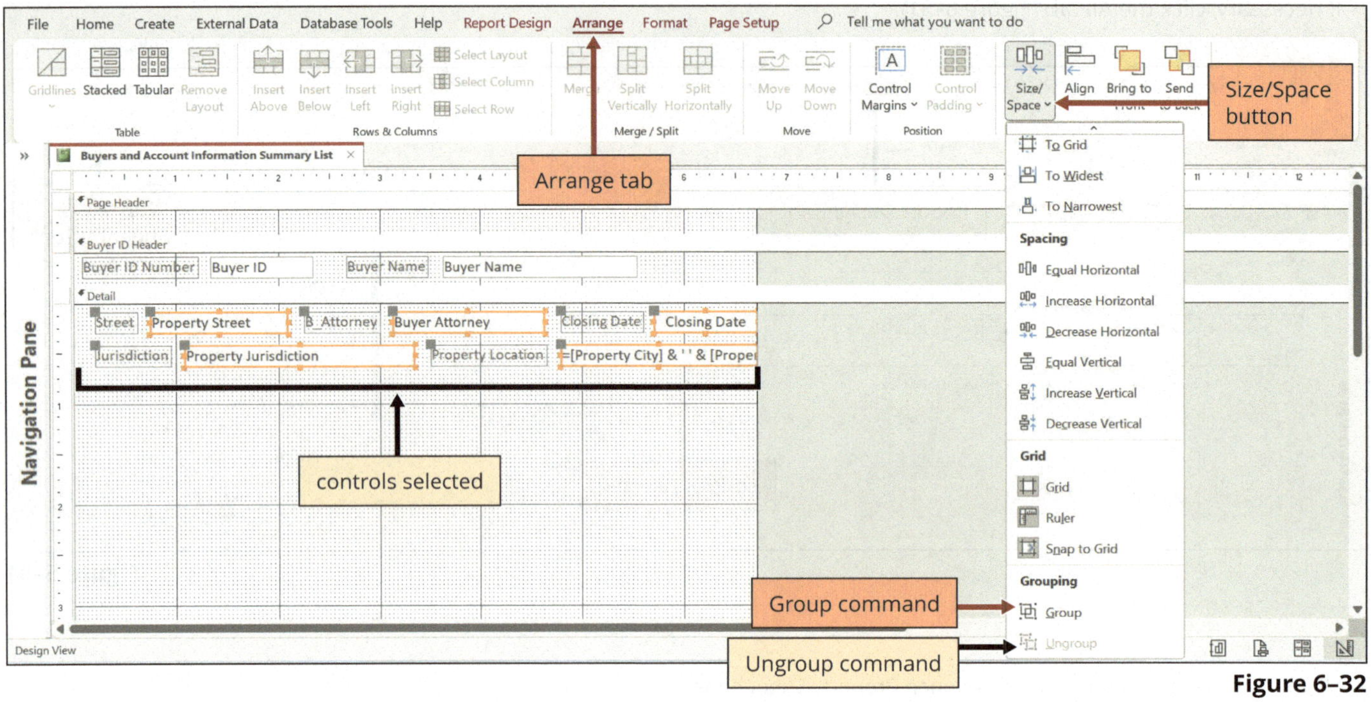

Figure 6–32

2

- Click Group on the Size/Space button menu to group the controls.
- Click outside the controls to deselect the group.

Q&A What if I make a mistake and group the wrong collection of controls?
Ungroup the controls using the following steps, and then group the correct collection of controls.

To Ungroup Controls

If you no longer need to simultaneously modify all the controls you have placed in a group, you can ungroup the controls. To do so, you would use the following steps.

1. Click any of the controls in a group to select the entire group.
2. Display the Arrange tab.
3. Click the Size/Space button (Arrange tab | Sizing & Ordering group) to display the Size/Space button menu.
4. Click the Ungroup button on the Size/Space button menu to ungroup the controls.

Consider This

Can you group controls in forms?

Yes. The process is identical to the process of grouping controls in reports.

To Modify Grouped Controls

To modify grouped controls, click any control in the group to select the entire group. **Why?** Any change you make then affects all controls in the group. The following steps bold the controls in the group, resize them, and then change the border style.

1

- Click any one of the grouped controls to select the group.
- Display the Format tab.
- Click the Bold button (Format tab | Font group) to bold all the controls in the group (Figure 6–33).

Q&A How do I change only one control in the group?
Double-click the control to select just the one control and not the entire group. You then can make any change you want to that control.

Do I need to use the Property Street field to select the group or could I use another field?
Any field in the group will work.

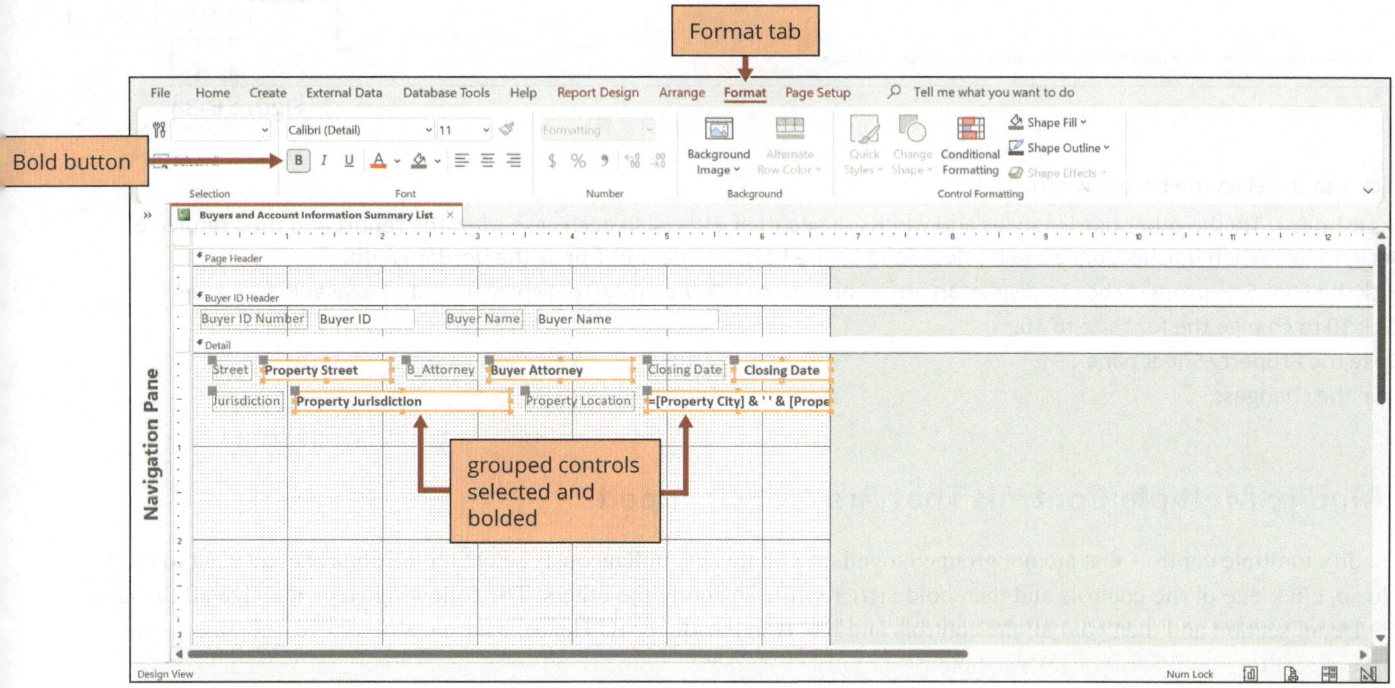

Figure 6–33

2

- Display the Report Design tab, and then click the Property Sheet button (Report Design tab | Tools group) to display the property sheet for the grouped controls.
- With the All tab (Property Sheet pane) selected, ensure the Border Style property is set to Solid. If it is not, click the Border Style property box to display an arrow, click the arrow to display the list of available border styles, and click Solid.
- Click the Border Width property box to display an arrow, and then click the arrow to display the list of available border widths (Figure 6–34).

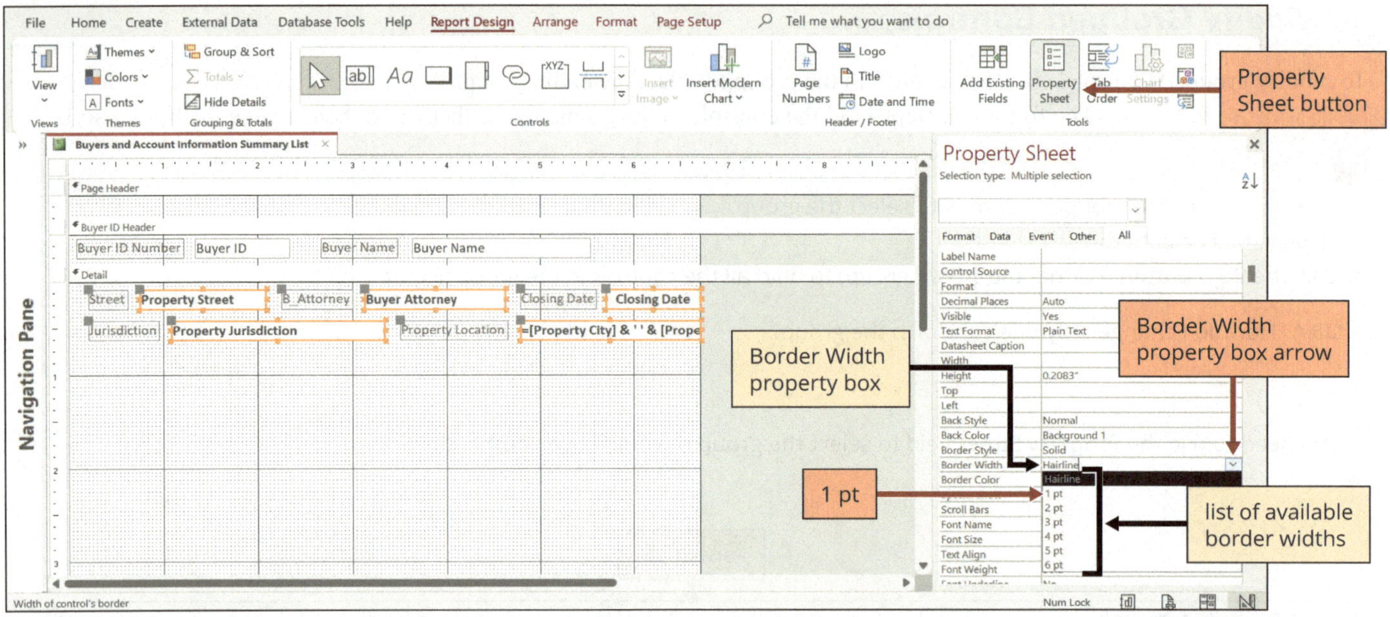

Figure 6–34

3

- Click 1 pt to select the border width.
- **Experiment:** Try the other border styles and widths to see their effects. In each case, view the report and then return to Design view. When finished, once again select Solid as the border style and 1 pt as the border width.
- Click the Font Size property box to display an arrow, and then click the arrow to display the list of available font sizes.
- Click 10 to change the font size to 10.
- Close the Property Sheet pane.
- Save the changes.

To Modify Multiple Controls That Are Not Grouped

To modify multiple controls that are not grouped together, you must simultaneously select all the controls you want to modify. To do so, click one of the controls and then hold SHIFT while selecting the others. The following steps italicize all the labels in the Detail section and then bold all the controls and labels in the Buyer ID Header section. **Why?** Text formatting makes it easier to visually group pieces of information in a report.

1

- Click the label (the control with the transparent background) for the Street control to select it.
- While pressing SHIFT, click the labels for all the other controls in the Detail section to select them.
- Display the Format tab.
- Click the Italic button (Format tab | Font group) to italicize the labels (Figure 6–35).

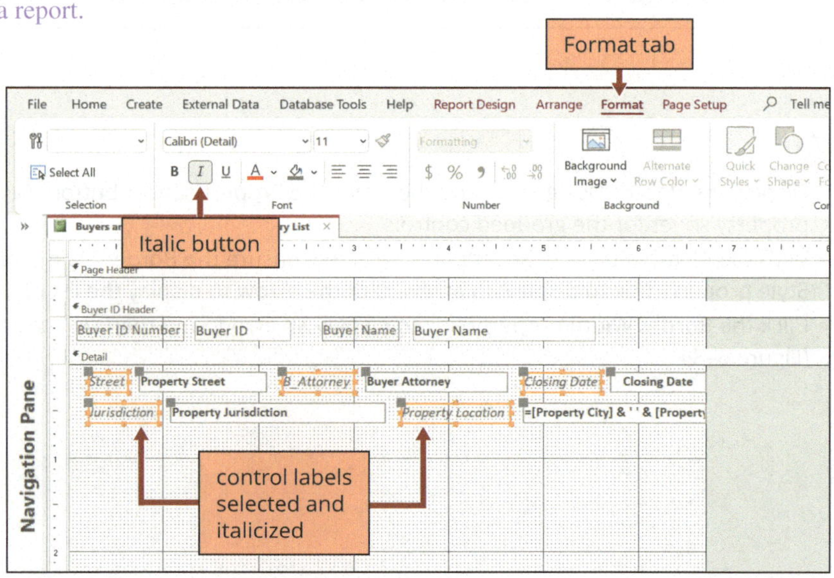

Figure 6–35

2

- Click in the vertical ruler to the left of the Buyer ID control to select all the controls in the Buyer ID Header section.

Q&A What exactly is selected when I click in the vertical ruler?
If you picture a horizontal line through the point you clicked, any control that intersects that horizontal line is selected.

- Use the buttons on the Arrange tab to align the controls on the top, if necessary.
- Display the Format tab, and then click the Bold button (Format tab | Font group) to bold all the selected controls (Figure 6–36).

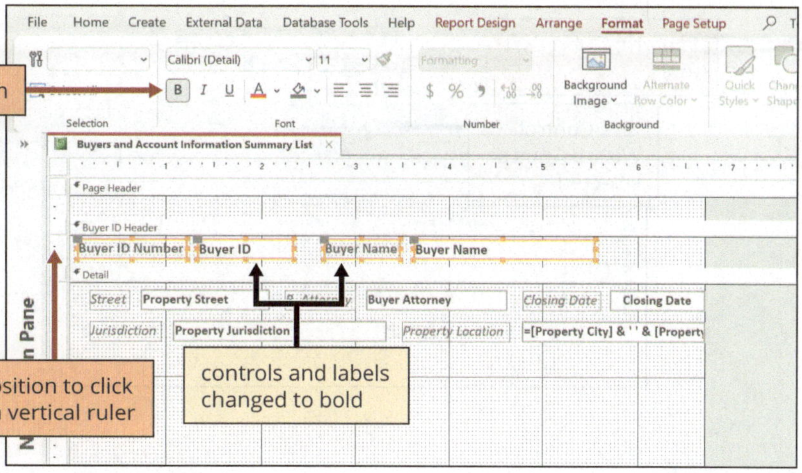

Figure 6–36

3

- View the report in Print Preview and then make any necessary adjustments.
- Close Print Preview and save the report.

Undoing and Saving

Remember that if you make a mistake, you can often correct it by clicking the Undo button on the Home tab. Clicking the Undo button usually will reverse your most recent change. You can also click the Undo button more than once to reverse multiple changes.

You should save your work frequently. That way, if you have problems that the Undo button will not fix, you can close the report without saving it and open it again. The report will be in exactly the state it was in the last time you saved it.

To Add a Subreport

To add a subreport to a report, you use the Subform/Subreport tool on the Report Design tab. The following steps add a subreport to display the workshop data, after first ensuring the 'Use Control Wizards' button is selected. **Why?** Provided the 'Use Control Wizards' button is selected, a wizard will guide you through the process of adding the subreport.

1

- If necessary, switch to Design view, and then display the Report Design tab.
- Click the More button, which is shown in Figure 6–37a (Report Design tab | Controls group), to display a gallery of available tools (Figure 6–37b).

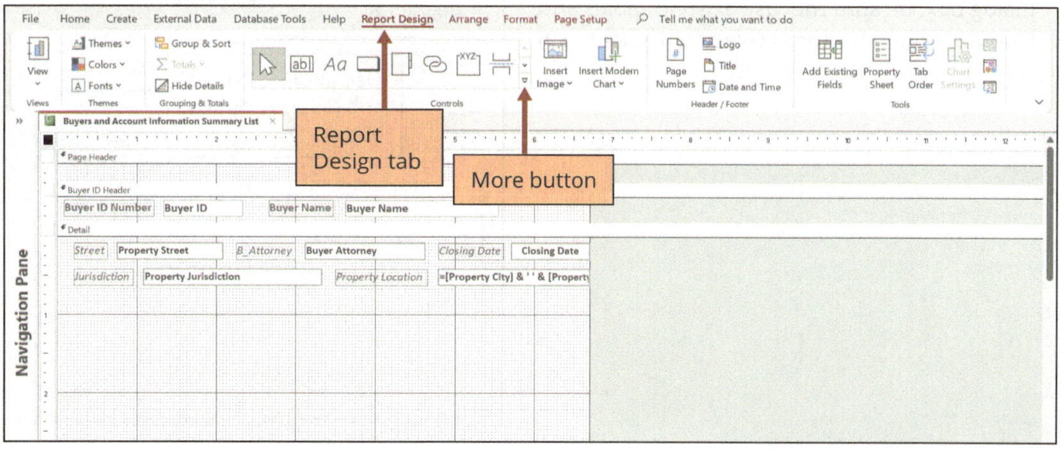

Figure 6–37a More Button

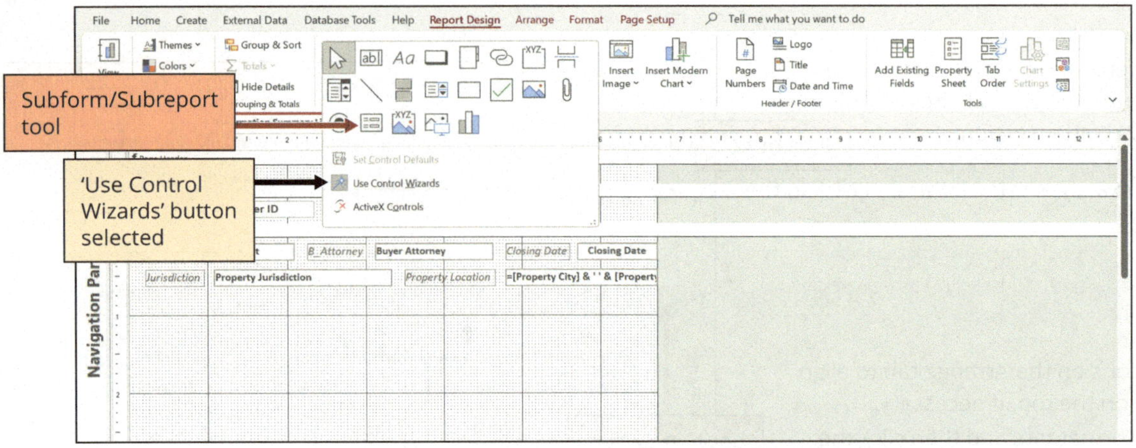

Figure 6–37b Design Tools Gallery

2

- Be sure the 'Use Control Wizards' button is selected, click the Subform/Subreport tool, and then move the pointer, which has changed to a plus sign with a subreport, to the approximate position shown in Figure 6–38.

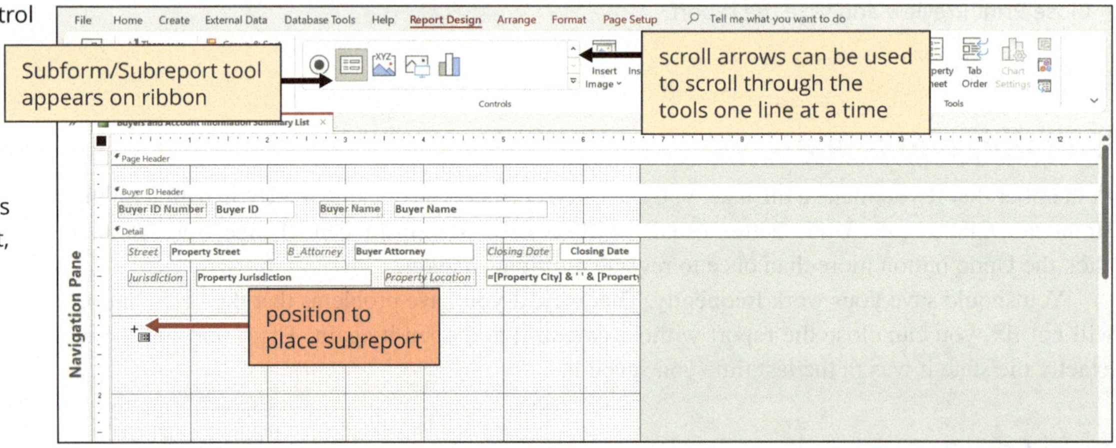

Figure 6–38

3

- Click the position shown in Figure 6–38 to place the subreport and display the SubReport Wizard dialog box. Be sure the 'Use existing Tables and Queries' option button is selected (Figure 6–39).

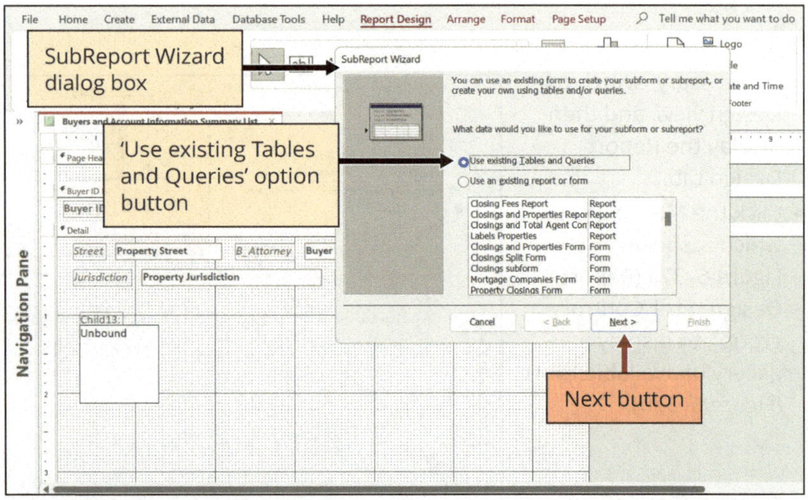

Figure 6–39

4

- Click the Next button.
- Click the Tables/Queries box arrow to display a list of the available tables and queries.
- Scroll down and click Query: Workshop Enrollments and Workshops to specify this query as the data source, and then click the 'Add All Fields' button to select all the fields in the query and add them to the subreport (Figure 6–40).

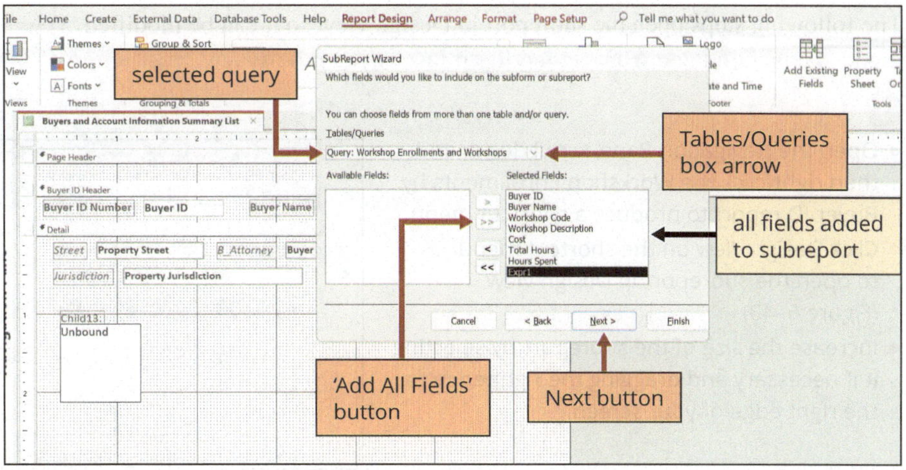

Figure 6–40

5

- Click the Next button and then ensure the 'Choose from a list.' option button is selected. If necessary, click 'Show Workshop Enrollments and Workshops for each record in Buyers and Account Information using Buyer ID.' (Figure 6–41).

Q&A What is the purpose of this dialog box?

You use this dialog box to indicate the fields that link the main report (referred to as a "form") to the subreport (referred to as a "subform"). If the fields have the same name, as they often will, you can simply select 'Choose from a list' and then accept the selection Access already has made.

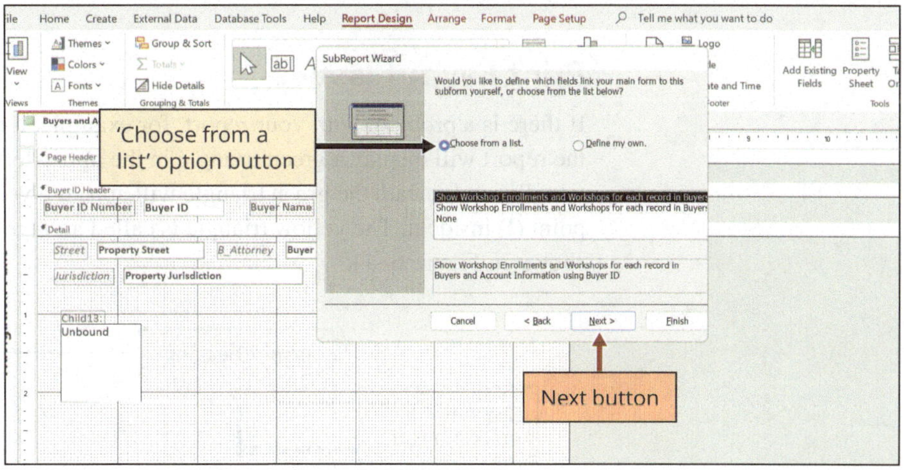

Figure 6–41

6

- Click the Next button, change the subreport name to **Workshop Enrollments by Buyer ID** and then click the Finish button to add the subreport to the Buyers and Account Information Summary List report (Figure 6–42).

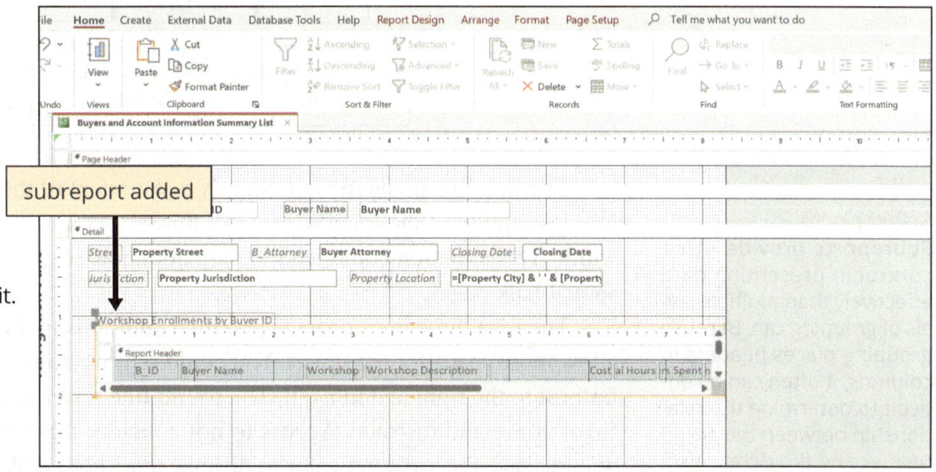

Figure 6–42

7

- Click outside the subreport to deselect it.
- Save your changes.
- Close the report.

Break Point: If you wish to take a break, this is a good place to do so. You can quit Access now. To resume at a later time, start Access, open the database called SC_AC_06_Partners.accdb, and continue following the steps from this location forward.

To Open the Subreport in Design View

The following steps open the subreport in Design view so it can be modified. **Why?** The subreport appears as a separate report in the Navigation Pane. You can modify it just as you modify any other report.

1

- Open the Navigation Pane, scroll down, and then right-click the Workshop Enrollments by Buyer ID report to produce a shortcut menu.
- Click Design View on the shortcut menu to open the subreport in Design view (Figure 6–43).
- Increase the size of the subreport by selecting it if necessary and dragging the right edge to the right edge of your screen.

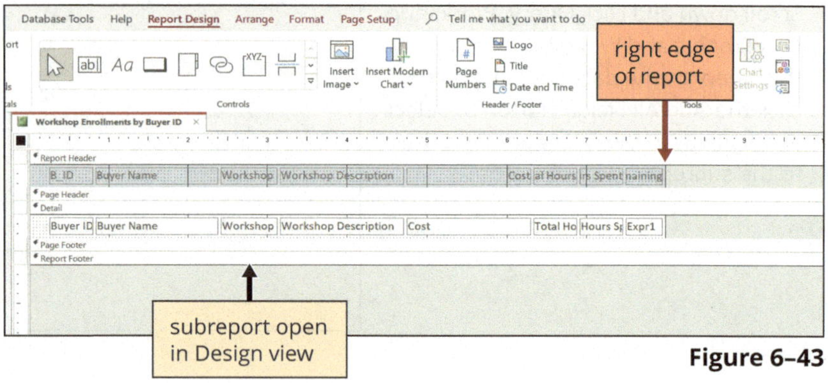

Figure 6–43

Print Layout Issues

If there is a problem with your report, for example, a report that is too wide for the printed page, the report will display a green triangle in the upper-left corner of the report selector button. Additionally, underneath the green triangle will appear a yellow triangular symbol with an exclamation point (!) inside it. The yellow triangle is called an **error indicator**. Clicking it produces the menu shown in Figure 6–44.

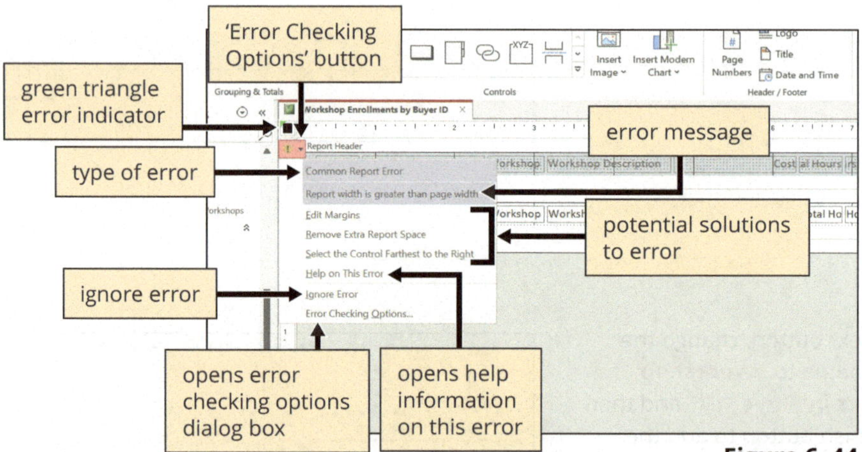

Figure 6–44

BTW
Subreports
Subreports provide more control in presenting data effectively than multiple levels of grouping can. Because grouping places headers in columns, it often can be difficult to determine the relationship between the group header and the detail. Also, you might want to present subreports side by side. You cannot do this with grouping.

The first line in the menu is simply a statement of the type of error that occurred. The second is a description of the specific error, in this case, the fact the report width is greater than the page width. This situation could lead to data not appearing where you expect it to, as well as printing some blank pages.

The next three lines provide potential solutions to the error. You could change the margins to allow more space for the report. You could remove some extra space. You could select the control farthest to the right and move it. The fourth line gives more detailed help on the error. The Ignore Error command instructs Access to not consider this situation an error. Selecting Ignore Error would cause the error indicator to disappear without making any changes. The final line displays the Error Checking Options dialog box, where you can make other changes.

Later in this module, you will fix the problem by changing the width of the report, so you do not need to take any action at this time.

To Modify the Controls in the Subreport

The query used to create the subreport contains three fields not needed for this report. The fields are needed in the query for another report, but they should not be listed in this subreport. The following steps modify the subreport by deleting the Buyer ID, Buyer Name, and Cost controls and revising the appearance of the column headings. **Why?** Because the Buyer ID appears in the main report, it does not need to be duplicated in the subreport.

1

- Close the Navigation Pane.
- Click the Buyer ID control in the Detail section to select the control. While holding SHIFT, click the Buyer Name control and the Cost control in the Detail section, and then click the Buyer ID control, the Buyer Name control, and the Cost control in the Report Header section to select all six controls.
- With six controls selected, press DEL to delete the controls.

2

- Break the heading for the Total Hours column over two lines by clicking in front of the word, Hours, to produce an insertion point and then pressing SHIFT+ENTER to move the second word to a second line.
- Break the headings for the Hours Spent and Hours Remaining columns over two lines using the same technique.
- Adjust the sizes and placement of the labels in the Report Header section to match those shown in Figure 6–45.

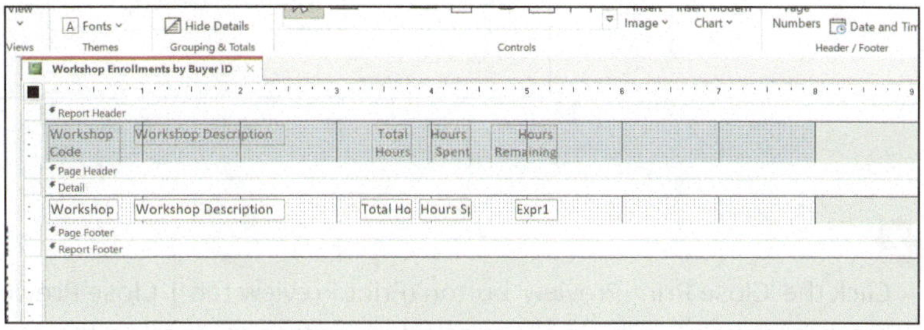

Figure 6–45

- Change the sizes and positions of the controls in the Detail section to match those in the figure by selecting the controls and dragging the sizing handles and by using the alignment controls (Arrange tab | Sizing & Ordering group).

Q&A Why does Expr1 appear in the Detail section under the Hours Remaining label?
Expr1 indicates that Hours Remaining is a calculated control.

Consider This

How can you adjust fields where some of the entries are too long to fit in the available space?

This problem can be addressed in several ways.

1. Move the controls to allow more space between controls. Then, drag the appropriate handles on the controls that need to be expanded to enlarge them.
2. Use the Font Size property to select a smaller font size. This will allow more data to fit in the same space.
3. Use the Can Grow property. By changing the value of this property from No to Yes, the data can be spread over two lines, thus allowing all the data to print. Access will split data at natural break points, such as commas, spaces, and hyphens.

To Change the Can Grow Property

The third suggested approach to handling entries that are too long is the easiest to use and also produces a very readable report. The following steps change the Can Grow property for the Workshop Description field. **Why?** Changing the Can Grow property allows Access to optimize the size of fields in reports.

1

- Click the View button arrow (Report Design tab | Views group), and then click Print Preview to preview the report (Figure 6–46). If an error message appears indicating the report is too wide, click OK.

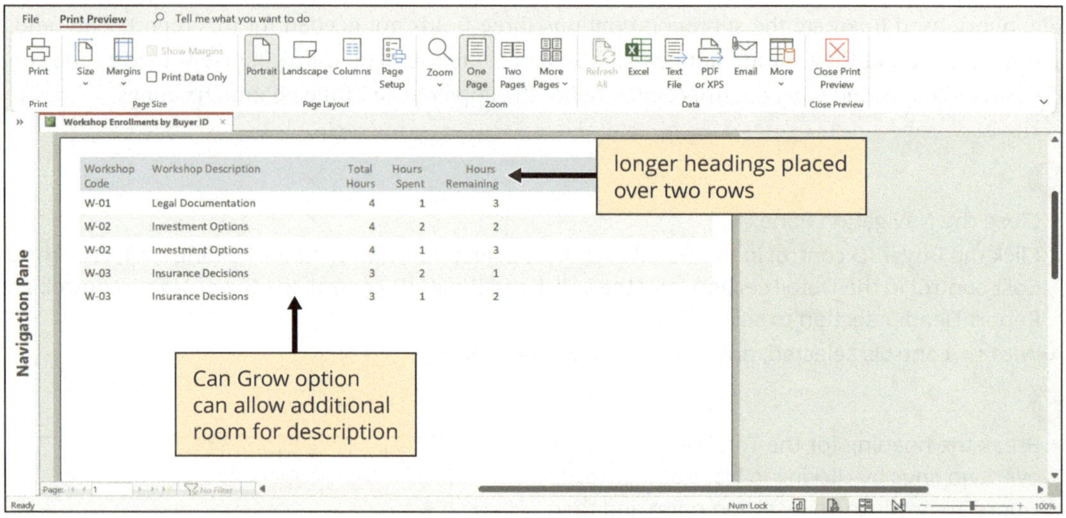

Figure 6–46

2

- Click the 'Close Print Preview' button (Print Preview tab | Close Preview group) to return to Design view.
- If necessary, click outside all the selected controls to deselect the controls.
- Click the Workshop Description control in the Detail section to select it.
- Click the Property Sheet button (Report Design tab | Tools group) to display the Property Sheet pane.
- With the All tab selected, scroll down until the Can Grow property appears, click the Can Grow property box to display the property arrow, and then click the Can Grow property box arrow to display the list of possible values for the Can Grow property (Figure 6–47).

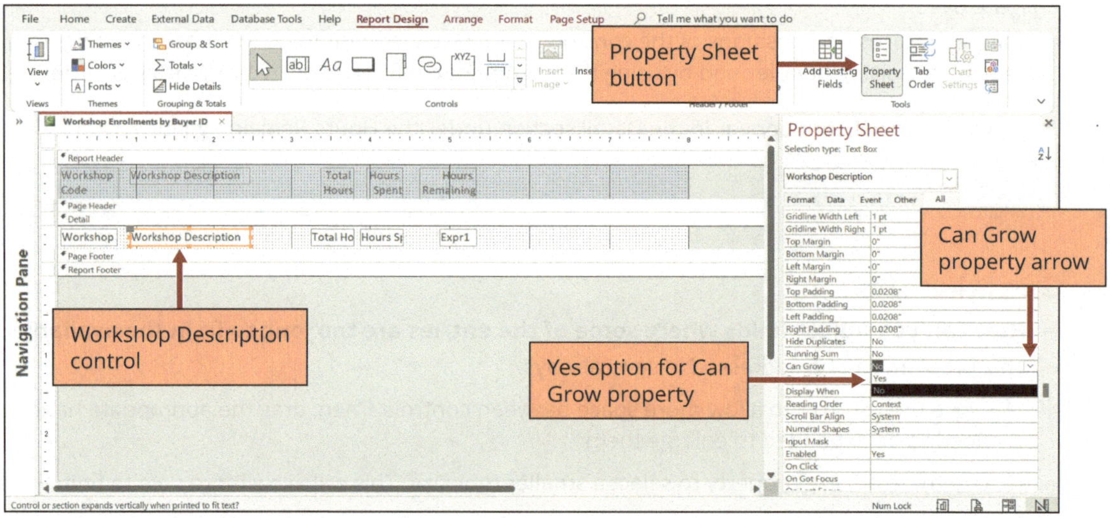

Figure 6–47

Q&A What is the effect of the Can Shrink property?

If the value of the Can Shrink property is set to Yes, Access will remove blank lines that occur when the field is empty.

3

- Click Yes in the list to allow the Workshop Description control to grow as needed.
- Close the Property Sheet pane.

To Change the Appearance of the Controls in the Subreport

Why? Partners paralegals prefer certain formatting for the subreport controls. The following steps change the controls in the Detail section to bold and the controls in the Report Header section to italic. They also change the background color in the Report Header section to white.

1

- Drag the right boundary of the subreport to the approximate position shown in Figure 6–48. The error indicator should disappear.

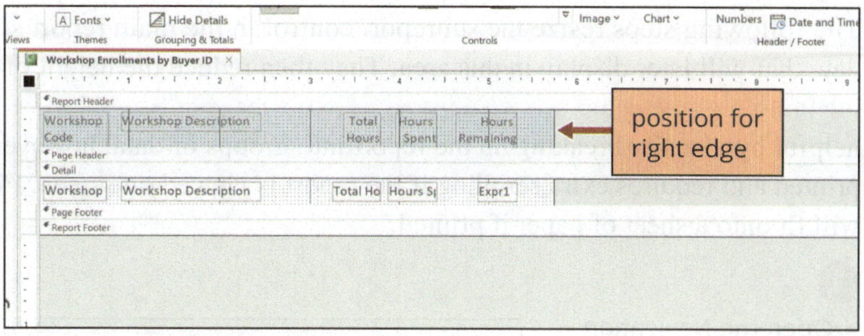

Figure 6–48

2

- Display the Format tab.
- Click the vertical ruler to the left of the controls in the Detail section to select the controls in that section, and then click the Bold button (Format tab | Font group) to bold the controls.
- Click the ruler to the left of the controls in the Report Header section to select the controls in that section, and then click the Italic button (Format tab | Font group) to italicize the controls.
- Click the title bar for the Report Header to select the header without selecting any of the controls in the header.
- Click the Background Color button arrow (Format tab | Font group) to display a color palette (Figure 6–49).

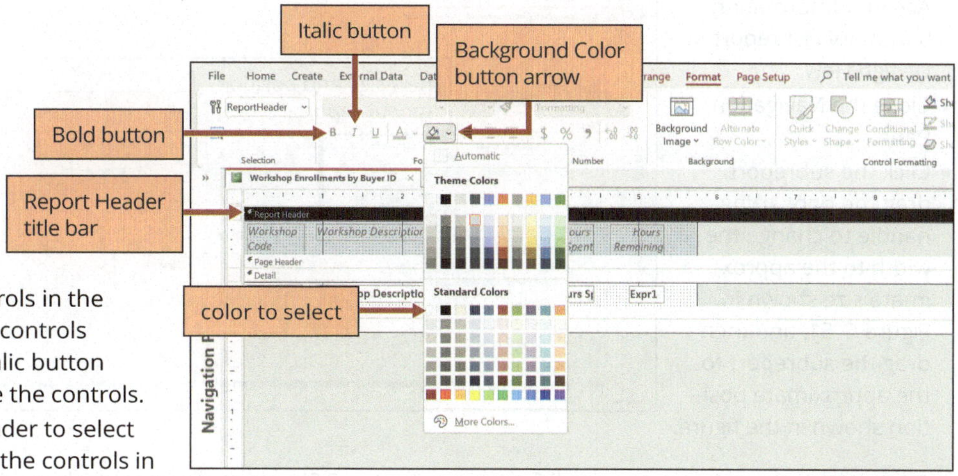

Figure 6–49

3

- Click White in the first row, first column of the Standard Colors to change the background color to white (Figure 6–50).

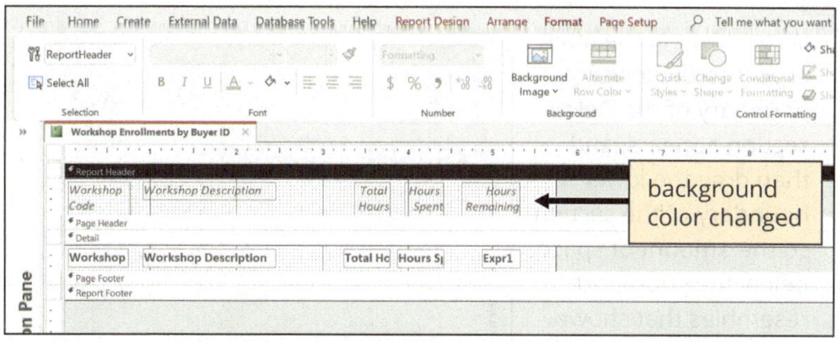

Figure 6–50

Q&A What is the difference between clicking a color in the Theme colors and clicking a color in the Standard Colors?

The theme colors are specific to the currently selected theme. The first column, for example, represents "background 1," one of the selected background colors in the theme. The various entries in the column represent different intensities of the color at the top of the column. The colors would be different if a different theme were selected. If you select one of the theme colors and a different theme is selected in the future, the color you selected would change to the color in the same location. On the other hand, if you select a standard color, a change of theme would have no effect on the color.

- Save the changes, and then close the subreport.

To Resize the Subreport and the Report in Design View

The following steps resize the subreport control in the main report so the control for the subreport will appropriately fit the data that will later display in this area. They then reduce the height of the detail section. **Why?** Any additional white space at the bottom of the detail section appears as extra space at the end of each detail line in the final report. Some extra space can be helpful by visually breaking up the report into groups of data; however, too much extra space just wastes paper if the report is printed and requires extra scrolling if the report is viewed on screen. Finally, the steps reduce the width of the main report so it will fit onto a sheet of paper if printed.

1

- Open the Navigation Pane.
- Open the Buyers and Account Information Summary List report in Design view.
- Close the Navigation Pane.
- Click the subreport, drag the right sizing handle to change the width to the approximate size shown in Figure 6–51, and then drag the subreport to the approximate position shown in the figure.

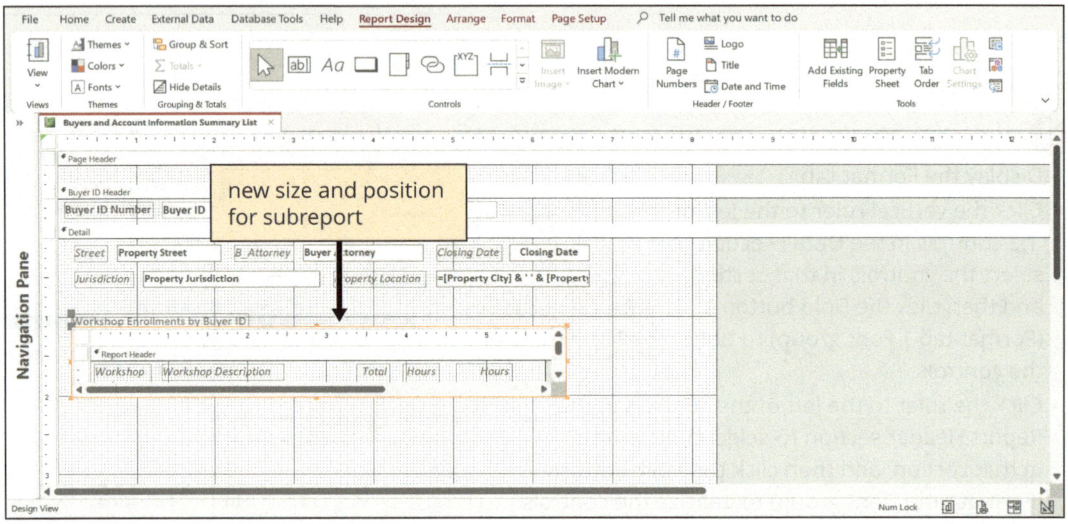

Figure 6–51

Q&A Why is the subreport so small from top to bottom? Shouldn't all the controls inside the subreport appear as well?
The rulers in the subreport control take up a lot of space in Design view that will later be used to display the subreport's data in Report view or Print Preview. Considering the data that will eventually be displayed in this area, the subreport does not need to be any taller. You can check that the subreport is tall enough without being too tall by switching to Report view or Print Preview as you make changes to the sizes and positions of all controls.

2

- Scroll down in the main report so the lower boundary of the Detail section appears, and then drag the lower boundary of the section so the amount of space below the subreport resembles that shown in Figure 6–52.

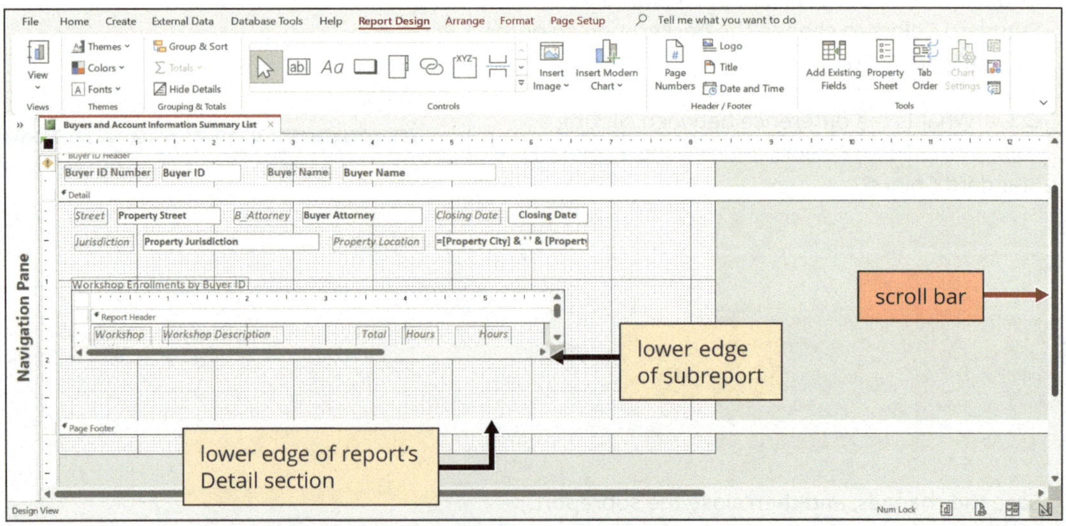

Figure 6–52

Q&A I scrolled down to see the lower boundary of the Detail section, and the controls are no longer on the screen. What is the easiest way to drag the boundary when the position to which I want to drag it is not visible?
You do not need to see the location to drag to it. As you get close to the top of the visible portion of the screen, Access will automatically scroll. You might find it easier, however, to drag the boundary near the top of the visible portion of the report, use the scroll bar to scroll up, and then drag some more. You might have to scroll more than once.

3

- Click the label for the subreport (the label that reads Workshop Enrollments by Buyer ID), and then press DEL to delete the label.
- Resize the report by dragging its right border to the location shown in Figure 6–53.

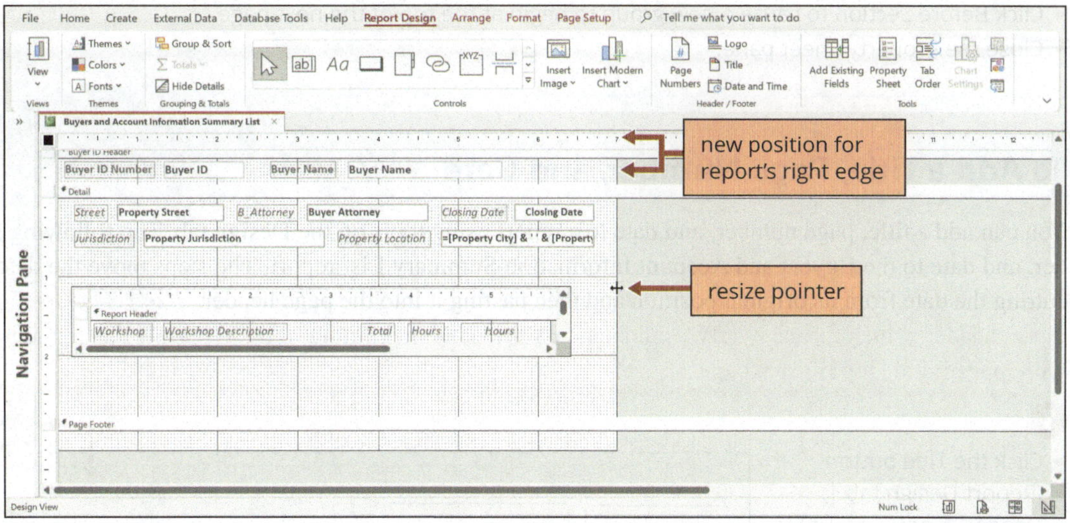

Figure 6–53

Q&A How does a report become the wrong size?

When you move a control and a portion of the control extends into the area to the right of the right boundary of the report, the report will be resized. The new, larger size will remain even if you move the control back to the left. Thus, it is possible that your report has a larger size than it did before. If this is the case, you need to drag the right boundary to resize the report.

To Modify Section Properties

The following steps make two modifications to the Buyer ID Header section. The first modification, which causes the contents of the Group Header section to appear at the top of each page, changes the Repeat Section property to Yes. **Why?** Without this change, the Buyer ID and name would only appear at the beginning of each buyer's account information. If the list of account information occupies more than one page, it would not be apparent on subsequent pages which buyer ID is associated with that information. The second modification changes the Force New Page property to Before Section, causing each section to begin at the top of a page.

1

- Click the Buyer ID Header bar to select the header, and then click the Property Sheet button (Report Design tab | Tools group) to display the Property Sheet pane.
- With the All tab selected, click the Repeat Section property box, click the arrow that appears, and then click Yes to cause the contents of the group header to appear at the top of each page of the report.
- Click the Force New Page property box, and then click the arrow that appears to display the menu of possible values (Figure 6–54).

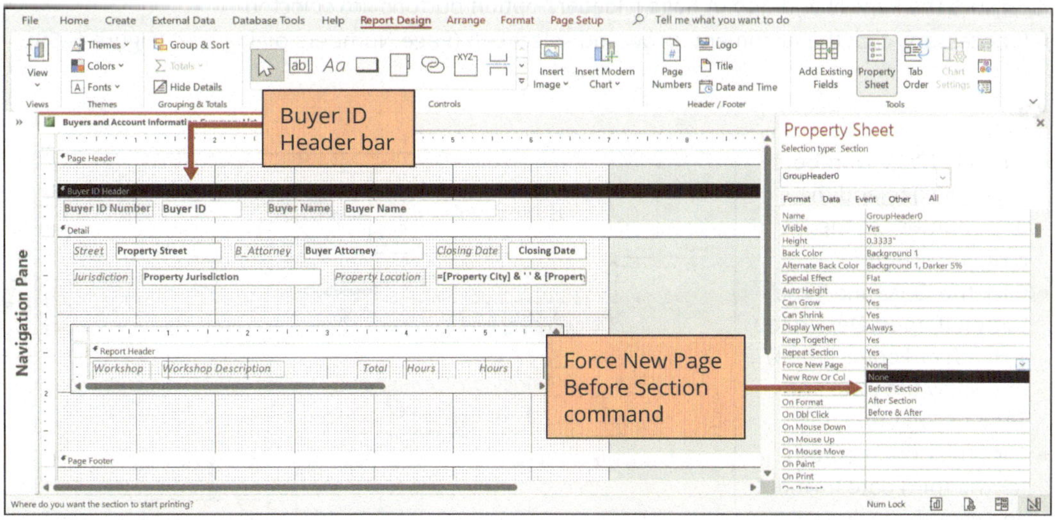

Figure 6–54

2

- Click Before Section to cause a new group to begin at the top of the next page.
- Close the Property Sheet pane.

To Add a Title, Page Number, and Date

You can add a title, page number, and date to a report using tools on the Design tab. The following steps add a title, page number, and date to the Buyers and Account Information Summary List report. The steps move the date to the page header by first cutting the date from its original position and then pasting it into the page header. **Why?** The date is automatically added to the report header, which means it only would appear once at the beginning of the report. If it is in the page header instead, the date will appear at the top of each page.

1

- Click the Title button (Report Design tab | Header / Footer group) to add a title.

Q&A The title is the same as the name of the report object. Can I change the report title without changing the name of the report object in the database?

Yes. The report title is a label, and you can change it using any of the techniques that you used for changing column headings and other labels.

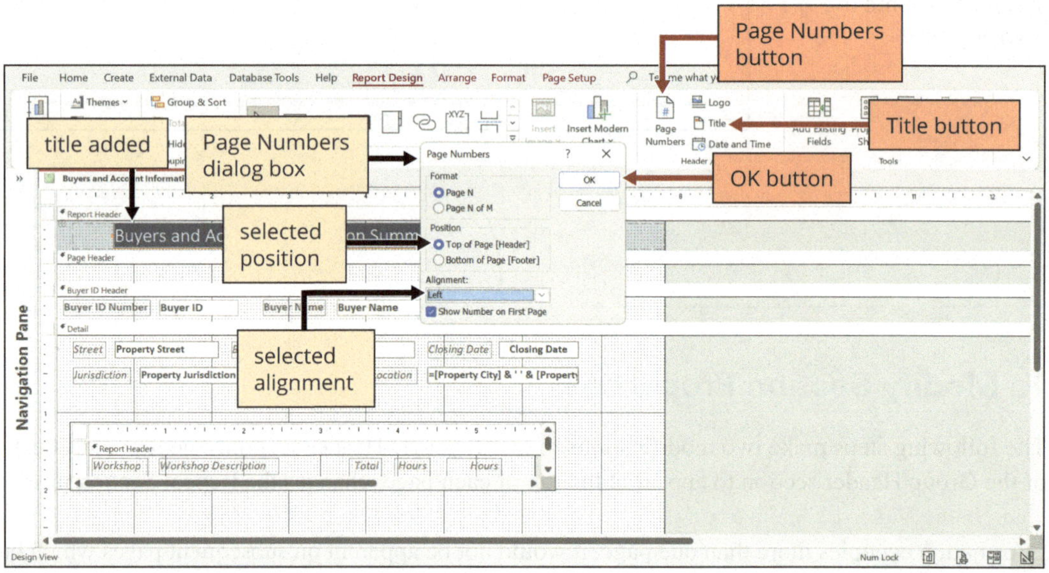

Figure 6–55

- Click the Page Numbers button (Report Design tab | Header / Footer group) to display the Page Numbers dialog box.
- Be sure the Page N and 'Top of Page [Header]' option buttons are selected.
- If necessary, click the Alignment arrow and select Left (Page Numbers dialog box) (Figure 6–55).

2

- Click OK (Page Numbers dialog box) to add the page number to the Header section.
- Click the 'Date and Time' button (Report Design tab | Header / Footer group) to display the Date and Time dialog box.
- Click the option button for the third date format and click the Include Time check box to remove the check mark (Figure 6–56).

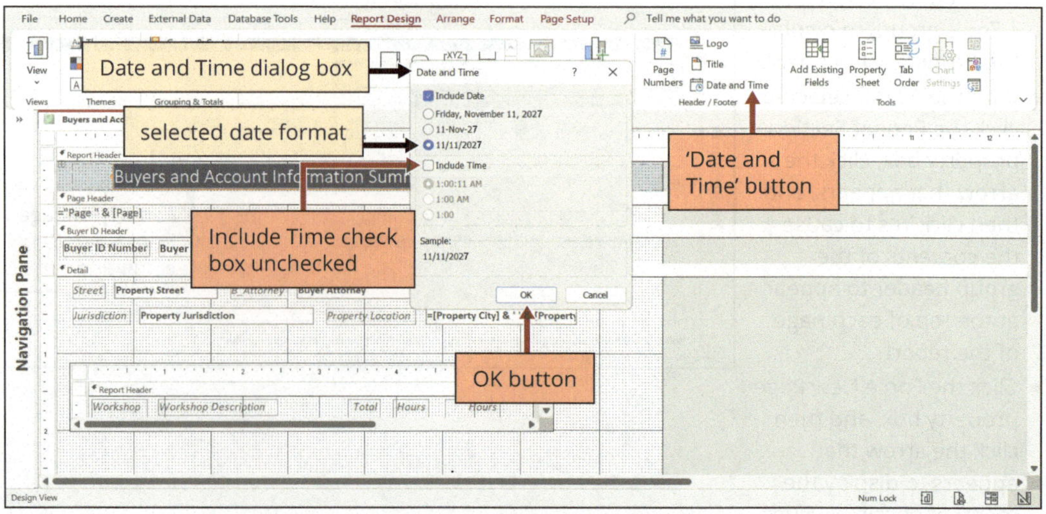

Figure 6–56

3

- Click the OK button (Date and Time dialog box) to add the date to the Report Header.
- Display the Home tab.
- If the Date control is not selected, click the Date control to select it (Figure 6–57).

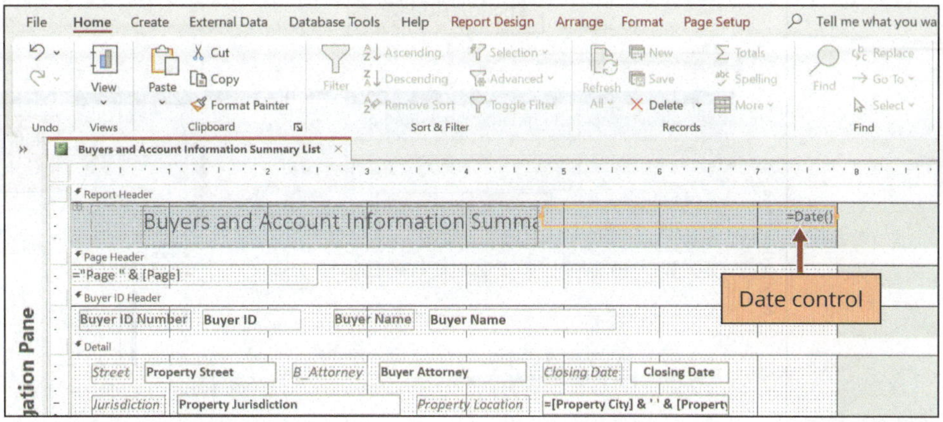

Figure 6–57

4

- With the control containing the date selected, click the Cut button (Home tab | Clipboard group) to cut the date, click the title bar for the Page Header to select the page header, and then click the Paste button (Home tab | Clipboard group) to paste the Date control at the beginning of the page header.

Q&A When I click the Cut button, the control disappears, but the Paste button grays out and won't work. How can I fix this?
You might have an error in your Access installation and should consider reinstalling Access. In the meantime, you can work around this limitation by copying the control instead of cutting it, and then the Paste button should still work. Make sure to delete the original control from the section where you intended to cut it from.

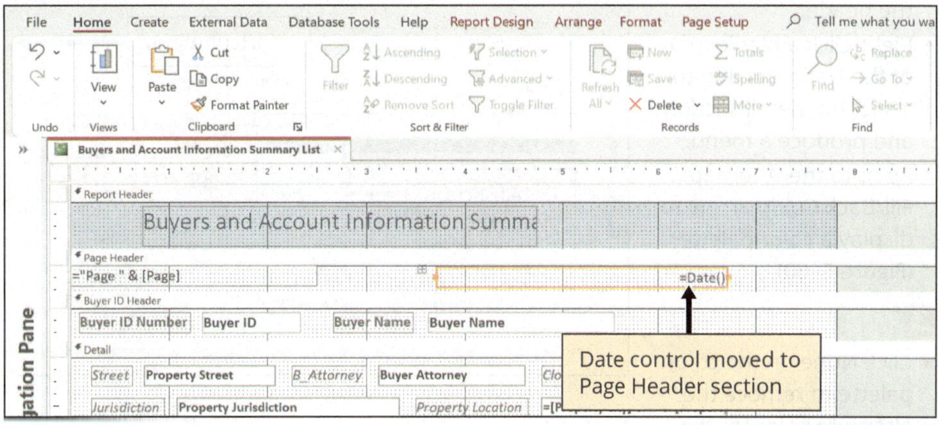

Figure 6–58

- Drag the Date control, which is currently sitting on top of the Page Number control, to the position shown in Figure 6–58.

To Remove the Header Background Color and the Alternate Color

The report header currently has a blue background, which is not what Partners paralegals want. In addition, the report has alternate colors, as you saw in Figure 6–46. An **alternate color** is a color different from the main color that appears on every other line in a datasheet or report. Using alternate colors can sometimes make a datasheet or report more readable but is not always desirable.

The following steps first remove the color from the report header. They then remove the alternate colors from the various sections in the report, starting with the Detail section. **Why?** Access automatically assigns alternate colors within the report. In reports with multiple sections, the alternate colors can be confusing. If you do not want these alternate colors, you must remove them.

1

- Right-click the title bar for the Report Header to select the header without selecting any of the controls in the header and to produce a menu.
- Point to the 'Fill/Back Color' arrow to display a color palette (Figure 6–59).

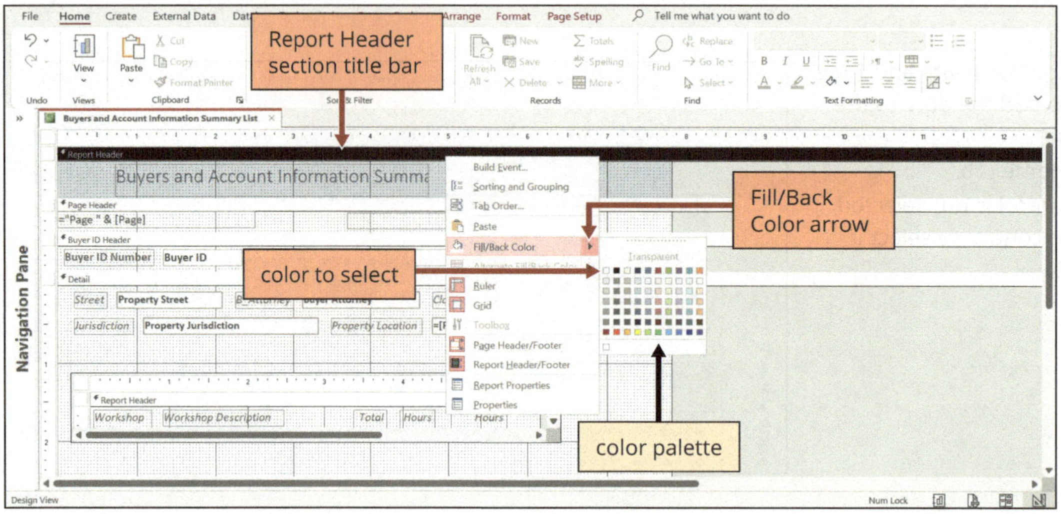

Figure 6–59

2

- Click White in the first row, first column of the color palette to change the background color for the header.
- Right-click a blank area of the Detail section to select the detail section and produce a menu.
- Point to the 'Alternate Fill/Back Color' arrow to display a color palette (Figure 6–60).

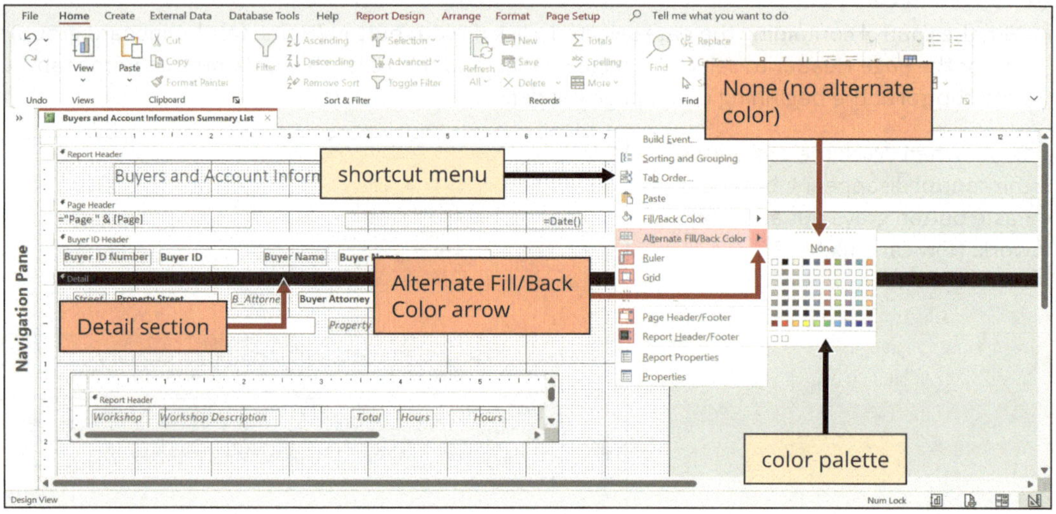

Figure 6–60

3

- Click None on the color palette to remove the alternate color for the Detail section.
- Save the report.

4

- To open the subreport in Design view from the report, click the subreport control, and then click the 'Subreport in New Window' button (Report Design tab | Tools group) (Figure 6–61).

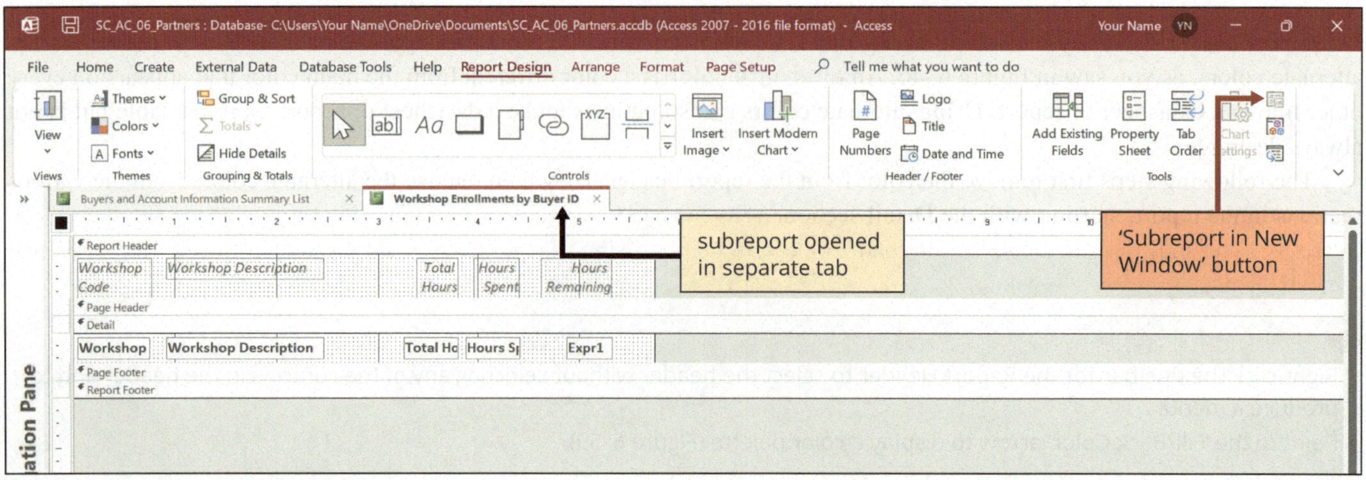

Figure 6–61

- Remove the header background color and the alternate color from the subreport using similar techniques as the changes you just made to the main report.
- Save and close the subreport.
- View the report in Print Preview (Figure 6–62).
- Close Print Preview, and then save and close the report.

Q&A How can I be sure I removed all the background colors where needed?

View the report in Print Preview to check no color appears in the report.

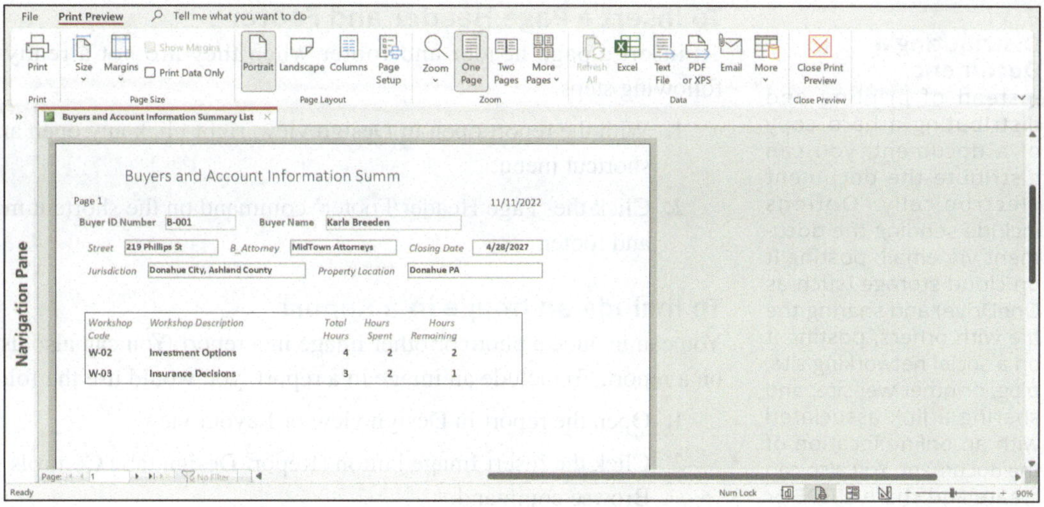

Figure 6–62

Headers and Footers

Access gives you some options for including or omitting headers and footers in your reports. They go together, so if you have a report header, you will also have a report footer. If you do not want one of the sections to appear, you can shrink its size so there is no room for any content, or you can remove the header and footer from your report altogether. If you later decide you want to include them, you once again can add them. You have similar options with page headers and page footers.

To Remove a Report Header and Footer

To remove a report header and footer, you would use the following steps.

1. With the report open in Design view, right-click any open area of the report to produce a shortcut menu.
2. Click the 'Report Header/Footer' command on the shortcut menu to remove the report header and footer.
3. If the Microsoft Access dialog box appears, asking if it is acceptable to delete any controls in the section, click Yes.

To Remove a Page Header and Footer

To remove a page header and footer, you would use the following steps.

1. With the report open in Design view, right-click any open area of the report to produce a shortcut menu.
2. Click the 'Page Header/Footer' command on the shortcut menu to remove the page header and footer.
3. If the Microsoft Access dialog box appears, asking if it is acceptable to delete any controls in the section, click Yes.

To Insert a Report Header and Footer

To insert a report header and footer when they are not already present, you would use the following steps.

1. With the report open in Design view, right-click any open area of the report to produce a shortcut menu.
2. Click the 'Report Header/Footer' command on the shortcut menu to insert a report header and footer.

BTW

Report Title Placement

You also can place a report title in a page header. One advantage of doing so is that the title will then print on each page of the report.

BTW

Page Breaks

You can force a page break to occur at a particular position in a report by adding a page break control to the report. To do so, click the Insert Page Break tool from the Controls gallery (Report Design tab | Controls group), move the pointer to the desired position, and click the position to place the page break.

BTW

White Space

In page layout and report design, white space is the space on a printed page that is left unmarked. This includes margins, spacing between records, and space around graphics. Not enough white space can make a report look cluttered and can be difficult to read. Too much white space wastes paper. Thoughtful use of white space can make a report more visually appealing and easier to interpret.

BTW
Distributing a Document
Instead of printing and distributing a hard copy of a document, you can distribute the document electronically. Options include sending the document via email; posting it on cloud storage (such as OneDrive) and sharing the file with others; posting it on a social networking site, blog, or other website; and sharing a link associated with an online location of the document. You also can create and share a PDF or XPS image of the document, so that users can view the file in Acrobat Reader or XPS Viewer instead of in Access.

To Insert a Page Header and Footer

To insert a page header and footer when they are not already present, you would use the following steps.

1. With the report open in Design view, right-click any open area of the report to produce a shortcut menu.
2. Click the 'Page Header/Footer' command on the shortcut menu to insert a page header and footer.

To Include an Image in a Report

You can include a photo or other image in a report. You can also use an image as the background on a report. To include an image in a report, you would use the following steps.

1. Open the report in Design view or Layout view.
2. Click the Insert Image button (Report Design tab | Controls group), and then click the Browse command.
3. Select the desired image and click OK.
4. Click the desired location to add the image to the report.

To Use an Image as Background for a Report

To include an image as a background for a report, you would use the following steps.

1. Open the report in Design view or Layout view.
2. Click anywhere in the report, click the Background Image button (Format tab | Background group), and then click the Browse command.
3. Select the desired image for the background and click OK.

To Publish a Report

You can make a report available as an external document by publishing the report as either a PDF or an XPS file. To do so, you would use the following steps.

1. Select the report to be published in the Navigation Pane.
2. Display the External Data tab.
3. Click the PDF or XPS button (External Data tab | Export group) to display the Publish as PDF or XPS dialog box.
4. Select the appropriate Save as type (either PDF or XPS).
5. Select either 'Standard (publishing online and printing)' or 'Minimum size (publishing online).'
6. If you want to publish only a range of pages, click the Options button, select the desired range, and click OK.
7. Click the Publish button to publish the report in the desired format.
8. If you want to save the export steps, click the 'Save export steps' check box (Expert – PDF dialog box), and then click the Save Export button. If not, click the Close button.

Break Point: If you wish to take a break, this is a good place to do so. You can quit Access now. To resume at a later time, start Access, open the database called SC_AC_06_Partners.accdb, and continue following the steps from this location forward.

Creating a Second Report

Partners would also like a report that groups accounts by Buyer ID and Workshop Costs. The report should include subtotals and a discount amount based on the total cost of workshops for each buyer. Finally, it should show the combined cost of the workshops less the discount. The discount amount is based on the total workshop cost. Buyers taking workshops in excess of $300 will receive a 20 percent discount on all workshops, and buyers taking workshops totaling $300 or less will not receive a discount.

BTW
Graphs
You can add graphs, called charts, to a report using the Chart tool. To add a chart to a report, click the Chart tool, move the pointer to the desired location, and click the position to place the chart. Follow the directions in the Chart Wizard dialog box to specify the data source for the chart, the values for the chart, and the chart type.

To Create a Second Report

The following steps create the Discount Report, select the record source, and specify grouping and sorting options.

1

- If necessary, close the Navigation Pane.
- Display the Create tab and then click the Report Design button (Create tab | Reports group) to create a report in Design view.

2

- Ensure the selector for the entire report, which is the box in the upper-left corner of the report, contains a black square indicating it is selected, and then click the Property Sheet button (Report Design tab | Tools group) to display the Property Sheet pane.

3

- With the All tab selected, click the Record Source property box arrow, and then click the Workshop Enrollments and Workshops query to select the query as the record source for the report.
- Close the Property Sheet pane.

4

- Click the Group & Sort button (Report Design tab | Grouping & Totals group) to display the 'Group, Sort, and Total' pane.
- Click the 'Add a group' button to display the list of available fields for grouping, and then click the Buyer ID field to group by Buyer ID. When you add a group, a header will appear above each Buyer ID. However, you also need a group footer.

5

- On the 'Group on Buyer ID' row (Group, Sort, and Total pane), click More.
- Click the arrow next to 'without a footer section' to display the options for the Buyer ID section footer.
- Click 'with a footer section' to add a Buyer ID section footer to the report.

6

- Click the 'Add a sort' button to display the list of available fields for sorting, and then click the Workshop Code field to sort workshops by the workshop code.
- Remove the 'Group, Sort, and Total' pane by clicking the Group & Sort button (Report Design tab | Grouping & Totals group).

7

- Save the report as **Discount Report** but do not close it yet.

Q&A Why save it at this point?

You do not have to save it at this point. It is a good idea to save often, however. Doing so will give you a convenient point from which to restart if you have problems. If you have problems, you could close the report without saving it. When you reopen the report, it will be in the state it was in when you last saved it.

To Add and Move Fields in a Report

As with the previous reports, you can add a field to the report by dragging the field from the field list. After adding a field to a report, you can adjust the placement of the field's label, separating it from the control to which it is attached by dragging the move handle in its upper-left corner. This technique does not work, however, if you want to drag the attached label to a section different from the section where the control is placed. If you want the label to be in a different section, you must select the label, cut the label, select the section to which you want to move the label, and then paste the label. You then can move the label to the desired location.

The following steps add the Buyer ID field to the Buyer ID Header section, and then they move the Buyer ID label to the Page Header section. **Why?** The label should appear at the top of each page, rather than in the group header.

1

- Click the 'Add Existing Fields' button (Report Design tab | Tools group) to display a field list. (Figure 6–63).

Q&A My field list displays 'Show only fields in the current record source,' not 'Show all tables,' as in the figure. What should I do?

Click the 'Show only fields in the current record source' link at the top of the field list to display only those fields in the Workshop Enrollments and Workshops query.

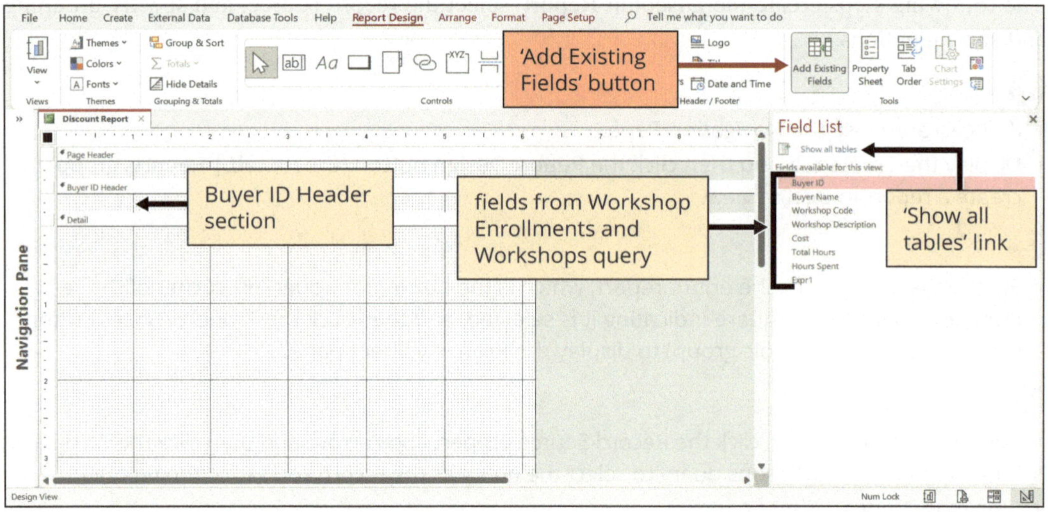

Figure 6–63

2

- Drag the Buyer ID field to the approximate position shown in Figure 6–64.

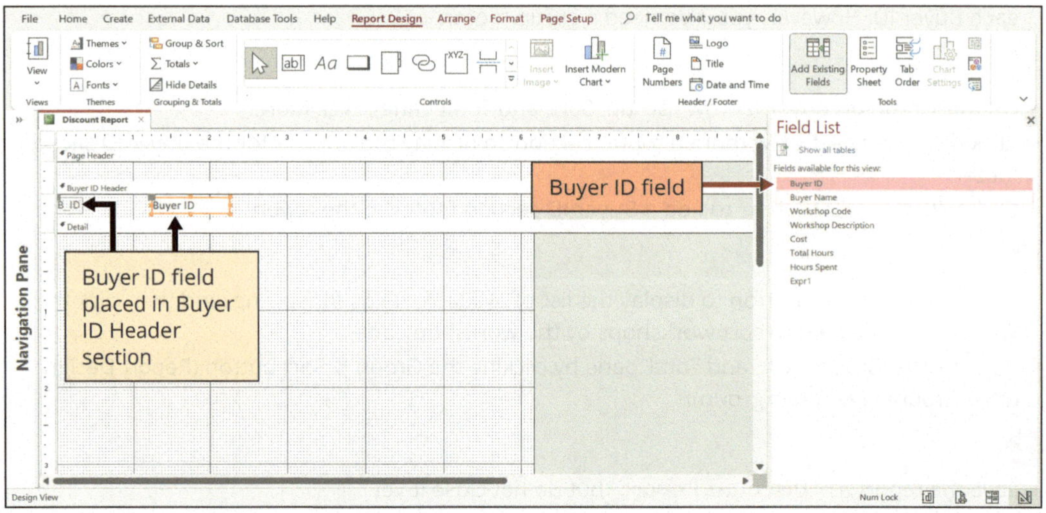

Figure 6–64

3

- Click the label for the Buyer ID control to select it (Figure 6–65).

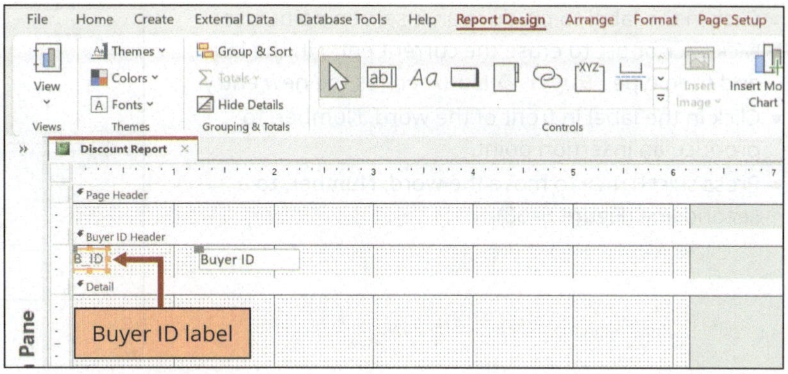

Figure 6–65

4

- Display the Home tab.
- Click the Cut button (Home tab | Clipboard group) to cut the label.
- Click the Page Header bar to select the page header (Figure 6–66).

Q&A Do I have to click the bar, or could I click somewhere else within the section?
You could also click within the section. Clicking the bar is usually safer, however. If you click in a section intending to select the section, but click within one of the controls in the section, you will select the control rather than the section. Clicking the bar always selects the section.

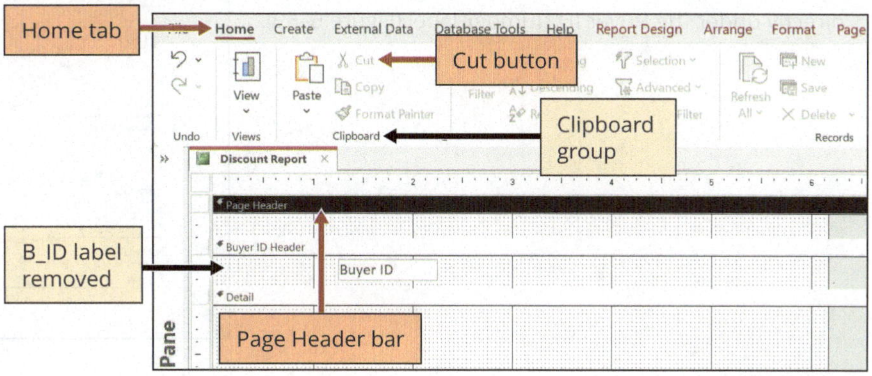

Figure 6–66

5

- Click the Paste button (Home tab | Clipboard group) to paste the label in the Page Header section (Figure 6–67).

Q&A When would I want to click the Paste button arrow rather than just the button?
Clicking the arrow displays the Paste button menu, which includes the Paste command and two additional commands. Paste Special allows you to paste data into different formats. Paste Append, which is available if you have cut or copied a record, allows you to paste the record to a table with a similar structure. If you want the simple Paste command, you can just click the button.

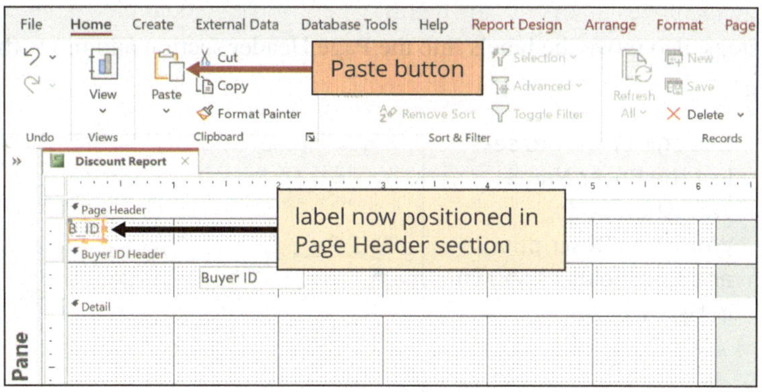

Figure 6–67

6

- Click in the label to produce an insertion point, use BACKSPACE or DEL to erase the current entry in the label, and then type **Buyer ID Number** as the new entry.
- Click in the label in front of the word, Number, to produce an insertion point.
- Press SHIFT+ENTER to move the word, Number, to a second line (Figure 6–68).

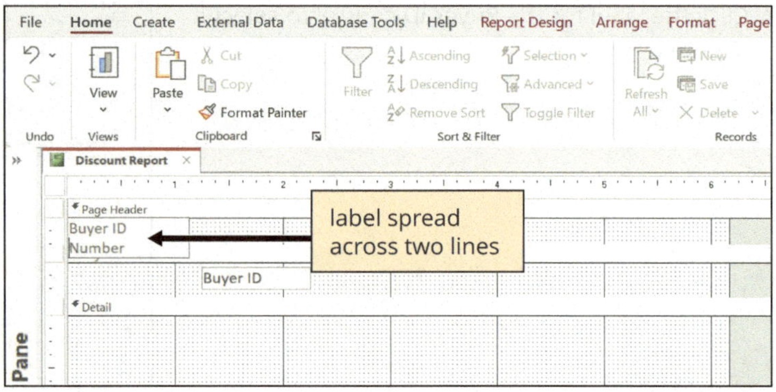

Figure 6–68

7

- Move the Buyer ID control to the left edge of the report, directly under the Buyer ID Number label (Figure 6–69).

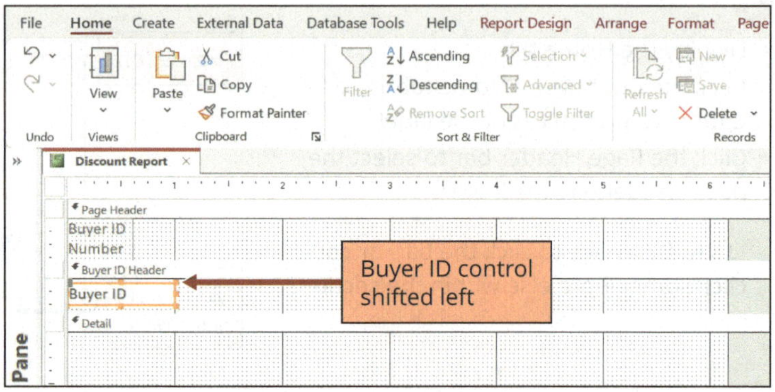

Figure 6–69

To Add the Remaining Fields

The following steps add all the remaining fields for the report by dragging them into the Detail section. **Why?** Dragging the fields moves them onto the report, where you can then relocate the controls and labels individually to the desired locations. The steps also move the labels into the Page Header section and move the controls containing the fields to the appropriate locations.

1

- Use CTRL or SHIFT to select the Buyer Name, Workshop Code, Workshop Description, and Cost fields as shown in Figure 6–70.

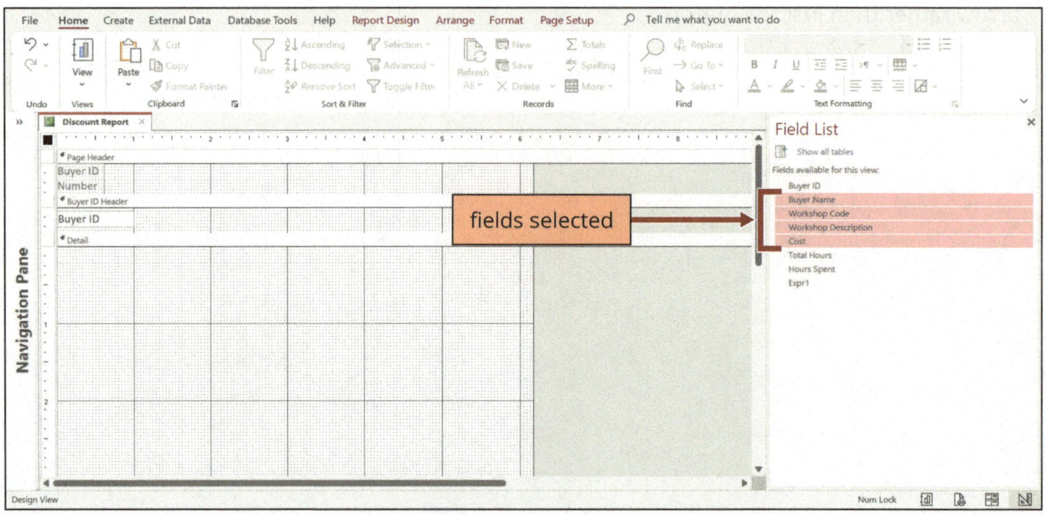

Figure 6–70

- Drag the Buyer Name, Workshop Code, Workshop Description, and Cost fields into the Detail section and close the Field List pane (Figure 6–71).

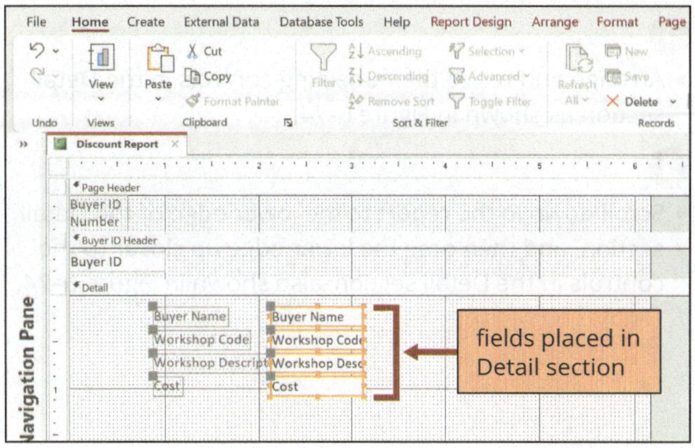

Figure 6–71

2

- One at a time, move the Buyer Name, Workshop Code, Workshop Description, and Cost label controls to the Page Header section, resize them, and break each label into two lines where appropriate (Figure 6–72).

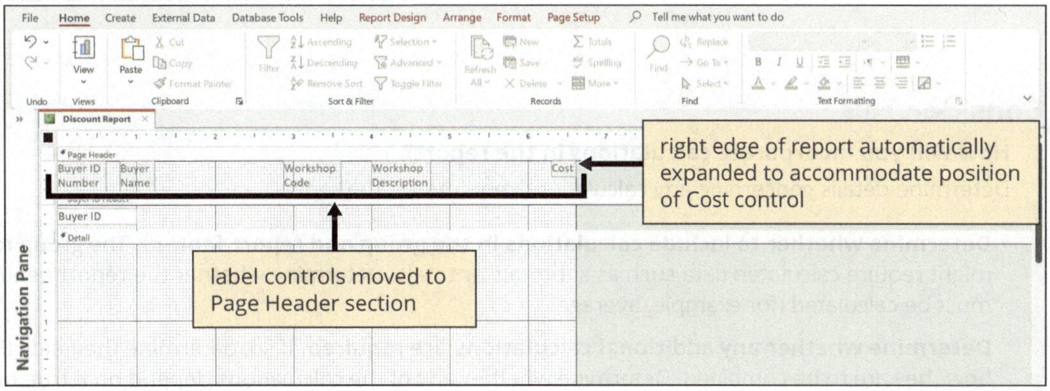

Figure 6–72

Q&A When I paste the label, it is always placed at the left edge, superimposing the Buyer ID label control. Can I change where Access places it?

Unfortunately, when you paste to a different section, Access places the control at the left edge. You will need to drag each control to its proper location after pasting it into the Page Header section.

How can I place the control accurately when there are no gridlines?

When you click the position for the control, Access will automatically expand the grid. You can then adjust the control using the grid.

Can I automatically cause controls to be aligned to the grid?

Yes. Click the Size/Space button (Arrange tab | Sizing & Ordering group), and then click Snap to Grid on the Size/Space menu. From that point on, any controls you add will be automatically aligned to the grid.

3

- Move and resize the Buyer Name control to its approximate position in the Buyer ID Header section, resizing the Buyer ID control as needed to fit the space (Figure 6–73).

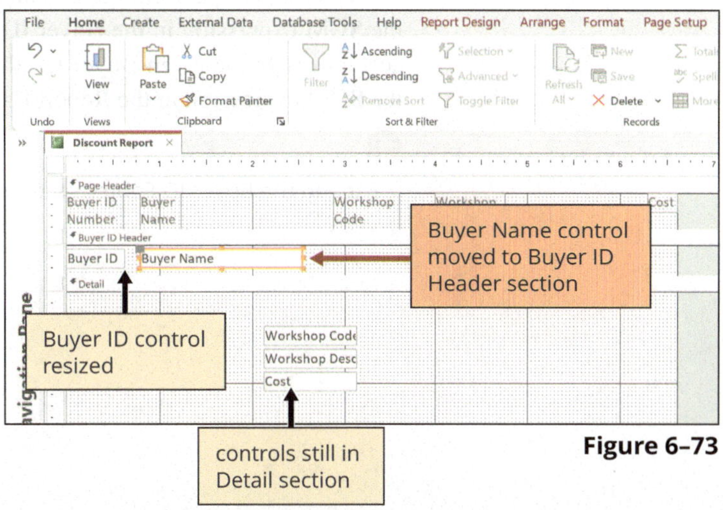

Figure 6–73

4

- Arrange and resize the remaining controls in the Detail section as shown in Figure 6–74.

5

- Scroll down in the report to the lower edge of the Detail section, and then drag the lower edge up closer to the controls in the Detail section, also shown in Figure 6–74.

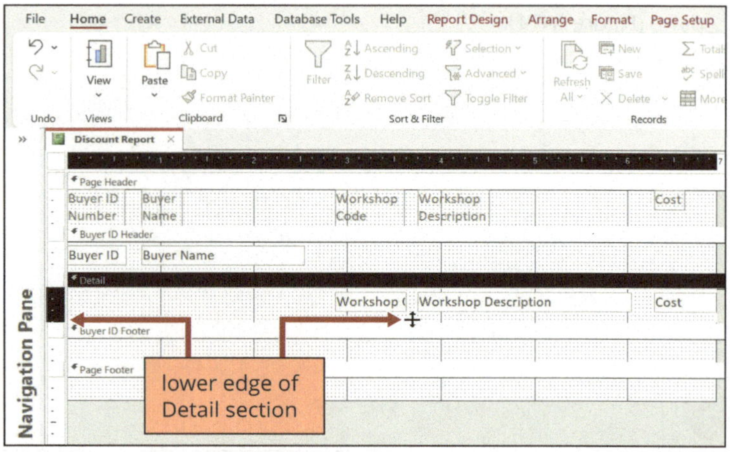

Figure 6–74

Consider This

How will you incorporate calculations in the report?

Determine details concerning any calculations required for the report.

- **Determine whether to include calculations in the group and report footers.** The group footers or report footers might require calculated data such as subtotals or totals. Determine whether the report needs other statistics that must be calculated (for example, average).
- **Determine whether any additional calculations are required.** If so, determine the fields that are involved and how they are to be combined. Determine whether any of the calculations depend on a true or false statement for a criterion, in which case the calculations are conditional.

BTW

Arguments

An argument is a piece of data on which a function operates. For example, in the expression =SUM([Cost]), Cost is the argument because the SUM function will calculate the total of Cost.

Totals and Subtotals

To add totals or other statistics to a footer, add a text box control. You can use any of the aggregate functions in a text box: COUNT, SUM, AVG (average), MAX (largest value), MIN (smallest value), STDEV (standard deviation), VAR (variance), FIRST, and LAST. To use a function, type an equal (=) sign, followed by the function name. You then include a set of parentheses containing the item for which you want to perform the calculation. If the item name contains spaces, such as Annual Total, you must enclose it in square brackets. For example, to calculate the sum of values of a field named Annual Total, the expression would be =SUM([Annual Total]).

Access will perform the calculation for the appropriate collection of records. If you enter the SUM expression in the Buyer ID Footer section, Access will only calculate the subtotal for accounts with the given Buyer ID; that is, it will calculate the appropriate subtotal. If you enter the SUM expression in the Report Footer section, Access will calculate the total for all accounts.

1

- Expand the Buyer ID Footer section by dragging the lower edge down (Figure 6–75).

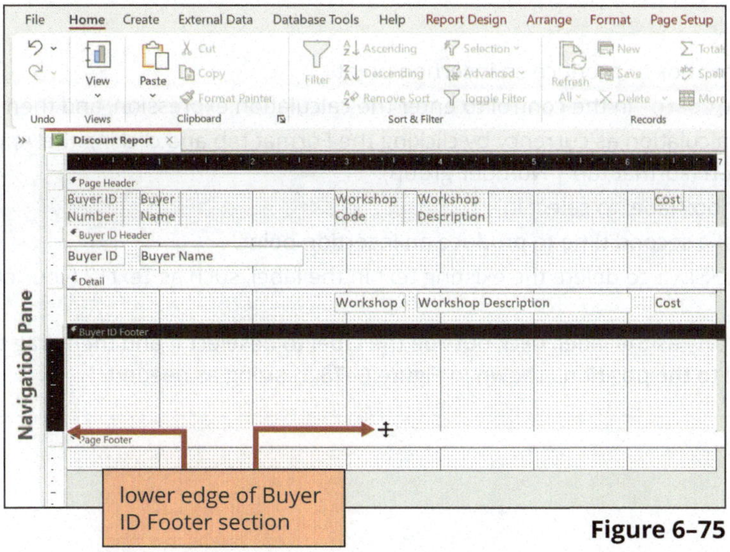

Figure 6–75

2

- Click the Text Box tool (Report Design tab | Controls group), and then point to the position shown in Figure 6–76.

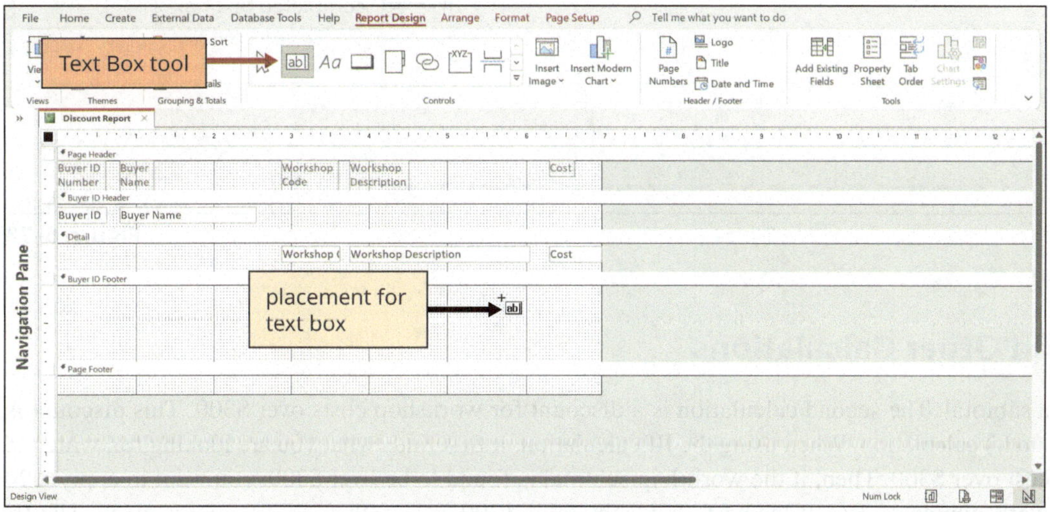

Figure 6–76

3

- Click the position shown in Figure 6–76 to place a text box (Figure 6–77).

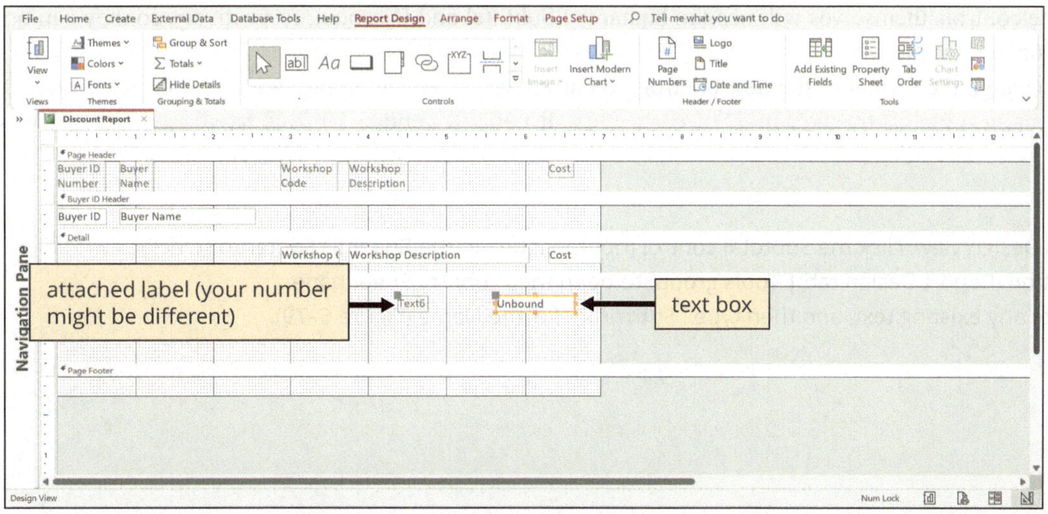

Figure 6–77

4

- Click in the text box to produce an insertion point.
- Type **=Sum([Cost])** in the control to enter the calculation expression, and then press ENTER.
- Format the calculation as currency by clicking the Format tab and clicking the 'Apply Currency Format' button (Format tab | Number group).
- Click the text box label to select it.
- Click the label a second time to produce an insertion point.
- Use DEL or BACKSPACE to delete the existing text in the label, such as Text12 (your number might be different).
- Type **Subtotal** as the label. Click outside the label to deselect it and then drag the control and the label to the positions shown in Figure 6–78, resizing as needed.

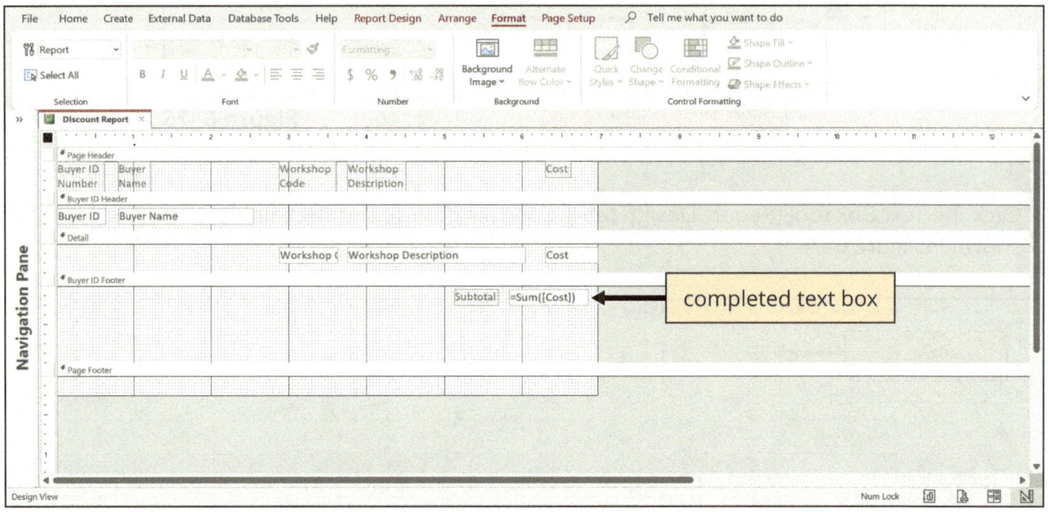

Figure 6–78

To Add Subtotals and Other Calculations

The preceding steps created a subtotal. The second calculation is a discount for workshop costs over $300. This discount is applied using the IIf (Immediate If) calculation. When using the IIf calculation, it first finds what you are looking for, which in this case is a total workshop cost over $300. Then, if the workshop subtotal is found to be over $300, you want to apply a 20 percent (.20) discount to the workshop costs. But, if the workshop subtotal is $300 or less, then no discount is given. The IIf calculation for this example would be entered manually in a control as follows: =IIf([subtotal]>300,[subtotal]*0.2,0) Notice that the subtotal field needs to be in square brackets. Also, note that there are commas after each part of the calculation. The results of the subtotal and the IIf calculations will both be displayed in the Buyer ID Footer section with the control labels Subtotal and Discount. Additionally, the controls themselves will need to be named Subtotal and Discount, respectively, so they can be referenced in calculations for other controls.

The following steps also change the format of the new controls to currency. **Why?** The requirements at Partners indicate the Discount Report should contain subtotals for the workshop costs and a discount for clients who are paying more than $300 for their workshop costs.

1

- With the Discount Report in Design view, click the Subtotal control (not the label) in the Buyer ID Footer to select it.
- Click the Property Sheet button (Report Design tab | Tools group) to open the Property Sheet pane.
- Click in the Name box, delete any existing text, and then type **Subtotal** for the Name (Figure 6–79).

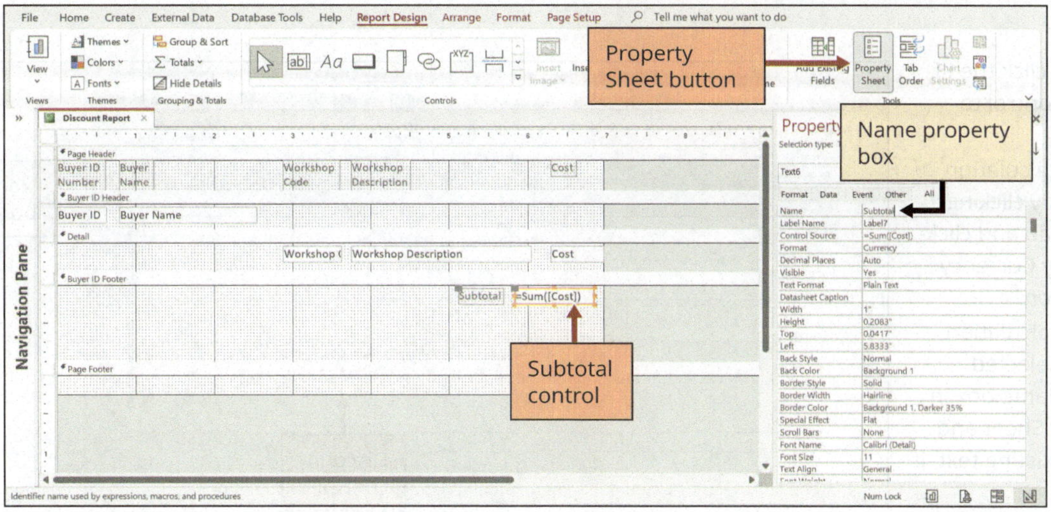

Figure 6–79

2

- Click the Text Box tool (Report Design tab | Controls group), and then click the position in the Buyer ID Footer section shown in Figure 6–80.

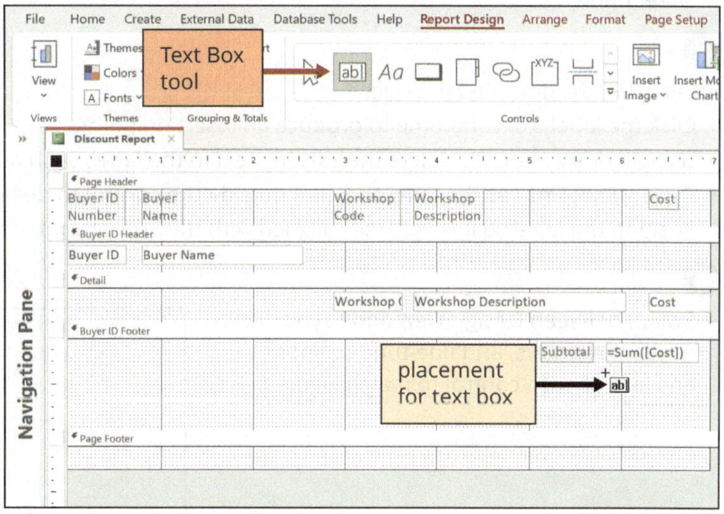

Figure 6–80

3

- Click the text box to produce an insertion point.
- Type **=IIf([Subtotal]>300,[Subtotal]*0.2,0)** in the control to enter the expression calculation, and then press ENTER (Figure 6–81).

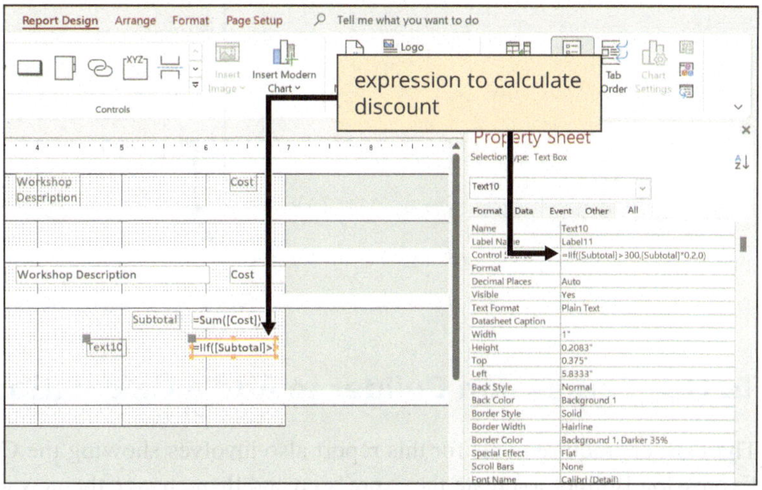

Figure 6–81

4

- If necessary, click the IIf calculation control to select it.
- Format the calculation as currency by clicking the Format tab and clicking the 'Apply Currency Format' button.
- With the IIf calculation control still selected, click in the Name box in the Property Sheet and delete any existing text, if necessary.
- Type **Discount** for the Name (Figure 6–82), and then close the Property Sheet pane.

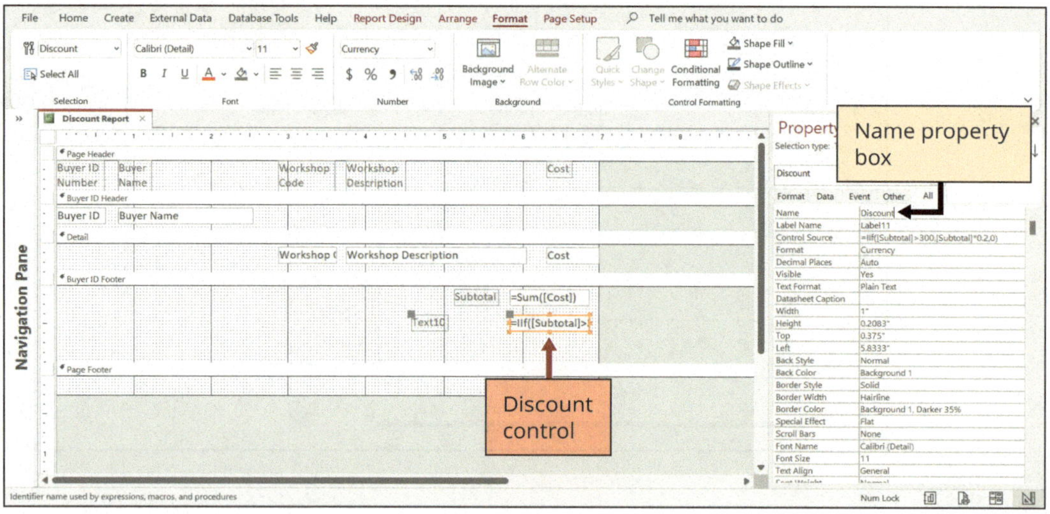

Figure 6–82

5

- Click the text box label to select it.
- Click the label a second time to produce an insertion point.
- Use DEL or BACKSPACE to delete the existing text in the label, such as Text18 (your number might be different).
- Type **Discount** as the label and click outside the control to deselect it.
- Position the label so it is vertically aligned with the Subtotal label and horizontally aligned with the Discount control.

6

- Switch between Design view and Layout view to see the results, and fine-tune the position and size of each control to match Figure 6–83.

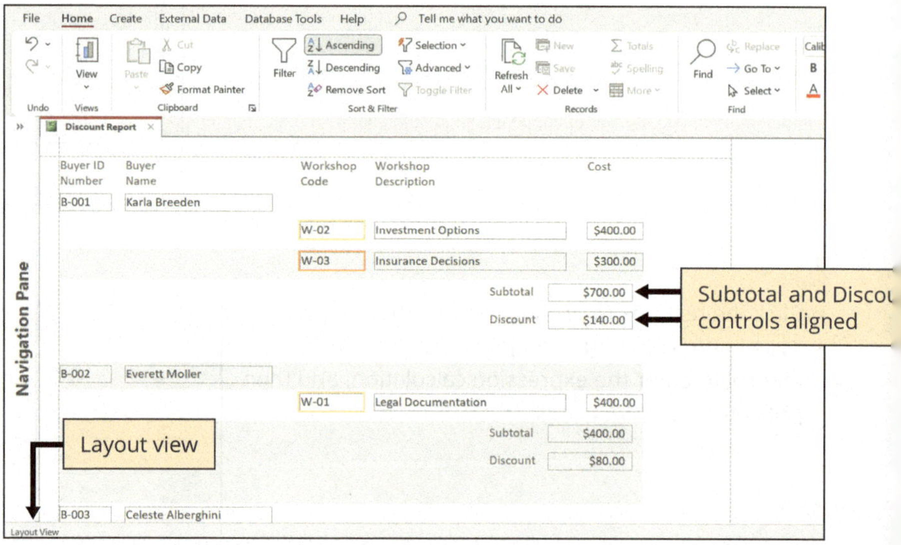

Figure 6–83

To Use Expression Builder to Add a Calculation

The Partners requirements for this report also involves showing the Cost subtotal less the Discount amount. These steps use Expression Builder to create the expression and then change the new control's properties. **Why?** Expression Builder is a convenient way to include a calculation.

1

- If necessary, return to Design view.
- Click the Text Box tool (Report Design tab | Controls group), and then click in the approximate position in the Buyer ID Footer section to place the control for the calculation (Figure 6–84).

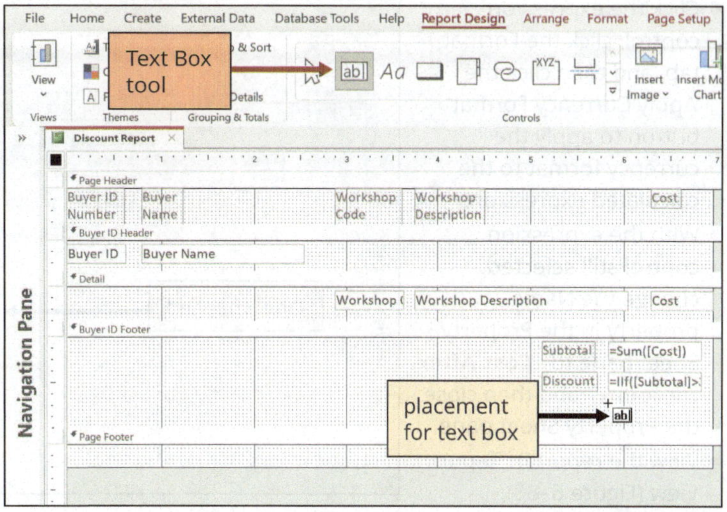

Figure 6–84

2

- Click the text box control, and then open the Property Sheet pane.
- On the All tab, click the Control Source property, and then click the Build button to display the Expression Builder dialog box.
- Type an equal sign (**=**) in the Expression Builder box.
- Click Discount Report in the Expression Elements category in the first column.
- Scroll down in the second column so that Subtotal appears, and then double-click the Subtotal control in the second column.
- Type a minus sign (**–**), scroll in the second column so that Discount appears, and then double-click the Discount control to add it to the expression (Figure 6–85).

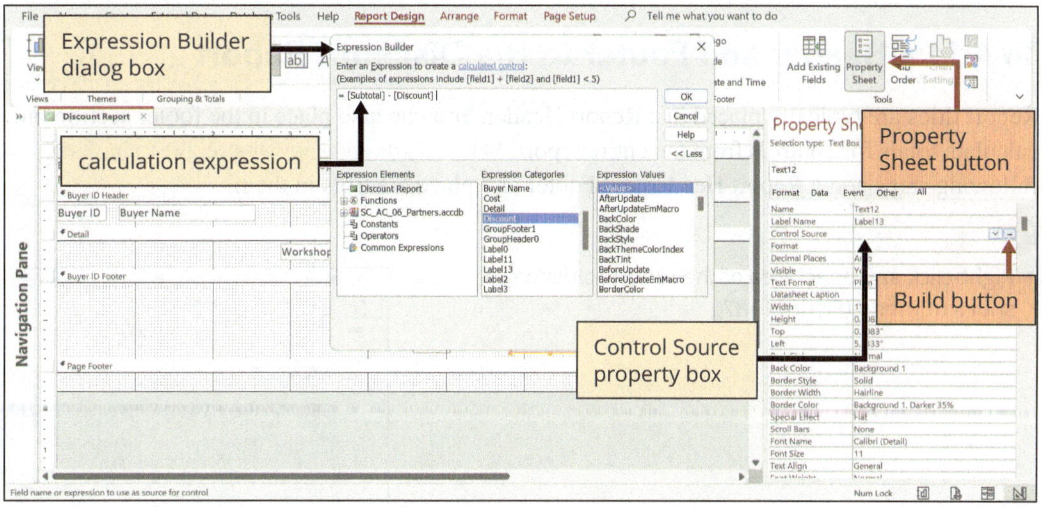

Figure 6–85

Q&A Why did I choose Control Source instead of Record Source?

You use Record Source to select the source of the records in a report, usually a table or a query. You use the Control Source property to specify the source of data for the control. This allows you to bind an expression or field to a control.

Are there other ways I could enter the expression?

Yes. You could just type the whole expression. On the other hand, you could select the function just as in these steps, and, when entering each argument, you could select the fields from the list of fields and click the desired operators.

3

- Click OK to close the Expression Builder dialog box.
- Click the label for the expression control, and then click the label for the expression control a second time to produce an insertion point.
- Use BACKSPACE or DEL to erase the current entry in the label, and then type **Cost After Discount** as the new entry.
- Use the move handle to reposition the label control as needed so it does not overlap the expression control.

4

- Click the expression control, click the Format tab, and then click the 'Apply Currency Format' button to apply the currency format to the calculated expression.
- With the expression control still selected, change the Name property in the Property Sheet pane to **Cost After Discount** and then close the Property Sheet pane.
- View the report in Report View (Figure 6–86).

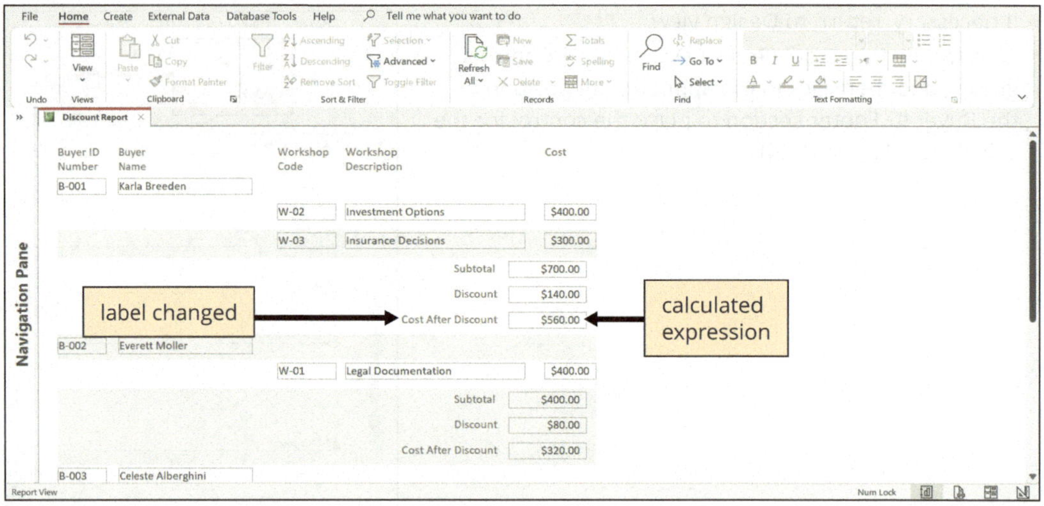

Figure 6–86

5

- Return to Design view and save your changes.

To Add a Header and Footer to the Discount Report

Report titles are typically placed in a Report Header. You can also place in the footer section one or more calculation fields that calculate totals for controls from the entire report. **Why?** Partners wants the report to include a total for all workshop costs. The following steps add a Report Header and Footer and place controls in them.

1

- Right-click any open area of the report to display a shortcut menu (Figure 6–87).

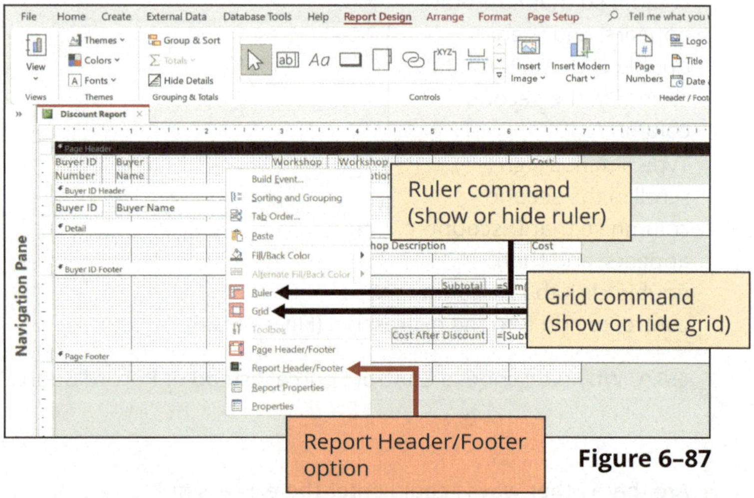

Figure 6–87

2

- Click 'Report Header/Footer' to display the Report Header and Footer sections.
- Click the Subtotal control in the Buyer ID Footer section to select the control and its label.
- Display the Home tab.
- Click the Copy button (Home tab | Clipboard group) to copy the selected controls to the Clipboard.
- Click the Report Footer bar to select the footer, and then click the Paste button (Home tab | Clipboard group) to paste a copy of the controls into the report footer (Figure 6–88).

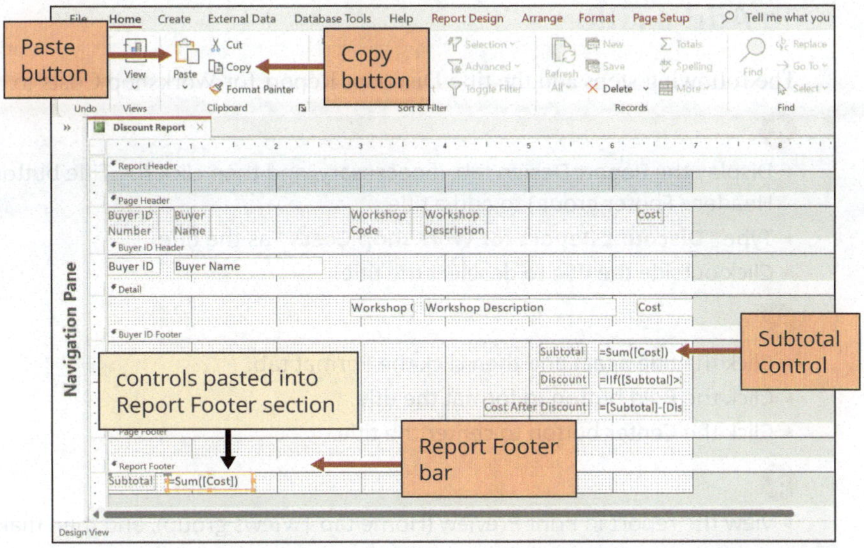

Figure 6–88

3

- Click the label in the Report Footer section to select the label, and then click a second time to produce an insertion point.
- Use BACKSPACE or DEL to erase the current contents, type **Total** to change the label, and then move the label and control to the positions shown in Figure 6–89.

4

- View your changes in Layout view, and then return to Design view and save the report.

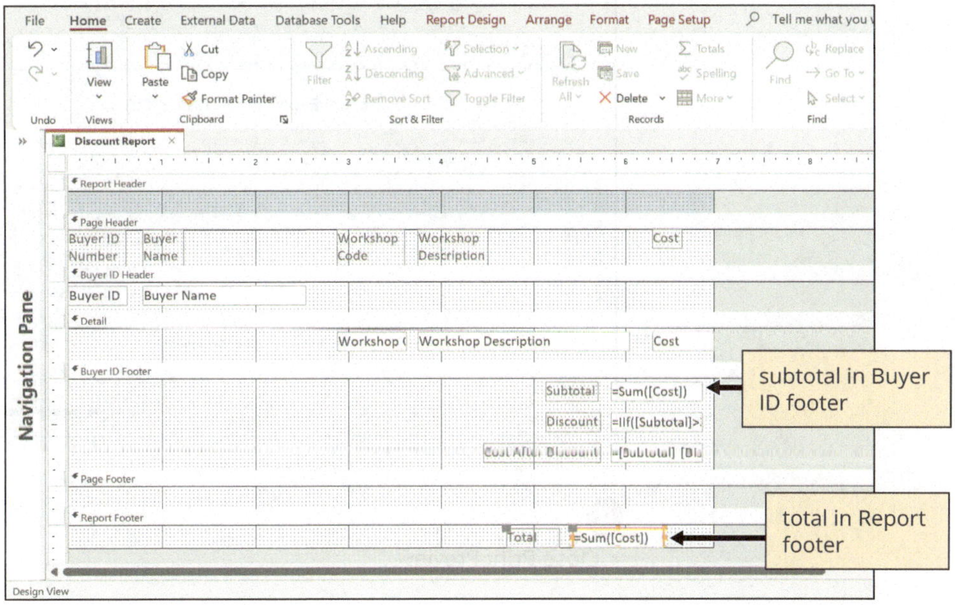

Figure 6–89

To Remove the Color from the Report Header

The following step removes the color from the Report Header section by changing the background color for the header to white.

1

- Right-click the report header to produce a menu.
- Point to the 'Fill/Back Color' arrow on the shortcut menu to display a color palette.
- Click White in the first row, first column to change the background color to white.

To Add a Title

The following steps add the title Discount Report for Workshop Costs to the report.

1

- Display the Report Design tab, if necessary, and then click the Title button (Report Design tab | Header / Footer group) to add a title.
- Type **Discount Report for Workshop Costs** as the title.
- Click outside the title to deselect the title.

2

- Click the title again and then click the Format tab.
- Click the Bold button to format the title.
- Click the Center button to center the title.

3

- View the report in Print Preview (Home tab | Views group), and then make any further adjustments to controls so all text is visible for all records and all controls are neatly aligned and organized, as shown in Figure 6–90.

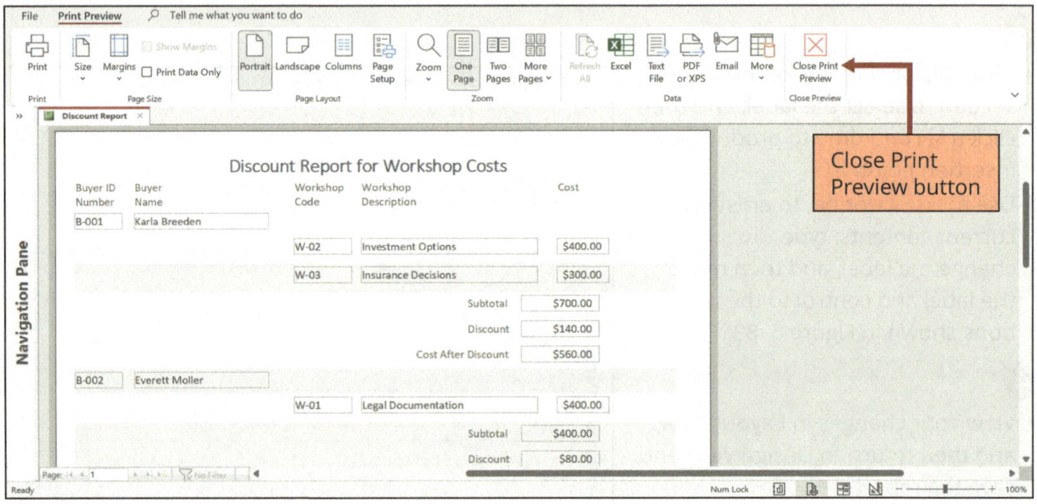

Figure 6–90

4

- Close Print Preview.

Obtaining Help on Functions

There are many functions included in Access that are available for a variety of purposes. To see the list of functions, display the Expression Builder. (See Figure 6–85 for one way to display the Expression Builder.) Double-click Functions in the first column and then click Built-In Functions. You can then scroll through the entire list of functions in the third column. Alternatively, you can click a function category in the second column, in which case the third column will only contain the functions in that category. To obtain detailed help on a function, highlight the function in the third column and click the Help button. The Help information presented will show the syntax of the function, that is, the specific rule for how you must type the function and any arguments. It will give you general comments on the function as well as examples illustrating the use of the function.

Page Setup Tab

You can use the buttons on the Page Setup tab to change margins, orientation, and other page setup characteristics of the report (Figure 6–91a). If you click the Margins button, you can choose from among some predefined margins or set your own custom margins (Figure 6–91b). If you click the Columns button, you will see the Page Setup dialog box with the Columns tab selected (Figure 6–91c). You can use this tab to specify multiple columns in a report as well as column spacing. You can specify orientation by clicking the Page tab (Figure 6–91d). You can also select paper size, paper source, and printer using this tab. Back on the ribbon, if you click the Page Setup button, you will see the Page Setup dialog box with the Print Options tab selected (Figure 6–91e). You can use this tab to specify custom margins.

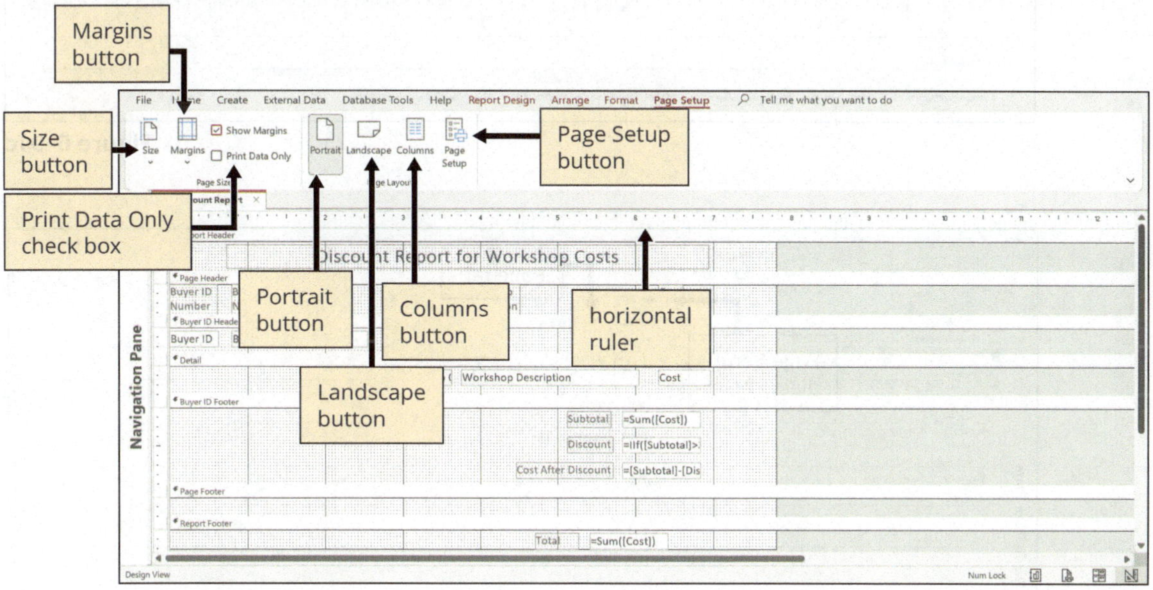

Figure 6–91a

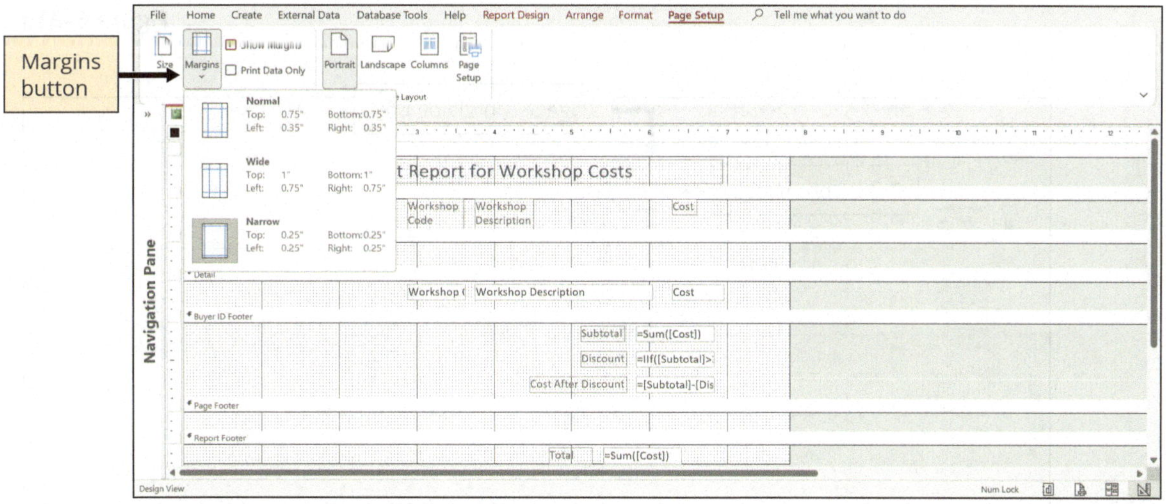

Figure 6–91b

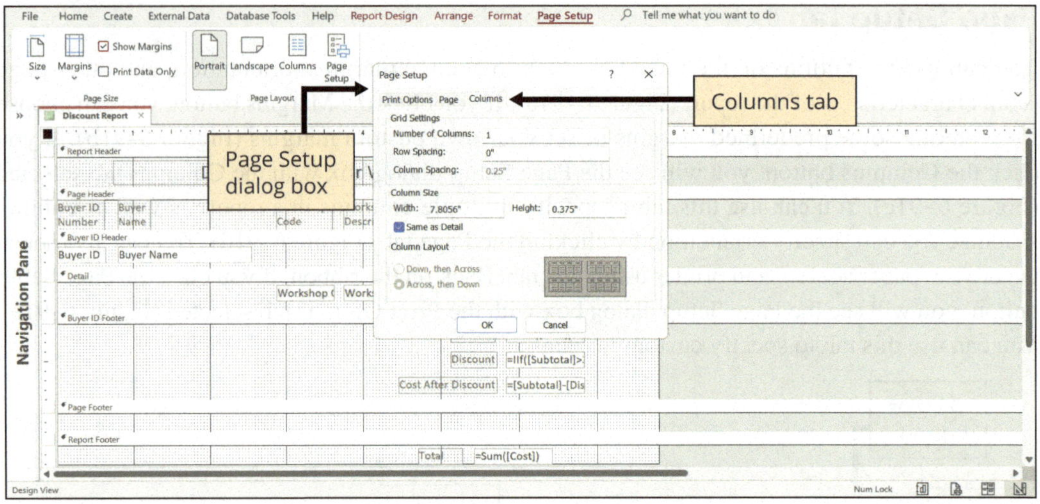

Figure 6–91c

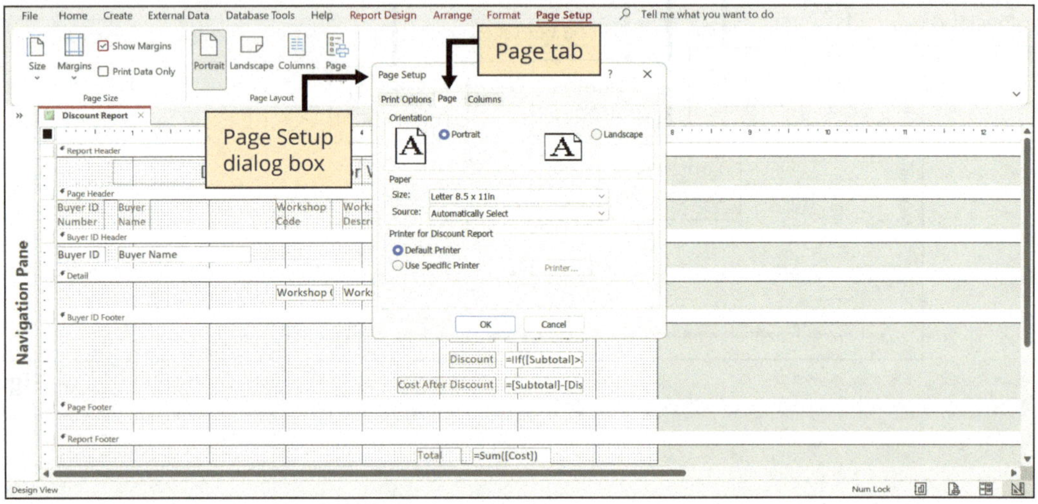

Figure 6–91d

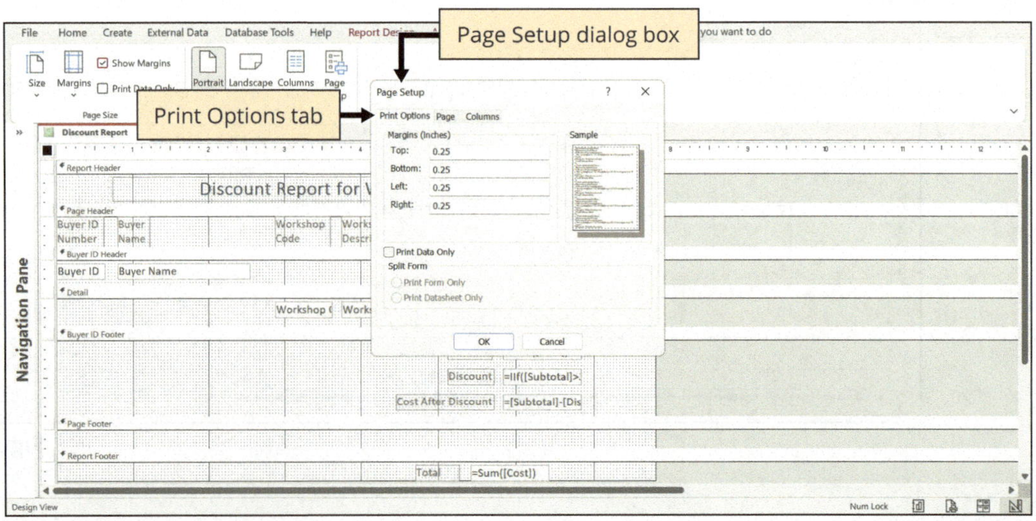

Figure 6–91e

To Change the Report Margins

Looking at the horizontal ruler in Figure 6–91a, you will notice the report width is nearly 8 inches. Because the report will probably print on standard 8½" × 11" paper, an 8-inch report with 1-inch margins on the left and right would result in a 10-inch width, which will not fit. To allow the report to fit on the page, you could change the orientation from Portrait to Landscape or you could reduce the margins. There are two ways to change the margins. You can click the Margins button on the Page Setup tab and then select one of the predefined options. If you want more control, you can click the Page Setup button to display the Page Setup dialog box. You can then specify your own margins, change the orientation, and also specify multiple columns if you want a multicolumn report.

The following step uses the Margins button to confirm Narrow margins is selected, as this option will provide the most printable space on the page.

1

- Display the Page Setup tab.
- Click the Margins button (Page Setup tab | Page Size group).
- If necessary, click Narrow to specify the Narrow margin option.

Fine-Tuning a Report

When you have finished a report, you should review several of its pages in Print Preview to make sure the layout is precisely what you want. You might find that you need to increase the size of a control, which you can do by selecting the control and dragging the appropriate sizing handle. You might decide to add a control, which you could do by using the appropriate tool in the Controls group or by dragging a field from the field list.

In both cases, if the control is located between other controls, you have a potential problem. You might not have enough space between the other controls to increase the size or to add an additional control. If the control is part of a control layout that you had when you modified earlier reports in Layout view, you can resize controls or add new fields, and the remaining fields automatically adjust for the change. In Design view with individual controls, you must make any necessary adjustments manually.

To Make Room for Resizing or Adding Controls

To make room for resizing a control or for adding controls, you would use the following steps.

1. Select all controls to the right of the control you want to resize, or to the right of the position where you want to add another control.
2. Drag any of the selected controls to the right to make room for the change.

To Save and Close a Report

Now that you have completed your work on your report, you should save the report and close it. The following steps first save your work on the report and then close the report.

1

- If instructed to do so by your instructor, change the title of the Discount Report to LastName Report where LastName is your last name.
- Click the Save button on the Quick Access Toolbar to save your work.
- Close the Discount Report.

2

- If desired, sign out of your Microsoft account.
- sam Exit Access.

Summary

In this module, you have learned to create and relate additional tables; create queries for a report; create reports in Design view; add fields and text boxes to a report; format controls; group and ungroup controls; modify multiple controls; add and modify a subreport; modify section properties; add a title, page number, and date; add subtotals; use a function in a text box; and publish a report.

Consider This: Plan Ahead

What decisions will you need to make when creating your own reports?

Use these guidelines as you complete the assignments in this module and create your own reports outside of this class.

1. Determine the intended audience and purpose of the report.
   a. Identify the user or users of the report and determine how they will use it.
   b. Specify the necessary data and level of detail to include in the report.
2. Determine the source of data for the report.
   a. Determine whether all the data is in a single table or whether it comes from multiple related tables.
3. Determine whether the data is stored in a query.
   a. You might need to create multiple versions of a report for a query where the criterion for a field changes, in which case, you would use a parameter query and enter the criterion when you run the report.
   b. If the data comes from multiple related tables, you might want to create a query and use the query as a source of data.
4. Determine the fields that belong on the report.
   a. Identify the data items that are needed by the user of the report.
5. Determine the organization of the report.
   a. The report might be enhanced by displaying the fields in a particular order and arranged in a certain way.
   b. Should the records in the report be grouped in some way?
   c. Should the report contain any subreports?
6. Determine any calculations required for the report.
   a. Should the report contain totals or subtotals?
   b. Are there any special calculations?
   c. Are there any calculations that involve criteria?
7. Determine the format and style of the report.
   a. What information should be in the report heading?
   b. Do you want a title and date?
   c. Do you want special background colors or alternate colors?
   d. Should the report contain an image?
   e. What should be in the body of the report?

Consider This

How should you submit solutions to critical thinking questions in the assignments?

Every assignment in this course contains one or more critical thinking questions. These questions require you to think beyond the assigned database. Present your responses to the questions in the format required by your instructor. Possible formats may include one or more of these options: write the answer; create a document that contains the answer; present your answer to the class; discuss your answer in a group; record the answer as audio or video using a webcam, smartphone, or portable media player; or post answers on a blog, wiki, or website.

Student Assignments

Apply Your Knowledge

Reinforce the skills and apply the concepts you learned in this module.

Creating a Report with a Subreport

Note: To complete this assignment, you will be required to use the Data Files. Please contact your instructor for information about accessing the Data Files.

Instructions: Start Access. Open the database, SC_AC_06-2.accdb, which is located in the Data Files folder. Enable the content.

Perform the following tasks:

1. Save the database using the file name, SC_AC_06_Construction. Enable the content.
2. In the Relationships window, delete the existing relationship between the Job Sites table and the Subcontractors table. Add the Accounting table to the window.
3. Create a one-to-many relationship (enforce referential integrity) between the Subcontractors table and the Accounting table using the Subcontractor Number field in both tables. Create a second one-to-many relationship (enforce referential integrity) between the Job Sites table and the Accounting table using the Job Site Number field in both tables. Save the relationships and close the Relationships window.
4. Create a query that joins the Subcontractors and Accounting tables. Include the Subcontractor Number, Subcontractor Name, and Specialty fields from the Subcontractors table. Include the Pymt ID, Amount Paid, Current Due, and JS # fields from the Accounting table. Sort the results by Subcontractor Number in Ascending order. Save the query as Subcontractors and Accounting. Run the query to confirm it shows all seven records from the Accounting table in the results, and then save and close the query.
5. Create the report shown in Figure 6–92. The report uses the Subcontractors and Accounting query as the basis for the main report and the Job Sites table as the basis for the subreport. Group by Subcontractor Number and sort by JS #. When stepping through the SubReport Wizard, link the subform to the main form using the job site number field on each side of the connection. Use the name Subcontractors and Job Sites Summary List for the report. The report title has a Text Align property value of Center. The Border Width property for the detail controls is 1 pt and the subreport name is Job Sites subreport. The report is similar in style to the Buyers and Account Information Summary List shown in Figure 6–1a.

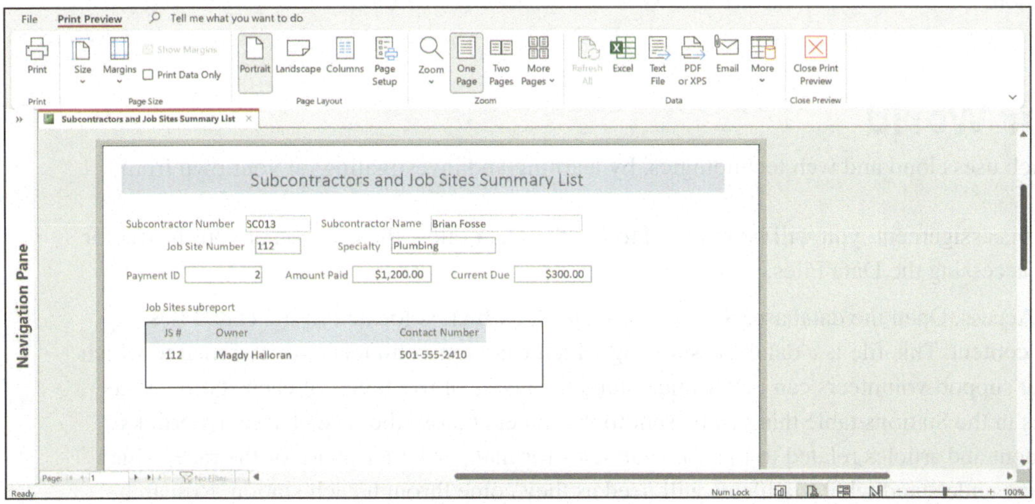

Figure 6–92

Continued on next page

6. If requested to do so by your instructor, change the title for the report to First Name Last Name Summary List where First Name and Last Name are your first and last names.
7. Submit the revised database in the format specified by your instructor.
8. **Consider This:** How would you change the font weight of the report title to bold?

Extend Your Knowledge

Extend the skills you learned in this module and experiment with new skills. You may need to use Help to complete the assignment.

Modifying Reports

Note: To complete this assignment, you will be required to use the Data Files. Please contact your instructor for information about accessing the Data Files.

Instructions: Start Access. Open the database, SC_AC_06-3.accdb, which is located in the Data Files folder. PicsPlus is a small photography cooperative that is seeking grant funding. As part of the grant application process, PicsPlus needs to make some design changes to a report in its database.

Perform the following tasks:

1. Save the database using the file name, SC_AC_06_PicsPlus. Enable the content.
2. Open the Photographer Balances Summary Report in Design view. Insert a date field (such as 14-Nov-27) in the report header. If necessary, arrange the date so it aligns with the right edge of the report.
3. Change the report title to Revised Photographer Balances Summary Report. Change the report header background to white. Use the Property Sheet to change the font of the title text to Calibri with a font weight of semi-bold. Make sure the entire title is visible and the title is left-aligned in the Report Header section.
4. Add a label to the report footer section. The label should contain text to indicate the end of the report, for example, End of Report or similar text.
5. Use conditional formatting to format the sum for each record with the Green 3 background color for all records where the value is equal to or greater than $1,000.00.
6. If requested to do so by your instructor, open the Photographer table and add your name to the table.
7. Submit the revised database in the format specified by your instructor.
8. **Consider This:** Do you think the borders surrounding the controls enhance or detract from the appearance of the Photographer Balances Summary Report? What other design changes would you suggest? Explain your position.

Expand Your World

Create a solution, which uses cloud and web technologies, by learning and investigating on your own from general guidance.

Note: To complete this assignment, you will be required to use the Data Files. Please contact your instructor for information about accessing the Data Files.

Instructions: Start Access. Open the database, SC_AC_06-4.accdb, which is located in the Data Files folder, and enable the content. This file is a database showing which triathlon volunteers are assigned to which support station. So that support volunteers can better understand the needs of triathletes at each station, you want to add hyperlinks in the Stations table that can be sent to volunteers before the race. These hyperlinks should connect to content and articles related to tips for triathletes for that particular phase of the race, which will also help volunteers understand what triathletes will need as they come through each station. Research how to add a hyperlink in an Access table. The race coordinators want specific websites for specific stations. You can use the information shown in Table 6–5, or you can research and find your own links that you think would be helpful for volunteers at each station. After placing the hyperlinks in the Stations table, add the hyperlink field to the Volunteers Stations Report.

Perform the following tasks:

1. Search the web to find how to add a hyperlink in an Access table and also in a report that was created previously.
2. Save the database using the file name, SC_AC_06_Triathlon. Enable the content. Create a new field with the Hyperlink Data Type called Information in the Stations table. Add the websites shown in Table 6–5 in the new field for the station indicated; alternatively, find another website for each station that would be helpful for volunteers at each station and add those websites instead.

Table 6–5 Stations and Associated Hyperlinks

Station Number	Suggested Hyperlink
BK1 and BK2	https://www.trigirl.co.uk/beginners/top-5-cycling-tips-for-beginner-triathletes/
RN1 and RN2	https://www.trainingpeaks.com/blog/five-steps-run-faster-triathlon/
SW1	https://www.formswim.com/blogs/all/triathlon-swimming-strokes

3. Open the Volunteers Stations Report in Design view and delete any alternate background color in the report.
4. Add the hyperlink field to the Volunteers Stations Report.
5. Review the report in Report view and verify the accuracy of the website hyperlinks.
6. Save your changes.
7. Submit the revised database in the format specified by your instructor.
8. **Consider This:** What steps did you select to create a hyperlink? What source did you use to learn this information? Justify your selection of the source.

In the Lab

Design and implement a solution using creative thinking and problem-solving skills.

Lab: Creating a Report for the Homegrown Nurse Staffing Agency Database

Note: To complete this assignment, you will be required to use the Data Files. Please contact your instructor for information about accessing the Data Files.

Problem: From time to time, equipment needs to be updated or replaced. Team managers, coaches, and administrators want to keep track of the changes as part of the database.

Perform the following tasks:

Part 1: Open the SC_AC_06-5.accdb database from the Data Files folder. Save the file with the name, SC_AC_06_Travel-Nurses, and enable the content. Use the concepts and techniques presented in this module to perform each of the following tasks. The agency needs to create a report to help track payments by traveler and assignment.

1. Create a query that includes fields from the Travelers table and the Assignments table (these tables are joined in a one-to-many relationship). Include the Traveler ID and Traveler Name fields from the Travelers table. Include the Assignment ID, Assignment Pay Rate, and Assignment Reimbursements fields from the Assignments table. Sort in Ascending order on Traveler ID. Save the query as Travelers and Pay Rates.

Continued on next page

2. Create the report shown in Figure 6–93. The report uses the Travelers and Pay Rates query as the basis for the main report and the Traveler Payments table as the basis for the subreport. Use the name Travelers and Payments Summary List as the name for the report and the name Traveler Payments as the name for the subreport. Change the Text Align property for the title to Center.

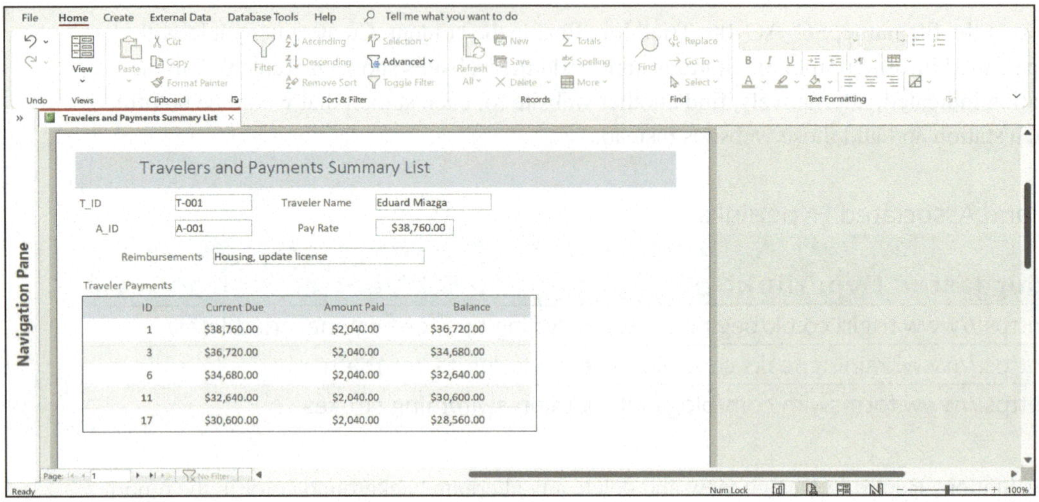

Figure 6–93

3. The page number and current date appear in the report footer section. Change the Can Grow property for the Traveler Name field to Yes.
4. If instructed to do so by your instructor, add a label to the report footer with your first and last name.
5. **Consider This:** Adding a subreport can provide quick reference to other database information. What are your thoughts about using the Traveler Payments table for the subreport? Do you think it is helpful or would you use another table or some other object in the subreport?

Submit your assignment in the format specified by instructor.

Part 2: Consider This: You made several decisions, such as creating a query, creating and modifying a report, and adding a subreport control. What was the rationale behind your decisions? Would you add any additional fields to this table?

Advanced Form Techniques

Objectives

After completing this module, you will be able to:

- Add a combo box that selects values
- Apply formatting characteristics with the Format Painter
- Modify content and design of a header or footer
- Insert an image in a form
- Add a command button to a form
- Add a combo box for searching
- Add a rectangle shape
- Modify a button's actions in a form
- Modify VBA (Visual Basic for Applications) code
- Add concatenated fields to a form
- Use tab controls to create a multipage form
- Insert a chart
- Modify a chart type
- Format a chart

Introduction

In other modules, you created basic forms using the Form Wizard, and you created more complex forms using Design view. In this module, you continue learning advanced design and formatting techniques for when you are working with forms. With the proper tools, forms can provide a valuable means of interacting with data in the database. You will create two new forms that include elements to increase functionality and display different types of information. The first form contains two combo boxes, one for selecting data from a related table and one for finding a record on the form. It also contains command buttons to accomplish various tasks.

The second form you will create is a **multipage form**, which is a form that contains more than one page of information. The form contains a tab control that allows you to access two different pages. Clicking the first tab displays a page containing a subform. Clicking the second tab displays a page containing two charts.

Project: Advanced Form Techniques

Clearnet wants two additional forms to use with its Carriers and Loads tables. The first form, Loads View and Update Form (Figure 7–1a), contains fields from the Loads table. The form has five command buttons: Next Record, Previous Record, Add Record, Delete Record, and Close Form. Clicking any of these buttons causes the action indicated on the button to occur.

The form also contains combo boxes for the Carrier and Shipper fields, which assists users in viewing who is involved in the load (Figure 7–1b).

To assist users in finding an account when they know the load number, the form also includes a combo box they can use for record navigation (Figure 7–1c). This combo box allows users to enter the load number in one of two ways: they can either type the number in the text field, or they can click the arrow to display a list and then select the load they want. Access will then locate the account and display that load's data in the form (Figure 7–1d).

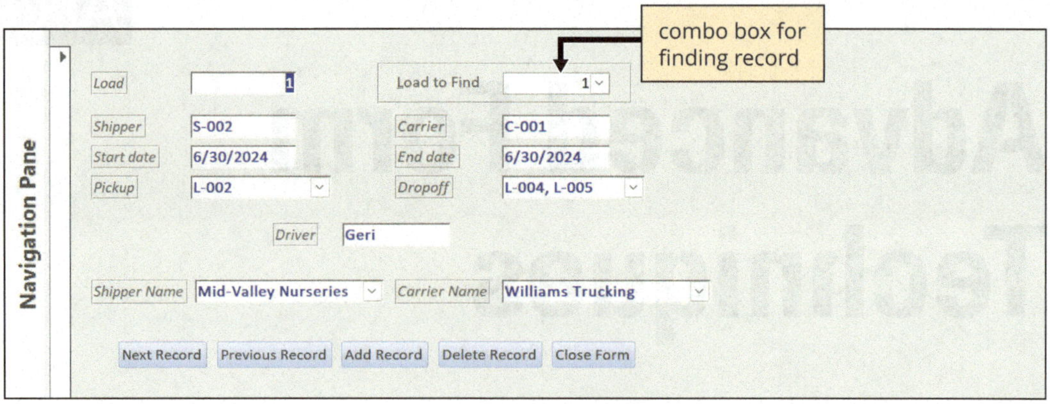

Figure 7–1a Loads View and Update Form

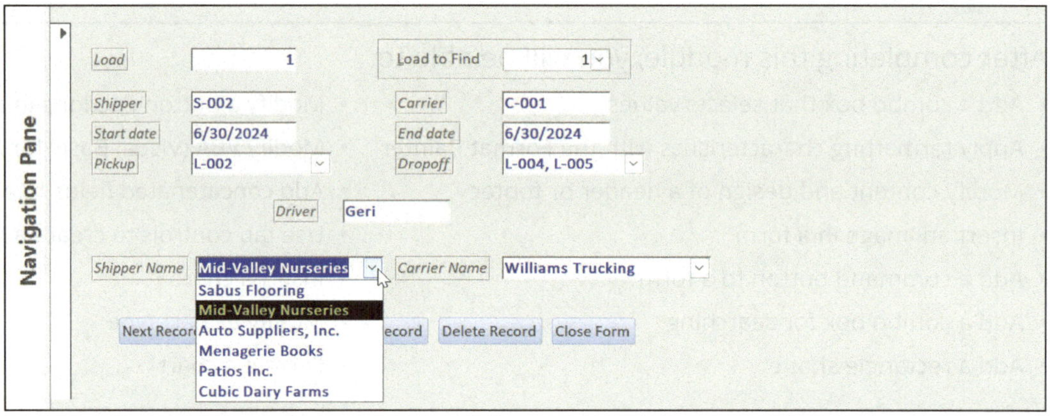

Figure 7–1b Shipper Combo Box

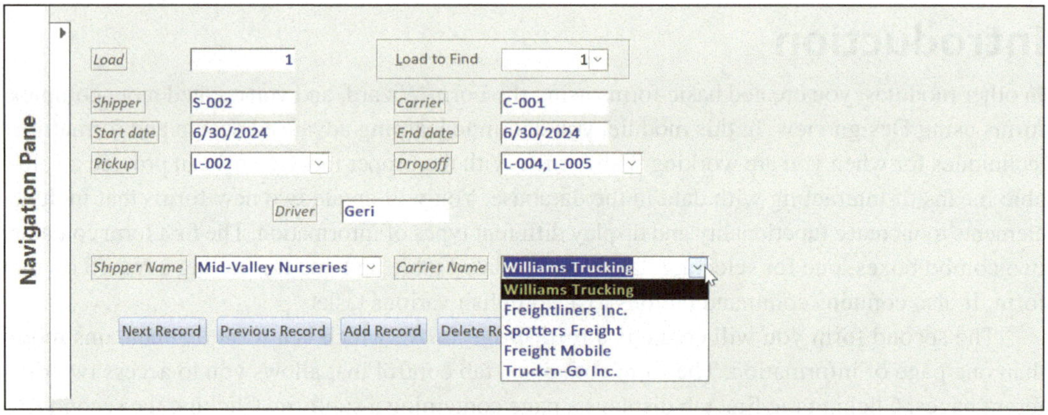

Figure 7–1c Carrier Combo Box

BTW

Drop-Down Boxes

Combo boxes also are called drop-down boxes because a list drops down when you click the combo box arrow. This is one of the primary differences between a combo box and a list box (which is a different type of control). The list box displays the list all the time, and you cannot type a different value into a list box. You simply click the value that you want from the list. With a combo box, however, the drop-down list only appears when you click the arrow, and you have the option of typing a different value into the box.

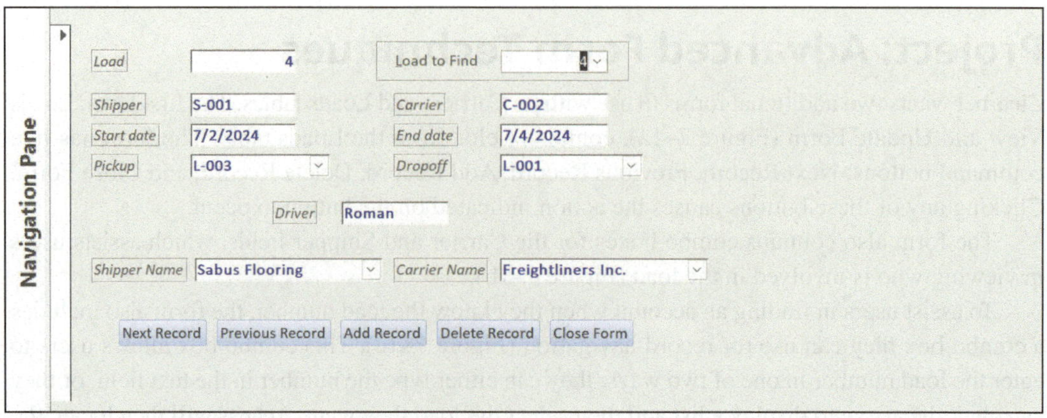

Figure 7–1d Load Data

For the second new form, Clearnet needs a multipage form that lists the payments by shipper. Each of the two pages that make up the form is displayed in its own tab. Selecting the first tab, the one labeled Datasheet, displays a subform listing information about rate confirmations and agent commissions for each shipper (Figure 7–2a).

Selecting the other tab, the one labeled Charts, displays two charts that illustrate data about the shipper's rate cons and agent commissions for each load (Figure 7–2b). In the pie chart, the slices of the pie represent the sum of rate confirmations for each bill status. They are color-coded, and the legend at the bottom indicates the meaning of the various colors. The size of the pie slice gives a visual representation of the portion of rate confirmations with that bill status. The chart also includes specific percentages. If you look at the purple slice in the Rate Confirmation Statuses chart, for example, you see the color represents Bill Sent statuses. This slice signifies 58 percent of the total. The columns in the second chart represent the amount of agent commission earned for each load sent by that shipper. Over time, this chart would start to show trends of agent commissions with each shipper.

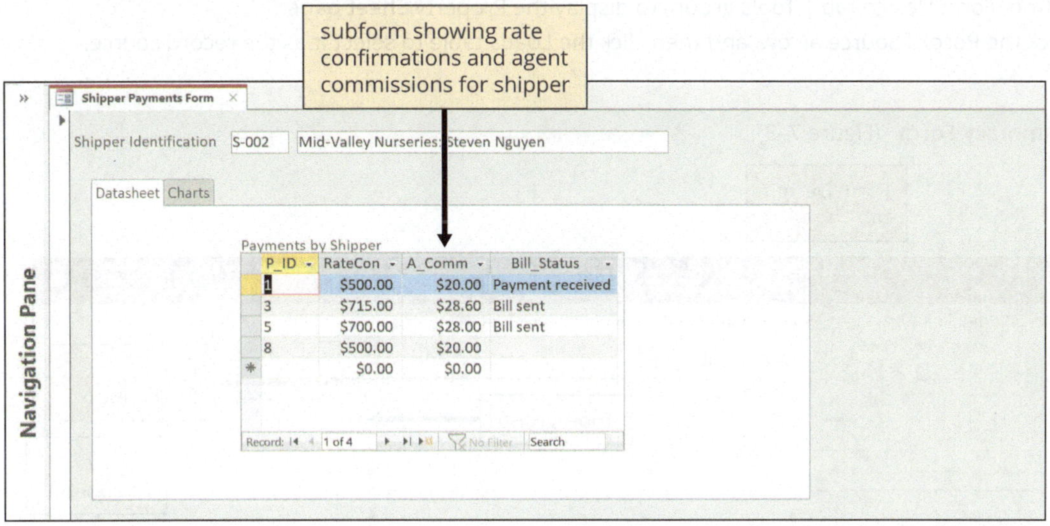

Figure 7–2a Datasheet

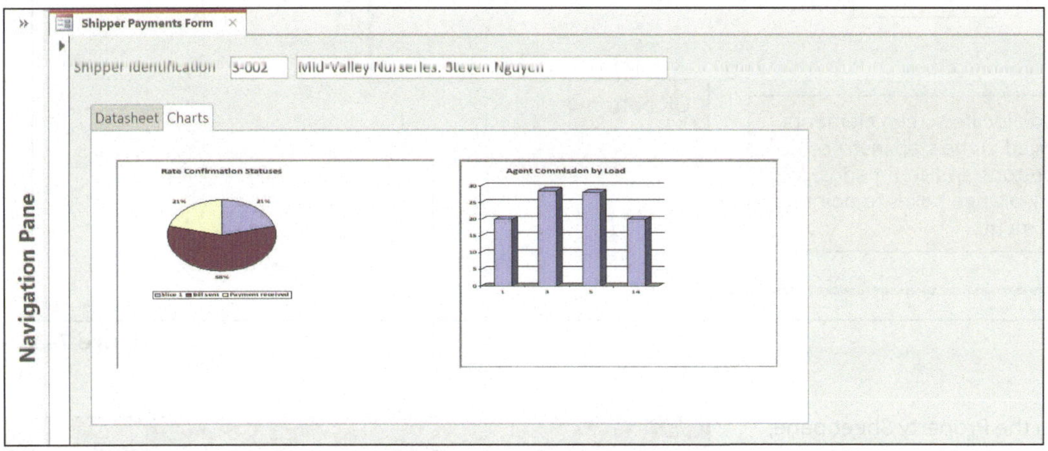

Figure 7–2b Charts

Creating a Form with Combo Boxes and Command Buttons

After planning a form, you might decide that including features such as combo boxes and command buttons will make the form easier to use. You can include such items while modifying the form in Design view.

BTW
Enabling the Content
For each of the databases you use in this module, you will need to enable the content.

To Create a Form in Design View

As you have previously learned, Access provides several ways to create a form, including tools such as the Form Wizard and the Form button. The following steps create a form in Design view. **Why?** Creating a form in Design view gives you the most flexibility in laying out the form. You will be presented with a blank design on which to place objects.

1

- sam Start Access. Open the database, SC_AC_07-1.accdb, which is located in the Data Files folder. Save the file to your hard disk, One Drive, or other storage location using the file name, **SC_AC_07_Clearnet**. Enable the content.
- Display the Create tab.
- Click the Form Design button (Create tab | Forms group) to create a new form in Design view.
- Close the Navigation Pane.

2

- Ensure the form selector, the box in the upper-left corner of the form, is selected.
- Click the Property Sheet button (Form Design tab | Tools group) to display the Property Sheet pane.
- With the All tab selected, click the Record Source arrow, and then click the Loads table to select it as the record source.

3

- Save the form as **Loads Summary Form** (Figure 7–3).

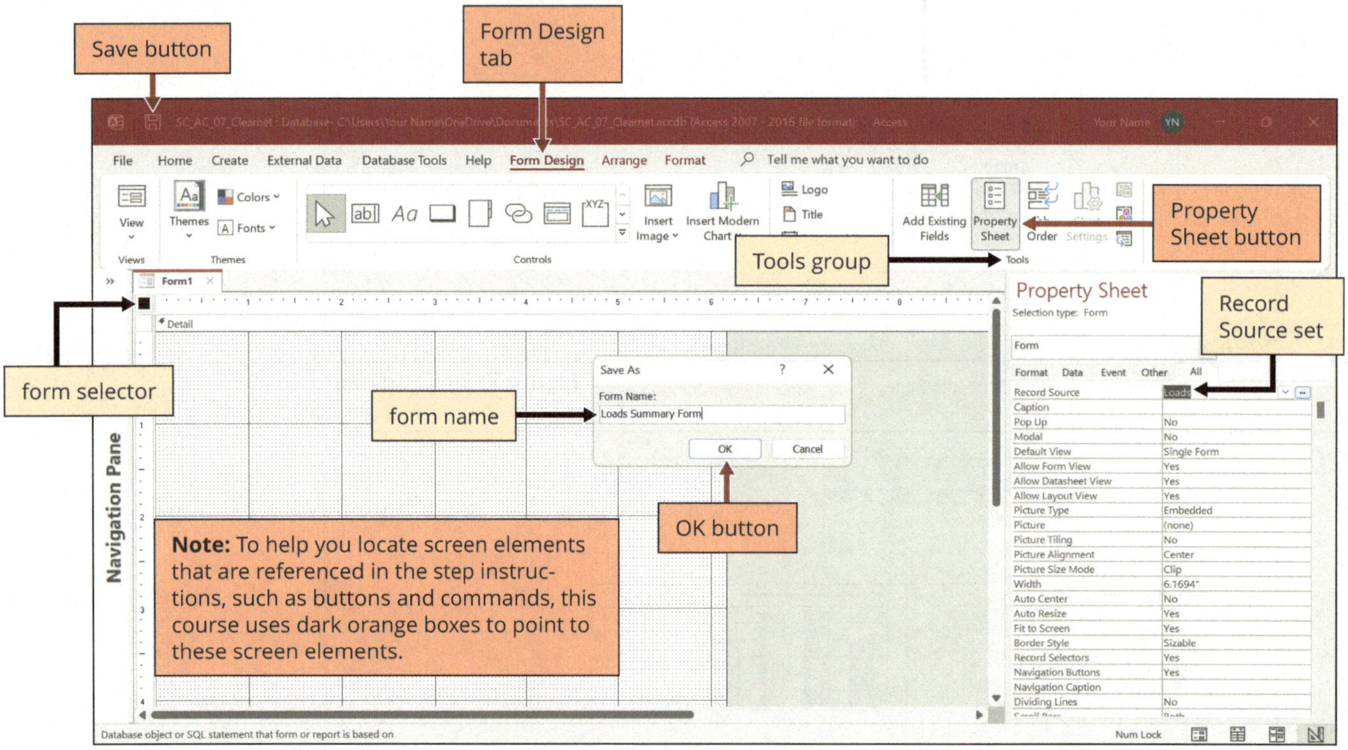

Figure 7–3

4

- Click the Caption property in the Property Sheet pane, and then type **Loads View and Update Form** as the new caption.
- Close the Property Sheet pane.
- Click the 'Add Existing Fields' button (Form Design tab | Tools group) to display the Field List pane (Figure 7–4).

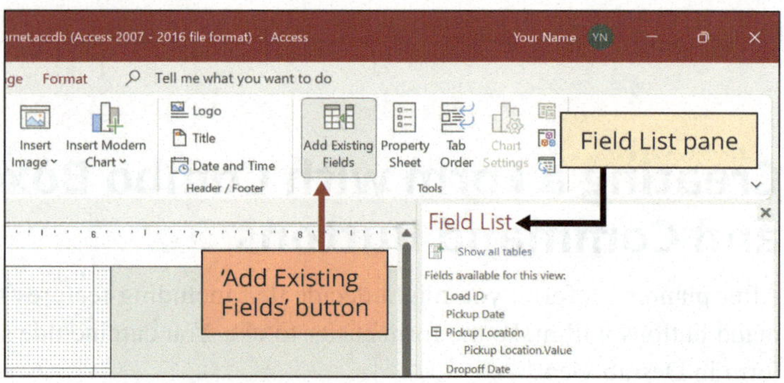

Figure 7–4

Q&A Why does the name on the tab not change to the new caption, Loads View and Update Form?

The name on the tab will change to the new caption in Form view. In Design view, you still see the name of the form object.

To Add Fields to the Form Design

After deciding which fields to add to the Loads View and Update Form, you can place them on the form by dragging the fields from the field list to the desired position. The following steps first display only the fields in the Loads table in the Field List pane, and then place the appropriate fields on the form.

BTW
The Ribbon and Screen Resolution
Access may change how the groups and buttons within the groups appear on the ribbon, depending on the computer's screen resolution. Thus, your ribbon might look different from the ones in this course if you are using a screen resolution other than 1920 x 1080.

1

- If necessary, click the 'Show only fields in the current record source' link at the top of the Field List pane to change the link to 'Show all tables' so the pane displays only the fields in the Loads table.
- Drag the Load ID field from the Field List pane to the top-left area of the form and adjust the location as necessary to match Figure 7–5.

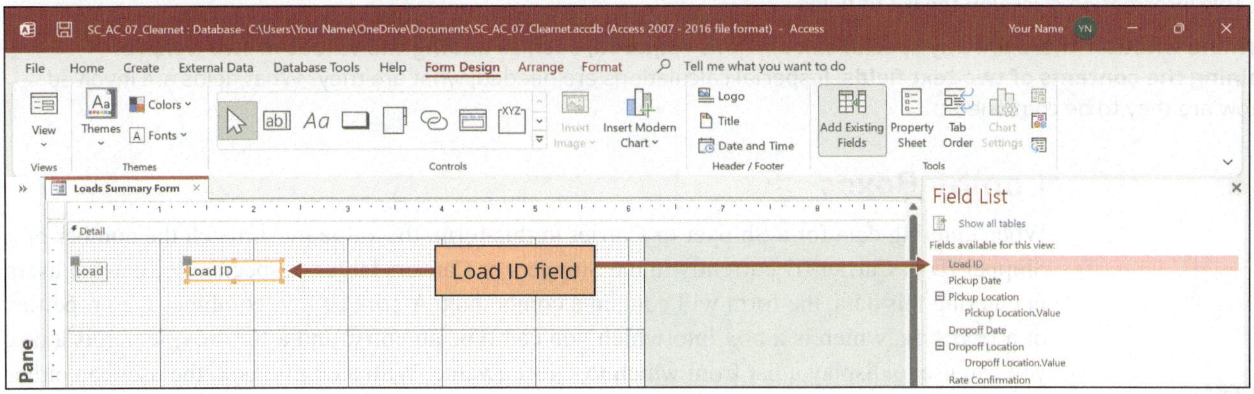

Figure 7–5

BTW
Touch Screen Differences
The Office and Windows interfaces may vary if you are using a touch screen. For this reason, you might notice the function or appearance of your touch screen differs slightly from this module's presentation.

2

- Use CTRL to select the Pickup Date, Pickup Location, Dropoff Date, Dropoff Location, Driver Name, Carrier, and Shipper fields in the Field List pane.
- Drag the selected fields to a position below the Load ID field.
- Close the Field List pane, and reposition the fields and their labels to the approximate positions shown in Figure 7–6. If controls for any of the fields are not aligned properly, align them by dragging them to the desired location or by using the alignment buttons on the Arrange tab.

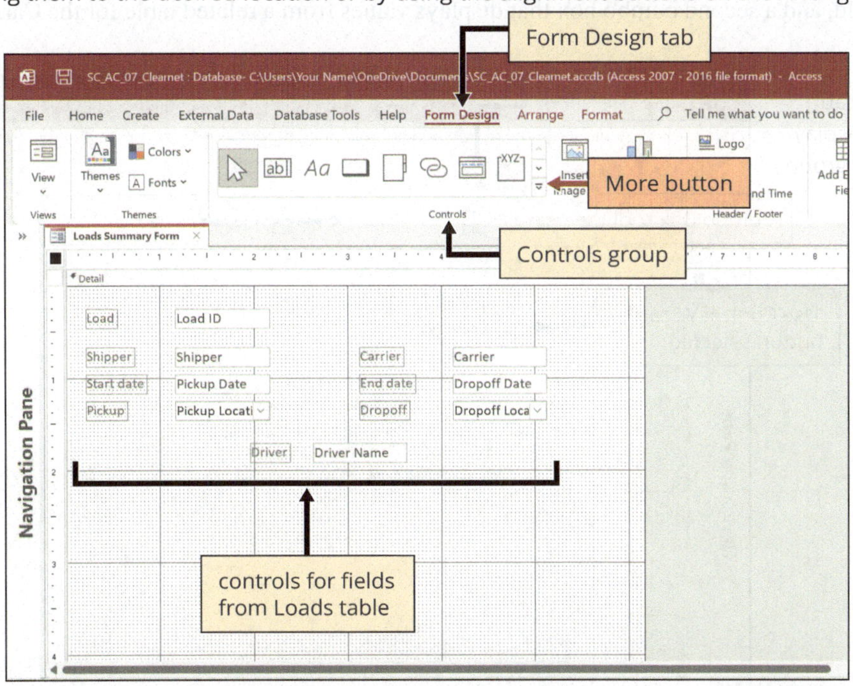

Figure 7–6

Q&A I added a field twice by mistake. Can I delete the control?

Yes, select the control and press DEL.

Consider This

How do you decide on the contents of a form?

To design and create forms, follow these general guidelines:

- **Determine the fields that belong on the form.** If you determine that data should be presented as a form, you then need to determine which tables and fields contain the data for the form.
- **Examine the requirements for the form in general to determine the tables.** Do the requirements only relate to data in a single table, or does the data come from multiple tables? How are the tables related?
- **Examine the specific requirements for the form to determine the fields necessary.** Look for all the data items that are specified for the form. Each item should correspond to a field in a table or be able to be computed from a field in a table. This information gives you the list of fields.
- **Determine whether there are any special calculations required, such as adding the values in two fields or combining the contents of two text fields.** If special calculations are needed, what are they? What fields are involved and how are they to be combined?

Combo Boxes

When entering data for a Shipper or Carrier in this form, the value must match the number of a Shipper ID or Carrier ID currently in the Shippers or Carriers tables, respectively. To assist users in entering this data, the form will contain a combo box. A **combo box** combines the properties of a **text box**, which is a box into which you can type an entry, and a **list box**, which is a box you can use to display a list from which to select a value. With a combo box, the user can either type the data or click the combo box arrow to display a drop-down list of possible values and then select an item from the list.

BTW
Combo Boxes
You also can create combo boxes for reports.

To Add a Combo Box That Selects Values

If you have determined that a combo box displaying values from a related table would be useful on your form, you can add the combo box to a form using the Combo Box tool in the Controls group on the Form Design tab. Why? A combo box that allows the user to select a value from a list is a convenient way to enter data. Before adding the combo box, you should make sure the 'Use Control Wizards' button is selected. The following steps place on the form one combo box that displays values from a related table for the Shipper field, and a second combo box that displays values from a related table for the Carrier field.

1

- Click the More button (Form Design tab | Controls group) (see Figure 7–6) to display all the available tools in the Controls group (Figure 7–7).

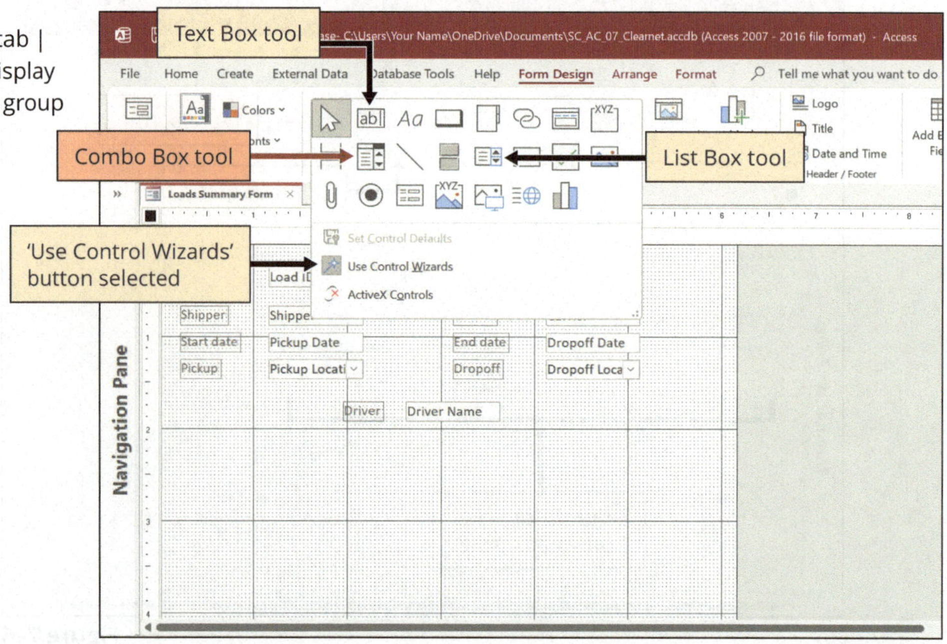

Figure 7–7

2

- With the 'Use Control Wizards' button in the Controls group on the Form Design tab selected, click the Combo Box tool (Form Design tab | Controls group), and then move the pointer, whose shape has changed to a small plus (+) symbol accompanied by a combo box, to the position shown in Figure 7–8.

BTW
Touch and Pointers
Remember that if you are using your finger on a touch screen, you will not see the pointer.

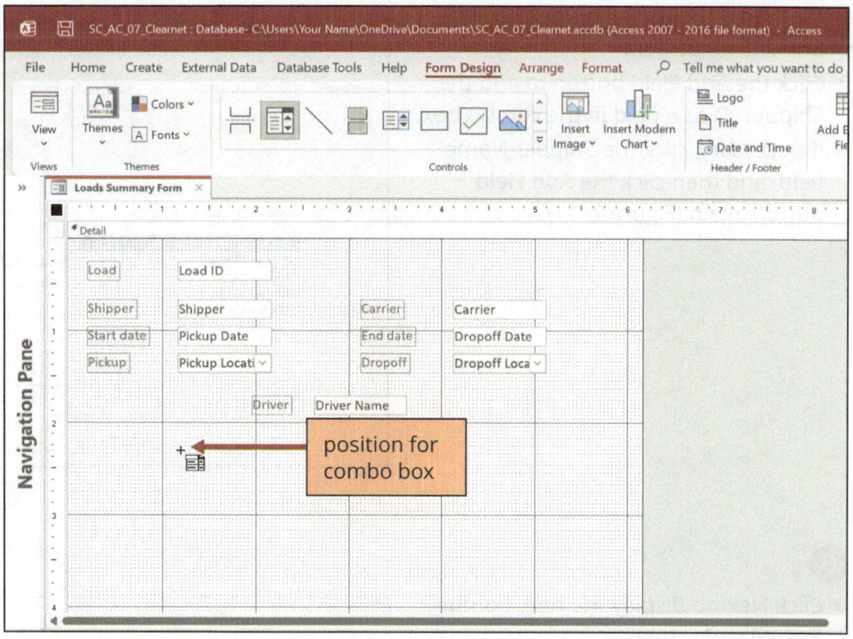

Figure 7–8

3

- Click the position shown in Figure 7–8 to place a combo box and display the Combo Box Wizard dialog box.
- If necessary, in the Combo Box Wizard dialog box, click the 'I want the combo box to get the values from another table or query.' option button (Figure 7–9).

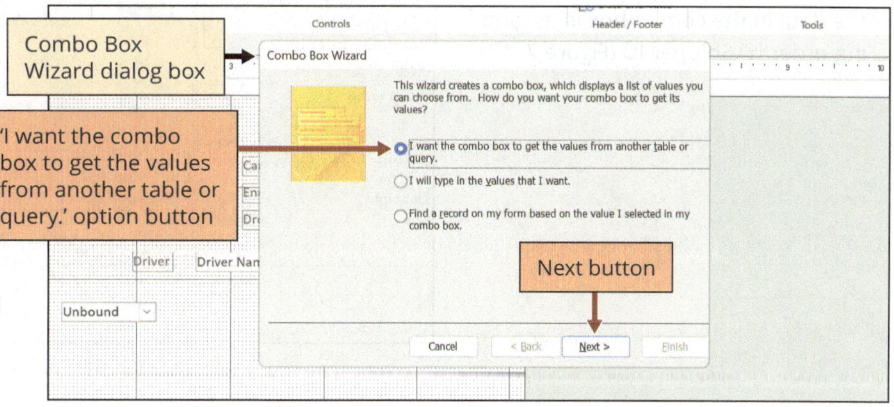

Figure 7–9

Q&A Why did I receive a security warning when I placed a combo box in the form?

Depending on your security settings, you might receive a warning when creating a combo box. Click the Open button to allow the Combo Box Wizard to initiate.

What is the purpose of the other options on the first screen in the Combo Box Wizard dialog box?

Use the second option if you want to type a list from which the user will choose. Use the third option if you want to use the combo box to search for a record. You will use this third option later in this module.

4

- Click Next, and then, with the Tables option button selected in the View area, click Table: Shippers (Figure 7–10) in the list of tables to specify that the combo box values will come from the Shippers table.

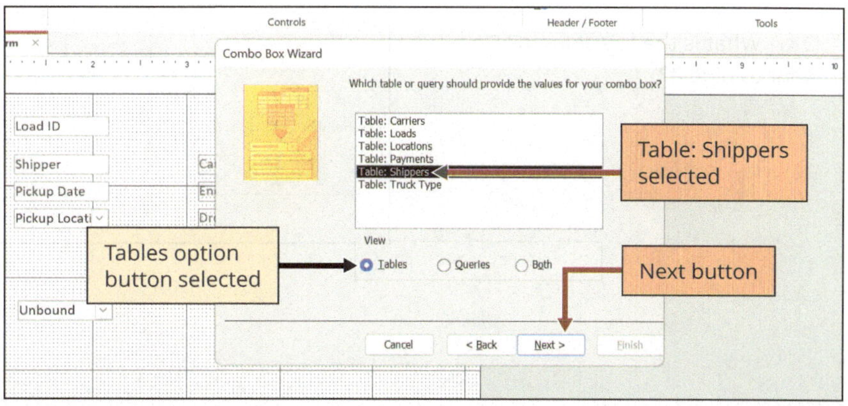

Figure 7–10

5

- Click Next to display the next Combo Box Wizard screen.
- Click the Add Field button to add the Shipper ID as a field in the combo box.
- If necessary, click the Shipper Name field, and then click the Add Field button again (Figure 7–11).

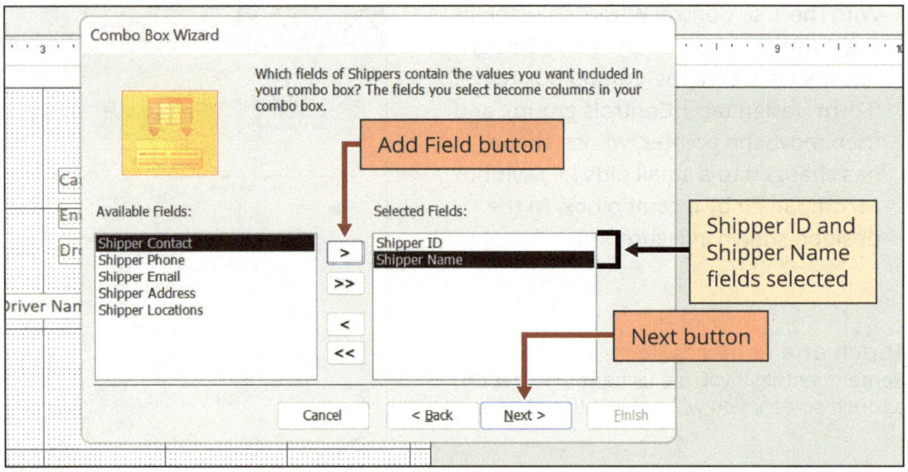

Figure 7–11

6

- Click Next to display the next Combo Box Wizard screen.
- Click the arrow in the first text box, and then select the Shipper ID field to sort the data in the combo box in ascending order by Shipper ID (Figure 7–12).

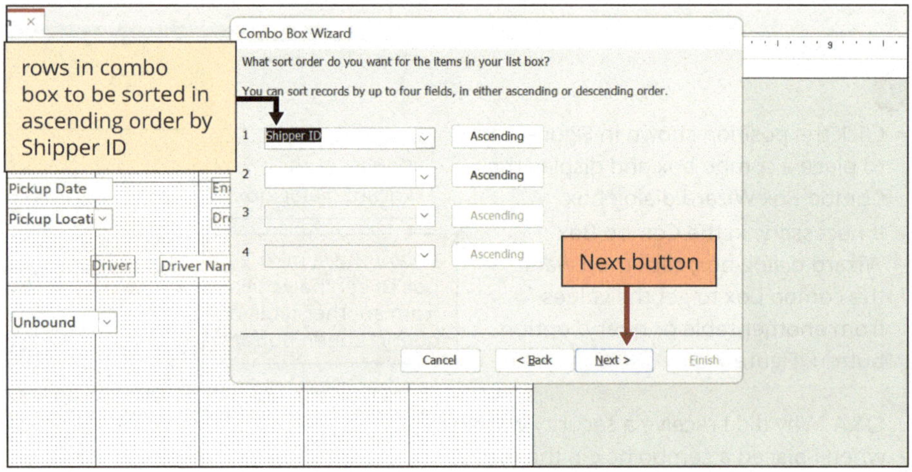

Figure 7–12

7

- Click Next to display the next Combo Box Wizard screen.
- Double-click the right edge of the Shipper Name column to autofit the column so all data is visible (Figure 7–13).

Q&A What is the key column? Do I want to hide it?

The key column would be the Shipper ID, which is the column that identifies a shipper name. Because the purpose of this combo box is to display the shipper's name, you want the Shipper IDs to be hidden.

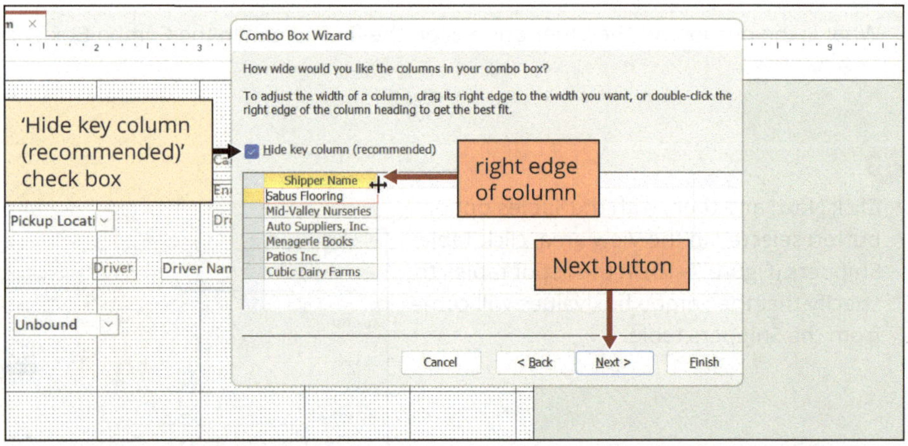

Figure 7–13

8

- Click Next to display the next Combo Box Wizard screen.
- Click the 'Store that value in this field:' option button.
- Because you want the value the user selects to be stored in the Shipper field in the Loads table, click the 'Store that value in this field:' box arrow, and then click Shipper (Figure 7–14).

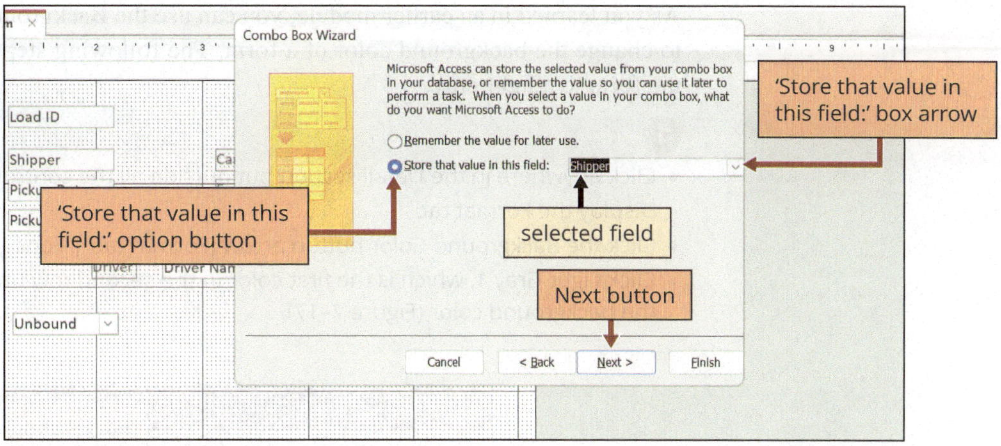

Figure 7–14

9

- Click Next to display the next Combo Box Wizard screen.
- Type **Shipper Name** as the label for the combo box, and then click the Finish button to place the combo box.

Q&A Could I change the label to something else?

Yes. If you prefer a different label, you could change it.

- Reposition and resize the Shipper Name control and label by dragging their move handles to match the sizes and positions shown in Figure 7–15.

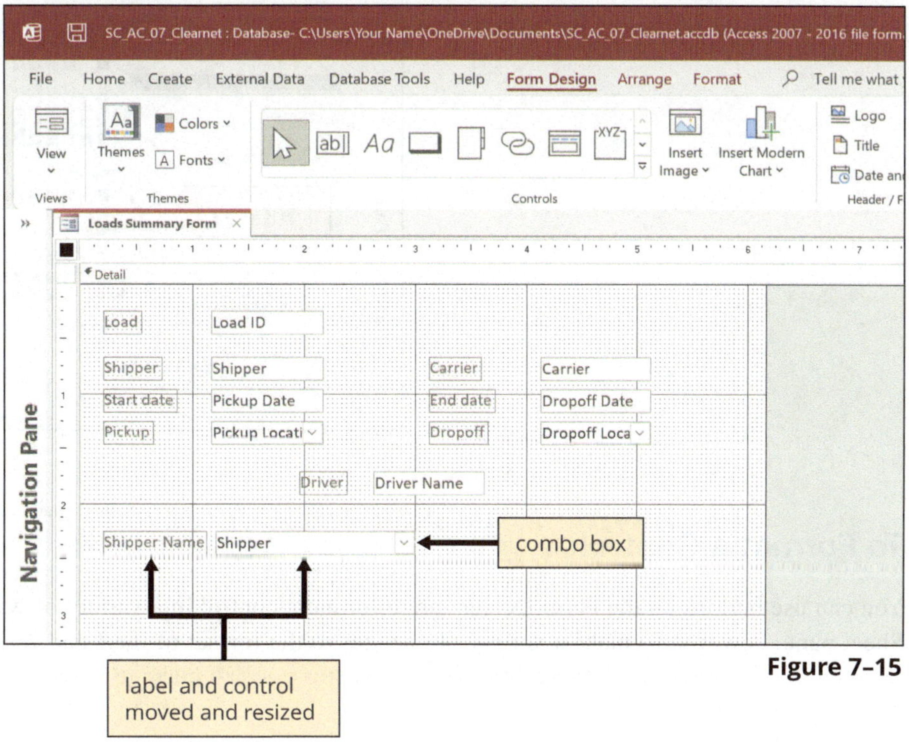

Figure 7–15

10

- Repeat steps 1–9 for the Carrier Name field from the Carriers table, with the following differences: select the Carriers table to provide the data for the combo box, type **Carrier Name** as the label for the Carrier Name combo box, and store the value in the Carrier field of the Loads table.
- Reposition and resize the combo box and label to match Figure 7–16.

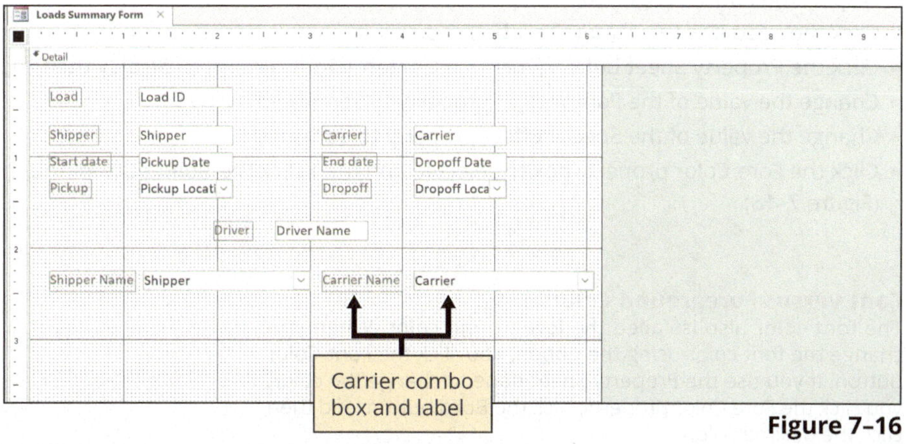

Figure 7–16

11

- Save your changes to the form.

To Use the Background Color Button

As you learned in an earlier module, you can use the Background Color button on the Format tab to change the background color of a form. The following step changes the background color of the form to a light gray.

1

- Click anywhere in the Detail section but outside all the controls to select the section.
- Display the Format tab.
- Click the Background Color button arrow (Format tab | Font group) to display a color palette.
- Click Light Gray 1, which is the first color in the second row under Standard Colors, to change the background color (Figure 7–17).

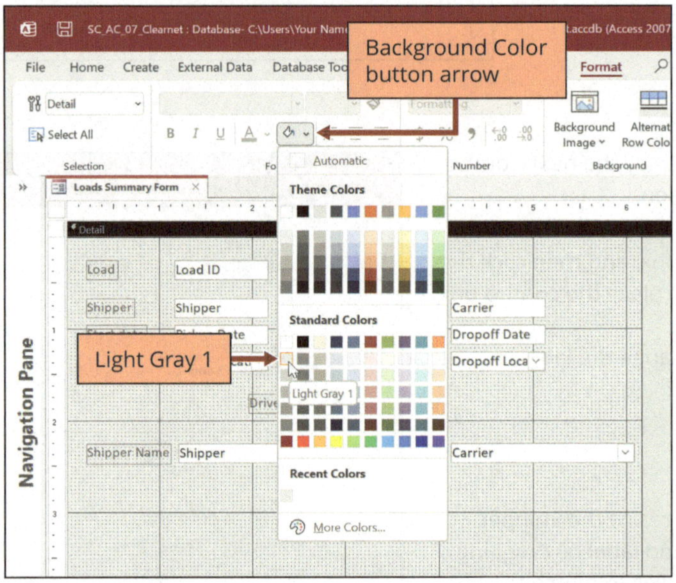

Figure 7–17

To Format a Control

You can use buttons on the Form Design tab to format a control in a variety of ways. The following steps use the Property Sheet pane, however, to make a variety of changes to the format of the Load ID control. **Why?** Using the Property Sheet pane gives you more options with the types of changes you can make to the form controls than you have with simply using the buttons.

1

- Display the Form Design tab.
- Click the Load ID control (not the label) to select it.
- Click the Property Sheet button (Form Design tab | Tools group) to display the Property Sheet pane.
- Change the value of the Font Weight property to Semi-bold.
- Change the value of the Special Effect property to Sunken.
- Click the Fore Color property box to select it, and then click the Build button (the three dots) to display a color palette (Figure 7–18).

BTW

Font versus Foreground Color

The font color also is called the foreground color. When you change the font color using the ribbon, you click the Font Color button. If you use the Property Sheet pane to change the color, you click the Fore Color property, click the Build button, and then click the desired color.

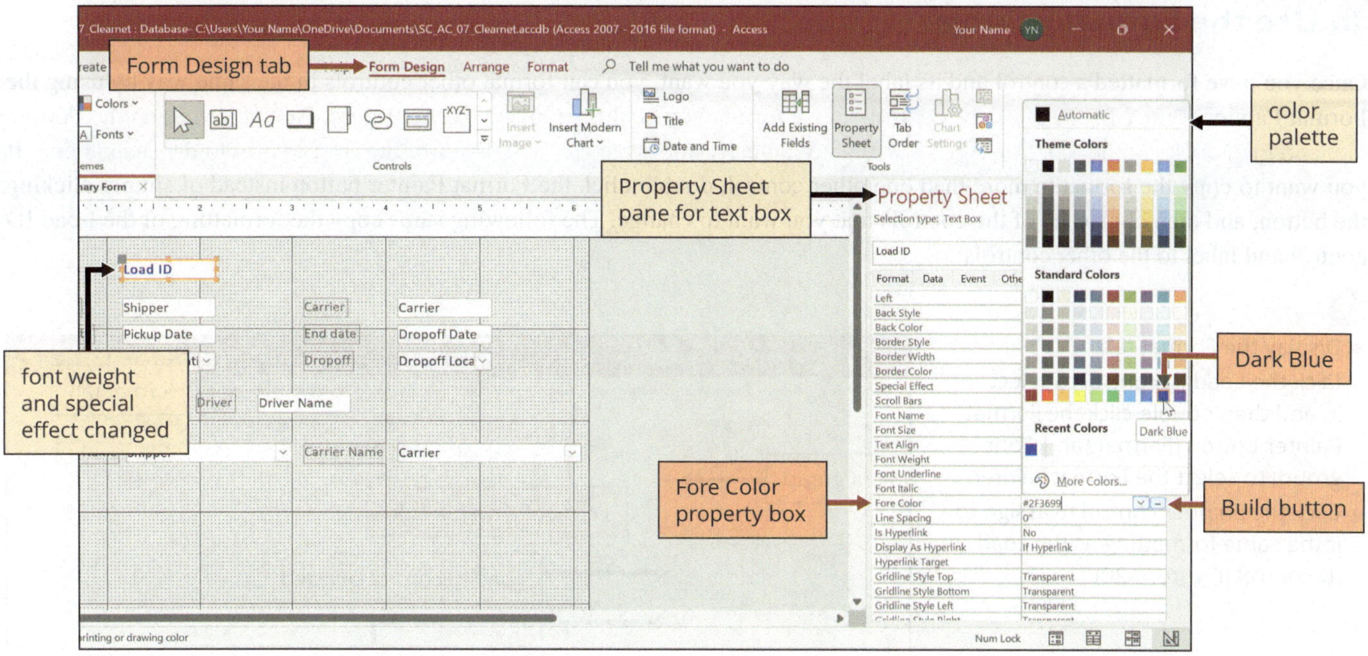

Figure 7–18

2

- Click Dark Blue (the second color from the right in the bottom row under Standard Colors) to select it as the fore color, which is the font color.

3

- Click the label for the Load ID field to select it.
- Change the value of the Font Italic property to Yes.
- Change the value of the Special Effect property to Etched (Figure 7–19).

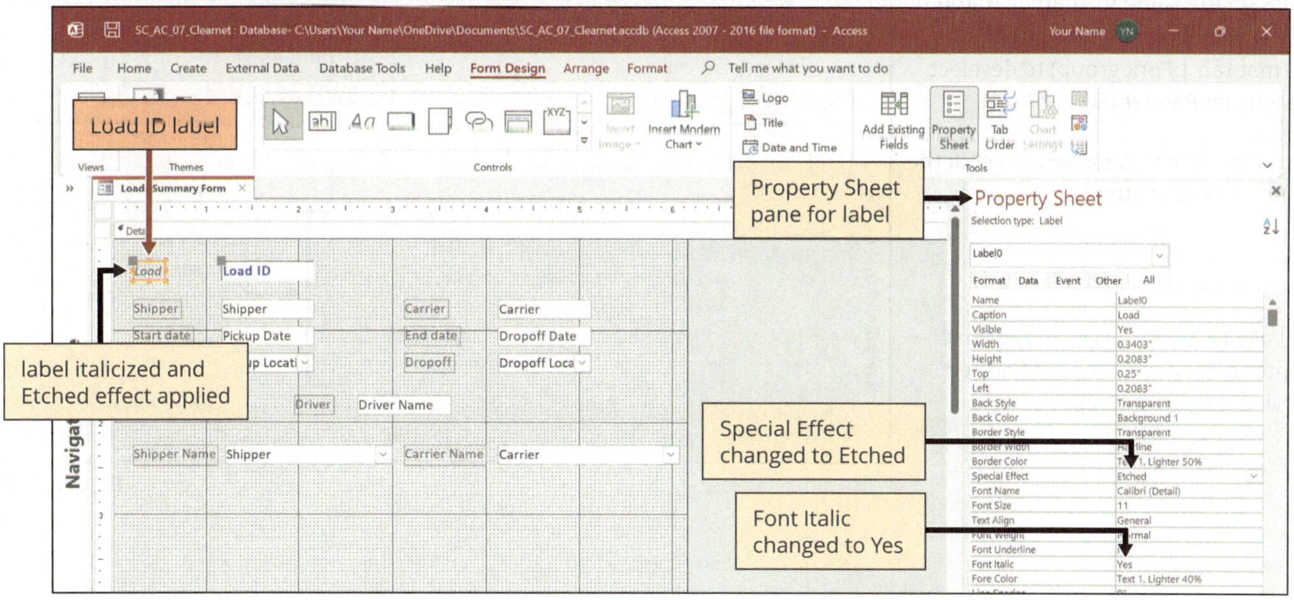

Figure 7–19

4

- Close the Property Sheet pane.

Q&A Should I not have closed the Property Sheet pane before selecting a different control?

You could have, but it is not necessary. The Property Sheet pane displayed on the screen always applies to the currently selected control or group of controls.

To Use the Format Painter

Once you have formatted a control and its label the way you want, you can format other controls in the same way by using the Format Painter. **Why?** If you click the control whose format you want to copy, click the Format Painter button on the Format tab, and then click another control, Access will automatically apply the characteristics of the first control to the second one. If you want to copy the format to more than one other control, double-click the Format Painter button instead of simply clicking the button, and then click each of the controls that you want to change. The following steps copy the formatting of the Load ID control and label to the other controls.

1

- Display the Format tab.
- Click the Load ID control to select it, and then double-click the Format Painter button (Format tab | Font group) to select the Format Painter.
- Click the Shipper control to assign to it the same formatting as the Load ID control (Figure 7–20).

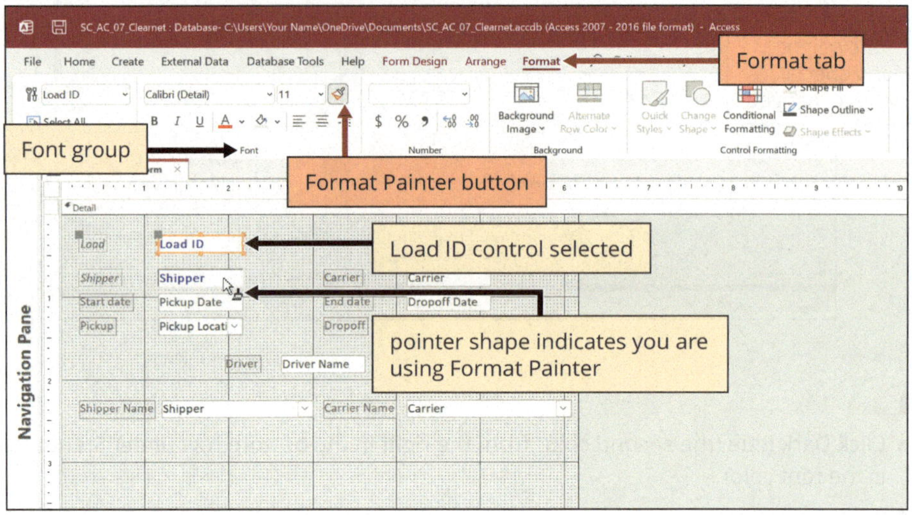

Figure 7–20

2

- Click all the other controls on the form to assign the same formatting to them.
- Click the Format Painter button (Format tab | Font group) to deselect the Format Painter (Figure 7–21).

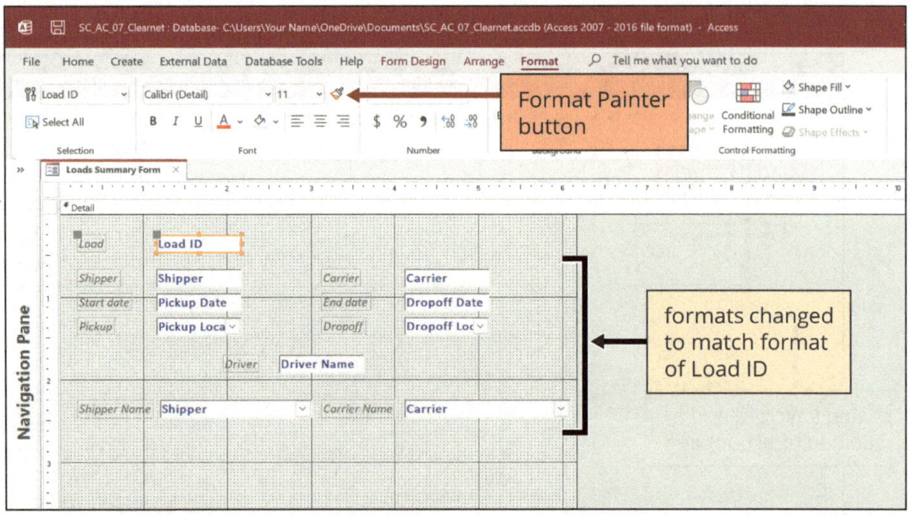

Figure 7–21

Q&A Does the order in which I click the other controls matter?

No. The only thing that is important is to click all the controls whose formatting you want to change.

Do I always have to click the Format Painter button when I have finished copying the formatting?

If you double-clicked the Format Painter button to enable you to copy the formatting to multiple controls, you need to click the Format Painter button again to turn off the copying or press ESC on your keyboard. If you single-clicked the Format Painter button to enable you to copy the formatting to a single control, you do not need to click the button again. As soon as you copy the formatting to a single control, the copying will be turned off.

3

- Save your changes to the form.

To View the Form

The following steps view the form in Form view and then return to Design view. **Why?** As you are working on the design of a form, it is a good idea to periodically view the form in Form view to see the effects of your changes.

1

- Display the Form Design tab.
- Click the View button (Form Design tab | Views group) to view the form in Form view.
- As needed, return to Design view, adjust the controls to display the entire field for each control, and then again check the design in Form view (Figure 7–22).

Q&A Why did I have to change from the Format tab to the Design tab?
The Format tab does not have a View button. Alternatively, you could use the view buttons in the status bar.

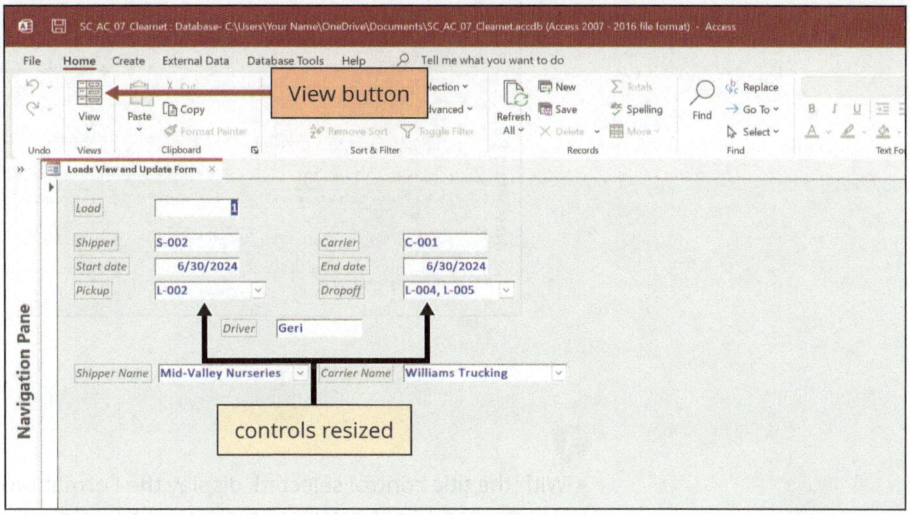

Figure 7–22

2

- Click the View button arrow (Home tab | Views group) to produce the View button menu.
- Click Design View on the View menu to return to Design view.

Q&A Could I simply click the View button to return to Design view?
No. When in Form view, the icon on the View button is the one for Layout view. Clicking the button would show you the form in Layout view, but you are working on the form in Design view.

Other Ways

1. Click Form View button on status bar to change to Form view
2. Click Design View button on status bar to change to Design view

To Add a Title and Expand the Form Header Section

The following steps insert the Form Header and Form Footer sections, and then add a title to the Form Header section. They also expand the Form Header section.

1

- Click the Title button (Form Design tab | Header / Footer group) to add a Form Header section and to add a control for the title to the Form Header section.

2

- Drag the lower boundary of the Form Header section down to the approximate position shown in Figure 7–23.

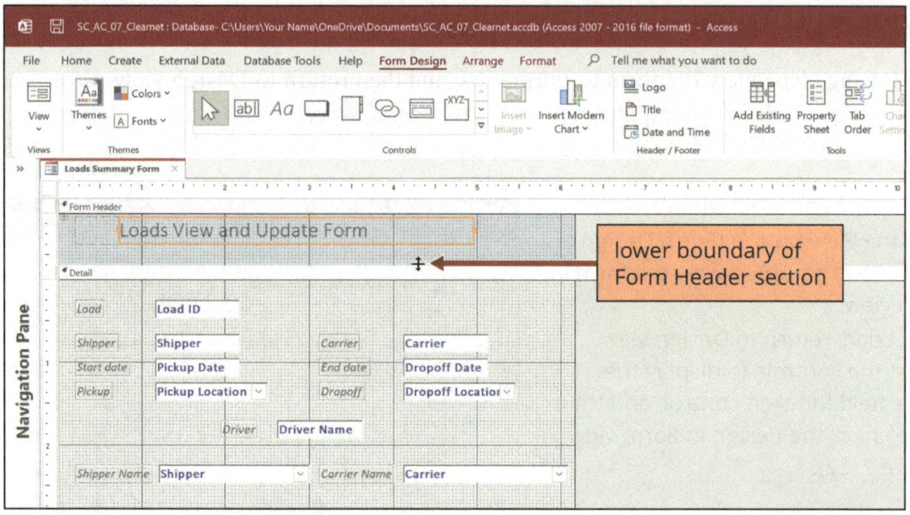

Figure 7–23

3

- With the title control selected, display the Format tab, and then click the Bold button (Format tab | Font group) to make the title bold.

To Change the Background Color of the Form Header

The background color of the form header in the form in Figure 7–1 is the same as the rest of the form. The following steps change the background color of the form header appropriately.

1

- Click anywhere in the Form Header section but outside the control to select the section.

2

- Click the Background Color button arrow (Format tab | Font group) to display a color palette.
- Click Light Gray 1, the first color in the second row under Standard Colors, to change the background color.

3

- Save your changes to the form.

Headers and Footers

Just as with reports, you have control over whether your forms contain a form header and footer. They go together, so if you have a form header, you will also have a form footer. If you do not want the header and footer sections to appear, you can shrink the size so there is no room for any content. You can also remove the sections from your form altogether. If you later decide you want to include them, you can once again add them. You have similar options with page headers and page footers, although typically page headers and page footers are only used with reports. If you had a very long form that spanned several pages on the screen, you might choose to use page headers and footers, but it is not common to do so.

To Remove a Form Header and Footer

To remove a form header and footer, you would use the following steps.

1. With the form open in Design view, right-click any open area of the form to produce a shortcut menu.

2. Click the Form Header/Footer command on the shortcut menu to remove the form header and footer.
3. If the Microsoft Access dialog box appears, asking if it is acceptable to delete any controls in the section, click Yes.

To Remove a Page Header and Footer

To remove a page header and footer, you would use the following steps.

1. With the form open in Design view, right-click any open area of the form to produce a shortcut menu.
2. Click the Page Header/Footer command on the shortcut menu to remove the page header and footer.
3. If the Microsoft Access dialog box appears, asking if it is acceptable to delete any controls in the section, click Yes.

To Insert a Form Header and Footer

To insert a form header and footer, you would use the following steps.

1. With the form open in Design view, right-click any open area of the form to produce a shortcut menu.
2. Click the Form Header/Footer command on the shortcut menu to insert a form header and footer.

To Insert a Page Header and Footer

To insert a page header and footer, you would use the following steps.

1. With the form open in Design view, right-click any open area of the form to produce a shortcut menu.
2. Click the Page Header/Footer command on the shortcut menu to insert a page header and footer.

Images

You can include an image such as a photo in a form. You can also use an image as the background for a form or as a logo.

To Include an Image in a Form

To include an image in a form, you would use the following steps.

1. Open the form in Design view or Layout view.
2. Click the Insert Image button (Form Design tab | Controls group), and then click the Browse command.
3. Select the desired image.
4. Click the desired location to add the image to the form.

To Use an Image as Background for a Form

To include an image as background for a form, you would use the following steps.

1. Open the form in Design view or Layout view.
2. Click anywhere in the form, click the Background Image button (Format tab | Background group), and then click the Browse command.
3. Select the desired image for the background.

To Add a Logo to a Form

To include an image as a logo for a form, you would use the following steps.

1. Open the form in Design view or Layout view.
2. Click anywhere in the form, and then click the Logo button (Form Design tab | Header / Footer group).
3. Select the desired image for the logo.

Break Point: If you wish to take a break, this is a good place to do so. You can quit Access now. To resume at a later time, start Access, open the database called SC_AC_07_Clearnet.accdb, open the Loads Summary Form in Design view, and continue following the steps from this location forward.

BTW
Record Order
When you use the Next Record button to move through the records, recall that the records are in order by Load ID, which is the primary key, and not in alphabetical order.

Command Buttons

Command buttons are buttons placed on a form that users can click to carry out specific actions. To add command buttons, you use the Button tool in the Controls group on the Form Design tab. When using the series of Command Button Wizard dialog boxes, you indicate the action that should be taken when the command button is clicked, for example, go to the next record. Within the Command Button Wizard, Access includes several categories of commonly used actions.

Consider This

When would you include command buttons in your form?

You can make certain actions more convenient for users by including command buttons. Buttons can carry out record navigation actions (for example, go to the next record), record operation actions (for example, add a record), form operation actions (for example, close a form), report operation actions (for example, print a report), application actions (for example, quit application), and some miscellaneous actions (for example, run a macro).

To Add Command Buttons to a Form

You might find that you can improve the functionality of your form by adding command buttons. *Why? Command buttons enable users to accomplish tasks with a single click.* Before adding the buttons, you should make sure the 'Use Control Wizards' button is selected.

In the Record Navigation action category, you will select the Go To Next Record action for one of the command buttons. From the same category, you will select the Go To Previous Record action for another. Other buttons will use the Add New Record and the Delete Record actions from the Record Operations category. The Close Form button will use the Close Form action from the Form Operations category.

The following steps add command buttons to move to the next record, move to the previous record, add a record, delete a record, and close the form.

1

- Scroll down a bit in the Loads Summary Form so you can see more of the space below the last fields in the Detail section.
- If necessary, display the Form Design tab, click the More button in the Controls gallery, and then ensure the 'Use Control Wizards' button is selected.
- Click the Button tool (Form Design tab | Controls group), and then move the pointer to the approximate position shown in Figure 7–24.

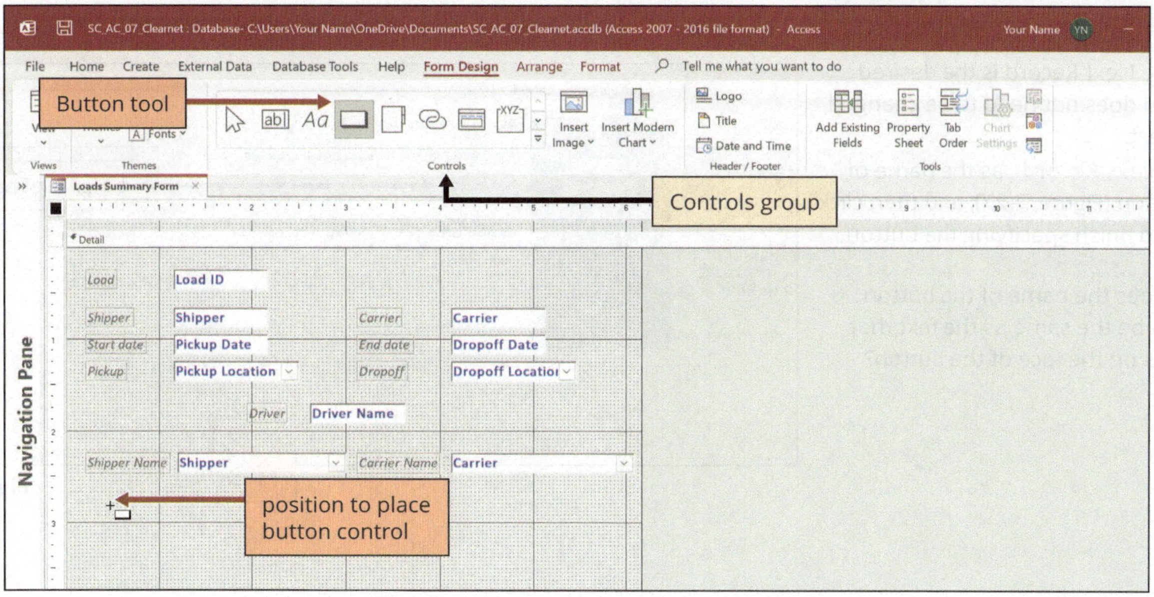

Figure 7–24

2

- Click the position shown in Figure 7–24 to display the Command Button Wizard dialog box.
- With Record Navigation selected in the Categories box, click Go To Next Record in the Actions box (Figure 7–25).

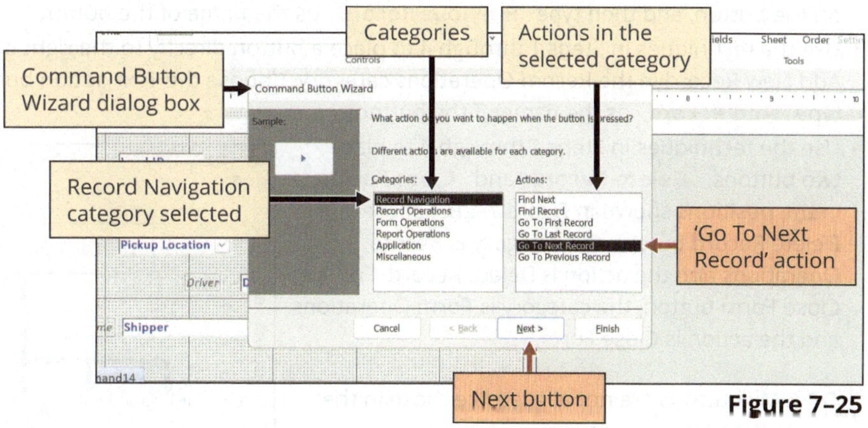

Figure 7–25

3

- Click Next to display the next Command Button Wizard screen.
- Click the Text option button (Figure 7–26).

Q&A What is the purpose of these option buttons?
Choose the first option button to place text on the button. You then can specify the text to be included or accept the default choice. Choose the second option button to place a picture on the button. You can then select a picture.

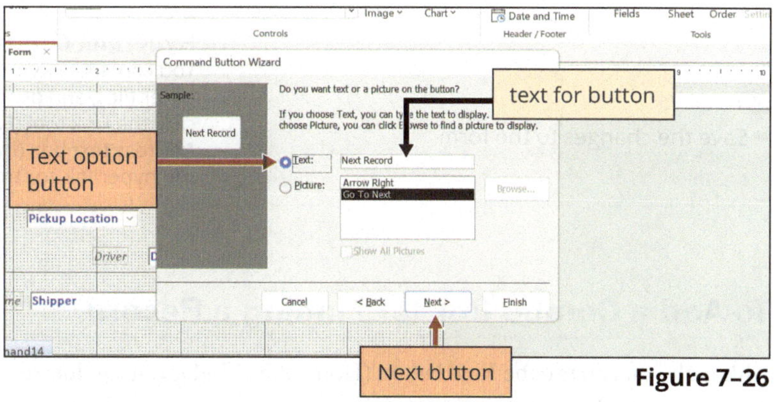

Figure 7–26

4

- Because Next Record is the desired text and does not need to be changed, click Next.
- Type **Next Record** as the name of the button (Figure 7–27), and then click Finish to finish specifying the button.

Q&A Does the name of the button have to be the same as the text that appears on the face of the button?
No. The text is what will appear on the screen. You use the name when you need to refer to the specific button. They can be different, but this can lead to confusion. Thus, many people will typically make them the same.

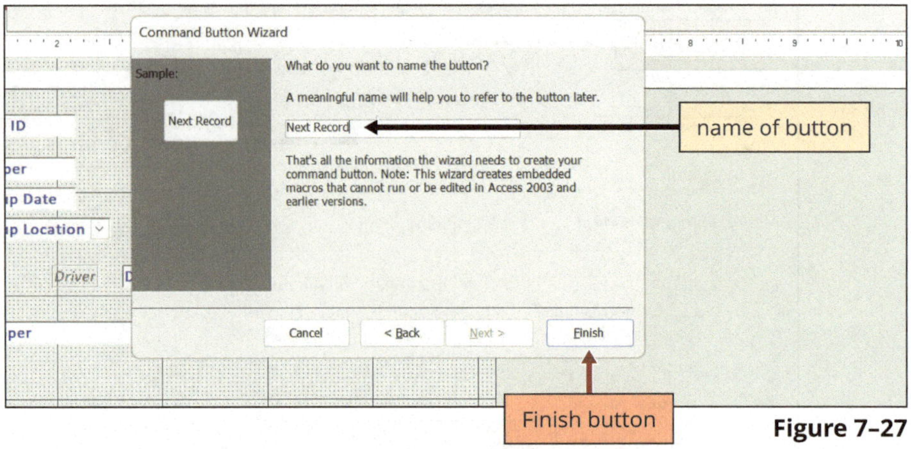

Figure 7–27

5

- Use the techniques in Steps 1 through 4 to place the Previous Record button directly to the right of the Next Record button. The action is Go To Previous Record in the Record Navigation category. Choose the Text option button and Previous Record on the button, and then type **Previous Record** as the name of the button.
- Use the techniques in Steps 1 through 4 to place a button directly to the right of the Previous Record button. The action is Add New Record in the Record Operations category. Choose the Text option button and Add Record on the button, and then type **Add Record** as the name of the button.
- Use the techniques in Steps 1 through 4 to place two buttons, **Delete Record** and **Close Form**, in the positions shown in Figure 7–28. For the Delete Record button, the category is Record Operations and the action is Delete Record. For the Close Form button, the category is Form Operations and the action is Close Form.

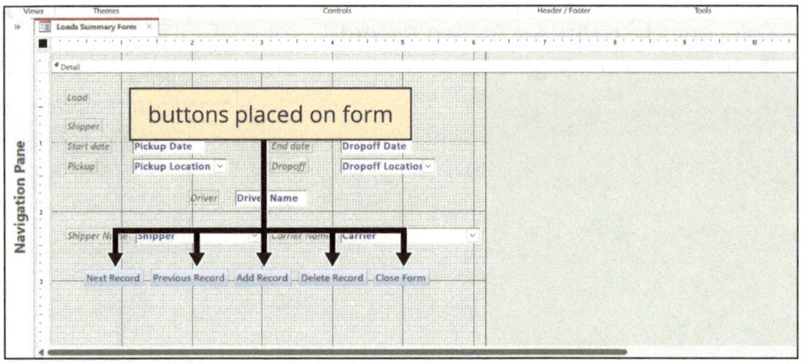

Figure 7–28

Q&A My buttons are not aligned like those in the figure. What should I do?
If your buttons are not aligned properly, you can drag them to the correct positions. You can also use the buttons in the Sizing & Ordering group on the Arrange tab.

6

- Save the changes to the form.

BTW
Hyperlink Controls
You can add a hyperlink to forms, which can be used to navigate to web pages, other files, and other locations within the current database. To add a hyperlink, click the Link tool (Form Design tab | Controls group), enter the hyperlink in the Address text box (Insert Hyperlink dialog box), and click OK. If necessary, move the hyperlink control to the desired location on the form.

To Add a Combo Box for Finding a Record

Although you can use the Find button (Home tab | Find group) to locate records on a form or a report, it is often more convenient to use a combo box. **Why?** You can click the combo box arrow to display a list and then select the desired entry from the list.

To create a combo box, use the Combo Box tool in the Controls group on the Design tab. Before the Combo Box will find records, Microsoft Access requires the form to be bound to an existing table or query. In this case, you will bind the form to a saved query. Once that is accomplished, the Combo Box Wizard will guide you through the steps of adding the combo box. The following steps create the query and then place a combo box for names on the form.

1

- Click the form selector in the upper left corner.
- Open the Property Sheet pane and select the Data tab, and then confirm the selection type is form.
- Click the build button for the Record Source property (Figure 7–29) to create a query based on the Loads table and open the Loads Summary Form: Query Builder tab.

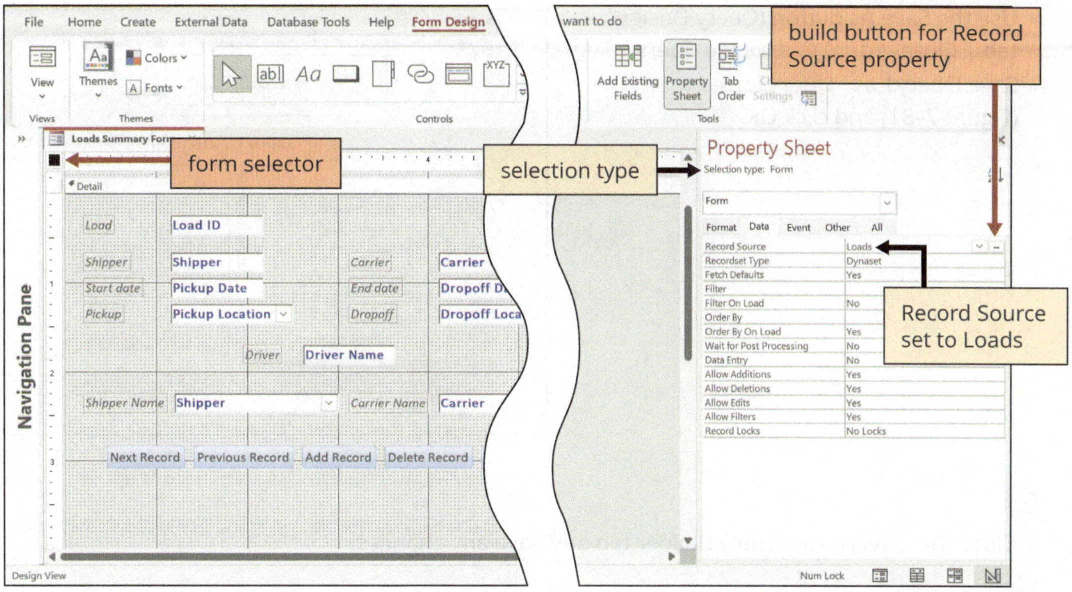

Figure 7–29

Q&A A warning dialog box opened. What should I do?

If you see a warning stating 'You invoked the Query Builder on a table. Do you want to create a query based on the table?' click Yes.

Why click the Data tab in the Property Sheet pane? Why not just use the All tab as we have before?

You can always use the All tab; however, if you know the category that contains the property in which you are interested, you can greatly reduce the number of properties that Access will display by clicking the tab for that category. This gives you fewer properties to search through to find the property you want. Whether you use the All tab or one of the other tabs is strictly a matter of personal preference.

2

- If necessary, close the Property Sheet pane.
- Create the query by adding the fields as shown in Figure 7–30.

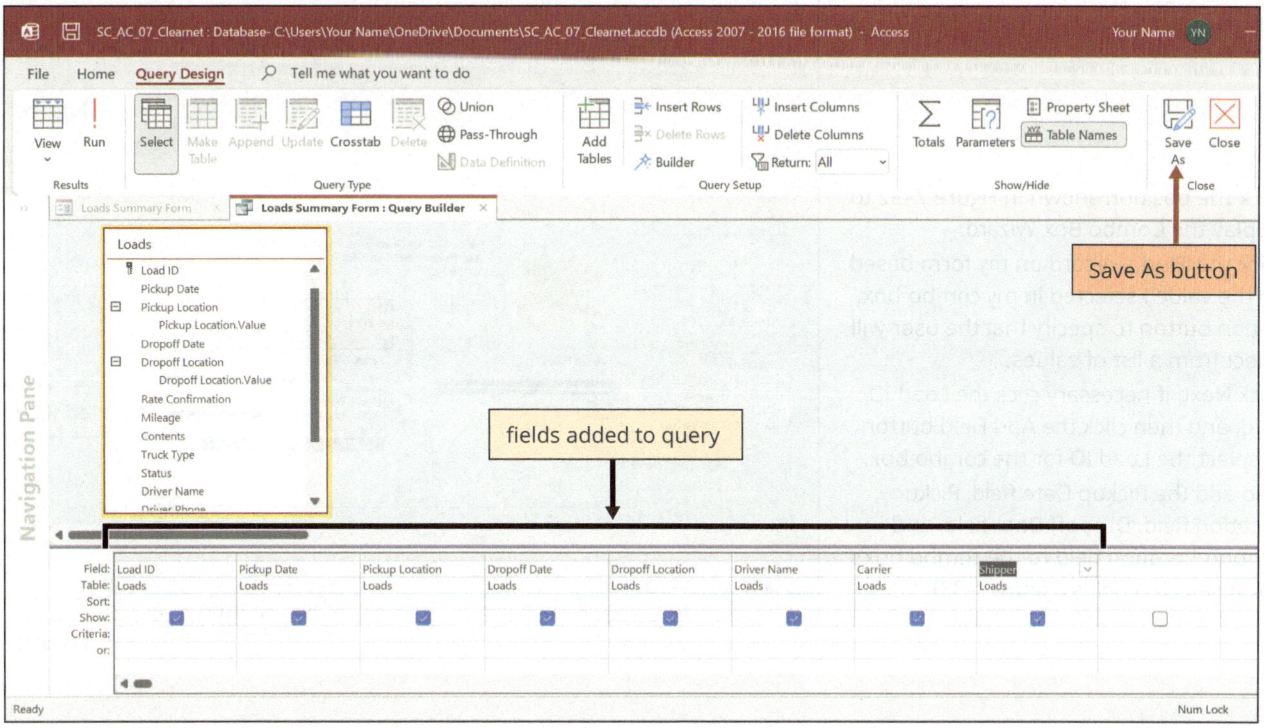

Figure 7–30

3

- Use the Save As button (Query Design tab | Close group) to save the query.
- Save Query1 as **Queryform** (Figure 7–31) and click OK.

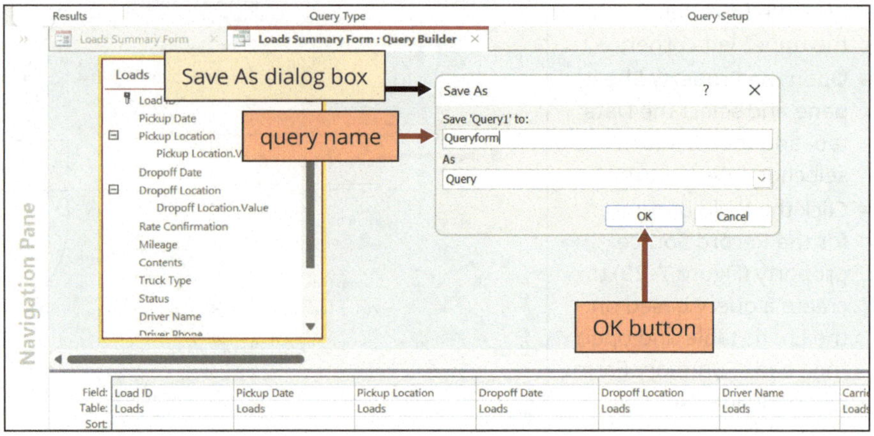

Figure 7–31

4

- Close the Queryform: Query Builder tab and save any changes.

5

- If necessary, display the Form Design tab.
- Click the More button (Form Design tab | Controls group) to display all the controls.
- With the 'Use Control Wizards' button selected, click the Combo Box tool (Form Design tab | Controls group), and then move the pointer, whose shape has changed to a small plus sign with a combo box, to the position shown in Figure 7–32.

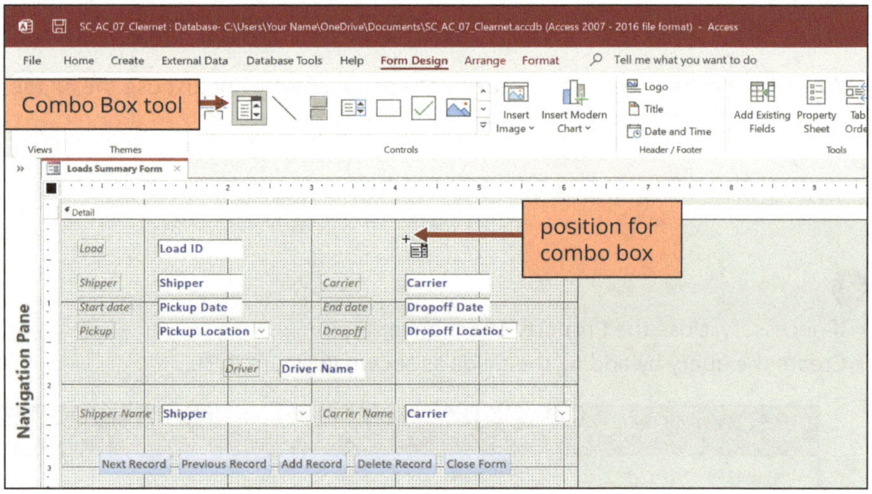

Figure 7–32

6

- Click the position shown in Figure 7–32 to display the Combo Box Wizard.
- Click the 'Find a record on my form based on the value I selected in my combo box.' option button to specify that the user will select from a list of values.
- Click Next, if necessary click the Load ID field, and then click the Add Field button to select the Load ID for the combo box.
- Also add the Pickup Date field, Pickup Location field, Dropoff Date field, and Dropoff Location field to the combo box's list of selected fields (Figure 7–33).

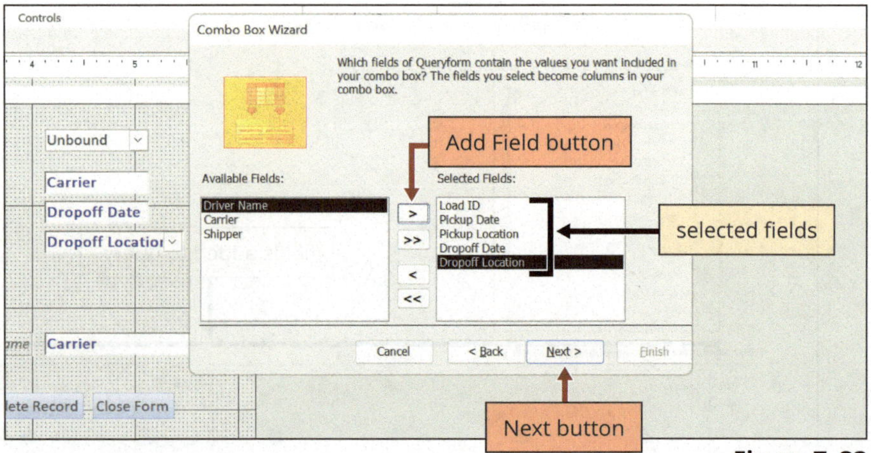

Figure 7–33

7

- Click Next.
- Adjust each column width for best fit (Figure 7–34).

Q&A What options do I have to resize each column to best fit the data?
You could either drag the right edge of each column to a position that allows all text in the column to be visible without using too much space, or you could double-click the right edge of each column so Access will choose the best fit for you.

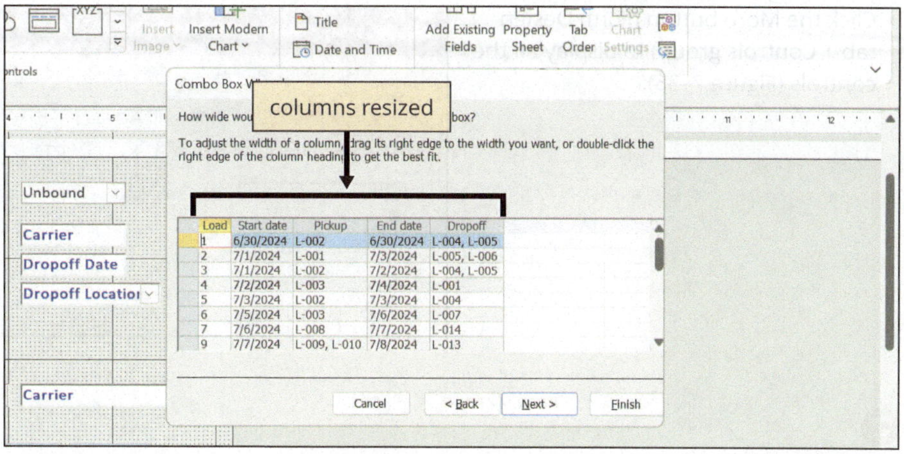

Figure 7–34

8

- Click Next, and then type **&Load to Find** as the label for the combo box.

Q&A What is the purpose of the ampersand in front of the letter, L?
The ampersand (&) in front of the letter, L, indicates that users can select the combo box by pressing ALT+L when using the form.

- Click Finish, and, as necessary, reposition and resize the control and label so your screen resembles Figure 7–35.

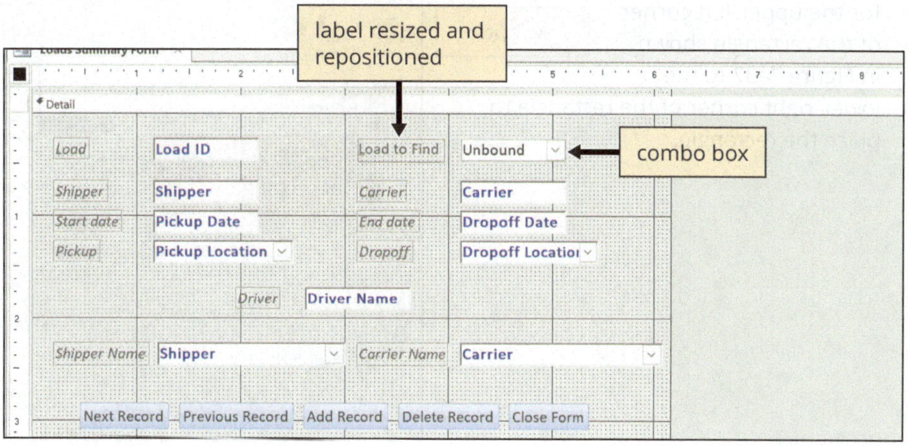

Figure 7–35

Q&A Why is the letter, L, underlined?
The underlined letter, L, in the word, Load, indicates that you can press ALT+L to select the combo box. It is underlined because you preceded the letter, L, with the ampersand.

Consider This

When would you include a combo box in your form?

A combo box is a combination of a text box, where users can type data, and a list box, where users can click an arrow to display a list. Would a combo box improve the functionality of the form? Is there a place where it would be convenient for users to enter data by selecting the data from a list, either a list of predefined items or a list of values from a related table? If users need to search for records, including a combo box can assist in the process.

To Place a Rectangle

The following steps use the Rectangle tool to place a rectangle around the combo box. **Why?** To emphasize an area of a form, you can place a rectangle around it as a visual cue.

1

- Click the More button (Form Design tab | Controls group) to display all the controls (Figure 7–36).

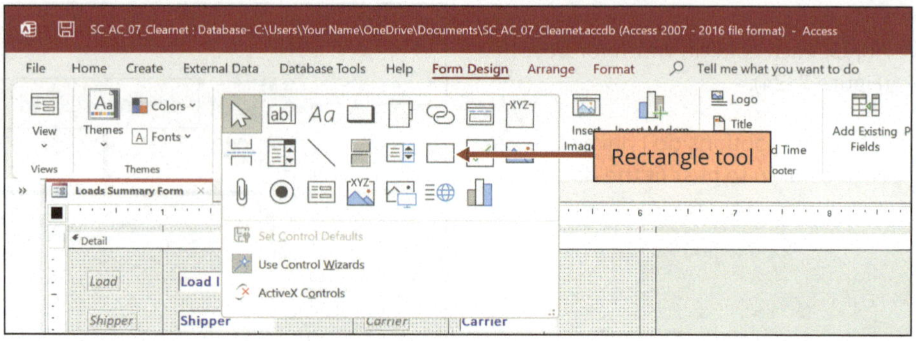

Figure 7–36

2

- Click the Rectangle tool, and then press and drag from the position for the upper-left corner of the rectangle shown in Figure 7–37 to the lower-right corner of the rectangle to place the rectangle.

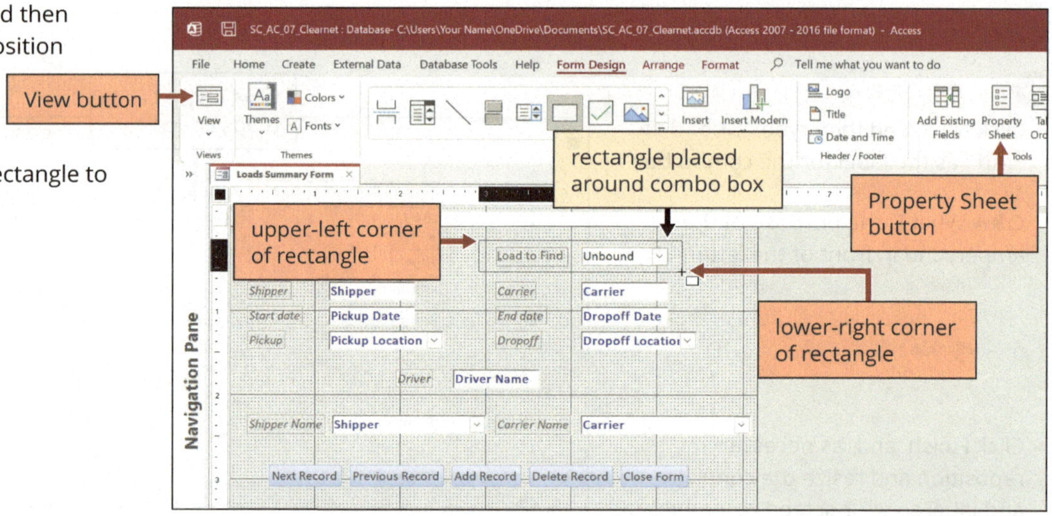

Figure 7–37

3

- Click the Property Sheet button (Form Design tab | Tools group) to display the property sheet for the rectangle, and click the All tab.
- If necessary, change the value of the Special Effect property to Etched.
- If necessary, change the value of the Back Style property to Transparent so the combo box will appear within the rectangle.
- Adjust any control widths to make all labels visible.
- Click the Pickup Date control (not the label) and change the Text Align property to Left (Property Sheet pane).
- Click the Dropoff Date control (not the label) and change the Text Align property to Left (Property Sheet pane).

Q&A What if the Back Style value is not Transparent ?

If the value is not Transparent, the rectangle will cover the combo box completely and the combo box will not be visible.

4

- Close the Property Sheet pane and save the form.
- Click the View button (Form Design tab | Views group) to switch to Form view (Figure 7–38). You will use this view to test the form.

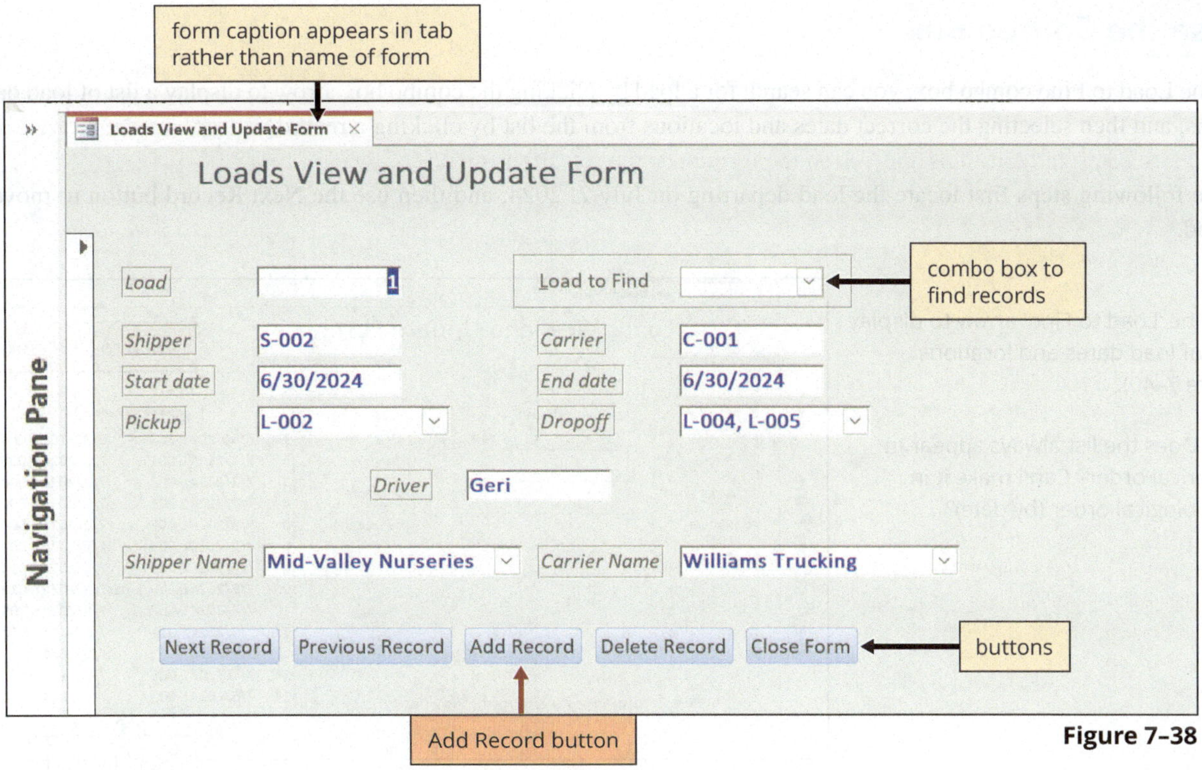

Figure 7–38

Using the Buttons

To move from record to record on the form, you can use the buttons to perform the actions you specify. To move forward to the next record, click the Next Record button. Click the Previous Record button to move back to the previous record. Clicking the Delete Record button would delete the record currently on the screen. Access will display a message requesting that you verify the deletion before the record is actually deleted. Clicking the Close Form button will remove the form from the screen.

To Test the Add Record Button

The following step uses the Add Record button. **Why?** Clicking the Add Record button will clear the contents of the form so you can add a new record.

1

- In Form view, click the Add Record button (Figure 7–39).
- **Experiment:** Try each of the other buttons to see their effects. Do not delete any records. After clicking the Close Form button, open the Navigation Pane if necessary, open the form once again, and then close the Navigation Pane.

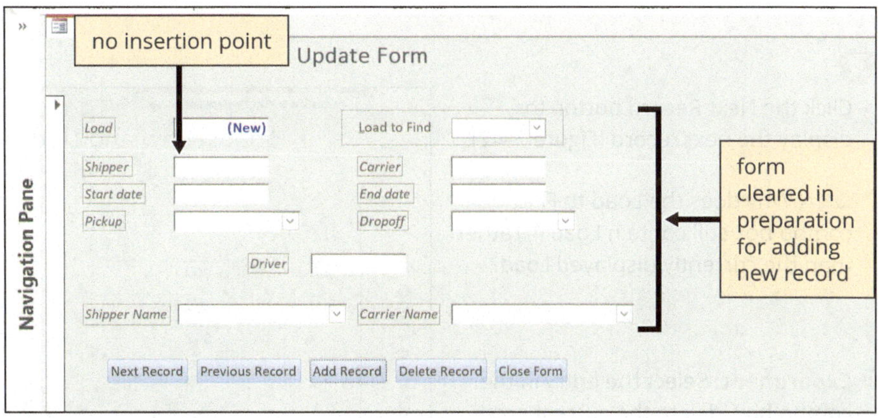

Figure 7–39

Q&A Why does the word, "(New)", appear in the Load field?

The value, (New), refers to the autonumber type field, which will automatically assign a new Load ID as you begin to fill in the form.

There is no insertion point in the Shipper field. How would I begin entering a new record?

To begin entering a record, you would have to click the Shipper field before you can start typing.

To Use the Combo Box

Using the Load to Find combo box, you can search for a load by clicking the combo box arrow to display a list of load dates and locations, and then selecting the correct dates and locations from the list by clicking a record. **Why?** The data for the selected load on those dates and locations appears on the form once the selection is made.

The following steps first locate the load departing on July 2, 2024, and then use the Next Record button to move to the next load.

1

- Click the 'Load to Find' arrow to display a list of load dates and locations (Figure 7–40).

Q&A Does the list always appear in numerical order? Can I make it in chronological order (by date)?
No, not always. You will change the combo box later so the records will always appear in chronological order.

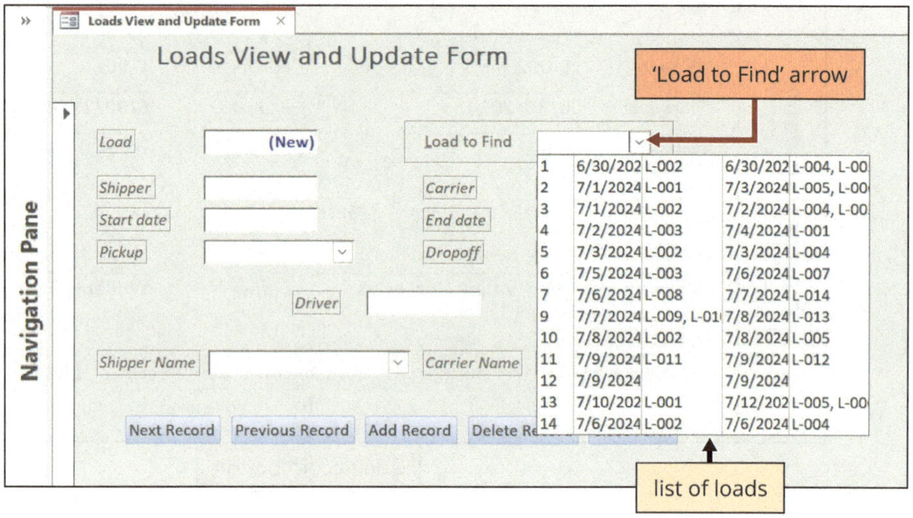

Figure 7–40

2

- Click 4 to display the data in the form for the load being picked up on 7/2/2024 (Figure 7–41).

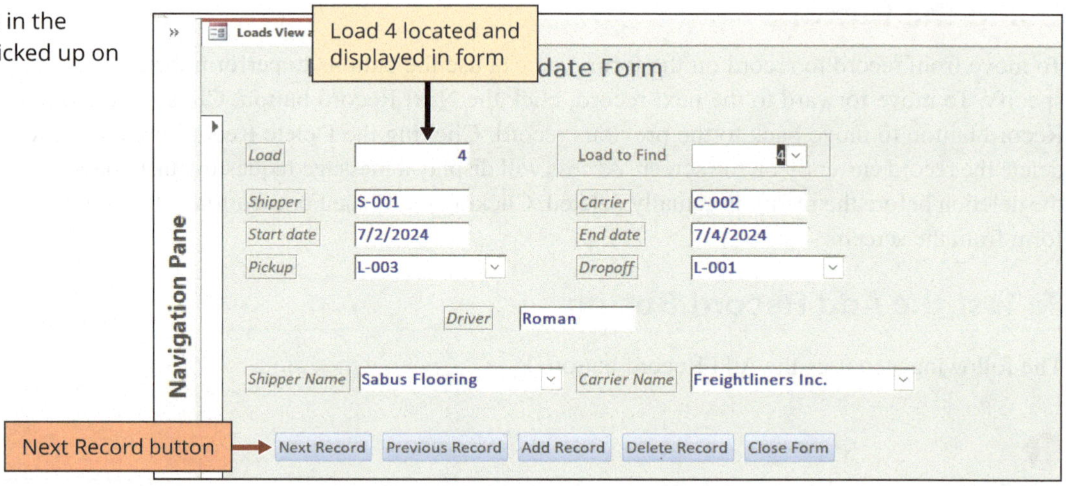

Figure 7–41

3

- Click the Next Record button to display the next record (Figure 7–42).

Q&A Why does the Load to Find combo box still contain Load 4, rather than the currently displayed Load?
This is a problem with the combo box. You will address this issue later.

- **Experiment:** Select the entry in the combo box, delete the current entry, enter the number, 7, and press TAB, to find the load departing on 7/6/2024.

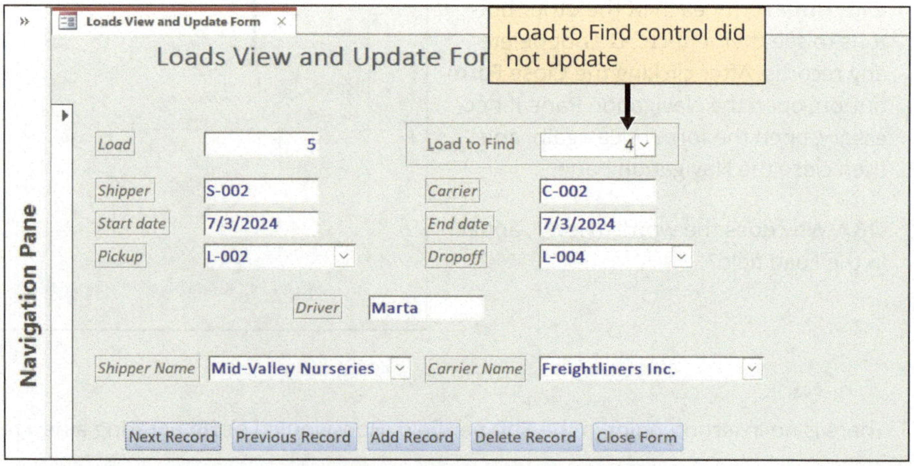

Figure 7–42

Issues with the Add Record Button

Although clicking the Add Record button does erase the contents of the form in preparation for adding a new record, there is a problem with it. After clicking the Add Record button, there should be an insertion point in the control for the first field you need to type into—the Shipper field—but there is not. To display an insertion point automatically when you click the Add Record button, you need to change the focus. A control is said to have the **focus** when it becomes active, that is, when it becomes able to receive user input through mouse, touch, or keyboard actions. At any point in time, only one item on the form has the focus. In addition to adding a new record, clicking the Add Record button needs to update the focus to the Shipper field.

BTW
Focus
Sometimes it is difficult to determine which object on the screen has the focus. If a field has the focus, an insertion point appears in the field. If a button has the focus, a small rectangle appears inside the button.

Macros

To correct the problem with the Add Record button not displaying an insertion point, you will update a **macro**, which is a series of actions that Access performs when a particular event occurs, in this case when the Add Record button is clicked. Access has already created the macro; you just need to add a single action to it.

Specifically, you need to add an action to the macro that will move the focus to the control for the Shipper field. The appropriate action is GoToControl. Like many actions, the GoToControl action requires additional information, called an argument or arguments. The argument for the GoToControl action is the name of the control, in this case, the Shipper control.

To Modify the Macro for the Add Record Button

The following steps modify the macro that is associated with the Add Record button. **Why?** Modifying the macro lets you add an action that changes the focus to the Shipper field. You will then complete an action that changes the focus to the control for the Shipper field.

1

- Click the View button arrow (Home tab | Views group), and then click Design View to return to Design view.

2

- Right-click the Add Record button to display a shortcut menu (Figure 7–43).

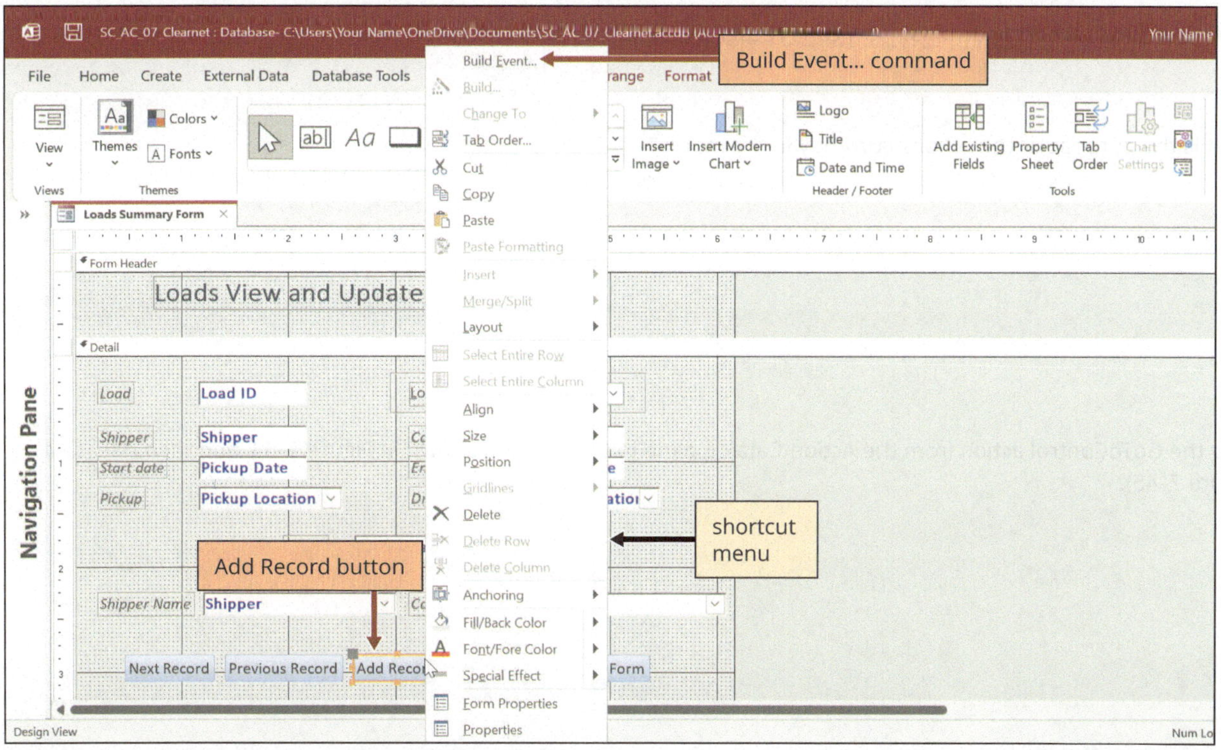

Figure 7–43

- Click Build Event… on the shortcut menu to display the macro associated with the On Click event that Access created automatically.
- If the Action Catalog pane, which lists all the available actions, does not appear, click the Action Catalog button (Macro Design tab | Show/Hide group) to display the Action Catalog pane.
- In the Action Catalog pane, if the expand indicator is an open triangle in front of Actions, click the triangle to display all actions.
- If the Database Objects expand indicator is an open triangle, click the expand indicator to display all actions associated with Database Objects (Figure 7–44).

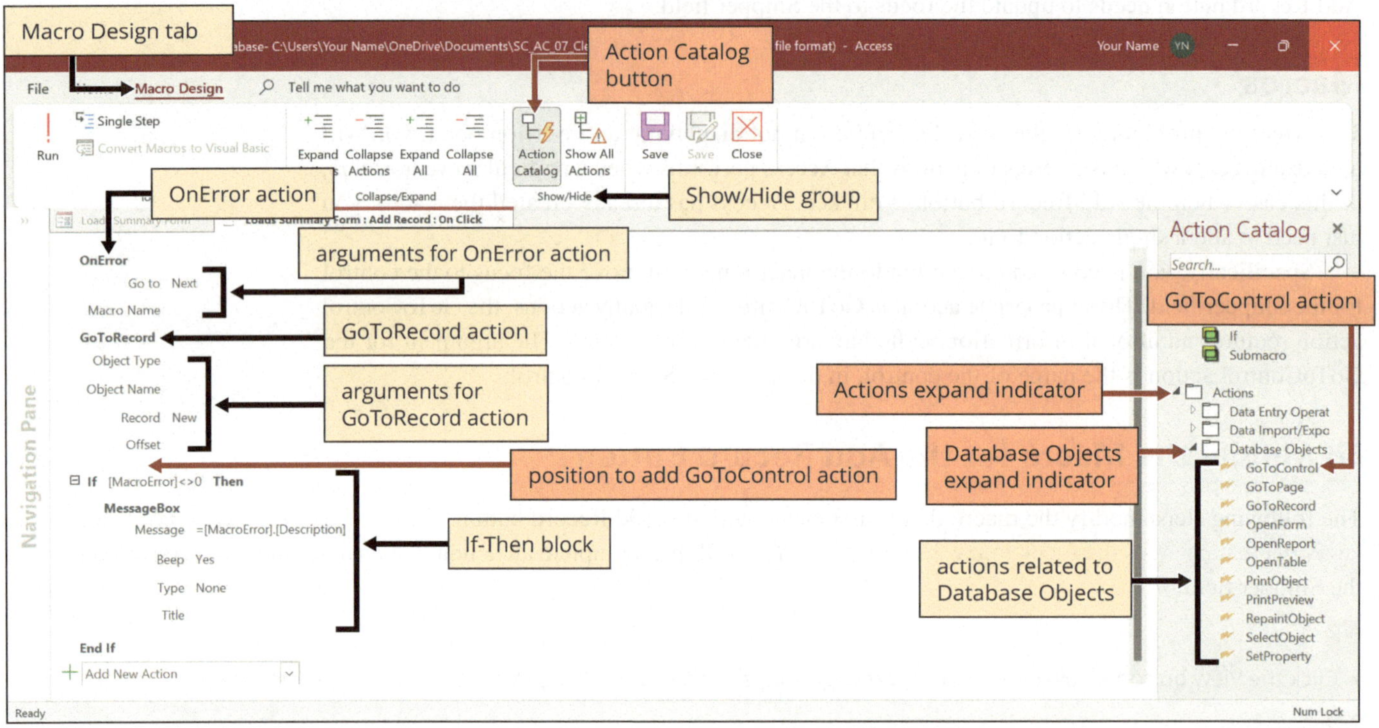

Figure 7–44

Q&A How can I recognize actions? How can I recognize the arguments of the actions?
The actions are in bold. The arguments for the action follow the action and are not bold. The value for an argument appears to the right of the argument. The value for the 'Go to' argument of the OnError action is Next, for example.

What is the purpose of the actions currently in the macro?
The first action indicates that, if there is an error, Access should proceed to the next action in the macro rather than immediately stopping the macro. The second action causes Access to go to the record indicated by the values in the arguments. The value, New, indicates that Access should go to a new record. Because the final action has a condition, the action will be executed only if the condition is true, that is, the error code contains a value other than 0. In that case, the MsgBox action will display a description of the error.

3

- Drag the GoToControl action from the Action Catalog pane to the position shown in Figure 7–44, and then release it (Figure 7–45).

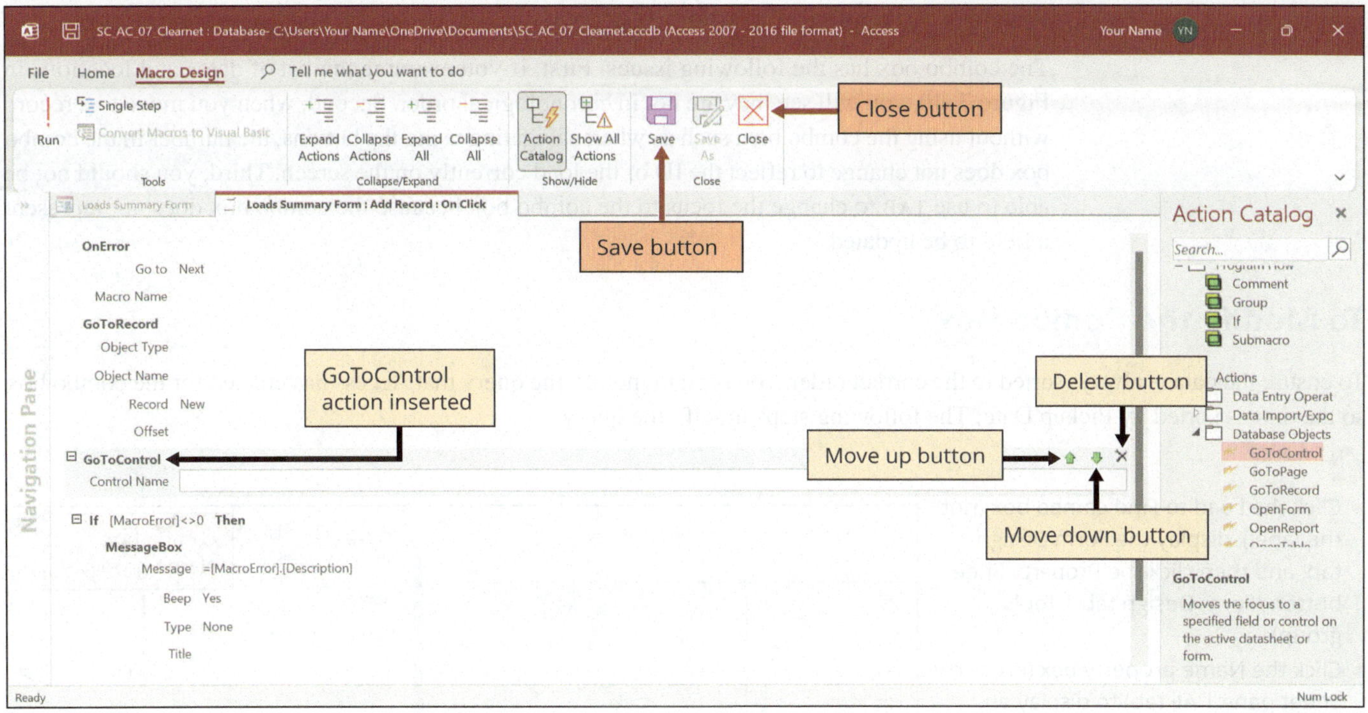

Figure 7–45

4

- Type **Shipper** as the Control Name argument (Figure 7–46).

Q&A What is the effect of the GoToControl action?

When Access executes this action, the focus will move to the control indicated in the Control Name argument, in this case, the Shipper control.

I added the GoToControl action to the wrong place in the macro. How do I move it?

To move it up in the list, click the Move up button. To move it down, click the Move down button.

I added the wrong action. What should I do?

Click the Delete button to delete the action you added, and then add the GoToControl action. If you decide you would rather start over instead, click Close (Macro Design tab | Close group) and then click the No button when asked if you want to save your changes. You can then begin again from Step 2.

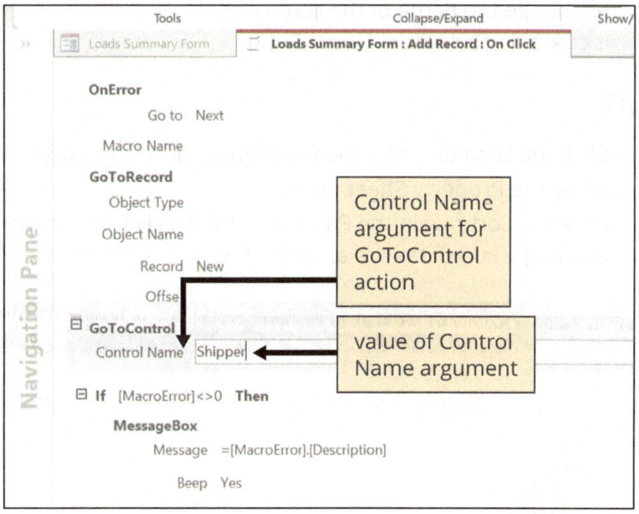

Figure 7–46

5

- Click the Save button (Macro Design tab | Close group) to save your changes.
- Click the Close button (Macro Design tab | Close group) to close the macro and return to the form design.

BTW

Events

Events are actions that have happened or are happening at the present time. An event can result from a user action. For example, one of the events associated with a button on a form is clicking the button. The corresponding event property is On Click. If you associate a macro with the On Click event property, the macro will execute any time you click the button. Using properties associated with events, you can instruct Access to run a macro, call a Visual Basic function, or run an event procedure in response to an event. You will learn more about Visual Basic later.

Issues with the Combo Box

The combo box has the following issues. First, if you examine the list of dates and locations in Figure 7–40, you will see they are not in chronological order. Second, when you move to a record without using the combo box, such as when navigating using the buttons, the number in the combo box does not change to reflect the ID of the load currently on the screen. Third, you should not be able to use TAB to change the focus to the combo box because the combo box does not represent a field to be updated.

To Modify the Combo Box

To ensure the data is always sorted in the correct order, you need to modify the query that Access has created for the combo box so the data is sorted by Pickup Date. The following steps modify the query.

1

- Click the Load to Find combo box (not the label), display the Form Design tab, and then click the Property Sheet button (Form Design tab | Tools group).
- Click the Name property box (Property Sheet pane | All tab) to display an insertion point, use DEL or BACKSPACE to remove the existing name, and then enter the new value, **Load_to_Find**, to change the name of the control so it contains no spaces (Figure 7–47).

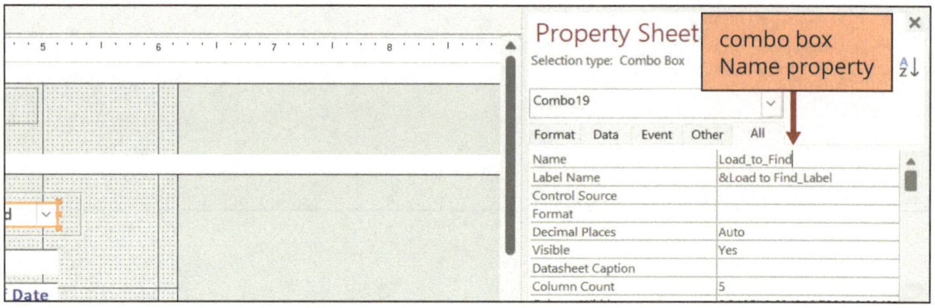

Figure 7–47

2

- Click the Data tab, click the Row Source property, and then click the Build button (the three dots) to display the Query Builder.
- Close the Property Sheet pane.
- Click the Sort row in the Pickup Date field, click the arrow that appears, and then click Ascending to change the order to ensure pickup dates are always listed in chronological order in the combo box (Figure 7–48).

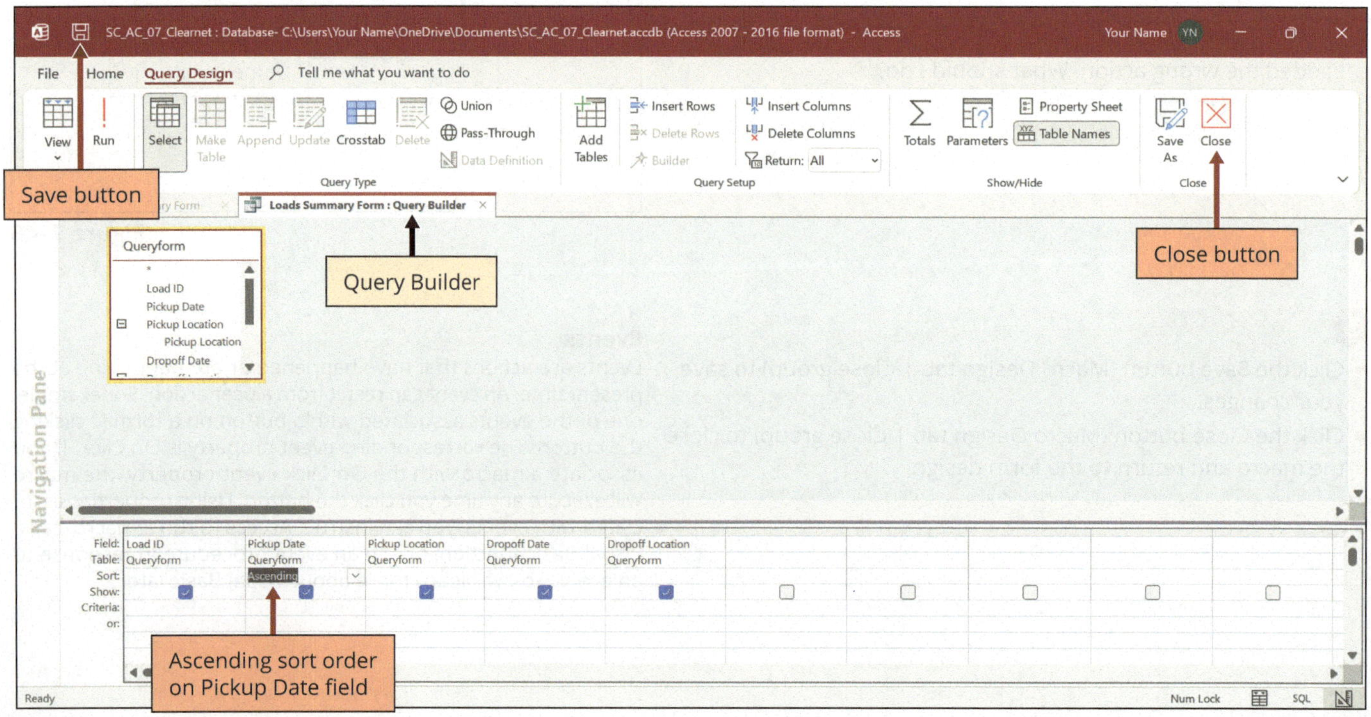

Figure 7–48

3

- Click Save on the Quick Access Toolbar to save your changes.
- Click the Close button (Query Design tab | Close group) to close the Query Builder tab.

To Correct Issues with the Combo Box

The form does not update the Load ID in the combo box to reflect the load currently on the screen unless the Load to Find box is used to find the load. The following steps first change the name of the Load ID control to remove the space, a requirement in VBA (Visual Basic for Applications), and then modify the query and the code associated with the On Current event property appropriately. **Why?** Modifying the VBA code lets you update the form actions appropriately. You can use different methods of changing control names so they do not contain spaces. One approach is to simply remove the space. This approach would change Load ID to LoadID, for example. The approach you will use is to insert an underscore (_) in place of the space. For example, you will change Load ID to Load_ID.

After changing the name of the Load ID control, the final step changes the Tab Stop property for the combo box from Yes to No.

BTW
VBA (Visual Basic for Applications)
Visual Basic for Applications (VBA) is a programming language that can be used with Access. As with other programming languages, programs in VBA consist of code, that is, a collection of statements, also called commands, which are instructions that will cause actions to take place when the program executes. VBA is included with all Microsoft Office apps.

1

- Click the control for the Load ID field (not the label).
- Open the Property Sheet pane.
- Click the All tab in the Property Sheet pane.
- In the Name property box, click the space immediately following the word, Load, press DEL to delete the space, and then type an underscore (_) to change the name to Load_ID (Figure 7–49).

Q&A Could I just erase the old name and type Load_ID?
Yes. Use whichever method you find most convenient.

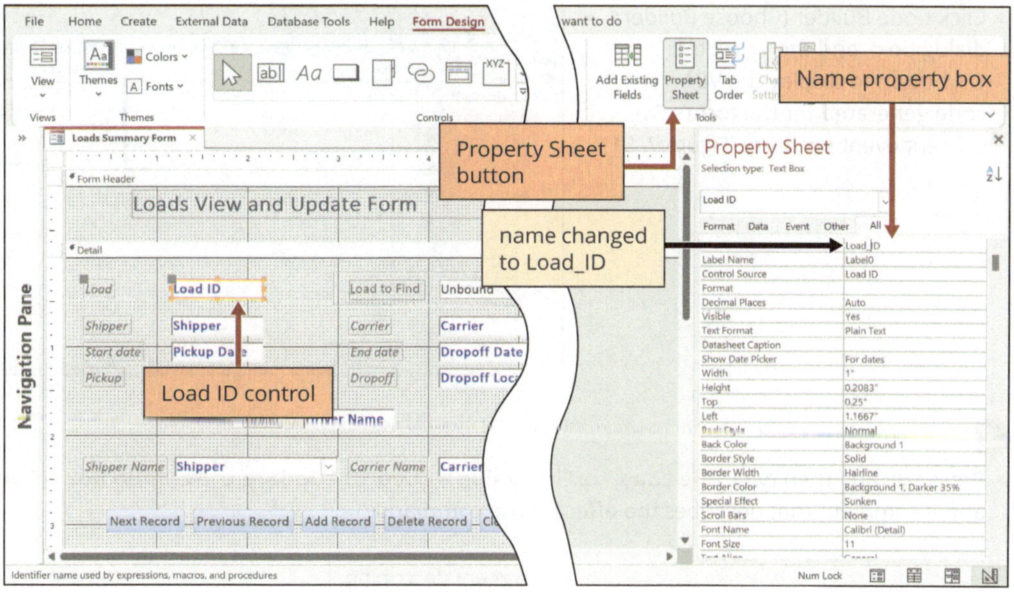

Figure 7–49

2

- Click the form selector (the box in the upper-left corner of the form) to select the form.
- In the Property Sheet pane, click the Event tab, and then click the On Current property box.
- Click the Build button (the three dots) to display the Choose Builder dialog box (Figure 7–50).

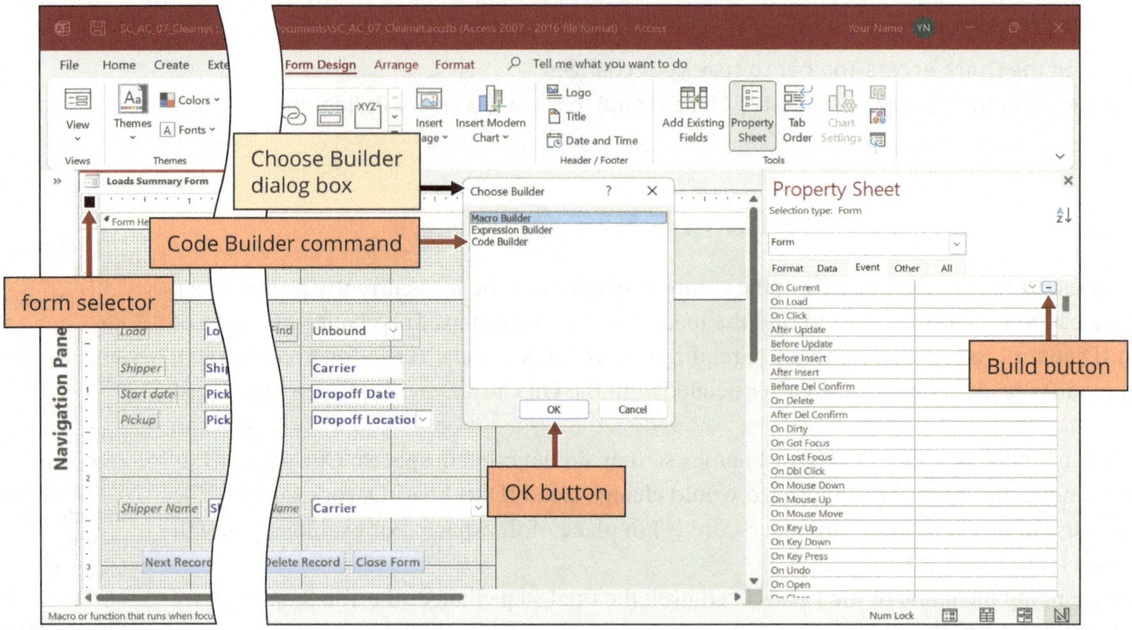

Figure 7–50

3

- Click Code Builder (Choose Builder dialog box), and then click the OK button to display the VBA code generated for the form's On Current event property (Figure 7–51).

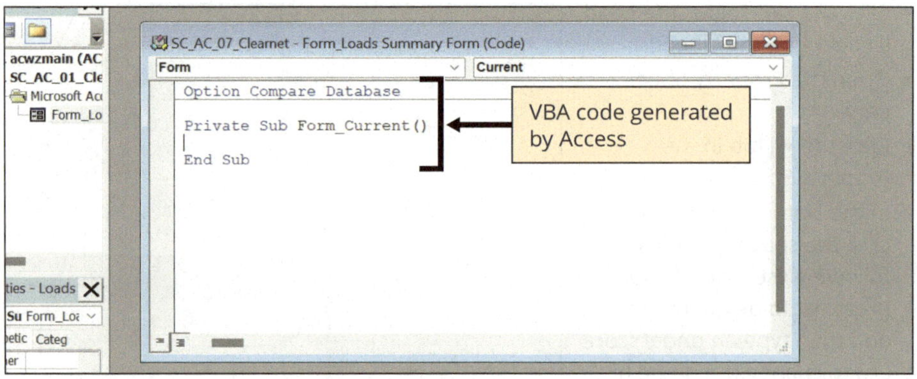

Figure 7–51

4

- Press TAB, and then type **Me.Load_to_Find.Value = Load_ID ' Update the combo box** (Figure 7–52) to create the command and a comment that describes the effect of the command.

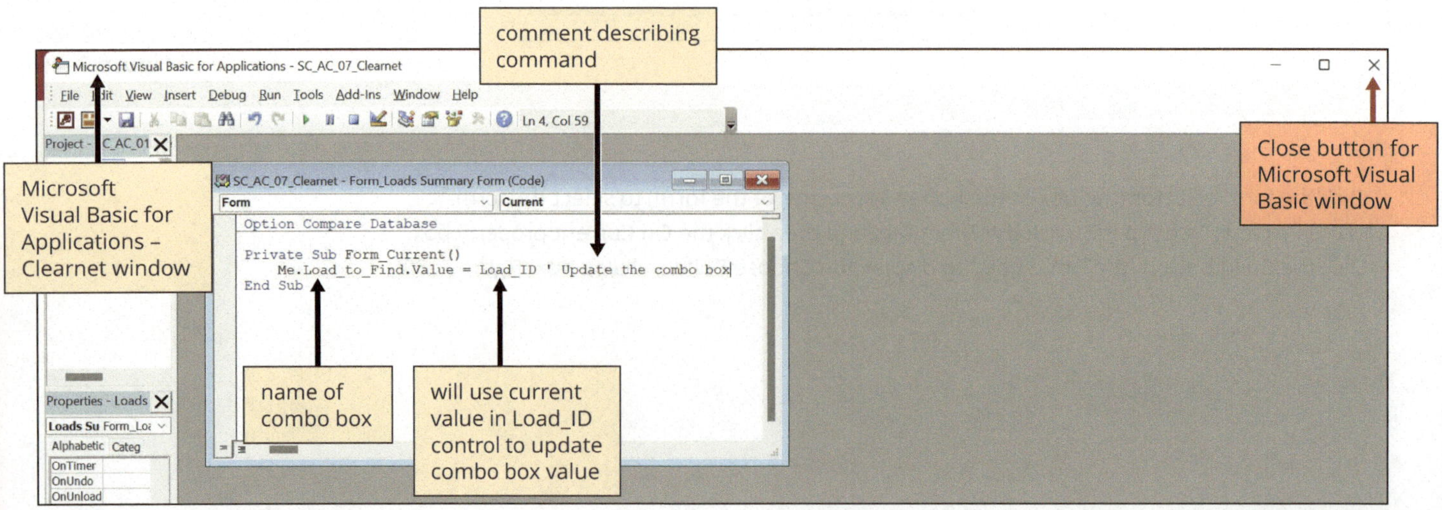

Figure 7–52

Q&A How would I construct a command like this in my own form?
Begin with the name you assigned to the combo box, followed by an equal sign, and then the name of the control containing the primary key of the table. The portion of the statement following the single quotation mark is a comment describing the purpose of the command. Comments are not read by the application and are provided by the programmer for future reference to help explain the purpose of the code; comments are helpful when troubleshooting or updating code later.

BTW
Comments in Macros
You can use the Comment action in the Action Catalog to place comments in macros.

BTW
Converting Macros to VBA Code
You can convert macros that are attached to forms to VBA (Visual Basic for Applications) code. To do so, open the form in Design view and click the 'Convert Form's Macros to Visual Basic' button. You also can convert macros that are attached to reports.

5

- Click Close for the Microsoft Visual Basic for Applications window.
- Click the Load to Find combo box (not the label).
- In the Property Sheet pane, click the Other tab, click the Tab Stop property box, and then click the Tab Stop property box arrow.
- Click No to change the value of the Tab Stop property, which skips over the combo box in the tab sequence.

To Adjust the Tab Stop Order

Currently, when pressing TAB to navigate through controls in the form, the focus skips from control to control in an illogical order. Setting the tab stop order can fix this problem. **Why?** Pressing tab is a convenient way to move through fields in a form during data entry, and the tab stop order should be set for logical navigation through the form. The following steps first provide descriptive names for the Shipper and Carrier combo boxes, and then they adjust the tab stop order.

1

- Click the Shipper Name combo box (not the label).
- In the Property Sheet pane, click the Name property box, and then change the Name value to **Shipper_Combo** (Figure 7–53).

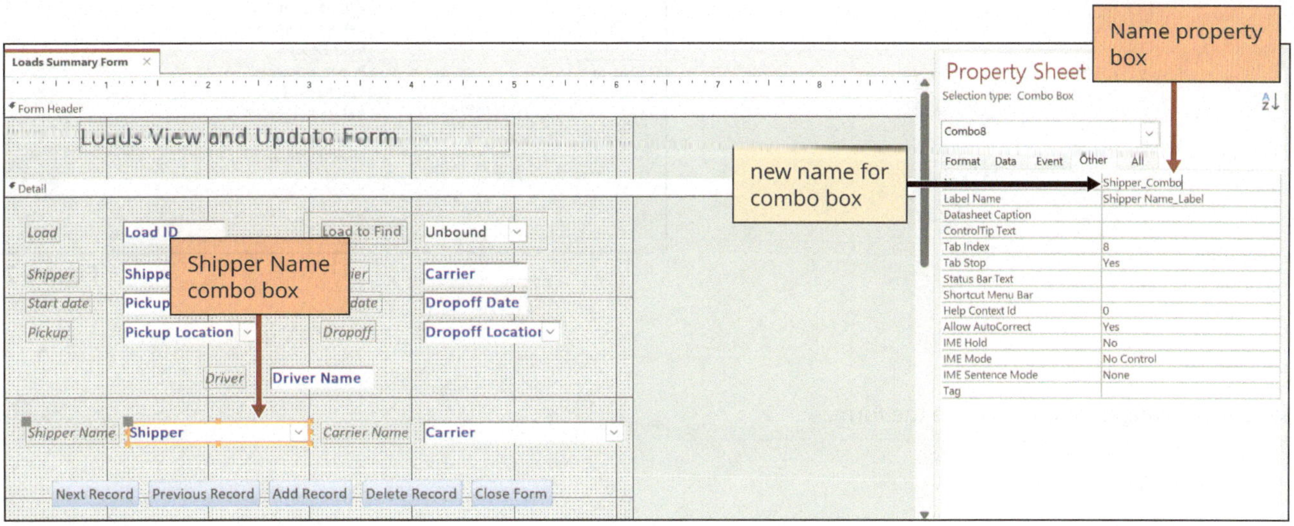

Figure 7–53

2

- Use the same technique to rename the Carrier combo box to **Carrier_Combo**, and then close the Property Sheet pane.

3

- Click the Tab Order button (Form Design tab | Tools group) to display the Tab Order dialog box.
- Click the box to the left of the Shipper row (Tab Order dialog box) to select Shipper, and then drag the left end of the row to move the Shipper row to just below the Load_ID row (Figure 7–54).

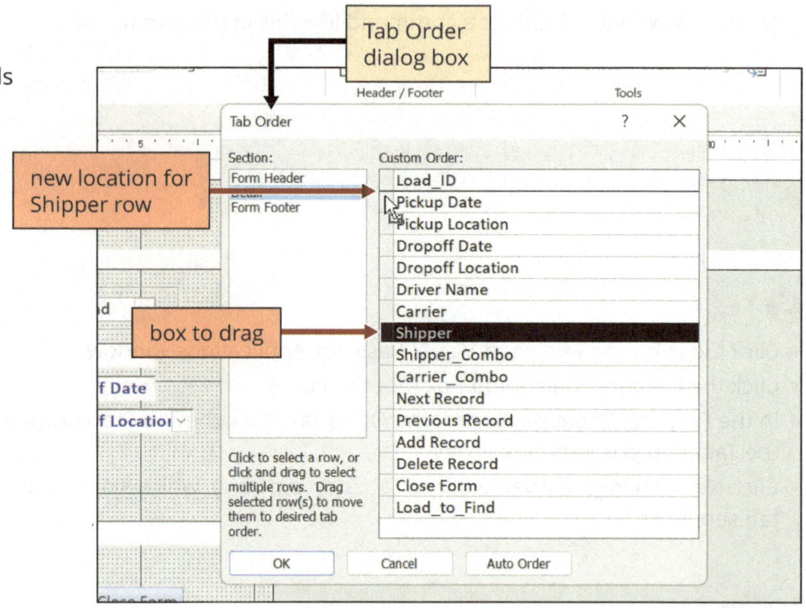

Figure 7–54

4

- Use the same technique to reorder all the rows to match the order shown in Figure 7–55.

Q&A I thought I removed the tab stop for the Load to Find combo box. Why is this control still listed in the Tab Stop dialog box?

The control is still listed simply because it exists in the form. However, it is disabled and will not receive focus as you tab through the form.

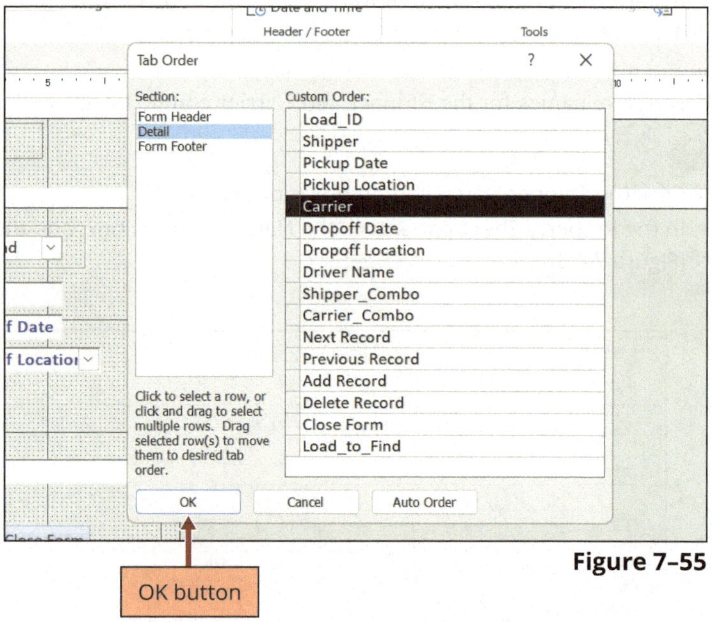

Figure 7–55

5

- Click OK.
- Save your changes, and then close the form.

Using the Modified Form

The problems with the Add Record button and the combo box are now corrected. When you click the Add Record button, an insertion point appears in the Shipper field (Figure 7–56a). When you click the Load to Find box arrow, the list of pickup dates is displayed in chronological order (Figure 7–56b). After using the Load to Find box to find a load (Figure 7–56c) and then clicking the Next Record button, the Load to Find box is updated with the correct Load ID (Figure 7–56d). When you press TAB while navigating through fields in the form, the tab stops occur in a logical order without including the Load to Find box.

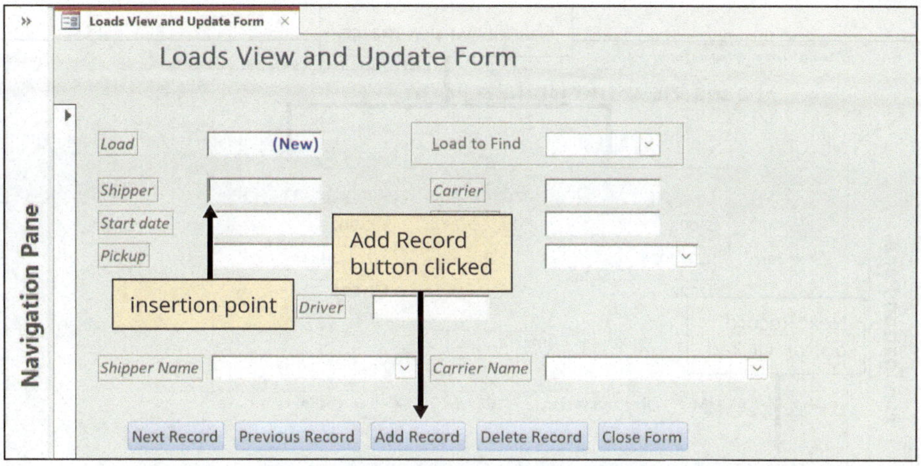

Figure 7–56a

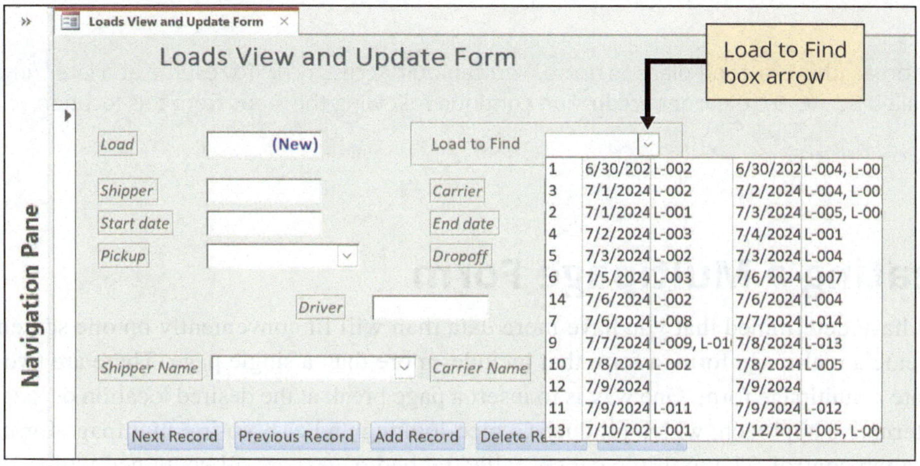

Figure 7–56b

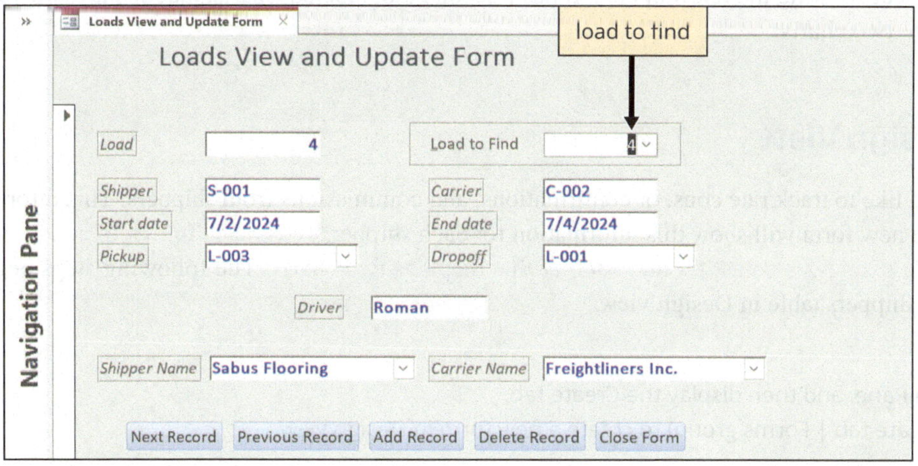

Figure 7–56c

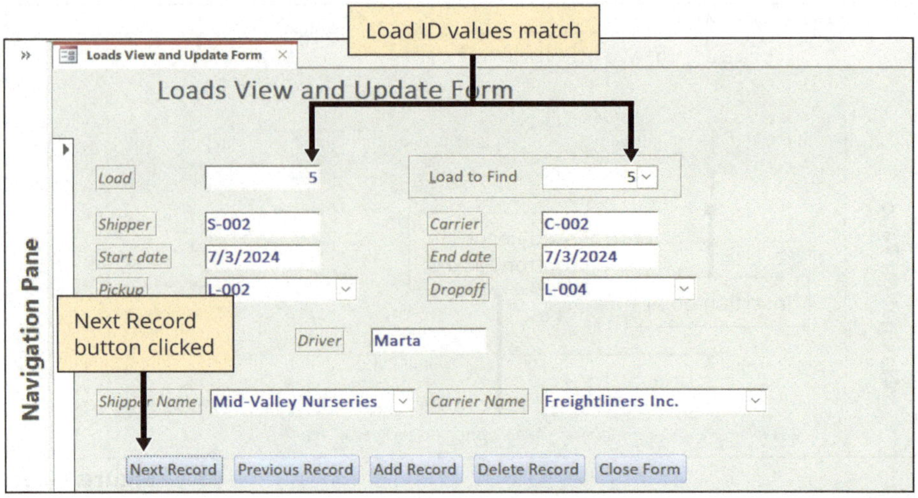

Figure 7–56d

Break Point: If you wish to take a break, this is a good place to do so. You can quit Access now. To resume at a later time, start Access, open the database called SC_AC_07_Clearnet.accdb, and continue following the steps from this location forward.

Creating a Multipage Form

If you have determined that you have more data than will fit conveniently on one screen, you can create a multipage form, a form that includes more than a single page. There are two ways to create a multipage form. One way is to insert a page break at the desired location or locations. An alternative approach, which produces a nice-looking and easy-to-use multipage form, is to insert a tab control. The multiple pages, called tabbed pages, are all contained within the tab control. To move from one page in the tab control to another, a user simply clicks the desired tab. The tab control shown in Figure 7–2, for example, has a tab labeled Datasheet that contains a datasheet showing the relevant data. It has a second tab, labeled Charts, that displays the relevant data in two charts.

To Create a Form in Design View

The management at Clearnet would like to track rate cons, or confirmations, and commissions from shippers. This information is stored in the Payments table. The new form will show this information for each shipper. **Why?** The form will contain the tab control including two tabs: one that displays a datasheet and another that displays two charts. The following steps begin the process by creating a form for the Shippers table in Design view.

1

- If necessary, close the Navigation Pane, and then display the Create tab.
- Click the Form Design button (Create tab | Forms group) to create a new form in Design view.

2

- Ensure the form selector — the box in the upper-left corner of the form — is selected.
- If necessary, click the Property Sheet button (Form Design tab | Tools group) to display the Property Sheet pane.
- Click the Data tab, click the Record Source property box arrow, and then click Shippers to select the Shippers table as the record source for the new form.
- Close the Property Sheet pane.

3

- Click the 'Add Existing Fields' button (Form Design tab | Tools group) to display the Field List pane, and then drag the Shipper ID field to the approximate position shown in Figure 7–57.

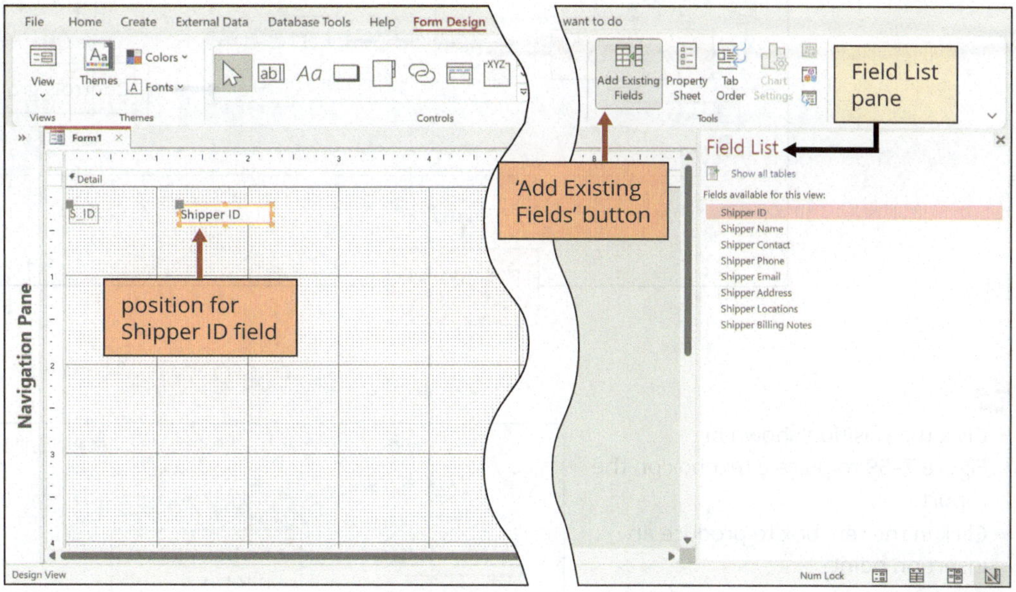

Figure 7–57

4

- Change the label for the Shipper ID field from S_ID to **Shipper Identification**.
- Resize and move the label and the Shipper ID control to match Figure 7–58.

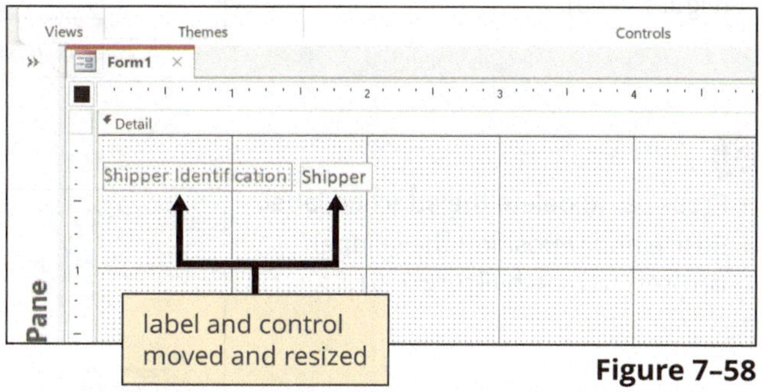

Figure 7–58

To Use the Text Box Tool with Concatenation

You can create a concatenated field by using the Text Box tool in the Controls group on the Design tab and then indicating the concatenation that is to be performed. **Why?** Concatenation means to combine objects in a series. The following steps add a concatenated field, involving two text fields, Shipper Name and Shipper Contact. Specifically, you will concatenate the shipper name, a colon, a single space, and the shipper's contact name.

1

- Click the Text Box tool (Form Design tab | Controls group), and then move the pointer, whose shape has changed to a small plus symbol (+) accompanied by a text box, to the position shown in Figure 7–59.

BTW

Concatenation

Concatenation is often used in computing to combine or merge two or more things. For example, if you have two separate fields, such as first name and last name, you can concatenate them to show a full name. You also can include punctuation between the fields, such as concatenating a city name, a comma, a space, and a state name.

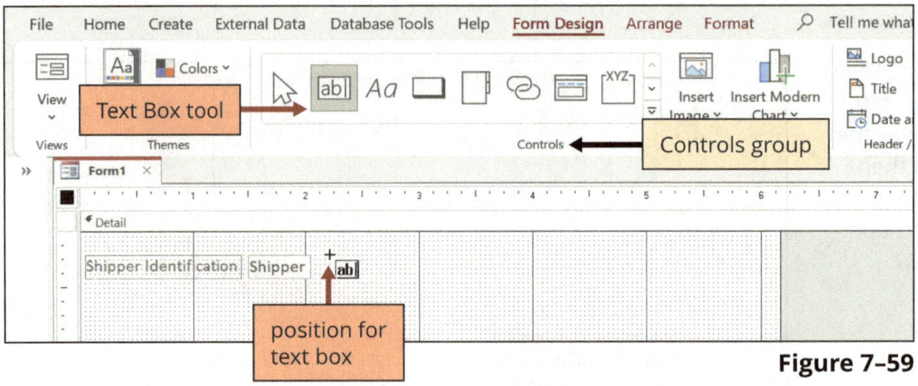

Figure 7–59

2

- Click the position shown in Figure 7–59 to place a text box on the report.
- Click in the text box to produce an insertion point.
- Type **=[Shipper Name] & ':' & ' ' & [Shipper Contact]** as the entry in the text box.
- Click the attached label to select it (Figure 7–60).

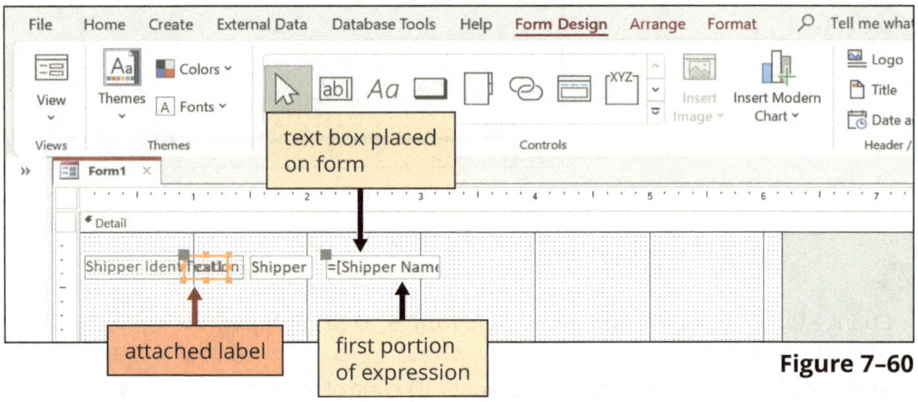

Figure 7–60

3

- Press DEL to delete the attached label.
- Resize and reposition the shipper controls to match Figure 7–61.

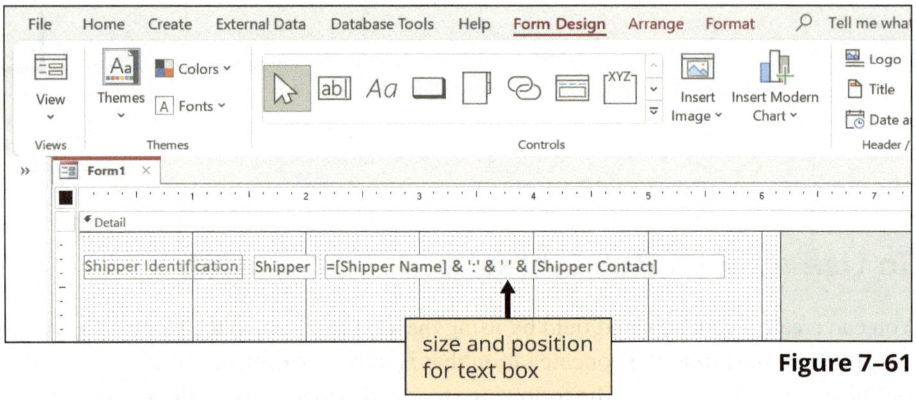

Figure 7–61

4

- Close the Field List pane.
- Save the form using the name, **Shipper Payments Form**.

To Use Tab Controls to Create a Multipage Form

To use tabs on a form, you need to insert a tab control. The following steps insert a tab control with two tabs: Datasheet and Charts. **Why?** Users will be able to click the Datasheet tab in the completed form to view rate confirmations and commissions in Datasheet view. Clicking the Charts tab will display two charts representing the similar data as in the Datasheet tab.

1

- Click the Tab Control tool (Form Design Tab | Controls group) and move the pointer to the approximate location shown in Figure 7–62.

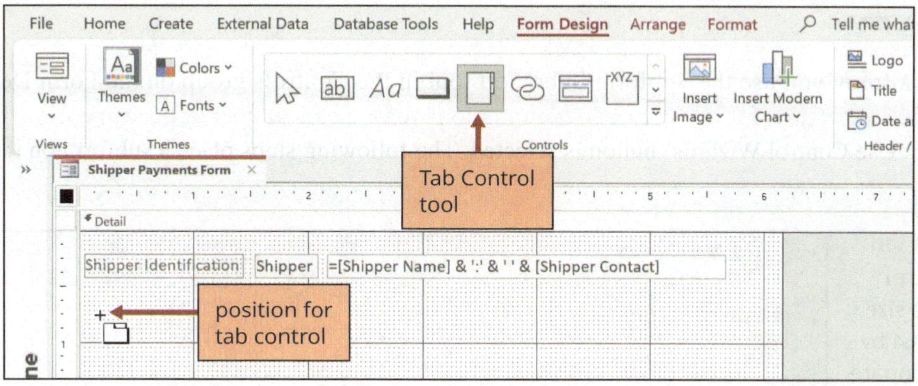

Figure 7–62

2

- Click the position shown in Figure 7–62 to place a tab control on the form.
- Click the left tab in the tab control, and then click the Property Sheet button (Form Design tab | Tools group) to display the Property Sheet pane.
- Click the Format tab.
- Set the value for the Caption property to **Datasheet** (Figure 7–63).

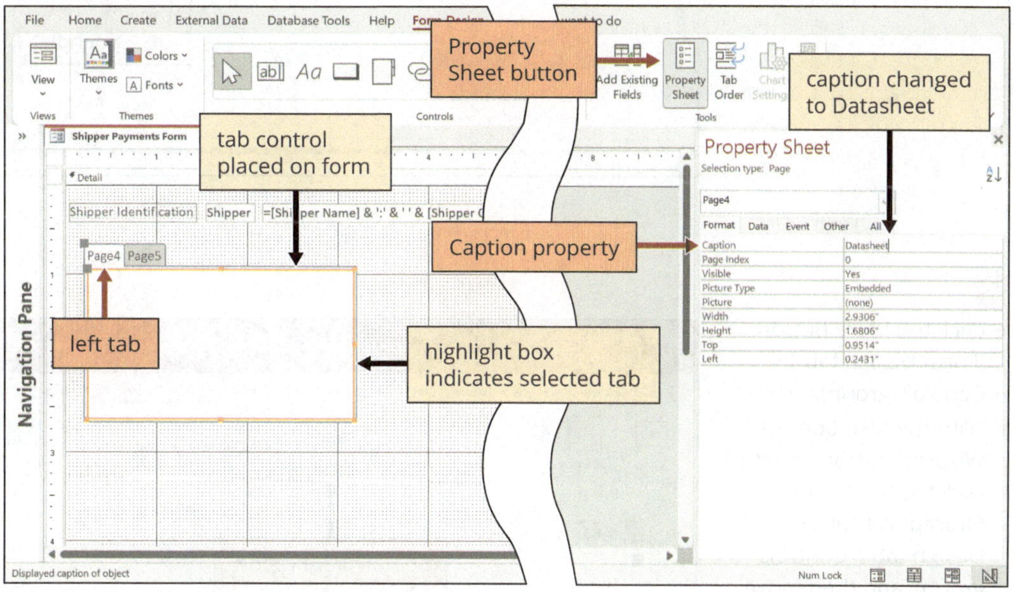

Figure 7–63

Q&A My property sheet looks different. What should I do?

Be sure you clicked the far-left tab before displaying the Property Sheet pane. The highlight should be within the border of the tab, as shown in the figure.

3

- Click the second tab in the tab control.
- Set the value for the Caption property to **Charts**, and then close the Property Sheet pane.

Consider This

When would you include a tab control in your form?

If the form contains more information than will conveniently fit on the screen at a time, consider adding a tab control. With a tab control, you can organize the information within a collection of tabbed pages. To access any of the tabbed pages, users need only click the corresponding tab.

BTW

Tab Control Order

You can change the order of tabs in a tab control. To do so, right-click any tab in the tab control and click Page Order on the shortcut menu. Use the Move Up and Move Down buttons to change to the desired order.

To Add a Subform

To add a subform to a form, you use the Subform/Subreport tool in the Controls group on the Form Design tab. **Why?** The subform enables you to show data for rate cons and commissions for a given shipper at the same time. Before doing so, you should make sure the 'Use Control Wizards' button is selected. The following steps place a subform on the Datasheet tab.

1

- Click the Datasheet tab.
- Resize the tab control to the approximate size shown in Figure 7–64 by dragging the appropriate sizing handles.

Q&A Why do I need to resize the tab control?
Because there needs to be enough room in the form to display all the datasheet columns and the two charts, you will need to make the tab control larger.

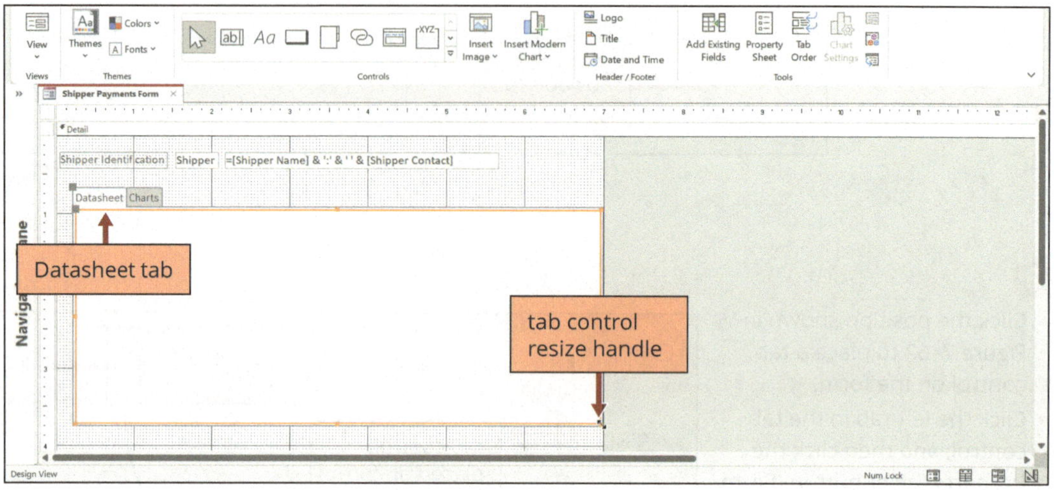

Figure 7–64

2

- Click the More button (Form Design tab | Controls group).
- With the 'Use Control Wizards' button selected, click the Subform/Subreport tool (Form Design tab | Controls group), and then move the pointer to the approximate position shown in Figure 7–65.

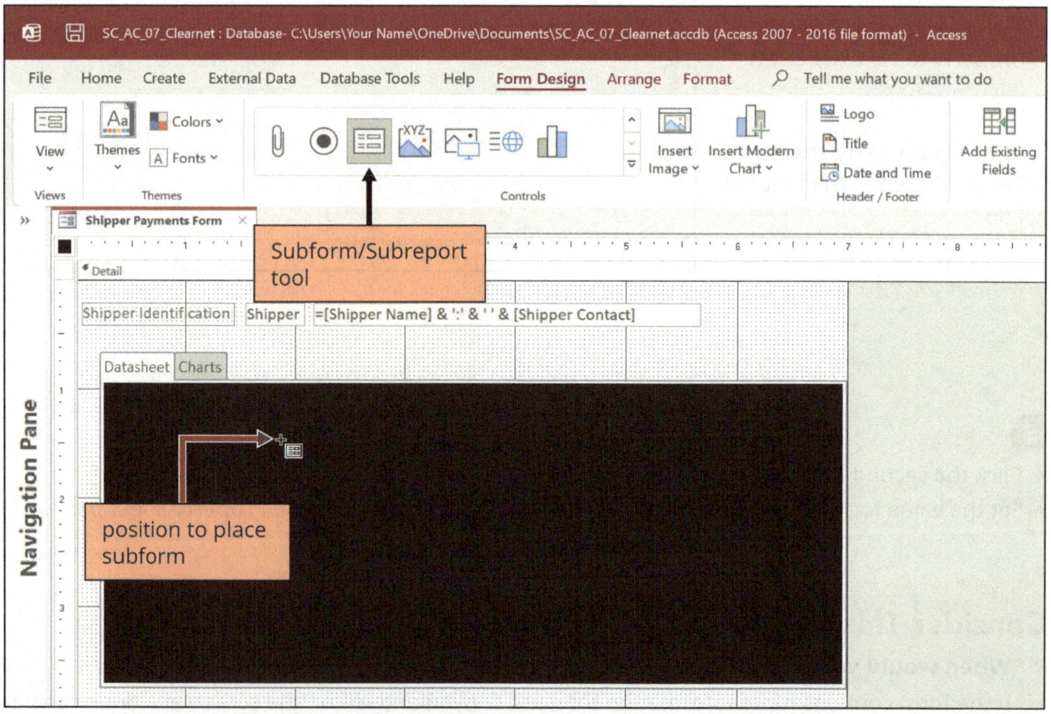

Figure 7–65

3

- Click the position shown in Figure 7–65 to open the SubForm Wizard dialog box.
- Be sure the 'Use existing Tables and Queries' option button is selected.
- Click Next to display the next SubForm Wizard screen.

- Click the Tables/Queries arrow, and then click the Payments table to indicate the fields for the subform will be selected from this table.
- If necessary, click the Payment ID field to select it, and then click the Add Field button.
- Use the same technique to add the Rate Confirmation field, Agent Commission field, Shipper Bill Status field, and Shipper ID field (Figure 7–66).

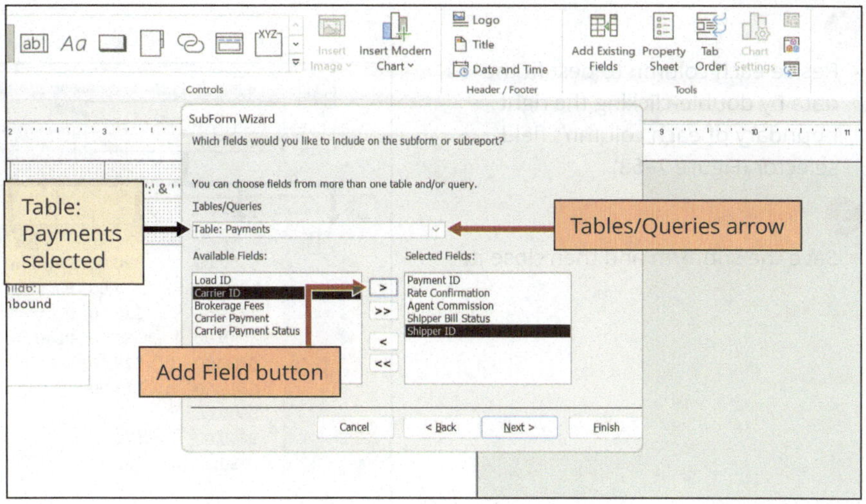

Figure 7–66

4

- Click Next.
- Be sure the 'Choose from a list' option button is selected.
- Click Next.
- Change the name of the subform to **Payments by Shipper**, and then click Finish to complete the creation of the sub-form (Figure 7–67).

5

- Save and close the Shipper Payments Form.

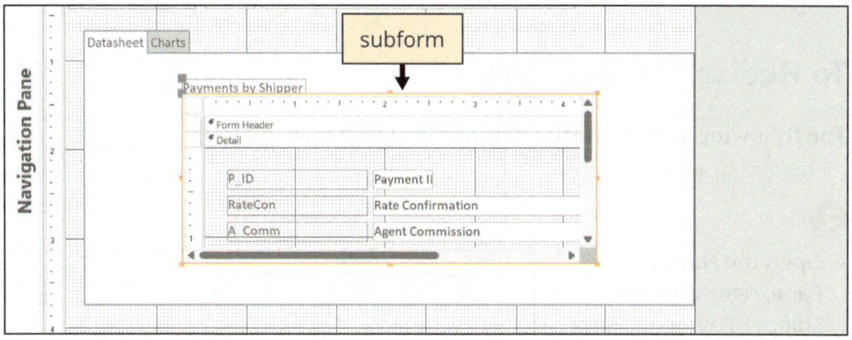

Figure 7–67

Consider This

When would you include a subform in your form?

If the fields for the form come from exactly two tables, a one-to-many relationship exists between the two tables, and the form is based on the "one" table, you will often place the data for the "many" table in a subform. If there are more than two tables involved, you might be able to create a query on which you can base the subform.

To Modify a Subform

The next task is to modify the subform. The first step is to remove the Shipper ID field from the subform. **Why?** The Shipper ID field needed to be included initially in the subform because it is the field that is used to link the data in the subform to the data in the main form. It is not supposed to appear in the form, however. In addition, the remaining columns need to be resized for best fit. The following step first removes the Shipper ID field. You then switch to Datasheet view to resize the remaining columns.

1

- Open the Navigation Pane, right-click the Payments by Shipper form, click Design View on the shortcut menu, and then close the Navigation Pane.
- Click the Shipper ID control, and then press DEL to delete the control.
- Switch to Datasheet view.

2

- Resize each column to best fit the data by double-clicking the right boundary of each column's field selector (Figure 7–68).

3

- Save the subform and then close it.

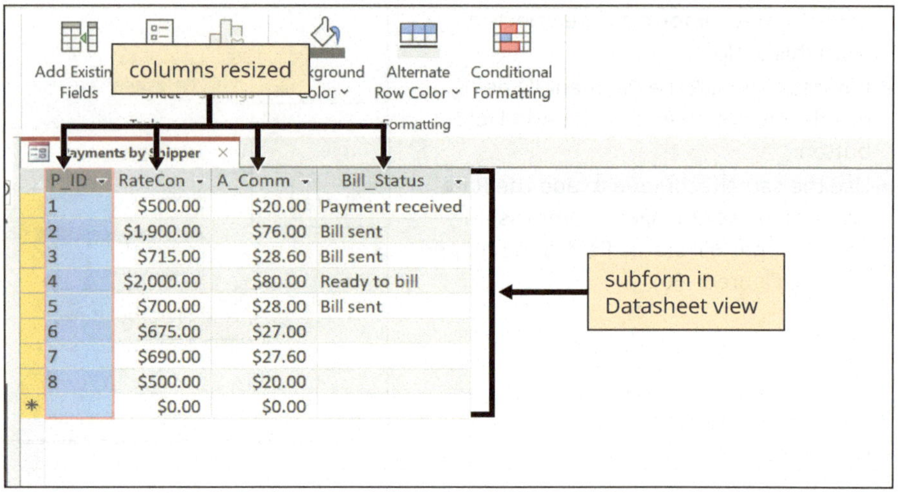

Figure 7–68

To Resize the Subform

The following step resizes the subform inside the tab control. **Why?** The size should enable the user to clearly view all the data without taking more room than needed.

1

- Open the Navigation Pane, right-click the Shipper Payments Form, and then click Design View on the shortcut menu.
- Close the Navigation Pane.
- Resize and reposition the subform to match Figure 7–69.

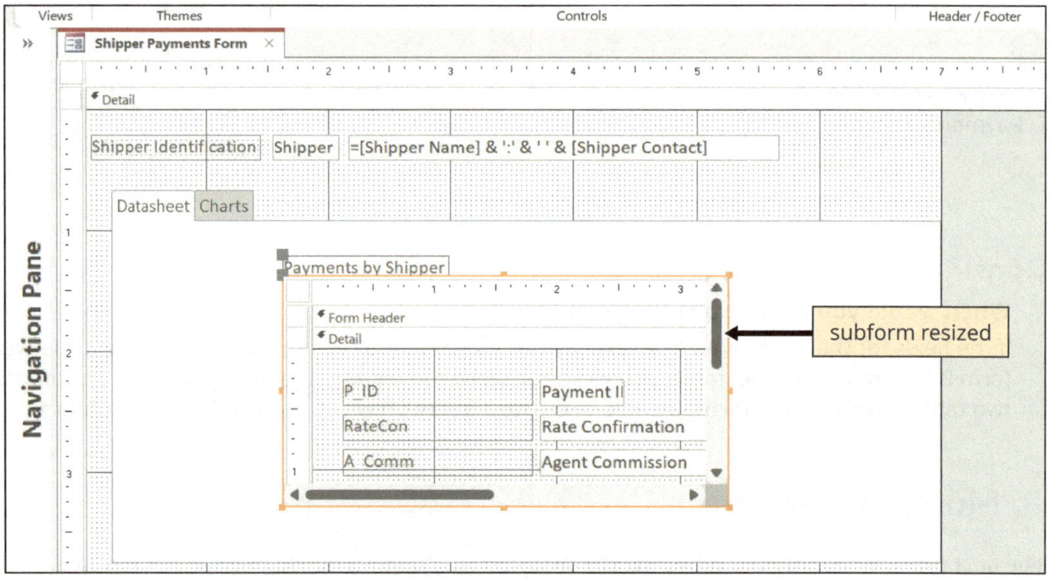

Figure 7–69

To Change the Background Color

The following steps change the background color of the form to a light gray.

1

- Click anywhere in the Detail section in the main form but outside all the controls to select the section.

2

- Display the Format tab.
- Click the Background Color button arrow (Format tab | Font group) to display a color palette (Figure 7–70).

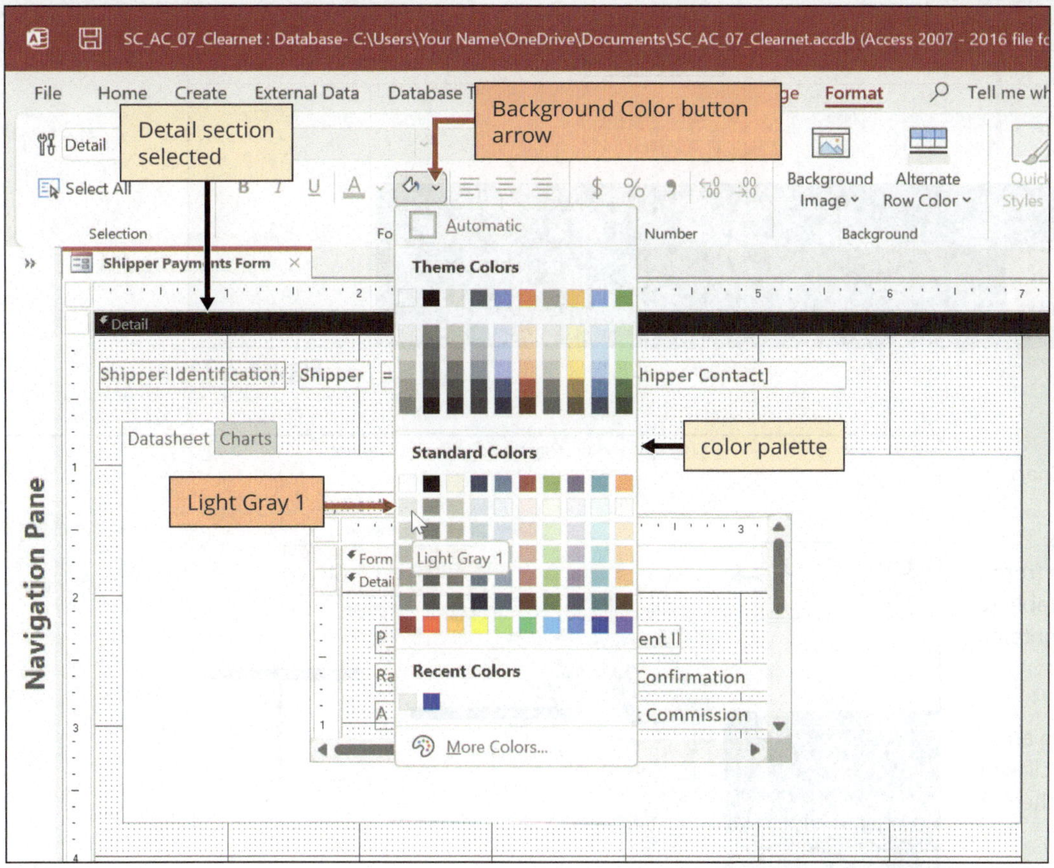

Figure 7–70

3

- Click Light Gray 1, the first color in the second row under Standard Colors, to change the background color.

To Insert Charts

Why? To visually represent data in a table or query, you can create a chart. To insert a chart, use the Chart tool on the Form Design tab. The Chart Wizard will then ask you to indicate the fields to be included on the chart and the type of chart you want to insert. The following steps insert a chart that visually represents the amount of payments from shippers.

1

- Display the Form Design tab.
- Click the Charts tab on the tab control to switch to that tab.
- Click the More button (Form Design tab | Controls group) to display the design tools.
- Click the Chart tool, and then move the pointer to the approximate position shown in Figure 7–71.

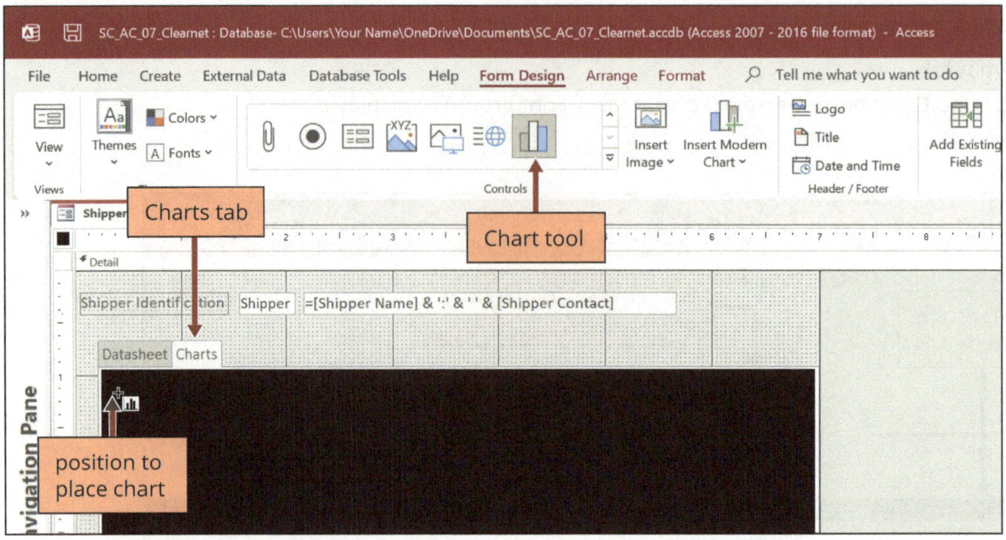

Figure 7–71

2

- Click the position shown in Figure 7–71 to display the Chart Wizard dialog box.
- The Chart Wizard dialog box indicates the data will come from a table; click the Payments table to indicate the specific table containing the desired fields.
- Click Next.
- Select the Rate Confirmation and Shipper Bill Status fields by clicking each one and then clicking the Add Field button (Figure 7–72).

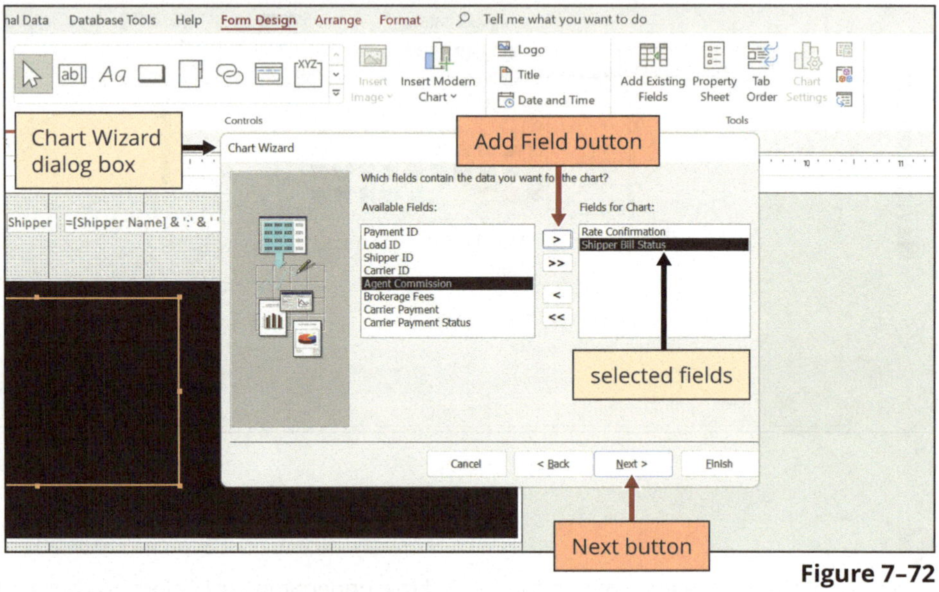

Figure 7–72

3

- Click Next.
- Click the Pie Chart type, the first chart in the bottom row (Chart Wizard dialog box) (Figure 7–73).
- **Experiment:** Click the other chart types and read the descriptions of chart types in the lower-right corner of the Chart Wizard dialog box. When finished, click the Pie Chart in the lower-left corner.

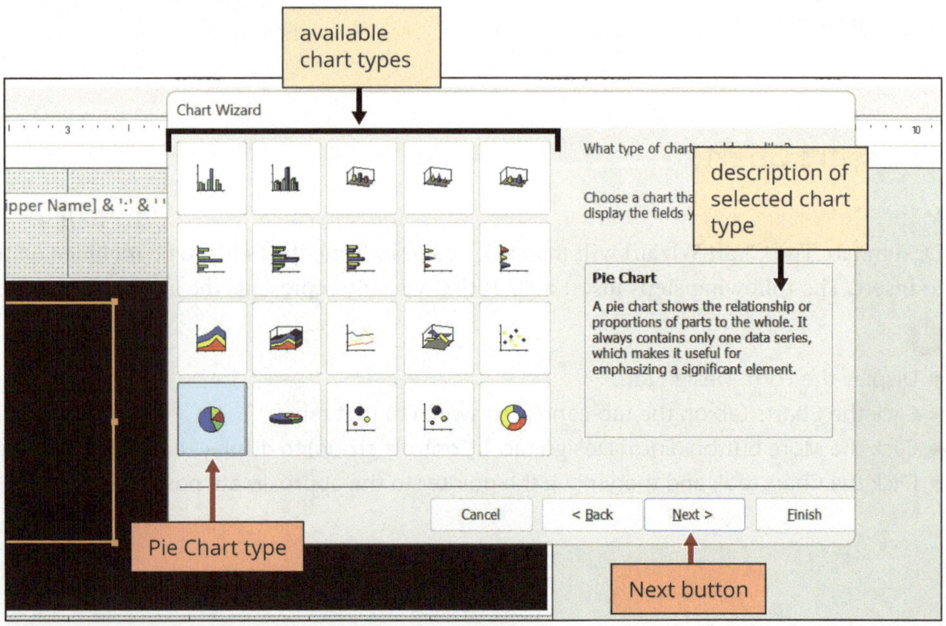

Figure 7–73

4

- Click Next to create the chart (Figure 7–74). Your screen might take several seconds to refresh.

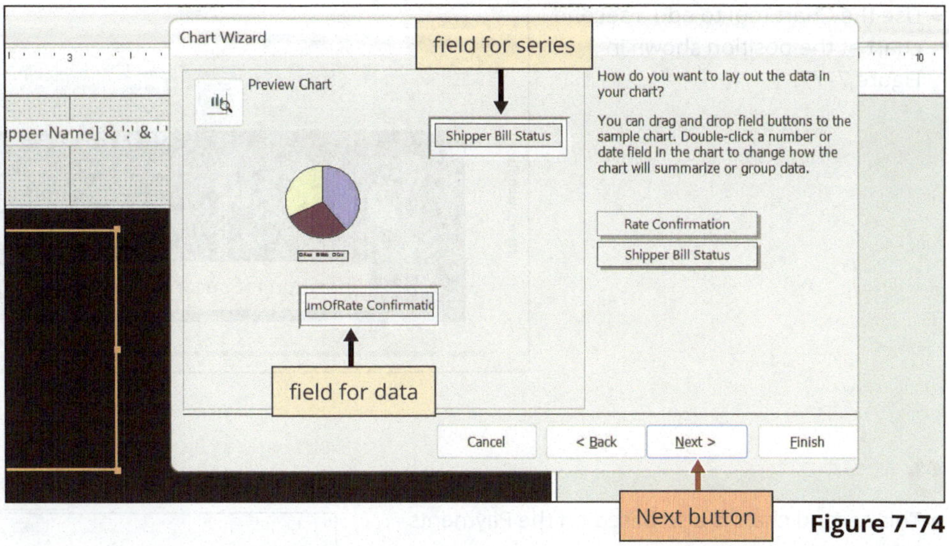

Figure 7–74

Q&A What do the chart positions represent? Can I change them?
The field under the chart represents the data that will be summarized by slices of the pie. The other field is used to indicate the series. In this example, the field for the series is the shipper bill status, and the sizes of the slices of the pie will represent the sum of the rate confirmations for each bill status. You can change these by dragging the fields to the desired locations.

These positions make sense for a pie chart. What if I selected a different chart type?
The items on this screen will be relevant to the chart type you select. Just as with the pie chart, the correct fields will often be selected automatically. If not, you can drag the fields to the correct locations.

5

- Click Next to select the layout Access has proposed (Figure 7–75).

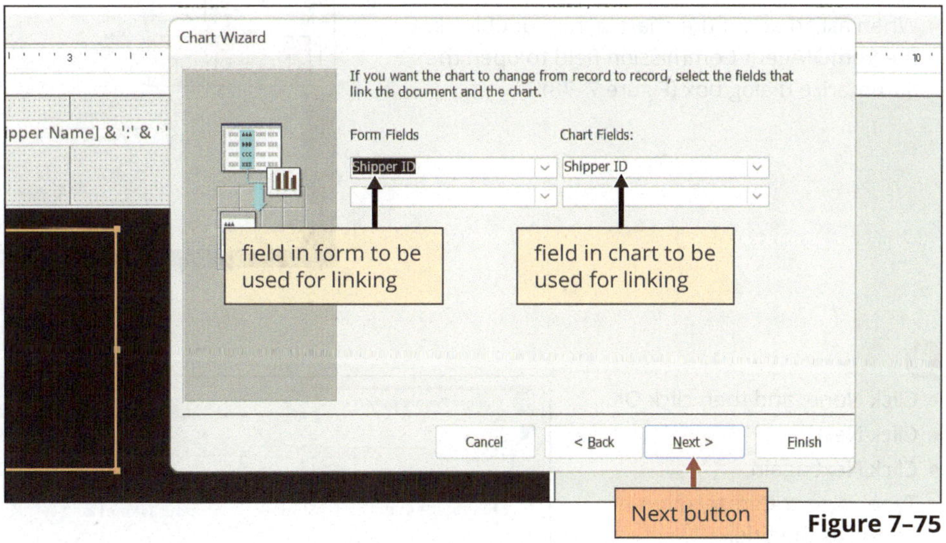

Figure 7–75

Q&A The Shipper ID field does not appear in my chart. Can I still use it to link the form and the chart?
Yes. Even though the Shipper ID does not appear, it is still included in the query on which the chart is based. In fact, it is essential that it is included so you can link the document (that is, the form) and the chart. Linking the document and the chart ensures the chart will accurately reflect the data for the correct shipper, that is, the shipper that currently appears in the form.

6

- Click Next, type **Rate Confirmation Statuses** as the title, and then click the Finish button (Figure 7–76).

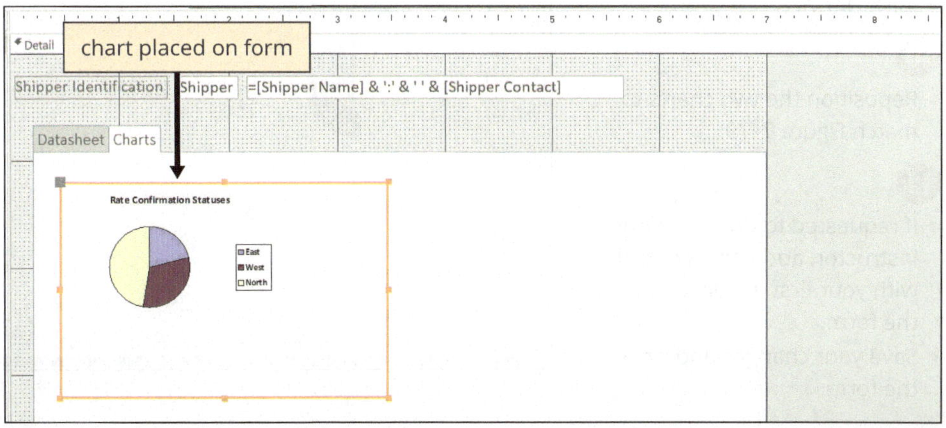

Figure 7–76

Q&A The data does not look right. What is wrong and what do I need to do to fix it?
The data in your chart might be fictitious, as in Figure 7–76. In that case, the data simply represents the general way the chart will look. When you view the actual form, the data represented in the chart should be correct.

7

- Use the Chart tool to add a second chart at the position shown in Figure 7–77.

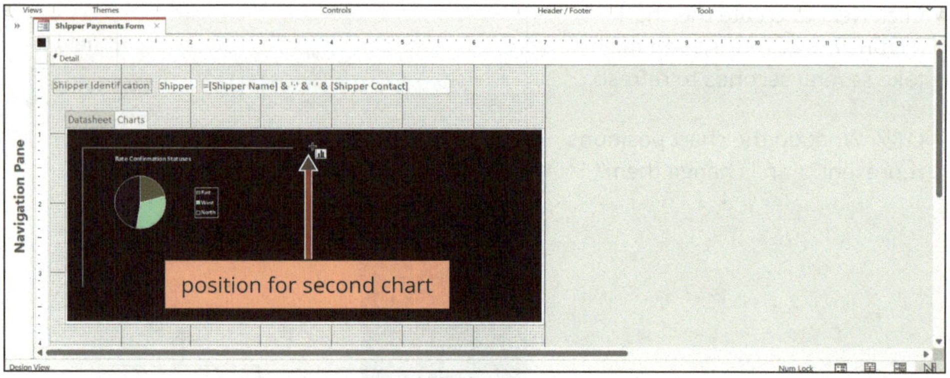

Figure 7–77

8

- This second chart is also based on the Payments table.
- Add the Load ID field and the Agent Commission field to the chart.
- Choose the Column Chart type, which is the default selection in the upper-left corner.
- When asked about the chart layout, double-click the SumOfAgent Commission field to open the Summarize dialog box (Figure 7–78).

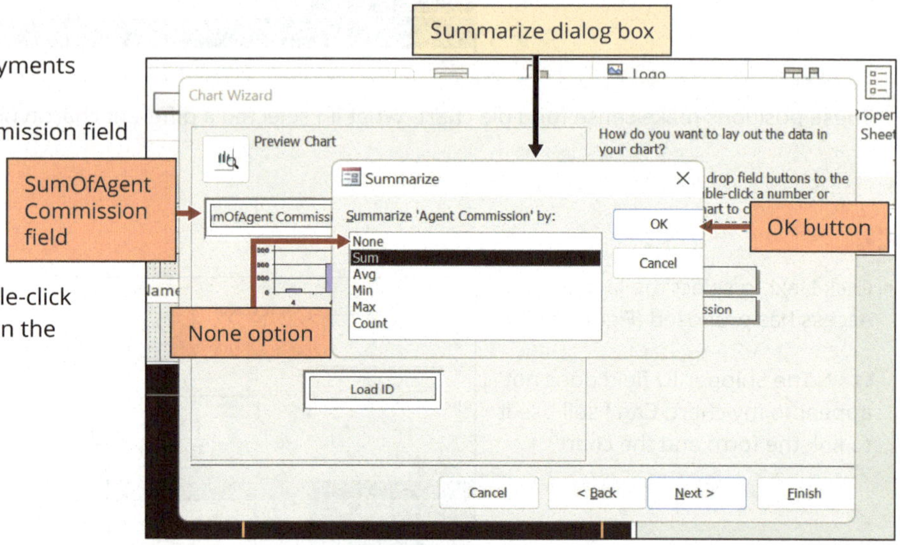

Figure 7–78

9

- Click None, and then click OK.
- Click Next.
- Click Next again.
- Type **Agent Commission by Load** as the title.
- Click the 'No, don't display a legend' option button.
- Click Finish.

10

- Reposition the two charts to match Figure 7–79.

11

- If requested to do so by your instructor, add a title control with your first and last name to the form.
- Save your changes and close the form.

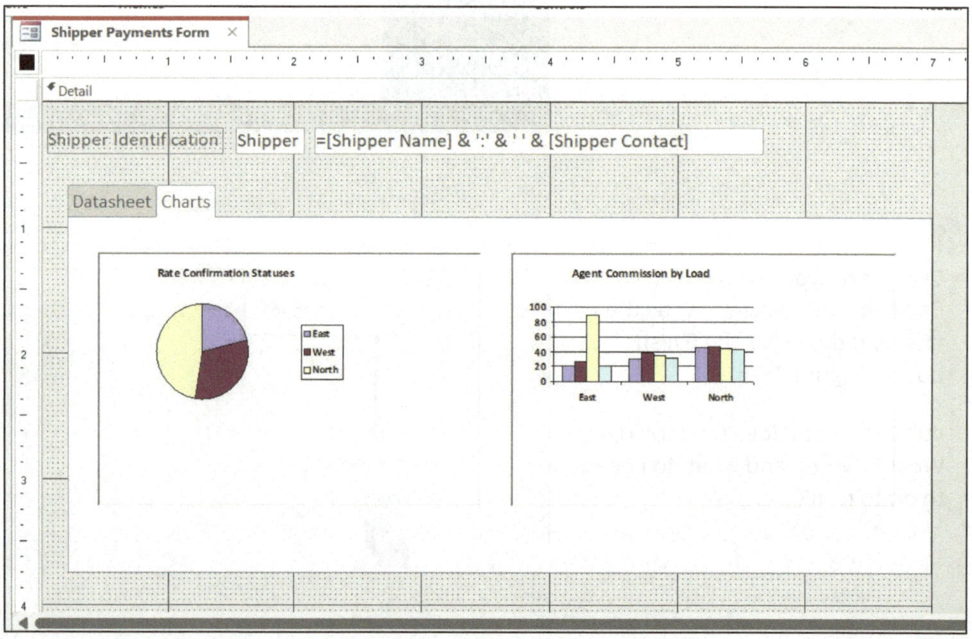

Figure 7–79

To Use the Form

You use this form just like the other forms you have created and used. When using the form, it is easy to move from one tabbed page to another. **Why?** Click each tab to navigate to the desired tabbed page. The following steps use the form to view the rate confirmation and agent commission data.

1

- Open the Navigation Pane, open the Shipper Payments Form in Form view, and then close the Navigation Pane (Figure 7–80). Ensure all headings are visible, and adjust any column widths if necessary.

Q&A What is the purpose of the navigation buttons in the subform?
These navigation buttons allow you to move within the records in the subform, that is, within the payment data for the shipper whose number and name appear at the top of the form.

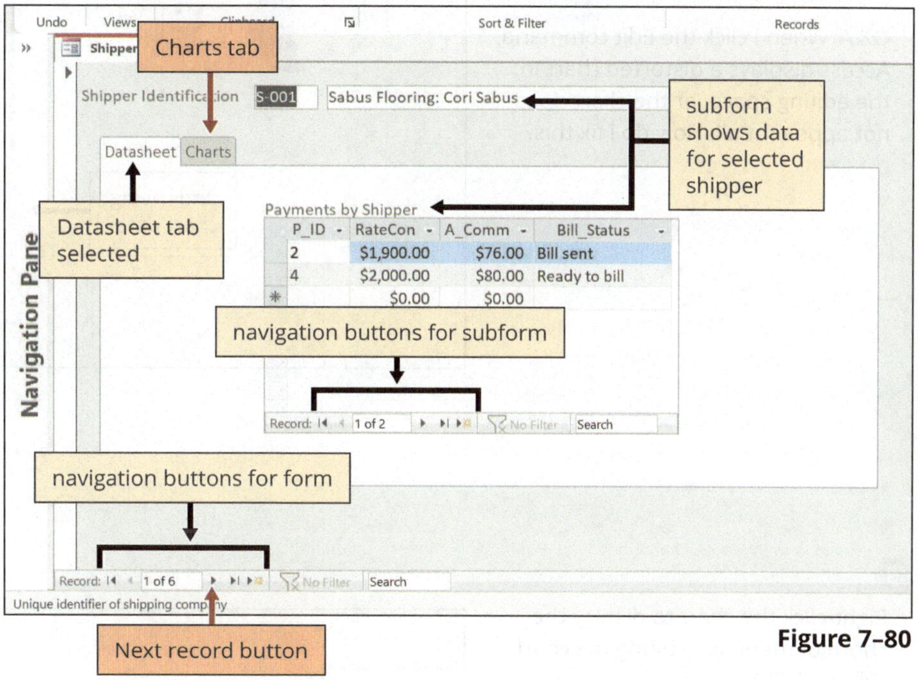

Figure 7–80

2

- Click the Charts tab to display the charts.
- Click the Next record button to navigate through other shipper records to see different chart data.

To Modify a Chart Type

When you first create a chart, you specify the chart type. You sometimes will later want to change the type. **Why?** You might find that a different chart type is a better way to represent the data. In addition, you have more options when you later change the chart type than when you first created the chart. You change the type by editing the chart and selecting the Chart Type command. The following steps change the chart type of the column chart by selecting a different style of column chart.

1

- Switch to Design view.
- Click the tab control, and then click the Charts tab to display the charts in Design view.
- Click the Agent Commission by Load chart to select it, and then right-click the chart to display a shortcut menu.
- Point to Chart Object on the shortcut menu to display the Chart Object submenu (Figure 7–81).

Q&A Does it matter where I right-click?
You should right-click within the rectangle but outside any of the items within the rectangle, in other words, in the white space.

My shortcut menu is very different. What should I do?
Click the View button arrow, then click Design View to ensure you are viewing the form in Design view, and then try again.

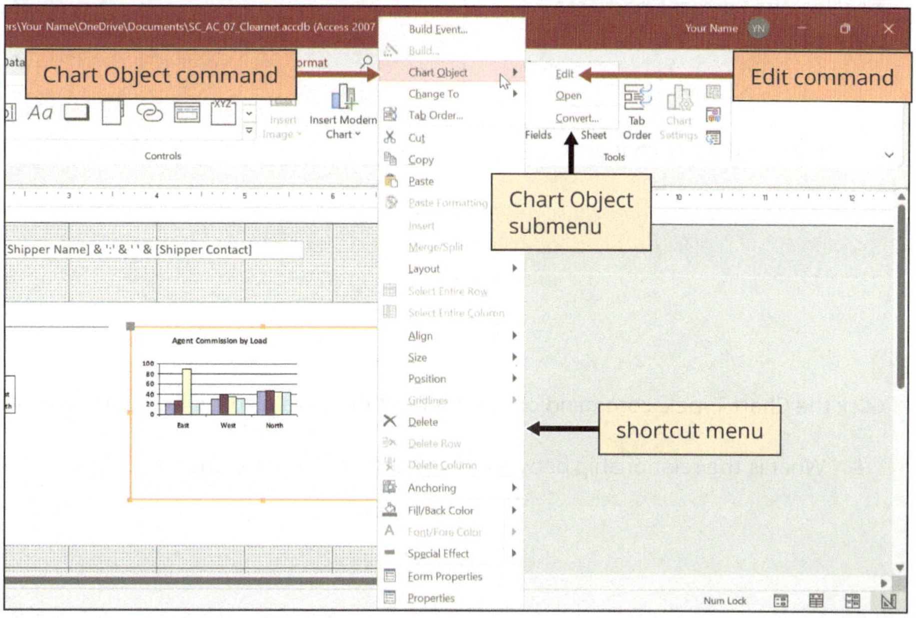

Figure 7–81

2

- Click Edit on the Chart Object submenu to edit the chart. Access will automatically display the underlying chart data in Datasheet view (Figure 7–82).

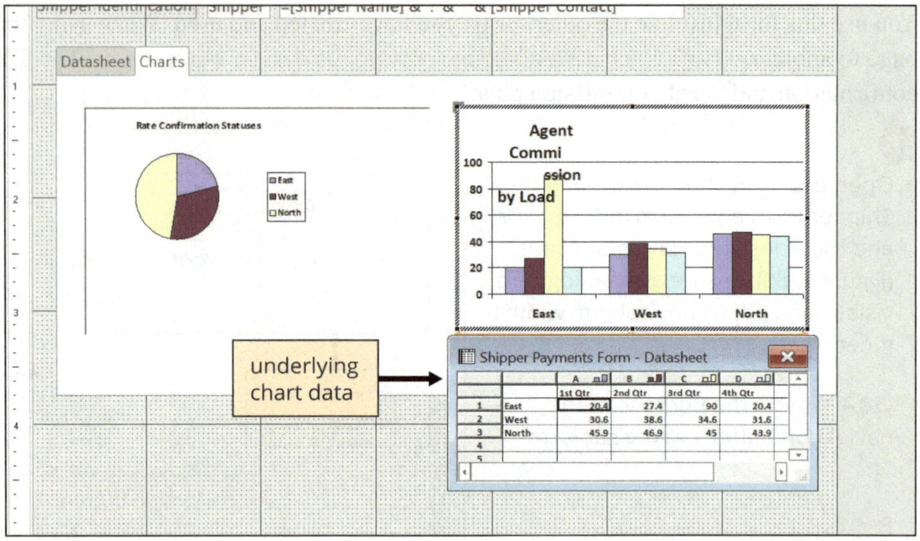

Figure 7–82

Q&A When I click the Edit command, Access displays a distorted chart in the editing space, or the chart does not appear at all. How do I fix this?
In some cases, you might need to use the Open command instead of the Edit command to get a usable interface for editing a chart. Click outside the chart editing space, again right-click the chart, point to Chart Object, and this time, click Open to display the Microsoft Graph window. The screen will look slightly different from the figures in this portion of the module; however, all the steps should work the same. When you are finished editing, you can close the Microsoft Graph window.

3

- Right-click the chart to display the shortcut menu for editing the chart (Figure 7–83).

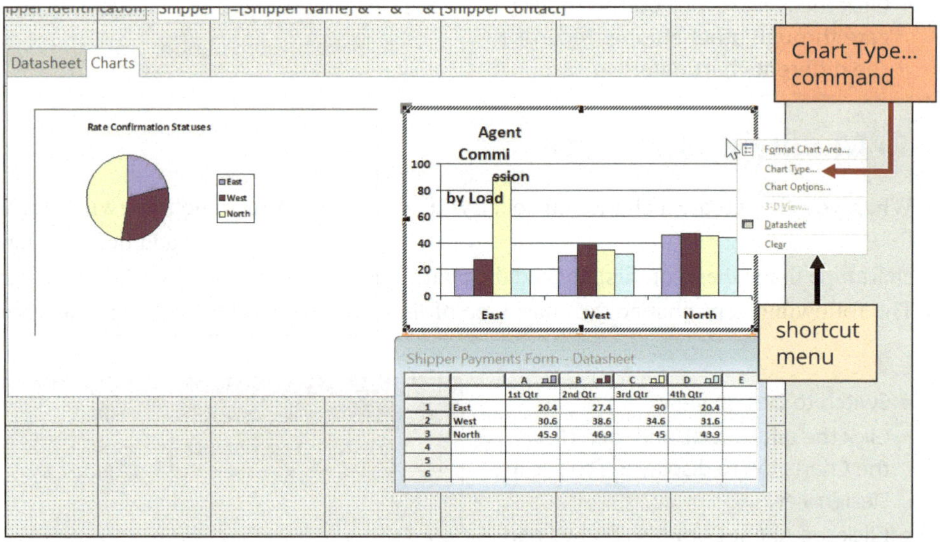

Figure 7–83

Q&A Does it matter where I right-click?
You should right-click within the rectangle but outside any of the items within the rectangle, in other words, in the white space.

What types of changes can I make if I select the Format Chart Area... command?
You can change things such as border style, color, fill effects, and fonts.

How do I make other changes?
By clicking Chart Options... on the shortcut menu, you can change titles, legends, and labels. For 3-D charts, by clicking 3-D View... on the shortcut menu, you can change the elevation and rotation of the chart. You can also format specific items on the chart, as you will see in the next section.

4

- Click the Chart Type... command on the shortcut menu to display the Chart Type dialog box (Figure 7–84).

Q&A What is the relationship between the Chart type and the Chart sub-type?
You can think of Chart types as categories of charts. There are column charts, bar charts, line charts, and so on. Once you have selected a category, the chart sub-types are charts in that category. If you have selected the Column chart category, for example, the charts within the category are the ones shown in the list of chart sub-types in Figure 7–85.

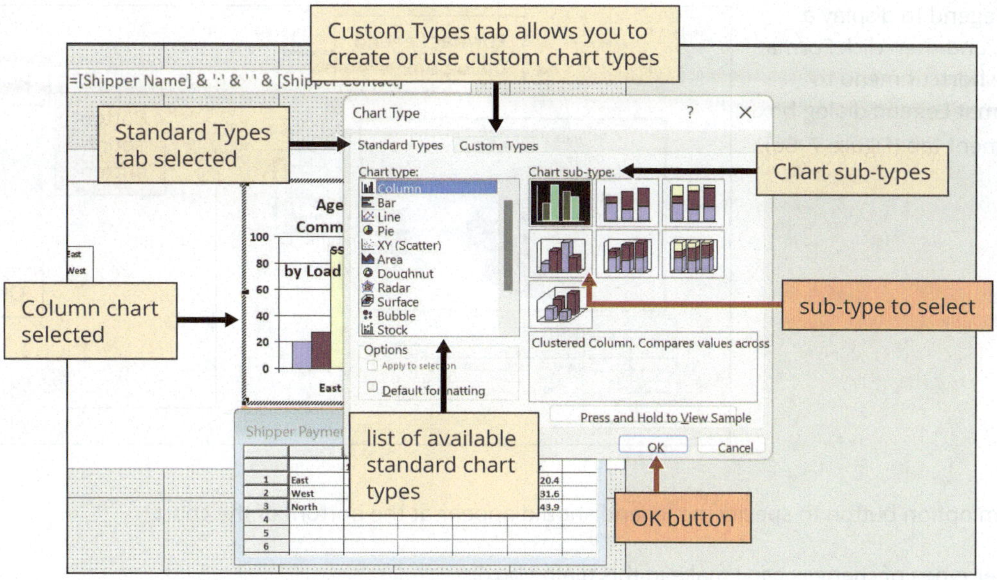

Figure 7–84

5

- Click the first chart sub-type in the second row of chart sub-types to select the 'Clustered column with a 3-D visual effect' chart sub-type.
- **Experiment:** Click each of the chart types and examine the chart sub-types associated with that chart type. When finished, select Column as the chart type and the first sub-type in the second row as the chart sub-type.
- Click the OK button to change the chart sub-type.
- Click outside the chart and the tab control to deselect the chart (Figure 7–85).

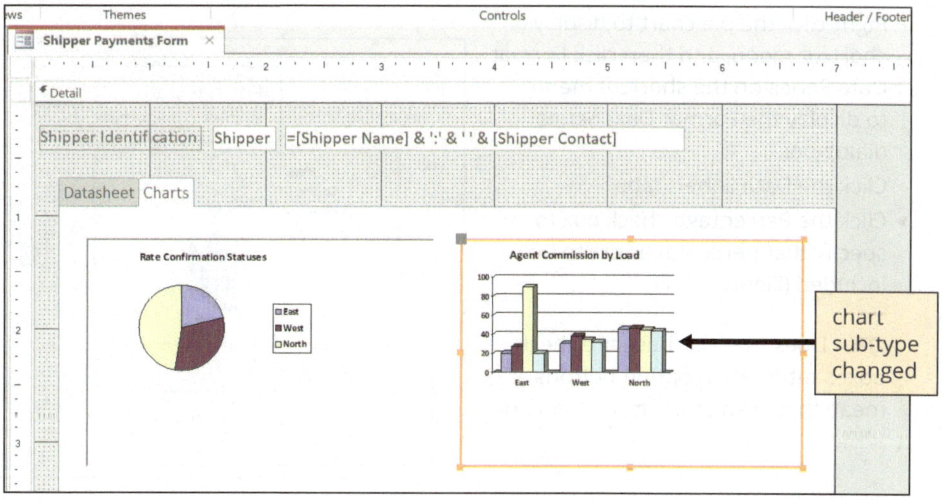

Figure 7–85

To Format a Chart

After right-clicking a chart, pointing to Chart Object, and then clicking Edit, you have many formatting options available. You can change the border style, color, fill effects, and fonts by using the Format Chart Area command. You can change titles, legends, and labels by using the Chart Options command. You can also format specific portions of a chart by right-clicking the portion you want to format and then clicking the appropriate command on the shortcut menu. The following steps use this technique to move the legend on the pie chart so it is at the bottom of the chart. They also include percentages in the chart. **Why?** Percentages provide valuable information in a pie chart.

1

- Right-click the Rate Confirmation Statuses chart to display a shortcut menu, point to Chart Object on the shortcut menu to display the Chart Object submenu, and then click Edit on the Chart Object submenu.

Q&A If the Edit command is not working well for me, will the Open command work here as before?
Yes, you can use the Open command here as an alternative to the Edit command, just as in the earlier steps. The Open command will open the Microsoft Graph window where you can make all the needed changes described in these steps. When you are finished editing, you can close the Microsoft Graph window.

- Right-click the legend to display a shortcut menu, and then click Format Legend on the shortcut menu to display the Format Legend dialog box.
- Click the Placement tab (Figure 7–86).

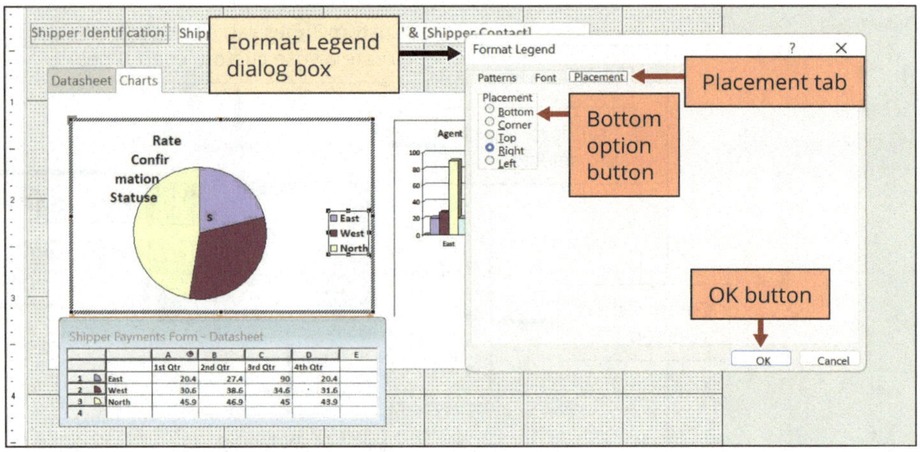

Figure 7–86

2

- Click the Bottom option button to specify the legend should appear at the bottom of the chart.

Q&A What other types of changes can I make in this dialog box?
Click the Patterns tab to change such things as border style, color, and fill effects. Click the Font tab to change the font and font characteristics.

- Click OK to place the legend at the location you selected.
- Right-click the pie chart to display a shortcut menu, and then click Format Data Series on the shortcut menu to display the Format Data Series dialog box.
- Click the Data Labels tab.
- Click the Percentage check box to specify that percentages are to be included (Figure 7–87).

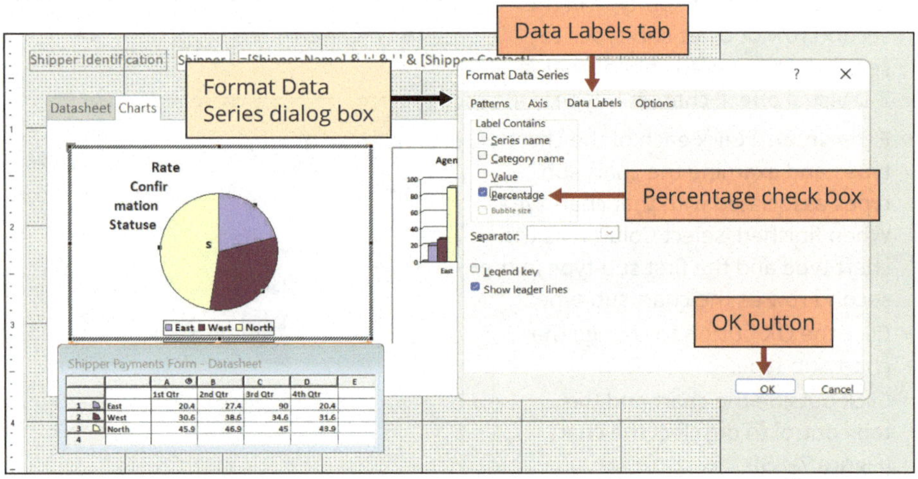

Figure 7–87

Q&A Does the fact these are check boxes rather than option buttons mean that I can select more than one?
Because these are check boxes, you can select as many as you want. Selecting too many can clutter the chart, however.

The tabs and options in the Format Data Series dialog box make sense for a pie chart, but what about other chart types?
The options you see will vary from one chart type to another. They will be relevant for the selected chart type.

3

- Click OK to include percentages on the chart.
- Click outside the chart and the tab control to deselect the chart.

4

- View the form in Form view to see the effect of your changes.
- Save and then close the form.
- If desired, sign out of your Microsoft account.
- sam Exit Access.

BTW
Distributing a Document
Instead of printing and distributing a hard copy of a document, you can distribute the document electronically. Options include sending the document via email; posting it on cloud storage (such as OneDrive) and sharing the file with others; posting it on a social networking site, blog, or other website; and sharing a link associated with an online location of the document. You also can create and share a PDF or XPS image of the document, so users can view the file in Acrobat Reader or XPS Viewer instead of in Access.

Consider This

What type of decisions should you make when considering whether to use a chart?

Do you want to represent data in a visual manner? If so, you can include a chart. If you decide to use a chart, you must determine which type of chart would best represent the data. If you want to represent total amounts, for example, a bar chart might be appropriate. If instead you want to represent portions of the whole, a pie chart might be better.

Summary

In this module you have learned how to create a form in Design view, add a combo box that displays information from a related table as well as a combo box that is used to find records on a form, format controls, add command buttons to a form, modify a button and a combo box, add a concatenated field to a form, use a tab control to create a multipage form, add and modify a subform, insert charts, change chart types, and format charts.

Consider This: Plan Ahead

What decisions will you need to make when creating your own forms?

Use these guidelines as you complete the assignments in this module and create your own forms outside of this class.

1. Determine the intended audience and the purpose of the form.
   a. Who will use the form?
   b. How will they use it?
   c. What data do they need?
   d. What level of detail do they need?
2. Determine the source of data for the form.
   a. Determine whether data comes from a single table or from multiple related tables.
   b. Which table or tables contain the data?
3. Determine the fields that belong on the form.
   a. What data items are needed by the user of the form?
4. Determine any calculations required for the form.
   a. Decide whether the form should contain any special calculations, such as adding two fields.
   b. Determine whether the form should contain any calculations involving text fields, such as concatenating (combining) the fields.
5. Determine the organization of the form.
   a. In what order should the fields appear?
   b. How should they be arranged?
   c. Does the form need multiple pages?
6. Determine any additional controls that should be on the form.
   a. Should the form contain a subform?
   b. Should the form contain a chart?
   c. Should the form contain command buttons to assist the user in performing various functions?
   d. Should the form contain a combo box to assist the user in searching for a record?
7. Determine the format and style of the form.
   a. What should be in the form heading?
   b. Do you want a title?
   c. Do you want an image?
   d. What should be in the body of the form?
   e. What visual characteristics, such as background color and special effects, should the various portions of the form have?

Consider This

How should you submit solutions to critical thinking questions in the assignments?

Every assignment in this course contains one or more critical thinking questions. These questions require you to think beyond the assigned database. Present your responses to the questions in the format required by your instructor. Possible formats might include one or more of these options: write the answer; create a document that contains the answer; present your answer to the class; discuss your answer in a group; record the answer as audio or video using a webcam, smartphone, or portable media player; or post answers on a blog, wiki, or website.

Student Assignments

Apply Your Knowledge

Reinforce the skills and apply the concepts you learned in this module.

Creating a Multipage Form for the Tutoring Services Database

Note: To complete this assignment, you will be required to use the Data Files. Please contact your instructor for information about accessing the Data Files.

Instructions: Start Access. Open the database, SC_AC_07-2.accdb, which is located in the Data Files folder. Enable the content.

Perform the following tasks:

1. Save the database using the file name, SC_AC_07_City-Tutoring. Enable the content.
2. Create the Amount Received and Current Due form shown in Figure 7–88. Concatenate the first and last name of the counselor, and change the control's background color to Light Gray 1 (the first color in row 2 of the Standard Colors). The Datasheet tab displays a subform listing information about payments from the counselor's students (Figure 7–88a). Data for the subform is based on the Accounting table. Data for the Chart tab is also based on the Accounting table and displays the amount received from each student for the specified counselor, in this case, the sum of amounts received by counselor Number 103, Enrique Estevez (Figure 7–88b).

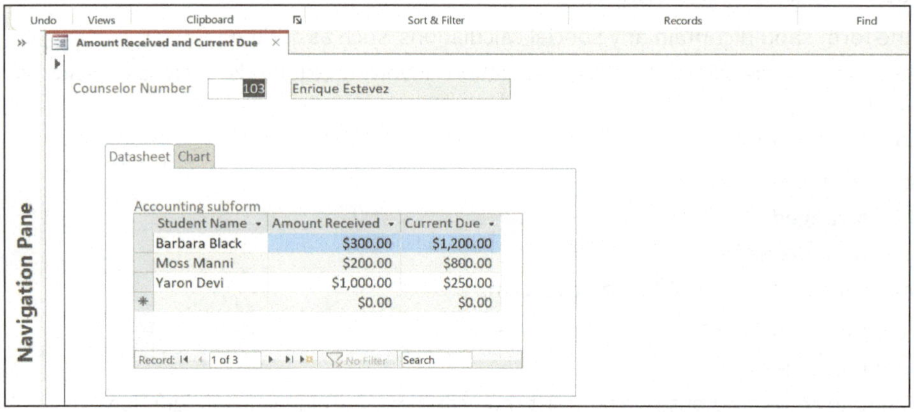

Figure 7–88a

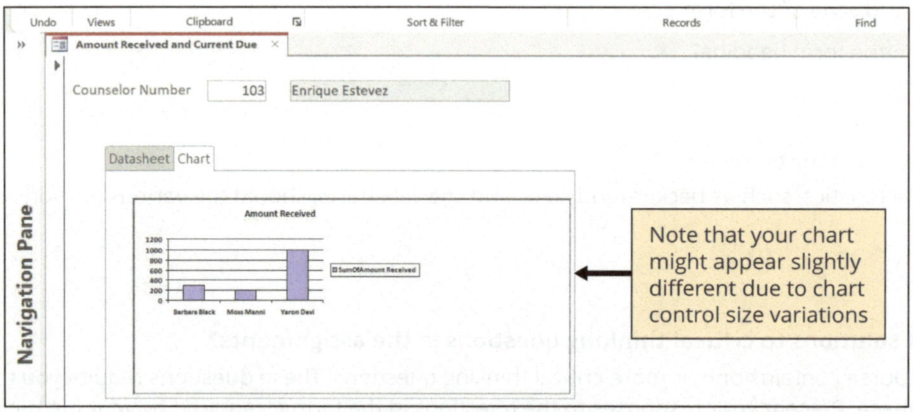

Figure 7–88b

3. If requested to do so by your instructor, rename the Amount Received and Current Due form as LastName Services Data where LastName is your last name.
4. Submit the revised database in the format specified by your instructor.
5. **Consider This:** How would you add a title to the Amount Received and Current Due form?

Extend Your Knowledge

Extend the skills you learned in this module and experiment with new skills. You may need to use Help to complete the assignment.

Modifying Forms

Note: To complete this assignment, you will be required to use the Data Files. Please contact your instructor for information about accessing the Data Files.

Instructions: Start Access. Open the database, SC_AC_07-3.accdb, which is located in the Data Files folder.

Perform the following tasks:

1. Save the database using the file name, SC_AC_07_Physical-Therapists. Enable the content.
2. Open the Technician Form in Design view. Insert the current date in the form header.
3. Bold the Technician Form title.
4. Change the font color of the title to Dark Red (Standard colors, first color in the last row).
5. Below the existing controls, add a tab control to the form (make room for the new control as needed). Change the caption for the first tab to Clients.
6. Add a subform to the Clients tab control. The Client table is the basis of the subform. Display the Client Name, Amount Paid, and Balance Due fields in a datasheet on the subform. Accept the default name for the subform and delete the label that appears above the datasheet. Resize the datasheet columns for best fit, and resize the datasheet control so all columns appear in the control.
7. Delete the other tab.
8. Add a command button to close the form and use the picture option to place the Exit Doorway picture on the button. Name the button Close Form.
9. Save the changes to the form.
10. If requested to do so by your instructor, open the Technician table in Datasheet view and change the first and last name of Technician 22 to your first and last name.
11. Submit the revised database in the format specified by your instructor.
12. **Consider This:** What chart would be appropriate to add to this form?

Expand Your World

Create a solution, which uses cloud and web technologies, by learning and investigating on your own from general guidance.

Note: To complete this assignment, you will be required to use the Data Files. Please contact your instructor for information about accessing the Data Files.

Instructions: Start Access. Open the database, SC_AC_07-4.accdb, which is located in the Data Files folder, and enable the content. Solutions IT Support needs a form to help them organize their technicians and clients. You will create a Summary Form to include a hyperlink. You will also include a combo box to find a field and link the box's code to the records displayed in the table by editing the VBA code.

Perform the following tasks:

1. Save the database using the file name, SC_AC_07_Solutions-IT-Support. Enable the content.
2. Create a form based on the Client table using Design view and save it as Summary Form.
3. At the top of the form, add the Client Number field and the Technician Number field.
4. Add any other fields you think are necessary from the Client table, such as the client's contact information.
5. Add a Client to Find combo box with an appropriate name of your choice for the subquery. Adjust the On Current VBA code so the client data changes to match the record when the records are advanced.

Continued on next page

6. Access any website containing royalty-free images, such as Unsplash.com or Pexels.com, and search for an image suitable to use as a background image to the form, and then add the background image to the Summary Form.
7. Add a hyperlink for a local computer repair website at the bottom of the form.
8. Access any website containing royalty-free images and search for an image suitable to use on a Close Form command button; for example, a Stop sign or a door. Save the image to a storage location of your choice.
9. Add a Close Form command button to the form using the image you downloaded. Note that if you found an image with a file extension other than .bmp, you will need to adjust settings in the Select Picture dialog box from Bitmaps (*.bmp) to All Files (*.*). The button might show only part of the image you chose; this is not a problem. Resize the button as needed.
10. Save your changes to the Summary Form.
11. Submit the revised database in the format specified by your instructor.
12. **Consider This:** What image did you choose as the background for your form? What image did you choose for the command button? Why did you make those choices?

In the Lab

Design and implement a solution using creative thinking and problem-solving skills.

Lab: Applying Advanced Form Techniques to the Great Outdoors Campground Database

Note: To complete this assignment, you will be required to use the Data Files. Please contact your instructor for information about accessing the Data Files.

Problem: The administrators at Great Outdoors Campground need a form to use to track staff members involved in each activity zone. They also need a form to track payments from campers for each camping event.

Perform the following tasks:

Part 1: Open the SC_AC_07-5.accdb database from the Data Files folder. Save the file with the name, SC_AC_07_Great-Outdoors, and enable the content. Use the concepts and techniques presented in this module to perform each of the following tasks.

1. Create a Staff Activities Summary Form that is similar in style and appearance to the form shown in Figure 7–1a. The form should include a combo box to search for activity zones by name, which should be listed in ascending order; give the subquery an appropriate name of your choice. Include command buttons to go to the next record, go to the previous record, add records, delete records, and close the form. The user should not be able to tab to the combo box. When the Add Record button is clicked, the focus should be the Activity Zone ID.
2. Create a query that joins the Campers, Enrollments, and Camper Payments tables. Include the Camper ID field from the Campers table, the Event field from the Enrollments table, and the Amount Paid and Balance Due fields from the Camper Payments table. Save the query using a name of your choice.
3. Create a form from the Campers table that is similar to the form shown in Figure 7–2a. The form should have two tabs, a Datasheet tab and a Charts tab. The Datasheet tab displays a subform listing the camper's event enrollments. Data for the subform is based on the query you created in Step 2; use an appropriate name of your choice for the subform. The Charts tab should include two charts that represent the amounts paid and balances due for each event. Data for the Charts tab is also based on the query created in Step 2.

Submit your assignment in the format specified by your instructor.

Part 2: **Consider This:** You made several decisions while creating these two forms. What was the rationale behind your decisions? What chart style did you choose for the two charts? Why? What other chart styles could you use to represent the data?

Index

A

B

C

E

F

N

O

P

Q

R

T

U

V

W

X

Y

Z

9 780357 881453